PHILIP'S

www.philips-maps.co.uk

First published in 2000 by Philip's,
a division of Octopus Publishing Group Ltd.
www.octopusbooks.co.uk
Endeavour House, 189 Shaftesbury Avenue
London WC2H 8JG
An Hachette UK Company
www.hachette.co.uk

Fourth edition 2010
First impression 2010

ISBN 978-1-84907-060-7 (pocket spiral)
ISBN 978-1-84907-061-4 (pocket paperback)

LONDA

© Philip's 2010

os Ordnance Survey®

This product includes mapping data licensed
from Ordnance Survey® with the permission
of the Controller of Her Majesty's Stationery
Office. © Crown copyright 2010. All rights
reserved. Licence number 100011710.

Contents

II **Key to map pages**

IV Administrative and Postcode boundaries

VI **Route planning**

XXIV **Key to map symbols**

1 **Street maps**

228 **Keys to enlarged map pages and symbols**

229 **Enlarged street maps**

271 **Index**

477 **List of numbered locations**

498 West End theatres and cinemas

500 Central London buses

502 Local rail and London Underground

Digital Data

The exceptionally high-quality mapping found in this atlas is available as digital data in TIFF format, which is easily convertible to other bitmapped (raster) image formats. The index is also available in digital form as a standard database table. It contains all the details found in the printed index together with the National Grid reference for the map square in which each entry is named.

For further information and to discuss your requirements, please contact
philips@mapsinternational.co.uk

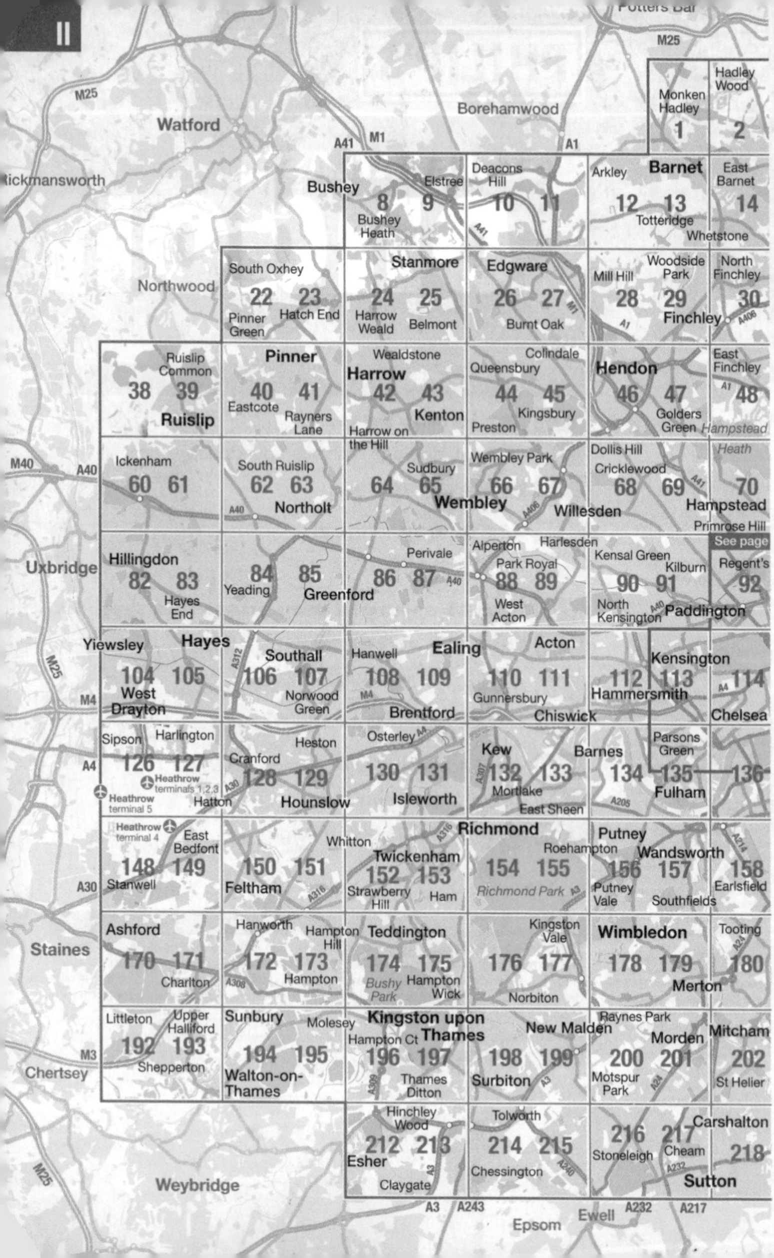

Potters Bar

M25

Monken Hadley **1** — Hadley Wood **2**

Watford

Borehamwood

M1 — A41

Rickmansworth — M25

Arkley — **Barnet** — East Barnet

Bushey **8** Elstree **9** — Deacons Hill **10** **11** — **12** Totteridge **13** — **14** Whetstone

Bushey Heath

Northwood

South Oxhey **22** **23** Hatch End — **Stanmore** **24** Harrow **25** Weald Belmont — **Edgware** **26** **27** Burnt Oak — Mill Hill **28** Woodside Park **29** **Finchley** North Finchley **30**

Pinner Green

Ruislip Common **38** **39** — **Pinner** **40** **41** Eastcote Rayners Lane — Wealdstone **Harrow** **42** **43** Kenton — Colindale Queensbury **44** **45** Kingsbury Preston — **Hendon** **46** **47** Golders Green — East Finchley **48** Hampstead Heath

Ruislip — Harrow on the Hill

Ickenham **60** **61** — South Ruislip **62** **63** **Northolt** — Sudbury **64** **65** **Wembley** — Wembley Park **66** **67** Willesden — Dollis Hill Cricklewood **68** **69** — **70** Hampstead Primrose Hill

M40 — A40

M40 — A40 — Hillingdon **82** **83** Hayes End — Yeading **84** **85** **Greenford** **86** **87** — Perivale — Alperton **88** **89** West Acton — Park Royal Harlesden — Kensal Green **90** **91** Kilburn — North Kensington **Paddington** **92** See page — Regent's

Uxbridge

Yiewsley **Hayes** **104** **105** West Drayton — **Southall** **106** **107** Norwood Green — Hanwell **108** **109** **Brentford** — **Ealing** **110** **111** Gunnersbury — **Acton** **112** **113** Chiswick Hammersmith — **Kensington** **114** Chelsea

M4

Sipson Harlington **126** **127** — Cranford **128** **129** Hatton **Hounslow** — Heston Osterley **130** **131** Isleworth — **Kew** **132** **133** Mortlake East Sheen — **Barnes** **134** **135** Fulham — Parsons Green **136**

A4 — M4

Heathrow terminals 1,2,3 — Heathrow terminal 5

Heathrow terminal 4 — East Bedfont **148** **149** Stanwell — **150** **151** **Feltham** — Whitton **Twickenham** **152** **153** Strawberry Hill Ham — **Richmond** **154** **155** Richmond Park — **Putney** Roehampton **156** **157** **Wandsworth** Putney Vale Southfields — **158** Earlsfield

A30

Ashford **170** **171** Charlton — Hanworth **172** **173** Hampton — Hampton Hill **Teddington** **174** **175** Bushy Park Hampton Wick — Kingston Vale **176** **177** Norbiton — **Wimbledon** **178** **179** **Merton** — Tooting **180**

Staines

Chertsey — Littleton **192** **193** Shepperton — Upper Halliford Sunbury **194** **195** **Walton-on-Thames** Molesey — **Kingston upon Thames** **196** **197** Hampton Ct Thames Ditton — **New Malden** **198** **199** **Surbiton** — Raynes Park **200** **201** Motspur Park **Morden** — **Mitcham** **202** St Helier

M3

Weybridge — Hinchley Wood **212** **213** **Esher** Claygate — Tolworth **214** **215** Chessington — **216** Stoneleigh **21** Cheam — Carshalton **218** **Sutton**

Epsom — Ewell — A3 A243 — A232 A217

M25

A10

A10

3 — Cockfosters

Clay Hill
4 5 — Enfield Town
Forty Hill

Enfield Wash
6 7 — Brimsdown
Enfield Lock

Enfield

Lough

Key to map pages

Herne

A23

160

Tulse Hill

Atlas pages at approximately 3 inches to 1 mile

Central London atlas coverage at approximately 6 inches to 1 mile
see page 228

Oakwood
Winchmore Hill
15 — Osidge
16 17 — **Southgate**

Ponders End
18 19

Lower Edmonton

Epping Forest
20 21
Chingford
Buckhurst Hill

Scale
0 1 2 3 4 5 km
0 1 2 3 miles

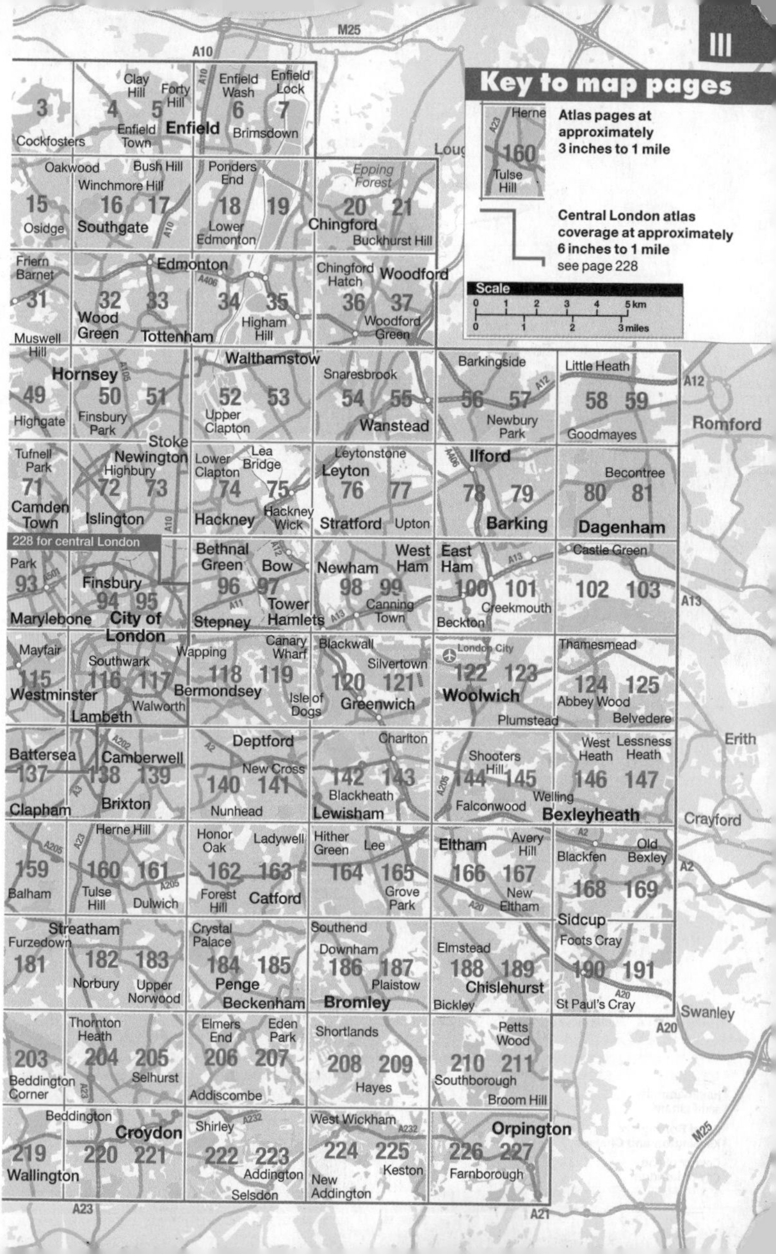

Friern Barnet
31 — Muswell Hill

Edmonton
32 33
Wood Green
Tottenham

34 35
Higham Hill

Chingford Hatch
36 37
Woodford
Woodford Green

A12

Romford

Hornsey
49 — Highgate
50 51 — Finsbury Park

Walthamstow
52 53
Upper Clapton

Snaresbrook
54 55
Wanstead

Barkingside
56 57
Newbury Park
Goodmayes

Little Heath
58 59

A12

Tufnell Park
71 — Camden Town
Stoke Newington
Highbury
72 73
Islington

Lower Clapton
74 75
Hackney
Lea Bridge
Hackney Wick

Leytonstone
Leyton
76 77
Stratford
Upton

Ilford
78 79
Barking

Becontree
80 81
Dagenham

228 for central London

Park
93 — **Marylebone**
Finsbury
94 95
City of London

Bethnal Green
96 97
Stepney
Bow
Tower Hamlets

West Ham
Newham
98 99
Canning Town

East Ham
100 101
Creekmouth
Beckton

Castle Green
102 103

A13

Mayfair
115 — **Westminster**
Southwark
116 117
Lambeth
Walworth

Wapping
118 119
Bermondsey
Isle of Dogs

Canary Wharf
Blackwall
120 121
Silvertown
Greenwich

London City
122 123
Woolwich
Plumstead

Thamesmead
124 125
Abbey Wood
Belvedere

Erith

Battersea
137 — Clapham
Camberwell
138 139
Brixton

Deptford
140 141
New Cross
Nunhead

Charlton
142 143
Blackheath
Lewisham

Shooters Hill
144 145
Falconwood
Welling

West Heath
146 147
Bexleyheath
Lessness Heath

Crayford

A2

Balham
159 — **Streatham**
Herne Hill
160 161
Tulse Hill
Dulwich

Honor Oak
162 163
Forest Hill
Ladywell
Catford

Hither Green
164 165
Lee
Grove Park

Eltham
166 167
New Eltham
Avery Hill

Blackfen
168 169
Sidcup
Old Bexley

A2

Furzedown
181 — **Norbury**
182 183
Upper Norwood

Crystal Palace
184 185
Penge
Beckenham

Southend
Downham
186 187
Plaistow
Bromley
Bickley

Elmstead
188 189
Chislehurst

Foots Cray
190 191
St Paul's Cray

Swanley

A20

Thornton Heath
203 — Beddington Corner
204 205
Selhurst

Elmers End
206 207
Addiscombe
Eden Park

Shortlands
208 209
Hayes

Petts Wood
210 211
Southborough
Broom Hill

A20

Beddington
219 — Wallington
Croydon
220 221

Shirley
222 223
Addington
Selsdon

West Wickham
224 225
New Addington
Keston

Orpington
226 227
Farnborough

A21

M25

A23

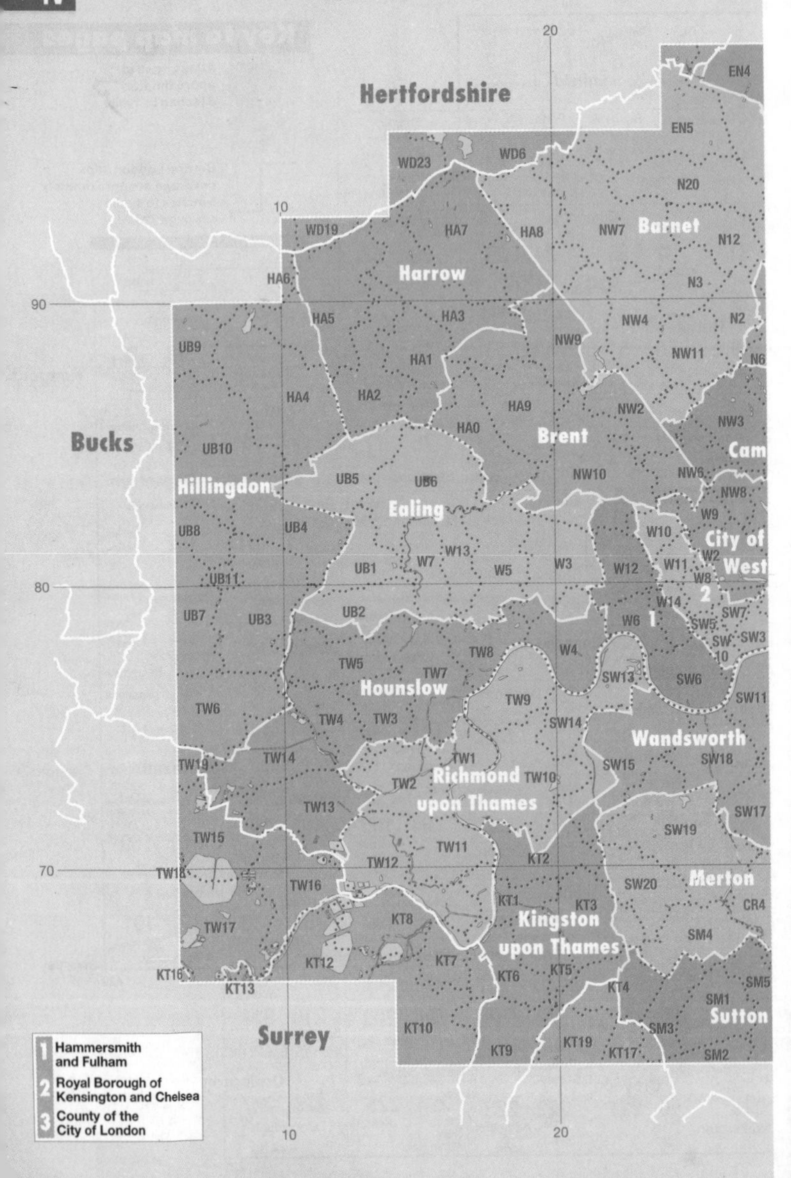
Hertfordshire
Bucks
Surrey
Barnet
Harrow
Brent
Hillingdon
Ealing
Hounslow
Richmond upon Thames
Wandsworth
Kingston upon Thames
Merton
Sutton
EN4
EN5
WD23
WD6
N20
WD19
HA7
HA8
NW7
N12
HA6
N3
HA5
HA3
NW4
N2
NW9
HA1
NW11
N6
UB9
HA4
HA2
HA9
NW2
NW3
HA0
UB10
NW10
NW6
UB5
UB6
NW8
W9
UB8
UB4
W10
W13
W2
UB1
W7
W5
W3
W12
W11
W8
UB11
W14
UB7
UB3
UB2
W6
SW7
SW5
SW3
SW10
W4
TW5
TW8
TW7
SW13
SW6
TW9
SW11
TW6
TW4
TW3
SW14
TW19
TW14
TW1
SW15
SW18
TW2
TW10
TW13
SW17
SW19
TW15
TW11
KT2
TW18
TW12
SW20
TW16
KT1
KT3
CR4
KT8
TW17
SM4
KT7
KT12
KT5
KT6
SM5
KT16
KT13
KT4
SM1
KT10
SM3
KT19
KT9
KT17
SM2
90
80
70
10
20
1 Hammersmith and Fulham
2 Royal Borough of Kensington and Chelsea
3 County of the City of London

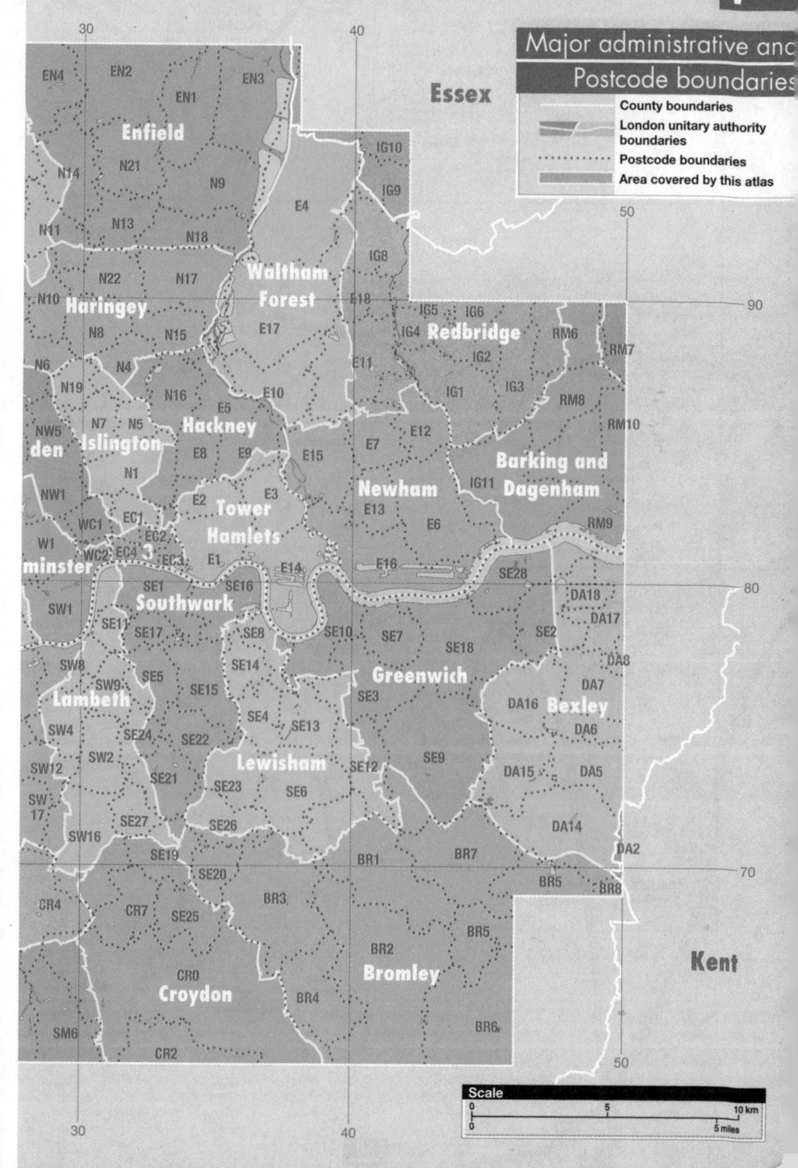

V

Essex

Kent

Scale

0   5   10 km

0   5 miles

EN4 EN2 EN1 EN3
Enfield
N14 N21 N9 IG10
N11 N13 N18 IG9
E4
N22 N17 IG8
N10 Haringey Waltham Forest E18 IG5 IG6
N8 N15 E17 IG4 Redbridge RM6
N6 N4 E11 IG2 RM7
N19 N16 E5 E10 IG1 IG3 RM8
NW5 N7 N5 Hackney E12 RM10
den Islington E8 E9 E15 E7 Barking and IG11 Dagenham
NW1 N1 E2 E3 Newham RM9
W1 WC1 EC1 Tower E13 E6
minster WC2 EC4 EC3 Hamlets E1 E16 SE28
SW1 SE1 SE16 Southwark SE18 SE2 DA18 DA17
SE11 SE17 SE8 SE10 SE7 Greenwich DA8
SW8 SE5 SE14 SE3 DA16 Bexley DA7
Lambeth SW9 SE15 SE4 SE13 DA6
SW4 SE24 SE22 Lewisham SE9 DA15 DA5
SW12 SW2 SE21 SE23 SE12 SE6 DA14 DA2
SW17 SE27 SE26 BR1 BR7 DA2
SW16 SE19 BR5 BR8
CR4 SE20 BR3
CR7 SE25 BR5
CR0 BR2 Bromley
Croydon BR4 BR6
SM6 CR2

Route planning

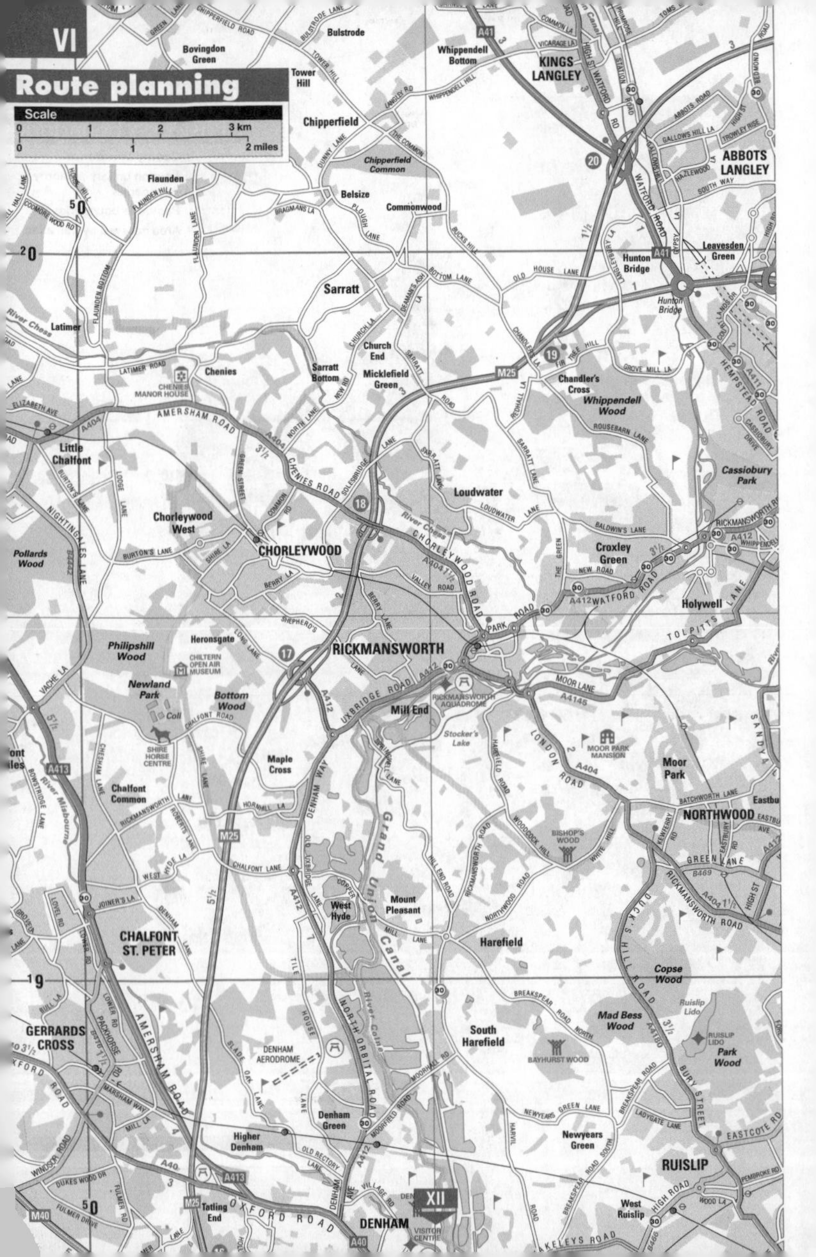

Scale
0 1 2 3 km
0 1 2 miles
Bulstrode
Bovingdon Green
Tower Hill
Whippendell Bottom
KINGS LANGLEY
Chipperfield
Chipperfield Common
ABBOTS LANGLEY
Flaunden
Belsize
Commonwood
Leavesden Green
Hunton Bridge
Sarratt
Latimer
Church End
Chenies
Sarratt Bottom
Micklefield Green
Chandler's Cross
Whippendell Wood
CHENIES MANOR HOUSE
Little Chalfont
Cassiobury Park
Loudwater
Chorleywood West
CHORLEYWOOD
Croxley Green
Pollards Wood
Holywell
Philipshill Wood
Heronsgate
RICKMANSWORTH
CHILTERN OPEN AIR MUSEUM
Newland Park
Bottom Wood
RICKMANSWORTH AQUADROME
Mill End
Stocker's Lake
SHIRE HORSE CENTRE
Maple Cross
MOOR PARK MANSION
Moor Park
Chalfont Common
NORTHWOOD
BISHOP'S WOOD
Grand Union Canal
West Hyde
Mount Pleasant
CHALFONT ST. PETER
Harefield
Copse Wood
Mad Bess Wood
Ruislip Lido
GERRARDS CROSS
South Harefield
DENHAM AERODROME
BAYHURST WOOD
RUISLIP LIDO
Park Wood
Denham Green
Higher Denham
Newyears Green
RUISLIP
Tatling End
DENHAM
VISITOR CENTRE
West Ruislip
XII
M25
M40
A40
A41
A404
A412
A413
A4145
A4180

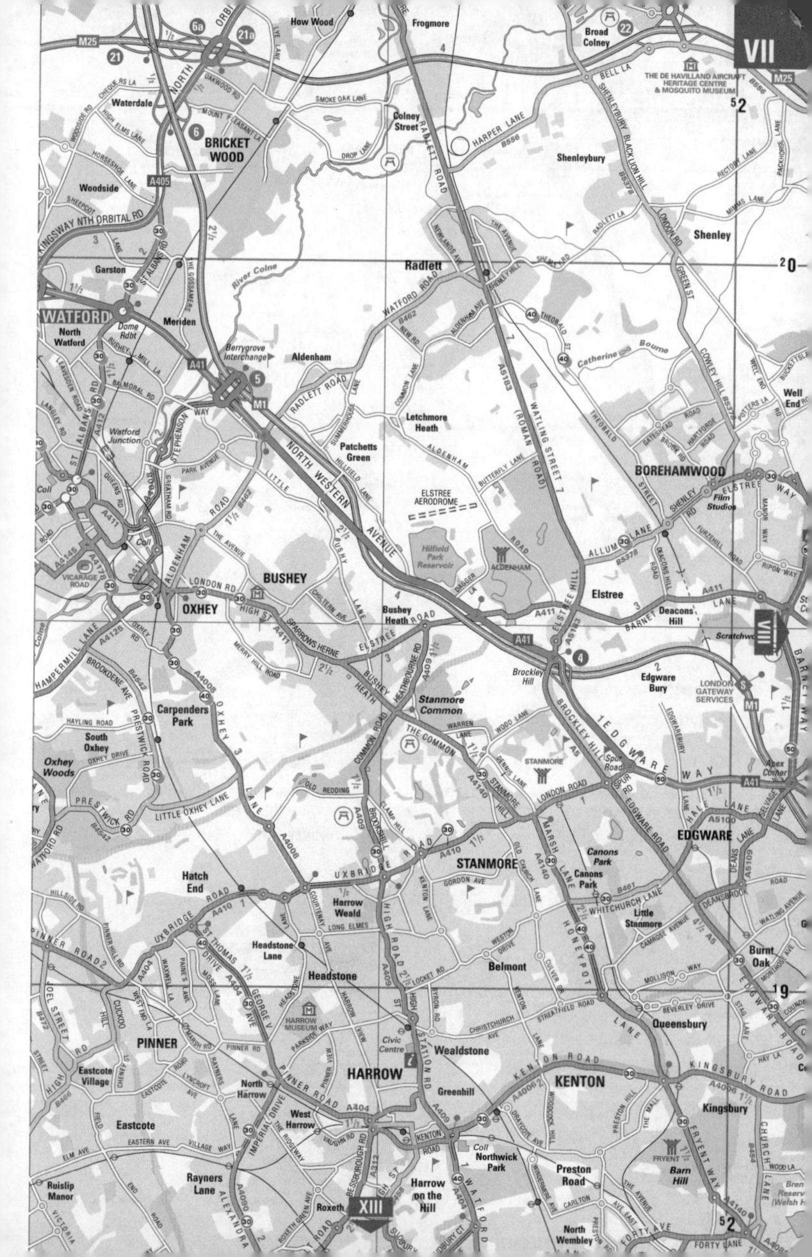

VII
M25
How Wood
Frogmore
Broad Colney
THE DE HAVILLAND AIRCRAFT HERITAGE CENTRE & MOSQUITO MUSEUM
BELL LA
SHENLEYBURY
BLACK LION HILL
Waterdale
CHEQUE RS LA
OAKWOOD RD
SMOKE OAK LANE
MOUNT PLEASANT LA
Colney Street
RADLETT ROAD
HARPER LANE
B556
Shenleybury
BRICKET WOOD
HIGH ELMS LANE
HORSESHOE LANE
DROP LANE
A405
Woodside
SHEEPCOT
KINGSWAY NTH ORBITAL RD
RECTORY LANE
PACKHORSE LANE
MIMMS LANE
B5378
LONDON RD
RADLETT LA
Shenley
Garston
ST ALBANS RD
THE GOSSAMERS
River Colne
Radlett
NEWLANDS AVE
THE AVENUE
SHENLEY HILL
GREEN ST
WATFORD
North Watford
Dome Rdbt
Meriden
WATFORD ROAD
B462
NEW RD
ALDENHAM AVE
THEOBALD ST
Catherine Bourne
COWLEY HILL
BUSHEY MILL LA
LEAVESDEN ROAD
BALMORAL RD
Berrygrove Interchange
Aldenham
A41
M1
RADLETT ROAD
COMMON LANE
A5183
WATLING STREET
(ROMAN ROAD)
WELL END
Well End
BUCKETTSLAND
POTTERS LA
LANGLEY RD
ST ALBANS RD
A412
STEPHENSON WAY
Watford Junction
Letchmore Heath
SUMMERHOUSE LANE
THEOBALD STREET
GATESHEAD ROAD
BROOK RD
HARTFORDE ROAD
Patchetts Green
NORTH WESTERN AVENUE
HILLFIELD LANE
ALDENHAM
PARK AVENUE
QUEENS RD
GREATHAM RD
LITTLE
ALDENHAM ROAD
BUTTERFLY LANE
ELSTREE AERODROME
BOREHAMWOOD
Film Studios
ELSTREE WAY
SHENLEY RD
MANOR WAY
FURZEHILL ROAD
Coll
A411
A4145
VICARAGE ROAD
A4178
THE AVENUE
BUSHEY LANE
Hilfield Park Reservoir
ALDENHAM
ALLUM LANE
B5378
DEACONS HILL
ROAD
RIPON WAY
LONDON RD
BUSHEY
OXHEY
HIGH ST
SPARROWS HERNE
CHILTERN AVE
Bushey Heath
DAGGER LA
ELSTREE HILL
Elstree
BARNET LANE
Deacons Hill
VIII
Scratchwood
HAMPERMILL LANE
A4125
OXHEY RD
BROOKDENE AVE
MERRY HILL ROAD
ELSTREE ROAD
HEATHBOURNE RD
A409
Brockley Hill
Edgware Bury
LONDON GATEWAY SERVICES
BARNET WAY
B4542
A4008
OXHEY LANE
Carpenders Park
BUSHEY HEATH
Stanmore Common
COMMON ROAD
BROCKLEY HILL
EDGWAREBURY
HAYLING ROAD
PRESTWICK ROAD
South Oxhey
OXHEY DRIVE
Oxhey Woods
WARREN LANE
THE COMMON
WOOD LANE
DENNIS LANE
STANMORE
A5
Spur Road
EDGWARE WAY
Apex Corner
A41
PRESTWICK RD
LITTLE OXHEY LANE
OLD REDDING
A4140
STANMORE HILL
LONDON ROAD
SPUR RD
EDGWARE ROAD
HALE LANE
A5100
SELVAGE LANE
WATFORD RD
CLAMP HILL
BROOKSHILL
A410
UXBRIDGE ROAD
STANMORE
OLD CHURCH LANE
MARSH LANE
Canons Park
EDGWARE
DEANS LANE
A5109
Hatch End
HILLSIDE RD
COURTENAY AVE
Harrow Weald
KENTON LANE
GORDON AVE
B461
WHITCHURCH LANE
Little Stanmore
DEANSBROOK ROAD
WATLING AVENUE
PINNER HILL RD
UXBRIDGE ROAD
A410
LONG ELMES
CAMROSE AVENUE
PINNER ROAD
ST THOMAS DRIVE
Headstone Lane
HIGH ROAD
WESTON DRIVE
HONEYPOT LANE
Burnt Oak
MONTROSE AVE
A404
WAXWELL LA
PAINE'S LANE
MOSS LANE
GEORGE V AVE
Headstone
LOCKET RD
Belmont
CULVER GR
MOLLISON WAY
JOEL STREET
CUCKOO HILL
WEST END LA
HEADSTONE
HARROW VIEW
BYRON RD
STREATFIELD ROAD
BEVERLEY DRIVE
STAG LANE
19
B472
HARROW MUSEUM
PARKSIDE WAY
Civic Centre
CHRISTCHURCH AVE
Queensbury
PINNER
MARSH RD
PINNER RD
RAYNERS LANE
Wealdstone
STATION RD
HAY LA
HIGH STREET
Eastcote Village
CHENEY ST
EASTCOTE RD
LYNCROFT AVE
North Harrow
PINNER VIEW
HARROW
KENTON ROAD
KENTON
KINGSBURY ROAD
B466
PINNER ROAD
Greenhill
A4006
PRESTON HILL
THE MALL
Kingsbury
Eastcote
FIELD END
EASTERN AVE
VILLAGE WAY
IMPERIAL DRIVE
West Harrow
THE RIDGEWAY
VAUGHAN RD
A404
KENTON ROAD
Coll
Northwick Park
DRAYCOTT AVE
WOODCOCK HILL
FRYENT
Barn Hill
CHURCH LANE
B454
ELM AVE
Rayners Lane
BESSBOROUGH RD
A312
Harrow on the Hill
WATFORD
Preston Road
WINDERMERE AVE
THE AVENUE
FRYENT WAY
WOOD LA
Ruislip Manor
ALEXANDRA
A4090
Roxeth
ROXETH GREEN AVE
XIII
North Wembley
CARLTON
AVE EAST
FORTY AVE
FORTY LANE
A4140
VICTORIA ROAD
SUDBURY CT

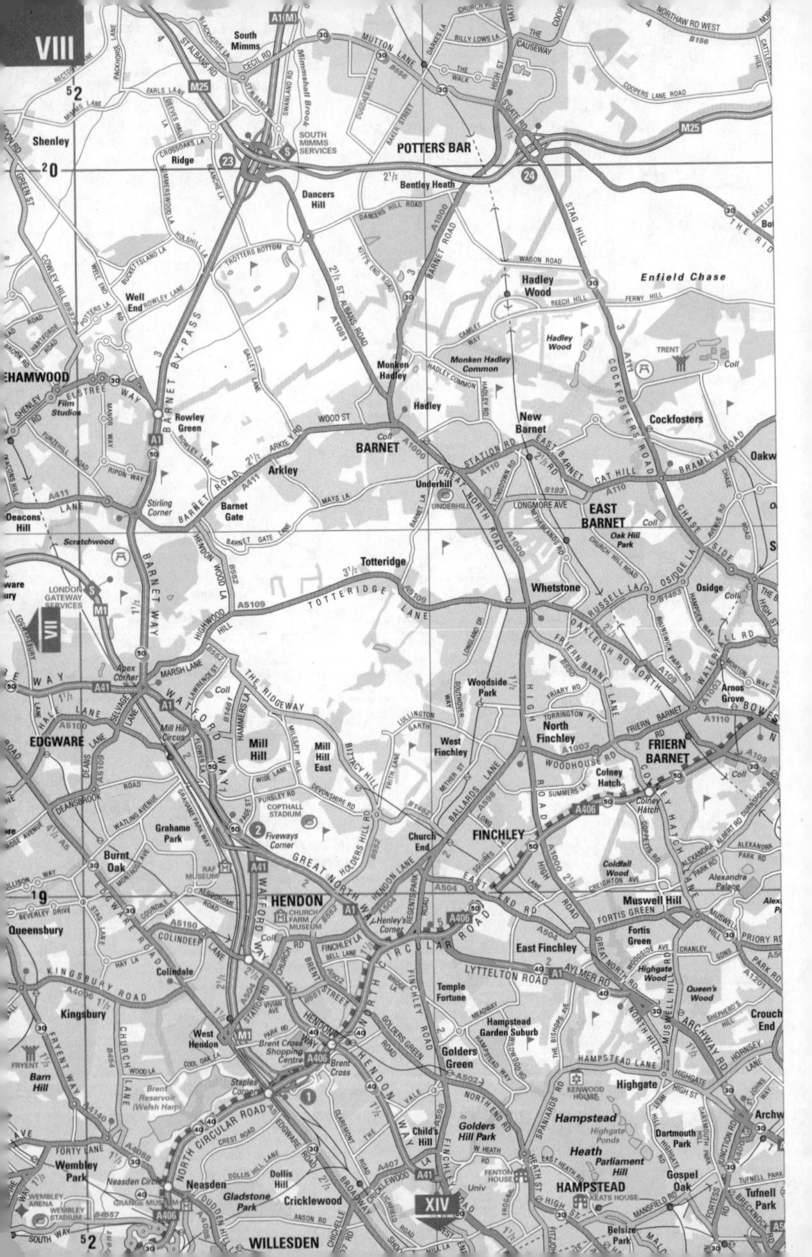
South Mimms
Potters Bar
Shenley
Ridge
South Mimms Services
Dancers Hill
Bentley Heath
Mimmshall Brook
Mutton Lane
The Causeway
Northaw Rd West
Coopers Lane Road
M25
A1(M)
Enfield Chase
Hadley Wood
Monken Hadley Common
Monken Hadley
Hadley
Trent
Cockfosters
Cockfosters Road
Stag Hill
Barnet Road
St. Albans Road
Barnet By-Pass
Well End
Rowley Green
Arkley
Barnet
Barnet Gate
Underhill
New Barnet
East Barnet
Oak Hill Park
Ehamwood
Elstree Way
Film Studios
Deacons Hill
Stirling Corner
Scratchwood
London Gateway Services
Totteridge
Totteridge Lane
Whetstone
Osidge
Oakleigh Rd North
Friern Barnet Lane
Apex Corner
Edgware
Mill Hill Circus
Mill Hill
Mill Hill East
Watford Way
The Ridgeway
Woodside Park
West Finchley
North Finchley
Friern Barnet
Arnos Grove
Colney Hatch
Copthall Stadium
Fiveways Corner
Grahame Park
Burnt Oak
RAF Museum
Hendon
Church Farm Museum
Church End
Finchley
Coldfall Wood
Alexandra Palace
Muswell Hill
Fortis Green
East Finchley
Henley's Corner
North Circular Road
Great North Way
Queensbury
Colindale
Kingsbury
Kingsbury Road
Temple Fortune
Lyttelton Road
Highgate Wood
Queen's Wood
Crouch End
Hampstead Garden Suburb
West Hendon
Brent Cross Shopping Centre
Brent Cross
Staples Corner
Brent Reservoir (Welsh Harp)
Golders Green
Barn Hill
Fryent Way
Hampstead Lane
Highgate
Kenwood House
Hampstead Heath
Highgate Ponds
Parliament Hill
Dartmouth Park
Golders Hill Park
Child's Hill
Fenton House
Wembley Park
Neasden
Neasden Circle
Dollis Hill
Gladstone Park
Cricklewood
Wembley Arena
Wembley Stadium
Grange Museum
Willesden
Hampstead
Keats House
Gospel Oak
Tufnell Park
Belsize Park
Archway Road
XIV
VIII

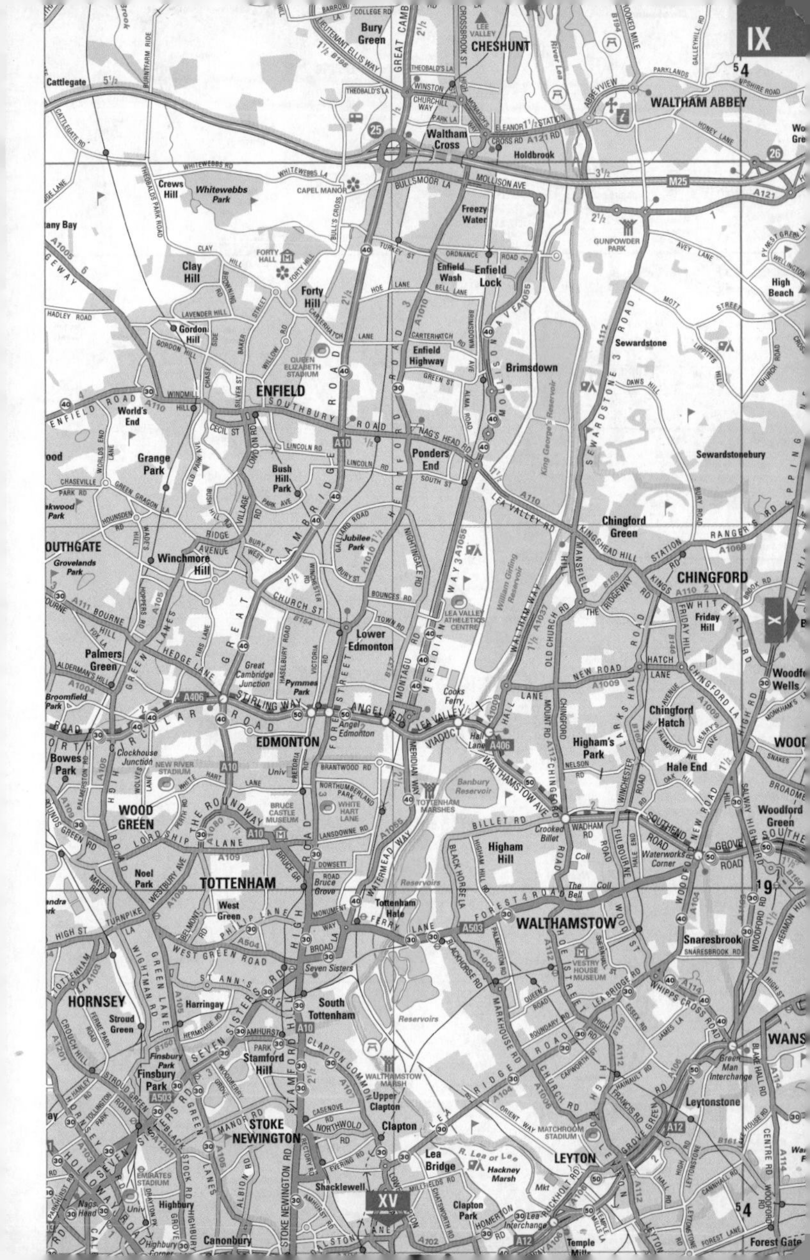
Bury Green
CHESHUNT
WALTHAM ABBEY
Cattlegate
Waltham Cross
Holdbrook
Crews Hill
Whitewebbs Park
CAPEL MANOR
M25
Freezy Water
GUNPOWDER PARK
Clay Hill
FORTY HALL
Forty Hill
Enfield Wash
Enfield Lock
High Beach
Gordon Hill
Enfield Highway
Brimsdown
Sewardstone
QUEEN ELIZABETH STADIUM
ENFIELD
World's End
Grange Park
Bush Hill Park
Ponders End
Sewardstonebury
King George's Reservoir
Chingford Green
Jubilee Park
Winchmore Hill
Grovelands Park
SOUTHGATE
William Girling Reservoir
CHINGFORD
Friday Hill
LEA VALLEY ATHLETICS CENTRE
Lower Edmonton
Palmers Green
Great Cambridge Junction
Pymmes Park
Cooks Ferry
Chingford Hatch
Woodford Wells
EDMONTON
Angel Edmonton
Bowes Park
Clockhouse Junction
NEW RIVER STADIUM
Higham's Park
Hale End
Banbury Reservoir
TOTTENHAM MARSHES
WOOD GREEN
BRUCE CASTLE MUSEUM
WHITE HART LANE
Woodford Green
Crooked Billet
Higham Hill
Waterworks Corner
Noel Park
TOTTENHAM
Bruce Grove
Reservoirs
West Green
Tottenham Hale
WALTHAMSTOW
Snaresbrook
Seven Sisters
VESTRY HOUSE MUSEUM
HORNSEY
Harringay
South Tottenham
Stroud Green
Finsbury Park
Stamford Hill
WALTHAMSTOW MARSH
Green Man Interchange
Upper Clapton
Leytonstone
STOKE NEWINGTON
Clapton
MATCHROOM STADIUM
LEYTON
Lea Bridge
Hackney Marsh
EMIRATES STADIUM
Shacklewell
Highbury
Nags Head
Clapton Park
Homerton
Lea Interchange
Canonbury
Temple Mills
Forest Gate
XV
X

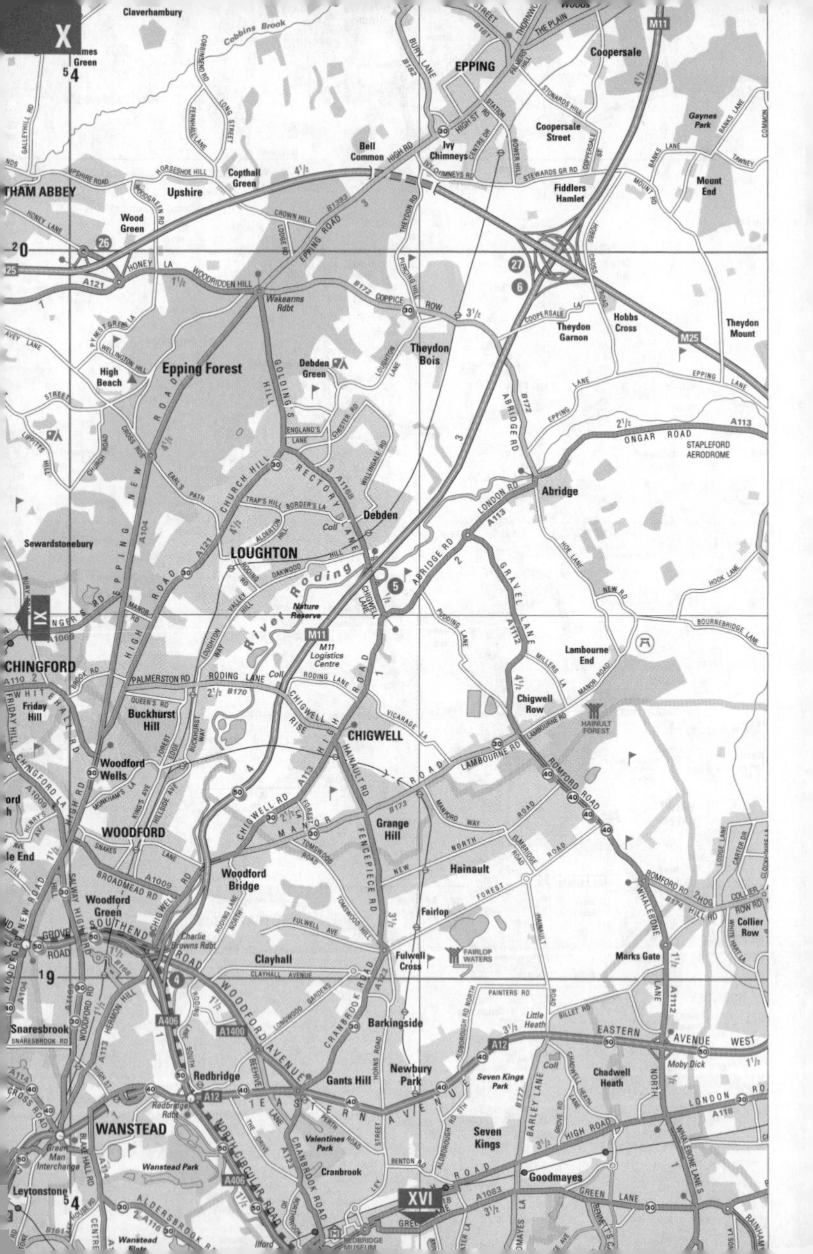
X
Claverhambury
EPPING
Coopersale
Coopersale Street
Gaynes Park
Bell Common
Ivy Chimneys
Copthall Green
Upshire
Fiddlers Hamlet
Mount End
WALTHAM ABBEY
Wood Green
Wakearms Rdbt
Theydon Garnon
Hobbs Cross
Theydon Mount
Epping Forest
High Beach
Debden Green
Theydon Bois
STAPLEFORD AERODROME
Abridge
Debden
Sewardstonebury
LOUGHTON
River Roding
Nature Reserve
M11 Logistics Centre
CHINGFORD
Lambourne End
Friday Hill
Buckhurst Hill
CHIGWELL
Chigwell Row
HAINAULT FOREST
Woodford Wells
WOODFORD
Grange Hill
Woodford Bridge
Hainault
Woodford Green
Fairlop
Charlie Browns Rdbt
Clayhall
Fulwell Cross
FAIRLOP WATERS
Marks Gate
Collier Row
Snaresbrook
Barkingside
Little Heath
Redbridge
Gants Hill
Newbury Park
Seven Kings Park
Chadwell Heath
Moby Dick
Redbridge Rdbt
WANSTEAD
Valentines Park
Seven Kings
Green Man Interchange
Wanstead Park
Cranbrook
Goodmayes
Leytonstone
XVI
IX
REDBRIDGE MUSEUM
Ilford
Wanstead Flats

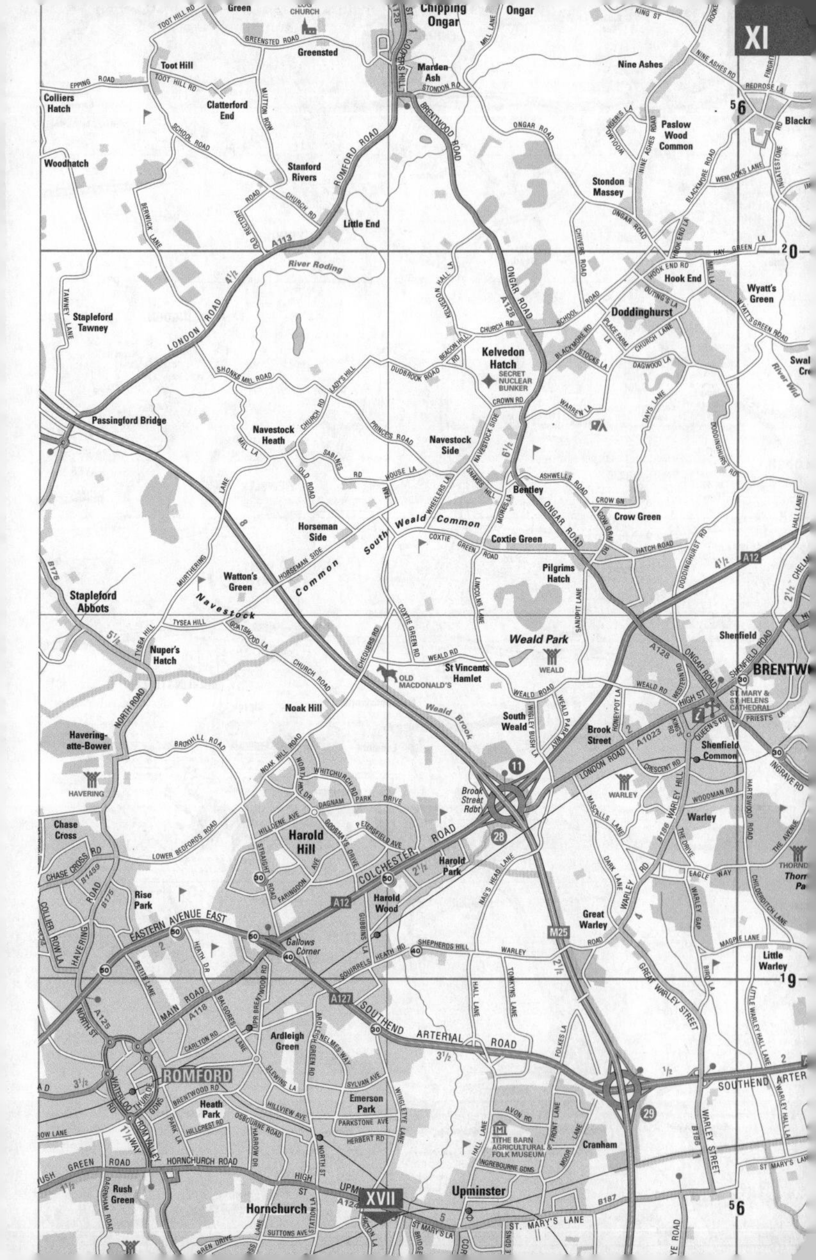
Chipping Ongar
Greenstead
Marden Ash
Nine Ashes
Toot Hill
Colliers Hatch
Clatterford End
Woodhatch
Stanford Rivers
Paslow Wood Common
Stondon Massey
Little End
River Roding
Hook End
Wyatt's Green
Doddinghurst
Stapleford Tawney
Kelvedon Hatch
SECRET NUCLEAR BUNKER
Passingford Bridge
Navestock Heath
Navestock Side
Bentley
Crow Green
Horseman Side
South Weald Common
Coxtie Green
Pilgrims Hatch
Watton's Green
Stapleford Abbots
Navestock Common
Weald Park
Nuper's Hatch
St Vincents Hamlet
OLD MACDONALD'S
Shenfield
BRENTW
ST. MARY & ST. HELENS CATHEDRAL
Noak Hill
Weald Brook
South Weald
Brook Street
Shenfield Common
Havering-atte-Bower
HAVERING
WARLEY
Brook Street Rdbt
Warley
Chase Cross
Harold Hill
Harold Park
Rise Park
Harold Wood
Great Warley
Gallows Corner
Little Warley
Ardleigh Green
ROMFORD
Emerson Park
Heath Park
TITHE BARN AGRICULTURAL & FOLK MUSEUM
Cranham
Rush Green
Hornchurch
Upminster
XVII
A113
A128
A12
A127
A1023
M25
A118
A125
B175
B1459
B186
B187
LONDON ROAD
ROMFORD ROAD
ONGAR ROAD
COLCHESTER ROAD
EASTERN AVENUE EAST
MAIN ROAD
SOUTHEND ARTERIAL ROAD
HORNCHURCH ROAD
ST. MARY'S LANE
56
20
19

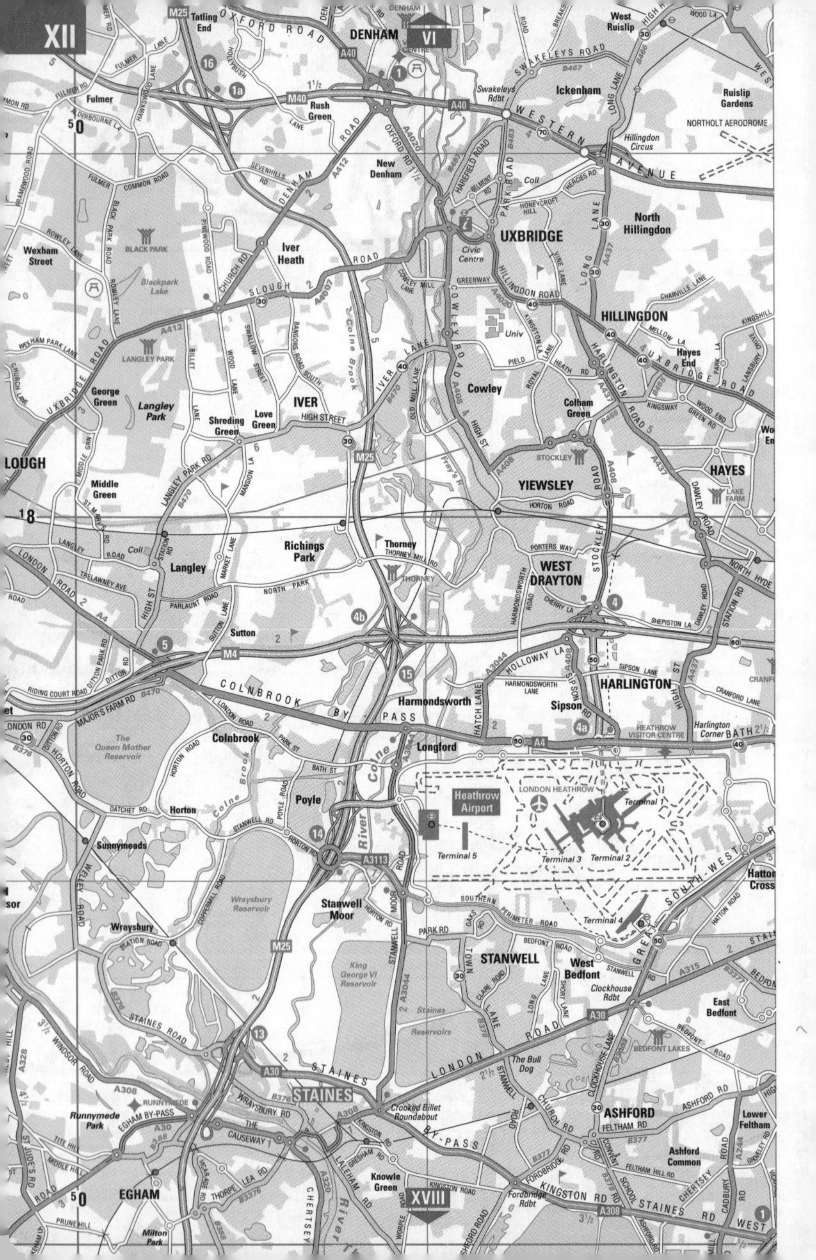
DENHAM
VI
West Ruislip
Tatling End
OXFORD ROAD
Fulmer
Rush Green
Ickenham
Ruislip Gardens
NORTHOLT AERODROME
WESTERN AVENUE
Hillingdon Circus
New Denham
North Hillingdon
UXBRIDGE
Civic Centre
Wexham Street
BLACK PARK
Blackpark Lake
Iver Heath
HILLINGDON
Hayes End
UXBRIDGE ROAD
LANGLEY PARK
George Green
Langley Park
IVER
Cowley
Colham Green
Shreding Green
Love Green
SLOUGH
Middle Green
YIEWSLEY
STOCKLEY
HAYES
LAKE FARM
Richings Park
Thorney
Langley
WEST DRAYTON
Sutton
HARLINGTON
COLNBROOK BY-PASS
Harmondsworth
Sipson
HEATHROW VISITOR CENTRE
Harlington Corner
Colnbrook
The Queen Mother Reservoir
Longford
Heathrow Airport
LONDON HEATHROW
Terminal 1
Terminal 2
Terminal 3
Terminal 4
Terminal 5
Poyle
Horton
Sunnymeads
Hatton Cross
Wraysbury Reservoir
Stanwell Moor
Wraysbury
STANWELL
West Bedfont
King George VI Reservoir
Clockhouse Rdbt
East Bedfont
Staines Reservoirs
BEDFONT LAKES
The Bull Dog
STAINES
RUNNYMEDE
Runnymede Park
Crooked Billet Roundabout
ASHFORD
Lower Feltham
Ashford Common
Knowle Green
XVIII
Fordbridge Rdbt
EGHAM
Milton Park

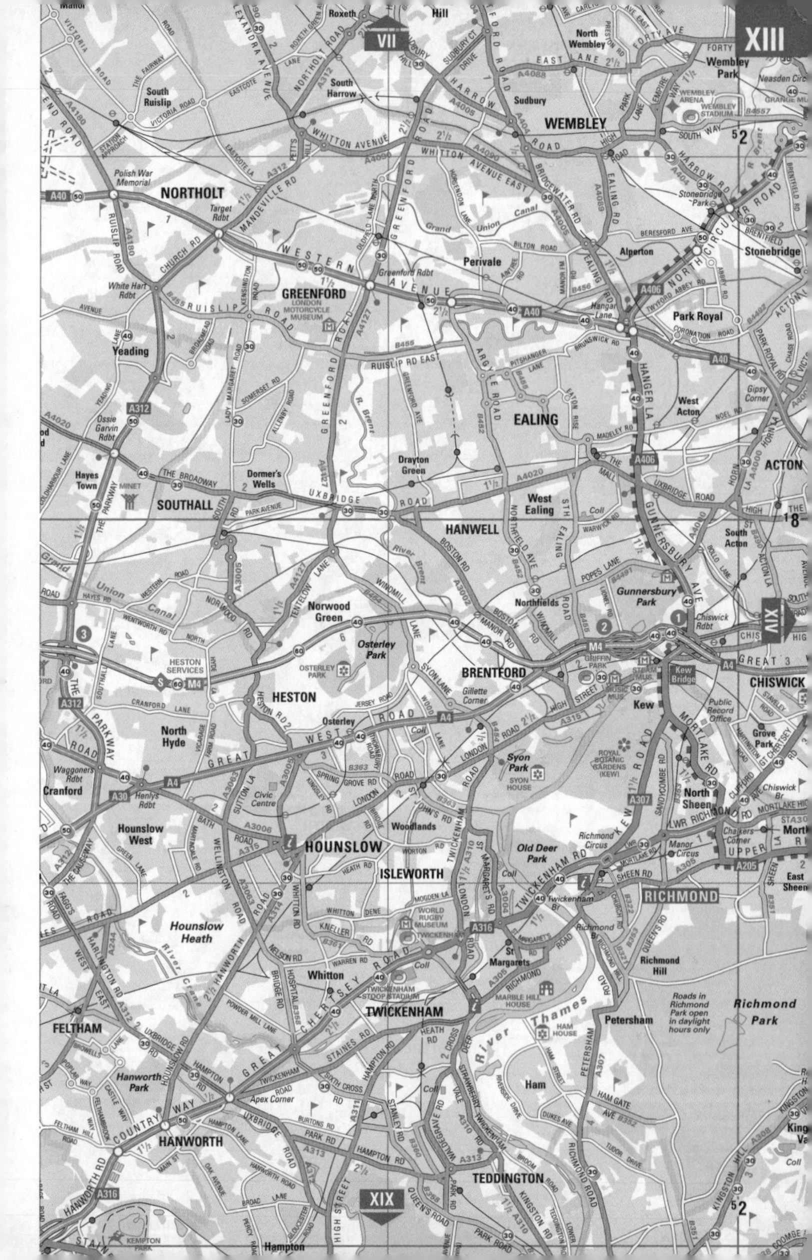
XIII
VII
XIX
XIV
WEMBLEY
NORTHOLT
GREENFORD
SOUTHALL
EALING
HANWELL
ACTON
HESTON
BRENTFORD
CHISWICK
HOUNSLOW
ISLEWORTH
RICHMOND
TWICKENHAM
FELTHAM
HANWORTH
TEDDINGTON
South Ruislip
South Harrow
North Wembley
Wembley Park
Sudbury
Alperton
Stonebridge
Perivale
Park Royal
Yeading
West Acton
Drayton Green
West Ealing
Hayes Town
Dormer's Wells
South Acton
Norwood Green
Osterley Park
Northfields
Gunnersbury Park
North Hyde
Cranford
Kew
Hounslow West
Woodlands
North Sheen
Old Deer Park
Hounslow Heath
Whitton
St Margarets
Richmond Hill
Petersham
Richmond Park
Hanworth Park
Ham
Hampton
Roads in Richmond Park open in daylight hours only
River Thames
Grand Union Canal

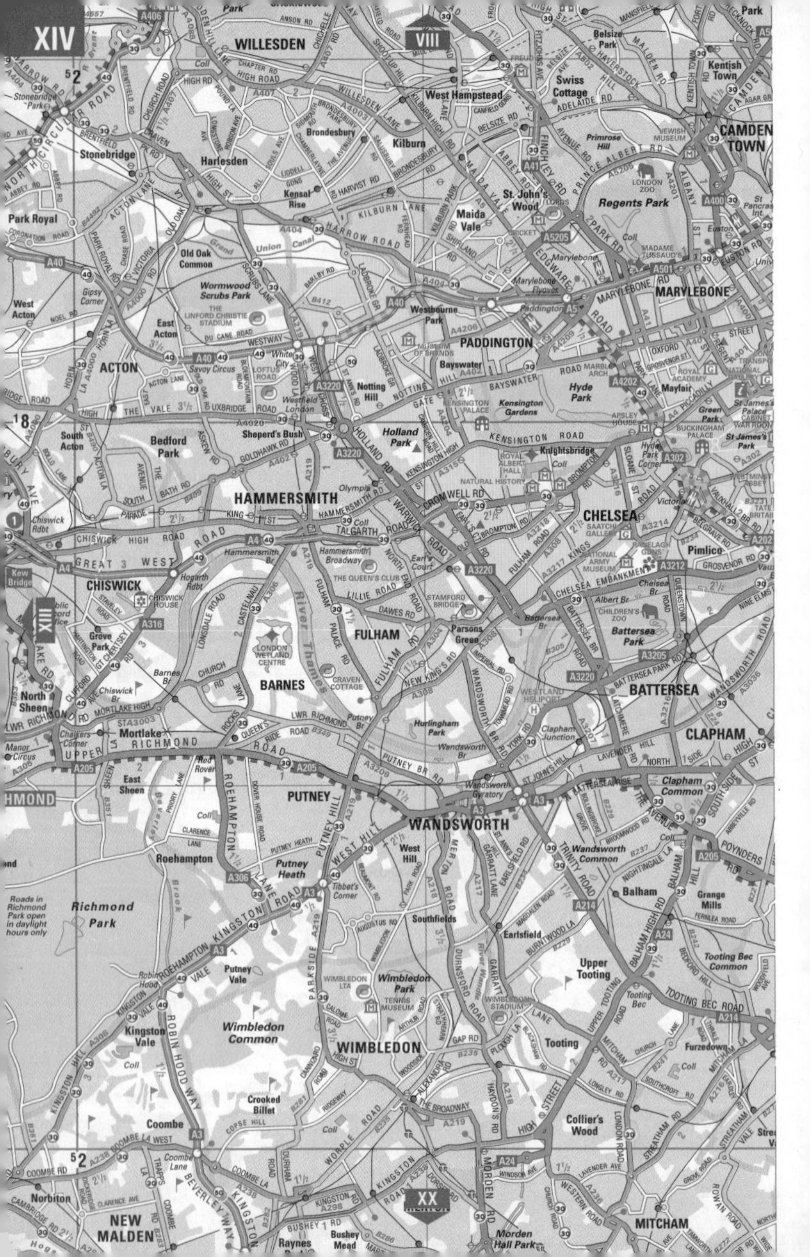

XIV
VIII
XX
WILLESDEN
West Hampstead
Swiss Cottage
Belsize Park
Kentish Town
CAMDEN TOWN
Primrose Hill
JEWISH MUSEUM
LONDON ZOO
Regents Park
Stonebridge
Harlesden
Brondesbury
Kilburn
Kensal Rise
St. John's Wood
Maida Vale
Park Royal
Old Oak Common
Wormwood Scrubs Park
Grand Union Canal
Marylebone
MARYLEBONE
MADAME TUSSAUD'S
Paddington
PADDINGTON
Westbourne Park
West Acton
East Acton
Gipsy Corner
ACTON
Savoy Circus
White City
Westfield London
Notting Hill
Bayswater
Hyde Park
Mayfair
Kensington Gardens
KENSINGTON PALACE
ROYAL ACADEMY
Green Park
St James's Palace
BUCKINGHAM PALACE
St James's Park
South Acton
Bedford Park
Sheperd's Bush
Holland Park
KENSINGTON ROAD
Knightsbridge
ROYAL ALBERT HALL
NATURAL HISTORY
Hyde Park Corner
Victoria
HAMMERSMITH
Olympia
CHELSEA
Pimlico
Chiswick Rdbt
Kew Bridge
CHISWICK
CHISWICK HOUSE
Hogarth Rdbt
Hammersmith Br
Hammersmith Broadway
THE QUEEN'S CLUB
Earl's Court
STAMFORD BRIDGE
NATIONAL ARMY MUSEUM
CHELSEA EMBANKMENT
Chelsea Br
Albert Br
CHILDREN'S ZOO
Battersea Park
Battersea Br
Grove Park
LONDON WETLAND CENTRE
River Thames
FULHAM
Parsons Green
Barnes Br
Chiswick Br
North Sheen
BARNES
CRAVEN COTTAGE
Hurlingham Park
WESTLAND HELIPORT
BATTERSEA
Clapham Junction
CLAPHAM
Mortlake
Chalkers Corner
Manor Circus
Putney Br
Wandsworth Br
East Sheen
PUTNEY
Wandsworth Gyratory
WANDSWORTH
Clapham Common
Roehampton
Putney Heath
West Hill
Wandsworth Common
Balham
Grange Mills
Tibbet's Corner
Southfields
Earlsfield
Richmond Park
Roads in Richmond Park open in daylight hours only
Upper Tooting
Tooting Bec Common
Putney Vale
Robin Hood
Wimbledon Park
WIMBLEDON LTA
TENNIS MUSEUM
WIMBLEDON STADIUM
Tooting Bec
Kingston Vale
Wimbledon Common
WIMBLEDON
Tooting
Furzedown
Crooked Billet
Coombe
Collier's Wood
Coombe Lane
Norbiton
NEW MALDEN
Raynes Park
Bushey Mead
Morden Hall Park
MITCHAM

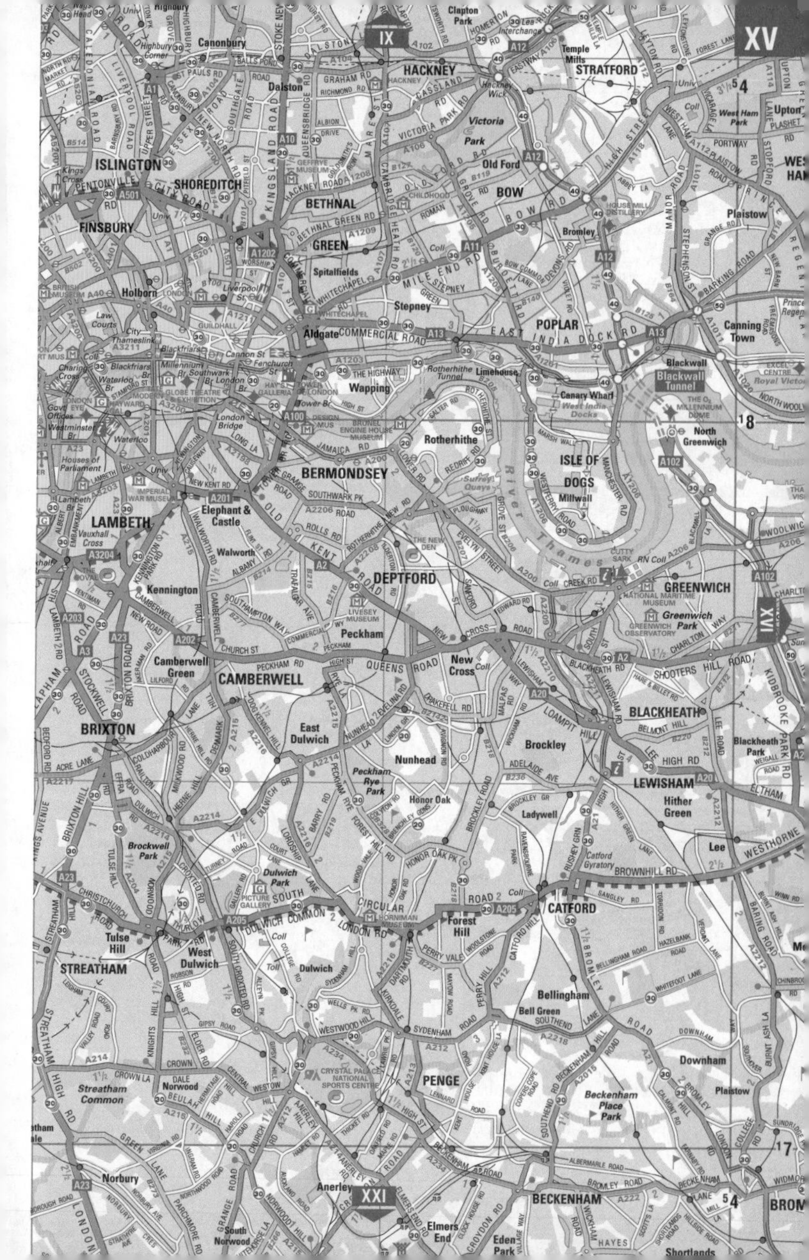

XV
IX
XVI
XXI
Clapton Park
Canonbury
Highbury Corner
Dalston
HACKNEY
Hackney Wick
Temple Mills
STRATFORD
West Ham Park
Upton
ISLINGTON
SHOREDITCH
Victoria Park
Old Ford
BOW
Plaistow
Kings Cross
PENTONVILLE
BETHNAL GREEN
FINSBURY
Bromley
Holborn
Spitalfields
Stepney
POPLAR
Canning Town
Law Courts
Liverpool St
Aldgate
Blackwall
Blackwall Tunnel
Fenchurch St
Wapping
Limehouse
Canary Wharf
West India Docks
London Bridge
Waterloo
Rotherhithe
North Greenwich
Houses of Parliament
BERMONDSEY
ISLE OF DOGS
Millwall
Surrey Quays
LAMBETH
Elephant & Castle
Walworth
River Thames
Vauxhall Cross
DEPTFORD
GREENWICH
Greenwich Park
Kennington
Peckham
New Cross
Camberwell Green
CAMBERWELL
BLACKHEATH
BRIXTON
East Dulwich
Nunhead
Brockley
Blackheath Park
Peckham Rye Park
Honor Oak
Ladywell
LEWISHAM
Hither Green
Brockwell Park
Dulwich Park
Lee
Catford Gyratory
Forest Hill
CATFORD
Tulse Hill
West Dulwich
STREATHAM
Dulwich
Bellingham
Bell Green
Downham
PENGE
Norwood
Streatham Common
Beckenham Place Park
Plaistow
Norbury
Anerley
BECKENHAM
South Norwood
Elmers End
Eden Park
Shortlands

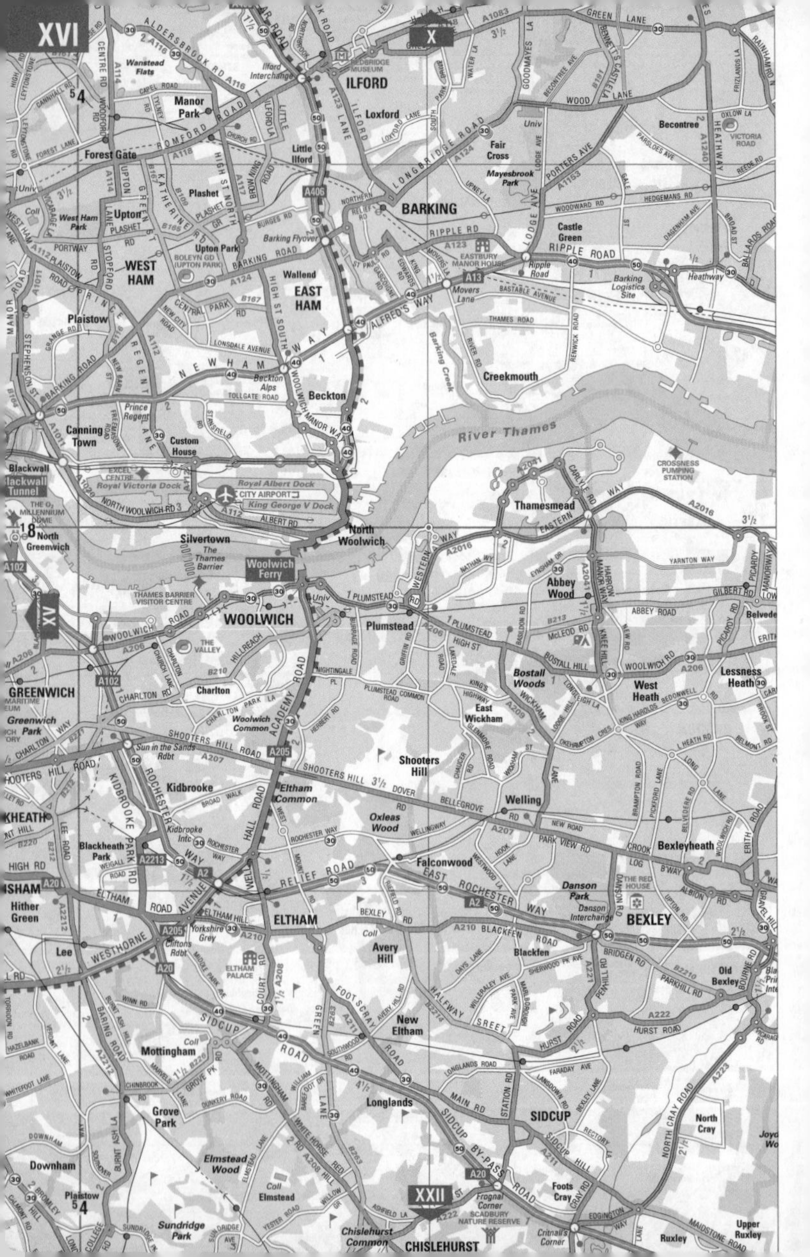
X
XV
XXII
Wanstead Flats
ALDERSBROOK RD
Ilford Interchange
REDBRIDGE MUSEUM
ILFORD
GREEN LANE
Manor Park
ROMFORD ROAD
Loxford
Forest Gate
Little Ilford
LONGBRIDGE ROAD
Fair Cross
Univ
Mayesbrook Park
Becontree
VICTORIA ROAD
HEATHWAY
PORTERS AVE
WOOD LANE
Plashet
West Ham Park
Upton
Upton Park
BOLEYN GD (UPTON PARK)
WEST HAM
BARKING
Barking Flyover
BARKING ROAD
RIPPLE RD
RIPPLE ROAD
Castle Green
EASTBURY MANOR HOUSE
Ripple Road
Barking Logistics Site
Heathway
Movers Lane
ALFRED'S WAY
Wallend
EAST HAM
Plaistow
BASTABLE AVENUE
THAMES ROAD
Barking Creek
NEWHAM WAY
Beckton Alps
Beckton
Creekmouth
Prince Regent
Canning Town
Custom House
River Thames
CROSSNESS PUMPING STATION
Blackwall
Blackwall Tunnel
EXCEL CENTRE
Royal Victoria Dock
Royal Albert Dock
CITY AIRPORT
King George V Dock
NORTH WOOLWICH RD
ALBERT RD
THE O2 MILLENNIUM DOME
North Greenwich
Silvertown
The Thames Barrier
THAMES BARRIER VISITOR CENTRE
North Woolwich
Woolwich Ferry
Thamesmead
EASTERN WAY
WESTERN WAY
YARNTON WAY
Abbey Wood
ABBEY ROAD
WOOLWICH
PLUMSTEAD
Plumstead
THE VALLEY
Charlton
GREENWICH
Greenwich Park
Woolwich Common
ACADEMY ROAD
Bostall Woods
East Wickham
West Heath
Lessness Heath
Belvedere
SHOOTERS HILL ROAD
Sun in the Sands Rdbt
Shooters Hill
Kidbrooke
Eltham Common
Oxleas Wood
Welling
Kidbrooke Intc
Blackheath Park
ROCHESTER WAY
Falconwood
Bexleyheath
RELIEF ROAD
EAST ROCHESTER WAY
Danson Park
Danson Interchange
THE RED HOUSE
BEXLEY
Hither Green
ELTHAM
Yorkshire Grey
Cliftons Rdbt
Lee
WESTHORNE
Avery Hill
BLACKFEN ROAD
Blackfen
Old Bexley
ELTHAM PALACE
New Eltham
SIDCUP ROAD
HURST ROAD
Mottingham
Longlands
SIDCUP
North Cray
NORTH CRAY ROAD
Grove Park
Downham
Elmstead Wood
Elmstead
SIDCUP BY-PASS ROAD
Foots Cray
Plaistow
Sundridge Park
Frognal Corner
SCADBURY NATURE RESERVE
Chislehurst Common
CHISLEHURST
Critnall's Corner
Ruxley
Upper Ruxley
MAIDSTONE ROAD

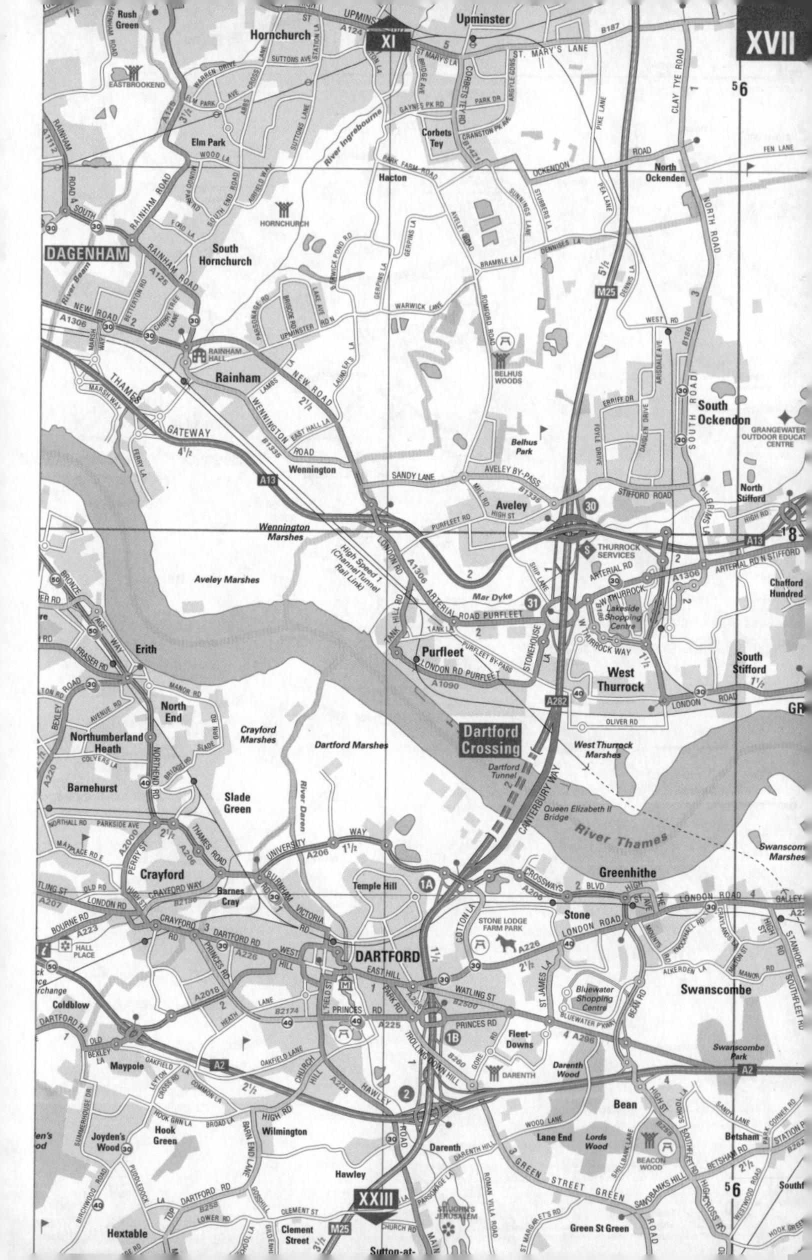
Upminster
Hornchurch
XI
Rush Green
Elm Park
Corbets Tey
North Ockenden
Hacton
DAGENHAM
South Hornchurch
Rainham
Wennington
Belhus Park
South Ockendon
North Stifford
Aveley
Wennington Marshes
Aveley Marshes
Purfleet
West Thurrock
South Stifford
Chafford Hundred
Erith
North End
Northumberland Heath
Crayford Marshes
Dartford Marshes
Dartford Crossing
West Thurrock Marshes
Queen Elizabeth II Bridge
River Thames
Barnehurst
Slade Green
Crayford
Barnes Cray
Temple Hill
Greenhithe
Stone
DARTFORD
Swanscombe
Bluewater Shopping Centre
Fleet-Downs
Darenth Wood
Maypole
Bean
Joyden's Wood
Hook Green
Wilmington
Darenth
Lane End
Lords Wood
Betsham
Hawley
XXIII
Hextable
Clement Street
Green St Green
Lakeside Shopping Centre
THURROCK SERVICES
Dartford Tunnel
High Speed 1 (Channel Tunnel Rail Link)
River Ingrebourne
River Darent
Mar Dyke
M25
A13
A2

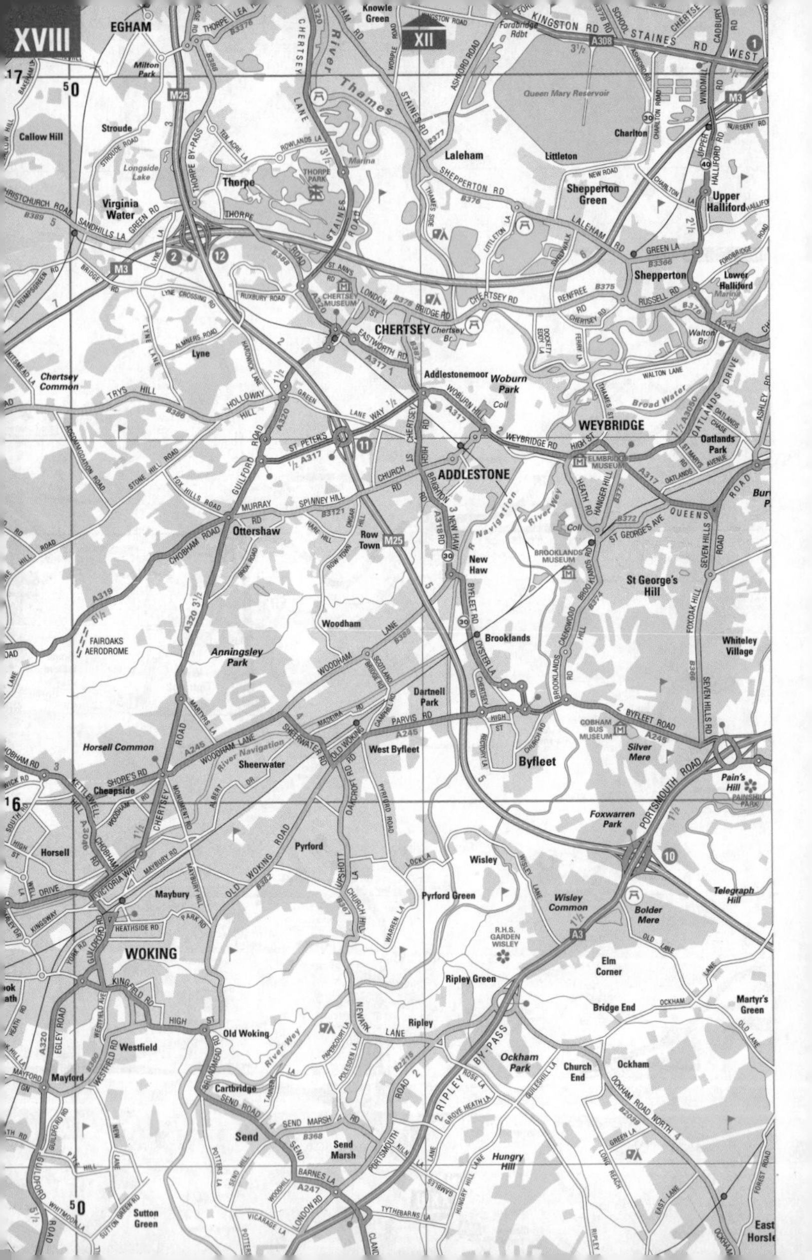
XVIII
XII
Egham
Milton Park
Callow Hill
Stroude
Longside Lake
Virginia Water
Thorpe
Thorpe Park
Marina
Knowle Green
River Thames
Queen Mary Reservoir
Laleham
Littleton
Charlton
Shepperton Green
Upper Halliford
Shepperton
Lower Halliford
Walton Br
Chertsey
Chertsey Br
Chertsey Museum
Lyne
Chertsey Common
Addlestonemoor
Woburn Park
Coll
Weybridge
Elmbridge Museum
Oatlands Park
Addlestone
Ottershaw
Row Town
New Haw
Brooklands Museum
St George's Hill
Woodham
Brooklands
Whiteley Village
Fairoaks Aerodrome
Anningsley Park
Dartnell Park
Horsell Common
Sheerwater
West Byfleet
Byfleet
Cobham Bus Museum
Silver Mere
Pain's Hill
Painshill Park
Cheapside
Horsell
Foxwarren Park
Pyrford
Wisley
Maybury
Pyrford Green
Wisley Common
Telegraph Hill
Bolder Mere
R.H.S. Garden Wisley
Woking
Elm Corner
Ripley Green
Martyr's Green
Bridge End
Ripley
Old Woking
Westfield
Ockham Park
Church End
Ockham
Mayford
Cartbridge
Send
Send Marsh
Hungry Hill
Sutton Green
East Horsle
River Wey
Wey Navigation
Broad Water
Basingstoke Canal
M25
M3
A3
A308
A317
A320
A319
A245
A247
A318
A3050
B3121
B375
B376
B377
B378
B388
B389
B3366
B365
B367
B368
B373
B374
B382
B385
B386
B387
B2039
B2215
KINGSTON RD
STAINES RD WEST
SHEPPERTON RD
LALEHAM RD
GREEN LA
RUSSELL RD
CHERTSEY RD
RENFREE RD
WALTON LANE
OATLANDS DRIVE
QUEENS ROAD
SEVEN HILLS ROAD
ST GEORGE'S AVE
BYFLEET ROAD
PORTSMOUTH ROAD
WEYBRIDGE RD
WOBURN HILL
HIGH ST
CHURCH RD
SPINNEY HILL
MURRAY RD
CHOBHAM ROAD
GUILDFORD ROAD
ST PETER'S WAY
STONE HILL ROAD
FOX HILLS ROAD
HOLLOWAY HILL
TRYS HILL
LYNE LANE
GUILDFORD ROAD
PARVIS RD
WOODHAM LANE
OLD WOKING ROAD
VICTORIA WAY
KINGFIELD RD
EGLEY ROAD
SEND ROAD
SEND MARSH RD
RIPLEY BY-PASS
NEWARK LANE
OCKHAM ROAD NORTH
OCKHAM LA
OLD LANE
HUNGRY HILL LANE
LONDON RD
BROADMEAD RD
THORPE BY-PASS
CHRISTCHURCH ROAD
SANDHILLS LA
CHERTSEY LANE
STAINES ROAD
EASTWORTH RD
LONDON ST
BRIDGE RD
ADDLESTONE

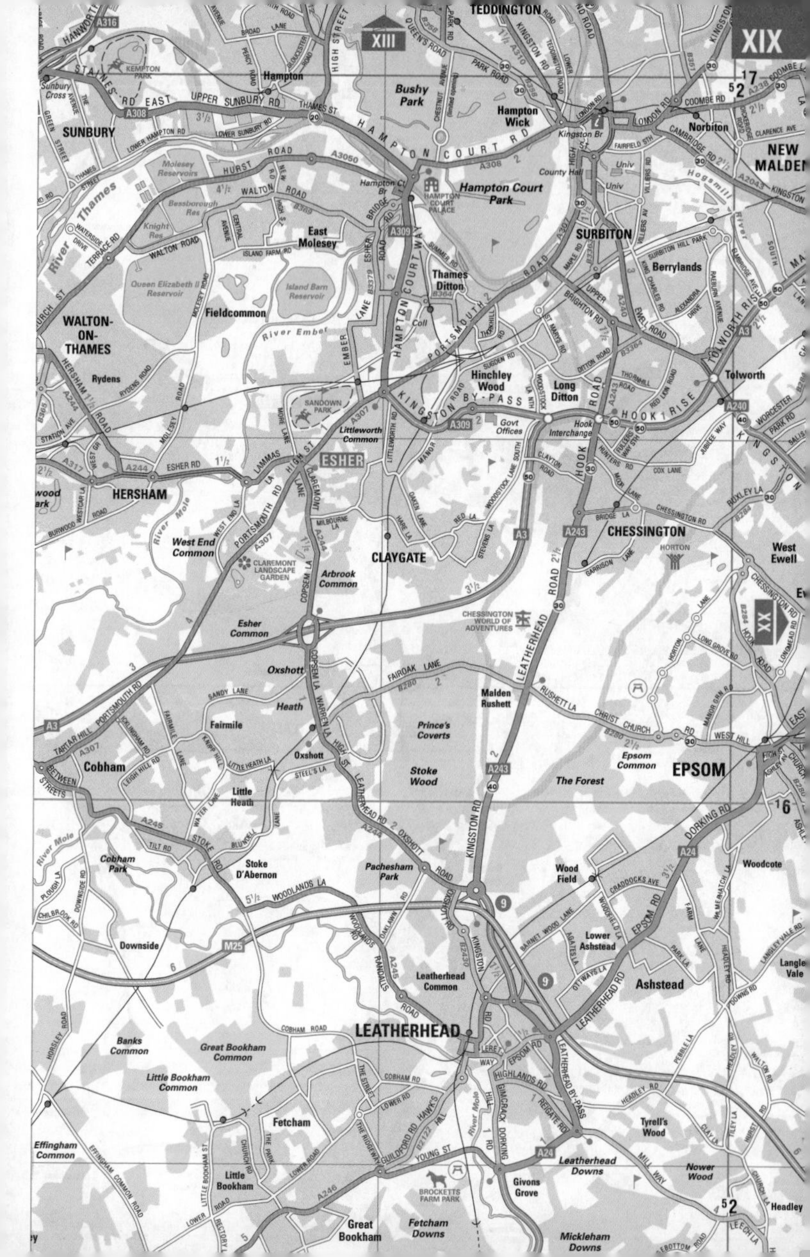
XIII
XIX
XX
TEDDINGTON
HANWORTH
A316
KEMPTON PARK
Sunbury Cross
STAINES RD EAST
UPPER SUNBURY RD
A308
SUNBURY
Hampton
HIGH STREET
THAMES ST
Bushy Park
QUEEN'S ROAD
PARK ROAD
Hampton Wick
HAMPTON COURT RD
KINGSTON ROAD
Kingston Br
LONDON RD
COOMBE RD
Norbiton
NEW MALDEN
CAMBRIDGE RD
CLARENCE AVE
FAIRFIELD STH
Univ
County Hall
Hogsmill River
KINGSTON
LOWER SUNBURY RD
LOWER HAMPTON RD
HURST ROAD
A3050
Molesey Reservoirs
WALTON ROAD
River Thames
Bessborough Res
Knight Res
Hampton Ct Br
HAMPTON COURT PALACE
Hampton Court Park
A308
WATERSIDE DRIVE
TERRACE RD
WALTON ROAD
East Molesey
ISLAND FARM RD
A309
HAMPTON COURT WAY
SUMMER RD
A307
SURBITON
SURBITON HILL PARK
Berrylands
Queen Elizabeth II Reservoir
Island Barn Reservoir
Thames Ditton
PORTSMOUTH RD
B364
Coll
UPPER BRIGHTON RD
EWELL ROAD
A240
TOLWORTH RISE
A3
Fieldcommon
River Ember
EMBER LANE
WALTON-ON-THAMES
Rydens
HERSHAM ROAD
A244
RYDENS ROAD
MOLESEY ROAD
SANDOWN PARK
Hinchley Wood
KINGSTON BY-PASS
Long Ditton
DITTON ROAD
HOOK ROAD
HOOK RISE
Tolworth
A240
WORCESTER PARK RD
STATION AVE
Littleworth Common
ESHER
A309
Govt Offices
Hook Interchange
A3
CLAYTON ROAD
HUNTERS RD
COX LANE
JUBILEE WAY
ESHER RD
A317
HERSHAM
LAMMAS LA
HIGH ST
CLAREMONT LANE
MILBOURNE LA
HARE LA
OAKEN LANE
RED LA
WOODSTOCK LANE SOUTH
A243
BRIDGE LA
CHESSINGTON
CHESSINGTON RD
RUXLEY LA
West Ewell
BURWOOD
River Mole
WEST END LA
PORTSMOUTH RD
West End Common
CLAREMONT LANDSCAPE GARDEN
Arbrook Common
CLAYGATE
STEVENS LA
GARRISON LANE
HORTON
COPSEM LA
Esher Common
CHESSINGTON WORLD OF ADVENTURES
LEATHERHEAD ROAD
CHESSINGTON RD
HOOK RD
LONG GROVE RD
Oxshott
FAIROAK LANE
B280
Malden Rushett
RUSHETT LA
SANDY LANE
Heath
COPSEM LA
WARREN LA
Fairmile
Prince's Coverts
CHRIST CHURCH RD
WEST HILL
TARTAR HILL
PORTSMOUTH RD
A307
Cobham
LEIGH HILL RD
LITTLE HEATH LA
Oxshott
Stoke Wood
Epsom Common
EPSOM
BETWEEN STREETS
STEEL'S LA
A243
The Forest
Little Heath
LEATHERHEAD RD
OXSHOTT ROAD
KINGSTON RD
DORKING RD
A24
River Mole
A245
WATER LANE
TILT RD
STOKE RD
Cobham Park
Stoke D'Abernon
Pachesham Park
Wood Field
Woodcote
CRADDOCKS AVE
EPSOM RD
WOODLANDS LA
PLOUGH LA
DOWNSIDE RD
CHILBROOK RD
OAKLAWN RD
RANDALLS RD
BARNET WOOD LANE
WOODFIELD LA
Lower Ashstead
M25
Downside
Leatherhead Common
OTTWAYS LA
Ashstead
LEATHERHEAD RD
Langley Vale
HORSLEY ROAD
COBHAM ROAD
LEATHERHEAD
LEATHERHEAD BY-PASS
PEBBLE LA
Banks Common
Great Bookham Common
EPSOM RD
HIGHLANDS RD
Little Bookham Common
COBHAM RD
THE STREET
LOWER RD
HAWK'S HILL
GIMCRACK DORKING RD
REIGATE RD
HEADLEY RD
Fetcham
Effingham Common
EFFINGHAM COMMON ROAD
CHURCH RD
THE PARK
GUILDFORD RD
THE RIDGEWAY
YOUNG ST
Tyrell's Wood
MILL WAY
Leatherhead Downs
Nower Wood
A246
Little Bookham
LITTLE BOOKHAM ST
LOWER ROAD
BROCKETTS FARM PARK
Givons Grove
Headley
Great Bookham
Fetcham Downs
Mickleham Downs
RECTORY LA
LEECH LA

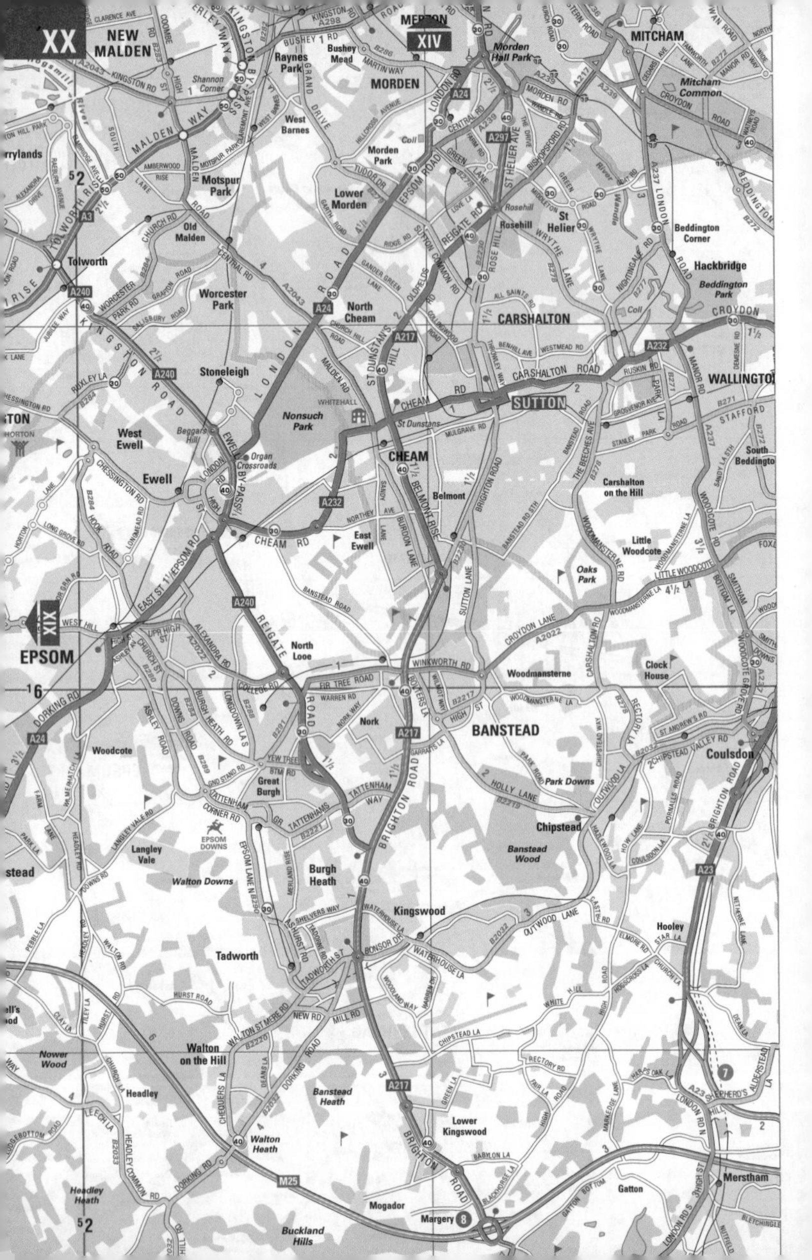
NEW MALDEN
MERTON
XIV
MITCHAM
Raynes Park
Bushey Mead
Morden Hall Park
Shannon Corner
MORDEN
Mitcham Common
West Barnes
Morden Park
Motspur Park
Lower Morden
Rosehill
St Helier
Old Malden
Beddington Corner
Tolworth
Hackbridge
Beddington Park
Worcester Park
North Cheam
CARSHALTON
Stoneleigh
WALLINGTON
SUTTON
Nonsuch Park
WHITEHALL
St Dunstans
West Ewell
Beggars Hill
Organ Crossroads
CHEAM
South Beddington
Ewell
Belmont
Carshalton on the Hill
East Ewell
Little Woodcote
Oaks Park
XIX
EPSOM
North Looe
Clock House
Woodmansterne
Nork
BANSTEAD
Woodcote
Coulsdon
Great Burgh
Park Downs
EPSOM DOWNS
Chipstead
Langley Vale
Banstead Wood
Walton Downs
Burgh Heath
Kingswood
Hooley
Tadworth
Walton on the Hill
Nower Wood
Headley
Banstead Heath
Lower Kingswood
Walton Heath
Merstham
Headley Heath
Gatton
Mogador
Margery
Buckland Hills
M25
A3
A24
A217
A232
A240
A23
A297
A2022

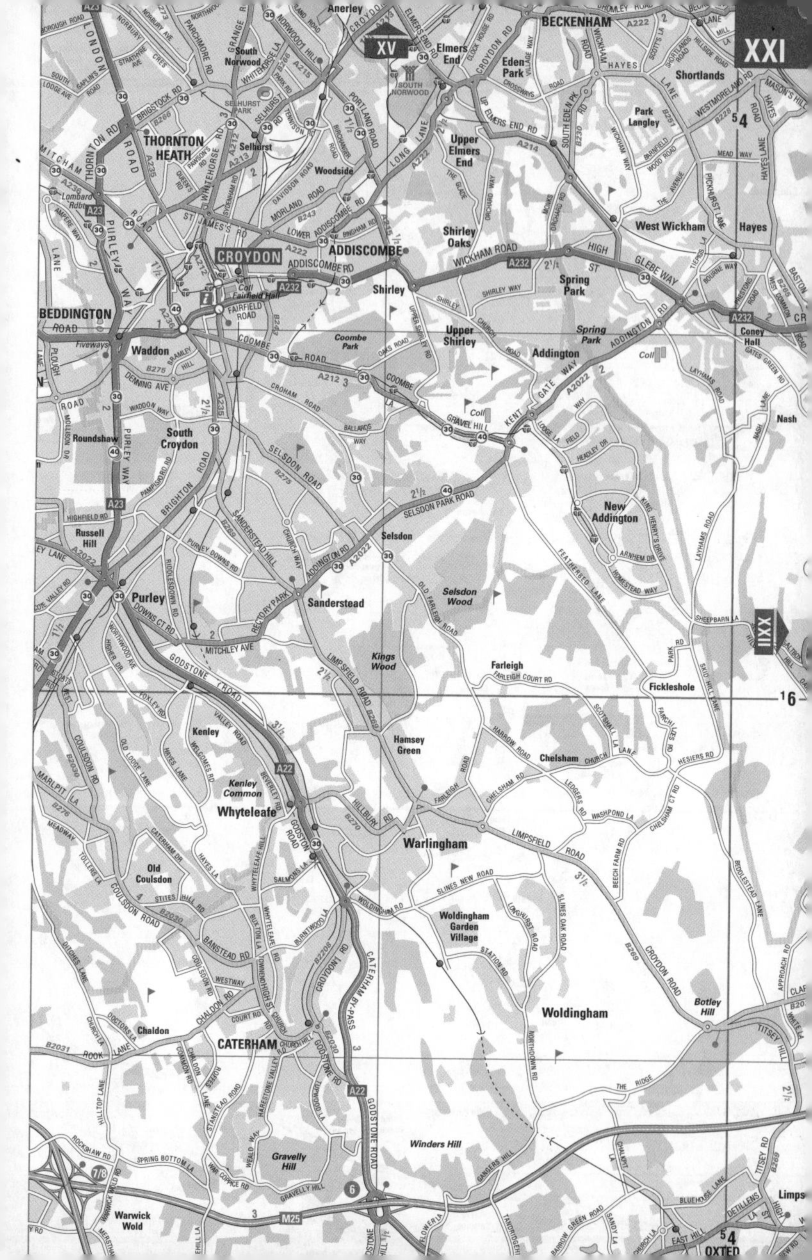
XXI
XV
XXII
BECKENHAM
Anerley
South Norwood
Elmers End
Eden Park
Shortlands
Park Langley
THORNTON HEATH
Selhurst
Woodside
Upper Elmers End
CROYDON
ADDISCOMBE
Shirley Oaks
West Wickham
Hayes
Shirley
Spring Park
Coney Hall
BEDDINGTON
Waddon
Coombe Park
Upper Shirley
Addington
Nash
Roundshaw
South Croydon
New Addington
Russell Hill
Selsdon
Purley
Sanderstead
Selsdon Wood
Kings Wood
Farleigh
Fickleshole
Kenley
Hamsey Green
Chelsham
Kenley Common
Whyteleafe
Warlingham
Old Coulsdon
Woldingham Garden Village
Woldingham
Botley Hill
Chaldon
CATERHAM
Winders Hill
Gravelly Hill
Warwick Wold
OXTED
A23
A232
A22
A2022
M25

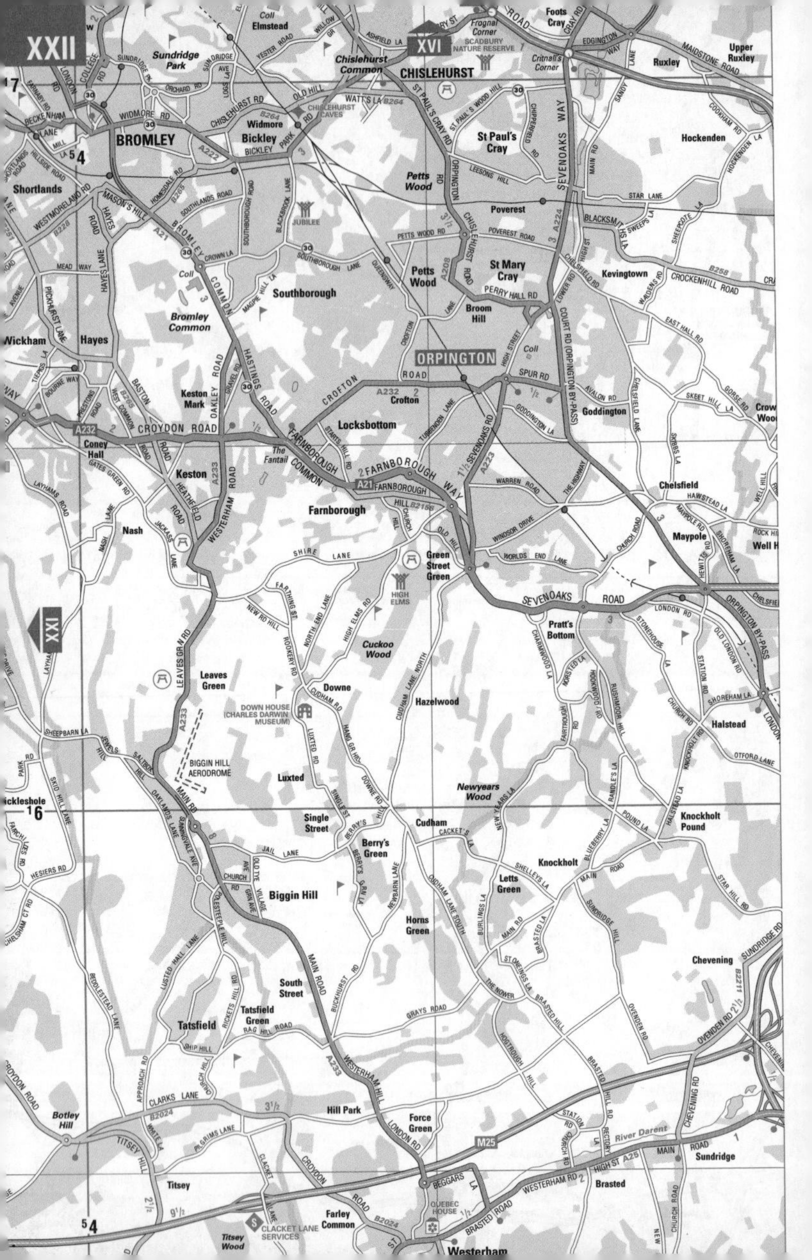
XVI
XXI
Coll
Elmstead
Sundridge
Park
Chislehurst
Common
CHISLEHURST
Frognal
Corner
SCADBURY
NATURE RESERVE
Foots
Cray
Critnall's
Corner
Upper
Ruxley
Ruxley
BROMLEY
Widmore
Bickley
CHISLEHURST
CAVES
St Paul's
Cray
Hockenden
Shortlands
Petts
Wood
Poverest
JUBILEE
St Mary
Cray
Kevingtown
Petts
Wood
Broom
Hill
Coll
Southborough
Bromley
Common
Wickham
Hayes
ORPINGTON
Coll
Keston
Mark
Crofton
Locksbottom
Goddington
Coney
Hall
The
Fantail
Keston
Chelsfield
Farnborough
Maypole
Nash
Green
Street
Green
HIGH
ELMS
Pratt's
Bottom
Cuckoo
Wood
Leaves
Green
Downe
Hazelwood
DOWN HOUSE
(CHARLES DARWIN
MUSEUM)
Halstead
BIGGIN HILL
AERODROME
Luxted
Newyears
Wood
Single
Street
Cudham
Knockholt
Pound
Berry's
Green
Knockholt
Letts
Green
Biggin Hill
Horns
Green
Chevening
South
Street
Tatsfield
Green
Tatsfield
Hill Park
Force
Green
Botley
Hill
Titsey
Brasted
Sundridge
Farley
Common
CLACKET LANE
SERVICES
Titsey
Wood
QUEBEC
HOUSE
Westerham
River Darent
M25
A21
A232
A233
A222
A223
A224
A208
A25
B264
B265
B228
B258
B2158
B2024
B2211
CROYDON ROAD
FARNBOROUGH WAY
SEVENOAKS ROAD
SEVENOAKS WAY
ORPINGTON BY-PASS
COURT RD (ORPINGTON BY-PASS)
MAIDSTONE ROAD
HASTINGS ROAD
OAKLEY ROAD
WESTERHAM ROAD
LEAVES GRN RD
MAIN RD
MAIN ROAD
WESTERHAM HILL
LONDON RD
HIGH STREET
SPUR RD
CROFTON ROAD
WIDMORE RD
BICKLEY PARK RD
CHISLEHURST RD
ST PAUL'S CRAY RD
ORPINGTON RD
CHISLEHURST ROAD
WINDSOR DRIVE
WORLDS END LANE
SHIRE LANE
CUDHAM LANE NORTH
CUDHAM LANE SOUTH
NEW YEARS LA
CLARKS LANE
PILGRIMS LANE
TITSEY HILL
WESTERHAM RD
HIGH ST
BRASTED ROAD
BEGGARS LA
OVENDEN ROAD
SUNDRIDGE RD
CHEVENING RD
STAR LANE
CROCKENHILL ROAD
EAST HALL RD
SKEET HILL LA
GORSE RD
OTFORD LANE
SHOREHAM LA
STAR HILL RD
SUNDRIDGE HILL
GRAYS ROAD
RAG HILL ROAD
SHIP HILL
CHURCH RD
JAIL LANE
CACKET'S LA
STONEHOUSE LA

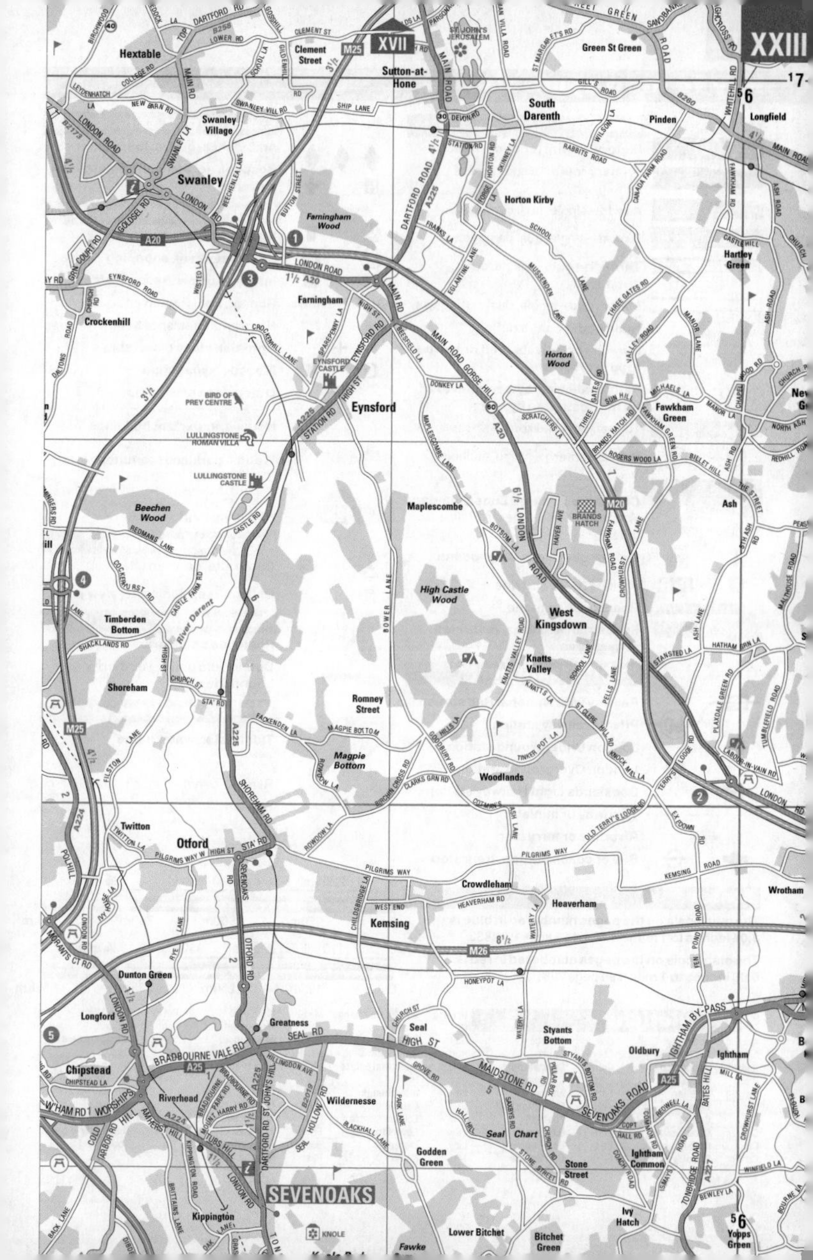
XXIII
XVII
Hextable
Clement Street
Sutton-at-Hone
St John's Jerusalem
Green St Green
South Darenth
Pinden
Longfield
Swanley Village
Swanley
Farningham Wood
Horton Kirby
Hartley Green
Crockenhill
Farningham
Eynsford Castle
Bird of Prey Centre
Eynsford
Lullingstone Roman Villa
Lullingstone Castle
Horton Wood
Fawkham Green
Ash
Beechen Wood
Maplescombe
Brands Hatch
High Castle Wood
West Kingsdown
Timberden Bottom
River Darent
Knatts Valley
Shoreham
Romney Street
Magpie Bottom
Woodlands
Twitton
Otford
Crowdleham
Heaverham
Kemsing
West End
Wrotham
Dunton Green
Longford
Greatness
Seal
Styants Bottom
Oldbury
Ightham
Chipstead
Riverhead
Wildernesse
Seal Chart
Godden Green
Stone Street
Ightham Common
SEVENOAKS
Kippington
Knole
Ivy Hatch
Lower Bitchet
Bitchet Green
Fawke
Yopps Green
M25
M20
M26
A20
A225
A224
A25
A227
B2173
B258
B260
B2019
London Road
Main Road
Dartford Road
Main Road Gorse Hill
Eynsford Road
Maidstone Road
Sevenoaks Road
Ightham By-Pass
Pilgrims Way
Bradbourne Vale Rd
Seal Rd
Tonbridge Road
Otford Road
Shoreham Rd
Kemsing Road
Honeypot La
Heaverham Rd
Ash Lane
Pells Lane
School Lane
Knatts Valley Road
Three Gates Rd
Valley Road
Mussenden Lane
Scratchers La
Rogers Wood La
Billet Hill
The Street
Manor Lane
Ash Road
Malthouse Road
Plaxdale Green Rd
Tumblefield Road
Labour-in-Vain Rd
Stansted La
Hatham Grn La
Crowhurst Lane
Fawkham Road
Haver Ave
Botsom La
Maplescombe Lane
Donkey La
Bower Lane
Beechen La
Button Street
Ship Lane
Swanley Vill Rd
Lower Rd
Top Dartford Rd
Clement St
Gildenhill
School La
Goldsel Rd
Grn Court Rd
Eynsford Road
Crockenhill Lane
Daltons Road
Church Rd
Redmans Lane
Cockerhurst Rd
Castle Farm Rd
Shacklands Rd
Church St
Filston Lane
Fackenden La
Magpie Bottom
Rowdow La
Birchin Cross Rd
Clarks Grn Rd
Cotmans Ash Lane
Old Terry's Lodge Rd
Terry's Lodge Rd
Knock Mill La
Tinker Pot La
St Clere Hill Rd
Knatts La
Hills La
Goodbury Rd
Childsbridge La
Watery La
Fen Pond Road
Pilgrims Way W
High St
Sta' Rd
Polhill
Morants Ct Rd
Twitton La
Rye Lane
Amherst Hill
Worships Hill
Chipstead La
Mount Harry Rd
Bradbourne Rd
St John's Hill
Hillingdon Ave
Seal Hollow Rd
Blackhall Lane
Park Lane
Grove Rd
Church St
Hall Rd
Church Rd
Saxbys Rd
Pillar Box Rd
Styants Bottom Rd
Coach Road
Common Rd
Redwell La
Mill La
Bates Hill
Crowhurst Lane
Winfield La
Bewley La
Bourne La
Tubs Hill
Kippington Road
Brittains Lane
Back Lane
Dartford Rd
Stone Street Rd
Gill's Road
Rabbits Road
Wilson La
Canada Farm Road
Horton Rd
Skinney La
Station Rd
Franks La
Eglantine Lane
Deion Rd
St Margaret's Rd
Sandbanks
Whitehill Rd
Castle Hill
Church Rd
Chapel Wood Rd
Michaels La
Manor La
North Ash Rd
Redhill Rd
Sun Hill
Brands Hatch Rd
Fawkham Green Rd
Ash Rd
Leydenhatch La
College Rd
New Barn Rd
Swanley La
Beechenlea Lane
Wisted La
Sparepenny La
Castle Rd
Beesfield La
Station Rd
Cheneys Rd
Ex-Down Rd

Key to map symbols

Roads

(22a) Motorway with junction number

Primary route – single, dual carriageway

A road – single, dual carriageway

B road – single, dual carriageway

Through-route – single, dual carriageway

Minor road – single, dual carriageway

Road under construction

Rural track, private road or narrow road in urban area

Path, bridleway, byway open to all traffic, restricted byway

Tunnel, covered road

(30) (30) Speed camera – single, multiple

Congestion Charge Zone boundary
Roads within the zone are outlined in green

Gate or obstruction, car pound

P P&R Parking, park and ride

Crooked Billet Road junction name

Pedestrianised area, restricted access area

Public transport

Railway with National Rail station

Private railway station

London Underground station

London Overground station

Docklands Light Railway station

Tramway or miniature railway

Riverbus or ferry pier

Bus or coach station, tram stop

Emergency services

Ambulance, police, fire station

Hospital, accident and emergency entrance

General features

Market, public amenity site

Sports stadium, shopping centre

Information centre, post office

VILLA House Roman, non-Roman antiquity

100 .304 House number, spot height – metres

Christian place of worship

Mosque, synagogue

Other place of worship

Houses, important buildings

Woods, parkland/common

123 Adjoining page number

Leisure facilities

Camp site, caravan site

Golf course, picnic site, view point

Boundaries

NW6 Postcode boundaries

Westminster County and unitary authority boundaries

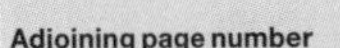

Water features

Barking Creek Tidal water, water name

River or canal – minor, major

Stream

Water

Scales

The map scale on the pages numbered in blue is
3.04 inches to 1 mile • 4.8cm to 1 km • 1 : 20833

0	220 yds	440yds	660yds	½ mile
0	250m	500m	750m	1km

The map scale on the pages numbered in red is
6.08 inches to 1 mile, see page 228

0	110 yds	220yds	330yds	¼ mile
0	125m	250m	375m	½km

Abbreviations

Acad	Academy	Coll	College	Drv Rng	Golf Driving Range	Meml	Memorial	Ret Pk	Retail Park
Allot Gdns	Allotments	Ct	Court	Gn	Green	Mon	Monument	Sch	School
Bndstd	Bandstand	Crem	Crematorium	Gd	Ground	Mus	Museum	Sh Ctr	Shopping Centre
Btcl	Botanical	Crkt	Cricket	Hort	Horticultural	Nat Res	Nature Reserve	Sp	Sports
Bwg Gn	Bowling	Ent	Enterprise	Ind Est	Industrial Estate	Obsy	Observatory	Stad	Stadium
Cemy	Cemetery	Ex H	Exhibition Hall	Inst	Institute	Pav	Pavilion	Sw Pool	Swimming Pool
Ctr	Centre	Fball	Football	Int	Interchange	Pk	Park	Tenn Cts	Tennis
C Ctr	Civic Centre	Gdns	Gardens	Ct	Law Court	Pl Fld	Playing Field	TH	Town Hall
CH	Club House	Glf C	Golf Course	L Ctr	Leisure Centre	Pal	Royal Palace	Trad Est	Trading Estate
Ctry Pk	Country Park	Glf Crs	Golf Course	LC	Level Crossing	PH	Public House	Univ	University
				Liby	Library	Recn Gd	Recreation Ground	YH	Youth Hostel
				Mkt	Market	Resr	Reservoir		

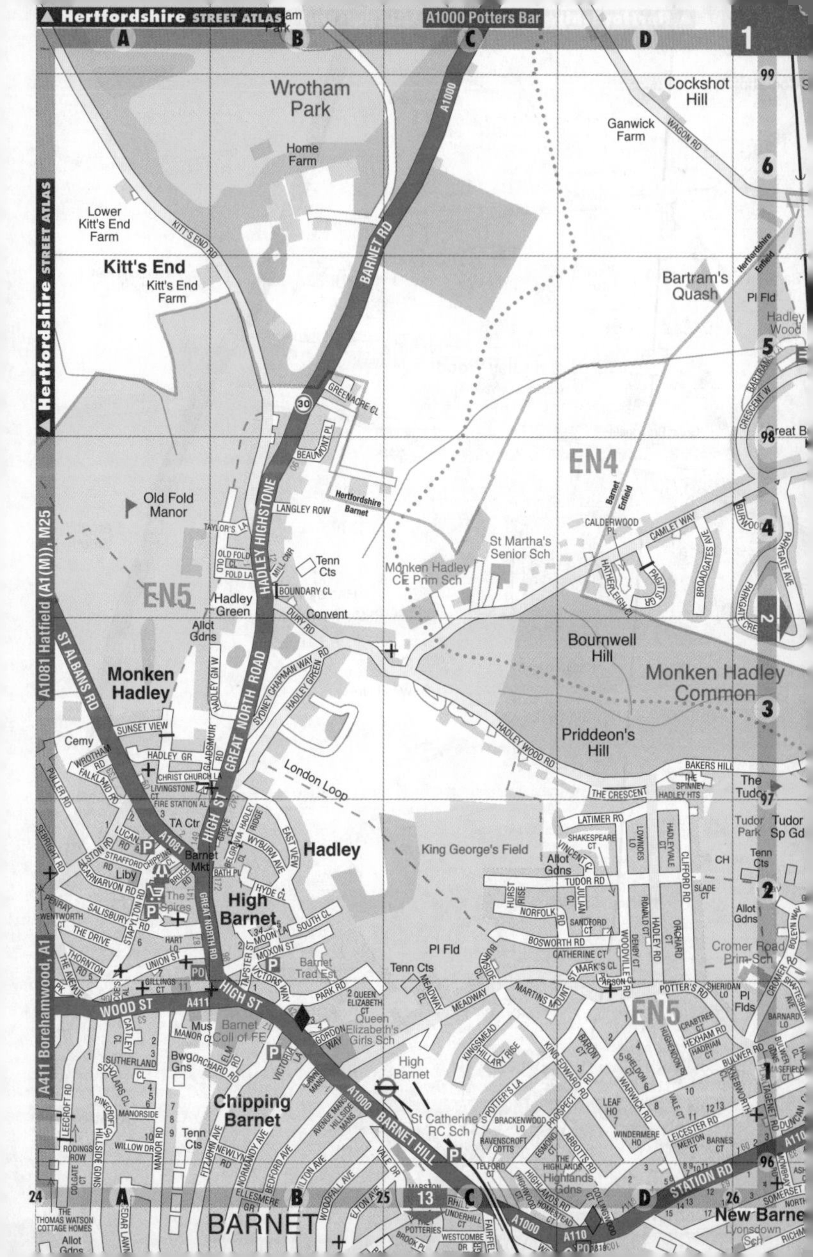
A1000 Potters Bar
Wrotham Park
Home Farm
Lower Kitt's End Farm
Kitt's End
Kitt's End Farm
KITT'S END RD
BARNET RD
A1000
Cockshot Hill
Ganwick Farm
WAGON RD
Bartram's Quash
Hertfordshire Enfield
Pl Fld
Hadley Wood
GREENACRE CL
BEAUMONT PL
Hertfordshire Barnet
LANGLEY ROW
TAYLOR'S LA
OLD FOLD CL
OLD FOLD LA
MILL CNR
BOUNDARY CL
HADLEY HIGHSTONE
Old Fold Manor
EN4
EN5
Barnet Enfield
CALDERWOOD PL
CAMLET WAY
St Martha's Senior Sch
Monken Hadley CE Prim Sch
Tenn Cts
HATHERLEIGH CL
PAGITTS GR
BROADGATES AVE
PARKGATE AVE
PARKGATE CRES
CRESCENT W
BARTRAMS LA
Great B
Hadley Green
Convent
DURY RD
Allot Gdns
Monken Hadley
HADLEY GN W
GREAT NORTH ROAD
SYDNEY CHAPMAN WAY
HADLEY GREEN RD
Bournwell Hill
Monken Hadley Common
Priddeon's Hill
HADLEY WOOD RD
BAKERS HILL
THE SPINNEY
HADLEY HTS
THE CRESCENT
The Tudor
Tudor Park
Tudor Sp Gd
ST ALBANS RD
SUNSET VIEW
Cemy
WROTHAM RD
FALKLAND RD
PULLER RD
HADLEY GR
GLADSMUIR RD
CHRIST CHURCH LA
LIVINGSTONE CT
FIRE STATION AL
London Loop
TA Ctr
A1081
HIGH ST
GROVE
BELGRAVIA
HADLEY RIDGE
WYBURN AVE
EAST VIEW
Hadley
King George's Field
LATIMER RD
SHAKESPEARE CT
VINCENT CL
LOWNDES LO
HADLEYVALE CT
CLIFFORD RD
CH
SEBRIGHT RD
ALSTON RD
LUCAN RD
STRAFFORD RD
CHIPPING CL
Barnet Mkt
BATH PL
HYDE CL
Allot Gdns
TUDOR RD
HURST RISE
JULIAN CL
NORFOLK RD
SANDFORD CT
RONALD CT
HADLEY RD
ORCHARD CT
SLADE CT
Tenn Cts
Allot Gdns
CARNARVON RD
Liby
BRUCE RD
The Spires
High Barnet
SOUTH CL
MOON LA
MOXON ST
PENRAY
WENTWORTH CT
SALISBURY RD
STAPYLTON RD
THE DRIVE
HART LO
TAPSTER ST
VICTORS WAY
Barnet Trad Est
Pl Fld
BOSWORTH RD
CATHERINE CT
ST MARK'S CL
DENBY CT
WOODVILLE RD
Cromer Road Prim Sch
THORNTON RD
THE AVENUE
UNION ST
PO
GILLINGS CT
PARK RD
QUEEN ELIZABETH CT
Tenn Cts
MEADWAY CL
MEADWAY
BURNSIDE CL
MARTINS MOUNT
PARSON CL
POTTER'S RD
SHERIDAN LO
Pl Flds
CROMER RD
SHAFTESBURY AVE
BARNARD LO
WOOD ST
A411
HIGH ST
Mus
MANOR CL
Barnet Coll of FE
GORDON WAY
Queen Elizabeth's Girls Sch
EN5
CRABTREE CT
HEXHAM RD
HADRIAN CT
BULWER RD
CATLEY
SUTHERLAND CL
SCHOLARS CL
Bwg Gns
ORCHARD RD
ELM
VICTORIA LA
LAWN MANS
High Barnet
KINGSMEAD
HILLARY RISE
KING EDWARD RD
BARON CT
SHELDON CT
HUGHENDON
WARWICK RD
KNEBWORTH
DUNCAN
PINECROFT CR
MANORSIDE
Chipping Barnet
A1000
BARNET HILL
AVENUE MANS
HILLSIDE MANS
St Catherine's RC Sch
POTTER'S LA
BRACKENWOOD LO
PROSPECT RD
LEAF HO
VALE CT
LEICESTER RD
MERTON CT
BARNES CT
WINDERMERE HO
LEECROFT RD
RODINGS ROW
WILLOW DR
HILLSIDE GDNS
MANOR RD
Tenn Cts
FITZJOHN AVE
NEWLYN RD
NORMANDY AVE
BEDFORD AVE
MILTON AVE
VALE DR
RAVENSCROFT COTTS
ESMOND CT
ABBOTTS RD
THE HIGHLANDS
Highlands Gdns
TELFORD CT
STATION RD
A110
MOWBRAY
SOMERSET
COLGATE CT
THE THOMAS WATSON COTTAGE HOMES
Allot Gdns
CEDAR LAWN
ELLESMERE GR
BARNET
WOODFALL AVE
ELTON AVE
MARSTON
THE POTTERIES
BROOK PL
UNDERHILL CT
WESTCOMBE DR
FAIRFIELD
HIGHWOOD CT
HIGHLANDS RD
HOMESTEAD
COLLINGWOOD
New Barnet
Lyonsdown Sch
RICHMOND
A1081 Hatfield (A1(M)), M25
A411 Borehamwood, A1
A B C D
99 98 97 96
6 5 4 3 2 1
24 25 26

13

2

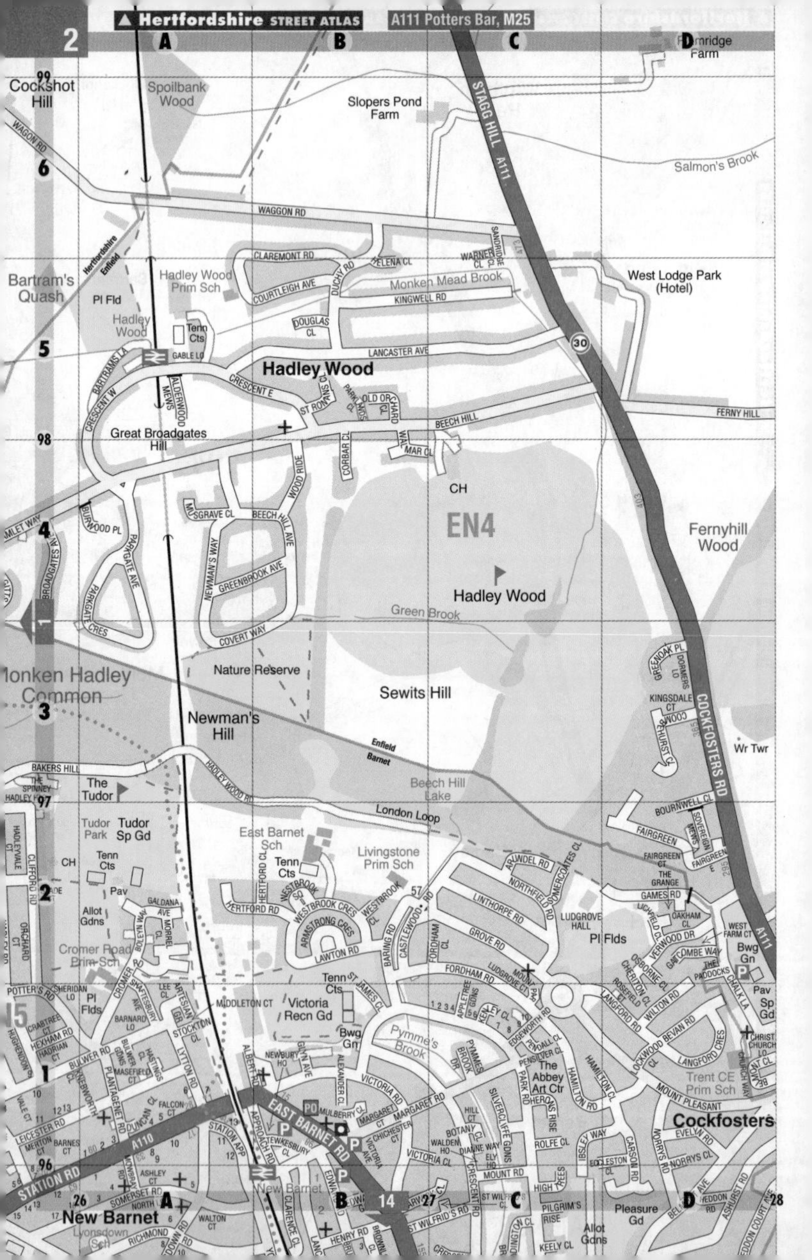
2
Hertfordshire STREET ATLAS
A111 Potters Bar, M25
A
B
C
D
Cockshot Hill
Spoilbank Wood
Slopers Pond Farm
Ferny Hill Farm
STAGG HILL
A111
WAGON RD
Salmon's Brook
WAGGON RD
Hertfordshire
Enfield
Bartram's Quash
Pl Fld
Hadley Wood Prim Sch
Hadley Wood
Tenn Cts
GABLE LO
CLAREMONT RD
COURTLEIGH AVE
DUCHY RD
HELENA CL
WARNER CL
SANDRIDGE CL
Monken Mead Brook
KINGWELL RD
DOUGLAS CL
LANCASTER AVE
West Lodge Park (Hotel)
Hadley Wood
BARTRAMS LA
CRESCENT W
CRESCENT E
ALDERWOOD MEWS
ST RONANS CL
PARK MOS CL
OLD ORCHARD CL
BEECH HILL
FERNY HILL
Great Broadgates Hill
CORBAR CL
WAL MAR CL
CH
WOOD RIDE
MUSGRAVE CL
BEECH HILL AVE
HAMLET WAY
BURWOOD PL
BROADGATES AVE
PARKGATE AVE
PARKGATE CRES
NEWMAN'S WAY
GREENBROOK AVE
COVERT WAY
EN4
Hadley Wood
Fernyhill Wood
Green Brook
Monken Hadley Common
Nature Reserve
Sewits Hill
Newman's Hill
GREENOAK PL
DORMERS
KINGSDALE CT
COOMBEHURST CL
COCKFOSTERS RD
Wr Twr
Enfield
Barnet
BAKERS HILL
THE SPINNEY
HADLEY WOOD RD
The Tudor
Beech Hill Lake
London Loop
BOURNWELL CL
SOVEREIGN MEWS
FAIRGREEN
FAIRGREEN CT
FAIRGREEN E
Tudor Park
Tudor Sp Gd
East Barnet Sch
Tenn Cts
Livingstone Prim Sch
ARUNDEL RD
NORTHFIELD RD
SOMERCOATES CL
THE GRANGE
GAMES RD
HADLEYVALE CT
CLIFFORD RD
ORCHARD CT
CH
Pav
Allot Gdns
GALDANA AVE
MORREL CL
BOLEYN WAY
HERTFORD CL
HERTFORD RD
WESTBROOK SQ
WESTBROOK CRES
WESTBROOK CL
ARMSTRONG CRES
LAWTON RD
BARING RD
CASTLEWOOD RD
FORDHAM CL
LINTHORPE RD
GROVE RD
LUDGROVE HALL
Pl Flds
LICHFIELD CL
OAKHAM CL
WEST FARM CT
VERWOOD DR
GATCOMBE WAY
Bwg Gn
THE PADDOCKS
A111
Cromer Road Prim Sch
CROMER RD
SHAFTESBURY AVE
LEE CL
ARTESIAN GR
FORDHAM RD
LUDGROVE CT
MOUNT PARK
Tenn Cts
ST JAMES CL
Victoria Recn Gd
MIDDLETON CT
POTTER'S RD
SHERIDAN LO
Pl Flds
BARNARD LO
STOCKTON CL
CRABTREE CT
HEXHAM RD
HADRIAN CT
HUGHENDON CT
BULWER RD
BULWER GDNS
MASEFIELD CT
HASTINGS CT
LYTTON RD
NEWBURY HO
GLYNN AVE
ALBERT RD
ALEXANDER CL
Bwg Gn
Pymme's Brook
APPLETREE GDNS
KENLEY CL
EDGEWORTH RD
PENDALL CL
PENSILVER CL
PYMMES BROOK DR
The Abbey Art Ctr
HAMILTON RD
HAMILTON CL
OSBORNE CL
CHERITON CL
ROSEFIELD CL
LANGFORD RD
WILTON RD
LOCKWOOD CL
BEVAN RD
LANGFORD CRES
CHALK LA
Pav
Sp Gd
CHRIST CHURCH LO
CHURCH WAY
Trent CE Prim Sch
MOUNT PLEASANT
KNEBWORTH CL
PLANTAGENET RD
DUNCAN CL
FALCON CT
VICTORIA RD
MARGARET RD
MULBERRY CL
MARGARET CT
CHICHESTER CT
HILL CT
BOTANY CL
WALDEN HO
DIANNE WAY
ELY HO
SILVERCLIFFE GDNS
PARK RD
HERONS RISE
ROLFE CL
IBSLEY WAY
CARSON RD
Cockfosters
EVELYN RD
NORRYS CL
MORRYS RD
LEICESTER RD
MERTON CT
BARNES CT
STATION APP
APPROACH RD
EAST BARNET RD
TEWKESBURY CL
VICTORIA AVE
VICTORIA CL
CRESCENT RD
MOUNT RD
ECCLESTON CL
HIGH TREES
STATION RD
A110
ASHLEY CT
SOMERSET RD
NORTH
New Barnet
New Barnet
A
B
C
D
26
27
28
14
15
EDWARD
HENRY RD
CLARENCE CL
WALTON CT
RICHMOND
Lyonsdown Sch
ST WILFRID'S RD
ST WILFRID'S
PILGRIM'S RISE
Pleasure Gd
Allot Gdns
KEELY CL
BELLE AVE
HEDDON RD
ASHURST RD
HEDDON COURT AVE
99
6
5
98
4
3
97
2
1
96
1

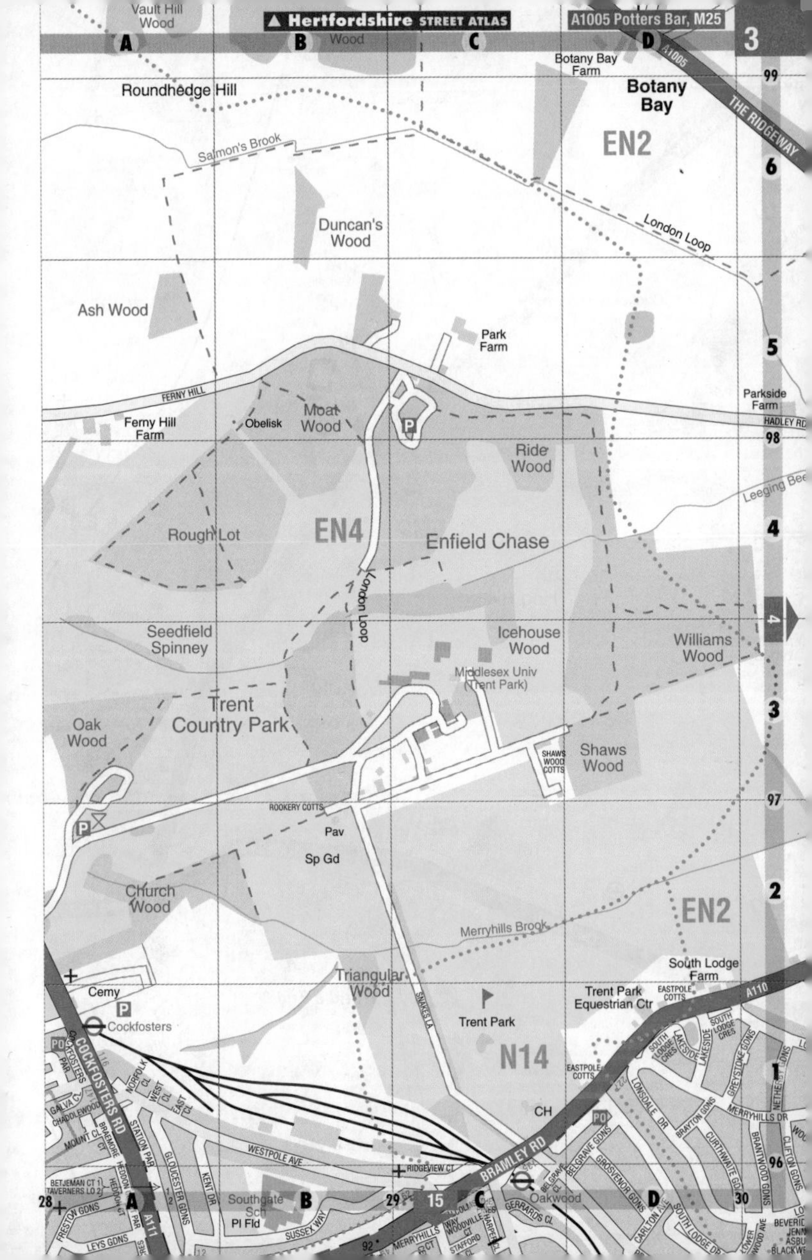
Vault Hill Wood
Wood
A
B
C
D
Botany Bay Farm
A1005
99
Roundhedge Hill
Botany Bay
THE RIDGEWAY
EN2
Salmon's Brook
6
Duncan's Wood
London Loop
Ash Wood
Park Farm
5
FERNY HILL
Parkside Farm
Ferny Hill Farm
Obelisk
Moat Wood
P
HADLEY RD
98
Ride Wood
Leeging Bee
EN4
Rough Lot
Enfield Chase
4
London Loop
4
Seedfield Spinney
Icehouse Wood
Williams Wood
Middlesex Univ (Trent Park)
3
Trent Country Park
Oak Wood
SHAWS WOOD COTTS
Shaws Wood
ROOKERY COTTS
97
P
Pav
Sp Gd
2
Church Wood
EN2
Merryhills Brook
South Lodge Farm
Triangular Wood
Cemy
Trent Park Equestrian Ctr
EASTPOLE COTTS
A110
SNAKES LA
P
Trent Park
Cockfosters
SOUTH LODGE CRES
LAKESIDE
GREYSTOKE GDNS
PO
COCKFOSTERS RD
COCKFOSTERS PAR
N14
EASTPOLE COTTS
1
NORFOLK CL
WEST CL
EAST CL
NETHERBY GDNS
GALVA CL
CHADDLEWOOD
LONSDALE DR
BRAYTON GDNS
MERRYHILLS DR
CH
PO
MOUNT CL
BRAEMORE CT
STATION PAR
GLOUCESTER GDNS
KENT DR
BELGRAVE GDNS
GROSVENOR GDNS
CURTHWAITE GDNS
BRANTWOOD GDNS
CLIFTON GDNS
WESTPOLE AVE
BRAMLEY RD
96
RIDGEVIEW CT
BETJEMAN CT
TAVERNERS LO
HEDDON CT
BELGRAVE CL
28
A
Southgate Sch
B
29
15
C
Oakwood
D
30
FRESTON GDNS
A111
PAR
Pl Fld
SUSSEX WAY
GERRARDS CL
CARLTON AVE
SOUTH LODGE DR
LOWER WOOD AVE
LEYS GDNS
92
MERRYHILLS CT
WAY
WOODVILLE CT
STAFFORD CT
HARPER CL
BEVERIDGE

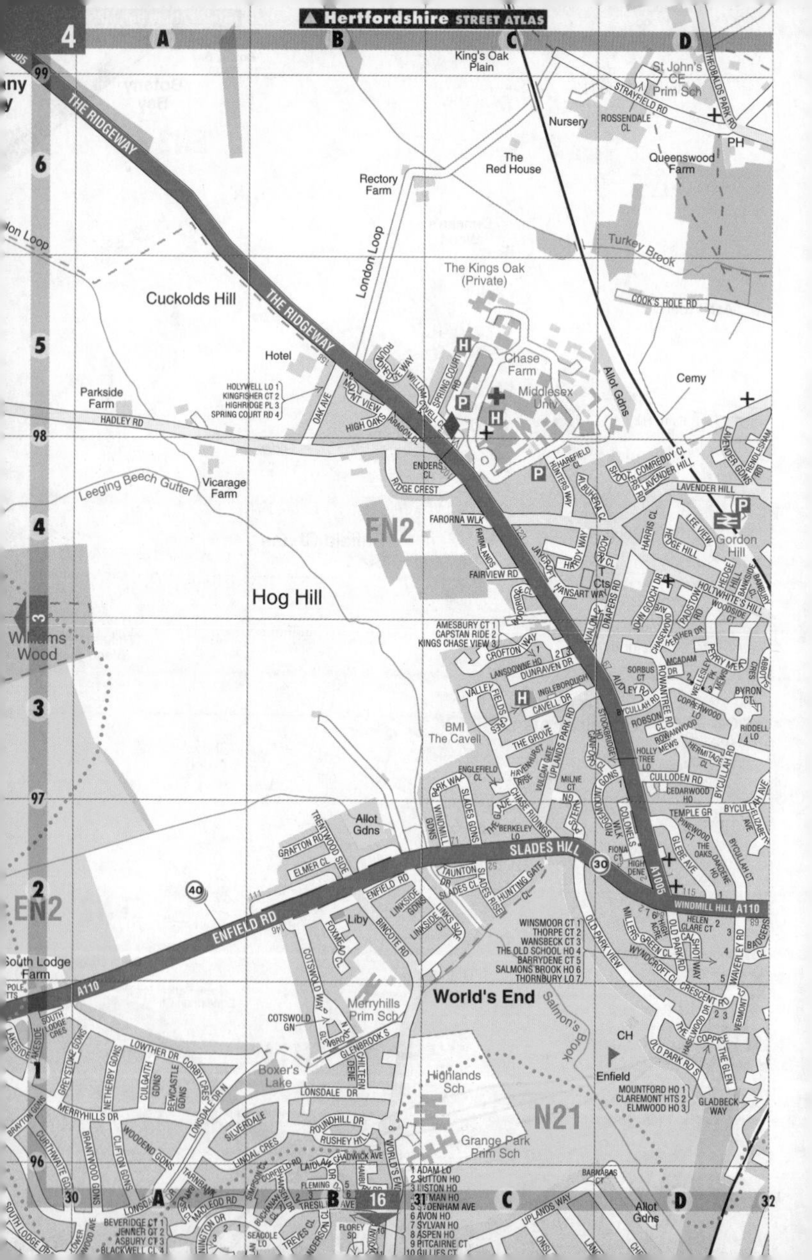

THE RIDGEWAY

King's Oak Plain

St John's CE Prim Sch

ROSSENDALE CL

Nursery

Queenswood Farm

PH

Rectory Farm

The Red House

London Loop

Turkey Brook

Cuckolds Hill

The Kings Oak (Private)

COOK'S HOLE RD

THE RIDGEWAY

Hotel

HOLYWELL LO 1
KINGFISHER CT 2
HIGHRIDGE PL 3
SPRING COURT RD 4

H

Chase Farm

Middlesex Univ

Cemy

Parkside Farm

HADLEY RD

HIGH OAKS

P

H

P

LAVENDER HILL

Leeging Beech Gutter

Vicarage Farm

ENDERS CL

EDGE CREST

Gordon Hill

EN2

FARORNA WLK

P

Hog Hill

FAIRVIEW RD

LEE VIEW

BYRON

AMESBURY CT 1
CAPSTAN RIDE 2
KINGS CHASE VIEW 3

CROFTON WAY

RIDDELL LO

Williams Wood

LANGDOWNE

DUNRAVEN DR

INGLEBOROUGH

SORBUS CT

H

VALLEY RD

CAVELL DR

ACADAM

ROBSON

BMI The Cavell

THE GROVE

HOLLY MEWS

CULLODEN RD

CEDARWOOD HO

ENGLEFIELD

MILNE

TEMPLE GR

PARK WAY

THE BERKELEY

SLADES GDNS

FIONA

BYCULLA

THE OAKS

Allot Gdns

GRAFTON GDNS

ELMER CL

SLADES HILL

30

WINDMILL HILL A110

HIGH DENE

ENFIELD RD

40

TAUNTON

HUNTING GATE

MILLERS GREEN CL

HELEN CLARE CT

WYNDHORPE

Liby

ENFIELD RD

LINSCOTT GDNS

BINCOTE RD

OLD PARK VIEW

WINSMOOR CT 1
THORPE CT 2
WANSBECK CT 3
THE OLD SCHOOL HO 4
BARRYDENE CT 5
SALMONS BROOK HO 6
THORNBURY LO 7

COTSWOLD WAY

South Lodge Farm

A110

SOUTH LODGE

LOWTHER DR

GLENBROOK

CHILTERN

COTSWOLD GN

Merryhills Prim Sch

Boxer's Lake

Highlands Sch

LONSDALE DR

World's End

Salmon's Brook

CH

Enfield

N21

MOUNTFORD HO 1
CLAREMONT HTS 2
ELMWOOD HO 3

GLADBECK WAY

EN2

MERRYHILLS DR

BRAINTWOOD GDNS

CLAY

WOODEND GDNS

SILVERDALE

LUCAS CRES

RYONHILL DR

RUSHEY HY

Grange Park Prim Sch

BARNABAS

UPLANDS WAY

Allot Gdns

30

A

BEVERIDGE CT 1
JINNER CT 2
ASBURY CT 3
BLACKWELL CL 4

B

16

C

D

32

1 ADAM LO
2 SUTTON HO
3 MAN HO
4 OAK HO
5 FORNHAM AVE
6 AVON HO
7 SYLVAN HO
8 ASPEN HO
9 RITCAIRNE CT
10 GILLIES CT

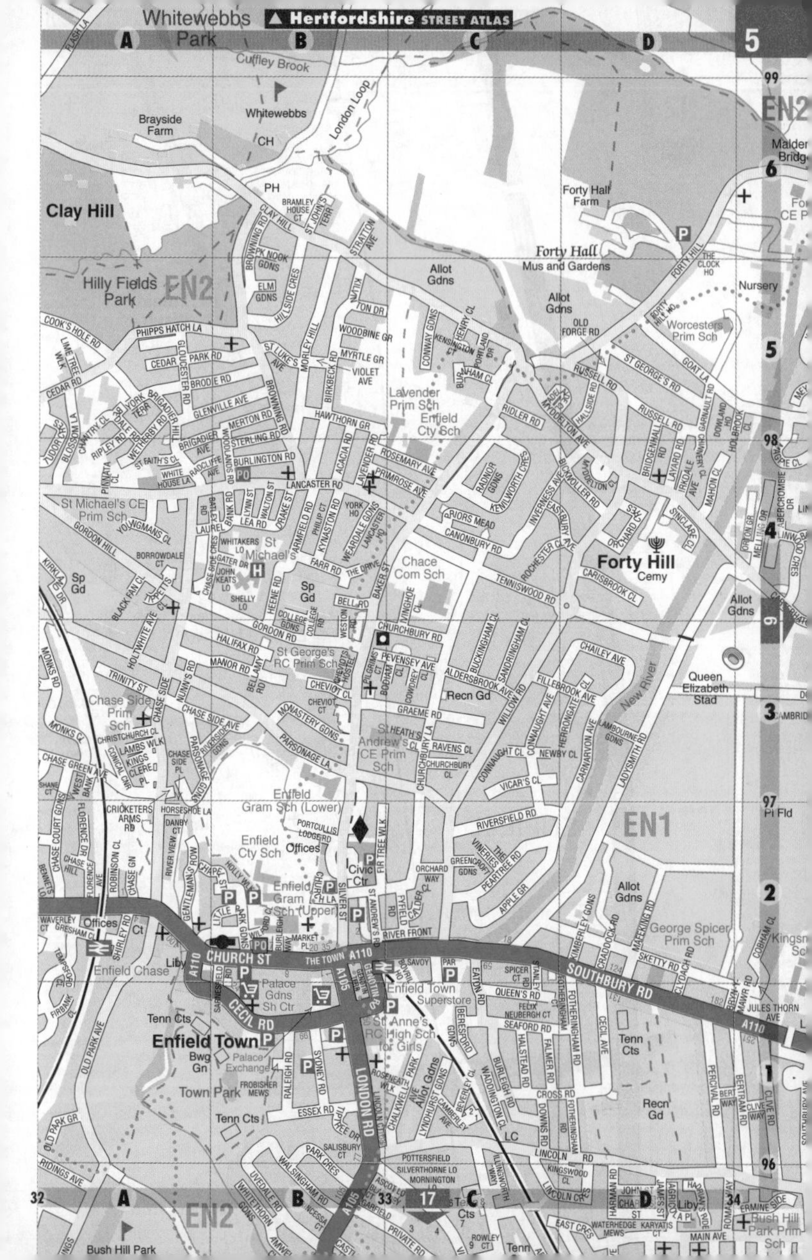
Whitewebbs Park
A
B
C
D
Cuffley Brook
Whitewebbs
Brayside Farm
CH
London Loop
PH
Clay Hill
Hilly Fields Park
EN2
BRAMLEY HOUSE CT
ST JOHN'S TERR
CLAY HILL
STRATTON AVE
BROWNING RD
PK NOOK GDNS
ELM GDNS
HILLSIDE CRES
Forty Hall Farm
Forty Hall
Mus and Gardens
Allot Gdns
FORTY HILL
THE CLOCK HO
Nursery
Worcesters Prim Sch
Malden Bridge
COOK'S HOLE RD
PHIPPS HATCH LA
CEDAR RD
CEDAR
PARK RD
GLOUCESTER RD
BRODIE RD
GLENVILLE AVE
MERTON RD
STERLING RD
BURLINGTON RD
BRIGADIER HILL
BRIGADIER AVE
WETHERBY RD
RIPLEY RD
CHANTRY CL
TUDOR CRES
BLOSSOM LA
LIME TREE WLK
ST LUKE'S AVE
MORLEY HILL
BIRKBECK RD
VIOLET AVE
WOODBINE GR
MYRTLE GR
TON DR
HAWTHORN GR
ACACIA RD
LAVENDER RD
ROSEMARY AVE
PRIMROSE AVE
Lavender Prim Sch
Enfield Cty Sch
CONWAY GDNS
KENSINGTON CT
HENRY CL
PORTLAND DR
BURNHAM CL
OLD FORGE RD
RUSSELL RD
ST GEORGE'S RD
GOAT LA
RIDLER RD
MYDDELTON AVE
HALLSIDE RD
BRIDGENHALL RD
LAYARD RD
IRKDALE AVE
MAHON CL
HOLBROOK CL
ABERCROMBIE DR
ORTON GR
MELLING DR
LINWOOD CRES
WHITE HOUSE LA
RADCLIFFE AVE
PINNATA CL
ST FAITH'S CL
LANCASTER RD
PO
St Michael's CE Prim Sch
YOUNGMANS CL
LAUREL
BANK RD
LYNN ST
WALTON ST
DRAKE ST
LEA RD
ARMFIELD RD
PHILIP CT
KYNASTON RD
YORK HO
WEARDALE GDNS
LANCASTER HO
RADNOR GDNS
KENILWORTH CRES
PRIORS MEAD
CANONBURY RD
INVERNESS AVE
EASTBURY AVE
ROCHESTER CL
BICKNOLLER RD
MYDDELTON CL
ORCHARD CL
SINCLARE CL
Forty Hill
Cemy
GORDON HILL
BORROWDALE CT
WHITAKERS LO
GATER DR
JOHN KEATS LO
St Michael's
H
SHELLY LO
Sp Gd
FARR RD
THE DRIVE
Chace Com Sch
TENNISWOOD RD
CARISBROOK CL
Allot Gdns
BLACK FAN CL
HOLTWHITE AVE
PETTS
HEENE RD
BELL RD
IVINGHOE CL
COLLEGE GDNS
COLLEGE RD
WESTON RD
BAKER ST
CHURCHBURY RD
GORDON RD
HALIFAX RD
St George's RC Prim Sch
BELLAMY RD
CHEVIOTS HOSTEL
PILGRIMS CT
PEVENSEY AVE
BODIAM CL
COWDREY CL
BUCKINGHAM CL
SANDRINGHAM CL
CHAILEY AVE
Queen Elizabeth Stad
New River
MANOR RD
TRINITY ST
NUNN'S RD
CHASE SIDE
CHEVIOT CL
CHEVIOT CT
ALDERSBROOK AVE
WILLOW RD
Recn Gd
FILLEBROOK AVE
CONNAUGHT AVE
HERRONGATE CL
GRAEME RD
Chase Side Prim Sch
CHASE SIDE AVE
MONASTERY GDNS
RIVERSIDE GDNS
PARSONAGE GDNS
PARSONAGE LA
MONKS RD
MONKS CL
CHRISTCHURCH CL
LAMBS WLK
KINGS
CLERE
CONICAL CNR
PL
CHASE SIDE PL
St Andrew's CE Prim Sch
HEATH'S CL
RAVENS CL
CHURCHBURY CL
CHURCHBURY LA
CONNAUGHT CL
NEWBY CL
VICAR'S CL
CARNARVON AVE
LAMBOURNE GDNS
LADYSMITH RD
CHASE GREEN AVE
WEST BANK
SHANE CT
CRICKETERS ARMS RD
HORSESHOE LA
DANBY CT
Enfield Gram Sch (Lower)
PORTCULLIS LODGE RD
RIVERSFIELD RD
EN1
CHASE COURT GDNS
FLORENCE DR
CHASE HILL
ROBINSON CL
CHASE GN
RIVER VIEW
GENTLEMAN'S ROW
CHAPEL ST
HOLLY WK
Enfield Cty Sch
Offices
Civic Ctr
FIR TREE WLK
THE VINERIES
PEARTREE RD
GREENCROFT GDNS
ORCHARD WAY CL
APPLE GR
BENNETS
AVE
Enfield Gram Sch (Upper)
CHURCH LA
SILVER ST
ST ANDREW'S RD
FYFIELD RD
CALDER CL
RIVER FRONT
KIMBERLEY GDNS
CRADDOCK RD
MAFEKING RD
George Spicer Prim Sch
COBHAM CL
Kingsm Sch
WAVERLEY
GRESHAM CL
Offices
SHIRLEY RD
Ct
LITTLE PARK GDNS
BURLEIGH WAY
MARKET PL
CHURCH ST
A110
THE TOWN
Liby
Enfield Chase
SARNESFIELD RD
Palace Gdns Sh Ctr
A105
GENOTIN TERR
GENOTIN RD
SAVOY
BOURNE HO
PAR
Enfield Town
Superstore
EATON RD
SPICER CT
STANLEY CT
QUEEN'S RD
FELIX NEUBERGH CT
SEAFORD RD
SOUTHBURY RD
SKETTY RD
CLYDACH RD
BRYN Y MAWR RD
JULES THORN AVE
TEMPSFORD
FIRBANK CL
CECIL RD
Tenn Cts
Enfield Town
Bwg Gn
Palace Exchange
OLD PARK AVE
RALEIGH RD
SYDNEY RD
LONDON RD
ST Anne's RC High Sch for Girls
BERESFORD GDNS
HALSTEAD RD
FALMER RD
FOTHERINGHAM RD
CECIL AVE
Tenn Cts
PERCIVAL RD
BERTRAM RD
BERT WAY
CLIVE WAY
CLIVE RD
Town Park
FROBISHER MEWS
ROSENEATH WLK
PARK AVE
CHALKWELL
Allot Gdns
LYNDHURST GDNS
CAMBERLEY AVE
BEVERLEY CL
BURLEIGH RD
WADDINGTON CL
DOWNS RD
CROSS RD
Recn Gd
ESSEX RD
TIPTREE DR
OLD PARK GR
LC
LINCOLN RD
SALISBURY CT
PARK CRES
POTTERSFIELD
SILVERTHORNE LO
MORNINGTON LO
ILLINGWORTH WAY
KINGSWOOD CL
LINCOLN CRES
RIDINGS AVE
WALSINGHAM RD
UVEDALE RD
WHITETHORN GDNS
ASCOT LO
GARFIELD
PRIVATE RD
ROWLEY CT
HARMAN RD
JOHN ST
CHARLES ST
JAMES ST
AGRICOLA PL
HADRIAN'S RIDE
ROMAN WAY
ERMINE SIDE
EAST CRES
WATERHEDGE MEWS
KARYATIS CT
MAIN AVE
Bush Hill Park Prim Sch
Bush Hill Park
EN2
99
98
97
96
6
5
4
3
2
1
Pl Fld
9
16
17
32
33
34

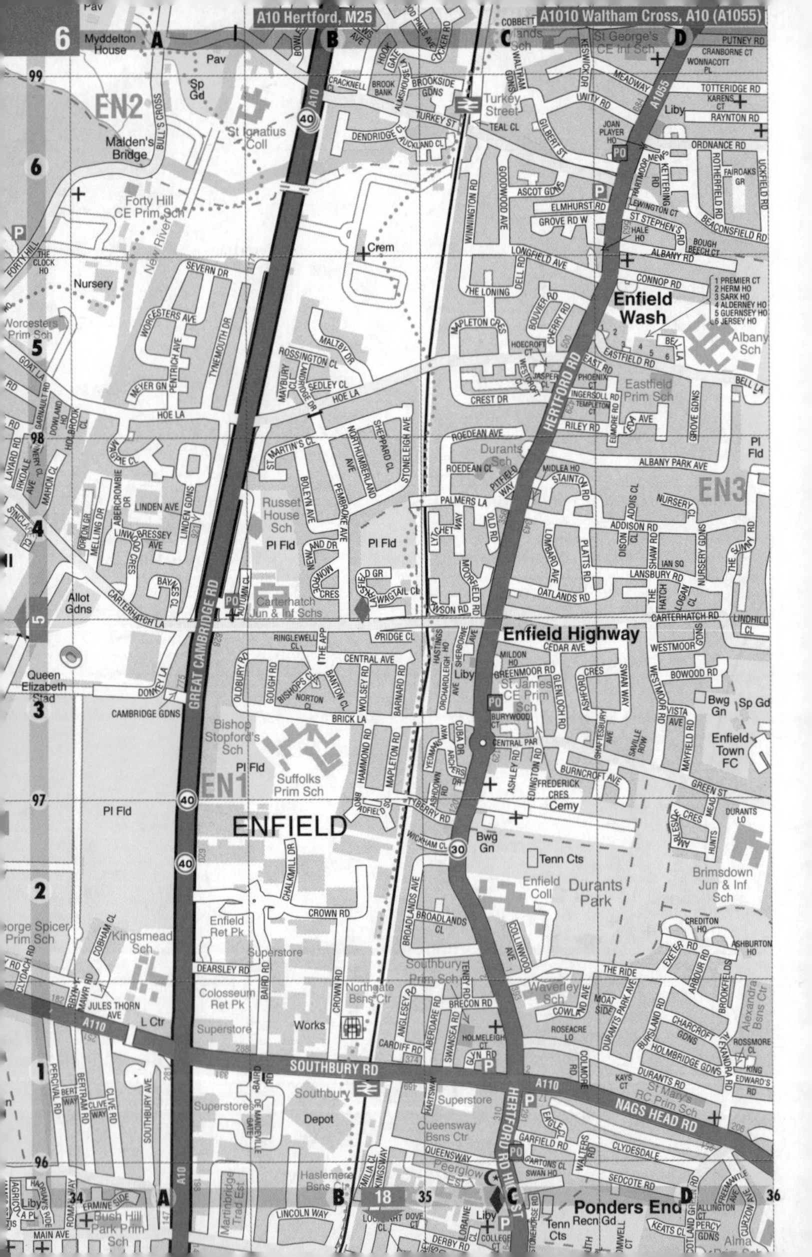
A10 Hertford, M25
A1010 Waltham Cross, A10 (A1055)
Myddelton House
Pav
Sp Gd
EN2
St Ignatius Coll
Malden's Bridge
BULL'S CROSS
Forty Hill CE Prim Sch
New River
FORTY HILL
THE CLOCK HO
Nursery
Worcesters Prim Sch
GOAT LA
SEVERN DR
WORCESTERS AVE
PENTRICH AVE
TYNEMOUTH DR
MEYER GN
HOE LA
GARNAULT RD
DOWLAND HO
HOLBROOK CL
MAGPIE CL
LAYARD RD
MAHON CL
ABERCROMBIE DR
LINDEN AVE
LINDEN GDNS
BRESSEY AVE
ORTON GR
MELLING DR
BAYNES CL
CARTERHATCH LA
Allot Gdns
Queen Elizabeth Stad
DONKEY LA
CAMBRIDGE GDNS
GREAT CAMBRIDGE RD
CRACKNELL CL
BROOK BANK
BROOKSIDE GDNS
TURKEY ST
Turkey Street
DENDRIDGE CL
AUCKLAND CL
Crem
MALTBY DR
ROSSINGTON CL
MAYBURY CL
SEDLEY CL
ST MARTIN'S CL
NORTHUMBERLAND AVE
SHEPPARD CL
STONELEIGH AVE
BOLEYN AVE
PEMBROKE AVE
Russet House Sch
Pl Fld
NEWLAND DR
MONROE CRES
Carterhatch Jun & Inf Schs
AUTUMN CL
WAGTAIL CL
RINGLEWELL CL
THE APP
BRIDGE CL
CENTRAL AVE
OLDBURY RD
GOUGH RD
BISHOPS CL
NORTON CL
BANTON CL
WOLSEY RD
BARNARD RD
BRICK LA
Bishop Stopford's Sch
Suffolks Prim Sch
HAMMOND RD
MAPLETON RD
EN1
ENFIELD
BROADFIELD SQ
CHALKMILL DR
CROWN RD
Enfield Ret Pk
Superstore
DEARSLEY RD
Colosseum Ret Pk
BAIRD RD
Northgate Bsns Ctr
Works
Kingsmead Sch
George Spicer Prim Sch
COBHAM CL
CLYDACH RD
BRYN-Y-MAWR RD
JULES THORN AVE
L Ctr
A110
SOUTHBURY RD
PERCIVAL RD
BERTRAM RD
BERT WAY
CLIVE WAY
CLIVE RD
SOUTHBURY AVE
Superstores
DE MANDEVILLE GATE
Southbury
Depot
Haslemere Bsns Ctr
Martinbridge Trad Est
LINCOLN WAY
KINGSWAY
AGRICOLA PL
Liby
ERMINE SIDE
Bush Hill Park Prim Sch
MAIN AVE
COBBETT
Ash Lands Sch
WALTHAM GDNS
KESWICK DR
St George's CE Inf Sch
MEADWAY
UNITY RD
GILBERT ST
TEAL CL
JOAN PLAYER HO
A1055
PUTNEY RD
CRANBORNE CT
WONNACOTT PL
TOTTERIDGE RD
KARENS CT
RAYNTON RD
ORDNANCE RD
HARTMOOR MEWS
KETTERING RD
ROTHERFIELD RD
FAIROAKS GR
BEACONSFIELD RD
GOODWOOD AVE
WINNINGTON RD
ASCOT GDNS
ELMHURST RD
GROVE RD W
LEWINGTON CT
ST STEPHEN'S RD
HALE HO
BOUGH BEECH CT
ALBANY RD
LONGFIELD AVE
DELL RD
CONNOP RD
THE LONING
Enfield Wash
1 PREMIER CT
2 HERM HO
3 SARK HO
4 ALDERNEY HO
5 GUERNSEY HO
6 JERSEY HO
BOUVIER RD
CHERRY RD
MAPLETON CRES
HOECROFT CT
WESTCROFT CT
JASPER CL
Albany Sch
BELL LA
EASTFIELD RD
EAST RD
PHOENIX CT
INGERSOLL RD
TEMPLETON CT
Eastfield Prim Sch
CREST DR
HERTFORD RD
RILEY RD
ELMORE RD
LEDA AVE
GROVE GDNS
ROEDEAN AVE
Durants Sch
ROEDEAN CL
PITFIELD WAY
MIDLEA HO
STAINTON RD
ALBANY PARK AVE
Pl Fld
EN3
PALMERS LA
ADDIS CL
NURSERY CL
LYTCHET WAY
OLD RD
ADDISON RD
LOMBARD AVE
PLATTS RD
DISON CL
SHAW RD
IAN SQ
NURSERY GDNS
THE SUNNY RD
MOORFIELD RD
LANSBURY RD
OATLANDS RD
THE HATCH
LOGAN CL
LAWSON RD
CARTERHATCH RD
LINDHILL CL
Enfield Highway
CEDAR AVE
HASTINGS HO
ORCHARDLEIGH AVE
SHERBORNE AVE
MILDON HO
GREENMOOR RD
WESTMOOR GDNS
WESTMOOR RD
BOWOOD RD
St James CE Prim Sch
ASHFORD CRES
SWAN WAY
GLENLOCH RD
SHAFTESBURY AVE
SAVILLE ROW
VISTA AVE
MAYFIELD RD
Bwg Gn
Sp Gd
Enfield Town FC
BURYWOOD CT
CENTRAL PAR
CUBA DR
YEOMANS WAY
ARCHERS DR
ASHDOWN RD
ASHLEY RD
EDINGTON RD
FREDERICK CRES
BURNCROFT AVE
GREEN ST
Cemy
TYBERRY RD
WICKHAM CL
AMBLESIDE CRES
MEAD
HUNTS
DURANTS LO
Tenn Cts
Enfield Coll
Durants Park
Brimsdown Jun & Inf Sch
BROADLANDS AVE
BROADLANDS CL
COLLINWOOD AVE
CREDITON HO
ASHBURTON HO
EXETER RD
ARBOUR RD
BROOKFIELDS
THE RIDE
Southbury Prim Sch
TENBY RD
Waverley Sch
COWLAND AVE
MOAT SIDE
DURANTS PARK AVE
BURSLAND RD
CHARCROFT GDNS
Alexandra Bsns Ctr
ANGLESEY RD
ABERDARE RD
SWANSEA RD
BRECON RD
HOLMELEIGH CT
GLYN RD
CARDIFF RD
ROSEACRE LO
COLMORE RD
HOLMBRIDGE GDNS
ALEXANDRA RD
ROSSMORE CL
KING EDWARD'S RD
KAYS CT
DURANTS RD
HARTSWAY
Superstore
Queensway Bsns Ctr
QUEENSWAY
Peerglow Est
EAGLE CL
GARFIELD RD
GARTONS CL
SWAN HO
WALTERS RD
CLYDESDALE
St Mary's RC Prim Sch
NAGS HEAD RD
SEDCOTE RD
FREEMANTLE ST
ALLINGTON CT
PERCY GDNS
CURZON AVE
HERTFORD RD
HIGH ST
EMILIA CL
LOCKHART CL
DOVE CT
LORAINE
COLLEGE CT
DERBY RD
STONEHORSE RD
Ponders End
Tenn Cts
Recn Gd
KEATS CL
Alma

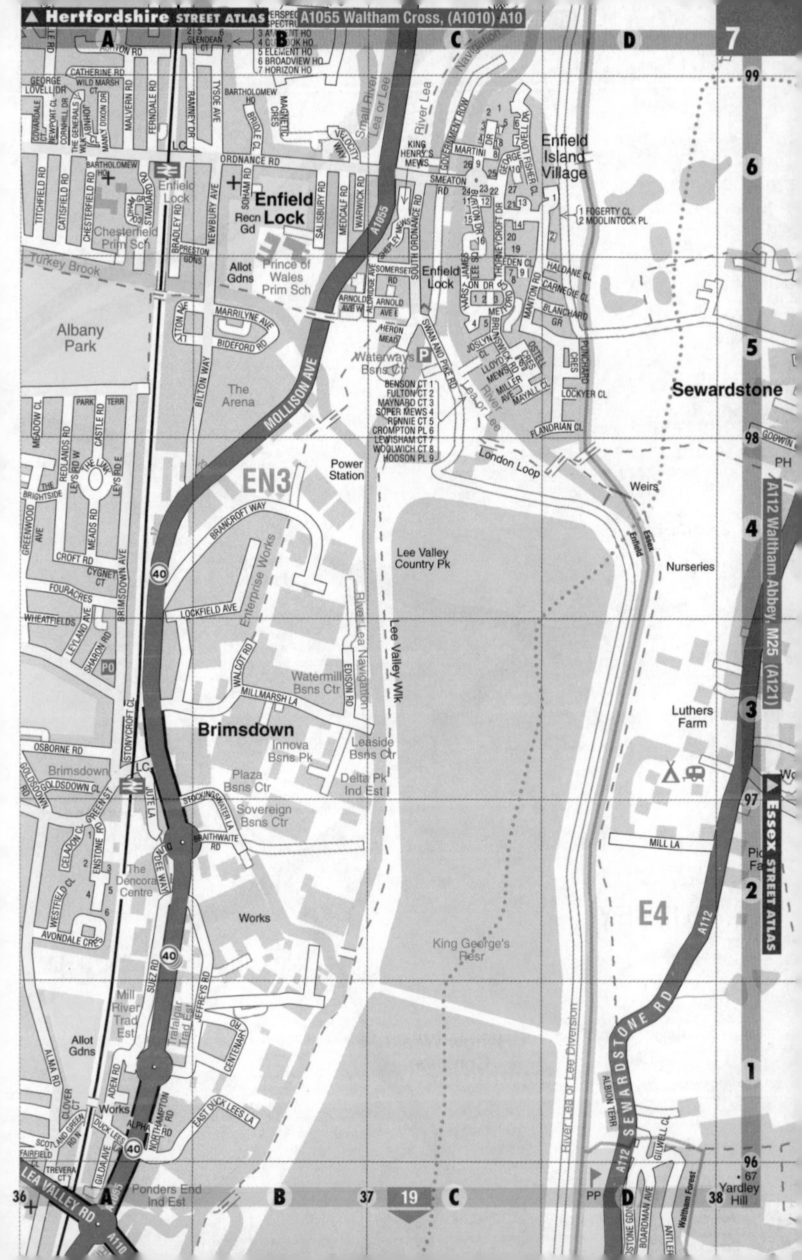
Enfield Lock
Enfield Island Village
Albany Park
Sewardstone
Brimsdown
EN3
E4
Lee Valley Country Pk
King George's Resr
Power Station
The Arena
Prince of Wales Prim Sch
Chesterfield Prim Sch
Waterways Bsns Ctr
Watermill Bsns Ctr
Innova Bsns Pk
Leaside Bsns Ctr
Plaza Bsns Ctr
Delta Pk Ind Est
Sovereign Bsns Ctr
The Dencora Centre
Mill River Trad Est
Trafalgar Trad Est
Ponders End Ind Est
Enterprise Works
Works
Allot Gdns
Recn Gd
Luthers Farm
Nurseries
Weirs
London Loop
Turkey Brook
River Lea
Small River Lea or Lee
River Lea Navigation
River Lea or Lee Diversion
Lee Valley Wlk
MOLLISON AVE
SEWARDSTONE RD
LEA VALLEY RD
ORDNANCE RD
SOUTH ORDNANCE RD
MILL LA
1 FOGERTY CL
2 MOOLINTOCK PL
BENSON CT 1
FULTON CT 2
MAYNARD CT 3
SOPER MEWS 4
RENNIE CT 5
CROMPTON PL 6
LEWISHAM CT 7
WOOLWICH CT 8
HODSON PL 9
3 AMETHYST HO
4 CUTBROOK HO
5 ELEMENT HO
6 BROADVIEW HO
7 HORIZON HO
A112 Waltham Abbey, M25 (A121)
▲ Essex STREET ATLAS
Yardley Hill

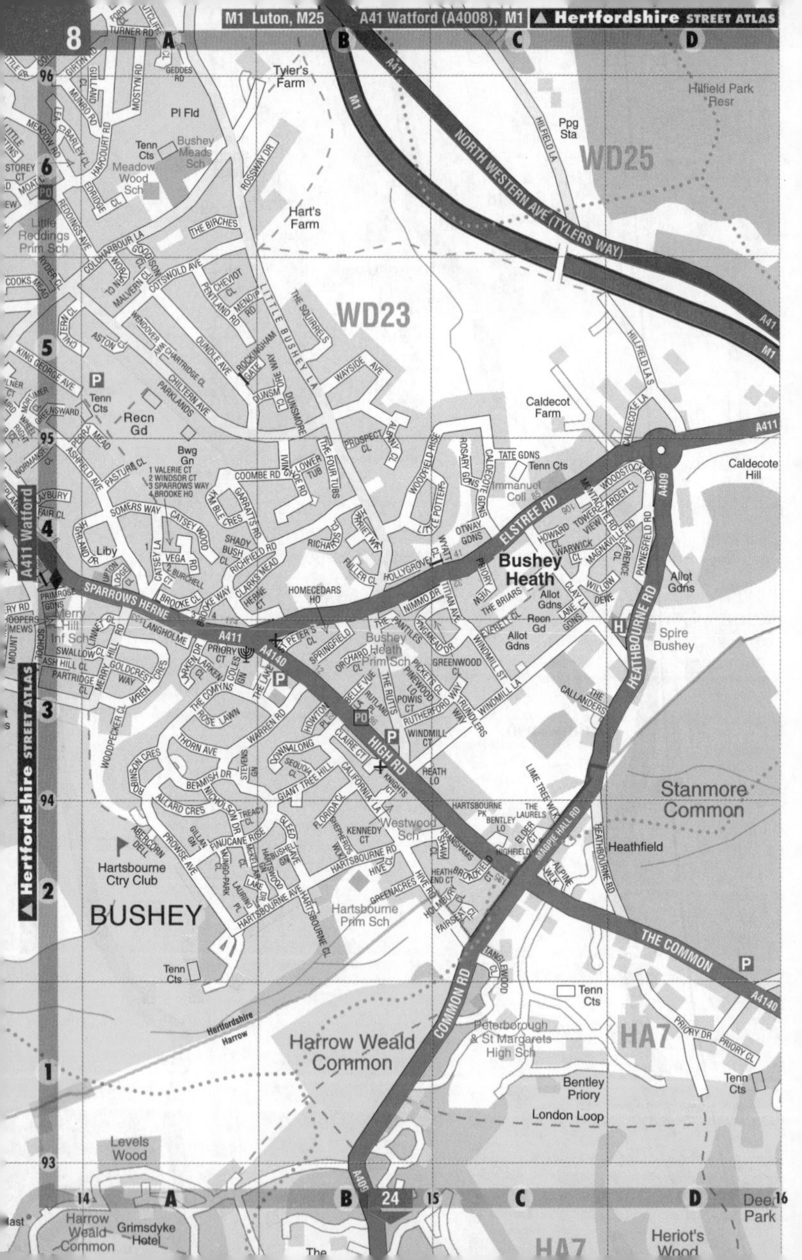
Tyler's Farm
Pl Fld
Bushey Meads Sch
Meadow Wood Sch
Little Reddings Prim Sch
Hart's Farm
WD23
WD25
Hilfield Park Resr
Ppg Sta
NORTH WESTERN AVE (TYLERS WAY)
Caldecot Farm
Caldecote Hill
Recn Gd
Bwg Gn
1 VALERIE CT
2 WINDSOR CT
3 SPARROWS WAY
4 BROOKE HO
Liby
Merry Hill Inf Sch
HOMECEDARS HO
Bushey Heath Prim Sch
Immanuel Coll
Bushey Heath
Allot Gdns
Spire Bushey
ELSTREE RD
HEATHBOURNE RD
SPARROWS HERNE
HIGH RD
Westwood Sch
Stanmore Common
Heathfield
Hartsbourne Ctry Club
BUSHEY
Hartsbourne Prim Sch
THE COMMON
COMMON RD
Harrow Weald Common
Peterborough & St Margarets High Sch
HA7
Bentley Priory
London Loop
Levels Wood
Harrow Weald Common
Grimsdyke Hotel
Heriot's Wood
Deer Park
Hertfordshire
Harrow

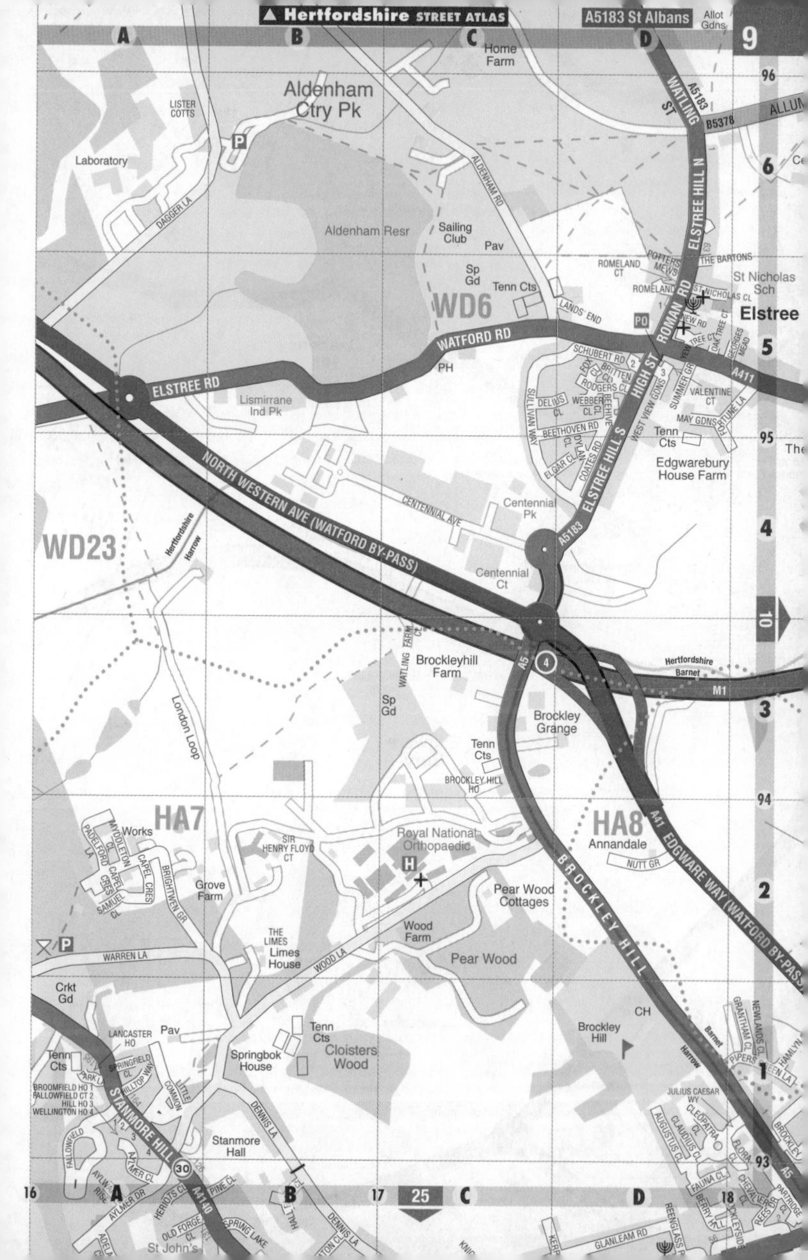
Aldenham Ctry Pk
Home Farm
LISTER COTTS
Laboratory
DAGGER LA
Aldenham Resr
Sailing Club
Pav
Sp Gd
Tenn Cts
ALDENHAM RD
WD6
WATLING ST
A5183
B5378
ELSTREE HILL N
ROMELAND CT
POTTERS MEWS
THE BARTONS
ROMELAND
ST NICHOLAS CL
St Nicholas Sch
Elstree
LANDS' END
WATFORD RD
ROMAN RD
NEW RD
PH
ELSTREE RD
Lismirrane Ind Pk
SCHUBERT RD
FOX CL
BRITTEN CL
RODGERS CL
DELIUS CL
WEBBER CL
BEEHIVE
SULLIVAN WAY
BEETHOVEN RD
DYLAN CL
ELGAR CL
COATES RD
HIGH ST
WEST VIEW GDNS
SUMMER GR
VALENTINE CT
MAY GDNS
FORTUNE LA
YEW TREE CT
OAK TREE CT
GEORGES MEAD
A411
Tenn Cts
Edgwarebury House Farm
ELSTREE HILL S
NORTH WESTERN AVE (WATFORD BY-PASS)
CENTENNIAL AVE
Centennial Pk
Centennial Ct
WD23
Hertfordshire
Harrow
WATLING FARM CL
Brockleyhill Farm
Sp Gd
A5
Hertfordshire
Barnet
M1
Brockley Grange
London Loop
Tenn Cts
BROCKLEY HILL HO
HA7
HA8
A41
EDGWARE WAY (WATFORD BY-PASS)
Annandale
NUTT GR
Works
MYDDLETON CL
PADELFORD LA
CAPEL CRES
BRIGHTWEN GR
SAMUEL CL
Grove Farm
SIR HENRY FLOYD CT
Royal National Orthopaedic
Pear Wood Cottages
BROCKLEY HILL
THE LIMES
Limes House
Wood Farm
WARREN LA
WOOD LA
Pear Wood
Crkt Gd
Pav
LANCASTER HO
Tenn Cts
Cloisters Wood
Springbok House
SPRINGFIELD CL
HILLTOP WAY
PARK LA
LITTLE COMMON
BROOMFIELD HO 1
FALLOWFIELD CT 2
HILL HO 3
WELLINGTON HO 4
STANMORE HILL
DENNIS LA
Stanmore Hall
FALLOWFIELD
AYLMER CL
AYLMER DR
HERIOTS CL
PINE CL
A4140
OLD FORGE CL
SPRING LAKE
St John's
Brockley Hill
CH
Barnet
Harrow
GRANTHAM CL
NEWLANDS CL
PIPERS GREEN LA
JULIUS CAESAR WY
CLEOPATRA CL
CLAUDIUS CL
AUGUSTUS CL
FLORA CL
FAUNA CL
BERRY HILL
CHEVALIER CL
REES DR
PARTRIDGE CL
REENGLASS RD
GLANLEAM RD
DENNIS LA
PO
H
30
4
10
16
17
18
93
94
95
96
1
2
3
4
5
6

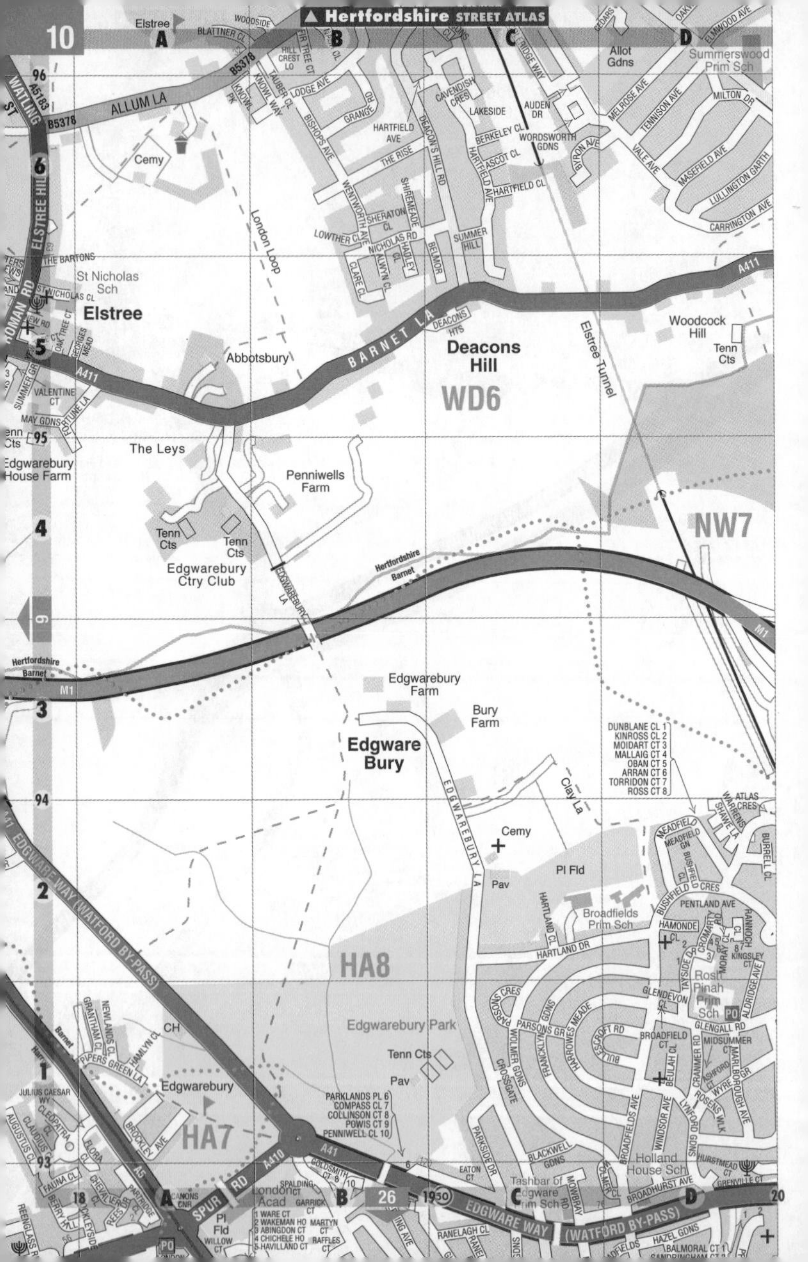
Elstree
A
B
C
D
Allot Gdns
Summerswood Prim Sch
ALLUM LA
B5378
WATLING ST
A5183
ELSTREE HILL
Cemy
London Loop
St Nicholas Sch
Elstree
Abbotsbury
BARNET LA
A411
Deacons Hill
WD6
Elstree Tunnel
Woodcock Hill
Tenn Cts
The Leys
Edgwarebury House Farm
Penniwells Farm
Edgwarebury Ctry Club
EDGWAREBURY LA
Hertfordshire
Barnet
NW7
M1
Edgwarebury Farm
Bury Farm
Edgware Bury
DUNBLANE CL 1
KINROSS CL 2
MOIDART CT 3
MALLAIG CT 4
OBAN CT 5
ARRAN CT 6
TORRIDON CT 7
ROSS CT 8
Clay La
Cemy
Pl Fld
Pav
Broadfields Prim Sch
HARTLAND DR
Rosh Pinah Prim Sch
EDGWARE WAY (WATFORD BY-PASS)
HA8
Edgwarebury Park
Tenn Cts
Pav
Edgwarebury
HA7
CH
PARKLANDS PL 6
COMPASS CL 7
COLLINSON CT 8
POWIS CT 9
PENNIWELL CL 10
Holland House Sch
Tashbar of Edgware Prim Sch
London Acad
1 WARE CT
2 WAKEMAN HO
3 ABINGDON CT
4 CHICHELE HO
5 HAVILLAND CT
A410
A41
A5
96
95
94
93
6
5
4
3
2
1
9
18
26
20
19 50

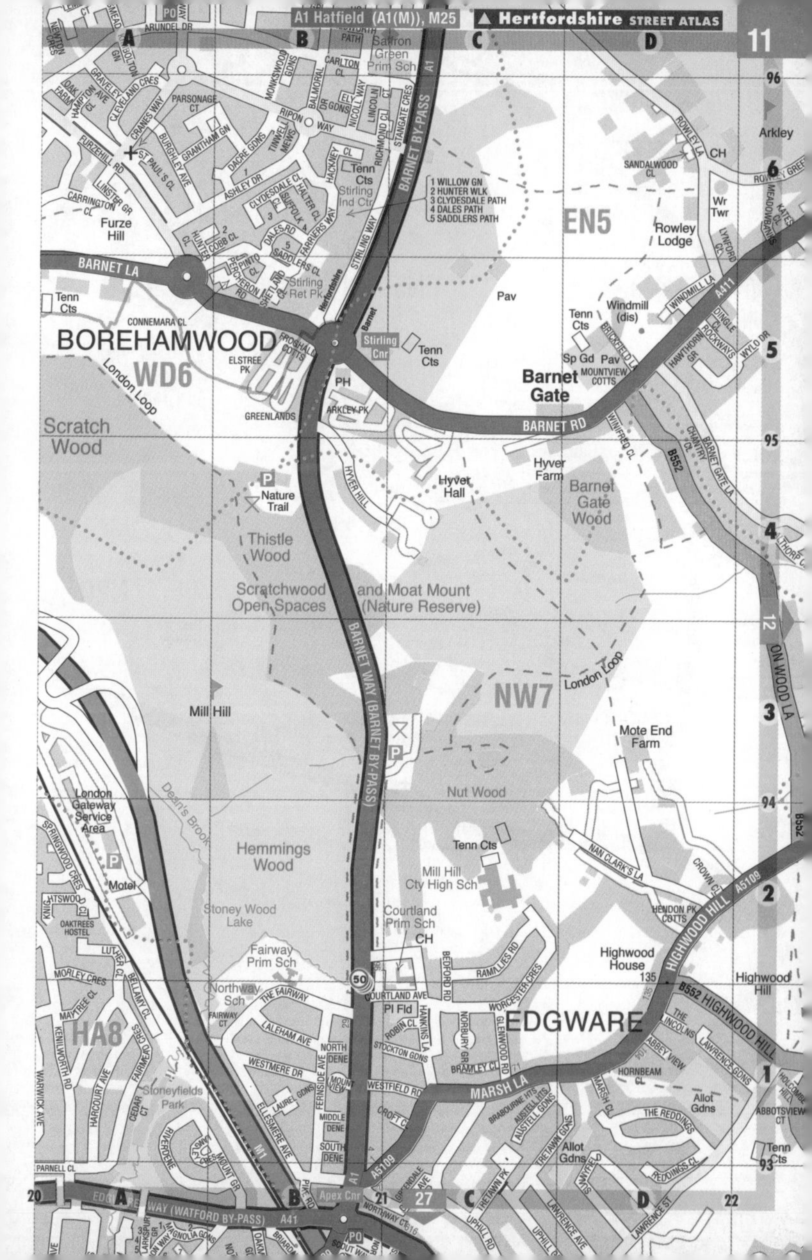
BOREHAMWOOD
WD6
EN5
NW7
HA8
EDGWARE
Barnet Gate
Furze Hill
Scratch Wood
Thistle Wood
Scratchwood and Moat Mount Open Spaces (Nature Reserve)
Mill Hill
Hemmings Wood
Nut Wood
Barnet Gate Wood
Hyver Farm
Hyver Hall
Rowley Lodge
Mote End Farm
Highwood House
Highwood Hill
Arkley
London Loop
BARNET LA
BARNET RD
BARNET BY-PASS
BARNET WAY (BARNET BY-PASS)
HIGHWOOD HILL
MARSH LA
EDGWARE WAY (WATFORD BY-PASS)
1 WILLOW GN
2 HUNTER WLK
3 CLYDESDALE PATH
4 DALES PATH
5 SADDLERS PATH
London Gateway Service Area
Stoney Wood Lake
Stoneyfields Park
Mill Hill Cty High Sch
Courtland Prim Sch
Fairway Prim Sch
Northway Sch
Saffron Green Prim Sch
Stirling Ind Ctr
Stirling Ret Pk
Stirling Cnr
Apex Cnr
Nature Trail
Windmill (dis)
Dean's Brook
OAKTREES HOSTEL
Motel
A
B
C
D
20
21
22
27
12
1
2
3
4
5
6
93
94
95
96

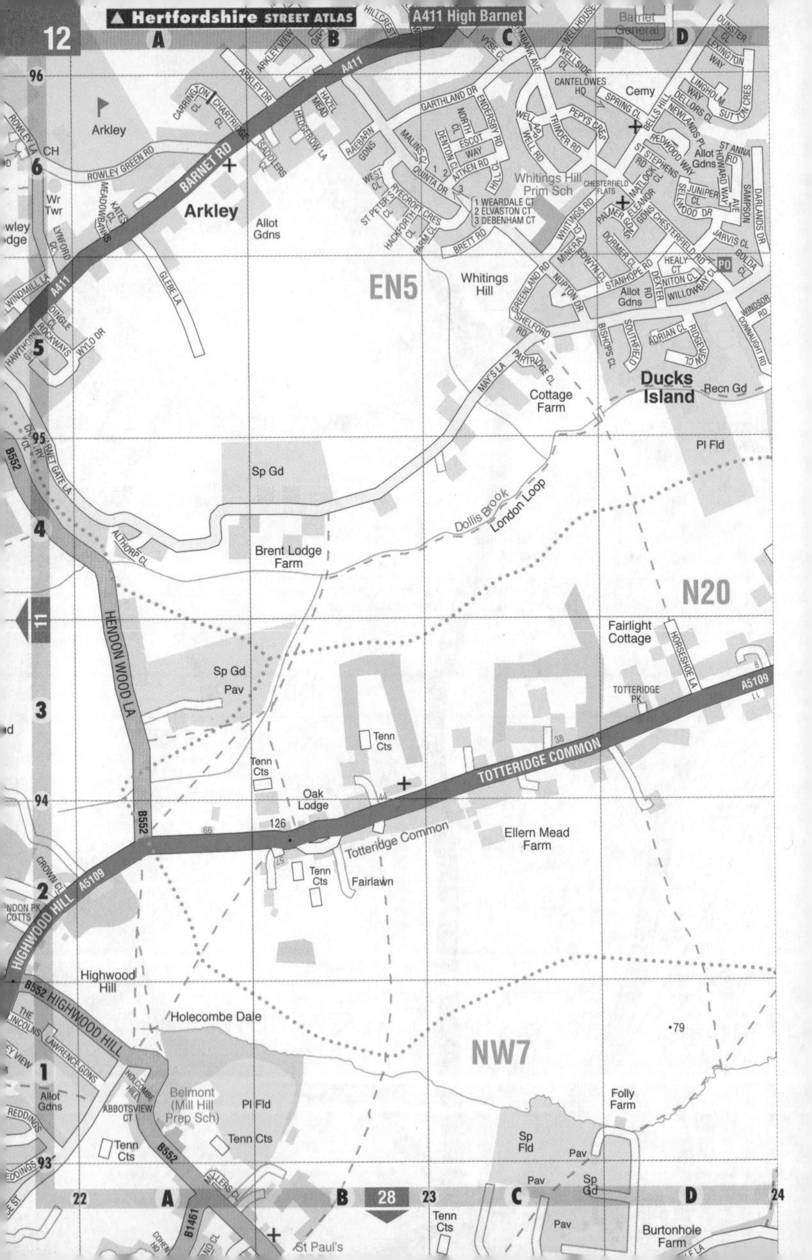
A411 High Barnet
A
B
C
D
96
Arkley
CH
6
Wr
Twr
Arkley
Allot
Gdns
EN5
Whitings
Hill
Cemy
Whitings Hill
Prim Sch
CANTELOWES
HQ
1 WEARDALE CT
2 ELVASTON CT
3 DEBENHAM CT
Allot
Gdns
Allot
Gdns
5
Ducks
Island
Recn Gd
Cottage
Farm
95
Pl Fld
Sp Gd
Dollis Brook
London Loop
4
Brent Lodge
Farm
N20
11
Fairlight
Cottage
Sp Gd
Pav
3
TOTTERIDGE
PK
A5109
Tenn
Cts
Tenn
Cts
TOTTERIDGE COMMON
94
Oak
Lodge
126
Totteridge Common
Ellern Mead
Farm
Tenn
Cts
Fairlawn
2
HIGHWOOD HILL
Highwood
Hill
B552 HIGHWOOD HILL
Holecombe Dale
NW7
•79
1
Allot
Gdns
Belmont
(Mill Hill
Prep Sch)
Pl Fld
Folly
Farm
Tenn
Cts
Tenn Cts
Sp
Fld
Pav
Pav
Sp
Gd
93
22
A
B
28
23
C
D
24
Tenn
Cts
Pav
Burtonhole
Farm
St Paul's
HENDON WOOD LA
BARNET RD
ROWLEY GREEN RD
B552

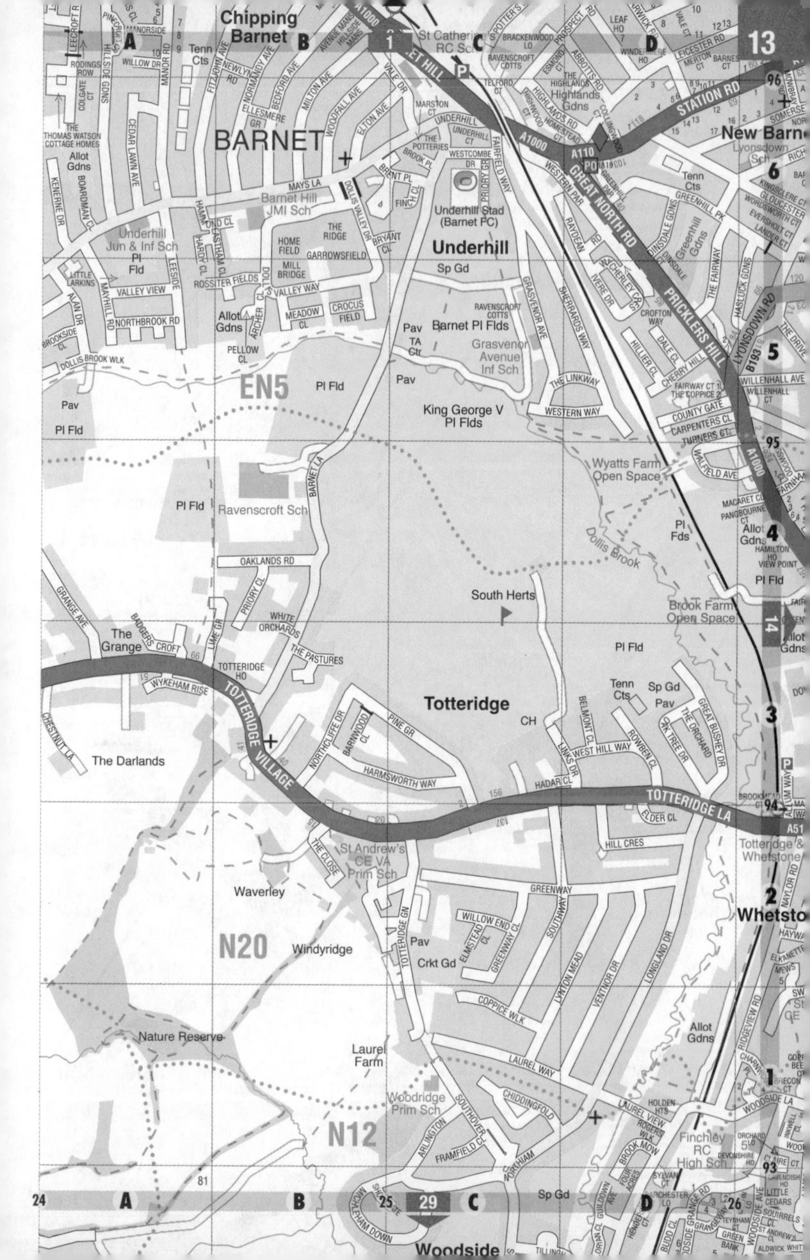
13
Chipping Barnet
BARNET
Underhill
New Barnet
EN5
Totteridge
N20
N12
Whetstone
Woodside
Barnet Hill JMI Sch
Underhill Jun & Inf Sch
Underhill Stad (Barnet FC)
Barnet Pl Flds
Grasvenor Avenue Inf Sch
King George V Pl Flds
Ravenscroft Sch
Wyatts Farm Open Space
Dollis Brook
South Herts
Brook Farm Open Space
The Grange
The Darlands
Waverley
Windyridge
Nature Reserve
Laurel Farm
Woodridge Prim Sch
St Andrew's CE VA Prim Sch
Finchley RC High Sch
Totteridge & Whetstone
TOTTERIDGE VILLAGE
TOTTERIDGE LA
GREAT NORTH RD
PRICKLERS HILL
STATION RD
LYONSDOWN RD
A1000
A110
A5109
B193
14
29
24
25
26
A
B
C
D

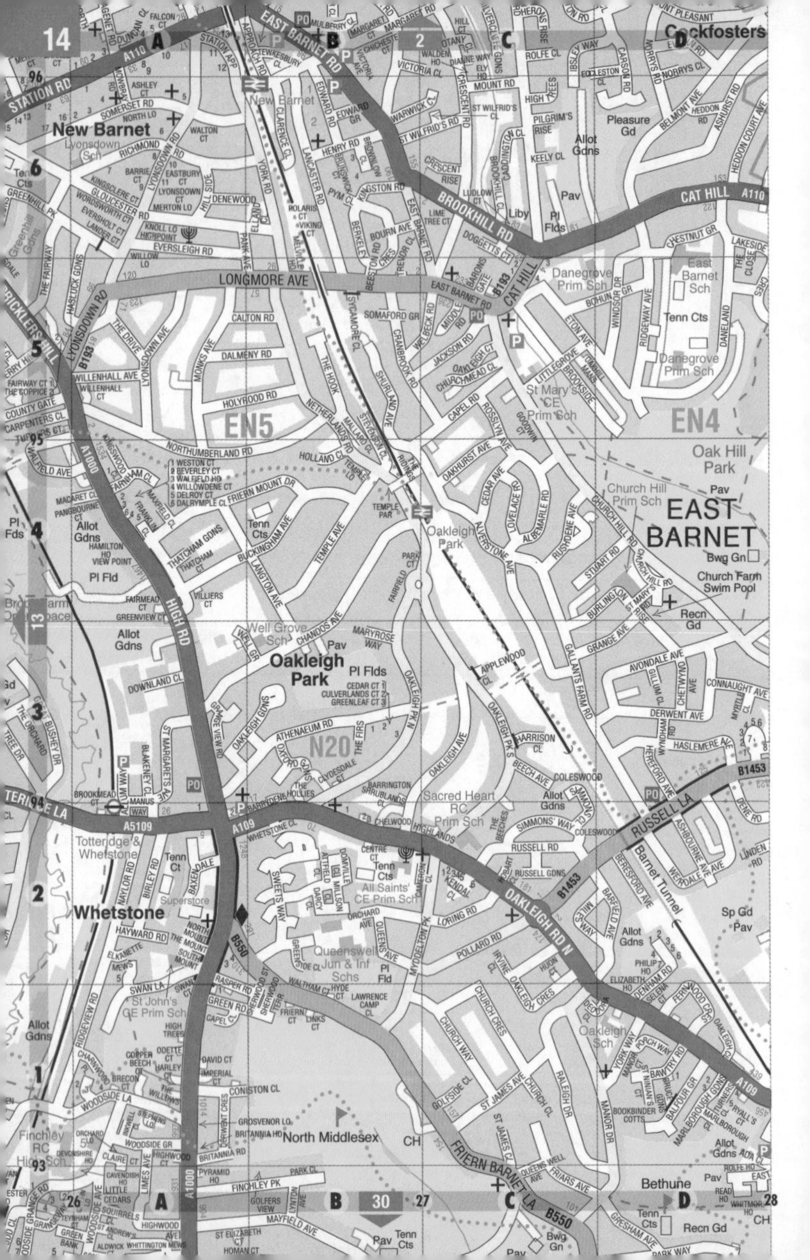
Cockfosters
New Barnet
EAST BARNET RD
STATION RD
A110
STATION APP
APPROACH RD
TEWKESBURY CL
MULBERRY CL
MARGARET CT
MARGARET RD
CHICHESTER CT
VICTORIA AVE
VICTORIA CL
OTANY CL
WALDEN HO
DIANNE WAY
ELY HO
MOUNT RD
HILL CT
ALVERCLIFFE GDNS
HERONS RISE
ROLFE CL
IBSLEY WAY
CARSON RD
NORRYS RD
NORRYS CL
ECCLESTON CL
HIGH TREES
PILGRIM'S RISE
KEELY CL
Pleasure Gd
Allot Gdns
BELMONT AVE
HEDDON RD
ASHURST RD
HEDDON COURT AVE
FALCON CT
DUNCAN CL
ASHLEY CT
SOMERSET RD
NORTH LO
WALTON CT
RICHMOND
Lyonsdown Sch
LYONSDOWN RD
BARRIE CT
EASTBURY CT
LYONSDOWN CT
MERTON LO
KINGSCLERE CT
GLOUCESTER CT
WORDSWORTH CT
EVERSHOLT CT
LANDER CT
DENEWOOD
HILL SIDE
KNOLL LO
HIGHPOINT
EVERSLEIGH RD
WILLOW LO
GREENHILL PK
Greenhill Gdns
Ten Cts
THE FAIRWAY
HASLUCK GDNS
ELLAND CL
PARK AVE
YORK RD
CLARENCE CL
LANCASTER RD
EDWARD RD
EDWARD GR
HENRY RD
BRUNSWICK CT
BROWNLOW
PYM CL
KINGSTON RD
BERKELEY
BOURN AVE
BEESTON RD
TREVOR CL
EAST BARNET RD
WARWICK CL
CRESCENT RD
ST WILFRID'S RD
ST WILFRID'S CL
CRESCENT RISE
CADDINGTON CL
BROOKHILL CL
LUDLOW CT
BROOKHILL RD
Liby
Pl Flds
Pav
CAT HILL
A110
CHESTNUT GR
LAKESIDE
THE CLOSE
LIME TREE CT
POLARIS CT
VIKING CT
MELVILLE HO
DOGGETTS CT
BARONS GATE
B193
Danegrove Prim Sch
East Barnet Sch
BOHUN GR
WINDSOR DR
RIDGEWAY AVE
Tenn Cts
DANELAND
ETON AVE
LONGMORE AVE
LYONSDOWN RD
SYCAMORE CL
SOMAFORD GR
CRANBROOK RD
WELBECK RD
MIDDLE RD
JACKSON RD
OAKLEIGH CT
CHURCHMEAD CL
LITTLEGROVE
BROOKSIDE
OAKHILL MANS
Danegrove Prim Sch
St Mary's CE Prim Sch
THE DRIVE
LYONSDOWN AVE
MONKS AVE
CALTON RD
DALMENY RD
HOLYROOD RD
THE HOOK
SHURLAND AVE
NETHERLANDS RD
MALLARD CL
STEVENSON CL
CAPEL RD
ROSSLYN AVE
GOODWIN CT
EN5
EN4
Oak Hill Park
STRICKLERS HILL
B193
WILLENHALL AVE
WILLENHALL CT
FAIRWAY CT
THE COPPICE
COUNTY GATE
CARPENTERS CL
NORTHUMBERLAND RD
HOLLAND CL
TEMPLE LO
THE RIDINGS
OAKHURST AVE
CEDAR AVE
LOVELACE RD
ALBEMARLE RD
Church Hill Prim Sch
EAST BARNET
A1000
KINGSWOOD
WALFIELD AVE
FARNHAM CL
1 WESTON CT
2 BEVERLEY CT
3 WALFIELD HO
4 WILLOWDENE CT
5 DELROY CT
6 DALRYMPLE CL
FRIERN MOUNT DR
MAXFIELD CL
FRANKLIN CL
MACARET CL
PANGBOURNE CT
Allot Gdns
HAMILTON HO
VIEW POINT
Pl Fld
Pl Fds
THATCHAM GDNS
THATCHAM CT
Tenn Cts
BUCKINGHAM AVE
TEMPLE AVE
TEMPLE PAR
Oakleigh Park
ALVERSTONE AVE
RUSHDENE AVE
CHURCH HILL RD
STUART RD
Bwg Gn
Church Farm Swim Pool
LANGTON AVE
PARK CT
FAIRFIELD CT
VILLIERS CT
FAIRMEAD CT
GREENVIEW CT
HIGH RD
13
Well Grove Sch
WELL GR
CHANDOS AVE
MARYROSE WAY
Pav
Oakleigh Park
Pl Flds
BURLINGTON RI
ST MARY'S RISE
CHURCH HILL RD
Recn Gd
GRANGE AVE
GALLANTS FARM RD
AVONDALE AVE
GILLUM CL
CHETWYND AVE
CONNAUGHT AVE
MYRTLE CL
DOWNLAND CL
CEDAR CT
CULVERLANDS CT
GREENLEAF CT
OAKLEIGH PK N
APPLEWOOD CL
DERWENT AVE
WYNDHAM RD
HASLEMERE AVE
GRANGE VIEW RD
OAKLEIGH GDNS
ATHENAEUM RD
THE FIRS
OAKLEIGH AVE
OAKLEIGH PK S
HARRISON CL
HEREFORD AVE
B1453
N20
GREAT BUSHEY DR
THE ORCHARD
ST MARGARETS AVE
BLAKENEY CL
ALLUM WAY
OXFORD GDNS
CLYDESDALE CT
BEECH AVE
COLESWOOD
BROOKMEAD CT
MANUS WAY
THE HOLLIES
BARRINGTON
SHRUBLANDS CL
Sacred Heart RC Prim Sch
Allot Gdns
SIMMONS CL
RUSSELL LA
DENE RD
TOTTERIDGE LA
A5109
A109
WHETSTONE CL
CHELWOOD
HIGHLANDS
THE BEECHES
SIMMONS' WAY
COLESWOOD
Totteridge & Whetstone
Tenn Ct
BAXENDALE
SWEETS WAY
ATTFIELD CL
DOMVILLE CL
MILLSON CL
DARCY CL
CENTRE CT
Tenn Cts
All Saints' CE Prim Sch
CAMERON CL
KENDAL CL
HOBART CL
RUSSELL RD
RUSSELL GDNS
B1453
BERESFORD AVE
Barnet Tunnel
ASHBOURNE AVE
WEIRDALE AVE
LINDEN RD
NAYLOR RD
BIRLEY RD
Superstore
Whetstone
NORTH MOUNT
HAYWARD RD
THE MOUNT
SOUTH MOUNT
ELKANETTE MEWS
B550
ORCHARD AVE
QUEENS AVE
MYDDELTON PK
LORING RD
OAKLEIGH RD N
MILLS WAY
BARFIELD AVE
Sp Gd
Pav
Allot Gdns
PHILIP HO
ELIZABETH HO
DENHAM RD
GREENSIDE CL
Queenswell Jun & Inf Schs
Pl Fld
POLLARD RD
IRVINE CL
HUON CT
SWAN LA
St John's CE Prim Sch
RASPER RD
GREEN RD
SHERWOOD ST
SHERWOOD TERR
WALTHAM CT
HYDE CT
LAWRENCE CAMP CL
CHURCH CRES
OAKLEIGH CRES
SELENA CT
FERNWOOD CRES
OAKLEIGH GDNS
RIDGEVIEW RD
CAPEL CT
FRIERN CT
LINKS CT
Allot Gdns
HIGH TREES
CHURCH WAY
Oakleigh Sch
DEODORA
YORK WAY
MANOR PL
BIRCH WAY
BAWTRY RD
CHARNWOOD
COPPER BEECH CT
ODETTE CT
HARLEY CT
DAVID CT
IMPERIAL CT
GOLFSIDE CL
ST JAMES AVE
CHURCH CL
RALEIGH DR
MANOR DR
ST NINIAN'S CT
BRUCE GDNS
BALFOUR GR
MARLBOROUGH GDNS
TURNERS CL
RYALL'S CT
A109
BRECON CT
THE WILLOWS
CONISTON CL
WOODSIDE LA
DERWENT CRES
GROSVENOR LO
BRITANNIA HO
North Middlesex
CH
BOOKBINDER COTTS
MARLBOROUGH CT
Finchley RC High Sch
ORCHARD LO
DEVONSHIRE HO
CLAIRE CT
WOODSIDE GR
HIGHWOOD CT
HIGHWOOD HO
BRITANNIA RD
CAVENDISH HO
LITTLE CEDARS
LIMES AVE
PYRAMID HO
PARK CL
FINCHLEY PK
ST JAMES CL
QUEENS WELL AVE
FRIARS AVE
FRIERN BARNET LA
Allot Gdns
ROLFE HO
Bethune
Pav
READ HO
WHITMOR HO
EAST
GRANGE AVE
GRANVILLE AVE
WOODSIDE AVE
SQUIRRELS
ST ANDREW'S CL
GREEN BANK
ALDWICK
WHITTINGTON MEWS
HIGHWOOD
GOLFERS VIEW
MAYFIELD AVE
ST ELIZABETH CT
HOMAN CT
Pav
Tenn Cts
LYNTON AVE
B550
Bwg Gn
Tenn Cts
Recn Gd
GRESHAM AVE
PARK WAY
CH
A1000
A
B
C
D
2
30
26
27
28
1
2
3
4
5
6
93
94
95
96

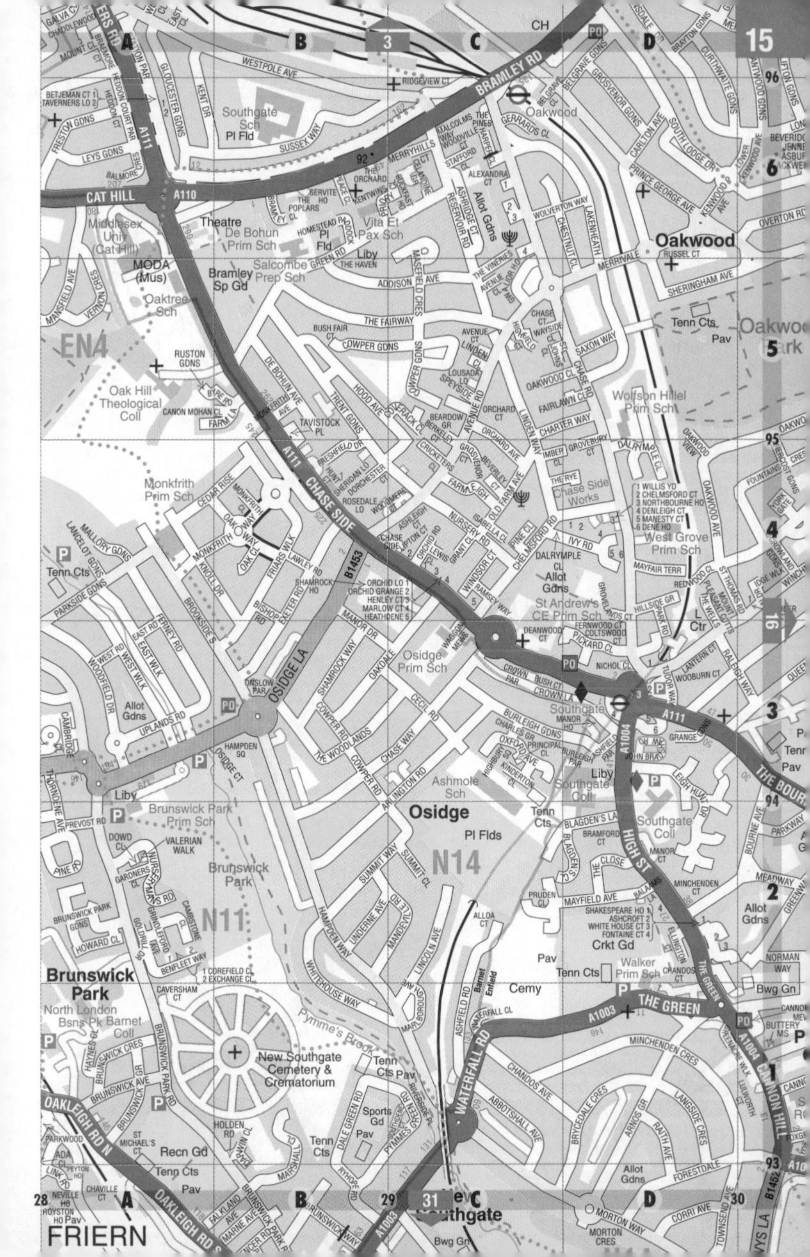
15
A
B
C
D
3
CH
WESTPOLE AVE
RIDGEVIEW CT
BRAMLEY RD
Oakwood
Southgate Sch
Pl Fld
SUSSEX WAY
GLOUCESTER GDNS
KENT DR
STATION PAR
HEDDON COURT PAR
BETJEMAN CT
TAVERNERS LO
FRESTON GDNS
LEYS GDNS
BALMORE CRES
MOUNT CL
CHADDLEWOOD
GALVA CL
A111
CAT HILL
A110
Theatre
De Bohun Prim Sch
Middlesex Univ (Cat Hill)
MODA (Mus)
Bramley Sp Gd
Salcombe Prep Sch
Oaktree Sch
Vita Et Pax Sch
Liby
THE HAVEN
GREEN RD
ADDISON AVE
HOMESTEAD PADDOCK
SERVITE HO
THE POPLARS
THE ORCHARD
KENTWINS
PRIORY CT
MERRYHILLS CT
MALCOLMS WAY
THE PINES
WOODVILLE CT
STAFFORD CT
HARPER CL
ALEXANDRA CT
GERRARDS CL
ASHRIDGE CT
RESERVOIR RD
Allot Gdns
WOLVERTON WAY
CHESTNUT CL
LAKENHEATH
MERRIVALE
RUSSEL CT
SHERINGHAM AVE
Oakwood
BELGRAVE GDNS
GROSVENOR GDNS
CARLTON AVE
SOUTH LODGE DR
PRINCE GEORGE AVE
KENWOOD AVE
OVERTON RD
BRAYTON GDNS
CURTHWAITE GDNS
96
6
5
4
3
2
1
95
94
93
Tenn Cts
Pav
Oakwood Park
Wolfson Hillel Prim Sch
EN4
MANSFIELD AVE
VERNON CRES
RUSTON GDNS
Oak Hill Theological Coll
CANON MOHAN CL
FARM LA
BYRE RD
MONKFRITH AVE
DE BOHUN AVE
TAVISTOCK PL
THE FAIRWAY
BUSH FAIR CT
COWPER GDNS
HOOD AVE
TRENT GDNS
MASEFIELD CRES
AVENUE CT
LINDEN CL
LOUSADA LO
SPEYSIDE
AVENUE RD
ORCHARD CT
ORCHARD AVE
BEARDOW GR
BERKELEY CT
COVERACK CL
CHASE CT
WAYSIDE
SAXON WAY
OAKWOOD CL
FAIRLAWN CL
CHARTER WAY
GROVEBURY CT
DALRYMPLE CL
CHASE RD
LINDEN WAY
THE VINERIES
Monkfrith Prim Sch
CEDAR RISE
MONKFRITH CL
OAK WAY
OAK CL
FRIARS WLK
LAWLEY RD
A111 CHASE SIDE
FRESHFIELD DR
SHERIDAN LO
DORCHESTER CT
ROSEDALE LO
WOODMERE CT
CRICKETERS CL
GROSVENOR CT
BEVERLEY CT
FARM LEIGH
OLD FARM AVE
THE RYE
Chase Side Works
1 WILLIS YD
2 CHELMSFORD CT
3 NORTHBOURNE HO
4 DENLEIGH CT
5 MANESTY CT
6 DENE HO
West Grove Prim Sch
OAKWOOD AVE
OAKWOOD VIEW
FOUNTAINS CRES
MALLORY GDNS
LANCELOT GDNS
Tenn Cts
PARKSIDE GDNS
MONKFRITH WAY
KNOLL DR
BROOKSIDE S
SHAMROCK HO
B1453
ORCHID LO 1
ORCHID GRANGE 2
HENLEY CT 3
MARLOW CT 4
HEATHDENE 5
EXETER RD
BISHOP RD
NURSERY RD
ISABELLA CL
PINE CL
CHELMSFORD RD
IVY RD
DALRYMPLE CL
Allot Gdns
MAYFAIR TERR
REDWOOD CL
ST THOMAS RD
HILLSIDE GR
PARK RD
GROVELANDS CT
St Andrew's CE Prim Sch
WINDSOR CT
RAMSEY WAY
MANOR DR
DEANWOOD CT
FERNWOOD CT
COLTSWOOD CT
PICKARD CL
NICHOL CL
L Ctr
16
LANTERN CL
WOOBURN CT
RALEIGH WAY
WEST RD
EAST RD
FERNEY RD
EAST WLK
WEST WLK
WOODFIELD DR
CAMBRIDGE
Allot Gdns
UPLANDS RD
ONSLOW PAR
OSIDGE LA
SHAMROCK WAY
OAKDALE
Osidge Prim Sch
WAGGON MEWS
CROWN LA
BUSH CT
CROWN PAR
Southgate
MANOR HO
TUDOR WAY
A111
GRANGE GDNS
JOHN BRADSHAW RD
CECIL RD
COWPER RD
THE WOODLANDS
CHASE WAY
ARLINGTON RD
BURLEIGH GDNS
CHARLES GR
PRINCIPAL CL
OXFORD AVE
HIGHBURY SQ
KINDERTON CL
BURLEIGH PAR
ASHFIELD PAR
A1004
Liby
Southgate Coll
LEIGH HUNT DR
THE BOURNE
BOURNE AVE
PARKWAY
Ashmole Sch
Osidge
Pl Flds
N14
HAMPDEN SQ
OSIDGE CT
THORNDENE AVE
Liby
PREVOST RD
Brunswick Park Prim Sch
DOWD CL
VALERIAN WALK
NURSERYMANS RD
GARDNERS CL
PINE RD
Brunswick Park
SUMMIT WAY
SUMMIT CL
Tenn Cts
BLAGDEN'S LA
BLAGDEN'S CL
BRAMFORD CT
THE CLOSE
Southgate Coll
MANOR CT
HIGH ST
MINCHENDEN CT
MEADWAY
Allot Gdns
PRUDEN CL
MAYFIELD AVE
BALAAMS LA
SHAKESPEARE HO 1
ASHCROFT 2
WHITE HOUSE CT 3
FONTAINE CT 4
Crkt Gd
ELLINGTON CT
BRUNSWICK PARK GDNS
HOWARD CL
N11
CAMBSTONE CL
GRINDLEFORD AVE
BENFLEET WAY
1 COREFIELD CL
2 EXCHANGE CL
HAMPDEN WAY
UNDERNE AVE
MANDEVILLE RD
LINCOLN AVE
ALLOA CT
Pav
Tenn Cts
Walker Prim Sch
CHANDOS CT
NORMAN WAY
Bwg Gn
Brunswick Park
North London Bsns Pk
Barnet Coll
CAVERSHAM CT
WHITEHOUSE WAY
MARLBOROUGH AVE
Barnet
Enfield
ASHFIELD RD
WATERFALL CL
Cemy
A1003
THE GREEN
CANNON MEWS
BUTTERY MS
Pymme's Brook
New Southgate Cemetery & Crematorium
HAYNES CL
BRUNSWICK CRES
BRUNSWICK GR
BRUNSWICK AVE
BRUNSWICK PARK RD
Tenn Cts Pav
MINCHENDEN CRES
GREENACRE WLK
A1004 CANNON HILL
CHANDOS AVE
ABBOTSHALL AVE
BRYCEDALE CRES
ARNOS GR
RAITH AVE
LANGSIDE CRES
LULWORTH
WATERFALL RD
OAKLEIGH RD N
PARKWOOD
ADA CL
PEYTON HO
LINK RD
ST MICHAEL'S CT
HOLDEN RD
DARWIN CL
Recn Gd
Tenn Cts
Pav
DALE GREEN RD
Sports Gd
Pav
SOUTHGATE CL
PYMMES GREEN RD
RIVERSIDE RD
Tenn Cts
MARSHALL CL
RYHOPE RD
FORESTDALE
Allot Gdns
TOWNSEND AVE
CORRI AVE
MORTON WAY
MORTON CRES
B1452
28
29
30
31
NEVILLE HO
CHAVILLE CT
ROYSTON HO
Pav
FALKLAND AVE
MARNE AVE
BRUNSWICK PARK RD
BRUNSWICK CRES
OAKLEIGH RD S
A1003
New Southgate
Bwg Gn
FRIERN

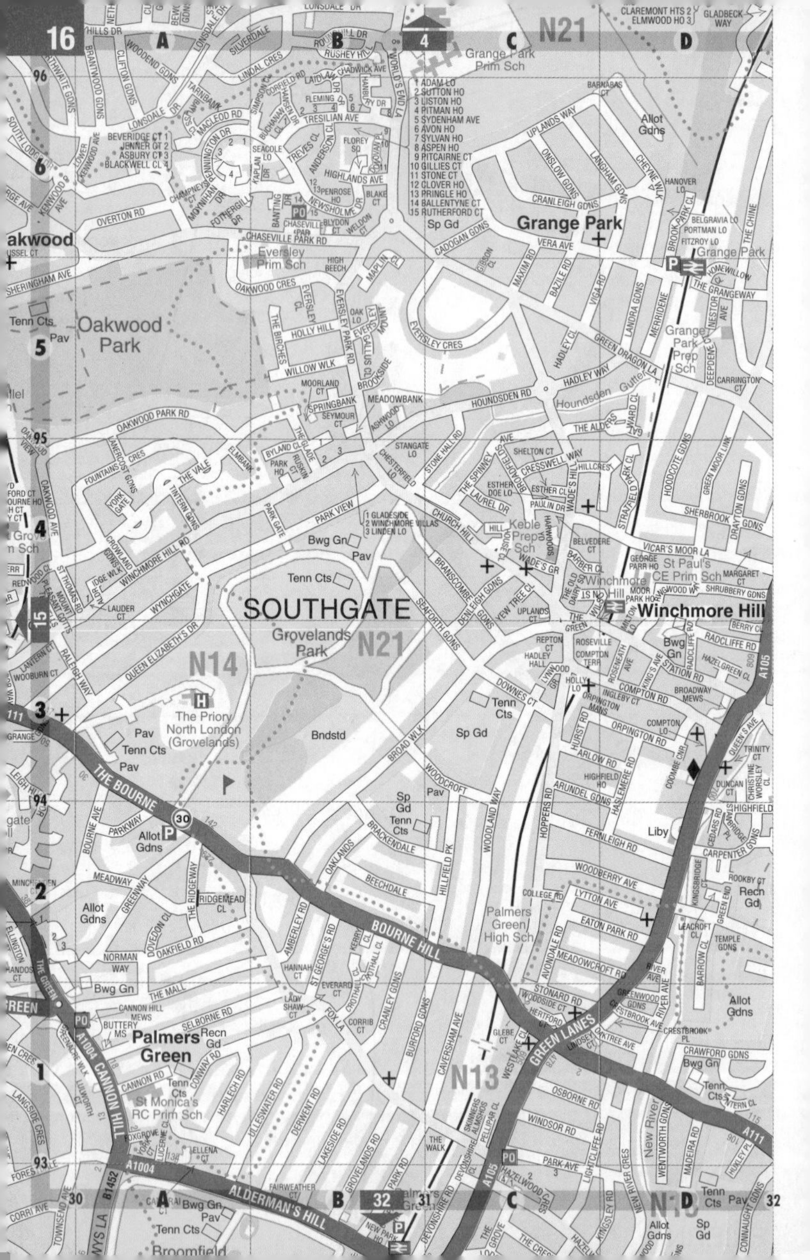
A
B
C
D
4
N21
96
95
94
93
6
5
4
3
2
1
15
30
31
32
Grange Park Prim Sch
CLAREMONT HTS 2
ELMWOOD HO 3
GLADBECK WAY
1 ADAM LO
2 SUTTON HO
3 LISTON HO
4 PITMAN HO
5 SYDENHAM AVE
6 AVON HO
7 SYLVAN HO
8 ASPEN HO
9 PITCAIRNE CT
10 GILLIES CT
11 STONE CT
12 CLOVER HO
13 PRINGLE HO
14 BALLENTYNE CT
15 RUTHERFORD CT
BEVERIDGE CT 1
JENNER CT 2
ASBURY CT 3
BLACKWELL CL 4
Grange Park
Oakwood
Oakwood Park
Eversley Prim Sch
SOUTHGATE
Grovelands Park
N14
The Priory North London (Grovelands)
Keble Prep Sch
St Paul's CE Prim Sch
Winchmore Hill
Grange Park Prep Sch
Houndsden Gutter
Palmers Green
Palmers Green High Sch
St Monica's RC Prim Sch
N13
New River
Broomfield
1 GLADESIDE
2 WINCHMORE VILLAS
3 LINDEN LO
LONSDALE DR
SILVERDALE
RUSHEY HILL
WORLD'S END LA
TRESILIAN AVE
HIGHLANDS AVE
CHASEVILLE PARK RD
OVERTON RD
SHERINGHAM AVE
OAKWOOD CRES
EVERSLEY PARK RD
EVERSLEY CRES
HOLLY HILL
WILLOW WLK
BROOKSIDE
MEADOWBANK
HOUNDSDEN RD
OAKWOOD PARK RD
PARK VIEW
CHURCH HILL
WINCHMORE HILL RD
QUEEN ELIZABETH'S DR
WYNCHGATE
CADOGAN GDNS
VERA AVE
GREEN DRAGON LA
HADLEY WAY
UPLANDS WAY
CRANLEIGH GDNS
CRESSWELL WAY
WADE'S HILL
VICAR'S MOOR LA
STATION RD
COMPTON RD
ORPINGTON RD
FERNLEIGH RD
WOODBERRY AVE
LYTTON AVE
EATON PARK RD
MEADOWCROFT RD
GREEN LANES
THE BOURNE
BOURNE HILL
BROAD WLK
WOODCROFT
WOODLAND WAY
CANNON HILL
ALDERMAN'S HILL
CAVERSHAM AVE
DEVONSHIRE RD
OSBORNE RD
WINDSOR RD
PARK AVE
A105
A111
A1004
B1452
Tenn Cts
Pav
Bwg Gn
Sp Gd
Allot Gdns
Bndstd
Recn Gd
Liby
PO

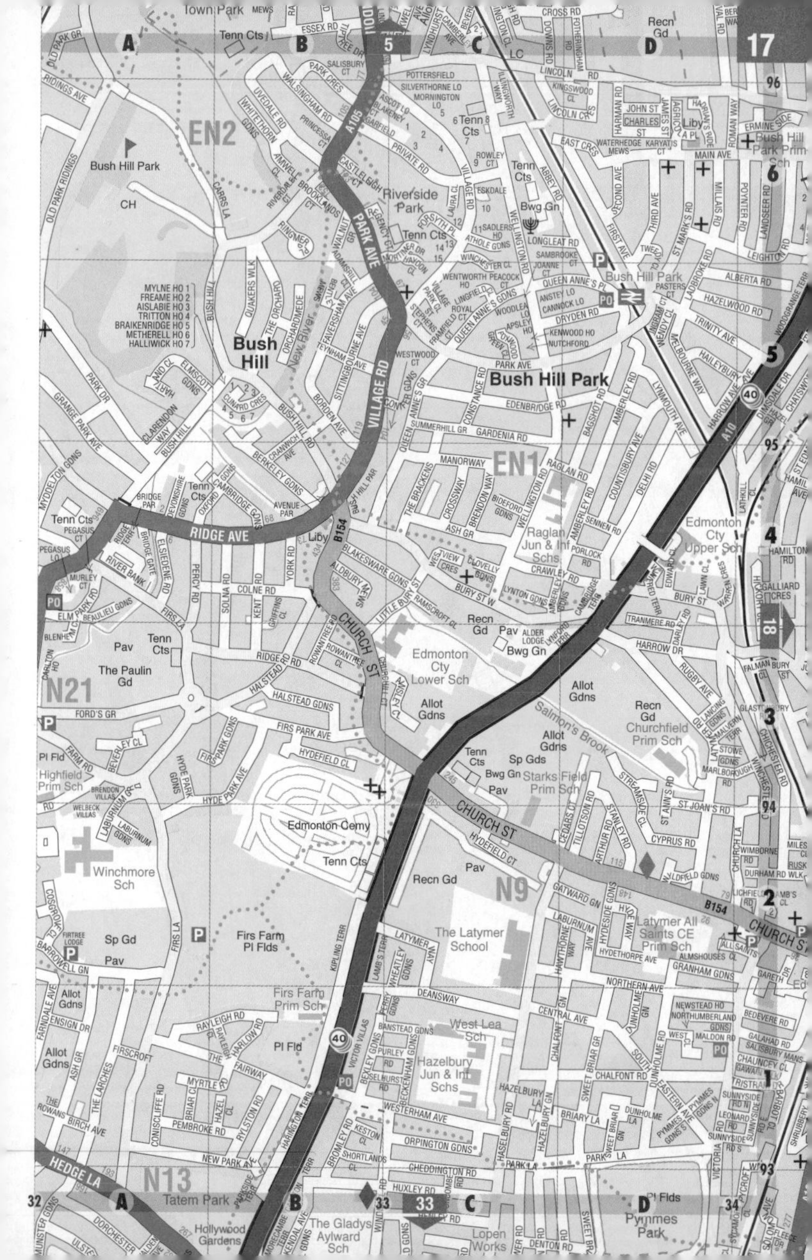
17
A
B
C
D
5
96
6
5
95
4
3
94
2
1
93
18
32
33
34
EN2
EN1
N21
N9
N13
Town Park
Tenn Cts
Recn Gd
Essex Rd
Tiptree Dr
Lyndhurst Ave
Camberley Ave
Cross Rd
Downs Rd
Fotheringham Rd
LC
Lincoln Rd
Lincoln Cres
Kingswood Cl
Old Park Gr
Ridings Ave
Old Park Ridings
Bush Hill Park
CH
Salisbury Ct
Park Cres
Walsingham Rd
Uvedale Rd
Whitethorn Gdns
Princessa Ct
Pottersfield
Silverthorne Lo
Mornington Lo
Ascot Lo
Blakeney Ct
Garfield
Private Rd
A105
Illingworth Way
Harman Rd
John St
Charles St
James St
Agricola Pl
Hadrians Ride
Roman Way
Liby
Waterhedge Mews
Karyatis Ct
East Cres
Ermine Side
Bush Hill Park Prim Sch
Main Ave
Second Ave
Third Ave
First Ave
St Mark's Rd
Millais Rd
Poynter Rd
Landseer Rd
Leighton Rd
Carrs La
Riverdale Ct
Annwell Cl
Brooklands Ct
Castleleigh Ct
Riverside Park
Rowley Ct
Eskdale
Village Rd
Laura Cl
Abbey Rd
Tenn Cts
Bwg Gn
Wellington Rd
Sadlers Ho
Athole Gdns
Longleat Rd
Sambrooke Ct
Joanne Ct
Winchester Cl
Park Ave
Regency Ct
Forsyth Pl
Walnut Gr
Ringmer Pl
Mortimer Dr
Haydon Ct
Wentworth Ho
Peacock Ct
Queen Anne's Pl
Anstey Lo
Cannock Lo
Dryden Rd
Bush Hill Park
PO
Pasters Ct
Ingram Ct
Wendy Cl
Ladbroke Rd
Alberta Rd
Hazelwood Rd
Trinity Ave
Haileybury Ave
Woodgrange Ter
Melbourne Way
Harrow Ave
Dimsdale Dr
Chatsworth
Mylne Ho 1
Freame Ho 2
Aislabie Ho 3
Tritton Ho 4
Braikenridge Ho 5
Metherell Ho 6
Halliwick Ho 7
Bush Hill
Quakers Wlk
The Orchard
Orchardmede
New River
Faversham Ave
Teynham Ave
Sittingbourne Ave
Village Park Cl
Stephens Ct
Framfield Ct
Lingfield Ct
Royal Ct
Queen Anne's Gdns
Woodlea Ho
Apsley Ho
Poynder Ct
Kenwood Ho
Nutchford
Westwood Ct
Elmscott Gdns
Hart and Cl
Cunard Cres
Park Dr
Grange Park Ave
Clarendon Way
Bush Hill Rd
Borden Ave
Village Rd
Conifer Gdns
Queen Anne's Gr
Constance Rd
Edenbridge Rd
Bagshot Rd
Amberley Rd
Lynmouth Ave
A10
Summerhill Gr
Gardenia Rd
Manorway
Raglan Rd
Countisbury Ave
Delhi Rd
Lathkill Cl
Hamilton
Myddelton Gdns
Cranwich Ave
Berkeley Gdns
Tenn Cts
Devonshire Gdns
Oxford Gdns
Cambridge Gdns
Bridge Par
Avenue Par
Bush Hill Par
The Brackens
Crossway
Brendon Way
Bideford Gdns
Ash Gr
Sennen Rd
Edmonton Cty Upper Sch
Pegasus Ct
Pegasus
Ridge Ave
Ridge Ter
Bridge Gate
Elsiedene Rd
B154
Liby
Blakesware Gdns
Aldbury Mews
Westview Cres
Clovelly Gdns
Raglan Jun & Inf Schs
Porlock Rd
Crawley Rd
Edward Cl
Lawn Cl
Warren Cres
Galliard
Murley Ct
River Bank
Percy Rd
Solna Rd
Kent Rd
York Rd
Colne Rd
Griffins Cl
Little Bury St
Bury St W
Lynton Gdns
Cambridge Terr
Bury St
Hickory Cl
Elm Park Rd
Beaulieu Gdns
Firs La
Ramscroft Cl
Recn Gd
Pav
Alder Lodge
Lynford Terr
Bwg Gn
Tranmere Rd
Darley Rd
Harrow Dr
Blenheim Cl
Carlton Ho
Pav
Tenn Cts
The Paulin Gd
Ridge Rd
Rowantree Rd
Rowantree Cl
Church St
Churchill Ct
Edmonton Cty Lower Sch
Falman Cl
Bury St
Halstead Rd
Halstead Gdns
Wisley Cl
Allot Gdns
Allot Gdns
Rugby Ave
Recn Gd
Churchfield Prim Sch
Lancing Gdns
Latymer Rd
Malvern Terr
Glastonbury
Ford's Gr
P
Firs Park Ave
Salmon's Brook
Allot Gdns
Stowe Gdns
Marlborough Rd
Chichester Rd
Winchester Rd
Beverley Cl
Farm Rd
Pl Fld
Firs Park Gdns
Hydefield Cl
Tenn Cts
Sp Gds
Bwg Gn
Starks Field Prim Sch
Highfield Prim Sch
Hyde Park Gdns
Hyde Park Ave
Pav
Streamside Cl
St Ann's Rd
St Joan's Rd
Brendon Villas
Welbeck Villas
Laburnum Gr
Laburnum Gdns
Edmonton Cemy
Church St
Hydefield Ct
Cedars Ct
Tillotson Rd
Arthur Rd
Stanley Rd
Cyprus Rd
Church La
Wimborne Rd
Miles
Rusk
Durham Rd
Winchmore Sch
Tenn Cts
Pav
Recn Gd
Oldfield Gdns
Lichfield Rd
Lamb's Cl
Cosgrove Cl
Firs La
P
Firs Farm Pl Flds
Kipling Terr
Gatward Gn
Laburnum Ave
Hydeside Gdns
Hyde Way
B154
Church St
Firtree Lodge
Sp Gd
Pav
Barrowell Gn
Latymer Way
Lamb's Terr
Wheatley Gdns
The Latymer School
Hawthorne Ave
Hydethorpe Ave
Latymer All Saints CE Prim Sch
All Saints Cl
Almshouses
Granham Gdns
Gareth Dr
Farndale Ave
Allot Gdns
Ensign Dr
Firs Farm Prim Sch
Perry Gdns
Deansway
Northern Ave
Central Ave
Chalfont Gn
Dunholme Gn
Newstead Ho
Northumberland Gdns
Bedevere Rd
Rayleigh Rd
Rayleigh Cl
Harlow Rd
Pl Fld
40
Victor Villas
Banstead Gdns
Bexley Gdns
Purley Rd
Selhurst Rd
Beckenham Gdns
West Lea Sch
Hazelbury Jun & Inf Schs
Sweet Briar Gr
Chalfont Rd
South Eastern Ave
Dunholme Rd
West Ct
Maldon Rd
Galahad Rd
Salisbury Mans
Chauncey Cl
Gawaine Cl
Tristram Dr
Allot Gdns
Ash Gr
The Larches
Firscroft
The Fairway
Myrtle Rd
Briar Cl
Hazel Cl
Rylston Rd
Coniscliffe Rd
The Rowans
Birch Ave
Pembroke Rd
PO
Harington Terr
Westerham Ave
Keston Cl
Bromley Rd
Hazelbury La
Hazelbury Gn
Briary La
Sweet Briar Gn
Dunholme La
Pymmes Gdns S
Pymmes Gdns N
Sunnyside Rd N
Leonard Rd
Sunnyside Rd E
Sunnyside Rd S
Barbot Cl
Shrubbery
Hedge La
New Park Ave
Orpington Gdns
Shortlands Cl
Gheddington Rd
Haselbury Rd
Park La
Victoria Rd
Pycroft Way
Tatem Park
Parkside Terr
Huxley Rd
Pl Flds
Pymmes Park
Munster Gdns
Dorchester
Ulster
Hollywood Gardens
Morecambe Terr
Kendal Ave
The Gladys Aylward Sch
Lopen Works
Denton Rd
Sweet Briar
Sycamore
Solomon Ave
Fleece

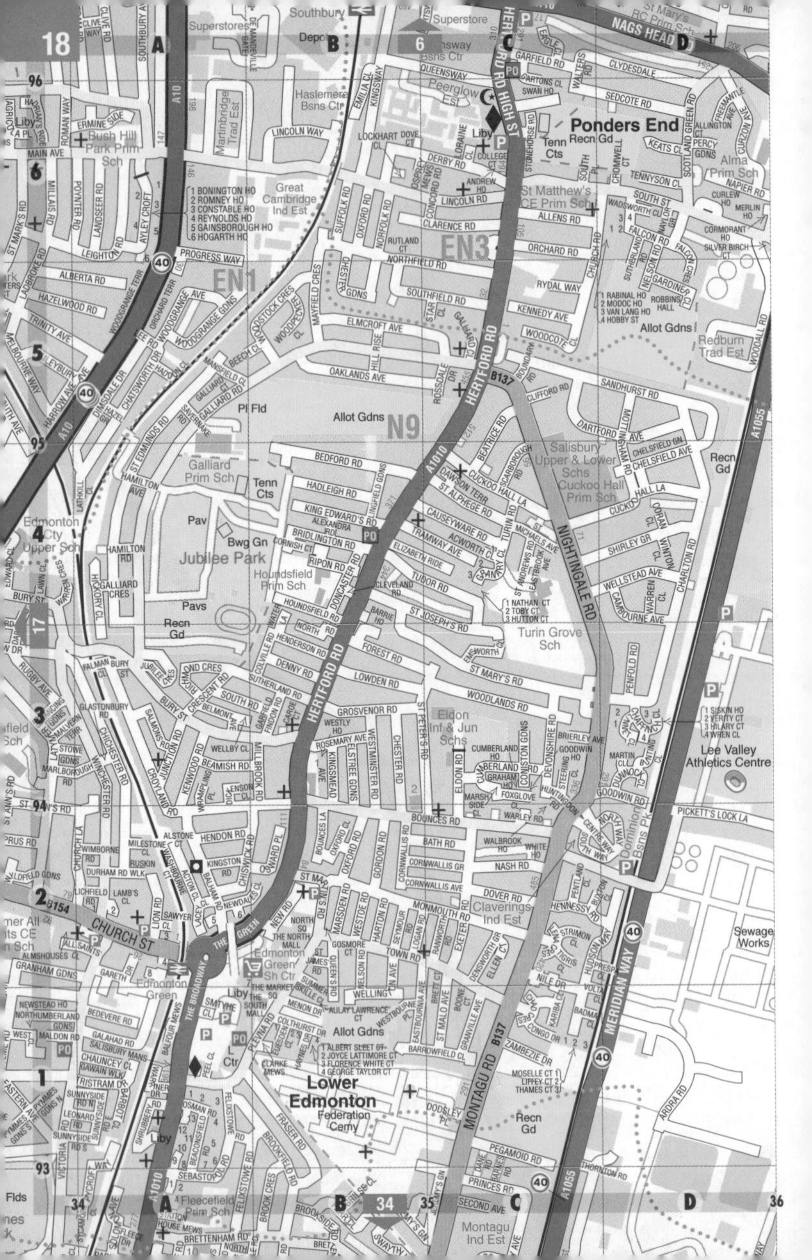

18
A
B
C
D
6
96
95
94
93
5
4
3
2
1
17
34
35
36
Southbury
Superstores
Superstore
Depot
NAGS HEAD RD
Ponders End
EN1
EN3
N9
A10
A1010
A1055
B137
B154
Haslemere Bsns Ctr
Martinbridge Trad Est
Great Cambridge Ind Est
Peerglow Est
Queensway Bsns Ctr
Bush Hill Park Prim Sch
Tenn Cts
Recn Gd
St Matthew's CE Prim Sch
Alma Prim Sch
Allot Gdns
Redburn Trad Est
Galliard Prim Sch
Pl Fld
Pav
Pavs
Bwg Gn
Jubilee Park
Houndsfield Prim Sch
Edmonton Cty Upper Sch
Salisbury Upper & Lower Schs
Cuckoo Hall Prim Sch
Turin Grove Sch
Eldon Inf & Jun Schs
Lee Valley Athletics Centre
Dominion Bsns Pk
Claverings Ind Est
Sewage Works
Edmonton Green Sh Ctr
Edmonton Green
Lower Edmonton
Federation Cemy
Montagu Ind Est
Fleecefield Prim Sch
HERTFORD RD
HIGH ST
NIGHTINGALE RD
MONTAGU RD
MERIDIAN WAY
CHURCH ST
THE BROADWAY
THE GREEN
SOUTHBURY AV
QUEENSWAY
GARFIELD RD
CLYDESDALE
SEDCOTE RD
KINGSWAY
LINCOLN WAY
LOCKHART CL
DERBY RD
LINCOLN RD
ALLENS RD
CLARENCE RD
NORTHFIELD RD
SOUTHFIELD RD
ORCHARD RD
RYDAL WAY
KENNEDY AVE
WOODCOTE
ELMCROFT AVE
OAKLANDS AVE
SANDHURST RD
CLIFFORD RD
DARTFORD AVE
CHELSFIELD AVE
BEDFORD RD
HADLEIGH RD
KING EDWARD'S RD
CUCKOO HALL LA
ST ALPHEGE RD
CAUSEYWARE RD
TRAMWAY AVE
ACWORTH CL
TUDOR RD
ST JOSEPH'S RD
FOREST RD
LOWDEN RD
ST MARY'S RD
WOODLANDS RD
GROSVENOR RD
SHIRLEY GR
WELLSTEAD AVE
CAMBOURNE AVE
PENFOLD RD
CHARLTON RD
PICKETT'S LOCK LA
GOODWIN RD
BOUNCES RD
BATH RD
CORNWALLIS GR
CORNWALLIS AVE
NASH RD
DOVER RD
MONMOUTH RD
TOWN RD
WELLINGTON
ALBERTA RD
HAZELWOOD RD
TRINITY AVE
MELBOURNE WAY
LEIGHTON RD
PROGRESS WAY
WOODGRANGE AVE
HAMILTON AVE
HAMILTON RD
GALLIARD CRES
BURY ST
RUGBY AVE
SOUTH RD
BELMONT AVE
WELLBY CL
BEAMISH RD
HENDON RD
KINGSTON RD
DURHAM RD WLK
GRANHAM GDNS
BEDEVERE RD
SALISBURY MANS
CHAUNCEY CL
GAWAIN WLK
TRISTRAM DR
PEGAMOID RD
PRINCES RD
SECOND AVE
THORNTON RD
ZAMBEZIE DR
CONGO DR
NILE DR
HUDSON WAY
ARDRA RD
DODSLEY PL
BARROWFIELD CL
FELIXSTOWE RD
BROOKFIELD RD
BROOK CRES
BRETTENHAM RD
FLEECEFIELD
1 BONINGTON HO
2 ROMNEY HO
3 CONSTABLE HO
4 REYNOLDS HO
5 GAINSBOROUGH HO
6 HOGARTH HO
1 RABINAL HO
2 MODOC HO
3 VAN LANG HO
4 HOBBY ST
1 NATHAN CT
2 TOBY CT
3 HUTTON CT
1 SISKIN HO
2 VERITY CT
3 HILARY CT
4 WREN CL
1 ALBERT SLEET CT
2 JOYCE LATTIMORE CT
3 FLORENCE WHITE CT
4 GEORGE TAYLOR CT
MOSELLE CT
LIFFEY CT
THAMES CT

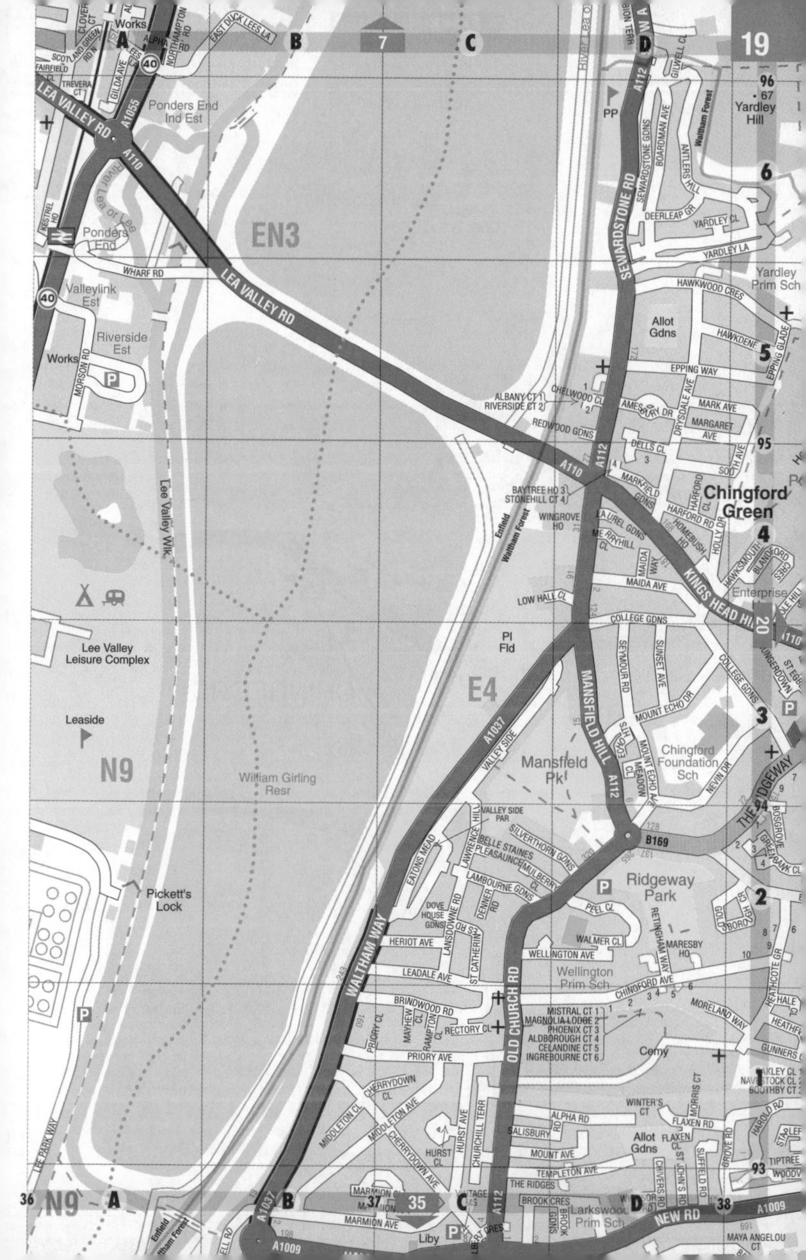

EN3
E4
N9
LEA VALLEY RD
Ponders End Ind Est
Ponders End
Valleylink Est
Riverside Est
Works
Lee Valley Wlk
Lee Valley Leisure Complex
Leaside
Pickett's Lock
William Girling Resr
SEWARDSTONE RD
Yardley Hill
Yardley Prim Sch
Allot Gdns
Chingford Green
KINGS HEAD HILL
Enterprise
MANSFIELD HILL
Mansfield Pk
Chingford Foundation Sch
Pl Fld
Ridgeway Park
THE RIDGEWAY
OLD CHURCH RD
WALTHAM WAY
Wellington Prim Sch
CHINGFORD AVE
Cemy
Allot Gdns
Larkswood Prim Sch
NEW RD
Liby
LEE PARK WAY

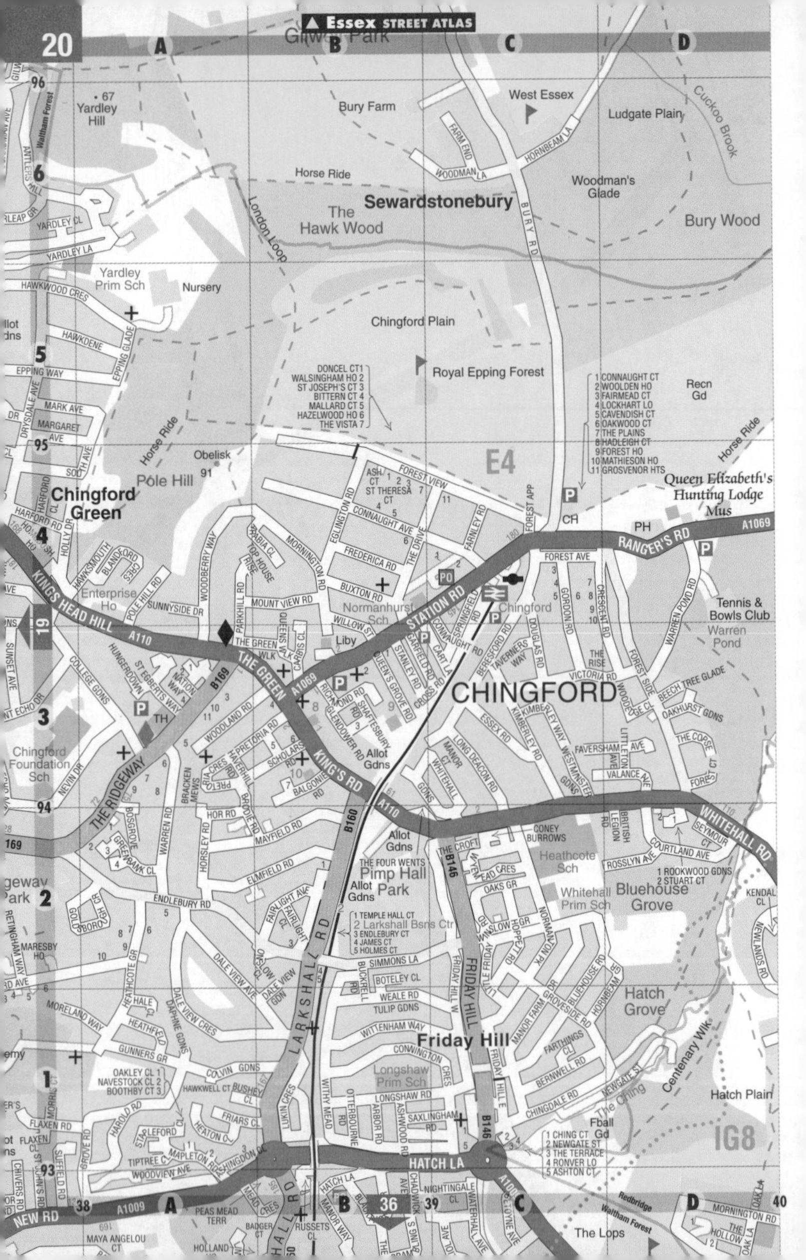
Gilwell Park
A
B
C
D
Bury Farm
West Essex
Ludgate Plain
Cuckoo Brook
FARM END
HORNBEAM LA
WOODMAN LA
Horse Ride
Woodman's Glade
Sewardstonebury
BURY RD
The Hawk Wood
London Loop
Bury Wood
67
Yardley Hill
Waltham Forest
ANTLERS HILL
YARDLEY CL
YARDLEY LA
Yardley Prim Sch
Nursery
HAWKWOOD CRES
HAWKDENE
EPPING GLADE
EPPING WAY
Chingford Plain
Royal Epping Forest
DONCEL CT 1
WALSINGHAM HO 2
ST JOSEPH'S CT 3
BITTERN CT 4
MALLARD CT 5
HAZELWOOD HO 6
THE VISTA 7
1 CONNAUGHT CT
2 WOOLDEN HO
3 FAIRMEAD CT
4 LOCKHART LO
5 CAVENDISH CT
6 OAKWOOD CT
7 THE PLAINS
8 HADLEIGH CT
9 FOREST HO
10 MATHIESON HO
11 GROSVENOR HTS
Recn Gd
MARK AVE
MARGARET AVE
DRYSDALE AVE
Horse Ride
Obelisk
91
Pole Hill
E4
Queen Elizabeth's Hunting Lodge Mus
FOREST VIEW
ASH CT
ST THERESA CT
EGLINTON RD
CONNAUGHT AVE
FOREST APP
CH
PH
RANGER'S RD
A1069
Chingford Green
HARFORD RD
HOLLY DR
HAWKSMOUTH
BLANDFORD CRES
POLE HILL RD
WOODBERRY WAY
ARABIA CL
TOP HOUSE RISE
MORNINGTON RD
FREDERICA RD
THE DRIVE
FARNLEY RD
FOREST AVE
Enterprise Ho
SUNNYSIDE DR
MOUNT VIEW RD
BUXTON RD
PO
Normanhurst Sch
STATION RD
Chingford
GORDON RD
CRESCENT RD
WARREN POND RD
Tennis & Bowls Club
Warren Pond
KINGS HEAD HILL
A110
19
PARKHILL RD
QUEENS WALK
CARBIS CL
WILLOW ST
Liby
THE GREEN WLK
THE GREEN
SPRINGFIELD RD
CONNAUGHT RD
DOUGLAS RD
THE RISE
FOREST SIDE
BEECH TREE GLADE
SUNSET AVE
COLLEGE GDNS
HUNGERDOWN
ST EGBERTS WAY
NATION WAY
B169
TH
WOODLAND RD
A1069
RICHMOND RD
SHAFTESBURY
QUEEN'S GROVE RD
STANLEY RD
GARFIELD RD
CART LA
CROSS RD
BERESFORD RD
TAVERNERS WAY
VICTORIA RD
CHINGFORD
ESSEX RD
KIMBERLEY RD
KIMBERLEY WAY
OAKHURST GDNS
THE COPSE
FOREST CT
Chingford Foundation Sch
NEVIN DR
PRETORIA RD
HAVERHILL
SCHOLARS RD
GLENDOWER RD
Allot Gdns
KING'S RD
BALGONIE RD
MANOR CT
WHITEHALL GDNS
LONG DEACON RD
WESTMINSTER GDNS
FAVERSHAM AVE
LITTLETON AVE
VALANCE AVE
94
THE RIDGEWAY
BRACKEN MEWS
WARREN RD
HOR RD
BRODIE RD
HORSLEY RD
MAYFIELD RD
B160
A110
Allot Gdns
BRITISH LEGION RD
WHITEHALL RD
SEYMOUR CT
COURTLAND AVE
BOSGROVE
GREENBANK CL
THE CROFT
CONEY BURROWS
Heathcote Sch
ROSSLYN AVE
1 ROOKWOOD GDNS
2 STUART CT
ELMFIELD RD
THE FOUR WENTS
Pimp Hall Park
B146
MEAD CRES
OAKS GR
Whitehall Prim Sch
Bluehouse Grove
KENDAL CL
ENDLEBURY RD
FAIRLIGHT AVE
FAIRLIGHT CL
Allot Gdns
1 TEMPLE HALL CT
2 Larkshall Bsns Ctr
3 ENDLEBURY CT
4 JAMES CT
5 HOLMES CT
WINSLOW GR
HOPPETT RD
NORMANTON PK
NEWLANDS RD
MARESBY HO
HEATHCOTE GR
DALE VIEW AVE
ONSLOW CL
DALE VIEW GDN
SIMMONS LA
BUCKRELL RD
BOTELEY CL
WEALE RD
TULIP GDNS
FRIDAY HILL W
FRIDAY HILL
LITTLE FRIDAY RD
BLUEHOUSE RD
HORNBEAM GR
Hatch Grove
MORELAND WAY
HALE CL
HEATHFIELD
DALE VIEW CRES
DAPHNE GDNS
LARKSHALL RD
WITTENHAM WAY
Friday Hill
MANOR FARM DR
GROVESIDE RD
CENTENARY WLK
GUNNERS GR
CONNINGTON CRES
FARTHINGS CL
OAKLEY CL 1
NAVESTOCK CL 2
BOOTHBY CT 3
COLVIN GDNS
HAWKWELL CT
BUSHEY CL
Longshaw Prim Sch
BERNWELL RD
NEWGATE ST
The Ching
Hatch Plain
HAROLD RD
LUKIN CRES
WITHY MEAD
OTTERBOURNE RD
ARBOR RD
LONGSHAW RD
ASHWOOD RD
SAXLINGHAM RD
CHINGDALE RD
FLAXEN RD
FLAXEN CL
STAPLEFORD CL
FRIARS CL
HEATON CL
Fball Gd
1 CHING CT
2 NEWGATE ST
3 THE TERRACE
4 RONVER LO
5 ASHTON CT
IG8
GROVE RD
SUFFIELD RD
MAPLETON RD
TIPTREE C
ASHINGDON CL
HATCH LA
93
CHIVERS RD
ST JOHN'S RD
WOODVIEW AVE
HATCH LA
CHADWICK AVE
NIGHTINGALE CL
WATERHALL AVE
A1009
Redbridge
Waltham Forest
OAKLA
38
NEW RD
A1009
A
PEAS MEAD TERR
MEAD CRES
B
36
39
C
D
40
MORNINGTON RD
THE HOLLOW
BADGER CT
RUSSETS CL
MANOR WAY
SETOYNE AVE
The Lops
MAYA ANGELOU CT
HOLLAND

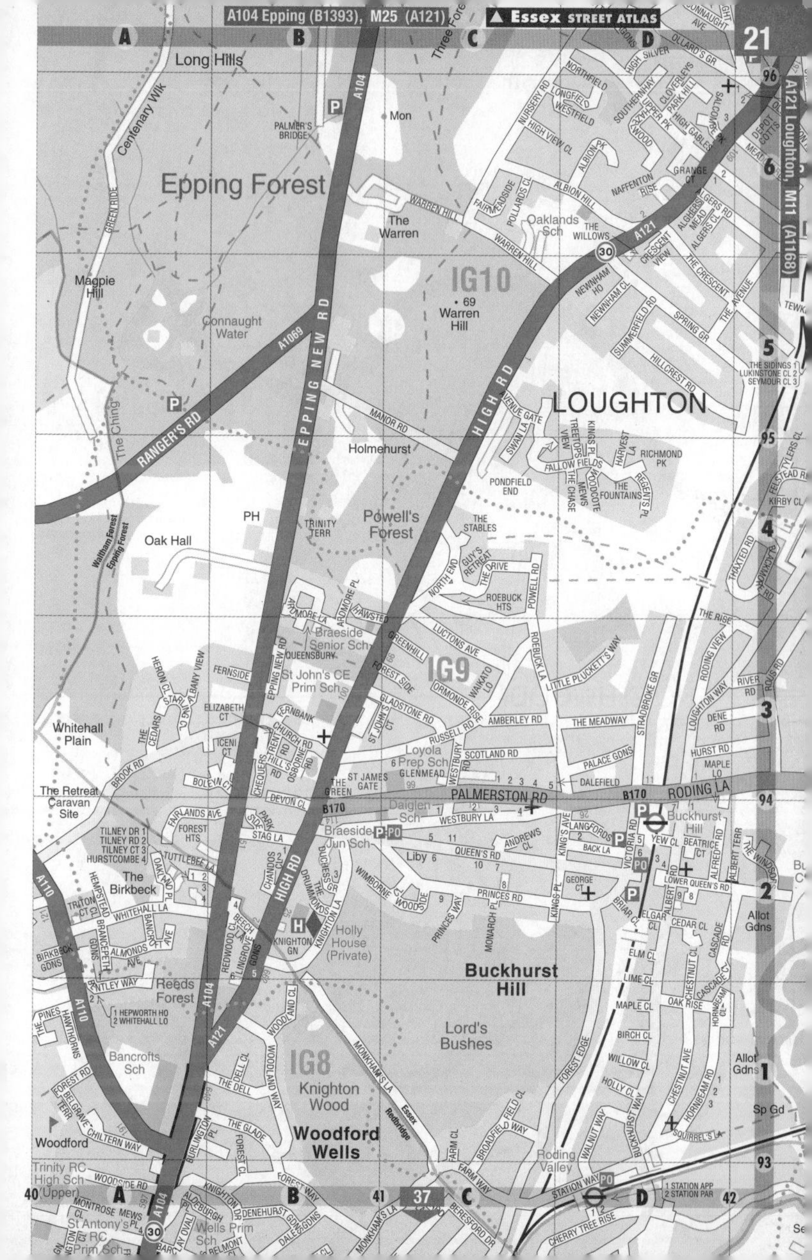

A104 Epping (B1393), M25 (A121)
Essex STREET ATLAS
21
A121 Loughton, M11 (A1168)
Long Hills
Centenary Wlk
Green Ride
Palmer's Bridge
Mon
Epping Forest
Warren Hill
The Warren
Magpie Hill
Connaught Water
A1069
Ranger's Rd
Epping New Rd
A104
IG10
69 Warren Hill
Oaklands Sch
The Willows
A121
High Rd
Manor Rd
Holmehurst
LOUGHTON
The Ching
Waltham Forest
Epping Forest
PH
Oak Hall
Trinity Terr
Powell's Forest
Pondfield End
The Stables
Guy's Retreat
The Drive
North End
Roebuck Hts
Powell Rd
Ardmore La
Ardmore Pl
Hawsted
Braeside Senior Sch
Queensbury
IG9
St John's CE Prim Sch
Luctons Ave
Greenhill
Forest Side
Ormonde Rise
Waikato Lo
Gladstone Rd
Russell Rd
Amberley Rd
The Meadway
Little Plucketts Way
Roebuck La
Stradbroke Gr
Whitehall Plain
Heron Cl
Albany View
Fernside
Elizabeth Ct
The Cedars
Iceni Ct
Church Rd
Loyola Prep Sch
Scotland Rd
Palace Gdns
Dalefield
Brook Rd
Boleyn Ct
Glenmead
St James Gate
The Green
Devon Cl
Palmerston Rd
B170
Roding La
The Retreat Caravan Site
Fairlands Ave
Forest Hts
Daiglen Sch
Westbury La
Stag La
Braeside Jun Sch
Queen's Rd
Liby
Andrews Cl
Langfords
Back La
Victoria Rd
Buckhurst Hill
Yew Cl
Beatrice Ct
Tilney Dr 1
Tilney Rd 2
Tilney Ct 3
Hurstcombe 4
Tuttlebee La
The Birkbeck
Chandos Cl
Duchess Gr
The Drummonds
Wimborne Cl
Woodside
Princes Rd
George Ct
Lower Queen's Rd
Albert Rd
Alfred Rd
Albert Terr
The Windsors
A110
Whitehall La
Triton Ct
Hempstead
Brancepeth Gdns
Almonds Ave
Bancroft Ave
Birkbeck Gdns
Beech La
Redwood Cl
Lingrove Gdns
Knighton La
Knighton Gn
Holly House (Private)
Princes Way
Monarch Pl
Kings Pl
Briar Cl
Elgar Cl
Cedar Cl
Cascade Rd
Allot Gdns
Bentley Way
Reeds Forest
1 Hepworth Ho
2 Whitehall Lo
The Pines
Hawthorns
Bancrofts Sch
Woodland Cl
Woodland Way
The Dell Cl
The Dell
IG8
Knighton Wood
Monkham's La
Essex
Redbridge
Buckhurst Hill
Lord's Bushes
Forest Edge
Elm Cl
Lime Cl
Maple Cl
Oak Rise
Chestnut Cl
Cascade Cl
Hornbeam Cl
Birch Cl
Willow Cl
Holly Cl
Chestnut Ave
Hornbeam Rd
Buckhurst Way
Squirrel's La
Sp Gd
Forest Rd
Belgrave Terr
Chiltern Way
Woodford
Burlington Pl
The Glade
Forest Cl
Woodford Wells
Farm Cl
Broadfield Cl
Broadfield Way
Walnut Way
Roding Valley
Farm Way
Station Way
1 Station App
2 Station Par
Trinity RC High Sch (Upper)
Woodside Rd
Montrose Mews
Knighton Dr
Forest Way
Denehurst Gdns
Aldeburgh Pl
Monkham's La
Beresford Dr
Cherry Tree Rise
St Antony's RC Prim Sch
Wells Prim Sch
Dale Gdns
Belmont
Nursery Rd
Northfield
Longfield
Westfield
High View Cl
High Silver
Ollard's Gr
Connaught Ave
Southernhay
Upper Pk
Cloverleys
Park Hill
High Gables
Salcombe Pk
Albion Pk
Albion Hill
Fairmeadside
Pollard's Cl
Naffenton Rise
Grange Ct
Algers Rd
Algers Mead
Algers Cl
Crescent View
The Crescent
The Avenue
Newnham Ho
Newnham Cl
Summerfield Rd
Spring Gr
Hillcrest Rd
The Sidings 1
Lukinstone Cl 2
Seymour Cl 3
Avenue Gate
Swan La
Treetops View
Kings Pl
Harvest La
Richmond Pk
Fallow Fields
The Chase
Mews
Woodcote
The Fountains
Regent's Pl
Tylers Cl
Felstead Rd
Kirby Cl
Thaxted Rd
Blackmore Rd
The Rise
Roding View
Loughton Way
River Rd
Rous Rd
Dene Rd
Hurst Rd
Maple Lo
Depot Cotts
Meadow
Tewk
Bu C
Se
A B C D
1 2 3 4 5 6
93 94 95 96
40 41 42
37
30

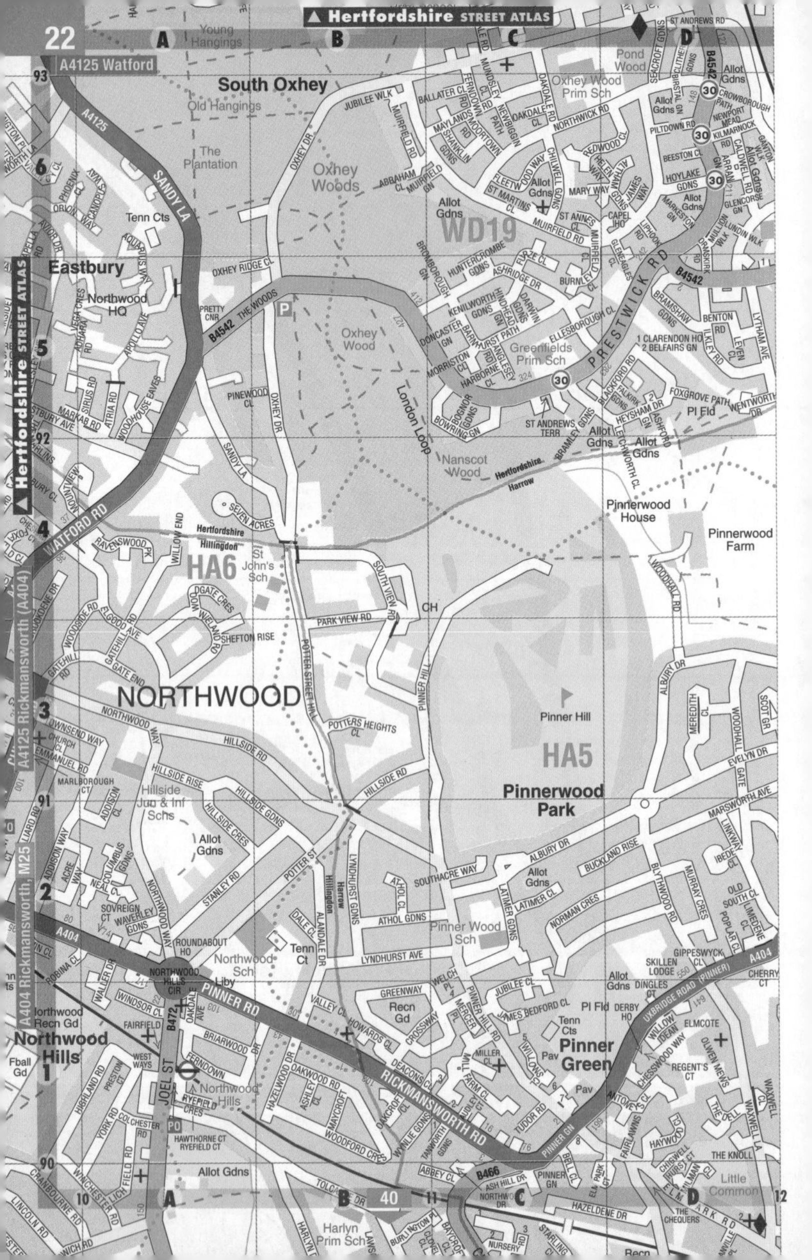
Hertfordshire STREET ATLAS
A4125 Watford
South Oxhey
Young Hangings
Old Hangings
The Plantation
Oxhey Woods
Oxhey Wood
Eastbury
Northwood HQ
Tenn Cts
SANDY LA
B4542 THE WOODS
OXHEY DR
OXHEY RIDGE CL
PRETTY CNR
PINEWOOD CL
London Loop
Nanscot Wood
WD19
Oxhey Wood Prim Sch
Pond Wood
Greenfields Prim Sch
PRESTWICK RD
B4542
JUBILEE WLK
MUIRFIELD RD
NORTHWICK RD
BALLATER CL
OAKDALE CL
MAYLANDS RD
ST MARTINS CL
MARY WAY
ST ANNES CL
CAPEL CL
HUNTERCROMBE GDNS
ASHRIDGE DR
KENILWORTH GDNS
DONCASTER GN
MORRISTON CL
HARBORNE CL
BOWRING GN
ELLESBOROUGH CL
BRAMSHAW GDNS
BENTON RD
1 CLARENDON HO
2 BELFAIRS GN
FOXGROVE PATH
ST ANDREWS TERR
HOYLAKE GDNS
PILTDOWN RD
BEESTON CL
CROWBOROUGH PATH
LYTHAM AVE
Allot Gdns
Pl Fld
Pinnerwood House
Pinnerwood Farm
Hertfordshire
Harrow
Hillingdon
SEVEN ACRES
HA6
St John's Sch
SOUTH VIEW RD
PARK VIEW RD
CH
SHEFTON RISE
WATFORD RD
NORTHWOOD
POTTER STREET HILL
POTTERS HEIGHTS CL
PINNER HILL
Pinner Hill
HA5
Pinnerwood Park
WOODHALL DR
ALBURY DR
EVELYN DR
MARSWORTH AVE
BUCKLAND RISE
SOUTHACRE WAY
LATIMER GDNS
NORMAN CRES
BLYTHWOOD RD
MURRAY CRES
HILLSIDE RD
HILLSIDE RISE
HILLSIDE GDNS
Hillside Jun & Inf Schs
NORTHWOOD WAY
STANLEY RD
POTTER ST
LYNDHURST GDNS
ATHOL GDNS
LYNDHURST AVE
Pinner Wood Sch
A4125 Rickmansworth (A404)
A404 Rickmansworth, M25
A404
ROUNDABOUT HO
NORTHWOOD HILLS CIR
Liby
Northwood Sch
Tenn Ct
PINNER RD
RICKMANSWORTH RD
UXBRIDGE ROAD (PINNER)
B472
JOEL ST
Northwood Hills
Northwood Recn Gd
Fball Gd
HIGHLAND RD
YORK RD
HAWTHORNE CT
RYEFIELD CT
Allot Gdns
Recn Gd
GREENWAY
CROSSWAY
JAMES BEDFORD CL
Tenn Cts
Pinner Green
Pav
ELMCOTE
REGENT'S CT
TUDOR RD
PINNER GN
HAZELDENE DR
THE KNOLL
Little Common
THE CHEQUERS
B466
Harlyn Prim Sch
NURSERY RD
STARLING CL
40
10
11
12
A
B
C
D
1
2
3
4
5
6
90
91
92
93

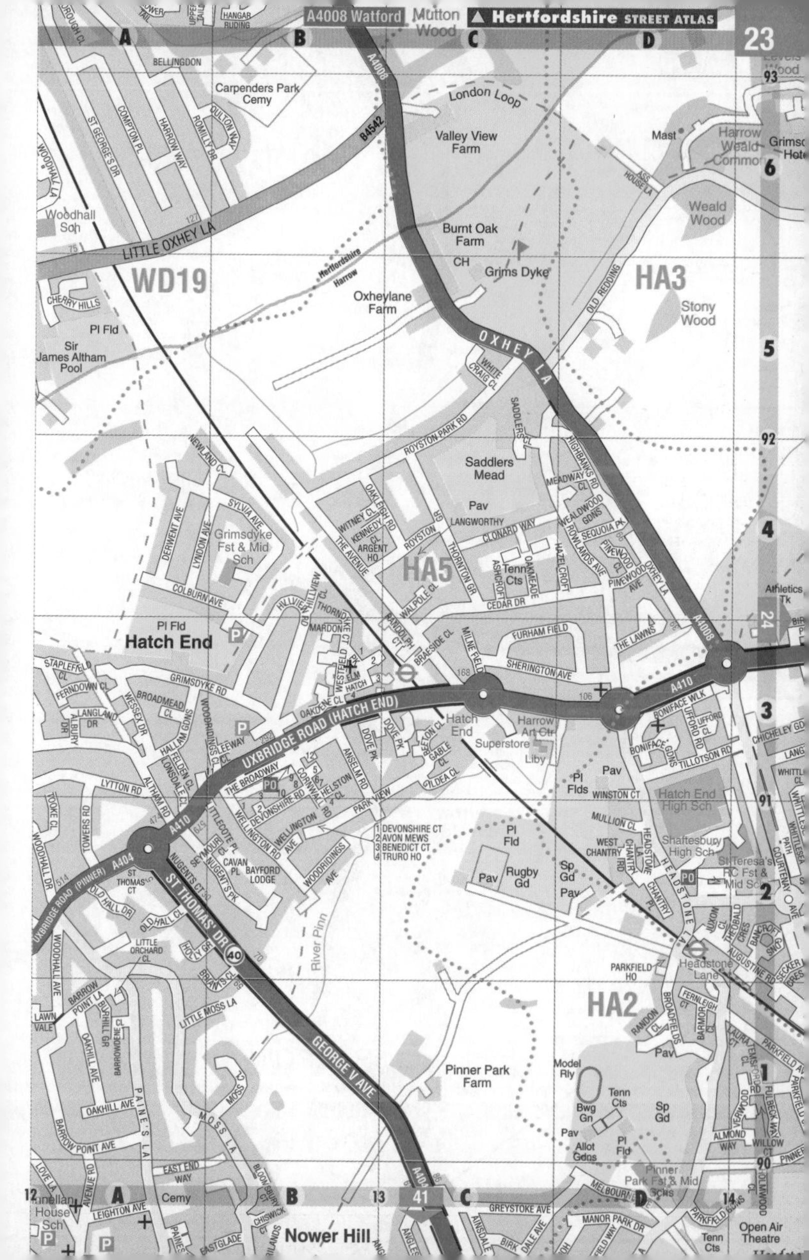

Carpenders Park Cemy
London Loop
Valley View Farm
Mast
Harrow Weald Common
Weald Wood
Woodhall Sch
LITTLE OXHEY LA
Burnt Oak Farm
Grims Dyke
WD19
HA3
Oxheylane Farm
Stony Wood
Sir James Altham Pool
OXHEY LA
Saddlers Mead
HA5
Grimsdyke Fst & Mid Sch
Hatch End
UXBRIDGE ROAD (HATCH END)
Harrow Art Ctr
Superstore
Liby
Hatch End High Sch
Shaftesbury High Sch
St Teresa's RC Fst & Mid Sch
Rugby Gd
Headstone Lane
HA2
GEORGE V AVE
ST THOMAS' DR
Pinner Park Farm
Model Rly
Pinner Park Fst & Mid Schs
Nower Hill
Open Air Theatre

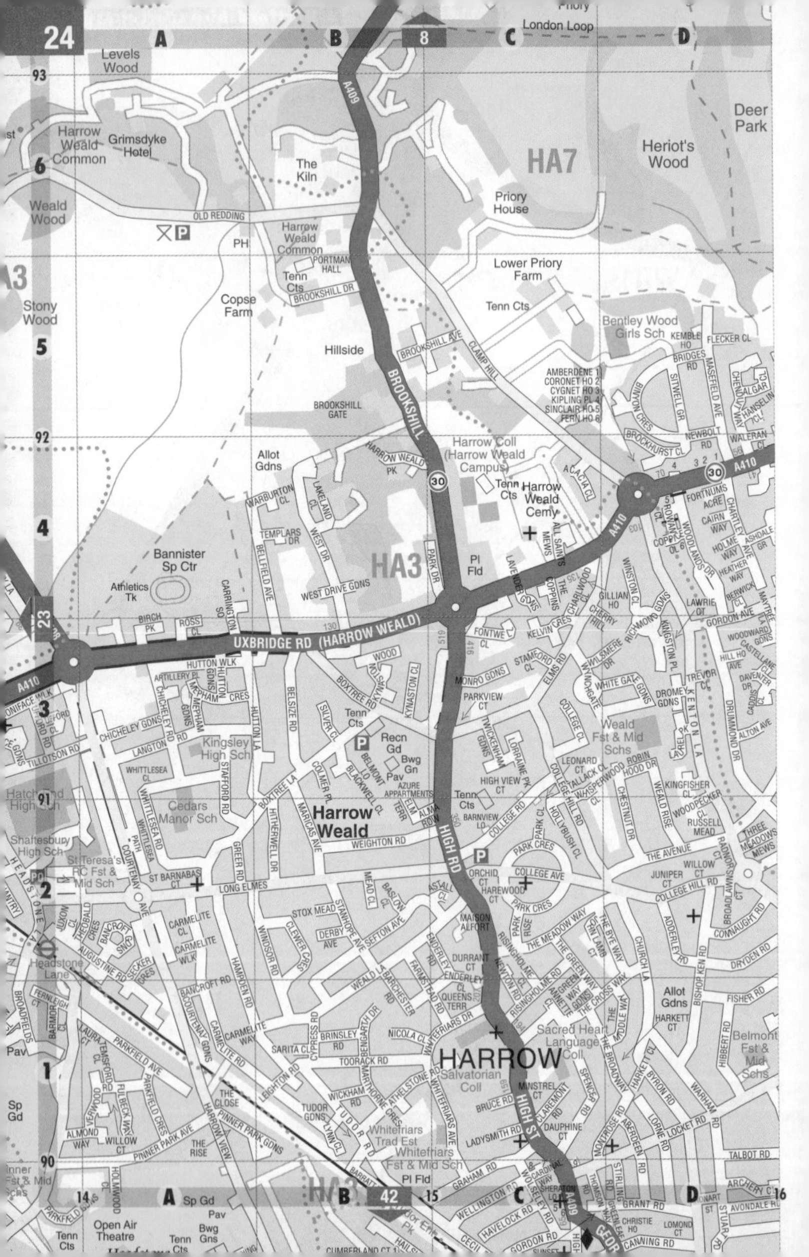

24
A
B
8
C
D
London Loop
Levels Wood
93
Harrow Weald Common
Grimsdyke Hotel
6
Weald Wood
OLD REDDING
PH
The Kiln
A409
HA7
Deer Park
Heriot's Wood
Priory House
Harrow Weald Common
PORTMAN HALL
Tenn Cts
BROOKSHILL DR
Lower Priory Farm
Tenn Cts
Stony Wood
Copse Farm
5
Hillside
BROOKSHILL AVE
CLAMP HILL
Bentley Wood Girls Sch
KEMBLE HO
FLECKER CL
BRIDGES RD
MASEFIELD AVE
AMBERDENE 1
CORONET HO 2
CYGNET HO 3
KIPLING PL 4
SINCLAIR HO 5
FERN HO 6
BROOKSHILL
BROOKSHILL GATE
SITWELL GR
BROCKHURST CL
NEWBOLT RD
WALERAN CL
92
Allot Gdns
HARROW WEALD PK
Harrow Coll (Harrow Weald Campus)
Tenn Cts
Harrow Weald Cemy
ACACIA CL
A410
FORTNUMS ACRE
CAIRN WAY
WARBURTON CL
LAKELAND CL
4
TEMPLARS DR
WEST DR
BELLFIELD AVE
HA3
PARK DR
Pl Fld
LAVENDER GDNS
ALL SAINTS MEWS
COPPINS
WINSTON CL
WOODLANDS DR
HOLME WAY
HEATHER WAY
BERWICK CL
Bannister Sp Ctr
Athletics Tk
CARRINGTON SQ
WEST DRIVE GDNS
GILLIAN HO
CHERRY HILL
CHARLWOOD CL
LAWRIE CT
GORDON AVE
WOODWARD GDNS
23
BIRCH PK
ROSS CL
UXBRIDGE RD (HARROW WEALD)
FONTWELL CL
KELVIN CRES
RICHMOND GDNS
KINGSTON PL
HILL HO AVE
CASTELLANE CL
A410
HUTTON WLK
ARTILLERY PL
HUTTON GDNS
WOOD
STAMFORD CL
ELMS RD
WILSMERE DR
MONRO GDNS
WHITE GATE GDNS
TREVOR CL
DAVENTER DR
3
MEPHAM CRES
MEPHAM GDNS
CHICHELEY RD
HUTTON LA
BELSIZE RD
BOXTREE RD
KYNASTON CL
PARKVIEW CT
WYNCHGATE
COLLEGE CL
DROMEY GDNS
KENTON LA
DRUMMOND DR
CHICHELEY GDNS
TILLOTSON RD
LANGTON RD
SILVER CL
Tenn Cts
Recn Gd
Bwg Gn
Pav
TWICKENHAM GDNS
LORRAINE PK
Weald Fst & Mid Schs
LAUREL PK
ALTON AVE
Kingsley High Sch
STAFFORD RD
BELMONT LO
BLACKWELL CL
LEONARD CT
TALLACK CL
WASPERWOOD CL
ROBIN HOOD DR
WHITTLESEA CL
AZURE APARTMENTS
HIGH VIEW CT
COLLEGE HILL RD
CHESTNUT DR
WEALD RISE
KINGFISHER CL
91
Hatch End High Sch
WHITTLESEA RD
Cedars Manor Sch
BOXTREE LA
COLMER PL
MARICAS AVE
ELM TERR
ALMA ROW
Tenn Cts
BARNVIEW LO
COLLEGE RD
WOODPECKER CL
RUSSELL MEAD
THREE MEADOWS MEWS
Shaftesbury High Sch
COURTENAY AVE
GREER RD
HITHERWELL DR
Harrow Weald
WEIGHTON RD
HIGH RD
PARK CL
PARK CRES
HOLLYBUSH CL
THE AVENUE
RADNOR
St Teresa's RC Fst & Mid Sch
ST BARNABAS CT
LONG ELMES
MEAD CL
ORCHID CT
COLLEGE AVE
JUNIPER CT
WILLOW CT
COLLEGE HILL RD
2
HEADSTONE
BASLOW CL
ASTALL CL
HAREWOOD CT
PARK CRES
BROADLAWNS CT
CONNAUGHT RD
JUXON CL
THEOBALD CRES
BANCROFT GDNS
CARMELITE CL
STOX MEAD
STANHOPE AVE
DERBY AVE
SEFTON AVE
MAISON ALFORT
PARK RISE
THE MEADOW WAY
THE BYE WAY
CHURCH LA
ADDERLEY RD
DRYDEN RD
Headstone Lane
AUGUSTINE RD
SECKER CRES
CARMELITE WLK
WINDSOR RD
CLEWER CRES
ENDERLEY RD
DURRANT CT
RISINGHOLME CL
THE GREEN WAY
BISHOP KEN RD
FISHER RD
BROADFIELDS
FERNLEIGH CT
BARMOR CL
BANCROFT RD
HAMPDEN RD
WEALD LA
BARCHESTER RD
FARMSTEAD RD
ENDERLEY CT
QUEENS TERR
NEWTON RD
RISINGHOLME RD
ANNETTE CL
GREEN WAY GDNS
THE CROSS WAY
MIDDLE WAY
Allot Gdns
HARKETT CT
Pav
LAURA CL
TEMSFORD CL
PARKFIELD AVE
COURTENAY GDNS
CARMELITE WAY
CARMELITE RD
CYPRESS RD
BRINSLEY RD
BENGARTH DR
NICOLA CL
WHITEFRIARS DR
Sacred Heart Language Coll
THE BROADWAY
HIBBERT RD
Belmont Fst & Mid Schs
1
SARITA CL
TOORACK RD
HARROW
Salvatorian Coll
HARKETT CL
BYRON RD
WARHAM RD
Sp Gd
ALMOND WAY
WILLOW CT
VERWOOD DR
FULBECK WAY
PARKFIELD CRES
THE CLOSE
HARROW VIEW
PINNER PARK GDNS
LEIGHTON RD
WICKHAM RD
MARTHORNE CRES
ATHELSTONE RD
WHITEFRIARS AVE
MINSTREL CT
BRUCE RD
HIGH ST
CLAREMONT RD
SPENCER RD
MONTROSE RD
ABERDEEN RD
LORNE RD
LOCKET RD
PINNER PARK AVE
THE RISE
TUDOR GDNS
TUDOR RD
LYNN CL
Whitefriars Trad Est
Whitefriars Fst & Mid Sch
LADYSMITH RD
DAUPHINE CT
TALBOT RD
90
Pinner Fst & Mid Schs
HOLMWOOD CL
GRAHAM RD
CARDINAL WAY
Pl Fld
STIRLING RD
ARCHERY CL
14
A
Sp Gd
B
42
15
C
SHERATON LO
THOMSON RD
D
16
PARKFIELD GDNS
Pav
WELLINGTON RD
WOLSELEY RD
A409
GRANT RD
GREENLEE WALK
AVONDALE RD
STUART RD
Open Air Theatre
Tenn Cts
Tenn Cts
Bwg Gns
HAVELOCK RD
CHRISTIE HO
LOMOND CT
CUMBERLAND CT
CECIL
GORDON RD
CANNING RD
GEORGE

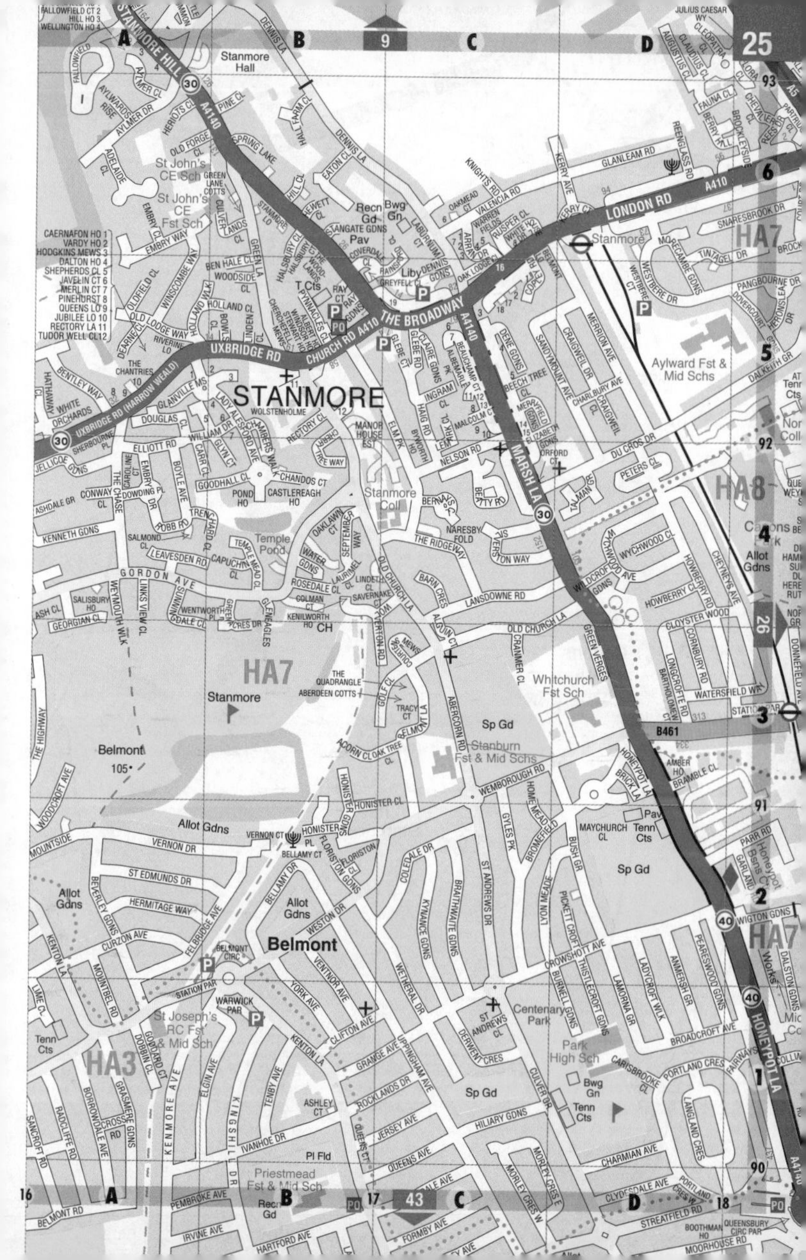

25
A
B
C
D
9
43
6
5
4
3
2
1
16
17
18
FALLOWFIELD CT 2
HILL HO 3
WELLINGTON HO 4
STANMORE HILL
DENNIS LA
JULIUS CAESAR WY
CLEOPATRA CL
AUGUSTUS CL
CLAUDIUS CL
FLORA CL
FAUNA CL
CHEVALIER CL
BERRY HILL
BROCKLEYSIDE
REES DR
PARTRIDGE
A5
93
Stanmore Hall
FALLOWFIELD
AYLMER CL
AYLMER DR
AYLWARDS RISE
ADELAIDE CL
HERIOTS CL
PINE CL
A4140
HALL FARM CL
OLD FORGE CL
SPRING LAKE
St John's CE Sch
St John's CE Fst Sch
GREEN LANE COTTS
CULVER LANDS
EATON CL
HILL CL
STANMORE LO
HEWETT CL
Recn Gd
Bwg Gn
LABURNUM CT
KNIGHTS RD
KERRY AVE
GLANLEAM RD
REENGLASS RD
OAKMEAD CT
VALENCIA RD
WARREN FIELDS
RUSPER CL
WHITE HO DR
ARRAN DR
KERRY CT
LONDON RD
A410
SNARESBROOK DR
HA7
BROCK
Stanmore
WESTBERE CT
MORECAMBE GDNS
TINTAGEL DR
WESTBERE DR
PANGBOURNE DR
DOVERCOURT
HERONSLEA DR
CAERNAFON HO 1
VARDY HO 2
HODGKINS MEWS 3
DALTON HO 4
SHEPHERDS CL 5
JAVELIN CT 6
MERLIN CT 7
PINEHURST 8
QUEENS LO 9
JUBILEE LO 10
RECTORY LA 11
TUDOR WELL CL 12
EMBRY CL
EMBRY WAY
GREEN LA
LANGATE GDNS
Pav
COVERDALE CL
RAINSFORD
Liby
DENNIS GDNS
OAK LODGE CL
GREYFELL CL
BELMONT
COPE
BEN HALE CL
WOODSIDE CL
HALSBURY CL
THE WOODLANDS
T Cts
RAY CT
RAY GDNS
PYNNACLES CL
OLDFIELD CL
WINSCOMBE WAY
HOLLAND WLK
HOLLAND CL
BOWLS
LINDEN CL
CHERCHEFELL MEWS
STEWART HO
WINDSOR HO
ALBERT HO
OLD LODGE WAY
DEARNE CL
RIVERINE LO
THE BROADWAY
CHURCH RD A410
UXBRIDGE RD
PO
GLEBE CT
GLEBE RD
CLAIRE GDNS
INGRAM CL
BEAUCHAMP CT
ALBEMARLE PK
DENE GDNS
BEECH TREE CL
SANDYMOUNT AVE
CRAIGWEIL DR
MERRION AVE
CHARLBURY AVE
CRAIGWEIL CL
Aylward Fst & Mid Schs
DALKEITH GR
THE CHANTRIES
HATHAWAY
BENTLEY WAY
WHITE ORCHARDS
UXBRIDGE RD (HARROW WEALD)
GLANVILLE MS
STANMORE
WOLSTENHOLME
LADY ALESFORD AVE
DOUGLAS CL
WILLIAM DR
CHAMBERS WALK
MANOR HOUSE EST
ELM PK
HAIG RD
BYWORTH HO
KIRK CL
LEM
MALCOLM CT
MERRYFIELD GDNS
ELIZABETH GDNS
MARSH LA
NELSON RD
ORFORD CT
DU CROS DR
PETERS CL
92
HA8
SHERBOURNE PL
JELLICOE GDNS
ELLIOTT RD
CAROLINE CT
EMBRY DR
BOYLE AVE
CARR CL
GLYN CT
RECTORY CL
CHERRY TREE WAY
CHANDOS CT
GOODHALL CL
POND HO
CASTLEREAGH HO
Stanmore Coll
BERNAYS CL
BEATTY RD
TALMAN GR
ASHDALE GR
CONWAY CL
THE CHASE
DOWDING PL
ROBB RD
TRENCHARD CL
KENNETH GDNS
SALMOND CL
Temple Pond
OAKLAWN CT
SEPTEMBER WAY
NARESBY FOLD
THE RIDGEWAY
VERSTON WAY
WYCHWOOD CL
WYCHWOOD AVE
WILDCROFT GDNS
HOWBERRY RD
CHEYNEYS AVE
Allot Gdns
LEAVESDEN RD
CAPUCHIN CL
TEMPLE MEAD CL
WATER GDNS
LAURIMEL CL
LINDETH CL
OLD CHURCH LA
BARN CRES
LANSDOWNE RD
HOWBERRY CL
GORDON AVE
SALISBURY HO
LINKS VIEW CL
SUNNINGDALE CL
WENTWORTH PL
GREENACRES DR
GLENEAGLES
ROSEDALE CL
GOLMAN CT
SAVERNAKE CT
TOM OVERTON RD
KENILWORTH HO
CH
CLOYSTER WOOD
CORNBURY RD
LONGCROFTE RD
BARTHOLOMEW CL
26
ASH CL
GEORGIAN CL
WEYMOUTH WLK
OLD CHURCH LA
ALCUIN CT
CRANMER CL
GREEN VERGES
COURTENAY MEWS
HA7
THE QUADRANGLE
ABERDEEN COTTS
GOLF CL
TRACY CT
BELMONT LA
ABERCORN RD
Whitchurch Fst Sch
WATERSFIELD WAY
STATION PAR
313
B461
Stanmore
Sp Gd
THE HIGHWAY
Belmont
105
ACORN CL
OAK TREE CL
Stanburn Fst & Mid Schs
HONEYPOT LA
BRICK LA
AMBER HO
BRAMBLE CL
HONISTER GDNS
HONISTER CL
WEMBOROUGH RD
HOME MEAD
91
WOODCROFT AVE
Allot Gdns
MOUNTSIDE
VERNON DR
VERNON CT
HONISTER PL
FLORISTON CL
BELLAMY CT
FLORISTON GDNS
COLEDALE DR
GYLES PK
BROMEFIELD
BUSH GR
MAYCHURCH CL
Tenn Cts
PARR RD
Honeypot Bsns C
GARLAND
ST EDMUNDS DR
BEVERLEY GDNS
HERMITAGE WAY
FELBRIDGE AVE
BELLAMY DR
Allot Gdns
WESTON DR
KYNANCE GDNS
BRAITHWAITE GDNS
ST ANDREWS DR
LYON MEADE
PICKETT CROFT
WIGTON GDNS
CURZON AVE
KENTON LA
MOUNTBEL RD
BELMONT CIRC
Belmont
VENTNOR AVE
WETHERAL DR
CROWSHOTT AVE
THISTLECROFT GDNS
BURNELL GDNS
LAMORNA GR
LADYCROFT WLK
ANMERSH GR
PEARSWOOD GDNS
DALSTON GDNS
Works
LIME CL
STATION PAR
WARWICK PAR
YORK AVE
St Joseph's RC Fst & Mid Sch
Tenn Cts
HA3
GODDARD CT
DOBBIN CL
CLIFTON AVE
KENTON LA
UPPINGHAM AVE
ST ANDREWS CL
DERWENT CRES
Centenary Park
Park High Sch
BROADCROFT AVE
FAIRWAYS
HONEYPOT LA
GRANGE AVE
ELGIN AVE
KENMORE AVE
KINGSHILL DR
TENBY AVE
ASHLEY CT
ROCKLANDS DR
Sp Gd
CULVER DR
Bwg Gn
Tenn Cts
CARISBROOKE CL
PORTLAND CRES
LANGLAND CRES
GRASMERE GDNS
CROSS RD
BORROWDALE AVE
RADCLIFFE RD
SANCROFT RD
JERSEY AVE
QUEENS CT
HILIARY GDNS
IVANHOE DR
Pl Fld
QUEENS AVE
MORLEY CRES
CHARMIAN AVE
90
A4140
Priestmead Fst & Mid Sch
PEMBROKE AVE
Recn Gd
BELMONT RD
IRVINE AVE
HARTFORD AVE
FORMBY AVE
MORLEY CRES E
MORLEY CRES W
CLYDESDALE AVE
PORTLAND CRES W
STREATFIELD RD
BOOTHMAN HO
QUEENSBURY CIRC PAR
MOORHOUSE RD

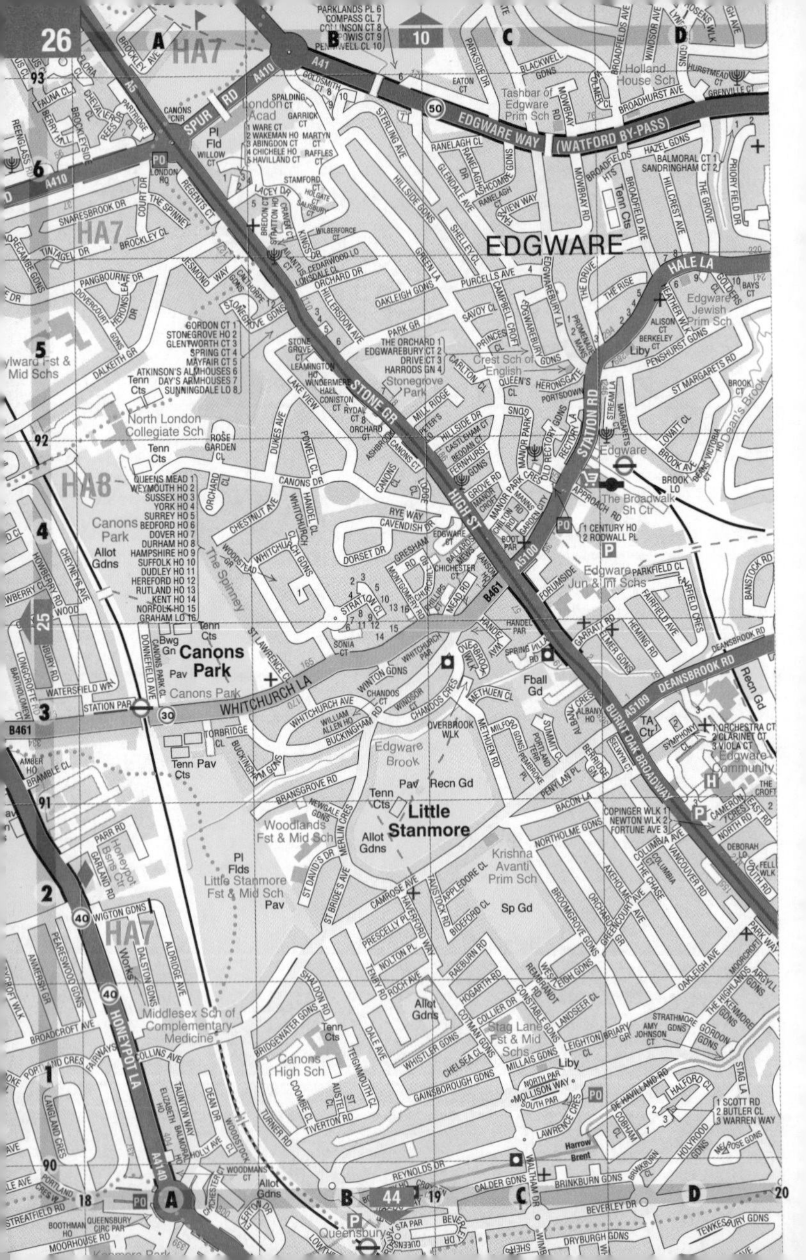

26
A
B
C
D
10
HA7
HA8
EDGWARE
Canons Park
Little Stanmore
SPUR RD
A410
A41
A5
EDGWARE WAY
(WATFORD BY-PASS)
STONE GR
HIGH ST
B461
A5100
STATION RD
HALE LA
BURNT OAK BROADWAY
A5109
DEANSBROOK RD
WHITCHURCH LA
HONEYPOT LA
A4140
Holland House Sch
Tashbar of Edgware Prim Sch
London Acad
North London Collegiate Sch
Stonegrove Park
Crest Sch of English
Edgware Jewish Prim Sch
The Broadwalk Sh Ctr
Edgware Jun & Inf Schs
Edgware Community
Edgware Brook
Woodlands Fst & Mid Sch
Krishna Avanti Prim Sch
Little Stanmore Fst & Mid Sch
Honeypot Bsns Ctr
Middlesex Sch of Complementary Medicine
Canons High Sch
Stag Lane Fst & Mid Schs
Queensbury
Recn Gd
Allot Gdns
Tenn Cts
Fball Gd
Sp Gd
Liby
25
44

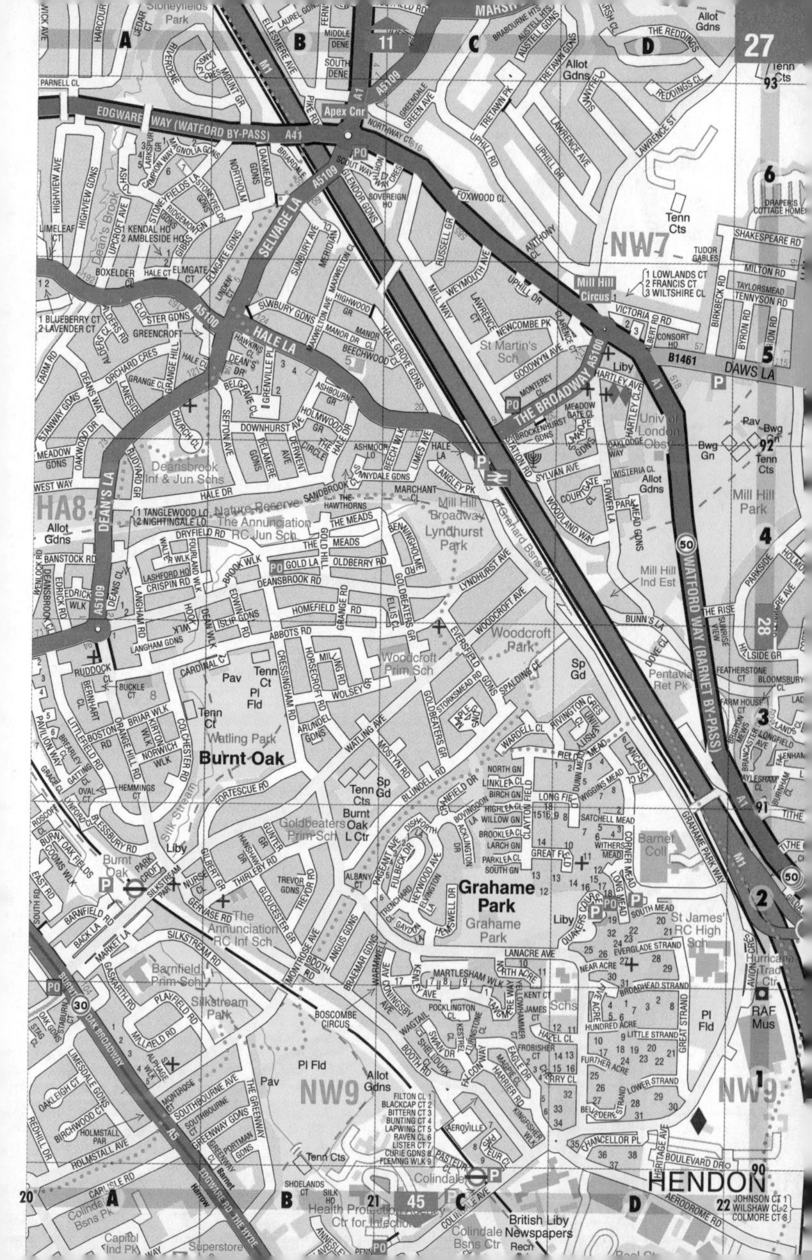
A
B
C
D
11
Stoneyfields Park
EDGWARE WAY (WATFORD BY-PASS)
A41
A5109
A1
Apex Cnr
PARNELL CL
ELLESMERE AVE
MIDDLE DENE
SOUTH DENE
THE REDDINGS
REDDINGS CL
Allot Gdns
BRABOURNE HTS
AUSTELL HTS
AUSTELL GDNS
TRETAWN GDNS
TRETAWN PK
UPHILL RD
LAWRENCE AVE
LAWRENCE ST
NORTHWAY CT
GREENDALE
GREEN AVE
HIGHVIEW AVE
HIGHVIEW GDNS
MAGNOLIA GDNS
LARKSPUR
CAMPION WAY
STONEYFIELDS LA
STONEYFIELDS GDNS
NORTHOLM
OAKMEAD GDNS
BRIARDALE
SCOUT WAY
GLENDOR GDNS
SOVEREIGN HO
SELVAGE LA
SUNBURY AVE
MERIDIAN
MAXWELTON CL
FOXWOOD CL
RUSSELL GR
ANTHONY CL
Tenn Cts
NW7
SHAKESPEARE RD
TUDOR GABLES
MILTON RD
TAYLORSMEAD
TENNYSON RD
DRAPER'S COTTAGE HOMES
1 LOWLANDS CT
2 FRANCIS CT
3 WILTSHIRE CL
Mill Hill Circus
VICTORIA RD
ALBERT RD
CONSORT HO
BIRKBECK RD
BYRON RD
B1461
DAWS LA
LIMELEAF CT
UPCROFT AVE
1 KENDAL HO
2 AMBLESIDE HO
RIDGEMONT GDNS
GIBBS GN
Dean's Brook
BOXELDER CL
HALE CT
ELMGATE CT
ELMGATE GDNS
LINDEN CT
SUNBURY GDNS
MAXWELTON AVE
HIGHWOOD GR
MANOR DR
MANOR CL
HALE GROVE GDNS
MILL WAY
WEYMOUTH AVE
UPHILL DR
LAWRENCE CT
NEWCOMBE PK
CLARENCE CT
St Martin's Sch
GOODWYN AVE
A5100
THE BROADWAY
MONTEREY CL
HARTLEY AVE
HARTLEY CL
Liby
1 BLUEBERRY CT
2 LAVENDER CT
ALDERS CL
ALDERS RD
CLOISTER GDNS
GREENCROFT
HALE LA
HAWKINS CL
DEAN'S DR
GRENVILLE PL
BEECHWOOD CL
FARM RD
DEANS WAY
ORCHARD CRES
GRANGE HILL
GRANGE CL
LANESIDE
BELGRAVE CL
ASHBOURNE GR
HOLMWOOD GR
THE CIRCLE
HALE DR
MEADOW GATE CL
BROCKENHURST GDNS
STATION RD
SYLVAN AVE
OAKLODGE WAY
WISTERIA CL
Univ of London Obsy
Pav
Bwg Gn
Tenn Cts
STANWAY GDNS
OAKWOOD DR
MEADOW GDNS
CHURCH CL
SEFTON AVE
DOWNHURST AVE
DELAMERE GDNS
DERWENT AVE
ASHMOOR LO
BEECH WLK
LIMES AVE
HALE LA
SUNNYDALE GDNS
LANGLEY PK
COURTGATE CL
FLOWER LA
Allot Gdns
Mill Hill Park
WEST WAY
DEAN'S LA
Deansbrook Inf & Jun Schs
RUDYARD GR
HALE DR
SANDBROOK CL
THE HAWTHORNS
MARCHANT CL
Mill Hill Broadway
WOODLAND WAY
PARK
MEAD GDNS
HA8
1 TANGLEWOOD LO
2 NIGHTINGALE LO
Nature Reserve
The Annunciation RC Jun Sch
THE MEADS
BENNINGHOLME RD
Lyndhurst Park
Grahard Bsns Ctr
Allot Gdns
DRYFIELD RD
WALTER WLK
FOURLAND WLK
BANSTOCK RD
WENLOCK RD
DEANSBROOK RD
EDRICK RD
EDRICK WLK
LASHFORD HO
CRISPIN RD
BROOK WLK
GOLD LA
GOLD HILL
OLDBERRY RD
GOLDBEATERS GR
LYNDHURST AVE
Mill Hill Ind Est
WATFORD WAY (BARNET BY-PASS)
50
DEANS CL
LANGHAM RD
HOOK WLK
DEAN WLK
EDWIN GDNS
ISLIP GDNS
HOMEFIELD RD
GRANGE RD
ELLIS CL
WOODCROFT AVE
BUNN'S LA
DOVE CL
SUNRISE VIEW
THE RISE
PARKSIDE
28
HILLSIDE GR
LANGHAM GDNS
ABBOTS RD
CARDINAL CT
Tenn Ct
CRESSINGHAM RD
HORSECROFT RD
MILLING RD
Woodcroft Prim Sch
EVERSFIELD GDNS
Woodcroft Park
Sp Gd
Pentavia Ret Pk
FEATHERSTONE CT
BLOOMSBURY CL
RUDDOCK CL
BUCKLE CT
BERNHART CL
Pav
Pl Fld
WOLSEY GR
STORKSMEAD RD
SPALDING CL
FARM HOUSE CT
BRISTON MEWS
LONGFIELD AVE
BRANCASTER RD
RIVINGTON CRES
UNIVERSITY CL
PAVILION WAY
BRIAR WLK
KIRTON WLK
NORWICH WLK
COLCHESTER RD
ARUNDEL GDNS
WATLING AVE
GOLDBEATERS GR
MAPLE CL
WARDELL CL
FIELD MEAD
LANCASTER CL
BREARLEY CL
LITTLEFIELD RD
BOSTON RD
ORANGE HILL RD
Watling Park
Burnt Oak
MOSTYN RD
BLUNDELL RD
DUNN MEAD
AYLESHAM CL
BURNHAM CL
GRACE CL
GATTING CL
OVAL CT
HEMMINGS CT
FORTESCUE RD
Tenn Cts
Sp Gd
Burnt Oak L Ctr
CRANFIELD DR
NORTH GN
LINKLEA CL
BIRCH GN
HIGHLEA CL
WILLOW GN
CLAYTON FIELD
LONG FIELD
WIGGINS MEAD
SATCHELL MEAD
91
TITHE
ROSCOFF CL
LYNFORD CL
BURNT OAK FIELDS
COOMBS WLK
BLESSBURY RD
Silk Stream
Goldbeaters Prim Sch
GUNTER GR
HANSHAW DR
BOVINGDON LA
DISHFORTH LA
ACKLINGTON DR
BROOKLEA CL
LARCH GN
PARKLEA CL
SOUTH GN
GREAT FIELD
WITHERS MEAD
CORNER MEAD
Barnet Coll
EAST RD
SOUTH RD
Burnt Oak
Liby
GILBERT GR
PARK CROFT
THIRLEBY RD
TREVOR GDNS
TREVOR RD
GLOUCESTER GR
ALBANY CT
PAGEANT AVE
FULBECK DR
HEYWOOD AVE
ELVINGTON LA
Grahame Park
LONG MEAD
GRAHAME PARK WAY
M1
50
SILKSTREAM PAR
NURSERY CL
GERVASE RD
The Annunciation RC Inf Sch
BARNFIELD RD
BACK LA
MARKET LA
TRENCHARD CL
GAYDON LA
HEMSWELL DR
Liby
QUAKERS COURSE
SOUTH MEAD
St James' RC High Sch
SILKSTREAM RD
GASKARTH RD
Barnfield Prim Sch
PLAYFIELD RD
Silkstream Park
MONTROSE AVE
BOOTH RD
ANGUS GDNS
BRAEMAR GDNS
WARMWELL AVE
LANACRE AVE
NORTH ACRE
MARTLESHAM WLK
KENLEY AVE
YELLOWHAMMER CT
NEAR ACRE
EVERGLADE STRAND
BROADHEAD STRAND
Hurricane Trad Ctr
AVION CRES
30
BURNT OAK BROADWAY
STABURN CT
STAG CL
OAK GDNS
MILLFIELD RD
ALPHAGE WLK
CONINGSBY AVE
BOSCOMBE CIRCUS
POCKLINGTON CL
WAGTAIL CL
SWAN DR
SHELDUCK CL
KESTREL CL
TURNSTONE CL
FALCON WAY
TANGMERE WAY
KENT CT
JAMES CT
HAZEL CL
FROBISHER CT
HUNDRED ACRE
FIVE ACRE
LITTLE STRAND
FURTHER ACRE
GREAT STRAND
Pl Fld
RAF Mus
LIMESDALE GDNS
OAKLEIGH CT
BIRCHWOOD CT
HOLMSTALL PAR
HOLMSTALL AVE
REDHILL DR
MONTROSE CT
SOUTHBOURNE AVE
SOUTHBOURNE CT
GREENWAY GDNS
PORTMAN GDNS
THE GREENWAY
Pav
Pl Fld
NW9
Allot Gdns
FILTON CL 1
BLACKCAP CT 2
BITTERN CT 3
BUNTING CT 4
LAPWING CT 5
RAVEN CL 6
LISTER CT 7
CURIE GDNS 8
FLEMING WLK 9
BOOTH RD
AEROVILLE
PASTEUR CL
PASTEUR DR
EAGLE DR
MAGPIE CL
HARRIER RD
KINGFISHER WLK
CHERRY CL
BELVEDERE STRAND
LOWER STRAND
NW9
CHANCELLOR PL
HERITAGE AVE
BOULEVARD DR
90
HENDON
1
Tenn Cts
Colindale
A5
EDGWARE RD THE HYDE
CARLISLE RD
Barnet
Harrow
20
A
B
21
45
C
D
22
SHOELANDS CT
SILK HO
COLINDALE AVE
JOHNSON CT 1
WILSHAW CL 2
COLMORE CT 3
AERODROME RD
Colindale Bsns Pk
Capitol Ind Pk
Superstore
Health Protection Agency Ctr for Infections
British Liby Newspapers
Colindale Bsns Ctr
Recn
ANNESLEY

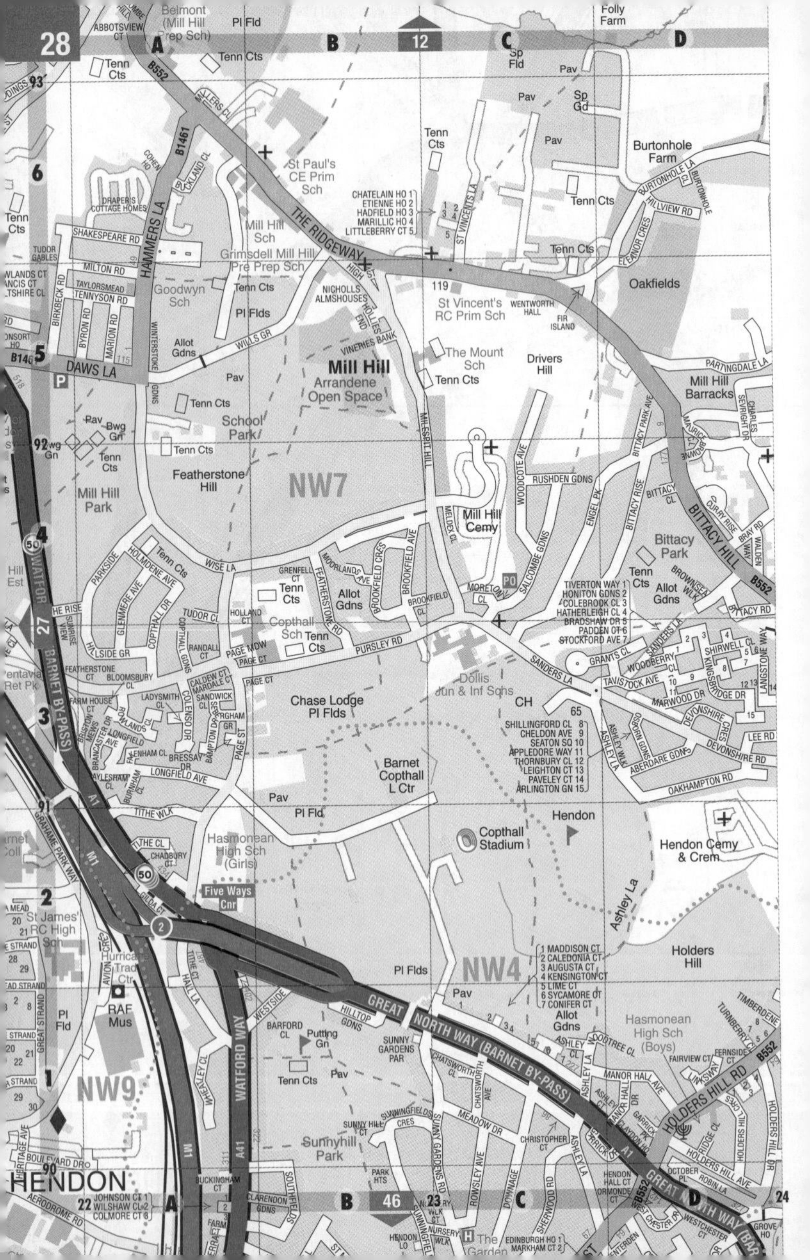
12
A
B
C
D
6
5
4
3
2
1
46
24
Belmont (Mill Hill Prep Sch)
Pl Fld
Folly Farm
Abbotsview Ct
Tenn Cts
B552
B1461
Millers Cl
Cohen Ho
Buckland Cl
Draper's Cottage Homes
Hammers La
Shakespeare Rd
Tudor Gables
Milton Rd
Taylorsmead
Tennyson Rd
Birkbeck Rd
Byron Rd
Marion Rd
Winterstoke Gdns
Goodwyn Sch
Daws La
B1461
St Paul's CE Prim Sch
Mill Hill Sch
Grimsdell Mill Hill Pre Prep Sch
The Ridgeway
High St
Nicholls Almshouses
Hollies End
Vineries Bank
Wills Gr
Allot Gdns
Pl Flds
Mill Hill
Arrandene Open Space
School Park
Pav
Bwg Gn
Mill Hill Park
Featherstone Hill
NW7
Sp Fld
Sp Gd
Burtonhole Farm
Burtonhole La
Burtonhole Cl
Hillview Rd
Eleanor Cres
Oakfields
Chatelain Ho 1
Etienne Ho 2
Hadfield Ho 3
Marillic Ho 4
Littleberry Ct 5
St Vincents La
119
St Vincent's RC Prim Sch
Wentworth Hall
Fir Island
The Mount Sch
Drivers Hill
Partingdale La
Mill Hill Barracks
Milespit Hill
Mill Hill Cemy
Meldex Cl
Woodcote Ave
Rushden Gdns
Salcombe Gdns
Engel Pk
Bittacy Park Ave
Bittacy Rise
Bittacy Cl
Bittacy Hill
Bittacy Park
Maurice Browne Ct
Charles Sevright Dr
Curry Rise
Bray Rd
Walden Way
Brownsea Wlk
Bittacy Rd
B552
Moreton Cl
PO
Wise La
Parkside
Holmdene Ave
Glenmere Ave
Copthall Dr
Copthall Gdns
Tudor Cl
Randall Ct
Hillside Gr
Sunrise View
The Rise
Featherstone Ct
Bloomsbury Cl
Grenfell Ct
Moorlands Ave
Brookfield Cres
Brookfield Ave
Brookfield Ct
Featherstone Rd
Holland Ct
Copthall Sch
Page Mdw
Page Ct
Pursley Rd
Dollis Jun & Inf Schs
Sanders La
CH
Tiverton Way 1
Honiton Gdns 2
Colebrook Cl 3
Hatherleigh Cl 4
Bradshaw Dr 5
Padden Ct 6
Stockford Ave 7
Grants Cl
Woodberry
Tavistock Ave
Shirwell Cl
Kingsbridge Dr
Langstone Way
Marwood Dr
Devonshire Cres
Devonshire Rd
Lee Rd
Osborn Gdns
Ashley Wlk
Ashley La
Aberdare Gdns
Oakhampton Rd
Shillingford Cl 8
Cheldon Ave 9
Seaton Sq 10
Appledore Way 11
Thornbury Cl 12
Leighton Ct 13
Paveley Ct 14
Arlington Gn 15
65
Chase Lodge Pl Flds
Barnet Copthall L Ctr
Hendon
Copthall Stadium
Hendon Cemy & Crem
Ladysmith Cl
Colenso Dr
Caldew Ct
Mardale Ct
Sandwick Cl
Farm House Ct
Briston Mews
Brancaster Dr
Rowlands Cl
Longfield Ave
Fakenham Cl
Bressay Dr
Bampton Dr
Page St
Aylesham Cl
Burnham Cl
Tithe Wlk
The Cl
Chadbury Ct
Hasmonean High Sch (Girls)
Five Ways Cnr
Gilda Ct
Watford Way
Barnet By-Pass
A1
M1
50
27
Grahame Park Way
Mill Hill Est
Pentavia Ret Pk
St James' RC High Sch
Hurricane Trad Ctr
Avion Cres
RAF Mus
Pl Fld
Great Strand
NW9
Heritage Ave
Boulevard Dr
HENDON
Aerodrome Rd
Johnson Ct 1
Wilshaw Cl 2
Colmore Ct 3
Buckingham Ct
Clarendon Gdns
Southfields
Tithe Ct
Hall La
Wheatley Cl
A41
Westside
Barford Cl
Putting Gn
Hilltop Gdns
Sunny Gardens Par
Sunny Hill Ct
Sunningfields Cres
Sunnyhill Park
Sunny Gardens Rd
Park Hts
Great North Way (Barnet By-Pass)
Chatsworth Cl
Chatsworth Ave
Meadow Dr
Rowsley Ave
Downage
Sherwood Rd
Christopher Ct
Ashley La
NW4
1 Maddison Ct
2 Caledonia Ct
3 Augusta Ct
4 Kensington Ct
5 Lime Ct
6 Sycamore Ct
7 Conifer Ct
Ashley Cl
Woodtree Cl
Manor Hall Ave
Manor Hall Dr
Claydon Ho
Garrick Pk
Garrick Dr
Holders Hill
Hasmonean High Sch (Boys)
Timberdene
Turnberry Ct
Fairview Ct
Fernside Ct
Linksway
Holders Hill Rd
Holders Hill Cres
Ridge Cl
Holders Hill Dr
Holders Hill Ave
October Pl
Robin La
Hendon Hall Ct
Ormonde Ct
Westchester Dr
Westchester Ct
Nursery Wlk
Hendon Lo
The Garden
Edinburgh Ho 1
Markham Ct 2
Grove Ho

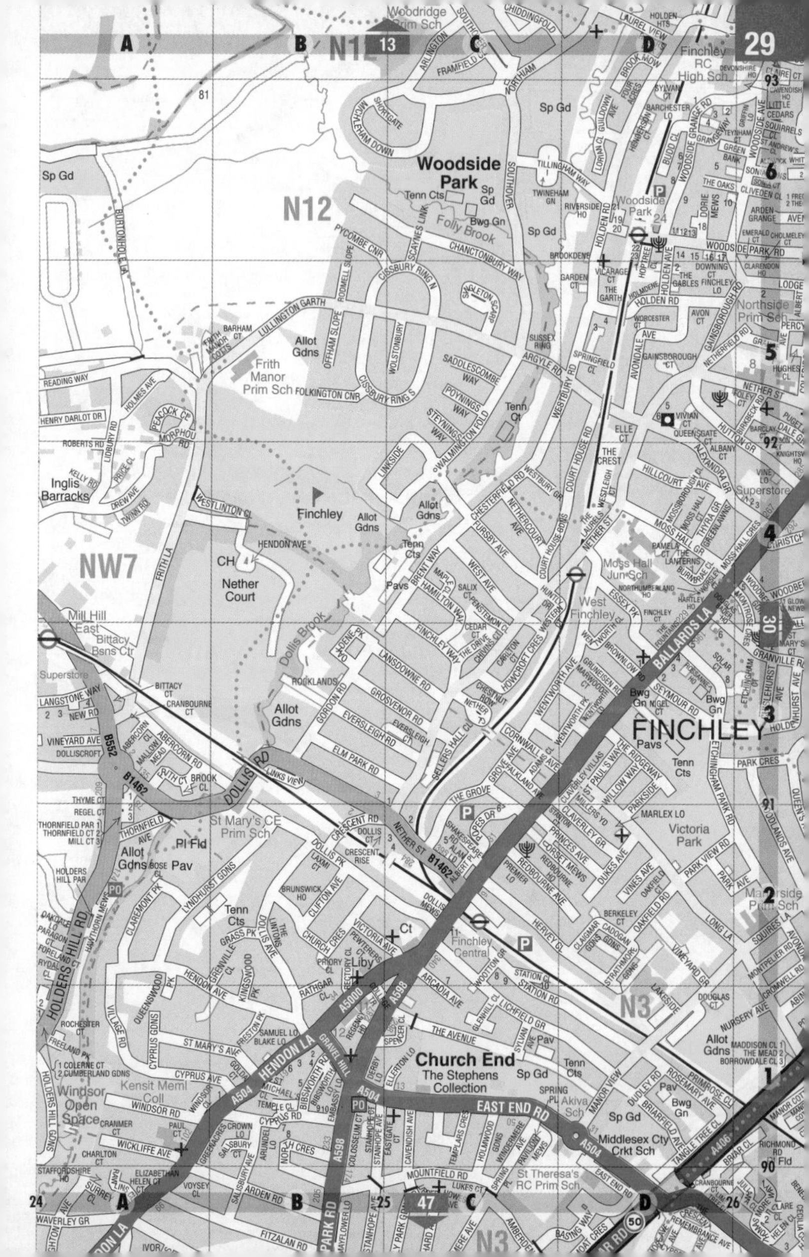

A
B
C
D
N12
13
Woodridge Prim Sch
Finchley RC High Sch
Sp Gd
Woodside Park
N12
Tenn Cts
Bwg Gn
Folly Brook
Woodside Park
Northside Prim Sch
Frith Manor Prim Sch
Allot Gdns
Inglis Barracks
Finchley
NW7
Nether Court
Mill Hill East
Bittacy Bsns Ctr
Superstore
Dollis Brook
Moss Hall Jun Sch
West Finchley
30
FINCHLEY
Pavs
Victoria Park
St Mary's CE Prim Sch
Pl Fld
Pav
Finchley Central
Liby
N3
Church End
The Stephens Collection
Kensit Meml Coll
Windsor Open Space
Akiva Sch
Middlesex Cty Crkt Sch
St Theresa's RC Prim Sch
Manorside Prim Sch
HOLDERS HILL RD
HENDON LA
GRAVEL HILL
EAST END RD
BALLARDS LA
NETHER ST
DOLLIS RD
REGENTS PARK RD
HOLDEN RD
WOODSIDE PARK RD
CISSBURY RING N
CISSBURY RING S
LULLINGTON GARTH
CHANCTONBURY WAY
ARGYLE RD
WESTBURY RD
COURT HOUSE RD
LANSDOWNE RD
GROSVENOR RD
EVERSLEIGH RD
ELM PARK RD
ARDEN RD
FITZALAN RD
MOUNTFIELD RD
THE AVENUE
LICHFIELD GR
STATION RD
HERVEY CL
ARCADIA AVE
MANOR VIEW
ETCHINGHAM PARK RD
NURSERY AVE
LONG LA
24
25
26
47
50

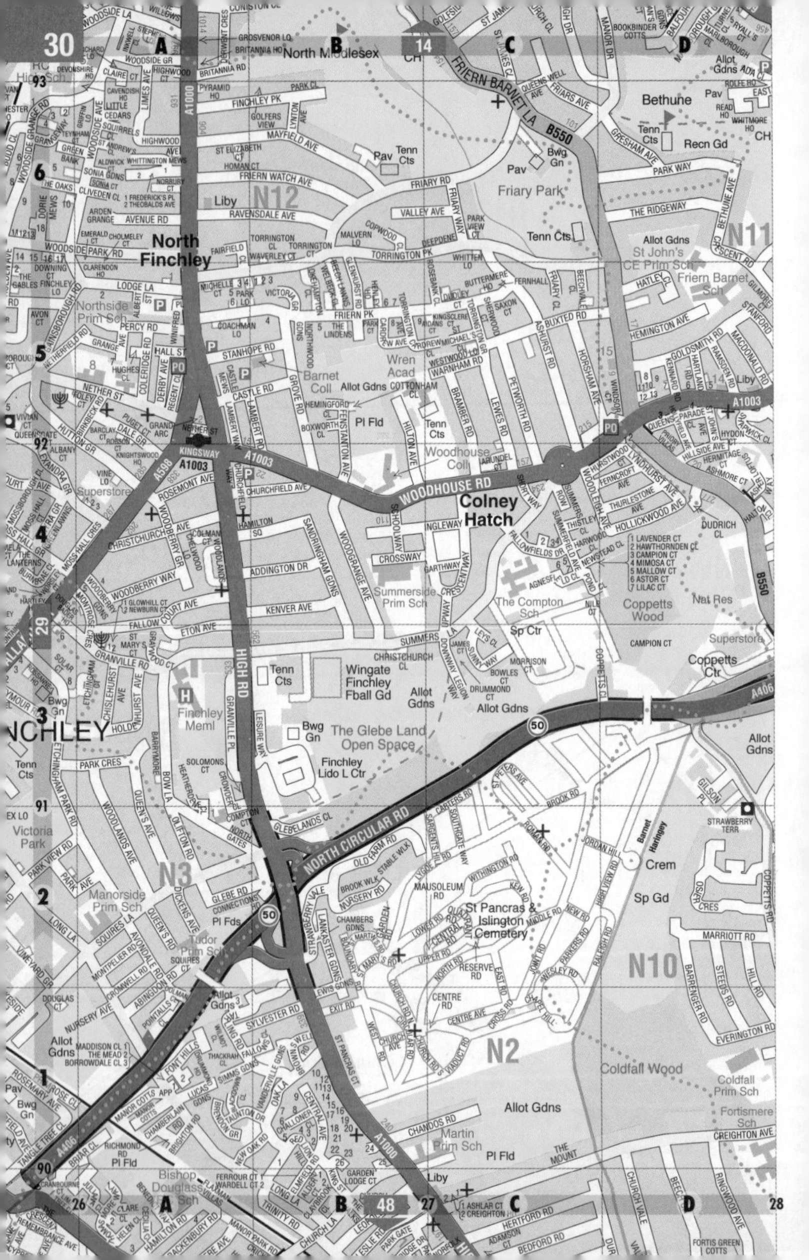
A
B
C
D
14
48
North Middlesex
FRIERN BARNET LA
B550
Bethune
Recn Gd
Tenn Cts
Pav
Bwg Gn
Friary Park
FRIARY RD
FRIARS AVE
QUEENS WELL AVE
GRESHAM AVE
PARK WAY
THE RIDGEWAY
BETHUNE AVE
N11
Allot Gdns
St John's CE Prim Sch
Friern Barnet Sch
HATLEY CL
HEMINGTON AVE
GOLDSMITH RD
MACDONALD RD
Liby
A1003
N12
FRIERN WATCH AVE
MAYFIELD AVE
FINCHLEY PK
GOLFERS VIEW
LYNTON AVE
PARK CL
RAVENSDALE AVE
VALLEY AVE
FRIARY WAY
PARK VIEW CT
TORRINGTON PK
TORRINGTON RD
WAVERLEY CT
MALVERN LO
COPWOOD CL
DEEPDENE
WHITTEN LO
BUTTERMERE HO
FERNHALL
FRIERN PK
BUXTED RD
HORSHAM AVE
ASHURST RD
PETWORTH RD
LEWES RD
BRAMBER RD
WARNHAM RD
Wren Acad
Barnet Coll
Allot Gdns
COTTONHAM CL
HEMINGFORD CL
BOXWORTH CL
Pl Fld
Tenn Cts
Woodhouse Coll
WOODHOUSE RD
Colney Hatch
FENSTANTON AVE
GROVE RD
LAMBERT RD
CASTLE RD
STANHOPE RD
North Finchley
A1000
WOODSIDE LA
WOODSIDE GR
WOODSIDE AVE
WOODSIDE PARK RD
HIGHWOOD AVE
LIMES AVE
BRITANNIA RD
PYRAMID HO
AVENUE RD
Liby
LODGE LA
Northside Prim Sch
PERCY RD
HALL ST
NETHER ST
KINGSWAY
A1003
A598
CHURCHFIELD AVE
ROSEMONT AVE
Superstore
WOODBERRY GR
CHRISTCHURCH AVE
WOODBERRY WAY
ADDINGTON DR
KENVER AVE
SANDRINGHAM GDNS
WOODGRANGE AVE
SCHOOLWAY
INGLEWAY
CROSSWAY
GARTHWAY
CRESCENTWAY
UPWAY
Summerside Prim Sch
The Compton Sch
Sp Ctr
Coppetts Wood
Nat Res
Superstore
Coppetts Ctr
CAMPION CT
FALLOWFIELDS DR
SUMMERFIELD AVE
NEWSTEAD CL
WOODLEIGH AVE
HOLLICKWOOD AVE
THURLESTONE AVE
HURSTWOOD CT
LYNDHURST AVE
DUDRICH CL
1 LAVENDER CT
2 HAWTHORNDEN CL
3 CAMPION CT
4 MIMOSA CT
5 MALLOW CT
6 ASTOR CT
7 LILAC CT
FALLOW COURT AVE
ETON AVE
SUMMERS LA
CHRISTCHURCH CL
HIGH RD
GRANVILLE RD
Wingate Finchley Fball Gd
Allot Gdns
Tenn Cts
Finchley Meml
Bwg Gn
The Glebe Land Open Space
Finchley Lido L Ctr
A406
50
NORTH CIRCULAR RD
FINCHLEY
Tenn Cts
Victoria Park
PARK CRES
ETCHINGHAM PARK RD
WOODLANDS AVE
QUEEN'S AVE
BOW LA
N3
Manorside Prim Sch
LONG LA
SQUIRES LA
DICKENS AVE
QUEEN'S RD
Tudor Prim Sch
Pl Fds
GLEBE RD
GLEBELANDS CL
OLD FARM RD
STABLE WLK
BROOK WLK
NURSERY RD
STRAWBERRY VALE
LANKASTER GDNS
MAUSOLEUM RD
WITHINGTON RD
St Pancras & Islington Cemetery
BROOK RD
ST PETERS AVE
JORDAN HILL
Barnet
Haringey
Crem
Sp Gd
HIGH VIEW RD
N10
MARRIOTT RD
BARRENGER RD
STEEDS RD
HILL RD
EVERINGTON RD
COPPETTS RD
Coldfall Wood
Coldfall Prim Sch
Fortismere Sch
CREIGHTON AVE
N2
Allot Gdns
CHANDOS RD
Martin Prim Sch
Pl Fld
THE MOUNT
CHURCH VALE
RINGWOOD AVE
Liby
1 ASHLAR CT
2 CREIGHTON AVE
HERTFORD RD
BEDFORD RD
FORTIS GREEN COTTS
ST PANCRAS CT
A1000
EAST END RD
NURSERY AVE
Allot Gdns
Pav
Bwg Gn
A406
Pl Fld
RICHMOND RD
Bishop Douglass Sch
TRINITY RD
CHURCH LA
26
27
28
1
2
3
4
5
6
90
91
92
93

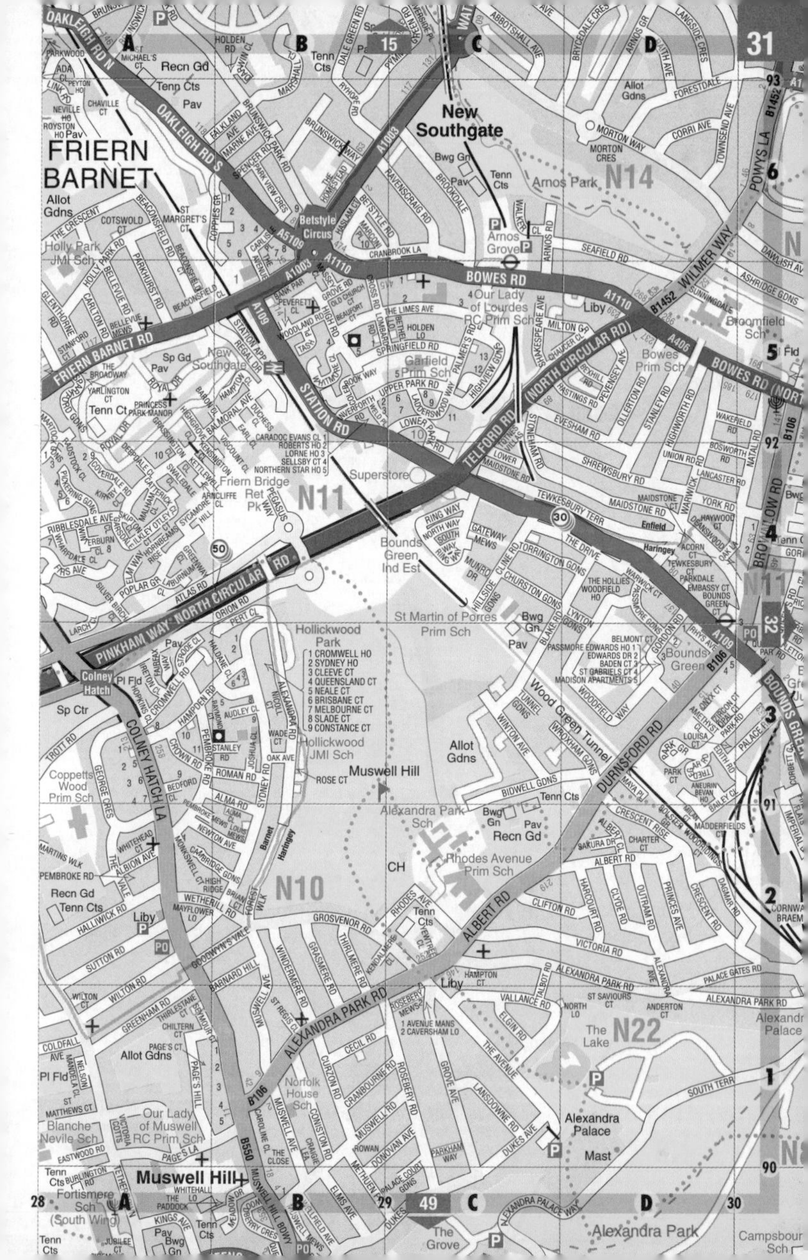
31
15
A
B
C
D
OAKLEIGH RD N
OAKLEIGH RD S
PARKWOOD
ST MICHAEL'S CT
HOLDEN RD
Recn Gd
Tenn Cts
Pav
ADA CL
PEYTON HO
LINK RD
CHAVILLE CT
NEVILLE HO
ROYSTON HO
FRIERN BARNET
Allot Gdns
Tenn Cts
DALE GREEN RD
RYHOPE RD
MARSHALL
BRUNSWICK PARK RD
FALKLAND AVE
MARNE AVE
SPENCER RD
PARK VIEW CRES
BRUNSWICK WAY
THE HOMESTEAD
A1003
New Southgate
ABBOTSHALL AVE
BRYCEDALE CRES
ARNOS GR
LANGSIDE CRES
FORESTDALE
Allot Gdns
MORTON WAY
MORTON CRES
CORRI AVE
TOWNSEND AVE
POWYS LA
B1452
N14
Arnos Park
Bwg Gn
Pav
Tenn Cts
BROOKDALE
RAVENSCRAIG RD
BETSTYLE RD
Betstyle Circus
A5109
A1110
CRANBROOK LA
Arnos Grove
ARNOS RD
WALKER CL
SEAFIELD RD
WILMER WAY
DAWLISH AV
ASHRIDGE GDNS
SUNNINGDALE
Broomfield Sch
THE CRESCENT
COTSWOLD CT
ST MARGARET'S CT
BEACONSFIELD RD
COPPIES GR
Holly Park JMI Sch
HOLLY PARK RD
BELLEVUE RD
PARKHURST RD
CARLTON RD
GLENTHORNE
BEACONSFIELD
BELLEVUE MEWS
STANFORD CT
FRIERN BARNET RD
BOWES RD
Our Lady of Lourdes RC Prim Sch
SHAKESPEARE AVE
MILTON GR
Liby
A1110
B1452
A406
Bowes Prim Sch
BOWES RD (NORTH
Fld
STATION APP
REGAL DR
New Southgate
Sp Gd
Pav
THE BROADWAY
YARLINGTON CT
Tenn Ct
PRINCESS PARK MANOR
ROYAL DR
A109
STATION RD
PEVERETT CL
WOODLAND RD
GROVE RD
OLD CHURCH CT
HIGH RD
BEAUFORT CT
CROSS RD
THE LIMES AVE
HOLDEN LO
SPRINGFIELD RD
Garfield Prim Sch
PALMER'S RD
HIGHVIEW GDNS
UPPER PARK RD
LOWER PARK RD
LAUDERSWOOD WAY
TELFORD RD (NORTH CIRCULAR RD)
CHAUCER CT
PEVENSEY AVE
BEXHILL RD
HASTINGS RD
OLLERTON RD
STANLEY RD
HIGHWORTH RD
WAKEFIELD RD
EVESHAM RD
SHREWSBURY RD
UNION RD
BOSWORTH RD
NATAL RD
LANCASTER RD
B106
CARADOC EVANS CL 1
ROBERTS HO 2
LORNE HO 3
SELLSBY CT 4
NORTHERN STAR HO 5
Superstore
Friern Bridge Ret Pk
PEGASUS WAY
N11
MAIDSTONE RD
TEWKESBURY TERR
Enfield
Haringey
YORK RD
HAYWOOD CT
BROWNLOW RD
RIBBLESDALE AVE
PICKERING GDNS
COVERDALE RD
SKIPTON CL
ILKLEY CT
HORNBEAMS RISE
SYCAMORE HILL
ARNCLIFFE CL
RING WAY
NORTH WAY
SOUTH WAY
GATEWAY MEWS
Bounds Green Ind Est
MUNRO DR
CLINE RD
TORRINGTON GDNS
THE DRIVE
ACORN CT
TEWKESBURY CT
PARKDALE
EMBASSY CT
BOUNDS GREEN CT
WHARFEDALE CL
FIRS AVE
POPLAR GR
ATLAS RD
SILVER BIRCH
PINKHAM WAY NORTH CIRCULAR RD
ORION RD
PERT CL
HILLSIDE GDNS
CHURSTON GDNS
THE HOLLIES
WOODFIELD HO
WARWICK CT
St Martin of Porres Prim Sch
Bwg Gn
Pav
LYNTON GDNS
BLAKE RD
Hollickwood Park
1 CROMWELL HO
2 SYDNEY HO
3 CLEEVE CT
4 QUEENSLAND CT
5 NEALE CT
6 BRISBANE CT
7 MELBOURNE CT
8 SLADE CT
9 CONSTANCE CT
PASSMORE EDWARDS HO 1
EDWARDS DR 2
BADEN CT 3
ST GABRIELS CT 4
MADISON APARTMENTS 5
Bounds Green
A109
B106
BOUNDS GREEN
32
Colney Hatch
Pl Fld
Sp Ctr
CROMWELL RD
HAMPDEN RD
STROUDE CL
AUDLEY CL
ALEXANDRA RD
NICOLL CT
WADE CT
Wood Green Tunnel
TUNNEL GDNS
WINTON AVE
WROXHAM GDNS
WOODFIELD WAY
DURNSFORD RD
AMETHYST CT
ONYX CT
PALACE RD
PARK CT
LOUISA CT
EDITH RD
TROTT RD
COLNEY HATCH LA
CROWN RD
PEMBROKE RD
STANLEY RD
ROMAN RD
JOSHUA CL
OAK AVE
ROSE CT
Hollickwood JMI Sch
Muswell Hill
Allot Gdns
MAYA PL
BIDWELL GDNS
Tenn Cts
ANEURIN BEVAN HO
BAILEY CL
Coppetts Wood Prim Sch
GEORGE CRES
BEDFORD
ALMA RD
SYDNEY RD
Alexandra Park Sch
Bwg Gn
Pav
Recn Gd
CRESCENT RISE
CHARTER CT
MADDERFIELDS CT
SAKURA DR
ALBERT CL
ALBERT RD
91
WHITEHEAD CT
NEWTON AVE
CAMBRIDGE GDNS
MARTINS WLK
ALBION AVE
THE VALE
PEMBROKE RD
Recn Gd
Tenn Cts
HALLIWICK RD
MONKSWELL CT
HIGH RIDGE
WETHERILL RD
MAYFLOWER LO
Barnet
Haringey
CH
Rhodes Avenue Prim Sch
N10
FOREST WLK
RHODES AVE
Tenn Cts
CLIFTON RD
HARCOURT RD
CLYDE RD
OUTRAM RD
PRINCES AVE
CRESCENT RD
DAGMAR RD
Liby
PO
SUTTON RD
GOODWYN'S VALE
BARNARD HILL
WINDERMERE RD
GRASMERE RD
THIRLMERE RD
GROSVENOR RD
KENDALMERE CL
YEWTREE CL
ALBERT RD
VICTORIA RD
ALEXANDRA PARK RD
PALACE GATES RD
WILTON RD
WILTON CT
GREENHAM RD
THIRLESTANE CT
SEYMOUR CT
CHILTERN CT
MUSWELL AVE
ST REGIS CL
HAMPTON CT
Liby
ROSEBERY MEWS
VALLANCE RD
ST SAVIOURS CT
NORTH LO
ANDERTON CT
1 AVENUE MANS
2 CAVERSHAM LO
ELGIN RD
Alexandra Palace
The Lake
N22
COLDFALL AVE
NELSON MANDELA CL
Pl Fld
Allot Gdns
PAGE'S CT
PAGE'S HILL
ST MATTHEWS CT
B106
CECIL RD
CURZON RD
CRANBOURNE RD
ROSEBERY RD
GROVE AVE
THE AVENUE
LANSDOWNE RD
SOUTH TERR
Norfolk House Sch
Our Lady of Muswell RC Prim Sch
Blanche Nevile Sch
VICTORIA COTTS
EASTWOOD RD
PAGE'S LA
B550
MUSWELL HILL
CAROLINE CL
THE CLOSE
CRAIGIE LEA
CONISTON RD
MUSWELL RD
ROWAN
DONOVAN AVE
PARKHAM WAY
METHUEN
PALACE COURT GDNS
DUKES AVE
Alexandra Palace
Mast
90
Tenn Cts
BURLINGTON RD
Muswell Hill
WHITEHALL LO
THE PADDOCK
Fortismere Sch (South Wing)
28
29
49
30
ELMS AVE
ALEXANDRA PALACE WAY
KINGS AVE
Pav
Bwg Gn
Tenn Cts
JUBILEE CT
MUSWELL HILL BDWY
The Grove
Alexandra Park
Campsbourne Sch
1
2
3
4
5
6
92
93

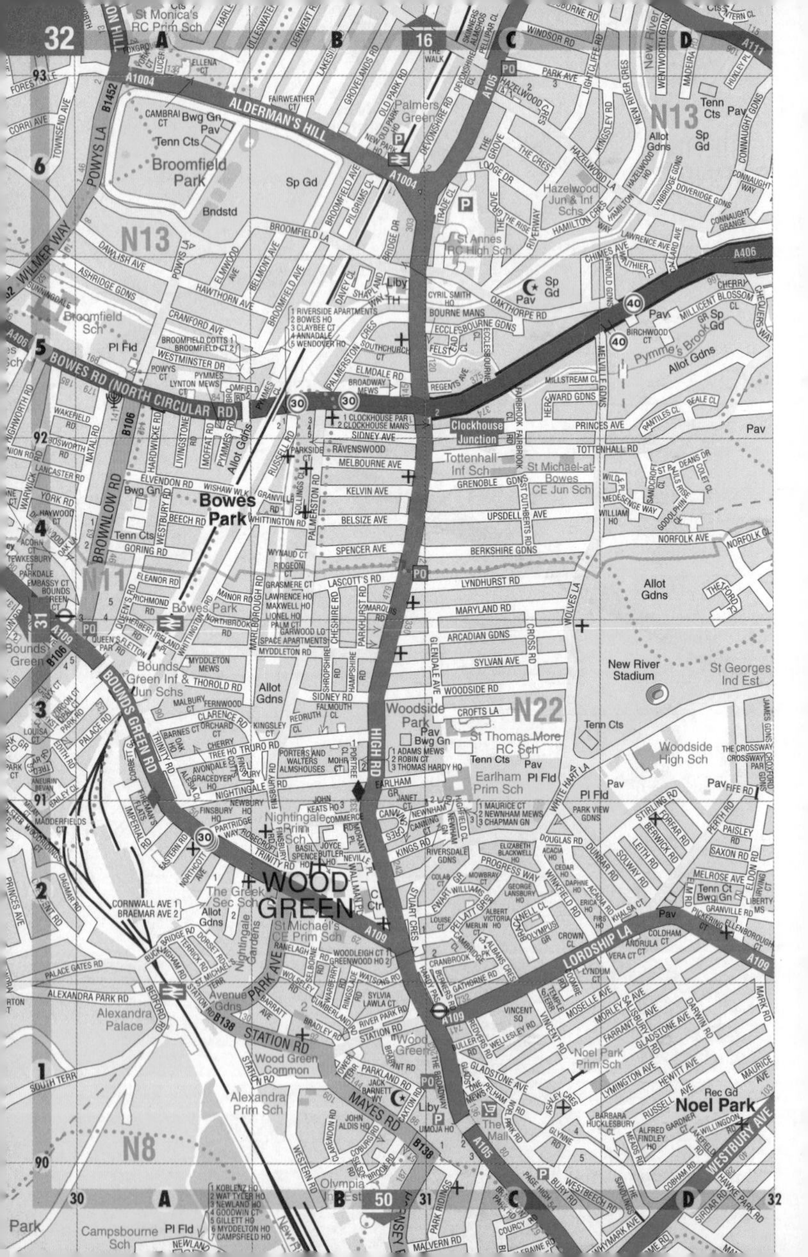
32
A
B
C
D
16
50
31
30
93
92
91
90
6
5
4
3
2
1
St Monica's RC Prim Sch
ALDERMAN'S HILL
A1004
B1452
POWYS LA
Broomfield Park
Bwg Gn
Pav
Tenn Cts
Sp Gd
Bndstd
N13
CAMBRAI CT
FAIRWEATHER CT
ELLENA CT
FORESDALE
CORRI AVE
TOWNSEND AVE
WILMER WAY
Palmers Green
DEVONSHIRE RD
GROVELANDS RD
OLD PARK RD
LAKESIDE
DERWENT RD
ILLESWATER
HARLECH
THE WALK
SKINNERS ALMSHOS
PELLIPAR CL
A105
PO
WINDSOR RD
PARK AVE
HAZELWOOD CRES
LIGHTCLIFFE RD
NEW RIVER CRES
KINGSLEY RD
THE GROVE
THE CREST
LODGE DR
HAZELWOOD LA
Hazelwood Jun & Inf Schs
HAMILTON CRES
THE RISE
RIVERWAY
TRADE CL
St Annes RC High Sch
New River
WENTWORTH GDNS
MADEIRA RD
A111
HUXLEY PL
Tenn Cts
Pav
Allot Gdns
Sp Gd
CONNAUGHT GDNS
CONNAUGHT WAY
CONNAUGHT GRANGE
DOVERIDGE GDNS
LYNBRIDGE GDNS
HAZELWOOD HO
HAMILTON WAY
LAWRENCE AVE
CALLARD AVE
CHIMES AVE
ARNOLD GDNS
WAUTHIER CL
A406
CHERRY
MILLICENT BLOSSOM CL
CHEQUERS WAY
Sp Gd
Pav
40
BIRCHWOOD CT
Pymme's Brook
Allot Gdns
MELVILLE GDNS
MILLSTREAM CL
HEREWARD GDNS
BEALE CL
PANTILES CL
PRINCES AVE
Pav
TOTTENHALL RD
OAKTHORPE RD
CYRIL SMITH HO
BOURNE MANS
ECCLESBOURNE GDNS
FELSTEAD CL
REGENTS AVE
Clockhouse Junction
BROOMFIELD AVE
PILGRIMS CL
BROOMFIELD LA
BRIDGE DR
DAVEY CL
SHAPLAND WAY
Liby
TH
1 RIVERSIDE APARTMENTS
2 BOWES HO
3 CLAYBEE CT
4 ANNADALE
5 WENDOVER HO
PALMERSTON CRES
SOUTHCHURCH CT
ELMDALE RD
BROADWAY MEWS
DAWLISH AVE
ASHRIDGE GDNS
ELMWOOD AVE
BELMONT AVE
HAWTHORN AVE
CRANFORD AVE
BROOMFIELD COTTS 1
BROOMFIELD CT 2
WESTMINSTER DR
POWYS CT
PYMMES MEWS
LYNTON CT
Broomfield Sch
Pl Fld
SUNNINGDALE
BOWES RD (NORTH CIRCULAR RD)
30
1 CLOCKHOUSE PAR
2 CLOCKHOUSE MANS
SIDNEY AVE
RAVENSWOOD
PARKSIDE
MELBOURNE AVE
Tottenhall Inf Sch
St Michael-at-Bowes CE Jun Sch
GRENOBLE GDNS
FAIRBROOK RD
KELVIN AVE
BELSIZE AVE
UPSDELL AVE
ST CUTHBERTS RD
SPENCER AVE
BERKSHIRE GDNS
NORFOLK AVE
NORFOLK CL
WILDE PL
MEDESENGE WAY
WILLIAM HO
SANDCROFT CL
ST PAULS RISE
DEANS DR
COLET CL
GODOLPHIN CL
HIGHWORTH RD
WAKEFIELD RD
BOSWORTH RD
NATAL RD
LANCASTER RD
WARWICK
YORK RD
HAYWOOD CT
B106
BROWNLOW RD
HARDWICKE RD
LIVINGSTONE RD
MOFFAT RD
PYMMES RD
Allot Gdns
ELVENDON RD
WISHAW WLK
Bwg Gn
WESTBURY RD
Bowes Park
BEECH RD
GRANVILLE RD
WHITTINGTON RD
RUSSELL RD
COLLINGS CL
PALMERSTON RD
Tenn Cts
GORING RD
ACORN CT
TEWKESBURY CT
PARKDALE
EMBASSY CT
BOUNDS GREEN CT
N11
ELEANOR RD
RICHMOND RD
MANOR RD
Bowes Park
NORTHBROOK RD
MARLBOROUGH RD
WYNAUD CT
RIDGEON CT
GRASMERE CT
LAWRENCE HO
MAXWELL HO
LIONEL HO
PALM CT
GARWOOD LO
SPACE APARTMENTS
LASCOTT'S RD
CHESHIRE RD
PARKHURST RD
MARQUIS RD
LYNDHURST RD
MARYLAND RD
ARCADIAN GDNS
CROSS RD
WOLVES LA
Allot Gdns
THETFORD CL
SYLVAN AVE
GLENDALE AVE
WOODSIDE RD
New River Stadium
St Georges Ind Est
A109
QUEEN'S RD
HERBERT RD
IRELAND PL
QUEEN'S PAR
FLETTON RD
Bounds Green
Bounds Green Inf & Jun Schs
MYDDLETON MEWS
THOROLD RD
MYDDLETON RD
SHROPSHIRE RD
HAMPSHIRE RD
Allot Gdns
SIDNEY RD
FALMOUTH CL
REDRUTH CL
KINGSLEY CT
Woodside Park
Pav
Bwg Gn
CROFTS LA
N22
St Thomas More RC Sch
Tenn Cts
Pav
Tenn Cts
Woodside High Sch
THE CROSSWAY
CROSSWAY PAR
JAMES GDNS
CROXFORD GDNS
BOUNDS GREEN RD
MALBURY CT
FERNWOOD
CLARENCE RD
ORCHARD CT
BARNES CT
OAK RD
CHERRY TREE HO
TRURO RD
TRINITY RD
CORBETT GR
AVONDALE CT
GRACEDYER HO
FINSBURY RD
PORTERS AND WALTERS ALMSHOUSES
MOHR CT
PORTREE CL
1 ADAMS MEWS
2 ROBIN CT
3 THOMAS HARDY HO
HIGH RD
Earlham Prim Sch
Pl Fld
WHITE HART LA
Pl Fld
Pav
Pav
FIFE RD
NIGHTINGALE RD
EARLHAM GR
JANET CT
NEWNHAM RD
HIGHFIELD CL
1 MAURICE CT
2 NEWNHAM MEWS
3 CHAPMAN GN
PARK VIEW GDNS
STIRLING RD
FORFAR RD
BERWICK RD
PERTH RD
PAISLEY RD
SAXON RD
FINSBURY HO
NEWBURY HO
PARTRIDGE WAY
ROSECROFT
JOHN KEATS HO
COMMERCE RD
Nightingale Prim Sch
CANNING CRES
KINGS RD
RIVERSDALE GDNS
ELIZABETH BLACKWELL HO
PROGRESS WAY
DOUGLAS RD
DUNBAR RD
SOLWAY RD
LEITH RD
ACACIA HO
CEDAR HO
DAPHNE HO
ERICA HO
FIRS HO
MELROSE AVE
Tenn Ct
Bwg Gn
ELM RD
ELDON RD
LIBERTY MS
GRANVILLE RD
IRVING CT
MADDERFIELDS CT
WOODRIDINGS
EASTERN RD
NORTHCOTT AVE
JOYCE BUTLER HO
BASIL SPENCE HO
NEVILLE PL
WALLMAN PL
WOOD GREEN
Ctr
COLAB CT
MOWBRAY CT
EWART GR
WILLIAMS CT
GEORGE LANSBURY HO
WINKFIELD RD
ACACIA RD
KHALSA CT
PICKERING CT
ELLENBOROUGH CT
Pav
A109
PRINCES AVE
DAGMAR RD
The Greek Sec Sch
CORNWALL AVE 1
BRAEMAR AVE 2
Allot Gdns
Nightingale Gardens
St Michael's CE Prim Sch
PARK AVE
STUART CRES
LOUISE CT
PELLATT GR
ALBERT VICTORIA HO
MERLIN HO
OLYMPUS
BRACKNELL CL
CROWN CL
ANDRULA CT
COLDHAM CT
VERA CT
LORDSHIP LA
LYNDUM CT
PALACE GATES RD
ALEXANDRA PARK RD
BUCKINGHAM RD
DORSET RD
TERRICK RD
ST MICHAEL'S TERR
STATION RD
BEDFORD RD
Avenue Gdns
BARRATT AVE
RANELAGH RD
WOLSELEY RD
SELBORNE RD
WARBERRY RD
RINGSLADE RD
WATSONS RD
WOODLEIGH CT 1
GREENWOOD HO 2
SYLVIA LAWLA CT
CUMBERLAND RD
RIVER PARK RD
STATION RD
BRADLEY RD
CRANBROOK
GATHORNE RD
BERNERS RD
MOSELLE AVE
MORLEY AVE
SALISBURY AVE
FARRANT AVE
GLADSTONE AVE
DARWIN RD
MARK RD
VINCENT SQ
VINCENT RD
TEMPLE TERR
COOMBE RD
WELLESLEY RD
REDVERS RD
FULLERS RD
Alexandra Palace
B138
STATION RD
Wood Green Common
Wood Green
BRAMPTON PARK RD
THE BROADWAY
GLADSTONE AVE
Noel Park Prim Sch
LYMINGTON AVE
HEWITT AVE
MAURICE AVE
SOUTH TERR
STATION RD
TOWER TERR
PARKLAND RD
JACK BARNETT WY
CAXTON RD
PO
Liby
UMOJA HO
The Mall
PELHAM RD
NOEL PARK RD
ASHLEY CRES
Rec Gd
Noel Park
BARBARA HUCKLESBURY CL
RUSSELL AVE
ALFRED FINDLEY HO
GARDINER CT
WILLINGDON RD
WESTBURY AVE
Alexandra Prim Sch
MAYES RD
JOHN ALDIS HO
CLARENDON RD
COBURG RD
B138
BROOK RD
WESTERN RD
N8
A105
GLYNNE RD
WESTBEECH RD
THE SANDLINGS
MEADS RD
LAKEFIELD RD
COBHAM RD
PAGE HIGH
BURY RD
HAWKE PARK RD
SIRDAR RD
Olympia Ind Est
1 KOBLENZ HO
2 WAT TYLER HO
3 NEWLAND HO
4 GOODWIN CT
5 GILLETT HO
6 MYDDELTON HO
7 CAMPSFIELD HO
Park
Campsbourne Sch
Pl Fld
NEWLAND
PARK RIDINGS
COURCY RD
MALVERN RD
WHYMARK AVE

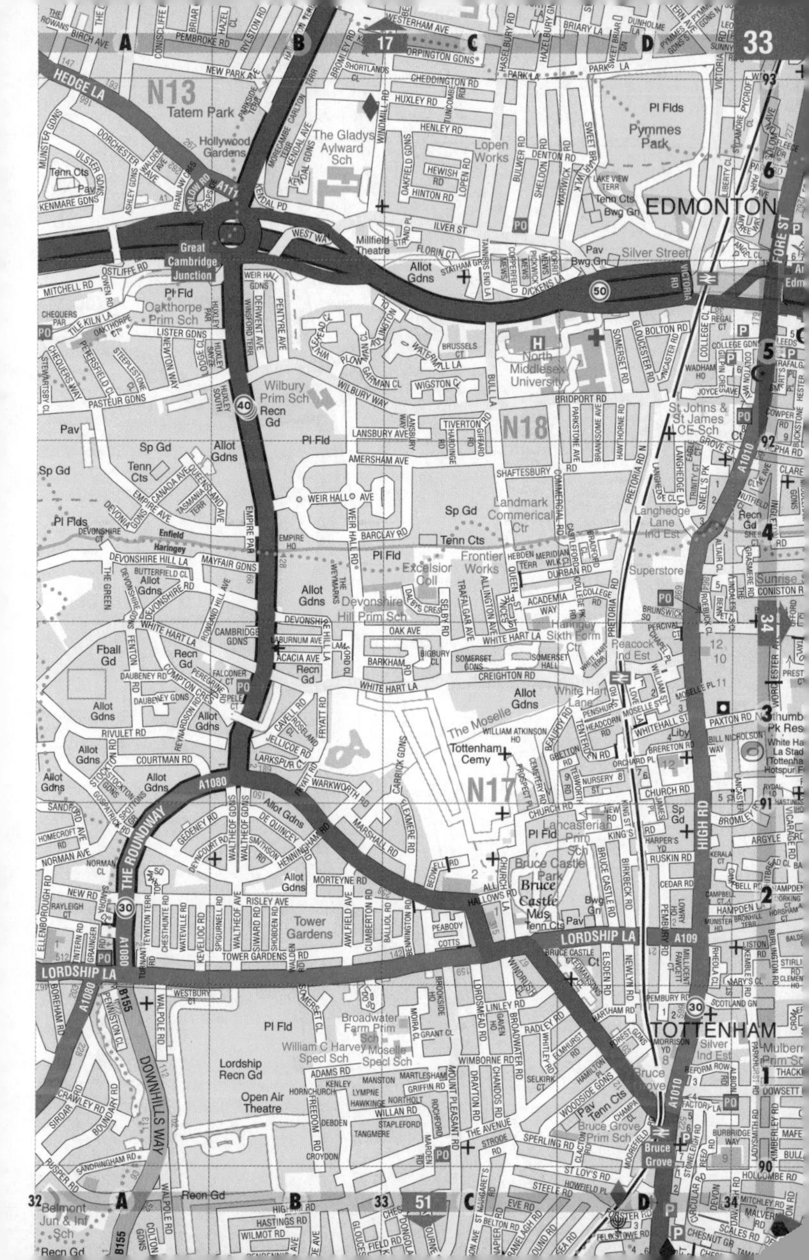
A
B
C
D
17
51
N13
N18
N17
Tatem Park
Hollywood Gardens
HEDGE LA
The Gladys Aylward Sch
Lopen Works
EDMONTON
Pymmes Park
Pl Flds
Tenn Cts
Bwg Gn
Silver Street
Great Cambridge Junction
Oakthorpe Prim Sch
Allot Gdns
Millfield Theatre
North Middlesex University
Wilbury Prim Sch
Recn Gd
St Johns & St James CE Sch
Landmark Commerical Ctr
Langhedge Lane Ind Est
Sp Gd
Frontier Works
Excelsior Coll
Devonshire Hill Prim Sch
Superstore
Haringey Sixth Form Ctr
Peacock Ind Est
White Hart Lane
The Moselle
Tottenham Cemy
Lancasterian Prim Sch
Bruce Castle Park
Bruce Castle Mus
Tower Gardens
Broadwater Farm Prim Sch
William C Harvey Specl Sch
Moselle Specl Sch
Lordship Recn Gd
Open Air Theatre
TOTTENHAM
Silver Ind Est
Bruce Grove
Bruce Grove Prim Sch
Belmont Jun & Inf Sch
Enfield
Haringey
WHITE HART LA
LORDSHIP LA
THE ROUNDWAY
HIGH RD
DOWNHILLS WAY
A1080
A111
A1010
A109
B155
40
50
30
32
33
34

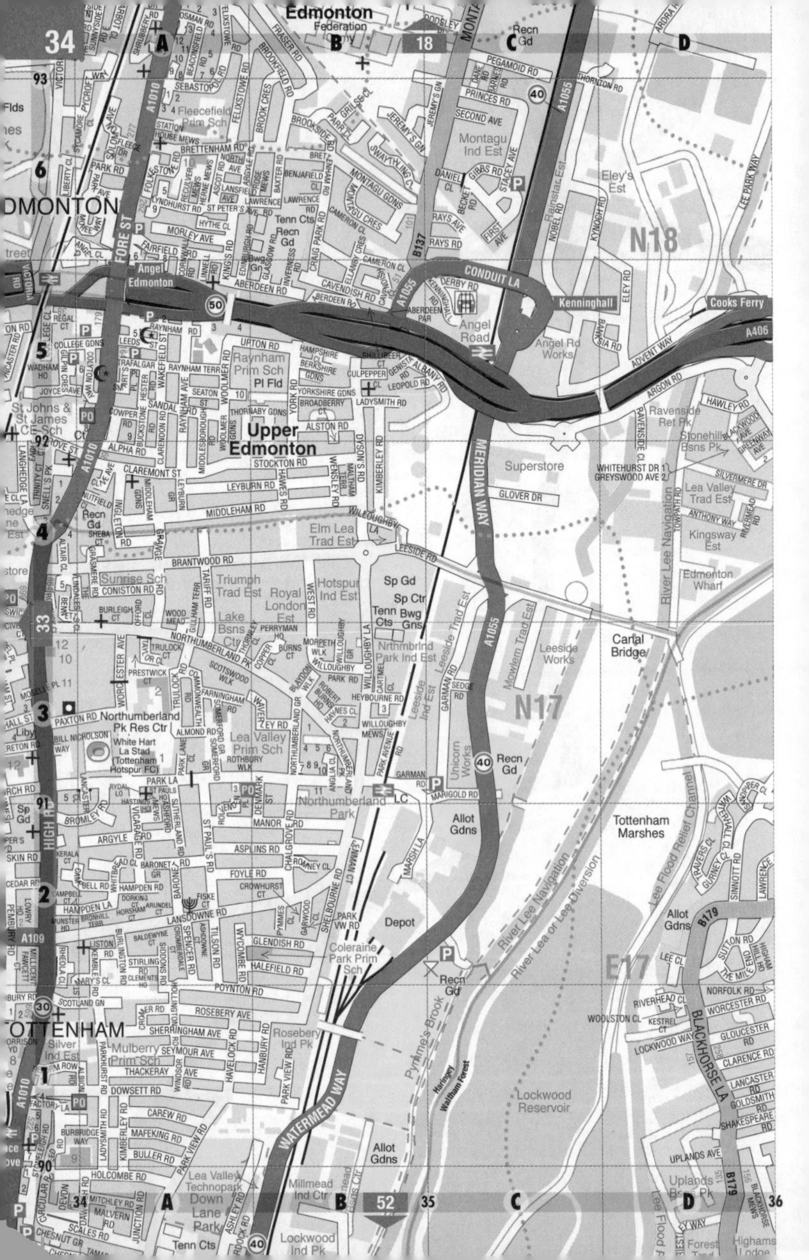
34
18
52
35
36
Edmonton
Upper Edmonton
Tottenham Marshes
N18
N17
E17
Angel Road
Cooks Ferry
Kenninghall
Lockwood Reservoir
Meridian Way
Watermead Way
Northumberland Park
River Lee Navigation
Lee Flood Relief Channel

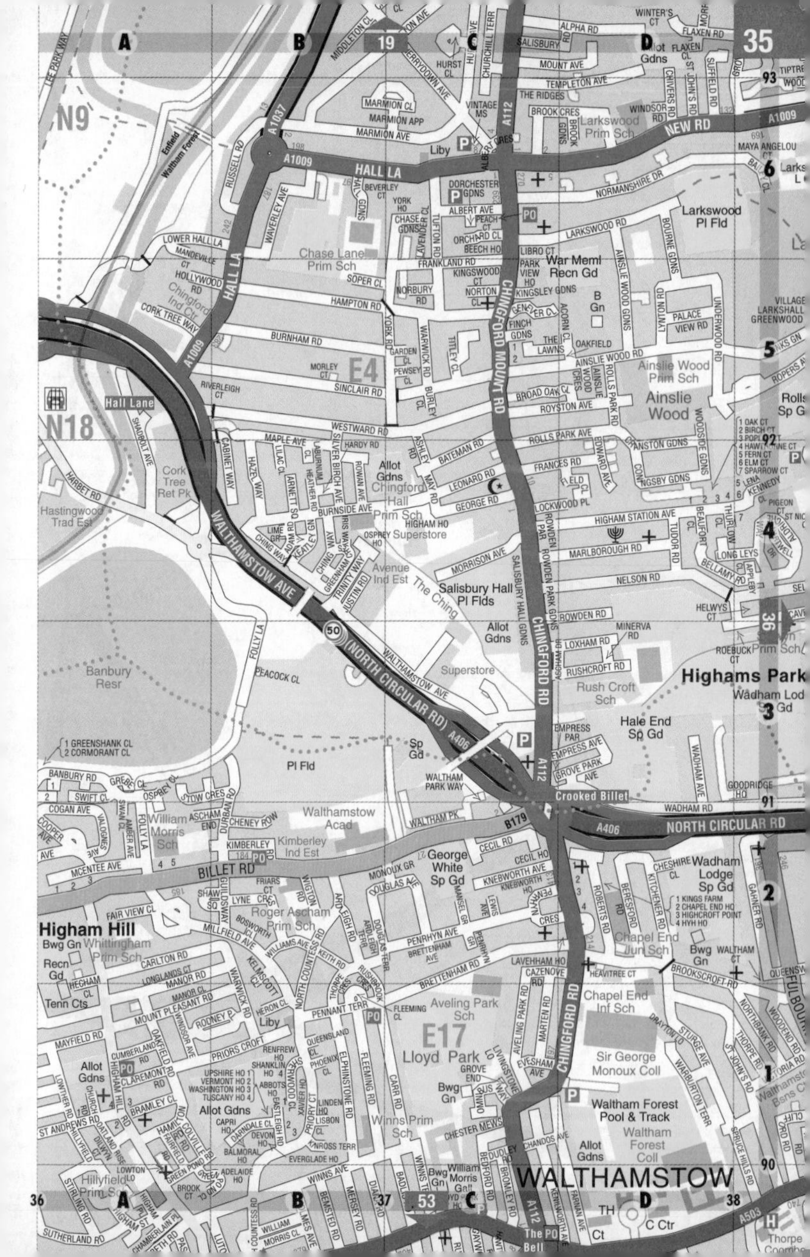

35
A
B
C
D
19
53
36
37
38
93
92
91
90
N9
N18
E4
E17
LEE PARK WAY
MIDDLETON CL
MERRYDOWN AVE
HURST CL
CHURCHILL TERR
ALPHA RD
SALISBURY RD
WINTER'S CT
FLAXEN RD
FLAXEN CL
Allot Gdns
MOUNT AVE
TEMPLETON AVE
THE RIDGES
CHIVERS RD
ST JOHN'S RD
SUFFIELD RD
TIPTREE
WOOD
MARMION CL
MARMION APP
MARMION AVE
VINTAGE MS
BROOK CRES
BROOK GDNS
Larkswood Prim Sch
WINDSOR RD
NEW RD
A1009
A1037
A112
Enfield
Waltham Forest
RUSSELL RD
HALL LA
Liby
ALBERT CRES
MAYA ANGELOU CT
Larks
BEVERLEY CT
YORK HO
CHASE GDNS
DORCHESTER GDNS
ALBERT AVE
PEACH CT
ORCHARD CL
BEECH HO
NORMANSHIRE DR
LARKSWOOD RD
Larkswood Pl Fld
WAVERLEY AVE
LOWER HALL LA
MANDEVILLE CT
HOLLYWOOD RD
Chingford Ind Ctr
CORK TREE WAY
Chase Lane Prim Sch
SOPER CL
HAMPTON RD
NORBURY RD
KINGSWOOD CT
NORTON CL
LAVENDER CT
TUFTON RD
FRANKLAND RD
LIBRO CT
PARK VIEW HO
War Meml Recn Gd
KINGSLEY GDNS
AINSLIE WOOD GDNS
BOURNE GDNS
LYNTON RD
UNDERWOOD RD
VILLAGE LARKSHALL GREENWOOD
B Gn
GENESTER CL
FINCH GDNS
THE LAWNS
ACORN CL
OAKFIELD
PALACE VIEW RD
BURNHAM RD
YORK RD
WARWICK RD
TITLEY CL
GARDEN CL
PEWSEY CL
MORLEY CT
SINCLAIR RD
BURLEY CL
CHINGFORD MOUNT RD
AINSLIE WOOD RD
ROLLS PARK RD
AINSLIE WOOD CRES
Ainslie Wood Prim Sch
Ainslie Wood
ROPERS AVE
Rolls Sp Gd
RIVERLEIGH CT
Hall Lane
BROAD OAK CL
ROYSTON AVE
WESTWARD RD
ASHLEY RD
BATEMAN RD
ROLLS PARK AVE
EDWARD AVE
ANSTON GDNS
WOODSIDE GDNS
1 OAK CT
2 BIRCH CT
3 POPLAR CT
4 HAWTHORNE CT
5 FERN CT
6 ELM CT
7 SPARROW CT
SHADBOLT AVE
CABINET WAY
MAPLE AVE
LILAC CL
LABURNUM CL
SILVER BIRCH AVE
HARDY RD
ROWAN AVE
HAZEL WAY
ARNETT SQ
HEATHER RD
Allot Gdns
Chingford Hall Prim Sch
MAY RD
FRANCES RD
FIELD CL
CONWAY
KINGSBY GDNS
LENA KENNEDY CL
LEONARD RD
GEORGE RD
LOCKWOOD PL
PIGEON CT
ST NICHOLAS
HARBET RD
Cork Tree Ret Pk
Hastingwood Trad Est
BURNSIDE AVE
LIME GR
ADAM RD
KEATLEY GN
CHING WAY
IRIS WAY
HIGHAM HO
OSPREY HO
Superstore
HIGHAM STATION AVE
BEAUFORT CL
THURLOW CL
TUDOR RD
ALDRIDGE WALK
ROWDEN PAR
ROWDEN PARK GDNS
MARLBOROUGH RD
LONG LEYS
GREENHAM CL
TRINITY WAY
JUSTIN RD
Avenue Ind Est
The Ching
MORRISON AVE
SALISBURY HALL GDNS
Salisbury Hall Pl Flds
NELSON RD
BELLAMY RD
APPLEBY CL
WALTHAMSTOW AVE
50
(NORTH CIRCULAR RD)
A406
HELWYS CT
ROWDEN RD
CHINGFORD RD
Allot Gdns
MINERVA RD
LOXHAM RD
ROEBUCK CT
Prim Sch
FOLLY LA
Banbury Resr
PEACOCK CL
Superstore
RUSHCROFT RD
Highams Park
Rush Croft Sch
Wadham Lodge Sp Gd
Hale End Sp Gd
1 GREENSHANK CL
2 CORMORANT CL
Sp Gd
EMPRESS PAR
EMPRESS AVE
GROVE PARK AVE
WADHAM AVE
Pl Fld
WALTHAM PARK WAY
Crooked Billet
GOODRIDGE HO
BANBURY RD
GREBE CL
SWIFT CL
OSPREY CL
STOW CRES
WADHAM RD
COGAN AVE
COOPER AVE
VALOGNES AVE
SWAN CL
AMBER AVE
William Morris Sch
ASCHAM END
CHENEY ROW
DURBAN RD
Walthamstow Acad
WALTHAM PK
B179
NORTH CIRCULAR RD
FOLLY LA
KIMBERLEY RD
Kimberley Ind Est
George White Sp Gd
CECIL RD
CECIL HO
MCENTEE AVE
BILLET RD
KNEBWORTH AVE
KNEBWORTH HO
Wadham Lodge Sp Gd
CHESHIRE CL
GAHNER RD
FRIARS CT
WIGTON RD
MONOUX GR
DOUGLAS AVE
LYNE CRES
SHAW SQ
GUILDSWAY
MANSEL GR
LEWIS AVE
PENRHYN CRES
ROBERTS RD
BERESFORD RD
KITCHENER RD
1 KINGS FARM
2 CHAPEL END HO
3 HIGHCROFT POINT
4 HYH HO
FAIR VIEW CL
Roger Ascham Prim Sch
BOSWORTH RD
ARDLEIGH RD
ARDLEIGH TERR
DOUGLAS TERR
Higham Hill
Bwg Gn
Whittingham Prim Sch
MILLFIELD AVE
WILLIAMS AVE
KEITH RD
PENRHYN AVE
PENRHYN GR
BRETTENHAM AVE
Chapel End Jun Sch
Bwg Gn
WALTHAM CT
QUEENSWOOD
Recn Gd
CARLTON RD
LONGLANDS CT
MANOR RD
KELMSCOTT CL
NORTH COUNTESS RD
RUSHBROOK CRES
THORPE CRES
BRETTENHAM RD
LAVEHHAM HO
CAZENOVE RD
HEAVITREE CT
BROOKSCROFT RD
FULBOURNE
HECHAM CL
Tenn Cts
MANOR CL
MOUNT PLEASANT RD
RODNEY P
WARWICK RD
HERON CL
PENNANT TERR
FLEEMING CL
Aveling Park Sch
Chapel End Inf Sch
DRAYTON RD
NORTHBANK RD
WOODEND RD
MAYFIELD RD
WINDSOR AVE
OAKFIELD RD
Liby
QUEENSLAND
RENFREW HO
SHANKLIN HO
PHOENIX CL
Lloyd Park
AVELING PARK RD
MARTEN RD
STURGE AVE
THORPE RD
ST JOHN'S RD
CUMBERLAND RD
PRIORS CROFT
ELPHINSTONE RD
FLEEMING RD
LIVINGSTONE LO
Sir George Monoux Coll
VICTORIA RD
Allot Gdns
HIGHAM HILL RD
CLAREMONT RD
UPSHIRE HO 1
VERMONT HO 2
WASHINGTON HO 3
TUSCANY HO 4
ABBOTS HO
FARWOOD CL
EASTLEIGH RD
XAVIER HO
CARR RD
GROVE END
EVESHAM AVE
Walthamstow Bsns Ctr
LOWTHER RD
CHURCH HILL
BRAMLEY CL
Allot Gdns
CAPRI HO
DARNDALE CL
DEVON HO
PRIORY CT
LINDEN HO
LISBON HO
Bwg Gn
Waltham Forest Pool & Track
WARBURTON TERR
ST ANDREWS RD
HILLYFIELD
OATLAND RISE
DILWYN CT
HAMILTON RD
FAIRFIELD RD
COLVILLE RD
BALMORAL HO
KINROSS TERR
Winns Prim Sch
CHESTER MEWS
CHANDOS AVE
Waltham Forest Coll
SPRUCE HILLS RD
LOWTON HO
GREEN POND RD
ADELAIDE HO
EVERGLADE HO
Allot Gdns
CLIFFORD RD
Hillyfield Prim Sch
BROOK CT
WINNS AVE
BADLIS RD
WINNS TERR
William Morris Gall
DUDLEY RD
BEDFORD RD
BROMLEY RD
WALTHAMSTOW
STIRLING RD
HIGHAM ST
COUNTESS RD
BEMSTED RD
MERSEY RD
DIANA RD
TH
C Ctr
A503
SUTHERLAND RD
CHAMBERLAIN PL
WILLIAM MORRIS CL
ELMES AVE
KENILWORTH AVE
FARNAN AVE
The Bell
Ct
Thorpe Coombe

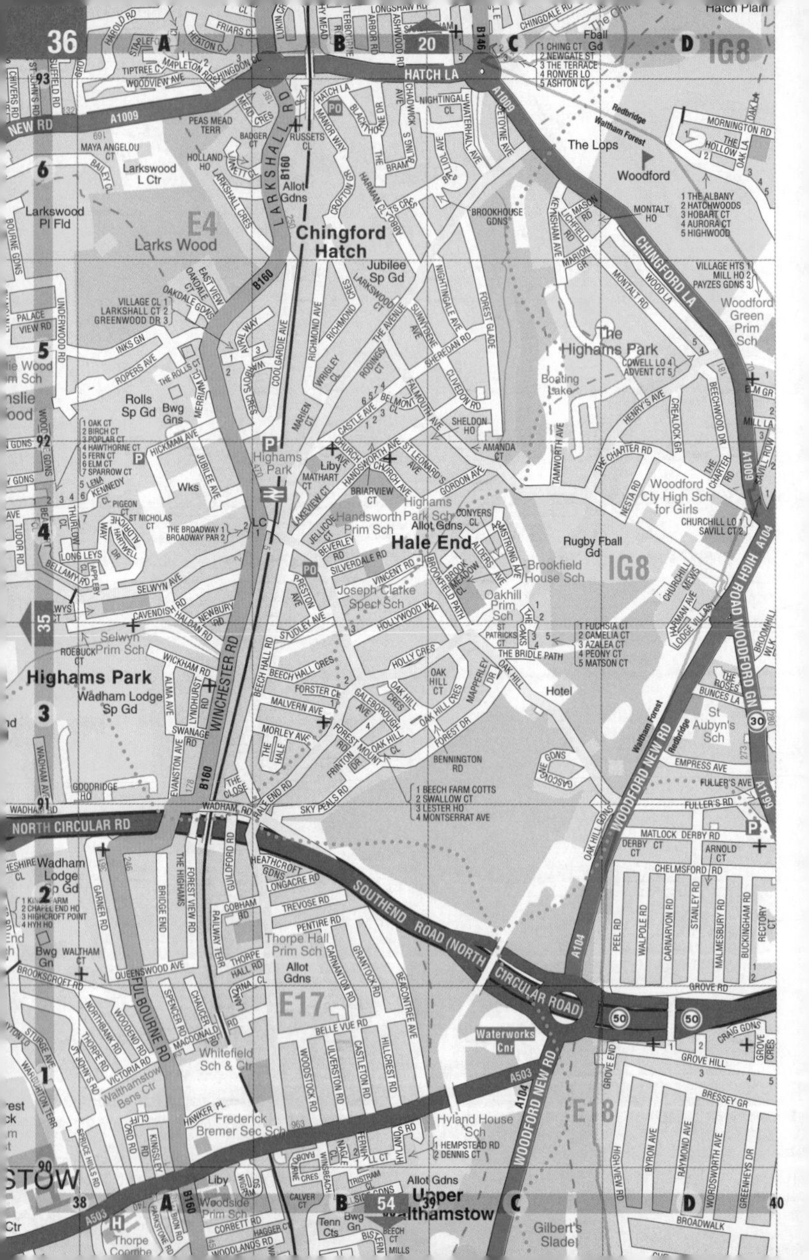
Chingford Hatch
Hale End
Highams Park
Larks Wood
The Highams Park
The Lops
Woodford
Upper Walthamstow
E4
E17
E18
IG8
NORTH CIRCULAR RD
SOUTHEND ROAD (NORTH CIRCULAR ROAD)
WOODFORD NEW RD
CHINGFORD LA
HIGH ROAD WOODFORD GN
WINCHESTER RD
LARKSHALL RD
HATCH LA
NEW RD
FULBOURNE RD
Waterworks Cnr
Rugby Fball Gd
Woodford Cty High Sch for Girls
Handsworth Prim Sch
Joseph Clarke Specl Sch
Brookfield House Sch
Oakhill Prim Sch
Selwyn Prim Sch
Thorpe Hall Prim Sch
Whitefield Sch & Ctr
Frederick Bremer Sec Sch
Hyland House Sch
Woodside Prim Sch
Wadham Lodge Sp Gd
Jubilee Sp Gd
Rolls Sp Gd
Larkswood L Ctr
Larkswood Pl Fld
St Aubyn's Sch
Woodford Green Prim Sch
Boating Lake
Allot Gdns
Hotel
Waltham Forest
Redbridge
A
B
C
D
1
2
3
4
5
6
20
35
54
38
39
40
90
91
92
93

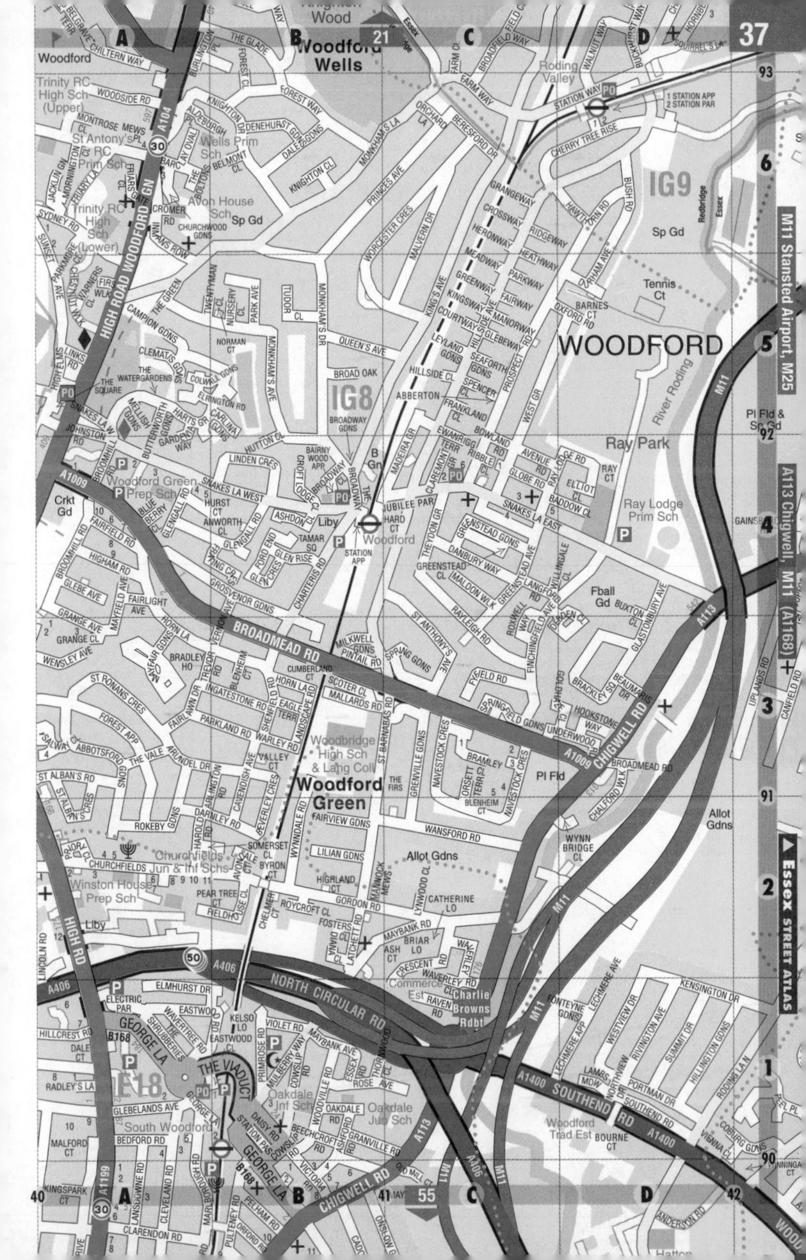
Woodford Wells
Woodford
Trinity RC High Sch (Upper)
St Antony's RC Prim Sch
Trinity RC High Sch (Lower)
Wells Prim Sch
Avon House Sch
Sp Gd
Roding Valley
STATION WAY
1 STATION APP
2 STATION PAR
CHERRY TREE RISE
IG9
IG8
WOODFORD
HIGH ROAD WOODFORD GN
A104
CHILTERN WAY
WOODSIDE RD
MONTROSE MEWS
KNIGHTON DR
DENEHURST GDNS
DALE GDNS
KNIGHTON CL
FOREST WAY
MONKHAM'S LA
ORCHARD LA
BERESFORD DR
FARM WAY
BROADFIELD WAY
PRINCES AVE
WORCESTER CRES
MALVERN DR
KING'S AVE
GRANGEWAY
CROSSWAY
HERONWAY
MEADWAY
GREENWAY
KINGSWAY
COURTWAY
RIDGEWAY
HEATHWAY
PARKWAY
FAIRWAY
MANORWAY
GLEBEWAY
HAWTHORN RD
BUSH RD
DURHAM AVE
OXFORD RD
BARNES CT
Tennis Ct
River Roding
Ray Park
Ray Lodge Prim Sch
Pl Fld & Sp Gd
M11
CAMPION GDNS
CLEMATIS GDNS
THE WATERGARDENS
THE SQUARE
COLWALL GDNS
ELRINGTON RD
NORMAN CT
QUEEN'S AVE
BROAD OAK
MONKHAM'S AVE
MONKHAM'S DR
TUDOR CL
PARK AVE
BROADWAY GDNS
LEYLAND GDNS
HILLSIDE CL
SEAFORTH GDNS
SPENCER CL
ABBERTON
FRANKLAND CL
PROSPECT RD
WEST GR
SNAKES LA W
JOHNSTON RD
A1009
SNAKES LA WEST
SNAKES LA EAST
Woodford Green Prep Sch
Crkt Gd
LINDEN CRES
HUTTON CL
BAIRNY WOOD APP
BROADWAY
Liby
Woodford
STATION APP
JUBILEE PAR
HARD CT
GLOBE RD
BADDOW CL
ELLIOT CL
RAY CT
BOWLAND RD
RIBBLE CL
EWANRIGG TERR
MADEIRA GR
CLAREMONT
GREENSTEAD GDNS
DANBURY WAY
GREENSTEAD CL
MALDON WLK
GREENSTEAD AVE
WILLINGALE CL
LANGFORD RD
Fball Gd
BUXTON CL
GLASTONBURY AVE
BROADMEAD RD
MILKWELL GDNS
PINTAIL RD
SPRING GDNS
ST ANTHONY'S AVE
RAYLEIGH RD
FYFIELD RD
SPRINGFIELD GDNS
UNDERWOOD RD
HOOKSTONE WAY
BRACKLEY SQ
BEAUMARIS DR
CHIGWELL RD
A113
FAIRFIELD RD
HIGHAM RD
GLEBE AVE
FAIRLIGHT AVE
GRANGE AVE
GRANGE CL
WENSLEY AVE
ST RONANS CRES
FOREST APP
ABBOTSFORD GDNS
THE VALE
ARUNDEL DR
MAYFAIR GDNS
BRADLEY HO
INGATESTONE RD
PARKLAND RD
WARLEY RD
VALLEY CT
CUMBERLAND CT
SCOTER CL
MALLARDS RD
HORN LA
EAGLE TERR
Woodbridge High Sch & Lang Coll
Woodford Green
THE FIRS
GRENVILLE GDNS
NAVESTOCK CRES
BRAMLEY CL
ORSETT TERR
BLENHEIM CT
Pl Fld
CHALFORD WLK
WYNN BRIDGE CL
Allot Gdns
ST ALBAN'S RD
ROKEBY GDNS
DARNLEY RD
FAIRVIEW GDNS
WANSFORD RD
LILIAN GDNS
HIGHLAND CT
SOMERSET CL
BYRON CT
Churchfields Jun & Inf Schs
CHURCHFIELDS
Winston House Prep Sch
PEAR TREE CT
ROYCROFT CL
GORDON RD
FOSTERS CL
CATHERINE LO
MAYBANK RD
BRIAR LO
ASH CT
CRESCENT RD
WAVERLEY RD
Commerce Est
RAVEN RD
Charlie Browns Rdbt
HIGH RD
A406
NORTH CIRCULAR RD
ELMHURST DR
ELECTRIC PAR
EASTWOOD CL
KELSO LO
VIOLET RD
MAYBANK AVE
GEORGE LA
B168
HILLCREST RD
DALE CT
RADLEY'S LA
E18
THE VIADUCT
GLEBELANDS AVE
South Woodford
MALFORD CT
BEDFORD RD
Oakdale Inf Sch
Oakdale Jun Sch
OAKDALE RD
ROSE AVE
BEECHCROFT RD
GRANVILLE RD
KINGSPARK CT
LANSDOWNE RD
CLEVELAND RD
CLARENDON RD
A1199
PULTENEY RD
PELHAM RD
A1400
SOUTHEND RD
KENSINGTON DR
LECHMERE AVE
WESTVIEW DR
RIVINGTON AVE
SUMMIT DR
HILLINGTON GDNS
RODING LA N
PORTMAN DR
LAMBS MDW
Woodford Trad Est
BOURNE CT
COBURG GDNS
UPLANDS RD
CANFIELD RD
M11 Stansted Airport, M25
A113 Chigwell, M11 (A1168)
▲ Essex STREET ATLAS
21
55
A
B
C
D
93
92
91
90
40
41
42
6
5
4
3
2
1

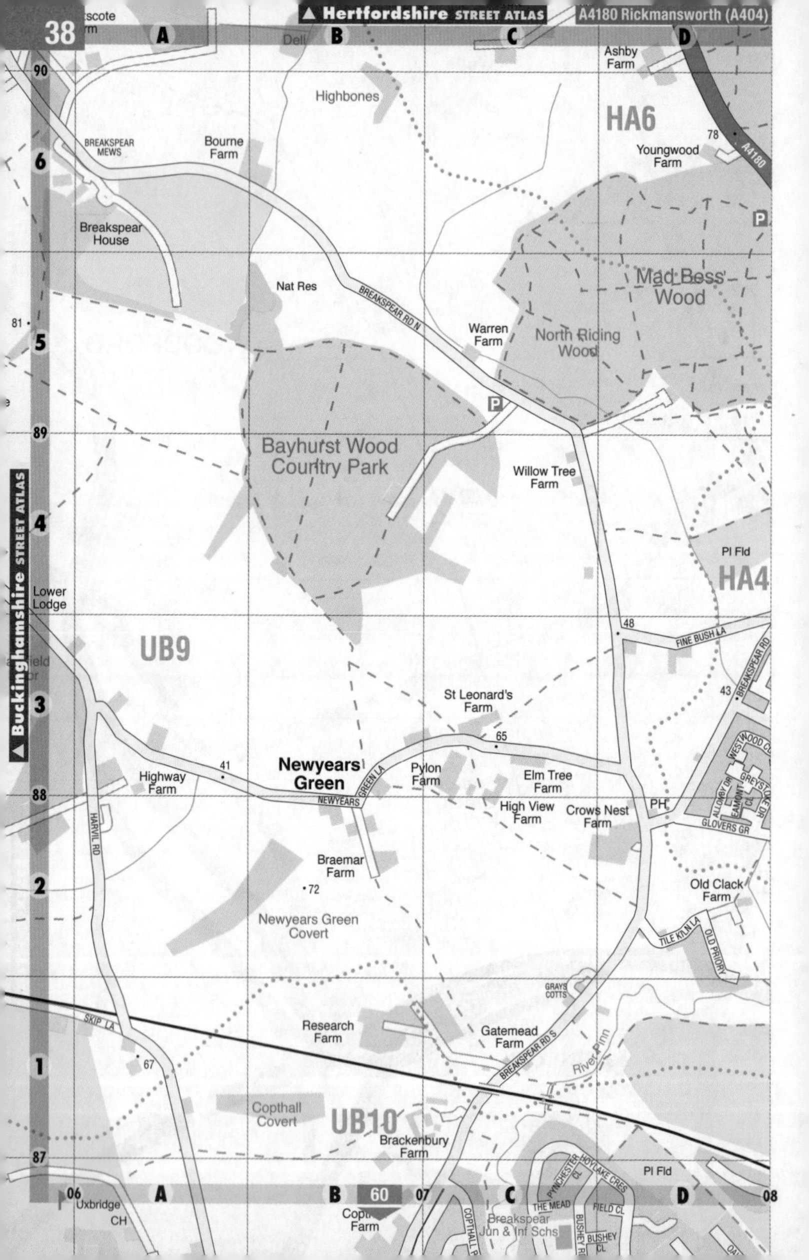

38

scote

Dell

A   B   C   D

90

Highbones

6   BREAKSPEAR
MEWS   Bourne
Farm

Breakspear
House   Nat Res

HA6

Ashby
Farm

78

Youngwood
Farm

A4180

81
5   Warren
Farm

BREAKSPEAR RD N.

Mad Bess
Wood

North Riding
Wood

89   Bayhurst Wood
Country Park

P

Willow Tree
Farm

4

Pl Fld

HA4

Lower
Lodge

48   FINE BUSH LA

43   BREAKSPEAR RD

field
or

UB9

3   St Leonard's
Farm

65

WOOD C

88   Highway
Farm   41   Newyears
Green

HARVIL RD

GREEN LA

NEWYEARS

Pylon
Farm

Elm Tree
Farm

High View   Crows Nest
Farm   Farm

PH

ELMANT
GRESCLE DR
WESTWOOD C

2   Braemar
Farm
72

GLOVERS GR

Old Clack
Farm

Newyears Green
Covert

TILE KILN LA   OLD PRIORY

SKIP LA

GRAYS
COTTS

1   67   Research
Farm

Gatemead
Farm

BREAKSPEAR RD S.

River Pinn

Copthall
Covert   Brackenbury
Farm

UB10

Pl Fld

87

06   A   Uxbridge
CH   B   60   07   Copt
Farm   THE MEAD

Breakspear
Jun & Inf Schs

C   D   08

WINCHESTER
HOLGATE CRES
FIELD CL

COPTHALL
BUSHEY CL
BUSHEY

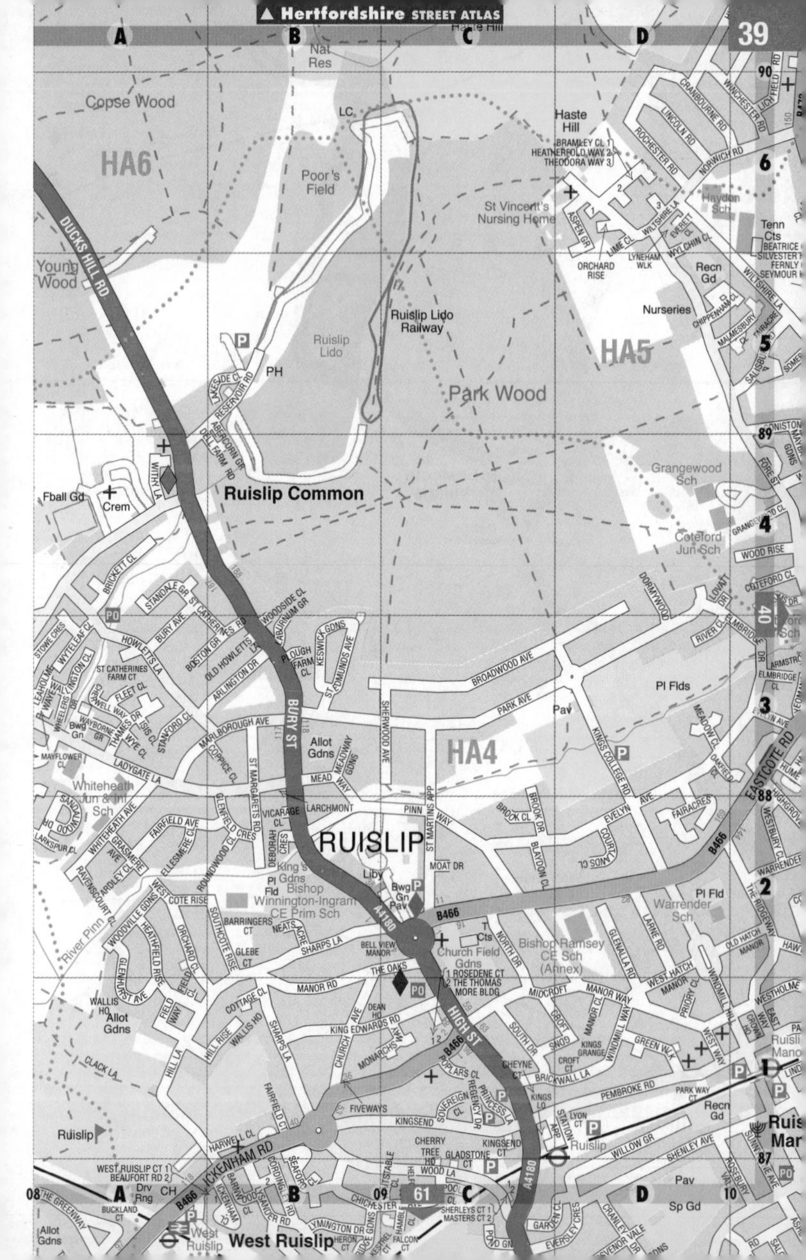
▲ Hertfordshire STREET ATLAS
39
A
B
C
D
Haste Hill
Nat Res
Copse Wood
HA6
LC
Poor's Field
Young Wood
DUCKS HILL RD
Ruislip Lido
Ruislip Lido Railway
PH
Park Wood
HA5
St Vincent's Nursing Home
BRAMLEY CL 1
HEATHERFOLD WAY 2
THEODORA WAY 3
CRANBOURNE RD
LINCOLN RD
ROCHESTER RD
WINCHESTER RD
NORWICH RD
Haydon Sch
Tenn Cts
BEATRICE
SILVESTER
FERNLY
SEYMOUR
ASPEN GR
ORCHARD RISE
LIME CL
WILTSHIRE LA
LYNEHAM WLK
WYCHIN CL
Recn Gd
Nurseries
CHIPPENHAM CL
MALMESBURY CL
FAIRACRE
SALISBURY
RESERVOIR RD
LAKESIDE CL
ABERCORN GR
DELL FARM RD
WITHY LA
Ruislip Common
Fball Gd
Crem
Grangewood Sch
Coteford Jun Sch
GRANGEWOOD CL
WOOD RISE
COTEFORD CL
BRICKETT CL
STANDALE GR
ST CATHERINES RD
WOODSIDE CL
LABURNUM GR
DORMYWOOD
LOVATT DR
RIVER CL
ELMBRIDGE DR
ELMBRIDGE CL
ARMSTRONG
PO
STOWE CRES
WYTELEAF CL
HOWLETTS LA
BURY AVE
BOSTON GR
OLD HOWLETTS LA
ARLINGTON DR
PLOUGH FARM CL
KESWICK GDNS
ST EDMUNDS AVE
BROADWOOD AVE
Pl Flds
LEAHOLME WAY
WALLINGTON CL
ST CATHERINES FARM CT
FLEET CL
CHERWELL WAY
WHEELERS DR
Bwg Gn
WAYBORNE GR
THAMES DR
ISIS CL
WYE CL
STANFORD CL
MARLBOROUGH AVE
BURY ST
SHERWOOD AVE
PARK AVE
Pav
MEADOW CL
KINGS COLLEGE RD
EASTCOTE RD
MAYFLOWER CL
LADYGATE LA
COPPICE CL
ST MARGARETS RD
Allot Gdns
MEADWAY GDNS
MEAD WAY
HA4
OAKFIELD CL
Whiteheath Jun & Inf Sch
SANDALWOOD DR
LARKSPUR CL
WHITEHEATH AVE
FAIRFIELD AVE
GLENFIELD CRES
VICARAGE CL
LARCHMONT
PINN WAY
ST MARTINS APP
BROOK CL
BROOK DR
EVELYN AVE
COURTLANDS CL
FAIRACRES
WESTBURY CL
B466
RUISLIP
GRASMERE AVE
ELLESMERE CL
ROUNDWOOD CL
DEBORAH CRES
MOAT DR
BLAYDON CL
ARDLEY CL
RAVENSCOURT CL
King's Gdns
Liby
Pl Fld
Bishop Winnington-Ingram CE Prim Sch
Bwg Gn
Pav
WARRENDER
THE RIDGEWAY
Warrender Sch
WEST COTE RISE
WOODVILLE GDNS
HEATHFIELD RISE
ORCHARD CL
SOUTHCOTE RISE
BARRINGERS CT
NEATS ACRE
A4180
River Pinn
GLEBE CT
SHARPS LA
BELL VIEW MANOR
Church Field Gdns
T Cts
Bishop Ramsey CE Sch (Annex)
NORTH DR
GLENALLA RD
LARNE RD
OLD HATCH MANOR
GLENHURST AVE
FIELD CL
THE OAKS
1 ROSEDENE CT
2 THE THOMAS MORE BLDG
MIDCROFT
MANOR WAY
WEST HATCH MANOR
WINDMILL HILL
WESTHOLME
WALLIS HO
Allot Gdns
FIELD WAY
COTTAGE CL
MANOR RD
DEAN HO
HIGH ST
CROFT GDNS
MANOR CL
PRIORY CL
EAST WAY
CROWN
HILL RISE
WALLIS HO
SHARPS LA
CHURCH AVE
KING EDWARDS RD
MONARCHS WAY
SOUTH DR
KINGS GRANGE
CROFT CT
GREEN WLK
WEST WAY
CLACK LA
HILL LA
POPLARS CL
CHEYNE CT
BRICKWALL LA
PEMBROKE RD
PARK WAY CT
FAIRFIELD CT
FIVEWAYS
SOVEREIGN CL
REGENCY DR
PRINCESS LA
KINGS LO
STATION APP
LYON CT
Recn Gd
Ruislip
KINGSEND
HARWELL CL
CHERRY TREE HO
KINGSEND CT
GLADSTONE CT
Ruislip
WILLOW GR
SHENLEY AVE
ROSEBURY VALE
SUNNINGDALE AVE
WEST RUISLIP CT 1
BEAUFORT RD 2
ICKENHAM RD
SEAFORD CL
CORDINGLEY RD
WOOD LA
POOL CL
Drv Rng
CH
08
09
61
10
Pav
Sp Gd
THE GREENWAY
BUCKLAND CT
LYSANDER RD
CHICHESTER AVE
SHERLEYS CT 1
MASTERS CT 2
GARDEN CL
EVERSLEY CRES
CRANLEY DR
Allot Gdns
West Ruislip
LYMINGTON DR
HERON CT
FALCON
KESTREL
POND GN
ST VENOR VALE
West Ruislip
6
5
89
4
40
3
88
2
1
87
Ruislip Manor

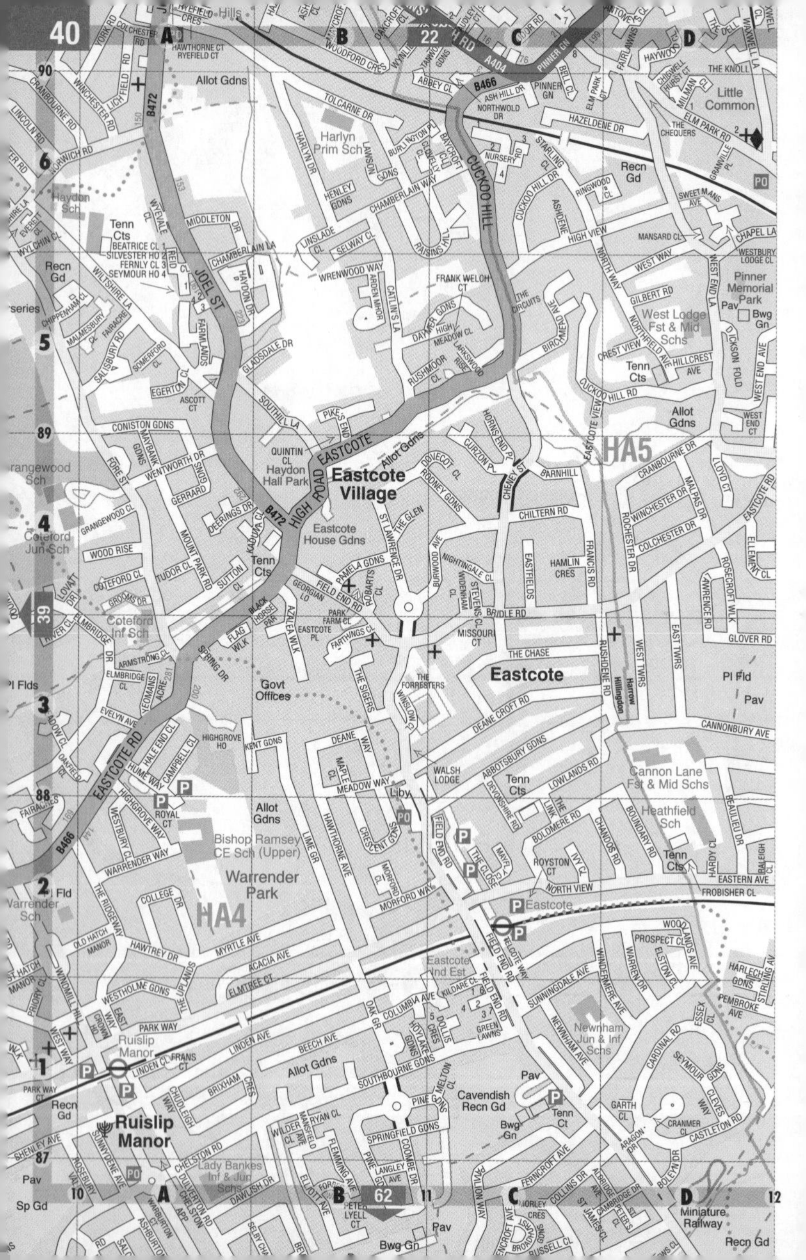

A
B
C
D
22
Eastcote Village
Eastcote
Ruislip Manor
HA4
HA5
JOEL ST
HIGH ROAD EASTCOTE
CUCKOO HILL
EASTCOTE RD
FIELD END RD
Harlyn Prim Sch
Haydon Sch
Haydon Hall Park
Eastcote House Gdns
Coteford Jun Sch
Coteford Inf Sch
Govt Offices
Bishop Ramsey CE Sch (Upper)
Warrender Park
Cannon Lane Fst & Mid Schs
Heathfield Sch
West Lodge Fst & Mid Schs
Pinner Memorial Park
Little Common
Newnham Jun & Inf Schs
Cavendish Recn Gd
Lady Bankes Inf & Jun Schs
Eastcote Ind Est
Miniature Railway
39
62
90
89
88
87
10
11
12

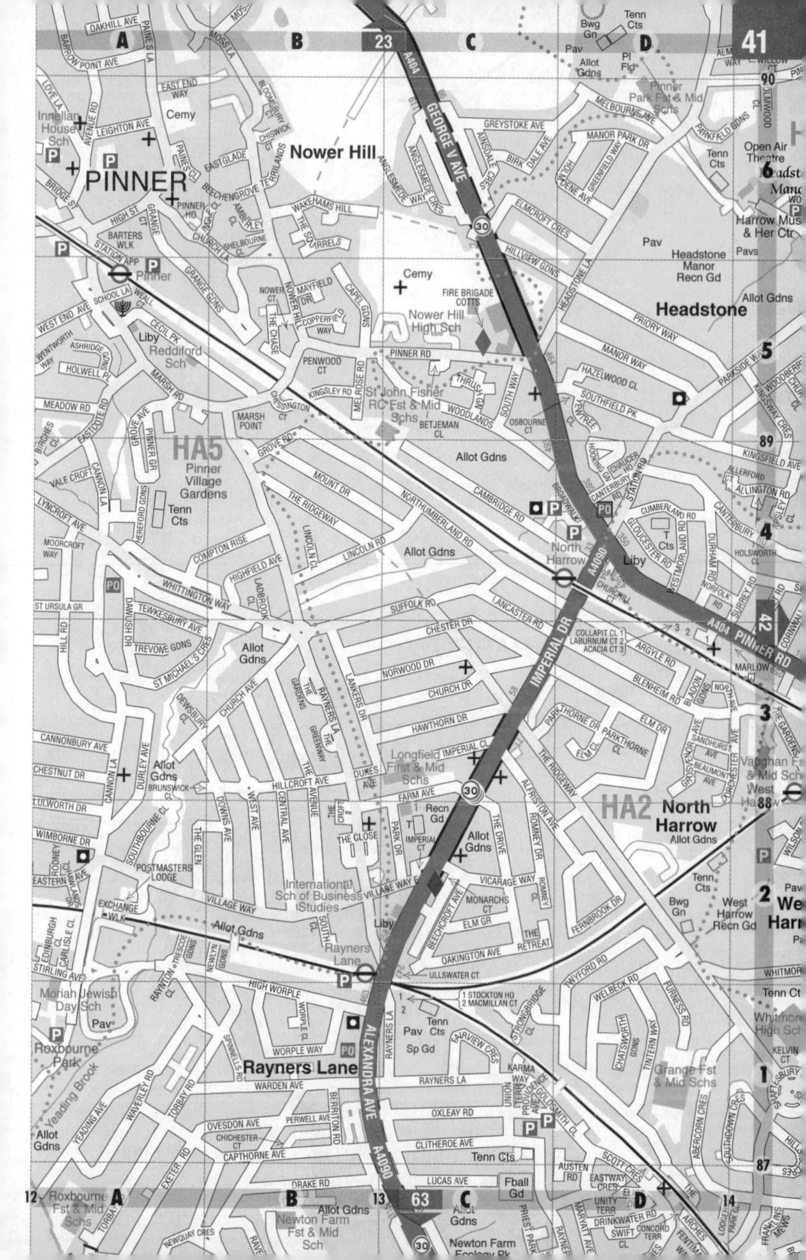

A
B
C
D
23
63
12
13
14
6
5
4
3
2
1
90
89
88
87
42
OAKHILL AVE
PAINE'S LA
BARROW POINT AVE
MOSS LA
LOVE LA
AVENUE RD
EAST END WAY
Cemy
BLOOMSBURY CT
CHISWICK CT
Innellan House Sch
LEIGHTON AVE
PAINES CL
EASTGLADE
TERRILANDS
Nower Hill
PINNER
BRIDGE ST
BEECHENGROVE
PINNER HO
AMBERLEY CL
WAKEHAMS HILL
THE SQUIRRELS
HIGH ST
GRANGE
BARTERS WLK
CHURCH LA
SHELBOURNE CL
STATION APP
Pinner
GRANGE GDNS
SCHOOL LA
WEALL CT
WEST END AVE
CECIL PK
Liby
Reddiford Sch
WENTWORTH WAY
ASHRIDGE GDNS
HOLWELL PL
MARSH RD
MEADOW RD
EASTCOTE RD
GROVE AVE
PINNER GR
BIRCHES CL
HA5
Pinner Village Gardens
VALE CROFT
CANNON LA
LYNCROFT AVE
HEREFORD GDNS
Tenn Cts
MOORCROFT WAY
COMPTON RISE
PO
WHITTINGTON WAY
ST URSULA GR
TEWKESBURY AVE
DAWLISH DR
HILL RD
TREVONE GDNS
ST MICHAEL'S CRES
NOWER CT
NOWER HILL
MAYFIELD DR
THE CHASE
COPPERFIELD WAY
CAPEL GDNS
PENWOOD CT
MELROSE RD
KINGSLEY RD
CHESSINGTON CT
MARSH POINT
GROVE RD
MOUNT DR
THE RIDGEWAY
LINCOLN CL
LINCOLN RD
NORTHUMBERLAND RD
HIGHFIELD AVE
LADBROOK CL
Allot Gdns
George V Ave
A404
ANGLESMEDE CRES
ANGLESMEDE WAY
GREYSTOKE AVE
AINSDALE CRES
BIRK DALE AVE
MANOR PARK DR
GREENFIELD WAY
HOLLY DENE AVE
ELMCROFT CRES
HILLVIEW GDNS
HEADSTONE LA
MELBOURNE AVE
Pinner Park Fst & Mid Schs
Bwg Gn
Tenn Cts
Pav
Pl Fld
PARKFIELD GDNS
Open Air Theatre
Headstone Manor
Harrow Mus & Her Ctr
Pavs
Headstone Manor Recn Gd
Headstone
PRIORY WAY
MANOR WAY
HAZELWOOD CL
SOUTHFIELD PK
YEWTREE CL
PARKSIDE WAY
KINGSWAY CRES
KINGSFIELD AVE
ALLERFORD CT
ALLINGTON RD
CANTERBURY RD
HOLSWORTH CL
Cemy
FIRE BRIGADE COTTS
Nower Hill High Sch
PINNER RD
THRUSH GN
SOUTH WAY
OSBOURNE CT
WOODLANDS
St John Fisher RC Fst & Mid Schs
BETJEMAN CL
CAMBRIDGE RD
HOOKING GN
CHAUCER CL
CANTERBURY RD
STATION RD
BROADWALK
North Harrow
A4090
CHURCHILL CT
CUMBERLAND RD
GLOUCESTER RD
WESTMORLAND RD
DURHAM RD
NORFOLK RD
SURREY RD
Cts
LANCASTER RD
SUFFOLK RD
CHESTER DR
COLLAPIT CL 1
LABURNUM CT 2
ACACIA CT 3
ARGYLE RD
BLENHEIM RD
A404 PINNER RD
MARLOW CT
CORNWALL
NORTH AVE
BLADON GDNS
IMPERIAL DR
NORWOOD DR
CHURCH DR
HAWTHORN DR
DEWSBURY CL
CHURCH AVE
THE GARDENS
RAYNERS LA
THE GREENWAY
LANKERS DR
PARKTHORNE DR
PARKTHORNE CL
ELM CL
ELM DR
THE RIDGEWAY
GROSVENOR AVE
SANDHURST AVE
BEAUMONT AVE
DORCHESTER AVE
Vaughan Fst & Mid Sch
West Harrow
HA2
North Harrow
CANNONBURY AVE
CHESTNUT DR
LULWORTH DR
WIMBORNE DR
DURLEY AVE
BRUNSWICK CL
SOUTHBOURNE CL
DOWNS AVE
WEST AVE
CENTRAL AVE
THE AVENUE
HILLCROFT AVE
DUKES AVE
Longfield First & Mid Schs
IMPERIAL CL
FARM AVE
Recn Gd
THE CROFT
THE CLOSE
PARK DR
IMPERIAL CT
ALFRISTON AVE
THE DRIVE
ROMNEY DR
RODNEY RD
RAWLANDS DR
EASTERN AVE
THE GLEN
POSTMASTERS LODGE
EXCHANGE WLK
VILLAGE WAY
International Sch of Business Studies
SOUTH CL
VILLAGE WAY E
BEECHCROFT AVE
MONARCHS CT
ELM GR
VICARAGE WAY
ROMNEY CL
THE RETREAT
FERNBROOK DR
OAKINGTON AVE
Bwg Gn
West Harrow Recn Gd
WILSON
EDINBURGH CL
CARLISLE CL
STIRLING AVE
RAYNTON CL
TRESCOE GDNS
NEWLYN GDNS
Rayners Lane
ULLSWATER CT
TWYFORD RD
1 STOCKTON HO
2 MACMILLAN CT
WHITMORE
Tenn Cts
Whitmore High Sch
Moriah Jewish Day Sch
Pav
HIGH WORPLE
WORPLE CL
WORPLE WAY
Roxbourne Park
SPINNELLS RD
Rayners Lane
ALEXANDRA AVE
RAYNERS LA
Pav
Sp Gd
FAIRVIEW CRES
STRONGBRIDGE CL
WELBECK RD
CHATSWORTH GDNS
TINTERN WAY
FURNESS RD
Grange Fst & Mid Schs
KELVIN CT
SHAFTESBURY
Yeading Brook
WAVERLEY RD
TORBAY RD
WARDEN AVE
KARMA WAY
UNION TERR
PROVIDENCE AVE
GOLDSMITH CL
ABERCORN CRES
SOUTHDOWN CRES
YEADING AVE
OVESDON AVE
PERWELL AVE
BERRITON RD
OXLEAY RD
CHICHESTER CT
CLITHEROE AVE
CAPTHORNE AVE
Tenn Cts
SCOTT CRES
EXETER RD
AUSTEN RD
EASTWAY CRES
DRAKE RD
LUCAS AVE
Fball Gd
Roxbourne Fst & Mid Schs
TORBAY
Newton Farm Fst & Mid Sch
NEWQUAY CRES
Allot Gdns
UNITY TERR
DRINKWATER RD
SWIFT CL
CONCORD TERR
PRIEST PARK
MARYATT AVE
Newton Farm Ecology Pk
ARCHES
LODGE PARK
FRANKLINS MEWS
30

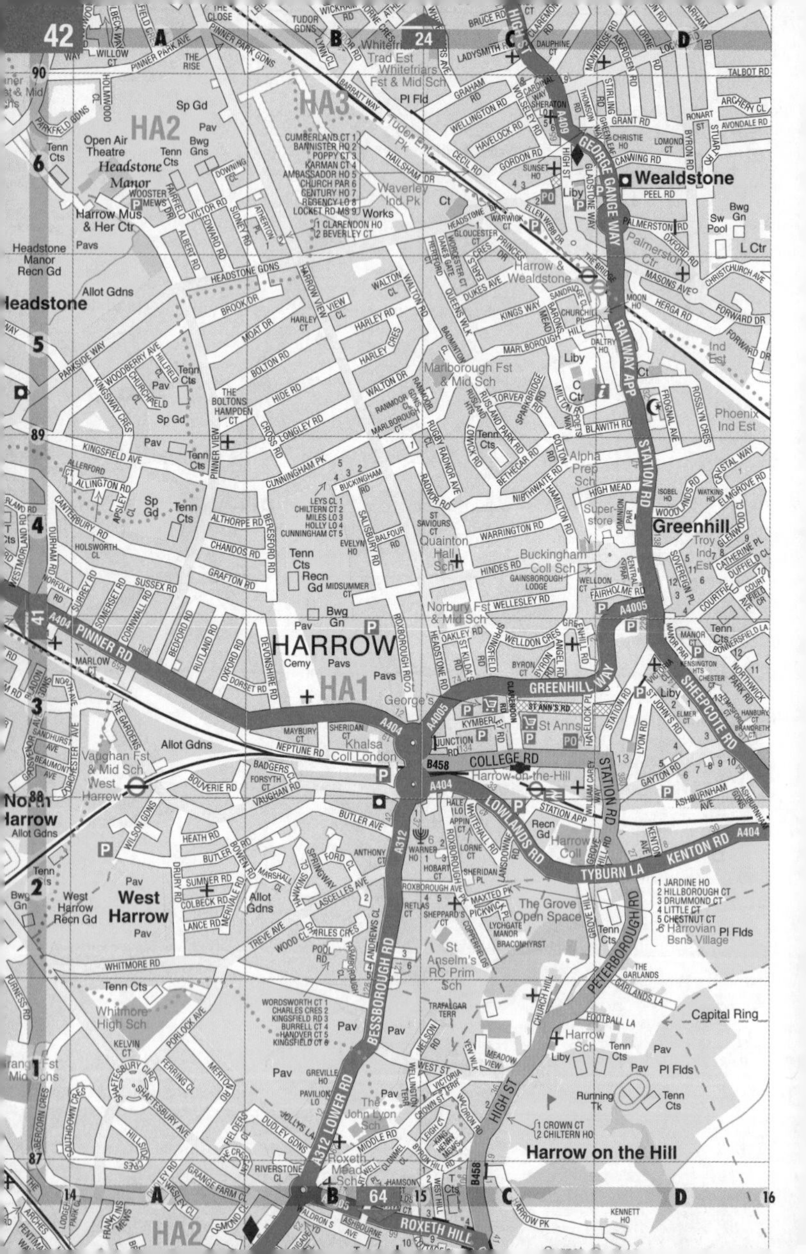
A
B
C
D
24
64
41
90
89
88
87
6
5
4
3
2
1
14
15
16
HA2
HA3
HA1
HARROW
Wealdstone
Greenhill
Headstone
West Harrow
North Harrow
Harrow on the Hill
Headstone Manor
Open Air Theatre
Harrow Mus & Her Ctr
Headstone Manor Recn Gd
Allot Gdns
Whitefriars Trad Est
Whitefriars Fst & Mid Sch
Tudor Ent Pk
Waverley Ind Pk
Works
Marlborough Fst & Mid Sch
Alpha Prep Sch
Quainton Hall Sch
Buckingham Coll Sch
Norbury Fst & Mid Sch
Vaughan Fst & Mid Sch
Khalsa Coll London
Harrow Coll
Harrow-on-the-Hill
Harrow & Wealdstone
West Harrow
Whitmore High Sch
St Anselm's RC Prim Sch
The John Lyon Sch
Roxeth Mead Sch
Harrow Sch
The Grove Open Space
West Harrow Recn Gd
Palmerston Ctr
Phoenix Ind Est
Troy Ind Est
Capital Ring
Running Tk
St Anns
Cemy
Super-store
C Ctr
Liby
Sw Pool
L Ctr
PINNER PARK AVE
PINNER PARK GDNS
THE RISE
HIGH ST
GEORGE GANGE WAY
RAILWAY APP
STATION RD
SHEEPCOTE RD
GREENHILL WAY
COLLEGE RD
LOWLANDS RD
TYBURN LA
KENTON RD
PINNER RD
BESSBOROUGH RD
LOWER RD
PETERBOROUGH RD
ROXETH HILL
HEADSTONE GDNS
HEADSTONE RD
CUNNINGHAM PK
KINGSFIELD AVE
WHITMORE RD
SHAFTESBURY CIRC
SHAFTESBURY AVE
HARROW VIEW
PINNER VIEW
LONGLEY RD
HIDE RD
BOLTON RD
MOAT DR
BROOK DR
HARLEY RD
WALTON RD
WALTON DR
KINGS WAY
MARLBOROUGH HILL
WELLINGTON RD
HAVELOCK RD
GORDON RD
CECIL RD
HAILSHAM DR
PEEL RD
PALMERSTON RD
MASONS AVE
HERGA RD
FORWARD DR
WARRINGTON RD
HINDES RD
WELLESLEY RD
WELLDON CRES
OAKLEY RD
DORSET RD
OXFORD RD
RUTLAND RD
BEDFORD RD
CORNWALL RD
SOMERSET RD
SUSSEX RD
GRAFTON RD
CHANDOS RD
ALTHORPE RD
CANTERBURY RD
NEPTUNE RD
BUTLER AVE
LASCELLES AVE
BOUVERIE RD
VAUGHAN RD
BADGERS CL
HEATH RD
SUMNER RD
COLBECK RD
LANCE RD
TREVE AVE
WOOD CL
CHARLES CRES
PORLOCK AVE
HILLSIDE CRES
DUDLEY GDNS
JOLLYS LA
MIDDLE RD
CHURCH HILL
FOOTBALL LA
GARLANDS LA
THE GARLANDS
ROXBOROUGH AVE
ROXBOROUGH PK
MAXTED PK
PICKWICK PL
CROWN ST
WEST ST
VICTORIA TERR
MEADOW VIEW
YEW WLK
GROVE HILL
LANSDOWNE RD
GAYTON RD
ASHBURNHAM AVE
NORTHWICK PARK RD
HIGH MEAD
NIBTHWAITE RD
BETHECAR RD
BLAWITH RD
TORVER RD
COLTON RD
HAMILTON RD
1 JARDINE HO
2 HILLBOROUGH CT
3 DRUMMOND CT
4 LITTLE CT
5 CHESTNUT CT
6 Harrovian Bsns Village
1 CROWN CT
2 CHILTERN HO
CUMBERLAND CT 1
BANNISTER HO 2
POPPY CT 3
KARMAN CT 4
AMBASSADOR HO 5
CHURCH PAR 6
CENTURY HO 7
REGENCY LO 8
LOCKET RD MS 9
1 CLARENDON HO
2 BEVERLEY CT
LEYS CL 1
CHILTERN CT 2
MILES LO 3
HOLLY LO 4
CUNNINGHAM CT 5
WORDSWORTH CT 1
CHARLES CRES 2
KINGSFIELD RD 3
BURRELL CT 4
HANOVER CT 5
KINGSFIELD CT 6
A404
A409
A4005
A312
B458

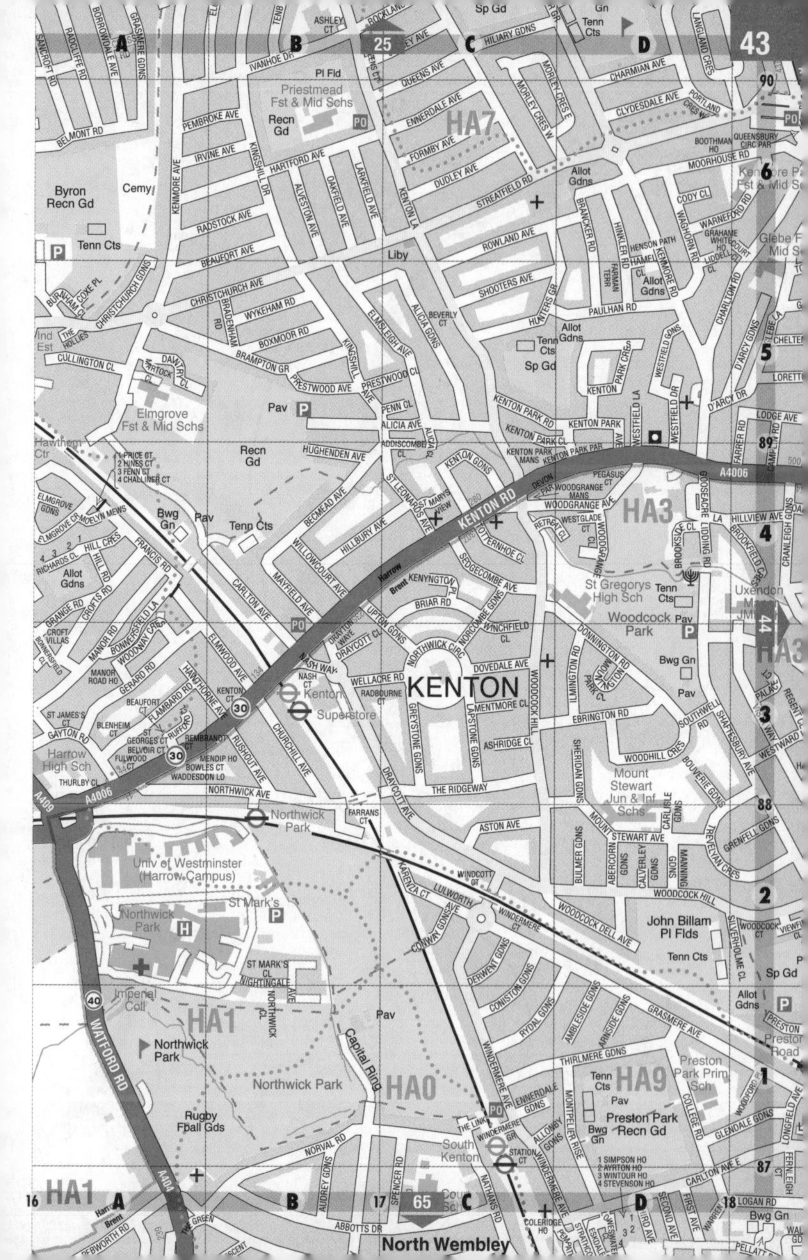
43
A
B
C
D
25
65
44
KENTON
North Wembley
HA7
HA3
HA1
HA0
HA9
KENTON RD
A4006
A409
A404
WATFORD RD
Priestmead Fst & Mid Schs
Recn Gd
Byron Recn Gd
Cemy
Tenn Cts
Elmgrove Fst & Mid Schs
Pav
Bwg Gn
Allot Gdns
Harrow High Sch
Liby
Sp Gd
St Gregorys High Sch
Woodcock Park
Mount Stewart Jun & Inf Schs
John Billam Pl Flds
Kenton
Superstore
Northwick Park
Univ of Westminster (Harrow Campus)
Northwick Park
St Mark's
Imperial Coll
Northwick Park
Rugby Fball Gds
Capital Ring
South Kenton
Preston Park Prim Sch
Preston Park Recn Gd
Preston Road
Uxendon Manor JMI
Kenmore Park Fst & Mid Schs
Glebe Fst & Mid Schs
Hawthorn Ctr
Wind Est
1 PRICE CT
2 HINES CT
3 FENN CT
4 CHALLINER CT
1 SIMPSON HO
2 AYRTON HO
3 WINTOUR HO
4 STEVENSON HO
IVANHOE DR
QUEENS AVE
PEMBROKE AVE
IRVINE AVE
RADSTOCK AVE
BEAUFORT AVE
CHRISTCHURCH AVE
CHRISTCHURCH GDNS
WYKEHAM RD
BOXMOOR RD
BRAMPTON GR
PRESTWOOD AVE
KINGSHILL DR
KINGSHILL AVE
KENMORE AVE
HARTFORD AVE
ALVESTON AVE
OAKFIELD AVE
LARKFIELD AVE
KENTON LA
ENNERDALE AVE
FORMBY AVE
DUDLEY AVE
STREATFIELD RD
ROWLAND AVE
SHOOTERS AVE
HUNTERS GR
ALICIA GDNS
ALICIA AVE
ELMSLEIGH AVE
HUGHENDEN AVE
BECMEAD AVE
HILLBURY AVE
WILLOWCOURT AVE
MAYFIELD AVE
CARLTON AVE
ELMWOOD AVE
CHURCHILL AVE
RUSHOUT AVE
NORTHWICK AVE
DRAYCOTT AVE
THE RIDGEWAY
ASTON AVE
NORTHWICK CIRC
GREYSTONE GDNS
LAPSTONE GDNS
ASHRIDGE CL
MENTMORE CL
DOVEDALE AVE
WOODCOCK HILL
EBRINGTON RD
ILMINGTON RD
DONNINGTON RD
SHERIDAN GDNS
WOODHILL CRES
SOUTHWELL RD
SHAFTESBURY AVE
BOUVERIE GDNS
TREVELYAN CRES
GRENFELL GDNS
MOUNT STEWART AVE
BULMER GDNS
WOODCOCK DELL AVE
GRASMERE AVE
THIRLMERE GDNS
WINDERMERE AVE
CONISTON GDNS
RYDAL GDNS
AMBLESIDE GDNS
ARNSIDE GDNS
DERWENT GDNS
CONWAY GDNS
LULWORTH AVE
KARENZA CT
NORVAL RD
AUDREY GDNS
SPENCER RD
NATHANS RD
ABBOTTS DR
MONTPELIER RISE
ALLONBY GDNS
COLLEGE RD
CARLTON AVE E
GLENDALE GDNS
LOGAN RD
FRANCIS RD
HILL RD
CROFTS RD
GRANGE RD
MANOR RD
GERARD RD
HAWTHORNE AVE
FLAMBARD RD
GAYTON RD
BELMONT RD
RADCLIFFE RD
BORROWDALE AVE
GRASMERE GDNS
SANCROFT RD
CHARMIAN AVE
CLYDESDALE AVE
MOORHOUSE RD
BRANCKER RD
HINKLER RD
KENMORE RD
WAGHORN RD
PAULHAN RD
CHARLTON RD
WESTFIELD LA
WESTFIELD DR
KENTON PARK RD
KENTON PARK AVE
D'ARCY DR
D'ARCY GDNS
LODGE AVE
GOOSEACRE LA
LIDDING RD
HILLVIEW AVE
BROOKFIELD CRES
CRANLEIGH GDNS
WOODGRANGE AVE
SEDGECOMBE AVE
BRIAR RD
UPTON GDNS
DRAYCOTT CL
WELLACRE RD
NASH WAY
WOODCOCK HILL
SILVERHOLME CL
PRESTON RD
WOODFORD PL
LONGFIELD AVE
FERNLEIGH CT
FIRST AVE
SECOND AVE
WARREN

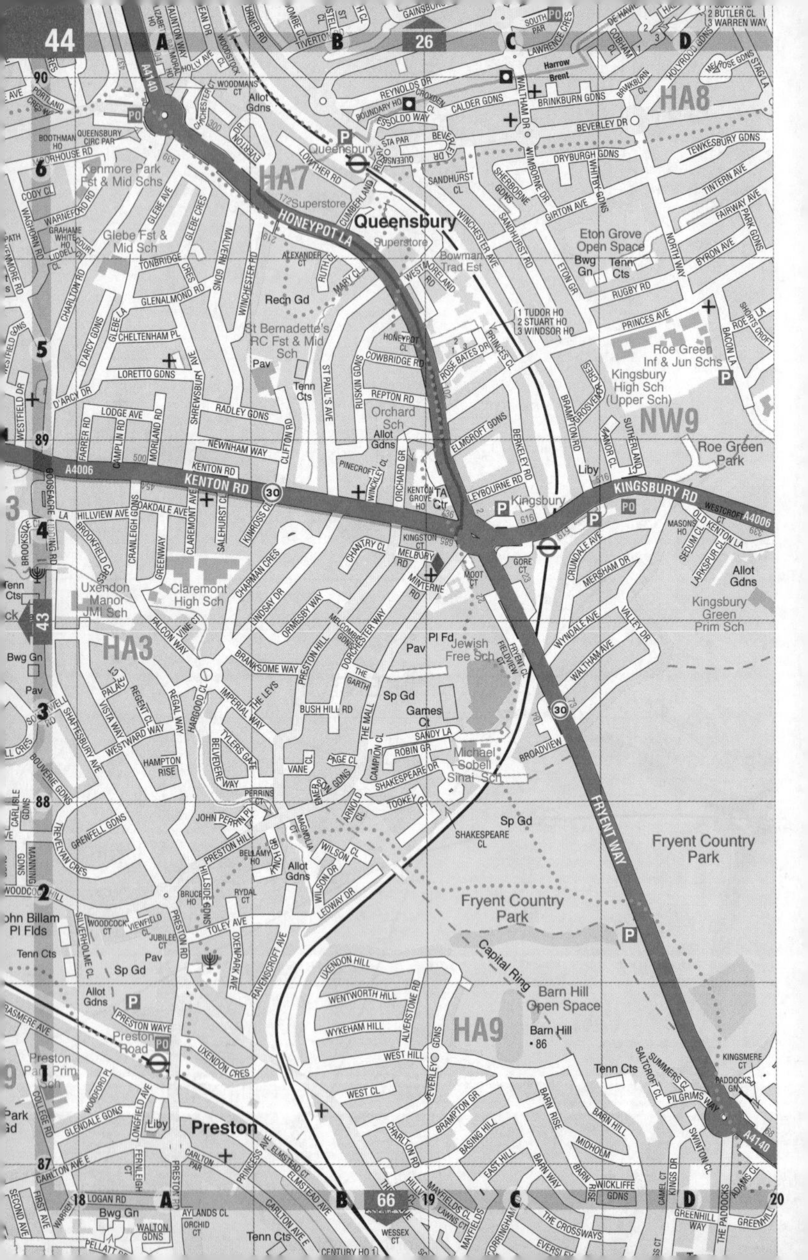
A
B
26
C
D
90
89
88
87
6
5
4
3
2
1
43
66
18
19
20
HA7
HA8
HA3
HA9
NW9
Queensbury
Kingsbury
Preston
Preston Road
A4140
A4006
HONEYPOT LA
KENTON RD
KINGSBURY RD
FRYENT WAY
TAUNTON WAY
HOLLY AVE
WOODSTOCK
WOODMANS CT
CHICHESTER CT
Allot Gdns
PORTLAND CRES
BOOTHMAN HO
QUEENSBURY CIRC PAR
MOORHOUSE RD
Kenmore Park Fst & Mid Schs
CODY CL
WARNEFORD RD
WAGHORN RD
GRAHAME WHITE HO
LIDDELL CL
COURT
Glebe Fst & Mid Sch
GLEBE AVE
GLEBE CRES
TONBRIDGE CRES
GLENALMOND RD
CHARLTON RD
D'ARCY GDNS
GLEBE LA
CHELTENHAM PL
LORETTO GDNS
D'ARCY DR
WESTFIELD DR
WESTFIELD GDNS
LODGE AVE
FARRER RD
CAMPLIN RD
MORLAND RD
SHREWSBURY AVE
RADLEY GDNS
NEWNHAM WAY
KENTON RD
MALVERN GDNS
WINCHESTER RD
EVERTON DR
LOWTHER RD
CUMBERLAND RD
Superstore
ALEXANDER CT
RUTHIN CL
MARY CL
Recn Gd
St Bernadette's RC Fst & Mid Sch
Pav
Tenn Cts
ST PAUL'S AVE
CLIFTON RD
RUSKIN GDNS
HONEYPOT CL
COWBRIDGE RD
REPTON RD
Orchard Sch
WESTMORELAND RD
Bowman Trad Est
ROSE BATES DR
PRINCES CL
1 TUDOR HO
2 STUART HO
3 WINDSOR HO
ELMCROFT GDNS
BERKELEY RD
LEYBOURNE RD
KENTON GROVE HO
TA Ctr
PINECROFT CT
WINCKLEY CL
ORCHARD GR
REYNOLDS DR
BOUNDARY HO
CROXDEN CL
ESSOLDO WAY
STA PAR
BEVERLEY DR
CALDER GDNS
BRINKBURN GDNS
BRINKBURN CL
WALTHAM DR
WIMBORNE DR
SANDHURST CL
SANDHURST RD
SHERBORNE GDNS
DRYBURGH GDNS
WHITBY GDNS
GIRTON AVE
WINCHESTER AVE
ETON GR
Eton Grove Open Space
Bwg Gn
TENKESBURY GDNS
TINTERN AVE
FAIRWAY AVE
PARK GDNS
BYRON AVE
NORTH WAY
RUGBY RD
PRINCES AVE
HOLYROOD GDNS
STAG LA
Roe Green Inf & Jun Schs
Kingsbury High Sch (Upper Sch)
BACON LA
SHORTS CROFT
ROE LA
GROSVENOR CRES
BRAMPTON RD
MANOR CL
SUTHERLAND CL
Roe Green Park
Liby
WESTCROFT CT
MASONS HO
OLD KENTON LA
SEDUM CL
LARKSPUR CL
Kingsbury Green Prim Sch
SOUTH PAR
LAWRENCE CRES
DE HAVILAND
COBHAM CL
2 BUTLER CL
3 WARREN WAY
Harrow
Brent
GAINSBOROUGH
TIVERTON
HILLVIEW AVE
OAKDALE AVE
CRANLEIGH GDNS
CLAREMONT AVE
SALEHURST CL
KINROSS CL
GREENWAY
BROOKFIELD CRES
BROOKSIDE CL
GOOSEACRE LA
Uxendon Manor JMI Sch
Claremont High Sch
CHAPMAN CRES
CHANTRY CL
LINDSAY DR
ORMESBY WAY
KINGSTON CT
MELBURY RD
MINTERNE RD
MOOT CT
GORE CT
CRUNDALE AVE
MERSHAM DR
WYNDALE AVE
VALLEY DR
WALTHAM AVE
FALCON WAY
VINE CT
BRANKSOME WAY
PRESTON HILL
MELCOMBE GDNS
DORCHESTER WAY
THE GARTH
Pl Fd
Jewish Free Sch
FRYENT CL
FIELDVIEW CT
Sp Gd
Games Ct
BUSH HILL RD
THE MALL
SANDY LA
ROBIN GR
Michael Sobell Sinai Sch
BROADVIEW
CAMPION CL
PAGE CL
VANE CL
SHAKESPEARE DR
TOOKEY CL
SHAKESPEARE CL
EMERSON GDNS
ARNOLD CL
PERRINS CT
Bwg Gn
HA3
PALACE CT
REGENT CL
VISTA WAY
REGAL WAY
HARGOOD CL
IMPERIAL WAY
THE LEYS
WESTWARD WAY
SHAFTESBURY AVE
SOMERWELL RD
HAMPTON RISE
TYLERS GATE
BELVEDERE WAY
BOUVERIE GDNS
CARLISLE GDNS
GRENFELL GDNS
TREVELYAN CRES
MANNING GDNS
JOHN PERRIN PL
PRESTON HILL
BELLAMY HO
KNIGHTS CT
MAGNOLIA CT
WILSON CL
WILSON DR
LEDWAY DR
Allot Gdns
HILLSIDE GDNS
BRUCE HO
RYDAL CT
TOLEY AVE
WOODCOCK HILL
John Billam Pl Flds
WOODCOCK CT
VIEWFIELD CL
JUBILEE CT
SILVERHOLME CL
PRESTON RD
OXENPARK AVE
RAVENSCROFT AVE
Fryent Country Park
Capital Ring
Barn Hill Open Space
Barn Hill • 86
UXENDON HILL
WENTWORTH HILL
WYKEHAM HILL
ALVERSTONE RD
WEST HILL
BEVERLEY GDNS
UXENDON CRES
PRESTON WAYE
GRASMERE AVE
Preston Park Prim Sch
COLLEGE RD
WOODFORD PL
GLENDALE GDNS
LONGFIELD AVE
Park Gd
FERNLEIGH CT
CARLTON AVE E
CARLTON PAR
PRINCESS AVE
ELMSTEAD AVE
ELMSTEAD CT
WEST CL
BRAMPTON GR
CHARLTON RD
BASING HILL
EAST HILL
BARN RISE
BARN WAY
BARN HILL
MIDHOLM
WICKLIFFE GDNS
SUMMERS CL
SALTCROFT CL
PILGRIMS WAY
SWINTON CL
KINGSMERE CT
PADDOCKS GN
ADAMS CL
THE PADDOCKS
KINGS DR
CAMEL CT
GREENHILL WAY
THE CROSSWAYS
CORRINGHAM
MAYFIELDS
MAYFIELDS CL
LAWNS CT
WESSEX CT
CENTURY HO
LOGAN RD
Bwg Gn
AYLANDS CL
ORCHID CT
WALTON GDNS
PELLATT RD
SECOND AVE
FIRST AVE
WARREN
Tenn Cts
CARLTON AVE E
Liby

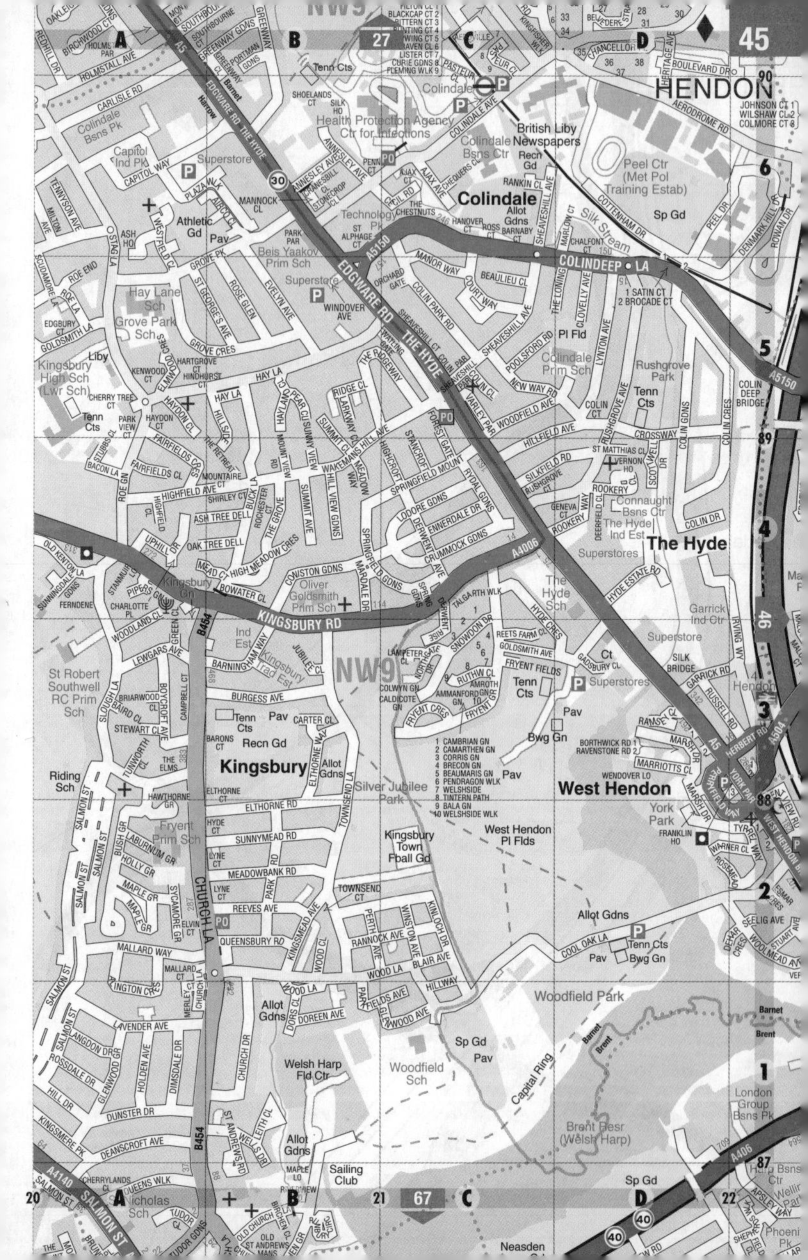
HENDON
Colindale
Kingsbury
West Hendon
The Hyde
NW9
27
67
A
B
C
D
20
21
22
90
89
88
87
1
2
3
4
5
6
46
Colindale Bsns Pk
Capitol Ind Pk
Superstore
Athletic Gd
Pav
Health Protection Agency Ctr for Infections
Tenn Cts
British Liby Newspapers
Colindale Bsns Ctr
Recn Gd
Peel Ctr (Met Pol Training Estab)
Sp Gd
Technology Pk
Allot Gdns
Silk Stream
Beis Yaakov Prim Sch
Hay Lane Sch
Grove Park Sch
Kingsbury High Sch (Lwr Sch)
Liby
Colindale Prim Sch
Pl Fld
Rushgrove Park
Connaught Bsns Ctr
The Hyde Ind Est
Superstores
Oliver Goldsmith Prim Sch
The Hyde Sch
Garrick Ind Ctr
Kingsbury Gn
Ind Est
Kingsbury Trad Est
St Robert Southwell RC Prim Sch
Recn Gd
Silver Jubilee Park
Bwg Gn
Riding Sch
Fryent Prim Sch
Kingsbury Town Fball Gd
West Hendon Pl Flds
York Park
Franklin Ho
Allot Gdns
Woodfield Park
Welsh Harp Fld Ctr
Woodfield Sch
Capital Ring
Brent Resr (Welsh Harp)
Sailing Club
London Group Bsns Pk
Harp Bsns Ctr
St Nicholas Sch
Neasden
Barnet
Brent
Harrow
EDGWARE RD THE HYDE
KINGSBURY RD
COLINDEEP LA
CHURCH LA
A5
A5150
A4006
B454
A4140
A406
A504
SALMON ST
1 CAMBRIAN GN
2 CAMARTHEN GN
3 CORRIS GN
4 BRECON GN
5 BEAUMARIS GN
6 PENDRAGON WLK
7 WELSHSIDE
8 TINTERN PATH
9 BALA GN
10 WELSHSIDE WLK
1 SATIN CT
2 BROCADE CT
JOHNSON CT 1
WILSHAW CL 2
COLMORE CT 3
BORTHWICK RD 1
RAVENSTONE RD 2
CARLISLE RD
CAPITOL WAY
HOLMSTALL AVE
GROVE PK
HAY LA
HIGHFIELD AVE
BURGESS AVE
ELTHORNE RD
SUNNYMEAD RD
MEADOWBANK RD
REEVES AVE
QUEENSBURY RD
MALLARD WAY
LAVENDER AVE
DUNSTER DR
DEANSCROFT AVE
COOL OAK LA
AERODROME RD
COTTENHAM DR
CROSSWAY
HILLFIELD AVE
WOODFIELD AVE
MANOR WAY
HYDE ESTATE RD
GARRICK RD
SPRINGFIELD MOUNT
WAKEMANS HILL AVE
BOWATER CL
BARNINGHAM WAY
LEWGARS AVE
FRYENT FIELDS
GOLDSMITH AVE
WOOD LA
RANNOCK AVE
WOODFIELD PARK
SEELIG AVE
WOOLMEAD AVE

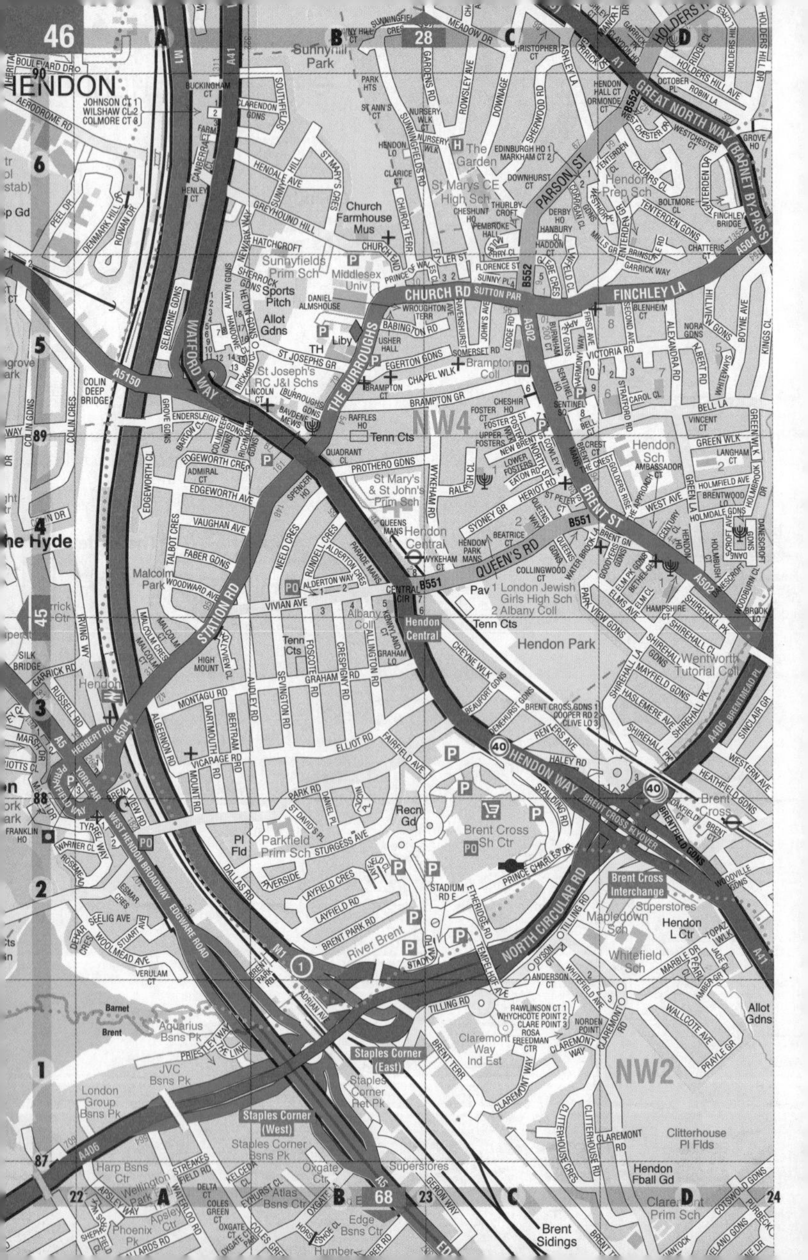
46
A
B
C
D
28
68
HENDON
NW4
NW2
Sunnyhill Park
Church Farmhouse Mus
Sunnyfields Prim Sch
Middlesex Univ
Sports Pitch
Allot Gdns
Liby
TH
St Joseph's RC J&I Schs
St Marys CE High Sch
The Garden
Hendon Prep Sch
Brampton Coll
Tenn Cts
St Mary's & St John's Prim Sch
Hendon Central
Hendon Sch
Malcolm Park
Albany Coll
Hendon Park
Pav
1 London Jewish Girls High Sch
2 Albany Coll
Wentworth Tutorial Coll
Brent Cross Sh Ctr
Brent Cross Interchange
Brent Cross
Recn Gd
Pl Fld
Parkfield Prim Sch
River Brent
Mapledown Sch
Whitefield Sch
Hendon L Ctr
Superstores
Allot Gdns
Claremont Way Ind Est
Staples Corner (East)
Staples Corner (West)
Staples Corner Ret Pk
Staples Corner Bsns Pk
Aquarius Bsns Pk
JVC Bsns Pk
London Group Bsns Pk
Harp Bsns Ctr
Wellington Park
Atlas Bsns Ctr
Oxgate Ctr
Edge Bsns Ctr
Phoenix Pk
Apsley Ctr
Clitterhouse Pl Flds
Hendon Fball Gd
Claremont Prim Sch
Brent Sidings
Barnet
Brent
The Hyde
Colin Deep Bridge
Silk Bridge
HENDON WAY
WATFORD WAY
THE BURROUGHS
STATION RD
CHURCH RD
FINCHLEY LA
QUEEN'S RD
BRENT ST
PARSON ST
NORTH CIRCULAR RD
GREAT NORTH WAY (BARNET BY-PASS)
WEST HENDON BROADWAY
EDGWARE ROAD
BRENT CROSS FLYOVER
A41
M1
A5150
A504
A502
B552
B551
A406
A5
A1
40
1
2
3
4
5
6
87
88
89
90
22
23
24
45

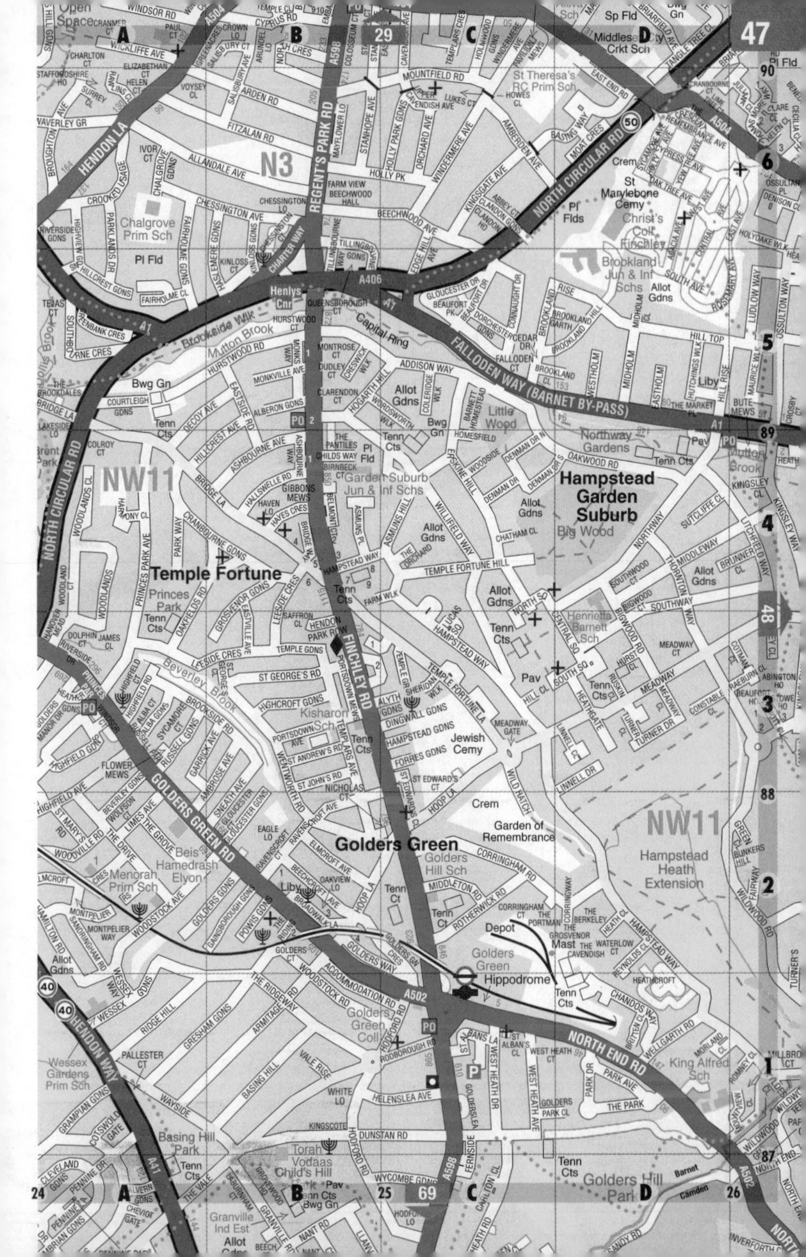

47
29
A
B
C
D
N3
NW11
NW11
Hampstead
Garden
Suburb
Temple Fortune
Golders Green
HENDON LA
REGENT'S PARK RD
FINCHLEY RD
GOLDERS GREEN RD
NORTH CIRCULAR RD
NORTH CIRCULAR RD
FALLODEN WAY (BARNET BY-PASS)
NORTH END RD
HENDON WAY
A598
A406
A1
A41
A502
A504
Henlys
Cnr
Capital Ring
Mutton Brook
Brookside Wlk
Beverley Brook
Chalgrove
Prim Sch
Pl Fld
St Theresa's
RC Prim Sch
Middlesex Cty
Crkt Sch
St
Marylebone
Cemy
Christ's
Coll
Finchley
Brookland
Jun & Inf
Schs
Allot
Gdns
Little
Wood
Northway
Gardens
Big Wood
Garden Suburb
Jun & Inf Schs
Princes
Park
Henrietta
Barnett
Sch
Kisharon
Sch
Jewish
Cemy
Crem
Garden of
Remembrance
Golders
Hill Sch
Beis
Hamedrash
Elyon
Menorah
Prim Sch
Hampstead
Heath
Extension
Golders
Green
Hippodrome
Depot
Mast
King Alfred
Sch
Golders
Green
Coll
Wessex
Gardens
Prim Sch
Basing Hill
Park
Torah
Vodaas
Child's Hill
Granville
Ind Est
Golders Hill
Park
Barnet
Camden
6
5
4
3
2
1
90
89
88
87
48
24
25
26
69

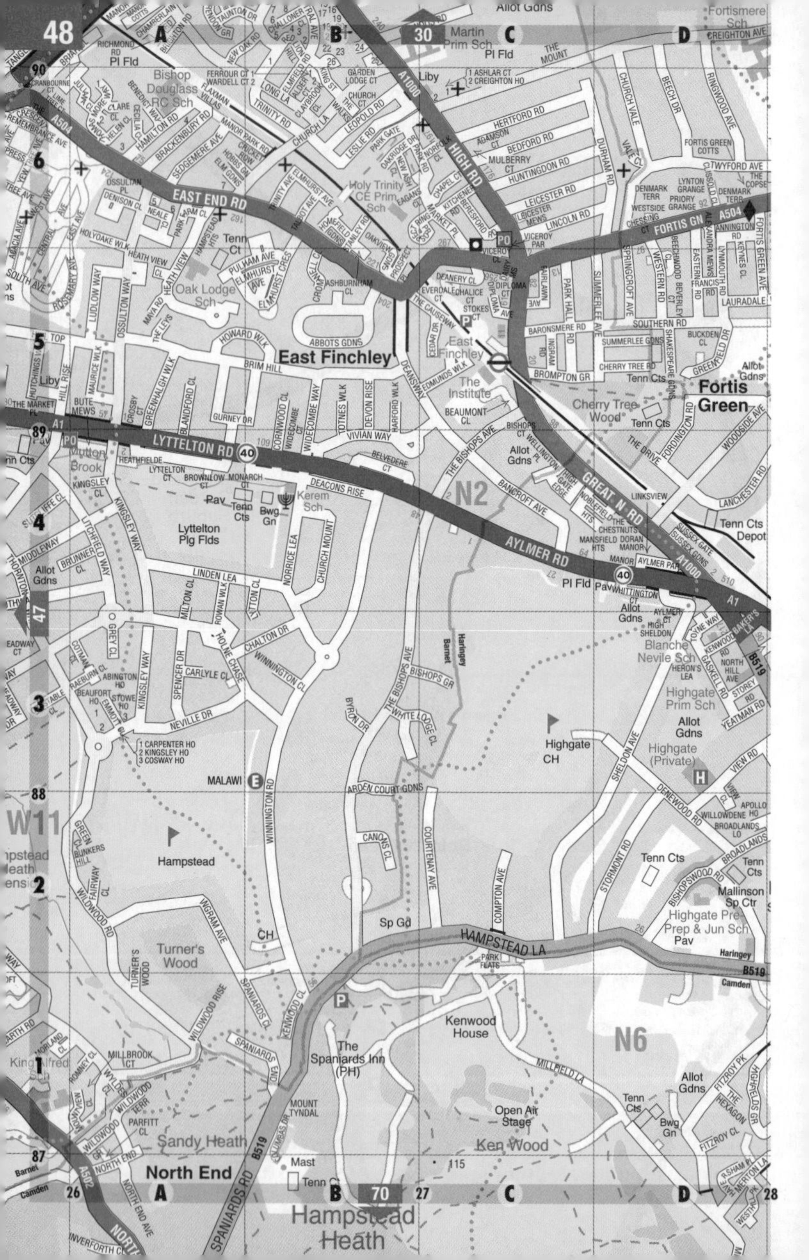

East Finchley
Fortis Green
N2
N6
W11
Hampstead
Highgate
Turner's Wood
Sandy Heath
Ken Wood
Kenwood House
The Spaniards Inn (PH)
Hampstead Heath
North End
EAST END RD
LYTTELTON RD
AYLMER RD
GREAT N RD
HIGH RD
FORTIS GN
HAMPSTEAD LA
SPANIARDS RD
THE BISHOPS AVE
WINNINGTON RD
Lyttelton Plg Flds
Cherry Tree Wood
Highgate Prim Sch
Blanche Nevile Sch
Holy Trinity CE Prim Sch
Bishop Douglass RC Sch
Oak Lodge Sch
Kerem Sch
Martin Prim Sch
Mallinson Sp Ctr
Highgate Pre-Prep & Jun Sch
The Institute
MALAWI
Open Air Stage
A
B
C
D
30
70
47
28
26
27
87
88
89
90

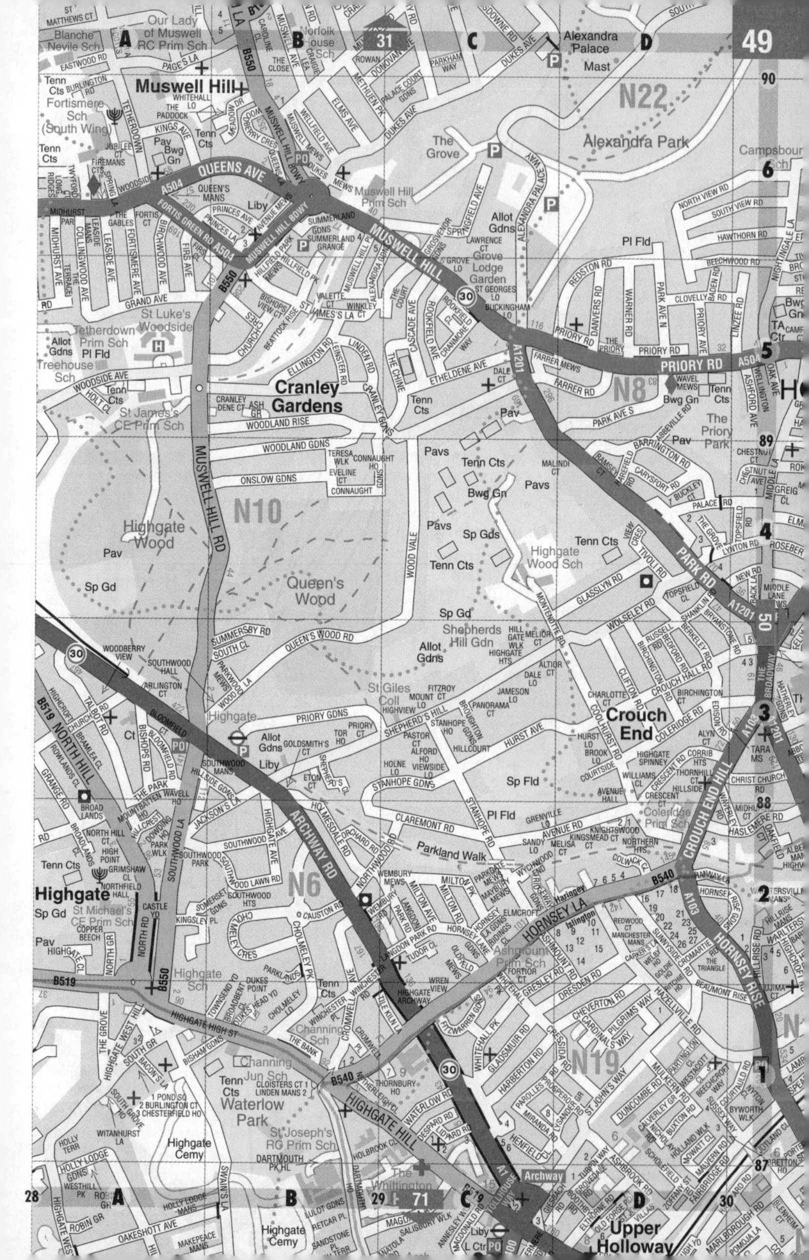

49
31
71
Muswell Hill
Alexandra Palace
Mast
N22
Alexandra Park
The Grove
Campsbourne Sch
Our Lady of Muswell RC Prim Sch
Blanche Nevile Sch
Norfolk House Sch
Fortismere Sch (South Wing)
Muswell Hill Prim Sch
QUEENS AVE
MUSWELL HILL
MUSWELL HILL BDWY
FORTIS GREEN RD
ALEXANDRA PALACE WAY
Allot Gdns
Grove Lodge Garden
PRIORY RD
N8
PARK AVE S
St Luke's Woodside
Tetherdown Prim Sch
Treehouse Sch
St James's CE Prim Sch
Cranley Gardens
WOODLAND RISE
WOODLAND GDNS
ONSLOW GDNS
N10
Highgate Wood
MUSWELL HILL RD
Queen's Wood
WOOD VALE
QUEEN'S WOOD RD
Highgate Wood Sch
Shepherds Hill Gdn
The Priory Park
PARK RD
TIVOLI RD
GLASSLYN RD
WOLSELEY RD
CROUCH HALL RD
Crouch End
COLERIDGE RD
HURST AVE
Coleridge Prim Sch
CROUCH END HILL
St Giles Coll
SHEPHERD'S HILL
PRIORY GDNS
Highgate
ARCHWAY RD
N6
Parkland Walk
CLAREMONT RD
AVENUE RD
HORNSEY LA
HORNSEY RISE
Ashmount Prim Sch
NORTH HILL
Highgate
St Michael's CE Prim Sch
Highgate Sch
HIGHGATE HIGH ST
Channing Sch
Channing Jun Sch
Waterlow Park
HIGHGATE HILL
St Joseph's RC Prim Sch
Highgate Cemy
The Whittington
N19
ST JOHN'S WAY
Archway
Upper Holloway
THE BROADWAY

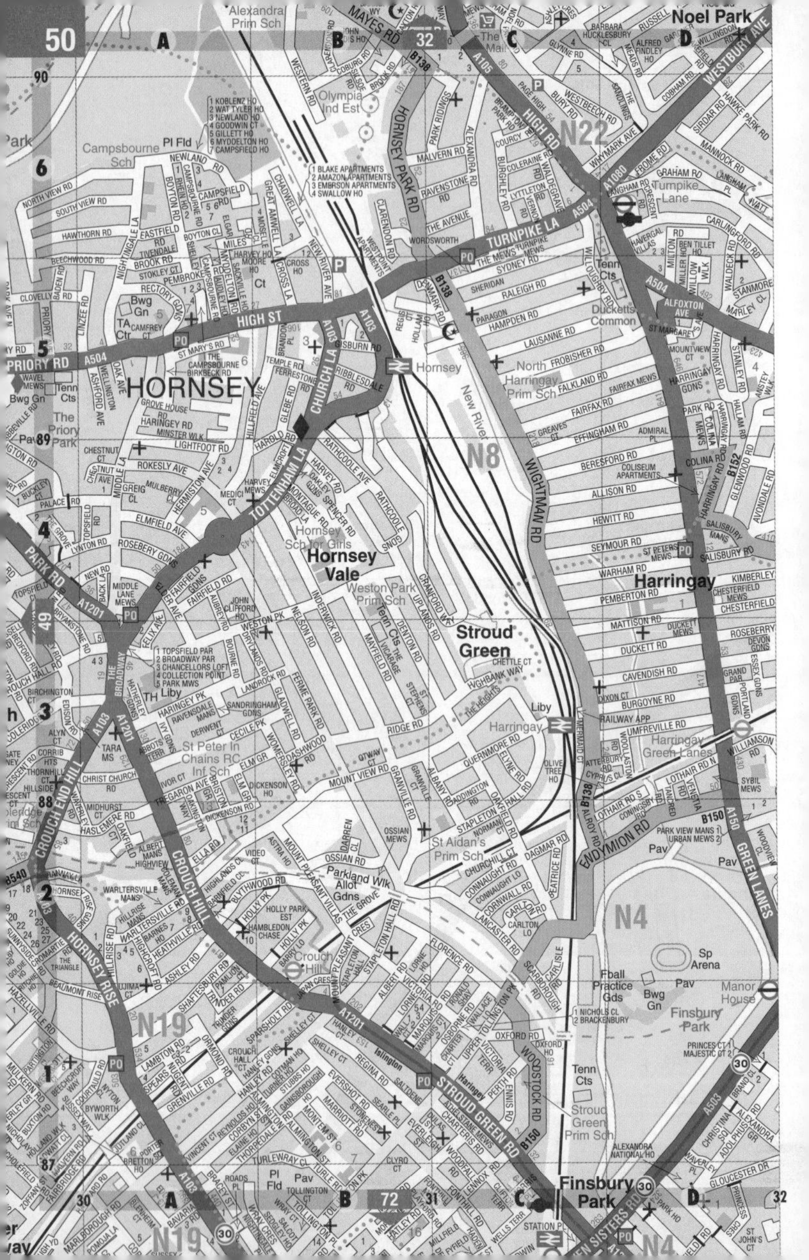
A
B
C
D
32
90
6
5
89
4
3
88
2
1
87
30
72
31
49
Noel Park
Alexandra Prim Sch
MAYES RD
The Mall
WESTBURY AVE
HIGH RD
N22
Olympia Ind Est
HORNSEY PARK RD
Campsbourne Sch
Pl Fld
1 KOBLENZ HO
2 WAT TYLER HO
3 NEWLAND HO
4 GOODWIN CT
5 GILLETT HO
6 MYDDELTON HO
7 CAMPSFIELD HO
1 BLAKE APARTMENTS
2 AMAZON APARTMENTS
3 EMBERSON APARTMENTS
4 SWALLOW HO
TURNPIKE LA
Turnpike Lane
WESTERN RD
ALEXANDRA RD
PARK RIDINGS
MALVERN RD
RAVENSTONE RD
THE AVENUE
WORDSWORTH
Tenn Cts
Ducketts Common
HIGH ST
PRIORY RD
HORNSEY
The Priory Park
Bwg Gn
TA Ctr
CHURCH LA
Hornsey
North Harringay Prim Sch
New River
N8
WIGHTMAN RD
TOTTENHAM LA
Hornsey Sch for Girls
Hornsey Vale
Weston Park Prim Sch
Stroud Green
Harringay
HARRINGAY RD
GREEN LANES
PARK RD
CROUCH END HILL
CROUCH HILL
THE BROADWAY
HORNSEY RISE
1 TOPSFIELD PAR
2 BROADWAY PAR
3 CHANCELLORS LOFT
4 COLLECTION POINT
5 PARK MWS
Liby
St Peter In Chains RC Inf Sch
St Aidan's Prim Sch
Parkland Wlk
Allot Gdns
Crouch Hill
N19
N4
ENDYMION RD
Sp Arena
Fball Practice Gds
Finsbury Park
Manor House
1 NICHOLS CL
2 BRACKENBURY
STROUD GREEN RD
Stroud Green Prim Sch
WOODSTOCK RD
Tenn Cts
SEVEN SISTERS RD
Finsbury Park
STATION PL

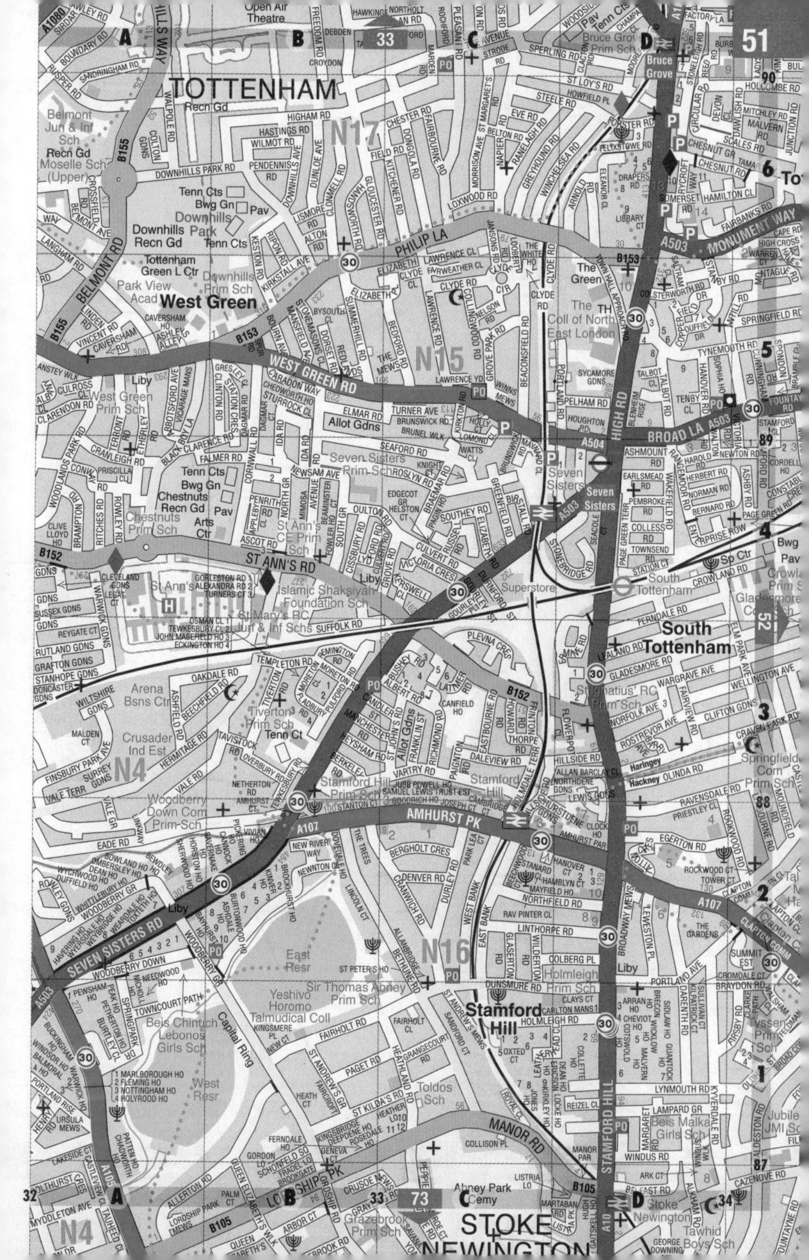
51
A
B
C
D
33
TOTTENHAM
N17
Bruce Grove
West Green
N15
The Green
The Coll of North East London
WEST GREEN RD
PHILIP LA
BROAD LA
HIGH RD
MONUMENT WAY
Seven Sisters
ST ANN'S RD
SEVEN SISTERS RD
South Tottenham
52
N4
AMHURST PK
N16
Stamford Hill
STAMFORD HILL
East Resr
West Resr
Capital Ring
MANOR RD
Abney Park Cemy
STOKE NEWINGTON
73
32
34
1
2
3
4
5
6
87
88
89
90

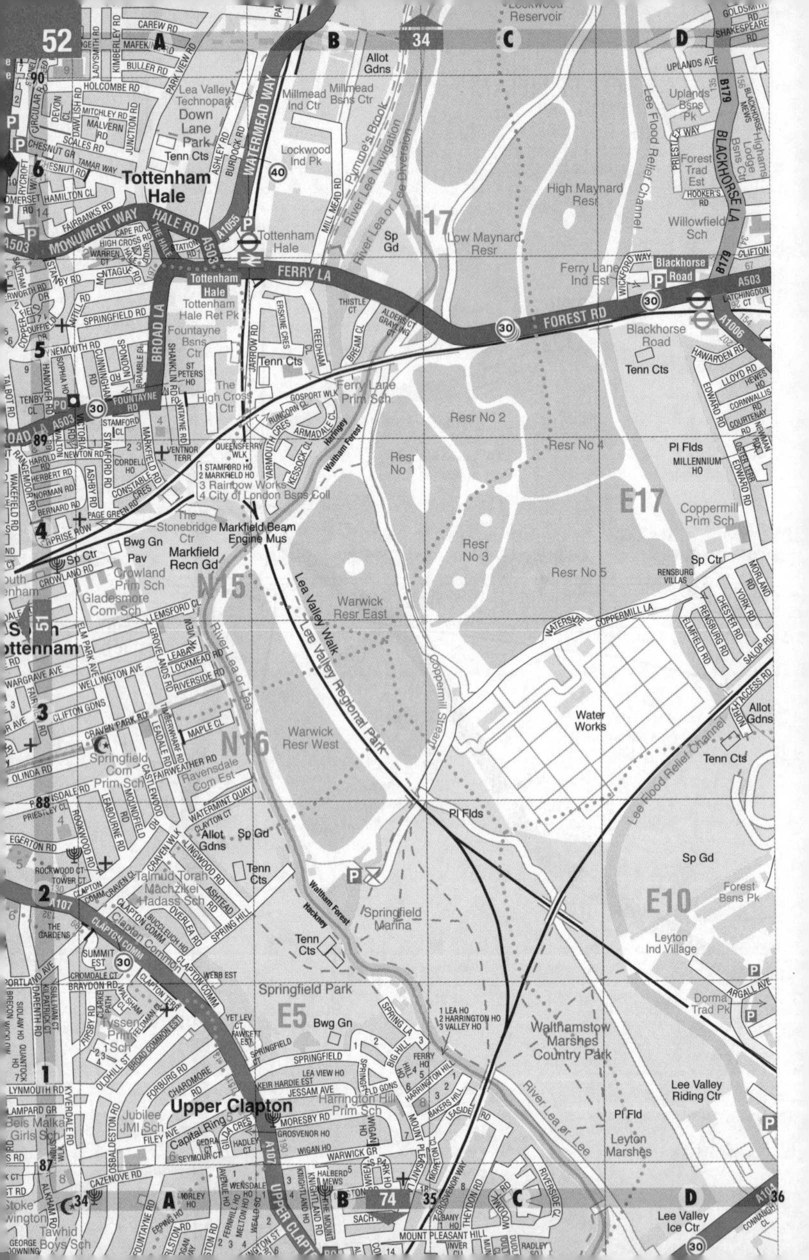
52
A
B
C
D
34
Lockwood Reservoir
Allot Gdns
Millmead Ind Ctr
Millmead Bsns Ctr
Lea Valley Technopark
Down Lane Park
Lockwood Ind Pk
Tenn Cts
Tottenham Hale
Pymme's Brook
River Lee Navigation
River Lea or Lee Diversion
WATERMEAD WAY
High Maynard Resr
Low Maynard Resr
Lee Flood Relief Channel
N17
Sp Gd
Tottenham Hale
MONUMENT WAY
HALE RD
FERRY LA
FOREST RD
A503
A1055
B179
BLACKHORSE LA
Uplands Bsns Pk
Forest Trad Est
Blackhorse Lodge Bsns Ctr
Willowfield Sch
Ferry Lane Ind Est
Blackhorse Road
Tottenham Hale Ret Pk
Fountayne Bsns Ctr
The High Cross Ctr
Ferry Lane Prim Sch
BROAD LA
Tenn Cts
Resr No 1
Resr No 2
Resr No 3
Resr No 4
Resr No 5
Pl Flds
E17
Coppermill Prim Sch
Sp Ctr
Stonebridge Ctr
Markfield Beam Engine Mus
Markfield Recn Gd
Bwg Gn
Pav
Crowland Prim Sch
Gladesmore Com Sch
South Tottenham
N15
Warwick Resr East
Warwick Resr West
Lea Valley Walk
Lee Valley Regional Park
Coppermill Stream
COPPERMILL LA
Water Works
Allot Gdns
Tenn Cts
N16
Springfield Com Prim Sch
Ravensdale Com Est
Allot Gdns
Sp Gd
Tenn Cts
Talmud Torah Machzikei Hadass Sch
Springfield Marina
Sp Gd
E10
Forest Bsns Pk
Leyton Ind Village
Dorma Trad Pk
Clapton Common
Springfield Park
E5
Bwg Gn
Walthamstow Marshes Country Park
Tyssen Prim Sch
Upper Clapton
Harrington Hill Prim Sch
Jubilee JMI Sch
Beis Malka Girls Sch
Capital Ring
Lee Valley Riding Ctr
Pl Fld
Leyton Marshes
River Lea or Lee
A107
UPPER CLAPTON
74
35
36
Lee Valley Ice Ctr
Tawhid Boys Sch
Stoke Newington

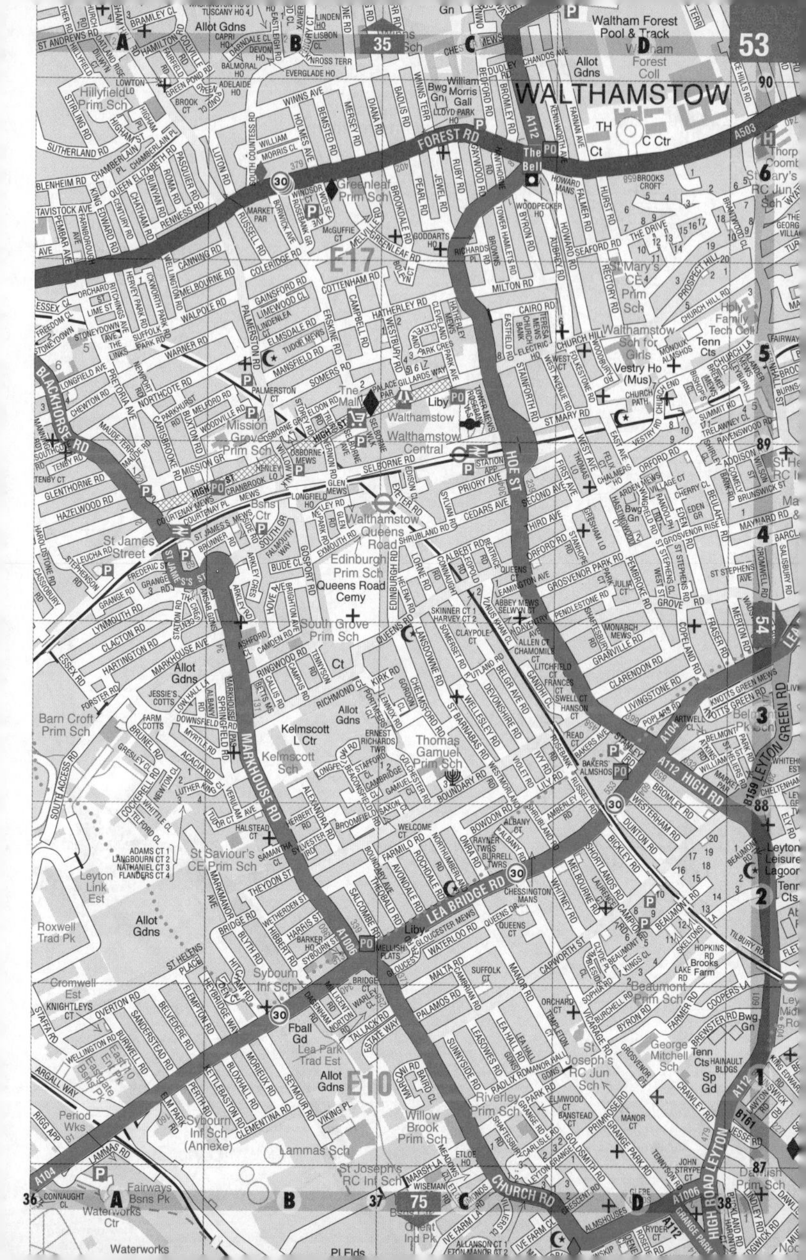
WALTHAMSTOW
Waltham Forest Pool & Track
Waltham Forest Coll
Allot Gdns
William Morris Gall
Lloyd Park
Forest Rd
A112
A503
The Bell
Hillyfield Prim Sch
Greenleaf Prim Sch
E17
Walthamstow Sch for Girls
Vestry Ho (Mus)
St Mary's CE Prim Sch
Holy Family Tech Coll
The Mall
Walthamstow Central
High St
Hoe St
Blackhorse Rd
Mission Grove Prim Sch
St James Street
Walthamstow Queens Road
Edinburgh Prim Sch
Queens Road Cemy
South Grove Prim Sch
Markhouse Rd
Kelmscott L Ctr
Kelmscott Sch
Thomas Gamuel Prim Sch
Barn Croft Prim Sch
St Saviour's CE Prim Sch
Leyton Link Est
Roxwell Trad Pk
Lea Bridge Rd
A104
A1006
A112 High Rd
Leyton Green Rd
Beaumont Prim Sch
George Mitchell Sch
Brooks Farm
Leyton Leisure Lagoon
Sybourn Inf Sch
Fball Gd
Lea Park Trad Est
E10
Willow Brook Prim Sch
Riverley Prim Sch
St Joseph's RC Jun Sch
St Joseph's RC Inf Sch
Lammas Sch
Sybourn Inf Sch (Annexe)
Period Wks
Fairways Bsns Pk
Waterworks Ctr
Church Rd
High Road Leyton
Dawlish Prim Sch
35
75
54
36
37
38
89
90
88
87

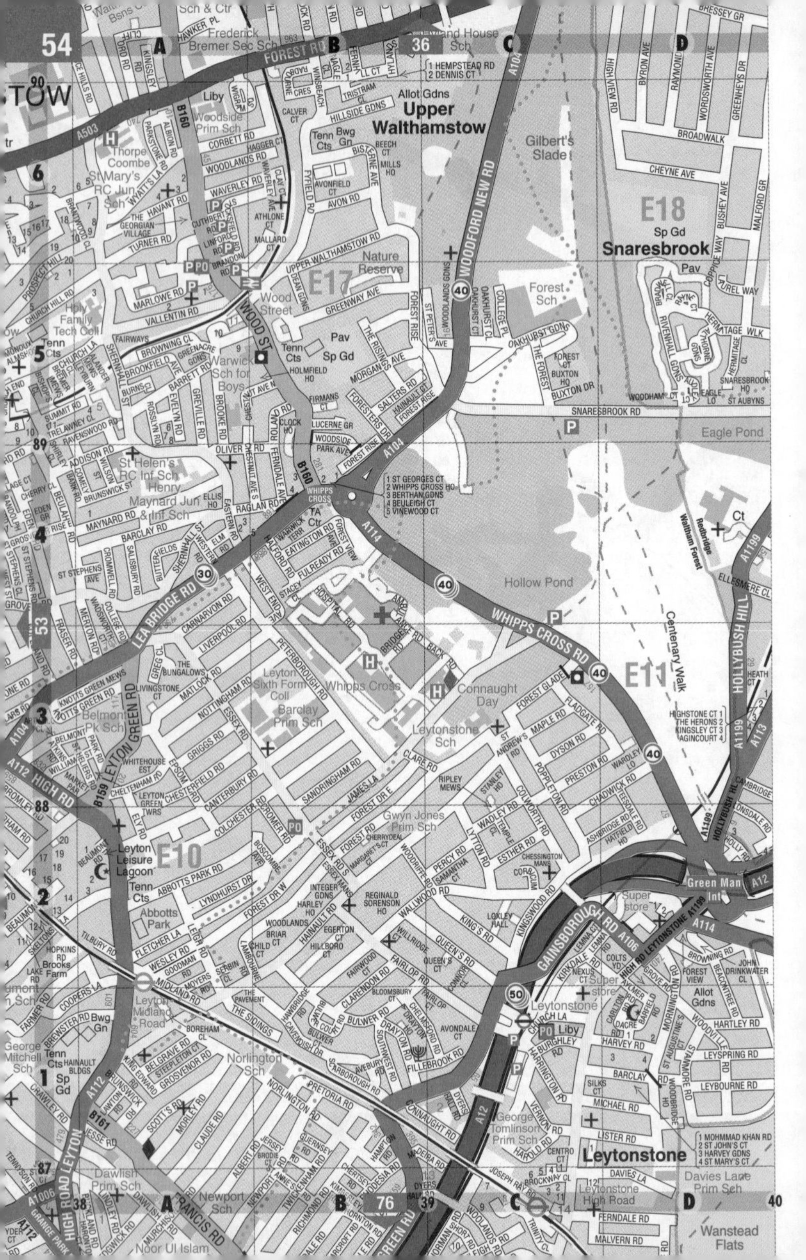
Upper Walthamstow
Snaresbrook
Leytonstone
E17
E18
E11
E10
FOREST RD
WOODFORD NEW RD
WHIPPS CROSS RD
LEA BRIDGE RD
HIGH RD LEYTON
GAINSBOROUGH RD
HOLLYBUSH HILL
SNARESBROOK RD
WOOD ST
LEYTON GREEN RD
HIGH RD LEYTONSTONE
Gilbert's Slade
Eagle Pond
Hollow Pond
Centenary Walk
Whipps Cross
Green Man Int
Nature Reserve
Wanstead Flats
Leyton Midland Road
Leyton Leisure Lagoon
Abbotts Park
Brooks Farm
Allot Gdns
Redbridge
Waltham Forest
36
76
53
A
B
C
D

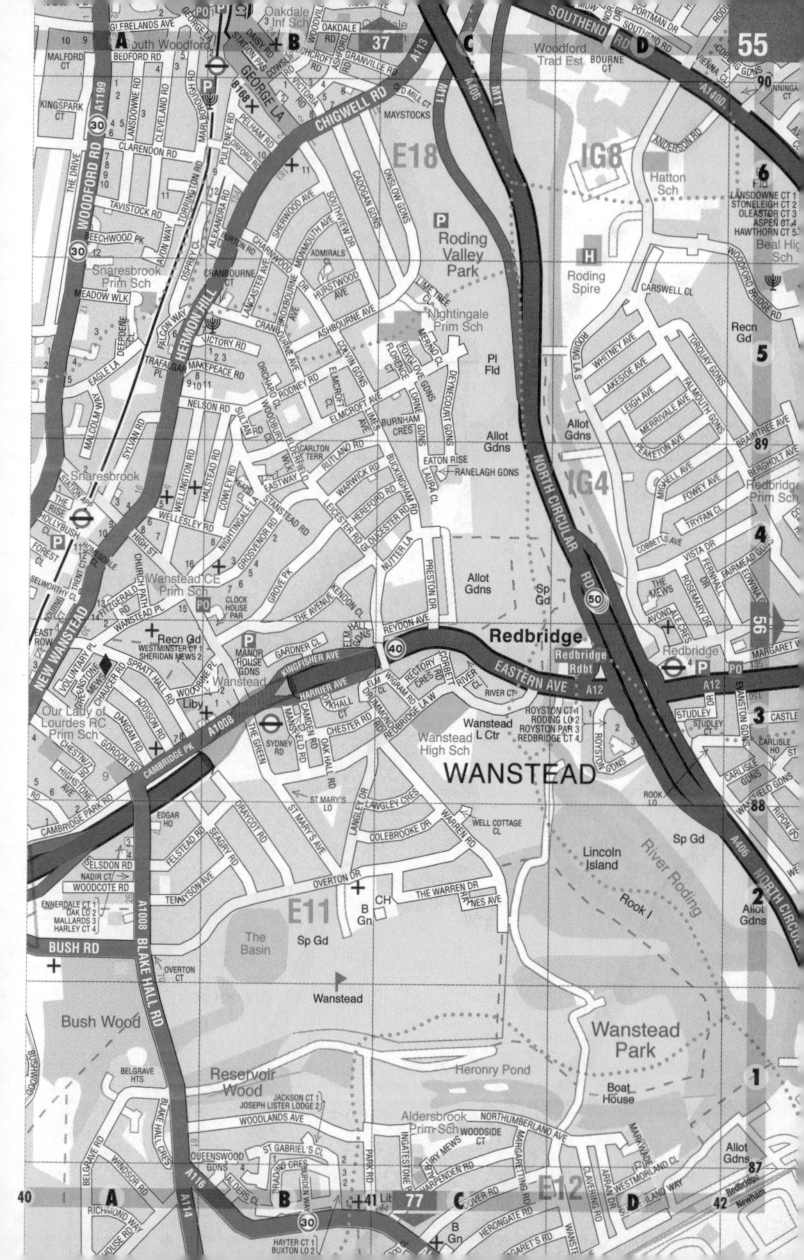
55
South Woodford
Oakdale Inf Sch
37
Woodford Trad Est
SOUTHEND RD
PORTMAN DR
GLEBELANDS AVE
BEDFORD RD
MALFORD CT
KINGSPARK CT
WOODFORD RD
A1199
LANSDOWNE RD
CLEVELAND RD
MARLBOROUGH RD
GEORGE LA
B168
CHIGWELL RD
A113
DAISY RD
COWSLIP RD
OAKDALE RD
GRANVILLE RD
VICTORIA RD
ASHFORD RD
MAYSTOCKS
CLARENDON RD
TAVISTOCK RD
TORRINGTON RD
PULTENEY RD
PELHAM RD
ORFORD RD
BEECHWOOD PK
Snaresbrook Prim Sch
MEADOW WLK
THE DRIVE
AVON WAY
OSPREY CL
ALEXANDRA RD
BURTON RD
CRANBOURNE CT
HERMON HILL
FALCON WAY
VICTORY RD
TRAFALGAR PL
MAKEPEACE RD
EAGLE LA
DEEPDENE CL
MALCOLM WAY
NELSON RD
SYLVAN RD
E18
CADOGAN GDNS
ONSLOW GDNS
SOUTHVIEW DR
SHERWOOD AVE
MONMOUTH AVE
CHARNWOOD DR
ADMIRALS CL
HURSTWOOD AVE
LANCASTER AVE
BROXBOURNE AVE
CRANBOURNE AVE
ASHBOURNE AVE
COLVIN GDNS
ORCHARD CL
RODNEY RD
ELMCROFT CL
ELMCROFT AVE
LIMES AVE
FOXGLOVE GDNS
FLORENCE CT
MERINO CL
LORNE GDNS
DEYNECOURT GDNS
BURNHAM CRES
LIME TREE CL
Nightingale Prim Sch
Roding Valley Park
Pl Fld
Allot Gdns
EATON RISE
RANELAGH GDNS
LAURA CL
M11
A406
IG8
Hatton Sch
ANDERSON RD
Roding Spire
CARSWELL CL
WOODFORD BRIDGE RD
Beal High Sch
LANSDOWNE CT 1
STONELEIGH CT 2
OLEASTOR CT 3
ASPEN CT 4
HAWTHORN CT 5
Recn Gd
RODING LA S
WHITNEY AVE
TORQUAY GDNS
LAKESIDE AVE
LEIGH AVE
FALMOUTH GDNS
MERRIVALE AVE
PEAKETON AVE
BRAINTREE AVE
BERGHOLT AVE
MICHELL AVE
FOWEY AVE
TRYFAN CL
Redbridge Prim Sch
COBBETTS AVE
VISTA DR
FERNHALL DR
ROSEMARY DR
FAIRMEAD GDNS
EDWINA GDNS
THE MEWS
AVONDALE CRES
IG4
NORTH CIRCULAR RD
Snaresbrook
STATION APP
THE RISE
HOLLYBUSH
FOREST CL
HOMESDALE CL
TRENT CT
SELWORTHY CL
WELLINGTON RD
HALSTEAD RD
COWLEY RD
KEATS CL
NIGHTINGALE LA
WELLESLEY RD
HIGH ST
CHURCH PATH
SULTAN RD
WOODBURY CL
ELDERFIELD WLK
EASTWAY
CARLTON TERR
RUTLAND RD
WARWICK RD
BUCKINGHAM RD
HEREFORD RD
LEICESTER RD
GLOUCESTER RD
STANSTEAD RD
GROSVENOR RD
NUTTER LA
PRESTON DR
Wanstead CE Prim Sch
CLOCK HOUSE PAR
GROVE PK
THE AVENUE
KENDON CL
ELM HALL GDNS
REYDON AVE
Sp Gd
Redbridge
Redbridge Rdbt
EASTERN AVE
A12
RIVER CT
RIVER CL
CORBETT
RECTORY CRES
WIGRAM RD
ROYSTON CT 1
RODING LO 2
ROYSTON PAR 3
REDBRIDGE CT 4
ROYSTON GDNS
Wanstead L Ctr
Wanstead High Sch
WANSTEAD
STUDLEY DR
STUDLEY CT
EVANSTON GDNS
CARLISLE GDNS
CARLISLE HO
WAKEFIELD GDNS
RIPON GDNS
ROOK LO
MARGARET WAY
CASTLE
56
NEW WANSTEAD
FITZGERALD RD
WANSTEAD PL
EAST ROW
VOLUNTARY PL
GREENSTONE MEWS
CHAUCER RD
SPRATT HALL RD
ADDISON RD
DANGAN RD
GORDON RD
Recn Gd
WESTMINSTER CT 1
SHERIDAN MEWS 2
MANOR HOUSE GDNS
GARDNER CL
KINGFISHER AVE
HARRIER AVE
WOODBINE PL
Wanstead
Liby
Our Lady of Lourdes RC Prim Sch
CHESTNUT DR
HIGHSTONE AVE
CAMBRIDGE PARK RD
CAMBRIDGE PK
A1008
THE GREEN
SYDNEY RD
MANSFIELD RD
CAMDEN RD
OAKHALL CT
CHESTER RD
DRUMMOND RD
ELM CL
REDBRIDGE LA W
OAK HALL RD
ST MARY'S LO
ST MARY'S AVE
LANGLEY DR
LANGLEY CRES
COLEBROOKE DR
WARREN RD
WELL COTTAGE CL
DRAYCOT RD
EDGAR HO
FELSTEAD RD
SEAGRY RD
ELSDON RD
NADIR CT
WOODCOTE RD
TENNYSON AVE
ENNERDALE CT 1
OAK LO 2
MALLARDS 3
HARLEY CT 4
OVERTON DR
THE WARREN DR
RAYNES AVE
E11
CH
B Gn
The Basin
Sp Gd
Lincoln Island
River Roding
Rook I
Sp Gd
Allot Gdns
NORTH CIRCULAR
BUSH RD
BLAKE HALL RD
OVERTON CT
Wanstead
Bush Wood
BUSHWOOD
BELGRAVE HTS
Reservoir Wood
Heronry Pond
Wanstead Park
Boat House
JACKSON CT 1
JOSEPH LISTER LODGE 2
WOODLANDS AVE
Aldersbrook Prim Sch
NORTHUMBERLAND AVE
WOODSIDE CT
BELGRAVE RD
WINDSOR RD
BLAKE HALL CRES
QUEENSWOOD GDNS
ST GABRIEL'S CL
BRADING CRES
BURDEN WAY
ALDERS CL
PARK RD
INGATESTONE RD
HARPENDEN RD
MARGARETTING RD
CLAVERING RD
ARRAN DR
MARKWADE CL
WESTMORLAND CL
E12
Allot Gdns
Redbridge
Newham
RICHMOND WAY
A116
A114
77
Lib
DOVER RD
HERONGATE RD
HAYTER CT 1
BUXTON LO 2
B Gn
40
41
42
A
B
C
D
1
2
3
4
5
6
87
88
89
90

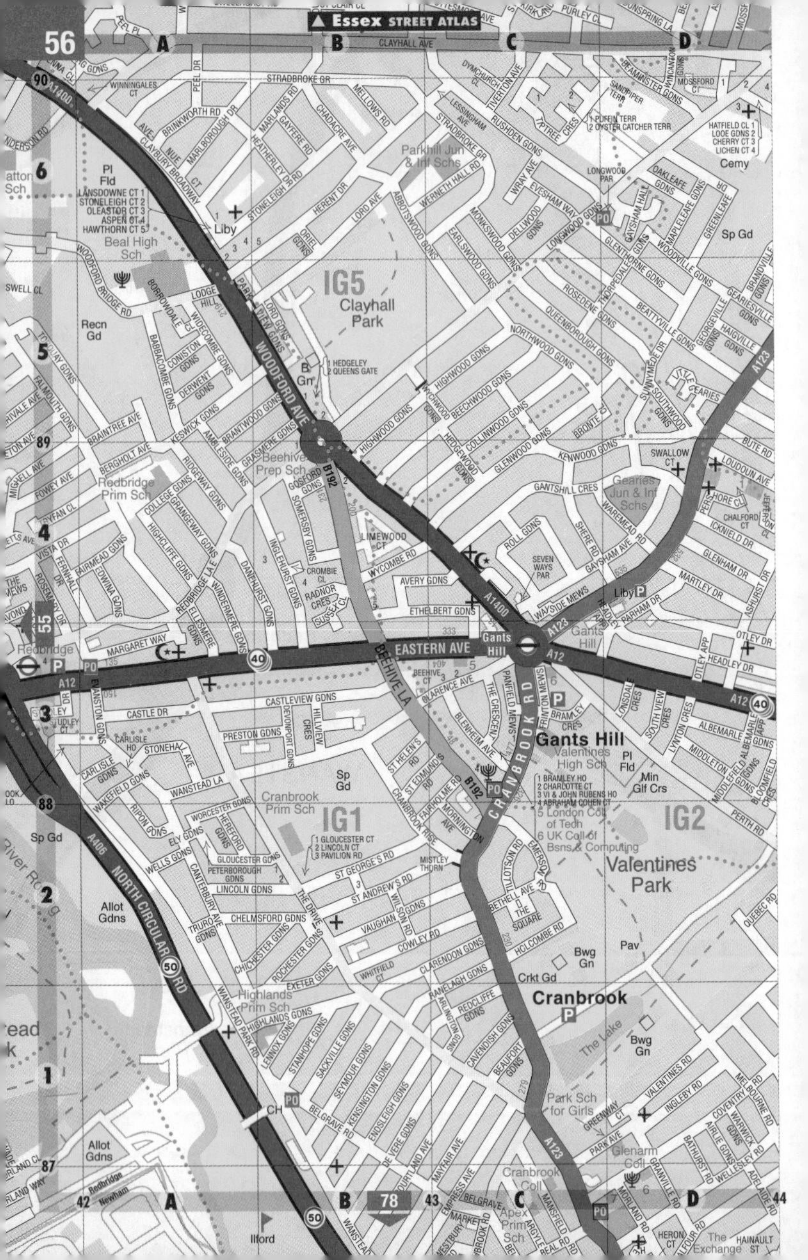
CLAYHALL AVE
PEEL PL
PURLEY CL
WINNINGALES CT
STRADBROKE GR
PEEL DR
BRINKWORTH RD
MARLBOROUGH DR
MARLANDS RD
GAYFERE RD
CHADACRE AVE
MELLOWS RD
HEATHERLEY DR
CLAYBURY BROADWAY
DYMCHURCH CL
TIVERTON AVE
LESSINGHAM AVE
STRADBROKE GR
RUSHDEN GDNS
TIPTREE CRES
SANDPIPER TERR
1 PUFFIN TERR
2 OYSTER CATCHER TERR
BEAMINSTER GDNS
WINCANTON GDNS
MOSSFORD CT
HATFIELD CL 1
LOOE GDNS 2
CHERRY CT 3
LICHEN CT 4
Cemy
Parkhill Jun & Inf Schs
WERNETH HALL RD
Pl Fld
LANSDOWNE CT 1
STONELEIGH CT 2
OLEASTOR CT 3
ASPEN CT 4
HAWTHORN CT 5
Liby
STONELEIGH RD
HERENT DR
LORD AVE
ORIEL GDNS
ABBOTSWOOD GDNS
WRAY AVE
EVESHAM WAY
LONGWOOD PAR
OAKLEAFE GDNS
GAYSHAM HALL
MAPLELEAFE GDNS
GREENLEAFE DR
MONKSWOOD GDNS
EARLSWOOD GDNS
DELLWOOD GDNS
LONGWOOD GDNS
GLENTHORNE GDNS
WOODVILLE GDNS
Sp Gd
Beal High Sch
WOODFORD BRIDGE RD
BORROWDALE CL
LODGE HILL
PARK VIEW GDNS
LORD GDNS
IG5
Clayhall Park
ROSEDENE GDNS
THORPEDALE GDNS
BEATTYVILLE GDNS
QUEENBOROUGH GDNS
NORTHWOOD GDNS
BRANDVILLE GDNS
GEARIESVILLE GDNS
GEORGEVILLE GDNS
HAIGVILLE GDNS
SUNNYMEDE DR
Recn Gd
TORQUAY GDNS
FALMOUTH GDNS
BABBACOMBE GDNS
WIDECOMBE GDNS
CONISTON GDNS
DERWENT GDNS
WOODFORD AVE
B Gn
1 HEDGELEY
2 QUEENS GATE
HIGHWOOD GDNS
WYCHWOOD GDNS
BEECHWOOD GDNS
LITTLE GEARIES
SOUTHWOOD GDNS
BRONTE CL
A123
BRAINTREE AVE
KESWICK GDNS
AMBLESIDE GDNS
BRANTWOOD GDNS
GRASMERE GDNS
HEDGEWOOD GDNS
COLLINWOOD GDNS
GLENWOOD GDNS
KENWOOD GDNS
SWALLOW CT
BUTE RD
LOUDOUN AVE
BERGHOLT AVE
Beehive Prep Sch
GOSFORD GDNS
B192
GANTSHILL CRES
Gearies Jun & Inf Schs
PERSHORE CL
CHALFORD CT
JEFFERSON CL
FOWEY AVE
Redbridge Prim Sch
COLLEGE GDNS
GRANGEWAY GDNS
RIDGEWAY GDNS
HIGHCLIFFE GDNS
SOMERSBY GDNS
LIMEWOOD CT
ROLL GDNS
SHERE RD
WAREMEAD RD
ICKNIELD DR
GLENHAM DR
TRYFAN CL
VISTA DR
FERNHALL DR
FAIRMEAD GDNS
EDWINA GDNS
ROSEMARY DR
INGLEHURST GDNS
DANEHURST GDNS
CROMBIE CL
WYCOMBE RD
SEVEN WAYS PAR
GAYSHAM AVE
MARTLEY DR
RADNOR CRES
SUSSEX CL
AVERY GDNS
ETHELBERT GDNS
A1400
WAYSIDE MEWS
HEADLEY APP
PARHAM DR
ASHURST DR
REDBRIDGE LA E
WINDERMERE GDNS
ELLESMERE GDNS
MARGARET WAY
Redbridge
EASTERN AVE
Gants Hill
A12
Gants Hill
OTLEY DR
OTLEY APP
HEADLEY DR
55
BEEHIVE LA
BEEHIVE CT
CLARENCE AVE
THE CRESCENT
PANFIELD MEWS
PRINTON MEWS
CRANBROOK RD
BRAMLEY CRES
LONSDALE CRES
SOUTH VIEW CRES
LYNTON CRES
ALBEMARLE GDNS
ALBEMARLE APP
CASTLEVIEW GDNS
CASTLE DR
EVANSTON GDNS
STUDLEY CT
DEVONPORT GDNS
HILLVIEW CRES
PRESTON GDNS
CARLISLE HO
STONEHALL AVE
BLENHEIM AVE
Gants Hill
Valentines High Sch
Pl Fld
Min Glf Crs
MIDDLETON GDNS
MIDDLEFIELD GDNS
BLOOMFIELD CRES
CARLISLE GDNS
WAKEFIELD GDNS
WANSTEAD LA
ST HELEN'S RD
ST EDMUND'S RD
Sp Gd
1 BRAMLEY HO
2 CHARLOTTE CT
3 VI & JOHN RUBENS HO
4 ABRAHAM COHEN CT
5 London Coll of Tech
6 UK Coll of Bsns & Computing
IG2
PERTH RD
Cranbrook Prim Sch
IG1
FAIRHOLME RD
CRANBROOK RISE
MORNINGTON AVE
WORCESTER GDNS
HEREFORD GDNS
RIPON GDNS
ELY GDNS
Sp Gd
1 GLOUCESTER CT
2 LINCOLN CT
3 PAVILION RD
WELLS GDNS
GLOUCESTER GDNS
PETERBOROUGH GDNS
ST GEORGE'S RD
MISTLEY THORN
TILLOTSON RD
EMERSON RD
Valentines Park
LINCOLN GDNS
ST ANDREW'S RD
WILSON RD
BETHELL AVE
THE SQUARE
QUEBEC RD
Allot Gdns
NORTH CIRCULAR RD
A406
CANTERBURY AVE
TRURO GDNS
CHELMSFORD GDNS
THE DRIVE
VAUGHAN GDNS
HOLCOMBE RD
COWLEY RD
Bwg Gn
Pav
CHICHESTER GDNS
ROCHESTER GDNS
CLARENDON GDNS
WHITFIELD CT
Crkt Gd
EXETER GDNS
RANELAGH GDNS
ARLINGTON GDNS
REDCLIFFE GDNS
Cranbrook
Highlands Prim Sch
HIGHLANDS GDNS
LENNOX GDNS
STANHOPE GDNS
SACKVILLE GDNS
SEYMOUR GDNS
KENSINGTON GDNS
CAVENDISH GDNS
BEAUFORT GDNS
The Lake
Bwg Gn
WANSTEAD PARK RD
ENDSLEIGH GDNS
Park Sch for Girls
VALENTINES RD
INGLEBY RD
MELBOURNE RD
COVENTRY RD
WARWICK GDNS
CH
BELGRAVE RD
DE VERE GDNS
GREENWAY CT
PARK AVE
AIRLIE GDNS
BATHURST RD
Allot Gdns
COURTLAND AVE
MAYFAIR AVE
Glenarm Coll
GRANVILLE RD
WELLESLEY RD
ADELAIDE RD
Redbridge
Newham
EMPRESS AVE
Cranbrook Coll
MANSFIELD RD
78
BELGRAVE
Apex Prim Sch
MARKET
ARGYLE RD
MORLAND RD
Ilford
WANSTEAD
HERON CT
The Exchange
HAINAULT ST

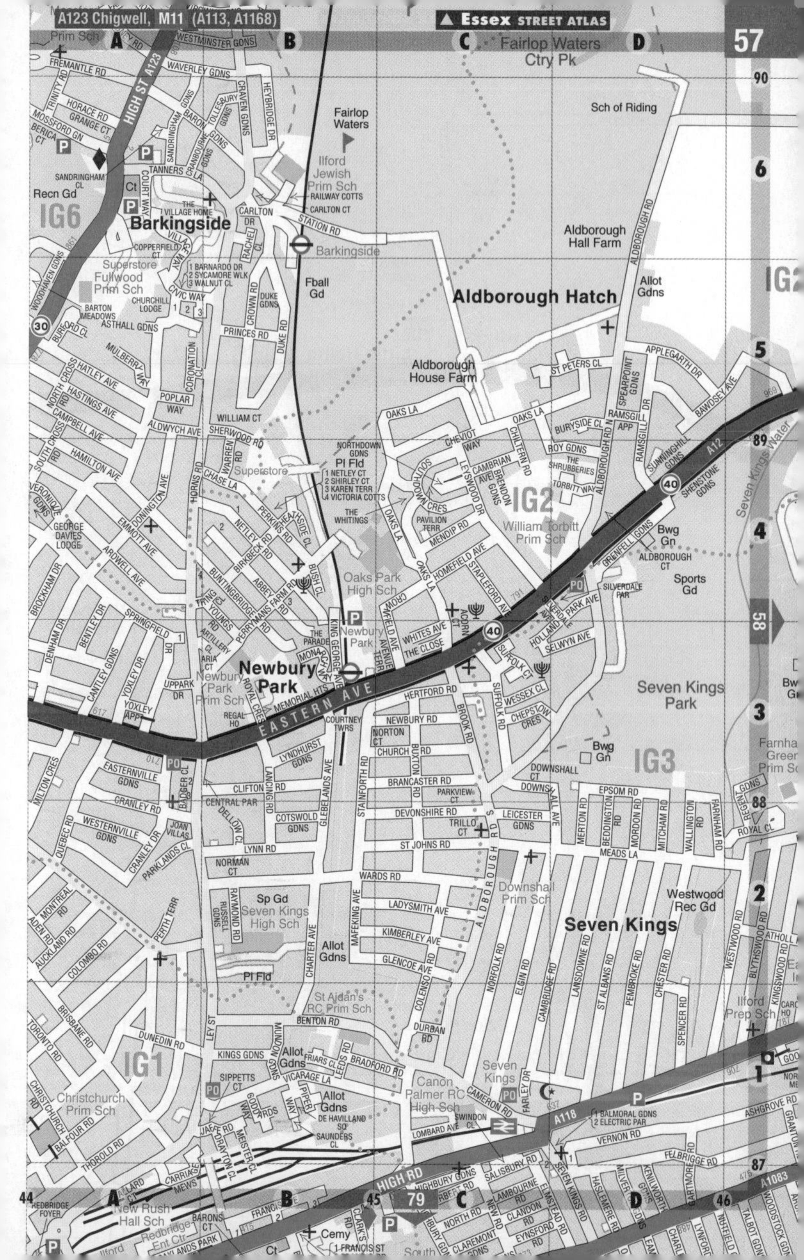
A123 Chigwell, M11 (A113, A1168)
Essex STREET ATLAS
57
Fairlop Waters Ctry Pk
Fairlop Waters
Ilford Jewish Prim Sch
Sch of Riding
Barkingside
IG6
Recn Gd
Superstore
Fullwood Prim Sch
Fball Gd
Aldborough Hall Farm
Aldborough Hatch
Allot Gdns
Aldborough House Farm
IG2
William Torbitt Prim Sch
Superstore
Pl Fld
Oaks Park High Sch
Newbury Park
Newbury Park Prim Sch
EASTERN AVE
Bwg Gn
Sports Gd
Seven Kings Park
Seven Kings Water
IG3
Sp Gd
Seven Kings High Sch
Allot Gdns
Pl Fld
Downshall Prim Sch
Westwood Rec Gd
Seven Kings
St Aidan's RC Prim Sch
IG1
Christchurch Prim Sch
Canon Palmer RC High Sch
Ilford Prep Sch
New Rush Hall Sch
Redbridge Ent Ctr
Cemy
HIGH RD
A12
A118
A1083
79
58

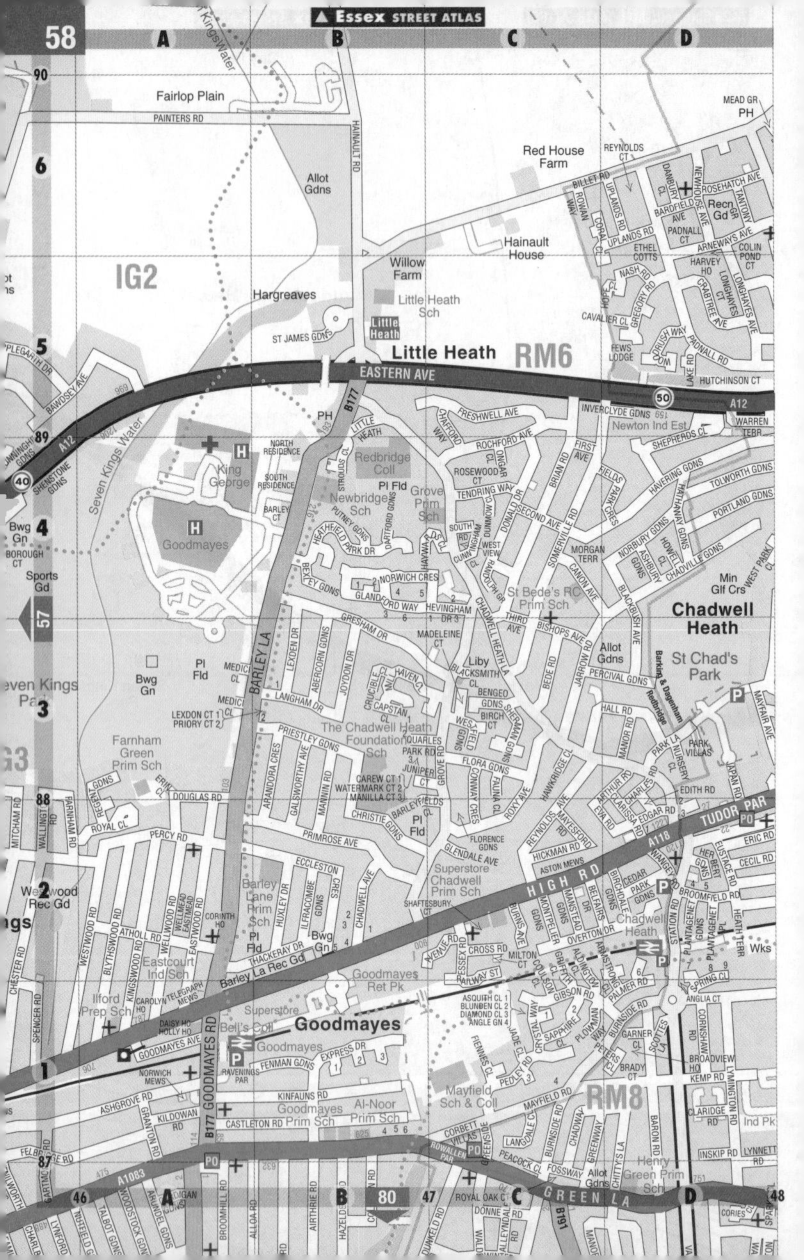

A   B   C   D

90

Fairlop Plain

PAINTERS RD

Allot
Gdns

Red House
Farm

REYNOLDS CT

MEAD GR
PH

6

IG2

Hargreaves

Willow
Farm

Hainault
House

Little Heath
Sch

BILLET RD

UPLANDS RD

ETHEL
COTTS

ROSEHATCH AVE

PADNALL CT

ARNEWAYS AVE

HARVEY
HO

COLIN
POND CT

LONGBARNS
AVE

ST JAMES GDNS

Little
Heath

NASH RD

CAVALIER CL

DEWS
LODGE

5

PLEGANTON RD

BOWDSEL AVE

SEVEN KINGS WATER

ST JAMES GDNS

Little Heath **RM6**

EASTERN AVE   B177

50   A12

HUTCHINSON CT

WARREN
TEBR

89

A12

SHERSTONE GDNS

King
George

H

NORTH
RESIDENCE

SOUTH
RESIDENCE

PH

LITTLE
HEATH

Redbridge
Coll

B177

Newbridge
Sch

Pl Fld

Grove
Prim Sch

FRESHWELL AVE

ROCHFORD AVE

ROSEWOOD CL

TENDRING WAY

FIRST
AVE

INVERCLYDE GDNS

Newton Ind Est

SHEPHERDS CT

HAVERING GDNS

TOLWORTH GDNS

PORTLAND GDNS

4

Bwg
Gn

BOROUGH
CT

Sports
Gd

H

Goodmayes

BARLEY
CT

ICHFIELD PARK DR

SOUTH
VIEW

WEST
VIEW

SECOND AVE

THIRD
AVE

SOMERVILLE GDNS

NORBURY GDNS

ASHBURY

CHADVILLE GDNS

Min
Glf Crs

**Chadwell
Heath**

40

57

Seven Kings
Par

Bwg
Gn

Pl
Fld

MEDICI
CL

MEDICI
CL

LEXDON CT 1
PRIORY CT 2

NORWICH CRES

GLAND CL

HEVINGHAM

MADELEINE
CT

Liby

HAVEN
CL

BENGEO

BIRCH

St Bede's RC
Prim Sch

BLACKSMITH

BISHOPS AVE

Allot
Gdns

PERCIVAL GDNS

St Chad's
Park

HALL RD

PARK VILLAS

PARK
LA

3

G3

Farnham
Green
Prim Sch

BARLEY LA

LEXDON DR

ABERCORN GDNS

LANGHAM DR

The Chadwell Heath
Foundation
Sch

QUARLES

PARK RD

JUNIPER

FLORA GDNS

CONYWAY

WANGROVE CL

EDITH RD

TUDOR PAR

A118   PO

ERIC RD

88

MITCHAM RD

WALLINGER

ROYAL CL

PERCY RD

CAREW CT 1
WATERMARK CT 2
MANILLA CT 3

DOUGLAS RD

PRIMROSE AVE

CHRISTIE

ECCLESTON
GDNS

BARLEYFIELDS

Pl
Fld

FLORENCE
GDNS

GLENDALE AVE

ASTON MEWS

SHAFTESBURY

REYNOLDS

MATTON RD

BETTONS

HIGH RD

CECIL RD

HERBERT RD

BROOMFIELD RD

2

Westwood
Rec Gd

Kings

CHESTER RD

SPENCER RD

WESTWOOD RD

BLYTHSWOOD RD

ATHOLL RD

KINGSWOOD RD

LAMBOURNE RD

EASTWOOD RD

CORINTH
RD

Barley
Lane
Prim Sch

HURLEY RD

ILFRACOMBE
GDNS

CHADWELL AVE

Bwg
Gn

Eastcourt
Ind Sch

Ilford
Prep Sch

DAISY HO
HOLLY HO

Superstore
Bell's Coll

Goodmayes
EXPRESS DR

RAILWAY ST

CROSS RD

MILTON

BRADY
CT

ANGLIA CT

CORNWALLIS RD

BROADVIEW

Wks

Chadwell
Heath

P

STATION RD

HIGHTERR

1

FELBRIG

NORWICH
MEWS

ASHGROVE RD

KILDOWAN
RD

GOODMAYES RD

THACKERAY DR

Barley La Rec Gd

Goodmayes
Ret Pk

Goodmayes

Goodmayes
FENMAN GDNS

KINFAUNS
RD

CASTLETON RD

Al-Noor
Goodmayes
Prim Sch

ASQUITH CL 1
BLUNDEN CL 2
DIAMOND CL 3
ANGLE GN 4

SAPPHIRE

PLOVER

GIBSON

PEDG

FERMES DR

Mayfield
Sch & Coll

MAYFIELD RD

CORBETT

PEACOCK CL

FOSSWAY

LANG

CHINNAM

BRENNAN

BARKIN RD

Henry
Green
Prim Sch

Allot
Gdns

CLARIDGE

RM8

KEMP RD

INSKIP RD

LYNNETT

Ind Pk

87

B177

A1083   GOODMAYES RD

46   A   80   47   GREEN LA   C   B191   48

ROYAL OAK   DONNE

CORIES

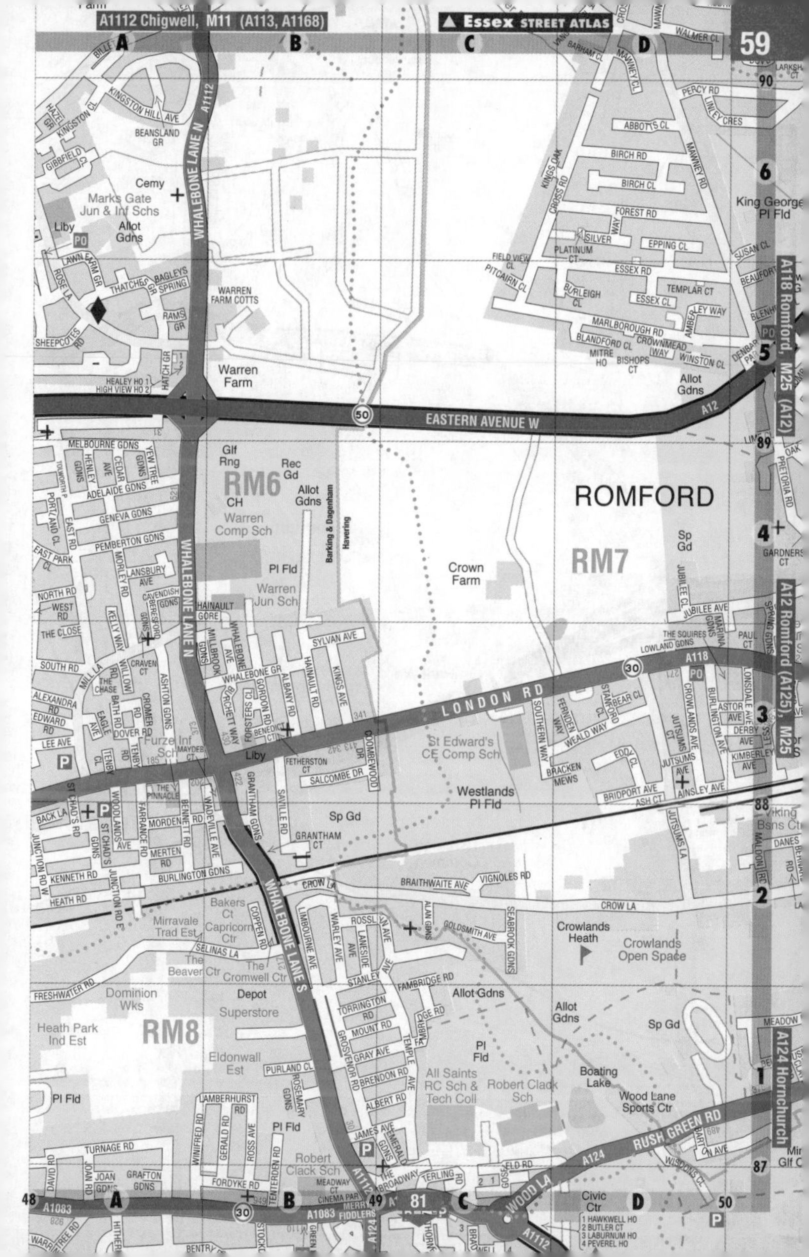
A1112 Chigwell, M11 (A113, A1168)
A
B
C
D
WALMER CL
BARHAM CL
MAWNEY CL
LARKSHALL CT
90
PERCY RD
LINLEY CRES
ABBOTTS CL
BIRCH RD
MAWNEY RD
BIRCH CL
KINGS OAK
CROSS RD
FOREST RD
WAY
SILVER
PLATINUM CT
EPPING CL
FIELD VIEW CL
PITCAIRN CL
ESSEX RD
BURLEIGH CL
TEMPLAR CT
ESSEX CL
LEY WAY
AMBER
MARLBOROUGH RD
BLANDFORD CL
CROWNMEAD WAY
MITRE HO
BISHOPS CT
WINSTON CL
SUSAN CL
BEAUFORT
BLENHEIM
DENBAR PAR
PO
6
King George Pl Fld
5
Allot Gdns
A118 Romford, M25 (A12)
BILLET
KINGSTON HILL AVE
KINGSTON CL
HAZEL GR
BEANSLAND GR
GIBBFIELD CL
A1112
WHALEBONE LANE N
Cemy
Marks Gate Jun & Inf Schs
Liby
PO
Allot Gdns
LAWN FARM GR
ROSE LA
THATCHES GR
BAGLEYS SPRING
WARREN FARM COTTS
RAMS GR
SHEEPCOTES RD
HATCH GR
HEALEY HO 1
HIGH VIEW HO 2
Warren Farm
50
EASTERN AVENUE W
A12
89
OAK
PRETORIA RD
MELBOURNE GDNS
HENLEY GDNS
AVE
CEDAR GDNS
YEW TREE GDNS
TOLWORTH P
Glf Rng
Rec Gd
RM6
CH
Allot Gdns
ADELAIDE GDNS
PORTLAND CL
EAST RD
GENEVA GDNS
Warren Comp Sch
Barking & Dagenham
Havering
ROMFORD
4
GARDNERS CT
PEMBERTON GDNS
EAST PARK CL
MORLEY RD
LANSBURY AVE
Pl Fld
Crown Farm
RM7
Sp Gd
JUBILEE CL
NORTH RD
WEST RD
CAVENDISH GDNS
BERESFORD GDNS
Warren Jun Sch
HAINAULT GORE
A12 Romford (A125), M25
JUBILEE AVE
SPRING GDNS
THE CLOSE
KELLY WAY
MILLBROOK GDNS
WHALEBONE AVE
SYLVAN AVE
THE SQUIRES
MARINA GDNS
PAUL CT
LOWLAND GDNS
SOUTH RD
MILL LA
WILLOW RD
CRAVEN CT
WHALEBONE GR
HAINAULT RD
KINGS AVE
30
A118
PO
THE CHASE
ALEXANDRA RD
EDWARD RD
BATH RD
CROMER RD
ASHTON GDNS
BIRCHETT WAY
FORSTERS CL
GORDON RD
ALBANY RD
LONDON RD
SOUTHERN WAY
FERNDEN WAY
STANFORD CL
BEAR CL
CROWLANDS AVE
BURLINGTON AVE
LONSDALE AVE
ASTOR AVE
3
DERBY AVE
EAGLE AVE
DOVER RD
BENEDICT CT
COOMBEWOOD DR
WEALD WAY
JUTSUMS CT
KIMBERLEY AVE
LEE AVE
TENBY CL
TENBY RD
Furze Inf Sch
MAYDEB CT
Liby
St Edward's CE Comp Sch
FETHERSTON CT
SALCOMBE DR
BRACKEN MEWS
EDD CL
JUTSUMS AVE
P
ST CHAD'S RD
THE PINNACLE
GRANTHAM GDNS
Westlands Pl Fld
BRIDPORT AVE
ASH CT
AINSLEY AVE
88
Viking Bsns Ctr
BACK LA
P
WOODLANDS AVE
FARRANCE RD
BENNETT RD
WADEVILLE AVE
MORDEN RD
SAVILLE RD
Sp Gd
GRANTHAM CT
JUTSUMS LA
MALDON RD
DANES
JUNCTION RD
ST CHAD'S GDNS
MERTEN RD
BURLINGTON GDNS
KENNETH RD
JUNCTION RD W
BRAITHWAITE AVE
VIGNOLES RD
CROW LA
2
HEATH RD
JUNCTION RD E
Bakers Ct
COPPEN RD
WHALEBONE LANE S
LIMBOURNE AVE
WARLEY AVE
ROSSLYN AVE
LANESIDE AVE
ALAN GDNS
GOLDSMITH AVE
SEABROOK GDNS
Crowlands Heath
Crowlands Open Space
Mirravale Trad Est
Capricorn Ctr
SELINAS LA
The Beaver Ctr
The Cromwell Ctr
STANLEY AVE
FAMBRIDGE RD
FRESHWATER RD
Dominion Wks
Depot
Allot Gdns
TORRINGTON RD
MOUNT RD
Allot Gdns
Superstore
FAMBRIDGE RD
Sp Gd
MEADOW
Heath Park Ind Est
RM8
GROSVENOR RD
GRAY AVE
TEMPLE AVE
Pl Fld
A124 Hornchurch
Eldonwall Est
PURLAND CL
BRENDON RD
All Saints RC Sch & Tech Coll
Robert Clack Sch
Boating Lake
1
Pl Fld
LAMBERHURST RD
ROSEMARY GDNS
ALBERT RD
Wood Lane Sports Ctr
WINIFRED RD
GERALD RD
ROSS AVE
Pl Fld
RUSH GREEN RD
JAMES AVE
EMERALD GDNS
P
A124
WISDONS CL
BARTON AVE
TURNAGE RD
TENTERDEN RD
Robert Clack Sch
DAVID RD
JOAN RD
JOAN GDNS
GRAFTON GDNS
THE BROADWAY
TERLING RD
GOSFIELD RD
A1112
MEADWAY CT
87
Mill Glf C
FORDYKE RD
48
A
B
CINEMA PAR
MERRY FIDDLERS
49
81
C
WOOD LA
Civic Ctr
D
50
A1083
30
A1083
A124
A1112
1 HAWKWELL HO
2 BUTLER CT
3 LABURNUM HO
4 PEVEREL HO
P
WARRINGTREE RD
HITHER
STOCK
GREEN
BENTRY
THORN
BRAD
WELL

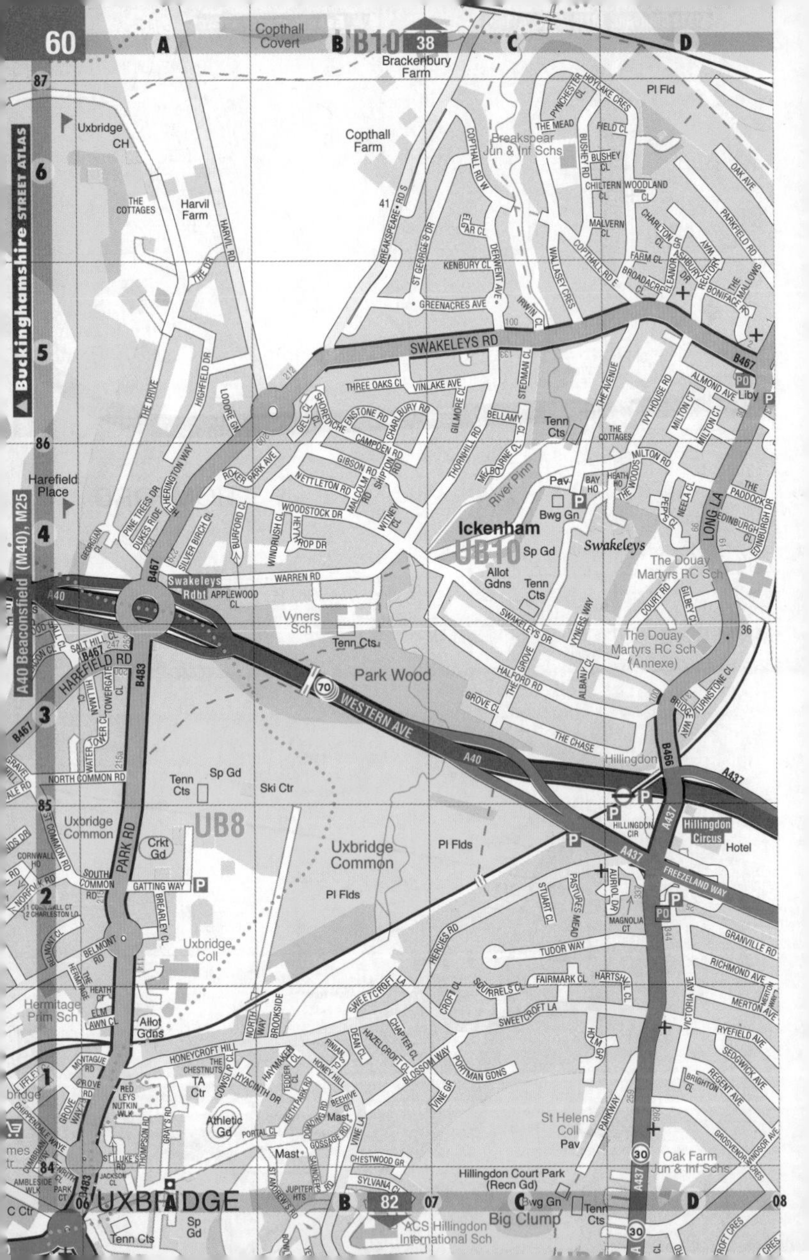
A
B
C
D
UB10
38
Copthall Covert
Brackenbury Farm
Pl Fld
87
Buckinghamshire STREET ATLAS
Uxbridge CH
Copthall Farm
PYNCHESTER CL
HOYLAKE CRES
THE MEAD
FIELD CL
Breakspear Jun & Inf Schs
BUSHEY RD
BUSHEY CL
CHILTERN CL
WOODLAND CL
OAK AVE
PARKFIELD RD
MALVERN CL
CHARLTON CL
THE COTTAGES
Harvil Farm
HARVIL RD
41
BREAKSPEARE RD S
COPTHALL RD W
ELGAR CL
ST GEORGE'S DR
DERWENT AVE
KENBURY CL
WALLASEY CRES
COPTHALL RD E
FARM CL
ELEANOR GR
ASHBURY DR
RECTORY WAY
BROADACRE CL
BONIFACE RD
THE MALLOWS
THE DR
GREENACRES AVE
IRWIN CL
SWAKELEYS RD
B467
THREE OAKS CL
VINLAKE AVE
GILMORE CL
STEDMAN CL
THE AVENUE
ALMOND AVE
IVY HOUSE RD
Liby
THE DRIVE
HIGHFIELD DR
LODORE GN
GELL CL
SHOREDITCH CL
ENSTONE RD
CHARLBURY RD
CAMPDEN RD
BELLAMY CL
Tenn Cts
THE COTTAGES
MILTON CT
86
HERINGTON WAY
ROKER PARK AVE
GIBSON RD
SHIPTON RD
THORNHILL RD
MELBOURNE CL
MILTON RD
NETTLETON RD
MALCOLM RD
River Pinn
Pav
BAY HO
HEATH HO
THE WOODS
Harefield Place
PINE TREES DR
DUKES RIDE
SILVER BIRCH CL
BURFORD CL
WOODSTOCK DR
WINDRUSH CL
HEYTHROP DR
WITNEY CL
Bwg Gn
PEPYS CL
NEELA CL
THE PADDOCK
EDINBURGH DR
EDINBURGH CL
LONG LA
Ickenham
UB10
Sp Gd
Swakeleys
The Douay Martyrs RC Sch
GEORGIAN CL
A40 Beaconsfield (M40), M25
WARREN RD
Allot Gdns
Swakeleys Rdbt
APPLEWOOD CL
Vyners Sch
A40
SALT HILL CL
SWAKELEYS DR
VYNERS WAY
COURT RD
GILBEY CL
Tenn Cts
The Douay Martyrs RC Sch (Annexe)
36
HAREFIELD RD
HILLMAN CL
TOWERGATE CL
B483
Park Wood
THE GROVE
HALFORD RD
ALBANY CL
TURNSTONE CL
70
WESTERN AVE
GROVE CL
BRIDGE WAY
3
WATER TOWER CL
THE CHASE
Hillingdon
B466
A437
NORTH COMMON RD
Tenn Cts
Sp Gd
Ski Ctr
85
ST COMMON RD
Uxbridge Common
UB8
HILLINGDON CIR
Hillingdon Circus
Hotel
CORNWALL HO
NORFOLK RD
Crkt Gd
Uxbridge Common
Pl Flds
Pl Flds
FREEZELAND WAY
SOUTH COMMON RD
GATTING WAY
PARK RD
BREARLEY CL
STUART CL
PASTURES MEAD
AURIOL DR
1 CORNWALL CT
2 CHARLESTON LD
MAGNOLIA CT
BELMONT CL
BELMONT RD
HERCIES RD
TUDOR WAY
GRANVILLE RD
Uxbridge Coll
RICHMOND AVE
THE HERMITAGE
HEATH CL
CROFT CL
SQUIRRELS CL
FAIRMARK CL
HARTSHILL CL
MERTON AVE
Hermitage Prim Sch
ELM LAWN CL
Allot Gdns
SWEETCROFT LA
SWEETCROFT LA
VICTORIA AVE
NORTH WAY
BROOKSIDE
DEAN CL
HAZELCROFT CL
CHAPTER CL
HOLM GR
RYEFIELD AVE
SEDGWICK AVE
HONEYCROFT HILL
MONTAGUE RD
THE CHESTNUTS
COWSLIP CL
HAYMAKER CL
HONEY HILL
FINIAN CL
BLOSSOM WAY
PORTMAN GDNS
BRIGHTON CL
REGENT AVE
1
IFFLEY
GROVE RD
GROVE WAY
RED LEYS
NUTKIN WLK
TA Ctr
HYACINTH DR
TEDDER CL
KEITH PARK RD
BEECHIVE CL
VINE GR
PARKWAY
CHIPPENDALE WAYE
THOMPSON RD
GRAY'S RD
Athletic Gd
DOWDING RD
Mast
VINE LA
St Helens Coll
Pav
GROSVENOR CRES
WINDSOR AVE
PORTAL CL
GOSSAGE RD
Mast
SAUNDERS RD
CHESTWOOD GR
Oak Farm Jun & Inf Schs
30
ST LUKE'S RD
JACKSON CL
84
AMBLESIDE WLK
PARK CT
ST ANDREW'S RD
JUPITER HTS
SYLVANA CL
Hillingdon Court Park (Recn Gd)
06
UXBRIDGE
B
82
07
C
Bwg Gn
Tenn Cts
D
08
C Ctr
Tenn Cts
Sp Gd
ACS Hillingdon International Sch
Big Clump
30

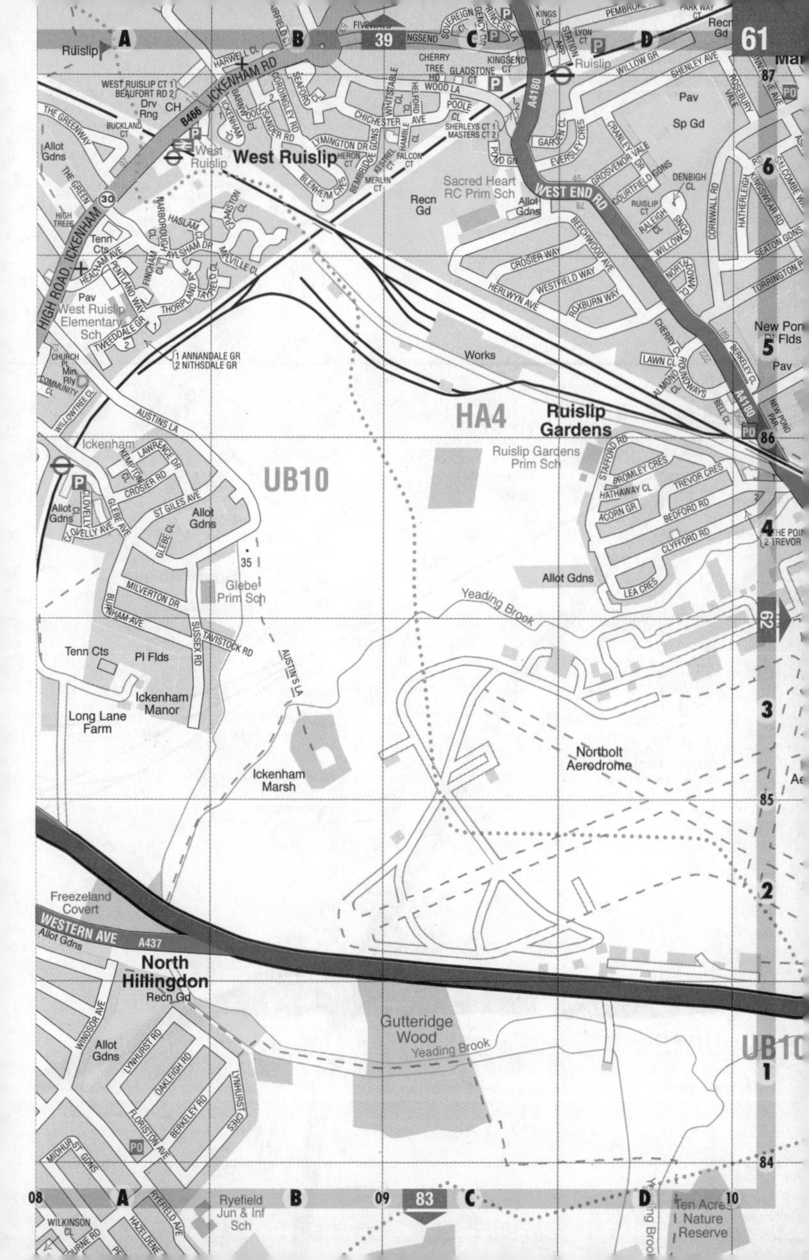
West Ruislip
Ruislip Gardens
Northolt Aerodrome
North Hillingdon
Ickenham Manor
Ickenham Marsh
Long Lane Farm
Gutteridge Wood
Freezeland Covert
HA4
UB10
WESTERN AVE
ICKENHAM RD
WEST END RD
HIGH ROAD, ICKENHAM
Yeading Brook
Works
Sacred Heart RC Prim Sch
Ruislip Gardens Prim Sch
Glebe Prim Sch
West Ruislip Elementary Sch
Ryefield Jun & Inf Sch
Ten Acres Nature Reserve
39
83
62

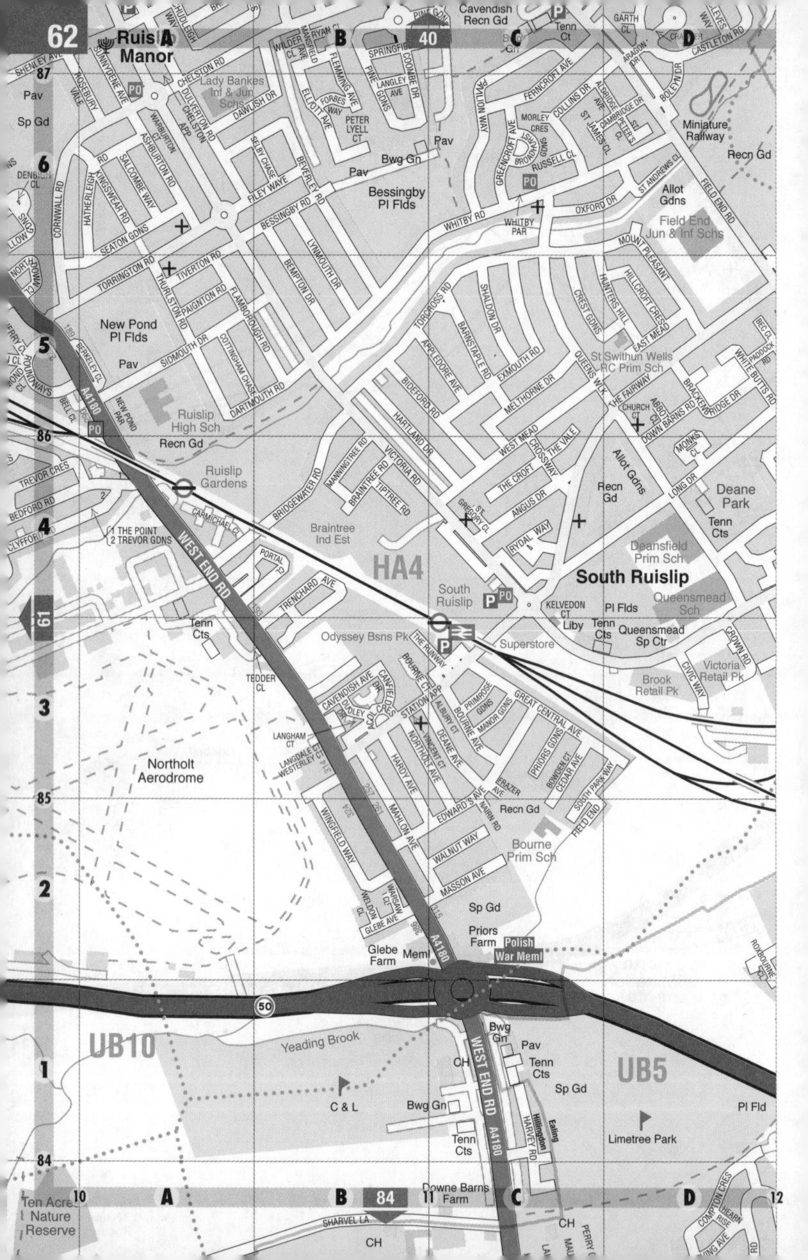

Ruislip Manor
Lady Bankes Inf & Jun Schs
Bessingby Pl Flds
Cavendish Recn Gd
Miniature Railway
Recn Gd
Allot Gdns
Field End Jun & Inf Schs
New Pond Pl Flds
Ruislip High Sch
Recn Gd
Ruislip Gardens
St Swithun Wells RC Prim Sch
Braintree Ind Est
HA4
South Ruislip
Deane Park
Deansfield Prim Sch
Queensmead Sch
Queensmead Sp Ctr
Odyssey Bsns Pk
Superstore
Victoria Retail Pk
Brook Retail Pk
Northolt Aerodrome
Bourne Prim Sch
Priors Farm
Polish War Meml
Glebe Farm
UB10
Yeading Brook
UB5
C & L
Limetree Park
Downe Barns Farm
Ten Acres Nature Reserve
WEST END RD
A4180
A40
SHARVEL LA

40
61
84

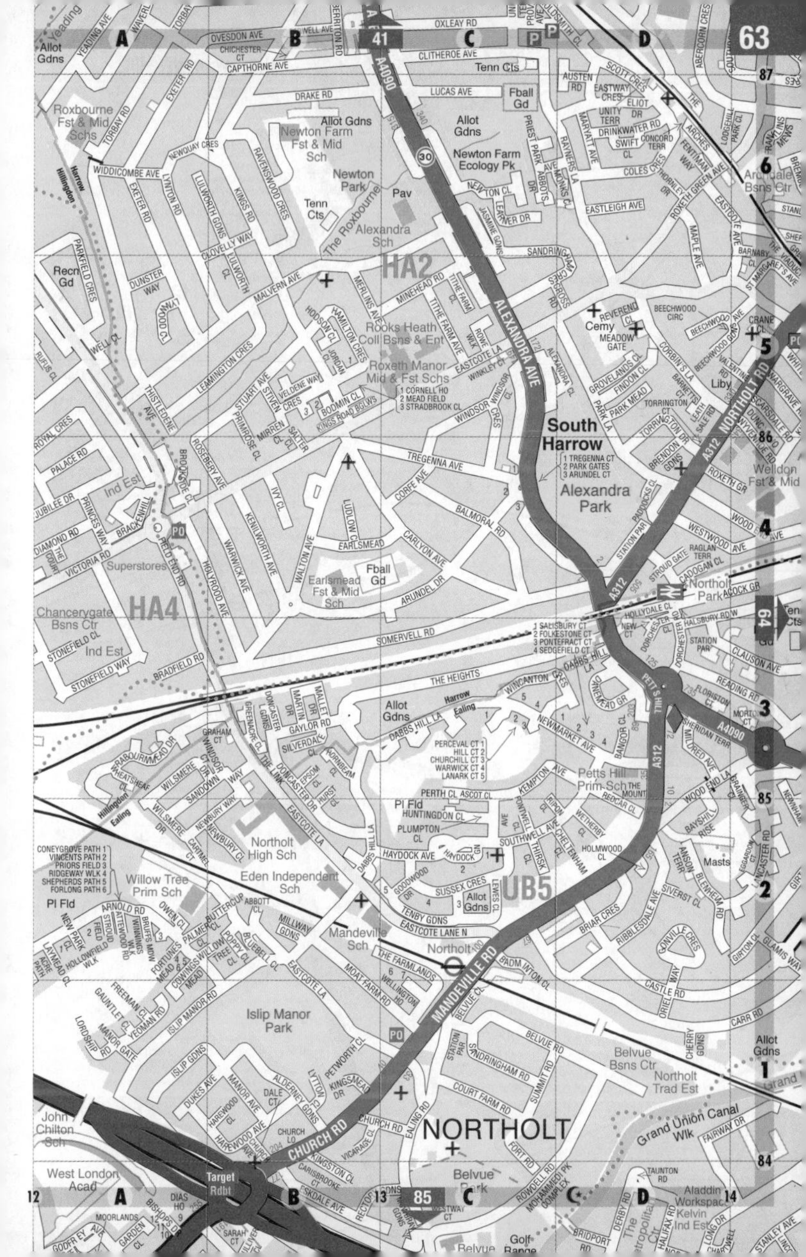

A
B
C
D
41
85
64
87
86
85
84
12
13
14
South Harrow
Alexandra Park
NORTHOLT
HA2
HA4
UB5
ALEXANDRA AVE
A4090
A312
NORTHOLT RD
MANDEVILLE RD
CHURCH RD
PETTS HILL
Target Rdbt
Roxbourne Fst & Mid Schs
Newton Farm Fst & Mid Sch
Newton Park
Newton Farm Ecology Pk
Alexandra Sch
Rooks Heath Coll Bsns & Ent
Roxeth Manor Mid & Fst Schs
Earlsmead Fst & Mid Sch
Chancerygate Bsns Ctr
Superstores
Ind Est
Northolt High Sch
Eden Independent Sch
Willow Tree Prim Sch
Mandeville Sch
Islip Manor Park
Petts Hill Prim Sch
Welldon Fst & Mid
Belvue Bsns Ctr
Northolt Trad Est
Grand Union Canal Wlk
Aladdin Workspace
Kelvin Ind Est
West London Acad
John Chilton Sch
Belvue Park
Northolt Park
Northolt
Archdale Bsns Ctr
Allot Gdns
Tenn Cts
Fball Gd
Recn Gd
Cemy
Liby
Pl Fld
Masts
OXLEAY RD
OVESDON AVE
CAPTHORNE AVE
CLITHEROE AVE
DRAKE RD
LUCAS AVE
WIDDICOMBE AVE
MALVERN AVE
LEMINGTON CRES
TREGENNA AVE
BALMORAL RD
CARLYON AVE
ARUNDEL DR
SOMERVELL RD
THE HEIGHTS
BRADFIELD RD
VICTORIA RD
EASTCOTE LA
EASTCOTE LANE N
ISLIP MANOR RD
COURT FARM RD
SANDRINGHAM RD
BELVUE RD
CASTLE RD
CARR RD
WESTWOOD AVE
READING RD
CLAUSON AVE
STATION PAR
1 TREGENNA CT
2 PARK GATES
3 ARUNDEL CT
1 SALISBURY CT
2 FOLKESTONE CT
3 PONTEFRACT CT
4 SEDGEFIELD CT
PERCEVAL CT 1
HILL CT 2
CHURCHILL CT 3
WARWICK CT 4
LANARK CT 5
1 CORNELL HO
2 MEAD FIELD
3 STRADBROOK CL
CONEYGROVE PATH 1
VINCENTS PATH 2
PRIORS FIELD 3
RIDGEWAY WLK 4
SHEPHERDS PATH 5
FORLONG PATH 6
Harrow
Hillingdon
Ealing

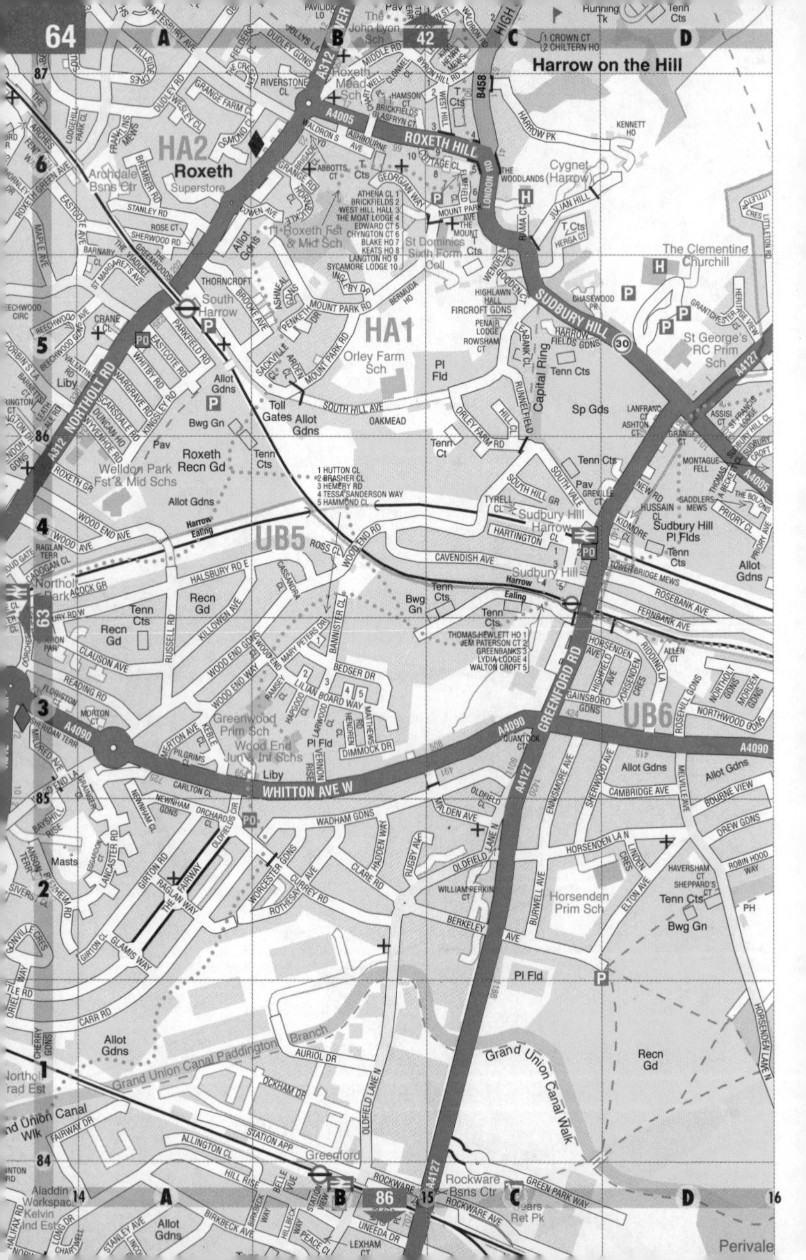
64
A
B
C
D
42
86
Harrow on the Hill
1 CROWN CT
2 CHILTERN HO
HA2
Roxeth
Superstore
Archdale Bsns Ctr
HA1
UB5
UB6
The John Lyon Sch
Roxeth Mead Sch
RIVERSTONE CL
GRANGE FARM CL
DUDLEY RD
DUDLEY GDNS
HILLSIDE CRES
WESLEY CL
OSMOND CL
BREMBER RD
STANLEY RD
ROSE CT
SHERWOOD RD
BARNABY CL
THE VIADUCT
ST MARGARET'S AVE
THE GREENWOODS
ROXETH GREEN AVE
EASTCOTE AVE
MAPLE AVE
A312
A4005
ROXETH HILL
ASHBOURNE
WALDRON S
HAMSON CT
BRICKFIELDS
GLASFRYN CT
BYRON HILL RD
WEST HILL
COTTAGE CL
GEORGIAN WAY
ELMFIELD
MOUNT PARK
THE MOUNT
B458
LONDON RD
HARROW PK
KENNETT HO
Cygnet (Harrow)
THE WOODLANDS
JULIAN HILL
HERGA CT
RAMA CT
ATHENA CL 1
BRICKFIELDS 2
WEST HILL HALL 3
THE MOAT LODGE 4
EDWARD CT 5
CHYNGTON CT 6
BLAKE HO 7
KEATS HO 8
LANGTON HO 9
SYCAMORE LODGE 10
11 Roxeth Fst & Mid Sch
St Dominics Sixth Form Coll
The Clementine Churchill
Allot Gdns
THORNCROFT
BROOKE AVE
ASHNEAL GDNS
PENKETH DR
MOUNT PARK RD
BERMUDA HO
HIGHLAWN HALL
FIRCROFT GDNS
PENAIR LODGE
ROWSHAM CT
WENDELL
GOODEN CT
SUDBURY HILL
CHASEWOOD PK
HARROW FIELDS GDNS
GRANTCHESTER
HERITAGE VIEW
St George's RC Prim Sch
A4127
South Harrow
PARKFIELD RD
EASTCOTE RD
WHITBY RD
WARGRAVE RD
SCARSDALE RD
DUNCAN HO
WYVENHOE RD
KINGSLEY RD
NORTHOLT RD
Liby
CRANE CL
BEECHWOOD GDNS
VALENTINE
Orley Farm Sch
SACKVILLE
ARDEN CL
Pl Fld
Capital Ring
Tenn Cts
Sp Gds
SOUTH HILL AVE
OAKMEAD
Toll Gates
Bwg Gn
Pav
Roxeth Recn Gd
Welldon Park Fst & Mid Schs
ROXETH GR
ORLEY FARM RD
HILL CL
RUNNELFIELD
LANFRANC CT
ASHTON CT
GRANGE CT
ASSISI CT
ST FRANCIS LODGE
SUDBURY HILL CL
MONTAGUE FELL
THOMAS A BECKET CL
SUDBURY CROFT
A4005
THE BOLTONS
PRIORY CL
SADDLERS MEWS
HUSSAIN CL
NEW RD
KIDMORE CL
Sudbury Hill Pl Flds
1 HUTTON CL
2 BRASHER CL
3 HEMERY RD
4 TESSA SANDERSON WAY
5 HAMMOND CL
SOUTH HILL GR
SOUTH VALE
GREVILLE CT
TYRELL CL
Sudbury Hill Harrow
HARTINGTON CL
Harrow
Ealing
WOOD END AVE
RAGLAN TERR
CADOGAN CL
Northolt Park
ACOCK GR
HALSBURY RD E
CASSANDRA
ROSS CL
WOOD END RD
CAVENDISH AVE
Sudbury Hill
TOWER BRIDGE MEWS
ROSEBANK AVE
FERNBANK AVE
Recn Gd
KILLOWEN AVE
RUSSELL RD
CLAUSON AVE
STATION PAR
READING RD
FLORISTON
MORTON CT
WOOD END GDNS
WOOD END WAY
MARY PETERS DR
BANNISTER CL
BEDSER DR
LILIAN BOARD WAY
RAMSEY CL
HAPGOOD CL
LARWOOD CL
HENDREN CL
MATTHEWS RD
DIMMOCK DR
THOMAS HEWLETT HO 1
JEM PATERSON CT 2
GREENBANKS 3
LYDIA LODGE 4
WALTON CROFT 5
HORSENDEN AVE
HIGHFIELD AVE
HORSENDEN CRES
RIDDING LA
ALLEN CT
GAINSBORO GDNS
ROSEHILL GDNS
NORTHOLT GDNS
MORDEN GDNS
NORTHWOOD GDNS
GREENFORD RD
A4090
QUANTOCK CT
SHERIDAN TERR
MILDRED AVE
MERTON AVE
KEBLE CL
PILGRIMS CL
Greenwood Prim Sch
Wood End Jun & Inf Schs
VERNON RISE
CARLTON CL
WHITTON AVE W
OLDFIELD CL
MALDEN AVE
ENNISMORE AVE
SHERWOOD AVE
CAMBRIDGE AVE
MELVILLE AVE
BOURNE VIEW
DREW GDNS
WOOD END LA
GRAINGER CL
NEWNHAM GDNS
NEWNHAM CL
ORCHARD CL
OLDFIELDS CIR
WADHAM GDNS
HADDEN WAY
RUGBY AVE
OLDFIELD LANE N
HORSENDEN LA N
LINDEN CRES
ELTON AVE
HAVERSHAM CT
SHEPPARD'S CT
ROBIN HOOD WAY
BAYSHILL RISE
EGGARDON CT
LANCASTER RD
Masts
ANSON TERR
PETHERAM RD
GIRTON RD
THE FAIRWAY
RAGLAN WAY
WORCESTER GDNS
CURREY RD
ROTHESAY AVE
CLARE RD
WILLIAM PERKIN CT
BURWELL AVE
Horsenden Prim Sch
PH
CONVILLE CRES
GIRTON CL
GLAMIS WAY
BERKELEY AVE
ORIEL WAY
CARR RD
CHERRY GDNS
Grand Union Canal Paddington Branch
AURIOL DR
Grand Union Canal Walk
OCKHAM DR
OLDFIELD LANE N
Grand Union Canal Wlk
FAIRWAY DR
STATION APP
ALLINGTON CL
Greenford
HILL RISE
BELLE VUE
STATION VIEW
ROCKWARE AVE
Rockware Bsns Ctr
GREEN PARK WAY
Aladdin Workspace
Kelvin Ind Est
HALIFAX RD
LONG DR
STANLEY AVE
BIRKBECK AVE
BIRKBECK WAY
HILLBECK WAY
PEACE CL
UNEEDA DR
LEXHAM CT
Perivale
HORSENDEN LANE N
14
15
16
87
86
85
84
6
5
4
3
2
1

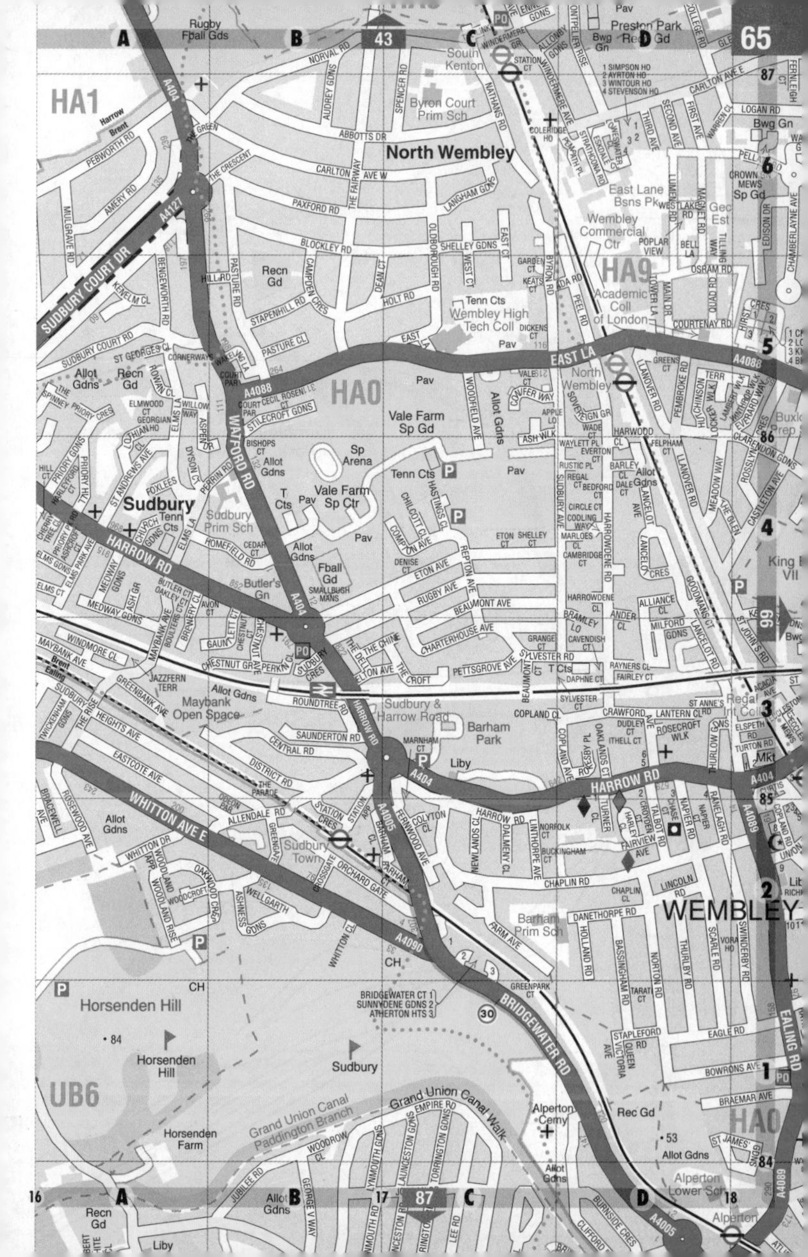

65
43
87
A
B
C
D
Rugby Fball Gds
Preston Park Rec Gd
South Kenton
Bwg Gn
HA1
HA9
HA0
UB6
North Wembley
Byron Court Prim Sch
NORVAL RD
AUDREY GDNS
SPENCER RD
NATHANS RD
ABBOTTS DR
THE GREEN
THE CRESCENT
PEBWORTH RD
AMERY RD
MULGRAVE RD
CARLTON AVE W
CARLTON AVE E
PAXFORD RD
LANGHAM GDNS
BLOCKLEY RD
SHELLEY GDNS
OLDBOROUGH RD
THE FAIRWAY
CAMPDEN CRES
PASTURE RD
DEAN CT
HOLT RD
STAPENHILL RD
PASTURE CL
HILL RD
WEST CT
EAST CT
BYRON RD
PEEL RD
ADA RD
Recn Gd
Tenn Cts
Wembley High Tech Coll
SUDBURY COURT DR
SUDBURY COURT RD
BENGEWORTH RD
KENELM CL
ST GEORGES CL
CORNERWAYS
WATFORD RD
A404
A4127
A4088
A4089
A4090
A4005
EAST LA
North Wembley
East Lane Bsns Pk
Wembley Commercial Ctr
Academic Coll of London
COURTENAY RD
OSRAM RD
LOGAN RD
CROWN MEWS
Sp Gd
EDISON DR
CHAMBERLAYNE AVE
FIRST AVE
SECOND AVE
THIRD AVE
WARREN CL
1 SIMPSON HO
2 AYRTON HO
3 WINTOUR HO
4 STEVENSON HO
WINDERMERE AVE
MONTPELIER RISE
COLERIDGE HO
STRATHCONA RD
ESKDALE CL
LOWESWATER CL
LUMEN RD
MAGNET RD
TILLING WAY
QUAD RD
MAIN DR
TOWER LA
POPLAR VIEW
BELL LA
Gec Est
Allot Gdns
Recn Gd
Pav
Vale Farm Sp Gd
Sp Arena
Vale Farm Sp Ctr
Tenn Cts
T Cts
Fball Gd
WOODFIELD AVE
CONIFER WAY
ASH WLK
SUDBURY AVE
HARROWDENE RD
LANCELOT AVE
LANCELOT CRES
LLANOVER RD
PEMBROKE RD
HUTCHINSON TERR
LOCKER WLK
LAMBERT WLK
WINTHROP WLK
EVERARD WAY
MEADOW WAY
THE GLEN
ROSSLYN CRES
CASTLETON AVE
CLARENDON GDNS
FELPHAM CT
HARWOOD CL
WAYLETT PL
EVERTON CT
RUSTIC PL
REGAL CT
BEDFORD CT
BARLEY CL
DALE CT
CIRCLE CT
CODLING WAY
MARLOES CL
CAMBRIDGE CT
ETON CT
SHELLEY CT
CHILCOTT CL
COMPTON AVE
HASTINGS CL
REPTON AVE
DENISE CT
ETON AVE
RUGBY AVE
BEAUMONT AVE
CHARTERHOUSE AVE
GRANGE CT
CAVENDISH CT
BRAMLEY LO
HARROWDENE CL
ANDER CL
ALLIANCE CL
MILFORD GDNS
GOODMANS CT
LANCELOT RD
ST JOHN'S RD
Sudbury
Sudbury Prim Sch
HARROW RD
HOMEFIELD RD
CEDAR CT
Butler's Gn
SMALLBUGH MANS
STILECROFT GDNS
CECIL ROSEN CT
BISHOPS CT
PERRIN RD
DYSON CT
ASPEN DR
WILLOW WAY
ELMS LA
ROWAN CL
ELMWOOD CT
GEORGIAN CT
LOTHIAN HO
ST ANDREWS AVE
FOXLEES
CHURCH GDNS
PRIORY CRES
PRIORY GDNS
PRIORY HILL
HARLEYFORD
PRIORY PK RD
ASHCROFT CT
ELMS PARK AVE
ELMS GDNS
ELMS CT
MEDWAY GDNS
MEDWAY
ASH GR
BUTLER CT
OAKLEY CT
BOULTERS CT
BREWERY CL
AVON CT
MAYBANK AVE
CHESTNUT AVE
CHESTNUT GR
PERKIN CL
SUDBURY CRES
THE DELL
THE CHINE
ELTON AVE
THE CROFT
PETTSGROVE AVE
SYLVESTER RD
BEAUMONT CT
DAPHNE CT
RAYNERS CL
FAIRLEY CT
WINDMORE CL
JAZZFERN TERR
GREENBANK AVE
Maybank Open Space
ROUNDTREE RD
Sudbury & Harrow Road
Barham Park
Liby
COPLAND CL
SYLVESTER CT
CRAWFORD AVE
LANTERN CL
ROSECROFT WLK
DUDLEY CT
ITHELL CT
THURLOW GDNS
ST ANNE'S RD
Regal Int Coll
ELSPETH RD
TURTON RD
Mkt
SUDBURY
TWICKENHAM GDNS
THE RISE
HEIGHTS AVE
EASTCOTE AVE
SAUNDERTON RD
CENTRAL RD
DISTRICT RD
THE PARADE
MARNHAM CT
WHITTON AVE E
BRACEWELL AVE
ROSEWOOD AVE
ALLENDALE RD
ODEON PAR
GREENGATE
STATION CRES
STATION APP
Sudbury Town
BARHAM CL
FERNWOOD AVE
COLYTON CL
HARROW RD
NEWLANDS CL
DALMENY CL
LINTHORPE AVE
NORFOLK CT
BUCKINGHAM CT
COPLAND AVE
OAKLANDS CT
TURNER CL
CROYDON CT
HARLEY CL
CHASE CT
TALBOT RD
NAPIER RD
NAPIER CT
RANELAGH RD
FAIRVIEW AVE
CHAPLIN RD
CHAPLIN CL
LINCOLN RD
WEMBLEY
WHITTON DR
WOODLAND APP
WOODLAND RISE
WOODCROFT
OAKWOOD CRES
ASHNESS GDNS
WELLGARTH
CROSSGATE
ORCHARD GATE
WHITTON CL
CH
Barham Prim Sch
FARM AVE
DANETHORPE RD
HOLLAND RD
BASSINGHAM RD
NORTON RD
THURLBY RD
SCARLE RD
SWINDERBY RD
VORA HO
TARATI CT
Horsenden Hill
Horsenden Hill
Sudbury
BRIDGEWATER CT 1
SUNNYDENE GDNS 2
ATHERTON HTS 3
GREENPARK CT
BRIDGEWATER RD
STAPLEFORD RD
QUEEN VICTORIA AVE
EAGLE RD
BOWRONS AVE
BRAEMAR AVE
EALING RD
Rec Gd
Alperton Cemy
Allot Gdns
ST JAMES' GDNS
Alperton Lower Sch
Alperton
Horsenden Farm
Grand Union Canal Paddington Branch
Grand Union Canal Walk
WOODROW CL
LYNMOUTH GDNS
LAUNCESTON GDNS
EMPIRE RD
TORRINGTON GDNS
JUBILEE RD
GEORGE V WAY
LEE RD
BURNSIDE CRES
CLIFFORD
Recn Gd
Liby
16
17
18
1
2
3
4
5
6
84
85
86
87

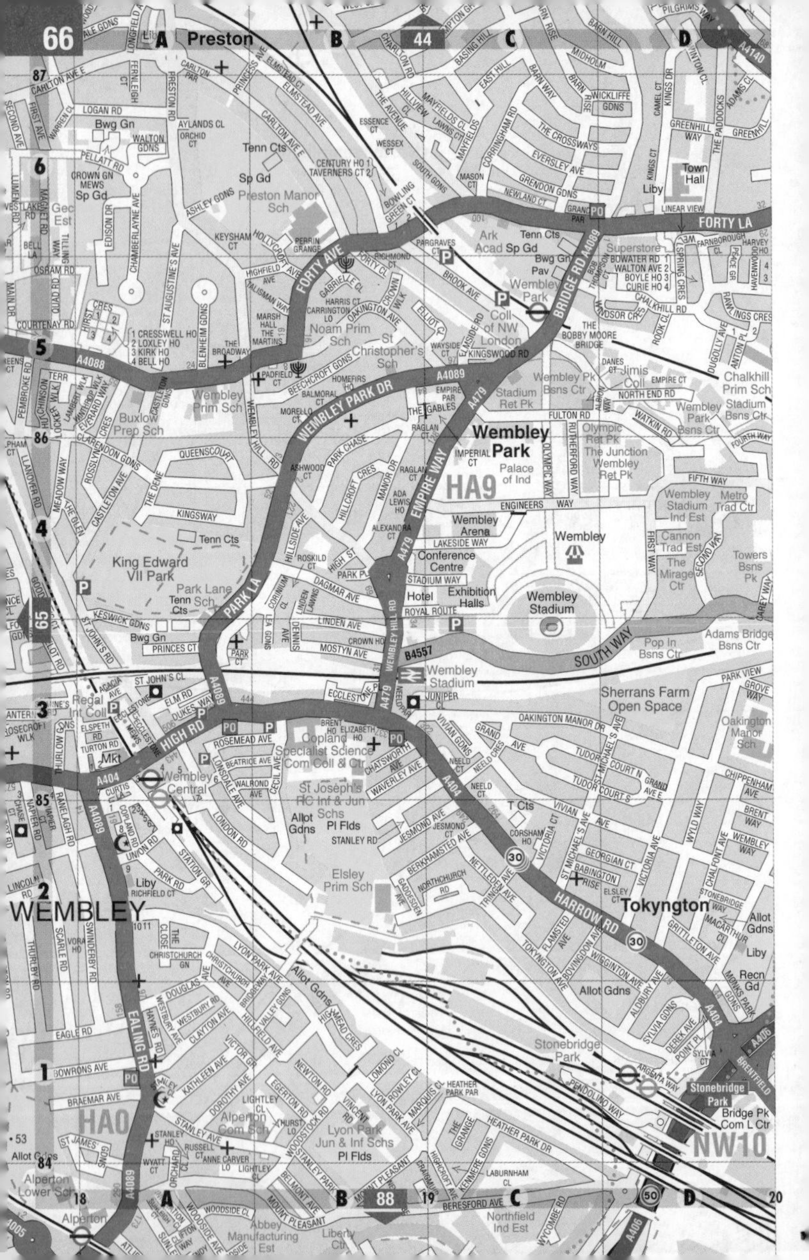

Preston
44
A
B
C
D
Wembley Park
HA9
Wembley
Wembley Stadium
Wembley Arena
Conference Centre
Exhibition Halls
Hotel
King Edward VII Park
Park Lane Sch
Preston Manor Sch
Wembley Prim Sch
Buxlow Prep Sch
Noam Prim Sch
St Christopher's Sch
Coll of NW London
Ark Acad Sp Gd
Copland Specialist Science Com Coll & Ctr
St Joseph's RC Inf & Jun Schs
Elsley Prim Sch
Alperton Com Sch
Lyon Park Jun & Inf Schs
Alperton Lower Sch
Chalkhill Prim Sch
Oakington Manor Sch
Sherrans Farm Open Space
Stonebridge Park
Tokyngton
Wembley Central
Wembley Stadium
Regal Int Coll
Town Hall
Superstore
Stadium Ret Pk
Wembley Pk Bsns Ctr
Olympic Ret Pk
The Junction Wembley Ret Pk
Palace of Ind
Wembley Stadium Ind Est
Metro Trad Ctr
Cannon Trad Est
The Mirage Ctr
Towers Bsns Pk
Adams Bridge Bsns Ctr
Pop In Bsns Ctr
Wembley Park Bsns Ctr
Stadium Bsns Ctr
Jimis Coll
Bridge Pk Com L Ctr
Abbey Manufacturing Est
Northfield Ind Est
Liberty Ctr
WEMBLEY
HA0
NW10
FORTY AVE
FORTY LA
WEMBLEY PARK DR
EMPIRE WAY
BRIDGE RD
PARK LA
HIGH RD
HARROW RD
EALING RD
WEMBLEY HILL RD
SOUTH WAY
ENGINEERS WAY
FIFTH WAY
FOURTH WAY
FIRST WAY
OLYMPIC WAY
FULTON RD
RUTHERFORD WAY
KINGSWAY
QUEENSCOURT
THE DENE
PRESTON RD
CARLTON AVE E
ELMSTEAD AVE
THE AVENUE
HILLVIEW
MAYFIELDS
CORRINGHAM RD
THE CROSSWAYS
EVERSLEY AVE
GRENDON GDNS
NEWLAND CT
BARN HILL
BARN RISE
MIDHOLM
WICKLIFFE GDNS
KINGS DR
GREENHILL WAY
THE PADDOCKS
CHALKHILL RD
RAWLINGS CRES
BOWATER RD
WALTON AVE
BROOK AVE
KINGSWOOD RD
NORTH END RD
WATKIN RD
LOGAN RD
CARLTON AVE E
CHAMBERLAYNE AVE
ST AUGUSTINE'S AVE
BLENHEIM GDNS
ASHLEY GDNS
CLARENDON GDNS
CASTLETON AVE
MEADOW WAY
LLANOVER RD
LINDEN AVE
MOSTYN AVE
DAGMAR AVE
HILLSIDE AVE
PARK CHASE
HILLCROFT CRES
MANOR DR
LAKESIDE WAY
STADIUM WAY
ROYAL ROUTE
ECCLESTONE PL
OAKINGTON MANOR DR
GRAND AVE
TUDOR COURT N
TUDOR COURT S
ST MICHAEL'S AVE
VIVIAN AVE
GEORGIAN CT
VICTORIA AVE
WYLD WAY
CHALFONT AVE
BRENT WAY
WEMBLEY WAY
CHIPPENHAM AVE
NEELD CRES
JESMOND AVE
BERKHAMSTED AVE
NORTHCHURCH RD
NETTLEDEN AVE
TRING AVE
FLAMSTED AVE
BOVINGDON AVE
WIGGINTON AVE
ALDBURY AVE
TOKYNGTON AVE
SYLVIA GDNS
DEREK AVE
GRITTLETON AVE
MONKS PARK
ROSEMEAD AVE
LONSDALE AVE
LONDON RD
CECIL AVE
CHATSWORTH AVE
WAVERLEY AVE
STANLEY RD
STATION GR
PARK RD
UNION RD
COPLAND RD
CURTIS LA
LYON PARK AVE
HIGHMEAD CRES
NEWTON RD
LOMOND CL
LYON ROWLEY CL
MARQUIS CL
HEATHER PARK DR
THE GRANGE
KENMERE GDNS
BERESFORD AVE
WOODSTOCK RD
EGERTON RD
VINCENT RD
DOROTHY AVE
KATHLEEN AVE
CLAYTON AVE
WESTBURY AVE
DOUGLAS AVE
BOWRONS AVE
BRAEMAR AVE
EAGLE RD
STANLEY AVE
MOUNT PLEASANT
BELMONT AVE
WOODSIDE AVE
SWINDERBY RD
SCARLE RD
THURLBY RD
RANELAGH RD
NAPIER RD
THURLOW GDNS
PENDOLINO WAY
ARGENTA WAY
BRENTFIELD
A4088
A4089
A479
A404
A406
B4557
A4140
A4005
Alperton
Stonebridge Park
Allot Gdns
Tenn Cts
Bwg Gn
Sp Gd
Liby
Mkt
Recn Gd
88

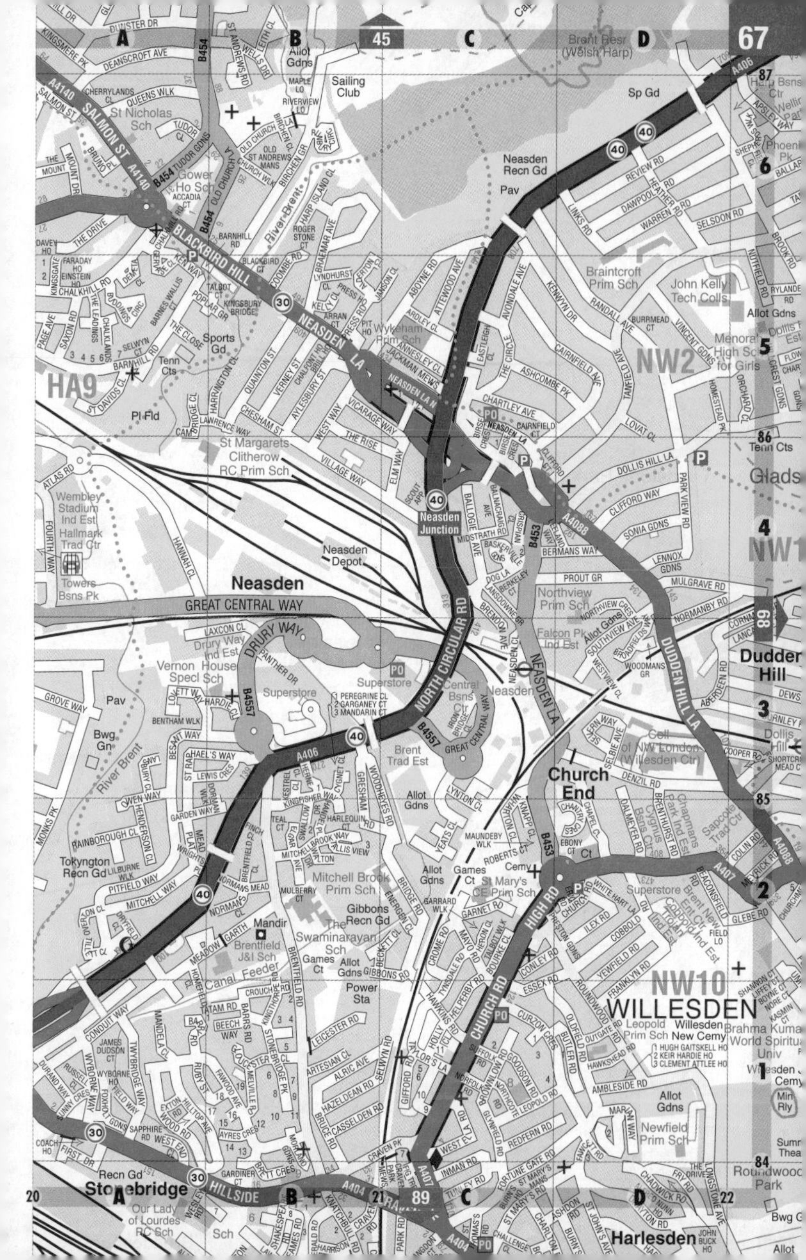

A
B
C
D
45
Brent Resr (Welsh Harp)
Sailing Club
Allot Gdns
Sp Gd
Neasden Recn Gd
Pav
St Nicholas Sch
Gower Ho Sch
SALMON ST
A4140
BLACKBIRD HILL
NEASDEN LA
Sports Gd
Tenn Cts
HA9
Pl Fld
St Margarets Clitherow RC Prim Sch
Wembley Stadium Ind Est
Hallmark Trad Ctr
Towers Bsns Pk
Neasden Depot
Neasden
GREAT CENTRAL WAY
Neasden Junction
NORTH CIRCULAR RD
A406
Braintcroft Prim Sch
John Kelly Tech Colls
Menorah High Sch for Girls
NW2
DOLLIS HILL LA
A4088
DUDDEN HILL LA
Northview Prim Sch
Falcon Pk Ind Est
Drury Way Ind Est
DRURY WAY
Vernon House Specl Sch
Superstore
Central Bsns Ctr
Brent Trad Est
Coll of NW London (Willesden Ctr)
Church End
Dudden Hill
Chapmans Park Ind Est
Sapcote Trad Ctr
Tokyngton Recn Gd
Mitchell Brook Prim Sch
Gibbons Recn Gd
Mandir
The Swaminarayan Sch
Brentfield J&I Sch
Canal Feeder
Power Sta
St Mary's CE Prim Sch
HIGH RD
CHURCH RD
NW10
WILLESDEN
Leopold Prim Sch
Willesden New Cemy
Brahma Kumaris World Spiritual Univ
Newfield Prim Sch
Roundwood Park
Stonebridge
HILLSIDE
Our Lady of Lourdes RC Sch
Harlesden
89
20
21
22
84
85
86
87
1
2
3
4
5
6

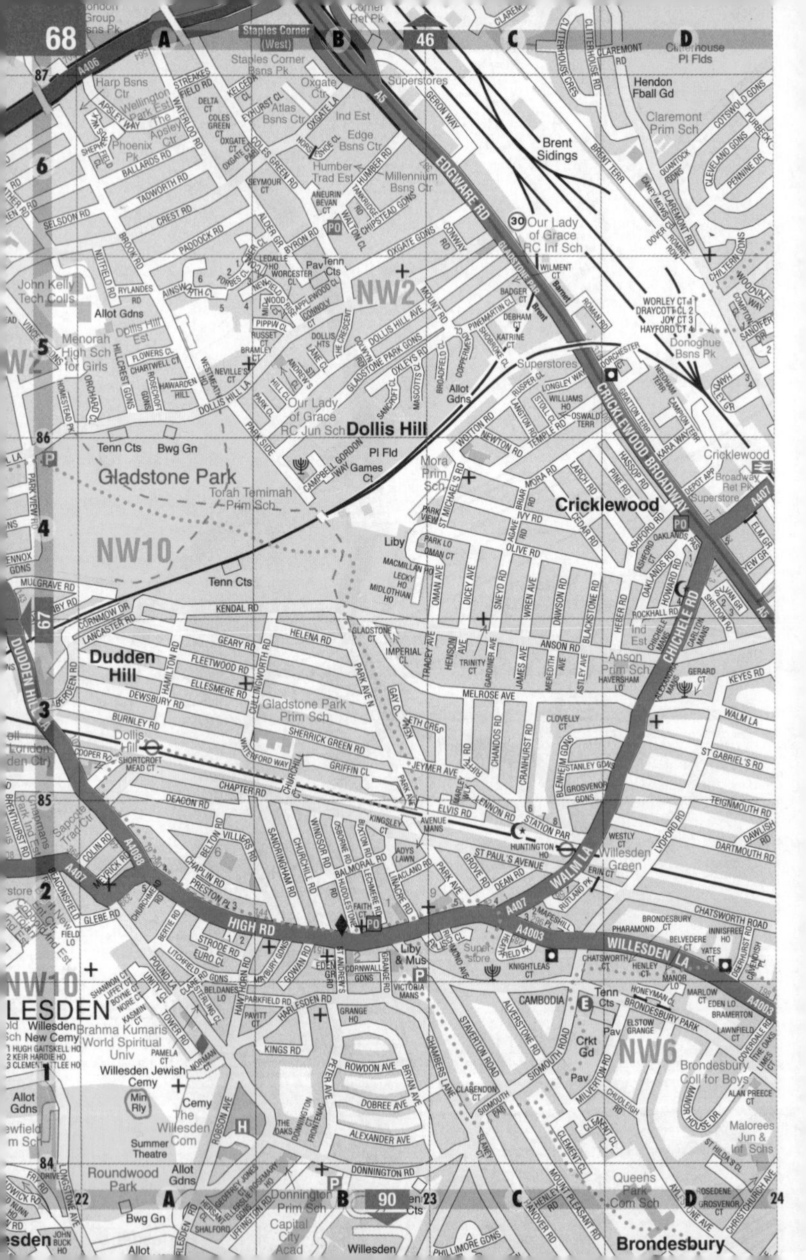

A
B
C
D
Staples Corner (West)
46
87
A406
London Group Bsns Pk
Staples Corner Bsns Pk
Corner Ret Pk
CLAREMONT RD
Clitterhouse Pl Flds
CLITTERHOUSE CRES
CLITTERHOUSE RD
Hendon Fball Gd
Claremont Prim Sch
COTSWOLD GDNS
PURBECK
Harp Bsns Ctr
Wellington Park Est
The Apsley Ctr
Phoenix Pk
APSLEY WAY
STREAKES FIELD RD
WATERLOO RD
DELTA CT
COLES GREEN CT
OXGATE CT
KELCEDA CL
EYHURST CL
Atlas Bsns Ctr
Oxgate Ctr
OXGATE LA
Ind Est
Edge Bsns Ctr
HORSESHOE CL
Superstores
GERON WAY
A5
Brent Sidings
BRENT TERR
QUANTOCK GDNS
CLEVELAND GDNS
PENNINE DR
6
BALLARDS RD
TADWORTH RD
COLES GREEN RD
SEYMOUR CT
Humber Trad Est
HUMBER RD
Millennium Bsns Ctr
EDGWARE RD
ANEURIN BEVAN CT
TANKRIDGE RD
CHIPSTEAD GDNS
WALTON CL
SELSDON RD
CREST RD
ALDER GR
PADDOCK RD
BYRON RD
PO
30
Our Lady of Grace RC Inf Sch
GLADSTONE PAR
CANEY MEWS
CLAREMONT RD
DOVER CL
ROMNEY ROW
CHILTERN GDNS
OXGATE GDNS
CONWAY RD
BROOK RD
NUTFIELD RD
John Kelly Tech Colls
RYLANDES RD
AINSWORTH CL
FORBES CL
LEDALLE HO
WORCESTER CL
Pav
Tenn Cts
NEWFIELD RISE
WOOD RISE
APPLEWOOD CL
CONNOLY
NW2
MOUNT RD
WILMENT CT
Barnet
Brent
BADGER CT
DEBHAM CT
ROMAN RD
WORLEY CT 1
DRAYCOTT CL 2
JOY CT 3
HAYFORD CT 4
WOODVALE WAY
COMPTON CL
SANDIFER DR
Allot Gdns
Dollis Hill Est
Menorah High Sch for Girls
PIPPIN CL
RUSSET CT
BRAMLEY CT
DOLLIS HTS
THE CRESCENT
COLWYN RD
DOLLIS HILL AVE
GLADSTONE PARK GDNS
OXLEYS RD
PINEMARTIN CL
SHOBROKE CL
KATRINE CT
COPPERMEAD CL
DORCHESTER CT
Donoghue Bsns Pk
5
FLOWERS CL
CHARTWELL CT
HILLCREST GDNS
WESTMEATH HO
NEVILLE'S CT
HAWARDEN HILL
ROSECROFT GDNS
ORCHARD CL
HOMESTEAD PK
DOLLIS HILL LA
HILL CL
ANDREW'S CL
LANE CL
PARK CL
SANCROFT CL
MASCOTTS CL
BROADFIELD CL
Allot Gdns
Superstores
RUSPER CL
LONGLEY WAY
WILLIAMS HO
STOLL CL
LANGTON RD
OSWALD TERR
TEMPLE RD
CRICKLEWOOD BROADWAY
GRATTON TERR
NEEDHAM TERR
CAMPION TERR
KARA WAY
Our Lady of Grace RC Jun Sch
Dollis Hill
86
PARK SIDE
CAMPBELL GORDON WAY
Pl Fld
Games Ct
WOTTON RD
NEWTON RD
Mora Prim Sch
Cricklewood
Tenn Cts
Bwg Gn
Gladstone Park
Torah Temimah Prim Sch
PARK VIEW RD
ST MICHAEL'S RD
MORA RD
BRIAR RD
LARCH RD
HASSOP RD
PINE RD
DEPOT APP
Broadway Ret Pk
Superstore
A407
Cricklewood
4
NW10
PARK VIEW
IVY RD
AGAVE RD
CEDAR RD
ASHFORD RD
OAKLANDS PAS
ELM GR
YEW GR
Liby
PARK LO
OMAN CT
OLIVE RD
LENNOX GDNS
MULGRAVE RD
MACMILLAN HO
LECKY HO
MIDLOTHIAN HO
OMAN AVE
DICEY AVE
SNEYD RD
WREN AVE
DAWSON RD
BLACKSTONE RD
HEBER RD
ASHFORD CT
OAKLANDS RD
HOWARD RD
CHICHELE RD
SHELDON RD
SYLVAN GR
Tenn Cts
67
KENDAL RD
CORNMOW DR
LANCASTER RD
ROCKHALL RD
HELENA RD
GLADSTONE CT
Ind Est
CHICHELE MANS
CARLTON MANS
A5
Dudden Hill
GEARY RD
CULLINGWORTH RD
IMPERIAL CL
TRACEY AVE
HENSON AVE
TRINITY CT
GARDINER AVE
JAMES AVE
MEREDITH AVE
ASTLEY AVE
ANSON RD
Anson Prim Sch
HAVERSHAM LO
ALEXANDRA MANS
GERARD CT
KEYES RD
DUDDEN HILL LA
FLEETWOOD RD
ELLESMERE RD
HAMILTON RD
ABERDEEN RD
DEWSBURY RD
PARK AVE N
GAY CL
MELROSE AVE
3
BURNLEY RD
Gladstone Park Prim Sch
KENNETH CRES
CHANDOS RD
CRANHURST RD
CLOVELLY CT
WALM LA
Dollis Hill
SHERRICK GREEN RD
WATERFORD WAY
BLENHEIM GDNS
STANLEY GDNS
ST GABRIEL'S RD
COOPER RD
SHORTCROFT MEAD CT
GRIFFIN CL
JEYMER AVE
RIFFEL RD
CHAPTER RD
CHURCHILL CT
PARK AVE
MARLEY WLK
LENNON RD
GROSVENOR GDNS
TEIGNMOUTH RD
85
BRENTHURST RD
Chapmans Park Ind Est
DEACON RD
ELVIS RD
STATION PAR
Sapcote Trad Ctr
BELTON RD
VILLIERS RD
SANDRINGHAM RD
CHURCHILL RD
WINDSOR RD
OSBORNE RD
BUXTON RD
KINGSLEY CT
AVENUE MANS
HUNTINGTON HO
Willesden Green
WESTLY CT
LYDFORD RD
DAWLISH RD
DARTMOUTH RD
COLIN RD
MEYRICK RD
A4088
CHAPLIN RD
BALMORAL RD
LECHMERE RD
ADYS LAWN
ACLAND RD
ST PAUL'S AVENUE
GROVE RD
DEAN RD
ERIN CT
RUTLAND PK
2
A407
BEACONSFIELD
PRESTON PL
CHURCHMEAD RD
HUDDLESTONE RD
LINACRE RD
PARK AVE
CHATSWORTH ROAD
GLEBE RD
BERTIE RD
HIGH RD
FAITH CT
PO
MAPESHILL PL
A4003
BRONDESBURY CT
PHARAMOND
BELVEDERE CT
INNISFREE HO
YATES CT
DEERHURST RD
CAVENDISH
STRODE RD
EURO CL
ST ANDREW'S
Liby & Mus
RICHMOND AVE
ELLIS CL
Superstore
HEATHFIELD PK
KNIGHTLEAS CT
WILLESDEN LA
CHATSWORTH CT
HENLEY CT
MANOR LO
MARLOW CT
EDEN LO
NW10
LESDEN
LITCHFIELD GDNS
POUND LA
UNITY CL
CLARE RD
STERLING CL
BELDANES LO
HAWTHORN RD
MAYBURY GDNS
GOWAN RD
EDEN GR
CORNWALL GDNS
GRANGE RD
VICTORIA MANS
P
CAMBODIA
Tenn Cts
HONEYMAN CL
BRONDESBURY PARK
BRAMERTON
A4003
SHANNON CT
LIFFEY CT
BOYNE CT
NORE CT
KASMIN CT
TOWER RD
PARKFIELD RD
HARLESDEN RD
PAVITT CT
GRANGE HO
STAVERTON ROAD
ALVERSTONE RD
SIDMOUTH ROAD
Crkt Gd
Pav
ELSTOW GRANGE
LAWNFIELD CT
COVERDALE RD
THE OAKS
LIMES CT
Willesden New Cemy
Brahma Kumaris World Spiritual Univ
1 HUGH GAITSKELL HO
2 KEIR HARDIE HO
3 CLEMENT ATTLEE HO
PAMELA CT
NORMAN CT
KINGS RD
NW6
Brondesbury Coll for Boys
Willesden Jewish Cemy
ROWDON AVE
BRYAN AVE
CHAMBERS LANE
MILVERTON RD
1
Allot Gdns
Min Rly
Cemy
The Willesden Com
ROBSON AVE
H
DOBREE AVE
CLARENDON CT
SIDMOUTH PAR
CLEMENT CL
CHUDLEIGH RD
MANOR HOUSE DR
ALAN PREECE CT
Newfield Prim Sch
Summer Theatre
THE OAKS
DONNINGTON CT
FRONTENAC
ALEXANDER AVE
PETER AVE
SLANEY CT
CLEMENT CL
Malorees Jun & Inf Schs
84
Roundwood Park
Allot Gdns
DONNINGTON RD
MOUNT PLEASANT RD
ST HILDA'S CL
LONGSTONE AVE
DRIVE
FRY RD
22
GEOFFREY JONES CT
HERSANT CL
ELLERSLIE GDNS
ROSEMARY HO
UFFINGTON RD
Donnington Prim Sch
90
23
Tenn Cts
HENLEY RD
HANOVER RD
Queens Park Com Sch
AYLESTONE AVE
ROSEDENE
GROSVENOR CT
CHRISTCHURCH AVE
24
CHADWICK RD
NUNN RD
Bwg Gn
SHALFORD
WILLESDEN RD
Capital City Acad
Willesden
PHILLIMORE GDNS
Brondesbury
Willesden
JOHN BUCK HO
Allot

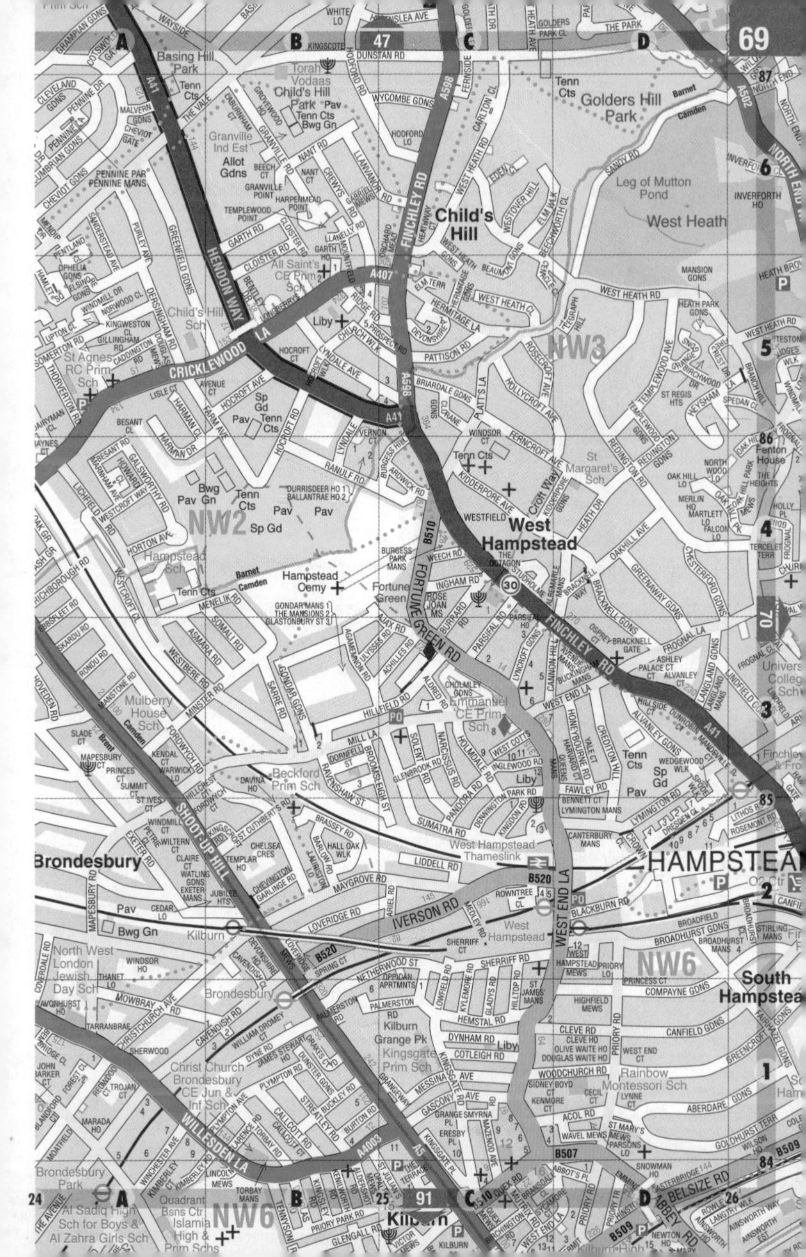
Basing Hill Park
Golders Hill Park
Child's Hill Park
Leg of Mutton Pond
West Heath
Child's Hill
West Hampstead
NW3
NW2
NW6
Hampstead Cemy
Fortune Green
Brondesbury
HAMPSTEAD
South Hampstead
Kilburn
Kilburn Grange Pk
West Hampstead Thameslink
FINCHLEY RD
HENDON WAY
CRICKLEWOOD LA
FORTUNE GREEN RD
WEST END LA
SHOOT-UP HILL
WILLESDEN LA
IVERSON RD
WEST HEATH RD
FROGNAL LA
BELSIZE RD
ABBEY RD
Barnet
Camden
Brent
47
91
70
24
25
26

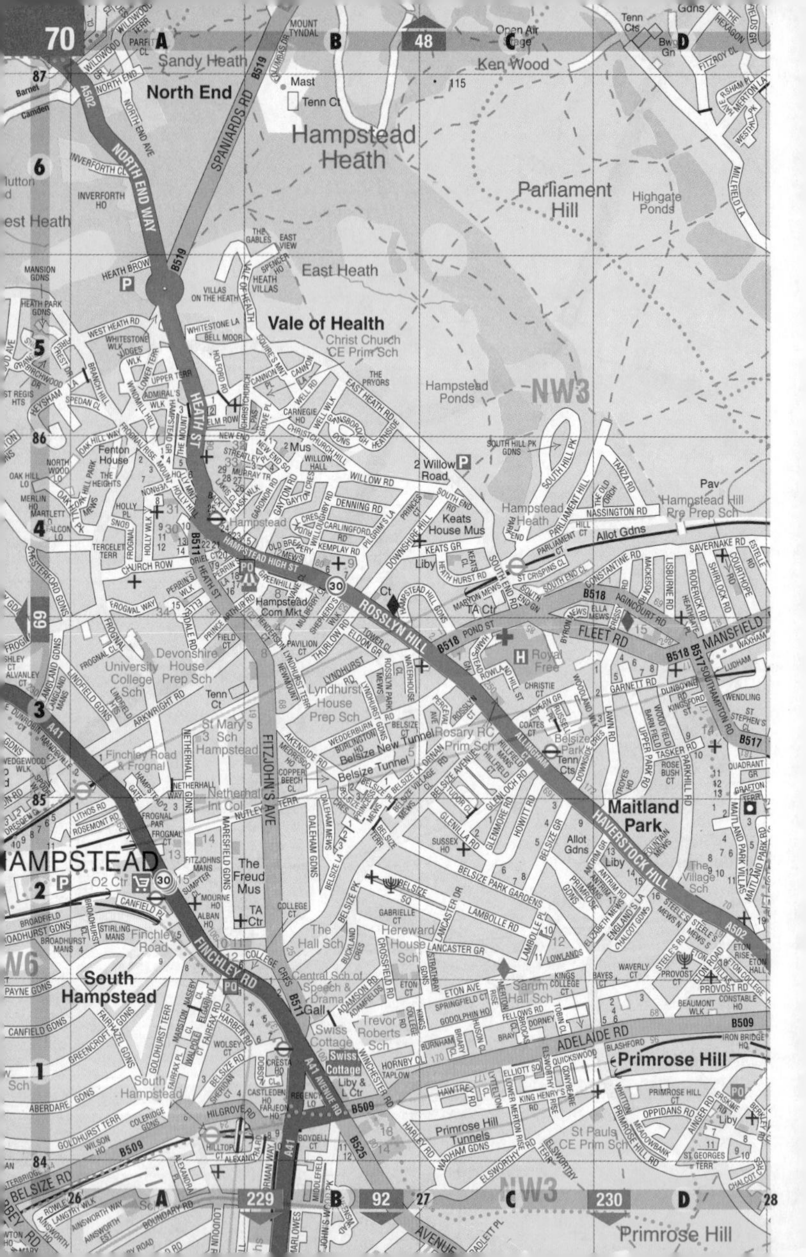
A
B
48
C
D
MOUNT TYNDAL
Open Air Stage
Tenn Cts
Bowl Gn
Sandy Heath
Ken Wood
87
Barnet
Camden
North End
Mast
Tenn Ct
115
Hampstead Heath
6
Parliament Hill
Highgate Ponds
INVERFORTH CL
INVERFORTH HO
NORTH END WAY
NORTH END AVE
NORTH END
WILDWOOD
SPANIARDS RD
B519
A502
West Heath
MILFIELD LA
FITZROY CL
HEXAGON
WESTHILL PK
MERTON LA
THE GABLES
EAST VIEW
SPENCER HO
HEATH VILLAS
East Heath
VALE OF HEALTH
MANSION GDNS
HEATH BROW
VILLAS ON THE HEATH
HEATH PARK GDNS
WEST HEATH RD
WHITESTONE LA
WHITESTONE WLK
BELL MOOR
Vale of Health
Christ Church CE Prim Sch
5
JUDGES' WLK
LOWER TERR
UPPER TERR
BRANCH HILL
BIRCHWOOD DR
HEYSHAM LA
SPEDAN CL
ADMIRAL'S WLK
HOLFORD RD
HEATH ST
CANNON PL
CANNON LA
SQUIRE'S MT
WELL RD
EAST HEATH RD
THE PRYORS
Hampstead Ponds
NW3
ELM ROW
CHRISTCHURCH PAS
CARNEGIE HO
WELL WLK
GAINSBOROUGH GDNS
HEATHSIDE
86
OAK HILL WAY
Fenton House
NORTH WOOD LO
OAK HILL LO
NEW END
NEW END SQ
STREATLEY PL
2 Mus
WILLOW HALL
CHRISTCHURCH HILL
SOUTH HILL PK GDNS
SOUTH HILL PK
TANZA RD
THE OLD ORCH
2 Willow Road
WILLOW RD
MERLIN HO
MARTLETT CT
THE HEIGHTS
OAK HILL PK
MURRAY TR
FLASK WLK
GARDNOR RD
GAYTON RD
GAYTON CRES
DENNING RD
SOUTH END RD
Pav
Hampstead Hill Pre Prep Sch
4
HOLLY PL
HOLLY WLK
FROGNAL
Hampstead
CARLINGFORD RD
WILLOUGHBY RD
PILGRIM'S LA
DOWNSHIRE HILL
Keats House Mus
Hampstead Heath
PARLIAMENT HILL
NASSINGTON RD
Allot Gdns
SAVERNAKE RD
ESTELLE RD
COURTHOPE RD
SHIRLOCK RD
RODERICK RD
TERCELET TERR
HAMPSTEAD HIGH ST
B511
OLD BREWERY MEWS
KEMPLAY RD
KEATS GR
KEATS CL
HEATH HURST RD
PARLIAMENT CT
ST CRISPINS CL
SOUTH END CL
CONSTANTINE RD
MACKESON RD
LISBURNE RD
CHURCH ROW
PO
Liby
30
PERRIN'S WLK
GREENHILL
Hampstead Com Mkt
ROSSLYN HILL
Ct
HAMPSTEAD HILL GDNS
MARYON MEWS
SOUTH END GN
TA Ctr
B518
AGINCOURT RD
HEATHGATE
69
FROGNAL WAY
PRINCE ARTHUR RD
SHEPHERD'S WLK
MULBERRY CL
THURLOW RD
ELDON GR
TOWER CL
POND ST
BYRON MEWS
ELLA MEWS
FLEET RD
MANSFIELD RD
B517
WAXHAM
FROGNAL CL
FIELD CT
PAVILION CT
LYNDHURST GDNS
LYNDHURST TERR
NEWMOUNT
HENDERSON CT
Devonshire House Prep Sch
University College Sch
Royal Free
H
CHRISTIE CT
WOODLAND WLK
GARNETT RD
DUNBOYNE RD
KINGSFORD ST
SOUTHAMPTON RD
LUDHAM
WENDLING
ST STEPHEN'S CL
ALVANLEY CT
LANGLAND GDNS
LINDFIELD GDNS
ARKWRIGHT RD
Tenn Ct
Lyndhurst House Prep Sch
ROSSLYN PARK MEWS
WATERHOUSE CL
ROSSLYN HILL
ASPERN GR
RUSSELL
LAWN RD
UPPER PARK RD
BARN FIELD
WOOD FIELD
3
A41
DUNROBIN CT
MANDEVILLE CT
St Mary's Sch Hampstead
NETHERHALL GDNS
FITZJOHN'S AVE
WEDDERBURN RD
BURLINGTON
BELSIZE CT
Belsize New Tunnel
Rosary RC Prim Sch
COATES CT
Belsize Park
Tenn Cts
ALLINGHAM
TASKER RD
ROSE BUSH CT
PARKHILL RD
B517
QUADRANT GR
Finchley Road & Frognal
AKENSIDE RD
MEDRESCO HO
COPPER BEECH CL
Belsize Tunnel
BELSIZE LA
BELSIZE AVENUE
HILLFIELD CT
GLENLOCH RD
DOWNSIDE CRES
TROYES HO
GRAFTON TERR
85
LITHOS RD
ROSEMONT RD
NETHERHALL WAY
Netherhall Int Col
NUTLEY TERR
DALEHAM MEWS
BELSIZE MEWS
TUDOR CL
GLENMORE RD
HOWITT RD
HAVERSTOCK HILL
Maitland Park
FROGNAL PAR
FROGNAL CT
MARESFIELD GDNS
DALEHAM GDNS
GLENILLA RD
SUSSEX HO
BELSIZE GR
Allot Gdns
ANTRIM GR
FOUNTAIN MEWS
MAITLAND PARK VILLAS
MAITLAND PARK RD
HAMPSTEAD
FITZJOHNS MANS
The Freud Mus
BELSIZE TERR
BELSIZE PARK GARDENS
ANTRIM MANS
ANTRIM RD
Liby
The Village Sch
2
O2 Ctr
SUMPTER CL
MOURNE HO
ALBAN HO
TA Ctr
COLLEGE CT
BELSIZE PK
BELSIZE SQ
GABRIELLE CT
LANCASTER DR
LAMBOLLE RD
LAMBOLLE PL
PRIMROSE GDNS
ELIZABETH MEWS
ENGLAND'S LA
CHALCOT GDNS
STEELE'S MEWS N
STEELE'S MEWS S
A502
BROADFIELD
BROADHURST GDNS
BROADHURST MANS
STIRLING MANS
CANFIELD PL
Finchley Road
FINCHLEY RD
COLLEGE CRES
The Hall Sch
BUCKLAND CRES
CROSSFIELD RD
Hereward House Sch
LANCASTER GR
LOWLANDS
WAVERLY CT
STEELE'S RD
ETON RISE
ETON HALL
NW6
South Hampstead
PAYNE GDNS
PO
Central Sch of Speech & Drama
ADAMSON RD
ADAMFIELDS
ETON CT
KINGS GDNS
STRATHRAY
ETON AVE
Sarum Hall Sch
KINGS COLLEGE CT
BAYES CT
PROVOST CT
ETON VILLAS
ETON COLLEGE RD
PROVOST RD
BEAUMONT WLK
CONSTABLE HO
CANFIELD GDNS
GREENCROFT GDNS
FAIRHAZEL GDNS
GOLDHURST TERR
MARSTON CL
NASEBY CL
ELGAR HO
FAIRFAX RD
HARBEN RD
B511
Gall
Swiss Cottage
Trevor Roberts Sch
SPRINGFIELD CT
GODOLPHIN HO
MERTON RISE
FELLOWS RD
DORNEY
TOBIN CL
B509
1
WOLSEY CT
FAIRFAX PL
WALPOLE CT
BELSIZE RD
CRESTA HO
DOBSON CL
A41 AVENUE RD
WINCHESTER RD
HORNBY CL
BURNHAM
BRIARY CT
HUSON CL
BROCAS CL
BRAY
ADELAIDE RD
BLASHFORD
QUICKSWOOD
IRON BRIDGE HO
Primrose Hill
Sch
South Hampstead
SHERIDAN CT
CASTLEDEN HO
REGENCY LO
Liby & L Ctr
TAPLOW
ELLIOTT SQ
CONYBEARE
HAWTREY RD
LYTTELTON CL
LOWER MERTON RISE
KING HENRY'S RD
WHITTON
PRIMROSE HILL CT
ERSKINE RD
BERKLEY RD
ABERDARE GDNS
COLERIDGE GDNS
HILGROVE RD
FARJEON HO
B509
Primrose Hill Tunnels
PRIMROSE HILL RD
OPPIDANS RD
AINGER RD
GOLDHURST TERR
WILSON HO
B509
HILLTOP
ALEXANDRA RD
BOYDELL CT
B525
HARLEY RD
WADHAM GDNS
ELSWORTHY RD
ELSWORTHY TERR
St Pauls CE Prim Sch
MEADOWBANK
ST GEORGES TERR
CHALCOT SQ
84
BELSIZE RD
MIDDLEFIELD
NW3
26
A
229
B
92
27
C
230
D
28
ROWLEY WAY
LANGTRY WLK
AINSWORTH WAY
AINSWORTH EST
BOUNDARY RD
LOUDOUN RD
MARLOWES
AVENUE
ADELAIDE RD
Primrose Hill

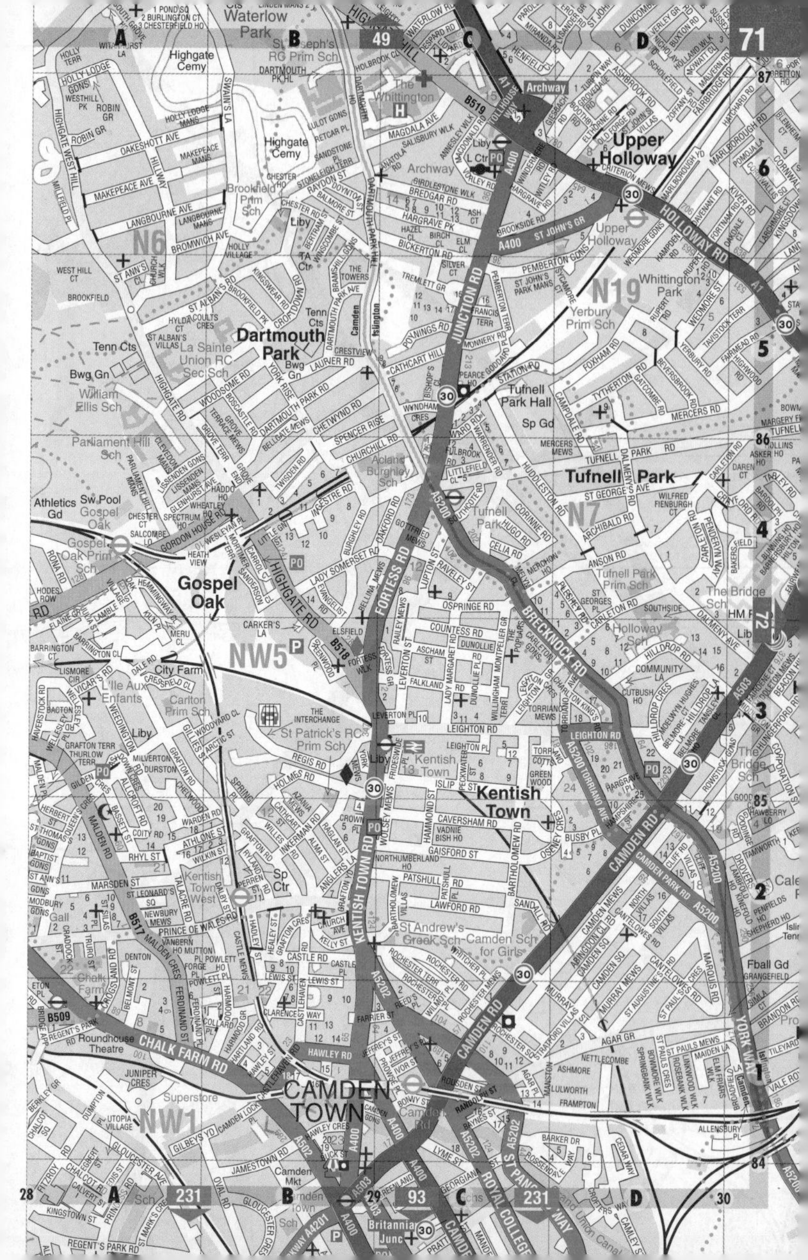

A
B
C
D
49
87
86
85
84
72
28
29
30
231
93
231
Waterlow Park
St Joseph's RC Prim Sch
Highgate Cemy
The Whittington
Archway
Upper Holloway
Holly Lodge Gdns
Westhill Pk
Robin Gr
Oakeshott Ave
Makepeace Ave
Langbourne Ave
Bromwich Ave
Holly Lodge Mans
Makepeace Mans
Langbourne Mans
Swain's La
Hillway
Highgate West Hill
Millfield Pl
Dartmouth Pk Hl
Dartmouth Park Hill
Magdala Ave
Salisbury Wlk
Lulot Gdns
Retcar Pl
Sandstone Pl
Stoneleigh Terr
Raydon St
Doynton St
Balmore St
Chester Rd
Brookfield Prim Sch
Holly Village
Bredgar Rd
Hargrave Pk
Bickerton Rd
Girdlestone Wlk
Junction Rd
St John's Gr
Holloway Rd
Whittington Park
Yerbury Prim Sch
N6
N19
N7
NW5
NW1
Dartmouth Park
La Sainte Union RC Sec Sch
William Ellis Sch
Parliament Hill Sch
Tenn Cts
Bwg Gn
Athletics Gd
Sw Pool
Gospel Oak
Gospel Oak Prim Sch
Highgate Rd
Gordon House Rd
York Rise
Laurier Rd
Dartmouth Park Rd
Chetwynd Rd
Spencer Rise
Churchill Rd
Acland Burghley Sch
Tufnell Park Hall
Tufnell Park
Tufnell Park Rd
St George's Ave
Anson Rd
Tufnell Park Prim Sch
Holloway Sch
Brecknock Rd
Fortess Rd
Lady Somerset Rd
Ospringe Rd
Countess Rd
Leighton Rd
City Farm
Carlton Prim Sch
L'Ile Aux Enfants
St Patrick's RC Prim Sch
Kentish Town
Kentish Town Rd
Caversham Rd
Gaisford St
Prince of Wales Rd
Malden Rd
Kentish Town West
Camden Rd
Camden Park Rd
Camden Sq
St Andrew's Greek Sch
Camden Sch for Girls
Chalk Farm Rd
Roundhouse Theatre
Superstore
Camden Town
Camden Mkt
Hawley Rd
Agar Gr
York Way
Fball Gd
The Bridge Sch
HM Prison
Caledonian Rd
Camden Rd
Britannia Junc
Royal College St
St Pancras Way
Gloucester Ave
Regent's Park Rd
A1
A400
A503
A5200
A5202
A502
B519
B518
B517
B509

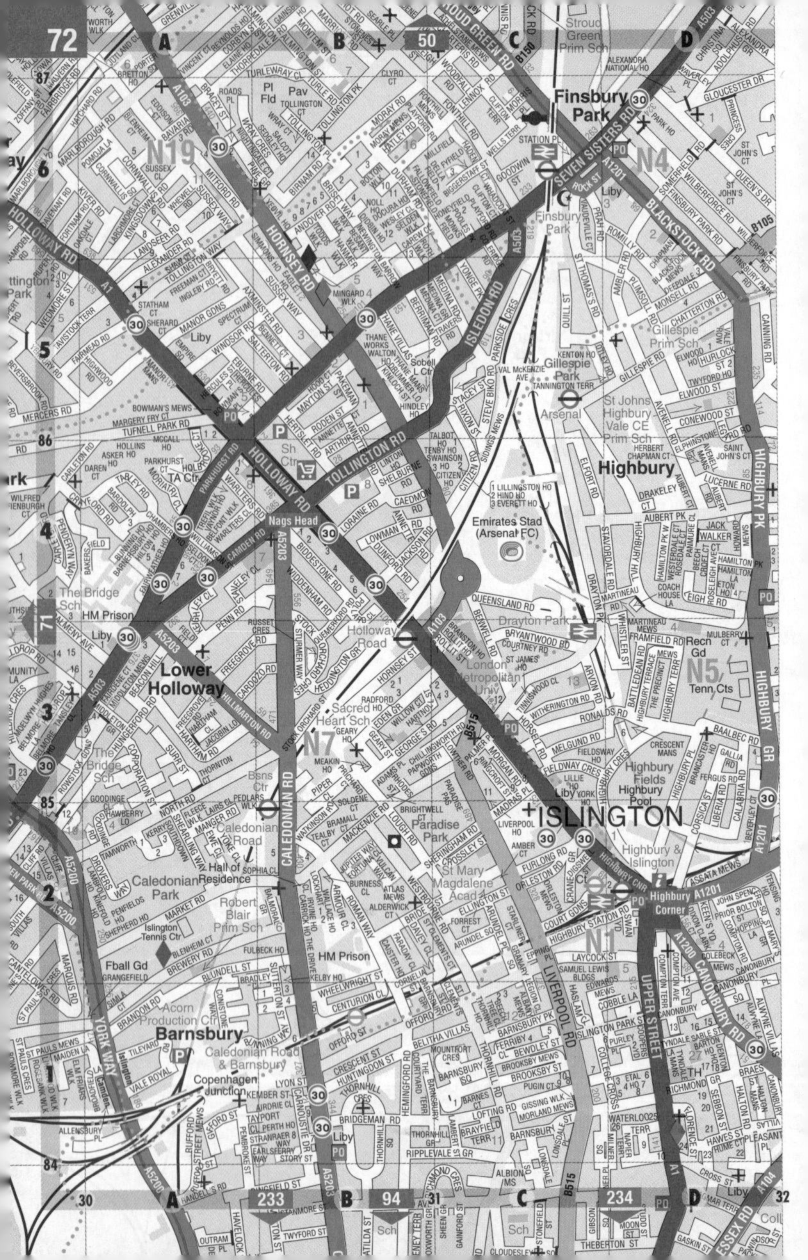

A
B
C
D
50
71
233
94
234
N19
N4
N7
N5
N1
Finsbury Park
Stroud Green Prim Sch
Alexandra National Ho
Seven Sisters Rd
Blackstock Rd
Hornsey Rd
Holloway Rd
Tollington Rd
Isledon Rd
Camden Rd
Caledonian Rd
Liverpool Rd
Upper Street
Canonbury Rd
Highbury Pk
Highbury Gr
York Way
Hillmarton Rd
Mitford Rd
Tufnell Park Rd
Mercers Rd
Seven Sisters Rd
Gillespie Park
Gillespie Prim Sch
Arsenal
St Johns Highbury Vale CE Prim Sch
Highbury
Emirates Stad (Arsenal FC)
Drayton Park
Holloway Road
London Metropolitan Univ
Nags Head
Sobell L Ctr
Lower Holloway
HM Prison
The Bridge Sch
Sacred Heart Sch
Caledonian Road
Caledonian Park
Hall of Residence
Paradise Park
St Mary Magdalene Acad
ISLINGTON
Highbury Fields
Highbury Pool
Highbury & Islington
Highbury Corner
Robert Blair Prim Sch
Islington Tennis Ctr
Fball Gd
Acorn Production Ctr
Barnsbury
Caledonian Road & Barnsbury
Copenhagen Junction
Tenn Cts
Recn Gd
Pl Fld
Pav
Liby
Sh Ctr
TA Ctr
Bsns Ctr
Sch
Coll
A1
A103
A503
A5203
A5200
A1201
A1200
A104
B515
B105
B150
87
86
85
84
30
31
32

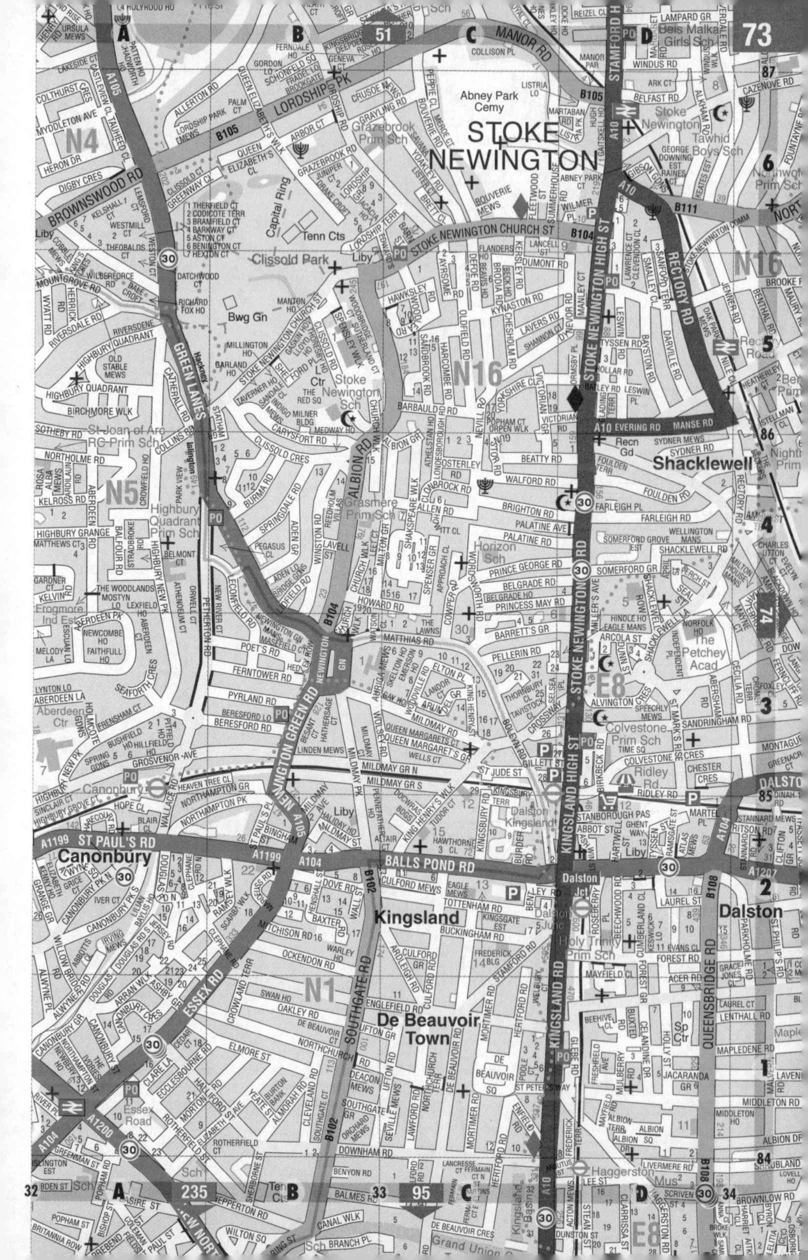

STOKE NEWINGTON
Abney Park Cemy
Stoke Newington
Shacklewell
Dalston
Kingsland
De Beauvoir Town
Canonbury
Clissold Park
N4
N16
N5
N1
E8
STOKE NEWINGTON HIGH ST
KINGSLAND HIGH ST
KINGSLAND RD
STOKE NEWINGTON RD
STOKE NEWINGTON CHURCH ST
GREEN LANES
NEWINGTON GREEN RD
ESSEX RD
ST PAUL'S RD
BALLS POND RD
SOUTHGATE RD
QUEENSBRIDGE RD
ALBION RD
RECTORY RD
LORDSHIP PK
BROWNSWOOD RD
MANOR RD
STAMFORD HILL
EVERING RD
MANSE RD
Grazebrook Prim Sch
Stoke Newington Sch
Grasmere Prim Sch
Highbury Quadrant Prim Sch
Horizon Sch
The Petchey Acad
Colvestone Prim Sch
Holy Trinity Prim Sch
Canonbury
Essex Road
Dalston Kingsland
Dalston Junc
Haggerston
Rectory Road
Stoke Newington
A
B
C
D
51
235
95
74
32
33
34
84
85
86
87

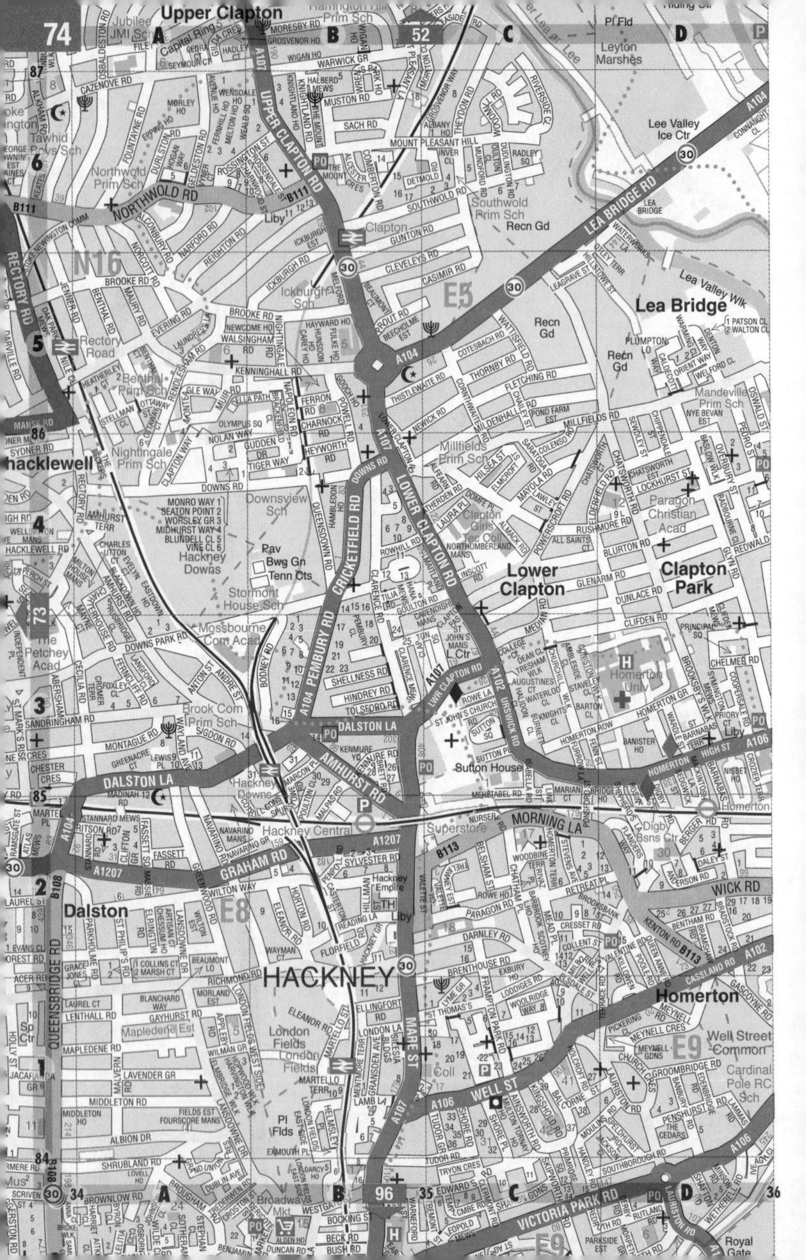
Upper Clapton
A
B
C
D
52
Leyton Marshes
Lee Valley Ice Ctr
Jubilee JMI Sch
Capital Ring
MORESBY RD
GROSVENOR HO
WIGAN HO
WARWICK GR
CAZENOVE RD
Tawhid Boys Sch
UPPER CLAPTON RD
A107
MUSTON RD
SACH RD
MOUNT PLEASANT HILL
MOUNT PLEASANT LA
THEYDON RD
RIVERSIDE CL
Northwold Prim Sch
NORTHWOLD RD
B111
ROSSINGTON ST
DURLSTON RD
GELDESTON RD
FOUNTAYNE RD
SOUTHWOLD RD
Southwold Prim Sch
Recn Gd
LEA BRIDGE RD
A104
Clapton
GUNTON RD
CLEVELEYS RD
CASIMIR RD
RECTORY RD
STOKE NEWINGTON COMM
NARFORD RD
REIGHTON RD
NORCOTT RD
N16
E5
BROOKE RD
ICKBURGH RD
Ickburgh Sch
MAURY RD
BENTHAL RD
JENNER RD
EVERING RD
Lea Bridge
Lea Valley Wlk
LEAGRAVE ST
WATTISFIELD RD
Rectory Road
NIGHTINGALE RD
WALSINGHAM RD
KENNINGHALL RD
NEWCOME HO
HAYWARD HO
BEECHOLME EST
COTESBACH RD
THORNBY RD
FLETCHING RD
THISTLEWAITE RD
Bentha Prim Sch
RENDLESHAM RD
NAPOLEON RD
FERRON RD
CHARNOCK RD
HEYWORTH RD
POWELL RD
GOOCH HO
NEWICK RD
MILDENHALL RD
MILLFIELDS RD
POND FARM EST
Mandeville Prim Sch
NYE BEVAN EST
OSWALD ST
PEDRO ST
Shacklewell
Nightingale Prim Sch
CLAPTON WAY
NOLAN WAY
GUDDEN DR
TIGER WAY
DOWNS RD
Millfields Prim Sch
LOWER CLAPTON RD
CRICKETFIELD RD
Downsview Sch
MONRO WAY 1
SEATON POINT 2
WORSLEY GR 3
MIDHURST WAY 4
BLUNDELL CL 5
VINE CL 6
RECTORY RD
AMHURST TERR
CHARLES DUTTON CT
Hackney Downs
Pav
Bwg Gn
Tenn Cts
Stormont House Sch
QUEENSDOWN RD
CLARENCE RD
Clapton Girls Tec Coll
MAYOLA RD
POWERSCROFT RD
ALL SAINTS CT
RUSHMORE RD
Paragon Christian Acad
CHATSWORTH RD
LOCKHURST ST
BLURTON RD
Lower Clapton
Clapton Park
GLENARM RD
DUNLACE RD
CLIFDEN RD
73
The Petchey Acad
Mossbourne Com Acad
DOWNS PARK RD
PEMBURY RD
A104
SHELLNESS RD
HINDREY RD
TOLSFORD RD
LWR CLAPTON RD
URSWICK RD
A102
Homerton Univ
HOMERTON GR
HOMERTON ROW
CHELMER RD
Brook Com Prim Sch
SANDRINGHAM RD
MONTAGUE RD
DALSTON LA
AMHURST RD
Sutton House
HOMERTON HIGH ST
A106
Liby
Hackney Downs
MORNING LA
Superstore
Hackney Central
GRAHAM RD
A1207
B113
Digby Bsns Ctr
WICK RD
Homerton
Dalston
Hackney Empire
TH
E8
PARAGON RD
DARNLEY RD
KENTON RD
HACKNEY
QUEENSBRIDGE RD
B108
RICHMOND RD
BRENTHOUSE RD
CASSLAND RD
Homerton
Sp Ctr
Mapledene Est
London Fields
ELEANOR RD
MARE ST
WELL ST
E9
Well Street Common
Cardinal Pole RC Sch
MAPLEDENE RD
LAVENDER GR
MIDDLETON RD
ALBION DR
SHRUBLAND RD
Pl Flds
Coll
LAURISTON RD
PENSHURST RD
SOUTHBOROUGH RD
VICTORIA PARK RD
BROWNLOW RD
96
Broadway Mkt
35
36
34
Royal Gate

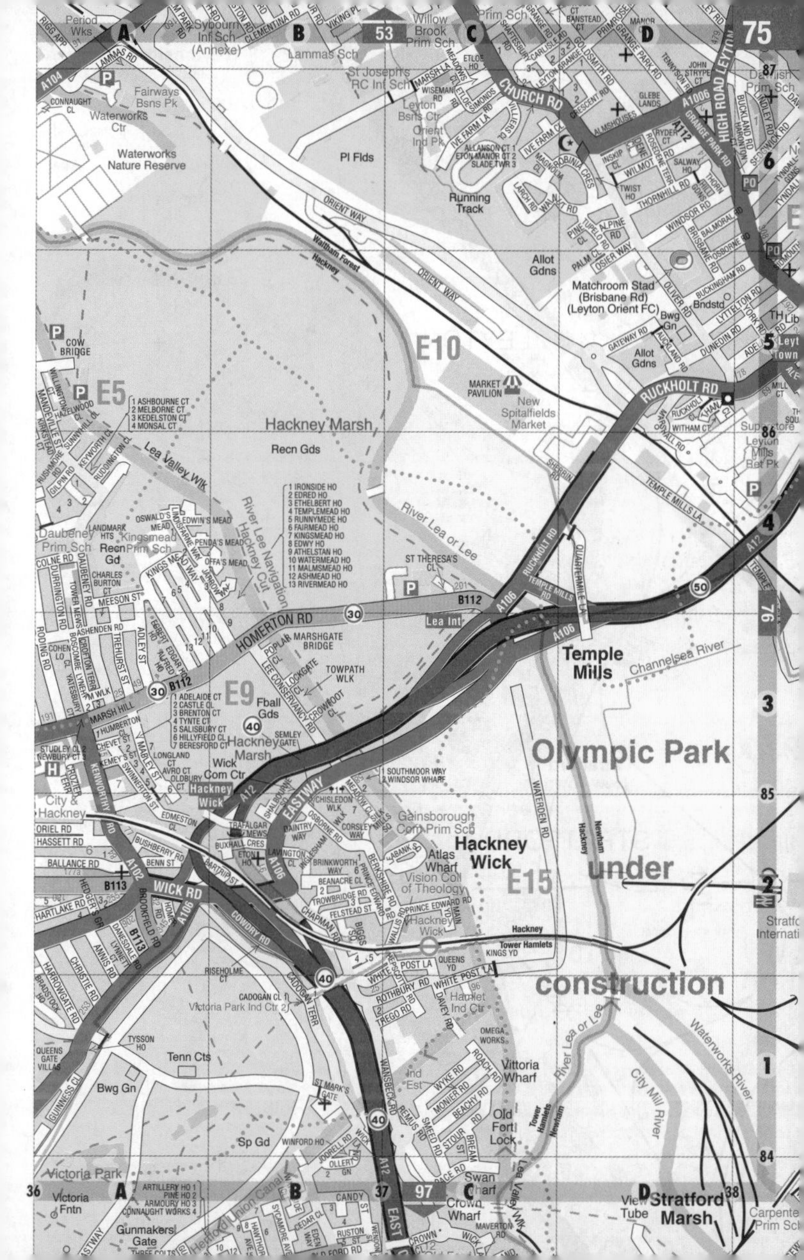
53
97
76
Hackney Marsh
Recn Gds
E10
E5
E9
E15
Olympic Park
under
construction
Temple Mills
Hackney Wick
Matchroom Stad
(Brisbane Rd)
(Leyton Orient FC)
Waterworks Nature Reserve
Fairways Bsns Pk
Waterworks Ctr
Pl Flds
Running Track
New Spitalfields Market
MARKET PAVILION
River Lee Navigation
Hackney Cut
River Lea or Lee
Lea Valley Wlk
Channelsea River
Waterworks River
City Mill River
HOMERTON RD
RUCKHOLT RD
ORIENT WAY
CHURCH RD
HIGH ROAD LEYTON
TEMPLE MILLS LA
EASTWAY
WICK RD
MARSH HILL
WATERDEN RD
Victoria Park
Tenn Cts
Bwg Gn
Sp Gd
Kingsmead Prim Sch
Daubeney Prim Sch
Gainsborough Com Prim Sch
Vision Coll of Theology
Atlas Wharf
Vittoria Wharf
Old Ford Lock
Swan Wharf
Crown Wharf
Stratford Marsh
Victoria Park Ind Ctr
Hamlet Ind Ctr
Lea Int
Hackney Wick
Wick Com Ctr
Fball Gds
Allot Gdns
Leyton Mills Ret Pk
Stratford International

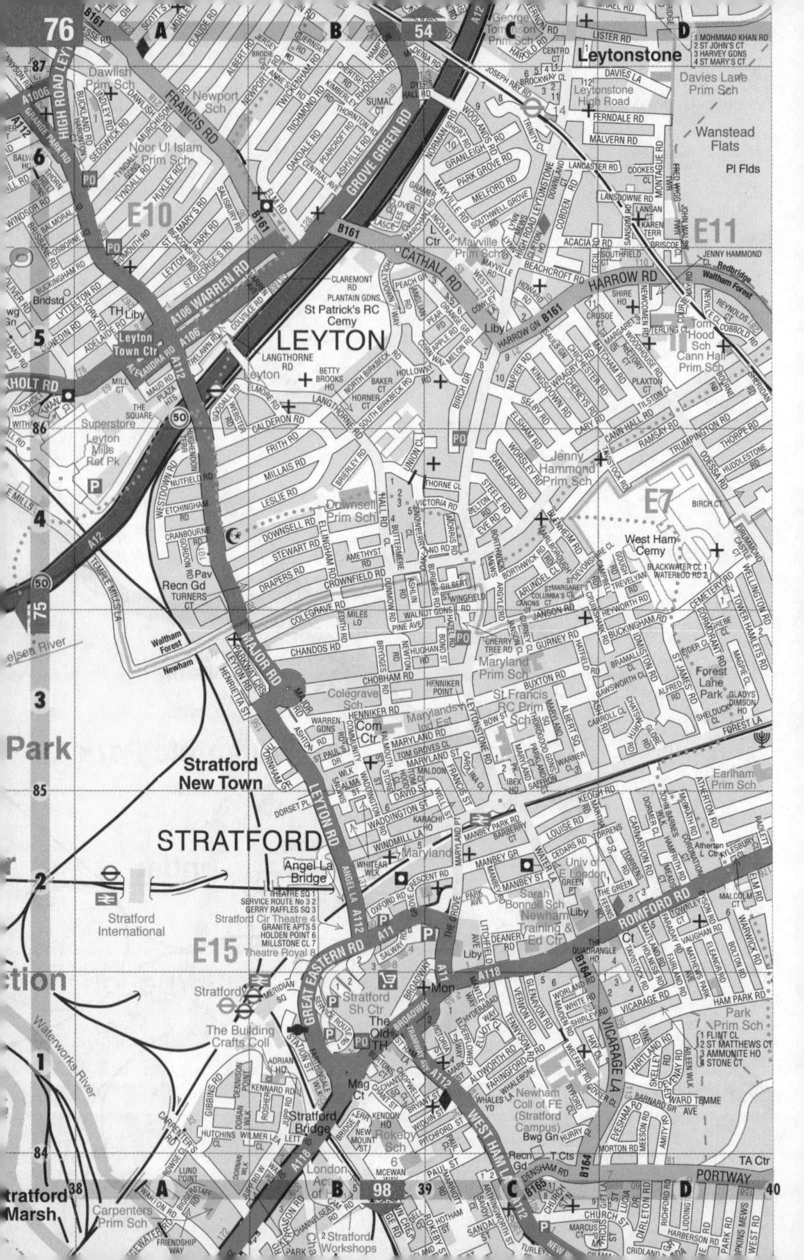
76
A
B
C
D
54
1 MOHMMAD KHAN RD
2 ST JOHN'S CT
3 HARVEY GDNS
4 ST MARY'S CT
Leytonstone
Leytonstone High Road
Davies Lane Prim Sch
Wanstead Flats
Pl Flds
Dawlish Prim Sch
Newport Sch
Noor Ul Islam Prim Sch
E10
E11
HIGH ROAD LEYTON
FRANCIS RD
GROVE GREEN RD
A106 WARREN RD
CATHALL RD
HARROW RD
Mayville Prim Sch
Redbridge
Waltham Forest
Tom Hood Sch
Cann Hall Prim Sch
St Patrick's RC Cemy
LEYTON
Leyton Town Ctr
Superstore
Leyton Mills Ret Pk
Jenny Hammond Prim Sch
E7
West Ham Cemy
Downsell Prim Sch
Recn Gd
MAJOR RD
Waltham Forest
Newham
Maryland Prim Sch
St Francis RC Prim Sch
Colegrave Sch
Forest Lane Park
Maryland Ind Est
Earlham Prim Sch
Stratford New Town
STRATFORD
LEYTON RD
Angel La Bridge
Stratford International
E15
Univ of E London
Sarah Bonnell Sch
Newham Training & Ed Ctr
ROMFORD RD
GREAT EASTERN RD
Stratford Sh Ctr
The Old TH
The Building Crafts Coll
Waterworks River
Stratford Bridge
Rokeby Sch
Newham Coll of FE (Stratford Campus)
WEST HAM LA
VICARAGE LA
Park Prim Sch
1 FLINT CL
2 ST MATTHEWS CT
3 AMMONITE HO
4 STONE CT
PORTWAY
London Acad of H
98
Carpenters Prim Sch
Stratford Workshops
Stratford Marsh
38
39
40

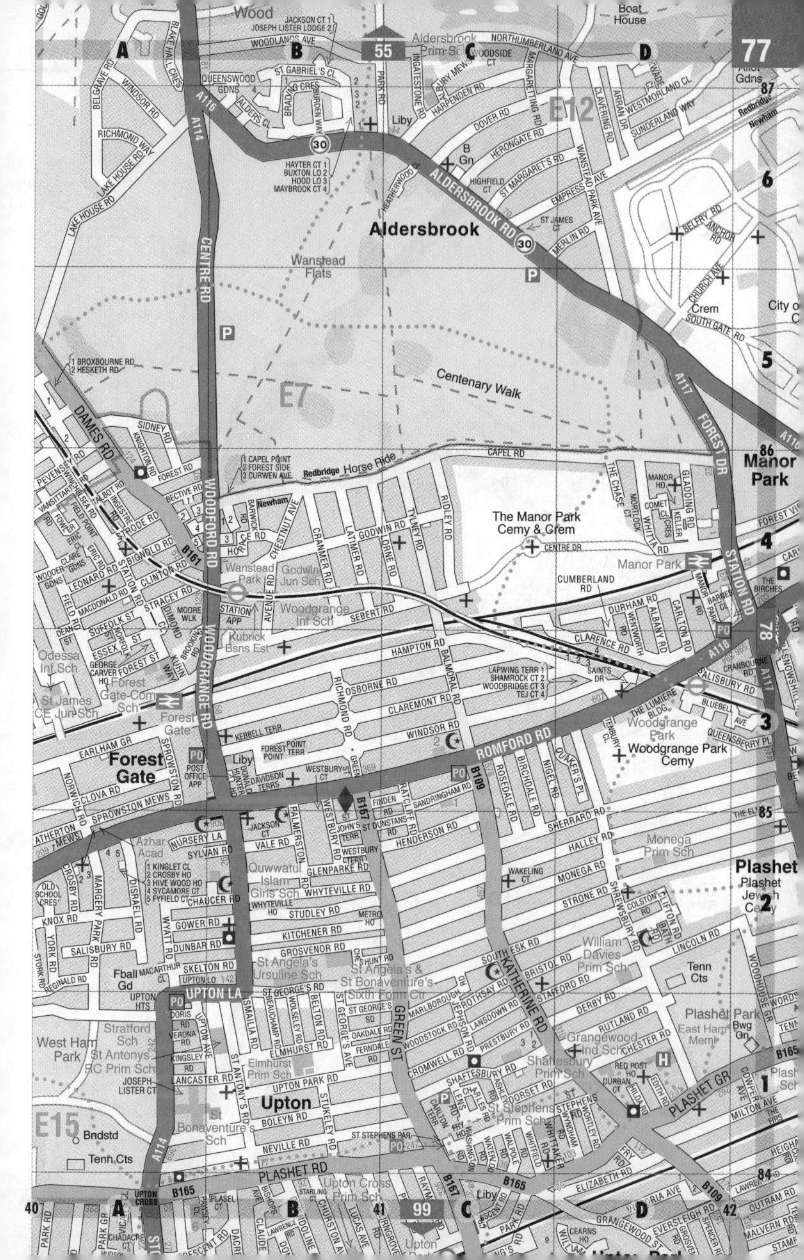
77
55
99
A
B
C
D
1
2
3
4
5
6
E12
E7
E15
Aldersbrook
Wanstead Flats
Centenary Walk
Manor Park
Forest Gate
Upton
Plashet
ALDERSBROOK RD
CENTRE RD
WOODFORD RD
WOODGRANGE RD
ROMFORD RD
FOREST DR
STATION RD
GREEN ST
KATHERINE RD
UPTON LA
PLASHET RD
PLASHET GR
DAMES RD
CAPEL RD
Redbridge Horse Ride
The Manor Park Cemy & Crem
Woodgrange Park Cemy
Plashet Jewish Cemy
Plashet Park
West Ham Park
Wanstead Park
Aldersbrook Prim Sch
Godwin Jun Sch
Woodgrange Inf Sch
Kubrick Bsns Est
Forest Gate Com Sch
Odessa Inf Sch
St James CE Jun Sch
Azhar Acad
Quwwatul Islam Girls Sch
St Angela's Ursuline Sch
St Angela's & St Bonaventure's Sixth Form Ctr
Monega Prim Sch
William Davies Prim Sch
Grangewood Ind Sch
Shaftesbury Prim Sch
St Stephens Prim Sch
Elmhurst Prim Sch
Stratford Sch
St Antonys RC Prim Sch
St Bonaventure's Sch
Upton Cross Prim Sch
East Ham Meml
Tenn Cts
Bndstd
Fball Gd

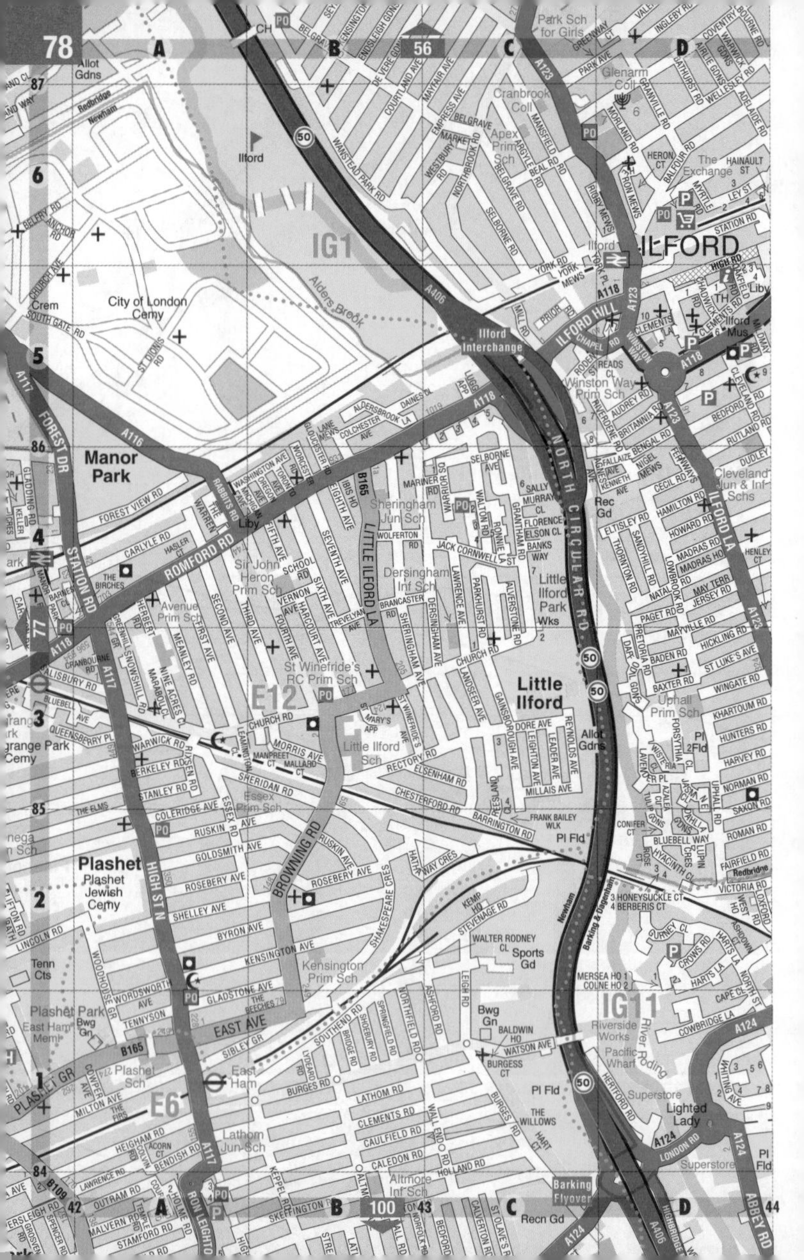

A
B
C
D
56
100
77
Allot Gdns
Redbridge
Newham
Ilford
IG1
Alders Brook
City of London Cemy
Crem
SOUTH GATE RD
ST DIONIS RD
BELFRY RD
ANCHOR RD
CHURCH AVE
FOREST DR
A117
A116
A118
A406
Manor Park
FOREST VIEW RD
STATION RD
ROMFORD RD
CARLYLE RD
HASLER CT
THE BIRCHES
MANOR PARK
BARNES CL
THE WARREN
RABBITS RD
Liby
WASHINGTON AVE
MICHIGAN AVE
OREGON AVE
TORONTO AVE
WORCESTER RD
GLOUCESTER RD
LANE MEWS
COLCHESTER AVE
ALDERSBROOK LA
DAINES CL
LUGG APP
FIFTH AVE
SEVENTH AVE
EIGHTH AVE
IBIS HO
B165
LITTLE ILFORD LA
Sheringham Jun Sch
WOLFERTON RD
MARINER RD
WARRIOR SQ
SELBORNE AVE
WALTON RD
RONNIE LA
GRANTHAM RD
SALLY MURRAY CL
FLORENCE ELSON CL
BANKS WAY
JACK CORNWELL ST
Dersingham Inf Sch
LAWRENCE AVE
PARKHURST RD
ALVERSTONE RD
Little Ilford Park
Wks
Sir John Heron Prim Sch
SCHOOL RD
VERNON AVE
HARCOURT AVE
SIXTH AVE
TREVELYAN AVE
BRANCASTER RD
SHERINGHAM AVE
DERSINGHAM AVE
Avenue Prim Sch
HERBERT RD
GREENHILL GR
MEANLEY RD
FIRST AVE
SECOND AVE
THIRD AVE
FOURTH AVE
CRANBOURNE RD
SALISBURY RD
SNOWSHILL RD
NINE ACRES CL
MARABOU CL
St Winefride's RC Prim Sch
E12
CHURCH RD
ST MARY'S APP
ST WINEFRIDE'S AVE
Little Ilford Sch
RECTORY RD
ELSENHAM RD
LANDSEER AVE
GAINSBOROUGH AVE
Little Ilford
DORE AVE
LEIGHTON AVE
LEADER AVE
REYNOLDS AVE
MILLAIS AVE
Allot Gdns
BLUEBELL AVE
QUEENSBERRY PL
Grange Park Cemy
WARWICK RD
RIXSEN RD
LEAMINGTON CL
MORRIS AVE
MANPREET CT
MALLARD CT
BERKELEY RD
STANLEY RD
SHERIDAN RD
CHESTERFORD RD
BARRINGTON RD
FRANK BAILEY WLK
Pl Fld
THE ELMS
COLERIDGE AVE
ESSEX RD
Essex Prim Sch
RUSKIN AVE
GOLDSMITH AVE
BROWNING RD
HATHAWAY CRES
Plashet
Plashet Jewish Cemy
ROSEBERY AVE
SHELLEY AVE
BYRON AVE
KENSINGTON AVE
SHAKESPEARE CRES
KEMP HO
STEVENAGE RD
WALTER RODNEY CL
Sports Gd
Newham
LINCOLN RD
Tenn Cts
WOODHOUSE GR
Kensington Prim Sch
WORDSWORTH AVE
GLADSTONE AVE
THE BEECHES
TENNYSON
EAST AVE
Plashet Park
East Ham Meml
Bwg Gn
B165
SIBLEY GR
SOUTHEND RD
SHOEBURY RD
SPRINGFIELD RD
NORTHFIELD RD
ASHFORD RD
LEIGH RD
BALDWIN HO
WATSON AVE
BURGESS CT
PLASHET GR
COWPER AVE
Plashet Sch
East Ham
E6
MILTON AVE
THE FIRS
LYDEARD RD
BRIDGE RD
BURGES RD
LATHOM RD
CLEMENTS RD
CAULFIELD RD
CALEDON RD
HOLLAND RD
WALL END RD
BURGES RD
THE WILLOWS
HART CT
HEIGHAM RD
COLVIN
ACORN CT
BENDISH RD
Lathom Jun Sch
LAWRENCE RD
B109
OUTRAM RD
HOLME RD
KEPPEL RD
ALTMORE
Altmore Inf Sch
SKEFFINGTON RD
MALVERN RD
STAMFORD RD
SPENCER RD
BEDFORD
CALVERTON RD
ST OLAVE'S RD
Recn Gd
Barking Flyover
A124
Park Sch for Girls
GREENWAY
PARK AVE
INGLEBY RD
COVENTRY
BOURNE RD
WARWICK GDNS
AIRLIE GDNS
CATHURST RD
WELLESLEY RD
ADELAIDE RD
Glenarm Coll
GRANVILLE RD
MORLAND RD
Cranbrook Coll
A123
MANSFIELD RD
Apex Prim Sch
ARGYLE RD
BEAL RD
BELGRAVE RD
SELBORNE RD
RIGBY MEWS
HERON CT
BALFOUR RD
The Exchange
HAINAULT ST
MYRTLE RD
LEY ST
STATION RD
ILFORD
Ilford
YORK RD
YORK MEWS
YORK PL
A118
HIGH RD
CHADWICK RD
OAKFIELD RD
CLEMENTS RD
CLEMENTS LA
ILFORD HILL
CHAPEL RD
WINSTON WAY
Ilford Mus
Ilford Interchange
MILL RD
PRIOR RD
RODEN ST
READS CL
Winston Way Prim Sch
AUDREY RD
BRITANNIA RD
CLEVELAND RD
BEDFORD RD
RUTLAND RD
DUDLEY
Cleveland Jun & Inf Schs
NORTH CIRCULAR RD
RIVERDENE RD
FALLAIZE AVE
KENNETH AVE
BENGAL RD
NIGEL MEWS
FERNWAYS
CECIL RD
Rec Gd
HAMILTON RD
HOWARD RD
ILFORD LA
ELTISLEY RD
THORNTON RD
SANDYHILL RD
LOWBROOK RD
MADRAS RD
MADRAS HO
HENLEY CT
MAY TERR
JERSEY RD
NATAL RD
PAGET RD
PRETORIA RD
MAYVILLE RD
HICKLING RD
BADEN RD
ST LUKE'S AVE
BAXTER RD
WINGATE RD
Uphall Prim Sch
KHARTOUM RD
HUNTERS RD
FORSYTHIA CL
WISTERIA CL
HARVEY RD
LAVENDER PL
JASMINE CL
UPHALL RD
NORMAN RD
AZALEA CL
DAHLIA GDNS
TULIP GDNS
SAXON RD
CONIFER CT
ROMAN RD
BLUEBELL WAY
LUPIN CRES
ROSE CT
HYACINTH CL
FAIRFIELD RD
Redbridge
VICTORIA RD
3 HONEYSUCKLE CT
4 BERBERIS CT
Barking & Dagenham
WEST HO
ASHDOWN
LOXFORD
GURNEY CL
CROWS RD
HARTS LA
NORTH ST
MERSEA HO 1
COLNE HO 2
CAPE CL
IG11
Riverside Works
River Roding
COWBRIDGE LA
Pacific Wharf
HERTFORD RD
Superstore
WHITING AVE
Lighted Lady
LONDON RD
Superstore
ABBEY RD
HIGHBRIDGE RD
Pl Fld

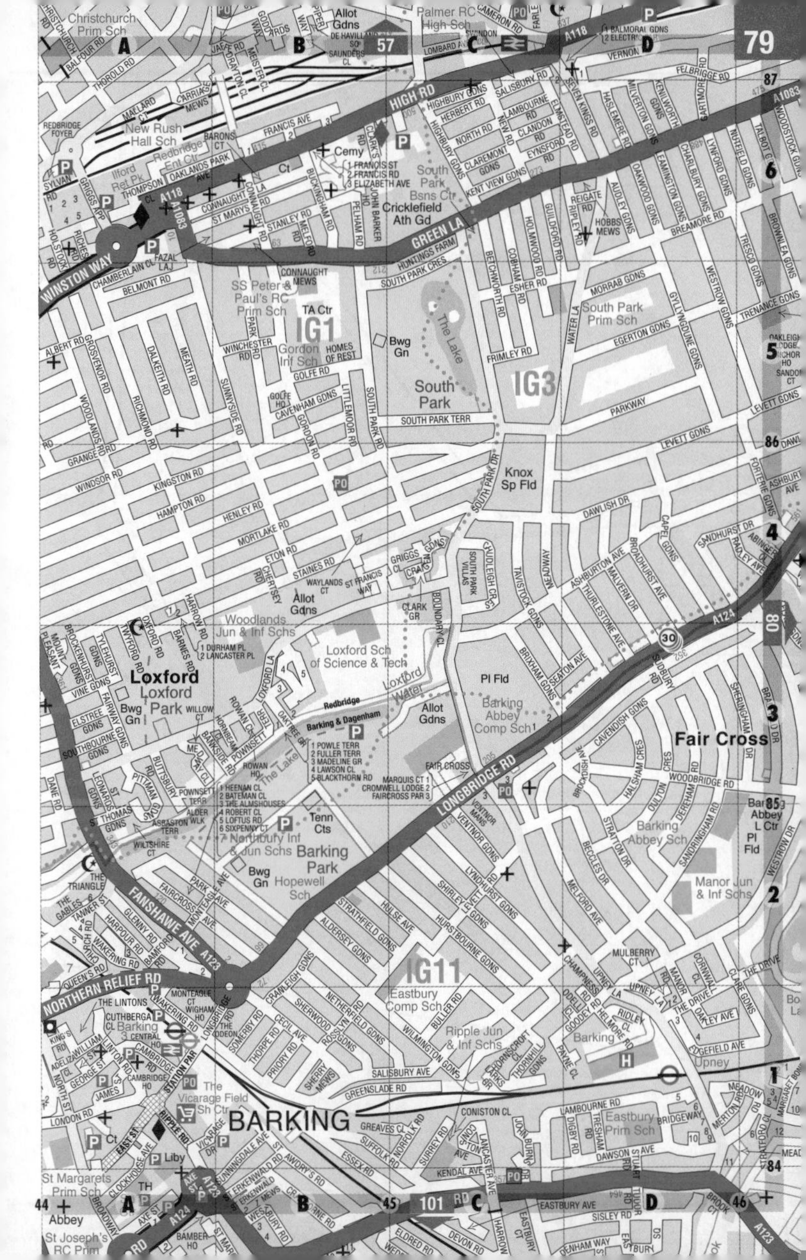

79
A
B
C
D
57
87
86
85
84
6
5
4
3
2
1
44
45
46
80
101
Christchurch Prim Sch
Palmer RC High Sch
Allot Gdns
HIGH RD
GREEN LA
A118
A1083
A124
A123
WINSTON WAY
New Rush Hall Sch
Redbridge Ent Ctr
Ilford Ret Pk
REDBRIDGE FOYER
Cemy
South Park Bsns Ctr
Cricklefield Ath Gd
SS Peter & Paul's RC Prim Sch
TA Ctr
IG1
Gordon Inf Sch
HOMES OF REST
Bwg Gn
The Lake
South Park
IG3
South Park Prim Sch
SOUTH PARK TERR
PARKWAY
LEVETT GDNS
Knox Sp Fld
SOUTH PARK DR
DAWLISH DR
ASHBURTON AVE
Allot Gdns
Woodlands Jun & Inf Schs
Loxford Sch of Science & Tech
Loxford Water
Loxford
Loxford Park
Redbridge
Barking & Dagenham
Pl Fld
Barking Abbey Comp Sch
Fair Cross
LONGBRIDGE RD
Barking Abbey Sch
Barking Abbey L Ctr
Manor Jun & Inf Schs
Tenn Cts
Northbury Inf & Jun Schs
Barking Park
Hopewell Sch
FANSHAWE AVE
NORTHERN RELIEF RD
IG11
Eastbury Comp Sch
Ripple Jun & Inf Schs
Barking
Upney
The Vicarage Field Sh Ctr
BARKING
Eastbury Prim Sch
St Margarets Prim Sch
Abbey
St Joseph's RC Prim
Liby
TH
EASTBURY AVE
KENDAL AVE
SALISBURY AVE
GREENSLADE RD
STATION PAR
RIPPLE RD
EAST ST
LONDON RD

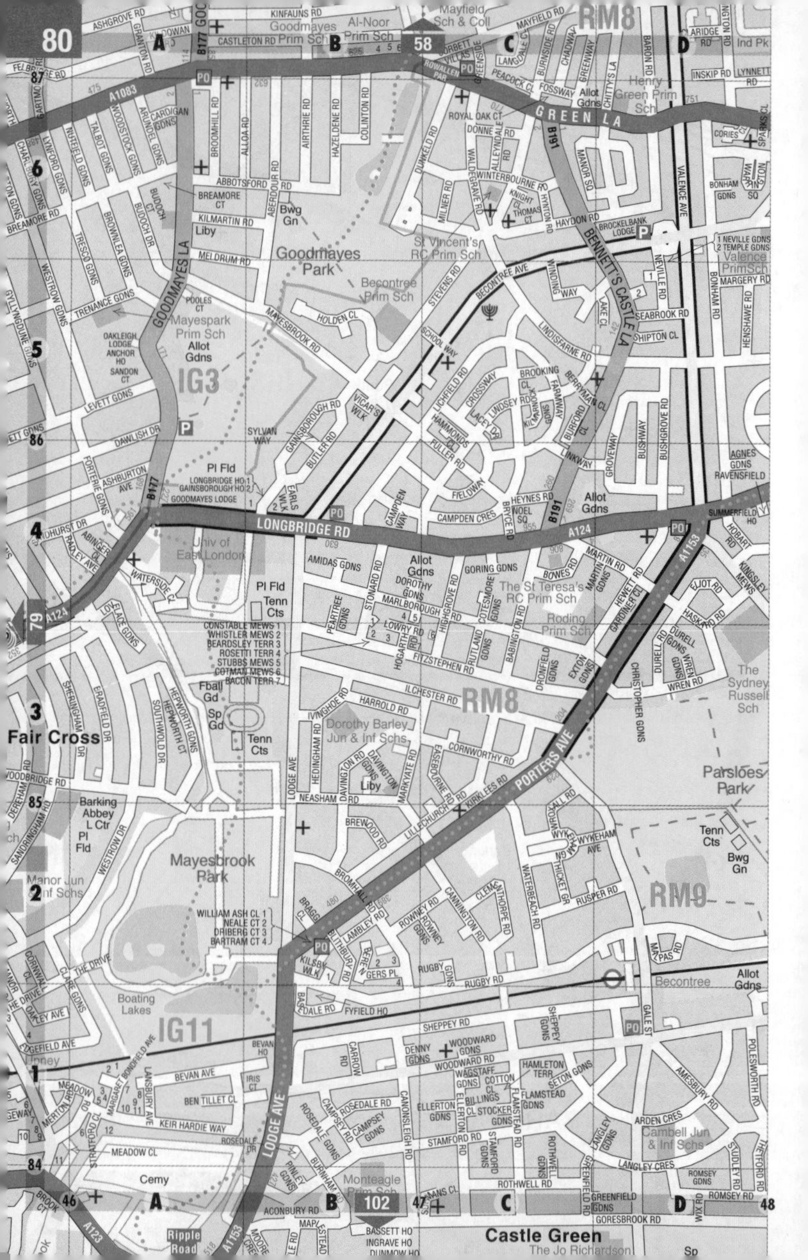

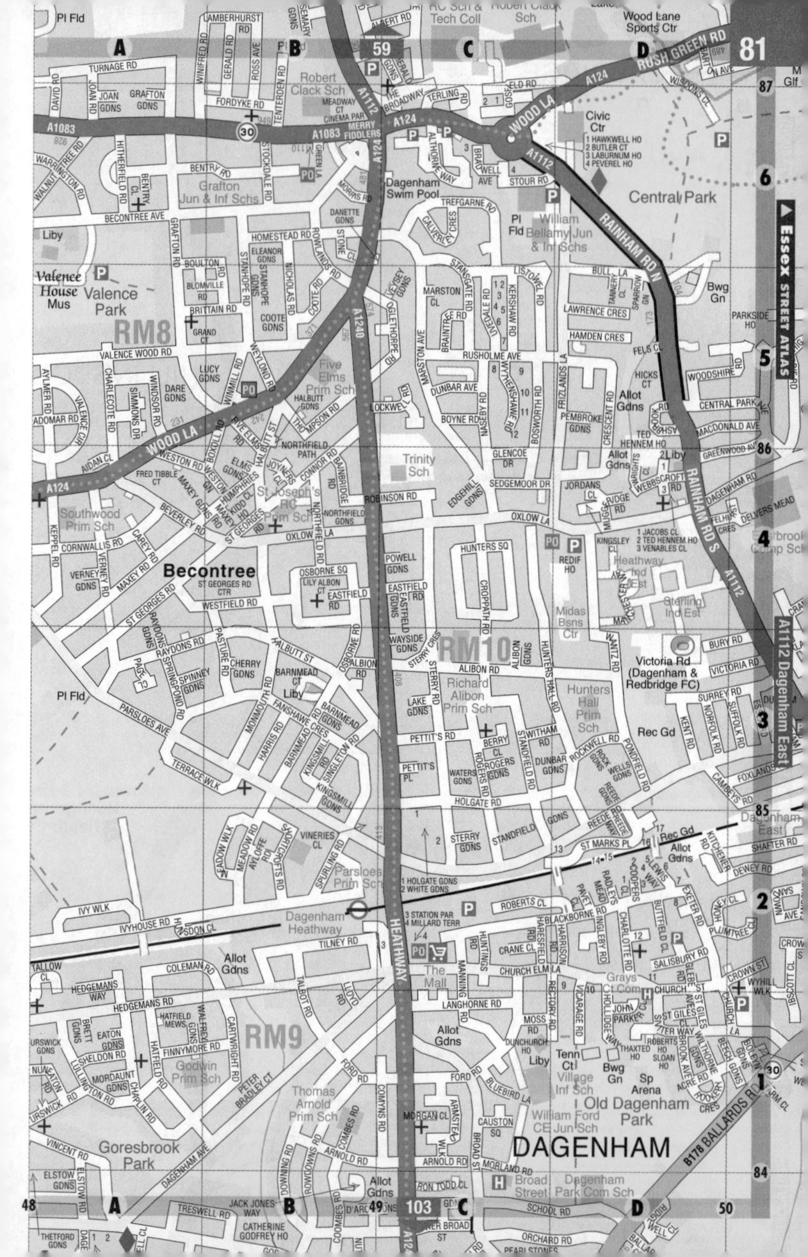
A
B
C
D
59
103
87
86
85
84
6
5
4
3
2
1
48
49
50
Essex STREET ATLAS
RM8
RM9
RM10
Becontree
DAGENHAM
Valence House Mus
Valence Park
Central Park
Goresbrook Park
Old Dagenham Park
Wood Lane Sports Ctr
Robert Clack Sch
Civic Ctr
1 HAWKWELL HO
2 BUTLER CT
3 LABURNUM HO
4 PEVEREL HO
Dagenham Swim Pool
William Bellamy Jun & Inf Schs
Grafton Jun & Inf Schs
Five Elms Prim Sch
Trinity Sch
St Joseph's RC Prim Sch
Southwood Prim Sch
Richard Alibon Prim Sch
Hunters Hall Prim Sch
Parsloes Prim Sch
Godwin Prim Sch
Thomas Arnold Prim Sch
William Ford CE Jun Sch
Village Inf Sch
Dagenham Park Com Sch
Victoria Rd (Dagenham & Redbridge FC)
Heathway Ind Est
Sterling Ind Est
Midas Bsns Ctr
Dagenham Heathway
Dagenham East
The Mall
Grays Ct Com
Allot Gdns
Rec Gd
Pl Fld
Liby
Bwg Gn
Sp Arena
1 JACOBS CL
2 TED HENNEM HO
3 VENABLES CL
1 HOLGATE GDNS
2 WHITE GDNS
3 STATION PAR
4 MILLARD TERR
A1083
A124
A1112
A1240
B178
WOOD LA
RUSH GREEN RD
RAINHAM RD N
RAINHAM RD S
A1112 Dagenham East
HEATHWAY
BALLARDS RD
BECONTREE AVE
VALENCE WOOD RD
OXLOW LA
ALIBON RD
PARSLOES AVE
ST GEORGES RD
WESTFIELD RD
HALBUTT ST
ROBINSON RD
TILNEY RD
CHURCH ELM LA
LANGHORNE RD
FORD RD
ARNOLD RD
SCHOOL RD
CHURCH ST
CHURCH LA
HEDGEMANS RD
IVYHOUSE RD
RUSHOLME AVE
OXLOW LA
HUNTERS HALL RD
VICTORIA RD
BURY RD
CENTRAL PARK AVE
MACDONALD AVE
DAGENHAM RD
DELVERS MEAD
SALISBURY RD
CROWN ST
VINCENT RD
ORCHARD RD
TRESWELL RD
JACK JONES WAY
CATHERINE GODFREY HO

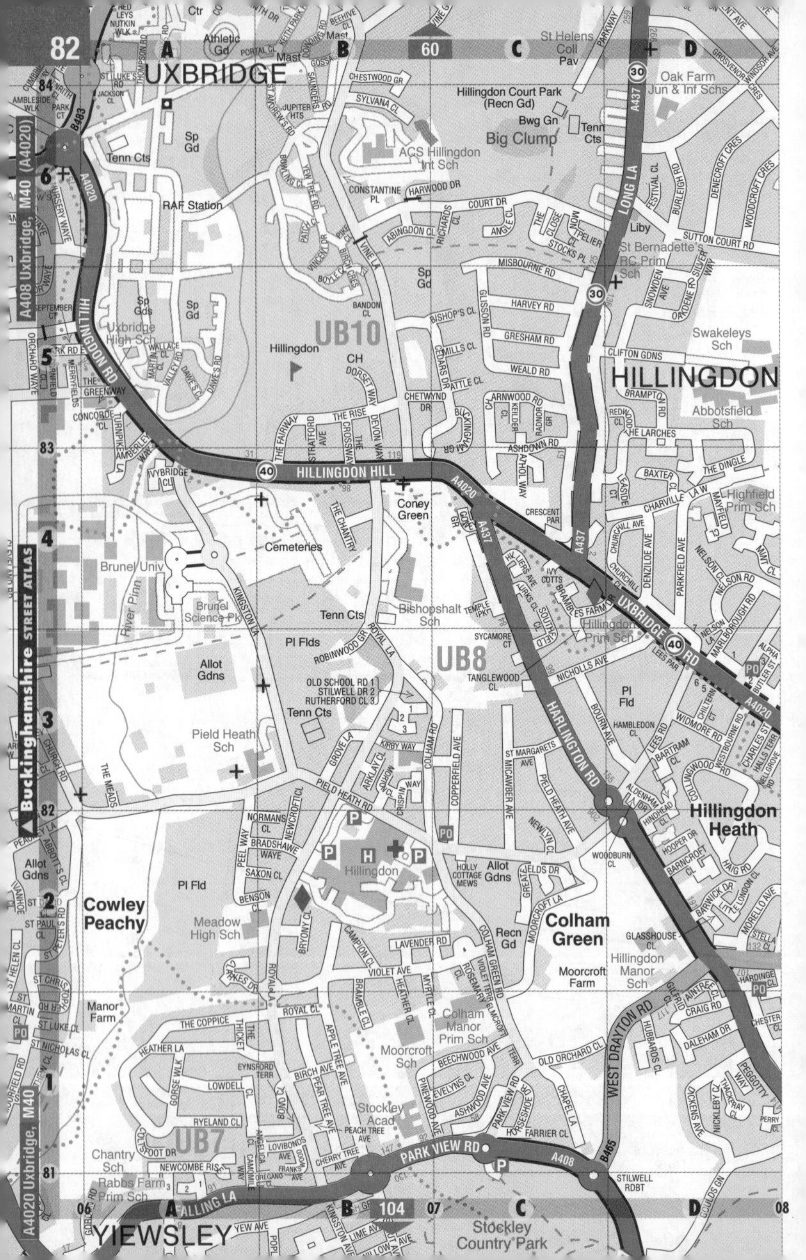
UXBRIDGE
HILLINGDON
Hillingdon Heath
Colham Green
Cowley Peachy
YIEWSLEY
UB10
UB8
UB7
HILLINGDON HILL
HILLINGDON RD
HARLINGTON RD
UXBRIDGE RD
LONG LA
PARK VIEW RD
FALLING LA
WEST DRAYTON RD
PIELD HEATH RD
COLHAM GREEN RD
KINGSTON LA
ROYAL LA
Brunel Univ
Brunel Science Pk
RAF Station
Cemeteries
Hillingdon Court Park (Recn Gd)
Big Clump
ACS Hillingdon Int Sch
St Bernadette's RC Prim Sch
Swakeleys Sch
Abbotsfield Sch
Highfield Prim Sch
Bishopshalt Sch
Hillingdon Prim Sch
Pield Heath Sch
Meadow High Sch
Colham Manor Prim Sch
Moorcroft Sch
Stockley Acad
Hillingdon Manor Sch
Chantry Sch
Rabbs Farm Prim Sch
Uxbridge High Sch
Oak Farm Jun & Inf Schs
Stockley Country Park
Moorcroft Farm
Manor Farm
Coney Green
A4020
A437
A408
B465
B483
A408 Uxbridge, M40 (A4020)
A4020 Uxbridge, M40
Buckinghamshire STREET ATLAS
60
104
A
B
C
D
06
07
08
81
82
83
84

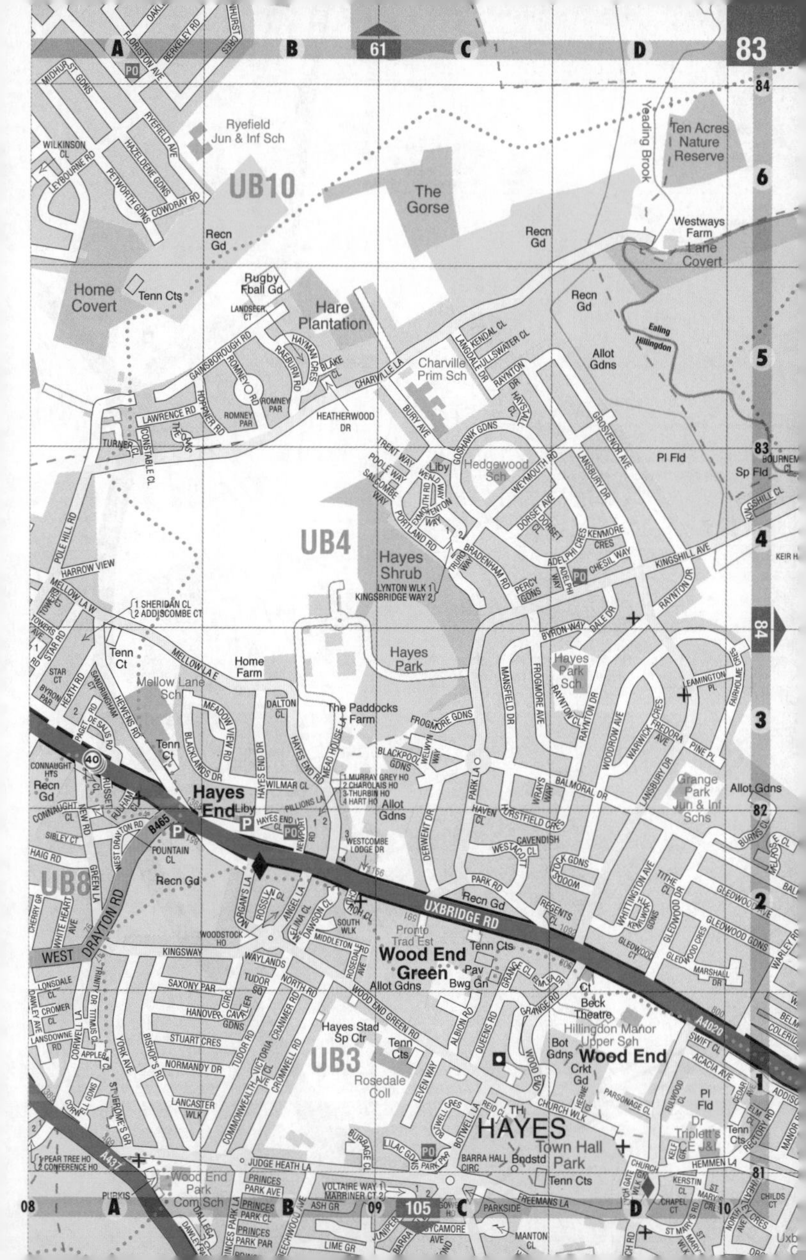
A
B
61
C
D
84
UB10
Ryefield Jun & Inf Sch
The Gorse
Yeading Brook
Ten Acres Nature Reserve
Westways Farm
Lane Covert
Recn Gd
Home Covert
Tenn Cts
Rugby Fball Gd
Hare Plantation
Ealing
Hillingdon
Allot Gdns
Charville Prim Sch
CHARVILLE LA
Hedgewood Sch
Pl Fld
Sp Fld
UB4
Hayes Shrub
Hayes Park
Home Farm
Mellow Lane Sch
The Paddocks Farm
Hayes Park Sch
KINGSHILL AVE
Grange Park Jun & Inf Schs
Hayes End
UXBRIDGE RD
Pronto Trad Est
Wood End Green
UB8
UB3
WEST DRAYTON RD
Hayes Stad Sp Ctr
Rosedale Coll
Beck Theatre
Hillingdon Manor Upper Sch
Wood End
Bot Gdns
Crkt Gd
HAYES
Town Hall Park
Dr Triplett's CE J&I
Wood End Park Com Sch
A4020
A437
B465
FREEMANS LA
08
09
105
10

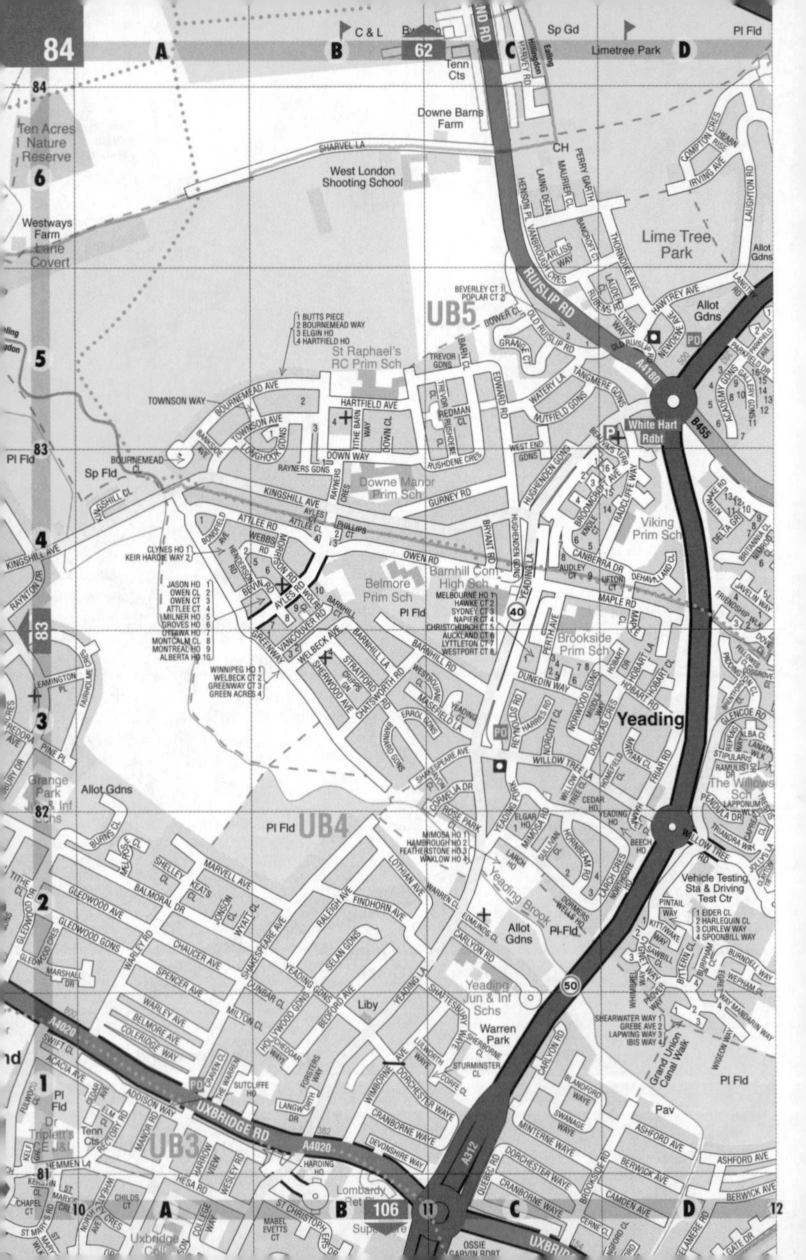

A
B
C
D
62
C & L
Tenn Cts
Sp Gd
Limetree Park
Pl Fld
Downe Barns Farm
Ten Acres Nature Reserve
SHARVEL LA
West London Shooting School
Westways Farm
Lane Covert
Lime Tree Park
UB5
St Raphael's RC Prim Sch
Downe Manor Prim Sch
Belmore Prim Sch
Barnhill Com High Sch
Viking Prim Sch
Brookside Prim Sch
Yeading
White Hart Rdbt
RUISLIP RD
A4180
B455
Sp Fld
KINGSHILL AVE
OWEN RD
UB4
Pl Fld
Grange Park Jun & Inf Schs
Allot Gdns
The Willows Sch
Vehicle Testing Sta & Driving Test Ctr
Yeading Brook
Yeading Jun & Inf Schs
Warren Park
Liby
Grand Union Canal Walk
Pav
A4020
UXBRIDGE RD
A312
UB3
Dr Triplett's CE J&I
Lombardy Ret Pk
106
Uxbridge Coll
OSSIE GARVIN RDBT
1 BUTTS PIECE
2 BOURNEMEAD WAY
3 ELGIN HO
4 HARTFIELD HO
BEVERLEY CT 1
POPLAR CT 2
CLYNES HO 1
KEIR HARDIE WAY 2
JASON HO 1
OWEN CL 2
OWEN CT 3
ATTLEE CT 4
MILNER HO 5
GROVES HO 6
OTTAWA HO 7
MONTCALM CL 8
MONTREAL HO 9
ALBERTA HO 10
WINNIPEG HO 1
WELBECK CT 2
GREENWAY CT 3
GREEN ACRES 4
MELBOURNE HO 1
HAWKE CT 2
SYDNEY CT 3
NAPIER CT 4
CHRISTCHURCH CT 5
AUCKLAND CT 6
LYTTLETON CT 7
WESTPORT CT 8
MIMOSA HO 1
HAMBROUGH HO 2
FEATHERSTONE HO 3
WAXLOW HO 4
1 EIDER CL
2 HARLEQUIN CL
3 CURLEW WAY
4 SPOONBILL WAY
SHEARWATER WAY 1
GREBE AVE 2
LAPWING WAY 3
IBIS WAY 4

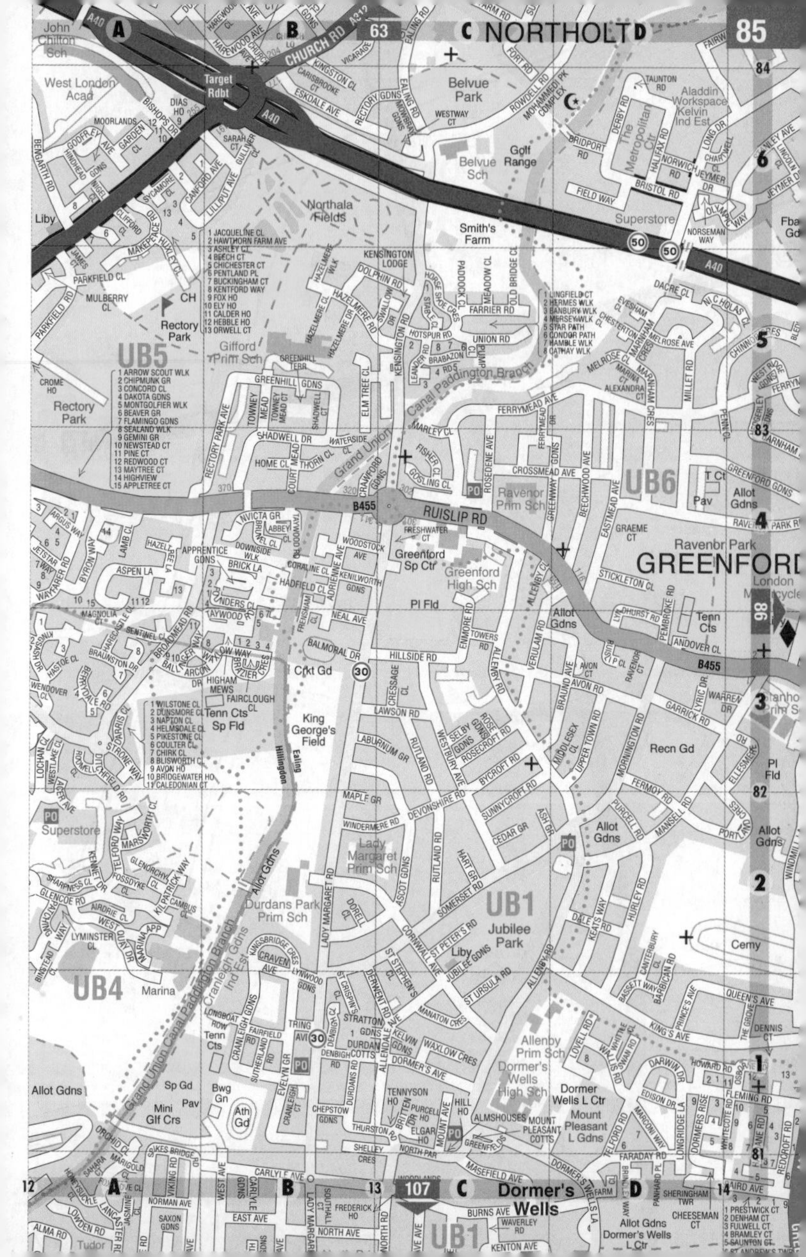
NORTHOLT
A
B
C
D
63
A40
A312
CHURCH RD
John Chilton Sch
West London Acad
Target Rdbt
Belvue Park
Belvue Sch
Golf Range
MOHAMMEDI PK COMPLEX
Aladdin Workspace
Kelvin Ind Est
The Metropolitan Ctr
Superstore
Northala Fields
Smith's Farm
Liby
Rectory Park
Gifford Prim Sch
UB5
CH
1 JACQUELINE CL
2 HAWTHORN FARM AVE
3 ASHLEY CT
4 BEECH CT
5 CHICHESTER CT
6 PENTLAND PL
7 BUCKINGHAM CT
8 KENTFORD WAY
9 FOX HO
10 ELY HO
11 CALDER HO
12 HEBBLE HO
13 ORWELL CT
1 ARROW SCOUT WLK
2 CHIPMUNK GR
3 CONCORD CL
4 DAKOTA GDNS
5 MONTGOLFIER WLK
6 BEAVER GR
7 FLAMINGO GDNS
8 SEALAND WLK
9 GEMINI GR
10 NEWSTEAD CT
11 PINE CT
12 REDWOOD CT
13 MAYTREE CT
14 HIGHVIEW
15 APPLETREE CT
1 LINGFIELD CT
2 HERMES WLK
3 BANBURY WLK
4 MERSEY WLK
5 STAR PATH
6 CONDOR PATH
7 HAMBLE WLK
8 CATHAY WLK
Grand Union Canal Paddington Branch
UB6
Ravenor Prim Sch
B455
RUISLIP RD
Greenford Sp Ctr
Greenford High Sch
Pl Fld
GREENFORD
Ravenor Park
Allot Gdns
Tenn Cts
Crkt Gd
King George's Field
Tenn Cts Sp Fld
1 WILSTONE CL
2 DUNSMORE CL
3 NAPTON CL
4 HELMSDALE CL
5 PIKESTONE CL
6 COULTER CL
7 CHIRK CL
8 BLISWORTH CL
9 AVON HO
10 BRIDGEWATER HO
11 CALEDONIAN CT
Recn Gd
Superstore
Lady Margaret Prim Sch
Durdans Park Prim Sch
UB1
Jubilee Park
Cemy
UB4
Marina
Cranleigh Gdns Ind Est
Allenby Prim Sch
Dormer's Wells High Sch
Dormer Wells L Ctr
Mount Pleasant L Gdns
Sp Gd
Pav
Bwg Gn
Mini Glf Crs
Ath Gd
Allot Gdns
107
Dormer's Wells
1 PRESTWICK CT
2 DENHAM CT
3 FULWELL CT
4 BRAMLEY CT
5 SAUNTON CT
Cheeseman CT
Allot Gdns
Dormer's Wells L Ctr
UB1
12
13
14
98

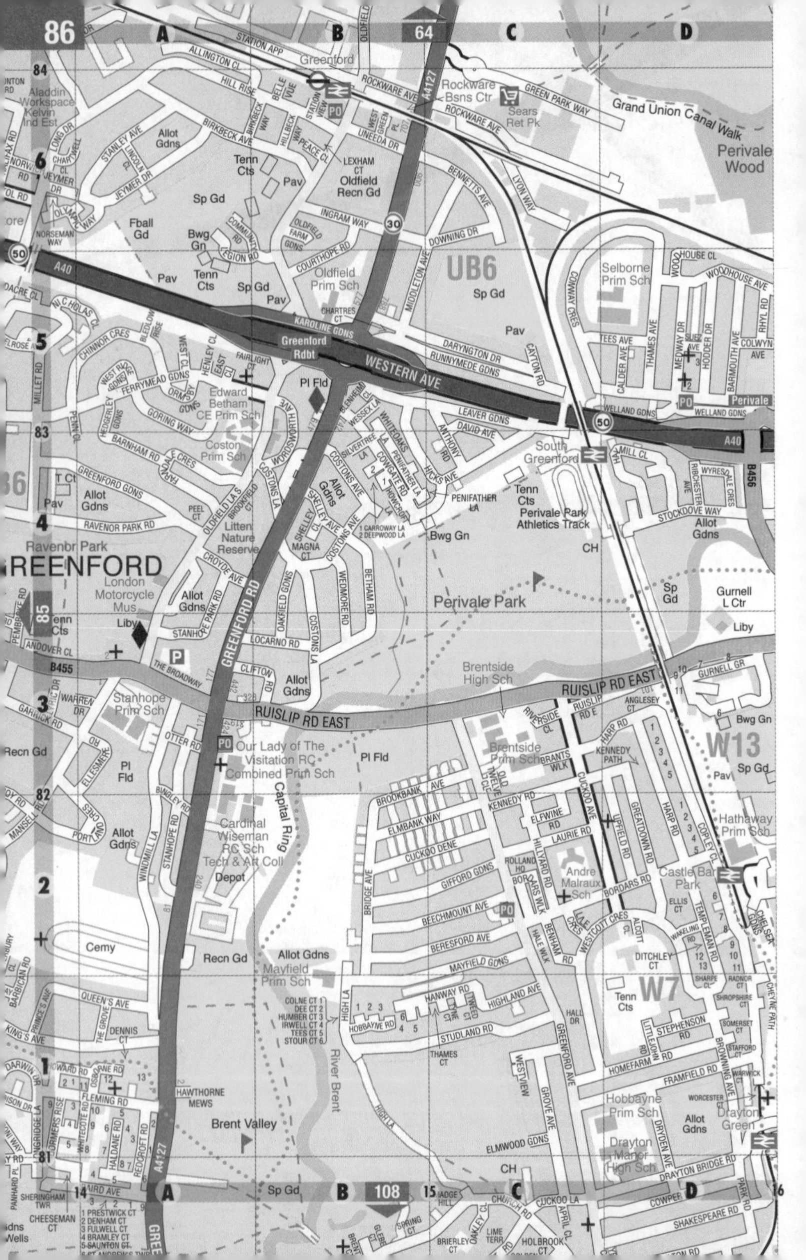
A
B
C
D
64
STATION APP
ALLINGTON CL
Greenford
HILL RISE
BELLE VUE
ROCKWARE AVE
Rockware Bsns Ctr
GREEN PARK WAY
Sears Ret Pk
Grand Union Canal Walk
Perivale Wood
Aladdin Workspace
Kelvin Ind Est
84
BIRKBECK AVE
STANLEY AVE
LINCOLN CL
Allot Gdns
HILLBECK WAY
PEACE CL
UNEEDA DR
LEXHAM CT
Oldfield Recn Gd
BENNETTS AVE
LYON WAY
JEYMER DR
Tenn Cts
Pav
Sp Gd
Fball Gd
Bwg Gn
INGRAM WAY
COMMUNITY RD
OLDFIELD FARM GDNS
LEGION RD
COURTHOPE RD
DOWNING DR
A4127
30
50
A40
NORSEMAN WAY
OLYMPIC WAY
6
UB6
Oldfield Prim Sch
MIDDLETON AVE
CONWAY CRES
Selborne Prim Sch
WOODHOUSE CL
WOODHOUSE AVE
CHARTRES CT
KAROLINE GDNS
Greenford Rdbt
WESTERN AVE
DARYNGTON DR
RUNNYMEDE GDNS
CAYTON RD
TEES AVE
THAMES AVE
CALDER AVE
MEDWAY DR
HODDER DR
BARMOUTH AVE
RHYL RD
COLWYN AVE
NICHOLAS GDNS
CHINNOR CRES
BLEDLOW RISE
WEST CL
HENLEY CL
EAST CL
FAIRLIGHT CT
5
WEST RIDGE GDNS
FERRYMEAD GDNS
ORMSBY GDNS
Edward Betham CE Prim Sch
Pl Fld
BLENHEIM CL
WESSEX LA
WHITEOAKS LA
LEAVER GDNS
DAVID AVE
ANTHONY RD
WELLAND GDNS
Perivale
MILLET RD
HEDGERLEY GDNS
GORING WAY
BARNHAM RD
FARRDALE CRES
Coston Prim Sch
WORDSWORTH AVE
SILVERTREE LA
PENIFATHER LA
COWGATE RD
HICKS AVE
South Greenford
HAMILL CL
RIBCHESTER AVE
WYRESDALE CRES
B456
83
GREENFORD GDNS
T Ct
Pav
Allot Gdns
PEEL CT
OLDFIELD LA S
BROOKFIELD CT
COSTONS LA
COSTONS AVE
SHELLEY AVE
HOWCROFT LA
PENIFATHER LA
1 CARROWAY LA
2 DEEPWOOD LA
Tenn Cts
Perivale Park Athletics Track
STOCKDOVE WAY
RAVENOR PARK RD
4
Litten Nature Reserve
MAGNA CT
Bwg Gn
CH
Ravenbr Park
GREENFORD
London Motorcycle Mus
CROYDE AVE
Allot Gdns
STANHOPE PARK RD
OAKFIELD GDNS
WEDMORE RD
BETHAM RD
Perivale Park
Sp Gd
Gurnell L Ctr
Liby
85
PEMBROKE RD
Tenn Cts
Liby
ANDOVER CL
GREENFORD RD
LOCARNO RD
COSTONS LA
CLIFTON RD
B455
THE BROADWAY
Brentside High Sch
RUISLIP RD EAST
GURNELL GR
WARREN DR
Stanhope Prim Sch
Allot Gdns
3
GARRICK RD
RUISLIP RD EAST
RIVERSIDE CL
RUISLIP RD E
ANGLESEY CT
Bwg Gn
OTTER RD
Our Lady of The Visitation RC Combined Prim Sch
Pl Fld
Brentside Prim Sch
BRANTS WLK
HARP RD
KENNEDY PATH
W13
Recn Gd
ELLESMERE RD
Pl Fld
OLD TWELVE CL
Pav
Sp Gd
82
MANSELL RD
PORTLAND CRES
Allot Gdns
BINGLEY RD
BROOKBANK AVE
KENNEDY RD
CUCKOO AVE
ELMBANK WAY
ELFWINE RD
LAURIE RD
UPFIELD RD
GREATDOWN RD
COPLEY CL
Hathaway Prim Sch
Cardinal Wiseman RC Sch Tech & Art Coll
Capital Ring
CUCKOO DENE
HILLYARD RD
Andre Malraux Sch
WINDMILL LA
STANHOPE RD
Depot
BRIDGE AVE
GIFFORD GDNS
ROLLAND HO
BORDARS WLK
BORDARS RD
Castle Bar Park
2
ELLIS CT
TEMPLEMAN RD
BEECHMOUNT AVE
BENHAM RD
LYLE CRES
WESTCOTT CRES
ALCOTT CL
WAKELING RD
Cemy
BERESFORD AVE
HALE WLK
CHELSEA GDNS
Recn Gd
Allot Gdns
Mayfield Prim Sch
MAYFIELD GDNS
DITCHLEY CT
BARBICAN RD
QUEEN'S AVE
PRINCE'S AVE
HANWAY RD
HIGHLAND AVE
W7
Tenn Cts
SHARPE CL
RADNOR CT
SHROPSHIRE CT
CHEYNE PATH
COLNE CT 1
DEE CT 2
HUMBER CT 3
IRWELL CT 4
TEES CT 5
STOUR CT 6
HIGH LA
HOBBAYNE RD
TWEED CT
TYNE CT
HALL DR
THE GROVE
DENNIS CT
KING'S AVE
STUDLAND RD
THAMES CT
STEPHENSON RD
LITTLEJOHN RD
SOMERSET CT
STAFFORD CT
River Brent
GREENFORD AVE
WESTVIEW
HOMEFARM RD
1
DARWIN DR
HOWARD RD
OSBORNE RD
FLEMING RD
HAWTHORNE MEWS
FRAMFIELD RD
BROWNING AVE
WARWICK CT
WORCESTER CT
FORMERS RISE
WHITECOTE RD
HALDANE RD
REDCROFT RD
Brent Valley
HIGH LA
GROVE AVE
Hobbayne Prim Sch
DRYDEN AVE
Allot Gdns
Drayton Green
81
LONGRIDGE LA
ELMWOOD GDNS
Drayton Manor High Sch
DRAYTON BRIDGE RD
CH
PANHARD PL
SHERINGHAM TWR
14
LAIRD AVE
Sp Gd
108
15
CHURCH RD
CUCKOO LA
APRIL CL
COWPER RD
PARK RD
16
CHEESEMAN CT
1 PRESTWICK CT
2 DENHAM CT
3 FULWELL CT
4 BRAMLEY CT
5 SAUNTON CT
GLEBE CL
SPRING CT
BRIERLEY CT
OAKLEY CL
LIME TERR
HOLBROOK CT
SHAKESPEARE RD

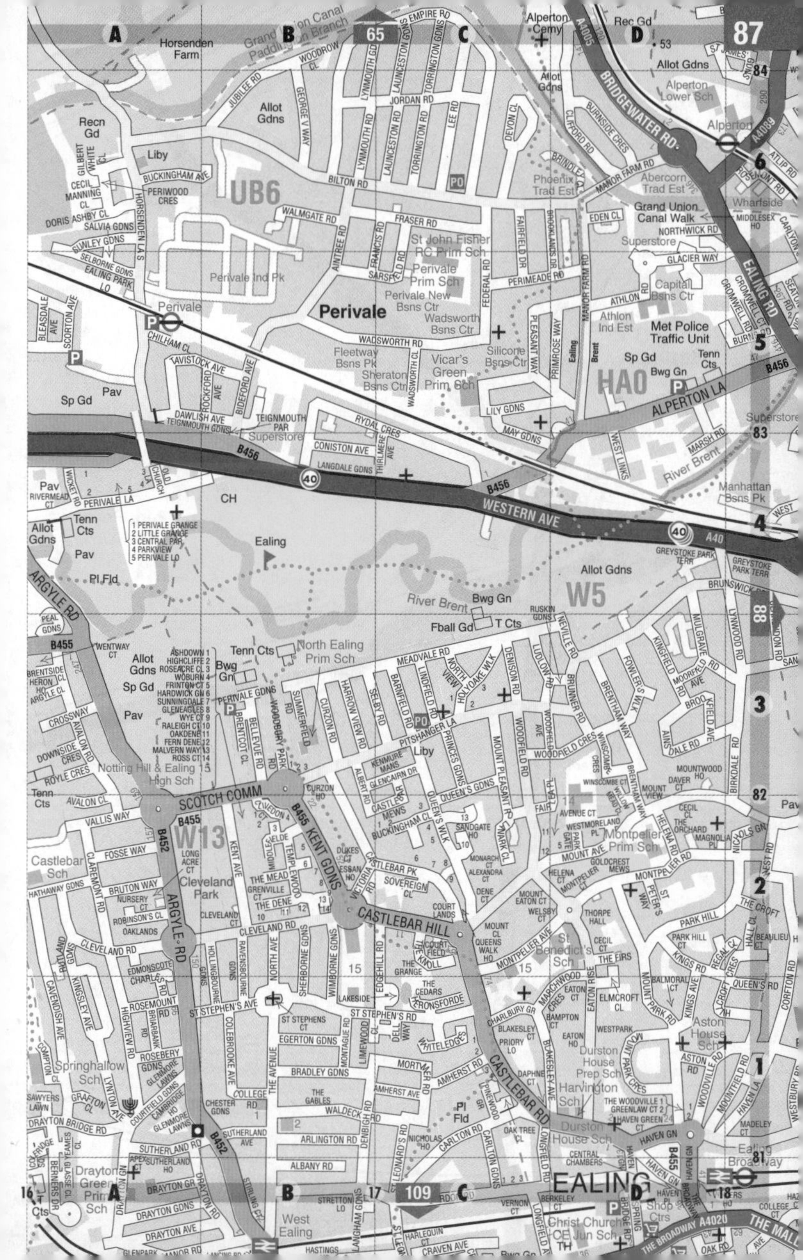
A
B
C
D
65
Horsenden Farm
Grand Union Canal Paddington Branch
Alperton Cemy
Rec Gd
Allot Gdns
Alperton Lower Sch
Alperton
BRIDGEWATER RD
Recn Gd
Liby
UB6
Allot Gdns
EMPIRE RD
WOODROW CL
JUBILEE RD
GEORGE V WAY
LYNMOUTH GD
LAUNCESTON GDNS
TORRINGTON GDNS
JORDAN RD
LAUNCESTON RD
TORRINGTON RD
LEE RD
DEVON CL
CLIFFORD RD
BURNSIDE CRES
BRINDLEY CL
MANOR FARM RD
Phoenix Trad Est
Abercorn Trad Est
Grand Union Canal Walk
Wharfside
MIDDLESEX HO
EDEN CL
NORTHWICK RD
Superstore
GLACIER WAY
EALING RD
GILBERT WHITE CL
BUCKINGHAM AVE
PERIWOOD CRES
CECIL MANNING CL
DORIS ASHBY CL
SALVIA GDNS
GUNLEY GDNS
SELBORNE GDNS
EALING PARK LO
HORSENDEN LA S
BILTON RD
WALMGATE RD
FRASER RD
AINTREE RD
FRANCIS RD
SARSFIELD RD
St John Fisher RC Prim Sch
Perivale Prim Sch
Perivale New Bsns Ctr
Wadsworth Bsns Ctr
FAIRFIELD DR
BROOKLANDS DR
PERIMEADE RD
FEDERAL RD
Perivale Ind Pk
Perivale
Capital Bsns Ctr
ATHLON RD
Athlon Ind Est
Met Police Traffic Unit
CROMWELL RD
BURNS RD
PLEASANT WAY
PRIMROSE WAY
Ealing
Brent
Sp Gd
Tenn Cts
Bwg Gn
HA0
ALPERTON LA
B456
BLEASDALE AVE
SCORTON AVE
CHILHAM CL
WADSWORTH RD
Fleetway Bsns Pk
Sheraton Bsns Ctr
Vicar's Green Prim Sch
Silicone Bsns Ctr
TAVISTOCK AVE
ROCKFORD AVE
BIDEFORD AVE
DAWLISH AVE
TEIGNMOUTH PAR
TEIGNMOUTH GDNS
Superstore
RYDAL CRES
CONISTON AVE
THIRLMERE AVE
LANGDALE GDNS
LILY GDNS
MAY GDNS
WEST LINKS
MARSH RD
River Brent
83
Manhattan Bsns Pk
Sp Gd
Pav
WICKET RD
RIVERMEAD CT
PERIVALE LA
OLD CHURCH LA
CH
40
WESTERN AVE
A40
Allot Gdns
Tenn Cts
Pav
1 PERIVALE GRANGE
2 LITTLE GRANGE
3 CENTRAL PAR
4 PARKVIEW
5 PERIVALE LO
Ealing
Pl Fld
GREYSTOKE PARK TERR
Allot Gdns
W5
BRUNSWICK RD
ARGYLE RD
River Brent
Bwg Gn
Fball Gd
T Cts
RUSKIN GDNS
88
PEAL GDNS
B455
WENTWAY CT
Allot Gdns
Sp Gd
Pav
ASHDOWN 1
HIGHCLIFFE 2
ROSEACRE CL 3
WOBURN 4
FRINTON CT 5
HARDWICK GN 6
SUNNINGDALE 7
GLENEAGLES 8
WYE CT 9
RALEIGH CT 10
OAKDENE 11
FERN DENE 12
MALVERN WAY 13
ROSS CT 14
Tenn Cts
Bwg Gn
North Ealing Prim Sch
MEADVALE RD
NEVILLE RD
BRUNNER RD
FOWLER'S WK
KINGSFIELD RD
MULGRAVE RD
LYNWOOD RD
BRENTSIDE
HERON CL
ARGYLE CL
CROSSWAY
AVALON RD
DOWNSIDE CRES
ROYLE CRES
PERIVALE GDNS
BRENTCOT CL
BELLEVUE RD
WOODBURY PARK RD
SUMMERFIELD RD
CURZON RD
HARROW VIEW RD
SELBY RD
BARNFIELD RD
LINDFIELD RD
NORTH VIEW
HOLYOAKE WLK
DENISON RD
LUDLOW RD
BRENTHAM WAY
MOORFIELD RD
BROOKFIELD AVE
AINSDALE RD
PITSHANGER LA
PRINCES GDNS
MOUNT PLEASANT RD
WOODFIELD RD
WOODFIELD AVE
WOODFIELD CRES
WINSCOMBE CRES
Liby
KENMURE MANS
GLENCAIRN DR
ALBERT RD
CASTLEBAR MEWS
QUEEN'S GDNS
QUEEN'S WLK
BUCKINGHAM CL
SANDGATE HO
Notting Hill & Ealing High Sch
Tenn Cts
AVALON CL
SCOTCH COMM
CURZON HO
B455
KENT GDNS
VALLIS WAY
W13
B452
BIRKDALE RD
MOUNTWOOD HO
DAVER CT
MOUNT VIEW
82
Pav
AVENUE CT
WESTMORELAND PL
PARK GATE
Montpelier Prim Sch
MOUNT AVE
GOLDCREST MEWS
HELENA RD
CECIL CL
THE ORCHARD
MAGNOLIA PL
NICHOLS GN
WEST RD
Castlebar Sch
CLAREMONT RD
FOSSE WAY
LONG ACRE CT
KENT AVE
Cleveland Park
DUKES CT
CASTLEBAR PK
SOVEREIGN CL
MONARCH CT
ALEXANDRA CT
DENE CT
HELENA CT
MONTPELIER CT
MONTPELIER RD
ST PETER'S WAY
THE CROFT
2
HATHAWAY GDNS
BRUTON WAY
NURSERY CT
ROBINSON'S CL
OAKLANDS
CLEVELAND CT
THE MEAD
GRENVILLE CT
THE DENE
TEMPLEWOOD
CASTLEBAR HILL
COURT LANDS
MOUNT EATON CT
WELSBY CT
THORPE HALL
PARK HILL
ARGYLE RD
CLEVELAND RD
CLEVELAND RD
RUTLAND GDNS
EDMONSCOTE
CHARLES RD
HOLLINGBOURNE GDNS
RAVENSBOURNE GDNS
NORTH AVE
SHERBORNE GDNS
WIMBORNE GDNS
EDGEHILL RD
COURTFIELD
THE KNOLL
THE GRANGE
MOUNT CL
QUEENS WALK HO
MONTPELIER AVE
St Benedict's Sch
CECIL CT
THE FIRS
PARK HILL CT
KINGS RD
REGAL CL
BEAULIEU
HALL CL
CAVENDISH AVE
KINGSLEY AVE
ROSEMOUNT RD
BRIARBANK RD
HIGHVIEW RD
ST STEPHEN'S AVE
COLEBROOKE AVE
ST STEPHENS CT
LAKESIDE
THE CEDARS
HERONSFORDE
MARCHWOOD CRES
EATON CT
EATON RISE
ELMCROFT CL
MOUNT PARK RD
BALMORAL CT
KINGS AVE
QUEEN'S RD
CORFTON RD
ST STEPHEN'S RD
EGERTON GDNS
LIMEWOOD CL
DELL WAY
WHITELEDGES
CHARLBURY GR
BLAKESLEY CT
PRIORY LO
BAMPTON CT
EATON HO
WESTPARK
Aston House Sch
ASTON RD
WOODVILLE RD
MOUNTFIELD RD
COMPTON CL
Springhallow Sch
ROSEBERY GDNS
GLENMORE LAWNS
BRADLEY GDNS
MORTIMER RD
AMHERST RD
CASTLEBAR RD
DAPHNE CT
BLAKESLEY AVE
Durston House Prep Sch
Harvington Sch
HAVEN LA
1
SAWYERS LAWN
GRAFTON CL
LYNTON AVE
COURTFIELD GDNS
CAMBRIDGE HO
GLENMORE LAWNS
CHESTER GDNS
COLLEGE RD
THE AVENUE
THE GABLES
WALDECK RD
AMHERST AVE
Pl Fld
PINEWOOD GR
THE WOODVILLE
GREENLAW CT
HAVEN GREEN CT
MADELEY CT
DRAYTON BRIDGE RD
SUTHERLAND RD
SUTHERLAND AVE
ARLINGTON RD
DENBIGH RD
ST LEONARD'S RD
NICHOLAS HO
CARLTON RD
CARLTON GDNS
OAK TREE CL
LONGFIELD RD
Durston House Sch
HAVEN GN
B455
HAVEN GN
CENTRAL CHAMBERS
Ealing Broadway
81
Drayton Green Prim Sch
APEX CT
SUTHERLAND HO
ALBANY RD
DRAYTON GR
DRAYTON GDNS
DRAYTON RD
DRAYTON AVE
B452
STIRLING RD
West Ealing
STRETTON LO
LANGHAM GDNS
109
VERNON CT
BERKELEY CT
EALING
Christ Church CE Jun Sch
BRIDGE RD
SPRING BRIDGE RD
Shop Ctrs
THE BROADWAY A4020
THE MALL
COLLEGE
OAK RD
HARLEQUIN CT
CRAVEN AVE
HASTINGS
16
17
18
Cts
BERNERS DR
GLASSE CL
YEAMES CL
A4005
A4089
84
6
5
4
3
B456
ATLIP RD
ROSEMONT RD
CARLYON
SEATON

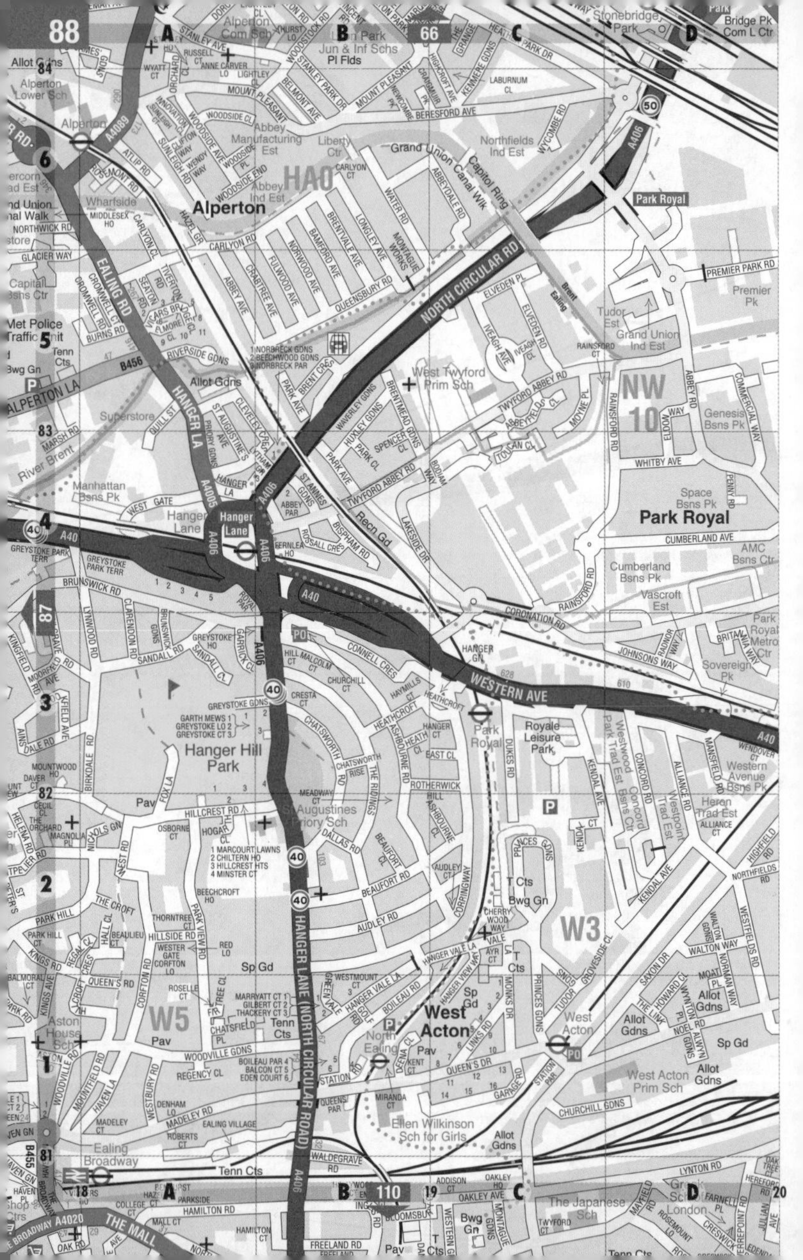
A
B
C
D
66
Alperton Com Sch
Jun & Inf Schs
Pl Flds
Stonebridge Park
Bridge Pk Com L Ctr
Allot Gdns
84
Alperton Lower Sch
STANLEY AVE
RUSSELL CT
ANNE CARVER LO
LIGHTLEY CL
WYATT CT
ORCHARD CL
MOUNT PLEASANT
BELMONT AVE
STANLEY PARK DR
WOODSTOCK RD
MOUNT PLEASANT
NEWCOMBE PK
CRAIGMUIR PK
HIGHCROFT AVE
THE GRANGE
KENMERE GDNS
HEATHER PARK DR
LABURNUM CL
BERESFORD AVE
WYCOMBE RD
50
A406
A4089
Alperton
6
INNOVATION CL
SUNLEIGH CT
WOODSIDE CL
WOODSIDE AVE
CLIFTON WAY
WENDY WAY
WOODSIDE PL
WOODSIDE END
SUNLEIGH RD
Abbey Manufacturing Est
Liberty Ctr
Grand Union Canal Wlk
Capitol Ring
Northfields Ind Est
HA0
CARLYON CT
Abbey Ind Est
ATLIP RD
ROSEMONT RD
Alperton
Wharfside
Grand Union Canal Walk
MIDDLESEX HO
NORTHWICK RD
CARLYON CL
HAZEL GR
CARLYON RD
WATER RD
ABBEYDALE RD
MONTAGUE WORKS
LONGLEY AVE
BRENTVALE AVE
BAMFORD AVE
NORWOOD AVE
FULWOOD AVE
CRABTREE AVE
ABBEY AVE
QUEENSBURY RD
Park Royal
GLACIER WAY
EALING RD
Capital Bsns Ctr
CROMWELL RD
CROMWELL CT
TIVERTON RD
SEATON CT
VICARS BR
ELMORE CL
BURNS RD
Met Police Traffic Unit
5
Tenn Cts
Bwg Gn
B456
RIVERSIDE GDNS
1 NORBRECK GDNS
2 BEECHWOOD GDNS
3 NORBRECK PAR
NORTH CIRCULAR RD
ELVEDEN PL
ELVEDEN RD
IVEAGH AVE
IVEAGH CL
Brent
Ealing
Tudor Est
Grand Union Ind Est
RAINSFORD CT
PREMIER PARK RD
Premier Pk
ALPERTON LA
Allot Gdns
HANGER LA
BRENT CRES
PARK AVE
West Twyford Prim Sch
TWYFORD ABBEY RD
NW 10
ABBEY RD
COMMERCIAL WAY
Genesis Bsns Pk
ELDON WAY
Superstore
QUILL ST
ST AUGUSTINE'S AVE
PRIORY GDNS
CLEVELEY CRES
WAVERLEY GDNS
BRENTMEAD GDNS
HUXLEY GDNS
SPENCER CL
PARK CL
ABBEYFIELDS CL
MOYNE PL
TOUCAN CL
RAINSFORD RD
83
MARSH RD
River Brent
LYTHAM
HANGER LA
ST ANNES GDNS
TWYFORD ABBEY RD
BODIAM WAY
WHITBY AVE
PERRY RD
Manhattan Bsns Pk
WEST GATE
Hanger Lane
Hanger Lane
A4005
ABBEY PAR
Space Bsns Pk
Park Royal
4
40
A40
A406
Recn Gd
LAKESIDE DR
CUMBERLAND AVE
AMC Bsns Ctr
GREYSTOKE PARK TERR
FERNLEA HO
ROSSALL CRES
BISPHAM RD
Cumberland Bsns Pk
BRUNSWICK RD
ROYAL PAR
RAINSFORD RD
Vascroft Est
87
LYNWOOD RD
CLARENDON RD
BRUNSWICK GDNS
A40
CORONATION RD
Park Royal Metro Ctr
KINGFIELD RD
GREYSTOKE HO
SANDALL RD
SANDALL CL
GARRICK CL
PO
HILL CT
MALCOLM CT
CONNELL CRES
HANGER GN
JOHNSONS WAY
RADNOR WAY
BRITANNIA WAY
MOORFIELD RD
CHURCHILL CT
HAYMILLS CT
HEATHCROFT
628
610
Sovereign Pk
WESTERN AVE
3
CRESTA CT
GREYSTOKE GDNS
GARTH MEWS 1
GREYSTOKE LO 2
GREYSTOKE CT 3
CHATSWORTH CT
HEATHCROFT
HANGER CT
ASHBOURNE AVE
Park Royal
Royale Leisure Park
Westwood Park Trad Est
CONCORD RD
ALLIANCE RD
MANSFIELD RD
WENDOVER CT
A40
AINSDALE RD
BIRKDALE RD
Hanger Hill Park
HEATH CL
EAST CL
DUKES RD
KENDAL AVE
Concord Bsns Ctr
Westpoint Trad Est
Western Avenue Bsns Pk
MOUNTWOOD HO
DAVER CT
82
CHATSWORTH RISE
THE RIDINGS
ROTHERWICK HILL
ASHBOURNE CL
Heron Trad Est
ALLIANCE CT
CECIL CL
FOX LA
Pav
MEADWAY CT
St Augustines Priory Sch
P
THE ORCHARD
MAGNOLIA PL
NICHOLS GN
HILLCREST RD
OSBORNE CT
HOGARTH CL
DALLAS RD
BEAUFORT CL
PRINCES GDNS
KENDAL CT
HIGHFIELD RD
HELENA RD
WEST RD
1 MARCOURT LAWNS
2 CHILTERN HO
3 HILLCREST HTS
4 MINSTER CT
40
103
AUDLEY CT
CORRINGWAY
T Cts
Bwg Gn
KENDAL AVE
NORTHFIELDS RD
2
BEECHCROFT HO
BEAUFORT RD
40
THE CROFT
PARK VIEW RD
THORNTREE CT
AUDLEY RD
CHERRY WOOD WAY
W3
PARK HILL
PARK HILL CT
HALL CL
BEAULIEU CT
HILLSIDE RD
WESTER GATE
CORFTON LO
RED LO
HANGER VALE LA
AYR CT
T Cts
GROVESIDE CL
WALTON GDNS
WALTON WAY
SAXON DR
NORMAN WAY
WESTFIELDS RD
KINGS RD
REGAL CL
CROFT CRES
Sp Gd
HANGER VIEW WAY
MONKS DR
PRINCES GDNS
GDNS
HOWARD CL
MOAT
BALMORAL CT
QUEEN'S RD
CORFTON RD
ROSELLE CT
FIR TREE CL
WESTMOUNT CT
GREEN VALE
HANGER VALE LA
BOILEAU RD
Sp Gd
TUDOR GDNS
WYNTON PL
Allot Gdns
KINGS AVE
MARRYATT CT 1
GILBERT CT 2
THACKERY CT 3
GOLF RD
West Acton
THE LINK
Allot Gdns
W5
CHATSFIELD PL
Tenn Cts
HANGER LANE (NORTH CIRCULAR ROAD)
West Acton
NOEL RD
ALWYN GDNS
Aston House Sch
Pav
North Ealing
Pav
LINKS RD
Sp Gd
1
WOODVILLE RD
WOODVILLE GDNS
BOILEAU PAR 4
BALCON CT 5
EDEN COURT 6
STATION RD
DENNA CL
KENT CT
QUEEN'S DR
STATION PAR
PO
West Acton Prim Sch
Allot Gdns
MOUNTFIELD RD
HAVEN LA
REGENCY CL
GARRAGE RD
WESTBURY RD
DENHAM LO
MADELEY RD
QUEENS PAR
MIRANDA CT
CHURCHILL GDNS
MADELEY CT
EALING VILLAGE
ROBERTS CT
Ellen Wilkinson Sch for Girls
Allot Gdns
B455
81
Ealing Broadway
WALDEGRAVE RD
Tenn Cts
LYNTON RD
18
A
B
110
19
ADDISON CT
OAKLEY HO
OAKLEY AVE
C
D
20
PARKSIDE
COLLEGE CT
HAMILTON RD
A406
BLOOMSBURY
WESTERN GDNS
MONTAGUE GDNS
Bwg Gn
The Japanese Sch
TWYFORD CT
MAYFIELD RD
Greek Sch London
ROSEMOUNT RD
FARNELL PL
CRESWICK
HEREFORD RD
JULIAN AVE
THE BROADWAY A4020
THE MALL
MALL CT
HAMILTON CT
FREELAND RD
OAK RD
Pav
T Cts
Tenn Cts

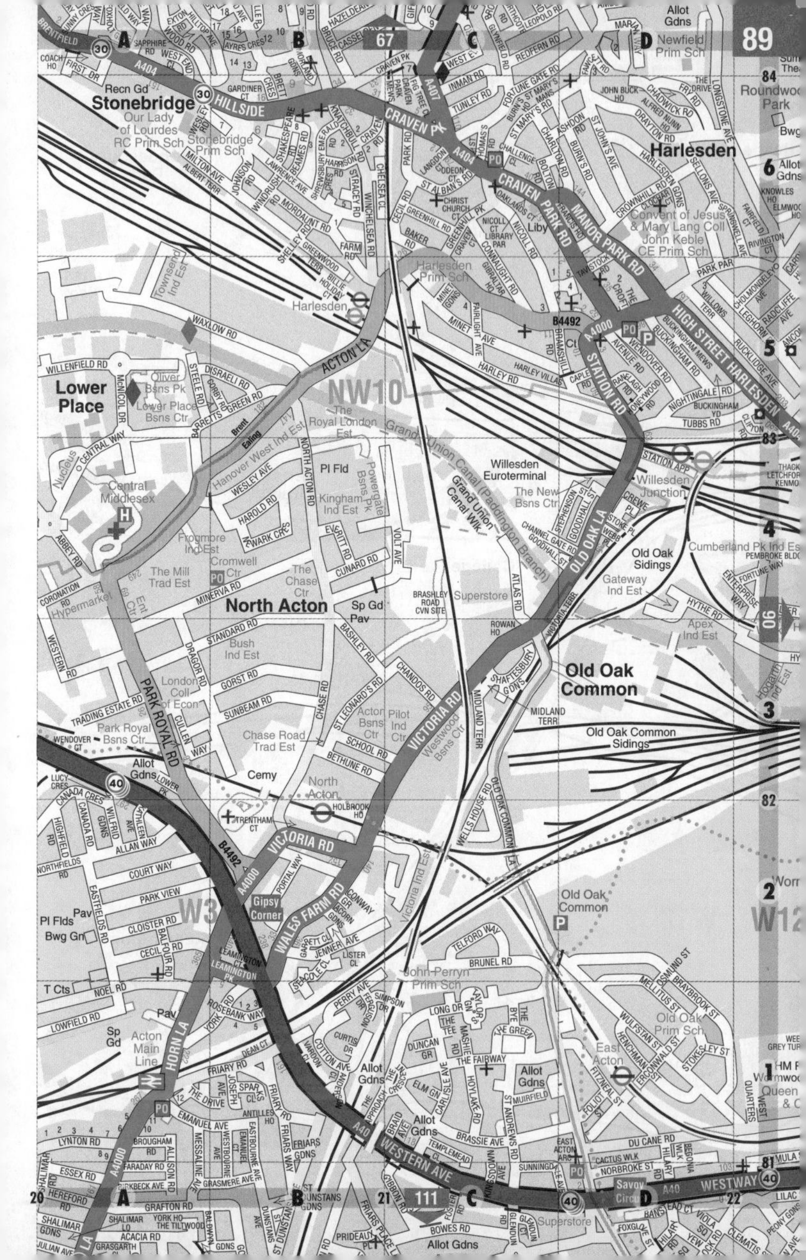

Stonebridge
Harlesden
Lower Place
North Acton
Old Oak Common
NW10
W3
W12
Recn Gd
Our Lady of Lourdes RC Prim Sch
Stonebridge Prim Sch
HILLSIDE
CRAVEN PK
CRAVEN PARK RD
MANOR PARK RD
HIGH STREET HARLESDEN
STATION RD
OLD OAK LA
VICTORIA RD
ACTON LA
PARK ROYAL RD
WALES FARM RD
HORN LA
WESTERN AVE
WESTWAY
A404
A407
A4000
B4492
A40
Newfield Prim Sch
Roundwood Park
Allot Gdns
Convent of Jesus & Mary Lang Coll
John Keble CE Prim Sch
Harlesden Prim Sch
Harlesden
Townsend Ind Est
WAXLOW RD
WILLENFIELD RD
Oliver Bsns Pk
Lower Place Bsns Ctr
The Royal London Est
Grand Union Canal
Grand Union Canal (Paddington Branch)
Grand Union Canal Wlk
Willesden Euroterminal
Willesden Junction
The New Bsns Ctr
Central Middlesex
Hanover West Ind Est
Kingham Ind Est
Powergate Bsns Pk
Pl Fld
Frogmore Ind Est
Cromwell Ctr
The Mill Trad Est
The Chase Ctr
Sp Gd Pav
Superstore
Old Oak Sidings
Gateway Ind Est
Cumberland Pk Ind Est
Apex Ind Est
Bush Ind Est
London Coll of Econ
Park Royal Bsns Ctr
Acton Bsns Ctr
Pilot Ind Ctr
Chase Road Trad Est
Westwood Bsns Ctr
Old Oak Common Sidings
Cemy
North Acton
Gipsy Corner
Victoria Ind Est
Old Oak Common
John Perryn Prim Sch
Old Oak Prim Sch
East Acton
Acton Main Line
Allot Gdns
Superstore
Savoy Circus
67
111
90
A B C D
84
83
82
81
20
21
22
1 2 3 4 5 6

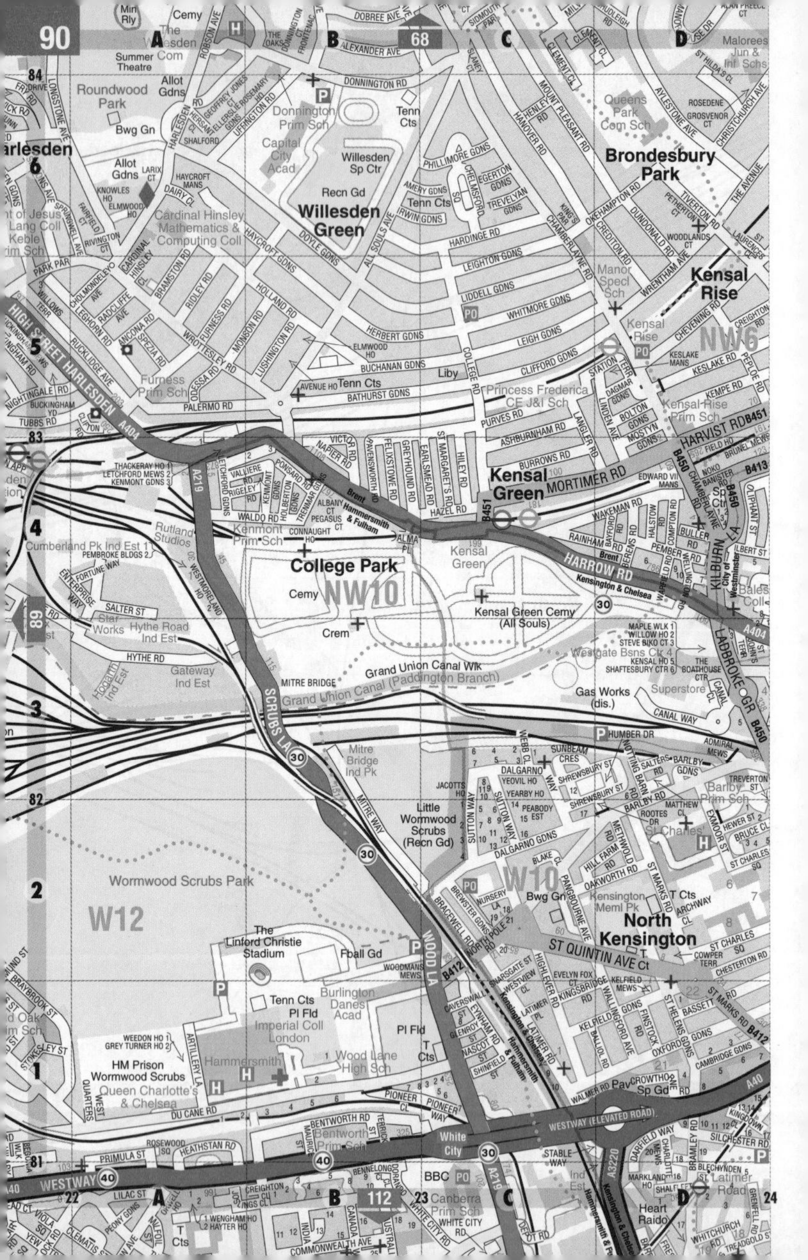

68
Willesden Green
Brondesbury Park
Kensal Rise
Kensal Green
College Park
NW10
NW6
W10
W12
North Kensington
Wormwood Scrubs Park
Kensal Green Cemy (All Souls)
Grand Union Canal (Paddington Branch)
Grand Union Canal Wlk
HM Prison Wormwood Scrubs
The Linford Christie Stadium
Little Wormwood Scrubs (Recn Gd)
HARROW RD
SCRUBS LA
WOOD LA
WESTWAY
HIGH STREET HARLESDEN
MORTIMER RD
LADBROKE GR
ST QUINTIN AVE
White City
BBC
112
89

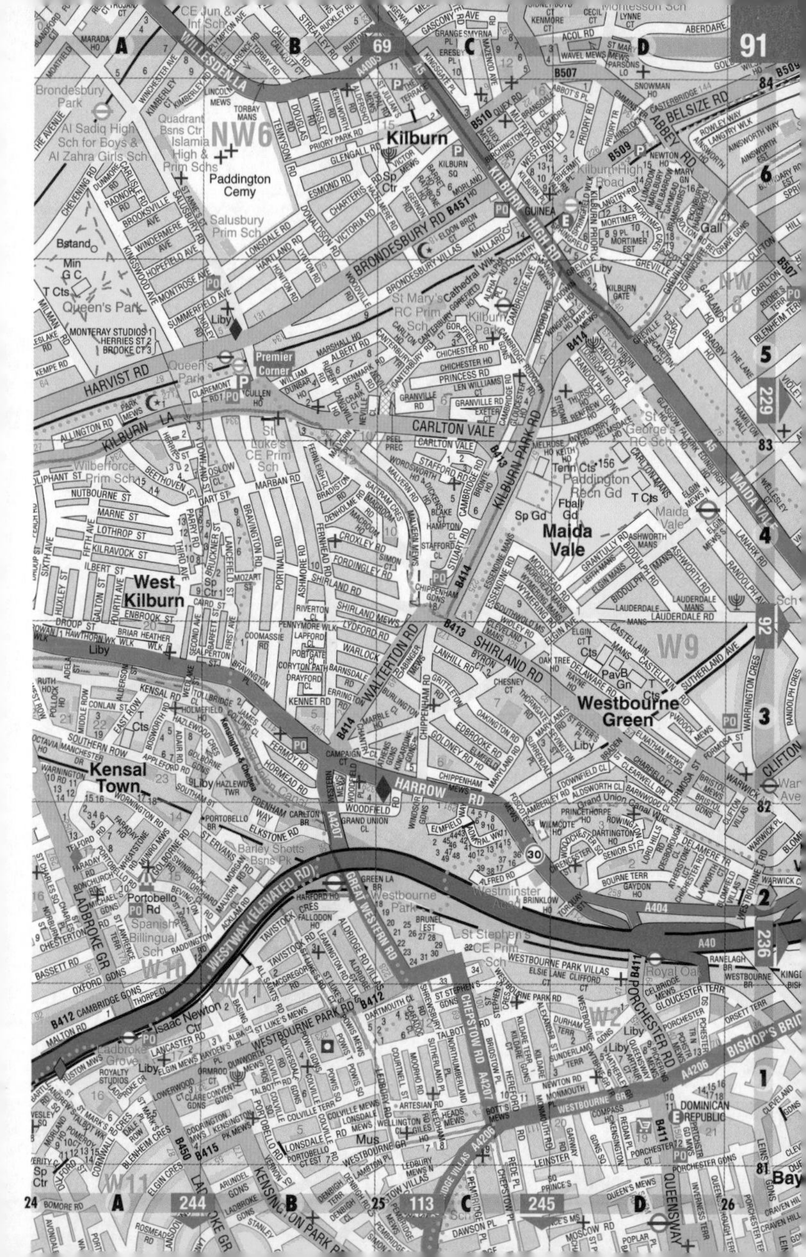
A
B
C
D
69
NW6
Kilburn
Brondesbury Park
Al Sadiq High Sch for Boys & Al Zahra Girls Sch
Quadrant Bsns Ctr
Islamia High & Prim Schs
Paddington Cemy
Salusbury Prim Sch
Queen's Park
Premier Corner
WILLESDEN LA
KILBURN HIGH RD
BELSIZE RD
ABBEY RD
BRONDESBURY RD
BRONDESBURY VILLAS
HARVIST RD
KILBURN LA
CARLTON VALE
KILBURN PARK RD
MAIDA VALE
Kilburn High Road
Kilburn Park
St Mary's RC Prim Sch
St Luke's CE Prim Sch
Wilberforce Prim Sch
St George's RC Sch
Paddington Recn Gd
Maida Vale
West Kilburn
W9
SHIRLAND RD
WALTERTON RD
HARROW RD
Westbourne Green
Kensal Town
Grand Union Canal
Barley Shotts Bsns Pk
Portobello Rd
Spanish Bilingual Sch
Westminster Acad
St Stephen's CE Prim Sch
Westbourne Park
Royal Oak
WESTWAY (ELEVATED RD)
GREAT WESTERN RD
LADBROKE GR
WESTBOURNE PARK RD
WESTBOURNE GR
CHEPSTOW RD
PORCHESTER RD
QUEENSWAY
BISHOP'S BRIDGE
Ladbroke Grove
W10
W11
W2
Isaac Newton Ctr
DOMINICAN REPUBLIC
Mus
229
92
236
244
113
245
6
5
4
3
2
1
84
83
82
81
24
25
26

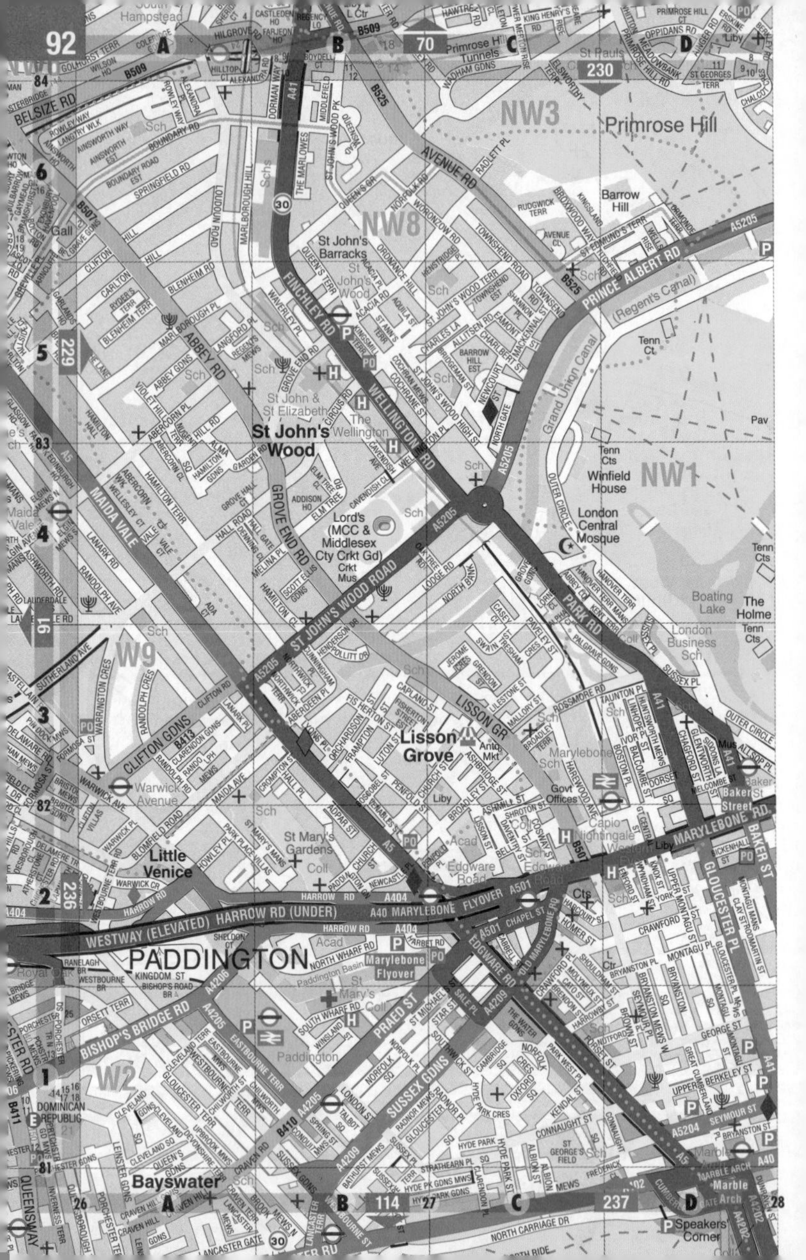

South Hampstead
A
B
C
D
70
230
229
91
236
114
237
26
27
28
84
83
82
81
6
5
4
3
2
1
B509
Primrose Hill Tunnels
St Pauls
NW3
Primrose Hill
Barrow Hill
NW8
St John's Barracks
St John's Wood
St John & St Elizabeth
The Wellington
St John's Wood
Lord's (MCC & Middlesex Cty Crkt Gd)
Crkt Mus
Winfield House
NW1
London Central Mosque
Boating Lake
The Holme
London Business Sch
Tenn Cts
Tenn Ct
Pav
W9
Lisson Grove
Marylebone
Govt Offices
Baker Street
Capio Nightingale
Edgware Road
Little Venice
Warwick Avenue
St Mary's Gardens
PADDINGTON
Paddington Basin
Paddington
Marylebone Flyover
St Mary's
W2
Bayswater
DOMINICAN REPUBLIC
Marble Arch
Speakers' Corner
Maida Vale
Gall
FINCHLEY RD
WELLINGTON RD
PARK RD
PRINCE ALBERT RD
AVENUE RD
ABBEY RD
MAIDA VALE
GROVE END RD
ST JOHN'S WOOD ROAD
LISSON GR
MARYLEBONE RD
BAKER ST
GLOUCESTER PL
EDGWARE RD
PRAED ST
SUSSEX GDNS
BISHOP'S BRIDGE RD
WESTWAY (ELEVATED) HARROW RD (UNDER)
A40 MARYLEBONE FLYOVER
HARROW RD
CLIFTON GDNS
NORTH CARRIAGE DR
BELSIZE RD
BOUNDARY RD
LOUDOUN ROAD
HAMILTON TERR
Grand Union Canal
(Regent's Canal)
OUTER CIRCLE
A5205
A41
A5
A404
A501
A4209
A4205
A4206
A5204
B525
B507
B410
B411
B413

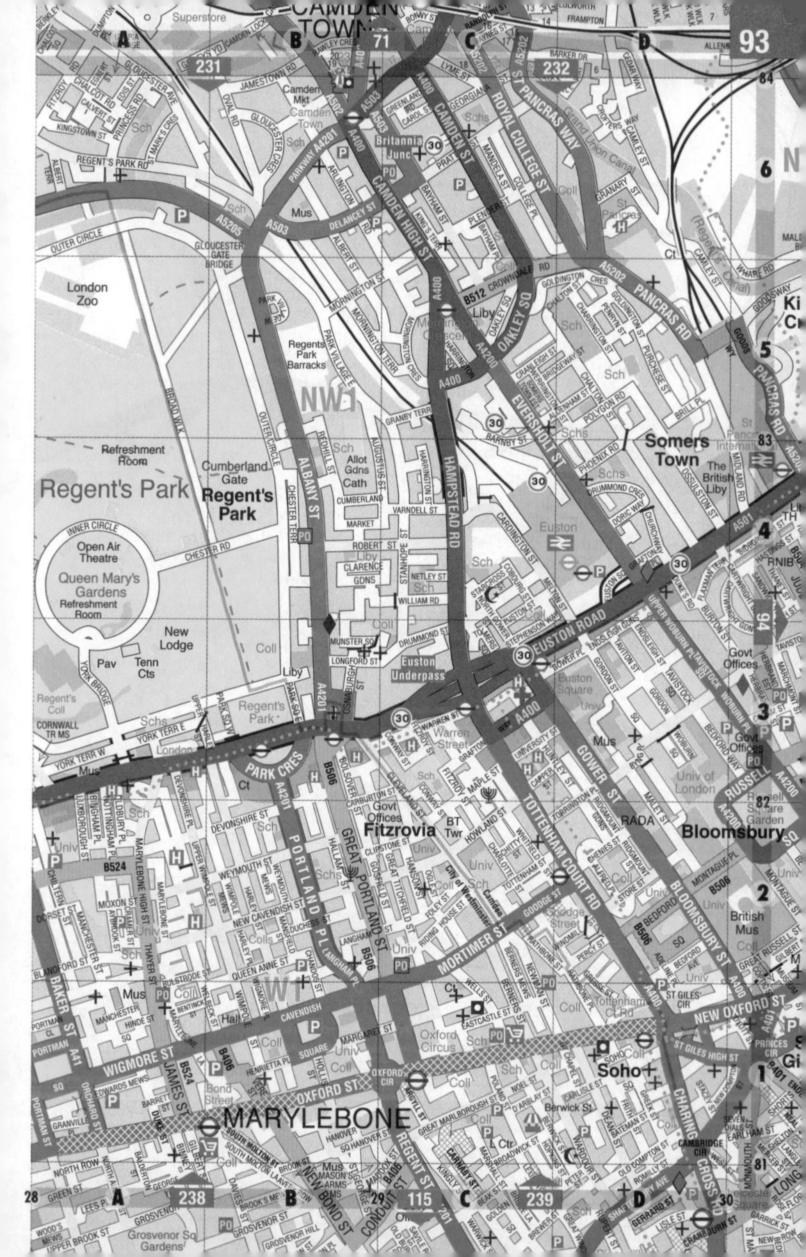

93
CAMDEN TOWN
A
B
C
D
231
71
232
Camden Mkt
Camden Town
Britannia Junc
Grand Union Canal
Regent's Canal
St Pancras
London Zoo
Regents Park Barracks
NW1
Mornington Crescent
Somers Town
The British Liby
St Pancras International
Euston
Refreshment Room
Cumberland Gate
Regent's Park
Open Air Theatre
Queen Mary's Gardens
New Lodge
Pav
Tenn Cts
Euston Underpass
Warren Street
Euston Square
Univ of London
Bloomsbury
British Mus
RADA
Fitzrovia
BT Twr
Govt Offices
Goodge Street
Tottenham Ct Rd
Oxford Circus
Soho
MARYLEBONE
Bond Street
W1
Regent's Park
Great Portland Street
ALBANY ST
HAMPSTEAD RD
EUSTON ROAD
CAMDEN HIGH ST
CAMDEN ST
ROYAL COLLEGE ST
ST PANCRAS WAY
PANCRAS RD
EVERSHOLT ST
TOTTENHAM COURT RD
GOWER ST
BLOOMSBURY ST
PORTLAND PL
GREAT PORTLAND ST
MORTIMER ST
OXFORD ST
CAVENDISH SQUARE
WIGMORE ST
BAKER ST
MARYLEBONE HIGH ST
REGENT ST
NEW BOND ST
CHARING CROSS RD
NEW OXFORD ST
ST GILES HIGH ST
RUSSELL SQ
PARK CRES
OUTER CIRCLE
INNER CIRCLE
CHESTER RD
BROAD WALK
JAMES ST
DUKE ST
CONDUIT ST
CARNABY ST
WARDOUR ST
BERWICK ST
28
238
29
115
239
30
6
5
4
3
2
1
84
83
82
81
94

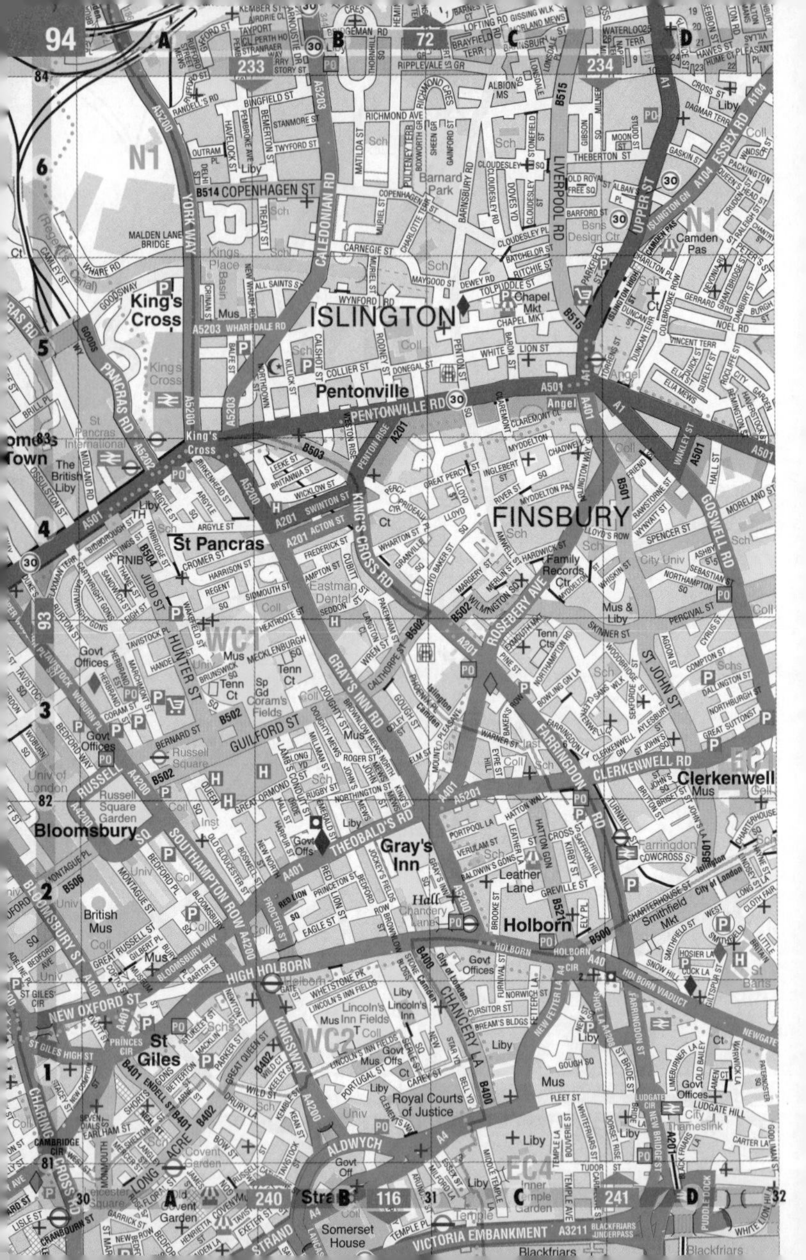

A
B
C
D
72
233
234
6
5
4
3
2
1
84
83
82
81
93
240
116
241
30
31
32
N1
ISLINGTON
Pentonville
FINSBURY
St Pancras
King's Cross
Bloomsbury
Clerkenwell
Gray's Inn
Holborn
St Giles
Camden Pas
Barnard Park
Chapel Mkt
Angel
WC1
WC2
EC1
EC4
Somerset House
Royal Courts of Justice
Lincoln's Inn Fields
Lincoln's Inn
Leather Lane
Smithfield Mkt
Family Records Ctr
Eastman Dental
Coram's Fields
Russell Square Garden
British Mus
The British Liby
St Pancras International
Kings Place Basin
Covent Garden
Farringdon
City Thameslink
Inner Temple Garden
Blackfriars
YORK WAY
CALEDONIAN RD
COPENHAGEN ST
LIVERPOOL RD
UPPER ST
ESSEX RD
PENTONVILLE RD
KING'S CROSS RD
GRAY'S INN RD
ROSEBERY AVE
FARRINGDON RD
GOSWELL RD
ST JOHN ST
CLERKENWELL RD
THEOBALD'S RD
SOUTHAMPTON ROW
HIGH HOLBORN
HOLBORN VIADUCT
NEW OXFORD ST
KINGSWAY
CHANCERY LA
ALDWYCH
STRAND
FLEET ST
VICTORIA EMBANKMENT
CHARING CROSS RD
LONG ACRE
GUILFORD ST
HUNTER ST
RUSSELL SQ
BLOOMSBURY ST
MIDLAND RD
PANCRAS RD
EUSTON RD
ARGYLE ST
RICHMOND AVE
WHITE LION ST
WHARFDALE RD
SWINTON ST
ACTON ST
NEWGATE
LUDGATE HILL
NEW BRIDGE ST
FARRINGDON ST
ST BRIDE ST
SHOE LA
NEW FETTER LA
CHARTERHOUSE ST

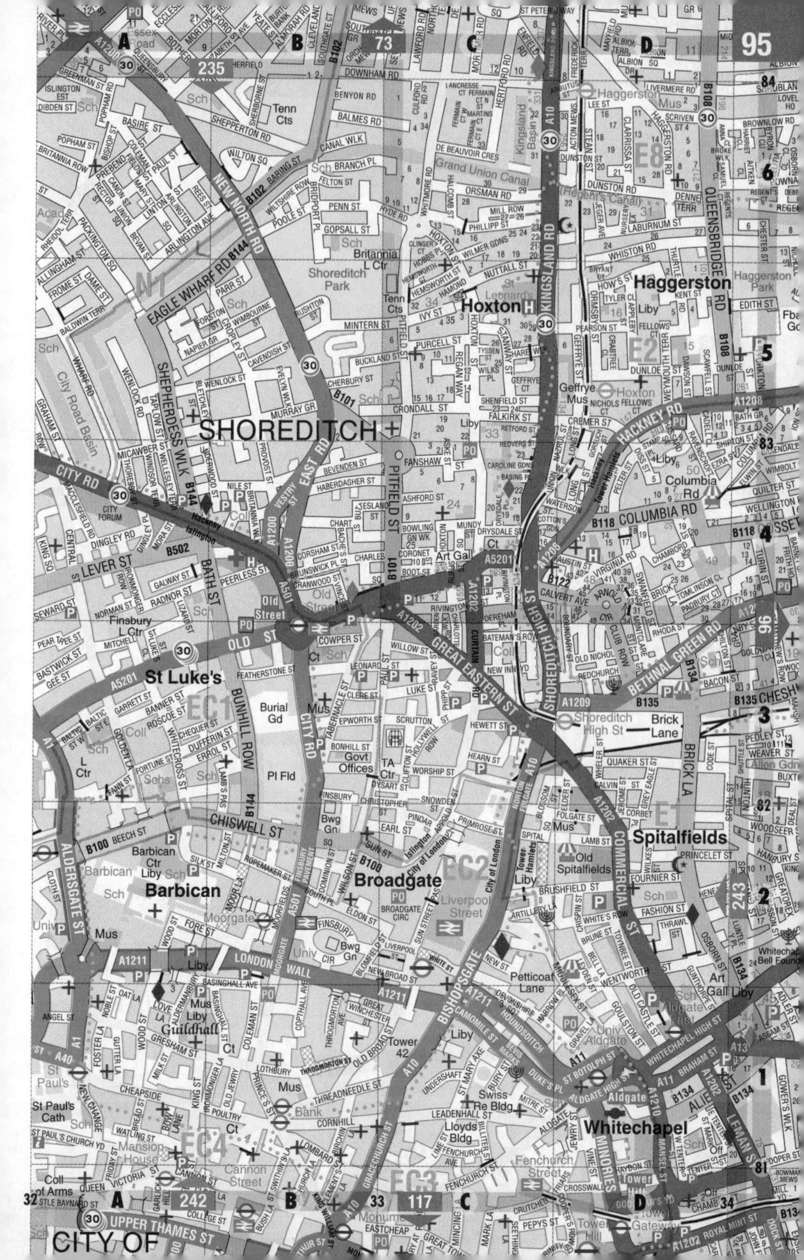

A
B
C
D
73
235
SHOREDITCH
Hoxton
Haggerston
St Luke's
Barbican
Broadgate
Spitalfields
Whitechapel
CITY OF
Shoreditch Park
Haggerston Park
Grand Union Canal
(Regent's Canal)
City Road Basin
Kingsland Basin
N1
E8
E2
E1
EC1
EC2
EC3
EC4
NEW NORTH RD
KINGSLAND RD
QUEENSBRIDGE RD
HACKNEY RD
COLUMBIA RD
CITY RD
OLD ST
LEVER ST
BATH ST
BUNHILL ROW
CHISWELL ST
BEECH ST
ALDERSGATE ST
LONDON WALL
MOORGATE
FINSBURY PAVEMENT
BISHOPSGATE
COMMERCIAL ST
GREAT EASTERN ST
SHOREDITCH HIGH ST
BETHNAL GREEN RD
BRICK LA
WHITECHAPEL HIGH ST
LEMAN ST
MINORIES
HOUNDSDITCH
UPPER THAMES ST
QUEEN VICTORIA ST
CHEAPSIDE
CANNON ST
EASTCHEAP
GRACECHURCH ST
FENCHURCH ST
LEADENHALL ST
THREADNEEDLE ST
CORNHILL
PITFIELD ST
EAST RD
SHEPHERDESS WLK
WHARF RD
EAGLE WHARF RD
ROYAL MINT ST
ALDGATE HIGH ST
Old Street
Liverpool Street
Moorgate
Aldgate
Aldgate East
Shoreditch High St
Fenchurch Street
Tower Hill
Tower Gateway
Cannon Street
Bank
Monument
Haggerston
Hoxton
Essex Road
Old Spitalfields
Petticoat Lane
Geffrye Mus
Barbican Ctr
Guildhall
Tower 42
Lloyds Bldg
Swiss Re Bldg
St Paul's Cath
Mansion House
Burial Gd
Pl Fld
Brick Lane
242
117
243
96

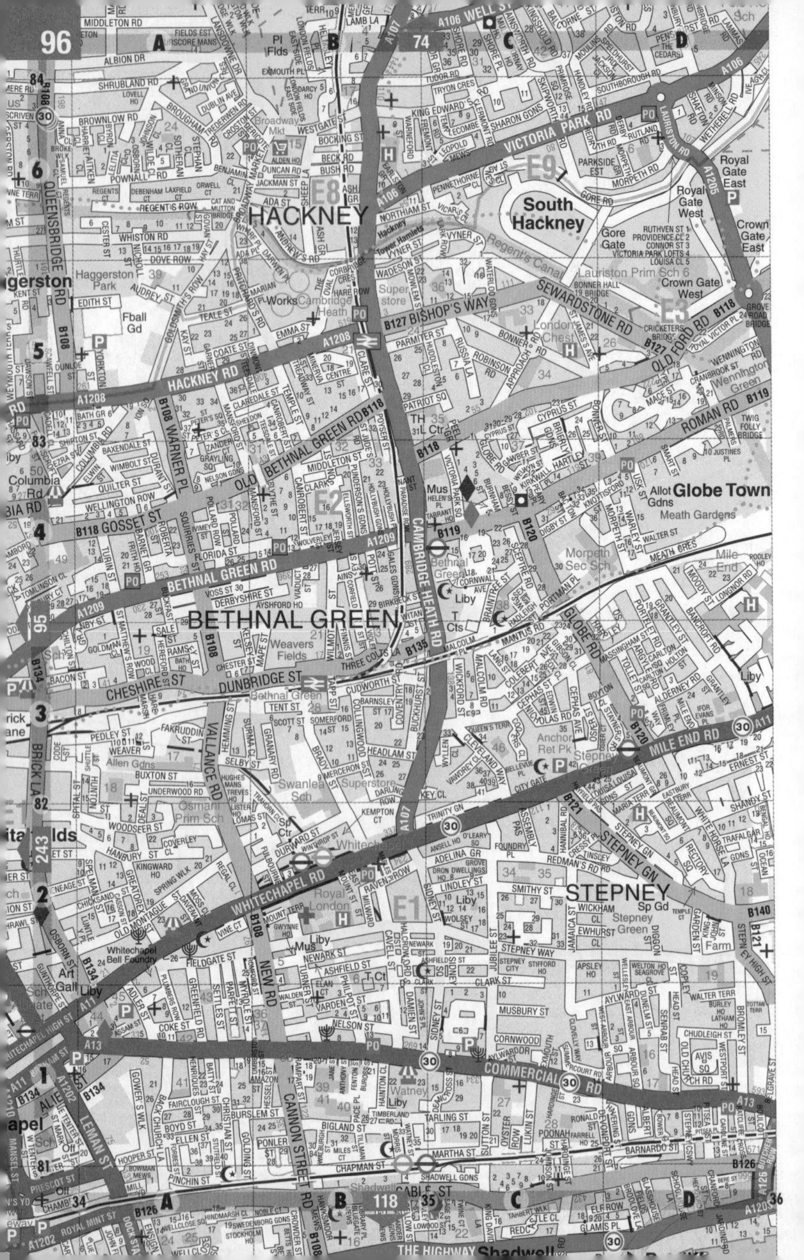

A
B
C
D
74
MIDDLETON RD
ALBION DR
SHRUBLAND RD
BROWNLOW RD
QUEENSBRIDGE RD
Haggerston
Haggerston Park
Fball Gd
HACKNEY
E8
Broadway Mkt
WESTGATE ST
BOCKING ST
BECK RD
BUSH RD
JACKMAN ST
REGENT'S ROW
WHISTON RD
DOVE ROW
AUDREY ST
EDITH ST
TEALE ST
EMMA ST
Cambridge Heath
Works
Super store
HACKNEY RD
A1208
A106
A107
WELL ST
TUDOR RD
TRYON CRES
VICTORIA PARK RD
E9
South Hackney
GORE RD
MORPETH RD
Royal Gate East
Royal Gate West
Gore Gate
Crown Gate East
Crown Gate West
Regent's Canal
Lauriston Prim Sch
SEWARDSTONE RD
B127 BISHOP'S WAY
London Chest
E3
OLD FORD RD
B118
ROMAN RD
B119
Wennington Green
TWIG FOLLY BRIDGE
CYPRUS ST
Globe Town
Allot Gdns
Meath Gardens
MEATH GRES
Mile End
Morpeth Sec Sch
BETHNAL GREEN RD
B108 WARNER PL
COLUMBIA RD
Columbia Rd
OLD BETHNAL GREEN RD
GOSSET ST
E2
CAMBRIDGE HEATH RD
A1209
Mus
Bethnal Green
Liby
BETHNAL GREEN
Weavers Fields
CHESHIRE ST
DUNBRIDGE ST
THREE COLTS LA
B135
B120
GLOBE RD
MILE END RD
95
BRICK LA
VALLANCE RD
Allen Gdns
Osmani Prim Sch
Swanlea Sch
Superstore
Whitechapel
WHITECHAPEL RD
Royal London
E1
Whitechapel Bell Foundry
Art Gall
NEW RD
A13
COMMERCIAL RD
CANNON STREET RD
Watney
STEPNEY
Stepney Green
STEPNEY WAY
Sp Gd
Farm
B140
B121
B126
A1202
LEMAN ST
B134
Shadwell
CABLE ST
THE HIGHWAY
118
35
36
34
243

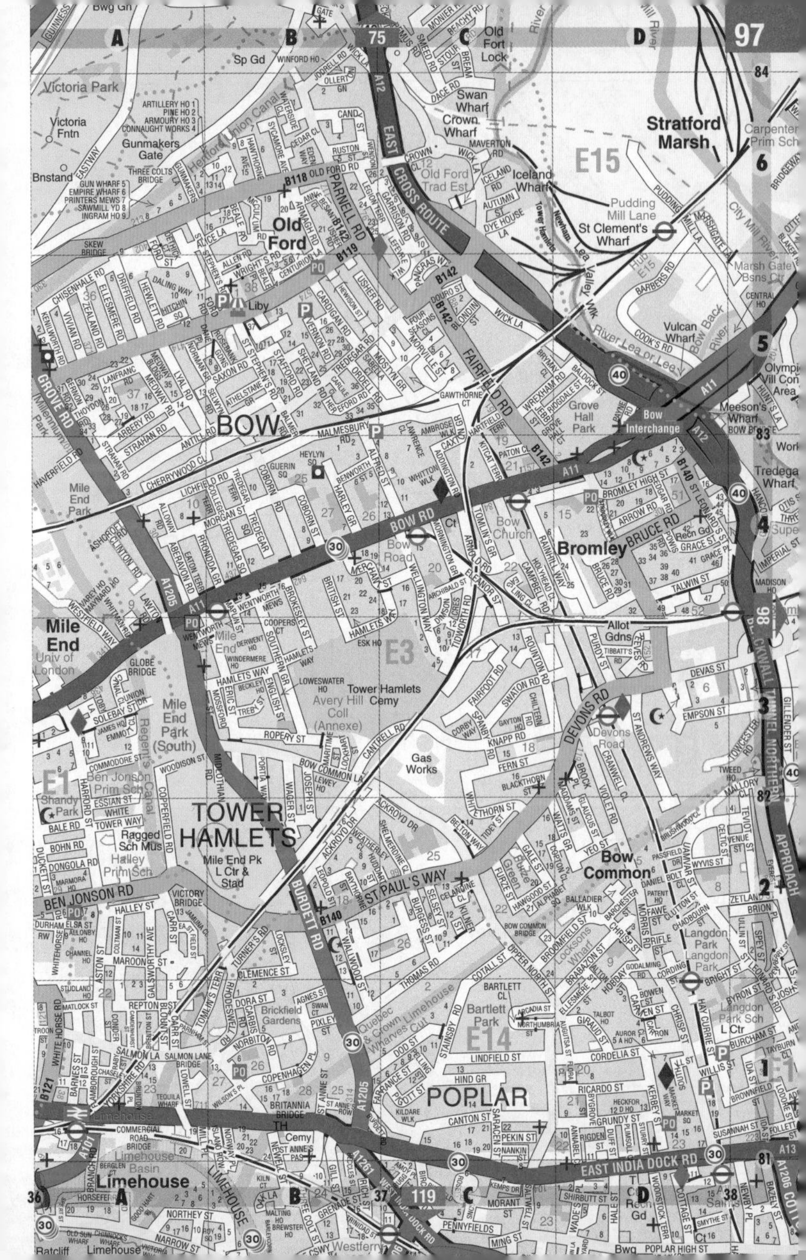
97
75
119
Victoria Park
Victoria Fntn
Gunmakers Gate
Hertford Union Canal
Old Ford
Old Ford Lock
Swan Wharf
Crown Wharf
Old Ford Trad Est
Iceland Wharf
Stratford Marsh
E15
Pudding Mill Lane
St Clement's Wharf
Marsh Gate Bsns Ctr
Vulcan Wharf
River Lea or Lee
Bow Back River
City Mill River
Lea Valley Wlk
Carpenters Prim Sch
Olympic Vill Con Area
Meeson's Wharf
Tredegar Wharf
Bow Interchange
Grove Hall Park
BOW
EAST CROSS ROUTE
FAIRFIELD RD
GROVE RD
BOW RD
Bow Road
Bow Church
Bromley
Mile End Park
Mile End
Univ of London
Globe Bridge
Mile End Park (South)
Regent's Canal
E3
Tower Hamlets Cemy
Avery Hill Coll (Annexe)
Gas Works
Devons Road
Allot Gdns
BLACKWALL TUNNEL NORTHERN APPROACH
E1
Shandy Park
Ben Jonson Prim Sch
Ragged Sch Mus
Halley Prim Sch
TOWER HAMLETS
Mile End Pk L Ctr & Stad
BURDETT RD
ST PAUL'S WAY
Bow Common
Langdon Park
Langdon Park Sch
Locksons Wharf
Bartlett Park
E14
POPLAR
Brickfield Gardens
Limehouse Cut
Quebec & Crown Wharves
Limehouse
Limehouse Basin
EAST INDIA DOCK RD
COMMERCIAL ROAD
Westferry
Ratcliff
A
B
C
D
84
83
82
81
6
5
4
3
2
1
36
37
38

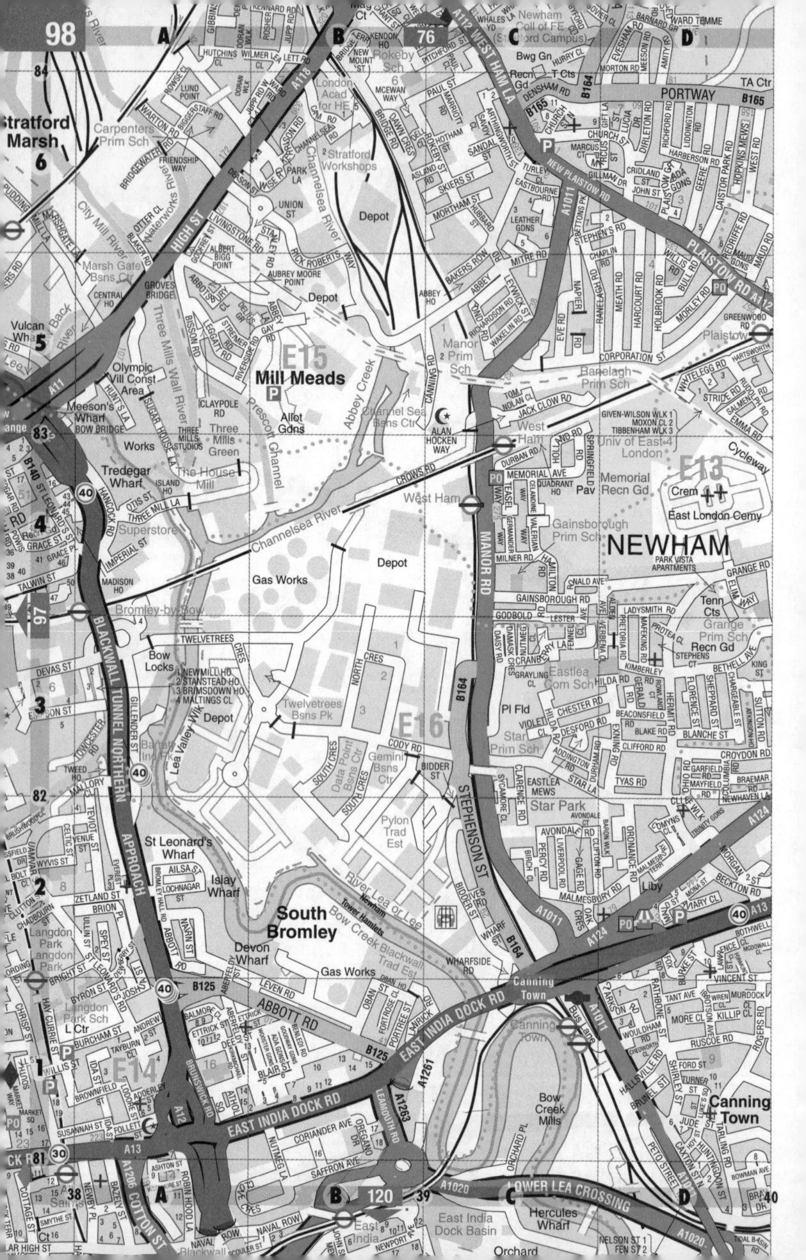

98
76
120
67
Stratford Marsh
Carpenters Prim Sch
London Acad for HE
Rokeby Sch
Stratford Workshops
Newham Coll of FE (Stratford Campus)
Bwg Gn
Recn Gd
T Cts
PORTWAY
TA Ctr
WEST HAM LA
NEW PLAISTOW RD
PLAISTOW RD
HIGH ST
Depot
Marsh Gate Bsns Ctr
Vulcan Wharf
Olympic Vill Const Area
Mill Meads
E15
Allot Gdns
Abbey Creek
Channel Sea Bsns Ctr
Manor Prim Sch
Ranelagh Prim Sch
Plaistow
Meeson's Wharf
BOW BRIDGE
Three Mills Green
Three Mills Wall River
Prescott Channel
The House Mill
Tredegar Wharf
Works
Superstore
Channelsea River
West Ham
Univ of East London
Memorial Recn Gd
Pav
E13
Crem
East London Cemy
Cycleway
Gainsborough Prim Sch
NEWHAM
Gas Works
Bromley-by-Bow
BLACKWALL TUNNEL NORTHERN APPROACH
Bow Locks
Twelvetrees Bsns Pk
Depot
Lea Valley Wlk
MANOR RD
Grange Prim Sch
Recn Gd
Tenn Cts
Eastlea Com Sch
Pl Fld
Star Prim Sch
E16
Data Point Bsns Ctr
Gemini Bsns Ctr
Pylon Trad Est
Star Park
STEPHENSON ST
St Leonard's Wharf
Islay Wharf
South Bromley
River Lea or Lee
Bow Creek
Devon Wharf
Gas Works
Blackwall Trad Est
Liby
EAST INDIA DOCK RD
Canning Town
Langdon Park
Langdon Park Sch
L Ctr
E14
Bow Creek Mills
Canning Town
LOWER LEA CROSSING
East India Dock Basin
Hercules Wharf
East India
All Saints
Orchard
Blackwall
A
B
C
D

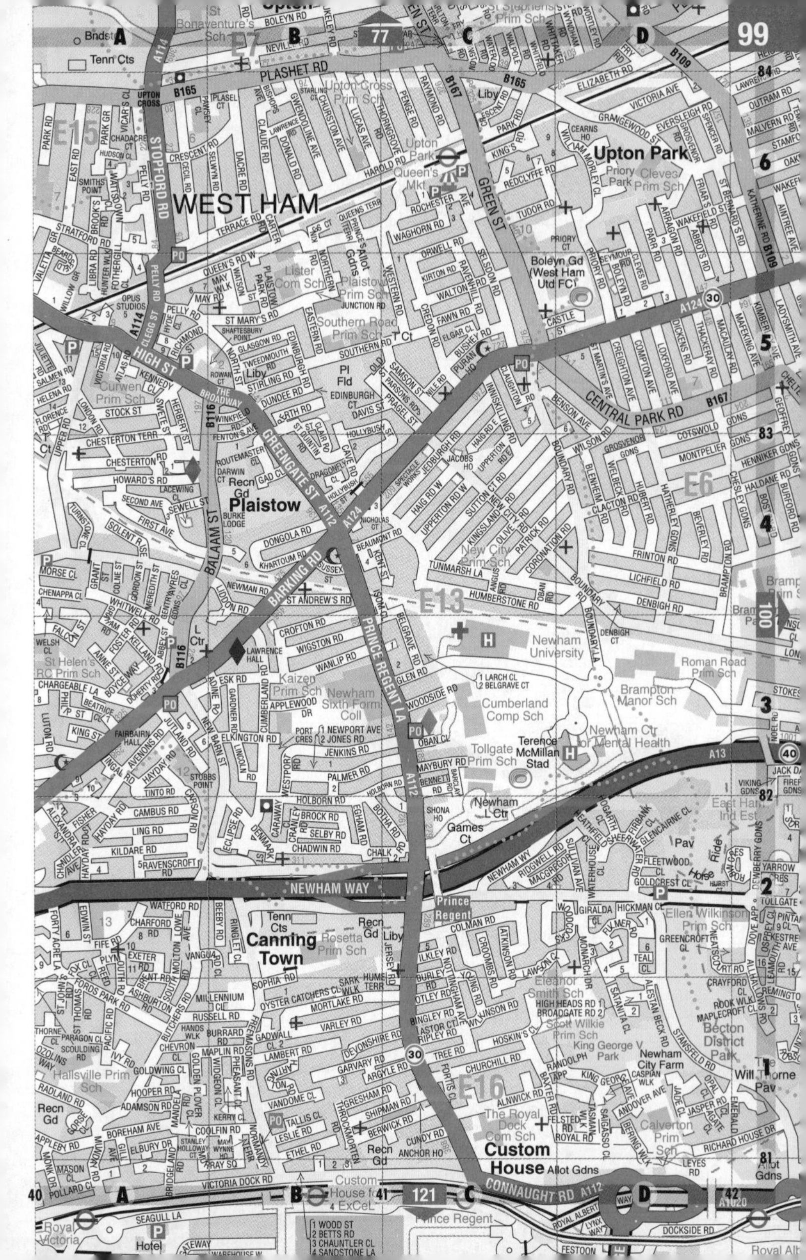

99
77
100
121
A
B
C
D
84
83
82
81
40
41
42
6
5
4
3
2
1
E7
E15
E13
E6
E16
WEST HAM
Upton Park
Plaistow
Canning Town
Custom House
Bonaventure's Sch
Tenn Cts
BOLEYN RD
NEVILLE RD
PLASHET RD
B165
B167
B109
A114
A124
A112
A13
A1020
B116
UPTON CROSS
STOPFORD RD
Upton Cross Prim Sch
ELIZABETH RD
VICTORIA AVE
GRANGEWOOD ST
EVERSLEIGH RD
LAWRENCE RD
GWENDOLINE AVE
CHURSTON AVE
LUCAS AVE
THORNGROVE
PENGE RD
RAYMOND RD
CLAUDE RD
DONALD RD
CRESCENT RD
SELWYN RD
DACRE RD
CECIL RD
HAROLD RD
Upton Park
Queen's Mkt
GREEN ST
Liby
PARK RD
KING'S RD
REDCLYFFE RD
TUDOR RD
Priory Park
Cleves Prim Sch
WAKEFIELD ST
ST BERNARD'S RD
KATHERINE RD
ARRAGON RD
PARR RD
ABBOTS RD
FRIAR'S RD
GROSVENOR RD
SPENCER RD
OUTRAM RD
MALVERN RD
STAMFORD RD
PARK RD
EAST RD
PARK GR
VICAR'S CL
SMITHS POINT
PELLY RD
STRATFORD RD
LIBRA RD
VALETTA GR
WILLOW GR
TERRACE RD
CARTER RD
QUEENS TERR
ROCHESTER AVE
WAGHORN RD
ORWELL RD
KIRTON RD
WALTON RD
FAWN RD
ELGAR CL
BUSHEY RD
SELSDON RD
RAVENHILL RD
CREDON RD
WESTERN RD
NORTHERN RD
Lister Com Sch
Plaistow Prim Sch
Allot Gdns
JUNCTION RD
Southern Road Prim Sch
SOUTHERN RD
EASTERN RD
EDINBURGH RD
ST MARY'S RD
QUEEN'S RD W
MAY WLK
OPUS STUDIOS
HIGH ST
THE BROADWAY
CLEGG ST
RICHMOND ST
GLASGOW RD
TWEEDMOUTH RD
STIRLING RD
DUNDEE RD
PERTH RD
Pl Fld
EDINBURGH CT
DAVIS ST
HOLLYBUSH ST
SAMSON ST
PARSONS RD
PRAGEL ST
NILE RD
PURAN HO
Boleyn Gd (West Ham Utd FC)
PRIORY CT
PRIORY RD
BOLEYN RD
CLEVES RD
CASTLE ST
CENTRAL PARK RD
BENSON AVE
CLAUGHTON RD
ST MARTIN'S AVE
CREIGHTON AVE
COMPTON AVE
LOXFORD AVE
DICKENS RD
THACKERAY RD
MACAULAY RD
MAFEKING AVE
KIMBERLEY AVE
LADYSMITH AVE
GEOFFREY GDNS
COTSWOLD GDNS
MONTPELIER GDNS
HENNIKER GDNS
HALDANE RD
CHESLEY GDNS
BURFORD RD
GROSVENOR GDNS
WELBECK RD
HUBERT RD
HATHERLEY GDNS
BEVERLEY RD
BLENHEIM RD
CLACTON RD
WILSON RD
BOUNDARY RD
INNISKILLING RD
HAIG RD E
UPPERTON RD E
JEDBURGH RD
JACOBS HO
HAIG RD W
UPPERTON RD W
SUTTON CT RD
KINGSLAND RD
NEW CITY RD
OLIVE RD
PATRICK RD
CORONATION RD
New City Prim Sch
TUNMARSH LA
HUMBERSTONE RD
ANGUS RD
OBAN RD
FRINTON RD
LICHFIELD RD
DENBIGH RD
DENBIGH CT
BRAMPTON RD
Newham University
Roman Road Prim Sch
Brampton Manor Sch
Cumberland Comp Sch
Newham Ctr for Mental Health
Terence McMillan Stad
Tollgate Prim Sch
Newham L Ctr
Games Ct
East Ham Ind Est
Pav
Horse Ride
FLEETWOOD CL
GOLDCREST CL
YARROW CRES
TOLLGATE RD
Ellen Wilkinson Prim Sch
GREENCROFT CL
CRAYFORD CL
ROOK WLK
MAPLECROFT CL
Becton District Park
Will Thorne Pav
Allot Gdns
RICHARD HOUSE DR
Calverton Prim Sch
JASPER RD
EMERALD SQ
OPAL CL
JADE CL
ANDOVER AVE
BERING WLK
Newham City Farm
CASPIAN WLK
King George V Park
Scott Wilkie Prim Sch
HIGH HEADS RD
BROADGATE RD
Eleanor Smith Sch
STANSFELD RD
ALESTAN BECK RD
SATANITA CL
MONARCH DR
WOODCOCK RD
GIRALDA CL
HICKMAN CL
TEAL CL
FULMER RD
RIDGWELL RD
MACGREGOR RD
SULLIVAN AVE
WATERHOUSE CL
HOGARTH CL
HEATHFIELD CL
FIRBANK CL
GLENCAIRNE CL
SHEERWATER RD
NEWHAM WY
NEWHAM WAY
Prince Regent
PRINCE REGENT LA
COLMAN RD
ATKINSON RD
CROOMBS RD
ILKLEY RD
BURLEY RD
OTLEY RD
BINGLEY RD
NOTTINGHAM AVE
YOUNG RD
WILKINSON RD
HOSKIN'S CL
TREE RD
CHURCHILL RD
FORTIS CL
RANDOLPH APP
BAXTER RD
ALNWICK RD
The Royal Dock Com Sch
FELSTED WLK
ROYAL RD
TASMAN WLK
SAIGASSO CL
CUNDY RD
ANCHOR HO
Recn Gd
BERWICK RD
SHIPMAN RD
GRESHAM RD
THROCKMORTEN RD
CONNAUGHT RD
Custom House for ExCeL
Prince Regent
ROYAL ALBERT WAY
DOCKSIDE RD
FESTOON WAY
Royal Victoria
SEAGULL LA
Hotel
GATEWAY
1 WOOD ST
2 BETTS RD
3 CHAUNTLER CL
4 SANDSTONE LA
VICTORIA DOCK RD
POLLARD CL
MASON CL
MONK DR
APPLEBY RD
MUNDAY RD
GILL AVE
ELBURY DR
BRIDGELAND RD
RAY SQ
ETHEL RD
LESLIE RD
TALLIS CL
VANDOME CL
ARGYLE RD
GARVARY RD
DEVONSHIRE RD
LAMBERT RD
GADWALL CL
VARLEY RD
MORTLAKE RD
OYSTER CATCHERS CL
SARK WLK
HUME TERR
SOPHIA RD
Tenn Cts
Rosetta Prim Sch
Liby
JERSEY RD
MILLENNIUM CL
RUSSELL RD
HANDS WLK
BURRARD RD
CHEVRON CL
MAPLIN RD
GOLDWING CL
WIDGEON CL
PHEASANT CL
HOOPER RD
ADAMSON RD
MANDELA RD
GOLDEN PLOVER CL
KERRY CL
COOLFIN RD
BOREHAM AVE
STANLEY HOLLOWAY CT
NORMANDY TERR
Recn Gd
Hallsville Prim Sch
RADLAND RD
OZOLINS WAY
SCOULDING RD
PARAGON CL
IVY RD
PACIFIC RD
ST THOMAS RD
ST JOHN'S RD
FORDS PARK RD
ASHBURTON RD
BUTCHERS RD
SOUTH MOLTON RD
EXETER RD
FIFE RD
REED CL
FOX CL
FORTY ACRE LA
EDWIN ST
CHARFORD RD
LOWE AVE
WATFORD RD
BEEBY RD
RINGLET CL
VANGUARD CL
RAVENSCROFT RD
KILDARE RD
LING RD
CAMBUS RD
CHANDLER AVE
HAYDAY RD
ALEXANDRA ST
FISHER ST
TINTO RD
STUBBS POINT
CARSON RD
JUTLAND RD
AVENONS RD
FAIRBAIRN HALL
INGAL RD
LUTON RD
KING ST
PHILIP ST
BEATRICE RD
CHARGEABLE LA
St Helen's RC Prim Sch
WELSH CL
FALCON ST
ANNE ST
BOYCE WAY
DOHERTY RD
KELLAND RD
FOSTER RD
WHITWELL RD
MEREDITH ST
GORDON ST
COLNE ST
GRANT ST
CHENAPPA CL
MORSE CL
SOLENT RISE
FIRST AVE
SECOND AVE
TURNSTONE CL
SEWELL ST
LACEWING CL
HOWARD'S RD
CHESTERTON RD
CHESTERTON TERR
STOCK ST
Curwen Prim Sch
SALMEN RD
HELENA RD
FLORENCE RD
UPPER RD
LONDON RD
KENNEDY CL
VICTORIA RD
ATLAS RD
HERBERT ST
SWETE ST
BALAAM ST
WINKFIELD RD
FENTON'S AVE
ROUTEMASTER CL
DARWIN CT
Recn Gd
BURKE LODGE
GREENGATE ST
BARKING RD
DONGOLA RD
KHARTOUM RD
NEWMAN RD
LIDDON RD
ST ANDREW'S RD
SUSSEX ST
L Ctr
LAWRENCE HALL
ESK RD
ADINE RD
GARDINER RD
NORTH ST
NEW BARN ST
ELKINGTON RD
LINCOLN RD
CUMBERLAND RD
Kaizen Prim Sch
APPLEWOOD DR
Newham Sixth Form Coll
PORT CRES
1 NEWPORT AVE
2 JONES RD
JENKINS RD
PALMER RD
WESTPORT RD
HOLBORN RD
CARAWAY CL
CRANLEY RD
BROCK RD
SELBY RD
CHADWIN RD
DENMARK ST
ECLIPSE RD
EGHAM RD
BOTHA RD
CHALK RD
CROFTON RD
WIGSTON RD
WANLIP RD
ISOM CL
BELGRAVE RD
GLEN RD
WOODSIDE RD
1 LARCH CL
2 BELGRAVE CT
OBAN CL
MAYBURY RD
BENNETT RD
BARCLAY RD
SHONA HO
BEAUMONT RD
KENT ST
NICHOLAS CT
SPECTACLE WORKS
DRAGONFLY CL
GAD CL
HOLLYBUSH ST
CAVE RD
ST QUINTIN RD
ST CLAIR RD
30
40

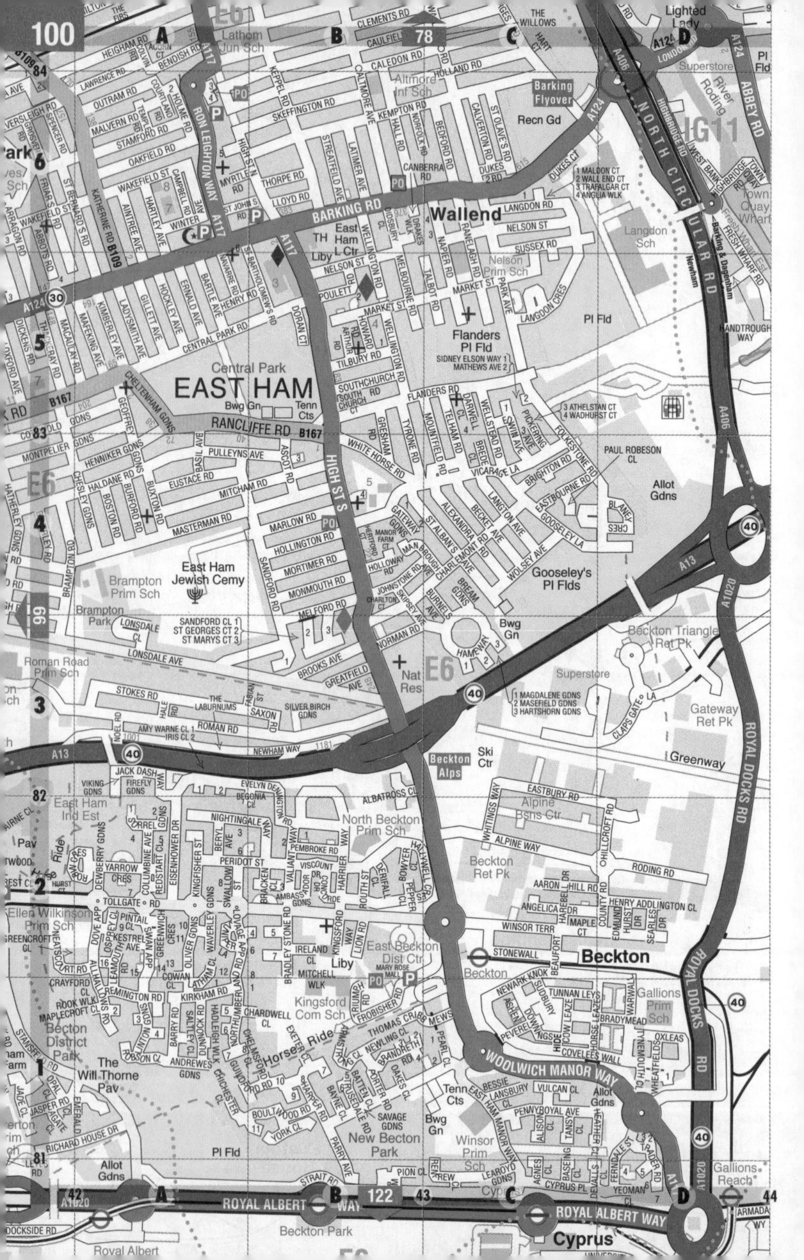
A
B
C
D
78
Lathom Jun Sch
CLEMENTS RD
CAULFIELD RD
CALEDON RD
HOLLAND RD
THE WILLOWS
HART CT
Lighted Lady
LONDON RD
A124
A406
Superstore
River Roding
ABBEY RD
Pl Fld
HEIGHAM RD
BENDISH RD
LAWRENCE RD
OUTRAM RD
MALVERN RD
STAMFORD RD
OAKFIELD RD
WAKEFIELD ST
CAMPBELL RD
HARTLEY AVE
AINTREE AVE
KATHERINE RD
B109
RON LEIGHTON WAY
A117
HIGH ST N
MYRTLE RD
THORPE RD
LLOYD RD
ST JOHNS RD
KEPPEL RD
SKEFFINGTON RD
CALTMORE AVE
Altmore Inf Sch
KEMPTON RD
HALL RD
NORFOLK RD
BEDFORD RD
CALVERTON RD
ST OLAVE'S RD
STREATFEILD AVE
LATIMER AVE
CANBERRA RD
DUKES RD
Barking Flyover
Recn Gd
DUKES CT
1 MALDON CT
2 WALL END CT
3 TRAFALGAR CT
4 ANGLIA WLK
NORTH CIRCULAR RD
HIGHBRIDGE RD
IG11
WEST BANK
TOWN QUAY
Town Quay Wharf
FRESH WHARF RD
Barking & Dagenham
Newham
Langdon Sch
LANGDON RD
NELSON ST
SUSSEX RD
Wallend
BARKING RD
Park
Sch
FRIARS RD
ST BERNARD'S RD
ABBOTS RD
ARRAGON RD
WINTER AVE
East Ham L Ctr
TH
Liby
NELSON ST
POULETT RD
WELLINGTON RD
DIDSBURY CL
DRAKES WLK
MELBOURNE RD
NAPIER RD
RANELAGH RD
TALBOT RD
Nelson Prim Sch
MARKET ST
PARK AVE
LANGDON CRES
Pl Fld
A124
30
DICKENS RD
THACKERAY RD
MACAULAY RD
MAFEKING AVE
KIMBERLEY AVE
LADYSMITH AVE
GILLETT AVE
HOCKLEY AVE
ERNALD AVE
BARTLE AVE
HENRY RD
NAVARRE RD
ST BARTHOLOMEW'S RD
DORAN CT
CENTRAL PARK RD
HOWARD RD
ARTHUR RD
TILBURY RD
Flanders Pl Fld
SIDNEY ELSON WAY 1
MATHEWS AVE 2
HANDTROUGH WAY
Central Park
EAST HAM
Bwg Gn
Tenn Cts
SOUTHCHURCH RD
SOUTH CHURCH CT
FLANDERS RD
DARWELL CL
WELLSTEAD RD
EDWIN AVE
PICKERING AVE
3 ATHELSTAN CT
4 WADHURST CT
B167
CHELTENHAM GDNS
GEOFFREY GDNS
RANCLIFFE RD
MONTPELIER GDNS
HENNIKER GDNS
PULLEYNS AVE
BASIL AVE
ASCOT RD
GRESHAM RD
TYRONE RD
MOUNTFIELD RD
TELHAM RD
BREDE CL
VICARAGE LA
BRIGHTON RD
FOLKESTONE RD
PAUL ROBESON CL
A406
E6
CHESLEY GDNS
HALDANE RD
EUSTACE RD
MITCHAM RD
HIGH ST S
WHITE HORSE RD
EASTBOURNE RD
Allot Gdns
HATHERLEY GDNS
BOSTON RD
BURFORD RD
BUXTON RD
MASTERMAN RD
MARLOW RD
HOLLINGTON RD
MORTIMER RD
MONMOUTH RD
GATEWAY GDNS
ST ALBAN'S AVE
ALEXANDRA RD
BECKET AVE
LANGTON AVE
BLANEY CRES
GOOSELEY LA
CHARLEMONT RD
WOLSEY AVE
40
A13
BRAMPTON RD
East Ham Jewish Cemy
Brampton Prim Sch
SANDFORD RD
HERTFORD CT
MANOR FARM CT
HOLLOWAY RD
BROUGH CT
JOHNSTONE RD
SKIPSEY AVE
BURNELS AVE
BREAM GDNS
Gooseley's Pl Flds
A1020
99
Brampton Park
LONSDALE CL
SANDFORD CL 1
ST GEORGES CT 2
ST MARYS CT 3
MELFORD RD
CHARLTON CT
NORMAN RD
Bwg Gn
HAMEWAY
Beckton Triangle Ret Pk
LONSDALE AVE
BROOKS AVE
GREATFIELD AVE
Nat Res
Superstore
Roman Road Prim Sch
STOKES RD
THE LABURNUMS
FABIAN ST
SAXON RD
SILVER BIRCH GDNS
1 MAGDALENE GDNS
2 MASEFIELD GDNS
3 HARTSHORN GDNS
CLAPS GATE LA
Gateway Ret Pk
ROYAL DOCKS RD
HALE RD
NOEL RD
ROMAN RD
AMY WARNE CL 1
IRIS CL 2
NEWHAM WAY
Beckton Alps
Ski Ctr
Greenway
JACK DASH WAY
FIREFLY GDNS
VIKING GDNS
EVELYN DENNINGTON RD
BEGONIA CL
ALBATROSS CL
EASTBURY RD
Alpine Bsns Ctr
East Ham Ind Est
SORREL GDNS
NIGHTINGALE WAY
North Beckton Prim Sch
WHITINGS WAY
HILLCROFT RD
Pav
DEWBERRY GDNS
COLUMBINE AVE
REDSTART CL
EISENHOWER DR
KINGFISHER ST
BERYL AVE
PEMBROKE RD
VALIANT WAY
HARRIER WAY
HALLYWELL CR
ALPINE WAY
RODING RD
Ride
YARROW CRES
PERIDOT ST
VISCOUNT DR
CONDOR DR
AMBASSADOR GDNS
BRACKEN CL
ROUTH ST
DERIFALL CL
BOWYER CL
PEPPER CL
Beckton Ret Pk
AARON HILL RD
HAREBELL DR
COUNTY RD
HENRY ADDLINGTON CL
TOLLGATE RD
SWALLOW ST
ANGELICA DR
MAPLE CT
EDMUND HURST DR
SEARLES DR
Ellen Wilkinson Prim Sch
DOVE APP
OSPREY CL
PINTAIL CL
KESTREL AVE
GREENWICH CRES
OLIVER GDNS
WAVERLEY GDNS
LOVAGE APP
BRADLEY STONE RD
KINGSFORD WAY
LION RD
East Beckton Dist Ctr
WINSOR TERR
BEAUFORT
GREENCROFT CL
NEATSCOURT RD
LEAMOUTH RD
SWAN APP
IRELAND CL
Liby
MARY ROSE MALL
STONEWALL
Beckton
ALLHALLOWS RD
COWAN CL
ATHAM CL
NORTHUMBERLAND RD
MITCHELL WLK
TRIUMPH RD
FROBISHER RD
Kingsford Com Sch
NEWARK KNOK
SUDBURY
TUNNAN LEYS
Gallions Prim Sch
CRAYFORD CL
REMINGTON RD
KIRKHAM RD
ROOK WLK
MAPLECROFT CL
Becton District Park
INTON GDNS
BARRY RD
SALTLEY CL
DUNNOCK RD
HADLEIGH WLK
CHARDWELL CL
EXETER RD
THOMAS CRIBB MEWS
ASHEN
DOWNINGS
COW LEAZE
HORSE LEAZE
WARWALL
BRADYMEAD
OXLEAS
TYNEMOUTH CL
WHEATFIELDS
COVELEES WALL
HIDE
PEVEREL
STANSFELD RD
The Will Thorne Pav
ROBSON CL
ANDREWES GDNS
CHICHESTER CL
CHELMSFORD CL
GUILDFORD RD
Horse Ride
NEWLING CL
BRANDRETH RD
PEARL CL
WOOLWICH MANOR WAY
Farm
OPAL CL
JADE CL
JASPER RD
AGATE CL
EMERALD
HARPER RD
BATTEN CL
TRUSEDALE RD
PORTER RD
OAKES CL
Tenn Cts
EAST HAM MANOR WAY
BESSIE LANSBURY CL
VULCAN CL
Allot Gdns
BOULTWOOD RD
YORK CL
BAYNE CL
SAVAGE GDNS
Bwg Gn
PENNYROYAL AVE
ALISON CL
TANSY CL
HEATHER CL
FERNDALE ST
TRADER RD
RICHARD HOUSE DR
Pl Fld
New Becton Park
Winsor Prim Sch
BASEING CL
DEVALLS CL
PARRY AVE
Allot Gdns
STRAIT RD
PION CL
REW CL
LEAROYD GDNS
AGNES CL
CYPRUS PL
YEOMAN CL
Gallions Reach
42
43
44
122
A1020
ROYAL ALBERT WAY
DOCKSIDE RD
Beckton Park
Royal Albert
Cyprus
ARMADA WY
6
5
4
3
2
1
84
83
82
81

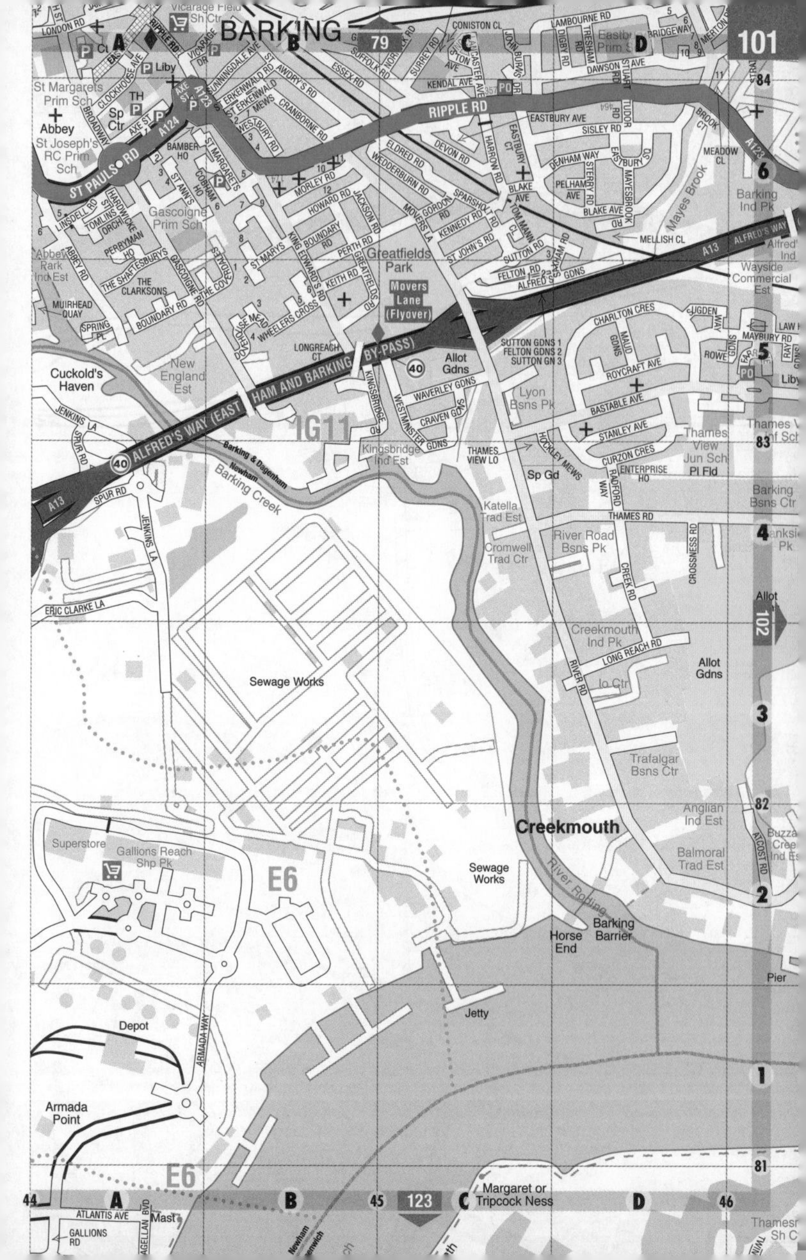
BARKING
79
Vicarage Field Sh Ctr
RIPPLE RD
ALFRED'S WAY (EAST HAM AND BARKING BY-PASS)
A13
A123
A124
ST PAULS RD
St Margarets Prim Sch
Abbey
St Joseph's RC Prim Sch
Gascoigne Prim Sch
Greatfields Park
Movers Lane (Flyover)
Allot Gdns
Cuckold's Haven
New England Est
IG11
Kingsbridge Ind Est
Barking Creek
Lyon Bsns Pk
Thames View Jun Sch
Sp Gd
Katella Trad Est
Cromwell Trad Ctr
River Road Bsns Pk
Creekmouth Ind Pk
THAMES RD
RIVER RD
LONG REACH RD
CREEK RD
Sewage Works
Trafalgar Bsns Ctr
Anglian Ind Est
Balmoral Trad Est
Creekmouth
River Roding
Barking Barrier
Horse End
Jetty
Superstore
Gallions Reach Shp Pk
E6
Depot
Armada Point
ARMADA WAY
Margaret or Tripcock Ness
ATLANTIS AVE
GALLIONS RD
Mast
Pier
Barking Ind Pk
Wayside Commercial Est
Barking Bsns Ctr
102
123
A B C D
44 45 46
81 82 83 84
1 2 3 4 5 6

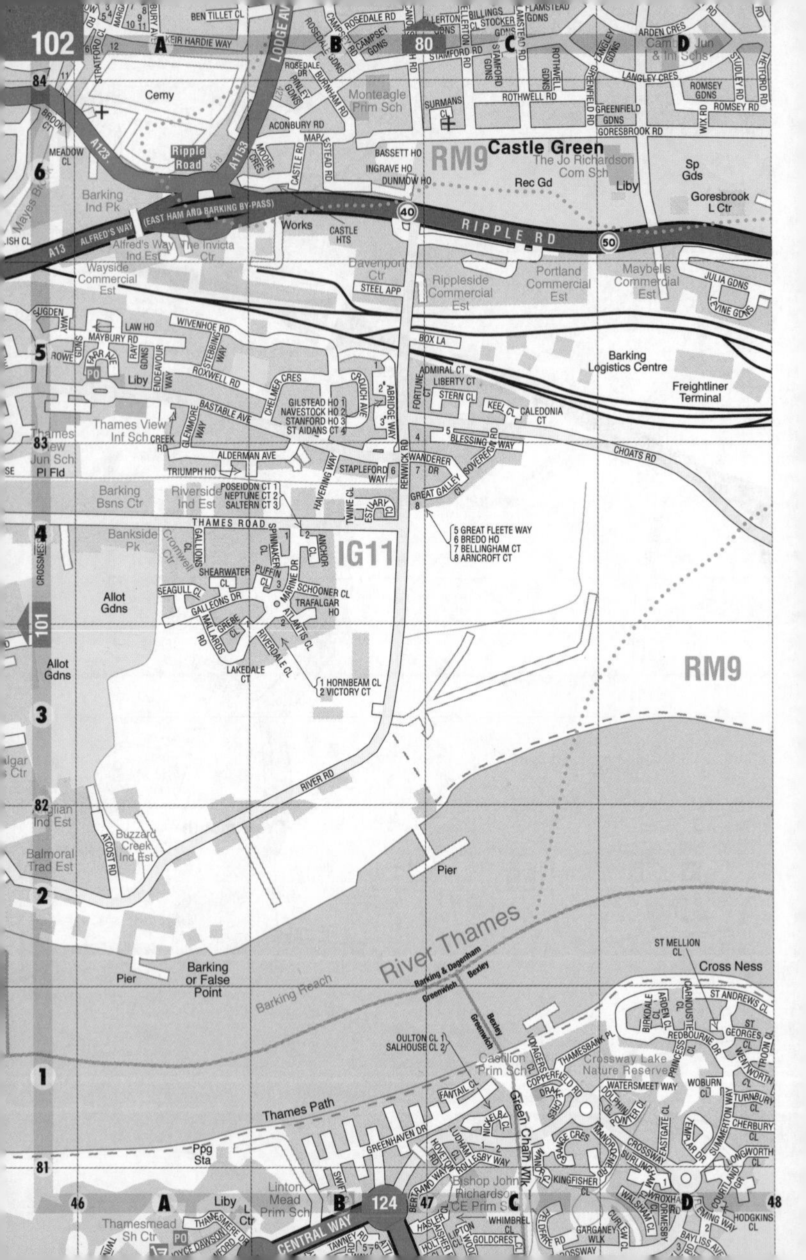
Castle Green
RM9
IG11
RM9
River Thames
Barking Reach
Cemy
Ripple Road
RIPPLE RD
ALFRED'S WAY
(EAST HAM AND BARKING BY-PASS)
Barking Ind Pk
Alfred's Way Ind Est
The Invicta Ctr
Wayside Commercial Est
Davenport Ctr
Rippleside Commercial Est
Portland Commercial Est
Maybells Commercial Est
Monteagle Prim Sch
The Jo Richardson Com Sch
Rec Gd
Liby
Sp Gds
Goresbrook L Ctr
Barking Logistics Centre
Freightliner Terminal
Thames View Inf Sch
Thames View Jun Sch
Pl Fld
Barking Bsns Ctr
Riverside Ind Est
Bankside Pk
Cromwell Ctr
Allot Gdns
Allot Gdns
Anglian Ind Est
Buzzard Creek Ind Est
Balmoral Trad Est
Pier
Pier
Barking or False Point
Cross Ness
Castilion Prim Sch
Crossway Lake Nature Reserve
Thames Path
Green Chain Wlk
Ppg Sta
Linton Mead Prim Sch
Bishop John Richardson CE Prim Sch
Thamesmead Sh Ctr
Barking & Dagenham
Bexley
Greenwich
POSEIDON CT 1
NEPTUNE CT 2
SALTERN CT 3
GILSTEAD HO 1
NAVESTOCK HO 2
STANFORD HO 3
ST AIDANS CT 4
5 GREAT FLEETE WAY
6 BREDO HO
7 BELLINGHAM CT
8 ARNCROFT CT
1 HORNBEAM CL
2 VICTORY CT
OULTON CL 1
SALHOUSE CL 2
80
101
124
A B C D
46 47 48
84 83 82 81
6 5 4 3 2 1

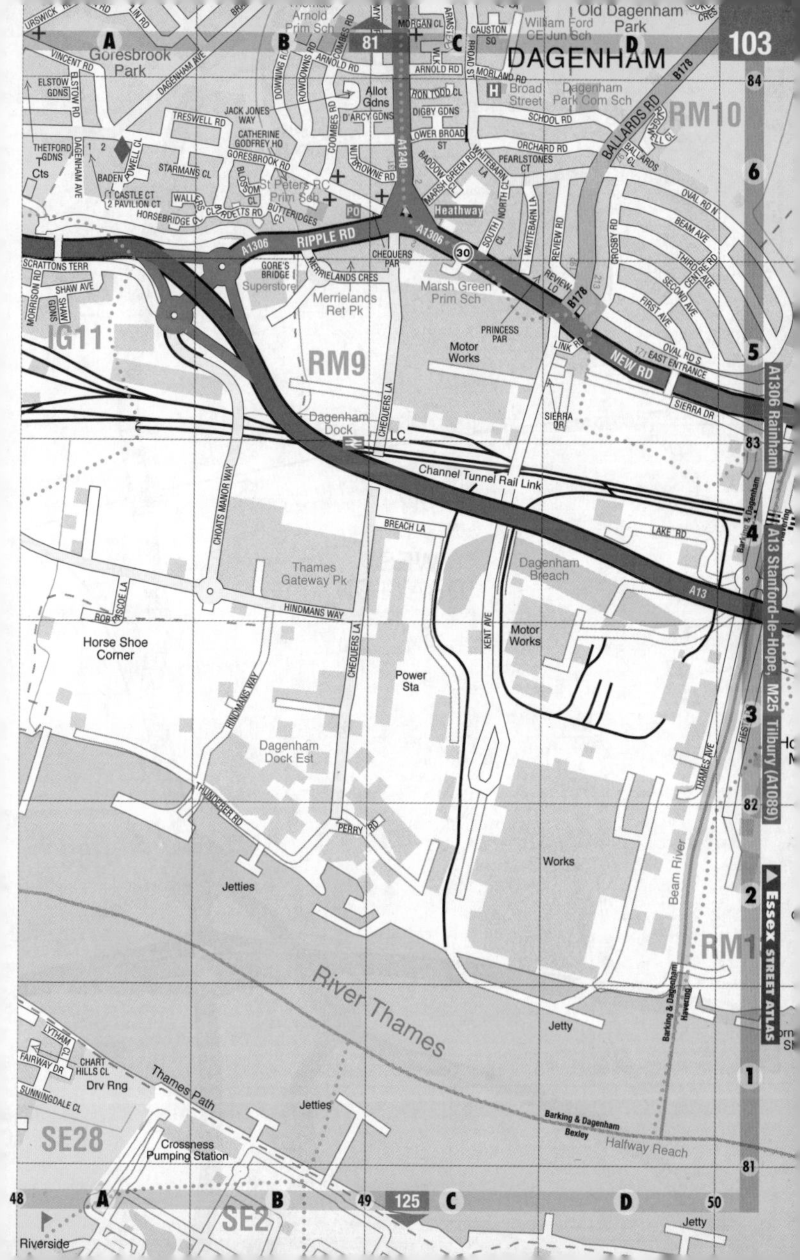
DAGENHAM
Old Dagenham Park
William Ford CE Jun Sch
Goresbrook Park
Arnold Prim Sch
Allot Gdns
Broad Street
Dagenham Park Com Sch
RM10
St Peters RC Prim Sch
Heathway
RIPPLE RD
A1306
A1240
B178
BALLARDS RD
Superstore
Merrielands Ret Pk
Marsh Green Prim Sch
IG11
RM9
Motor Works
NEW RD
Dagenham Dock
LC
Channel Tunnel Rail Link
A13
Thames Gateway Pk
Dagenham Breach
Horse Shoe Corner
HINDMANS WAY
CHOATS MANOR WAY
CHEQUERS LA
KENT AVE
Power Sta
Dagenham Dock Est
Works
Jetties
Beam River
RM13
River Thames
Jetty
Thames Path
Drv Rng
SE28
Crossness Pumping Station
Barking & Dagenham
Bexley
Halfway Reach
SE2
Riverside
A1306 Rainham
A13 Stanford-le-Hope, M25 Tilbury (A1089)
Essex STREET ATLAS
81
125
48
49
50
84
83
82
81
A
B
C
D
1
2
3
4
5
6

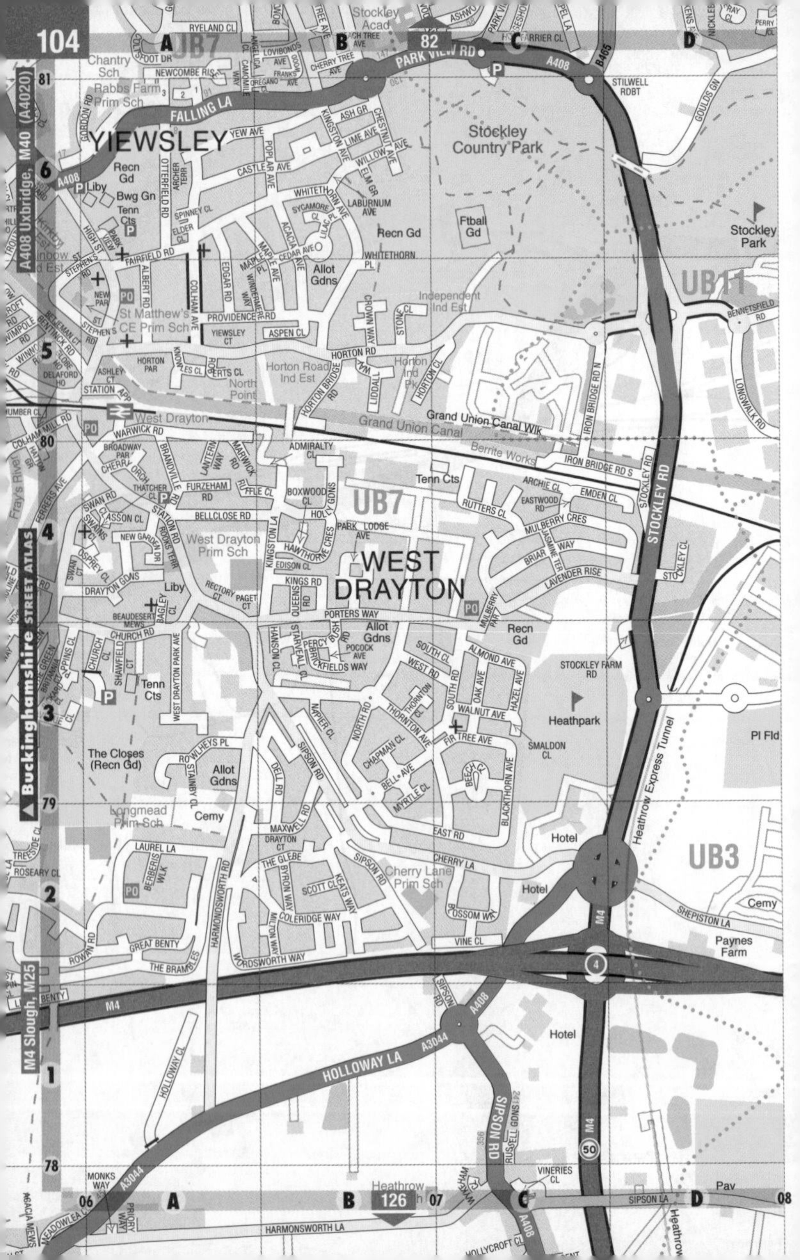
82
126
A408 Uxbridge, M40 (A4020)
Buckinghamshire STREET ATLAS
M4 Slough, M25
YIEWSLEY
WEST DRAYTON
UB7
UB11
UB3
Stockley Country Park
Stockley Park
Stockley Acad
Chantry Sch
Rabbs Farm Prim Sch
RYELAND CL
COLTSFOOT DR
NEWCOMBE RISE
LOVIBONDS AVE
FRANKS AVE
OREGANO
CAMOMILE WAY
ANGELICA CL
CHERRY TREE AVE
PEACH TREE AVE
PARK VIEW RD
A408
B465
STILWELL RDBT
GOULDS GN
FALLING LA
GORDON RD
YEW AVE
ASH GR
KINGSTON AVE
CHESTNUT AVE
LIME AVE
WILLOW AVE
ELM GR
CASTLE AVE
POPLAR AVE
OTTERFIELD RD
ARCHER TERR
Recn Gd
Liby
Bwg Gn
Tenn Cts
WHITETHORN AVE
LABURNUM AVE
SYCAMORE CL
LILAC PL
ACACIA AVE
CEDAR AVE
MAPLE AVE
MAPLE PL
WINDERMERE WAY
SPINNEY CL
ELDER CL
FAIRFIELD RD
HIGH ST
PARK VIEW
ST STEPHEN'S RD
NEW PAR
ALBERT RD
COLHAM AVE
EDGAR RD
WHITETHORN PL
Allot Gdns
Ftball Gd
CROWN WAY
STONE CL
Independent Ind Est
BENNETSFIELD RD
PROVIDENCE RD
St Matthew's CE Prim Sch
ST STEPHEN'S RD
YIEWSLEY CT
ASPEN CL
HORTON RD
HORTON PAR
KNOWLES CL
ROBERTS CL
Horton Road Ind Est
North Point
HORTON BRIDGE RD
LIDDALL WAY
Horton Ind Pk
HORTON CL
IRON BRIDGE RD N
LONGWALK RD
ASHLEY CT
STATION APP
BETJEMAN CL
BENTINCK RD
WIMPOLE RD
WINNOCK RD
DELAFORD RD
HUMBER CL
COLHAM MILL RD
West Drayton
Grand Union Canal
Grand Union Canal Wlk
WARWICK RD
BROADWAY PAR
CHERRY ORCH
BRANDVILLE RD
LANTERN WAY
MARWICK RD
ADMIRALTY CL
Berrite Works
IRON BRIDGE RD S
STOCKLEY RD
Tenn Cts
ARCHIE CL
EMDEN CL
EASTWOOD RD
RUTTERS CL
THATCHER CL
FURZEHAM RD
RUFFLE CL
BOXWOOD CL
HOLLY GDNS
SWAN RD
SWAINS CL
ASSON CL
BELLCLOSE RD
KINGSTON LA
PARK LODGE AVE
MULBERRY CRES
BRIAR WAY
JASMINE TER
LAVENDER RISE
STOCKLEY CL
Fray's River
FERRERS AVE
STATION RD
NEW GARDEN DR
ROOKS TERR
West Drayton Prim Sch
HAWTHORNE CRES
EDISON CL
OSPREY CL
SWAN CT
DRAYTON GDNS
Liby
RECTORY CT
PAGET CT
KINGS RD
QUEENS RD
BAGLEY CL
BEAUDESERT MEWS
PORTERS WAY
MULBERRY PAR
Recn Gd
CHURCH RD
HANSON CL
STARVEALL CL
PERCY RD
BUSH RD
POCOCK AVE
BRICKFIELDS WAY
Allot Gdns
STOCKLEY FARM RD
CHURCH CL
SHAWFIELD CT
WEST DRAYTON PARK AVE
Tenn Cts
SOUTH CL
ALMOND AVE
WEST RD
SOUTH RD
OAK AVE
HAZEL AVE
Heathpark
NAPIER CL
NORTH RD
THORNTON AVE
THORNTON CL
WALNUT AVE
SMALDON CL
Heathrow Express Tunnel
Pl Fld
The Closes (Recn Gd)
ROWLHEYS PL
STAINBY CL
Allot Gdns
SIPSON RD
DELL RD
CHAPMAN CL
BELL AVE
FIR TREE AVE
BEECH CL
BLACKTHORN AVE
MYRTLE CL
Longmead Prim Sch
Cemy
MAXWELL RD
DRAYTON CT
EAST RD
Hotel
TRESIDE CL
LAUREL LA
BERBERIS WLK
HARMONDSWORTH RD
THE GLEBE
BYRON WAY
SCOTT CL
KEATS WAY
SIPSON RD
CHERRY LA
Cherry Lane Prim Sch
ROSEARY CL
Hotel
BLOSSOM WAY
Cemy
SHEPISTON LA
COLERIDGE WAY
MILTON WAY
ROWAN RD
GREAT BENTY
THE BRAMBLES
WORDSWORTH WAY
VINE CL
Paynes Farm
M4
4
BENTY
SIPSON RD
A408
Hotel
HOLLOWAY CL
HOLLOWAY LA
A3044
SIPSON RD
RUSSELL GDNS
50
MONKS WAY
PRIORY WAY
WYKEHAM CL
VINERIES CL
Heathrow
SIPSON LA
Pav
ACACIA MEWS
MEADOWLEA CL
HARMONDSWORTH LA
HOLLYCROFT CL
06
07
08
81
80
79
78
A B C D
1 2 3 4 5 6

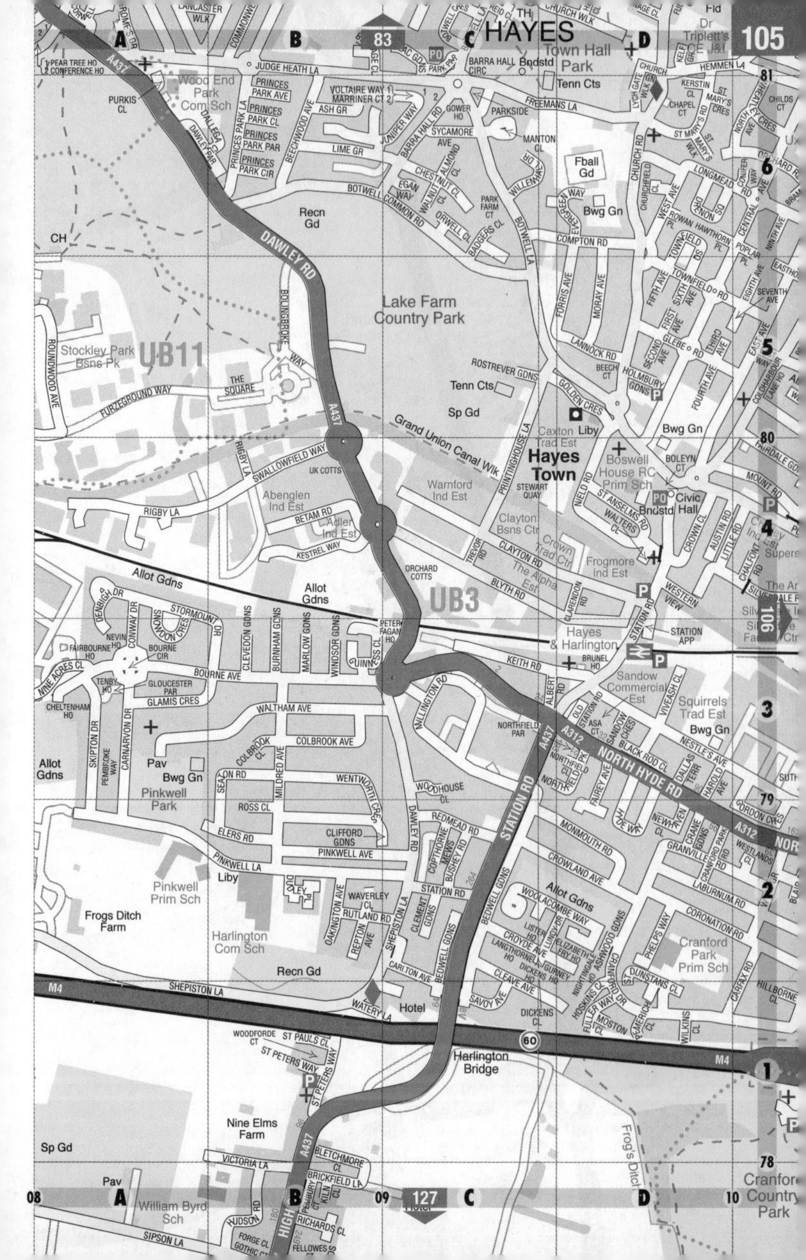
A
B
83
C
D
Wood End Park Com Sch
PURKIS CL
JUDGE HEATH LA
PRINCES PARK AVE
PRINCES PARK CL
PRINCES PARK PAR
PRINCES PARK CIR
PRINCES PARK LA
DAWLEY PAR
BEECHWOOD AVE
ASH GR
LIME GR
VOLTAIRE WAY
MARRINER CT
JUNIPER WAY
BARRA HALL RD
BARRA HALL CIRC
GOWER HO
SYCAMORE AVE
CHESTNUT CL
ALMOND CL
EGAN WAY
WALNUT CL
BOTWELL COMMON RD
ORWELL CL
PARK FARM CT
BADGERS CL
BOTWELL LA
Town Hall Park
Tenn Cts
FREEMANS LA
PARKSIDE
MANTON CL
WILLENHALL DR
Fball Gd
EVERGREEN WAY
Bwg Gn
COMPTON RD
CHURCH RD
CHURCHFIELD CL
LYCH GATE WLK
KERSTIN CL
CHAPEL CT
ST MARY'S RD
ST MARY'S CRES
HEMMEN LA
CHILDS CT
LONGMEAD RD
CONIFER WAY
CENTRAL AVE
WEST AVE
ROWAN PL
HAWTHORN PL
POPLAR PL
NINTH AVE
TOWNFIELD RD
TOWNFIELD SQ
FIFTH AVE
FIRST AVE
SIXTH AVE
EIGHTH AVE
SEVENTH AVE
SECOND AVE
GLEBE RD
THIRD AVE
EAST AVE
FOURTH AVE
81
6
5
80
4
3
79
2
1
78
Recn Gd
CH
DAWLEY RD
A437
BOLINGBROKE WAY
Lake Farm Country Park
Stockley Park Bsns Pk
UB11
ROUNDWOOD AVE
THE SQUARE
FURZEGROUND WAY
FORRIS AVE
MORAY AVE
LANNOCK RD
ROSTREVER GDNS
BEECH CT
HOLMBURY GDNS
GOLDEN CRES
Tenn Cts
Sp Gd
Liby
Caxton Trad Est
Hayes Town
Grand Union Canal Wlk
PRINTINGHOUSE LA
RIGBY LA
SWALLOWFIELD WAY
UK COTTS
Abenglen Ind Est
Warnford Ind Est
STEWART QUAY
Boswell House RC Prim Sch
BOLEYN CT
Civic Hall
Bndstd
NIELD RD
ST ANSELMS RD
WALTERS CL
MOUNT RD
FAIRDALE GDNS
BETAM RD
Adler Ind Est
KESTREL WAY
Clayton Bsns Ctr
Crown Trad Ctr
TREVOR RD
CLAYTON RD
The Alpha Est
Frogmore Ind Est
CROWN CL
AUSTIN RD
LITTLE RD
CHALFONT RD
Allot Gdns
ORCHARD COTTS
BLYTH RD
CLARENDON RD
WESTERN VIEW
STATION RD
UB3
DENBIGH DR
STORMOUNT DR
SNOWDON CRES
NEVIN HO
CONWAY DR
CLEVEDON GDNS
BURNHAM GDNS
MARLOW GDNS
WINDSOR GDNS
PETER FAGAN HO
GUINNESS CL
Hayes & Harlington
STATION APP
106
FAIRBOURNE HO
BOURNE CIR
NINE ACRES CL
TENBY HO
GLOUCESTER PAR
BOURNE AVE
GLAMIS CRES
KEITH RD
BRUNEL HO
ALBERT RD
Sandow Commercial Est
VIVEASH CL
Squirrels Trad Est
CHELTENHAM HO
WALTHAM AVE
MILLINGTON RD
NORTHFIELD PAR
OLD STATION RD
ASA CT
SANDOW CRES
A312
NORTH HYDE RD
BLACK ROD CL
NESTLE'S AVE
COLBROOK CL
COLBROOK AVE
SKIPTON DR
PEMBROKE WAY
CARNARVON DR
Pav
Bwg Gn
SEATON RD
MILDRED AVE
WENTWORTH CRES
WOODHOUSE CL
NORTHFIELD CL
FAIREY AVE
DALLAS TERR
HAROLD AVE
Pinkwell Park
ROSS CL
HYDE WAY
NEWHAVEN CL
CRANE GDNS
GORDON CRES
Allot Gdns
ELERS RD
CLIFFORD GDNS
DAWLEY RD
REDMEAD RD
MONMOUTH RD
GRANVILLE RD
CRANFORD PARK RD
WESTLANDS CL
PINKWELL LA
PINKWELL AVE
COPTHORNE MEWS
BUSHEY RD
CROWLAND AVE
LABURNUM RD
Liby
Pinkwell Prim Sch
DUDLEY PL
WAVERLEY CL
STATION RD
BEDWELL GDNS
WOOLACOMBE WAY
CORONATION RD
Frogs Ditch Farm
OAKINGTON AVE
RUTLAND RD
CLEMENT GDNS
LISTER HO
LUNDY DR
ELIZABETH FRY HO
ASHWOOD GDNS
PHELPS WAY
Cranford Park Prim Sch
Harlington Com Sch
REPTON AVE
SHEPISTON LA
CROYDE AVE
LANGTHORNE HO
DICKENS HO
GURNEY
NIGHTINGALE HO
CARRAX RD
Recn Gd
CARLTON AVE
CLEAVE AVE
ST DUNSTANS CL
HILLBORNE CL
M4
SHEPISTON LA
WATERY LA
Hotel
SAVOY AVE
DICKENS CL
HOSKINS CL
CRANFORD DR
FULLER WAY
MOSTON CL
PEMERICH CL
WILKINS CL
WOODFORDE CT
ST PAULS CL
ST PETERS WAY
60
Harlington Bridge
Frog's Ditch
Nine Elms Farm
Sp Gd
VICTORIA LA
BLETCHMORE CL
BRICKFIELD LA
Pav
PEMBURY CT
KILN CL
William Byrd Sch
HUDSON RD
HIGH
RICHARDS CL
SIPSON LA
FORGE CL
GOTHIC CT
FELLOWES
08
09
127
10
Cranford Country Park

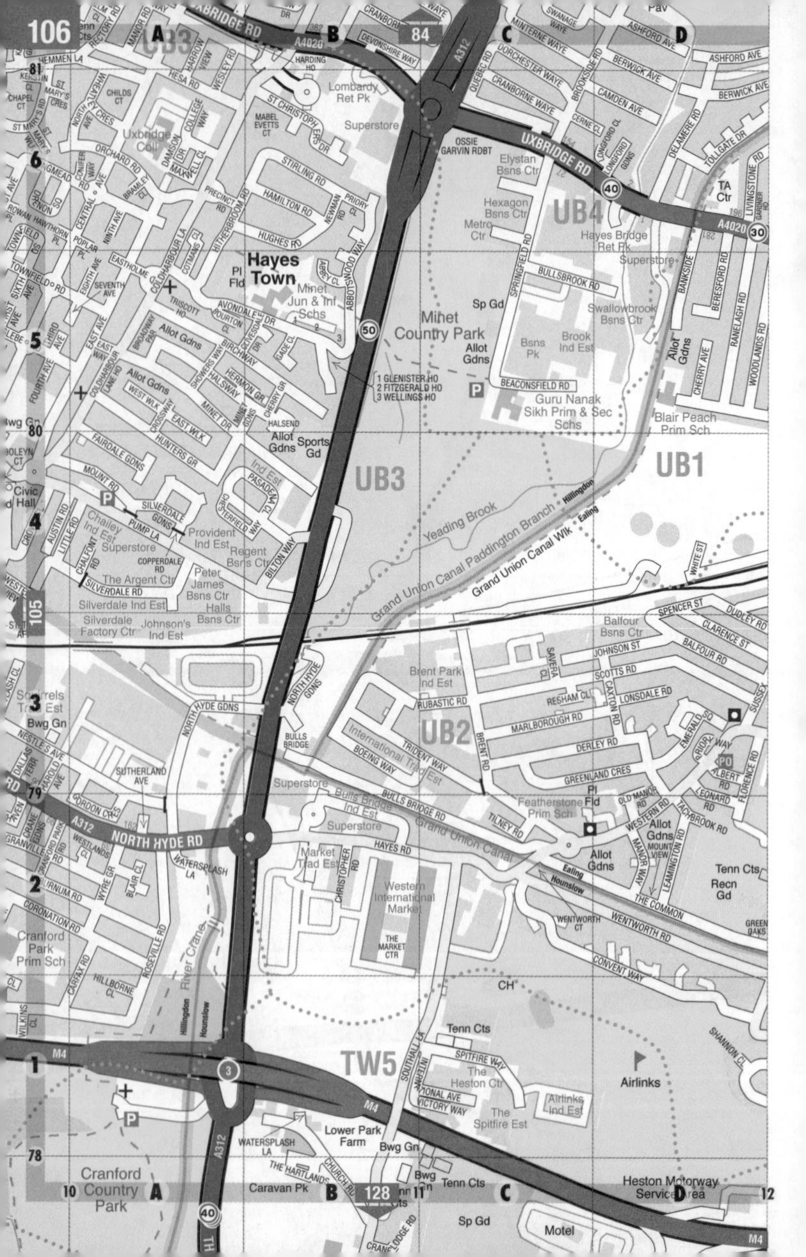

UXBRIDGE RD
A4020
84
Lombardy Ret Pk
Superstore
OSSIE GARVIN RDBT
Elystan Bsns Ctr
Hexagon Bsns Ctr
Metro Ctr
UB4
UB3
Uxbridge Coll
Hayes Town
Minet Jun & Inf Schs
Minet Country Park
Hayes Bridge Ret Pk
Swallowbrook Bsns Ctr
Brook Ind Est
Bsns Pk
Guru Nanak Sikh Prim & Sec Schs
Blair Peach Prim Sch
1 GLENISTER HO
2 FITZGERALD HO
3 WELLINGS HO
UB1
Yeading Brook
Grand Union Canal Paddington Branch
Grand Union Canal Wlk
Chailey Ind Est
Provident Ind Est
Regent Bsns Ctr
The Argent Ctr
Peter James Bsns Ctr
Halls Bsns Ctr
Silverdale Ind Est
Silverdale Factory Ctr
Johnson's Ind Est
Civic Hall
105
Balfour Bsns Ctr
Brent Park Ind Est
UB2
International Trad Est
Squirrels Trad Est
Bulls Bridge Ind Est
Market Trad Est
Western International Market
THE MARKET CTR
Featherstone Prim Sch
Grand Union Canal
NORTH HYDE RD
A312
Cranford Park Prim Sch
River Crane
TW5
M4
The Heston Ctr
Airlinks Ind Est
The Spitfire Est
Airlinks
Lower Park Farm
Cranford Country Park
Caravan Pk
128
Heston Motorway Service Area
Motel
Tenn Cts
Recn Gd

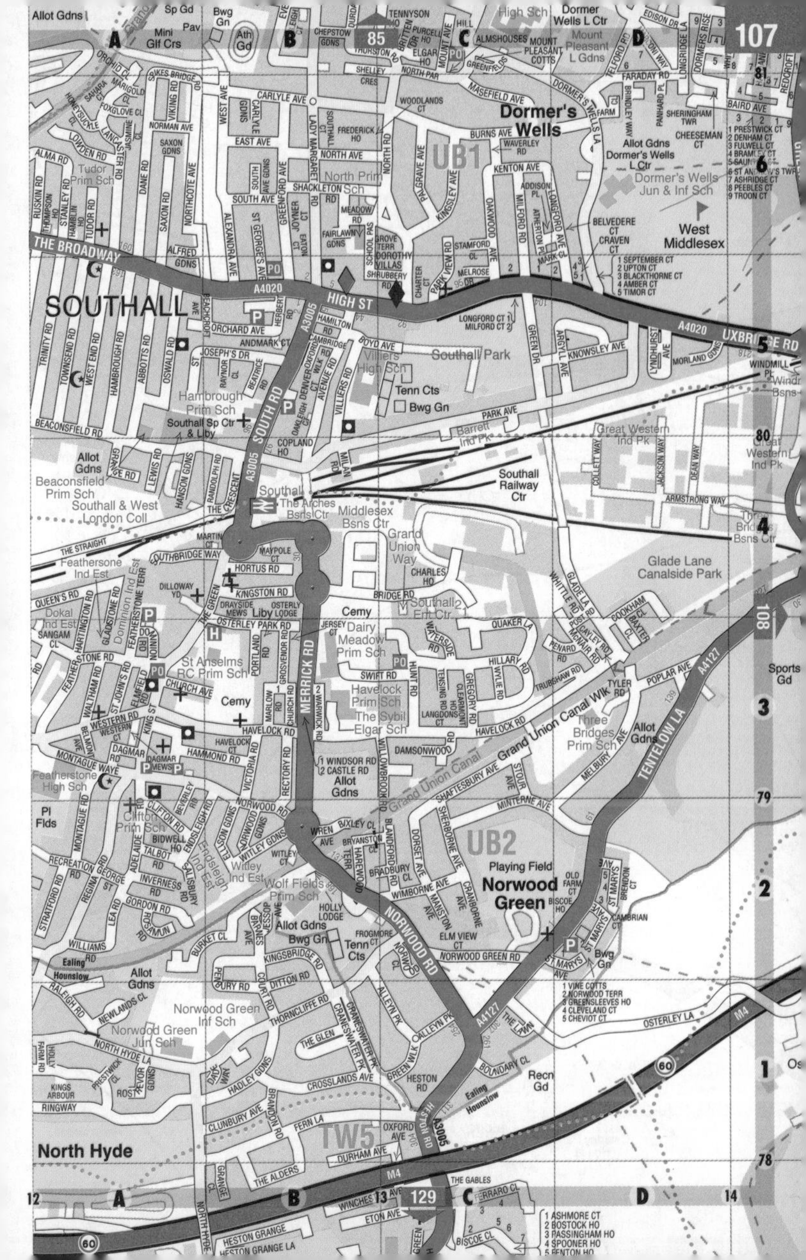

107
85
129
A
B
C
D
12
13
14
81
80
79
78
6
5
4
3
2
1
108
SOUTHALL
Dormer's Wells
Norwood Green
North Hyde
UB1
UB2
TW5
THE BROADWAY
HIGH ST
A4020
UXBRIDGE RD
A3005
SOUTH RD
MERRICK RD
NORWOOD RD
HESTON RD
A4127
TENTELOW LA
M4
60
Grand Union Canal
Grand Union Canal Wlk
Allot Gdns
Sp Gd
Pav
Bwg Gn
Mini Glf Crs
Ath Gd
High Sch
Dormer Wells L Ctr
Mount Pleasant L Gdns
ALMSHOUSES
MOUNT PLEASANT COTTS
Tudor Prim Sch
North Prim Sch
Allot Gdns Dormer's Wells L Ctr
Dormer's Wells Jun & Inf Sch
West Middlesex
Southall Park
Villiers High Sch
Tenn Cts
Bwg Gn
Hambrough Prim Sch
Southall Sp Ctr & Liby
Barrett Ind Pk
Great Western Ind Pk
Southall Railway Ctr
Beaconsfield Prim Sch
Southall & West London Coll
Southall
The Arches Bsns Ctr
Middlesex Bsns Ctr
Grand Union Way
Glade Lane Canalside Park
Three Bridges Bsns Ctr
Feathersone Ind Est
Dominion Ind Est
Dokal Ind Est
Liby
Cemy
Dairy Meadow Prim Sch
Southall Ent Ctr
St Anselms RC Prim Sch
Havelock Prim Sch
The Sybil Elgar Sch
Three Bridges Prim Sch
Allot Gdns
Sports Gd
Featherstone High Sch
Pl Flds
Clifton Prim Sch
Endsleigh Ind Est
Witley Ind Est
Wolf Fields Prim Sch
Playing Field
Allot Gdns
Bwg Gn
Tenn Cts
Norwood Green Inf Sch
Norwood Green Jun Sch
Recn Gd
Ealing
Hounslow
1 SEPTEMBER CT
2 UPTON CT
3 BLACKTHORNE CT
4 AMBER CT
5 TIMOR CT
1 PRESTWICK CT
2 DENHAM CT
3 FULWELL CT
4 BRAMLEY CT
5 SAUNTON CT
6 ST ANDREW'S TWR
7 ASHRIDGE CT
8 PEEBLES CT
9 TROON CT
1 WINDSOR RD
2 CASTLE RD
1 VINE COTTS
2 NORWOOD TERR
3 GREENSLEEVES HO
4 CLEVELAND CT
5 CHEVIOT CT
1 ASHMORE CT
2 BOSTOCK HO
3 PASSINGHAM HO
4 SPOONER HO
LONGFORD CT 1
MILFORD CT 2

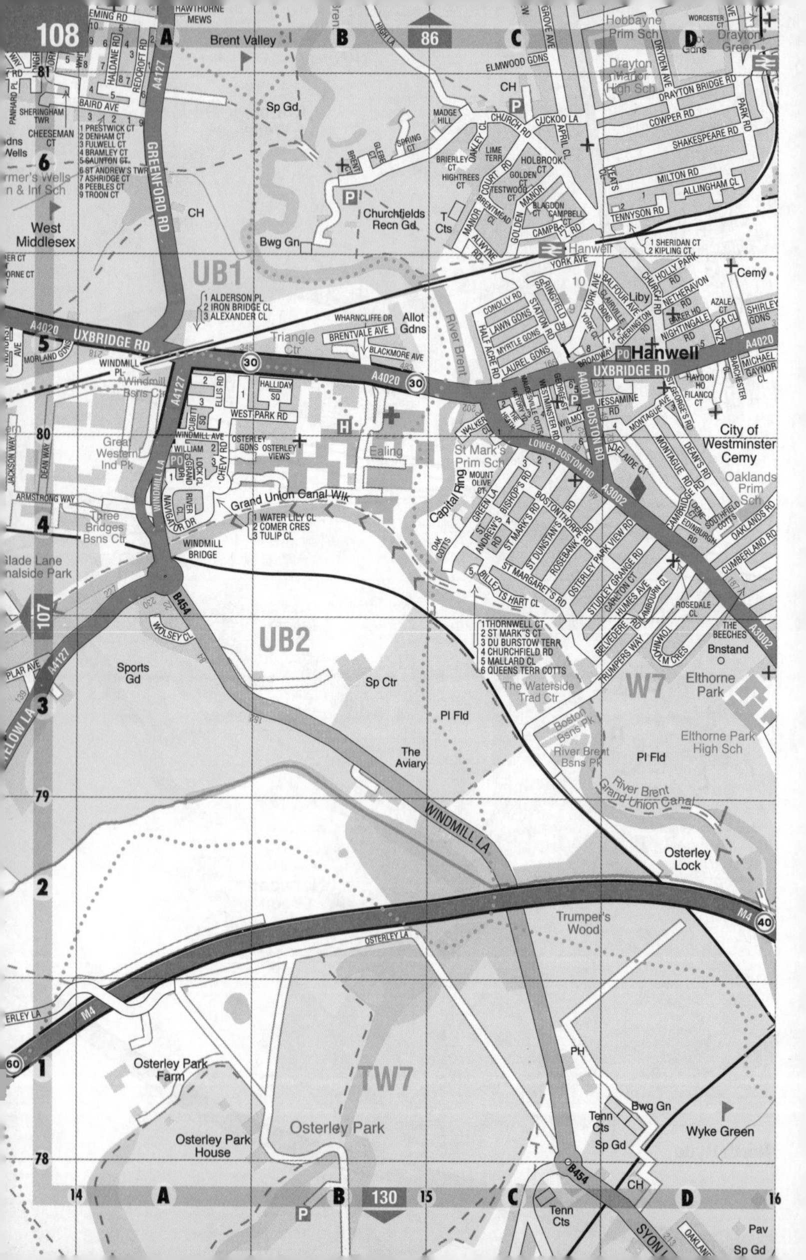

Brent Valley
86
Hobbayne Prim Sch
Drayton Green
Drayton Manor High Sch
UB1
UB2
W7
TW7
Hanwell
Uxbridge Rd
Greenford Rd
Windmill La
Boston Rd
Churchfields Recn Gd
West Middlesex
Great Western Ind Pk
Three Bridges Bsns Ctr
Grand Union Canal Wlk
Ealing
St Mark's Prim Sch
City of Westminster Cemy
Oaklands Prim Sch
Elthorne Park
Elthorne Park High Sch
The Waterside Trad Ctr
Boston Bsns Pk
River Brent Bsns Pk
Osterley Lock
Trumper's Wood
The Aviary
Osterley Park
Osterley Park House
Osterley Park Farm
Wyke Green
107
130

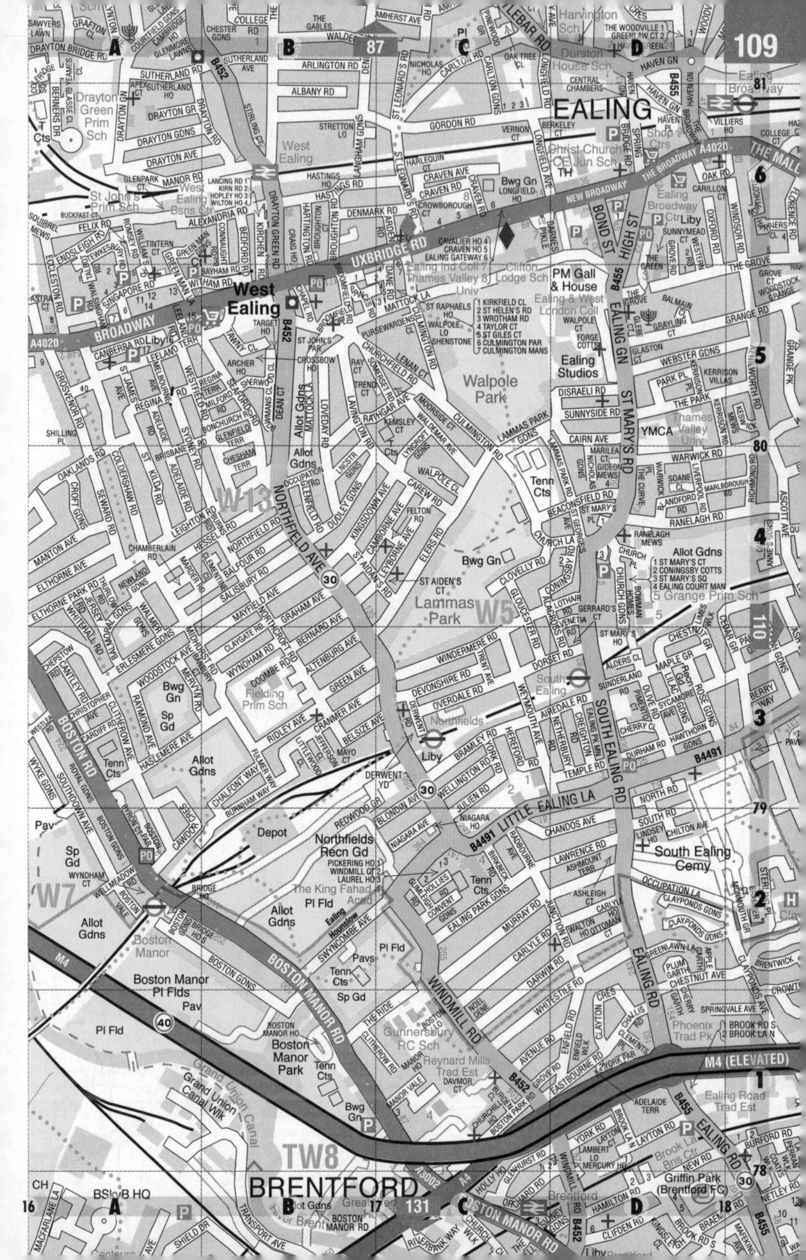

EALING
West Ealing
BRENTFORD
W13
W5
W7
TW8
87
131
110
A
B
C
D
16
17
18
81
80
79
78
6
5
4
3
2
1
Drayton Green Prim Sch
St John's Prim Sch
West Ealing Bsns Ctr
Christ Church CE Jun Sch
Harvington Sch
Durston House Sch
Ealing Broadway Ctr
Ealing Broadway
PM Gall & House
Ealing & West London Coll
Ealing Studios
Walpole Park
Lammas Park
Thames Valley Univ
YMCA
Ealing Ind Coll
Clifton Lodge Sch
Fielding Prim Sch
Grange Prim Sch
South Ealing
Northfields
Northfields Recn Gd
The King Fahad Acad
South Ealing Cemy
Boston Manor
Boston Manor Pl Flds
Boston Manor Park
Gunnersbury RC Sch
Reynard Mills Trad Est
Phoenix Trad Pk
Ealing Road Trad Est
Brook La Bns Ctr
Griffin Park (Brentford FC)
BSkyB HQ
Grand Union Canal
Grand Union Canal Wlk
Depot
Allot Gdns
Tenn Cts
Bwg Gn
Pl Fld
Sp Gd
Pav
Liby
UXBRIDGE RD
BROADWAY
NEW BROADWAY
THE BROADWAY
THE MALL
A4020
B452
B455
B4491
A3002
A4
M4
M4 (ELEVATED)
NORTHFIELD AVE
BOSTON RD
BOSTON MANOR RD
SOUTH EALING RD
ST MARY'S RD
EALING GN
HIGH ST
BOND ST
EALING RD
WINDMILL RD
LITTLE EALING LA
CULMINGTON RD
DRAYTON GREEN RD
GORDON RD
MATTOCK LA
GROSVENOR RD
OCCUPATION LA

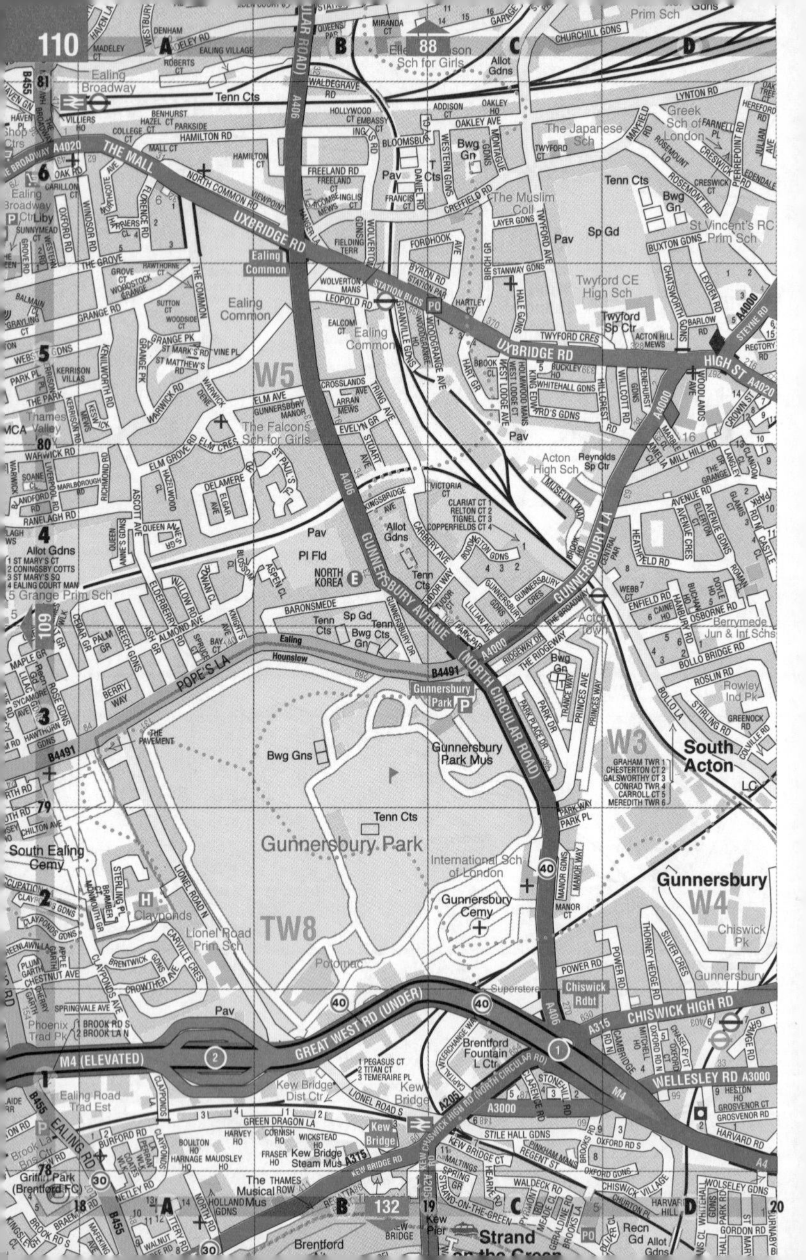

A
B
C
D
88
Ellen Wilkinson Sch for Girls
Ealing Broadway
Tenn Cts
The Japanese Sch
Greek Sch of London
THE MALL
UXBRIDGE RD
NORTH COMMON RD
The Muslim Coll
Twyford CE High Sch
Twyford Sp Ctr
St Vincent's RC Prim Sch
Ealing Common
W5
The Falcons Sch for Girls
Acton High Sch
Reynolds Sp Ctr
HIGH ST
GUNNERSBURY AVENUE (NORTH CIRCULAR ROAD)
GUNNERSBURY LA
Acton Town
W3
South Acton
Berrymede Jun & Int Schs
Rowley Ind Pk
POPE'S LA
Gunnersbury Park
Gunnersbury Park Mus
Gunnersbury Park
International Sch of London
Gunnersbury Cemy
Gunnersbury
W4
Chiswick Pk
South Ealing Cemy
Clayponds
Lionel Road Prim Sch
TW8
GREAT WEST RD (UNDER)
M4 (ELEVATED)
CHISWICK HIGH RD
Chiswick Rdbt
Brentford Fountain L Ctr
Kew Bridge Dist Ctr
Kew Bridge
WELLESLEY RD A3000
Kew Bridge Steam Mus
The Musical Mus
Griffin Park (Brentford FC)
Ealing Road Trad Est
Phoenix Trad Pk
EALING RD
109
132
Kew Pier
Strand on the Green
Brentford
18
19
20

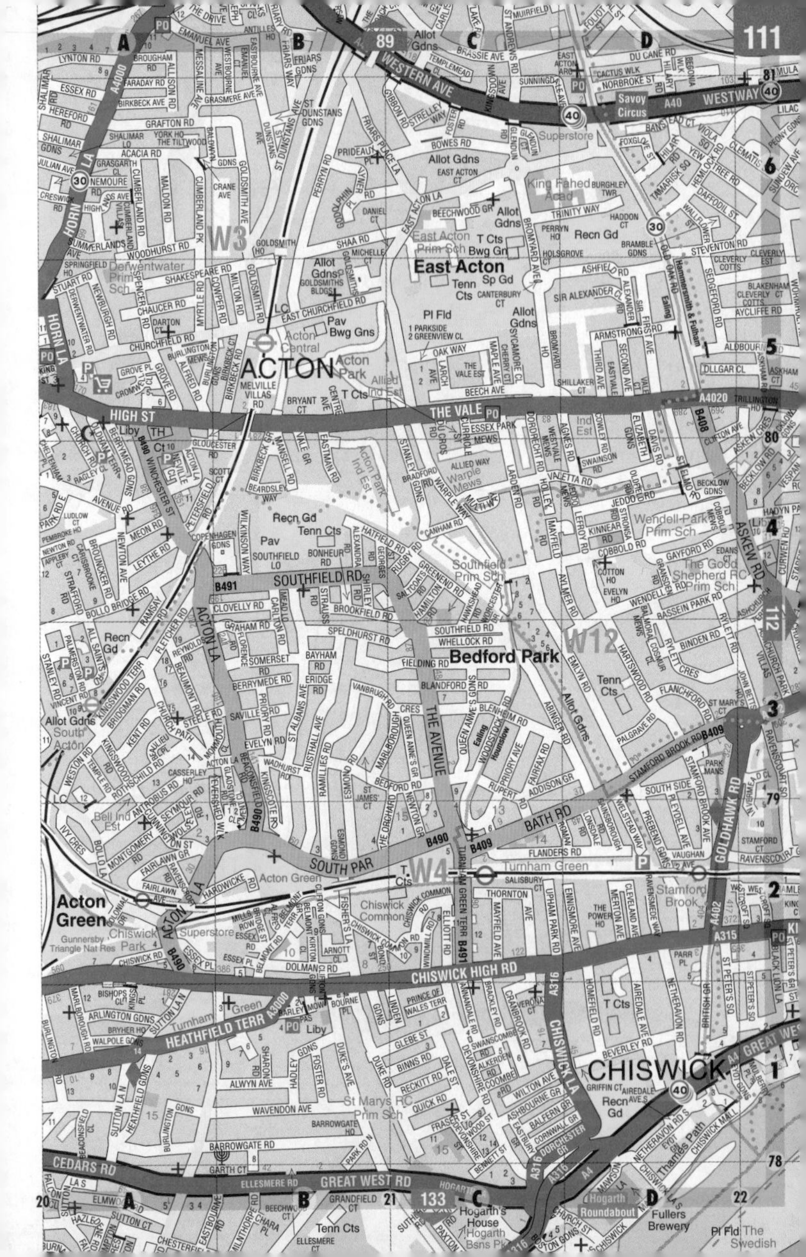
111
A
B
C
D
89
WESTERN AVE
A40
WESTWAY
Savoy Circus
W3
ACTON
Acton Central
Acton Park
East Acton
HIGH ST
THE VALE
A4020
SOUTHFIELD RD
B491
Bedford Park
W12
THE AVENUE
BATH RD
B409
SOUTH PAR
B490
W4
Turnham Green
Stamford Brook
Acton Green
Chiswick Park
Chiswick Common
CHISWICK HIGH RD
HEATHFIELD TERR
A3000
CHISWICK LA
A316
CHISWICK
GREAT WEST RD
CEDARS RD
A4
Hogarth Roundabout
Fullers Brewery
Hogarth's House
GOLDHAWK RD
A402
ASKEW RD
STAMFORD BROOK RD
HORN LA
A4000
112
133
20
21
22
1
2
3
4
5
6
78
79
80
81

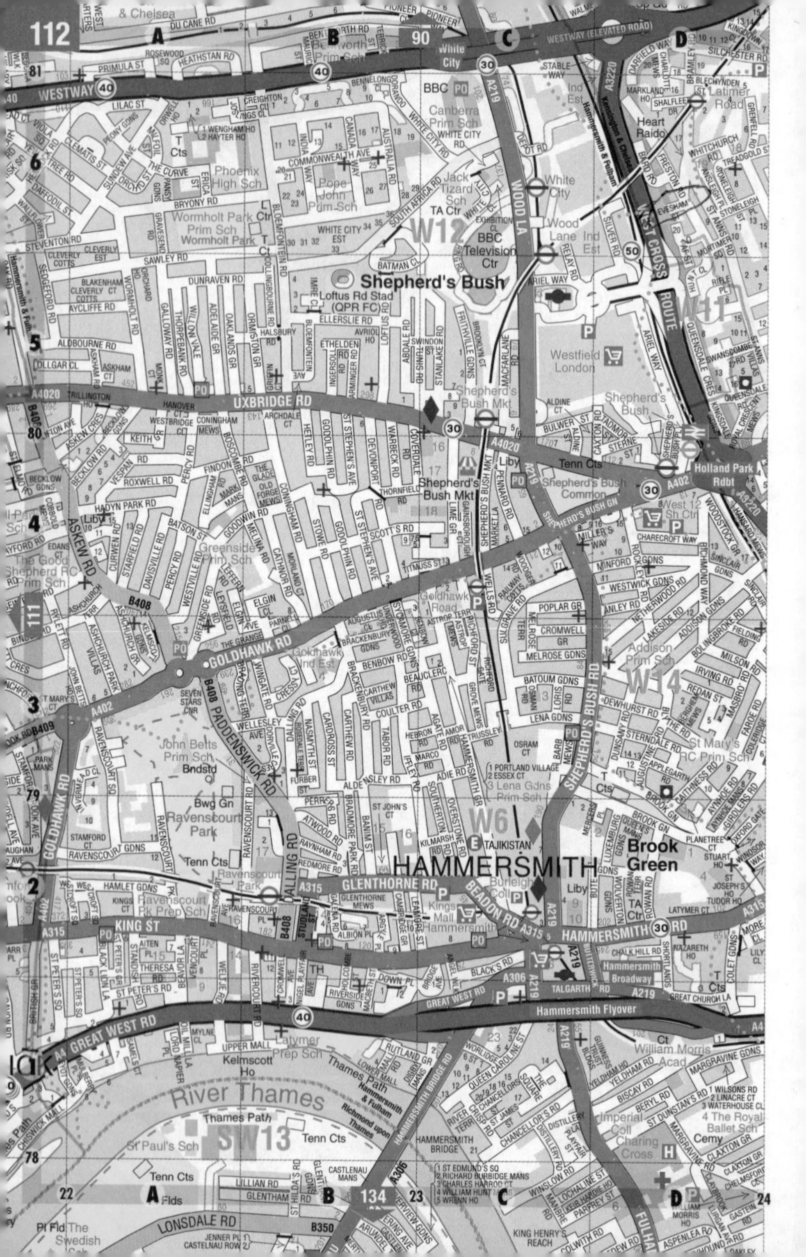
WESTWAY (ELEVATED ROAD)
WESTWAY
DU CANE RD
White City
BBC
Canberra Prim Sch
Phoenix High Sch
Pope John Prim Sch
Wormholt Park Prim Sch
Wormholt Park
WHITE CITY EST
W12
BBC Television Ctr
Shepherd's Bush
Loftus Rd Stad (QPR FC)
Westfield London
Heart Raido
Latimer Road
WEST CROSS ROUTE
W11
UXBRIDGE RD
Shepherd's Bush Mkt
Shepherd's Bush Common
SHEPHERD'S BUSH GN
Holland Park Rdbt
West 12 Sh Ctr
Greenside Prim Sch
GOLDHAWK RD
Goldhawk Road
Goldhawk Ind Est
Addison Prim Sch
W14
St Mary's RC Prim Sch
John Betts Prim Sch
Ravenscourt Park
PADDENSWICK RD
SHEPHERD'S BUSH RD
W6
HAMMERSMITH
Brook Green
GLENTHORNE RD
Kings Mall
HAMMERSMITH RD
KING ST
Hammersmith Broadway
TALGARTH RD
Hammersmith Flyover
GREAT WEST RD
Latymer Prep Sch
Kelmscott Ho
River Thames
Thames Path
SW13
St Paul's Sch
HAMMERSMITH BRIDGE
William Morris Acad
Imperial Coll Charing Cross
LONSDALE RD
The Swedish
A
B
C
D
1
2
3
4
5
6
90
111
134
22
23
24
78
79
80
81

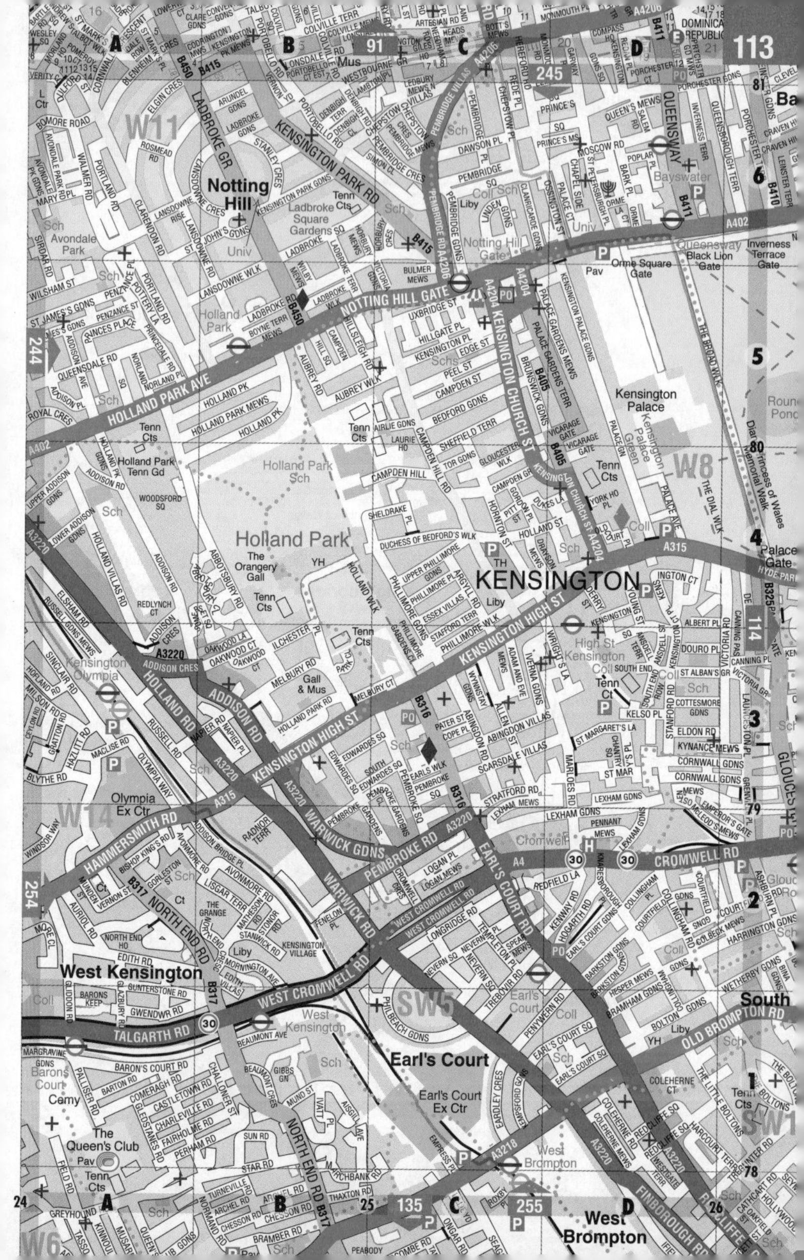
A
B
C
D
91
245
244
114
254
135
255
W11
W8
W14
SW5
Notting Hill
Kensington
West Kensington
Earl's Court
West Brompton
South
Ladbroke Square Gardens
Avondale Park
Holland Park
Holland Park Tenn Gd
The Orangery Gall
Kensington Palace
Kensington Palace Green
Kensington Olympia
Olympia Ex Ctr
Earl's Court Ex Ctr
The Queen's Club
Bayswater
Queensway
Notting Hill Gate
High St Kensington
Queensway Black Lion Gate
Orme Square Gate
Inverness Terrace Gate
Palace Gate
Diana Princess of Wales Memorial Walk
THE BROAD WLK
THE DIAL WLK
LADBROKE GR
KENSINGTON PARK RD
PEMBRIDGE VILLAS
PORTOBELLO RD
WESTBOURNE GR
QUEENSWAY
MOSCOW RD
PEMBRIDGE RD A4206
NOTTING HILL GATE
HOLLAND PARK AVE
KENSINGTON CHURCH ST
KENSINGTON PALACE GDNS
CAMPDEN HILL RD
HOLLAND WLK
KENSINGTON HIGH ST
HOLLAND RD
ADDISON RD
ADDISON CRES
HAMMERSMITH RD
NORTH END RD
WARWICK GDNS
WARWICK RD
PEMBROKE RD
EARL'S COURT RD
CROMWELL RD
WEST CROMWELL RD
TALGARTH RD
OLD BROMPTON RD
FINBOROUGH RD
REDCLIFFE SQ
GLOUCESTER RD
A4
A315
A402
A3220
A4204
A4206
A3218
B450
B415
B411
B405
B316
B317
B325
B410
24
25
26
78
79
80
81
1
2
3
4
5
6

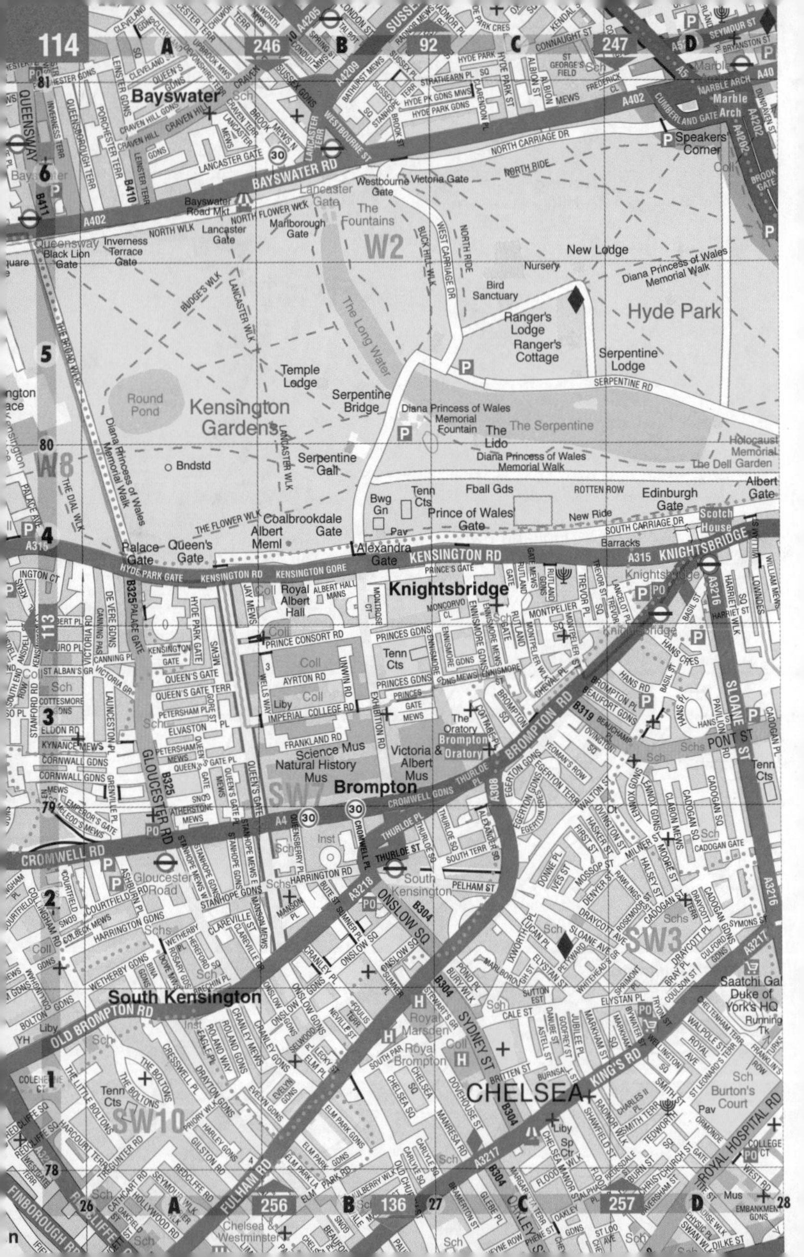
A
B
C
D
246
92
247
256
136
257
Bayswater
BAYSWATER RD
QUEENSWAY
LANCASTER GATE
NORTH CARRIAGE DR
NORTH RIDE
Westbourne Gate
Victoria Gate
Speakers' Corner
Marble Arch
MARBLE ARCH
CUMBERLAND GATE
CONNAUGHT ST
SEYMOUR ST
BRYANSTON ST
Bayswater Road Mkt
Lancaster Gate
Marlborough Gate
The Fountains
W2
Inverness Terrace Gate
Black Lion Gate
Queensway
NORTH FLOWER WLK
NORTH WLK
BUDGE'S WLK
LANCASTER WLK
THE BROAD WLK
The Long Water
BUCK HILL WLK
WEST CARRIAGE DR
Bird Sanctuary
Nursery
New Lodge
Diana Princess of Wales Memorial Walk
Hyde Park
Ranger's Lodge
Ranger's Cottage
Serpentine Lodge
SERPENTINE RD
Temple Lodge
Serpentine Bridge
Round Pond
Kensington Gardens
Diana Princess of Wales Memorial Fountain
The Lido
The Serpentine
Holocaust Memorial
The Dell Garden
Bndstd
Serpentine Gall
W8
THE DIAL WLK
ROTTEN ROW
Fball Gds
Tenn Cts
Bwg Gn
Prince of Wales' Gate
Edinburgh Gate
Albert Gate
New Ride
SOUTH CARRIAGE DR
Scotch House
Barracks
THE FLOWER WLK
Coalbrookdale Gate
Albert Meml
Palace Gate
Queen's Gate
Alexandra Gate
KENSINGTON RD
KENSINGTON GORE
HYDE PARK GATE
KNIGHTSBRIDGE
Knightsbridge
Royal Albert Hall
PRINCE CONSORT RD
PRINCES GDNS
EXHIBITION RD
IMPERIAL COLLEGE RD
Science Mus
Natural History Mus
Victoria & Albert Mus
Brompton
Brompton Oratory
The Oratory
BROMPTON RD
SW7
CROMWELL RD
CROMWELL GDNS
GLOUCESTER RD
Gloucester Road
QUEEN'S GATE
HARRINGTON RD
THURLOE ST
THURLOE PL
South Kensington
ONSLOW SQ
PELHAM ST
SLOANE ST
SLOANE AVE
PONT ST
HANS PL
CADOGAN SQ
SW3
SYDNEY ST
Royal Marsden
Royal Brompton
CHELSEA
KING'S RD
South Kensington
OLD BROMPTON RD
THE BOLTONS
SW10
FULHAM RD
ROYAL HOSPITAL RD
Saatchi Gal
Duke of York's HQ
Burton's Court
FINBOROUGH RD
Chelsea & Westminster
EMBANKMENT GDNS

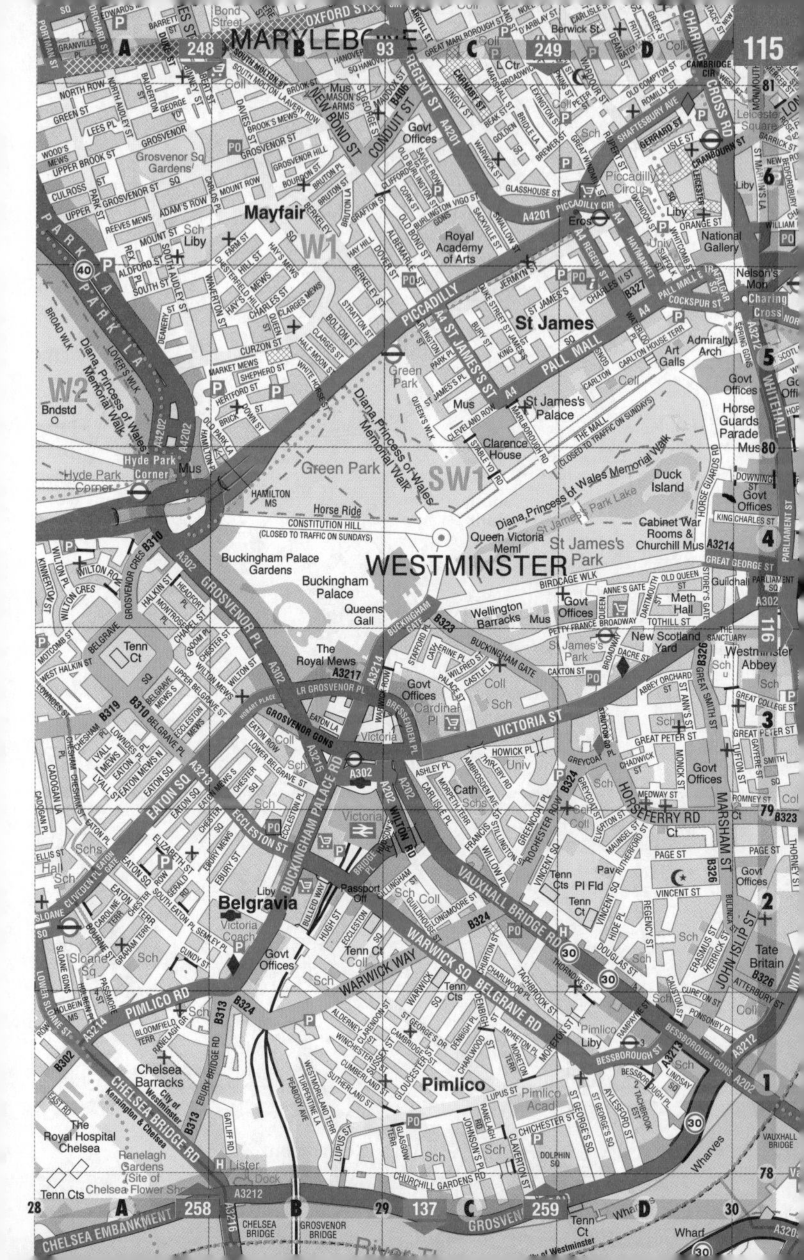
MARYLEBONE
248
93
249
A
B
C
D
Mayfair
W1
W2
SW1
St James
WESTMINSTER
Belgravia
Pimlico
Oxford St
Regent St
New Bond St
Conduit St
Carnaby St
Wardour St
Shaftesbury Ave
Charing Cross Rd
Gerrard St
Cranbourn St
Leicester Square
Piccadilly Circus
Piccadilly Cir
Eros
Haymarket
Grosvenor Sq Gardens
Grosvenor St
Mount St
Park Lane
Park St
South Audley St
Curzon St
Berkeley Sq
Piccadilly
Royal Academy of Arts
Jermyn St
St James's St
Pall Mall
Trafalgar Sq
Cockspur St
National Gallery
Nelson's Mon
Charing Cross
Admiralty Arch
Art Galls
Whitehall
Horse Guards Parade
Govt Offices
Downing St
Horse Guards Rd
Duck Island
Cabinet War Rooms & Churchill Mus
King Charles St
Great George St
Parliament St
Green Park
Diana, Princess of Wales Memorial Walk
Constitution Hill
(Closed to traffic on Sundays)
Horse Ride
The Mall
St James's Palace
Clarence House
Hyde Park Corner
Hyde Park
Bndstd
Broad Wlk
Lover's Wlk
Hamilton Ms
Queen Victoria Meml
St James's Park
St James's Park Lake
Buckingham Palace Gardens
Buckingham Palace
Queens Gall
Birdcage Wlk
Wellington Barracks
Mus
Petty France
Broadway
New Scotland Yard
Tothill St
Meth Hall
Guildhall
Westminster Abbey
The Sanctuary
Great Smith St
Great College St
Great Peter St
Victoria St
Buckingham Gate
Grosvenor Pl
The Royal Mews
Lr Grosvenor Pl
Grosvenor Gdns
Buckingham Palace Rd
Victoria
Wilton Rd
Vauxhall Bridge Rd
Horseferry Rd
Marsham St
John Islip St
Tate Britain
Atterbury St
Bessborough Gdns
Vauxhall Bridge
Wharves
Wharf
Eaton Sq
Belgrave Sq
Tenn Ct
Wilton Cres
Halkin St
Chapel St
Upper Belgrave St
Eccleston St
Ebury St
Elizabeth St
Victoria Coach
Passport Off
Sloane Sq
Lower Sloane St
Pimlico Rd
Chelsea Barracks
Ebury Bridge Rd
Chelsea Bridge Rd
City of Westminster
Kensington & Chelsea
The Royal Hospital Chelsea
Ranelagh Gardens (Site of Chelsea Flower Show)
Warwick Way
Warwick Sq
Belgrave Rd
Lupus St
Pimlico Acad
Churchill Gardens Rd
Claverton St
Dolphin Sq
Grosvenor Rd
Chelsea Embankment
Chelsea Bridge
Grosvenor Bridge
Lister
Dock
Tenn Cts
28
29
30
258
137
259
81
80
79
78
116
1
2
3
4
5
6
40
30
A4
A4201
A4202
A302
A3212
A3214
A3216
A3217
A3213
A3215
A202
B310
B319
B313
B302
B323
B324
B326
B327

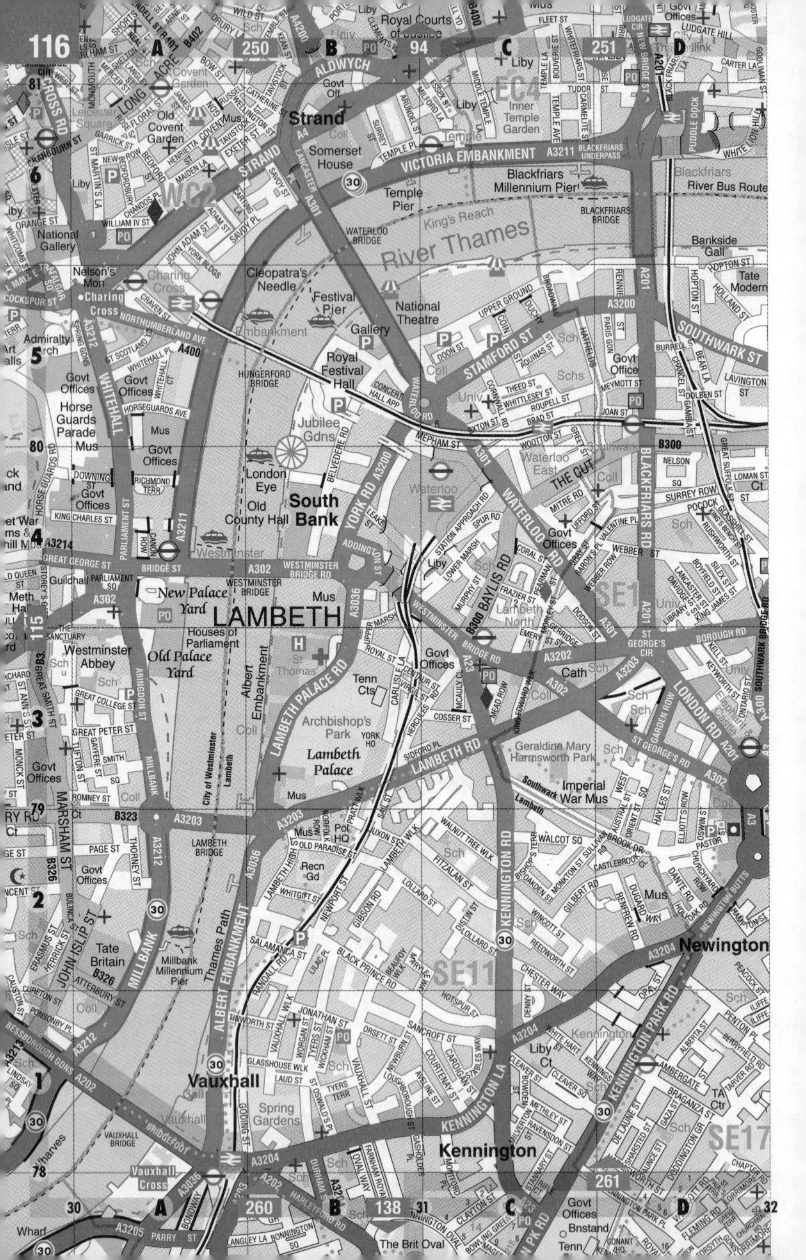
250
94
251
Royal Courts of Justice
Aldwych
Strand
Somerset House
Covent Garden
Old Covent Garden
Leicester Square
Long Acre
Cross Rd
Cranbourn St
National Gallery
Nelson's Mon
Charing Cross
Trafalgar Sq
Cockspur St
Northumberland Ave
Admiralty Arch
Whitehall
Horse Guards Parade
Horseguards Ave
Downing St
King Charles St
Great George St
Bridge St
Parliament St
Westminster
New Palace Yard
LAMBETH
Houses of Parliament
Old Palace Yard
Westminster Abbey
Great College St
Great Peter St
Great Smith St
Marsham St
Millbank
Tate Britain
Millbank Millennium Pier
Abingdon St
Lambeth Bridge
Thames Path
Albert Embankment
Lambeth Palace Rd
Lambeth Palace
Archbishop's Park
St Thomas'
Lambeth Rd
Lambeth High St
Vauxhall
Vauxhall Bridge
Vauxhall Cross
Spring Gardens
Bessborough Gdns
Victoria Embankment
Temple
Temple Pier
Inner Temple Garden
Fleet St
EC4
WC2
Blackfriars Millennium Pier
Blackfriars Bridge
Blackfriars River Bus Route
River Thames
King's Reach
Waterloo Bridge
Cleopatra's Needle
Festival Pier
Embankment
Hungerford Bridge
Royal Festival Hall
National Theatre
Jubilee Gdns
London Eye
Old County Hall
South Bank
Waterloo
Waterloo East
The Cut
Waterloo Rd
Stamford St
Upper Ground
Bankside Gall
Tate Modern
Southwark St
Blackfriars Rd
St George's Cir
SE1
Borough Rd
London Rd
Baylis Rd
Lambeth North
Westminster Bridge Rd
York Rd
Kennington Rd
Geraldine Mary Harmsworth Park
Imperial War Mus
Elephant & Castle
Newington
Newington Butts
Kennington Park Rd
Kennington
Kennington La
SE11
SE17
The Brit Oval
Harleyford Rd
260
138
261
A
B
C
D

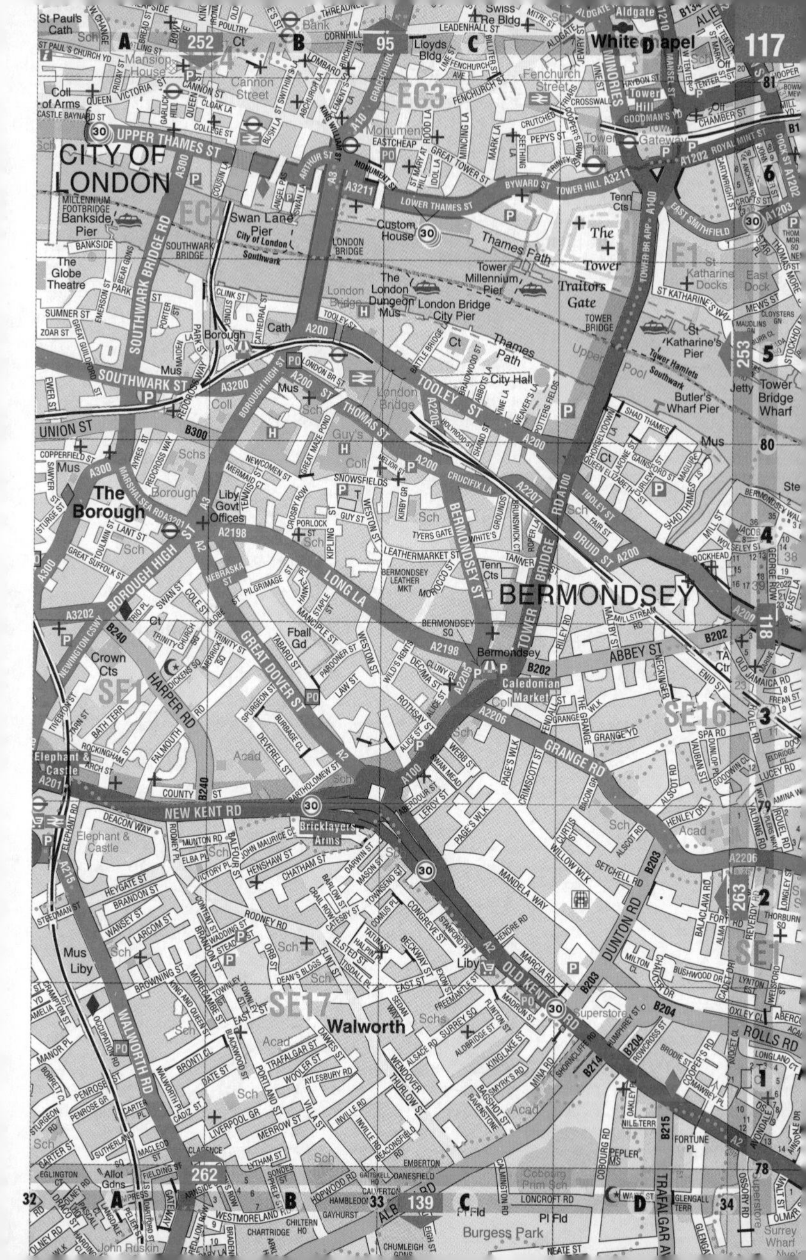
A
B
C
D
252
95
White Chapel
St Paul's Cath
Mansion House
Bank
Cannon Street
Lloyds Bldg
Swiss Re Bldg
Aldgate
EC3
EC4
Fenchurch Street
Coll of Arms
Monument
Tower Hill
Tower Gateway
CITY OF LONDON
UPPER THAMES ST
LOWER THAMES ST
BYWARD ST
TOWER HILL A3211
ROYAL MINT ST
EAST SMITHFIELD
MINORIES
E1
Millennium Footbridge
Bankside Pier
The Globe Theatre
Swan Lane Pier
City of London
Southwark
Southwark Bridge
London Bridge
Custom House
Thames Path
Tower Millennium Pier
The Tower
Traitors Gate
Tower Bridge
St Katharine Docks
East Dock
St Katharine's Pier
Tower Hamlets
Butler's Wharf Pier
Tower Bridge Wharf
Jetty
Upper Pool
The London Dungeon Mus
London Bridge City Pier
City Hall
Borough
Cath
SOUTHWARK BRIDGE RD
SOUTHWARK ST
UNION ST
TOOLEY ST
ST THOMAS ST
Guy's
CRUCIFIX LA
SHAD THAMES
DRUID ST
The Borough
BOROUGH HIGH ST
MARSHALSEA RD
LONG LA
BERMONDSEY ST
TOWER BRIDGE RD
BERMONDSEY
Bermondsey Leather Mkt
Bermondsey Sq
Bermondsey
Caledonian Market
ABBEY ST
GRANGE RD
SE16
SE1
Crown Cts
HARPER RD
GREAT DOVER ST
Fball Gd
Elephant & Castle
NEW KENT RD
Bricklayers Arms
OLD KENT RD
MANDELA WAY
DUNTON RD
SE17
Walworth
WALWORTH RD
Superstore
ROLLS RD
Burgess Park
Cobourg Prim Sch
TRAFALGAR AV
262
139
32
33
34
118
253
263
80
79
78
81
6
5
4
3
2
1

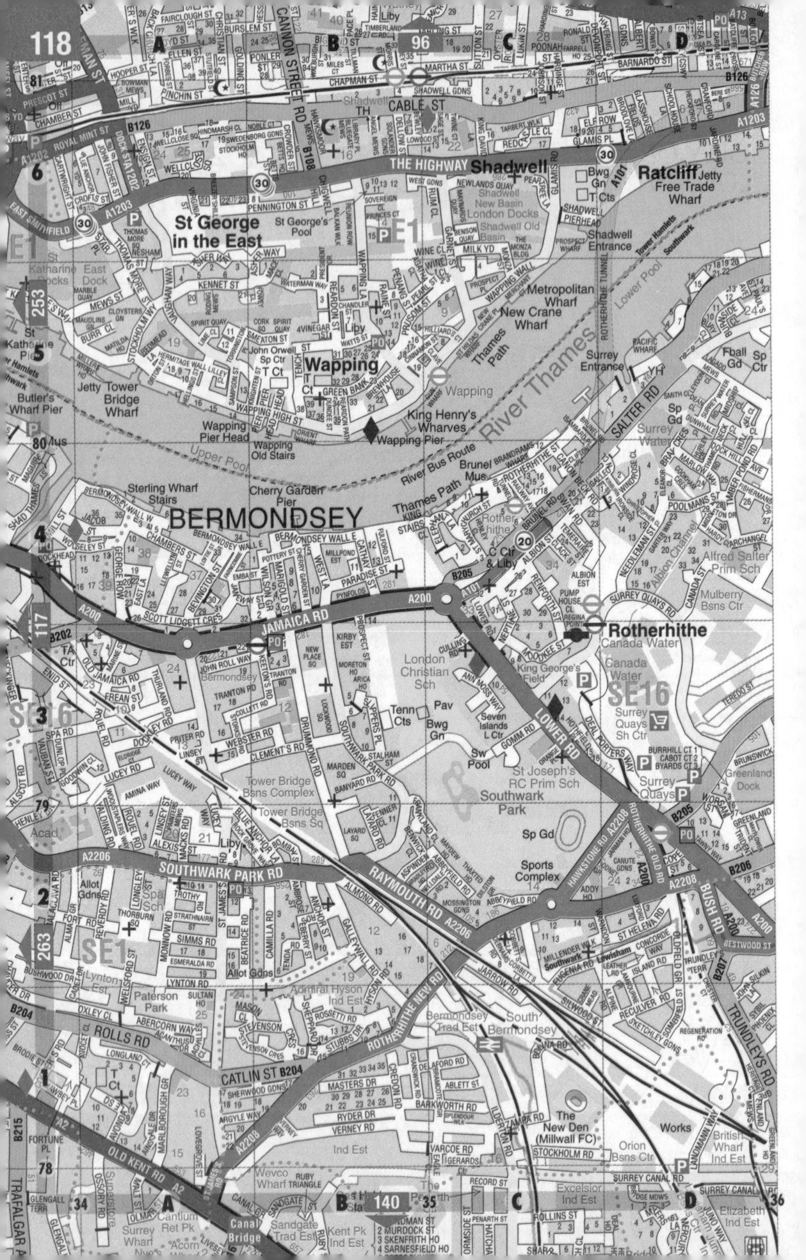
118
A
B
C
D
96
6
5
4
3
2
1
253
117
263
140
80
79
78
81
34
35
36
CABLE ST
THE HIGHWAY
Shadwell
Ratcliff
Jetty
Free Trade
Wharf
Shadwell
New Basin
London Docks
Shadwell Old
Basin
Shadwell
Entrance
St George
in the East
St George's
Pool
St
Katharine
Docks
East
Dock
E1
Wapping
Metropolitan
Wharf
New Crane
Wharf
Thames
Path
River Thames
Lower Pool
Upper Pool
Surrey
Entrance
Jetty Tower
Bridge
Wharf
Butler's
Wharf Pier
Wapping
Pier Head
Wapping
Old Stairs
King Henry's
Wharves
Wapping Pier
River Bus Route
Brunel
Mus
Sterling Wharf
Stairs
Cherry Garden
Pier
BERMONDSEY
ROTHERHITHE TUNNEL
SALTER RD
Surrey
Water
JAMAICA RD
Rotherhithe
Canada Water
London
Christian
Sch
Tenn
Cts
Pav
Bwg
Gn
Seven
Islands
L Ctr
King George's
Field
SE16
Surrey
Quays
Sh Ctr
Alfred Salter
Prim Sch
Mulberry
Bsns Ctr
Albion Channel
St Joseph's
RC Prim Sch
Southwark
Park
Sw
Pool
Sp Gd
Sports
Complex
LOWER RD
Greenland
Dock
Surrey
Quays
Tower Bridge
Bsns Complex
Tower Bridge
Bsns Sq
SOUTHWARK PARK RD
RAYMOUTH RD
SE1
Lynton
Est
Paterson
Park
Admiral Hyson
Ind Est
Bermondsey
Trad Est
South
Bermondsey
ROTHERHITHE NEW RD
ROLLS RD
CATLIN ST
OLD KENT RD
The
New Den
(Millwall FC)
Works
British
Wharf
Ind Est
Orion
Bsns Ctr
Ind Est
Excelsior
Ind Est
Wevco
Wharf
Cantium
Ret Pk
Surrey
Wharf
Sandgate
Trad Est
Kent Pk
Ind Est
Elizabeth
Ind Est
TRUNDLEYS RD
BUSH RD
Canal
Bridge
SURREY CANAL RD
STOCKHOLM RD

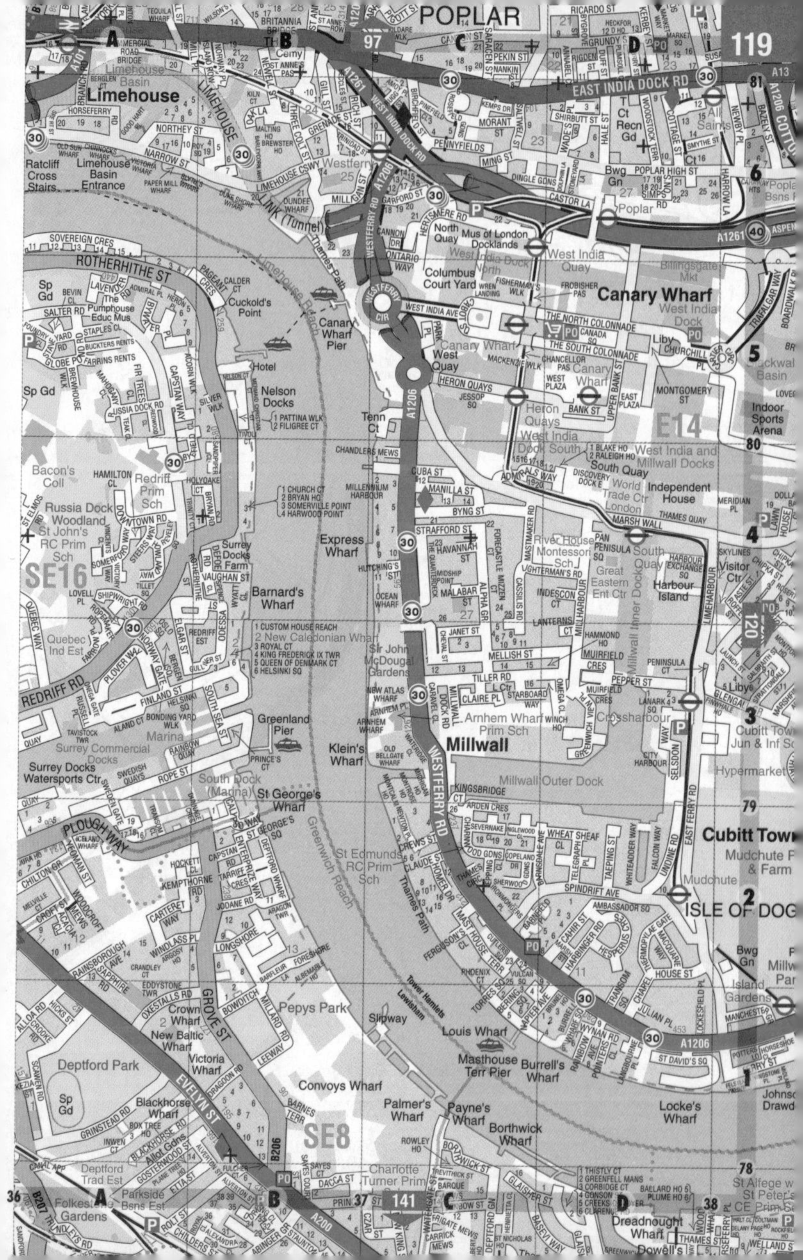
POPLAR
Limehouse
Limehouse Basin
Ratcliff Cross Stairs
Limehouse Basin Entrance
LIMEHOUSE LINK (Tunnel)
NARROW ST
EAST INDIA DOCK RD
WEST INDIA DOCK RD
POPLAR HIGH ST
PENNYFIELDS
Westferry
West India Quay
Mus of London Docklands
North Quay
Columbus Court Yard
Canary Wharf
Canary Wharf Pier
WESTFERRY CIR
WEST INDIA AVE
THE NORTH COLONNADE
THE SOUTH COLONNADE
West India Dock
Billingsgate Mkt
Blackwall Basin
Heron Quays
West India Dock South
South Quay
MARSH WALL
Independent House
World Trade Ctr London
Indoor Sports Arena
E14
ROTHERHITHE ST
Cuckold's Point
Limehouse Reach
Nelson Docks
Hotel
Tenn Ct
Express Wharf
Barnard's Wharf
Sir John McDougal Gardens
Klein's Wharf
Millwall
Millwall Outer Dock
Millwall Inner Dock
Harbour Island
Crossharbour
Arnhem Wharf Prim Sch
WESTFERRY RD
Greenwich Reach
St Edmunds RC Prim Sch
Thames Path
Mudchute
ISLE OF DOGS
Cubitt Town
Mudchute Park & Farm
Island Gardens
Louis Wharf
Masthouse Terr Pier
Burrell's Wharf
Locke's Wharf
Tower Hamlets
Lewisham
SE16
Russia Dock Woodland
Redriff Prim Sch
Bacon's Coll
Surrey Docks Farm
Quebec Ind Est
REDRIFF RD
Greenland Pier
Surrey Commercial Docks
Surrey Docks Watersports Ctr
South Dock (Marina)
St George's Wharf
PLOUGH WAY
EVELYN ST
GROVE ST
Deptford Park
Crown Wharf
New Baltic Wharf
Victoria Wharf
Pepys Park
Slipway
Convoys Wharf
Palmer's Wharf
Payne's Wharf
Borthwick Wharf
Blackhorse Wharf
SE8
Deptford Trad Est
Charlotte Turner Prim Sch
Folkestone Gardens
Parkside Bsns Est
Dreadnought Wharf
St Alfege with St Peter's CE Prim Sch
97
141
120
36
37
38

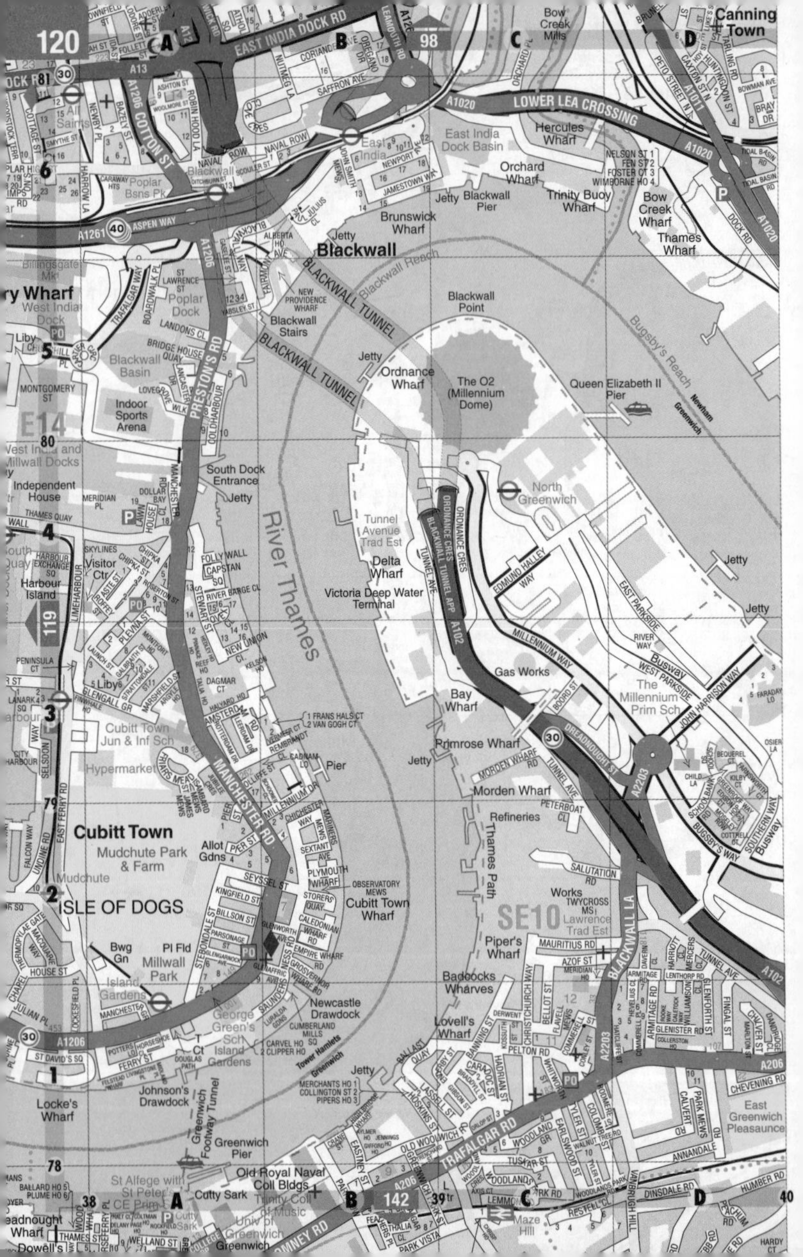

98
119
142
Canning Town
Bow Creek Mills
EAST INDIA DOCK RD
LEAMOUTH RD
LOWER LEA CROSSING
A1020
A13
A12
A1206
COTTON ST
ROBIN HOOD LA
NUTMEG LA
SAFFRON AVE
CORIANDER AVE
OREGANO DR
ORCHARD PL
Hercules Wharf
East India Dock Basin
East India
Orchard Wharf
Trinity Buoy Wharf
Bow Creek Wharf
Thames Wharf
PETO STREET N
CAXTON ST N
TARLING RD
HUNTINGDON ST
BOWMAN AVE
BRAY DR
TIDAL BASIN RD
DOCK RD
A1011
NELSON ST 1
FEN ST 2
FOSTER CT 3
WIMBORNE HO 4
All Saints
NEWBY PL
BAZELY ST
COTTAGE ST
SMYTHE ST
HARROW LA
Poplar Bsns Pk
NAVAL ROW
Blackwall
JOHN SMITH MEWS
NEWPORT AVE
JAMESTOWN WAY
Jetty
Blackwall Pier
Brunswick Wharf
Blackwall
A1261
ASPEN WAY
Billingsgate Mkt
TRAFALGAR WAY
BOARDWALK PL
ST LAWRENCE ST
Poplar Dock
YABSLEY ST
FAIRMONT AVE
ALBERTA HO
NEW PROVIDENCE WHARF
Blackwall Stairs
BLACKWALL TUNNEL
Blackwall Reach
Blackwall Point
Bugsby's Reach
Canary Wharf
West India Dock
LANDONS CL
BRIDGE HOUSE QUAY
Blackwall Basin
LANCASTER DR
LOVEGROVE WLK
PRESTON'S RD
COLDHARBOUR
Indoor Sports Arena
MONTGOMERY ST
E14
West India and Millwall Docks
Jetty
Ordnance Wharf
The O2 (Millennium Dome)
Queen Elizabeth II Pier
Newham
Greenwich
South Dock Entrance
Independent House
MERIDIAN PL
DOLLAR BAY
LAWN HOUSE CL
MANCHESTER RD
THAMES QUAY
River Thames
Tunnel Avenue Trad Est
Delta Wharf
Victoria Deep Water Terminal
ORDNANCE CRES
BLACKWALL TUNNEL APP
TUNNEL AVE
A102
North Greenwich
EDMUND HALLEY WAY
EAST PARKSIDE
MILLENNIUM WAY
RIVER WAY
WEST PARKSIDE
Busway
JOHN HARRISON WAY
The Millennium Prim Sch
Jetty
Harbour Exchange
Visitor Ctr
Harbour Island
SKYLINES
CHIPKA ST
ASTE ST
ROFFEY ST
ROGERSTON ST
LIMEHARBOUR
FOLLY WALL
CAPSTAN SQ
RIVER BARGE CL
STEWART ST
NEW UNION CL
PLEVNA ST
MONTFORT PL
LAUNCH ST
GALBRAITH ST
STRATTONDALE ST
MARSHFIELD ST
PENINSULA CT
GLENGALL GR
DAGMAR CT
KELSON HO
Gas Works
BOORD ST
Bay Wharf
DREADNOUGHT ST
A2203
Primrose Wharf
1 FRANS HALS CT
2 VAN GOGH CT
VERMEER CT
REMBRANDT CL
AMSTERDAM RD
ROTTERDAM DR
Cubitt Town Jun & Inf Sch
Hypermarket
FRIARS MEAD
JUBILEE CRES
CADMAN CL
Pier
Jetty
MORDEN WHARF RD
Morden Wharf
PETERBOAT CL
Refineries
SCHOOLBANK RD
BUGSBY'S WAY
SOUTHERN WAY
MILLENNIUM DR
CHICHESTER WAY
MARINERS MEWS
SEXTANT AVE
Cubitt Town
Mudchute Park & Farm
Allot Gdns
PIER ST
SEYSSEL ST
PLYMOUTH WHARF
OBSERVATORY MEWS
Cubitt Town Wharf
STORERS QUAY
CALEDONIAN WHARF RD
EMPIRE WHARF RD
KINGFIELD ST
BILLSON ST
PARSONAGE ST
STEBONDALE ST
GLENWORTH AVE
Mudchute
ISLE OF DOGS
EAST FERRY RD
UNDINE RD
FALCON WAY
SELSDON WAY
Bwg Gn
Pl Fld
Millwall Park
HOUSE ST
THERMOPYLAE GATE
MACQUARIE WAY
CHAPEL
JULIAN PL
Island Gardens
MANCHESTER GR
SAUNDERS NESS RD
GROSVENOR WHARF RD
Newcastle Drawdock
CUMBERLAND MILLS SQ
CARVEL HO 1
CLIPPER HO 2
Tower Hamlets
Greenwich
George Green's Sch
Island Gardens
A1206
ST DAVID'S SQ
POTTERS LODGE
HORSESHOE CL
FERRY ST
DOUGLAS PATH
Locke's Wharf
Johnson's Drawdock
Greenwich Footway Tunnel
Greenwich Pier
Thames Path
SALUTATION RD
Works
TWYCROSS MS
SE10
Lawrence Trad Est
Piper's Wharf
MAURITIUS RD
AZOF ST
BLACKWALL LA
Badcocks Wharves
Lovell's Wharf
CHRISTCHURCH WAY
BELLOT ST
DERWENT
BANNING ST
PELTON RD
BALLAST QUAY
CARADOC ST
HADRIAN ST
WHITWORTH ST
MERCERS CL
TUNNEL AVE
HARRIOTT CL
LENTHORP RD
ARMITAGE RD
GLENFORTH ST
FINGAL ST
WILLIAMSON
GLENISTER RD
CALVERT RD
PARK MEWS
CHEVENING RD
A206
East Greenwich Pleasaunce
MERCHANTS HO 1
COLLINGTON ST 2
PIPERS HO 3
Jetty
HOSKINS ST
LASSELL ST
TRAFALGAR RD
OLD WOOLWICH RD
EASTNEY ST
WOODLAND GR
EARLSWOOD ST
COLOMB ST
TUSKAR ST
WOODLANDS PARK RD
VANBRUGH HILL
ANNANDALE RD
DINSDALE RD
HUMBER RD
St Alfege with St Peter's CE Prim Sch
Old Royal Naval Coll Bldgs
Trinity Coll of Music
Cutty Sark
Univ of Greenwich
Maze Hill
RESTELL CL
PARK VISTA
THALIA CL
ROMNEY RD
BALLARD HO 5
PLUME HO 6
Dreadnought Wharf
THAMES ST
WELLAND ST
Dowell's
Greenwich
A
B
C
D
1
2
3
4
5
6
38
39
40
78
79
80
81

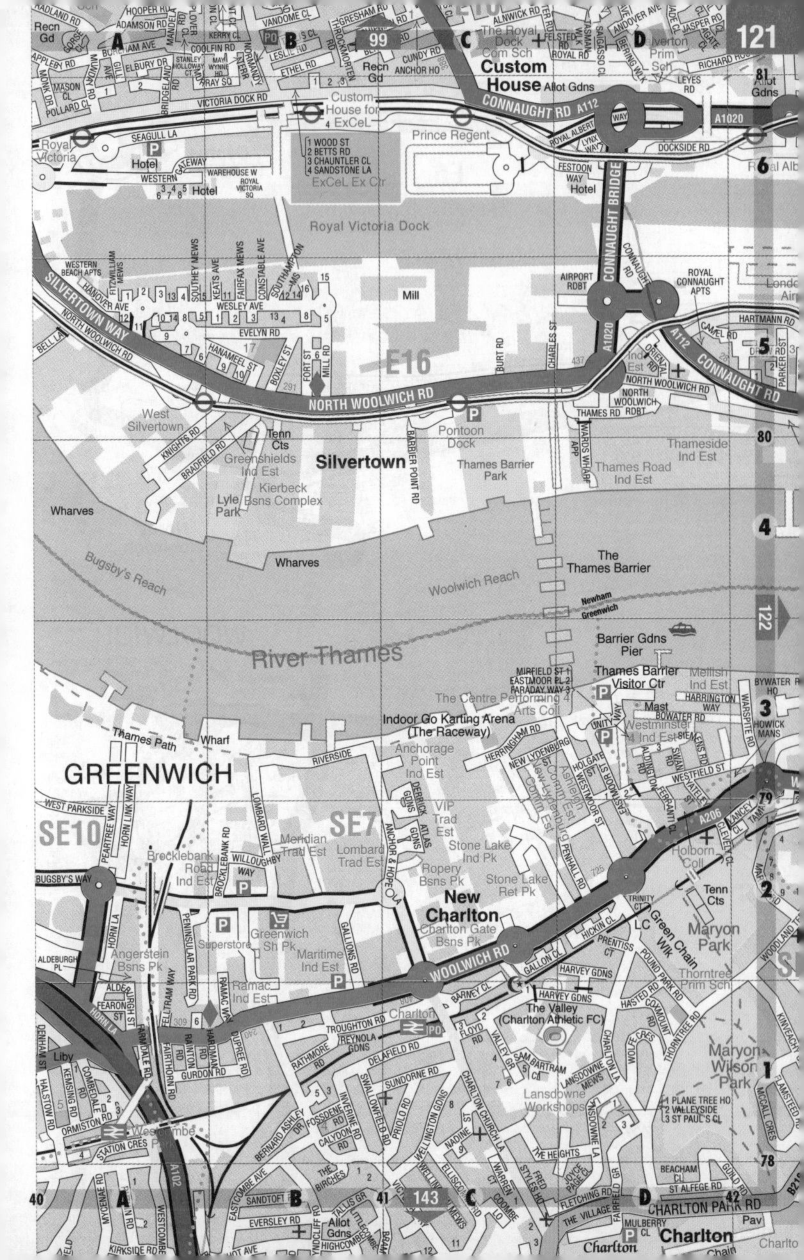
121
A
B
C
D
99
122
143
81
80
79
78
6
5
4
3
2
1
40
41
42
Custom House
Custom House for ExCeL
ExCeL Ex Ctr
Prince Regent
Royal Victoria
Royal Victoria Dock
CONNAUGHT RD
CONNAUGHT BRIDGE
A112
A1020
VICTORIA DOCK RD
SEAGULL LA
WESTERN GATEWAY
DOCKSIDE RD
ROYAL ALBERT WAY
Hotel
1 WOOD ST
2 BETTS RD
3 CHAUNTLER CL
4 SANDSTONE LA
The Royal Dock Com Sch
Allot Gdns
Recn Gd
AIRPORT RDBT
ROYAL CONNAUGHT APTS
HARTMANN RD
Mill
E16
SILVERTOWN WAY
NORTH WOOLWICH RD
WESLEY AVE
EVELYN RD
HANAMEEL ST
West Silvertown
Silvertown
Tenn Cts
Greenshields Ind Est
Kierbeck Bsns Complex
Lyle Park
Pontoon Dock
Thames Barrier Park
Thames Road Ind Est
Thameside Ind Est
NORTH WOOLWICH RDBT
THAMES RD
Wharves
Bugsby's Reach
Woolwich Reach
River Thames
The Thames Barrier
Newham
Greenwich
Barrier Gdns Pier
Thames Barrier Visitor Ctr
Mellish Ind Est
MIRFIELD ST 1
EASTMOOR PL 2
FARADAY WAY 3
The Centre Performing Arts Coll
Indoor Go Karting Arena (The Raceway)
Anchorage Point Ind Est
Thames Path
Wharf
GREENWICH
SE10
SE7
RIVERSIDE
WEST PARKSIDE
BUGSBY'S WAY
Brocklebank Road Ind Est
Meridian Trad Est
Lombard Trad Est
VIP Trad Est
Stone Lake Ind Pk
Stone Lake Ret Pk
Ropery Bsns Pk
New Charlton
Charlton Gate Bsns Pk
Greenwich Sh Pk
Superstore
Maritime Ind Est
Angerstein Bsns Pk
Ramac Ind Est
WOOLWICH RD
A206
Westminster Ind Est
Mast
Holborn Coll
Tenn Cts
Maryon Park
Green Chain Wlk
Thorntree Prim Sch
The Valley (Charlton Athletic FC)
Charlton
Lansdowne Workshops
Maryon Wilson Park
1 PLANE TREE HO
2 VALLEYSIDE
3 ST PAUL'S CL
Westcombe Park
Liby
A102
CHARLTON PARK RD
Allot Gdns
Charlton
Pav

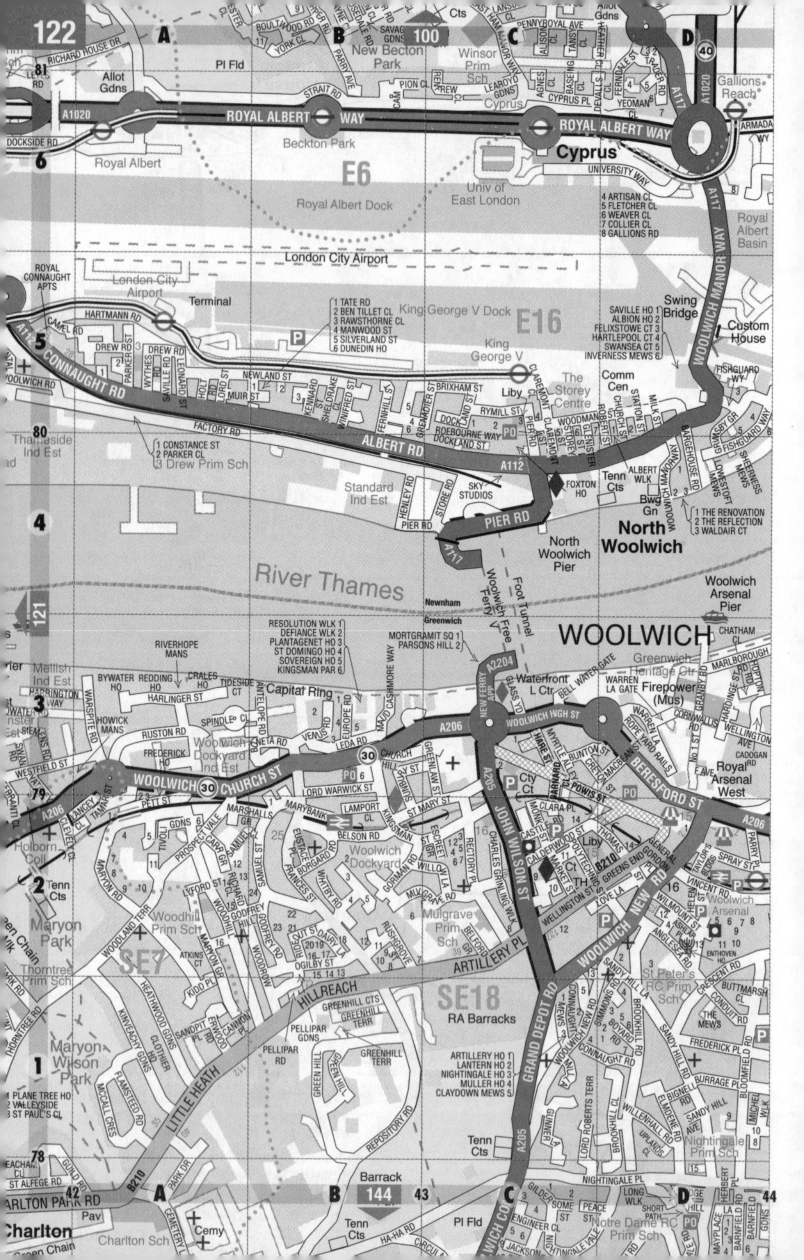
A
B
C
D
100
New Becton Park
Winsor Prim Sch
Pl Fld
Allot Gdns
RICHARD HOUSE DR
BOULTWOOD RD
YORK CL
PARRY AVE
SAVAGE GDNS
PENNYROYAL AVE
STRAIT RD
PION CL
REW CL
LEAROYD GDNS
CYPRUS PL
YEOMAN CL
A1020
ROYAL ALBERT WAY
A117
Gallions Reach
Beckton Park
Royal Albert
DOCKSIDE RD
Cyprus
UNIVERSITY WAY
E6
Royal Albert Dock
Univ of East London
4 ARTISAN CL
5 FLETCHER CL
6 WEAVER CL
7 COLLIER CL
8 GALLIONS RD
Royal Albert Basin
London City Airport
ROYAL CONNAUGHT APTS
London City Airport
Terminal
1 TATE RD
2 BEN TILLETT CL
3 RAWSTHORNE CL
4 MANWOOD ST
5 SILVERLAND ST
6 DUNEDIN HO
King George V Dock
E16
Swing Bridge
Custom House
SAVILLE HO 1
ALBION HO 2
FELIXSTOWE CT 3
HARTLEPOOL CT 4
SWANSEA CT 5
INVERNESS MEWS 6
HARTMANN RD
CAMEL RD
DREW RD
A112
CONNAUGHT RD
WOOLWICH MANOR WAY
King George V
NEWLAND ST
MUIR ST
BRIXHAM ST
RYMILL ST
DOCKLAND ST
ROEBOURNE WAY
Liby
The Storey Centre
Comm Cen
WOODMAN ST
FISHGUARD WY
FACTORY RD
ALBERT RD
1 CONSTANCE ST
2 PARKER CL
3 Drew Prim Sch
Thameside Ind Est
Standard Ind Est
SKY STUDIOS
FOXTON HO
Tenn Cts
ALBERT WLK
Bwg Gn
1 THE RENOVATION
2 THE REFLECTION
3 WALDAIR CT
PIER RD
North Woolwich Pier
North Woolwich
River Thames
Woolwich Free Ferry
Foot Tunnel
Woolwich Arsenal Pier
Newnham
Greenwich
WOOLWICH
RESOLUTION WLK 1
DEFIANCE WLK 2
PLANTAGENET HO 3
ST DOMINGO HO 4
SOVEREIGN HO 5
KINGSMAN PAR 6
MORTGRAMIT SQ 1
PARSONS HILL 2
CHATHAM CL
Greenwich Heritage Ctr
Firepower (Mus)
RIVERHOPE MANS
Mellish Ind Est
Capital Ring
Waterfront L Ctr
A2204
BELL WATER GATE
WARREN LA GATE
MARLBOROUGH
HARLINGER ST
HARRINGTON WAY
HOWICK MANS
RUSTON RD
Woolwich Dockyard Ind Est
FREDERICK HO
A206
WOOLWICH HIGH ST
WOOLWICH CHURCH ST
CORNWALLIS RD
WELLINGTON AVE
Royal Arsenal West
BERESFORD ST
WESTFIELD ST
LORD WARWICK ST
LAMPORT CL
POWIS ST
Cty Ct
Liby
BELSON RD
Woolwich Dockyard
JOHN WILSON ST
B210
GREENS END
Holborn Coll
Tenn Cts
Maryon Park
Woodhill Prim Sch
SE7
Mulgrave Prim Sch
ARTILLERY PL
WOOLWICH NEW RD
Woolwich Arsenal
St Peter's RC Prim Sch
HILLREACH
SE18
RA Barracks
Thorntree Prim Sch
Maryon Wilson Park
LITTLE HEATH
GRAND DEPOT RD
ARTILLERY HO 1
LANTERN HO 2
NIGHTINGALE HO 3
MULLER HO 4
CLAYDOWN MEWS 5
1 PLANE TREE HO
2 VALLEYSIDE
3 ST PAUL'S CL
Nightingale Prim Sch
Tenn Cts
A205
NIGHTINGALE PL
Barrack
144
43
42
44
CHARLTON PARK RD
Charlton
Charlton Sch
Cemy
Pl Fld
Notre Dame RC Prim Sch
Tenn Cts

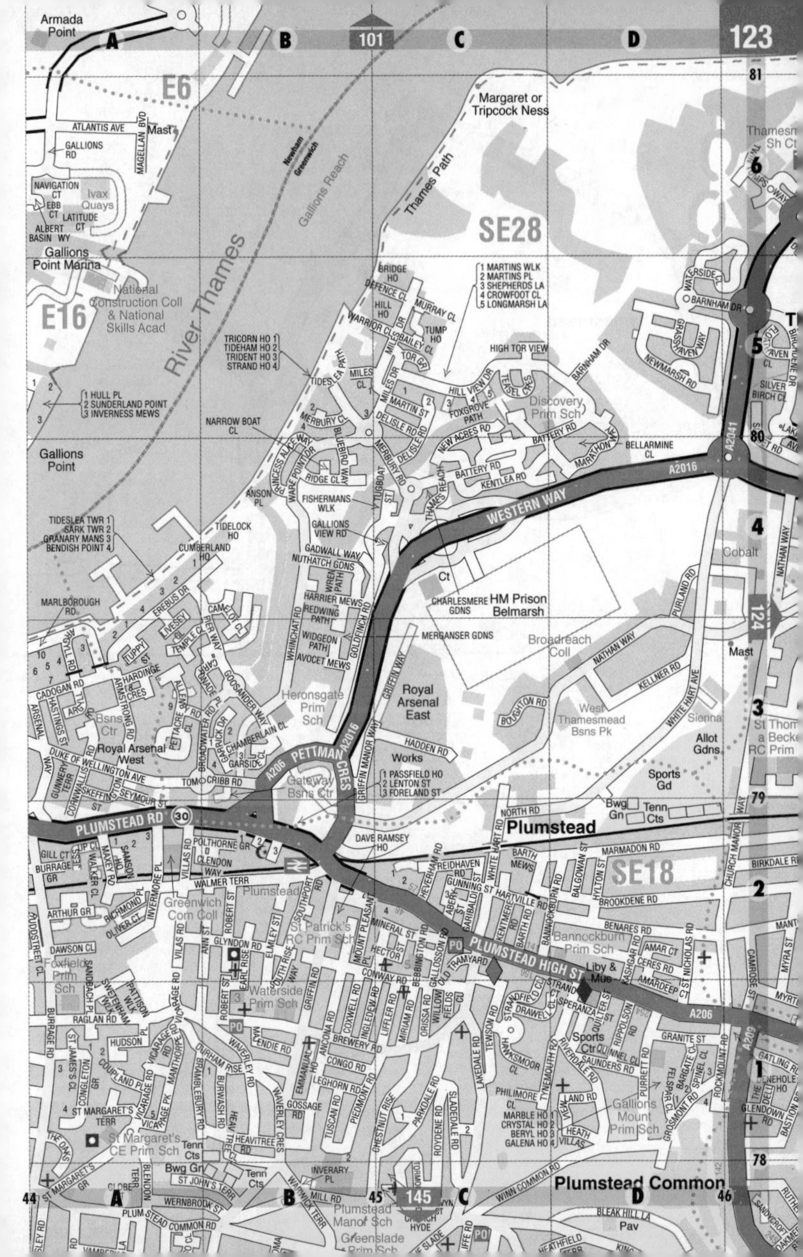
123
101
145
124
A
B
C
D
81
80
79
78
44
45
46
Armada Point
E6
E16
SE28
SE18
Margaret or Tripcock Ness
Thames Path
Gallions Reach
Newham
Greenwich
River Thames
ATLANTIS AVE
MAGELLAN BVD
Mast
GALLIONS RD
NAVIGATION CT
EBB CT
LATITUDE CT
ALBERT BASIN WY
Ivax Quays
Gallions Point Marina
National Construction Coll & National Skills Acad
Gallions Point
1 HULL PL
2 SUNDERLAND POINT
3 INVERNESS MEWS
TRICORN HO 1
TIDEHAM HO 2
TRIDENT HO 3
STRAND HO 4
BRIDGE HO
DEFENCE CL
HILL HO
MURRAY CL
WARRIOR CL
BAILEY CL
TUMP HO
TOR GR
MILES DR
MILES CL
TIDESLEA PATH
MARTIN ST
DELISLE RD
MERBURY CL
MERBURY RD
BLUEBIRD WAY
NARROW BOAT CL
PRINCESS ALICE WAY
WARE POINT DR
RIDGE CL
ANSON PL
FISHERMANS WLK
TUGBOAT ST
GALLIONS VIEW RD
TIDELOCK HO
CUMBERLAND HO
1 MARTINS WLK
2 MARTINS PL
3 SHEPHERDS LA
4 CROWFOOT CL
5 LONGMARSH LA
HIGH TOR VIEW
HILL VIEW DR
TEASEL CRES
FOXGROVE PATH
BARNHAM DR
Discovery Prim Sch
NEW ACRES RD
BATTERY RD
KENTLEA RD
MARATHON WAY
BELLARMINE CL
THAMES REACH
WESTERN WAY
A2016
A2041
WATERSIDE CL
BARNHAM DR
GRASSHAVEN WAY
NEWMARSH RD
Thamesm Sh Ct
SILVER BIRCH CL
TIDESLEA TWR 1
SARK TWR 2
GRANARY MANS 3
BENDISH POINT 4
GADWALL WAY
NUTHATCH GDNS
WREN PATH
HARRIER MEWS
REDWING PATH
WIDGEON PATH
AVOCET MEWS
WHINCHAT RD
GOLDFINCH RD
MERGANSER GDNS
Ct
CHARLESMERE GDNS
HM Prison Belmarsh
Broadreach Coll
Cobalt
NATHAN WAY
PURLAND RD
Mast
MARLBOROUGH RD
EREBUS DR
ARGYLL RD
TUPPY ST
LIVESEY CL
TEMPLE CL
CAMELOT CL
PIER WAY
HARDINGE CRES
ARMSTRONG RD
CADOGAN RD
HASTINGS ST
ARSENAL WAY
Bsns Ctr
Royal Arsenal West
GOOSANDER WAY
CARRONADE PL
ALLENBY RD
PETTACRE CL
BROADWATER RD
GARRICK DR
CHAMBERLAIN CL
GARSIDE CL
Heronsgate Prim Sch
GRIFFIN WAY
Royal Arsenal East
HADDEN RD
Works
NATHAN WAY
KELLNER RD
BOUGHTON RD
West Thamesmead Bsns Pk
WHITE HART AVE
Sienna
Allot Gdns
Sports Gd
DUKE OF WELLINGTON AVE
CORNWALLIS RD
GUNNERY TERR
SKEFFINGTON ST
SEYMOUR ST
TOM CRIBB RD
PETTMAN CRES
A206
Gateway Bsns Ctr
GRIFFIN MANOR WAY
1 PASSFIELD HO
2 LENTON ST
3 FORELAND ST
Bwg Gn
Tenn Cts
NORTH RD
Plumstead
PLUMSTEAD RD
30
GILL CT
BURRAGE GR
MAXEY RD
SAMSON HO
POLTHORNE GR
CLENDON WAY
VILLAS RD
INVERMORE PL
WALMER TERR
Plumstead
DAVE RAMSEY HO
MARMADON RD
BIRKDALE RD
REIDHAVEN RD
BARTH MEWS
GUNNING ST
HARTVILLE RD
BROOKDENE RD
BALGOWAN ST
HYLTON ST
CHURCH MANOR WAY
ARTHUR GR
RICHMOND PL
OLIVER CT
Greenwich Com Coll
DAWSON CL
Foxfield Prim Sch
SANDBACH PL
SWETENHAM WLK
PATTISON WLK
VILAS RD
ANN ST
ROBERT ST
GLYNDON RD
ELMLEY ST
SOUTH RISE WAY
SOUTHPORT RD
St Patrick's RC Prim Sch
MOUNT PLEASANT
MINERAL ST
HECTOR ST
CONWAY RD
PLUMSTEAD HIGH ST
PO
Bannockburn Prim Sch
BENARES RD
AMAR CT
CERES RD
AMARDEEP CT
Liby & Mus
ST NICHOLAS RD
CAMROSE ST
MYRTL
Waterside Prim Sch
GRIFFIN RD
COXWELL RD
INGLEDEW RD
LIFFLER RD
MIRIAM RD
BEBBINGTON RD
GALLOSSON RD
WILLOW FIELDS CL
OLD TRAMYARD
STRANDFIELD CL
DRAWELL CL
SPERANZA ST
QUILTER ST
RIPPOLSON RD
A206
GRANITE ST
RAGLAN RD
HUDSON PL
BURRAGE RD
ST JAMES'S CL
CONGLETON GR
COUPLAND PL
VICARAGE RD
MANTHORPE RD
DURHAM RISE
BRAMBLEBURY RD
WAVERLEY RD
MACKENDIE RD
ANCONA RD
BREWERY RD
CONGO RD
LEGHORN RD
EMMANUEL HO
TUSCAN RD
PIEDMONT RD
GOSSAGE RD
WAVERLEY CRES
CHESTNUT RISE
PARKDALE RD
ROYDENE RD
SLADEDALE RD
LAKEDALE RD
TEWSON RD
HAWKSMOOR CL
TYNEMOUTH RD
RIVERDALE RD
Sports Ctr
QUINNEL CL
SAUNDERS RD
PURRETT RD
GALLIONS Mount Prim Sch
BARGATE CL
SPINEL CL
FELSPAR CL
GROSMONT RD
ROCKMOUNT RD
A209
GATLING RD
DENEHOLE HO
THE DELL
GLENDOWN RD
BASTION
PHILIMORE CL
MARBLE HO 1
CRYSTAL HO 2
BERYL HO 3
GALENA HO 4
NEW LAND RD
HEATH VILLAS
ST MARGARET'S TERR
VICARAGE PK
BURWASH RD
HEAVITREE RD
HEAVITREE CL
THE OAKS
St Margaret's CE Prim Sch
Tenn Cts
Bwg Gn
ST JOHN'S TERR
Tenn Cts
INVERARY PL
ST MARGARET'S GR
GLOBE
BLENDON TERR
WERNBROOK ST
PLUMSTEAD COMMON RD
MILL RD
WARWICK TERR
Plumstead Manor Sch
Greenslade Prim Sch
WINN COMMON RD
Plumstead Common
BLEAK HILL LA
Pav
HEATHFIELD
St Thom a Beck RC Prim
SANDYCROFT

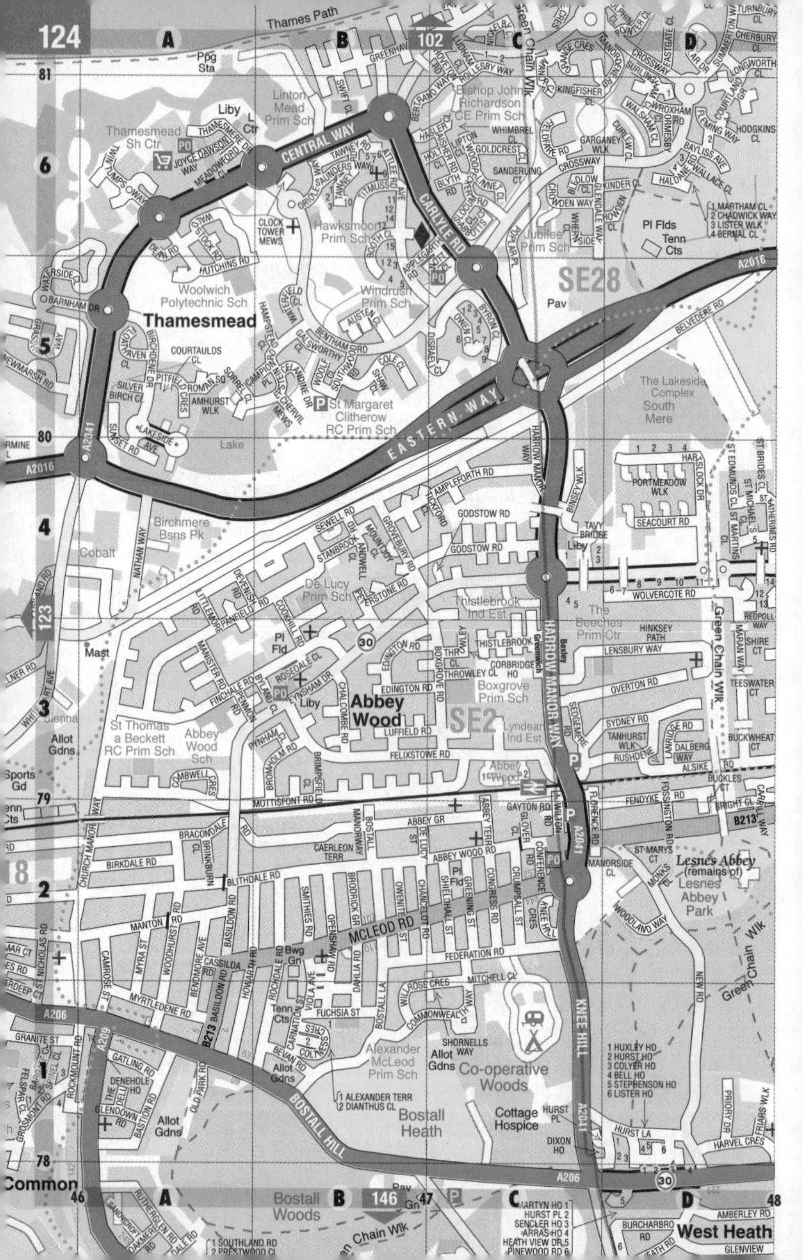
A
B
C
D
102
Thames Path
Ppg Sta
Thamesmead Sh Ctr
Liby
L Ctr
Linton Mead Prim Sch
Bishop John Richardson CE Prim Sch
CENTRAL WAY
CARLYLE RD
JOYCE DAWSON WAY
MEADOWFORD CL
THAMESMERE DR
TWIN TUMPS WAY
WALDSTOCK RD
HUTCHINS RD
DEAN RD
CLOCK TOWER MEWS
Hawksmoor Prim Sch
Woolwich Polytechnic Sch
Windrush Prim Sch
Thamesmead
WATERSIDE CL
BARNHAM DR
GRASSMERE CL
NEWMARSH RD
FLORIAN AVE
BIRCHDENE DR
COURTAULDS CL
PITFIELD CRES
ROMAN SQ
SORREL CL
SILVER BIRCH CL
AMHURST WLK
LAKESIDE AVE
SUNSET RD
Lake
St Margaret Clitherow RC Prim Sch
CAMPION PL
GALSWORTHY
BENTHAM RD
SOUTHWOOD RD
WOOLF CL
COLE CL
SHAW CL
AUSTEN CL
OWEN CL
BYRON CL
DISRAELI CL
CELANDINE DR
CHERVIL MEWS
HAMPSTEAD RD
WATERFIELD CL
BOOTH CL
APPLEGARTH RD
TITMUSS
ATTLEE RD
SAUNDERS WAY
TAWNEY RD
ORIOLE WAY
SWIFT CL
GREENHAVEN DR
LUDHAM CL
ROLLESBY WAY
HOVETON RD
BERTRAND WAY
HASLER CL
HOLT CL
BLYTH RD
LIPTON CL
GOLDCREST CL
WHIMBREL CL
SANDERLING CT
KINGFISHER CL
GARGANEY WLK
FELDFARE RD
CROSSWAY
GRANGE CRES
MANOR DENE RD
EASTGATE CL
WROXHAM RD
WALSHAM CL
ORMESBY
CURLEW CL
BARDLOW CL
GLENDALE WAY
CROWDEN WAY
KINDER CL
HOWDEN CL
WHERNSIDE CL
POPLAR PL
Jubilee Prim Sch
SE28
Pav
Pl Flds
Tenn Cts
CHERBURY CL
LONGWORTH CL
SUMMERTON WAY
TURNBURY CL
COURTLAND GR
FLEMING WAY
HODGKINS CL
BAYLISS AVE
WALLACE CL
HALDANE RD
1 MARTHAM CL
2 CHADWICK WAY
3 LISTER WLK
4 BERNAL CL
A2016
BELVEDERE RD
EASTERN WAY
The Lakeside Complex
South Mere
HARROW MANOR WAY
ERMINE RD
A2041
Birchmere Bsns Pk
Cobalt
NATHAN WAY
AMPLEFORTH RD
TICKFORD CL
GODSTOW RD
BINSEY WLK
TAVY BRIDGE
PORTMEADOW WLK
HARTSLOCK DR
SEACOURT RD
ST EDMUNDS CL
ST MICHAEL'S CL
ST MARTINS CL
ST KATHERINES RD
ST BRIDES CL
SEWELL RD
STANBROOK RD
MOUNTJOY CL
ANDWELL CL
GROVEBURY RD
De Lucy Prim Sch
PETERSTONE RD
WOLVERCOTE RD
Thistlebrook Ind Est
The Beeches Prim Ctr
HINKSEY PATH
LENSBURY WAY
THISTLEBROOK
THROWLEY CL
CORBRIDGE HO
EDINGTON RD
BOXGROVE RD
Boxgrove Prim Sch
OVERTON RD
SEDGEMERE
SYDNEY RD
TANHURST WLK
LANRIDGE RD
DALBERG WAY
RUSHDENE
ALSIKE
Green Chain Wlk
MARAN WAY
REDPOLL WAY
SHIRE CT
TEESWATER CT
BUCKWHEAT CT
BUCKLES CT
CARRILL WAY
BRIGHT CL
123
DEVENISH RD
LITTLEMORE RD
PANFIELD RD
COOKHILL RD
Pl Fld
Mast
MANISTER RD
FINCHALE RD
BYLAND CL
PENMON RD
ROSEDALE CL
EYNSHAM DR
CHALCOMBE RD
Liby
Abbey Wood
SE2
Lyndean Ind Est
LUFFIELD RD
FELIXSTOWE RD
WHITEHART AVE
Sienna
St Thomas a Beckett RC Prim Sch
Abbey Wood Sch
Allot Gdns
Sports Gd
Tenn Cts
PYNHAM CL
BROMHOLM RD
BRIMPSFIELD CL
MOTTISFONT RD
CUMBWELL CRES
Abbey Wood
GAYTON RD
WILTON RD
FLORENCE RD
FENDYKE RD
FOSSINGTON RD
B213
ABBEY GR
DE LUCY ST
ABBEY TERR
ABBEY WOOD RD
GLOVER CL
CONFERENCE RD
CHURCH MANOR WAY
BRACONDALE RD
BRINKBURN CL
CAERLEON TERR
BOSTALL MANORWAY
ST MARYS CT
MANORSIDE CL
MONKS CL
Lesnes Abbey (remains of)
Lesnes Abbey Park
WOODLAND WAY
BIRKDALE RD
BLITHDALE RD
SMITHIES RD
BRODRICK GR
OWENITE ST
CHANCELOT RD
SHIELDHALL ST
GREENING ST
CONGRESS RD
CRUMPSALL ST
KNEE HILL CRES
MCLEOD RD
MANTON RD
WOODHURST RD
MYRA ST
CAMROSE ST
BENDMORE AVE
CASSILDA RD
BASILDON RD
HOWARTH RD
ROCHDALE RD
Bwg Gn
OPENSHAW RD
DAHLIA RD
FEDERATION RD
MITCHELL CL
WILLROSE CRES
COMMONWEALTH WAY
SHORNELLS WAY
KNEE HILL
NEW RD
ST NICHOLAS RD
MYRTLEDENE RD
A206
A209
GRANITE ST
GATLING RD
DENEHOLE HO
THE DELL
GLENDOWN RD
BASTION RD
OLD PARK RD
ROCKMOUNT RD
SPINEL CL
FELSPAR CL
GROSMONT RD
Allot Gdns
VIOLA AVE
CARNATION ST
FUCHSIA ST
COLTNESS CRES
BEVAN RD
BOSTALL LA
Alexander McLeod Prim Sch
Co-operative Woods
1 ALEXANDER TERR
2 DIANTHUS CL
Bostall Heath
BOSTALL HILL
Cottage Hospice
HURST PL
DIXON HO
1 HUXLEY HO
2 HURST HO
3 COLYER HO
4 BELL HO
5 STEPHENSON HO
6 LISTER HO
HURST LA
PRIORY DR
HARVEL CRES
FRIARS WLK
Common
46
47
48
78
79
80
81
146
Bostall Woods
Green Chain Wlk
RUTHERGLEN RD
SANDYCROFT
OAKMERE RD
DALE RD
1 SOUTHLAND RD
2 PRESTWOOD CL
MARTYN HO 1
HURST PL 2
SENCLER HO 3
ARRAS HO 4
HEATH VIEW DR 5
PINEWOOD RD 6
BURCHARBRO RD
West Heath
AMBERLEY RD
GLENVIEW
30

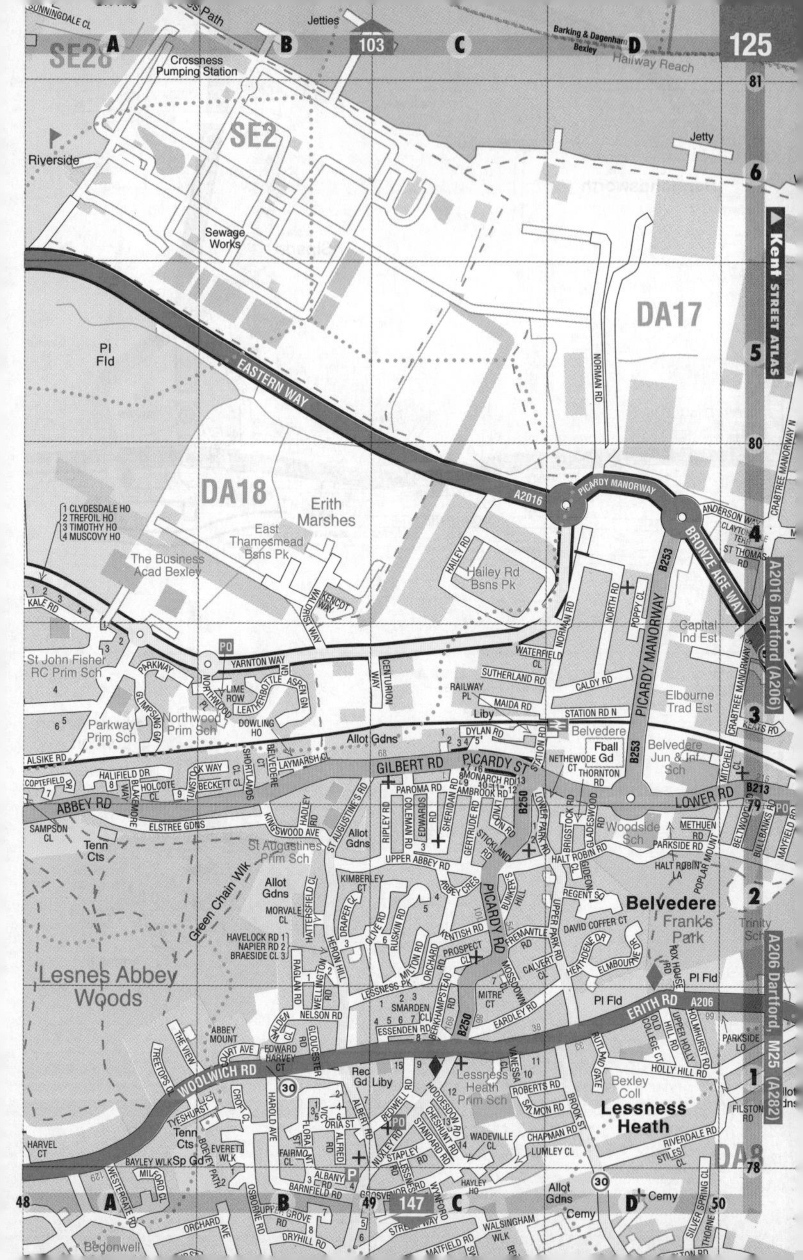

Jetties
103
Barking & Dagenham
Bexley
Halfway Reach
Crossness Pumping Station
SE28
SE2
Riverside
Jetty
Sewage Works
Kent STREET ATLAS
DA17
NORMAN RD
Pl Fld
EASTERN WAY
A2016
PICARDY MANORWAY
DA18
Erith Marshes
East Thamesmead Bsns Pk
1 CLYDESDALE HO
2 TREFOIL HO
3 TIMOTHY HO
4 MUSCOVY HO
The Business Acad Bexley
HAILEY RD
Hailey Rd Bsns Pk
ANDERSON WAY
BRONZE AGE WAY
ST THOMAS RD
CRABTREE MANORWAY N
A2016 Dartford (A206)
KALE RD
KENCOT WAY
WALDRIST WAY
Capital Ind Est
St John Fisher RC Prim Sch
PARKWAY
YARNTON WAY
CENTURION WAY
WATERFIELD CL
SUTHERLAND RD
CALDY RD
NORTH RD
POPPY CL
B253
NORTHWOOD PL
LIME ROW
LEATHERBOTTLE GN
ASPEN GN
GLIMPSING GN
Northwood Prim Sch
Parkway Prim Sch
RAILWAY PL
MAIDA RD
STATION RD N
Liby
Belvedere
Elbourne Trad Est
CRABTREE MANORWAY S
KEATS RD
DOWLING HO
DYLAN RD
Allot Gdns
Fball Gd
Belvedere Jun & Inf Sch
ALSIKE RD
HALIFIELD DR
TUNSTOCK WAY
BECKETT CL
SHORTLANDS CL
BELVEDERE CT
LAYMARSH CL
GILBERT RD
PICARDY ST
MONARCH RD
AMBROOK RD
STATION RD
NETHEWODE CT
THORNTON RD
COPTEFIELD DR
HOLCOTE CL
BLAKEMORE WAY
PAROMA RD
MITCHELL CL
LOWER RD
B213
ABBEY RD
SAMPSON CL
ELSTREE GDNS
KINGSWOOD AVE
HADLEY CT
ST AUGUSTINE'S RD
RIPLEY RD
COLEMAN RD
EDWARDS RD
SHERIDAN RD
GERTRUDE RD
LYNDON RD
B250
LOWER PARK RD
BRIGSTOCK RD
GLADESWOOD RD
Woodside Sch
METHUEN RD
PARKSIDE RD
BELTWOOD RD
BULLBANKS RD
MAYFIELD RD
Tenn Cts
St Augustines Prim Sch
Allot Gdns
UPPER ABBEY RD
STICKLAND RD
HALT ROBIN RD
HALT ROBIN LA
POPLAR MOUNT
Green Chain Wlk
Allot Gdns
HATTERSFIELD CL
KIMBERLEY CT
ABBEY CRES
BUNKER'S HILL
GIDEON CL
REGENT SQ
Belvedere
Frank's Park
Trinity Sch
MORVALE CL
DRAPER CL
PICARDY RD
UPPER PARK RD
DAVID COFFER CT
HAVELOCK RD 1
NAPIER RD 2
BRAESIDE CL 3
HERON HILL
CLIVE RD
RUSKIN RD
MILTON RD
ORCHARD RD
KENTISH RD
PROSPECT CL
FREMANTLE RD
MOSSDOWN CL
CALVERT CL
HEATHDENE DR
ELMBOURNE DR
FOX HOUSE RD
Pl Fld
A206 Dartford, M25 (A282)
Lesnes Abbey Woods
RAGLAN RD
WELLINGTON RD
LESSNESS PK
SMARDEN CL
BERKHAMPSTEAD RD
MITRE CT
EARDLEY RD
Pl Fld
ERITH RD
A206
OLD COLLEGE CT
HILL RD
UPPER HOLLY HILL RD
HOLMHURST RD
PARKSIDE LO
NELSON RD
WALDEN CL
GLOUCESTER RD
ESSENDEN RD
THE VIEW
ABBEY MOUNT
COURT AVE
EDWARD HARVEY CT
RUTLAND GATE
HOLLY HILL RD
TREETOPS CL
WOOLWICH RD
Rec Gd
Liby
Lessness Heath Prim Sch
VANESSA CL
ROBERTS RD
SALMON RD
Bexley Coll
Lessness Heath
FILSTON RD
TYESHURST CL
CROFT CL
HAROLD AVE
VICTORIA ST
FLORA ST
ALFRED RD
ALBERT RD
BEDWELL RD
NUXLEY RD
HODDESDON RD
CHESHUNT RD
STANDARD RD
BROOK ST
HARVEL CT
Tenn Cts
BOEVEY PATH
EVERETT WALK
FAIRMONT CL
STAPLEY RD
WADEVILLE CL
CHAPMAN RD
LUMLEY CL
RIVERDALE RD
STILES CL
DA8
BAYLEY WLK
Sp Gd
WESTERGATE RD
MILFORD CL
ALBANY RD
BARNFIELD RD
LESSNESS RD
HAYLEY HO
Allot Gdns
Cemy
78
48
A
B
49
147
C
D
50
GROSVENOR RD
OSBORNE RD
UPPER GROVE RD
STREAM WAY
WYNFORD
Cemy
ORCHARD AVE
DRYHILL RD
WALSINGHAM WLK
SILVER SPRING CL
THORNE CL
MATFIELD RD
Bedonwell
SUNNINGDALE CL
81
80
79

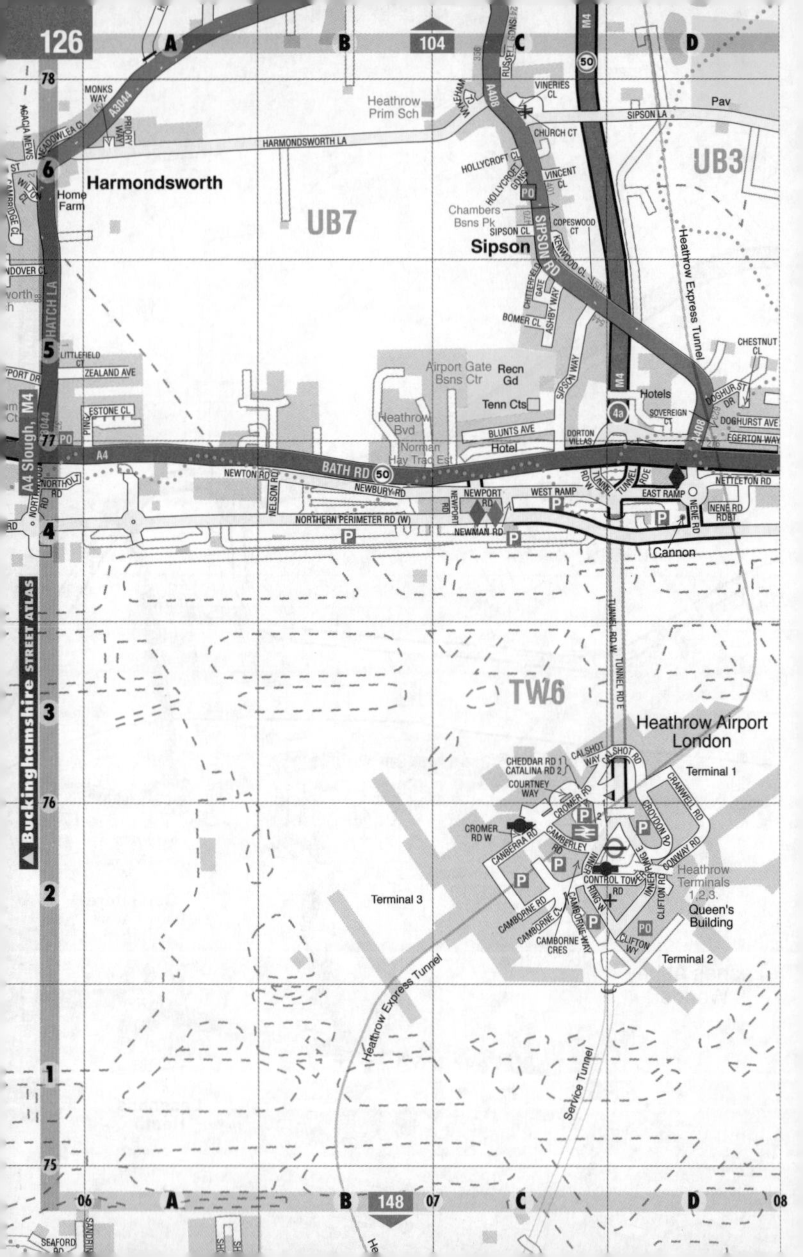
104
A
B
C
D
Harmondsworth
Home Farm
UB7
Heathrow Prim Sch
Sipson
Chambers Bsns Pk
UB3
Heathrow Express Tunnel
Airport Gate Bsns Ctr
Recn Gd
Tenn Cts
Heathrow Bvd
Norman Hay Trad Est
Hotel
Hotels
BATH RD
A4
A4 Slough, M4
NORTHERN PERIMETER RD (W)
WEST RAMP
EAST RAMP
Cannon
TW6
TUNNEL RD W
TUNNEL RD E
Heathrow Airport London
Terminal 1
Terminal 2
Terminal 3
Heathrow Terminals 1,2,3.
Queen's Building
Service Tunnel
HARMONDSWORTH LA
SIPSON LA
SIPSON RD
HATCH LA
ZEALAND AVE
BLUNTS AVE
NEWPORT RD
NEWMAN RD
NEWBURY RD
NEWTON RD
NELSON RD
NETTLETON RD
NENE RD
DOGHURST AVE
EGERTON WAY
CHESTNUT CL
Pav
Buckinghamshire STREET ATLAS
148
06
07
08

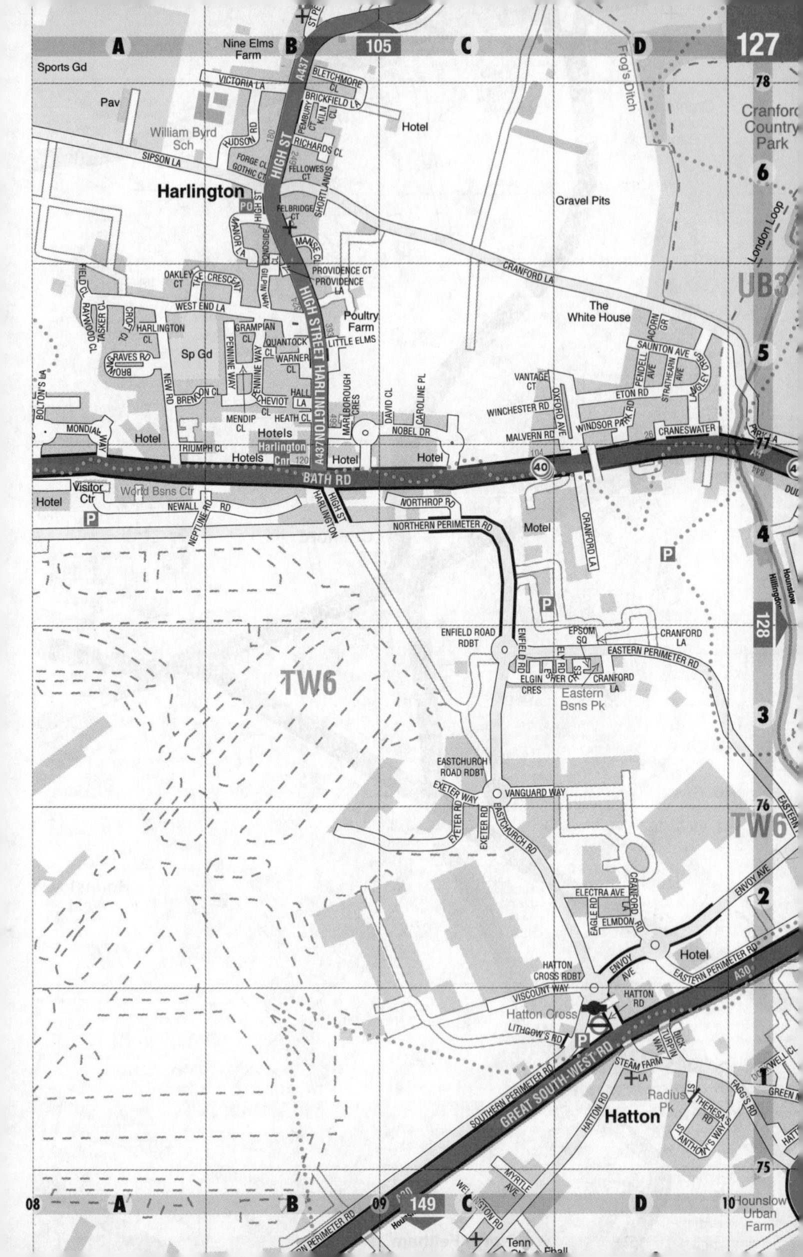

127
105
149
128
A
B
C
D
78
77
76
75
6
5
4
3
2
1
08
09
10
Nine Elms Farm
Sports Gd
Pav
William Byrd Sch
Harlington
Hotel
Gravel Pits
Frog's Ditch
Cranford Country Park
London Loop
UB3
VICTORIA LA
BLETCHMORE CL
BRICKFIELD LA
PEMBURY CT
KILN CL
HUDSON RD
HIGH ST
A437
RICHARDS CL
SIPSON LA
FORGE CL
GOTHIC CT
FELLOWES CT
SHORTLANDS
PO
FELBRIDGE CT
MANOR LA
PONDSIDE CL
MANSE CL
GILPIN WAY
PROVIDENCE CT
PROVIDENCE LA
CRANFORD LA
OAKLEY CT
THE CRESCENT
WEST END LA
HIGH STREET HARLINGTON
Poultry Farm
The White House
ACORN GR
RAYWOOD CL
TASKER CL
CROFT CL
HARLINGTON CL
GRAMPIAN CL
QUANTOCK CL
LITTLE ELMS
WARNER CL
SAUNTON AVE
PENDELL AVE
STRATHEARN AVE
LANGLEY CRES
Sp Gd
PENNINE WAY
BROWNING CL
GRAVES RD
NEW RD
BRENDON CL
CHEVIOT CL
HALL LA
HEATH CL
MARLBOROUGH CRES
DAVID CL
CAROLINE PL
VANTAGE CT
OXFORD AVE
ETON RD
WINDSOR PARK RD
WINCHESTER RD
MALVERN RD
CRANESWATER
PARK LA
BOLTON'S LA
MONDIAL WAY
MENDIP CL
Hotels
Harlington Cnr
NOBEL DR
TRIUMPH CL
BATH RD
A4
40
Visitor Ctr
World Bsns Ctr
NEWALL RD
NEPTUNE RD
HARLINGTON HIGH ST
NORTHROP RD
NORTHERN PERIMETER RD
Motel
CRANFORD LA
P
Hounslow
Hillingdon
TW6
ENFIELD ROAD RDBT
ENFIELD RD
EPSOM SQ
ELY RD
EASTERN PERIMETER RD
ELGIN CRES
FISHER CL
CRANFORD LA
Eastern Bsns Pk
EASTCHURCH ROAD RDBT
EXETER WAY
VANGUARD WAY
EXETER RD
EASTCHURCH RD
ELECTRA AVE
EAGLE RD
ELMDON RD
ENVOY AVE
HATTON CROSS RDBT
VISCOUNT WAY
HATTON RD
Hatton Cross
LITHGOW'S RD
GREAT SOUTH-WEST RD
A30
DICK TURPIN WAY
STEAM FARM LA
Radius Pk
SOUTHERN PERIMETER RD
HATTON RD
Hatton
ST THERESA'S RD
ST ANTHONY'S WAY
FAGG'S RD
GREEN
MYRTLE AVE
WELLINGTON RD
Hounslow Urban Farm
Tenn

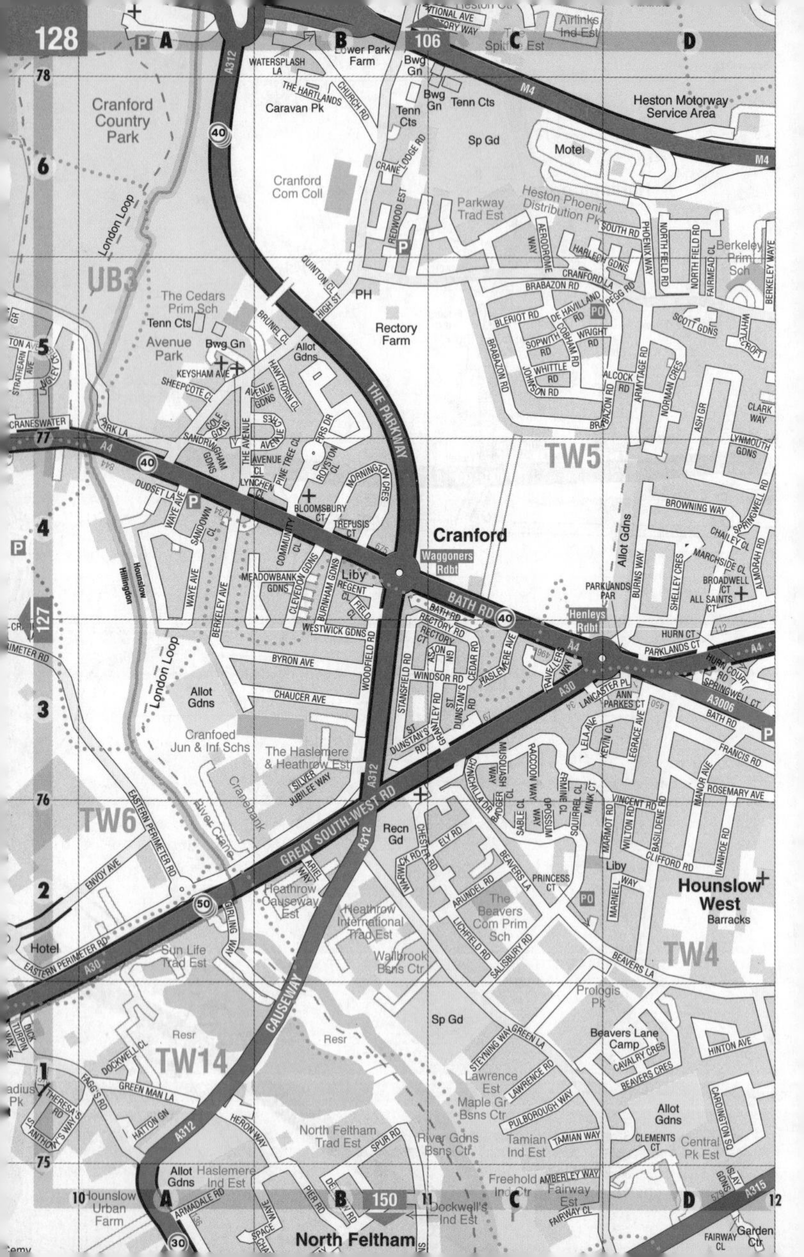
A
B
C
D
106
78
6
5
77
4
3
76
2
1
75
127
150
10
11
12
Cranford Country Park
London Loop
UB3
The Cedars Prim Sch
Tenn Cts
Avenue Park
Bwg Gn
KEYSHAM AVE
SHEEPCOTE CL
CRANESWATER
PARK LA
A4
DUDSET LA
WAYE AVE
SANDOWN CL
Hillingdon
Hounslow
BERKELEY AVE
Allot Gdns
Cranfoed Jun & Inf Schs
TW6
EASTERN PERIMETER RD
ENVOY AVE
Hotel
A30
TURPIN
DOCKWELL CL
TW14
FAGG'S RD
GREEN MAN LA
THERESA RD
ST ANTHONY'S WAY
HATTON GN
Resr
Hounslow Urban Farm
ARMADALE RD
A312
WATERSPLASH LA
Lower Park Farm
THE HARTLANDS
CHURCH RD
Caravan Pk
Cranford Com Coll
CRANE LODGE RD
REDWOOD EST
QUINTON CL
HIGH ST
PH
BRUNEL CL
Allot Gdns
HAWTHORN CL
AVENUE GDNS
AVENUE CRES
COLE GDNS
SANDRINGHAM GDNS
THE AVENUE
AVENUE CL
LYNCHEN CL
PINE TREE CL
FIRS DR
ROYSTON CL
MORNINGTON CRES
BLOOMSBURY CT
TREFUSIS CT
COMMUNITY CL
MEADOWBANK GDNS
CLEVEDON GDNS
BURNHAM GDNS
Liby
REGENT CL
FIELD CL
WESTWICK GDNS
WOODFIELD RD
BYRON AVE
CHAUCER AVE
The Haslemere & Heathrow Est
SILVER JUBILEE WAY
Cranebank
River Crane
GREAT SOUTH-WEST RD
ARIEL WAY
Heathrow Causeway Est
GIRLING WAY
Sun Life Trad Est
CAUSEWAY
HERON WAY
North Feltham Trad Est
SPUR RD
Allot Gdns
Haslemere Ind Est
PIER RD
SPACE WAYE
North Feltham
THE PARKWAY
Rectory Farm
Cranford
Waggoners Rdbt
BATH RD
RECTORY RD
RECTORY GN
ASKON
STANSFIELD RD
WINDSOR RD
CEDAR RD
HASLEMERE AVE
GRANTLEY RD
ST DUNSTAN'S RD
TRAVELLERS WAY
Recn Gd
CHESTER RD
WARWICK RD
ELY RD
ARUNDEL RD
LICHFIELD RD
SALISBURY RD
BEAVERS LA
The Beavers Com Prim Sch
Heathrow International Trad Est
Wallbrook Bsns Ctr
Sp Gd
STEYNING WAY
GREEN LA
Lawrence Est
LAWRENCE RD
Maple Gr Bsns Ctr
PULBOROUGH WAY
River Gdns Bsns Ctr
Tamian Ind Est
TAMIAN WAY
Freehold Ind Ctr
AMBERLEY WAY
Fairway Est
FAIRWAY CL
Dockwell's Ind Est
Airlinks Ind Est
Spitfire Est
M4
Bwg Gn
Tenn Cts
Sp Gd
Heston Motorway Service Area
Motel
Parkway Trad Est
Heston Phoenix Distribution Pk
AERODROME WAY
SOUTH RD
PHOENIX WAY
HARLECH GDNS
CRANFORD LA
PEGG RD
BRABAZON RD
BLERIOT RD
DE HAVILLAND RD
SOPWITH RD
COBHAM RD
WRIGHT RD
WHITTLE RD
JOHNSON RD
ALCOCK RD
ARMYTAGE RD
NORMAN CRES
TW5
Allot Gdns
BURNS WAY
SHELLEY CRES
PARKLANDS PAR
Henleys Rdbt
HURN CT
PARKLANDS CT
LANCASTER PL
ANN PARKES CT
LELA AVE
KEVIN CL
LEGRACE AVE
MUSQUASH WAY
RACCOON WAY
CHINCHILLA DR
BADGER CL
SABLE CL
OPOSSUM WAY
ERMINE CL
SQUIRREL CL
MINK CT
MARMOT RD
WILTON RD
VINCENT RD
BASILDENE RD
CLIFFORD RD
PRINCESS CT
Liby
MARNELL WAY
PO
TW4
Prologis Pk
Beavers Lane Camp
CAVALRY CRES
BEAVERS CRES
Allot Gdns
CLEMENTS CT
Central Pk Est
CARDINGTON SQ
ISLAY GDNS
A315
FAIRWAY CL
Garden Ctr
NORTH FIELD RD
FAIRMEAD CL
Berkeley Prim Sch
BERKELEY WAYE
SCOTT GDNS
WHYTECROFT
ASH GR
CLARK WAY
LYNMOUTH GDNS
BROWNING WAY
SPRINGWELL RD
CHAILEY CL
MARCHSIDE CL
BROADWELL CT
ALL SAINTS CT
ALMORAH RD
HURN COURT RD
SPRINGWELL CT
A3006
BATH RD
FRANCIS RD
MANOR AVE
ROSEMARY AVE
IVANHOE RD
Hounslow West
Barracks
HINTON AVE

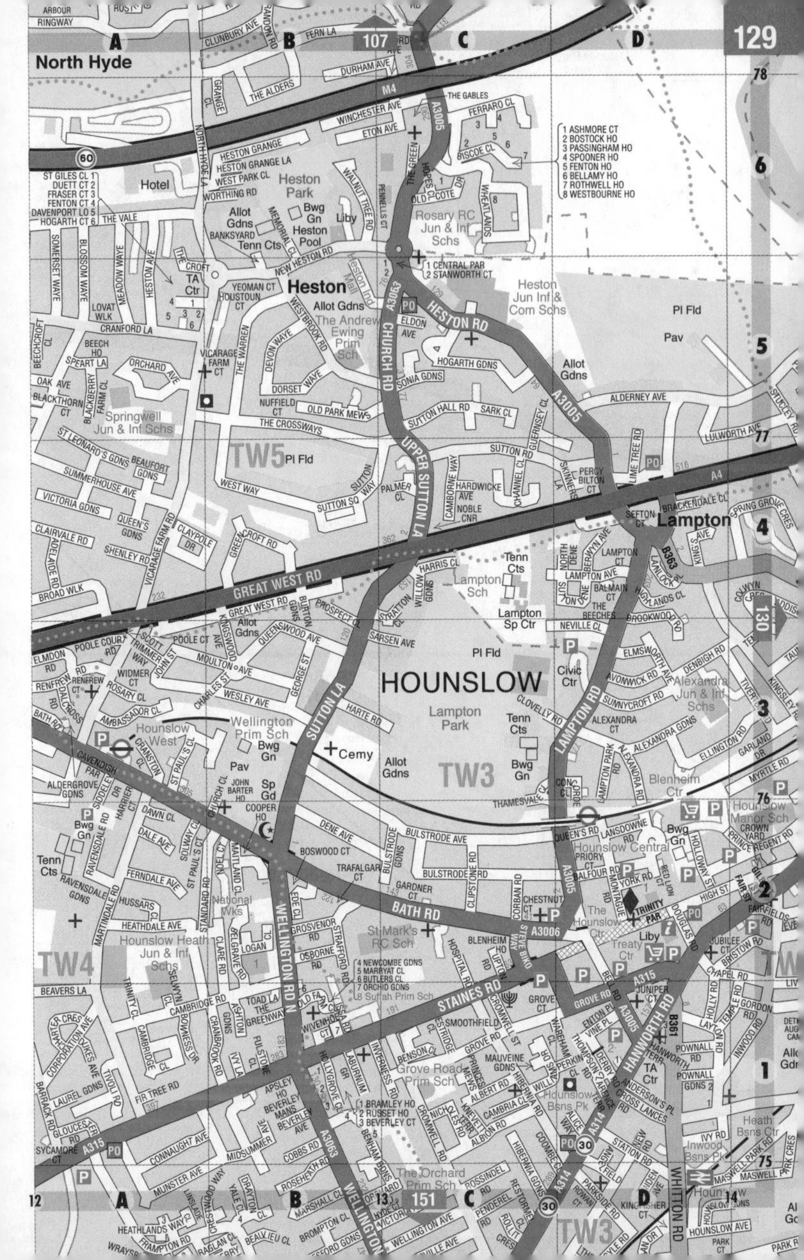

North Hyde
Heston
Lampton
HOUNSLOW
TW5
TW3
TW4
Heston Park
Lampton Park
Hounslow West
Hounslow Central
GREAT WEST RD
BATH RD
STAINES RD
HESTON RD
CHURCH RD
UPPER SUTTON LA
SUTTON LA
WELLINGTON RD N
LAMPTON RD
HANWORTH RD
WHITTON RD
1 ASHMORE CT
2 BOSTOCK HO
3 PASSINGHAM HO
4 SPOONER HO
5 FENTON HO
6 BELLAMY HO
7 ROTHWELL HO
8 WESTBOURNE HO
ST GILES CL 1
DUETT CT 2
FRASER CT 3
FENTON CT 4
DAVENPORT LO 5
HOGARTH CT 6
1 CENTRAL PAR
2 STANWORTH CT
4 NEWCOMBE GDNS
5 MARRYAT CL
6 BUTLERS CL
7 ORCHID GDNS
8 Suffah Prim Sch
1 BRAMLEY HO
2 RUSSET HO
3 BEVERLEY CT
107
130
151

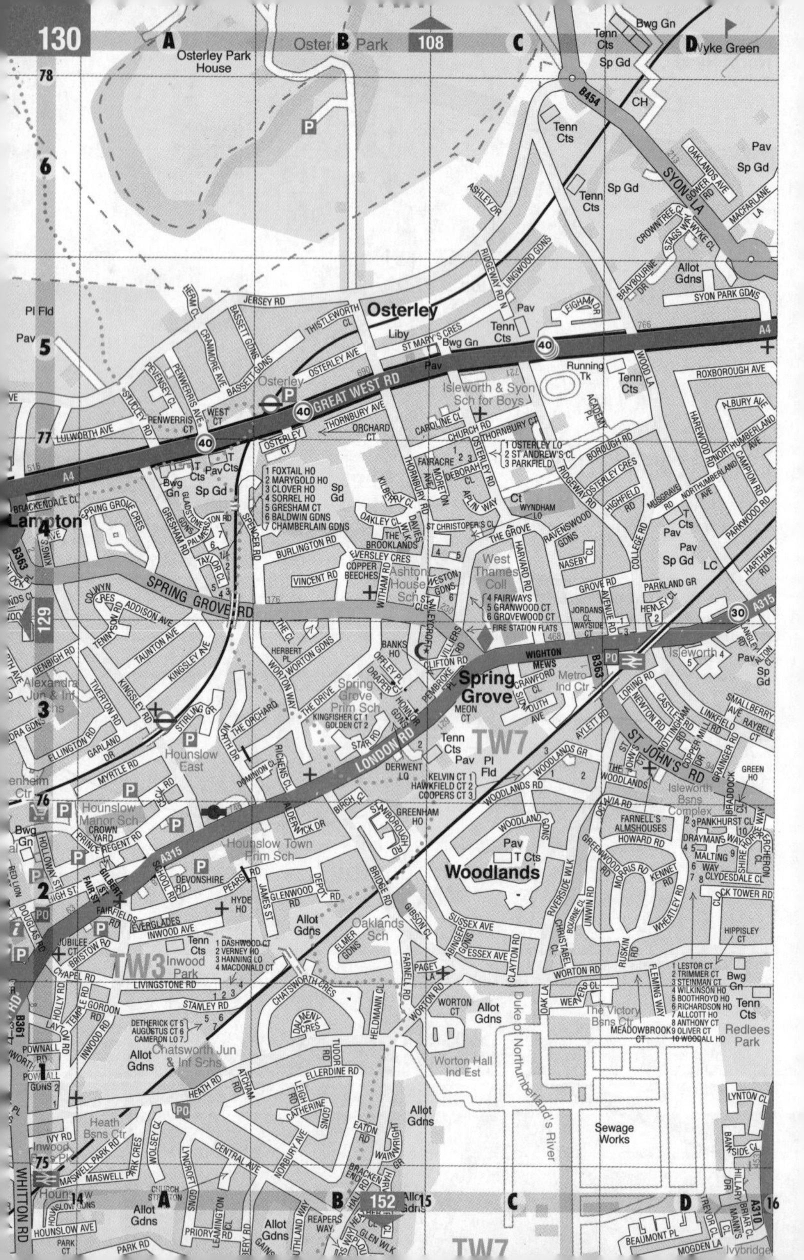
Osterley Park House
Osterley Park
108
Bwg Gn
Tenn Cts
Sp Gd
Wyke Green
B454
CH
Pav
OAKLANDS AVE
GOWER RD
MACFARLANE LA
SYON LA
CROWNTREE CL
STAGS WAY
WYKE CL
Allot Gdns
BRAYBOURNE DR
SYON PARK GDNS
ASHLEY DR
RIDGEWAY RD N
LINGWOOD GDNS
LEIGHAM DR
Osterley
JERSEY RD
HERM CL
BASSETT GDNS
THISTLEWORTH CL
CRANMORE AVE
Liby
ST MARY'S CRES
Pl Fld
A4
Running Tk
WOOD LA
ROXBOROUGH AVE
OSTERLEY AVE
GREAT WEST RD
Isleworth & Syon Sch for Boys
ACADEMY PL
ALBURY AVE
HAREWOOD RD
NORTHUMBERLAND AVE
PEVENSEY CL
PENWERRIS AVE
STUCLEY RD
WEST CT
PENWERRIS CT
THORNBURY AVE
ORCHARD CT
CAROLINE CL
CHURCH RD
THORNBURY CT
LULWORTH AVE
OSTERLEY CT
1 OSTERLEY LO
2 ST ANDREW'S CL
3 PARKFIELD
BOROUGH RD
OSTERLEY CRES
CAMPION RD
1 FOXTAIL HO
2 MARYGOLD HO
3 CLOVER HO
4 SORREL HO
5 GRESHAM CT
6 BALDWIN GDNS
7 CHAMBERLAIN GDNS
FAIRACRE
MORETON AVE
DEBORAH CL
OSTERLEY RD
RIDGEWAY RD
HIGHFIELD RD
MUSGRAVE RD
NORTHUMBERLAND AVE
PARKWOOD RD
BRACKENDALE CL
SPRING GROVE CRES
GLADSTONE GDNS
PALMERSTON RD
KILBERRY CL
APLIN WAY
WYNDHAM LO
Lampton
GRESHAM RD
SPENCER RD
OAKLEY CL
DAVIES WLK
THE BROOKLANDS
ST CHRISTOPHER'S CL
THE GROVE
RAVENSWOOD GDNS
COLLEGE RD
KINGS AVE
B363
TAYLOR CL
BURLINGTON RD
EVERSLEY CRES
West Thames Coll
HARVARD RD
NASEBY CL
HARTHAM RD
COPPER BEECHES
WITHAM RD
WESTON GDNS
VINCENT RD
Ashton House Sch
GROVE RD
AVENUE RD
PARKLAND GR
COLWYN CRES
ADDISON AVE
SPRING GROVE RD
4 FAIRWAYS
5 GRANWOOD CT
6 GROVEWOOD CT
STANLEYCROFT CL
HEMLEY CL
A315
129
TENNYSON RD
TAUNTON AVE
THE CL
JORDANS CL
WAYSIDE CT
FIRE STATION FLATS
DENBIGH RD
KINGSLEY AVE
HERBERT PL
WORTON GDNS
BANKS HO
VILLIERS RD
WIGHTON MEWS
Isleworth
Alexandra Jun & Inf Schs
TIVERTON RD
KINGSLEY RD
WORTON WAY
OFFLEY PL
DRAPER CL
CLIFTON RD
PEMBROKE PL
Spring Grove
CRAWFORD CL
SIDMOUTH AVE
Metro Ind Ctr
LORING RD
SMALLBERRY AVE
Spring Grove Prim Sch
HONNOR GDNS
NEWTON RD
CASTLE RD
LINKFIELD
RAYBELL CT
STIRLING GR
THE ORCHARD
THE DRIVE
MEON CT
NOTTINGHAM RD
COPPER MILL DR
GARLAND DR
ELLINGTON RD
NORTH DR
KINGFISHER CT 1
GOLDEN CT 2
STAR RD
TW7
ST JOHN'S CT
ST JOHN'S RD
GRAINGER RD
Hounslow East
DOMINION CL
RICHENS CL
LONDON RD
DERWENT LO
Tenn Cts
WOODLANDS GR
AYLETT RD
GREEN HO
MYRTLE RD
KELVIN CT 1
HAWKFIELD CT 2
COOPERS CT 3
WOODLANDS RD
THE WOODLANDS
Isleworth Bsns Complex
BRADDOCK CL
Hounslow Manor Sch
BECK RD
ALDERWICK DR
BIRCH CL
STAMBOROUGH RD
GREENHAM HO
OCTAVIA RD
FARNELL'S ALMSHOUSES
PANKHURST CL
CROWN YARD
PRINCE REGENT RD
Hounslow Town Prim Sch
WOODLAND GDNS
HOWARD RD
DRAYMANS WAY
SHIRE HORSE WAY
HOLLOWAY ST
SCHOOL RD
DEVONSHIRE HO
PEARS RD
DEPOT RD
GREENWOOD RD
MORRIS RD
KENNET RD
MALTING WAY
CLYDESDALE CL
Woodlands
RED LION
HIGH ST
FAIR ST
GILBERT ST
GLENWOOD RD
JAMES ST
BRIDGE RD
RIVERSIDE WLK
UNWIN RD
WHEATLEY RD
CLOCK TOWER RD
DOUGLAS RD
FAIRFIELDS RD
HYDE HO
EVERGLADES
INWOOD AVE
Allot Gdns
Oaklands Sch
GIBSON CL
SUSSEX AVE
ABINGER GDNS
ESSEX AVE
CLAYTON RD
CHRISTABEL CL
BOURNE CL
RUSKIN RD
HIPPISLEY CT
JUBILEE CT
BRISTOW RD
1 DASHWOOD CT
2 VERNEY HO
3 HANNING LO
4 MACDONALD CT
ELMER GDNS
PAGET LA
WORTON RD
FLEMING WAY
1 LESTOR CT
2 TRIMMER CT
3 STEINMAN CT
4 WILKINSON HO
5 BOOTHROYD HO
6 RICHARDSON HO
7 ALLCOTT HO
8 ANTHONY CT
9 OLIVER CT
10 WOODALL HO
TW3
Inwood Park
CHAPEL RD
LIVINGSTONE RD
CHATSWORTH CRES
HEIDMANN CL
FARNELL RD
WORTON CT
OAK LA
WEAVERS CL
The Victory Bsns Ctr
MEADOWBROOK CT
Redlees Park
STANLEY RD
GORDON RD
HOLLY RD
TEMPLE RD
DETHERICK CT 5
AUGUSTUS CT 6
CAMERON LO 7
DALMENY CRES
TUDOR RD
Duke of Northumberland's River
B361
LAYTON RD
INWOOD RD
POWNALL RD
POWNALL GDNS
Chatsworth Jun & Inf Schs
Worton Hall Ind Est
ELLERDINE RD
HEATH RD
ATCHAM RD
LEIGH RD
CATHERINE GDNS
LYNTON CL
Heath Bsns Ctr
IVY RD
WOLSEY CL
LYNCROFT GDNS
CENTRAL AVE
NORBURY AVE
EATON RD
WAINWRIGHT GR
Sewage Works
BANKSIDE CL
Inwood Bsns Pk
MASWELL PARK RD
MASWELL PARK CRES
BRACKEN END
HILLARY DR
Hounslow
CHURCH STRETTON
152
WHITTON RD
HOUNSLOW GDNS
HOUNSLOW AVE
LEAMINGTON CL
PRIORY RD
REAPERS WAY
GLEN WLK
TREVOR CL
BRIAR CL
MANN'S CL
A310
BEAUMONT PL
MOGDEN LA
PARK CT
PARK RD
Ivybridge
A
B
C
D
78
77
76
75
6
5
4
3
2
1
14
15
16

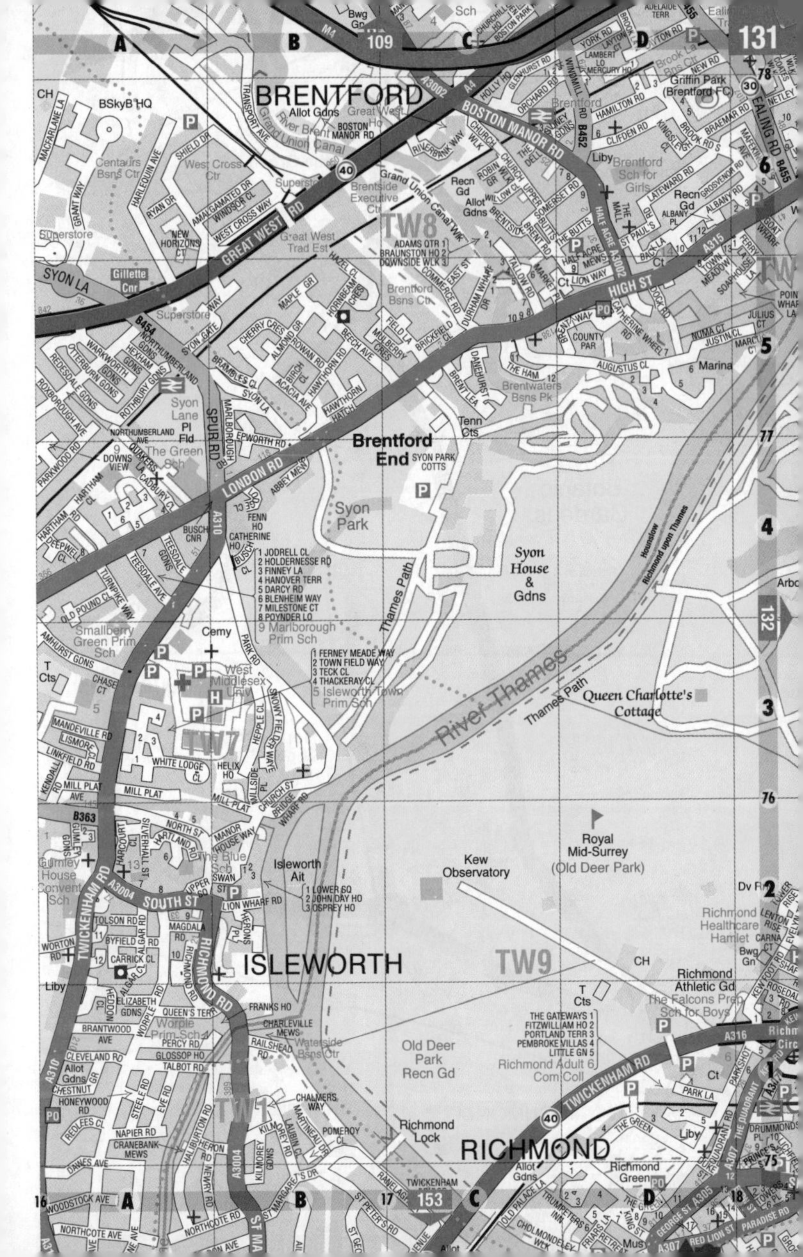
BRENTFORD
Brentford End
ISLEWORTH
RICHMOND
TW8
TW7
TW9
TW1
Syon Park
Syon House & Gdns
Queen Charlotte's Cottage
River Thames
Thames Path
Royal Mid-Surrey (Old Deer Park)
Kew Observatory
Old Deer Park Recn Gd
Richmond Lock
Isleworth Ait
Griffin Park (Brentford FC)
Brentford Sch for Girls
BSkyB HQ
Centaurs Bsns Ctr
West Cross Ctr
Brentside Executive Ctr
Great West Trad Est
Brentford Bsns Ctr
Brentwaters Bsns Pk
Syon Lane Pl Fld
The Green Sch
Smallberry Green Prim Sch
West Middlesex Univ
Marlborough Prim Sch
Isleworth Town Prim Sch
The Blue Sch
Gumley House Convent Sch
Worple Prim Sch
Waterside Bsns Ctr
Richmond Healthcare Hamlet
Richmond Athletic Gd
The Falcons Prep Sch for Boys
Richmond Adult Com Coll
Richmond Green
Grand Union Canal
River Brent
GREAT WEST RD
LONDON RD
BOSTON MANOR RD
HIGH ST
TWICKENHAM RD
SOUTH ST
RICHMOND RD
SPUR RD
SYON LA
HALF ACRE
EALING RD
A4
A315
A3002
A310
A3004
A316
A307
A305
B454
B452
B455
B363
M4
109
153
132
1 JODRELL CL
2 HOLDERNESSE RD
3 FINNEY LA
4 HANOVER TERR
5 DARCY RD
6 BLENHEIM WAY
7 MILESTONE CT
8 POYNDER LO
1 FERNEY MEADE WAY
2 TOWN FIELD WAY
3 TECK CL
4 THACKERAY CL
1 LOWER SQ
2 JOHN DAY HO
3 OSPREY HO
ADAMS QTR 1
BRAUNSTON HO 2
DOWNSIDE WLK 3
THE GATEWAYS 1
FITZWILLIAM HO 2
PORTLAND TERR 3
PEMBROKE VILLAS 4
LITTLE GN 5
A B C D
1 2 3 4 5 6
75 76 77 78
16 17 18

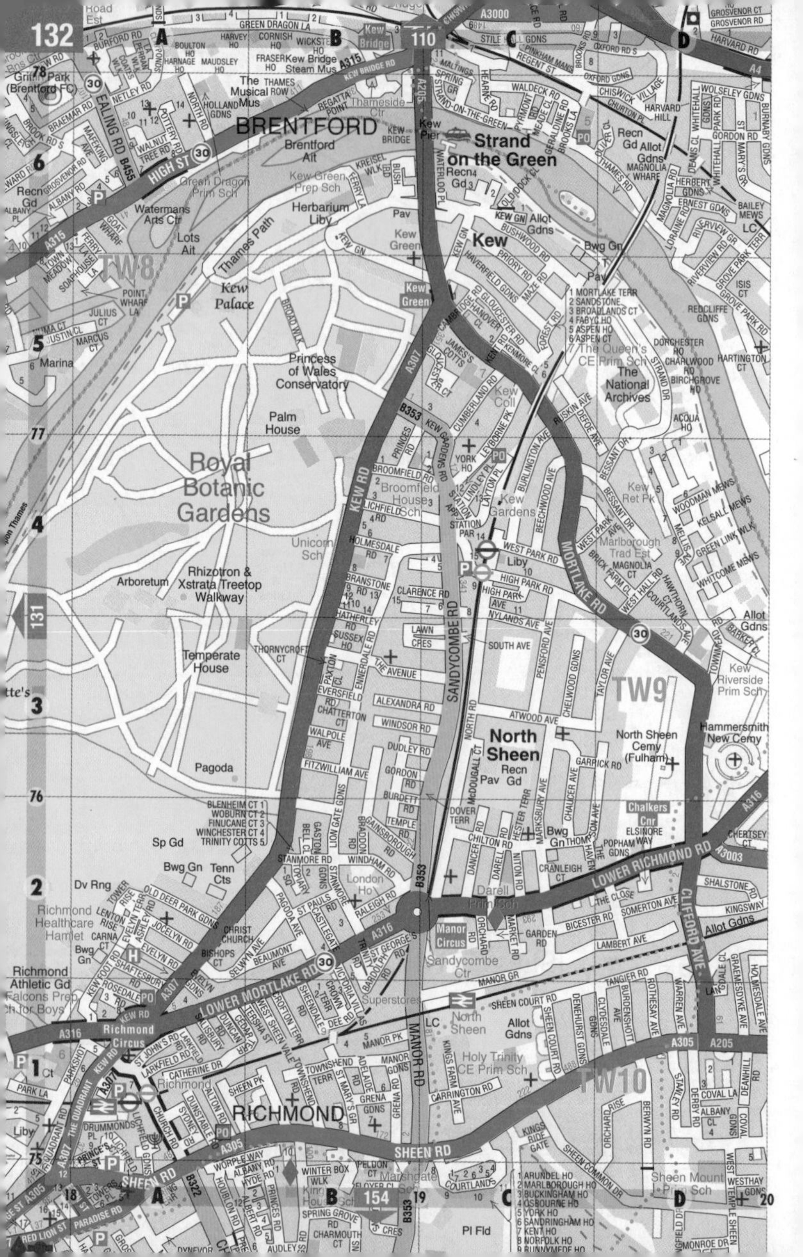

110
BRENTFORD
Strand on the Green
Kew Bridge
Kew Bridge Steam Mus
The Musical Mus
Brentford Ait
Griffin Park (Brentford FC)
Watermans Arts Ctr
Lots Ait
Kew Green Prep Sch
Herbarium Liby
Kew Green
Kew
Kew Palace
Thames Path
TW8
Marina
Princess of Wales Conservatory
Palm House
Royal Botanic Gardens
Rhizotron & Xstrata Treetop Walkway
Arboretum
Temperate House
Pagoda
Unicorn Sch
Broomfield House Sch
The Queen's CE Prim Sch
The National Archives
Kew Coll
Kew Gardens
Kew Ret Pk
Marlborough Trad Est
Kew Riverside Prim Sch
TW9
North Sheen
Hammersmith New Cemy
North Sheen Cemy (Fulham)
Chalkers Cnr
London Ho
Darell Prim Sch
Manor Circus
Sandycombe Ctr
Superstores
North Sheen
Holy Trinity CE Prim Sch
TW10
Richmond Healthcare Hamlet
Richmond Athletic Gd
Falcons Prep Sch for Boys
Richmond Circus
Richmond
RICHMOND
Sheen Mount Prim Sch
Marshgate Sch
Kings House Sch
131
154
KEW RD
SANDYCOMBE RD
MORTLAKE RD
LOWER RICHMOND RD
LOWER MORTLAKE RD
CLIFFORD AVE
MANOR RD
SHEEN RD
HIGH ST
EALING RD
A B C D
1 ARUNDEL HO
2 MARLBOROUGH HO
3 BUCKINGHAM HO
4 OSBOURNE HO
5 YORK HO
6 SANDRINGHAM HO
7 KENT HO
8 NORFOLK HO
9 RUNNYMEDE HO
1 MORTLAKE TERR
2 SANDSTONE
3 BROADLANDS CT
4 FABYC HO
5 ASPEN HO
6 ASPEN CT
1 BLENHEIM CT
2 WOBURN CT
3 FINUCANE CT
4 WINCHESTER CT
5 TRINITY COTTS

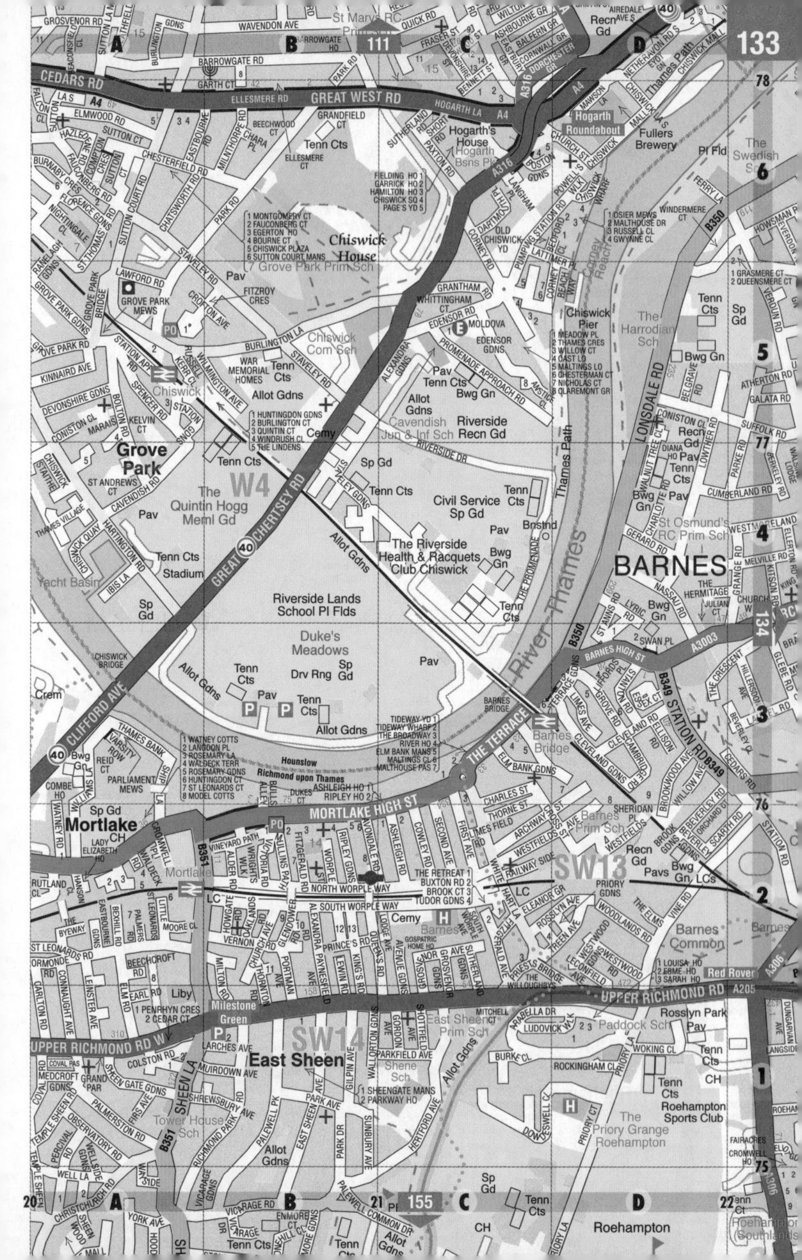
133
A
B
C
D
111
78
6
5
77
4
134
3
76
2
1
75
20
21
155
22
GROSVENOR RD
WAVENDON AVE
St Marys RC Prim Sch
QUICK RD
ASHBOURNE GR
BALFERN GR
CORNWALL GR
AIRDALE AVE S
Recn Gd
NETHERAVON RD S
CHISWICK MALL
BARROWGATE RD
BARROWGATE HO
CEDARS RD
GARTH CT
ELLESMERE RD
GREAT WEST RD
HOGARTH LA
A4
A316
DORCHESTER GR
Thames Path
Eyot
ELMWOOD RD
SUTTON CT
BEECHWOOD CT
GRANDFIELD CT
Tenn Cts
ELLESMERE CT
CHARA PL
Hogarth Roundabout
Hogarth's House
Hogarth Bsns Pk
Fullers Brewery
Pl Fld
The Swedish Sch
CHESTERFIELD RD
CHATSWORTH RD
SUTTON COURT RD
PARK RD
MILNTHORPE RD
EASTBOURNE RD
BURNABY CRES
FAUCONBERG RD
FLORENCE GDNS
NIGHTINGALE CL
FIELDING HO 1
GARRICK HO 2
HAMILTON HO 3
CHISWICK SQ 4
PAGE'S YD 5
CHURCH ST
CHISWICK WHARF
POWELL'S WLK
FERRY LA
WINDERMERE CT
B350
1 OSIER MEWS
2 MALTHOUSE DR
3 RUSSELL CL
4 GWYNNE CL
1 MONTGOMERY CT
2 FAUCONBERG CT
3 EGERTON HO
4 BOURNE CT
5 CHISWICK PLAZA
6 SUTTON COURT MANS
7 Grove Park Prim Sch
Chiswick House
OLD CHISWICK YD
PUMPING STATION RD
LATTIMER PL
Corney Reach
1 GRASMERE CT
2 QUEENSMERE CT
VERDUN RD
LAWFORD RD
GROVE PARK MEWS
STAVELEY RD
FITZROY CRES
CROFTON AVE
Pav
GRANTHAM RD
WHITTINGHAM CT
EDENSOR RD
MOLDOVA
EDENSOR GDNS
Chiswick Pier
1 MEADOW PL
2 THAMES CRES
3 WILLOW CT
4 OAST LO
5 MALTINGS LO
6 CHESTERMAN CT
7 NICHOLAS CT
8 CLAREMONT GR
The Harrodian Sch
Tenn Cts
Sp Gd
Bwg Gn
BELGRAVE RD
ATHERTON RD
GALATA RD
GROVE PARK RD
GROVE PARK GDNS
GROVE PARK BRIDGE
BURLINGTON LA
Chiswick Com Sch
STATION APP
WAR MEMORIAL HOMES
ALEXANDRA GDNS
PROMENADE APPROACH RD
AMSTICE CL
KINNAIRD AVE
DEVONSHIRE GDNS
Chiswick
WILMINGTON AVE
Allot Gdns
Cavendish Jun & Inf Sch
Riverside Recn Gd
LONSDALE RD
CONISTON CL
Recn Gd
SUFFOLK RD
1 HUNTINGDON GDNS
2 BURLINGTON CT
3 QUINTIN CT
4 WINDRUSH CL
5 THE LINDENS
Cemy
KELVIN CT
BOLTON RD
MARAIS
Grove Park
RIVERSIDE DR
DIANA HO
WALNUT TREE CL
LOWTHER RD
PARKE RD
BERKELEY RD
Tenn Cts
W4
ST ANDREWS CT
CAVENDISH RD
The Quintin Hogg Meml Gd
GREAT CHERTSEY RD
Sp Gd
Civil Service Sp Gd
Thames Path
CUMBERLAND RD
THAMES VILLAGE
CHISWICK QUAY
HARTINGTON RD
40
Allot Gdns
The Riverside Health & Racquets Club Chiswick
Bnstnd
THE PROMENADE
St Osmund's RC Prim Sch
GERARD RD
WESTMORELAND
ELLERTON RD
MELVILLE RD
KITSON RD
Yacht Basin
IBIS LA
Stadium
River Thames
BARNES
THE HERMITAGE
NASSAU RD
GRANGE RD
Riverside Lands School Pl Flds
LYRIC RD
ST ANNS RD
JULIAN CT
SWAN PL
BARNES HIGH ST
A3003
Duke's Meadows
CHISWICK BRIDGE
Drv Rng
THE CRESCENT
HILLERSDON AVE
GLEBE RD
Crem
STATION RD
B349
TERRACE GDNS
LIMES AVE
GROVE RD
STANTON RD
ESSEX CT
CLEVELAND RD
ELLISON RD
BEVERLEY CL
BARNES BRIDGE
CLIFFORD AVE
THAMES BANK
VARSITY ROW
TIDEWAY YD 1
TIDEWAY WHARF 2
THE BROADWAY 3
RIVER HO 4
ELM BANK MANS 5
MALTINGS CL 6
MALTHOUSE PAS 7
THE TERRACE
Barnes Bridge
CLEVELAND GDNS
BROOKWOOD AVE
WILLOW AVE
CEDARS RD
1 WATNEY COTTS
2 LANGDON PL
3 ROSEMARY LA
4 WALDECK TERR
5 ROSEMARY GDNS
6 HUNTINGDON CT
7 ST LEONARDS CT
8 MODEL COTTS
Hounslow
Richmond upon Thames
REID CT
PARLIAMENT MEWS
COMBE HO
ASHLEIGH HO 1
RIPLEY HO 2
DUKES CT
ELM BANK GDNS
CHARLES ST
THORNE ST
SHERIDAN PL
BEVERLEY RD
ORCHARD CL
SCARTH RD
MORTLAKE HIGH ST
Sp Gd
Mortlake
CH
LADY ELIZABETH HO
CROMWELL PL
WALDECK RD
VINEYARD PATH
WRIGHTS WLK
VICTORIA RD
MULLINS PATH
FITZGERALD RD
WORPLE ST
RIPLEY GDNS
AVONDALE RD
ASHLEIGH RD
COWLEY RD
SECOND AVE
FIRST AVE
LIMES FIELD
ARCHWAY ST
CROSS ST
WESTFIELDS AVE
WESTFIELDS
Barnes Prim Sch
BROOK GDNS
BEVERLEY GDNS
STATION RD
Recn Gd
Pavs
Bwg Gn
LCs
SW13
B351
Mortlake
RUTLAND
HANSON
ALDER RD
THE RETREAT 1
BUXTON RD 2
BROOK CT 3
TUDOR GDNS 4
NORTH WORPLE WAY
SOUTH WORPLE WAY
RAILWAY SIDE
WHITE HART LA
PRIORY GDNS
THE ELMS
VINE RD
LC
EASTBOURNE GDNS
BEXHILL RD
PALMERS RD
ST LEONARDS RD
LITTLE MOORE CL
THE BYEWAY
HOWGATE RD
OAKLANDS AVE
CHURCH AVE
GLENDOWER RD
ALEXANDRA RD
Cemy
Barnes
SOUTH WORPLE AVE
ELEANOR GR
ROSSLYN AVE
TREEN AVE
WESTWOOD GDNS
WOODLANDS RD
Barnes Common
VERNON RD
PRINCE'S RD
QUEEN'S RD
LODGE AVE
GOSPATRIC HOME RD
AVENUE GDNS
GROSVENOR AVE
GROSVENOR GDNS
SUTHERLAND GDNS
FITZGERALD AVE
PRIESTS BRIDGE
LECONFIELD AVE
WESTWOOD
1 LOUISA HO
2 EDME HO
3 SARAH HO
Red Rover
A306
ST LEONARDS RD
ORMONDE RD
BEECHCROFT RD
MILTON RD
THORNTON RD
PORTMAN AVE
PAYNESFIELD AVE
LEWIN RD
KING'S RD
THE WILLOUGHBYS
UPPER RICHMOND RD
A205
CARLTON RD
CONNAUGHT AVE
LEINSTER AVE
ELM RD
EARL RD
Liby
1 PENRHYN CRES
2 CEDAR CT
Milestone Green
WALLORTON GDNS
GORDON AVE
SHOTTFIELD AVE
MITCHELL CT
East Sheen Prim Sch
ARABELLA DR
LUDOVICK WLK
Paddock Sch
Rosslyn Park
Pav
DUNGARVAN
LANGSIDE
UPPER RICHMOND RD W
LARCHES AVE
SW14
PARKFIELD AVE
Allot Gdns
WOKING CL
Tenn Cts
COVAL PAS
COLSTON RD
MUIRDOWN AVE
East Sheen
Shene Sch
BURKE CL
ROCKINGHAM CL
PRIORY LA
MEDCROFT GDNS
GRAND PAR
SHEEN GATE GDNS
SHEEN LA
SHREWSBURY AVE
GILPIN AVE
1 SHEENGATE MANS
2 PARKWAY HO
CH
Tenn Cts
Roehampton Sports Club
COVAL RD
TEMPLE SHEEN RD
PALMERSTON RD
FIRS AVE
PARK AVE
DOWNESWELL CL
PRIORY CT
ROEHAMPTON
PERCIVAL RD
OBSERVATORY RD
Tower House Sch
RICHMOND PARK RD
PALEWELL PK
EAST SHEEN AVE
PARK DR
SUNBURY AVE
HERTFORD AVE
The Priory Grange Roehampton
FAIRACRES
CROMWELL HO
WELLSIDE GDNS
WELL LA
B351
VICARAGE GDNS
Allot Gdns
TEMPLE SHEEN
WAYSIDE
Sp Gd
CHRISTCHURCH RD
VICARAGE RD
ENMORE GDNS
PALEWELL COMMON DR
Tenn Cts
SHEEN WOOD
YORK AVE
VICARAGE DR
CH
Roehampton
Tenn Cts
Tenn Ct
Roehampton Southlands
PRIORY LA

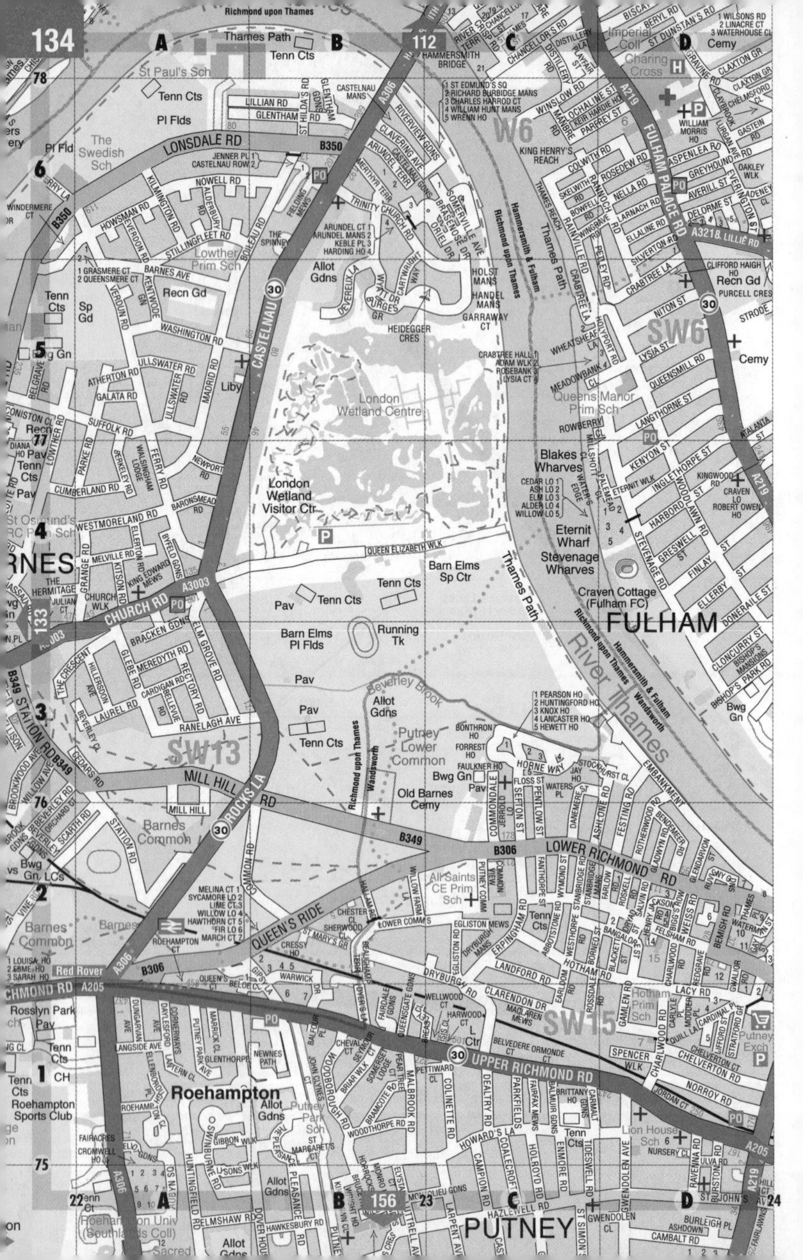
Richmond upon Thames
Thames Path
Tenn Cts
St Paul's Sch
Pl Flds
The Swedish Sch
LONSDALE RD
HAMMERSMITH BRIDGE
W6
Imperial Coll
Charing Cross
FULHAM PALACE RD
KING HENRY'S REACH
CASTELNAU
Lowther Prim Sch
BARNES AVE
Recn Gd
WASHINGTON RD
Allot Gdns
London Wetland Centre
London Wetland Visitor Ctr
QUEEN ELIZABETH WLK
Hammersmith & Fulham
Richmond upon Thames
SW6
Queens Manor Prim Sch
Blakes Wharves
Eternit Wharf
Stevenage Wharves
Craven Cottage (Fulham FC)
FULHAM
BARNES
CHURCH RD
Barn Elms Sp Ctr
Barn Elms Pl Flds
Running Tk
Beverley Brook
Putney Lower Common
River Thames
Wandsworth
SW13
MILL HILL RD
ROCKS LA
Old Barnes Cemy
Barnes Common
LOWER RICHMOND RD
QUEEN'S RIDE
All Saints CE Prim Sch
Red Rover
UPPER RICHMOND RD
SW15
Hotham Prim Sch
Roehampton
Putney Park Sch
Lion House Sch
Putney Exch
Roehampton Sports Club
Roehampton Univ (Southlands Coll)
PUTNEY
112
133
156

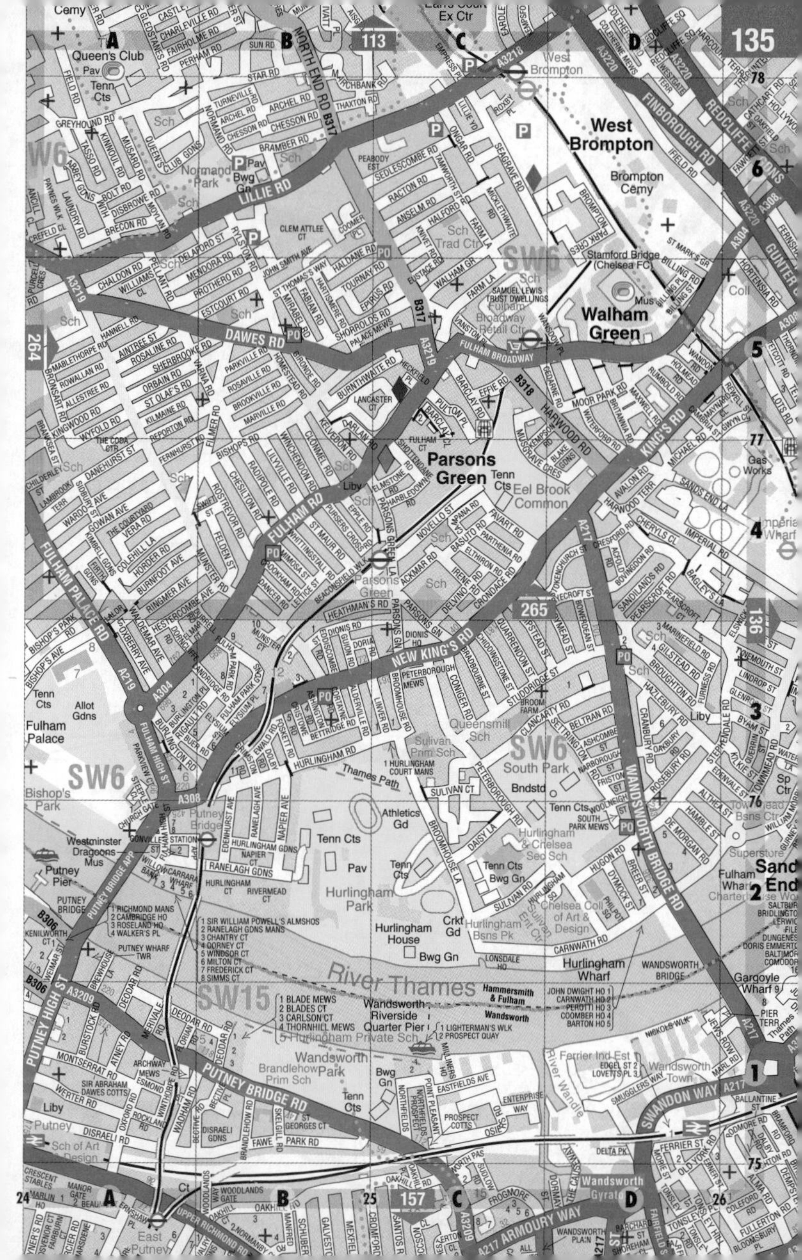
113
A
B
C
D
West Brompton
Brompton Cemy
Queen's Club
Normand Park
Walham Green
Stamford Bridge (Chelsea FC)
Parsons Green
Eel Brook Common
Fulham Broadway
Gas Works
Imperial Wharf
South Park
Hurlingham Park
Hurlingham House
Hurlingham & Chelsea Sec Sch
Chelsea Coll of Art & Design
Fulham Palace
Bishop's Park
Westminster Dragoons Mus
Putney Pier
Putney Bridge
River Thames
SW6
SW15
Hammersmith & Fulham
Wandsworth
Wandsworth Riverside Quarter Pier
Wandsworth Park
Ferrier Ind Est
River Wandle
Wandsworth Town
Wandsworth Gyratory
Sands End
Fulham Wharf
Gargoyle Wharf
Hurlingham Wharf
East Putney
Putney
LILLIE RD
DAWES RD
FULHAM RD
FULHAM PALACE RD
NEW KING'S RD
KING'S RD
WANDSWORTH BRIDGE RD
PUTNEY BRIDGE RD
PUTNEY HIGH ST
UPPER RICHMOND RD
SWANDON WAY
A217 ARMOURY WAY
FINBOROUGH RD
REDCLIFFE GDNS
NORTH END RD
HARWOOD RD
HURLINGHAM RD
264
265
136
157
24
25
26
1
2
3
4
5
6
77
76
75
78

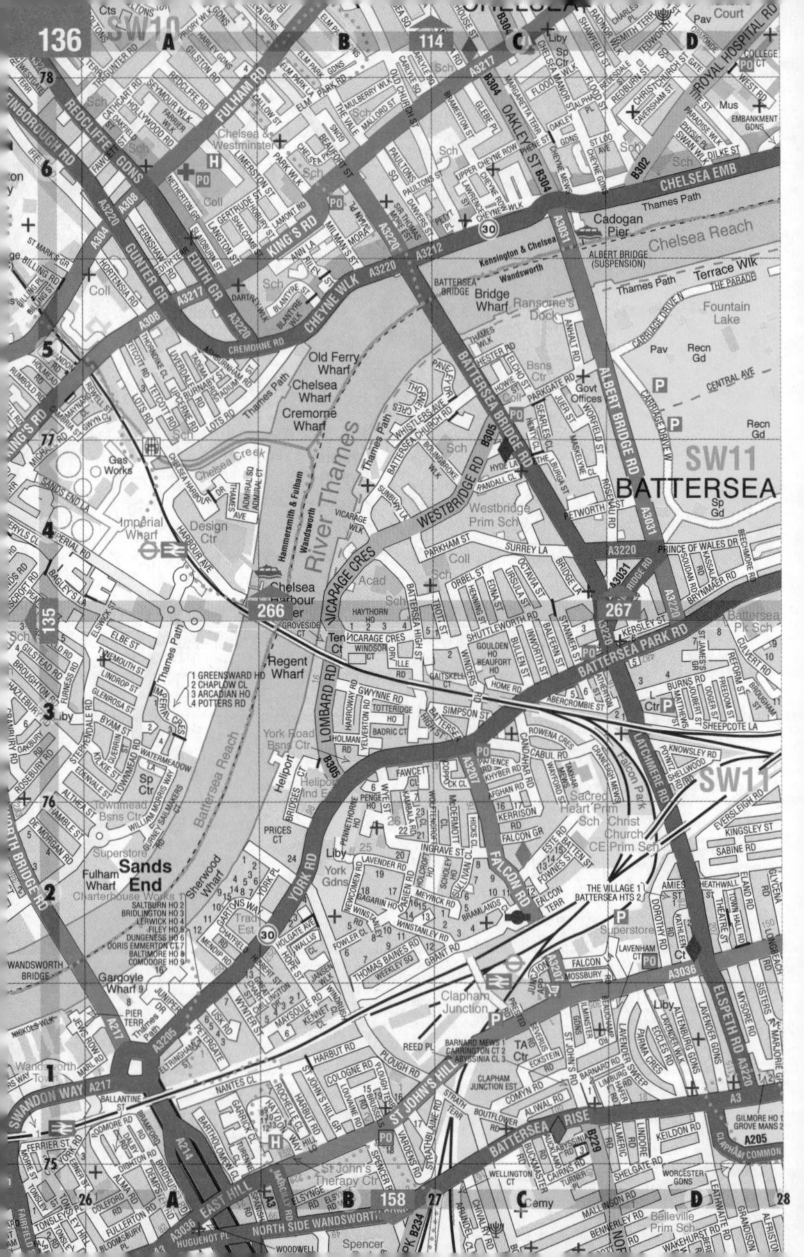

136
SW10
A
B
C
D
114
CHELSEA
6
5
4
3
2
1
78
77
76
75
26
27
28
135
266
267
158
REDCLIFFE GDNS
FULHAM RD
FINBOROUGH RD
GUNTER GR
EDITH GR
KING'S RD
CHEYNE WLK
CREMORNE RD
OAKLEY ST
CHELSEA EMB
ROYAL HOSPITAL RD
Chelsea & Westminster
Coll
Sch
Cadogan Pier
Chelsea Reach
ALBERT BRIDGE (SUSPENSION)
Thames Path
Terrace Wlk
THE PARADE
Fountain Lake
Pav
Recn Gd
CENTRAL AVE
CARRIAGE DRIVE N
CARRIAGE DRIVE W
Kensington & Chelsea
Wandsworth
BATTERSEA BRIDGE
Bridge Wharf
Ransome's Dock
Old Ferry Wharf
Chelsea Wharf
Cremorne Wharf
River Thames
Hammersmith & Fulham
Gas Works
Chelsea Creek
Imperial Wharf
Design Ctr
HARBOUR AVE
Chelsea Harbour Pier
BATTERSEA BRIDGE RD
ALBERT BRIDGE RD
Govt Offices
Bsns Ctr
SW11
BATTERSEA
Sp Gd
WESTBRIDGE RD
Westbridge Prim Sch
VICARAGE CRES
SURREY LA
PARKHAM ST
PRINCE OF WALES DR
BATTERSEA HIGH ST
BATTERSEA PARK RD
Battersea Pk Sch
Regent Wharf
LOMBARD RD
York Road Bsns Ctr
Heliport
Battersea Reach
Sands End
Fulham Wharf
Charterhouse Works
Sherwood Wharf
Townmead Bsns Ctr
Superstore
YORK RD
WANDSWORTH BRIDGE
Gargoyle Wharf
Thames Path
Falcon Park
Sacred Heart Prim Sch
Christ Church CE Prim Sch
FALCON RD
THE VILLAGE 1
BATTERSEA HTS 2
Clapham Junction
LATCHMERE RD
ELSPETH RD
LAVENDER SWEEP
ST JOHN'S HILL
BATTERSEA RISE
CLAPHAM COMMON
SWANDON WAY
EAST HILL
NORTH SIDE WANDSWORTH COMMON
St John's Therapy Ctr
Cemy
Belleville Prim Sch
Spencer
1 GREENSWARD HO
2 CHAPLOW CL
3 ARCADIAN HO
4 POTTERS RD
SALTBURN HO 2
BRIDLINGTON HO 3
LERWICK HO 4
FILEY HO 5
DUNGENESS HO 6
DORIS EMMERTON CT 7
BALTIMORE HO 8
COMODORE HO 9
BARNARD MEWS 1
CARRINGTON CT 2
ABYSSINIA CL 3
GILMORE HO 1
GROVE MANS 2
A3220
A3217
A308
A3212
A3031
A3205
A3207
A3036
A217
A214
A205
A3
B304
B305
B302
B229
B234

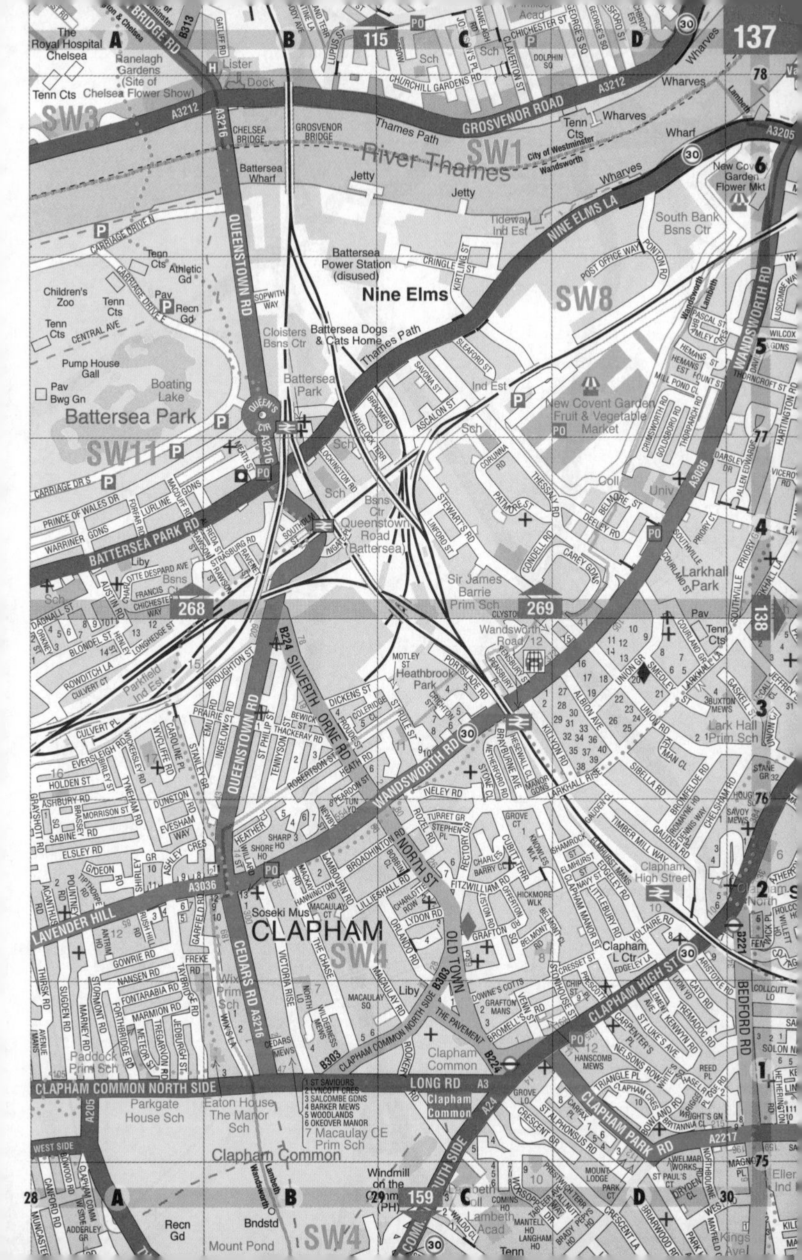
115
The Royal Hospital Chelsea
Ranelagh Gardens (Site of Chelsea Flower Show)
Lister
Dock
Tenn Cts
SW3
A3212
A3216
CHELSEA BRIDGE
GROSVENOR BRIDGE
CHURCHILL GARDENS RD
CHICHESTER ST
CLAVERTON ST
DOLPHIN SQ
GROSVENOR ROAD
Wharves
Wharf
Thames Path
River Thames
SW1
City of Westminster
Wandsworth
A3205
Battersea Wharf
Jetty
New Covent Garden Flower Mkt
South Bank Bsns Ctr
NINE ELMS LA
Tideway Ind Est
CARRIAGE DRIVE N
CARRIAGE DRIVE E
CARRIAGE DR S
QUEENSTOWN RD
Battersea Power Station (disused)
CRINGLE ST
KIRTLING ST
POST OFFICE WAY
PONTON RD
Children's Zoo
Athletic Gd
Recn Gd
SOPWITH WAY
Nine Elms
SW8
CENTRAL AVE
Cloisters Bsns Ctr
Battersea Dogs & Cats Home
Pump House Gall
Boating Lake
Battersea Park
QUEEN'S CIR
SW11
WANDSWORTH RD
SLEAFORD ST
SAVONA ST
ASCALON ST
Ind Est
New Covent Garden Fruit & Vegetable Market
BROADMEAD
HAVELOCK TERR
LOCKINGTON RD
PRINCE OF WALES DR
WARRINER GDNS
BATTERSEA PARK RD
Queenstown Road (Battersea)
CORUNNA RD
THESSALY RD
STEWART'S RD
LINFORD ST
PATMORE ST
CONDELL RD
CAREY GDNS
DEELEY RD
BELMORE ST
Coll
Univ
A3036
SOUTHVILLE
PRIORY CT
Larkhall Park
Sir James Barrie Prim Sch
268
269
138
Wandsworth Road
Parkfield Ind Est
B224
SILVERTHORNE RD
Heathbrook Park
PORTSLADE RD
UNION GR
SMEDLEY ST
LARKHALL LA
Lark Hall Prim Sch
LAVENDER HILL
A3036
CEDARS RD
A3216
CLAPHAM
Soseki Mus
SW4
NORTH ST
OLD TOWN
B303
CLAPHAM COMMON NORTH SIDE
THE PAVEMENT
Clapham Common
CLAPHAM MANOR ST
Clapham L Ctr
Clapham High Street
CLAPHAM HIGH ST
BEDFORD RD
B221
Clapham North
LONG RD
A3
A205
A24
Paddock Prim Sch
Parkgate House Sch
Eaton House The Manor Sch
1 ST SAVIOURS
2 LYNCOTT CRES
3 SALCOMBE GDNS
4 BARKER MEWS
5 WOODLANDS
6 OKEOVER MANOR
7 Macaulay CE Prim Sch
Clapham Common
CLAPHAM PARK RD
A2217
WEST SIDE
Windmill on the Common (PH)
Lambeth Coll
Lambeth Acad
Recn Gd
Bndstd
Mount Pond
159
SW4
28
29
30
A
B
C
D
1
2
3
4
5
6
75
76
77
78

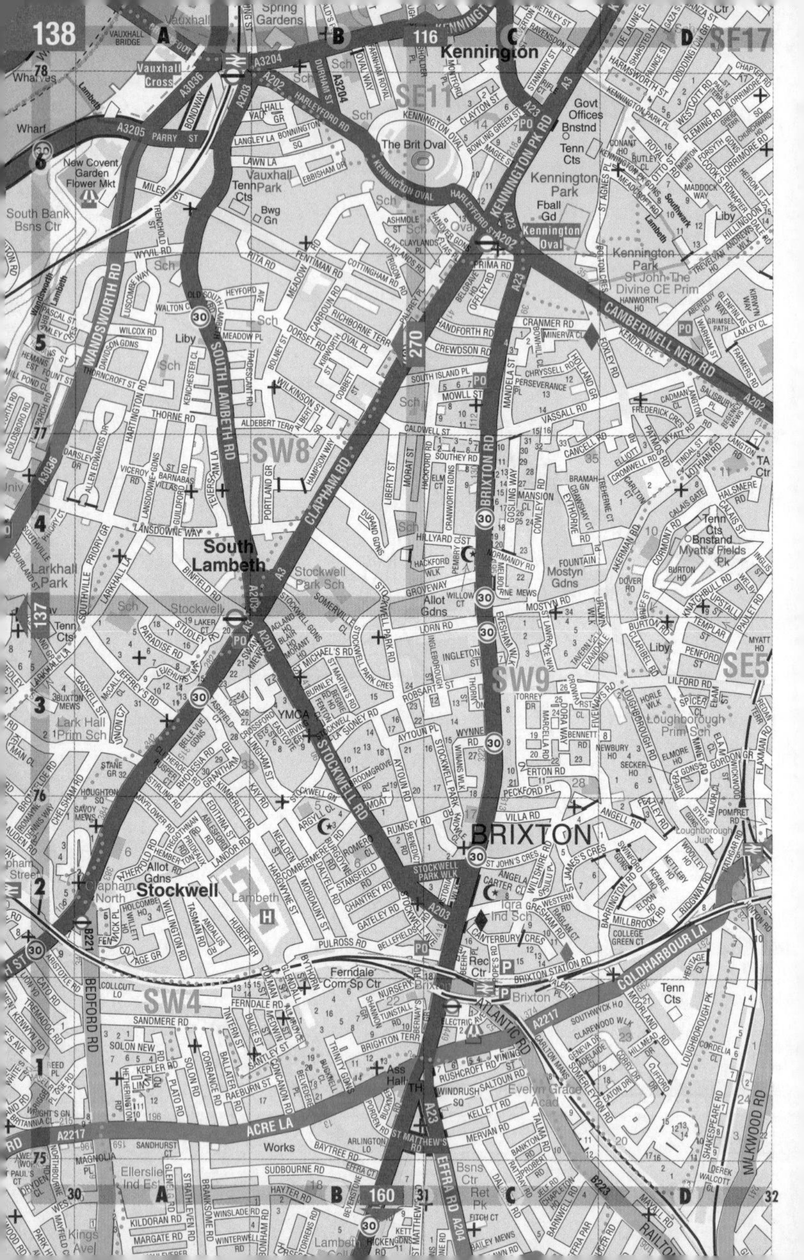
A
B
C
D
116
SE17
Vauxhall
Vauxhall Bridge
Vauxhall Cross
Spring Gardens
Kennington
Wharves
Wharf
New Covent Garden Flower Mkt
South Bank Bsns Ctr
SE11
The Brit Oval
Kennington Oval
Kennington Park
Kennington Park Rd
Govt Offices Bnstnd
Tenn Cts
Fball Gd
Vauxhall Park
Bwg Gn
Harleyford Rd
Kennington Oval
St John The Divine CE Prim
Camberwell New Rd
Southwark
Lambeth
Wandsworth Rd
South Lambeth Rd
Clapham Rd
Brixton Rd
SW8
270
Liby
Sch
Wyvil Rd
Fentiman Rd
Richborne Terr
Dorset Rd
Crewdson Rd
Handforth Rd
Vassall Rd
Lansdowne Way
South Lambeth
Stockwell Park Sch
Larkhall Park
137
Stockwell
Groveway
Allot Gdns
Mostyn Gdns
Myatt's Fields Pk
Lorn Rd
SW9
SE5
YMCA
Stockwell Rd
Loughborough Prim Sch
Lark Hall Prim Sch
Villa Rd
BRIXTON
Loughborough Junc
Stockwell Park Wlk
Clapham North
Stockwell
Lambeth
Iqra Ind Sch
Coldharbour La
Rec Ctr
Brixton Station Rd
Ferndale Com Sp Ctr
Brixton
Atlantic Rd
SW4
Bedford Rd
Ferndale Rd
Sandmere Rd
Electric Av
Ass Hall
TH
Evelyn Grace Acad
Acre La
A2217
Works
Ellerslie Ind Est
Effra Rd
Bsns Ctr
Ret Pk
Milkwood Rd
Loughborough Pk
Railton Rd
160
31
30
32
75
76
77
78
1
2
3
4
5
6

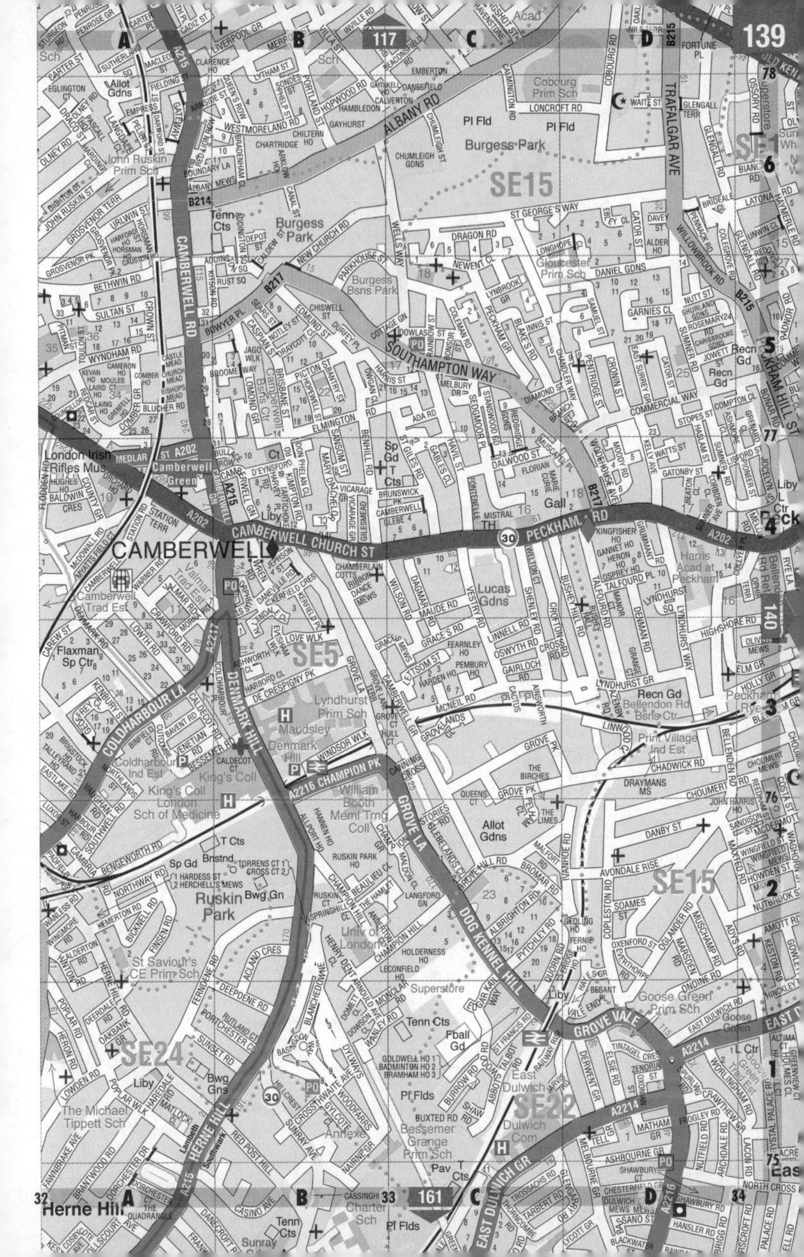

117
A
B
C
D
CAMBERWELL
SE15
SE5
SE24
SE22
SE15
Burgess Park
Burgess Park
Cobourg Prim Sch
Pl Fld
Pl Fld
ALBANY RD
CAMBERWELL RD
A215
B214
B217
B215
A202
A2216
A2214
A2217
TRAFALGAR AVE
WILLOWBROOK RD
SOUTHAMPTON WAY
PECKHAM RD
CAMBERWELL CHURCH ST
CAMBERWELL GROVE
DENMARK HILL
COLDHARBOUR LA
CHAMPION PK
GROVE LA
DOG KENNEL HILL
GROVE VALE
EAST DULWICH GR
HERNE HILL
RYE LA
PECKHAM HILL ST
COMMERCIAL WAY
ST GEORGE'S WAY
NEW CHURCH RD
WELLS WAY
PARKHOUSE ST
BOWYER PL
WYNDHAM RD
CAMBERWELL NEW RD
MEDLAR ST
Camberwell Green
London Irish Rifles Mus
Camberwell Trad Est
Flaxman Sp Ctr
Coldharbour Ind Est
King's Coll
King's Coll London Sch of Medicine
Maudsley
Denmark Hill
Lyndhurst Prim Sch
William Booth Meml Trng Coll
Univ of London
Ruskin Park
St Saviour's CE Prim Sch
John Ruskin Prim Sch
Gloucester Prim Sch
Burgess Bsns Park
Camberwell Bsns Ctr
Lucas Gdns
Allot Gdns
Harris Acad at Peckham
Bellendon Rd Bsns Ctr
Prim Village Ind Est
Goose Green Prim Sch
Goose Green
Goose Green Trad Est
East Dulwich
Dulwich Com
Bessemer Grange Prim Sch
The Michael Tippett Sch
Charter Sch
Herne Hill
Peckham Rye
Superstore
Tenn Cts
Fball Gd
Pl Flds
Annexe
Liby
Gall
Recn Gd
161
140
32
33
34
1
2
3
4
5
6
75
76
77
78

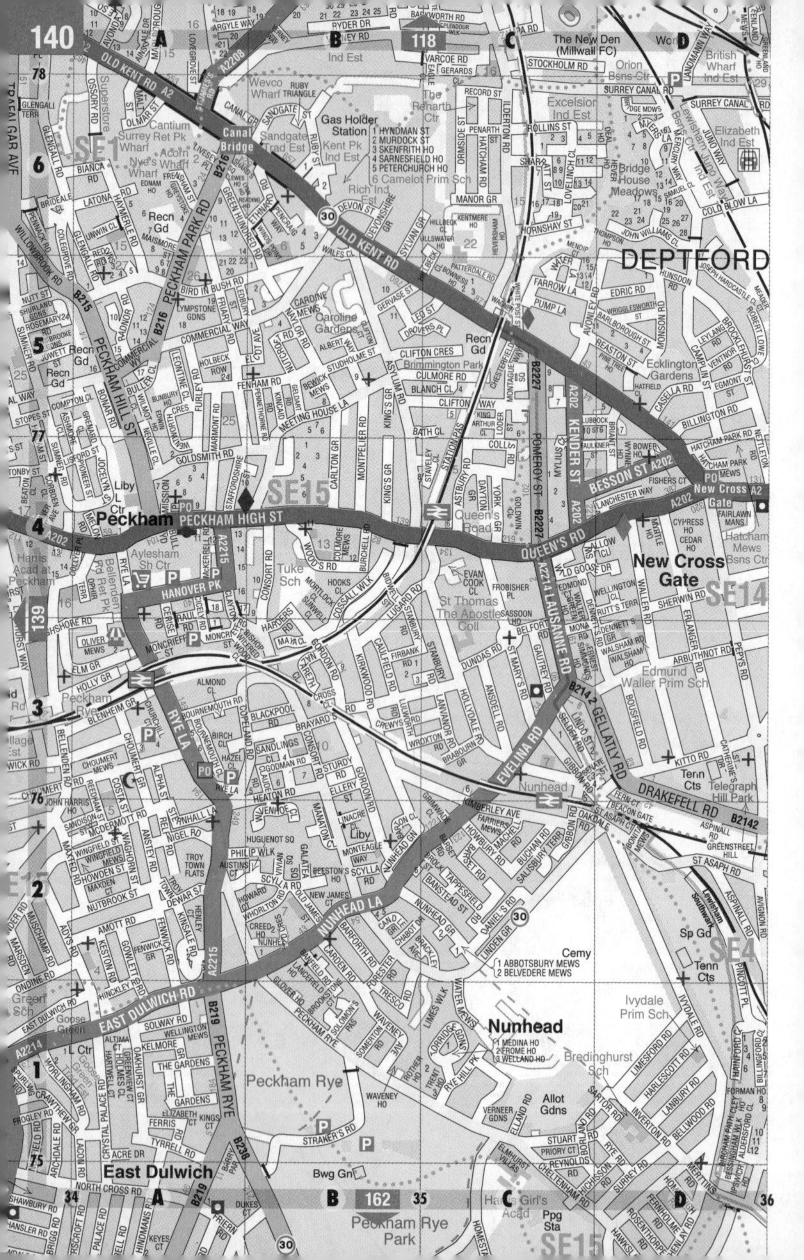
A
B
C
D
118
162
139
34
35
36
75
76
77
78
1
2
3
4
5
6
The New Den
(Millwall FC)
DEPTFORD
Peckham
New Cross Gate
Nunhead
East Dulwich
Peckham Rye
Peckham Rye Park
SE1
SE15
SE14
SE4
OLD KENT RD A2
OLD KENT RD
Canal Bridge
PECKHAM PARK RD
PECKHAM HILL ST
PECKHAM HIGH ST
QUEEN'S RD
HANOVER PK
RYE LA
EVELINA RD
LAUSANNE RD
GELLATLY RD
DRAKEFELL RD
NUNHEAD LA
EAST DULWICH RD
PECKHAM RYE
KENDER ST
BESSON ST A202
POMEROY ST
COMMERCIAL WAY
STATION PAS
ASYLUM RD
SURREY CANAL RD
ILDERTON RD
Gas Holder Station
1 HYNDMAN ST
2 MURDOCK ST
3 SKENFRITH HO
4 SARNESFIELD HO
5 PETERCHURCH HO
6 Camelot Prim Sch
Caroline Gardens
Brimmington Park
Ecklington Gardens
Excelsior Ind Est
Orion Bsns Ctr
British Wharf Ind Est
Elizabeth Ind Est
Bridge House Meadows
Cantium Surrey Ret Pk
Aylesham Sh Ctr
Bellenden Rd Ret Pk
Tuke Sch
St Thomas The Apostle Coll
Queen's Road
Edmund Waller Prim Sch
Tenn Cts
Telegraph Hill Park
Nunhead
Cemy
1 ABBOTSBURY MEWS
2 BELVEDERE MEWS
1 MEDINA HO
2 FROME HO
3 WELLAND HO
Ivydale Prim Sch
Bredinghurst Sch
Allot Gdns
Sp Gd
Goose Green
Bwg Gn
Harris Girl's Acad
Ppg Sta
Hatcham Mews Bsns Ctr
Recn Gd
Liby

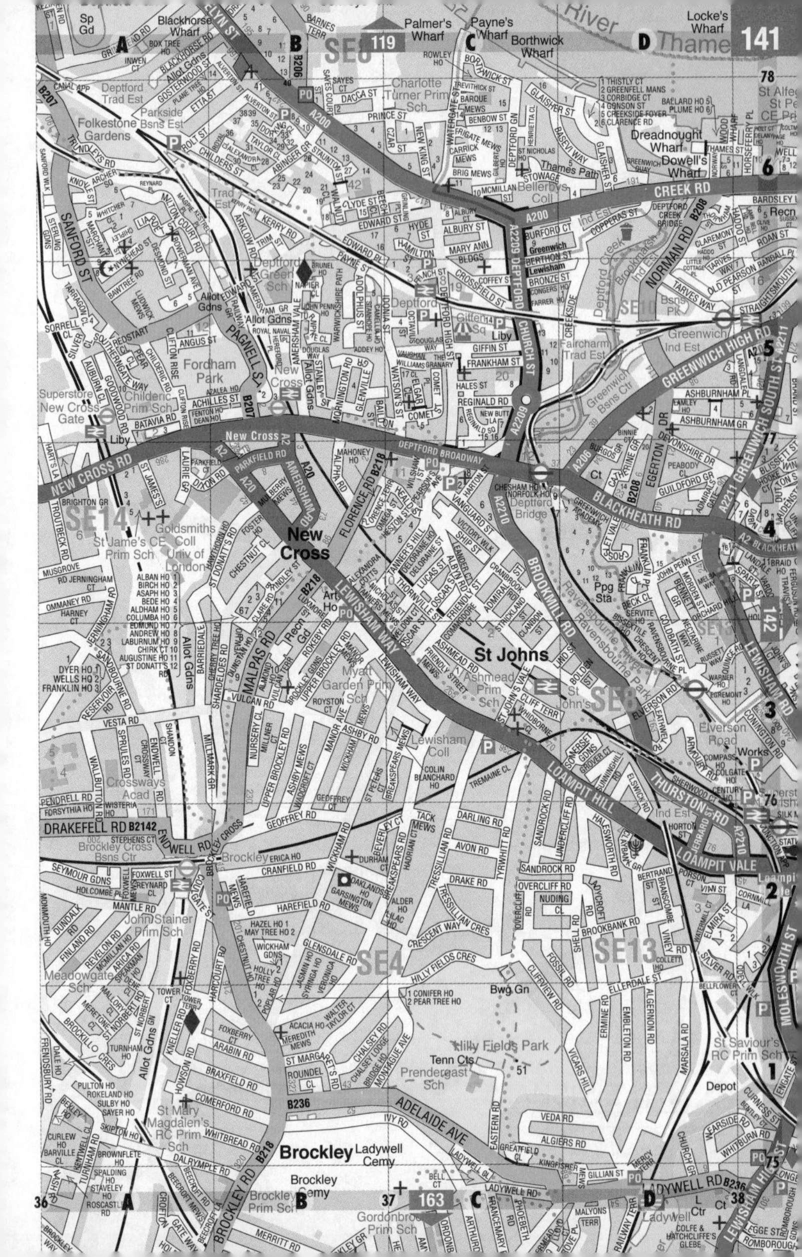
River Thames
Locke's Wharf
Palmer's Wharf
Payne's Wharf
Borthwick Wharf
Blackhorse Wharf
119
SE8
Deptford Trad Est
Parkside Bsns Est
Folkestone Gardens
Charlotte Turner Prim Sch
Dreadnought Wharf
Dowell's Wharf
St Alfege
78
6
CREEK RD
Bellerbys Coll
Thames Path
SANFORD ST
Deptford Green Sch
Deptford
Giffen Sq
Liby
Faircharm Trad Est
Greenwich Ind Est
Greenwich Bsns Ctr
SE10
GREENWICH HIGH RD
5
Fordham Park
Childeric Prim Sch
Superstore
New Cross Gate
New Cross
NEW CROSS RD
DEPTFORD BROADWAY
BLACKHEATH RD
77
4
SE14
Goldsmiths Coll Univ of London
St James's CE Prim Sch
New Cross
LEWISHAM WAY
Deptford Bridge
BROOKMILL RD
Ravensbourne Park
St Johns
Myatt Garden Prim Sch
Ashmead Prim Sch
St John's
SE8
Elverson Road
142
LEWISHAM RD
3
Lewisham Coll
Crossways Acad
LOAMPIT HILL
THURSTON RD
LOAMPIT VALE
76
DRAKEFELL RD B2142
Brockley Cross Bsns Ctr
Brockley
John Stainer Prim Sch
Meadowgate Sch
SE4
SE13
Hilly Fields Park
Bwg Gn
Tenn Cts
Prendergast Sch
2
MOLESWORTH ST
St Saviour's RC Prim Sch
Depot
1
St Mary Magdalen's RC Prim Sch
ADELAIDE AVE
Brockley
Ladywell Cemy
Brockley Cemy
BROCKLEY RD
LADYWELL RD
Ladywell
75
36
A
Brockley Prim Sch
B
37
163
C
Gordonbrock Prim Sch
D
38

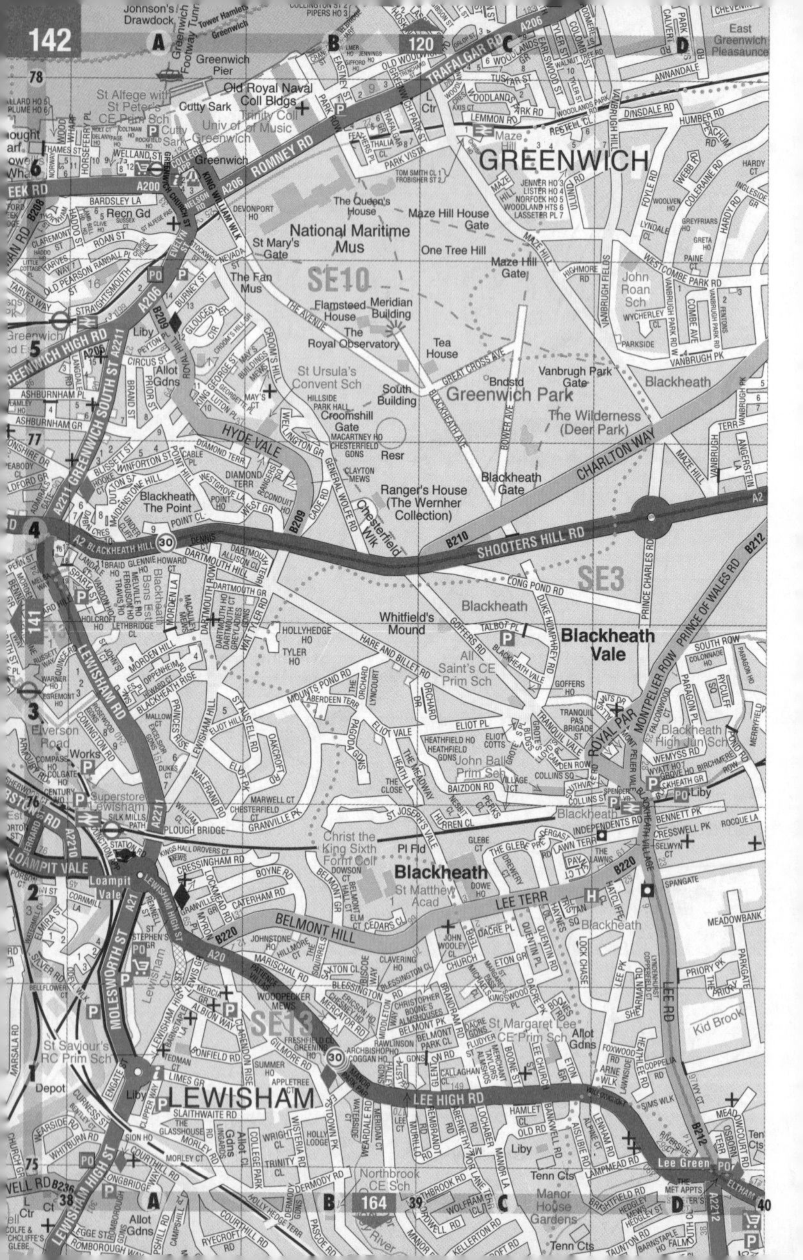

142
A
B
120
C
D
GREENWICH
SE10
SE3
SE13
LEWISHAM
Blackheath
Blackheath Vale
Greenwich Park
National Maritime Mus
The Queen's House
Old Royal Naval Coll Bldgs
Cutty Sark
Greenwich Pier
Greenwich Footway Tunnel
Johnson's Drawdock
East Greenwich Pleasaunce
St Alfege with St Peter's CE Prim Sch
Trinity Coll Univ of of Music
Maze Hill
Maze Hill House Gate
Maze Hill Gate
One Tree Hill
St Mary's Gate
The Fan Mus
Flamsteed House
Meridian Building
The Royal Observatory
Tea House
South Building
Croomshill Gate
Resr
St Ursula's Convent Sch
Vanbrugh Park Gate
The Wilderness (Deer Park)
Blackheath Gate
Ranger's House (The Wernher Collection)
Chesterfield Wlk
John Roan Sch
Bndstd
Whitfield's Mound
All Saint's CE Prim Sch
John Ball Prim Sch
Blackheath High Jun Sch
Christ the King Sixth Form Coll
St Matthew Acad
St Margaret Lee CE Prim Sch
Northbrook CE Sch
St Saviour's RC Prim Sch
Elverson Road
Lewisham
Loampit Vale
Lewisham Ctr
Superstore
Works
Depot
Allot Gdns
Pl Fld
Kid Brook
Tenn Cts
Manor House Gardens
Lee Green
Recn Gd
ROMNEY RD
TRAFALGAR RD
KING WILLIAM WLK
GREENWICH HIGH RD
GREENWICH SOUTH ST
GREENWICH CHURCH ST
CREEK RD
HYDE VALE
CROOM'S HILL
THE AVENUE
GREAT CROSS AVE
BLACKHEATH AVE
BOWER AVE
CHARLTON WAY
MAZE HILL
VANBRUGH PARK
VANBRUGH HILL
WESTCOMBE PARK RD
SHOOTERS HILL RD
BLACKHEATH HILL
DARTMOUTH ROW
LEWISHAM HILL
LEWISHAM RD
PRINCE CHARLES RD
PRINCE OF WALES RD
MONTPELIER ROW
ROYAL PAR
LONG POND RD
GOFFERS RD
HARE AND BILLET RD
ELIOT VALE
MOUNTS POND RD
TRANQUIL VALE
BLACKHEATH VILLAGE
LEE TERR
BELMONT HILL
LEE HIGH RD
LEE RD
MOLESWORTH ST
LEWISHAM HIGH ST
LOAMPIT VALE
A2
A20
A200
A206
A21
A2211
A2212
A2210
B209
B210
B212
B220
B236
B208
30
141
164
78
77
76
75
6
5
4
3
2
1
38
39
40

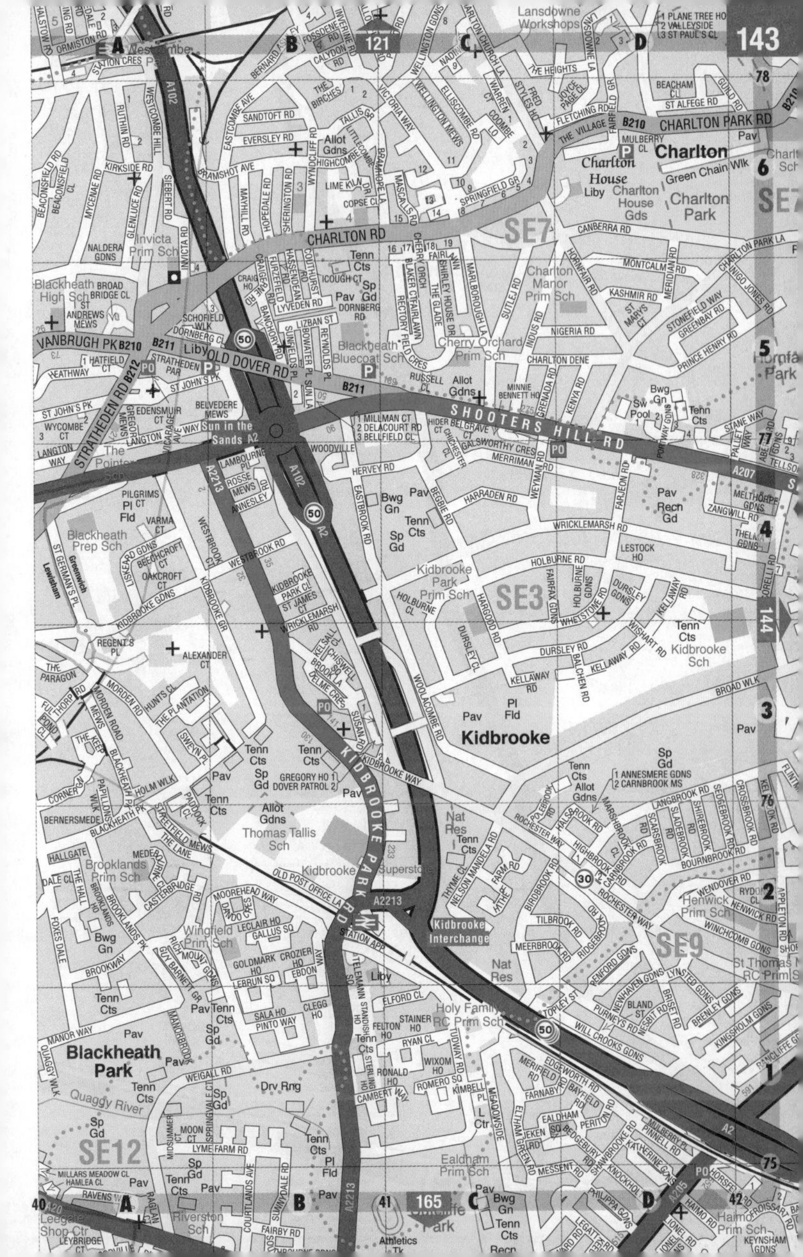
A
B
C
D
121
165
144
78
77
76
75
6
5
4
3
2
1
40
41
42
Westcombe Park
Lansdowne Workshops
1 PLANE TREE HO
2 VALLEYSIDE
3 ST PAUL'S CL
ORMISTON RD
STATION CRES
WESTCOMBE HILL
RUTHIN RD
BEACONSFIELD RD
BEACONSFIELD CL
MYCENAE RD
KIRKSIDE RD
GLENLUCE RD
SIEBERT RD
INVICTA RD
A102
EASTCOMBE AVE
SANDTOFT RD
EVERSLEY RD
BRAMSHOT AVE
MAYHILL RD
HOPEDALE RD
SHERINGTON RD
WYNDCLIFF RD
BERNARD ASHLEY
FOSSDENE
INVERINE RD
CALYDON RD
THE BIRCHES
VICTORIA WAY
TALLIS GR
LITTLECOMBE
HIGHCOMBE
Allot Gdns
LIME KILN DR
COPSE CL
BRAMHOPE LA
MASCALLS RD
WELLINGTON GDNS
WELLINGTON MEWS
ELLISCOMBE RD
CHARLTON CHURCH LA
NADINE
WARREN CT
COOMBE LO
FRED STYLES HO
THE HEIGHTS
JOYCE PAGE CL
LANSDOWNE LA
FAIRFIELD GR
FLETCHING RD
THE VILLAGE
B210
CHARLTON PARK RD
BEACHAM CL
ST ALFEGE RD
GUILD RD
MULBERRY CL
Charlton
Charlton House
Liby
Charlton House Gds
Green Chain Wlk
Charlton Park
SE7
SPRINGFIELD GR
CHARLTON RD
CANBERRA RD
CHARLTON PARK LA
Tenn Cts
NALDERA GDNS
Invicta Prim Sch
Blackheath High Sch
BROAD BRIDGE CL
ST ANDREWS MEWS
CRAIGHOLM
CRAIGERNE RD
FURZEFIELD RD
HASSENDEAN RD
COUTHURST RD
ICOUGH CT
LYVEDEN RD
Pav
Sp Gd
DORNBERG RD
CHERRY ORCH
BLAKER CT
FAIRLAWN
SHIRLEY HOUSE DR
THE GLADE
RECTORY FIELD CRES
MARLBOROUGH LA
SUTLEJ RD
HORNFAIR RD
Charlton Manor Prim Sch
MONTCALM RD
MERIDIAN RD
KASHMIR RD
ST MARYS CT
STONEFIELD WAY
GREENBAY RD
INIGO JONES RD
PRINCE HENRY RD
NIGERIA RD
INDUS RD
SCHOFIELD WLK
DORNBERG CL
LIZBAN ST
SUNFIELDS PL
BOWATER PL
REYNOLDS PL
BANCHORY RD
Blackheath Bluecoat Sch
Cherry Orchard Prim Sch
CHARLTON DENE
VANBRUGH PK
B210
B211
Liby
OLD DOVER RD
1 HATFIELD CT
HEATHWAY
STRATHEDEN PAR
STRATHEDEN RD
B212
ST JOHN'S PK
ST JOHN'S PK
EDENSMUIR CT
BELVEDERE MEWS
WYCOMBE CT
GREGORY MEWS
LANGTON WAY
VICARAGE AVE
Sun in the Sands A2
The Pointer Sch
RUSSELL CL
Allot Gdns
MINNIE BENNETT HO
GRENADA RD
KENYA RD
Bwg Gn
Sw Pool
PORTWAY GDNS
STANE WAY
PALLET WAY
SHOOTERS HILL RD
1 MILLMAN CT
2 DELACOURT RD
3 BELLFIELD CL
HIDER CT
BELGRAVE CT
CHICHESTER CL
GALSWORTHY CRES
PO
MERRIMAN RD
WEYMAN RD
FARJEON RD
A207
TELLSON
MELTHORPE GDNS
ZANGWILL RD
WOODVILLE
HERVEY RD
LAMBOURNE PL
ROSSE MEWS
ANNESLEY RD
A2213
A2
EASTBROOK RD
BEGBIE RD
HARRADEN RD
Rech Gd
WRICKLEMARSH RD
THELMA GDNS
PILGRIMS CT
Pl Fld
VARMA CT
Blackheath Prep Sch
ST GERMAN'S PL
Lewisham
Greenwich
ISKEARD GDNS
BEECHCROFT CT
OAKCROFT CT
WESTBROOK CT
WESTBROOK RD
KIDBROOKE GDNS
KIDBROOKE GR
KIDBROOKE PARK CL
ST JAMES CT
HOLBURNE RD
LESTOCK HO
Kidbrooke Park Prim Sch
HOLBURNE CL
HARGOOD RD
SE3
FAIRFAX GDNS
HOLBURNE GDNS
WHETSTONE RD
DURSLEY GDNS
KELLAWAY RD
WISHART RD
DURSLEY CL
DURSLEY RD
BALCHEN RD
KELLAWAY RD
Kidbrooke Sch
CORELLI RD
REGENT'S PL
ALEXANDER CT
THE PARAGON
MORDEN RD
MORDEN ROAD MEWS
THORPE CL
HUNTS CL
THE PLANTATION
KELSALL CL
CHISWELL SQ
BROOK LA
DELME CRES
SUSAN RD
WOOLACOMBE RD
BROAD WLK
Kidbrooke
THE KEEP
BLACKHEATH PK
SWEYN PL
HOLM WLK
PAPILLONS WLK
CORNER GN
BERNERSMEDE
PADDOCK CL
KIDBROOKE PARK RD
KIDBROOKE WAY
GREGORY HO 1
DOVER PATROL 2
Thomas Tallis Sch
Nat Res
1 ANNESMERE GDNS
2 CARNBROOK MS
LANGBROOK RD
SEDGEBROOK RD
CROSSBROOK RD
FLINTMILL
POLEBROOK RD
ROCHESTER WAY
HALSBROOK RD
MARSHBROOK CL
HIGHBROOK RD
SCARSBROOK RD
SLADEBROOK RD
SHIREBROOK RD
CARNBROOK RD
BOURNBROOK RD
NELSON MANDELA RD
THYME CL
FARM RD
HITHER
BIRDBROOK RD
STREETFIELD MEWS
THE LANE
HALLGATE
MEDEBOURNE CL
Brooklands Prim Sch
DALE CL
THE HALL
BROOKLANDS HO
CASTERBRIDGE RD
Kidbrooke Superstore
OLD POST OFFICE LA
MOOREHEAD WAY
DANDO CRES
LECLAIR HO
GALLUS SQ
Wingfield Prim Sch
Kidbrooke Interchange
STATION APP
TILBROOK RD
RIDGEBROOK RD
MEERBROOK RD
WENDOVER RD
RYDON CL
HENWICK RD
Henwick Prim Sch
WINCHCOMB GDNS
APPLETON RD
SE9
St Thomas More RC Prim Sch
FOXES DALE
BROOKLANDS PK
GUY BARNETT GR
RICH MOUNT GDNS
GOLDMARK HO
CROZIER HO
EBDON WAY
LEBRUN SQ
BROOKWAY
RENFORD GDNS
NEWHAVEN GDNS
LYNSTED GDNS
BRISET RD
BLAND ST
NESBIT RD
BRENLEY GDNS
PURNEYS RD
KINGSHOLM GDNS
MANOR WAY
MANORBROOK
SALA HO
PINTO WAY
CLEGG HO
ELFORD CL
STAINER HO
FELTON HO
TELEMANN SQ
STANDISH HO
STERLING HO
Holy Family RC Prim Sch
TOPLEY ST
WILL CROOKS GDNS
RANCLIFFE GDNS
Blackheath Park
QUAGGY WLK
WEIGALL RD
Drv Rng
RYAN CL
WIXOM HO
RONALD HO
ROMERO SQ
KIMBELL PL
TUDWAY RD
CAMBERT WAY
L Ctr
MEADOWSIDE
MERIFIELD RD
FARNABY RD
EDGEWORTH RD
BAYFIELD RD
Quaggy River
MIDSUMMER AVE
MOON CT
SPRINGVALE CT
LYME FARM RD
SE12
EALDHAM SQ
JEKEN RD
PERITON RD
BEDGEBURY RD
SHAWBROOKE RD
KATHERINE GDNS
MULBERRY PL
PINNELL RD
KNOCKHOLT RD
Eltham Green Rd
MESSENT RD
Eldham Prim Sch
MILLARS MEADOW CL
HAMLEA CL
RAVENS WAY
RAGLAN
COURTLANDS AVE
SUNNYDALE RD
Leegate Shop Ctr
LEYBRIDGE CT
Riverston Sch
FAIRBY RD
Athletics Tk
Park
PHILIPPA GDNS
A205
HORSFELD RD
HAIMO RD
Haimo Prim Sch
FROISSART RD
KEYNSHAM GDNS
LEGATT RD
LIONEL RD
Recn

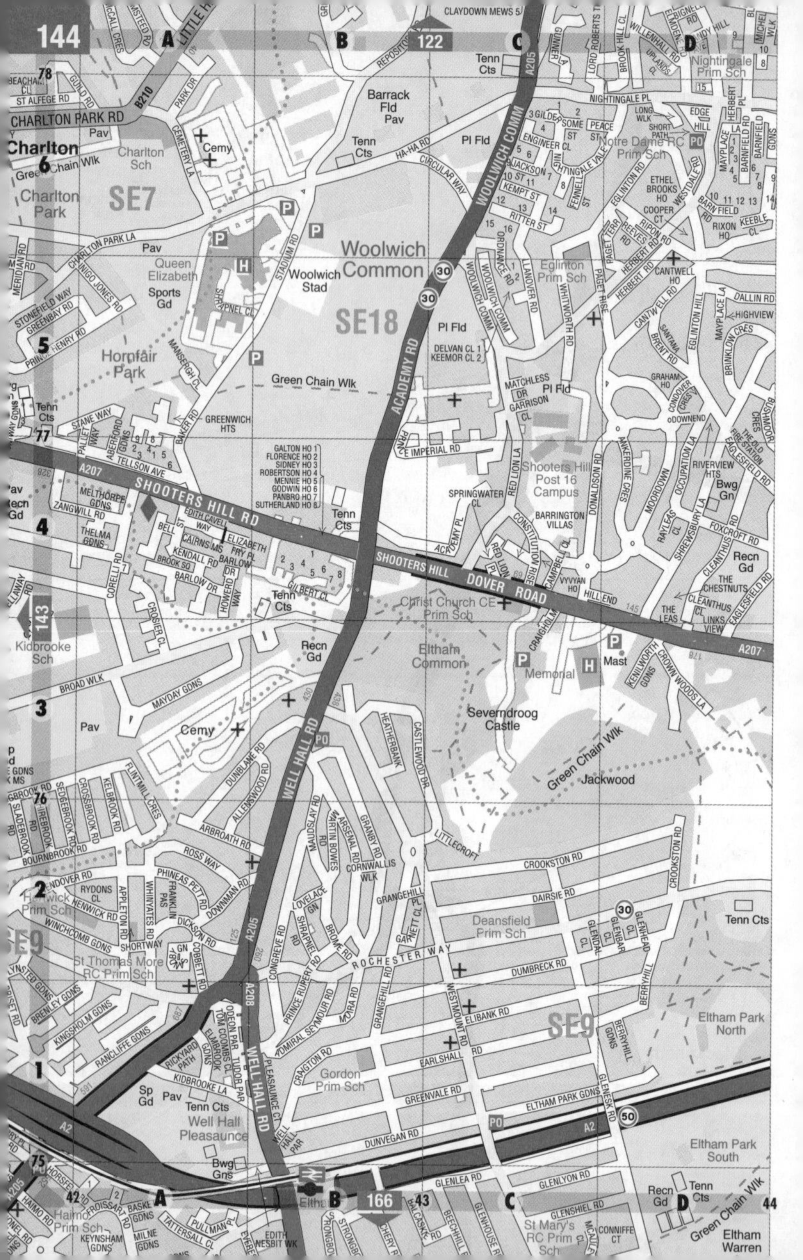

A
B
C
D
122
CLAYDOWN MEWS
Tenn Cts
Barrack Fld Pav
Nightingale Prim Sch
NIGHTINGALE PL
CHARLTON PARK RD
ST ALFEGE RD
Charlton
Charlton Sch
Cemy
Green Chain Wlk
Charlton Park
SE7
CEMETERY LA
PARK DR
HA-HA RD
CIRCULAR WAY
Pl Fld
WOOLWICH COMM
GILDERSOME ST
PEACE ST
ENGINEER CL
NIGHTINGALE VALE
Notre Dame RC Prim Sch
JACKSON ST
KEMPT ST
RITTER ST
EGLINTON RD
WESTDALE RD
ETHEL BROOKS HO
COOPER CT
BARNFIELD RD
KEEBLE CL
RIXON HO
CHARLTON PARK LA
Pav
Queen Elizabeth
Sports Gd
Woolwich Stad
Woolwich Common
STADIUM RD
SHRAPNEL CL
SE18
Eglinton Prim Sch
ORDNANCE RD
LLANOVER RD
WHITWORTH RD
PAGET RISE
HERBERT RD
CANTWELL HO
CANTWELL RD
EGLINTON HILL
DALLIN RD
HIGHVIEW
BRINKLOW CRES
STONEFIELD WAY
GREENBAY RD
PRINCE HENRY RD
Hornfair Park
MANSERGH CL
ACADEMY RD
DELVAN CL
KEEMOR CL
Green Chain Wlk
MATCHLESS DR
GARRISON CL
Pl Fld
GRAHAM HO
CONDOVER CRES
DOWNEND
Tenn Cts
STANE WAY
GREENWICH HTS
BAKER RD
TELLSON AVE
GALTON HO
FLORENCE HO
SIDNEY HO
ROBERTSON HO
MENNIE HO
GODWIN HO
PANBRO HO
SUTHERLAND HO
IMPERIAL RD
Shooters Hill Post 16 Campus
RED LION LA
DONALDSON RD
MOORDOWN
OCCUPATION LA
RIVERVIEW HTS
Bwg Gn
A207
SHOOTERS HILL RD
MELTHORPE GDNS
ZANGWILL RD
THELMA GDNS
EDITH CAVELL WAY
ELIZABETH FRY PL
CAIRNS MS
KENDALL RD
BROOK SQ
BARLOW DR
SPRINGWATER CL
BARRINGTON VILLAS
CONSTITUTION RISE
SHOOTERS HILL
DOVER ROAD
VYVYAN HO
HILL END
FOXCROFT RD
Recn Gd
THE CHESTNUTS
CLEANTHUS RD
EAGLESFIELD RD
THE LEAS
LINKS VIEW
143
Kidbrooke Sch
CROSIER CL
Tenn Cts
GILBERT CL
Christ Church CE Prim Sch
Recn Gd
Eltham Common
CRAIGHOLM
Memorial
Mast
KENILWORTH GDNS
CROWN WOODS LA
BROAD WLK
MAYDAY GDNS
Pav
Cemy
Severndroog Castle
Green Chain Wlk
Jackwood
WELL HALL RD
HEATHERBANK
CASTLEWOOD DR
DUNBLANE RD
ALLENSWOOD RD
FLINTMILL CRES
ARBROATH RD
BOURNBROOK RD
SEDGEBROOK RD
CROSSBROOK RD
KELBROOK RD
MAUDSLAY RD
ARSENAL RD
MARTIN BOWES RD
GRANBY RD
CORNWALLIS WLK
LITTLECROFT
CROOKSTON RD
ROSS WAY
PHINEAS PETT RD
FRANKLIN PAS
DOWNMAN RD
GRANGEHILL PL
DAIRSIE RD
Tenn Cts
Horn Park Prim Sch
ENDOVER RD
RYDONS CL
HENWICK RD
APPLETON RD
WHINYATES RD
DICKSON RD
LOVELACE GN
SHRAPNEL RD
BROOME RD
GARNETT CL
Deansfield Prim Sch
GLENDALE CL
GLENBAR CL
GLENHEAD CL
WINCHCOMB GDNS
SHORTWAY
SE9
St Thomas More RC Prim Sch
COBBETT RD
CONGREVE RD
PRINCE RUPERT RD
ROCHESTER WAY
DUMBRECK RD
BERRYHILL
A205
A208
BRENLEY GDNS
KINGSHOLM GDNS
RANCLIFFE GDNS
RICKYARD PATH
ODEON PAR
TOM COOMBS CL
ELMBROOK GDNS
TUDOR PAR
ADMIRAL SEYMOUR RD
MOIRA RD
GRANGEHILL RD
WESTMOUNT RD
ELIBANK RD
BERRYHILL GDNS
Eltham Park North
CRAIGTON RD
Gordon Prim Sch
EARLSHALL RD
KIDBROOKE LA
PLEASAUNCE CT
GREENVALE RD
ELTHAM PARK GDNS
GLENESK RD
Sp Gd
Pav
Tenn Cts
Well Hall Pleasaunce
A2
WELL HALL PAR
DUNVEGAN RD
Eltham Park South
Bwg Gns
GLENLEA RD
GLENLYON RD
Recn Gd
Tenn Cts
Green Chain Wlk
Haimo Prim Sch
HAIMO RD
TATTERSALL CL
PULLMAN PL
EDITH NESBIT WK
166
Eltham
GLENSHIEL RD
St Mary's RC Prim Sch
CONNIFFE CT
Eltham Warren
KEYNSHAM GDNS
MILNE GDNS

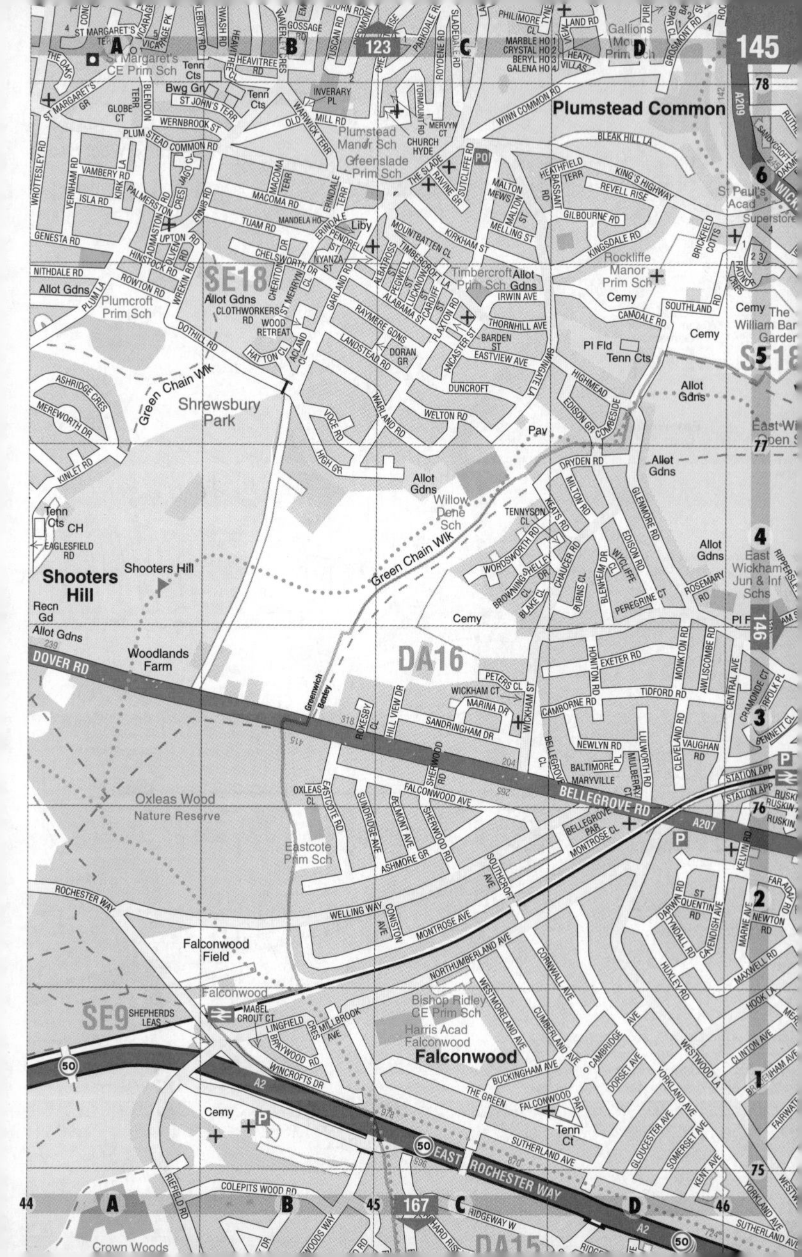
123
A
B
C
D
78
ST MARGARET'S TERR
St Margaret's CE Prim Sch
THE OAKS
ST MARGARET'S GR
GLOBE CT
BLENDON TERR
Bwg Gn
Tenn Cts
HEAVITREE RD
HEAVITREE CL
WAVERLEY CRES
GOSSAGE RD
TUSCAN RD
INVERARY PL
MILL RD
OLD MILL RD
WARWICK TERR
ST JOHN'S TERR
WERNBROOK ST
PLUMSTEAD COMMON RD
Plumstead Manor Sch
Greenslade Prim Sch
CHURCH HYDE
TORMOUNT RD
MERVYN CT
ROYDENE RD
SLADEDALE RD
PARKDALE RD
PHILIMORE CL
MARBLE HO
CRYSTAL HO
BERYL HO
GALENA HO
HEATH VILLAS
Gallions Mount Prim Sch
GROSMONT RD
WINN COMMON RD
Plumstead Common
BLEAK HILL LA
A209
WROTTESLEY RD
VERNHAM RD
VAMBERY RD
ISLA RD
KIRK LA
PALMERSTON CRES
JAGO CL
ENNIS RD
MACOMA TERR
MACOMA RD
ERINDALE TERR
THE SLADE
RAVINE GR
SUTCLIFFE RD
PO
MALTON MEWS
MALTON ST
HEATHFIELD TERR
BASSANT RD
KING'S HIGHWAY
REVELL RISE
St Paul's Acad
Superstore
GENESTA RD
ADMASTON RD
UPTON RD
TUAM RD
MANDELA HO
ERINDALE
Liby
PENDRELL ST
NYANZA ST
MOUNTBATTEN CL
KIRKHAM ST
MELLING ST
GILBOURNE RD
KINGSDALE RD
BRICKFIELD COTTS
HINSTOCK RD
OLVEN RD
NITHDALE RD
ROWTON RD
WREKIN RD
SE18
CHELSWORTH DR
CHERITON DR
ST MERRYN CL
GARLAND RD
ALBATROSS ST
PEGWELL ST
LUCKNOW ST
TIMBERCROFT LA
CARDIFF ST
ALABAMA ST
Timbercroft Prim Sch
Allot Gdns
Rockliffe Manor Prim Sch
RADNOR CRES
Allot Gdns
PLUM LA
Plumcroft Prim Sch
CLOTHWORKERS RD
WOOD RETREAT
RAYMERE GDNS
FLAXTON RD
IRWIN AVE
Cemy
THORNHILL AVE
SOUTHLAND RD
CAMDALE RD
Cemy
The William Barefoot Garden
DOTHILL RD
ACLAND CL
HATTON CL
LANDSTEAD RD
DORAN GR
ANCASTER ST
BARDEN ST
EASTVIEW AVE
Pl Fld
Tenn Cts
5
ASHRIDGE CRES
MEREWORTH DR
Green Chain Wlk
Shrewsbury Park
WARLAND RD
DUNCROFT
SWINGATE LA
HIGHMEAD
EDISON GR
COMBESIDE
Allot Gdns
VOCE RD
WELTON RD
Pav
East Wickham Open Space
77
KINLET RD
HIGH GR
Allot Gdns
Willow Dene Sch
DRYDEN RD
MILTON RD
GLENMORE RD
Allot Gdns
Tenn Cts
CH
EAGLESFIELD RD
TENNYSON CL
KEATS RD
WORDSWORTH RD
EDISON RD
4
Shooters Hill
Shooters Hill
Recn Gd
Allot Gdns
WORDSWORTH RD
BROWNING CL
SHELLEY DR
CHAUCER RD
BLAKE CL
BURNS CL
BLENHEIM DR
WYCLIFFE CL
PEREGRINE CT
ROSEMARY RD
Allot Gdns
East Wickham Jun & Inf Schs
Cemy
DOVER RD
Woodlands Farm
DA16
HONITON RD
EXETER RD
MONKTON RD
AWLISCOMBE RD
146
PETERS CL
WICKHAM CT
WICKHAM ST
TIDFORD RD
CENTRAL AVE
CRAMONDE CT
Greenwich
Bexley
ROKESBY CL
HILL VIEW DR
MARINA DR
SANDRINGHAM DR
CAMBORNE RD
3
BENNETT CL
NEWLYN RD
CLEVELAND RD
VAUGHAN RD
BELLEGROVE CL
BALTIMORE PL
MARYVILLE
MULBERRY CT
LULWORTH RD
SHERWOOD RD
STATION APP
OXLEAS CL
EASTCOTE RD
SUNDRIDGE AVE
BELMONT AVE
FALCONWOOD AVE
BELLEGROVE RD
A207
RUSKIN
76
Oxleas Wood Nature Reserve
Eastcote Prim Sch
ASHMORE GR
SHERWOOD RD
SOUTHCROFT AVE
BELLEGROVE PAR
MONTROSE CL
P
KELVIN RD
ROCHESTER WAY
WELLING WAY
CONISTON AVE
MONTROSE AVE
DARWIN RD
ST QUENTIN RD
CAVENDISH AVE
TYNDALL RD
MARNE AVE
NEWTON RD
2
Falconwood Field
NORTHUMBERLAND AVE
CORNWALL AVE
HUXLEY RD
MAXWELL RD
Falconwood
SE9
SHEPHERDS LEAS
MABEL CROUT CT
LINGFIELD CRES
MILLBROOK AVE
BRAYWOOD RD
Bishop Ridley CE Prim Sch
Harris Acad Falconwood
WESTMORELAND AVE
CUMBERLAND AVE
CAMBRIDGE AVE
HOOK LA
WESTWOOD LA
CLINTON AVE
Falconwood
50
A2
WINCROFTS DR
BUCKINGHAM AVE
THE GREEN
FALCONWOOD PAR
DORSET AVE
YORKLAND AVE
GLOUCESTER AVE
SOMERSET AVE
1
Cemy
P
Tenn Ct
EAST ROCHESTER WAY
SUTHERLAND AVE
KENT AVE
75
RIEFIELD RD
COLEPITS WOOD RD
44
45
167
46
RIDGEWAY W
Crown Woods
DA15
SUTHERLAND AVE

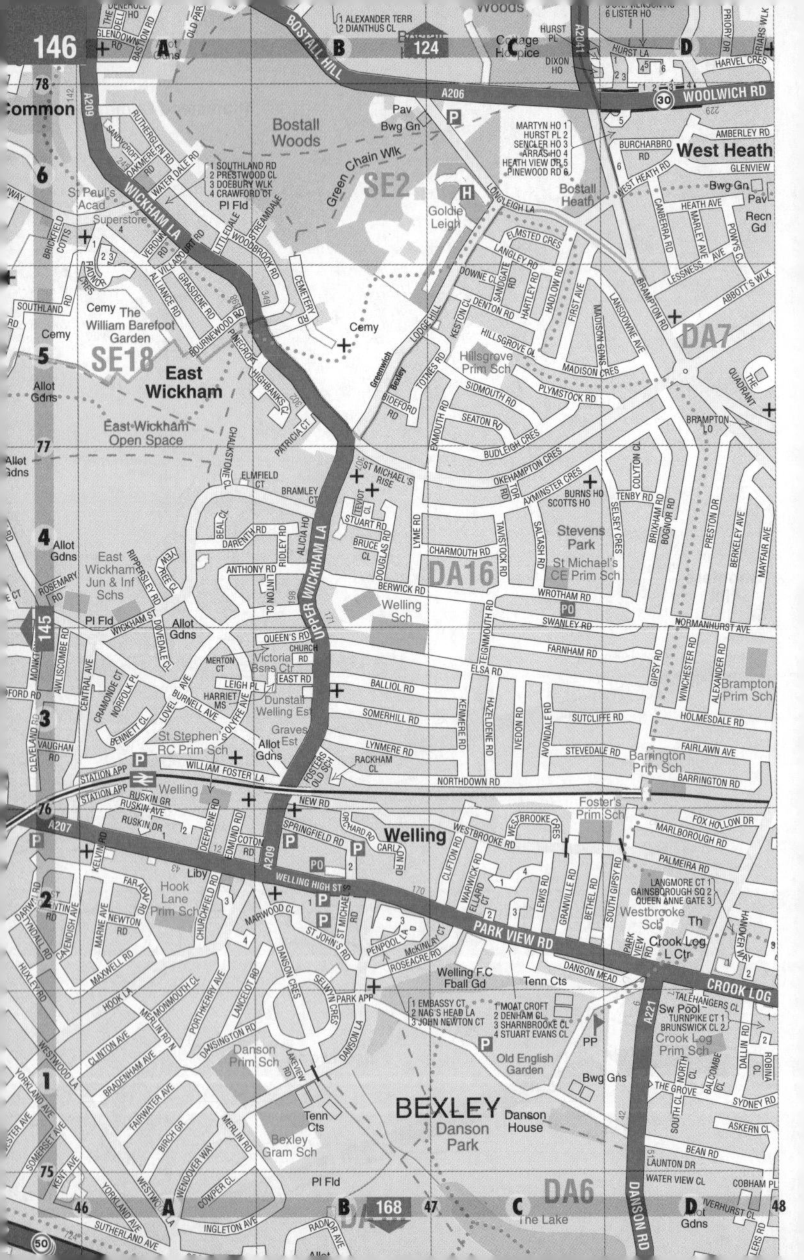

A
B
C
D
124
145
168
Bostall Hill
Woolwich Rd
A206
A209
A207
A2041
A221
Bostall Woods
Green Chain Wlk
SE2
SE18
DA7
DA16
DA6
Goldie Leigh
Bostall Heath
West Heath
Cottage Hospice
Common
St Paul's Acad
Superstore
The William Barefoot Garden
Cemy
East Wickham
East Wickham Open Space
East Wickham Jun & Inf Schs
Allot Gdns
Pl Fld
Wickham La
Upper Wickham La
Long Leigh La
Lodge Hill
Hillsgrove Prim Sch
Stevens Park
St Michael's CE Prim Sch
Welling Sch
Victoria Bsns Ctr
Dunstall Welling Est
Graves Est
St Stephen's RC Prim Sch
Welling
Foster's Prim Sch
Barrington Prim Sch
Brampton Prim Sch
Hook Lane Prim Sch
Welling High St
Park View Rd
Crook Log
Crook Log L Ctr
Crook Log Prim Sch
Westbrooke Sch
Welling F.C Fball Gd
Tenn Cts
Danson Prim Sch
Bexley Gram Sch
BEXLEY
Danson Park
Danson House
Old English Garden
Bwg Gns
The Lake
Danson Rd
Recn Gd
Sw Pool
1 SOUTHLAND RD
2 PRESTWOOD CL
3 DOEBURY WLK
4 CRAWFORD CT
MARTYN HO 1
HURST PL 2
SENCLER HO 3
ARRAS HO 4
HEATH VIEW DR 5
PINEWOOD RD 6
1 ALEXANDER TERR
2 DIANTHUS CL
LANGMORE CT 1
GAINSBOROUGH SQ 2
QUEEN ANNE GATE 3
1 EMBASSY CT
2 NAG'S HEAD LA
3 JOHN NEWTON CT
1 MOAT CROFT
2 DENHAM CL
3 SHARNBROOKE CL
4 STUART EVANS CL
TURNPIKE CT 1
BRUNSWICK CL 2
78
77
76
75
46
47
48

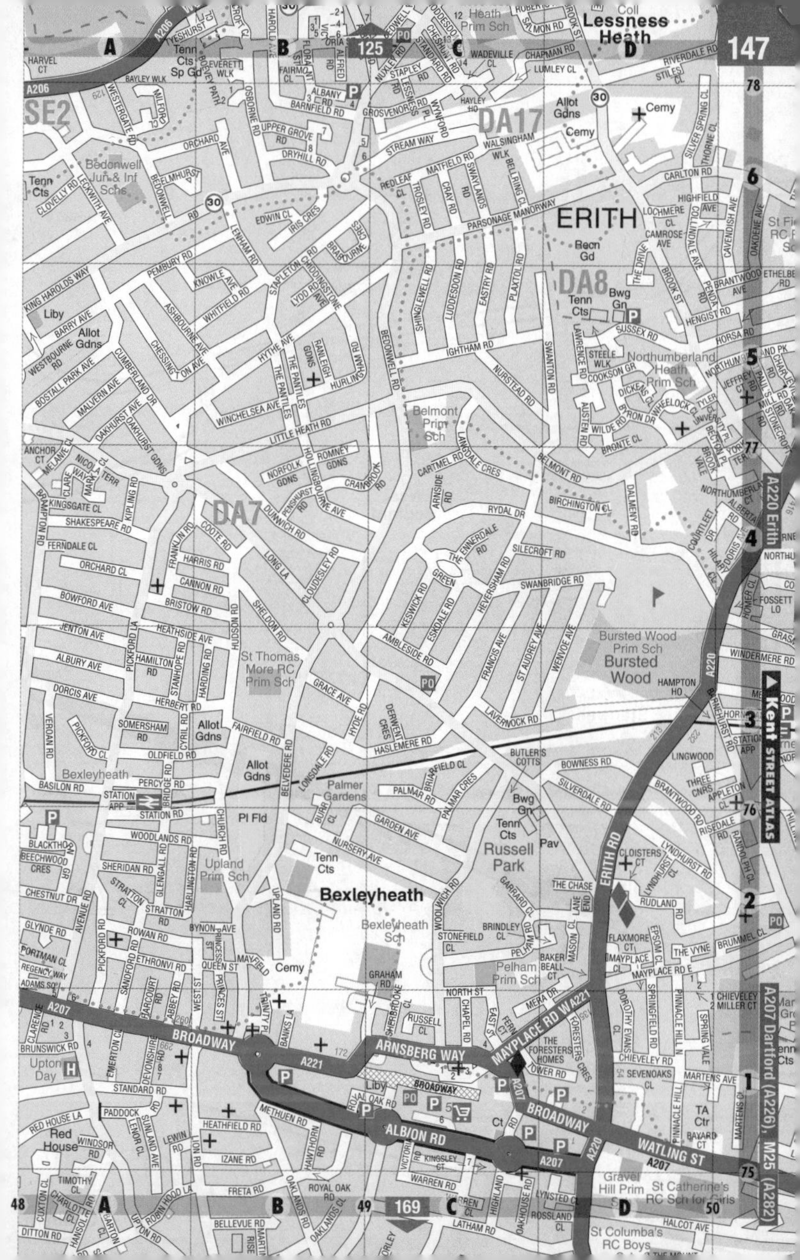
147
125
169
A
B
C
D
48
49
50
78
77
76
75
6
5
4
3
2
1
Lessness Heath
Coll
Heath Prim Sch
SE2
DA17
DA8
DA7
ERITH
Bexleyheath
Bexleyheath Sch
Bedonwell Jun & Inf Schs
Belmont Prim Sch
St Thomas More RC Prim Sch
Upland Prim Sch
Northumberland Heath Prim Sch
Bursted Wood Prim Sch
Bursted Wood
Pelham Prim Sch
Russell Park
Palmer Gardens
Allot Gdns
Tenn Cts
Tenn Cts Sp Gd
Recn Gd
Bwg Gn
Cemy
Liby
Pl Fld
Pav
Red House
Upton Day
TA Ctr
Gravel Hill Prim Sch
St Catherine's RC Sch for Girls
St Columba's RC Boys
A206
A207
A220
A221
A220 Erith
A207 Dartford (A226), M25 (A282)
Kent STREET ATLAS
HARVEL CT
BAYLEY WLK
WESTERGATE RD
MILFORD CL
EVERETT WLK
HAROLD AVE
FLORANCE ST
FAIRMOUNT CL
ALBANY RD
ALFRED RD
BARNFIELD RD
OSBORNE RD
UPPER GROVE RD
DRYHILL RD
ORCHARD AVE
STREAM WAY
GROSVENOR RD
STAPLEY RD
NUXLEY RD
LESSNESS PL
WYNFORD
WADEVILLE CL
CHAPMAN RD
LUMLEY CL
RIVERDALE RD
STILES CL
HAYLEY HO
WALSINGHAM WLK
SILVER SPRING CL
THORNE CL
CARLTON RD
HIGHFIELD AVE
LOCHMERE CL
CAMROSE AVE
COLLINDALE AVE
CAVENDISH AVE
OAKDENE AVE
THE DRIVE
BROOK ST
PENDA RD
BRANTWOOD AVE
HENGIST RD
HORSA RD
SUSSEX RD
STEELE WLK
COOKSON GR
LAWRENCE RD
AUSTEN RD
WILDE RD
BYRON DR
DICKENS CL
WHEELOCK CL
TYLER
UNIVERSITY PL
BRONTE CL
BECTON PL
BROOK VALE
YORK TER
NORTHUMBERLAND CT
ALBERTA
COURTLEET DR
HILARY CL
DORIS AVE
DALMENY RD
BIRCHINGTON CL
BELMONT RD
REDLEAF CL
TROSLEY RD
MATFIELD RD
CRAY RD
SWAYLANDS RD
BELLRING CL
PARSONAGE MANORWAY
SHINGLEWELL RD
LUDDESDON RD
EASTRY RD
PLAXTOL RD
IGHTHAM RD
NURSTEAD RD
SWANTON RD
EDWIN CL
IRIS CRES
BRABOURNE CRES
LENHAM RD
PEMBURY RD
KNOWLE AVE
WHITFIELD RD
ASHBOURNE AVE
CHESSINGTON AVE
STAPLETON RD
CHIDDINGSTONE AVE
LYDD RD
HYTHE AVE
THE PANTILES
RANLEIGH GDNS
HURLINGHAM RD
BEDONWELL RD
WINCHELSEA AVE
LITTLE HEATH RD
HOLLINGBOURNE AVE
ROMNEY GDNS
NORFOLK GDNS
CRANBROOK RD
PENSHURST RD
DUNWICH RD
CARTMEL RD
LANGDALE CRES
ARNSIDE RD
RYDAL DR
THE GREEN
ENNERDALE RD
SILECROFT RD
SWANBRIDGE RD
HEVERSHAM RD
KESWICK RD
ESKDALE RD
AMBLESIDE RD
FRANCIS AVE
ST AUDREY AVE
WENVOE AVE
LAVERNOCK RD
KING HAROLDS WAY
BARRY AVE
WESTBOURNE RD
BOSTALL PARK AVE
CUMBERLAND DR
MALVERN AVE
OAKHURST AVE
OAKHURST GDNS
CLOVELLY RD
LECKWITH AVE
ELMHURST
ANCHOR CT
MELANIE CL
NICOLA TERR
CLARE WAY
MARK CL
KINGSGATE CL
KIPLING RD
SHAKESPEARE RD
BRAMPTON RD
FERNDALE CL
ORCHARD CL
BOWFORD AVE
JENTON AVE
ALBURY AVE
DORCIS AVE
VEROAN RD
PICKFORD CL
PICKFORD LA
HAMILTON RD
STANHOPE RD
HARDING RD
HEATHSIDE AVE
FRANKLIN RD
COOTE RD
HARRIS RD
CANNON RD
BRISTOW RD
HUDSON RD
LONG LA
SHELDON RD
CLOUDESLEY RD
HERBERT RD
SOMERSHAM RD
CYRIL RD
OLDFIELD RD
FAIRFIELD RD
GRACE AVE
HYDE RD
DERWENT CRES
HASLEMERE RD
BELVEDERE RD
LONSDALE RD
BASILON RD
PERCY RD
BRIDGE RD
STATION APP
STATION RD
WOODLANDS RD
CHURCH RD
BLACKTHORN GR
BEECHWOOD CRES
SHERIDAN RD
GLENGALL RD
HARLINGTON RD
CHESTNUT DR
AVENUE RD
STRATTON CL
STRATTON RD
GLYNDE RD
PORTMAN CL
REGENCY WAY
ADAMS SQ
PICKFORD RD
ROWAN RD
SANDFORD RD
ETHRONVI RD
BYNON AVE
PRINCESS ST
QUEEN ST
PRINCES ST
WEST ST
MAYFIELD
TRINITY PL
BANKS LA
UPLAND RD
BURR CL
NURSERY AVE
GARDEN AVE
PALMAR RD
PALMAR CRES
BRIARFIELD CL
BUTLER'S COTTS
BOWNESS RD
SILVERDALE RD
BRANTWOOD RD
LINGWOOD
THREE CNRS
APPLETON CL
RISEDALE RD
RANDOLPH CL
LYNDHURST RD
LYNDHURST CL
CLOISTERS CT
RUDLAND RD
ERITH RD
BARNEHURST RD
HAMPTON HO
WINDERMERE RD
FOSSETT LO
HOMER CL
THE CHASE
GARRARD CL
LANE END
MASON CL
BRINDLEY CL
PELHAM RD
STONEFIELD CL
WOOLWICH RD
BAKER BEALL CT
FLAXMORE CT
MAYPLACE CL
MAYPLACE RD E
MAYPLACE RD W
EPSOM CL
THE VYNE
BRUMMEL CL
CHIEVELEY
MILLER CT
DOROTHY EVANS CL
SPRINGFIELD RD
PINNACLE HILL N
SPRING VALE
CHIEVELEY RD
SEVENOAKS CL
MARTENS AVE
MARTENS CL
PINNACLE HILL
BAYARD CT
WATLING ST
MERA DR
FORESTERS CRES
THE FORESTERS HOMES
TOWER RD
NORTH ST
CHAPEL RD
EAST ST
FERN CT
GRAHAM RD
SHERBROOKE CL
RUSSELL CL
ARNSBERG WAY
BROADWAY
ALBION RD
ROYAL OAK RD
METHUEN RD
HAWTHORN RD
VICTORIA RD
KINGSLEY CT
WARREN RD
WARREN CL
HIGHLAND RD
OAKHOUSE RD
LYNSTED CL
ROSSLAND CL
HALCOT AVE
LATHAM RD
OAKLANDS RD
OAKLANDS CL
ROYAL OAK RD
FRETA RD
BELLEVUE RD
IZANE RD
LION RD
LEWIN RD
HEATHFIELD RD
SUNLAND AVE
LENOR CL
PADDOCK CL
STANDARD RD
RED HOUSE LA
WINDSOR RD
TIMOTHY CL
CHARLOTTE CL
HANSOL RD
CUXTON CL
DITTON RD
CARTON CL
ROBIN HOOD LA
UPTON RD
BRUNSWICK RD
CLARENCE RD
EMERTON CL
DEVONSHIRE RD
HARCOURT RD
ABBEY RD
JEFFREY CT
PAUL'S RD
MILL RD
STONECROFT
THE ENNERDALE
NORTHUMBERLAND PK
ETHELBERT RD
St Fi RC P Sc
STATION APP
PO
P
H
30

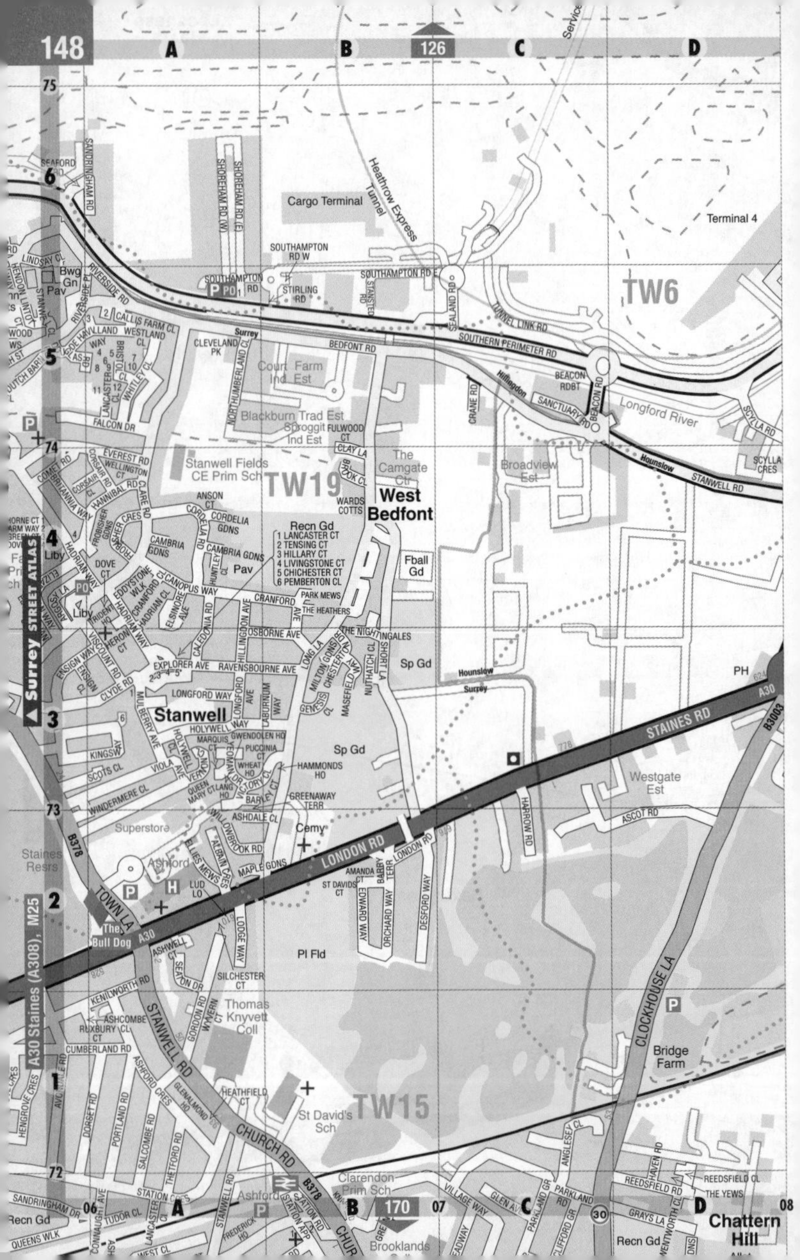
A
B
126
C
D
Surrey STREET ATLAS
Cargo Terminal
Heathrow Express Tunnel
Terminal 4
TW6
SOUTHAMPTON RD W
SOUTHAMPTON RD
STIRLING RD
SOUTHAMPTON RD E
STANSTED RD
SEALAND RD
TUNNEL LINK RD
SOUTHERN PERIMETER RD
SHOREHAM RD (W)
SHOREHAM RD (E)
SANDRINGHAM RD
SEAFORD RD
LINDSAY CL
HENDON
Bwg Gn
Pav
RIVERSIDE RD
RIVERSIDE PL
CALLIS FARM CL
DE HAVILLAND WAY
WESTLAND CL
BRISTOL CL
WHITLEY CL
LANCASTER CL
FALCON DR
CLEVELAND PK
NORTHUMBERLAND CL
BEDFONT RD
Court Farm Ind Est
Blackburn Trad Est
Spoggit Ind Est
FULWOOD CT
CLAY LA
BROOK CL
The Camgate Ctr
CRANE RD
BEACON RDBT
BEACON RD
SANCTUARY RD
Longford River
SCYLLA RD
SCYLLA CRES
Hounslow
STANWELL RD
Broadview Est
EVEREST RD
WELLINGTON CT
COMET RD
CORSAIR RD
CORSAIR CL
BRITANNIA WAY
HANNIBAL RD
CLARE RD
Stanwell Fields CE Prim Sch
TW19
ANSON CT
CORDELIA CT
CORDELIA GDNS
CORDELIA RD
WARDS COTTS
West Bedfont
Recn Gd
1 LANCASTER CT
2 TENSING CT
3 HILLARY CT
4 LIVINGSTONE CT
5 CHICHESTER CT
6 PEMBERTON CL
FROBISHER GDNS
FROBISHER CRES
CAMBRIA GDNS
HUNTLEY CL
Pav
Fball Gd
HADRIAN WAY
Liby
DOVE CT
EDDYSTONE WLK
CRAMFORD CL
HADRIAN CL
ELSINORE AVE
CANOPUS WAY
CRANFORD AVE
PARK MEWS
THE HEATHERS
TRIDENT HO
HERON CT
VISCOUNT RD
CALEDONIA RD
HILLINGDON AVE
OSBORNE AVE
LONG LA
THE NIGHTINGALES
SHORT LA
NUTHATCH CL
MASEFIELD WAY
MILTON GDNS
CHESTERTON DR
GENESIS CL
Sp Gd
ENSIGN WAY
ENSIGN CL
EXPLORER AVE
RAVENSBOURNE AVE
CLYDE RD
LONGFORD WAY
LONGFORD AVE
LABURNUM WAY
MULBERRY AVE
Stanwell
HOLYWELL WAY
KINGSWAY
MARQUIS CT
GWENDOLEN HO
PUCCINIA CT
YEOMAN DR
WHEAT HO
HOLYWELL CL
VERNON CL
HAMMONDS HO
SCOTS CL
VIOLA AVE
QUEEN MARY CT
LANG HO
VICTORY CL
BARLEY CT
GREENAWAY TERR
WINDERMERE CL
ASHDALE CL
Sp Gd
Superstore
WILLOWBROOK RD
Cemy
B378
Staines Resrs
Ashford
ELLIES MEWS
ALBAIN CRES
MAPLE GDNS
LONDON RD
LUD LO
TOWN LA
The Bull Dog
A30
LODGE WAY
AMANDA CT
ST DAVIDS CT
BARRY TERR
EDWARD WAY
ORCHARD WAY
DESFORD WAY
Pl Fld
Hounslow
Surrey
STAINES RD
A30
B3003
PH
HARROW RD
Westgate Est
ASCOT RD
ASHWELL CT
SEATON DR
SILCHESTER CT
KENILWORTH RD
ASHCOMBE
RUXBURY CL
CUMBERLAND RD
STANWELL RD
GORDON RD
WYVERN CL
Thomas Knyvett Coll
CLOCKHOUSE LA
Bridge Farm
A30 Staines (A308), M25
HENGROVE CRES
AVONDALE RD
DORSET RD
PORTLAND RD
ASHFORD CRES
SALCOMBE RD
THETFORD RD
GLENALMOND HO
HEATHFIELD CT
St David's Sch
TW15
CHURCH RD
B378
ANGLESEY CL
HAVEN RD
REEDSFIELD CL
REEDSFIELD RD
THE YEWS
Clarendon Prim Sch
STATION CRES
STANWELL RD
LANCASTER CL
Ashford
STATION RD
STATION APP
FREDERICK HO
170
VILLAGE WAY
GLEN AVE
PARKLAND GR
PARKLAND RD
CLIFFORD GR
GRAYS LA
WENTWORTH CL
SANDRINGHAM DR
TUDOR CL
CONNAUGHT AVE
QUEENS WLK
WEST CL
Recn Gd
Brooklands
Recn Gd
Chattern Hill
06
07
08
75
74
73
72
1
2
3
4
5
6

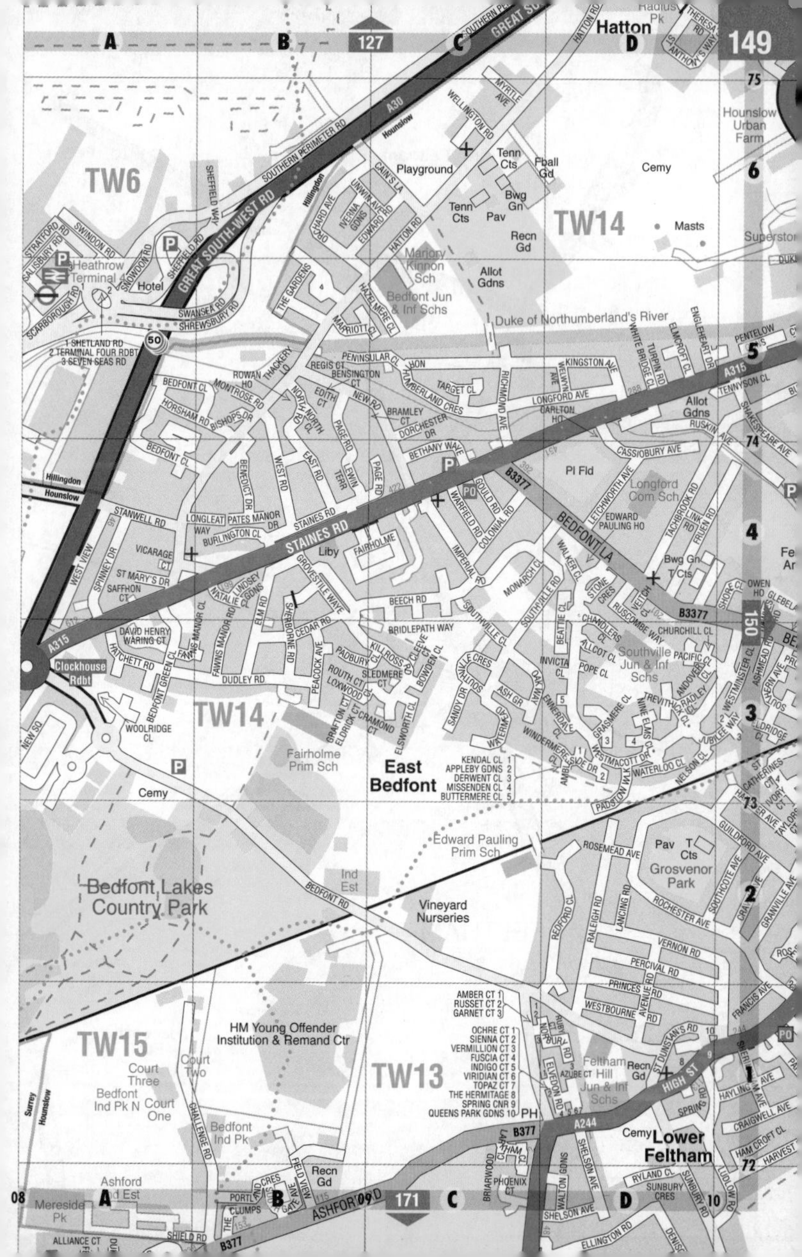

149
127
171
A
B
C
D
Hatton
TW6
TW14
TW15
TW13
Heathrow Terminal 4
Hotel
Playground
Tenn Cts
Fball Gd
Cemy
Bwg Gn
Pav
Recn Gd
Masts
Hounslow Urban Farm
Superstore
Marjory Kinnon Sch
Bedfont Jun & Inf Schs
Allot Gdns
Duke of Northumberland's River
GREAT SOUTH-WEST RD
SOUTHERN PERIMETER RD
A30
Hounslow
Hillingdon
SHEFFIELD WAY
SHEFFIELD RD
SWANSEA RD
SHREWSBURY RD
SWINDON RD
STRATFORD RD
SALISBURY RD
SNOWDON RD
SCARBOROUGH RD
1 SHETLAND RD
2 TERMINAL FOUR RDBT
3 SEVEN SEAS RD
ORCHARD AVE
IVERNA GDNS
UNWIN AVE
CAIN'S LA
EDWARD RD
HATTON RD
WELLINGTON RD
MYRTLE AVE
THE GARDENS
HAZELMERE CL
MARRIOTT CL
PENINSULAR CL
HUMBERLAND CRES
TARGET CL
RICHMOND AVE
WELWYN AVE
KINGSTON AVE
WHITE BRIDGE CL
TURPIN RD
ELMCROFT CL
ENGLEHEART DR
PENTELOW GDNS
A315
TENNYSON CL
SHAKESPEARE AVE
RUSKIN AVE
Allot Gdns
LONGFORD AVE
CARLTON HO
CASSIOBURY AVE
Pl Fld
Longford Com Sch
LETCHWORTH AVE
EDWARD PAULING HO
TACHBROOK RD
LINK RD
FRUEN RD
B3377
BEDFONT LA
Bwg Gn
T Cts
ROWAN HO
THACKERY LO
REGIS CT
BENSINGTON CT
BEDFONT CL
MONTROSE RD
HORSHAM RD
BISHOPS DR
EDITH CT
NORTH RD
NORTH CL
NEW RD
BRAMLEY CT
DORCHESTER DR
BETHANY WAVE
PAGE RD
LEWIN TERR
EAST RD
WEST RD
BENEDICT DR
GOULD RD
WARFIELD RD
COLONIAL RD
IMPERIAL RD
STAINES RD
STANWELL RD
LONGLEAT WAY
PATES MANOR DR
BURLINGTON CL
STAINES RD
FAIRHOLME
Liby
VICARAGE CT
WEST VIEW
SPINNEY DR
ST MARY'S DR
SAFFHON CT
NATALIE CL
LINDSEY GDNS
GROVESTILE WAYE
SHERBORNE RD
BEECH RD
MONARCH CL
SOUTHVILLE RD
WALKER CL
STONE CRES
RUSCOMBE WAY
VEITCH CL
OWEN HO
GLEBELANDS
SHORE CL
150
CHURCHILL CL
PACIFIC CL
Southville Jun & Inf Schs
ANDOVER CL
RADLEY CL
TREVITHICK CL
WESTMINSTER CL
ASHMEAD RD
SOUTHVILLE CL
BEATTIE CL
CHANDLERS CL
ALLCOT CL
POPE CL
INVICTA CL
DAVID HENRY WARING CT
HATCHETT RD
BEDFONT GREEN CL
FAWNS MANOR CL
FAWNS MANOR RD
ELM RD
CEDAR RD
PEACOCK AVE
PADBURY
KILLROSS RD
CLEEVE CT
BOWDEN CL
BRIDLEPATH WAY
SLEDMERE CT
ROUTH CT
LOXWOOD CL
GRAFTON CL
ELDRICK CT
CRAMOND CT
ELSWORTH CL
DUDLEY RD
SOUTHVILLE CRES
SANDY DR
ASH GR
OAK WAY
ENNERDALE CL
WATERMERE CL
WINDERMERE CL
GRASMERE CL
NINE ELMS CL
JUBILEE WAY
WESTMACOTT DR
NELSON CL
WATERLOO CL
PADSTOW WLK
Clockhouse Rdbt
WOOLRIDGE CL
NEW SQ
TW14
Fairholme Prim Sch
East Bedfont
KENDAL CL 1
APPLEBY GDNS 2
DERWENT CL 3
MISSENDEN CL 4
BUTTERMERE CL 5
Cemy
Edward Pauling Prim Sch
Bedfont Lakes Country Park
Ind Est
BEDFONT RD
Vineyard Nurseries
ROSEMEAD AVE
Pav
T Cts
Grosvenor Park
ROCHESTER AVE
SOUTHCOTE AVE
GUILDFORD AVE
GRANVILLE AVE
ST CATHERINES CT
IVORY CT
TAYLORS CT
REDFORD CL
RALEIGH RD
LANCING RD
VERNON RD
PERCIVAL RD
PRINCES RD
AVENUE RD
WESTBOURNE RD
FRANCIS AVE
AMBER CT 1
RUSSET CT 2
GARNET CT 3
OCHRE CT 1
SIENNA CT 2
VERMILLION CT 3
FUSCIA CT 4
INDIGO CT 5
VIRIDIAN CT 6
TOPAZ CT 7
THE HERMITAGE 8
SPRING CNR 9
QUEENS PARK GDNS 10
PH
RUBY CL
NORBURY RD
ELVEDON RD
AZURE CT
Feltham Hill Jun & Inf Schs
Recn Gd
ST DUNSTAN'S RD
HIGH ST
SPRING RD
HAYLING AVE
SHERIDAN AVE
CRAIGWELL AVE
HAM CROFT CL
HARVEST
HM Young Offender Institution & Remand Ctr
Court Two
Court Three
Court One
Bedfont Ind Pk N
Bedfont Ind Pk
Surrey
Hounslow
CHALLENGE RD
B377
A244
LARCH CL
BRIARWOOD
PHOENIX CT
WALTON GDNS
SHELSON AVE
Cemy
Lower Feltham
RYLAND CL
SUNBURY CRES
SUNBURY RD
LUDLOW RD
Ashford Ind Est
Mereside Pk
ALLIANCE CT
PORTLAND CRES
CLUMPS
FIELD VIEW
Recn Gd
ASHFORD RD
SHIELD RD
ELLINGTON RD
08
09
10
75
74
73
72
6
5
4
3
2
1

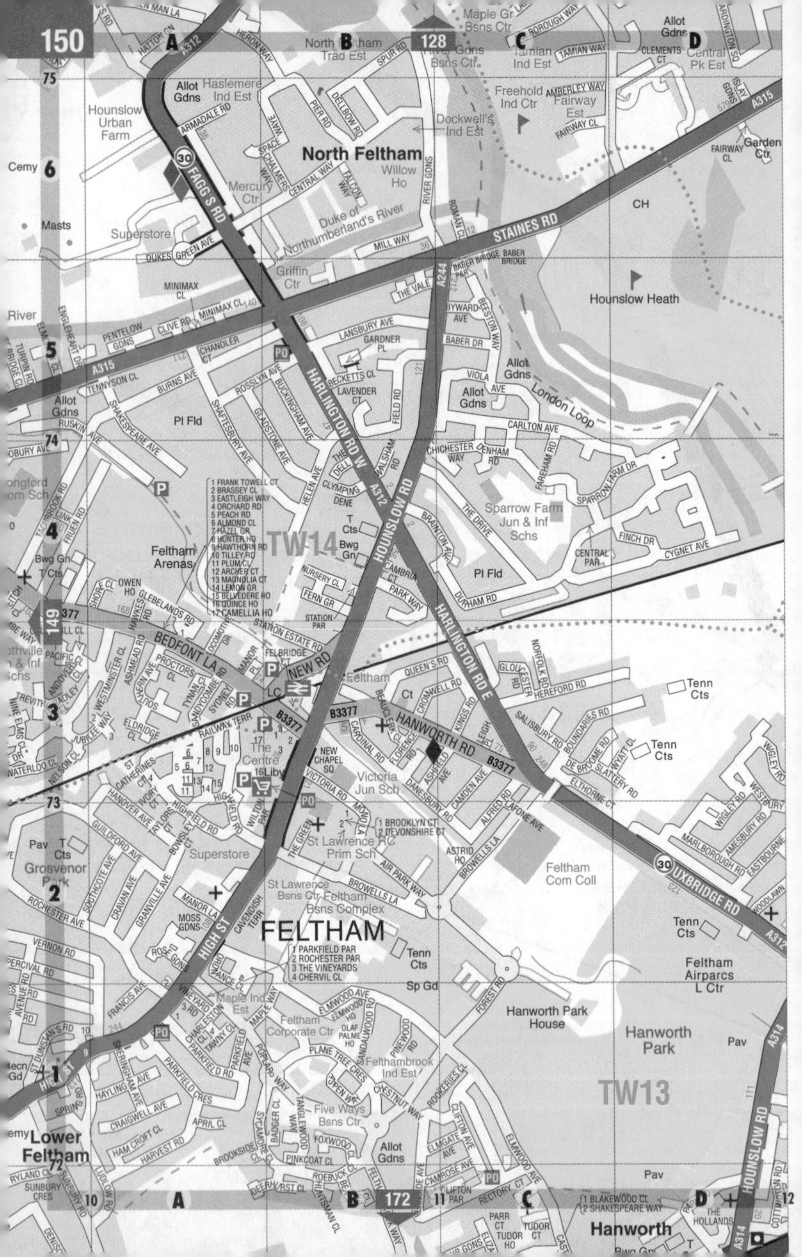

150
A
B
128
C
D
North Feltham Trad Est
River Gdns Bsns Ctr
Maple Gr Bsns Ctr
Tamian Ind Est
Allot Gdns
Central Pk Est
CLEMENTS CT
HATTON GN
HERON WAY
SPUR RD
BOROUGH WAY
TAMIAN WAY
ISLAY GDNS
Allot Gdns
Haslemere Ind Est
Hounslow Urban Farm
ARMADALE RD
PIER RD
DELLBOW RD
SPACE WAYE
Freehold Ind Ctr
AMBERLEY WAY
Fairway Est
FAIRWAY CL
Dockwell's Ind Est
A315
Garden Ctr
FAIRWAY CL
North Feltham
Willow Ho
Cemy
Mercury Ctr
CHALMERS WAY
CENTRAL WAY
FALCON WAY
FAGG'S RD
RIVER GDNS
ROMAN CL
CH
Masts
Superstore
Duke of Northumberland's River
MILL WAY
STAINES RD
DUKES GREEN AVE
Griffin Ctr
BABER BRIDGE PAR
BABER BRIDGE
THE VALE
A244
Hounslow Heath
MINIMAX CL
River
PENTELOW GDNS
CLIVE RD
CHANDLER CT
LANSBURY AVE
BYWARD AVE
BEESTON WAY
GARDNER PL
BABER DR
PO
A315
ENGLEHEART DR
TURPIN RD
TENNYSON CL
BURNS AVE
ROSSLYN AVE
BECKETTS CL
LAVENDER CT
FIELD RD
Allot Gdns
VIOLA AVE
London Loop
Allot Gdns
RUSKIN AVE
SHAKESPEARE AVE
Pl Fld
SHAFTESBURY AVE
GLADSTONE AVE
BUCKINGHAM AVE
HARLINGTON RD W
CARLTON AVE
CHICHESTER WAY
DENHAM RD
FAREHAM RD
SPARROW FARM DR
THE DELL
WALSHAM RD
HELEN AVE
CLYMPING DENE
A312
HOUNSLOW RD
THE DRIVE
Sparrow Farm Jun & Inf Schs
1 FRANK TOWELL CT
2 BRASSEY CL
3 EASTLEIGH WAY
4 ORCHARD RD
5 PEACH RD
6 ALMOND CL
7 HAZEL GR
8 HUNTER HO
9 HAWTHORN RD
10 TILLEY RD
11 PLUM CL
12 ARCHER CT
13 MAGNOLIA CT
14 LEMON GR
15 BELVEDERE HO
16 QUINCE HO
17 CAMELLIA HO
TW14
T Cts
Bwg Gn
Feltham Arenas
BRAINTON AVE
FINCH DR
CENTRAL PAR
CYGNET AVE
Pl Fld
CAMBRIA CT
PARK WAY
NURSERY CL
FERN GR
DURHAM RD
HARLINGTON RD E
Bwg Gn
T Cts
OWEN HO
GLEBELANDS RD
SHORE CL
149
B377
STATION PAR
STATION ESTATE RD
HAWKES
BEDFONT LA
PACIFIC CL
ANDOVER CL
WESTMINSTER CL
ASHMEAD RD
PROCTORS CL
LOCOMOTIVE DR
MANOR PL
FELBRIDGE CT
NEW RD
Feltham
QUEEN'S RD
NORFOLK RD
GLOUCESTER RD
HEREFORD RD
Tenn Cts
CROMWELL RD
Ct
KINGS RD
BEAUCLERC
TREVITHICK
HADLEY
SOUTHERN AVE
TYNAN CL
SANDYCOMBE RD
SYDNEY RD
LC
B3377
HANWORTH RD
SALISBURY RD
BOUNDARIES RD
NINE ELMS CL
JUBILEE WAY
ELDRIDGE CL
RAILWAY TERR
CARDINAL RD
FLORENCE RD
LEIGH RD
DE BROME RD
WYATT CL
Tenn Cts
WIGLEY RD
NEW CHAPEL SQ
The Centre
Liby
ASHFIELD AVE
SLATTERY RD
WATERLOO CL
NELSON CL
ST CATHERINES CT
IVORY CT
VICTORIA RD
Victoria Jun Sch
DANESBURY RD
CAMDEN AVE
ELTHORNE CT
WESTBURY RD
73
HANOVER AVE
TAYLORS CT
HIGHFIELD RD
WILTON PAR
PO
MONMOUTH
ALFRED RD
LAFONE AVE
AMESBURY RD
MARLBOROUGH RD
EASTBOURNE
1 BROOKLYN CT
2 DEVONSHIRE CT
Pav
T Cts
Grosvenor Park
GUILDFORD AVE
BOWSLEY CT
Superstore
THE GREEN
St Lawrence RC Prim Sch
ASTRID HO
BROWELLS LA
Feltham Com Coll
UXBRIDGE RD
SOUTHCOTE AVE
CRAVAN AVE
GRANVILLE AVE
AIR PARK WAY
ROCHESTER AVE
MANOR LA
St Lawrence Bsns Ctr Feltham Bsns Complex
BROWELLS LA
WOODLAWN
Tenn Cts
MOSS GDNS
CAVENDISH TERR
HIGH ST
FELTHAM
A312
VERNON RD
PERCIVAL RD
ROSE GDNS
1 PARKFIELD PAR
2 ROCHESTER PAR
3 THE VINEYARDS
4 CHERVIL CL
Tenn Cts
Feltham Airparcs L Ctr
Sp Gd
ORDNANCE CL
FRANCIS AVE
VINEYARD RD
Maple Ind Est
MAPLE WAY
ELMWOOD AVE
ELMWOOD HO
SANDALWOOD RD
FOREST RD
Hanworth Park House
AVENUE RD
ST DUNSTAN'S RD
CHARLESTON CL
TAWNY CL
PARKFIELD AVE
Feltham Corporate Ctr
OLAF PALME HO
PINEWOOD RD
Hanworth Park
Pav
A314
PO
SHERINGHAM AVE
PARKFIELD RD
POPLAR WAY
PLANE TREE CRES
Felthambrook Ind Est
ROOKERIES CL
HIGH ST
HAYLING AVE
PARKFIELD CRES
ASPEN WAY
CHESTNUT WAY
TW13
SPRINGS
CRAIGWELL AVE
APRIL CL
Five Ways Bsns Ctr
BADGER CL
TANGLEWOOD WAY
CLIFTON AVE
HOUNSLOW RD
Lower Feltham
HAM CROFT CL
HARVEST RD
BROOKSIDE
SYCAMORE CL
FOXWOOD CL
Allot Gdns
ELMGATE AVE
ELMWOOD AVE
PINKCOAT CL
ROEBUCK CL
CAMROSE AVE
PO
Pav
RYLAND CL
SUNBURY CRES
SUNBURY RD
LUDLOW RD
DEERHURST CL
HUNTSMAN CL
CLIFTON PAR
RECTORY CT
1 BLAKEWOOD CL
2 SHAKESPEARE WAY
THE HOLLANDS
COTTINGTON RD
10
A
B
172
11
C
D
12
PARR CT
TUDOR CT
TUDOR HO
Hanworth
75
6
5
74
4
3
2
1
72

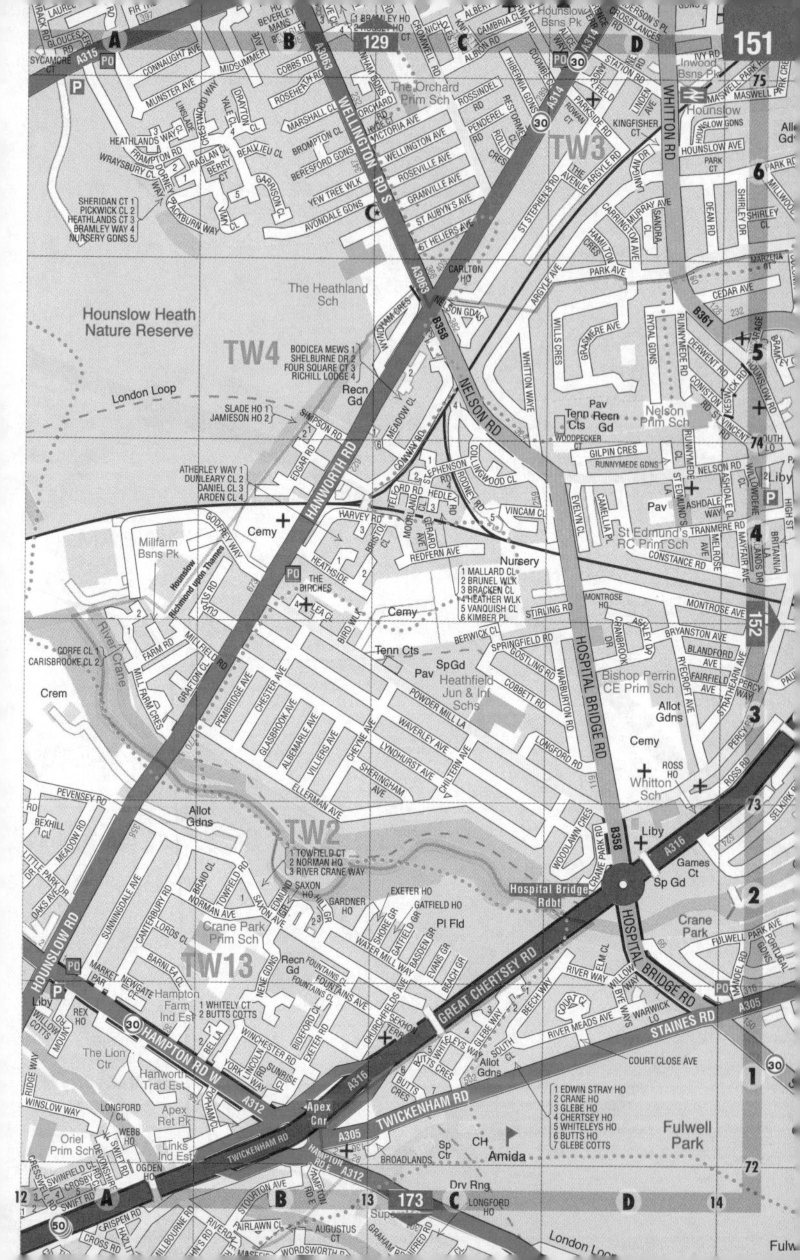
151
129
173
152
A
B
C
D
1
2
3
4
5
6
72
73
74
75
12
13
14
TW2
TW3
TW4
TW13
Hounslow Heath Nature Reserve
London Loop
The Heathland Sch
The Orchard Prim Sch
Hounslow Bsns Pk
Inwood Bsns Pk
Hounslow
Nelson Prim Sch
St Edmund's RC Prim Sch
Bishop Perrin CE Prim Sch
Heathfield Jun & Inf Schs
Whitton Sch
Crane Park Prim Sch
Oriel Prim Sch
Millfarm Bsns Pk
Hampton Farm Ind Est
Hanworth Trad Est
Apex Ret Pk
Links Ind Est
The Lion Ctr
Hospital Bridge Rdbt
Apex Cnr
Crane Park
Fulwell Park
River Crane
Crem
Cemy
Nursery
Allot Gdns
Recn Gd
Tenn Cts
Pav
SpGd
Pl Fld
Games Ct
Sp Ctr
Drv Rng
Amida
Liby
HANWORTH RD
WELLINGTON RD S
NELSON RD
HOSPITAL BRIDGE RD
WHITTON RD
GREAT CHERTSEY RD
TWICKENHAM RD
STAINES RD
HAMPTON RD W
HOUNSLOW RD
POWDER MILL LA
CONNAUGHT AVE
MIDSUMMER AVE
MUNSTER AVE
VICTORIA AVE
WELLINGTON AVE
ROSEVILLE AVE
GRANVILLE AVE
ST AUBYN'S AVE
ST HELIERS AVE
AVONDALE GDNS
YEW TREE WLK
ARGYLE AVE
PARK AVE
CEDAR AVE
GRASMERE AVE
WHITTON WAYE
WILLS CRES
GILPIN CRES
RUNNYMEDE GDNS
CONSTANCE RD
MONTROSE AVE
BRYANSTON AVE
WAVERLEY AVE
LYNDHURST AVE
ELLERMAN AVE
CHILTERN AVE
LONGFORD RD
COBBETT RD
REDFERN AVE
HARVEY RD
GODFREY WAY
MILLFIELD RD
FARM RD
PEVENSEY RD
SUNNINGDALE AVE
CANTERBURY RD
NORMAN AVE
WINSLOW WAY
RIVER MEADS AVE
COURT CLOSE AVE
BROADLANDS
SHERIDAN CT 1
PICKWICK CL 2
HEATHLANDS CT 3
BRAMLEY WAY 4
NURSERY GDNS 5
BODICEA MEWS 1
SHELBURNE DR 2
FOUR SQUARE CT 3
RICHILL LODGE 4
SLADE HO 1
JAMIESON HO 2
ATHERLEY WAY 1
DUNLEARY CL 2
DANIEL CL 3
ARDEN CL 4
1 MALLARD CL
2 BRUNEL WLK
3 BRACKEN CL
4 HEATHER WLK
5 VANQUISH CL
6 KIMBER PL
CORFE CL 1
CARISBROOKE CL 2
1 TOWFIELD CT
2 NORMAN HO
3 RIVER CRANE WAY
1 WHITELY CT
2 BUTTS COTTS
1 EDWIN STRAY HO
2 CRANE HO
3 GLEBE HO
4 CHERTSEY HO
5 WHITELEYS HO
6 BUTTS HO
7 GLEBE COTTS
London Loop

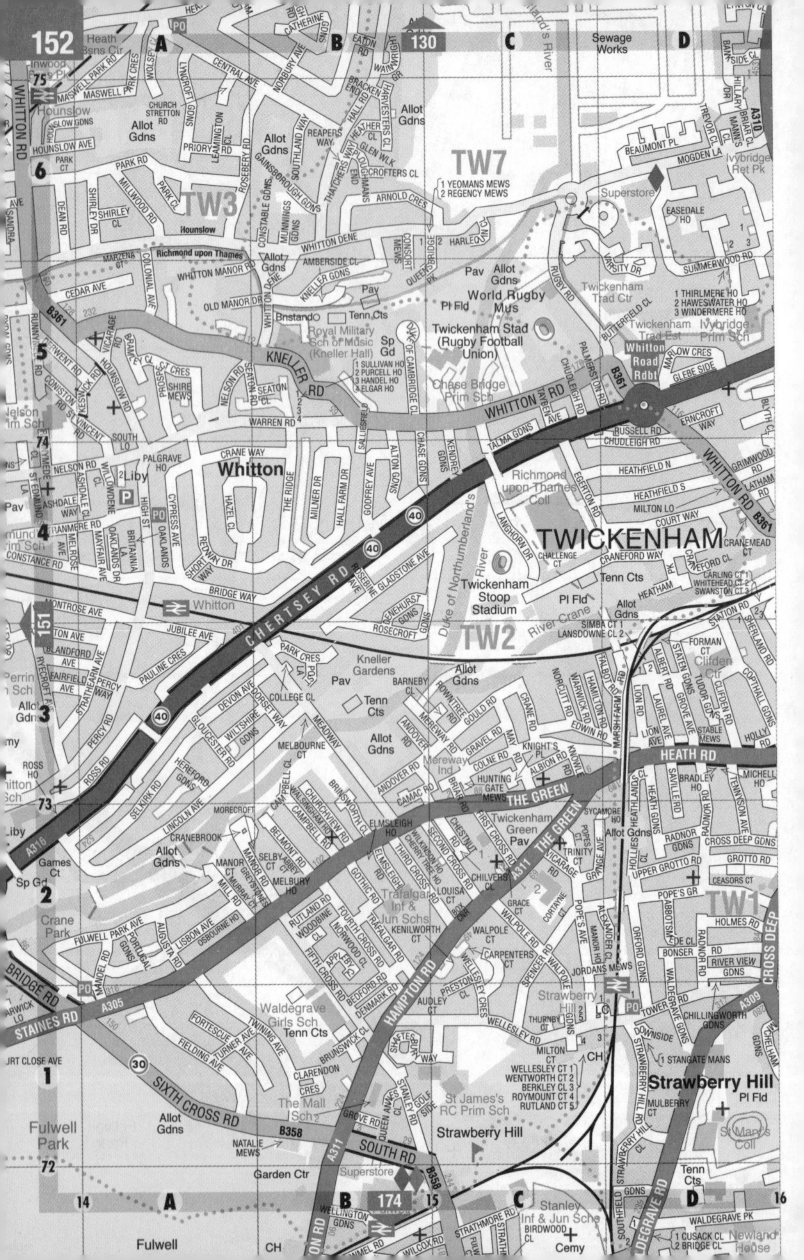
130
174
151
A
B
C
D
14
15
16
1
2
3
4
5
6
72
73
74
75
TW7
TW3
TW2
TW1
TWICKENHAM
Whitton
Strawberry Hill
Fulwell
Fulwell Park
Heath Bsns Ctr
Inwood Bsns Pk
Hounslow
Richmond upon Thames
Sewage Works
Duke of Northumberland's River
River Crane
WHITTON RD
MASWELL PARK RD
MASWELL PARK CRES
HOUNSLOW GDNS
HOUNSLOW AVE
PARK CT
PARK RD
CENTRAL AVE
CHURCH STRETTON RD
LYNGROFT GDNS
LEAMINGTON CL
PRIORY RD
ROSEBERY RD
NORBURY AVE
CATHERINE GDNS
EATON RD
WAINWRIGHT GR
BRACKEN END
HALL RD
HARVESTERS CL
SOUTHLAND WAY
REAPERS WAY
HEATHER CL
GLEN WLK
CROFTERS CL
PLOUGHMANS END
THATCHERS WAY
GAINSBOROUGH GDNS
CONSTABLE GDNS
MUNNINGS GDNS
ARNOLD CRES
1 YEOMANS MEWS
2 REGENCY MEWS
MILLWOOD RD
SHIRLEY DR
SHIRLEY CL
DEAN RD
PARK CL
WHITTON DENE
AMBERSIDE CL
KNELLER GDNS
CONSORT MEWS
QUEENSBRIDGE PK
HARLEQUIN CL
MARZENA CT
COLONIAL AVE
WHITTON MANOR RD
CEDAR AVE
OLD MANOR DR
Allot Gdns
Pav
Tenn Cts
Bnstand
Royal Military Sch of Music (Kneller Hall)
Sp Gd
DUKE OF CAMBRIDGE CL
World Rugby Mus
Pl Fld
Twickenham Stad (Rugby Football Union)
Chase Bridge Prim Sch
KNELLER RD
1 SULLIVAN HO
2 PURCELL HO
3 HANDEL HO
4 ELGAR HO
B361
RUNNYMEDE RD
DERWENT RD
CONISTON RD
KESWICK RD
VICARAGE RD
HOUNSLOW RD
BRAMCOTE CL
PROSPECT CRES
SHIRE MEWS
NELSON RD
SEATON RD
SEATON CL
WARREN RD
SALLIESFIELD
ST VINCENT RD
SOUTH LO
Nelson Prim Sch
RUGBY RD
VARSITY DR
SUMMERWOOD RD
EASEDALE HO
Twickenham Trad Ctr
BUTTERFIELD CL
Twickenham Trad Est
1 THIRLMERE HO
2 HAWESWATER HO
3 WINDERMERE HO
Ivybridge Prim Sch
Ivybridge Ret Pk
Superstore
BEAUMONT PL
MOGDEN LA
TREVOR CL
MANN'S CL
BRIAR CL
HILLARY DR
BANKSIDE CL
A310
Whitton Road Rdbt
MARLOW CRES
GLEBE SIDE
PALMERSTON RD
CHUDLEIGH RD
TAYBEN AVE
ERNCROFT WAY
RUSSELL RD
BLYTH CL
GRIMWOOD RD
LATHAM RD
HEATHFIELD N
HEATHFIELD S
MILTON LO
COURT WAY
EGERTON RD
TALMA GDNS
Richmond upon Thames Coll
LANGHORN DR
CHALLENGE CT
CRANEFORD WAY
CRANEMEAD CT
CARLING CT
WHITEHEAD CT
SWANSTON CT
HEATHAM PK
Twickenham Stoop Stadium
NELSON RD
CRANE WAY
PALGRAVE HO
Liby
ASHDALE CL
ASHDALE WAY
WILLOWDENE CL
ST EDMUND'S LA
HIGH ST
CYPRESS AVE
HAZEL CL
THE RIDGE
MILNER DR
HALL FARM DR
GODFREY AVE
ALTON GDNS
CHASE GDNS
KENDREY GDNS
CHERTSEY RD
CRANMERE RD
MELROSE AVE
MAYFAIR AVE
OAKLANDS DR
BRITANNIA LA
OAKLANDS AVE
REDWAY DR
SHORT WAY
CONSTANCE RD
BRIDGE WAY
MONTROSE AVE
JUBILEE AVE
ROSEBINE AVE
GLADSTONE AVE
DENEHURST GDNS
ROSECROFT GDNS
BLANDFORD AVE
FAIRFIELD AVE
STRATHEARN AVE
PERCY WAY
PAULINE CRES
PARK CRES
POST LA
Kneller Gardens
SIMBA CT
LANSDOWNE CL
STATION RD
SHERLAND RD
FORMAN CT
Clifden Ctr
RYECROFT AVE
PERCY RD
ROSS RD
ROSS HO
DEVON AVE
DORSET WAY
COLLEGE CL
GLOUCESTER RD
WILTSHIRE GDNS
MEADWAY
MELBOURNE CT
BARNEBY CL
ROWNTREE RD
MEREWAY RD
GOULD RD
CRANE RD
NORCUTT RD
WARWICK RD
HAMILTON RD
TALBOT RD
MARSH FARM RD
EDWIN RD
ANDOVER RD
GRAVEL RD
MAY RD
KNIGHT'S PL
ALBION RD
KNOWLE RD
COLNE RD
HUNTING GATE MEWS
Mereway Ind
CAMAC RD
HEATH RD
THE GREEN
ALBERT RD
STATEN GDNS
GROVE AVE
LION RD
LAUREL AVE
TUDOR GDNS
CLIFDEN RD
COPTHALL GDNS
STABLE MEWS
HOLLY RD
LION AVE
BRADLEY HO
MICHELL HO
TENNYSON AVE
HEREFORD GDNS
SELKIRK RD
LINCOLN AVE
MORECROFT
CRANEBROOK
CAMPBELL CL
WALSINGHAM HO
CHURCHVIEW RD
BRINSWORTH CL
ELMSLEIGH HO
ELMSLEIGH RD
WILKINSON HO
CHERRY TREE HO
SECOND CROSS RD
THIRD CROSS RD
CHESTNUT RD
FIRST CROSS RD
Twickenham Green
BELMONT RD
SELBY CT
ABBEY CT
MELBURY HO
GOTHIC RD
Trafalgar Inf & Jun Schs
LOUISA CT
BOX CNR
CHILVERS CL
A311
GRACE CT
CORTAYNE CT
VICARAGE RD
TRINITY CT
POPES CT
GRANGE AVE
SYCAMORE HO
HEATHLANDS CL
HEATH GDNS
HOLLIES CL
RADNOR GDNS
RADNOR RD
SAVILLE RD
CROSS DEEP GDNS
GROTTO RD
UPPER GROTTO RD
CEASORS CT
POPE'S GR
ABBOTSMEDE CL
HOLMES RD
BONSER RD
RIVER VIEW GDNS
CROSS DEEP
Games Ct
Sp Gd
MANOR CT
MANOR RD
MURRAY CT
GREYSTONES
MILL RD
Crane Park
FULWELL PARK AVE
PORTUGAL GDNS
AUGUSTA RD
LISBON AVE
OSBOURNE HO
MANOEL RD
RUTLAND RD
WOODBINE CL
FOURTH CROSS RD
NORWOOD CL
TRAFALGAR RD
APPLEBY CL
FIFTH CROSS RD
BEDFORD RD
DENMARK RD
KENILWORTH CT
WALPOLE CT
WALPOLE RD
CARPENTERS CT
SPENCER RD
POPE'S AVE
MANOR HO
ALEXANDER CL
JORDANS MEWS
ORFORD GDNS
WALDEGRAVE GDNS
PRESTON CL
WELLESLEY CRES
HAMPTON RD
AUDLEY CT
BRIDGE RD
STAINES RD
A305
WARWICK LO
Waldegrave Girls Sch
FORTESCUE AVE
TURNER AVE
TWINING AVE
FIELDING AVE
BRUNSWICK CL
SHAFTESBURY WAY
THURNBY CT
WELLESLEY RD
MILTON CT
WELLESLEY CT
WENTWORTH CT
BERKLEY CL
ROYMOUNT CT
RUTLAND CT
Strawberry Hill GDNS
TOWER RD
CHILLINGWORTH GDNS
DOWNSIDE
1 STANGATE MANS
STRAWBERRY HILL RD
STRAWBERRY HILL CL
MULBERRY CT
A309
CHELHAM GDNS
COURT CLOSE AVE
SIXTH CROSS RD
B358
CLARENDON CRES
The Mall Sch
GROVE RD
QUEEN ANNES CL
STANLEY RD
GOLF SIDE
St James's RC Prim Sch
NATALIE MEWS
SOUTH RD
Garden Ctr
Pl Fld
St Mary's Coll
Tenn Cts
WELLINGTON GDNS
WILCOX RD
STRATHMORE RD
Stanley Inf & Jun Schs
BIRDWOOD CL
Cemy
SOUTHFIELD GDNS
WALDEGRAVE RD
WALDEGRAVE PK
1 CUSACK CL
2 BRIDGE CL
Newland House
CH
PO

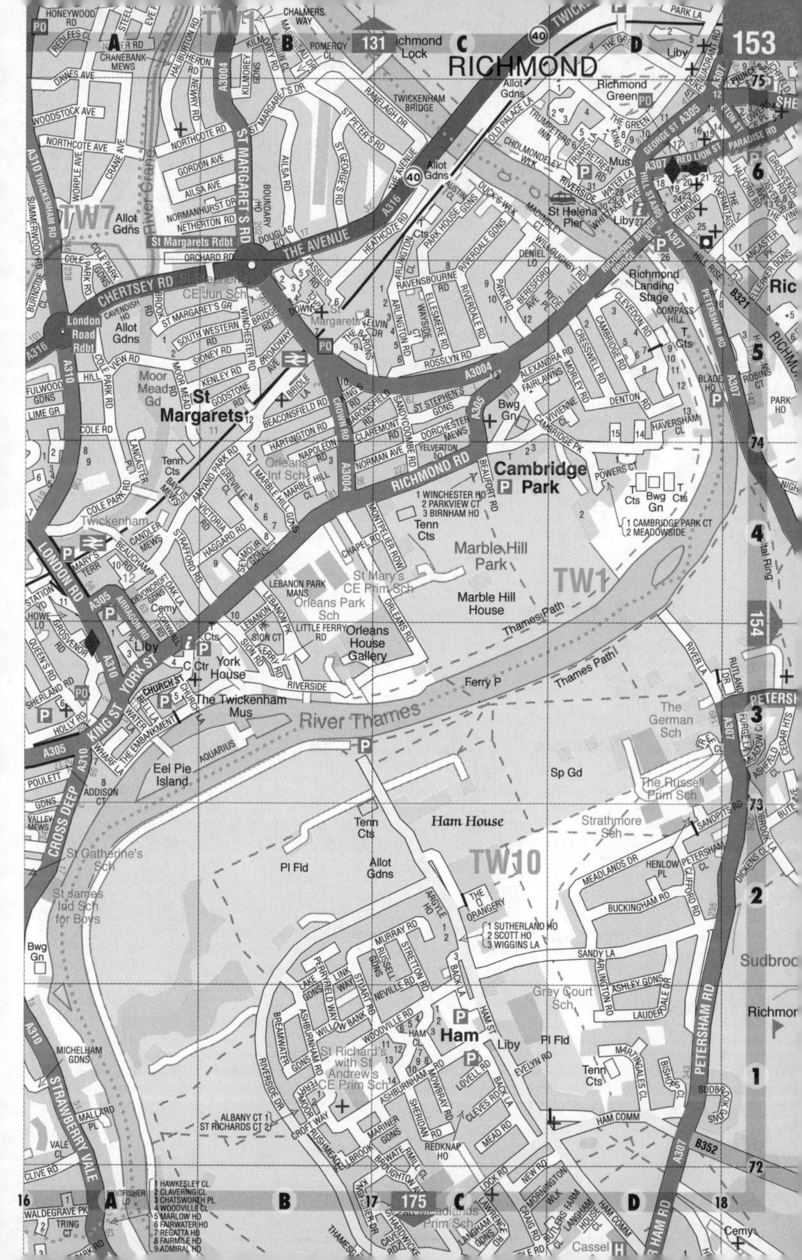
RICHMOND
Richmond Lock
Richmond Green
Twickenham Bridge
St Margarets
Cambridge Park
Marble Hill Park
Marble Hill House
Orleans House Gallery
York House
The Twickenham Mus
River Thames
Eel Pie Island
Ham House
Ham
TW1
TW7
TW10
Thames Path
St Helena Pier
Richmond Landing Stage
St Margarets Rdbt
London Road Rdbt
Twickenham
The German Sch
The Russell Prim Sch
Strathmore Sch
Grey Court Sch
St Richard's with St Andrew's CE Prim Sch
Orleans Park Sch
St Mary's CE Prim Sch
Orleans Inf Sch
St Stephen's CE Jun Sch
St Catherine's Sch
St James Ind Sch for Boys
Moor Mead Gd
River Crane
THE AVENUE
CHERTSEY RD
RICHMOND RD
ST MARGARET'S RD
LONDON RD
CROSS DEEP
STRAWBERRY VALE
PETERSHAM RD
YORK ST
KING ST
HAM ST
SANDY LA
RIVERSIDE
RIVERSIDE DR
HAM COMM
A305
A307
A310
A316
A3004
B321
B352
131
154
175

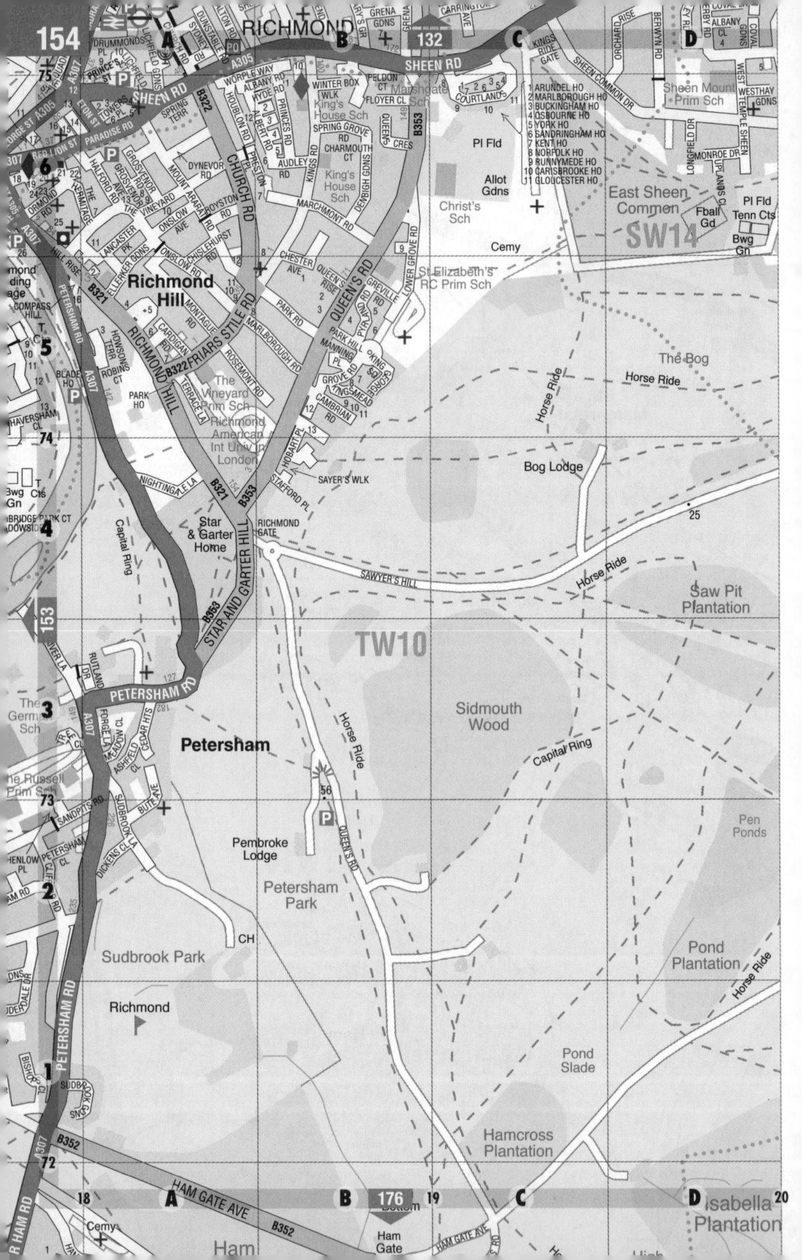
RICHMOND
132
SHEEN RD
Richmond Hill
Petersham
Sheen Mount Prim Sch
East Sheen Common
SW14
King's House Sch
Christ's Sch
Cemy
Allot Gdns
Pl Fld
St Elizabeth's RC Prim Sch
The Vineyard Prim Sch
Richmond American Int Univ in London
Star & Garter Home
The Bog
Horse Ride
Bog Lodge
SAWYER'S HILL
Saw Pit Plantation
TW10
Sidmouth Wood
Capital Ring
Pembroke Lodge
Petersham Park
Sudbrook Park
Richmond
Pen Ponds
Pond Plantation
Pond Slade
Hamcross Plantation
Isabella Plantation
HAM GATE AVE
Ham Gate
Ham
153
176
PETERSHAM RD
RICHMOND HILL
QUEEN'S RD
STAR AND GARTER HILL
CHURCH RD
FRIARS STILE RD
1 ARUNDEL HO
2 MARLBOROUGH HO
3 BUCKINGHAM HO
4 OSBOURNE HO
5 YORK HO
6 SANDRINGHAM HO
7 KENT HO
8 NORFOLK HO
9 RUNNYMEDE HO
10 CARISBROOKE HO
11 GLOUCESTER HO

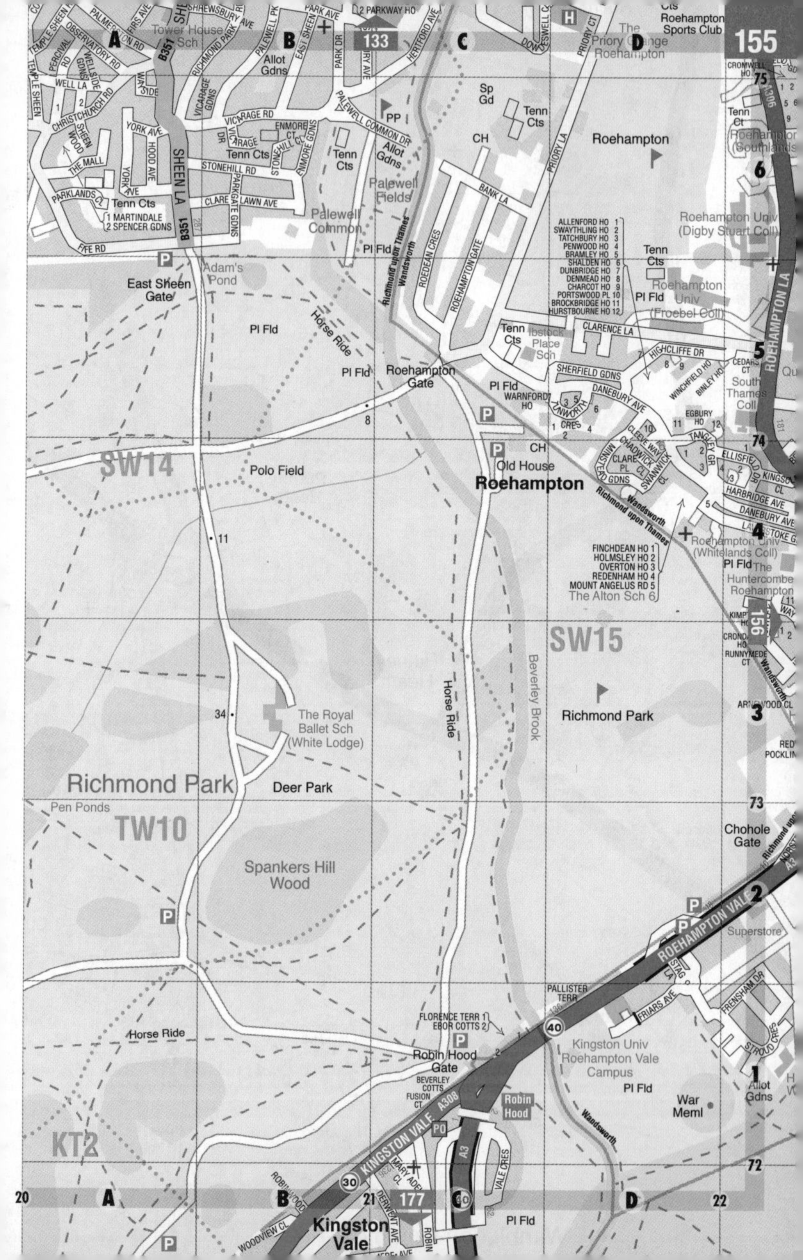
A
B
C
D
133
Roehampton Sports Club
The Priory Grange Roehampton
Tower House Sch
Allot Gdns
Sp Gd
Tenn Cts
CH
Roehampton
Roehampton Univ (Digby Stuart Coll)
Palewell Fields
Palewell Common
Pl Fld
Richmond upon Thames
Wandsworth
ALLENFORD HO 1
SWAYTHLING HO 2
TATCHBURY HO 3
PENWOOD HO 4
BRAMLEY HO 5
SHALDEN HO 6
DUNBRIDGE HO 7
DENMEAD HO 8
CHARCOT HO 9
PORTSWOOD PL 10
BROCKBRIDGE HO 11
HURSTBOURNE HO 12
Roehampton Univ (Froebel Coll)
East Sheen Gate
Adam's Pond
Horse Ride
Roehampton Gate
Ibstock Place Sch
South Thames Coll
SW14
Polo Field
Old House
Roehampton
FINCHDEAN HO 1
HOLMSLEY HO 2
OVERTON HO 3
REDENHAM HO 4
MOUNT ANGELUS RD 5
The Alton Sch 6
Roehampton Univ (Whitelands Coll)
The Huntercombe Roehampton
SW15
Beverley Brook
The Royal Ballet Sch (White Lodge)
Richmond Park
Deer Park
Pen Ponds
TW10
Spankers Hill Wood
Chohole Gate
Superstore
ROEHAMPTON VALE
PALLISTER TERR
FLORENCE TERR 1
EBOR COTTS 2
Kingston Univ Roehampton Vale Campus
Robin Hood Gate
War Meml
Allot Gdns
BEVERLEY COTTS
FUSION CT
Robin Hood
KINGSTON VALE
A308
A3
A306
B351
SHEEN LA
ROEHAMPTON LA
KT2
177
Kingston Vale
20
21
22
72
73
74
75

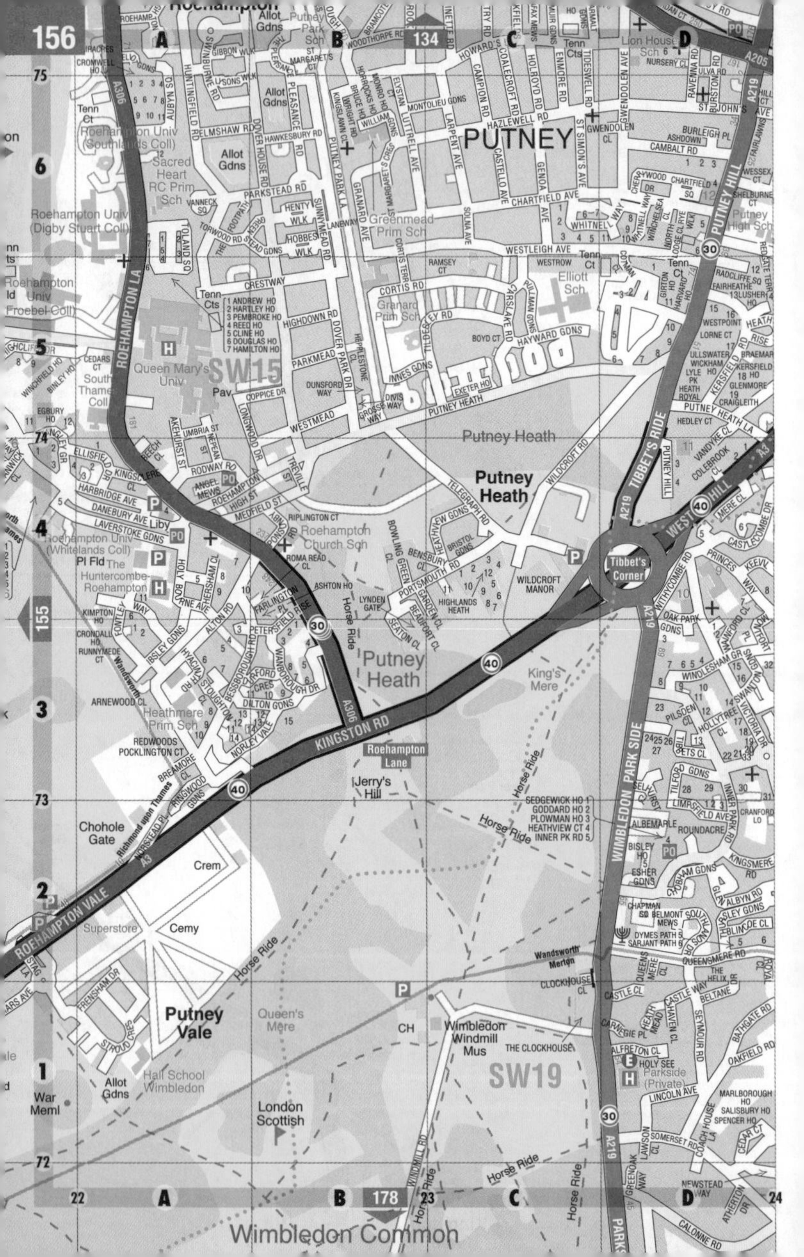

156
A
B
134
C
D
PUTNEY
Putney Heath
Tibbet's Corner
SW15
SW19
Roehampton
Roehampton Univ (Southlands Coll)
Roehampton Univ (Digby Stuart Coll)
Roehampton Univ (Froebel Coll)
Roehampton Univ (Whitelands Coll)
Queen Mary's Univ
Sacred Heart RC Prim Sch
Greenmead Prim Sch
Granard Prim Sch
Elliott Sch
Roehampton Church Sch
Heathmere Prim Sch
Putney High Sch
Lion House Sch
South Thames Coll
The Huntercombe-Roehampton
WILDCROFT MANOR
King's Mere
Queen's Mere
Roehampton Lane
Jerry's Hill
Chohole Gate
Putney Vale
Crem
Cemy
Superstore
Hall School Wimbledon
War Meml
London Scottish
Wimbledon Windmill Mus
THE CLOCKHOUSE
Parkside (Private)
Wimbledon Common
ROEHAMPTON LA
KINGSTON RD
ROEHAMPTON VALE
PUTNEY HILL
TIBBET'S RIDE
WIMBLEDON PARK SIDE
WEST HILL
PUTNEY HEATH
PUTNEY PARK LA
DOVER HOUSE RD
DOVER PARK DR
HIGHDOWN RD
PARKMEAD
WESTMEAD
CHARTFIELD AVE
WESTLEIGH AVE
HAZLEWELL RD
CAMBALT RD
TELEGRAPH RD
WILDCROFT RD
PORTSMOUTH RD
QUEENSMERE RD
CASTLE WAY
SEYMOUR RD
LINCOLN AVE
CALONNE RD
WINDMILL RD
Horse Ride
A306
A219
A3
A205
155
178
75
74
73
72
22
23
24
Wandsworth
Merton
Richmond upon Thames

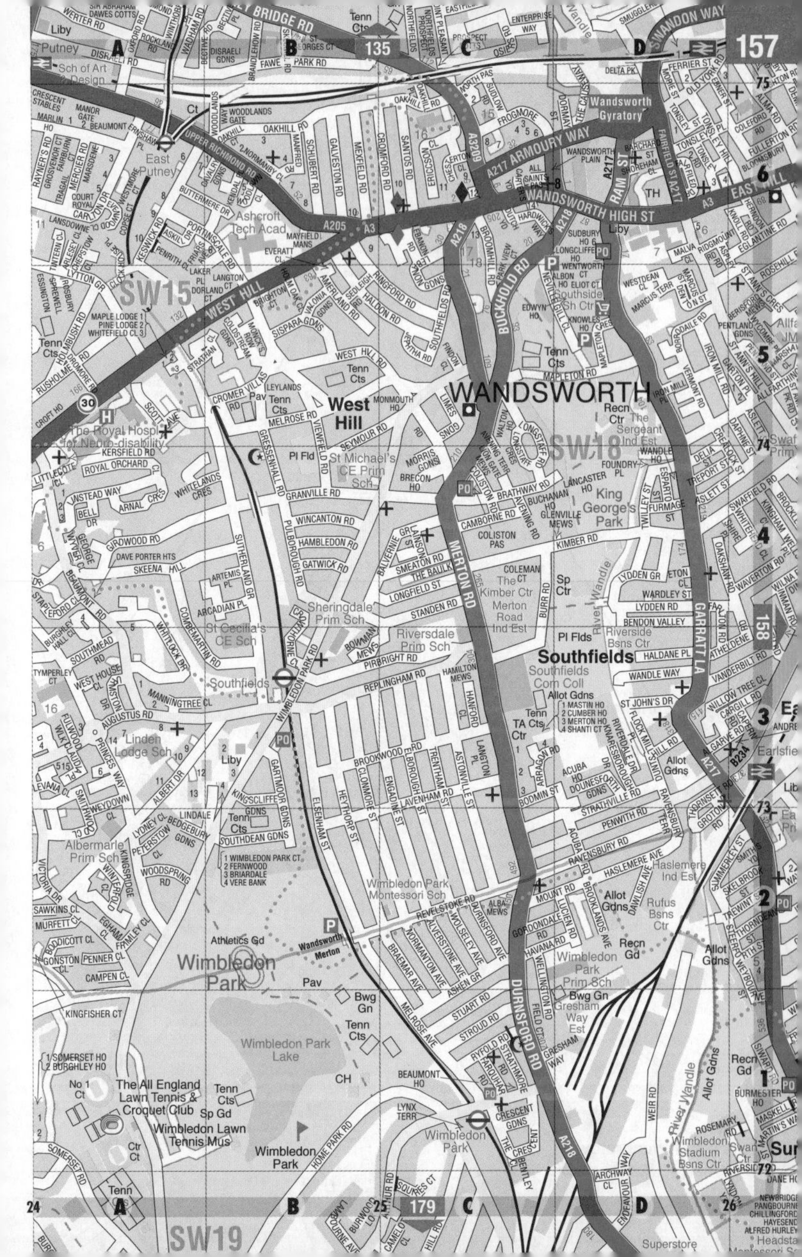

157
135
179
158
A
B
C
D
1
2
3
4
5
6
24
25
26
75
74
73
72
SW15
SW18
SW19
WANDSWORTH
West Hill
Southfields
Putney
East Putney
Wandsworth Gyratory
WANDSWORTH HIGH ST
WANDSWORTH PLAIN
A217 ARMOURY WAY
UPPER RICHMOND RD
WEST HILL
A205
A3
A218
A3209
A217
B234
SWANDON WAY
EAST HILL
MERTON RD
BUCKHOLD RD
GARRATT LA
DURNSFORD RD
WIMBLEDON PARK RD
RAM ST
FAIRFIELD ST
OLD YORK RD
ALMA RD
FERRIER ST
DELTA PK
ENTERPRISE WAY
SMUGGLERS WAY
FROGMORE
DORMAY ST
THE CAUSEWAY
SUDLOW RD
OAKHILL RD
OAKHILL PL
SANTOS RD
CROMFORD RD
MEXFIELD RD
GALVESTON RD
SCHUBERT RD
MANFRED RD
ERICSSON CL
WOODLANDS WAY
WOODLANDS GATE
NORMANBY CL
DISRAELI RD
DISRAELI GDNS
FAWE PARK RD
WERTER RD
OXFORD RD
ROCKLAND RD
WADHAM RD
BRANDLEHOW RD
NORTHFIELDS
PROSPECT CTS
OSIERS RD
WINTHORPE RD
Sch of Art & Design
CRESCENT STABLES
MANOR GATE
MARLIN HO
BEAUMONT
ERNSHAW PL
RAYNER'S RD
GROSVENOR CT
FAIRBURN CT
MERCIER RD
MARSDENE
TRAGAIL
COURT ROYAL
CARLTON DR
WESTMORE CT
COPSE CT
LANSDOWNE
BUTTERMERE DR
KESWICK RD
ASKILL DR
PENRITH CL
PORTINSCALE RD
FRIARS AVE
KENDAL PL
Ashcroft Tech Acad
MAYFIELD MANS
EVERATT CL
LAKER PL
LANGTON CT
DORLAND CT
TINTERN CL
LYTTON GR
ESSINGTON
SPREWELL
ROSEBURY
HOLMBUSH RD
MAPLE LODGE
PINE LODGE
WHITEFIELD CL
Tenn Cts
DROMORE RD
RUSHOLME RD
CROFT HO
The Royal Hospl for Neuro-disability
KERSFIELD RD
ROYAL ORCHARD
LITTLECOTE CL
UNSTEAD WAY
BELL DR
ARNAL CRES
WHITELANDS CRES
GIRDWOOD RD
DAVE PORTER HTS
SKEENA HILL
GEORGE WYVER CL
BEAUMONT RD
STAPLEFORD CL
BURGHLEY HALL CL
SOUTHMEAD RD
TYMPERLEY CT
WEST HOUSE CL
WHITLOCK DR
COMBEMARTIN RD
ARTEMIS PL
ARCADIAN PL
SUTHERLAND GR
St Cecilia's CE Sch
MANNINGTREE CL
AUGUSTUS RD
Linden Lodge Sch
PRINCES WAY
FULWOOD
WILKS
CLAUDIA PL
LEVANA CL
SMITHWOOD CL
WEYDOWN CL
Albermarle Prim Sch
KINGSRIDGE
WINTERFOLD CL
VICTORIA DR
SAWKINS CL
MURFETT CL
BODDICOTT CL
GONSTON CL
PENNER CL
CAMPEN CL
EGHAM CL
FRIMLEY CL
ALBERT DR
LYDNEY CL
BEDGEBURY GDNS
PETERSTOW CL
WOODSPRING RD
LINDALE
Liby
KINGSCLIFFE GDNS
GARTMOOR GDNS
SOUTHDEAN GDNS
1 WIMBLEDON PARK CT
2 FERNWOOD
3 BRIARDALE
4 VERE BANK
STRATHAN CL
COLDSTREAM GDNS
MONK'S ROW
CROMER VILLAS RD
LEYLANDS
Pav
MELROSE RD
GRESSENHALL RD
VIEWFIELD RD
SEYMOUR RD
Pl Fld
St Michael's CE Prim Sch
GRANVILLE RD
WINCANTON RD
HAMBLEDON RD
GATWICK RD
PULBOROUGH RD
Sheringdale Prim Sch
BOWMAN MEWS
Riversdale Prim Sch
PIRBRIGHT RD
REPLINGHAM RD
HAMILTON MEWS
HANFORD CL
BRIGHTON CT
HOLM OAK CL
VALONIA GDNS
SISPARA GDNS
AMERLAND RD
SEDLEIGH RD
RINGFORD RD
HALDON RD
SOUTHFIELDS RD
WEST HILL RD
MONMOUTH HO
LIMES GDNS
MORRIS GDNS
BRECON HO
BALVERNIE GR
LANSON ST
SMEATON RD
THE BAULK
LONGFIELD ST
STANDEN RD
ELSENHAM ST
HEYTHORP ST
BROOKWOOD RD
CLONMORE ST
ELBOROUGH ST
ENGADINE ST
TRENTHAM ST
ASTONVILLE ST
LAVENHAM RD
LANGTON PL
Wimbledon Park Montessori Sch
REVELSTOKE RD
ALBA MEWS
BRAEMAR AVE
NORMANTON AVE
ALVERSTONE AVE
WOLSELEY AVE
DURNSFORD AVE
ASHEN GR
MELROSE AVE
STUART RD
STROUD RD
RYFOLD RD
FARQUHAR RD
STRATHMORE
BEAUMONT HO
LYNX TERR
CRESCENT GDNS
THE CRESCENT
THE CL
BENTLEY
Wimbledon Park
Athletics Gd
Wandsworth
Merton
Bwg Gn
Wimbledon Park Lake
CH
KINGFISHER CT
1 SOMERSET HO
2 BURGHLEY HO
No 1 Ct
The All England Lawn Tennis & Croquet Club
Sp Gd
Wimbledon Lawn Tennis Mus
SOMERSET RD
Ctr Ct
HOME PARK RD
ARTHUR RD
SQUIRES CT
LAMBOURNE AVE
BURWOOD
CAMELOT
HILL RD
BROOMHILL RD
PARK VIEW CT
NEVILLE GILL CL
SUDBURY HO
LONGCLIFFE HO
WENTWORTH CT
ALBON HO
ELIOT CT
Southside Sh Ctr
EDWYN HO
KNOWLES HO
MAPLETON CRES
MAPLETON RD
FINDON CL
SPATHA RD
WALTON LODGE
LONGSTAFF RD
LONGSTAFF CRES
AVENING TERR
LION GATE MEWS
COLISTON RD
BRATHWAY RD
AVENING RD
BUCHANAN HO
LANCASTER HO
GLENVILLE MEWS
CAMBORNE RD
COLISTON PAS
KIMBER RD
King George's Park
COLEMAN CT
The Kimber Ctr
Merton Road Ind Est
BURR RD
Sp Ctr
River Wandle
Pl Flds
Riverside Bsns Ctr
Southfields Com Coll
Allot Gdns
1 MASTIN HO
2 CUMBER HO
3 MERTON HO
4 SHANTI CT
TA Ctr
ARRAGON RD
BODMIN ST
ACUBA HO
DOUNESFORTH GDNS
ACUBA RD
STRATHVILLE RD
PENWITH RD
RAVENSBURY RD
RAVENSBURY TERR
HASLEMERE AVE
Haslemere Ind Est
DAWLISH AVE
Rufus Bsns Ctr
MOUNT RD
LUCIEN RD
BROOKLANDS AVE
GORDONDALE RD
HAVANA RD
WELLINGTON RD
FIELD CT
Recn Gd
Wimbledon Park Prim Sch
Gresham Way Est
GRESHAM WAY
WEIR RD
ARCHWAY CL
ENDEFAVOUR WAY
Superstore
Wimbledon Stadium Bsns Ctr
ST JOHN'S DR
FLOCK MILL PL
RIVERDALE DR
KNARESBOROUGH DR
SUMMERLEY ST
SKELBROOK ST
TREWINT ST
ROSEMARY
BURMESTER HO
MASKELL
Recn Ctr
The Sergeant Ind Est
WANDLE HO
FOUNDRY PL
TWILLEY ST
ESPARTO ST
FURMAGE ST
IRON MILL PL
IRON MILL RD
VERMONT RD
BORRODAILE RD
WESTDEAN CL
MARCUS TERR
MARCUS CT
MALVA
RIDGMOUNT
EGLANTINE RD
ROSEHILL
ST ANN'S CRES
PENTLAND GDNS
GARTON PL
ST ANN'S HILL
ALLFARTHING
DAPHNE ST
ASLETT ST
CRESSFORD
DELIA ST
TREPORT ST
SWAFFIELD RD
KINGHAM CL
OAKSHAW RD
WAVERTON RD
LYDDEN GR
LYDDEN RD
WARDLEY ST
BENDON VALLEY
HALDANE PL
WANDLE WAY
VANDERBILT RD
WILLOW TREE CL
CARGILL RD
ALGARVE RD
Earlsfield
THORNSETT RD
GROTON RD
TONSLEY HILL
TONSLEY PL
COLEFORD RD
FULLERTON RD
BLOOMSBURY
HERNDON RD
KNOLL RD
TH
SHOREHAM CL
BARCHARD ST
ALL SAINTS PAS
HARDWICKS WAY
CHESTERTON CL
LEBANON GDNS

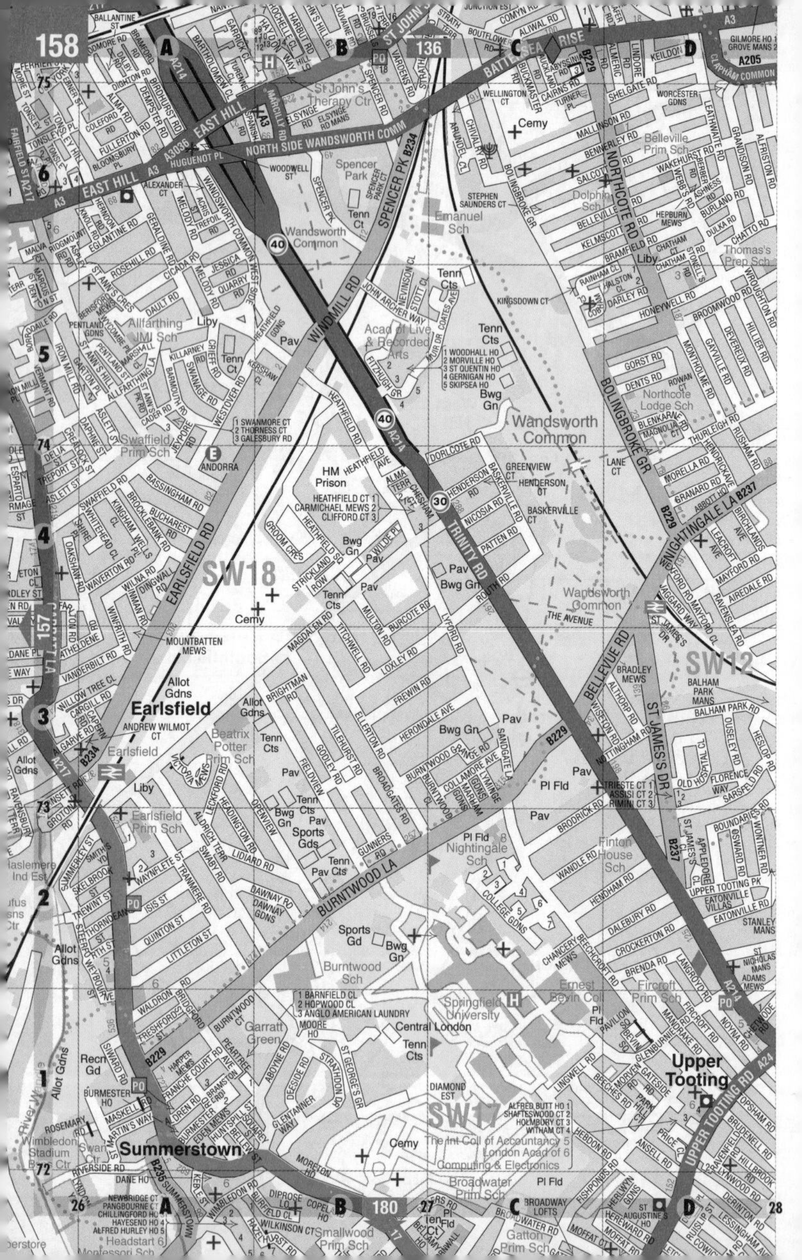
158
A
B
C
D
136
180
157
26
27
28
75
74
73
72
6
5
4
3
2
1
SW18
SW12
SW17
Earlsfield
Summerstown
Upper Tooting
Wandsworth Common
Spencer Park
HM Prison
Emanuel Sch
Allfarthing JMI Sch
Swaffield Prim Sch
Beatrix Potter Prim Sch
Earlsfield Prim Sch
Nightingale Sch
Burntwood Sch
Springfield University
Ernest Bevin Coll
Fircroft Prim Sch
Finton House Sch
Northcote Lodge Sch
Belleville Prim Sch
Dolphin Sch
Thomas's Prep Sch
Acad of Live & Recorded Arts
St John's Therapy Ctr
Garratt Green
Central London
The Int Coll of Accountancy 5
London Acad of 6 Computing & Electronics
Broadwater Prim Sch
Gatton Prim Sch
Smallwood Prim Sch
Headstart 6 Montessori Sch
Wimbledon Stadium Bus Ctr
Haslemere Ind Est
Swan Ctr
Allot Gdns
Recn Gd
Sports Gds
Cemy
Liby
Pav
Tenn Cts
Bwg Gn
Pl Fld
ANDORRA
DIAMOND EST
EAST HILL
NORTH SIDE WANDSWORTH COMM
WANDSWORTH COMMON WEST SIDE
BATTERSEA RISE
ST JOHN'S HILL
SPENCER PK
WINDMILL RD
EARLSFIELD RD
TRINITY RD
NORTHCOTE RD
BOLINGBROKE GR
NIGHTINGALE LA
BELLEVUE RD
ST JAMES'S DR
BURNTWOOD LA
GARRATT LA
UPPER TOOTING RD
MAGDALEN RD
THE AVENUE
CLAPHAM COMMON
A3
A205
A214
A217
A24
A3036
B229
B234
B235
B237
1 SWANMORE CT
2 THORNESS CT
3 GALESBURY RD
1 WOODHALL HO
2 MORVILLE HO
3 ST QUENTIN HO
4 GERNIGAN HO
5 SKIPSEA HO
HEATHFIELD CT 1
CARMICHAEL MEWS 2
CLIFFORD CT 3
TRIESTE CT 1
ASSISI CT 2
RIMINI CT 3
1 BARNFIELD CL
2 HOPWOOD CL
3 ANGLO AMERICAN LAUNDRY
ALFRED BUTT HO 1
SHAFTESWOOD CT 2
HOLMBURY CT 3
WITHAM CT 4
NEWBRIDGE CT 1
PANGBOURNE CT 2
CHILLINGFORD HO 3
HAYESEND HO 4
ALFRED HURLEY HO 5

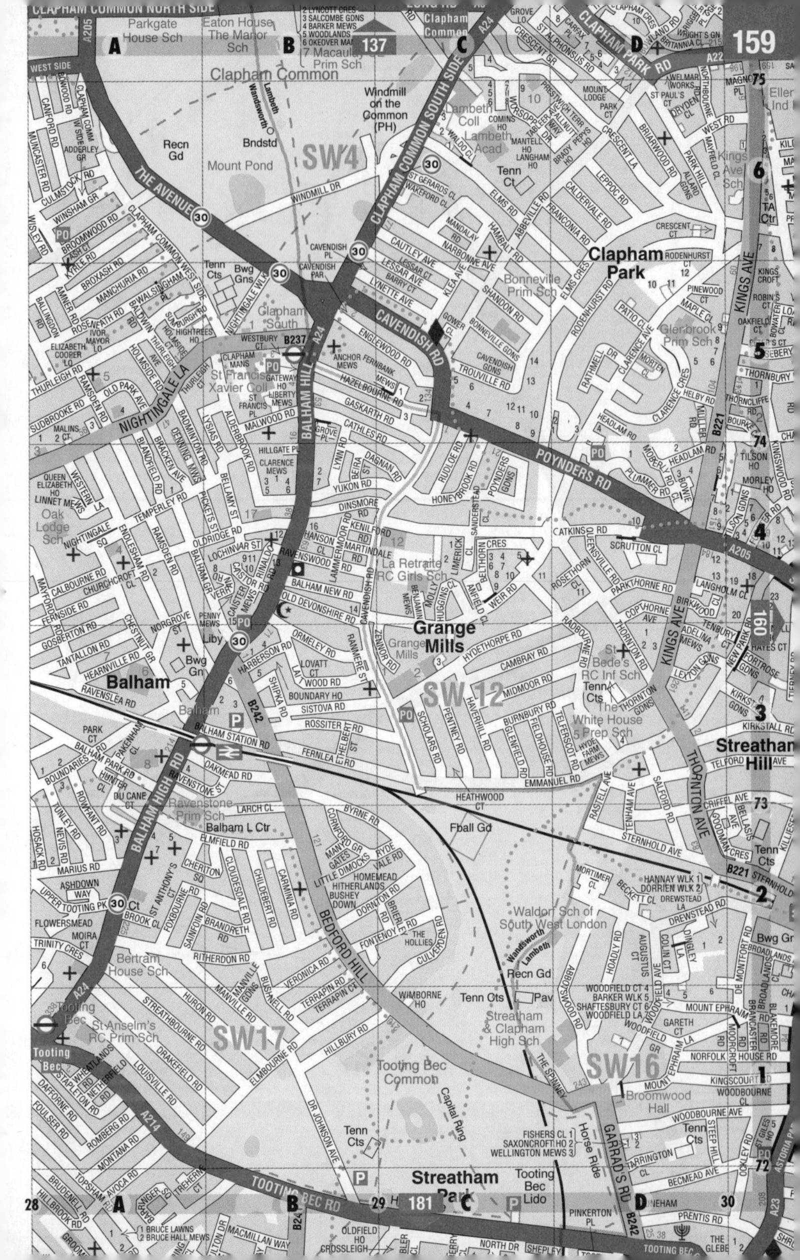

CLAPHAM COMMON NORTH SIDE
Parkgate House Sch
Eaton House The Manor Sch
2 LYNCOTT CRES
3 SALCOMBE GDNS
4 BARKER MEWS
5 WOODLANDS
6 OKEOVER MANOR
7 Macaulay C of E Prim Sch
137
Clapham Common
A
B
C
D
A205
A24
WEST SIDE
Clapham Common
Windmill on the Common (PH)
Lambeth
Wandsworth
Bndstd
Recn Gd
Mount Pond
SW4
WINDMILL DR
THE AVENUE
CLAPHAM COMMON SOUTH SIDE
CLAPHAM CRES
CLAPHAM PARK RD
A3
CRESCENT GR
ST ALPHONSUS RD
GROVE LO
CARFAX PL
Lambeth Coll
Lambeth Acad
Tenn Ct
MOUNT LODGE
PARK CT
CRESCENT LA
BRIARWOOD RD
LEPPOC RD
CALDERVALE RD
FRANCONIA RD
ELMS RD
ABBEVILLE RD
ST GERARDS CL
WAKEFORD CL
MANDALAY RD
NARBONNE AVE
CAUTLEY AVE
LESSAR AVE
BARRY CT
LYNETTE AVE
HAMBALT RD
KLEA AVE
Bonneville Prim Sch
SHANDON RD
BONNEVILLE GDNS
CAVENDISH GDNS
TROUVILLE RD
ELMS CRES
RODENHURST RD
Clapham Park
CRESCENT CT
PINEWOOD CT
MAPLE CL
PATIO CL
Glenbrook Prim Sch
CLARENCE AVE
MORTEN CL
RATHMELL DR
CLARENCE CRES
HELBY RD
HEADLAM RD
WELMAR WORKS
ST PAUL'S CT
DRYDEN CL
NORTHBOURNE
MAYFIELD CL
WEST RD
PARK HILL
ALLARD GDNS
Kings Ave Sch
TA Ctr
Ellerslie Ind Est
KINGS AVE
KINGS CROFT
ROBIN'S CT
OAKFIELD CT
THORNBURY
BOURKE CL
KINGSWOOD RD
TILSON HO
MORLEY HO
TILSON GDNS
MAGNOLIA PL
Clapham South
CAVENDISH PL
CAVENDISH PAR
CAVENDISH RD
GOWER CL
Tenn Cts
Bwg Gns
NIGHTINGALE WLK
BROOMWOOD RD
KYRLE RD
BROXASH RD
MANCHURIA RD
WALSINGHAM PL
ROSENEATH RD
IVOR MAYOR LO
ELIZABETH COOPER LO
HIGHTREES HO
HOLMSIDE RD
THURLEIGH RD
NIGHTINGALE LA
WESTBURY CT
CLAPHAM MANS
B237
St Francis Xavier Coll
GATEWAY HO
LIBERTY MEWS
ST FRANCIS PL
BALHAM HILL
ANCHOR MEWS
FERNBANK MEWS
ENGLEWOOD RD
HAZELBOURNE RD
GASKARTH RD
MALWOOD RD
CATHLES RD
GROVE PL
HILLGATE PL
CLARENCE MEWS
LYNN RD
BEIRA ST
DAGNAN RD
YUKON RD
POYNDERS RD
POYNDERS GDNS
RUDLOE RD
HONEYBROOK RD
SANDERSTEAD CL
CATKINS RD
SCRUTTON CL
QUEENSVILLE RD
ROSETHORN CL
PARKTHORNE RD
COPTHORNE AVE
LANGHOLM CL
A205
B221
160
HAYES CT
FORTROSE GDNS
NEW PARK RD
TENBURY CT
ADELINA MEWS
LEYTON GDNS
KIRKSTALL GDNS
KIRKSTALL RD
Streatham Hill
TELFORD AVE
CULMSTOCK RD
WINSHAM GR
CANFORD RD
MUNCASTER RD
ADDERLEY GR
WISLEY RD
AMNER RD
BALLINGDON
SUDBROOKE RD
RAMSDEN RD
OLD PARK AVE
MALINS CT
QUEEN ELIZABETH HO
LINNET MEWS
WESTERN LA
Oak Lodge Sch
NIGHTINGALE SQ
TEMPERLEY RD
BELLAMY ST
PICKETS ST
DINSMORE RD
KENILFORD RD
HANSON CL
MARTINDALE RD
LOCHINVAR ST
OLDRIDGE RD
ENDLESHAM RD
BALHAM GR
RAVENSWOOD RD
BALHAM NEW RD
OLD DEVONSHIRE RD
La Retraite RC Girls Sch
CAVENDISH RD
LIMERICK CL
BELTHORN CRES
WEIR RD
ANFIELD CL
HUGGINS CL
BENJAMIN MEWS
Grange Mills
HYDETHORPE RD
CAMBRAY RD
MIDMOOR RD
RADBOURNE RD
THORNTON RD
St Bede's RC Inf Sch
Tenn Cts
The White House Prep Sch
THORNTON GDNS
HYDE FARM MEWS
THORNTON AVE
CALBOURNE RD
CHURCHCROFT CL
MAYFORD RD
FERNSIDE RD
GOSBERTON RD
TANTALLON RD
HEARNVILLE RD
CHESTNUT GR
NORGROVE ST
PENNY MEWS
Liby
Bwg Gn
Balham
RAVENSLEA RD
HARBERSON RD
ORMELEY RD
LOVATT CT
LAITWOOD RD
BOUNDARY HO
SISTOVA RD
SHIPKA RD
B242
ZENNOR RD
RANMERE ST
SW 12
SCHOLARS RD
PENTNEY RD
HAVERHILL RD
BURNBURY RD
GLENFIELD RD
FIELDHOUSE RD
TELFERSCOT RD
ROSSITER RD
ETHELBERT ST
FERNLEA RD
BALHAM STATION RD
OAKMEAD RD
EMMANUEL RD
HEATHWOOD CT
RASTELL AVE
TENHAM AVE
SALFORD RD
CRIFFEL AVE
GOODMAN CRES
BELLASIS AVE
STERNHOLD AVE
HANNAY WLK 1
DORRIEN WLK 2
DREWSTEAD LA
DREWSTEAD RD
PARK CT
PAKENHAM CL
BALHAM PARK RD
BOUNDARIES RD
HUNTER CL
RAVENSTONE ST
DU CANE CT
Ravenstone Prim Sch
LARCH CL
Balham L Ctr
ELMFIELD RD
BALHAM HIGH RD
BYRNE RD
CORNFORD GR
MANY GATES
LITTLE DIMOCKS
RYDE VALE RD
HOMEMEAD
HITHERLANDS
BUSHEY DOWN
DORNTON RD
BRIERLEY RD
THE HOLLIES
FONTENOY RD
CULVERDEN RD
Fball Gd
MORTIMER CL
BECKETT CL
Waldorf Sch of South West London
HOADLY RD
AUGUSTUS CT
COLIN CT
DINGLEY LA
DE MONTFORT RD
BROADLANDS
BRANCASTER
BLAKEMORE
Bwg Gr
ROWFANT RD
TUNLEY RD
NEVIS RD
HOSACK RD
MARIUS RD
ASHDOWN WAY
UPPER TOOTING PK
Ct
FLOWERSMEAD
MOIRA CT
TRINITY CRES
BROOK CL
CHERITON SQ
ST ANTHONY'S CT
FOXBOURNE RD
SAINFOIN RD
BRANDRETH RD
CLOUDESDALE RD
CHILDEBERT RD
CARMINIA RD
RITHERDON RD
BEDFORD HILL
Bertram House Sch
MANVILLE GDNS
MANVILLE RD
BUSHNELL RD
VERONICA RD
TERRAPIN RD
TERRAPIN CT
WIMBORNE HO
Recn Gd
Tenn Cts
Pav
Wandsworth
Lambeth
ABBOTSWOOD RD
WOODFIELD CT 4
BARKER WLK 5
SHAFTESBURY CT 6
WOODFIELD LA
WOODFIELD AVE
WOODFIELD GR
GARETH CT
MOUNT EPHRAIM LA
MOUNT EPHRAIM RD
MOORCROFT RD
NORFOLK HOUSE RD
KINGSCOURT RD
WOODBOURNE CL
WOODBOURNE AVE
Broomwood Hall
Streatham & Clapham High Sch
THE SPINNEY
SW16
Tooting Bec
St Anselm's RC Prim Sch
HURON RD
STREATHBOURNE RD
SW17
DRAKEFIELD RD
LOUISVILLE RD
ELMBOURNE RD
HILLBURY RD
Tooting Bec Common
Capital Ring
DR JOHNSON AVE
Tenn Cts
WHEATLANDS
STAPLETON RD
NETHERFIELD
DAFFORNE RD
ROMBERG RD
FOULSER RD
MONTANA RD
A214
TOPSHAM RD
AVOCA RD
BRUDENELL RD
HILLBROOK RD
BARRINGER SQ
TREHERNE CT
TOOTING BEC RD
1 BRUCE LAWNS
2 BRUCE HALL MEWS
MACMILLAN WAY
B24
OLDFIELD HO
CROSSLEIGH
Streatham Park
181
Tooting Bec Lido
Horse Ride
FISHERS CL 1
SAXONCROFT HO 2
WELLINGTON MEWS 3
GARRAD'S RD
B242
PINKERTON PL
TARRINGTON CL
BECMEAD AVE
STEEP HILL
OCKLEY RD
PRENTIS RD
THE GLEBE
NORTH DR
SHEPLEY
A23
28
29
30
72
73
74
75

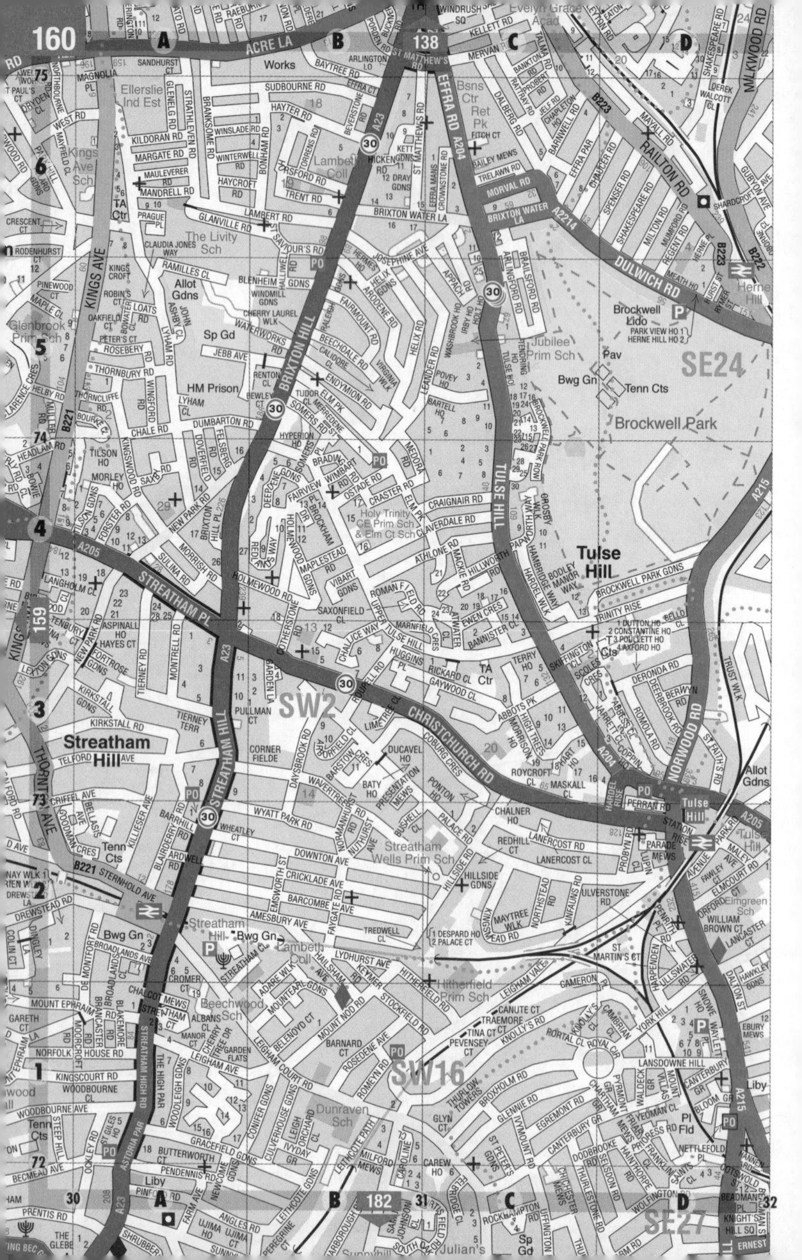

160
A
B
C
D
138
ACRE LA
ST MATTHEW'S RD
Works
EFFRA RD
Bsns Ctr
Ret Pk
MAGNOLIA PL
Ellerslie Ind Est
KILDORAN RD
MARGATE RD
MANDRELL RD
Kings Ave Sch
Lambeth Coll
SUDBOURNE RD
HAYTER RD
BRIXTON WATER LA
LAMBERT RD
GLANVILLE RD
The Livity Sch
MORVAL RD
DULWICH RD
RAILTON RD
MILKWOOD RD
Brockwell Lido
SE24
Brockwell Park
Tenn Cts
Bwg Gn
Pav
Jubilee Prim Sch
KINGS AVE
Allot Gdns
Sp Gd
HM Prison
JEBB AVE
BRIXTON HILL
TULSE HILL
Tulse Hill
Glenbrook Prim Sch
STREATHAM PL
CHRISTCHURCH RD
Holy Trinity CE Prim Sch & Elm Ct Sch
BROCKWELL PARK GDNS
TRINITY RISE
SW2
Streatham Hill
STREATHAM HILL
NORWOOD RD
Allot Gdns
Streatham Wells Prim Sch
WYATT PARK RD
DOWNTON AVE
CRICKLADE AVE
BARCOMBE AVE
AMESBURY AVE
STERNHOLD AVE
Lambeth Coll
Hitherfield Prim Sch
Beechwood Sch
LEIGHAM COURT RD
SW16
Dunraven Sch
KNOLLY'S RD
ROYAL CIR
LANSDOWNE HILL
Elmgreen Sch
Liby
Pl Fld
Tenn Cts
182
SE27
30
31
32

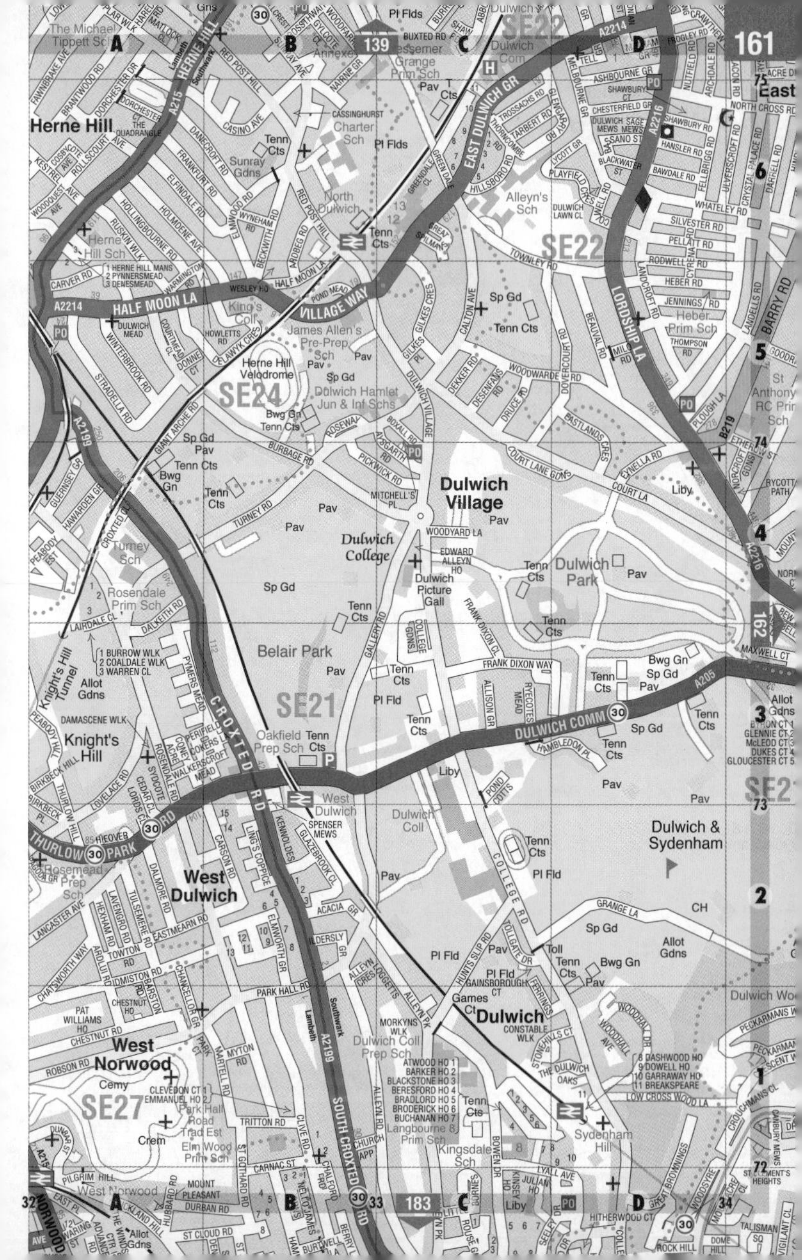

161
A
B
C
D
139
183
SE22
SE24
SE21
SE27
Herne Hill
Dulwich Village
Dulwich College
West Dulwich
West Norwood
Knight's Hill
Dulwich
Dulwich & Sydenham
Dulwich Park
Belair Park
Herne Hill Velodrome
Dulwich Picture Gall
Alleyn's Sch
Charter Sch
North Dulwich
James Allen's Pre-Prep Sch
Dulwich Hamlet Jun & Inf Schs
Rosendale Prim Sch
Turney Sch
Herne Hill Sch
Heber Prim Sch
St Anthony RC Prim Sch
Oakfield Prep Sch
Dulwich Coll
Dulwich Coll Prep Sch
Langbourne Prim Sch
Kingsdale Sch
Elm Wood Prim Sch
Rosemead Prep Sch
Sydenham Hill
Knight's Hill Tunnel
Park Hall Road Trad Est
HALF MOON LA
VILLAGE WAY
EAST DULWICH GR
LORDSHIP LA
DULWICH COMM
CROXTED RD
SOUTH CROXTED RD
HERNE HILL
THURLOW PARK RD
COLLEGE RD
GALLERY RD
DULWICH VILLAGE
COURT LA
GRANGE LA
RED POST HILL
TURNEY RD
BURBAGE RD
CALTON AVE
WOODWARDE RD
DOVERCOURT RD
BARRY RD
ACACIA GR
PARK HALL RD
HUNTS SLIP RD
FRANK DIXON WAY
ALLISON GR
GIPSY HILL
LOW CROSS WOOD LA
A2214
A215
A2199
A2216
A205
B219
Tenn Cts
Sp Gd
Pav
Pl Flds
Bwg Gn
Allot Gdns
Liby
Cemy
Crem

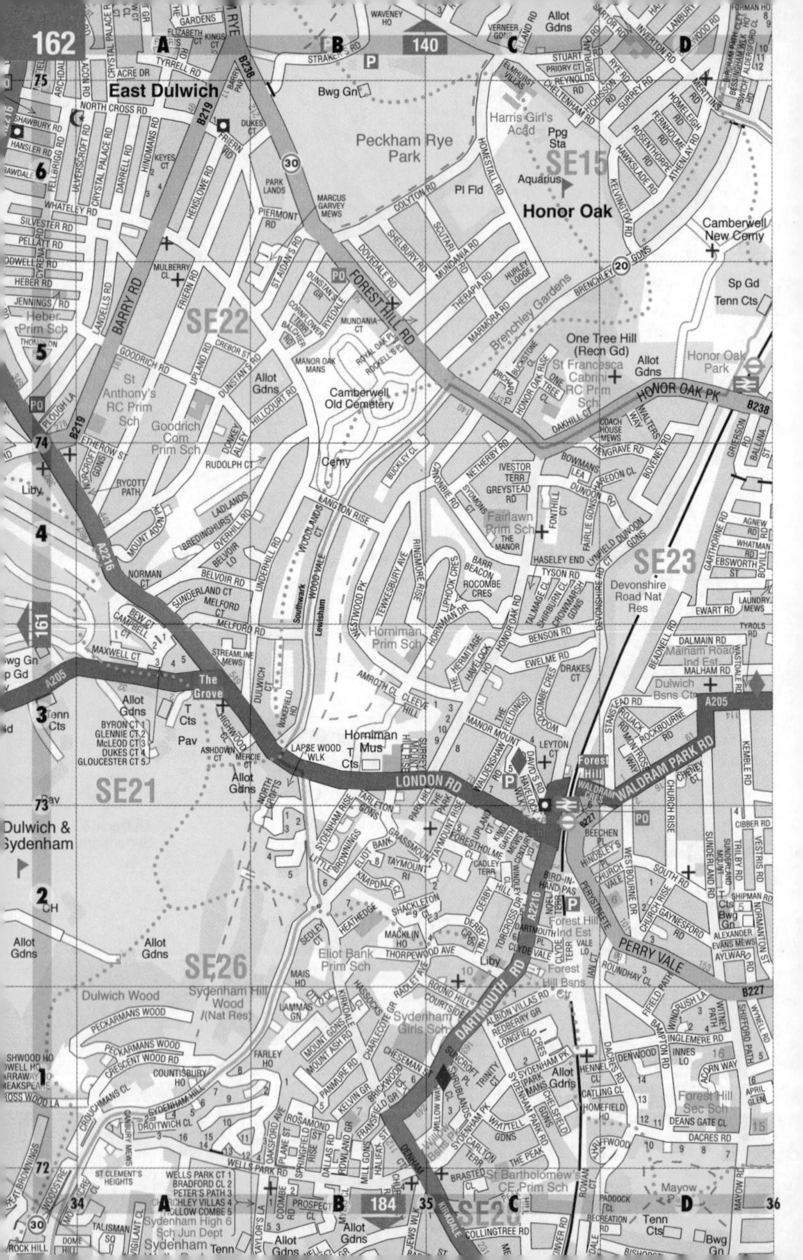
East Dulwich
Peckham Rye Park
Honor Oak
SE15
SE22
SE23
SE21
SE26
Camberwell Old Cemetery
Camberwell New Cemy
One Tree Hill (Recn Gd)
Honor Oak Park
Brenchley Gardens
Harris Girl's Acad
Horniman Mus
Horniman Prim Sch
Forest Hill
Dulwich & Sydenham
Dulwich Wood
Sydenham Hill Wood (Nat Res)
Eliot Bank Prim Sch
Sydenham Girls Sch
Forest Hill Sec Sch
Devonshire Road Nat Res
St Anthony's RC Prim Sch
Goodrich Com Prim Sch
Heber Prim Sch
Fairlawn Prim Sch
St Francesca Cabrini RC Prim Sch
St Bartholomew's CE Prim Sch
Sydenham High Sch Jun Dept
Forest Hill Ind Est
Forest Hill Bsns Ctr
Dulwich Bsns Ctr
Malham Road Ind Est
Mayow Pk
LONDON RD
DARTMOUTH RD
HONOR OAK PK
FOREST HILL RD
BARRY RD
PERRY VALE
WALDRAM PARK RD
SYDENHAM HILL
WELLS PARK RD
KIRKDALE
A2216
A205
B238
B219
B227
140
161
184
A
B
C
D
1
2
3
4
5
6
34
35
36
72
73
74
75

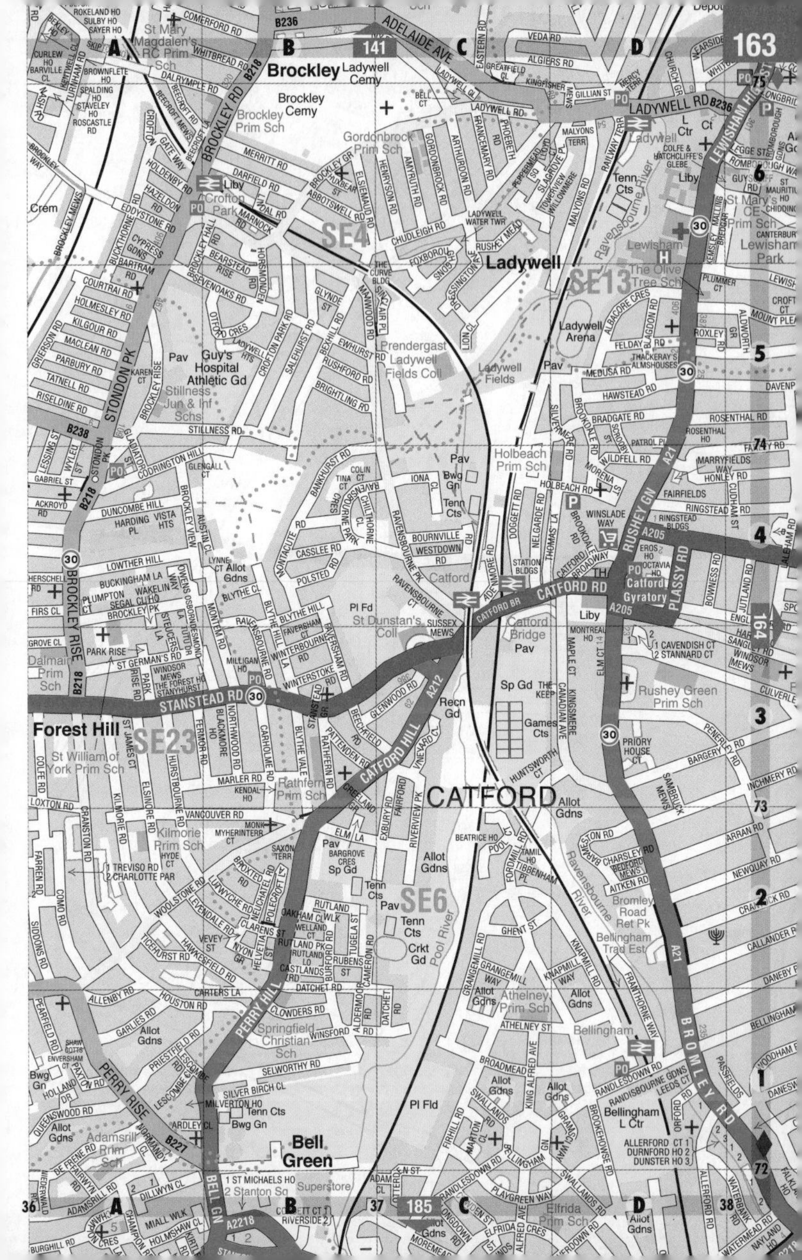

163
141
164
185
Brockley
Ladywell Cemy
Brockley Cemy
Brockley Prim Sch
St Mary Magdalen's RC Prim Sch
Gordonbrock Prim Sch
Crofton Park
SE4
Ladywell
SE13
Lewisham
The Olive Tree Sch
Ladywell Arena
Ladywell Fields
Prendergast Ladywell Fields Coll
Guy's Hospital Athletic Gd
Stillness Jun & Inf Schs
Holbeach Prim Sch
Catford
Catford Gyratory
St Dunstan's Coll
Catford Bridge
Rushey Green Prim Sch
Forest Hill
SE23
St William of York Prim Sch
Rathfern Prim Sch
Kilmorie Prim Sch
CATFORD
SE6
Bromley Road Ret Pk
Bellingham Trad Est
Athelney Prim Sch
Bellingham
Springfield Christian Sch
Bellingham L Ctr
Adamsrill Prim Sch
Bell Green
Superstore
Elfrida Prim Sch
Dalmain Prim Sch
St Mary's CE Prim Sch
Lewisham Park
Crem
ADELAIDE AVE
LADYWELL RD
BROCKLEY RD
STONDON PK
BROCKLEY RISE
STANSTEAD RD
CATFORD RD
CATFORD HILL
RUSHEY GN
BROMLEY RD
LEWISHAM HILL
PERRY HILL
PERRY RISE
BELL GN
PLASSY RD
RAVENSBOURNE PK
Ravensbourne River
Pool River
B236
B218
B238
B227
A21
A205
A212
A2218
A
B
C
D
1
2
3
4
5
6
36
37
38
72
73
74
75

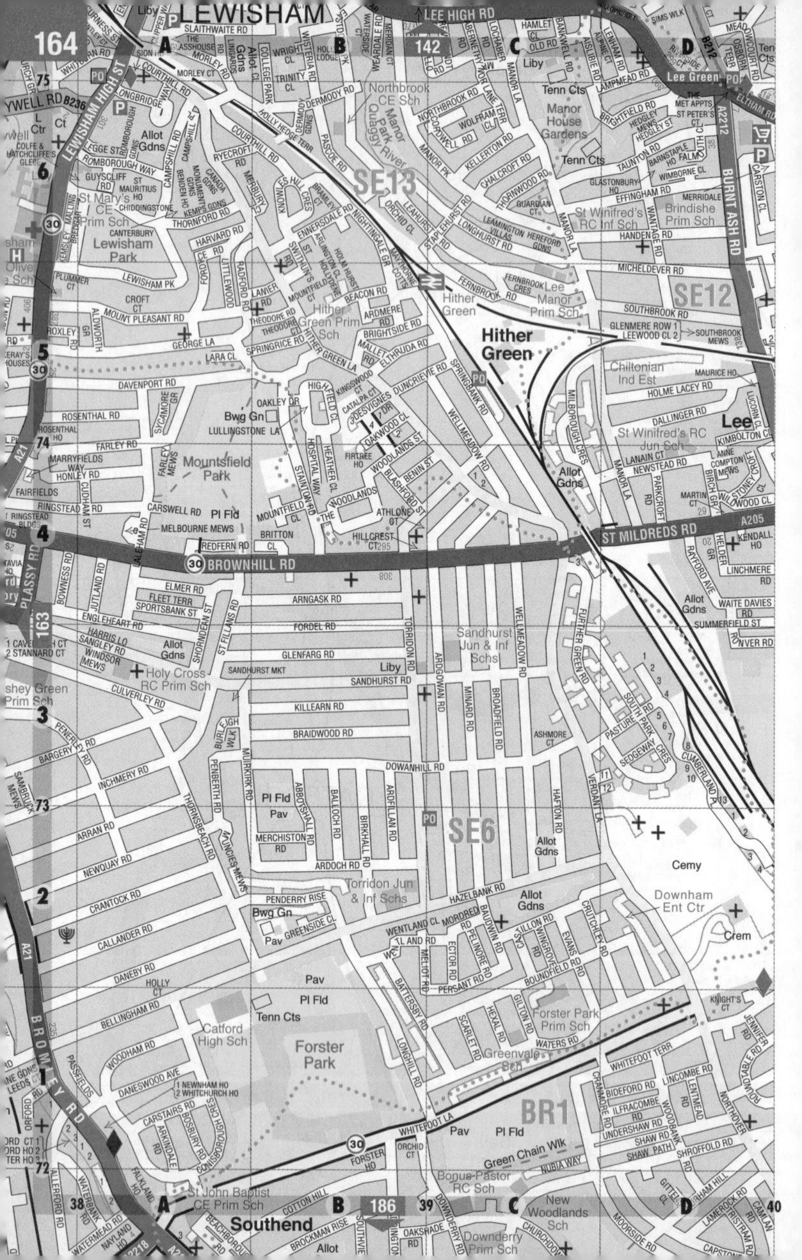
164
LEWISHAM
LEE HIGH RD
142
A
B
C
D
SE13
SE12
SE6
BR1
Lee Green
Lee
Hither Green
Southend
LEWISHAM HIGH ST
BURNT ASH RD
BROWNHILL RD
ST MILDREDS RD
BROMLEY RD
PLASSY RD
WHITEFOOT LA
Lewisham Park
Mountsfield Park
Forster Park
Manor House Gardens
Manor Park
Quaggy River
Northbrook CE Sch
St Mary's CE Prim Sch
St Winifred's RC Inf Sch
Brindishe Prim Sch
Lee Manor Prim Sch
Hither Green Prim Sch
Chiltonian Ind Est
St Winifred's RC Jun Sch
Sandhurst Jun & Inf Schs
Holy Cross RC Prim Sch
Torridon Jun & Inf Schs
Catford High Sch
Forster Park Prim Sch
Greenvale Sch
Bonus Pastor RC Sch
St John Baptist CE Prim Sch
New Woodlands Sch
Downderry Prim Sch
Downham Ent Ctr
Cemy
Crem
Green Chain Wlk
Allot Gdns
Pl Fld
Pav
Tenn Cts
Bwg Gn
Liby
A21
A205
A2212
B212
B236
30
163
186
39
38
40
75
74
73
72

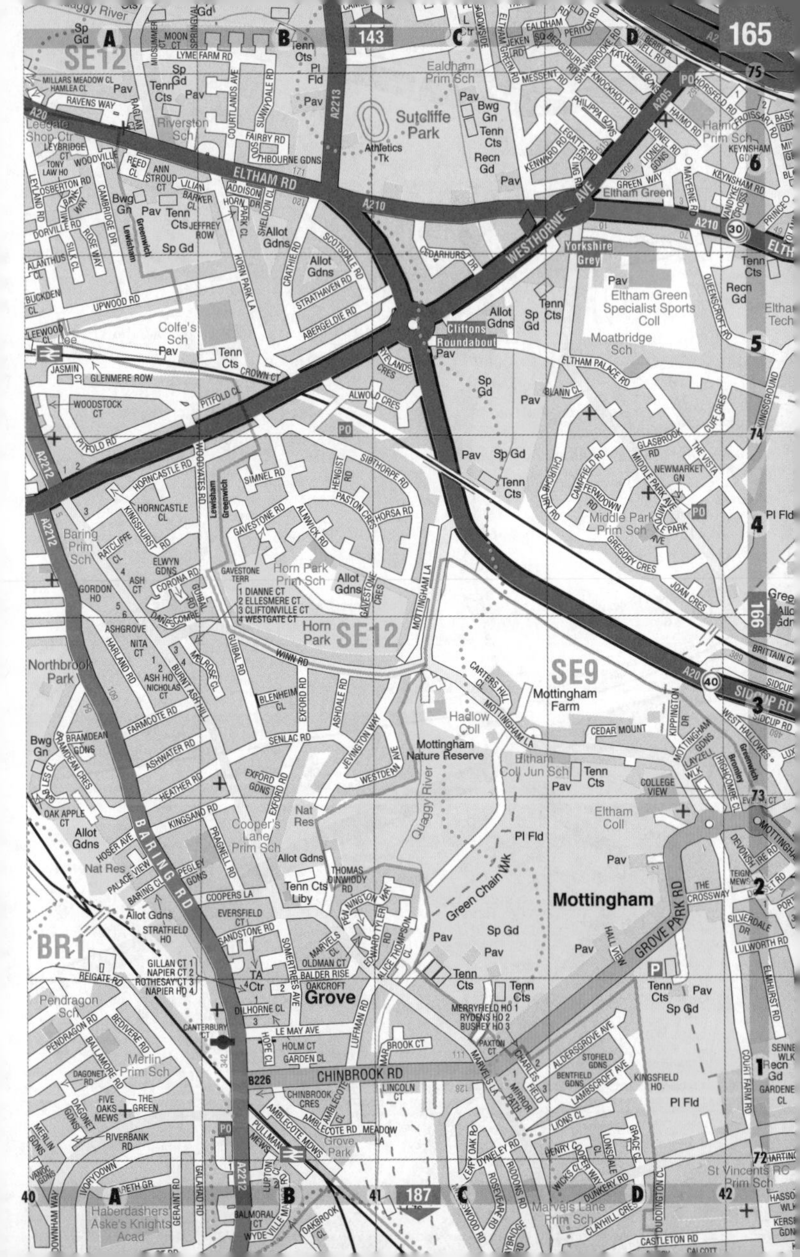

165
143
166
187
A
B
C
D
SE12
SE9
BR1
Quaggy River
ELTHAM RD
A20
A210
A2213
A2212
A205
WESTHORNE AVE
Sutcliffe Park
Athletics Tk
Eltham Prim Sch
Riverston Sch
Leegate Shop Ctr
Colfe's Sch
Cliftons Roundabout
Yorkshire Grey
Eltham Green Specialist Sports Coll
Moatbridge Sch
Haimo Prim Sch
Eltham Green
ELTHAM PALACE RD
Middle Park Prim Sch
Horn Park Prim Sch
Horn Park
Baring Prim Sch
Northbrook Park
Hadlow Coll
Mottingham Nature Reserve
Mottingham Farm
Eltham Coll Jun Sch
Eltham Coll
Quaggy River
Green Chain Wk
Mottingham
Cooper's Lane Prim Sch
BARING RD
GROVE PARK RD
CHINBROOK RD
B226
Grove Park
Pendragon Sch
Merlin Prim Sch
Haberdashers Aske's Knights Acad
Marvels Lane Prim Sch
St Vincents RC Prim Sch
SIDCUP RD
MOTTINGHAM LA
SIBTHORPE RD
WINN RD
MOTTINGHAM LA
UPWOOD RD
GLENMERE ROW
HORN PARK LA
BURNT ASH HILL
COURT FARM RD
1 DIANNE CT
2 ELLESMERE CT
3 CLIFTONVILLE CT
4 WESTGATE CT
GILLAN CT 1
NAPIER CT 2
ROTHESAY CT 3
NAPIER HO 4
MERRYFIELD HO 1
RYDENS HO 2
BUSHEY HO 3
40
41
42
72
73
74
75

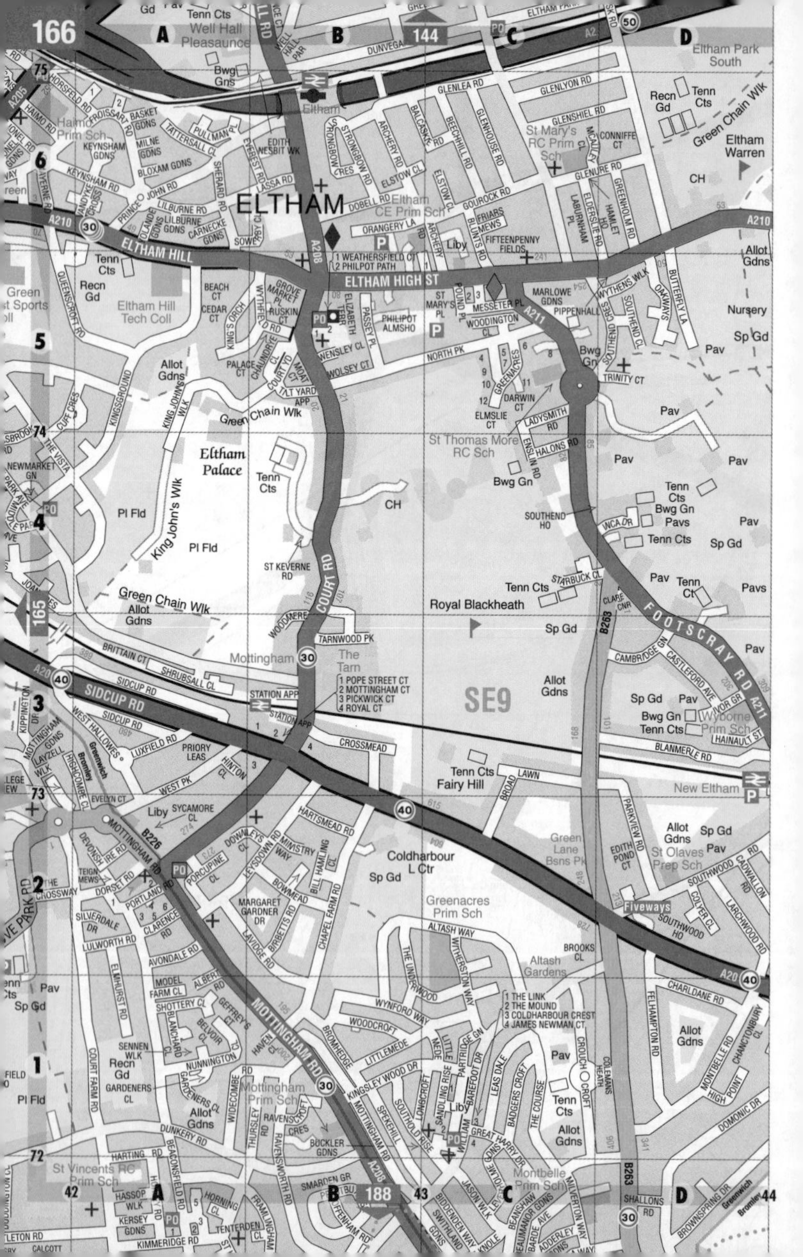
166
A
B
C
D
144
Well Hall Pleasaunce
Tenn Cts
Bwg Gns
DUNVEGAN
A2
Eltham Park South
Eltham
HORSFIELD RD
FROISSART RD
BASKET GDNS
HAIMO RD
Haimo Prim Sch
KEYNSHAM GDNS
MILNE GDNS
TATTERSALL CL
PULLMAN PL
EDITH NESBIT WK
EVEREST RD
KEYNSHAM RD
BLOXAM GDNS
SHERARD RD
LASSA RD
JOHN RD
LILBURNE RD
LILBURNE GDNS
CARNECKE GDNS
SOWE
ELTHAM
STRONGBOW RD
STRONGBOW CRES
ARCHERY RD
BALCASKIE RD
BEECHILL RD
GLENHOUSE RD
GLENLEA RD
GLENLYON RD
GLENSHIEL RD
ELSTOW CL
ELSTOW RD
DOBELL RD
Eltham CE Prim Sch
St Mary's RC Prim Sch
McAULEY CL
CONNIFFE CT
GLENURE RD
LABURNHAM PL
ELDERSLIE RD
HAMLET HO
GREENHOLM RD
GOUROCK RD
FRIARS MEWS
BLUNTS RD
FIFTEENPENNY FIELDS
ORANGERY LA
Liby
Recn Gd
Tenn Cts
Green Chain Wlk
Eltham Warren
CH
A210
ELTHAM HILL
A208
1 WEATHERSFIELD CT
2 PHILPOT PATH
ELTHAM HIGH ST
Tenn Cts
Recn Gd
Eltham Hill Tech Coll
QUEENSCROFT RD
BEACH CT
CEDAR CT
KING'S ORCH
WYTHFIELD RD
GROVE MARKET PL
RUSKIN CT
ELIZABETH TERR
PASSEY PL
PHILIPOT ALMSHO
ST MARY'S PL
POUND PL
MESSETER PL
WOODINGTON CL
MARLOWE GDNS
PIPPENHALL
WYTHENS WLK
SOUTHEND CRES
SOUTHEND CL
OAKWAYS
BUTTERFLY LA
Allot Gdns
Nursery
Sp Gd
Pav
WENSLEY CL
WOLSEY CT
NORTH PK
GREENACRES
A211
Bwg Gn
TRINITY CT
Allot Gdns
KINGSGROUND
KING JOHN'S WLK
PALACE CT
CHAUNDRYE CL
COURT YD
MOAT CT
TILT YARD APP
Green Chain Wlk
DARWIN CT
ELMSLIE CT
LADYSMITH RD
St Thomas More RC Sch
HALONS RD
ENSLIN RD
Bwg Gn
CUFF CRES
THE VISTA
NEWMARKET GN
Eltham Palace
Tenn Cts
CH
King John's Wlk
Pl Fld
Pl Fld
ST KEVERNE RD
SOUTHEND HO
WCA DR
Tenn Cts
Bwg Gn
Pavs
Sp Gd
COURT RD
Tenn Cts
STARBUCK CL
Royal Blackheath
CLARE CNR
FOOTSCRAY RD
Green Chain Wlk
Allot Gdns
WOODMERE
TARNWOOD PK
The Tarn
Mottingham
B263
Sp Gd
165
BRITTAIN CT
SHRUBSALL CL
A20
SIDCUP RD
SIDCUP RD
1 POPE STREET CT
2 MOTTINGHAM CT
3 PICKWICK CT
4 ROYAL CT
STATION APP
SE9
Allot Gdns
CAMBRIDGE GN
CASTLEFORD AVE
IVOR GR
Wyborne Prim Sch
HAINAULT ST
KIPPINGTON DR
MOTTINGHAM GDNS
LAYZELL WLK
WEST HALLOWES
LUXFIELD RD
PRIORY LEAS
HINTON CL
CROSSMEAD
BLANMERLE RD
Tenn Cts
Fairy Hill
BROAD LAWN
New Eltham
HIGHCOMBE CL
EVELYN CT
WEST PK
Liby
SYCAMORE CL
B226
MOTTINGHAM RD
DEVONSHIRE RD
HARTSMEAD RD
DOWNLEYS CL
LEYSDOWN RD
MIMSTRY WAY
BILL HAMLING CL
Coldharbour L Ctr
Sp Gd
Green Lane Bsns Pk
EDITH POND CT
PARKVIEW RD
Allot Gdns
Sp Gd
Pav
St Olaves Prep Sch
SOUTHWOOD RD
CADWALLON RD
TEIGN MEWS
THE CROSSWAY
DORSET RD
PORTLAND RD
PORCUPINE CL
BOWMEAD
MARGARET GARDNER DR
BIRBETTS RD
CHAPEL FARM RD
Greenacres Prim Sch
Fiveways
SOUTHWOOD HO
COLYER CL
LARCHWOOD RD
SILVERDALE DR
CLARENCE RD
LULWORTH RD
AVONDALE RD
LAVIDGE RD
ALTASH WAY
THE UNDERWOOD
WITHERSTON WAY
BROOKS CL
Altash Gardens
ELMHURST RD
MODEL FARM CL
ALBERT RD
SHOTTERY CL
BLANCHARD CL
BELVOIR CL
GEFFREY'S CT
WYNFORD WAY
1 THE LINK
2 THE MOUND
3 COLDHARBOUR CREST
4 JAMES NEWMAN CT
CHARLDANE RD
A20
Pav
Sp Gd
COURT FARM RD
SENNEN WLK
Recn Gd
NUNNINGTON CL
GARDENERS CL
HAVEN CL
WOODCROFT
BROMHEDGE
LITTLEMEDE
LITTLE MEDE
PARTRIDGE GN
BAREFOOT DR
LEAS DALE
Pav
CROUCH CROFT
COLEMANS HEATH
FELHAMPTON RD
Allot Gdns
CHANCTONBURY CL
MONTBELLE RD
HIGH POINT
Pl Fld
WIDECOMBE RD
Mottingham Prim Sch
RAVENSCROFT CRES
KINGSLEY WOOD DR
SPEKEHILL
SOUTHOLD RISE
LONGCROFT
SANDLING RISE
WILLIAM BAREFOOT DR
BADGERS CROFT
THE COURSE
Tenn Cts
Liby
Allot Gdns
DOMONIC DR
Allot Gdns
DUNKERY RD
THURSLEY RD
RAVENSWORTH RD
BUCKLER GDNS
GREAT HARRY DR
LEVEHURST WAY
JASON WLK
Montbelle Prim Sch
B263
HARTING RD
BEACONSFIELD RD
St Vincents RC Prim Sch
42
HASSOP WLK
KERSEY GDNS
HORNING CL
TENTERDEN CL
FRAMLINGHAM CRES
SMARDEN GR
188
43
BIDDENDEN WAY
SWITHLAND GDNS
BEANSHAW
BEAUMANOR GDNS
BARDE AVE
ADDERLEY GDNS
MILVERTON WAY
SHALLONS RD
BROWNSPRING DR
Greenwich
Bromley
44
KIMMERIDGE RD
72
73
74
75

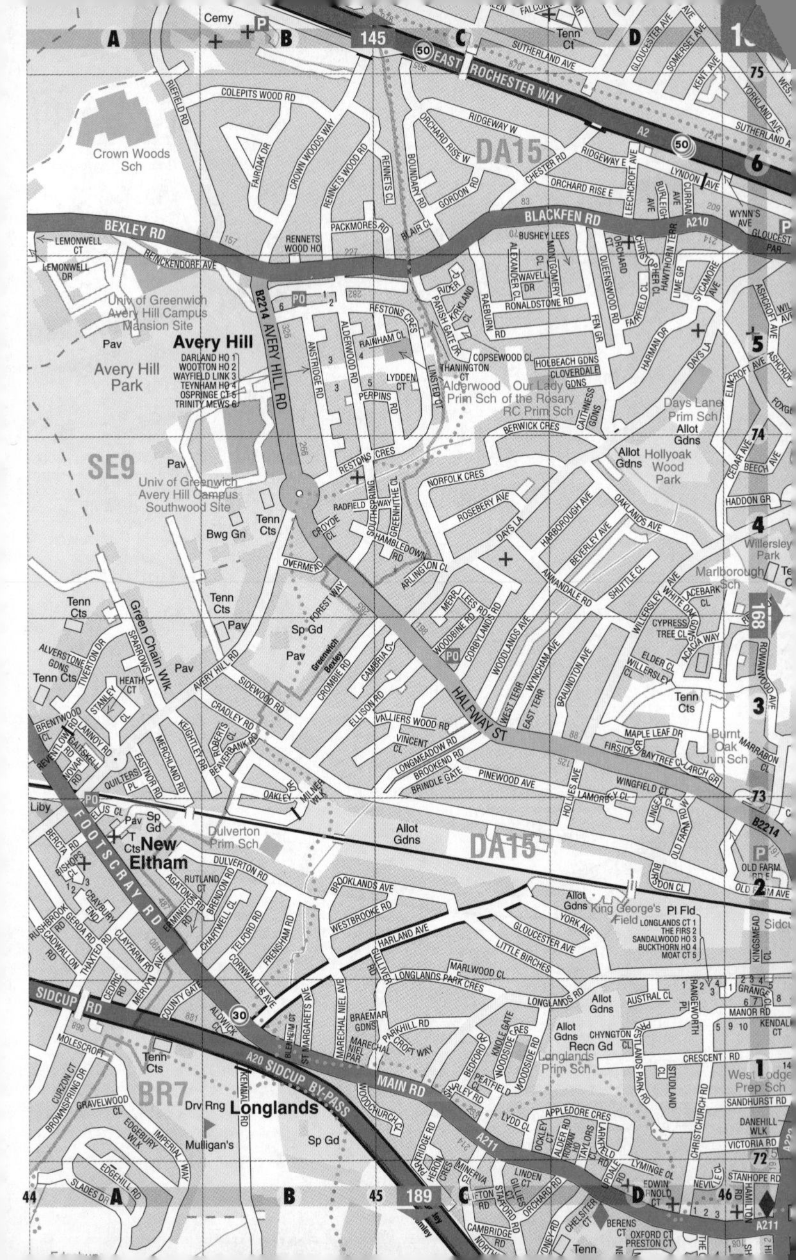

A
B
C
D
145
Cemy
Tenn Ct
50
EAST ROCHESTER WAY
SUTHERLAND AVE
GLOUCESTER AVE
SOMERSET AVE
KENT AVE
YORKLAND AVE
SUTHERLAND AVE
75
6
RIEFIELD RD
COLEPITS WOOD RD
Crown Woods Sch
FAIROAK DR
CROWN WOODS WAY
RENNETS WOOD RD
RENNETS CL
BOUNDARY RD
ORCHARD RISE W
RIDGEWAY W
DA15
CHESTER RD
RIDGEWAY E
LEECHCROFT AVE
A2
LYNDON AVE
ORCHARD RISE E
BURLEIGH AVE
CURRAN AVE
GORDON RD
WYNN'S AVE
BEXLEY RD
BLACKFEN RD
A210
GLOUCESTER PAR
PACKMORES RD
RENNETS WOOD HO
BLAIR CL
LEMONWELL CT
LEMONWELL DR
REINCKENDORF AVE
BUSHEY LEES
ALEXANDER CL
MONTGOMERY CL
WAVELL DR
QUEENSWOOD RD
ORCHARD CT
CHRISTOPHER CL
HAWTHORN TERR
LIME GR
SYCAMORE AVE
ASHCROFT AVE
B2214
PO
RESTONS CRES
RIDER CL
PARISH GATE DR
KIRKLAND CL
RONALDSTONE RD
RAEBURN RD
FEN GR
FAIRFIELD CL
Univ of Greenwich Avery Hill Campus Mansion Site
Pav
Avery Hill
DARLAND HO 1
WOOTTON HO 2
WAYFIELD LINK 3
TEYNHAM HO 4
OSPRINGE CT 5
TRINITY MEWS 6
AVERY HILL RD
ANSTRIDGE RD
ALDERWOOD RD
RAINHAM CL
LYDDEN CT
PERPINS RD
LINSTED CT
THANINGTON CT
COPSEWOOD CL
HOLBEACH GDNS
CLOVERDALE GDNS
HARMAN DR
DAYS LA
5
Avery Hill Park
Alderwood Prim Sch
Our Lady of the Rosary RC Prim Sch
CAITHNESS GDNS
Days Lane Prim Sch
Allot Gdns
ELMCROFT AVE
FOXGLOVE
BERWICK CRES
SE9
Univ of Greenwich Avery Hill Campus Southwood Site
RESTONS CRES
Hollyoak Wood Park
74
CEDAR AVE
BEECH AVE
HADDON GR
RADFIELD WAY
SOUTHSPRING
GREENHITHE CL
NORFOLK CRES
ROSEBERY AVE
HARBOROUGH AVE
OAKLANDS AVE
Bwg Gn
Tenn Cts
CROYDE CL
HAMBLEDOWN RD
BEVERLEY AVE
4
Willersley Park
Marlborough Sch
OVERMEAD
ARLINGTON CL
ANNANDALE RD
SHUTTLE CL
WILLERSLEY AVE
WHITE OAK GDNS
LACEBARK CL
168
FOREST WAY
Green Chain Wlk
Sp Gd
MERRILEES RD
CORBYLANDS RD
CYPRESS TREE CL
ACACIA WAY
ROWANWOOD AVE
Greenwich
Bexley
WOODBINE RD
WOODLANDS AVE
WYNCHAM AVE
BRAUNDTON AVE
ELDER CL
WILLERSLEY
ALVERSTONE GDNS
TIVERTON DR
SPARROWS LA
AVERY HILL RD
SIDEWOOD RD
CROMBIE RD
CAMBRIA CL
HEATH CT
STANLEY CL
ELLISON RD
HALFWAY ST
WEST TERR
EAST TERR
3
BRENTWOOD CL
LANNOY RD
CRADLEY RD
KEIGHTLEY DR
VALLIERS WOOD RD
VINCENT CL
MAPLE LEAF DR
FIRSIDE GR
BAYTREE CL
LARCH GR
Burnt Oak Jun Sch
MARRABON CL
REVENTLOW RD
GAITSKELL
NOVAR
ROBERTS CL
BEAVERBANK RD
LONGMEADOW RD
BROOKEND RD
BRINDLE GATE
PINEWOOD AVE
QUILTERS PL
EASTNOR RD
MERCHLAND RD
HOLMES AVE
WINGFIELD CT
LAMORBEY CL
LINGEY CL
OLD FARM RD W
73
OAKLEY
MILNER WLK
Liby
ELLIS CL
FOOTSCRAY RD
Allot Gdns
B2214
Dulverton Prim Sch
New Eltham
DA15
BERCTA RD
BISHOPS CL
DULVERTON RD
RUTLAND CT
AGATON RD
BRENDON RD
BROOKLANDS AVE
BURSDON CL
OLD FARM RD E
OLD FARM AVE
2
CRAYBURY END
RUSHBROOK RD
GERDA RD
CADWALLON RD
EMMINGTON CL
CHARTWELL CL
TELFORD RD
FRENSHAM RD
WESTBROOKE RD
HARLAND AVE
YORK AVE
King George's Field
Pl Fld
LONGLANDS CT 1
THE FIRS 2
SANDALWOOD HO 3
BUCKTHORN HO 4
MOAT CT 5
KINGSMEAD
GLOUCESTER AVE
LITTLE BIRCHES
CLAYFARM RD
THAXTED RD
MERVYN AVE
CORNWALLIS AVE
GULLIVER RD
MARLWOOD CL
LONGLANDS PARK CRES
LONGLANDS RD
CEDRIC RD
COUNTY GATE
SIDCUP RD
30
ALDWICK CL
BLENHEIM CT
ST MARGARETS AVE
MARECHAL NIEL AVE
BRAEMAR GDNS
MARECHAL NIEL PAR
PARKHILL RD
CROFT WAY
KNOLE GATE
WOODSIDE CRES
WOODSIDE RD
AUSTRAL CL
CHYNGTON CL
Recn Gd
RANGEWORTH PL
GRANGE CL
MANOR RD
KENDALE CT
MOLESCROFT
A20 SIDCUP BY-PASS
MAIN RD
BEDFORD RD
PEATFIELD CL
Longlands Prim Sch
STUDLAND
CRESCENT RD
1
West Lodge Prep Sch
CURZON CT
BROWNSPRING DR
Tenn Cts
BR7
KEMNAL RD
WOODCHURCH CL
A211
GRAVELWOOD CL
Drv Rng
Longlands
CHRISTCHURCH RD
SANDHURST RD
EDGEBURY WLK
IMPERIAL WAY
Mulligan's
APPLEDORE CRES
LYDD CL
DANEHILL WLK
VICTORIA RD
72
PARTRIDGE RD
HERON CRES
MINERVA CL
LINDEN CT
OCKLEY CT
ALDER RD
ROWAN HO
TAYLORS CL
LARKFIELD
UPDALE RD
LYMINGE CL
EDWIN ARNOLD CT
NEVILLE CL
STANHOPE RD
HAMILTON RD
EDGEHILL RD
SLADES DR
44
45
189
46
CLIFTON RD
STAFFORD RD
GILLIES CT
ORCHARD RD
CAMBRIDGE RD
CHELSITER CT
BERENS CT
OXFORD CT
PRESTON CT
Tenn

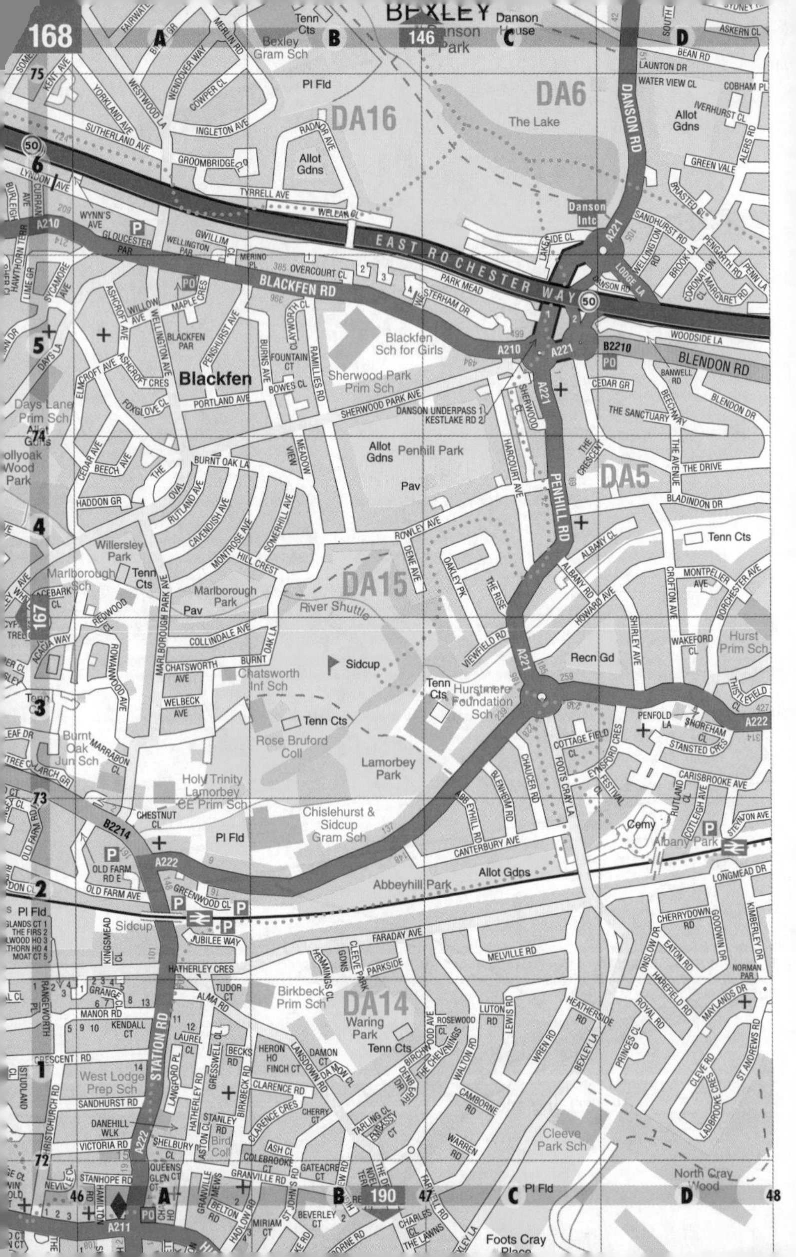
168
A
B
C
D
146
190
167
BEXLEY
Danson House
Danson Park
Tenn Cts
Bexley Gram Sch
Pl Fld
DA16
DA6
DA5
DA15
DA14
The Lake
Allot Gdns
Blackfen
Danson Intc
EAST ROCHESTER WAY
BLACKFEN RD
BLENDON RD
DANSON RD
PENHILL RD
STATION RD
A210
A221
A222
A211
B2210
B2214
FAIRWATER
BIRCH GR
MERLIN RD
WENDOVER WAY
COWPER CL
WESTWOOD LA
YORKLAND AVE
KENT AVE
SUTHERLAND AVE
INGLETON AVE
RADNOR AVE
GROOMBRIDGE CL
TYRRELL AVE
WELLAN CL
LYNDON AVE
CURRAN AVE
BURLEIGH
WYNN'S AVE
GLOUCESTER PAR
GWILLIM CL
WELLINGTON PAR
MERINO PL
OVERCOURT CL
PARK MEAD
WESTERHAM DR
HAWTHORN TERR
LIME GR
SYCAMORE AVE
ASHCROFT AVE
WILLOW AVE
WELLINGTON AVE
MAPLE CRES
PENSHURST AVE
BLACKFEN PAR
BURNS AVE
CLAYWORTH CL
FOUNTAIN CT
RAMILLIES RD
BOWES CL
Blackfen Sch for Girls
Sherwood Park Prim Sch
SHERWOOD PARK AVE
DANSON UNDERPASS 1
KESTLAKE RD 2
SHERWOOD CL
LAKESIDE CL
LODGE LA
DANSON RD
SANDHURST RD
WELLINGTON RD
BROOK LA
PENGARTH RD
PENN LA
CORONATION CL
MARGARET RD
WOODSIDE LA
BANWELL RD
CEDAR GR
BLENDON DR
THE SANCTUARY
BEECHWAY
THE CRESCENT
THE AVENUE
THE DRIVE
BLADINDON DR
DAYS LA
ELMCROFT AVE
ASHCROFT CRES
FOXGLOVE CL
PORTLAND AVE
Days Lane Prim Sch
Hollyoak Wood Park
CEDAR AVE
BEECH AVE
THE OVAL
BURNT OAK LA
MEADOW VIEW
Allot Gdns
Penhill Park
Pav
HARCOURT AVE
HADDON GR
RUTLAND AVE
CAVENDISH AVE
SOMERHILL AVE
MONTROSE AVE
HILL CREST
ROWLEY AVE
DENE AVE
OAKLEY PK
THE RISE
ALBANY CL
ALBANY RD
HOWARD AVE
SHIRLEY AVE
CROFTON AVE
MONTPELIER AVE
DORCHESTER AVE
Willersley Park
Marlborough Sch
Marlborough Park
River Shuttle
MARLBOROUGH PARK AVE
REDWOOD CL
ACACIA WAY
ROWANWOOD AVE
COLLINDALE AVE
BURNT OAK LA
CHATSWORTH AVE
Chatsworth Inf Sch
Sidcup
VIEWFIELD RD
Hurstmere Foundation Sch
Recn Gd
WAKEFORD CL
Hurst Prim Sch
THISTLEFIELD CL
WELBECK AVE
Rose Bruford Coll
Lamorbey Park
Burnt Oak Jun Sch
MARRABON CL
LARCH GR
Holy Trinity Lamorbey CE Prim Sch
CHESTNUT CL
Chislehurst & Sidcup Gram Sch
COTTAGE FIELD CL
FOOTS CRAY LA
CHAUCER RD
BLENHEIM RD
ABBEYHILL RD
EYNSFORD CRES
FESTIVAL CL
PENFOLD LA
SHOREHAM CL
STANSTED CRES
CARISBROOKE AVE
RUTLAND CL
COTLEIGH AVE
STEYNTON AVE
Cemy
Albany Park
CANTERBURY AVE
OLD FARM RD
OLD FARM RD E
OLD FARM AVE
Pl Fld
Allot Gdns
Abbeyhill Park
GREENWOOD CL
LONGMEAD DR
Sidcup
JUBILEE WAY
KINGSMEAD CL
FARADAY AVE
HEMMINGS CL
CLEEVE PARK GDNS
PARKSIDE
MELVILLE RD
CHERRYDOWN RD
GOODWIN DR
KIMBERLEY DR
ONSLOW DR
EATON RD
NORMAN PAR
HATHERLEY CRES
TUDOR CT
ALMA RD
GRANGE CL
MANOR RD
KENDALL CT
Birkbeck Prim Sch
Waring Park
Tenn Cts
LUTON RD
LEWIS RD
ROSEWOOD CL
BIRCHWOOD AVE
THE CHEVENINGS
HEATHERSIDE RD
HAREFIELD RD
MAYLANDS DR
ROYAL RD
PRINCES CL
LAUREL CL
LANGFORD PL
GRESSWELL CL
BECKS RD
HERON HO
FINCH CT
DAMON CT
LANSDOWNE RD
DAMON CL
DENBEARY DR
WALTON RD
WREN RD
BEXLEY LA
CLEVE RD
LADBROOKE CRES
ST ANDREWS RD
CRESCENT RD
STUDLAND
West Lodge Prep Sch
CHRISTCHURCH RD
SANDHURST RD
HATHERLEY RD
BIRKBECK RD
CLARENCE RD
CLARENCE CRES
CHERRY CT
TARLING CL
EMBASSY CT
CAMBORNE RD
Cleeve Park Sch
DANEHILL WLK
STANLEY RD
Bird Coll
VICTORIA RD
SHELBURY CL
ASTON CL
ASH CL
COLEBROOKE CT
GATEACRE CT
WARREN RD
North Cray Wood
STANHOPE RD
QUEENS GLEN CT
GRANVILLE MEWS
GRANVILLE RD
ST JOHNS RD
NOEL TERR
THE DRIVE
FAIRFIELD RD
BELTON RD
HADLOW RD
MIRIAM CT
BEVERLEY CT
CHARLES CL
THE LAWNS
Foots Cray Place
RANGEWORTH PL
HAMILTON RD
NEVILLE CL
46
47
48
72
73
74
75
1
2
3
4
5
6

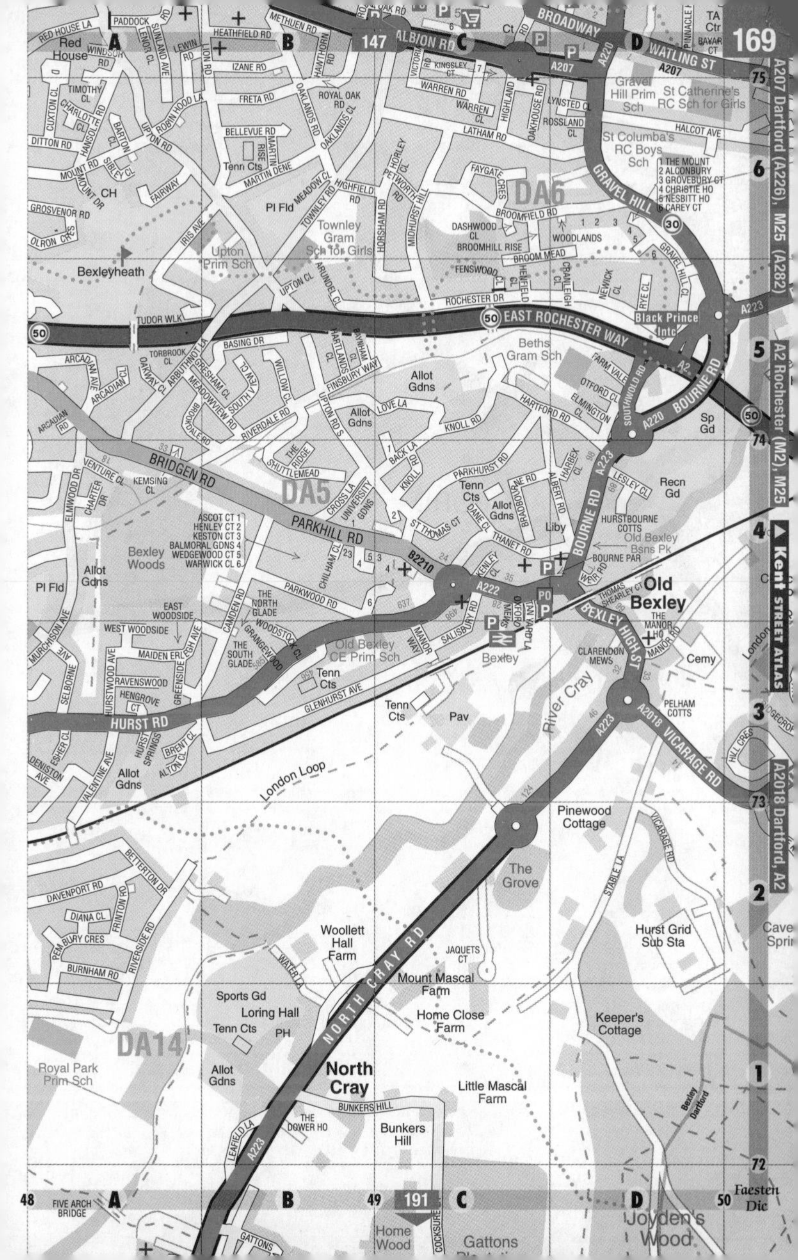
169
A
B
C
D
147
191
48
49
50
75
6
5
74
4
3
73
2
1
72
A207 Dartford (A226), M25 (A282)
A2 Rochester (M2), M25
Kent STREET ATLAS
A2018 Dartford, A2
RED HOUSE LA
PADDOCK
LENOR CL
SUNLAND AVE
Red House
WINDSOR RD
HEATHFIELD RD
LEWIN RD
LION RD
METHUEN RD
HAWTHORN RD
ALBION RD
ROYAL OAK RD
BROADWAY
WATLING ST
A207
A220
TA Ctr
PINNACLE
BAYARD CT
Ct
TIMOTHY CL
CHARLOTTE CL
CUXTON CL
HANSOL RD
BARTON CL
IZANE RD
FRETA RD
ROBIN HOOD LA
UPTON RD
OAKLANDS RD
OAKLANDS CL
VICTORIA RD
KINGSLEY CT
WARREN RD
WARREN CL
HIGHLAND RD
OAKHOUSE RD
LYNSTED CL
ROSSLAND CL
Gravel Hill Prim Sch
St Catherine's RC Sch for Girls
HALCOT AVE
St Columba's RC Boys Sch
1 THE MOUNT
2 ALCONBURY
3 GROVEBURY CT
4 CHRISTIE HO
5 NESBITT HO
6 CAREY CT
DITTON RD
BELLEVUE RD
MARTIN RISE
LATHAM RD
HORLEY CL
PETWORTH RD
MOUNT RD
MOUNT DR
SIBLEY CL
Tenn Cts
MARTIN DENE
FAYGATE CRES
DA6
GRAVEL HILL
CH
FAIRWAY
MEADOW CL
HIGHFIELD RD
TOWNLEY RD
HORSHAM RD
MIDHURST HILL
BROOMFIELD RD
GROSVENOR RD
Pl Fld
Townley Gram Sch for Girls
DASHWOOD CL
BROOMHILL RISE
WOODLANDS
OLRON CRES
IRIS AVE
Upton Prim Sch
BROOM MEAD
GRAVEL HILL CL
Bexleyheath
FENSWOOD CL
HENFIELD CL
CRANLEIGH CL
NEWICK CL
RYE CL
UPTON CL
ARUNDEL CL
ROCHESTER DR
A223
TUDOR WLK
EAST ROCHESTER WAY
Black Prince Intc
50
BASING DR
BAYNHAM CL
HARTLANDS CL
TORBROOK CL
Beths Gram Sch
FARM VALE
ARCADIAN AVE
ARCADIAN CL
OAKWAY CL
ARBUTHNOT LA
GRESHAM CL
SOUTH VIEW CL
WILLOW CL
FINSBURY WAY
Allot Gdns
OTFORD CL
SOUTHWOLD RD
A2
BOURNE RD
MEADOWVIEW RD
RIVERDALE RD
UPTON RD S
LOVE LA
HARTFORD RD
ELMINGTON CL
ARCADIAN RD
BROOKDALE RD
KNOLL RD
A220
Sp Gd
BACK LA
THE RIDGE
SHUTTLEMEAD
PARKHURST RD
HARBEX CL
BRIDGEN RD
VENTURE CL
KEMSING CL
ELMWOOD DR
CHARTER DR
DA5
CROSS LA
UNIVERSITY GDNS
Tenn Cts
BRADBOURNE RD
ALBERT RD
LESLEY CL
Recn Gd
HURSTBOURNE COTTS
ASCOT CT 1
HENLEY CT 2
KESTON CT 3
BALMORAL GDNS 4
WEDGEWOOD CT 5
WARWICK CL 6
PARKHILL RD
ST THOMAS CT
DANE CL
THANET RD
Liby
Old Bexley Bsns Pk
Bexley Woods
CHILHAM CL
B2210
KENLEY CL
BOURNE PAR
WEIR RD
Pl Fld
PARKWOOD RD
A222
THOMAS SHEARLEY CT
Old Bexley
PO
EAST WOODSIDE
CAMDEN RD
THE NORTH GLADE
SALISBURY RD
OXFORD MEWS
TAN YARD LA
BEXLEY HIGH ST
THE MANOR HO
MANOR RD
WEST WOODSIDE
WOODSTOCK CL
GRANGEWOOD
MANOR WAY
Old Bexley CE Prim Sch
Bexley
CLARENDON MEWS
Cemy
London
MURCHISON AVE
MAIDEN ERLEGH AVE
THE SOUTH GLADE
SELBORNE AVE
HURSTWOOD AVE
RAVENSWOOD
GREENSIDE
Tenn Cts
GLENHURST AVE
River Cray
PELHAM COTTS
HENGROVE CT
Pav
A2018
VICARAGE RD
HURST RD
ESHER CL
HURST SPRINGS
BRENT CL
ALTON CL
HILL CRES
DENISTON AVE
VALENTINE AVE
London Loop
Pinewood Cottage
VICARAGE RD
BETTERTON DR
The Grove
STABLE LA
DAVENPORT RD
FRINTON RD
DIANA CL
Woollett Hall Farm
Hurst Grid Sub Sta
PEMBURY CRES
RIVERSIDE RD
NORTH CRAY RD
JAQUETS CT
BURNHAM RD
WATER LA
Mount Mascal Farm
Sports Gd
Loring Hall
Home Close Farm
Keeper's Cottage
Tenn Cts
PH
DA14
Royal Park Prim Sch
Allot Gdns
North Cray
Little Mascal Farm
Bexley
Dartford
BUNKERS HILL
THE DOWER HO
LEAFIELD LA
Bunkers Hill
FIVE ARCH BRIDGE
Home Wood
COCKSURE LA
Gattons
GATTONS
Joyden's Wood
Faesten Dic

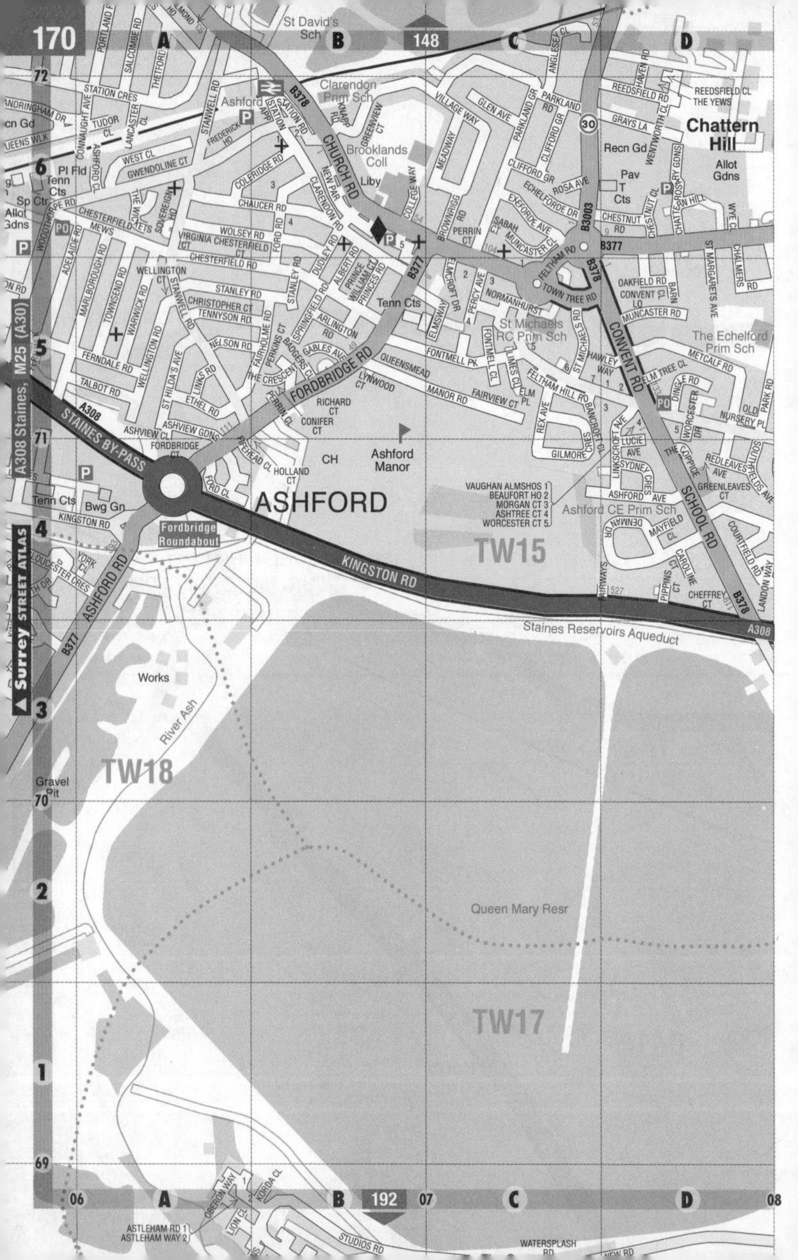

ASHFORD
Chattern Hill
TW15
TW18
TW17
Queen Mary Resr
Staines Reservoirs Aqueduct
KINGSTON RD
STAINES BY-PASS
Fordbridge Roundabout
Ashford Manor
Brooklands Coll
Clarendon Prim Sch
St David's Sch
St Michaels RC Prim Sch
The Echelford Prim Sch
Ashford CE Prim Sch
CHURCH RD
FORDBRIDGE RD
CONVENT RD
SCHOOL RD
ASHFORD RD
FELTHAM HILL RD
TOWN TREE RD
Works
River Ash
Gravel Pit
VAUGHAN ALMSHOS 1
BEAUFORT HO 2
MORGAN CT 3
ASHTREE CT 4
WORCESTER CT 5
ASTLEHAM RD 1
ASTLEHAM WAY 2
A308 Staines, M25 (A30)
Surrey STREET ATLAS
148
192

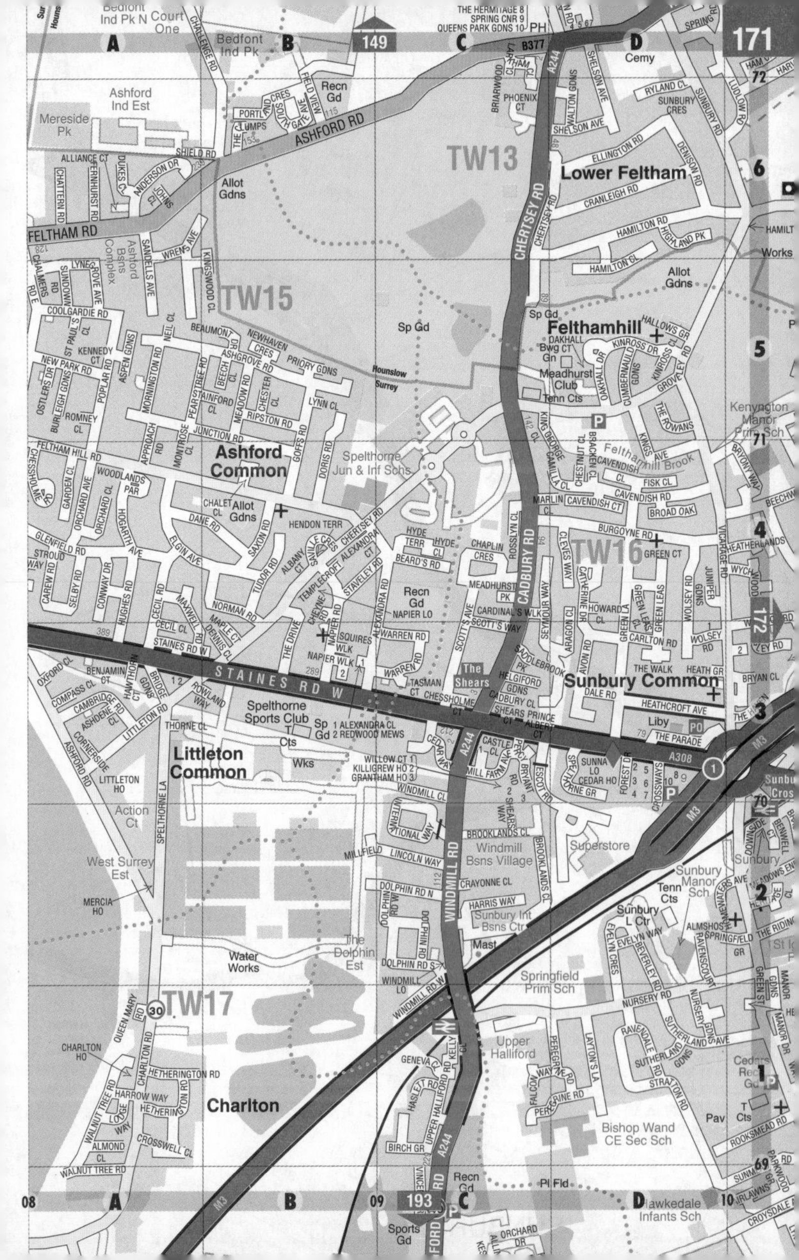

149
A
B
C
D
TW13
Lower Feltham
Feltham Hill
TW15
Ashford Common
TW16
Sunbury Common
Littleton Common
TW17
Charlton
Upper Halliford
Bedfont Ind Pk
Ashford Ind Est
Mereside Pk
Ashford Bsns Complex
Allot Gdns
Recn Gd
Sp Gd
Spelthorne Jun & Inf Schs
Spelthorne Sports Club
Meadhurst Club
Tenn Cts
Kenyngton Manor Prim Sch
Feltham Hill Brook
Windmill Bsns Village
Sunbury Int Bsns Ctr
Superstore
Sunbury Manor Sch
Sunbury L Ctr
Springfield Prim Sch
Bishop Wand CE Sec Sch
Hawkedale Infants Sch
The Dolphin Est
Water Works
West Surrey Est
Action Ct
The Shears
Hounslow
Surrey
ASHFORD RD
FELTHAM RD
FELTHAM HILL RD
CHERTSEY RD
CADBURY RD
STAINES RD W
WINDMILL RD
A244
A308
B377
M3
172
193
08
09
10
1
2
3
4
5
6

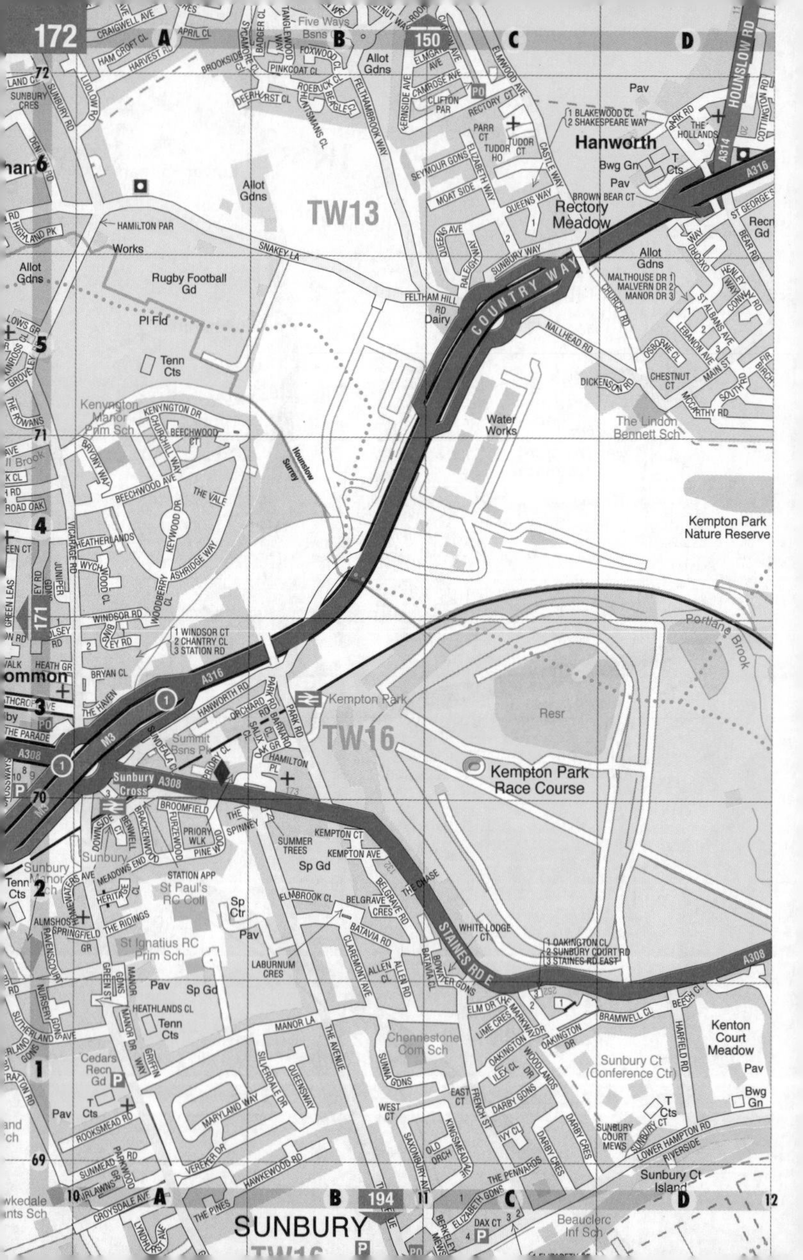
A
B
C
D
150
Five Ways Bsns Ctr
CRAIGWELL AVE
APRIL CL
HAM CROFT CL
HARVEST RD
BROOKSIDE
BADGER CL
SYCAMORE CL
TANGLEWOOD WAY
FOXWOOD CL
PINKCOAT CL
Allot Gdns
ELMGATE AVE
CAMROSE AVE
CLIFTON PAR
FERNSIDE AVE
CLIFTON AVE
ELMWOOD AVE
RECTORY CT
PO
72
LUDLOW RD
SUNBURY CRES
SUNBURY RD
DEERHURST CL
ROEBUCK CL
BEAGLE CL
HUNTSMANS CL
FELTHAMBROOK WAY
PARR CT
TUDOR HO
TUDOR CT
1 BLAKEWOOD CL
2 SHAKESPEARE WAY
Pav
PARK RD
THE HOLLANDS
HOUNSLOW RD
A314
COTTINGTON RD
Hanworth
Bwg Gn
T Cts
A316
6
SEYMOUR GDNS
ELIZABETH WAY
CASTLE WAY
MOAT SIDE
QUEENS WAY
BROWN BEAR CT
Rectory Meadow
ST GEORGE'S
Recn Gd
Allot Gdns
TW13
HAMILTON PAR
HIGHLAND PK
QUEENS AVE
RALEIGH WAY
SUNBURY WAY
OXFORD WAY
BEAR RD
Works
SNAKEY LA
Allot Gdns
MALTHOUSE DR 1
MALVERN DR 2
MANOR DR 3
HENLEY WAY
Allot Gdns
Rugby Football Gd
COUNTRY WAY
FELTHAM HILL RD
Dairy
CHURCH RD
ST ALBANS AVE
CONWAY RD
Pl Fld
5
KINROSS CL
GROVELEY RD
NALLHEAD RD
LEBANON AVE
OSBORNE CL
Tenn Cts
CHESTNUT CT
MAIN ST
DICKENSON RD
SOUTH RD
FIR RD
BIRCH
THE ROWANS
Kenyngton Manor Prim Sch
KENYNGTON DR
BEECHWOOD CT
CHURCHILL WAY
Water Works
McCARTHY RD
The Lindon Bennett Sch
71
BRYONY WAY
Hounslow
Surrey
BEECHWOOD AVE
THE VALE
KEYWOOD DR
ROAD OAK
Kempton Park Nature Reserve
4
VICARAGE RD
HEATHERLANDS
ASHRIDGE WAY
JUNIPER GDNS
WYCHWOOD CL
WOODBERRY CL
GREEN LEAS
171
WINDSOR RD
1 WINDSOR CT
2 CHANTRY CL
3 STATION RD
Portlane Brook
HEATH GR
BRYAN CL
Common
3
THE HAVEN
HANWORTH RD
PARK RD
ORCHARD RD
BARNARD CL
SALIX CL
OAK GR
Kempton Park
TW16
Resr
THE PARADE
A308
M3
Summit Bsns Pk
SUNDEALA CL
PRIORY CL
HAMILTON PL
Kempton Park Race Course
Sunbury Cross
A308
173
70
BROOMFIELD
DOWNSIDE CT
BENWELL CT
BRACKENWOOD
FURZEWOOD
PRIORY WLK
PINE WOOD
THE SPINNEY
SUMMER TREES
KEMPTON CT
KEMPTON AVE
Sunbury
Sunbury Manor Sch
MEADOWS END
STATION APP
Sp Gd
THE CHASE
132
2
Tenn Cts
WATERS AVE
HERITAGE CL
St Paul's RC Coll
Sp Ctr
ELMBROOK CL
BELGRAVE CRES
BELGRAVE RD
ALMSHOUSES
SPRINGFIELD GR
THE RIDINGS
Pav
BATAVIA RD
STAINES RD E
WHITE LODGE CT
1 OAKINGTON CL
2 SUNBURY COURT RD
3 STAINES RD EAST
A308
RAVENSCOURT
St Ignatius RC Prim Sch
LABURNUM CRES
CLAREMONT AVE
ALLEN CL
ALLEN RD
BATAVIA CL
BOWYER GDNS
NURSERY GDNS
GREEN ST
GDNS
MANOR
Pav
Sp Gd
HEATHLANDS CL
ELM DR
THE MARKWAY
BEECH CL
BRAMWELL CL
HARFIELD RD
Kenton Court Meadow
SUTHERLAND AVE
GDNS
Tenn Cts
MANOR DR
WAY
GRIFFIN
MANOR LA
THE AVENUE
Chennestone Com Sch
LIME CRES
OAKINGTON DR
OAKINGTON DR
1
Cedars Recn Gd
SILVERDALE DR
QUEENSWAY
SUNNA GDNS
ILEX CL
WOODLANDS DR
Sunbury Ct (Conference Ctr)
Pav
Bwg Gn
MARYLAND WAY
EAST CT
WEST CT
FRENCH ST
DARBY GDNS
T Cts
Pav
T Cts
ROOKSMEAD RD
KINGSMEAD AVE
SAXONBURY AVE
OLD ORCH
IVY CL
DARBY CRES
SUNBURY COURT MEWS
SUNBURY CT
LOWER HAMPTON RD
RIVERSIDE
69
SUNMEAD RD
PARKWOOD GR
VEREKER DR
HAWKEWOOD RD
THE PENNARDS
DARBY CRES
Sunbury Ct Island
10
FAIRLAWNS
CROYSDALE AVE
THE PINES
194
11
ELIZABETH GDNS
12
SUNBURY
BERKELEY MEWS
DAX CT
Beauclerc Inf Sch
LYNDHURST AVE
TW16
P
PO

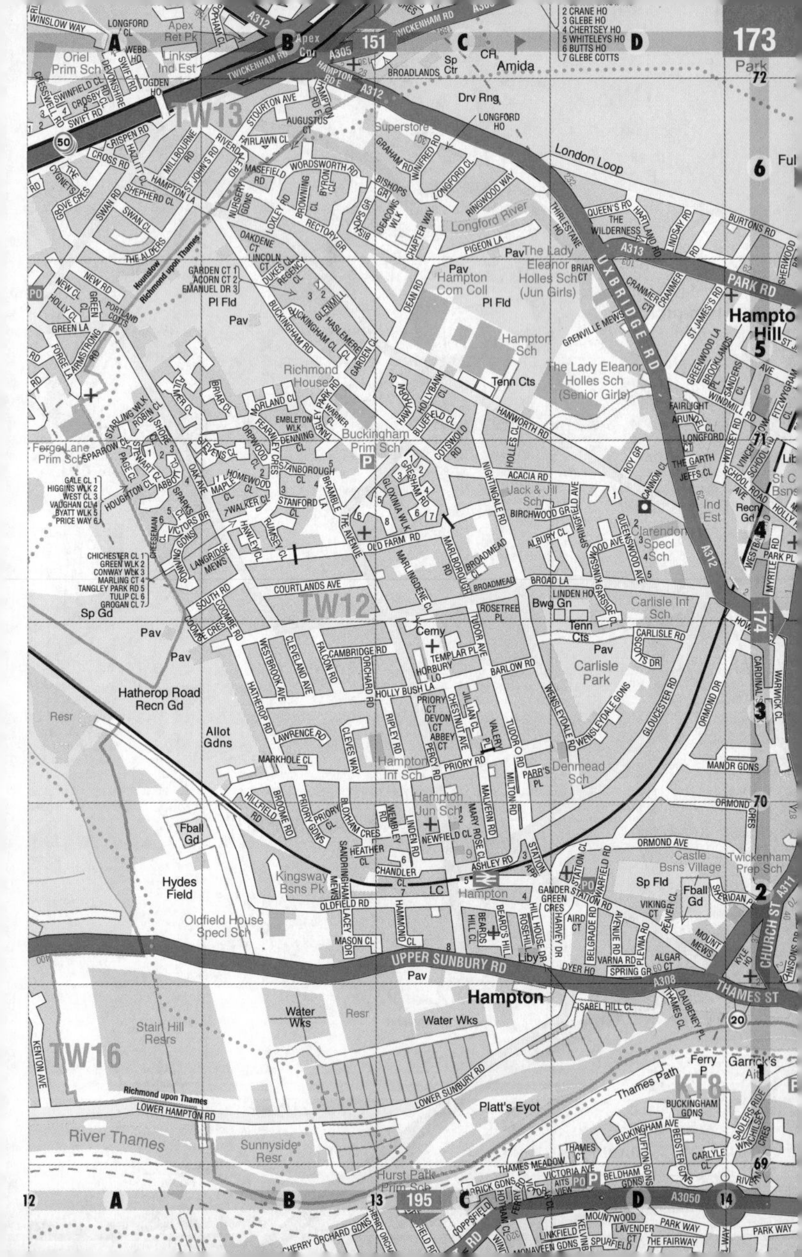

2 CRANE HO
3 GLEBE HO
4 CHERTSEY HO
5 WHITELEYS HO
6 BUTTS HO
7 GLEBE COTTS
A
B
C
D
151
WINSLOW WAY
LONGFORD CL
Apex Ret Pk
Apex Cnr
Links Ind Est
Oriel Prim Sch
TWICKENHAM RD
A312
A305
HAMPTON RD E
BROADLANDS
Sp Ctr
CH
Amida
Park
72
Drv Rng
TW13
STOURTON AVE
AUGUSTUS CT
Superstore
LONGFORD HO
London Loop
6
Ful
FAIRLAWN CL
GRAHAM RD
WINIFRED RD
LONGFORD CL
RINGWOOD WAY
CRISPEN RD
HAZLITT CL
MILLBOURNE RD
ST JOHN'S RD
RIVERDALE RD
MASEFIELD RD
WORDSWORTH RD
BYRON CL
BROWNING CL
LOXLEY RD
BISHOPS GR
DEACONS WLK
CHAPTER WAY
Longford River
THIRLESTANE HO
QUEEN'S RD
THE WILDERNESS
HARTLAND RD
LINDSAY RD
BURTONS RD
SHERWOOD
CROSS RD
HAMPTON LA
SHEPHERD CL
SWAN RD
SWAN CL
THE CYGNETS
GROVE CRES
NURSERY GDNS
RECTORY GR
PIGEON LA
A313
Pav
The Lady Eleanor Holles Sch (Jun Girls)
BRIAR CT
UXBRIDGE RD
CRANMER CT
CRANMER
PARK RD
THE ALDERS
NEW RD
NEW CL
HOLLY CL
GREEN
PORTLAND COTTS
GREEN LA
FORGE LA
ARMSTRONG RD
Hounslow
Richmond upon Thames
OAKDENE CT
LINCOLN CT
DUKES CT
REGENCY CL
GARDEN CT 1
ACORN CT 2
EMANUEL DR 3
Pl Fld
Pav
GLENMILL
HASLEMERE
BUCKINGHAM CL
BUCKINGHAM RD
GARDEN CL
DEAN RD
Hampton Com Coll
Pl Fld
Hampton Sch
GRENVILLE MEWS
ST JAMES'S RD
GREENWOOD LA
BROOKLANDS PL
Hampton Hill
5
Richmond House
HOLLYBANK CL
Tenn Cts
The Lady Eleanor Holles Sch (Senior Girls)
SANDERS CL
AVE
FITZWYGRAM
8
FAIRLIGHT
ARUNDEL CL
LONGFORD CT
WINDMILL RD
WOLSEY RD
VINCENT ROW
71
TULMER CL
BRIAR CL
MORLAND CL
EMBLETON WLK
FEARNLEY CRES
DENNING CL
WARNER CL
TANGLEY PARK RD
Buckingham Prim Sch
BLUEFIELD CL
COTSWOLD RD
HANWORTH RD
STARLING WLK
ROBIN CL
SPARROW CL
Forge Lane Prim Sch
STEWART CL
PAGE CL
ABBOTT CL
HOUGHTON CL
SHORE CL
OAK AVE
STEVENS CL
ORPWOOD CL
STANBOROUGH CL
BRAMBLE LA
GRESHAM RD
GLOXINIA WLK
NIGHTINGALE RD
HOLLES CL
ACACIA RD
ROY GR
CANNON CL
THE GARTH
JEFFS CL
SCHOOL RD
SCHOOL ROAD AVE
Lib
St C Bsns
GALE CL 1
HIGGINS WLK 2
WEST CL 3
VAUGHAN CL 4
BYATT WLK 5
PRICE WAY 6
SPARKS CL
MAPLE CL
HOMEWOOD CL
WALKER CL
STANFORD CL
Jack & Jill Sch
BIRCHWOOD GR
SPRINGFIELD AVE
Ind Est
Recn Gd
HOLLY
CHEESEMAN CL
VICTORS DR
SONNING GDNS
LANGRIDGE MEWS
HAWLEY CL
RUMSEY CL
THE AVENUE
OLD FARM RD
MARLINGDENE CL
MARLBOROUGH RD
BROADMEAD
ALBURY CL
KINGSWOOD AVE
QUEENSWOOD AVE
Clarendon Specl Sch
A312
4
WESTBANK RD
PARK PL
CHICHESTER CL 1
GREEN WLK 2
CONWAY WLK 3
MARLING CT 4
TANGLEY PARK RD 5
TULIP CL 6
GROGAN CL 7
SOUTH RD
COURTLANDS AVE
BROADMEAD
BROAD LA
GARSIDE CL
LINDEN HO
Bwg Gn
Carlisle Inf Sch
MYRTLE RD
Sp Gd
COOMBE CRES
COOMBE RD
TW12
ROSETREE PL
TUDOR AVE
Tenn Cts
CARLISLE RD
174
Pav
Pav
WESTBROOK AVE
CLEVELAND AVE
FALCON RD
CAMBRIDGE RD
ORCHARD RD
Cemy
TEMPLAR PL
HORBURY LO
BARLOW RD
Pav
SCOTTS DR
Carlisle Park
GLOUCESTER RD
ORMOND DR
CARDINALS WAY
WARWICK CL
Hatherop Road Recn Gd
HATHEROP RD
HOLLY BUSH LA
PRIORY CT
DEVON CT
ABBEY CT
CHESTNUT AVE
JILLIAN CL
VALERY PL
WENSLEYDALE RD
WENSLEYDALE GDNS
3
Resr
Allot Gdns
LAWRENCE RD
RIPLEY RD
PERCY RD
CLEVES WAY
TUDOR RD
MARKHOLE CL
Hampton Inf Sch
PRIORY RD
MILTON RD
PARR'S PL
Denmead Sch
MANOR GDNS
HILLFIELD RD
BROOME RD
PRIORY GDNS
PRIORY CL
BLOXHAM CRES
WEMBLEY RD
LINDEN RD
Hampton Jun Sch
MARY ROSE CL
MALVERN RD
ORMOND CRES
70
Fball Gd
SANDRINGHAM MEWS
HEATHER CL
NEWFIELD CL
ASHLEY RD
STATION APP
STATION CL
WARFIELD RD
ORMOND AVE
Castle Bsns Village
Twickenham Prep Sch
Hydes Field
Kingsway Bsns Pk
CHANDLER CL
LC
Hampton
Sp Fld
Fball Gd
2
SHERIDAN PL
A311
OLDFIELD RD
LACEY DR
HAMMOND CL
BEARDS HILL CL
BEARD'S HILL
ROSEHILL
HILL HOUSE DR
GANDER GREEN CRES
HARVEY DR
AIRD CT
BELGRADE RD
AVENUE RD
PLEVNA RD
VIKING CT
BEAVER CL
MOUNT MEWS
CHURCH ST
Oldfield House Specl Sch
MASON CL
UPPER SUNBURY RD
Pav
Liby
DYER HO
VARNA RD
SPRING GR
ALGAR CL
KYLE HO
JOHNSONS DR
A308
THAMES ST
Hampton
ISABEL HILL CL
THAMES CL
DAUBENEY PL
Water Wks
Resr
Water Wks
20
Stain Hill Resrs
TW16
KENTON AVE
LOWER SUNBURY RD
Ferry P
Garrick's Ait
1
KT8
Thames Path
Richmond upon Thames
LOWER HAMPTON RD
Platt's Eyot
BUCKINGHAM GDNS
River Thames
BUCKINGHAM AVE
BEDSTER GDNS
TUFTON GDNS
SADLERS RIDE
WINCHILSEA CRES
Sunnyside Resr
THAMES CT
CARLYLE CL
69
THAMES MEADOW
VICTORIA AVE
BELDHAM GDNS
AITS VIEW
Hurst Park Prim Sch
GARRICK GDNS
HOTHAM CL
FERRY RD
PO
P
A3050
12
A
B
13
195
C
D
14
COPPSFIELD
MOUNTWOOD
LAVENDER CT
PARK WAY
THE FAIRWAY
LINKFIELD
KELVIN
SPURFIELD
MONAVEEN GDNS
CHERRY ORCHARD GDNS
PARK WAY

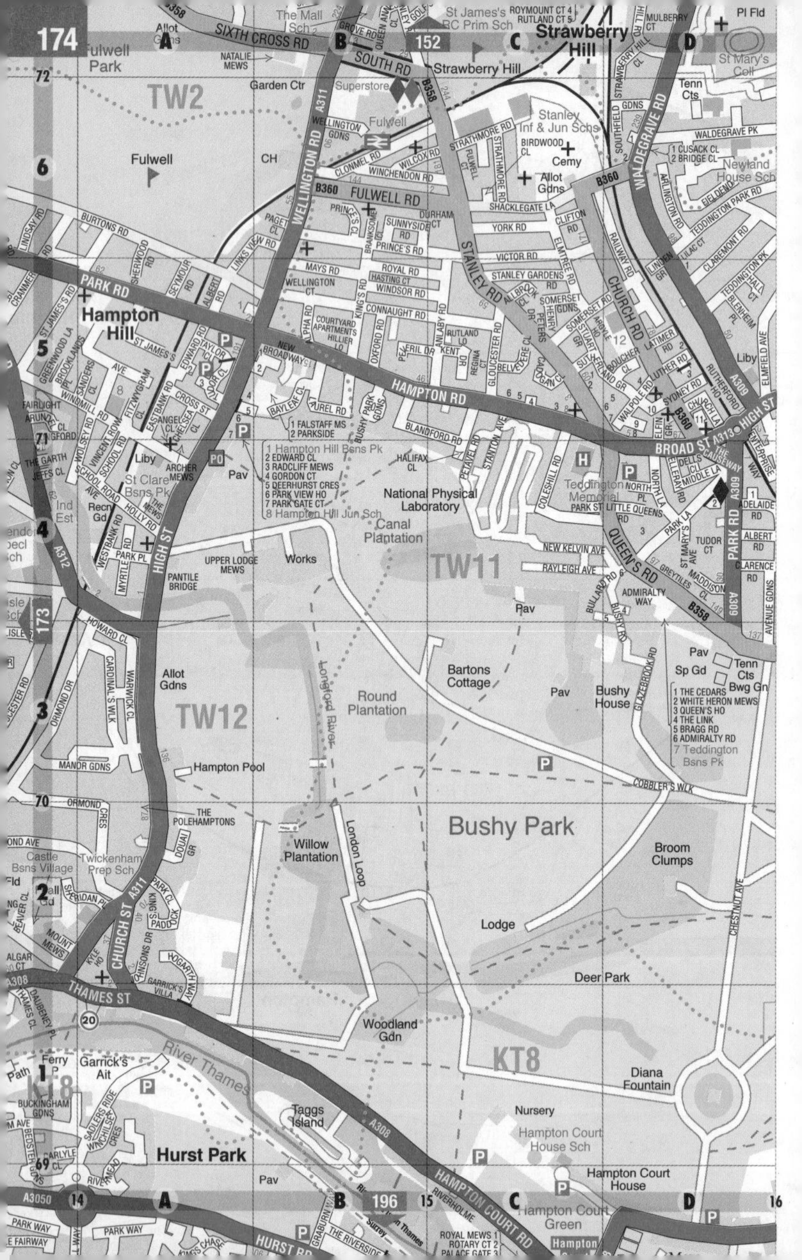

174
A
B
C
D
152
Fulwell Park
TW2
Fulwell
CH
SIXTH CROSS RD
SOUTH RD
NATALIE MEWS
Garden Ctr
Superstore
Fulwell
Strawberry Hill
St James's RC Prim Sch
The Mall Sch
ROYMOUNT CT 4
RUTLAND CT 5
MULBERRY CT
Pl Fld
St Mary's Coll
Tenn Cts
Stanley Inf & Jun Schs
WALDEGRAVE PK
WALDEGRAVE RD
1 CUSACK CL
2 BRIDGE CL
Newland House Sch
STRAWBERRY HILL RD
SOUTHFIELD GDNS
BIRDWOOD CL
Cemy
Allot Gdns
SHACKLEGATE LA
STRATHMORE RD
FULWELL CT
WELLINGTON GDNS
WILCOX RD
CLONMEL RD
WINCHENDON RD
B360
FULWELL RD
WELLINGTON RD
A311
B358
PAGET CL
PRINCE'S CL
BRANKSOME
SUNNYSIDE RD
DURHAM CT
PRINCE'S RD
YORK RD
CLIFTON RD
VICTOR RD
STANLEY RD
STANLEY GARDENS RD
ELMTREE RD
RAILWAY RD
CHURCH RD
LINDEN GR
LILAC CT
CLAREMONT RD
TEDDINGTON PARK RD
TEDDINGTON PK
FIELDEND
ARLINGTON RD
BURTONS RD
LINDSAY RD
LINKS VIEW RD
MAYS RD
ROYAL RD
HASTING CT
WINDSOR RD
WELLINGTON CT
KING'S RD
CONNAUGHT RD
ALLBROOK CL
PETERS
SOMERSET GDNS
HENRY
SOMERSET RD
PARK RD
SHERWOOD RD
SEYMOUR RD
ALBERT RD
CRANMER
Hampton Hill
ST JAMES'S RD
GREENWOOD LA
BROOKLANDS PL
SANDERS CL
ST JAMES'S AVE
FITZWYGRAM CL
EDWARD CL
TAYLOR CL
TUDOR CL
EASTBANK RD
CROSS ST
NEW BROADWAY
COURTYARD APARTMENTS
HILLIER LO
ALPHA RD
OXFORD RD
ANLABY RD
RUTLAND LO
ERIL DR
KENT DR
REGINA CT
GLOUCESTER RD
BELVEDERE CL
CADOGAN CL
STUART GR
SUTHERLAND GR
BOUCHER CL
LATIMER RD
LUTHER RD
RUTHERFORD HO
ELMFIELD AVE
Liby
HAMPTON RD
BAYLEAF CL
LAUREL RD
BUSHY PARK GDNS
1 FALSTAFF MS
2 PARKSIDE
BLANDFORD RD
WALPOLE RD
SYDNEY RD
CHURCH LA
A313
HIGH ST
A309
ENTERPRISE WAY
BROAD ST
THE CAUSEWAY
FAIRLIGHT
WINDMILL RD
ARUNDEL CL
LONGFORD
WOLSEY RD
VINCENT ROW
SCHOOL RD
ANGEL CL
CHELSEA CL
THE GARTH
JEFFS CL
Liby
ARCHER MEWS
PO
Pav
1 Hampton Hill Bsns Pk
2 EDWARD CL
3 RADCLIFF MEWS
4 GORDON CT
5 DEERHURST CRES
6 PARK VIEW HO
7 PARK GATE CT
8 Hampton Hill Jun Sch
HALIFAX CL
PETAVEL RD
STANTON AVE
COLESHILL RD
Teddington Memorial
NORTH PL
NORTH LA
ELLERAY RD
DELLS CL
MIDDLE LA
ADELAIDE RD
PARK ST
LITTLE QUEENS RD
St Clare Bsns Pk
SCHOOL ROAD AVE
THE MEWS
HOLLY RD
Ind Est
Recn Gd
National Physical Laboratory
Canal Plantation
TW11
NEW KELVIN AVE
RAYLEIGH AVE
QUEEN'S RD
PARK LA
ST MARY'S AVE
TUDOR CT
ALBERT RD
CLARENCE RD
GREYTILES
MADDISON CL
WESTBANK RD
PARK PL
MYRTLE RD
HIGH ST
UPPER LODGE MEWS
Works
PANTILE BRIDGE
A312
173
BULLARD RD
BUSHY RD
ADMIRALTY WAY
Pav
B358
AVENUE GDNS
HOWARD CL
CARDINAL'S WLK
WARWICK CL
ORMOND DR
Allot Gdns
TW12
Longford River
Round Plantation
Bartons Cottage
Pav
Bushy House
GLAZEBROOK RD
Pav
Sp Gd
Tenn Cts
Bwg Gn
1 THE CEDARS
2 WHITE HERON MEWS
3 QUEEN'S HO
4 THE LINK
5 BRAGG RD
6 ADMIRALTY RD
7 Teddington Bsns Pk
MANOR GDNS
Hampton Pool
COBBLER'S WLK
ORMOND CRES
THE POLEHAMPTONS
Bushy Park
Willow Plantation
London Loop
Broom Clumps
Castle Bsns Village
Twickenham Prep Sch
DOUAI GR
SHERIDAN PL
BEAVER CL
MOUNT MEWS
CHURCH ST
PARK CL
KING'S PADDOCK
KYLE HO
JOHNSONS DR
HOGARTH WAY
GARRICK'S VILLA
Lodge
CHESTNUT AVE
Deer Park
ALGAR CT
A308
THAMES ST
DAUBENEY PL
THAMES CL
20
Woodland Gdn
KT8
Ferry
Garrick's Ait
River Thames
Diana Fountain
KT8
BUCKINGHAM GDNS
SADLERS RIDE
WINCHILSEY CRES
Taggs Island
Nursery
Hampton Court House Sch
BEDSTER GDNS
CARLYLE CL
RIVERMEAD
Hurst Park
Pav
HAMPTON COURT RD
RIVERHOLME
Hampton Court House
A3050
14
196
15
16
Hampton Court Green
PARK WAY
FAIRWAY
KINGS CHASE
HURST RD
GRABURN WAY
THE RIVERSIDE
Surrey
ROYAL MEWS 1
ROTARY CT 2
PALACE GATE 3
Hampton
72
6
5
71
4
3
70
2
1
69

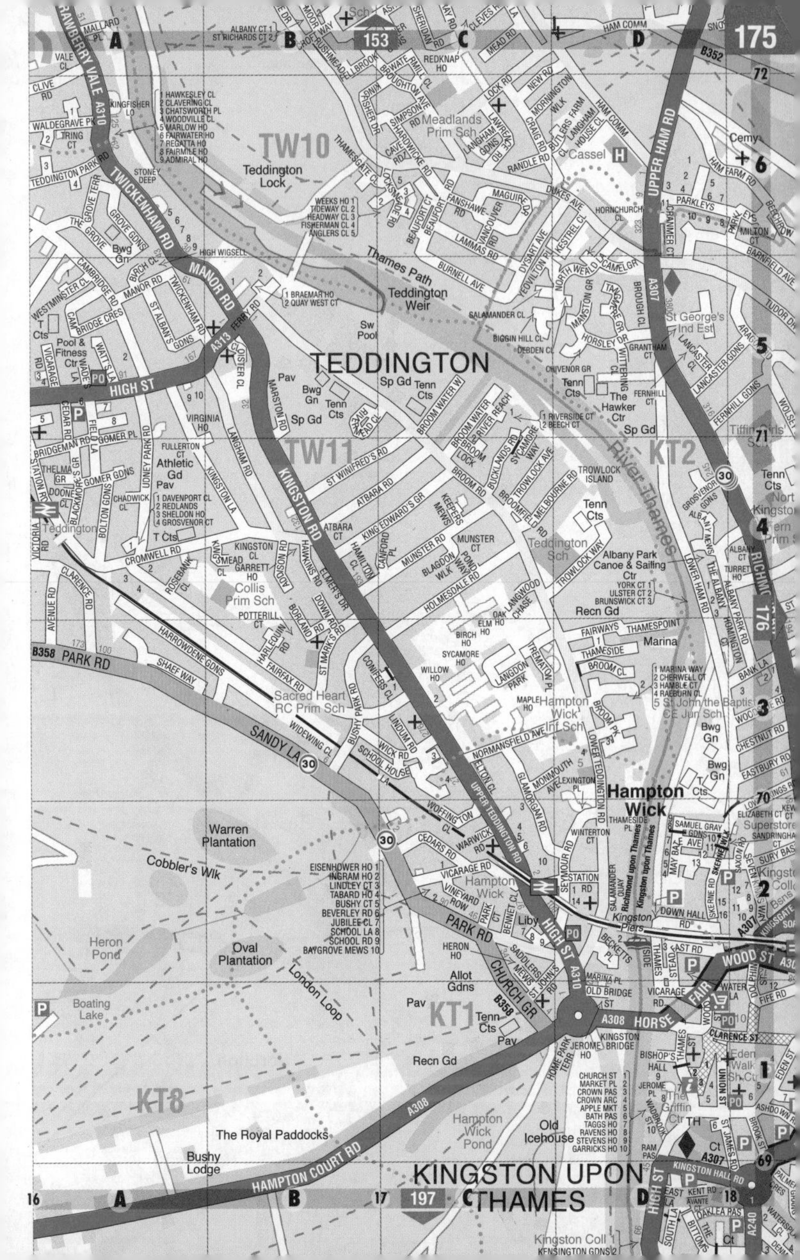
TEDDINGTON
TW10
TW11
KT2
KT1
KT8
Teddington Lock
Teddington Weir
Thames Path
River Thames
Meadlands Prim Sch
Cassel
Collis Prim Sch
Sacred Heart RC Prim Sch
Teddington Sch
Hampton Wick Inf Sch
St John the Baptist CE Jun Sch
Hampton Wick
Warren Plantation
Oval Plantation
Cobbler's Wlk
Heron Pond
Boating Lake
London Loop
The Royal Paddocks
Bushy Lodge
Hampton Wick Pond
Old Icehouse
KINGSTON UPON THAMES
Kingston Bridge
Kingston Piers
Albany Park Canoe & Sailing Ctr
Trowlock Island
St George's Ind Est
The Hawker Ctr
Pool & Fitness Ctr
Athletic Gd
Teddington
HIGH ST
KINGSTON RD
UPPER TEDDINGTON RD
UPPER HAM RD
TWICKENHAM RD
MANOR RD
PARK RD
SANDY LA
HAMPTON COURT RD
HORSE FAIR
WOOD ST
CLARENCE ST
LOWER HAM RD
LOWER TEDDINGTON RD
BROOM RD
CROMWELL RD
A310
A313
A307
A308
B358
B352
153
176
197
A
B
C
D
1
2
3
4
5
6
16
17
18
69
70
71
72

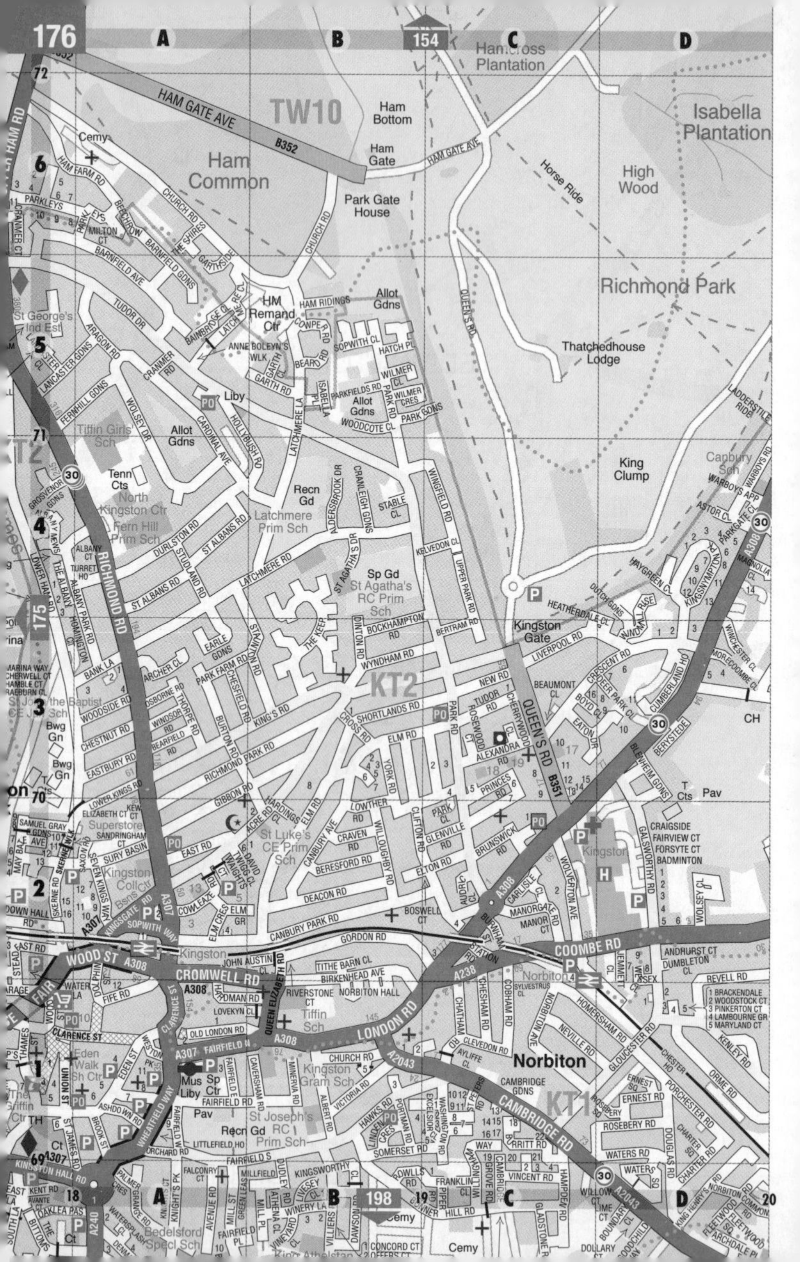
A
B
154
C
D
Hamcross Plantation
HAM GATE AVE
B352
TW10
Ham Bottom
Ham Gate
Isabella Plantation
Ham Common
Horse Ride
High Wood
Park Gate House
CHURCH RD
Richmond Park
QUEEN'S RD
HM Remand Ctr
HAM RIDINGS
Allot Gdns
Thatchedhouse Lodge
ANNE BOLEYN'S WLK
SOPWITH CL
HATCH PL
LATCHMERE LA
PARKFIELDS RD
WOODCOTE CL
PARK GDNS
LADDERSTILE RIDE
St George's Ind Est
LANCASTER GDNS
TUDOR DR
CARDINAL AVE
HOLLYBUSH RD
Tiffin Girls Sch
Allot Gdns
Liby
North Kingston Ctr
Fern Hill Prim Sch
Tenn Cts
Recn Gd
Latchmere Prim Sch
STABLE CL
WINGFIELD RD
King Clump
Canbury Sch
WARBOYS APP
ASTOR CL
PARKGATE CL
RICHMOND RD
LATCHMERE RD
ST ALBANS RD
Sp Gd
St Agatha's RC Prim Sch
KELVEDON CL
UPPER PARK RD
HEATHERDALE CL
HAYGREEN CL
KINGSNYMPTON PK
MAGNOLIA CL
175
Kingston Gate
LIVERPOOL RD
BOCKHAMPTON RD
BERTRAM RD
WYNDHAM RD
KT2
NEW RD
BEAUMONT CL
CRESCENT RD
CUMBERLAND HO
WINCHESTER CL
MORECOMBE CL
KING'S RD
SHORTLANDS RD
TUDOR RD
QUEEN'S RD
B351
DEER PARK CL
BERYSTEDE
CH
St John the Baptist CE Jun Sch
Bwg Gn
CHESTNUT RD
EASTBURY RD
RICHMOND PARK RD
ELM RD
PARK RD
ALEXANDRA RD
PRINCES RD
EATON DR
BLENHEIM GDNS
T Cts
Pav
LOWER KINGS RD
GIBBON RD
LOWTHER RD
CRAVEN RD
CLIFTON RD
PARK CL
GLENVILLE RD
BRUNSWICK RD
CRAIGSIDE
FAIRVIEW CT
FORSYTE CT
BADMINTON
Superstore
St Luke's CE Prim Sch
BERESFORD RD
ELTON RD
Kingston
GALSWORTHY RD
WOLVERTON AVE
Kingston Coll Bsns Ctr
DEACON RD
CANBURY PARK RD
BOSWELL CT
A308
MANORGATE RD
WOLSEY CL
A307
KINGSGATE RD
SOPWITH WAY
GORDON RD
Kingston
COOMBE RD
ANDHURST CT
DUMBLETON CL
WOOD ST
A308
CROMWELL RD
JOHN AUSTIN CL
TITHE BARN CL
BIRKENHEAD AVE
STATION RD
A238
Norbiton
REVELL RD
RIVERSTONE CT
NORBITON HALL
CHATHAM RD
CHESHAM RD
COBHAM RD
NORBITON AVE
HOMERSHAM RD
1 BRACKENDALE
2 WOODSTOCK CT
3 PINKERTON CT
4 LAMBOURNE GR
5 MARYLAND CT
FIFE RD
Tiffin Sch
LONDON RD
CLARENCE ST
OLD LONDON RD
QUEEN ELIZABETH RD
NEVILLE RD
GLOUCESTER RD
KENLEY RD
Eden Walk Sh Ctr
FAIRFIELD N
A2043
CLEVEDON RD
AYLIFFE CL
Norbiton
CHESTER HO
ORME RD
UNION ST
Mus Liby
Sp Ctr
CHURCH RD
Kingston Gram Sch
CAMBRIDGE GDNS
KT1
ERNEST SQ
ERNEST RD
PORCHESTER RD
The Griffin Ctr
WHEATFIELD WAY
Pav
Recn Gd
St Joseph's RC Prim Sch
VICTORIA RD
CAMBRIDGE RD
ROSEBERY RD
CHARTER SQ
LITTLEFIELD HO
FAIRFIELD S
SOMERSET RD
BURRITT RD
WATERS RD
DOUGLAS RD
CHARTER RD
KINGSTON HALL RD
KINGSWORTHY CL
VINCENT RD
FRANKLIN CL
WATERS SQ
A
B
198
C
D
Cemy
HILL RD
GLADSTONE RD
KING HENRY'S RD
NORBITON COMMON RD
FLEETWOOD SQ
ARCHDALE PL
Bedelsford Specl Sch
CONCORD CT
Cemy
DOLLARY

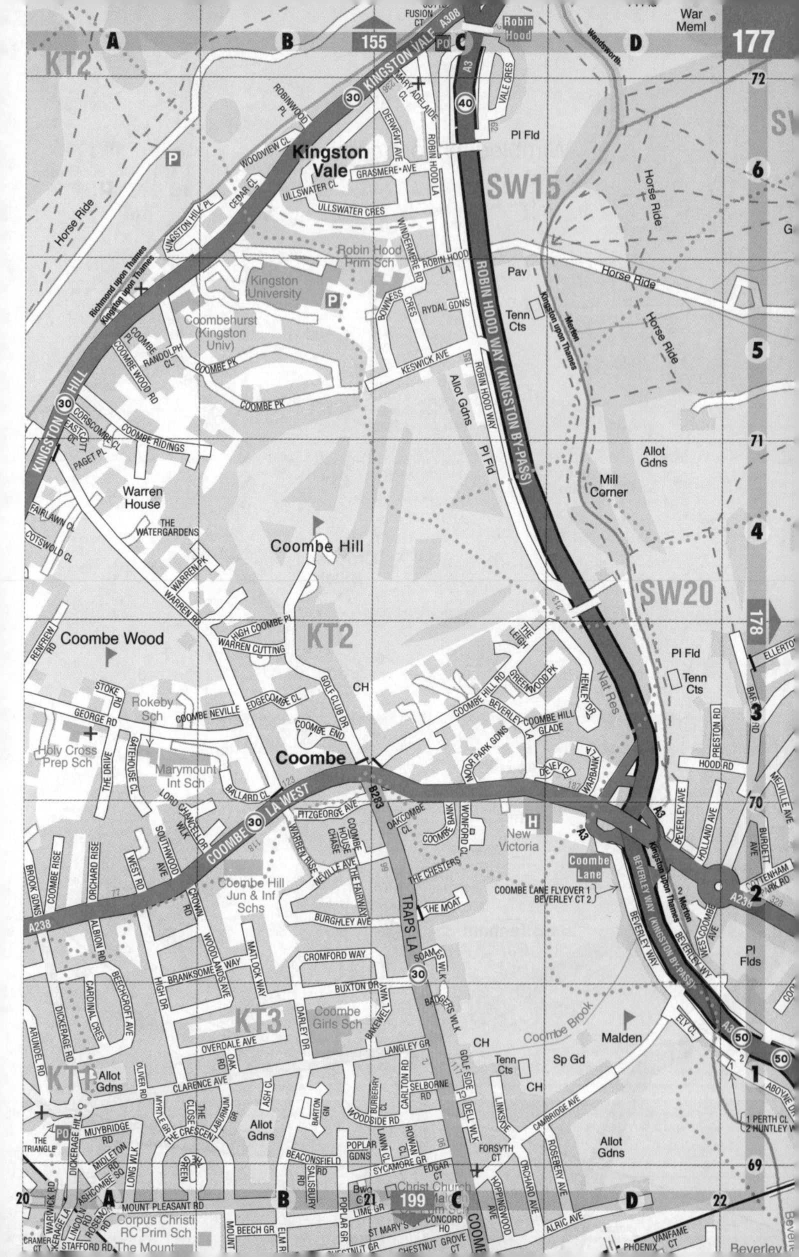

A
B
C
D
155
KT2
Robin Hood
War Meml
Wandsworth
KINGSTON VALE
A308
A3
ROBINWOOD PL
MARY ADELAIDE CL
DERWENT AVE
ROBIN HOOD LA
VALE CRES
Pl Fld
Kingston Vale
WOODVIEW CL
GRASMERE AVE
ULLSWATER CL
ULLSWATER CRES
SW15
Horse Ride
CEDAR CL
KINGSTON HILL PL
WINDERMERE RD
Robin Hood Prim Sch
ROBIN HOOD LA
Richmond upon Thames
Kingston upon Thames
Kingston University
BOWNESS CRES
RYDAL GDNS
ROBIN HOOD WAY (KINGSTON BY-PASS)
Pav
Tenn Cts
Merton
Coombehurst (Kingston Univ)
COOMBE PL
RANDOLPH CL
COOMBE PK
KESWICK AVE
COOMBE WOOD RD
Allot Gdns
ROBIN HOOD WAY
KINGSTON HILL
CORSCOMBE CL
EASTCOTT
COOMBE RIDINGS
PAGET PL
Pl Fld
Allot Gdns
Mill Corner
Warren House
FAIRLAWN CL
THE WATERGARDENS
Coombe Hill
COTSWOLD CL
WARREN PK
SW20
WARREN RD
178
RENFREW RD
Coombe Wood
HIGH COOMBE PL
WARREN CUTTING
KT2
THE LEIGH
GREENWOOD PK
HENLEY DR
Nat Res
Pl Fld
Tenn Cts
ELLERTON
STOKE RD
Rokeby Sch
EDGECOMBE CL
GOLF CLUB DR
CH
COOMBE HILL RD
BEVERLEY
COOMBE HILL GLADE
GEORGE RD
COOMBE NEVILLE
COOMBE END
PRESTON RD
Holy Cross Prep Sch
THE DRIVE
GATEHOUSE CL
Marymount Int Sch
Coombe
MOOR PARK GDNS
DENEY CL
WARBANK LA
HOOD RD
BALLARD CL
LORD CHANCELLOR WLK
COOMBE LA WEST
B283
FITZGEORGE AVE
OAKCOMBE CL
COOMBE BANK
WONFORD CL
New Victoria
BEVERLEY AVE
HOLLAND AVE
MELVILLE AVE
BURDETT AVE
SOUTHWOOD AVE
WARREN RISE
COOMBE HOUSE CHASE
COOMBE
NEVILLE AVE
THE FAIRWAY
THE CHESTERS
Coombe Lane
Kingston upon Thames
COTTENHAM PARK RD
BROOK GDNS
COOMBE RISE
ORCHARD RISE
WEST RD
CROWN RD
Coombe Hill Jun & Inf Schs
THE MOAT
COOMBE LANE FLYOVER 1
BEVERLEY CT 2
BEVERLEY WAY (KINGSTON BY-PASS)
A238
ALBION RD
WOODLANDS AVE
MATLOCK WAY
BURGHLEY AVE
TRAPS LA
WEST COOMBE AVE
BEVERLEY WY
Pl Flds
BEVERLEY WAY
CROMFORD WAY
SOAMES WLK
BRANKSOME WAY
BEECHCROFT AVE
CARDINAL CRES
DICKERAGE RD
HIGH DR
BUXTON DR
BAKEWELL WAY
BADGERS WLK
Coombe Girls Sch
KT3
DARLEY DR
Coombe Brook
Malden
ARUNDEL RD
OVERDALE AVE
LANGLEY GR
CH
ELY CL
KT1
Allot Gdns
OLIVER RD
OAK RD
CLARENCE AVE
ASH CL
Tenn Cts
Sp Gd
GOLF SIDE CL
CARLTON RD
SELBORNE RD
BURBERRY CL
CH
ABOYNE DR
MYRTLE GR
THE CLOSE
LABURNUM GR
BARTON GN
WOODSIDE RD
DELL WLK
LINKSIDE
CAMBRIDGE AVE
1 PERTH CL
2 HUNTLEY WAY
THE TRIANGLE
MUYBRIDGE RD
DICKERAGE HILL
THE CRESCENT
Allot Gdns
POPLAR GDNS
LAWN CL
ROWAN CL
ROSEBERY AVE
Allot Gdns
MIDLETON RD
ASHCOMBE SQ
LONG WLK
GREEN
BEACONSFIELD RD
SYCAMORE GR
EDGAR CT
FORSYTH CT
ORCHARD AVE
HOPPINGWOOD AVE
SALISBURY RD
Christ Church
WARWICK RD
LINCOLN
ROSEMOUNT
MOUNT PLEASANT RD
POPLAR GR
LIME GR
199
ALRIC AVE
Corpus Christi RC Prim Sch
MOUNT
BEECH GR
ELM RD
ST MARY'S CT
CONCORD HO
GROVE CT
PHOENIX CT
VANFAME CT
STAFFORD RD
The Mount
72
6
5
71
4
3
70
2
1
69
20
21
22

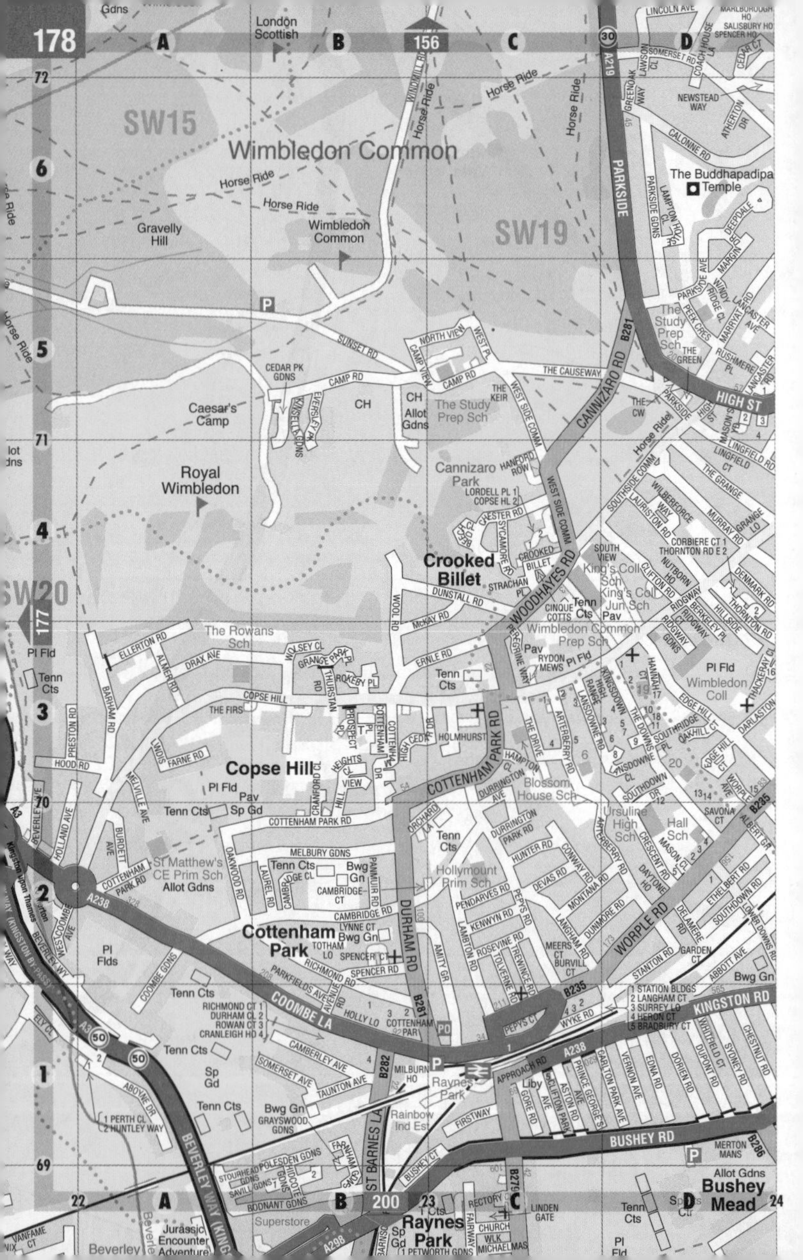
A
B
C
D
156
London Scottish
SW15
Wimbledon Common
Horse Ride
Gravelly Hill
Wimbledon Common
SW19
PARKSIDE
The Buddhapadipa Temple
SUNSET RD
CAMP RD
THE CAUSEWAY
CANNIZARO RD
Caesar's Camp
The Study Prep Sch
Cannizaro Park
Royal Wimbledon
Crooked Billet
WOODHAYES RD
WEST SIDE COMM
SW20
177
The Rowans Sch
Wimbledon Common Prep Sch
COPSE HILL
Copse Hill
COTTENHAM PARK RD
Blossom House Sch
Ursuline High Sch
Wimbledon Coll
St Matthew's CE Prim Sch
Hollymount Prim Sch
DURHAM RD
WORPLE RD
Cottenham Park
COOMBE LA
KINGSTON RD
BEVERLEY WAY
Raynes Park
Rainbow Ind Est
BUSHEY RD
ST BARNES LA
200
Bushey Mead
Raynes Park
Jurassic Encounter Adventure
22
23
24
72
6
5
71
4
3
70
2
1
69

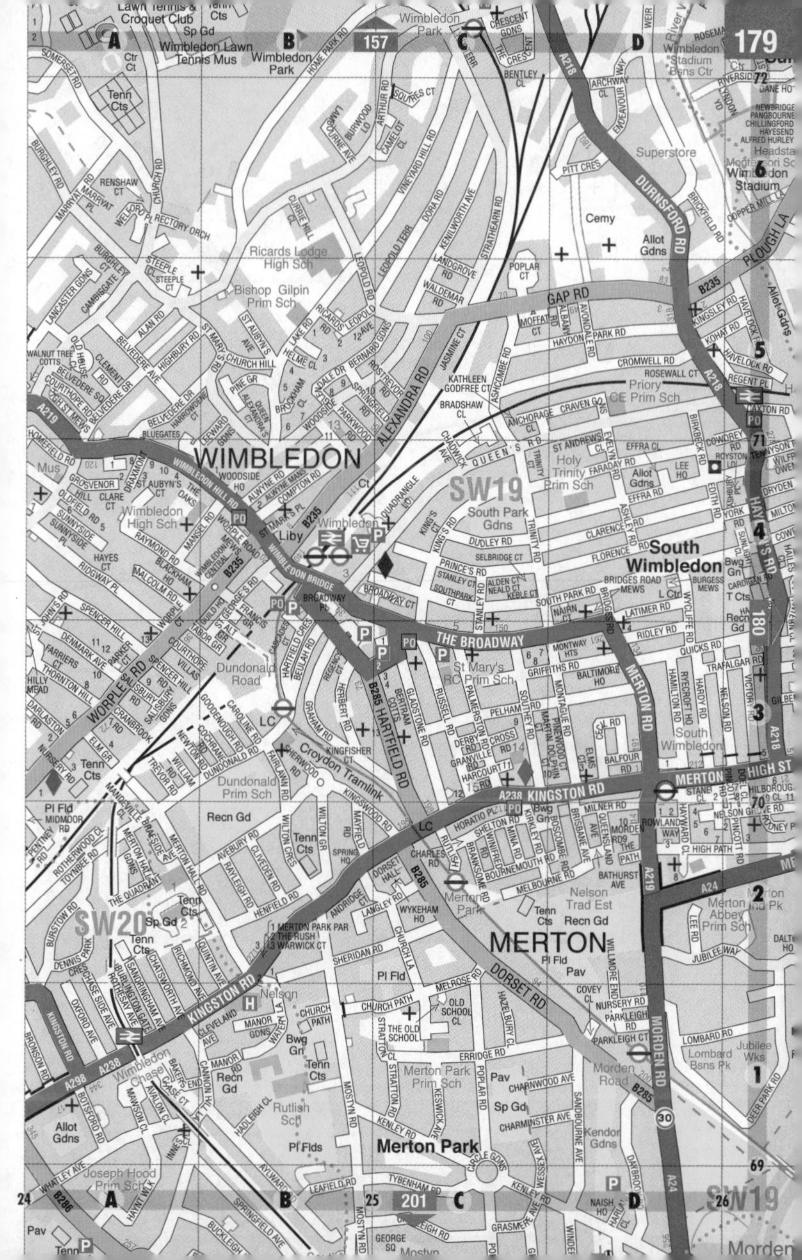
157
A
B
C
D
Wimbledon Lawn Tennis Mus
Lawn Tennis & Croquet Club
Wimbledon Park
Wimbledon Stadium Bsns Ctr
Wimbledon Stadium
Superstore
Cemy
Allot Gdns
DURNSFORD RD
PLOUGH LA
GAP RD
Ricards Lodge High Sch
Bishop Gilpin Prim Sch
WIMBLEDON
SW19
ALEXANDRA RD
WIMBLEDON HILL RD
WIMBLEDON BRIDGE
THE BROADWAY
Wimbledon
Liby
Wimbledon High Sch
South Park Gdns
Holy Trinity Prim Sch
Priory CE Prim Sch
South Wimbledon
WORPLE RD
Dundonald Road
Dundonald Prim Sch
Croydon Tramlink
HARTFIELD RD
St Mary's RC Prim Sch
MERTON RD
KINGSTON RD
MERTON HIGH ST
Recn Gd
Tenn Cts
SW20
Merton Park
MERTON
Nelson Trad Est
Merton Abbey Prim Sch
DORSET RD
MORDEN RD
Morden Road
Lombard Bsns Pk
Jubilee Wks
Merton Park Prim Sch
Rutlish Sch
Kendor Gdns
Nelson
Wimbledon Chase
Allot Gdns
Joseph Hood Prim Sch
Merton Park
A218
A219
A238
A24
A298
B235
B285
B286
6
5
4
3
2
1
72
71
70
69
24
25
201
26

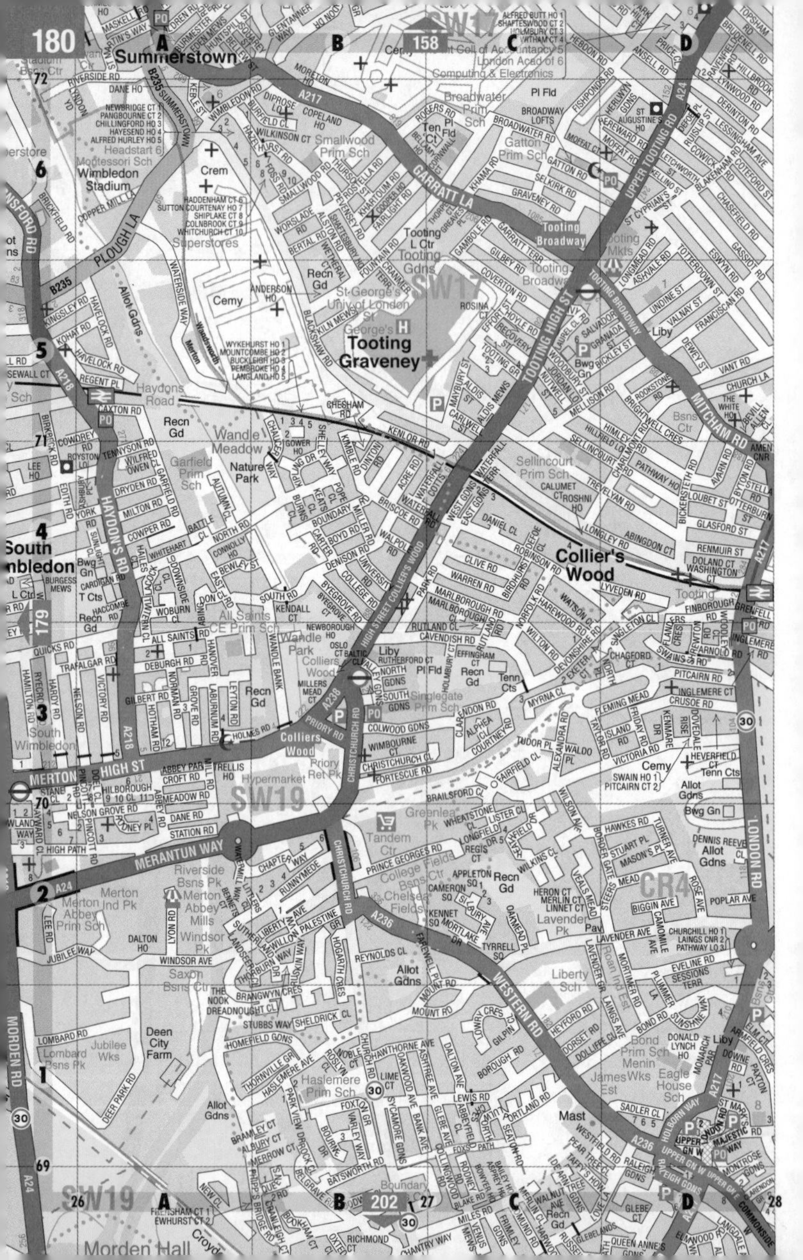
Summerstown
Wimbledon Stadium
SW17
158
Tooting Graveney
Tooting Broadway
Collier's Wood
South Wimbledon
SW19
CR4
179
202
Colliers Wood
Morden Hall
GARRATT LA
UPPER TOOTING RD
TOOTING HIGH ST
HIGH STREET COLLIER'S WOOD
MITCHAM RD
LONDON RD
HAYDON'S RD
MERTON HIGH ST
MERANTUN WAY
CHRISTCHURCH RD
WESTERN RD
PLOUGH LA
MORDEN RD
A
B
C
D
1
2
3
4
5
6
26
27
28
69
70
71
72

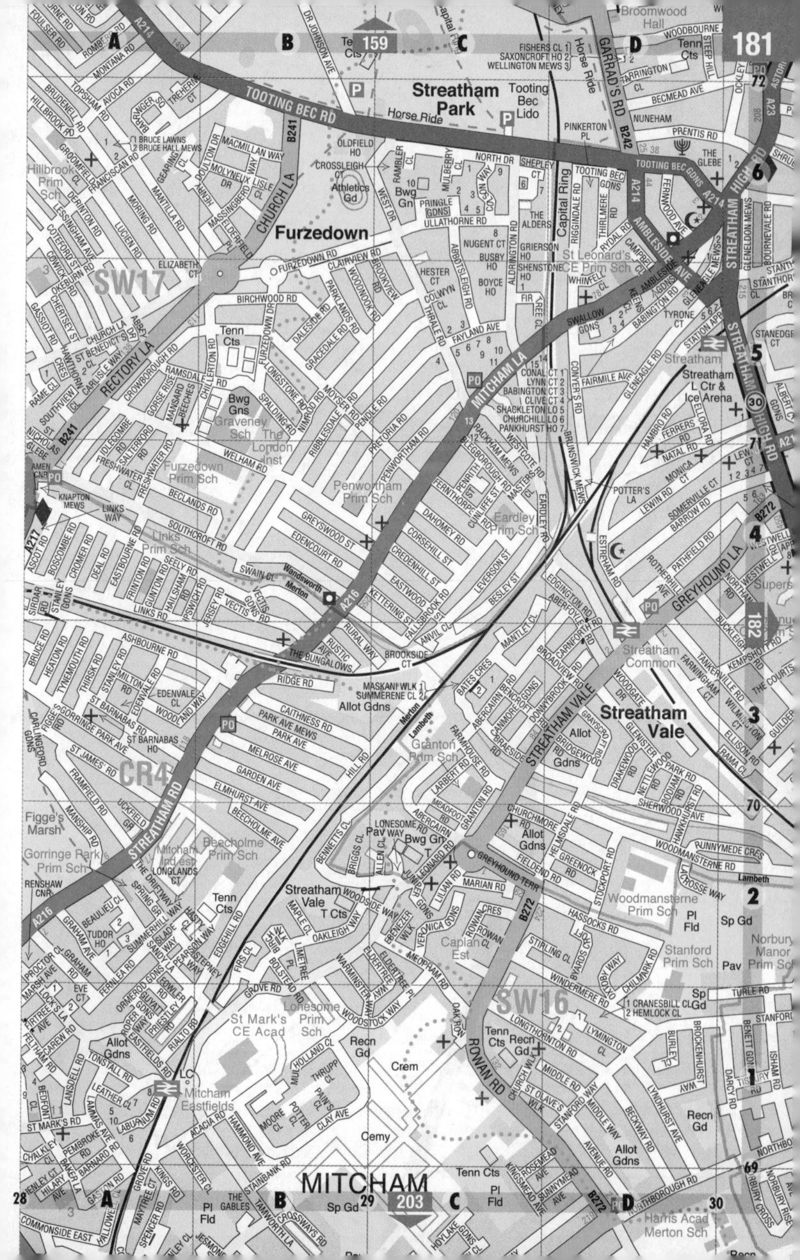
A
B
C
D
159
Streatham Park
Tooting Bec Lido
TOOTING BEC RD
Horse Ride
GARRAD'S RD
Broomwood Hall
Furzedown
SW17
CHURCH LA
RECTORY LA
Hillbrook Prim Sch
Capital Ring
MITCHAM LA
Athletics Gd
Tenn Cts
Bwg Gns
Graveney Sch
The London Inst
Furzedown Prim Sch
Links Prim Sch
Penwortham Prim Sch
Eardley Prim Sch
St Leonard's CE Prim Sch
Streatham
Streatham L Ctr & Ice Arena
STREATHAM HIGH RD
GREYHOUND LA
Streatham Common
Streatham Vale
STREATHAM VALE
Allot Gdns
Granton Prim Sch
CR4
STREATHAM RD
Figge's Marsh
Gorringe Park Prim Sch
Mitcham Ind Est
Beecholme Prim Sch
Streatham Vale T Cts
Caplan Est
Woodmansterne Prim Sch
Stanford Prim Sch
Norbury Manor Prim Sch
SW16
Lonesome Prim Sch
St Mark's CE Acad
Recn Gd
Crem
Cemy
Mitcham Eastfields
MITCHAM
Harris Acad Merton Sch
ROWAN RD
182
203
28
29
30
6
5
4
3
2
1
72
71
70
69

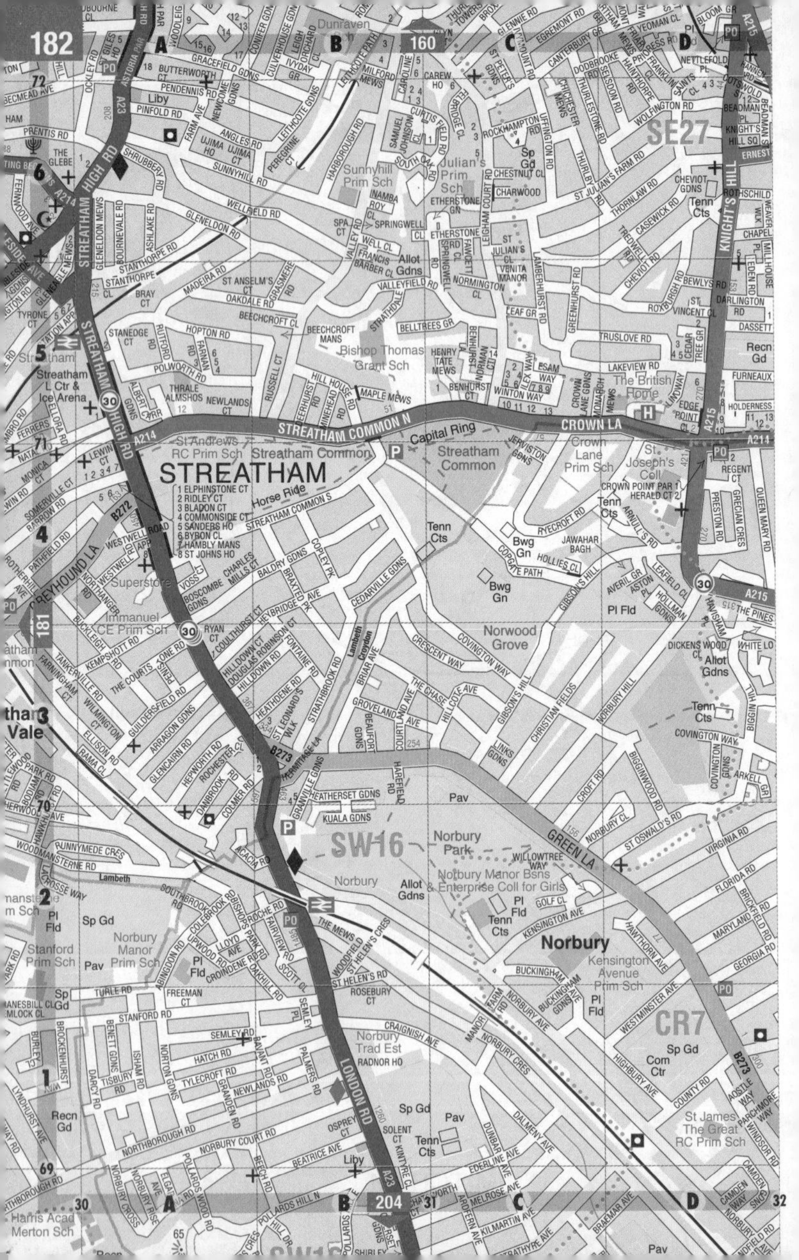

182
A
B
160
C
D
SE27
STREATHAM
SW16
CR7
Norbury
Streatham Common
Norwood Grove
Norbury Park
STREATHAM HIGH RD
STREATHAM COMMON N
CROWN LA
GREEN LA
LONDON RD
KNIGHT'S HILL
GREYHOUND LA
A23
A214
A215
B272
B273
Capital Ring
Horse Ride
1 ELPHINSTONE CT
2 RIDLEY CT
3 BLADON CT
4 COMMONSIDE CT
5 SANDERS HO
6 BYRON CL
7 HAMBLY MANS
8 ST JOHNS HO
Bishop Thomas Grant Sch
St Andrews RC Prim Sch
Sunnyhill Prim Sch
Julian's Prim Sch
Crown Lane Prim Sch
St Joseph's Coll
The British Home
Streatham L Ctr & Ice Arena
Superstore
Immanuel CE Prim Sch
Norbury Manor Bsns & Enterprise Coll for Girls
Norbury Manor Prim Sch
Stanford Prim Sch
Kensington Avenue Prim Sch
St James The Great RC Prim Sch
Harris Acad Merton Sch
Norbury Trad Est
Sp Gd
Pl Fld
Tenn Cts
Bwg Gn
Allot Gdns
Recn Gd
Pav
Liby
181
204
30
31
32

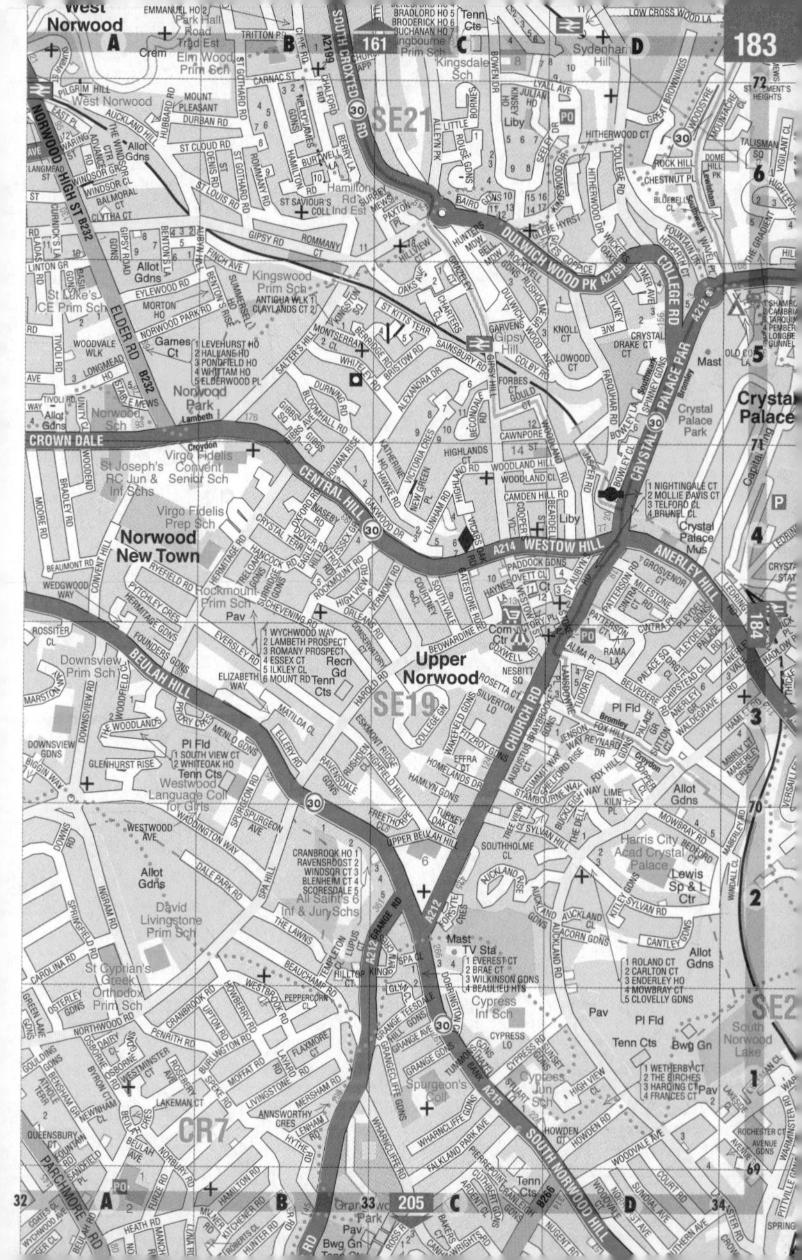

West Norwood
Crem
Elm Wood Prim Sch
Park Hall Road Trad Est
161
SOUTH CROXTED RD
Kingsdale Sch
SE21
Sydenham Hill
LOW CROSS WOOD LA
PILGRIM HILL
West Norwood
NORWOOD HIGH ST B232
AUCKLAND HILL
MOUNT PLEASANT
DURBAN RD
ST CLOUD RD
ST GOTHARD RD
CARNAC ST
CHALFORD RD
ST SAVIOUR'S COLL
Hamilton Rd Ind Est
GIPSY RD
ROMMANY CT
Allot Gdns
Kingswood Prim Sch
St Luke's CE Prim Sch
ELDER RD
EYLEWOOD RD
NORWOOD PARK RD
Games Ct
1 LEVEHURST HO
2 HALLANE HO
3 PONDFIELD HO
4 WHITTAM HO
5 ELDERWOOD PL
Norwood Park
Norwood Sch
CROWN DALE
DULWICH WOOD PK A2199
COLLEGE RD
HITHERWOOD CT
Liby
PO
BAIRD GDNS
HUNTERS MDW
GIPSY HILL
Gipsy Hill
SAINSBURY RD
ST KITTS TERR
WHITELEY RD
ALEXANDRA DR
CRYSTAL PALACE PAR
Crystal Palace Park
Crystal Palace
Mast
Virgo Fidelis Convent Senior Sch
St Joseph's RC Jun & Inf Schs
Virgo Fidelis Prep Sch
CENTRAL HILL
Norwood New Town
WESTOW HILL A214
1 NIGHTINGALE CT
2 MOLLIE DAVIS CT
3 TELFORD CL
4 BRUNEL CL
Crystal Palace Mus
ANERLEY HILL
184
Rockmount Prim Sch
Pav
1 WYCHWOOD WAY
2 LAMBETH PROSPECT
3 ROMANY PROSPECT
4 ESSEX CT
5 ILKLEY CL
6 MOUNT RD
Recn Gd
Tenn Cts
Upper Norwood
SE19
BEULAH HILL
Downsview Prim Sch
CHURCH RD
Pl Fld
1 SOUTH VIEW CT
2 WHITEOAK HO
Westwood Language Coll for Girls
UPPER BEULAH HILL
CRANBROOK HO 1
RAVENSROOST 2
WINDSOR CT 3
BLENHEIM CT 4
SCORESDALE 5
All Saint's Inf & Jun Schs
David Livingstone Prim Sch
Harris City Acad Crystal Palace
Lewis Sp & L Ctr
Allot Gdns
Mast
TV Sta
1 EVEREST CT
2 BRAE CT
3 WILKINSON GDNS
4 BEAULIEU HTS
1 ROLAND CT
2 CARLTON CT
3 ENDERLEY HO
4 MOWBRAY CT
5 CLOVELLY GDNS
St Cyprian's Greek Orthodox Prim Sch
Cypress Inf Sch
Spurgeon's Coll
Cypress Jun Sch
Pav
Pl Fld
Tenn Cts
Bwg Gn
South Norwood Lake
SE25
1 WETHERBY CT
2 THE BIRCHES
3 HARDING CT
4 FRANCES CT
CR7
SOUTH NORWOOD HILL
A215
GRANGE RD A212
Grangewood Park
205
32
33
34
A
B
C
D
1
2
3
4
5
6

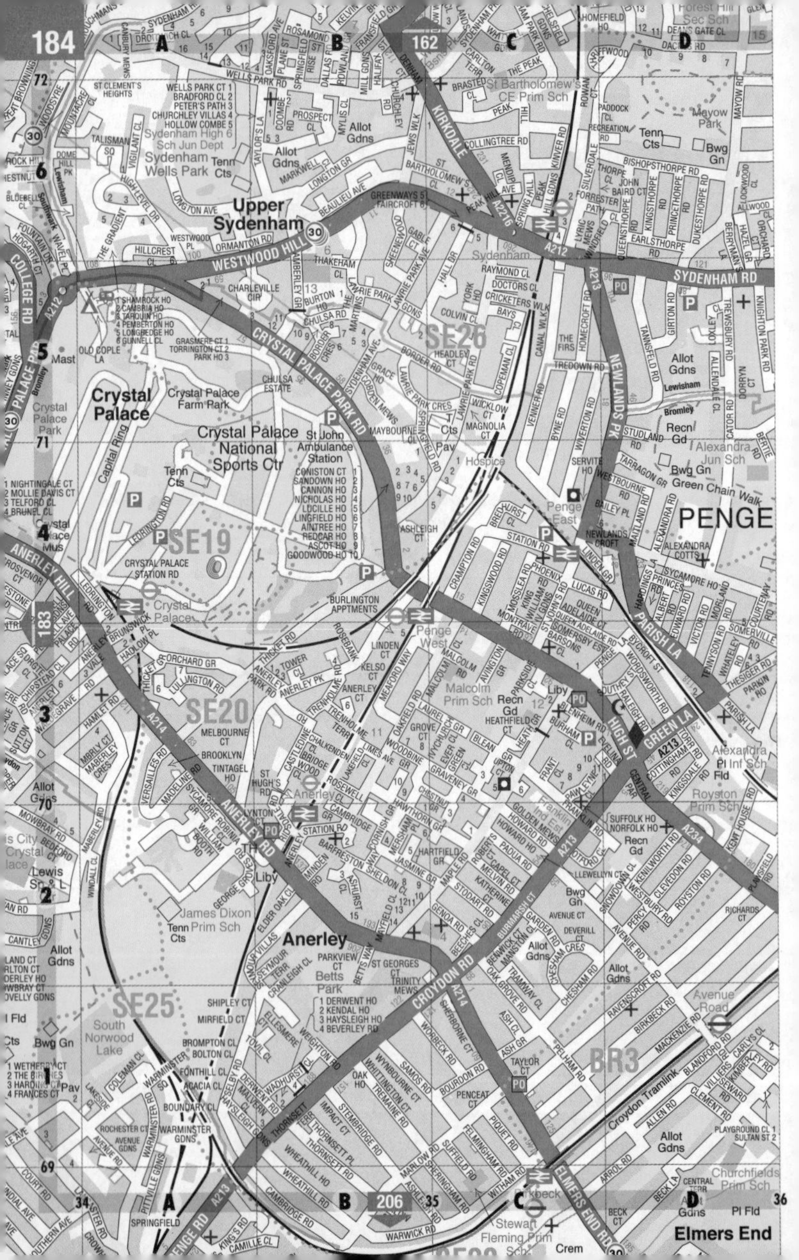

184
A
B
C
D
162
Upper Sydenham
Sydenham Wells Park
Sydenham High Sch Jun Dept
St Bartholomew's CE Prim Sch
Mayow Park
Crystal Palace
Crystal Palace Farm Park
Crystal Palace National Sports Ctr
Crystal Palace Park
St John Ambulance Station
Crystal Palace Mus
SE19
SE26
SE20
SE25
BR3
PENGE
Penge East
Penge West
Crystal Palace
Anerley
Sydenham
Malcolm Prim Sch
Alexandra Jun Sch
Alexandra Inf Sch
Royston Prim Sch
Green Chain Walk
Franklin Ind Est
James Dixon Prim Sch
South Norwood Lake
Betts Park
Avenue Road
Croydon Tramlink
Churchfields Prim Sch
Stewart Fleming Prim Sch
Birkbeck
Elmers End
Capital Ring
WESTWOOD HILL
SYDENHAM RD
CRYSTAL PALACE PARK RD
ANERLEY HILL
ANERLEY RD
CROYDON RD
HIGH ST
GREEN LA
PARISH LA
NEWLANDS PK
KIRKDALE
COLLEGE RD
PALACE PDE
ELMERS END RD
PENGE RD
A212
A213
A214
A216
A234
183
206
34
35
36
72
71
70
69

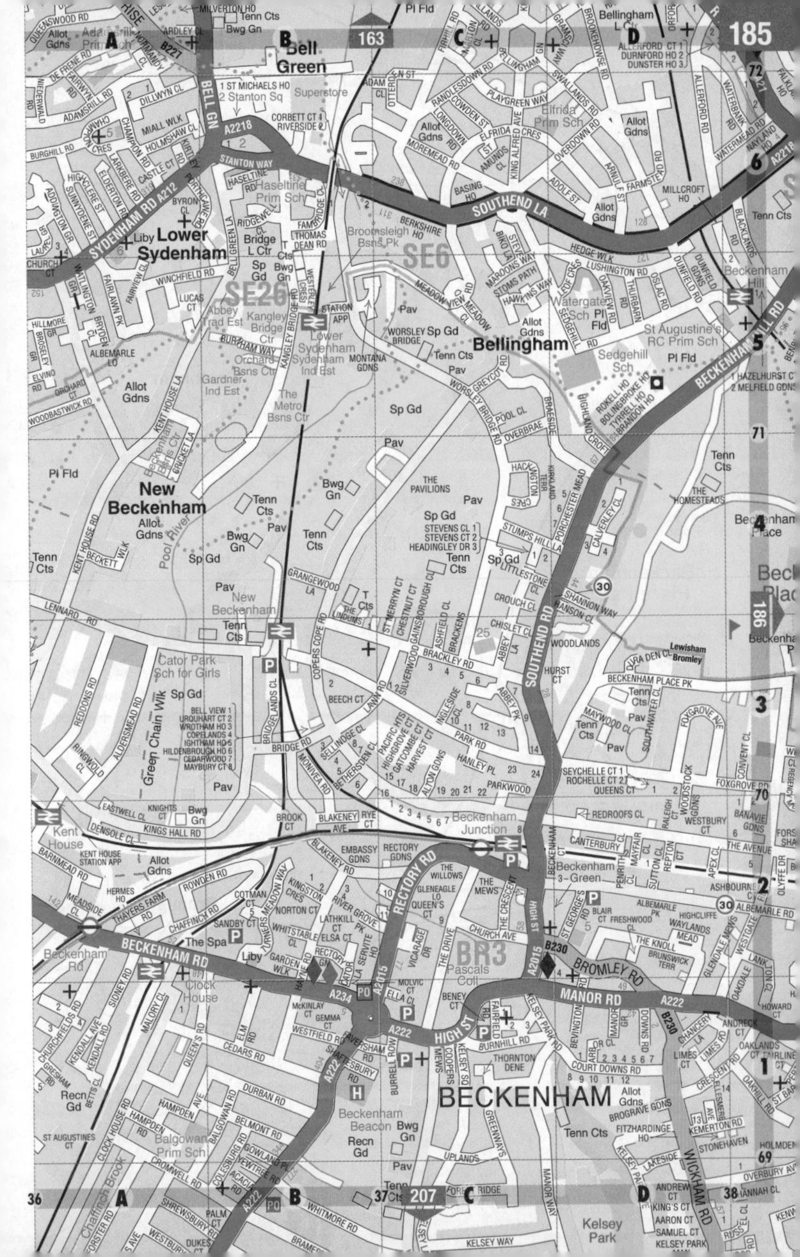

Bell Green
Lower Sydenham
Bellingham
New Beckenham
BECKENHAM
SE26
SE6
BR3
163
186
207
A
B
C
D
36
37
38
72
71
70
69
6
5
4
3
2
1
QUEENSWOOD RD
MILVERTON HO
Tenn Cts
Bwg Gn
PI Fld
Bellingham L Ctr
Adamsrill Prim Sch
ARDLEY CL
B227
NORMANDY CL
BELL GN
1 ST MICHAELS HO
2 Stanton Sq
Superstore
CORBETT CT 1
RIVERSIDE 2
A2218
STANTON WAY
SYDENHAM RD A212
Haseltine Prim Sch
HASELTINE RD
RIDGEWELL CL
Bridge L Ctr
THOMAS DEAN RD
Broomsleigh Bsns Pk
SOUTHEND LA
BERKSHIRE HO
Elfrida Prim Sch
ALLERFORD CT 1
DURNFORD HO 2
DUNSTER HO 3
ALLERFORD RD
WATERBANK RD
WATERMEAD RD
MILLCROFT HO
PLAYGREEN WAY
SWALLANDS RD
BELLINGHAM GN
BROOKEHOWSE RD
RANDLESDOWN RD
COWDEN ST
LONGDOWN RD
MOREMEAD RD
ELFRIDA CRES
KING ALFRED AVE
OVERDOWN RD
ADOLF ST
FARMSTEAD RD
Allot Gdns
BASING HO
Beckenham Hill
HEDGE WLK
LUSHINGTON RD
THURBARN RD
OSLAC RD
DUNFIELD RD
DUNFIELD GDNS
MAROONS WAY
STOMS PATH
HAWKINS WAY
Watergate Sch
St Augustine's RC Prim Sch
Sedgehill Sch
BECKENHAM HILL RD
1 HAZELHURST CT
2 MELFIELD GDNS
ROKELL HO
BOLINGBROKE HO
TYRRELL HO
BRANDON HO
HIGHLAND CROFT
MEADOWVIEW RD
WORSLEY BRIDGE RD
Sp Gd
Pav
GREYCOT RD
POOL CL
OVERBRAE
BRAESIDE
WINCHFIELD RD
Abbey Trad Est
Kangley Bridge Ctr
KANGLEY BRIDGE RD
STATION APP
Lower Sydenham
Sydenham Ind Est
MONTANA GDNS
BURNHAM WAY
Orchard Bsns Ctr
Gardner Ind Est
The Metro Bsns Ctr
ALBEMARLE LO
HILLMORE GR
BROSELEY GR
ELVINO RD
ORCHARD GR
WOODBASTWICK RD
KENT HOUSE LA
Beckenham Bsns Ctr
CRICKET LA
Pool River
THE PAVILIONS
HACKINGTON CRES
KIRKLAND TERR
PORCHESTER MEAD
STEVENS CL 1
STEVENS CT 2
HEADINGLEY DR 3
STUMPS HILL LA
LITTLESTONE CL
CALVERLEY CL
THE HOMESTEADS
Beckenham Place
SHANNON WAY
HANSON CL
CROUCH CL
CHISLET CL
WOODLANDS
HURST CT
SOUTHEND RD
Lewisham
Bromley
DURA DEN CL
BECKENHAM PLACE PK
KENT HOUSE RD
BECKETT WLK
Tenn Cts
Pl Fld
Bwg Gn
LENNARD RD
GRANGEWOOD LA
THE LINDUMS
New Beckenham
Cator Park Sch for Girls
COPERS COPE RD
ST MERRYN CT
CHESTNUT CT
GAINSBOROUGH CL
SILVERWOOD
ASHFIELD CL
BRACKENS
BRACKLEY RD
ABBEY LA
ABBEY PK
BEECH CT
LAWN RD
PARK RD
INGLESIDE CL
HANLEY PL
PARKWOOD
REDDONS RD
ALDERSMEAD RD
RINGWOLD CL
Green Chain Wlk
BELL VIEW 1
URQUHART CT 2
WROTHAM HO 3
COPELANDS 4
IGHTHAM HO 5
HILDENBROUGH HO 6
CEDARWOOD 7
MAYBURY CT 8
BRIDGELANDS CL
BRIDGE RD
SELLINDGE CL
BETHERSDEN CL
MONIVEA RD
PACIFIC HTS
HIGHGROVE CT
GATCOMBE CT
HARVEST CT
ALTON GDNS
MAYWOOD CL
SOUTHWATER CL
FOXGROVE AVE
CONVENT CL
SEYCHELLE CT 1
ROCHELLE CT 2
QUEENS CT
RALEIGH CT
WOODSTOCK GDNS
WESTBURY CT
BANAVIE GDNS
FOXGROVE RD
REDROOFS CL
EASTWELL CL
KNIGHTS CT
KINGS HALL RD
DENSOLE CL
Kent House
BROOK CT
BLAKENEY AVE
RYE CT
Beckenham Junction
CANTERBURY CL
PENRITH CL
MAYFAIR CL
SUTTON CL
REPTON CT
APEX CL
THE AVENUE
BARNMEAD RD
KENT HOUSE STATION APP
HERMES HO
ROWDEN RD
THAYERS FARM RD
MEADSIDE CL
CHAFFINCH RD
SANDBY CT
COTMAN CT
TURNERS MEADOW WAY
KINGSTON CRES
NORTON CT
RIVER GROVE PK
LATHKILL CT
WHITSTABLE CL
ELSA CT
EMBASSY GDNS
RECTORY GDNS
BLAKENEY RD
RECTORY RD
THE WILLOWS
GLENEAGLE LO
QUEEN'S CT
THE MEWS
THE CRESCENT
CHURCH AVE
BECKENHAM CT
Beckenham Green
ST GEORGE'S RD
BLAIR CT
FRESHWOOD CL
ALBEMARLE PK
HIGHCLIFFE
WAYLANDS MEAD
ALBEMARLE RD
ASHBOURNE CT
THE KNOLL
BRUNSWICK TERR
GLENDALE MEWS
WESTGATE
LANKTON CL
OAKDALE
HOWARD CT
BECKENHAM RD
The Spa
Liby
Beckenham Rd
Clock House
GARDEN WLK
RECTORY GN
HAYNE RD
CATOR RD
LA SERVITE HO
A2015
A234
VICARAGE DR
THE DRIVE
Pascals Coll
HIGH ST
B230
BROMLEY RD
MANOR RD
A222
McKINLAY CT
GEMMA CT
ELLA CL
MOLVIC CT
BENEY CT
FAIRFIELD RD
KELSEY PARK RD
BEVINGTON RD
DOWNS RD
CHANCERY LA
LIMES RD
LIMES CT
ANDRECK CT
OAKLANDS CT
FAIRLINE CT
CRESCENT RD
OAKHILL RD
KEMERTON RD
STONEHAVEN
HOLMDENE
OVERBURY AVE
HANNAH CL
WICKHAM RD
CHURCHFIELDS RD
KENDALL AVE
KENDALL RD
SIDNEY RD
MALORY CL
QUEEN'S RD
ELM RD
WESTFIELD RD
CEDARS RD
FAVERSHAM RD
SHAFTESBURY RD
BURRELL ROW
COOPERS MEWS
KELSEY SQ
BURNHILL RD
THORNTON DENE
COURT DOWNS RD
Allot Gdns
BROGRAVE GDNS
FITZHARDINGE HO
LAKESIDE
Recn Gd
GRESHAM RD
BETTS CL
CLOCK HOUSE RD
HAMPDEN AVE
HAMPDEN RD
BALGOWAN RD
DURBAN RD
BELMONT RD
Balgowan Prim Sch
COLESBURG RD
GOWLAND PL
YEWTREE RD
ACACIA RD
Beckenham Beacon
Bwg Gn
Recn Gd
UPLANDS
GREENWAYS
MANOR WAY
Tenn Cts
ST AUGUSTINES CT
CROMWELL RD
Chaffinch Brook
FORSTER RD
SHREWSBURY RD
WESTBURY RD
PALM CT
DUKES CT
WHITMORE RD
BRAMERTON RD
FOREST RIDGE
KELSEY WAY
Kelsey Park
ANDREW CT
KING'S CT
AARON CT
SAMUEL CT
KELSEY PARK
RUSSELL CL
KENWOOD DR

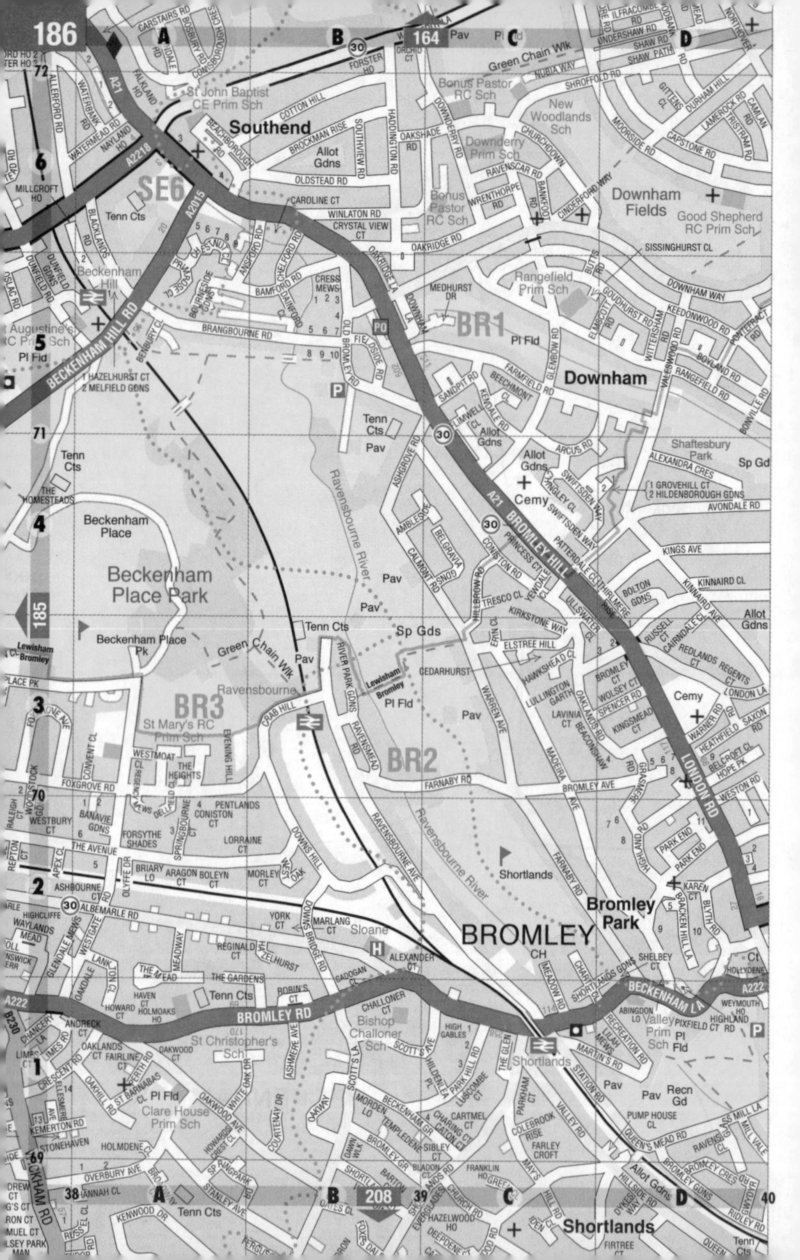

186
164
208
185
A
B
C
D
Southend
SE6
BR1
BR2
BR3
Downham
Downham Fields
BROMLEY
Bromley Park
Shortlands
Beckenham Place Park
Beckenham Place
Beckenham Place Pk
Beckenham Hill
Ravensbourne
Ravensbourne River
Green Chain Wlk
St John Baptist CE Prim Sch
Bonus Pastor RC Sch
New Woodlands Sch
Downderry Prim Sch
Good Shepherd RC Prim Sch
Rangefield Prim Sch
St Augustine's RC Prim Sch
St Mary's RC Prim Sch
St Christopher's Sch
Bishop Challoner Sch
Clare House Prim Sch
Valley Prim Sch
Shaftesbury Park
Sloane
Lewisham
Bromley
BECKENHAM HILL RD
BROMLEY HILL
LONDON RD
BROMLEY RD
BECKENHAM LA
A21
A2218
A2015
A222
B230
BRANGBOURNE RD
DOWNHAM WAY
OAKRIDGE RD
OLDSTEAD RD
WINLATON RD
CRYSTAL VIEW CT
FOXGROVE RD
ALBEMARLE RD
THE AVENUE
FARNABY RD
BROMLEY AVE
RAVENSBOURNE AVE
DOWNS HILL
WARREN AVE
MADEIRA AVE
SHORTLANDS GDNS
STATION RD
VALLEY RD
QUEEN'S MEAD RD
KINGS AVE
AVONDALE RD
ALEXANDRA CRES
RANGEFIELD RD
KEEDONWOOD RD
BOYLAND RD
CAPSTONE RD
MOORSIDE RD
DURHAM HILL
SHROFFOLD RD
CINDERFORD WAY
CHURCHDOWN
HILLSIDE RD
BROMLEY GDNS
OVERBURY AVE
HOLMDENE CL
KENWOOD DR
HAZELWOOD HO
Tenn Cts
Allot Gdns
Pl Fld
Pav
Sp Gds
Sp Gd
Cemy
Recn Gd
CH
38
39
40
69
70
71
72

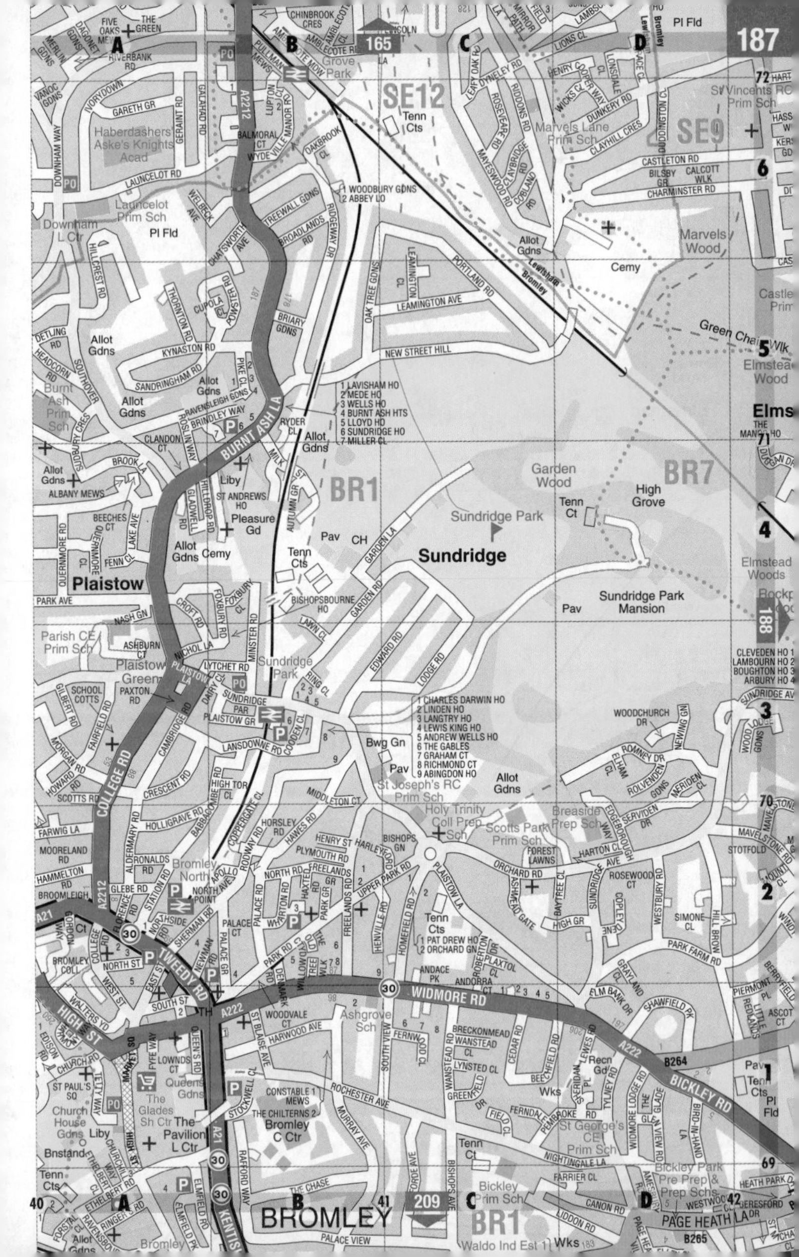

SE12
SE9
BR1
BR7
Grove Park
Haberdashers' Aske's Knights Acad
Launcelot Prim Sch
Downham L Ctr
Marvels Lane Prim Sch
St Vincents RC Prim Sch
Marvels Wood
Cemy
Allot Gdns
Green Chain Wlk
Elmstead Wood
Garden Wood
High Grove
Sundridge Park
Sundridge
Sundridge Park Mansion
Plaistow
Burnt Ash Prim Sch
Parish CE Prim Sch
Plaistow Green
Pleasure Gd
Elmstead Woods
St Joseph's RC Prim Sch
Holy Trinity Coll Prep Sch
Scotts Park Prim Sch
Breaside Prep Sch
Bromley North
Bromley Coll
Ashgrove Sch
Queens Gdns
The Glades Sh Ctr
The Pavilion L Ctr
Church House Gdns
Bromley C Ctr
St George's CE Prim Sch
Bickley Park Pre Prep & Prep Schs
Bickley Prim Sch
BURNT ASH LA
COLLEGE RD
WIDMORE RD
BICKLEY RD
TWEEDY RD
HIGH ST
PAGE HEATH LA
BROMLEY
165
188
209
1 LAVISHAM HO
2 MEDE HO
3 WELLS HO
4 BURNT ASH HTS
5 LLOYD HO
6 SUNDRIDGE HO
7 MILLER CL
1 CHARLES DARWIN HO
2 LINDEN HO
3 LANGTRY HO
4 LEWIS KING HO
5 ANDREW WELLS HO
6 THE GABLES
7 GRAHAM CT
8 RICHMOND CT
9 ABINGDON HO
CLEVEDEN HO
LAMBOURN HO
BOUGHTON HO
ARBURY HO
1 WOODBURY GDNS
2 ABBEY LO
1 PAT DREW HO
2 ORCHARD GN

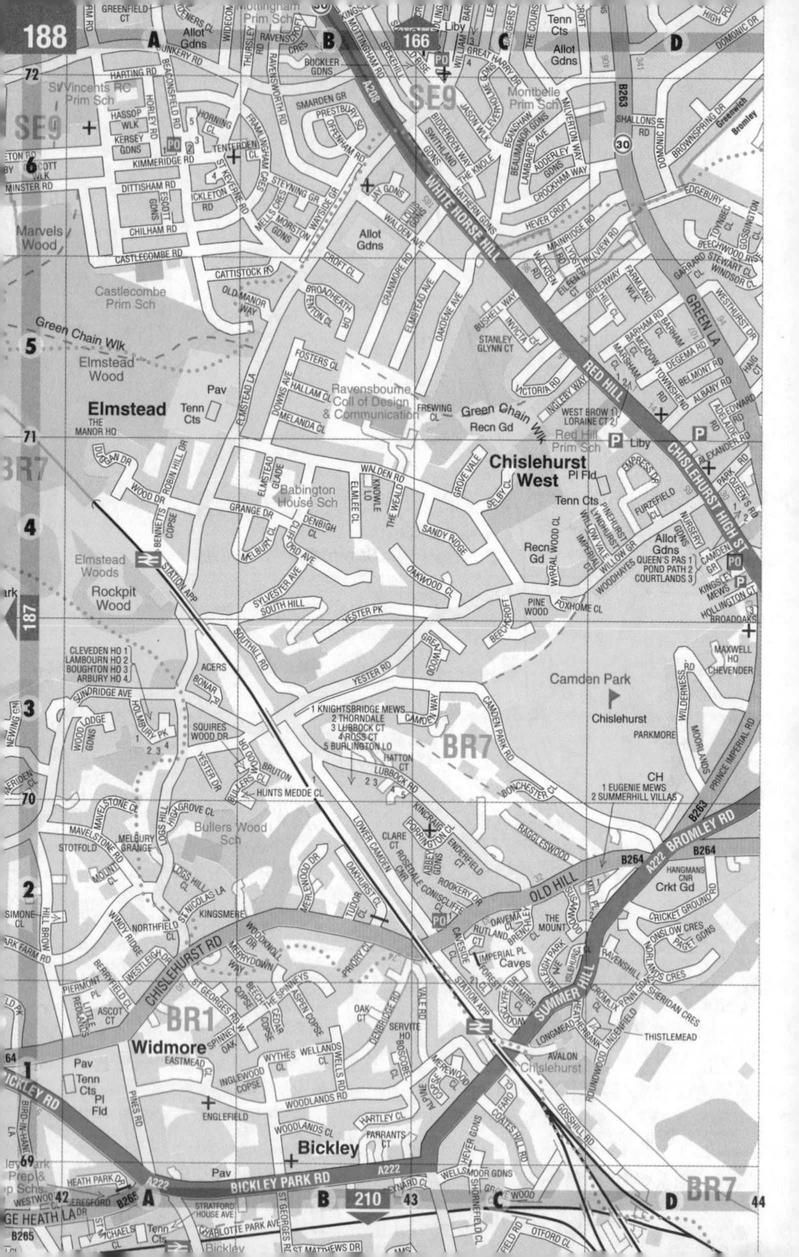
188
A
B
C
D
166
210
187
72
6
5
71
4
3
70
2
1
69
64
42
43
44
SE9
BR7
BR1
Elmstead
Chislehurst West
Widmore
Bickley
Chislehurst
Allot Gdns
Mottingham Prim Sch
Liby
Tenn Cts
GREENFIELD CT
BUNKERY RD
HARTING RD
BEACONSFIELD RD
St Vincents RC Prim Sch
HASSOP WLK
KERSEY GDNS
HORLEY RD
HORNING CL
TENTERDEN CL
KIMMERIDGE RD
DITTISHAM RD
ICKLETON RD
ESCOTT GDNS
CHILHAM RD
CASTLECOMBE RD
CATTISTOCK RD
ST KEVERNE RD
MINSTER RD
Marvels Wood
Castlecombe Prim Sch
OLD MANOR WAY
Green Chain Wlk
Elmstead Wood
THURSLEY RD
RAVENSCROFT CRES
RAVENSWORTH RD
BUCKLER GDNS
SMARDEN GR
PRESTBURY SQ
OFFENHAM RD
FRAMLINGHAM CRES
STEYNING GR
MELLS CRES
MORSTON GDNS
WAYSIDE GR
MOTTINGHAM RD
SPEKEHILL
A208
WHITE HORSE HILL
JAY GDNS
LOUIS GDNS
WALDEN AVE
BIDDENDEN WAY
SWITHLAND GDNS
JASON WLK
THE KNOLE
HATHERN GDNS
Montbelle Prim Sch
GREAT HARRY DR
BEANSHAW
BEAUMANOIR GDNS
LAMBARDE AVE
ADDERLEY GDNS
MILVERTON WAY
CROCKHAM WAY
HEVER CROFT
B263
SHALLONS RD
DOMONIC DR
BROWNSPRING DR
Greenwich
Bromley
EDGEBURY
TOYNBEC CL
GOSSINGTON CL
BEECHWOOD RISE
STEWART CL
WINDSOR CL
GARRARD CL
WESTHURST DR
GREEN LA
CROFT CL
BROADHEATH DR
FENTON CL
CRANMORE RD
ELMSTEAD AVE
OAKDENE AVE
MAINRIDGE RD
WALKDEN RD
EILEEN CT
HILLVIEW RD
GREENWAY
FARMLAND WLK
HILL CL
BUSHELL WAY
INVICTA CL
STANLEY GLYNN CT
BARHAM RD
BARHAM CL
MEADOW RD
MARSHAM CL
DEGEMA RD
TOWNSHEND RD
BELMONT RD
ALBANY RD
HAIG CT
EDWARD RD
ADELAIDE RD
RED HILL
VICTORIA RD
INGLEBY WAY
WEST BROW 1
LORAINE CT 2
Red Hill Prim Sch
FOSTERS CL
DOWNS AVE
HALLAM CL
MELANDA CL
Ravensbourne Coll of Design & Communication
FREWING CL
Green Chain Wlk
Recn Gd
ELMSTEAD LA
Pav
THE MANOR HO
DUNGAN DR
ROBIN HILL DR
WOOD DR
BENNETTS COPSE
ELMSTEAD GLADE
Babington House Sch
KNOWLE LO
ELMLEE CL
THE WEALD
WALDEN RD
GROVE VALE
SELBY CL
GRANGE DR
DENBIGH CL
MELBURY CL
CLIFFORD AVE
SANDY RIDGE
Pl Fld
EMPRESS DR
PINEHURST
LYNDHURST
WILLOW VALE
IMPERIAL WAY
WRRAL WOOD CL
FURZEFIELD CL
NURSERY GDNS
ALEXANDER RD
PARK RD
QUEEN'S RD
CHISLEHURST HIGH ST
WILLOW GR
WOODHAYES
QUEEN'S PAS 1
POND PATH 2
COURTLANDS 3
CAMDEN GR
KINGSLEY MEWS
HOLLINGTON CT
BROADOAKS
Elmstead Woods
Rockpit Wood
STATION APP
SYLVESTER AVE
SOUTH HILL
YESTER PK
OAKWOOD CL
PINE WOOD
FOXHOME CL
BEECHCROFT
GREAT WOOD
SOUTHILL RD
YESTER RD
CLEVEDEN HO 1
LAMBOURN HO 2
BOUGHTON HO 3
ARBURY HO 4
SUNDRIDGE AVE
ACERS
BONAR PL
Camden Park
MAXWELL HO
CHEVENDER
WILDERNESS RD
MOORLANDS
PARKMORE
PRINCE IMPERIAL RD
WOOD LODGE GDNS
HOLMBURY PK
SQUIRES WOOD DR
1 KNIGHTSBRIDGE MEWS
2 THORNDALE
3 LUBBOCK CT
4 ROSS CT
5 BURLINGTON LO
CAMDEN WAY
CAMDEN PARK RD
HATTON CT
LUBBOCK RD
YESTER DR
WOOD DR
BULLERS CL
BRUTON CL
HUNTS MEDDE CL
BONCHESTER CL
CH
1 EUGENIE MEWS
2 SUMMERHILL VILLAS
MAVELSTONE CL
MAVELSTONE RD
GROVE CL
LOGS HILL
Bullers Wood Sch
STOTFOLD
MELBURY GRANGE
LOWER CAMDEN
KINCRAIG
PORRINGTON CL
CLARE CT
ROSEDALE CNR
ABBEY GDNS
ENDERFIELD CT
RAGGLESWOOD
BROMLEY RD
A222
B264
HANGMANS CNR
Crkt Gd
MOUNT CL
LOGS HILL CL
ST NICOLAS LA
MERLEWOOD DR
OAKHURST CL
TUDOR CL
CONISCLIFFE
ROOKERY DR
OLD HILL
SUSAWOOD
MILL PL
CRICKET GROUND RD
ONSLOW CRES
PAGET GDNS
SIMONE CL
HILL BROW
WINDY RIDGE
NORTHFIELD CL
KINGSMERE
WOODKNOLL DR
MERRYDOWN WAY
CHISLEHURST RD
PRIORY CL
DAVEMA CL
RUTLAND CT
BRENCHLEY
THE MOUNT
OAKLEIGH PARK AVE
IMPERIAL PL
Caves
ISLEHURST CL
RAVENSHILL
NORLANDS CRES
PARK FARM RD
WESTLEIGH DR
BERRYFIELD CL
PIERMONT PL
LITTLE REDLANDS
ASCOT CT
ST GEORGES RD W
COPSE
BEECH COPSE
THE SPINNEYS
ASPEN COPSE
CEDAR COPSE
OAK CT
DENBRIDGE RD
VALE RD
SERVITE HO
BOSCOBEL
CAVESIDE CL
STATION APP
FOREST CL
CHISLEHURST
SUMMER HILL
CROMLIX CL
PENN GDNS
SHERIDAN CRES
HEATHERBANK
LINDENFIELD
THISTLEMEAD
LONGMEAD
Widmore
SPINNEY OAK
EASTMEAD
WYTHES CL
WELLANDS CL
WELLS RD
AVALON
Chislehurst
ROUNDWOOD
BICKLEY RD
BIRD-IN-HAND LA
Pav
Tenn Cts
Pl Fld
PINES RD
INGLEWOOD COPSE
ENGLEFIELD
WOODLANDS RD
MEREWOOD CL
COPSE
ALPINE
FARO CL
COATES HILL RD
GOSSHILL RD
HARTLEY CL
WOODLANDS CL
FARRANTS CT
Bickley
HEVER GDNS
HEATH PARK DR
Bickley Park Prep Sch
BICKLEY PARK RD
WELLSMOOR GDNS
HEATH LA
WESTWOOD CL
BERESFORD
B265
STRATFORD HOUSE AVE
ST GEORGES RD
SHORNEFIELD CL
WOOD
CHARLOTTE PARK AVE
ST MICHAELS CL
ST MATTHEWS DR
OTFORD CL
Bickley

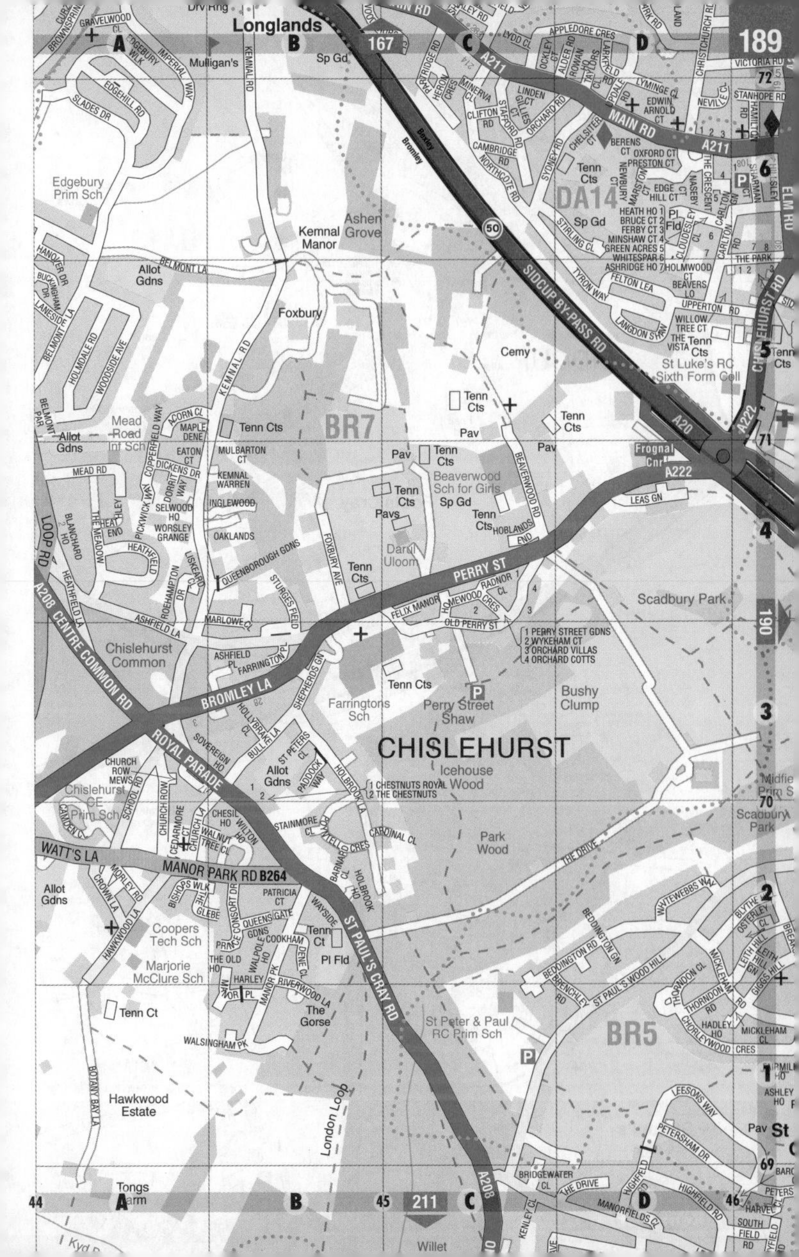
Longlands
167
Mulligan's
Sp Gd
Edgebury Prim Sch
Kemnal Manor
Ashen Grove
Allot Gdns
Foxbury
BR7
DA14
SIDCUP BY-PASS RD
MAIN RD
A211
Tenn Cts
Cemy
St Luke's RC Sixth Form Coll
Frognal Cnr
A20
A222
Mead Road Inf Sch
Beaverwood Sch for Girls
Darul Uloom
PERRY ST
Scadbury Park
190
Chislehurst Common
BROMLEY LA
CENTRE COMMON RD
LOOP RD
A208
Farringtons Sch
Perry Street Shaw
Bushy Clump
CHISLEHURST
Icehouse Wood
ROYAL PARADE
Chislehurst CE Prim Sch
WATT'S LA
MANOR PARK RD B264
Park Wood
THE DRIVE
Coopers Tech Sch
Marjorie McClure Sch
ST PAUL'S CRAY RD
St Peter & Paul RC Prim Sch
BR5
Hawkwood Estate
London Loop
Tongs Farm
1 PERRY STREET GDNS
2 WYKEHAM CT
3 ORCHARD VILLAS
4 ORCHARD COTTS
1 CHESTNUTS ROYAL
2 THE CHESTNUTS
44
45
46
211
Willet

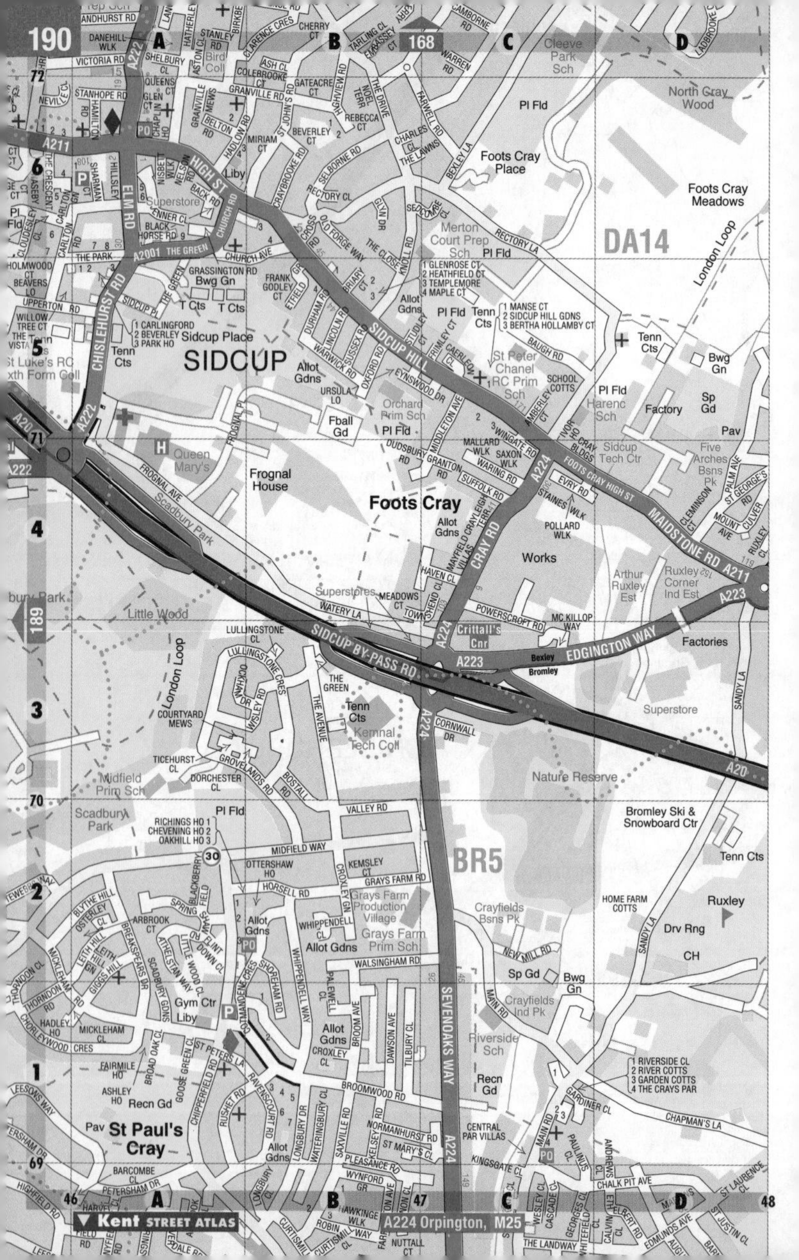

190
168
A
B
C
D
189
Kent STREET ATLAS
A224 Orpington, M25
46
47
48
72
71
70
69
6
5
4
3
2
1
SIDCUP
Foots Cray
St Paul's Cray
DA14
BR5
HIGH ST
ELM RD
CHISLEHURST RD
SIDCUP HILL
FOOTS CRAY HIGH ST
MAIDSTONE RD
CRAY RD
SIDCUP BY-PASS RD
EDGINGTON WAY
SEVENOAKS WAY
A20
A211
A222
A223
A224
A2001
THE GREEN
CHURCH RD
CHURCH AVE
VICTORIA RD
STANHOPE RD
GRANVILLE RD
SELBORNE RD
RECTORY CL
RECTORY LA
OLD FORGE WAY
FROGNAL AVE
Frognal House
Queen Mary's
Sidcup Place
Scadbury Park
Little Wood
London Loop
Foots Cray Place
Foots Cray Meadows
North Cray Wood
Cleeve Park Sch
Merton Court Prep Sch
St Peter Chanel RC Prim Sch
Orchard Prim Sch
Harenc Sch
Sidcup Tech Ctr
Five Arches Bsns Pk
Arthur Ruxley Est
Ruxley Corner Ind Est
Crittall's Cnr
Superstores
Superstore
Works
Factory
Factories
Kemnal Tech Coll
Nature Reserve
Bromley Ski & Snowboard Ctr
Ruxley
Drv Rng
Grays Farm Production Village
Grays Farm Prim Sch
Crayfields Bsns Pk
Crayfields Ind Pk
Riverside Sch
Midfield Prim Sch
MIDFIELD WAY
GRAYS FARM RD
VALLEY RD
WALSINGHAM RD
BROOMWOOD RD
NEW MILL RD
SANDY LA
CHAPMAN'S LA
MAIN RD
KINGSGATE CL
CHALK PIT AVE
ST LAURENCE CL
CORNWALL DR
POWERSCROFT RD
WATERY LA
Bexley
Bromley

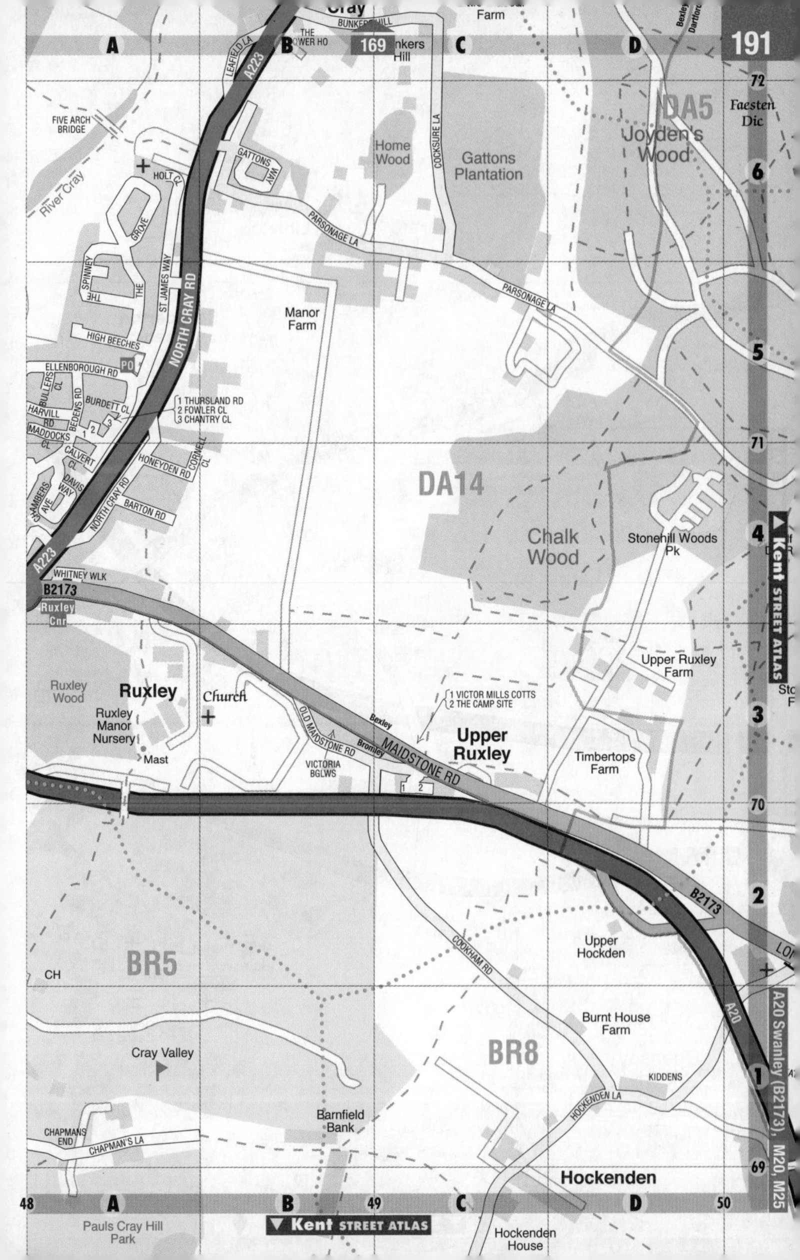
A
B
C
D
169
Bunkers Hill
BUNKERS HILL
THE TOWER HO
Farm
72
Faesten Dic
DA5
Joyden's Wood
6
FIVE ARCH BRIDGE
River Cray
LEAFIELD LA
A223
GATTONS WAY
Home Wood
COCKSURE LA
Gattons Plantation
HOLT CL
THE GROVE
THE SPINNEY
ST JAMES WAY
NORTH CRAY RD
PARSONAGE LA
Manor Farm
HIGH BEECHES
ELLENBOROUGH RD
PO
BULLERS CL
BEDENS RD
HARVILL RD
BURDETT CL
MADDOCKS CL
CALVERT CL
1 THURSLAND RD
2 FOWLER CL
3 CHANTRY CL
HONEYDEN RD
CORNELL CL
5
71
DA14
DAVIS WAY
CHAMBERS AVE
BARTON RD
Chalk Wood
Stonehill Woods Pk
4
WHITNEY WLK
B2173
Ruxley Cnr
Upper Ruxley Farm
Ruxley Wood
Ruxley
Church
1 VICTOR MILLS COTTS
2 THE CAMP SITE
3
Ruxley Manor Nursery
Mast
OLD MAIDSTONE RD
VICTORIA BGLWS
Bexley
Bromley
MAIDSTONE RD
Upper Ruxley
Timbertops Farm
70
2
Upper Hockden
COOKHAM RD
CH
BR5
A20
Burnt House Farm
Cray Valley
BR8
KIDDENS
1
HOCKENDEN LA
Barnfield Bank
CHAPMANS END
CHAPMAN'S LA
69
Hockenden
48
49
50
Kent STREET ATLAS
A20 Swanley (B2173), M20, M25
Pauls Cray Hill Park
Hockenden House

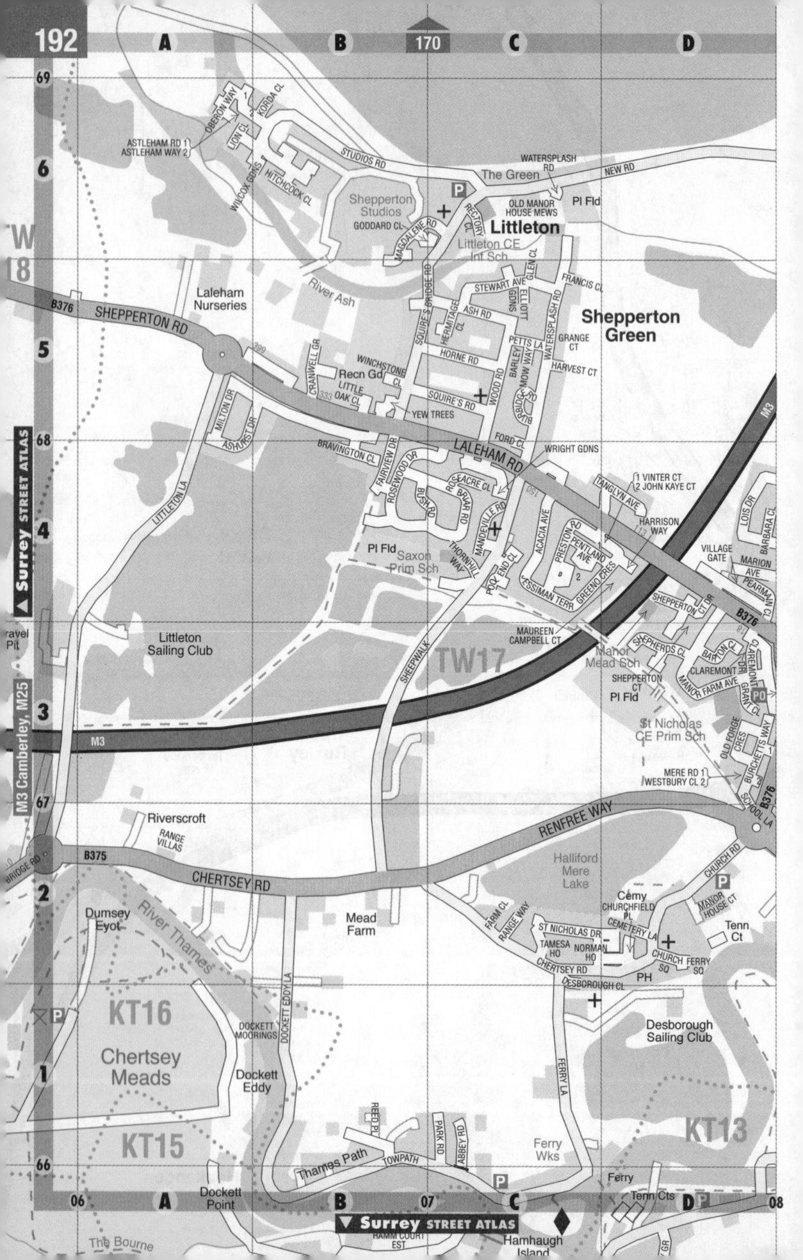

A
B
170
C
D
Surrey STREET ATLAS
M3 Camberley, M25
Littleton
Shepperton Green
Shepperton Studios
STUDIOS RD
The Green
NEW RD
WATERSPLASH RD
OLD MANOR HOUSE MEWS
Pl Fld
OBERON WAY
KORDA CL
LION CL
ASTLEHAM RD 1
ASTLEHAM WAY 2
WILCOX GDNS
HITCHCOCK CL
GODDARD CL
MAGDALENE RD
RECTORY CL
Littleton CE Inf Sch
River Ash
SQUIRE'S BRIDGE RD
STEWART AVE
GLEN CL
ELLIOTT GDNS
FRANCIS CL
HERMITAGE CL
ASH RD
WATERSPLASH RD
PETTS LA
GRANGE CT
HARVEST CT
HORNE RD
Laleham Nurseries
B376
SHEPPERTON RD
CRANWELL GR
WINCHSTONE CL
Recn Gd
LITTLE OAK CL
SQUIRE'S RD
YEW TREES
WOOD RD
BARLEY MOW WAY
BURBIDGE RD
FORD CL
MILTON DR
ASHURST DR
BRAVINGTON CL
FAIRVIEW DR
ROSEWOOD DR
LALEHAM RD
WRIGHT GDNS
ROSEACRE CL
BRIAR RD
BUSH RD
MANDEVILLE RD
ACACIA AVE
PRESTON RD
PENTLAND AVE
TANGLYN AVE
1 VINTER CT
2 JOHN KAYE CT
HARRISON WAY
LOIS DR
BARBARA CL
VILLAGE GATE
MARION AVE
PEARMAIN CL
LITTLETON LA
Pl Fld
Saxon Prim Sch
THORNHILL WAY
POOL END CL
JESSIMAN TERR
GREENO CRES
SHEPPERTON CT DR
B376
M3
Littleton Sailing Club
MAUREEN CAMPBELL CT
SHEEPWALK
TW17
Manor Mead Sch
SHEPHERDS CL
BARTON CL
CLAREMONT DR
CLAREMONT
MANOR FARM AVE
GRANT CL
SHEPPERTON CT
Pl Fld
St Nicholas CE Prim Sch
OLD FORGE CRES
BURCHETTS WAY
MERE RD 1
WESTBURY CL 2
SCHOOL LA
Riverscroft
RANGE VILLAS
RENFREE WAY
B375
CHERTSEY RD
BRIDGE RD
Halliford Mere Lake
CHURCH RD
Cemy
CHURCHFIELD PL
MANOR HOUSE CT
Tenn Ct
Dumsey Eyot
River Thames
Mead Farm
FARM CL
RANGE WAY
ST NICHOLAS DR
CEMETERY LA
TAMESA HO
NORMAN HO
CHURCH SQ
FERRY SQ
CHERTSEY RD
PH
DESBOROUGH CL
KT16
DOCKETT MOORINGS
DOCKETT EDDY LA
Desborough Sailing Club
Chertsey Meads
Dockett Eddy
FERRY LA
REED PL
PARK RD
ABBEY RD
KT15
KT13
Ferry Wks
Thames Path
TOWPATH
Ferry
Tenn Cts
Dockett Point
06
07
08
69
6
5
68
4
3
67
2
1
66
HAMM COURT EST
Hamhaugh Island
The Bourne

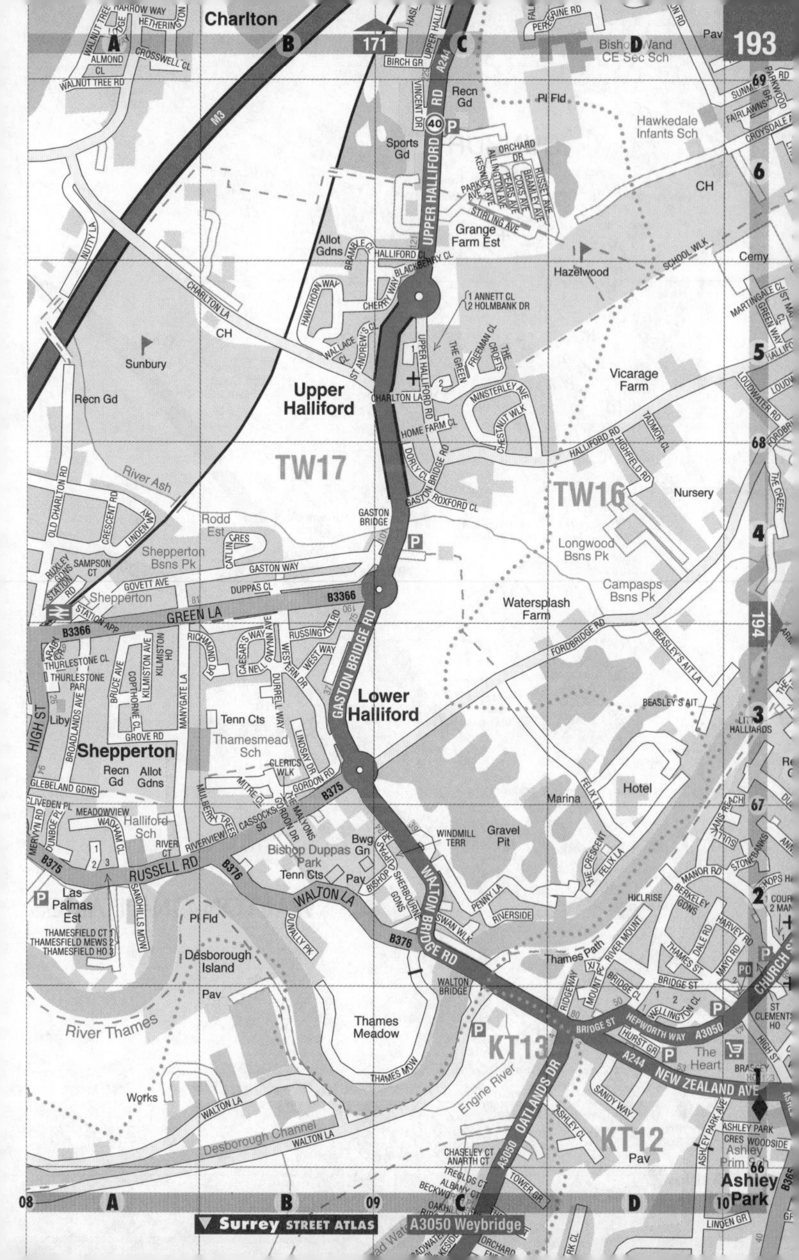

Charlton
A
B
171
C
D
Bishop Wand CE Sec Sch
Pav
HARROW WAY
HETHERINGTON
WALNUT TREE
ALMOND CL
CROSSWELL CL
WALNUT TREE RD
BIRCH GR
UPPER HALLIFORD
A244
VINCENT DR
Recn Gd
PEREGRINE RD
Pl Fld
Hawkedale Infants Sch
PARKWOOD
SUMMER GR
FAIRLAWNS
CROYSDALE AV
M3
40
Sports Gd
UPPER HALLIFORD RD
ORCHARD DR
ALLINGTON AVE
KESWICK AVE
PEARS AVE
COXS AVE
BRAMLEY AVE
RUSSET AVE
PARK AVE
STIRLING AVE
6
CH
NUTTY LA
Allot Gdns
BRAMBLE CL
HALLIFORD CL
BLACKBERRY CL
Grange Farm Est
Hazelwood
SCHOOL WLK
Cemy
CHARLTON LA
HAWTHORN WAY
CHERRY WAY
1 ANNETT CL
2 HOLMBANK DR
MARTINGALE CL
GREEN WAY
CH
WALLACE CL
ST ANDREW'S CL
FREEMAN CL
THE CROFTS
THE GREEN
Sunbury
5
Vicarage Farm
Upper Halliford
CHARLTON LA
MINSTERLEY AVE
LOUDWATER RD
Recn Gd
HOME FARM CL
CHESTNUT WLK
HALLIFORD RD
HIGHFIELD RD
TADMOR CL
68
TW17
DORLY CL
GASTON BRIDGE RD
TW16
Nursery
THE CREEK
River Ash
OLD CHARLTON RD
CRESCENT RD
LINDEN WAY
GASTON ROXFORD CL
GASTON BRIDGE
Rodd Est
CATLIN CRES
4
Longwood Bsns Pk
Shepperton Bsns Pk
BUXLEY GDNS
SAMPSON CT
GASTON WAY
STATION RD
GOVETT AVE
DUPPAS CL
Shepperton
B3366
Campasps Bsns Pk
Watersplash Farm
STATION APP
GREEN LA
194
B3366
ARABY CT
THURLESTONE CL
THURLESTONE PAR
RICHMOND DR
KILMISTON AVE
KILMISTON HO
CAESAR'S WAY
NELL GWYNN AVE
RUSSINGTON RD
WESTERN DR
WEST WAY
FORDBRIDGE RD
BEASLEY'S AIT LA
BRUCE AVE
COPTHORNE CL
BROADLANDS AVE
MANYGATE LA
DURRELL WAY
GASTON BRIDGE RD
Lower Halliford
BEASLEY'S AIT
HIGH ST
Liby
Tenn Cts
LITTLE HALLIARDS
3
GROVE RD
Thamesmead Sch
LINDSAY DR
Shepperton
Recn Gd
Allot Gdns
CLERICS WLK
GORDON RD
FELIX LA
Hotel
GLEBELAND GDNS
MITRE CL
Marina
B375
CLIVEDEN PL
MEADOWVIEW
MULBERRY TREES
THE MALYONS
GORDON DR
CASSOCKS SQ
67
MERVYN RD
DUNBOE PL
WADHAM CL
Halliford Sch
RIVER CT
RIVERVIEW
Bwg Gn
WINDMILL TERR
Gravel Pit
THE CRESCENT
FELIX LA
Bishop Duppas Park
B375
RUSSELL RD
B376
Tenn Cts
Pav
BISHOP DUPPAS PK
SHERBOURNE GDNS
WALTON BRIDGE RD
MANOR RD
STONEBANKS
BERKELEY GDNS
HILLRISE
2
Las Palmas Est
SANDHILLS MDW
WALTON LA
PENNY LA
RIVERSIDE
SWAN WLK
HARVEY RD
DALE RD
Pl Fld
THAMESFIELD CT 1
THAMESFIELD MEWS 2
THAMESFIELD HO 3
DUNALLY PK
B376
Desborough Island
Thames Path
RIVER MOUNT
MOUNT PL
RIDGEWAY
THAMES ST
MAYO RD
BRIDGE CL
BRIDGE ST
WALTON BRIDGE
Pav
WELLINGTON CL
ST CLEMENTS HO
River Thames
BRIDGE ST
HEPWORTH WAY
A3050
CHURCH ST
Thames Meadow
KT13
HURST GR
The Heart
HIGH ST
A244
NEW ZEALAND AVE
BRASSEY
1
Engine River
OATLANDS DR
SANDY WAY
THAMES MDW
Works
WALTON LA
ASHLEY CL
ASHLEY PARK AVE
ASHLEY PARK CRES
WOODSIDE
Desborough Channel
WALTON LA
A3050
KT12
Ashley Prim Sch
CHASELEY CT
ANARTH CT
TOWER GR
Pav
66
TREGLOS CT
ALBANY CT
Ashley Park
08
A
B
09
C
D
10
B365
LINDEN GR
ORCHARD

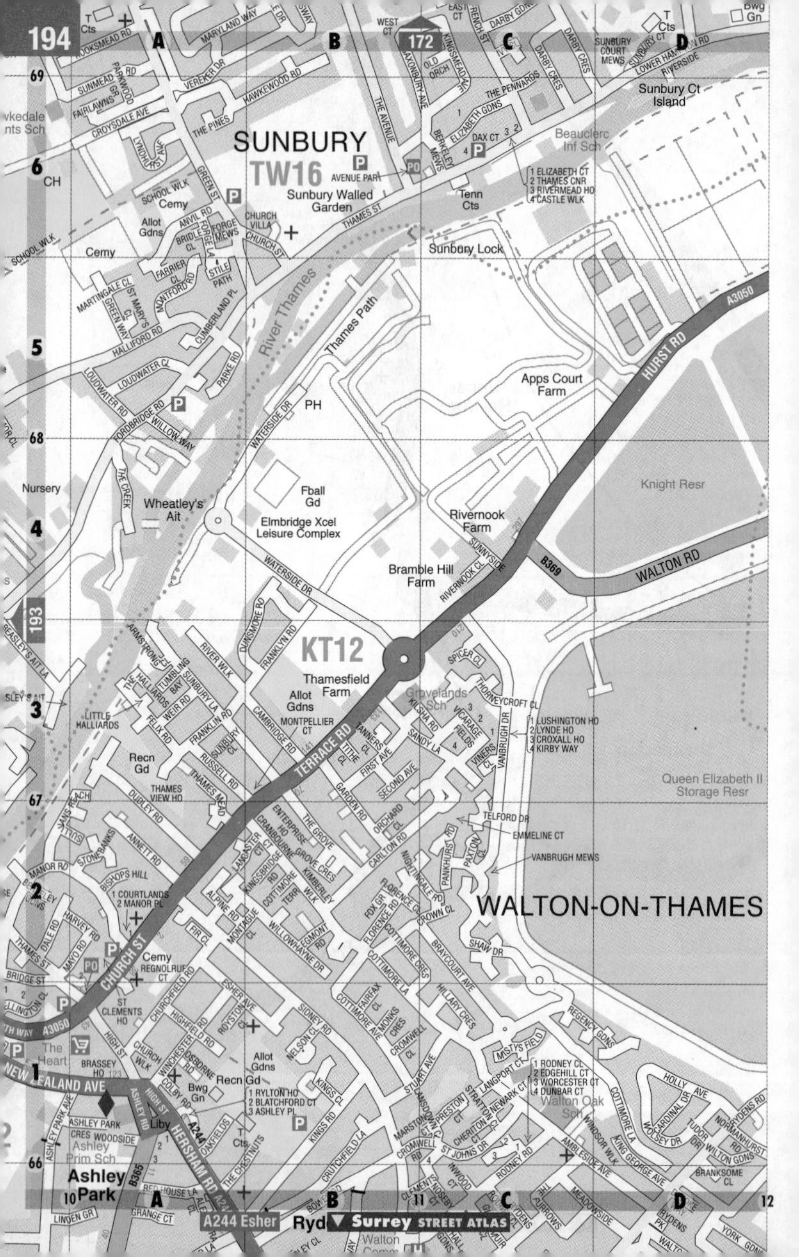

194
A
B
C
D
172
SUNBURY
TW16
Sunbury Walled Garden
AVENUE PARK
THAMES ST
Tenn Cts
1 ELIZABETH CT
2 THAMES CNR
3 RIVERMEAD HO
4 CASTLE WLK
Beauclerc Inf Sch
Sunbury Ct Island
SUNBURY COURT MEWS
LOWER HAMPTON RD
RIVERSIDE
THE PENNARDS
DARBY CRES
DARBY GDNS
ELIZABETH GDNS
DAX CT
BERKELEY MEWS
KINGSMEAD AVE
SAXONBURY AVE
THE AVENUE
OLD ORCH
WEST CT
EAST CT
FRENCH ST
MARYLAND WAY
HAWKEWOOD RD
VEREKER DR
THE PINES
CROYSDALE AVE
FAIRLAWNS
SUNMEAD RD
PARKWOOD GR
BROOKSMEAD RD
LYNDHURST AVE
GREEN ST
SCHOOL WLK
Cemy
Allot Gdns
ANVIL RD
BRIDLE CL
FORGE LA
FORGE MEWS
CHURCH VILLA
CHURCH ST
FARRIER CL
STILE PATH
MONTFORD RD
MARTINGALE CL
ST MARY'S CL
GREEN WAY
CUMBERLAND PL
HALLIFORD RD
LOUDWATER CL
LOUDWATER RD
PARKE RD
FORDBRIDGE RD
WILLOW WAY
River Thames
Sunbury Lock
Thames Path
WATERSIDE DR
PH
Apps Court Farm
HURST RD
A3050
Knight Resr
Nursery
THE CREEK
Wheatley's Ait
Fball Gd
Elmbridge Xcel Leisure Complex
Rivernook Farm
SUNNYSIDE
RIVERNOOK CL
Bramble Hill Farm
B369
WALTON RD
193
KT12
Thamesfield Farm
Allot Gdns
MONTPELLIER CT
Grovelands Sch
SPICER CL
THORNEYCROFT CL
VANBRUGH DR
1 LUSHINGTON HO
2 LYNDE HO
3 CROXALL HO
4 KIRBY WAY
Queen Elizabeth II Storage Resr
ARMSTRONG CL
TUMBLING BAY
THE HALLIARDS
LITTLE HALLIARDS
WEIR RD
FELIX RD
SUNBURY LA
RIVER WLK
DUNSMORE RD
FRANKLYN RD
FRANKLIN RD
CAMBRIDGE RD
TERRACE RD
TANNERS CL
TITHE CL
FIRST AVE
SECOND AVE
KILSHA RD
SANDY LA
VICARAGE FIELDS
VINERS CL
Recn Gd
RUSSELL RD
SUNBURY CL
THAMES VIEW HO
THAMES MEAD
DUDLEY RD
ANNETT RD
STONEBANKS
BISHOPS HILL
MANOR RD
1 COURTLANDS
2 MANOR PL
ENTERPRISE HO
CRANBOURNE CT
LANCASTER CT
THE GROVE
GARDEN RD
ORCHARD CL
CARLTON RD
TELFORD DR
EMMELINE CT
VANBRUGH MEWS
PANKHURST RD
PAXTON CL
GROVE CRES
KINGSBRIDGE RD
COTTIMORE TERR
KIMBERLEY WLK
ALPINE RD
MONTAGUE CL
WILLOWHAYNE DR
EGMONT RD
FOX GR
FLORENCE RD
FLORENCE CL
NIGHTINGALE RD
CROWN CL
COTTIMORE CRES
COTTIMORE LA
BRAYCOURT AVE
SHAW DR
WALTON-ON-THAMES
HARVEY RD
OALE RD
MAYO RD
THAMES ST
BRIDGE ST
CHURCH ST
Cemy
REGNOLRUF CT
FIR CL
CHURCHFIELD RD
ESHER AVE
ROYSTON AVE
HIGHFIELD RD
ST CLEMENTS HO
HIGH ST
FAIRFAX CL
MONKS CRES
CROMWELL CL
HILLARY CRES
REGENCY GDNS
SIDNEY RD
NELSON CL
The Heart
BRASSEY HO
NEW ZEALAND AVE
CHURCH WLK
WINCHESTER RD
OSBORNE RD
Recn Gd
Allot Gdns
1 RYLTON HO
2 BLATCHFORD CT
3 ASHLEY PL
KINGS CL
KINGS RD
STUART AVE
MISTYS FIELD
LANGPORT CT
1 RODNEY CL
2 EDGEHILL CT
3 WORCESTER CT
4 DUNBAR CT
Walton Oak Sch
HOLLY AVE
CARDINAL DR
WOLSEY DR
TUDOR DR
NORMANHURST RD
RYDENS RD
WILTON GDNS
BRANKSOME CL
ASHLEY PARK AVE
ASHLEY PARK CRES
WOODSIDE
Ashley Prim Sch
Ashley Park
ASHLEY RD
HIGH ST
Liby
COLBY RD
Bwg Gn
A244
HERSHAM RD
OAKFIELDS
T Cts
THE CHESTNUTS
CRUTCHFIELD LA
MARSTON CT
CROMWELL RD
ST JOHNS DR
PRESTON CT
CHERITON CT
STRATTON CT
NEWARK CT
RODNEY RD
AMBLESIDE AVE
WINDSOR WLK
COTTIMORE LA
KING GEORGE AVE
THE FURROWS
MEADOWSIDE
B365
RED HOUSE LA
GRANGE CT
LINDEN GR
A244 Esher
Ryd
Surrey STREET ATLAS
10
11
12
66
67
68
69
1
2
3
4
5
6

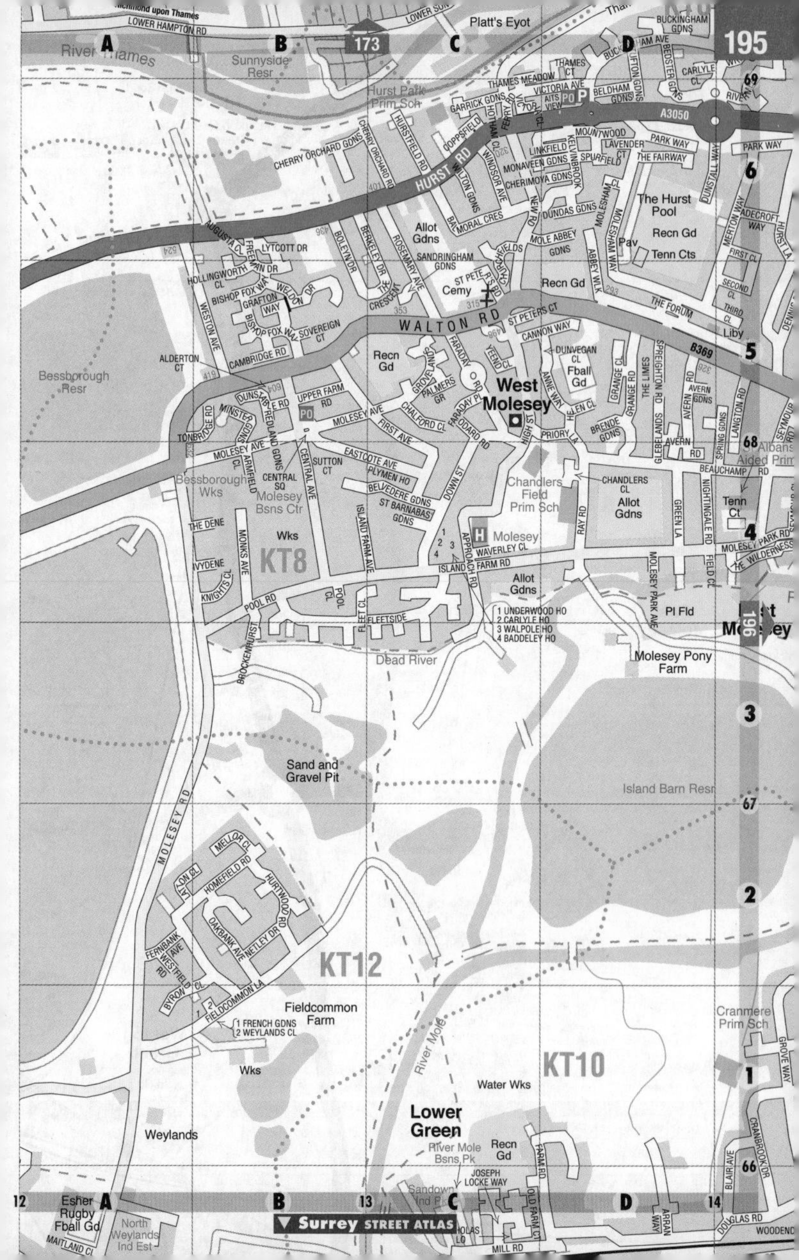

River Thames
Sunnyside Resr
Platt's Eyot
Hurst Park Prim Sch
HURST RD
A3050
WALTON RD
B369
West Molesey
The Hurst Pool
Recn Gd
Tenn Cts
Allot Gdns
Cemy
Bessborough Resr
Bessborough Wks
Molesey Bsns Ctr
KT8
Chandlers Field Prim Sch
Molesey
Pl Fld
East Molesey
Molesey Pony Farm
Dead River
Sand and Gravel Pit
Island Barn Resr
MOLESEY RD
KT12
Fieldcommon Farm
Wks
Weylands
River Mole
KT10
Water Wks
Lower Green
River Mole Bsns Pk
Sandown Ind Pk
Cranmere Prim Sch
Esher Rugby Fball Gd
North Weylands Ind Est
1 UNDERWOOD HO
2 CARLYLE HO
3 WALPOLE HO
4 BADDELEY HO
1 FRENCH GDNS
2 WEYLANDS CL

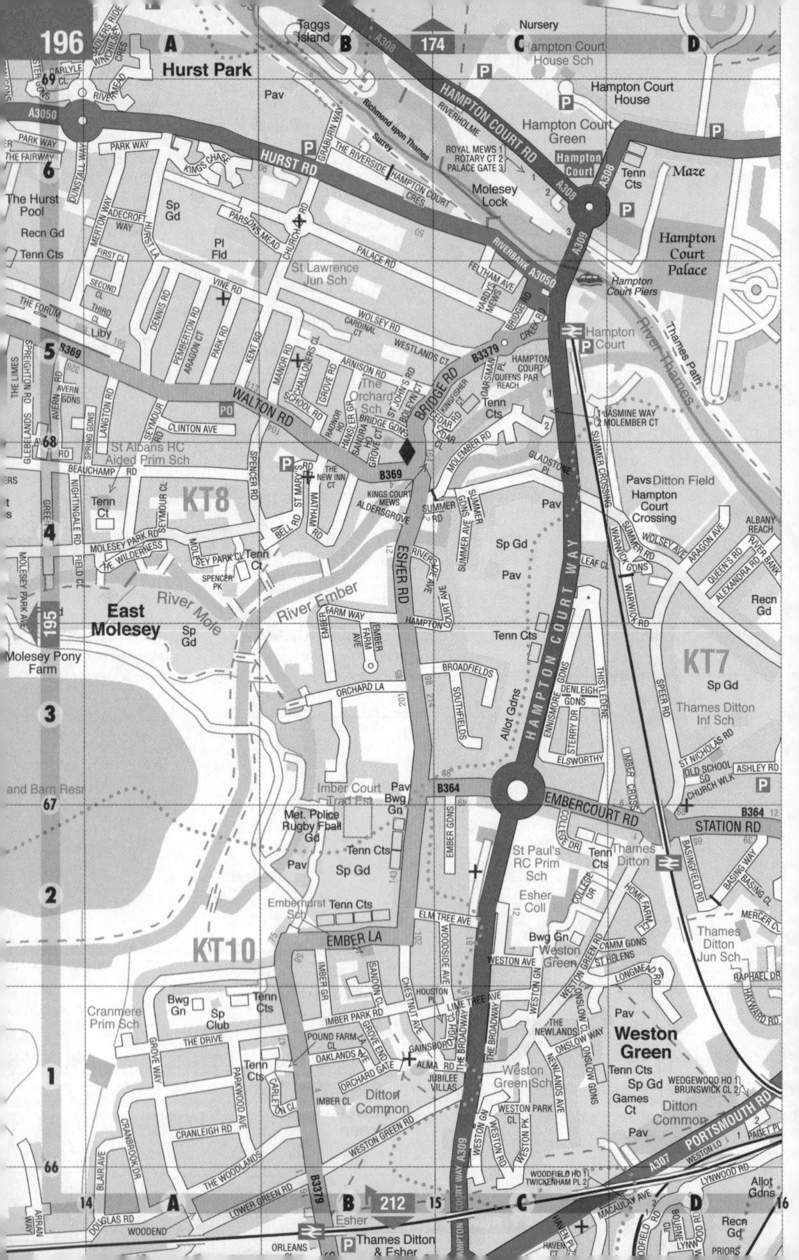

174
Taggs Island
Nursery
Hampton Court House Sch
Hurst Park
Hampton Court House
Hampton Court Green
Hampton Court
Molesey Lock
Tenn Cts
Maze
Hampton Court Palace
Hampton Court Piers
River Thames
Thames Path
HAMPTON COURT RD
HURST RD
Richmond upon Thames
Surrey
The Hurst Pool
Recn Gd
Tenn Cts
Sp Gd
Pl Fld
St Lawrence Jun Sch
Liby
WALTON RD
The Orchard Sch
St Albans RC Aided Prim Sch
KT8
East Molesey
Molesey Pony Farm
River Mole
River Ember
ESHER RD
HAMPTON COURT WAY
Ditton Field
Hampton Court Crossing
KT7
Thames Ditton Inf Sch
Imber Court Trad Est
Met. Police Rugby Fball Gd
Emberhurst Sch
KT10
St Paul's RC Prim Sch
Esher Coll
Thames Ditton
Thames Ditton Jun Sch
EMBERCOURT RD
STATION RD
Cranmere Prim Sch
Ditton Common
Weston Green
Weston Green Sch
PORTSMOUTH RD
Esher
Thames Ditton & Esher
212
195

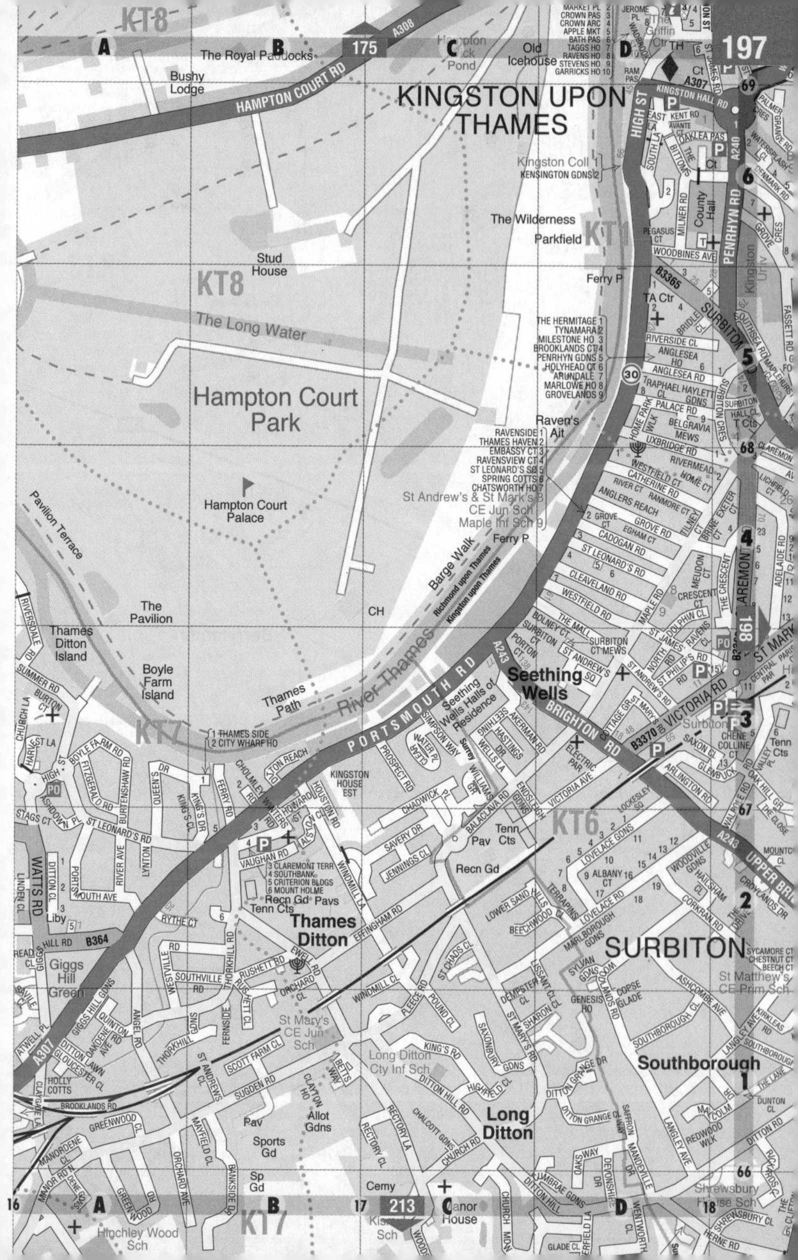
KINGSTON UPON THAMES
Hampton Court Park
Hampton Court Palace
The Long Water
The Royal Paddocks
Bushy Lodge
Stud House
Old Icehouse
The Wilderness
Parkfield
The Pavilion
Thames Ditton Island
Boyle Farm Island
Pavilion Terrace
River Thames
Thames Path
Barge Walk
Raven's Ait
Seething Wells
Thames Ditton
SURBITON
Southborough
Long Ditton
HAMPTON COURT RD
PORTSMOUTH RD
BRIGHTON RD
VICTORIA RD
PENRHYN RD
HIGH ST
KT8
KT7
KT6
KT1
175
198
213

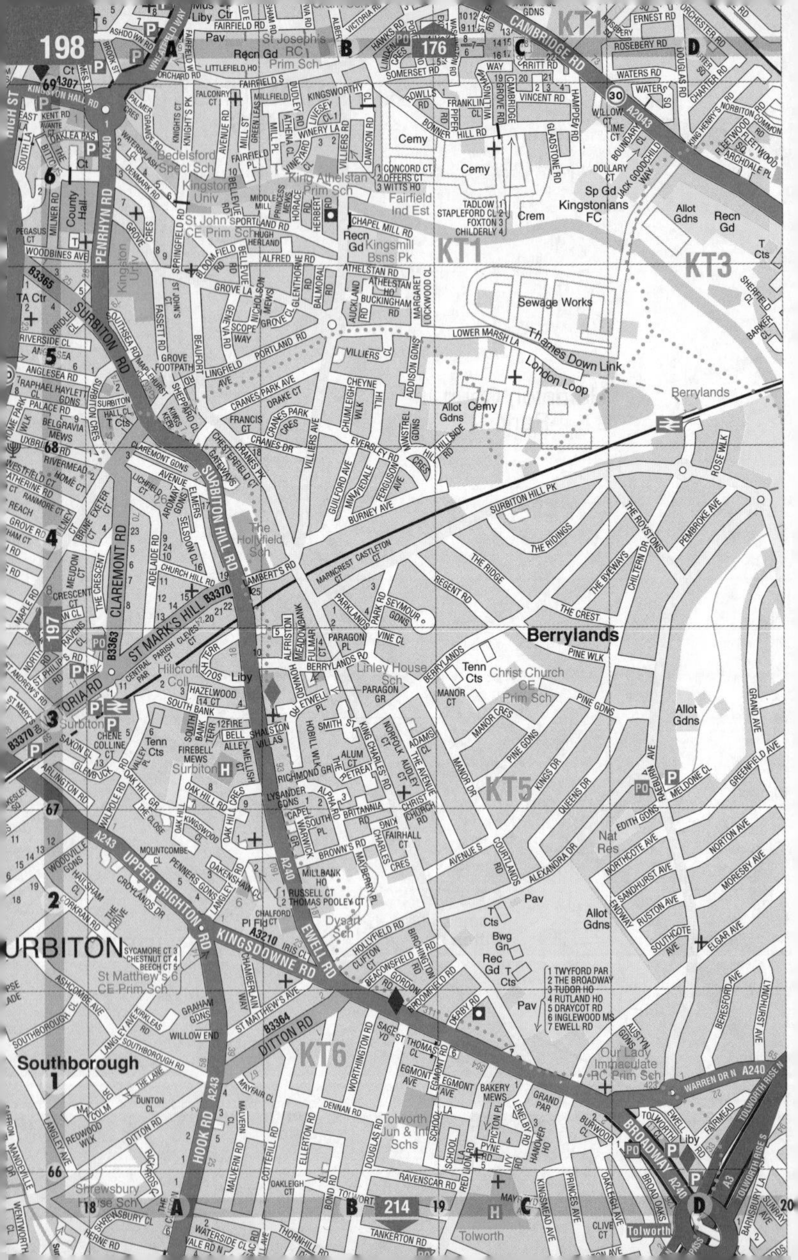
KT1
KT3
KT5
KT6
176
197
214
Recn Gd
St Joseph's RC Prim Sch
Bedelsford Specl Sch
Kingston Univ
County Hall
King Athelstan Prim Sch
Fairfield Ind Est
St John's CE Prim Sch
Kingsmill Bsns Pk
Cemy
Crem
Kingstonians FC
Sp Gd
Allot Gdns
Sewage Works
Thames Down Link
London Loop
Berrylands
The Hollyfield Sch
Hillcroft Coll
Linley House Sch
Christ Church CE Prim Sch
Tenn Cts
Surbiton
Surbiton H
Nat Res
Dysart Sch
SURBITON
St Matthew's CE Prim Sch
Southborough
Our Lady Immaculate RC Prim Sch
Tolworth Jun & Inf Schs
Shrewsbury House Sch
Tolworth
FAIRFIELD RD
CAMBRIDGE RD
PENRHYN RD
SURBITON RD
SURBITON HILL RD
CLAREMONT RD
ST MARK'S HILL
VICTORIA RD
EWELL RD
UPPER BRIGHTON RD
KINGSDOWNE RD
DITTON RD
HOOK RD
BROADWAY
ALEXANDRA DR
KINGS DR
QUEENS DR
MANOR DR
SURBITON HILL PK
LOWER MARSH LA
PORTLAND RD
VILLIERS AVE
CRANES PARK AVE
BERRYLANDS RD
THE RIDGE
THE CREST
PINE GDNS
ELGAR AVE
WARREN DR N
TOLWORTH RISE N
A240
A243
A2043
A3210
B3363
B3364
B3365
B3370
1 TWYFORD PAR
2 THE BROADWAY
3 TUDOR HO
4 RUTLAND HO
5 DRAYCOT RD
6 INGLEWOOD MS
7 EWELL RD
1 CONCORD CT
2 OFFERS CT
3 WITTS HO
TADLOW 1
STAPLEFORD CL 2
FOXTON 3
CHILDERLY 4
1 RUSSELL CT
2 THOMAS POOLEY CT
SYCAMORE CT 3
CHESTNUT CT 4
BEECH CT 5

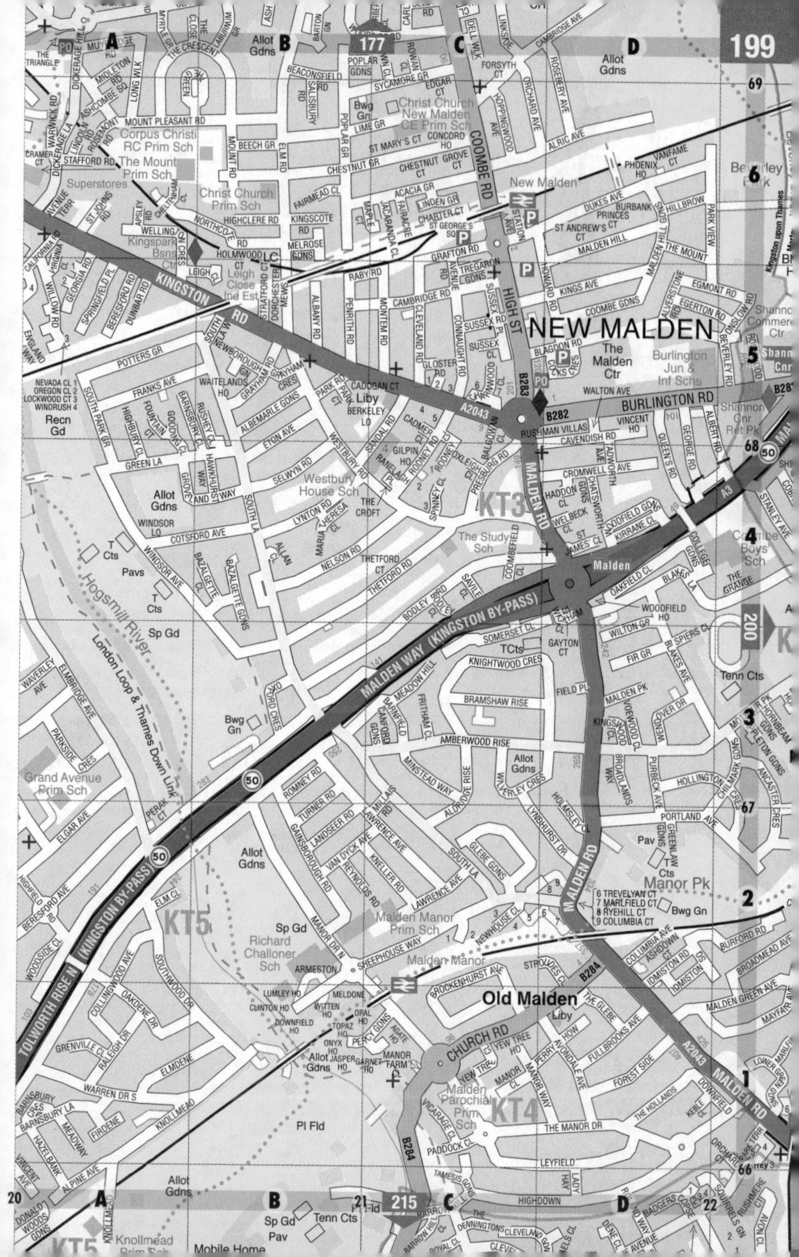
199
177
200
215
A
B
C
D
20
21
22
69
6
5
4
3
2
1
68
67
66
NEW MALDEN
Old Malden
New Malden
Malden Manor
Malden
KT3
KT4
KT5
THE TRIANGLE
MUYBRIDGE RD
DICKERAGE HILL
MYRTLE GR
THE CRESCENT
THE CLOSE
LABURNUM
Allot Gdns
BARTON GN
POPLAR GDNS
ROWAN CL
SYCAMORE GR
BEACONSFIELD RD
SALISBURY RD
EDGAR CT
FORSYTH CT
DELL WLK
LINKSIDE
CAMBRIDGE AVE
ROSEBERY AVE
ORCHARD AVE
HOPPINGWOOD AVE
COOMBE RD
Christ Church New Malden CE Prim Sch
Bwg Gn
LIME GR
ST MARY'S CT
CONCORD HO
CHESTNUT GR
CHESTNUT CT
GROVE CT
ALRIC AVE
MIDDLETON RD
ASHCOMBE SQ
LONG WLK
MOUNT PLEASANT RD
Corpus Christi RC Prim Sch
The Mount Prim Sch
MOUNT RD
BEECH GR
ELM RD
POPLAR GR
WARWICK RD
LINCOLN AVE
ROSEMONT RD
DICKERAGE LA
CRAMER CT
STAFFORD RD
Superstores
Christ Church Prim Sch
AVENUE TERR
ST JOHNS RD
CHELTENHAM AVE
APSLEY RD
WELLINGTON CRES
NORTHCOTE RD
HIGHCLERE RD
KINGSCOTE RD
FAIRMEAD CL
ACACIA GR
LINDEN GR
MAPLE CT
JACARANDA CL
FAIRACRE
CHARTER CT
ST GEORGE'S SQ
PHOENIX HO
VANFAME CT
DUKES AVE
BURBANK
PRINCES CT
HILLBROW
ST ANDREW'S CT
MALDEN HILL
MALDEN HILL GDNS
PARK VIEW
THE MOUNT
STATION AVE
Kingspark Bsns Ctr
HOLMWOOD CT
LC
LEIGH CL
Leigh Close Ind Est
MELROSE GDNS
RABY RD
GRAFTON RD
TREGARON GDNS
AVENUE
HIGH ST
HOWARD RD
KINGS AVE
COOMBE GDNS
ALVERSTONE RD
EGMONT RD
EGERTON RD
ONSLOW RD
Beverley Park
Kingston upon Thames
Shannon Commerce Ctr
CALIFORNIA RD
VIRGINIA CL
WILLOW RD
GEORGIA RD
SPRINGFIELD PL
BERESFORD RD
DUNBAR RD
KINGSTON RD
DORCHESTER MEWS
STRATFORD CT
ALBANY RD
PENRITH RD
MONTEM RD
CAMBRIDGE RD
CLEVELAND RD
CONNAUGHT RD
SUSSEX CL
SUSSEX RD
SUSSEX PL
ENGLAND WAY
NEVADA CL 1
OREGON CL 2
LOCKWOOD CT 3
WINDRUSH 4
Recn Gd
POTTERS GR
SOUTH LAWN
NEWBOROUGH GN
GRAYHAM RD
GRAYHAM CRES
WAITELANDS HO
FRANKS AVE
PARK RD
PARK CT
CADOGAN CT
Liby
BERKELEY LO
GLOSTER RD
HARWOOD RD
BLAGDON RD
COCKS CRES
The Malden Ctr
Burlington Jun & Inf Schs
BEVERLEY RD
A2043
B283
B282
B281
PO
WALTON AVE
BURLINGTON RD
Shannon Cnr Ret Pk
SOUTH PARK GR
HIGHBURY CL
FOUNTAIN CT
BARNSBURY CL
GOODING CL
RUSHEY CL
ALBEMARLE GDNS
ETON AVE
SANDAL RD
WESTBURY RD
CADMER CL
RODNEY RD
RODNEY CL
OXLEIGH CL
BALGOWAN CL
RUSHMAN VILLAS
VINCENT HO
CAVENDISH RD
QUEEN'S RD
GEORGE RD
ALBERT RD
GREEN LA
HAWKHURST WAY
GROVELAND WAY
SELWYN RD
GILPIN HO
RANELAGH PL
SPINNEY CL
PRESBURG RD
MALDEN RD
CROMWELL AVE
TADWORTH AVE
CHATSWORTH GDNS
HADDON CL
WELBECK CL
ST JAMES' CL
WOODFIELD GDNS
KIRRANE CL
COLLEGE GDNS
A3
STANLEY AVE
Westbury House Sch
THE CROFT
LYNTON RD
MARIA THERESA CL
WINDSOR LO
COTSFORD AVE
The Study Sch
COOMBEFIELD CL
Coombe Boys' Sch
THE GRANGE
T Cts
Pavs
WINDSOR AVE
BAZALGETTE CL
BAZALGETTE GDNS
ALLAN CL
NELSON RD
THETFORD CT
THETFORD RD
SAVILE CL
BODLEY RD
BODLEY CL
OAKFIELD CL
BLAKES LA
WOODFIELD HO
Hogsmill River
Sp Gd
London Loop & Thames Down Link
MALDEN WAY (KINGSTON BY-PASS)
SOMERSET CL
WICKHAM CL
GAYTON CT
WILTON GR
SPIERS CL
TCts
FIR GR
BLAKES AVE
Tenn Cts
KNIGHTWOOD CRES
WAVERLEY AVE
ELMBRIDGE AVE
OXFORD CRES
MEADOW HILL
BARNFIELD
FRITHAM CL
BRAMSHAW RISE
FIELD PL
MALDEN PK
KINGSWOOD CL
VOEWOOD CL
WOMERSLEY
OVER DR
HORNBEAM GDNS
Bwg Gn
CANFORD GDNS
AMBERWOOD RISE
PARKSIDE CRES
Grand Avenue Prim Sch
PERAK CT
ROMNEY RD
MINSTEAD WAY
ALDRIDGE RISE
WAVERLEY CRES
BROADLANDS WAY
PURBECK AVE
CHILMARK GDNS
APPLETON GDNS
ANCASTER CRES
HOLLINGTON CRES
ELGAR AVE
TURNER RD
MILLAIS RD
LAWRENCE AVE
HOLMSLEY CL
LYNDHURST DR
PORTLAND AVE
Pav
GREENLAW GDNS
T Cts
Manor Pk
GAINSBOROUGH RD
LANDSEER RD
VAN DYCK AVE
REYNOLDS RD
KNELLER RD
SOUTH LA
GLEBE GDNS
6 TREVELYAN CT
7 MARLFIELD CT
8 RYEHILL CT
9 COLUMBIA CT
HIGHFIELD RD
BERESFORD AVE
KINGSTON BY-PASS
ELM CL
Malden Manor Prim Sch
NEWHOUSE CL
COLUMBIA AVE
ASHDOWN CT
BURFORD RD
BROADMEAD AVE
Richard Challoner Sch
MANOR DR N
SHEEPHOUSE WAY
ARMESTON
STROUDES CL
B284
IDMISTON RD
IDMISTON SQ
WOODSIDE CL
TOLWORTH RISE N
COLLINGWOOD AVE
SOUTHWOOD DR
OAKDENE DR
LUMLEY HO
MELDONE
CLINTON HO
WITTEN HO
OPAL HO
DOWNFIELD HO
TOPAZ HO
PERCY GDNS
AGATE HO
BROCKENHURST AVE
THE GLEBE
MALDEN GREEN AVE
MAYFAIR AVE
GRENVILLE CL
RALEIGH DR
ONYX HO
JASPER HO
GARNET HO
MANOR FARM CL
CHURCH RD
YEW TREE HO
YEW TREE
PERRY HOW
AVONDALE AVE
FULLBROOKS AVE
FOREST SIDE
ELMDENE
WARREN DR S
Malden Parochial Prim Sch
MANOR CL
MANOR WAY
THE HOLLANDS
DOWNFIELD
KEBLE CL
LOWER GREEN GDNS
BARNSBURY CRES
BARNSBURY LA
FIRDENE
MEADWAY
HAZELBANK
KNOLLMEAD
Pl Fld
VICARAGE CL
PADDOCK CL
THE MANOR DR
LEYFIELD
ORCHARD CT
PARK TERR
VINCENT AVE
ALPINE AVE
TAMESIS GDNS
HAY
LADY
HIGHDOWN
BADGERS COPSE
SQUIRRELS GN
RUSHMERE CT
DONALD WOODS GDNS
Sp Gd
Tenn Cts
Pav
Knollmead Prim Sch
Mobile Home
BARROW HILL
THE DENNINGTONS
CLEVELAND GDNS
ROYAL CL
DENE CL
AVON CL

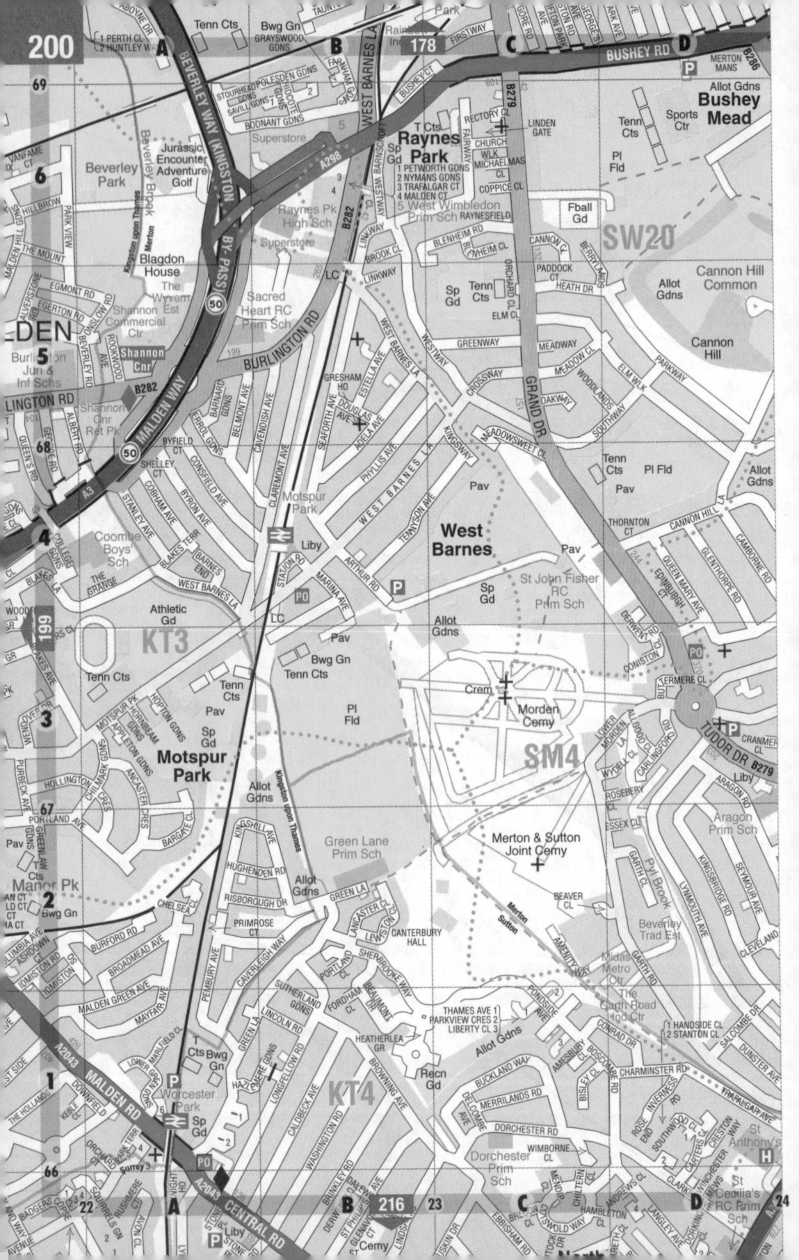

200
178
216
199
A
B
C
D
BUSHEY RD
BEVERLEY WAY (KINGSTON BY-PASS)
WEST BARNES LA
Raynes Park
Bushey Mead
SW20
Cannon Hill Common
Cannon Hill
Beverley Park
Jurassic Encounter Adventure Golf
Blagdon House
Shannon Commercial Ctr
Shannon Cnr
Shannon Cnr Ret Pk
Raynes Pk High Sch
Sacred Heart RC Prim Sch
Burlington Jun & Inf Schs
BURLINGTON RD
MALDEN WAY
GRAND DR
West Barnes
Motspur Park
St John Fisher RC Prim Sch
Morden Cemy
SM4
KT3
KT4
Coombe Boys' Sch
Athletic Gd
Merton & Sutton Joint Cemy
Green Lane Prim Sch
Aragon Prim Sch
Beverley Trad Est
Midas Metro Ctr
The Garth Road Ind Ctr
Dorchester Prim Sch
TUDOR DR
MALDEN RD
CENTRAL RD
Worcester Park
Manor Pk
St Anthony's
St Cecilia's RC Prim Sch
5 West Wimbledon Prim Sch
1 PETWORTH GDNS
2 NYMANS GDNS
3 TRAFALGAR CT
4 MALDEN CT
THAMES AVE 1
PARKVIEW CRES 2
LIBERTY CL 3
1 HANDSIDE CL
2 STANTON CL
1 PERTH CL
2 HUNTLEY WAY
69
68
67
66
22
23
24

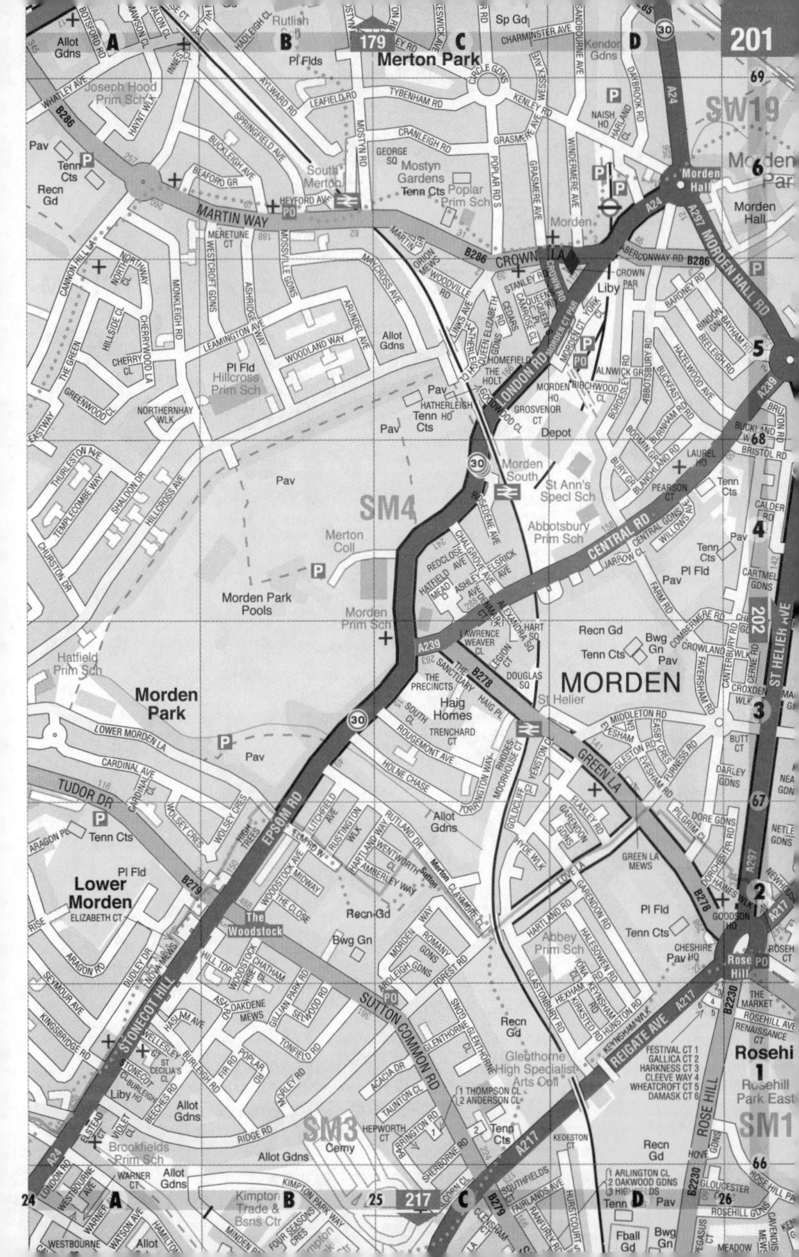
201
179
A
B
C
D
Merton Park
Allot Gdns
Botsford Rd
Rutlish Sch
Hadleigh Cl
Sp Gd
Charminster Ave
Sandbourne Ave
Kendor Gdns
Pl Flds
Joseph Hood Prim Sch
Whatley Ave
Haynt Wlk
Innes Cl
Aylward Rd
Leafield Rd
Tybenham Rd
Circle Gdns
Kenley Rd
Daybrook Rd
Naish Ho
Harland Cl
SW19
69
B286
Springfield Ave
Buckleigh Ave
Cranleigh Rd
Grasmere Ave
Windermere Ave
Mostyn Rd
Pav
Tenn Cts
Recn Gd
Beaford Gr
South Merton
George Sq
Mostyn Gardens
Poplar Prim Sch
Poplar Rd S
Morden Hall
Morden Hall
6
Heyford Ave
PO
Martin Way
A24
A297
Morden
Meretune Ct
Westcroft Gdns
Mossville Gdns
Martin Gr
Orion Mews
Woodville Rd
B286
Crown La
Aberconway Rd
Morden Hall Rd
Cannon Hill La
Northway
North Cl
Monkleigh Rd
Ashridge Way
Mancross Ave
Links Ave
Queen Elizabeth Gdns
Cedars Rd
Stanley Rd
Camrose Cl
Queens Rd
Crown Rd
Morden Ct Par
York Cl
Liby
Crown Par
Bardney Rd
Bindon Gn
Bayham Rd
Beeleigh Rd
Hillside Cl
Cherrywood La
Leamington Ave
Woodland Way
Arundel Ave
Allot Gdns
The Green
Cherry Cl
Pl Fld
Hillcross Prim Sch
Hatherleigh Cl
Homefield
The Holt
London Rd
Alnwick Gr
Abbotsbury Rd
Bordesley Rd
Buckfast Rd
Hazelwood Ave
5
A239
Greenwood Cl
Northernhay Wlk
Eastway
Hatherleigh Ho
Goodwood Cl
Morden Ho
Birchwood Cl
Grosvenor Ct
Depot
Bodmin Gr
Burnham Rd
Buckland Wlk
Bruton Rd
68
Bristol Rd
Thurleston Ave
Templecombe Way
Shaldon Dr
Hillcross Ave
30
Morden South
St Ann's Specl Sch
Bury Gr
Blanchland Rd
Laurel Ho
Pearson Ct
Calder Rd
Churston Dr
SM4
Rosedene Ave
Abbotsbury Prim Sch
Central Rd
Central Gdns
Willows Ave
4
Merton Coll
Chalgrove Ave
Redclose Ave
Elsrick Ave
Jarrow Cl
Cartmel Gdns
Hatfield Mead
Ashley Ave
Denmark Ct
Alexandra Sq
Farm Rd
Morden Park Pools
Morden Prim Sch
Recn Gd
Bwg Gn
Combermere Rd
Crowland Wlk
Canterbury Rd
Cerne Rd
202
St Helier Ave
Lawrence Weaver Cl
Legion Ct
Hart Sq
Douglas Sq
The Sanctuary
The Precincts
B278
Faversham Rd
Hatfield Prim Sch
Morden Park
Haig Homes
Haig Pl
MORDEN
St Helier
Croxden Wlk
3
South Cl
Trenchard Ct
Middleton Rd
Evesham Gn
Easby Cres
Lower Morden La
Rougemont Ave
Egleston Rd
Furness Rd
Butt Ct
Holne Chase
Torrington Way
Rhodes Moorhouse Ct
Yenston Cl
Green La
Evesham Rd
Darley Gdns
Cardinal Ave
Cardinal Cl
Tudor Dr
Wolsey Cres
High Trees
Epsom Rd
Litchfield Ave
Rustington Wlk
Rutland Dr
Goldcliff Cl
Flaxley Rd
Garendon Gdns
Pilgrim Cl
Dore Gdns
67
Aragon Pl
Tenn Cts
Elmbrook Rd
Hartland Way
Wentworth Cl
Merton
Sutton
Amberley Way
Hyde Wlk
Green La Mews
Dorchester Rd
Netley Gdns
A297
Lower Morden
B279
Woodstock Ave
Midway
The Close
Claymore Cl
Love La
Garendon Rd
Haines Wlk
2
A217
Elizabeth Ct
Rise
The Woodstock
Recn Gd
Morden Way
Romany Gdns
Hartland Rd
Abbey Prim Sch
Halesowen Rd
Goodson Ho
Aragon Rd
Bwg Gn
Pav
Cheshire Ho
Rose Hill
Seymour Ave
Budley Dr
Nova Mews
Hill Top
Woodstock Rise
Chatham Cl
Ardleigh Gdns
Forest Rd
Iona Cl
Keynsham Rd
Glastonbury Rd
Hexham Rd
Kirksted Rd
Hunston Rd
Keynsham Wlk
The Market
Rosehill Ave
Renaissance Ct
Kingsbridge Rd
Stonecot Hill
Haslam Ave
Oakdene Mews
Gillian Park Rd
Selwood Rd
Tonfield Rd
Sutton Common Rd
Glenthorne Gdns
Glenthorne Cl
Recn Gd
Reigate Ave
B2230
Festival Ct 1
Gallica Ct 2
Harkness Ct 3
Cleeve Way 4
Wheatcroft Ct 5
Damask Ct 6
Rosehi
1
Wellesley Ct
St Cecilia's Cl
Stonecot Cl
Burleigh Rd
Fir Rd
Poplar Rd
Glenthorne High Specialist Arts Coll
Liby
Burleigh Ho
Beeches Rd
Allot Gdns
Morley Rd
Acacia Dr
Taunton Cl
1 Thompson Cl
2 Anderson Cl
Rose Hill
Rosehill Park East
SM1
Elstead Ct
Violet Cl
Brookfields Prim Sch
Ridge Rd
SM3
Hepworth Ct
Cemy
Barrington Rd
Sherborne Rd
Tenn Cts
A217
Kedeston Ct
Recn Gd
Hove Gdns
66
Allot Gdns
Warner Ct
Allot Gdns
Kimpton Trade & Bsns Ctr
Kimpton Park Way
Four Seasons Cres
Minden Rd
Hamilton
Southfields
Fairlands Ave
Ranfurly Rd
Hurstcourt
1 Arlington Cl
2 Oakwood Gdns
3 Highfields
Tenn
Pav
Gloucester
Rosehill Gdns
Rose Hill Pk
24
London Rd
Westbourne Ave
Warner Ave
Watson Ave
Westbourne
Allot
25
217
26
Clensham
B279
Fball Gd
Bwg Gn
Pegasus
Meadow
Cavendish Mews

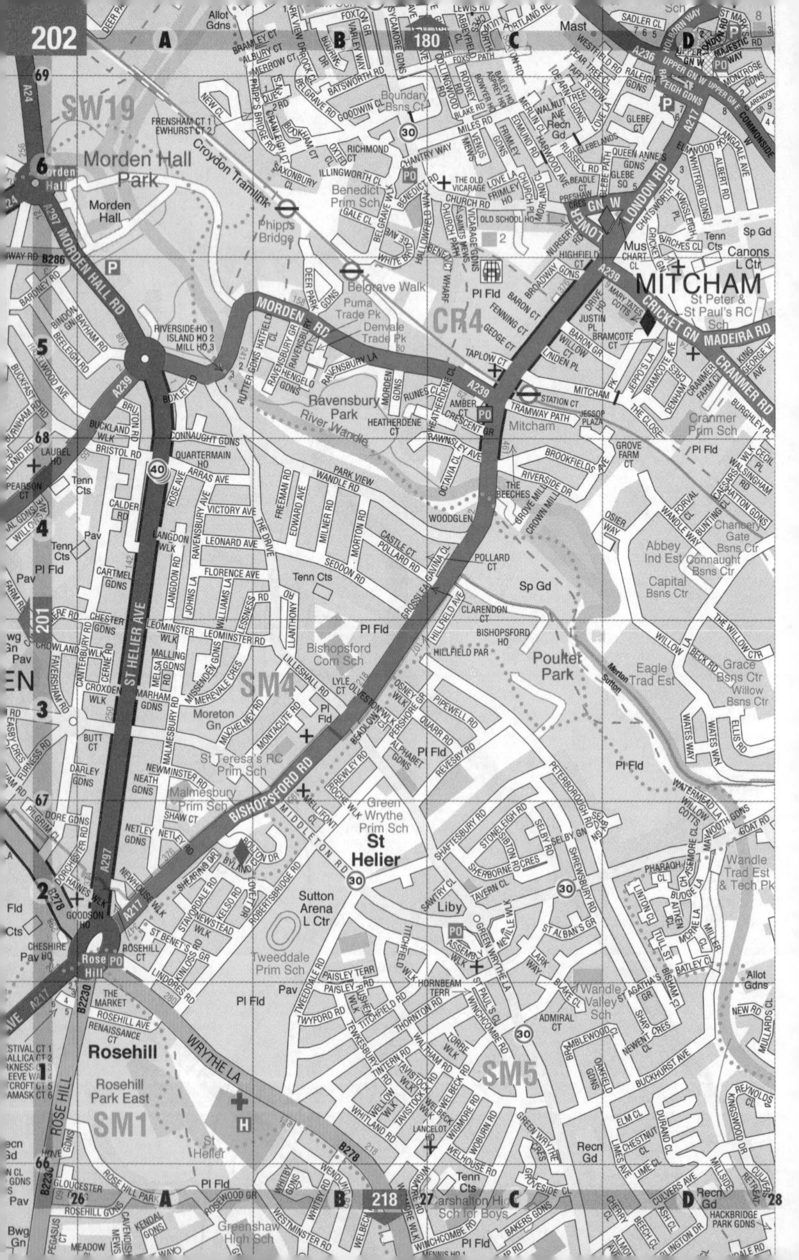
A
B
180
C
D
SW19
Morden Hall Park
Morden Hall
Croydon Tramlink
Phipps Bridge
Belgrave Walk
Boundary Bsns Ct
Benedict Prim Sch
Puma Trade Pk
Denvale Trade Pk
CR4
MITCHAM
St Peter & St Paul's RC Sch
Cranmer Prim Sch
Ravensbury Park
River Wandle
Mitcham
Abbey Ind Est
Connaught Bsns Ctr
Capital Bsns Ctr
Chancery Gate Bsns Ctr
Poulter Park
Eagle Trad Est
Grace Bsns Ctr
Willow Bsns Ctr
Bishopsford Com Sch
SM4
Moreton Gn
St Teresa's RC Prim Sch
Malmesbury Prim Sch
Green Wrythe Prim Sch
St Helier
Sutton Arena L Ctr
Tweeddale Prim Sch
Wandle Valley Sch
Wandle Trad Est & Tech Pk
Rosehill
Rosehill Park East
SM1
SM5
St Helier
Carshalton High Sch for Boys
Greenshaw High Sch
MORDEN HALL RD
MORDEN RD
ST HELIER AVE
BISHOPSFORD RD
WRYTHE LA
LONDON RD
CRICKET GN
MADEIRA RD
CRANMER RD
MITCHAM PK
ROSE HILL
GREEN WRYTHE LA
BUCKHURST AVE
MIDDLETON RD
WANDLE RD
RIVERSIDE DR
MILES RD
CHURCH RD
ROSEHILL AVE
ROSE HILL PARK
26
27
28
218
201
69
68
67
66
6
5
4
3
2
1

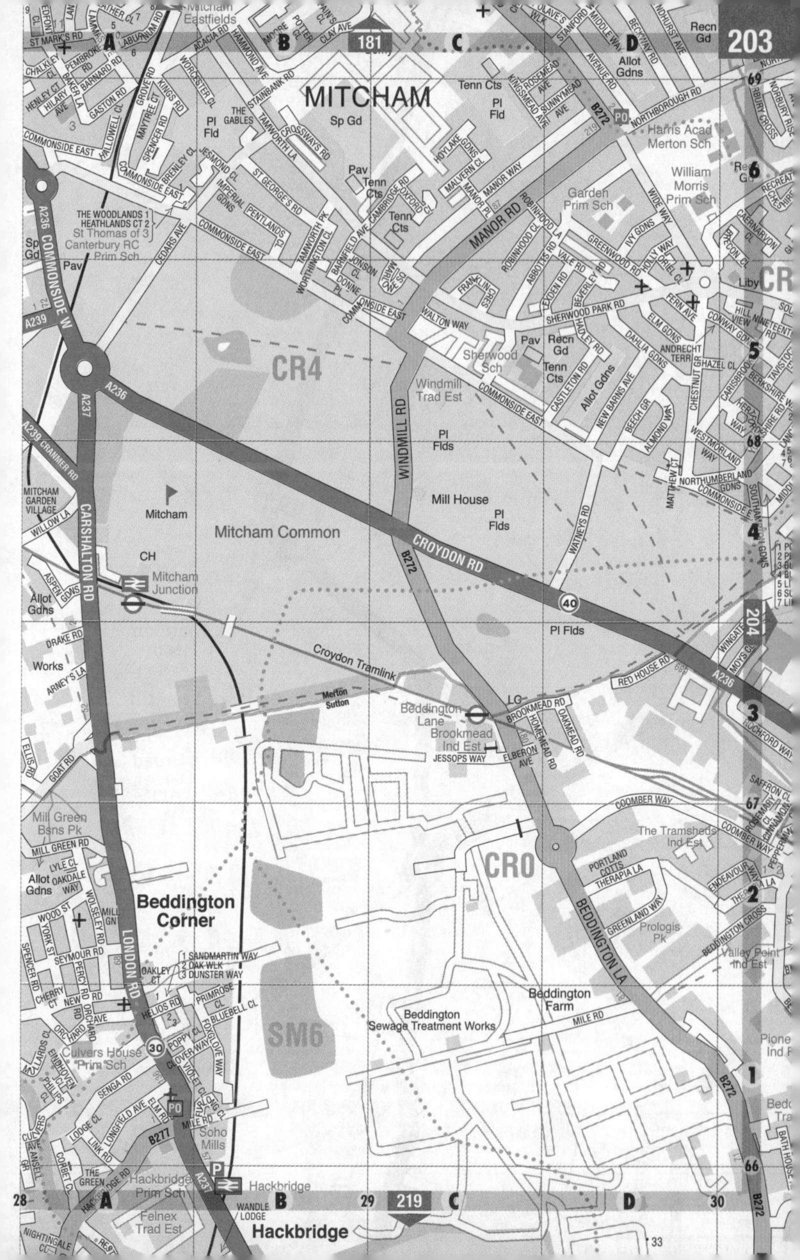

A
B
C
D
181
MITCHAM
Mitcham Eastfields
Sp Gd
Pl Fld
Tenn Cts
Allot Gdns
Recn Gd
Harris Acad Merton Sch
William Morris Prim Sch
Garden Prim Sch
THE WOODLANDS 1
HEATHLANDS CT 2
St Thomas of Canterbury RC Prim Sch
COMMONSIDE EAST
COMMONSIDE W
CARSHALTON RD
MANOR RD
WINDMILL RD
CROYDON RD
CR4
Windmill Trad Est
Pl Flds
Mill House
Mitcham
Mitcham Common
CH
Mitcham Junction
Croydon Tramlink
Merton
Sutton
Beddington Lane
Brookmead Ind Est
Sherwood Sch
Works
Mill Green Bsns Pk
The Tramsheds Ind Est
CR0
Prologis Pk
Valley Point Ind Est
Beddington Corner
1 SANDMARTIN WAY
2 OAK WLK
3 DUNSTER WAY
Beddington Farm
Beddington Sewage Treatment Works
SM6
Culvers House Prim Sch
Soho Mills
Hackbridge Prim Sch
Hackbridge
Felnex Trad Est
LONDON RD
BEDDINGTON LA
A236
A237
A239
B272
B277
204
219
28
29
30
1
2
3
4
5
6
66
67
68
69

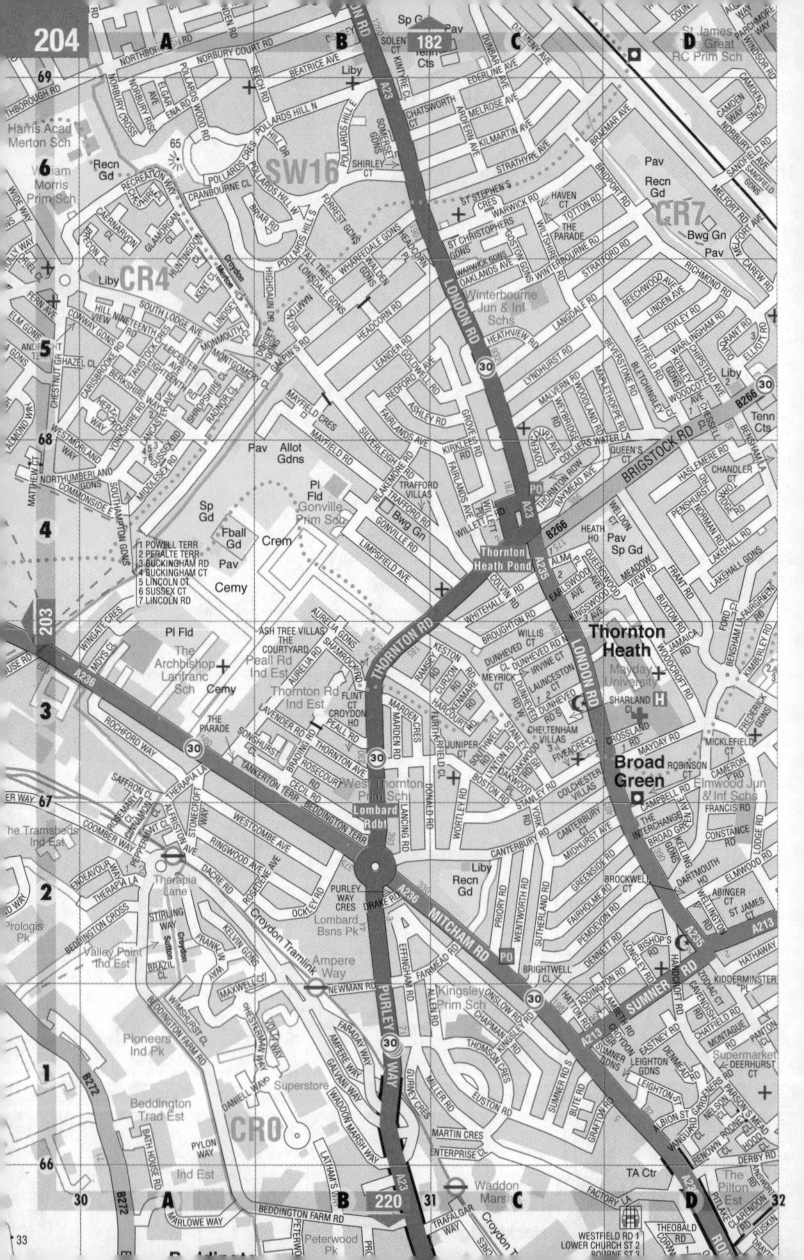

204
A
B
C
D
182
203
220
30
31
32
33
69
68
67
66
6
5
4
3
2
1
SW16
CR4
CR7
CR0
LONDON RD
A23
A235
A236
A213
B266
B272
NORBURY COURT RD
NORTHBOROUGH RD
BEATRICE AVE
POLLARDS HILL N
POLLARDS WOOD RD
NORBURY CROSS
NORBURY RISE
ELGAR AVE
ENA RD
BEECH RD
Liby
Harris Acad Merton Sch
Recn Gd
William Morris Prim Sch
RECREATION WAY
CRANBOURNE CL
POLLARDS CRES
POLLARDS HILL W
POLLARDS HILL S
POLLARDS HILL E
SOMERSET GDNS
SHIRLEY CT
SOLENT CT
KINTYRE CL
Tenn Cts
Sp Gd
Pav
DALMENY AVE
DUNBAR AVE
EDERLINE AVE
CHATSWORTH CT
MELROSE AVE
ARDFERN AVE
KILMARTIN AVE
STRATHYRE AVE
BRAEMAR AVE
St James the Great RC Prim Sch
CAMDEN WAY
NORBURY AVE
SANDFIELD RD
SANDFIELD GDNS
MELFORT RD
MELFORT AVE
Bwg Gn
CAREW RD
RICHMOND RD
BRIDPORT RD
HAVEN CT
TOTTON RD
THE PARADE
WARWICK RD
ST STEPHEN'S CRES
ST CHRISTOPHERS GDNS
WILTSHIRE RD
GOSTON GDNS
WINTERBOURNE RD
STRATFORD RD
WARWICK GDNS
OAKLANDS AVE
Winterbourne Jun & Inf Schs
FORREST GDNS
WHARFEDALE GDNS
HEADCORN PL
WALDEN GDNS
TALL TREES
LONSDALE GDNS
BRIAR RD
HIGHDAUN DR
CAERNARVON CL
GLAMORGAN CL
BRECON CL
HUNTINGDON CL
KENT CL
LINDSEY CL
MONMOUTH CL
HILL VIEW
NINETEENTH RD
SOUTH LODGE AVE
CONWAY GDNS
FERN AVE
ELM GDNS
CHESTNUT GR
HAZEL CL
CARISBROOKE RD
BERKSHIRE WAY
TAVISTOCK CRES
LEICESTER AVE
EIGHTEENTH RD
MONTGOMERY CL
SHROPSHIRE CL
RADNOR CL
LANCASTER AVE
YORKSHIRE RD
HERTFORD WAY
WESTMORLAND WAY
SUSSEX RD
MIDDLESEX RD
NORTHUMBERLAND GDNS
COMMONSIDE E
MATTHEW CT
SOUTHAMPTON GDNS
ALMOND WAY
DORSET GDNS
GALPIN'S RD
NAMTON DR
HEADCORN RD
LEANDER RD
GOLDWELL RD
REDFORD AVE
ASHLEY RD
FAIRLANDS AVE
MAYFIELD CRES
MAYFIELD RD
SILVERLEIGH RD
BLAKEMORE RD
KIRKLEES RD
GROVE RD
TRAFFORD VILLAS
TRAFFORD RD
HEATHVIEW RD
LANGDALE RD
LYNDHURST RD
MALVERN RD
WETBRIDGE RD
WOODLAND RD
MAPLETHORPE RD
BEVERSTONE RD
BLETCHINGLEY CL
NUTFIELD RD
BEECHWOOD AVE
LINDEN AVE
FOXLEY RD
WARLINGHAM RD
CHIPSTEAD AVE
KENLEY GDNS
WOODCOTE AVE
GRANT RD
ELLIOTT RD
CHESSELL CL
BRIGSTOCK RD
QUEEN'S CT
COLLIERS WATER LA
DOVERCOURT AVE
THORNTON ROW
RAYMEAD AVE
HASLEMERE RD
CHANDLER CT
PENSHURST RD
NORMAN RD
TORRIDGE RD
LAKEHALL RD
LAKEHALL GDNS
BENSHAM LA
Tenn Cts
Pav
Allot Gdns
Pl Fld
Gonville Prim Sch
Sp Gd
Fball Gd
Crem
Cemy
GONVILLE RD
LIMPSFIELD AVE
WILLETT RD
WILLETT PL
Thornton Heath Pond
PO
HEATH HO
WELDON CT
Pav
Sp Gd
MEADOW VIEW RD
FRANT RD
BUXTON RD
QUEENSWOOD AVE
EARLSWOOD AVE
KINGSWOOD AVE
ALMA PL
COLVIN RD
WHITEHALL RD
BROUGHTON RD
1 POWELL TERR
2 PERALTE TERR
3 BUCKINGHAM RD
4 BUCKINGHAM CT
5 LINCOLN CT
6 SUSSEX CT
7 LINCOLN RD
WINGATE CRES
MOYS CL
Pl Fld
The Archbishop Lanfranc Sch
Cemy
ASH TREE VILLAS
THE COURTYARD
AURELIA GDNS
AURELIA RD
SHAMROCK RD
Peall Rd Ind Est
Thornton Rd Ind Est
THORNTON RD
FLINT CT
CROYDON HO
LAVENDER RD
PEALL RD
THORNTON AVE
ROSECOURT RD
BRADING RD
CECIL RD
SONGHURST CL
THE PARADE
ROCHFORD WAY
TANKERTON TERR
BEDDINGTON TERR
West Thornton Prim Sch
Lombard Rdbt
KESTON RD
RAMSEY RD
CURZON RD
KENMARE RD
HARCOURT RD
MARDEN CRES
MARDEN RD
FURTHERFIELD CL
JUNIPER CT
SOUTHWELL RD
LYNTON RD
BOSTON RD
DONALD RD
LANCING RD
WORTLEY RD
STANLEY RD
OAKWOOD RD
OAKWOOD PL
YORK RD
WILLIS CT
DUNHEVED RD N
DUNHEVED RD W
DUNHEVED RD S
DUNHEVED CL
MEYRICK CT
IRVINE CT
LAUNCESTON CT
CHELTENHAM VILLAS
FIVEACRE CL
COLCHESTER VILLAS
Thornton Heath
Mayday University
SHARLAND CL
CROSSLAND RD
MAYDAY RD
WOODCROFT RD
JAMAICA RD
KIMBERLEY RD
FAIRGREEN RD
FORD CL
BENSHAM LA
FREDERICK GDNS
MICKLEFIELD CT
Broad Green
ROBINSON CT
CAMERON RD
Elmwood Jun & Inf Schs
CAMPBELL RD
THE INTERCHANGE
BROAD GREEN AVE
KELLING GDNS
FRANCIS RD
CONSTANCE RD
LODGE RD
ELMWOOD RD
DARTMOUTH HO
ABINGER CT
ST JAMES CT
WELLINGTON RD
CANTERBURY RD
CANTERBURY CT
MIDHURST AVE
GREENSIDE RD
FAIRHOLME RD
PEMDEVON RD
BROCKWELL CT
THERAPIA LA
SAFFRON CL
ROSEMARY CL
CINNAMON CL
PEPPERMINT CL
ALFRISTON AVE
STONECROFT WAY
WESTCOMBE AVE
RINGWOOD AVE
ROSEDENE AVE
DACRE RD
OCKLEY RD
COOMBER WAY
The Tramsheds Ind Est
ENDEAVOUR WAY
Therapia Lane
Liby
Recn Gd
PRIORY RD
WENTWORTH RD
SUTHERLAND RD
PURLEY WAY CRES
DRAKE RD
MITCHAM RD
Lombard Bsns Pk
Croydon Tramlink
Prologis Pk
BEDDINGTON CROSS
STIRLING WAY
Valley Point Ind Est
FRANKLIN WAY
KELVIN GDNS
BRAZIL CL
MAXWELL CL
Ampere Way
NEWMAN RD
EFFINGHAM RD
FAIRMEAD RD
ALLEN RD
Kingsley Prim Sch
ONSLOW RD
CHAPMAN RD
KINGSLEY RD
DENNETT RD
BRIGHTWELL CL
HATTON RD
ADDINGTON RD
LAMBETH RD
LONGLEY RD
BISHOP'S RD
HANDCROFT RD
SUMNER RD
HATHAWAY RD
KIDDERMINSTER RD
ZODIAC CT
CAVENDISH CT
CHATFIELD RD
MONTAGUE RD
PANTON CL
Supermarket
DEERHURST CT
EASTNEY RD
DENMEAD RD
CROYDON GR
SUMNER GDNS
LEIGHTON GDNS
LEIGHTON ST
ALBION ST
GARDENERS RD
NELSON CL
PARSON'S MEAD
RODNEY CL
VANGUARD CL
RENOWN CL
HOOD CL
DERBY RD
WIMSHURST CL
BEDDINGTON FARM RD
CHESTERMAN WAY
VOLTA WAY
FARADAY WAY
AMPERE WAY
GALVANI WAY
WADDON MARSH WAY
PURLEY WAY
GURNEY CRES
MILLER RD
THOMSON CRES
EUSTON RD
SUMNER RD S
BUTE RD
GRAFTON RD
MARTIN CRES
ENTERPRISE CL
Pioneers Ind Pk
Superstore
DANIELL WAY
Beddington Trad Est
PYLON WAY
BATH HOUSE RD
Ind Est
LATHAM'S WAY
Waddon Marsh
FACTORY LA
TA Ctr
The Pilton Est
PITLAKE
ANSWORTH CL
CLARENDON RD
RUSKIN
MARLOWE WAY
BEDDINGTON FARM RD
TRAFALGAR WAY
Peterwood Pk
WESTFIELD RD 1
LOWER CHURCH ST 2
THEOBALD RD

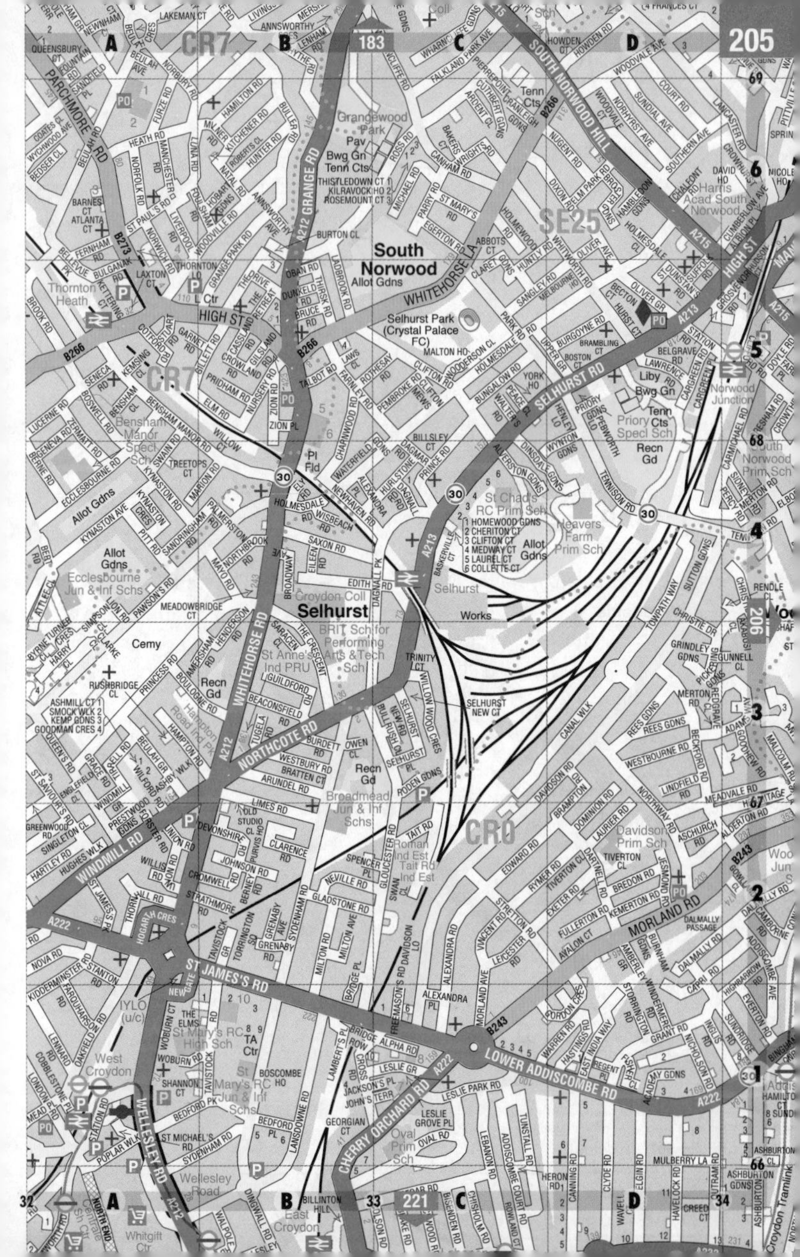

205
183
A
B
C
D
CR7
SE25
CR0
South Norwood
Selhurst
Thornton Heath
Norwood Junction
West Croydon
East Croydon
SOUTH NORWOOD HILL
WHITEHORSE LA
WHITEHORSE RD
SELHURST RD
GRANGE RD
PARCHMORE RD
HIGH ST
NORTHCOTE RD
WINDMILL RD
ST JAMES'S RD
LOWER ADDISCOMBE RD
MORLAND RD
CHERRY ORCHARD RD
WELLESLEY RD
BENSHAM MANOR RD
KYNASTON AVE
CANAL WLK
TOWPATH WAY
Grangewood Park
Selhurst Park (Crystal Palace FC)
Harris Acad South Norwood
Bensham Manor Specl Sch
Ecclesbourne Jun & Inf Schs
Croydon Coll
BRIT Sch for Performing Arts & Tech Sch
St Anne's Ind PRU
Broadmead Jun & Inf Schs
Roman Ind Est
Tait Rd Ind Est
Davidson Prim Sch
St Chad's RC Prim Sch
Heavers Farm Prim Sch
Priory Specl Sch
South Norwood Prim Sch
St Mary's RC High Sch
St Mary's RC Jun & Inf Schs
Oval Prim Sch
Wellesley Road
Whitgift Ctr
Centrale Sh Ctr
Hampton Road Ind Pk
Selhurst Works
Allot Gdns
Cemy
Recn Gd
206
221
32
33
34
66
67
68
69

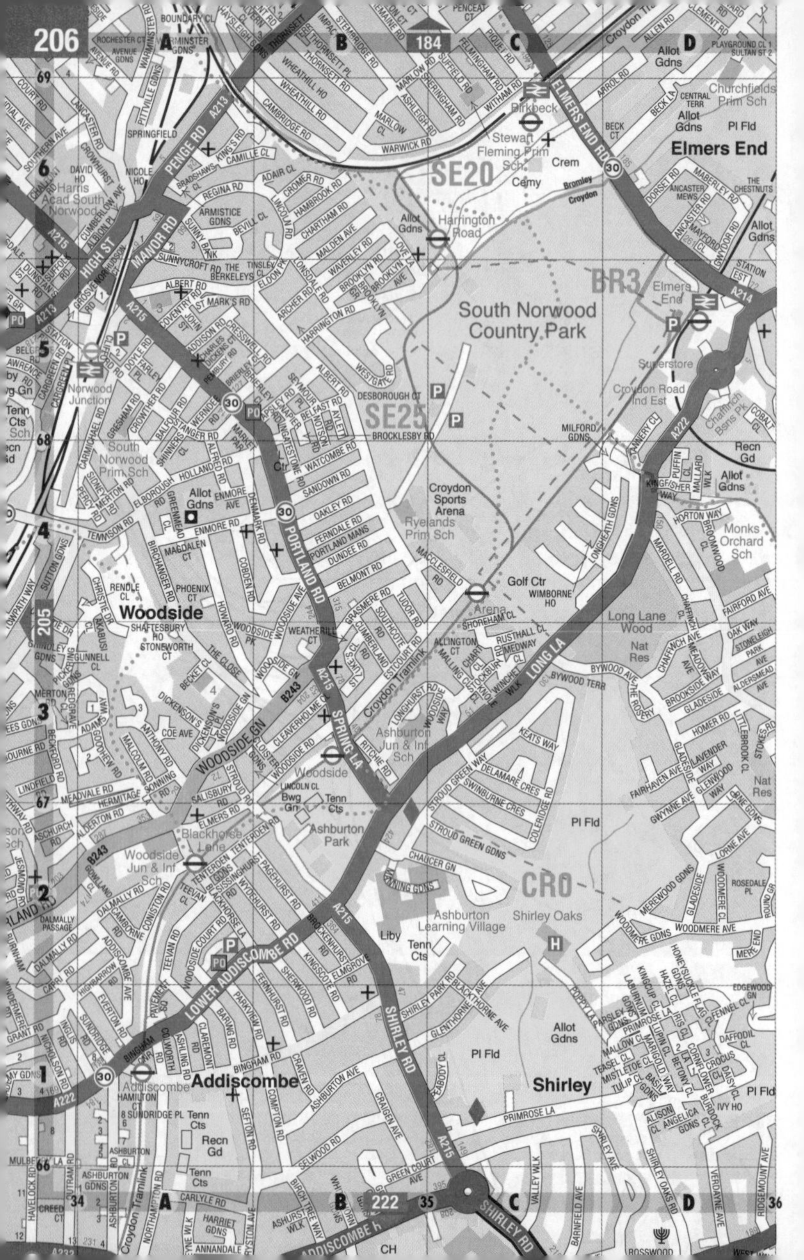
184
A
B
C
D
Elmers End
SE20
BR3
SE25
CR0
Birkbeck
Stewart Fleming Prim Sch
Crem
Cemy
Harrington Road
South Norwood Country Park
Elmers End
Superstore
Croydon Road Ind Est
Chaffinch Bsns Pk
Churchfields Prim Sch
Allot Gdns
Pl Fld
Recn Gd
Monks Orchard Sch
Harris Acad South Norwood
Norwood Junction
South Norwood Prim Sch
Croydon Sports Arena
Ryelands Prim Sch
Golf Ctr
Arena
Long Lane Wood
Nat Res
Woodside
Ashburton Jun & Inf Sch
Ashburton Park
Blackhorse Lane
Woodside Jun & Inf Sch
Ashburton Learning Village
Shirley Oaks
Liby
Tenn Cts
Bwg Gn
Addiscombe
Shirley
Croydon Tramlink
PENGE RD
HIGH ST
MANOR RD
PORTLAND RD
SPRING LA
LONG LA
ELMERS END RD
WOODSIDE GN
LOWER ADDISCOMBE RD
SHIRLEY RD
SOUTH NORWOOD HILL
A213
A215
A214
A222
B243
205
222
34
35
36
69
68
67
66
6
5
4
3
2
1

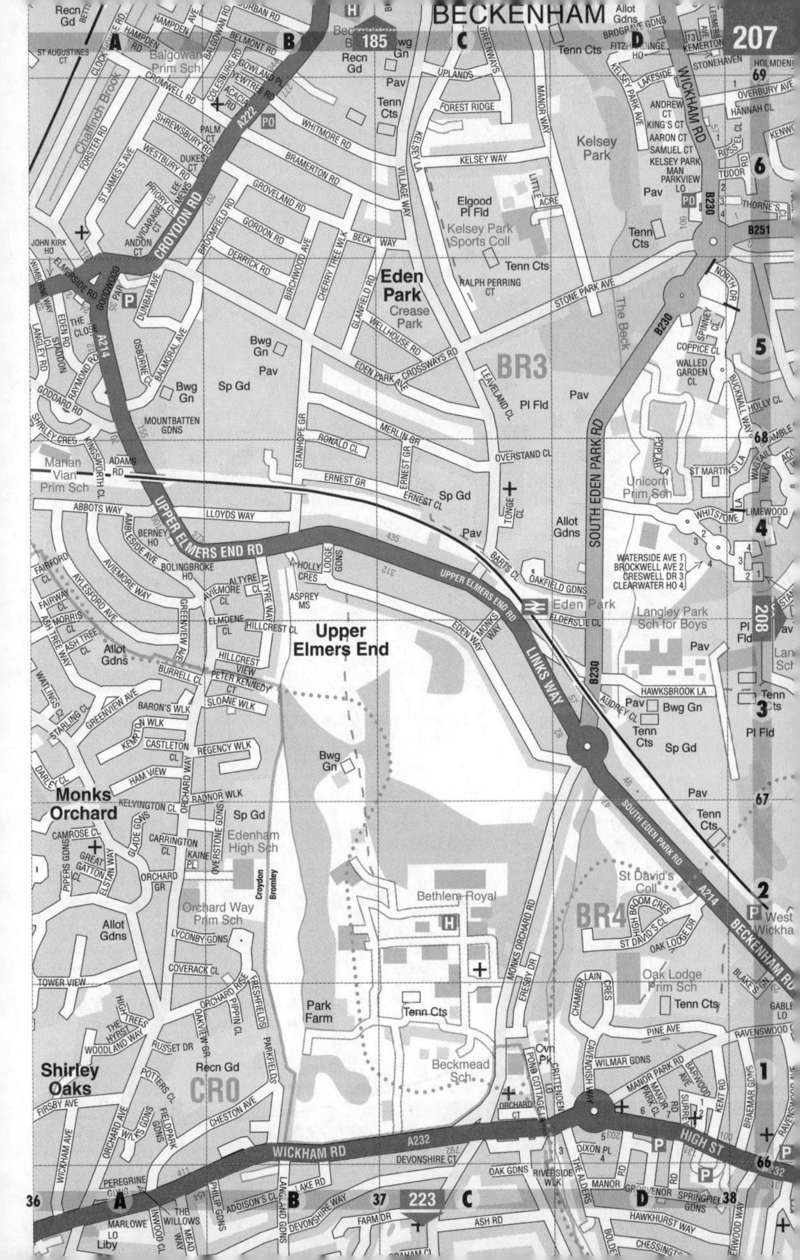
BECKENHAM
185
208
223
A
B
C
D
36
37
38
69
6
5
68
4
3
67
2
1
66
Eden Park
Crease Park
BR3
BR4
CR0
Upper Elmers End
Monks Orchard
Shirley Oaks
Kelsey Park
Elgood Pl Fld
Kelsey Park Sports Coll
Balgowan Prim Sch
Marian Vian Prim Sch
Unicorn Prim Sch
Langley Park Sch for Boys
Edenham High Sch
Orchard Way Prim Sch
Bethlem Royal
St David's Coll
Oak Lodge Prim Sch
Beckmead Sch
Park Farm
Eden Park
CROYDON RD
UPPER ELMERS END RD
SOUTH EDEN PARK RD
LINKS WAY
WICKHAM RD
HIGH ST
BECKENHAM RD
A222
A214
A232
B230
B251
WATERSIDE AVE 1
BROCKWELL AVE 2
CRESWELL DR 3
CLEARWATER HO 4

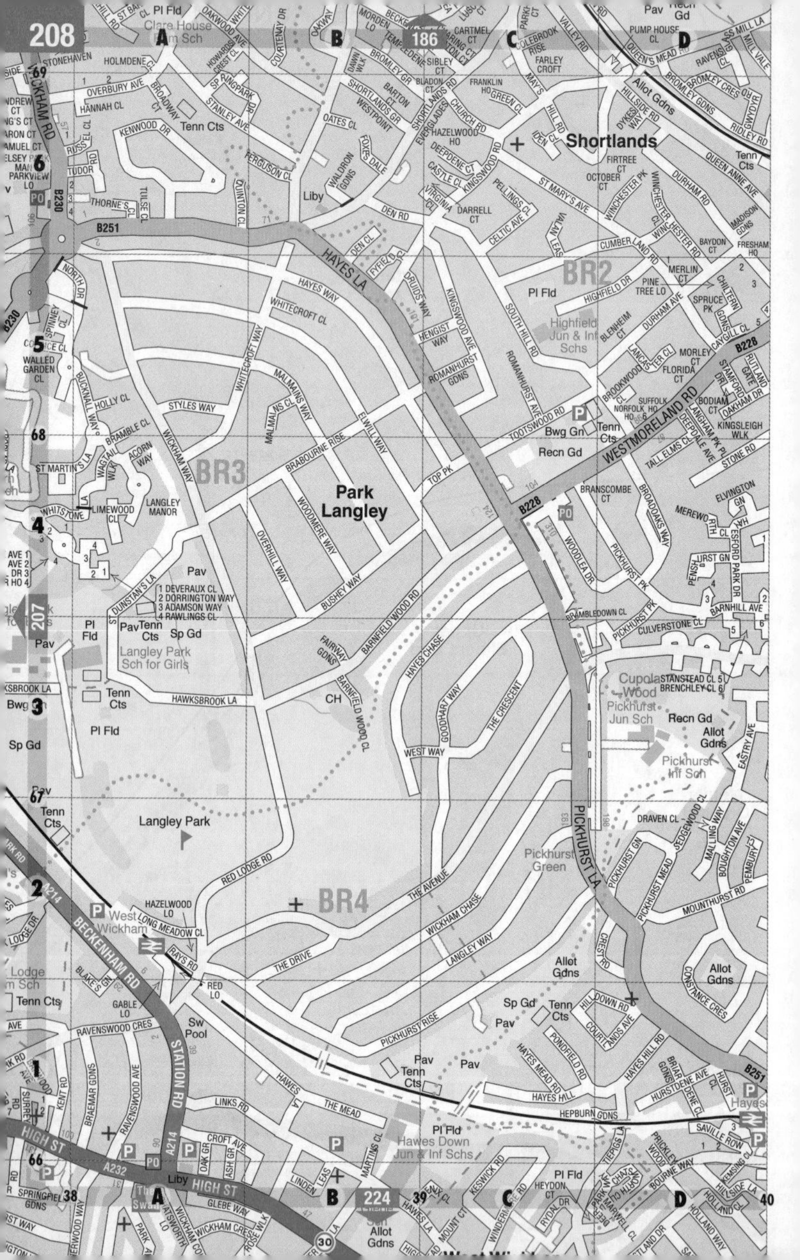
Park Langley
Shortlands
BR2
BR3
BR4
Langley Park
Pickhurst Green
Cupola Wood
Highfield Jun & Inf Schs
Langley Park Sch for Girls
Pickhurst Jun Sch
Pickhurst Inf Sch
Hawes Down Jun & Inf Schs
West Wickham
HAYES LA
WESTMORELAND RD
PICKHURST LA
WICKHAM RD
BECKENHAM RD
STATION RD
HIGH ST
186
207
224

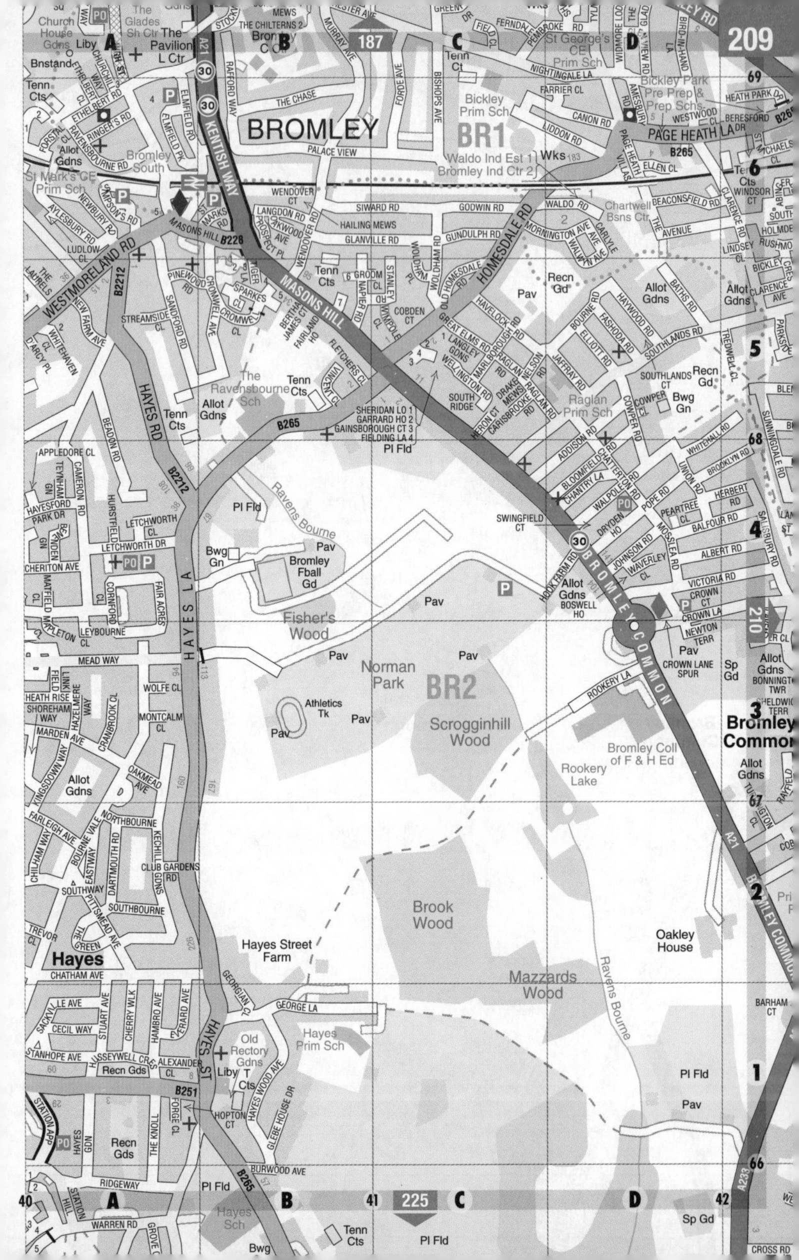
BROMLEY
BR1
BR2
Hayes
Bromley Common
KENTISH WAY
MASONS HILL
BROMLEY COMMON
HAYES LA
HAYES ST
HAYES RD
WESTMORELAND RD
HOMESDALE RD
PAGE HEATH LA
Norman Park
Scrogginhill Wood
Brook Wood
Mazzards Wood
Fisher's Wood
Ravens Bourne
Rookery Lake
Oakley House
Hayes Street Farm
Bromley Coll of F & H Ed
Raglan Prim Sch
The Ravensbourne Sch
Hayes Prim Sch
Bickley Prim Sch
St Mark's CE Prim Sch
Bromley Fball Gd
Athletics Tk
187
225
210

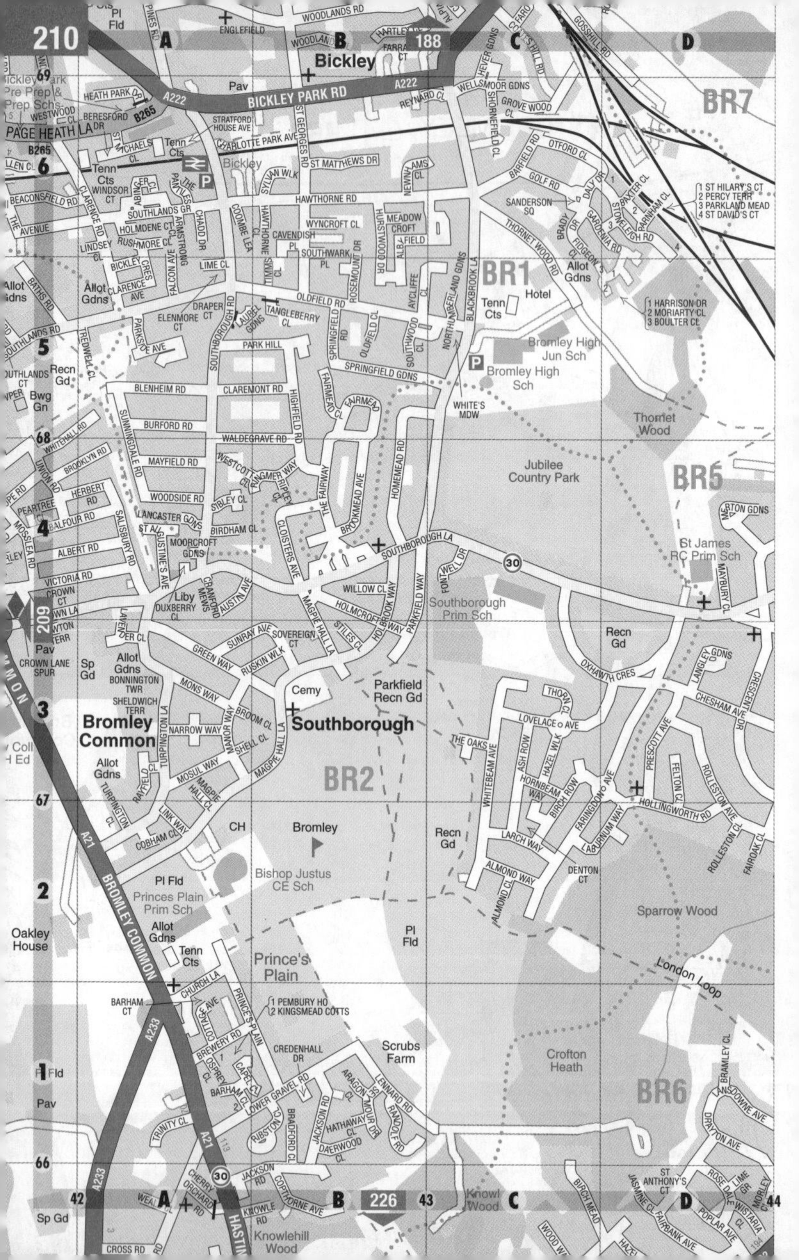

210
A
B
C
D
188
226
209
Bickley
Southborough
Bromley Common
BR1
BR2
BR5
BR6
BR7
BICKLEY PARK RD
A222
B265
PAGE HEATH LA
WOODLANDS RD
ENGLEFIELD
PINES RD
HARTLEY
FARRAN CT
Pav
Pl Fld
Bickley Park Pre Prep & Prep Schs
HEATH PARK DR
WESTWOOD
BERESFORD DR
STRATFORD HOUSE AVE
CHARLOTTE PARK AVE
ST GEORGES RD
REYNARD CL
WELLSMOOR GDNS
HEVER GDNS
SHORNEFIELD CL
GROVE WOOD CL
GOSSHILL RD
Tenn Cts
ST MICHAELS CL
Bickley
ST MATTHEWS DR
SYLVAN WLK
NEWNHAMS CL
BARFIELD RD
OTFORD CL
GOLF RD
SANDERSON SQ
DALY DR
BAXTER CL
PARNHAM CL
1 ST HILARY'S CT
2 PERCY TERR
3 PARKLAND MEAD
4 ST DAVID'S CT
WINDSOR CT
THE PANTILES
BEACONSFIELD RD
CLARENCE RD
HAWTHORNE RD
THE AVENUE
SOUTHLANDS GR
HOLMDENE CT
ARMSTRONG
CHADD DR
COOMBE LEA
HAWTHORNE CL
WYNCROFT CL
CAVENDISH PL
SOUTHWARK PL
HURSTWOOD DR
MEADOW CROFT
ALBYFIELD
THORNET WOOD RD
BRADY DR
GARDENIA RD
STONELEIGH RD
FIDGEON CL
LINDSEY CL
RUSHMORE CL
BICKLEY CRES
CLARENCE AVE
FALCON AVE
LIME CL
ROSEMOUNT DR
AYCLIFFE CL
NORTHUMBERLAND GDNS
BLACKBROOK LA
Allot Gdns
Hotel
BATHS RD
DRAPER CT
ELENMORE CT
SOUTHBOROUGH RD
LAUREL GDNS
TANGLEBERRY CL
OLDFIELD RD
SPRINGFIELD RD
OLDFIELD CL
SOUTHWOOD CL
1 HARRISON DR
2 MORIARTY CL
3 BOULTER CL
SOUTHLANDS RD
TREDWELL CL
PARKSIDE AVE
PARK HILL
SPRINGFIELD GDNS
Bromley High Jun Sch
Bromley High Sch
Recn Gd
Bwg Gn
BLENHEIM RD
CLAREMONT RD
HIGHFIELD RD
FAIRMEAD CL
FAIRMEAD
WHITE'S MDW
Thornet Wood
BURFORD RD
SUNNINGDALE RD
WALDEGRAVE RD
WHITEHALL RD
BROOKLYN RD
UNION RD
MAYFIELD RD
WESTCOTT CL
RINGMER WAY
RIPLEY CL
THE FAIRWAY
BROOKMEAD AVE
HOMEMEAD RD
Jubilee Country Park
HERBERT RD
WOODSIDE RD
SIBLEY CL
PEARTREE CL
BALFOUR RD
SALISBURY RD
LANCASTER GDNS
ST AUGUSTINE'S AVE
BIRDHAM CL
CLOISTERS AVE
MOORCROFT GDNS
SOUTHBOROUGH LA
MERTON GDNS
St James RC Prim Sch
MOSSLEA RD
ALBERT RD
FONTWELL DR
MAYBURY CL
VICTORIA RD
CROWN CT
CROWN LA
CRANFORD MEWS
AUSTIN AVE
Liby
DUXBERRY CL
MAGPIE HALL LA
WILLOW CL
HOLBROOK WAY
PARKFIELD WAY
Southborough Prim Sch
NEWTON TERR
HOLMCROFT WAY
STILES CL
Pav
CROWN LANE SPUR
LAVENDER CL
SUNRAY AVE
SOVEREIGN CT
Recn Gd
OXHAWTH CRES
LANGLEY GDNS
CRESCENT DR
Sp Gd
Allot Gdns
BONNINGTON TWR
GREEN WAY
RUSKIN WLK
Cemy
Parkfield Recn Gd
THORN CL
CHESHAM AVE
SHELDWICH TERR
MONS WAY
BROOM CL
LOVELACE AVE
PRESCOTT AVE
NARROW WAY
MANOR WAY
SHELL CL
THE OAKS
WHITEBEAM AVE
ASH ROW
HAZEL WLK
FELTON CL
ROLLESTON AVE
TURPINGTON LA
MOSUL WAY
MAGPIE HALL CL
HORNBEAM WAY
BIRCH ROW
FARINGDON AVE
HOLLINGWORTH RD
RAYFIELD CL
TURPINGTON CL
LINK WAY
CH
Bromley
Recn Gd
LARCH WAY
LABURNUM WAY
ROLLESTON CL
FAIROAK CL
COBHAM CL
ALMOND WAY
DENTON CT
ALMOND CL
A21
BROMLEY COMMON
Pl Fld
Princes Plain Prim Sch
Bishop Justus CE Sch
Sparrow Wood
Oakley House
Allot Gdns
Tenn Cts
Pl Fld
Prince's Plain
London Loop
CHURCH LA
BARHAM CT
1 PEMBURY HO
2 KINGSMEAD COTTS
A233
COTTAGE AVE
PRINCE'S PLAIN
BREWERY RD
OSPREY CL
CREDENHALL DR
Scrubs Farm
Crofton Heath
BRAMLEY CL
CAPEL CT
LOWER GRAVEL RD
BARHAM CL
ARAGON CL
SEYMOUR DR
LENNARD RD
RANDOLF RD
LANSDOWNE AVE
TRINITY CL
RIBSTON CL
BRADFORD CL
JACKSON RD
HATHAWAY CL
DAERWOOD CL
DRAYTON AVE
JACKSON RD
CHERRY ORCHARD RD
COPTHORNE AVE
KNOWLE RD
Knowl Wood
BIRCH MEAD
ST ANTHONY'S CT
ROSE DALE
LIME GR
MORLEY CL
JASMINE CL
FAIRBANK AVE
POPLAR AVE
WISTARIA CL
WEALD CL
HASTINGS
Sp Gd
Knowlehill Wood
CROSS RD
WOOD WAY
69
68
67
66
42
43
44
6
5
4
3
2
1
30

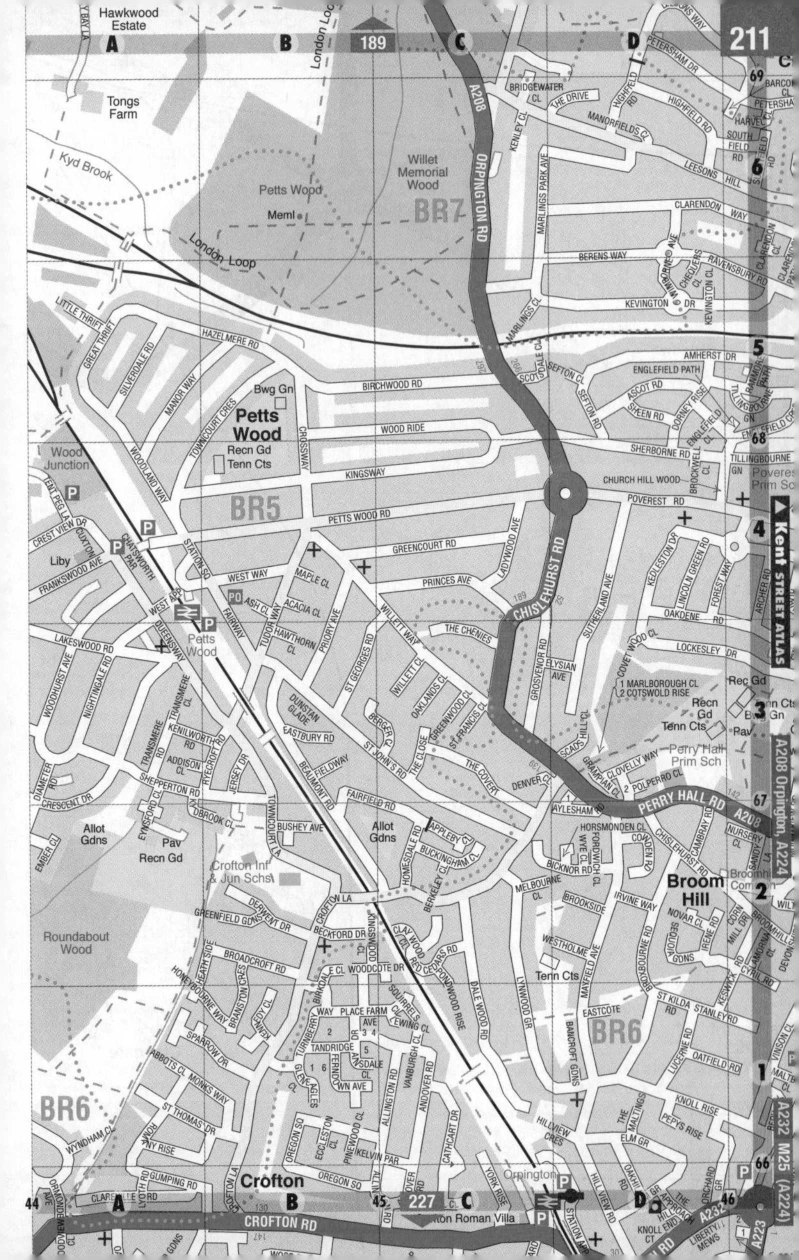

Hawkwood Estate
Tongs Farm
Kyd Brook
Petts Wood
Meml
Willet Memorial Wood
London Loop
BR7
ORPINGTON RD
A208
189
BRIDGEWATER CL
THE DRIVE
HIGHFIELD RD
MANORFIELDS CL
PETERSHAM DR
LEESONS WAY
LEESONS HILL
HIGHFIELD RD
KENLEY CL
MARLINGS PARK AVE
CLARENDON WAY
BERENS WAY
RAVENSBURY RD
CHEQUERS CL
KEVINGTON DR
KEVINGTON CL
MARLINGS CL
LITTLE THRIFT
GREAT THRIFT
HAZELMERE RD
SILVERDALE RD
MANOR WAY
TOWNCOURT CRES
Bwg Gn
Petts Wood
Recn Gd
Tenn Cts
CROSSWAY
BIRCHWOOD RD
WOOD RIDE
KINGSWAY
SCOTSDALE CL
SEFTON CL
AMHERST DR
ENGLEFIELD PATH
ASCOT RD
SHEEN RD
DORNEY RISE
SHERBORNE RD
TILLINGBOURNE GN
CHURCH HILL WOOD
Poverest Prim Sch
POVEREST RD
BR5
PETTS WOOD RD
GREENCOURT RD
PRINCES AVE
LADYWOOD AVE
CHISLEHURST RD
WEST WAY
MAPLE CL
ACACIA CL
ASH CL
HAWTHORN CL
TUDOR WAY
PRIORY AVE
FAIRWAY
STATION SQ
WEST APP
QUEENSWAY
Petts Wood
Wood Junction
TENT PEG LA
CREST VIEW DR
CUXTON
CHATSWORTH PAR
Liby
FRANKSWOOD AVE
LAKESWOOD RD
WOODHURST AVE
NIGHTINGALE RD
TRANSMERE RD
TRANSMERE CL
KENILWORTH RD
RYECROFT RD
ADDISON CL
JERSEY DR
SHEPPERTON RD
DIAMETER RD
CRESCENT DR
EYNSFORD CL
Allot Gdns
Pav
Recn Gd
EMBER CL
WILLETT WAY
THE CHENIES
ST GEORGES RD
WILLETT CL
OAKLANDS CL
GREENWOOD CL
ST FRANCIS CL
DUNSTAN GLADE
EASTBURY RD
BERGER CL
ST JOHN'S RD
THE CLOSE
THE COVERT
BEAUMONT RD
FIELDWAY
FAIRFIELD RD
TOWNCOURT LA
BUSHEY AVE
Allot Gdns
HOMESDALE RD
APPLEBY CL
BUCKINGHAM CL
BERKELEY CL
Crofton Inf & Jun Schs
GROSVENOR RD
ELYSIAN AVE
SUTHERLAND AVE
KEDLESTON DR
LINCOLN GREEN RD
FOREST WAY
OAKDENE RD
LOCKESLEY DR
COVET WOOD CL
1 MARLBOROUGH CL
2 COTSWOLD RISE
Rec Gd
Recn Gd
Tenn Cts
Pav
SCADS HILL CL
GRAMPIAN CL
CLOVELLY WAY
POLPERRO CL
Perry Hall Prim Sch
DENVER CL
AYLESHAM RD
PERRY HALL RD
A208
HORSMONDEN CL
WYE CL
FORDWICH CL
COWDEN RD
CHISLEHURST RD
CAMBRAY RD
NURSERY CL
SANDY LA
BICKNOR RD
MELBOURNE CL
BROOKSIDE
IRVINE WAY
Broom Hill
NOVAR CL
SEQUOIA GDNS
IRENE RD
CORN MILL DR
BROOMHILL RD
LAMORNA CL
CYRIL RD
WESTHOLME
MAYFIELD AVE
BROXBOURNE RD
KESWICK RD
Tenn Cts
LYNWOOD GR
ST KILDA RD
STANLEY RD
EASTCOTE
BANCROFT GDNS
BR6
LUCERNE RD
OATFIELD RD
KNOLL RISE
PEPYS RISE
THE MALTINGS
ELM GR
HILLVIEW CRES
OAKHILL RD
ORCHARD GR
HILL VIEW RD
APPROACH RD
KNOLL END CT
LIBERTY MEWS
Roundabout Wood
GREENFIELD GDNS
DERWENT DR
CROFTON LA
BECKFORD DR
KINGSWOOD CL
CLAY WOOD CL
RED CEDARS RD
PONDWOOD RISE
DALE WOOD RD
HEATH SIDE
BROADCROFT RD
HONEYBOURNE WAY
BRANSTON CRES
KENNEDY CL
WOODCOTE DR
SQUIRRELS CL
TURNBERRY WAY
PLACE FARM AVE
EWING CL
TANDRIDGE DR
FERNDOWN AVE
SPARROW DR
ABBOTS CL
MONKS WAY
ST THOMAS' DR
GLENEAGLES CL
VANBURGH CL
ANDOVER RD
ALLINGTON RD
CATHCART DR
YORK RISE
BR6
WYNDHAM CL
OREGON SQ
ECCLESTON CL
PINEWOOD CL
KELVIN PAR
OREGON SQ
Crofton
GUMPING RD
LYNDHURST
CLAREVILLE RD
ORMONDE AVE
CROFTON RD
Crofton Roman Villa
Orpington
STATION APP
A232
A223
44
45
46
66
67
68
69
A
B
C
D
1
2
3
4
5
6
227
▲ Kent STREET ATLAS
A208 Orpington, A224
A232 M25 (A224)

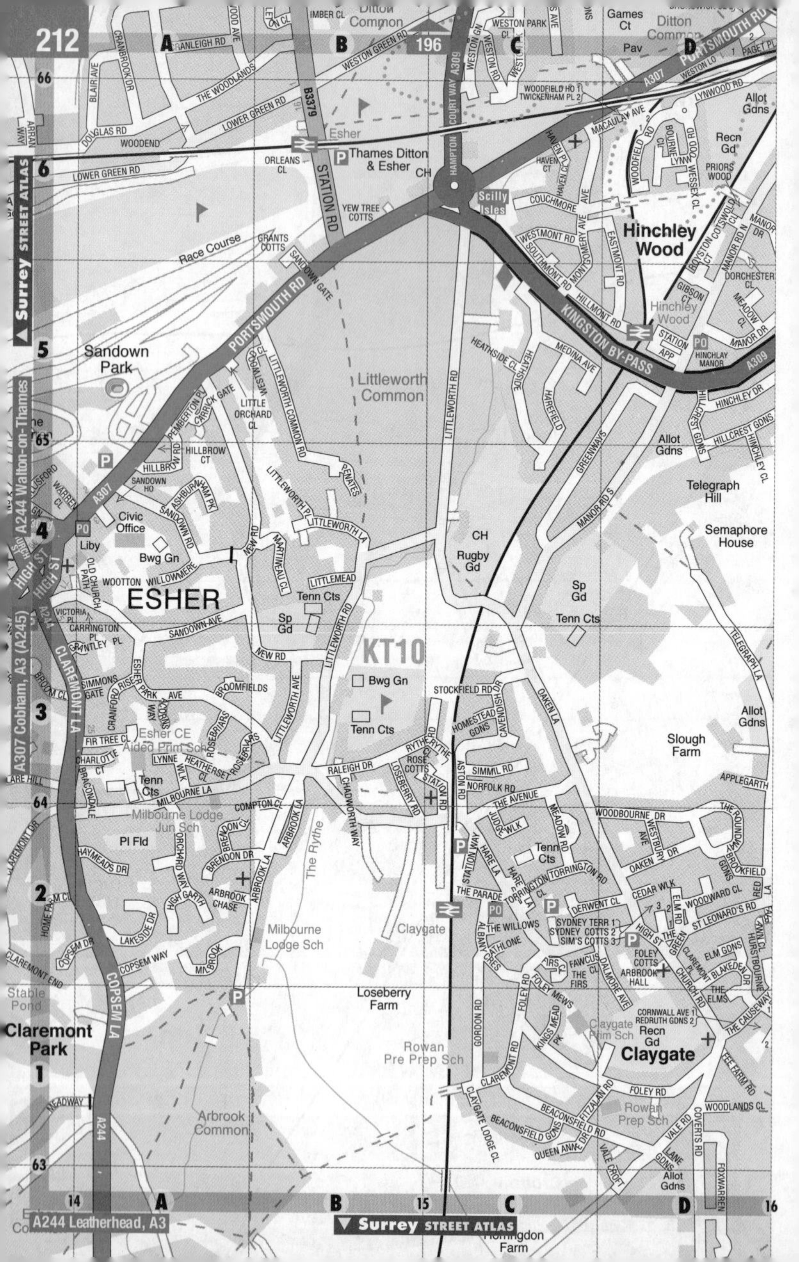

196
Surrey STREET ATLAS
A244 Walton-on-Thames
A307 Cobham, A3 (A245)
A244 Leatherhead, A3
Surrey STREET ATLAS
A
B
C
D
66
6
5
65
4
3
64
2
1
63
14
15
16
Ditton Common
Games Ct
Pav
PORTSMOUTH RD
PAGET PL
WESTON LO
CRANLEIGH RD
CRANBROOK DR
BLAIR AVE
THE WOODLANDS
WESTON GREEN RD
LOWER GREEN RD
DOUGLAS RD
WOODEND
ARRAN WAY
IMBER CL
B3379
Esher
Thames Ditton & Esher
ORLEANS CL
STATION RD
CH
HAMPTON COURT WAY
A309
WESTON PARK CL
WESTON GN
WOODFIELD HO 1
TWICKENHAM PL 2
MACAULAY AVE
LYNWOOD RD
Allot Gdns
Recn Gd
WOODFIELD RD
BOURNE CL
LYNWOOD RD
WESSEX CL
PRIORS WOOD
HAVEN PL
HAVEN CT
Scilly Isles
COUCHMORE AVE
WESTMONT RD
SOUTHMONT RD
MONTGOMERY AVE
EASTMONT RD
HILLMONT RD
Hinchley Wood
ROYSTON CT
COTSWOLD CL
MANOR RD N
MANOR DR
DORCHESTER CL
GIBSON CT
MEADOW CL
STATION APP
PO
HINCHLAY MANOR
KINGSTON BY-PASS
LOWER GREEN RD
YEW TREE COTTS
Race Course
GRANTS COTTS
SANDOWN GATE
Sandown Park
PORTSMOUTH RD
A307
Littleworth Common
LITTLEWORTH RD
HEATHSIDE CL
HEATHSIDE
MEDINA AVE
HAREFIELD
HINCHLEY DR
HILLCREST GDNS
HINCHLEY CL
Allot Gdns
GREENWAYS
Telegraph Hill
Semaphore House
MANOR RD S
PEMBERTON PL
CARRICK GATE
LITTLE ORCHARD CL
WESTWOOD CL
LITTLEWORTH COMMON RD
PENATES
LITTLEWORTH PL
LITTLEWORTH LA
HILLBROW RD
HILLBROW CT
SANDOWN HO
ASHBURNHAM PK
SANDOWN RD
WARREN CL
Civic Office
Liby
Bwg Gn
WILLOWMERE
NEW RD
MARTINEAU CL
LITTLEMEAD
Tenn Cts
Sp Gd
CH
Rugby Gd
Sp Gd
Tenn Cts
HIGH ST
WOOTTON
OLD CHURCH PATH
ESHER
VICTORIA PL
CARRINGTON PL
BENTLEY PL
SANDOWN AVE
NEW RD
KT10
Bwg Gn
TELEGRAPH LA
CLAREMONT LA
SIMMONS GATE
BROOM CL
CRANFORD RISE
ESHER PARK AVE
ACORNS WAY
BROOMFIELDS
LITTLEWORTH AVE
STOCKFIELD RD
CAVENDISH DR
HOMESTEAD GDNS
OAKEN LA
Allot Gdns
Slough Farm
Esher CE Aided Prim Sch
FIR TREE CL
CHARLOTTE CT
BRACONDALE
LYNNE WLK
HEATHERSET CL
ROSEBRIARS
Tenn Cts
RYTHE RD
RYTHE CL
RALEIGH DR
ROSE COTTS
LOSEBERRY RD
STATION RD
ASTON RD
SIMMIL RD
NORFOLK RD
APPLEGARTH
MILBOURNE LA
COMPTON CL
CHADWORTH WAY
THE AVENUE
JUDGE WLK
MEADOW RD
WOODBOURNE DR
WESTBURY AVE
THE ROUNDWAY
Milbourne Lodge Jun Sch
Pl Fld
HAYMEADS DR
ORCHARD WAY
BRENDON CL
BRENDON DR
ARBROOK LA
The Rythe
STATION WAY
HARE LA
Tenn Cts
OAKEN DR
BROOKFIELD GDNS
CLAREMONT DR
HOME FARM CL
HIGH GARTH
ARBROOK CHASE
THE PARADE
TORRINGTON CL
TORRINGTON RD
CEDAR WLK
ELM RD
WOODWARD CL
ST LEONARD'S RD
LAKESIDE DR
Milbourne Lodge Sch
Claygate
THE WILLOWS
DERWENT CL
SYDNEY TERR 1
SYDNEY COTTS 2
SIM'S COTTS 3
HIGH ST
THE GREEN
COPSEM DR
CLAREMONT END
COPSEM WAY
MILLBROOK
ALBANY CRES
ATHLONE
FIRS CL
FAWCUS CL
THE FIRS
DALMORE AVE
FOLEY COTTS
ARBROOK HALL
CLAREMONT CL
CHURCH RD
ELM GDNS
BLAKEDEN DR
HURSTBOURNE
THE ELMS
THE CAUSEWAY
Stable Pond
Claremont Park
COPSEM LA
Loseberry Farm
FOLEY RD
FOLEY MEWS
KINGS MEAD PK
Claygate Prim Sch
CORNWALL AVE 1
REDRUTH GDNS 2
Recn Gd
Claygate
Rowan Pre Prep Sch
GORDON RD
CLAREMONT RD
FITZALAN RD
FOLEY RD
FEE FARM RD
MEADWAY
A244
Arbrook Common
CLAYGATE LODGE CL
BEACONSFIELD RD
BEACONSFIELD GDNS
QUEEN ANNE'S DR
VALE RD
VALE CROFT
Rowan Prep Sch
COVERTS RD
WOODLANDS CL
LANE GDNS
Allot Gdns
FOXWARREN
Horringdon Farm

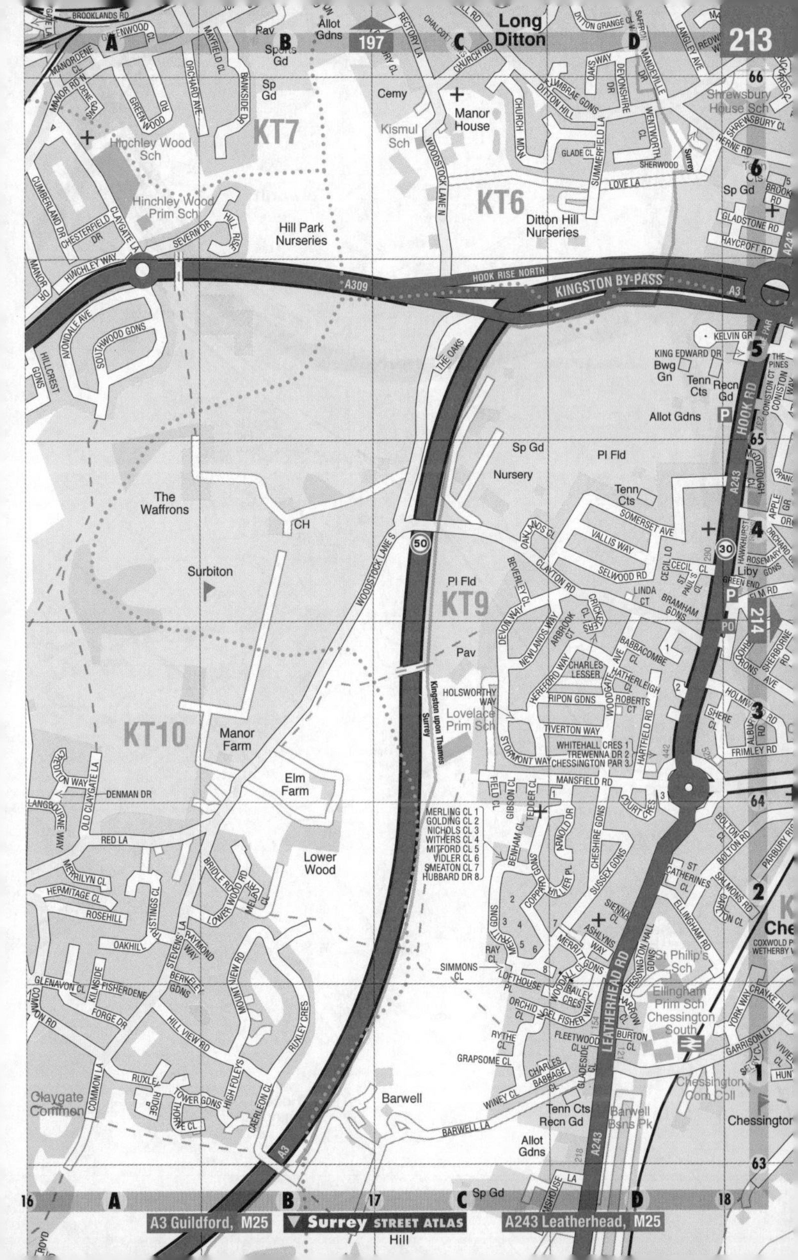
Long Ditton
KT7
KT6
KT9
KT10
Hinchley Wood Sch
Hinchley Wood Prim Sch
Hill Park Nurseries
Ditton Hill Nurseries
Manor House
Kismul Sch
Cemy
Shrewsbury House Sch
The Waffrons
Surbiton
Manor Farm
Elm Farm
Lower Wood
Barwell
Claygate Common
Lovelace Prim Sch
St Philip's Sch
Ellingham Prim Sch
Chessington South
Chessington Com Coll
Chessington
Barwell Bsns Pk
KINGSTON BY-PASS
HOOK RISE NORTH
LEATHERHEAD RD
HOOK RD
WOODSTOCK LANE S
WOODSTOCK LANE N
A3 Guildford, M25
Surrey STREET ATLAS
A243 Leatherhead, M25

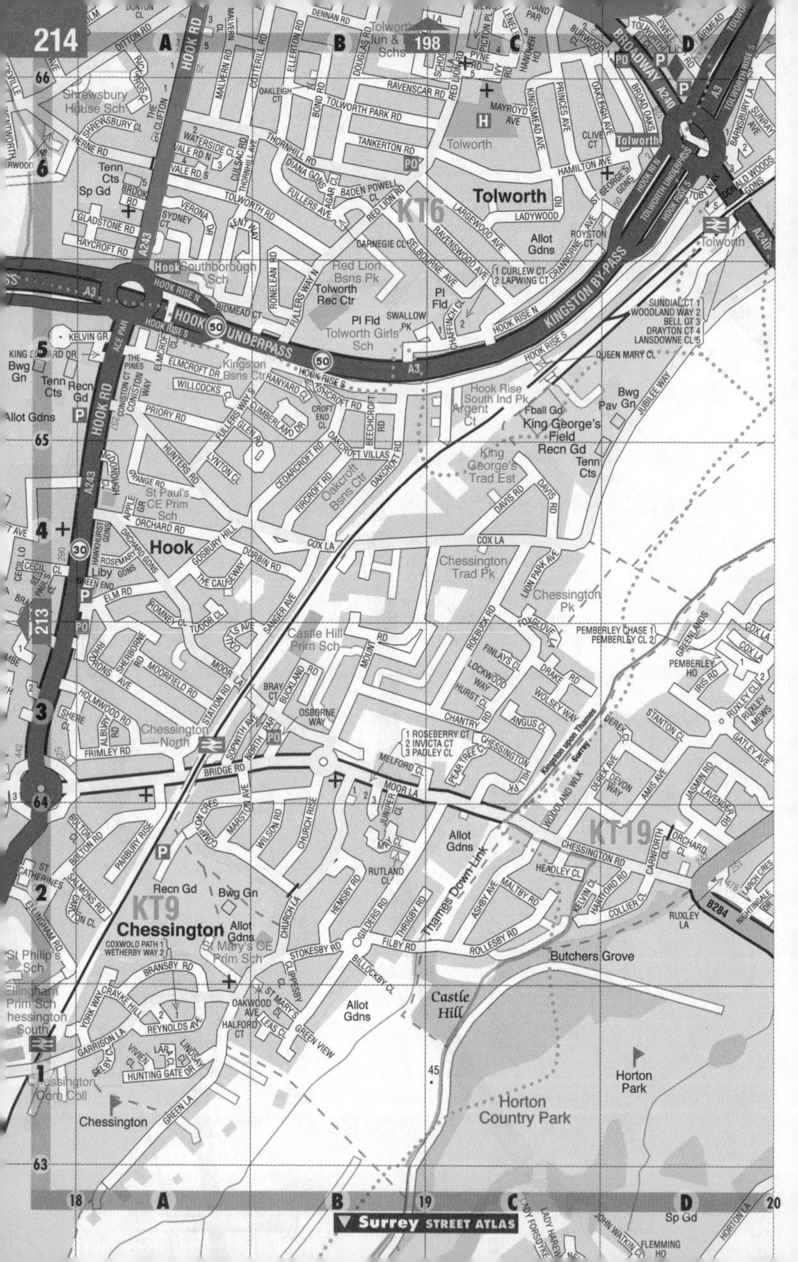
214
198
A
B
C
D
66
65
64
63
18
19
20
6
5
4
3
2
1
213
Surrey STREET ATLAS
HOOK RD
A243
DITTON RD
MALVERN RD
COTTERILL RD
ELLERTON RD
DENNAN RD
Tolworth Jun & Schs
DOUGLAS RD
BOND RD
OAKLEIGH
RAVENSCAR RD
TOLWORTH PARK RD
TANKERTON RD
PYNE RD
RED LION RD
IVY RD
HANOVER HO
PICTON PL
BURWOOD CL
BROADWAY
A240
TOLWORTH CL
EWELL RD
FAIRMEAD
Liby
PO
P
H
MAYROYD AVE
KINGSMEAD AVE
PRINCES AVE
OAKLEIGH AVE
BROAD OAKS
CLIVE CT
Tolworth
HAMILTON AVE
ST GEORGE'S GDNS
A3
TOLWORTH RISE S
BARNSBURY LA
SUNRAY AVE
HOOK RISE N
TOLWORTH UNDERPASS
HOOK RISE S
TOBY WAY
DONALD WOODS GDNS
Shrewsbury House Sch
RICHARDS CL
THE CLIFTON
SHREWSBURY CL
HERNE RD
WATERSIDE CL
VALE RD N
VALE RD S
CULSAC RD
THORNHILL AVE
THORNHILL RD
DIANA GDNS
AGAR CL
BADEN POWELL CL
FULLERS AVE
Tenn Cts
Sp Gd
BROOK RD
GLADSTONE RD
HAYCROFT RD
SYDNEY CT
VERONA DR
TOLWORTH RD
KENT WAY
KT6
Tolworth
LARGEWOOD AVE
LADYWOOD RD
RAVENSWOOD AVE
SELBOURNE AVE
CARNEGIE CL
Allot Gdns
ROYSTON CT
CRANBORNE AVE
1 CURLEW CT
2 LAPWING CT
KINGSTON BY-PASS
Hook
Southborough Sch
RONELEAN RD
FULLERS WAY N
Red Lion Bsns Pk
Tolworth Rec Ctr
Pl Fld
SWALLOW PK
CHAFFINCH CL
BIDMEAD CT
HOOK UNDERPASS
50
Tolworth Girls' Sch
SUNDIAL CT 1
WOODLAND WAY 2
BELL CT 3
DRAYTON CT 4
LANSDOWNE CL 5
QUEEN MARY CL
KELVIN GR
ACE PAR
KING EDWARD DR
Bwg Gn
Tenn Cts
Recn Gd
Allot Gdns
THE PINES
ELMCROFT DR
CONISTON CT
CONISTON WAY
Kingston Bsns Ctr
RANYARD CL
ASHCROFT RD
WILLCOCKS CL
PRIORY RD
FULLERS WAY S
CUMBERLAND DR
GLEN RD
CROFT END CL
BEECHCROFT RD
Hook Rise South Ind Pk
Argent Ct
Fball Gd
King George's Field
Recn Gd
Bwg Gn
Pav
JUBILEE WAY
Tenn Cts
HUNTERS RD
LYNTON CL
CEDARCROFT RD
FIRCROFT RD
OAKCROFT VILLAS
OAKCROFT RD
Oakcroft Bsns Ctr
King George's Trad Est
DAVIS RD
McDONOUGH CL
GRANGE RD
St Paul's CE Prim Sch
APPLE GR
ORCHARD RD
HAWKHURST GDNS
ORCHARD GDNS
30
Hook
GOSBURY HILL
DURBIN RD
COX LA
Chessington Trad Pk
LION PARK AVE
Chessington Pk
CECIL CL
ROSEMARY GDNS
Liby
GREEN END
ELM RD
THE CAUSEWAY
ROMNEY CL
TUDOR CL
SANGER AVE
Castle Hill Prim Sch
MOUNT RD
ROEBUCK RD
FOXGLOVE LA
FINLAYS CL
LOCKWOOD WAY
DRAKE RD
WOLSEY WAY
HURST CL
CHANTRY RD
ANGUS CL
PEMBERLEY CHASE 1
PEMBERLEY CL 2
GREENLANDS
PEMBERLEY HO
COX LA
IRIS RD
RUXLEY CL
RUXLEY MEWS
STANTON CL
GATLEY AVE
DEREK CL
SHERBORNE RD
MOORFIELD RD
COLEMANS AVE
MOOR LA
STATION RD
BRAY CT
BUCKLAND RD
OSBORNE WAY
1 ROSEBERRY CT
2 INVICTA CT
3 PADLEY CL
PEAR TREE CL
CHESSINGTON HILL PK
Kingston upon Thames
Surrey
HOLMWOOD RD
SHERE CL
ALBURY RD
Chessington North
FRIMLEY RD
SOPWITH AVE
NORTH PAR
BRIDGE RD
MELFORD CL
MOOR LA
JUNIPER CL
DEREK AVE
DEVON WAY
AMIS AVE
JASMIN RD
LAVENDER RD
WOODLAND WLK
KT19
BOLTON CL
BOLTON RD
PARBURY RISE
COMPTON CRES
MARSTON AVE
WILSON RD
CHURCH RISE
MAY CL
Allot Gdns
CHESSINGTON RD
ORCHARD CL
CARNFORTH CL
HEADLEY CL
RUTLAND CL
ST CATHERINES
SALMONS RD
CARLTON CL
ELLINGHAM RD
Recn Gd
Bwg Gn
KT9
Chessington
Allot Gdns
CHURCH LA
HEMSBY RD
GILDERS RD
THRIGBY RD
Thames Down Link
ASHBY AVE
MALTBY RD
KELVIN CL
HARTFORD RD
COLLIER CL
B284
RUXLEY LA
NIGHTINGALE DR
LARCH CRES
COXWOLD PATH 1
WETHERBY WAY 2
St Mary's CE Prim Sch
STOKESBY RD
FILBY RD
ROLLESBY RD
Butchers Grove
St Philip's Sch
BRANSBY RD
CLIPPESBY CL
BILLOCKBY CL
Ellingham Prim Sch
Chessington South
YORK WAY
CRAYKE HILL
REYNOLDS AVE
OAKWOOD AVE
ST MARY'S CL
Allot Gdns
Castle Hill
HALFORD CT
LEAS CL
GREEN VIEW
GARRISON LA
SELBY CL
VIVIEN CL
LARA CL
LINDSAY
HUNTING GATE DR
Chessington Com Coll
45
Horton Park
Horton Country Park
Chessington
GREEN LA
LADY FORSDYKE
LADY HAREWOOD
JOHN WATKIN CL
FLEMMING HO
Sp Gd
HORTON LA

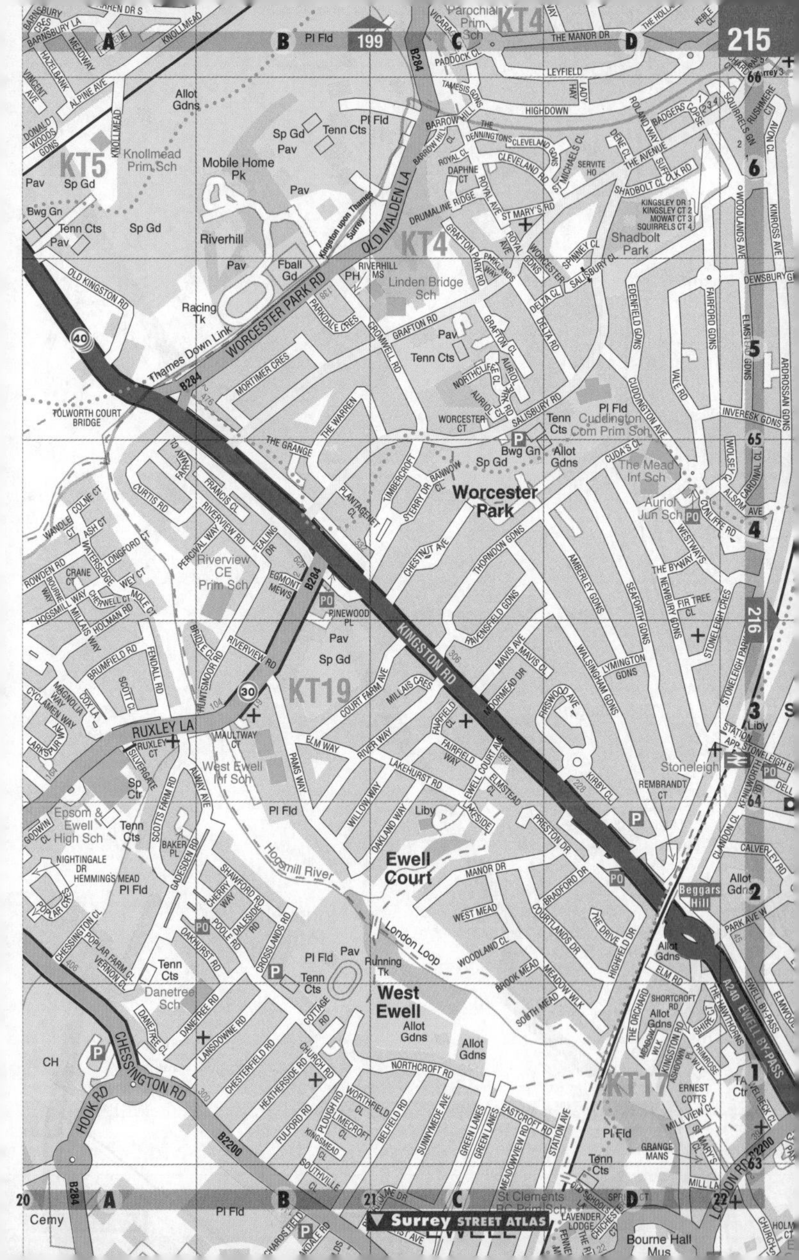

199
A
B
C
D
KT4
KT5
KT19
KT17
Allot Gdns
Knollmead Prim Sch
Mobile Home Pk
Riverhill
Racing Tk
Thames Down Link
WORCESTER PARK RD
OLD MALDEN LA
Kingston upon Thames
Surrey
Linden Bridge Sch
THE MANOR DR
LEYFIELD
HIGHDOWN
BARROW HILL
CLEVELAND RD
THE AVENUE
Shadbolt Park
SERVITE HO
KINGSLEY DR 1
KINGSLEY CT 2
MOWAT CT 3
SQUIRRELS CT 4
OLD KINGSTON RD
TOLWORTH COURT BRIDGE
GRAFTON RD
SALISBURY RD
Cuddington Com Prim Sch
The Mead Inf Sch
Auriol Jun Sch
Worcester Park
KINGSTON RD
Riverview CE Prim Sch
RUXLEY LA
West Ewell Inf Sch
Epsom & Ewell High Sch
Stoneleigh
Beggars Hill
Hogsmill River
Ewell Court
London Loop
Running Tk
West Ewell
Danetree Sch
CHESSINGTON RD
HOOK RD
A240 EWELL BY-PASS
216
Cemy
St Clements RC Prim Sch
Bourne Hall Mus
20
21
22
Surrey STREET ATLAS

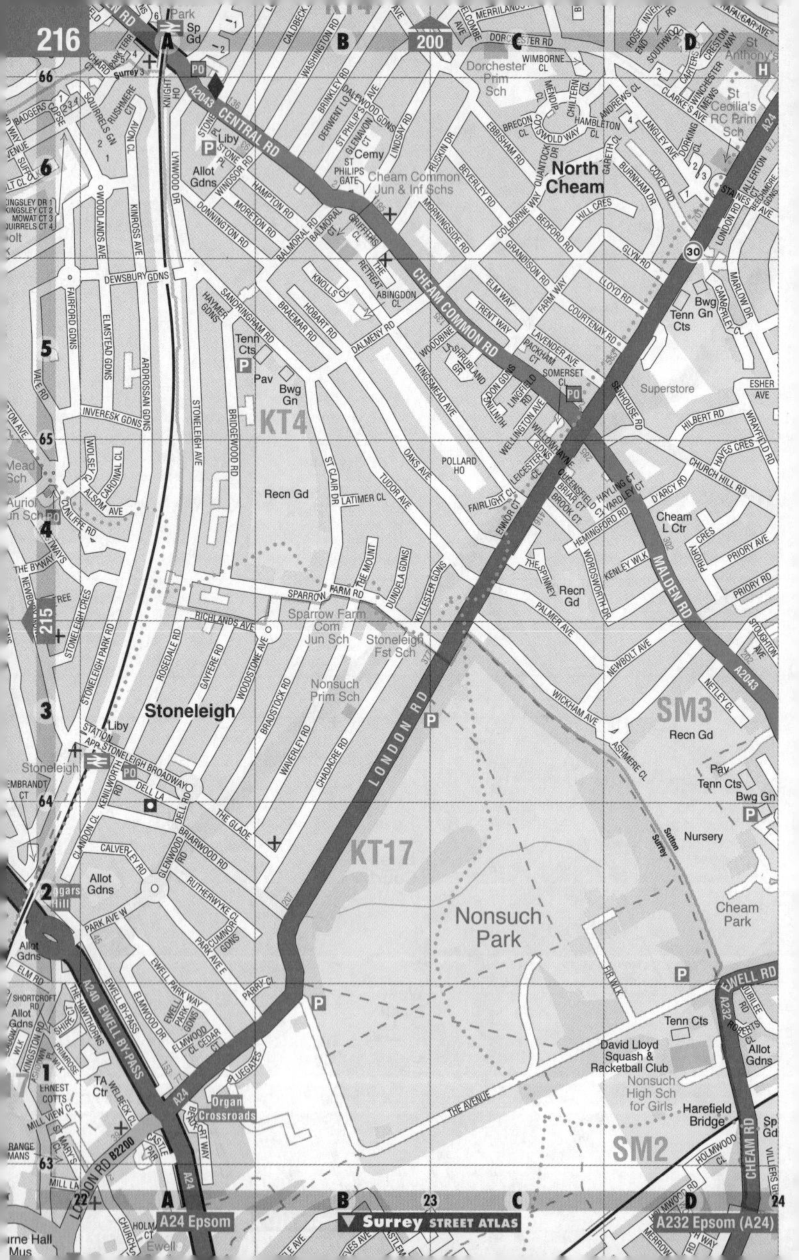

216
A
B
C
D
200
Park
Sp Gd
PO
Surrey
A2043
CENTRAL RD
KNIGHT HO
STONE PL
Liby
Allot Gdns
LYNWOOD DR
WINDSOR RD
HAMPTON RD
MORETON RD
DONNINGTON RD
BALMORAL RD
BALMORAL CT
GRIFFITHS CL
CALDBECK
WASHINGTON RD
BRINKLEY RD
DERWENT LO
DALEWOOD GDNS
ST PHILIPS AVE
GLENAVON CT
LINDSAY RD
Cemy
ST PHILIPS GATE
Cheam Common Jun & Inf Schs
MERRILANDS
WELCOMBE AVE
DORCHESTER RD
Dorchester Prim Sch
WIMBORNE CL
MENDIP CL
CHILTERN CL
BRECON CL
COTSWOLD WAY
HAMBLETON CL
QUANTOCK DR
EBBISHAM RD
RUSKIN DR
BEVERLEY RD
MORNINGSIDE RD
North Cheam
COLBORNE WAY
BEDFORD RD
GRANDISON RD
HILL CRES
GARETH CL
BURNHAM DR
COVEY RD
ANDREWS CL
GLYN RD
ROSE END
SOUTHWOOD
CARTERS CL
CRESTON WAY
TRAFALGAR AVE
St Anthony's
H
WINCHESTER MEWS
CLARKE'S AVE
St Cecilia's RC Prim Sch
LANGLEY AVE
DORKING CL
A24
ALLERTON CT
STAINES CT
BEECHMORE AVE
LONDON RD
30
66
BADGERS COPSE
SQUIRRELS GN
RUSHMERE CT
AVON CL
KINGSLEY DR
KINGSLEY CT
MOWAT CT
SQUIRRELS CT
WOODLANDS AVE
KINROSS AVE
6
DEWSBURY GDNS
FAIRFORD GDNS
ELMSTEAD GDNS
ARDROSSAN GDNS
HAYMER GDNS
SANDRINGHAM RD
BRAEMAR RD
HOBART RD
KNOLLS CL
THE RETREAT
ABINGDON CL
DALMENY RD
CHEAM COMMON RD
ELM WAY
TRENT WAY
FARM WAY
LLOYD RD
COURTENAY RD
LAVENDER AVE
PACKHAM CT
WOODBINE LA
SHRUBLAND GR
KINGSMEAD AVE
HUNTINGDON GDNS
LINGFIELD RD
SOMERSET CL
SENHOUSE RD
Superstore
Bwg Gn
Tenn Cts
CAMBERLEY CL
MARLOW DR
ESHER AVE
HILBERT RD
WRAYFIELD RD
HAYES CRES
CHURCH HILL RD
D'ARCY RD
5
VALE RD
INVERESK GDNS
STONELEIGH AVE
BRIDGEWOOD RD
Pav
KT4
65
WOLSEY CL
CARDINAL CL
ALSOM AVE
Mead Sch
Auriol Jun Sch
CUNLIFFE RD
4
Recn Gd
ST CLAIR DR
LATIMER CL
TUDOR AVE
OAKS AVE
POLLARD HO
WELLINGTON AVE
WILLOWHAYNE GDNS
LEICESTER CL
FAIRLIGHT CL
ENNOR CT
QUEENSFIELD CT
BRIAR CT
BROOK CT
HAYLING CT
YARDLEY CT
HEMINGFORD RD
WORDSWORTH DR
KENLEY WLK
MALDEN RD
Cheam L Ctr
PRIORY CRES
PRIORY AVE
PRIORY RD
THE BYWAY
NEWBOLT AVE
215
STONELEIGH CRES
STONELEIGH PARK RD
THE MOUNT
DUNDELA GDNS
KILLESTER GDNS
SPARROW FARM RD
RICHLANDS AVE
THE SPINNEY
PALMER AVE
Sparrow Farm Com Jun Sch
Stoneleigh Fst Sch
ROSEDALE RD
GAYFERE RD
WOODSTONE AVE
BRADSTOCK RD
Nonsuch Prim Sch
STOUGHTON AVE
A2043
NETLEY CL
3
Stoneleigh
STATION APP
LONDON RD
WICKHAM AVE
SM3
ASHMERE CL
WAVERLEY RD
CHADACRE RD
STONELEIGH BROADWAY
KENILWORTH RD
DELL LA
DELL RD
Stoneleigh
REMBRANDT CT
64
THE GLADE
BRIARWOOD RD
CLANDON CL
CALVERLEY RD
GLENWOOD RD
RUTHERWYKE CL
KT17
Sutton
Surrey
Nursery
Pav
Tenn Cts
Bwg Gn
2
Beggars Hill
Allot Gdns
PARK AVE W
CUMNOR GDNS
PARK AVE E
Nonsuch Park
Cheam Park
ELM RD
SHORTCROFT RD
THE HAWTHORNS
A240
EWELL BY-PASS
EWELL PARK WAY
EWELL PARK GDNS
ELMWOOD DR
ELMWOOD CL
CEDAR CT
PARRY CL
FIR WLK
EWELL RD
A232
JUBILEE RD
ROBERTS CL
Tenn Cts
David Lloyd Squash & Racketball Club
Allot Gdns
SHIRE CT
KINGSTON RD
PRIMROSE WLK
1
ERNEST COTTS
TA Ctr
WELBECK CL
MILL VIEW CL
BLUEGATES
Organ Crossroads
THE AVENUE
Nonsuch High Sch for Girls
Harefield Bridge
ST MARY'S
B2200
CASTLE PAR
BEAUFORT WAY
SM2
HOLMWOOD CL
CHEAM RD
Sp Gd
VILLIERS
GRANGE MANS
63
MILL LA
LONDON RD
22
23
24
A24 Epsom
Surrey STREET ATLAS
A232 Epsom (A24)
HOLMWOOD RD
CHURCH
HOLM CT
Ewell
Bourne Hall Mus

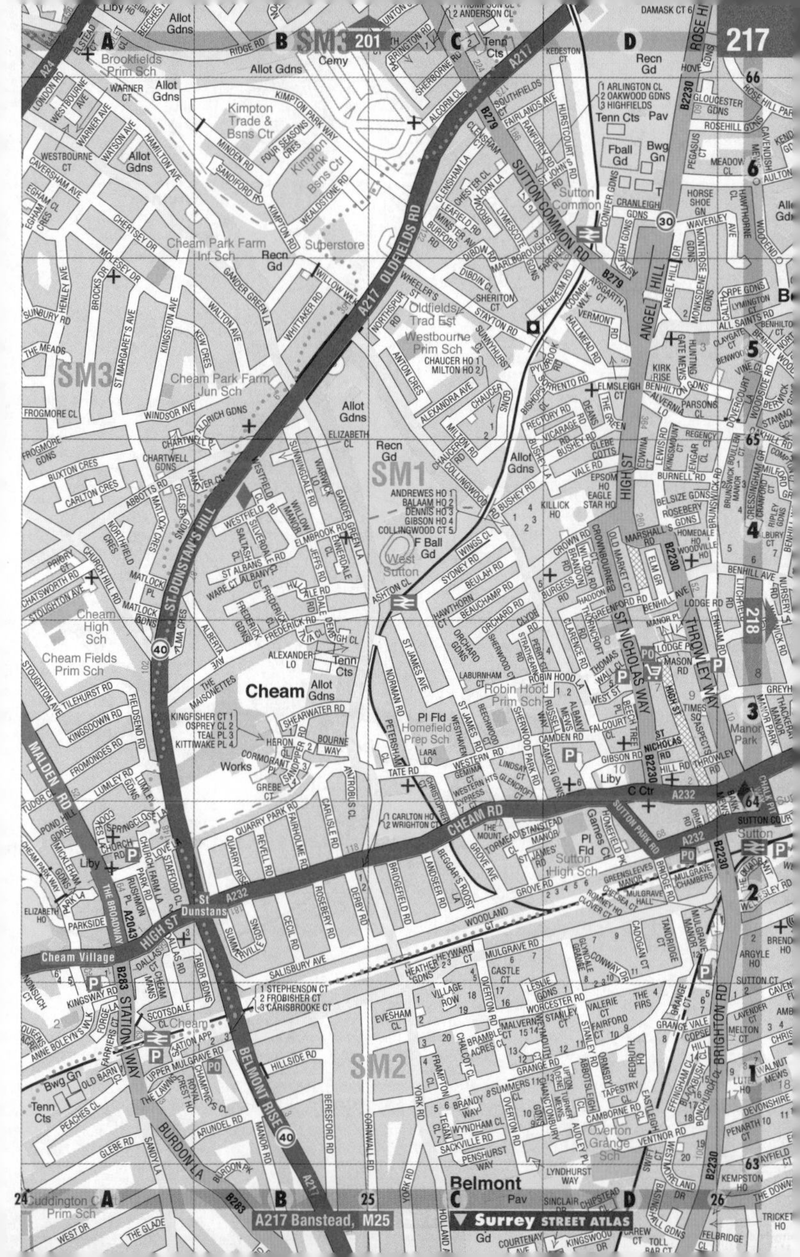

217
A
B
C
D
SM3
201
218
Brookfields Prim Sch
Allot Gdns
Cemy
Tenn Cts
Recn Gd
Liby
RIDGE RD
ELSTEAD CT
2 ANDERSON CL
DAMASK CT
ROSE HILL
HOVE GDNS
66
ROSE HILL PARK
GLOUCESTER GDNS
ROSEHILL GDNS
CAVENDISH MEWS
MEADOW CL
AULTON
WARNER CT
WARNER AVE
WESTBOURNE AVE
LONDON RD
A24
WATSON AVE
HAMILTON AVE
WESTBOURNE CT
CAVERSHAM AVE
EGHAM CL
EGHAM CRES
Kimpton Trade & Bsns Ctr
KIMPTON PARK WAY
FOUR SEASONS CRES
Kimpton Link Bsns Ctr
MINDEN RD
SANDIFORD RD
KIMPTON RD
WEALDSTONE RD
SHERBORNE RD
ALCORN CL
A217
KEDESTON CT
SOUTHFIELDS
FAIRLANDS AVE
HURSTCOURT RD
RANFURLY RD
1 ARLINGTON CL
2 OAKWOOD GDNS
3 HIGHFIELDS
Tenn Cts
Pav
Fball Gd
Bwg Gn
B2230
B279
SUTTON COMMON RD
Sutton Common
CLENSHAM LA
CLENSHAM CT
CHESTER CL
LEAFIELD RD
MINSTER AV
BURFORD RD
LYMESCOTE GDNS
ST JOHN'S RD
CONIFER GDNS
CRANLEIGH GDNS
HIGH GDNS
30
WAVERLEY AVE
PEGASUS CT
HORSE SHOE GN
MONTROSE GDNS
HAWTHORNE AVE
WOODEND
6
CHERTSEY DR
Cheam Park Farm Inf Sch
Superstore
Recn Gd
MOLESEY DR
HENLEY AVE
BROCKS DR
SUNBURY RD
GANDER GREEN LA
WALTON AVE
KINGSTON AVE
KEW CRES
ST MARGARET'S AVE
WHITTAKER RD
WILLOW WK
OLDFIELDS RD
DIBDIN RD
DIBDIN CL
MARLBOROUGH RD
FARRIER PL
WHEELER'S ST
NORTHSPUR RD
Oldfields Trad Est
Westbourne Prim Sch
SHERITON CT
STAYTON RD
SUNNYHURST CL
ANTON CRES
CHAUCER HO 1
MILTON HO 2
COOMBE WLK
AYSGARTH CT
BLENHEIM RD
VERMONT RD
HALLMEAD RD
ANGEL HILL
ANGEL HILL DR
MONKSDENE
CALTHORPE GDNS
LYMINGTON CT
ALL SAINTS RD
BENHILTON CT
HUNTING GATE MEWS
CLAYGATE CT
BENWOOD
5
THE MEADS
SM3
Cheam Park Farm Jun Sch
FROGMORE CL
WINDSOR AVE
ALDRICH GDNS
Allot Gdns
ALEXANDRA AVE
CHAUCER GDNS
PYLBROOK RD
SORRENTO RD
BISHOPSFORD CL
ELMSLEIGH CT
KIRK RISE
BENHILTON GDNS
ALVERNIA LO
PARSONS CL
DOVERCOURT LA
WOODSIDE RD
BERWICK
FROGMORE GDNS
CHARTWELL PL
CHARTWELL GDNS
ELIZABETH CL
SUNNINGDALE RD
WARWICK LO
Recn Gd
SM1
MILTON RD
RECTORY RD
VICARAGE RD
BUSHEY RD
GLEBE COTTS
THE GREEN
DEANS
REGENCY CT
LEWIS RD
KINGSMOUNT CT
JENGAR CL
EDWINA CT
BRUNSWICK BOULLEN CT
MANOR CL
65
BUXTON CRES
CARLTON CRES
ABBOTTS RD
MATLOCK CRES
HANOVER CL
WESTFIELD RD
CHAUCER RD
COLLINGWOOD RD
Allot Gdns
VALE RD
BURNELL RD
EPSOM HO
EAGLE STAR HO
ANDREWES HO 1
BALAAM HO 2
DENNIS HO 3
GIBSON HO 4
COLLINGWOOD CT 5
BUSHEY LA
KILLICK HO
BELSIZE GDNS
ROSEBERY GDNS
CRESSINGHAM GR
MILFORD GDNS
NORTHFIELD CRES
WESTFIELD CL
SALTASH CL
SILVERDALE CL
WILLOW MANOR
ELMBROOK RD
ENNERDALE CL
F Ball Gd
West Sutton
WINGS CL
CROWN RD
CROWNBOURNE CT
MARSHALL'S RD
B2230
HOMEDALE HO
WOODVILLE HO
4
PRIORY CT
CHURCH HILL RD
CHATSWORTH RD
MATLOCK PL
MATLOCK RD
STOUGHTON AVE
ST ALBANS RD
WARE CT
ALBANY CT
JEFFS RD
SYDNEY RD
BEULAH RD
WILCOX RD
BRANDON RD
BURGESS RD
OLD MARKET CT
ELM GR
BENHILL AVE
LITCHFIELD
NURSERY
ST DUNSTAN'S HILL
FREDERICK GDNS
FREDERICK RD
FREDERICK CL
ASHTON CL
HAWTHORN CT
BEAUCHAMP RD
ORCHARD RD
HADDON RD
GREENFORD RD
ST NICHOLAS WAY
THROWLEY WAY
LODGE RD
LENHAM RD
MANOR PL
LODGE PL
Cheam High Sch
Cheam Fields Prim Sch
40
ALMA CRES
ALBERTA AVE
HIGH CL
ALEXANDER LO
Tenn Cts
ST JAMES AVE
NORMAN RD
ORCHARD GDNS
SHERWOOD CT
CLYDE
STRATHEARN RD
PERRY CT
CLARENCE RD
THORNCROFT
THOMAS WALL CL
PO
MASON RD
TILEHURST RD
STOUGHTON AVE
FIELDSEND RD
THE MAISONETTES
Cheam
Allot Gdns
LABURNHAM CT
ROBIN HOOD LA
Robin Hood Prim Sch
WEST ST
BEECH TREE PL
HIGH ST
TIMES SQ
ASPECTS
Manor Park
3
KINGSDOWN RD
FROMONDES RD
KINGFISHER CT 1
OSPREY CL 2
TEAL PL 3
KITTIWAKE PL 4
SHEARWATER RD
HERON CT
BOURNE WAY
SANDPIPER RD
CORMORANT PL
Works
GREBE CT
PETERSHAM CL
Pl Fld
Homefield Prep Sch
LARA LO
ST JAMES RD
WESTHAVEN
BEECHWOOD CT
RUSSELL CT
SHERWOOD PARK RD
ALBANY MEWS
CAMDEN RD
FALCOURT CL
GIBSON RD
ST NICHOLAS RD
HILL RD
THROWLEY RD
MALDEN RD
LUMLEY RD
TUDOR CL
POND HILL GDNS
SPRINGCLOSE LA
CHURCH FARM LA
LOVE LA
STAFFORD CL
QUARRY PARK RD
FAIRHOLME RD
CARLISLE RD
ANTROBUS CL
TATE RD
CHRISTOPHER CT
WESTERN RD
GEMIMA CT
WESTERN HTS
CYPRESS CT
LINDSAY CT
GLENCROFT CT
CAMDEN GDNS
Liby
C Ctr
A232
CHALK PIT WAY
BANK MEWS
64
CHEAM RD
1 CARLTON HO
2 WRIGHTON CT
THE MOUNT
TORMEAD CL
STANSTEAD MANOR
Games Ct
SUTTON PARK RD
HOMEFIELD PK
Sutton
SUTTON COURT
CHEAM PARK WAY
MICKLEHAM GDNS
CHURCH RD
Liby
QUARRY RISE
REVELL RD
ROSEBERY RD
DERBY RD
BRIDGEFIELD RD
LANDSEER RD
BEGGAR'S ROOST LA
GROVE AVE
ST JAMES' RD
Pl Fld
Sutton High Sch
GREENSLEEVES MANOR
BRIDGE RD
MULGRAVE CHAMBERS
THE QUADRANT
2
WELLESLEY RD
PARK LA
PARK RD
RUSHMON PL
THE BROADWAY
A2043
ELIZABETH HO
PARKSIDE
HIGH ST
St Dunstans
GROVE RD
CHELSEA CT
ROMNEY HO
CLOVER CT
MULGRAVE HALL
WOODLAND CT
Cheam Village
DALLAS CT
DALLAS RD
CHEAM MANS
TABOR GDNS
SUMMERVILLE GDNS
CECIL RD
SALISBURY AVE
HEYWARD CT
HEATHER GDNS
MULGRAVE RD
CASTLE CT
GLYNDALE GRANGE
CONWAY DR
CADOGAN CT
TANDRIDGE CT
MULGRAVE MANOR
ARGYLE HO
BRENDON
B283
NONSUCH CT
KINGSWAY RD
STATION WAY
SCOTSDALE CL
1 STEPHENSON CT
2 FROBISHER CT
3 CARISBROOKE CT
VILLAGE ROW
OVERTON RD
LESLIE GDNS
WORCESTER RD
VALERIE CT
THE FIRS
SUTTON CT
QUEENS ACRE
ANNE BOLEYN'S WLK
FORGE LA
FARRIERS CT
Cheam
STATION APP
UPPER MULGRAVE RD
EVESHAM CL
BRAMBLE ACRES CL
MALVERN CT
STANLEY CT
STANLEY RD
FAIRFORD CT
GRANGE CT
GRANGE VALE
COPSE HILL
BRIGHTON RD
LAVENDER CT
MELTON CT
HILLSIDE RD
BELMONT RISE
SM2
CHALCOT CL
FRAMPTON CL
GRANGE RD
WEYMOUTH CT
ABBOTSLEIGH RD
ORMSBY
REDRUTH HO
TAPESTRY CL
EFFINGHAM CL
BLACKBUSH CL
BONCHURCH CL
WALNUT MEWS
1
Bwg Gn
OLD BARN
ROYAL CREST HO
CHAMPNEYS CL
THE LAWNS
SUMMERS CL
DENE
TURNER MEWS
UPTON
CHANCTONBURY GDNS
Tenn Cts
PEACHES CL
BRANDY WAY
TEGAN
WYNDHAM CL
CAMBORNE RD
EASTLEIGH
DEVONSHIRE
PENARTH CT
ARUNDEL RD
MANOR RD
BERESFORD RD
CORNWALL RD
YORK RD
SACKVILLE RD
PENSHURST WAY
AUDLEY PL
Overton Grange Sch
VENTNOR RD
WESTMORELAND DR
SWIFT CT
GLEBE RD
SANDY LA
BURDON LA
BURDON PK
Belmont
LYNDHURST WAY
KEMPSTON HO
63
FAYFIELD CT
Cuddington C... Prim Sch
24
25
26
Pav
SINCLAIR DR
CHIPSTEAD CL
BASINGHALL GDNS
THE DOWNS
WEST DR
THE GLADE
HOLLAND AVE
A217 Banstead, M25
Surrey STREET ATLAS
Gd
COURTENAY AVE
KINGSWOOD DR
CAREW CT
TOLL BAR CT
FELBRIDGE CL
TRICKETT HO

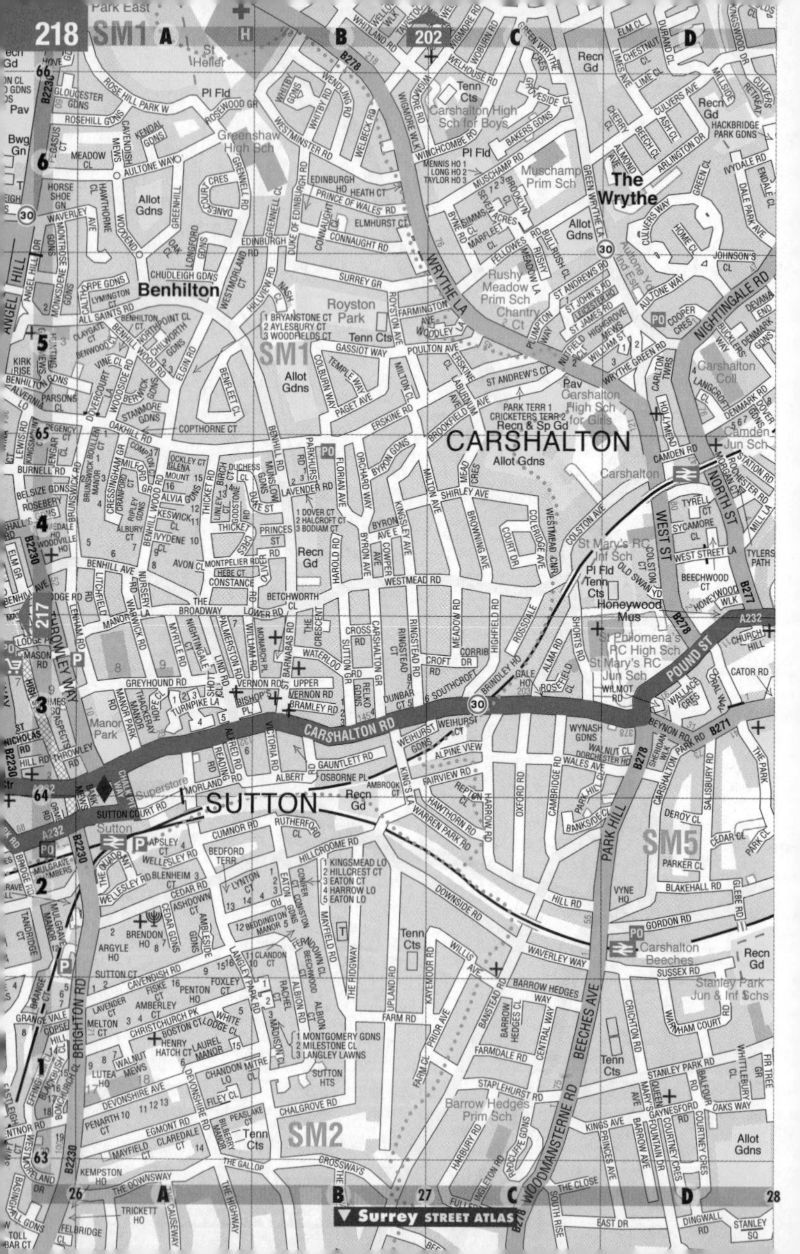

218
SM1
A
B
C
D
202
217
Park East
St Helier
Benhilton
Royston Park
CARSHALTON
The Wrythe
SUTTON
SM1
SM2
SM5
Carshalton High Sch for Boys
Greenshaw High Sch
Muschamp Prim Sch
Rushy Meadow La Prim Sch
Carshalton High Sch for Girls
Carshalton Coll
Camden Jun Sch
St Mary's RC Inf Sch
Honeywood Mus
St Philomena's RC High Sch
St Mary's RC Jun Sch
Barrow Hedges Prim Sch
Stanley Park Jun & Inf Schs
Carshalton
Carshalton Beeches
Sutton
Manor Park
Superstore
Allot Gdns
Recn Gd
Tenn Cts
Pl Fld
ROSE HILL PARK W
ROSEHILL GDNS
GLOUCESTER GDNS
AULTONE WAY
WESTMINSTER RD
WHITLAND RD
WIGMORE RD
WIGMORE WLK
WINCHCOMBE RD
WELHOUSE RD
WOBURN RD
GREEN WRYTHE LA
GREEN WRYTHE CRES
MUSCHAMP RD
WRYTHE LA
WRYTHE GREEN RD
CULVERS AVE
CULVERS WAY
NIGHTINGALE RD
ST ANDREWS RD
HEATH CT
PRINCE OF WALES' RD
ELMHURST CT
CONNAUGHT RD
SURREY GR
GASSIOT WAY
POULTON AVE
ST ANDREW'S CT
ERSKINE RD
BROOKFIELD AVE
COPTHORNE CT
OAKHILL RD
BENHILL WOOD RD
ELGIN RD
ALL SAINTS RD
LAVENDER RD
SHIRLEY AVE
COLSTON AVE
WESTMEAD RD
WEST ST
NORTH ST
STATION RD
CAMDEN RD
THE BROADWAY
LOWER RD
MANOR LA
GREYHOUND RD
BENHILL AVE
CARSHALTON RD
POUND ST
A232
B278
B277
B271
B2230
THROWLEY WAY
HIGH ST
GAUNTLETT RD
ALBERT RD
OSBORNE PL
WARREN PARK RD
HAWTHORN RD
ALPINE VIEW
FAIRVIEW RD
CUMNOR RD
RUTHERFORD CL
HILLCROOME RD
SUTTON COURT RD
BRIGHTON RD
CAVENDISH RD
CHRISTCHURCH PK
DEVONSHIRE AVE
DEVONSHIRE RD
MAYFIELD RD
LANGLEY PARK RD
THE RIDGWAY
UPLAND RD
DOWNSIDE RD
WAVERLEY WAY
BARROW HEDGES WAY
BANSTEAD RD
FARMDALE RD
STAPLEHURST RD
WOODMANSTERNE RD
BEECHES AVE
PARK HILL
GORDON RD
HILL RD
BLAKEHALL RD
SUSSEX RD
STANLEY PARK RD
GAYNESFORD RD
KINGS AVE
THE GALLOP
CROSSWAYS
THE DOWNSWAY
CHALGROVE RD
EGMONT RD
CLAREDALE
26
27
28
63
64
65
66

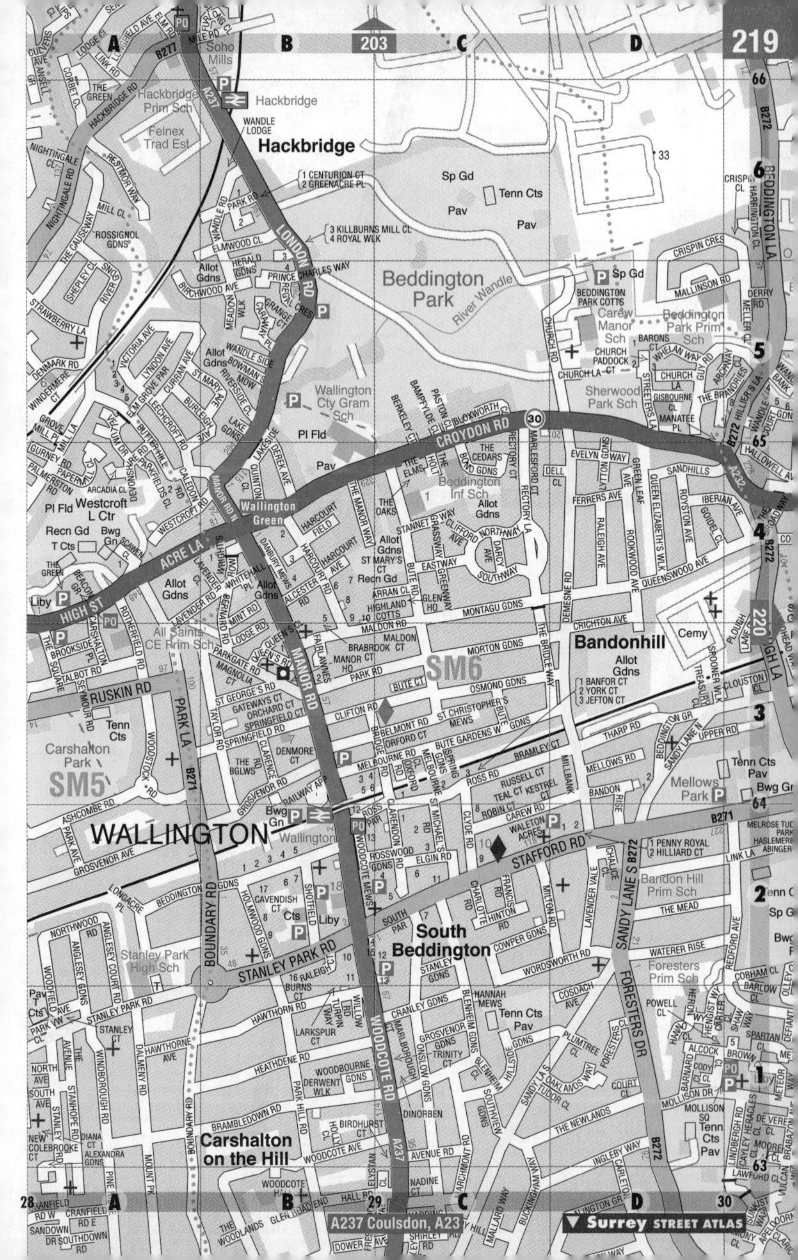

219
203
A
B
C
D
Hackbridge
Soho Mills
Hackbridge Prim Sch
Felnex Trad Est
WANDLE LODGE
B277
A237
MILE RD
HACKBRIDGE RD
NIGHTINGALE RD
NIGHTINGALE CL
RESTMOR WAY
MILL CL
ROSSIGNOL GDNS
THE CAUSEWAY
SHEPLEY CL
RIVER GDNS
STRAWBERRY LA
DENMARK RD
WINDERMERE CT
GROVE MILL PL
GURNEY RD
PAPERMILL CL
PALMERSTON RD
ARCADIA CL
Pl Fld
Westcroft L Ctr
Recn Gd
Bwg Gn
T Cts
Liby
HIGH ST
ACRE LA
1 CENTURION CT
2 GREENACRE PL
3 KILLBURNS MILL CL
4 ROYAL WLK
PARK RD
WANDLE RD
ELMWOOD CL
HERALD GDNS
PRINCE CHARLES WAY
LONDON RD
Allot Gdns
BIRCHWOOD AVE
MEADOW WLK
REGAL CRES
GRANGE CT
CARAWAY PL
WANDLE SIDE
BOWMAN'S MDW
RIVERSIDE CL
LAKE GDNS
VICTORIA AVE
LYNDON AVE
CURRAN AVE
ST MARY AVE
BURLEIGH AVE
ELM GROVE PAR
LEECHCROFT RD
BUTTER HILL
PARKFIELDS CL
CALEDON RD
WESTCROFT RD
Wallington Green
MANOR RD N
QUINTON CL
LAKESIDE
DEREK AVE
Sp Gd
Tenn Cts
Pav
Beddington Park
River Wandle
Wallington Cty Gram Sch
Pl Fld
CROYDON RD
THE MANOR WAY
HARCOURT FIELD
HARCOURT AVE
HARCOURT RD
ALCESTER RD
DANBURY MEWS
BERKELEY CT
BAMPFYLDE CL
PASTON CL
BLOXWORTH CL
THE ELMS
THE OAKS
HOLT
BOND GDNS
THE CEDARS
Beddington Inf Sch
RECTORY CT
RECTORY LA
MARLESFORD CT
Allot Gdns
STANNET WAY
GRASSWAY
CLIFFORD AVE
NORTHWAY
DARCY AVE
SOUTHWAY
EASTWAY
GREENWAY
ST MARY'S CT
Recn Gd
ARRAN CL
BUTE RD
GLEN HO
HIGHLAND COTTS
MONTAGU GDNS
MALDON RD
MALDON CT
BRABROOK CT
MANOR CT HO
FAIRLAWNES
QUEEN'S CL
QUEEN'S RD
MANOR RD
PARK RD
MORTON GDNS
OSMOND GDNS
BUTE CT
SM6
CHURCH RD
Carew Manor Sch
CHURCH PADDOCK CT
BEDDINGTON PARK COTTS
CHURCH LA
BARONS CT
WHELAN WAY
CHURCH LA
STREETERS LA
GISBOURNE CL
MANATEE PL
Sherwood Park Sch
Beddington Park Prim Sch
CRISPIN CRES
MALLINSON RD
CRISPIN CL
HARRINGTON CL
BEDDINGTON LA
B272
DERRY RD
MELLER CL
GUY RD
ARCHWAY
THE BRANDRIES
HILLIER'S LA
WANDLE CT
HALLOWELL AV
A232
THE BROAD WAY
DELL CL
EVELYN WAY
LYTTON GDNS
GREEN LEAF AVE
SANDHILLS
FERRERS AVE
RALEIGH AVE
ROOKWOOD AVE
QUEEN ELIZABETH'S WLK
ROYSTON AVE
GOIDEL CL
IBERIAN AVE
QUEENSWOOD AVE
DEMESNE RD
THE BRIDLE WAY
CRICHTON AVE
Bandonhill
Allot Gdns
Cemy
PLOUGH LANE CL
220
SPOONER WLK
TREASURY CL
CLOUSTON CL
1 BANFOR CT
2 YORK CT
3 JEFTON CT
ST CHRISTOPHER'S MEWS
BUTE GDNS
BUTE GARDENS W
BRAMLEY CT
THARP RD
BEDDINGTON GR
SANDY LANE N
UPPER RD
MELLOWS RD
BANDON RISE
Tenn Cts
Pav
Mellows Park
Bwg Gr
MILLBANK
THE SQUARE
BROOKSIDE
CARSHALTON PL
ROTHERFIELD RD
All Saints CE Prim Sch
LAVENDER RD
LAVENDER CL
BERNARD RD
WHITEHALL PL
MINT RD
LODGE RD
PARKGATE RD
MAGNOLIA CT
TALBOT RD
SEYMOUR RD
RUSKIN RD
PARK LA
B271
ST GEORGE'S RD
GATEWAYS CT
ORCHARD CT
SPRINGFIELD CT
SPRINGFIELD RD
CLIFTON RD
BELMONT RD
ORFORD CT
BRIDGE RD
CLARENCE RD
THE BGLWS
DENMORE CT
TAYLOR RD
GROSVENOR RD
RAILWAY APP
MELBOURNE RD
OXFORD RD
MELBOURNE CL
SPRING GDNS
ROSS RD
RUSSELL CT
TEAL CT
KESTREL CT
ROBIN CT
CAREW RD
WALETON ACRES
Tenn Cts
Carshalton Park
SM5
WOODSTOCK RD
ASHCOMBE RD
PARK AVE
GROSVENOR AVE
WALLINGTON
Wallington
Bwg Gn
ROSS PAR
CLARENDON RD
ST MICHAEL'S RD
CLYDE RD
WOODCOTE MEWS
ROSSWOOD GDNS
ELGIN RD
STAFFORD RD
CHALICE CL
B272
1 PENNY ROYAL
2 HILLIARD CT
LINK LA
MELROSE TUD PARK
HASLEMERE
ABINGER
Bandon Hill Prim Sch
THE MEAD
REDFORD AVE
LONGACRE PL
BEDDINGTON GDNS
BOUNDARY RD
CAVENDISH CT
HOLMWOOD GDNS
SHOTFIELD
Cts
Liby
SOUTH PAR
South Beddington
CHARLOTTE RD
FRANCIS RD
HINTON RD
MILTON RD
LAVENDER VALE
SANDY LANE S
COWPER GDNS
WORDSWORTH RD
WATERER RISE
Foresters Prim Sch
NORTHWOOD RD
ANGLESEY COURT RD
ANGLESEY GDNS
WOODFIELD AVE
Stanley Park High Sch
STANLEY PARK RD
RALEIGH CT
BURNS CT
STANLEY GDNS
HANNAH MEWS
BLENHEIM GDNS
COSDACH AVE
FORESTERS DR
FORESTERS CL
POWELL CL
HERON CT
HENGIST WY
CARTER CL
SHAW WAY
COBHAM CL
BARLOW CL
SPARTAN CL
BROWN CL
ALCOCK CL
CODY CL
BARNARD CL
MOLLISON DR
MOLLISON SQ
Tenn Cts
Pav
LINDBERGH RD
CAYLEY CL
HERACLES CL
DE VERE CL
MODRE CL
BRABAZON AVE
LAWFORD CL
VULCAN
METEOR
Pav
Cts
PARK VW
STANLEY PARK RD
STANLEY CT
HAWTHORN RD
TURPIN WAY
WILLOW RD
LARKSPUR CT
WOODCOTE RD
CRANLEY GDNS
GROSVENOR GDNS
TRINITY CT
MARLBOROUGH CT
ONSLOW GDNS
BLENHEIM CL
HILLSIDE GDNS
Tenn Cts
Pav
PLUMTREE CL
OAKLANDS WAY
TUDOR CL
COURT CL
THE AVENUE
NORTH AVE
SOUTH AVE
STANHOPE RD
WINDBOROUGH RD
DALMENY RD
HAWTHORNE AVE
HEATHDENE RD
WOODBOURNE GDNS
DERWENT WLK
PARK HILL RD
BRAMBLEDOWN RD
BIRDHURST CT
HOLLY CL
DINORBEN
SOUTHVIEW GDNS
SANDY LA S
THE NEWLANDS
NEW COLEBROOKE CT
DIANA CT
ALEXANDRA GDNS
Carshalton on the Hill
WOODCOTE AVE
ELYSTAN CL
AVENUE RD
MARCHMONT RD
INGLEBY WAY
CARLETON AVE
BUCKINGHAM WAY
MOUNT PK
PINE RD
NADINE CT
WOODCOTE HALL
HALL RD
MALLARD WAY
CRANFIELD RD W
CRANFIELD RD E
SANDOWN DR
SOUTHDOWN RD
GLEN ROAD END
THE WOODLANDS
DOWER AVE
A237 Coulsdon, A23
Surrey STREET ATLAS
28
29
30
63
64
65
66
1
2
3
4
5
6

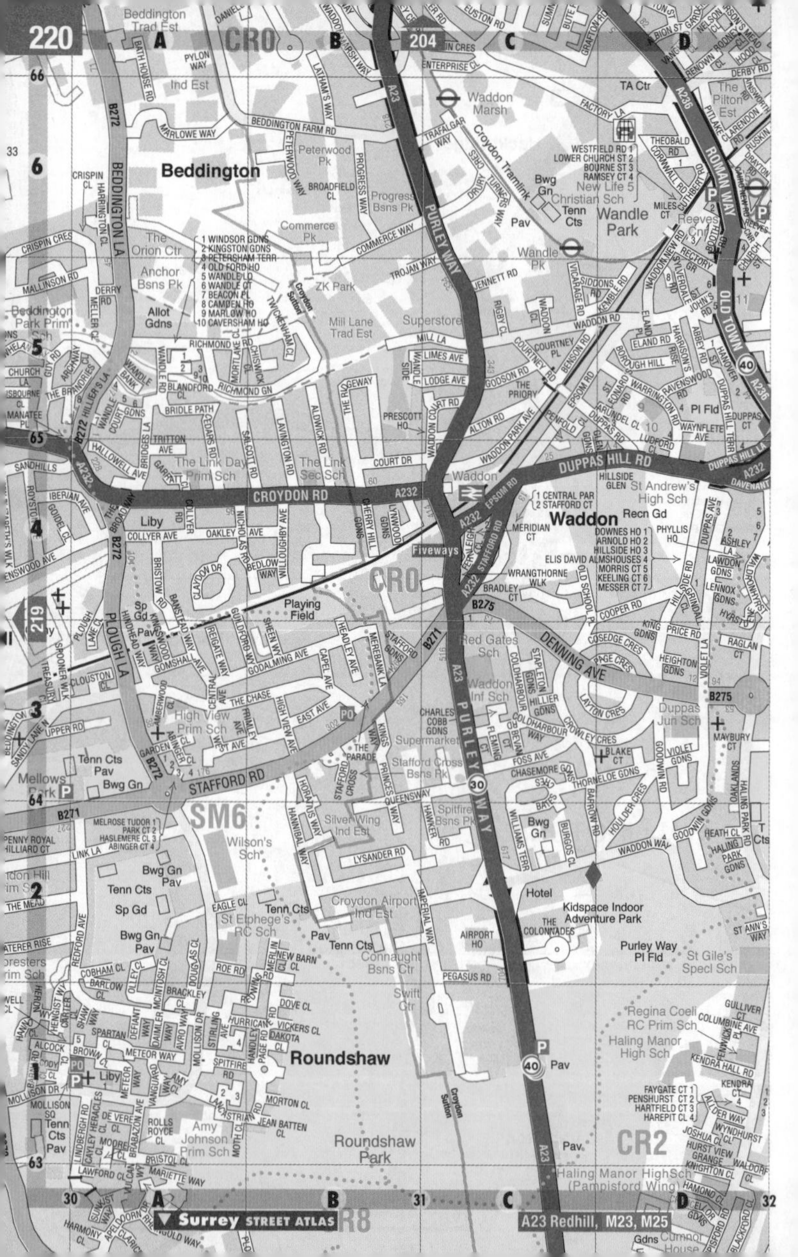
A
B
C
D
CR0
204
66
6
5
65
4
3
64
2
1
63
30
31
32
Beddington Trad Est
Beddington
Ind Est
PYLON WAY
BATH HOUSE RD
B272
BEDDINGTON LA
MARLOWE WAY
BEDDINGTON FARM RD
PETERWOOD WAY
LATHAM'S WAY
Peterwood Pk
PROGRESS WAY
BROADFIELD CL
Progress Bsns Pk
Commerce Pk
COMMERCE WAY
TROJAN WAY
ZK Park
Mill Lane Trad Est
Superstore
A23
PURLEY WAY
ENTERPRISE CL
EUSTON RD
Waddon Marsh
Croydon Tramlink
TRAFALGAR WAY
FACTORY LA
TA Ctr
WESTFIELD RD 1
LOWER CHURCH ST 2
BOURNE ST 3
RAMSEY CT 4
New Life 5
Christian Sch
Bwg Gn
Tenn Cts
Wandle Park
Pav
Wandle Pk
A236
ROMAN WAY
OLD TOWN
The Pilton Est
THEOBALD RD
CORNWALL RD
MILES CT
Reeves Cnr
CRISPIN CL
HARRINGTON CL
CRISPIN CRES
MALLINSON RD
DERRY RD
MELLER CL
Beddington Park Prim Sch
The Orion Ctr
Anchor Bsns Pk
1 WINDSOR GDNS
2 KINGSTON GDNS
3 PETERSHAM TERR
4 OLD FORD HO
5 WANDLE HO
6 WANDLE CT
7 BEACON PL
8 CAMDEN HO
9 MARLOW HO
10 CAVERSHAM HO
Allot Gdns
TWICKENHAM CL
RICHMOND RD
RICHMOND GN
MORTLAKE CL
CHISWICK CL
WANDLE RD
BLANDFORD CL
BRIDLE PATH
CEDARS RD
SALCOTT RD
LAVINGTON RD
ALDWICK RD
THE RIDGEWAY
MILL LA
LIMES AVE
LODGE AVE
WANDLE SIDE
PRESCOTT HO
WADDON COURT RD
ALTON RD
GODSON RD
THE PRIORY
COURTNEY RD
COURTNEY PL
BENSON RD
WADDON RD
RIGBY CL
WADDON CL
VICARAGE RD
SIDDONS RD
KEMBLE RD
JENNETT RD
WADDON PARK AVE
EPSOM RD
PENFOLD CL
DUPPAS RD
ARUNDEL CL
ST LEONARD'S RD
WARRINGTON RD
ELAND RD
BOROUGH HILL
HARRISON'S RISE
ABBEY RD
ST JOHN'S RD
HANOVER ST
RAVENSWOOD CL
DUPPAS HILL TERR
Pl Fld
WAYNFLETE AVE
LUDFORD CL
DUPPAS CT
40
CHURCH ST
RECTORY GR
SYLVERDALE RD
WADDON NEW RD
TRITTON AVE
HALLOWELL AVE
GARRATT CL
BRIDGES LA
The Link Day Prim Sch
The Link Sec Sch
COURT DR
Waddon
A232
CROYDON RD
DUPPAS HILL RD
DUPPAS HILL LA
DAVENANT RD
HILLSIDE GLEN
St Andrew's High Sch
Recn Gd
1 CENTRAL PAR
2 STAFFORD CT
MERIDIAN CT
Waddon
DOWNES HO 1
ARNOLD HO 2
HILLSIDE HO 3
ELIS DAVID ALMSHOUSES 4
MORRIS CT 5
KEELING CT 6
MESSER CT 7
PHYLLIS HO
ASHLEY LA
LAWDON GDNS
LENNOX GDNS
SANDHILLS
ROYSTON AVE
IBERIAN AVE
GOIDEL CL
ENSWOOD AVE
THE BROADWAY
Liby
COLLYER AVE
COLLYER RD
OAKLEY AVE
NICHOLAS RD
BEDLOW WAY
WILLOUGHBY AVE
CHERRY HILL GDNS
LYNWOOD GDNS
Fiveways
FERNLEIGH CL
STAFFORD RD
WRANGTHORNE WLK
BRADLEY CT
OLD SCHOOL PL
COOPER RD
HILLSIDE RD
GRINDAL CL
CLAYDON DR
BRISTOW RD
BANSTEAD WAY
Playing Field
219
PLOUGH LA
PLOUGH LANE CL
HINDHEAD WAY
KINGSWOOD WAY
Sp Gd
Pav
GOMSHALL AVE
REIGATE WAY
GUILDFORD WAY
SHEEN WAY
GODALMING AVE
CAPEL AVE
HEADLEY AVE
MERERANK LA
STAFFORD GDNS
B271
B275
Red Gates Sch
DENNING AVE
COSEDGE CRES
PAGE CRES
KING GDNS
PRICE RD
HEIGHTON GDNS
VIOLET LA
RAGLAN CT
CLOUSTON CL
SPOONER WLK
TREASURY CL
UPPER RD
SANDY LANE N
CENTRAL AVE
THE CHASE
FRIMLEY AVE
HIGH VIEW AVE
EAST AVE
WEST AVE
PO
High View Prim Sch
AMBERWOOD CL
GARDEN CL
ABINGER CL
Waddon Inf Sch
COLDHARBOUR RD
STAPLETON GDNS
HILLIER GDNS
CHARLES COBB GDNS
FLEMING CT
BEVAN CT
COLDHARBOUR WAY
LAYTON CRES
CROWLEY CRES
Duppas Jun Sch
MAYBURY CT
Supermarket
THE PARADE
STAFFORD CROSS
KINGS WAY
PRINCES WAY
Stafford Cross Bsns Pk
FOSS AVE
CHASEMORE GDNS
BLAKE CT
THORNELOE GDNS
GOODWIN RD
VIOLET GDNS
Tenn Cts Pav
Mellows Park
Bwg Gn
STAFFORD RD
30
HORATIUS WAY
QUEENSWAY
HAWKER RD
BATES CRES
BARROW RD
HOULDER CRES
OAKLANDS
HALING PARK RD
SM6
MELROSE TUDOR 1
PARK CT 2
HASLEMERE CL 3
ABINGER CT 4
PENNY ROYAL
HILLIARD CT
LINK LA
Wilson's Sch
HANNIBAL WAY
Silver Wing Ind Est
Spitfire Bsns Pk
WILLIAMS TERR
BURGOS CL
GOODWIN GDNS
HEATH CL
HALING PARK GDNS
LYSANDER RD
WADDON WAY
Bwg Gn Pav
Tenn Cts
Sp Gd
THE MEAD
EAGLE CL
St Elphege's RC Sch
Croydon Airport Ind Est
IMPERIAL WAY
Hotel
Kidspace Indoor Adventure Park
THE COLONNADES
AIRPORT HO
ST ANN'S WAY
CATERER RISE
Bwg Gn Pav
REDFORD AVE
Pav
Tenn Cts
Connaught Bsns Ctr
Purley Way Pl Fld
St Gile's Specl Sch
COBHAM CL
BARLOW CL
OILLEY CL
MCINTOSH CL
DOUGLAS CL
ROE RD
MERLIN CL
NEW BARN CL
PEGASUS RD
BRACKLEY CL
DOVE CL
HURRICANE RD
VICKERS CL
DAKOTA CL
Swift Ctr
HERON CT
HENGIST WAY
CARTER
SHAW WAY
DEFIANT WAY
DAIMLER WAY
AVRO WAY
MOLLISON DR
STIRLING WAY
HANDLEY PAGE RD
Regina Coeli RC Prim Sch
Haling Manor High Sch
GULLIVER CT
COLUMBINE AVE
FENWICK PL
SPARTAN CL
ALCOCK CL
BROWN CL
METEOR WAY
SPITFIRE RD
Roundshaw
P
Pav
KENDRA HALL RD
KENDRA CT
COBY CL
Liby
METEOR WAY
AMY WAY
MORTON CL
FAYGATE CT 1
PENSHURST CT 2
HARTFIELD CT 3
HAREPIT CL 4
ALLDER WAY
MOLLISON SQ
Tenn Cts Pav
LINDBERGH RD
CAYLEY CL
HERACLES CL
DE VERE CL
BRABAZON AVE
ROLLS ROYCE CL
LANCASTRIAN RD
JEAN BATTEN CL
MOTH CL
Amy Johnson Prim Sch
Roundshaw Park
Pav
CR2
WYNDHURST CL
JOSHUA CL
HURST VIEW GRANGE
KNIGHTON CL
WALDORF CL
MOORE CL
BRISTOL CL
LAWFORD CL
VULCAN WAY
MARIETTE WAY
HAMOND CL
Haling Manor High Sch (Pampisford Wing)
Surrey STREET ATLAS
A23 Redhill, M23, M25
SUNKIST WAY
HARMONY CL
APELDOORN DR
Gdns
Cumnor House

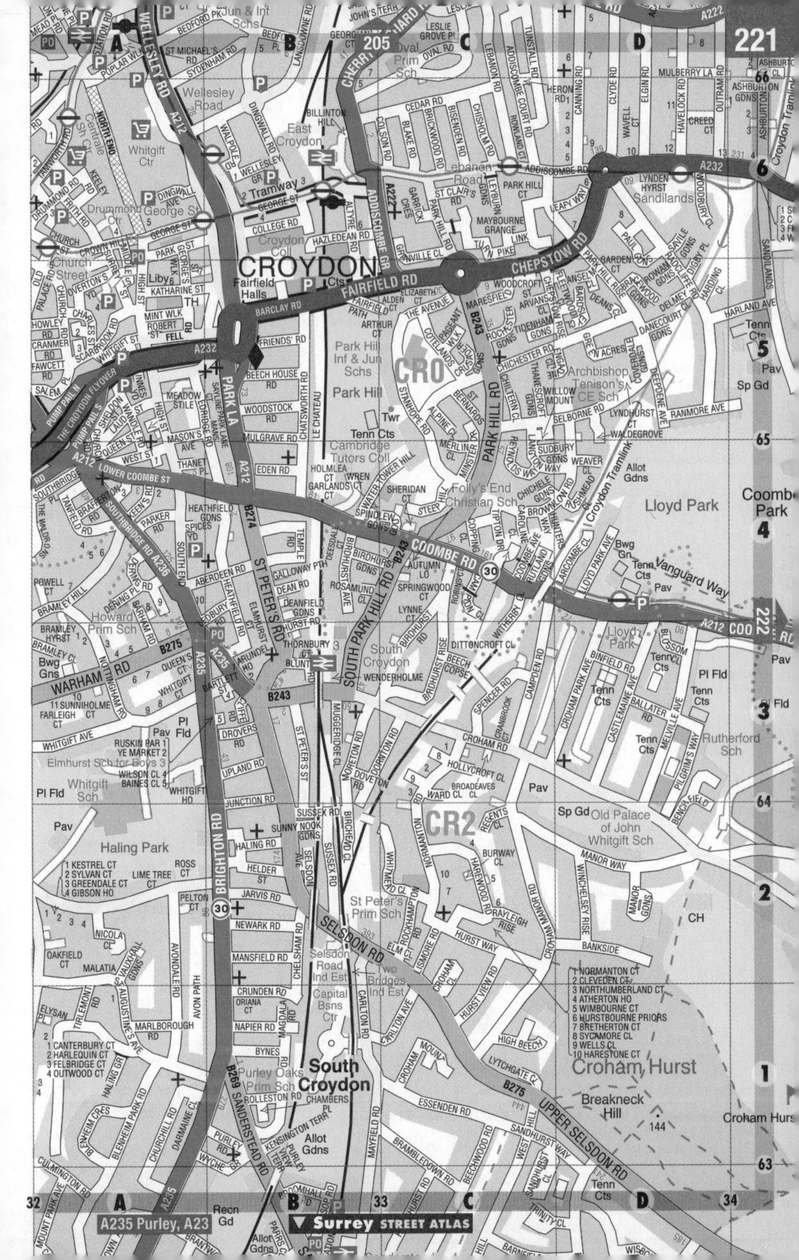
A
B
C
D
205
Wellesley Road
WELLESLEY RD
A212
Jun & Inf Schs
Oval Prim Sch
OVAL RD
LESLIE GROVE PL
LEBANON RD
TUNSTALL RD
ADDISCOMBE COURT RD
CANNING RD
CLYDE RD
ELGIN RD
MULBERRY LA
ASHBURTON GDNS
Croydon Tramlink
CEDAR RD
COLSON RD
BLAKE RD
BRICKWOOD RD
BISENDEN RD
CHISHOLM RD
ROWLAND CT
HERON RD
WAVELL CT
HAVELOCK RD
CREED CT
OUTRAM RD
East Croydon
BILLINTON HILL
Whitgift Ctr
Centrale Sh Ctr
NORTH END
TAMWORTH RD
KEELEY
DRUMMOND RD
FRITH RD
Drummond Ctr
George St
GEORGE ST
Tramway
COLLEGE RD
Croydon Coll
HAZLEDEAN RD
ALTYRE RD
ADDISCOMBE GR
A222
GARRICK CRES
PARK HILL RD
ST CLAIR'S RD
Lebanon Road
ADDISCOMBE RD
PARK HILL CT
LEYBURN GDNS
MAYBOURNE GRANGE
LEAFY WAY
LINK
TURN PIKE
A232
LYNDEN HYRST
Sandilands
WOODBURY CL
SANDILANDS
CHEPSTOW RD
CROYDON
Church Street
CROWN HILL
PARK ST
ST GEORGE'S WK
HIGH ST
Liby
KATHARINE ST
TH
MINT WLK
ROBERT ST
FELL RD
Fairfield Halls
BARCLAY RD
FAIRFIELD RD
Cts
ELIZABETH CT
FAIRFIELD PATH
ALDEN CT
ARTHUR CT
THE AVENUE
WOODCROFT
ST ARVANS CL
MARESFIELD
GARDEN CT
PARK HILL RISE
HOWLEY RD
CRANMER RD
FAWCETT RD
SALEM PL
OLD PALACE RD
CHURCH RD
CHARLES ST
SCARBROOK RD
WHITGIFT ST
FRIENDS' RD
PARK LA
B243
PUMP PAIL N
THE CROYDON FLYOVER
PUMP PAIL S
BEECH HOUSE RD
WOODSTOCK RD
MULGRAVE RD
MEADOW STILE
MASON'S AVE
WEST ST
THANET
EDEN RD
CHATSWORTH RD
LE CHATEAU
Park Hill Inf & Jun Schs
Park Hill
CR0
Twr
Tenn Cts
Cambridge Tutors Coll
COTELANDS
PAGEANT WLK
STANHOPE RD
ALPINE CL
ST BERNARDS
MERLIN CL
MINSTER DR
ROCHESTER GDNS
TIDENHAM GDNS
CHICHESTER RD
CHILTERN CL
THANESCROFT GDNS
WILLOW MOUNT
Archbishop Tenison's CE Sch
SELBORNE RD
LYNDHURST CT
RANMORE AVE
DANECOURT GDNS
DEEPDENE AVE
WALDEGROVE
HARLAND AVE
Sp Gd
Pav
5
65
A212
LOWER COOMBE ST
SOUTHBRIDGE RD
SOUTHBRIDGE PL
TANFIELD RD
BRAFFERTON RD
HEATHFIELD GDNS
SPICES YD
PARKER RD
SOUTH END
B274
HOLMLEA CT
GARLANDS CT
WREN CT
WATER TOWER HILL
SHERIDAN CT
SPINDLEWOOD GDNS
STEEP HILL
Folly's End Christian Sch
COPPING CL
TIPTON DR
CAROLINE CT
BROWNLOW RD
HUNTERS WAY
SUDBURY GDNS
LANGTON WAY
WEAVER CL
Allot Gdns
Lloyd Park
Coombe Park
4
COOMBE RD
A236
ST PETER'S RD
TEMPLE RD
GALLOWAY PTH
DEAN RD
DEANFIELD GDNS
BIRDHURST RD
BIRDHURST GDNS
BIRDHURST AVE
ROSAMUND CL
AUTUMN LO
SPRINGWOOD CT
LYNNE CT
30
COOMBE AVE
RUTLAND GDNS
LARCOMBE CL
LLOYD PARK AVE
Bwg Gn
Tenn Cts
Vanguard Way
POWELL CT
BRAMLEY HILL
ABERDEEN RD
Howard Prim Sch
DERING PL
BARHAM RD
BRAMLEY HYRST
BRAMLEY CL
Bwg Gns
WARHAM RD
B275
QUEEN'S CT
WHITGIFT CT
NOTTINGHAM RD
11 SUNNIHOLME
FARLEIGH CT
A235
ARUNDEL HO
ELMHURST
HURST RD
THORNBURY CT
BLUNT
South Croydon
BIRDHURST RISE
BEECH COPSE
DITTONCROFT CL
WENDERHOLME
SOUTH PARK HILL RD
MUGGERIDGE CL
WITHERBY CL
CAMPDEN RD
SPENCER RD
CRANBROOK
CROHAM RD
CROHAM PARK AVE
BINFIELD RD
CASTLEMAINE AVE
BALLATER RD
MELVILLE AVE
Pl Fld
222
A212
WHITGIFT AVE
RUSKIN PAR 1
YE MARKET 2
Elmhurst Sch for Boys 3
WILSON CL 4
BAINES CL 5
Pav
Pl Fld
DROVERS RD
UPLAND RD
ST PETER'S ST
MORETON RD
DORNTON RD
DOVETON RD
HOLLYCROFT CL
BROADEAVES CL
WARD CL
Rutherford Sch
PILGRIM'S WAY
3
Whitgift Sch
WHITGIFT HO
JUNCTION RD
SUSSEX RD
SUNNY NOOK GDNS
BIRCHEND CL
NORMANTON RD
CR2
REGENTS CL
Sp Gd
Old Palace of John Whitgift Sch
BENCHFIELD
64
Haling Park
HALING RD
HELDER ST
SELSDON AVE
WHITMEAD CL
BURWAY CL
HAREWOOD RD
MANOR WAY
WINCHELSEY RISE
MANOR GDNS
1 KESTREL CT
2 SYLVAN CT
3 GREENDALE CT
4 GIBSON HO
LIME TREE CT
ROSS CT
JARVIS RD
PELTON CT
BRIGHTON RD
St Peter's Prim Sch
ROCKHAMPTON RD
RAYLEIGH RISE
CROHAM MANOR RD
2
CH
NICOLA CL
OAKFIELD CT
MALATIA
VAUXHALL GDNS
AVONDALE RD
NEWARK RD
CHELSHAM RD
SELSDON RD
ELM CL
LISMORE RD
HURST WAY
CROHAM CL
BANKSIDE
MANSFIELD RD
Selsdon Road Ind Est
Two Bridges Ind Est
HURST VIEW RD
1 NORMANTON CT
2 CLEVEDEN CT
3 NORTHUMBERLAND CT
4 ATHERTON HO
5 WIMBOURNE CT
6 HURSTBOURNE PRIORS
7 BRETHERTON CT
8 SYCAMORE CL
9 WELLS CL
10 HARESTONE CT
ELYSAN PL
TIRLEMONT RD
AUGUSTINE'S AVE
MARLBOROUGH RD
AVON PATH
CRUNDEN RD
ORIANA CT
NAPIER RD
MAGDALA RD
Capital Bsns Ctr
CARLTON AVE
CARLTON RD
1 CANTERBURY CT
2 HARLEQUIN CT
3 FELBRIDGE CT
4 OUTWOOD CT
BYNES RD
B269
SANDERSTEAD RD
Purley Oaks Prim Sch
South Croydon
ROLLESTON RD
CHAMBERS PL
CROHAM MOUNT
HIGH BEECH
LYTCHGATE CL
Croham Hurst
1
Breakneck Hill
144
UPPER SELSDON RD
Croham Hurst
HALING GR
BLENHEIM CRES
BLENHEIM PARK RD
CHURCHILL RD
DARMAINE CL
PURLEY RD
WYCHE GR
KENSINGTON TERR
PURLEY VIEW TERR
Allot Gdns
MAYFIELD RD
ESSENDEN RD
BRAMBLEDOWN RD
BEECHWOOD RD
WEST HILL
SANDHURST WAY
SANDHURST CL
Tenn Cts
63
CULMINGTON RD
MOUNT PARK AVE
32
A
B
33
C
D
34
A235 Purley, A23
Recn Gd
BROOMHALL RD
Surrey STREET ATLAS
TRINITY CL

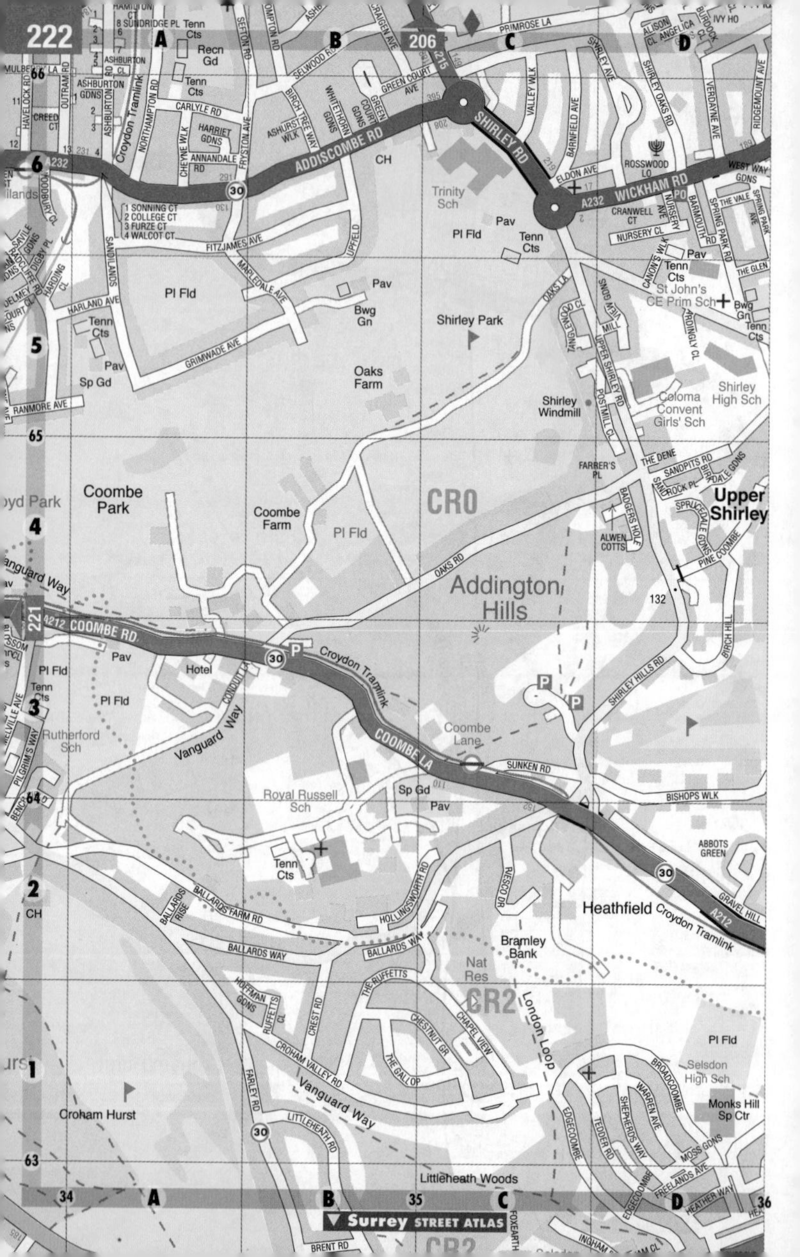

Addiscombe Rd
Shirley Rd
Wickham Rd
Shirley Park
Coombe Park
Coombe Farm
Addington Hills
Upper Shirley
Coombe Rd
Coombe La
Croydon Tramlink
Vanguard Way
Royal Russell Sch
Heathfield
Bramley Bank
London Loop
Croham Hurst
Littleheath Woods
CR0
CR2

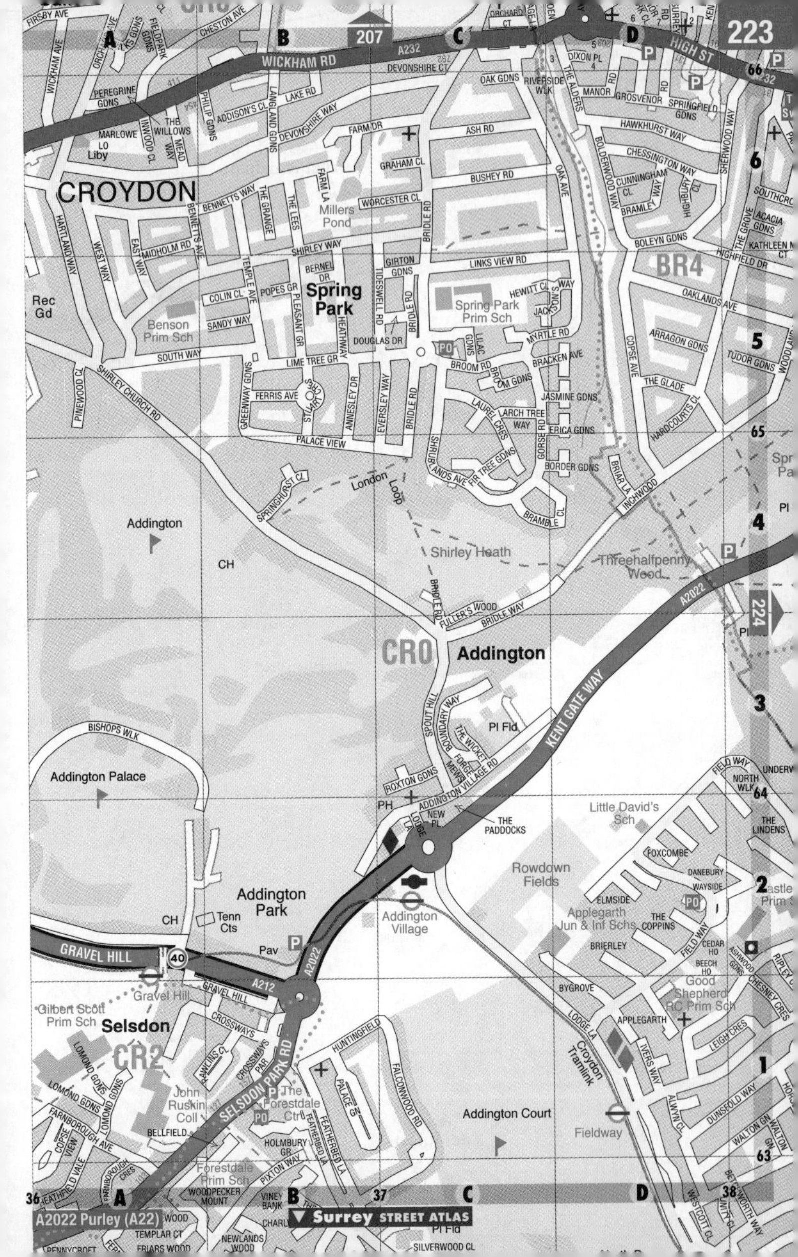
CROYDON
Spring Park
Addington
Shirley Heath
Threehalfpenny Wood
BR4
CR0
CR2
Addington Palace
Addington Park
Addington Village
Selsdon
Addington Court
Fieldway
Rowdown Fields
Millers Pond
Benson Prim Sch
Spring Park Prim Sch
Little David's Sch
Applegarth Jun & Inf Schs
Good Shepherd RC Prim Sch
Gilbert Scott Prim Sch
John Ruskin Coll
Forestdale Prim Sch
The Forestdale Ctr
Gravel Hill
Croydon Tramlink
London Loop
Rec Gd
WICKHAM RD
A232
HIGH ST
GRAVEL HILL
A212
A2022
KENT GATE WAY
SELSDON PARK RD
SHIRLEY CHURCH RD
ADDINGTON VILLAGE RD
SPOUT HILL
BRIDLE RD
LODGE LA
FIELD WAY
207
224
A2022 Purley (A22)
Surrey STREET ATLAS

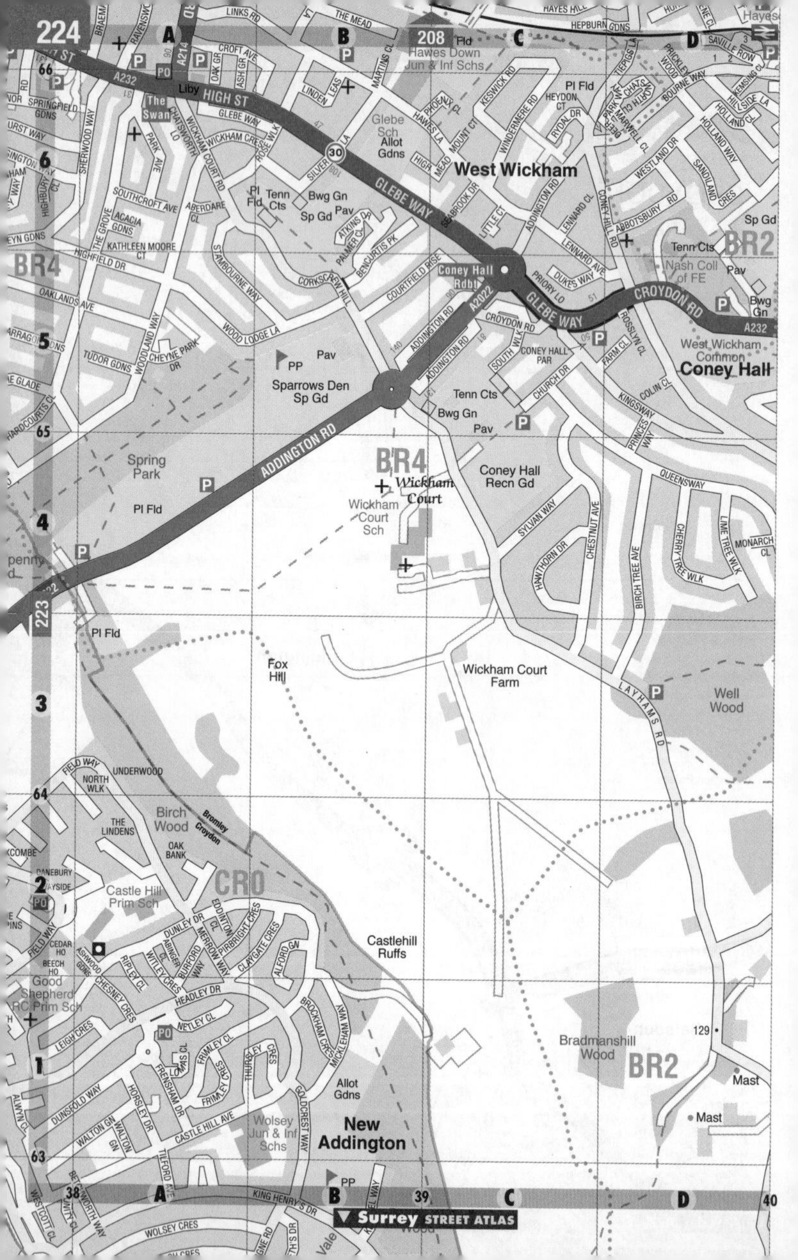
West Wickham
Coney Hall
New Addington
HIGH ST
GLEBE WAY
CROYDON RD
ADDINGTON RD
Coney Hall Rdbt
Spring Park
Sparrows Den Sp Gd
Wickham Court
Wickham Court Sch
Coney Hall Recn Gd
Wickham Court Farm
Fox Hill
Well Wood
Birch Wood
Castle Hill Prim Sch
Castlehill Ruffs
Bradmanshill Wood
Wolsey Jun & Inf Schs
Good Shepherd RC Prim Sch
West Wickham Common
Nash Coll of FE
Hawes Down Jun & Inf Schs
Glebe Sch
LAYHAMS RD
QUEENSWAY
KINGSWAY
SYLVAN WAY
CHESTNUT AVE
BIRCH TREE AVE
HAWTHORN DR
CHERRY TREE WLK
LIME TREE WLK
MONARCH CL
FIELD WAY
UNDERWOOD
KING HENRY'S DR
WOLSEY CRES
CASTLE HILL AVE
GOLDCREST WAY
MICKLEHAM WAY
BROCKHAM CRES
HEADLEY DR
NETLEY CL
CHESNEY CRES
BR4
BR2
CR0
Bromley
Croydon

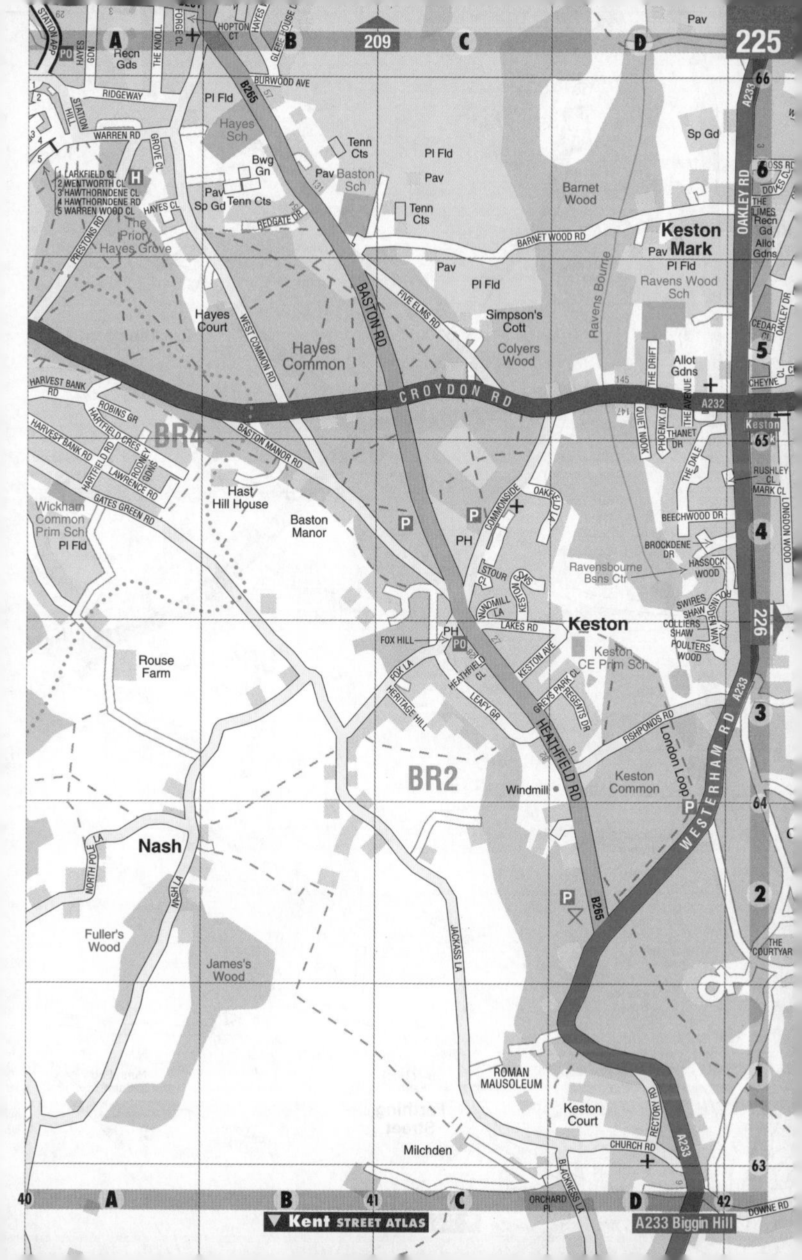

209
226
A
B
C
D
Recn Gds
Pl Fld
Hayes Sch
Tenn Cts
Bwg Gn
Pav
Baston Sch
Sp Gd
Barnet Wood
Keston Mark
Ravens Wood Sch
Hayes Court
Hayes Common
Simpson's Cott
Colyers Wood
CROYDON RD
BASTON RD
BR4
BR2
Hast Hill House
Baston Manor
Wickham Common Prim Sch
Keston
Keston CE Prim Sch
Rouse Farm
Keston Common
Windmill
Nash
Fuller's Wood
James's Wood
ROMAN MAUSOLEUM
Keston Court
Milchden
WESTERHAM RD
HEATHFIELD RD
London Loop
Ravensbourne Bsns Ctr
OAKLEY RD
Kent STREET ATLAS
A233 Biggin Hill

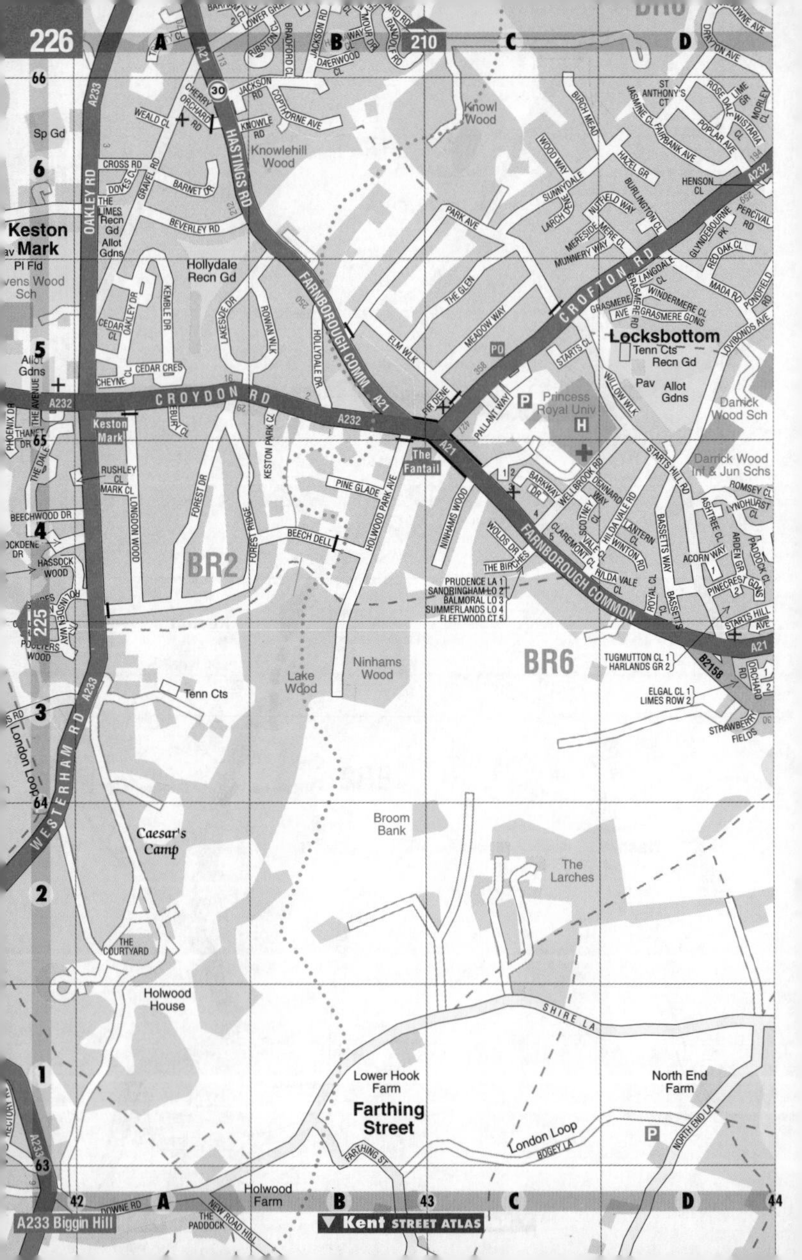
A
B
C
D
210
66
6
5
65
4
3
64
2
1
63
42
43
44
225
30
A21
A233
A232
B2158
Keston Mark
Locksbottom
Farthing Street
BR2
BR6
Sp Gd
Pl Fld
Allot Gdns
Knowl Wood
Knowlehill Wood
Hollydale Recn Gd
The Limes Recn Gd
Tenn Cts Recn Gd
Pav
Princess Royal Univ
The Fantail
Darrick Wood Sch
Darrick Wood Inf & Jun Schs
Ninhams Wood
Lake Wood
Tenn Cts
Caesar's Camp
Broom Bank
The Larches
The Courtyard
Holwood House
Lower Hook Farm
North End Farm
Holwood Farm
London Loop
OAKLEY RD
HASTINGS RD
FARNBOROUGH COMM
FARNBOROUGH COMMON
CROYDON RD
CROFTON RD
WESTERHAM RD
JACKSON RD
COPTHORNE AVE
KNOWLE RD
CHERRY ORCHARD RD
WEALD CL
CROSS RD
GRAVEL RD
DOVES CL
BARNET DR
BEVERLEY RD
KEMBLE DR
OAKLEY DR
CEDAR CL
CEDAR CRES
CHEYNE CL
LAKESIDE DR
ROWAN WLK
HOLLYDALE DR
KESTON PARK CL
FOREST DR
FOREST RIDGE
LONGDON WOOD
RUSHLEY CL
MARK CL
BEECHWOOD DR
HASSOCK WOOD
PHOENIX DR
THE AVENUE
THANET DR
THE DALE
PINE GLADE
BEECH DELL
HOLWOOD PARK AVE
PARK AVE
THE GLEN
MEADOW WAY
ELM WLK
FIR DENE
PALLANT WAY
NINHAMS WOOD
WOLDS DR
THE BIRCHES
BARKWAY DR
WELLBROOK RD
DENNARD WAY
SCOTNEY CL
CLAREMONT CL
VALE CL
HILDA VALE RD
HILDA VALE CL
WINTON RD
LANTERN CL
BASSETTS WAY
BASSETTS CL
ROYAL CL
STARTS HILL RD
STARTS CL
WILLOW WLK
WOOD WAY
SUNNYDALE
LARCH DENE
MERESIDE WAY
MERE CL
MUNNERY WAY
NUTFIELD WAY
BURLINGTON CL
HAZEL GR
BIRCH MEAD
ST ANTHONY'S CT
JASMINE CL
FAIRBANK AVE
ROSE DALE
LIME GR
WISTARIA CL
POPLAR AVE
HENSON CL
GLYNDEBOURNE PK
PERCIVAL RD
RED OAK CL
MADA RD
PONDFIELD RD
LOVIBONDS AVE
LANGDALE CL
WINDERMERE CL
GRASMERE AVE
GRASMERE RD
GRASMERE GDNS
ROMSEY CL
LYNDHURST CL
ASHTREE CL
ARDEN GR
PADDOCK CL
ACORN WAY
PINECREST GDNS
STARTS HILL AVE
ORCHARD RD
STRAWBERRY FIELDS
DRAYTON AVE
PRUDENCE LA 1
SANDRINGHAM LO 2
BALMORAL LO 3
SUMMERLANDS LO 4
FLEETWOOD CT 5
TUGMUTTON CL 1
HARLANDS GR 2
ELGAL CL 1
LIMES ROW 2
SHIRE LA
BOGEY LA
NORTH END LA
FARTHING ST
DOWNE RD
NEW ROAD HILL
THE PADDOCK
BRADFORD CL
RIBSTON CL
LOWER GRAVEL RD
DAERWOOD CL
JACKSON RD
RANDOLF RD
A233 Biggin Hill
▼ Kent STREET ATLAS

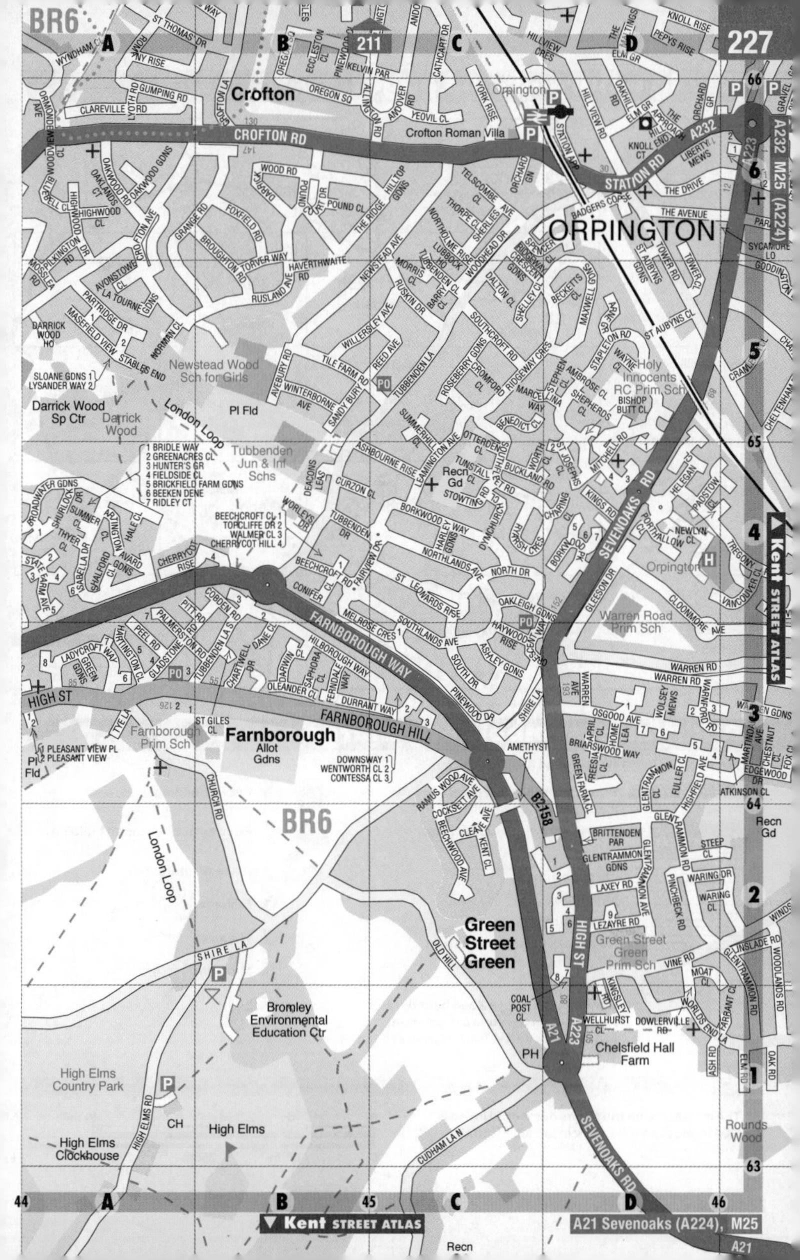
BR6
A
B
C
D
211
Crofton
CROFTON RD
Crofton Roman Villa
Orpington
ORPINGTON
STATION RD
A232
A232 M25 (A224)
Newstead Wood Sch for Girls
Darrick Wood Sp Ctr
Darrick Wood
London Loop
Pl Fld
Tubbenden Jun & Inf Schs
1 BRIDLE WAY
2 GREENACRES CL
3 HUNTER'S GR
4 FIELDSIDE CL
5 BRICKFIELD FARM GDNS
6 BEEKEN DENE
7 RIDLEY CT
BEECHCROFT CL 1
TOPCLIFFE DR 2
WALMER CL 3
CHERRYCOT HILL 4
SLOANE GDNS 1
LYSANDER WAY 2
Holy Innocents RC Prim Sch
Recn Gd
FARNBOROUGH WAY
FARNBOROUGH HILL
SEVENOAKS RD
Warren Road Prim Sch
Kent STREET ATLAS
HIGH ST
Farnborough
Farnborough Prim Sch
Allot Gdns
DOWNSWAY 1
WENTWORTH CL 2
CONTESSA CL 3
1 PLEASANT VIEW PL
2 PLEASANT VIEW
B2158
Green Street Green
Green Street Green Prim Sch
Bromley Environmental Education Ctr
Chelsfield Hall Farm
High Elms Country Park
High Elms
High Elms Clockhouse
Rounds Wood
A21
A223
44
45
46
63
64
65
66
A21 Sevenoaks (A224), M25
▼ Kent STREET ATLAS

228

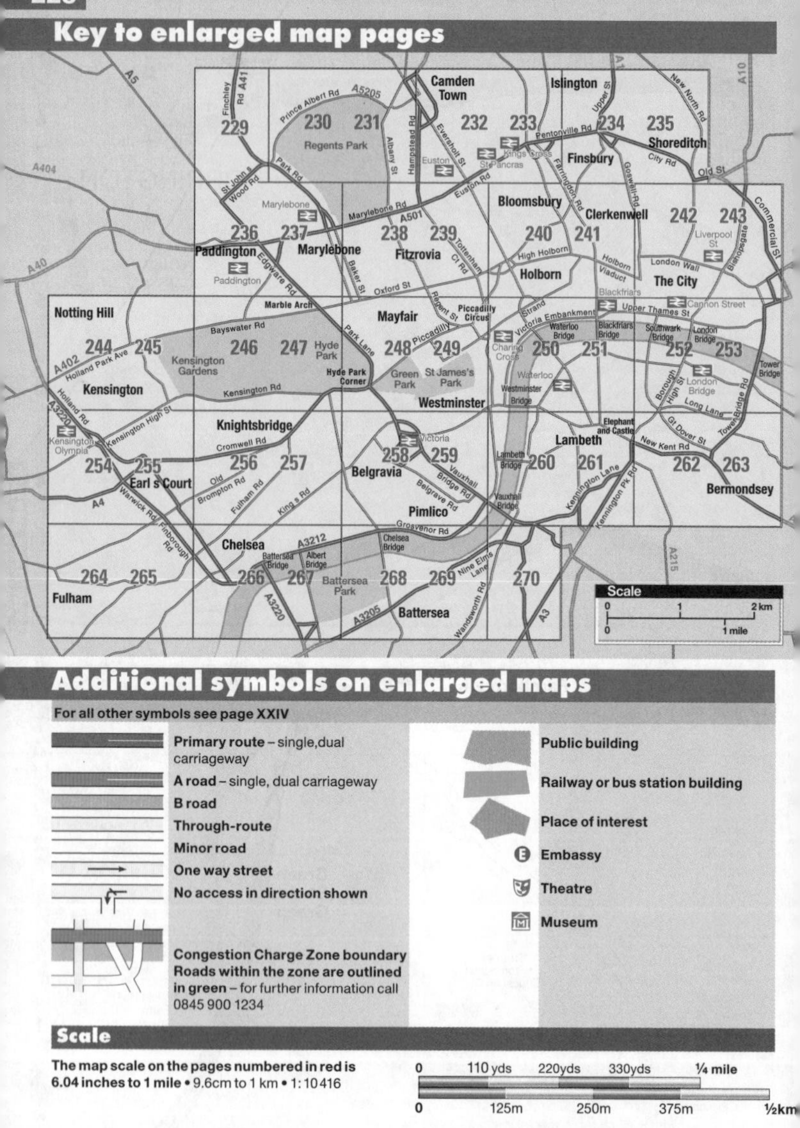

Additional symbols on enlarged maps

For all other symbols see page XXIV

- Primary route – single, dual carriageway
- A road – single, dual carriageway
- B road
- Through-route
- Minor road
- One way street
- No access in direction shown
- Congestion Charge Zone boundary
  Roads within the zone are outlined in green – for further information call 0845 900 1234

- Public building
- Railway or bus station building
- Place of interest
- **E** Embassy
- Theatre
- **M** Museum

Scale

The map scale on the pages numbered in red is 6.04 inches to 1 mile • 9.6cm to 1 km • 1:10416

| 0 | 110 yds | 220yds | 330yds | ¼ mile |
| 0 | 125m | 250m | 375m | ½km |

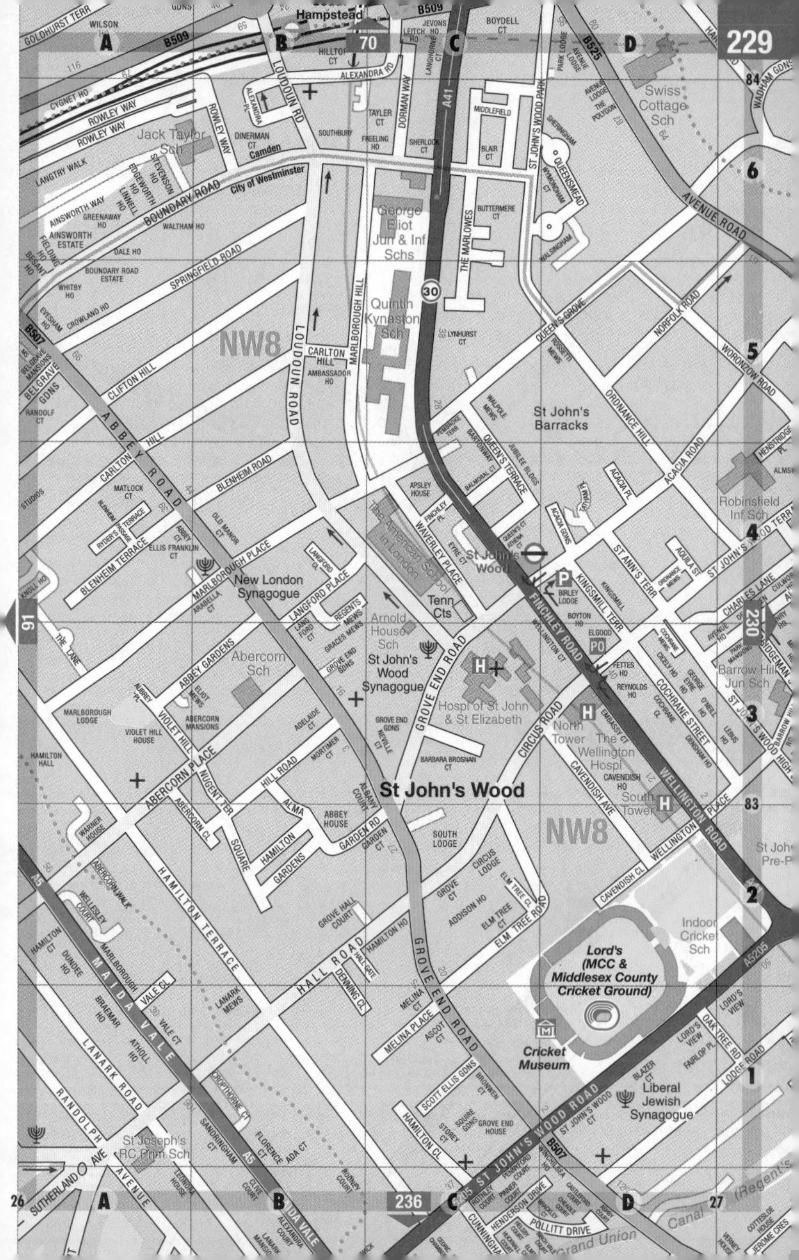
Hampstead
Swiss Cottage Sch
Jack Taylor Sch
George Eliot Jun & Inf Schs
Quintin Kynaston Sch
NW8
St John's Barracks
Robinsfield Inf Sch
New London Synagogue
The American School in London
St John's Wood
Tenn Cts
Arnold House Sch
St John's Wood Synagogue
Abercorn Sch
Hospl of St John & St Elizabeth
North Tower
The Wellington Hospl
South Tower
Barrow Hill Jun Sch
St John's Wood
Lord's (MCC & Middlesex County Cricket Ground)
Indoor Cricket Sch
Cricket Museum
Liberal Jewish Synagogue
St Joseph's RC Prim Sch
ABBEY ROAD
FINCHLEY ROAD
WELLINGTON ROAD
GROVE END ROAD
ST JOHN'S WOOD ROAD
MAIDA VALE
AVENUE ROAD
LOUDOUN ROAD
BOUNDARY ROAD
SPRINGFIELD ROAD
QUEEN'S GROVE
ACACIA ROAD
HAMILTON TERRACE
CIRCUS ROAD
Grand Union Canal (Regent's

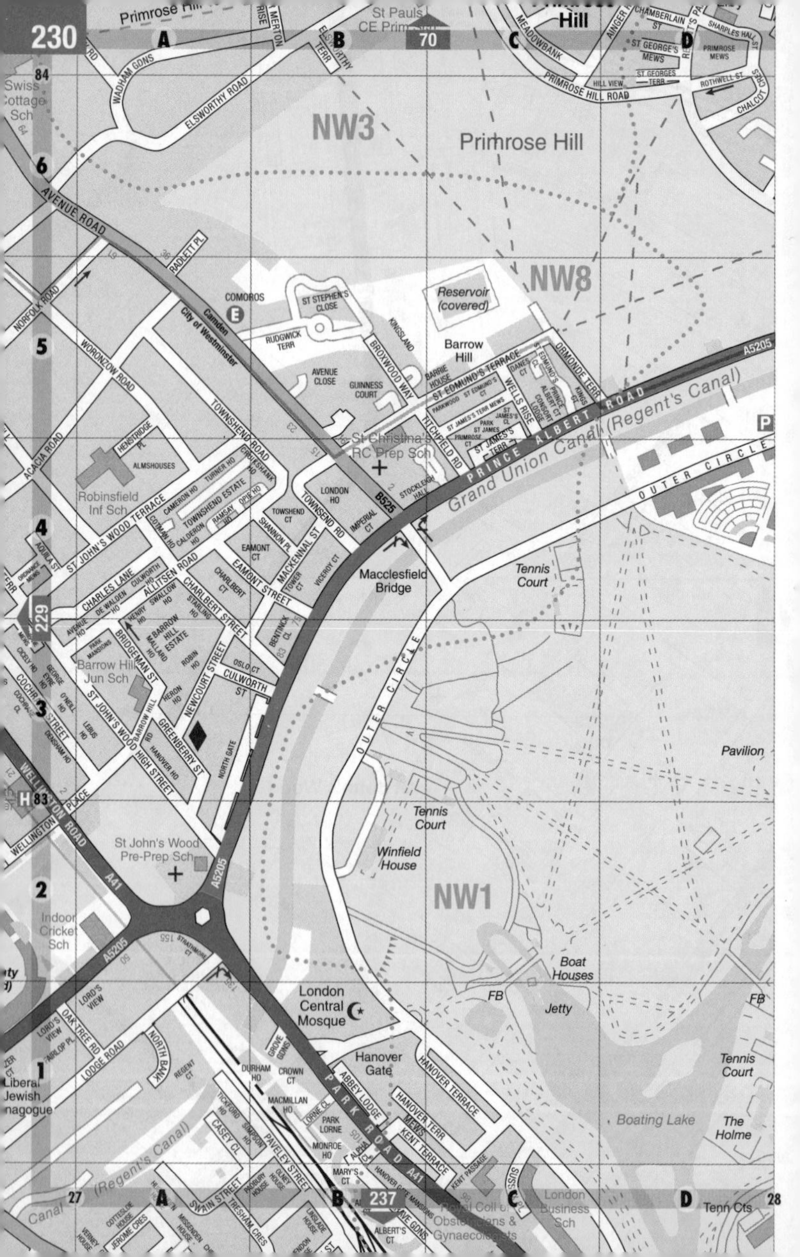
Primrose Hill
St Pauls CE Primary
70
Hill
A
B
C
D
MERTON RISE
ELSWORTHY TERR
MEADOWBANK
AINGER RD
CHAMBERLAIN ST
ST GEORGE'S MEWS
ST GEORGES TERR
HILL VIEW
PRIMROSE MEWS
SHARPLES HALL ST
ROTHWELL ST
CHALCOT CRES
PRIMROSE HILL ROAD
WADHAM GDNS
ELSWORTHY ROAD
Swiss Cottage Sch
84
NW3
Primrose Hill
6
AVENUE ROAD
RADLETT PL
NW8
COMOROS
ST STEPHEN'S CLOSE
RUDGWICK TERR
KINGSLAND
BROXWOOD WAY
Reservoir (covered)
Barrow Hill
Camden
City of Westminster
NORFOLK ROAD
5
WORONZOW ROAD
AVENUE CLOSE
GUINNESS COURT
BARRIE HOUSE
ST EDMUND'S TERRACE
DANES CT
ST EDMUND'S CL
ORMONDE TERR
PRINCE ALBERT CT
CONSORT LODGE
KINGS CT
WELLS RISE
PARKWOOD
ST JAMES'S TERR MEWS
PRIMROSE CT
ST JAMES'S TERR
A5205
PRINCE ALBERT ROAD
Grand Union Canal (Regent's Canal)
P
OUTER CIRCLE
TOWNSHEND ROAD
ACACIA ROAD
HENSTRIDGE PL
ALMSHOUSES
Robinsfield Inf Sch
St Christina's RC Prep Sch
FITCHFIELD RD
STOCKLEIGH HALL
LONDON HO
B525
IMPERIAL CT
CAMERON HO
TURNER HO
CRUICKSHANK HO
TOWNSHEND ESTATE
OPIE HO
RAMSAY HO
CALDERON HO
COTMAN HO
TOWSHEND CT
SHANNON PL
TOWNSEND RD
4
AQUILA ST
ST JOHN'S WOOD TERRACE
ORDNANCE MEWS
EAMONT CT
MACKENNAL ST
EAMONT STREET
TOWER CT
VICEROY CT
Macclesfield Bridge
Tennis Court
CHARLES LANE
DE WALDEN HO
CULWORTH HO
ALLITSEN ROAD
CHARLBERT CT
CHARLBERT STREET
SWALLOW HO
STARLING HO
229
AVENUE HO
HENRY HO
BARROW HILL ESTATE
MALLARD HO
BENTINCK CL
PARK MANSIONS
BRIDGEMAN ST
ROBIN HO
OSLO CT
CULWORTH ST
Barrow Hill Jun Sch
NEWCOURT STREET
HERON HO
GEORGE EYRE HO
O'NEILL HO
COCHRANE STREET
COCHRANE CL
3
LEBUS HO
ST JOHN'S WOOD HIGH STREET
BARROW HILL RD
GREENBERRY ST
HANOVER HO
NORTH GATE
OUTER CIRCLE
DENSHAM HO
Pavilion
WELLINGTON PLACE
WELLINGTON ROAD
83
H
Tennis Court
Winfield House
St John's Wood Pre-Prep Sch
A41
A5205
2
NW1
Indoor Cricket Sch
STRATHMORE CT
Boat Houses
FB
Jetty
LORD'S VIEW
OAK TREE RD
FAIRLOP PL
LODGE ROAD
NORTH BANK
REGENT CT
London Central Mosque
GROVE GDNS
DURHAM HO
CROWN CT
Hanover Gate
HANOVER TERRACE
1
Liberal Jewish Synagogue
MACMILLAN HO
ABBEY LODGE
HANOVER TERR MEWS
KENT TERRACE
LORNE CL
PARK LORNE
PARK ROAD
TICKFORD HO
SIMPSON HO
CASEY CL
PAVELEY STREET
MONROE HO
ALPHA CL
Boating Lake
The Holme
Tennis Court
(Regent's Canal)
KENT PASSAGE
MARY'S CT
HANOVER GATE MANSIONS
Canal
27
SWAIN STREET
PADBURY HOUSE
OLNEY HOUSE
237
London Business Sch
Royal Coll of Obstetricians & Gynaecologists
Tenn Cts
28
COTTESLOE HOUSE
MISSENDEN HOUSE
JEROME CRES
TRESHAM CRES
LINSLADE HOUSE
ALBERT'S CT
CAVE GDNS
VERNEY HOUSE

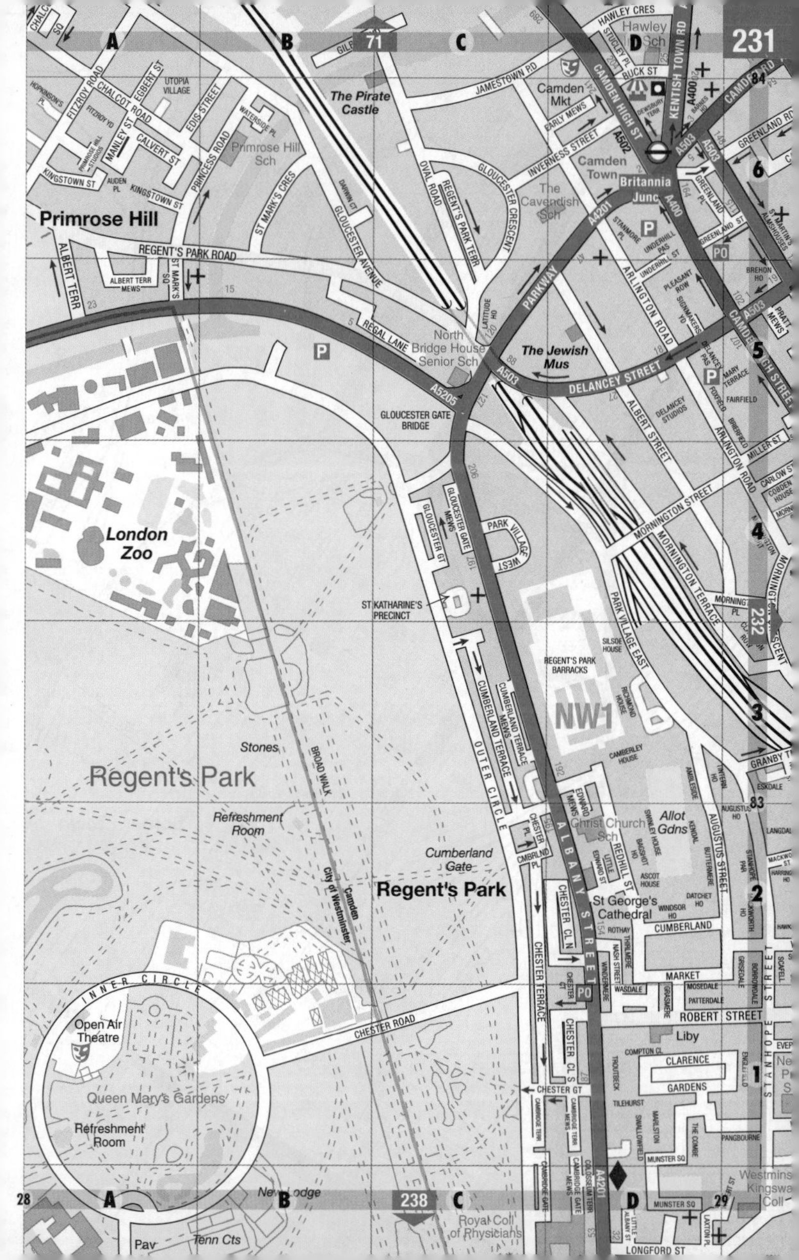
A
B
71
C
D
Hawley Sch
HAWLEY CRES
STUCKLEY PL
BUCK ST
KENTISH TOWN RD
CAMDEN HIGH ST
Camden Mkt
JAMESTOWN RD
EARLY MEWS
INVERNESS STREET
A502
Camden Town
Britannia Junc
A503
A400
A4201
DEWSBURY TERR
BARNES HO
CAMDEN RD
GREENLAND RD
GREENLAND ST
ALMSHOUSES
ST MARTIN'S
BREHON HO
PRATT MEWS
84
6
5
4
3
2
1
CHALCOT SQ
FITZROY ROAD
CHALCOT ROAD
EGBERT ST
UTOPIA VILLAGE
EDIS STREET
HOPKINSON'S PL
FITZROY YD
MANLEY ST
CALVERT ST
PRIMROSE HILL STUDIOS
KINGSTOWN ST
AUDEN PL
PRINCESS ROAD
WATERSIDE PL
Primrose Hill Sch
Primrose Hill
The Pirate Castle
DARWIN CT
ST MARK'S CRES
GLOUCESTER AVENUE
OVAL ROAD
REGENT'S PARK TERR
GLOUCESTER CRESCENT
The Cavendish Sch
STANMORE PL
UNDERHILL PAS
UNDERHILL ST
PLEASANT ROW
SIGNMAKERS YD
ARLINGTON ROAD
REGENT'S PARK ROAD
ALBERT TERR
ALBERT TERR MEWS
ST MARK'S SQ
PARKWAY
LATITUDE HO
REGAL LANE
North Bridge House Senior Sch
The Jewish Mus
DELANCEY STREET
DELANCEY PAS
MARY TERRACE
FAIRFIELD
DELANCEY STUDIOS
ALBERT STREET
A5205
GLOUCESTER GATE BRIDGE
MILLER ST
CARLOW ST
COBDEN HOUSE
MORNINGTON STREET
MORNINGTON TERRACE
MORNINGTON CRESCENT
MORNINGTON PL
London Zoo
GLOUCESTER GT
GLOUCESTER GATE MEWS
PARK VILLAGE WEST
ST KATHARINE'S PRECINCT
PARK VILLAGE EAST
SILSOE HOUSE
REGENT'S PARK BARRACKS
RICHMOND HOUSE
NW1
CAMBERLEY HOUSE
232
CUMBERLAND TERRACE
CUMBERLAND TERRACE MEWS
OUTER CIRCLE
GRANBY TER
ESKDALE
83
Stones
BROAD WALK
Regent's Park
Refreshment Room
CHESTER PL
EDWARD MEWS
Christ Church Sch
Allot Gdns
AMBLESIDE
KENDAL
AUGUSTUS HO
AUGUSTUS STREET
BUTTERMERE
LANGDALE
STANHOPE PAR
Cumberland Gate
CMBRLND PL
ALBANY STREET
LITTLE EDWARD ST
REDHILL ST
BAGSHOT HO
SWINLEY HOUSE
ASCOT HOUSE
DATCHET HO
WINDSOR HO
City of Westminster
Camden
CHESTER CL N
St George's Cathedral
ROTHAY
THIRLMERE
CUMBERLAND
MARKET
NASH STREET
WINDERMERE
WASDALE
GRASMERE
MOSEDALE
PATTERDALE
GRISEDALE
BORROWDALE
SCAFELL
STANHOPE STREET
INNER CIRCLE
Open Air Theatre
CHESTER ROAD
CHESTER TERRACE
CHESTER CT
PO
ROBERT STREET
CHESTER CL S
Liby
COMPTON CL
CLARENCE GARDENS
TROUTBECK
CHESTER GT
TILEHURST
SWALLOWFIELD
MARLSTON
THE COMBE
PANGBOURNE
Queen Mary's Gardens
CAMBRIDGE TERR
CAMBRIDGE TERR MEWS
CAMBRIDGE GATE MEWS
CAMBRIDGE GATE
COLOSSEUM TERR
MUNSTER SQ
Westminster Kingsway Coll
New Lodge
238
28
29
Royal Coll of Physicians
Pav
Tenn Cts
LITTLE ALBANY ST
LAXTON PL
LONGFORD ST

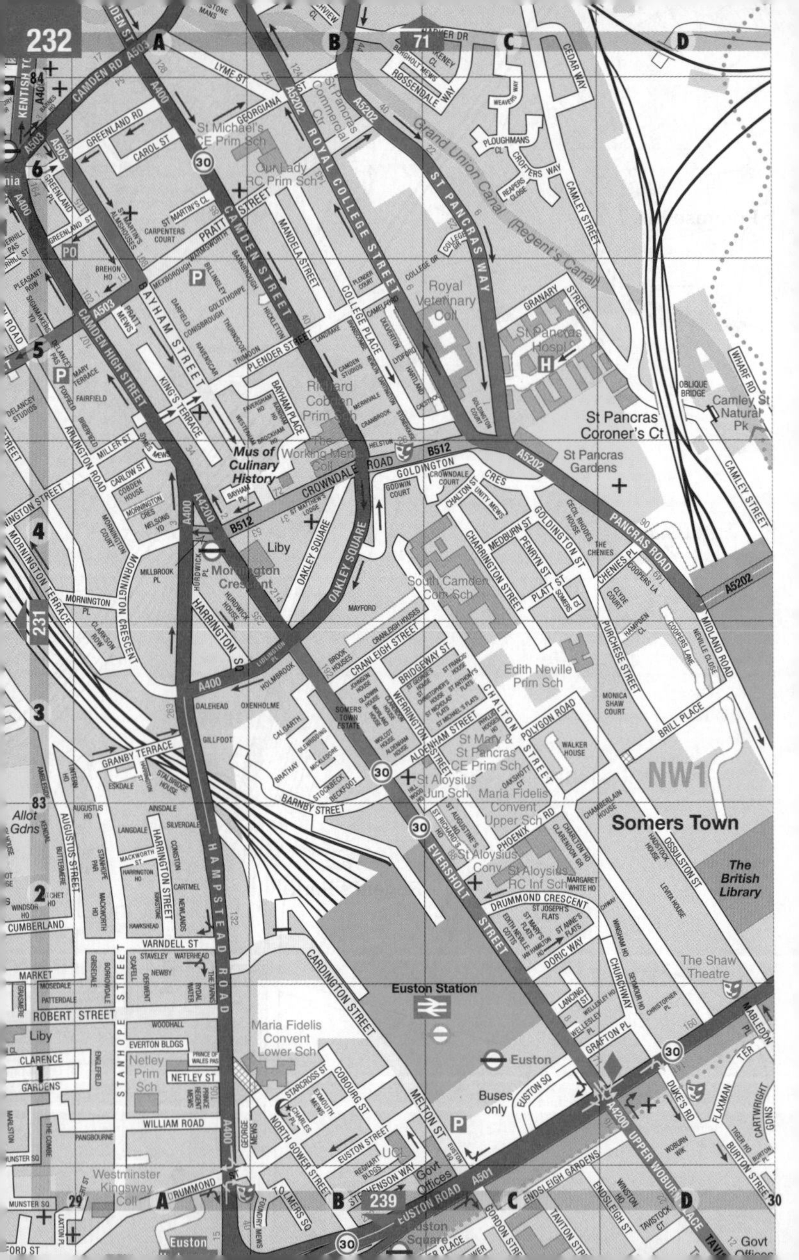
232
A
B
C
D
71
CAMDEN RD
A503
LYME ST
GEORGIANA ST
GREENLAND RD
CAROL ST
St Michael's CE Prim Sch
Our Lady RC Prim Sch
St Pancras Commercial Ctr
A5202
ROYAL COLLEGE STREET
ST PANCRAS WAY
Grand Union Canal (Regent's Canal)
BERGHOLT MEWS
ROSSENDALE WAY
WEAVERS WAY
PLOUGHMANS CL
CROFTERS WAY
REAPERS CLOSE
CEDAR WAY
CAMLEY STREET
KENTISH TOWN
GREENLAND PL
GREENLAND ST
ST MARTIN'S CL
ST MARTIN'S ALMSHOUSES
CARPENTERS COURT
PRATT STREET
CAMDEN STREET
MANDELA STREET
PLENDER COURT
COLLEGE GR
COLLEGE PL
Royal Veterinary Coll
GRANARY STREET
St Pancras Hospl
PO
BREHON HO
MEXBOROUGH
BILLINGLEY
BARNSBOROUGH
P
BAYHAM STREET
PRATT MEWS
DARFIELD
CONISBROUGH
GOLDTHORPE
THURNSCOE
RAVENSCAR
HICKLETON
TRIMDON
CAMDEN HIGH STREET
PLENDER STREET
LANDRAKE
CAMELFORD
DULVERTON
LYDFORD
HARTLAND
CAMDEN STUDIOS
GOLDINGTON COURT
PLEASANT ROW
SIGNMAKERS YD
DELANCEY PAS
DELANCEY STUDIOS
MARY TERRACE
FAIRFIELD
KING'S TERRACE
FAVERSHAM HO
BAYHAM PLACE
BROCKHAM HO
Richard Cobden Prim Sch
MERRIVALE
CRANBROOK
STONEHOUSE
OBLIQUE BRIDGE
WHARF RD
Camley St Natural Pk
St Pancras Coroner's Ct
ARLINGTON ROAD
MILLER ST
SYMES MEWS
Mus of Culinary History
The Working Men's Coll
HELSTON
B512
CROWNDALE ROAD
GOLDINGTON CRES
CROWNDALE COURT
St Pancras Gardens
A5202
CARLOW ST
COBDEN HOUSE
MORNINGTON CRES
NELSONS YD
BAYHAM PL
ST MATTHEW'S LODGE
GODWIN COURT
CHALTON ST
UNITY MEWS
MORNINGTON STREET
MORNINGTON COURT
A400
A4200
OAKLEY SQUARE
Liby
CECIL RHODES HOUSE
THE CHENIES
PANCRAS ROAD
MORNINGTON TERRACE
MILLBROOK PL
HURDWICK PL
Mornington Crescent
MEDBURN ST
PENRYN ST
GOLDINGTON ST
CHENIES PL
COOPERS LA
CLYDE COURT
A5202
MORNINGTON PL
CLARKSON ROW
MORNINGTON CRESCENT
HARRINGTON SQ
HURDWICK HOUSE
South Camden Com Sch
CHARRINGTON STREET
PLATT ST
SOMERS CL
MAYFORD
HAMPDEN CL
COOPERS LANE
NEVILLE CLOSE
MIDLAND ROAD
231
CRANLEIGH HOUSES
CRANLEIGH STREET
BRIDGEWAY ST
BROOK HOUSES
Edith Neville Prim Sch
PURCHESE STREET
HOLMBROOK
DALEHEAD
OXENHOLME
JOHNSON HOUSE
GLADWIN HOUSE
WERRINGTON STREET
CHALTON STREET
POLYGON ROAD
MONICA SHAW COURT
BRILL PLACE
SOMERS TOWN ESTATE
ALDENHAM STREET
CALGARTH
GILLFOOT
GRANBY TERRACE
St Mary & St Pancras CE Prim Sch
WALKER HOUSE
NW1
ESKDALE
STALBRIDGE HOUSE
BRAYHAY
MICKLEDORE
STOCKBECK
BECKFOOT
St Aloysius Jun Sch
Maria Fidelis Convent Upper Sch
OAKSHOTT CT
30
BARNBY STREET
CHAMBERLAIN HOUSE
Allot Gdns
AUGUSTUS HO
AINSDALE
SILVERDALE
LANGDALE
HARRINGTON STREET
AUGUSTUS STREET
PHOENIX RD
Somers Town
EVERSHOLT STREET
St Aloysius Conv
St Aloysius RC Inf Sch
HADSTOCK HOUSE
OSSULSTON ST
The British Library
MACKWORTH ST
HAMPSTEAD ROAD
CONISTON
CARTMEL
NEWLANDS
MARGARET WHITE HO
LEVITA HOUSE
WINDSOR HO
CUMBERLAND
HAWKSHEAD
DRUMMOND CRESCENT
ST JOSEPH'S FLATS
ST ANNE'S FLATS
DORIC WAY
VARNDELL ST
STAVELEY
WATERHEAD
NEWBY
CHURCHWAY
MARKET
MOSEDALE
PATTERDALE
STANHOPE STREET
CARDINGTON STREET
Euston Station
The Shaw Theatre
ROBERT STREET
WOODHALL
LANCING ST
WELLESLEY PL
Liby
EVERTON BLDGS
Maria Fidelis Convent Lower Sch
PRINCE OF WALES PAS
GRAFTON PL
CLARENCE GARDENS
Netley Prim Sch
NETLEY ST
Euston
STARCROSS ST
COBOURG ST
EXMOUTH MEWS
CHARLES PL
MELTON ST
EUSTON SQ
Buses only
DUKE'S RD
MABLEDON PL
FLAXMAN TER
CARTWRIGHT GDNS
WILLIAM ROAD
PANGBOURNE
NORTH GOWER STREET
GEORGE MEWS
EUSTON STREET
UCL
A4200
UPPER WOBURN PLACE
WOBURN WLK
TIGER HO
BURTON STREET
MUNSTER SQ
Westminster Kingsway Coll
DRUMMOND ST
REGNART BLDGS
STEPHENSON WAY
Govt Offices
EUSTON ROAD
A501
ENDSLEIGH GARDENS
WINSTON HO
ENDSLEIGH ST
TAVISTOCK CT
29
TOLMERS SQ
239
GORDON ST
TAVITON ST
LAXTON PL
FOUNDRY MEWS
Euston Square
Govt Offices
1
2
3
4
5
6

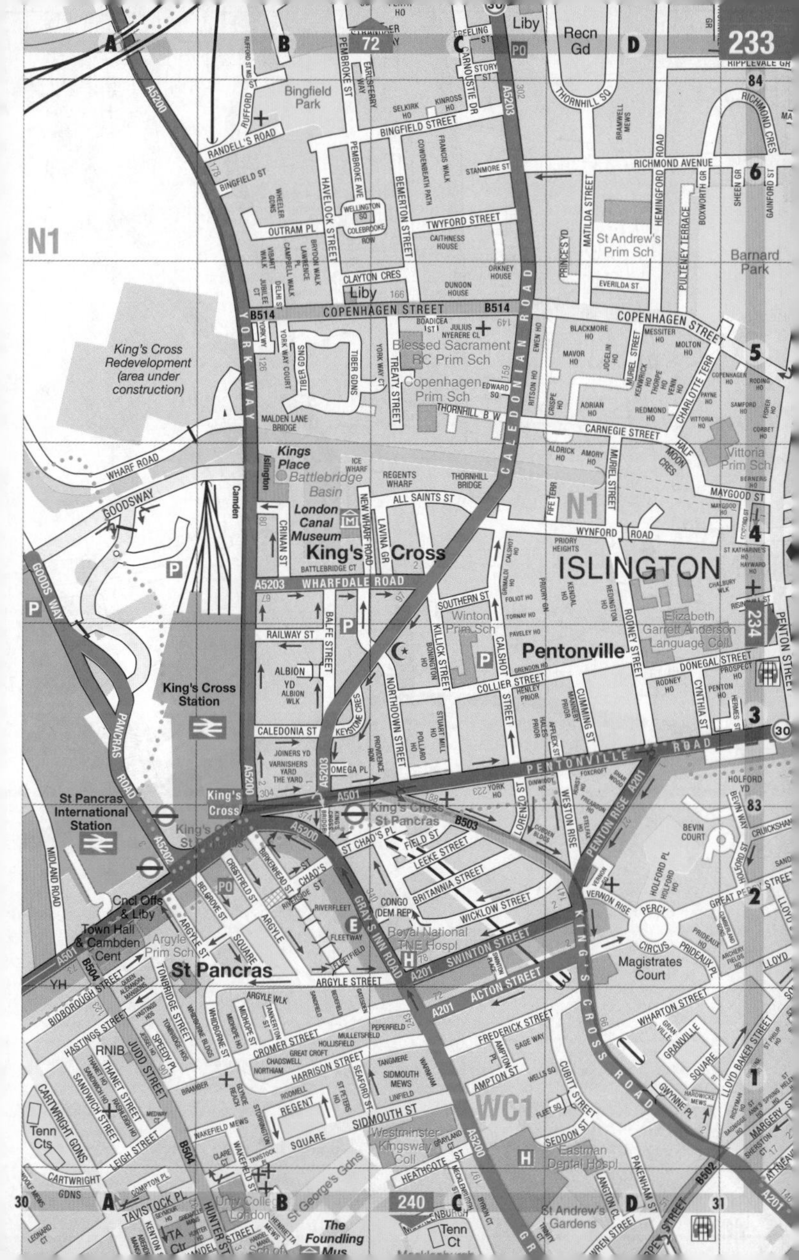
A
B
C
D
72
Liby
Recn Gd
PO
RIPPLEVALE GR
84
RICHMOND CRES
6
5
4
3
2
1
N1
RUFFORD ST
RANDELL'S ROAD
Bingfield Park
PEMBROKE ST
EARLSFERRY WAY
FREELING ST
CARNOUSTIE DR
STORY ST
SELKIRK HO
KINROSS HO
A5203
A5200
THORNHILL SQ
BRAMWELL MEWS
BINGFIELD STREET
BINGFIELD ST
HAVELOCK STREET
PEMBROKE AVE
WELLINGTON SQ
COLEBROOKE ROW
BEMERTON STREET
COWDENBEATH PATH
FRANCIS WALK
STANMORE ST
RICHMOND AVENUE
HEMINGFORD ROAD
BOXWORTH GR
SHEEN GR
GAINFORD ST
MATILDA STREET
St Andrew's Prim Sch
PULTENEY TERRACE
Barnard Park
WHEELER GDNS
OUTRAM PL
TWYFORD STREET
CAITHNESS HOUSE
ORKNEY HOUSE
DUNOON HOUSE
PRINCE'S YD
EVERILDA ST
VIBART WALK
CAMPBELL WALK
BRYDON WALK
LAWRENCE PL
JUBILEE CT
DELHI ST
CLAYTON CRES
COPENHAGEN STREET
B514
YORK WAY
CALEDONIAN ROAD
King's Cross Redevelopment (area under construction)
YORK WAY COURT
TIBER GDNS
YORK WAY CT
TREATY STREET
BOADICEA ST
JULIUS NYERERE CL
Blessed Sacrament RC Prim Sch
Copenhagen Prim Sch
EDWARD SQ
THORNHILL B W
RITSON HO
EWEN HO
BLACKMORE HO
MAVOR HO
JOCELIN HO
ADRIAN HO
MURIEL STREET
KENWRICK HO
THORPE HO
VENN HO
MESSITER HO
MOLTON HO
REDMOND HO
CHARLOTTE TERR
COPENHAGEN HO
RODING HO
PAYNE HO
SAMFORD HO
FISHER HO
VITTORIA HO
CORBET HO
CRISPE HO
MALDEN LANE BRIDGE
WHARF ROAD
CARNEGIE STREET
HALF MOON CRES
Vittoria Prim Sch
Kings Place
Islington
ICE WHARF
Battlebridge Basin
REGENTS WHARF
THORNHILL BRIDGE
ALDRICK HO
AMORY HO
BERNERS HO
MAYGOOD ST
MAYGOOD HO
GOODSWAY
Camden
London Canal Museum
NEW WHARF ROAD
ALL SAINTS ST
FIFE TERR
N1
WYNFORD ROAD
CRINAN ST
LAVINA GR
King's Cross
BATTLEBRIDGE CT
CALSHOT HO
PRIORY HEIGHTS
ISLINGTON
ST KATHARINE'S HO
HAYWARD HO
CHALBURY WLK
RISINGHILL ST
GOODS WAY
A5203 WHARFDALE ROAD
GRIMALDI HO
FOLIOT HO
TORNAY HO
PAVELEY HO
PRIORY GN
KENDAL HO
REDINGTON HO
RODNEY STREET
SOUTHERN ST
Winton Prim Sch
Elizabeth Garrett Anderson Language Coll
234
PENTON STREET
BALFE STREET
RAILWAY ST
KILLICK STREET
BONINGTON HO
Pentonville
ALBION YD
ALBION WLK
King's Cross Station
NORTHDOWN STREET
CALSHOT STREET
GRENDON HO
COLLIER STREET
HENLEY PRIOR
DONEGAL STREET
PROSPECT HO
RODNEY HO
PENTON HO
CYNTHIA ST
HERMES ST
MANNEBY PRIOR
CUMMING ST
HALES PRIOR
AFFLECK ST
PANCRAS ROAD
CALEDONIA ST
KEYSTONE CRES
STUART MILL HO
POLLARD HO
PROVIDENCE ROW
JOINERS YD
VARNISHERS YARD
THE YARD
OMEGA PL
PENTONVILLE ROAD
30
FOXCROFT
SHARWOOD
YORK HO
DINWIDDY HO
WESTON RISE
HURST HO
FREARSON HO
PENTON RISE
A201
HOLFORD YD
BEVIN WAY
83
CRUICKSHANK
A501
King's Cross
St Pancras International Station
King's Cross St Pancras
B503
LORENZO ST
COBDEN BLDGS
BEVIN COURT
MIDLAND ROAD
A5202
ST CHAD'S PL
FIELD ST
LEEKE STREET
BRITANNIA STREET
HOLFORD PL
HOLFORD ST
GREAT PERCY STREET
CRESTFIELD ST
BIRKENHEAD ST
CHAD'S ST
RIVERSIDE ST
RIVERFLEET
GRAY'S INN ROAD
CONGO (DEM REP)
WICKLOW STREET
VERNON RISE
PERCY CIRCUS
PRIDEAUX PL
CUMBERLAND GDNS
ARCHERY FIELDS HO
LLOYD
Cncl Offs & Liby
BELGROVE ST
ARGYLE SQUARE
FLEETWAY
Royal National TNE Hospl
SWINTON STREET
SWINTON PLACE
KING'S CROSS ROAD
Magistrates Court
Town Hall & Cambden Cent
Argyle Prim Sch
St Pancras
ARGYLE STREET
ACTON STREET
A501
B504
YH
BIDBOROUGH STREET
QUEEN ALEXANDRA MANSIONS
TONBRIDGE STREET
ARGYLE WLK
TANKERTON ST
SANDFIELD
BEDEFIELD
GATESDEN
WHARTON STREET
GRANVILLE SQUARE
LLOYD BAKER STREET
HASTINGS STREET
HASTINGS HO
TONBRIDGE HO
WHIDBORNE BLDGS
WHIDBORNE ST
MIDHOPE HO
MIDHOPE ST
PEPERFIELD
FREDERICK STREET
SAGE WAY
RNIB
JUDD STREET
SPEEDY PL
CROMER STREET
GREAT CROFT
MULLETSFIELD
HOLLISFIELD
AMPTON PL
AMPTON ST
WELLS SQ
THANET HO
SANDWICH HO
THANET STREET
SANDWICH STREET
RASHLEIGH HO
CHADSWELL
NORTHIAM
HARRISON STREET
SEAFORD ST
TANGMERE
SIDMOUTH MEWS
WARNHAM
LINFIELD
WC1
CUBITT STREET
GWYNNE PL
HARDWICKE MEWS
RICEYMAN HO
BASINGEE
ST ANN'S HO
SPRING HO
ST HELENS
MARGERY ST
SHERSTON CT
CARTWRIGHT GDNS
Tenn Cts
BRAMBER
GLYNDE REACH
RODMELL
REGENT SQUARE
ST PETERS HO
SIDMOUTH ST
FLEET SQ
MEDWAY CT
LEIGH STREET
WAKEFIELD MEWS
STORRINGTON
Westminster Kingsway Coll
GRAYLAND CT
SEDDON ST
Eastman Dental Hospl
PAKENHAM ST
B502
ATTNEAVE
CARTWRIGHT GDNS
COMPTON PL
CLARE CT
TAVISTOCK PL
WAKEFIELD ST
St George's Gdns
HEATHCOTE ST
MECKLENBURGH
BYRON CT
LANGTON CL
30
A
B
240
C
D
31
TAVISTOCK PL
SEYMOUR HO
GRENVILLE MEWS
HUNTER ST
Univ Coll London
HENRIETTA MEWS
The Foundling Mus
Tenn Ct
St Andrew's Gardens
WREN STREET
KENTON ST
TA Ctr
LEONARD CT

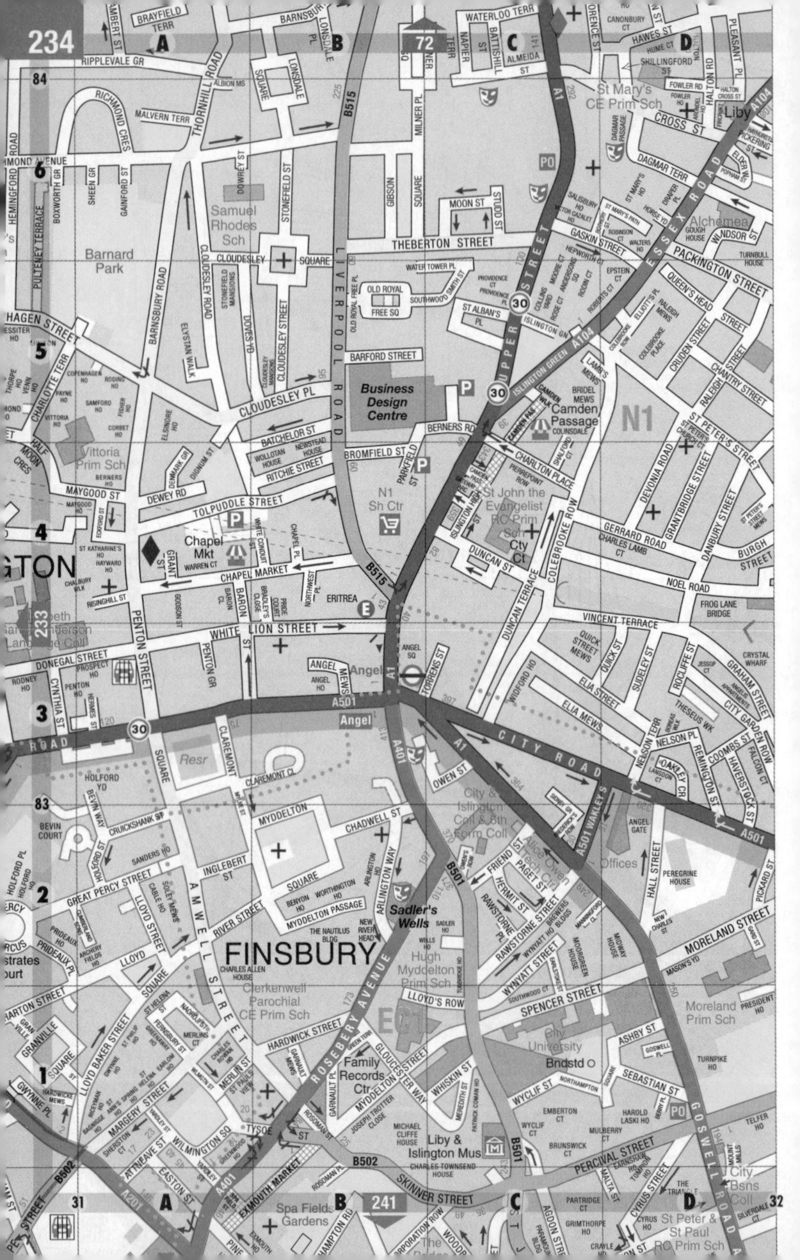

BRAYFIELD TERR
RIPPLEVALE GR
RICHMOND CRES
MALVERN TERR
THORNHILL ROAD
ALBION MS
LONSDALE
SQUARE
B515
72
MILNER PL
WATERLOO TERR
NAPIER
BATTISHILL ST
ALMEIDA ST
A1
HAWES ST
HUME CT
SHILLINGFORD ST
FOWLER RD
HALTON RD
PLEASANT PL
St Mary's CE Prim Sch
CROSS ST
Liby
A104
DAGMAR TERR
DAGMAR PASSAGE
PO
HEMINGFORD ROAD
BOXWORTH GR
SHEEN GR
GAINFORD ST
PULTENEY TERRACE
Barnard Park
Samuel Rhodes Sch
DOWREY ST
STONEFIELD ST
GIBSON SQUARE
MOON ST
STUDD ST
THEBERTON STREET
SALISBURY HO
VICTOR CAZALET HO
ST MARY'S PATH
DRAPER PL
HORSE YD
ESSEX ROAD
Alchemea
GOUGH HOUSE
WINDSOR ST
GASKIN STREET
HEPWORTH CT
PACKINGTON STREET
TURNBULL HOUSE
CLOUDESLEY SQUARE
LIVERPOOL ROAD
BARNSBURY ROAD
CLOUDESLEY ROAD
STONEFIELD MANSIONS
DOVES YD
CLOUDESLEY STREET
ELYSTAN WALK
WATER TOWER PL
OLD ROYAL FREE SQ
OLD ROYAL FREE PL
SOUTHWOOD SMITH ST
PROVIDENCE CT
ST ALBAN'S PL
COLLINS YARD
MOORE CT
ANDERSONS SQ
RODIN CT
EPSTEIN CT
QUEEN'S HEAD STREET
UPPER STREET
30
ISLINGTON GN
ISLINGTON GREEN
RALEIGH MEWS
COLEBROOKE PLACE
CRUDEN STREET
COPENHAGEN STREET
CHARLOTTE TERR
BARFORD STREET
Business Design Centre
P
LAMB'S MEWS
BRIDEL MEWS
CAMDEN WLK
CAMDEN PAS
Camden Passage
COLINSDALE
N1
RALEIGH STREET
CHANTRY STREET
CLOUDESLEY PL
BATCHELOR ST
WOLLOTAN HOUSE
NEWSTEAD HOUSE
RITCHIE STREET
BERNERS RD
BROMFIELD ST
PARKFIELD ST
CHARLTON PLACE
PIERREPOINT ROW
SHALFORD CT
ST PETER'S STREET
DEVONIA ROAD
GRANTBRIDGE STREET
Vittoria Prim Sch
HALF MOON CRES
MAYGOOD ST
DEWEY RD
DENMARK GR
DIGNUM ST
TOLPUDDLE STREET
N1 Sh Ctr
St John the Evangelist RC Prim Sch
Cty Ct
COLEBROOKE ROW
GERRARD ROAD
CHARLES LAMB CT
DANBURY STREET
BURGH STREET
Chapel Mkt
GRANT ST
WARREN CT
WHITE CONDUIT ST
CHAPEL PL
CHAPEL MARKET
NORTHWEST PL
DUNCAN ST
DUNCAN TERRACE
NOEL ROAD
FROG LANE BRIDGE
RISINGHILL ST
PENTON STREET
GODSON ST
BARON CL
BARON ST
BRADLEY'S CLOSE
PRIDE COURT
ERITREA
E
VINCENT TERRACE
QUICK STREET MEWS
QUICK ST
SUDELEY ST
ROCLIFFE ST
CRYSTAL WHARF
WHITE LION STREET
DONEGAL STREET
PROSPECT HO
PENTON GR
ANGEL MEWS
ANGEL SQ
Angel
TORRENS ST
WIDFORD HO
ELIA STREET
ELIA MEWS
GRAHAM STREET
CITY GARDEN ROW
THESEUS WK
CYNTHIA ST
A501
Angel
CLAREMONT
A401
NELSON TERR
NELSON PL
REMINGTON ST
COOMBS ST
HAVERSTOCK ST
FALCON CT
ROAD
Resr
SQUARE
CLAREMONT CL
OWEN ST
CITY ROAD
OAKLEY CR
HOLFORD YD
BEVIN WAY
MYDDELTON
CHADWELL ST
City & Islington Coll & 6th Form Coll
WAKLEY ST
ANGEL GATE
A501
83
BEVIN COURT
CRUICKSHANK ST
SANDERS HO
HOLFORD ST
INGLEBERT ST
ARLINGTON WAY
B501
FRIEND ST
PAGET ST
Alice Owen Tech Ctr
Offices
HALL STREET
PEREGRINE HOUSE
PICKARD ST
HOLFORD PL
GREAT PERCY STREET
AMWELL STREET
SQUARE
BENYON HO
WORTHINGTON HO
MYDDELTON PASSAGE
Sadler's Wells
HERMIT ST
RAWSTORNE PL
RAWSTORNE STREET
MORELAND STREET
LLOYD STREET
RIVER STREET
THE NAUTILUS BLDG
NEW RIVER HEAD
SADLER HO
MIDWAY HOUSE
PRIDEAUX PL
LLOYD
FINSBURY
Hugh Myddelton Prim Sch
WYNYATT STREET
MOORGREEN HOUSE
MASON'S YD
CHARLES ALLEN HOUSE
Clerkenwell Parochial CE Prim Sch
ROSEBERY AVENUE
LLOYD'S ROW
SPENCER STREET
Moreland Prim Sch
PRESIDENT HO
GRANVILLE SQUARE
LLOYD BAKER STREET
FERNSBURY ST
MERLIN ST
HARDWICK STREET
EC1
City University
ASHBY ST
TURNPIKE HO
Family Records Ctr
GLOUCESTER WAY
MYDDELTON STREET
WHISKIN ST
Bndstd
SEBASTIAN ST
WYCLIF ST
NORTHAMPTON SQUARE
GWYNNE PL
MARGERY STREET
WILMINGTON SQ
TYSOE ST
GARNAULT PL
ROSOMAN ST
JOSEPH TROTTER CLOSE
MICHAEL CLIFFE HOUSE
Liby & Islington Mus
EMBERTON CT
HAROLD LASKI HO
PO
TELFER HO
WYCLIF CT
BRUNSWICK CT
MULBERRY CT
PERCIVAL STREET
GOSWELL ROAD
B502
ATTNEAVE ST
EASTON ST
A201
EXMOUTH MARKET
B502
CHARLES TOWNSEND HOUSE
SKINNER STREET
MALTA ST
CYRUS STREET
THE TRIANGLE
City Bsns Coll
31
A
B
241
C
D
32
Spa Fields Gardens
PARTRIDGE CT
GRIMTHORPE HO
St Peter & St Paul RC Prim Sch
SILVERDALE CT
84
6
5
4
3
2
1
233

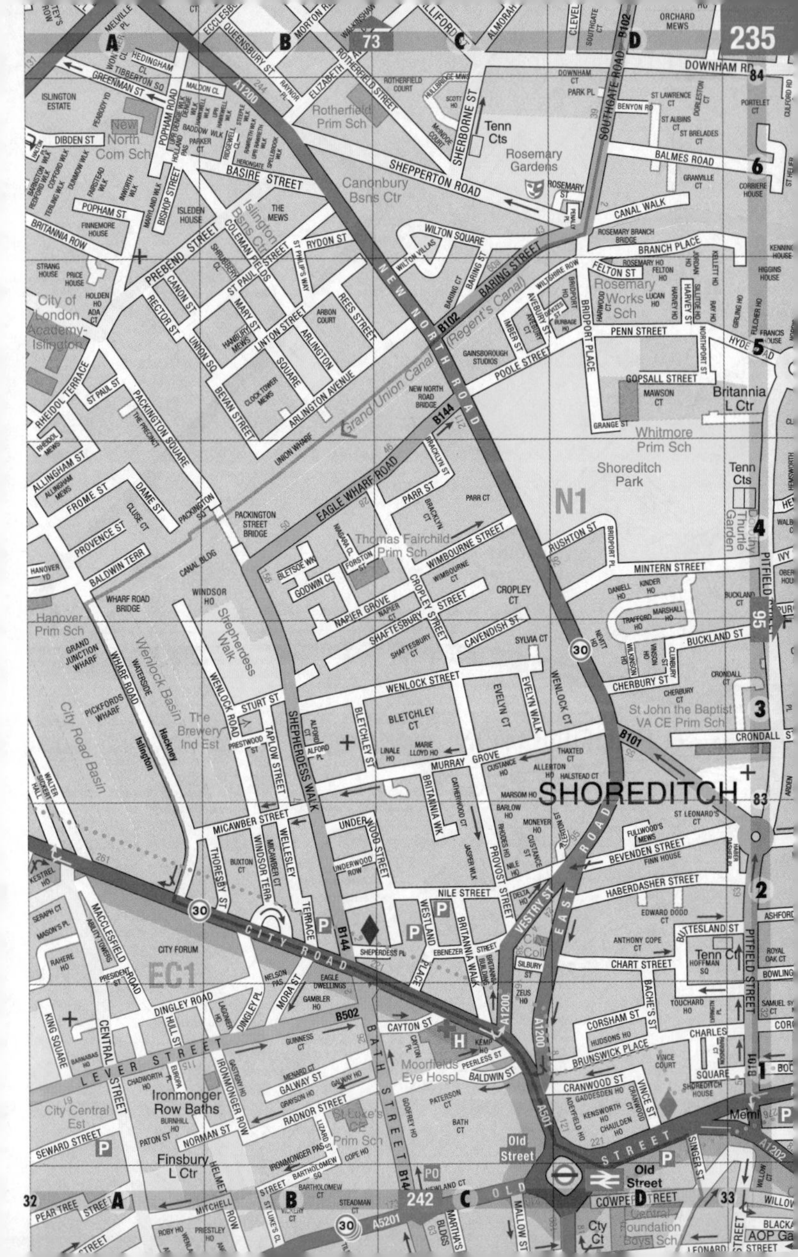
235
A
B
C
D
73
84
6
5
4
3
2
1
83
32
33
242
95
30
MELVILLE PL
WONTNER CL
HEDINGHAM CL
TIBBERTON SQ
GREENMAN ST
ISLINGTON ESTATE
PEABODY YD
DIBDEN ST
New North Com Sch
MALDON CL
POPHAM ROAD
HOLLAND PAS
BADDOW WLK
PARKER CT
BASIRE STREET
BISHOP STREET
POPHAM ST
FINNEMORE HOUSE
BRITANNIA ROW
ISLEDEN HOUSE
MARYLAND WLK
ECCLESBOURNE
QUEENSBURY ST
MORTON RD
RAYNOR PL
ELIZABETH AVE
ROTHERFIELD STREET
ROTHERFIELD COURT
Rotherfield Prim Sch
WALKINSHAW
HULLBRIDGE MWS
SCOTT HO
McINDOE COURT
SHERBORNE ST
Tenn Cts
SHEPPERTON ROAD
Canonbury Bsns Ctr
Rosemary Gardens
ROSEMARY ST
PENNLY PL
ORCHARD MEWS
SOUTHGATE CT
SOUTHGATE ROAD
B102
DOWNHAM RD
DOWNHAM CT
PARK PL
BENYON RD
ST LAWRENCE CT
DORLESTON CT
ST AUBINS CT
ST BRELADES CT
PORTELET CT
CULFORD RD
BALMES ROAD
GRANVILLE CT
CORBIERE HOUSE
ST HELIER
CANAL WALK
ROSEMARY BRANCH BRIDGE
BRANCH PLACE
KENNING HOUSE
HIGGINS HOUSE
WILTON SQUARE
WILTON VILLAS
BARING CT
BARING ST
BARING STREET
NEW NORTH ROAD
A1200
THE MEWS
Islington Bsns Ctr
PREBEND STREET
COLEMAN FIELDS
RYDON ST
ST PHILIP'S WAY
ST PAUL STREET
SHRUBBERY CL
CANON ST
RECTOR ST
STRANG HOUSE
PRICE HOUSE
HOLDEN HO
ADA CT
City of London Academy-Islington
MARY ST
HANBURY MEWS
LINTON STREET
ARBON COURT
REES STREET
ARLINGTON
UNION SQ
SQUARE
ARLINGTON AVENUE
CLOCK TOWER MEWS
BEVAN STREET
UNION WHARF
Grand Union Canal
(Regent's Canal)
NEW NORTH ROAD BRIDGE
B144
GAINSBOROUGH STUDIOS
POOLE STREET
IMBER ST
AVEBURY ST
DEVIZES ST
BURBAGE HO
WILTSHIRE ROW
BRIDPORT HO
FELTON ST
Rosemary Works Sch
ROSEMARY HO
FELTON HO
LUCAN HO
HARWOOD CT
HARVEY ST
KELLETT HO
RAY HO
GIRLING HO
FULCHER HO
FRANCIS HOUSE
PENN STREET
NORTHPORT ST
HYDE ROAD
BRIDPORT PLACE
GOPSALL STREET
MAWSON CT
GRANGE ST
Britannia L Ctr
Whitmore Prim Sch
Shoreditch Park
N1
Tenn Cts
Dorothy Thurtle Garden
RHEIDOL TERRACE
RHEIDOL MEWS
ST PAUL ST
PACKINGTON SQUARE
THE PRECINCT
ALLINGHAM ST
ALLINGHAM MEWS
FROME ST
DAME ST
CLUSE CT
PROVENCE ST
PACKINGTON SQ
PACKINGTON STREET BRIDGE
EAGLE WHARF ROAD
BRACKLYN ST
PARR ST
PARR CT
BRACKLYN CT
HANOVER YD
BALDWIN TERR
CANAL BLDG
WHARF ROAD BRIDGE
WINDSOR HO
Hanover Prim Sch
GRAND JUNCTION WHARF
WHARF ROAD
WATERSIDE
Wenlock Basin
Shepherdess Walk
BLETSOE WK
NIAGARA CL
FORSTON ST
Thomas Fairchild Prim Sch
WIMBOURNE STREET
WIMBOURNE CT
GODWIN CL
NAPIER GROVE
NAPIER CT
CROPLEY STREET
SHAFTESBURY STREET
SHAFTESBURY CT
CROPLEY CT
CAVENDISH ST
SYLVIA CT
RUSHTON ST
BRIDPORT PL
MINTERN STREET
DANIELL HO
KINDER HO
TRAFFORD HO
MARSHALL HO
NEVITT HO
WILKINSON HO
VINSON HO
CLUNBURY ST
BUCKLAND ST
BUCKLAND CT
CHERBURY ST
CRONDALL CT
CHERBURY CT
CRONDALL ST
St John the Baptist VA CE Prim Sch
PITFIELD ST
IVY
WALBROOK
HEMSWORTH
City Road Basin
PICKFORDS WHARF
Hackney
Islington
WENLOCK ROAD
The Brewery Ind Est
STURT ST
PRESTWOOD ST
TAPLOW STREET
SHEPHERDESS WALK
ALFORD CT
ALFORD PL
WENLOCK STREET
BLETCHLEY CT
BLETCHLEY ST
LINALE HO
MARIE LLOYD HO
EVELYN CT
EVELYN WALK
WENLOCK CT
MURRAY GROVE
CUSTANCE HO
THAXTED CT
ALLERTON HO
HALSTEAD CT
B101
BRITANNIA WK
CATHERWOOD CT
MARSOM HO
BARLOW HO
MONEYER HO
RHODES HO
CUSTANCE ST
NILE HO
SHOREDITCH
ST LEONARD'S CT
FULLWOOD'S MEWS
BEVENDEN STREET
FINN HOUSE
HABERDASHER PL
WALTER SICKERT HALL
KESTREL HO
MICAWBER STREET
THORESBY ST
BUXTON CT
WINDSOR TERR
MICAWBER CT
WELLESLEY TERRACE
UNDERWOOD STREET
UNDERWOOD ROW
JASPER WLK
PROVOST STREET
NILE STREET
EAST ROAD
VESTRY ST
DELTA HO
HABERDASHER STREET
EDWARD DODD CT
ASHFORD
SERAPH CT
MASON'S PL
ABILITY TOWERS
MACCLESFIELD ROAD
RAHERE HO
PRESIDENT ST
CITY FORUM
EC1
CITY ROAD
B144
SHEPHERDESS PL
WESTLAND PLACE
EBENEZER STREET
BRITANNIA WALK
BRITANNIA BUILDING
City Coll
SILBURY ST
ZEUS HO
ANTHONY COPE CT
BUTTESLAND ST
CHART STREET
HOFFMAN SQ
Tenn Ct
ROYAL OAK CT
BOWLING
NELSON PAS
EAGLE DWELLINGS
GAMBLER HO
MORA ST
DINGLEY ROAD
DINGLEY PL
LADDMER HO
HULL ST
KING SQUARE
BARNABAS HO
CENTRAL STREET
B502
CAYTON ST
CAYTON PL
H
KEMP HO
TOUCHARD HO
BACHE'S ST
SAMUEL ST CT
CORSHAM ST
HUDSONS HO
CHARLES SQUARE
BRUNSWICK PLACE
VINCE COURT
LEVER STREET
CHADWORTH HO
EUROPA HO
GASTIGNY HO
IRONMONGER ROW
GUINNESS CT
MENARD CT
GALWAY ST
GALWAY HO
GRAYSON HO
Moorfields Eye Hospl
PEERLESS ST
BALDWIN ST
CRANWOOD ST
GADDESDEN HO
ADEYFIELD HO
KENSWORTH HO
CHAULDEN HO
CRANWOOD ST
VINCE ST
SHOREDITCH HOUSE
A1200
A501
A1202
Ironmonger Row Baths
City Central Est
BURNHILL HO
PATON ST
NORMAN ST
RADNOR STREET
St Luke's CE Prim Sch
GODFREY HO
PATERSON CT
BATH CT
BATH STREET
LIZARD ST
COPE HO
IRONMONGER PAS
BARTHOLOMEW SQ
SEWARD STREET
Finsbury L Ctr
HELMET ROW
Old Street
Old Street
OLD STREET
SINGER ST
WILLOW CT
WILLOW
Meml
PEAR TREE STREET
MITCHELL HO
ROBY HO
PRIESTLEY HO
ST LUKE'S CL
STREET
BARTHOLOMEW CT
VICKERY CT
STEADMAN CT
NEWLAND CT
MALLOW ST
MARTHA'S BLDGS
COWPER STREET
Cty Ct
Central Foundation Boys' Sch
LEONARD ST
BLACKALL
AOP Ga
A5201

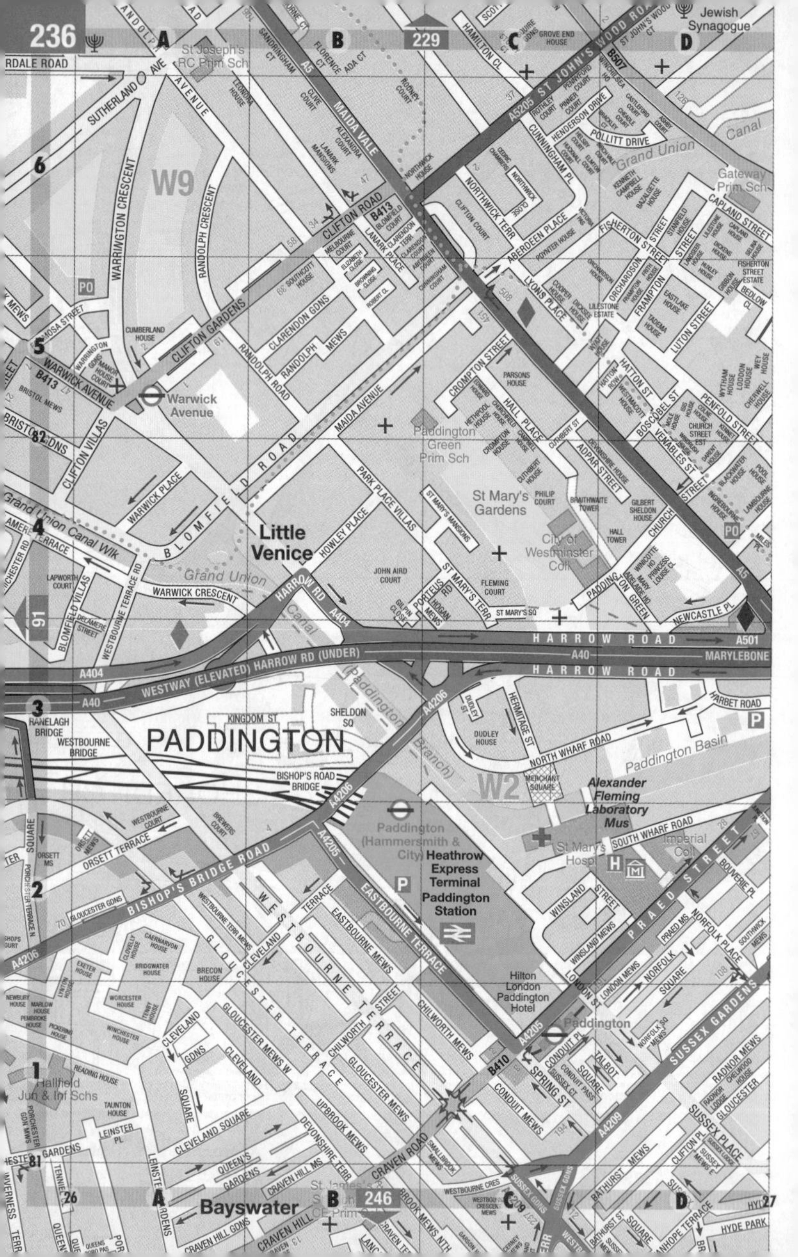
A
B
C
D
229
6
5
4
3
2
1
W9
W2
Little Venice
PADDINGTON
Bayswater
Warwick Avenue
Paddington
Paddington Green Prim Sch
St Mary's Gardens
City of Westminster Coll
Alexander Fleming Laboratory Mus
St Mary's Hosp
Imperial Coll
Heathrow Express Terminal
Paddington Station
Hilton London Paddington Hotel
Hallfield Jun & Inf Schs
St Joseph's RC Prim Sch
Gateway Prim Sch
Jewish Synagogue
Grand Union Canal
Grand Union Canal Wlk
Paddington Basin
MAIDA VALE
CLIFTON ROAD
CLIFTON GARDENS
WARWICK AVENUE
WARRINGTON CRESCENT
RANDOLPH CRESCENT
RANDOLPH ROAD
MAIDA AVENUE
BLOMFIELD ROAD
ST JOHN'S WOOD ROAD
HARROW ROAD
WESTWAY (ELEVATED) HARROW RD (UNDER)
NORTH WHARF ROAD
SOUTH WHARF ROAD
PRAED STREET
BISHOP'S BRIDGE ROAD
EASTBOURNE TERRACE
WESTBOURNE TERRACE
GLOUCESTER TERRACE
SUSSEX GARDENS
CRAVEN ROAD
91
246
26
27

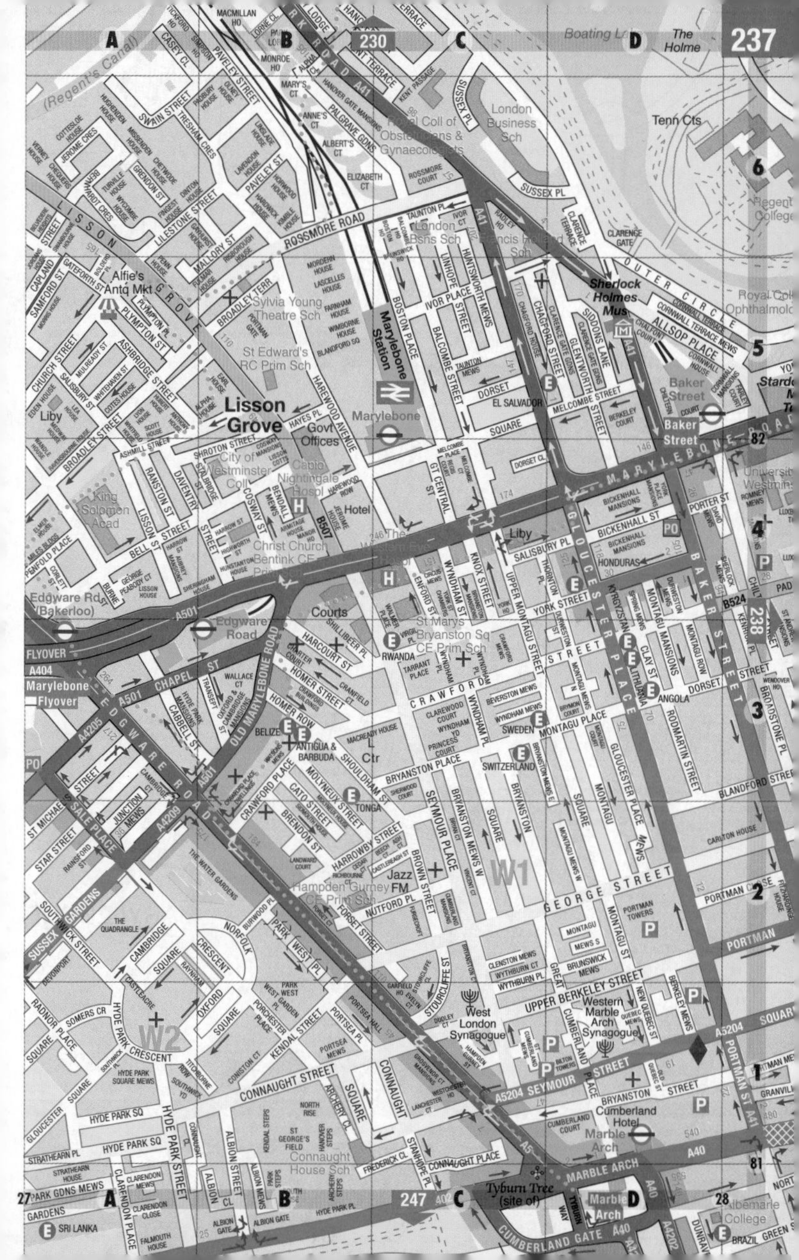
A
B
C
D
230
Boating Lake
The Holme
(Regent's Canal)
MACMILLAN HO
CASEY CL
SIMPSON HO
PAVELEY STREET
MONROE HO
LODGE
PARK ROAD
A41
KENT TERRACE
KENT PASSAGE
SUSSEX PL
London Business Sch
Tenn Cts
SWAIN STREET
TRESHAM CRES
MARY'S CT
ANNE'S CT
HANOVER GATE MANSIONS
PALGRAVE GDNS
ALBERT'S CT
Royal Coll of Obstetricians & Gynaecologists
ELIZABETH CT
ROSSMORE COURT
COTTESLOE HOUSE
JEROME CRES
HUGHENDEN HOUSE
MISSENDEN HOUSE
PADBURY HOUSE
OLNEY HOUSE
LINSLADE HOUSE
LAVENDON HOUSE
GRENDON ST
PAVELEY ST
HORWOOD HOUSE
6
Regent's College
SUSSEX PL
BERWHARDT CRES
TURVILLE HOUSE
WYCOMBE HOUSE
CHETWODE HOUSE
DINTON HOUSE
FINGEST HOUSE
LILESTONE STREET
HARDWICK HOUSE
KIMBLE HOUSE
LISSON GROVE
ROSSMORE ROAD
TAUNTON PL
IVOR CT
London Bsns Sch
Francis Holland Sch
CLARENCE TERRACE
CLARENCE GATE
OUTER CIRCLE
MALLORY ST
RISBOROUGH HOUSE
PENN HOUSE
CAPLAND
SAMFORD ST
GATEFORTH ST
BOLSOVER ST
Alfie's Antq Mkt
BROADLEY TERR
MORDERN HOUSE
LASCELLES HOUSE
FARNHAM HOUSE
WIMBORNE HOUSE
BLANDFORD SQ
BOSTON PLACE
LINHOPE STREET
HUNTSWORTH MEWS
IVOR PLACE
CHAGFORD STREET
CHAGFORD HOUSE
CLARENCE GATE GDNS
GLENTWORTH STREET
SIDDONS LANE
Sherlock Holmes Mus
CORNWALL TERRACE
CORNWALL TERRACE MEWS
ALLSOP PLACE
CHALFONT COURT
Royal Coll Ophthalmol
5
Stardome
PLYMPTON PL
PLYMPTON ST
Sylvia Young Theatre Sch
PORTMAN GATE
Marylebone Station
BALCOMBE STREET
TAUNTON MEWS
DORSET
EL SALVADOR
SQUARE
MELCOMBE STREET
BERKELEY COURT
Baker Street
CHURCH STREET
MULREADY ST
ASHBRIDGE STREET
St Edward's RC Prim Sch
HAREWOOD AVENUE
SALISBURY ST
WHITEHAVEN ST
COTES HOUSE
EARL HOUSE
ALPHA HOUSE
Lisson Grove
HAYES PL
Marylebone
Liby
BROADLEY STREET
ASHMILL STREET
SHROTON STREET
COSWAY MANSIONS
Govt Offices
MELCOMBE PLACE
DORSET CL
MARYLEBONE ROAD
82
University of Westminster
City of Westminster Coll
Capio Nightingale Hospl
HAREWOOD ROW
GT CENTRAL ST
174
BICKENHALL MANSIONS
YORK PLACE MANSIONS
PORTER ST
ROMNEY MEWS
King Solomon Acad
RANSTON ST
DAVENTRY STREET
STALBRIDGE ST
COSWAY ST
BENDALL MEWS
JEROME HOUSE
Hotel
B507
GLOUCESTER PLACE
BICKENHALL ST
PO
4
LISSON ST
BELL STREET
HARROW ST
HIGHWORTH ST
HUNSTANTON HOUSE
The Western Eye Hospl
Christ Church Bentinck CE Prim Sch
Liby
SALISBURY PL
HONDURAS
BAKER STREET
P
PENFOLD PLACE
GEORGE PEABODY CT
LISSON HOUSE
SHERINGHAM HOUSE
ENFORD ST
WYNDHAM ST
KNOX STREET
UPPER MONTAGU STREET
THORNTON PL
YORK STREET
KYRGYZSTAN
MONTAGU MANSIONS
B524
238
Edgware Rd (Bakerloo)
A501
Edgware Road
Courts
SHILLIBEER PL
HARCOURT ST
WALMER PLACE
St Marys Bryanston Sq CE Prim Sch
CRAWFORD MEWS
STREET
CLAY ST
MONTAGU ROW
FLYOVER
A404
Marylebone Flyover
CHAPEL ST
OLD MARYLEBONE ROAD
WALLACE CT
TRANSEPT ST
HOMER STREET
CRANFIELD CT
RWANDA
TARRANT PLACE
WYNDHAM PL
CRAWFORD
LITHUANIA
ANGOLA
DORSET
STREET
3
EDGWARE ROAD
A4205
CABBELL ST
HYDE PARK MANSIONS
BELIZE
HOMER ROW
ANTIGUA & BARBUDA
MACREADY HOUSE
L Ctr
CLAREWOOD COURT
WYNDHAM YD
PRINCESS COURT
BEVERSTON MEWS
WYNDHAM MEWS
SWEDEN
MONTAGU PLACE
SWITZERLAND
RODMARTIN STREET
BROADSTONE PL
PO
STREET
CAMBRIDGE CT
JUNCTION MEWS
A4209
SHOULDHAM ST
MOLYNEUX STREET
CATO STREET
CRAWFORD PLACE
BRYANSTON PLACE
SHERWOOD COURT
TONGA
SEYMOUR PLACE
BRYANSTON MEWS W
BRYANSTON SQUARE
MONTAGU SQUARE
GLOUCESTER PLACE MEWS
BLANDFORD STREET
ST MICHAELS ST
SALE PLACE
STAR STREET
RAINSFORD ST
BRENDON ST
HARROWBY STREET
LANDWARD COURT
BROWN STREET
Jazz FM
W1
GEORGE STREET
CARLTON HOUSE
PORTMAN CLOSE
2
SUSSEX GARDENS
THE WATER GARDENS
Hampden Gurney CE Prim Sch
NUTFORD PL
FORSET STREET
PORTMAN TOWERS
PORTMAN
THE QUADRANGLE
CAMBRIDGE SQUARE
NORFOLK CRESCENT
PARK WEST PL
MONTAGU MEWS S
BRUNSWICK MEWS
CLENSTON MEWS
WYTHBURN CT
WYTHBURN PL
GREAT CUMBERLAND PLACE
SOUTHWICK STREET
RAYNHAM
OXFORD SQUARE
PARK WEST
STOURCLIFFE ST
UPPER BERKELEY STREET
Western Marble Arch Synagogue
NEW QUEBEC ST
BERKELEY MEWS
RADNOR PLACE
SOMERS CR
HYDE PARK CRESCENT
W2
PORCHESTER PLACE
KENDAL STREET
PORTSEA PL
PORTSEA HALL
West London Synagogue
A5204
SQUARE
PORTMAN ST A41
SOUTHWICK PL
HYDE PARK SQUARE MEWS
TITCHBORNE ROW
CONISTON CT
PORTSEA MEWS
CONNAUGHT SQUARE
CONNAUGHT
SEYMOUR STREET
BRYANSTON STREET
1
GLOUCESTER SQUARE
HYDE PARK SQ
HYDE PARK STREET
CONNAUGHT STREET
ARCHERY CL
NORTH RISE
ST GEORGE'S FIELD
LANCHESTER CT
Cumberland Hotel
Marble Arch
CUMBERLAND COURT
STRATHEARN PL
STRATHEARN HOUSE
Connaught House Sch
STANHOPE PL
FREDERICK CL
CONNAUGHT PLACE
A5
A40
81
27
PARK GDNS MEWS
CLARENDON MEWS
CLARENDON PLACE
ALBION STREET
ALBION MEWS
247
Tyburn Tree (site of)
MARBLE ARCH
Marble Arch
28
Albemarle College
GARDENS
CLARENDON CLOSE
ALBION CL
HYDE PARK PL
TYBURN WAY
SRI LANKA
FALMOUTH HOUSE
ALBION GATE
CUMBERLAND GATE
A40
BRAZIL
GREEN ST

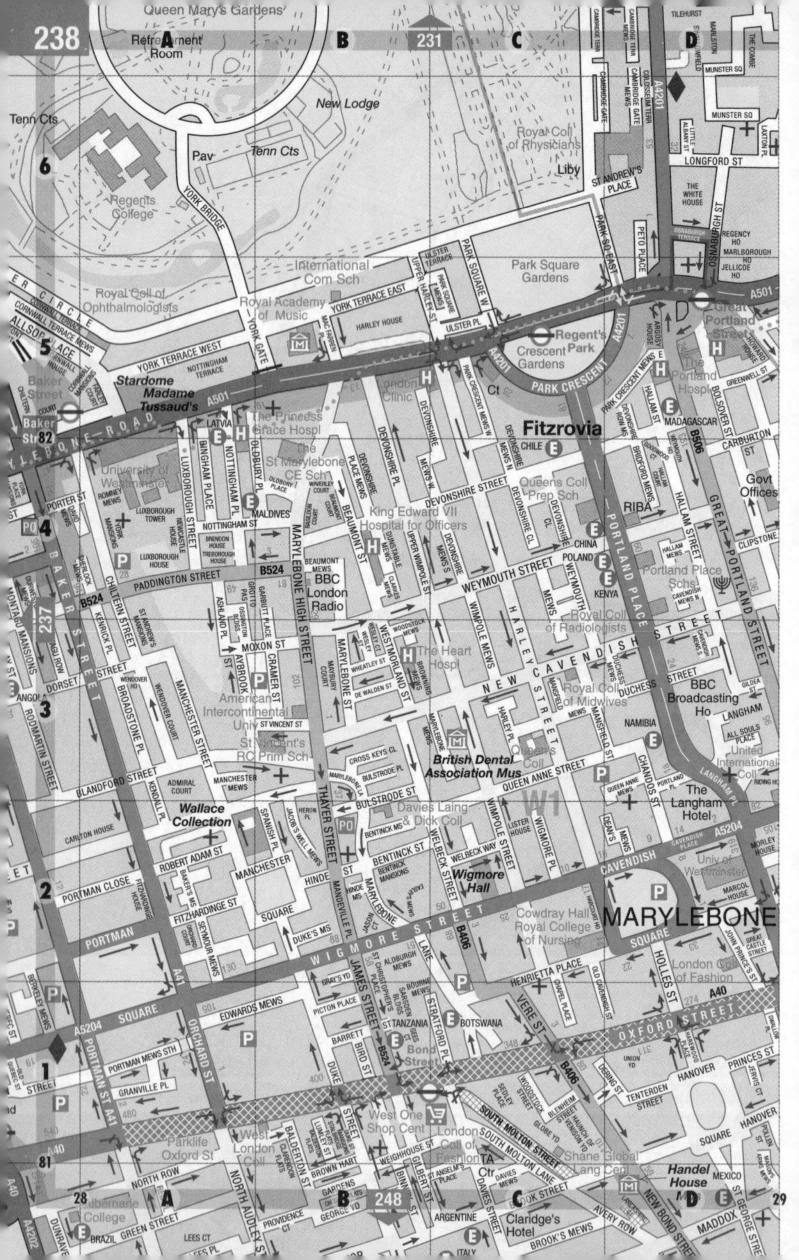
A
B
231
C
D
Queen Mary's Gardens
Refreshment Room
New Lodge
Tenn Cts
Pav
Tenn Cts
Regents College
YORK BRIDGE
Royal Coll of Physicians
Liby
CAMBRIDGE TERR
CAMBRIDGE TERR MEWS
CAMBRIDGE GATE
CAMBRIDGE GATE MEWS
COLOSSEUM TERR
A4201
TILEHURST
MARLSTON
THE COMBE
MUNSTER SQ
LITTLE ALBANY ST
LAXTON PL
LONGFORD ST
ST ANDREW'S PLACE
THE WHITE HOUSE
OSNABURGH ST
OSNABURGH TERRACE
PARK SQ EAST
PETO PLACE
REGENCY HO
MARLBOROUGH HO
JELLICOE HO
Park Square Gardens
International Com Sch
ULSTER TERRACE
UPPER HARLEY ST
PARK SQUARE MEWS
PARK SQUARE W
A501
Great Portland Street
Royal Coll of Ophthalmologists
OUTER CIRCLE
CORNWALL TERRACE
CORNWALL TERRACE MEWS
ALLSOP PLACE
Royal Academy of Music
YORK TERRACE EAST
HARLEY HOUSE
MAC FARREN PL
ULSTER PL
Regent's Park
Crescent Gardens
A4201
YORK GATE
YORK TERRACE WEST
NOTTINGHAM TERRACE
Stardome
Madame Tussaud's
Baker Street
CHILTERN COURT
MARYLEBONE ROAD
London Clinic
PARK CRESCENT MEWS W
PARK CRESCENT
ARGOSY HOUSE
PARK CRESCENT MEWS E
The Portland Hospl
GREENWELL ST
HOWARD HOUSE
BOLSOVER ST
LATVIA
The Princess Grace Hospl
The St Marylebone CE Sch
DEVONSHIRE PLACE MEWS
DEVONSHIRE PL
DEVONSHIRE MEWS W
DEVONSHIRE MEWS N
Fitzrovia
CHILE
DEVONSHIRE ROW MS
HALLAM ST
MADAGASCAR
B506
CARBURTON ST
University of Westminster
LUXBOROUGH STREET
BINGHAM PLACE
NOTTINGHAM PL
OLDBURY PL
OLDBURY PLACE
WAVERLEY COURT
GOODWOOD CT
BRIDFORD MEWS
HALLAM COURT
WEYMOUTH MEWS
DEVONSHIRE STREET
Queens Coll Prep Sch
Govt Offices
PORTER ST
DAVID MEWS
YORK MANSIONS
ROMNEY MEWS
LUXBOROUGH TOWER
MALDIVES
NOTTINGHAM ST
BASILDON COURT
BEAUMONT COURT
King Edward VII Hospital for Officers
DEVONSHIRE CL
DEVONSHIRE CL
RIBA
GREAT PORTLAND STREET
CLIPSTONE
PO
BAKER STREET
NEWCASTLE HOUSE
BRENDON HOUSE
TREBOROUGH HOUSE
BEAUMONT ST
DUNSTABLE MEWS
UPPER WIMPOLE ST
DEVONSHIRE MEWS S
CHINA
POLAND
PORTLAND PLACE
HALLAM STREET
HALLAM MEWS
SHERLOCK MEWS
LUXBOROUGH HOUSE
B524
BEAUMONT MEWS
BBC London Radio
WEYMOUTH STREET
WEYMOUTH MEWS
KENYA
Portland Place Schs
CAVENDISH MEWS N
DUNSTAN MEWS
MONTAGU MANSIONS
237
B524
PADDINGTON STREET
GROTTO PAS
OSSINGTON BLDGS
GARBUTT PLACE
MARYLEBONE HIGH STREET
CLARKES MEWS
ASHLAND PL
KENRICK PL
CHILTERN STREET
ST ANDREW'S MANSIONS
MOXON ST
WESLEY CT
WESTMORLAND ST
WOODSTOCK MEWS
The Heart Hospl
WIMPOLE MEWS
HARLEY STREET
Royal Coll of Radiologists
NEW CAVENDISH STREET
CAVENDISH MEWS S
AGU ROW
DORSET STREET
WENDOVER HO
AYBROOK ST
CRAMER ST
MAYBURY COURT
MARYLEBONE ST
WHEATLEY ST
BROWNING MEWS
DE WALDEN ST
MANSFIELD MEWS
DUCHESS MEWS
DUCHESS STREET
Royal Coll of Midwives
BBC Broadcasting Ho
GILDEA ST
ANGOLA
BROADSTONE PL
WENDOVER COURT
MANCHESTER STREET
American Intercontinental Univ
ST VINCENT ST
MARYLEBONE MEWS
HARLEY PL
NAMIBIA
LANGHAM
ALL SOULS PLACE
RODMARTIN STREET
St Vincent's RC Prim Sch
CROSS KEYS CL
BULSTRODE PL
British Dental Association Mus
Queen's Coll
MANSFIELD ST
CHANDOS ST
United International Coll
LANGHAM PL
RIDING HO
BLANDFORD STREET
KENDALL PL
ADMIRAL COURT
MANCHESTER MEWS
MARYLEBONE LA
THAYER STREET
BULSTRODE ST
QUEEN ANNE STREET
QUEEN ANNE MEWS
PORTLAND PL
The Langham Hotel
Wallace Collection
CARLTON HOUSE
SPANISH PL
JACOB'S WELL MEWS
HERON PL
Davies Laing & Dick Coll
W1
WIMPOLE STREET
LISTER HOUSE
WIGMORE PL
DEAN'S MEWS
A5204
MORLEY HOUSE
BENTINCK MS
PO
WELBECK STREET
WELBECK WAY
CAVENDISH PLACE
ROBERT ADAM ST
BAKER'S MS
MANCHESTER SQUARE
HINDE ST
MANDEVILLE PL
BENTINCK ST
BENTINCK MANSIONS
Wigmore Hall
CAVENDISH SQUARE
Univ of Westminster
PORTMAN CLOSE
FITZHARDINGE HOUSE
FITZHARDINGE ST
HINDE MS
MARYLEBONE LANE
EASLEY'S MEWS
Cowdray Hall
Royal College of Nursing
HARCOURT HO
MARYLEBONE
MARCOL HOUSE
JOHN PRINCE'S ST
GREAT CASTLE STREET
ORCHARD COURT
SEYMOUR MEWS
DUKE'S MS
JASON CT
WIGMORE STREET
B406
PORTMAN SQUARE
A41
ST CHRISTOPHER'S PLACE
ALDBURGH MEWS
London Coll of Fashion
HOLLES ST
BERKELEY MEWS
GRAY'S YD
JAMES STREET
SARSDEN BLDGS
BOURNE MEWS
HENRIETTA PLACE
CHAPEL PLACE
OLD CAVENDISH ST
A40
A5204
EDWARDS MEWS
PICTON PLACE
TANZANIA
BOTSWANA
VERE ST
OXFORD STREET
SWALLOW PL
BARRETT ST
BIRD ST
GEES CT
STRATFORD PL
B524
Bond Street
B406
UNION YD
HAREWOOD PLACE
PRINCES ST
PORTMAN MEWS STH
ORCHARD ST
DUKE ST
DERING ST
HANOVER ST
JERVIS CT
PORTMAN ST A41
GRANVILLE PL
TENTERDEN STREET
WOODSTOCK STREET
SEDLEY PLACE
BLENHEIM STREET
HAUNCH OF VENISON YD
GLOBE YD
SOUTH MOLTON STREET
SOUTH MOLTON LANE
HANOVER SQUARE
POLLEN ST
Parklife Oxford St
West London Coll
West One Shop Cent
LUMLEY ST
BALDERTON FLATS
CLARENDON FLATS
London Coll of Fashion
Shane Global Lang Cent
A40
NORTH ROW
BROWN HART GARDENS
WEIGHOUSE ST
GILBERT ST
BINNEY ST
ST ANSELM'S PLACE
DAVIES MEWS
TA Ctr
Handel House
MEXICO
MASON'S ARMS MEWS
A40
Albemarle College
NORTH AUDLEY ST
PROVIDENCE CT
GEORGE YD
248
ARGENTINE
DAVIES STREET
BROOK STREET
Claridge's Hotel
AVERY ROW
LANCASHIRE CT
NEW BOND STREET
MADDOX ST
ST GEORGE STREET
A4202
DUNRAVEN
BRAZIL
GREEN STREET
LEES CT
BROOK'S MEWS
ITALY
6
5
4
3
2
1
28
29
82
81

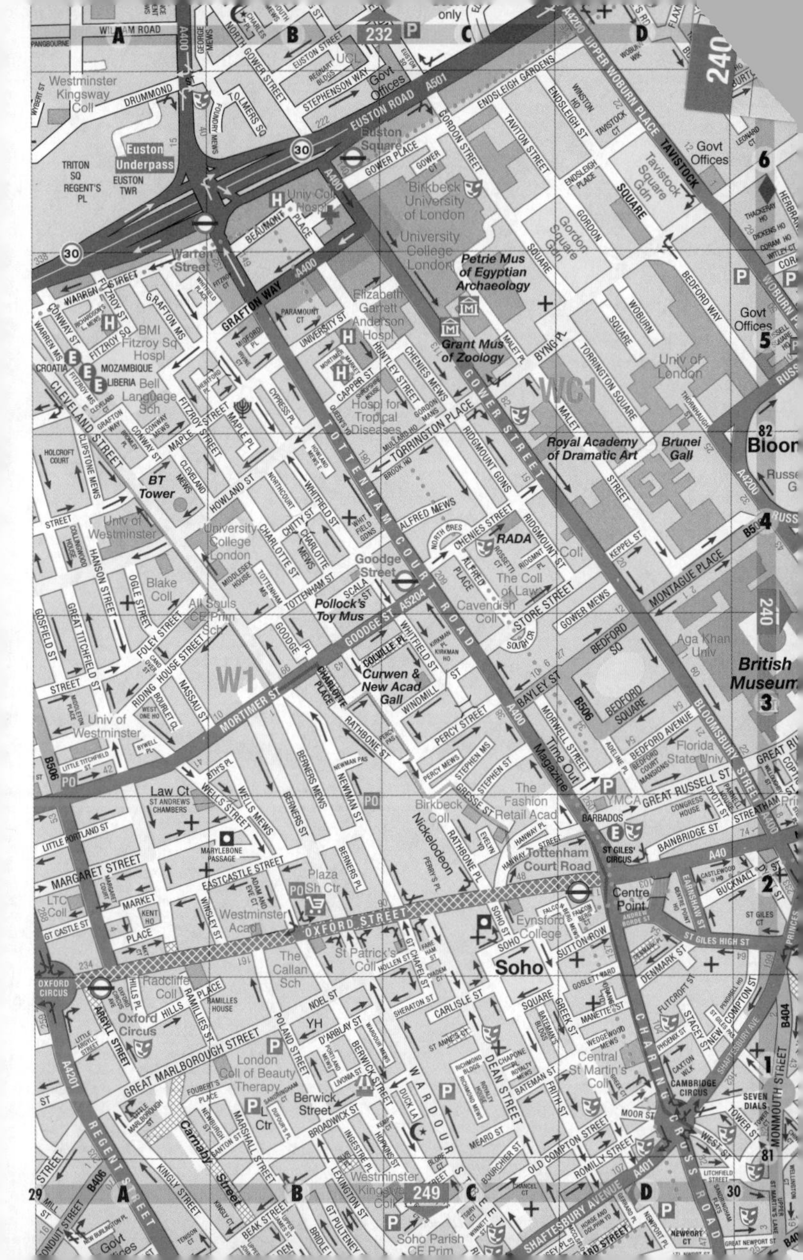

232
240
249
A
B
C
D
6
5
4
3
2
1
29
30
81
82
WILLIAM ROAD
PANGBOURNE
Westminster Kingsway Coll
DRUMMOND ST
TOLMERS SQ
FOUNDRY MEWS
EUSTON STREET
UCL
REGNART BLDGS
STEPHENSON WAY
Govt Offices
EUSTON ROAD
A501
A400
A4200
UPPER WOBURN PLACE
Euston Square
Euston Underpass
TRITON SQ
REGENT'S PL
EUSTON TWR
ENDSLEIGH GARDENS
ENDSLEIGH ST
ENDSLEIGH PLACE
TAVISTOCK CT
TAVISTOCK SQUARE
Tavistock Square Gdn
GORDON STREET
TAVITON STREET
GOWER PLACE
GOWER CT
Birkbeck University of London
University College London
Univ Coll Hospl
BEAUMONT PLACE
Warren Street
GRAFTON WAY
Petrie Mus of Egyptian Archaeology
Grant Mus of Zoology
Gordon Square Gdn
GORDON SQUARE
WOBURN SQUARE
BEDFORD WAY
Govt Offices
Univ of London
TORRINGTON SQUARE
BYNG PL
MALET PL
MALET STREET
WC1
Royal Academy of Dramatic Art
Brunei Gall
Bloom
Russe
WARREN STREET
FITZROY ST
CONWAY ST
FITZROY SQ
BMI Fitzroy Sq Hospl
CROATIA
MOZAMBIQUE
LIBERIA
Bell Language Sch
CLEVELAND STREET
GRAFTON MS
MIDFORD PL
PARAMOUNT CT
UNIVERSITY ST
Elizabeth Garrett Anderson Hospl
HUNTLEY STREET
CHENIES MEWS
CAPPER ST
Hospl for Tropical Diseases
GORDON MANS
TORRINGTON PLACE
GOWER STREET
RIDGMOUNT GDNS
MAPLE ST
MAPLE PL
CONWAY MEWS
FITZROY STREET
CLEVELAND MEWS
HOLCROFT COURT
CLIPSTONE MEWS
BT Tower
HOWLAND ST
WHITFIELD ST
TOTTENHAM COURT ROAD
ALFRED MEWS
CHENIES STREET
RADA
RIDGMOUNT ST
Coll
KEPPEL ST
MONTAGUE PLACE
Univ of Westminster
University College London
CHARLOTTE ST
CHITTY ST
CHARLOTTE MEWS
Goodge Street
ALFRED PLACE
The Coll of Law
Cavendish Coll
STORE STREET
GOWER MEWS
BEDFORD SQ
BEDFORD SQUARE
Aga Khan Univ
British Museum
HANSON STREET
OGLE STREET
Blake Coll
All Souls CE Prim Sch
TOTTENHAM ST
SCALA ST
Pollock's Toy Mus
GOODGE ST
A5204
GOSFIELD ST
GREAT TITCHFIELD STREET
FOLEY STREET
RIDING HOUSE STREET
NASSAU ST
W1
GOODGE PL
COLVILLE PL
WHITFIELD ST
Curwen & New Acad Gall
CHARLOTTE PLACE
WINDMILL ST
BAYLEY ST
B506
MORWELL STREET
BLOOMSBURY STREET
BEDFORD AVENUE
Florida State Univ
MORTIMER ST
Univ of Westminster
BOURLET CL
RATHBONE ST
PERCY STREET
PERCY MEWS
STEPHEN MS
STEPHEN ST
Time Out Magazine
ADELINE PL
GREAT RUSSELL ST
LITTLE TITCHFIELD ST
PO
Law Ct
ST ANDREWS CHAMBERS
WELLS STREET
WELLS MEWS
BERNERS MEWS
NEWMAN ST
BERNERS ST
Birkbeck Coll
Nickelodeon
GRESSE ST
The Fashion Retail Acad
YMCA
BARBADOS
CONGRESS HOUSE
DYOTT ST
STREATHAM ST
LITTLE PORTLAND ST
MARYLEBONE PASSAGE
RATHBONE PL
PERRY'S PL
HANWAY PL
HANWAY ST
Tottenham Court Road
ST GILES' CIRCUS
BAINBRIDGE ST
A40
MARGARET STREET
EASTCASTLE STREET
BERNERS PL
Plaza Sh Ctr
Centre Point
EARNSHAW ST
BUCKNALL ST
CASTLEWOOD HO
LTC Coll
MARKET PLACE
GT CASTLE ST
WINSLEY ST
Westminster Acad
OXFORD STREET
SOHO ST
Eynsford College
SUTTON ROW
ST GILES CT
ST GILES HIGH ST
OXFORD CIRCUS
Radcliffe Coll
HILLS PL
RAMILLIES PLACE
RAMILLIES ST
The Callan Sch
St Patrick's Coll
HOLLEN ST
SOHO SQUARE
Soho
GREEK ST
DENMARK ST
FLITCROFT ST
STACEY ST
NEW COMPTON ST
Oxford Circus
ARGYLL STREET
GREAT MARLBOROUGH STREET
NOEL ST
YH
D'ARBLAY ST
POLAND STREET
BERWICK STREET
WARDOUR STREET
SHERATON ST
CARLISLE ST
ST ANNE'S CT
DEAN STREET
MANETTE ST
CHARING CROSS ROAD
SHAFTESBURY AVE
B404
A4201
London Coll of Beauty Therapy
FOUBERT'S PLACE
Berwick Street
BROADWICK ST
RICHMOND MEWS
BATEMAN ST
FRITH ST
Central St Martin's Coll
PHOENIX ST
CAXTON WLK
CAMBRIDGE CIRCUS
SEVEN DIALS
MONMOUTH STREET
MARSHALL STREET
Carnaby Street
INGESTRE PL
HOPKINS ST
DUCK LA
MEARD ST
OLD COMPTON STREET
MOOR ST
ROMILLY STREET
TOWER ST
WEST ST
REGENT STREET
B406
KINGLY STREET
LEXINGTON ST
Westminster Kingsway Coll
BOURCHIER ST
A401
SHAFTESBURY AVENUE
LITCHFIELD STREET
SANDRINGHAM FLATS
CONDUIT STREET
NEW BURLINGTON PL
BEAK STREET
GT PULTENEY
Soho Parish CE Prim
NEWPORT CT
GREAT NEWPORT ST
Govt Offices

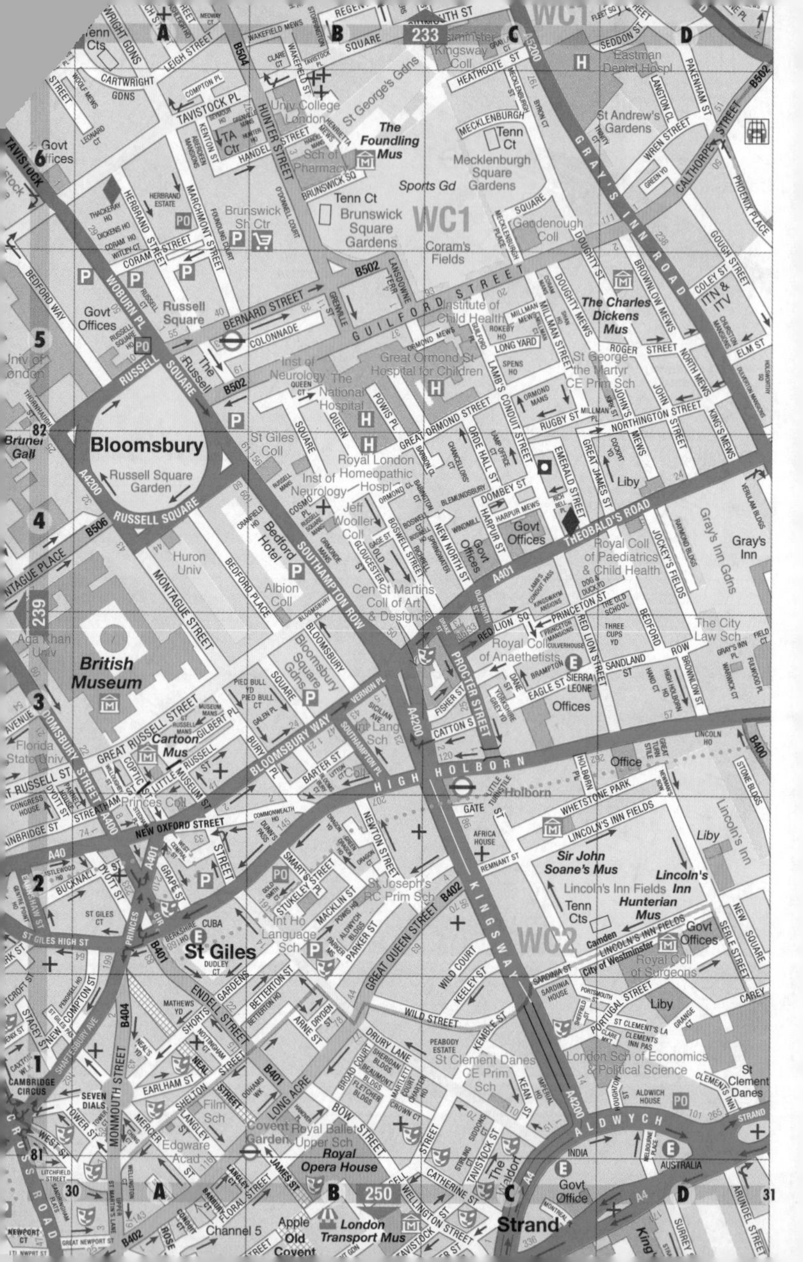

233
WC1
Bloomsbury
Russell Square Garden
RUSSELL SQUARE
British Museum
239
The Foundling Mus
Brunswick Square Gardens
Mecklenburgh Square Gardens
Coram's Fields
Sports Gd
Goodenough Coll
GUILFORD STREET
Great Ormond St Hospital for Children
The National Hospital
Royal London Homeopathic Hospl
The Charles Dickens Mus
St Andrew's Gardens
Eastman Dental Hospl
GRAY'S INN ROAD
THEOBALD'S ROAD
Gray's Inn
Gray's Inn Gdns
Royal Coll of Paediatrics & Child Health
The City Law Sch
SOUTHAMPTON ROW
Bloomsbury Square Gdns
BLOOMSBURY WAY
HIGH HOLBORN
Holborn
NEW OXFORD STREET
KINGSWAY
LINCOLN'S INN FIELDS
Sir John Soane's Mus
Lincoln's Inn
Hunterian Mus
Royal Coll of Surgeons
London Sch of Economics & Political Science
WC2
St Giles
SHAFTESBURY AVE
CAMBRIDGE CIRCUS
SEVEN DIALS
MONMOUTH STREET
LONG ACRE
Covent Garden
Royal Opera House
Royal Ballet Upper Sch
DRURY LANE
GREAT QUEEN STREET
St Clement Danes CE Prim Sch
ALDWYCH
The Waldorf
Strand
250
London Transport Mus
Channel 5
Apple
Old Covent
CHARING CROSS ROAD
30
31
81
82

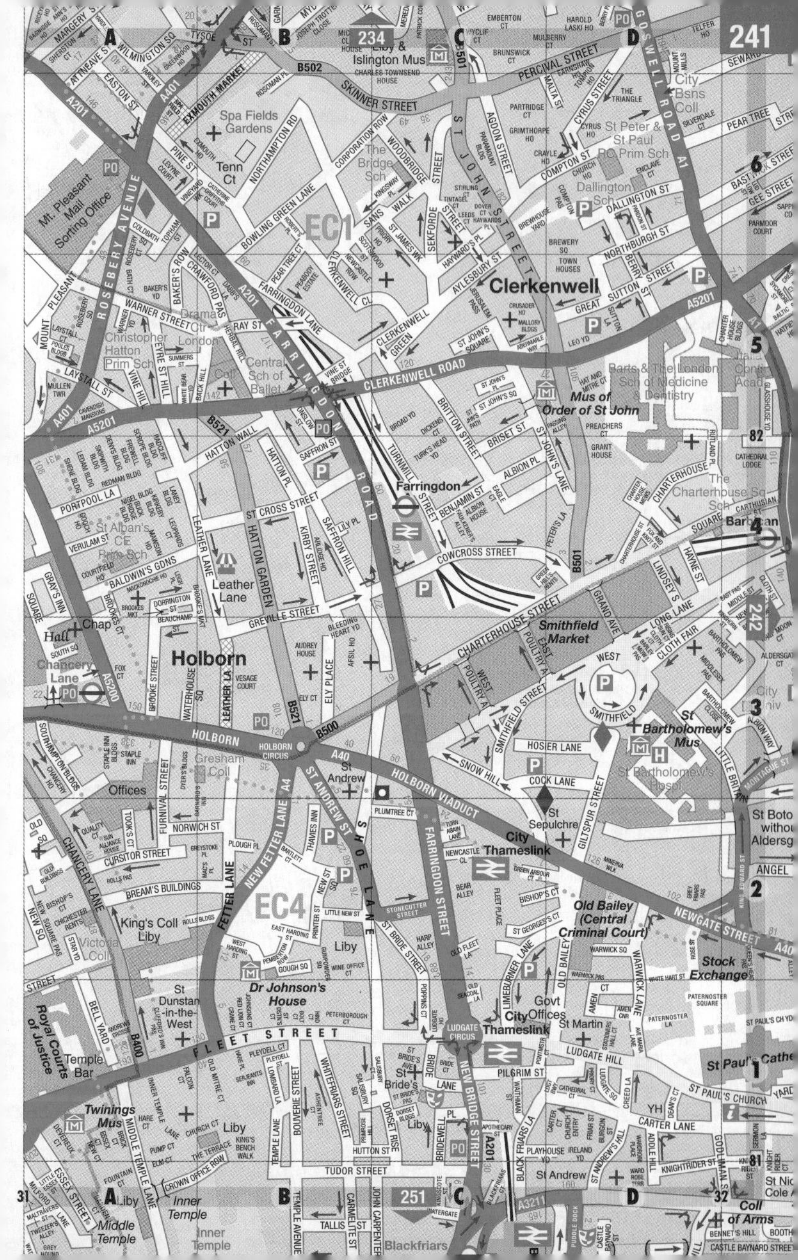
234
Liby & Islington Mus
B502
SKINNER STREET
PERCIVAL STREET
GOSWELL ROAD
A1
City Bsns Coll
Spa Fields Gardens
EXMOUTH MARKET
NORTHAMPTON RD
CORPORATION ROW
The Bridge Sch
WOODBRIDGE STREET
ST JOHN STREET
AGDON STREET
CYRUS STREET
St Peter & St Paul RC Prim Sch
COMPTON ST
Dallington Sch
DALLINGTON ST
NORTHBURGH ST
PEAR TREE
Mt. Pleasant Mail Sorting Office
ROSEBERY AVENUE
A401
A201
Tenn Ct
PINE ST
BOWLING GREEN LANE
EC1
SANS WALK
ST JAMES WK
SEKFORDE STREET
AYLESBURY ST
Clerkenwell
GREAT SUTTON ST
A5201
BERRY ST
FARRINGDON LANE
FARRINGDON ROAD
CLERKENWELL GREEN
CLERKENWELL ROAD
WARNER STREET
RAY ST
Drama Ctr London
Christopher Hatton Prim Sch
Central Sch of Ballet
MOUNT PLEASANT
LAYSTALL ST
VINE HILL
EYRE ST HILL
ST JOHN'S SQUARE
Barts & The London Sch of Medicine & Dentistry
Mus of Order of St John
BRITTON STREET
TURNMILL STREET
BRISET ST
ALBION PL
ST JOHN'S LANE
HATTON WALL
SAFFRON ST
HATTON PL
PORTPOOL LA
Farringdon
CHARTERHOUSE SQUARE
The Charterhouse Sq Sch
Barbican
ST CROSS STREET
St Alban's CE Prim Sch
VERULAM ST
LEATHER LANE
HATTON GARDEN
KIRBY STREET
SAFFRON HILL
COWCROSS STREET
B501
BALDWIN'S GDNS
GRAY'S INN SQUARE
Leather Lane
GREVILLE STREET
CHARTERHOUSE STREET
Smithfield Market
LINDSEY ST
LONG LANE
CLOTH FAIR
Chap
Hall
Holborn
Chancery Lane
A5200
BROOKE STREET
FOX CT
VESAGE COURT
ELY PLACE
WEST POULTRY A
EAST POULTRY A
GRAND AVE
WEST SMITHFIELD
242
HOLBORN
HOLBORN CIRCUS
B500
B521
A40
SMITHFIELD STREET
HOSIER LANE
COCK LANE
St Bartholomew's Mus
St Bartholomew's Hospl
LITTLE BRITAIN
Gresham Coll
Offices
St Andrew
HOLBORN VIADUCT
SNOW HILL
St Sepulchre
GILTSPUR STREET
St Boto without Aldersg
ANGEL
FURNIVAL STREET
NORWICH ST
CHANCERY LANE
CURSITOR STREET
NEW FETTER LANE
ST ANDREW ST
SHOE LANE
FARRINGDON STREET
City Thameslink
BREAM'S BUILDINGS
FETTER LANE
EC4
NEW ST SQ
FLEET PLACE
Old Bailey (Central Criminal Court)
NEWGATE STREET
King's Coll Liby
Victoria Coll
ST BRIDE STREET
Liby
Stock Exchange
Dr Johnson's House
St Dunstan-in-the-West
OLD BAILEY
LIMEBURNER LANE
WARWICK LANE
Govt Offices
City Thameslink
St Martin
Royal Courts of Justice
BELL YARD
Temple Bar
B400
FLEET STREET
LUDGATE CIRCUS
LUDGATE HILL
St Paul's Cathe
PILGRIM ST
St Bride's
BRIDE LANE
NEW BRIDGE STREET
ST PAUL'S CHURCH YARD
Twinings Mus
Liby
WHITEFRIARS STREET
BOUVERIE STREET
DORSET RISE
CARTER LANE
YH
HUTTON ST
A201
PLAYHOUSE YD
St Andrew
TUDOR STREET
KNIGHTRIDER ST
251
A3211
Inner Temple
Middle Temple
Liby
TALLIS ST
Blackfriars
Coll of Arms
St Nic Cole A
CASTLE BAYNARD STREET

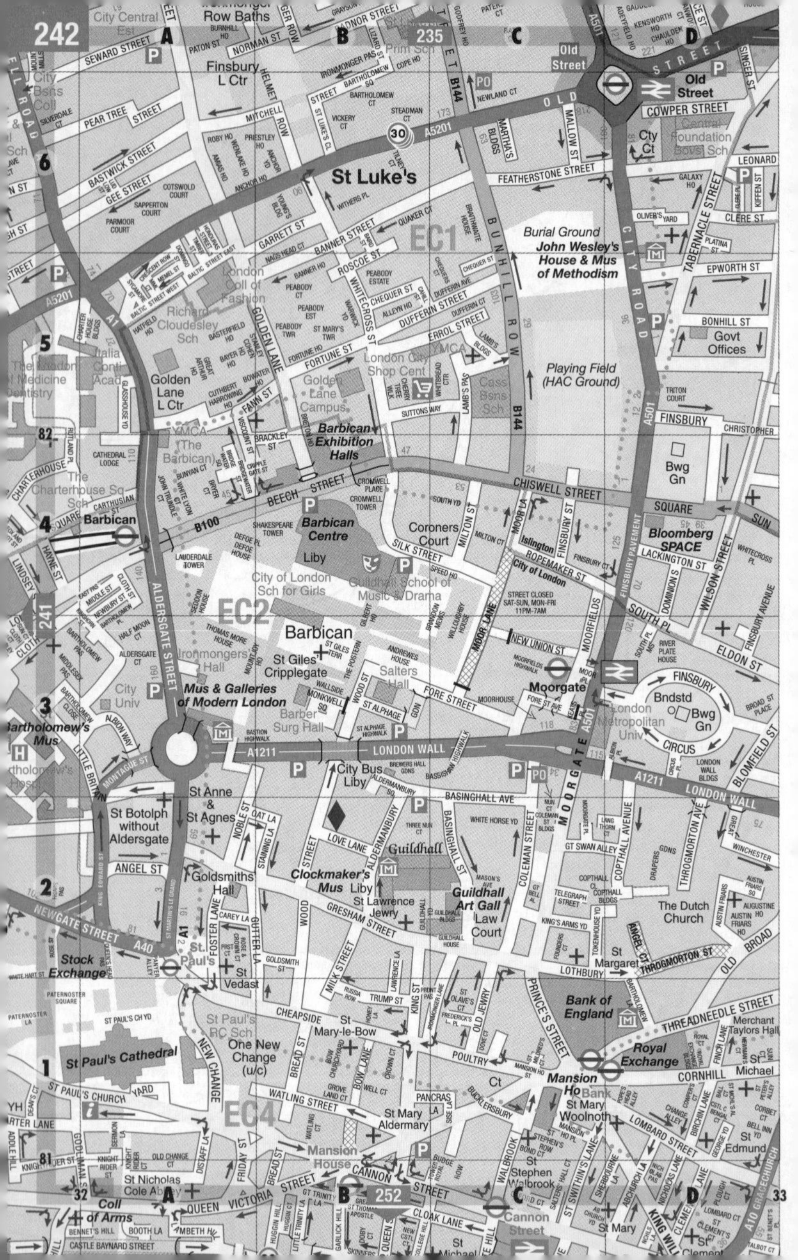
A
B
C
D
235
252
241
32
33
1
2
3
4
5
6
Old Street
Old Street
St Luke's
EC1
EC2
EC4
Finsbury L Ctr
City Bsns Coll
Golden Lane L Ctr
Burial Ground
John Wesley's House & Mus of Methodism
Playing Field (HAC Ground)
Govt Offices
City Ct
Central Foundation Boys' Sch
London Coll of Fashion
Richard Cloudesley Sch
Golden Lane Campus
London City Shop Cent
Cass Bsns Sch
Barbican Exhibition Halls
YMCA (The Barbican)
The Charterhouse Sq Sch
Barbican
Barbican Centre
Liby
City of London Sch for Girls
Guildhall School of Music & Drama
Coroners Court
Bwg Gn
Bloomberg SPACE
Islington
City of London
STREET CLOSED SAT-SUN, MON-FRI 11PM-7AM
Moorgate
Bndstd
London Metropolitan Univ
St Giles Cripplegate
Ironmongers Hall
Salters Hall
Barber Surg Hall
Mus & Galleries of Modern London
City Univ
Bartholomew's Mus
St Botolph without Aldersgate
St Anne & St Agnes
Goldsmiths Hall
City Bus Liby
Guildhall
Clockmaker's Mus
Liby
St Lawrence Jewry
Guildhall Art Gall
Law Court
The Dutch Church
St Margaret
Bank of England
Royal Exchange
Merchant Taylors Hall
St Michael
Stock Exchange
St. Paul's
St Vedast
St Paul's RC Sch
St Paul's Cathedral
One New Change (u/c)
St Mary-le-Bow
St Mary Aldermary
Mansion Ho
Bank
St Mary Woolnoth
St Edmund
Mansion House
St Nicholas Cole Abbey
St Stephen Walbrook
Cannon Street
Coll of Arms
St Mary
St Clement
OLD STREET
CITY ROAD
BUNHILL ROW
ALDERSGATE STREET
GOLDEN LANE
WHITECROSS ST
BEECH STREET
CHISWELL STREET
LONDON WALL
MOORGATE
MOOR LANE
FORE STREET
WOOD ST
NEWGATE STREET
CHEAPSIDE
POULTRY
CANNON STREET
QUEEN VICTORIA STREET
THREADNEEDLE STREET
CORNHILL
LOMBARD STREET
PRINCE'S STREET
GRESHAM STREET
COLEMAN STREET
FINSBURY PAVEMENT
FINSBURY SQUARE
FINSBURY CIRCUS
FEATHERSTONE STREET
TABERNACLE STREET
BASINGHALL ST
ALDERMANBURY
MILK STREET
BREAD ST
FRIDAY ST
WATLING STREET
NEW CHANGE
ST PAUL'S CHURCH YARD
KING EDWARD ST
ST MARTIN'S LE GRAND
GOSWELL ROAD
SEWARD STREET
PEAR TREE STREET
BASTWICK STREET
GEE STREET
ROPEMAKER ST
SILK STREET
MOORFIELDS
ELDON ST
BLOMFIELD ST
THROGMORTON ST
OLD BROAD ST
GRACECHURCH

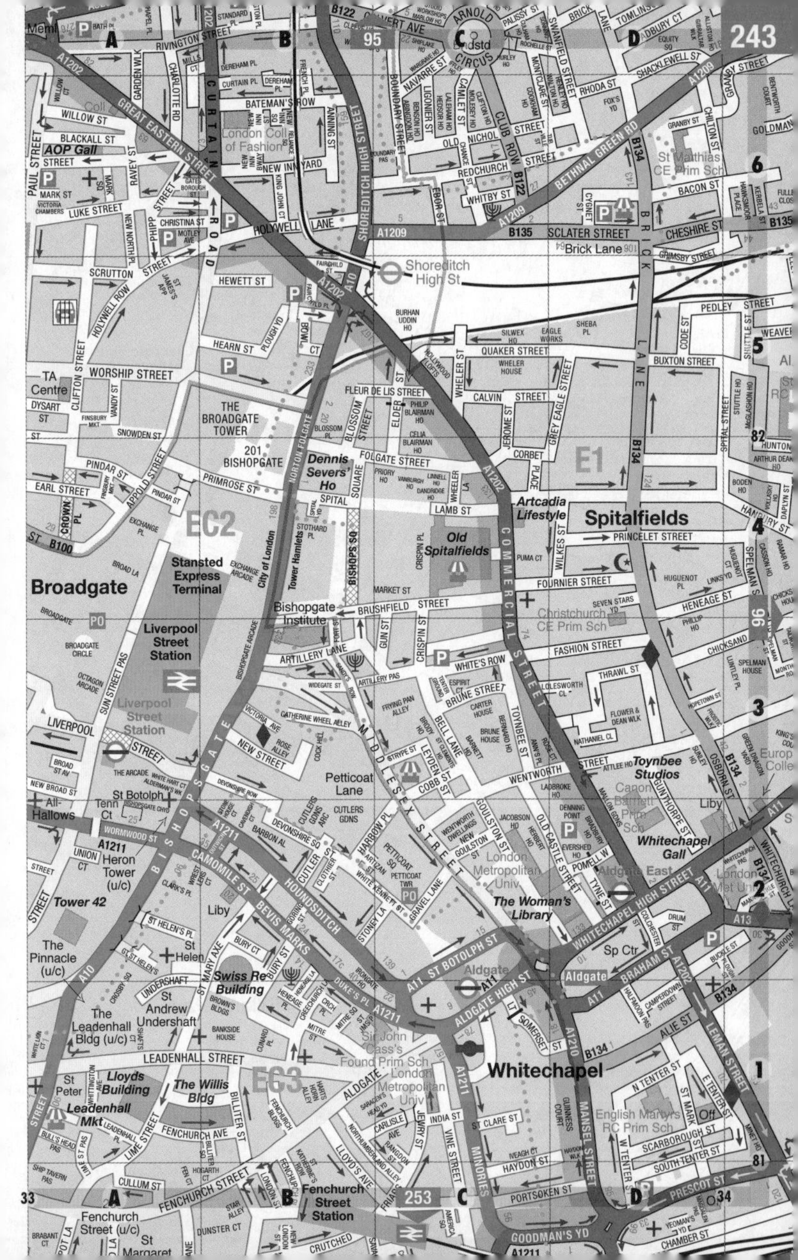

243
A
B
C
D
95
ARNOLD CIRCUS
RIVINGTON STREET
CALVERT AVE
GREAT EASTERN STREET
CURTAIN ROAD
CHARLOTTE RD
GARDEN WLK
WILLOW ST
BLACKALL ST
AOP Gall
PAUL STREET
MARK ST
LUKE STREET
RAVEY ST
CHRISTINA ST
MOTLEY AVE
HOLYWELL LANE
PHIPP STREET
SCRUTTON STREET
HOLYWELL ROW
HEWETT ST
CURTAIN PL
BATEMAN'S ROW
London Coll of Fashion
NEW INN YARD
ANNING ST
KING JOHN CT
SHOREDITCH HIGH STREET
BOUNDARY STREET
NAVARRE ST
LIGONIER ST
CAMLET ST
CLUB ROW
OLD NICHOL STREET
REDCHURCH STREET
WHITBY ST
EBOR ST
SWANFIELD STREET
MONTCLARE ST
RHODA ST
SHACKLEWELL ST
BRICK LANE
TOMLINSONS
GRANBY STREET
BETHNAL GREEN RD
A1209
B122
B134
B135
SCLATER STREET
CHESHIRE ST
BACON ST
GRIMSBY STREET
St Matthias CE Prim Sch
Brick Lane
Shoreditch High St
A1202
A10
WORSHIP STREET
TA Centre
CLIFTON STREET
DYSART ST
HEARN ST
PLOUGH YD
BOWL CT
QUAKER STREET
WHELER ST
WHELER HOUSE
CALVIN STREET
GREY EAGLE STREET
PEDLEY STREET
BUXTON STREET
CODE ST
WEAVER
THE BROADGATE TOWER
201 BISHOPGATE
SNOWDEN ST
PINDAR ST
APPOLD STREET
EARL STREET
PRIMROSE ST
NORTON FOLGATE
FLEUR DE LIS STREET
BLOSSOM STREET
ELDER ST
FOLGATE STREET
Dennis Severs' Ho
SPITAL SQUARE
LAMB ST
CORBET PLACE
JEROME ST
E1
Artcadia Lifestyle
Spitalfields
PRINCELET STREET
HANBURY ST
EC2
Broadgate
Stansted Express Terminal
City of London
Tower Hamlets
BISHOPS SQ
Old Spitalfields
CRISPIN PL
PUMA CT
WILKES ST
FOURNIER STREET
MARKET ST
Bishopgate Institute
BRUSHFIELD STREET
Christchurch CE Prim Sch
HENEAGE ST
FASHION STREET
CHICKSAND
PO
Liverpool Street Station
SUN STREET PAS
BROADGATE CIRCLE
OCTAGON ARCADE
ARTILLERY LANE
WHITE'S ROW
BRUNE STREET
THRAWL ST
FLOWER & DEAN WLK
96
Liverpool Street Station
LIVERPOOL STREET
BISHOPSGATE
VICTORIA AVE
NEW STREET
CATHERINE WHEEL ALLEY
FRYING PAN ALLEY
MIDDLESEX STREET
BELL LANE
TOYNBEE ST
WENTWORTH STREET
Toynbee Studios
Petticoat Lane
COBB ST
OSBORN ST
GUNTHORPE ST
Canon Barnett Prim Sch
Whitechapel Gall
All-Hallows
Tenn Ct
St Botolph
WORMWOOD ST
A1211
CAMOMILE ST
HOUNDSDITCH
DEVONSHIRE SQ
CUTLER ST
GOULSTON ST
London Metropolitan Univ
The Woman's Library
Aldgate East
WHITECHAPEL HIGH STREET
Heron Tower (u/c)
Tower 42
Liby
BEVIS MARKS
ST BOTOLPH ST
Aldgate
A11
Sp Ctr
BRAHAM ST
The Pinnacle (u/c)
St Helen
Swiss Re Building
DUKE'S PL
ALDGATE HIGH ST
St Andrew Undershaft
The Leadenhall Bldg (u/c)
LEADENHALL STREET
EC3
Sir John Cass's Found Prim Sch
London Metropolitan Univ
Whitechapel
ALIE ST
LEMAN STREET
Lloyds Building
The Willis Bldg
St Peter
Leadenhall Mkt
ALDGATE
FENCHURCH AVE
BILLITER ST
LIME STREET
MINORIES
MANSEL STREET
English Martyrs RC Prim Sch
SCARBOROUGH ST
SOUTH TENTER ST
CULLUM ST
FENCHURCH STREET
Fenchurch Street Station
253
PORTSOKEN ST
PRESCOT ST
GOODMAN'S YD
Fenchurch Street (u/c)
St Margaret
CRUTCHED
CHAMBER ST
1
2
3
4
5
6
33
34

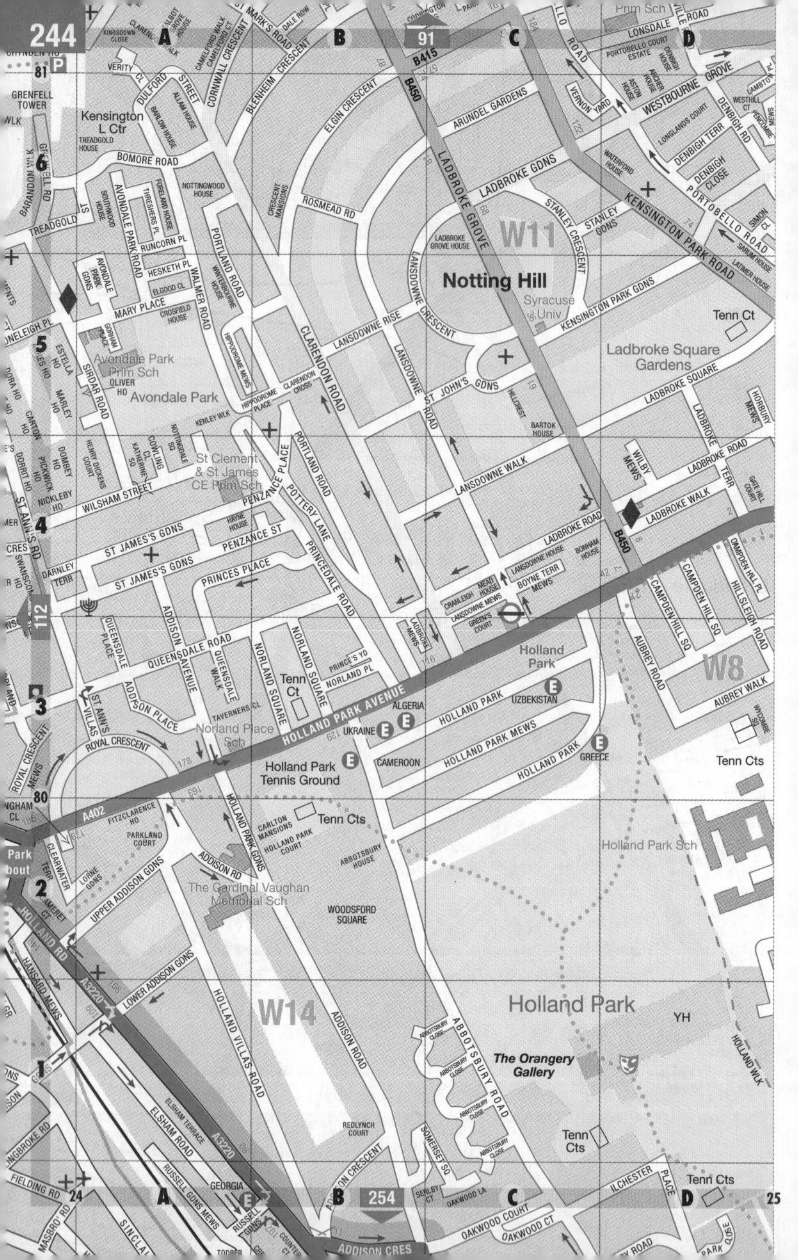

Notting Hill
W11
W8
W14
Holland Park
Holland Park Avenue
Ladbroke Grove
Kensington Park Road
Westbourne Grove
Portobello Road
Lansdowne Crescent
Ladbroke Square Gardens
Avondale Park
Avondale Park Prim Sch
Kensington L Ctr
Grenfell Tower
St Clement & St James CE Prim Sch
Norland Place Sch
Holland Park Tennis Ground
The Cardinal Vaughan Memorial Sch
Holland Park Sch
The Orangery Gallery
Syracuse Univ
Clarendon Road
Addison Road
Abbotsbury Road
Holland Villas Road
Holland Park Gdns
Royal Crescent
St Ann's Rd
Holland Rd
Elsham Road
Addison Cres
Oakwood Court
Ilchester Place
Holland Wlk
Ladbroke Road
Ladbroke Walk
Campden Hill Sq
Aubrey Road
Aubrey Walk
Hillsleigh Road
Lansdowne Walk
Lansdowne Rise
St John's Gdns
Stanley Crescent
Ladbroke Gdns
Arundel Gardens
Elgin Crescent
Blenheim Crescent
Rosmead Rd
Pottery Lane
Portland Road
Princedale Road
Penzance Place
Queensdale Road
Norland Square
Woodsford Square
Walmer Road
Bomore Road
Wilsham Street
Ukraine
Algeria
Cameroon
Uzbekistan
Greece
Georgia
91
112
254
A
B
C
D
1
2
3
4
5
6
24
25
80
81

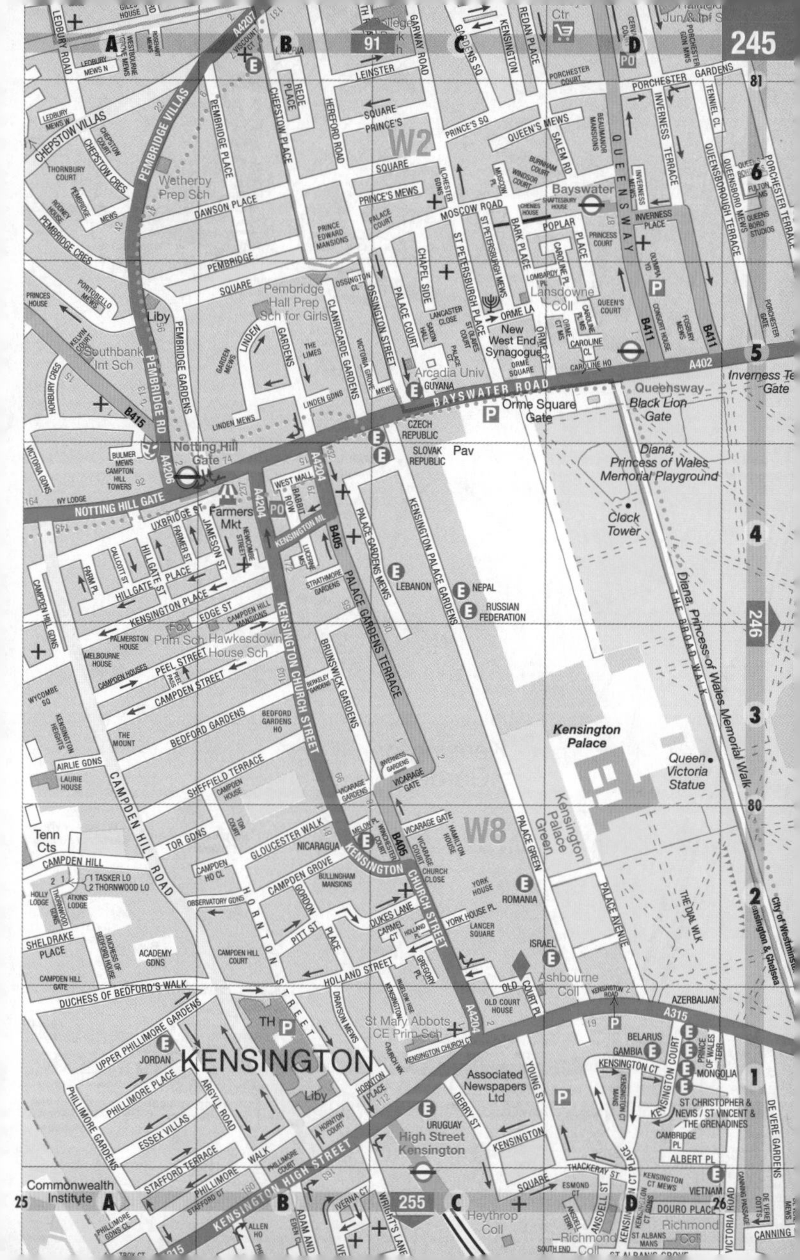
A
B
C
D
91
W2
W8
KENSINGTON
LEDBURY ROAD
LEDBURY MEWS N
LEDBURY MEWS W
WESTBOURNE GROVE MEWS
CHEPSTOW VILLAS
CHEPSTOW CRES
CHEPSTOW COURT
THORNBURY COURT
RODNEY HOUSE
PEMBRIDGE MEWS
PEMBRIDGE CRES
PEMBRIDGE VILLAS
PEMBRIDGE PLACE
PEMBRIDGE SQUARE
PEMBRIDGE GARDENS
PEMBRIDGE RD
Wetherby Prep Sch
DAWSON PLACE
PORTOBELLO MEWS
PRINCES HOUSE
KELVIN COURT
Southbank Int Sch
HORBURY CRES
Liby
Notting Hill Gate
NOTTING HILL GATE
BULMER MEWS
CAMPTON HILL TOWERS
IVY LODGE
VICTORIA GDNS
B415
A4206
A4207
VISCOUNT CT
LIBERIA
REDE PLACE
CHEPSTOW PLACE
HEREFORD ROAD
LEINSTER SQUARE
PRINCE'S SQUARE
PRINCE'S MEWS
GARWAY ROAD
PRINCE EDWARD MANSIONS
PALACE COURT
Pembridge Hall Prep Sch for Girls
LINDEN GARDENS
LINDEN MEWS
LINDEN GDNS
GARDEN MEWS
THE LIMES
CLANRICARDE GARDENS
VICTORIA GROVE MEWS
OSSINGTON CL
OSSINGTON STREET
GUYANA
Arcadia Univ
BAYSWATER ROAD
CZECH REPUBLIC
SLOVAK REPUBLIC
Pav
Orme Square Gate
ICHESTER GDNS
GARDENS SQ
KENSINGTON
REDAN PLACE
PORCHESTER COURT
PORCHESTER GARDENS
PORCHESTER TERRACE
PRINCE'S SQ
QUEEN'S MEWS
SALEM RD
BEAUMANOR MANSIONS
BURNHAM COURT
WINDSOR COURT
MOSCOW PL
MOSCOW ROAD
CHENIES HOUSE
SHAFTESBURY HOUSE
Bayswater
QUEENSWAY
INVERNESS TERRACE
INVERNESS MEWS
INVERNESS PLACE
OLYMPIA YD
CONSORT HOUSE
FOSBURY MEWS
QUEENSBOROUGH TERRACE
QUEENSBORO MEWS
QUEENS BORO STUDIOS
TENNIEL CL
FULTON MS
PORCHESTER GATE
BARK PLACE
POPLAR PLACE
PRINCESS COURT
CHAPEL SIDE
ST PETERSBURGH PLACE
ST PETERSBURGH MEWS
CAROLINE PL
CAROLINE PL MS
CAROLINE CL
CAROLINE HO
LOMBARDY PL
Lansdowne Coll
QUEEN'S COURT
LANCASTER CLOSE
SAXON HALL
PALACE CT
ST OLAVES COURT
ORME LA
ORME CT
ORME CT MS
ORME SQUARE
New West End Synagogue
B411
A402
Inverness Terrace Gate
Queensway Black Lion Gate
Diana, Princess of Wales Memorial Playground
Clock Tower
Diana, Princess of Wales Memorial Walk
THE BROAD WALK
Kensington Palace
Kensington Palace Green
Queen Victoria Statue
THE DIAL WLK
City of Westminster
Kensington & Chelsea
WEST MALL
RABBIT ROW
KENSINGTON ML
LUCERNE MS
STRATHMORE GARDENS
A4204
B405
PALACE GARDENS MEWS
PALACE GARDENS TERRACE
KENSINGTON PALACE GARDENS
LEBANON
NEPAL
RUSSIAN FEDERATION
UXBRIDGE ST
FARMER ST
JAMESON ST
NEWCOMBE STREET
Farmers Mkt
FARM PL
CALLCOTT ST
HILLGATE ST
HILLGATE PLACE
KENSINGTON PLACE
EDGE ST
CAMPDEN HILL MANSIONS
CAMPDEN HILL GDNS
PALMERSTON HOUSE
Fox Prim Sch
Hawkesdown House Sch
MELBOURNE HOUSE
PEEL STREET
PEEL PASS
CAMPDEN HOUSES
CAMPDEN STREET
WYCOMBE SQ
KENSINGTON HEIGHTS
THE MOUNT
BEDFORD GARDENS
BEDFORD GARDENS HO
KENSINGTON CHURCH STREET
BERKELEY GARDENS
BRUNSWICK GARDENS
AIRLIE GDNS
LAURIE HOUSE
SHEFFIELD TERRACE
CAMPDEN HOUSE
INVERNESS GARDENS
VICARAGE GATE
VICARAGE GARDENS
VICARAGE COURT
HAMILTON HOUSE
TOR COURT
TOR GDNS
GLOUCESTER WALK
NICARAGUA
MELON PL
WINCHESTER COURT
CAMPDEN HILL ROAD
Tenn Cts
CAMPDEN HILL
1 TASKER LO
2 THORNWOOD LO
HOLLY LODGE
THORNWOOD GDNS
ATKINS LODGE
CAMPDEN HO CL
CAMPDEN GROVE
BULLINGHAM MANSIONS
CHURCH CLOSE
GORDON PLACE
OBSERVATORY GDNS
HORNTON STREET
DUKES LANE
PITT ST
CARMEL CT
HOLLAND PL
YORK HOUSE
YORK HOUSE PL
LANCER SQUARE
ROMANIA
PALACE GREEN
PALACE AVENUE
ISRAEL
SHELDRAKE PLACE
DUCHESS OF BEDFORD HOUSE
ACADEMY GDNS
CAMPDEN HILL COURT
CAMPDEN HILL GATE
HOLLAND STREET
GREGORY PL
DUCHESS OF BEDFORD'S WALK
Ashbourne Coll
OLD COURT PL
OLD COURT HOUSE
KENSINGTON ROAD
AZERBAIJAN
A315
TH
DRAYSON MEWS
KENSINGTON CHURCH CT
St Mary Abbots CE Prim Sch
UPPER PHILLIMORE GARDENS
JORDAN
PHILLIMORE PLACE
PHILLIMORE GARDENS
ESSEX VILLAS
ARGYLL ROAD
CHURCH WK
HORNTON PLACE
HORNTON COURT
Associated Newspapers Ltd
DERRY ST
YOUNG ST
BELARUS
GAMBIA
KENSINGTON CT
KENSINGTON COURT
KENSINGTON CT MANS
PRINCE OF WALES TERR
MONGOLIA
ST CHRISTOPHER & NEVIS / ST VINCENT & THE GRENADINES
CAMBRIDGE PL
ALBERT PL
DE VERE GARDENS
URUGUAY
High Street Kensington
KENSINGTON SQUARE
THACKERAY ST
KENSINGTON CT PLACE
KENSINGTON CT MEWS
VIETNAM
STAFFORD TERRACE
PHILLIMORE WALK
PHILLIMORE COURT
KENSINGTON HIGH STREET
Commonwealth Institute
STAFFORD CT
PHILLIMORE GDNS CL
ALLEN HO
ADAM AND EDEN CL
IVERNA CT
WRIGHT'S LANE
255
Heythrop Coll
ESMOND CT
ANSDELL TERR
ANSDELL ST
Richmond Coll
DOURO PLACE
VICTORIA ROAD
CANNING PASSAGE
DE VERE COTTS
CANNING
ST ALBANS MANS
SOUTH END
246
25
26

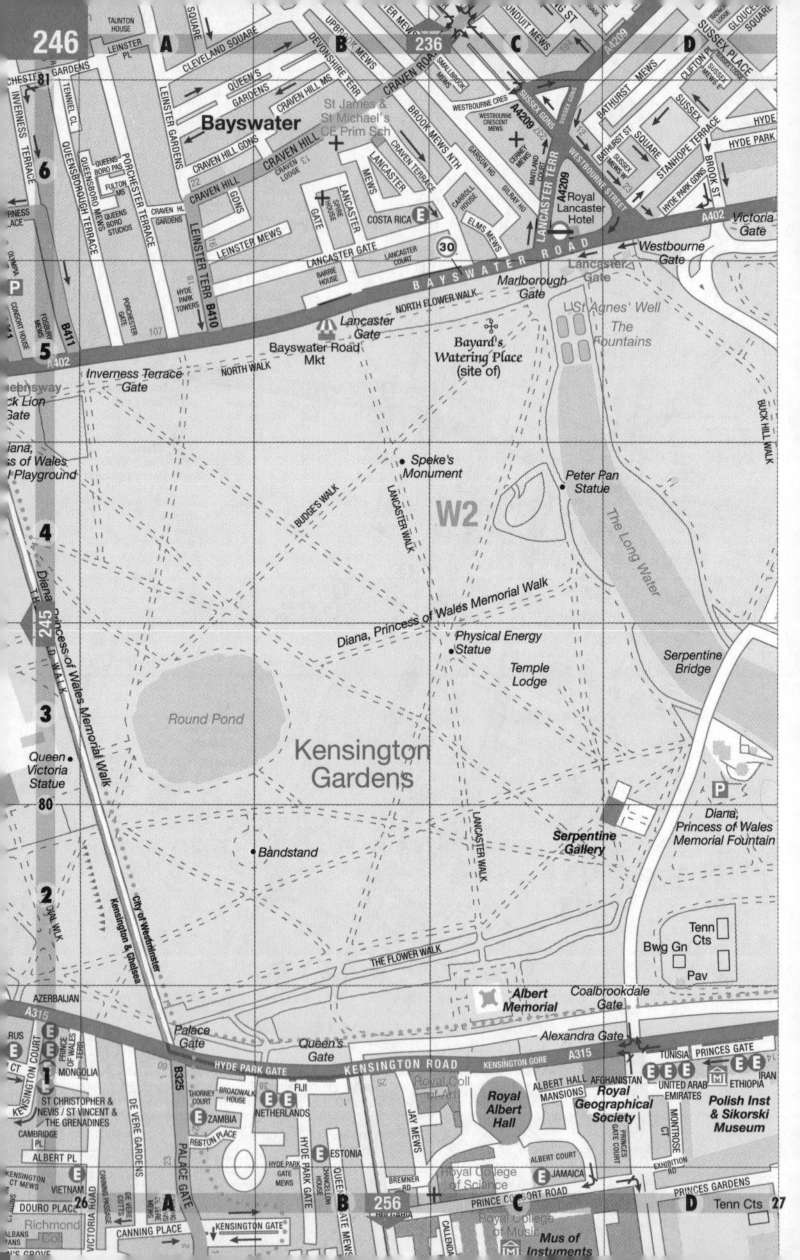

246
A
B
236
C
D
Bayswater
St James & St Michael's CE Prim Sch
CLEVELAND SQUARE
QUEEN'S GARDENS
LEINSTER GARDENS
CRAVEN HILL GDNS
CRAVEN HILL
CRAVEN ROAD
CRAVEN TERRACE
DEVONSHIRE TERR
UPBROOK MEWS
BROOK MEWS NTH
LANCASTER MEWS
LANCASTER GATE
LEINSTER MEWS
LEINSTER TERR
PORCHESTER TERRACE
QUEENSBOROUGH TERRACE
INVERNESS TERRACE
TENNIEL CL
WESTBOURNE CRES
SUSSEX GDNS
LANCASTER TERR
WESTBOURNE STREET
BATHURST MEWS
SUSSEX SQUARE
STANHOPE TERRACE
HYDE PARK GDNS
SUSSEX PLACE
CLIFTON PL
HYDE PARK
BROOK ST
Royal Lancaster Hotel
COSTA RICA
BAYSWATER ROAD
A402
A4209
B410
B411
Victoria Gate
Westbourne Gate
Lancaster Gate
Marlborough Gate
NORTH FLOWER WALK
Bayswater Road Mkt
Bayard's Watering Place (site of)
St Agnes' Well
The Fountains
Inverness Terrace Gate
NORTH WALK
BUCK HILL WALK
Speke's Monument
Peter Pan Statue
BUDGE'S WALK
LANCASTER WALK
W2
The Long Water
Diana, Princess of Wales Memorial Walk
Physical Energy Statue
Temple Lodge
Serpentine Bridge
Round Pond
Kensington Gardens
Queen Victoria Statue
Serpentine Gallery
Diana, Princess of Wales Memorial Fountain
Bandstand
Kensington & Chelsea
City of Westminster
THE FLOWER WALK
Tenn Cts
Bwg Gn
Pav
Albert Memorial
Coalbrookdale Gate
Palace Gate
Queen's Gate
Alexandra Gate
A315
HYDE PARK GATE
KENSINGTON ROAD
KENSINGTON GORE
PRINCES GATE
AZERBAIJAN
MONGOLIA
ST CHRISTOPHER & NEVIS / ST VINCENT & THE GRENADINES
NETHERLANDS
FIJI
ZAMBIA
ESTONIA
REFUGEE PLACE
Royal Coll of Art
Royal Albert Hall
ALBERT HALL MANSIONS
AFGHANISTAN
Royal Geographical Society
TUNISIA
UNITED ARAB EMIRATES
ETHIOPIA
IRAN
Polish Inst & Sikorski Museum
JAMAICA
ALBERT COURT
Royal College of Science
Royal College of Music
Mus of Instuments
PRINCE CONSORT ROAD
PRINCES GARDENS
VIETNAM
ALBERT PL
DE VERE GARDENS
PALACE GATE
B325
JAY MEWS
HYDE PARK GATE
VICTORIA ROAD
DOURO PLACE
CANNING PLACE
KENSINGTON GATE
256
Tenn Cts
27
26

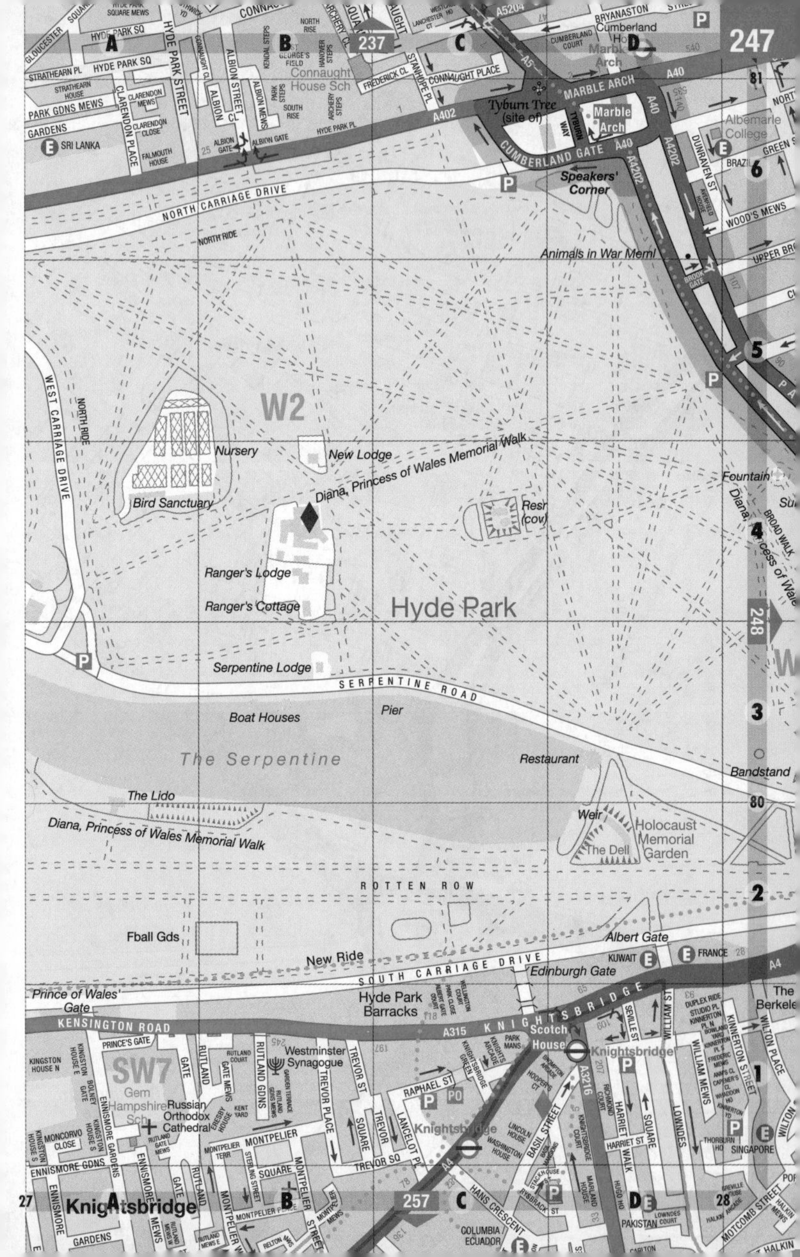
A
B
C
D
237
HYDE PARK SQ
HYDE PARK STREET
STRATHEARN PL
PARK GDNS MEWS
GARDENS
SRI LANKA
CLARENDON PLACE
ALBION STREET
ALBION GATE
Connaught House Sch
CONNAUGHT PLACE
FREDERICK CL
STANHOPE PL
HYDE PARK PL
BRYANASTON
Cumberland Ho
Marble Arch
MARBLE ARCH
Tyburn Tree (site of)
TYBURN WAY
CUMBERLAND GATE
Speakers' Corner
Albemarle College
DUNRAVEN ST
WOOD'S MEWS
UPPER BRO
NORTH CARRIAGE DRIVE
NORTH RIDE
Animals in War Meml
W2
WEST CARRIAGE DRIVE
Nursery
New Lodge
Diana, Princess of Wales Memorial Walk
Bird Sanctuary
Resr (cov)
Fountain
BROAD WALK
Ranger's Lodge
Ranger's Cottage
Hyde Park
248
Serpentine Lodge
SERPENTINE ROAD
Boat Houses
Pier
The Serpentine
Restaurant
Bandstand
The Lido
Weir
Holocaust Memorial Garden
The Dell
ROTTEN ROW
Fball Gds
Albert Gate
New Ride
KUWAIT
FRANCE
SOUTH CARRIAGE DRIVE
Edinburgh Gate
Prince of Wales' Gate
Hyde Park Barracks
KNIGHTSBRIDGE
KENSINGTON ROAD
A315
Scotch House
Knightsbridge
SW7
PRINCE'S GATE
RUTLAND GATE
Westminster Synagogue
TREVOR PLACE
TREVOR ST
Russian Orthodox Cathedral
RAPHAEL ST
BASIL STREET
WILLIAM ST
WILLIAM MEWS
KINNERTON STREET
WILTON PLACE
HARRIET WALK
LOWNDES SQUARE
SINGAPORE
ENNISMORE GARDENS
ENNISMORE GDNS
MONTPELIER SQUARE
MONTPELIER STREET
TREVOR SQ
HANS CRESCENT
COLUMBIA / ECUADOR
PAKISTAN
257
MOTCOMB STREET

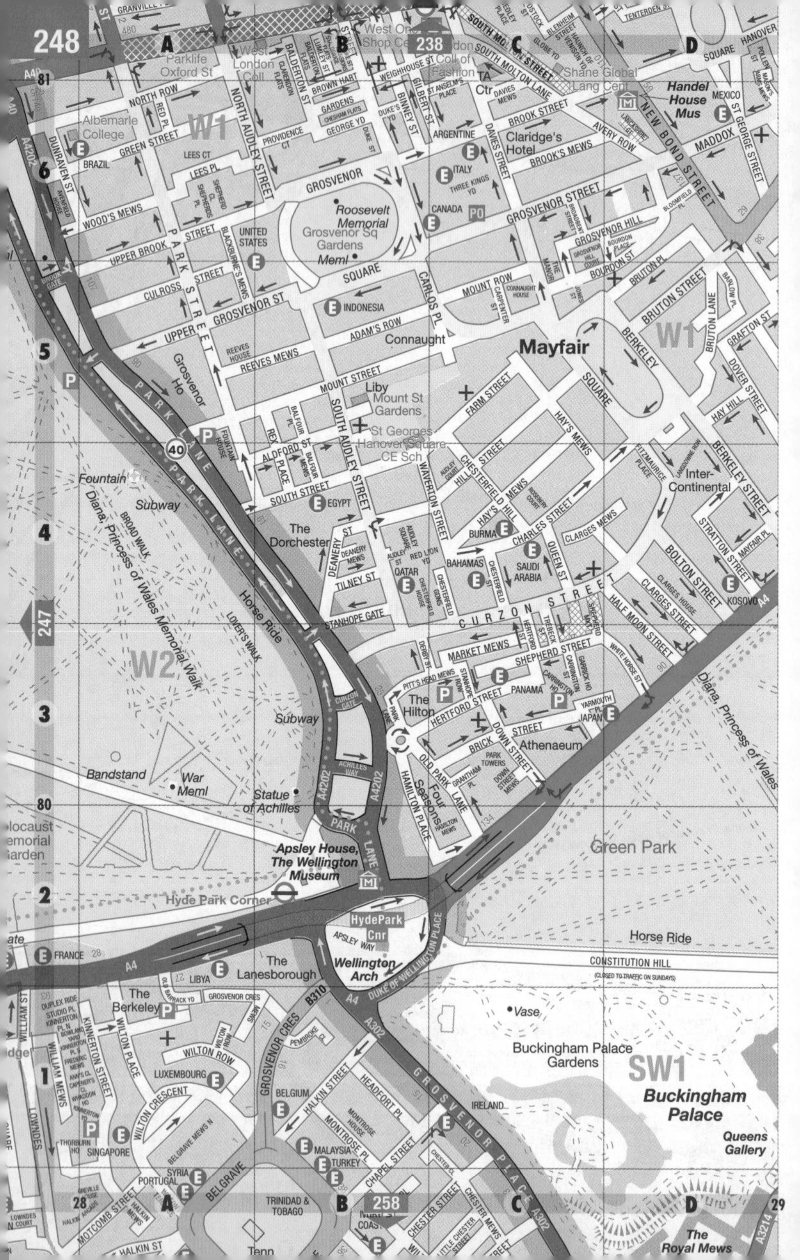
A
B
238
C
D
Parklife Oxford St
West London Coll
West One Shop Centre
London Coll of Fashion
GRANVILLE PL
NORTH ROW
RED PL
NORTH AUDLEY STREET
BALDERTON ST
BALDERTON FLATS
CLARENDON FLATS
LUMLEY ST
LUMLEY FLATS
BROWN HART GARDENS
CHESHAM FLATS
GEORGE YD
DUKE ST
DUKE'S YD
WEIGHHOUSE ST
BINNEY ST
GILBERT ST
ST ANSELM'S PLACE
TA Ctr
DAVIES MEWS
SOUTH MOLTON STREET
SOUTH MOLTON LANE
GLOBE YD
BLENHEIM STREET
HAUNCH OF VENISON YD
TENTERDEN ST
Shane Global Lang Cent
HANOVER SQUARE
POLLEN ST
MASON'S ARMS MEWS
Handel House Mus
MEXICO
ST GEORGE STREET
MADDOX ST
NEW BOND STREET
LANCASHIRE CT
AVERY ROW
BROOK STREET
Claridge's Hotel
BROOK'S MEWS
DAVIES STREET
ARGENTINE
ITALY
THREE KINGS YD
CANADA
PO
Albemarle College
W1
DUNRAVEN ST
BRAZIL
GREEN STREET
LEES CT
LEES PL
SHEPHERDS PL
SHEPHERDS CL
GROSVENOR
PROVIDENCE CT
Roosevelt Memorial
Grosvenor Sq Gardens
Meml
WOOD'S MEWS
AVENFIELD HOUSE
UPPER BROOK STREET
PARK STREET
UNITED STATES
BLACKBURNE'S MEWS
CULROSS STREET
UPPER GROSVENOR ST
SQUARE
INDONESIA
CARLOS PL
MOUNT ROW
CARPENTER ST
CONNAUGHT HOUSE
GROSVENOR STREET
BROADBENT STREET
GROSVENOR HILL
GROSVENOR HILL COURT
BOURDON PLACE
BOURDON ST
THE MANOR
JONES ST
BLOOMFIELD PL
BRUTON PL
BRUTON STREET
BARLOW PL
BRUTON LANE
GRAFTON ST
BERKELEY
SQUARE
W1
BROOK GATE
REEVES HOUSE
REEVES MEWS
ADAM'S ROW
Connaught
Mayfair
Grosvenor Ho
PARK LANE
MOUNT STREET
Liby
Mount St Gardens
St Georges Hanover Square CE Sch
FOUNTAIN HOUSE
BALFOUR PL
REX PLACE
ALDFORD ST
BALFOUR MEWS
SOUTH AUDLEY STREET
SOUTH STREET
EGYPT
FARM STREET
HAY'S MEWS
CHESTERFIELD HILL
HILL STREET
AUDLEY COURT
WAVERTON STREET
ROSEBERY COURT
CHARLES STREET
FITZMAURICE PLACE
LANSDOWNE ROW
Inter-Continental
BERKELEY STREET
HAY HILL
DOVER STREET
Fountain
Subway
BROAD WALK
Diana, Princess of Wales Memorial Walk
The Dorchester
DEANERY ST
DEANERY MEWS
AUDLEY SQUARE
AUDLEY ST
RED LION YD
QATAR
BURMA
BAHAMAS
CHESTERFIELD ST
SAUDI ARABIA
QUEEN ST
CLARGES MEWS
STRATTON STREET
MAYFAIR PL
BOLTON STREET
CLARGES STREET
CLARGES HOUSE
KOSOVO
A4
TILNEY ST
CHESTERFIELD GDNS
CHESTERFIELD HOUSE
STANHOPE GATE
CURZON STREET
HERTFORD ST
TREBECK ST
SHEPHERD MKT
HALF MOON STREET
LOVER'S WALK
Horse Ride
247
W2
DERBY ST
MARKET MEWS
SHEPHERD STREET
CARRINGTON STREET
GARRICK HO
WHITE HORSE ST
PITT'S HEAD MEWS
STANHOPE ROW
PANAMA
CARRINGTON HO
CURZON GATE
The Hilton
PARK LANE
HERTFORD STREET
YARMOUTH PL
JAPAN
Subway
DOWN STREET
BRICK STREET
Athenaeum
ACHILLES WAY
OLD PARK LANE
PARK TOWERS
GRANTHAM PL
DOWN STREET MEWS
HAMILTON PLACE
Four Seasons
HAMILTON MEWS
Bandstand
War Meml
Statue of Achilles
A4202
Holocaust Memorial Garden
Green Park
Apsley House, The Wellington Museum
Hyde Park Corner
HydePark Cnr
APSLEY WAY
DUKE OF WELLINGTON PLACE
Horse Ride
CONSTITUTION HILL
(CLOSED TO TRAFFIC ON SUNDAYS)
FRANCE
LIBYA
The Lanesborough
Wellington Arch
The Berkeley
OLD BARRACK YD
GROSVENOR CRES
GROSVENOR CRES MEWS
B310
A302
Vase
WILLIAM ST
DUPLEX RIDE
STUDIO PL
KINNERTON PL N
BOWLAND YARD
KINNERTON PL S
FREDERIC MEWS
KINNERTON STREET
WILTON PLACE
WILTON ROW
PEMBROKE CL
Buckingham Palace Gardens
SW1
WILLIAM MEWS
ANN'S CL
CAPENER'S CL
WHADDON HO
KINNERTON YD
LUXEMBOURG
WILTON CRESCENT
BELGRAVE MEWS N
HALKIN STREET
HEADFORT PL
GROSVENOR PLACE
BELGIUM
MONTROSE HOUSE
MONTROSE PL
IRELAND
Buckingham Palace
Queens Gallery
LOWNDES
THORBURN HO
SINGAPORE
MALAYSIA
TURKEY
CHAPEL STREET
CHESTER CL
SYRIA
PORTUGAL
BELGRAVE
GREVILLE HOUSE
HALKIN ARCADE
MOTCOMB STREET
HALKIN MEWS
TRINIDAD & TOBAGO
258
CHESTER STREET
CHESTER MEWS
A302
The Royal Mews
A3214
LOWNDES COURT
HALKIN ST
LITTLE CHESTER STREET
28
29
81
80
6
5
4
3
2
1
40

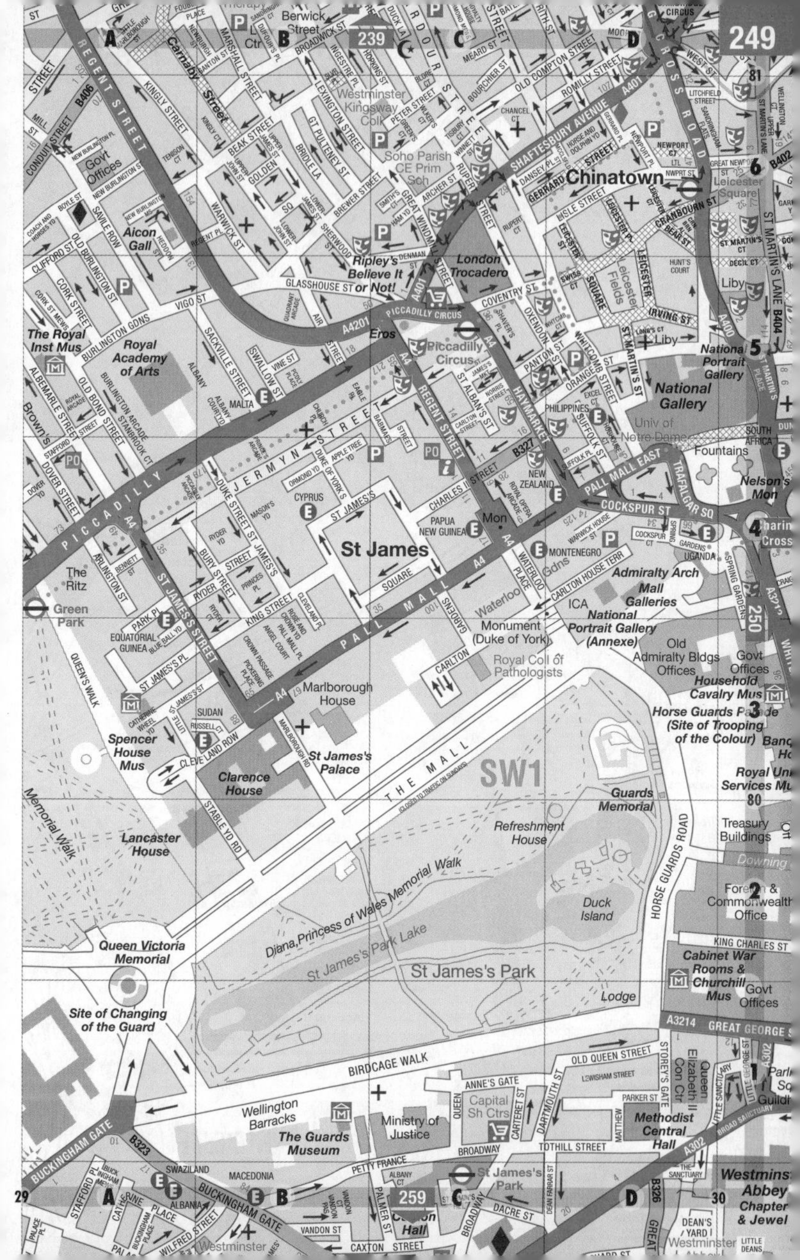

249
239
259
250
Regent Street
Carnaby Street
Berwick Street
Broadwick St
Wardour Street
Old Compton Street
Shaftesbury Avenue
Charing Cross Road
Chinatown
Gerrard Street
Leicester Square
Leicester Fields
Cranbourn St
St Martin's Lane
Westminster Kingsway Colk
Soho Parish CE Prim Sch
Govt Offices
Aicon Gall
Savile Row
Old Burlington St
Cork Street
Clifford St
Conduit Street
Beak Street
Golden Sq
Brewer Street
Great Windmill Street
Ripley's Believe It or Not!
London Trocadero
Glasshouse St
Vigo St
Burlington Gdns
Royal Academy of Arts
The Royal Inst Mus
Albemarle Street
Old Bond Street
Dover Street
Sackville Street
Piccadilly Circus
Piccadilly
Eros
Coventry St
Haymarket
Jermyn Street
Duke Street St James's
St James's Street
St James
St James's Square
Pall Mall
Pall Mall East
Cockspur St
Trafalgar Sq
National Portrait Gallery
National Gallery
Univ of Notre Dame
Fountains
Nelson's Mon
Charing Cross
The Ritz
Green Park
Arlington St
King Street
Charles II Street
Waterloo Place
Waterloo Gdns
Carlton House Terr
Admiralty Arch
Mall Galleries
ICA
National Portrait Gallery (Annexe)
Monument (Duke of York)
Royal Coll of Pathologists
Old Admiralty Bldgs Offices
Govt Offices
Household Cavalry Mus
Horse Guards Parade (Site of Trooping of the Colour)
Royal United Services Mus
Treasury Buildings
Marlborough House
St James's Palace
Clarence House
Lancaster House
Spencer House Mus
Queen's Walk
Cleveland Row
Stable Yd Rd
The Mall
SW1
Guards Memorial
Refreshment House
Horse Guards Road
Duck Island
Diana, Princess of Wales Memorial Walk
St James's Park Lake
St James's Park
Queen Victoria Memorial
Site of Changing of the Guard
Memorial Walk
Lodge
Foreign & Commonwealth Office
King Charles St
Cabinet War Rooms & Churchill Mus
Great George St
Birdcage Walk
Old Queen Street
Queen Anne's Gate
Wellington Barracks
The Guards Museum
Ministry of Justice
Capital Sh Ctrs
Dartmouth St
Tothill Street
Broadway
Petty France
Buckingham Gate
St James's Park
Queen Elizabeth II Con Ctr
Methodist Central Hall
Storey's Gate
Broad Sanctuary
Westminster Abbey Chapter & Jewel
Caxton Street
Palmer St
Dacre St
Vandon St
Wilfred Street
Catherine Place
Stafford Pl
Malta
Cyprus
Papua New Guinea
New Zealand
Montenegro
Philippines
Uganda
South Africa
Equatorial Guinea
Sudan
Swaziland
Macedonia
Albania
29
30

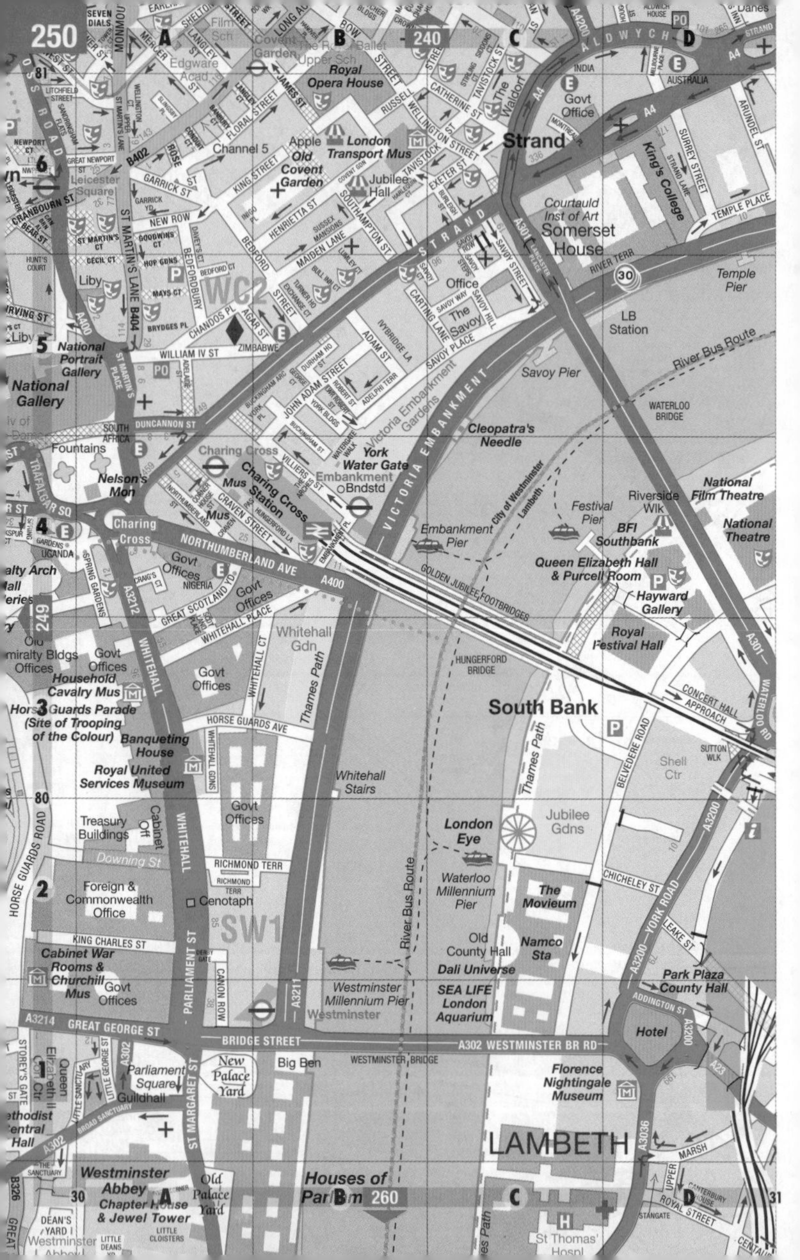
Royal Opera House
London Transport Mus
Old Covent Garden
Jubilee Hall
Strand
The Waldorf
Govt Office
INDIA
AUSTRALIA
ALDWYCH
King's College
Courtauld Inst of Art
Somerset House
Temple Pier
Temple Place
River Terr
LB Station
The Savoy
Savoy Place
Savoy Pier
River Bus Route
Waterloo Bridge
Leicester Square
Cranbourn St
St Martin's Lane
Garrick St
New Row
Bedfordbury
WC2
Chandos Pl
Agar St
William IV St
National Portrait Gallery
National Gallery
Duncannon St
South Africa
Fountains
Nelson's Mon
Trafalgar Sq
Charing Cross
Charing Cross Station
Craven Street
Northumberland Ave
Embankment
Bndstd
York Water Gate
Victoria Embankment
Victoria Embankment Gardens
Cleopatra's Needle
Embankment Pier
Golden Jubilee Footbridges
Festival Pier
Riverside Wlk
National Film Theatre
National Theatre
BFI Southbank
Queen Elizabeth Hall & Purcell Room
Hayward Gallery
Royal Festival Hall
Hungerford Bridge
South Bank
Belvedere Road
Concert Hall Approach
Waterloo Rd
Shell Ctr
Jubilee Gdns
London Eye
Waterloo Millennium Pier
The Movieum
Namco Sta
Old County Hall
Dali Universe
SEA LIFE London Aquarium
Chicheley St
York Road
Leake St
Park Plaza County Hall
Addington St
Hotel
Westminster Br Rd
Florence Nightingale Museum
LAMBETH
Upper Marsh
Royal Street
St Thomas' Hospl
Great Scotland Yd
Whitehall Place
Whitehall
Whitehall Gdn
Thames Path
Govt Offices
Old Admiralty Bldgs
Household Cavalry Mus
Horse Guards Parade (Site of Trooping of the Colour)
Horse Guards Ave
Banqueting House
Royal United Services Museum
Whitehall Stairs
Treasury Buildings
Cabinet Off
Downing St
Richmond Terr
Foreign & Commonwealth Office
Cenotaph
SW1
King Charles St
Cabinet War Rooms & Churchill Mus
Parliament St
Canon Row
Westminster Millennium Pier
Westminster
Great George St
Bridge Street
Westminster Bridge
Big Ben
New Palace Yard
Parliament Square
Guildhall
Queen Elizabeth II Conf Ctr
Methodist Central Hall
Broad Sanctuary
Westminster Abbey
Chapter House & Jewel Tower
Old Palace Yard
Houses of Parliament
St Margaret St
Little Cloisters
Dean's Yard

240
249
260

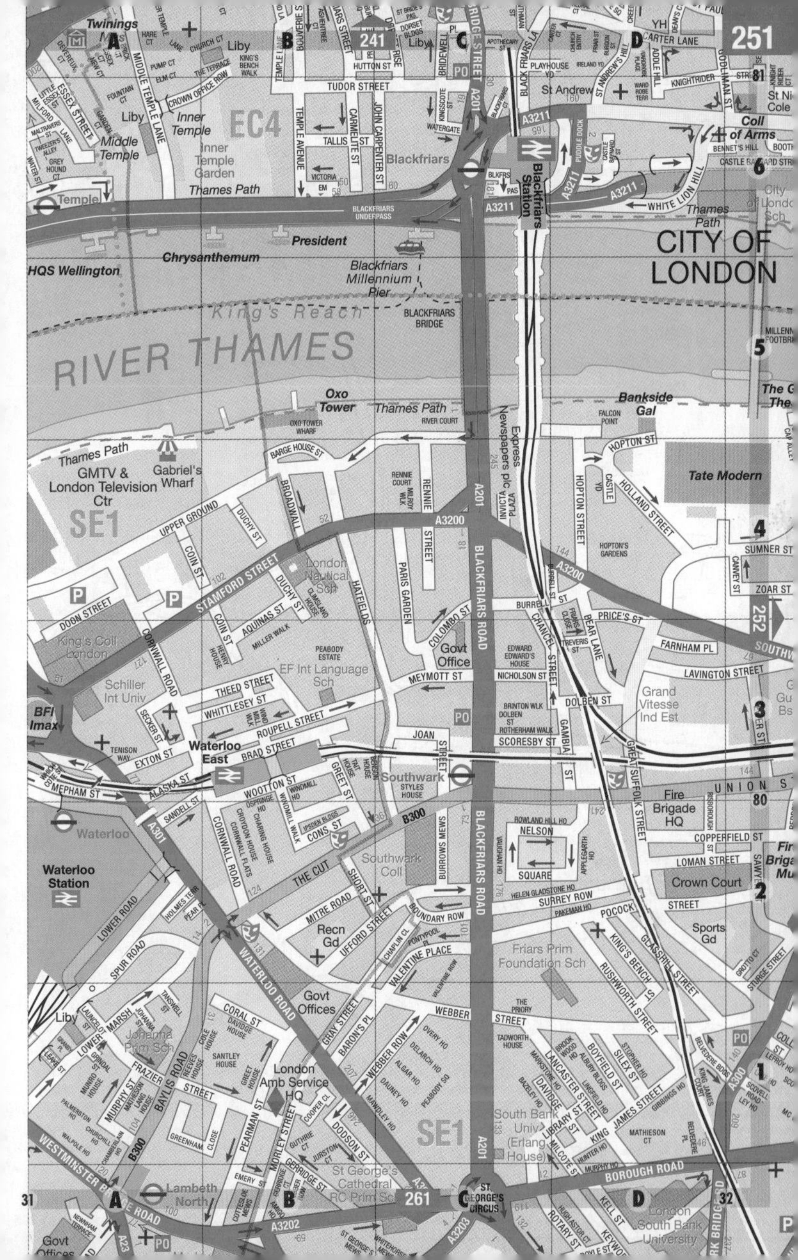

CITY OF LONDON
RIVER THAMES
King's Reach
EC4
SE1
Twinings
Inner Temple
Middle Temple
Inner Temple Garden
Thames Path
Temple
Blackfriars
Blackfriars Station
Blackfriars Millennium Pier
BLACKFRIARS BRIDGE
BLACKFRIARS UNDERPASS
President
Chrysanthemum
HQS Wellington
St Andrew
Coll of Arms
Oxo Tower
OXO TOWER WHARF
Bankside Gal
Tate Modern
GMTV & London Television Ctr
Gabriel's Wharf
Express Newspapers plc
London Nautical Sch
King's Coll London
Schiller Int Univ
EF Int Language Sch
Govt Office
Grand Vitesse Ind Est
BFI Imax
Waterloo East
Southwark
Waterloo
Waterloo Station
Fire Brigade HQ
Southwark Coll
Crown Court
Recn Gd
Sports Gd
Friars Prim Foundation Sch
Govt Offices
Johanna Prim Sch
London Amb Service HQ
South Bank Univ (Erlang House)
St George's Cathedral RC Prim Sch
Lambeth North
ST GEORGE'S CIRCUS
London South Bank University
STAMFORD STREET
BLACKFRIARS ROAD
WATERLOO ROAD
THE CUT
UNION ST
BOROUGH ROAD
WESTMINSTER BRIDGE ROAD
NELSON SQUARE
A201
A3200
A3211
A301
B300
A3202
A3203
A300
A23
241
252
261

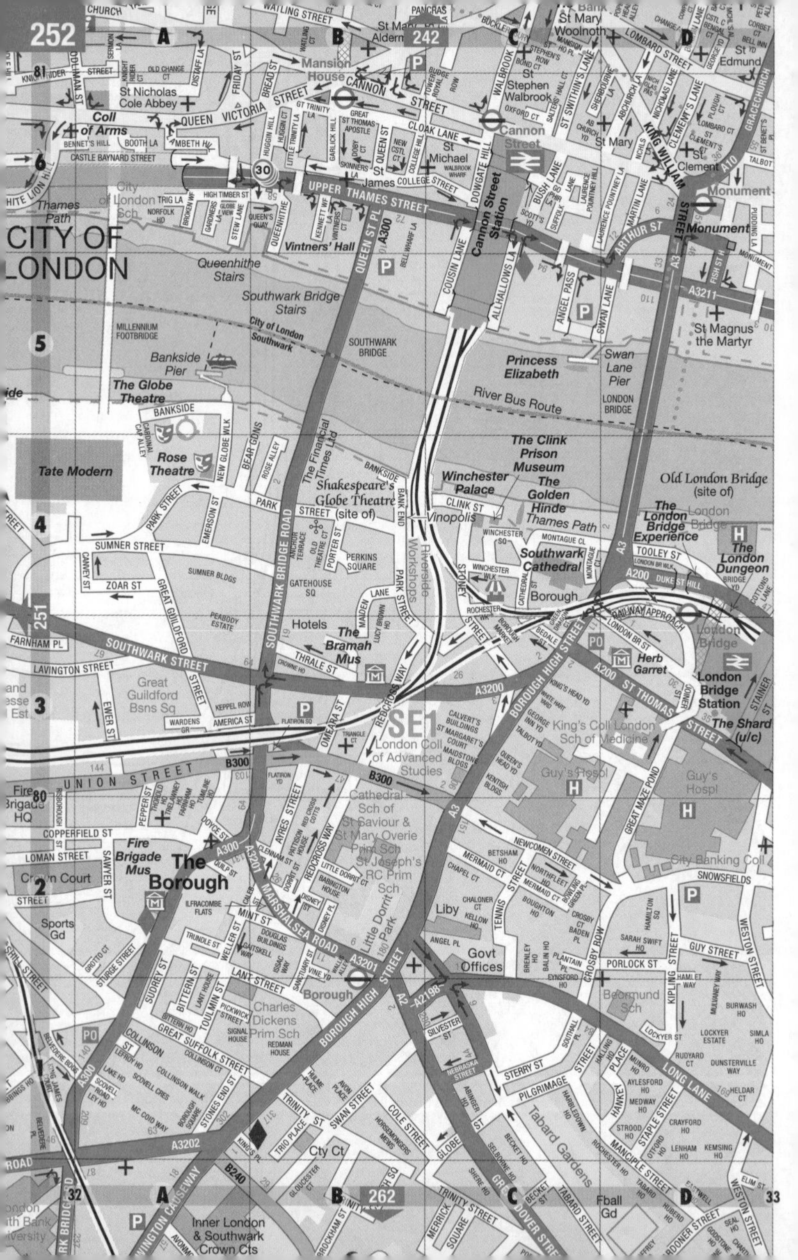

CITY OF LONDON
SE1
The Borough
Mansion House
Cannon Street
Queen Victoria Street
Upper Thames Street
Cannon Street Station
Monument
St Magnus the Martyr
St Nicholas Cole Abbey
Coll of Arms
St Stephen Walbrook
St Mary Woolnoth
St Edmund
St Clement
St Michael
St James
St Mary
Vintners' Hall
Queenhithe Stairs
Southwark Bridge Stairs
City of London
Southwark
Southwark Bridge
Millennium Footbridge
Bankside Pier
The Globe Theatre
Tate Modern
Rose Theatre
Princess Elizabeth
Swan Lane Pier
London Bridge
River Bus Route
Thames Path
The Clink Prison Museum
Winchester Palace
The Golden Hinde
The Financial Times Ltd
Shakespeare's Globe Theatre (site of)
Vinopolis
Old London Bridge (site of)
The London Bridge Experience
The London Dungeon
Southwark Cathedral
Borough
Riverside Workshops
Hotels
The Bramah Mus
Herb Garret
London Bridge Station
The Shard (u/c)
King's Coll London Sch of Medicine
Guy's Hospl
London Coll of Advanced Studies
Cathedral Sch of St Saviour & St Mary Overie Prim Sch
St Joseph's RC Prim Sch
Little Dorrit Park
Liby
Govt Offices
Charles Dickens Prim Sch
Fire Brigade Mus
Fire Brigade HQ
Crown Court
Sports Gd
Great Guildford Bsns Sq
City Banking Coll
Bermund Sch
Tabard Gardens
Fball Gd
Cty Ct
Inner London & Southwark Crown Cts
Southwark Street
Southwark Bridge Road
Borough High Street
Union Street
Marshalsea Road
Great Suffolk Street
Long Lane
Snowsfields
Weston Street
Tooley St
St Thomas Street
Great Maze Pond
Newcomen Street
Park Street
Sumner Street
Bankside
A3
A300
A3200
A3201
A3202
A3211
A200
A2
A2198
B300
B240
242
251
262
A B C D
1 2 3 4 5 6

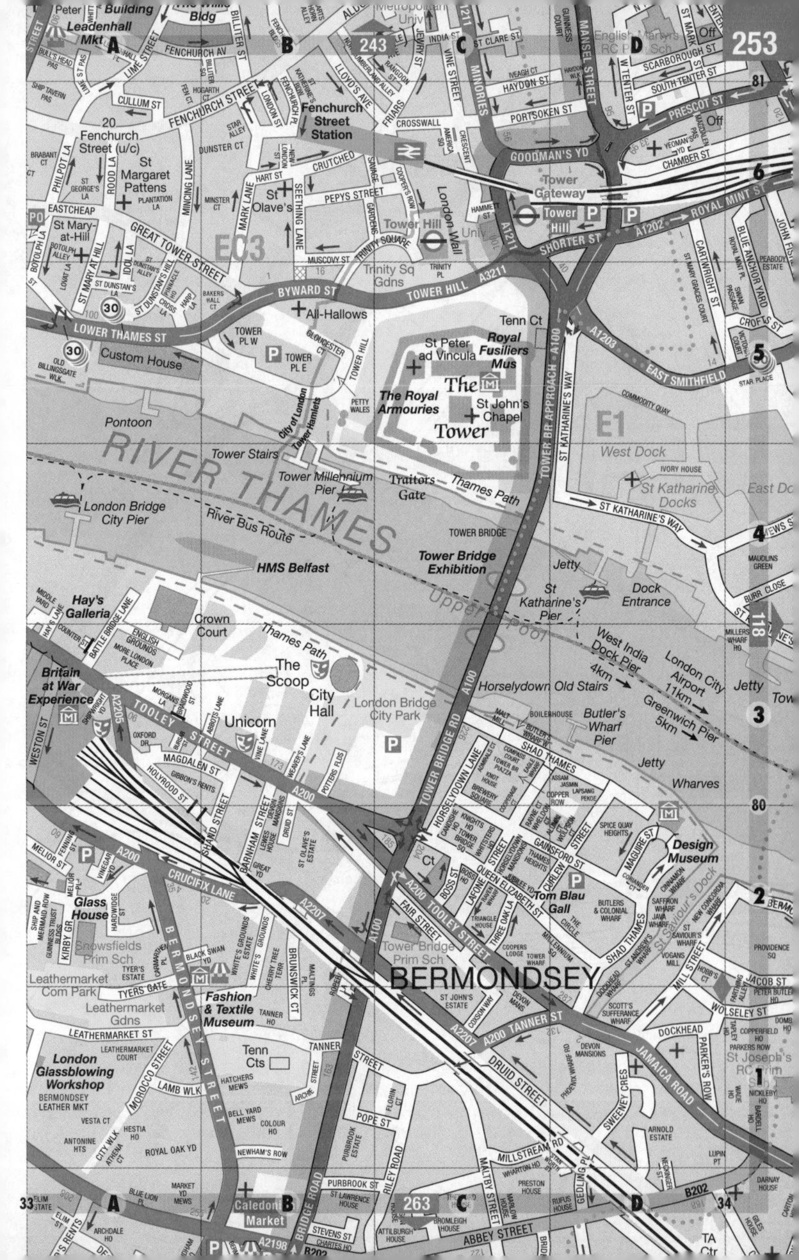
Leadenhall Mkt
Fenchurch Street (u/c)
St Margaret Pattens
Fenchurch Street Station
FENCHURCH AV
FENCHURCH STREET
BILLITER ST
LIME STREET
CULLUM ST
MINCING LANE
MARK LANE
SEETHING LANE
CRUTCHED
PEPYS STREET
St Olave's
COOPER'S ROW
London Wall
MINORIES
VINE STREET
JEWRY ST
INDIA ST
ST CLARE ST
HAYDON ST
PORTSOKEN ST
CROSSWALL
GOODMAN'S YD
MANSEL STREET
English Martyrs RC Prim Sch
SCARBOROUGH ST
SOUTH TENTER ST
PRESCOT ST
CHAMBER ST
Tower Gateway
Tower Hill
Tower Hill
SHORTER ST
ROYAL MINT ST
A1202
EASTCHEAP
St Mary-at-Hill
GREAT TOWER STREET
EC3
BYWARD ST
TOWER HILL
A3211
Trinity Sq Gdns
TRINITY SQUARE
MUSCOVY ST
LOWER THAMES ST
All-Hallows
Custom House
TOWER PL W
TOWER PL E
Tenn Ct
St Peter ad Vincula
Royal Fusiliers Mus
The Royal Armouries
The Tower
St John's Chapel
TOWER BR APPROACH
A100
ST KATHARINE'S WAY
EAST SMITHFIELD
A1203
E1
West Dock
IVORY HOUSE
St Katharine Docks
Pontoon
RIVER THAMES
Tower Stairs
Tower Millennium Pier
Traitors Gate
Thames Path
London Bridge City Pier
River Bus Route
TOWER BRIDGE
Tower Bridge Exhibition
HMS Belfast
Jetty
St Katharine's Pier
Dock Entrance
Upper Pool
Hay's Galleria
Crown Court
Thames Path
West India Dock Pier 4km
London City Airport 11km
Greenwich Pier 5km
Britain at War Experience
The Scoop
City Hall
London Bridge City Park
Horselydown Old Stairs
Butler's Wharf Pier
Unicorn
TOOLEY STREET
TOWER BRIDGE RD
SHAD THAMES
Jetty
Wharves
MAGDALEN ST
A200
SHAND STREET
GARNHAM STREET
HORSELYDOWN LANE
GAINSFORD ST
Design Museum
MAGUIRE ST
Glass House
CRUCIFIX LANE
A2207
QUEEN ELIZABETH ST
Tom Blau Gall
St Saviour's Dock
Snowsfields Prim Sch
Leathermarket Com Park
Leathermarket Gdns
TYERS GATE
BERMONDSEY STREET
Fashion & Textile Museum
Tower Bridge Prim Sch
BERMONDSEY
A200 TANNER ST
JAMAICA ROAD
DOCKHEAD
PARKER'S ROW
MILL STREET
JACOB ST
WOLSELEY ST
LEATHERMARKET ST
London Glassblowing Workshop
BERMONDSEY LEATHER MKT
MOROCCO STREET
LAMB WLK
Tenn Cts
DRUID STREET
St Joseph's RC Prim Sch
POPE ST
RILEY ROAD
ROYAL OAK YD
NEWHAM'S ROW
MILLSTREAM RD
BRIDGE ROAD
PURBROOK ST
MALTBY STREET
Caledonian Market
ABBEY STREET
B202
A2198
A B C D
243
263
118
33
34
81
80
1 2 3 4 5 6

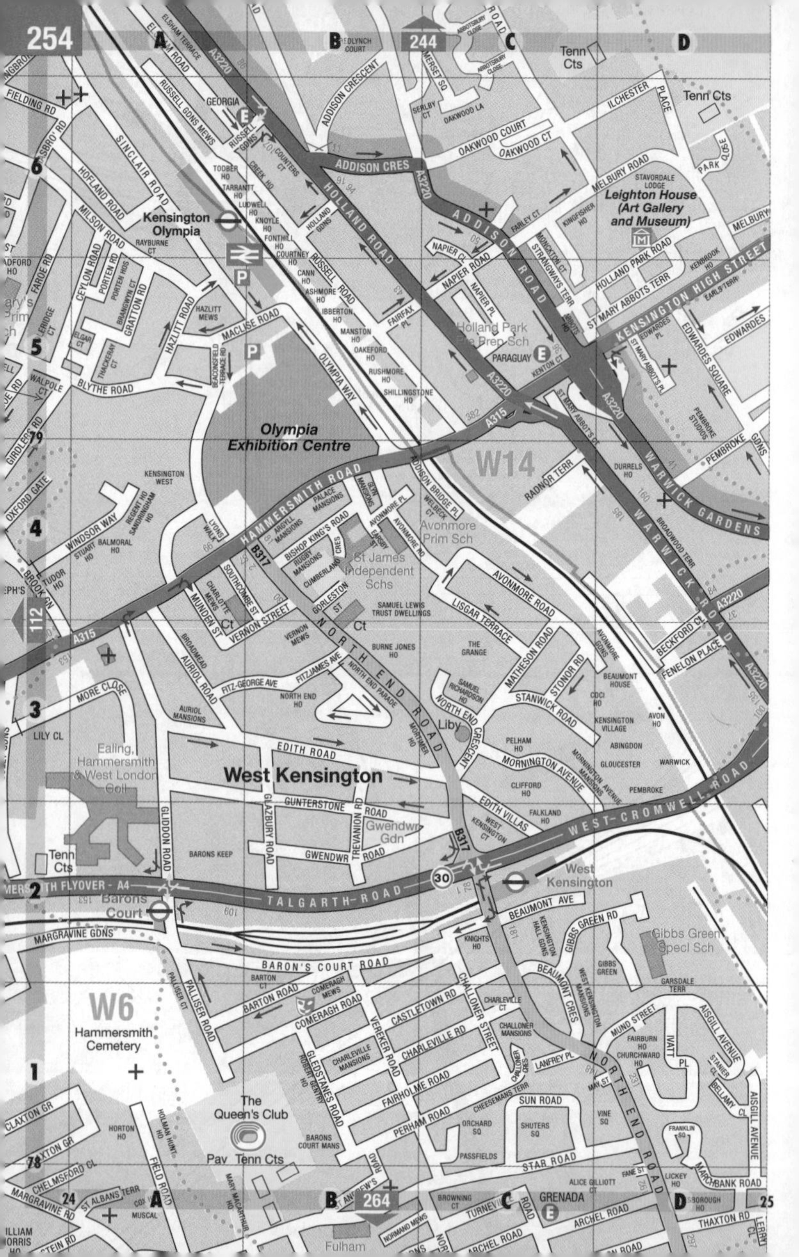

254
A
B
C
D
244
264
112
25
24
Tenn Cts
Leighton House (Art Gallery and Museum)
Kensington Olympia
Olympia Exhibition Centre
W14
W6
West Kensington
Holland Park Pre Prep Sch
Avonmore Prim Sch
St James Independent Schs
Ealing, Hammersmith & West London Coll
Gibbs Green Specl Sch
Hammersmith Cemetery
The Queen's Club
Pav Tenn Cts
Barons Court
Fulham
HOLLAND ROAD
ADDISON ROAD
ADDISON CRES
ADDISON CRESCENT
KENSINGTON HIGH STREET
WARWICK GARDENS
WARWICK ROAD
HAMMERSMITH ROAD
NORTH END ROAD
WEST CROMWELL ROAD
TALGARTH ROAD
EDITH ROAD
GUNTERSTONE ROAD
GWENDWR ROAD
BARON'S COURT ROAD
MARGRAVINE GDNS
AVONMORE ROAD
LISGAR TERRACE
MATHESON ROAD
STANWICK ROAD
MORNINGTON AVENUE
BLYTHE ROAD
MACLISE ROAD
OLYMPIA WAY
RUSSELL ROAD
SINCLAIR ROAD
HOFLAND ROAD
MILSON ROAD
GLIDDON ROAD
PALLISER ROAD
COMERAGH ROAD
CHALLONER STREET
CASTLETOWN RD
CHARLEVILLE RD
FAIRHOLME ROAD
PERHAM ROAD
VEREKER ROAD
GLEDSTANES ROAD
SUN ROAD
STAR ROAD
ARCHEL ROAD
MARCHBANK ROAD
AISGILL AVENUE
MELBURY ROAD
ILCHESTER PLACE
OAKWOOD COURT
EDWARDES SQUARE
PEMBROKE GDNS
A3220
A315
A4
B317

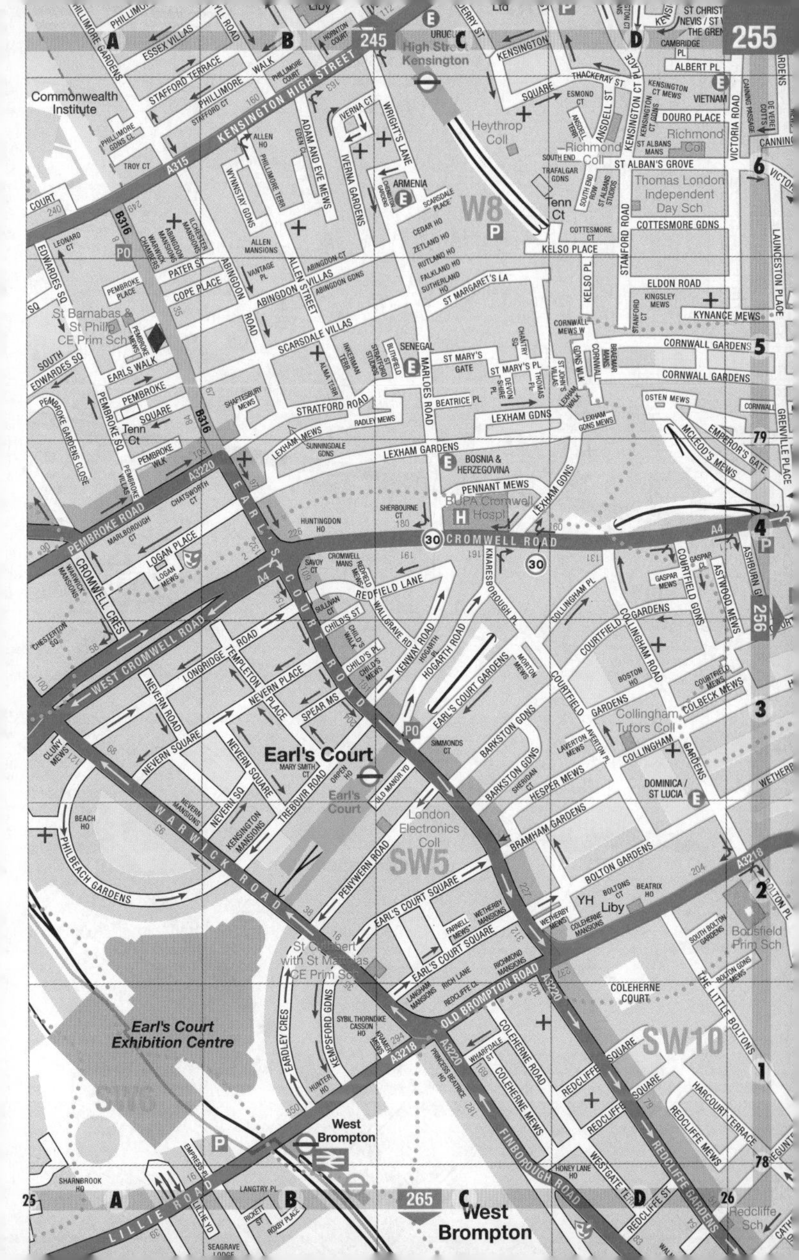
255
245
256
265
A
B
C
D
1
2
3
4
5
6
25
26
78
79
W8
SW5
SW10
High Street Kensington
Commonwealth Institute
Kensington High Street
A315
B316
A3220
A4
A3218
Phillimore Gardens
Essex Villas
Stafford Terrace
Phillimore Walk
Phillimore Gdns Cl
Troy Ct
Stafford Ct
Allen Ho
Adam and Eve Mews
Iverna Ct
Iverna Gardens
Wright's Lane
Wynnstay Gdns
Phillimore Terr
Allen Mansions
Allen Street
Abingdon Road
Abingdon Villas
Abingdon Ct
Abingdon Gdns
Vantage Pl
Pater St
Cope Place
Pembroke Place
Ilchester Mansions
Abingdon Mansions
Warwick Chambers
Edwardes Sq
South Edwardes Sq
Leonard Ct
St Barnabas & St Philip CE Prim Sch
Earls Walk
Pembroke Square
Pembroke Sq
Pembroke Gardens Close
Pembroke Walk
Pembroke Villas
Tenn Ct
Scarsdale Villas
Shaftesbury Mews
Stratford Road
Radley Mews
Lexham Mews
Sunningdale Gdns
Alma Terr
Inkerman Terr
Blithfield St
Stratford Studios
Senegal
Marloes Road
St Mary's Gate
St Mary's Pl
Devonshire Pl
Thomas Pl
Chantry Sq
Beatrice Pl
Lexham Gdns
Lexham Gardens
Lexham Walk
Lexham Gdns Mews
St Margaret's La
Cedar Ho
Zetland Ho
Rutland Ho
Falkland Ho
Sutherland Ho
Armenia
Scarsdale Place
Kensington Square
Thackeray St
Esmond Ct
Ansdell St
Ansdell Terr
Heythrop Coll
Richmond Coll
South End
Trafalgar Gdns
St Alban's Grove
South End Row
St Albans Studios
Cottesmore Ct
Cottesmore Gdns
Kelso Place
Kelso Pl
Stanford Road
Eldon Road
Kingsley Mews
Stanford Ct
Kynance Mews
Thomas London Independent Day Sch
Kensington Ct Place
Kensington Ct Mews
Kensington Ct Gdns
St Albans Mans
Albert Pl
Cambridge Pl
Douro Place
Vietnam
Victoria Road
Canning Passage
De Vere Cotts
Launceston Place
Cornwall Mews W
Cornwall Gdns Walk
Braemar Mans
Cornwall Gardens
St John's Villas
Osten Mews
McLeod's Mews
Emperor's Gate
Grenville Place
Ashburn Gdns
Bosnia & Herzegovina
Pennant Mews
BUPA Cromwell Hospl
Sherbourne Ct
Huntingdon Ho
Cromwell Road
Pembroke Road
Chatsworth Ct
Marlborough Ct
Logan Place
Logan Mews
Cromwell Cres
Warwick Mansions
Chesterton Sq
Earl's Court Road
Savoy Ct
Cromwell Mans
Redfield Mews
Redfield Lane
Sullivan Ct
Child's St
Child's Walk
Child's Pl
Child's Mews
Wallgrave Rd
Kenway Road
Hogarth Pl
Hogarth Road
Knaresborough Pl
Collingham Pl
Courtfield Gardens
Courtfield Gdns
Gaspar Cl
Gaspar Mews
Astwood Mews
Collingham Gardens
Collingham Road
Boston Ho
Courtfield Mews
Colbeck Mews
Collingham Tutors Coll
Laverton Mews
Laverton Pl
Dominica / St Lucia
Earl's Court Gardens
Morton Mews
Barkston Gdns
Sheridan Ct
Hesper Mews
Bramham Gardens
Bolton Gardens
Boltons Ct
Beatrix Ho
YH
Liby
South Bolton Gardens
Bolton Gdns Mews
Bousfield Prim Sch
The Little Boltons
Harcourt Terrace
Redcliffe Mews
Redcliffe Square
Redcliffe Gardens
Redcliffe St
Redcliffe Sch
Coleherne Court
West Cromwell Road
Longridge Road
Templeton Place
Nevern Place
Nevern Road
Nevern Square
Nevern Sq
Nevern Mansions
Spear Ms
Kensington Mansions
Trebovir Road
Mary Smith Ct
Orpen Ho
Old Manor Yd
Earl's Court
Simmonds Ct
London Electronics Coll
Cluny Mews
Beach Ho
Philbeach Gardens
Warwick Road
Penywern Road
Earl's Court Square
Farnell Mews
Wetherby Mansions
Wetherby Mews
Coleherne Mansions
Richmond Mansions
Langham Mansions
Rich Lane
Redcliffe Cl
Old Brompton Road
St Cuthbert with St Matthias CE Prim Sch
Eardley Cres
Kempsford Gdns
Sybil Thorndike Casson Ho
Kramer Mews
Hunter Ho
Earl's Court Exhibition Centre
SW6
Princess Beatrice Ho
Wharfdale St
Coleherne Road
Coleherne Mews
Finborough Road
Westgate Ter
Honey Lane Ho
West Brompton
Empress Pl
Sharnbrook Ho
Lillie Road
Lillie Yd
Langtry Pl
Rickett St
Roxby Place
Seagrave Lodge

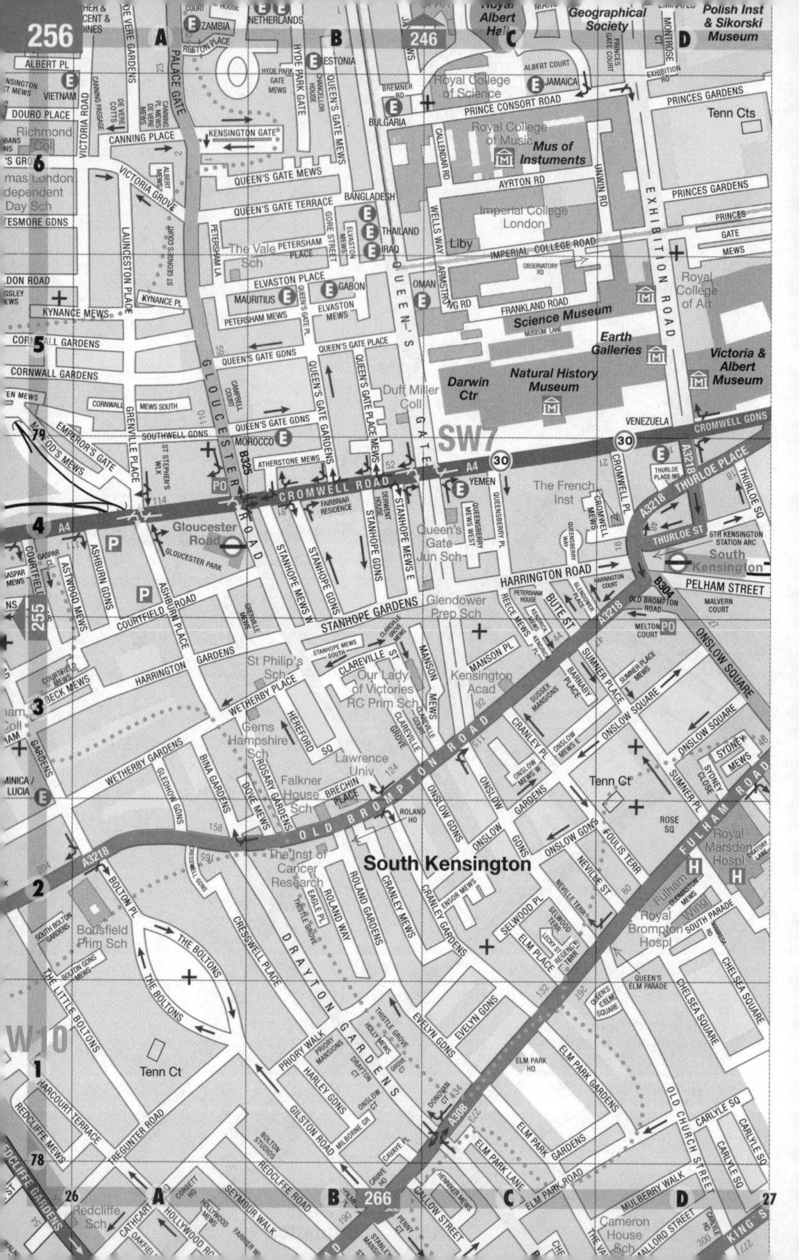

A
B
C
D
246
Royal Albert Hall
Geographical Society
Polish Inst & Sikorski Museum
ZAMBIA
NETHERLANDS
ESTONIA
VIETNAM
BULGARIA
JAMAICA
ALBERT PL
DOURO PLACE
DE VERE GARDENS
PALACE GATE
RESTON PLACE
HYDE PARK GATE
QUEEN'S GATE MEWS
CANNING PLACE
CANNING PASSAGE
VICTORIA ROAD
KENSINGTON GATE
Richmond Coll
Royal College of Science
PRINCE CONSORT ROAD
ALBERT COURT
PRINCES GARDENS
EXHIBITION RD
MONTROSE CT
Tenn Cts
Royal College of Music
Mus of Instuments
CALLENDAR RD
AYRTON RD
UNWIN RD
EXHIBITION ROAD
6
VICTORIA GROVE
QUEEN'S GATE TERRACE
BANGLADESH
Imperial College London
Liby
IMPERIAL COLLEGE ROAD
WELLS WAY
THAILAND
IRAQ
GORE STREET
PETERSHAM LA
LAUNCESTON PLACE
ST GEORGE'S CT
The Vale Sch
PETERSHAM PLACE
ELVASTON PLACE
GABON
MAURITIUS
OMAN
FRANKLAND ROAD
Science Museum
Royal College of Art
KYNANCE PL
KYNANCE MEWS
PETERSHAM MEWS
ELVASTON MEWS
QUEEN'S GATE
CORNWALL GARDENS
5
QUEEN'S GATE GDNS
QUEEN'S GATE PLACE
Earth Galleries
Victoria & Albert Museum
Natural History Museum
Darwin Ctr
Duff Miller Coll
GLOUCESTER ROAD
CAMPBELL COURT
CORNWALL MEWS SOUTH
EMPEROR'S GATE
SOUTHWELL GDNS
MOROCCO
QUEEN'S GATE GARDENS
QUEEN'S GATE PLACE MEWS
SW7
VENEZUELA
CROMWELL GDNS
30
ST STEPHEN'S WLK
GRENVILLE PLACE
B325
ATHERSTONE MEWS
CROMWELL ROAD
A4
YEMEN
The French Inst
CROMWELL PL
THURLOE PLACE
A3218
THURLOE SQ
4
Gloucester Road
GLOUCESTER PARK
PO
P
ASHBURN GDNS
ASTWOOD MEWS
COURTFIELD GDNS
FAIRBRIAR RESIDENCE
STANHOPE MEWS W
STANHOPE GDNS
STANHOPE MEWS E
DERWENT HOUSE
QUEENSBERRY MEWS WEST
QUEENSBERRY PL
Queen's Gate Jun Sch
THURLOE ST
STH KENSINGTON STATION ARC
South Kensington
PELHAM STREET
HARRINGTON ROAD
B304
255
COURTFIELD ROAD
ASHBURN PLACE
GRENVILLE MEWS
STANHOPE GARDENS
Glendower Prep Sch
REECE MEWS
BUTE ST
OLD BROMPTON ROAD
MALVERN COURT
MELTON COURT
ONSLOW SQUARE
HARRINGTON GARDENS
St Philip's Sch
CLAREVILLE ST
MANSON MEWS
MANSON PL
Kensington Acad
SUMNER PLACE
3
BECK MEWS
WETHERBY PLACE
Our Lady of Victories RC Prim Sch
HEREFORD SQ
Gems Hampshire Sch
CLAREVILLE GROVE
CRANLEY PL
ONSLOW MEWS E
SYDNEY MEWS
WETHERBY GARDENS
GLEDHOW GDNS
BINA GARDENS
ROSARY GARDENS
Lawrence Univ
Falkner House Sch
BRECHIN PLACE
DOVE MEWS
ONSLOW GDNS
ONSLOW GARDENS
Tenn Ct
SUMNER PL
SYDNEY CLOSE
FULHAM ROAD
ROSE SQ
158
OLD BROMPTON ROAD
ROLAND HO
The Inst of Cancer Research
South Kensington
FOULIS TERR
NEVILLE ST
Royal Marsden Hospl
2
A3218
BOLTON PL
CRESSWELL GDNS
EAGLE PL
THISTLE GROVE
ROLAND WAY
ROLAND GARDENS
CRANLEY MEWS
CRANLEY GARDENS
ENSOR MEWS
SELWOOD PL
SELWOOD TERR
NEVILLE TERR
ELM PLACE
LECKY ST
REGENCY TERR
Fulham Wing
Royal Brompton Hospl
SOUTH PARADE
DUDMASTON MEWS
SOUTH BOLTON GARDENS
Bousfield Prim Sch
THE BOLTONS
CRESSWELL PLACE
DRAYTON GARDENS
BOLTON GDNS MEWS
THE LITTLE BOLTONS
QUEEN'S ELM PARADE
QUEEN'S ELM SQUARE
CHELSEA SQUARE
W10
1
Tenn Ct
PRIORY WALK
PRIORY MANSIONS
HARLEY GDNS
DRAYTON CT
HOLLY MEWS
GROVE CT
THISTLE GROVE
EVELYN GDNS
ELM PARK HO
ELM PARK GARDENS
OLD CHURCH STREET
HARCOURT TERRACE
REDCLIFFE MEWS
TREGUNTER ROAD
GILSTON ROAD
ONSLOW CT
MILBORNE GR
DONOVAN CT
A308
CARLYLE SQ
78
BOLTON STUDIOS
REDCLIFFE ROAD
CAVAYE PL
ELM PARK LANE
ELM PARK ROAD
MULBERRY WALK
26
A
B
266
C
D
27
REDCLIFFE GARDENS
Redcliffe Sch
CATHCART
HOLLYWOOD ROAD
HOLLYWOOD MEWS
SEYMOUR WALK
CALLOW STREET
HENNIKER MEWS
Cameron House Sch
CARLYLE HO
KING'S

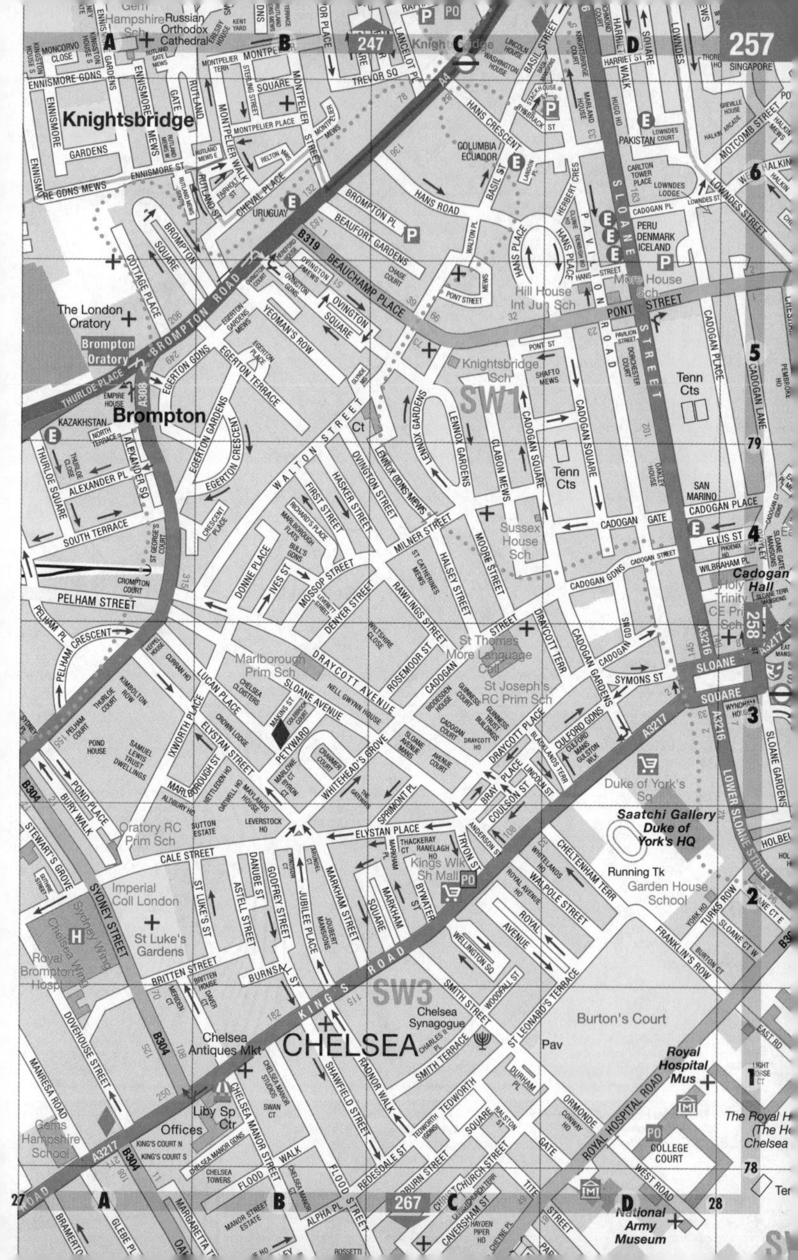
Knightsbridge
Brompton
CHELSEA
SW1
SW3
Russian Orthodox Cathedral
The London Oratory
Brompton Oratory
Columbia Ecuador
Uruguay
Kazakhstan
Pakistan
Peru
Denmark
Iceland
San Marino
Singapore
Hill House Int Jun Sch
More House Sch
Knightsbridge Sch
Sussex House Sch
Tenn Cts
Marlborough Prim Sch
St Thomas More Language Coll
St Joseph's RC Prim Sch
Cadogan Hall
Holy Trinity CE Pri Sch
Duke of York's Sq
Saatchi Gallery
Duke of York's HQ
Running Tk
Garden House School
Oratory RC Prim Sch
Imperial Coll London
St Luke's Gardens
Royal Brompton Hospl
Sydney Wing
Chelsea Wing
Kings Wlk Sh Mall
Chelsea Synagogue
Chelsea Antiques Mkt
Liby Sp Ctr
Offices
Gems Hampshire School
Burton's Court
Pav
Royal Hospital Mus
The Royal H (The H Chelsea
College Court
National Army Museum
Brompton Road
Beauchamp Place
Pont Street
Sloane Street
Sloane Square
Lower Sloane Street
King's Road
Walton Street
Draycott Avenue
Sloane Avenue
Fulham Road
Sydney Street
Royal Hospital Road
Cadogan Square
Cadogan Place
Cadogan Gardens
Hans Crescent
Hans Road
Hans Place
Lowndes Street
Egerton Gardens
Egerton Crescent
Egerton Terrace
Pelham Street
Pelham Crescent
Thurloe Place
Thurloe Square
Ennismore Gardens
Montpelier Square
Montpelier Street
Ovington Square
Ovington Street
Lennox Gardens
Milner Street
Moore Street
Elystan Street
Elystan Place
Cale Street
Smith Street
St Leonard's Terrace
Royal Avenue
Cheltenham Terr
Flood Street
Oakley Street
Chelsea Manor Street
Shawfield Street
Radnor Walk
Tedworth Square
Franklin's Row
Turks Row
West Road
247
267
258
A308
A3216
A3217
B304
B319
A4

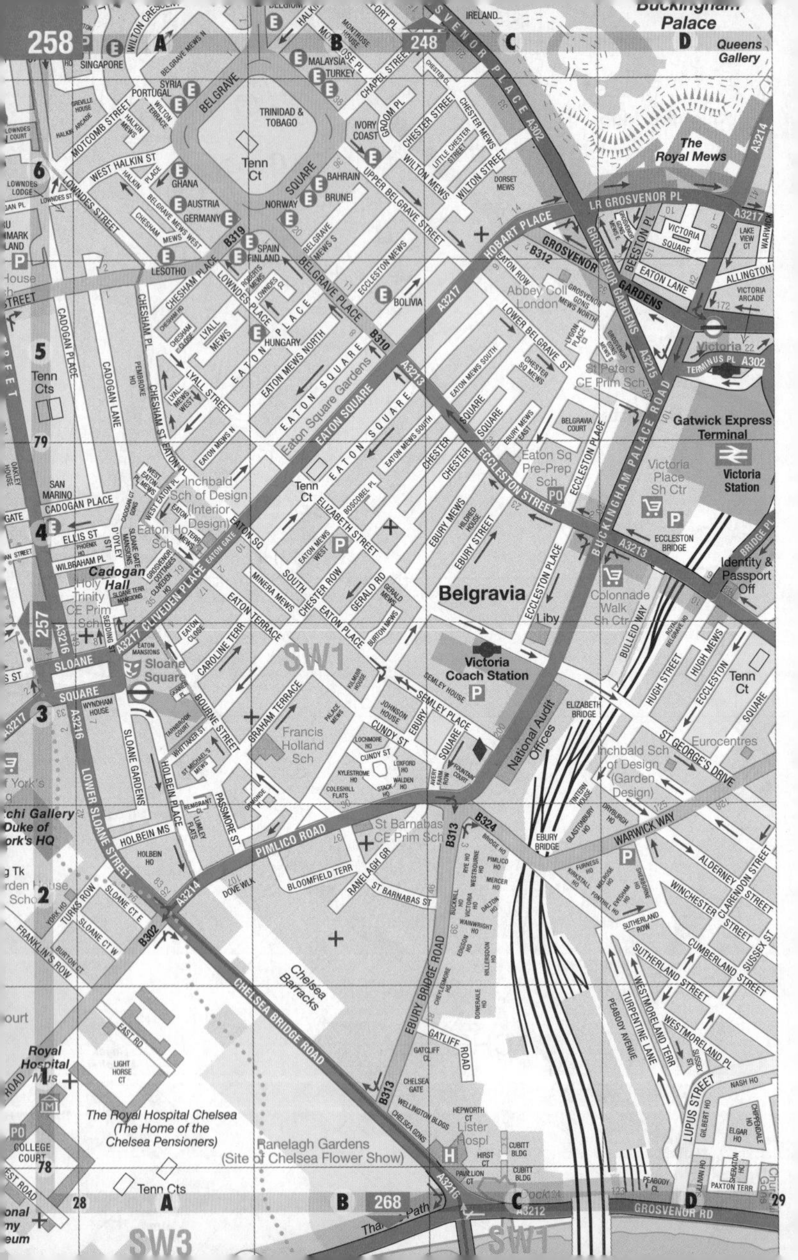
Buckingham Palace
Queens Gallery
The Royal Mews
A B C D
248
268
257
Belgravia
SW1
SW3
Belgrave Square
Trinidad & Tobago
Tenn Ct
Singapore
Syria
Portugal
Malaysia
Turkey
Ivory Coast
Ghana
Austria
Germany
Lesotho
Spain
Finland
Norway
Bahrain
Brunei
Bolivia
Hungary
Belgium
Ireland
Grosvenor Place A302
Lr Grosvenor Pl
Victoria Square
Beeston Pl
Eaton Lane
Allington
Victoria Arcade
Lake View Ct
Warwick
A3217
A3214
Hobart Place
Grosvenor Gardens
Terminus Pl A302
Victoria
Gatwick Express Terminal
Victoria Station
Victoria Place Sh Ctr
Eccleston Bridge
Identity & Passport Off
Buckingham Palace Road
A3213
A3215
Colonnade Walk Sh Ctr
Bulleid Way
Hugh Street
Hugh Mews
Eccleston Square
St George's Drive
Eurocentres
Inchbald Sch of Design (Garden Design)
Warwick Way
Alderney Street
Clarendon Street
Winchester Street
Cumberland Street
Sussex St
Sutherland Street
Westmoreland Terr
Westmoreland Pl
Turpentine Lane
Peabody Avenue
Lupus Street
Nash Ho
Grosvenor Rd
A3212
Chester Square
Eaton Square
Eaton Square Gardens
Chesham Place
Lowndes Place
Lowndes Street
Lyall Street
Lyall Mews
Eaton Place
Eaton Mews North
Eaton Mews South
Elizabeth Street
Ebury Street
Ebury Mews
Eccleston Street
Eccleston Place
Lower Belgrave St
Upper Belgrave Street
Belgrave Place
Chester Street
Chester Mews
Wilton Street
Wilton Mews
Chapel Street
Groom Pl
Abbey Coll London
St Peters CE Prim Sch
Eaton Sq Pre-Prep Sch
Belgravia Court
Liby
Victoria Coach Station
Semley Place
Elizabeth Bridge
National Audit Offices
Ebury Bridge
Ebury Bridge Road
B313
B324
Pimlico Road
A3214
St Barnabas CE Prim Sch
Bloomfield Terr
Ranelagh Gr
St Barnabas St
Chelsea Barracks
Chelsea Bridge Road
Gatliff Road
Lister Hospl
Ranelagh Gardens (Site of Chelsea Flower Show)
The Royal Hospital Chelsea (The Home of the Chelsea Pensioners)
Royal Hospital
Light Horse Ct
East Rd
College Court
Tenn Cts
Thames Path
A3216
Lower Sloane Street
Sloane Square
Sloane Gardens
Holbein Place
Holbein Ms
Bourne Street
Graham Terrace
Francis Holland Sch
Caroline Terr
Eaton Terrace
Cliveden Place
Eaton Gate
Cadogan Hall
Holy Trinity CE Prim Sch
Inchbald Sch of Design (Interior Design)
Eaton Ho Sch
Cadogan Place
Cadogan Lane
Chesham St
Pembroke Ho
Ellis St
Wilbraham Pl
D'Oyley
San Marino
Motcomb Street
West Halkin St
Halkin Arcade
Wilton Crescent
Franklin's Row
Turks Row
Sloane Ct E
Sloane Ct W
Burton Ct
B302
Cundy St
Johnson House
Minera Mews
Gerald Rd
Chester Row
South Eaton Place
28 29 78 79

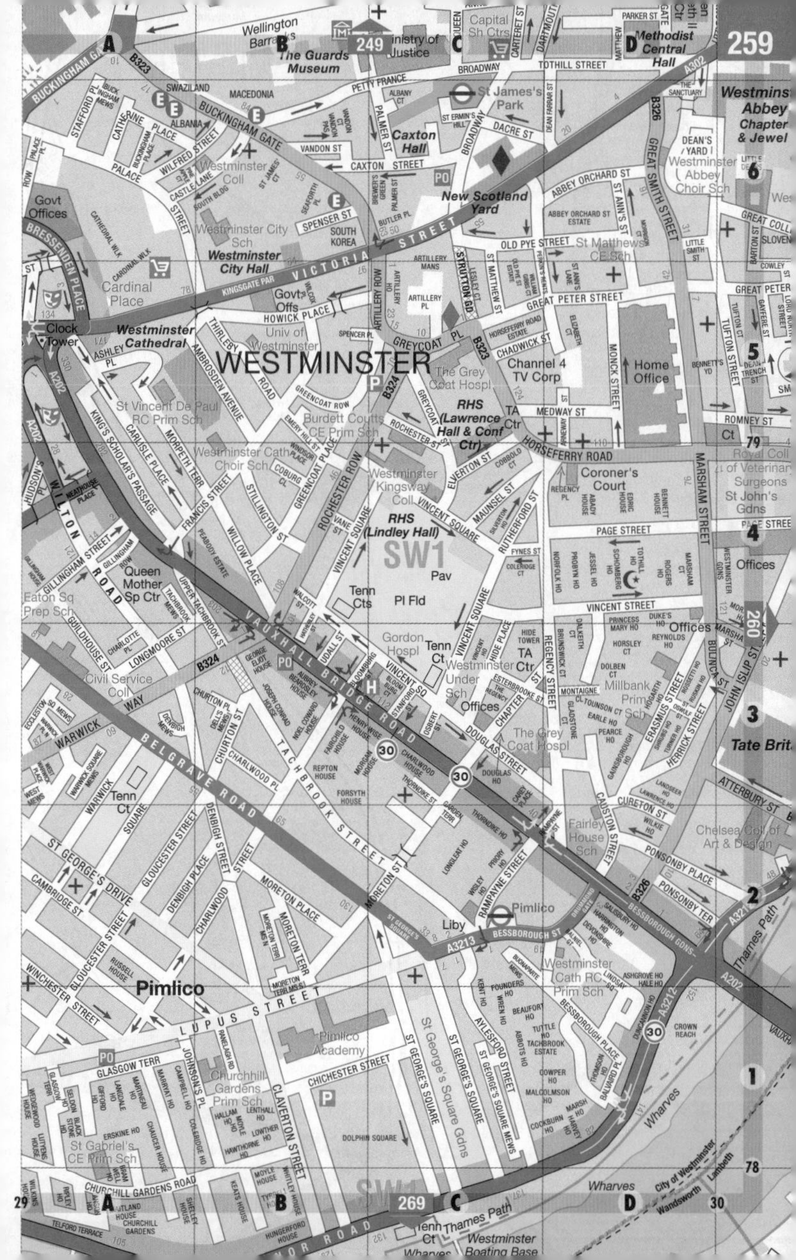

259
249
260
269
A
B
C
D
6
5
4
3
2
1
79
78
29
30
Wellington Barracks
The Guards Museum
Ministry of Justice
Capital Sh Ctrs
Methodist Central Hall
Westminster Abbey Chapter & Jewel
Westminster Abbey Choir Sch
BUCKINGHAM GATE
PETTY FRANCE
BROADWAY
TOTHILL STREET
St James's Park
Caxton Hall
CAXTON STREET
New Scotland Yard
Westminster Coll
Westminster City Sch
Westminster City Hall
VICTORIA STREET
Govt Offices
Cardinal Place
BRESSENDEN PLACE
Clock Tower
Westminster Cathedral
Univ of Westminster
WESTMINSTER
GREAT SMITH STREET
ABBEY ORCHARD ST
OLD PYE STREET
St Matthews CE Sch
GREAT PETER STREET
Channel 4 TV Corp
Home Office
MONCK STREET
MARSHAM STREET
HORSEFERRY ROAD
The Grey Coat Hospl
RHS (Lawrence Hall & Conf Ctr)
St Vincent De Paul RC Prim Sch
Burdett Coutts CE Prim Sch
Westminster Cath Choir Sch
Westminster Kingsway Coll
RHS (Lindley Hall)
VINCENT SQUARE
SW1
Coroner's Court
PAGE STREET
VINCENT STREET
Royal Coll of Veterinary Surgeons
St John's Gdns
Offices
Queen Mother Sp Ctr
Eaton Sq Prep Sch
Civil Service Coll
VAUXHALL BRIDGE ROAD
BELGRAVE ROAD
WILTON ROAD
Gordon Hospl
Westminster Under Sch
Millbank Prim Sch
Tate Brit
Chelsea Coll of Art & Design
Fairley House Sch
Pimlico
Liby
BESSBOROUGH ST
Westminster Cath RC Prim Sch
ST GEORGE'S DRIVE
LUPUS STREET
Pimlico Academy
Churchill Gardens Prim Sch
St Gabriel's CE Prim Sch
CHURCHILL GARDENS ROAD
CLAVERTON STREET
St George's Square Gdns
DOLPHIN SQUARE
Thames Path
Wharves
Westminster Boating Base
City of Westminster
Lambeth
Wandsworth

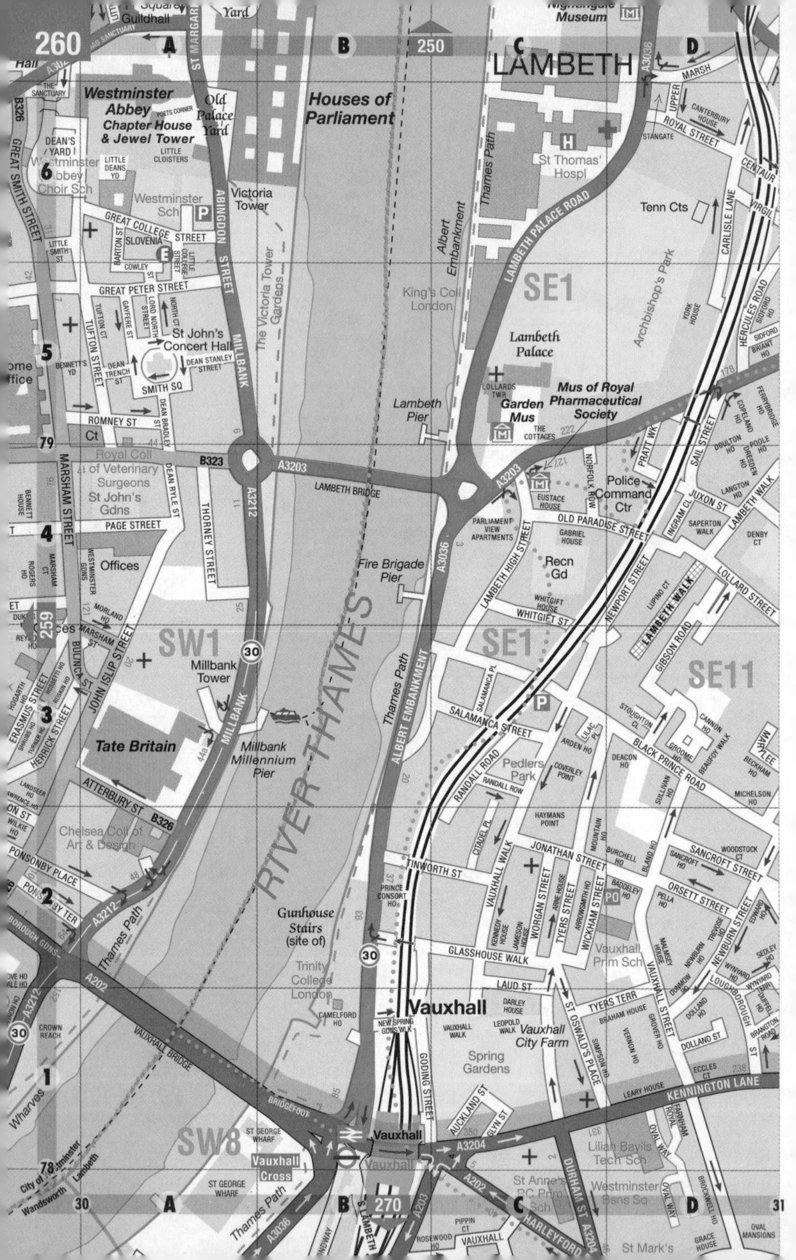
LAMBETH
Westminster Abbey
Chapter House & Jewel Tower
Houses of Parliament
Old Palace Yard
Victoria Tower
Westminster Sch
St Thomas' Hospl
Lambeth Palace
Archbishop's Park
Mus of Royal Pharmaceutical Society
Garden Mus
St John's Concert Hall
SMITH SQ
GREAT PETER STREET
GREAT COLLEGE STREET
GREAT SMITH STREET
ABINGDON STREET
MILLBANK
LAMBETH PALACE ROAD
Albert Embankment
King's Coll London
Lambeth Pier
LAMBETH BRIDGE
Royal Coll of Veterinary Surgeons
St John's Gdns
MARSHAM STREET
HORSEFERRY ROAD
PAGE STREET
THORNEY STREET
Offices
SW1
SE1
SE11
Millbank Tower
Tate Britain
Millbank Millennium Pier
RIVER THAMES
Fire Brigade Pier
Thames Path
ALBERT EMBANKMENT
LAMBETH HIGH STREET
OLD PARADISE STREET
Recn Gd
Police Command Ctr
LAMBETH WALK
BLACK PRINCE ROAD
SALAMANCA STREET
Pedlers Park
JONATHAN STREET
VAUXHALL WALK
Chelsea Coll of Art & Design
ATTERBURY ST
PONSONBY PLACE
Gunhouse Stairs (site of)
Trinity College London
Vauxhall
Vauxhall City Farm
Spring Gardens
VAUXHALL BRIDGE
KENNINGTON LANE
Lilian Baylis Tech Sch
Westminster Bsns Sq
SW8
Vauxhall Cross
St Anne's RC Prim Sch
DURHAM ST
HARLEYFORD
Wharves
City of Westminster
Lambeth
Wandsworth

250
259
270

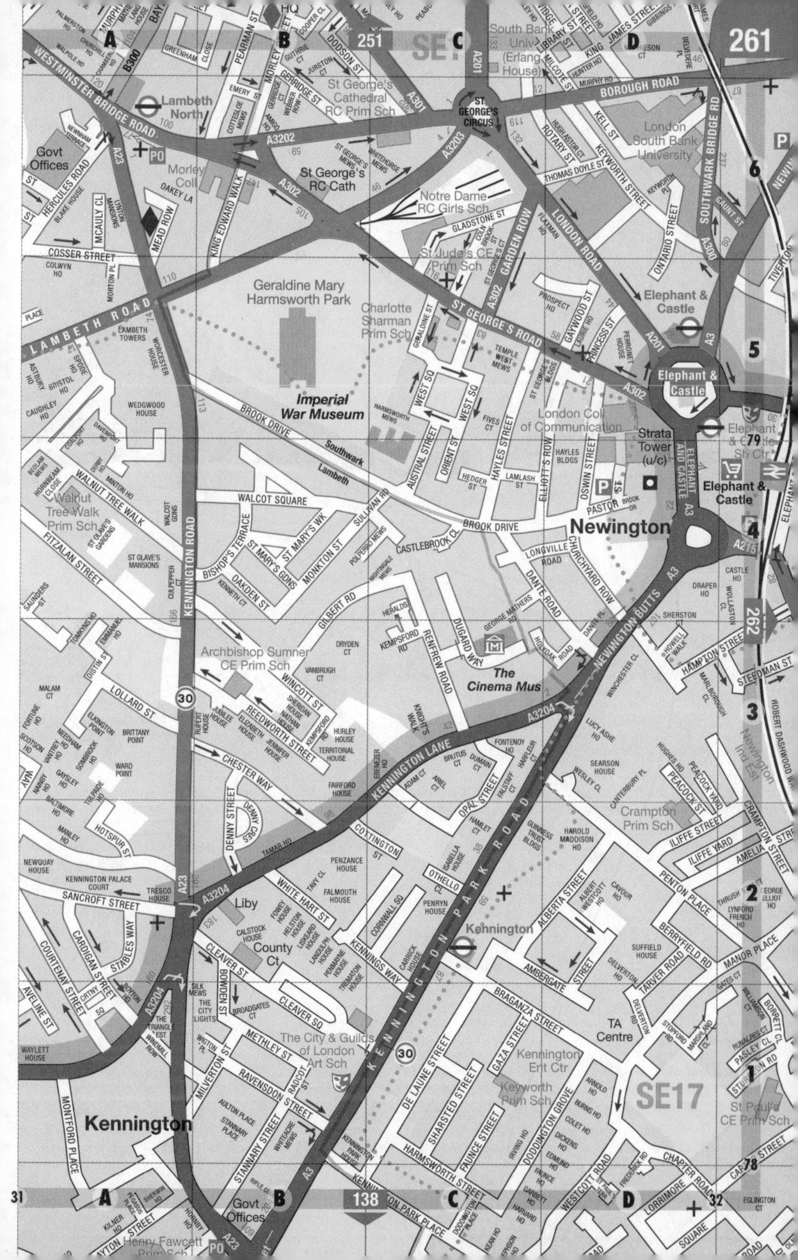
SE1
251
A
B
C
D
Westminster Bridge Road
Lambeth North
Govt Offices
Hercules Road
Morley Coll
St George's Cathedral RC Prim Sch
St George's Circus
St George's RC Cath
South Bank Univ (Erlang House)
Borough Road
London South Bank University
Southwark Bridge Rd
London Road
Notre Dame RC Girls Sch
St Jude's CE Prim Sch
Geraldine Mary Harmsworth Park
Imperial War Museum
Charlotte Sharman Prim Sch
St George's Road
Elephant & Castle
Lambeth Road
Kennington Road
Brook Drive
Walcot Square
Walnut Tree Walk
Walnut Tree Walk Prim Sch
London Coll of Communication
Strata Tower (u/c)
Newington
Newington Butts
Archbishop Sumner CE Prim Sch
The Cinema Mus
Kennington Lane
Kennington Park Road
Kennington
Liby
County Ct
Crampton Prim Sch
Newington Ind Est
TA Centre
Kennington Ent Ctr
Keyworth Prim Sch
The City & Guilds of London Art Sch
SE17
St Paul's CE Prim Sch
Kennington
Govt Offices
Henry Fawcett Prim Sch
138
262
31
32
A
B
C
D
6
5
4
3
2
1

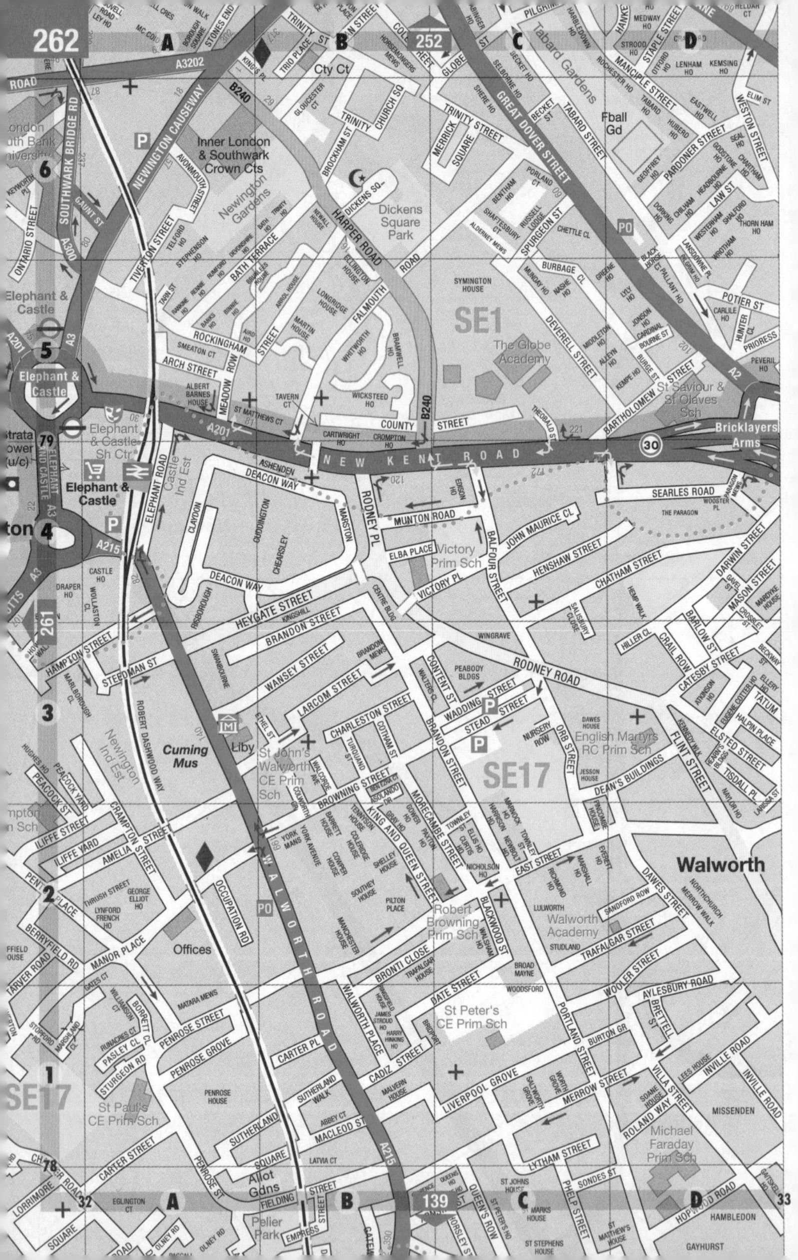
262
A
B
C
D
252
A3202
B240
City Ct
Trinity St
Trio Place
Kings Pl
Gloucester Ct
Trinity Church Sq
Horsemongers Mews
Globe St
Pilgrimage St
Tabard Gardens
Merrick Square
Trinity Street
Great Dover Street
Tabard Street
Selborne Ho
Becket Ho
Becket St
Shere Ho
Hambledon Ho
Rochester Ho
Manciple Street
Staple Street
Medway Ho
Strood Ho
Otford Ho
Lenham Ho
Kemsing Ho
Eastwell Ho
Weston Street
Elim St
Fball Gd
Tabard Ho
Hubert Ho
Pardoner Street
Geoffrey Ho
Godstone Ho
Seal Ho
Chartham Ho
Headbourne Ho
Law St
Dorking Ho
Chilham Ho
Westerham Ho
Shalford Ho
Thorn Ham Ho
Wrotham Ho
Lansdowne Pl
Pilgrim Ho
Black Horse Ct
Pallant Ho
Potier St
Carlile Ho
Hunter Cl
Prioress
Peveril Ho
A2
PO
Road
Southwark Bridge Rd
London South Bank University
6
Keyworth Pl
Gaunt St
Ontario Street
A300
Newington Causeway
Avonmouth Street
Inner London & Southwark Crown Cts
Newington Gardens
P
Tiverton Street
Telford Ho
Stephenson Ho
Bath Terrace
Devonshire Ho
Rumford Ho
Trinity Ho
Bath Ho
Newall House
Dickens Sq
Harper Road
Dickens Square Park
Brockham St
Portland Ct
Bentham Ho
Russell Lodge
Shaftesbury Ct
Spurgeon St
Chettle Cl
Alderney Mews
Burbage Cl
Munday Ho
Nashe Ho
Greene Ho
Lyly Ho
Road
Eglinton House
Arrol House
Longridge House
Martin House
Falmouth
Symington House
SE1
The Globe Academy
Deverell Street
Middleton Ho
Jonson Ho
Cardinal Bourne St
Alleyn Ho
Kempe Ho
Burge St
Bartholomew Street
St Saviour & St Olaves Sch
Elephant & Castle
5
A201
A3
Rockingham
Street
Smeaton Ct
Arch Street
Meadow Row
Albert Barnes House
St Matthews Ct
Tavern Ct
Whitworth Ho
Bramwell Ho
Wicksteed Ho
County Street
B240
Cartwright Ho
Crompton Ho
Theobald St
Bricklayers Arms
30
New Kent Road
Elephant & Castle Sh Ctr
Strata Tower (u/c)
79
Elephant and Castle
Elephant Road
Castle Ind Est
Ashenden
Deacon Way
Claydon
Cuddington
Chearsley
Marston
Rodney Pl
Edison Ho
Munton Road
Searles Road
Paragon Mews
Wooster Pl
The Paragon
4
A215
Elba Place
Victory Prim Sch
Victory Pl
Balfour Street
John Maurice Cl
Henshaw Street
Chatham Street
Darwin Street
Castle Ho
Draper Ho
Wollaston Cl
Risborough
Deacon Way
Heygate Street
Kingshill
Brandon Street
Centre Bldg
Wingrave
Salisbury Close
Hemp Walk
Mason Street
Gaywood St
Mardyke House
Crosslet St
Barlow St
Hiller Cl
Crail Row
Catesby Street
Beckway St
261
Hampton Street
Steedman St
Swanbourne
Wansey Street
Brandon Mews
Peabody Bldgs
Content St
Walters Cl
Rodney Road
Atkinson Ho
Eugene Cotter Ho
Ellery St
Tatum St
Marlborough Cl
3
Robert Dashwood Way
Newington Ind Est
Cuming Mus
Liby
Ethel St
Larcom Street
Charleston Street
Cotham St
Wadding Street
Stead Street
Nursery Row
Orb Street
Dawes House
English Martyrs RC Prim Sch
Kennedy Wlk
Halpin Place
Elsted Street
Tisdall Pl
Hughes Ho
Peacock Yard
Peacock St
St John's Walworth CE Prim Sch
Walcorde Ave
Turquand St
Browning Street
Brandon Street
SE17
Jesson House
Dean's Buildings
Flint Street
Naylor Ho
Larissa St
Iliffe Street
Iliffe Yard
Crampton Street
Amelia Street
York Mans
York Avenue
Barrett House
Tennyson House
Coleridge House
Cowper House
King and Queen Street
Gray Ho
Gower Ho
Paxton Ho
Morecambe Street
Townley St
Ellis Ho
Curtis Ho
Nicholson Ho
Marlbrook Ho
Harrison Ho
Newbolt Ho
Pinchose House
Everett Ho
Walworth
East Street
Marshall Ho
Richmond Ho
Dawes Street
Northchurch
Merrow Walk
2
Penton Place
Thrush Street
George Elliot Ho
Lynford French Ho
Occupation Rd
PO
Walworth Road
Shelley House
Southey House
Pilton Place
Manchester House
Robert Browning Prim Sch
Blackwood St
Walsham Ho
Lulworth
Walworth Academy
Sandford Row
Trafalgar Street
Studland
Berryfield Rd
Tarver Road
Manor Place
Offices
Gates Ct
Williamson Ct
Borrett Cl
Matara Mews
Bronti Close
Trafalgar House
Broad Mayne
Woodsford
Wooler Street
Aylesbury Road
Brettell St
Stopford Rd
Marshland Cl
Runacres Ct
Pasley Cl
Penrose Street
Penrose Grove
Carter Pl
Walworth Place
Stainsfield House
James Stroud Ho
Harry Hinkins Ho
Date Street
Bridport
St Peter's CE Prim Sch
Portland Street
Burton Gr
Inville Road
1
SE17
Sturgeon Rd
St Paul's CE Prim Sch
Penrose House
Cadiz Street
Sutherland Walk
Malvern House
Liverpool Grove
Saltwood Grove
Worth Grove
Merrow Street
Soane House
Villa Street
Lees House
Missenden
Roland Way
Michael Faraday Prim Sch
Abbey Ct
Macleod St
Sutherland Square
Latvia Ct
A215
Lytham Street
Sondes St
78
Carter Street
Chester Road
Lorrimore
32
Eglington Ct
A
Penrose St
Allot Gdns
Fielding Street
B
139
Queen's Row
St Johns House
C
Phelp Street
D
Hopwood Road
33
Gatesill Ho
Pelier Park
Empress Street
Olney Rd
Square
Marks House
St Peters Ho
St Stephens House
St Matthew's House
Hambledon
Gayhurst

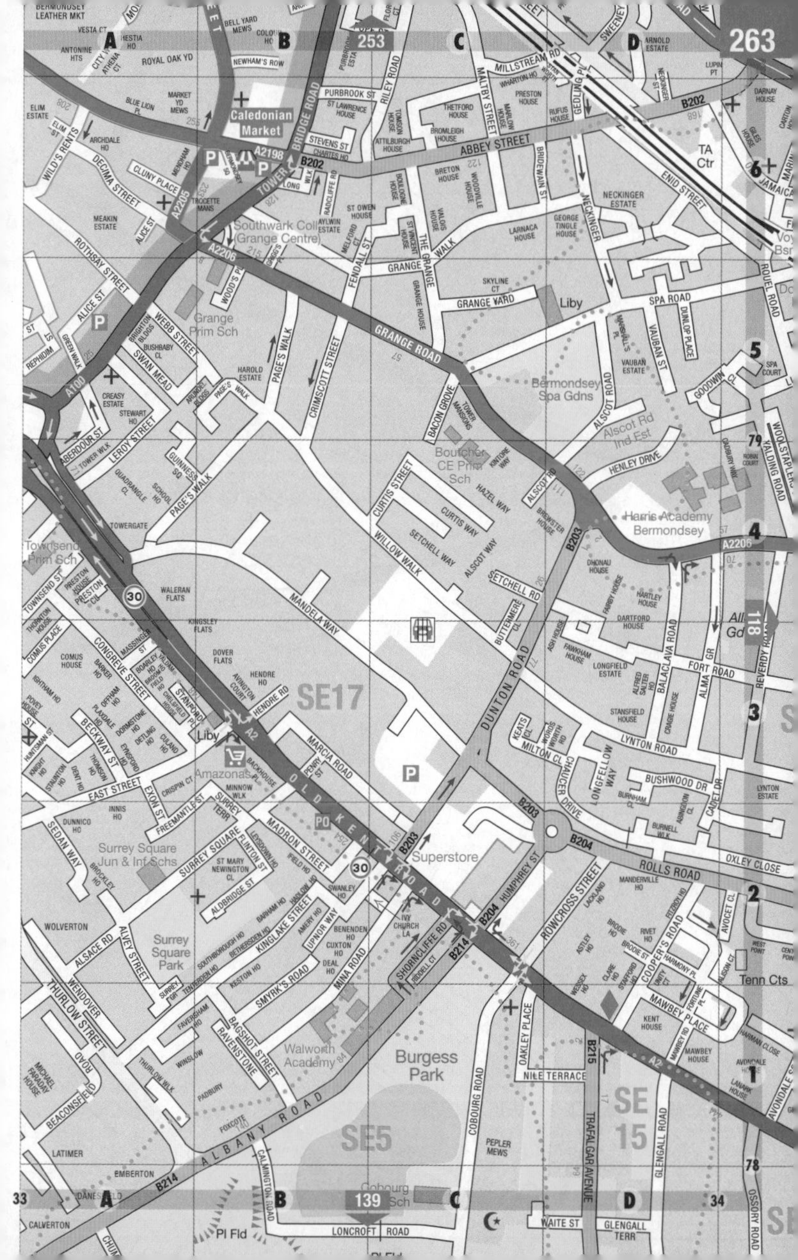
263
253
118
139
A
B
C
D
1
2
3
4
5
6
33
34
78
79
BERMONDSEY LEATHER MKT
VESTA CT
HESTIA HO
ANTONINE HTS
ROYAL OAK YD
BELL YARD MEWS
NEWHAM'S ROW
Caledonian Market
BLUE LION PL
MARKET YD MEWS
ELIM ESTATE
ARCHDALE HO
WILD'S RENTS
DECIMA STREET
CLUNY PLACE
MENDHAM HO
TROCETTE MANS
MEAKIN ESTATE
ALICE ST
ROTHSAY STREET
TOWER BRIDGE ROAD
PURBROOK ST
ST LAWRENCE HOUSE
STEVENS ST
CHARTES HO
RILEY ROAD
TOMSON HOUSE
ATTILBURGH HOUSE
MALTBY STREET
MILLSTREAM RD
WHARTON HO
PRESTON HOUSE
MARLOW HOUSE
RUFUS HOUSE
GEDLING PL
SWEENEY
ARNOLD ESTATE
LUPIN PT
DARNAY HOUSE
CARTON
THETFORD HOUSE
BROMLEIGH HOUSE
ABBEY STREET
B202
A2198
A2205
A2206
BRETON HOUSE
WOODVILLE HOUSE
BRIDEWAIN ST
NECKINGER
NECKINGER ESTATE
ENID STREET
TA Ctr
JAMAICA
LONG WALK
RADCLIFFE HO
BOULOGNE HOUSE
ST OWEN HOUSE
AYLWIN ESTATE
VALOIS HOUSE
LARNACA HOUSE
GEORGE TINGLE HOUSE
Southwark Coll (Grange Centre)
MELFORD CT
FENDALL ST
ST VINCENT HOUSE
THE GRANGE
GRANGE WALK
GRANGE HOUSE
SKYLINE CT
GRANGE YARD
Liby
SPA ROAD
ROUEL ROAD
WOOD'S PL
Grange Prim Sch
WEBB STREET
BRIGHTON BLDGS
BUSHBABY CL
SWAN MEAD
PAGE'S WALK
CRIMSCOTT STREET
GRANGE ROAD
MARSHALL'S PL
VAUBAN ST
DUNLOP PLACE
VAUBAN ESTATE
SPA COURT
GOODWIN CL
Bermondsey Spa Gdns
ALSCOT ROAD
Alscot Rd Ind Est
HENLEY DRIVE
WOOLSTAPLERS
YALDING ROAD
ROBIN COURT
CADBURY WAY
HAROLD ESTATE
ARUNDEL BLDGS
BACON GROVE
TOWER MANSIONS
Boutcher CE Prim Sch
KINTORE WAY
HAZEL WAY
ALSCOT RD
BREWSTER HOUSE
Harris Academy Bermondsey
GREEN WALK
REPHIDIM ST
CREASY ESTATE
STEWART HO
LEROY STREET
ABERDOUR ST
TOWER WLK
QUADRANGLE CL
GUINNESS SQ
SCHOOL HO
TOWERGATE
A100
Townsend Prim Sch
CURTIS STREET
CURTIS WAY
SETCHELL WAY
ALSCOT WAY
WILLOW WALK
B203
DHONAU HOUSE
FAIRBY HOUSE
HARTLEY HOUSE
DARTFORD HOUSE
SETCHELL RD
BUTTERMERE CL
ASH HOUSE
FAWKHAM HOUSE
LONGFIELD ESTATE
BALACLAVA ROAD
ALMA GR
FORT ROAD
REVERDY RD
TOWNSEND ST
PRESTON HOUSE
PRESTON CL
THORNTON HOUSE
WALERAN FLATS
KINGSLEY FLATS
MANDELA WAY
30
COMUS PLACE
COMUS HOUSE
CONGREVE STREET
MASSINGER ST
DOVER FLATS
HENDRE HO
AVINGTON COURT
HENDRE RD
SE17
DUNTON ROAD
KEATS CL
WORDSWORTH RD
STANSFIELD HOUSE
CRAIGIE HOUSE
ALFRED SALTER HO
ISHTHAM HO
POVEY HOUSE
BARKER HO
OFFHAM HO
PLAYDALE HO
DORMSTONE HO
DETLING HO
EYNSFORD HO
CULAND HO
STANFORD PL
BOARLEY HO
MILTON CL
CHAUCER DRIVE
LONGFELLOW WAY
LYNTON ROAD
HUNTSMAN ST
BECKWAY ST
KNIGHT HO
STAUNTON HO
DENT HO
THOMSON HOUSE
Amazonas
BACKHOUSE PL
MINNOW WLK
MARCIA ROAD
PENRY ST
A2
OLD KENT ROAD
BUSHWOOD DR
BURNHAM CL
ABINGDON CL
CADET DR
LYNTON ESTATE
EAST STREET
EXON ST
CRISPIN CT
INNIS HO
DUNNICO HO
SEDAN WAY
FREEMANTLE ST
SURREY TERR
MADRON STREET
PO
B204
BURNELL WLK
ROLLS ROAD
OXLEY CLOSE
Surrey Square Jun & Inf Schs
SURREY SQUARE
FLINTON ST
ST MARY NEWINGTON CL
ALDBRIDGE ST
LEYSDOWN HO
IFIELD HO
Superstore
HUMPHREY ST
ROWCROSS STREET
MANDERVILLE HO
LACKLAND HO
BROCKLEY HO
SWANLEY HO
BARHAM HO
HADLOW HO
KINGLAKE STREET
UPNOR WAY
BENENDEN HO
CUXTON HO
DEAL HO
IVY CHURCH LA
B214
SHORNCLIFFE RD
BRODIE HO
RIVET HO
BRODIE ST
COOPER'S ROAD
AVOCET CL
WEST POINT
WOLVERTON
ALSACE RD
ALVEY STREET
Surrey Square Park
SOUTHBOROUGH HO
BETHERSDEN HO
AMERY HO
MINA ROAD
RIDDELL CT
ASTLEY HO
WESSEX HO
CLARE HO
STAFFORD HO
HARMONY PL
UNITY CT
ALISON CT
Tenn Cts
WENDOVER
THURLOW STREET
TENTERDEN HO
SURREY GR
KESTON HO
SMYRK'S ROAD
FAVERSHAM HO
BAGSHOT STREET
RAVENSTONE
OAKLEY PLACE
MAWBEY PLACE
FORTUNE PL
KENT HOUSE
HARMAN CLOSE
WINSLOW
THURLOW WLK
Walworth Academy
Burgess Park
COBOURG ROAD
B215
MAWBEY HO
MAWBEY HOUSE
AVONDALE HO
LANARK HOUSE
AVONDALE SQ
MICHAEL FARADAY HOUSE
BEACONSFIELD ROAD
PADBURY
NILE TERRACE
TRAFALGAR AVENUE
SE 15
GLENGALL ROAD
FOXCOTE
ALBANY ROAD
SE5
PEPLER MEWS
LATIMER
EMBERTON
DANESFIELD
CALMINGTON ROAD
Cobourg Sch
CALVERTON
Pl Fld
LONCROFT ROAD
WAITE ST
GLENGALL TERR
OSSORY ROAD

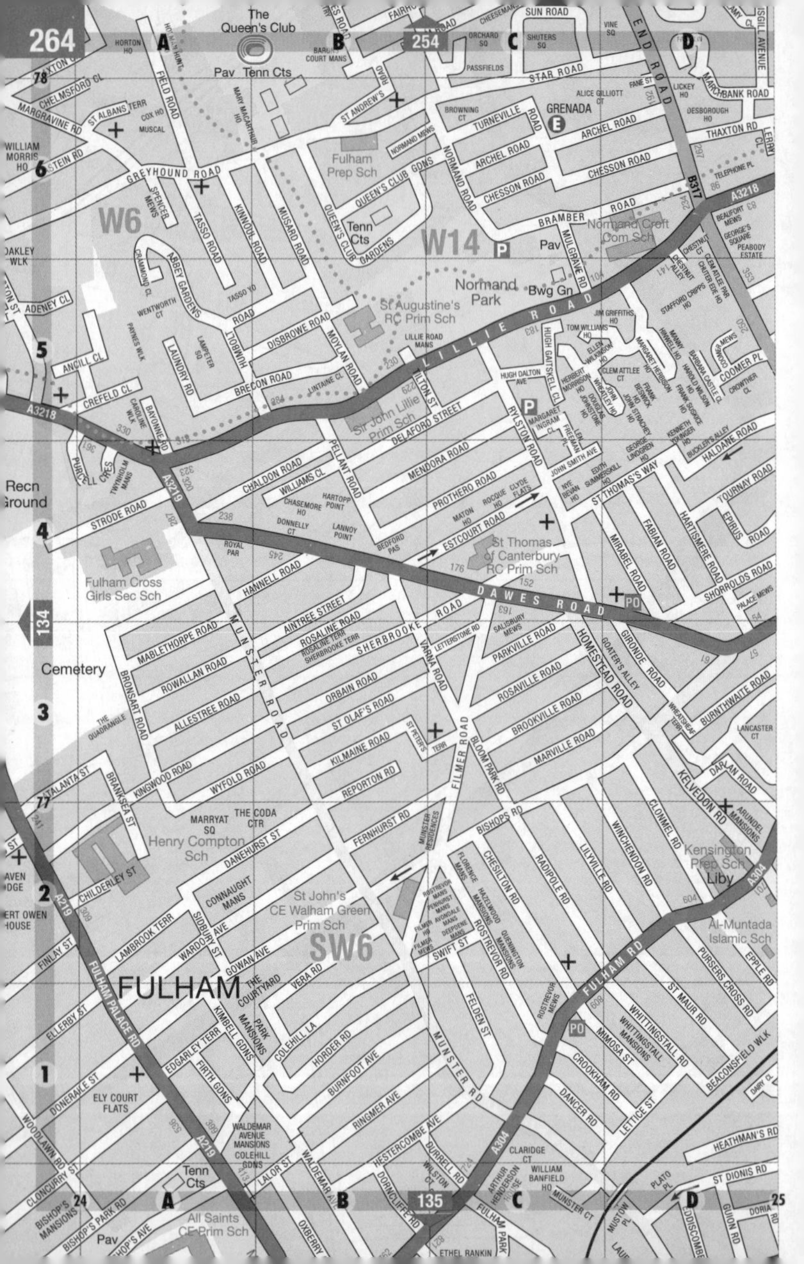
A
B
C
D
254
The Queen's Club
Pav Tenn Cts
W6
W14
SW6
FULHAM
GREYHOUND ROAD
LILLIE ROAD
DAWES ROAD
FULHAM PALACE RD
FULHAM RD
MUNSTER ROAD
NORTH END ROAD
GRENADA
Fulham Prep Sch
Normand Park
Normand Croft Com Sch
St Augustine's RC Prim Sch
Sir John Lillie Prim Sch
St Thomas of Canterbury RC Prim Sch
Fulham Cross Girls Sec Sch
Henry Compton Sch
St John's CE Walham Green Prim Sch
Kensington Prep Sch
Al-Muntada Islamic Sch
All Saints CE Prim Sch
Recn Ground
Cemetery
Liby
134
135
24
25
1
2
3
4
5
6
A3218
A3219
A219
A304
B317

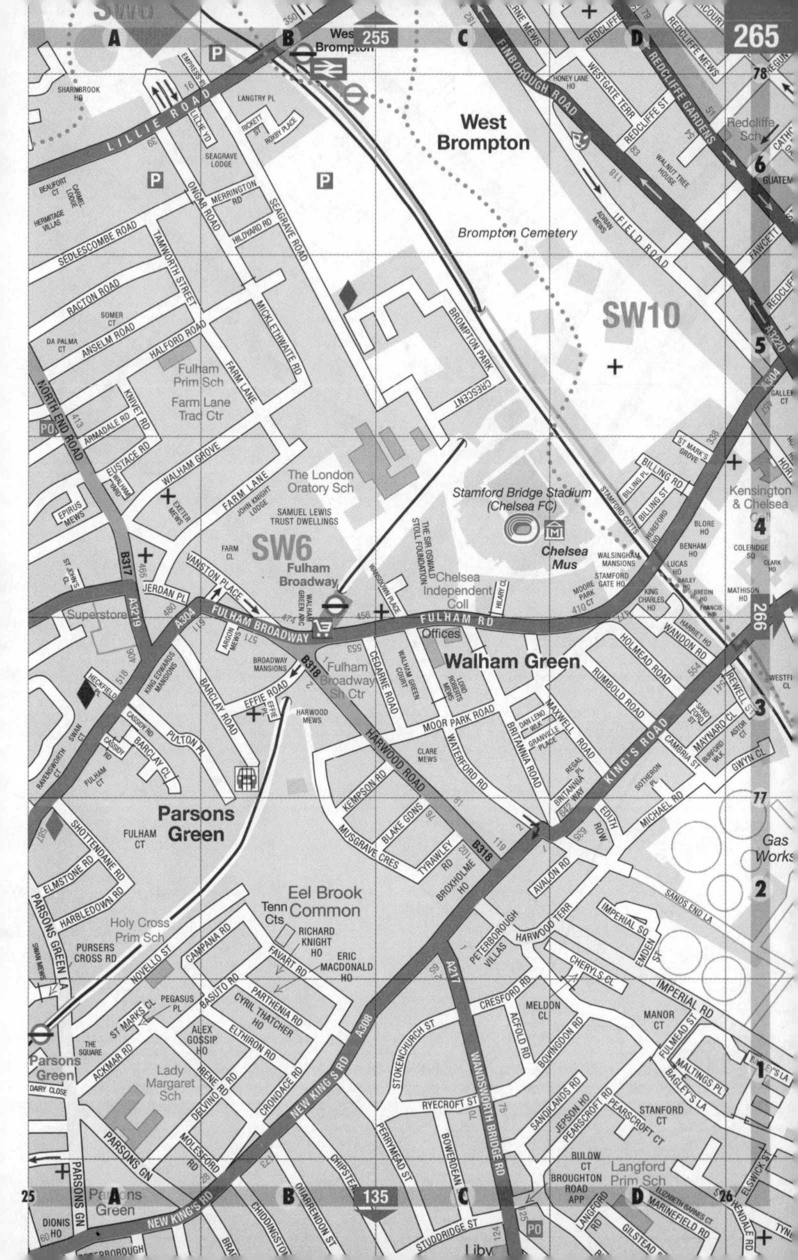
West Brompton
Brompton Cemetery
SW10
SW6
Fulham Broadway
Walham Green
Parsons Green
Eel Brook Common
Stamford Bridge Stadium (Chelsea FC)
Chelsea Mus
Chelsea Independent Coll
The London Oratory Sch
Samuel Lewis Trust Dwellings
Fulham Prim Sch
Farm Lane Trad Ctr
Fulham Broadway Sh Ctr
Superstore
Offices
Holy Cross Prim Sch
Lady Margaret Sch
Langford Prim Sch
Kensington & Chelsea Coll
Redcliffe Sch
Gas Works
Lillie Road
Seagrave Road
Brompton Park Crescent
Finborough Road
Redcliffe Gardens
Ifield Road
Sedlescombe Road
Racton Road
Anselm Road
Halford Road
Tamworth Street
Farm Lane
Mickelthwaite Rd
North End Road
Walham Grove
Vanston Place
Fulham Broadway
Fulham Rd
Harwood Road
King's Road
New King's Rd
Wandsworth Bridge Rd
Moor Park Road
Waterford Rd
Britannia Road
Maxwell Road
Rumbold Road
Holmead Road
Wandon Rd
Billing Rd
Imperial Rd
Sands End La
Parsons Green La
Parsons Gn
Musgrave Cres
Cedarne Road
Barclay Road
Effie Road
Novello St
Campana Rd
Favart Rd
Parthenia Rd
Elthiron Rd
Crondace Rd
Stokenchurch St
Ryecroft St
Peterborough Villas
Harwood Terr
Cresford Rd
Bovingdon Rd
Pearscroft Rd
Studdridge St
A3219
A304
B317
B318
A217
A308
A3220
255
135
266

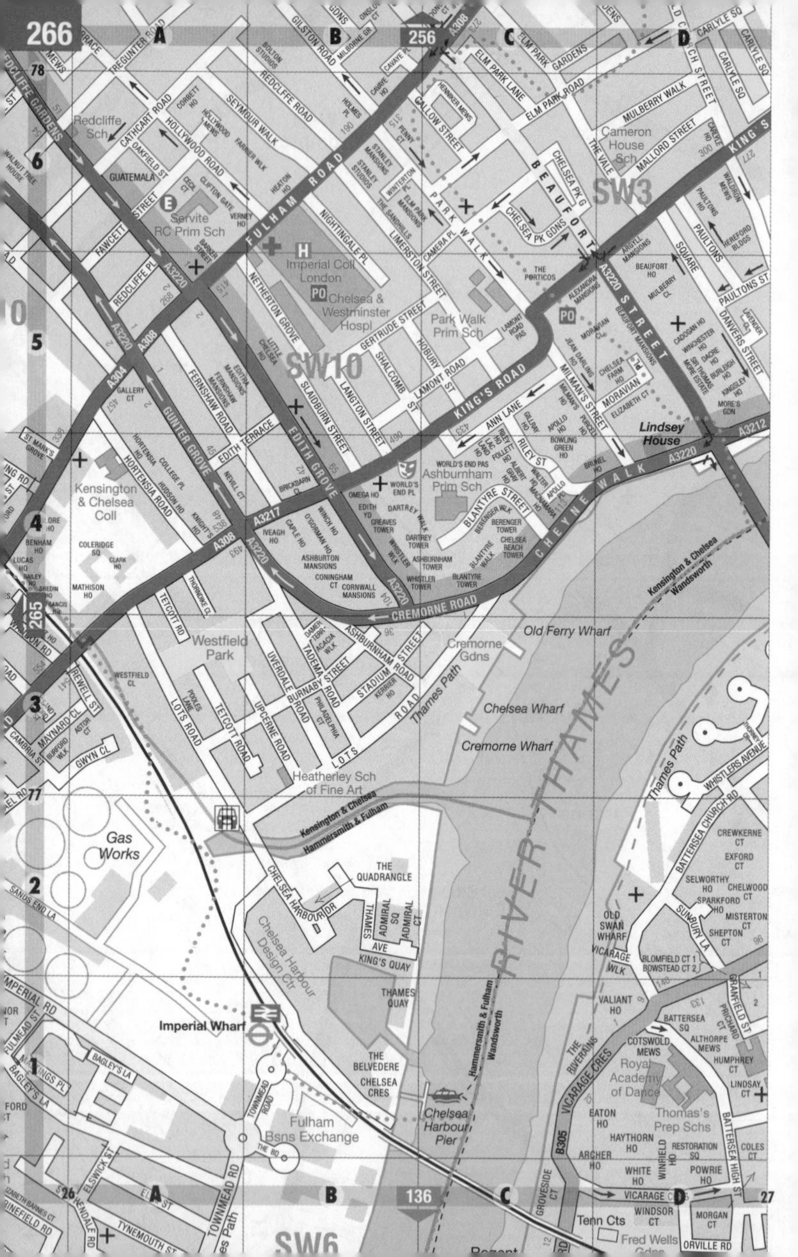

A
B
C
D
256
78
6
5
4
3
2
1
77
265
136
26
27
SW3
SW10
SW6
FULHAM ROAD
KING'S ROAD
CHEYNE WALK
CREMORNE ROAD
EDITH GROVE
GUNTER GROVE
LOTS ROAD
RIVER THAMES
Thames Path
Redcliffe Sch
Servite RC Prim Sch
Imperial Coll London
Chelsea & Westminster Hospl
Park Walk Prim Sch
Ashburnham Prim Sch
Cameron House Sch
Kensington & Chelsea Coll
Westfield Park
Heatherley Sch of Fine Art
Cremorne Gdns
Old Ferry Wharf
Chelsea Wharf
Cremorne Wharf
Gas Works
Chelsea Harbour Design Ctr
Imperial Wharf
Fulham Bsns Exchange
Chelsea Harbour Pier
Royal Academy of Dance
Thomas's Prep Schs
Tenn Cts
Fred Wells
Lindsey House
Kensington & Chelsea
Hammersmith & Fulham
Wandsworth
REDCLIFFE GARDENS
TREGUNTER ROAD
GILSTON ROAD
REDCLIFFE ROAD
SEYMOUR WALK
HOLLYWOOD ROAD
CATHCART ROAD
ELM PARK GARDENS
ELM PARK LANE
ELM PARK ROAD
CARLYLE SQ
MULBERRY WALK
MALLORD STREET
THE VALE
CALLOW STREET
PARK WALK
BEAUFORT STREET
LIMERSTON STREET
NETHERTON GROVE
NIGHTINGALE PL
GERTRUDE STREET
HOBURY ST
LAMONT ROAD
LANGTON STREET
SLAIDBURN STREET
SHALCOMB ST
MILMAN'S STREET
ANN LANE
RILEY ST
BLANTYRE STREET
PAULTONS SQUARE
DANVERS STREET
FERNSHAW ROAD
EDITH TERRACE
HORTENSIA ROAD
TETCOTT RD
UVERDALE ROAD
BURNABY STREET
ASHBURNHAM ROAD
STADIUM STREET
UPCERNE ROAD
TETCOTT ROAD
CHELSEA HARBOUR DR
KING'S QUAY
THAMES QUAY
THAMES AVE
THE QUADRANGLE
THE BELVEDERE
CHELSEA CRES
IMPERIAL RD
TOWNMEAD ROAD
BAGLEY'S LA
SANDS END LA
VICARAGE CRES
BATTERSEA CHURCH RD
BATTERSEA HIGH ST
WHISTLERS AVENUE
SUNBURY LA
GRANFIELD ST
OLD SWAN WHARF
VICARAGE WLK
COTSWOLD MEWS
BATTERSEA SQ
THE RIVERAINS
GROVESIDE CT
TYNEMOUTH ST
ELSWICK ST
ORVILLE RD
A308
A3220
A304
A3217
A3212
B305

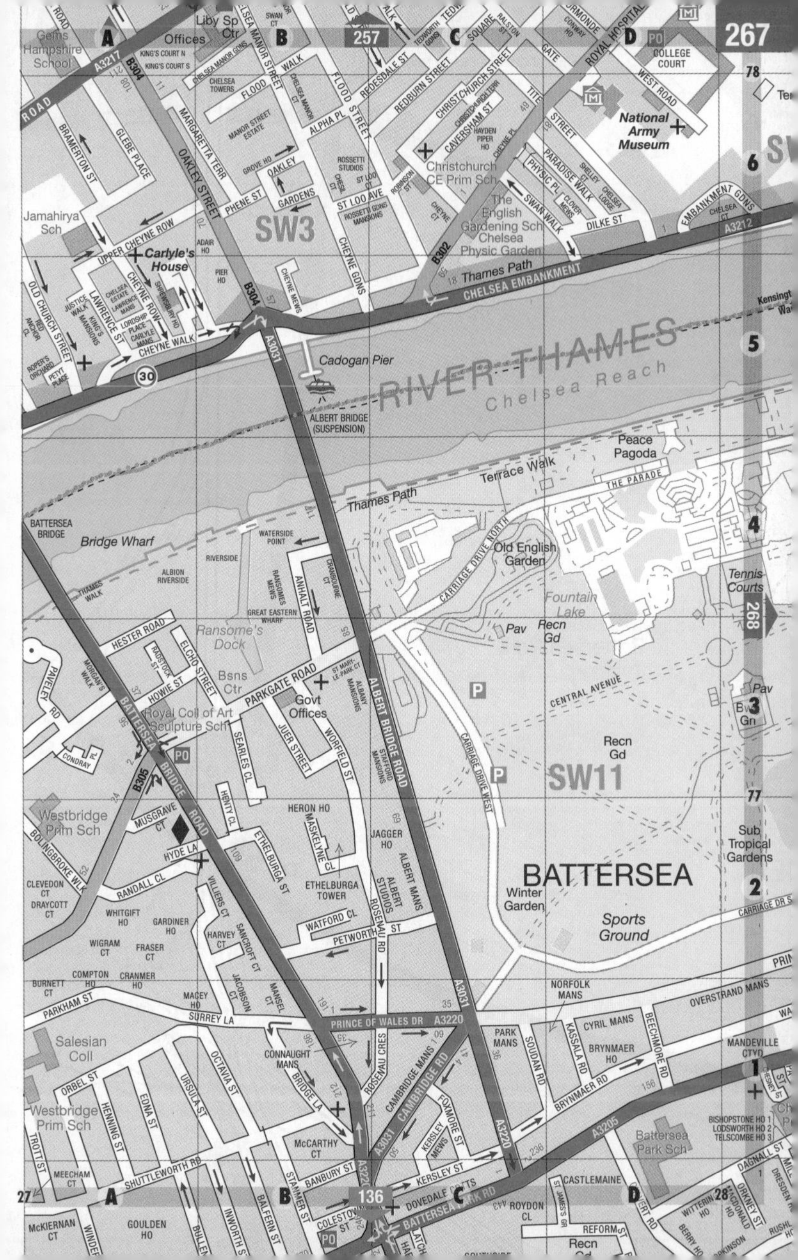

Gems Hampshire School
Liby
Sp Ctr
Offices
257
KING'S COURT N
KING'S COURT S
CHELSEA MANOR GDNS
CHELSEA TOWERS
CHELSEA MANOR STREET
FLOOD WALK
FLOOD STREET
REDESDALE ST
TEDWORTH GDNS
TEDWORTH SQUARE
ROYAL HOSPITAL ROAD
COLLEGE COURT
WEST ROAD
National Army Museum
BRAMERTON ST
GLEBE PLACE
MARGARETTA TERR
OAKLEY STREET
MANOR STREET ESTATE
GROVE HO
OAKLEY GARDENS
ALPHA PL
ROSSETTI STUDIOS
REDBURN STREET
CHRISTCHURCH STREET
CAVERSHAM ST
Christchurch CE Prim Sch
TITE STREET
PARADISE WALK
SWAN WALK
PHYSIC PL
DILKE ST
EMBANKMENT GDNS
CHELSEA CT
A3212
PHENE ST
ST LOO AVE
ROSSETTI GDNS MANSIONS
CHEYNE GDNS
CHEYNE CT
The English Gardening Sch
Chelsea Physic Garden
Thames Path
CHELSEA EMBANKMENT
B302
SW3
Jamahirya Sch
UPPER CHEYNE ROW
Carlyle's House
ADAIR HO
PIER HO
B304
CHEYNE MEWS
OLD CHURCH STREET
LAWRENCE ST
CHEYNE ROW
CHEYNE WALK
JUSTICE WALK
LORDSHIP PLACE
CARLYLE MANS
ROPER'S ORCHARD
PETYT PLACE
RED ANCHOR CL
A3031
Cadogan Pier
RIVER THAMES
Chelsea Reach
ALBERT BRIDGE (SUSPENSION)
Peace Pagoda
Terrace Walk
THE PARADE
BATTERSEA BRIDGE
Bridge Wharf
WATERSIDE POINT
RIVERSIDE
ALBION RIVERSIDE
THAMES WALK
RANSOMES MEWS
GREAT EASTERN WHARF
ANHALT ROAD
CRANBOURNE CT
CARRIAGE DRIVE NORTH
Old English Garden
Fountain Lake
Tennis Courts
268
HESTER ROAD
RADSTOCK ST
ELCHO STREET
Ransome's Dock
Pav
Recn Gd
HOWIE ST
Bsns Ctr
PARKGATE ROAD
ST MARY-LE-PARK CT
ALBANY MANSIONS
Govt Offices
MORGAN'S WALK
PAVELEY RD
BATTERSEA BRIDGE ROAD
Royal Coll of Art Sculpture Sch
CONDRAY PL
SEARLES CL
JUER STREET
WORFIELD ST
ALBERT BRIDGE ROAD
STAFFORD MANSIONS
CENTRAL AVENUE
CARRIAGE DRIVE WEST
SW11
B305
Westbridge Prim Sch
MUSGRAVE CT
HYDE LA
HENTY CL
ETHELBURGA ST
HERON HO
MASKELYNE CL
JAGGER HO
ALBERT MANS
ALBERT STUDIOS
Sub Tropical Gardens
BATTERSEA
Winter Garden
Sports Ground
CARRIAGE DR S
BOLINGBROKE WLK
CLEVEDON CT
DRAYCOTT CT
RANDALL CL
VILLIERS CT
ETHELBURGA TOWER
ROSENAU RD
WHITGIFT HO
GARDINER HO
HARVEY CT
SANCROFT CT
WATFORD CL
PETWORTH ST
WIGRAM CT
FRASER CT
COMPTON HO
CRANMER HO
BURNETT CT
MACEY HO
JACOBSON CT
MANSEL CT
NORFOLK MANS
OVERSTRAND MANS
PARKHAM ST
SURREY LA
PRINCE OF WALES DR
A3220
PARK MANS
SOUDAN RD
KASSALA RD
CYRIL MANS
BEECHMORE RD
BRYNMAER HO
MANDEVILLE CTYD
Salesian Coll
CONNAUGHT MANS
ORBEL ST
OCTAVIA ST
URSULA ST
ROSENAU CRES
CAMBRIDGE MANS
CAMBRIDGE RD
BRYNMAER RD
BRIDGE LA
FOXMORE ST
HENNING ST
EDNA ST
KERSLEY MEWS
A3205
BISHOPSTONE HO
LODSWORTH HO
TELSCOMBE HO
Battersea Park Sch
TROTT ST
McCARTHY CT
MEECHAM CT
SHUTTLEWORTH RD
BANBURY ST
KERSLEY ST
CASTLEMAINE
DAGNALL ST
ORKNEY ST
DRESDEN RD
136
DOVEDALE COTTS
BATTERSEA PARK RD
ST JAMES'S GR
ROYDON CL
REFORM ST
Recn
McKIERNAN CT
GOULDEN HO
BULLEN ST
INWORTH ST
BALFERN ST
STANMER ST
COLESTON ST
MCDONALD HO
WITTERING HO
BERRY HO
RUSHILL

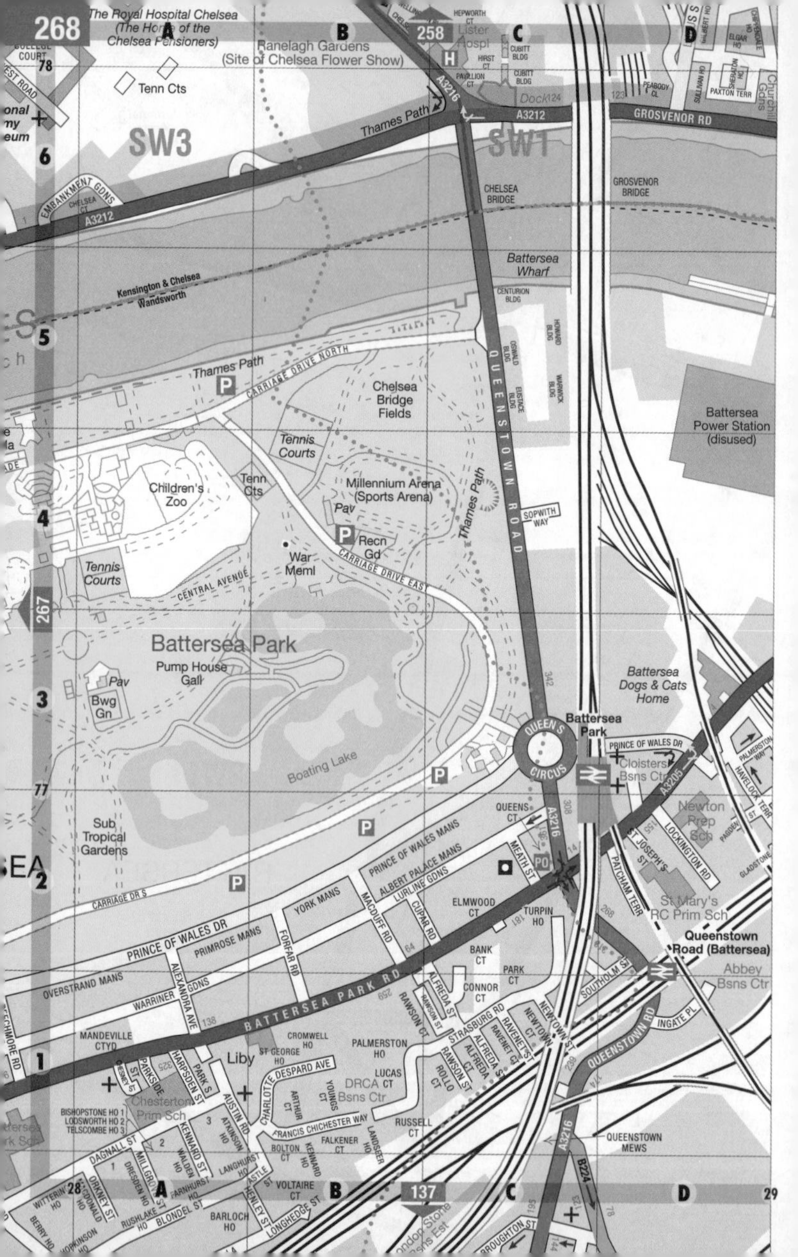
268
The Royal Hospital Chelsea
(The Home of the Chelsea Pensioners)
A
B
C
D
258
Ranelagh Gardens
(Site of Chelsea Flower Show)
Lister Hospl
HEPWORTH CT
CUBITT BLDG
HIRST CT
PAVILLION CT
Tenn Cts
Dock
A3216
A3212
GROSVENOR RD
PEABODY CL
PAXTON TERR
SULLIVAN HO
ELGAR HO
Thames Path
SW3
SW1
EMBANKMENT GDNS
CHELSEA CT
CHELSEA BRIDGE
GROSVENOR BRIDGE
Battersea Wharf
Kensington & Chelsea
Wandsworth
CENTURION BLDG
HOWARD BLDG
OSWALD BLDG
EUSTACE BLDG
WARWICK BLDG
QUEENSTOWN ROAD
Battersea Power Station (disused)
CARRIAGE DRIVE NORTH
Chelsea Bridge Fields
Tennis Courts
Millennium Arena (Sports Arena)
Children's Zoo
Tenn Cts
Pav
Recn Gd
SOPWITH WAY
War Meml
CARRIAGE DRIVE EAST
CENTRAL AVENUE
Tennis Courts
267
Battersea Park
Pump House Gall
Pav
Bwg Gn
Battersea Dogs & Cats Home
Battersea Park
QUEEN'S CIRCUS
PRINCE OF WALES DR
Cloisters Bsns Ctr
A3205
PALMERSTON WAY
HAVELOCK TERR
Boating Lake
Sub Tropical Gardens
QUEENS CT
Newton Prep Sch
LOCKINGTON RD
ST JOSEPH'S ST
PAGDEN ST
GLADSTONE TERR
PRINCE OF WALES MANS
ALBERT PALACE MANS
LURLINE GDNS
MEATH ST
PO
PATCHAM TERR
St Mary's RC Prim Sch
CARRIAGE DR S
YORK MANS
MACDUFF RD
CUPAR RD
ELMWOOD CT
TURPIN HO
Queenstown Road (Battersea)
PRINCE OF WALES DR
PRIMROSE MANS
FORFAR RD
ALEXANDRA AVE
BANK CT
PARK CT
SOUTHOLM ST
Abbey Bsns Ctr
OVERSTRAND MANS
WARRINER GDNS
BATTERSEA PARK RD
ALFREDA ST
CONNOR CT
RAWSON CT
STRASBURG RD
RAVENET ST
NEWTOWN ST
QUEENSTOWN RD
INGATE PL
MANDEVILLE CTYD
CROMWELL HO
PALMERSTON HO
ST GEORGE HO
Liby
DESPARD AVE
CHARLOTTE
LUCAS CT
DRCA Bsns Ctr
ROLLO CT
PARKSIDE
HARPSDEN ST
PARK ST
AUSTIN RD
Chesterton Prim Sch
ARTHUR CT
YOUNGS CT
BISHOPSTONE HO 1
LODSWORTH HO 2
TELSCOMBE HO 3
FRANCIS CHICHESTER WAY
RUSSELL CT
QUEENSTOWN MEWS
DAGNALL ST
KENNARD ST
ATKINSON HO
WALDEN HO
BOLTON CT
FALKENER CT
LANDSEER
B224
MILLGROVE ST
DRESDEN HO
LANGHURST HO
ASTLE ST
VOLTAIRE CT
ORKNEY ST
FARNHURST HO
HENLEY ST
137
WITTERING HO
MACDONALD HO
RUSHLAKE HO
BLONDEL ST
BARLOCH HO
LONGHEDGE ST
London Stone Bsns Est
BROUGHTON ST
BERRY HO
HOPKINSON HO
29

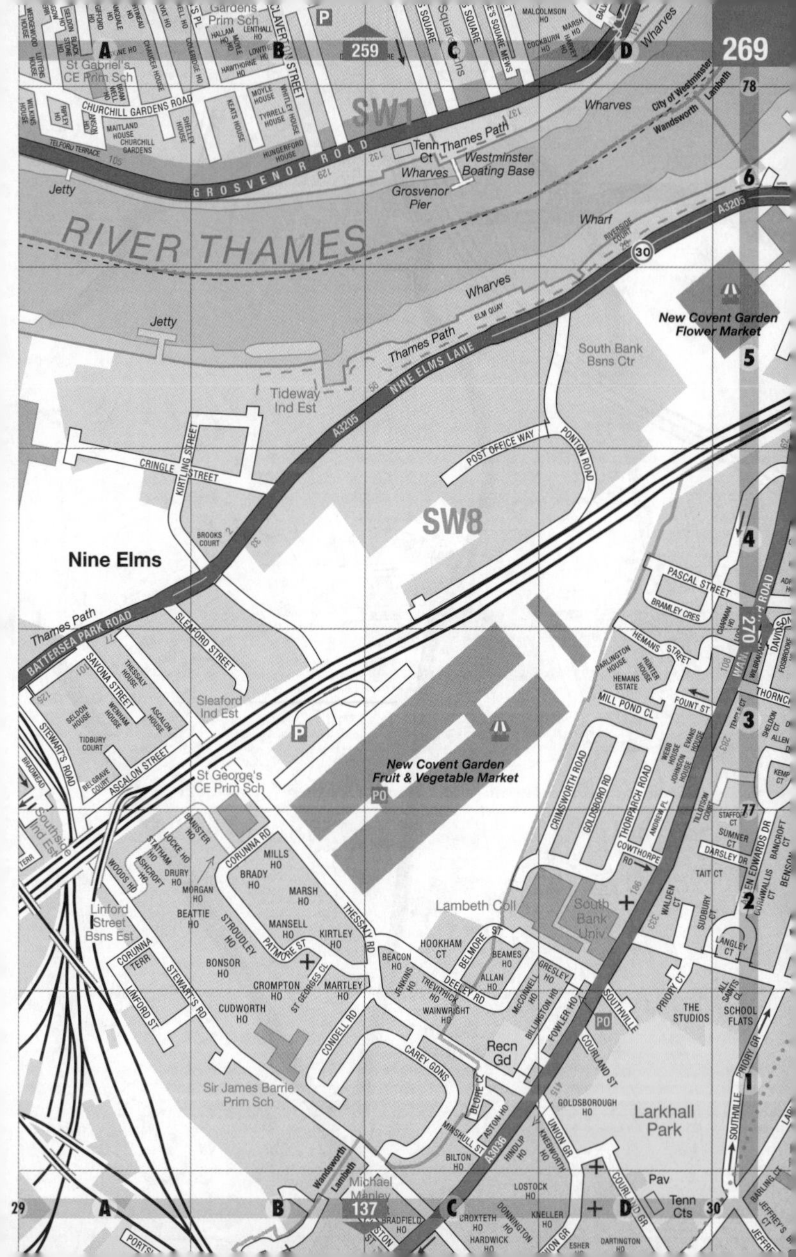

RIVER THAMES
SW1
SW8
Nine Elms
GROSVENOR ROAD
NINE ELMS LANE
BATTERSEA PARK ROAD
CHURCHILL GARDENS ROAD
CLAVERTON STREET
Grosvenor Pier
Westminster Boating Base
Tideway Ind Est
South Bank Bsns Ctr
New Covent Garden Flower Market
New Covent Garden Fruit & Vegetable Market
Sleaford Ind Est
St George's CE Prim Sch
St Gabriel's CE Prim Sch
Linford Street Bsns Est
Lambeth Coll
South Bank Univ
Sir James Barrie Prim Sch
Larkhall Park
Recn Gd
Thames Path
POST OFFICE WAY
PONTON ROAD
CRINGLE STREET
KIRTLING STREET
SLEAFORD STREET
SAVONA STREET
ASCALON STREET
STEWART'S ROAD
PASCAL STREET
HEMANS STREET
CRIMSWORTH ROAD
GOLDSBORO RD
THORPARCH ROAD
CORUNNA RD
THESSALY RD
PATMORE ST
DEELEY RD
CAREY GDNS
CONDELL RD
PRIORY GR
SOUTHVILLE
COURLAND ST
UNION GR
Pav
Tenn Cts

259
137
270

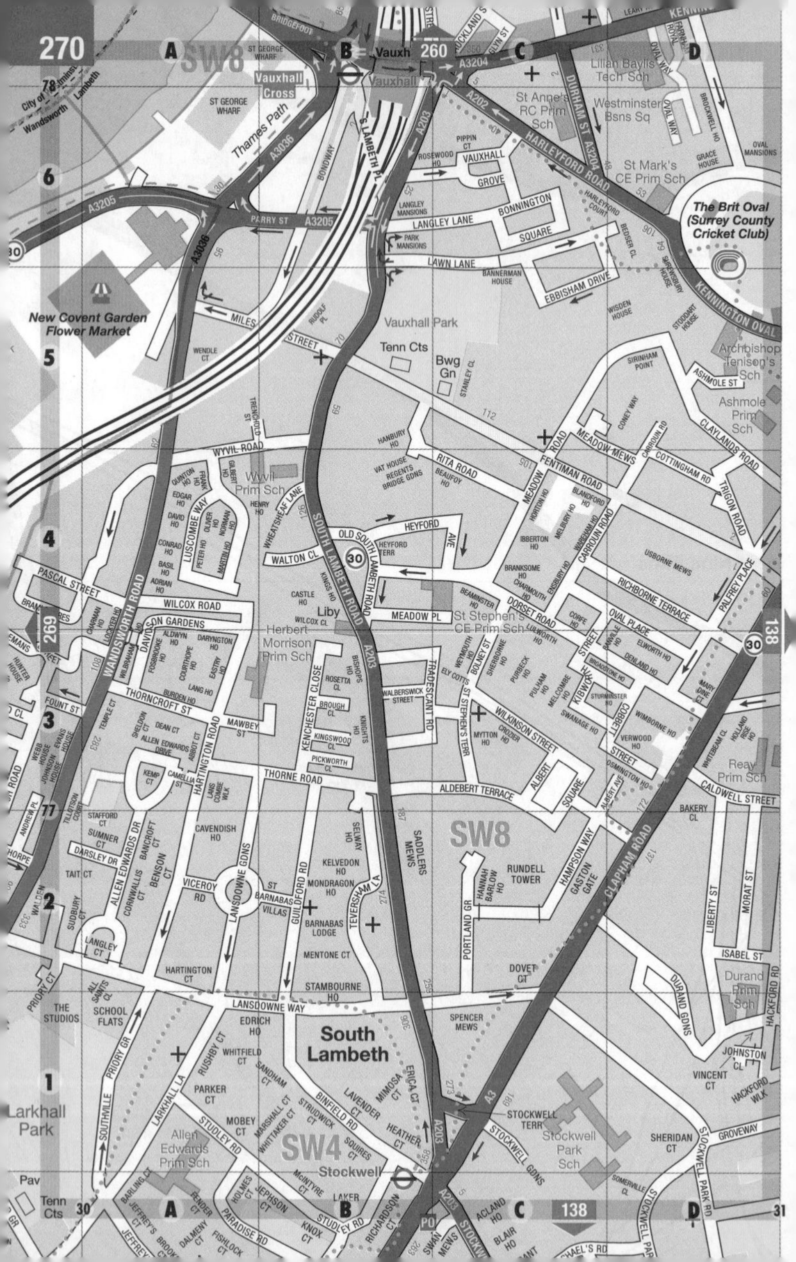
270
A
B
C
D
SW8
78
6
5
4
3
77
2
1
City of Westminster
Lambeth
Wandsworth
Bridgefoot
St George Wharf
Vauxhall Cross
Vauxhall
260
A3204
Stockland St
Glyn St
Leary
Kennington
Lillian Baylis Tech Sch
Farnham Royal
Oval Way
Durham St
St Anne's RC Prim Sch
Westminster Bsns Sq
Brockwell Ho
Oval Mansions
A202
Harleyford Road
St Mark's CE Prim Sch
Grace House
The Brit Oval (Surrey County Cricket Club)
Thames Path
A3036
Bondway
S. Lambeth Pl
A203
Pippin Ct
Rosewood Ho
Vauxhall Grove
Bonnington Square
Langley Mansions
Langley Lane
Park Mansions
Lawn Lane
Bannerman House
Ebbisham Drive
Harleyford Court
Bedser Cl
Shrewsbury House
Kennington Oval
Wisden House
Stoddart House
A3205
Parry St
New Covent Garden Flower Market
Miles Street
Rudolf Pl
Vauxhall Park
Tenn Cts
Bwg Gn
Stanley Cl
Wendle Ct
Sirinham Point
Ashmole St
Archbishop Tenison's Sch
Ashmole Prim Sch
Claylands Road
Coney Way
Meadow Mews
Meadow Road
Carroun Rd
Cottingham Rd
Trenchold St
Wyvil Road
Hanbury Ho
Rita Road
Fentiman Road
Trigon Road
Quinton Ho
Frank Ho
Gilbert Ho
Wyvil Prim Sch
Vat House
Regents Bridge Gdns
Beaufoy Ho
Horton Ho
Blandford Ho
Edgar Ho
David Ho
Luscombe Way
Oliver Ho
Norman Ho
Henry Ho
Wheatsheaf Lane
South Lambeth Road
Heyford Ave
Heyford Terr
Melbury Ho
Wareham Ho
Carroun Road
Usborne Mews
Conrad Ho
Basil Ho
Adrian Ho
Peter Ho
Martin Ho
Walton Cl
Old South Lambeth Road
Ibberton Ho
Branksome Ho
Charmouth Ho
Ensbury Ho
Richborne Terrace
Palfrey Place
Pascal Street
Wilcox Road
Castle Ho
Kings Ho
Liby
Wilcox Cl
Meadow Pl
Beaminster Ho
St Stephen's CE Prim Sch
Dorset Road
Corfe Ho
Oval Place
Lulworth Ho
Elworth Ho
Denland Ho
269
Brambles
Davidson Gardens
Charman Ho
Lockyer Ho
Wilbraham Ho
Aldwyn Ho
Daryngton Ho
Fosbrooke Ho
Courthope Ho
Eastry Ho
Lang Ho
Burden Ho
Herbert Morrison Prim Sch
Bishops Ho
Rosetta Cl
Brough Cl
Kingswood Cl
Pickworth Cl
Knights Ho
Kenchester Close
Walberswick Street
Tradescant Rd
Ely Cotts
Weymouth Ho
Bolney St
Sherborne Ho
Purbeck Ho
Pulham Ho
Melcombe Ho
Swanage Ho
Broadstone Ho
Sturminster Ho
Kibworth
Cobbett Street
Wimborne Ho
Verwood Ho
Mary Dine Ct
138
Hunter House
Wandsworth Road
Fount St
Thorncroft St
Temple Ct
Sheldon Ct
Dean Ct
Allen Edwards Drive
Abbot Ct
Hartington Road
Mawbey St
St Stephen's Terr
Wilkinson Street
Mytton Ho
Crozier Ho
Osmington Ho
Whitebeam Cl
Holland Rise Ho
Reay Prim Sch
Webb House
Johnson House
Evans House
Kemp Ct
Camellia St
Thorne Road
Aldebert Terrace
Albert Square
Albert Ave
Caldwell Street
Bakery Cl
Tillotson Court
Andrew Pl
Stafford Ct
Sumner Ct
Darsley Dr
Lans Combe Wlk
Cavendish Ho
Selway Ho
Saddlers Mews
SW8
Rundell Tower
Hampson Way
Gaston Gate
Clapham Road
Liberty St
Morat St
Tait Ct
Allen Edwards Dr
Bancroft Ct
Benson Ct
Cornwallis Ct
Viceroy Rd
Lansdowne Gdns
St Barnabas Villas
Guildford Rd
Kelvedon Ho
Mondragon Ho
Barnabas Lodge
Teversham La
Hannah Barlow Ho
Portland Gr
Sudbury Ct
Walden
Langley Ct
Hartington Ct
Mentone Ct
Stambourne Ho
Dovet Ct
Isabel St
Durand Gdns
Durand Prim Sch
Hackford Rd
Priory Ct
All Saints Cl
The Studios
School Flats
Lansdowne Way
Edrich Ho
South Lambeth
Spencer Mews
Johnston Cl
Vincent Ct
Hackford Wlk
Rushby Ct
Whitfield Ct
Sandham Ct
Priory Gr
Larkhall La
Parker Ct
Mimosa Ct
Erica Ct
Lavender Ct
Binfield Rd
Stockwell Terr
Stockwell Park Sch
Sheridan Ct
Groveway
Larkhall Park
Southville
Allen Edwards Prim Sch
Studley Rd
Mobey Ct
Marshall Ct
Whittaker Ct
Strudwick Ct
Heather Ct
Squires Ct
SW4
Stockwell
Stockwell Gdns
Somerville Cl
Stockwell Park Rd
Pav
Tenn Cts
Barling Ct
Render Ct
Holmes Ct
Jephson Ct
McIntyre Ct
Laker Ct
Richardson Ct
Jeffrey's Ct
Dalmeny Ct
Paradise Rd
Knox Ct
Studley Rd
Fishlock Ct
Brook
PO
Swan Mews
Acland Ho
Blair Ho
Stockwell
Michael's Rd
30
31

Place name May be abbreviated on the map ➤ Church Rd **6** Beckenham BR2....53 C6 **228** C6

Location number Present when a number indicates the place's position in a crowded area of mapping

Locality, town or village Shown when more than one place has the same name

Postcode district District for the indexed place

Map page number and grid square References to the large-scale maps on pages 229–270 are underlined in red

Cities, towns and villages are listed in CAPITAL LETTERS. **Public and commercial buildings** are highlighted in magenta. **Places of interest** are highlighted in blue with a star★

Abbreviations used in the index

Acad	Academy	Ct	Court	Hts	Heights	Pl	Place
App	Approach	Ctr	Centre	Ind	Industrial	Prec	Precinct
Arc	Arcade	Ctry	Country	Inst	Institute	Prom	Promenade
Ave	Avenue	Cty	County	Int	International	Rd	Road
Bglw	Bungalow	Dr	Drive	Intc	Interchange	Recn	Recreation
Bldg	Building	Dro	Drove	Junc	Junction	Ret	Retail
Bsns, Bus	Business	Ed	Education	L	Leisure	Sh	Shopping
Bvd	Boulevard	Emb	Embankment	La	Lane	Sq	Square
Cath	Cathedral	Est	Estate	Liby	Library	St	Street
Cir	Circus	Ex	Exhibition	Mdw	Meadow	Sta	Station
Cl	Close	Gd	Ground	Meml	Memorial	Terr	Terrace
Cnr	Corner	Gdn	Garden	Mkt	Market	TH	Town Hall
Coll	College	Gn	Green	Mus	Museum	Univ	University
Com	Community	Gr	Grove	Orch	Orchard	Wk, Wlk	Walk
Comm	Common	H	Hall	Pal	Palace	Wr	Water
Cott	Cottage	Ho	House	Par	Parade	Yd	Yard
Cres	Crescent	Hospl	Hospital	Pas	Passage		
Cswy	Causeway	HQ	Headquarters	Pk	Park		

Index of towns, villages, streets, hospitals, industrial estates, railway stations, schools, shopping centres, universities and places of interest

176 Gall★ NW5.......71 A2
201 Bishopgate EC2 **243** B4

A

Aaron Ct BR3......207 C6
Aaron Hill Rd E6....100 C2
Abady Ho SW1.....259 D4
Abberley Mews **9**
  SW8.......137 B2
Abberton IG8.......37 C5
Abbess Cl
  11 Newham E6 ....100 A2
  Streatham SW2....160 D3
Abbeville Mews **3**
  SW4.......137 D1
Abbeville Rd
  Clapham Pk SW4 ..159 C6
  Hornsey N8 ....49 D5
Abbey Ave HA0.....88 A5
Abbey Bsns Ctr
  SW8.......137 B4 **268** C2
Abbey Cl Hayes UB3 ..106 B5
  Northolt UB5 ....85 B4
  Pinner HA5...........40 C6
Abbey Coll London
  SW1.....115 B3 **258** C5
Abbey Cres DA17 ...125 C2
Abbey Ct
  6 Bedford Pk W12 ..111 C3
  Camberwell SE17....**262** B1
  Church End N3......47 C6

Abbey Ct continued
  5 Edgware HA8 ....26 C5
  Hampton TW12 ....173 C3
  St John's Wood NW8 **229** A4
Abbeydale Rd HA0....88 C6
Abbey Dr SW17.....181 A5
Abbeyfield Cl CR4....180 C1
Abbeyfield Rd SE16 ..118 C2
Abbeyfields Cl NW10...88 C5
Abbey Gdns
  10 Bermondsey
    SE16.......118 A2
  Chislehurst BR7....188 C2
  St John's Wood
    NW8 ....92 A5 **229** B3
  West Kensington
    W6 .....135 A4 **264** A5
Abbey Gr SE2......124 B2
Abbeyhill Rd DA15 ..168 C2
Abbey Ho
  Newham E15 ......98 C5
  St John's Wood NW8 ..229 A4
Abbey Ind Est
  Ealing NW10 ......88 B6
  Mitcham CR4 ......202 D4
Abbey La
  Beckenham BR3....185 C3
  Mill Meads E15 ....98 B5
Abbey Lane Commercial
  Est **1** E15 ......98 C5
Abbey Lo
  Bromley SE12.....187 B6

Abbey Lo continued
  Ealing W5 ....109 C6
  Lisson Gr NW8 ....**230** B1
Abbey Manufacturing Est
  HA0.......88 B6
Abbey Mews
  Brentford TW7....131 B4
  Walthamstow E17...53 C4
Abbey Mount DA17 ..125 B1
Abbey Orchard St
  SW1 .....115 D3 **259** D6
Abbey Orchard Street Est
  SW1.......**259** D6
Abbey Par
  Ealing NW10 ......88 B4
  Merton SW19.....180 A3
Abbey Park Ind Est
  IG11.......101 A6
Abbey Pk BR3 .....185 C3
Abbey Prim Sch
  SM4.......201 C2
Abbey Rd
  Barking IG11......101 A6
  Bexley DA7.......147 A1
  Croydon CR0 .....220 D5
  Enfield EN1 ......17 C6
  Erith DA17 ....125 A3
  Ilford IG2.........57 B4
  Lower Halliford TW17 192 C1
  Merton SW19.....180 A3
  Newham E15 ......98 C5
  St John's Wood
    NW8 ....92 A5 **229** A4

Abbey Rd continued
  Wembley NW10......88 D5
Abbey Sports Ctr
  IG11.......101 A6
Abbey St
  Bermondsey
    SE1 .....117 D3 **263** C6
  Newham E13 ......99 A3
Abbey Terr SE2 .....124 C2
Abbey Trad Est SE26..185 B5
Abbey View NW7.....11 D1
Abbey Wlk KT8 .....195 D5
ABBEY WOOD 124 B3
Abbey Wood Rd SE2 ..124 C2
Abbey Wood Sch
  SE2.......124 A3
Abbey Wood Sta
  SE2.......124 C3
Abbot Cl **1** SW8....270 A3
Abbot CI HA4........62 C5
Abbot Ho **14** E14 ..119 D6
Abbotsbury Cl
  Kensington
    W14 ....113 B4 **244** C1
  Mill Meads E15 .....98 A5
Abbotsbury Gdns
  HA5.......40 C3
Abbotsbury Ho W14. **244** B2
Abbotsbury Mews
  SE15.......140 C2
Abbotsbury Prim Sch
  SM4.......201 D4

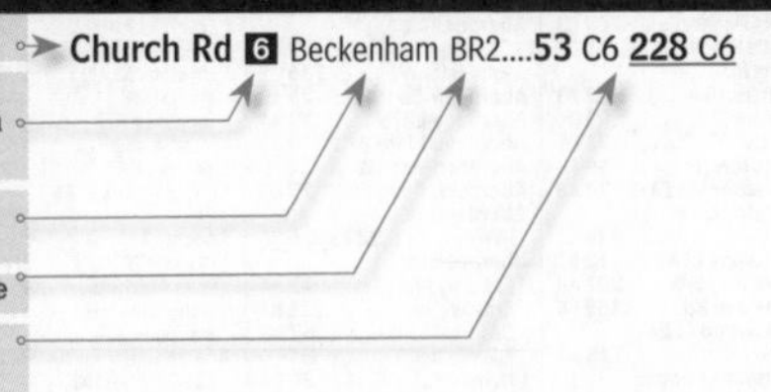

176–Abb

Abbotsbury Rd
  Coney Hatch BR2,
    BR4.......224 D6
  Kensington
    W14 ....113 B4 **244** C1
  Morden SM4 ......201 D5
Abbots Cl BR5 .....211 A1
Abbots Ct SE25 .....205 C6
Abbots Dr HA2........63 C6
Abbotsfield Sch **1**UB10 82 C5
Abbotsford Ave N15...51 A5
Abbotsford Gdns IG8 ..37 A3
Abbotsford Rd IG3....80 B6
Abbots Gdns N2.......48 B5
Abbots Gn CR0,CR2 ..222 D2
Abbots Green 222 D2
Abbotshade Rd **12**
  SE16.......118 C5
Abbotshall Ave N14...15 C1
Abbotshall Rd SE6..164 B2
Abbots Ho
  Kensington W14....**254** C5
  Pimlico SW1......**259** C1
  Walthamstow E17...35 B1
Abbots La
  SE1.......117 C5 **253** B3
Abbotsleigh Cl SM2..217 D1
Abbotsleigh Rd
  SW16.......181 C5

Abbotsmede Cl TW1 152 D2
Abbots Pk SW2 160 C3
Abbot's Pl NW6 91 D6
Abbots Rd
Burnt Oak HA8 27 B3
Newham E6 99 D6
Abbot St E8 73 D2
Abbots Terr N8 50 A3
Abbotstone Ho 4 E5 74 A6
Abbotstone Rd SW15 134 C2
Abbotsview Ct NW7 12 A1
Abbots Way BR3 207 A4
Abbotswell Rd SE4 163 B6
Abbotswood Cl 7 DA17 125 A3
Abbotswood Gdns IG5 56 B6
Abbotswood Rd
London SE22 139 C1
Streatham SW16 159 D1
Abbotswood Way UB3 106 B5
Abbott Ave SW20 178 D2
Abbott Cl
Hampton TW12 173 A4
Northolt UB5 63 B2
Abbott Ho SW12 158 D4
Abbott Rd E14 98 B1
Abbotts Cl
Canonbury N1 73 A2
Romford RM7 59 D6
Woolwich SE28 124 C6
Abbotts Cres
Chingford E4 36 B6
Enfield EN2 4 D3
Abbotts Ct HA2 64 B6
Abbotts Dr HA0 65 B6
Abbotts Park Rd E10 54 A2
Abbotts Rd Barnet EN5 1 D1
Cheam SM3 217 A4
Mitcham CR4 203 C5
Southall UB1 107 A5
Abbotts Wharf 4 E14 97 C1
Abbott's Wlk DA7 146 D5
Abchurch La EC2, EC4 117 B6 252 D6
Abchurch Yd EC4 252 C6
Abdale Rd W12 112 B5
Abel Ho
7 Kennington SE11 138 C6
1 Woolwich SE18 123 A2
Abenglen Ind Est UB3 105 B4
Aberavon Rd E3 97 A4
Abercairn Rd SW16 181 C3
Aberconway Rd SM4 201 D5
Abercorn Cl
Finchley NW7 29 A3
St John's Wood NW8 92 A4 229 A2
Abercorn Cres HA2 41 D1
Abercorn Dell WD23 8 A2
Abercorn Gdns
Harrow HA3 43 D2
Ilford RM6 58 B3
Abercorn Gr HA4 39 B5
Abercorn Mans NW8 229 B3
Abercorn Mews 10 TW10 132 B1
Abercorn Pl NW8 92 A5 229 A3
Abercorn Rd
Finchley NW7 29 A3
Stanmore HA7 25 C3
Abercorn Sch NW8 92 A5 229 B3
Abercorn Trad Est HA0 87 D6
Abercorn Way SE1 118 A1
Abercorn Wlk NW8 92 A4 229 A2
Abercrombie Dr EN1 6 A4
Abercrombie Ho 1 W12 112 B6
Abercrombie St SW11 136 C3
Aberdale Ct 22 SE16 118 D4
Aberdare Cl BR4 224 A6
Aberdare Gdns
Finchley NW7 28 D3
South Hampstead NW6 69 D1
Aberdare Rd EN3 6 C1
Aberdeen Cotts HA7 25 C3
Aberdeen Ct
Canonbury N5 73 A3
Paddington W2 236 C5
Aberdeen Ctr N5 73 A3
Aberdeen La N5 73 A3
Aberdeen Mans WC1 240 A6
Aberdeen Par N18 34 B5
Aberdeen Pk N5 73 A3
Aberdeen Pl NW8 92 B3 236 C6
Aberdeen Rd
Canonbury N5 73 A4
Croydon CR0 221 B4
Dudden Hill NW10 67 D3
Edmonton N18 34 B5
Harrow HA3 24 D1
Aberdeen Terr SE3 142 B3
Aberdour Rd IG3 80 B6
Aberdour St SE1 117 C2 263 A4
Aberfeldy Ho SE5 138 D5
Aberfeldy St E14 98 A1
Aberford Gdns SE18 144 A4
Aberfoyle Rd SW16 181 D4
Abergeldie Rd SE12 165 B5
Abernethy Rd SE13 142 C1
Abersham Rd E8 73 D3
Abery St SE18 123 C2
Ability Plaza 8 E8 73 D1
Ability Twrs EC1 235 A2
Abingdon W14 254 D3
Abingdon Cl
Fulham SE1 263 D2
Hillingdon UB10 82 B6
Kentish Town NW1 71 D2
North Cheam KT4 216 B5
Wimbledon SW19 180 A4
Abingdon Ct
Earl's Ct W8 255 B5
Edgware HA8 26 A6
Upper Tooting SW17 180 D4
Abingdon Gdns W8 255 B5
Abingdon Ho
Bromley BR1 187 B3
Spitalfields E2 243 C6
Abingdon Lo
2 Barnet EN5 1 A1
Bromley BR2 186 D1
Abingdon Mans W8 255 A6
Abingdon Rd
Finchley N3 30 A1
Kensington W8 113 C3 255 B5
Thornton Heath SW16 182 A2
Abingdon St SW1 116 A3 260 A6
Abingdon Villas W8 113 C3 255 B5
Abinger Cl
Barking IG11 80 A4
Bickley BR1 210 A6
New Addington CR0 224 A2
Wallington SM6 220 A3
Abinger Ct
3 Ealing W5 109 C6
Thornton Heath CR0 204 D2
Wallington SM6 220 A3
Abinger Gdns TW7 130 C2
Abinger Gr SE8 141 B6
Abinger Ho
Borough The SE1 252 C1
2 Kingston u T KT2 176 D3
Abinger Mews W9 91 C3
Abinger Rd W4 111 C3
Abington Ho NW11 48 A3
Ablett St SE16 118 C1
Abney Gdns 5 N16 73 D6
Abney Park Cemetery★ N16 73 C6
Abney Park Ct N16 73 D6
Aborfield 6 NW5 71 C3
Aboyne Dr SW20 178 A1
Aboyne Rd
Neasden NW10 67 C5
Wandsworth SW17 158 B1
Abraham Cl WD19 22 B6
Abraham Cohen Ct IG1 56 C3
Abraham Fisher Ho 2 E12 78 C3
Abridge Way IG11 102 B5
Abyssinia Cl SW11 136 C1
Abyssinia Rd SW11 136 C1
Acacia Ave
Brentford TW8 131 B5
East Finchley N2 47 D6
Hayes UB3 83 D1
Littleton TW17 192 C4
Ruislip HA4 40 B2
Tottenham N17 33 B3
Wembley HA9 66 A3
Yiewsley UB7 104 B6
Acacia Bsns Ctr 1 E11 76 C5
Acacia Cl
Penge SE20 184 A1
Petts Wood BR5 211 B4
Rotherhithe SE8 119 A2
Stanmore HA7 24 C4
Acacia Ct Harrow HA1 41 D3
5 West Norwood SW16 182 C5
Acacia Dr SM3 201 C1
Acacia Gdns
St John's Wood NW8 229 D4
West Wickham BR4 224 A6
Acacia Gr
Dulwich SE21 161 B2
Kingston u T KT3 199 C6
Acacia Ho
Brockley SE4 141 B1
1 New Malden KT3 199 C5
Stoke Newington N16 73 B6
Wood Green N22 32 C2
Acacia Lo 6 N3 29 B1
Acacia Pl NW8 92 B5 229 D4
Acacia Rd Acton W3 111 A6
Beckenham BR3 207 B6
Enfield EN2 5 B4
Hampton TW12 173 C4
Leyton E11 76 C6
Mitcham CR4 181 B1
St John's Wood NW8 92 B5 229 D4
Thornton Heath SW16 182 A2
Walthamstow E17 53 A3
Wood Green N22 32 C2
Acacias Lo EN4 14 B6
Acacias The EN4 14 B6
Acacia Way DA15 167 D3
Acacia Wlk SW10 266 B3
Academia Way N17 33 C4
Academic Coll of London HA0 65 D5
Academy Ct 13 E2 96 C4
Academy Gdns
Croydon CR0 205 D1
Kensington W8 245 A2
Northolt UB5 84 D5
Academy Pl
Hounslow TW7 130 C5
Woolwich SE18 144 C4
Academy Rd SE18 144 B5
Academy Sch The 9 NW3 70 B4
Academy The 2 N19 49 C1
Acad of Live & Recorded Arts SW18 158 B5
Acanthus Dr SE1 118 A1
Acanthus Rd SW11 137 A2
Accadia Ct NW9 67 A6
Accommodation Rd NW11 47 B1
Ace Par KT9 214 A5
Acer Ave UB4 85 A2
Acer Ct
2 Cricklewood NW2 68 D4
3 Enfield EN3 7 A2
Acer Rd E8 73 D1
Acers BR7 188 A3
Acfold Rd SW6 265 C1
Achilles Cl SE1 118 A1
Achilles Ho 16 E2 96 B5
Achilles Rd NW6 69 C3
Achilles St SE14 141 A5
Achilles Way W1 248 B3
Acklam Rd W10 91 B2
Acklington Dr NW9 27 C2
Ackmar Rd SW6 135 C4 265 A1
Ackroyd Dr E3 97 C2
Ackroyd Rd SE23 163 A4
Acland Burghley Sch NW5 71 B4
Acland Cl SE18 145 B5
Acland Cres SE5 139 B2
Acland Ho SW9 138 B3
Acland Rd NW2 68 B2
Acock Gr UB5 64 A4
Acol Cres HA4 62 B3
Acol Ct 3 NW6 69 C1
Acol Rd NW6 69 D1
Aconbury Rd RM9 102 B6
Acorn Cl Chingford E4 35 D5
Chislehurst BR7 189 A5
Enfield EN2 4 D4
1 Hampton TW12 173 D4
Stanmore HA7 25 B3
Acorn Ct 5 Bow E3 97 C5
Hampton TW12 173 B5
Ilford IG2 57 C4
Upton Pk E6 78 A1
Wood Green N11 31 D4
Acorn Gdns
North Acton W3 89 B2
South Norwood SE19 183 D2
Acorn Gr
Harlington UB3 127 D5
Ruislip HA4 61 D4
Acorn Par 7 SE15 140 B5
Acorn Production Ctr N7 72 A1
Acorns The 21 SW19 156 D3
Acorns Way KT10 212 A3
Acorn Way
Beckenham BR3 208 A4
Forest Hill SE23 162 D1
Orpington BR6 226 D4
Acorn Wharf SE15 140 A6
Acorn Wlk SE16 119 A5
Acqua Ho TW9 132 D5
Acre Dr SE22 140 A1
Acrefield Ho 4 NW4 46 D5
Acre La Brixton SW2 138 B1
Wallington SM5 219 A4
Acre Path UB5 63 A2
Acre Rd
Dagenham RM10 81 D1
Kingston u T KT2 176 B2
Mitcham SW19 180 B4
Acre Way HA6 22 A2
Acris St SW18 158 A6
ACS Hillingdon International Sch UB10 82 B6
Action Ct TW15 171 A2
ACTON 111 B5
Acton Bsns Ctr NW10 89 B3
Acton Central Ind Est 4 W3 110 D5
Acton Central Sta W3 111 B5
Acton Cl N9 18 A2
ACTON GREEN 111 A2
Acton High Sch W3 110 C4
Acton Hill Mews W3 110 D5
Acton Ho 5 Acton W3 89 A1
16 Haggerston E8 95 D6
Acton La
Acton Green W4 111 A2
Acton W3 111 A4
Harlesden NW10 89 B5
Acton Main Line Sta W3 89 A1
Acton Mews E8 95 D6
Acton Park Ind Est W3 111 B4
Acton St WC1 94 B4 233 C1
Acton Town Sta W3 110 C4
Acton Vale Ind Pk W3 111 D5
Acton & West London Coll 16 W3 110 D5
Acuba Ho SW18 157 D3
Acuba Rd SW18 157 D2
Acworth Cl N9 18 C4
Acworth Ho 1 SE18 144 D6
Ada Ct Islington N1 235 A5
St John's Wood W9 92 A4 229 B1
Ada Gdns
Plaistow E15 98 D6
South Bromley E14 98 B1
Ada Ho 23 E2 96 A6
Adair Cl SE25 206 B6
Adair Ho SW3 267 B6
Adair Rd W10 91 A3
Adair Twr 7 W10 91 A3
Ada Kennedy Ct 6 SE10 142 A5
Ada Lewis Ho HA9 66 B4
Adam Cl SE6 185 C6
Adam Ct
Newington SE11 261 C3
15 Sutton SM1 218 A4
Adam & Eve Ct W1 239 B2
Adam & Eve Mews W8 113 C3 255 B6
Adamfields NW3 70 B1
Adam Lo N21 16 B6
Adam Rd E4 35 B4
Adams Bridge Bsns Ctr HA9 66 D3
Adams Cl Finchley N3 29 C3
Surbiton KT5 198 B3
Wembley Pk NW9 66 D6
Adams Ct E17 53 A3
Adams Gardens Est 5 SE16 118 C4
Adams Ho
3 South Bromley E14 98 B1
3 Streatham SW16 181 C5
Adams Mews
Upper Tooting SW17 158 D2
Wood Green N22 32 B3
Adamson Ct N2 48 C6
Adamson Rd
Hampstead NW3 70 B1
Newham E16 99 A1
Adamson Way BR3 208 A4
Adams Pl N7 72 B3
Adams Qtr TW8 131 C6
Adams Rd
Beckenham BR3 207 A4
Tottenham N17 33 B1
Adamsrill Cl EN1 17 B5
Adamsrill Prim Sch SE26 163 A1
Adamsrill Rd SE26 185 A6
Adam's Row W1 115 A6 248 B5
Adams Sq DA6 147 A2
Adam St WC2 116 A6 250 B5
Adams Way CR0 206 A3
Adams Wlk 11 KT1 176 A1
Adam Wlk SW6 134 C5
Ada Pl E2 96 A6
Ada Rd
Camberwell SE5 139 C5
Wembley HA0, HA9 65 D5
Adare Wlk SW16, SW2 160 B2
Ada St E8 96 B6
Adcot Wlk 6 BR6 227 D4
Adderley Gdns SE9 188 C6
Adderley Gr SW11 159 A6
Adderley Rd HA3 24 D2
Adderley St E14 98 A1
Addey Ho SE8 141 B5
Addey & Stanhope Sch 11 SE14 141 C4
ADDINGTON 223 C3
Addington Ct 7 SW14 133 B2
Addington Dr N12 30 B4
Addington Gr SE26 185 A6
Addington Ho 13 SW9 138 B3
Addington Rd Bow E3 97 C4
Newham E16 98 C3
Stroud Green N4 50 C3
Thornton Heath CR0 204 C1
West Wickham BR4 224 C6
West Wickham BR4, CR0 224 B4
Addington Sq SE5 139 B5
Addington St SE1 116 B4 250 D1
Addington Village Rd CR0 223 C3
Addington Village Sta CR0 223 C2
Addis Cl EN3 6 D4
ADDISCOMBE 206 A1
Addiscombe Ave CR0 206 A2
Addiscombe Cl HA3 43 C4
Addiscombe Court Rd CR0 221 C6
Addiscombe Ct UB10 83 A3
Addiscombe Rd CR0 222 B6

Addiscombe Sta
CR0 206 A1
Addis Ho 13 E1 96 C2
Addison Ave
Hounslow TW3 130 A4
Notting Hill
W11 113 A5 244 A3
Southgate N14 15 C5
Addison Bridge Pl
W14 113 B2 254 C4
Addison Cl
Northwood HA6 22 A2
Orpington BR5 211 A3
Addison Cres
W14 113 A3 254 B6
Addison Ct
3 Belmont SM2 217 D1
Ealing W5 110 C6
Twickenham TW1 153 A3
Addison Dr SE12 165 B6
Addison Gdns
Hammersmith W14 112 D3
Kingston u T KT5 198 B5
Addison Gr W4 111 C3
Addison Ho
NW8 92 B4 229 C2
Addison Park Mans 12
W14 112 D4
Addison Pl
Notting Hill
W11 113 A5 244 A3
Southall UB1 107 C6
Addison Prim Sch
W14 112 D3
Addison Rd
Bromley BR2 209 D4
Croydon SE25 206 A5
Enfield EN3 6 D4
Kensington
W14 113 B3 254 C6
Teddington TW11 175 B4
Walthamstow E17 54 A4
Wanstead E11 55 A3
Addison's Cl CR0 223 B6
Addison Way
Hampstead Garden Suburb
NW11 47 C5
Hayes UB3 84 A1
Northwood HA6 22 A2
Addle Hill EC4 241 D1
Addlestone Ho 4
W10 90 C2
Addy Ho SE16 118 C2
Adecroft Way KT8 196 A6
Adela Ave KT3 200 B5
Adela Ho 9 W6 112 C1
Adelaide Ave SE4 141 C1
Adelaide Cl
Brixton SW9 138 C1
Enfield EN1 5 C5
Stanmore HA7 25 A6
Adelaide Ct
15 Beckenham BR3 185 C3
Hackney E5 75 A3
Hanwell W7 108 D4
St John's Wood NW8 229 B3
Adelaide Gdns RM6 59 A4
Adelaide Gr W12 112 A5
Adelaide Ho E17 53 B6
Adelaide Rd
Ashford TW15 170 A6
Chislehurst BR7 188 D5
Ealing W13 109 A4
Heston TW5 129 A4
Ilford IG1 78 D6
Kingston u T KT6 198 A4
Leyton E10 76 A5
Primrose Hill NW3 70 C1
Richmond TW9 132 B1
Southall UB2 107 A2
Teddington TW11 174 D4
2 Wandsworth
SW18 157 C6
Adelaide St WC2 250 A5
Adelaide Terr TW8 109 D1
Adela St W10 91 A3
Adelina Gr E1 96 C2
Adelina Mews SW12 159 D3
Adeline Pl
WC1 93 D2 239 D3
Adelphi Cres UB4 83 D4
Adelphi Ct
19 Finchley N2 30 B1
20 Rotherhithe SE16 118 D4
Adelphi Terr WC2 250 B5
Adelphi Way UB4 83 D4
Adeney Cl W6 134 D6
Aden Gr N16 73 B4
Aden Ho 15 E1 96 D2
Aden Lo N16 73 B4
Adenmore Rd SE6 163 C4
Aden Rd Enfield EN3 7 A1
Ilford IG1 57 A2
Adeyfield Ho EC1 235 D1
Adhara Rd HA6 22 A5
Adie Rd W6 112 C3
Adine Rd E13 99 B3
Adisham Ho 4 E5 74 B3
Adler Ind Est UB3 105 B4
Adler St E1 96 A1
Adley St E5 75 A3
Adlington Cl N18 33 C5
Admaston Rd SE18 145 A6
Admiral Ct
Barking IG11 102 C5
Carshalton SM5 202 C1
Chelsea
SW10 136 A4 266 B2
Hendon NW4 46 A4
Marylebone W1 238 A3
Admiral Ho TW11 175 A6
Admiral Hyson Ind Est
SE16 118 B1
Admiral Mews W10 90 D3
Admiral Pl
Harringay N8 50 D5
Rotherhithe SE16 119 A5
Admirals Cl E18 55 B5
Admirals Ct
Bermondsey SE1 253 C3
3 Newham E6 100 D1
32 Putney SW19 156 D3
Admiral Seymour Rd
SE9 144 B1
Admirals Gate SE10 141 D4
Admiral Sq
SW10 136 A4 266 B2
Admiral St SE8 141 C4
Admirals Way E14 119 C4
Admiral's Wlk NW3 70 A5
Admiralty Arch★
SW1 249 D4
Admiralty Cl
1 London SE8 141 C4
West Drayton UB7 104 B4
Admiralty Rd TW11 174 D4
Admiralty Way
TW11 174 D4
Admiral Wlk W9 91 C2
Adolf St SE6 185 D6
Adolphus Rd N4 50 D1
Adolphus St SE8 141 B5
Adomar Rd RM8 81 A5
Adpar St W2 92 B2 236 C4
Adrian Ave NW2 46 B1
Adrian Bolt Ho 2 E2 96 B4
Adrian Cl EN5 12 D5
Adrian Ho
Islington N1 233 D5
South Lambeth SW8 270 A4
Stratford E15 76 B1
Adrian Mews SW10 265 D6
Adriatic Bldg 18 E14 119 A6
Adriatic Ho 18 E1 96 D3
Adrienne Ave UB1 85 B4
Adron Ho 13 SE16 118 C2
Adstock Ho 5 N1 72 D1
Advance Rd SE27 183 A6
Advent Ct IG8 36 D5
Adventurers Ct 17
E14 120 B6
Advent Way N18 34 D5
Adyar Ct 7 SW19 179 A3
Adys Lawn NW2 68 B2
Adys Rd SE15 139 D2
Aegean Apts 7 E16 121 A6
Aegon Ho 3 E14 119 D3
Aerodrome Rd NW4,
NW9 45 D6
Aerodrome Way
TW5 128 C6
Aeroville NW9 27 C1
Affleck St N1 233 D3
Afghan Rd SW11 136 C3
Africa Ho WC2 240 C2
Afsil Ho EC1 241 B3
Aga Khan Univ WC1 239 D3
Agamemnon Rd NW6 69 B3
Agar Cl KT6 214 B6
Agar Gr NW1 71 D1
Agar Ho 6 KT1 198 A6
Agar Pl NW1 71 C1
Agar St WC2 250 B5
Agate Cl E16 99 D1
Agate Ho
New Malden KT4 199 C1
12 Penge SE26 184 B5
Agate Rd W6 112 C3
Agatha Cl E1 118 C5
Agaton Rd SE9 167 A2
Agave Rd NW2 68 C4
Agdon St EC1 94 D3 241 C6
Agincourt E11 54 D3
Agincourt Rd NW3 70 D4
Agnes Ave IG1 78 D4
Agnes Cl E6 122 C6
Agnes Ct 11 SW18 136 B1
Agnesfield Cl N12 30 C4
Agnes Gdns RM8 80 D4
Agnes Ho 13 W11 112 D6
Agnes Rd W3 111 D4
Agnes St E14 97 B1
Agnew Rd SE23 162 D4
Agricola Pl EN1 17 D6
Aicon Gall★ SW1 249 A6
Aidan Cl RM8 81 A4
Aidans Ct N12 30 C5
Aigburth Mans 5
SW9 138 C5
Ailantus Ct HA8 26 B5
Aileen Wlk E15 76 D1
Ailsa Ave TW1 153 B6
Ailsa Rd TW1 153 B6
Ailsa St E14 98 A2
Ainger Rd NW3 70 D1
Ainsdale NW1 232 A2
Ainsdale Cl BR6 211 B1
Ainsdale Cres HA5 41 C6
Ainsdale Dr SE1 118 A1
Ainsdale Rd W5 87 D3
Ainsley Ave RM7 59 D3
Ainsley Cl N9 17 C3
Ainsley St E2 96 B4
Ainslie Ct 2 HA0 88 A5
Ainslie Ho 1 E4 35 C5
Ainslie Wlk 8 SW12 159 B4
Ainslie Wood Cres
E4 35 D5
Ainslie Wood Gdns
E4 35 D5
Ainslie Wood Prim Sch
E4 35 D5
Ainslie Wood Rd E4 35 D5
Ainsty St 20 SE16 118 C4
Ainsworth Cl
Camberwell SE5 139 C3
Dollis Hill NW2 68 A5
Ainsworth Est
NW8 92 A6 229 A6
Ainsworth Ho NW8 91 D6
Ainsworth Rd
Croydon CR0 220 D6
Hackney E9 74 C1
Ainsworth Way
NW8 92 A6 229 A6
Aintree Ave E6 100 A6
Aintree Cl UB8 82 D2
Aintree Ho SE26 184 B4
Aintree Rd UB6 87 B5
Aintree St
SW6 135 A5 264 B4
Airborne Ho 10 SM6 219 B4
Airco Cl NW9 45 B6
Aird Ct TW12 173 D2
Aird Ho SE1 262 A5
Airdrie Cl
Barnsbury N1 72 B1
Hayes UB4 85 A2
Airedale Ave W4 111 D1
Airedale Ave S W4 111 D1
Airedale Rd
Balham SW12 158 D4
Ealing W5 109 D3
Airlie Gdns Ilford IG1 56 D1
Kensington
W8 113 C5 245 A3
Airlinks Ind Est TW5 106 C1
Air Park Way TW13 150 B2
Airport Gate Bsns Ctr
UB7 126 C5
Airport Ho CR0 220 C2
Airport Rdbt E16 121 D5
Air St W1 249 B5
Airthrie Rd IG3 80 B6
Aisgill Ave
SW5 113 B1 254 D1
Aisher Rd SE28 124 C6
Aislabie Ho N21 17 B5
Aislibie Rd SE12 142 C1
Aiten Pl W6 112 A2
Aithan Ho 15 E14 97 B1
Aitken Cl
Carshalton CR4 202 D2
Hackney E8 96 A6
Aitken Rd Barnet EN5 12 C6
Catford SE6 163 D2
Aits View KT8 195 D6
Ajax Ave NW9 45 C6
Ajax Ct NW9 45 C6
Ajax Ho 15 E2 96 B5
Ajax Rd NW6 69 C3
Akabusi Cl SE25 206 A3
Akbar Ho 7 E14 119 D2
Akehurst St SW15 156 A4
Akenside Ct 3 NW3 70 B3
Akenside Rd NW3 70 B3
Akerman Rd
Brixton SW9 138 D4
Kingston u T KT6 197 C3
Akintaro Ho 7 SE8 141 B6
Akiva Sch N3 29 D1
Alabama St SE18 145 C5
Alacross Rd W5 109 D4
Aladdin Workspace
UB6 85 D6
Alamaro Lo 5 SE10 120 D3
Alandale Dr HA5 22 B2
Aland Ct SE16 119 A3
Alander Mews E17 54 A5
Alan Dr EN5 13 A5
Alan Gdns RM7 59 C2
Alan Hocken Way
E15 98 C5
Alan Lo N3 29 C2
Alan Preece Ct NW6 68 D1
Alan Rd SW19 179 A5
Alanthus Cl SE12 165 A5
Alaska Bldg 12 SE13 141 D4
Alaska St SE1 251 A3
Alastor Ho 10 E14 120 A3
Alba Cl UB4 84 D3
Albacore Cres SE13 163 D5
Alba Gdns NW11 47 A3
Albain Cres TW15 148 A2
Alba Mews SW18,
SW19 157 C2
Alban Ho
Hampstead NW3 70 A2
New Cross SE14 141 B4
Albans Cl SW16 160 A1
Albany W1 249 A5
Albany Cl Bushey WD23 8 B5
Ickenham UB10 60 C3
Mortlake SW14 132 D1
Sidcup DA5 168 D4
West Green N15 51 A5
Albany Coll NW4 46 C4
Albany Coll Hendry Ho
NW4 46 B4
Albany Cres
Claygate KT10 212 C2
Edgware HA8 26 C3
Albany Ct
Ashford TW15 171 B4
Cheam SM1 217 B4
Chingford E4 19 D5
College Pk NW10 90 B4
Finchley N12 29 D4
Grahame Pk HA8 27 B2
Kingston u T KT2 176 A4
NW8 229 C3
Richmond TW10 153 B1
Surbiton KT6 197 D2
Walthamstow E10 53 C2
Westminster SW1 259 C6
8 Whitechapel E1 96 A1
Albany Ctyd W1 249 B5
Albany Ho
6 Brentford TW8 132 A6
Edgware HA8 26 C3
Upper Clapton E5 74 C6
Albany Mans SW11 267 B3
Albany Mews
Camberwell SE5 139 A6
Islington N1 72 C1
Kingston u T KT2 175 D4
Plaistow BR1 187 A4
Sutton SM1 217 D3
Albany Par 4 TW8 132 A6
Albany Park Ave EN3 6 D4
Albany Park Rd KT2 176 A4
Albany Park Sta
DA14 168 D2
Albany Pas 12 TW10 154 A6
Albany Pk Canoe &
Sailing Ctr KT2 175 D4
Albany Pl TW8 131 D6
Albany Rd
Brentford TW8 131 D6
Camberwell SE5 139 C6
Chislehurst BR7 188 D5
Dagenham RM6 59 B3
Ealing W13 109 B6
Enfield EN3 6 D5
Erith DA17 147 B6
Leyton E10 53 C2
Manor Pk E12 77 D4
New Malden KT3 199 B5
Richmond TW10 154 A6
Sidcup DA5 168 C4
Stroud Green N4 50 C3
Upper Edmonton N18 34 C5
Walthamstow E17 53 A3
Wimbledon SW19 179 D5
Albany Reach KT7 196 D4
Albany Sch EN3 6 D5
Albany St
NW1 93 B4 231 D2
Albany Terr 6
TW10 154 B6
Albany The
Kingston u T KT2 175 D4
Woodford IG8 36 D6
Albany View IG9 21 A3
Albany Wlk N15 50 D5
Alba Pl W11 91 B1
Albatross 31 NW9 27 D1
Albatross Cl E6 100 B3
Albatross St SE18 145 C5
Albemarle SW19 156 D2
Albemarle App IG2 56 D3
Albemarle Ave TW2 151 B3
Albemarle Coll W1 247 D6
Albemarle Gdns
Ilford IG2 56 D3
New Malden KT3 199 B5
Albemarle Ho
2 Brixton SW9 138 C2
Rotherhithe SE8 119 B2
Albemarle Lo SE26 185 A5
Albemarle Mans
NW3 69 D4
Albemarle Pk
Beckenham BR3 185 D2
Stanmore HA7 25 C5
Albemarle Prim Sch
SW19 157 A2
Albemarle Rd
Beckenham BR2,
BR3 186 A2
East Barnet EN4 14 C4
Albemarle St
W1 115 C6 249 A5
Albemarle Way EC1 241 C5
Alberon Gdns NW11 47 B5
Alberta Ave SM1 217 B3
Alberta Ct 1 TW10 154 B6
Alberta Ho
Blackwall E14 120 A5
Hayes UB4 84 B4
Alberta Rd EN1 18 A5
Alberta St
SE17 116 D1 261 D2
Albert Ave
Chingford E4 35 C6
South Lambeth SW8 270 C3
Albert Barnes Ho
SE1 262 A5
Albert Basin Way
E16 123 A6
Albert Bigg Point
E15 98 A6
Albert Bridge Rd
SW11 136 D5 267 C3
Albert Carr Gdns
SW16 182 A5
Albert Cl
11 Hackney E9 96 B6
Wood Green N22 31 D2
Albert Cotts 2 E1 96 A2
Albert Cres E4 35 C6
Albert Ct
Knightsbridge SW7 246 C1
9 Putney SW19 157 A3
Albert Dr SW19 157 A3
Albert Emb
SE1 116 A2 260 B3

Albert Gate Ct SW1 247 C1
Albert Gdns E1 96 D1
Albert Gr SW20 178 D2
Albert Gray Ho SW10 266 C4
Albert Hall Mans
SW7 114 B4 246 C1
Albert Ho
Stanmore HA7 25 B5
5 Wanstead E18 55 B6
2 Woolwich SE28 123 A3
Albert Mans
Battersea SW11 267 C2
Hornsey N8 50 A2
Albert Meml★
SW7 114 B4 246 C1
Albert Mews W8 256 A6
Albert Palace Mans
SW11 268 B2
Albert Pl Finchley N3 29 C2
Kensington
W8 113 D4 245 D1
Albert Rd
Ashford TW15 170 B5
Bromley Comm BR2 209 D4
Buckhurst Hill IG9 21 D2
Chislehurst SE9 166 A1
Croydon SE25 206 B5
Dagenham RM8 59 C1
Ealing W5 87 B3
East Barnet EN4 2 A1
Erith DA17 125 B1
Finsbury Pk N4 50 B2
Hampton TW12 174 A5
Harrow HA2 42 A6
Hayes UB3 105 C3
Hendon NW4 46 D5
Hounslow TW3 129 C1
Ilford IG1 79 A5
Kilburn NW6 91 B5
Kingston u T KT1 176 B1
Leyton E10 54 A1
Mill Hill NW7 27 D5
Mitcham CR4 202 D6
Newham E16 122 B4
New Malden KT3 199 D5
Penge SE20 184 D4
Richmond TW10 154 B6
Sidcup DA5 169 D4
Southall UB2 106 D3
South Tottenham N15 51 C3
Sutton SM1 218 B3
Teddington TW11 174 D4
Twickenham TW1 152 D3
Walthamstow E17 53 C4
4 Wanstead E18 55 B6
Wood Green N22 31 C2
Yiewsley UB7 104 A5
Albert's Ct NW1 237 B6
Albert Sleet Ct N9 18 B1
Albert Sq Leyton E15 76 C3
South Lambeth
SW8 138 B5 270 C3
Albert St
Camden Town
NW1 93 B6 231 D5
North Finchley N12 30 A5
Albert Starr Ho 7
SE8 118 D2
Albert Studios SW11 267 C2
Albert Terr
Buckhurst Hill IG9 21 D2
Camden Town
NW1 93 A6 231 A5
Stonebridge NW10 89 A6
Albert Terr Mews
NW1 231 A5
Albert Victoria Ho
N22 32 C2
Albert Way SE15 140 B5
Albert Westcott Ho
SE17 261 D2
Albert Whicher Ho 3
E17 54 A5
Albert Wlk E16 122 D4
Albion Ave
Clapham SW8 137 D3
Muswell Hill N10 31 A2
Albion Cl W2 247 B6
Albion Coll
WC1 94 A2 240 B3
Albion Ct
7 Hammersmith
W6 112 B2
Albion Ct *continued*
Sutton SM2 218 B1
2 Woolwich SE18 122 A2
Albion Dr E8 74 A1
Albion Est SE16 118 C4
Albion Gate W2 247 B6
Albion Gdns 1 W6 112 B2
Albion Gr N16 73 C4
Albion Hill IG10 21 D6
Albion Ho
17 Deptford SE8 141 C5
EC1 241 C4
Newham E16 122 D5
Albion Mews
Bayswater
W2 114 C6 247 B6
6 Hammersmith W6 112 B2
Islington N1 234 A6
Albion Pk IG10 21 D6
Albion Pl
Broadgate EC2 242 D3
Clerkenwell EC1 241 C4
Hammersmith W6 112 B2
South Norwood SE25 206 A6
Albion Prim Sch 34
SE16 118 C4
Albion Rd
Bexley DA6 147 C1
Dagenham RM10 81 B3
Hayes UB3 83 C1
Hounslow TW3 129 C1
Kingston u T KT2 177 A2
Stoke Newington N16 73 B4
Sutton SM2 218 B1
Tottenham N17 34 A1
Twickenham TW2 152 C3
Walthamstow E17 54 A6
Albion Riverside
SW11 267 A4
Albion Sq E8 73 D1
Albion St
Bayswater
W2 114 C6 247 B6
Rotherhithe SE16 118 C4
Thornton Heath CR0 204 D1
Albion Terr
Hackney E8 73 D1
Sewardstone E4 7 D1
Albion Villas Rd SE23,
SE26 162 C1
Albion Way
Barbican EC1 242 A3
Lewisham SE13 142 A1
Wembley HA9 66 C5
Albion Wlk N1 233 B3
Albion Works Studios 14
E8 74 A3
Albion Yd N1 233 B3
Albon Ho SW18 157 D5
Albrighton Rd SE5,
SE22 139 C2
Albuhera Cl EN2 4 C4
Albury Ave
Bexleyheath DA7 147 A3
Hounslow TW7 130 D5
Albury Bldgs SE1 251 D1
Albury Cl TW12 173 D4
Albury Ct
4 Croydon CR0 221 A4
Deptford SE8 141 C6
Mitcham CR4 180 B1
6 Northolt UB5 84 C4
Ruislip HA4 62 C3
Sutton SM1 218 A4
Albury Dr HA5 22 D3
Albury Lo 7 SW2 160 B4
Albury Mews E12 77 C6
Albury Rd KT9 214 A3
Albury St SE8 141 C6
Albyfield BR1 210 B6
Albyn Rd SE8 141 C4
Alcester Cres E5 74 B6
Alcester Ct 4 SM6 219 B4
Alcester Rd SM6 219 B4
Alchemea Coll of Audio
Engineering
N1 94 D6 234 D6
Alcock Cl SM6 219 D1
Alcock Rd TW5 128 D5
Alconbury DA6 169 D6
Alconbury Rd E5 74 A6
Alcorn Cl SM3 217 C6
Alcott Cl W7 86 D2
Aldborough Ct
Chingford E4 19 D1
Ilford IG2 57 D4
ALDBOROUGH
HATCH 57 C5
Aldborough Rd IG2 57 D6
Aldborough Rd N
IG2 57 D4
Aldborough Rd S IG3 57 C2
Aldbourne Rd W12 112 A5
Aldbridge St
SE17 117 C1 263 B2
Aldburgh Mews W1 238 B2
Aldbury Ave HA9 66 D1
Aldbury Ho SW3 257 A3
Aldbury Mews N9 17 B4
Aldebert Terr
SW8 138 B5 270 C3
Aldeburgh Cl 16 E5 74 B6
Aldeburgh Pl
Greenwich SE10 121 A2
Woodford IG8 37 A6
Aldeburgh St SE10 121 A1
Alden Ave E15 98 D4
Alden Ct
South Croydon CR0 221 C5
Wimbledon SW19 179 C4
Aldenham Ctry Pk
WD6 9 B6
Aldenham Dr UB8 82 D3
Aldenham Ho NW1 232 B3
Aldenham Rd WD6 9 C6
Aldenham St
NW1 93 D5 232 C3
Alden Ho E8 96 B6
Aldensley Rd W6 112 B3
Alderbrook Prim Sch 17
SW12 159 B4
Alderbrook Rd
SW12 159 B5
Alderbury Rd SW13 134 A6
Alder Ct
East Finchley N2 48 B6
3 West Norwood
SW16 182 C5
Alder Gr NW2 68 B6
Aldergrove Gdns
TW4 129 A3
Aldergrove Ho 3 E5 74 A6
Alder Ho
Camberwell SE15 139 D6
1 Maitland Pk NW3 70 D2
St Johns SE4 141 C2
Alderley Ho 36 SW8 137 D3
Alder Lo SW6 134 D4
Alder Lodge N9 17 C3
Alderman Ave IG11 102 A4
Aldermanbury
EC2 95 A1 242 B2
Aldermanbury Sq
EC2 242 B3
Alderman Ct 13 N11 30 D5
Alderman Judge Mall 6
KT1 176 A1
Alderman's Hill N13 32 B6
Alderman's Wlk EC2 243 A3
Aldermary Rd BR1 187 A2
Aldermead 2 TW3 129 D1
Alder Mews 12 N19 71 C6
Aldermoor Rd SE6 163 B1
Alderney Ave TW5 129 D5
Alderney Gdns UB5 63 B1
Alderney Ho
20 Canonbury N1 73 A2
Enfield EN3 6 D5
Alderney Mews SE1 262 C6
Alderney Rd E1 96 D3
Alderney St
SW1 115 B1 258 D2
Alder Rd
Mortlake SW14 133 B2
Sidcup DA14 167 D1
Alders Ave IG8 36 C4
ALDERSBROOK 77 C6
Aldersbrook Ave EN1 5 C3
Aldersbrook Dr KT2 176 B4
Aldersbrook La E12 78 B5
Aldersbrook Prim Sch
E12 77 C6
Aldersbrook Rd E11,
E12 77 C6
Alders Cl Ealing W5 109 D3
Edgware HA8 27 A5
Wanstead E11 77 B6
Alders Ct N17 52 B5
Aldersey Gdns IG11 79 B2
Aldersford Cl SE4 140 D1
Aldersgate Ct EC1 242 A3
Aldersgate St
EC1 95 A2 242 A3
Aldersgrove KT8 196 B4
Aldersgrove Ave SE9,
SE12 165 D1
Aldershot Rd NW6 91 B6
Aldersmead Ave
CR0 206 D3
Aldersmead Rd BR3 185 A3
Alderson Pl UB2 108 A5
Alderson St W10 91 A3
Alders Rd HA8 27 A5
Alders The
Feltham TW13 173 A6
Heston TW5 129 B6
Southgate N21 16 C5
Streatham SW16 181 C6
West Wickham BR4 223 D6
Alderton 9 KT2 176 D2
Alderton Cl NW10 67 B5
Alderton Cres NW4 46 B4
Alderton Ct KT8 195 B5
Alderton Rd
Croydon CR0 206 A2
Herne Hill SE24 139 A2
Alderton Way NW4 46 B4
Alderville Rd SW6 135 B3
Alderwick Ct N7 72 B2
Alderwick Dr TW3 130 B2
Alder Wlk IG11 79 A2
Alderwood Mews EN4 2 A5
Alderwood Prim Sch
SE9 167 C5
Alderwood Rd SE9 167 B5
Aldford St
W1 115 A5 248 B4
Aldgate EC3 95 C1 243 B1
Aldgate East Sta
E1 95 D1 243 D2
Aldgate High St
EC3 95 D1 243 C1
Aldgate Sta
EC3 95 D1 243 C1
Aldham Hall 1 E11 55 A3
Aldham Ho SE4 141 B4
Aldine Ct W12 112 C5
Aldine St W12 112 C4
Aldington Cl RM8 58 C1
Aldington Ct 1 E8 74 A1
Aldington Rd SE18 121 D3
Aldis Mews
3 Holdbrook EN3 7 C6
Upper Tooting SW17 180 C5
Aldis St SW17 180 C5
Aldred Rd NW6 69 C3
Aldren Rd SW17 158 A1
Aldriche Way E4 36 A4
Aldrich Gdns SM3 217 B5
Aldrich Terr SW18 158 A2
Aldrick Ho N1 233 D4
Aldridge Ave
Edgware HA8 10 D1
Holdbrook EN3 7 C5
Ruislip HA4 62 D6
Stanmore HA7 26 A2
Aldridge Ct W11 91 B2
Aldridge Rd Villas
W11 91 B2
Aldridge Rise KT3 199 C3
Aldridge Wlk N14 16 A4
Aldrington Rd SW16 181 C6
Aldsworth Cl W9 91 D3
Aldwich Ho WC2 240 D1
Aldwick Cl SE9 167 B1
Aldwick Ct N12 30 A6
Aldwick Rd CR0 220 B4
Aldworth Gr SE13 164 A5
Aldworth Rd E15 76 C1
Aldwych WC2 94 B1 240 D1
Aldwych Ave IG6 57 A5
Aldwych Bldgs WC2 240 B2
Aldwyn Ho SW8 270 A3
Alers Rd DA6 168 D6
Alesia Cl N22 32 A3
Alestan Beck Rd E16 99 D1
Alexa Ct 4 SM2 217 C2
Alexander Ave NW10 68 B1
Alexander Cl
Barnet EN4 2 B1
Hayes BR2 209 A1
Sidcup DA15 167 C5
Southall UB2 108 A5
Twickenham TW2 152 D2
Alexander Ct
Beckenham BR3 186 B2
Greenwich SE3 143 B3
Alexander Ct *continued*
Stanmore HA7 44 B6
14 Surbiton KT6 197 D2
Wandsworth SW18 158 A6
Alexander Evans Mews
SE23 162 D2
Alexander Fleming
Laboratory Mus★
W2 236 D2
Alexander Ho
8 Kingston u T
KT2 176 A2
15 Millwall E14 119 C3
16 Sutton SM2 218 A2
Alexander Lo SM1 217 B3
Alexander McLeod Prim
Sch SE2 124 B1
Alexander Mews 2
W2 91 D1
Alexander Pl SW7 257 A4
Alexander Rd
Bexley DA7 146 D3
Chislehurst BR7 188 D5
Upper Holloway N19 72 A6
Alexander Sq
SW3 114 C2 257 A4
Alexander St W2 91 C1
Alexander Terr SE2 124 B1
Alexandra Ave
Battersea SW11 268 A1
Harrow HA2 63 C5
Southall UB1 107 B6
Sutton SM1 217 C5
Wood Green N22 31 D2
Alexandra Bsns Ctr
EN3 6 D1
Alexandra Cl
Ashford TW15 171 B3
Deptford SE8 141 B6
Harrow HA2 63 D5
Alexandra Cotts
New Cross SE14 141 B4
Penge SE20 184 D4
Alexandra Cres BR1 186 D4
Alexandra Ct
Ashford TW15 171 B4
Ealing W5 87 C2
Greenford UB6 85 D5
Hounslow TW3 129 D3
Paddington W9 236 B6
4 Shacklewell N16 73 D4
5 Shepherd's Bush
W12 112 A4
Southgate N14 15 C6
Wembley HA9 66 B4
Alexandra Dr
Surbiton KT5 198 C2
West Norwood SE19 183 C5
Alexandra Gdns
Chiswick W4 133 C5
Cranley Gdns N10 49 B5
Hounslow TW3 129 D3
Wallington SM5 219 A1
Alexandra Gr
Finchley N12 29 D4
Finsbury Pk N4 50 D1
Alexandra Ho 13
W6 112 C1
Alexandra Inf Sch
19 Kingston u T
KT2 176 C3
Penge BR3 184 D3
Alexandra Jun & Inf Schs
TW3 129 D3
Alexandra Jun Sch
SE26 184 D4
Alexandra Mans
Chelsea SW3 266 C5
Cricklewood NW2 68 D3
6 Hampstead NW6 69 C3
9 Shepherd's Bush
W12 112 C5
Alexandra Mews N2 48 D6
Alexandra National Ho
N4 72 D6
Alexandra Pal★ N22 31 D1
Alexandra Palace Sta
N22 32 A1
Alexandra Palace Way
N10 49 C6
Alexandra Park Rd N10,
N22 31 D2
Alexandra Park Sch
N11 31 C2
Alexandra Pl
Croydon CR0 205 C1

Alexandra Pl *continued*
South Norwood SE25 ... 205 B4
St John's Wood NW8 ... 92 A6 229 B6
Alexandra Prim Sch N22 ... 32 B1
Alexandra Rd
Acton W4 ... 111 B4
Ashford TW15 ... 171 C4
10 Brentford TW8 ... 131 D6
Croydon CR0 ... 205 C2
Dagenham RM6 ... 59 A3
Edmonton N9 ... 18 B4
Enfield EN3 ... 6 D1
Hampstead NW8 ... 70 B1
Hendon NW4 ... 46 D5
Hornsey N8, N22 ... 50 C6
Hounslow TW3 ... 129 D3
Kingston u T KT2 ... 176 C3
Leyton E10 ... 76 A5
Mitcham SW19 ... 180 C3
Mortlake SW14 ... 133 B2
Muswell Hill N10 ... 31 B3
Penge SE26 ... 184 D4
Richmond TW9 ... 132 B3
Thames Ditton KT7 ... 196 D4
Tottenham N15 ... 51 B4
Twickenham TW1 ... 153 C5
Wallend E6 ... 100 C4
Walthamstow E17 ... 53 B2
Wanstead E18 ... 55 B6
Wimbledon SW19 ... 179 C5
Alexandra Sch HA2 ... 63 C6
Alexandra Sq SM4 ... 201 C4
Alexandra St
5 Deptford SE14 ... 141 A5
Newham E16 ... 99 A2
Alexandra Wlk 8 SE19 ... 183 C5
Alexandria Rd W13 ... 109 B6
Alex Gossip Ho SW6 265 A1
Alexis St SE16 ... 118 A2
Al Falah Sch 7 E5 ... 74 B5
Alfearn Rd E5 ... 74 C4
Alfie's Antique Mkt★ NW8 ... 92 C3 237 A5
Alford Ct
18 Belmont SM2 ... 217 D1
Shoreditch N1 ... 235 B3
Alford Gn CR0 ... 224 B2
Alford Ho
Crouch End N6 ... 49 C3
6 Woolwich SE18 ... 144 D6
Alford Pl N1 ... 235 B3
Alfoxton Ave N8, N15 ... 50 D5
Alfreda Ct SW11 ... 268 C1
Alfreda St SW11 ... 137 B4 268 C1
Alfred Butt Ho SW17 ... 158 D1
Alfred Cl W4 ... 111 B2
Alfred Findley Ho N22 ... 32 D1
Alfred Gdns UB1 ... 107 A6
Alfred Ho E9 ... 75 A3
Alfred Hurley Ho SW17 ... 180 A6
Alfred Mews W1, WC1 ... 239 C4
Alfred Nunn Ho NW10 ... 89 D6
Alfred Pl WC1 ... 93 C2 239 C4
Alfred Prior Ho 7 E12 ... 78 C4
Alfred Rd Acton W3 ... 111 A5
Buckhurst Hill IG9 ... 21 D2
Croydon SE25 ... 206 A4
Erith DA17 ... 125 B1
Feltham TW13 ... 150 C2
Kingston u T KT1 ... 198 B6
Leyton E15 ... 76 D3
Paddington W2 ... 91 C2
Sutton SM1 ... 218 A3
Alfred Salter Ho SE1 263 D3
Alfred Salter Prim Sch SE16 ... 118 D4
Alfred's Gdns IG11 ... 101 C5
Alfred St E3 ... 97 B4
Alfred's Way (East Ham & Barking By-Pass) IG11 ... 101 B5
Alfred's Way Ind Est IG11 ... 102 A6
Alfred Villas 9 E17 ... 54 A5
Alfreton Cl SW19 ... 156 D1
Alfriston KT5 ... 198 B3
Alfriston Ave
Harrow HA2 ... 41 C2
Thornton Heath CR0 ... 204 A2
Alfriston Cl 5 KT5 ... 198 B3
Alfriston Rd SW11 ... 158 D6
Algar Cl
Isleworth TW7 ... 131 A2
Stanmore HA7 ... 24 D5
Algar Ct TW12 ... 173 D2
Algar Ho SE1 ... 251 C1
Algar Rd TW7 ... 131 A2
Algarve Rd SW18 ... 157 D3
Algernon Rd
Hendon NW4 ... 46 A3
Kilburn NW6 ... 91 C6
Lewisham SE13 ... 141 D1
Algers Cl IG10 ... 21 D6
Algers Rd IG10 ... 21 D6
Alghers Mead IG10 ... 21 D6
Algiers Rd SE13 ... 141 C1
Alguin Ct HA7 ... 25 C3
Alibon Gdns RM10 ... 81 C3
Alibon Rd RM10 ... 81 C3
Alice Cl 13 EN5 ... 2 A1
Alice Ct 10 N3 ... 29 C2
Alice Gilliott Ct W14 264 D6
Alice La E3 ... 97 B6
Alice Mews 3 TW11 ... 174 D5
Alice Owen Tech Ctr EC1 ... 234 C2
Alice Shepherd Ho 12 E14 ... 120 A4
Alice St SE1 ... 117 C3 263 A5
Alice Thompson Cl SE12 ... 165 C2
Alice Walker Cl 8 SE24 ... 138 D1
Alice Way TW3 ... 129 D1
Alicia Ave HA3 ... 43 C5
Alicia Cl HA3 ... 43 C5
Alicia Gdns HA3 ... 43 C5
Alicia Ho DA16 ... 146 B4
Alie St E1 ... 95 D1 243 D1
Alington Cres NW9 ... 45 A1
Alison Cl
Croydon CR0 ... 206 D1
Newham E6 ... 100 C1
Alison Ct HA8 ... 26 D5
Aliwal Rd SW11 ... 136 C1
Alkerden Rd W4 ... 111 C1
Al Khair Prim & Sec Sch 7 CR0 ... 205 C1
Alkham Rd N16 ... 73 D6
Allam Ho W11 ... 244 A6
Allan Barclay Cl N15 ... 51 D3
Allanbridge N16 ... 51 C2
Allan Cl KT3 ... 199 B4
Allandale Ave N3 ... 47 B6
Allan Ho SW8 ... 269 C2
Allanson Ct E10 ... 75 C6
Allan Way W3 ... 89 A2
Allard Cres WD23 ... 8 A2
Allard Gdns SW4 ... 159 D6
Allardyce St SW4, SW9 ... 138 B1
Allbrook Cl TW11 ... 174 C5
Allbrook Ho 4 SW15 ... 156 A4
Allcot Cl TW14 ... 149 D3
Allcott Ho TW7 ... 130 D2
Allcroft Rd NW5 ... 71 A2
Allder Way CR2 ... 220 D1
Allenby Cl UB6 ... 85 C4
Allenby Prim Sch UB1 ... 85 C1
Allenby Rd
Forest Hill SE23 ... 163 A1
Southall UB1 ... 85 C3
Woolwich SE28 ... 123 A3
Allen Cl
Streatham CR4 ... 181 C2
Sunbury TW16 ... 172 B2
Allen Ct
Greenford UB6 ... 64 D3
Walthamstow E17 ... 53 C3
Allendale Ave UB1 ... 85 C1
Allendale Cl
Camberwell SE5 ... 139 B4
Forest Hill SE26 ... 184 D5
Allendale Rd UB6 ... 65 B2
Allen Edwards Dr SW8 ... 138 A4 270 A2
Allen Edwards Prim Sch SW4 ... 138 A4 270 A1
Allenford Ho SW15 ... 155 D5
All England Lawn Tennis & Croquet Club The SW19 ... 157 A1
Allen Ho W8 ... 255 B6
Allen Mans W8 ... 255 B6
Allen Rd Old Ford E3 ... 97 B5
Penge BR3 ... 184 D1
Stoke Newington N16 ... 73 C4
Sunbury TW16 ... 172 B1
Thornton Heath CR0 ... 204 C1
Allensbury Pl
7 Camden Town NW1 ... 71 D1
Camden Town NW1 ... 72 A1
Allens Rd EN3 ... 18 C6
Allen St W8 ... 113 C3 255 B5
Allenswood 12 SW19 ... 157 A3
Allenswood Rd SE9 ... 144 B3
Allerdale Ho 7 N4 ... 51 B2
Allerford Ct
Catford SE6 ... 163 D1
Harrow HA2 ... 42 A4
Allerford Rd SE6 ... 185 D6
Allerton Ct
5 Hendon NW4 ... 28 D1
North Cheam SM3 ... 216 D6
Allerton Ho
4 Merton SW19 ... 180 A3
Shoreditch N1 ... 235 D3
Allerton Rd N16 ... 73 A6
Allerton St N1 ... 235 D2
Allerton Wlk 11 N7 ... 72 B6
Allestree Rd SW6 ... 135 A5 264 A3
Alleyn Cres SE21 ... 161 B2
Alleyndale Rd RM8 ... 80 C6
Alleyn Ho
Bermondsey SE1 ... 262 C5
St Luke's EC1 ... 242 B5
Alleyn Pk
Dulwich SE21 ... 161 C1
Southall UB2 ... 107 C1
Alleyn Rd SE21 ... 161 C1
Alleyn's Sch SE22 ... 161 C6
Allfarthing JMI Sch SW18 ... 158 A5
Allfarthing La SW18 ... 158 A5
Allgood Cl SM4 ... 200 D3
Allgood St 10 E2 ... 95 D5
Allhallows La EC4 ... 252 C5
Allhallows Rd E6 ... 100 A1
All Hallows Rd N17 ... 33 C2
Alliance Cl HA0 ... 65 D4
Alliance Ct Acton W3 ... 88 D2
Ashford TW15 ... 171 A6
Alliance Rd Acton W3 ... 88 D3
East Wickham SE18 ... 146 A5
1 Newham E16 ... 99 C2
Allied Ind Est W3 ... 111 C5
Allied Way W3 ... 111 C4
Allingham Cl W7 ... 108 D6
Allingham Ct NW3 ... 70 C3
Allingham Mews N1 235 A4
Allingham St N1 ... 95 A5 235 A4
Allington Ave
Tottenham N17 ... 33 C4
Upper Halliford TW17 193 C6
Allington Cl
Greenford UB6 ... 64 A1
3 Wimbledon SW19 ... 178 D5
Allington Ct
6 Clapham SW8 ... 137 C3
Croydon CR0 ... 206 C3
Enfield EN3 ... 18 D6
Allington Rd
Harrow HA2 ... 42 A4
Hendon NW4 ... 46 B3
Kensal Rise W10 ... 91 A5
Orpington BR6 ... 211 C1
Allington St SW1 ... 258 D5
Allison Cl SE10 ... 142 A4
Allison Gr SE21 ... 161 C3
Allison Rd Acton W3 ... 111 A6
Harringay N8 ... 50 D4
Alliston Ho 27 E2 ... 95 D4
Allitsen Rd NW8 ... 92 C5 230 A4
All Nations Ho 10 E8 ... 74 B1
Allnutt Way SW4 ... 159 D6
Alloa Ct N14 ... 15 C2
Alloa Rd IG3 ... 80 A6
Allom Ct 11 SW4 ... 138 A3
Allonby Dr HA4 ... 38 D2
Allonby Gdns HA9 ... 43 C1
Allonby Ho E14 ... 97 A2
Alloway Rd E3 ... 97 A4
Allport Ho SE5 ... 139 B2
Allport Mews 44 E1 ... 96 C3
All Saints' Benhilton CE Prim Sch 3 SM1 ... 217 D5
All Saints CE Prim Sch
8 Fulham SW6 ... 135 A3
Merton SW19 ... 180 A3
Putney SW15 ... 134 C2
All Saints' CE Prim Sch
Blackheath Vale SE3 ... 142 C3
Child's Hill NW2 ... 69 B5
East Barnet N20 ... 14 B2
Wallington SM5 ... 219 A3
All Saints Church 9 N19 ... 71 D5
All Saints' Cl N9 ... 18 A2
All Saints Ct
Heston TW5 ... 128 D4
Lower Clapton E5 ... 74 C4
10 Shadwell E1 ... 118 C6
All Saints Dr SE3 ... 142 D3
All Saints Ho 2 W11 ... 91 B2
All Saint's Inf & Jun Schs SE19 ... 183 C2
All Saints Mews HA3 ... 24 C4
All Saints Pas SW18 ... 157 C6
All Saints RC Sch & Tech Coll RM8 ... 59 C1
All Saints Rd
Merton SW19 ... 180 A3
Notting Hill W11 ... 91 B1
Sutton SM1 ... 218 A5
All Saints' Rd W3 ... 111 A3
All Saints St N1 ... 94 B5 233 C4
All Saints Sta E14 ... 119 D6
All Saints Twr 19 E10 ... 53 D2
Allsop Pl NW1 ... 92 D3 237 D5
All Souls Ave NW10 ... 90 B6
All Souls CE Prim Sch W1 ... 93 C2 239 A4
All Souls Pl W1 ... 238 D3
Allum La WD6 ... 10 A6
Allum Way N20 ... 14 A3
Allwood Cl SE26 ... 184 D6
Alma Ave E4 ... 36 A3
Alma Birk Ho 1 NW6 ... 69 B1
Almack Rd E5 ... 74 C4
Alma Cl N10 ... 31 B2
Alma Cres SM1 ... 217 A3
Alma Gr SE1 ... 117 D2 263 D3
Alma Ho
7 Brentford TW8 ... 132 A6
2 Edmonton N9 ... 34 A6
Alma Pl
College Pk NW10 ... 90 B4
Penge SE19 ... 183 D3
Thornton Heath CR7 ... 204 C4
Alma Prim Sch
21 Bermondsey SE16 ... 118 A2
Enfield EN3 ... 18 D6
Alma Rd
Carshalton SM5 ... 218 C3
Enfield EN3 ... 7 A1
Muswell Hill N10 ... 31 B3
Sidcup DA14 ... 168 A1
Southall UB1 ... 107 A6
Thames Ditton KT10, KT7 ... 196 C1
Wandsworth SW18 ... 158 A6
Alma Row HA3 ... 24 B2
Alma Sq NW8 ... 92 A4 229 B2
Alma St
Camden Town NW5 ... 71 B2
Stratford New Town E15 ... 76 B2
Alma Terr
Earl's Ct W8 ... 255 B5
Wandsworth SW18 ... 158 B4
Almeida St 10 N1 ... 72 D1
Almeric Rd SW11 ... 136 D1
Almer Rd SW20 ... 178 A3
Almington St N4 ... 50 B1
Almond Ave
Carshalton SM5 ... 218 D6
Ealing W5 ... 110 A3
Uxbridge UB10 ... 60 D5
West Drayton UB7 ... 104 C3
Almond Cl
Bromley BR2 ... 210 C2
Charlton TW17 ... 171 A1
Feltham TW14 ... 150 A3
Almond Cl *continued*
Hayes UB3 ... 105 C6
Peckham SE15 ... 140 A3
Ruislip HA4 ... 61 D5
Almond Gr TW8 ... 131 B5
Almond Ho SE4 ... 141 B3
Almond Rd
Bermondsey SE16 ... 118 B2
Tottenham N17 ... 34 A3
Almonds Ave IG9 ... 21 A2
Almond Way
Bromley BR2 ... 210 C2
Harrow HA2 ... 24 A1
Mitcham CR4 ... 203 D5
Almorah Rd
De Beauvoir Town N1 ... 73 B1
Heston TW5 ... 128 D4
Almshouse La EN1 ... 6 B6
Almshouses
Edmonton N9 ... 17 D2
Leyton E10 ... 75 D6
Southall UB1 ... 85 C1
Sunbury TW16 ... 171 D2
Almshouses The IG11 ... 79 A2
Al-Muntada Islamic Sch SW6 ... 135 B4 264 D2
Alnmouth Ct 10 UB1 ... 86 A1
Al-Noor Prim Sch IG3 ... 58 B1
Alnwick 8 N17 ... 34 B3
Alnwick Gr SM4 ... 201 D5
Alnwick Rd
Eltham SE12 ... 165 B4
Newham E16 ... 99 C1
Alonso Ho 4 DA17 ... 125 C1
ALPERTON ... 88 A6
Alperton Com Sch HA0 ... 66 B1
Alperton La UB6 ... 87 D5
Alperton Lower Sch HA0 ... 87 D6
Alperton St W10 ... 91 B3
Alperton Sta HA0 ... 88 A6
Alphabet Gdns SM5 ... 202 B3
Alphabet Sq E3 ... 97 C2
Alpha Bsns Ctr E17 ... 53 B4
Alpha Cl NW8 ... 92 C4 230 B1
Alpha Ct 6 NW5 ... 71 B2
Alpha Est The UB3 ... 105 C4
Alpha Gr E14 ... 119 C4
Alpha Ho
19 Brixton SW4 ... 138 B1
Kilburn NW6 ... 91 C5
Lisson Gr NW8 ... 237 B5
Alpha Pl
Chelsea SW3 ... 136 C6 267 B6
Kilburn NW6 ... 91 C5
Alpha Prep Sch HA1 ... 42 C4
Alpha Rd Chingford E4 ... 19 D1
Croydon CR0 ... 205 C1
Edmonton N18 ... 34 A4
Enfield EN3 ... 7 A1
Hillingdon UB10 ... 82 D3
New Cross SE14 ... 141 B4
Surbiton KT5 ... 198 B3
Teddington TW12 ... 174 B5
Alpha St SE15 ... 140 A3
Alphea Cl SW19 ... 180 C3
Alpine Ave KT5 ... 215 A6
Alpine Bsns Ctr E6 ... 100 C2
Alpine Cl CR0 ... 221 C5
Alpine Copse BR1 ... 188 C1
Alpine Ct SE12 ... 142 D1
Alpine Gr 37 E9 ... 74 C1
Alpine Rd
Deptford SE16 ... 118 D1
Leyton E10 ... 75 D6
Walton-on-T KT12 ... 194 A2
Alpine View SM5 ... 218 C3
Alpine Way E6 ... 100 C2
Alpine Wlk HA7 ... 8 C2
Alric Ave
Kingston u T KT3 ... 199 D6
Willesden NW10 ... 67 B1
Al-risaala Sec Sch 1 SW17 ... 180 D6
Alroy Rd N4 ... 50 C2
Alsace Rd SE17 ... 117 C1 263 A2

Al Sadiq High Sch for Boys & Al Zahra Girls Sch NW6 91 A6
Alscot Rd
SE1 117 D3 263 D5
Alscot Road Ind Est
SE1 263 D5
Alscot Way SE1 263 C4
Alsike Rd DA18 125 A3
Alsom Ave KT19, KT4 216 A4
Alston Cl KT7 197 B2
Alston Ct 2 EN5 1 A2
Alstone Ct N9 18 A2
Alston Rd
Edmonton N18 34 B5
High Barnet EN5 1 A2
Upper Tooting SW17 180 B6
Altair Cl N17 33 D4
Altair Ct N1 73 B2
Altash Way SE9 166 C2
Altenburg Ave W13 109 B3
Altenburg Gdns
SW11 136 D1
Alt Gr SW19 179 B3
Altham Gdns WD19 22 D6
Altham Rd HA5 23 A3
Althea St SW6 135 D2
Althorne Gdns E18 54 D5
Althorne Way RM10 81 C6
Althorp Cl EN5 12 A4
Althorpe Mews
SW11 266 D1
Althorpe Rd HA1 42 A4
Althorp Rd SW17 158 D3
Altima Ct SE22 140 A1
Altior Ct N6 49 C3
Altmore Ave E6 100 B6
Altmore Inf Sch E6 100 B6
Alton Ave HA7 24 D3
Alton Cl
Isleworth TW7 130 D3
Sidcup DA5 169 A3
Alton Ct 18 BR3 185 C3
Alton Gdns
Beckenham BR3 185 C3
Twickenham TW2 152 B4
Alton Ho 3 E3 97 D4
Alton Rd
Croydon CR0 220 C5
Richmond TW10, TW9 132 A1
Roehampton SW15 156 A3
Tottenham N17 51 B6
Alton Sch The SW15 155 D4
Alton St E14 97 D2
Altyre Cl BR3 207 B4
Altyre Rd CR0 221 B6
Altyre Way BR3 207 B4
Alum Ct KT5 198 B3
Alumni Ct SE1 253 D2
Alvanley Ct NW3 69 D3
Alvanley Gdns NW6 69 D3
Alvanley Ho 14 SW9 138 C4
Alvernia Lo SM1 217 D5
Alverstone Ave
East Barnet EN4 14 C4
Wimbledon SW18, SW19 157 C2
Alverstone Gdns
SE9 167 A3
Alverstone Ho 11
SE11 138 C6
Alverstone Rd
Little Ilford E12 78 C4
New Malden KT3 199 D5
Wembley HA9 44 B1
Willesden NW2 68 C1
Alverston Gdns
SE25 205 C4
Alverton St SE8 141 B6
Alveston Ave HA3 43 B6
Alveston Sq 5 E18 37 A1
Alvey St SE17 263 A2
Alvia Gdns SM1 218 A4
Alvington Cres E8 73 D3
Alway Ave KT19 215 B3
Alwen Cotts CR0 222 D4
Alwold Cres SE12 165 C5
Alwyn Ave W4 111 B1
Alwyn Cl
Borehamwood WD6 10 B5
New Addington CR0 223 D1
Alwyne La N1 72 D1
Alwyne Mans SW19 179 B4
Alwyne Pl N1 73 A1
Alwyne Rd
Canonbury N1 73 A1
Ealing W7 108 C6
Wimbledon SW19 179 B4
Alwyne Sq N1 73 A2
Alwyne Villas N1 72 D1
Alwyn Gdns Acton W3 88 D1
Hendon NW9 46 A5
Alyn Ct N8 49 D3
Alyth Gdns NW11 47 C3
Alzette Ho 11 E2 96 D5
Amalgamated Dr
TW8 131 B6
Amanda Ct
Ashford TW15 148 B2
Chingford E4 36 C4
Aman Dalvi Ho 2
SW18 157 A4
Amar Ct SE18 123 D2
Amardeep Ct SE18 123 D1
Amazon Apartments
N8 50 B6
Amazonas
SE1 117 C2 263 B3
Amazon St E1 96 B1
Ambassador Cl TW3 129 A3
Ambassador Ct
9 Hampstead NW6 69 C3
Hendon NW4 46 D4
Ambassador Gdns
E6 100 B2
Ambassador Ho
Harrow HA3 42 C6
St John's Wood NW8 229 B5
Ambassador Sq E14 119 D2
Amber Ave E17 35 A2
Amber Ct
Feltham TW13 149 C1
Islington N7 72 C2
Mitcham CR4 202 C5
Southall UB1 107 D5
Amberden Ave N3 47 C6
Amberdene HA7 24 D4
Ambergate St
SE17 116 D1 261 D2
Amber Gr NW2 46 D1
Amber Ho HA7 25 D3
Amberley Cl
2 Orpington BR6 227 D3
Pinner HA5 41 B6
Amberley Ct
2 Brixton SW9 138 D2
Sidcup DA14 190 C5
Sutton SM2 218 A1
Amberley Gdns
Enfield EN1 17 C4
Worcester Pk KT19 215 D4
Amberley Gr
Croydon CR0 205 D2
Penge SE26 184 B5
Amberley Ho
8 Barnet EN5 1 D1
7 Ealing W7 108 C5
Amberley Rd
Buckhurst Hill IG9 21 C3
Enfield EN1 17 D5
Palmers Green N13 16 B2
Walthamstow E10 53 D2
Westbourne Green W9 91 C2
West Heath SE2 146 D6
Amberley Way
Heston TW4 150 C6
Morden SM4 201 B2
Romford RM7 59 D5
Uxbridge UB10 82 A5
Amberside Cl TW2 152 B5
Amber Wharf 29 E2 95 D6
Amberwood Cl SM6 220 A3
Amberwood Rise
KT3 199 C3
Amblecote Cl SE12 165 B1
Amblecote Mdws
SE12 165 B1
Amblecote Rd SE12 165 B1
Ambler Prim Sch 2
N4 72 D6
Ambler Rd N4 72 D5
Ambleside
Catford BR1 186 B4
13 Putney SW19 157 A3
Regent's Pk NW1 231 D3
Ambleside Ave
Beckenham BR3 207 A4
Streatham SW16 181 D6
Ambleside Ave *continued*
Walton-on-T KT12 194 C1
Ambleside Cl
Lower Clapton E9 74 C3
5 Tottenham N17 51 D6
Walthamstow E10 53 D2
Ambleside Cres EN3 6 D2
Ambleside Dr TW14 149 D3
Ambleside Gdns
Redbridge IG4 56 A4
Streatham SW16 181 D5
Sutton SM2 218 A2
Wembley HA9 43 D1
Ambleside Ho HA8 27 A5
Ambleside Point 1
SE15 140 C5
Ambleside Rd
Bexleyheath DA7 147 C3
Willesden NW10 67 D1
Ambrook Ct SM1 218 B3
Ambrook Rd DA17 125 C3
Ambrosden Ave
SW1 115 C3 259 B5
Ambrose Ave NW11 47 B3
Ambrose Cl
6 Newham E6 100 B2
Orpington BR6 227 D5
Ambrose Ho 9 E14 97 C2
Ambrose Mews 2
SW11 136 D3
Ambrose St SE16 118 B2
Ambrose Wlk E3 97 C5
Ambulance Rd E11 54 B4
AMC Bsns Ctr NW10 88 D4
Amelia Cl W3 110 D4
Amelia Ho 5 W6 112 C1
Amelia St
SE17 117 A1 262 A2
Amen Cnr
Holborn EC4 241 D1
Streatham SW17 181 A4
Amen Ct EC4 94 D1 241 D1
Amenity Way SM4 200 C2
American Intercontinental Univ
W1 93 A2 238 B3
American Sch in London The NW8 92 B5 229 C4
American Univ in London The 3 N7 72 B5
America Sq EC3 253 C6
America St SE1 252 A3
Amerland Rd SW18 157 B5
Amersham Ave N18 33 B4
Amersham Gr SE14 141 B5
Amersham Rd
New Cross SE14 141 B4
Thornton Heath CR0 205 B3
Amersham Vale SE14,
SE8 141 B5
Amery Gdns NW10 90 B6
Amery Ho SE17 263 B2
Amery Rd HA1 65 A6
Amesbury Ave SW2 160 B2
Amesbury Cl KT4 200 C1
Amesbury Ct EN2 4 C3
Amesbury Dr E4 19 D5
Amesbury Rd
Bromley BR1 209 D6
Dagenham RM9 80 D1
Feltham TW13 150 D2
Amesbury Twr 4
SW8 137 C3
Ames Cotts 12 E3 97 A2
Ames Ho 10 E2 96 D5
Amethyst Cl 1 EN3 7 A2
Amethyst Cl N11 31 D3
Amethyst Ct BR6 227 C3
Amethyst Rd E15 76 B4
Amherst Ave W13 87 C1
Amherst Dr BR5 211 D5
Amherst Gdns 2
W13 87 C1
Amherst Rd W13 87 C1
Amhurst Ct N4 51 B2
Amhurst Gdns TW7 131 A3
Amhurst Par N16 51 D2
Amhurst Pk N4, N16 51 C2
Amhurst Rd E8, N16 74 A4
Amhurst Terr E8 74 A4
Amhurst Wlk SE28 124 A5
Amias Ho EC1 242 A6
Amidas Gdns RM8 80 B4
Amiel St 15 E1 96 C3
Amies St SW11 136 D2
Amigo Ho SE1 261 B6
Amina Way SE16 118 A3
Amis Ave KT19 214 D3
Amity Gr SW20 178 C2
Amity Rd E15 76 D1
Ammanford Gn NW9 45 C3
Ammonite Ho 3 E15 76 D1
Amner Rd SW11 159 A5
Amora 8 HA7 25 C6
Amor Rd W6 112 C3
Amory Ho N1 233 D4
Amott Rd SE15 140 A2
Amoy Pl E14 119 C6
Ampere Way Sta
CR0 204 B1
Ampleforth Rd SE2 124 C4
Ampton Pl WC1 233 C1
Ampton St
WC1 94 B4 233 C1
Amroth Cl SE23 162 B3
Amroth Gn NW9 45 C3
Amstel Ct 12 SE15 139 D5
Amsterdam Rd E14 120 A3
Amundsen Ct 7
E14 119 C1
Amundsen Ho 6
NW10 67 B1
Amwell Cl EN2 17 B6
Amwell St EC1 94 C4 234 A2
Amyand Cotts 12
TW1 153 B5
Amyand Park Gdns 2
TW1 153 B4
Amyand Park Rd
TW1 153 B4
Amy Cl SM6 220 A1
Amy Johnson Ct HA8 26 D1
Amy Johnson Prim Sch
SM6 220 A1
Amyruth Rd SE4 163 C6
Amy Warne Cl E6 100 A3
Anarth Ct KT13 193 C1
Anatola Rd N19 71 C6
Ancaster Cres KT3 200 A3
Ancaster Mews CR0 206 D6
Ancaster Rd BR3 206 D6
Ancaster St SE18 145 C5
Anchorage Cl SW19 179 C5
Anchorage Point 1
E14 119 C4
Anchorage Point Ind Est
SE7 121 C3
Anchor Bsns Pk CR0,
SM6 220 A5
Anchor Cl IG11 102 B4
Anchor Ct
Bexley DA7 147 A4
5 Enfield EN1 17 C6
Anchor Ho Ilford IG3 80 A5
Newham E16 99 C1
St Luke's EC1 242 A6
Anchor & Hope La
SE7 121 C2
Anchor Mews SW12 159 B5
Anchor Rd E12 77 D6
Anchor Ret Pk E1 96 C3
Anchor St SE16 118 B2
Anchor Terr SE1 252 B4
Anchor Yd EC1 242 B6
Ancill Cl W6 135 A6 264 A5
Ancona Rd
Plumstead SE18 123 B1
Willesden Green NW10 90 A5
Andace Pk BR1 187 C2
Andalus Rd SW9 138 A2
Andaman Ho 3 E1 97 A2
Ander Cl HA0 65 D4
Andersens Wharf 9
E14 97 B1
Anderson Cl
Morden SM3 201 C1
North Acton W3 89 B1
Southgate N21 16 B6
Anderson Ct NW2 46 C2
Anderson Dr TW15 171 A6
Anderson Ho
1 Barking IG11 101 B5
10 Blackwall E14 120 A6
Upper Tooting SW17 180 B5
Anderson Rd
Homerton E9 74 D2
Redbridge IG8 55 D6
Anderson's Pl TW3 129 D1
Andersons Sq N1 234 C5
Anderson St SW3 257 C2
Anderson Way
Erith DA17 125 D4
Anderson Way *continued*
Erith DA17 125 D4
Anderton Cl SE5 139 B2
Anderton Ct N22 31 D1
Andhurst Ct KT2 176 D2
Andmark Ct UB1 107 B5
Andon Ct BR3 207 A6
Andorra Ct BR1 187 C2
Andover Ave E16 99 D1
Andover Cl
East Bedfont TW14 149 D3
Greenford UB6 85 D3
Andover Ho 5 N7 72 B6
Andover Pl NW6 91 D5
Andover Rd
Finsbury Pk N7 72 B6
Orpington BR6 211 C1
Twickenham TW2 152 B3
Andoversford Ct 2
SE15 139 C6
Andrecht Terr CR4 203 D5
Andreck Ct BR3 186 A1
Andre Malraux Sch
W7 86 C2
Andre St E8 74 A3
Andrew Borde St
WC2 239 D2
Andrew Ct
Beckenham BR3 207 D6
2 Forest Hill SE23 162 D2
Andrewes Ct 2 W7 108 C5
Andrewes Gdns E6 100 A1
Andrewes Ho
Barbican EC2 242 B3
Sutton SM1 217 C4
Andrew Ewing Prim Sch
The TW5 129 B5
Andrew Ho
Enfield EN3 18 C6
New Cross SE4 141 B3
Putney SW15 156 A6
Andrew Logan's
Glasshouse★ SE1 253 A2
Andrew Marvell Ho 12
N16 73 C4
Andrew Pl SW8 269 D2
Andrew Reed Ho 3
SW18 157 A4
Andrews Cl
Buckhurst Hill IG9 21 C2
Harrow HA1 42 B2
North Cheam KT4 216 D6
Sidcup BR5 190 D1
Andrews Crosse
WC2 241 A1
Andrew's Rd E8 96 B6
Andrew St E14 98 A1
Andrews Wharf 14 E8 96 B6
Andrews Wlk SE17 138 D6
Andrew Wells Ho
BR1 187 B3
Andrew Wilmot Ct
SW18 158 A3
Andridge Ct SW19 179 B2
Andringham Lo 4
BR1 187 B2
Andrula Ct N22 32 D2
Andwell Cl SE2 124 B4
ANERLEY 184 B2
Anerley Ct SE20 184 B3
Anerley Gr SE19 183 D3
Anerley Hill SE19 183 D4
Anerley Park Rd
SE20 184 B3
Anerley Pk SE20 184 B3
Anerley Rd SE20 184 B2
Anerley Sta SE20 184 B2
Anerley Station Rd
SE20 184 B2
Anerley Vale SE19 184 A3
Aneurin Bevan Ct
NW2 68 B6
Aneurin Bevan Ho
N11 31 D3
Anfield Cl SW12 159 C4
Angel EC1 94 D5 234 D3
Angela Carter Cl
SW9 138 C2
Angela Ct 2 SE23 162 C3
Angela Davis Ind Est 20
SW9 138 D1
Angel Cl
Edmonton N18 34 A6
Hampton TW12 174 A5
Angel Corner Par 6
N18 34 A6

Angel Ct
Broadgate EC2 242 D2
St James SW1 249 B3
5 Willesden NW2 68 A2
Angel Edmonton N18 34 A5
Angelfield TW3 151 D6
Angel Gate EC1 234 D2
Angel Hill SM1 217 D5
Angel Hill Dr SM1 217 D5
Angel Ho N1 234 B3
Angelica Cl UB7 82 B1
Angelica Dr E6 100 C2
Angelica Gdns CR0 206 D1
Angelina Ho 2 SE15 140 A4
Angelis Appartments N1 234 D3
Angel La Hayes UB3 83 B2
Stratford E15 76 B2
Angell Park Gdns 4 SW9 138 C2
Angell Rd SW9 138 D2
Angel Mews
Finsbury N1 234 B3
Putney SW15 156 A4
Stepney E1 118 B6
Angel Pas EC4 117 B6 252 C5
Angel Pl
Borough The SE1 252 C2
1 Edmonton N18 34 A5
Angel Rd Harrow HA1 42 C3
Thames Ditton KT7 197 A1
Angel Rd (North Circular Rd) N18 34 B5
Angel Rd Works N18 34 C5
Angel Road Sta N18 34 C5
Angel Sq N1 234 B3
Angel St EC1 95 A1 242 A2
Angel Sta EC1 94 C5 234 B3
Angel Wlk W6 112 C2
Angerstein Bsns Pk SE10 121 A2
Angerstein La SE3 142 D4
Anglebury 5 W2 91 C1
Angle Cl UB10 82 C6
Angle Gn RM8 58 C1
Anglers Cl TW10 175 C6
Anglers La NW5 71 B2
Anglers Reach KT6 197 D4
Anglesea Ave 4 SE18 122 D2
Anglesea Ho KT1 197 D5
Anglesea Mews 12 SE18 122 D2
Anglesea Rd
Kingston u T KT1 197 D5
Woolwich SE18 122 D2
Anglesey Cl TW15 148 C1
Anglesey Court Rd SM5 219 A2
Anglesey Ct W7 86 D3
Anglesey Gdns SM5 219 A2
Anglesey Ho 13 E14 97 C1
Anglesey Rd
Enfield EN3 6 B1
South Oxhey WD19 22 C5
Anglesmede Cres HA5 41 C6
Anglesmede Way HA5 41 C6
Angles Rd SW16 182 A6
Anglia Cl N17 34 B3
Anglia Ct RM8 58 D1
Anglia Ho 13 E14 97 A1
Anglian Ind Est IG11 101 D2
Anglian Rd E11 76 B5
Anglia Wlk E6 100 C6
Anglo American Laundry SW17 158 A1
Anglo Rd 16 E3 97 B5
Angrave Ct 4 E8 95 D6
Angrave Pas 5 E8 95 D6
Angus Cl KT9 214 C3
Angus Dr HA4 62 C4
Angus Gdns NW9 27 B2
Angus Ho 12 SW12 159 D4
Angus Rd E13 99 C4
Angus St SE14 141 A5
Anhalt Rd SW11 136 C5 267 B4
Animals in War Meml* W1 247 D6
Ankerdine Cres SE18 144 D4
Anlaby Rd TW11 174 C5
Anley Rd W14 112 D4
Anmersh Gr HA7 25 D2
Annabel Cl E14 97 D1
Anna Cl E8 95 D6
Annadale N22 32 B5
Annandale Gr UB10 61 A5
Annandale Rd
Chiswick W4 111 C1
Croydon CR0 222 A6
Greenwich SE10 120 D1
Sidcup DA15 167 D4
Anna Neagle Cl 2 E7 77 A4
Anne Boleyn's Wlk
Belmont SM3 217 A1
Kingston u T KT2 176 A5
Anne Compton Mews SE12 164 D4
Anne Goodman Ho 3 E1 96 C1
Anne Kerr Ct 18 SW15 156 D5
Anne's Ct NW8 237 B6
Annesley Ave NW9 45 B6
Annesley Cl NW10 67 C5
Annesley Dr CR0 223 B5
Annesley Ho
31 Brixton SW9 138 C4
15 Kennington SW9 138 C5
Annesley Rd SE3 143 B4
Annesley Wlk N19 71 C6
Annesmere Gdns SE3 143 D2
Anne St E13 99 A3
Annett Cl TW17 193 C5
Annette Cl HA3 24 C1
Annette Cres 16 N1 73 A1
Annette Ct N7 72 B5
Annette Rd N7 72 B4
Annette White Lo 20 N2 30 B1
Annett Rd KT12 194 A2
Anne Way KT8 195 D5
Annie Besant Cl E3 97 B6
Annie Taylor Ho 2 E12 78 C4
Anning St EC2 243 B6
Annington Rd N2 48 D6
Annis Rd E9 75 A2
Ann La SW10 136 B6 266 C5
Ann Moss Way SE16 118 C3
Ann Parkes Ct TW5 128 D3
Ann's Cl SW1 248 A1
Ann's Pl E1 243 C3
Ann St SE18 123 B2
Ann Stroud Ct SE12 165 A6
Annsworthy Ave CR7 205 B6
Annsworthy Cres CR7 183 B1
Annunciation RC Inf Sch The HA8 27 B2
Annunciation RC Jun Sch The HA8 27 B4
Ansar Gdns E17 53 B4
Ansdell Rd SE15 140 C3
Ansdell St W8 113 D3 255 D6
Ansdell Terr W8 113 D3 255 D6
Ansell Gr SM5 203 A1
Ansell Ho E1 96 C2
Ansell Rd SW17 158 D1
Anselm Cl CR0 221 D5
Anselm Rd
Hatch End HA5 23 B3
West Brompton SW6 135 C6 265 A5
Ansford Rd BR1, SE6 186 B6
Ansleigh Pl W11 112 D6
Anson 30 NW9 27 D1
Anson Ct TW19 148 A4
Anson Ho
Pimlico SW1 269 A6
6 Tower Hamlets E1 97 A3
Anson Pl SE28 123 B4
Anson Prim Sch NW2 68 D3
Anson Rd
Cricklewood NW2 68 C3
Tufnell Pk N7 71 D4
Anson Terr UB5 63 D2
Anstey Ct 6 W3 110 D4
Anstey Ho 7 E9 96 C6
Anstey Lo EN1 17 C5
Anstey Rd SE15 140 A2
Anstey Wlk N15 51 A5
Anstice Cl W4 133 C5
Anstridge Rd SE9 167 B5
Antelope Rd SE18 122 B3
Antenor Ho 11 E2 96 B5
Anthony Cl NW7 27 C6
Anthony Cope Ct N1 235 D2
Anthony Ct
Harrow HA1 42 B2
Isleworth TW7 130 D2
Anthony Ho NW8 237 A5
Anthony Kendal Ho 4 E5 74 B5
Anthony Rd
Croydon SE25 206 A3
East Wickham DA16 146 A4
Greenford UB6 86 C4
Anthony St E1 96 B1
Antigua Wlk SE19 183 B5
Antilles Bay 19 E14 120 A4
Antilles Ho W3 89 B1
Antill Rd Mile End E3 97 A4
Tottenham Hale N15 52 A5
Antill Terr 5 E1 96 D1
Antlers Hill E4 19 D6
Anton Cres SM1 217 C5
Antoneys Cl HA5 22 D1
Antonine Hts SE1 253 A1
Anton Pl HA9 66 D5
Anton St E8 74 A3
Antony Ho
4 Deptford SE14 140 D5
2 Rotherhithe SE16 118 C2
Antrim Gr NW3 70 D2
Antrim Ho SW11 137 A2
Antrim Mans NW3 70 D2
Antrim Rd NW3 70 D2
Antrobus Cl SM1 217 B3
Antrobus Rd W4 111 A3
Anvil Cl SW16 181 C3
Anvil Ho 10 N9 18 A1
Anvil Rd TW16 194 A6
Anworth Cl IG8 37 B4
AOP Gall* EC2 243 A6
Apex Cl BR3 185 D2
Apex Cnr
Edgware NW7 27 B6
Twickenham TW13 151 B1
Apex Ct W13 87 A1
Apex Ind Est NW10 89 D3
Apex Lo 10 EN5 14 A6
Apex Prim Sch
3 Barking IG11 79 A1
Ilford IG1 78 C6
Apex Ret Pk TW13 151 B1
Aphrodite Ct 11 E14 119 C2
Aplin Ct 4 SM1 217 D2
Aplin Way TW7 130 C4
Apollo Ave
Bromley BR1 187 B2
Loughton HA6 22 A5
Apollo Bldg 2 E14 119 C2
Apollo Ho
Chelsea SW10 266 C5
32 Hackney E2 96 B5
Highgate N6 48 D2
Apollo Ind Bsns Ctr 29 SE8 140 D6
Apollo Pl
Chelsea SW10 266 C4
6 Leyton E11 76 C5
Apollo Studios 18 NW5 71 D3
Apollo Way 1 SE18 123 B3
Apostle Way CR7 182 D1
Apothecary St EC4 241 C1
Appach Rd SW2 160 C5
Appin Ct HA1 42 C2
Appleby Cl
Chingford E4 36 A4
Hayes UB3, UB8 83 A1
Orpington BR5 211 C2
Twickenham TW2 152 B2
West Green N15 51 B4
Appleby Ct W3 111 A4
Appleby Gdns TW14 149 D3
Appleby Rd
Hackney E8 74 A1
Newham E16 99 A1
Appleby St E2 95 D5
Appledore Ave HA4 62 C5
Appledore Cl
Bromley BR2 209 A4
Edgware HA8 26 C2
Upper Tooting SW12, SW17 158 D2
Appledore Cres DA14 167 D1
Appledore Way NW7 28 D3
Appleford 8 NW5 71 C3
Appleford Ho 6 W10 91 A3
Appleford Rd W10 91 A3
Applegarth
Claygate KT10 212 D3
New Addington CR0 223 D1
Apple Garth TW8 109 D2
Applegarth Dr IG2 57 D5
Applegarth Ho
Borough The SE1 251 D2
9 Camberwell SE15 140 A5
Applegarth Inf Sch CR0 223 D2
Applegarth Jun Sch CR0 223 D2
Applegarth Rd
Hammersmith W14 112 D3
Woolwich SE28 124 C6
Apple Gr
Chessington KT9 214 A4
Enfield EN1 5 C2
Apple Lo HA0 65 C5
Apple Mkt KT1 175 D1
Apple Mkt* WC2 250 B6
Apple Rd E11 76 C5
Appleshaw Ho 4 SE5 139 C2
Appleton Ct 30 E8 74 B3
Appleton Gdns KT3 200 A3
Appleton Rd SE9 144 A2
Appleton Sq CR4 180 C2
Apple Tree Ave UB7 82 B1
Appletree Cl 5 SE20 184 B2
Appletree Ct
Lewisham SE13 142 B1
Northolt UB5 85 A4
Appletree Gdns EN4 2 C1
Apple Tree Yd SW1 249 B4
Applewood Cl
Dollis Hill NW2 68 B5
Ickenham UB10 60 A4
Oakleigh Pk N20 14 C3
Applewood Dr E13 99 B3
Appold St EC2 95 C2 243 A4
Appollo Ct 7 SW9 138 C4
Apprentice Gdns UB5 85 B4
Apprentice Way 5 E5 74 B4
Approach Cl N16 73 C4
Approach Rd
Ashford TW15 171 A4
Bethnal Green E2 96 C5
East Molesey KT8 195 C4
Edgware HA8 26 C4
Merton SW20 178 C1
New Barnet EN4, EN5 2 B1
Approach The
Acton W3 89 B1
Enfield EN1 6 B3
Hendon NW4 46 D4
Orpington BR6 227 D6
Aprey Gdns NW4 46 C5
April Cl Ealing W7 108 C6
Feltham TW13 150 A1
Orpington BR6 227 D3
April Ct 20 E2 96 A5
April Glen SE23 162 D1
April St E8 73 D4
Apsley Cl HA2 42 A4
Apsley Ct SM2 218 A2
Apsley Ctr The NW2 68 A6
Apsley Ho Enfield EN1 17 C5
Hounslow TW4 129 B1
Stepney E1 96 C2
St John's Wood NW8 229 C4
Apsley Ho, The Wellington Mus* SW1 115 A4 248 B2
Apsley Rd
Croydon SE25 206 B5
Kingston u T KT3 199 A6
Apsley Way
Dollis Hill NW2 68 A6
Mayfair W1 248 B2
Aquarius TW1 153 B3
Aquarius Bsns Pk NW2 46 A1
Aquarius Way HA6 22 A6
Aquila St NW8 92 B5 229 D4
Aquinas St SE1 116 C5 251 B3
Arabella Ct NW8 229 B4
Arabella Dr SW15 133 C1
Arabia Cl E4 20 B4
Arabian Ho 3 E1 97 A3
Arabin Rd SE4 141 B1
Aragon Ave KT7 196 D4
Aragon Cl
Ashford TW16 171 D3
Bromley BR2 210 B1
Enfield EN2 4 B5
Aragon Ct
Beckenham BR3 186 A2
East Molesey KT8 196 A5
Aragon Dr HA4 40 D1
Aragon Pl SM4 201 A2
Aragon Prim Sch SM4 200 D2
Aragon Rd
Kingston u T KT2 176 A5
West Barnes SM4 201 A2
Aragon Twr SE8 119 B2
Arakan Ho 4 N16 73 B4
Aral Ho 14 E1 96 D3
Arandora Cres RM6 58 B2
Aranya Ct 3 E17 35 A1
Arapiles Ho 6 E14 98 B1
Arbery Rd E3 97 A5
Arbon Ct N1 235 B5
Arbor Cl BR3 185 D1
Arbor Ct N16 73 B6
Arborfield Cl SW2 160 B3
Arborfield Ho 7 E14 119 C6
Arbor Rd E4 20 B1
Arbour Ho 3 E1 96 D1
Arbour Rd EN3 6 D2
Arbour Sq E1 96 D1
Arbroath Rd SE9 144 A2
Arbrook Chase KT10 212 A2
Arbrook Ct
Chessington KT9 213 D3
St Paul's Cray BR5 190 A2
Arbrook Hall KT10 212 D2
Arbrook La KT10 212 B2
Arbury Ho BR1 188 A3
Arbury Terr 3 SE26 162 B1
Arbuthnot La DA5 169 A5
Arbuthnot Rd SE14 140 D3
Arbutus St E8 95 D6
Arcade Ho 7 NW11 47 B4
Arcade The
Broadgate EC2 243 A3
2 Eltham SE9 166 C5
1 Tufnell Pk N7 72 A4
Walthamstow E17 53 C5
Arcadia Ave N3 29 C2
Arcadia Centre The W5 109 D6
Arcadia Cl SM5 219 A4
Arcadian Ave DA5 169 A5
Arcadian Cl DA5 169 A5
Arcadian Gdns N22 32 C3
Arcadian Ho SW6 136 A3
Arcadian Pl SW18 157 B4
Arcadian Rd DA5 169 A5
Arcadia St E14 97 C1
Arcadia Univ W2 113 D6 245 C5
Archangel St SE16 118 D4
Archbishop Coggan Ho SE13 142 B1
Archbishop Lanfranc Sch The CR0 204 A3
Archbishop's Pl 1 SW2 160 B4
Archbishop Sumner CE Prim Sch SE11 116 C2 261 B3
Archbishop Tenison's CE Sch CR0 221 D5
Archbishop Tenison's Sch SE11 138 B6 270 D5
Archdale Bsns Ctr HA2 64 A6
Archdale Ct W12 112 B5
Archdale Ho SE1 263 A6
Archdale Pl KT3 198 D6
Archdale Rd SE22 139 D1
Archdeacon Cambridge's CE Prim Sch 2 TW2 152 C2
Archel Rd W14 135 B6 264 C6
Archer Cl Barnet EN5 13 B5

Archer Cl *continued*
Kingston u T KT2 ... 176 A3
Archer Ct TW13 ... 150 A3
Archer Ho
[1] Battersea SW11 ... 136 B3
Ealing W13 ... 109 B5
[24] Hoxton N1 ... 95 C6
[1] New Cross SE14 ... 141 A4
Notting Hill W11 ... 244 D6
Archer Mews TW12 ... 174 A4
Archer Rd SE25 ... 206 B5
Archers Ct [3] CR2 ... 221 A3
Archers Dr EN3 ... 6 C3
Archers Lo [22] SE16 ... 118 A1
Archer Sq SE14 ... 141 A6
Archer St W1 ... 249 C6
Archer Terr UB7 ... 104 A6
Archery Cl
Harrow HA3 ... 42 D6
Paddington W2 ... 237 B1
Archery Fields Ho
WC1 ... 234 A2
Archery Rd SE9 ... 166 B6
Archery Stps W2 ... 247 B6
Arches Bsns Ctr The
UB2 ... 107 B4
Arches The
Harrow HA2 ... 63 D6
Strand WC2 ... 250 B4
Archgate Bsns Ctr [1]
N12 ... 30 A5
Archibald Mews W1 248 C5
Archibald Rd N7 ... 71 D4
Archibald St E3 ... 97 C4
Archie Cl UB7 ... 104 C4
Archie St SE1 ... 253 B1
Arch St SE1 ... 117 A3 262 A5
Archway N19 ... 71 C6
Archway Bsns Ctr [5]
N19 ... 71 D5
Archway Cl
North Kensington
W10 ... 90 D2
[2] Upper Holloway
N19 ... 71 C6
Wallington SM6 ... 220 A5
Wimbledon SW19 ... 179 D6
Archway Hts [5] N19 ... 49 C1
Archway L Ctr N19 ... 71 C6
Archway Mews
SW15 ... 135 A1
Archway Rd N6 ... 49 B2
Archway St SW13,
SW14 ... 133 C2
Archway Sta N19 ... 71 C6
Arcola St E8 ... 73 D3
Arcon Dr UB5 ... 85 A3
Arctic St NW5 ... 71 B3
Arcus Rd BR1 ... 186 C4
Ardbeg Rd SE24 ... 161 B6
Arden [17] SW19 ... 156 D3
Arden Cl
Bushey Heath WD23 ... 8 D4
Erith SE28 ... 102 D1
Harrow HA1 ... 64 B5
Twickenham TW2 ... 151 B4
Arden Court Gdns N2 . 48 B3
Arden Cres
Dagenham RM9 ... 80 D1
Millwall E14 ... 119 C2
Arden Gr BR6 ... 226 D4
Arden Grange N12 ... 30 A6
Arden Ho
[21] Hoxton N1 ... 95 C5
[29] Stockwell SW9 ... 138 A3
Vauxhall SE11 ... 260 C3
Arden Mews E17 ... 53 D4
Arden Mhor HA5 ... 40 B5
Arden Rd Ealing W13 ... 109 C6
Finchley N3 ... 47 B6
Ardent Cl SE25 ... 205 C6
Ardent Ho [30] E3 ... 97 A5
Ardfern Ave SW16 ... 204 C6
Ardfillan Rd SE6 ... 164 B2
Ardgowan Rd SE6 ... 164 C3
Ardilaun Rd N5 ... 73 A4
Ardingly Cl CR0 ... 222 D5
Ardleigh Gdns SM3 ... 201 C2
Ardleigh Ho [4] IG11 ... 101 A6
Ardleigh Rd
Kingsland N1 ... 73 C2
Walthamstow E17 ... 35 B2
Ardleigh Terr E17 ... 35 B2
Ardley Cl
Forest Hill SE6 ... 163 A1
Neasden NW10 ... 67 C5
Ruislip HA4 ... 39 A2
Ardlui Rd SE27 ... 161 A2
Ardmay Gdns KT6 ... 198 A4
Ardmere Rd SE13 ... 164 B5
Ardmore La IG9 ... 21 B4
Ardmore Pl IG9 ... 21 B4
Ardoch Rd SE6 ... 164 B2
Ardra Rd N9 ... 18 D1
Ardrossan Gdns KT4 . 216 A5
Ardshiel Cl [6] SW15 . 134 D2
Ardwell Ave IG6 ... 57 A4
Ardwell Rd SW2 ... 160 A2
Ardwick Rd NW2 ... 69 C4
Arena Bsns Ctr N4 ... 51 A3
Arena Est N4 ... 50 D3
Arena Sta SE25 ... 206 C4
Arena The EN3 ... 7 B5
Ares Ct [16] E14 ... 119 C2
Arethusa Ho [8] E14 . 119 D2
Argali Ho [3] DA18 ... 125 A3
Argall Ave E10 ... 52 D1
Argall Way E10 ... 53 A1
Argenta Way NW10 ... 66 D1
Argent Ct KT6 ... 214 C5
Argent Ctr The UB3 . 106 A4
Argent Ho HA5 ... 23 B4
Argo Bsns Ctr [7]
NW6 ... 91 C4
Argon Mews SW6 ... 265 B3
Argon Rd N18 ... 34 D5
Argos Ct [5] SW9 ... 138 C4
Argos Ho [8] E2 ... 96 B5
Argosy Ho
Fitzrovia W1 ... 238 D5
Rotherhithe SE8 ... 119 A2
Argus Way UB5 ... 85 A4
Argyle Cl W13 ... 87 A3
Argyle Ho
Cubitt Town E14 ... 120 A3
Richmond TW10 ... 153 C2
Sutton SM2 ... 218 A2
Teddington TW11 ... 174 C5
Argyle Mans [4] NW2 ... 68 D4
Argyle Pl W6 ... 112 B2
Argyle Prim Sch
WC1 ... 94 A4 233 A2
Argyle Rd Ealing W13 ... 87 A2
Edmonton N18 ... 34 A6
Harrow HA2 ... 41 D3
Hounslow TW3 ... 151 D6
Ilford IG1 ... 78 C6
Leyton E15 ... 76 C4
Newham E16 ... 99 B1
Stepney E1 ... 96 D3
Tottenham N17 ... 34 A2
Woodside Pk N12 ... 29 C5
Argyle Sq
WC1 ... 94 A4 233 B2
Argyle St WC1 . 94 A4 233 B2
Argyle Way SE16 ... 118 A1
Argyle Wlk WC1 ... 233 B1
Argyll Ave UB1 ... 107 D5
Argyll Cl SW9 ... 138 B2
Argyll Ct [15] SW2 ... 160 A4
Argyll Gdns HA8 ... 26 D2
Argyll Mans
Chelsea SW3 ... 266 D6
West Kensington W14 254 B4
Argyll Rd
Kensington
W8 ... 113 C4 245 B1
Woolwich SE18 ... 123 A3
Argyll St W1 ... 93 C1 239 A1
Aria Ct IG2 ... 57 A3
Arica Ho SE16 ... 118 B3
Arica Rd SE4 ... 141 A2
Ariel Ct
[5] Belvedere DA17 ... 125 C1
[5] Hammersmith
W12 ... 112 A3
Newington SE11 ... 261 C3
Ariel Rd NW6 ... 69 C2
Ariel Way
Hounslow TW4 ... 128 B2
Shepherd's Bush W11,
W12 ... 112 D5
Aristotle Rd SW4 ... 137 D2
Arizona Bldg [10]
SE13 ... 141 D4
Ark Acad HA9 ... 65 C6
Arkansas Ho [21] N19 ... 49 D2
Ark Ct N16 ... 73 D6
Arkell Gr SW16 ... 182 D3
Arkindale Rd SE6 ... 164 A1
Arklay Cl UB8 ... 82 B3
ARKLEY ... 12 A6
Arkley Cres E17 ... 53 B4
Arkley Dr EN5 ... 12 B6
Arkley Pk EN5 ... 11 B5
Arkley Rd E17 ... 53 B4
Arklow Ho SE17 ... 139 B6
Arklow Mews [4]
KT6 ... 214 A6
Arklow Rd SE14 ... 141 B6
Arklow Road Trad Est
SE14 ... 141 B6
Arkwright Ho [23]
SW2 ... 160 A4
Arkwright Mans [1]
NW3 ... 70 A3
Arkwright Rd NW3 ... 70 A3
Arlesey Cl SW15 ... 157 A6
Arlesford Rd SW9 ... 138 A2
Arless Ho [8] HA1 ... 42 D4
Arlidge Ho EC1 ... 241 B4
Arlingford Rd SW2 ... 160 C5
Arlington N12 ... 13 C1
Arlington Ave
N1 ... 95 A6 235 B5
Arlington Cl
Lewisham SE13 ... 164 B6
Sidcup DA15 ... 167 C4
Sutton SM1 ... 217 C6
Twickenham TW1 ... 153 C5
Arlington Ct
[13] Acton W3 ... 110 D5
Highgate N6 ... 49 A3
[4] Twickenham TW1 . 153 C5
Arlington Dr
Carshalton SM5 ... 218 D6
Ruislip HA4 ... 39 B3
Arlington Gdns
Acton Green W4 ... 111 A1
Ilford IG1 ... 56 C1
Arlington Gn NW7 ... 28 D3
Arlington Ho
[3] Deptford SE8 ... 141 B6
Finsbury EC1 ... 234 B2
[1] Shepherd's Bush
W12 ... 112 B5
Arlington Lo SW2 ... 138 B1
Arlington Park Mans [1]
W4 ... 111 A1
Arlington Pl [7] SE10 . 142 A5
Arlington Rd
Ashford TW15 ... 170 B5
Camden Town
NW1 ... 93 B6 231 D5
Ealing W13 ... 87 B1
Osidge N14 ... 15 C3
Richmond TW10 ... 153 D2
Surbiton KT6 ... 197 D3
Teddington TW11 ... 174 D6
Twickenham TW1 ... 153 C5
Woodford IG8 ... 37 B3
Arlington Sq
N1 ... 95 A6 235 B5
Arlington St
SW1 ... 115 C5 249 A4
Arlington Way
EC1 ... 94 C4 234 B2
Arliss Way UB5 ... 84 C6
Arlow Rd N21 ... 16 C3
Armada Ct [11] SE8 ... 141 C6
Armadale Cl N17 ... 52 B5
Armadale Rd
Feltham TW14 ... 150 A6
West Brompton SW6 . 265 A5
Armada St [10] SE8 ... 141 C6
Armada Way
Newham E6 ... 101 B1
Newham E16 ... 122 D6
Armagh Rd E3 ... 97 B6
Armeston KT3 ... 199 B2
Armfield Cl KT8 ... 195 B4
Armfield Cotts [3]
SW19 ... 180 D1
Armfield Cres CR4 ... 180 D1
Armfield Rd EN2 ... 5 B4
Arminger Rd W12 ... 112 B5
Armistice Gdns
SE25 ... 206 A6
Armitage Ho
NW1 ... 92 C2 237 B4
Armitage Rd
Golders Green NW11 ... 47 B1
Greenwich SE10 ... 120 D1
Armour Cl N7 ... 72 B2
Armoury Ho E3 ... 97 A6
Armoury Rd SE8 ... 141 D3
Armoury Way SW18 ... 157 C6
Armsby Ho [17] E1 ... 96 C2
Armstead Wlk RM10 ... 81 C1
Armstrong Ave IG8 ... 36 C4
Armstrong Cl
Bickley BR1 ... 210 A6
Dagenham RM8 ... 58 D2
Newham E6 ... 100 B1
Pinner HA5 ... 40 A3
Walton-on-T KT12 ... 194 A3
Armstrong Cres EN4 ... 2 B2
Armstrong Ho [8]
SW15 ... 156 D5
Armstrong Rd
East Acton W3 ... 111 D5
Feltham TW13 ... 173 A5
Knightsbridge SW7 ... 256 C5
[10] Willesden NW0 ... 67 C1
Woolwich SE18 ... 123 A3
Armstrong Way UB2 107 D4
Armytage Rd TW5 ... 128 D5
Arnal Cres SW18 ... 157 A4
Arncliffe NW6 ... 91 D6
Arncliffe Cl N11 ... 31 A4
Arncroft Ct IG11 ... 102 B4
Arndale Wlk [6]
SW18 ... 157 D6
Arndell Ho [16] SM1 ... 218 A4
Arne Gr BR6 ... 227 D5
Arne Ho SE11 ... 260 C2
Arne St WC2 ... 94 A1 240 B1
Arnett Sq E4 ... 35 B4
Arneways Ave RM6 ... 58 D6
Arneway St SW1 ... 259 D5
Arne Wlk SE3 ... 142 D1
Arnewood Cl SW15 ... 156 A3
Arney's La CR4 ... 203 A3
Arngask Rd SE6 ... 164 B4
Arnhem Pl E14 ... 119 C3
Arnhem Way [3]
SE22 ... 161 C6
Arnhem Wharf E14 . 119 C3
Arnhem Wharf Prim Sch
E14 ... 119 C3
Arnison Rd KT8 ... 196 B5
Arnold Ave E EN3 ... 7 C5
Arnold Ave W EN3 ... 7 B5
Arnold Cir E2 ... 95 D4
Arnold Cl HA3 ... 44 B2
Arnold Cres TW7 ... 152 B6
Arnold Ct E18 ... 36 D2
Arnold Dr KT9 ... 213 D2
Arnold Est SE1 ... 253 D1
Arnold Gdns N13 ... 32 D5
Arnold Ho
Croydon CR0 ... 220 D4
Newington SE17 ... 261 D1
[9] Stoke Newington
N16 ... 73 C5
Arnold House Sch
NW8 ... 92 B5 229 C3
Arnold Rd Bow E3 ... 97 C4
Dagenham RM10 ... 81 C1
Mitcham SW17 ... 180 D3
Northolt UB5 ... 63 A2
Tottenham N15 ... 51 D6
Arnos Gr N14 ... 15 D1
Arnos Grove Ct [4]
N11 ... 31 C5
Arnos Grove Sta N11 ... 31 C6
Arnos Rd N11 ... 31 C6
Arnot Ho [27] SE5 ... 139 A5
Arnott Cl
Acton Green W4 ... 111 B2
Thamesmead SE28 ... 124 C5
Arnould Ave SE5 ... 139 B1
Arnsberg Way DA6,
DA7 ... 147 C1
Arnside Gdns HA9 ... 43 D1
Arnside Ho [2] SE17 ... 139 B6
Arnside Rd DA7 ... 147 C4
Arnside St SE17 ... 139 A6
Arnulf St SE6 ... 185 D6
Arnull's Rd SW16 ... 182 D4
Arodene Rd SW2 ... 160 B5
Arosa Rd [8] TW1 ... 153 D5
Arragon Gdns
Streatham SW16 ... 182 A3
West Wickham BR4 ... 223 D5
Arragon Rd
Newham E6 ... 99 D6
[4] Twickenham TW1 . 153 A3
Wandsworth SW18 ... 157 C3
Arran Cl SM6 ... 219 C4
Arran Ct Edgware HA8 ... 10 D2
Arran Ct *continued*
[32] Hendon NW9 ... 27 D1
Neasden NW10 ... 67 B5
Arrandene Ho [3]
BR5 ... 190 B1
Arran Dr
Stanmore HA7 ... 25 C6
Wanstead E12 ... 77 D6
Arran Ho
[5] Canary Wharf
E14 ... 120 A5
Stoke Newington N16 ... 51 D1
Arran Mews W5 ... 110 B5
Arran Rd SE6 ... 164 A2
Arran Wlk N1 ... 73 A1
Arras Ave SM4 ... 202 A4
Arras Ho SE2 ... 146 D6
Arrol Ho SE1 ... 262 B5
Arrol Rd BR3 ... 206 D6
Arrowe Ct [6] E5 ... 74 B4
Arrow Ho [23] N1 ... 95 C6
Arrow Rd E3 ... 97 D4
Arrow Scout Wlk
UB5 ... 85 A4
Arrowsmith Ho SE11 260 C2
Arsenal Rd SE9 ... 144 B2
Arsenal Sta N5 ... 72 C5
Arsenal Way SE18 ... 123 A3
Arta Ho [26] E1 ... 96 C1
Artcadia Lifestyle★
EC2 ... 243 C4
Artemis Ct [14] E14 ... 119 C2
Artemis Pl SW18 ... 157 B4
Arterberry Rd SW20,
SW19 ... 178 D2
Artesian Cl NW10 ... 67 B1
Artesian Gr EN5 ... 2 A1
Artesian Rd W2 ... 91 C1
Artesian Wlk [4] E11 ... 76 C5
Arthingworth St E15 ... 98 C6
Arthur Ct
Battersea SW11 ... 268 B1
[10] North Kensington
W10 ... 90 D1
Paddington W2 ... 91 D1
South Croydon CR0 ... 221 B5
Arthur Deakin Ho [1]
E1 ... 96 A2
Arthurdon Rd SE4 ... 163 C6
Arthur Gr SE18 ... 123 A2
Arthur Henderson Ho
[9] Crouch End N19 ... 49 D2
[9] Fulham SW6 ... 135 B3
Arthur Newton Ho [19]
SW11 ... 136 B2
Arthur Rd
Dagenham RM6 ... 58 D3
Edmonton N9 ... 17 D2
[6] Kingston u T KT2 ... 176 C3
Lower Holloway N7 ... 72 B4
Newham E6 ... 100 B5
West Barnes KT3 ... 200 B4
Wimbledon SW19 ... 179 C6
Arthur Ruxley Est
DA14 ... 190 D4
Arthur St
EC4 ... 117 B6 252 D6
Arthur Wade Ho [7]
E2 ... 95 D4
Arthur Walls Ho [3]
E12 ... 78 C5
Artichoke Hill [8] E1 ... 118 B6
Artichoke Mews [5]
SE5 ... 139 B4
Artichoke Pl SE5 ... 139 B4
Artillery Cl IG2 ... 57 A3
Artillery Ho Bow E3 ... 97 A6
Westminster SW1 ... 259 C5
Woolwich SE18 ... 122 C1
Artillery La
Broadgate
E1 ... 95 C2 243 B3
North Kensington W12 ... 90 A1
Artillery Pas E1 ... 243 B3
Artillery Pl
Harrow Weald HA3 ... 24 A3
Westminster SW1 ... 259 C5
Woolwich SE18 ... 122 C2
Artillery Row SW1 ... 259 C5
Artington Cl BR6 ... 227 A4
Artisan Cl E16 ... 122 D6
Artisan Ct E8 ... 74 A2
Artisan Mews [9]
NW10 ... 90 D4
Artisan Quarter [10]
NW10 ... 90 D4

Artizan St E1 .... 243 B2
Arton Wilson Ho 12 SW15 ....156 A6
Art Pilgrim★ NW3 ....70 B1
Artsdepot★ N12 ......30 A5
Arts Educational Sch The 14 W4 ....111 C2
Artwell Cl E10 ....53 D3
Arundale KT1 ....197 D5
Arundel Ave SM4 ....201 B5
Arundel Bldgs SE1 .. 263 B5
Arundel Cl
Croydon CR0 .... 220 D5
Hampton TW12 ..... 173 D5
Leyton E15 ....76 C4
Sidcup DA5 ....169 B5
Wandsworth SW11 .. 158 C6
Arundel Ct
Barnes SW13 ....134 B6
4 Beckenham BR2 .. 186 C1
2 Bexley DA6 ...... 147 A1
Chelsea SW3 .... 257 B2
Colney Hatch N12 .....30 C4
3 Croydon CR0 ..... 220 D5
Harrow HA2 ....63 C4
Putney SW15 ....156 D6
Tottenham N17 ....34 A2
Arundel Dr
Borehamwood WD6....11 A6
Harrow HA2 ....63 C4
Woodford IG8 ....37 A3
Arundel Gdns
Burnt Oak HA8 ....27 B3
Ilford IG3 ....80 A6
Notting Hill W11 .....113 B6 244 C6
Southgate N21 ....16 C3
Arundel Gr N16 ....73 C3
Arundel Ho
Croydon CR0 .... 221 B3
Islington N1 ...94 D6 234 D6
Richmond TW10 ..... 154 C6
3 South Acton W3 .. 110 D4
Arundel Lo
Church End N3 ....29 B1
9 Upper Holloway N19 ....72 A6
Arundel Mans
Barnes SW13 ....134 B6
Fulham SW6 .... 264 D2
Arundel Pl N1, N7 .....72 C2
Arundel Rd
Belmont SM2 ....217 B1
Cockfosters EN4 ....2 C2
Hounslow TW4 ...... 128 C2
Kingston u T KT1 .... 177 A1
Thornton Heath CR0 ..205 B3
Arundel Sq N7 ....72 C2
Arundel St WC2 ....116 B6 250 D6
Arundel Terr SW13 ...134 B6
Arungford Mews 12 SW2 ....160 C6
Arun Ho 5 KT2 ....175 D2
Arvon Rd N5 ....72 C3
Asa Ct UB3 ....105 D3
Asaph Ho SE14 ....141 B4
Asbaston Terr IG11....79 A2
Asbury Ct N21 ....16 A6
Ascalon Ct 16 SW2 ....160 B4
Ascalon Ho SW8 .... 269 A3
Ascalon St SW8 ....137 C5 269 A3
Ascham Dr E4 ....35 C3
Ascham End E17 ....35 A2
Ascham St NW5 ......71 C3
Aschurch Rd CR0 ... 205 D2
Ascot Cl
Borehamwood WD6....10 C6
Northolt UB5 ....63 C3
Ascot Ct
8 Brixton SW4 ..... 138 A1
Bromley BR1 .... 188 A1
Old Bexley DA5 ......169 B4
St John's Wood NW8 . 229 C1
Ascot Gdns Enfield EN3.. 6 C6
Southall UB1 ....85 C2
Ascot Ho
6 Acton Green W4 ... 111 A1
1 Paddington W9 .....91 C2
Penge SE26 ....184 B4
Regent's Pk NW1 .... 231 D2
Ascot Lo Enfield EN1 ...17 B6
Paddington NW6 ......91 D5
Ascot Par 9 SW4 ....138 A1
Ascot Pl 12 HA7 ....25 C5
Ascot Rd
East Bedfont TW14 .. 148 D2
Edmonton N18 ....34 A6
Newham E6 ....100 B4
Orpington BR5 ...... 211 D5
Streatham SW17 .... 181 A4
Tottenham N15 ......51 B4
Ascott Ave W5 ....110 A4
Ascott Ct HA5 ....40 A5
Ashbourne Ave
East Barnet N20 ....14 D2
Erith DA7 .... 147 A5
Harrow HA2 ....64 B6
Temple Fortune NW11 ..47 B4
Wanstead E18 ....55 B5
Ashbourne Cl
Ealing W5 ....88 C2
18 Woodside Pk N12 ...29 D6
Ashbourne Coll W8........ 113 D4 245 C1
Ashbourne Ct
Beckenham BR3..... 186 A2
Clapton Pk E5 ....75 A4
13 Woodside Pk N12 ...29 D6
Ashbourne Gr
Chiswick W4 .... 111 C1
East Dulwich SE22... 139 D1
Edgware NW7 ....27 B5
Ashbourne Lo 2 N13 .32 C6
Ashbourne Par 2 NW11 ....47 B5
Ashbourne Rd
Ealing W5 ....88 B3
Mitcham CR4 .... 181 A3
Ashbourne Rise BR6 .227 C4
Ashbourne Terr 1 SW19 ....179 C3
Ashbourne Way NW11 ....47 B4
Ashbridge Ct 3 W6 ..112 B3
Ashbridge Rd E11 .....54 D2
Ashbridge St NW8 ....92 C3 237 A5
Ashbrook HA8 ....26 B4
Ashbrook Rd
Dagenham RM10 ......81 D5
Upper Holloway N19 ...71 D6
Ashburn Ct BR1 ....187 A3
Ashburn Gdns SW7 . 256 A4
Ashburnham Ave HA1 ....42 D3
Ashburnham Cl N2 ...48 B5
Ashburnham Gdns HA1 ....42 D3
Ashburnham Gr SE10 ....141 D5
Ashburnham Pk KT10 ....212 A4
Ashburnham Pl SE10 ....141 D5
Ashburnham Prim Sch SW10 ....266 C4
Ashburnham Rd
Chelsea SW10 .....136 A5 266 B3
Kensal Rise NW10 .....90 C5
Richmond TW10 ......153 B1
Ashburnham Retreat 4 SE10 ....141 D5
Ashburnham Twr SW10 ....266 C4
Ashburn Pl SW7 ....114 A2 256 A3
Ashburton Ave
Croydon CR0 ....206 B1
Ilford IG3 ....79 D4
Ashburton Cl CR0....206 A1
Ashburton Ct 1 HA5..40 D6
Ashburton Gdns CR0 ....222 A6
Ashburton Ho
Enfield EN3 ....6 D2
2 Wallington SM6 .. 219 D3
Ashburton Jun & Inf Sch CR0 ....206 B3
Ashburton Learning Village CR9 ....206 B2
Ashburton Mans SW10 ....266 B4
Ashburton Rd
Croydon CR0 .... 222 A6
Newham E16 ....99 A1
Ruislip HA4 ....62 A6
Ashburton Terr 2 E13 ....99 A5
Ashbury Dr UB10 .....60 D5
Ashbury Gdns RM6....58 D4
Ashbury Pl SW19 ....180 A4
Ashbury Rd SW11....137 A2
Ashby Ave KT19, KT9..214 C2
Ashby Ct NW8 ...... 236 D6
Ashby Gr N1 ....73 A1
Ashby Grange 7 SM6 ....219 C2
Ashby Ho
6 Brixton SW9 ..... 138 D3
17 Islington N1 ....73 A1
3 Northolt UB5 ....85 B3
14 Surbiton KT6 ..... 198 A3
Ashby Mews
10 Clapham Pk SW2 ....160 A6
New Cross SE4 ....141 B3
Ashby Rd
New Cross SE4 ....141 B3
South Tottenham N15...52 A4
Ashby St EC1 ..94 D4 234 D1
Ashby Way UB7 ......126 C5
Ashby Wlk CR0 ....205 A3
Ashchurch Ct 2 W12 ....112 A3
Ashchurch Gr W12...112 A3
Ashchurch Park Villas W12 ....112 A3
Ashchurch Terr W12 ....112 A3
Ash Cl
Carshalton SM5 ..... 218 D6
Edgware HA8 ....27 A6
Kingston u T KT3 .....177 B1
Penge SE20 .... 184 C1
Petts Wood BR5 ......211 B4
Sidcup DA14 ....168 B1
Stanmore HA7 ....25 A4
Ashcombe Ave KT6 . 197 D2
Ashcombe Cl TW15 ..148 A1
Ashcombe Ct 4 SW15 ....157 A6
Ashcombe Gdns HA8..26 C6
Ashcombe Ho 39 E3 ..97 D4
Ashcombe Pk NW2 ...67 C5
Ashcombe Rd
Wallington SM5 ..... 219 A2
Wimbledon SW19 ..... 179 C5
Ashcombe Sq KT3 ...199 A6
Ashcombe St SW6 ... 135 D3
Ashcroft
Hatch End HA5 ....23 C4
Osidge N14 ....15 D2
Ashcroft Ave DA15 ...168 A5
Ashcroft Cres DA15 ..168 A5
Ashcroft Ct
5 Eltham SE9 ...... 166 C5
Wembley HA0 ....65 A4
3 Whetstone N20 ......14 B2
Ashcroft Ho SW8 ... 269 A2
Ashcroft Rd Bow E3 ...97 A4
Chessington KT9 .....214 B5
Ashcroft Sq 8 W6 ...112 C2
Ashcroft Tech Acad SW15 ....157 B6
Ash Ct Chingford E4 ....20 B4
Clapham SW11 ......159 A6
Lee SE12 .... 165 A4
Marylebone W1 ..... 237 C2
Romford RM7 ....59 D3
6 Rotherhithe SE16 . 119 A5
Upper Holloway N19 ...71 C6
West Ewell KT19 .... 215 A4
2 West Norwood SW16 ....182 C5
9 Wimbledon SW19. 179 A3
Woodford E18 ....37 C2
Ashdale Cl
Stanwell TW19 ...... 148 A2
Twickenham TW2..... 152 A4
Ashdale Gr HA7 ....24 D4
Ashdale Ho N4 ....51 B2
Ashdale Rd SE12 ....165 B3
Ashdale Way TW2 .... 151 D4
Ashdene
6 Deptford SE15 ....140 B5
Pinner HA5 ....40 C6
Ashdene Cl TW15 ....171 A3
Ashdon Cl IG8 ....37 B4
Ashdon Rd NW10 ......89 D6
Ashdown Ealing W13 ...87 B2
Putney SW15 .... 156 D6
Ashdown Cl 13 BR3 . 185 D1
Ashdown Cres NW5 ...71 A3
Ashdown Ct
Dulwich SE22 .... 162 A3
Ashdown Ct *continued*
Ilford IG1 ....78 D2
New Malden KT4 .... 199 D2
Sutton SM2 .... 218 A2
Ashdowne Ct N17 .....34 A2
Ashdown Ho 7 E5 ....74 A6
Ashdown Pl
Ewell KT17 .... 215 D1
Thames Ditton KT7... 197 A2
Ashdown Rd
Enfield EN3 ....6 C3
Hillingdon UB10 ......82 C5
Kingston u T KT1 .... 176 A1
Ashdown Way SW17 .159 A2
Ashdown Wlk 20 E14 ....119 C2
Ashe Ho 9 TW1 .... 153 D5
Ashen E6 ....100 C1
Ashenden SE17 ..... 262 B4
Ashenden Rd E5 ......75 A3
Ashen Gr SW19 ......157 C2
Ashentree Ct EC4 .... 241 B1
Asher Loftus Way N11 ....30 D4
Asher Way E1 ....118 A6
Ashfield Ave
Bushey WD23 ....8 A4
Feltham TW13 ....150 B3
Ashfield Cl
Beckenham BR3..... 185 C3
Richmond TW10 ..... 154 A3
Ashfield Ct SW9 .....138 A3
Ashfield Ho 5 N5.....73 A3
Ashfield La BR7 ......189 A3
Ashfield Par N14 ......15 D3
Ashfield Pl BR7 ......189 B3
Ashfield Rd
East Acton W3 ...... 111 D5
New Southgate N14....15 C1
Tottenham N4 ....51 A3
Ashfield St E1 ....96 C2
4 Whitechapel E1 .....96 B2
Ashfield Yd 21 E1 .....96 C2
ASHFORD 170 B4
Ashford Ave
Ashford TW15 ...... 170 D4
Hayes UB4 ....84 D1
Hornsey N8 ....50 A5
Ashford Bsns Complex TW15 ....171 A6
Ashford CE Prim Sch TW15 ....170 D4
Ashford Cl
Ashford TW15 ...... 170 A6
Walthamstow E17 .....53 B3
ASHFORD COMMON 171 B4
Ashford Cres EN3......6 C3
Ashford Ct
Cricklewood NW2 .....68 D4
Edgware HA8 ....10 D1
Ashford Gn WD19 .....22 D5
Ashford Ho
14 Brixton SW9 ..... 138 D1
11 Deptford SE8 .....141 B6
Ashford Hospl TW15 148 A2
Ashford Ind Est TW15 ....171 A6
Ashford Mews N17....34 A2
Ashford Rd
Cricklewood NW2 .....68 D4
Feltham TW13, TW15..171 B6
Littleton TW15, TW17. 171 A3
Staines TW18....... 170 A4
Wallend E6 ....78 C1
Woodford E18 ....37 B1
Ashford St N1 ....95 C4
Ashford Sta TW15....170 B6
Ash Gr
Cranley Gardens N10...49 B5
Cricklewood NW2 .....69 A4
Ealing W5 ....110 A3
East Bedfont TW14 ... 149 C3
Edmonton N13 ....17 A1
Enfield EN1 ....17 C4
Hackney E8 ....96 B6
Hayes UB3 ....105 B6
Heston TW5 ....128 D5
Penge SE20 ....184 C1
Southall UB1 ....85 C2
Wembley HA0 ....65 A4
West Wickham BR4 .. 208 A1
Yiewsley UB7 ....104 B6
Ashgrove SE12 ....165 A3
Ashgrove Ct 2 W9.....91 C2
Ashgrove Ho SW1... 259 D2
Ashgrove Rd
Ashford TW15 ....171 B5
Catford BR1 ....186 B4
Ashgrove Sch BR1 ...187 B1
Ash Hill Dr HA5 ....40 C6
Ash Ho
3 Canary Wharf E14 ....120 A4
Fulham SE1 .... 263 D3
Kenton NW9 ....45 A6
Lewisham SE12 ..... 165 A3
2 Teddington TW11 .. 175 C3
Ashingdon Cl E4......20 A1
Ashington 1 NW5 ....71 B2
Ashington Ho 16 E1....96 B3
Ashington Rd SW6...135 B3
Ashlake Rd SW16 ....182 A6
Ashland Pl W1...... 238 A4
Ashlar Ct N2 ....48 C6
Ashlar Pl SE18 ...... 122 D2
Ashleigh Commercial Est SE7 ....121 D3
Ashleigh Ct
Ealing W5 .... 109 D2
Osidge N14 ....15 C4
Penge SE26 ....184 B4
Ashleigh Gdns SM1 . 217 D6
Ashleigh Ho
Mortlake SW14 ..... 133 C2
1 Streatham SW16 ..182 B6
Ashleigh Point 8 SE26 ....162 D1
Ashleigh Rd
Mortlake SW14 ..... 133 C2
Penge SE20 ....206 B6
Ashley Ave SM4 ....201 C4
Ashley Cl Hendon NW4 .28 C1
Oatlands Pk KT12, KT13 ....193 D1
Pinner Green HA5 .....22 B1
Ashley Cres
Clapham SW11 ..... 137 A2
Wood Green N22 ......32 C1
Ashley Ct
Hampstead NW3 ......69 D3
Hendon NW4 ....28 C1
19 Kingsland N16 .....73 C3
New Barnet EN5 ....14 A6
Northolt UB5 ....85 A6
Stanmore HA7 ....25 B1
Yiewsley UB7....... 104 A5
Ashley Dr
Borehamwood WD6....11 B6
Hounslow TW7....... 130 C6
Twickenham TW2.... 151 D3
Ashley Gdns
Edmonton N13 ....33 A6
Orpington BR6...... 227 C3
Richmond TW10 ..... 153 D2
Wembley HA9 ....66 A6
Ashley Ho BR5 ....190 A1
Ashley La
Croydon CR0 .... 220 D4
Edgware NW7 ....28 D3
Hendon NW4 ....28 C1
Ashley Park Ave KT12 ....193 D1
Ashley Park Cres KT12 ....194 A1
Ashley Pl
Walton-on-T KT12 ... 194 A1
Westminster SW1 ..... 115 C3 259 A5
Ashley Prim Sch KT12 ....194 A1
Ashley Rd
Chingford E4 ....35 C4
Enfield EN3 ....6 C3
Hampton TW12 ..... 173 C2
Hornsey N19 ....50 A2
Richmond TW9 ....132 A2
Thames Ditton KT7... 196 D3
Thornton Heath CR7 ...204 B5
Tottenham Hale N17 ...52 A6
Upton E7 ....77 C1
Walton-on-T KT12 ... 194 A1
Wimbledon SW19 ....179 D4
Ashleys Alley N15 ....51 A5
Ashley Wlk NW7 ....28 D3
Ashling Ho 2 N17 ....33 D1
Ashling Rd CR0 ....206 A1
Ashlin Rd E15 ....76 B4

Ash Lo
2 Ashford TW16 171 D3
Fulham SW6 134 D4
Ashlone Rd SW15 134 D2
Ashlyns Way KT9 213 D2
Ashmead 4 N14 15 C6
Ashmead Bsns Ctr 2
E16 98 B3
Ashmead Gate BR1 187 C2
Ashmead Ho E9 75 A3
Ashmead Mews 1
SE8 141 C3
Ashmead Prim Sch
SE8 141 C3
Ashmead Rd
East Bedfont TW14 150 A3
St Johns SE8 141 C3
Ashmere Ave BR3 186 B1
Ashmere Cl SM3 216 D3
Ashmere Gr 11 SW2,
SW4 138 A1
Ashmere Ho 10 SW2 138 A1
Ashmill Ct CR0 205 A3
Ashmill St
NW8 92 C2 237 A4
Ashmole Prim Sch
SW8 138 B6 270 D5
Ashmole Sch N14 15 C3
Ashmole St
SW8 138 B6 270 D5
Ashmoor Lo NW7 27 B4
Ashmore NW1 71 D1
Ashmore Cl SE15 139 D5
Ashmore Ct
Catford SE6 164 C3
Colney Hatch N11 30 D4
Heston TW5 129 C6
Ashmore Gr DA16 145 C2
Ashmore Ho W14 254 B5
Ashmore Rd W9 91 B4
Ashmount Prim Sch
N19 49 C2
Ashmount Rd
Crouch End N19 49 D2
South Tottenham N15 51 D4
Ashmount Terr W5 109 D2
Ashneal Gdns HA1 64 B5
Ashness Gdns UB6 65 B2
Ashness Rd SW11 158 D6
Ashpark Ho 4 E14 97 B1
Ash Rd Cheam SM3 201 B1
Croydon CR0 223 C6
Littleton TW17 192 C5
Orpington BR6 227 D1
Plashet E15 76 D3
Ashridge Cl HA3 43 C3
Ashridge Cres SE18 145 A5
Ashridge Ct
Southall UB1 108 A6
Southgate N14 15 C6
Ashridge Dr WD19 22 C5
Ashridge Gdns
Bowes Pk N13 32 A5
Pinner HA5 41 A5
Ashridge Ho DA14 189 D6
Ashridge Way
Ashford TW16 172 A4
Merton SM4 201 B5
Ash Row BR2 210 C3
Ashtead Ct 15 SW19 156 D3
Ashtead Rd E5 52 A2
Ashton Cl SM1 217 C4
Ashton Ct
1 Beckenham BR3 185 B2
Chingford E4 20 C1
Harrow HA1 64 D5
Ashton Gdns
Dagenham RM6 59 A3
Hounslow TW4 129 B1
Ashton Ho
13 Kennington SW9 138 C5
Roehampton SW15 156 B4
Ashton House Sch
TW7 130 B4
Ashton Rd E15 76 B3
Ashton St E14 120 A6
Ashtree Ave CR4 180 B1
Ashtree Cl BR6 226 D4
Ash Tree Cl
Croydon CR0 207 A3
1 Surbiton KT6 198 A1
Ashtree Ct TW15 170 D5
Ash Tree Dell NW9 45 B4

Ash Tree Villas CR0 204 B3
Ash Tree Way CR0 207 A3
Ashurst Cl SE20 184 B2
Ashurst Dr
Ilford IG2, IG6 57 A4
Littleton TW17 192 A4
Ashurst Lo 4 N5 72 D3
Ashurst Rd
Cockfosters EN4 14 D6
Colney Hatch N12 30 C5
Ashurst Wlk CR0 222 B6
Ashvale Rd SW17 180 D5
Ashview Cl TW15 170 A5
Ashview Gdns TW15 170 A5
Ashville Rd E11 76 B6
Ashwater Rd SE12 165 A3
Ashway Ctr 5 KT2 176 A2
Ashwell Cl 8 E6 100 A1
Ashwell Ct TW15 148 A2
Ashwin St E8 73 D2
Ash Wlk HA0 65 C4
Ashwood Ave UB8 82 C1
Ashwood Ct HA9 66 B4
Ashwood Gdns
Hayes UB3 105 D2
New Addington CR0 224 A2
Ashwood Ho 10 NW4 46 C5
Ashwood Lo
9 New Barnet EN5 13 D6
Southgate N21 16 B5
Ashwood Pk 6 SM2 217 C1
Ashwood Rd E4 20 B1
Ashworth Cl SE5 139 B3
Ashworth Mans W9 91 D4
Ashworth Rd W9 91 D4
Aske Ho 2 N1 95 C4
Asker Ho N7 72 A4
Askern Cl DA6 146 D1
Aske St N1 95 C4
Askew Cres W12 112 A4
Askew Mans 14
W12 112 A4
Askew Rd W12 112 A4
Askham Ct W12 112 A5
Askham Lo 5 SE12 165 A4
Askham Rd W12 112 A5
Askill Dr SW15 157 A6
Asland Rd E15 98 B6
Aslett St SW18 158 A4
Asmara Rd NW2 69 A3
Asmuns Hill NW11 47 C4
Asmuns Pl NW11 47 B4
Asolando Dr SE17 262 B3
Aspect Ho 7 E14 120 A4
Aspects SM1 217 D3
Aspen Cl Ealing W5 110 B4
13 Upper Holloway
N19 71 C6
Yiewsley UB7 104 B5
Aspen Copse BR1 188 B1
Aspen Ct 10 Acton W3 89 A1
12 Hackney E8 74 A3
Redbridge IG5 56 A6
Richmond TW9 132 C5
Aspen Dr HA0 65 A5
Aspen Gdns
Ashford TW15 171 A5
2 Hammersmith W6 112 B1
Mitcham CR4 203 A4
Aspen Gn DA18 125 B3
Aspen Gr HA5 39 D6
Aspen Ho
8 Deptford SE15 140 C6
4 Maitland Pk NW3 70 D2
Richmond TW9 132 C5
2 Sidcup DA15 168 A1
Southgate N21 16 B6
Aspen La UB5 85 A4
Aspenlea Rd W6 134 D6
Aspen Lo 1 SW19 179 B4
Aspen Way
Canary Wharf E14 120 A6
Feltham TW13 150 B1
Aspern Gr NW3 70 C3
Aspinall Ho SW12 160 A3
Aspinall Rd SE4 140 D2
Aspinden Rd SE16 118 B2
Aspire Bld 10 SW15 157 B6
Aspley Rd SW18 157 D6
Asplins Rd N17 34 B2
Asprey Ho CR4 202 C6
Asprey Mews BR3 207 B4
Asquith Cl RM8 58 C1
Assam SE1 253 D3
Assam St E1 96 A1
Assata Mews N1 72 D2

Assembly Pas E1 96 C2
Assembly Wlk SM5 202 C2
Assheton-Bennett Ho 15
KT6 198 A4
Ass House La HA3 23 D6
Assisi Ct
Upper Tooting
SW12 158 D3
Wembley HA0 64 D5
Assunah Sch 8 N17 33 D1
Astall Cl HA3 24 C2
Astbury Bsns Pk 5
SE15 140 C4
Astbury Ho SE11 261 A5
Astbury Rd SE15 140 C4
Astell St SW3 114 C1 257 B2
Aster Ct 3 HA8 27 A6
Aster Ho 3 SE13 142 A3
Aste St E14 120 A4
Astey's Row 1 N1 73 A1
Asthall Gdns IG6 57 A5
Astins Ho 4 E17 53 D5
Astleham Rd TW17 192 A6
Astleham Way TW17 192 A6
Astle St SW11 137 A3
Astley Ave NW2 68 C3
Astley Ho Fulham SE1 263 D2
39 Paddington W2 91 C2
8 West Norwood
SE27 183 A6
Aston Ave HA3 43 C2
Aston Cl Bushey WD23 8 A5
Sidcup DA14 168 A1
Aston Ct
Stoke Newington N4 73 A6
3 Wimbledon SW19 178 C3
10 Woodford IG8 37 A4
Aston Gn TW5 128 C3
Aston Ho
Notting Hill W11 244 D6
South Lambeth SW8 269 C1
Aston House Sch W5 87 D1
Aston Mews RM6 58 C2
Aston Pl SW16 182 D4
Aston Rd
Claygate KT10 212 C3
Ealing W5 87 D1
Merton SW20 178 C1
Aston St E14 97 A2
Astonville St SW18 157 C3
Astor Ave RM7 59 D3
Astor Cl KT2 176 D4
Astor Ct
Colney Hatch N12 30 C4
Newham E16 99 C1
Walham Green SW6 266 A3
Astoria Mans 18
SW16 160 A1
Astoria Par SW16 160 A1
Astoria Wlk SW9 138 C2
Astra Ct W13 109 A5
Astra Ho 4 Bow E3 97 B4
Hornsey N4 50 B2
Astrid Ho TW13 150 C2
Astrop Mews W6 112 C3
Astrop Terr W6 112 C4
Astwood Mews SW7 256 A4
Asylum Rd SE15 140 B5
Atalanta St
SW6 134 D5 264 A3
Atbara Ct TW11 175 B4
Atbara Rd TW11 175 B4
Atcham Rd TW3 130 A1
Atcost Rd IG11 102 A2
Atheldene Rd SW18 158 A3
Athelney Prim Sch
SE6 163 C1
Athelney St SE6 163 C1
Athelstan Ct E6 100 C5
Athelstane Gr E3 97 B5
Athelstane Mews N4 50 C1
Athelstan Gdns 8
NW6 69 A1
Athelstan Ho
Hackney Wick E9 75 B3
Kingston u T KT1 198 B5
Stoke Newington N16 73 C4
Athelstan House Sch 9
TW12 173 C2
Athelstan Rd KT1 198 B5
Athelstan Way BR5 190 A2
Athelstone Rd HA3 24 B1
Athena Cl Harrow HA2 64 C6
Kingston u T KT1 198 B6
Athena Ct
Bermondsey SE1 253 A1

Athena Ct *continued*
St John's Wood NW8 229 C4
Athenaeum Pl 3 N10 49 B6
Athenaeum Rd N20 14 B3
Athenia Ho 7 E14 98 B1
Athenlay Rd SE15 162 D6
Athenoeum Ct N5 73 A4
Athens Gdns W9 91 C3
Atherden Rd E5 74 C4
Atherfield Ct SW18 157 D5
Atherfold Rd SW9 138 A2
Atherley Way TW4 151 B4
Atherstone Ct W2 91 D2
Atherstone Mews
SW7 114 A2 256 B4
Atherton Dr SW19 178 D6
Atherton Ho CR2 221 C2
Atherton Hts HA0 65 C2
Atherton L Ctr E15 76 D2
Atherton Mews E7 77 A2
Atherton Pl
Harrow HA2 42 B6
Southall UB1 107 C6
Atherton Rd
Barnes SW13 134 A5
Stratford E7 76 D2
Atherton St SW11 136 C3
Athlone KT10 212 C2
Athlone Cl 24 E5 74 B3
Athlone Ct
Lewisham SE6 164 B4
Upper Walthamstow
E17 54 B6
Athlone Ho
16 Camden Town
NW5 71 A2
9 Stepney E1 96 C1
Athlone Rd SW2 160 C4
Athlone St NW5 71 A2
Athlon Ind Est HA0 87 D5
Athlon Rd HA0 87 D5
Athol Cl HA5 22 B2
Athol Ct 15 N4 72 B6
Athole Gdns EN1 17 C6
Athole Terr CR7 183 A1
Athol Gdns HA5 22 B2
Atholl Ho W9 229 A1
Atholl Rd IG3 58 A2
Athol Sq E14 98 A1
Athol Way UB10 82 C4
Atkins Ct
13 Old Ford E3 97 B6
Woolwich SE7 122 A2
Atkins Dr BR4 224 B6
Atkins Lo W8 245 A2
Atkinson Ct 3 E10 53 D2
Atkinson Ho
11 Battersea SW11 137 A3
Battersea SW11 268 A1
15 Hackney E2 96 A5
Newham E13 98 D3
Walworth SE17 262 D3
Atkinson Rd E16 99 C2
Atkinson's Almhouses
HA8 26 B5
Atkins Rd
Streatham SW4,
SW12 159 D4
Walthamstow E10 53 D3
Atlanta Bldg 8
SE13 141 D4
Atlanta Ct CR7 205 A6
Atlantic Ct 19 E14 120 B6
Atlantic Ho
5 Putney SW15 157 B6
4 Tower Hamlets E1 97 A2
Atlantic Rd SW2, SW9,
SE24 138 C1
Atlantis Ave E16 123 A6
Atlantis Cl IG11 102 B4
Atlas Bsns Ctr NW2 68 B6
Atlas Cres HA8 10 D2
Atlas Gdns SE7 121 C2
Atlas Mews
Dalston E8 73 D2
Islington N7 72 B2
Atlas Rd
Friern Barnet N11 31 A4
Newham E13 99 A5
North Acton NW10 89 C4
Wembley HA9 67 A4
Atlip Rd HA0 88 A6
Atney Rd SW15 135 A1
Atria Rd HA6 22 A5
Atrium 9 IG9 21 D2
Atterbury Rd N4 50 D3

Atterbury St
SW1 116 A2 260 A3
Attewood Ave NW10 67 C5
Attewood Rd UB5 63 A2
Attfield Cl N20 14 B2
Attilburgh Ho SE1 263 C6
Attleborough Ct 4
SE21 162 B2
Attle Cl UB10 82 C5
Attlee Cl Hayes UB4 84 B4
Thornton Heath CR7 205 A4
Attlee Ct UB4 84 B4
Attlee Ho E1 243 D3
Attlee Rd Hayes UB4 84 B4
Thamesmead SE28 124 B6
Attlee Terr 3 E17 53 D5
Attneave St WC1 234 A1
Atwater Cl SW2 160 C3
Atwell Pl KT7 197 A1
Atwell Rd 6 SE15 140 A3
Atwood Ave TW9 132 C3
Atwood Ho SE21 161 C1
Atwood Rd W6 112 B2
Aubert Ct N5 72 D4
Aubert Pk N5 72 D4
Aubert Rd N5 72 D4
Aubrey Beardsley Ho
SW1 259 B3
Aubrey Mans NW1 237 A4
Aubrey Moore Point
E15 98 A5
Aubrey Pl NW8 229 A3
Aubrey Rd Hornsey N8 50 A4
Kensington
W14 113 B5 244 D3
Walthamstow E17 53 D6
Aubrey Wlk
W14 113 B5 244 D3
Auburn Cl SE14 141 A5
Aubyn Hill SE27 183 B6
Aubyn Sq SW15 156 A6
Auckland Cl Enfield EN1 6 B6
South Norwood SE19 183 D2
Auckland Ct UB4 84 C3
Auckland Gdns
SE19 183 D2
Auckland Hill SE27 183 A6
Auckland Ho 11
W12 112 B6
Auckland Rd
Clapham SW11 136 C1
Ilford IG1 57 A2
Kingston u T KT1 198 B5
Leyton E10 75 D5
South Norwood SE19 183 D2
Auckland Rise SE19 183 C2
Auckland St SE11 260 C1
Audax 29 NW9 27 D1
Auden Dr WD6 10 C6
Auden Pl NW1 231 A6
Audley Cl
8 Clapham SW11 137 A2
Muswell Hill N10 31 B3
Audley Ct Ealing W5 88 C2
Mayfair W1 248 C4
Northolt UB5 84 C4
Pinner Green HA5 22 C1
Snaresbrook E11, E18 54 D5
Surbiton KT5 198 B3
Twickenham TW2 152 B1
Audley Dr 3 E16 121 B5
Audley Gdns IG3 79 D6
Audley Ho N8 50 A5
Audley Pl SM2 217 D1
Audley Rd Ealing W5 88 B2
Enfield EN2 4 D3
Hendon NW4 46 B3
Richmond TW10 154 B6
Audley Sq W1 248 B4
Audley St W1 248 B4
Audrey Cl BR3 207 D3
Audrey Gdns HA0 65 B6
Audrey Ho EC1 241 B3
Audrey Rd IG1 78 D5
Audrey St E2 96 A5
Audric Cl KT2 176 C2
Augurs La 3 E13 99 B4
Augusta Cl KT8 195 B6
Augusta Ct NW4 28 C1
Augusta Rd TW2 152 A2
Augusta St E14 97 D1
Augustine Ho
Broadgate EC2 242 D2
New Cross SE4 141 B4
Augustine Rd
Hammersmith W14 112 D3

Augustine Rd *continued*
Harrow Weald HA3 .... 24 A2
Augustines Ct E9 .... 74 C3
Augustus Cl
Brentford TW8 .... 131 D5
Hammersmith W12 .... 112 B3
Stanmore HA7 .... 9 D1
Augustus Ct
Feltham TW13 .... 173 B6
Isleworth TW3 .... 130 A1
8 Putney SW19 .... 157 A3
South Norwood SE19 .... 183 C3
Streatham SW16 .... 159 D2
Augustus Ho NW1 .... 232 A2
Augustus Rd
33 Putney SW19 .... 156 D3
Putney SW19 .... 157 A3
Augustus St
NW1 .... 93 B4 231 D2
Aulay Lawrence Ct
N9 .... 18 B1
Aultone Way
Carshalton SM5 .... 218 D5
Sutton SM1 .... 218 A6
Aultone Yd Ind Est
SM5 .... 218 D5
Aulton Pl SE11 .... 261 B1
Aura Ho 3 TW9 .... 132 D4
Aurelia Gdns CR0 .... 204 B3
Aurelia Rd CR0 .... 204 B3
Auriga Mews N1 .... 73 B3
Auriol Cl KT4 .... 215 C5
Auriol Dr
Greenford UB6 .... 64 B1
Hillingdon UB10 .... 60 D2
Auriol Jun Sch KT19 .... 215 D4
Auriol Mans W14 .... 254 A3
Auriol Park Rd KT4 .... 215 C5
Auriol Rd
W14 .... 113 A2 254 A3
Aurora Bldg 4 E14 .... 120 A5
Aurora Ct IG8 .... 36 D6
Aurora Ho E14 .... 97 D1
Austell Gdns NW7 .... 11 C1
Austell Hts NW7 .... 11 C1
Austen Cl SE28 .... 124 B5
Austen Ho 5 NW6 .... 91 C4
Austen Rd Erith DA8 .... 147 D5
Harrow HA2 .... 63 D6
Austin Ave BR1, BR2 .... 210 A4
Austin Cl
Forest Hill SE23 .... 163 B4
Twickenham TW1 .... 153 C6
Austin Ct
9 Enfield EN1 .... 17 C6
9 Newham E6 .... 99 C6
Austin Friars EC2 .... 242 D2
Austin Friars Ho EC2 .... 242 D2
Austin Friars Sq EC2 .... 242 D2
Austin Ho
6 Brixton SW2 .... 160 B6
19 Kingston u T KT6 .... 198 A4
1 New Cross SE14 .... 141 B5
Austin Rd
Battersea
SW11 .... 137 A4 268 A1
Hayes UB3 .... 105 D4
Austins Ct SE15 .... 140 A2
Austins La UB10 .... 61 A5
Austin St E2 .... 95 D4
Austral Cl DA15 .... 167 D1
Australia Rd W12 .... 112 B6
Austral St
SE11 .... 116 D2 261 C4
Austyn Gdns KT5 .... 198 D1
Autumn Cl Enfield EN1 .... 6 A4
Wimbledon SW19 .... 180 A4
Autumn Gr BR1 .... 187 B4
Autumn Lo CR2 .... 221 C4
Autumn Rise 9 W4 .... 111 B1
Autumn St E3 .... 97 C6
Avalon BR7 .... 188 C1
Avalon Cl Ealing W13 .... 87 A2
Enfield EN2 .... 4 C3
Merton SW20 .... 179 A1
Avalon Ct CR0 .... 205 D2
Avalon Rd Ealing W13 .... 87 A3
Parsons Green
SW6 .... 135 D4 265 C2
Avante Ct KT1 .... 197 D6
Avard Gdns BR6 .... 227 A4
Avarn Rd SW17 .... 180 D4
Avebury Ct N1 .... 235 C5
Avebury Rd
Leytonstone E11 .... 54 B1
Merton SW19 .... 179 B2

Avebury Rd *continued*
Orpington BR6 .... 227 B5
Avebury St N1 .... 235 C5
Aveley Ct 15 E5 .... 74 B6
Aveley Mans 1 IG11 .... 78 D1
Aveline St
SE11 .... 116 C1 261 A1
Aveling Ho 12 N19 .... 71 C5
Aveling Park Rd E17 .... 35 C1
Aveling Park Sch E17 .... 35 C1
Ave Maria La EC4 .... 241 D1
Avenell Mans N5 .... 72 D4
Avenell Rd N5 .... 72 D5
Avenfield Ho W1 .... 247 D6
Avening Rd SW18 .... 157 C4
Avening Terr SW18 .... 157 C4
Avenons Rd E13 .... 99 A3
Avenue Cl
Cranford TW5 .... 128 B4
Primrose Hill
NW8 .... 92 C6 230 B5
Southgate N14 .... 15 C5
Avenue Cres
Cranford TW5 .... 128 B5
South Acton W3 .... 110 D4
Avenue Ct
Chelsea SW3 .... 257 C3
Cricklewood NW2 .... 69 A5
Ealing W5 .... 87 D2
Penge SE20 .... 184 C2
Redbridge IG5 .... 56 A6
Southgate N14 .... 15 C5
Avenue Elmers KT6 .... 198 A4
Avenue Gate IG10 .... 21 C5
Avenue Gdns
Cranford TW5 .... 128 B5
Mortlake SW14 .... 133 C2
South Acton W3 .... 110 D4
South Norwood SE25 .... 184 A1
Teddington TW11 .... 174 D4
Avenue Hall N6 .... 49 D3
Avenue Ho
St John's Wood
NW8 .... 230 A3
Upper Clapton N16 .... 74 A6
Willesden Green NW10 .... 90 B5
Avenue House Sch 2
W13 .... 87 B1
Avenue Ind Est E4 .... 35 B4
Avenue Lo 12 NW8 .... 70 B1
Avenue Mans
Barnet EN5 .... 1 B1
Clapham SW11 .... 137 A1
Hampstead NW3 .... 69 D3
Muswell Hill N10 .... 31 C1
Willesden NW2 .... 68 B2
Avenue Mews N10 .... 49 B6
Avenue Par
Southgate N21 .... 17 B4
Sunbury TW16 .... 194 B6
Avenue Park Rd SE21,
SE27 .... 160 D2
Avenue Prim Sch E12 .... 78 A3
Avenue Rd
Bexley DA6, DA7 .... 147 A2
Brentford TW8 .... 109 C1
Crouch End N6 .... 49 D2
Feltham TW13 .... 149 D1
Forest Gate E7 .... 77 B4
Hampton TW12 .... 173 D2
Harlesden NW10 .... 89 D5
Hounslow TW7 .... 130 D4
Ilford RM6 .... 58 C2
Kingston u T KT1 .... 198 A6
Mitcham SW16 .... 181 D1
New Malden KT3 .... 199 C5
North Finchley N12 .... 30 A6
Penge BR3, SE20 .... 184 D2
Pinner HA5 .... 41 A6
Primrose Hill
NW8 .... 92 C6 230 A6
South Acton W3 .... 110 D4
Southall UB1 .... 107 B5
Southgate N14 .... 15 C5
South Norwood SE25 .... 184 A1
Teddington TW11 .... 175 A4
Tottenham N15 .... 51 B4
Wallington SM6 .... 219 C1
Wimbledon SW20 .... 178 B1
Woodford IG8 .... 37 C4
Avenue Road Sta
BR3 .... 184 D1
Avenue S KT5 .... 198 C2
Avenue Terr
Ilford IG2 .... 57 C3
Kingston u T KT3 .... 199 A6

Avenue The Barnet EN5 .... 1 A2
Beckenham BR3 .... 186 A2
Bedford Pk W4 .... 111 C3
Bromley BR1 .... 209 D6
Brondesbury Pk NW6 .... 91 A6
8 Buckhurst Hill IG9 .... 21 C2
Chingford E4 .... 36 B5
Clapham SW4 .... 159 A6
Claygate KT10 .... 212 C3
Cranford TW5 .... 128 A4
Ealing W13 .... 87 B1
Finchley N3 .... 29 C1
Friern Barnet N11 .... 31 B5
Greenwich SE10 .... 142 B5
Hampton TW12 .... 173 B4
Harrow HA3 .... 24 D2
Hatch End HA5 .... 23 B4
Hornsey N8 .... 50 C6
Hounslow TW3 .... 151 D6
Isleworth TW1 .... 153 B6
Keston Mark BR2 .... 225 D5
Loughton IG10 .... 21 D5
Muswell Hill N10 .... 31 C1
4 New Malden KT4 .... 200 A1
Orpington BR6 .... 227 D6
Pinner HA5 .... 41 B3
Richmond TW9 .... 132 B3
Sidcup DA5 .... 168 D4
South Croydon CR0 .... 221 C5
Stoneleigh KT17, SM3 .... 216 C1
St Paul's Cray BR5 .... 190 B3
Sunbury TW16 .... 172 B1
Surbiton KT5 .... 198 B3
Tottenham N17 .... 33 C1
Uxbridge UB10 .... 60 D5
Wallington SM5 .... 219 A1
Wandsworth SW18,
SW12 .... 158 C4
Wanstead E11 .... 55 B4
Wembley HA9 .... 44 B1
West Wickham BR4 .... 208 C2
Worcester Pk KT4 .... 215 D6
Averil Gr SW16 .... 182 D4
Averill St W6 .... 134 D6
Avern Gdns KT8 .... 195 D5
Avern Rd KT8 .... 195 D5
Avery Ct 1 SE20 .... 184 B3
Avery Farm Row
SW1 .... 258 C3
Avery Gdns IG2 .... 56 B4
AVERY HILL 167 B5
Avery Hill Coll (Mile End
Annexe) E3 .... 97 B3
Avery Hill Rd SE9 .... 167 B3
Avery Row
W1 .... 115 B6 248 D6
Aviary Cl E16 .... 98 D2
Aviemore Cl BR3 .... 207 B4
Aviemore Way BR3 .... 207 A4
Avignon Rd SE4 .... 140 D2
Avingdor Ct 10 W3 .... 111 A5
Avington Ct SE1 .... 263 B3
Avington Gr SE20 .... 184 C3
Avion Cres NW7, NW9 .... 28 A2
Avis Sq E1 .... 96 D1
Avoca Rd SW17 .... 181 A6
Avocet Cl SE1 .... 118 A1
Avocet Mews SE28 .... 123 B3
Avon Cl Hayes UB4 .... 84 C3
Sutton SM1 .... 218 A4
Worcester Pk KT4 .... 216 A6
Avon Ct 1 Acton W3 .... 89 A1
11 Chingford E4 .... 20 A3
Greenford UB6 .... 85 D3
North Finchley N12 .... 29 D5
10 Putney SW15 .... 157 A6
Wembley HA0 .... 65 A4
Avondale N22 .... 32 A3
Avondale Ave
Barnet EN4 .... 14 D3
Finchley N12 .... 29 D5
Hinchley Wood KT10 .... 213 A5
Neasden NW2 .... 67 C5
New Malden KT4 .... 199 D1
Avondale Cres
Enfield EN3 .... 7 A2
Redbridge IG4 .... 55 D4
Avondale Ct
Canning Town E16 .... 98 C2
Leytonstone E11 .... 54 C1
9 Sutton SM2 .... 218 A1
Woodford E18 .... 37 B2
Avondale Dr UB3 .... 106 B5
Avondale Gdns TW4 .... 151 B6

Avondale Ho
11 Bermondsey
SE1 .... 118 A1
6 Mortlake SW14 .... 133 B2
Avondale Mans SW6 .... 264 C2
Avondale Park Gdns
W11 .... 113 A6 244 A5
Avondale Park Prim Sch
W11 .... 113 A6 244 A5
Avondale Park Rd
W11 .... 113 A6 244 A6
Avondale Pavement 7
SE1 .... 118 A1
Avondale Rd
Bexley DA16 .... 146 C3
Bromley BR1 .... 186 D4
Chislehurst SE9 .... 166 A2
Finchley N3 .... 30 A2
Harringay N15 .... 50 D4
Harrow HA3 .... 42 D6
Mortlake SW14 .... 133 B2
Newham E16 .... 98 C2
South Croydon CR2 .... 221 A2
Southgate N13 .... 16 C2
Walthamstow E17 .... 53 C2
Wimbledon SW19 .... 179 D5
Avondale Rise SE15 .... 139 D2
Avondale Sq SE1 .... 118 A1
Avonfield Ct E17 .... 54 B6
Avon Ho
2 Islington N1 .... 72 C1
7 Kingston u T KT2 .... 175 D2
Northolt UB5 .... 85 A3
Southgate N21 .... 16 B6
14 Stoke Newington
N16 .... 73 B4
West Kensington W14 .... 254 D3
Avon House Sch IG8 .... 37 A6
Avonhurst Ho NW6 .... 69 A1
Avonley Rd SE14 .... 140 C5
Avon Mews HA5 .... 23 B2
Avonmore Gdns
W14 .... 254 D3
Avonmore Pl W14 .... 254 B4
Avonmore Prim Sch
W14 .... 113 A2 254 B4
Avonmore Rd
W14 .... 113 B2 254 C4
Avonmouth St SE1 .... 262 A6
Avon Path CR0 .... 221 A1
Avon Pl SE1 .... 252 B1
Avon Rd
Ashford TW16 .... 171 D3
Greenford UB6 .... 85 D3
St Johns SE4 .... 141 C2
Upper Walthamstow
E17 .... 54 B6
Avonstowe Cl BR6 .... 227 A5
Avon Way E18 .... 55 A6
Avonwick Rd TW3 .... 129 D3
Avril Way E4 .... 36 A5
Avriol Ho W12 .... 112 B5
Avro Ct E9 .... 75 A3
Avro Way SM6 .... 220 A1
Awlfield Ave N17 .... 33 B2
Awliscombe Rd
DA16 .... 145 D3
Axeholm Ave HA8 .... 26 D2
Axe St IG11 .... 101 A6
Axford Ho SW2 .... 160 D3
Axiom Apartments 5
BR2 .... 209 B5
Axis Ct
7 Bermondsey
SE16 .... 118 A4
Greenwich SE10 .... 142 C6
Axminster Cres
DA16 .... 146 C4
Axminster Rd N7 .... 72 B5
Axon Pl 5 IG1 .... 79 A6
Aybrook St
W1 .... 93 A2 238 A3
Aycliffe Cl BR1 .... 210 B5
Aycliffe Rd W12 .... 112 A5
Ayerst Ct 1 E10 .... 54 A2
Aylands Cl HA9 .... 66 A6
Aylesbury Cl E7 .... 76 D2
Aylesbury Ct SM1 .... 218 A5
Aylesbury Ho 13
SE15 .... 140 A6
Aylesbury Rd
Bromley BR2 .... 209 A6
Walworth
SE17 .... 117 B1 262 D1

Aylesbury St
Clerkenwell
EC1 .... 94 D3 241 C5
Neasden NW10 .... 67 B5
Ayles Ct UB4 .... 84 B4
Aylesford Ave BR3 .... 207 A4
Aylesford Ho SE1 .... 252 D1
Aylesford St
SW1 .... 115 D1 259 C1
Aylesham Cl NW7 .... 28 A3
Aylesham Rd BR6 .... 211 D2
Aylesham Sh Ctr
SE15 .... 140 A4
Ayles Rd UB4 .... 84 B4
Aylestone Ave NW6 .... 90 D6
Aylestone Ct 10 HA0 .... 66 A2
Aylett Rd
Croydon SE25 .... 206 B5
Isleworth TW7 .... 130 C3
Ayley Croft EN1 .... 18 A6
Ayliffe Cl KT1 .... 176 C1
Aylmer Cl HA7 .... 25 A6
Aylmer Ct N2 .... 48 D4
Aylmer Dr HA7 .... 25 A6
Aylmer Ho SE10 .... 120 B1
Aylmer Par N2 .... 48 D4
Aylmer Rd
Acton W12 .... 111 D4
Dagenham RM8 .... 81 A5
East Finchley N2 .... 48 C4
Leytonstone E11 .... 54 D1
Ayloffe Rd RM9 .... 81 B2
Aylsham Dr UB10 .... 61 A6
Aylton Est 28 SE16 .... 118 C4
Aylward Fst & Mid Schs
HA7 .... 25 D5
Aylward Rd
Forest Hill SE23 .... 162 D2
Merton SW20 .... 201 B6
Aylwards Rise HA7 .... 25 A6
Aylward St E1 .... 96 D1
Aylwin Est SE1 .... 263 B6
Aynhoe Mans W14 .... 112 D2
Aynhoe Rd W14 .... 112 D3
Ayr Ct W3 .... 88 C2
Ayres Cl E13 .... 99 A4
Ayres Cres NW10 .... 67 B1
Ayres St SE1 .... 117 A4 252 B2
Ayrsome Rd N16 .... 73 C5
Ayrton Gould Ho 9
E2 .... 96 D4
Ayrton Ho HA9 .... 65 D6
Ayrton Rd
SW7 .... 114 B3 256 C6
Aysgarth Ct SM1 .... 217 D5
Aysgarth Rd SE21 .... 161 C4
Ayshford Ho E1 .... 96 B4
Ayston Ho 19 SE8 .... 118 D2
Aytoun Ct 17 SW9 .... 138 B3
Aytoun Pl SW9 .... 138 B3
Aytoun Rd SW9 .... 138 B3
Azalea Cl Ealing W7 .... 108 D5
Ilford IG1 .... 78 D3
Azalea Ct
Chingford IG8 .... 36 C3
Ealing W7 .... 108 D5
Azalea Ho
2 Feltham TW13 .... 150 B3
New Cross SE14 .... 141 B5
Azalea Wlk HA5 .... 40 B3
Azania Mews NW5 .... 71 B2
Azenby Rd SE15 .... 139 D3
Azhar Acad E7 .... 77 A2
Azof St SE10 .... 120 C2
Azov Ho 10 E1 .... 97 A3
Aztec Ct 8 N16 .... 73 C2
Azure Apartments
HA3 .... 24 B3
Azure Ct TW13 .... 149 D1
Azure Ho 28 E2 .... 96 A4

B

Baalbec Rd N5 .... 72 D3
Babbacombe Cl KT9 .... 213 D3
Babbacombe Gdns
IG4 .... 56 A5
Babbacombe Rd
BR1 .... 187 A2
Baber Bridge Par
TW14 .... 150 C5
Baber Dr TW14 .... 150 C5

Babington Ct
Bloomsbury WC1 240 B4
Streatham SW16 181 D5
Babington Ho SE1 252 B2
Babington House Sch
BR7 188 B4
Babington Rd
Dagenham RM8 80 C4
Hendon NW4 46 B5
Streatham SW16 181 D5
Babington Rise HA9 66 C2
Babmaes St SW1 249 C5
Bacchus Wlk 12 N1 95 C5
Bache's St N1 95 B4 235 D1
Back Church La E1 96 A1
Back Hill EC1 241 B5
Backhouse Pl SE1 263 B3
Back La
Brentford TW8 131 D6
Buckhurst Hill IG9 21 D2
Burnt Oak HA8 27 A2
Dagenham RM6 59 A2
Hampstead NW3 70 A4
Hornsey N8 50 A4
Richmond TW10 153 C2
Sidcup DA5 169 C4
Backley Gdns SE25 206 A3
Back Rd
Leytonstone E11 54 C3
Sidcup DA14 190 A6
Teddington TW11 174 C3
Bacon Gr
SE1 117 D3 263 C5
Bacon La
Edgware HA8 26 C2
Queensbury NW9 44 D5
Bacon's Coll SE16 119 A4
Bacon's La N6 49 A1
Bacon St E2 95 D3 243 D6
Bacon Terr RM8 80 B3
Bacton NW5 71 A3
Bacton St E2 96 C4
Baddeley Cl 11 EN3 7 C6
Baddeley Ho
East Molesey KT8 195 C4
Vauxhall SE11 260 D2
Baddow Cl
Dagenham RM10 103 C6
Woodford IG8 37 D4
Baddow Wlk N1 235 A6
Baden Ct N11 31 D3
Baden Pl SE1 252 C2
Baden Powell Cl
Dagenham RM9 103 A6
Surbiton KT6 214 B6
Baden Powell Ho 11
DA17 125 C3
Baden Powell Sch 8
E5 74 B5
Baden Rd Hornsey N8 49 D5
Ilford IG1 78 D3
Badger Cl
Feltham TW13 150 B1
Hounslow TW4 128 C2
Ilford IG2 57 A2
Badger Ct
Chingford E4 36 B6
Dollis Hill NW2 68 C5
Badgers Cl
Ashford TW15 170 B5
Enfield EN2 4 D2
Harrow HA1 42 B3
Hayes UB3 105 C6
Badgers Copse
Orpington BR6 227 D6
Worcester Pk KT4 215 D6
Badgers Croft
Barnet N20 13 A3
Chislehurst SE9 166 C1
Badgers Hole CR0 222 D4
Badgers Wlk KT3 177 C1
Badlis Rd E17 53 C6
Badma Cl N9 18 C1
Badminton KT2 176 D2
Badminton Cl
Harrow HA1 42 C5
Northolt UB5 63 C2
Badminton Ct 5 N4 51 A2
Badminton Ho SE22 139 C1
Badminton Mews 9
E16 121 A5
Badminton Rd
SW12 159 A5
Badric Ct SW11 136 B3
Badsworth Rd 3
SE5 139 A4
Bagley Cl UB7 104 A4
Bagley's La
SW6 135 D4 265 D1
Bagleys Spring RM6 59 A5
Bagnigge Ho WC1 234 A1
Bagshot Ho NW1 231 D2
Bagshot Rd EN1 17 D5
Bagshot St
SE17 117 C1 263 B1
Baildon 27 E2 96 C5
Baildon St SE8 141 B5
Bailey Cl Chingford E4 36 A6
Wood Green N11 31 D3
Woolwich SE28 123 C5
Bailey Cres KT9 213 D1
Bailey Ct
4 Chingford E4 36 B5
9 Shepherd's Bush
W12 112 A4
Bailey Ho
Mitcham CR4 202 C6
11 Penge SE26 184 B5
Walham Green SW10 265 D4
Bailey Mews
Brixton SW2 160 C6
Chiswick W4 132 D6
Bailey Pl SE26 184 D4
Bainbridge cl KT2 176 A5
Bainbridge Rd RM9 81 B4
Bainbridge St WC1 239 D2
Baines Cl CR2 221 B3
Bain Ho 23 SW9 138 A3
Baird Ave UB1 108 A6
Baird Cl
Kingsbury NW9 45 A3
Walthamstow E10 53 C1
Baird Gdns SE19 183 C6
Baird Ho
12 Belvedere DA17 125 C3
29 Shepherd's Bush
W12 112 B6
Baird Rd EN1 6 B1
Baird St EC1 242 B6
Bairny Wood App IG8 37 B4
Baizdon Rd SE3 142 C3
Baker Beall Ct DA7 147 D2
Baker Ct E11 76 B5
Baker Ho
12 Bromley E3 97 D4
Ealing W7 108 D5
Baker La CR4 203 A6
Baker Pl KT19 215 A2
Baker Rd
Harlesden NW10 89 C6
Kidbrooke SE18 144 A4
Bakers' Almshouses
E10 53 D3
Bakers Ave E17 53 D3
Bakers Ct RM8 59 B2
Bakers Ct SE25 205 C6
Bakers End SW20 179 A1
Bakers Field N7 72 A4
Bakers Gdns SM5 218 C6
Bakers Hall Ct EC3 253 B5
Bakers Hill Barnet EN5 1 D3
Upper Clapton E5 52 C1
Bakers Ho W5 109 D5
Baker's La N6 48 D3
Bakers Mews 9
BR6 227 D2
Baker's Mews W1 238 A2
Bakers Pas 22 NW3 70 A4
Bakers Rents 13 E2 95 D4
Bakers Row E15 98 C5
Baker's Row
EC1 94 C3 241 A5
Baker St Enfield EN1 5 B4
Marylebone
W1 92 D2 237 D4
Baker Street
W1 92 D2 237 D4
Baker Street Sta
NW1 92 D3 237 D5
Baker's Yd EC1 241 A5
Bakery Cl SW9 270 D3
Bakery Mews KT6 198 C1
Bakewell Way KT3 177 C1
Balaam Ho SM1 217 C4
Balaam L Ctr E13 99 A3
Balaams La N14 15 D2
Balaam St E13 99 B4
Balaclava Rd
Bermondsey
SE1 117 D2 263 D3
Kingston u T KT6 197 C2
Bala Gn NW9 45 C3
Balcaskie Rd SE9 166 B6
Balchen Rd SE3 143 D3
Balchier Rd SE22 162 B5
Balcombe Cl DA6 146 D1
Balcombe Ho
Lisson Gr NW1 237 C6
3 Streatham SW2 160 B3
Balcombe St
NW1 92 D3 237 C5
Balcon Ct W5 88 B1
Balcorne St E9 74 C1
Balder Rise SE12 165 B2
Balderton Flats W1 238 B1
Balderton St
W1 93 A1 238 B1
Baldewyne Ct N17 34 A2
Baldock Ho 31 SE5 139 A3
Baldock St E3 97 D5
Baldrey Ho 1 SE10 120 D1
Baldry Gdns SW16 182 B4
Baldwin Cres SE5 139 A4
Baldwin Gdns TW3 130 A4
Baldwin Ho
15 Streatham SW2 160 C3
Wallend E12 78 C1
Baldwin Rd SW12 159 A5
Baldwin's Gdns
EC1 94 C2 241 A4
Baldwin St EC1 235 C1
Baldwin Terr
N1 95 A5 235 A4
Baldwyn Gdns W3 111 B6
Balearic Apts 3
E16 121 A6
Bale Rd E1 97 A2
Bales Coll W10 90 D4
Balfern Gr W4 111 C1
Balfern St SW11 136 C3
Balfe St N1 94 A5 233 B3
Balfour Ave W7 108 D5
Balfour Bsns Ctr
UB2 106 D3
Balfour Gr N20 14 D1
Balfour Ho 4 W10 90 D2
Balfour Mews
Edmonton N9 18 A1
Mayfair W1 248 B4
Balfour Pl
Mayfair W1 248 B5
Putney SW15 134 B1
Balfour Rd
Bromley Comm BR2 209 D4
Croydon SE25 206 A5
Ealing W13 109 B4
Harrow HA1 42 B4
Highbury N5 73 A4
Hounslow TW3 129 D2
Ilford IG1 57 A1
Merton SW19 179 D3
North Acton W3 89 A2
Southall UB2 106 D3
Wallington SM5 218 D1
Balfour St
SE17 117 B2 262 C4
Balfron Twr 4 E14 98 A1
Balgonie Rd E4 20 B3
Balgowan Cl KT3 199 C5
Balgowan Prim Sch
BR3 185 A1
Balgowan Rd BR3 185 B1
Balgowan St SE18 123 D2
BALHAM 159 A3
Balham Gr SW12 159 A4
Balham High Rd SW12,
SW17 159 A3
Balham Hill SW12 159 B5
Balham L Ctr SW12 159 B2
Balham New Rd
SW12 159 B4
Balham Park Mans
SW12 158 D3
Balham Park Rd SW12,
SW17 159 A3
Balham Rd N9 18 A2
Balham Sta SW12 159 B3
Balham Station Rd
SW12 159 B3
Balin Ho SE1 252 C2
Balkan Wlk E1 118 B6
Balladier Wlk E14 97 D2
Ballamore Rd BR1 165 A1
Ballance Rd E9 75 A2
Ballantine St SW18 136 A1
Ballantrae Ho NW2 69 B4
Ballantyne Cl 5
SE9 188 A6
Ballard Cl KT2 177 B3
Ballard Ho SE10 141 D6
Ballards Cl RM10 103 D6
Ballards Farm Rd CR0,
CR2 222 A2
Ballards La N3 29 D3
Ballards Mews HA8 26 C4
Ballards Rd
Dagenham RM10 103 D6
Dollis Hill NW2 68 A6
Ballards Rise CR2 222 A2
Ballards Way CR0,
CR2 222 B2
Ballast Quay SE10 120 B1
Ballater Cl WD19 22 C6
Ballater Rd
Brixton SW2, SW4 138 A1
South Croydon CR2 221 D3
Ball Ct EC3 242 D1
Ballentyne Ct N21 16 B6
Ballina St SE23 162 D4
Ballin Ct 14 E14 120 A4
Ballingdon Rd SW11 159 A5
Ballinger Point 18 E3 97 D4
Ballinger Way UB5 85 A3
Balliol Ave E4 36 C6
Balliol Ho 11 SW15 156 D5
Balliol Rd
Bexley DA16 146 B3
North Kensington W10 90 D1
Tottenham N17 33 C2
Balloch Rd SE6 164 B2
Ballogie Ave NW10 67 C4
Ballow Cl 15 SE5 139 C5
Ball's Pond Pl 3 N1 73 B2
Ball's Pond Rd N1 73 C2
Balmain Cl W5 109 D5
Balmain Ct TW3 129 D4
Balman Ho 3 SE16 118 D2
Balmer Rd E3 97 B5
Balmes Rd N1 95 B6 235 D6
Balmoral Ave
Beckenham BR3 207 A5
Friern Barnet N11 31 B5
Balmoral Cl 1
SW15 156 D5
Balmoral Cres KT8 195 C6
Balmoral Ct
18 Belmont SM2 217 C1
Ealing W5 87 D1
Edgware HA8 26 D6
Grove Pk SE12 187 B6
North Cheam KT4 216 B6
21 Rotherhithe SE16 118 D5
St John's Wood NW8 229 C4
Wembley HA9 66 B5
West Norwood SE27 183 A6
Balmoral Dr
Borehamwood WD6 11 B6
Hayes UB4 83 D3
Southall UB1 85 B3
Balmoral Gdns
Ealing W13 109 A3
Ilford IG3 57 D1
Old Bexley DA5 169 B4
Balmoral Gr N7 72 B2
Balmoral Ho
2 Isle Of Dogs
E14 119 D3
Stanmore HA7 26 A1
Stoke Newington N4 51 A1
Walthamstow E17 35 B1
West Kensington W14 254 A4
Balmoral Lo BR6 226 C4
Balmoral Mews
W12 111 D3
Balmoral Rd
Forest Gate E7 77 C3
Harrow HA2 63 C4
Kingston u T KT1 198 B5
Leyton E10 75 D6
North Cheam KT4 216 B6
Willesden NW2 68 B2
Balmoral Trad Est
IG11 101 D2
Balmore Cl E14 98 A1
Balmore Cres EN4 15 A6
Balmore St N19 71 B6
Balmuir Gdns SW15 134 C1
Balnacraig Ave NW10 67 C4
Balniel Gate SW1 259 D2
Balsam Ho 9 E14 119 D6
Baltic Apts 5 E16 121 A6
Baltic Cl SW19 180 B3
Baltic Ho 7 SE5 139 A3
Baltic St E
EC1 95 A3 242 A5
Baltic St W
EC1 95 A3 242 A5
Baltimore Ho
Clapham SW18 136 A1
Kennington SE11 261 A2
Merton SW19 179 D3
Baltimore Pl DA16 145 D3
Balvaird Pl SW1 259 D1
Balvernie Gr SW18 157 C4
Bamber Ho IG11 101 A6
Bamber Rd 5 SE15 139 D4
Bamborough Gdns 12
W12 112 C4
Bamburgh 9 N17 34 B3
Bamford Ave HA0 88 B5
Bamford Rd
Barking IG11 79 A2
Catford BR1 186 B5
Bampfylde Cl SM6 219 C5
Bampton Ct W5 87 D1
Bampton Dr NW7 28 A3
Bampton Rd SE23 162 D1
Banavie Gdns BR3 186 A2
Banbury Cl EN2 4 D4
Banbury Ct
11 Belmont SM2 217 C1
Ealing W13 109 A3
Strand WC2 250 A6
Banbury Ho 5 E9 74 D1
Banbury Rd
Higham Hill E17 35 A3
Homerton E9 74 D1
Banbury St 3 SW11 136 C3
Banbury Wlk UB5 85 C5
Banchory Rd SE3 143 B5
Bancroft Ave
East Finchley N2 48 C4
Woodford IG9 21 A2
Bancroft Cl TW15 170 C5
Bancroft Ct
Northolt UB5 84 C6
South Lambeth SW8 270 A2
Bancroft Gdns
Harrow Weald HA3 24 A2
Orpington BR6 211 D1
Bancroft Ho 11 E1 96 C3
Bancroft Rd
Bethnal Green E1 96 D3
Harrow Weald HA3 24 A1
Bancrofts Sch IG8 21 A1
Bandon Cl UB10 82 B5
BANDONHILL 219 D3
Bandon Hill Prim Sch
SM6 219 D2
Bandon Rise SM6 219 D3
Banff Ho 1 NW3 70 C2
Banfield Rd SE15 140 B2
Banfor Ct SM6 219 C3
Bangabandhu Prim Sch
38 E2 96 C4
Bangalore St SW15 134 D2
Bangor Cl UB5 63 D3
Banim St W6 112 B2
Banister Ho
Hackney E9 74 D3
Nine Elms SW8 269 B2
9 West Kilburn W10 91 A4
Banister Rd W10 90 D4
Bank Ave CR4 180 B1
Bank Bldgs 13 SW16 181 C5
Bank Ct SW11 268 C2
Bank End SE1 252 B4
Bankfoot Rd BR1 186 C6
Bankhurst Rd SE6 163 B4
Bank La
Kingston u T KT2 176 A3
Roehampton SW15 155 C6
Bank Mews SM1 218 A2
Bank of England★
EC2 242 C1
Bank of England Mus★
EC2 95 B1 242 C1
Bank Par N11 31 B5
Banks Ho
Isleworth TW7 130 C3
Newington SE1 262 A5
Banksia Rd N18 34 D5
Bankside
Borough The
SE1 117 A6 252 A5

Bankside *continued*
Borough The SE1 252 B4
Enfield EN2 4 D4
Southall UB1 106 D5
South Croydon CR2 221 D2
Bankside Ave
1 Lewisham SE13 142 A2
Northolt UB5 84 A5
Bankside Cl
Carshalton SM5 218 C2
Isleworth TW7 130 D1
Bankside Dr KT7 213 B6
Bankside Gall★ SE1 116 D6 251 D5
Bankside Ho EC3 243 B1
Bankside Pier SE1 117 A6 252 A5
Bankside Pk IG11 102 A4
Bankside Rd IG1 79 B3
Bankside Way 6 SE19 183 C4
Banks La DA6 147 B1
Bank St E14 119 D5
Bank Sta EC3 95 B1 242 D1
Banks Way E12 78 C4
Banksyard TW5 129 B6
Bank The N6 49 B1
Bankton Rd SW2 138 C1
Bankwell Rd SE13 142 C1
Banner Ct 5 SE16 118 C2
Banner Ho EC1 242 B5
Bannerman Ho SW8 270 C5
Banner St EC1 95 A3 242 B6
Banning Ho 4 SW19 156 D3
Banning St SE10 120 C1
Bannister Cl
Greenford UB6 64 B3
Streatham SW2 160 C3
Bannister Ho
28 Deptford SE14 140 D6
Harrow HA3 42 C6
Bannister Sports Ctr HA3 24 A4
Bannockburn Prim Sch SE18 123 D2
Bannockburn Rd SE18 123 D2
Bannow Cl KT19 215 C4
Banqueting Ho★ SW1 250 A3
Banstead Ct
East Acton W12 111 D6
Stoke Newington N4 51 A1
Walthamstow E10 53 D1
Banstead Gdns N9 17 C1
Banstead Rd SM5 218 C1
Banstead St SE15 140 C2
Banstead Way SM6 220 A3
Banstock Rd HA8 26 D4
Banting Dr N21 16 B6
Banting Ho 6 NW2 68 A5
Bantock Ct 1 N20 14 D2
Bantock Ho 8 W10 91 A4
Banton Cl EN1 6 B3
Bantry Ho 13 E1 96 D3
Bantry St SE5 139 B5
Banville Ho SW8 270 D3
Banwell Rd DA5 168 D5
Banyan Ho 8 NW3 69 D2
Banyard Rd SE16 118 B3
Baptist Gdns NW5 71 A2
Barandon Wlk 6 W11 112 D6
Barbanel Ho 26 E1 96 C3
Barbara Brosnan Ct NW8 229 C3
Barbara Castle Cl SW6 264 D5
Barbara Cl TW17 192 D4
Barbara Hucklesbury Cl N22 32 D1
Barbara Martin Ho 1 N11 31 C5
Barbara Rudolph Ct 5 N19 50 A2
Barbara Ward Ct 3 E11 76 C6
Barbauld Rd N16 73 C5
Barber Beaumont Ho 21 E1 96 D4
Barber Cl N21 16 C4
Barberry Ct E15 76 C2
Barbers Alley 1 E13 99 B4
Barbers Rd E15 97 D5
BARBICAN 95 A2
Barbican★ EC2 95 A2 242 B3
Barbican Ctr★ EC2 95 A2 242 B4
Barbican Rd UB1 85 D1
Barb Mews W6 112 C3
Barbon Alley EC3 243 B2
Barbon Cl WC1 240 C4
Barbot Cl N9 18 A1
Barbrook Ho E9 74 C2
Barchard St SW18 157 D6
Barchester Cl W7 108 D5
Barchester Lo N12 29 D6
Barchester Rd HA3 24 B1
Barchester St E14 97 D2
Barclay Cl SW6 135 C5 265 A3
Barclay Ct N12 30 A5
Barclay Ho 21 E9 74 C1
Barclay Oval IG8 37 A6
Barclay Prim Sch E10 54 B3
Barclay Rd
Edmonton N18 33 B4
Leyton E11 54 D1
Newham E13 99 C3
Parsons Green SW6 135 C5 265 B3
South Croydon CR0 221 B5
Walthamstow E17 54 A4
Barcombe Ave SW2 160 B2
Barcom Trad Est 1 CR0 204 A2
Bardell Ho 17 SE1 118 A4
Barden St SE18 145 C5
Bardfield Ave RM6 58 D6
Bardney Rd SM4 201 D5
Bardolph Rd
Richmond TW9 132 B2
Tufnell Pk N7 72 A4
Bard Rd W10 112 D6
Bardsey Pl 41 E1 96 C3
Bardsey Wlk 5 N1 73 A2
Bardsley Cl CR0 221 D5
Bardsley Ho 6 SE10 142 A6
Bardsley La SE10 142 A6
Barents Ho 10 E1 96 D3
Barfett St W10 91 B3
Barfield Ave N20 14 D2
Barfield Rd
Bromley BR1, BR7 210 C6
Leytonstone E11 54 D1
Barfleur La SE8 119 B2
Barford Cl NW4 28 A2
Barford Ho 23 E3 97 B5
Barford St N1 94 C6 234 B5
Barforth Rd SE15 140 B2
Barfreston Way SE20 184 B2
Bargate Cl
New Malden KT3 200 A2
Plumstead Comm SE18 123 D1
Bargehouse Rd E16 122 D4
Barge House St SE1 251 B4
Barge La 10 E3 97 B6
Bargery Rd SE6 163 D3
Bargrove Cl 8 SE20 184 A3
Bargrove Cres SE6 163 B2
Barham Cl
Chislehurst BR7 188 D5
Keston Mark BR2 210 A1
Wembley HA0 65 C2
Barham Ct
8 Croydon CR2 221 A4
Keston Mark BR2 210 A1
Wembley HA0 65 C2
Woodside Pk N12 29 B5
Barham Ho SE17 263 B2
Barham Prim Sch HA0 65 C2
Barham Rd
Chislehurst BR7 188 D5
Croydon CR2 221 A3
Wimbledon SW20 178 A3
Baring Cl SE12 165 A2
Baring Ct N1 235 C5
Baring Ho 15 E14 97 C1
Baring Prim Sch SE12 165 A4
Baring Rd Barnet EN4 2 B2
Croydon CR0 206 A1
Grove Pk SE12 165 A2
Baring St N1 95 B6 235 C5
Barker Cl
Kingston u T KT3 198 D5
Richmond TW9 132 D3
Barker Dr NW1 71 D1
Barker Ho
Dulwich SE21 161 C1
3 Harringay N15 50 D5
Walthamstow E17 53 B2
Walworth SE17 263 A3
Barker Mews SW4 137 B1
Barker St SW10 266 A6
Barker Wlk SW16 159 D1
Barkham Rd N17 33 C3
BARKING 79 B1
Barking Abbey Comp Sch (Sports & Humanities Coll)) IG11 79 C3
Barking Abbey L Ctr IG11 80 A2
Barking Abbey (ruins of)★ IG11 101 A6
Barking Abbey Sch (Sports & Humanities Coll) IG11 79 D2
Barking Bsns Ctr IG11 102 A4
Barking Flyover IG11 78 D1
Barking Hospl IG11 79 D1
Barking Ind Pk IG11 102 A6
Barking Rd
East Ham E6 100 B6
Plaistow E13 99 B4
BARKINGSIDE 57 A6
Barkingside Sta IG6 57 B6
Barking Sta IG11 79 A1
Bark Pl W2 113 D6 245 C6
Barkston Gdns SW5 113 D2 255 C3
Barkway Cl BR6 226 C4
Barkway Ct N4 73 A6
Barkwith Ho 27 SE14 140 D6
Barkworth Rd SE16 118 C1
Barlborough St SE14 140 D5
Barlby Gdns W10 90 D3
Barlby Prim Sch W10 90 D3
Barlby Rd W10 90 D2
Barley Cl Bus WD23 8 A6
Wembley HA9 65 D4
Barleycorn Way E14 119 B6
Barley Ct Ilford IG3 58 B4
Stanwell TW19 148 A3
Barleyfields Cl RM6 58 C2
Barley La IG3 58 B3
Barley Lane Prim Sch RM6 58 B2
Barley Mow Pas
Chiswick W4 111 B1
Clerkenwell EC1 241 D3
Barley Mow Way TW17 192 C5
Barley Shotts Bsns Pk W10 91 B2
Barling 6 NW1 71 B1
Barling Ct 1 SW4 138 A3
Barlings Ho 2 SE4 140 D1
Barloch Ho 14 SW11 137 A3
Barlow Cl SM6 220 A1
Barlow Dr SE18 144 A4
Barlow Ho
14 Bermondsey SE16 118 B2
Notting Hill W11 244 A6
Shoreditch N1 235 C2
Barlow Pl W1 248 D5
Barlow Rd Acton W3 110 D5
Brondesbury NW6 69 B2
Hampton TW12 173 C3
Barlow St SE17 117 B2 262 D3
Barmeston Rd SE6 163 D2
Barmor Cl HA2 23 D1
Barmouth Ave UB6 86 D5
Barmouth Ho 6 N7 72 B6
Barmouth Rd
Croydon CR0 222 D6
Wandsworth SW18 158 A5
Barnabas Ct N21 16 D6
Barnabas Ho EC1 235 A1
Barnabas Lo SW8 270 B2
Barnabas Rd E9 74 D3
Barnaby Cl HA2 64 A6
Barnaby Ct NW9 45 C6
Barnaby Pl SW7 256 C3
Barnard Cl
Chislehurst BR7 189 B2
Sunbury TW16 172 B3
Wallington SM6 219 D1
Barnard Cl *continued*
Woolwich SE18 122 C3
Barnard Ct SW16 160 B1
Barnard Gdns
Hayes UB4 84 B3
West Barnes KT3 200 A5
Barnard Gr E15 76 D1
Barnard Hill N10 31 B2
Barnard Ho 17 E2 96 B4
Barnard Lo
New Barnet EN5 2 A1
10 Paddington W9 91 C2
Barnard Mews SW11 136 C1
Barnardo Dr IG6 57 A5
Barnardo Gdns 1 E1 118 D6
Barnardo St E1 96 D1
Barnard Rd
Clapham SW11 136 C1
Enfield EN1 6 B3
Mitcham CR4 181 A1
Barnard's Inn EC4 241 B2
Barnbrough NW1 232 A5
Barnby Sq 1 E15 98 C6
Barnby St
Somers Town NW1 93 C4 232 B2
2 West Ham E15 98 C6
Barn Cl
Ashford TW15 170 D5
19 Kentish Town NW5 71 D3
Northolt UB5 84 C5
Barn Cres HA7 25 C4
Barncroft Cl UB8 82 D2
Barn Croft Prim Sch E17 53 A3
Barneby Cl TW2 152 C3
Barnehurst Rd DA7 147 D3
Barn Elms Sp Ctr SW15 134 C4
Barnersbury Ho N7 72 A4
BARNES 133 D4
Barnes Ave
Barnes SW13 134 A5
Southall UB2 107 B2
Barnes Bridge Sta SW13 133 C3
Barnes Cl E12 77 D4
Barnes Common★ SW13 134 A2
Barnes Ct Barnet EN5 1 D1
Islington N1 72 C1
3 Newham E16 99 C2
South Norwood CR7 205 A6
Woodford IG8 37 D5
Wood Green N22 32 A3
Barnes End KT3 200 A4
Barnes High St SW13 133 D3
Barnes Ho
8 Barking IG11 101 B6
14 Bethnal Green E2 96 C5
Camden Town NW1 231 D6
26 Deptford SE14 140 D6
Hornsey N19 50 A2
Barnes Hospl SW14 133 C2
Barnes Prim Sch SW13 133 D2
Barnes Qtr 6 TW8 131 C5
Barnes Rd
Edmonton N18 34 C6
Ilford IG1 79 A3
Barnes St E14 97 A1
Barnes Sta SW13 134 A2
Barnes Terr SE8 119 B1
Barnes Wallis Ct HA9 67 A5
BARNET 13 B6
Barnet By-Pass WD6 11 C6
Barnet Coll (Grahame Park) NW9 27 D2
Barnet Coll (North London Bsns Pk) N11 15 A1
Barnet Coll (Stanhope Rd) N12 30 B5
Barnet Coll (Wood St) EN5 1 B1
Barnet Dr BR2 226 A6
BARNET GATE 11 C5
Barnet Gate La EN5 11 D4
Barnet Gr E2 96 A4
Barnet Hill EN5 1 C1
Barnet Hill JMI Sch EN5 13 B6
Barnet Ho 35 SE5 139 A3
Barnet La
Barnet EN5, N20 13 B4
Borehamwood WD6 10 B5
Barnet Mus★ EN5 1 A1
Barnet Rd Barnet EN5 1 B5
Edgware EN5 11 C5
Barnett Ho E1 243 C3
Barnett Homestead NW11 47 C5
Barnet Trad Est EN5 1 B2
Barnetts Ct HA2 63 D5
Barnett St 18 E1 96 B1
Barnet Way (Barnet By-Pass) EN5, NW7, WD6 11 B3
Barnet Wood Rd BR2 225 C6
Barney Cl SE7 121 C1
Barnfield KT3 199 C3
Barn Field NW3 70 D3
Barnfield Ave
Croydon CR0 222 C6
Kingston u T KT2 176 A5
Mitcham CR4 203 B6
Barnfield Cl
London N4 50 A2
Wandsworth SW17 158 A1
Barnfield Gdns
Kingston u T KT2 176 A5
Shooters Hill SE18 144 D6
Barnfield Pl E14 119 C2
Barnfield Prim Sch HA8 27 A2
Barnfield Rd
Burnt Oak HA8 27 A2
Ealing W5 87 C3
Erith DA17 147 B6
Shooters Hill SE18 144 D6
Barnfield Wood Cl BR3 208 B3
Barnfield Wood Rd BR3 208 B3
Barnham Dr SE28 123 D5
Barnham Rd UB6 86 A4
Barnham St SE1 253 B2
Barnhill HA5 40 C4
Barn Hill HA9 44 D1
Barnhill Ave BR2 208 D4
Barnhill Com High Sch UB4 84 C4
Barnhill Ct UB4 84 B4
Barnhill La UB4 84 B3
Barnhill Rd Hayes UB4 84 C3
Wembley HA9 67 A5
Barnhurst Path WD19 22 C5
Barningham Way NW9 45 B3
Barnlea Cl TW13 151 A2
Barnmead Ct RM9 81 B3
Barnmead Gdns RM9 81 B3
Barnmead Rd
Dagenham RM9 81 B3
Penge BR3 185 A2
Barn Rise HA9 66 C6
BARNSBURY 72 A1
Barnsbury Cl KT3 199 A5
Barnsbury Cres KT5 199 A1
Barnsbury Gr N7 72 B1
Barnsbury Ho 12 SW4 159 D5
Barnsbury La KT5 199 A1
Barnsbury Pk N1 72 C1
Barnsbury Rd N1 94 C6 234 A5
Barnsbury Sq N1 72 C1
Barnsbury St N1 72 C1
Barnsbury Terr N1 72 B1
Barnscroft SW20 200 B6
Barnsdale Ave E14 119 C2
Barnsdale Rd W9 91 B3
Barnsley St E1 96 B3
Barn St N16 73 C6
Barnstaple Ho SE12 164 D6
Barnstaple La SE13 142 A1
Barnstaple Rd HA4 62 C5
Barnston Wlk N1 235 A6
Barnview Lo HA3 24 C2
Barn Way HA9 66 C6
Barnwell Ho 1 SE5 139 C4
Barnwell Rd SW2 160 C6
Barnwood Cl
Barnet N20 13 B3
Ruislip HA4 61 B6
Westbourne Green W9 91 D3

Baron Cl
Friern Barnet N11 31 B5
Islington N1 234 A4
Baron Ct Barnet EN5 1 D1
Mitcham CR4 202 C5
Baroness Rd 5 E2 95 D4
Baronet Gr N17 34 A2
Baronet Rd N17 34 A2
Baron Gdns IG6 57 A6
Baron Gr CR4 202 C5
Baron Ho 6 SW19 180 B2
Baron Rd RM8 58 D1
Barons 14 BR3 185 D1
Barons Court Mans
W14 254 B1
Baron's Court Rd
W14 113 A1 254 B2
Barons Court Sta
W14 113 A1 254 A2
Barons Ct Ilford IG1 79 B6
Kingsbury NW9 45 B3
Wallington SM6 219 D5
Baronsfield Rd TW1 153 B5
Barons Gate
East Barnet EN4 14 C5
13 South Acton W4 111 A3
Barons Keep
W14 113 A1 254 A2
Barons Lo 9 E14 120 A2
Barons Mead HA1 42 C5
Baronsmead Rd
SW13 134 A4
Baronsmede W5 110 B4
Baronsmere Ct 9 EN5 1 A1
Baronsmere Rd N2 48 C5
Baron's Pl
SE1 116 C4 251 B1
Baron St N1 94 C5 234 A4
Barons The TW1 153 B5
Baron's Wlk CR0 207 A3
Baron Wlk E16 98 D2
Barque Mews SE8 141 C6
Barrack Rd TW4 129 A1
Barradell Ho 15
W14 112 D3
Barra Hall Cir UB3 83 C1
Barra Hall Rd UB3 105 C6
Barrass Cl 7 EN3 7 C6
Barratt Ave N22 32 B1
Barratt Ho 15 N1 72 D1
Barratt Ind Pk
Poplar E3 98 A3
Southall UB1 107 C5
Barratt Way HA3 42 B6
Barr Beacon SE23 162 C4
Barrenger Rd N10 30 D1
Barret Ho NW6 91 C6
Barrett Ct 2 NW10 89 C5
Barrett Rd E17 54 A5
Barrett's Gr N16 73 C3
Barretts Green Rd
NW10 89 B5
Barrett St W1 93 A1 238 B1
Barrhill Rd SW2 160 A2
Barrie Ct EN5 14 A6
Barriedale SE14 141 A3
Barrie Ho Acton W3 111 A4
Bayswater W2 246 B5
Edmonton N9 18 B4
Primrose Hill NW8 230 B5
8 Stoke Newington
N16 73 C5
Barrier Gdns Pier
SE18 121 D3
Barrier Point Rd
E16 121 C4
Barringers Ct HA4 39 B2
Barringer Sq SW17 181 A6
Barrington N20 14 B3
Barrington Cl NW5 71 A3
Barrington Ct
9 Acton W3 110 D4
Kentish Town NW5 71 A3
4 Muswell Hill N10 31 B1
31 South Lambeth
SW9 138 A3
Barrington Prim Sch
DA7 146 D3
Barrington Rd
Bexley DA7 146 D3
Brixton SW9 138 D2
Cheam SM3 201 C1
Hornsey N8 49 D4
Barrington Rd *continued*
Little Ilford E12 78 C2
Barrington Villas
SE18 144 C4
Barrington Wlk 9
SE19 183 C4
Barrow Ave SM5 218 D1
Barrow Cl N21 16 D2
Barrow Ct 6 SE6 164 D3
Barrowdene Cl HA5 23 A1
Barrowell Gn N21 17 A2
Barrowfield Cl N9 18 C1
Barrowgate Ho W4 111 B1
Barrowgate Rd W4 111 B1
Barrow Hedges Cl
SM5 218 C1
Barrow Hedges Prim Sch
SM5 218 C1
Barrow Hedges Way
SM5 218 C1
Barrow Hill KT4 215 C6
Barrow Hill Cl KT4 215 C6
Barrow Hill Est
NW8 92 C5 230 A3
Barrow Hill Jun Sch
NW8 92 C5 230 A3
Barrow Hill Rd NW8 230 A3
Barrow Point Ave
HA5 23 A1
Barrow Point La HA5 23 A1
Barrow Rd
Croydon CR0 220 C3
Streatham SW16 181 D4
Barrow Wlk 1 TW8 109 C1
Barrs Rd NW10 67 B1
Barry Ave Erith DA7 147 A5
South Tottenham N15 51 D3
Barry Cl BR6 227 C5
Barry Ct SW4 159 C5
Barrydene N20 14 B2
Barrydene Ct EN2 4 D2
Barry Ho 4 SE16 118 B1
Barry Lo N4 50 B2
Barrymore N12 30 A3
Barry Par SE22 140 A1
Barry Rd
London SE22 162 A6
Newham E6 100 A1
Willesden NW10 67 A1
Barry Terr TW15 148 B2
Barset Rd SE15 140 C2
Barsons Cl SE20 184 C3
Barston Rd SE27 161 A1
Barstow Cres SW2 160 B3
Bartell Ho SW2 160 C5
Barter St WC1 94 A2 240 B3
Barters Wlk HA5 41 A6
Barth Mews SE18 123 C2
Bartholomew Cl
Barbican EC1 242 A3
Wandsworth SW18 136 A1
Bartholomew Ct
16 Blackwall E14 120 B6
Edgware HA8 25 D3
St Luke's EC1 242 B6
Bartholomew Ho
22 Camberwell SE5 139 A3
Enfield EN3 7 A6
Bartholomew La EC2 242 D1
Bartholomew Pas
EC1 241 D3
Bartholomew Pl EC1 242 A3
Bartholomew Rd
NW5 71 C2
Bartholomew Sq
18 Bethnal Green E1 96 B3
St Luke's EC1 242 B6
Bartholomew St
SE1 117 B3 262 D5
Bartholomew Villas
NW5 71 C2
Barth Rd SE18 123 C2
Bartle Ave E6 100 A5
Bartle Rd W11 91 A1
Bartlett Cl E14 97 C1
Bartlett Ct EC4 241 B2
Bartletts Cotts 4 EN5 1 A2
Bartletts Ho 10 RM10 81 D2
Bartlett St CR2 221 B3
Bartok Ho W11 244 C5
Barton Ave RM7 59 D1
Barton Cl Bexley DA6 169 A6
Hackney E9 74 C3
Hendon NW4 46 A5
2 Newham E6 100 B1
Peckham SE15 140 B2
Barton Cl *continued*
Shepperton TW17 192 D3
Barton Ct
Beckenham BR2 208 B6
10 South Lambeth
SW4 138 A3
3 Sutton SM1 217 D2
West Kensington W14 254 B2
Barton Gn KT3 177 B1
Barton Ho
8 Bromley E3 97 D4
Islington N1 72 D1
Sands End SW6 135 D2
Barton Mdws IG6 57 A5
Barton Rd
Sidcup DA14 191 A4
West Kensington
W14 113 A1 254 B1
Barton St SW1 260 A6
Bartons The WD6 9 D5
Bartonway NW8 229 C4
Bartram Cl UB8 82 D3
Bartram Ct RM9 80 B2
Bartram Rd SE4 163 A5
Bartrams La EN4 2 A5
Bartrip St E9 75 B2
Barts Cl BR3 207 C4
Barts & The London Sch
of Medicine & Dentistry
EC1 94 D3 241 D5
Barville Cl SE4 141 A1
Barwell Bsns Pk
KT9 213 D1
Barwell Ho 7 E2 96 A3
Barwell La KT9 213 C1
Barwick Dr UB8 82 D2
Barwick Ho 7 W3 111 A4
Barwick Rd E7 77 B4
Barwood Ave BR4 207 D1
Bascome St 13 SW2 160 C5
Basden Gr TW13 151 C2
Base Apartments 8
N1 73 A1
Basedale Rd RM9 80 B1
Baseing Cl E6 122 C6
Baseline Business
Studios 18 W11 112 D6
Basevi Way SE8 141 D6
Bashley Rd NW10 89 B3
Basil Ave E6 100 A4
Basil Ct 11 EN5 2 A1
Basildene Rd TW4,
TW5 128 D2
Basildon Ct W1 238 B4
Basildon Rd SE2 124 A1
Basil Gdns
Croydon CR0 206 D1
West Norwood SE27 183 A5
Basil Ho
South Lambeth SW8 270 A4
22 Whitechapel E1 96 A1
Basil Mans SW1 247 C1
Basilon Rd DA7 147 A3
Basil Spence Ho N22 32 B2
Basil St
Knightsbridge
SW1 114 D4 247 C1
Knightsbridge SW1,
SW3 114 D3 257 C6
Basin App 20 E14 97 A1
Basing Cl KT7 196 D2
Basing Ct 18 SE15 139 D4
Basingdon Way SE5 139 B1
Basing Dr DA5 169 B5
Basingfield Rd KT7 196 D2
Basinghall Ave
EC2 95 B1 242 C2
Basinghall St
EC2 95 B1 242 C2
Basing Hill
London NW11 47 B1
Wembley HA9 44 C1
Basing Ho
7 Barking IG11 101 B6
Catford SE6 185 C6
Basing House Yd 22
E2 95 C4
Basing Pl E2 95 C4
Basing St W11 91 B1
Basing Way
London N3 47 D6
Thames Ditton KT7 196 D2
Basire St N1 95 A6 235 B6
Baskerville Ct
South Norwood
SE25 205 C4
Baskerville Ct *continued*
Wandsworth SW18 158 C4
Baskerville Gdns
NW10 67 C4
Baskerville Rd
SW18 158 C4
Basket Gdns SE9 166 A6
Basle Ho 3 E15 76 C3
Baslow Cl HA3 24 B2
Baslow Wlk E5 74 D4
Basnett Rd 9 SW11 137 A2
Basque Ct 21 SE16 118 D4
Bassano St SE22 161 D6
Bassant Rd SE18 145 D6
Bassein Park Rd
W12 111 D4
Bassett Gdns TW7 130 A5
Bassett Ho RM9 102 B6
Bassett House Sch 22
W10 90 D1
Bassett Rd W10 90 D1
Bassetts Cl BR6 226 D4
Bassett St NW5 71 A2
Bassetts Way BR6 226 D4
Bassett Way UB1 85 D1
Bassingbourn Ho 3
N1 72 D1
Bassingham Rd
Wandsworth SW18 158 A4
Wembley HA0 65 D2
Bassishaw Highwalk
EC2 242 C3
Basswood Cl 5
SE15 140 B2
Bastable Ave IG11 102 A5
Basterfield Ho EC1 242 A5
Bastion Highwalk
EC2 242 A3
Bastion Rd SE18, SE2 124 A1
Baston Manor Rd BR2,
BR4 225 B4
Baston Rd BR2 225 B5
Baston Sch BR2 225 B6
Bastwick St
EC1 95 A3 242 A6
Basuto Rd
SW6 135 C4 265 B1
Batavia Cl TW16 172 C2
Batavia Ho 1 SE14 141 A5
Batavia Mews 3
SE14 141 A5
Batavia Rd
Deptford SE14 141 A5
Sunbury TW16 172 B2
Batchelor St
N1 94 C6 234 B5
Bateman Cl IG11 79 A2
Bateman Ho 8
SE17 138 D6
Bateman Rd E4 35 C4
Bateman's Bldgs W1 239 C1
Bateman's Row
EC2 95 C3 243 B6
Bateman St
W1 93 D1 239 C1
Bates Cres
Croydon CR0 220 C3
Streatham SW16 181 C3
Bateson St 3 SE18 123 C2
Bate St 10 E14 119 B6
Bath Cl SE15 140 B5
Bath Ct Finsbury EC1 235 C1
3 Forest Hill SE26 162 A1
Holborn EC1 241 A5
Bathgate Ho 8
SW9 138 D4
Bathgate Rd SW19 156 D1
Bath Gr E2 96 A5
Bath Ho
Bethnal Green E2 96 A3
Borough The SE1 262 B6
Bath House Rd CR0 204 A1
Bath Pas KT1 175 D1
Bath Pl Barnet EN5 1 B2
14 Hammersmith W6 112 C1
11 Shoreditch EC2 95 C4
Bath Rd Acton W4 111 C2
Cranford TW3, TW4,
TW5 128 C4
Dagenham RM6 59 A3
Harlington TW6, UB7,
TW5 127 B4
Harmondsworth TW6,
UB7 126 B4
Lower Edmonton N9 18 C2
Upton E7 77 D2
Baths Rd BR1, BR2 209 D5
Bath St EC1 95 B4 235 C1
Bath Terr
SE1 117 A3 262 A6
Bathurst Ave SW19 179 D2
Bathurst Gdns NW10 90 B5
Bathurst Ho 2 W12 112 B6
Bathurst Mews
W2 114 B6 246 D6
Bathurst Rd IG1 56 D1
Bathurst St W2 246 D6
Bathway 11 SE18 122 C2
Batley Cl CR4 202 D2
Batley Pl 3 N16 73 D5
Batley Rd Enfield EN2 5 B4
Shacklewell N16 73 D5
Batman Cl W12 112 B5
Batoum Gdns W6 112 C3
Batson Ho 29 E1 96 A1
Batson St W12 112 A4
Batsworth Rd CR4 202 B6
Battenburg Wlk 10
SE19 183 C5
Batten Cl E6 100 B1
Batten Ho
7 London SW4 159 C6
8 Walthamstow E17 53 D6
10 West Kilburn W10 91 A4
Batten St SW11 136 C2
Battersby Rd SE6 164 B1
BATTERSEA 136 D4
Battersea Bridge Rd
SW11 136 C5 267 A3
Battersea Bsns Ctr
SW11 137 A2
Battersea Church Rd
SW11 136 B4 266 D2
Battersea Dogs & Cats
Home SW8 137 B5 268 D3
Battersea High St
SW11 136 B3
Battersea Hts SW11 136 D2
Battersea Park★
SW11 137 A5 268 A3
Battersea Park Rd SW11,
SW8 267 D1
Battersea Park Sch
SW11 136 D4 267 D1
Battersea Park Sta
SW8 137 B5 268 C3
Battersea Power
Station(dis)
SW8 137 B6 268 D6
Battersea Rise
SW11 136 C1
Battersea Sq SW11 266 D1
Battery Rd SE28 123 C4
Battishill St 9 N1 72 D1
Battlebridge Ct NW1 233 B4
Battle Bridge La
SE1 117 C5 253 A3
Battle Cl SW19 180 A4
Battledean Rd N5 72 D3
Battle Ho 8 SE15 140 A6
Battle House Mews 7
EN5 2 A1
Batty St E1 96 A1
Baty Ho SW2 160 B3
Baudwin Rd SE6 164 C2
Baugh Rd DA14 190 C5
Baulk The SW18 157 C4
Bavant Rd SW16 182 B1
Bavaria Rd N19 72 A6
Bavdene Mews NW4 46 B5
Bavent Rd SE5 139 A3
Bawdale Rd SE22 161 D6
Bawdsey Ave IG2 57 D5
Bawtree Rd SE14 141 A5
Bawtry Rd N20 14 D1
Baxendale N20 14 A2
Baxendale St E2 96 A4
Baxter Cl
Bromley BR1 210 D6
Hillingdon UB10 82 D4
Southall UB2 107 D3
Baxter Ho 11 E3 97 D4
Baxter Rd
Edmonton N18 34 B6
Ilford IG1 78 D3
Islington N1 73 B2
Newham E16 99 C1
Bayard Ct DA7 147 D1
Baycliffe Ho 8 E9 74 D2
Baycroft Cl HA5 40 C6
Bay Ct Ealing W5 110 A3
7 Stepney E1 96 D3

Baydon Ct BR2 ... 208 D6
Bayer Ho EC1 ... 242 A5
Bayes Ct NW3 ... 70 D1
Bayeux Ho 10 SE7 ... 143 C6
Bayfield Ho 3 SE4 .. 140 D1
Bayfield Rd SE9 ... 143 D1
Bayford Lodge HA5 ... 23 B2
Bayford Rd NW10 ... 90 D4
Bayford St Ind Ctr 4 E8 ... 74 B1
Bayford St 5 E8 ... 74 B1
Baygrove Mews KT1 .175 C2
Bayham Pl NW1 ... 93 C6 232 B5
Bayham Rd
Acton W4 ... 111 B3
Ealing W13 ... 109 B5
Morden SM4 ... 202 A5
Bayham St NW1 ... 93 C6 232 A5
Bay Ho UB10 ... 60 C4
Bayhurst Ho N4 ... 51 A2
Bayhurst Wood Country Park UB9 ... 38 B4
Bayleaf Cl TW12 ... 174 B5
Bayley St WC1 ... 239 C3
Bayley Wlk SE2 ... 125 A1
Baylis Mews TW1 ... 153 A4
Baylis Rd SE1 ... 116 C4 251 A1
Bayliss Ave SE28 ... 124 D6
Bayliss Cl
4 Southall UB1 ... 85 D1
Southgate N21 ... 16 A6
Bayne Cl E6 ... 100 B1
Baynes Cl EN1 ... 6 A4
Baynes Mews 2 NW3 ... 70 B2
Baynes St NW1 ... 71 C1
Baynham Cl DA5 ... 169 B5
Bayon Ho 27 N19 ... 49 D2
Bayonne Rd W6 ... 264 A5
Bays Cl SE26 ... 184 C5
Bays Ct HA8 ... 26 D5
Bayshill Rise UB5 ... 63 D2
Bayston Rd N16 ... 73 D5
BAYSWATER ... 114 A6
Bayswater Rd W2 ... 114 B6 246 C5
Bayswater Rd Mkt* W2 ... 114 A6 246 B5
Bayswater Sta W2 ... 113 D6 245 D6
Bayton Ct 2 E8 ... 74 A1
Baytree Cl
Bromley BR1 ... 187 D2
Sidcup DA15 ... 167 D3
Baytree Ho E4 ... 19 D4
Baytree Rd SW2 ... 138 B1
Bazalgette Cl KT3 ... 199 B4
Bazalgette Gdns KT3 ... 199 B4
Bazalgette Ho NW8 ... 236 D6
Bazeley Ho SE1 ... 251 C1
Bazely St E14 ... 120 A6
Bazile Rd N21 ... 16 C5
BBC Television Ctr W12 ... 112 C5
Beacham Cl SE7 ... 143 D6
Beachborough Rd BR1 ... 186 A6
Beachcroft Ave UB1 .107 B5
Beachcroft Rd E11 ... 76 C5
Beach Ct SE9 ... 166 A5
Beach Gr TW13 ... 151 C2
Beach Ho SW5 ... 255 A2
Beachy Rd E3 ... 75 C1
Beaconfield Terrace Rd W14 ... 254 A5
Beacon Gate SE14 .. 140 D2
Beacon Gr SM5 ... 219 A4
Beacon Hill N7 ... 72 A3
Beacon Ho
11 Camberwell SE5 .. 139 C5
7 Isle Of Dogs E14 . 119 D1
10 Penge SE26 ... 184 B5
South Lambeth SW8 . 269 C2
Beacon Pl CR0 ... 220 A5
Beacon Rd
Harlington TW19, TW6 ... 148 C5
Hither Green SE13 ... 164 B5
Beacon Rdbt TW6 ... 148 C5
Beacons Cl 10 E6 ... 100 A2
Beaconsfield Cl
Acton Green W4 ... 111 A1
Beaconsfield Cl *continued*
Friern Barnet N11 ... 31 A5
Greenwich SE3 ... 143 A6
Beaconsfield Ct N11 ... 31 A5
Beaconsfield Gdns KT10 ... 212 C1
Beaconsfield Par 1 SE9 ... 188 A6
Beaconsfield Prim Sch UB2 ... 107 A5
Beaconsfield Rd
Acton W4 ... 111 B3
Bromley BR1 ... 209 D6
Claygate KT10 ... 212 C1
Ealing W5 ... 109 D4
Edmonton N9 ... 18 A1
Elmstead SE9 ... 188 A6
Enfield EN3 ... 6 D6
Friern Barnet N11 ... 31 A6
Greenwich SE3 ... 143 A5
Hayes UB4 ... 106 C5
Kingston u T KT3 ... 177 B1
Leyton E10 ... 76 A5
Newham E16 ... 98 D3
Southall UB1 ... 107 A5
South Tottenham N15 ... 51 C5
Surbiton KT5 ... 198 B2
Thornton Heath CR0 ... 205 B3
Twickenham TW1 ... 153 B5
Walthamstow E17 ... 53 B3
Walworth SE17 ... 117 C1 263 A1
Willesden NW10 ... 67 D2
Beaconsfield Wlk SW6 ... 135 B4 264 D1
Beaconshaw BR1 ... 186 C3
Beacontree Ave E17 ... 36 B1
Beacontree Rd E11 ... 54 D2
Beadle Ct CR4 ... 202 C6
Beadlow Cl SM4 ... 202 B3
Beadman Pl SE27 ... 182 D6
Beadman St SE27 ... 182 D6
Beadnell Rd SE23 ... 162 D3
Beadon Rd
Bromley BR2 ... 209 A4
Hammersmith W6 ... 112 C2
Beaford Gr SW20 ... 201 B6
Beagle Cl TW13 ... 172 B6
Beak St W1 ... 115 C6 249 B6
Beal Cl DA16 ... 146 A4
Beale Cl N13 ... 32 D5
Beale Ho 7 SW9 ... 138 B3
Beale Pl E3 ... 97 B5
Beale Rd E3 ... 97 B6
Beal High Sch IG5 ... 56 A5
Beal Rd IG1 ... 78 C6
Beam Ave RM10 ... 103 D6
Beames Ho SW8 ... 269 C2
Beames Rd NW10 ... 89 B6
Beaminster Ct N15 ... 51 B4
Beaminster Gdns IG6 56 D6
Beaminster Ho SW8 270 C4
Beamish Dr WD23 ... 8 A3
Beamish Ho 7 SE16 .118 C2
Beamish Rd N9 ... 18 A3
Beanacre Cl E9 ... 75 B2
Bean Rd DA6 ... 146 D1
Beanshaw SE9 ... 188 C6
Beansland Gr RM6 ... 59 A6
Bear Alley EC4 ... 241 C2
Bear Cl RM7 ... 59 D3
Bear Croft Ho 6 SW6 ... 135 B3
Beardell St SE19 ... 183 D4
Beardow Gr N14 ... 15 C5
Beard Rd KT2 ... 176 B5
Beardsfield E13 ... 99 A5
Beard's Hill TW12 ... 173 C2
Beards Hill Cl TW12 ... 173 C2
Beardsley Terr RM8 ... 80 B3
Beardsley Way W3 ... 111 B4
Beard's Rd TW15, TW16 ... 171 C4
Bearfield Rd KT2 ... 176 A3
Bear Gdns SE1 ... 117 A5 252 A4
Bear La SE1 . 116 D5 251 D3
Bear Rd TW13 ... 172 D6
Bear St WC2 ... 249 D6
Bearstead Rise SE4 ... 163 B6
Bearsted Terr 7 BR3 ... 185 C2
Beasley's Ait TW17 .. 193 D3
Beasley's Ait La TW16, TW17 ... 193 D3
Beaton Cl SE15 ... 139 D4
Beatrice Ave
Thornton Heath SW16 ... 182 B1
Wembley HA9 ... 66 A3
Beatrice Cl
Newham E13 ... 99 A3
Pinner HA5 ... 40 A5
Beatrice Ct
Buckhurst Hill IG9 ... 21 D2
Hendon NW4 ... 46 C4
Beatrice Ho
1 Brixton SW2 ... 160 B6
Forest Hill SE6 ... 163 C2
4 Hammersmith W6 112 C1
2 Stepney E1 ... 96 D2
Beatrice Lo 3 N12 ... 30 A4
Beatrice Pl W8 ... 255 C5
Beatrice Rd
Bermondsey SE1 ... 118 A2
Edmonton N9 ... 18 C4
Finsbury Pk N4 ... 50 C2
2 Richmond TW10 ... 154 B6
Southall UB1 ... 107 B5
Walthamstow E17 ... 53 C4
Beatrice Tate Sch 33 E2 ... 96 B4
Beatrice Webb Ho 4 E3 ... 97 A5
Beatrix Ho SW5 ... 255 D2
Beatrix Potter Prim Sch SW18 ... 158 A3
Beatson Wlk 23 SE16 ... 118 D5
Beattie Cl TW14 ... 149 D3
Beattie Ho SW8 ... 269 B2
Beattock Rise N10 ... 49 B5
Beatty Ho 16 E14 ... 119 C4
Beatty Rd
Stanmore HA7 ... 25 C4
Stoke Newington N16 .73 C4
Beattyville Gdns IG6 .56 D5
Beauchamp Cl 17 W4 ... 111 A3
Beauchamp Ct HA7 ... 25 C5
Beauchamp Pl SW3 ... 114 C3 257 B5
Beauchamp Rd
Clapham SW11 ... 136 D1
East Molesey KT8 ... 196 A4
South Norwood SE19 .. 183 B2
Sutton SM1 ... 217 C4
Twickenham TW1 ... 153 A4
Upton E7 ... 77 B1
Beauchamp St EC1 . 241 A3
Beauchamp Terr SW15 ... 134 B2
Beauclerc Inf Sch TW16 ... 194 C6
Beauclerc Rd W6 ... 112 B3
Beauclere Ho 1 SM2 ... 218 A1
Beauclerk Cl TW13 ... 150 B3
Beauclerk Ho 10 SW16 ... 160 A1
Beaudesert Mews UB7 ... 104 A4
Beaufort E6 ... 100 C2
Beaufort Ave HA3 ... 43 B6
Beaufort Cl
Chingford E4 ... 35 D4
Ealing W5 ... 88 B2
Putney SW19 ... 156 B4
Beaufort Ct
Friern Barnet N11 ... 31 B5
Harrow HA3 ... 43 A3
3 New Barnet EN5 ... 14 A6
Richmond TW10 ... 175 C6
West Brompton SW6 . 265 A6
Beaufort Dr NW11 ... 47 C5
Beaufort Gdns
Hendon NW4 ... 46 C3
Heston TW5 ... 129 A4
Ilford IG1 ... 56 C1
Knightsbridge SW3 ... 114 C3 257 B6
South Norwood SW16 182 B3
Beaufort Ho
Ashford TW15 ... 170 D5
Battersea SW11 ... 136 C3
Chelsea SW3 ... 266 D5
Hampstead Garden Suburb NW11 ... 48 A3
20 Millwall E14 ... 119 C4
Pimlico SW1 ... 259 C1
8 South Tottenham N15 ... 51 D5
Beaufort Ho *continued*
1 Wimbledon SW20 . 178 D2
Beaufort Mans SW3 . 266 D5
Beaufort Mews SW6 264 D6
Beaufort Pk NW11 ... 47 C5
Beaufort Rd Ealing W5 . 88 B2
Kingston u T KT1, KT5, KT6 ... 198 A5
Richmond TW10 ... 175 C6
Ruislip HA4 ... 61 B6
Twickenham TW1 ... 153 C4
Beaufort St SW3 ... 136 B6 266 C6
Beaufort Way KT17 ... 216 A1
Beaufoy Ho
South Lambeth SW8 . 270 C4
3 West Norwood SE27 ... 160 D1
Beaufoy Rd
11 London SW8 ... 137 B2
Tottenham N17 ... 33 C3
Beaufoy Wlk SE11 ... 116 B2 260 D3
Beaulieu Ave
Forest Hill SE26 ... 184 B6
1 Newham E16 ... 121 B5
Beaulieu Cl
Camberwell SE5 ... 139 B2
Colindale NW9 ... 45 C5
Hounslow TW4 ... 151 B6
Mitcham CR4 ... 181 A2
14 Twickenham TW1 . 153 D5
Beaulieu Ct W5 ... 88 A2
Beaulieu Dr HA5 ... 40 D2
Beaulieu Gdns N21 ... 17 A4
Beaulieu Ho 6 NW4 .. 28 D1
Beaulieu Hts CR7 ... 183 C2
Beaulieu Pl W4 ... 111 A3
Beaumanor Gdns SE9 ... 188 C6
Beaumanor Mans W2 ... 245 D6
Beaumaris 5 N11 ... 32 A4
Beaumaris Dr IG8 ... 37 D3
Beaumaris Gn NW9 ... 45 C3
Beaumaris Twr 2 W3 ... 110 D4
Beaumont SW15 ... 157 A6
Beaumont Ave
Harrow HA2 ... 41 D3
Richmond TW9 ... 132 B2
Wembley HA0 ... 65 C4
West Kensington W14 ... 113 B1 254 C2
Beaumont Bldgs WC2 ... 240 B1
Beaumont Cl
East Finchley N2 ... 48 C5
Kingston u T KT2 ... 176 C3
Beaumont Cres W14 ... 113 B1 254 C1
Beaumont Ct
10 Acton Green W4 .. 111 A1
16 Hendon NW9 ... 27 D1
Lower Clapton E5 ... 74 B5
Marylebone W1 ... 238 B4
7 Mile End E1 ... 97 A4
6 Mitcham CR4 ... 181 A1
Wembley HA0 ... 65 C3
17 Wimbledon SW19 . 178 D3
Beaumont Dr
Ashford TW15 ... 171 B5
New Malden KT4 ... 200 B2
Beaumont Gdns NW3 .69 C5
Beaumont Gr E1 ... 96 D3
Beaumont Ho
12 Leyton E10 ... 53 D2
1 Streatham SW2 .. 160 A3
West Kensington W14 254 D3
Wimbledon SW19 ... 157 C1
Beaumont Lo E8 ... 74 A2
Beaumont Pl
Barnet EN5 ... 1 B4
Fitzrovia NW1, WC1, W1 ... 93 C3 239 B6
Isleworth TW7 ... 152 D6
Beaumont Prim Sch E10 ... 53 D1
Beaumont Rd
Leyton E10 ... 53 D2
Newham E13 ... 99 B4
Orpington BR5 ... 211 B3
Putney SW15, SW19 . 157 A4
South Acton W4 ... 111 A3
South Norwood SE19 . 183 A4
Beaumont Rise N19 ... 49 D1
Beaumont Sq E1 ... 96 D2
Beaumont St W1 ... 238 B4
Beaumont Terr 1 SE13 ... 164 C4
Beaumont Wlk NW3 ... 70 D1
Beauvais Terr UB5 ... 84 D4
Beauvale 6 NW1 ... 71 A1
Beauval Rd SE22 ... 161 D5
Beaverbank Rd SE9 .. 167 B3
Beaver Cl
Hampton TW12 ... 173 D2
9 Penge SE20 ... 184 A3
West Barnes SM4 ... 200 C2
Beaver Ctr The RM8 ... 59 A2
Beaver Gr UB5 ... 85 A4
Beavers Com Prim Sch The TW4 ... 128 C2
Beavers Cres TW4 .. 128 D1
Beavers La TW4 ... 128 C2
Beavers Lo DA14 ... 189 D5
Beaverwood Rd BR7 .189 C4
Beaverwood Sch for Girls BR7 ... 189 C4
Beavis Ho N16 ... 73 C5
Beavor La W6 ... 112 A1
Bebbington Rd SE18 .123 C2
Beblets Cl 4 BR6 ... 227 D3
Bec Cl HA4 ... 62 D5
Beccles Dr IG11 ... 79 D2
Beccles St E14 ... 119 B6
Bechervaise Ct 2 E10 ... 53 D1
Beck Cl SE13 ... 141 D4
Beck Ct BR3 ... 206 D6
BECKENHAM ... 185 C1
Beckenham Beacon Hospl BR3 ... 185 B1
Beckenham Bsns Ctr BR3 ... 185 A4
Beckenham Ct BR3 .. 185 C2
Beckenham Gdns N9 .. 17 C1
Beckenham Gr BR2 .. 186 B1
Beckenham Hill Rd BR3, SE6 ... 186 A5
Beckenham Hill Sta SE6 ... 186 A5
Beckenham Junction Sta BR3 ... 185 C2
Beckenham La BR1, BR2 ... 186 D1
Beckenham Place Pk BR3 ... 185 D3
Beckenham Rd
Penge BR3 ... 185 A2
West Wickham BR3, BR4 ... 208 A2
Beckenham Rd Sta BR3 ... 185 A2
Beckers The N16 ... 74 A4
Becket Ave E6 ... 100 C4
Becket Cl
Croydon SE25 ... 206 A3
2 Merton SW19 ... 179 D2
Becket Fold 10 HA1 ... 42 D4
Becket Ho SE1 ... 252 C1
Becket Rd N18 ... 34 C6
Becket St SE1 ... 262 C6
Beckett Cl
Abbey Wood DA17 ... 125 B3
Streatham SW16 ... 159 D2
Willesden NW10 ... 67 C2
Beckett Ho
28 London SW9 ... 138 A3
15 Stepney E1 ... 96 C2
Becketts Cl
Feltham TW14 ... 150 B5
Orpington BR6 ... 227 D5
Becketts Pl KT1 ... 175 D2
Beckett Wlk BR3 ... 185 A4
Beckfoot NW1 ... 232 B3
Beckford Cl W14 ... 254 D3
Beckford Dr BR5 ... 211 B2
Beckford Ho 18 N16 ... 73 C3
Beckford Prim Sch NW6 ... 69 B3
Beckford Rd CR0 ... 205 D3
Beckham Ho SE11 .. 260 D3
Beck Ho
4 Edmonton N18 ... 34 A5
Stoke Newington N16 .. 73 C5
Beckington 18 NW5 ... 71 A2
Beck La BR3 ... 206 D6
Beckley Ho E3 ... 97 B3

Becklow Gdns
Chiswick W12 111 D4
[1] Shepherd's Bush W12 112 A4
Becklow Mews [7] W12 112 A4
Becklow Rd W12 112 A4
Beckmead Sch BR3 207 C1
Beck Rd E8 96 B6
Mitcham CR4 202 D3
Beck River Pk [10] BR3 185 C2
Becks Rd DA14 168 A1
BECKTON 100 D2
Beckton Alps E6 100 C3
Beckton Alps Ski Ctr E6 100 C3
Beckton Park Sta E6 122 B6
Beckton Rd E16 98 D2
Beckton Ret Pk E6 100 C2
Beckton Sta E6 100 C2
Beckton Triangle Ret Pk E6 100 D3
Beck Way BR3 207 B6
Beckway Rd SW16 181 D1
Beckway St SE17 117 C2 263 A3
Beckwith Ho [22] E2 96 B5
Beckwith Rd SE24 161 B6
Beclands Rd SW17 181 A4
Becmead Ave
Harrow HA3 43 B4
Streatham SW16 181 D6
Becondale Rd SE19 183 C5
BECONTREE 81 A4
Becontree Ave RM8 80 C5
Becontree Prim Sch RM8 80 B5
Becontree Sta RM9 80 D2
Bective Pl SW15 135 B1
Bective Rd
Forest Gate E7 77 A4
Putney SW15 135 B1
Becton Pl DA8 147 D5
Bedale Rd EN2 5 A5
Bedale St SE1 252 C3
Beddan Ct HA8 26 C4
BEDDINGTON 220 A6
BEDDINGTON CORNER 203 A2
Beddington Cross CR0 204 A2
Beddington Farm Rd CR0 204 A1
Beddington Gdns SM5, SM6 219 A2
Beddington Gn BR5 189 D2
Beddington Gr SM6 219 D3
Beddington Inf Sch SM6 219 C4
Beddington La
Wallington CR0 203 D2
Wallington CR0 220 A6
Beddington Lane Sta CR0 203 C3
Beddington Manor SM2 218 B2
Beddington Park Cotts SM6 219 D5
Beddington Park Prim Sch CR0 219 D5
Beddington Rd
Ilford IG3 57 D2
St Paul's Cray BR5 189 D2
Beddington Terr CR0 204 B2
Beddington Trad Est CR0 204 A1
Bede Cl HA5 22 D2
Bedefield WC1 233 B1
Bede Ho London SE14 141 B4
[5] Putney SW15 156 D5
Bedelsford Specl Sch KT1 198 A6
Bedens Rd DA14 191 A5
Bede Rd RM6 58 C3
Bedevere Rd N9 18 A1
Bedfont Cl
East Bedfont TW14 149 A5
Mitcham CR4 181 A1
Bedfont Green Cl TW14 149 A3
Bedfont Ind Pk TW15 149 B1
Bedfont Ind Pk N TW15 149 A1
Bedfont Jun & Inf Schs TW14 149 C5
Bedfont La TW14, TW13 149 D4
Bedfont Lakes Ctry Pk TW14 149 A2
Bedfont Rd
East Bedfont TW13, TW14 149 B2
Stanwell TW19 148 B5
Bedford Ave
Barnet EN5 13 B6
Bloomsbury WC1 93 D2 239 D3
Hayes UB4 84 B1
Bedfordbury WC2 116 A6 250 A5
Bedford Cl
Chiswick W4 133 D6
Muswell Hill N10 31 A3
Bedford Cnr [3] W4 111 C2
Bedford Court Mans WC1 239 D3
Bedford Ct
[6] Richmond TW9 132 B1
South Norwood SE19 183 D2
St James WC2 250 A5
Wembley HA0 65 D4
Bedford Gardens Ho W8 245 B3
Bedford Gdns W8 113 C5 245 B3
Bedford Hill SW12 159 B2
Bedford Ho
[2] Acton W4 111 C2
Edgware HA8 26 B3
[7] Stockwell SW4 138 A1
Bedford Mews SE6 163 D2
BEDFORD PARK 111 C3
Bedford Park Cnr [5] W4 111 C2
Bedford Park Mans [4] W4 111 B2
Bedford Pas SW6 264 B4
Bedford Pk CR0 205 A1
Bedford Pl
Bloomsbury WC1 94 A2 240 A4
Croydon CR0 205 B1
Bedford Rd
Acton W4 111 C3
Barking E6 100 C6
Crouch End N8 49 D3
Ealing W13 109 B6
East Finchley N2 48 C6
Edgware NW7 11 C1
Edmonton N9 18 B4
Harrow HA1 42 A3
Ilford IG1 78 D5
North Cheam KT4 216 C6
Ruislip HA4 61 D4
Sidcup DA15 167 C1
South Tottenham N15 51 C5
Stockwell SW2, SW4 138 A1
Twickenham TW2 152 B1
Walthamstow E17 53 C6
Woodford E18 37 A1
Wood Green N22 32 A1
Bedford Row WC1 94 B2 240 D3
Bedford Sq WC1 93 D2 239 D3
Bedford St WC2 116 A6 250 B5
Bedford Terr SM2 218 A2
Bedford Villas [3] SM5 218 D5
Bedford Way WC1 93 D3 239 D5
Bedgebury Gdns SW19 157 A2
Bedgebury Rd SE9 143 D1
Bedivere Rd BR1 165 A1
Bedlam Mews SE11 261 A4
Bedlow Cl NW8 236 D5
Bedlow Way CR0 220 B4
Bedonwell Inf Sch DA17 147 A6
Bedonwell Jun Sch DA17 147 A6
Bedonwell Rd
Bexley DA17 147 A6
Bedonwell Rd *continued*
Erith DA7 147 C5
Bedser Cl
Kennington SE11 270 D6
South Norwood CR7 205 A6
Bedser Ct [7] SW4 138 A3
Bedser Dr UB6 64 B3
Bedster Gdns KT8 195 D6
Bedwardine Rd SE19 183 C3
Bedwell Ct [4] RM6 58 D2
Bedwell Gdns UB3 105 C2
Bedwell Ho [18] SW9 138 C3
Bedwell Rd
Belvedere DA17 125 C1
Tottenham N17 33 C2
Beeby Rd E16 99 B2
Beech Ave Acton W3 111 C5
Brentford TW8 131 B5
[4] Chigwell IG9 21 B2
East Barnet N20 14 C3
Ruislip HA4 40 B1
Sidcup DA15 168 A4
Beech Cl
Ashford TW15 171 B5
Carshalton SM5 218 D6
Deptford SE8 141 B6
Enfield N9 18 B5
Putney SW15 156 A4
Sunbury TW16 172 D1
West Drayton UB7 104 C3
Wimbledon SW19 178 C4
Beech Copse
Bickley BR1 188 B1
South Croydon CR2 221 C3
Beechcroft
Chislehurst West BR7 188 C3
[3] Kingston u T KT2 176 D2
Beechcroft Ave
Golders Green NW11 47 B2
Harrow HA2 41 C2
Kingston u T KT1, KT3 177 A1
Beechcroft Cl
Heston TW5 129 A5
Orpington BR6 227 B4
Streatham SW16 182 B5
Beechcroft Ct
[3] Golders Green NW11 47 B2
Greenwich SE3 143 A4
[8] Woodside Pk N12 29 D6
Beech Croft Ct N5 72 D4
Beechcroft Gdns HA9 66 B5
Beechcroft Ho W5 88 A2
Beechcroft Lo [6] SM2 218 A1
Beechcroft Mans SW16 182 B5
Beechcroft Rd
Chessington KT9 214 B5
Mortlake SW14 133 A2
Orpington BR6 227 B4
Upper Tooting SW17 158 C2
Woodford E18 37 B1
Beechcroft Way N19 49 D1
Beech Ct
Beckenham BR3 185 B3
[3] Buckhurst Hill IG9 21 D2
Child's Hill NW2 69 B6
Hayes UB3 105 D5
[6] Ilford E12 78 C5
Marylebone W1 237 C2
Northolt UB5 85 A6
[43] Notting Hill W2 91 C2
[7] Rotherhithe SE16 119 A5
Surbiton KT6 198 A2
Teddington TW11 175 C4
Walthamstow E17 54 B6
[4] West Norwood SW16 182 C5
Beechdale N21 16 B2
Beechdale Rd SW2 160 B5
Beech Dell BR2, BR6 226 B4
Beechdene [4] SE15 140 B4
Beech Dr N2 48 D6
Beechen Cliff Way [2] TW7 130 D3
Beechengrove HA5 41 B6
Beechen Pl SE23 162 C2
Beeches Ave SM5 218 C1
Beeches Cl SE20 184 C2
Beeches Ct BR1 187 A4
Beeches Prim Ctr The SE2 124 C3
Beeches Rd
Cheam SM3 201 A1
Upper Tooting SW17 158 D1
Beeches The
Ealing W7 108 D4
East Barnet N20 14 C2
East Ham E12 78 B1
Hounslow TW3 129 D4
Mitcham CR4 202 C4
[1] Upper Holloway N19 50 A1
Beechey Ho [30] E1 118 B5
Beech Farm Cotts IG8 36 B3
Beechfield Cotts [5] BR1 187 C1
Beechfield Ct [7] CR2 221 A4
Beechfield Rd
Bromley BR1 187 C1
Forest Hill SE6 163 B3
Harringay N4 51 A3
Beech Gdns
Dagenham RM10 81 D1
Ealing W5 110 A3
Beech Gr
Kingston u T KT3 199 B6
Mitcham CR4 203 D5
Beech Hall Cres E4 36 B3
Beech Hall Rd E4 36 B3
Beech Hill EN4 2 C5
Beech Hill Ave EN4 2 B4
Beechhill Rd SE9 166 C6
Beech Ho Chingford E4 35 C6
Hayes UB4 84 D2
Heston TW5 129 A5
[6] Maitland Pk NW3 70 D2
New Addington CR0 223 D2
[22] Rotherhithe SE16 118 C4
[7] Sidcup DA15 168 A1
[5] Stoke Newington N16 73 B6
[12] Wallington SM6 219 C2
Beech House Rd CR0 221 B5
Beech La IG9 21 B2
Beech Lawns N12 30 B5
Beechmont Cl BR1 186 C5
Beechmore Gdns SM3 216 D6
Beechmore Rd SW11 136 D4 267 D1
Beechmount Ave W7 86 C2
Beecholme [15] N12 29 D6
Beecholme Ave CR4 181 B2
Beecholme Est E5 74 B5
Beecholme Prim Sch CR4 181 B2
Beech Rd
Bowes Pk N11 32 A4
East Bedfont TW14 149 C4
Thornton Heath SW16 204 B6
Beechrow KT2 176 A6
Beech St EC2 95 A2 242 B4
Beech Tree Cl
Islington N1 72 C1
Stanmore HA7 25 C5
Beech Tree Glade E4 20 D3
Beech Tree Pl SM1 217 D3
Beechvale Cl N12 30 C5
Beechway DA5 168 D5
Beech Way
Twickenham TW2 151 C1
Willesden NW10 67 B1
Beech Wlk NW7 27 C4
Beechwood Ave
Ashford TW16 172 A4
East Finchley N3 47 C6
Greenford UB6 85 D4
Harrow HA2 63 D5
Hayes UB3 105 B6
Hillingdon UB8 82 C1
Orpington BR6 227 C2
Richmond TW9 132 C4
Ruislip HA4 61 D6
Thornton Heath CR7 204 D5
Beechwood Circ HA2 63 D5
Beechwood Cl
Edgware NW7 27 C5
Fortis Green N2 48 D5
Surbiton KT6 197 D2
Beechwood Cres DA7 147 A2
Beechwood Ct
Ashford TW16 172 A5
Beechwood Ct *continued*
Carshalton SM5 218 D4
Cheam SM1 217 C3
Chiswick W4 133 B6
Stamford Hill N16 51 C2
Sutton SM2 218 B2
Beechwood Dr
Keston BR2 225 D4
Woodford IG8 36 D5
Beechwood Gdns
Ealing NW10 88 B4
Harrow HA2 63 D5
Ilford IG5 56 C5
Beechwood Gr W3 111 C6
Beechwood Hall N3 47 B6
Beechwood Ho [23] E2 96 A5
Beechwood Mews [2] N9 18 A2
Beechwood Pk E18 55 A6
Beechwood Rd
Dalston E8 73 D2
London N8 50 A5
South Croydon CR2 221 C1
Beechwood Rise BR7 188 D6
Beechwood Sch SW16 160 A1
Beechwoods Ct [5] SE19 183 D5
Beechworth Cl NW3 69 C6
Beecroft La SE4 163 A6
Beecroft Mews SE4 163 A6
Beecroft Rd SE4 163 A6
Beehive Cl Dalston E8 73 D1
Elstree WD6 9 D5
Hillingdon UB10 60 B1
Beehive Ct IG1 56 B3
Beehive La IG1 56 B3
Beehive Pl SW9 138 C2
Beehive Prep Sch IG4 56 B4
Beeken Dene BR6 227 A4
Beeleigh Rd SM4 201 D5
Beeston Cl
[5] Dalston E8 74 A3
South Oxhey WD19 22 D6
Beeston Pl SW1 258 D6
Beeston Rd EN4 14 B5
Beeston's Ho SE15 140 B2
Beeston Way TW14 150 C5
Beethoven Rd WD6 9 D5
Beethoven St W10 91 A4
Beeton Cl HA5 23 C3
Begbie Ho SW9 138 B3
Begbie Rd SE3 143 C4
Beggars Hill KT17 215 D2
Beggar's Roost La SM1 217 C2
Begonia Cl E6 100 B3
Begonia Pl [1] TW12 173 C4
Begonia Wlk W12 89 D1
Beira St SW12 159 B4
Beis Chinuch Lebonos Girls Sch N4 51 A2
Beis Hamedrash Elyon NW11 47 A2
Beis Malka Girls Sch N16 51 D1
Beis Rochel d'Satmar Girls Sch [1] N16 51 C2
Beis Soroh Schneirer (Sch) [4] NW4 46 A3
Beis Yaakov Prim Sch NW9 45 B6
Bekesbourne St [17] E14 97 A1
Belcroft Cl BR1 186 D3
Beldanes Lo NW10 68 A1
Beldham Gdns KT8 195 D6
Belenoyd Ct SW16 160 B1
Belfairs Dr RM6 58 C2
Belfairs Gn WD19 22 D5
Belfast Rd
Croydon SE25 206 B5
Stoke Newington N16 73 D6
Belfield Rd KT19 215 C1
Belfont Wlk N7 72 A4
Belford Gr SE18 122 C2
Belford Ho [7] E8 95 D6
Belfort Rd SE15 140 C3
Belfry Cl [33] SE16 118 B1
Belfry Rd E12 77 D6
Belgrade Ho N16 73 C4
Belgrade Rd
Hampton TW12 173 D2
Stoke Newington N16 73 C4

Belgrave Cl
1 Acton W3 111 A4
Burnt Oak NW7 27 B5
Southgate N14 15 C6
Belgrave Cres TW16 172 B2
Belgrave Ct
8 Acton Green W4 111 A1
Charlton SE3 143 C5
22 Limehouse E14 119 B6
Newham E13 99 C3
Nine Elms SW8 269 A3
Belgrave Gdns
Kilburn NW8 91 D6
Southgate N14 3 D1
1 Stanmore HA7 25 C5
St John's Wood NW8 229 A5
Belgrave Ho SW9 138 C5
Belgrave Hts E11 55 A1
Belgrave Mans NW8 229 A5
Belgrave Market IG1 78 C6
Belgrave Mews N
SW1 248 A1
Belgrave Mews S
SW1 115 A3 258 B6
Belgrave Mews W
SW1 258 A6
Belgrave Pl
SW1 115 A3 258 B5
Belgrave Rd
Barnes SW13 133 D5
Hounslow TW4 129 B2
Leyton E10 54 A1
Mitcham CR4 202 B6
Newham E13 99 C3
Redbridge IG1 56 B1
South Norwood SE25 205 D5
Sunbury TW16 172 B2
Walthamstow E17 53 C3
Wanstead E11 55 A1
Westminster
SW1 115 C2 259 A3
Belgrave Sq
SW1 115 A3 258 A6
Belgrave St E1 96 D1
Belgrave Terr IG8 21 A1
Belgrave Wlk CR4 202 B6
Belgrave Wlk Sta
CR4 202 B5
Belgrave Yd SW1 258 C5
BELGRAVIA 115 B2
Belgravia Cl EN5 1 B2
Belgravia Ct SW1 258 C5
Belgravia Gdns BR1 186 C4
Belgravia Ho
11 London SW4 159 D5
1 Teddington TW11 175 C3
Belgravia Lo N21 16 D6
Belgravia Mews
KT1 197 D5
Belgrove St WC1 233 B2
Belham Wlk 13 SE5 139 B4
Belinda Rd 8 SW9 138 D2
Belitha Villas N1 72 C1
Bel La TW13 151 B1
Bellamy Cl
Edgware HA8 11 A1
13 Millwall E14 119 C4
Uxbridge UB10 60 C5
West Kensington SW5 254 D1
Bellamy Ct HA7 25 B2
Bellamy Dr HA7 25 B2
Bellamy Ho
Harrow HA3 44 A2
Heston TW5 129 C6
Upper Tooting SW17 180 B6
Bellamy Rd
Chingford E4 35 D4
Enfield EN2 5 B3
Bellamy's Ct 16
SE16 118 D5
Bellamy St SW12 159 B4
Bellarmine Cl SE28 123 D4
Bellasis Ave SW2 160 A2
Bell Ave UB7 104 B3
Bell Cl Pinner HA5 40 C6
Ruislip HA4 61 D5
Bellclose Rd UB7 104 A4
Bell Ct Hendon NW4 46 C5
Ladywell SE13 163 C6
Tolworth KT5 214 D6
Bell Dr SW18 157 A4
Bellefields Rd SW9 138 B2
Bellegrove Cl DA16 145 D3
Bellegrove Par
DA16 145 D2
Bellegrove Rd DA16 145 D3
Bellenden Prim Sch 5
SE15 140 A2
Bellenden Rd SE15 139 D3
Bellenden Rd Ret Pk
SE15 140 A4
Bellendon Road Bsns Ctr
SE15 139 D3
Bellerbys Coll SE8 141 C6
Belle Staines Pleasaunce
E4 19 C2
Belleville Prim Sch
SW11 158 D6
Belleville Rd SW11 158 D6
Belle Vue UB6 86 B6
Belle Vue Gdns SW9 138 A3
Belle Vue La WD23 8 B3
Bellevue Mews N11 31 A5
Bellevue Pk CR7 205 A5
Bellevue Pl E1 96 C3
Bellevue Rd
Barnes SW13 134 A3
Bexley DA6 169 B6
Ealing W13 87 B3
Friern Barnet N11 31 A5
Kingston u T KT1 198 A6
Upper Tooting SW17 158 D3
Belle Vue Rd
Chingford E17 36 B1
8 Hendon NW4 46 C5
Bellew St SW17 158 A1
Bellfield CR0 223 B1
Bellfield Ave HA3 24 B4
Bellfield Cl SE3 143 B5
Bell Flats 4 NW2 68 A2
Bellflower Cl 2 E6 100 A2
Bellflower Ct SE13 141 D1
Bellgate Mews NW5 71 B5
Bell Gn SE26 185 B6
Bellgrave Lo 9 W4 110 D1
BELL GREEN 163 B1
Bell Green La SE26 185 B6
Bell Ho
6 Dagenham RM10 81 D2
Greenwich SE10 142 A6
15 Streatham SW2 160 C4
Wembley HA9 66 A5
West Heath SE2 124 D1
Bellina Mews NW5 71 C4
Bell Ind Est 2 W4 111 A2
BELLINGHAM 185 C5
Bellingham 10 N17 34 B3
Bellingham Ct IG11 102 B4
Bellingham Gn SE6 163 C1
Bellingham L Ctr
SE6 163 D1
Bellingham Rd SE6 164 A1
Bellingham Sta SE6 163 D1
Bellingham Trad Est
SE6 163 D2
Bell Inn Yd EC3 242 D1
Bell La Enfield EN3 6 D5
Hendon NW4 46 D5
Newham E16 121 A5
Spitalfields E1 95 D2 243 C3
Twickenham TW1 153 A3
Wembley HA9 65 D6
Bell Lane Prim Sch 7
NW4 46 D5
Bell Language Sch
W1 93 C3 239 A5
Bellmaker Ct 13 E3 97 C2
Bell Mdw SE19 183 C6
Bell Moor NW3 70 A5
Bellmore Ct 5 CR0 205 D1
Bello Cl SE24, SW2 160 D3
Bellot Gdns 1 SE10 120 C1
Bellot St SE10 120 C1
Bell Rd
East Molesey KT8 196 B4
Enfield EN1 5 B4
Hounslow TW3 129 D1
Bellring Cl DA17 147 C6
Bell's Coll IG3 58 A1
Bells Hill EN5 12 D6
Bell St
Kidbrooke SE18 144 A4
Paddington
NW1 92 C2 237 A4
Bell The E17 53 C6
Bell View BR3 185 B3
Bellview Ct 1 TW3 129 D1
Bell View Manor HA4 39 C2
Bell Water Gate
SE18 122 C3
Bell Wharf La EC4 252 B6
Bellwood Rd SE15 140 D1
Bell Yard Mews SE1 253 B1
Bell Yd WC2 94 C1 241 A1
BELMONT 25 B2
Belmont Ave
Bowes Pk N13 32 B5
Cockfosters EN4 14 D6
Edmonton N9 18 A3
Falconwood DA16 145 C2
Southall UB2 107 A3
Tottenham N17 51 A6
Wembley HA0 88 B6
West Barnes KT3 200 A5
Belmont Circ HA3 25 B2
Belmont Cl
Chingford E4 36 B5
Clapham SW4 137 C2
Cockfosters EN4 2 D1
Totteridge N20 13 D3
Uxbridge UB8 60 A2
Woodford IG8 37 B6
Belmont Ct
Highbury N5 73 A4
6 Stamford Hill N16 51 C1
Temple Fortune NW11 47 B4
1 Whetstone N20 14 A1
Wood Green N11 31 D3
Belmont Fst & Mid Schs
HA3 24 D1
Belmont Gr
Chiswick W4 111 B2
Lewisham SE13 142 B2
Belmont Hall Ct
SE13 142 B2
Belmont Hill SE13 142 B2
Belmont Jun & Inf Sch
N22 51 A6
Belmont La
Chislehurst BR7 189 A5
Stanmore HA7 25 C3
Belmont Lo
Harrow HA3 24 B3
Stanmore HA7 25 C6
Belmont Mews
SW19 156 D2
Belmont (Mill Hill Prep Sch) NW7 12 A1
Belmont Par
Chislehurst BR7 189 A5
2 Temple Fortune
NW11 47 B4
Belmont Park Cl
SE13 142 C1
Belmont Park Rd E10 53 D3
Belmont Pk SE13 142 C1
Belmont Pk Sch E10 54 A3
Belmont Prim Sch
10 Chiswick W4 111 B2
Erith DA8 147 C5
Belmont Rd
Beckenham BR3 185 B1
Chislehurst BR7 188 D5
Clapham SW4 137 C2
Croydon SE25 206 B4
Erith DA8 147 D4
Harrow HA3 43 A6
Ilford IG1 79 A5
London W4 111 B2
Twickenham TW2 152 B2
Uxbridge UB8 60 A2
Wallington SM6 219 C3
West Green N15, N17 51 A5
Belmont Rise SM1,
SM2 217 B1
Belmont St NW1 71 A1
Belmont Terr W4 111 B2
Belmor WD6 10 C5
Belmore Ave UB4 84 A1
Belmore Ho N7 71 D3
Belmore La N7 71 D3
Belmore Prim Sch
UB4 84 B4
Belmore St
SW8 137 D4 269 C2
Beloe Cl SW15 134 A1
Belper Ct 11 E5 74 D4
Belsham St E9 74 C2
Belsize Ave
Bowes Pk N13 32 B4
Ealing W13 109 B3
Maitland Pk NW3 70 C3
Belsize Court Garages 1
NW3 70 B3
Belsize Cres NW3 70 B2
Belsize Ct NW3 70 B3
Belsize Gdns SM1 217 D4
Belsize Gr NW3 70 C2
Belsize La NW3 70 B3
Belsize Mews NW3 70 B2
Belsize Park Gdns
NW3 70 C2
Belsize Park Mews 1
NW3 70 B2
Belsize Park Sta NW3 70 C3
Belsize Pk NW3 70 B2
Belsize Pl NW3 70 B3
Belsize Rd
Harrow HA3 24 B3
Kilburn NW6 91 D6
Belsize Sq NW3 70 B2
Belsize Terr NW3 70 B2
Belson Rd SE18 122 B2
Beltane Dr SW19 156 D1
Belthorn Cres SW12 159 C4
Belton Rd Leyton E11 76 C4
Sidcup DA14 190 A6
Tottenham N17 51 C6
Upton E7 77 B1
Willesden NW2 68 A2
Belton Way E3 97 C2
Beltran Rd SW6 135 D3
BELVEDERE 125 D2
Belvedere Ave
SW19 179 A5
Belvedere Bldgs SE1 251 D1
Belvedere Cl TW11 174 C5
Belvedere Ct
Abbey Wood DA17 125 B3
Brondesbury NW2 68 D2
7 Clapham Pk SW4 159 D5
East Finchley N2 48 B4
8 Kingston u T KT2 176 C3
Putney SW15 134 C1
33 Shoreditch N1 95 C6
Southall UB1 107 D6
Southgate N21 16 C4
Belvedere Dr SW19 179 A5
Belvedere Gdns KT8 195 C4
Belvedere Gr SW19 179 A5
Belvedere Ho TW14 150 A3
Belvedere Htss NW8 237 A6
Belvedere Jun & Inf Sch
DA17 125 D3
Belvedere Mews
Greenwich SE3 143 B5
Nunhead SE15 140 C2
Belvedere Pl
Brixton SW2 138 B1
Lambeth SE1 251 D1
Belvedere Rd
Bexleyheath DA7 147 B3
Erith SE2, SE28 124 D5
Hanwell W7 108 D3
Lambeth SE1 116 B5 250 D3
Penge SE19 183 D3
Walthamstow E10 53 A1
Belvedere Sq SW19 179 A5
Belvedere Sta DA17 125 D3
Belvedere Strand
NW9 27 D1
Belvedere The SW10 266 B1
Belvedere Way HA3 44 A3
Belvoir Cl SE9 166 A1
Belvoir Ct HA3 43 A3
Belvoir Lo SE22 162 A4
Belvoir Rd SE22 162 A4
Belvue Bsns Ctr UB5 63 D1
Belvue Cl UB5 63 C1
Belvue Rd UB5 63 C1
Belvue Sch UB5 85 C6
Bembridge Cl NW6 69 A1
Bembridge Gdns HA4 61 B6
Bembridge Ho
9 Deptford SE8 119 B2
Wandsworth SW18 157 D5
Bemersyde Point 6
E13 99 B4
Bemerton St
N1 94 B6 233 C6
Bemish Rd SW15 134 D2
Bempton Dr HA4 62 B5
Bemsted Rd E17 53 B6
Benabo Ct 6 E8 74 A3
Benares Rd SE18,
SE2 123 D2
Benbow Ct W6 112 B3
Benbow Ho 12 SE8 141 C6
Benbow Rd W6 112 B3
Benbow St SE8 141 C6
Benbury Cl BR1 186 A5
Bence Ho 13 SE8 119 A2
Bench Field CR2 221 D3
Bencroft Rd SW16 181 C3
Bencurtis Pk BR4 224 B6
Bendall Mews NW1 237 B4
Bendemeer Rd
SW15 134 D2
Benden Ho SE13 164 A6
Bendish Point SE28 123 A4
Bendish Rd E6 78 A1
Bendmore Ave SE2 124 A2
Bendon Valley
SW18 157 D4
Benedict Cl
9 Erith DA17 125 A3
Orpington BR6 227 C5
Benedict Ct
Dagenham RM9 59 B3
Pinner HA5 23 B2
Benedict Dr TW14 149 B4
Benedict House Sch 15
DA15 168 A1
Benedict Prim Sch
CR4 202 B6
Benedict Rd
London SW9 138 B2
Mitcham CR4 202 B6
Benedict Way N2 48 A6
Benedict Wharf CR4 202 C6
Benenden Gn BR2 209 A4
Benenden Ho SE17 263 B2
Benett Gdns SW16 182 A1
Beney Ct BR3 185 C1
Ben Ezra Ct SE17 262 B3
Benfleet Cl SM1 218 A5
Benfleet Ct 6 E8 95 D6
Benfleet Way N11 15 A2
Bengal Ct EC3 242 D1
Bengal Ho E1 96 D2
Bengal Rd IG1 78 D5
Bengarth Dr HA3 24 B1
Bengarth Rd UB5 85 A6
Bengeo Gdns RM6 58 C3
Bengeworth Rd
Camberwell SE5 139 A2
Harrow HA1 65 A5
Ben Hale Cl HA7 25 B5
Benham Cl KT9 213 C2
Benham Gdns TW3,
TW4 151 B6
Benham Ho SW10 265 D4
Benham Rd W7 86 C2
Benham's Pl 11 NW3 70 A4
Benhill Ave SM1 218 A4
Benhill Rd
London SE5 139 B4
Sutton SM1 218 B4
Benhill Wood Rd
SM1 218 A4
BENHILTON 218 A5
Benhilton Ct SM1 218 A5
Benhilton Gdns
SM1 217 D5
Benhurst Ct
Ealing W5 110 A6
12 Penge SE20 184 B2
West Norwood SW16 182 C5
Benhurst La SW16 182 C5
Benington Ct N4 73 A6
Benin St SE13 164 B4
Benjafield Cl N18 34 B6
Benjamin Cl E8 96 A6
Benjamin Ct
4 Ealing W7 108 C5
4 Erith DA17 147 B6
Littleton TW15 171 A3
Benjamin Franklin House ★ SW1 250 A4
Benjamin Ho 12 W3 110 D5
Benjamin Mews
SW12 159 C4
Benjamin St EC1 241 C4
Ben Jonson Ct 30 N1 95 C5
Ben Jonson Prim Sch
E1 97 A3
Ben Jonson Rd E1 97 A2
Benledi Rd E14 98 B1
Bennelong Cl W12 90 B1
Bennerley Rd SW11 158 D6
Bennet Cl KT1 175 C2
Bennets Ct SW19 180 A2
Bennetsfield Rd
UB11 104 D5
Bennet's Hill EC4 251 D6
Bennets Lo EN2 5 A2

Bennett Cl
Twickenham TW4 151 A6
Welling DA16 146 A3
Bennett Ct
Hampstead NW6 69 D2
Lower Holloway N7 72 B5
7 South Acton W3 110 D4
Bennett Gr SE13 141 D4
Bennett Ho
2 Streatham SW4 159 D4
Westminster SW1 259 D4
Bennett Pk SE3 142 D2
Bennett Rd
Brixton SW9 138 C3
Dagenham RM6 59 A2
Newham E13 99 C3
Bennetts Ave
Croydon CR0 223 A6
Greenford UB6 86 C6
Bennett's Castle La
RM8 80 D5
Bennetts Cl
Mitcham CR4, SW16 181 B2
Tottenham N17 33 D4
Bennetts Copse BR7 188 A4
Bennett St
Chiswick W4 111 C1
St James SW1 249 A4
Bennetts Way CR0 223 B6
Bennett's Yd SW1 259 D5
Benn Ho
Bethnal Green E2 96 A4
7 Greenwich SE7 121 C1
Benningholme Rd
HA8 27 C4
Bennington Rd
Chingford IG8 36 C3
Tottenham N17 33 C2
Benn St E9 75 A2
Benns Wlk 8 TW9 132 A1
Bensbury Cl SW15 156 C4
Bensham Cl CR7 205 A5
Bensham Gr CR7 183 A1
Bensham La CR0,
CR7 204 D3
Bensham Manor Rd
CR7 205 A5
Bensham Manor Specl
Sch CR7 205 A4
Bensington Ct TW14 149 B5
Bensley Cl 7 N11 30 D5
Ben Smith Way 21
SE16 118 A3
Benson Ave E13, E6 99 D5
Benson Cl
Hillingdon UB8 82 A2
Hounslow TW3 129 C1
Benson Ct
Holdbrook EN3 7 C5
South Lambeth SW8 270 A2
1 Tufnell Pk N19 71 C4
Benson Ho
Lambeth SE1 251 B3
1 Richmond TW10 153 C1
Shoreditch E2 243 C6
Benson Prim sch
CR0 223 A5
Benson Quay E1 118 C6
Benson Rd
Croydon CR0 220 C5
Forest Hill SE23 162 C3
Bentall Sh Ctr The 10
KT1 176 A1
Bentfield Gdns SE9 165 D1
Benthal Ct N16 74 A5
Benthal Prim Sch
N16 74 A5
Benthal Rd N16 74 A5
Bentham Ct 11 N1 73 A1
Bentham Ho SE1 262 C6
Bentham Rd
Homerton E9 74 D2
Woolwich SE28 124 B5
Bentham Wlk NW10 67 A3
Ben Tillet Cl E16 122 B5
Ben Tillet Ho N15 50 D6
Bentinck Cl NW8 230 B3
Bentinck Ho
4 Richmond TW10 153 C1
4 Shepherd's Bush
W12 112 B6
Bentinck Mans W1 238 B2
Bentinck Mews W1 238 B2
Bentinck Rd UB7 104 A5
Bentinck St
W1 93 A1 238 B2
Bentley Cl SW19 157 C1
Bentley Ct SE13 142 A1
Bentley Dr
Child's Hill NW2 69 B5
Ilford IG2 57 A3
Bentley Ho 6 Bow E3 97 C3
4 Camberwell SE5 139 C4
Bentley Lo WD23 8 C2
Bentley Mews EN1 17 B5
Bentley Rd N1 73 C2
Bentley Way
Stanmore HA7 25 A5
Woodford IG8 21 A1
Bentley Wood Girls Sch
HA7 24 D5
Benton Rd
Ilford IG1, IG2 57 B1
South Oxhey WD19 22 D5
Benton's La SE27 183 A6
Benton's Rise SE27 183 B5
Bentry Cl RM8 81 A6
Bentry Rd RM8 81 B6
Bentworth Ct 1 E2 96 A3
Bentworth Prim Sch
W12 90 B1
Bentworth Rd W12 90 B1
Ben Uri Gall* NW8 91 D6
Benwell Ct TW16 172 A2
Benwell Rd N7 72 C3
Benwick Cl SE16 118 B2
Benwick Ct SE20 184 C2
Benwood Ct SM1 218 A5
Benworth St E3 97 B4
Benyon Ho EC1 234 B2
Benyon Rd N1 95 B6 235 D6
Benyon Wharf 31 E8 95 C6
Beormund Sch
SE1 117 B4 252 D1
Bequerel Ct SE10 120 D3
Berberis Ct IG1 78 D2
Berberis Ho 17 E3 97 C2
Berberis Wlk UB7 104 A2
Berber Par 8 SE18 144 A4
Berber Pl 2 E14 119 C6
Berber Rd SW11 158 D6
Berberry Cl 5 HA8 27 A6
Bercta Rd SE9 167 A2
Berebinder Ho 21 E3 97 B5
Berengers Pl RM9 80 B2
Berenger Twr SW10 266 C4
Berenger Wlk SW10 266 C4
Berens Ct DA14 189 D6
Berens Rd NW10 90 D4
Berens Way BR5,
BR7 211 D6
Beresford Ave
Ealing W7 86 C2
Friern Barnet N20 14 D2
Tolworth KT5 199 A2
Twickenham TW1 153 C5
Wembley HA0 88 C6
Beresford Ct
Homerton E9 75 A3
11 Twickenham TW1 153 C5
Beresford Dr
Bickley BR1 210 A6
Woodford IG8 37 C6
Beresford Gdns
Dagenham RM6 59 A4
Enfield EN1 5 C1
Hounslow TW4 151 B6
Beresford Ho
Dulwich SE21 161 C1
15 Stockwell SW4 138 A1
Beresford Lo N4 73 B3
Beresford Rd
Belmont SM2 217 B1
Canonbury N5 73 B3
Chingford E4 20 C3
East Finchley N2 48 C6
Harringay N8 50 D4
Harrow HA1 42 B4
Kingston u T KT2 176 B2
New Malden KT3 199 A5
Southall UB1 106 D5
Walthamstow E17 35 D2
Beresford Sq 1
SE18 122 D2
Beresford Square Mkt
SE18 122 D2
Beresford Terr 3 N5 73 A3
Bere St E1 118 D6
Berestede Rd 4
W6 111 D1
Bergen Ho 1 SE5 139 A3
Bergenia Ho 1
TW13 150 B3
Bergen Sq SE16 119 A3
Berger Cl BR5 211 C3
Berger Prim Sch 30
E9 74 D2
Berger Rd E9 74 D2
Berghem Mews
W14 112 D3
Bergholt Ave IG4 56 A4
Bergholt Cres N16 51 C2
Bergholt Mews 4
NW1 71 D1
Berglen Ct E14 119 A6
Berica Ct IG6 57 A6
Bering Sq E14 119 C1
Bering Wlk E16 99 D1
Berisford Mews
SW18 158 A5
Berkeley Ave
Cranford TW4 128 A3
Erith DA16 146 D4
Northolt UB6 64 C2
Berkeley Cl
Borehamwood WD6 10 C6
Broom Hill BR5 211 C2
2 Kingston u T KT2 176 A3
Ruislip HA4 62 A5
Berkeley Cres EN4 14 B6
Berkeley Ct
Ealing W5 109 C6
Edgware HA8 26 D5
Finchley N3 29 D2
1 Golders Green
NW11 47 B2
Marylebone NW1 237 D5
Southgate N14 15 C5
Wallington SM6 219 C4
Willesden NW10 67 C4
Berkeley Dr KT8 195 C6
Berkeley Gdns
Claygate KT10 213 A2
Kensington W8 245 B3
Southgate N21 17 B4
Walton-on-T KT12 193 D2
Berkeley Ho
17 Bow E3 97 C4
11 Brentford TW8 131 D6
8 Deptford SE8 119 B1
Berkeley Lo Enfield EN2 4 C2
New Malden KT3 199 C5
Berkeley Mews
Marylebone W1 237 D1
Sunbury TW16 194 C6
Berkeley Pl SW19 178 D4
Berkeley Prim Sch
TW5 128 D5
Berkeley Rd
Barnes SW13 134 A4
Crouch End N8 49 D3
Hillingdon UB10 61 A1
Manor Pk E12 78 A3
Queensbury NW9 44 C4
Stamford Hill N15 51 B3
Berkeley Sq
W1 115 B6 248 D5
Berkeley St
W1 115 B5 248 D4
Berkeleys The SE25 206 A5
Berkeley The NW11 47 D2
Berkeley Waye TW5 128 D5
Berkeley Wlk 1 N7 72 B6
Berkhampstead Rd
DA17 125 C1
Berkhamsted Ave
HA9 66 C2
Berkley Cl TW2 152 C1
Berkley Ct 8 TW1 153 A4
Berkley Gr NW1 71 A1
Berkley Rd NW1 70 D1
Berkshire Ct 1 W7 86 D3
Berkshire Gdns
Bowes Pk N13 32 C4
Upper Edmonton N18 34 B5
Berkshire Ho
Catford SE6 185 C6
St Giles WC2 240 A2
Berkshire Rd E9 75 B2
Berkshire Way CR4 204 A5
Bermans Way NW10 67 D4
BERMONDSEY 118 A4
Bermondsey Leather Mkt
SE1 253 A1
Bermondsey Sq SE1 263 B6
Bermondsey St
SE1 117 C4 253 A1
Bermondsey Sta
SE16 118 B3
Bermondsey Trad Est
SE16 118 C1
Bermondsey Wall E
SE16 118 B4
Bermondsey Wall W SE1,
SE16 118 A4
Bermuda Ho HA1 64 B5
Bernal Cl SE28 124 D6
Bernard Angell Ho 4
SE10 142 B6
Bernard Ashley Dr
SE7 121 B1
Bernard Ave W13 109 B3
Bernard Cassidy St 2
E16 98 D2
Bernard Gdns SW19 179 B5
Bernard Ho E1 243 C3
Bernard Rd
South Tottenham
N15 51 D4
Wallington SM5, SM6 219 B4
Bernard Shaw Ct 5
NW1 71 C1
Bernard Shaw Ho 2
NW10 89 B6
Bernard St
WC1 94 A3 240 B5
Bernays Cl HA7 25 C4
Bernay's Gr SW9 138 B1
Bernel Dr CR0 223 B5
Berne Rd CR7 205 A4
Berners Dr W13 109 A6
Berners Ho N1 234 A4
Bernersmede SE3 143 A2
Berners Mews
W1 93 C2 239 B3
Berners Pl W1 239 B2
Berners Rd
Islington N1 234 C5
Wood Green N22 32 C1
Berners St W1 93 C1 239 B2
Berner Terr 27 E1 96 A1
Berney Ho BR3 207 A4
Berney Rd CR0 205 B2
Bernhard Baron Ho 23
E1 96 A1
Bernhardt Cres NW8 237 A6
Bernhart Cl HA8 27 A3
Bernie Grant Ho 40
E9 74 C1
Bernwell Rd E4 20 C1
Bernwood Ho 6 N4 51 B2
Berridge Gn HA8 26 C3
Berridge Mews NW6 69 C3
Berridge Rd SE19 183 C5
Berriman Rd N7 72 B5
Berrite Works UB7 104 C4
Berriton Rd HA2 41 B1
Berrybank Cl 4 E4 20 A2
Berry Cl
Dagenham RM10 81 C3
Southgate N21 16 D3
Berry Cotts 2 E14 97 A1
Berry Ct TW4 151 B6
Berrydale Rd UB4 85 A3
Berryfield Cl BR1 188 A1
Berry Field Cl 8 E17 53 D5
Berryfield Rd
SE17 116 D1 261 D2
Berryhill SE9 144 D1
Berry Hill HA7 25 D6
Berryhill Gdns SE9 144 D1
Berry Ho
10 Battersea SW11 136 D3
25 Bethnal Green E1 96 B3
Berry La SE21 183 B6
BERRYLANDS 198 C3
Berrylands
Surbiton KT5 198 C3
West Barnes SW20 200 C5
Berrylands Ct 16
SM2 217 D1
Berrylands Rd KT5 198 B3
Berrylands Sta KT5 198 D5
Berryman Cl RM8 80 C5
Berryman's La SE26 184 D6
Berrymead Gdns
W3 111 A4
Berrymede Inf Sch
W3 110 D4
Berrymede Jun Sch
W3 110 D4
Berrymede Rd W4 111 B3
Berry Pl EC1 234 D1
Berry St EC1 241 D5
Berry Way W5 110 A3
Bertal Rd SW17 180 B6
Bertha Hollamby Ct
DA14 190 C5
Bertha James Ct
BR2 209 B5
Bertha Neubergh Ho 1
SE5 139 A4
Berthan Gdns E17 54 B4
Berthon St SE8 141 C6
Bertie Rd
Penge SE26 184 D4
Willesden NW10 68 A2
Bertram Cotts SW19 179 C3
Bertram Rd Enfield EN1 6 A1
Hendon NW4 46 A3
Kingston u T KT2 176 C3
Bertram St N19 71 B6
Bertrand Ho 11
SW16 160 A1
Bertrand St SE13 141 D2
Bertrand Way SE28 124 C6
Bert Rd CR7 205 A4
Bert Reilly Ho 1
SE18 123 B1
Bertrum House Sch
SW17 159 A2
Bert Way EN1 5 D1
Berwick Ave UB4 106 D6
Berwick Cl
Harrow HA7 24 D4
Twickenham TW2 151 C3
Berwick Cres DA15 167 C5
Berwick Ct 8 BR3 185 C2
Berwick Gdns SM1 218 A5
Berwick Ho 10 N2 30 B1
Berwick Rd
Newham E16 99 C1
Tottenham N22 32 D2
Welling DA16 146 B4
Berwick St
W1 93 C1 239 B1
Berwick Street Mkt*
W1 93 C1 239 B1
Berwyn Ave TW3 129 D4
Berwyn Ho 3 N16 51 D1
Berwyn Rd
Mortlake SW14,
TW10 132 D1
Streatham SE24 160 D3
Beryl Ave E6 100 A2
Beryl Harding Ho 3
SW19 178 D3
Beryl Ho SE18 123 D1
Beryl Rd W6 112 D1
Berystede KT2 176 D3
Besant Cl NW2 69 A5
Besant Ct
Canonbury N1 73 B3
15 Thamesmead
SE28 124 B6
Besant Ho NW8 229 A5
Besant Pl SE22 139 D1
Besant Rd NW2 69 A4
Besant Way NW10 67 A3
Besant Wlk N7 72 B6
Besford Ho 26 E2 96 A5
Besley St SW16 181 C4
Bessant Dr TW9 132 D4
Bessborough Gdns
SW1 115 D1 259 D2
Bessborough Pl
SW1 115 D1 259 D2
Bessborough Rd
Harrow HA1 42 B1
Roehampton SW15 156 A3
Bessborough St
SW1 115 D1 259 C2
Bessborough Wks
KT8 195 B4
Bessemer Ct 7 NW1 71 C1
Bessemer Grange Prim
Sch SE5 139 C1
Bessemer Park Ind Est
3 SE24 138 D1
Bessemer Rd SE5 139 A3
Bessie Lansbury Cl
E6 100 C1
Bessingby Rd HA4 62 B6
Bessingham Wlk
SE4 162 D6

Besson St SE14 140 D4
Bessy St E2 96 C4
Bestwood St SE8 118 D2
Beswick Mews 1 NW6 69 D2
Betam Rd UB3 105 B4
Beta Pl 20 SW4 138 B1
Betchworth Cl SM1 218 B3
Betchworth Ho 8 N7 71 D3
Betchworth Rd IG3 79 C5
Betham Rd UB6 86 B4
Bethany Ct 8 DA6 147 A1
Bethany Waye TW14 149 C4
Bethecar Rd HA1 42 C4
Bethel Cl NW4 46 D4
Bethell Ave Ilford IG1 56 C2
Newham E13, E16 98 D3
Bethel Lo N11 31 C5
Bethel Rd DA16 146 C2
Bethersden Cl BR3 185 B3
Bethersden Ho SE17 263 B2
Bethesda Ct 5 SE20 184 C3
Beth Jacob Gram Sch 6 NW4 46 D5
Bethlehem Ho 13 E14 119 B6
Bethlem Royal Hospl BR3 207 C2
BETHNAL GREEN 96 B4
Bethnal Green Rd
Bethnal Green E2 96 A4
Shoreditch E1, E2 95 D3 243 D6
Bethnal Green Sta
Bethnal Green E1 96 B3
Bethnal Green E2 96 C4
Bethnal Green Tech Coll 49 E2 95 D4
Beths Gram Sch DA5 169 D5
Bethune Ave N11 30 D6
Bethune Rd
North Acton NW10 89 B3
Stamford Hill N16 51 C2
Bethwin Rd SE5 139 A5
Betjeman Cl HA5 41 C5
Betjeman Ct EN4 15 A6
Betony Cl CR0 206 D1
Betoyne Ave E4 36 C6
Betsham Ho SE1 252 C2
Betspath Ho 6 N11 31 C5
Betstyle Circus N11 31 B6
Betstyle Ho 2 N10 31 A3
Betstyle Rd N11 31 B6
Betterton Dr DA14 169 A2
Betterton Ho WC2 240 B1
Betterton St WC2 94 A1 240 B1
Bettons Pk E15 98 C6
Bettridge Rd SW6 135 B3
Betts Cl BR3 185 A1
Betts Ho E1 118 B6
Betts Mews E17 53 B3
Betts Rd E16 121 B6
Betts St E1 118 B6
Betts Way
Long Ditton KT6 197 B1
Penge SE20 184 B2
Bettswood Ct 15 SE20 184 B2
Betty Brooks Ho E11 76 B5
Betty Layward Prim Sch 1 N16 73 B5
Betty May Gray Ho 2 E14 120 A2
Beulah Ave CR7 183 A1
Beulah Cl HA8 10 D1
Beulah Cres CR7 183 A1
Beulah Gr CR0 205 A3
Beulah Hill SE19 183 A3
Beulah Inf Sch 2 CR7 205 A6
Beulah Jun Sch 1 CR7 205 A6
Beulah Rd
Merton SW19 179 B3
South Norwood CR7 205 A6
Sutton SM1 217 C4
Walthamstow E17 53 D4
Beuleigh Ct E17 54 B4
Bevan Ave IG11 80 A1
Bevan Ct
Croydon CR0 220 C3
10 Twickenham TW1 153 D5
Bevan Ho IG11 80 B1
Bevan Rd
Cockfosters EN4 2 D1
Plumstead Comm SE2 124 B1
Bevan St N1 95 A6 235 B5
Bev Callender Cl 4 SW8 137 B2
Bevenden St N1 95 B4 235 D2
Bevercote Wlk 1 DA17 147 B6
Beveridge Ct
Southgate N21 16 A6
1 Thamesmead SE28 124 B6
Beveridge Rd 1 NW10 67 C1
Beverley DA14 190 A5
Beverley Ave
Hounslow TW4 129 B1
Sidcup DA15 167 D4
Wimbledon SW20 177 D2
Beverley Cl
Barnes SW13 134 A3
Chessington KT9 213 C4
Edmonton N21 17 A3
Enfield EN1 5 C1
6 Wandsworth SW11 136 B1
Beverley Cotts SW15 155 C1
Beverley Cres IG8 37 B2
Beverley Ct
9 Acton Green W4 111 A1
5 Acton W12 111 C4
Brockley SE4 141 B2
6 Cheam SM2 217 C2
Chingford Hatch E4 35 B6
Fortis Green N2 48 D5
Harrow HA2 42 B6
Hounslow TW4 129 B1
Islington N5 72 D2
Northolt UB5 84 C5
Oakleigh Pk N20 14 A4
Oakwood N14 15 C4
Sidcup DA14 190 B6
Wimbledon SW20 177 D2
Beverley Dr HA8 44 C6
Beverley Gdns
Barnes SW13 133 D2
Hendon NW11 47 A2
2 New Malden KT4 200 A1
Stanmore HA7 25 A2
Wembley HA9 44 C1
Beverley Ho 5 BR1 186 B5
Beverley Hyrst 10 CR0 221 D6
Beverley La KT2 177 C3
Beverley Lo 6 TW10 154 A6
Beverley Mans TW4 129 B1
Beverley Path 9 SW13 133 D3
Beverley Rd
Barnes SW13 133 D2
Chingford E4 36 B4
Chiswick W4 111 D1
Dagenham RM9 81 A4
Keston Mark BR2 226 A6
Mitcham CR4 203 D5
Newham E6 99 D4
North Cheam KT4 216 C6
Penge SE20 184 B1
Ruislip HA4 62 B6
Southall UB2 107 A3
Sunbury TW16 171 D2
Teddington KT1 175 C2
West Barnes KT3 200 A5
Beverley Trad Est SM4 200 D2
Beverley Way KT3, SW20, KT2 177 D2
Beverley Way (Kingston By-Pass) KT3, SW20 200 A6
Beverly Ct HA3 43 C5
Beversbrook Rd N19 71 D5
Beverstone Rd
London SW2 160 B6
Thornton Heath CR7 204 D5
Beverston Mews NW1 237 C3
Bevill Allen Cl SW17 180 D5
Bevill Cl SE25 206 A6
Bevin Cl SE16 119 A5
Bevin Ct WC1 233 D2
Bevington Prim Sch 15 W10 91 A2
Bevington Rd
Beckenham BR3 185 D1
Kensal Town W10 91 A2
Bevington St SE16 118 A4
Bevin Ho
35 Bethnal Green E2 96 C4
8 Bow E3 97 C4
Bevin Rd UB4 84 B4
Bevin Sq SW17 158 D1
Bevin Way WC1 234 A2
Bevis Marks EC3 95 C1 243 B2
Bewcastle Gdns EN2 4 A1
Bew Ct SE21 162 A4
Bewdley Ho N4 51 A2
Bewdley St N1 72 C1
Bewick Mews SE15 140 B5
Bewick St SW8 137 B3
Bewley Ct SW2 160 B5
Bewley Ho 7 E1 118 B6
Bewley St Stepney E1 118 B6
Wimbledon SW19 180 A4
Bewlys Rd SE27 182 D5
Bexhill Cl TW13 151 A2
Bexhill Rd
Catford SE4 163 B5
Mortlake SW14 133 A2
Wood Green N11 31 D5
Bexhill Wlk 6 E15 98 C6
BEXLEY 146 B1
Bexley Coll (Erith Rd Campus) DA17 125 D1
Bexley Gdns
Edmonton N9 17 B1
Ilford RM6 58 B4
Bexley Gram Sch DA16 146 B1
BEXLEYHEATH 147 B2
Bexleyheath Sch DA8 147 C2
Bexleyheath Sta DA7 147 A3
Bexley High St DA5 169 D3
Bexley Ho SE4 141 A1
Bexley La DA14 168 C1
Bexley Rd SE9 167 A6
Bexley Sta DA5 169 C3
Beynon Rd SM5 218 D3
BFI Imax (Cinema) SE1 116 C5 251 A3
BFI Southbank★ SE1 250 D4
Bglws The SM6 219 B3
Bianca Rd SE1, SE15 140 A6
Bibsworth Lo N3 29 B1
Bibsworth Rd N3 29 B1
Bicester Rd TW9 132 D2
Bickenhall Mans W1 237 D4
Bickenhall St W1 92 D2 237 D4
Bickersteth Rd SW17 180 D4
Bickerton Rd N19 71 C6
BICKLEY 188 B1
Bickley Cres BR1 210 A5
Bickley Ct
10 Merton SW19 179 C3
1 Stanmore HA7 25 C6
Bickley Park Rd BR1, BR7 210 B6
Bickley Pk Pre Prep Sch BR1 209 D6
Bickley Pk Prep Sch BR1 209 D6
Bickley Prim Sch BR1 209 C6
Bickley Rd
Bromley BR1 187 D1
Leyton E10 53 D2
Bickley St SW17 180 D5
Bickley Sta BR1 210 A6
Bicknell Ho 34 E1 96 A1
Bicknell Rd SE5 139 A2
Bicknoller Rd EN1 5 D4
Bicknor Ho 2 E5 74 B3
Bicknor Rd BR6 211 D2
Bidborough Cl 3 BR2 208 D4
Bidborough St N1, WC1 94 A4 233 A1
Biddenden Way SE9 188 C6
Biddenham Ho 18 SE16 118 D2
Bidder St E16 98 C2
Biddesden Ho SW3 257 C3
Biddestone Rd N7 72 B4
Biddulph Ho 22 SE18 122 B2
Biddulph Mans W9 91 D4
Biddulph Rd W9 91 D4
Bideford Ave UB6 87 B5
Bideford Cl
Edgware HA8 26 C2
Twickenham TW13 151 B1
Bideford Gdns EN1 17 C4
Bideford Rd
Catford BR1 164 D1
East Wickham DA16 146 B5
Enfield EN3 7 B5
Ruislip HA4 62 B5
Bidmead Ct KT6 214 A5
Bidwell Gdns N11 31 C3
Bidwell Ho
Southall UB2 107 A2
3 Willesden NW2 68 A5
Bidwell St SE15 140 B4
Big Ben★ SW1 250 B1
Bigbury Cl N17 33 C3
Biggerstaff Rd E15 98 A6
Biggerstaff St N4 72 C6
Biggin Ave CR4 180 D2
Biggin Hill SE19 182 D3
Biggin Hill Cl KT2 175 C5
Biggin Way SE19 183 A3
Bigginwood Rd SW16 182 D2
Bigg's Row SW15 134 D2
Biggs Sq E9 75 B2
Big Hill E5 52 B1
Bigland Green Prim Sch 41 E1 96 B1
Bigland St E1 96 B1
Bignell Rd SE18 122 D1
Bignold Rd E7 77 A4
Bigwood Ct NW11 47 D4
Bigwood Rd NW11 47 D3
Biko Ho 1 NW10 67 B1
Bilberry Ho 18 E3 97 C2
Bilberry Manor SM2 218 A1
Billet Rd Ilford RM6 58 C6
Walthamstow E17 35 B2
Billetts Hart Cl W7 108 C4
Bill Hamling Cl SE9 166 B2
Billie Holiday Ct NW10 89 B5
Billingford Cl SE4 140 D1
Billing Ho 7 E1 96 D1
Billingley NW1 232 A5
Billing Pl SW10 135 D5 265 D4
Billing Rd SW10 135 D5 265 D4
Billings Cl RM9 80 C1
Billingsgate Mkt E14 119 D5
Billing St SW10 135 D5 265 D4
Billington Ho SW8 269 D1
Billington Rd SE14 140 D5
Billinton Hill CR0 221 B6
Billiter Sq EC3 243 B1
Billiter St EC3 95 C1 243 B1
Bill Nicholson Way N17 33 D3
Billockby Cl KT9 214 B2
Billsley Ct SE25 205 C5
Billson St E14 120 A2
Bilsby Gr SE9 187 D6
Bilton Ho SW8 269 C1
Bilton Rd UB6 87 B6
Bilton Twrs W1 237 D1
Bilton Way Enfield EN3 7 B5
Hayes UB3 106 B4
Bina Gdns SW5 114 A2 256 A3
Binbrook Ho 13 W10 90 C2
Bincote Rd EN2 4 B2
Binden Rd W12 111 D3
Bindon Gn SM4 201 D5
Binfield Ct SE5 139 A3
Binfield Rd
London SW4 138 A4 270 B1
South Croydon CR2 221 D3
Bingfield St N1 94 B6 233 C6
Bingham Cnr CR0 206 A1
Bingham Pl W1 93 A2 238 A4
Bingham Point 11 SE18 122 D2
Bingham Rd CR0 206 B1
Bingham St N1 73 B2
Bingley Rd
Ashford TW16 172 A3
Newham E16 99 C1
Southall UB6 86 A2
Binley Ho SW15 155 D5
Binney St W1 93 A1 238 B1
Binnie Ct SE10 141 D5
Binnie Ho SE1 262 A5
Binns Rd W4 111 C1
Binns Terr 3 W4 111 C1
Binsey Wlk 3 SE2 124 C4
Binstead Cl UB4 85 A2
Binstead Ho SW18 157 D5
Binyon Cres HA7 24 D5
Binyon Ho 8 N16 73 C4
Birbeck Ho 4 N19 49 D1
Birbetts Rd SE9 166 B2
Bircham Path SE4 140 D1
Birchanger Rd SE25 206 A4
Birch Ave
Edmonton N13 17 A1
Hillingdon UB7 82 B1
Birch Cl
Brentford TW8 131 B5
Buckhurst Hill IG9 21 D1
Hounslow TW3 130 B3
Newham E16 98 C2
Peckham SE15 140 A3
Romford RM7 59 D6
Teddington TW11 175 A5
Upper Holloway N19 71 C6
Birch Cres UB10 82 B6
Birch Ct Chingford E4 35 D4
Forest Gate E7 76 D4
Ilford RM6 58 C3
Sutton SM1 218 A4
9 Wallington SM6 219 B4
7 Woodside Pk N12 29 D6
Birchdale Gdns RM6 58 D2
Birchdale Rd E7 77 C3
Birchdene Dr SE28 124 A5
Birchdown Ho 32 E3 97 D4
Birchen Cl NW9 67 B6
Birchend Cl CR2 221 B2
Birchen Gr NW9 67 B6
Birches Cl
Mitcham CR4 202 D6
Pinner HA5 41 A4
Birches The
2 Beckenham BR2 208 D5
Bushey WD23 8 A6
Camberwell SE5 139 C3
Greenwich SE7 143 B6
Manor Pk E12 78 A4
Orpington BR6 226 C4
Southgate N21 16 B5
South Norwood SE25 183 D1
Twickenham TW4 151 B4
Birchfield Ho 3 E14 119 C6
Birchfield St E14 119 C6
Birch Gn NW9 27 C3
Birch Gr Acton W3 110 C6
Bexley DA16 146 A1
Lewisham SE12 164 D4
Leyton E11 76 C5
Upper Halliford TW17 171 C1
Birchgrove Ho TW9 132 D5
Birch Hill CR0 222 D3
Birch Ho
New Cross Gate SE14 141 B4
Teddington TW11 175 C3
8 Tulse Hill SW2 160 C5
Birchington Cl DA7 147 D4
Birchington Ct
Crouch End N8 49 D3
2 Kilburn NW6 91 D6
Birchington Ho 1 E5 74 B3
Birchington Rd
Crouch End N8 49 D3
Kilburn NW6 91 C6
Surbiton KT5 198 B2
Birchin La EC3 242 D1
Birchlands Ave SW12 158 D4
Birch Mead BR2, BR6 226 C6
Birchmead Ave HA5 40 C5
Birchmere Bsns Pk SE2 124 A4

Birchmere Lo 18 SE16 118 B1
Birchmere Row SE3 142 D3
Birchmore Wlk N5 73 A5
Birch Pk HA3 24 A3
Birch Rd
  Feltham TW13 172 D5
  Romford RM7 59 D6
Birch Row BR2 210 C3
Birch Tree Ave BR4 224 D4
Birch Tree Ho 16 SE7 143 C6
Birch Tree Way CR0 222 B6
Birch Vale Ct NW8 236 D6
Birchway UB3 106 A5
Birch Wlk CR4 181 B2
Birchwood Ave
  Beckenham BR3 207 B5
  Hackbridge SM5, SM6 219 B5
  Muswell Hill N10 49 A6
  Sidcup DA14 168 C1
Birchwood Cl SM4 201 D5
Birchwood Ct
  Burnt Oak HA8 27 A1
  Edmonton N13 32 D5
Birchwood Dr NW3 69 D5
Birchwood Gr TW12 173 C4
Birchwood Rd
  Orpington BR5 211 C5
  Streatham SW17 181 B5
Birdbrook Rd SE3 143 C2
Birdcage Wlk
  SW1 115 D4 249 C1
Bird Coll DA14 168 A1
Birdham Cl BR1 210 A4
Birdhurst Ave CR2 221 B4
Birdhurst Ct SM6 219 C1
Birdhurst Gdns CR2 221 B4
Birdhurst Rd
  London SW18 158 A6
  Mitcham SW19 180 C4
  South Croydon CR2 221 C3
Birdhurst Rise CR2 221 C3
Bird In Bush Rd
  SE15 140 A5
Bird-in-Hand La
  BR1 187 D1
Bird-In-Hand Pas
  SE23 162 C2
Bird In Hand Yd 24
  NW3 70 A4
Birdsall Ho 5 SE5 139 C2
Birdsfield La 12 E3 97 B6
Bird St W1 238 B1
Bird Wlk TW2 151 B3
Birdwood Ave 4
  SE13 164 B5
Birdwood Cl TW11 174 C6
Birkbeck Ave
  Acton W3 111 A6
  Greenford UB6 86 A6
Birkbeck Coll
  W1 93 D1 239 C2
Birkbeck Ct W3 111 B5
Birkbeck Gdns IG8 21 A2
Birkbeck Gr W3 111 B4
Birkbeck Hill SE21 160 D3
Birkbeck Mews 5
  E8 73 D3
Birkbeck Pl SE21 161 A2
Birkbeck Prim Sch
  DA14 168 B1
Birkbeck Rd
  Acton W3 111 B5
  Dalston E8 73 D3
  Ealing W5 109 C2
  Edgware NW7 27 D5
  Enfield EN2 5 B5
  Hornsey N8 50 A5
  Ilford IG2 57 B4
  North Finchley N12 30 A5
  Penge BR3 184 D1
  Sidcup DA14 168 A1
  Tottenham N17 33 D2
  Wimbledon SW19 179 D4
Birkbeck St E2 96 B4
Birkbeck Sta SE20 206 C6
Birkbeck Univ of London
  WC1 93 D3 239 C6
Birkbeck Way UB6 86 B6
Birkdale Ave HA5 41 C6
Birkdale Cl
  30 Bermondsey
  SE16 118 B1
  Crofton BR6 211 B2
  Erith SE28 102 D1
Birkdale Ct 3 UB1 86 A1
Birkdale Gdns CR0 222 D4
Birkdale Rd
  Abbey Wood SE2 124 A2
  Ealing W5 88 A3
Birkenhead Ave KT2 176 B2
Birkenhead Ho 11 N7 72 C3
Birkenhead St
  WC1 94 A4 233 B2
Birkhall Rd SE6 164 B2
Birkwood Cl SW12 159 D4
Birley Lo NW8 229 D4
Birley Rd N20 14 A2
Birley St SW11 137 A3
Birnam Rd N4 72 B6
Birnbeck Ct NW11 47 B4
Birnham Ho TW1 153 C4
Birrell Ho 9 SW9 138 B3
Birse Cres NW10 67 C4
Birstal Gn WD19 22 D6
Birstall Rd N15 51 C4
Birtwhistle Ho 5 E3 97 B6
Biscay Ho 11 E1 96 D3
Biscay Rd W6 112 D1
Biscoe Cl TW5 129 C6
Biscoe Ho UB2 107 D2
Biscoe Way SE13 142 B2
Biscott Ho 3 E3 97 D3
Bisenden Rd CR0 221 C6
Bisham Cl CR4 202 D1
Bisham Gdns N6 49 A1
Bishop Butt Cl BR6 227 D5
Bishop Challoner
  Collegiate Sch 28
  E1 96 C1
Bishop Challoner Sch
  BR2 186 B1
Bishop Ct 20 SW2 160 C5
Bishop Douglass RC Sch
  N2 48 A6
Bishop Duppa's
  Almshouses 7
  TW10 154 A6
Bishop Duppas Pk
  TW17 193 C2
Bishop Fox Way KT8 195 B5
Bishop Gilpins Prim Sch
  SW19 179 B5
Bishop John Robinson
  CE Prim Sch SE28 124 C6
Bishop Justus CE Sch
  BR2 210 A2
Bishop Ken Rd HA3 24 D2
Bishop King's Rd
  W14 113 A2 254 B4
Bishop Perrin CE Prim
  Sch TW2 151 D3
Bishop Ramsey CE Sch
  (Annexe) HA4 39 D2
Bishop Ramsey CE Sch
  (Upper) HA4 40 A2
Bishop Rd N14 15 B4
Bishop Ridley CE Prim
  Sch DA16 145 C1
Bishops Ave
  Borehamwood WD6 10 B6
  Bromley BR1 209 C6
  Ilford RM6 58 C3
  Newham E13 99 B6
Bishop's Ave SW6 135 A3
Bishops Ave The N2 48 B3
Bishopsbourne Ho
  BR1 187 B3
Bishop's Bridge Rd
  W2 92 A1 236 A2
Bishops Cl
  Acton Green W4 111 A1
  Barnet EN5 12 D5
  Enfield EN1 6 B3
  New Eltham SE9 167 A2
  Richmond TW10 153 D1
  Sutton SM1 217 C5
Bishop's Cl
  Dartmouth Pk N19 71 C5
  Hillingdon UB10 82 C5
  Walthamstow E17 53 D5
Bishopscourt 8
  CR0 221 D6
Bishops Ct
  1 Ashford TW16 171 D3
  13 Bayswater W2 91 D1
Bishops Ct *continued*
  East Finchley N2 48 C5
  Richmond TW9 132 A2
  Romford RM7 59 D5
  Wembley HA0 65 B4
Bishop's Ct
  Holborn EC4 241 C2
  Holborn WC2 241 A2
Bishopsdale Ho 8
  NW6 91 C6
Bishops Dr
  East Bedfont TW14 149 B5
  Northolt UB5 85 A6
Bishopsford Com Sch
  SM4 202 B3
Bishopsford Ho
  SM4 202 C3
Bishopsford Rd SM4 202 B3
Bishopsgate
  EC2 95 C1 243 A2
Bishopsgate Arc E1 243 B3
Bishopsgate Churchyard
  EC2 243 A2
Bishopsgate Inst
  EC2 95 C2 243 B3
Bishops Gn BR1 187 C2
Bishops Gr
  East Finchley N2 48 C3
  Feltham TW12 173 B6
Bishop's Hall KT1 175 D1
Bishopshalt Sch UB8 82 B4
Bishops Hill KT12 194 A2
Bishops Ho SW8 270 B3
Bishop's Mans SW6 134 D3
Bishops Mead SE5 139 A5
Bishops Park Rd
  SW16 182 A2
Bishop's Park Rd
  SW6 134 D3
Bishop's Pl SM1 218 A3
Bishops Rd
  Fulham
  SW6 135 B4 264 C2
  Highgate N6 49 A3
Bishop's Rd
  Hanwell W7 108 C4
  Hayes UB3 83 A1
  Thornton Heath CR0 204 D2
Bishops Sq E1 243 B4
Bishop St N1 95 A6 235 A6
Bishop's Terr
  SE11 116 C2 261 B4
Bishopsthorpe Rd
  SE26 184 D6
Bishopstone Ho 4
  SW11 137 A3
Bishop Stopford's Sch
  EN1 6 B3
Bishops View Ct N10 49 B5
Bishop's Way E2 96 C5
Bishops Wlk
  Chislehurst BR7 189 A2
  South Croydon CR0,
  CR9 223 A3
Bishopswood Rd N6 48 D2
Bishop Thomas Grant
  Sch SW16 182 B5
Bishop Wand CE Sec Sch
  TW16 171 D1
Bishop Wilfred Wood Cl
  SE15 140 A3
Bishop Wilfred Wood Ct
  3 E13 99 C5
Bishop Winnington-
  Ingram CE Prim Sch
  HA4 39 B2
Bisley Cl KT4 200 C1
Bisley Ho SW19 156 D2
Bispham Rd NW10 88 B4
Bissextile Ho SE13 141 D3
Bisson Rd E15 98 A5
Bisterne Ave E17 54 B6
Bittacy Bsns Ctr NW7 29 A3
Bittacy Cl NW7 28 D4
Bittacy Ct NW7 29 A3
Bittacy Hill NW7 28 D4
Bittacy Park Ave
  NW7 28 D5
Bittacy Rd NW7 28 D4
Bittacy Rise NW7 28 D4
Bittern Cl UB4 84 D2
Bittern Ct Chingford E4 20 B4
  7 Deptford SE8 141 C6
  Hendon NW9 27 C1
Bittern Ho SE1 252 A1
Bittern St SE1 252 A1
Bittoms The KT1 197 D6
Bixley Cl UB2 107 B2
Blackall St EC2 243 A6
Blackberry Cl TW17 193 C5
Blackberry Farm Cl
  TW5 129 A5
Blackberry Field
  BR5 190 A2
Blackbird Ct NW9 67 B5
Blackbird Hill NW9 67 B5
Blackborne Rd RM10 81 D2
Black Boy La N15 51 A4
Blackbrook La BR1,
  BR2 210 C5
Blackburn 28 NW9 27 D1
Blackburn Ct 21
  SW2 160 C5
Blackburne's Mews
  W1 248 A5
Blackburn Rd NW6 69 D2
Blackburn Trad Est
  TW19 148 B5
Blackburn Way TW4 151 A6
Blackbush Ave RM6 58 D4
Blackbush Cl SM2 217 D1
Blackcap Ct NW9 27 C1
Blackdown Cl N2 30 A1
Blackdown Ho E8 74 A4
Blackett St SW15 134 D2
Black Fan Cl EN2 5 A4
BLACKFEN 168 A5
Blackfen Par DA15 168 A5
Blackfen Rd DA15 168 B5
Blackfen Sch for Girls
  DA15 168 B5
Blackford Rd WD19 22 D5
Blackfriars Bridge
  EC4 251 C5
Blackfriars Ct EC4 251 C6
Black Friars La
  EC4 94 D1 241 C1
Blackfriars Pas EC4 251 C6
Blackfriars Pier EC4 251 C6
Blackfriars Rd
  SE1 116 D5 251 C3
Blackfriars Underpass
  EC4 116 C6 251 B6
Blackham Ho SW19 179 A4
BLACKHEATH 142 C2
Blackheath★ SE3 142 C4
Blackheath Ave SE3 142 C5
Blackheath Bluecoat Sch
  SE3 143 B5
Blackheath Bsns Est
  SE10 142 A4
Blackheath Gr SE3 142 D3
Blackheath High Jun Sch
  SE3 142 D3
Blackheath High Sch
  SE3 143 A5
Blackheath Hill
  SE10 142 A4
Blackheath Hospl
  SE3 142 C2
BLACKHEATH
  PARK 143 A1
Blackheath Pk SE3 143 A2
Blackheath Prep Sch
  SE3 143 A4
Blackheath Rd SE10 141 D4
Blackheath Rise
  SE13 142 A3
Blackheath Sta SE3 142 D2
BLACKHEATH
  VALE 142 D3
Blackheath Vale
  SE3 142 C3
Blackheath Village
  SE3 142 D3
Black Horse Ct SE1 262 D6
Blackhorse La
  Croydon CR0 206 A2
  Higham Hill E17 34 D1
Blackhorse La Sta
  CR0 206 A2
Blackhorse Mews
  E17 52 D6
Black Horse Par HA5 40 B4
Blackhorse Rd
  Deptford SE8 141 A6
  Walthamstow E17 53 A5
Black Horse Rd
  DA14 190 A6
Blackhorse Road E17 52 D5
Blackhorse Road Sta
  E17 52 D5
Blacklands Dr UB4 83 A3
Blacklands Rd SE6 186 A6
Blacklands Terr SW3 257 D3
Black Lion La W6 112 A2
Black Lion Mews 4
  W6 112 A2
Blackmore Ave UB1 108 B5
Blackmore Dr NW10 66 D1
Blackmore Ho
  Forest Hill SE23 163 B3
  Islington N1 233 D5
  2 Wandsworth
  SW18 157 D6
Blackmore's Gr
  TW11 175 A4
Blackmore Twr 1
  W3 111 A3
Blackness La BR2 225 D1
Blackpool Gdns UB4 83 C3
Blackpool Rd SE15 140 B3
Black Prince Intc
  DA6 169 D5
Black Prince Rd SE1,
  SE11 116 B2 260 D3
Black Rod Cl UB3 105 D3
Black Roof Ho 9
  SE5 138 D4
Blackshaw Rd SW17 180 B5
Blacksmith Cl RM6 58 C3
Blacksmiths Ho 7
  E17 53 C5
Black's Rd W6 112 C2
Blackstock Ho 2 N5 72 D5
Blackstock Mews N4 72 D5
Blackstock Rd N4, N5 72 D6
Blackstone Ho
  Dulwich SE21 161 C1
  Pimlico SW1 259 A1
Blackstone Rd NW2 68 C4
Black Swan Yd SE1 253 A2
Blackthorn Ave UB7 104 C3
Blackthorn Ct
  20 Camberwell
  SE15 139 D5
  Heston TW5 129 A5
  4 Leyton E15 76 B4
  6 West Norwood
  SW16 182 C5
Blackthorne Ave
  CR0 206 C1
Blackthorne Ct
  2 Littleton TW15 171 A3
  Southall UB1 107 D5
Blackthorne Dr E4 36 B6
Blackthorn Gr DA7 147 A2
Blackthorn Rd IG1 79 B3
Blackthorn St E3 97 C3
Blacktree Mews 11
  SW9 138 C2
BLACKWALL 120 B6
Blackwall Sta E14 120 A6
Blackwall Trad Est
  E14 98 B2
Blackwall Tunnel E14,
  SE10 120 B5
Blackwall Tunnel App
  SE10 120 C4
Blackwall Tunnel
  Northern Approach E14,
  E3 98 A3
Blackwall Way E14 120 A6
Blackwater Cl E7 76 D4
Blackwater Ho NW8 236 D4
Blackwater St SE22 161 D6
Blackwell Cl
  10 Clapton Pk E5 74 D4
  Harrow HA3 24 B3
  Southgate N21 16 A6
Blackwell Gdns HA8 10 C1
Blackwell Ho 3
  SW4 159 D5
Blackwood Ho 11 E1 96 B3
Blackwood St
  SE17 117 B1 262 C2
Blade Ho TW1 153 D5
Blade Mews SW15 135 B1
Bladen Ho 4 E1 96 D1
Blades Ct
  4 Hammersmith
  W6 112 B1
  Putney SW15 135 B1
Blades Ho 12 SE11 138 C6
Blades Lo 16 SW2 160 C5
Bladindon Dr DA5 168 D4
Bladon Ct
  Beckenham BR2 208 C6

Bladon Ct *continued*
Streatham SW16 182 A4
Bladon Gdns HA2 41 D3
Blagden's Cl N14 15 D2
Blagden's La N14 15 D2
Blagdon Ct W7 108 C6
Blagdon Rd
London SE13 163 D5
New Malden KT3 199 D5
Blagdon Wlk TW11 175 C4
Blagrove Rd 1 W10 91 B2
Blair Ave London NW9 45 C2
Thames Ditton KT10 212 A6
Blair Cl
Avery Hill DA15 167 C6
Canonbury N1 73 A2
Hayes UB3 106 A2
Blair Ct
Beckenham BR3 185 D2
8 Carshalton SM5 218 D5
7 Catford SE6 164 D3
St John's Wood NW8 229 C6
Blairderry Rd SW2 160 A2
Blairgowrie Ct 13 E14 98 B1
Blair Ho SW9 138 B3
Blair Peach Prim Sch
UB1 106 D5
Blair St E14 98 B1
Blake Apartments N8 50 B6
Blake Ave IG11 101 D6
Blake Cl Bexley DA16 145 C4
Carshalton SM5 202 C1
Hayes UB4 83 B5
Blake Coll W1 93 C2 239 A4
Blake Ct
8 Bermondsey SE16 118 B1
9 Clapham SW8 137 C3
Croydon CR2 220 D3
Kilburn NW6 91 C4
Southgate N21 16 B6
Blakeden Dr KT10 212 D2
Blake Gdns
SW6 135 D4 265 C2
Blake Hall Cres E11 55 A1
Blakehall Rd SM5 218 D2
Blake Hall Rd E11 55 A2
Blake Ho
6 Beckenham BR3 185 D4
2 Deptford SE8 141 C6
Harrow HA1 64 C6
Isle Of Dogs E14 119 D4
1 Kentish Town N19 71 D3
Lambeth SE1 261 A6
14 Stoke Newington N16 73 C4
Blake Lo N3 29 B1
Blake Mews 15 TW9 132 C4
Blakemore Rd
Streatham SW16 160 A1
Thornton Heath CR7 204 B4
Blakemore Way
DA17 125 A3
Blakeney Ave BR3 185 B2
Blakeney Cl
5 Camden Town NW1 71 D1
4 Dalston E8 74 A3
Whetstone N20 14 A3
Blakeney Ct EN2 17 B6
Blakeney Rd BR3 185 B2
Blakenham Ct W12 112 A5
Blakenham Rd
SW17 180 D6
Blaker Ct SE7 143 C5
Blake Rd
Croydon CR0 221 C6
Mitcham CR4 202 C6
Newham E16 98 D3
Wood Green N11 31 C3
Blaker Rd E15 98 A6
Blakes Ave KT3 199 D3
Blakes Cl W10 90 C2
Blake's Gn BR4 208 A1
Blakes La KT3 199 D4
Blakesley Ave W5 87 C1
Blakesley Ct W5 87 C1
Blakesley Ho 4 E12 78 C5
Blake's Rd SE15 139 C5
Blakes Terr KT3 200 A4
Blakesware Gdns N9 17 B4
Blakewood Cl TW13 172 C6
Blakewood Ct 5
SE20 184 B3
Blanca Ho 16 N1 95 C5
Blanchard Cl SE9 166 A1
Blanchard Gr EN3 7 D5
Blanchard Ho
Chislehurst BR7 189 A4
7 Twickenham TW1 153 D5
Blanchard Way E8 74 A2
Blanch Cl SE15 140 C5
Blanchedowne SE5 139 B1
Blanche Nevile Sch
Highgate N6 48 D3
Muswell Hill N10 31 A1
Blanche St E16 98 D3
Blanchland Rd SM4 201 D4
Blandfield Rd SW12 159 A4
Blandford Ave
2 Beckenham BR3 185 A1
Twickenham TW2 151 D3
Blandford Cl
London N2 48 A5
Romford RM7 59 D5
Wallington CR0 220 A5
Blandford Cres E4 20 A4
Blandford Ct
Brondesbury Pk NW6 69 A1
6 De Beauvoir Town N1 73 C1
Blandford Ho SW8 270 C4
Blandford Rd
Acton W4 111 C3
Ealing W5 109 D4
Penge BR3 184 D1
Southall UB2 107 C2
Teddington TW11 174 C5
Blandford Sq NW1 237 B5
Blandford St
W1 93 A2 238 A3
Blandford Waye UB4 84 C1
Bland Ho SE11 260 D2
Bland St SE9 143 D1
Blaney Cres E6 100 D4
Blanmerle Rd SE9 166 D3
Blann Cl SE9 165 D5
Blantyre St
SW10 136 B5 266 C4
Blantyre Twr SW10 266 C4
Blantyre Wlk
SW10 136 B5 266 C4
Blashford NW3 70 D1
Blashford St SE13 164 B4
Blasker Wlk 8 E14 119 D1
Blatchford Ct KT12 194 A1
Blatchford Ho 8
RM10 81 C5
Blawith Rd HA1 42 D5
Blaxland Ho 12 W12 112 B6
Blaydon Cl HA4 39 C2
Blaydon Ct 4 UB5 63 C2
Blaydon Wlk N17 34 B3
Blazer Ct NW8 229 D1
Bleak Hill La SE18 145 D6
Blean Gr SE20 184 C3
Bleasdale Ave UB6 87 A5
Blechynden Ho 17
W10 90 D1
Blechynden St W10 112 D6
Bledlow Cl SE28 124 C6
Bledlow Rise UB6 86 A5
Bleeding Heart Yd
EC1 241 B3
Blegborough Rd
SW16 181 C4
Blemundsbury WC1 240 C4
Blendon Dr DA5 168 D5
Blendon Path 9
BR1 186 D3
Blendon Rd DA5 168 D5
Blendon Terr SE18 145 A6
Blendworth Point 4
SW15 156 B3
Blenheim 26 SW19 156 D3
Blenheim Ave IG2 56 C3
Blenheim Bsns Ctr
CR4 180 D1
Blenheim Centre 7
SE20 184 D3
Blenheim Cl
Edmonton N21 17 A3
Eltham SE12 165 B3
Greenford UB6 86 B5
Wallington SM6 219 C1
West Barnes SW20 200 C6
Blenheim Cres
Notting Hill W11 91 A1
Notting Hill W11 244 B6
Ruislip HA4 61 B6
South Croydon CR2 221 A1
Blenheim Ct
Barnsbury N7 72 A2
Beckenham BR2 208 D5
5 Hampton TW12 173 C2
Harrow HA3 43 A3
Hendon NW4 46 D5
Longlands DA14 167 B1
Richmond TW9 132 B2
17 Rotherhithe SE16 118 D5
South Norwood SE19 183 C2
Sutton SM2 218 A2
Upper Holloway N19 72 A6
Woodford IG8 37 B3
Blenheim Ctr TW3 129 D2
Blenheim Dr DA16 145 D4
Blenheim Gdns
Clapham Pk SW2 160 B5
Dollis Hill NW2 68 C3
Kingston u T KT2 176 D3
Wallington SM6 219 C1
Wembley HA9 66 A5
Blenheim Gr SE15 140 A3
Blenheim Ho
6 Edmonton N9 18 A1
Hounslow TW3 129 C2
8 Woolwich SE18 123 A3
Blenheim Par 2
UB10 82 D3
Blenheim Park Rd
CR2 221 A1
Blenheim Pas NW8 229 A4
Blenheim Pl TW11 174 D5
Blenheim Rd
Acton W4 111 C3
Bromley BR1, BR2 210 A5
Harrow HA2 41 D3
Leyton E15 76 C4
Newham E6 99 D4
Northolt UB5 63 D2
Penge SE20 184 C3
Sidcup DA15 168 C3
St John's Wood NW8 92 A5 229 B4
Sutton SM1 217 D5
Walthamstow E17 53 A6
West Barnes SW20 200 C6
Blenheim Rise N15 51 D5
Blenheim St W1 238 C1
Blenheim Terr
NW8 92 A5 229 A4
Blenheim Way TW7 131 A4
Blenkarne Rd SW11 158 D5
Bleriot 27 NW9 27 D1
Bleriot Rd TW5 128 C5
Blessbury Rd HA8 27 A2
Blessed Dominic RC Sch
NW9 27 D1
Blessed Sacrament RC Prim Sch N1 94 B6 233 C5
Blessington Cl SE13 142 B2
Blessington Rd SE13 142 B1
Blessing Way IG11 102 C5
Bletchingley Cl CR7 204 D5
Bletchington Ct 2
DA17 125 C2
Bletchley Ct N1 235 C3
Bletchley St
N1 95 A5 235 B3
Bletchmore Cl UB3 105 B1
Bletsoe Wlk N1 235 B4
Blewbury Ho 3 SE2 124 C4
Blick Ho 1 SE16 118 C3
Bligh Ho 4 SE27 183 A6
Blincoe Cl SW19 156 D2
Blissett St SE10 142 A4
Blissland Ct 5 N12 30 A4
Bliss Mews 14 W10 91 A4
Blisworth Cl UB4 85 A3
Blisworth Ho 12 E2 96 A6
Blithbury Rd RM9 80 B2
Blithdale Rd SE2 124 A2
Blithfield St W8 255 C5
Blockley Rd HA0 65 B6
Bloemfontein Ave
W12 112 B5
Bloemfontein Rd
W12 112 B6
Blomfield Ct
Battersea SW11 266 D2
Paddington W9 236 B6
Blomfield Ho 4
E14 119 D6
Blomfield Mans 3
W12 112 C5
Blomfield Rd
W9 92 A2 236 A4
Blomfield St
EC2 95 B2 242 D3
Blomfield Villas W9 236 A4
Blomville Rd RM8 81 A5
Blondel St SW11 137 A3
Blondin Ave W5 109 C3
Blondin St E3 97 C5
Bloomburg St SW1 259 B3
Bloomfield Cres IG2 56 D3
Bloomfield Ct N6 49 A3
Bloomfield Ho 19 E1 96 A2
Bloomfield Pl W1 248 D6
Bloomfield Rd
Bromley Comm BR2 209 D4
Highgate N6 49 A3
Kingston u T KT1 198 A6
Woolwich SE18 122 D1
Bloomfield Terr
SW1 115 A1 258 B2
Bloom Gr SE27 160 D1
Bloomhall Rd SE19 183 B5
Bloom Park Rd SW6 264 C3
Bloomsberg Space★
EC1 242 D4
BLOOMSBURY 93 D2
Bloomsbury Cl
Ealing W5 110 B6
Edgware NW7 28 A3
Bloomsbury Ct
Cranford TW5 128 B4
Leytonstone E11 54 B1
Pinner HA5 41 B6
St Giles WC1 240 B3
Bloomsbury Ho 10
SW4 159 D5
Bloomsbury International Language Sch WC1 94 A2 240 B3
Bloomsbury Pl
London SW18 158 A6
St Giles WC1 240 B3
Bloomsbury Sq
WC1 94 A2 240 B3
Bloomsbury St
WC1 93 D2 239 D3
Bloomsbury Way
WC1 94 A2 240 B3
Blore Cl SW8 269 C1
Blore Ct W1 249 C6
Blore Ho SW10 265 D4
Blossom Cl
Dagenham RM9 103 B6
Ealing W5 110 A4
South Croydon CR2 221 D3
Blossom House Sch
SW20 178 C3
Blossom La EN2 5 A4
Blossom Pl E1 243 B5
Blossom St E1 95 C3 243 B5
Blossom Way
Hillingdon UB10 60 B1
West Drayton UB7 104 C2
Blossom Waye TW5 129 A5
Blount St E14 97 A1
Bloxam Gdns SE9 166 A6
Bloxhall Rd E10 53 B1
Bloxham Cres TW12 173 B2
Bloxworth Cl SM6 219 C5
Blucher Rd SE5 139 A5
Blue Anchor Alley 4
TW9 132 A1
Blue Anchor La
SE16 118 B2
Blue Anchor Yd E1 118 A6
Blue Ball Yd SW1 249 A3
Bluebell Ave E12 78 A3
Bluebell Cl
Forest Hill SE26 183 D6
Hackbridge SM6 203 B1
10 Hackney E9 96 C6
Northolt UB5 63 B2
Orpington BR6 227 A6
Bluebell Ct 4 N12 14 A1
Bluebell Way IG1 78 D2
Blueberry Cl IG8 37 A4
Blueberry Ct
Edgware HA8 27 A5
3 Enfield EN2 4 D3
Bluebird La RM10 81 C1
Bluebird Way SE28 123 B4
Bluefield Cl TW12 173 C5
Blue Gate Fields Jun & Inf Schs 22 E1 118 C6
Bluegate Mews E1 118 B6
Bluegates
Stoneleigh KT17 216 A1
Bluegates *continued*
Wimbledon SW19 179 A5
Bluehouse Rd E4 20 C1
Blue Lion Pl SE1 263 A6
Blue Point Ct 2 HA1 42 D4
Blueprint Apartments 15
SW12 159 B4
Blue Sch The TW7 131 A2
Blundell Cl E8 74 A4
Blundell Rd HA8 27 C3
Blundell St N7 72 A2
Blunden Cl RM8 58 C1
Blunt Rd CR0 221 B3
Blunts Ave UB7 126 C5
Blunts Rd SE9 166 C6
Blurton Rd E5 74 D4
Blydon Ct N21 16 B6
Blyth Cl
4 Cubitt Town E14 120 B2
Twickenham TW1 152 D5
Blythe Cl SE23 163 B4
Blythe Hill
Forest Hill SE6 163 B4
St Paul's Cray BR5 190 A2
Blythe Hill La SE6 163 B3
Blythe Ho 8 SE11 138 C6
Blythe Mews 2
W14 112 D3
Blythendale Ho 34 E2 96 A5
Blythe Rd
W14 113 A3 254 A5
Blythe St E2 96 B4
Blytheswood Pl 4
SW16 182 B6
Blythe Vale SE6 163 B3
Blythewood 5 SM1 218 B3
Blyth Rd
Bromley BR1 186 D2
Hayes UB3 105 C4
Walthamstow E17 53 B2
Woolwich SE28 124 C6
Blyth's Wharf E14 119 A6
Blythswood Rd IG3 58 A2
Blythwood Pk 10
BR1 186 D2
Blythwood Rd
London N4 50 A2
Pinner HA5 22 D2
BMI Fitzroy Square Hospl W1 93 C3 239 A5
BMI The Cavell Hospl
EN2 4 C3
Bnois Jerusalem Girls Sch 2 N16 51 B2
Boades Mews 3
NW3 70 B4
Boadicea St N1 233 C5
Boardman Ave E4 19 D6
Boardman Cl EN5 13 A6
Boardwalk Pl E14 120 A5
Boarhound 25 NW9 27 D1
Boarley Ho SE17 263 A3
Boatemah Wlk 21
SW9 138 C3
Boathouse Ctr The
W10 90 D3
Boathouse Wlk 24
SE15 139 D5
Boat Lifter Way 19
SE16 119 A2
Bob Anker Cl 1 E13 99 A4
Bobbin Cl SW4 137 C2
Bobby Moore Bridge The
HA9 66 C5
Bob Marley Way 11
SE24 138 C1
Bobov Foundation Sch
4 N16 51 D2
Bob Thompson Ct
HA9 66 D5
Bockhampton Rd
KT2 176 B3
Bocking St E8 96 B6
Boddicott Cl SW19 157 A2
Boddington Gdns
W3 110 C4
Boddington Ho 2
SE14 140 C4
Bodeney Ho 10 SE5 139 C4
Boden Ho 4 E1 96 A2
Bodiam Cl EN1 5 C3
Bodiam Ct
Beckenham BR2 208 D5

Bodiam Ct *continued*
Sutton SM1 . . . . . 218 B4
Bodiam Rd SW16 . . . 181 D3
Bodiam Way NW10. . . 88 B4
Bodicea Mews TW4 . . 151 C5
Bodington Ct 2
W12 . . . . . 112 D4
Bodley Cl KT3 . . . . 199 C4
Bodley Manor Way
SE24. . . . . 160 C4
Bodley Rd KT3. . . . 199 C4
Bodmin 26 NW9 . . . 27 D1
Bodmin Cl HA2 . . . 63 B5
Bodmin Gr SM4. . . . 201 D4
Bodmin St SW18. . . 157 C3
Bodnant Gdns SW20 . 200 B6
Bodney Rd E5, E8 . . . 74 B3
Boeing Way UB2. . . . 106 B3
Boevey Path DA17 . . 125 B1
Bogart Ct 13 E14. . . 119 C6
Bognor Gdns WD19 . . 22 C5
Bognor Rd DA16. . . . 146 D4
Bohemia Pl 1 E8. . . . 74 B2
Bohn Rd E1. . . . . 97 A2
Bohun Gr EN4 . . . . 14 D5
Boileau Par W5. . . . 88 B1
Boileau Rd
Barnes SW13. . . . 134 B6
Ealing W5. . . . . 88 B1
Boilerhouse SE1. . . 253 C3
Boisseau Ho 31 E1. . . 96 C2
Bolden St SE8 . . . 141 D3
Boldero Pl NW8 . . . 237 A5
Bolderwood Way
BR4. . . . . 223 D6
Boldmere Rd HA5. . . 40 C2
Boleyn Ave EN1 . . . 6 B4
Boleyn Ct
Beckenham BR3. . . . 186 A2
Buckhurst Hill IG9 . . 21 B3
East Molesey KT8 . . 196 B5
Hayes UB3. . . . 105 D4
Walthamstow E17 . . 53 C5
Boleyn Dr
East Molesey KT8 . . 195 B6
Ruislip HA4 . . . . 62 D6
Boleyn Gdns BR4 . . 223 D6
Boleyn Ground (Upton Park) (West Ham Utd FC) E13, E6. . . . 99 D5
Boleyn Rd Newham E6 . 99 D5
Stoke Newington N16 . . 73 C3
Upton E7 . . . . . 77 B1
Boleyn Way EN5 . . . 2 A2
Bolina Rd SE16 . . . 118 C1
Bolingbroke Gr
SW11. . . . . 158 D5
Bolingbroke Ho
Beckenham BR3. . . . 207 A4
Catford BR3. . . . 185 D5
Bolingbroke Rd
W14. . . . . 112 D3
Bolingbroke Way UB3, UB11. . . . 105 B5
Bolingbroke Wlk
SW11 . . . . 136 C4 267 A2
Bollo Bridge Rd W3. . 111 A4
Bollo Ct 2 W3. . . . 111 A3
Bollo La W3 . . . . 110 D3
Bolney Ct KT6 . . . . 197 D4
Bolney Gate SW7 . . . 247 A1
Bolney St
SW8. . . . . 138 B5 270 C3
Bolsover St
W1. . . . . 93 B3 238 D5
Bolstead Rd CR4. . . . 181 B2
Bolster Gr N22. . . . 31 D2
Bolt Ct EC4 . . . . 241 B1
Boltmore Cl NW4 . . . 46 D6
Bolton Cl
Chessington KT9 . . . 214 A2
Penge SE20. . . . 184 A1
Bolton Cres SE5 . . . 138 D5
Bolton Ct SW11. . . . 268 B1
Bolton Dr SM4. . . . 202 B2
Bolton Gdns
Bromley BR1 . . . . 186 D4
Kensal Rise NW10. . . . 90 D5
South Kensington SW5 . . . 113 D1 255 D2
Teddington TW11. . . . 175 A4
Bolton Gdns Mews
SW10. . . . . 256 A2
Bolton Ho 4 SE10 . . . 120 C1
Bolton Pl SW5. . . . 256 A2
Bolton Rd
Chessington KT9 . . . 214 A2
Chiswick W4 . . . . 133 A5
Edmonton N18. . . . 33 D5
Harlesden NW10. . . . 89 C6
Harrow HA1. . . . 42 B5
Kilburn NW8 . . . . 91 D6
Stratford E15. . . . 76 D2
Boltons Ct SW5. . . . 255 D2
Bolton's La TW6, UB7. . . . . 127 A5
Bolton St W1 . 115 B5 248 D4
Boltons The
Harrow HA1. . . . 42 A5
South Kensington SW10 . . . 114 A1 256 A2
6 Stratford E15 . . . 76 D2
Wembley HA0 . . . . 64 D4
Woodford IG8 . . . . 37 A6
Bolton Studios SW10 256 B1
Bolton Wlk N7. . . . 72 B6
Bombay Ct 8 SE16 . . 118 C4
Bombay St SE16 . . . 118 B2
Bomer Cl UB7 . . . . 126 C5
Bomore Rd
W11 . . . . 113 A6 244 A6
Bonar Pl BR7 . . . . 188 A3
Bonar Rd SE15. . . . 140 A5
Bonchester Cl BR7. . . 188 C3
Bonchurch Cl SM2. . . 217 D1
Bonchurch Rd
Ealing W13. . . . . 109 B5
Kensal Town W10. . . . 91 A2
Bond Cl UB7. . . . . 82 B1
Bond Ct EC4. . . . 242 C1
Bondfield Ave UB4. . . . 84 A4
Bondfield Rd 4 E6 . . 100 B2
Bond Gdns SM6. . . . 219 C4
Bond Ho 4 NW6. . . . 91 B5
Bonding Yard Wlk
SE16. . . . . 119 A3
Bond Prim Sch CR4. 180 D1
Bond Rd
Mitcham CR4 . . . . 180 D1
Surbiton KT6 . . . . 214 B6
Bond St Chiswick W4 . . 111 B2
Ealing W5. . . . . 109 D6
Stratford E15. . . . 76 C3
Bond Street Sta
W1. . . . . 93 A1 238 B1
Bondway
SW8. . . . . 138 A6 270 B6
Boneta Rd SE18. . . . 122 B3
Bonfield Rd SE13 . . . 142 A1
Bonham Gdns RM8 . . . 80 D6
Bonham Ho W11. . . . 244 C4
Bonham Rd
Brixton SW2. . . . 160 B6
Dagenham RM8. . . . 80 D5
Bonheur Rd W4. . . . 111 B4
Bonhill St EC2 . 95 B3 242 D5
Boniface Gdns HA3 . . 23 D3
Boniface Rd UB10. . . . 60 D5
Boniface Wlk HA3 . . . 23 D3
Bonington Ho
Enfield EN1 . . . . 18 A6
Pentonville N1. . . . 233 C3
Bonita Mews SE15 . . 140 D2
Bonne Marche Terr Mews 18 SE27 . . . 183 C6
Bonner Hill Rd KT1. . . 198 C6
Bonner Ho 3 SW15. . 156 A6
Bonner Prim Sch 39
E2. . . . . 96 C4
Bonner Rd E2 . . . . 96 C5
Bonnersfield Cl HA1 . . 43 A3
Bonnersfield La
Greenhill HA1 . . . . 42 D3
Kenton HA1, HA3. . . . 43 A3
Bonner St E2 . . . . 96 C5
Bonneville Gdns
SW4. . . . . 159 C5
Bonneville Prim Sch
SW4. . . . . 159 C5
Bonnington Ct 14
UB5. . . . . 84 D5
Bonnington Ho 9
SM2 . . . . . 217 D2
Bonnington Sq
SW8. . . . . 138 B6 270 C6
Bonnington Twr
BR2. . . . . 210 A3
Bonny St NW1 . . . . 71 C1
Bonser Rd TW1 . . . . 152 D2
Bonsor Ho SW8. . . . 269 B2
Bonsor St SE5 . . . . 139 C5
Bonthron Ho SW15. . . 134 C3
Bonus Pastor RC Sch
BR1. . . . . 186 C6
Bonville Gdns 17
NW4. . . . . 46 A5
Bonville Rd BR1 . . . . 186 D5
Bookbinder Cotts
N20. . . . . 14 D1
Booker Cl 11 E3. . . . 97 B2
Booker Rd 5 N18. . . . 34 A5
Bookham Ct CR4. . . . 202 B6
Boone Ct N9. . . . . 18 C1
Boones Rd SE13 . . . . 142 C1
Boone St SE13. . . . 142 C1
Boord St SE10 . . . . 120 C3
Boothby Ct E4. . . . 20 A1
Boothby Ho 2
SW16. . . . . 181 C5
Boothby Rd N19 . . . . 71 D6
Booth Cl
10 Hackney E9. . . . 96 B6
Thamesmead SE28 . . . 124 B6
Booth Ho
9 Brentford TW8 . . . 131 C5
2 Streatham SW2 . . . 160 C4
Booth La EC4 . . . . 252 A6
Boothman Ho HA3. . . . 43 D6
Booth Rd
Croydon CR0 . . . . 220 D6
Hendon NW9 . . . . 27 C1
Boothroyd Ho TW7. . . 130 D2
Booth's Pl W1 . . . . 239 B3
Boot Par HA8. . . . . 26 C4
Boot St N1 . . . . . 95 C4
Bordars Rd W7 . . . . 86 D2
Bordars Wlk W7 . . . . 86 C2
Bordeaux Ho 1 E15 . . 76 C3
Borden Ave EN1 . . . . 17 B5
Border Cres SE26 . . . 184 B5
Border Gate CR4. . . . 180 D2
Border Gdns CR0 . . . 223 D4
Border Rd SE26. . . . 184 B5
Bordesley Rd SM4 . . 201 D5
Bordeston Ct 11
TW8 . . . . . 131 C5
Bordley Ct 4 N20. . . . 14 D2
Bordon Wlk 5
SW15 . . . . . 156 A4
Boreas Wlk N1 . . . . 234 D3
Boreham Ave E16. . . . 99 A1
Boreham Cl E11 . . . . 54 A1
Boreham Rd N22 . . . . 33 A1
BOREHAMWOOD 11 A5
Boreman Ho 11
SE10. . . . . 142 A6
Borgard Rd SE18. . . . 122 B2
Borkwood Pk BR6 . . 227 D4
Borkwood Way BR6. . 227 C4
Borland Rd
London SE15 . . . . 140 C1
Teddington TW11. . . . 175 B3
Borneo St SW15 . . . . 134 C2
Borough High St
SE1. . . . . 117 B5 252 C4
Borough Hill CR0 . . . 220 D5
Borough Mkt★
SE1. . . . . 117 B5 252 C3
Borough Rd
Hounslow TW7. . . . 130 D4
7 Kingston u T KT2. . . 176 C3
Lambeth SE1 116 D3 261 D6
Mitcham CR4 . . . . 180 C1
Borough Sq SE1 . . . . 252 A1
Borough Sta
SE1. . . . . 117 A4 252 B1
BOROUGH THE. . . . 117 A4
Borrett Cl
SE17. . . . . 117 A1 262 A1
Borrodaile Rd SW18 157 D5
Borrowdale NW1 . . . 232 A1
Borrowdale Ave HA3 . . 25 A1
Borrowdale Cl
Finchley N2 . . . . 30 A1
Redbridge IG4. . . . 56 A5
Borrowdale Ct EN2 . . . 5 A4
Borthwick Mews E15 . 76 C4
Borthwick Rd
Leyton E15. . . . . 76 C4
London NW9 . . . . 45 D3
Borthwick St SE8 . . . 119 C1
Borwick Ave E17. . . . 53 B6
Bosbury Rd SE6. . . . 164 A1
Boscastle Rd NW5 . . . 71 B5
Boscobel Cl BR1 . . . . 188 B1
Boscobel Ho 4 E8. . . . 74 B2
Boscobel Pl SW1 . . . 258 B4
Boscobel St
NW8. . . . . 92 B3 236 D5
Boscombe Ave E10 . . . 54 B2
Boscombe Circus
NW9. . . . . 27 B1
Boscombe Cl E5. . . . 75 A3
Boscombe Gdns
SW16 . . . . . 182 A4
Boscombe Ho CR0 . . . 205 B1
Boscombe Rd
Merton SW19. . . . 179 D2
North Cheam KT4. . . . 200 D1
Shepherd's Bush W12 112 A4
Streatham SW17 . . . . 181 A4
Bose Cl N3 . . . . . 29 A2
Bosgrove E4. . . . . 20 A2
Boss Ho SE1. . . . . 253 C2
Boss St SE1. . . . . 253 C2
Bostall Hill SE2 . . . . 124 B1
Bostall La SE2 . . . . 124 B1
Bostall Manorway
SE2. . . . . 124 B2
Bostall Park Ave
DA7. . . . . 147 A5
Bostall Rd BR5. . . . 190 B3
Bostock Ho TW5 . . . . 129 C6
Boston Bsns Pk W7 . 108 C3
Boston Ct
South Norwood SE25 . . . . 205 D5
Sutton SM2 . . . . 218 A1
Boston Gdns
Brentford TW8. . . . 109 B2
Chiswick W4 . . . . 133 C6
Boston Gr HA4. . . . 39 A3
Boston Ho
24 Camberwell SE5. . 139 A3
Earl's Ct SW5. . . . 255 D3
Lisson Gr NW1. . . . 237 C6
Boston Lo W13 . . . . 109 C1
Boston Manor Ho
TW8. . . . . 109 B1
Boston Manor Rd
TW8. . . . . 131 B6
Boston Manor Sta
TW8. . . . . 109 A2
Boston Par W7 . . . . 109 A2
Boston Park Rd
TW8. . . . . 109 C1
Boston Pl
NW1. . . . . 92 D3 237 C5
Boston Rd
Burnt Oak HA8. . . . 27 A3
Ealing W7. . . . . 109 A3
Newham E6 . . . . 100 A4
Thornton Heath CR0 . 204 C3
3 Walthamstow E17. . . 53 C3
Bostonthorpe Rd
W7 . . . . . 108 C4
Boston Vale W7. . . . 109 A2
Bosun Cl 22 E14 . . . 119 C4
Boswell Ct
Bloomsbury WC1. . . . 240 B4
9 Hammersmith W14 . . . . 112 D3
Kingston u T KT2 . . . 176 C2
Boswell Ho
Bloomsbury WC1. . . . 240 B4
Bromley Comm BR2. . 209 D4
5 Streatham SW16 . . 181 C5
Boswell Rd CR7. . . . 205 A5
Boswell St
WC1. . . . . 94 A2 240 B4
Boswood Ct TW4. . . . 129 B2
Bosworth Cl E17. . . . 35 B2
Bosworth Ho 4 W10. . 91 A3
Bosworth Rd
Barnet EN5 . . . . 1 C2
Dagenham RM10. . . . 81 C5
Kensal Town W10. . . . 91 A3
Wood Green N11. . . . 31 D4
Botany Bay La BR7. . . 189 A1
Botany Cl EN4 . . . . 2 C1
Boteley Cl E4. . . . . 20 B2
Botham Cl 6 HA8. . . . 27 A3
Botha Rd E13. . . . . 99 C2
Bothwell Cl E16. . . . 98 D2
Bothwell St 4 W6 . . 134 D6
Botolph Alley EC3. . . 253 A6
Botolph La EC3 . . . . 253 A6
Botsford Rd SW20 . . . 179 A1
Bott's Mews W2 . . . . 91 C1
Botwell Common Rd
UB3. . . . . 105 C6
Botwell Cres UB3 . . . . 83 C1
Botwell House RC Prim Sch UB3 . . . . 105 D4
Botwell La UB3 . . . . 105 C6
Boucher Cl TW11 . . . 174 D5
Bouchier Ho 6 N2. . . . 30 B1
Bough Beech Ct EN3. . . 6 D6
Boughton Ave BR2. . . 208 D2
Boughton Ho
Borough The SE1 . . . 252 C2
Bromley BR1 . . . . 188 A3
Boughton Rd SE28 . . . 123 C3
Boulcott St E1. . . . . 96 D1
Boulevard Dr NW9. . . . 27 D1
Boulevard The
Chelsea SW6. . . . 266 B1
4 Upper Tooting SW17 . . . . 159 A2
Boullen Ct SM1. . . . 218 A4
Boulogne Ho SE1 . . . 263 C6
Boulogne Rd CR0 . . . 205 A3
Boulter Cl BR1. . . . 210 C5
Boulter Ho 4 SE14 . . 140 C4
Boulters Ct HA0 . . . . 65 A4
Boulton Ho TW8 . . . . 110 A1
Boulton Rd RM8 . . . . 81 B6
Boultwood Rd E6 . . . . 100 B1
Bounces La N9 . . . . 18 B2
Bounces Rd N9. . . . 18 C2
Boundaries Mans 3
SW12. . . . . 159 A3
Boundaries Rd
Feltham TW13 . . . . 150 C3
Upper Tooting SW12 . 159 A3
Boundary Ave E17 . . . 53 B2
Boundary Bsns Ct
CR4 . . . . . 202 B6
Boundary Cl
Barnet EN5 . . . . 1 B4
Ilford IG3. . . . . 79 C4
Kingston u T KT1 . . . 198 D6
Penge SE20. . . . 184 A1
Southall UB2 . . . . 107 C1
Boundary Ct
3 Edmonton N18 . . . . 33 D4
9 New Southgate N11 31 B6
Boundary Ho
Balham SW12 . . . . 159 B3
1 Camberwell SE5. . 139 A5
Edgware HA8. . . . 44 B6
Isleworth TW1. . . . 153 B6
15 Notting Hill W11. . 112 D5
Boundary La
Camberwell SE17. . . . 139 A6
Newham E13, E6 . . . . 99 D3
Boundary Pas E2 . . . 243 C6
Boundary Rd
Avery Hill DA15 . . . 167 C6
Barking IG11 . . . . 101 A5
London N2 . . . . . 30 B2
Mitcham SW19 . . . . 180 B4
Newham E13 . . . . 99 D4
Pinner HA5. . . . . 40 D2
Ponders End N9. . . . 18 C5
St John's Wood NW8 . . . . 92 A6 229 B6
Tottenham N22 . . . . 33 A1
Wallington SM5, SM6. 219 A1
Walthamstow E17 . . . 53 C3
Boundary Road Est
NW8. . . . . 92 A6 229 A5
Boundary Row SE1. . 251 C2
Boundary St
E2. . . . . 95 D3 243 C6
Boundary Way CR0 . . 223 C3
Boundfield Rd SE6. . . 164 C2
Bounds Green Ct
N11. . . . . 31 D4
Bounds Green Ind Est
N11 . . . . . 31 C4
Bounds Green Jun & Inf Schs N11 . . . . 32 A3
Bounds Green Rd
London N11 . . . . 31 D4
Wood Green N22. . . . 32 A3
Bounds Green Sta
N11 . . . . . 31 D3
Bourbon Ho 9 SE6 . . 186 A6
Bourchier St W1. . . . 249 C6
Bourdillon Ct 2
SE9. . . . . 166 A2
Bourdon Pl W1 . . . . 248 D6
Bourdon Rd SE20 . . . 184 C1
Bourdon St
W1. . . . . 115 B6 248 D5

- Bourke Cl
  - London SW4 160 A5
  - Willesden NW10 67 C2
- Bourlet Cl W1 239 A3
- Bourn Ave
  - Hillingdon UB8 82 C3
  - New Barnet EN4 14 B6
  - West Green N15 51 B5
- Bournbrook Rd SE3, SE9 143 D2
- Bourne Ave
  - Hayes UB3 105 B3
  - Palmers Green N14 16 A2
  - Ruislip HA4 62 C3
- Bourne Cir UB3 105 A3
- Bourne Cl
  - Hinchley Wood KT7 212 D6
  - Isleworth TW7 130 C2
- Bourne Ct
  - Chiswick W4 133 A6
  - Ruislip HA4 62 B3
  - Wanstead E11 55 A4
  - Woodford IG8 37 D1
- Bourne Dr CR4 180 B1
- Bourne Gdns E4 35 D6
- Bourne Hill N13 16 B2
- Bourne Ho
  - 4 Ashford TW15 170 C5
  - 3 Buckhurst Hill IG9 21 D1
  - 5 Clapham SW4 137 C1
  - 1 Dollis Hill NW2 68 A5
- Bourne Mans N13 32 C5
- Bournemead Ave UB5 84 A5
- Bournemead Cl UB5 84 A4
- Bournemead Way UB5 84 B5
- Bourne Mews W1 238 B1
- Bournemouth Cl SE15 140 A3
- Bournemouth Ct 6 SM1 218 A3
- Bournemouth Rd
  - London SE15 140 A3
  - Merton SW19 179 C2
- Bourne Par DA5 169 D4
- Bourne Pl W4 111 B1
- Bourne Prim Sch HA4 62 C2
- Bourne Rd
  - Bexley DA5 169 D5
  - Bromley BR2 209 D5
  - Hornsey N8 50 A3
  - Leyton E7, E11 76 D5
- Bournes Ho 4 N15 51 C3
- Bourneside 5 N14 15 D3
- Bourneside Cres 6 N14 15 D3
- Bourneside Gdns SE6 186 A5
- Bourne St
  - Belgravia SW1 115 A2 258 A3
  - Croydon CR0 220 D6
- Bourne Terr W2 91 D2
- Bourne The N14 16 A3
- Bourne Vale BR2 209 A2
- Bournevale Rd SW16 182 A6
- Bourne View UB6 64 D3
- Bourne Way
  - Cheam SM1 217 B3
  - Coney Hall BR2, BR4 224 D6
  - West Ewell KT19 215 A4
- Bournewood Rd SE18 146 A5
- Bournville Rd SE6 163 C4
- Bournwell Cl EN4 2 D3
- Bourton Cl UB3 106 A5
- Bousfield Prim Sch SW10 114 A1 256 A2
- Bousfield Rd SE14 140 D3
- Boutcher CE Prim Sch SE1 117 D2 263 C4
- Boutflower Rd SW11 136 C1
- Bouverie Ct 4 SW16 182 A5
- Bouverie Gdns HA3 43 D3
- Bouverie Mews N16 73 C6
- Bouverie Pl W2 236 D2
- Bouverie Rd
  - Harrow HA1 42 A3
  - Stoke Newington N16 73 C6
- Bouverie St EC4 94 C1 241 B1
- Bouvier Rd EN3 6 C5
- Boveney Rd SE23 162 D4
- Bovill Rd SE23 162 D4
- Bovingdon Ave HA9 66 C2
- Bovingdon Cl 4 N19 71 C6
- Bovingdon La NW9 27 C2
- Bovingdon Rd SW6 135 D4 265 D1
- Bovril Ho EN1 5 C2
- BOW 97 B5
- Bowater Cl
  - Clapham Pk SW2 160 A5
  - Kingsbury NW9 45 B4
- Bowater Gdns TW16 172 C2
- Bowater Ho EC1 242 B5
- Bowater Pl SE3 143 B5
- Bowater Rd
  - Greenwich SE18 121 D3
  - Wembley HA9 66 D5
- Bow Brook The 20 E2 96 D5
- Bow Church Sta E3 97 C4
- BOW COMMON 97 D2
- Bow Common La E3 97 B3
- Bowden Cl TW14 149 C3
- Bowden Ct HA4 62 C3
- Bowden Ho 29 E3 97 D4
- Bowden St SE11 116 C1 261 B1
- Bowditch SE8 119 B1
- Bowdon Rd E17 53 C2
- Bowen Ct 2 N5 72 D4
- Bowen Dr SE21 161 C1
- Bowen Rd HA1 42 A2
- Bowen St E14 97 D1
- Bower Ave SE3 142 C5
- Bower Cl UB5 84 C5
- Bowerdean St SW6 135 D3
- Bower Ho SE14 140 D4
- Bowerman Ave SE14 141 A6
- Bowerman Ct 1 N19 71 D6
- Bowers Ho 5 IG11 78 D1
- Bower St E1 96 D1
- Bowers Wlk 1 E6 100 B1
- Bowery Ct 16 RM10 81 D2
- Bowes Cl DA15 168 B5
- Bowes Ho N13 32 B5
- Bowes-Lyon Hall 13 E16 121 A5
- Bowes Lyon Ho 2 TW10 153 C1
- BOWES PARK 32 A4
- Bowes Park Sta N22 32 A3
- Bowes Prim Sch N11 31 D5
- Bowes Rd Acton W3 111 C6
  - Dagenham RM8 80 C4
  - New Southgate N11 31 C5
  - Walton-on-T KT12 194 B1
- Bowes Rd (North Circular Rd) N13 32 A5
- Bowfell Rd W6 134 C6
- Bowford Ave DA7 147 A4
- Bowhill Cl SW9 138 C5
- Bow Ho 1 E3 97 C4
- Bowie Cl SW4 159 D4
- Bow La
  - Barbican EC2, EC4 95 A1 242 B1
  - Finchley N12 30 A3
- Bowland Ho N4 51 A2
- Bowland Rd
  - London SW4 137 D1
  - Woodford IG8 37 C4
- Bowland Yd SW1 247 D1
- Bowl Ct EC2 243 B5
- Bowles Ct
  - Finchley N12 30 C3
  - Harrow HA3 43 A3
- Bowles Rd 1 SE1 140 A6
- Bowley Cl SE19 183 D4
- Bowley Ho 6 SE16 118 A3
- Bowley La SE19 183 D5
- Bowling Cl UB10 82 B6
- Bowling Green Cl SW19 156 B4
- Bowling Green Ct HA9 66 B6
- Bowling Green Ho SW10 266 C4
- Bowling Green La EC1 94 C3 241 B6
- Bowling Green Pl SE1 252 C2
- Bowling Green Row 1 SE18 122 B2
- Bowling Green St SE11 138 C6
- Bowling Green Wlk N1 95 C4
- Bowls Cl HA7 25 B5
- Bowman Ave E16 120 D6
- Bowman Homes W5 109 D4
- Bowman Mews
  - St George in t East E1 118 A6
  - Wandsworth SW18 157 B3
- Bowmans Cl W13 109 B5
- Bowmans Lea SE23 162 C4
- Bowman's Meadow SM6 219 B5
- Bowman's Mews N7 72 A5
- Bowman's Pl N7 72 A5
- Bowman Trad Est NW9 44 C5
- Bowmar Lo 13 EN5 1 D1
- Bowmead SE9 166 B2
- Bowmore Wlk NW1 71 D1
- Bowness Cl 5 E8 73 D2
- Bowness Cres KT2, SW15 177 C5
- Bowness Dr TW4 129 A1
- Bowness Ho SE15 140 C5
- Bowness Rd
  - Catford SE6 163 D4
  - Erith DA7 147 D3
- Bowood Rd
  - Clapham SW11 159 A6
  - Enfield EN3 6 D3
- Bow Rd E3 97 C4
- Bowring Gn WD19 22 C5
- Bow Road Sta E3 97 C4
- Bowrons Ave HA0 65 D1
- Bowry Ho 14 E14 97 B2
- Bow Sec Sch 19 E3 97 C4
- Bowsley Ct TW13 150 A2
- Bowsprit Point 1 E14 119 C3
- Bow St
  - St Giles WC2 94 A1 240 B1
  - Stratford E15 76 C3
- Bowstead Ct SW11 266 D1
- Bow Triangle Bsns Ctr 17 E3 97 C3
- Bowyer Cl E6 100 B2
- Bowyer Ho
  - Mitcham CR4 202 C6
  - 27 Shoreditch N1 95 C6
  - Wandsworth SW18 157 D5
- Bowyer Pl SE5 139 A5
- Bowyer St 15 SE5 139 A5
- Boxall Rd SE21 161 C5
- Box Cnr TW2 152 C2
- Boxelder Cl HA8 27 A5
- Boxgrove Prim Sch SE2 124 C3
- Boxgrove Rd SE2 124 C3
- Box La IG11 102 C5
- Boxley Ho 3 E5 74 B3
- Boxley Rd SM4 202 A5
- Boxley St E16 121 B5
- Boxmoor Ho
  - 16 Hackney E2 96 A6
  - 9 Shepherd's Bush W11 112 D5
- Boxmoor Rd HA3 43 B5
- Boxoll Rd RM9 81 B5
- Boxshall Ho 7 SE18 144 D6
- Box Tree Ho SE8 119 A1
- Boxtree La HA3 24 B3
- Boxtree Rd HA3 24 B3
- Boxwood Cl UB7 104 B4
- Boxworth Cl N12 30 B5
- Boxworth Gr N1 94 B6 233 D6
- Boyard Rd SE18 122 D1
- Boyce Ho
  - Streatham SW16 181 C5
  - 1 West Kilburn W10 91 B4
- Boyce Way E13 99 A3
- Boycroft Ave NW9 45 A3
- Boyd Ave UB1 107 B5
- Boyd Cl KT2 176 C3
- Boyd Ct SW15 156 C5
- Boydell Ct NW8 70 B1
- Boyden Ho 8 E17 54 A6
- Boyd Rd SW19 180 B4
- Boyd St E1 96 A1
- Boyfield St SE1 116 D4 251 D1
- Boyland Rd BR1 186 D5
- Boyle Ave HA7 25 A4
- Boyle Cl UB10 82 B5
- Boyle Farm Rd KT7 197 A3
- Boyle Ho
  - 13 Belvedere DA17 125 C3
  - Wembley HA9 66 D5
- Boyle St W1 249 A6
- Boyne Ave NW4 46 D5
- Boyne Ct NW10 68 A1
- Boyne Ho 10 E5 74 B6
- Boyne Rd
  - Dagenham RM10 81 C5
  - Lewisham SE13 142 B2
- Boyne Terr Mews W11 113 B5 244 C4
- Boyson Rd 10 SE17 139 B6
- Boyton Cl London N8 50 A6
  - Stepney E1 96 D3
- Boyton Ho
  - Kennington SE11 261 A1
  - St John's Wood NW8 229 D4
- Boyton Rd N8 50 A6
- Brabant Ct EC3 253 A6
- Brabant Rd N22 32 B1
- Brabazon Ave SM6 220 A1
- Brabazon Rd
  - Heston TW5 128 D5
  - Northolt UB5 85 C5
- Brabazon St E14 97 D2
- Brabner Ho 3 E2 96 A4
- Brabourne Cl 7 SE19 183 C5
- Brabourne Cres DA7 147 B6
- Brabourne Hts NW7 11 C1
- Brabourne Rise BR3 208 B4
- Brabourn Gr SE15 140 C3
- Brabrook Ct SM6 219 B3
- Brabstone Ho 2 UB6 86 D5
- Bracer Ho 1 N1 95 C5
- Bracewell Ave UB6 65 A2
- Bracewell Rd W10 90 C2
- Bracewood Gdns CR0 221 D5
- Bracey Mews 1 N4 72 A6
- Bracey St N4 72 A6
- Bracken Ave
  - Balham SW12 159 A4
  - Croydon CR0 223 C5
- Brackenbridge Dr HA4 62 D5
- Brackenbury N4 50 B1
- Brackenbury Gdns W6 112 B3
- Brackenbury Prim Sch 4 W6 112 B3
- Brackenbury Rd
  - East Finchley N2 48 A6
  - Hammersmith W6 112 B3
- Bracken Cl
  - Ashford TW16 171 D4
  - Newham E6 100 B2
  - Twickenham TW4 151 C4
- Brackendale
  - Kingston u T KT1 176 D1
  - Southgate N21 16 B2
- Brackendale Cl TW5 129 D4
- Brackendale Ct 2 BR3 185 C3
- Bracken End TW7 152 B6
- Brackenfield Cl E5 74 B5
- Bracken Gdns SW13 134 A3
- Brackenhill HA4 63 A4
- Bracken Hill Cl 5 BR1 186 D2
- Bracken Hill La BR1 186 D2
- Bracken Ho 15 E3 97 C2
- Bracken Mews
  - Chingford E4 20 A3
  - Romford RM7 59 D3
- Brackens BR3 185 C3
- Brackens The EN1 17 C4
- Bracken The E4 20 A2
- Brackenwood TW16 172 A2
- Brackenwood Lo EN5 1 C1
- Brackley Ave SE15 140 C2
- Brackley Cl SM6 220 A1
- Brackley Ct NW8 236 D6
- Brackley Rd
  - Beckenham BR3 185 C3
  - Chiswick W4 111 C1
- Brackley Sq IG8 37 D3
- Brackley St EC1 242 B4
- Brackley Terr 6 W4 111 C1
- Bracklyn Ct N1 235 C4
- Bracklyn St N1 235 C4
- Bracknell Cl N22 32 C2
- Bracknell Gate NW3 69 D3
- Bracknell Gdns NW3 69 D4
- Bracknell Way NW3 69 D4
- Bracondale KT10 212 A3
- Bracondale Rd SE2 124 A2
- Braconhyrst HA1 42 C2
- Bradbeer Ho 24 E2 96 C4
- Bradbourne Ct 11 SM2 217 D2
- Bradbourne Rd DA5 169 C4
- Bradbourne St SW6 135 C3
- Bradbury Cl UB2 107 B2
- Bradbury Ct
  - 4 Barnet EN5 1 D1
  - 2 Greenwich SE3 143 A5
  - Merton SW20 178 C1
- Bradbury Ho E1 243 D2
- Bradbury St 28 N16 73 C3
- Bradby Ho NW8 91 D5
- Braddock Cl TW7 130 D3
- Braddon Rd TW9 132 B2
- Braddyll St SE10 120 C1
- Bradenham 11 SE17 139 B6
- Bradenham Ave DA16 146 A1
- Bradenham Cl SE17 139 B6
- Bradenham Rd
  - Harrow HA3 43 B5
  - Hayes UB4 83 C4
- Braden St W9 91 D3
- Bradfield Ct 14 NW1 71 B1
- Bradfield Dr IG11 80 A3
- Bradfield Ho 15 SW8 137 D3
- Bradfield Rd
  - Newham E16 121 B4
  - Ruislip HA4 63 A3
- Bradford Cl
  - Bromley BR2 210 B1
  - Forest Hill SE26 184 B6
  - Tottenham N17 33 D4
- Bradford Dr KT19 215 D2
- Bradford Ho 4 W14 112 D3
- Bradford Rd
  - Acton W3 111 C4
  - Ilford IG1 57 C1
- Bradgate Rd SE6 163 D5
- Brading Cres E11 77 B6
- Brading Rd
  - Streatham SW2 160 B4
  - Thornton Heath CR0 204 B3
- Brading Terr W12 112 A3
- Bradiston Rd W9 91 B4
- Bradley Cl N7 72 B2
- Bradley Ct CR0 220 C4
- Bradley Gdns W13 87 B1
- Bradley Ho
  - Bermondsey SE16 118 B2
  - 1 Bromley E3 97 D4
  - Twickenham TW1 152 D3
  - Woodford IG8 37 A3
- Bradley Mews SW12 158 D3
- Bradley Rd Enfield EN3 7 A6
  - Upper Norwood SE19 183 A4
  - Wood Green N22 32 B1
- Bradley's Cl N1 234 B4
- Bradley Stone Rd E6 100 B2
- Bradlord Ho SE21 161 C1
- Bradman Row 7 HA8 27 A3
- Bradmead SW8 137 C5 269 A3
- Bradmore Ct 2 EN3 7 A2
- Bradmore Park Rd W6 112 B2
- Bradon 24 NW9 27 D1
- Bradshaw Cl SW19 179 C4
- Bradshaw Dr NW7 28 D3
- Bradshawe Waye UB8 82 B2
- Bradshaws Cl SE25 206 A6
- Bradsole Ho 13 BR3 185 C3
- Brad St SE1 116 C5 251 B3
- Bradstock Ho E9 75 A1
- Bradstock Rd
  - Homerton E9 74 D2
  - Stoneleigh KT17 216 B3
- Bradwell Ave RM10 81 C6
- Bradwell Cl E18 54 D5

Bradwell Ho
8 Kilburn NW6 91 D6
9 Walthamstow E17 53 D6
Bradwell Mews 5 N18 34 A6
Bradwell St 24 E1 96 D4
Brady Ct RM8 58 D1
Brady Dr BR1 210 C6
Brady Ho
London SW4 159 D6
South Lambeth SW8 269 B2
Bradymead E6 100 D1
Brady St E1 96 B3
Braeburn Ct 1 EN4 2 C1
Brae Ct
2 Kingston u T KT2 176 C2
South Norwood SE25 183 C2
Braefoot Ct SW15 156 D6
Braemar SW15 156 D5
Braemar Ave
Thornton Heath CR7 204 D6
Welsh Harp NW10 67 B6
Wembley HA0 66 A1
Wimbledon SW18, SW19 157 C2
Wood Green N22 32 A2
Braemar Ct
4 Brentford TW8 131 D6
5 Catford SE6 164 D3
Braemar Gdns
Hendon NW9 27 B2
Longlands DA15 167 B1
West Wickham BR4 208 A1
Braemar Ho
Richmond TW11 175 B5
St John's Wood W9 229 A1
Braemar Mans W8 255 D5
Braemar Rd
Brentford TW8 131 D6
Newham E13 98 D3
North Cheam KT4 216 B5
South Tottenham N15 51 C4
Braemore Ct EN4 3 A1
Braeside BR3 185 D5
Braeside Ave SW19 179 A2
Braeside Cl HA5 23 C3
Braeside Jun Sch IG9 21 C2
Braeside Rd SW16 181 C3
Braeside Senior Sch IG9 21 B3
Braes St N1 72 D1
Braesyde Cl DA17 125 B2
Brafferton Rd CR0 221 A4
Braganza St SE17 116 D1 261 C1
Bragg Cl RM8 80 B2
Bragg Rd TW11 174 D4
Braham Ho SE11 260 D1
Braham St E1 243 D2
Brahma Kumaris World Spiritual Univ NW10 68 A1
Braid Ave W3 89 C1
Braid Cl TW13 151 B2
Braid Ho SE10 142 A4
Braidwood Ho 2 CR7 204 D5
Braidwood Rd SE6 164 B3
Braidwood St SE1 117 C5 253 A3
Braikenridge Ho N21 17 B5
Brailsford Cl SW19 180 C3
Brailsford Rd SW2 160 C5
Braintcroft Prim Sch NW2 67 D5
Brainton Ave TW14 150 C4
Braintree Ave IG4 56 A5
Braintree Ho 6 E1 96 C3
Braintree Ind Est HA4 62 B4
Braintree Rd
Dagenham RM10 81 C5
Ruislip HA4 62 B4
Braintree St E2 96 C4
Braithwaite Ave RM7 59 C2
Braithwaite Gdns HA7 25 C2
Braithwaite Ho EC1 242 C6
Braithwaite Rd EN3 7 B2
Braithwaite Twr W2 236 C4
Brake Shear Ho 1 EN5 1 B2
Bramah Gn SW9 138 C4
Bramah Mus of Tea & Coffee The* SE1 252 B3
Bramalea Cl N6 49 A3
Bramall Cl E15 76 D3
Bramall Ct N7 72 B2
Bramber WC1 233 A1
Bramber Ct TW8 110 A2
Bramber Ho 9 KT2 176 A2
Bramber Rd
Colney Hatch N12 30 C5
Fulham W14 135 B6 264 C6
Bramble Acres Cl SM2 217 C1
Bramblebury Rd SE18 123 A1
Bramble Cl
Beckenham BR3 208 A4
Croydon CR0 223 D4
Hillingdon UB8 82 B1
South Tottenham N15 52 A5
Stanmore HA7 25 D3
Upper Halliford TW17 193 B6
Brambledown 8 N4 50 A2
Brambledown Cl BR2, BR4 208 C4
Brambledown Rd
South Croydon CR2 221 C1
Wallington SM5, SM6 219 B1
Bramble Gdns W12 111 D6
Bramble Ho 16 E3 97 C2
Bramble La TW12 173 B4
Brambles Cl TW7, TW8 131 B5
Brambles Farm Dr UB10 82 C4
Brambles The
West Drayton UB7 104 A2
8 Wimbledon SW19 179 B5
Bramblewood Cl SM5 202 C1
Brambling Ct
25 Deptford SE8 141 B6
South Norwood SE25 205 D5
Bramblings The E4 36 B6
Bramcote Ave CR4 202 D5
Bramcote Ct CR4 202 D5
Bramcote Gr SE16 118 C1
Bramcote Rd SW15 134 B1
Bramdean Cres SE12 165 A3
Bramdean Gdns SE12 165 A3
Bramerton NW6 68 D1
Bramerton Rd BR3 207 B6
Bramerton St SW3 136 C6 267 A6
Bramfield Ct N4 73 A6
Bramfield Rd SW11 158 D6
Bramford Ct N14 15 D2
Bramford Rd SW18 136 A1
Bramham Gdns
Chessington KT9 213 D4
South Kensington SW5 113 D1 255 D2
Bramham Ho SE22 139 C1
Bramhope La SE7 143 B6
Bramlands Cl SW11 136 C2
Bramley Ave TW17 193 C6
Bramley Cl
Croydon CR2 221 A3
East Barnet N14 15 B6
Edgware NW7 11 C1
Hayes UB3 106 A6
Higham Hill E17 35 A1
Orpington BR6 210 D1
Pinner HA5 39 D6
Twickenham TW2 152 A5
Woodford IG8 37 C3
Bramley Cres
Ilford IG2 56 C3
Nine Elms SW8 137 D5 269 D4
Bramley Ct
2 Barnet EN4 2 C1
7 Chingford E4 20 A3
Dollis Hill NW2 68 B5
Feltham TW14 149 C5
Hither Green SE13 164 B6
Mitcham CR4 180 B1
Southall UB1 108 A6
Wallington SM6 219 C3
Welling DA16 146 B4
Bramley Gdns WD19 22 C5
Bramley Hill CR2 221 A4
Bramley Ho
Hounslow TW3 129 B1
Ilford IG2 56 C3
1 Kingston u T KT2 176 D3
19 North Kensington W10 90 D1
Roehampton SW15 155 D5
Bramley House Ct EN2 5 B6
Bramleyhyrst CR2 221 A3
Bramley Lo HA0 65 D4
Bramley Rd
Ealing W5 109 C3
North Kensington W10 90 D1
Southgate N14 15 C6
Sutton SM1 218 B3
Bramley Way
Hounslow TW4 151 B6
West Wickham BR4 223 D6
Brampton WC1 240 C3
Brampton Cl 14 E5 74 B6
Brampton Coll NW4 46 C5
Brampton Ct NW4 46 B5
Brampton Gr
Harrow HA3 43 B5
Hendon NW4 46 C5
Wembley HA9 44 C1
Brampton La 6 NW4 46 C5
Brampton Lo DA7 146 D5
Brampton Manor Sch E6 99 D3
Brampton Park Rd N22 50 C6
Brampton Prim Sch
Bexley DA7 146 D3
Newham E6 100 A4
Brampton Rd
Bexleyheath DA7 147 A4
Croydon CR0 205 D3
Harringay N15 51 A4
Hillingdon UB10 82 D5
Newham E6 99 D4
Queensbury NW9 44 C5
Bramshaw Gdns WD19 22 D5
Bramshaw Rd E9 74 D2
Bramshaw Rise KT3 199 C3
Bramshill Gdns NW5 71 B5
Bramshill Rd NW10 89 D5
Bramshot Ave SE7 143 B6
Bramshott Ct 3 KT6 198 A3
Bramshurst NW8 91 D6
Bramston Rd
Harlesden NW10 90 A5
Wandsworth SW17 158 A1
Bramwell Cl TW16 172 D1
Bramwell Ho
Borough The SE1 262 B5
Chelsea SW1 269 A6
Bramwell Mews N1 233 D6
Brancaster Dr NW7 28 A3
Brancaster Ho
22 Globe Town E1 96 D4
Islington N5 72 D3
Brancaster Rd
Ilford E12 78 B4
Newbury Pk IG2 57 C3
Streatham SW16 160 A1
Brancepeth Gdns IG9 21 A2
Branch Hill NW3 70 A5
Branch Ho 13 SM1 218 A4
Branch Pl N1 95 B6 235 D6
Branch Rd E14 119 A6
Branch St SE15 139 C5
Brancker Rd HA3 43 D6
Brancroft Way EN3 7 B4
Brandan Ho 11 HA1 42 D4
Brand Cl N4 50 D1
Branden Lo 13 W4 111 A1
Brandlehow Prim Sch SW15 135 B1
Brandlehow Rd SW15 135 B1
Brandon Ho BR3 185 D5
Brandon Mews
Barbican EC2 242 C4
Walworth SE17 262 B3
Brandon Pl N8 50 B5
Brandon Rd
Barnsbury N7 72 A1
Southall UB2 107 B1
Sutton SM1 217 D4
Walthamstow E17 54 A6
Brandon St SE17 117 A2 262 B3
Brandram Rd SE13 142 C1
Brandrams Wharf SE16 118 C4
Brandreth Ct HA1 42 D3
Brandreth Rd
Newham E6 100 B1
Upper Tooting SW17 159 B2
Brandries The SM6 219 D5
Brand St SE10 142 A5
Brandville Gdns IG6 56 D5
Brandville Rd UB7 104 A4
Brandy Way SM2 217 C1
Brangbourne Rd BR1 186 A5
Brangton Rd SE11 260 D1
Brangwyn Cres SW19 180 B1
Brangwyn Ct W14 254 A5
Branham Ho 1 SE18 122 D1
Branksea St SW6 135 A5 264 A3
Branksome Ave N18 33 D5
Branksome Cl
Teddington TW11 174 B6
Walton-on-T KT12 194 D1
Branksome Ct 6 N2 48 A6
Branksome Ho SW8 270 C4
Branksome Rd
London SW2 160 A6
Merton SW19 179 C2
Branksome Way
Harrow HA3 44 B3
Kingston u T KT3 177 B2
Bransby Ct 4 N16 73 C4
Bransby Rd KT9 214 A2
Branscombe NW1 232 B5
Branscombe Ct BR2 208 C4
Branscombe Gdns N21 16 C4
Branscombe St SE13 141 D2
Bransdale Cl NW6 91 C6
Bransgrove Rd HA8 26 B3
Branston Cres BR5 211 B1
Branstone Ct 9 TW9 132 B4
Branstone Rd TW9 132 B4
Branston Ho N7 72 C3
Brants Wlk W7 86 C3
Brantwood Ave
Erith DA8 147 D5
Isleworth TW7 131 A1
Brantwood Cl E17 53 D6
Brantwood Gdns
Enfield EN2 16 A6
Redbridge IG4 56 A5
Brantwood Ho 9 SE5 139 A5
Brantwood Rd
Erith DA7 147 D3
Herne Hill SE24 161 A6
Tottenham N17 34 A4
Brasenose Dr SW13 134 C6
Brasher Cl UB6 64 B3
Brashley Road Cvn Site NW10 89 C4
Brassett Point 3 E15 98 C6
Brassey Cl TW14 150 A3
Brassey Ho
1 Millwall E14 119 D2
Walton-on-T KT12 194 A1
Brassey Rd NW6 69 B2
Brassey Sq SW11 137 A2
Brassie Ave W3 89 C1
Brass Talley Alley 31 SE16 118 D4
Brasted Cl
Bexley DA6 168 D6
Forest Hill SE26 184 C6
Brasted Lo 11 BR3 185 C3
Brathay NW1 232 B3
Brathway Rd SW18 157 C4
Bratley St 11 E1 96 A3
Bratten Ct CR0 205 B3
Braund Ave UB6 85 D3
Braundton Ave DA15 167 D3
Braunston Dr UB4 85 A3
Braunston Ho TW8 131 C6
Bravington Cl TW17 192 B4
Bravington Pl W9 91 B3
Bravington Rd W9 91 B4
Brawne Ho 12 SE17 138 D6
Braxfield Rd SE4 141 B1
Braxted Pk SW16 182 B4
Bray NW3 70 C1
Brayard's Rd SE15 140 B3
Braybourne Dr TW7 130 D5
Braybrooke Gdns SE19 183 C3
Braybrook St W12 89 D1
Brayburne Ave SW4 137 C3
Braycourt Ave KT12 194 C2
Bray Cres SE16 118 D4
Bray Ct
Chessington KT9 214 B3
Streatham SW16 182 A5
Braydon Rd N16 52 A1
Bray Dr E16 120 D6
Brayfield Terr N1 72 C1
Brayford Sq 12 E1 96 C1
Bray Pl SW3 114 D2 257 C3
Bray Rd NW7 28 D4
Brayton Gdns EN2 3 D1
Braywick Ct 9 KT2 176 C3
Braywood Rd SE9 145 B1
Brazier Cres UB5 85 B3
Brazil Cl CR0 204 A2
Breach La RM9 103 C4
Bread St EC2, EC4 242 B1
Breakspeare SE21 161 D1
Breakspear Jun & Inf Schs UB10 60 C6
Breakspear Rd HA4, UB9 38 D3
Breakspear Road N UB9 38 B5
Breakspear Road S UB9, UB10 38 C1
Breakspears Dr BR5 190 A2
Breakspears Mews SE4 141 C3
Breakspears Rd SE4 141 C2
Breakwell Ct 16 W10 91 A3
Bream Cl N17 52 B5
Bream Gdns E6 100 C4
Breamore Cl SW15 156 A3
Breamore Ct IG3 80 A6
Breamore Ho 21 SE15 140 A5
Breamore Rd IG3 79 D6
Bream's Bldgs EC4 94 C1 241 A2
Bream St E3 75 C1
Breamwater Gdns TW10 153 B1
Brearley Cl
Burnt Oak HA8 27 A3
Uxbridge UB8 60 A2
Breaside Prep Sch BR1 187 D2
Breasley Cl SW15 134 B1
Brechin Pl SW7 114 A2 256 B3
Brecknock Prim Sch 18 N7 71 D2
Brecknock Rd N19 71 D3
Breckonmead BR1 187 C1
Brecon Cl
Mitcham CR4 204 A6
North Cheam KT4 216 C6
Brecon Ct
7 Eltham SE9 166 C5
Whetstone N12 14 A1
Brecon Gn NW9 45 C3
Brecon Ho
Stamford Hill N16 51 D1
Wandsworth SW18 157 C4
Brecon Rd Enfield EN3 6 C1
Fulham W6 135 A6 264 B5
Brede Cl E6 100 C4
Bredel Ho 1 E14 97 C2
Bredgar SE13 163 D6
Bredgar Rd N19 71 C6
Bredhurst Cl SE20 184 C4
Bredinghurst SE22 162 A4
Bredinghurst Sch SE15 140 D1
Bredin Ho SW10 265 D4
Bredo Ho IG11 102 B4
Bredon Ct HA8 26 B6
Bredon Rd CR0 205 D2
Breer St SW6 135 D2
Breezer's Ct 22 E1 118 A6
Breezer's Hill E1 118 A6
Brehon Ho NW1 232 A5
Bremans Row 1 SW18 158 A2
Bremer Rd HA2 64 A6
Bremer Mews E17 53 D5
Bremner Rd SW7 256 B6

Brenchley Cl
Chislehurst BR7 188 C2
Hayes BR2 208 D3
Brenchley Gdns SE15, SE22, SE23 162 D5
Brenchley Rd BR5 189 D1
Bren Ct 27 EN3 7 C6
Brenda Rd SW17 158 D2
Brende Gdns KT8 195 D5
Brendon Ave NW10 67 C4
Brendon Cl
Esher KT10 212 A2
Harlington UB7 127 A5
Brendon Ct
3 London N20 14 C2
Southall UB2 107 D2
Brendon Dr KT10 212 A2
Brendon Gdns
Harrow HA2 63 D4
Ilford IG2 57 C4
Brendon Gr N2 30 A1
Brendon Ho
Marylebone W1 238 A4
Sutton SM2 218 A2
Brendon Rd
Dagenham RM8 59 C1
New Eltham SE9 167 B2
Brendon St
W1 92 C1 237 B2
Brendon Villas N21 17 A3
Brendon Way EN1 17 C4
Brenley Cl CR4 203 A6
Brenley Gdns SE9 143 D1
Brenley Ho SE1 252 C2
Brennands Ct 14 N19 71 C5
Brent Adult Comm Education Service Coll 9 NW10 89 B6
Brent Cl DA5 169 A3
Brentcot Cl W13 87 B3
Brent Cres NW10 88 B5
Brent Cross Flyover NW2, NW4 46 D2
Brent Cross Gdns NW4 46 D3
Brent Cross Interchange NW2, NW4 46 D2
Brent Cross Sh Ctr NW4 46 C2
Brent Cross Sta NW11 46 D2
Brent Ct
5 Acton W12 111 C3
Ealing W7 108 B6
Hendon NW11 46 D2
Brentfield NW10 66 D1
Brentfield Cl NW10 67 B2
Brentfield Gdns NW2 46 D2
Brentfield Ho 7 NW10 67 B1
Brentfield Jun & Inf Sch NW10 67 B2
Brentfield Rd NW10 67 B2
BRENTFORD 131 B6
Brentford Bsns Ctr TW8 131 C5
Brentford Cl UB4 84 D3
BRENTFORD END 131 C4
Brentford Fountain L Ctr W4 110 C1
Brentford Ho 6 TW1 153 B4
Brentford Sch for Girls TW8 131 D6
Brentford Sta TW8 131 C6
Brent Gn NW4 46 D4
Brentham Way W5 87 D3
Brent Ho
3 Catford BR1 186 B5
16 Hackney E9 74 C2
Wembley HA9 66 B3
Brenthouse Rd E9 74 C2
Brenthurst Rd NW10 67 D2
Brent Knoll Sch 15 SE26 162 D1
Brent Lea TW8 131 C5
Brent Mans NW4 46 C4
Brentmead Cl W7 108 C6
Brentmead Gdns NW10 88 B5
Brentmead Pl NW11 46 D3
Brent Mus★ NW10 68 B2
Brent New Ent Ctr NW10 67 D2
Brenton Ct E9 75 A3
Brenton St E14 97 A1
Brent Park Ind Est UB2 106 C3
Brent Park Rd NW4 46 B2
Brent Pl EN5 13 B6
Brent Rd
Brentford TW8 131 C6
Newham E16 99 A2
Southall UB2 106 C3
Woolwich SE18 144 D5
Brentside TW8 131 C6
Brentside Cl W13 87 A3
Brentside Executive Ctr TW8 131 B6
Brentside High Sch W7 86 C3
Brentside Prim Sch W7 86 C3
Brent St NW4 46 C4
Brent Trad Est NW10 67 C3
Brentvale Ave
Southall UB1 108 B5
Wembley HA0 88 B6
Brent View Rd NW9 46 A2
Brentwaters Bsns Pk TW8 131 C5
Brent Way
Brentford TW8 131 D5
Finchley N3 29 C4
Wembley HA9 66 D2
Brentwick Gdns TW8 110 A2
Brentwood Cl SE9 167 A3
Brentwood Ho 2 SE18 143 D5
Brentwood Lo NW4 46 D4
Brereton Ho 4 SW2 160 C4
Brereton Rd N17 33 D3
Bressay Dr NW7 28 A3
Bressenden Pl SW1 115 C3 259 A6
Bressey Ave EN1 6 A4
Bressey Gr E18 36 D1
Bretherton Ct CR2 221 C2
Breton Ho
Bermondsey SE1 263 C6
St Luke's EC2 242 B5
Brett Cl
15 Northolt UB5 84 D4
Stoke Newington N16 73 C6
Brett Cres NW10 89 B6
Brett Ct N9 18 C2
Brettell St SE17 262 D1
Brettenham Ave E17 35 C2
Brettenham Prim Sch 10 N18 34 A6
Brettenham Rd
Edmonton N18 34 A6
Walthamstow E17 35 C2
Brett Ho 1 SW15 156 D4
Brett House Cl 2 SW15 156 D4
Brettinghurst 8 SE1 118 A1
Bretton Ho N19 50 A1
Brett Pas 28 E8 74 B3
Brett Rd Barnet EN5 12 C6
Hackney E8 74 B3
Brewers Bldgs EC1 234 C2
Brewers Ct W2 236 A2
Brewer's Gn SW1 259 C6
Brewers Hall Gdns EC2 242 B3
Brewers La 11 TW9 153 D6
Brewer St W1 115 C6 249 B6
Brewery Cl HA0 65 A4
Brewery Ind Est The N1 235 B3
Brewery Mews Bsns Ctr 1 TW7 131 A2
Brewery Rd
Islington N7 72 A2
Keston Mark BR2 210 A1
Plumstead SE18 123 B1
Brewery Sq
Bermondsey SE1 253 C3
Clerkenwell EC1 241 D6
Brewhouse La
Putney SW15 135 A2
Wapping E1 118 B5
Brewhouse Rd 3 SE18 122 B2
Brewhouse Wlk SE16 119 A5
Brewhouse Yd EC1 241 C6
Brewood Rd RM8 80 B2
Brewster Gdns W10 90 C2
Brewster Ho
Bermondsey SE1 263 D4
Poplar E14 119 B6
Brewster Rd E10 53 D1
Brian Ct N10 31 B2
Brian Rd RM6 58 C4
Briant Ho SE1 260 D5
Briants Cl HA5 23 B1
Briant St SE14 140 D5
Briar Ave SW16 182 B3
Briarbank Rd W13 87 A1
Briar Cl
Buckhurst Hill IG9 21 D2
Edmonton N13 17 A1
Finchley N2 30 A1
Hampton TW12 173 B5
Isleworth TW7 152 D6
Briar Cres UB5 63 D2
Briar Ct 7 Bow E3 97 C5
Cheam SM3 216 C4
9 Dalston E8 73 D1
Hampton TW12 173 D5
Leytonstone E11 54 B2
Briardale
Edgware HA8 27 B6
Wandsworth SW19 157 B3
Briardale Gdns NW3 69 C5
Briardale Ho 12 N16 51 C1
Briarfield Ave N3 29 D1
Briarfield Cl DA7 147 C3
Briar Gdns BR2 208 D1
Briaris Cl 11 N17 34 B3
Briar La CR0 223 D4
Briar Lo E18 37 C2
Briar Rd
Cricklewood NW2 68 C4
Harrow HA3 43 C4
Littleton TW17 192 C4
Thornton Heath SW16 204 B6
Twickenham TW2 152 C3
Briars The WD23 8 C4
Briarswood Way BR6 227 D3
Briar The 11 SM1 218 A4
Briarview Ct E4 36 B4
Briar Way UB7 104 C4
Briar Wlk
Burnt Oak HA8 27 A3
Putney SW15 134 B1
West Kilburn W10 91 A3
Briarwood Cl
Feltham TW13 149 C1
Kingsbury NW9 45 A3
Briarwood Ct 5 KT4 200 A1
Briarwood Dr HA6 22 A1
Briarwood Rd
London SW4 159 D6
Stoneleigh KT17 216 A2
Briary Cl NW3 70 C1
Briary Ct
10 Canning Town E16 98 D1
Sidcup DA14 190 B5
Briary Gdns BR1 187 B5
Briary Gr HA8 26 D1
Briary La N9 17 D1
Briary Lo BR3 186 A2
Brickbarn Cl SW10 266 B4
Brick Ct EC4 241 A1
Brickett Cl HA4 39 A4
Brick Farm Cl TW9 132 D4
Brickfield Cl TW8 131 C5
Brickfield Cotts SE18 145 D6
Brickfield Farm Gdns BR6 227 A4
Brickfield La
Edgware EN5 11 D5
Harlington UB3 127 B6
Brickfield Rd
South Norwood CR7, SW16 182 D2
Wimbledon SW19 179 D6
Brickfields HA2 64 B6
Brickfields Way UB7 104 B3
Brick La Enfield EN1 6 B3
Northolt UB5 85 B4
Shoreditch E2 95 D4
Spitalfields E1 95 D3 243 D5
Stanmore HA7 25 D3
Brick Lane Mkt★ E2 95 D3 243 D6
Bricklayers Arms SE1 262 D5
Brick St W1 115 B5 248 C3
Brickwall La HA4 39 D1
Brickwood Cl SE26 162 B1
Brickwood Rd CR0 221 C6
Brickworth Ho 26 SW9 138 C4
Brideale Cl SE15 139 D6
Bride Ct EC4 241 C1
Bride La EC4 94 D1 241 C1
Bridel Mews N1 234 C5
Bride St N7 72 B2
Bridewain St SE1 263 C6
Bridewell Pl
Holborn EC4 241 C1
20 Wapping E1 118 B5
Bridford Mews W1 238 D4
Bridge Acad The E2 95 D6
Bridge App NW3 71 A1
Bridge Ave Ealing W7 86 B2
Hammersmith W6 112 C1
Bridge Avenue Mans 1 W6 112 C1
Bridge Bsns Ctr The 2 UB2 107 C4
Bridge Cl Enfield EN1 6 B3
13 North Kensington W10 90 D1
Teddington TW11 174 D6
Walton-on-T KT12 193 D1
Bridge Ct
9 Blackwall E14 120 B6
Leyton E10 53 B2
2 Walton-on-T KT12 193 D1
7 Willesden NW10 67 C1
Bridge Dr N13 32 B6
Bridge End E17 36 A2
Bridge End Cl 4 KT2 176 C2
Bridge Field Ho 7 W2 91 D1
Bridgefield Rd SM1 217 C2
Bridgefoot SE1 116 A1 260 B1
Bridge Gate N21 17 A4
Bridge Gdns
Canonbury N16 73 B4
East Molesey KT8 196 B5
Littleton TW15 171 A3
Bridge Ho
Brockley SE4 141 B1
1 Camden Town NW1 71 A1
Ealing TW8 109 A2
Homerton E9 74 D3
Woolwich SE28 123 C5
Bridge Ho S TW8 109 A2
Bridge House Quay E14 120 A5
Bridge La
Battersea SW11 136 C4 267 B1
Temple Fortune NW11 47 B4
Bridgeland Rd E16 121 A6
Bridgelands Cl BR3 185 B3
Bridge L Ctr SE26 185 B6
Bridgeman Ho 19 E9 74 C1
Bridgeman Rd
Islington N1 72 B1
Teddington TW11 175 A4
Bridgeman St NW8 92 C5 230 A3
Bridge Meadows SE14 140 D6
Bridgend Rd SW18 136 A1
Bridgenhall Rd EN1 5 D4
Bridgen Ho 9 E1 96 B1
Bridgen Rd DA5 169 A4
Bridge Par
7 Croydon CR0 220 D5
Edmonton N21 17 A4
Bridge Pk
7 London SW18 157 C6
Wembley NW10 66 D1
Bridge Pk Com L Ctr NW10 66 D1
Bridge Pl
Belgravia SW1 115 B2 258 D4
Croydon CR0 205 B1
Bridgepoint Lofts 2 E7 77 C1
Bridgeport Pl 4 E1 118 A5
Bridge Rd
Beckenham BR3 185 B3
Bexleyheath DA7 147 A3
Bridge Rd *continued*
Chessington KT9 214 A3
East Ham E6 78 B1
East Molesey KT8 196 C5
Isleworth TW3, TW7 130 B2
Southall UB2 107 C4
Stratford Marsh E15 98 B6
Sutton SM2 217 D2
Twickenham TW1 153 B5
Wallington SM6 219 C3
Walthamstow E17 53 B2
Wembley HA9 66 C5
Willesden NW10 67 C2
Wood Green N22 32 A2
Bridge Row CR0 205 B1
Bridge Sch The
Clerkenwell EC1 94 D3 241 C6
Lower Holloway N7 72 A3
Bridges Ct SW11 136 B3
Bridges Ho 15 SE5 139 B5
Bridges La CR0 220 A4
Bridges Rd
Stanmore HA7 24 D5
Wimbledon SW19 179 D4
Bridges Road Mews SW19 179 D4
Bridge St
Chiswick W4 111 B2
Pinner HA5 41 A6
Richmond TW10 153 D6
Walton-on-T KT12 193 D2
Westminster SW1 116 A4 250 B1
Bridge Terr E15 76 B1
Bridge The HA3 42 D5
Bridgetown Cl 5 SE19 183 C5
Bridgeview 2 W6 112 C1
Bridgewater Cl BR7 211 C6
Bridgewater Ct HA0 65 C2
Bridgewater Gdns HA8 26 B1
Bridgewater Ho UB5 85 A3
Bridgewater Rd
Ruislip HA4 62 B4
Stratford Marsh E15 98 A6
Wembley HA0 65 C1
Bridgewater Sq EC2 242 A4
Bridgewater St EC2 242 A4
Bridgeway
Barking IG11 79 D1
Wembley HA0 66 B1
Bridge Way
London NW11 47 B4
Twickenham TW2 152 A4
Uxbridge UB10 60 D3
Bridgeway St NW1 93 C5 232 B3
Bridge Wharf 18 E2 96 D5
Bridge Wharf Rd TW7 131 B2
Bridgewood Cl SE20 184 B3
Bridgewood Rd
North Cheam KT17, KT4 216 A4
Streatham SW16 181 D3
Bridge Yd SE1 252 D4
Bridgford St SW17, SW18 158 A1
Bridgman Rd W4 111 A3
Bridgnorth Ho 10 SE15 140 A6
Bridgwater Ho W2 236 A2
Bridle Cl Enfield EN3 7 B6
Kingston u T KT1 197 D5
Sunbury TW16 194 A6
West Ewell KT19 215 B3
Bridle La
Marylebone W1 115 C6 249 B6
Twickenham TW1 153 B5
Bridle Path CR0 220 A5
Bridle Path The IG8 36 C3
Bridlepath Way TW14 149 C3
Bridle Rd
Addington CR0 223 C4
Claygate KT10 213 B2
Croydon CR0 223 C6
Pinner HA5 40 C4

Bridle Way
Addington CR0 223 C3
Orpington BR6 227 A4
Bridle Way The SM6 219 C3
Bridlington Ho
SW18 136 A1
Bridlington Rd N9 18 B4
Bridport SE17 262 B1
Bridport Ave RM7 59 D3
Bridport Ho
6 Edmonton N18 34 A5
Shoreditch N1 235 D5
Bridport Pl N1 95 B6 235 D5
Bridport Rd
Edmonton N18 33 D5
Greenford UB6 85 D6
Thornton Heath CR7 204 D6
Bridstow Pl W2 91 C1
Brief St SE5 138 D4
Brierfield NW1 232 A5
Brierley CR0 223 D2
Brierley Ave N9 18 C3
Brierley Cl SE25 206 A5
Brierley Ct W7 108 C6
Brierley Rd Leyton E11 76 B4
Upper Tooting SW12 159 C2
Brierly Gdns E2 96 C5
Brigade Cl HA2 64 B6
Brigade St SE3 142 D3
Brigadier Ave EN2 5 A4
Brigadier Hill EN2 5 A5
Briggeford Cl 5 E5 74 A6
Briggs Cl CR4 181 B2
Briggs Ho 20 E2 95 D4
Bright Cl DA17 124 D2
Bright Ct 8 SE28 124 C5
Brightfield Rd SE12 164 D6
Brightling Rd SE4 163 B5
Brightlingsea Pl 5
E14 119 B6
Brightman Rd SW18 158 B3
Brighton Ave E17 53 B4
Brighton Bldgs SE1 263 A5
Brighton Cl UB10 60 D1
Brighton Ct SW15 157 B5
Brighton Dr 3 UB5 63 C2
Brighton Gr SE14 141 A4
Brighton Ho 7 SE5 139 B4
Brighton Rd
Belmont SM2 217 D1
Finchley N2 30 A1
South Croydon CR2 221 B2
Stoke Newington N16 73 C4
Surbiton KT6 197 D3
Sutton SM2 218 A1
Wallend E6 100 C4
Brighton Terr SW9 138 B1
Brightside Rd SE13 164 B5
Brightside The EN3 7 A4
Bright St E14 97 D2
Brightwell Cl CR0 204 C1
Brightwell Cres
SW17 180 D5
Brightwell Ct N7 72 B3
Brightwells 1 SW6 135 D3
Brightwen Gr HA7 9 A2
Brig Mews SE8 141 C6
Brigstock Ho SE5 139 A3
Brigstock Par 1
CR7 204 C4
Brigstock Rd
Belvedere DA17 125 D2
Thornton Heath CR7 204 D4
Brill Ho NW10 67 B5
Brill Pl NW1 93 D5 232 D3
Brim Hill N2 48 B5
Brimpsfield Cl SE2 124 B3
BRIMSDOWN 7 B3
Brimsdown Ave EN3 7 A4
Brimsdown Ho E3 98 A3
Brimsdown Jun & Inf
Sch EN3 6 D2
Brimsdown Sta EN3 7 A3
Brimstone Ho 4 E15 76 C1
Brindishe Prim Sch
SE12 164 D6
Brindle Gate DA15 167 C3
Brindley Cl
Bexleyheath DA7 147 D2
Wembley HA0 87 D6
Brindley Ho
Carshalton SM1 218 C3
37 Notting Hill W2 91 C2
Brindley Ho *continued*
22 Streatham SW12 160 A4
Brindley St SE14 141 B4
Brindley Way
Bromley BR1 187 B5
Southall UB1 107 D6
Brindwood Rd E4 19 C1
Brine Ct KT6 197 D4
Brine Ho 11 E3 97 A5
Brinkburn Cl
Abbey Wood SE2 124 A2
Edgware HA8 44 D6
Brinkburn Gdns HA8 44 C6
Brinkley 18 KT1 176 C1
Brinkley Rd KT4 216 B6
Brinklow Cres SE18 144 D5
Brinklow Ho W2 91 D2
Brinkworth Rd IG5 56 A6
Brinkworth Way E9 75 B2
Brinsdale Rd NW4 46 D6
Brinsley Ho 17 E1 96 C1
Brinsley Rd HA3 24 B1
Brinsley St 35 E1 96 B1
Brinsworth Cl TW2 152 B2
Brinton Wlk SE1 251 C3
Brion Pl E14 98 A2
Brisbane Ave SW19 179 D2
Brisbane Ct N10 31 B3
Brisbane Ho 3 W12 112 B6
Brisbane Rd
Ealing W13 109 A4
Ilford IG1 57 A1
Leyton E10 75 D6
Brisbane St SE5 139 B5
Briscoe Cl E11 76 D6
Briscoe Rd SW19 180 B4
Briset Rd SE9 143 D1
Briset St EC1 94 D3 241 C5
Briset Way N7 72 B6
Bristol Cl
Stanwell TW19 148 A5
Twickenham TW4 151 C4
Wallington SM6 220 A1
Bristol Ct 11 TW19 148 A5
Bristol Gdns
Putney SW15 156 C4
Westbourne Green W9 91 D3
Bristol Ho
1 Barking IG11 80 A1
SE11 261 A5
Bristol Mews W9 91 D3
Bristol Park Rd 1
E17 53 A5
Bristol Rd
Greenford UB6 85 D6
Morden SM4 202 A4
Upton E7 77 D2
Briston Gr N8 50 A3
Briston Mews NW7 28 A3
Bristowe Cl 24 SW2 160 C5
Bristow Rd
Bexleyheath DA7 147 A4
Hounslow TW3 130 A2
Wallington CR0 220 A4
West Norwood SE19 183 C5
Britannia Building
N1 235 C2
Britannia Cl
London SW4 137 D1
Northolt UB5 84 D4
Britannia Gate 11
E16 121 A5
Britannia Ho N20 14 A1
Britannia Junc NW1 231 D6
Britannia La TW2 152 A4
Britannia L Ctr N1 95 C6
Britannia Rd
Ilford IG1 78 D5
23 Millwall E14 119 C2
Surbiton KT5 198 B2
Walham Green
SW6 135 D5 265 C3
Whetstone N12 14 A1
Britannia Row
N1 95 A6 235 A6
Britannia St
WC1 94 B4 233 C2
Britannia Village Prim
Sch 17 E16 121 B5
Britannia Way NW10 88 D3
Britannia Wlk N1 235 C2
British Coll of
Osteopathic Medicine
NW3 70 A2
British Dental
Association Mus★
W1 238 C3
British Gr W4 111 D1
British Grove Pas 2
W4 111 D1
British Grove S 3
W4 111 D1
British Home The
(Hospl) SE27 182 D5
British Legion Rd E4 20 D2
British Library
Newspapers NW9 45 C6
British Library The★
WC1 93 D4 232 D2
British Mus★
WC1 94 A2 240 A3
British Optical
Association Mus★
SW1 250 A4
British St E3 97 B4
British Wharf Ind Est
SE14 140 D6
Britley Ho 16 E14 97 B1
Brit Oval The (Surrey
Cnty Crkt Club)
SE11 138 C6 270 D6
BRIT Performing Arts &
Tech Sch SE25 205 B3
Brittage Rd 11 NW10 67 C1
Brittain Ct SE9 166 A3
Brittain Rd RM8 81 B5
Brittany Ho SW15 134 C1
Brittany Point SE11 261 A3
Britten Cl Elstree WD6 9 D5
Golders Green NW11 47 D1
Brittenden Cl 1
BR6 227 D2
Brittenden Par BR6 227 D2
Britten Dr UB1 85 C1
Britten Ho SW3 257 B2
Britten St
SW3 114 C1 257 A2
Britton Cl SE6 164 B4
Britton St EC1 94 D3 241 C5
Brixham Cres HA4 40 A1
Brixham Gdns IG3 79 C3
Brixham Rd DA16 146 D4
Brixham St E16 122 C5
BRIXTON 138 C2
Brixton Day Coll 6
SW9 138 A2
Brixton Hill SW2 160 B5
Brixton Hill Ct 5
SW2 160 B6
Brixton Hill Pl SW2 160 A4
Brixton Mkt★ SW9 138 C1
Brixton Oval 7 SW2 138 C1
Brixton Rd SW9 138 C4
Brixton Rec Ctr
SW9 138 C2
Brixton Sta SW9 138 C1
Brixton Station Rd
SW9 138 C2
Brixton Water La
SW2 160 B6
Broadacre Cl UB10 60 D5
Broadbent Cl N6 49 B1
Broadbent St W1 248 C6
Broadberry Ct N18 34 B5
Broadbridge Cl SE3 143 A5
Broad Common Est
N16 52 A1
Broadcoombe CR2 222 D1
Broadcroft Ave HA7 25 D1
Broadcroft Rd BR5 211 B2
Broad Ct WC2 240 B1
Broadeaves Cl CR2 221 C3
Broadfield NW6 69 D2
Broadfield Cl
Croydon CR0 220 B6
Dollis Hill NW2 68 C5
Broadfield Ct
Bushey WD23 8 C2
Edgware HA8 10 D1
Broadfield La NW1 72 A1
Broadfield Rd SE6 164 C3
Broadfields
Harrow HA2 23 D1
Thames Ditton KT8 196 C3
Broadfields Ave
Edgware HA8 10 D1
Southgate N21 16 C4
Broadfields Hts HA8 26 D6
Broadfields Prim Sch
HA8 10 C2
Broadfield Sq EN1 6 B3
Broadfields Way
NW10 67 D3
Broadfield Way IG9 21 C1
Broadford Ho 12 E1 97 A3
BROADGATE 95 C2
Broadgate
EC2 95 C2 243 A4
Broadgate Circ
EC2 95 C2 243 A3
Broadgate Rd E16 99 D1
Broadgates Ave EN4 1 D4
Broadgates Ct SE11 261 B1
Broadgates Rd
SW18 158 B3
Broadgate Twr The
EC2 243 B5
BROAD GREEN 204 D3
Broad Green Ave
CR0 204 D2
Broadhead Strand
NW9 27 D2
Broadheath Dr BR7 188 B5
Broadhinton Rd
SW4 137 C2
Broadhurst Ave
Edgware HA8 26 D6
Ilford IG3 79 D4
Broadhurst Cl
Hampstead NW6 70 A2
9 Richmond TW10 154 B6
Broadhurst Gdns
Hampstead NW6 69 D2
Ruislip HA4 62 C6
Broadhurst Mans
NW6 69 D2
Broad La
Broadgate EC2 243 A4
Hampton TW12 173 C4
Hornsey Vale N8 50 B4
South Tottenham N15 51 D5
South Tottenham N15 52 A5
Broadlands
Feltham TW13 151 C1
Highgate N6 49 A2
Broadlands Ave
Enfield EN3 6 B2
Shepperton TW17 193 A3
Streatham SW16 160 A2
Broadlands Cl
Enfield EN3 6 C2
Highgate N6 49 A2
Streatham SW16 160 A2
Broadlands Ct TW9 132 C5
Broadlands Lo N6 48 D2
Broadlands Mans 2
SW16 160 A2
Broadlands Rd
Grove Pk BR1 187 B6
Highgate N6 48 D2
Broadlands Way
KT3 199 D3
Broad Lawn SE9 166 C3
Broadlawns Ct HA3 24 D2
Broadley St
NW8 92 C2 237 A4
Broadley Terr
NW1 92 C3 237 B5
Broadmayne SE17 262 C2
Broadmead
Catford SE6 163 C1
Hampton TW12 173 C4
West Kensington W14 254 A3
Broadmead Ave KT4 200 A2
Broadmead Cl
Hampton TW12 173 C4
Pinner HA5 23 A3
Broadmead Ct 6 IG8 37 A4
Broadmead Inf Sch
CR0 205 B2
Broadmead Jun Sch
CR0 205 B3
Broadmead Rd
Northolt UB5 85 A3
Woodford IG8 37 B3
Broad Oak
Ashford TW16 171 D4
Woodford IG8 37 B5
Broad Oak Cl
Chingford E4 35 C5
St Paul's Cray BR5 190 A1
Broadoak Ct 8
SW9 138 C2
Broadoak Ho 11 NW6 91 D6
Broadoaks BR7 188 D4
Broad Oaks KT6 214 D6
Broadoaks Way BR2 208 D4
Broadreach Coll
SE28 123 D3
Broad St Ave EC2 243 A3
Broad Sanctuary
SW1 250 A1
Broad St
Dagenham RM10 81 C1
Teddington TW11 174 D4
Broadstone Ho SW8 270 C3
Broadstone Pl W1 238 A3
Broad Street NHS Walk-
in Ctr RM10 103 C6
Broad Street Pl EC2 242 D3
Broadview NW9 44 C3
Broadview Est TW19 148 C4
Broadview Ho RM8 58 D1
Broadview Rd SW16 181 D3
Broadwalk
Harrow HA2 41 D4
Snaresbrook E18 54 D6
Broadwalk Ho SW7 246 A1
Broadwalk La NW11 47 B2
Broadwalk Sh Ctr The
HA8 26 D4
Broadwall
SE1 116 C5 251 B4
Broadwater Farm Prim
Sch N17 33 B1
Broadwater Gdns
BR6 227 A4
Broadwater Prim Sch
SW17 180 C6
Broadwater Rd
Plumstead SE18 123 B3
Tottenham N17 33 C1
Upper Tooting SW17 180 C6
Broadway
Barking IG11 101 A6
Bexley DA6 147 C1
Bexleyheath DA6 147 B1
Hanwell W7 108 C5
Stratford E15 76 B1
Tolworth KT6 198 D1
West Ealing W13 109 A5
Westminster
SW1 115 D3 259 C6
Broadway Arc 3
W6 112 C2
Broadway Ave
Thornton Heath CR0 205 B4
Twickenham TW1 153 B5
Broadway Bldgs 5
W7 108 C5
Broadway Cl IG8 37 B4
Broadway Ct
Beckenham BR3 208 A6
Wimbledon SW19 179 C4
Broadway Ctr The 6
W6 112 C2
Broadway Gdns
Mitcham CR4 202 C5
Woodford IG8 37 B4
Broadway Ho 2 E8 96 B6
Broadway Ho 5
SW19 179 C3
Broadway Lofts
SW17 180 C6
Broadway Mans SW6 265 B3
Broadway Market E8 96 B6
Broadway Market Mews
21 E8 96 A6
Broadway Mews
Bowes Pk N13 32 B5
Southgate N21 16 D3
Stamford Hill E5 51 D2
Broadway Mkt E8 96 B6
Broadway Par
Chingford E4 36 A4
Hayes UB3 106 A5
Hornsey N8 50 A3
West Drayton UB7 104 A4
Broadway Pl SW19 179 B4
Broadway Ret Pk
NW2 68 D4
Broadway Sh Ctr 5
DA6 147 C1
Broadway The
Barnes SW13 133 C3
Bedington CR0 220 A4
Cheam SM3 217 A2
Chingford E4 36 B4
Dagenham RM8 81 C6
Ealing W5 109 D6
Edgware NW7 27 D5
Edmonton N9 18 A1

Broadway The *continued*
Friern Barnet N11 ... 31 A5
Greenford UB6 ... 86 A3
Harrow HA3 ... 24 D1
Hornsey N8 ... 50 A3
Merton SW19 ... 179 C3
Newham E13 ... 99 B5
Pinner HA5 ... 23 B3
South Acton W3 ... 110 C4
Southall UB1 ... 107 A6
2 Southgate N14 ... 15 D3
Stanmore HA7 ... 25 C5
Sutton SM1 ... 218 A4
Thames Ditton KT10 ... 196 C1
Tolworth KT6 ... 198 C1
Wembley HA9 ... 66 A5
Woodford IG8 ... 37 B4
Wood Green N22 ... 32 C1
Broadway Wlk 4 E14 ... 119 C3
Broadwell Ct TW5 ... 128 D4
Broadwick St W1 ... 93 C1 239 B1
Broad Wlk
Eltham SE3, SE18 ... 144 A3
Heston TW5 ... 129 A4
Mayfair W1 ... 115 A5 248 A4
Regent's Pk NW1 ... 93 A5 231 B3
Richmond TW9 ... 132 B5
Southgate N21 ... 16 B3
Broad Wlk The W8 ... 113 D5 245 D3
Broadwood Ave HA4 ... 39 C3
Broadwood Terr W14 ... 254 D4
Broad Yd EC1 ... 241 C5
Brocade Ct NW9 ... 45 D5
Brocas Cl NW3 ... 70 C1
Brockbridge Ho SW15 ... 155 D5
Brockdene Dr BR2 ... 225 D4
Brockdish Ave IG11 ... 79 D3
Brockelbank Lo RM8 ... 80 D6
Brockenhurst KT8 ... 195 B3
Brockenhurst Ave KT4 ... 199 C1
Brockenhurst Gdns
Edgware NW7 ... 27 C5
Ilford IG1 ... 79 A3
Brockenhurst Mews 9 N18 ... 34 A6
Brockenhurst Rd CR0 ... 206 B2
Brockenhurst Way SW16 ... 181 D1
Brocket Ho 16 SW8 ... 137 D3
Brockham Cl SW19 ... 179 B5
Brockham Cres CR0 ... 224 B1
Brockham Ct
17 Belmont SM2 ... 217 D1
8 South Croydon CR2 ... 221 A3
Brockham Dr
Ilford IG2 ... 57 A4
Streatham SW2 ... 160 B4
Brockham Ho
Camden Town NW1 ... 232 B5
11 Streatham SW2 ... 160 B4
Brockham St SE1 ... 262 B6
Brockhurst Cl HA7 ... 24 D4
Brockhurst Ho N4 ... 51 B2
Brockill Cres SE4 ... 141 A1
Brocklebank Ho 7 E16 ... 122 C5
Brocklebank Rd
Greenwich SE7 ... 121 B2
Wandsworth SW18 ... 158 A4
Brocklebank Road Ind Est SE7 ... 121 A2
Brocklehurst St SE14 ... 140 D5
Brocklesby Rd SE25 ... 206 B5
BROCKLEY ... 141 B1
Brockley Ave HA7 ... 10 A1
Brockley Cl HA7 ... 26 A6
Brockley Cross SE4 ... 141 B2
Brockley Cross Bsns Ctr SE4 ... 141 A2
Brockley Gdns SE4 ... 141 B3
Brockley Gr SE4 ... 163 B6
Brockley Hall Rd SE4 ... 163 A6
Brockley Hill HA7, HA8 ... 9 D2
Brockley Hill Ho HA7 ... 9 C3
Brockley Ho SE17 ... 263 A2
Brockley Mews SE4 ... 163 A6
Brockley Pk SE23 ... 163 A4
Brockley Prim Sch SE4 ... 163 B6
Brockley Rd SE4 ... 163 B6
Brockley Rise SE23 ... 163 A4
Brockleyside HA7 ... 26 A6
Brockley Sta SE4 ... 141 A2
Brockley View SE23 ... 163 A4
Brockley Way SE4 ... 163 A6
Brockman Rise BR1 ... 186 B6
Brockmer Ho 5 E1 ... 118 B6
Brock Pl E3 ... 97 D3
Brock Rd E13 ... 99 B2
Brocks Dr SM3 ... 217 A5
Brockshot Cl 1 TW8 ... 131 D6
Brock St SE15 ... 140 C2
Brockway Cl E11 ... 76 C6
Brockweir 28 E2 ... 96 C5
Brockwell Ave BR3 ... 207 D4
Brockwell Cl BR5 ... 211 D4
Brockwell Ct
2 London SW2 ... 160 C6
Thornton Heath CR0 ... 204 D2
Brockwell Ho SE11 ... 270 D6
Brockwell Lido SE24 ... 160 D5
Brockwell Park★ SE24 ... 160 D5
Brockwell Park Gdns SE24 ... 160 D4
Brockwell Park Row SW2 ... 160 C5
Brockworth 8 KT2 ... 176 D2
Broderick Ho SE21 ... 161 C1
Brodia Rd N16 ... 73 C5
Brodick Ho 12 E3 ... 97 B5
Brodie Ct E10 ... 54 B1
Brodie Ho
Bermondsey SE1 ... 263 D2
7 Wallington SM6 ... 219 B4
Brodie Rd
Chingford E4 ... 20 A2
Enfield EN2 ... 5 A5
Brodie St SE1 ... 117 D1 263 D2
Brodlove La E1 ... 118 D6
Brodrick Gr SE2 ... 124 B2
Brodrick Rd SW17 ... 158 C2
Brody Ho E1 ... 243 C3
Brograve Gdns BR3 ... 185 D1
Broken Wharf EC4 ... 252 A6
Brokesley St E3 ... 97 B4
Broke Wlk Hackney E8 ... 95 D6
1 Hackney E8 ... 96 A6
Bromar Rd SE5 ... 139 C2
Bromborough Gn WD19 ... 22 C5
Bromefield HA7 ... 25 C2
Bromehead St 8 E1 ... 96 C1
Bromell's Rd SW4 ... 137 C1
Brome Rd SE9 ... 144 B2
Bromfelde Rd SW4 ... 137 D3
Bromfield Ct 20 SE16 ... 118 A3
Bromfield St N1 ... 234 B4
Bromhall Rd RM8 ... 80 B2
Bromhedge SE9 ... 166 B1
Bromholm Rd SE2 ... 124 B3
Bromleigh Ct 1 SE21, SE22 ... 162 B2
Bromleigh Ho SE1 ... 263 C6
BROMLEY BR1 ... 186 C2
E3 ... 97 D4
Bromley Ave BR1 ... 186 C3
Bromley-by-Bow Sta E3 ... 98 A4
Bromley Coll BR1 ... 187 A2
Bromley Coll of F & H Ed (Rookery Lane Campus) BR2 ... 209 D3
Bromley Comm BR2 ... 209 D4
BROMLEY COMMON ... 210 A3
Bromley Cres
Beckenham BR2 ... 208 D6
Ruislip HA4 ... 61 D4
Bromley Ct BR1 ... 186 D3
Bromley Gdns BR2 ... 208 D6
Bromley Gr BR2 ... 186 B1
Bromley Hall Rd E14 ... 98 A2
Bromley High Jun Sch BR1 ... 210 C5
Bromley High Sch BR1 ... 210 C5
Bromley High St E3 ... 97 D4
Bromley Hill BR1 ... 186 C4
Bromley Ho 5 BR1 ... 187 A2
Bromley Ind Ctr BR1 ... 209 D6
Bromley La BR7 ... 189 B3
Bromley Lo 2 W3 ... 89 A1
Bromley Manor Mans 3 BR1 ... 209 A6
Bromley North Sta BR1 ... 187 A2
BROMLEY PARK ... 186 D2
Bromley Pk 11 BR1 ... 186 D2
Bromley Pl W1 ... 239 A4
Bromley Rd
Beckenham BR3 ... 185 D2
Bromley BR2, BR3 ... 186 B1
Catford SE6 ... 163 D1
Chislehurst BR7 ... 188 D2
Edmonton N18 ... 17 B1
Leyton E10 ... 53 D3
Tottenham N17 ... 34 A2
Walthamstow E17 ... 53 C6
Bromley Road Inf Sch 5 BR3 ... 185 D2
Bromley Road Ret Pk SE6 ... 163 D2
Bromley Ski & Snowboard Ctr BR5 ... 190 D1
Bromley South Sta BR2 ... 209 A6
Bromley St E1 ... 96 D1
BROMPTON ... 114 B3
Brompton Arc SW1 ... 247 D1
Brompton Cl
Hounslow TW4 ... 151 B6
Penge SE20 ... 184 A1
Brompton Ct 4 HA7 ... 25 C6
Brompton Gr N2 ... 48 C5
Brompton Ho 3 N9 ... 34 A6
Brompton Oratory SW3 ... 114 C3 257 A5
Brompton Park Cres SW6 ... 135 D6 265 C5
Brompton Pl SW3 ... 114 C3 257 B6
Brompton Rd SW3 ... 114 C3 257 A5
Brompton Sq SW3 ... 114 C3 257 A6
Bromstone Ho 19 SW9 ... 138 C4
Bromwich Ave N6 ... 71 A6
Bromwich Ho 3 TW10 ... 154 A5
Bromyard Ave W3 ... 111 C6
Bromyard Ho
Acton W3 ... 111 C5
3 Peckham SE15 ... 140 B5
Bron Ct NW6 ... 91 C6
BRONDESBURY ... 69 A2
Brondesbury Coll for Boys 10 NW6 ... 69 A1
Brondesbury Ct NW2 ... 68 D2
Brondesbury Mews 11 NW6 ... 69 C1
BRONDESBURY PARK ... 90 D6
Brondesbury Park Sta NW6 ... 91 A6
Brondesbury Pk NW6 ... 68 D1
Brondesbury Rd NW6 ... 91 C5
Brondesbury Sta NW6 ... 69 B1
Brondesbury Villas NW6 ... 91 C5
Bronhill Terr N17 ... 34 A2
Bronsart Rd SW6 ... 135 A5 264 A3
Bronson Rd SW20 ... 179 A1
Bronte Cl Erith DA8 ... 147 D5
1 Forest Gate E7 ... 77 A4
Ilford IG2 ... 56 C5
Bronte Ct 8 W14 ... 112 D3
Bronte Ho
Kilburn NW6 ... 91 C4
6 Stoke Newington N16 ... 73 C3
Bronti Cl SE17 ... 117 A1 262 B2
Bronwen Ct NW8 ... 229 C1
Bronze Age Way DA17 ... 125 D4
Bronze St SE8 ... 141 C5
Brook Ave
Dagenham RM10 ... 81 D1
Edgware HA8 ... 26 D4
Wembley HA9 ... 66 C5
Brook Bank EN1 ... 6 B6
Brookbank Ave W7 ... 86 B2
Brookbank Rd SE13 ... 141 D2
Brook Cl Acton W3 ... 110 C5
Finchley N12 ... 29 A3
Ruislip HA4 ... 39 C2
Stanwell TW19 ... 148 B4
Upper Tooting SW17 ... 159 A2
West Barnes SW20 ... 200 B6
Brook Com Prim Sch E8 ... 74 A3
Brook Cres
Chingford E4 ... 35 D6
Edmonton N9 ... 34 B6
Brook Ct
Barking IG11 ... 101 D6
Beckenham BR3 ... 185 B2
5 Brentford TW8 ... 131 D6
Cheam SM3 ... 216 C4
Edgware HA8 ... 26 D5
2 Leyton E11 ... 76 C5
Mortlake SW14 ... 133 C2
Walthamstow E17 ... 53 A6
Brookdale N11 ... 31 C6
Brookdale Rd
Catford SE6 ... 163 D4
Lewisham SE6 ... 163 D5
Sidcup DA5 ... 169 A5
Walthamstow E17 ... 53 C6
Brookdales The NW4 ... 47 A5
Brookdene N12 ... 29 D6
Brookdene Rd SE18, SE2 ... 123 D2
Brook Dr Harrow HA1 ... 42 A5
Newington SE11 ... 116 D2 261 C4
Ruislip HA4 ... 39 C2
Brooke Ave HA2 ... 64 A5
Brooke Cl WD23 ... 8 A4
Brooke Ct Kilburn W10 ... 91 A5
7 Kingston u T KT2 ... 175 D6
Brooke Ho
Bushey WD23 ... 8 A4
4 New Cross Gate SE14 ... 141 A4
Brookehowse Rd SE6 ... 163 D1
Brookend Rd DA15 ... 167 C3
Brooke Rd
Shacklewell E5, N16 ... 74 A5
Walthamstow E17 ... 54 A5
Brookes Ct EC1 ... 241 A4
Brooke's Mkt EC1 ... 241 B4
Brooke St EC1 ... 94 C2 241 A3
Brooke Way WD23 ... 8 A4
Brookfield
Dartmouth Pk N6 ... 71 A5
1 Finsbury Pk N4 ... 72 C6
Brookfield Ave
Carshalton SM1, SM5 ... 218 C5
Ealing W5 ... 87 D3
Mill Hill NW7 ... 28 B4
Walthamstow E17 ... 54 A5
Brookfield Cl NW7 ... 28 B4
Brookfield Cres
Harrow HA3 ... 44 A4
Mill Hill NW7 ... 28 B4
Brookfield Ct
Greenford UB6 ... 86 A4
1 London N12 ... 29 D6
Brookfield Gdns KT10 ... 212 D2
Brookfield Ho 23 E2 ... 96 B5
Brookfield House Sch IG8 ... 36 C4
Brookfield Path IG8 ... 36 C4
Brookfield Pk NW5 ... 71 B5
Brookfield Prim Sch
Cheam SM3 ... 201 A1
Dartmouth Pk N19 ... 71 B6
Brookfield Rd
Acton W4 ... 111 B4
Edmonton N9 ... 18 B1
Homerton E9 ... 75 A2
Brookfields EN3 ... 6 D1
Brookfields Ave CR4 ... 202 C4
Brookgate N16 ... 73 B6
Brook Gate W1 ... 114 D6 247 D5
Brook Gdns
Barnes SW13 ... 133 D2
Brook Gdns *continued*
Chingford E4 ... 35 D6
Kingston u T KT2 ... 177 A2
Brook Gn W6 ... 112 D2
BROOK GREEN ... 112 D2
Brook Green Flats 11 W14 ... 112 D3
Brookhill Cl
East Barnet EN4 ... 14 C6
Woolwich SE18 ... 122 D1
Brookhill Ct 2 EN4 ... 14 C5
Brookhill Rd
East Barnet EN4 ... 14 C6
Woolwich SE18 ... 122 D1
Brook Ho
3 Clapham Pk SW4 ... 159 C6
Ealing W3 ... 110 C4
3 Edmonton N9 ... 18 A1
4 Hammersmith W6 ... 112 C2
Marylebone WC1 ... 239 C4
4 Twickenham TW1 ... 153 A4
Brook Hos NW1 ... 232 B3
Brookhouse Gdns E4 ... 36 C6
Brook House Sixth Form Coll 5 E5 ... 74 B5
Brook Ind Est UB4 ... 106 C5
Brooking Cl RM8 ... 80 C5
Brooking Rd E7 ... 77 A3
Brook La Bexley DA5 ... 168 D5
Greenwich SE3 ... 143 B3
Plaistow BR1 ... 187 A4
Brook La N 3 TW8 ... 131 D6
Brookland Cl NW11 ... 47 C5
Brookland Garth NW11 ... 47 D5
Brookland Hill NW11 ... 47 D5
Brookland Jun & Inf Schs NW11 ... 47 D5
Brookland Rise NW11 ... 47 C5
Brooklands Ave
New Eltham DA15 ... 167 B2
Wandsworth SW18 ... 157 D2
Brooklands Cl TW16 ... 171 C2
Brooklands Coll TW15 ... 170 B6
Brooklands Court Apartments 3 NW6 ... 69 B1
Brooklands Ct
10 Clapham SW8 ... 137 C3
Enfield N21 ... 17 B6
Kingston u T KT1 ... 197 D5
2 London NW6 ... 69 B1
2 Mitcham CR4 ... 180 B1
Brooklands Dr UB6 ... 87 D6
Brooklands Ho SE3 ... 143 A2
Brooklands Pk SE3 ... 143 A2
Brooklands Pl TW12 ... 173 D5
Brooklands Prim Sch SE3 ... 143 A2
Brooklands Rd KT7 ... 197 A1
Brooklands The TW7 ... 130 B4
Brook Lane Bns Ctr TW8 ... 109 D1
Brooklea Cl NW9 ... 27 C2
Brook Lo
Crouch End N8 ... 49 D3
Edgware HA8 ... 26 D4
Hendon NW4 ... 46 D4
Brooklyn SE20 ... 184 A3
Brooklyn Ave SE25 ... 206 B5
Brooklyn Cl SM5 ... 218 C6
Brooklyn Ct
Feltham TW13 ... 150 B2
Shepherd's Bush W12 ... 112 C5
Brooklyn Gr SE25 ... 206 B5
Brooklyn Rd
Bromley BR2 ... 210 A4
Croydon SE25 ... 206 B5
Brookmarsh Ind Est SE10 ... 141 D5
Brook Mdw N12 ... 13 D1
Brook Mead KT19 ... 215 C2
Brookmead Ave BR1, BR2 ... 210 B4
Brookmead Ct N20 ... 14 A2
Brookmead Ind Est CR4 ... 203 C3
Brook Meadow Cl IG8 ... 36 C4
Brookmead Rd CR0 ... 203 C3

Brook Mews N
W2........114 A6 246 B6
Brookmill Rd SE8.....141 C4
Brook Park Cl N21....16 D6
Brook Pl EN5.........13 C6
Brook Rd
Buckhurst Hill IG9....21 A3
Dollis Hill NW2.......68 A6
Finchley N12..........30 C3
Hornsey N8...........50 A5
Ilford IG2............57 C3
South Norwood CR7,..205 A5
Surbiton KT6.........198 A4
Twickenham TW1.....153 A5
Wood Green N22......50 B6
Brook Ret Pk HA4.....62 D3
Brook Road S
Brentford TW8........109 D1
Brentford TW8........131 D6
Brooks Ave E6......100 B3
Brooksbank Ho E9 ..269 B4
Brooksbank St E9 ..74 C2
Brooksby Ho N1.....72 C1
Brooksby Mews N1..72 C1
Brooksby St N1......72 C1
Brooksby's Wlk E9 ..74 D3
Brooks Cl SE9......166 C2
Brookscroft E17....53 D6
Brookscroft Rd E17...35 D2
Brooks Ct ①
③ London SW4......138 A3
Nine Elms SW8......269 B4
Brooks Farm★ E10...53 D2
Brookshill HA3......24 B5
Brookshill Ave HA3..24 B5
Brookshill Dr HA3...24 B5
Brookshill Gate HA3..24 B5
Brooks Ho ⑤ SW2..160 C3
Brookside
Barnet EN5...........13 A5
Feltham TW13.......150 A1
Harrow HA3..........43 D4
South Harrow HA2,
HA4................63 A4
Brookside Cres ①
KT4................200 A1
Brookside Gdns EN1...6 C6
Brookside Ho N17...33 C3
Brookside Prim Sch
UB4................84 C4
Brookside Rd
Edmonton N9.........34 B6
Hayes UB4...........82 D6
Temple Fortune NW11..47 B3
Upper Holloway N19...71 C6
Brookside S EN4....15 A4
Brookside Way CR0..206 D3
Brooks La W4.......110 C1
Brook's Mans ⑤ IG3..58 B1
Brook's Mews
W1........115 B6 248 D5
Brook's Par ⑧ IG3...58 B1
Brook Sq SE18......144 A4
Brooks Rd W4.......110 C1
Brook's Rd E13.....99 A6
Brook St
Bayswater
W2........114 B6 246 D6
Erith DA8...........147 D5
Kingston u T KT1....176 A1
Mayfair W1..115 B6 248 C6
⑦ Tottenham N17....33 C3
Brookstone Ct SE15..140 B1
Brooksville Ave NW6..91 A6
Brook Vale DA8.....147 D4
Brookview Ct EN1...17 C6
Brookview Rd SW16..181 C5
Brookville Rd
SW6........135 B5 264 C3
Brookway SE3.......143 A2
Brook Wlk
Burnt Oak HA8.......27 B4
Finchley N2..........30 B2
Brookwood Ave
SW13...............133 D3
Brookwood Cl BR2..208 D5

Brookwood Ho ⑦..251 D1
Brookwood Rd
Hounslow TW3.......129 D2
Wandsworth SW18....157 C3
Broom Ave BR5.....190 B1
Broom Cl
Bromley Comm BR2...210 A3
Teddington KT1,
TW11...............175 D3
Broomcroft Ave UB5..84 C4
Broome Cl ⑧ TW9..132 C4
Broome Ho ⑦ E5...74 B3
Broome Rd TW12...173 B2
Broome Way SE5...139 B5
Broom Farm SW6...155 C3
Broomfield
⑦ Camden Town
NW1...............71 A1
Sunbury TW16......172 A2
Walthamstow E17....53 B2
Broomfield Ave N13..32 B5
Broomfield Cotts
N13................32 A5
Broomfield Ct N13....32 A5
Broomfield Ho
Stanmore HA7.........9 A1
⑪ St Paul's Cray BR5 .190 B1
Walworth SE17......263 A3
Broomfield House Sch
TW9................132 B4
Broomfield La N13...32 B6
Broomfield Pl W13..109 B5
Broomfield Rd
Beckenham BR3......207 B6
Bexley DA6..........169 C6
Bowes Pk N13.......32 A5
Dagenham RM6......58 D2
Ealing W13.........109 B5
Richmond TW9.......132 B4
Surbiton KT5........198 B1
Teddington TW11....175 C4
Broomfields KT10....212 A3
Broomfield St N14...31 D5
Broomfield St E14...97 D2
Broom Gdns CR0....223 C5
Broomgrove Gdns
HA8................26 C2
Broomgrove Rd
SW9................138 B3
BROOM HILL......211 D2
Broomhill Ct ② IG8..37 A4
Broomhill Rd
Broom Hill BR6.......211 D2
Ilford IG3............58 A5
Wandsworth SW18...157 C6
Woodford IG8........37 A4
Broomhill Rise DA6..169 C6
Broomhill Wlk IG8...36 D3
Broomhouse La
SW6................135 C2
Broomhouse Rd
SW6................135 C3
Broomleigh BR1....187 A2
Broomloan La SM1..217 C6
Broom Lock TW11..175 C4
Broom Mead DA6...169 C6
Broom Pk KT1.......175 C4
Broom Rd
Croydon CR0........223 C5
Teddington TW11....175 C4
Broomsleigh Bsns Pk
SE26...............185 B5
Broomsleigh St NW6..69 B3
Broom Water TW11..175 C4
Broom Water W
TW11...............175 C4
Broomwood Cl CR0 .206 D4
Broomwood Hall (Lower
Sch) ⑧ SW12.......243 B1
Broomwood Hall Sch
(Lower Sch) SW16 .159 A5
Broomwood Hall Sch
(Upper Sch) ⑧
SW12...............159 A4
Broomwood Rd
London SW11.......159 A6
St Paul's Cray BR5...190 B1
Broseley Gr SE26....185 A5
Broster Gdns SE25..205 D6
Brougham Rd
Acton W3............89 A1
Hackney E8..........96 A6
Brough Cl
Kingston u T KT2....175 D5
South Lambeth SW8 .270 B3

Broughton Ave
London N3...........47 A6
Richmond TW10......175 C6
Broughton Ct W13..109 B6
Broughton Dr ⑩
SW9................138 D1
Broughton Gdns N6..49 C3
Broughton Ho ⑩
SW19...............179 A3
Broughton Rd
Ealing W13..........109 B6
Orpington BR6......227 B6
Sands End SW6......135 D3
Thornton Heath CR7 .204 C3
Broughton Road App ②
SW6................135 D3
Broughton St SW8..137 B3
Broucker Rd W33...111 A4
Browells La TW3....150 B2
Brown Bear Ct
TW13...............172 D6
Brown Cl SM6.......220 A1
Browne Ho
⑥ Deptford SE8.....141 C5
⑤ Penge SE26......184 B5
Brownfield St E14....98 A1
Brownflete Ho SE4..141 A1
Browngraves Rd
UB7................127 A5
Brown Hart Gdns
W1........248 B6 *265 C1*
Brownhill Rd SE6....164 A4
Browning Ave
Carshalton SM1.....218 C4
Ealing W7...........86 D1
North Cheam KT4....200 B1
Browning Cl
Bexley DA16........145 C4
Feltham TW12.......173 B6
Paddington W9......236 B5
Walthamstow E17....54 A5
Browning Ct W14...264 C6
Browning Ho
⑨ London SE14....141 A4
⑦ Shepherd's Bush
W12................90 C1
⑩ Stoke Newington
N16................73 C4
Browning Mews W1 ..238 B3
Browning Rd
Enfield EN2...........5 B5
Leytonstone E11....54 D2
Plashet E12.........78 B2
Browning St
SE17........117 A2 *262 B3*
Browning Way TW5 .128 C4
Brownlea Gdns IG3...80 A6
Brownlow CEI H4....14 B6
Brownlow Cl
Barnet EN4..........14 E1
⑤ Hampstead Garden Suburb
N2................48 A4
Brownlow Ho ⑩
SE16...............118 A4
Brownlow Lo ⑪ N11..32 A4
Brownlow Mews
WC1........94 B3 *240* C5
Brownlow Rd
Bowes Pk N11.......32 A4
⑧ Ealing W13......109 A5
Finchley N3..........29 D3
⑦ Forest Gate E7...77 A4
Hackney E8..........96 A6
South Croydon CR0..221 D4
Willesden NW10.....67 C1
Brownlow St
WC1........94 B2 *240* D5
Brownrigg Rd TW15..170 C6
Brown's Bldgs EC3..*243* B1
Brownsea Wlk NW7..128 D4
Brownspring Dr SE9 .166 D1
Browns Rd E17.......53 C6
Brown's Rd KT5, KT6 .198 B2
Brown St W1..92 D1 *237* C2
Brownswell Rd N20..30 B1
Brownswood Rd N4 .73 A6
Broxash Rd SW11....159 B5
Broxbourne Ave E18..55 B5
Broxbourne Ho ① E3 .97 D3
Broxholme Cl
SE25...............205 B5
Broxholme Ho SW6 .265 C2

Broxholm Rd SE27,
SW16...............160 C1
Broxted Rd SE6......163 B2
Broxwood Way
NW8........92 C6 *230* B5
Bruce Ave TW17....193 A3
Bruce Castle Ct N17 .33 C2
Bruce Castle Mus★
N17................33 C2
Bruce Castle Rd N17 .33 C2
Bruce Cl
North Kensington
W10................90 D2
Welling DA16.......146 B4
Bruce Ct DA15.......189 D6
Bruce Gdns N20....14 E1
Bruce Glasier Ho ⑧
N19................49 D2
Bruce Gr N17.........33 D1
Bruce Grove N17.....33 D1
Bruce Grove Prim Sch
N17................33 D1
Bruce Grove Sta N17..33 D1
Bruce Hall Mews
SW17...............181 A6
Bruce Ho
④ Clapham Pk
SW4................159 D5
⑤ Greenhill HA1....42 D4
⑦ North Kensington
W10................90 D2
Preston HA3.........44 A2
Putney SW15.......156 B6
Bruce Lawns SW17..181 A6
Bruce Rd Barnet EN5..1 A2
Bromley E3...........97 D4
Harrow HA3.........24 C1
Mitcham CR4........181 A3
South Norwood SE25..205 B5
Willesden NW10.....67 B1
Bruckner St W10.....91 B4
Brudenell Rd SW17..181 A6
Bruffs Meadow UB5..63 A2
Bruges PI ⑯ NW1...71 C1
Brumfield Rd KT19...215 A3
Brune Ho E1.........*242* A3
Brunei Gall★ WC1 .*239* D4
Brunel Cl
Cranford TW5.......128 B5
Northolt TW5........85 B4
Penge SE19.........163 A5
Brunel Ct ⑬ SW13..133 D3
Brunel Est W2.......91 C2
Brunel Ho
Chelsea SW10......266 D4
④ Gospel Oak NW5..71 B4
Hayes UB3..........105 D3
Millwall E14........119 D1
New Cross SE8......141 B5
⑫ Streatham SW2...160 A4
Brunel Mews NW10...90 C6
Brunel Mus★ SE16..118 C4
Brunel Rd Acton W3..89 C2
Walthamstow E17...53 A4
Wapping SE16......118 C5
Brunel Science Pk
UB8................95 C2
Brunel St E16........98 D1
Brunel Univ UB8.....81 C1
Brunel Wlk
South Tottenham N15..51 C5
⑤ Twickenham TW2..151 C4
Brune St E1..95 D2 *243* C2
Brunel Ho ① E2.....95 D5
Brunner Cl NW11.....48 A4
Brunner Ho SE6.....186 A6
Brunner Rd Ealing W5..87 D3
Walthamstow E17....53 B4
Bruno Cl E8..........74 A2
Brunswick Ave N11..15 A1
Brunswick Cl
Bexley DA6..........146 D1
Pinner HA5..........41 A3
Thames Ditton KT7..196 D1
Brunswick Cres N11 .15 A1
Brunswick Ct
Bermondsey
SE1.......117 C4 *253* B2
Finsbury EC1........*234* C1
Kingston u T KT2....175 D4
New Barnet EN4......14 B6
② Penge SE19.......184 A3
Westminster SW1...*259* D3

Brunswick Ct continued
② Wimbledon SW19 .179 A3
Brunswick Gdns
Ealing W5...........88 A3
Kensington
W8........113 C5 *245* B3
Brunswick Gr N11...15 A1
Brunswick Ho
Church End N3.......29 B2
④ Haggerston E2....95 D5
Lisson Gr NW1......*237* C6
Brunswick Lo ⑥ E4 .20 A2
Brunswick Manor
SM1................218 A4
Brunswick Mews
Marylebone W1....*237* D2
Streatham SW16...181 D4
BRUNSWICK PARK ...15 A1
Brunswick Park Gdns
N11................15 A2
*Brunswick Park Prim
Sch*
Brunswick Pk N14...15 A2
㉒ Camberwell SE5..139 B5
Brunswick Park Rd
N11................15 A2
Brunswick Pl SE5...139 C4
Brunswick Pl
Penge SE19.........184 A3
Shoreditch N1 .95 B4 *235* D1
Brunswick Quay
SE16...............118 D3
Brunswick Rd
Bexley DA6.........147 A1
Ealing W5...........88 A4
Holdbrook EN3.......7 C5
Kingston u T KT2...176 C2
Leyton E10..........54 A1
Poplar E14..........98 A1
South Tottenham N15..51 C4
South Tottenham N15..51 C5
Sutton SM1.........217 D4
Brunswick Sh Ctr
WC1........94 A3 *240* B6
Brunswick Sq
St Pancras
WC1........94 A3 *240* B6
Tottenham N17......33 D4
Brunswick St E17....54 A4
Brunswick Terr BR3 .185 D2
Brunswick Villas ②
SE5................139 C4
Brunswick Way N11..31 B6
Brunton Pl E14......97 A1
Brushfield St
E1..............95 D2 *243* C4
Brushwood Lo ⑦
DA17...............125 C2
Brussels Rd SW11...159 B1
Bruton Cl BR7......188 B3
Bruton La
W1........115 B6 *248* D5
Bruton Pl
W1........115 B6 *248* D5
Bruton Rd SM4.....202 A5
Bruton St
W1........115 B6 *248* D5
Bruton Way W13....87 A2
Brutus Ct SE11....*261* C3
Bryan Ave NW10....68 B1
Bryan Cl TW16.....172 A3
Bryan Ct W1.......*237* C2
Bryan Ho SE16......119 B4
Bryan Rd SE16......119 B4
Bryanston Ave TW2 .151 D3
Bryanston Cl UB2....107 B2
Bryanston Ct SW1...*237* C2
Bryanstone Ct SM1..218 A5
Bryanstone Rd N8...49 D4
Bryanston Ho ①②
SE15...............139 B4
Bryanston Mans W1 *237* C4
Bryanston Mews E
W1................*237* D2
Bryanston Mews W
W1................*237* C2
Bryanston Pl
W1........92 D1 *237* C2
Bryanston Sq
W1........92 D1 *237* C2
Bryanston St
W1........92 D1 *237* C2
Bryant Cl EN5.......13 B6
Bryant Ct Acton W3..111 B3
Haggerston E2......95 D5

Bryant Rd UB5 84 C4
Bryant St E15 76 C1
Bryantwood Rd N5, N7 72 C3
Brycedale Cres N14 15 D1
Bryce Ho 25 SE14 140 D6
Bryce Rd RM8 80 C4
Brydale Ho 2 SE16 118 D2
Bryden Cl SE26 185 A5
Brydges Pl WC2 250 A5
Brydges Rd E15 76 B3
Brydon Wlk N1 233 B6
Bryer Ct EC2 242 A4
Bryett Rd N7 72 A5
Bryher Ho W4 111 A1
Brymay Cl E3 97 C5
Brymon Ct W1 237 D3
Brynmaer Ho SW11 267 D1
Brynmaer Rd SW11 136 D4 267 D1
Bryn-y-Mawr Rd EN1 5 D1
Bryony Cl UB8 82 B2
Bryony Rd W12 112 A6
Bryony Way TW16 172 A4
B Sky B Hq TW7 131 A6
BT Twr★ W1 93 C2 239 A4
Buccleuch Ho E5 52 A2
Buchanan Cl N21 16 B6
Buchanan Ct 16 SE16 118 D2
Buchanan Gdns NW10 90 B5
Buchanan Ho
Dulwich SE21 161 C1
Wandsworth SW18 157 C4
Buchan Ho W3 110 D4
Buchan Rd SE15 140 C2
Bucharest Rd SW18 158 A4
Buckden Cl
Fortis Green N2 48 D5
Lee SE12 165 A5
Buckfast Ct W13 109 A6
Buckfast Ho N14 15 C6
Buckfast Rd SM4 201 D5
Buckfast St E2 96 A4
Buck Hill Wlk W2 114 B6 246 D5
Buckhold Rd SW18 157 C5
Buckhurst Ave CR4, SM5 202 D1
Buckhurst Ct 7 IG9 21 D2
BUCKHURST HILL 21 C2
Buckhurst Hill Ho 3 IG9 21 B2
Buckhurst Hill Sta IG9 21 D2
Buckhurst Ho 15 N7 71 D3
Buckhurst St E1 96 B3
Buckhurst Way IG9 21 D1
Buckingham Ave
East Molesey KT8 173 D1
Falconwood DA16 145 C1
Feltham TW14 150 B5
Oakleigh Pk N20 14 B4
South Norwood CR7 182 C2
St James SW1 250 B5
Wembley UB6 87 A6
Buckingham Cl
Broom Hill BR5 211 C2
Ealing W5 87 C2
Enfield EN1 5 C3
Hampton TW12 173 B5
Buckingham College Prep Sch 1 HA2 41 C2
Buckingham College Sch HA1 42 C4
Buckingham Ct
2 Ealing W7 86 D3
Hendon NW4 46 A6
Mitcham CR4 204 A4
Northolt UB5 85 A6
Wembley HA0 65 C2
Buckingham Dr BR7 189 A5
Buckingham Gate SW1 115 C3 259 B6
Buckingham Gdns
East Molesey KT8 173 D1
Edgware HA8 26 B3
South Norwood CR7 182 C1
Buckingham Gr UB10 82 C5
Buckingham Ho
1 Acton W3 88 C1
Finsbury Pk N4 51 A1
Richmond TW10 154 C6
Buckingham La SE23 163 A4
Buckingham Lo N10 49 C5
Buckingham Mans NW6 69 D3
Buckingham Mews
Harlesden NW10 89 D5
7 Kingsland N1 73 C2
Westminster SW1 259 A6
Buckingham Pal★ SW1 115 C4 249 A1
Buckingham Palace Rd SW1 115 B2 258 D4
Buckingham Par 10 HA7 25 C5
Buckingham Pl SW1 259 A6
Buckingham Prim Sch TW12 173 B5
Buckingham Rd
Edgware HA8 26 B3
Hampton TW12, TW13 173 B5
Harlesden NW10 89 D5
Harrow HA1 42 B4
Ilford IG1 79 B6
Kingsland N1 73 C2
Kingston u T KT1 198 B5
Leyton E10 75 D5
Mitcham CR4 204 A4
Richmond TW10 153 D2
Stratford E15 76 D3
Wanstead E11 55 C4
Woodford E18 36 D2
Wood Green N22 32 A2
Buckingham St WC2 250 B5
Buckingham Way SM6 219 C1
Buckingham Yd NW10 89 D5
Buck La NW9 45 B4
Buckland Cl NW7 28 A6
Buckland Cres NW3 70 B2
Buckland Ct
6 Shoreditch N1 95 C5
Uxbridge UB10 61 A6
Buckland Ho 3 N1 72 C1
Buckland Rd
Chessington KT9 214 B3
Leyton E10 76 A6
Orpington BR6 227 C4
Buckland Rise HA5 22 D2
Bucklands Rd TW11 175 C4
Buckland St N1 95 B5 235 D3
Buckland Way KT4 200 C1
Buckland Wlk
2 Acton W3 111 A4
Morden SM4 202 A5
Buckle Ct HA8 27 A3
Buckleigh Ave SW20 201 B6
Buckleigh Ho SW17 180 B5
Buckleigh Rd SW16 182 A3
Buckleigh Way SE19 183 D3
Buckler Gdns SE9 166 B1
Buckler's Alley SW6 264 D4
Bucklersbury EC2, EC4 242 C1
Bucklers' Way SM5 218 D5
Buckles Ct DA17 124 D2
Buckle St
15 Whitechapel E1 96 A1
Whitechapel E1 243 D2
Buckley Cl SE23 162 B4
Buckley Ct
5 Brondesbury NW6 69 B1
London N8 49 D4
Buckley Ho W3 110 C5
Buckley Rd NW6 69 B1
Buckmaster Cl 1 SW9 138 C2
Buckmaster Ho 1 N7 72 B4
Buckmaster Rd SW11 136 C1
Bucknall St WC1 240 A2
Bucknall Way BR3 208 A5
Bucknell Cl SW2 138 B1
Buckner Rd SW2 138 B1
Buckrell Rd E4 20 B2
Buckridge Bldg EC1 241 A4
Buckshead Ho 19 W2 91 C2
Buck St NW1 71 B1
Buckstone Cl SE23 162 C5
Buckstone Rd N18 34 A5
Buckters Rents SE16 119 A5
Buckthorne Rd SE4 163 A6
Buckthorn Ho DA15 167 D1
Buckwheat Ct DA18 124 D3
Budd Cl N12 29 D6
Buddings Circ HA9 67 A5
Bude Cl E17 53 B4
Budge La CR4 202 D2
Budge Row EC4 242 C1
Budge's Wlk W2 114 A5 246 B4
Budleigh Cres DA16 146 C4
Budleigh Ho 19 SE15 140 A5
Budoch Ct IG3 80 A6
Budoch Dr IG3 80 A6
Buer Rd SW6 135 A3
Bugsby's Way SE10 120 D2
Buick Ho 4 E3 97 C3
Building 36 7 SE18 123 A3
Building 47 6 SE18 123 A3
Building 48 5 SE18 123 A3
Building 49 4 SE18 123 A3
Building 50 3 SE18 123 A3
Building Crafts Coll The E15 76 B1
Bulbarrow NW8 91 D6
Bulganak Rd CR7 205 A5
Bulinca St SW1 115 D2 259 D3
Bullace Row SE5 139 B4
Bullard Rd TW11 174 D4
Bullards Pl 13 E2 96 D4
Bull Dog The (Juct) TW15 148 A2
Bulleid Way SW1 115 B2 258 D3
Bullen Ho 13 E1 96 B3
Bullen St SW11 136 C3
Buller Cl SE15 140 A5
Buller Rd Barking IG11 79 C1
Kensal Green NW10 90 D4
South Norwood CR7 205 B6
Tottenham N17 34 A1
Wood Green N22 32 C1
Bullers Cl DA14 191 A5
Bullers Wood Dr BR7 188 B3
Bullers Wood Sch BR7 188 A2
Bullescroft Rd HA8 10 D1
Bullfinch Ct 4 SE21 161 B2
Bullingham Mans W8 245 B2
Bull Inn Ct WC2 250 B5
Bullivant St 9 E14 120 A6
Bull La
Chislehurst BR7 189 B3
Dagenham RM10 81 D5
Edmonton N18 33 C5
Bull Rd E15 98 D5
Bullrush Cl
Carshalton SM5 218 C6
Thornton Heath CR0 205 C3
Bulls Alley SW14 133 B3
Bulls Bridge Ind Est UB2 106 B2
Bulls Bridge Rd UB2 106 B2
Bullsbrook Rd UB4 106 C5
Bull's Cross EN1, EN2 6 A6
Bull's Gdns SW3 257 B4
Bulls Head Pas EC3 243 A1
Bull Yd SE15 140 A4
Bulmer Gdns HA3 43 D2
Bulmer Mews W11 113 C5 245 A4
Bulow Ct 3 SW6 135 D3
Bulstrode Ave TW3 129 C2
Bulstrode Gdns TW3 129 C2
Bulstrode Pl W1 238 B3
Bulstrode Rd TW3 129 C2
Bulstrode St W1 93 A1 238 B2
Bulwer Court Rd E11 54 B1
Bulwer Ct E11 54 B1
Bulwer Gdns EN5 2 A1
Bulwer Rd
Edmonton N18 33 C6
Leytonstone E11 54 B1
New Barnet EN5 2 A1
Bulwer St W12 112 C5
Bunbury Ho SE15 140 A5
Bunces La IG8 36 D3
Bungalow Rd SE25 205 C5
Bungalows The
Leyton E10 54 A3
Mitcham SW16 181 B3
Bunhill Row EC1 95 B3 242 C5
Bunhouse Pl SW1 258 B2
Bunkers Hill
London NW11 48 A2
North Cray DA14 169 B1
Bunker's Hill DA17 125 C2
Bunning Ho N7 72 A4
Bunning Way N7 72 B1
Bunn's La NW7 27 D4
Bunsen Ho 2 E3 97 A5
Bunsen St 3 E3 97 A5
Buntingbridge Rd IG2 57 B4
Bunting Cl London N9 18 D3
Mitcham CR4 202 D4
Bunting Ct NW9 27 C1
Bunton St SE18 122 C3
Bunyan Ct EC2 242 A4
Bunyan Rd E17 53 A6
Buonaparte Mews SW1 259 C2
Burbage Cl
Bermondsey SE1 117 B3 262 C5
Hayes UB3 83 B1
Burbage Ho
16 Deptford SE14 140 D6
Shoreditch N1 235 D5
Burbage Rd SE21, SE24 161 B4
Burbage Sch 34 N1 95 C5
Burbank KT3 199 D6
Burberry Cl KT3 177 C1
Burberry Ct 8 N3 29 D3
Burbidge Rd TW17 192 C5
Burbridge Way N17 34 A1
Burcham St E14 98 A1
Burcharbro Rd SE2 146 D6
Burchell Ct WD23 8 A4
Burchell Ho SE11 260 D2
Burchell Rd
Leyton E10 53 D1
London SE15 140 B4
Burcher Gale Gr 5 SE15 139 D5
Burchetts Way TW17 192 D3
Burchett Way RM6 59 B3
Burcote Rd SW18 158 B4
Burden Cl TW8 109 C1
Burden Ho SW8 270 A3
Burdenshott Ave TW10 132 D1
Burden Way E11 77 B6
Burder Cl N1 73 C2
Burder Rd N1 73 C2
Burdett Ave SW20 178 A2
Burdett Cl
2 Ealing W7 108 D5
Sidcup DA14 191 A5
Burdett Coutts & Townshend CE Prim Sch SW1 115 D2 259 D3
Burdett Mews 4 W2 91 D1
Burdett Rd
Richmond TW9 132 B2
Thornton Heath CR0 205 B3
Tower Hamlets E3 97 B2
Burdetts Rd RM9 103 B6
Burdock Cl CR0 206 D1
Burdock Rd N17 52 A6
Burdon Ct 3 E8 74 A2
Burdon La SM2 217 A1
Bure Ct 17 EN5 13 D6
Burfield Cl SW17 180 B6
Burford Cl
Dagenham RM8 80 C5
Ickenham UB10 60 A4
Ilford IG6 57 A5
Burford Ct SE8 141 C6
Burford Gdns N13 16 B1
Burford Ho
1 Brentford TW8 110 A1
11 South Lambeth SW9 138 B3
Burford Rd
Brentford TW8 110 A1
Bromley BR1 210 A5
Forest Hill SE6 163 B2
Newham E6 100 A4
New Malden KT4 200 A2
5 Stratford Marsh E15 98 B6
Sutton SM1 217 C6
Burford Way CR0 224 A2
Burford Wlk SW6 265 D3
Burgate Ct 9 SW9 138 C2
Burges Gr SW13 134 B5
Burges Rd E6 78 B1
Burgess Ave NW9 45 B3
Burgess Bsns Pk SE5 139 B5
Burgess Cl 4 TW13 173 A6
Burgess Ct
2 London N20 14 D2
3 Southall UB1 85 D1
Wallend E12 78 C1
Burgess Hill NW2 69 C4
Burgess Ho 3 SE5 139 A5
Burgess Mews SW19 179 D4
Burgess Park Mans NW6 69 C4
Burgess Rd
Leyton E15 76 C4
Sutton SM1 217 D4
Burgess St E14 97 C2
Burge St SE1 262 D5
Burgh House & Hampstead Mus★ NW3 70 D4
Burghill Rd SE26 185 A6
Burghley Ave
Borehamwood WD6 11 A6
Kingston u T KT3 177 B2
Burghley Ct SW19 179 A5
Burghley Hall Cl SW19 157 A3
Burghley Ho SW19 157 A1
Burghley Pl CR4 202 D5
Burghley Rd
Camden Town NW5 71 B4
Leytonstone E11 54 C1
London N8 50 C6
Wimbledon SW19 179 A6
Burghley Twr W3 111 D6
Burgh St N1 94 D5 234 D4
Burgon St EC4 241 D1
Burgos Cl CR0 220 C2
Burgos Gr SE10 141 D4
Burgoyne Rd
Ashford TW16 171 D4
Brixton SW9 138 B2
Harringay N4 50 D3
South Norwood SE25 205 D5
Burham Cl SE20 184 C3
Burhan Uddin Ho E1 243 C5
Burhill Gr HA5 23 A1
Buriton Ho 9 SW15 156 B3
Burke Cl SW15 133 C1
Burke Ho 1 SW11 136 B1
Burke Lodge E13 99 B4
Burke St E16 98 D2
Burket Cl UB2 107 B2
Burland Rd SW11 158 D6
Burleigh Ave
Bexley DA15 167 D6
Hackbridge SM6 219 B5
Burleigh Cl RM7 59 D5
Burleigh Coll W6 112 C2
Burleigh Ct N17 34 A4
Burleigh Gdns
Ashford TW15 171 A5
Osidge N14 15 C3
Burleigh Ho
Cheam SM3 201 A1
Chelsea SW3 266 D5
5 North Kensington W10 90 D2
Burleigh Lo 3 SW19 179 D3
Burleigh Par N14 15 D3
Burleigh Pl SW15 156 D6
Burleigh Rd
Cheam SM3 201 A1
Enfield EN1 5 C1
Hillingdon UB10 82 D6
Burleigh St WC2 250 C6
Burleigh Way EN2 5 B2
Burleigh Wlk SE6 164 A3
Burley Cl Chingford E4 35 C5
Mitcham SW16 181 D1
Burley Ho E1 96 D1
Burley Rd E16 99 C2
Burlington Apartments SE20 184 B3
Burlington Arc W1 249 A5

Burlington Ave
Richmond TW9 ...... 132 C4
Romford RM7 .... 59 D3
Burlington Cl
East Bedfont TW14 ... 149 B4
5 Newham E6 ..... 100 A1
Orpington BR6 ...... 226 D6
Paddington W9 .... 91 C3
Pinner HA5 .... 40 B6
Burlington Ct
Chiswick W4 .... 133 A5
Highgate N6 .... 49 A1
Burlington Danes Acad
W12 .... 90 B1
Burlington Gate
SW20 .... 179 A1
Burlington Gdns
Acton Green W4 ...... 111 A1
Acton W3 .... 111 A5
Dagenham RM6 .... 59 A2
4 Fulham SW6 ..... 135 A3
Marylebone
W1 ...... 115 C6 249 A5
Burlington Ho NW3 .... 70 B3
Burlington Inf Sch
KT3 .... 199 D5
Burlington Jun Sch
KT3 .... 199 D5
Burlington La W4 .... 133 B5
Burlington Lo BR7 ... 188 B3
Burlington Lodge
SW6 .... 135 A3
Burlington Mews
Acton W3 .... 111 A5
2 Putney SW15 ..... 157 B6
Burlington Park Ho 6
HA7 .... 25 C6
Burlington Pl
Fulham SW6 .... 135 A3
Woodford IG8 .... 21 A1
Burlington Rd
Acton Green W4 ..... 111 A1
Enfield EN2 .... 5 B4
Fulham SW6 .... 135 A3
Hounslow TW7 .... 130 B4
Muswell Hill N10 ...... 49 A6
New Malden KT3 ..... 199 D5
South Norwood CR7 ... 183 B1
Tottenham N17 .... 34 A2
Burlington Rise EN4 .. 14 D4
Burma Rd N16 .... 73 B4
Burmarsh 6 NW5 ..... 71 A2
Burmarsh Ct SE20 ... 184 C2
Burma Terr 11 SE19 .. 183 C5
Burmester Ho SW17 .. 158 A1
Burmester Rd SW17 .. 158 A1
Burnaby Cres W4 .... 133 A6
Burnaby Ct 31 SE16 .. 118 A4
Burnaby Gdns W4 .. 132 D6
Burnaby St
SW10 ...... 136 A5 266 B3
Burnand Ho 3 W14 . 112 D3
Burnbrae Cl N12 ...... 29 D4
Burnbury Rd SW12 ... 159 C3
Burncroft Ave EN3 ..... 6 C3
Burndell Way UB4 .... 84 D2
Burne Jones Ho
W14 .... 254 B3
Burnell Ave
Richmond TW10 ..... 175 C5
Welling DA16 .... 146 A3
Burnell Gdns HA7 ..... 25 D1
Burnell Ho 18 SW2 ... 160 C3
Burnell Rd SM1 ..... 217 D4
Burnell Wlk SE1 .... 263 D2
Burnels Ave E6 ...... 100 C4
Burness Cl N7 .... 72 B2
Burne St NW1 ...... 237 A4
Burnett Cl E9 .... 74 C3
Burnett Ct SW11 ..... 267 A1
Burnett Ho 6 SE13 .. 142 A3
Burney Ave KT5 ..... 198 B4
Burney Ho 4 SW16 .. 181 C5
Burney St SE10 ...... 142 A5
Burnfoot Ave
SW6 .... 135 A4 264 B1
Burnham NW3 .... 70 C1
Burnham Ave UB10 ... 61 A4
Burnham Cl
Bermondsey SE1 .... 263 D3
Enfield EN1 .... 5 C5
Harrow HA3 .... 43 A5
Hendon NW7 .... 28 A3
Burnham Cres E11 .... 55 C5
Burnham Ct
Bayswater W2 ...... 245 D6
Hendon NW4 .... 46 C5
15 Stanmore HA7 ..... 25 C5
Burnham Dr KT4 .... 216 D6
Burnham Est 8 E2 .... 96 C4
Burnham Gdns
Cranford TW4 .... 128 B4
Croydon CR0 .... 205 D2
Hayes UB3 .... 105 B3
Burnham Rd
Chingford Hatch E4 .... 35 B5
Dagenham RM9 ..... 102 B6
Morden SM4 .... 201 D5
Sidcup DA14 .... 169 A2
Burnham St
Bethnal Green E2 ...... 96 C4
Kingston u T KT2 .... 176 C2
Burnham Way
Ealing W13 .... 109 B3
Penge SE26 .... 185 B5
Burnhill Ho EC1 ..... 235 A1
Burnhill Rd BR3 ..... 185 C1
Burnley Cl WD19 ...... 22 C5
Burnley Rd
London SW9 .... 138 B3
Willesden NW10 ...... 68 A3
Burnsall St
SW3 .... 114 C1 257 B2
Burns Ave
Blackfen DA15 .... 168 B5
Feltham TW14 ...... 150 A5
Ilford RM6 .... 58 C2
Southall UB1 .... 107 C6
Burns Cl Bexley DA16 145 D4
Hayes UB4 .... 84 A2
Mitcham SW17 ...... 180 B4
Walthamstow E17 ..... 54 A5
Burns Ct
Tottenham N17 .... 34 B3
Wallington SM6 ...... 219 B1
Burns Ho
18 Bethnal Green E2 ... 96 C4
Bexley DA16 .... 146 C4
1 Islington N7 .... 72 B2
Kennington SE17 ..... 261 D1
11 Stoke Newington
N16 .... 73 C4
Burn's Ho NW10 ...... 89 C6
Burnside Ave E4 ...... 35 B4
Burnside Cl Barnet EN5 . 1 C2
Rotherhithe SE16 ..... 118 D5
Twickenham TW1 ..... 153 A5
Burnside Cres HA0 .... 87 D6
Burnside Ct 1 SM6 .. 219 A5
Burnside Rd RM8 ..... 58 D1
Burns Rd
Battersea SW11 .... 136 D3
Ealing W13 .... 109 B4
Wembley HA0 .... 88 A5
Burn's Rd NW10 ...... 89 D6
Burns Way TW5 ..... 128 D4
Burnt Ash Hill
Lee SE12 .... 164 D5
Lewisham SE12 ...... 165 A3
Burnt Ash Hts BR1 ... 187 B5
Burnt Ash La BR1,
SE12 .... 187 B5
Burnt Ash Prim Sch
BR1 .... 187 A5
Burnt Ash Rd SE12 .. 164 D6
Burnthwaite Rd
SW6 .... 135 B5 264 D3
BURNT OAK 27 B3
Burnt Oak Broadway
HA8 .... 26 D3
Burnt Oak Fields HA8 . 27 A2
Burnt Oak Jun Sch
DA15 .... 168 A3
Burnt Oak La DA15 ... 168 B3
Burnt Oak L Ctr HA8 .. 27 B2
Burnt Oak Sta HA8 .... 27 A2
Burntwood Cl SW18 . 158 C3
Burntwood Ct SW17 . 158 A1
Burntwood Grange Rd
SW18 .... 158 C3
Burntwood La SW17 . 158 B2
Burntwood Sch
SW17 .... 158 B2
Burntwood View 6
SE19 .... 183 D5
Buross St E1 .... 96 B1
Burpham Cl UB4 ...... 84 D2
Burrage Ct 17 SE16 . 118 D2
Burrage Gr SE18 .... 123 A2
Burrage Pl SE18 .... 122 D1
Burrage Rd SE18 .... 123 A1
Burrard Ho 11 E2 ..... 96 C5
Burrard Rd
Newham E16 .... 99 B1
West Hampstead NW6 . 69 C4
Burr Cl
Bexleyheath DA7 ..... 147 B2
St George in t East E1 118 A5
Burrell Cl
Croydon CR0 .... 207 A3
Edgware HA8 .... 10 D2
Burrell Ct HA1 .... 42 B2
Burrell Ho 4 TW1 ... 153 B4
Burrell Row BR3 ..... 185 C1
Burrells 9 BR3 ..... 185 D1
Burrell St
SE1 .... 116 D5 251 C4
Burrell's Wharf Sq
E14 .... 119 D1
Burrell Twrs E10 ...... 53 C2
Burrhill Ct SE16 ..... 118 D3
Burritt Rd KT1 ...... 176 C1
Burrmead Ct NW2 ..... 67 D5
Burroughs Gdns NW4 46 B5
Burroughs The NW4 .. 46 B5
Burrow Ho 19 SW9 ... 138 B3
Burrow Rd SE22 ..... 139 C1
Burrows Mews SE1 . 251 C2
Burrows Rd NW10 .... 90 C4
Burrow Wlk SE21 .... 161 A4
Burr Rd SW18 .... 157 C4
Bursar St SE1 ...... 253 A3
Bursdon Cl DA15 .... 167 D2
Bursland Rd EN3 .... 6 D1
Burslem St E1 .... 96 A1
Bursted Wood Prim Sch
DA7 .... 147 D3
Burstock Rd SW15 .. 135 A1
Burston Rd SW15 ... 156 D6
Burstow Rd SW20 ... 179 A2
Burtenshaw Rd KT7 . 197 A3
Burtley Cl N4 .... 51 A1
Burton Bank N1 ...... 73 B1
Burton Cl
Chessington KT9 .... 213 D1
South Norwood CR7 ... 205 B6
Burton Ct
Chelsea SW3 .... 257 D2
10 Friern Barnet N11 ... 30 D5
Thames Ditton KT7 ... 197 A3
Burton Dr EN3 .... 7 C6
Burton Gdns TW5 ... 129 B4
Burton Gr SE17 ..... 262 C1
Burton Ho
8 Bermondsey
SE16 .... 118 B4
Brixton SE5 .... 138 D4
Penge SE26 .... 184 B5
Burtonhole Cl NW7 ... 28 D6
Burtonhole La
Finchley NW7, NW12 ... 29 A6
Mill Hill NW7 .... 28 D6
Burton La 3 SW9 ... 138 C3
Burton Lo 6 SW15 ... 157 B6
Burton Mews SW1 .. 258 B3
Burton Pl WC1 ...... 232 D1
Burton Rd
7 Brixton SW9 ..... 138 C3
Brixton SW9 .... 138 D3
Brondesbury NW6 ..... 69 B1
Kingston u T KT2 .... 176 A3
Wanstead E18 .... 55 B6
Burtons Ct E15 .... 76 B1
Burtons Rd TW12 ... 174 A6
Burton St
WC1 .... 93 D3 239 D6
Burtonwood Ho N4 ... 51 B2
Burt Rd E16 .... 121 C5
Burtt Ho 6 N1 .... 95 C4
Burtwell La SE21,
SE27 .... 183 B6
Burvill Ct SW20 ..... 178 C2
Burwash Ho SE1 .... 252 D1
Burwash Rd SE18 ... 123 B1
Burway Cl CR2 ...... 221 C2
Burwell 2 KT1 ...... 176 C1
Burwell Ave UB6 ...... 64 C2
Burwell Cl 27 E1 ...... 96 B1
Burwell Rd E10 .... 53 A1
Burwell Wlk 14 E3 .... 97 C3
Burwood Ave
Hayes BR2 .... 225 B6
Pinner HA5 .... 40 C4
Burwood Cl KT6 ..... 198 C1
Burwood Ho 11
SW9 .... 138 D1
Burwood Lo SW19 ... 179 B6
Burwood Pl Barnet EN4 . 2 A4
Paddington W2 ..... 237 B2
Bury Ave Hayes UB4 ... 83 C5
Ruislip HA4 .... 39 A3
Bury Cl SE16 .... 118 D5
Bury Ct EC3 .... 243 B2
Buryfield Ct 23 SE8 . 118 D2
Bury Gr SM4 .... 201 D4
Bury Hall Villas N9 .... 17 D4
Bury Pl WC1 ... 94 A2 240 B3
Bury Rd Chingford E4 ... 20 C6
Dagenham RM10 ...... 81 D3
Hornsey N22 .... 50 C6
Bury St W N9 .... 17 C4
Buryside Cl IG2 ...... 57 D5
Bury St Edmonton N9 ... 18 A3
Ruislip HA4 .... 39 B3
St James
SW1 ...... 115 C5 249 B4
Whitechapel
EC3 .... 95 C1 243 B2
Bury Wlk
SW3 .... 114 C1 257 A2
Burywood Ct EN3 ...... 6 C3
Busbridge Ho 24 E14 .. 97 C2
Busby Ho SW16 ..... 181 C6
Busby Mews 5 NW1 .. 71 D2
Busby Pl NW5 .... 71 D2
Busch Cl TW7 .... 131 B4
Busch Cnr TW7 ...... 131 B4
Bushbaby Cl SE1 .... 263 A5
Bushberry Rd E9 ...... 75 A2
Bush Cl IG2 .... 57 B4
Bush Cotts 12 SW18 . 157 C6
Bush Ct London N14 .... 15 C3
7 Shepherd's Bush
W12 .... 112 D4
Bushell Cl SW2 ..... 160 B2
Bushell Gn WD23 ...... 8 B2
Bushell Ho 3 SE27 .. 183 A6
Bushell St 18 E1 ..... 118 A5
Bushell Way BR7 .... 188 C5
BUSHEY 8 A2
Bushey Ave
Crofton BR5 .... 211 B2
Snaresbrook E18 ...... 54 D6
Bushey Cl
Chingford E4 .... 20 A1
Ickenham UB10 .... 60 C6
Bushey Ct SW20 ..... 178 B1
Bushey Down SW12 .. 159 B2
Bushey Hall SE5 .... 139 D4
BUSHEY HEATH 8 C4
Bushey Heath Prim Sch
WD23 .... 8 B3
Bushey Hill Rd SE5 .. 139 D4
Bushey Ho SE12 ..... 165 C1
Bushey La SM1 ...... 217 C4
Bushey Lees DA15 .. 167 D5
BUSHEY MEAD 200 D6
Bushey Meads Sch
WD23 .... 8 A6
Bushey Rd
Croydon CR0 .... 223 C6
Hayes UB3 .... 105 C2
Ickenham UB10 .... 60 C6
Newham E13 .... 99 C5
South Tottenham N15 ... 51 C3
Sutton SM1 .... 217 C4
West Barnes SW20 .. 178 D1
Bushey Way BR3 .... 208 B4
Bush Fair Ct N14 ...... 15 B5
Bushfield Cl HA8 ...... 10 D2
Bushfield Cres HA8 ... 10 D2
Bushfield Ho N5 ...... 73 A3
Bush Gr London NW9 ... 45 A2
Stanmore HA7 .... 25 D2
Bushgrove Rd RM8 ... 80 D5
BUSH HILL 17 B5
Bush Hill N21 .... 17 A5
Bush Hill Par EN1 ..... 17 B4
BUSH HILL PARK 17 C5
Bush Hill Park Prim Sch
EN1 .... 18 A6
Bush Hill Park Sta
EN1 .... 17 D5
Bush Hill Rd
Enfield N21 .... 17 B5
Harrow HA3 .... 44 B3
Bush Ind Est NW10 .... 89 B3
Bush La EC4 .. 117 B6 252 C6
Bushmead Cl 7 N15 .. 51 D5
Bushmoor Cres
SE18 .... 144 D5
Bushnell Rd SW17 ... 159 B1
Bush Rd
Bermondsey SE8 .... 118 D2
Hackney E8 .... 96 B6
Littleton TW17 ...... 192 B4
Richmond TW9 ...... 132 B6
Wanstead E11 .... 55 A2
Woodford IG9 .... 37 D6
Bushway RM8 .... 80 D5
Bushwood E11 .... 55 A1
Bushwood Dr
SE1 .... 117 D2 263 D3
Bushwood Rd TW9 .. 132 C6
Bushy Ct KT1 .... 175 C2
Bushy Park Gdns
TW12 .... 174 B5
Bushy Park Rd
TW11 .... 175 B3
Bushy Rd TW11 ..... 174 D3
Business Acad Bexley
The DA18 .... 125 A4
Business Design Ctr★
N1 .... 94 C6 234 B5
Buspace Studios 3
W10 .... 91 A3
Butcher Row E1 ...... 96 D1
Butchers Rd E16 ...... 99 A1
Bute Ave TW10 ...... 154 A2
Bute Ct SM6 .... 219 C3
Bute Gardens W
SM6 .... 219 C3
Bute Gdns
Hammersmith W6 ... 112 D2
Wallington SM6 ..... 219 C3
Bute House Prep Sch 2
W6 .... 112 D2
Bute Mews NW11 ..... 48 A4
Bute Rd Ilford IG6 ..... 56 D4
Thornton Heath CR0 . 204 C1
Wallington SM6 ..... 219 C4
Bute St SW7 .. 114 B2 256 C4
Bute Wlk 18 N1 .... 73 B2
Butfield Ho 6 E9 ..... 74 C2
Butler Ave HA1 .... 42 B2
Butler Cl HA8 .... 26 D1
Butler Ct
Dagenham RM8 .... 81 C6
Wembley HA0 .... 65 A4
Butler Ho
32 Bethnal Green E2 ... 96 C4
5 Brixton SW9 ..... 138 D4
11 Poplar E14 .... 97 B1
Butler Pl SW1 ...... 259 C6
Butler Rd
Dagenham RM8 .... 80 B4
Harrow HA1 .... 42 A2
Willesden NW10 ...... 67 D1
Butlers Cl TW3 ...... 129 B1
Butlers & Colonial Wharf
SE1 .... 253 D2
Butler's Cotts DA7 .. 147 C3
Butlers Farm Cl
TW10 .... 175 D6
Butler St
33 Bethnal Green E2 ... 96 C4
Hillingdon UB10 .... 82 D3
Butler's Wharf W
SE1 .... 253 C3
Butley Ct 8 E3 .... 97 A5
Butt Ct SM4 .... 202 A3
Buttercup Cl UB5 ..... 63 B2
Butterfield Cl
1 Bermondsey
SE16 .... 118 B4
Tottenham N17 .... 33 A4
Twickenham TW1 .... 152 D5
Butterfield Ho 4 EN2 ... 4 D3
Butterfield Mews 15
SE18 .... 144 D6
Butterfields E17 ...... 54 A4
Butterfield Sq 10 E6 . 100 B1
Butterfly Ct 1 E6 .... 100 B4
Butterfly La SE9 .... 166 D5
Butterfly Wlk 2 SE5 . 139 B4
Butter Hill SM5, SM6 . 219 A4
Butteridges Cl RM9 .. 103 B6
Buttermere NW1 ... 231 D2
Buttermere Cl
Bermondsey SE1 .... 263 C3
East Bedfont TW14 .. 149 D3
Leyton E11 .... 76 B4
West Barnes SM4 ... 200 D3
Buttermere Ct NW8 . 229 C6

Buttermere Dr
SW15 . . . . 157 A6
Buttermere Ho
London N12 . . . . 30 C5
13 Tower Hamlets E3. . . 97 B4
Buttermere Wlk 9
E8 . . . . 73 D2
Butterwick W6 . . . . . . 112 C2
Butterworth Ct
SW16 . . . . 160 A1
Butterworth Gdns
IG8 . . . . 37 A5
Buttery Mews N4 . . . . 16 A1
Buttesland St
N1 . . . . 95 B4 235 D2
Buttfield Cl RM10 . . . . 81 D2
Buttmarsh Cl SE18 . . 122 D1
Buttsbury Rd IG1 . . . . 79 A3
Butts Cotts TW13 . . . . 151 B1
Butts Cres TW13 . . . . 151 C1
Butts Ho TW13 . . . . . . 151 C1
Butts Piece UB5 . . . . . 84 B5
Butts Rd BR1 . . . . 186 C5
Butts The TW8 . . . . . 131 D6
Buxhall Cres E9 . . . . . . 75 B2
Buxlow Prep Sch
HA9 . . . . 66 A5
Buxted Rd
Camberwell SE22 . . . . 139 C1
Colney Hatch N12 . . . . 30 C5
Dalston E8 . . . . 73 D1
Buxton Cl London N9 . . 18 C2
Woodford IG8 . . . . 37 D4
Buxton Cres SM3 . . . . 217 A4
Buxton Ct
1 Leyton E11 . . . . 54 D2
Shoreditch N1 . . . . . . 235 B2
Buxton Dr
Kingston u T KT3 . . . . 177 B1
Leytonstone E11 . . . . . 54 C5
Buxton Gdns W3 . . . . 110 D6
Buxton Ho
Leytonstone E11 . . . . . 54 C5
3 London SW11 . . . . . 136 B1
Buxton Lo E11 . . . . 77 B6
Buxton Mews SW4 . . 137 D3
Buxton Rd
Chingford E4 . . . . 20 B4
Ilford IG2 . . . . 57 C3
Mortlake SW14 . . . . . 133 C2
Newham E6 . . . . 100 A4
Stratford E15 . . . . 76 C3
Thornton Heath CR7 . 204 D4
Upper Holloway N19 . . 49 D1
Walthamstow E17 . . . . 53 A5
Willesden NW2 . . . . . . 68 B2
Buxton St E1 . . 95 D3 243 D5
Buzzard Creek Ind Est
IG11 . . . . 102 A2
Byam Shaw Sch of Art 8
N19 . . . . 71 D6
Byam St SW6 . . . . 136 A3
Byards Croft SW16 . . 181 D2
Byards Ct SE16 . . . . . 118 D3
Byas Ho 6 E3 . . . . 97 B4
Byatt Wlk TW12 . . . . . 173 A4
Bychurch End 11
TW11 . . . . 174 D5
Bycroft Rd UB1 . . . . . . 85 C3
Bycroft St SE20 . . . . . 184 D3
Bycullah Ave EN2 . . . . . 4 D3
Bycullah Ct EN2 . . . . . . 4 D2
Bycullah Rd EN2 . . . . . . 4 D3
Byefield Cl SE16 . . . . 119 A4
Byegrove Ct SW19 . . . 180 B4
Byegrove Rd SW19 . . . 180 B4
Byelands Cl 12 SE16 . 118 D5
Bye The W3 . . . . 89 C1
Bye Ways TW2 . . . . . . 151 D1
Byeways The KT5 . . . 198 D4
Byeway The SW14 . . . 133 A2
Bye Way The HA3 . . . . 24 D2
Byfeld Gdns SW13 . . . 134 A4
Byfield Ct KT3 . . . . . . 200 A5
Byfield Rd TW7 . . . . . . 131 A2
Byford Cl E15 . . . . 76 C1
Bygrove CR0 . . . . 223 D1
Bygrove Prim Sch 21
E14 . . . . 97 D1
Bygrove St E14 . . . . . . 97 D1
Byland Cl
Abbey Wood SE2 . . . . 124 B3
Carshalton SM4 . . . . . 202 B2
Southgate N21 . . . . 16 B4
Byne Rd
Carshalton SM5 . . . . . 218 C6
Byne Rd *continued*
Forest Hill SE26 . . . . . 184 C5
Bynes Rd CR2 . . . . . . 221 B1
Byng Pl WC1 . . . 93 D3 239 C5
Byng St E14 . . . . 119 C4
Bynon Ave DA7 . . . . . 147 B2
Byre Rd N14 . . . . 15 B5
Byrne Cl 2 CR0 . . . . . 204 D3
Byrne Ho 11 SW2 . . . . 160 B6
Byrne Rd SW12 . . . . . 159 B2
Byron Ave
Borehamwood WD6 . . . . 10 C6
Cranford TW4 . . . . 128 B3
Plashet E12 . . . . 78 A2
Queensbury NW9 . . . . . 44 D6
Sutton SM1 . . . . 218 B4
West Barnes KT3 . . . . 200 A4
Woodford E18 . . . . 36 D1
Byron Ave E SM1 . . . . 218 B4
Byron Cl
Feltham TW12 . . . . . . 173 B6
Forest Hill SE26 . . . . . 185 A6
Hackney E8 . . . . 96 A6
Streatham SW16 . . . . 182 A4
Thamesmead SE28 . . . 124 C5
Walton-on-T KT12 . . . 195 A1
Byron Court Prim Sch
HA0 . . . . 65 C6
Byron Ct Chelsea SW3 257 B3
Dulwich SE21 . . . . 162 A3
Ealing W7 . . . . 109 A2
Enfield EN2 . . . . 4 D3
3 Hampstead NW6 . . . 70 A1
Harrow HA1 . . . . 42 C3
4 New Barnet EN5 . . . . . 2 A1
Paddington W9 . . . . . . 91 C3
1 Richmond TW10 . . 175 D6
South Norwood CR7 . . 183 A1
St Pancras WC1 . . . . . 240 C6
11 Wanstead E11 . . . . . 55 A5
Woodford E18 . . . . 37 B2
Byron Dr
East Finchley N2 . . . . . 48 B3
Erith DA8 . . . . 147 D5
Byron Gdns SM1 . . . . 218 B4
Byron Hill Rd HA1,
HA2 . . . . 64 C6
Byron Ho 5 BR3 . . . . 185 D4
Byron Mews
Hampstead NW3 . . . . . 70 C4
2 Maida Vale W9 . . . . . 91 C3
Byron Par UB10 . . . . . . 83 A3
Byron Rd
Dollis Hill NW2 . . . . 68 B6
Ealing W5 . . . . 110 B5
Edgware NW7 . . . . 28 A5
Harrow HA1 . . . . 42 C3
Leyton E10 . . . . 53 D1
Walthamstow E17 . . . . 53 C6
Wealdstone HA3 . . . . . 24 D1
Wembley HA0 . . . . 65 C5
Byron St E14 . . . . 98 A1
Byron Way Hayes UB4 . . 83 D3
Northolt UB5 . . . . 85 A4
West Drayton UB7 . . . 104 B2
Bysouth Cl N15 . . . . . . 51 B5
Bythorn St SW9 . . . . . 138 B1
Byton Rd SW17 . . . . . 180 D4
Byward Ave TW14 . . . 150 C5
Byward St
EC3 . . . . 117 C6 253 B5
Bywater Ho SE18 . . . . 122 A3
Bywater Pl SE16 . . . . . 119 A5
Bywater St
SW3 . . . . 114 D1 257 C2
Byway The KT19 . . . . 215 D4
Bywell Pl W1 . . . . 239 A3
Bywood Ave CR0 . . . . 206 D3
Bywood Terr CR0 . . . . 206 C3
Byworth Ho HA7 . . . . . 25 C4
Byworth Wlk N19 . . . . . 50 A1

C

Cabbell St
NW1 . . . . 92 C2 237 A3
Cabinet Off SW1 . . . . 250 A2
Cabinet War Rooms &
Churchill Mus★
SW1 . . . . 115 D4 249 D2
Cabinet Way E4 . . . . . . 35 B4
Cable Ho WC1 . . . . . . 234 A2
Cable Pl SE10 . . . . . . 142 A4
Cable St E1 . . . . 118 B6
Cabot Ct SE16 . . . . . . 118 D3
Cabot Sq E14 . . . . 119 C5
Cabot Way 3 E6 . . . . . . 99 D6
Cabul Rd SW11 . . . . . 136 C3
Cactus Cl SE5 . . . . 139 C3
Cactus Wlk W12 . . . . . . 89 D1
Cadbury Cl
Ashford TW16 . . . . . . 171 C3
Isleworth TW7 . . . . . . 131 A4
Cadbury Rd TW16 . . . 171 C4
Cadbury Way 1
SE16 . . . . 118 A2
Caddington Cl EN4 . . . . 14 C6
Caddington Rd NW2 . . 69 A5
Caddis Cl HA7 . . . . 24 D3
Cadell Cl E2 . . . . 95 D5
Cadell Ho 12 E2 . . . . . . 95 D5
Cade Rd SE10 . . . . 142 B4
Cader Rd SW18 . . . . . 158 A5
Cadet Dr
SE1 . . . . 117 D1 263 D2
Cade Tyler Ho 10
SE10 . . . . 142 A4
Cadiz St
SE17 . . . . 117 A1 262 B1
Cadley Terr SE23 . . . . 162 C2
Cadman Cl SW9 . . . . . 138 D5
Cadmer Cl KT3 . . . . . 199 C5
Cadmore Ho 4 N1 . . . . 72 D1
Cadmus Cl 9 SW4 . . . 137 D2
Cadmus Ct 6 SW9 . . . 138 C4
Cadnam Lo E14 . . . . . 120 B3
Cadnam Point 15
SW15 . . . . 156 B3
Cadogan Cl
Beckenham BR3 . . . . . 186 B1
Hackney Wick E9 . . . . . 75 B1
Harrow HA2 . . . . 63 D4
Teddington TW11 . . . . 174 C5
Cadogan Ct
Chelsea SW3 . . . . 257 C3
New Malden KT3 . . . . 199 C5
Sutton SM2 . . . . 217 D2
Cadogan Ct Gdns
SW1 . . . . 258 A4
Cadogan Gate
SW1 . . . . 114 D2 257 D4
Cadogan Gdns
Chelsea
SW3 . . . . . . 114 D2 257 D3
Finchley N3 . . . . 29 D2
Southgate N21 . . . . 16 C6
Wanstead E18 . . . . 55 B6
Cadogan Hall★ SW1 258 A4
Cadogan Ho SW3 . . . 266 D5
Cadogan La
SW1 . . . . 115 A3 258 A5
Cadogan Pl
SW1 . . . . 114 D3 257 D5
Cadogan Rd
Kingston u T KT6 . . . . 197 D4
Woolwich SE18 . . . . . 122 D3
Woolwich SE18 . . . . . 123 A3
Cadogan Sq
SW1 . . . . 114 D3 257 D5
Cadogan St
SW3 . . . . 114 D2 257 C3
Cadogan Terr E9 . . . . . 75 B1
Cadoxton Ave 3 N15 . . 51 D3
Cadwallon Rd SE9 . . . 167 A2
Caedmon Rd N7 . . . . . 72 B4
Caerleon Cl
Claygate KT10 . . . . . . 213 B1
Sidcup DA14 . . . . 190 C5
Caerleon Terr SE2 . . . 124 B2
Caernafon Ho HA7 . . . . 25 A5
Caernarvon Cl CR4 . . 204 A6
Caernarvon Ct 3
KT5 . . . . 198 B4
Caernarvon Ho W2 . . 236 A2
Caesar Ct 25 E2 . . . . . . 96 D5
Caesar's Way TW17 . . 193 B3
Caesars Wlk CR4 . . . 202 D4
Cahill St EC1 . . . . . . 242 B5
Cahir St E14 . . . . 119 D2
Cain Ct 2 W5 . . . . 87 C2
Caine Ho W3 . . . . 110 D4
Cain's La TW14 . . . . . 149 C6
Caird St W10 . . . . 91 B4
Cairn Ave W5 . . . . . . 109 D5
Cairndale Cl BR1 . . . 186 D3
Cairnfield Ave NW2 . . . 67 D5
Cairnfield Ct NW2 . . . . 67 C5
Cairngorm Cl 3
TW11 . . . . 175 A5
Cairn Ho 3 SW19 . . . 180 C3
Cairns Ho 3 N7 . . . . . . 72 B4
Cairns Mews SE18 . . . 144 A4
Cairns Rd SW11 . . . . . 158 C6
Cairn Way HA7 . . . . . . 24 D4
Cairo New Rd CR0 . . 220 D6
Cairo Rd E17 . . . . 53 C5
Caister Ho N7 . . . . 72 B2
Caistor Ho
10 Balham SW12 . . . . 159 B4
5 West Ham E15 . . . . . 98 D6
Caistor Mews SW12 . . 159 B4
Caistor Park Rd E15 . . 98 D6
Caistor Rd SW12 . . . . 159 B4
Caithness Gdns
DA15 . . . . 167 D5
Caithness Ho N1 . . . . 233 C6
Caithness Rd
Hammersmith W14 . . 112 D3
Mitcham CR4 . . . . 181 B3
Calabria Rd N5 . . . . . . 72 D3
Calais Gate SE5 . . . . . 138 D4
Calais St SE5 . . . . 138 D4
Calbourne Rd SW12 . . 159 A4
Calcott Wlk SE9 . . . . . 187 D6
Calcraft Ho 10 E2 . . . . 96 C5
Caldbeck Ave KT4 . . . 200 B1
Caldecot Ct SE5 . . . . 139 A3
Caldecote 3 KT1 . . . . 176 C1
Caldecote Gdns WD23 . . 8 C4
Caldecote La WD23 . . . . 8 D5
Caldecot Rd SE5 . . . . 139 A3
Caldecott Way E5 . . . . 74 D5
Calder Ave UB6 . . . . . . 86 D5
Calder Cl EN1 . . . . 5 C2
Calder Ct SE16 . . . . . 119 B5
Calder Gdns HA8 . . . . . 44 C6
Calder Ho UB5 . . . . 85 A6
Calderon Ho NW8 . . . 230 A4
Calderon Pl 20 W10 . . . 90 C2
Calderon Rd E11 . . . . . 76 B5
Calder Rd SM4 . . . . . 202 A4
Caldervale Rd SW4 . . 159 D6
Calderwood Pl EN4 . . . . 1 D4
Calderwood St SE18 . 122 C2
Caldew Ct NW7 . . . . . . 28 A3
Caldew St SE5 . . . . . . 139 B5
Caldicote Gn NW9 . . . . 45 C3
Caldon Ho 2 UB5 . . . . 85 B3
Caldwell Rd WD19 . . . . 22 D6
Caldwell St
SW9 . . . . 138 B5 270 D3
Caldy Rd DA17 . . . . . 125 D3
Caldy Wlk 19 N1 . . . . . 73 A2
Caleb St SE1 . . . . 252 B2
Caledonia Ct
Barking IG11 . . . . 102 C5
Hendon NW4 . . . . 28 C1
Caledonia Ho 15 E14 . . 97 A1
Caledonian Cl 1 IG3 . . 58 B1
Caledonian Ct UB5 . . . 85 A3
Caledonian Market
SE1 . . . . 117 C3 263 B6
Caledonian Rd
Islington N1 . . . 94 B6 233 C5
Lower Holloway N7 . . . 72 B2
Caledonian Road &
Barnsbury Sta N7 . . . 72 B1
Caledonian Road Sta
N7 . . . . 72 B2
Caledonian Sq 6
NW1 . . . . 71 D2
Caledonian Wharf Rd
E14 . . . . 120 B2
Caledonia Rd TW19 . . 148 A3
Caledonia St N1 . . . . 233 B3
Caledon Rd
East Ham E6 . . . . 78 B1
Hackbridge SM5, SM6 219 A4
Cale St SW3 . . 114 C1 257 A2
Caletock Way SE10 . . 120 D1
Calgarth NW1 . . . . . . 232 B3
Calgary Ct 30 SE16 . . 118 C4
Caliban Twr 9 N1 . . . . 95 C5
Calico Ho 4 SW11 . . . 136 A2
Calico Row 5 SW11 . 136 A2
Calidore Cl SW2 . . . . 160 B5
California Bldg 2
SE13 . . . . 141 D4
California La WD23 . . . 8 B3
California Rd KT3 . . . 199 A6
Callaby Terr 11 N1 . . . 73 B2
Callaghan Cl SE13 . . . 142 C1
Callahan Cotts 8 E1 . . 96 C2
Callander Rd SE6 . . . 164 A2
Callanders The WD23 . . 8 C3
Callan Sch The
W1 . . . . 93 C1 239 B2
Callard Ave N13 . . . . . 32 D6
Callcott Ct NW6 . . . . . 69 B1
Callcott Rd NW6 . . . . . 69 B1
Callcott St W8 . . . . . . 245 A4
Callendar Rd SW7 . . . 256 C6
Callingham Cl 13 E14 . 97 B2
Callingham Ho 1
SW4 . . . . 138 A2
Callis Farm Cl TW19 . 148 A5
Callis Rd E17 . . . . 53 B3
Callonfield 3 E17 . . . . 53 A5
Callow St
SW3 . . . . 136 B6 266 C6
Calmington Rd SE5 . . 139 C6
Calmont Rd BR1 . . . . 186 C4
Calonne Rd SW19 . . . 178 D6
Calshot Ho N1 . . . . . 233 C4
Calshot Rd TW6 . . . . 126 D3
Calshot St N1 . . 94 B5 233 C3
Calshot Way
Enfield EN2 . . . . 4 D2
Harlington TW6 . . . . . 126 C3
Calstock NW1 . . . . . . 232 C5
Calstock Ho SE11 . . . 261 B2
Calthorpe Gdns
Edgware HA8 . . . . 26 B5
Sutton SM1 . . . . 218 A5
Calthorpe St
WC1 . . . . 94 B3 240 D6
Calton Ave SE21 . . . . 161 C5
Calton Rd EN5 . . . . 14 B5
Calumet Ct SW17 . . . 180 C4
Calver 13 NW5 . . . . 71 B4
Calver Ct E17 . . . . 54 B6
Calverley Cl BR3 . . . . 185 D4
Calverley Cres RM10 . . 81 C6
Calverley Gdns HA3 . . . 43 D2
Calverley Gr N19 . . . . . 49 D1
Calverley Rd KT17 . . . 216 A2
Calvert Ave E2 . . . . 95 D4
Calvert Cl
Belvedere DA17 . . . . . 125 D2
Sidcup DA14 . . . . 191 A4
Calvert Ct
1 London N19 . . . . 49 C1
5 Richmond TW9 . . . . 132 B1
Calvert Ho 9 W12 . . . 112 B6
Calverton SE5 . . . . . . 139 C6
Calverton Prim Sch
E16 . . . . 99 D1
Calverton Rd E6 . . . . 100 C6
Calvert Rd SE10 . . . . . 120 D1
Calvert's Bldgs SE1 . 252 C3
Calvert St
NW1 . . . . 93 A6 231 A6
Calvin St E1 . . . 95 D3 243 C5
Calydon Rd SE7 . . . . . 121 B1
Calypso Cres 6
SE15 . . . . 139 D5
Calypso Way SE8,
SE16 . . . . 119 B2
Camac Rd TW2 . . . . . 152 B3
Camarthen Gn NW9 . . . 45 C3
Cambalt Ho 3
SW15 . . . . 156 D6
Cambalt Rd SW15 . . . 156 D6
Cambay Ho 7 E1 . . . . . 97 A3
Cambell Jun & Inf Schs
RM9 . . . . 80 D1
Camber Ho 4 SE15 . . 140 C6
Camberley Ave
Enfield EN1 . . . . 5 C1
Wimbledon SW20 . . . 178 B1
Camberley Cl SM3 . . . 216 D5
Camberley Ct 15
SM2 . . . . 217 D1
Camberley Ho NW1 . . 231 D3
Camberley Rd TW6 . . . 126 C2
Cambert Way SE9 . . . 143 B1
CAMBERWELL 139 A4
Camberwell Bsns Ctr
SE5 . . . . 139 B5
Camberwell Church St
SE5 . . . . 139 B4
Camberwell Coll of Arts
16 Camberwell SE5 . . 139 C4
25 Camberwell SE15 . 139 D5
Camberwell Glebe
SE5 . . . . 139 C4
Camberwell Gn SE5 . . 139 B4
Camberwell Gr SE5 . . 139 C3
Camberwell Green
SE5 . . . . 139 A4

Camberwell New Rd SW9 . . . 138 D5
Camberwell Rd SE5 . . 139 A5
Camberwell Station Rd SE5 . . . 139 A4
Camberwell Trad Est SE5 . . . 139 A4
Cambeys Rd RM10 . . . 81 D3
Cambisgate SW19 . . . 179 A5
Camborne Ave W13 . . 109 C4
Camborne Cl TW6 . . . 126 C2
Camborne Cres TW6 . . . 126 C2
Camborne Rd
Belmont SM2 . . . 217 D1
Bexley DA16 . . . 145 D3
Croydon CR0 . . . 206 A2
Harmondsworth TW6 126 C2
Sidcup DA14 . . . 168 C1
Wandsworth SW18 . . 157 C4
West Barnes SM4 . . . 200 D4
Camborne Way
Harlington TW6 . . . 126 C2
Heston TW5 . . . 129 C4
Cambourne Ave N9 . . . 18 D4
Cambourne Mews 6 W11 . . . 91 A1
Cambrai Ct N13 . . . 32 A6
Cambray Rd
Broom Hill BR6 . . . 211 D2
Streatham SW12 . . . 159 C3
Cambria 6 BR3 . . . 185 D1
Cambria Cl
Hounslow TW3 . . . 129 C1
Sidcup DA15 . . . 167 C3
Cambria Ct TW14 . . . 150 B4
Cambria Gdns TW19 . 148 A4
Cambria Ho
Forest Hill SE26 . . . 184 A6
14 Limehouse E14 . . . 97 A1
Cambria Lo 3 SW15 . . . 157 B6
Cambrian Ave IG2 . . . 57 C4
Cambrian Cl SE27 . . . 160 D1
Cambrian Ct UB2 . . . 107 D2
Cambrian Gn NW9 . . . 45 C4
Cambrian Rd
Leyton E10 . . . 53 C1
Richmond TW10 . . . 154 B5
Cambria Rd SE5 . . . 139 A2
Cambria St SW6 . . . 135 D5 265 D3
Cambridge Ave
Falconwood DA16 . . . 145 D1
Greenford UB6 . . . 64 D3
Kilburn NW6 . . . 91 C5
Kingston u T KT3, SW20 . . . 177 D1
Cambridge Barracks Rd 11 SE18 . . . 122 B2
Cambridge Cir WC2 . . . 93 D1 239 D1
Cambridge Cl
East Barnet EN4 . . . 15 A3
Hounslow TW4 . . . 129 A1
Walthamstow E17 . . . 53 B3
Willesden NW10 . . . 67 A5
Wimbledon SW20 . . . 178 B2
Wood Green N22 . . . 32 C2
Cambridge Cotts TW9 . . . 132 C6
Cambridge Cres
20 Bethnal Green E2 . . . 96 B5
Teddington TW11 . . . 175 A5
Cambridge Ct
4 Barnet EN5 . . . 1 B2
26 Bethnal Green E2 . . . 96 B5
7 Hammersmith W6 112 C2
2 Kilburn NW6 . . . 91 C5
Marylebone W2 . . . 237 A3
Stamford Hill N16 . . . 51 C2
Wembley HA0 . . . 65 D4
Wimbledon SW20 . . . 178 B2
Cambridge Dr
Lee SE12 . . . 165 A6
Ruislip HA4 . . . 62 D6
Cambridge Gate NW1 . . . 238 C6
Cambridge Gate Mews NW1 . . . 238 D6
Cambridge Gdns
Enfield EN1 . . . 6 A3
Kilburn NW6 . . . 91 C5
Cambridge Gdns *continued*
Kingston u T KT1 . . . 176 C1
Muswell Hill N10 . . . 31 B2
North Kensington W10 . . 91 A1
Southgate N21 . . . 17 B4
Tottenham N17 . . . 33 B3
Cambridge Gn SE9 . . . 166 D3
Cambridge Gr
Hammersmith W6 . . . 112 B2
Penge SE20 . . . 184 B2
Cambridge Grove Rd
13 Kingston u T KT1 . . . 176 C1
Kingston u T KT1 . . . 198 C6
Cambridge Heath Rd E1, E2 . . . 96 B4
Cambridge Heath Sta E2 . . . 96 B5
Cambridge Ho
Barking IG11 . . . 79 A1
Ealing W13 . . . 87 A1
Fulham SW6 . . . 135 A2
2 Teddington TW11 . . . 175 A5
8 Woolwich SE18 . . . 122 B2
Cambridge Mans SW11 . . . 267 C1
Cambridge Par EN1 . . . 6 A4
CAMBRIDGE PARK . . 153 C4
Cambridge Park Ct TW1 . . . 153 D4
Cambridge Park Rd E11 . . . 55 A2
Cambridge Pas 9 E9 . 74 C1
Cambridge Pk
Twickenham TW1 . . . 153 D5
Wanstead E11 . . . 55 A3
Cambridge Pl W8 . . . 245 D1
Cambridge Rd
Barking IG11 . . . 79 A1
Barnes SW13 . . . 133 D3
Battersea SW11 . . . 136 D4 267 C1
Carshalton SM5 . . . 218 C3
3 Chingford E4 . . . 20 B3
East Molesey KT8 . . . 195 B5
Hampton TW12 . . . 173 B3
Hanwell W7 . . . 108 D4
Harrow HA2 . . . 41 C4
Hounslow TW4 . . . 129 A1
Ilford IG3 . . . 57 C1
Kilburn NW6 . . . 91 C4
Kilburn NW6 . . . 91 C5
Kingston u T KT1 . . . 176 C1
Leytonstone E11 . . . 54 D3
Littleton TW15 . . . 171 A3
Mitcham CR4 . . . 203 C6
New Malden KT3 . . . 199 C5
Penge SE20 . . . 206 B6
Plaistow BR1 . . . 187 A3
Richmond TW9 . . . 132 C5
Sidcup DA14 . . . 189 C6
Southall UB1 . . . 107 B5
Teddington TW11 . . . 175 A5
Twickenham TW1 . . . 153 D5
Walton-on-T KT12 . . . 194 B3
Wimbledon SW20 . . . 178 B2
Cambridge Rd N W4 . . . 110 D1
Cambridge Rd S 3 W4 . . . 110 D1
Cambridge Row SE18 . . . 122 D1
Cambridge Sch 15 W6 . . . 112 B2
Cambridge Sq W2 . . . 92 C1 237 A2
Cambridge St SW1 . . . 115 C1 259 A2
Cambridge Terr
Edmonton N9 . . . 17 D4
Regent's Pk NW1 . . . 231 C1
Cambridge Terr Mews NW1 . . . 231 D1
Cambridge Tutors Coll CR0 . . . 221 C4
Cambstone Cl N11 . . . 15 A2
Cambus Cl UB4 . . . 85 A2
Cambus Rd E16 . . . 99 A2
Cam Ct 2 SE15 . . . 139 D6
Camdale Rd SE18 . . . 145 D5
Camden Ave
Feltham TW13 . . . 150 C3
Hayes UB4 . . . 106 D6
Camden Cl BR7 . . . 189 A2
Camden Coll of English 8 NW1 . . . 71 A1
Camden Ct 9 DA17 . . 125 C1
Camden Gdns
Camden Town NW1 . . . 71 B1
Sutton SM1 . . . 217 D3
Thornton Heath CR7 . 204 D6
Camden Gr BR7 . . . 188 D4
Camden High St NW1 . . . 93 C6 232 A5
Camden Hill Rd SE19 . . . 183 C4
Camden Ho
6 Deptford SE8 . . . 119 B1
Wallington CR6 . . . 220 A5
Camdenhurst St E14 . . 97 A1
Camden Jun Sch SM5 . . . 218 D4
Camden Lock Pl NW1 71 B1
Camden Mews NW1 . . 71 D2
Camden Mkt* NW1 . . . 93 B6 231 D6
Camden Park Rd
Camden Town NW1 . . . 71 D2
Chislehurst West BR7 188 C3
Camden Pas* N1 . . . 94 D6 234 C5
Camden Rd
Camden Town NW1 . . . 93 B6 231 D6
Carshalton SM5 . . . 218 D4
Old Bexley DA5 . . . 169 B4
Sutton SM1 . . . 217 D3
Walthamstow E17 . . . 53 B3
Wanstead E11 . . . 55 B3
Camden Road Sta NW1 . . . 71 C1
Camden Row SE3 . . . 142 C3
Camden Sch for Girls The NW5 . . . 71 C2
Camden Sq NW1 . . . 71 D2
Camden St NW1 . . . 93 C6 232 B5
Camden Studios NW1 . . . 232 B5
Camden Terr 17 NW1 . . 71 D2
CAMDEN TOWN . . . 71 B1
Camden Town Sta NW1 . . . 93 B6 231 D6
Camden Way
Chislehurst West BR7 . . . 188 C3
Thornton Heath CR7 . 204 D6
Camden Wlk N1 . . . 234 C5
Cameford Ct 20 SW12 . . . 160 A4
Camelford NW1 . . . 232 B5
Camelford Ct 15 W11 . . 91 A1
Camelford Ho SE1 . . 260 B1
Camelford Wlk 13 W11 . . . 91 A1
Camel Gr KT2 . . . 175 D5
Camelia Ct IG8 . . . 36 C4
Camellia Ct 20 BR3 . . . 185 C3
Camellia Ho
Feltham TW13 . . . 150 A3
New Cross SE8 . . . 141 B5
Camellia Pl TW2 . . . 151 D4
Camellia St SW8 . . . 270 A3
Camelot Cl
Plumstead SE18 . . . 123 B4
Wimbledon SW19 . . . 179 C6
Camelot Ho 15 NW1 . . . 71 D2
Camelot Prim Sch SE15 . . . 140 B6
Camel Rd E16 . . . 121 D5
Camera Pl SW10 . . . 266 C6
Camera Press Gall The* SE1 . . . 253 C2
Cameret Ct 6 W11 . 112 D4
Cameron Cl
East Barnet N20 . . . 14 C2
Edmonton N18 . . . 34 B5
Cameron Cres HA8 . . . 26 D2
Cameron Ct 3 SW19 . . . 157 A3
Cameron Ho
8 Bromley BR1 . . . 186 D2
Camberwell SE5 . . . 139 A5
St John's Wood NW8 . 230 A4
Cameron House Sch SW10 . . . 266 D6
Cameron Lo TW3 . . . 130 A1
Cameron Pl SW16 . . . 160 C2
Cameron Rd
Bromley BR2 . . . 209 A4
Forest Hill SE6 . . . 163 B2
Ilford IG3 . . . 57 C1
Cameron Rd *continued*
Thornton Heath CR0 . 204 D3
Cameron Sq CR4 . . . 180 C2
Camerton Cl 8 E8 . . . 73 D2
Camfrey Ct N8 . . . 50 A5
Camgate Ctr The TW19 . . . 148 B4
Camilla Cl TW16 . . . 171 D4
Camilla Ct 12 SM2 . . . 217 C1
Camilla Rd SE16 . . . 118 B2
Camille Cl SE25 . . . 206 A6
Camlan Rd BR1 . . . 186 D6
Camlet St E2 . . . 243 C6
Camlet Way EN4 . . . 1 D4
Camley St Natural Pk* NW1 . . . 232 D5
Camley St NW1 . . . 93 D5 232 D4
Camm 23 NW9 . . . 27 D1
Camm Gdns
5 Kingston u T KT1 . . . 176 B1
Thames Ditton KT7 . . . 196 D2
Camomile Ave CR4 . . 180 D2
Camomile St EC3 . . . 95 C1 243 B2
Camomile Way UB7 . . . 82 A1
Campaign Ct W9 . . . 91 B3
Campana Rd SW6 . . . 135 C4 265 B2
Campasps Bsns Pk TW16 . . . 193 D4
Campbell Ave IG6 . . . 57 A5
Campbell Cl
Ruislip HA4 . . . 40 A3
Shooters Hill SE18 . . . 144 C4
Streatham SW16 . . . 181 D6
Twickenham TW2 . . . 152 B3
Campbell Croft HA8 . . . 26 C5
Campbell Ct
Dulwich SE21 . . . 162 A3
Ealing W7 . . . 108 C6
Kingsbury NW9 . . . 45 A3
South Kensington SW7 . . . 256 A5
Tottenham N17 . . . 33 D2
Campbell Gordon Way NW2 . . . 68 B4
Campbell Ho
Paddington W2 . . . 236 C5
Pimlico SW1 . . . 259 A1
30 Shepherd's Bush W12 . . . 112 B6
6 Wallington SM6 . . . 219 B4
Campbell Rd Bow E3 . . 97 C4
Ealing W7 . . . 108 C6
Newham E6 . . . 100 A6
Stratford E15 . . . 76 D4
Thornton Heath CR0 . 204 D3
Tottenham N17 . . . 34 A2
Twickenham TW2 . . . 152 B2
Walthamstow E17 . . . 53 B5
Campbell Wlk N1 . . . 233 B6
Campdale Rd N7 . . . 71 D5
Campden Cres
Dagenham RM8 . . . 80 C4
Wembley HA0 . . . 65 B5
Campden Gr W8 . . . 113 C4 245 B2
Campden Hill W8 . . . 113 C4 245 A2
Campden Hill Ct W8 245 B2
Campden Hill Gate W8 . . . 245 A2
Campden Hill Gdns W8 . . . 245 A4
Campden Hill Mans W8 . . . 245 B4
Campden Hill Pl W14 . . . 244 D4
Campden Hill Rd W8 . . . 113 C4 245 A2
Campden Hill Sq W14 . . . 113 B5 244 D4
Campden Ho 4 NW6 . 70 B1
Campden Hos W8 . . . 245 A3
Campden House Cl W8 . . . 245 B2
Campden Rd
Ickenham UB10 . . . 60 B4
South Croydon CR2 . . 221 C3
Campden St W8 . . . 113 C5 245 A3
Campden Way RM8 . . . 80 B4
Campe Ho 1 N10 . . . 31 A3
Campen Cl SW19 . . . 157 A2
Camperdown St E1 . 243 D1
Campfield Rd SE9 . . . 165 D4
Campion Cl
Harrow HA3 . . . 44 B3
Hillingdon UB8 . . . 82 B2
Newham E6 . . . 122 B6
South Croydon CR2 . . 221 C4
Campion Ct
London N12 . . . 30 C4
10 Wembley HA0 . . . 88 A5
Campion Gdns IG8 . . . 37 A5
Campion Ho 15 N16 . . . 73 C3
Campion Pl SE28 . . . 124 B5
Campion Rd
Hounslow TW7 . . . 130 D4
Leyton E10 . . . 53 D2
Putney SW15 . . . 156 C6
Campion Terr NW2 . . . 68 D5
Campion Way HA8 . . . 27 A6
Camplin Rd HA3 . . . 44 A4
Camplin St SE14 . . . 140 D5
Camp Rd SW19 . . . 178 C5
Campsbourne Ho 3 N8 . . . 50 A5
Campsbourne Rd
Hornsey N8 . . . 50 A5
Hornsey N8 . . . 50 A6
Campsbourne Sch N8 . . . 50 A6
Campsbourne The N8 . . . 50 A5
Campsey Gdns RM9 . . . 80 B1
Campsey Rd RM9 . . . 80 B1
Campsfield Ho N8 . . . 50 A6
Campsfield Rd N8 . . . 50 A6
Campshill Pl SE13 . . . 164 A6
Campshill Rd SE13 . . . 164 A6
Camp Site The BR8 . . . 191 C3
Campton Hill Twrs W8 . . . 245 A4
Campus Rd E17 . . . 53 B3
Camp View SW19 . . . 178 B5
Cam Rd E15 . . . 98 B6
Camrose Ave
Edgware HA8 . . . 26 B2
Erith DA8 . . . 147 D6
Feltham TW13 . . . 172 C6
Camrose Cl
Croydon CR0 . . . 207 A2
Morden SM4 . . . 201 C5
Camrose St SE2 . . . 124 A2
Camsey Ho 8 SW2 . . 160 B6
Canada Ave N18 . . . 33 A4
Canada Cres W3 . . . 89 A3
Canada Gdns SE13 . . . 164 A6
Canada Rd W3 . . . 89 A2
Canada Sq E14 . . . 119 D5
Canada St SE16 . . . 118 D4
Canada Water Sta SE16 . . . 118 D3
Canada Way W12 . . . 112 B6
Canadian Ave SE6 . . 163 D3
Canal App SE8 . . . 141 A6
Canal Bldg N1 . . . 235 A4
Canal Bridge SE15 . . . 140 A6
Canal Bvd 7 NW1 . . . 71 D2
Canal Cl Mile End E1 . . . 97 A3
North Kensington W10 . 90 D3
Canal Gr SE15 . . . 140 B6
Canal Head Public Sq 1 SE15 . . . 140 A4
Canal Path 22 E2 . . . 95 D6
Canalside Studios 29 N1 . . . 95 C6
Canal St SE5 . . . 139 B6
Canal Way W10 . . . 90 D3
Canal Wlk
Croydon CR0 . . . 205 D3
Forest Hill SE26 . . . 184 C5
Shoreditch N1 . 95 B6 235 D6
CANARY WHARF . . . 119 D5
Canary Wharf* E14 . 119 D5
Canary Wharf Pier (River Bus) E14 . . . 119 B5
Canary Wharf Sta E14 . . . 119 D5
Canary Wharf Sta (DLR) E14 . . . 119 C5
Canberra Cl NW4 . . . 46 A6
Canberra Dr UB4 . . . 84 C4
Canberra Ho 7 HA4 . . . 40 C1
Canberra Prim Sch W12 . . . 112 B6
Canberra Rd
Charlton SE7 . . . 143 D6
Ealing W13 . . . 109 A5
Erith DA7 . . . 146 D6

Canberra Rd *continued*
Harlington TW6 . . . . . **126** C2
Newham E6 . . . . **100** B6
Canbury 2000 Bsns Pk 3 KT2 . . . . **176** A2
Canbury Ave KT2 . . . . **176** B2
Canbury Ct 3 KT2 . . . **176** A3
Canbury Mews SE26 . **162** A1
Canbury Park Rd KT2 . . . . **176** B2
Canbury Sch KT2 . . . **176** D4
Cancell Rd SW9 . . . . **138** C4
Candahar Rd SW11 . . **136** C3
Candida Ct 9 NW1 . . . **71** B1
Candishe Ho SE1 . . . **253** C2
Candle Gr SE15 . . . . . **140** B2
Candlelight Ct 5 E15 . . . . **76** D2
Candlemakers 24 SW11 . . . . **136** B2
Candler Mews TW1 . . **153** A4
Candler St N15 . . . . **51** B3
Candover St W1 . . . . **239** A3
Candy St E3 . . . . **97** B6
Caney Mews NW2. . . . . **68** D6
Canfield Dr HA4 . . . . . . **62** B3
Canfield Gdns NW6 . . . **69** D1
Canfield Ho N15 . . . . . . **51** C3
Canfield Pl NW6 . . . . . . **70** A2
Canford Ave UB5. . . . . . **85** A6
Canford Cl EN2 . . . . **4** C3
Canford Gdns KT3 . . . **199** C3
Canford Pl TW11 . . . . . **175** C4
Canford Rd SW11 . . . . **159** A6
Canham Rd
Acton W3 . . . . **111** C4
South Norwood SE25. **205** C6
Canmore Gdns SW16 . . . . **181** C3
Cann Hall Prim Sch E11. . . . . **76** D5
Cann Hall Rd E11 . . . . . **76** D4
Cann Ho W14. . . . . **254** B5
Canning Cres N22 . . . . . **32** B2
Canning Cross SE5. . . **139** C3
Canning Ct N22. . . . . . . **32** B2
Canning Ho 23 W12 . . **112** B6
Canning Pas W8 . . . . **114** A3 **256** A6
Canning Pl W8 . . . . **114** A3 **256** A6
Canning Pl Mews W8 . . . . **256** A6
Canning Rd
Croydon CR0 . . . . **221** D6
Harrow HA3. . . . . **42** D6
Highbury N5. . . . . **72** D5
Walthamstow E17 . . . . . **53** A6
West Ham E15. . . . . **98** C5
Cannington 14 NW5. . . **71** A2
Cannington Rd RM9. . . **80** C2
CANNING TOWN **99** B2
Canning Town E16 . . . . . **98** C1
Canning Town Sta E16. . . . . **98** C1
Cannizaro Rd SW19. . **178** D5
Cannock Ho N4. . . . . . . **51** B2
Cannock Lo EN1 . . . . . . **17** C5
Cannonbury Ave HA5 . **40** D3
Cannon Cl
Hampton TW12 . . . . . . **173** D4
West Barnes SW20 . . **200** C6
Cannon Dr 21 E14. . . . **119** C6
Cannon Hill
Palmers Green N14. . . . **16** A1
West Hampstead NW6 . **69** C3
Cannon Hill La SM4, SW20 . . . . **201** A5
Cannon Hill Mews N14. . . . . **16** A1
Cannon Ho
Lambeth SE11 . . . . . . **260** D3
Penge SE26 . . . . **184** B4
Cannon La
Hampstead NW3. . . . . . **70** B5
Pinner HA5. . . . . **41** A3
Cannon Lane Fst & Mid Schs HA5 . . . . **40** D3
Cannon Pl
Hampstead NW3. . . . . . **70** B5
Woolwich SE7 . . . . . . **122** A1
Cannon Rd Erith DA7 . **147** B4
Palmers Green N14. . . . **16** A1
Cannon St
EC4. . . . . **117** A6 **252** B6
Cannon Street Rd E1. . **96** B1
Cannon Street Sta EC4 . . . . **117** B6 **252** C6
Cannon Trad Est HA9. . **66** D4
Cannon Way KT8. . . . **195** D5
Cannon (W End of General Roy's Base Line)★ TW6. . . . . **126** D4
Cannon Wharf Bsns Ctr 12 SE8. . . . . **119** A2
Canon Ave RM6. . . . . . . **58** C4
Canon Barnett Prim Sch E1. . . . . **95** D1 **243** D2
Canon Beck Rd SE16. . . . . **118** C4
Canonbie Rd SE23 . . . **162** C4
CANONBURY **73** A2
Canonbury Bsns Ctr N1. . . . . **235** B6
Canonbury Cres N1. . . **73** A1
Canonbury Ct 21 N1 . . . **72** D1
Canonbury Gr N1. . . . . **73** A1
Canonbury Hts 6 N1 . **73** B2
Canonbury La N1 . . . . . **72** D1
Canonbury Pk N N1. . . **73** A2
Canonbury Pk S N1. . . **73** A2
Canonbury Pl N1 . . . . . **72** D2
Canonbury Prim Sch 4 N1 . . . . **72** D2
Canonbury Rd
Enfield EN1 . . . . **5** C4
Islington N1. . . . . **72** D1
Canonbury Sq N1. . . . . **72** D1
Canonbury St N1 . . . . . **73** A1
Canonbury Sta N1, N5 **73** A3
Canonbury Villas N1 . . **72** D1
Canonbury Yd E 26 N1. . . . . **73** A2
Canon Mohan Cl N14 . **15** B5
Canon Murnane Rd SE1. . . . . **263** C5
Canon Palmer RC High Sch IG3. . . . . **57** C1
Canon Rd BR1 . . . . . . **209** D6
Canon Row SW1 . . . . **116** A4 **250** A1
Canons Cl
East Finchley N2 . . . . . . **48** B2
Edgware HA8. . . . . **26** B4
Canons Cnr HA8 . . . . **26** A6
Canons Ct
Edgware HA8. . . . . **26** B4
Leyton E15. . . . . **76** C4
Canons Dr HA8 . . . . **26** B4
Canons High Sch HA8 . . . . **26** B1
Canons L Ctr CR4 . . . **202** D5
Canonsleigh Rd RM9. . **80** B1
CANONS PARK. **26** A3
Canons Park Cl HA8. . . **26** A3
Canons Park Sta HA8 . **26** A3
Canon St N1. . . . **95** A6 **235** A5
Canon's Wlk CR0 . . . **222** D5
Canopus Way
Northwood HA6. . . . . . . **22** A6
Stanwell TW19. . . . . . **148** A4
Canrobert St E2 . . . . . . **96** B4
Cantelowes Ho EN5. . . **12** D6
Cantelowes Rd NW1 . . **71** D2
Canterbury SE13. . . . . **164** A6
Canterbury Ave
Redbridge IG1. . . . . **56** A2
Sidcup DA15. . . . . **168** C2
Canterbury Cl
Beckenham BR3. . . . . **185** D2
16 Camberwell SE5. . **139** A3
7 Newham E6 . . . . . . **100** B1
North Cheam KT4. . . . . **216** D6
Southall UB6 . . . . **85** D2
Canterbury Cres SW9 . . . . **138** C2
Canterbury Ct
Acton W3 . . . . **111** C5
4 Ashford TW15. . . . . **170** B6
Eltham SE12. . . . . **165** B1
15 Hendon NW9 . . . . . . **27** D1
Kilburn NW6 . . . . **91** C5
South Croydon CR2 . . **221** A1
Thornton Heath CR0 . **204** C2
Canterbury Gr SE27, SW16 . . . . **160** C1
Canterbury Hall KT4 . **200** B2
Canterbury Ho
2 Barking IG11 . . . . . . **80** A1
6 Bromley E3. . . . . **97** D4
Lambeth SE1 . . . . **260** D6
Canterbury Ind Pk 15 SE15. . . . . **140** C6
Canterbury Mans NW6. . . . . **69** D2
Canterbury Pl SE17 . **261** D3
Canterbury Rd
Feltham TW13 . . . . . . **151** A2
Harrow HA1, HA2 . . . . . **42** A4
Kilburn NW6 . . . . **91** C5
Leyton E10. . . . . **54** A3
Morden SM4 . . . . **202** A3
Thornton Heath CR0 . **204** C2
Canterbury Terr NW6 . **91** C5
Cantium Ret Pk SE1. **140** A6
Cantley Gdns
Ilford IG2. . . . . **57** A3
South Norwood SE19. **183** D2
Cantley Rd W7. . . . . . . **109** A3
Canton St E14 . . . . **97** C1
Cantrell Rd E3. . . . . **97** C3
Cantwell Ho SE18 . . . **144** D5
Cantwell Rd SE18 . . . **144** D5
Canute Ct SW16 . . . . . **160** C1
Canute Gdns SE16 . . **118** D2
Canute Ho 1 TW8 . . . **131** C5
Canvey St SE1 . . . . . . **252** A4
Cape Cl IG11 . . . . **78** D1
Cape Henry Ct 15 E14. . . . . **120** B6
Capel KT5 . . . . **198** B2
Capel Ave SM6. . . . . . . **220** B3
Capel Cl
Keston Mark BR2. . . . **210** A1
Whetstone N20 . . . . **14** A1
Capel Cres HA7. . . . . **9** A2
Capel Ct SE20. . . . . . . **184** C2
Capel Gdns Ilford IG3. . **79** D4
Pinner HA5. . . . . **41** B5
Capel Ho
17 Hackney E9. . . . . **74** C1
South Oxhey WD19 . . . . **22** D6
Capella Ho 1 SE7 . . . **143** B6
Capel Lo
5 Richmond TW9 . . . **132** B4
12 Streatham SW2 . . . **160** B4
Capel Point E7 . . . . **77** B4
Capel Rd
East Barnet EN4. . . . . . . **14** C5
Forest Gate E7, E12. . . . **77** C4
Capener's Cl SW1. . . **248** A1
Cape Rd N17 . . . . **52** A6
Capern Rd SW18. . . . . **158** A3
Cape Yd 6 E1 . . . . **118** A5
Capio Nightingale Hospl NW1. . . . . **92** C2 **237** B4
Capital Bsns Ctr
South Croydon CR0 . . . **221** B1
Wembley HA0 . . . . **87** D5
Capital City Acad NW10. . . . . **90** B6
Capital East Apts 8 E16. . . . . **121** A6
Capital Ind Est
Belvedere DA17. . . . . . **125** D3
Mitcham CR4 . . . . **202** D4
Capital Interchange Way TW8 . . . . **110** C1
Capital Sh Ctrs SW1 **249** C1
Capital Wharf 14 E1. . **118** A5
Capitol Ind Pk NW9. . . **45** A6
Capitol Way NW9 . . . . . **45** A6
Capland Ho NW8 . . . **236** D6
Capland St NW8 . . . . **92** B3 **236** D6
Caplan Est CR4 . . . . . **181** C2
Caple Ho SW10 . . . . . . **266** B4
Caple Rd NW10 . . . . **89** D5
Capper St WC1. . . . . **93** C3 **239** B5
Caprea Cl UB4 . . . . **84** D2
Capricorn Ctr RM8. . . . **59** B2
Capri Ho E17 . . . . **35** B1
Capri Rd CR0 . . . . **205** D2
Capstan Cl RM6. . . . . . . **58** B3
Capstan Ho 6 E14. . . . **120** A2
Capstan Rd SE8. . . . . . **119** B2
Capstan Ride EN2. . . . . . . **4** C3
Capstan Sq E14. . . . . . **120** A4
Capstan Way SE16 . . . **119** A5
Capstone Rd BR1 . . . . **186** D6
Capthorne Ave HA2 . . . **41** B1
Capuchin Cl HA7. . . . . . **25** B4
Capulet Mews 1 E16. . . . . **121** A5
Capworth St E10. . . . . . **53** D2
Caradoc Cl W2 . . . . **91** C1
Caradoc Evans Cl N11. . . . . **31** B5
Caradoc St SE10 . . . . . **120** C1
Caradon Cl 4 E11 . . . . **76** C6
Caradon Ct 7 TW1. . . **153** C5
Caradon Way N15. . . . . **51** B5
Cara Ho 10 N1. . . . . **72** C1
Caranday Villas 5 W11 . . . . **112** D5
Caravel Cl E14. . . . . . . **119** C3
Caravelle Gdns 1 UB5. . . . . **84** D4
Caravel Mews 14 SE8 . . . . **141** C6
Caraway Cl E13. . . . . **99** B2
Caraway Hts E14. . . . . **120** A6
Caraway Pl SM6 . . . . . **219** B5
Carberry Rd 12 SE19 . **183** C4
Carbery Ave W3 . . . . . **110** B4
Carbis Cl E4 . . . . **20** B3
Carbis Rd E14 . . . . **97** B1
Carbroke Ho 9 E9. . . . . **96** C6
Carburton St W1 . . . . **93** B3 **238** D5
Cardale St 1 E14 . . . . **120** A3
Cardamom Ct 1 E12. . **78** C4
Carden Rd SE15. . . . . . **140** B2
Cardiff Ho 9 SE15 . . . **140** A6
Cardiff Rd Ealing W7 . . **109** A3
Enfield EN3 . . . . **6** B1
Cardiff St SE18 . . . . . . **145** C5
Cardigan Ct 3 W7 . . . . **86** D3
Cardigan Gdns IG3 . . . **80** A6
Cardigan Rd
Barnes SW13. . . . . . . **134** A3
Bow E3. . . . . **97** B5
Richmond TW10. . . . . **154** A5
Wimbledon SW19 . . . **180** A4
Cardigan St SE11. . . . . . . **116** C1 **261** A2
Cardigan Wlk 19 N1. . . **73** A1
Cardinal Ave
Kingston u T KT2 . . . . **176** A4
West Barnes SM4 . . . **201** A3
Cardinal Bourne St SE1. . . . . **262** D5
Cardinal Cap Alley SE1. . . . . **252** A5
Cardinal Cl
Burnt Oak HA8. . . . . **27** B3
Chislehurst BR7. . . . . . **189** B2
West Barnes SM4 . . . **201** A3
Worcester Pk KT19, KT4 . . . . **216** A4
Cardinal Cres KT3 . . . **177** A1
Cardinal Ct KT8. . . . . . **196** B5
Cardinal Dr KT12. . . . . **194** D1
Cardinal Hinsley Cl NW10. . . . . **90** A5
Cardinal Hinsley Mathematics & Computing Coll NW10. . . . . **90** A6
Cardinal Pl SW15 . . . **134** D1
Cardinal Pl SW1. . . . . . . **115** C3 **259** A5
Cardinal Pole RC Sch
London E9 . . . . **74** D1
London E9 . . . . **75** A3
Cardinal Rd
Feltham TW13 . . . . **150** B3
Ruislip HA4 . . . . **40** D1
Cardinal Road Inf Sch 5 TW13. . . . . **150** B3
Cardinals Way N19. . . . **49** D1
Cardinal's Wlk
Ashford TW16 . . . . . . **171** C4
Hampton TW12 . . . . . **174** A3
Cardinal Vaughan Meml Sch The W14. . . . . . **244** A2
Cardinal Way HA3. . . . **42** C6
Cardinal Wiseman RC Sch UB6 . . . . **86** A2
Cardinal Wlk SW1 . . . **259** A5
Cardine Mews SE15. . **140** B5
Cardington Sq TW4 . **128** D1
Cardington St NW1. . . . . **93** C4 **232** B1
Cardozo Rd N7 . . . . **72** A3
Cardrew Ave N12 . . . . . **30** B5
Cardrew Cl N12. . . . . . . **30** B5
Cardrew Ct 8 N12. . . . . **30** B5
Cardross St W6. . . . . . **112** B3
Cardwell Prim Sch 25 SE18. . . . . **122** B2
Cardwell Rd 3 N7 . . . . **72** A4
Career Ct 11 SE16. . . **118** D4
Carew Cl N7. . . . . **72** B6
Carew Ct
15 Deptford SE14 . . . **140** D6
Ilford RM6 . . . . **58** B3
Carew Ho
West Norwood SW16 . . . . **160** C1
23 Woolwich SE18. . . . **122** B2
Carew Manor Sch SM6. . . . . **219** D5
Carew Rd
Ashford TW15 . . . . . . **171** A4
Ealing W13. . . . . **109** C4
Mitcham CR4 . . . . **181** A1
Thornton Heath CR7 . **204** D5
Tottenham N17 . . . . **34** A1
Wallington SM6 . . . . . **219** C2
Carew St SE5 . . . . **139** A3
Carey Ct Bexley DA6 . **169** D6
20 Camberwell SE5. . **139** A5
Carey Gdns SW8 . . . . . . **137** D4 **269** C1
Carey Ho E5 . . . . **74** B5
Carey La EC2 . . . . **242** A2
Carey Pl SW1 . . . . **259** C3
Carey Rd RM9 . . . . **81** A4
Carey St WC2 . . **94** B1 **240** D1
Carey Way HA9 . . . . **66** D4
Carfax Pl SW4 . . . . . . **137** D1
Carfax Rd UB3 . . . . . . **106** A2
Carfree Cl 5 N1 . . . . . . **72** C1
Cargill Rd SW18 . . . . . **158** A3
Cargreen Pl SE25 . . . **205** D5
Cargreen Rd SE25. . . **205** D5
Cargrey Ho 9 HA7. . . . . **25** C5
Carholme Rd SE23 . . . **163** B3
Carillon Ct W5. . . . . . . **109** D6
Carinthia Ct 5 SE8 . . **119** A2
Carisbrook 2 N10. . . . . **31** B1
Carisbrook Cl EN1 . . . . . **5** D4
Carisbrooke Ave DA5. . . . . **168** D3
Carisbrooke Cl
Stanmore HA7 . . . . **25** D1
Twickenham TW4. . . . **151** A4
Carisbrooke Ct
Acton W3 . . . . **111** A4
Belmont SM2. . . . . **217** B1
Northolt UB5 . . . . **85** B6
1 Streatham SW16 . . **160** B1
Carisbrooke Gdns SE15. . . . . **139** D5
Carisbrooke Ho
10 Kingston u T KT2 . . . . **176** A2
Richmond TW10. . . . . **154** C6
Carisbrooke Rd
Bromley BR2 . . . . **209** C5
Mitcham CR4 . . . . **204** A5
Walthamstow E17 . . . . . **53** A4
Carker's La
Crouch End N19. . . . . . . **49** B2
Gospel Oak NW5 . . . . . . **71** B3
Carleton Ave SM6. . . **219** D1
Carleton Cl KT10. . . . . **196** B1
Carleton Gdns N19. . . . **71** C3
Carleton Ho 4 N8 . . . . **50** A4
Carleton Rd N7. . . . . . . **71** D4
Carley Ct 6 N12 . . . . . . **30** B5
Carlile Cl E3. . . . . **97** B5
Carlile Ho SE1. . . . . . . **262** D5
Carlina Gdns IG8 . . . . . **37** B5
Carling Ct TW1 . . . . . . **152** D4
Carlingford DA14 . . . . **190** A5
Carlingford Gdns CR4. . . . . **181** A3
Carlingford Rd
Hampstead NW3 . . . . . . **70** B4
London N15 . . . . **50** D6
West Barnes SM4 . . . . **200** D3
Carlisle Ave Acton W3. . **89** C1
Whitechapel EC3 . . . . **243** C1
Carlisle Cl
Kingston u T KT2 . . . . **176** C2
Pinner HA5. . . . . **41** A2
Carlisle Gdns
Harrow HA3. . . . . **43** D2
Redbridge IG1. . . . . **56** A3
Carlisle Ho
6 Dartmouth Pk NW5 . . . . **71** C5
Redbridge IG1. . . . . **56** A3

Carlisle Inf Sch TW12 173 D4
Carlisle La SE1 116 B3 260 D6
Carlisle Lo 1 N3 29 B1
Carlisle Pl London N11 31 B6
Westminster SW1 115 C3 259 A5
Carlisle Rd
Cheam SM1 217 B2
Finsbury Pk N4 50 C2
Hampton TW12 173 D3
Hendon NW9 45 A6
Kilburn NW6 91 A6
Leyton E10 53 C1
Carlisle St W1 93 D1 239 C1
Carlisle Way SW17 181 A5
Carlisle Wlk 6 E8 73 D2
Carlos Pl W1 115 B6 248 C5
Carlow St NW1 232 A4
Carlson Ct SW15 135 B1
Carlton Ave
Feltham TW14 150 C5
Harrow HA3 43 B4
Hayes UB3 105 C2
South Croydon CR2 221 C1
Southgate N14 15 D6
Carlton Ave E HA9 65 D6
Carlton Ave W HA0 65 B6
Carlton Cl
Chessington KT9 213 D2
Child's Hill NW3 69 C6
Edgware HA8 26 C5
Northolt UB5 64 A3
Carlton Cres SM3 217 A4
Carlton Ct
Brixton SW9 138 D4
Ealing W7 108 D4
Finchley N3 29 C3
Ilford IG6 57 B6
Kilburn NW6 91 D5
11 Penge SE20 184 B2
South Norwood SE19 183 D2
8 Willesden NW2 68 C2
Carlton Dr Ilford IG6 57 B6
Putney SW15 157 A6
Carlton Gdns
Ealing W5 109 C6
St James SW1 115 D5 249 C3
Carlton Gn DA14 189 D6
Carlton Gr SE15 140 B4
Carlton Hill NW8 92 A5 229 A4
Carlton Ho
Cheam SM1 217 B2
Edmonton N21 17 A3
Feltham TW14 149 D5
Hounslow TW4 151 C5
8 Kilburn NW6 91 B5
Kilburn NW6 91 C5
Marylebone W1 237 D2
Carlton House Terr SW1 115 D5 249 D4
Carlton Lo N4 50 C2
Carlton Mans
Brixton SW9 138 C1
Cricklewood NW2 68 D3
Kensington W14 244 B2
Maida Vale W9 91 D4
7 South Hampstead NW6 69 C1
Stamford Hill N16 51 D1
Carlton Par HA9 44 A1
Carlton Park Ave SW20 178 D1
Carlton Prim Sch NW5 71 A3
Carlton Rd Acton W4 111 B4
Ashford TW16 171 D3
Ealing W5 87 C1
Erith DA8 147 D6
Finsbury Pk N4 50 C2
Friern Barnet N11 31 A5
Higham Hill E17 35 A2
Kingston u T KT3 177 C1
Leytonstone E11 54 D1
Manor Pk E12 77 D4
Mortlake SW14 133 A1
Sidcup DA14 189 D6
South Croydon CR2 221 B1
Walton-on-T KT12 194 B2
Welling DA16 146 B2
Carlton Sq E1 96 D3
Carlton St SW1 249 C5
Carltons The 5 SW15 157 A6
Carlton Terr
Edmonton N18 33 B6
Forest Hill SE26 162 C1
Upton E7 77 C1
Wanstead E11 55 B4
Carlton Tower Pl SW1 257 D6
Carlton Twrs SM5 218 D5
Carlton Vale NW6 91 C5
Carlton Vale Inf Sch 12 NW6 91 B4
Carlwell St SW17 180 C5
Carlyle Ave
Bromley BR1 209 D6
Southall UB1 107 B6
Carlyle Cl
East Molesey KT8 173 D1
Hampstead Garden Suburb N2 48 A3
Carlyle Gdns UB1 107 B6
Carlyle Ho
4 Camberwell SE5 139 A5
Chelsea SW3 266 D6
Ealing W5 109 D2
East Molesey KT8 195 C4
12 Stoke Newington N16 73 C5
Carlyle Lo 6 EN5 14 A6
Carlyle Mans SW3 267 A5
Carlyle Mews 24 E1 96 D3
Carlyle Pl SW15 134 D1
Carlyle Rd
Croydon CR0 222 A6
Ealing W5 109 C2
Manor Pk E12 78 A4
1 Stonebridge NW10 89 B6
Woolwich SE28 124 C6
Carlyle's Ho★ SW3 267 A5
Carlyle Sq SW3 114 B1 256 D1
Carlyon Ave HA2 63 C4
Carlyon Cl HA0 88 A6
Carlyon Ct HA0 88 B6
Carlyon Mans 1 HA0 88 A5
Carlyon Rd Hayes UB4 84 C2
Wembley HA0 88 A6
Carlys Cl BR3 184 D1
Carmalt Gdns SW15 134 C1
Carmarthen Ct 4 W7 86 D3
Carmarthen Ho 8 SW15 156 C4
Carmarthen Pl SE1 253 A2
Carmel Ct
Kensington W8 245 C2
Wembley Pk HA9 66 D6
Carmelite Cl HA3 24 A2
Carmelite Rd HA3 24 A1
Carmelite St EC4 116 C6 251 B6
Carmelite Way HA3 24 A1
Carmelite Wlk HA3 24 A2
Carmel Lo SW6 265 A6
Carmen St E14 97 D1
Carmichael Cl
8 London SW11 136 B2
Ruislip HA4 62 A4
Carmichael Ct 5 SW13 133 D3
Carmichael Ho
17 Dulwich SE21 183 C6
6 Poplar E14 120 A6
Carmichael Mews SW18 158 B4
Carmichael Rd SE25 206 A5
Carminia Rd SW17 159 B2
Carnaby St★ W1 93 C1 239 A1
Carnac St SE21, SE27 161 B1
Carna Ct TW9 132 A2
Carnanton Rd E17 36 B2
Carnarvon Ave EN1 5 D3
Carnarvon Dr UB3 105 A3
Carnarvon Rd
Barnet EN5 1 A2
Leyton E10 54 A4
Stratford E15 76 D2
Woodford E18 36 D2
Carnation St SE2 124 B1
Carnbrook Mews SE3 143 D2
Carnbrook Rd SE3 143 D2
Carnecke Gdns SE9 166 A6
Carnegie Cl
Holdbrook EN3 7 D5
Surbiton KT6 214 B6
Carnegie Ho NW3 70 B5
Carnegie Pl SW19 156 D1
Carnegie St N1 94 B6 233 D5
Carnforth Cl KT19 214 D2
Carnforth Rd SW16 181 D3
Carnicot Ho 9 SE15 140 B4
Carnoustie Cl SE28 102 D1
Carnoustie Dr N1 72 B1
Carnwath Ho SW6 135 D2
Carnwath Rd SW6 135 D2
Caroe Ct N9 18 B3
Carol Cl NW4 46 D5
Carole Ho 13 SE20 184 B2
Carolina Cl E15 76 C3
Carolina Rd CR7 183 A2
Caroline Cl
Bayswater W2 245 D5
Hounslow TW7 130 C5
Muswell Hill N10 31 B1
South Croydon CR0 221 C4
Streatham SW16 160 B1
Caroline Ct
Ashford TW15 170 D4
Catford SE6 186 B6
Stanmore HA7 25 A4
17 Surbiton KT6 197 D2
23 Woodside Pk N12 29 D6
Caroline Gdns E2 95 C4
Caroline Ho
Bayswater W2 245 D5
20 Hammersmith W6 112 C1
Caroline Martyn Ho 8 N19 49 D2
Caroline Pl
Bayswater W2 245 D5
Clapham SW11 137 A3
Harlington UB3 127 C5
Caroline Pl Mews W2 245 D5
Caroline Rd SW19 179 B3
Caroline St E1 96 D1
Caroline Terr SW1 115 A2 258 A3
Caroline Wlk W6 264 A5
Carol St NW1 93 C6 232 A6
Carolyn Ho IG3 58 A1
Caronia Ct 4 SE16 119 A2
Carpenter Gdns N21 16 D2
Carpenter Ho
London NW11 48 A3
11 Tower Hamlets E14 97 C2
5 Tufnell Pk N19 71 D4
Carpenters Cl EN5 13 D5
Carpenters Ct
Camden Town NW1 232 A6
5 Dagenham RM10 81 D2
Twickenham TW2 152 C2
Carpenter's Pl SW4 137 D1
Carpenters Prim Sch E15 98 A6
Carpenter St W1 248 C5
Carradale Ho 2 E14 98 A1
Carrara Cl 18 SW9 138 D1
Carrara Wharf SW6 135 A2
Carr Cl HA7 25 A4
Carr Gr SE18 122 A2
Carriage Dr E SW11 137 A5 268 B4
Carriage Drive E SW11 137 A5 268 B4
Carriage Drive N SW11, SW8 137 A6 268 B5
Carriage Dr N
Battersea SW8, SW11 136 D5 267 C4
Battersea SW8, SW11 137 A6 268 B5
Carriage Dr S SW11 137 A4 268 A2
Carriage Dr W SW11 136 D5 267 C3
Carriage Mews IG1 79 A6
Carriage Pl 14 SW16 181 C5
Carrick Cl TW7 131 A2
Carrick Gate KT10 212 A5
Carrick Gdns N17 33 C3
Carrick Ho
Islington N7 72 B2
Kennington SE11 261 C2
Carrick Mews SE8 141 C6
Carrill Way DA17 124 D3
Carrington Ave
Borehamwood WD6 10 D6
Hounslow TW3 151 D6
Carrington Cl
Barnet EN5 12 A6
Borehamwood WD6 11 A6
Croydon CR0 207 A2
Carrington Ct
London SW11 136 C1
3 New Malden KT3 199 C5
Southgate N21 16 D5
Carrington Gdns 4 E7 77 A4
Carrington Ho
Mayfair W1 248 C3
7 Merton SW19 179 C3
Carrington Lo
3 Richmond TW10 154 A6
Wembley HA9 66 B5
Carrington Pl KT10 212 A4
Carrington Rd TW10 132 C1
Carrington Sq HA3 24 A3
Carrington St W1 248 C3
Carrol Cl NW5 71 B4
Carroll Cl E15 76 D3
Carroll Ct Acton W3 110 D3
4 Shacklewell E5 74 A5
Carroll Ho W2 246 C6
Carronade Pl SE18 123 B3
Carron Cl E14 97 D1
Carroun Rd SW8 138 B5 270 C4
Carroway La UB6 86 B4
Carrow Rd RM9 80 B1
Carr Rd Northolt UB5 64 A1
Walthamstow E17 35 C1
Carrs La N21 17 B6
Carr St 5 E14 97 A1
CARSHALTON 218 C4
Carshalton Beeches Sta SM5 218 D2
Carshalton Coll SM5 218 D5
Carshalton Gr SM1 218 B3
Carshalton High Sch for Boys SM5 218 C6
Carshalton High Sch for Girls SM5 218 C5
CARSHALTON ON THE HILL 219 B1
Carshalton Park Rd SM5 218 D3
Carshalton Pl SM5 219 A3
Carshalton Rd
Mitcham CR4 203 A4
Sutton SM1, SM5 218 B3
Carshalton Sta SM5 218 D4
Carslake Rd SW15 156 C5
Carson Rd
Cockfosters EN4 2 D1
Dulwich SE21 161 B2
Newham E16 99 A2
Carstairs Rd SE6 164 A1
Carston Cl SE12 164 D6
Carswell Cl IG4 55 D5
Carswell Rd SE6 164 A4
Carter Cl NW9 45 B3
Carter Ct EC4 241 D1
Carteret Ho 8 W12 112 B6
Carteret St SW1 249 C1
Carteret Way SE8 119 A2
Carterhatch Jun & Inf Schs EN1 6 B4
Carterhatch La EN1 6 A4
Carterhatch Rd EN3 6 D4
Carter Ho
11 London SW2 160 C6
Spitalfields E1 243 C3
Carter La EC4 94 D1 241 D1
Carter Pl SE17 117 A1 262 B1
Carter Rd
Mitcham SW19 180 B4
Newham E13 99 B6
Carters Cl
10 Kentish Town NW5 71 D2
North Cheam KT4 200 D1
Carters Hill Cl SE9 165 C3
Carters La SE23 163 B1
Carters Rd N2 30 C3
Carter St SE17 117 A1 262 A1
Carter's Yd SW18 157 C6
Carthew Rd W6 112 B3
Carthew Villas W6 112 B3
Carthusian St EC1 242 A4
Cartier Circ E14 120 A5
Carting La WC2 116 A6 250 B5
Cart La E4 20 C3
Cartmel NW1 232 A2
Cartmel Cl N17 34 B3
Cartmel Ct
Beckenham BR2 186 C1
Northolt UB5 63 A2
Cartmel Gdns SM4 202 A4
Cartmel Rd DA7 147 C4
Carton Ho
4 Bermondsey SE16 118 A3
2 Dollis Hill NW2 68 A5
12 Shepherd's Bush W11 112 D6
Cartoon Mus The★ WC1 94 A2 240 A3
Cartwright Gdns WC1 94 A4 233 A1
Cartwright Ho SE1 262 B5
Cartwright Rd RM9 81 B1
Cartwright St E1 117 D6 253 D5
Cartwright Way SW13 134 B5
Carvel Ho E14 120 A1
Carver Cl 15 W4 111 A3
Carver Rd SE24 161 A5
Carville Cres TW8 110 A2
Caryl Ho 6 SW19 156 D3
Cary Rd E11 76 C5
Carysfort Rd
Canonbury N16 73 B4
London N8 49 D4
Casby Ho 7 SE16 118 A3
Cascade Ave N10 49 C5
Cascade Cl IG9 21 D2
Cascade Rd IG9 21 D2
Cascadia Ho 22 KT1 176 C1
Casella Rd SE14 140 D5
Casewick Rd SE27 182 D6
Casey Cl NW8 92 C4 230 B1
Casimir Rd E5 74 C5
Casino Ave SE24 161 B6
Caspian Ho 10 E1 96 D2
Caspian St SE5 139 B5
Caspian Wlk E16 99 D1
Cassandra Cl UB5 64 B4
Cassandra Ct 7 NW2 68 C2
Cass Bsns Sch EC1 95 B3 242 C5
Casselden Rd NW10 67 B1
Cassel Hospl TW10 175 D6
Cassell Ho 21 SW9 138 A3
Casserley Ho W4 111 B3
Cass Ho 23 E9 74 D2
Cassidy Rd SW6 265 A3
Cassilda Rd SE2 124 A2
Cassilis Rd
Millwall E14 119 C4
Twickenham TW1 153 B5
Cassinghurst SE24 161 B6
Cassiobury Ave TW14 149 D4
Cassiobury Rd E17 53 A4
Cassland Rd
Homerton E9 74 D2
South Norwood CR7 205 B5
Casslee Rd SE6 163 B4
Cassocks Sq TW17 193 B2
Casson Ho 11 E1 96 A2
Casson St E1 96 A2
Castalia Sq 6 E14 120 A4
Castellain Mans W9 91 D3
Castellain Rd W9 91 D3
Castellane Cl HA7 24 D3
Castell Ho 11 SE8 141 C5
Castello Ave SW15 156 C6
Castelnau SW13 134 B5
Castelnau Gdns SW13 134 B6
Castelnau Mans SW13 134 B6
Castelnau Row SW13 134 B6
Casterbridge
Kilburn NW6 91 D6
3 Notting Hill W11 91 C1
Casterbridge Rd SE3 143 A2
Casterton St E8 74 B2
Castile Rd SE18 122 C2

Castilion Prim Sch SE28 102 C1
Castillon Rd SE6 164 C2
Castlands Rd SE6 163 B2
Castleacre W2 237 A1
Castle Ave
  Chingford E4 36 B5
  Yiewsley UB7 104 B6
Castlebar Ct 5 W5 87 C2
Castlebar Hill W5 87 C2
Castlebar Mews W5 87 C2
Castle Bar Park Sta W7 86 D2
Castlebar Pk W5 87 B2
Castlebar Rd W5 87 C1
Castlebar Sch W13 87 A2
Castle Baynard St EC4 117 A6 252 A6
Castlebrook Cl SE11 116 D2 261 C4
Castle Bsns Village TW12 173 D2
Castle Cl
  12 Acton W3 111 A4
  Ashford TW16 171 C3
  Beckenham BR2 208 C6
  Homerton E9 75 A3
  South Acton W3 110 D4
  Wimbledon SW19 156 D1
Castlecombe Dr SW19 156 D4
Castlecombe Prim Sch SE9 188 A5
Castlecombe Rd SE9 188 A6
Castle Ct
  Belmont SM2 217 C2
  City of London EC3 242 D1
  Dagenham RM9 103 A6
  Forest Hill SE26 185 A6
  Morden SM4 202 B4
Castleden Ho NW6 70 B1
Castledine Rd SE20 184 B3
Castle Dr IG4 56 A3
Castleford Ave SE9 166 D3
Castleford Cl N17 33 D4
Castleford Ct NW8 236 D6
Castlefrank Ho 20 N1 95 C4
Castlegate TW9 132 B2
CASTLE GREEN 102 C6
Castleham Ct HA8 26 C4
Castlehaven Rd NW1 71 B1
Castle Hill Ave CR0 224 A1
Castle Hill Prim Sch
  Chessington KT9 214 B3
  New Addington CR0 224 A2
Castle Ho
  17 Belmont SM2 217 C1
  3 Chingford E4 36 B5
  Newington SE1 262 A4
  South Lambeth SW8 270 B4
Castle Hts RM9 102 B6
Castle Ind Est SE17 262 A4
Castle La SW1 115 C3 259 A6
Castleleigh Ct EN2 17 B6
Castlemaine 8 SW11 136 D3
Castlemaine Ave CR2 221 D3
Castlemaine St 2 E1 96 B2
Castle Mead SE5 139 A5
Castle Mews
  Camden Town NW1 71 B2
  North Finchley N12 30 A5
Castle Par KT17 216 A1
Castle Pl
  8 Acton W4 111 C2
  Camden Town NW1 71 B2
Castle Point 4 E13 99 C5
Castle Rd
  Camden Town NW1 71 B2
  Dagenham RM9 102 B6
  Enfield EN3 7 A5
  Isleworth TW7 130 D3
  North Finchley N12 30 B5
  Northolt UB5 63 D1
  Southall UB2 107 B3
Castlereagh Ho HA7 25 B4
Castlereagh St W1 237 C2
Castle St E6 99 C5
Castleton Ave HA9 66 A4
Castleton Cl CR0 207 A3
Castleton Ct KT5 198 B4
Castleton Gdns HA9 66 A5
Castleton Ho 3 E14 120 A2
Castleton Rd
  Chingford E17 36 B1
  Ilford IG3 58 B1
  Mitcham CR4 203 D5
  Mottingham SE12, SE9 187 D6
  Ruislip HA4 40 D1
Castletown Rd W14 113 A1 254 B1
Castleview Cl N4 73 A6
Castleview Gdns IG1 56 B3
Castle Way
  Feltham TW13 172 C6
  Wimbledon SW19 156 D1
Castle Wlk TW16 194 C6
Castlewood Dr SE9 144 B3
Castlewood Ho WC1 239 D2
Castlewood Rd
  Barnet EN4 2 B2
  Stamford Hill N16 52 A3
Castle Yd Highgate N6 49 A2
  Lambeth SE1 251 D4
  18 Richmond TW10 153 D6
Castor La E14 119 D6
Catalina Rd TW6 126 C2
Catalpa Ct SE13 164 B5
Caterham Rd SE13 142 B2
Catesby Ho 25 E9 74 C1
Catesby St SE17 117 B2 262 D3
CATFORD 163 C3
Catford Br SE6 163 C4
Catford Bridge Sta SE6 163 C4
Catford Broadway SE6 163 D4
Catford Gyratory SE6 163 D4
Catford High Sch SE6 164 A1
Catford Hill SE6 163 C3
Catford Rd SE6 163 C4
Catford Sh Ctr SE6 163 D4
Catford Sta SE6 163 C4
Cathall L Ctr E11 76 C6
Cathall Rd E11 76 B5
Cathay Ho SE16 118 B4
Cathay St 12 SE16 118 B4
Cathay Wlk UB5 85 C5
Cathcart Dr BR6 211 C1
Cathcart Hill N19 71 C5
Cathcart Rd SW10 136 A6 266 A6
Cathcart St NW5 71 B2
Cathedral Ct EC4 241 D1
Cathedral Lo EC1 242 A4
Cathedral Sch of St Saviour & St Mary Overie Prim Sch SE1 117 A4 252 B2
Cathedral St SE1 117 B5 252 C4
Cathedral Wlk SW1 259 A6
Catherall Rd N5, N16 73 A5
Catherine Baird Ct 12 SW12 159 B4
Catherine Ct
  Barnet EN5 1 D2
  1 Ilford IG2 57 A3
  2 Southgate N14 15 C6
  3 Wimbledon SW19 179 B5
Catherine Dr
  Ashford TW16 171 D4
  Richmond TW9 132 A1
Catherine Gdns TW3 130 B1
Catherine Godfrey Ho RM9 103 B6
Catherine Gr SE10 141 D4
Catherine Griffiths Ct EC1 241 B6
Catherine Ho
  Isleworth TW7 131 B4
  16 Shoreditch N1 95 C6
Catherine Lo E18 37 C2
Catherine Pl
  Harrow HA1 42 D4
  Westminster SW1 115 C3 259 A6
Catherine Rd
  Enfield EN3 7 A6
  Kingston u T KT6 197 D4
Catherine St WC2 116 B6 250 C6
Catherine Wheel Alley E1 243 B3
Catherine Wheel Rd TW8 131 D5
Catherine Wheel Yd SW1 249 A3
Catherwood Ct N1 235 C3
Cat Hill EN4 14 D6
Cathles Rd SW12 159 B5
Cathnor Rd W12 112 B4
Catisfield Rd EN3 7 A6
Catlin Cres TW17 193 B4
Catling Cl SE23 162 D1
Catlin's La HA5 40 B5
Catlin St SE16 118 B1
Catman Ho N4 50 B1
Caton Ct BR2 186 C1
Cato Rd SW4 137 D1
Cator La BR3 185 B2
Cator Park Sch for Girls BR3 185 A3
Cator Rd
  Penge SE20, SE26 184 D5
  Wallington SM5 218 D3
Cator St
  Camberwell SE15 139 D5
  Camberwell SE15 139 D6
Cato St W1 92 C1 237 B2
Catsey La WD23 8 A4
Catsey Wood WD23 8 A4
Catterick Cl N11 31 A4
Cattistock Rd SE9 188 B5
Cattley Cl EN5 1 A1
Catton St WC1 240 C3
Caughley Ho SE11 261 A5
Caulfield Ct 15 NW1 71 C1
Caulfield Rd
  East Ham E6 78 B1
  London SE15 140 B3
Causeway TW14, TW4 128 B1
Causeway The
  Carshalton SM5 219 A6
  Chessington KT9 214 A4
  Claygate KT10 212 D1
  East Finchley N2 48 C5
  Teddington TW11 174 D4
  Wandsworth SW18 157 D6
  Wimbledon SW19 178 C5
Causeyware Rd N9 18 C4
Causton Cotts 3 E14 97 A1
Causton Ho SE5 139 A5
Causton Rd N6 49 B2
Causton Sq RM10 81 C1
Causton St SW1 115 D1 259 D2
Cautley Ave SW4 159 C6
Cavalier Cl RM6 58 D5
Cavalier Gdns UB3 83 B1
Cavalier Ho W5 109 C6
Cavalry Cres TW4 128 D1
Cavalry Gdns SW15 157 B6
Cavan Pl HA5 23 B2
Cavaye Ho SW10 266 B6
Cavaye Pl SW10 256 B1
Cavell Ct 5 N19 71 C6
Cavell Dr EN2 4 C3
Cavell Ho 8 N1 95 C6
Cavell Rd N17 33 B3
Cavell St E1 96 B2
Cavendish Ave
  Ealing W13 87 A1
  Falconwood DA16 145 D2
  Finchley N3 29 C1
  Harrow HA1 64 C4
  Ruislip HA4 62 B3
  Sidcup DA15 168 A4
  St John's Wood NW8 92 B5 229 D3
  West Barnes KT3 200 B5
  Woodford IG8 37 B3
Cavendish Cl
  Ashford TW16 171 D4
  Brondesbury NW6 69 B2
  Edmonton N18 34 B5
  Hayes UB4 83 C2
  3 Putney SW15 157 A6
  St John's Wood NW8 92 B4 229 D2
Cavendish Coll WC1 93 D2 239 C4
Cavendish Cres WD6 10 C6
Cavendish Ct
  Ashford TW16 171 D4
  Catford SE6 163 D3
  5 Chingford E4 20 C4
  Wallington SM6 219 B2
  Wembley HA0 65 D3
Cavendish Ct *continued*
  Whitechapel EC2 243 B2
Cavendish Dr
  Claygate KT10 212 C3
  Edgware HA8 26 B4
  Leytonstone E11 54 B1
Cavendish Gdns
  Barking IG11 79 D3
  Clapham Pk SW4 159 C5
  Dagenham RM6 59 A4
  Ilford IG1 56 C1
Cavendish Ho
  London N12 30 A6
  5 Muswell Hill N10 31 A3
  3 Richmond TW10 153 C1
  South Lambeth SW8 270 A2
  St John's Wood NW8 229 D3
  Twickenham TW1 153 A5
Cavendish Jun & Inf Sch W4 133 C5
Cavendish Mans
  2 Clapham Pk SW12 159 C5
  Hackney E5 74 C3
  Holborn EC1 241 A5
  8 West Hampstead NW6 69 C3
Cavendish Mews SM1 218 A6
Cavendish Mews N W1 238 D4
Cavendish Mews S W1 238 D3
Cavendish Par
  Balham SW12 159 B5
  Hounslow TW4 129 A3
Cavendish Pl
  Balham SW4 159 B5
  Bromley BR1 210 B6
  Brondesbury NW2 68 D2
  Marylebone W1 238 D2
Cavendish Rd
  Ashford TW16 171 D4
  Brondesbury NW6 69 B1
  Chingford E4 36 A4
  Chiswick W4 133 A4
  Clapham Pk SW12 159 C5
  Edmonton N18 34 B5
  Harringay N4 50 D3
  Mitcham SW19 180 C3
  New Malden KT3 199 D5
  Sutton SM2 218 A1
  Thornton Heath CR0 204 D1
Cavendish Sch 14 SE16 118 C2
Cavendish Sch The NW1 93 B6 231 D6
Cavendish Sq W1 93 B1 238 D2
Cavendish St N1 95 B5 235 C3
Cavendish Terr
  Feltham TW13 150 A2
  11 Tower Hamlets E3 97 B4
Cavendish The NW11 47 D2
Cavendish Way BR4 207 D1
Cavenham Gdns IG1 79 B5
Cave Rd Newham E13 99 B4
  Richmond TW10 175 C6
Caverleigh Way KT4 200 B2
Caversham Ave
  Cheam SM3 217 A6
  Palmers Green N13 16 C1
Caversham Ct N11 15 A1
Caversham Ho
  8 Kingston u T KT1 176 A1
  7 Peckham SE15 140 A6
  Wallington CR0 220 A5
  West Green N15 51 A5
Caversham Lo N10 31 C1
Caversham Rd
  Kentish Town NW5 71 C2
  Kingston u T KT1 176 B1
  West Green N15 51 A5
Caversham St SW3 136 D6 267 C6
Caverswall St W12 90 C1
Caveside Cl BR7 188 C2
Cavour Ho SE17 261 D2
Cawdor Cres W7 109 A2
Cawnpore St SE19 183 C5
Cawston Ct 8 BR1 186 D3
Caxton Gr E3 97 C4
Caxton Hall ★ SW1 259 C6
Caxton Mews 9 TW8 131 D5
Caxton Rd
  Shepherd's Bush W12 112 D4
  Southall UB2 106 D3
  Wimbledon SW19 180 A5
  Wood Green N22 32 B1
Caxton St N E16 98 D1
Caxton St SW1 115 D3 259 C6
Caxton Trad Est UB3 105 C5
Caxton Wlk WC2 239 D1
Cayford Ho 1 NW3 70 D3
Caygill Cl BR2 208 D5
Cayley Cl SM6 220 A1
Cayley Prim Sch 22 E14 97 A1
Cayley Rd UB2 107 D3
Cayton Pl EC1 235 C1
Cayton Rd UB6 86 C5
Cayton St EC1 235 C1
Cazenove Mans 1 N16 74 A6
Cazenove Rd
  Stoke Newington N16 74 A6
  Walthamstow E17 35 C2
Cearns Ho E6 99 D6
Ceasors Ct TW1 152 D2
Cecil Ave Barking IG11 79 B1
  Enfield EN1 5 D1
  Wembley HA9 66 B3
Cecil Cl
  Chessington KT9 213 D4
  Ealing W5 87 D2
  Littleton TW15 171 A3
Cecil Ct
  Chelsea SW10 266 A6
  12 Croydon CR0 221 D6
  Ealing W5 87 D2
  South Hampstead NW6 69 D1
  St James WC2 250 A5
Cecile Pk N8 50 A3
Cecil Ho E17 35 C2
Cecilia Cl N2 48 A6
Cecilia Rd E8 74 A3
Cecil Lo KT9 213 D4
Cecil Manning Cl UB6 87 A6
Cecil Mans 2 SW17 159 A2
Cecil Pk HA5 41 A5
Cecil Pl CR4 202 D4
Cecil Rd Acton W3 89 A2
  Ashford TW15 171 A4
  Cheam SM1, SM2 217 B2
  Colindale NW9 45 C6
  Dagenham RM6 58 D2
  Enfield EN2 5 B1
  Harlesden NW10 89 C6
  Harrow HA3 42 C6
  Hounslow TW3 130 A3
  Ilford IG1 78 D4
  Leyton E11 76 C5
  Merton SW19 179 D3
  Muswell Hill N10 31 B1
  Newham E13 99 A6
  Osidge N14 15 C3
  Thornton Heath CR0 204 B3
  Walthamstow E17 35 C2
Cecil Rhodes Ho NW1 232 C4
Cecil Rosen Ct HA0 65 B5
Cecil Way BR2 209 A1
Cedar Ave
  Dagenham RM6 59 A4
  East Barnet EN4 14 C4
  Enfield EN3 6 C3
  Hayes UB3 84 A1
  Ruislip HA4 62 C3
  Sidcup DA15 168 A4
  Twickenham TW2 152 A5
  Yiewsley UB7 104 B6
Cedar Cl
  Buckhurst Hill IG9 21 D2
  East Molesey KT8 196 C5
  Keston Mark BR2 226 A5
  Kingston u T KT2 177 B6
  Old Ford E3 97 B6
  Wallington SM5 218 D2
  West Norwood SE21 161 A2
Cedar Copse BR1 188 B1
Cedar Cres BR2 226 A5

Cedarcroft Rd KT9 ... 214 B4
Cedar Ct
7 Brentford TW8 ... 131 D6
19 Charlton SE7 ... 143 C6
Edgware HA8 ... 11 A1
Eltham SE9 ... 166 A5
Finchley N3 ... 29 C3
Islington N1 ... 73 A1
Marylebone W1 ... 237 B2
Mortlake SW14 ... 133 A1
1 Muswell Hill N10 ... 31 B1
5 New Southgate N11 31 C5
Oakleigh Pk N20 ... 14 B3
Stoneleigh KT17 ... 216 A1
3 Sutton SM2 ... 218 A2
6 Wanstead E11 ... 55 B4
Wembley HA0 ... 65 B4
Wimbledon SW19 ... 156 D1
5 Woodford E18 ... 37 A2
Cedar Dr
Hampstead Garden Sub NW11 ... 47 C5
London N2 ... 48 C5
Pinner HA5 ... 23 C4
Cedar Gdns SM2 ... 218 A2
Cedar Gr Ealing W5 ... 110 A3
Sidcup DA5 ... 168 D5
Southall UB1 ... 85 C2
Cedar Grange 10 EN1 . 17 C6
Cedar Ho
Ashford TW16 ... 171 D3
5 Cubitt Town E14 .. 120 A4
Hayes UB4 ... 84 C3
Kensington W8 ... 255 C6
New Addington CR0 .. 223 D2
New Cross Gate SE14 140 D4
5 Richmond TW9 ... 132 D4
16 Rotherhithe SE16 . 118 D4
Wood Green N22 ... 32 C2
Cedar Hts TW10 ... 154 A3
Cedarhurst BR1 ... 186 C3
Cedarhurst Dr SE9 ... 165 C6
Cedar Lawn Ave EN5 .. 13 A6
Cedar Lo
Brondesbury NW2 ... 69 B2
Fulham SW6 ... 134 D4
Cedarmore Ct BR7 ... 189 A2
Cedar Mount SE9 ... 165 D3
Cedarne Rd SW6 ... 135 D5 265 C3
Cedar Park Gdns RM6 ... 58 D2
Cedar Park Rd EN2 ... 5 A5
Cedar Pk Gdns SW19 ... 178 B5
Cedar Pl 3 SE7 ... 121 C1
Cedar Rd
Bromley BR1 ... 187 C1
Cranford TW5 ... 128 C3
Cricklewood NW2 ... 68 C4
Croydon CR0 ... 221 C6
East Bedfont TW14 ... 149 B3
East Molesey KT8 ... 196 C5
Enfield EN2 ... 5 A5
Sutton SM2 ... 218 A2
Teddington TW11 ... 175 A5
Tottenham N17 ... 33 D2
Cedar Rise N14 ... 15 A4
Cedars Ave
Mitcham CR4 ... 203 A6
Walthamstow E17 ... 53 C4
Cedars Cl
Hendon NW4 ... 46 D6
Lewisham SE13 ... 142 B2
Cedars Ct
Edmonton N9 ... 17 D2
Putney SW15 ... 156 A5
Cedars Dr UB10 ... 82 C5
Cedars Ho
21 London SW2 ... 138 B1
15 Walthamstow E17 ... 53 D6
5 West Norwood SE27 ... 182 D5
Cedars Manor Sch HA3 ... 24 A2
Cedars Mews SW4 ... 137 B1
Cedars Prim Sch The TW5 ... 128 A5
Cedars Rd
Barnes SW13 ... 134 A3
Beckenham BR3 ... 185 B1
Clapham SW4 ... 137 B1
Cedars Rd *continued*
4 Lower Edmonton N9 ... 18 A2
Morden SM4 ... 201 C5
Stratford E15 ... 76 C2
Teddington KT8 ... 175 C2
Wallington CR0 ... 220 A4
Winchmore Hill N21 ... 16 D2
Cedars The
Buckhurst Hill IG9 ... 21 A3
Ealing W13 ... 87 C1
Hackney E9 ... 74 D1
4 Kingston u T KT2 .. 176 D2
Teddington TW11 ... 174 D4
Wallington SM6 ... 219 C4
Cedar Terr
9 Dagenham RM8 ... 58 D2
Richmond TW9 ... 132 A1
Cedar Tree Gr SE27 .. 182 D5
Cedarville Gdns SW16 ... 182 B4
Cedar Way
Ashford TW16 ... 171 C3
Camden Town NW1 ... 93 D6 232 C6
Cedar Wlk KT10 ... 212 D2
Cedarwood BR3 ... 185 B3
Cedarwood Ho EN2 ... 4 D3
Cedarwood Lo HA8 ... 26 B5
Cedra Ct N16 ... 52 A1
Cedric Chambers NW8 ... 236 C6
Cedric Rd SE9 ... 167 A1
Celadon Cl EN3 ... 7 A2
Celandine Cl E3, E14 .. 97 C2
Celandine Ct E4 ... 19 D1
Celandine Dr
Dalston E8 ... 73 D1
Woolwich SE28 ... 124 B5
Celandine Gr N14 ... 15 C6
Celandine Way E15 ... 98 C4
Celbridge Mews W2 .. 91 D1
Celestial Gdns SE13 .. 142 B1
Celia Blairman Ho E1 ... 243 C4
Celia Ct 7 TW9 ... 132 B4
Celia Ho 10 N1 ... 95 C5
Celia Rd N19 ... 71 C4
Celtic Ave BR2 ... 208 C6
Celtic St E14 ... 97 D2
Cemetery La
Lower Halliford TW17 ... 192 D2
Woolwich SE7 ... 144 A6
Cemetery Rd
East Wickham SE2 ... 146 B5
Forest Gate E7 ... 76 D4
Tottenham N17 ... 33 C3
Cenacle Cl NW3 ... 69 C5
Cenotaph* SW1 ... 250 A2
Centaur Ct 3 TW8 ... 110 A1
Centaurs Bsns Pk TW7 ... 131 A6
Centaur St SE1 ... 116 B3 260 D6
Centenary Rd EN3 ... 7 B1
Centennial Ave WD6 ... 9 C4
Centennial Ct WD6 ... 9 C4
Centennial Pk HA7, WD6 ... 9 C4
Central Ave
Battersea SW11 ... 136 D5 267 D3
East Finchley N2 ... 47 D6
East Molesey KT8 ... 195 B4
Edmonton N9 ... 17 D1
Enfield EN1 ... 6 B3
Finchley N2 ... 30 B1
Hayes UB3 ... 106 A6
Isleworth TW3, TW7 . 130 A1
Leyton E11 ... 76 B6
Pinner HA5 ... 41 B2
Wallington SM6 ... 220 A3
Welling DA16 ... 146 A3
Central Bsns Ctr NW10 ... 67 C3
Central Chambers W5 ... 109 D6
Central Cir NW4 ... 46 B4
Central Ct 2 SE18 ... 122 D2
Centrale Ctr CR0 ... 221 A6
Centrale Sta CR0 ... 221 A6
Central Foundation Boys' Sch EC2 ... 95 B3 242 D6
Central Foundation Lower Girls Sch The 10 E3 ... 97 A4
Central Foundation Upper Girls Sch The 27 E3 ... 97 B4
Central Gdns SM4 .. 201 D4
Central Hill SE19 ... 183 B4
Central Ho
Barking IG11 ... 79 A1
Mill Meads E15 ... 98 A5
Central Mans
8 London NW4 ... 46 B4
1 Streatham SW16 . 182 A6
Central Middlesex Hospl NW10 ... 89 A4
Central Par
Croydon CR0 ... 220 C4
Ealing UB6 ... 87 A4
Enfield EN3 ... 6 C3
Feltham TW14 ... 150 C4
Harrow HA1 ... 42 D4
Heston TW5 ... 129 C5
Ilford IG2 ... 57 B3
Penge SE20 ... 184 D3
South Acton W3 ... 110 D4
2 Streatham SW16 . 182 A6
Surbiton KT6 ... 198 A3
8 Walthamstow E17 ... 53 C5
Central Park Ave RM10 ... 81 D5
Central Park Prim Sch 7 E6 ... 99 D5
Central Park Rd E6 ... 99 D5
Central Par Villas BR5 ... 190 C1
Central Pk Est TW4 . 128 D1
Central Public Health Laboratories NW9 ... 45 C6
Central Rd Finchley N2 . 30 C2
Morden SM4 ... 201 D4
Wembley HA0 ... 65 B3
Worcester Pk KT4 ... 216 A6
Central St Martins Coll EC1 ... 94 C3 241 B5
Central St Martin's Coll of Art & Design W1 ... 93 D1 239 D1
Central St Martins Coll of Art & Design (The London Inst) WC1 ... 94 B2 240 C3
Central Sch of Ballet EC1 ... 94 C3 241 B5
Central Sch of Speech & Drama NW3 ... 70 B1
Central Sq
East Molesey KT8 ... 195 B5
Hampstead Garden Suburb NW11 ... 47 D3
4 Wembley HA9 ... 66 A3
Central St EC1 95 A4 235 A1
Central Terr BR3 ... 206 D6
Central Way
Feltham TW14 ... 150 B6
Lower Place NW10 ... 89 A4
Sutton SM5 ... 218 C1
Thamesmead SE28 ... 124 B6
Centre Acad 2 SW11 ... 136 B1
Centre Ave Acton W3 . 111 B5
Finchley N2 ... 30 C1
Centre Bldg SE17 ... 262 B4
Centre Common Rd BR7 ... 189 A3
Centre Court Sh Ctr 3 SW19 ... 179 B4
Centre Ct N20 ... 14 B2
Centre Dr E7 ... 77 C4
Centre Hts 5 NW3 ... 70 B1
Centre Point 3 SE1 .. 118 A1
Centre Point Ho WC2 ... 239 D2
Centre Rd
Dagenham RM10 ... 103 D5
Finchley N2 ... 30 C1
Wanstead E7, E11 ... 77 A6
Centre St E2 ... 96 B5
Centre The TW13 ... 150 B3
Centre The Performing Arts Coll SE18 ... 121 D3
Centreway 4 IG1 ... 79 A6
Centre Way N9 ... 18 D2
Centro Ct E11 ... 54 C1
Centurian Sq 9 SE18 ... 144 A4
Centurian Way DA18 ... 125 C3
Centurion Bldg SW8 268 C5
Centurion Cl N7 ... 72 B1
Centurion Ct
Hackbridge SM6 ... 219 B6
7 Woolwich SE18 ... 122 B2
Centurion La E3 ... 97 B5
Centurion Lodge 2 RM10 ... 81 D2
Centurion Way DA18 ... 125 C3
Century Cl NW4 ... 46 D4
Century Ho
Edgware HA8 ... 26 C3
Harrow HA3 ... 42 C6
Lewisham SE13 ... 141 D3
Wembley HA9 ... 66 B6
Century Rd E17 ... 53 A6
Century Yd SE23 ... 162 C2
Cephas Ave E1 ... 96 C3
Cephas Ho 9 E1 ... 96 C3
Cephas St E1 ... 96 C3
Ceres Ct 12 KT1 ... 176 A1
Ceres Rd SE18 ... 123 D2
Cerise Rd SE15 ... 140 A4
Cerne Cl UB4 ... 106 C6
Cerne Rd SM4 ... 202 A3
Cerney Mews W2 ... 246 C6
Cervantes Ct 12 W2 ... 91 D1
Cester St E2 ... 96 A6
Ceylon Rd
6 Hammersmith W14 ... 112 D3
Kensington W14 ... 254 A5
Chabot Dr SE15 ... 140 B2
Chace Com Sch EN1 ... 5 C4
Chadacre Ave IG5 ... 56 B6
Chadacre Ct E15 ... 99 A6
Chadacre Ho 10 SW9 ... 138 D1
Chadacre Rd KT17 ... 216 B3
Chadbourn St E14 ... 97 D2
Chadbury Ct NW7 ... 28 A2
Chad Cres N9 ... 18 C1
Chadd Dr BR1 ... 210 A6
Chadd Gn 2 E13 ... 99 A6
Chaddlewood EN4 ... 3 A1
Chadston Ho 17 N1 ... 72 D1
Chadswell WC1 ... 233 B1
Chadview Ct 2 RM6 .. 58 D2
Chadville Gdns RM6 .. 58 D4
Chadway RM8 ... 58 C1
Chadwell Ave RM6 ... 58 B2
CHADWELL HEATH ... 58 D4
Chadwell Heath Foundation Sch The RM6 ... 58 B3
Chadwell Heath Ind Pk RM8 ... 58 D1
Chadwell Heath La RM6 ... 58 C3
Chadwell Heath Sta RM6 ... 58 D2
Chadwell La N8 ... 50 B6
Chadwell Prim Sch RM6 ... 58 C2
Chadwell St EC1 ... 94 C4 234 B2
Chadwick Ave
Chingford E4 ... 36 B6
Enfield N21 ... 4 B1
Wimbledon SW19 ... 179 C4
Chadwick Cl
12 Ealing W7 ... 86 D2
Roehampton SW15 ... 155 D4
Teddington TW11 ... 175 A4
Chadwick Ct 4 SE28 ... 124 B5
Chadwick Pl KT6 ... 197 C3
Chadwick Rd
Harlesden NW10 ... 89 D6
Ilford IG1 ... 78 D5
Leytonstone E11 ... 54 D3
Peckham SE15 ... 139 D3
Chadwick St SW1 ... 115 D3 259 C5
Chadwick Way SE28 . 124 D6
Chadwin Rd E13 ... 99 B2
Chadworth Ho
Finsbury EC1 ... 235 A1
Finsbury Pk N4 ... 51 A1
Chadworth Way KT10 ... 212 B3
Chaffey Ho 6 SE7 ... 121 C1
Chaffinch Ave CR0 .. 206 D3
Chaffinch Bsns Pk CR0 ... 206 D5
Chaffinch Cl
Croydon CR0 ... 206 D3
Edmonton N9 ... 18 D3
Tolworth KT6 ... 214 C5
Chaffinch Rd BR3 ... 185 A2
Chafford Way RM6 ... 58 C5
Chagford Ct SW19 ... 180 C3
Chagford Ho
38 Bromley E3 ... 97 D4
Marylebone NW1 ... 237 C5
Chagford St NW1 ... 92 D3 237 D5
Chailey Ave EN1 ... 5 D3
Chailey Cl TW5 ... 128 D4
Chailey Ind Est UB3 . 106 A4
Chailey St E5 ... 74 C5
Chalbury Ho 8 SW9 . 138 B1
Chalbury Wlk N1 ... 234 A4
Chalcombe Rd SE2 .. 124 B3
Chalcot Cl SM2 ... 217 C1
Chalcot Cres NW1 ... 92 D6 230 D6
Chalcot Gdns NW3 ... 70 D2
Chalcot Mews SW16 . 160 A1
Chalcot Rd NW1 ... 93 A6 231 A6
Chalcot Sch 21 NW1 .. 71 B1
Chalcot Sq NW1 ... 71 A1
Chalcott Gdns KT6 .. 197 C1
Chalcroft Rd SE13 ... 164 C6
Chaldon Rd SW6 ... 135 A5 264 B4
Chale Rd SW2 ... 160 A5
Chalet Cl TW15 ... 171 B4
Chalfont Ave HA9 ... 66 D2
Chalfont Ct
3 Belvedere DA17 .. 125 C1
12 Harrow HA1 ... 42 D3
Hendon NW9 ... 45 D6
Marylebone NW1 ... 237 D5
Chalfont Gn N9 ... 17 C1
Chalfont Ho
2 Bermondsey SE16 ... 118 B3
Willesden NW10 ... 67 B5
Chalfont Rd
Edmonton N9 ... 17 D1
Hayes UB3 ... 106 A4
South Norwood SE25 . 205 D6
Chalfont Way W13 ... 109 B3
Chalfont Wlk 5 HA5 .. 22 C1
Chalford 7 NW3 ... 70 A2
Chalford Cl KT8 ... 195 C5
Chalford Ct Ilford IG2 . 56 D4
15 Putney SW15 ... 156 D5
Surbiton KT6 ... 198 B2
Chalford Rd SE21 ... 183 B6
Chalford Wlk IG8 ... 37 D3
Chalgrove Ave SM4 .. 201 C4
Chalgrove Gdns N3 ... 47 A6
Chalgrove Prim Sch N3 ... 47 A6
Chalgrove Rd
Sutton SM2 ... 218 B1
Tottenham N17 ... 34 B2
Chalice Cl SM6 ... 219 D2
Chalice Ct N2 ... 48 C5
Chalkenden Cl SE20 . 184 B3
Chalkers Cnr TW9 ... 132 D2
Chalk Farm Rd NW1 .. 71 A1
Chalk Farm Sta NW3 . 71 A1
Chalkhill Prim Sch HA9 ... 66 D5
Chalkhill Rd HA9 ... 67 A5
Chalk Hill Rd W6 ... 112 D2
Chalk La EN4 ... 2 D1
Chalklands HA9 ... 67 A5
Chalkley Cl CR4 ... 181 A1
Chalkmill Dr EN1 ... 6 B2
Chalk Pit Ave BR5 ... 190 C1
Chalk Pit Way SM1 .. 218 A3
Chalk Rd E13 ... 99 C2
Chalkstone Cl DA16 . 146 A4
Chalkwell Ho 10 E1 ... 96 D1
Chalkwell Park Ave EN1 ... 5 C1
Challenge Cl NW10 ... 89 C6
Challenge Ct TW2 ... 152 C4
Challenge Rd TW15 .. 149 B1
Challenger Ho 7 E14 ... 119 A6
Challice Way SW2 ... 160 B3
Challiner Ct HA1 ... 43 A4
Challin St 1 SE20 ... 184 C2

Challis Rd TW8 109 D1
Challoner Cl N2 30 B1
Challoner Cres W14 254 C1
Challoner Ct BR2 186 B1
Challoner Mans W14 254 C1
Challoners Cl KT8 196 B5
Challoner St
W14 113 B1 254 C1
Chalmers Ho
13 London SW11 136 A2
Walthamstow E17 53 D4
Chalmers Rd TW15 170 D5
Chalmers Rd E
TW15 171 A5
Chalmers Way
Feltham TW14 150 B6
Isleworth TW1 131 B1
Chalmer's Wlk 14
SE17 138 D6
Chalner Ho SW2 160 C3
Chaloner Ct SE1 252 C2
Chalsey Lodge SE4 141 B1
Chalsey Rd SE4 141 B1
Chalton Dr N2 48 B3
Chalton St
NW1 93 D5 232 C3
Chamberlain Cl
Ilford IG1 79 A5
Plumstead SE18 123 B3
Chamberlain Cotts
SE5 139 B4
Chamberlain Cres
BR4 207 D1
Chamberlain Gdns
TW3 130 A4
Chamberlain Ho 6
E1 118 C6
Chamberlain La HA5 40 A5
Chamberlain Pl E17 53 A6
Chamberlain Rd
Ealing W13 109 A4
Finchley N2 30 A1
Chamberlain St 7
NW1 70 D1
Chamberlain Way
Pinner HA5 40 B6
Surbiton KT6 198 A2
Chamberlain Wlk 5
TW13 173 A6
Chamberlayne Ave
HA9 66 A6
Chamberlayne Mans 3
NW10 90 D4
Chamberlayne Rd
NW10 90 C6
Chambers Ave DA14 191 A4
Chambers Bsns Pk
UB7 126 C6
Chambers Gdns N2 30 B2
Chambers Ho 2
SW16 181 C6
Chambers La NW10 68 C1
Chambers Pl CR2 221 B1
Chambers Rd N7 72 A4
Chambers St SE16 118 A4
Chamber St
E1 117 D6 253 D6
Chambers Walk HA7 25 B5
Chambon Pl 7 W6 112 A2
Chambord Ho 24 E2 95 D4
Chambord St E2 95 D4
Chamomile Ct E17 53 C3
Champa Cl N17 33 D1
Champion Cres
SE26 185 A6
Champion Gr SE5 139 B2
Champion Hill SE5 139 B2
Champion Pk SE5 139 B3
Champion Rd SE26 185 A6
Champlain Ho 26
W12 112 B6
Champness Cl 9
SE27 183 B6
Champness Rd IG11 79 D1
Champneys Cl SM2 217 B1
Champneys Ct N21 16 A6
Chancel Ct W1 249 C6
Chancellor Gr SE21 161 A1
Chancellor Ho
South Kensington
SW7 256 B6
29 Wapping E1 118 B5
Chancellor Pas E14 119 C5
Chancellor Pl NW9 27 D1
Chancellors' Ct WC1 240 C4
Chancellors Loft N8 50 A3
Chancellor's Rd W6 112 C1
Chancellors St W6 112 C1
Chancellors Wharf 21
W6 112 C1
Chancelot Rd SE2 124 B2
Chancel St
SE1 116 D5 251 C3
Chancery Bldgs 14
E1 118 C6
Chancerygate Bsns Ctr
HA4 63 A3
Chancery Gate Bsns Ctr
CR4 202 D4
Chancery Ho WC2 241 A3
Chancery La
Beckenham BR3 185 D1
Holborn EC4 94 C1 241 A2
Chancery Lane Sta
WC1 94 C2 241 A3
Chancery Mews
SW17 158 C2
Chance St E2 243 C6
Chanctonbury Cl
SE9 166 D1
Chanctonbury Gdns
SM2 217 D1
Chanctonbury Way
N12 29 C6
Chanderia Ct 5
CR0 221 A5
Chand Ho 7 N12 30 A5
Chandler Ave E16 99 A2
Chandler Cl TW12 173 C2
Chandler Ct
Feltham TW14 150 A5
Thornton Heath CR7 204 D4
2 Tolworth KT5 198 D1
8 Wallington SM6 219 B2
Chandlers Cl
East Bedfont TW14 149 D4
East Molesey KT8 195 D4
Chandlers Field Prim Sch KT8 195 C4
Chandlers Mews
E14 119 C4
Chandler St E1 118 B5
Chandlers Way 11
SE24 160 C4
Chandler Way SE15 139 D5
Chandlery Ho 26 E1 96 A1
Chandon Lo SM2 218 A1
Chandos Ave
Ealing W5 109 D2
New Southgate N14 15 C1
Oakleigh Pk N20 14 B3
Walthamstow E17 35 C1
Chandos Bsns Ctr 11
SM6 219 C2
Chandos Cl IG9 21 B2
Chandos Cres HA8 26 C3
Chandos Ct
Edgware HA8 26 B3
Palmers Green N14 15 D2
Stanmore HA7 25 B4
Chandos Pl
WC2 116 A6 250 A5
Chandos Rd
Cricklewood NW2 68 C3
Finchley N2 30 C1
Harrow HA1 42 A4
Old Oak Comm NW10 89 C3
Pinner HA5 40 D2
Stratford New Town
E15 76 B3
Tottenham N17 33 C1
Chandos St
W1 93 B2 238 D3
Chandos Way NW11 47 D1
Change Alley EC3 242 D1
Channel Cl TW5 129 C4
Channel Gate Rd
NW10 89 C4
Channel Ho E14 97 A2
Channel Sea Bsns Ctr
E15 98 B5
Channelsea Rd E15 98 B6
Channing Jun Sch
N6 49 A1
Channing Sch N6 49 B1
Channon Ct 3 KT6 198 A4
Chantrey Rd SW9 138 B2
Chantries The HA7 25 A5
Chantry Cl
2 Abbey Wood
SE2 124 C3
Edgware NW7 11 D4
Chantry Cl *continued*
Enfield EN2 5 A5
Harrow HA3 44 B4
Sidcup DA14 191 A5
Sunbury TW16 172 A3
West Kilburn W9 91 B3
Chantry Cres NW10 67 D2
Chantry Ct SM5 218 C5
Chantry Ct SW6 135 A2
Chantry La BR2 209 D4
Chantry Pl HA3 23 D2
Chantry Rd
Chessington KT9 214 C3
Harrow HA3 23 D2
Chantry Sch UB7 104 A6
Chantry Sq
W8 113 D3 255 C5
Chantry St N1 94 D6 234 D5
Chantry The UB8 82 B4
Chantry Way CR4 202 B6
Chant Sq E15 76 B1
Chant St E15 76 B1
Chapel Cl NW10 67 D2
Chapel Ct
Borough The SE1 252 C2
East Finchley N2 48 C6
Hayes UB3 105 D6
Chapel End Ho E17 35 D2
Chapel End Inf Sch
E17 35 D2
Chapel End Jun Sch
E17 35 D2
Chapel Farm Rd SE9 166 B2
Chapel Hill N2 30 C1
Chapel House St
E14 119 D2
Chapel La
5 Dagenham RM6 58 D2
Hillingdon UB8 82 C1
Pinner HA5 40 D6
Chapel Mill Rd KT1 198 B6
Chapel Mkt★
N1 94 C5 234 A4
Chapel Pl
Islington N1 234 B4
Marylebone W1 238 C1
12 Shoreditch EC2 95 C4
Tottenham N17 33 D3
Chapel Rd
Bexleyheath DA7 147 C1
Ealing W13 109 B5
Hounslow TW3 129 D2
Ilford IG1 78 D5
Twickenham TW1 153 B4
West Norwood SE27 182 D6
Chapel Side
W2 113 D6 245 C5
Chapel St Enfield EN2 5 B2
Paddington
NW1 92 C2 237 A3
Westminster
SW1 115 A4 248 B1
Chapel View CR2 222 C1
Chapel Wlk NW4 46 C5
Chapleton Ho SW2 160 C6
Chaplin Cl
Lambeth SE1 251 C2
Wembley HA0 65 D2
Chaplin Cres TW16 171 C4
Chaplin Ho
6 London SW9 138 C1
Sidcup DA14 190 A6
Chaplin Rd
Dagenham RM9 81 A1
3 Tottenham N17 51 D6
Wembley HA0 65 D2
West Ham E15 98 D6
Willesden NW2 68 A2
Chaplow Cl SW6 136 A3
Chapman Cl UB7 104 B3
Chapman Cres HA3 44 B3
Chapman Gn N22 32 C2
Chapman Ho
26 Stepney E1 96 B1
2 West Norwood
SE27 160 D1
Chapman Rd
Belvedere DA17 125 D1
Hackney Wick E9 75 B2
Thornton Heath CR0 204 C1
Chapmans End BR5 191 A1
Chapman's La BR5 190 D1
Chapmans Park Ind Est
NW10 67 D2
Chapman Sq SW19 156 D2
Chapman St E1 118 B6
Chapone Pl W1 239 C1
Chapter Cl
Hillingdon UB10 60 B1
16 South Acton W4 111 A3
Chapter House & Jewel Twr★ SW1 260 A6
Chapter Rd
Kennington
SE17 116 D1 261 D1
Willesden NW2 68 A3
Chapter St SW1 259 C3
Chapter Way
Hampton TW12 173 C6
Mitcham SW19 180 B2
Chara Pl W4 133 B6
Charcot Ho SW15 155 D5
Charcroft Ct 11
W14 112 D4
Charcroft Gdns EN3 6 D1
Chard Ho 7 N7 72 B6
Chardin Ho 30 SW9 138 C4
Chardin Rd 11 W4 111 C2
Chardmore Rd N16 52 A1
Chardwell Cl E6 100 B1
Charecroft Way
W12 112 D4
Charfield Ct W9 91 D3
Charford Rd E16 99 A2
Chargeable La E13 99 A3
Chargeable St E16 98 D3
Chargrove Cl 24
SE16 118 D4
Charing Cl BR6 227 D4
Charing Cross
SW1 116 A5 250 A4
Charing Cross Hospl
W6 112 D1
Charing Cross Rd
WC2 93 D1 239 D1
Charing Cross Sta
WC2 116 A5 250 B4
Charing Ct BR2 186 C1
Charing Ho SE1 251 B2
Chariot Cl 3 E3 97 C6
Charlbert Ct NW8 230 A4
Charlbert St
NW8 92 C5 230 A4
Charlbury Ave HA7 25 D5
Charlbury Gdns IG3 79 D6
Charlbury Gr W5 87 C1
Charlbury Ho 1 E12 78 C5
Charlbury Rd UB10 60 B5
Charldane Rd SE9 166 D1
Charlecote Gr SE26 162 B1
Charlecote Rd RM8 81 A5
Charlemont Rd E6 100 C4
Charles Allen Ho
EC1 234 A2
Charles Auffray Ho 30
E1 96 C2
Charles Babbage Cl
KT9 213 C1
Charles Barry Cl
SW4 137 C2
Charles Bradlaugh Ho 2
N17 34 B3
Charles Burton Ct E5 75 A4
Charles Cl DA14 190 B6
Charles Cobb Gdns
CR0 220 C3
Charles Coveney Rd 4
SE15 139 D4
Charles Cres HA1 42 B2
Charles Ct 5 TW11 174 C5
Charles Darwin Ho
8 Bethnal Green E2 96 B4
Bromley BR1 187 B3
Charles Dickens Ct
SE25 206 A5
Charles Dickens Ho 1
E2 96 B4
Charles Dickens Mus The★ WC1 94 B3 240 D5
Charles Dickens Prim Sch SE1 117 A4 252 A1
Charles Edward Brooke Sch 11 SW9 138 D4
Charles Edward Brooke Sch (Dennen Site) 10
SE5 138 D4
Charlesfield SE12 165 C1
Charles Flemwell Mews
7 E16 121 A5
Charles Goddard Ho 3
HA0 65 D3
Charles Gr N14 15 C3
Charles Grinling Wlk
SE18 122 C2
Charles Haller St 25
SW2 160 C4
Charles Harrod Ct
SW13 134 C6
Charles Ho
Southall UB2 107 C4
1 Tottenham N17 33 D3
Charles Hobson Ho 4
NW10 67 C1
Charles Hocking Ho 8
W3 111 A4
Charles II Pl
SW3 114 D1 257 C1
Charles II St
SW1 115 D5 249 C4
Charles La
NW8 92 C5 230 A4
Charles Lamb Ct N1 234 D4
Charles Lesser KT9 213 D3
Charles Mackenzie Ho 7
SE16 118 A2
Charlesmere Gdns
SE28 123 C4
Charles Mills Ct
SW16 182 A4
Charles Pl NW1 232 B1
Charles Rd
Dagenham RM6 58 D3
Ealing W13 87 A1
Merton SW19 179 C2
Upton E7 77 C1
Charles Rowan Ho
WC1 234 A1
Charles Sevright Dr
NW7 28 D5
Charles Sq N1 95 B4 235 D1
Charles St
Barnes SW13 133 C3
Croydon CR0 221 A5
Enfield EN1 17 D6
Hillingdon UB10 82 D3
Hounslow TW3 129 B3
Mayfair W1 115 B5 248 C4
Newham E16 121 C5
Charles Staunton Ho 3
SE27 183 B6
Charleston Cl TW13 150 A1
Charleston St SE17 262 B3
Charles Townsend Ho
EC1 241 C6
Charles Utton Ct E8 74 A4
Charles Whincup Rd 2
E16 121 B5
Charlesworth Ho 6
E14 97 C1
Charleville Cir SE26 184 A5
Charleville Ct SW5 254 C1
Charleville Mans
W14 254 B1
Charleville Mews
TW7 131 B1
Charleville Rd
W14 113 B1 254 C1
Charlie Browns Rdbt
E18 37 C1
Charlmont Rd SW17 180 D4
Charlotte Cl DA6 169 A6
Charlotte Ct
Crouch End N8 49 D3
Esher KT10 212 A3
10 Hammersmith W6 112 A2
Ilford IG2 56 C3
11 Wembley HA0 66 A2
Charlotte Despard Ave
SW11 137 A4 268 B1
Charlotte Ho 12 W6 112 C1
Charlotte Mews
Marylebone W1 239 B4
North Kensington W10 90 D1
West Kensington W14 254 A4
Charlotte Par SE23 163 A2
Charlotte Park Ave
BR1 210 A6
Charlotte Pl
Kenton NW9 45 A4
Marylebone W1 239 B3
Westminster SW1 259 A3
Charlotte Rd
Barnes SW13 133 D4
Dagenham RM10 81 D2

Charlotte Rd *continued*
Shoreditch
EC2 . . . . 95 C3 243 A6
Wallington SM6 . . . . . 219 C2
Charlotte Row SW4 . . 137 C2
Charlotte Sharman Prim Sch SE11 . . 116 D3 261 C5
Charlotte Sq 5
TW10 . . . . 154 B5
Charlotte St
W1 . . . . 93 C2 239 B4
Charlotte Terr
N1 . . . . 94 B6 233 D5
Charlotte Turner Prim Sch SE8 . . . . 141 C6
CHARLTON 143 D6 171 B1
Charlton Church La
SE7 . . . . 121 C1
Charlton Cl UB10 . . . . . 60 D6
Charlton Cres IG11 . 101 D5
Charlton Ct
Finchley N3 . . . . 29 A1
25 Hackney E2 . . . . 95 D6
17 Kentish Town N7 . . . . 71 D3
Newham E6 . . . . 100 B4
Charlton Dene SE7 . . 143 D5
Charlton Gate Bsns Pk
SE7 . . . . 121 C2
Charlton Ho
5 Brentford TW8 . . . 132 A6
Charlton TW17 . . . . 171 A1
Somers Town NW1 . . . 232 C2
Charlton King's Rd
NW5 . . . . 71 D3
Charlton La
Greenwich SE7 . . . . . . 121 D1
Upper Halliford TW17 . 193 B5
Upper Halliford TW17 193 C5
Charlton Lo 1 NW11 . . 47 B3
Charlton Manor Prim Sch SE7 . . . . 143 D5
Charlton Park La
SE7 . . . . 144 A6
Charlton Park Rd
SE7 . . . . 143 D6
Charlton Pl
N1 . . . . 94 D5 234 C4
Charlton Rd
Charlton TW17 . . . . . . 171 A1
Edmonton N9 . . . . 18 D4
Greenwich SE3, SE7 . . 143 B6
Harlesden NW10 . . . . . . 89 C6
Harrow HA3 . . . . 43 D5
Wembley HA9 . . . . 44 B1
Charlton Sch SE7 . . . 144 A6
Charlton Sta SE7 . . . 121 C1
Charlton Way SE10, SE3 . . . . 142 C4
Charlwood Cl HA3 . . . . 24 C4
Charlwood Ho
Richmond TW9 . . . . . . 132 D5
1 Streatham SW2 . . . 160 B3
Westminster SW1 . . . 259 C3
Charlwood Pl
SW1 . . . . 115 C2 259 B3
Charlwood Rd
SW15 . . . . 134 D1
Charlwood St
SW1 . . . . 115 C1 259 B2
Charlwood Terr 5
SW15 . . . . 134 D1
Charman Ho
18 London SW2 . . . . . 160 C5
South Lambeth SW8 . 270 A4
Charmian Ave HA7 . . . . 25 D1
Charmian Ho 19 N1 . . . 95 C5
Charminster Ave
SW19 . . . . 179 D1
Charminster Ct 3
KT6 . . . . 197 D2
Charminster Rd
Mottingham SE12, SE9 . . . . 187 D6
North Cheam KT4 . . . . 200 D1
Charmouth Ct TW10 . 154 B6
Charmouth Ho SW8 . 270 C4
Charmouth Rd DA16 . 146 C4
Charnock Ho 22
W12 . . . . 112 B6
Charnock Rd E5 . . . . . . 74 B5
Charnwood Ave
SW19 . . . . 179 D1
Charnwood Cl KT3 . . . 199 C5
Charnwood Dr E18 . . . . 55 B5
Charnwood Gdns
E14 . . . . 119 C2
Charnwood Ho 9 E5 . . 74 B6
Charnwood Pl N20 . . . 14 A1
Charnwood Rd
Hillingdon UB10 . . . . 82 C5
South Norwood SE25 . . 205 B5
Charnwood St E5 . . . . . 74 B6
Charolais Ho UB4 . . . . 83 B2
Charrington Ho 42
E1 . . . . 96 C3
Charrington Rd 2
CR0 . . . . 221 A6
Charrington St
NW1 . . . . 93 D5 232 C4
Charsley Rd SE6 . . . . 163 D2
Chart Cl Bromley BR2 . 186 C2
Croydon CR0 . . . . 206 C3
Mitcham CR4 . . . . 202 D5
Charter Ave IG2 . . . . . 57 B2
Charter Bldgs 14
SE10 . . . . 141 D4
Charter Cres TW4 . . . 129 A1
Charter Ct
Finsbury Pk N4 . . . . 50 C1
Kingston u T KT3 . . . . 199 C6
Marylebone W1 . . . . . 237 B3
Southall UB1 . . . . 107 C5
Wood Green N22 . . . . . . 31 D2
Charter Dr DA5 . . . . . 169 A4
Charter Ho WC2 . . . . 240 B1
Charterhouse Ave
HA0 . . . . 65 C3
Charterhouse Bldgs
EC1 . . . . 242 A5
Charterhouse Mews
EC1 . . . . 241 D4
Charterhouse Rd E8 . . 74 A3
Charterhouse Sq
EC1 . . . . 94 D2 241 D4
Charterhouse Square Sch The EC1 . . 94 D2 241 D4
Charterhouse St EC1 241 C3
Charterhouse Works
SW18 . . . . 136 A1
Charteris Rd
Finsbury Pk N4 . . . . 50 C1
Kilburn NW6 . . . . 91 B6
Woodford IG8 . . . . 37 B4
Charteris Sp Ctr NW6 . 91 C6
Charter Rd KT1 . . . . . 198 D6
Charter Rd The IG8 . . . 36 D4
Charter Sch SE24 . . . . 161 B6
Charters Cl SE19 . . . . 183 C5
Charter Sq KT1 . . . . . 176 D1
Charter Way
London NW3 . . . . 47 B5
Southgate N14 . . . . 15 D5
Chartes Ho SE1 . . . . . 263 B6
Chartfield Ave
SW15 . . . . 156 C6
Chartfield Sq SW15 . 156 D6
Chartham Ct 12
SW9 . . . . 138 C2
Chartham Gr SE27 . . 160 D1
Chartham Ho SE1 . . . 262 D6
Chartham Rd SE25 . . 206 B6
Chart Hills Cl SE28 . . 103 A1
Chart Ho 7 SW19 . . . 180 D1
Chart House The 5
E14 . . . . 119 D1
Chartley Ave
Harrow HA7 . . . . 24 D4
Neasden NW2 . . . . 67 C5
Charton Cl 5 DA17 . . 147 B6
Chartres Ct UB6 . . . . . 86 B5
Chartridge SE17 . . . . 139 B6
Chartridge Cl
Barnet EN5 . . . . 12 A6
Bushey WD23 . . . . 8 A5
Chartridge Ct 6 HA7 . 25 C5
Chart St N1 . . . . 95 B4 235 D2
Chartwell 25 SW19 . . 156 D3
Chartwell Bsns Ctr
BR1 . . . . 209 D6
Chartwell Cl
2 Croydon CR0 . . . . . 205 B1
Greenford UB6 . . . . 85 D6
Sidcup SE9 . . . . 167 B2
Chartwell Ct
10 Barnet EN5 . . . . 1 A1
Dollis Hill NW2 . . . . 68 A5
Chartwell Ct *continued*
2 Woodford IG8 . . . . . . 37 A3
Chartwell Dr BR6 . . . . 227 B3
Chartwell Gdns SM3 . 217 A4
Chartwell Lo 5 BR3 . 185 C3
Chartwell Pl
Cheam SM3 . . . . 217 B4
Harrow HA2 . . . . 64 B6
Chartwell Way 3
SE20 . . . . 184 B2
Charville Ct 8 HA1 . . . 42 D3
Charville La UB4 . . . . . 83 C5
Charville La W UB10 . . 82 D4
Charville Prim Sch
UB4 . . . . 83 C5
Charwood SW16 . . . . 182 C6
Chase Bridge Prim Sch
TW2 . . . . 152 C5
Chase Court Gdns EN2 . 5 A2
Chase Ct
Chelsea SW3 . . . . 257 C5
Isleworth TW7 . . . . . . 131 A3
Merton SW20 . . . . 179 A1
Southgate N14 . . . . 15 C5
Wembley HA0 . . . . 65 D2
Chase Ctr The NW10 . . 89 B4
Chase Farm Hospl EN2 4 C5
Chasefield Rd SW17 180 D6
Chase Gdns
Chingford E4 . . . . 35 C6
Twickenham TW2 . . . . 152 B4
Chase Gn EN2 . . . . 5 A2
Chase Green Ave EN2 . . 5 A3
Chase Hill EN2 . . . . 5 A2
Chase La IG6 . . . . 57 B4
Chase Lane Prim Sch
E4 . . . . 35 B6
Chaseley Ct
Gunnersbury W4 . . . . 110 D1
Oatlands Pk KT13 . . . . 193 C1
Chaseley St E14 . . . . . . 97 A1
Chasemore Cl CR4 . . 202 D2
Chasemore Gdns
CR0 . . . . 220 C3
Chasemore Ho SW6 . 264 B4
Chase Rd
North Acton NW10 . . . . 89 B3
Southgate N14 . . . . 15 D5
Chase Ridings EN2 . . . . 4 C3
Chase Road Trad Est
NW10 . . . . 89 B3
Chase Side
East Barnet N14 . . . . . . 15 B4
Enfield EN2 . . . . 5 A3
Chase Side Ave
Enfield EN2 . . . . 5 A3
Merton SW20 . . . . 179 A1
Chase Side Cres EN2 . . 5 A4
Chase Side Pl EN2 . . . . 5 A3
Chase Side Prim Sch
EN2 . . . . 5 A3
Chase Side Works
N14 . . . . 15 D4
Chase The
Bromley BR1 . . . . 209 B6
Clapham SW4 . . . . 137 B2
Dagenham RM6 . . . . . . 59 A3
Eastcote HA5 . . . . 40 C3
Edgware HA8 . . . . 26 D2
Erith DA7 . . . . 147 D2
Ickenham UB10 . . . . 60 C3
Loughton IG10 . . . . 21 D4
Manor Pk E12 . . . . 77 D4
Pinner HA5 . . . . 41 B5
South Norwood SW16 182 C3
Stanmore HA7 . . . . 25 A4
Sunbury TW16 . . . . . . 172 B2
Wallington CR0, SM6 . . 220 B3
Chaseville Par N21 . . . 16 B6
Chaseville Park Rd
N21 . . . . 16 B6
Chase Way N14 . . . . . . 15 C3
Chasewood Ave EN2 . . . 4 D3
Chasewood Ct 4
NW7 . . . . 27 B5
Chasewood Pk HA1 . . . 64 C5
Chateau The 4
SM5 . . . . 218 D5
Chatelain Ho NW7 . . . . 28 C6
Chater Ho 6 E2 . . . . . . 96 D4
Chatfield Rd
London SW11 . . . . 136 A2
Thornton Heath CR0 . 204 D1
Chatham Ave BR2 . . . 209 A2
Chatham Cl
Cheam SM3 . . . . 201 B2
Chatham Cl *continued*
Hampstead Garden Suburb
NW11 . . . . 47 C4
Woolwich SE18 . . . . . . 122 B3
Chatham Ct SW11 . . . 158 D6
Chatham Ho
7 London SE5 . . . . . . 139 C3
6 Wallington SM6 . . . 219 B3
21 Woolwich SE18 . . . 122 B2
Chatham Pl E9 . . . . 74 C2
Chatham Rd
Clapham SW11 . . . . . 158 D6
Kingston u T KT1, KT2 . 176 C1
Walthamstow E17 . . . . . 53 A6
1 Woodford E18 . . . . . . 36 D1
Chatham St
SE17 . . . . 117 B2 262 D4
Chatsfield Pl W5 . . . . . 88 A1
Chatsworth Ave
Grove Pk BR1 . . . . 187 B6
Hendon NW4 . . . . 28 C1
Merton SW20 . . . . 179 A1
Sidcup DA15 . . . . 168 A3
Wembley HA9 . . . . 66 B3
Chatsworth Cl
Coney Hall BR2, BR4 . . . . 224 D6
Hendon NW4 . . . . 28 C1
Chatsworth Cres TW3, TW7 . . . . 130 B2
Chatsworth Ct
Brondesbury NW2 . . . . . 68 D2
Clapton Pk E5 . . . . 74 D4
Earl's Ct W8 . . . . 255 A4
5 Stanmore HA7 . . . . . 25 C5
Thornton Heath SW16 . . . . 204 B6
Chatsworth Dr EN1 . . . 18 A5
Chatsworth Est E5 . . . . 74 D4
Chatsworth Gdns
Acton W3 . . . . 110 D5
Harrow HA2 . . . . 41 D1
New Malden KT3 . . . . 199 D4
Chatsworth Ho
2 Bromley BR2 . . . . . 209 A5
Kingston u T KT6 . . . . 197 D4
Chatsworth Inf Sch
Isleworth TW3 . . . . . . 130 A1
Sidcup DA15 . . . . 168 A3
Chatsworth Jun Sch
TW3 . . . . 130 A1
Chatsworth Lo
1 Chiswick W4 . . . . . . 111 B1
West Wickham BR4 . . 224 A6
Chatsworth Par BR5 . 211 A4
Chatsworth Pl
Mitcham CR4 . . . . 202 D6
Teddington TW11 . . . . 175 A6
Chatsworth Rd
Brondesbury NW2 . . . . . 68 D2
Cheam SM3 . . . . 217 A4
Chiswick W4 . . . . 133 A6
Clapton Pk E5 . . . . 74 D4
Ealing W5 . . . . 88 B3
Hayes UB4 . . . . 84 B3
South Croydon CR0 . . . 221 B5
Stratford E15 . . . . 76 D3
Chatsworth Rise W5 . . 88 B3
Chatsworth Way
SE27 . . . . 161 A1
Chattenden Ho 8 N4 . 51 B2
Chatteris Ct NW4 . . . . . 46 D6
CHATTERN HILL 170 D6
Chattern Hill TW15 . . 170 D6
Chattern Rd TW15 . . . 171 A6
Chatterton Ct TW9 . . . 132 B3
Chatterton Rd
Bromley Comm BR2 . . 209 D4
Highbury N4 . . . . 72 D5
Chatton Ct 5 NW9 . . . . 46 A5
Chatto Rd SW11 . . . . 158 D6
Chaucer Ave
Cranford TW4 . . . . 128 B3
Hayes UB4 . . . . 84 A2
Richmond TW9 . . . . . . 132 C3
Chaucer Cl N11 . . . . . . 31 D5
Chaucer Ct
14 New Barnet EN5 . . . . 13 D6
17 Stoke Newington N16 . . . . 73 C4
Chaucer Dr
SE1 . . . . 117 D2 263 D3
Chaucer Gdns SM1 . . 217 C5
Chaucer Gn CR0 . . . . . 206 C2
Chaucer Ho
Harrow HA2 . . . . 41 D4
Chaucer Ho *continued*
Pimlico SW1 . . . . 259 A1
Sutton SM1 . . . . 217 C5
2 West Norwood SE27 . . . . 183 A6
Chaucer Rd
Acton W3 . . . . 111 A5
Ashford TW15 . . . . 170 B6
Bexley DA16 . . . . 145 D4
Chingford E17 . . . . 36 A1
Herne Hill SE24 . . . . . 160 D6
Sidcup DA15 . . . . 168 C3
Sutton SM1 . . . . 217 C4
Upton E7 . . . . 77 A2
Wanstead E11 . . . . 55 A3
Chaucer Way SW17 . . 180 B5
Chaulden Ho EC1 . . . . 235 D1
Chauncey Cl N9 . . . . . . 18 A1
Chaundrye Cl SE9 . . . . 166 B5
Chauntler Cl E16 . . . . 121 B6
Chaville Ct N11 . . . . . . 31 A6
Cheadle Ct NW8 . . . . . 236 D6
Cheadle Ho 17 E14 . . . . 97 B1
CHEAM 217 B3
Cheam Common Inf Sch
KT4 . . . . 216 B6
Cheam Common Jun Sch
KT4 . . . . 216 B6
Cheam Common Rd
KT4 . . . . 216 C5
Cheam Court Flats 1
SM3 . . . . 217 A2
Cheam Fields Prim Sch
SM3 . . . . 217 A3
Cheam High Sch
SM3 . . . . 217 A4
Cheam L Ctr SM3 . . . 216 D4
Cheam Mans SM3 . . . 217 A1
Cheam Park Farm Inf Sch SM3 . . . . 217 A5
Cheam Park Farm Jun Sch SM3 . . . . 217 A5
Cheam Park Way
SM3 . . . . 217 A2
Cheam Rd
Belmont SM2, SM3 . . . 216 D1
Cheam SM1 . . . . 217 C2
Cheam St 6 SE15 . . . 140 B2
Cheam Sta SM2 . . . . 217 A1
Cheam Village SM3 . . 217 A2
Cheapside
Barbican EC2 . . 95 A1 242 B1
Edmonton N13 . . . . 33 A6
Chearsley SE17 . . . . . 262 B4
Cheddar Cl 1 N11 . . . . 31 A4
Cheddar Rd TW6 . . . . 126 C3
Cheddar Waye UB4 . . . 84 B1
Cheddington Ho 9
E2 . . . . 96 A6
Cheddington Rd N18 . . 33 C6
Chedworth Cl E16 . . . . 98 D1
Chedworth Ho
London N15 . . . . 51 B5
2 Stoke Newington E5 74 A6
Cheeseman Cl
TW12 . . . . 173 A4
Cheeseman Ct UB1 . 107 D6
Cheesemans Terr
W14 . . . . 254 C1
Cheffrey Ct TW15 . . . 170 D4
Cheldon Ave NW7 . . . . 28 D3
Chelford Rd BR1 . . . . 186 B5
Chelmer Cres IG11 . . . 102 B5
Chelmer Ct E18 . . . . . . 37 B2
Chelmer Rd E9 . . . . 74 D3
Chelmsford Cl
Fulham W6 . . . . 134 D6
Newham E6 . . . . 100 B1
Chelmsford Ct N14 . . . 15 D4
Chelmsford Gdns IG1 56 B2
Chelmsford Ho 5 N7 . 72 B4
Chelmsford Rd
Leytonstone E11 . . . . . 54 B1
London N14 . . . . 15 C4
Walthamstow E17 . . . . . 53 C3
Woodford E18 . . . . 36 D2
Chelmsford Sq NW10 . 90 C6
CHELSEA 114 C1
Chelsea Antiques Mkt★
SW3 . . . . 114 C1 257 B1
Chelsea Barracks★
SW1 . . . . 115 A1 258 B1
Chelsea Bridge
SW1 . . . . 137 B6 268 C6
Chelsea Bridge Rd
SW1 . . . . 115 A1 258 B1

Chelsea Cl
Edgware HA8 26 C1
Hampton TW12 174 A5
New Malden KT4 200 A2
Stonebridge NW10 89 B6
Chelsea Cloisters
SW3 257 B3
Chelsea Coll of Art & Design
SW1 116 A1 260 A2
Chelsea Cres
Brondesbury NW2 69 B2
Chelsea SW10 266 B1
Chelsea Ct
Chelsea SW3 268 A6
6 Chingford E4 20 A3
Sutton SM2 217 D2
Chelsea Emb
SW3 136 D6 267 C5
Chelsea Est SW3 267 A5
Chelsea Farm Ho
SW10 266 D5
Chelsea Fields
SW19 180 B2
Chelsea Gate SW1 258 B1
Chelsea Gdns
Cheam SM3 217 A4
Chelsea SW1 258 B1
Ealing W13 86 D2
Chelsea Harbour Design Ctr SW10 266 B2
Chelsea Harbour Dr
SW10 136 A4 266 B2
Chelsea Harbour Pier
SW10 266 C1
Chelsea Ind Coll
SW6 256 C3
Chelsea Lo SW3 267 D6
Chelsea Manor Ct
SW3 267 B6
Chelsea Manor Gdns
SW3 257 B1
Chelsea Manor St
SW3 114 C1 257 B1
Chelsea Manor Studios
SW3 257 B1
Chelsea Mus* SW6 265 D4
Chelsea Park Gdns
SW3 136 B6 266 C6
Chelsea Physic Gdn*
SW1 267 C6
Chelsea Reach Twr
SW10 266 C4
Chelsea Sp Ctr
SW3 114 C1 257 B1
Chelsea Sq
SW3 114 B1 256 D1
Chelsea Twrs SW3 267 B6
Chelsea & Westminster Hospl SW10 136 A6 266 B5
Chelsfield Ave N9 18 D4
Chelsfield Gdns
SE26 162 C1
Chelsfield Gn N9 18 D4
Chelsfield Ho SE17 263 A3
Chelsfield Point 3
E9 74 D1
Chelsham Ho 1
SW4 137 D2
Chelsham Rd
London SW4 137 D2
South Croydon CR2 221 B2
Chelsiter Ct DA14 189 D6
Chelston App HA4 62 A6
Chelston Ct 2 E11 55 B4
Chelston Rd HA4 40 A1
Chelsworth Dr SE18 145 B6
Cheltenham Ave 10
TW1 153 A4
Cheltenham Cl
Kingston u T KT3 199 A6
Northolt UB5 63 D2
Cheltenham Ct 8
HA7 25 C5
Cheltenham Gdns
E6 100 A5
Cheltenham Ho UB3 105 A3
Cheltenham Pl
10 Acton W3 110 D5
Acton W3 111 A4
Harrow HA3 44 A5
1 South Acton W3 110 D4
Cheltenham Rd
Leyton E10 54 A3
London SE15 162 C6
Cheltenham Terr
SW3 114 D1 257 D2
Cheltenham Villas
CR7 204 C3
Chelverton Ct SW15 134 D1
Chelverton Rd
SW15 134 D1
Chelwood
Gospel Oak NW5 71 A3
London N20 14 B2
Chelwood Cl E4 19 D5
Chelwood Ct
Battersea SW11 266 D2
9 South Croydon
CR2 221 A3
Chelwood Gdns
TW9 132 C3
Chelwood Ho W2 236 D1
Chelwood Lo N12 30 A4
Chenappa Cl E13 99 A4
Chenduit Way HA7 24 D5
Chene Colline Ct
KT6 198 A3
Cheney Ct SE23 162 D3
Cheney Row E17 35 B2
Cheneys Rd E11 76 C5
Cheney St HA5 40 C4
Chenies Ho W2 245 C6
Chenies Mews WC1 239 C5
Chenies Pl NW1 232 D4
Chenies St
WC1 93 D2 239 C5
Chenies The
Orpington BR6 211 C3
Somers Town NW1 232 D4
Cheniston Gdns W8 255 C6
Chennestone Prim Sch
TW16 172 B1
Chepstow Cl SW15 157 A6
Chepstow Cres
Ilford IG3 57 C3
Notting Hill
W11 113 C6 245 A6
Chepstow Ct W11 245 A6
Chepstow Gdns UB1 85 B1
Chepstow Pl
W2 113 C6 245 B6
Chepstow Rd
Croydon CR0 221 D6
Ealing W7 109 A3
Paddington W2 91 C1
Chepstow Rise CR0 221 C5
Chepstow Villas
W11 113 C6 245 A6
Chequers IG9 21 B3
Chequers Cl
London NW9 45 C6
Orpington BR5 211 D5
Chequers Ct
7 Croydon CR0 205 D1
St Luke's EC1 242 C5
Chequers Ho NW8 237 A6
Chequers La RM9 103 C5
Chequers Par
Dagenham RM9 103 C6
Edmonton N13 33 A5
Chequer St
EC1 95 A3 242 B5
Chequers The HA5 40 D6
Chequers Way N13 32 D5
Cherbury Cl SE28 102 D1
Cherbury Ct N1 235 D3
Cherbury St
N1 95 B5 235 D3
Cherchefells Mews
HA7 25 B5
Cherimoya Gdns
KT8 195 D6
Cherington Rd W7 108 D5
Cheriton Ave BR2 209 A4
Cheriton Cl
Cockfosters EN4 2 D1
10 Ealing W5 87 C2
Cheriton Ct
4 Lee SE12 165 A4
South Norwood SE25 205 C4
Walton-on-T KT12 194 C1
Cheriton Dr SE18 145 B6
Cheriton Ho 9 E5 74 B3
Cheriton Sq SW17 159 A2
Cherry Ave UB1 106 D5
Cherry Blossom Cl
N13 32 D5
Cherry Cl
Carshalton SM5 218 D6
Ealing W5 109 D3
Cherry Cl *continued*
Merton SM4 201 A5
Ruislip HA4 61 D5
7 Streatham SW2 160 C4
Walthamstow E17 53 D4
Cherrycot Hill BR6 227 B4
Cherrycot Rise BR6 227 A4
Cherry Cres TW8 131 B5
Cherry Croft Gdns 3
HA5 23 B3
Cherry Ct Acton W3 111 C5
Hackbridge CR4 203 A1
Ilford IG6 56 D6
Pinner HA5 22 D2
5 Rotherhithe SE16 119 A5
Sidcup DA14 168 B1
Cherrydeal Ct E11 54 B2
Cherrydown Ave E4 19 C1
Cherrydown Cl E4 19 C1
Cherrydown Rd
DA14 168 D2
Cherry Garden Ho 7
SE16 118 B4
Cherry Garden Sch 20
SE16 118 A2
Cherry Garden St
SE16 118 B4
Cherry Garth TW8 109 D1
Cherry Gdns
Dagenham RM9 81 B3
Northolt UB5 63 D1
Cherry Gr Hayes UB3 106 B5
Hillingdon UB8 83 A2
Cherry Hill
New Barnet EN5 13 D5
Stanmore HA3 24 C4
Cherry Hill Gdns
CR0 220 B4
Cherry Hills WD19 23 A5
Cherry La UB7 104 C2
Cherrylands Cl NW9 67 A6
Cherry Lane Prim Sch
UB7 104 B2
Cherry Laurel Wlk
SW2 160 B5
Cherry Orch
Charlton SE7 143 C6
West Drayton UB7 104 A4
Cherry Orchard Gdns
7 Croydon CR0 205 B1
East Molesey KT8 195 B6
5 South Croydon
CR0 221 B6
Cherry Orchard Prim Sch
SE7 143 C5
Cherry Orchard Rd
Croydon CR0 205 C1
East Molesey KT8 195 C6
Keston Mark BR2 226 A6
Cherry Rd EN3 6 C5
Cherry Tree Ave UB7 82 B1
Cherry Tree Cl
11 Hackney E9 96 C6
Wembley HA0 65 A4
Cherry Tree Ct
1 Camden Town
NW1 71 C1
17 Charlton SE7 143 C6
Kingsbury NW9 45 A5
11 Peckham SE15 140 B4
3 Woodford E18 36 D1
Cherry Tree Dr
SW16 160 A1
Cherry Tree Hill N6 48 D4
Cherrytree Ho 8
W10 90 D4
Cherry Tree Ho
London SE14 141 B3
Ruislip HA4 39 C1
Twickenham TW2 152 B2
Wood Green N22 32 A3
Cherry Tree Rd
London N2 48 D5
Stratford E15 76 C3
Cherry Tree Rise IG9 37 D6
Cherry Trees Sch The 22
E3 97 C4
Cherry Tree Terr
SE1 253 B2
Cherry Tree Way HA7 25 B4
Cherry Tree Wlk
Beckenham BR3 207 B5
Coney Hall BR4 224 D4
St Luke's EC1 242 B5
Cherry Way
Upper Halliford
TW17 193 C5
West Ewell KT19 215 B2
Cherry Wlk BR2 209 A1
Cherrywood Cl
Bow E3 97 A4
Kingston u T KT2 176 C3
Cherrywood Ct 1
TW11 175 A5
Cherrywood Dr
SW15 156 D6
Cherrywood La SM4,
SW20 201 A5
Cherry Wood Way
W5 88 C2
Chertsey Ct SW14 132 D2
Chertsey Dr SM3 217 A6
Chertsey Ho
Feltham TW13 151 C1
37 Shoreditch E2 95 D4
Chertsey Rd
Ashford TW15,
TW16 171 B4
Feltham TW13, TW16 171 C6
Ilford IG1 79 B4
Leyton E11 76 B6
Lower Halliford TW17 192 C2
Shepperton TW17 192 A2
Twickenham TW2 152 B4
Chertsey St SW17 181 A5
Chervil Cl TW13 150 A1
Chervil Mews SE28 124 B5
Cherwell Ct
Teddington KT1 175 D3
West Ewell KT19 215 A4
Cherwell Ho NW8 236 D5
Cherwell Way HA4 39 A3
Cheryls Cl
SW6 135 D4 265 D2
Cheseman St SE26 162 B1
Chesfield Rd KT2 176 A3
Chesham Ave BR2,
BR5 210 D3
Chesham Cl SW1 258 A5
Chesham Cres SE20 184 C2
Chesham Ct SW18 158 B4
Chesham Flats W1 248 B6
Chesham Ho SW1 258 A5
Chesham Mews SW1 258 A6
Chesham Pl
SW1 115 A3 258 A5
Chesham Rd
Kingston u T KT1,
KT2 176 C1
Mitcham SW19 180 B4
Penge SE20 184 C2
Chesham St
Westminster
SW1 115 A3 258 A5
Willesden NW10 67 B5
Chesham Terr W13 109 B4
Cheshire Cl
Chingford E17 35 D2
Mitcham CR4, SW16 204 A6
Cheshire Gdns KT9 213 D2
Cheshire Ho SM4 201 D2
Cheshire Rd N22 32 B4
Cheshire St
E2 95 D3 243 D6
Cheshir Ho NW4 46 C5
Chesholm Rd N16 73 C5
Cheshunt Ho
Hendon NW4 46 C6
9 Kilburn NW6 91 D6
Cheshunt Rd
Belvedere DA17 125 C1
Upton E7 77 B2
Chesil Ct
17 Bethnal Green E2 96 C5
Chelsea SW3 267 B6
Chesil Ho BR7 189 B2
Chesilton Rd
SW6 135 B4 264 C2
Chesil Way UB4 83 D4
Chesley Gdns E6 100 A4
Chesney Cres CR0 224 A1
Chesney Ct W9 91 C3
Chesney Ho SE13 142 B1
Chesney St SW11 268 A1
Chesnut Gr N17 51 D6
Chesnut Rd N17 51 D6
Chessell Cl CR7 204 D5
Chessholme Ct
TW16 171 C3
Chessholme Rd
TW15 171 A4
Chessing Ct N2 48 D6
CHESSINGTON 214 A2
Chessington Ave
Church End N3 47 B6
Erith DA7 147 A5
Chessington Cl
KT19 215 A2
Chessington Com Coll
KT9 213 D1
Chessington Ct
London N3 47 B6
Pinner HA5 41 B5
Chessington Hall Gdns
KT9 213 D1
Chessington Hill Pk
KT9 214 C3
Chessington Ho 19
SW8 137 D3
Chessington Lo N3 47 B6
Chessington Mans
Leyton E10 53 C2
Leytonstone E11 54 C2
Chessington North Sta
KT9 214 A3
Chessington Par
KT9 213 D3
Chessington Pk KT9 214 C4
Chessington Rd
KT19 215 B1
Chessington South Sta
KT9 213 D1
Chessington Trade Pk
KT9 214 C4
Chessington Way
BR4 223 D6
Chesson Rd
W14 135 B6 264 D6
Chessum Ho E8 74 A2
Chesswood Way HA5 22 D1
Chestbrook Ct 12
EN1 17 C6
Chester Ave
Richmond TW10 154 B5
Twickenham TW2 151 B3
Chester Cl
Ashford TW15 171 B5
Barnes SW13 134 B2
Hayes UB8 82 D1
Knightsbridge SW1 248 C1
1 Richmond TW10 154 B5
Sutton SM1 217 C6
Chester Close N
NW1 231 D2
Chester Close S
NW1 231 D1
Chester Cres E8 73 D3
Chester Ct
2 Acton W3 88 C1
Bermondsey SE8 118 D1
4 Camberwell SE5 139 B5
Gospel Oak NW5 71 A4
Harrow HA1 42 D3
Regent's Pk NW1 231 D1
Chester Dr HA2 41 C3
Chesterfield Ct
Ashford TW15 170 A6
Kingston u T KT6 198 A4
Lewisham SE13 142 A2
Chesterfield Dr
KT10 213 A6
Chesterfield Flats
EN5 12 D6
Chesterfield Gdns
Greenwich SE10 142 B5
Harringay N4 50 D4
Mayfair W1 248 C4
Chesterfield Gr
SE22 161 D6
Chesterfield Hill
W1 115 B5 248 C4
Chesterfield Ho
Highgate N6 49 A1
Mayfair W1 248 B4
6 Streatham SW16 181 C5
Chesterfield Lo N21 16 B4
Chesterfield Mews
Ashford TW15 170 A6
Harringay N4 50 D4
Chesterfield Prim Sch
EN3 7 A6

310 Che–Chi

Chesterfield Rd
Ashford TW15 . . . . . . 170 A5
Barnet EN5 . . . . 12 D6
Chiswick W4 . . . . 133 A6
Enfield EN3 . . . . 7 A6
Finchley N3 . . . . 29 C4
Leyton E10 . . . . 54 A3
West Ewell KT19 . . . . 215 B1
Chesterfield St W1 . . 248 C4
Chesterfield Way
Hayes UB3 . . . . 106 A4
Peckham SE15 . . . . . . 140 C5
Chesterford Gdns
NW3 . . . . 69 D4
Chesterford Ho 4
SE18 . . . . 143 D5
Chesterford Rd E12 . . . 78 B3
Chester Gate NW1 . . 231 D1
Chester Gdns
Ealing W13 . . . . 87 B1
Enfield EN3 . . . . 18 B5
Morden SM4 . . . . 202 A3
Chester Ho
5 Barnet EN5 . . . . 1 D1
Dartmouth Pk N19 . . . . . 71 B6
1 Deptford SE8 . . . . . 141 B6
Kingston u T KT1 . . . . 176 D1
Chesterman Ct W4 . . . 133 C5
Chester Mews
Belgravia SW1 . . . . . . 258 C6
Walthamstow E17 . . . . . 35 C1
Chester Pl NW1 . . . . . 231 C2
Chester Rd
Avery Hill DA15 . . . . . 167 C6
Dartmouth Pk N19 . . . . . 71 B6
Edmonton N9 . . . . 18 B3
Hounslow TW4 . . . . . . 128 B2
Ilford IG3 . . . . 57 D2
Newham E16 . . . . 98 C3
Regent's Pk
NW1 . . . . 93 B4 231 C2
Tottenham N17 . . . . 51 C6
Upton E7 . . . . 77 D1
Walthamstow E17 . . . . . 52 D4
Wanstead E11 . . . . 55 B3
Wimbledon SW19,
SW20 . . . . 178 C4
Chester Row
SW1 . . . . 115 A2 258 B4
Chester Sq
SW1 . . . . 115 B2 258 C4
Chester Sq Mews
SW1 . . . . 258 C5
Chester St
Bethnal Green E2 . . . . . 96 A3
Westminster
SW1 . . . . . . 115 A3 258 B6
Chesters The KT3 . . . . 177 C2
Chester Terr
NW1 . . . . 93 B4 231 C2
Chesterton Cl
Greenford UB6 . . . . 85 D5
Wandsworth SW18 . . . 157 C6
Chesterton Ct W3 . . . 110 D3
Chesterton Dr TW19 . 148 B3
Chesterton Ho
20 Battersea SW11 . . . 136 B2
3 Kensal Town W10 . . . 91 A2
3 Sutton SM1 . . . . . . 218 A4
Chesterton Prim Sch
SW11 . . . . . . 137 A4 268 A1
Chesterton Rd
Kensal Town W10 . . . . . 91 A2
Newham E13 . . . . 99 A4
Chesterton Sq W8 . . 255 A3
Chesterton Terr
6 Kingston u T
KT1 . . . . 176 C1
Newham E13 . . . . 99 A4
Chester Way
SE11 . . . . 116 C2 261 B3
Chesthunte Rd N17 . . . . 33 A2
Chestnut Alley SW6 . 264 D5
Chestnut Ave
Brentford TW8 . . . . . . 109 D2
Buckhurst Hill IG9 . . . . . 21 D1
Coney Hall BR4 . . . . . 224 C4
Edgware HA8 . . . . 26 B4
Forest Gate E7 . . . . 77 B4
Hampton TW12 . . . . . 173 C3
Hornsey N8 . . . . 50 A4
Kingston u T KT8,
KT11 . . . . 174 D2
Chestnut Ave *continued*
11 Mortlake SW14 . . . . 133 B2
Thames Ditton KT10 . . . 196 B1
Wembley HA0 . . . . 65 B3
Worcester Pk KT19 . . 215 C4
Yiewsley UB7 . . . . 104 B6
Chestnut Ave N E17 . . . 54 B5
Chestnut Ave S E17 . . . 54 B4
Chestnut Cl
Buckhurst Hill IG9 . . . . . 21 D2
Carshalton SM5 . . . . . 202 D1
Catford SE6 . . . . 186 A6
Chattern Hill TW15 . . . 170 D6
Harlington UB7 . . . . . 126 D5
Hayes UB3 . . . . 105 C6
New Cross Gate SE14 . 141 B4
Sidcup DA15 . . . . 168 A2
Southgate N14 . . . . 15 D6
1 Stoke Newington
N16 . . . . 73 B6
Sunbury Comm TW16 . 171 D4
West Norwood SW16 . 182 C6
Chestnut Ct
Beckenham BR3 . . . . . 185 C3
7 Cheam SM2 . . . . . . 217 C2
5 Croydon CR0 . . . . . 221 A4
Feltham TW13 . . . . . . 172 D5
Harrow HA1 . . . . 42 C2
Hornsey N8 . . . . 50 A4
Hounslow TW3 . . . . . . 129 C2
Kingston u T KT3 . . . . 199 C6
Surbiton KT6 . . . . 198 A2
Wembley HA0 . . . . 65 B3
West Brompton SW6 . 264 D6
Chestnut Dr
Bexley DA7 . . . . 147 A2
Harrow HA3 . . . . 24 D2
Pinner HA5 . . . . 41 A3
Wanstead E11 . . . . 55 A3
Chestnut Gr
Cockfosters EN4 . . . . . . 14 D6
Ealing W5 . . . . 109 D3
Isleworth TW7 . . . . . . 131 A1
Kingston u T KT3 . . . . 199 B6
Mitcham CR4 . . . . 203 D5
Penge SE20 . . . . 184 C3
South Croydon CR2 . . . 222 B1
Upper Tooting SW12 . 159 A3
Wembley HA0 . . . . 65 B3
Chestnut Grove Sch 6
SW12 . . . . 159 A3
Chestnut Ho
1 Acton W4 . . . . 111 C2
Brockley SE4 . . . . 141 B2
7 Maitland Pk NW3 . . . 70 D2
West Norwood SE27 . . 161 A1
Chestnut La N20 . . . . . . 13 A3
Chestnut Pl SE19 . . . . 183 D6
Chestnut Rd
Ashford TW15 . . . . . . 170 D6
Kingston u T KT2 . . . . 176 A3
Twickenham TW2 . . . . 152 C2
West Barnes SW20 . . . 178 D1
West Norwood SE21,
SE27 . . . . 161 A1
Chestnut Rise SE18 . . 123 C1
Chestnut Row N3 . . . . . 29 C3
Chestnuts Ct 3 E17 . . . 54 A6
Chestnuts Prim Sch
N15 . . . . 51 A4
Chestnuts Royal
BR7 . . . . 189 B3
Chestnuts The
Chislehurst BR7 . . . . . . 189 B3
Colindale NW9 . . . . 45 C6
East Finchley N2 . . . . . . 48 D4
7 Erith DA17 . . . . 125 B1
1 Highbury N5 . . . . 72 D4
Penge BR3 . . . . 206 D6
8 Pinner HA5 . . . . 23 B3
Shooters Hill SE18 . . . 144 D4
Uxbridge UB10 . . . . 60 A1
Walton-on-T KT12 . . . . 194 B1
Chestnut Way TW13 . . 150 B1
Chestnut Wlk
Upper Halliford
TW17 . . . . 193 C5
Woodford IG8 . . . . 37 A5
Cheston Ave CR0 . . . . 207 B1
Chestwood Gr UB10 . . . 60 B1
Chettle Cl SE1 . . . . . . 262 C6
Chettle Ct N8 . . . . 50 C3
Chetwode Ho NW8 . . 237 A6
Chetwode Rd SW17 . . 158 D1
Chetwood Wlk 13
E6 . . . . 100 A2
Chetwynd Ave EN4 . . . . 14 D3
Chetwynd Dr UB10 . . . . 82 B5
Chetwynd Rd NW5 . . . . 71 B5
Cheval Ct SW15 . . . . . . 134 B1
Chevalier Cl HA7 . . . . . . 26 A6
Cheval Pl
SW7 . . . . 114 C3 257 B6
Cheval St E14 . . . . 119 C3
Chevender BR7 . . . . . . 188 D3
Cheveney Wlk 2
BR2 . . . . 209 A6
Chevening Ho BR5 . . . 190 A2
Chevening Rd
Cubitt Town SE10 . . . . 120 D1
Kilburn NW6 . . . . 91 A6
South Norwood SE19 . . 183 B4
Chevenings The
DA14 . . . . 168 C1
Cheverell Ho 25 E2 . . . . 96 A5
Cheverton Rd N19 . . . . . 49 D1
Chevet St E9 . . . . 75 A3
Chevington NW2 . . . . . . 69 B2
Cheviot 4 N17 . . . . 34 B3
Cheviot Cl
Bushey WD23 . . . . 8 A5
Enfield EN1 . . . . 5 B3
Harlington UB3 . . . . . . 127 B5
Cheviot Ct
16 Deptford SE14 . . . 140 C5
Enfield EN2 . . . . 5 B3
Southall UB2 . . . . 107 D2
Cheviot Gate NW2 . . . . 69 A6
Cheviot Gdns
Cricklewood NW2 . . . . . 69 A6
West Norwood SE27 . 182 D6
Cheviot Ho N16 . . . . . . 51 D1
Cheviot Rd SE27 . . . . . 182 D5
Cheviots Hostel EN1 . . . 5 B3
Cheviot Way IG2 . . . . . . 57 C5
Chevron Cl E16 . . . . 99 A1
Chevy Rd UB2 . . . . 108 A4
Chewton Rd E17 . . . . . . 53 A5
Cheylesmore Ho
SW1 . . . . 258 C2
Cheyne Ave
Snaresbrook E18 . . . . . . 54 D6
Twickenham TW2 . . . . 151 B3
Cheyne Cl
6 Hendon NW4 . . . . . . 46 B4
Keston Mark BR2 . . . . 226 A5
Cheyne Ct
Chelsea SW3 . . . . 267 C6
1 Croydon CR0 . . . . . 221 D6
Ruislip HA4 . . . . 39 C1
4 Wallington SM6 . . . 219 B2
Cheyne Gdns
SW3 . . . . 136 C6 267 B5
Cheyne Hill KT5 . . . . . 198 B5
Cheyne Mews
SW3 . . . . 136 C6 267 B5
Cheyne Park Dr BR4 . 224 A5
Cheyne Path W7 . . . . . . 86 D1
Cheyne Pl SW3 . . . . . 267 C6
Cheyne Rd TW15 . . . . 171 B4
Cheyne Row
SW3 . . . . 136 C6 267 A5
Cheyne Wlk
Chelsea
SW10 . . . . . . 136 B5 266 C4
Croydon CR0 . . . . 222 A6
Hendon NW4 . . . . 46 C3
Southgate N21 . . . . 16 D6
Cheyney Ho 2 E9 . . . . . 74 D2
Cheyneys Ave HA8 . . . . 25 D4
Chichele Gdns CR0 . . 221 C4
Chichele Ho HA8 . . . . . 26 B6
Chichele Mans NW2 . . . 68 D3
Chichele Rd NW2 . . . . . 68 D3
Chicheley Gdns HA3 . . . 24 A3
Chicheley Rd HA3 . . . . . 24 A3
Chicheley St SE1 . . . . 250 D2
Chichester Ave HA4 . . . 61 B6
Chichester Cl
Hampton TW12 . . . . . 173 B4
Kidbrooke SE3 . . . . . . 143 C4
Newham E6 . . . . 100 A1
Chichester Ct
Barnet EN4 . . . . 2 B1
2 Camden Town NW1 . . 71 C1
Edgware HA8 . . . . 26 C4
Harrow HA2 . . . . 41 B1
Northolt UB5 . . . . 85 A6
3 Sidcup DA5 . . . . . . 169 C4
Stanmore HA7 . . . . 44 A6
Stanwell TW19 . . . . . . 148 A3
Chichester Gdns IG1 . . 56 B2
Chichester Ho
Kilburn NW6 . . . . 91 C5
2 Kingston u T KT2 . . 176 D2
Chichester Mews
SE27 . . . . 182 C6
Chichester Rd
Bayswater W2 . . . . 91 D2
Edmonton N9 . . . . 18 A3
Kilburn NW6 . . . . 91 C5
Leyton E11 . . . . 76 C5
South Croydon CR0 . . 221 C5
Chichester Rents
WC2 . . . . 241 A2
Chichester St
SW1 . . . . 115 C1 259 B1
Chichester Way
Cubitt Town E14 . . . . . 120 B2
Feltham TW14 . . . . . . 150 C4
Chicksand Ho 14 E1 . . . 96 A2
Chicksand St
E1 . . . . 95 D2 243 D3
Chicksand Street E1 . . 96 A2
Chiddingfold N12 . . . . . 13 C1
Chiddingstone SE13 . 164 A6
Chiddingstone Ave
DA7 . . . . 147 B5
Chiddingstone St
SW6 . . . . 135 C3
Chieveley Par DA7 . . 147 D2
Chieveley Rd DA7 . . . 147 D1
Chignell Pl 7 W13 . . . 109 A5
Chigwell Ct 1 E9 . . . . . 75 A2
Chigwell Hill E1 . . . . . 118 B6
Chigwell Hurst Ct
HA5 . . . . 40 D6
Chigwell Rd
Wanstead E18 . . . . 55 B6
Woodford IG8 . . . . 37 D3
Chiham Ho 5 SE15 . . 140 C6
Chilchester Ct 3
BR3 . . . . 207 D6
Chilcombe Ho 6
SW15 . . . . 156 A4
Chilcot Cl 13 E14 . . . . . 97 D1
Chilcott Cl HA0 . . . . 65 C4
Child Ct E11 . . . . 54 B2
Childebert Rd SW17 . 159 B2
Childeric Prim Sch
SE14 . . . . 141 A5
Childeric Rd SE14 . . . 141 A5
Childerley St
SW6 . . . . 135 A4 264 A2
Childerly KT1 . . . . 198 C6
Childers St SE8 . . . . . 141 B6
Chld La SE10 . . . . 120 D3
Childrens House Upper
Sch 15 N1 . . . . 73 C2
Childs Ct UB3 . . . . 106 A6
CHILD'S HILL 69 C6
Child's Hill Sch NW2 . . 69 A5
Childs La 11 SE19 . . . 183 C4
Child's Mews SW5 . . 255 B3
Child's Pl SW5 . . . . . . 255 B3
Child's St SW5 . . . . . . 255 B3
Childs Way NW11 . . . . . 47 B4
Child's Wlk SW5 . . . . 255 B3
Chilham Cl
Old Bexley DA5 . . . . . 169 B4
Wembley UB6 . . . . 87 A5
Chilham Ct 13 SW9 . . 138 C2
Chilham Ho SE1 . . . . . 262 D6
Chilham Rd SE9 . . . . . 188 A6
Chilham Way BR2 . . . . 209 A2
Chillerton Rd SW17 . . 181 B5
Chillingford Ho
SW17 . . . . 180 A6
Chillington Dr SW11 . 136 B1
Chillingworth Gdns
TW1 . . . . 152 D1
Chillingworth Rd N7 . . 72 C3
Chilmark Gdns KT3 . . 200 A3
Chilmark Rd SW16 . . 181 D2
Chiltern Ave
Bushey WD23 . . . . 8 A5
Twickenham TW2 . . . . 151 C3
Chiltern Cl Bus WD23 . . 8 A5
Ickenham UB10 . . . . 60 C6
North Cheam KT4 . . . . 216 C6
South Croydon CR0 . . 221 C5
Chiltern Ct
15 Deptford SE14 . . . 140 C5
6 East Barnet N20 . . . . 14 C2
11 Eltham SE9 . . . . . . 166 C5
Harrow HA1 . . . . 42 B4
Hillingdon UB8 . . . . 82 D3
Marylebone NW1 . . . . 237 D5
Chiltern Ct *continued*
Muswell Hill N10 . . . . . . 31 A1
1 New Barnet EN5 . . . . 14 A6
Chiltern Dene EN2 . . . . . 4 B1
Chiltern Dr KT5 . . . . . 198 D4
Chiltern Gdns
Beckenham BR2 . . . . . 208 D5
Cricklewood NW2 . . . . . 68 D5
Chiltern Ho
Camberwell SE17 . . . . 139 B6
Ealing W5 . . . . 88 A2
5 Edmonton N9 . . . . . . 18 A1
Harrow HA1 . . . . 42 C1
4 Kensal Town W10 . . . 91 A2
5 Stamford Hill N16 . . . 51 D1
Chiltern Pl 18 E5 . . . . . 74 B6
Chiltern Rd Bow E3 . . . . 97 C3
Ilford IG2 . . . . 57 C4
Pinner HA5 . . . . 40 C4
Chiltern St
W1 . . . . 93 A2 238 A4
Chilterns The BR1 . . . . 187 B1
Chiltern Way IG8 . . . . . 21 A1
Chilthorne Cl SE6 . . . . 163 B4
Chilton Ave W5 . . . . . . 109 D2
Chilton Gr SE8 . . . . . . 119 A2
Chiltonian Ind Est
SE12 . . . . 164 D5
Chilton Rd
Edgware HA8 . . . . 26 C4
Richmond TW9 . . . . . . 132 C2
Chilton St E2 . . 95 D3 243 D6
Chiltons The 1 E18 . . . . 37 A1
Chilvers Cl TW2 . . . . . 152 C2
Chilver St SE10 . . . . . 120 D1
Chilwell Gdns WD19 . . 22 C6
Chilworth Ct 8
SW19 . . . . 156 D3
Chilworth Gdns
SM1 . . . . 218 A5
Chilworth Mews
W2 . . . . 92 B1 236 C1
Chilworth St
W2 . . . . 92 A1 236 B1
Chimes Ave N13 . . . . . . 32 D6
Chimes Sh Ctr The
UB8 . . . . 60 A1
Chimney Ct 23 E1 . . . . 118 B5
Chimneys Ct 2
SW19 . . . . 178 C3
China Ct 1 E1 . . . . 118 B5
China Hall Mews 16
SE16 . . . . 118 C3
China Mews 17 SW2 . 160 B4
Chinbrook Cres
SE12 . . . . 165 B1
Chinbrook Rd SE12 . . 165 B1
Chinchilla Dr TW4 . . . 128 C3
Chindit Ho 11 N16 . . . . 73 B4
Chine The London N10 . . 49 C5
Southgate N21 . . . . 16 D6
Wembley HA0 . . . . 65 B3
Ching Ct Chingford E4 . . 20 C1
St Giles WC2 . . . . 240 A1
Chingdale Rd E4 . . . . . . 20 C1
CHINGFORD 20 C3
Chingford Ave E4 . . . . . 19 D2
Chingford CE Inf Sch 10
E4 . . . . 20 B3
Chingford CE Jun Sch 9
E4 . . . . 20 B3
Chingford Foundation
Sch E4 . . . . 19 D3
CHINGFORD GREEN . . 20 A4
Chingford Hall Com Prim
Sch E4 . . . . 35 B4
CHINGFORD HATCH . . 36 B6
Chingford Ind Ctr E4 . . 35 A5
Chingford La IG8 . . . . . 36 D5
Chingford Mount Rd
E4 . . . . 35 C5
Chingford Rd
Highams Pk E4 . . . . 35 C3
Walthamstow E17 . . . . . 35 D1
Chingford Sta E4 . . . . . 20 C4
Chingley Cl BR1 . . . . . 186 C4
Ching Way E4 . . . . 35 B4
Chinnery Cl EN1 . . . . 5 D4
Chinnocks Wharf
E14 . . . . 119 A6
Chinnor Cres UB6 . . . . . 86 A5
Chipka St E14 . . . . 120 A4
Chipley St SE14 . . . . . 141 A6
Chipmunk Gr UB5 . . . . . 85 A4
Chippendale Ho
SW1 . . . . 258 D1

Chippendale St E5....74 D5
Chippenham 4 KT1 .176 B1
Chippenham Ave
HA9..................66 D3
Chippenham CI HA5 .39 C5
Chippenham Gdns
NW6.................91 C4
Chippenham Mews
W9.................91 C3
Chippenham Rd W9..91 C3
Chipperfield Rd BR5 .190 A1
CHIPPING BARNET...1 B1
Chipping-CI EN5.......1 A2
Chip St SW4........137 D1
Chipstead Ave CR7..204 D5
Chipstead CI SE19 .183 D3
Chipstead Gdns NW2 .68 B6
Chipstead Ho 4
SW2................160 A3
Chipstead St SW6..135 C3
Chirk CI UB4..........85 A3
Chirk Ct SE4........141 B3

Chisenhale Prim Sch
E3....................97 A5
Chisenhale Rd E3....97 A5
Chisholm Ct 1 W6..112 A1
Chisholm Rd
Croydon CR0......221 C6
13 Richmond TW10..154 B5
Chisledon Wlk E9....75 B2
CHISLEHURST.......189 C3
Chislehurst Ave N12 .30 A3
Chislehurst CE Prim Sch
BR7................189 A3
Chislehurst High St
BR7................188 D4
Chislehurst Rd
Bromley BR1, BR7..188 A4
Broom Hill BR6......211 D2
Orpington BR5, BR6,
BR7................211 D2
Richmond TW10....154 A6
Sidcup DA14.......190 A5
Chislehurst & Sidcup
Gram Sch DA15 ..168 B2
Chislehurst Sta BR7.188 C1
CHISLEHURST
WEST.............188 C1
Chislet 1 NW5.......71 A2
Chislet Rd 3 BR5...185 C3
Chisley Rd 1 N15....51 C3
Chiswell Sq SE3....143 B3
Chiswell St
Barbican EC1...95 B2 242 C4
Camberwell SE5....139 B5
CHISWICK...........111 D1
Chiswick & Bedford Park
Prep Sch 13 W4....111 C1
Chiswick CI CR0....220 B5
Chiswick Common Rd
W4.................111 B2
Chiswick Com Sch
W4.................133 B5
Chiswick Ct HA5.....41 B6
Chiswick Green Studios
1 W4.............111 B2
Chiswick High Rd
W4.................111 C2
Chiswick High Road
(North Circular Rd)
W4.................110 C1
Chiswick Ho *W4..133 B6
Chiswick La W4......133 C1
Chiswick La S W4..133 C1
Chiswick Mall W4...111 D1
Chiswick Park Sta
W4.................111 A2
Chiswick Pier W4...133 D5
Chiswick Pk W4.....110 D2
Chiswick Plaza W4..133 A6
Chiswick Quay W4...133 A3
Chiswick Rd
Acton W4..........111 A2
Edmonton N9.......18 A2
Chiswick Rdbt W4 ..110 C1
Chiswick Sq W4....133 C1
Chiswick Sta W4....133 C5
Chiswick Staithe
W4.................133 A4
Chiswick Terr 6
W4.................111 A2
Chiswick Village
W4.................133 D2
Chiswick Wharf W4. 133 D6
Chitterfield Gate
UB7................126 C5

Chitty's La RM8......80 D6
Chitty St W1.....93 C2 239 B4
Chivalry Rd SW11..158 C6
Chivelston 27 SW19. 156 D3
Chivenor Gr KT2....175 D5
Chivers Rd E4........35 C6
Chivins Ct N3........29 C3
Choats Manor Way
RM9................103 B4
Choats Rd IG11.....102 D4
Chobham Gdns
SW19..............156 D2
Chobham Rd E15.....51 C1
Cholmeley Cres N6...49 B2
Cholmeley Ct N12....30 A6
Cholmeley Lo N6.....49 B1
Cholmeley Pk N6.....49 B2
Cholmeley Rd N6.....49 B2
Cholmley Gdns NW6..69 C3
Cholmley Rd KT7...197 B3
Cholmondeley Wlk
TW9................153 C6
Chopin's Ct 13 E1..118 B5
Chopwell CI E15.....76 B1
Chorleywood Cres
BR5................190 A1
Choument Gr SE15..140 A3
Choument Mews
SE15...............140 A3
Choumert Rd SE15..139 D3
Choumert Sq 4
SE15...............140 A3
Chow Sq 8 E8......73 D3
Chrisp Ho SE10....142 C6
Chrisp St E14........97 D1
Christabel CI TW7..130 C2
Christ Church TW9..132 A2
Christ Church Ave
Brondesbury NW6...69 A1
Finchley N12........30 A4
Harrow HA1.........42 D5
Harrow HA3.........43 A5
5 Teddington TW11.175 A5
Wembley HA0.......66 A2
Christ Church Bentinck
CE Prim Sch
NW1..........92 C2 237 B4
Christ Church
Brondesbury CE Jun &
Inf Sch NW6......69 B1
Christ Church CE Jun
Sch W5.............109 D6
Christ Church CE Prim
Sch SW3...136 D3 267 C6
Christ Church CE Prim
Sch
Battersea SW11 ...136 C2
18 Camberwell SW9..138 C4
Cubitt Town SE10...120 C1
6 Forest Hill SE23 .162 D2
Shooters Hill SE18..144 C4
Surbiton KT5.......198 C3
Christ Church CE Prim
Sch, Hampstead
NW3...............70 B5
Christchurch CE Sch
E1..........95 D3 243 D1
Christchurch Ct
Enfield EN2..........5 A3
Finchley N12........30 B3
Mitcham SW19....180 B3
Christ Church Ct UB4..84 C3
Christ Church Ct
1 Brondesbury Pk
NW6................69 A1
Harlesden NW10....89 C6
Christchurch Gdns
HA3.................43 A5
Christ Church Gn HA0 .66 A2
Christchurch Hill
NW3.................70 B4
Christ Church Ho 2
SW2................160 A3
Christ Church La EN5..1 C3
Christ Church Lo EN5 .2 D1
Christ Church New
Malden CE Prim Sch
KT3................199 C6
Christchurch Pas
NW3.................70 A5
Christ Church Pk
SM2................218 A1
Christchurch Prim Sch
IG1..................57 A1

Christ Church Prim Sch
KT3................199 C6
Christchurch Rd
Ilford IG1............57 A1
Mitcham SW19....180 B3
Mortlake SW14.....155 A6
Sidcup DA15.......167 D1
Streatham SW2....160 C5
Christ Church Rd
1 Beckenham BR3..185 C1
Hornsey N8.........50 A3
Surbiton KT5.......198 B3
Christ Church Sch
NW1.........93 B4 231 D2
Christchurch Sq 2
E9....................96 C6
Christchurch St
SW3.........136 D3 267 C6
Christ Church Streatham
CE Prim Sch 8
SW2................160 B3
Christchurch Terr
SW3................267 C6
Christchurch Way
SE10...............120 C2
Christian Ct SE16...119 B5
Christian Fields
SW16..............182 B3
Christian St E1......96 A1
Christie Ct
Maitland Pk NW3....70 C3
2 Upper Holloway
N19.................72 A6
Christie Dr SE25...206 A4
Christie Gdns RM6..58 B2
Christie Ho
Bexley DA6.........169 D2
2 Cubitt Town SE10 .120 D1
Harrow HA1.........42 D6
4 West Wickham
BR4................207 D1
Christie Rd E9.......75 A2
Christina Sq N1......50 D1
Christina St EC2...243 A6
Christine Worsley CI
N21.................17 A1
Christopher Ave W7 .109 A3
Christopher Boone's
Almshouses 3
SE13.............142 B1
Christopher CI
Bexley DA15.......167 B8
Rotherhithe SE16...118 D4
Christopher Ct
Ashford TW15.....170 A5
12 Barnet EN5.......2 D2
6 Croydon CR0...206 A1
Hendon NW4........28 C1
23 Sutton SM5....218 A4
Sutton SM1.......217 C3
Christopher France Ho
1 E1.................97 A4
Christopher Gdns
RM9.................80 D3
Christopher Hatton Prim
Sch EC1...94 C3 241 C6
Christopher Lo 2 N6 .49 C2
Christopher PI NW1 .232 D1
Christopher Rd UB2 .106 B2
Christopher St
EC2.........95 B3 242 D5
Christ's Coll Finchley
NW11................47 C6
Christ's Sch TW10 .. 154 C6
Christ the King RC Prim
Sch N4..............72 B6
Christ the King Sixth
Form Coll SE13 ..142 B2
Christ the Redeemer
Bible Coll 11 E15...76 C2
Chryssell Rd SW9..138 C4
Chubworthy St 1
SE14................141 A6
13 Chudleigh 11 DA14..190 B6
Chudleigh Cres IG3..79 C4
Chudleigh Gdns
SM1................218 A5
Chudleigh Rd
Hampstead NW6....68 D1
London SE4........163 C6
Twickenham TW2...152 D4
Chudleigh St E1.....96 D1
Chudleigh Way HA4..40 A1
Chulsa Rd SE26....184 B5
Chumleigh Gdns
SE5................139 C6

Chumleigh St SE5 .139 C6
Chumleigh Wlk KT5 .198 B5
Church App SE21...161 B1
Church Ave
Beckenham BR3....185 C2
Camden Town NW1...71 B2
Chingford E4........36 B4
Finchley N2.........30 B2
Mortlake SW14.....133 B2
Northolt UB5........63 B1
Pinner HA5..........41 B3
Ruislip HA4..........39 B1
Sidcup DA14.......190 B5
Southall UB2.......107 A3
Wanstead E12.......77 D5
Churchbank E17.....53 C5
Churchbury CI EN1...5 C3
Churchbury La EN1...5 C3
Churchbury Rd
Eltham SE9.........165 D4
Enfield EN1...........5 C3
Church CI
Edgware HA8........27 A5
Friern Barnet N20...14 C1
Hayes UB4...........84 B3
Hounslow TW4.....129 B3
Kensington W8.....245 C2
West Drayton UB7..104 A3
Church Cres
Church End N3......29 B2
Cranley Gdns N10...49 B5
Friern Barnet N20 ..14 C1
Hackney E9.........74 D1
Churchcroft CI
SW12..............159 A4
Church Ct
East Finchley N2....48 B6
Forest Hill SE26....185 A5
Harmondsworth UB7 .126 C6
Holborn EC4......241 B1
16 Richmond TW10 ..153 D6
Rotherhithe SE16...119 B4
Ruislip HA4..........39 B1
5 West Norwood
SE27................182 D6
Churchdale Ct 1
W4.................110 D1
Churchdown BR1..186 C6
Church Dr
Coney Hall BR4....224 C5
Harrow HA2.........41 C3
Welsh Harp NW9...45 A1
Church End La E11 .80 C2
12 Barnet EN5.......2 C1
13 Croydon SW9...138 C4
CHURCH END N3....29 C1
NW10................67 D3
Church End E17....241 C1
Church Entry EC4..241 D1
Church Estate
Almshouses 8
TW9...............132 B2
Church Farmhouse
Mus * NW4..........46 B6
Church Farm La
SM3................217 A2
Church Farm Swimming
Pool EN4...........14 D4
Churchfield Ave N12 .30 A4
Churchfield CI
Harrow HA2.........41 C3
Hayes UB3.........105 D6
Churchfield Ho W2 .236 C5
Churchfield Mans
SW6................135 A3
Churchfield PI
TW17...............192 D2
Churchfield Prim Sch
N9...................17 D3
Churchfield Rd
Acton W3..........111 A3
Ealing W13.........109 C5
Hanwell W7........108 C4
Walton-on-T KT12 .194 A1
Welling DA16.......146 A2
Churchfields
East Molesey KT8 ..195 C4
Greenwich SE10 ..142 A6
Woodford IG8.......37 C3
Churchfields Ave
TW13...............151 C1
Churchfields Jun & Inf
Sch E18............36 D1
Churchfields Prim Sch
BR3................206 D6
Churchfields Rd
BR3................185 A1

Churchill Way N12 .30 A4
Church Garth 4 N19..71 D6
Church Gate SW6 ..135 A2
Church Gdns
Ealing W5...........109 D4
Wembley HA0.......65 A4
Church Gn
Brixton SW9.......138 C3
Hayes UB3...........83 D1
Church Gr
London SE13.......163 D6
Teddington KT1 ...175 C1
Church Hill
Harrow HA1.........42 C1
Southgate N21......16 C4
Wallington SM5....218 D3
Walthamstow E17...53 D5
Wimbledon SW19 ..179 B5
Woolwich SE18....122 B3
Churchhill Gardens Prim
Sch SW1....1 C1 259 B1
Church Hill Prim Sch
EN4.................14 D4
Church Hill Rd
Cheam SM1, SM3...217 A4
East Barnet EN4....14 D4
Kingston u T KT6 ..198 A4
Walthamstow E17...53 D5
Church Hill Wood
BR5................211 D6
Church Ho EC1....241 D6
Church Hyde SE18 .145 C6
Churchill Ave
Harrow HA3.........43 B3
Hillingdon UB10....82 D4
Churchill CI
East Bedfont TW14 .149 D3
Hillingdon UB10....82 D4
Churchill Ct Ealing W5 .88 B3
Edmonton N9........17 B3
4 Farnborough BR6. 227 A3
Finsbury Pk N4.....50 C2
Harrow HA2.........41 D4
7 Ilford IG1..........78 D5
Northolt UB5........63 C3
Peckham SE15.....140 A3
Willesden NW2......68 B3
9 Woolwich SE18 .122 B2
Churchill Gdns
Acton W3............88 C1
Pimlico SW1..137 C6 269 A6
Churchill Gdns Rd
SW1..........137 C6 269 A6
Churchill Ho
Brentford TW8.....109 C1
Mitcham CR4.......180 D2
Churchill Lo
Streatham SW16...181 D5
Woodford IG8........36 D4
Churchill Lodge IG6..57 A5
Churchill Mews IG8..36 D4
Churchill PI
Canary Wharf E14 ..119 D5
Harrow HA1.........42 C5
Churchill Rd
Edgware HA8........26 C4
Gospel Oak NW5....71 B4
Newham E16.........99 C1
South Croydon CR2 .221 A1
Willesden NW2......68 B2
Churchill Terr E4.....19 C1
Church Way
Ashford TW17.....172 A4
Bromley BR1.......187 A1
Churchill Wlk E9....74 C3
Church La
Chessington KT9 ..214 B2
Chislehurst BR7...189 A2
Dagenham RM10...81 D1
Ealing W5...........109 D4
East Finchley N2....48 B6
Edmonton N9.......18 A2
Enfield EN1..........5 B2
Harrow HA3.........24 D2
Hornsey N8...........50 B5
Keston Mark BR2..210 A1
Kingsbury NW9....45 B2
Leytonstone E11....54 C1
Merton SW19......179 C2
Pinner HA5..........41 B6
Teddington TW11...174 D5
Thames Ditton KT7..197 A3
Tottenham N17......33 C2

Church La continued
Twickenham TW1.... 153 A3
Upper Tooting SW17 . 181 A5
Wallington SM6 .... 219 D5
Walthamstow E17 .. 123 D5
Churchlands Way 3
KT4 .... 216 D6
Churchley Rd SE26... 184 B6
Churchley Villas
SE26 .... 184 B6
Church Lo UB5 ...... 63 B1
Church Manor Way SE18,
SE2 .... 124 A2
Church Mdw KT6 .. 213 C6
Church Mead SE5 .. 139 A5
Churchmead Ci EN4 . 14 C5
Churchmead Rd
NW10 .... 68 A2
Churchmore Rd
SW16 .... 181 D2
Church Mount N2 ... 48 B4
Church Paddock Ct
SM6 .... 219 C5
Church Par
3 Ashford TW15 ... 170 B6
Harrow HA3 .... 42 C6
Church Path
Merton SW19 ...... 179 C1
Mitcham CR4 ...... 202 D2
South Acton W4 ... 111 A3
Walthamstow E17 .. 53 D5
Wanstead E11 ..... 55 A4
Church Pl Ealing W5 . 109 D4
Mitcham CR4 ...... 202 C6
St James SW1 ..... 249 B5
Uxbridge UB10 .... 61 A5

Church Rd Acton W3 . 110 B6
Ashford TW15 ..... 170 B6
Barking IG11 ...... 79 A2
Barnes SW13 ...... 134 A4
Beckenham BR2 ... 208 C6
Bexleyheath DA7 .. 147 B2
Buckhurst Hill IG9 .. 21 B3
3 Canonbury N1 .... 15 A2
Cheam SM3 .... 217 A2
Claygate KT10 .... 212 D2
Cranford TW5 ..... 128 B6
Croydon CR0 ...... 221 A5
Ealing W7 .... 108 C6
East Molesey KT8 .. 196 A6
Enfield EN3 .... 18 C6
Farnborough BR6 .. 227 A3
Feltham TW13 ..... 172 D5
Hayes UB3 .... 105 D6
Hendon NW4 ...... 46 C5
Heston TW5 .... 129 C5
Higham Hill E17 ... 35 A1
Highgate N6 ...... 49 A3
Hillingdon UB8 .... 82 A3
Hounslow TW7 .... 130 C5
Ilford IG2 .... 57 C3
Keston BR2 .... 225 D1
Kingston u T KT1 .. 176 B1
Leyton E10 .... 75 C6
Long Ditton KT6 ... 197 C1
Lower Halliford TW17 192 D2
Manor Pk E12 ..... 78 A3
Mitcham CR4 ...... 202 D6
Mitcham CR4, SW19 . 180 B1
New Malden KT4 ... 199 C1
Northolt UB5 ...... 85 A6
Richmond TW10,
Richmond TW10,
TW9 .... 154 A6
Sidcup DA14 ...... 190 A6
Southall UB2 ...... 107 B3
South Norwood SE19. 183 C3
Stanmore HA7 .... 25 B5
Teddington TW11 .. 174 D5
Tottenham N17 .... 33 D3
Wallington SM6 ... 219 D5
Welling DA16 ..... 146 B3
West Drayton UB7 .. 104 A3
West Ewell KT19 .. 215 B1
Willesden NW10 ... 67 C1
Church Rd N N2 .... 30 B2
Church Rd S N2 .... 30 B2
Church Rise
Chessington KT9 .. 214 B2
Forest Hill SE23 ... 162 D2

Church Row
Chislehurst BR7 .... 189 A2
Hampstead NW3 .... 70 A4
Church Row Mews
BR7 .... 189 A3
Church Sq TW17 .... 192 D2
Church St
Chiswick W4 ...... 133 D6
Croydon CR0 ...... 220 D6
Croydon CR0 ...... 221 A6
Dagenham RM10 ... 81 D2
Edmonton N9 ...... 17 C2
Enfield EN2 .... 5 B2
Hampton TW12 .... 174 A2
Isleworth TW7 .... 131 B3
Kingston u T KT1 .. 175 D1
Lisson Gr NW8 9 2 C3 237 A5
Newham E16 ...... 122 D5
Sunbury TW16 .... 194 B6
Twickenham TW1 .. 153 A3
West Ham E15 .... 98 D6
Church Stretton Rd
TW3 .... 152 A6
Church Studios 16
NW1 .... 71 D2
Church Terr
Hendon NW4 ...... 46 B6
Lewisham SE13 ... 142 C2
2 Richmond TW10 . 153 D6
Church Vale
Forest Hill SE23 .. 162 D2
Muswell Hill N2 ... 48 D6
Churchview Rd TW2 152 B2
Church Villa TW16... 194 B6
Churchward Ho
Camberwell SE17 .. 138 D6
West Kensington SW5 254 D1
Churchway N1 ...... 232 D2
Church Way
Cockfosters EN4 .... 2 D1
Friern Barnet N20 .. 14 C1
Church Wlk
Barnes SW13 ...... 134 A4
Brentford TW8 .... 131 C6
Canonbury N16 ... 73 B4
Child's Hill NW2 ... 69 B5
Dartmouth Pk N6... 71 A5
Hayes UB3 .... 83 D1
Mitcham SW16 .... 181 C1
2 Richmond TW9 .. 154 A2
Thames Ditton KT7 . 196 D3
Walton-on-T KT12 .. 194 A1
Welsh Harp NW9 ... 67 B6
West Barnes SW20 . 200 C6
Churchwood Gdns
IG8 .... 37 A6
Churchyard Row
SE11 .... 116 D2 261 D4
Churnfield 4 N4 .... 72 C6
Churston Cl SE23 .. 99 B6
Churston Cl 10 SW2 160 C3
Churston Dr SM4 .. 201 A4
Churston Gdns N11 . 31 C4
Churston Mans WC1 240 D5
Churton Pl
SW1 .... 115 C2 259 B3
Churton St
SW1 .... 115 C2 259 B3
Chute Ho 6 SW9 ... 138 C3
Chuter Ede Ho SW6 264 D5
Chyngton Cl DA15 . 167 D1
Chyngton Ct HA1 .. 64 C6
Cibber Rd SE23 .... 162 D2
Cicada Rd SW18 ... 158 A6
Cicely Ho NW8 .... 229 D3
Cicely Rd SE15 .... 140 A4
Cinderford Way BR1 186 C6
Cinema Mus The ★
SE11 .... 261 C3
Cinema Par RM8.... 81 B6
Cinnabar Wharf Central
16 E1 .... 118 A5
Cinnabar Wharf East
3 E1 .... 118 A5
Cinnabar Wharf West
7 E1 .... 118 A5
Cinnamon Cl
8 Camberwell
SE15 .... 139 D5
Thornton Heath CR0 . 204 A2

Cinnamon Row 3
SW11 .... 136 A2
Cinnamon St E1 .... 118 B5
Cinnamon Wharf
SE1 .... 253 D2
Cinque Cotts SW3 . 178 C4
Cintra Ct SE19 ..... 183 D4
Cintra Pk SE19 ..... 183 D3
Circle Ct HA0 ...... 65 D4
Circle Gdns SW19 .. 179 C1
Circle Ho 14 E14 ... 98 B1
Circle The
Bermondsey SE1 ... 253 D2
Burnt Oak NW7 .... 27 B4
Neasden NW2 ..... 67 C5
Circuits The HA5 ... 40 C5
Circular Rd London N2 . 30 B2
Tottenham N17 .... 51 A6
Circular Way SE18 . 144 C6
Circus Lo NW8 ..... 229 C2
Circus Mews 1 W1 . 237 C4
Circus Pl EC2 ...... 245 C3
Circus Rd
NW8 .... 92 B5 229 C3
Circus St SE10 ..... 142 A5
Cirencester St W2 .. 91 D2
Cirrus Cl 3 SM6 ... 220 A1
Cissbury Ho 6 SE26 . 162 A1
Cissbury Rd N15 ... 51 C4
Cissbury Ring N N12 . 29 C5
Cissbury Ring S N12 . 29 B5
Citadel Pl SE11 .... 260 C2
Citizen Ho N7 ..... 72 C4
Citizen Rd N7 ..... 72 C4
Citron Terr 4 SE15 . 140 B2
Citrus Ho 14 SE8 ... 119 B1
City Banking Coll
SE1 .... 117 B4 252 D2
City Bsns Coll
EC1 .... 94 D4 234 D1
City Bsns Ctr 59
SE16 .... 118 C4
City Business Coll
EC1 .... 235 C2
City Cll London
WC1 .... 240 D3
City Forum
EC1 .... 95 A4 235 A2
City Garden Row
N1 .... 94 D5 234 D4
City Gate E1 .... 96 C3
City & Guilds of London
Art Sch The
SE1 .... 116 C1 261 B1
City & Hackney Ctr for
Mental Health (Hospl)
N1 .... 75 A3
City Hall ★
SE1 .... 117 C5 253 B3
City Harbour E14 ... 119 D3
City Hts SE8 ...... 119 C2
City & Islington 6th Form
Coll EC1 .... 94 D4 234 D2
City & Islington Coll (Ctr
for Applied Sciences)
EC1 .... 235 C2
City & Islington Coll (Ctr
for Bsns, Arts &
Technology) **11** N7 . 72 A4
City & Islington Coll (Ctr
for Health, Social &
Child Care) **7** N7 .. 72 A4
City & Islington Coll (Ctr
for Lifelong Learning)
11 N4 .... 72 D6
City Law Sch The
EC1 .... 240 D3
City Lights The SE11 261 B1
CITY OF LONDON ... 117 A6
**City of London Acad-
Islington** N1 95 A6 235 A5
City of London Acad The
SE1 .... 118 A1
City of London Bsns Coll
N15 .... 52 A5
City of London
Information Ctr ★
EC4 .... 241 D1
City of London Sch
EC4 .... 117 A6 252 A6
City of London Sch for
Girls EC2 .. 95 A2 242 B4
City of Westminster Coll
W2 .... 92 B2 236 C4

**City of Westminster Coll,
Cosway Street Ctr**
NW1 .... 92 C2 237 B4
**City of Westminster Coll,
Maida Vale Ctr 1**
W9 .... 91 D4
**City of Westminster Coll,
Queens Park Ctr 10**
W9 .... 91 C4
City Prospect 5
SE19 .... 183 C4
City Rd EC1 .. 95 A4 235 B2
City Thameslink Sta
EC4 .... 94 D1 241 C1
City University
EC1 .... 94 D4
City View 3 IG1 .... 79 A6
City Wharf Ho KT7 . 197 B3
City Wlk SE1 ...... 253 A1
Civic Way Ilford IG6 . 57 A5
Ruislip HA4 .... 62 D3
Civil Service Coll
SW1 .... 115 C2 259 A3
Clabon Mews
SW1 .... 114 D2 257 C4
Clack St SE16 ..... 118 C4
Clacton Rd
Newham E6 ...... 99 D4
Tottenham N17 .... 51 A3
Walthamstow E17 .. 53 A3
Claigmar Gdns N3 . 29 D2
Claire Ct
Brondesbury NW2 .. 69 A2
Bushey WD23 .... 8 B4
5 Finsbury Pk N4 .. 72 C4
Whetstone N12 ... 14 A1
Claire Gdns HA7 ... 25 C5
Claire Pl E14 ..... 119 C3
Clairvale Rd TW5 .. 129 A4
Clairview Rd SW16... 181 B5
Clairville Gdns W7 . 108 C5
Clairville Point 12
SE23 .... 162 D1
Clamp Hill HA7 .... 24 C5
Clancarty Rd SW6 . 135 C3
Clandon Cl
South Acton W3 ... 110 D4
Stoneleigh KT17... 216 A2
Clandon Ct
Plaistow BR1 ..... 187 A4
Sutton SM2 .... 218 B2
Clandon Gdns N3 .. 29 D5
Clandon Ho
East Finchley N3 ... 47 C6
12 Kingston u T KT2 . 175 C1
Clandon Rd IG3 .... 79 C6
Clandon St SE8 ... 141 C3
Clanfield Ho 12
SW15 .... 156 A3
Clanricarde Gdns
W2 .... 113 C6 245 B5
CLAPHAM 137 B2
Clapham Common ★
SW4 .... 137 B1
Clapham Common North
Side SW4 .... 137 A1
Clapham Common South
Side SW4 .... 159 C6
Clapham Common Sta
SW4 .... 137 C2
Clapham Common
West Side
Clapham SW4,
SW11 .... 136 D1
Clapham SW11 ... 159 A6
**Clapham Computer &
Secretarial Coll 10**
SW11 .... 158 D2
Clapham Court Terr 2
SW4 .... 160 A6
Clapham Cres SW4 . 137 D2
Clapham Ct 8 SW4 . 160 A6
Clapham High Street Sta
SW4 .... 137 D2
Clapham High St
SW4 .... 137 D2
Clapham Junction Est
SW11 .... 136 C1
Clapham Junction Sta
SW11 .... 136 C1
Clapham L J Day Sch 1
SW4 .... 137 C2
Clapham Manor Ct 1
SW4 .... 137 C2
Clapham Manor Prim
Sch 6 SW4 ...... 137 C2

Clapham Manor St
SW4 .... 137 D2
Clapham Mans SW4 . 159 B5
Clapham North Bsns Ctr
10 SW4 .... 137 D2
Clapham North Sta
SW4 .... 138 A2
CLAPHAM PARK 159 D6
Clapham Park Rd
SW4 .... 137 D1
Clapham Park Terr 4
SW2 .... 160 A6
Clapham Rd
SW9 .... 138 B5 270 A4
Clapham South Sta
SW4 .... 159 B5
Claps Gate La E6 ... 100 D3
Clapton Comm E5 .. 52 A2
Clapton Girls Tec Coll
E5 .... 74 C4
CLAPTON PARK 74 D4
Clapton Pas E5 .... 74 C3
Clapton Sq E5 ..... 74 C3
Clapton Terr E5 .... 52 A1
Clapton Way E5 .... 74 A4
Clara Grant Ho 10
E14 .... 119 C3
Clara Grant Prim Sch
18 E3 .... 97 C3
Clara Pl SE18 ..... 122 C2
Clare Ct
Borehamwood WD6 .. 10 B5
New Cross SE9 .... 48 A6
Clare Cnr SE9 ..... 166 D4
Clare Ct
Chislehurst BR7.... 188 B2
St Pancras WC1 ... 233 B1
Wimbledon SW19 .. 179 A4
Claredale Ct SM2 .. 218 A1
Claredale Ho 8 E2 .. 96 B5
Claredale St E2 .... 96 A5
Clare Gdns
Barking IG11 ..... 80 A1
Forest Gate E7 .... 77 A4
Notting Hill W11 ... 91 A1
Clare Ho
Bermondsey SE1 ... 263 D2
8 Burnt Oak HA8 ... 27 A1
5 Ealing W7 ...... 108 C5
6 Old Ford E3 ..... 97 B6
Clare House Prim Sch
BR3 .... 186 A1
Clare La N1 .... 73 A1
Clare Lawn Ave
SW14 .... 155 B6
Clare Mews SW6 .. 265 C3
Clare Mkt WC2 .... 240 D1
Claremont
1 Putney SW15 ... 157 A6
Shepperton TW17 . 192 D3
Claremont Ave
Harrow HA3 ...... 44 A4
Sunbury TW16 .... 172 B2
West Barnes SW3 . 200 B4
Claremont Cl
Finsbury N1 .. 94 C5 234 B3
Newham E16 ..... 122 C5
Orpington BR6 .... 227 A3
6 Streatham SW2 . 160 B3
Claremont Ct 11 Why . 91 B5
Claremont Dr TW17 . 192 D3
Claremont Gdns
Ilford IG3 .... 79 C6
Kingston u T KT6 .. 198 A4
Claremont Gr
Chiswick W4 ..... 133 C5
Woodford IG8 .... 37 C4
Claremont High Sch
HA3 .... 44 A4
Claremont Ho 16
SM2 .... 217 C1
Claremont Hts EN2 . 4 D1
Claremont La KT10 . 212 A3
Claremont Lo 12
SW19 .... 178 D3
Claremont Pk N3 .. 29 A2
Claremont Pl KT10 . 212 D2
Claremont Prim Sch
NW2 .... 68 D6
Claremont Rd
Bromley BR1 ..... 210 B5
Claygate KT10 .... 212 C1
Croydon CR0 ..... 206 A1
Ealing W13 .... 87 A2
Forest Gate E7 .... 77 C3

Claremont Rd *continued*
Hadley Wood EN4 2 B6
Harrow HA3 24 C1
Hendon NW2 68 D6
Higham Hill E17 35 A1
Highgate N6 49 C2
Kingston u T KT6 198 A4
Leyton E7 76 B5
Teddington TW11 174 D6
Twickenham TW1 153 C5
West Kilburn W9 91 B5
Claremont Sq N1 94 C5 234 A3
Claremont St
Edmonton N18 34 A4
Greenwich SE10 141 D6
Newham E16 122 C4
Claremont Terr KT7 197 B2
Claremont Way NW2 46 C1
Claremont Way Ind Est NW2 46 C1
Clarence Ave
Bromley BR1, BR2 210 A5
Clapham Pk SW4 159 D5
Ilford IG2 56 C3
Kingston u T KT3 177 B1
Clarence Cl
Bushey WD23 8 D4
New Barnet EN4 14 B6
Clarence Cres
Clapham Pk SW4 159 D5
Sidcup DA14 168 B1
Clarence Ct
Edgware NW7 27 D5
10 Hammersmith W6 112 B2
5 North Finchley N12 30 B5
Clarence Gate NW1 237 D6
Clarence Gate Gdns NW1 237 D5
Clarence Gdns NW1 93 B4 231 D1
Clarence Ho SE17 139 A6
Clarence Ho★ SW1 115 C5 249 B3
Clarence La SW15 155 D5
Clarence Mews
Balham SW12 159 B4
Hackney E5 74 B3
1 Rotherhithe SE16 118 D5
Clarence Pl 25 E5 74 B3
Clarence Rd
Bexley DA6 147 A1
Brentford W4 110 C1
Bromley BR1, BR2 210 A6
Brondesbury NW6 69 B1
Chislehurst SE9 166 A2
Enfield EN3 18 C6
Greenwich SE8 141 D6
Harringay N15 51 A4
Higham Hill E17 34 D1
Lower Clapton E5 74 B4
Manor Pk E12 77 D3
Newham E16 98 C3
Richmond TW9 132 C4
Sidcup DA14 168 B1
Sutton SM1 217 D3
Teddington TW11 175 A4
Thornton Heath CR0 205 B2
Wallington SM6 219 B3
Wimbledon SW19 179 D4
Wood Green N22 32 A3
Clarence St
Kingston u T KT1, KT2 176 A1
5 Richmond TW9 132 A1
Southall UB2 106 D3
Clarence Terr
Hounslow TW3 129 D1
Lisson Gr NW1 237 D6
Clarence Way NW1 71 B1
Clarence Wlk 9 SW4 138 A3
Clarendon Cl
Bayswater W2 247 A6
38 Hackney E9 74 C1
Clarendon Cres TW2 152 B1
Clarendon Cross W11 244 B5
Clarendon Ct
London NW11 47 B5
Mitcham SM4 202 C4
Paddington W9 236 B6
1 Richmond TW9 132 C4
Willesden NW2 68 C1
Clarendon Dr SW15 134 C1
Clarendon Flats W1 238 B1
Clarendon Gdns
Hendon NW4 46 B6
Paddington W9 92 A3 236 B5
Redbridge IG1 56 B2
Wembley HA9 66 A4
Clarendon Gr
Mitcham CR4 202 D6
Somers Town NW1 232 C2
Clarendon Ho
Harrow HA2 42 B6
North Finchley N12 30 A5
Somers Town NW1 232 B3
South Oxhey WD19 22 D5
Clarendon Mews
Bayswater W2 247 A6
Old Bexley DA5 169 D3
Clarendon Pl W2 114 C6 247 A6
Clarendon Prim Sch TW15 170 B6
Clarendon Rd
Ashford TW15 170 B6
Croydon CR0 220 D6
Ealing W5 88 A3
Edmonton N18 34 A5
Harrow HA1 42 C3
Hayes UB3 105 D4
Hornsey N8 50 B6
Leytonstone E11 54 B1
Mitcham SW19 180 C3
Notting Hill W11 113 A6 244 B5
Wallington SM6 219 C2
Walthamstow E17 53 D3
Wanstead E18 55 A6
West Green N15 51 A5
Wood Green N22 32 B1
Clarendon Rise SE13 142 A1
Clarendon Specl Sch TW12 173 D4
Clarendon St SW1 115 B1 258 D2
Clarendon Terr W9 236 B6
Clarendon Way
Enfield N21 17 A5
Orpington BR5, BR7 211 D6
Clarendon Wlk 11 W11 91 A1
Clarens St SE6 163 B2
Clare Pl SW15 155 D4
Clare Point NW2 46 D1
Clare Rd
Hounslow TW4 129 B2
Leytonstone E11 54 B3
New Cross Gate SE14 141 B4
Northolt UB6 64 B2
Stanwell TW19 148 A4
Willesden NW10 68 A1
Clare St E2 96 B5
Claret Gdns SE25 205 C5
Clareville Ct SW7 256 B3
Clareville Gr SW7 114 A2 256 B3
Clareville Grove Mews SW7 256 B3
Clareville Rd BR5 227 A6
Clareville St SW7 114 A2 256 B3
Clare Way DA7 147 A4
Clarewood Ct W1 237 C3
Clarewood Wlk SW9 138 C1
Clarges Ho W1 248 D4
Clarges Mews W1 115 B5 248 C4
Clarges St W1 115 B5 248 D4
Clariat Ct W3 110 C4
Claribel Rd SW9 138 D3
Clarice Ct NW4 46 B6
Claridge Ct SW6 264 C1
Claridge Rd RM8 58 D1
Clarinet Ct HA8 26 D3
Clarissa Ho 7 E14 97 D1
Clarissa Rd RM6 58 D2
Clarissa St E8 95 D6
Clark Ct 17 NW10 67 B1
Clarke Cl CR0 205 A3
Clarke Ho
2 London SW4 137 C2
5 Richmond TW10 153 C1
Clarke Mans 9 IG11 79 D1
Clarke Mews N9 18 B1
Clarke Path N16 52 A1
Clarke's Ave KT4, SM3 216 D6
Clarkes Dr UB8 82 A2
Clarkes Mews W1 238 B4
Clark Gr IG3 79 C4
Clark Ho SW10 266 A4
Clark Lawrence Ct 10 SW11 136 B2
Clarks Mead WD23 8 B4
Clarkson Rd E16 98 D1
Clarkson Row NW1 232 A3
Clarkson St E2 96 B4
Clarksons The IG11 101 A5
Clark's Pl EC2 243 A2
Clark's Rd IG1 79 B6
Clark St E1 96 C2
Clark Way TW5 128 D5
Classic Mans 33 E9 74 C1
Classinghall Ho 14 SW15 156 D5
Classon Cl UB7 104 A4
Claude Rd Leyton E10 54 A1
London SE15 140 B3
Newham E13 99 B6
Claude St E14 119 C2
Claudia Jones Way SW2 160 A5
Claudia Pl SW19 157 A3
Claudius Cl HA7 9 D1
Claughton Rd E13 99 C5
Clauson Ave UB5 64 A3
Clavell St 8 SE10 142 A6
Claverdale Rd SW2 160 C4
Clavering Ave SW13 134 B6
Clavering Cl TW1 175 A6
Clavering Ho SE13 142 B1
Clavering Rd E12 77 D6
Claverings Ind Est N9 18 C2
Claverley Gr N3 29 D2
Claverley Villas N3 29 D3
Claverton St SW1 115 C1 259 B1
Clave St E1 118 C5
Claxton Gr W6 112 D1 254 A1
Clay Ave CR4 181 B1
Claybank Gr SE13 141 D2
Claybee Ct N22 32 B5
Claybourne Mews 2 SE19 183 D3
Claybridge Rd SE12 187 C6
Claybrook Cl N2 48 B6
Claybrook Rd W6 134 D6
Claybury Broadway IG5 56 A6
Clay Ct E17 54 B6
Claydon SE17 262 A4
Claydon Dr CR0 220 A4
Claydon Ho NW4 28 D1
Claydown Mews SE18 122 C1
Clayfarm Rd SE9 167 A2
CLAYGATE 212 D1
Claygate Cres CR0 224 B2
Claygate Ct SM1 218 A5
Claygate La
Hinchley Wood KT10 213 A6
Thames Ditton KT7 197 A1
Claygate Lodge Cl KT10 212 C1
Claygate Prim Sch KT10 212 C1
Claygate Rd W13 109 B3
Claygate Sta KT10 212 C2
CLAYHALL 56 B6
Clayhall Ct 20 E3 97 B5
CLAY HILL 5 A6
Clay Hill EN2 5 B6
Clayhill Cres SE12, SE9 187 D6
Clay La Bushey WD23 8 C4
Stanwell TW19 148 B4
Claylands Ct SE19 183 B5
Claylands Pl SW8 138 C5
Claylands Rd SW8 138 B6 270 D5
Claymill Ho 2 SE18 123 A1
Claymore Cl SM3, SM4 201 C2
Claymore Ct 4 E17 35 A2
Claypole Ct E17 53 C4
Claypole Dr TW5 129 A4
Claypole Rd E15 98 A5
Clayponds Ave TW8 110 A2
Clayponds Gdns W5 109 D2
Clayponds Hospl W5 110 A2
Clayponds La TW8 110 A1
Clays Ct N16 51 D1
Clay St W1 92 D2 237 D3
Clayton 22 NW9 27 D1
Clayton Ave HA0 66 A1
Clayton Bsns Ctr UB3 105 C4
Clayton Cl 3 E6 100 B1
Clayton Cres
Brentford TW8 109 D1
Islington N1 233 C5
Clayton Ct
1 Higham Hill E17 35 A1
Stamford Hill N16 52 A2
Clayton Field NW9 27 C2
Clayton Ho
22 Hackney E9 74 C1
Long Ditton KT7 197 B1
Clayton Mews SE10 142 B4
Clayton Rd
Chessington KT10, KT9 213 D4
Hayes UB3 105 C4
Isleworth TW7 130 C2
Peckham SE15 140 A4
Clayton St SE11 138 C6
Clayton Terr UB4 84 D2
Claytonville Terr DA17 125 D4
Clay Wood Cl BR6 211 C2
Clayworth Cl DA15 168 B5
Cleanthus Cl SE18 144 D4
Cleanthus Rd SE18 144 D4
Clearbrook Way 13 E1 96 C1
Clearmont Ho UB2 107 C3
Clearwater Ho BR3 207 D4
Clear Water Ho 9 TW10 154 A6
Clearwater Pl KT6 197 C3
Clearwater Terr 4 W11 112 D4
Clearwell Dr W9 91 D3
Cleave Ave
Hayes UB3 105 C2
Orpington BR6 227 C2
Cleaveland Rd KT6 197 D4
Cleaver Ho 6 NW3 70 D1
Cleaverholme Cl SE25 206 B3
Cleaver Sq SE11 116 C1 261 B1
Cleaver St SE11 116 C1 261 B2
Cleave's Almshos 1 KT2 176 A1
Cleeve Ct
East Bedfont TW14 149 C3
Muswell Hill N10 31 B3
Cleeve Hill SE23 162 B3
Cleeve Ho 15 E2 95 C4
Cleeve Park Gdns DA14 168 B2
Cleeve Park Sch DA14 168 C1
Cleeve Way
Cheam SM1 201 D1
Roehampton SW15 155 D4
Cleeve Workshops 14 E2 95 C4
Clegg Ho SE3 143 B1
Clegg St Newham E13 99 A5
16 Wapping E1 118 B5
Cleland Ho 19 E2 96 C5
Clematis Gdns IG8 37 A5
Clematis St W12 112 A6
Clem Atlee Par SW6 264 D5
Clem Attlee Ct SW6 135 B6 264 D5
Clemence St E14 97 B2
Clement Attlee Ho NW10 67 D1
Clement Ave SW4 137 D1
Clement Cl Acton W4 111 B2
Hampstead NW6 68 C1
Clement Danes Ho 2 W12 90 B1
Clement Gdns UB3 105 C2
Clement Ho
14 Deptford SE8 119 A2
17 North Kensington W10 90 C2
Clementhorpe Rd RM9 80 C2
Clementina Rd E10 53 B1
Clementine Churchill Hospl The HA1 64 D5
Clementine Cl W13 109 B4
Clementine Wlk 4 IG8 37 A3
Clement Rd
Penge BR3 184 D1
Wimbledon SW19 179 A5
Clements Ave 1 E16 121 A6
Clements Cl 19 N12 29 D6
Clements Ct
Hounslow TW4 128 D1
5 Ilford IG1 78 D5
Clements Ho N17 34 A2
Clements Inn WC2 94 B1 240 D1
Clements Inn Pas WC2 240 D1
Clements La IG1 78 D5
Clement's La EC2, EC4 117 B6 252 D6
Clements Pl TW8 109 D1
Clements Rd
East Ham E6 78 B1
Ilford IG1 78 D5
Clement's Rd SE16 118 B3
Cleminson Ct DA14 190 D4
Clemson Ho 9 E8 95 D6
Clendon Way SE18 123 B2
Clennam St SE1 252 B2
Clensham Ct SM3 217 C6
Clensham La SM1 217 C6
Clenston Mews W1 237 C2
Clent Ho 4 N16 51 D1
Cleopatra Cl HA7 9 D1
Cleopatra's Needle★ WC2 116 B6 250 C5
Clephane Rd 13 N1 73 A2
Clephane Rd N N1 73 A2
Clephane Rd S N1 73 B2
Clere Pl EC2 242 D6
Clere St EC2 95 B3 242 D6
Clerics Wlk TW17 193 B3
CLERKENWELL 94 D3
Clerkenwell Cl EC1 94 C3 241 B5
Clerkenwell Gn EC1 94 D3 241 C5
Clerkenwell Parochial CE Prim Sch EC1 94 C4 234 A1
Clerkenwell Rd EC1 94 D3 241 C5
Clermont Rd E9 96 C6
Cleveden Ct CR2 221 C3
Cleveden Ho BR1 188 A3
Clevedon Ct
Battersea SW11 267 A2
Dulwich SE21 161 B1
Clevedon Gdns
Cranford TW5 128 B4
Hayes UB3 105 B3
Clevedon Ho 4 SM1 218 A4
Clevedon Mans NW5 71 A4
Clevedon Rd
Kingston u T KT1 176 C1
Penge SE20 184 D2
Twickenham TW1 153 D5
Cleve Ho NW6 69 D1
Cleveland Ave
Chiswick W4 111 D2
Hampton TW12 173 B3
Merton SW20 179 B1
Cleveland Cres WD6 11 A6
Cleveland Ct
Ealing W13 87 B2
Marylebone W1 239 B5
Southall UB2 107 D2
Cleveland Gdns
Barnes SW13 133 D3
Harringay N4, N15 51 A4
Hendon NW2 68 D6
Paddington W2 92 A1 236 A1
Worcester Pk KT4 215 D6
Cleveland Gr 39 E1 96 C3
Cleveland Ho 7 N2 30 B1

Cleveland Inf Sch IG1 78 D5
Cleveland Jun Sch IG1 78 D5
Cleveland Mans
- 8 Brixton SW9 138 C5
- 4 Brondesbury NW6 69 B1
- Paddington W9 91 C3
Cleveland Mews W1 239 A4
Cleveland Park Ave E17 53 C5
Cleveland Park Cres E17 53 C5
Cleveland Pk TW19 148 A5
Cleveland Pl SW1 249 B4
Cleveland Rd
- Barnes SW13 133 D3
- Bexley DA16 145 D3
- Ealing W13 87 B2
- Edmonton N9 18 B4
- Ilford IG1 78 D5
- Isleworth TW7 131 A1
- Islington N1 73 B1
- New Malden KT3 199 C5
- 14 South Acton W4 111 A3
- Wanstead E18 55 A6
- Worcester Pk KT4 215 C6
Cleveland Rise SM4 200 D2
Cleveland Row SW1 115 C5 249 B3
Cleveland Sq W2 92 A1 236 A1
Cleveland St W1 93 C3 239 A5
Cleveland Terr W2 92 A1 236 B2
Cleveland Way E1 96 C3
Cleveley Cres W5 88 B5
Cleveleys Rd E5 74 B5
Clevely Cl SE7 121 D2
Clevendon Cl N16 73 D5
Cleve Rd
- Sidcup DA14 168 D1
- South Hampstead NW6 69 D1
Cleverly Cotts W12 111 D5
Cleverly Est W12 112 A6
Cleves Ct KT6 198 A3
Cleves Prim Sch E6 99 D6
Cleves Rd Newham E6 99 D5
- Richmond TW10 153 C1
Cleves Way
- Ashford TW16 171 D4
- Hampton TW12 173 B3
- Ruislip HA4 40 D1
Clewer Cres HA3 24 B2
Clewer Ct 2 E10 53 C1
Clewer Ho 6 SE2 124 D4
Cley Ho SE4 140 D1
Clichy Ho 32 E1 96 C2
Clifden Centre (Richmond Adult & Com Coll) TW1 152 D3
Clifden Ho 6 TW8 131 D6
Clifden Mews E5 74 D3
Clifden Rd
- Brentford TW8 131 D6
- Homerton E5 74 D3
- Twickenham TW1 152 D3
Cliff Ct 14 NW1 71 D2
Cliffe Ho 4 SE10 120 D1
Cliffe Rd CR2 221 B3
Cliffe Wlk 2 SM1 218 A3
Clifford Ave
- Elmstead BR7 188 B4
- Mortlake SW14 133 A3
- Mortlake SW14, TW9 132 D2
- Wallington SM6 219 C4
Clifford Cl UB5 85 A6
Clifford Ct
- Bayswater W2 91 D2
- Wandsworth SW18 158 B4
- Willesden NW10 67 C4
Clifford Dr SW9 138 D1
Clifford Gdns
- Hayes UB3 105 B2
- Kensal Green NW10 90 C5
Clifford Gr TW15 170 C6
Clifford Haigh Ho SW6 134 D5
Clifford Ho
- 2 Beckenham BR3 185 D4
- West Kensington W14 254 C3
Clifford Lo 5 N3 29 B1
Clifford Rd Barnet EN5 1 D2
- Chingford E17 36 A1
- Croydon SE25 206 A5
- Hounslow TW4 128 D2
- Newham E16 98 D3
- Ponders End N9 18 C5
- Richmond TW10 153 D2
- Wembley HA0 87 D6
Clifford's Inn Pas EC4 241 A1
Clifford St W1 115 C6 249 A5
Clifford Way NW10 67 D4
Cliff Rd NW1 71 D2
Cliff Road Studios 13 NW1 71 D2
Cliffsend Ho 23 SW9 138 C4
Cliff Terr SE8 141 C3
Cliffview Rd SE13 141 C2
Cliff Villas NW1 71 D2
Cliff Wlk E16 98 D2
Clifton Ave
- Church End N3 29 B2
- Feltham TW13 150 C1
- Shepherd's Bush W12 111 D5
- Stanmore HA7 25 B1
- Walthamstow E17 52 D6
- Wembley HA9 66 B2
Clifton Cl 8 BR6 227 A3
Clifton Cres SE15 140 B5
Clifton Ct
- 1 Beckenham BR3 185 D2
- Finsbury Pk N4 72 C6
- Paddington NW8 236 C6
- Peckham SE15 140 B5
- Putney SW15 156 D6
- South Norwood SE25 205 C4
- 9 Stanwell TW19 148 A5
- Surbiton KT5 198 B2
- 3 Woodford IG8 37 A4
Clifton Gate SW10 266 A6
Clifton Gdns
- Chiswick W4 111 B2
- Enfield EN2 16 A6
- Hillingdon UB10 82 D5
- Paddington W9 92 A3 236 A5
- South Tottenham N15 51 D3
- 2 Temple Fortune NW11 47 B3
Clifton Gr E8 74 A2
Clifton Hill NW8 92 A6 229 A5
Clifton Ho Leyton E11 76 C6
- Shoreditch E2 243 C6
Clifton Lodge Sch W5 109 C6
Clifton Mans 4 SW9 138 C1
Clifton Mews SE25 205 C5
Clifton Par TW13 172 C6
Clifton Park Ave SW20 178 C1
Clifton Pl
- Paddington W2 236 D1
- Rotherhithe SE16 118 C4
Clifton Prim Sch UB2 107 A2
Clifton Rd
- Bexley DA16 146 C2
- Crouch End N8 49 D3
- Finchley N3 30 A2
- Greenford UB6 86 B3
- Harlesden NW10 90 A5
- Harlington TW6 126 D2
- Harrow HA3 44 B4
- Ilford IG2 57 B3
- Isleworth TW7 130 C3
- Kingston u T KT2 176 B2
- Newham E16 98 C2
- Paddington W9 92 A3 236 B6
- Sidcup DA14 189 C6
- Southall UB2 107 A2
- South Norwood SE25 205 C5
- Teddington TW11 174 C6
- Upton E7 77 D2
- Wallington SM6 219 B3
- Wimbledon SW19 178 D4
- Wood Green N22 31 C2
Clifton Rise SE14 141 A5
Cliftons Roundabout SE9, SE12 165 C5
Clifton St EC2 95 C3 243 A5
Clifton Terr N4 72 C6
Clifton The KT6 214 A6
Clifton Villas W9 92 A2 236 A4
Cliftonville Ct SE12 165 A3
Clifton Way
- Harlington TW6 126 D2
- Peckham SE15 140 C5
- Wembley HA0 88 A6
Climsland Ho SE1 251 B4
Clinch Ct 11 E16 99 A2
Cline Ho SW15 156 A6
Cline Rd N11 31 C4
Clinger Ct N1 95 C6
Clink Prison Mus The★ SE1 252 C4
Clink St SE1 117 B5 252 C4
Clinton Ave
- Bexley DA16 146 A1
- East Molesey KT8 196 A5
Clinton Ho
- New Malden KT3 199 B1
- 6 Surbiton KT6 197 D2
Clinton Rd Bow E3 97 A4
- Forest Gate E7 77 A4
- West Green N15 51 B5
Clipper Appts 12 SE10 142 A6
Clipper Cl 3 SE16 118 D4
Clipper Ho E14 120 A1
Clipper Way SE13 142 A1
Clippesby Cl KT9 214 B2
Clipstone Ho 10 SW15 156 A6
Clipstone Mews W1 239 A4
Clipstone Rd TW3 129 C2
Clipstone St W1 93 C2 239 A4
Clissold Cl N2 48 D6
Clissold Cres N16 73 B4
Clissold Ct N4 73 A6
Clissold Ho 4 N16 73 B6
Clissold Rd N16 73 B5
Clitheroe Ave HA2 41 C1
Clitheroe Rd SW9 138 A3
Clitherow Ave W7 109 A3
Clitherow Rd TW8 109 C1
Clitterhouse Cres NW2 46 C1
Clitterhouse Rd NW2 46 C1
Clive Ave N18 34 A4
Clive Ct
- Paddington W9 236 B6
- Streatham SW16 181 D5
- Tolworth KT6 214 C6
Cliveden Cl N12 30 A6
Cliveden Ho SW1 258 A4
Cliveden Pl
- Belgravia SW1 115 A2 258 A4
- Shepperton TW17 193 A3
Cliveden Rd SW19 179 B2
Clivedon Ct
- Ealing W13 87 B2
- 6 New Barnet EN5 2 A1
Clivedon Rd E4 36 C5
Clive Ho
- 18 Clapham SW8 137 D3
- 3 Croydon CR0 205 D1
- Greenwich SE10 142 A6
Clive Lloyd Ho N15 51 A4
Clive Lo NW4 46 D3
Clive Rd
- Belvedere DA17 125 C2
- Enfield EN1 6 A1
- Feltham TW14 150 A5
- Mitcham SW19 180 C4
- Teddington TW1 175 A6
- West Norwood SE21, SE27 161 B1
Clivesdale Dr UB3 106 B5
Clive Way EN1 6 A1
Cloak La EC4 117 B6 252 C6
Clochar Ct NW10 89 D6
Clock Ct 2 E11 55 B5
Clock Ho
- Stamford Hill N16 51 D2
- Walthamstow E17 54 B5
Clock Ho The EN2 5 D6
Clockhouse Ave IG11 101 A6
Clockhouse Cl SW19 156 C2
Clock House Ct 1 BR3 185 A1
Clockhouse Junc N13 32 C5
Clockhouse La TW14, TW15 148 D2
Clockhouse Mans N13 32 C5
Clockhouse Par N13 32 C5
Clock House Par E11 55 B3
Clockhouse Pl SW15 157 A5
Clock House Rd BR3 185 A1
Clockhouse Rdbt TW14 149 A3
Clock House Sta BR3 185 A2
Clockhouse The SW19 156 C1
Clockmakers' Mus★ EC2 95 A1 242 B2
Clocktower Mews 6 W7 108 C5
Clock Tower Mews
- Islington N1 235 B5
- Thamesmead SE28 124 B6
Clock Tower Pl 1 N7 72 A2
Clock Tower Rd TW7 130 D2
Clock View Cres 2 N7 72 A2
Cloister Cl TW11 175 B5
Cloister Gdns
- Croydon SE25 206 B3
- Edgware HA8 27 A5
Cloister Rd Acton W3 89 A2
- Child's Hill NW2 69 B6
Cloisters Ave BR1, BR2 210 B4
Cloisters Ct
- Erith DA7 147 D2
- Highgate N6 49 B1
Cloisters Ho 8 SW19 179 C3
Cloisters The 22 SW9 138 C4
Clonard Way HA5 23 C4
Clonbrock Rd N16 73 C4
Cloncurry St SW6 134 D3
Clone Ct 4 W12 111 C3
Clone The 5 KT2 176 D3
Clonmel Cl HA2 42 B1
Clonmell Rd N17 51 B6
Clonmel Rd
- Fulham SW6 135 B4 264 D2
- Teddington TW11 174 B6
Clonmore St SW18 157 B3
Cloonmore Ave BR6 227 D4
Clorane Gdns NW3 69 C5
Close The
- Beckenham BR3 207 A5
- Cheam SM3 201 B2
- Chingford E4 36 A3
- Cockfosters EN4 14 D6
- Croydon SE25 206 A3
- Dagenham RM6 59 A3
- Eastcote HA5 40 C2
- Harrow HA2 24 A1
- Hillingdon UB10 82 C6
- Hounslow TW7 130 B3
- Ilford IG2 57 C3
- Kingston u T KT3 177 A1
- Lewisham SE3 142 B3
- Mitcham CR4 202 D5
- Mortlake TW9 132 D2
- Muswell Hill N10 31 B1
- 1 Old Bexley DA5 169 C4
- Palmers Green N14 15 D2
- Petts Wood BR5 211 C3
- Rayners La HA5 41 B2
- Sidcup DA14 190 B5
- Surbiton KT6 198 A3
- Totteridge N20 13 B2
- Wembley HA0 66 A2
- Wembley Pk HA9 67 A5
Cloth Ct EC1 241 D3
Cloth Fair EC1 94 D2 241 D3
Clothier Ho SE7 122 A1
Clothier St EC3 243 B2
Cloth St EC1 95 A2 242 A4
Clothworkers Rd SE18 145 B5
Cloudesdale Rd SW17 159 B2
Cloudesley Cl DA14 189 D6
Cloudesley Mans N1 234 B5
Cloudesley Pl N1 94 C6 234 B5
Cloudesley Rd
- Erith DA7 147 B4
- Islington N1 94 C6 234 A5
Cloudesley Sq N1 94 C6 234 B6
Cloudesley St N1 94 C6 234 B5
Clouston Cl SM6 220 A3
Clova Rd E7 77 A3
Clove Cres E14 120 B6
Clovelly Ave
- London NW9 45 D5
- Uxbridge UB10 61 A4
Clovelly Cl Pinner HA5 40 C6
- Uxbridge UB10 61 A4
Clovelly Ct NW2 68 C3
Clovelly Gdns
- Enfield EN1 17 C4
- South Norwood SE19 183 D2
Clovelly Ho W2 236 A2
Clovelly Rd
- Acton W4 111 B4
- Ealing W5 109 C4
- Erith DA7 147 A6
- Hornsey N8 49 D5
- Hounslow TW3 129 C3
Clovelly Way
- Harrow HA2 63 B6
- Orpington BR6 211 D3
- Stepney E1 96 C1
Clover Cl E11 76 B6
Clover Ct Enfield EN3 7 A1
- Sutton SM2 217 D2
Cloverdale Gdns DA15 167 D5
Clover Ho
- Hounslow TW3 130 A4
- Southgate N21 16 B6
Cloverleys IG10 21 D6
Clover Mews SW3 267 D6
Clover Way SM6 203 A1
Clove St 9 E13 99 A3
Clowders Rd SE6 163 B1
Clowes Ho 3 SW4 138 A1
Clowns Mus★ E8 95 D6
Clowser Cl 4 SM1 218 A3
Cloysters Gn E1 118 A5
Cloyster Wood HA8 25 D4
Club Gardens Rd BR2 209 A2
Club Row E2 95 D3 243 C6
Clumps The TW15 171 B6
Clunbury Ave UB2 107 B1
Clunbury St N1 235 D3
Clunie Ho SW1 257 D6
Cluny Mews SW5 255 A3
Cluny Pl SE1 117 C3 263 A6
Cluse Ct N1 235 A4
Clutton St E14 97 D2
Clydach Rd EN1 5 D1
Clyde Cir N15 51 C5
Clyde Ct NW1 232 D4
Clyde Flats SW6 264 C4
Clyde Ho 9 KT2 175 D2
Clyde Pl E10 53 D2
Clyde Rd
- Croydon CR0 221 D6
- South Tottenham N15 51 C5
- Stanwell TW19 148 A3
- Sutton SM1 217 C3
- Wallington SM6 219 C2
- Wood Green N22 31 D2
Clydesdale EN3 6 D1
Clydesdale Ave HA7 43 D6
Clydesdale Cl
- Borehamwood WD6 11 B6
- Isleworth TW7 130 D2
Clydesdale Ct N20 14 B3
Clydesdale Gdns TW10 132 D1
Clydesdale Ho
- Abbey Wood DA18 125 A4
- 4 Notting Hill W11 91 B1
Clydesdale Path WD6 11 B6
Clydesdale Rd W11 91 B1
Clyde St SE8 141 B6
Clyde Terr SE23 162 C2
Clyde Vale SE23 162 C2
Clyde Works 10 SM6 219 C2
Clyfford Rd HA4 61 D4
Clymping Dene TW14 150 B4

Clynes Ho
6 Dagenham RM10 81 C5
3 Globe Town E2 96 D4
Hayes UB4 84 A4
Clyro Ct N4 50 B1
Clyston St SW8 137 C3
Clytha Ct SE27 183 A6
Coach Ho NW10 67 A1
Coach & Horses Yd W1 249 A6
Coach House La
Highbury N5 72 D4
Wimbledon SW19 156 D1
Coach House Mews SE23 162 D5
Coach House Yd 5 NW3 70 B4
Coachmaker Mews 5 SW9 138 A2
Coachman Lo N12 30 A5
Coalbrook Mans 3 SW12 159 B3
Coaldale Wlk SE21 161 A4
Coalecroft Rd SW15 156 C6
Coalport Ho SE11 261 A4
Coal Post Cl BR6 227 D2
Coatbridge Ho 8 N1 72 B1
Coates Ave SW18 158 C5
Coates Cl CR7 205 A6
Coates Ct NW3 70 C3
Coates Hill Rd BR1 188 C1
Coates Rd WD6 9 D4
Coate St E2 96 A5
Coates Wlk TW8 110 A1
Cobalt SE2 124 A4
Cobalt Cl CR0 206 D5
Cobb Cl WD6 11 A6
Cobbett Rd
Kidbrooke SE9 144 A2
Twickenham TW2 151 C3
Cobbetts Ave IG4 55 D4
Cobbett St SW8 138 B5 270 D3
Cobble La N1 72 D1
Cobble Mews N4, N5 73 A5
Cobbler's Wlk TW11 174 D3
Cobblestone Pl CR0 205 A1
Cobbold Ct SW1 259 C4
Cobbold Ind Est NW10 67 D2
Cobbold Mews W12 111 D4
Cobbold Rd
Bedford Pk W12 111 D4
Leyton E11 76 D5
Willesden NW10 67 D2
Cobb's Hall 1 SW6 134 D6
Cobbs Rd TW4 129 B1
Cobb St E1 243 C3
Cobden Bldgs WC1 233 C2
Cobden Ct
Bromley BR2 209 C5
9 Thamesmead SE28 124 C5
Cobden Ho
11 Bethnal Green E2 96 A4
Regent's Pk NW1 232 A4
Cobden Mews SE26 184 B5
Cobden Rd
Croydon SE25 206 A4
Leyton E11 76 C6
Orpington BR6 227 B4
Cobham 21 NW9 27 D1
Cobham Ave KT3 200 A4
Cobham Cl
2 Blackfen DA15 168 B5
Bromley BR2 210 A2
Clapham SW11 158 C5
Edgware HA8 26 D1
Enfield EN1 6 A2
Wallington SM6 220 A2
Cobham Ct CR4 180 B1
Cobham Ho IG11 101 A6
Cobham Mews 3 NW1 71 D1
Cobham Pl DA6 168 D6
Cobham Rd
Chingford E17 36 A2
Harringay N22 50 D6
Heston TW5 128 C5
Ilford IG3 79 C5
Kingston u T KT1, KT2 176 C1
Cobland Rd SE12 187 C6
Coborn Mews 9 E3 97 B4
Coborn Rd E3 97 B4
Coborn St E3 97 B4
Cobourg Prim Sch SE5 139 D6
Cobourg Rd SE5 139 D6
Cobourg St NW1 93 C4 232 B1
Coburg Cl SW1 259 B4
Coburg Cres SW2 160 C3
Coburg Dwellings 11 E1 118 C6
Coburg Gdns IG5 37 D1
Coburg Rd N22 32 B1
Cochrane Cl NW8 229 D3
Cochrane Ct 3 E10 53 C1
Cochrane Ho 15 E14 119 C4
Cochrane Mews NW8 92 B5 229 D3
Cochrane Rd SW19 179 B3
Cochrane St NW8 92 B5 229 D3
Coci Ho W14 254 D3
Cockburn Ho SW1 259 D1
Cockerell Rd E17 53 A3
COCKFOSTERS 2 D1
Cockfosters Par EN4 3 A1
Cockfosters Rd EN4 2 D3
Cockfosters Sta EN4 3 A1
Cock Hill E1 243 B3
Cock La EC1 94 D2 241 D3
Cockpit Yd WC1 240 D4
Cocks Cres KT3 199 D5
Cocksett Ave BR6 227 C2
Cockspur Ct SW1 249 D4
Cockspur St SW1 115 D5 249 D4
Cocksure La DA14 191 C6
Coda Ctr The SW6 135 A4 264 B2
Code St E1 95 D3 243 D5
Codicote Ho 22 SE8 118 D2
Codicote Terr N4 73 A6
Codling Cl 12 E1 118 A5
Codling Way HA0 65 D4
Codrington Ct 3 SE16 119 A5
Codrington Hill SE23 163 A4
Codrington Ho 7 E1 96 B3
Codrington Mews W11 91 A1
Cody Cl Harrow HA3 43 D6
Wallington SM6 219 D1
Cody Rd E16 98 B3
Coe Ave SE25 206 A3
Coe's Alley EN5 1 A1
Coffey St SE8 141 C5
Cogan Ave E17 35 A2
Cohen Ho NW7 28 A6
Cohen Lo E5 75 A3
Coin St SE1 116 C5 251 A4
Coity Rd NW5 71 A2
Cokers La SE21 161 B3
Coke St E1 96 A1
Colab Ct N22 32 C2
Colas Mews 7 NW6 91 C6
Colbeck Mews SW5 113 D2 255 D3
Colbeck Rd HA1 42 A2
Colberg Pl N16 51 D2
Colbert 1 SE5 139 D4
Colborne Ct 8 SW19 179 D2
Colborne Ho 8 E14 119 C6
Colborne Way KT4 216 C6
Colbrook Ave UB3 105 B3
Colbrook Cl UB3 105 B3
Colburn Ave HA5 23 A4
Colburn Way SM1 218 B5
Colby Rd
Walton-on-T KT12 194 A1
West Norwood SE19 183 C5
Colchester Ave E12 78 B5
Colchester Dr HA5 40 D4
Colchester Ho 17 SW8 137 D3
Colchester Rd
Burnt Oak HA8 27 A3
Leyton E10 54 A2
Pinner HA6 22 A1
Walthamstow E17 53 C3
Colchester St E1 243 D2
Colchester Villas CR7 204 C3
Coldbath Sq EC1 241 A6
Coldbath St SE13 141 D3
Cold Blow La SE14 140 D6
Coldershaw Rd W13 109 A4
Coldfall Ave N10 31 A1
Coldfall Prim Sch N10 30 D1
Coldham Ct N22 32 D2
Coldham Gr EN3 7 A6
Coldharbour E14 120 A5
Coldharbour Crest SE9 166 C1
Coldharbour Ind Est SE5 139 A3
Coldharbour La
Brixton SW9 138 D2
Bushey WD23 8 A6
Hayes UB3 106 A5
Coldharbour Lane Ho UB3 106 A5
Coldharbour Pl SE5 139 B3
Coldharbour Rd CR0 220 C3
Coldharbour Sports Ctr SE9 166 B2
Coldharbour Way CR0 220 C3
Coldstream Gdns SW18 157 B5
Colebeck Mews N1 72 D2
Colebert Ave E1 96 C3
Colebert Ho 21 E1 96 C3
Colebrook Cl
Edgware NW7 28 D3
Putney SW19 156 D4
Colebrook Ct SW3 257 B3
Colebrooke Ave W13 87 B1
Colebrooke Ct DA14 190 B6
Colebrooke Dr E11 55 C2
Colebrooke Pl N1 234 D5
Colebrooke Row
Islington N1 233 B6
Islington N1 94 D5 234 C4
Islington N1 234 D5
Colebrook Ho 1 E14 97 D1
Colebrook Rd SW16 182 A2
Colebrook Rise BR2 186 C1
Colebrook Way N11 31 B5
Coleby Path 21 SE5 139 B5
Colechurch Ho 9 SE1 118 A1
Cole Cl SE28 124 B5
Cole Court Lo 9 TW1 153 A4
Coledale Dr HA7 25 C2
Colefax Bldg 12 E1 96 A1
Coleford Rd SW18 158 A6
Cole Gdns TW5 128 A5
Colegrave Rd E15 76 B3
Colegrave Sch E15 76 B3
Colegrove Rd SE15 139 D6
Coleherne Ct SW10 113 D1 255 D1
Coleherne Mans SW5 255 D2
Coleherne Mews SW10 113 D1 255 C1
Coleherne Rd SW10 113 D1 255 C1
Colehill Gdns SW6 264 A1
Colehill La SW6 135 A4 264 B1
Cole Ho SE1 251 B1
Coleman Cl SE25 184 A1
Coleman Ct SW18 157 C4
Coleman Fields N1 95 A6 235 B6
Coleman Mans N19 50 A2
Coleman Rd
Belvedere DA17 125 C2
Camberwell SE5 139 C5
Dagenham RM9 81 A2
Colemans Heath SE9 166 D1
Coleman St EC2 95 B1 242 C2
Coleman Street Bldgs EC2 242 C2
Colenso Dr NW7 28 A3
Colenso Rd Ilford IG2 57 C2
Lower Clapton E5 74 C4
Cole Park Gdns TW1 153 A5
Cole Park Rd TW1 153 A5
Cole Park View 2 TW1 153 A5
Colepits Wood Rd SE9 167 B6
Coleraine Park Prim Sch N17 34 B2
Coleraine Rd
Greenwich SE3 142 D6
Hornsey N8, N22 50 C6
Cole Rd TW1 153 A5
Coleridge Ave
Carshalton SM1 218 C4
Plashet E12 78 A2
Coleridge Cl SW8 137 B3
Coleridge Ct
Hammersmith W14 112 D3
15 New Barnet EN5 13 D6
2 Richmond TW10 175 D6
Coleridge Gdns NW6 70 A1
Coleridge Ho
Pimlico SW1 259 B1
Walworth SE17 262 B2
Wembley HA9 65 D6
Coleridge Prim Sch N8 49 D2
Coleridge Rd
Ashford TW15 170 B6
Crouch End N8 49 D3
Croydon CR0 206 C2
Finsbury Pk N4, N7 72 C6
North Finchley N12 30 A5
Walthamstow E17 53 B5
Coleridge Sq
Chelsea SW10 266 A4
Ealing W13 87 A1
Coleridge Way
Borehamwood WD6 10 C6
Hayes UB4 84 A1
West Drayton UB7 104 B2
Coleridge Wlk NW11 47 C5
Colerne Ct NW4 29 A1
Colesburg Rd BR3 185 B1
Coles Cres HA2 63 D6
Coles Ct SW11 266 D1
Coles Gn WD23 8 A3
Coles Green Ct NW2 68 A6
Coles Green Rd NW2 68 B6
Coleshill Flats SW1 258 B3
Coleshill Rd TW11 174 C4
Cole St SE1 117 A4 252 B1
Colestown St 4 SW11 136 C3
Coleswood N20 14 C3
Colesworth Ho 1 HA8 27 A1
Colet Cl N13 32 D4
Colet Gdns W14 112 D2
Colet Ho SE17 261 D1
Colette Ct 5 SE16 118 D4
Coley St WC1 94 B3 240 D5
Colfe & Hatchcliffe's Glebe SE13 163 D6
Colfe Rd SE23 163 A3
Colfe's Sch SE12 165 A5
Colgate Ct EN5 13 A6
Colgate Ho SE13 141 D3
Colgate Pl 10 EN3 7 C6
Colham Ave UB7 104 A5
COLHAM GREEN 82 C2
Colham Green Rd UB8 82 C2
Colham Manor Prim Sch UB8 82 C1
Colham Rd UB8 82 B3
Colina Mews N8, N15 50 D5
Colina Rd N8, N15 50 D4
Colin Blanchard Ho SE4 141 C3
Colin Cl Colindale NW9 45 C5
Coney Hall BR4 224 D5
Croydon CR0 223 B5
Colin Cres NW9 45 D5
Colin Ct
Forest Hill SE6 163 B4
Hendon NW9 45 D5
Streatham SW16 159 D2
COLINDALE 45 C6
Colindale Ave NW9 45 C6
Colindale Bsns Ctr NW9 45 C6
Colindale Bsns Pk NW9 45 A6
Colindale Prim Sch NW9 45 D5
Colindale Sta NW9 45 C6
Colindeep Gdns NW4 46 A5
Colindeep La NW9, NW4 45 D5
Colin Dr NW9 45 D4
Colinette Rd SW15 134 C1
Colin Gdns NW9 45 D5
Colin Par NW9 45 C5
Colin Park Rd NW9 45 C5
Colin Pond Ct RM6 58 D6
Colin Rd NW10 68 A2
Colinsdale N1 234 C5
Colinton Rd IG3 80 B6
Colin Winter Ho 45 E1 96 C3
Coliseum Apartments N8 50 D4
Coliston Pas SW18 157 C4
Coliston Rd SW18 157 C4
Collamore Ave SW18 158 C3
Collapit Cl HA1 41 D3
Collard Pl NW1 71 B1
Collard's Almshouses 1 E17 54 A4
Collcutt Lo SW4 138 A1
Collection Point N8 50 A3
College App SE10 142 A6
College Ave HA3 24 C2
College Cl
Edmonton N18 33 D5
Hackney E5 74 C3
Harrow HA3 24 C3
Twickenham TW2 152 B3
College Cres NW3 70 B2
College Cross N1 72 C1
College Ct
Chelsea SW3 114 D1 257 D1
Croydon CR0 222 A6
Ealing W5 110 A6
Enfield EN3 18 C6
3 Hammersmith W6 112 C1
Hampstead NW3 70 B2
College Dr Ruislip HA4 40 A2
Thames Ditton KT7 196 C2
College Fields Bsns Ctr SW19 180 B2
College Gdns
Chingford E4 20 A3
Dulwich SE21 161 C3
Edmonton N18 34 A5
Enfield EN2 5 B4
New Malden KT3 199 D4
Redbridge IG4 56 A4
Upper Tooting SW17 158 C2
College Gn SE19 183 C3
College Gr NW1 232 C6
College Green Ct SW9 138 D2
College Hill EC4 252 B6
College Hill Rd HA3 24 C3
College La NW5 71 B4
College Mews 5 SW18 157 D6
College of North West London HA9 65 C5
COLLEGE PARK 90 B4
College Park Cl SE13 142 B1
College Park Rd N17 33 D4
College Park Sch 20 W2 91 D1
College Pl
Camden Town NW1 93 C6 232 B5
Chelsea SW10 266 A4
Walthamstow E17 54 C5
College Pt 3 E15 76 D2
College Rd
Dulwich SE19, SE21 161 C2
Ealing W13 87 B1
Enfield EN2 5 B3
Harrow HA1 42 C3
Harrow Weald HA3 24 C2
Hounslow TW7 130 D4
Kensal Green NW10 90 C5
Mitcham SW19 180 B4
Plaistow BR1 187 A3
South Croydon CR0 221 B6
Southgate N21 16 C2
Tottenham N17 33 D4
Walthamstow E17 54 A4
Wembley HA9 43 D1
College Rdbt 1 KT1 198 A6
College St EC4 117 A6 252 B6
College Terr Bow E3 97 B4
Church End N3 29 B1
College View SE9 165 D3

College Way
Ashford TW15 170 B6
Hayes UB3 106 A6
College Wlk 10 KT1 198 A6
Collent Ho 12 E9 74 C2
Collent St E9 74 C2
Collerston Ho SE10 120 D1
Colless Rd N15 51 D4
Collette Ct SE25 205 C4
Collette Ho N16 51 D1
Collett Ho SE13 141 D2
Collett Rd SE16 118 A3
Collett Way UB2 107 D4
Colley Ho 12 N7 71 D3
Collier Cl
Newham E16 122 D6
West Ewell KT19 214 D2
Collier Dr HA8 26 C1
Colliers Shaw BR2 225 D3
Collier St N1 94 B5 233 C3
Colliers Water La
CR7 204 C4
Colliers Wood SW19 180 B3
COLLIER'S WOOD 180 C4
Collier's Wood Sta
SW19 180 B3
Collindale Ave
Erith DA8 147 D6
Sidcup DA15 168 A3
Collingbourne Rd
W12 112 B5
Collingham Gdns
SW5 113 D2 255 D3
Collingham Pl
SW5 113 D2 255 D4
Collingham Rd
SW5 113 D2 255 D3
Collingham Tutors Coll
SW5 113 D2 255 D3
Collings Cl N22 32 B4
Collington Ho 2
SE7 143 B6
Collington St SE10 120 B1
Collingtree Rd SE26 184 C6
Collingwood Ave
London N10 49 A5
Tolworth KT5 199 A1
Collingwood Cl
2 Penge SE20 184 B2
Twickenham TW2,
TW4 151 C4
Collingwood Ct
London NW4 46 C4
New Barnet EN5 13 D6
Sutton SM1 217 C4
Collingwood Ho
27 Bethnal Green E1 96 B3
Marylebone W1 239 A4
Collingwood Rd
Hillingdon UB8 82 D3
Mitcham CR4 202 C6
South Tottenham N15 51 C5
Sutton SM1 217 C4
Collingwood Sch 7
SM6 219 B3
Collingwood St E1 96 B3
Collins Ave HA7 26 A1
Collins Ct Dalston E8 74 A2
1 Loughton IG10 21 D6
Collins Dr HA4 62 C6
Collins Ho
8 Barking IG11 78 D1
6 Cubitt Town SE10 120 D1
4 Poplar E14 120 A6
Collinson Ct
Borough The SE1 252 A1
Edgware HA8 26 B6
Collinson Ho 14
SE15 140 A5
Collinson St SE1 252 A1
Collinson Wlk SE1 252 A1
Collins Rd N5, N16 73 A4
Collins Sq SE3 142 D3
Collins St SE3 142 C3
Collins Yd N1 234 C5
Collinwood Ave EN3 6 C2
Collinwood Gdns IG5 56 C5
Collison Pl N16 51 C1
Collis Prim Sch
TW11 175 B4
Coll of Arms★
EC4 117 A6 252 A6
Coll of Central London
The EC2 243 A6
Coll of Law The
(Bloomsbury)
EC1 93 D2 239 C4
Coll of Law The
(Moorgate)
EC1 95 B3 242 C5
Coll of North East
London The N15 51 D5
Coll of NW London 18
NW6 91 C6
Coll of NW London
(Willesden Centre)
NW10 67 D3
Coll of Optometrists The
SW1 250 A4
Coll Sharp Ct 42 E2 95 D4
Coll's Rd SE15 140 C4
Collyer Ave CR0 220 A4
Collyer Pl SE15 140 A4
Collyer Rd CR0 220 A4
Colman Ct London N12 30 A4
Stanmore HA7 25 B4
Colman Rd E16 99 C2
Colmans Wharf 5
E14 97 D2
Colmar Cl 3 E1 96 D3
Colmer Pl HA3 24 B3
Colmer Rd SW16 182 A3
Colmore Ct NW4 46 A6
Colmore Mews SE15 140 B4
Colmore Rd EN3 6 C1
Colnbrook Ct SW17 180 B6
Colnbrook St SE1 261 C6
Colne Ct Ealing W7 86 B1
West Ewell KT19 215 A4
Colne Ho Barking IG11 78 D2
Paddington NW8 236 D5
Colne Rd
Clapton Pk E5 75 A4
Southgate N21 17 B4
Twickenham TW1,
TW2 152 C3
Colne St E13 99 A4
COLNEY HATCH 30 C4
Colney Hatch N10 31 A3
Colney Hatch La N10 31 A3
Cologne Rd SW11 136 B1
Coloma Convent Girl's
Sch CR0 222 D5
Colombo Rd IG1 57 A2
Colombo St SE1 251 C3
Colomb St SE10 120 C1
Colonades The 4
SE5 139 B4
Colonels Wlk EN2 4 D2
Colonial Ave TW2 152 A5
Colonial Dr W4 111 A2
Colonial Rd TW14 149 C4
Colonnade WC1 240 B5
Colonnade Ho SE3 142 D3
Colonnades The
Croydon CR0 220 C2
6 Hackney E8 74 B2
Colonnade The 12
SE8 119 B2
Colonnade Wlk Sh Ctr
SW1 258 D4
Colorado Bldg 9
SE13 141 D4
Colosseum Ct N3 29 B1
Colosseum Ret Pk EN1 6 A1
Colosseum Terr
NW1 238 D6
Colour Ho SE1 253 B1
Colroy Ct NW4 47 A4
Colson Rd CR0 221 C6
Colson Way SW16 181 C6
Colstead Ho 22 E1 96 B1
Colsterworth Rd N15 51 D5
Colston Ave SM1,
SM5 218 C4
Colston Ct SM5 218 D4
Colston Rd
Mortlake SW14 133 A1
Upton E7 77 D2
Colthurst Cres N4 73 A6
Colthurst Dr N9 18 B1
Coltman Ho SE10 142 A6
Coltman St E14 97 A2
Colt Mews 5 EN3 7 C6
Coltness Cres SE2 124 B1
Colton Gdns N17 51 A6
Colton Rd HA1 42 C4
Coltsfoot Dr UB7 82 A1
Coltswood Ct N14 15 D3
Colts Yd E11 54 D2
Columba Ho SE14 141 B4
Columbas Dr NW3 48 B1
Columbia Ave
Edgware HA8 26 D2
New Malden KT4 199 D2
Ruislip HA4 40 B1
Columbia Ct
Edgware HA8 26 D2
New Malden KT3 199 D2
Columbia Ho 18 E3 97 C4
Columbia Point 7
SE16 118 C3
Columbia Prim Sch 50
E2 95 D4
Columbia Rd
9 Hackney E2 96 A5
Newham E13 98 D3
Shoreditch E2 95 D4
Columbia Road Flower
Mkt★ E2 95 D4
Columbine Ave
Croydon CR2 220 D1
Newham E6 100 A2
Columbus Gdns HA6 22 A2
Colveiw Ct SE9 165 D3
Colverson Ho 14 E1 96 C2
Colvestone Cres E8 73 D3
Colvestone Prim Sch
E8 73 D3
Colville Gdns W11 91 B1
Colville Ho
32 Bethnal Green E2 96 C5
Notting Hill W11 91 B1
Colville Mews W11 91 B1
Colville Pl W1 239 B3
Colville Prim Sch 5
W11 91 B1
Colville Rd
Edmonton N9 18 B3
Higham Hill E17 35 A1
Leyton E11 76 A5
Notting Hill W11 91 B1
South Acton W3 110 D3
Colville Sq W11 91 B1
Colville Terr W11 91 B1
Colvin Cl SE26 184 C5
Colvin Gdns
Chingford E4 20 A1
Wanstead E11 55 B5
Colvin Rd
Thornton Heath
CR7 204 C4
Upton Pk E6 78 A1
Colwall Gdns IG8 37 A5
Colwall Ho 18 SW9 138 B3
Colwell Rd SE22 161 D6
Colwick Cl N6 49 D2
Colwith Rd W6 134 C6
Colwood Gdns
SW19 180 B3
Colworth Gr SE17 262 B3
Colworth Rd
Croydon CR0 206 A1
Leytonstone E11 54 C2
Colwyn Ave UB6 86 D5
Colwyn Cl SW16 181 C5
Colwyn Cres TW3 130 A4
Colwyn Gn NW9 45 C3
Colwyn Ho SE1 261 A5
Colwyn Rd NW2 68 B5
Colyer Cl SE9 166 D2
Colyer Ho SE2 124 D1
Colyton Cl
Erith DA16 146 D4
Wembley HA0 65 C2
Colyton La 14 SW16 182 C5
Colyton Rd SE22 162 B6
Colyton Way N18 34 A5
Combe Ave SE3 142 D5
Combedale Rd SE10 121 A1
Combe Ho
Mortlake SW14 133 A3
20 Paddington W2 91 C2
Combe Lane Sta
CR0 222 C3
Combemartin Rd
SW18 157 A3
Combe Mews 4
SE3 142 D5
Comber Cl NW2 68 B6
Comber Gr SE5 139 A5
Comber Grove Prim Sch
34 SE5 139 A5
Comber Ho SE5 139 A5
Combermere Rd
London SW9 138 B2
Morden SM4 201 D4
Comberton 10 KT1 176 C1
Comberton Rd E5 74 B6
Combeside SE18 145 D5
Combes Rd RM9 81 B1
Combe The NW1 231 D1
Combwell Cres SE2 124 A3
Com Coll Hackney The
17 E8 96 B6
Comely Bank Rd E17 54 A4
Comeragh Mews
W14 254 B1
Comeragh Rd
W14 113 A1 254 B1
Comer Cres UB2 108 A4
Comerford Rd SE4 141 B1
Comer Ho 10 EN5 2 A1
Comet Cl E12 77 D4
Comet Pl SE8 141 C5
Comet St SE8 141 C5
Comfort St 6 SE15 139 C6
Comins Ho SW4 159 C6
Commerce Est E18 37 C1
Commerce Pk CR0 220 B6
Commerce Rd
Brentford TW8 131 C5
Wood Green N22 32 B2
Commerce Way CR0 220 B6
Commercial Rd
Edmonton N18 33 C4
Stepney E1 96 C1
Whitechapel E1 96 A1
Commercial St
E1 95 D2 243 C4
Commercial Way
Peckham SE15 140 A5
Wembley NW10 88 D5
Commerell Pl SE10 120 D1
Commerell St SE10 120 C1
Commodity Quay E1 253 D5
Commodore Ct SE8 141 C4
Commodore Ho 7
E14 120 A6
Commodore St E1 97 A3
Commondale SW15 134 C2
Common La KT10 213 A1
Common Rd
Barnes SW13 134 A2
Claygate KT10 213 A1
Stanmore HA7 8 C1
Commonside BR2 225 C4
Commonside Ct
SW16 182 A4
Commonside E CR4 203 B6
Commonside W CR4 203 A6
Common The
Ealing W5 110 A5
Southall UB2 106 D2
Stanmore HA7 8 D2
1 Stratford E15 76 D2
Common View
SW15 134 C2
Commonwealth Ave
Hayes UB3 83 B1
25 Shepherd's Bush
W12 112 B6
21 Shepherd's Bush
W12 112 B6
Commonwealth Ho
WC1 240 B2
Commonwealth Rd
N17 34 A3
Commonwealth Way
SE2 124 C1
Community Cl
Cranford TW5 128 B4
Uxbridge UB10 61 A5
Community La N7 71 D3
Community Rd
Greenford UB6 86 A6
Stratford New Town
E15 76 B3
Comodore Ho SW18 136 A1
Como Rd SE23 163 A2
Compania Bldg 12
E1 118 D6
Compass Cl
Edgware HA8 26 B6
Littleton TW15 171 A3
Compass Ct SE1 253 C3
Compass Hill TW10 153 D5
Compass Ho
Bayswater W2 91 D1
London SE8 141 D3
Compass Point 10
E14 119 C6
Compayne Gdns
NW6 69 D1
Compton Ave
Islington N1 72 D2
London N6 48 C2
Newham E6 99 D5
Wembley HA0 65 C4
Compton Cl
5 Burnt Oak HA8 27 A3
Camberwell SE15 139 D5
Cricklewood NW11 68 D5
Ealing W13 87 A1
Esher KT10 212 B3
Regent's Pk NW1 231 D1
Compton Cres
Chessington KT9 214 A2
Chiswick W4 133 A6
Northolt UB5 84 D6
Tottenham N17 33 A3
Compton Ct
London N12 30 A2
Sutton SM1 218 A4
9 West Norwood
SE19 183 C5
Compton Ho SW11 267 A2
Compton Lo N21 16 D3
Compton Pas EC1 241 D6
Compton Pl
Bloomsbury WC1 240 A6
South Oxhey WD19 23 A6
Compton Rd
Croydon CR0 206 B1
Hayes UB3 105 D6
Islington N1 72 D2
Kensal Green NW10 90 D4
Southgate N21 16 D3
Wimbledon SW19 179 B4
Compton Rise HA5 41 B4
Compton Sch The
N12 30 C4
Compton St
EC1 94 D3 241 D6
Compton Terr
Islington N1 72 D2
Southgate N21 16 C3
Comreddy Cl EN2 4 D4
Comus Ho SE17 263 A3
Comus Pl
SE17 117 C2 263 A3
Comyn Rd SW11 136 C1
Comyns Cl E16 98 D2
Comyns Rd RM9 81 C1
Comyns The WD23 8 A3
Conal Ct SW16 181 D5
Conant Ho SE11 138 D6
Conant Mews 1 E1 118 A6
Concanon Rd SW2,
SW4 138 B1
Concert Hall App
SE1 116 B5 250 D3
Concord Bsns Ctr
W3 88 D2
Concord Cl UB5 85 A4
Concord Ct KT1 198 B6
Concorde Cl
Hounslow TW3 129 D3
Uxbridge UB10 82 A5
Concorde Dr E6 100 B2
Concorde Way SE16 118 D2
Concord Ho
Kingston u T KT3 199 C6
5 Tottenham N17 33 D3
Concordia Wharf 10
E14 120 A5
Concord Rd Acton W3 88 D3
Enfield EN3 18 C6
Concord Terr HA2 63 D6
Concourse The
32 Edgware NW9 27 D2
7 Edmonton N9 18 A2
Condell Rd
SW8 137 C4 269 B1
Conder St E14 97 A1
Condor Path UB5 85 C5
Condover Cres SE18 144 D5
Condray Pl SW11 267 A3
Conduit Ct WC2 250 A6
Conduit Ho SE10 142 B4
Conduit La
London N18 34 C5
South Croydon CR0 222 A3
Conduit Mews
W2 92 B1 236 C1
Conduit Pas W2 236 C1

Conduit Pl W2 236 C1
Conduit Rd SE18 122 D1
Conduit St
W1 115 C6 249 A6
Conduit Way NW10 67 A1
Conewood St N5 72 D5
Coney Acre SE21 161 A3
Coney Burrows E4 20 C2
Coney Gr UB8 82 C4
Coneygrove Path
UB5 63 A2
CONEY HALL 224 D5
Coney Hall Par BR4 224 C5
Coney Hall Rdbt
BR4 224 C5
Coney Hill Rd BR4 224 D6
Coney Way SW8 270 D5
Conference Cl 3 E4 20 A2
Conference Ho UB8 83 A1
Conference Rd SE2 124 C2
Congers Ho SE8 141 C5
Congleton Gr SE18 123 A1
Congo Dr N9 18 C1
Congo Rd SE18 123 B1
Congress Ho WC1 239 D2
Congress Rd SE2 124 C2
Congreve Ho 10 N16 73 C3
Congreve Rd SE9 144 B2
Congreve St
SE17 117 C2 263 A3
Congreve Wlk 6 E16 99 D2
Conical Cnr EN2 5 A3
Conifer Cl BR6 227 B4
Conifer Ct
Ashford TW15 170 B5
Hendon NW4 28 C1
Ilford IG1 78 D2
23 Putney SW19 156 D3
Sutton SM2 218 B2
Conifer Gdns
Enfield EN1 17 C5
Streatham SW16 160 B1
Sutton SM1 217 D6
Conifer Ho SE4 141 B1
Conifers Cl TW11 175 C3
Conifer Way
Hayes UB3 106 A6
Wembley HA0 65 C5
Coniger Rd SW6 135 C3
Coningham Ct SW10 266 B4
Coningham Mews
W12 112 A5
Coningham Rd W12 112 B4
Coningsby Ave NW9 27 C1
Coningsby Cotts
W5 109 D4
Coningsby Ct 4
CR4 181 A1
Coningsby Gdns E4 35 D4
Coningsby Rd
Ealing W5 109 D4
Harringay N4 50 D2
Conington Rd SE13 142 A3
Conisbee Ct 3 N14 15 C6
Conisborough Cres
SE6 164 A1
Conisbrough NW1 232 A5
Coniscliffe Cl BR7 188 C2
Coniscliffe Rd N13 17 A1
Coniston NW1 232 A2
Coniston Ave
Barking IG11 79 C1
Ealing UB6 87 B4
Falconwood DA16 145 C2
Coniston Cl
Barking IG11 79 C1
Barnes SW13 133 D5
Chiswick W4 133 A5
West Barnes SM4 200 D3
Whetstone N20 14 A1
Coniston Ct
Beckenham BR3 186 A2
Chessington KT9 214 A5
Edgware HA8 26 B5
4 Finchley NW7 29 A3
Marylebone W2 237 B1
Penge SE26 184 B4
6 Rotherhithe SE16 118 D4
3 Wallington SM6 219 B4
Conistone Way N7 72 A1
Coniston Gdns
Edmonton N9 18 C3
Kingsbury NW9 45 B4
Pinner HA5 40 A5
Redbridge IG4 56 A5
Sutton SM2 218 B2
Coniston Gdns *continued*
Wembley HA9 43 C1
Coniston Ho
14 Bow E3 97 B4
18 Camberwell SE5 139 A5
Coniston Rd
Catford BR1 186 C4
Croydon CR0 206 A2
Muswell Hill N10 31 B1
Tottenham N17 34 A4
Twickenham TW2 151 D5
Coniston Way KT9 214 A5
Coniston Wlk E9 74 C3
Conlan St W10 91 A3
Conley Rd NW10 67 C2
Conley St SE10 120 C1
Connaught Ave
Ashford TW15 170 A6
Barnet EN4 14 D3
Chingford E4 20 B4
Enfield EN1 5 C3
Hounslow TW4 129 A1
Mortlake SW14 133 A1
Connaught Bridge
E16 121 D6
Connaught Bsns Ctr
London NW9 45 D4
Mitcham CR4 202 D4
Wallington CR0 220 B2
Connaught Cl
Carshalton SM1 218 B6
Enfield EN1 5 C3
Hillingdon UB8 83 A3
Lea Bridge E10 75 A6
Marylebone W2 237 B1
Connaught Ct
1 Chingford E4 20 C4
9 Walthamstow E17 53 D5
Connaught Day Hospl
E11 54 C3
Connaught Dr NW11 47 C5
Connaught Gdns
Cranley Gdns N10 49 B4
Edmonton N13 32 D6
Morden SM4 202 A5
Connaught Grange
N13 32 D6
Connaught Ho
College Pk NW10 90 B4
London N10 49 B4
Mayfair W1 248 C5
Connaught House Sch
W2 92 C1 237 B1
Connaught Hts UB10 83 A3
Connaught La IG1 79 B6
Connaught Lo N4 50 C2
Connaught Mans
Battersea SW11 267 B1
3 Brixton SW9 138 C1
15 Canonbury N16 73 B4
Fulham SW6 264 A2
Connaught Mews
Ilford IG1 79 B6
Woolwich SE18 122 C1
Connaught Pl W2 237 C1
Connaught Rd
Barnet EN5 12 D5
Carshalton SM1 218 B6
Chingford E4 20 C3
Ealing W13 109 B6
Finsbury Pk N4 50 C2
Harlesden NW10 89 C5
Harrow HA3 24 D2
Ilford IG1 79 B6
Leytonstone E11 54 B1
Newham E16 121 D5
New Malden KT3 199 C5
5 Richmond TW10 154 B6
Teddington TW11,
TW12 174 B5
Walthamstow E17 53 C4
Woolwich SE18 122 D1
Connaught Sch for Girls
2 E11 54 C1
Connaught Sch for Girls
(Annexe) 13 E11 76 C6
Connaught Sq
W2 92 D1 237 C1
Connaught St
W2 92 C1 237 B1
Connaught Way N13 32 D6
Connaught Works E3 97 A6
Connections Ho N2 30 B2
Connell Cres W5 88 B3
Connell Ct 6 SE14 140 D6
Connell Ho 6 SM6 219 C2
Connemara Cl WD6 11 B5
Conniffe Ct SE9 166 D6
Connington 5 KT1 176 C1
Connington Cres E4 20 B1
Connolly Ho SW19 180 A4
Connoly Ct NW2 68 B5
Connop Rd EN3 6 D5
Connor Cl E11 54 C2
Connor Ct SW11 268 C1
Connor Rd RM9 81 B4
Connor St E9 96 D6
Conolly Rd W7 108 C5
Conrad Dr KT4 200 D1
Conrad Ho
8 Limehouse SE16 119 A6
South Lambeth SW8 270 A4
12 Stoke Newington
N16 73 C3
Conrad Twr W3 110 D3
Conroy Ct 6 DA14 190 A6
Conservatory Ct
SE19 183 C3
Consfield Ave KT3 200 A4
Consort Ho
Bayswater W2 245 D5
Edgware NW7 27 D5
Consort Lo NW8 230 C5
Consort Mews TW7 152 B6
Consort Rd SE15 140 B3
Cons St SE1 251 B2
Constable Ave E16 121 B5
Constable Cl
12 Friern Barnet N11 30 D5
Hampstead Garden Suburb
NW11 47 D3
Hayes UB4 83 A5
Constable Cres N15 52 A4
Constable Ct 11
SE16 118 B1
Constable Gdns
Edgware HA8 26 C1
Isleworth TW7 152 B6
Constable Ho
Enfield EN1 18 A6
25 Millwall E14 119 C4
13 Northolt UB5 84 D5
Primrose Hill NW3 70 D1
Constable Mews
Bromley BR1 187 B1
Dagenham RM8 80 B4
Constable Wlk SE21 161 C1
Constance Cres BR2 208 D1
Constance Ct N10 31 B3
Constance Rd
Enfield EN1 17 C5
Sutton SM1 218 A4
Thornton Heath CR0 204 D2
Twickenham TW2 151 D4
Constance St E16 122 A5
Constant Ho 26 E14 119 D6
Constantine Ho
SW2 160 D3
Constantine Pl UB10 82 B6
Constantine Rd NW3 70 C4
Constitution Hill
W1 115 B4 248 D2
Constitution Rise
SE18 144 C4
Consul Ho 5 E3 97 C3
Content St
SE17 117 B2 262 C3
Contessa Cl BR6 227 C3
Control Tower Rd
TW6 126 D2
Convair Wlk 11 UB5 84 D4
Convent Cl BR3 186 A3
Convent Gdns
Ealing W5 109 C2
Notting Hill W11 91 B1
Convent Hill SE19 183 A4
Convent Lo TW15 170 D5
Convent of Jesus & Mary
Language Coll
NW10 89 D6
Convent of Jesus & Mary
RC Inf Sch 9 NW2 68 C2
Convent Rd TW15 170 D5
Convent Way UB2 106 D2
Conway Cl HA7 25 A4
Conway Cres
Dagenham RM6 58 C3
Greenford UB6 86 C5
Conway Dr
Ashford TW15 171 A4
Hayes UB3 105 A3
Sutton SM2 217 D2
Conway Gdns
Enfield EN2 5 C5
Mitcham CR4 204 A5
Wembley HA9 43 C2
Conway Gr W3 89 B2
Conway Ho
Chelsea SW3 257 D1
5 Millwall E14 119 D2
6 Streatham SW2 160 A3
Conway Mews W1 239 A5
Conway Prim Sch 5
SE18 123 C2
Conway Rd
Dollis Hill NW2 68 C6
Feltham TW13 172 D5
Harlington TW6 126 D2
Harringay N15 51 A4
Palmers Green N14 16 A1
Plumstead SE18 123 C2
Twickenham TW4 151 C4
Wimbledon SW20 178 C2
Conway St W1 93 C3 239 A5
Conway Wlk TW12 173 B4
Conybeare NW3 70 C1
Conyers Cl IG8 36 C4
Conyer's Rd SW16 181 D5
Conyer St 21 E3 97 A5
Cooden Cl BR1 187 B3
Cookes Cl E11 76 D6
Cookes La SM3 217 A2
Cooke St 2 IG11 101 A6
Cookham Cl UB2 107 D4
Cookham Cres SE16 118 D4
Cookham Dene Cl
BR7 189 B2
Cookham Ho E2 243 C6
Cookham Rd BR8,
DA14 191 C2
Cookhill Rd SE2 124 B3
Cooks Ferry N18 34 D5
Cook's Hole Rd EN2 5 A5
Cookson Gr DA8 147 D5
Cook's Rd
Camberwell SE17 138 D6
Stratford Marsh E15 97 D5
Coolfin Rd E16 99 B1
Coolgardie Ave E4 36 B5
Coolgardie Rd
TW15 171 A5
Coolhurst Rd N8 49 D3
Cool Oak La NW9 45 D2
Coomassie Rd W9 91 B3
COOMBE 177 B3
Coombe Ave CR0 221 C4
Coombe Bank KT2,
KT3 177 C2
Coombe Boys' Sch
KT3 200 A4
Coombe Cl
Edgware HA8 26 B1
Hounslow TW3 129 C1
Coombe Cnr N21 16 D3
Coombe Cres TW12 173 A3
Coombe Ct 2 BR3 185 B2
Coombe Dr HA4 40 B1
Coombe End KT2 177 B3
Coombefield Cl KT3 199 C4
Coombe Gdns
New Malden KT3 199 D5
Wimbledon SW20 178 A2
Coombe Girls Sch
KT3 177 B1
Coombe Hill Glade
KT2 177 C3
Coombe Hill Inf Sch
KT2 177 B2
Coombe Hill Jun Sch
KT2 177 B2
Coombe Hill Rd KT2 177 C3
Coombe Ho 13 N7 71 D3
Coombe House Chase
KT3 177 B2
Coombehurst Cl EN4 2 D3
Coombehurst (Kingston
University) KT2 177 A5
Coombe La CR0 222 B3
Coombe Lane Flyover
SW20 177 D2
Coombe La W KT2 177 B2
Coombe Lea BR1 210 A6
Coombe Lo SE7 143 C6
Coombe Neville KT2 177 B3
Coombe Pk KT2 177 B5
Coombe Pl KT2 177 A5
Coombe Rd
Bushey WD23 8 B4
Coombe Rd *continued*
Chiswick W4 111 C1
Ealing W13 109 B3
Forest Hill SE26 184 B6
Hampton TW12 173 B4
New Malden KT3 199 C6
Norbiton KT2 176 C2
South Croydon CR0,
CR2 221 C4
Willesden NW10 67 B5
Wood Green N22 32 C2
Coomber Ho SW6 135 D2
Coombe Ridings
KT2 177 A5
Coombe Rise KT2 177 A2
Coomber Way CR0 203 D3
Coombes Rd RM9 103 B6
Coombe Wlk SM1 217 D5
Coombewood Dr
RM6 59 B3
Coombe Wood Rd
KT2 177 A5
Coombs St N1 234 D3
Coomer Mews SW6 264 D5
Coomer Pl
SW6 135 B6 264 D5
Cooms Wlk HA8 27 A2
Cooperage Cl 5 N17 33 D4
Cooperage The SE1 253 C3
Cooper Ave E17 35 A2
Cooper Cl SE1 251 B1
Cooper Cres SM5 218 D5
Cooper Ct SE18 144 D6
Cooper Ho
Hounslow TW4 129 B2
Paddington NW8 236 C5
Upper Tooting SW17 180 B6
7 West Norwood
SW27 182 D5
Cooper Rd
Croydon CR0, CR9 220 D4
Hendon NW4 46 D3
Willesden NW10 68 A3
Coopersale Cl 3 IG8 37 C3
Coopersale Rd E9 74 D3
Coopers Cl
Bethnal Green E1 96 C3
Dagenham RM10 81 D2
Coopers Ct
9 Acton W3 111 A5
4 Friern Barnet N20 14 D1
Isleworth TW7 130 D3
Tower Hamlets E3 97 B3
Coopers La
Grove Pk SE12 165 B2
London E10 54 A1
Somers Town NW1 232 D3
Cooper's Lane Prim Sch
SE12 165 B2
Coopers Lo SE1 253 C2
Coopers Mews BR3 185 C1
Cooper's Rd
SE1 117 D1 263 D2
Cooper's Row
EC3 117 D6 253 C6
Cooper St 10 E16 98 D2
Coopers Tech Sch
BR7 189 A2
Coopers Yd N1 72 D1
Cooper's Yd SE19 183 C4
Coote Gdns RM8 81 B5
Coote Rd
Dagenham RM8 81 B5
Erith DA7 147 B4
Cope Ho EC1 235 B1
Copeland Dr E14 119 C2
Copeland Ho
Lambeth SE11 260 D5
Upper Tooting SW17 180 B6
Copeland Rd
London SE15 140 B3
Walthamstow E17 53 D3
Copelands BR3 185 B3
Copeman Cl SE26 184 C5
Copenhagen Gdns
W4 111 B4
Copenhagen Ho N1 234 A5
Copenhagen Pl E14 97 B1
Copenhagen Prim Sch
N1 94 B6 233 C5
Copenhagen St
N1 94 B6 233 C5
Cope Pl W8 113 C3 255 A5

Copers Cope Rd BR3 185 B3
Cope St SE16 118 D2
Copeswood Ct UB7 126 C5
Copford Wlk N1 235 A6
Copgate Path SW16 182 C4
Copinger Wlk HA8 26 D2
Copland Ave HA0 65 D3
Copland Cl HA0 65 C3
Copland Ho UB1 107 B4
Copland Mews 8 HA0 66 A2
Copland Rd HA0 66 A2
Copland Specialist Science Com Coll HA9 66 B3
Copleston Rd SE15 139 D2
Copley Cl
15 Camberwell SE17 138 D6
Ealing W7 86 D2
Copley Dene BR1 187 D2
Copley Pk SW16 182 B4
Copley Rd HA7 25 C5
Copley St E1 96 D2
Coppard Gdns KT9 213 C2
Coppedhall 2 SE21 161 B2
Coppelia Rd SE3 142 D1
Coppen Rd RM8 59 B2
Copperas St SE8 141 D6
Copper Beech N6 49 A2
Copperbeech Cl NW3 70 B3
Copper Beech Ct N20 14 A1
Copper Beeches TW7 130 B4
Copper Cl
Penge SE19 183 D3
Tottenham N17 34 B3
Copperdale Rd UB3 106 A4
Copperfield Ave UB8 82 C3
Copperfield Ct
Blackheath SE3 142 D2
Ilford IG6 57 A6
Copperfield Dr N15 51 D5
Copperfield Ho 12 SE1 118 A4
Copperfield Mews N18 33 C5
Copperfield Rd
Stepney E3 97 A2
Thamesmead SE28 102 C1
Copperfields
5 Beckenham BR3 186 A2
Harrow HA1 42 C2
Copperfields Ct W3 110 C4
Copperfield St SE1 117 A4 252 A2
Copperfield Way
Chislehurst BR7 189 A4
Pinner HA5 41 B5
Coppergate Cl BR1 187 B2
Coppermead Cl NW2 68 C5
Copper Mews 19 W4 111 A3
Copper Mill Dr TW7 130 D3
Coppermill La E17 52 D4
Copper Mill La SW17 180 A6
Coppermill Prim Sch E17 52 D4
Copper Row SE1 253 C3
Copperwood Lo EN2 4 D3
Coppetts Cl N12 30 D3
Coppetts Ctr N12 30 D3
Coppetts Rd N10 30 D2
Coppetts Wood Prim Sch N10 31 A2
Coppice Cl
Beckenham BR3 207 D5
Harrow HA7 24 D4
Ruislip HA4 39 B3
West Barnes SW20 200 C6
Coppice Dr SW15 156 B5
Coppice The
Ashford TW15 170 D4
Enfield EN2 4 D1
Hillingdon UB7 82 A1
New Barnet EN5 13 D5
Coppice Way E18 54 D6
Coppice Wlk N20 13 C1
Coppies Gr N11 31 B6
Copping Cl CR0 221 C4
Coppin Ho SW2 160 D3
Coppins The
2 Ilford RM6 58 B2
New Addington CR0 223 D2
Stanmore HA3 24 C4
Coppock Cl SW11 136 C3
Coppsfield KT8 195 C6
Copse Ave BR4 223 D5
Copse Cl SE7 143 B6
Copse Ct SW15 157 A6
Copse Glade KT6 197 D1
COPSE HILL 178 B3
Copse Hill
Belmont SM2 217 D1
Wimbledon SW19 178 C4
Wimbledon SW20 178 B3
Copsem Dr KT10 212 A2
Copsem La KT10 212 A1
Copsem Way KT10 212 A2
Copse The
Chingford E4 20 D3
Muswell Hill N2 48 D6
Copse View CR2 223 A1
Copsewood Cl DA15 167 C5
Coptefield Dr DA17 125 A3
Copthall Ave EC2 95 B1 242 D2
Copthall Bldgs EC2 242 D2
Copthall Cl EC2 242 C2
Copthall Dr NW7 28 A4
Copthall Gdns
Hendon NW7 28 A3
Twickenham TW1 152 D3
Copthall L Ctr NW4 28 B2
Copthall Rd E UB10 60 C5
Copthall Rd W UB10 60 C6
Copthall Sch NW7 28 B3
Copthall Stadium NW4 28 C2
Copthorne Ave
Bromley BR2 226 B6
Streatham SW12 159 D4
Copthorne Chase 3 TW15 170 B6
Copthorne Cl TW17 193 A3
Copthorne Ct SM1 218 A5
Copthorne Mews UB3 105 C2
Coptic St WC1 94 A2 240 A3
Copton Cl E3 97 C2
Copwood Cl N12 30 B6
Coral Apts 6 E16 121 A6
Coral Cl RM6 58 C6
Coral Ho 5 E1 97 A3
Coraline Cl UB1 85 B4
Coralline Wlk 4 SE2 124 C4
Coral Row 14 SW11 136 A2
Coral St SE1 116 C4 251 B1
Coram Ho
Bloomsbury WC1 240 A6
9 Chiswick W4 111 C1
Coram Mans WC1 240 C5
Coram St WC1 94 A3 240 A5
Coran Cl N9 18 D4
Corban Rd TW3 129 C2
Corbar Cl EN4 2 B4
Corbden Cl SE15 139 D4
Corbet Cl CR4, SM6 219 A6
Corbet Ct EC3 242 D1
Corbet Ho N1 234 A5
Corbet Pl E1 95 D2 243 C4
Corbett Ct SE26 185 B6
Corbett Gr N22 32 A3
Corbett Ho SW10 266 A6
Corbett Rd
Walthamstow E17 54 A6
Wanstead E11 55 C3
Corbett's La SE16 118 C2
Corbetts Pas 8 SE16 118 C2
Corbett Villas RM8 58 C1
Corbicum E11 54 C2
Corbidge Ct SE8 141 D6
Corbiere Ct SW19 178 D4
Corbiere Ho 5 N1 95 C6
Corbin Ho 7 E3 97 D4
Corbin's La HA2 63 D5
Corbridge 5 N17 34 B3
Corbridge Cres E2 96 B5
Corbridge Ho SE2 124 C3
Corby Cres EN2 4 A1
Corbylands Rd DA15 167 C3
Corbyn St N4, N19 50 A1
Corby Rd NW10 89 B5
Corby Way E3 97 C3
Cordelia Cl SE24 138 D1
Cordelia Gdns TW19 148 A4
Cordelia Ho 26 N1 95 C5
Cordelia Rd TW19 148 A4
Cordelia St E14 97 D1
Cordell Ho N15 51 D4
Cordingley Rd HA4 61 B6
Cording St E14 97 D2
Cordwainers Ct 18 E9 74 C1
Cordwainers Wlk 9 E13 99 A5
Cordwain Ho 7 N18 34 A5
Cordwell Rd SE13 164 C6
Corefield Cl N11 15 A2
Corelli Rd SE3 144 A4
Corfe Ave HA2 63 C4
Corfe Cl Hayes UB4 84 C1
Twickenham TW4 151 A3
Corfe Ho SW8 270 C4
Corfe Lodge 15 SE21 161 B2
Corfe Twr 6 W3 111 A4
Corfield Rd N21 16 B6
Corfield St E2 96 B4
Corfton Lo W5 88 A2
Corfton Rd W5 88 A2
Coriander Ave E14 98 B1
Coriander Ct SE1 253 D2
Cories Cl RM8 80 D6
Corigan Ct 6 E11 76 C6
Corinium Cl HA9 66 B4
Corinne Rd N19 71 C4
Corinth Ho IG3 58 A2
Cork St Mews W1 249 A5
Corkscrew Hill BR4 224 B5
Cork Sq E1 118 B5
Cork St W1 115 C6 249 A5
Cork Tree Ho 3 SW27 182 D5
Cork Tree Ret Pk N18 35 A4
Cork Tree Way E4 35 A5
Corlett St NW1 237 A4
Cormont Rd SE5 138 D4
Cormorant Cl E17 35 A3
Cormorant Ct
36 Deptford SE8 141 B6
13 Dulwich SE21 161 B2
Cormorant Ho EN3 18 D6
Cormorant Pl SM1 217 B3
Cormorant Rd E7 76 D3
Cornbury Ho 5 SE8 141 B6
Cornbury Rd HA8 25 D3
Cornel Ho 4 DA15 168 A1
Cornelia Dr UB4 84 C3
Cornelia St N7 72 B2
Cornelion Cotts 1 SM6 219 B3
Cornelius Ct 4 N12 30 A5
Cornell Bldg 9 E1 96 A1
Cornell Cl DA14 191 A4
Cornell Ct 4 EN3 7 A2
Cornell Ho HA2 63 B5
Corner Fielde SW2 160 B3
Corner Gn SE3 143 A3
Corner House St WC2 250 A4
Corner Mead NW9 27 D2
Cornerside TW15 171 A3
Cornerstone Ct 13 E1 96 A3
Cornerways
Harrow HA1 65 A5
Putney SW15 134 A1
Corney Rd W4 133 C6
Corney Reach Way W4 133 C5
Cornflower La CR0 206 D1
Cornflower Terr SE22 162 B5
Cornford Cl BR2 209 A4
Cornford Gr SW12 159 B2
Cornhill EC3 95 B1 242 D1
Cornhill Dr EN3 7 A6
Cornick Ho 7 SE16 118 B3
Cornish Ct N9 18 B4
Cornish Gr SE20 184 B2
Cornish Ho
Brentford TW8 110 B1
7 Camberwell SE17 138 D6
Cornmill La SE13 142 A2
Cornmow Dr NW10 68 A3
Cornshaw Rd RM8 58 D1
Cornthwaite Rd E5 74 C5
Cornwall Ave
Bethnal Green E2 96 C4
Claygate KT10 212 D1
Cornwall Ave *continued*
Falconwood DA16 145 D2
Finchley N3 29 C3
Southall UB1 85 C2
Wood Green N22 32 A2
Cornwall Cl IG11 79 D2
Cornwall Cres W11 91 A1
Cornwall Ct
5 Ealing W7 86 D3
5 Pinner HA5 23 B3
Upper Tooting SW17 180 C6
Cornwall Dr BR5 190 C3
Cornwall Flats SE1 251 B2
Cornwall Gdns
Kensington SW7 113 D3 255 D5
Willesden NW10 68 B2
Cornwall Gdns Wlk SW7 255 D5
Cornwall Gr W4 111 C1
Cornwall Ho
Marylebone NW1 237 D5
3 Putney SW15 156 C4
Cornwallis Ave
London N9 18 C2
New Eltham SE9 167 B2
Cornwallis Ct SW8 270 A2
Cornwallis Gr N9 18 C2
Cornwallis Ho 24 W12 112 B6
Cornwallis Rd
Dagenham RM9 81 A4
Edmonton N9 18 B2
Upper Holloway N19 72 A6
Walthamstow E17 52 D5
Woolwich SE18 122 D3
Woolwich SE18 123 A3
Cornwallis Sq
3 Finsbury Park N4 72 C6
London N19 72 A6
Cornwallis Wlk SE9 144 B2
Cornwall Mans
Chelsea SW10 266 B4
Marylebone NW1 237 D5
Cornwall Mews S SW7 256 A5
Cornwall Mews W SW7 255 D5
Cornwall Rd
Belmont SM2 217 B1
Croydon CR0 220 D6
Edmonton N18 34 A5
Finsbury Pk N4 50 C2
Harrow HA1 42 A3
Lambeth SE1 116 C4 251 B2
Pinner HA5 23 B3
Ruislip HA4 61 D6
Twickenham TW1 153 A3
West Green N15 51 B4
Cornwall Sq SE11 261 C2
Cornwall St 4 E1 118 B6
Cornwall Terr NW1 237 D5
Cornwall Terrace Mews NW1 237 D5
Corn Way E11 76 C5
Cornwood Cl N2 48 B5
Cornwood Dr E1 96 C1
Cornworthy Rd RM8 80 C3
Corona Rd SE12 165 A4
Coronation Ave 1 N16 73 D4
Coronation Cl
Bexley DA5 168 D5
Ilford IG6 57 A5
Coronation Ct
10 North Kensington W10 90 C2
Stratford E15 76 D2
Coronation Rd
Acton NW10 88 C3
Hayes UB3 105 D2
Newham E13 99 C4
Coronet Ho HA7 24 D4
Coronet Par 9 HA0 66 A2
Coronet St N1 95 C4
Corporation Ave TW4 129 A1
Corporation Row EC1 241 B6
Corporation St
Lower Holloway N7 72 A3
West Ham E15 98 D5
Corpus Christi RC Prim Sch
10 Brixton SW2 160 B6
Kingston u T KT3 199 A6
Corrance Rd SW2, SW4 138 A1
Corri Ave N14 31 D6
Corrib Ct N13 16 B1
Corrib Dr SM1 218 C3
Corrib Hts N8 49 D3
Corrigan Cl NW4 46 C6
Corringham Ct NW11 47 C2
Corringham Ho 11 E1 96 D1
Corringham Rd
London NW11 47 C2
Wembley HA9 66 C6
Corringway Ealing W5 88 C2
Golders Green NW11 47 D2
Corris Gn NW9 45 C3
Corry Dr SW9 138 D1
Corry Ho 2 E14 119 D6
Corsair Cl TW19 148 A4
Corsair Rd TW19 148 A4
Corscombe Cl KT2 177 A5
Corsehill St SW16 181 C4
Corsell Ho 5 TW8 131 C5
Corsham Ho HA9 66 C2
Corsham St N1 95 B4 235 D1
Corsica St N5 72 D2
Corsley Way E9 75 B2
Cortayne Ct TW2 152 C2
Cortayne Rd SW6 135 B3
Cortis Rd SW15 156 B5
Cortis Terr SW15 156 B5
Corunna Rd SW8 137 C4 269 B2
Corunna Terr SW8 269 A2
Corvette Sq 5 SE10 142 B6
Corwell Gdns UB8 83 A1
Corwell La UB8 83 A1
Coryton Path W9 91 B3
Cosbycote Ave SE24 161 A6
Cosdach Ave SM6 219 D1
Cosedge Cres CR0, CR9 220 D3
Cosgrove Cl
Edmonton N21 17 A2
Hayes UB4 84 D3
Cosgrove Ho 11 E2 96 A6
Cosmo Pl WC1 240 B4
Cosmur Cl W12 111 D3
Cossall Wlk SE15 140 B4
Cossar Mews 10 SW2 160 C6
Cosser St SE1 116 C3 261 A6
Costa St SE15 140 A3
Coston Prim Sch UB6 86 A4
Costons Ave UB6 86 B4
Costons La UB6 86 B4
Coston Wlk 4 SE4 140 D1
Cosway Ho NW11 48 A3
Cosway Mans NW1 237 B4
Cosway St NW1 92 C2 237 B4
Cotall St E14 97 C2
Coteford Cl HA5 40 A4
Coteford Inf Sch HA5 40 A3
Coteford Jun Sch HA5 39 D4
Coteford St SW17 181 A6
Cotelands CR0 221 C5
Cotesbach Rd E5 74 C5
Cotes Ho NW8 237 A5
Cotesmore Gdns RM8 80 C4
Cotford Rd CR7 205 A5
Cotham St SE17 262 B3
Cotherstone Rd SW2 160 B3
Cotleigh Ave DA5 168 D2
Cotleigh Rd NW6 69 C1
Cotman Cl
London NW11 48 A3
Putney SW15 156 D6
Cotman Ct BR3 185 B2
Cotmandene Cres BR5 190 A1
Cotman Gdns HA8 26 C1
Cotman Ho
5 Northolt UB5 84 D5
St John's Wood NW8 230 A4
Cotman Mews RM8 80 C3
Cotmans Cl UB3 106 A5
Coton Rd DA16 146 A2
Cotrill Gdns E8 74 B2
Cotsford Ave KT3 199 B4
Cotswold Ave WD23 8 A5

Cotswold Cl
Hinchley Wood
KT10 212 D6
Kingston u T KT2 177 A4
Cotswold Ct
London N11 31 A6
St Luke's EC1 242 A6
3 Wembley UB6 86 D5
Cotswold Gate NW2 47 A1
Cotswold Gdns
Hendon NW2 68 D6
Ilford IG2 57 B2
Newham E6 99 D5
Cotswold Gn EN2 4 B1
Cotswold Ho N16 51 D1
Cotswold Mews
SW11 266 D1
Cotswold Rd TW12 173 C4
Cotswold Rise BR6 211 D3
Cotswold St SE27 182 D6
Cotswold Way
Enfield EN2 4 B2
North Cheam KT4 216 C6
Cottage Ave BR2 210 A1
Cottage Cl
Harrow HA2 64 C6
Ruislip HA4 39 B1
Cottage Field Cl
DA14 168 C3
Cottage Gn SE5 139 B5
Cottage Gr
London SW9 138 A2
Surbiton KT6 197 D3
Cottage Pl
SW3 114 C3 257 A5
Cottage Rd KT19 215 B1
Cottage St E14 119 D6
Cottages The
Ickenham UB10 60 A6
Lambeth SE1 260 C5
Uxbridge UB10 60 D5
Cottage Wlk 2 N16 73 D5
Cottenham Dr
London NW9 45 D6
Wimbledon SW20 178 B3
Cottenham Ho 5
N19 72 A6
Cottenham Par
SW20 178 B1
COTTENHAM PARK 178 B2
Cottenham Park Rd
SW20 178 C3
Cottenham Pl SW20 178 B3
Cottenham Rd E17 53 B5
Cotterill Rd KT6 198 B1
Cottesbrook St 9
SE14 141 A5
Cottesloe Ho NW8 237 A6
Cottesloe Mews SE1 261 B6
Cottesmore Ct W8 255 D6
Cottesmore Gdns
W8 113 D3 255 D6
Cottimore Ave KT12 194 B1
Cottimore Cres
KT12 194 B2
Cottimore La KT12 194 B2
Cottimore Terr KT12 194 B2
Cottingham Chase
HA4 62 A5
Cottingham Rd
Penge SE20 184 D3
South Lambeth
SW8 138 B5 270 D4
Cottington Rd TW13 172 D6
Cottington St SE11 261 C2
Cotton Ave W3 89 B1
Cotton Cl
Dagenham RM9 80 C1
12 Leyton E11 76 C6
Cottongrass Cl 1
CR0 206 D1
Cottonham Cl N12 30 B5
Cotton Hill BR1 186 B6
Cotton Ho
Bedford Pk W12 111 D4
18 Streatham SW12 160 A4
Cotton Row SW11 136 B2
Cotton's Gdns E2 95 C4
Cottons La SE1 252 D4
Cotton St E14 120 A6
Cottrell Ct SE10 120 D2
Cotts Cl 13 W7 86 D2
Couchman Ho 8
SW4 159 C5
Couchmore Ave
KT10 212 C6

Coulgate St SE4 141 A2
Coulsdon Ct 4 N8 49 D4
Coulsdon Ho 5
SW2 160 A3
Coulson Cl RM8 58 C1
Coulson St
SW3 114 D1 257 C2
Coulter Cl UB4 85 A3
Coulter Rd W6 112 B3
Coulthurst Ct SW16 182 A3
Coults Cres NW5 71 A5
Councillor St SE5 139 A5
Counters Ct W14 254 B6
Counter St SE1 253 A3
Countess Rd NW5 71 C3
Countisbury Ave EN1 17 D4
Countisbury Ho
SE26 162 A1
Country Way TW13,
TW16 172 C5
County Gate
Longlands SE9 167 A1
New Barnet EN5 13 D5
County Gr SE5 139 A4
County Ho
22 Herne Hill SE24 138 D1
9 South Lambeth
SW9 138 C4
County Par TW8 131 D5
County Rd
Newham E6 100 D2
South Norwood CR7 182 D1
County St
SE1 117 A3 262 B5
Coupland Pl SE18 123 A1
Courcy Rd N8, N22 50 C6
Courier Ho 17 SW2 160 C4
Courland Gr SW8 137 D3
Courland St
SW8 137 D4 269 D1
Course The SE9 166 C1
Courtauld Ho 12 E2 96 A5
Courtauld Inst of Art*
WC2 250 C6
Courtauld Rd N19 50 A1
Courtaulds Cl SE28 124 A5
Court Ave DA17 125 B1
Court Cl Harrow HA3 44 A6
Twickenham TW13,
TW2 151 D1
Wallington SM6 219 D1
Court Close Ave TW13,
TW2 151 D1
Court Cres KT9 213 D2
Court Downs Rd
BR3 185 D1
Court Dr
Carshalton SM1 218 C4
Edgware HA7 26 A6
Hillingdon UB10 82 C6
Wallington CR0 220 B4
Courtenay Ave
Harrow HA3 24 A2
Highgate N6 48 C2
Courtenay Dr BR3 186 B1
Courtenay Gdns HA3 24 A1
Courtenay Mews E17 53 A4
Courtenay Pl E17 53 A4
Courtenay Rd
Leyton E11 76 D5
North Cheam KT4,
SM3 216 C5
Penge BR3, SE20 184 D4
Walthamstow E17 52 D5
Courtenay Rd HA9 65 D5
Courtenay Sq SE11 261 A1
Courtenay St
SE11 116 C1 261 A2
Courtens Mews HA7 25 C3
Court Farm Ave
KT19 215 B3
Court Farm Ind Est
TW19 148 B5
Court Farm Rd
Chislehurst SE9 166 A1
Northolt UB5 63 C1
Courtfield W13 87 C2
Courtfield Ave HA1 42 D4
Courtfield Cres HA1 42 D4
Courtfield Gdns
Ealing W13 87 A1
Ruislip HA4 61 D6
South Kensington
SW5 113 D2 255 D3
Courtfield Ho EC1 241 A4

Courtfield Mews
SW7 255 D3
Courtfield Rd
Ashford TW15 170 D4
South Kensington
SW7 114 A2 256 A3
Courtfield Rise BR4 224 B5
Courtgate Cl NW7 27 D4
Court Gdns N7 72 C2
Courthill Rd SE13 142 A1
Courthope Ho
14 Rotherhithe
SE16 118 C3
South Lambeth SW8 270 A3
Courthope Rd
Gospel Oak NW3 70 D4
Greenford UB6 86 B5
Wimbledon SW19 179 A5
Courthope Villas
SW19 179 A3
Court House Gdns
N3 29 C4
Court House Rd N12 29 D4
Court La SE21 161 D4
Courtland Ave
Chingford E4 20 D2
Edgware NW7 11 C1
Redbridge IG1 78 B6
South Norwood SW16 182 B3
Courtland Gr SE28 124 D6
Courtland Prim Sch
NW7 11 C2
Courtland Rd E6 100 A6
Courtlands
11 Beckenham BR3 185 D1
8 Belmont SM2 217 D1
Chislehurst BR7 188 D4
Ealing W5 87 C2
Richmond TW10 154 C6
5 Upper Clapton E5 52 B1
Walton-on-T KT12 194 A2
Courtlands Ave
Hampton TW12 173 B4
Hayes BR2 208 D1
Lee SE12 165 B6
Richmond TW9 132 D3
Courtlands Cl HA4 39 D2
Courtlands Dr KT19 215 D2
Courtlands Rd KT5 198 C2
Court Lane Gdns
SE21 161 C4
Courtleet Dr DA8 147 D4
Courtleigh 6 NW11 47 B4
Courtleigh Ave EN4 2 B5
Courtleigh Gdns
NW11 47 A5
Court Lo 11 DA17 125 C1
Courtman Rd N17 33 A3
Court Mans 8 W6 112 A2
Court Mead UB5 85 B4
Courtmead Cl SE24 161 A5
Courtnell St W2 91 C1
Courtney Cl SE19 183 C4
Courtney Cres SM5 218 D1
Courtney Ct N7 72 C3
Courtney Ho
1 Hendon NW4 46 C5
Kensington W14 254 B6
Courtney Pl CR0 220 C5
Courtney Rd
Croydon CR0 220 C5
Islington N7 72 C3
Mitcham SW19 180 C3
Courtney Twrs IG2 57 B3
Courtney Way TW6 126 C2
Court One TW15 149 A1
Court Par HA0 65 B5
Courtrai Rd SE23 163 A5
Court Rd Eltham SE9 166 B4
Southall UB2 107 B1
South Norwood SE25 205 D6
Uxbridge UB10 60 D4
Court Royal SW15 157 A6
Courtside
Crouch End N8 49 D3
Forest Hill SE23 162 C1
Court St
2 Bromley BR1 187 A1
3 Stepney E1 96 B2
Courts The SW16 182 A3
Court The London N10 49 C5
Ruislip HA4 63 A4
Court Three TW15 149 A1
Court Two TW15 149 A1
Courtville Ho 12 W10 91 A4
Courtway IG8 37 C5

Court Way Acton W3 89 A2
Colindale NW9 45 C5
Ilford IG6 57 A6
Twickenham TW1,
TW2 152 D4
Courtyard Apartments
TW11 174 B5
Courtyard Mews
BR5 190 A3
Courtyard The
Fulham
SW6 135 A4 264 A1
Islington N1 72 B1
Keston BR2 226 A2
Thornton Heath CR0 204 B3
13 Wandsworth
SW18 136 B1
Court Yd SE9 166 B5
Cousin La
EC4 117 B6 252 C5
Cousins Cl 2 UB7 104 A6
Cousins Ct 2 NW9 46 A5
Couthurst Rd SE3 143 B5
Coutts Ave KT9 214 A3
Couzens Ho 8 E3 97 B2
Coval Gdns SW14 132 D1
Coval La SW14 132 D1
Coval Pas SW14 133 A1
Coval Rd SW14 133 A1
Covardale Ct EN3 7 A6
Covelees Wall E6 100 C1
Covell Ct 16 SE8 141 C5
Covent Garden Sta
WC2 94 A1 240 B1
Coventry Cl
Kilburn NW6 91 C6
9 Newham E6 100 B1
Coventry Rd
Bethnal Green E1 96 B3
Croydon SE25 206 A5
Ilford IG1 56 D1
Coventry St W1 249 C5
Coverack Cl
Croydon CR0 207 A2
Southgate N14 15 C5
Coverdale Cl HA7 25 B5
Coverdale Gdns
CR0 221 D5
Coverdale Rd
Brondesbury NW2 69 A2
Friern Barnet N11 31 A4
Hammersmith W12 112 B4
Hampstead NW6 68 D1
Coverdales The
IG11 101 B5
Coverham Ho 5
SE4 140 D1
Coverley Cl E1 96 A2
Coverley Point SE11 260 C3
Coverton Rd SW17 180 C5
Coverts Rd KT10 212 D1
Covert The BR6 211 C3
Covert Way EN4 2 A3
Covet Wood Cl BR5 211 D3
Covey Cl SW19 179 D1
Covey Rd KT4, SM3 216 D6
Covington Gdns
SW16 182 D3
Covington Way
South Norwood
SW16 182 C3
South Norwood
SW16 182 D3
Cowan Cl E6 100 A2
Cowan Ct 14 NW10 67 B1
Cowan Lo 6 IG8 37 C4
Cowbridge La IG11 78 D1
Cowbridge Rd HA3 44 B5
Cowcross St
EC1 94 D2 241 C4
Cowdenbeath Path
N1 233 C6
Cowden Rd BR6 211 D2
Cowden St SE6 185 C6
Cowdray Hall Royal Coll
of Nursing
W1 93 B1 238 C2
Cowdray Ho 22
SE22 139 C2
Cowdray Rd UB10 83 A6
Cowdrey Cl EN1 5 C3
Cowdrey Rd SW19 180 A5
Cowdry Rd E9 75 B2
Cowell Lo E4 36 D5
Cowen Ave HA2 64 B6
Cowen Ho 4 SE18 144 D6

Cowgate Rd UB6 86 B4
Cowick Rd SW17 180 D6
Cowings Mead UB5 63 A2
Cowland Ave EN3 6 C1
Cow Leaze E6 100 C1
Cowleaze Rd KT2 176 A2
Cowley Ct 8 E18 37 A1
Cowley La E11 76 C5
COWLEY PEACHY 82 A2
Cowley Pl NW4 46 C4
Cowley Rd
Brixton SW9 138 C4
East Acton W3 111 D5
16 Kennington SW9 138 C5
Mortlake SW14 133 C2
Redbridge IG1 56 B2
Wanstead E11 55 B4
Cowley St SW1 260 A5
Cowling Cl W11 244 A4
Cowper Ave
Sutton SM1 218 B4
Upton Pk E6 78 A1
Cowper Cl
Bexley DA16 168 A6
Bromley BR2 209 D5
Cowper Gdns
Southgate N14 15 C5
Wallington SM6 219 C2
Cowper Ho
Pimlico SW1 259 D1
Walworth SE17 262 B2
Cowper Rd Acton W3 111 B5
6 Belvedere DA17 125 C2
Bromley BR2 209 D5
Ealing W7 108 D6
East Barnet N14 15 B3
Edmonton N18 34 A5
Kingston u T KT2 176 B5
Stoke Newington N16 73 C4
Wimbledon SW19 180 A4
Cowper's Ct EC3 242 D1
Cowper St EC1,
EC2 95 B3 242 D6
Cowper Terr W10 90 D2
Cowslip Cl UB10 60 A1
Cowslip Rd E18 37 B1
Cowthorpe Rd SW8 269 D2
Cox Ct 3 EN4 2 C1
Coxe Pl HA3 43 A5
Cox Ho W6 264 A6
Cox La
Chessington KT9 214 B4
West Ewell KT19 215 A3
Coxmount Rd SE7 121 D1
Coxs Ave TW17 193 C6
Coxson Way SE1 253 C1
Coxwell Rd
Plumstead SE18 123 B1
South Norwood SE19 183 C3
Coxwold Path KT9 214 A1
Coysh Ct 8 SW15 157 A6
Crabbs Croft Cl 7
BR6 227 A3
Crab Hill BR3 186 B3
Crabtree Ave
Dagenham RM6 58 D5
Wembley HA0 88 B5
Crabtree Cl E2 95 D5
Crabtree Ct EN5 1 D1
Crabtree Hall SW6 134 C5
Crabtree La SW6 134 D5
Cracknell Cl EN1 6 B6
Craddock Rd EN1 5 D2
Craddock St NW5 71 A2
Cradley Rd SE9 167 B3
Cragie Ho SE1 263 D3
Craig Dr UB8 82 D1
Craigen Ave CR0 206 B1
Craigen Gdns IG1,
IG3 79 C4
Craigerne Rd SE3 143 B5
Craig Gdns E18 36 D1
Craig Ho Ealing W13 109 B6
Greenwich SE3 143 B5
Craigholm SE18 144 C4
Craigie Lea N10 31 B1
Craigleith SW15 156 D5
Craigmuir Pk HA0 88 B6
Craignair Rd SW2 160 C4
Craignish Ave SW16 182 B1
Craig Park Rd N18 34 B6
Craig Rd TW10 175 C6
Craig's Ct SW1 250 A4

Craigside KT2 ... 176 D2
Craigton Rd SE9 ... 144 B1
Craigweil Cl HA7 ... 25 D5
Craigweil Dr HA7 ... 25 D5
Craigwell Ave TW13 ... 150 A1
Craik Ct NW6 ... 91 B5
Crail Row SE17 ... 117 B2 262 D3
Crales Ho SE18 ... 122 A3
Cramer Ct KT3 ... 199 A6
Cramer St W1 ... 93 A2 238 B3
Cramhurst Ho 3 SM1 ... 218 B3
Crammond Cl W6 ... 264 A5
Cramond Ct TW14 ... 149 C3
Cramonde Ct DA16 ... 146 A3
Crampton Prim Sch SE17 ... 116 D1 261 D2
Crampton Rd SE20 ... 184 C4
Crampton St SE17 ... 117 A1 262 A2
Cranberry Cl 2 UB5 ... 84 D5
Cranberry La E16 ... 98 C3
Cranborne Ave
Southall UB2 ... 107 C2
Tolworth KT6, KT9 ... 214 C5
Cranborne Rd IG11 ... 101 B6
Cranborne Waye
Hayes UB4 ... 84 B1
Hayes UB4 ... 106 C6
Cranbourn Alley WC2 ... 249 D6
Cranbourne Cl SW16 ... 204 A6
Cranbourne Ct
East Finchley N2 ... 47 D6
2 Edgware HA8 ... 26 D5
Finchley NW7 ... 29 A3
SW11 ... 267 B4
Walton-on-T KT12 ... 194 B2
Wanstead E18 ... 55 B5
Cranbourne Dr HA5 ... 40 D4
Cranbourne Gdns
Ilford IG6 ... 57 A6
Temple Fortune NW11 ... 47 B4
Cranbourne Rd
Leyton E15 ... 76 A4
London N10 ... 31 B1
Manor Pk E12 ... 78 A3
Northwood HA6 ... 39 D6
Cranbourn Ho 6 SE16 ... 118 B4
Cranbourn Pas 5 SE16 ... 118 B4
Cranbourn St WC2 ... 115 D6 249 D6
CRANBROOK ... 56 C1
Cranbrook NW1 ... 232 B5
Cranbrook Cl BR2 ... 209 A3
Cranbrook Coll (Boys) IG1 ... 78 C6
Cranbrook Ct
8 Brentford TW8 ... 131 D6
South Croydon CR2 ... 221 C3
Cranbrook Dr
Thames Ditton KT10 ... 196 A1
Twickenham TW2 ... 151 D3
Cranbrook Ho
5 Hackney E5 ... 74 B3
South Norwood SE19 ... 183 B2
Cranbrook La N11 ... 31 B6
Cranbrook Mews E17 ... 53 B4
Cranbrook Pk N22 ... 32 C2
Cranbrook Prim Sch IG1 ... 56 B2
Cranbrook Rd
Chiswick W4 ... 111 C1
Erith DA7 ... 147 B4
Hounslow TW4 ... 129 B1
Ilford IG1, IG2 ... 56 C3
New Barnet EN4 ... 14 B5
South Norwood CR7 ... 183 A1
St Johns SE8 ... 141 C4
Wimbledon SW19 ... 179 A3
Cranbrook Rise IG1 ... 56 B2
Cranbrook St E2 ... 96 D5
Cranbury Rd SW6 ... 135 D3
Crandale Ho 8 E5 ... 74 B3
Crandley Ct SE8 ... 119 A2
Crane Ave Acton W3 ... 111 A6
Isleworth TW7 ... 153 A6
Cranebank TW4 ... 128 B2
Cranebank Mews TW1 ... 131 A1
Cranebrook TW2 ... 152 A2
Crane Cl
Dagenham RM10 ... 81 C2
Harrow HA2 ... 64 A5
Crane Ct
7 Acton W12 ... 111 C4
Holborn EC4 ... 241 B1
West Ewell KT19 ... 215 A4
Craneford Cl TW2 ... 152 D4
Craneford Way TW2 ... 152 D4
Crane Gdns UB3 ... 105 D2
Crane Gr N7 ... 72 C2
Crane Ho 24 Bow E3 ... 97 A5
9 Catford BR1 ... 186 B5
Feltham TW13 ... 151 C1
10 Peckham SE15 ... 139 D4
Crane Lodge Rd TW5 ... 128 B6
Crane Mead SE16 ... 118 D2
Crane Mead Ct TW1 ... 152 D4
Crane Park Prim Sch TW13 ... 151 B2
Crane Park Rd TW2 ... 151 D2
Crane Rd
Stanwell TW19 ... 148 C5
Twickenham TW2 ... 152 C3
Cranesbill Cl
Kenton NW9 ... 45 B6
Mitcham SW16 ... 181 D1
Cranes Dr KT5 ... 198 B5
Cranes Park Ave KT5, KT6 ... 198 B5
Cranes Park Cres KT5 ... 198 B5
Cranes Pk KT5, KT6 ... 198 A4
Crane St
Greenwich SE10 ... 120 B1
6 Peckham SE15 ... 139 D4
Craneswater TW6 ... 127 D5
Craneswater Pk UB2 ... 107 B1
Cranes Way WD6 ... 11 A6
Crane Way TW2 ... 152 A4
Cranfield Ct
Marylebone NW1 ... 237 B3
2 Woodford IG8 ... 37 A6
Cranfield Dr NW9 ... 27 C3
Cranfield Ho WC1 ... 240 B4
Cranfield Rd SE4 ... 141 B2
CRANFORD ... 128 C4
Cranford Ave
Bowes Pk N13 ... 32 A5
Stanwell TW19 ... 148 B4
Cranford Cl
Stanwell TW19 ... 148 A4
Wimbledon SW20 ... 178 B3
Cranford Com Coll TW5 ... 128 B6
Cranford Cotts 8 E1 ... 118 D6
Cranford Ct SM1 ... 218 A4
Cranford Ctry Pk TW5 ... 128 A6
Cranford Dr UB3 ... 105 D2
Cranford Jun & Inf Schs TW4 ... 128 B3
Cranford La
Harlington TW6 ... 127 D4
Harlington UB3 ... 127 C5
Heston TW5 ... 128 C5
Cranford Lo SW19 ... 156 D2
Cranford Mews BR2 ... 210 A4
Cranford Park Prim Sch UB3 ... 105 D2
Cranford Park Rd UB3 ... 105 D2
Cranford Rd TW6 ... 127 D2
Cranford Rise KT10 ... 212 A3
Cranford St E1 ... 118 D6
Cranford Way N8 ... 50 C4
Cranhurst Rd NW2 ... 68 C3
Cranleigh W11 ... 244 C4
Cranleigh Cl
Bexley DA5 ... 169 D5
Penge SE20 ... 184 B1
Cranleigh Ct
1 Barnet EN5 ... 1 D1
Mitcham CR4 ... 202 B6
Richmond TW9 ... 132 C2
Southall UB1 ... 85 B1
4 Stamford Hill N16 ... 51 C1
Cranleigh Gardens Ind Est UB1 ... 85 B2
Cranleigh Gdns
Barking IG11 ... 79 B2
Harrow HA3 ... 44 A4
Kingston u T KT2 ... 176 B4
Southall UB1 ... 85 B1
Southgate N21 ... 16 C6
South Norwood SE25 ... 205 C6
Sutton SM1 ... 217 D6
Cranleigh Ho SW20 ... 178 B1
Cranleigh Hos NW1 ... 232 B3
Cranleigh Mews SW11 ... 136 D3
Cranleigh Rd
Feltham TW13 ... 171 D6
Harringay N15 ... 51 A4
Merton SW19 ... 201 C6
Thames Ditton KT10 ... 196 A1
Cranleigh St NW1 ... 93 C5 232 B3
Cranley Dene Ct N10 ... 49 B5
Cranley Dr Ilford IG2 ... 57 A2
Ruislip HA4 ... 61 D6
CRANLEY GARDENS ... 49 B5
Cranley Gdns
London N10 ... 49 B5
Palmers Green N13 ... 16 B1
South Kensington SW7 ... 114 B1 256 C2
Wallington SM6 ... 219 C1
Cranley Mews SW7 ... 114 A1 256 B2
Cranley Par 2 SE9 ... 188 A6
Cranley Pl SW7 ... 114 B2 256 C3
Cranley Rd Ilford IG2 ... 57 A2
Newham E13 ... 99 B2
Cranmer Ave W13 ... 109 B3
Cranmer Cl
Ruislip HA4 ... 40 D1
Stanmore HA7 ... 25 C3
West Barnes SM4 ... 200 D3
Cranmer Ct
Chelsea SW3 ... 257 B3
Church End N3 ... 29 A1
Hampton TW12 ... 173 D5
Kingston u T KT2 ... 175 D6
Cranmere Prim Sch KT10 ... 196 A1
Cranmer Farm Cl CR4 ... 202 D5
Cranmer Ho SW11 ... 267 A2
Cranmer Prim Sch CR4 ... 202 D5
Cranmer Rd
Brixton SW9 ... 138 C5
Croydon CR0 ... 221 A5
Edgware HA8 ... 10 D1
Forest Gate E7 ... 77 B4
Hampton TW12 ... 173 D5
Hayes UB3 ... 83 B1
Kingston u T KT2 ... 176 A5
Mitcham CR4 ... 202 D5
Cranmer Terr SW17 ... 180 B5
Cranmore Ave TW7 ... 130 A5
Cranmore Rd
Catford BR1 ... 164 D1
Elmstead BR7 ... 188 B5
Cranmore Way N10 ... 49 C5
Cranston Cl
Hounslow TW3, TW4 ... 129 A3
Uxbridge UB10 ... 61 B6
Cranston Ct 6 N20 ... 14 D2
Cranston Gdns E4 ... 35 D4
Cranston Rd SE23 ... 163 A2
Cranswick Rd SE16 ... 118 B1
Crantock Rd SE6 ... 164 A2
Cranwell Cl E3 ... 97 D3
Cranwell Ct
Croydon CR0 ... 222 D6
6 Hendon NW9 ... 27 D3
Cranwell Gr TW17 ... 192 B5
Cranwell Rd TW6 ... 126 D3
Cranwich Ave N21 ... 17 B4
Cranwich Rd N16 ... 51 C2
Cranwood Ct EC1 ... 235 D1
Cranwood St EC1 ... 95 B4 235 D1
Cranworth Cres 7 E4 ... 20 B3
Cranworth Gdns SW9 ... 138 C4
Cranworth Ho 6 N7 ... 72 B4
Craster Rd SW2 ... 160 B4
Craston Ho 2 SE5 ... 139 C3
Crathie Rd SE12 ... 165 B5
Crathorne Ho N2 ... 30 B1
Cravan Ave TW13 ... 150 A2
Craven Ave
Ealing W5 ... 109 C6
Southall UB1 ... 85 B2
Craven Cl Hayes UB4 ... 84 A1
Stamford Hill N16 ... 52 A2
Craven Cottage (Fulham FC) SW6 ... 134 D4
Craven Ct
Dagenham RM6 ... 59 A3
Edgware HA8 ... 26 B6
Harlesden NW10 ... 89 C6
Southall UB1 ... 107 D5
Craven Gdns
Barking IG11 ... 101 C5
Ilford IG6 ... 57 B6
Wimbledon SW19 ... 179 D5
Craven Hill W2 ... 114 A6 246 B6
Craven Hill Gdns W2 ... 114 A6 246 A6
Craven Hill Mews W2 ... 246 B6
Craven Ho Ealing W5 ... 109 C6
16 Finchley N2 ... 30 B1
2 Mortlake SW14 ... 133 B2
Craven Lo
Bayswater W2 ... 246 B6
Fulham SW6 ... 134 D4
Craven Mews 6 SW11 ... 137 A2
Craven Park Mews NW10 ... 89 C6
Craven Park Rd
Harlesden NW10 ... 89 C6
South Tottenham N15 ... 52 A3
Craven Pas WC2 ... 250 A4
Craven Pk NW10 ... 89 C6
Craven Rd
Croydon CR0 ... 206 B1
Ealing W5 ... 109 C6
Kingston u T KT2 ... 176 B2
Paddington W2 ... 92 A1 236 B1
Stonebridge NW10 ... 89 B6
Craven St WC2 ... 116 A5 250 A4
Craven Terr W2 ... 114 A6 246 B6
Craven Wlk E5, N16 ... 52 A2
Crawford Ave HA0 ... 65 D3
Crawford Bldgs NW1 ... 237 B3
Crawford Cl TW7 ... 130 C3
Crawford Ct SE18 ... 146 A6
Crawford Gdns
Edmonton N13 ... 16 D1
Northolt UB5 ... 85 B4
Crawford Mews W1 ... 237 C3
Crawford Pas EC1 ... 241 B5
Crawford Pl W1 ... 92 C2 237 B3
Crawford Place Dwellings NW1 ... 237 B3
Crawford Point 4 E16 ... 98 D1
Crawford Prim Sch SE5 ... 139 A4
Crawford Rd SE5 ... 139 A3
Crawford St
Marylebone W1 ... 92 D2 237 C3
16 Willesden NW10 ... 67 B1
Crawley Rd
Enfield EN1 ... 17 D4
Leyton E10 ... 53 D1
Tottenham N22 ... 33 A1
Crawshay Ct SW9 ... 138 C4
Crawshay Ho 13 N16 ... 73 B4
Crawthew Gr SE22 ... 139 D1
Cray Bldgs DA14 ... 190 C4
Craybrooke Rd DA14 ... 190 B6
Craybury End SE9 ... 167 A2
Crayfields Bsns Pk BR5 ... 190 C2
Crayfields Ind Pk BR5 ... 190 C1
Crayford Cl E6 ... 100 A1
Crayford Ho
Bermondsey SE1 ... 252 D1
5 Lower Holloway N7 ... 72 A4
Crayford Rd N7 ... 72 A4
Crayke Hill KT9 ... 214 A1
Crayle Ho EC1 ... 241 D6
Crayleigh Terr DA14 ... 190 C4
Crayonne Cl TW16 ... 171 C2
Cray Rd Erith DA17 ... 147 C6
Sidcup DA14 ... 190 C4
Crays Par The BR5 ... 190 C1
Crealock Gr IG8 ... 36 D5
Crealock St SW18 ... 157 D5
Creasy Est SE1 ... 263 A5
Crebor St SE22 ... 162 A5
Credenhall Dr BR2 ... 210 B1
Credenhill Ho 2 SE15 ... 140 B5
Credenhill St SW16 ... 181 C4
Crediton Hill NW6 ... 69 D3
Crediton Ho EN3 ... 6 D2
Crediton Rd NW10 ... 90 D6
Crediton Way KT10 ... 213 A3
Credon Rd
Bermondsey SE16 ... 118 B1
Newham E13 ... 99 C5
Creechurch La EC3 ... 243 B1
Creechurch Pl EC3 ... 243 B1
Creed Ct 5 E1 ... 97 A4
Creed Ho SE15 ... 140 B2
Creed La EC4 ... 241 D1
Creek Ho W14 ... 254 B6
CREEKMOUTH ... 101 D2
Creekmouth Ind Pk IG11 ... 101 D3
Creek Rd
Barking IG11 ... 101 D4
East Molesey KT8 ... 196 C5
Greenwich SE10, SE8 ... 141 D6
Creek Road Ind Est SE8 ... 141 D6
Creekside SE8 ... 141 D5
Creekside Foyer SE8 ... 141 D6
Creek The TW16 ... 194 A4
Creeland Gr SE6 ... 163 B3
Crefeld Cl W6 ... 135 A6 264 A5
Creffield Rd W3, W5 ... 110 C6
Creighton Ave
London N2, N10 ... 30 D1
Newham E6 ... 99 D5
Creighton Cl W12 ... 112 B6
Creighton Ho N2 ... 48 C6
Creighton Rd
Ealing W5 ... 109 D3
Kensal Rise NW6 ... 90 D5
Tottenham N17 ... 33 C3
Cremer Bsns Ctr 8 E2 ... 95 D5
Cremer Ho 9 SE8 ... 141 C5
Cremer St E2 ... 95 D5
Cremorne Rd SW10 ... 136 B5 266 C4
Creon Ct 3 SW9 ... 138 C4
Crescent EC3 ... 253 C6
Crescent Arc 1 SE10 ... 142 A6
Crescent Court Bsns Ctr 1 E16 ... 98 B3
Crescent Ct
Clapham Pk SW4 ... 159 D6
Crouch End N8 ... 49 D3
Kingston u T KT6 ... 197 D4
14 Sidcup DA15 ... 168 A1
Crescent Dr BR5 ... 211 A3
Crescent E EN4 ... 2 A5
Crescent Gdns
Ruislip HA4 ... 40 B2
Wimbledon SW19 ... 157 C1
Crescent Gr
London SW4 ... 137 C1
Mitcham CR4 ... 202 C5
Crescent Ho
London SE13 ... 141 D3
5 Wimbledon SW20 ... 178 D2
Crescent La SW4 ... 159 D6
Crescent Mans
Islington N5 ... 72 D3
Notting Hill W11 ... 244 B6
Crescent Par UB10 ... 82 C4
Crescent Pl SW3 ... 257 B4
Crescent Rd
Beckenham BR3 ... 185 D1
Chingford E4 ... 20 C4
Church End N3 ... 29 B2
Crouch End N8 ... 49 D3
Dagenham RM10 ... 81 D5
East Barnet EN4 ... 14 C6
Edmonton N9 ... 18 A3
Enfield EN2 ... 4 D1
Friern Barnet N11 ... 30 D6
Harringay N15 ... 50 D6

Crescent Rd *continued*
Kingston u T KT2 176 D3
Leyton E10 75 D6
Plaistow BR1 187 A3
Shepperton TW17 193 A4
Sidcup DA15 167 D1
Upton Pk E6 99 C6
West Ham E13 99 A6
Wimbledon SW20 178 D2
Woodford E18 37 C2
Wood Green N22 31 D2
Woolwich SE18 122 D2
Crescent Rise
East Barnet EN4 14 C6
3 Finchley N3 29 C2
Wood Green N22 31 D2
Crescent Row EC1 242 A5
Crescent St N1 72 B1
Crescent Stables
SW15 157 A6
Crescent The
Acton W3 89 C1
Ashford TW15 170 B5
Barnes SW13 134 A3
Barnet EN5 1 D3
Beckenham BR3 185 C2
Bexley DA5 168 C4
Coombe KT3 177 A1
Dollis Hill NW2 68 B5
East Finchley N2 47 D6
East Molesey KT8 195 C5
Friern Barnet N11 31 A6
Harlington UB7 127 B5
Harrow HA2 42 A1
Ilford IG2 56 C3
Loughton IG10 21 D5
Lower Halliford TW17 193 D2
Sidcup DA14 189 D6
Southall UB1 107 A4
Surbiton KT6 198 A4
Sutton SM1 218 B3
Thornton Heath CR0 205 B3
Walthamstow E17 53 A4
Wembley HA0 65 B6
West Wickham BR4 208 C3
Wimbledon SW19 157 C1
Crescent View IG10 21 D6
Crescent W EN4 2 A5
Crescentway N12 30 C4
Crescent Way
London SE4 141 C2
Orpington BR6 227 C3
South Norwood SW16 182 C3
Crescent Wood Rd SE21, SE26 162 A1
Cresford Rd
SW6 135 D4 265 C1
Crespigny Rd NW4 46 B3
Cressage Cl UB1 85 C3
Cressage Ho 9
TW8 132 A6
Cressall Ho 14 E14 119 C3
Cresset Ho 8 E9 74 C2
Cresset Rd E9 74 C2
Cresset St SW4 137 D2
Cressfield Cl NW5 71 A3
Cressida Rd N19 49 D1
Cressingham Ct 1
DA17 125 C3
Cressingham Gr
SM1 218 A4
Cressingham Rd
Burnt Oak HA8 27 B3
Lewisham SE13 142 A2
Cressington Cl 4
N16 73 C3
Cress Mews BR1 186 B5
Cresswell Gdns SW5 256 A2
Cresswell Ho HA9 66 A5
Cresswell Pk SE3 142 D2
Cresswell Pl
SW10 114 A1 256 B2
Cresswell Rd
Croydon SE25 206 A5
Feltham TW13 173 A6
Twickenham TW1 153 D5
Cresswell Way N21 16 C4
Cressy Ct
Hammersmith W6 112 B3
6 Stepney E1 96 C2
36 Stepney E1 96 C2
Cressy Ho SW13 134 B2
Cressy Hos 7 E1 96 C2
Cressy Pl E1 96 C2
Cressy Rd NW3 70 D4
Cresta Ct W5 88 B3
Cresta Ho 7 Bow E3 97 C3
Hampstead NW6 70 B1
Crestbrook Ave N13 16 D1
Crestbrook Pl N13 16 D1
Crest Ct NW4 46 C4
Crest Dr EN3 6 C5
Crestfield St N1, WC1 233 B2
Crest Gdns HA4 62 C5
Crest Ho 3 TW15 170 C5
Creston Way KT4 200 D1
Crest Rd
Dollis Hill NW2 68 A6
Hayes BR2 208 D2
South Croydon CR2 222 B1
Crest Sch of English
HA8 26 C5
Crest The
Edmonton N13 32 C6
Finchley N12 29 D4
Hendon NW4 46 C4
Surbiton KT5 198 C4
10 West Norwood
SW27 182 D5
Crestview NW5 71 B5
Crest View HA5 40 D5
Crest View Dr BR5 211 A4
Crestway SW15 156 B5
Crestwood Way
TW4 151 A6
Creswell Dr BR3 207 D4
Creswick Ct W3 110 D6
Creswick Rd W3 110 D6
Creswick Wlk
7 Bow E3 97 C4
Temple Fortune NW11 47 B5
Creton St SE18 122 C3
Crewdson Rd SW9 138 C5
Crewe Pl NW10 89 D4
Crewkerne Ct SW11 266 D2
Crews St E14 119 C2
Crewys Rd
Child's Hill NW2 69 B6
London SE15 140 B3
Crichton Ave SM6 219 D4
Crichton Rd SM5 218 D1
Crichton St SW8 137 C3
Cricket Ct 2 E6 100 B4
Cricketers Arms Rd
EN2 5 A3
Cricketers Cl
Chessington KT9 213 D4
Oakwood N14 15 C4
Cricketers Mews 4
SW18 157 D6
Cricketers Terr SM5 218 C5
Cricketers Wlk SE26 184 C5
Cricketfield Rd E5 74 B4
Cricket Gn CR4 202 D5
Cricket Green Specl Sch
1 CR4 202 C6
Cricket Ground Rd
BR7 188 D2
Cricket La BR3 185 A4
Cricket Row N2 48 B6
Cricklade Ave SW2 160 B2
CRICKLEWOOD 68 D4
Cricklewood Broadway
NW2 68 D4
Cricklewood La NW2 69 B5
Cricklewood Sta
NW2 68 D4
Cridland St E15 98 D6
Crieff Ct 3 TW11 175 C3
Crieff Rd SW18 158 A5
Criffel Ave SW2 159 D3
Crimscott St
SE1 117 C3 263 B5
Crimsworth Rd
SW8 137 D5 269 D3
Crinan St N1 94 A5 233 B4
Cringle St
SW8 137 C5 269 A4
Cripplegate St EC1 242 B4
Cripps Gn UB4 84 B3
Crispe Ho
4 Barking IG11 101 B5
Islington N1 233 D5
Crispen Rd TW13 173 A6
Crispian Cl NW10 67 C4
Crispin Cl SM6 220 A6
Crispin Cres SM6 219 D6
Crispin Ct SE17 263 A3
Crispin Mews 10
NW11 47 B4
Crispin Pl E1 243 C4
Crispin Rd HA8 27 A4
Crispin St E1 95 D2 243 C3
Crispin Way UB8 82 B3
Crisp Rd W6 112 C1
Cristowe Rd SW6 135 B3
Criterion Bldgs KT7 197 B2
Criterion Mews N19 71 D6
Crittall's Cnr DA14 190 C3
Crittenden Lo BR4 207 C1
Crockerton Rd
SW17 158 D2
Crockham Way SE9 188 C6
Crocus Cl CR0 206 D1
Crocus Field EN5 13 B5
Croft Ave BR4 208 A1
Croft Cl Edgware NW7 11 C1
Elmstead BR7 188 B5
Erith DA17 125 B1
Harlington UB7 127 A5
Hillingdon UB10 60 C1
Croft Ct London SE13 164 A5
Ruislip HA4 39 D1
Croftdown Rd NW5 71 B5
Croft End Cl KT9 214 B5
Crofters Cl TW7 152 B6
Crofters Ct 9 SE8 119 A2
Crofters Way
NW1 93 D6 232 C6
Croft Gdns
Ealing W7 109 A4
Ruislip HA4 39 D1
Croft Ho
Putney SW15 157 A5
11 West Kilburn W10 91 A4
Croft Lodge Cl IG8 37 B4
Croft Mews 3 N12 14 A1
CROFTON 227 B6
Crofton Ave
Chiswick W4 133 B5
Orpington BR6 227 A6
Sidcup DA5 168 D4
Crofton Gate Way
SE4 163 A6
Crofton Gr E4 36 B6
Crofton Inf Sch BR5 211 B2
Crofton Jun Sch
BR5 211 B2
Crofton La BR5, BR6 211 B2
Crofton Park Rd
SE4 163 B5
Crofton Park Sta
SE4 163 A6
Crofton Rd
Camberwell SE5 139 C3
Locksbottom BR6 226 C5
Newham E13 99 B3
Crofton Roman Villa★
BR6 227 C6
Crofton Terr
Homerton E5 75 A3
Richmond TW9 132 B1
Crofton Way
Enfield EN2 4 C3
New Barnet EN5 13 D5
Croft Rd
Carshalton SM1 218 C3
Enfield EN3 7 A4
Merton SW19 180 A3
Plaistow BR1 187 A4
South Norwood SW16 182 C3
Crofts Ho 21 E2 96 A5
Croftside The 3
SE25 206 A6
Crofts La N22 32 C3
Crofts Rd HA1 43 A4
Crofts St E1 118 A6
Croft St SE8 119 A2
Crofts The TW17 193 C5
Croft The Barnet EN5 1 A1
Chingford E4 20 C2
Ealing W5 88 A2
Edgware HA8 26 D3
Harlesden NW10 89 D5
Heston TW5 129 A5
New Malden KT3 199 C4
Pinner HA5 41 B2
Ruislip HA4 62 C4
Wembley HA0 65 C3
Croft Villas HA1 43 A3
Croft Way
Richmond TW10 153 B1
Sidcup DA15 167 C1
Crogsland Rd NW1 71 A1
Croham Cl CR2 221 C1
Croham Manor Rd
CR2 221 C2
Croham Mount CR2 221 C1
Croham Park Ave
CR2 221 D3
Croham Rd CR2 221 C3
Croham Valley Rd
CR2 222 B1
Croindene Rd SW16 182 A2
Crokesley Ho 2 HA8 27 A1
Cromartie Rd N19 49 D2
Cromarty Ct 7 BR1 187 C1
Cromarty Ho 8 E1 97 A2
Cromarty Rd HA8 10 D2
Cromberdale Ct N17 34 A2
Crombie Cl IG4 56 B4
Crombie Mews 5
SW11 136 C3
Crombie Rd DA15 167 B3
Cromdale Ct N16 51 D2
Crome Ho UB5 85 A5
Cromer Cl UB8 83 A1
Cromer Ct
Streatham SW16 160 A1
Wandsworth SW18 157 B5
Crome Rd NW10 67 C2
Cromer Mans 6
SM1 217 D3
Cromer Pl 5 BR6 211 B1
Cromer Rd Barnet EN5 2 A2
Croydon SE25 206 B6
Dagenham RM6 59 A3
Harlington TW6 126 C3
Leyton E10 54 B2
Streatham SW17 181 A4
Tottenham N17 34 A1
Woodford IG8 37 A6
Cromer Rd W TW6 126 C2
Cromer Road Prim Sch
EN5 2 A2
Cromer St
WC1 94 A4 233 B1
Cromer Terr
Dalston E8 74 A3
3 Ilford RM6 58 B4
Cromer Villas Rd
SW18 157 B5
Cromford Cl BR6 227 C5
Cromford Path 1 E5 74 D4
Cromford Rd SW18 157 C6
Cromford Way KT3 177 B2
Cromlix Cl BR7 188 D1
Crompton Ct SW3 257 A4
Crompton Ho
Borough The SE1 262 B5
Paddington W2 236 C5
South Lambeth SW8 269 B1
Crompton Pl EN3 7 C5
Crompton St
W2 92 B3 236 C5
Cromwell Ave
Bromley BR2 209 B5
Hammersmith W6 112 B2
Highgate N6 49 B1
New Malden KT3 199 D4
Cromwell Cl
Acton W3 111 A5
Bromley BR2 209 B5
East Finchley N2 48 B5
2 Gunnersbury W4 110 D1
Walton-on-T KT12 194 B1
Cromwell Cres
SW5 113 C2 255 A4
Cromwell Ct
Enfield EN3 18 D6
15 Kingston u T KT2 176 C3
Wembley HA0 88 A5
Cromwell Ctr
Barking IG11 102 A4
North Acton NW10 89 B4
Cromwell Ctr The
RM8 59 B2
Cromwell Est E10 53 A1
Cromwell Gdns
SW7 114 B3 256 D5
Cromwell Gr W6 112 C3
Cromwell Ho
Battersea SW11 268 B1
2 Croydon CR0 220 D5
Muswell Hill N10 31 B3
Putney SW15 134 A1
Cromwell Hospl (BUPA)
SW5 113 D2 255 C4
Cromwell Lo
Barking IG11 79 C3
40 Bethnal Green E1 96 C3
Cromwell Mans SW5 255 B4
Cromwell Mews
SW7 256 D4
Cromwell Pl
5 Acton W3 111 A5
Barbican EC1 242 B4
Highgate N6 49 B1
Mortlake SW14 133 A2
South Kensington
SW7 114 B2 256 D4
Cromwell Rd
Beckenham BR3 207 A6
Brixton SW9 138 D4
Feltham TW13 150 B3
Finchley N3 30 A2
Hayes UB3 83 B1
Hounslow TW3 129 C1
Kingston u T KT2 176 A2
Muswell Hill N10 31 A3
South Kensington
SW7 256 B4
Teddington TW11 175 A4
Thornton Heath CR0 205 B2
Upton E7 77 C1
Walthamstow E17 54 A4
Walton-on-T KT12 194 B1
Wembley HA0 88 A5
Wimbledon SW19 179 D5
Worcester Pk KT4 215 C5
Cromwell St TW3 129 C1
Cromwell Trad Ctr
IG11 101 C4
Cromwell Twr EC2 242 B4
Crondace Rd
SW6 135 C4 265 B1
Crondall Ct 7 N1 95 C5
Crondall Ho SW15 156 A3
Crondall Pl 15 N1 95 C5
Crondall St N1 95 C5
Crone Ct 5 NW6 91 B5
Cronin St SE15 139 D5
CROOKED BILLET 178 C4
Crooked Billet
Chingford E4 35 C3
Wimbledon SW19 178 C4
Crooked Billet Yd 18
E2 95 C4
Crooked Usage N3 47 A6
Crooke Rd SE8 119 A1
Crookham Rd
SW6 135 B4 264 C1
Crook Log DA6 146 D1
Crook Log L Ctr
DA7 146 D2
Crook Log Prim Sch
DA6 146 D1
Crookston Rd SE9 144 C2
Croombs Rd E16 99 C2
Croom's Hill SE10 142 B5
Croom's Hill Gr
SE10 142 A5
Cropley Ct N1 235 C4
Cropley St N1 95 B5 235 C4
Croppath Rd RM10 81 C4
Cropthorne Ct W9 229 B1
Crosbie 10 NW9 27 D1
Crosbie Ho 20 E17 53 D6
Crosby Cl TW13 173 A6
Crosby Ct
Borough The SE1 252 C2
East Finchley N2 48 A5
7 New Southgate N11 31 B6
Crosby Ho
18 Cubitt Town E14 120 A3
Forest Gate E7 77 A2
Crosby Rd
Dagenham RM10 103 D6
Upton E7 77 A2
Crosby Row
SE1 117 B4 252 C2
Crosby Sq EC3 243 A2
Crosby Wlk
3 Dalston E8 73 D2
Streatham SE24 160 C4
Crosfield Ct 3 W10 90 D1
Crosfield Ho W11 244 A5
Crosier Cl SE3 144 A3
Crosier Rd UB10 61 A4
Crosier Way HA4 61 C5
Crosland Pl 5
SW11 137 A2
Crossbow Ho
Ealing W13 109 B5
15 Shoreditch N1 95 C6
Crossbrook Rd SE3 144 A2
Cross Cl SE15 140 B3

Cross Ct London SE5 . . 139 B2
11 Thamesmead SE28 . . . . 124 B6
Cross Deep TW1 . . . . . 153 A2
Cross Deep Gdns TW1 . . . . 152 D2
Crossfield Rd
Hampstead NW3 . . . . . . 70 B2
London N17 . . . . 51 A6
Crossfield St SE8 . . . . 141 C5
Crossford St SW9 . . . . 138 B3
Crossgate
Edgware HA8 . . . . 10 C1
Wembley UB6 . . . . 65 B2
Crossharbour Sta E14 . . . . 119 D3
Cross Ho N8 . . . . 50 B5
Cross Keys Cl
5 Edmonton N9 . . . . . . 18 A2
Marylebone W1 . . . . . 238 B3
Cross La
City of London EC3 . . . 253 A5
Hornsey N8 . . . . 50 B5
Old Bexley DA5 . . . . . . 169 B4
Cross Lances Rd TW3 . . . . 129 D1
Crossland Rd CR7 . . . 204 D3
Crosslands Ave
Ealing W5 . . . . 110 B5
Southall UB2 . . . . 107 B1
Crosslands Rd KT19 . . 215 B2
Crossleigh Ct
3 New Cross SE14 . . . 141 B5
Streatham SW16 . . . . . . 181 B6
Crosslet St SE17 . . . . 262 D4
Crosslet Vale SE10 . . 141 D4
Crossley St N7 . . . . 72 C2
Crossman Hos 19 SW12 . . . . 160 A4
Crossmead SE9 . . . . 166 B3
Crossmead Ave UB6 . . 85 C4
Crossmount Ho 13 SE5 . . . . 139 A5
Crossness Rd IG11 . . 101 D4
Cross Rd Belmont HA3 . . 25 A1
Camberwell SE5 . . . . 139 C3
Chingford E4 . . . . 20 C3
Croydon CR0 . . . . 205 B1
Enfield EN1 . . . . 5 C1
Feltham TW13 . . . . . . 173 A6
Finchley N2 . . . . 30 C1
Friern Barnet N11 . . . . . 31 B5
Harrow HA1 . . . . 42 B4
Ilford RM6 . . . . 58 C2
Keston Mark BR2 . . . . 226 A6
Kingston u T KT2 . . . . . 176 B3
Merton SW19 . . . . 179 C3
Romford RM7 . . . . 59 C6
Sidcup DA14 . . . . 190 B6
South Harrow HA2 . . . . . 63 D5
Sutton SM1 . . . . 218 B3
Wood Green N22 . . . . . . 32 C3
Cross St
2 Edmonton N18 . . . . . 34 A5
Hampton TW12 . . . . . 174 A5
Islington N1 . . . 94 D6 234 D6
Mortlake SW13 . . . . . . 133 C2
Crossthwaite Ave SE5, SE24 . . . . 139 B1
Crosstrees Ho 7 E14 . . . . 119 C3
Crosswall EC3 . . . . 117 D6 253 C6
Crossway
Dagenham RM8 . . . . 80 C5
Ealing W13 . . . . 87 A3
Enfield EN1 . . . . 17 C4
Finchley N12 . . . . 30 B4
Hayes UB3 . . . . 106 A5
Hendon NW9 . . . . 45 D5
Kingsland E8, N16 . . . . . 73 C3
Petts Wood BR5 . . . . . . 211 B4
Pinner HA5 . . . . 22 B1
Ruislip HA4 . . . . 62 C4
Thamesmead SE28 . . 102 D1
West Barnes KT3, SW20 . . . . 200 C5
Woodford IG8 . . . . 37 C6
Crossway Ct SE4 . . . . . 141 A3
Crossway Par N22 . . . . 32 D3
Crossways
Ashford TW16 . . . . 171 D3
South Croydon CR2 . . . 223 B1
Crossways *continued*
Sutton SM2 . . . . 218 B1
Crossways Acad SE4 . . . . 141 A3
Crossways Par CR2 . . 223 B1
Crossways Rd
Beckenham BR3 . . . . . 207 C5
Mitcham CR4 . . . . 203 B6
Crossways The
Heston TW5 . . . . 129 B5
Wembley HA9 . . . . 66 C6
Crossway The
Chislehurst SE9 . . . . . 165 D2
Hillingdon UB10 . . . . 82 B5
Tottenham N22 . . . . 32 D3
Cross Way The HA3 . . . 24 C1
Crosswell Cl TW17 . . . 171 A1
Croston St E8 . . . . 96 A6
Crothall Cl N13 . . . . 16 B1
Crouch Ave IG11 . . . . . 102 B5
Crouch Cl BR3 . . . . 185 C4
Crouch Croft SE9 . . . . 166 C1
CROUCH END 49 D3
Crouch End Hill N8 . . . 49 D2
Crouch Hall Ct N19 . . . 50 A1
Crouch Hall Rd N8 . . . . 49 D3
Crouch Hill N4, N8, N19 . . . . 50 A2
Crouch Hill Sta N4 . . . . 50 B2
Crouchmans Cl SE21, SE26 . . . . 162 A1
Crouch Rd NW10 . . . . . . 67 B1
Crowborough Ct W13 . . . . 109 C6
Crowborough Path WD19 . . . . 22 D6
Crowborough Rd SW17 . . . . 181 A5
Crowden Way SE28 . . 124 C6
Crowder Cl N12 . . . . 30 A3
Crowder St E1 . . . . 118 B6
Crowfield Ho N5 . . . . . . 73 A4
Crowfoot Cl
Hackney Wick E9 . . . . . . 75 B3
Woolwich SE28 . . . . . 123 C5
Crowhurst SE25 . . . . . 206 A6
Crowhurst Cl SW9 . . . 138 C3
Crowhurst Ct N17 . . . . . 34 B2
Crowhurst Ho 21 SW9 . . . . 138 B3
Crow La RM7, RM8 . . . . . 59 D2
Crowland Ave UB3 . . . 105 D2
Crowland Gdns N14 . . . 16 A4
Crowland Ho NW8 . . . 229 A5
Crowland Prim Sch N15 . . . . 52 A4
Crowland Rd
South Norwood CR7 . . . 205 B5
South Tottenham N15 . . . 51 D4
Crowlands Ave RM7 . . . 59 D3
Crowland Terr N1 . . . . . 73 B1
Crowland Wlk SM4 . . . 202 A3
Crowley Cres CR0 . . . . 220 C3
Crowline Wlk 1 N1 . . . 73 A2
Crowmarsh Gdns SE23 . . . . 162 C4
Crown Arc KT1 . . . . . . 175 D1
Crown Bldgs 4 E4 . . . . 20 B3
Crownbourne Ct SM1 . . . . 217 D4
Crown Cl Bow E3 . . . . . . 97 C6
Edgware NW7 . . . . 11 D2
Hampstead NW6 . . . . . . 69 D2
Hayes UB3 . . . . 105 D4
Walton-on-T KT12 . . . 194 C2
Wood Green N22 . . . . . . 32 C2
Crown Close Bsns Ctr 12 E3 . . . . 97 C6
Crown Ct
Bromley BR1 . . . . 209 D4
City of London EC4 . . . 242 B1
Harrow HA2 . . . . 42 C1
Lee SE12 . . . . 165 B5
11 Muswell Hill N10 . . . . 31 A3
4 Putney SW15 . . . . . 134 D1
St Giles WC2 . . . . 240 B1
St John's Wood NW8 . . 230 B1
3 Twickenham TW1 . . . 153 B4
Crown Dale SE19 . . . . 183 A5
Crowndale Ct NW1 . . . 232 C4
Crowndale Rd NW1 . . . . 93 C5 232 B4
Crowne Ho SE1 . . . . . . 252 B3
Crownfield Ave IG2 . . . 57 C4
Crownfield Rd E15 . . . . 76 B4
Crowngate Ho 33 E3 . . 97 B5
Crown Hill CR0 . . . . . . 221 A5
Crownhill Rd NW10 . . . 89 D6
Crown Ho Ruislip HA4 . . 40 A1
Wembley HA9 . . . . 66 B3
3 Woolwich SE18 . . . . 123 A2
Crown La
Bromley Comm BR2 . . 209 D4
Chislehurst BR7 . . . . . 189 A2
Merton SM4 . . . . 201 C6
Osidge N14 . . . . 15 C3
South Norwood SE19, SW16 . . . . 182 C5
Crown Lane Gdns SE27 . . . . 182 C5
Crown Lane Prim Sch SE27 . . . . 182 D5
Crown Lane Spur BR2 . . . . 209 D3
Crownleigh Ct SW2 . . 160 C6
Crown Lo
Chelsea SW3 . . . . 257 B3
Finchley N3 . . . . 29 B1
Crownmead Way RM7 . . . . 59 D5
Crown Mews
2 Newham E13 . . . . . . 99 C6
9 Stepney E1 . . . . 96 D2
Crown Mill CR4 . . . . . . 202 C4
Crown Office Row EC4 . . . . 251 A6
Crown Par
London N14 . . . . 15 C3
Morden SM4 . . . . 201 D5
Crown Pas
Kingston u T KT1 . . . . 175 D1
St James SW1 . . . . . . 249 B3
Crown Pl
Broadgate EC2 . . . . . . 243 A4
Kentish Town NW5 . . . . . 71 B2
Crown Point Par SE19 . . . . 182 D4
Crown Rd Enfield EN1 . . . 6 B2
Ilford IG6 . . . . 57 B5
Kingston u T KT3 . . . . 177 A2
Morden SM4 . . . . 201 D5
Muswell Hill N10 . . . . . . 31 A3
Ruislip HA4 . . . . 62 D3
Sutton SM1 . . . . 217 D4
Twickenham TW1 . . . . . 153 B5
Crown Reach SW1 . . . 259 D1
Crown St Acton W3 . . . 110 D5
Camberwell SE5 . . . . . 139 A5
Dagenham RM10 . . . . . . 81 D2
Harrow HA2 . . . . 42 C1
Crownstone Ct 1 SW2 . . . . 160 C6
Crownstone Rd SW2 . . . . 160 C6
Crown Terr TW9 . . . . . . 132 B1
Crown Trad Ctr UB3 . 105 C4
Crowntree Cl TW7 . . . 130 D6
Crown Way UB7 . . . . . 104 B5
Crown Wlk HA9 . . . . 66 B5
Crown Woods La SE18 . . . . 144 D3
Crown Woods Sch SE9 . . . . 167 A6
Crown Woods Way SE9 . . . . 167 B6
Crown Yard TW3 . . . . . 130 A2
Crowshott Ave HA7 . . . 25 D2
Crows Rd
Barking IG11 . . . . 78 D2
Mill Meads E3, E15 . . . . . 98 B4
Crowther Ave TW8 . . . 110 A2
Crowther Cl SW6 . . . . 135 B6 264 D5
Crowther Rd SE25 . . . 206 A5
Crowthorne Cl SW18 . . . . 157 B3
Crowthorne Rd W10 . . 90 D1
Croxall Ho KT12 . . . . . 194 C3
Croxden Cl HA8 . . . . 44 C6
Croxden Wlk SM4 . . . . 202 A3
Croxford Gdns N22 . . . . 32 D3
Croxley Cl BR5 . . . . . . 190 B1
Croxley Gn BR5 . . . . . . 190 B2
Croxley Rd W9 . . . . 91 B4
Croxted Cl SE21 . . . . . 161 A4
Croxted Rd SE21, SE24 . . . . 161 B3
Croxteth Ho 11 SW8 . 137 D3
Croxton 17 KT1 . . . . . . 176 C1
Croyde Ave
Greenford UB6 . . . . 86 A4
Hayes UB3 . . . . 105 C2
Croyde Cl DA15 . . . . . . 167 B4
Croyden Ct HA0 . . . . 65 D2
CROYDON 221 B5
Croydon N17 . . . . 33 B1
Croydon Airport Ind Est CR0 . . . . 220 B2
Croydon Coll CR0 . . . . 221 B6
Croydon Coll Annexe 10 CR0 . . . . 205 B1
Croydon Coll (Selhurst Tertiary Ctr) SE25 . . 205 B4
Croydon Flyover The CR0 . . . . 221 A5
Croydon Gr CR0 . . . . 204 D1
Croydon Ho
Lambeth SE1 . . . . 251 B2
Thornton Heath CR0 . . 204 B3
Croydon Prim Independant Sch 8 CR0 . . . . 205 C1
Croydon Rd
Bandonhill CR0, SM5, SM6 . . . . 219 C5
Beckenham BR3 . . . . . 207 A6
Coney Hall BR2, BR4 . 224 D5
Harlington TW6 . . . . . 126 D2
Keston Mark BR2, BR4, BR6 . . . . 225 C5
Mitcham CR0, CR4 . . . 203 C4
Newham E13 . . . . 98 D3
Penge SE20 . . . . 184 C2
Waddon CR0 . . . . 220 B4
Croydon Rd Ind Est BR3 . . . . 206 D5
Croydon's Sports Arena SE25 . . . . 206 C4
Croydon Valley Trade Pk 2 CR0 . . . . 204 A2
Croyland Rd N9 . . . . 18 A3
Croylands Dr KT6 . . . . 198 A2
Croysdale Ave TW16 . 194 A6
Crozier Ho
Blackheath Pk SE3 . . . 143 B2
South Lambeth SW8 . 270 C3
Crozier Terr E9 . . . . 74 D3
Crucible Cl RM6 . . . . . . 58 B3
Crucifix La SE1 . . . . 117 C4 253 A2
Cruden Ho 15 Bow E3 . . 97 B5
11 Camberwell SE17 . 138 D6
Cruden St N1 . . 94 D6 234 D5
Cruickshank St WC1 234 A2
Cruikshank Ho NW8 230 B4
Cruikshank Rd E15 . . . . 76 C3
Crummock Gdns NW9 . . . . 45 C4
Crumpsall St SE2 . . . . 124 C2
Crundale Ave NW9 . . . . 44 C4
Crunden Rd CR2 . . . . . 221 B1
Crusader Gdns CR0 . . . 221 C5
Crusader Ho EC1 . . . 241 C5
Crusader Ind Est N4 . . . 51 A3
Crusoe Ct E11 . . . . 76 D5
Crusoe Mews N16 . . . . 73 B6
Crusoe Rd CR4 . . . . . 180 D3
Crutched Friars EC3 . . . . 117 C6 253 B6
Crutchfield La KT12 . . 194 B1
Crutchley Rd SE6 . . . . 164 C2
Crystal Ct SE19 . . . . . 183 D5
Crystal Ctr The 1 HA1 . . . . 42 D4
Crystal Ho SE18 . . . . . 123 D1
CRYSTAL PALACE . . . 184 A5
Crystal Palace Farm Pk★ SE20 . . . . 184 A5
Crystal Palace Mus★ SE19 . . . . 183 D4
Crystal Palace National Sports Ctr SE19 . . . 184 A4
Crystal Palace Par SE19 . . . . 183 D5
Crystal Palace Park Rd SE26 . . . . 184 B5
Crystal Palace Rd SE22 . . . . 162 A6
Crystal Palace Sta SE19 . . . . 184 A4
Crystal Palace Station Rd SE19 . . . . 184 A4
Crystal Terr SE19 . . . . 183 B4
Crystal View Ct BR1 . . 186 B6
Crystal Way
Dagenham RM8 . . . . 58 C1
Harrow HA1 . . . . 42 D4
Crystal Wharf N1 . . . 234 D3
Cuba Dr EN3 . . . . 6 C3
Cuba St E14 . . . . 119 C4
Cubitt Bldg SW1 . . . . . 258 C1
Cubitt Ho 4 SW4 . . . . 159 C5
Cubitt Sq UB2 . . . . 108 A5
Cubitt St WC1 . . 94 B4 233 D1
Cubitt Terr SW4 . . . . . . 137 C2
CUBITT TOWN 120 A2
Cubitt Town Jun & Inf Sch E14 . . . . 120 A3
Cuckoo Ave W7 . . . . 86 C3
Cuckoo Dene W7 . . . . . 86 B2
Cuckoo Hall La N9 . . . . 18 D4
Cuckoo Hall Prim Sch N9 . . . . 18 C4
Cuckoo Hill HA5 . . . . . . 40 C6
Cuckoo Hill Dr HA5 . . . 40 C6
Cuckoo Hill Rd HA5 . . . 40 D5
Cuckoo La W7 . . . . 108 C6
Cuda's Cl KT19 . . . . . . 215 D4
Cuddington SE17 . . . 262 B4
Cuddington Ave KT19, KT4 . . . . 215 D5
Cuddington Com Prim Sch KT4 . . . . 215 D5
Cudham La N BR6 . . . . 227 C1
Cudham St SE6 . . . . . . 164 A4
Cudworth Ho SW8 . . 269 B1
Cudworth St E1 . . . . 96 B3
Cuff Cres SE9 . . . . 165 D5
Cuffley Ho 3 W10 . . . . 90 C2
Cuff Point 12 E2 . . . . . 95 D4
Culand Ho SE17 . . . . . 263 A3
Culford Gdns SW3 . . . . . 114 D2 257 D3
Culford Gr N1 . . . . 73 C2
Culford Mans SW3 . . 257 D3
Culford Mews N1 . . . . . 73 C2
Culford Rd
Kingsland N1 . . . . 73 C2
Shoreditch N1 . . . . 95 C6
Culgaith Gdns EN2 . . . . . 4 A1
Culham Ho
21 Paddington W2 . . . . . 91 C2
33 Shoreditch E2 . . . . . . 95 D4
Cullen Ho W9 . . . . 91 B5
Cullen Way NW10 . . . . . 89 A3
Culling Rd SE16 . . . . . 118 C3
Cullington Cl HA3 . . . . . 43 A5
Cullingworth Rd NW10 . . . . 68 B3
Culloden Cl 21 SE16 . . 118 A1
Culloden Prim Sch 16 E14 . . . . 98 A1
Culloden Rd EN2 . . . . 4 D3
Cullum St EC3 . . . . . . 253 A6
Culmington Mans W13 . . . . 109 C6
Culmington Par W13 . . . . 109 C6
Culmington Rd
Ealing W13, W5 . . . . . 109 C5
South Croydon CR2 . . 221 A1
Culmore Rd SE15 . . . . 140 C5
Culmstock Rd SW11 . 159 A6
Culpepper Cl N18 . . . . . 34 B5
Culpepper Ct SE11 . . 261 A4
Culross Bldgs NW1 . 233 A4
Culross Cl N15 . . . . 51 A5
Culross St W1 . . . . 115 A6 248 A5
Culsac Rd KT6 . . . . 214 A6
Culver Ct SW18 . . . . . 157 D5
Culverden Rd SW12 . . 159 C2
Culver Gr HA7 . . . . 25 C1
Culverhouse WC1 . . . 240 C3
Culverhouse Gdns SW16 . . . . 160 B1
Culverin Ct 1 N7 . . . . . 72 B3
Culverlands Cl HA7 . . . 25 B6
Culverlands Ct N20 . . . 14 B3
Culverley Rd SE6 . . . . 164 A3
Culvers Ave SM5 . . . . 218 D6
Culvers House Prim Sch CR4 . . . . 203 A1
Culvers Retreat SM5 . . . . 218 D6
Culverstone Cl BR2 . 208 D4
Culvers Way SM5 . . . 218 D6
Culvert Ct SW11 . . . . . 137 A3
Culverton Ct 8 DA14 . . . . 190 A6
Culvert Pl SW11 . . . . . 137 A3
Culvert Rd
London SW11 . . . . 136 D3
South Tottenham N15 . . . 51 C4

Culworth Ho NW8 230 A4
Culworth St NW8 230 A3
Cumber Ho SW18 157 C3
Cumberland Ave
Falconwood DA16 145 D1
Wembley NW10 88 D4
Cumberland Bsns Pk NW10 88 D4
Cumberland Cl
Dalston E8 73 D2
2 Twickenham TW1 153 B5
8 Wimbledon SW20 178 D3
Cumberland Comp Sch E13 99 C3
Cumberland Cres W14 254 B4
Cumberland Ct
4 Croydon CR0 205 B1
7 Finchley N3 29 B1
Harrow HA1 42 C6
Marylebone W1 237 D1
Woodford IG8 37 B3
Cumberland Dr
Chessington KT9 214 B5
Erith DA7 147 A5
Hinchley Wood KT10 213 A6
Cumberland Gate W1 114 D6 247 D6
Cumberland Gdns
Church End NW4 29 A1
Finsbury WC1 234 A2
Cumberland Ho
Edmonton N9 18 C3
Kingston u T KT2 176 D3
Paddington W9 236 A5
1 Putney SW15 156 C4
Woolwich SE28 123 B4
Cumberland Mans
Marylebone W1 237 C2
7 West Hampstead NW6 69 C3
Cumberland Market NW1 93 B4 231 D2
Cumberland Mills Sq E14 120 B1
Cumberland Park Ind Est NW10 90 A4
Cumberland Pk W3 111 A6
Cumberland Pl
Catford SE6 164 D3
Regent's Pk NW1 231 C2
Sunbury TW16 194 A5
Cumberland Rd
Acton W3 111 A6
Ashford TW15 148 A1
Barnes SW13 134 A4
Beckenham BR2 208 D6
Croydon SE25 206 B3
Edmonton N9 18 C3
Hanwell W7 108 D4
Harrow HA1 41 D4
Higham Hill E17 35 A1
Manor Pk E12 77 D4
Newham E13 99 B3
Richmond TW9 132 C5
Stanmore HA7, HA8 44 B6
Wood Green N22 32 B1
Cumberland St SW1 115 B1 258 D2
Cumberland Terr NW1 231 C3
Cumberland Terrace Mews NW1 231 C3
Cumberland Villas W3 111 A6
Cumberland Wharf 12 SE16 118 C4
Cumberlow Ave SE25 206 A6
Cumbernauld Gdns TW16 171 D5
Cumberton Rd N17 33 B2
Cumbrae Gdns KT6 213 D6
Cumbrian Gdns NW2 69 A6
Cuming Mus★ SE17 262 A3
Cumming St N1 233 D3
Cumnor Cl 23 SW9 138 B3
Cumnor Gdns KT17 216 A2
Cumnor Rd SM2 218 A2
Cunard Cres N21 17 B5
Cunard Pl EC3 243 B1
Cunard Rd NW10 89 B4
Cunard Wlk 3 SE16 119 A2
Cundy Rd E16 99 C1
Cundy St SW1 115 A2 258 B3
Cunliffe Rd KT19 215 D4
Cunliffe St SW16 181 C4
Cunningham Cl
Dagenham RM6 58 C4
West Wickham BR4 223 D6
Cunningham Ct
Harrow HA1 42 B4
Paddington W2 236 C5
Cunningham Ho 16 SE5 139 B5
Cunningham Pk HA1 42 B4
Cunningham Pl NW8 92 B3 236 C6
Cunningham Rd N15 52 A5
Cunnington St W4 111 A2
Cupar Rd SW11 268 B2
Cupola Cl BR1 187 B5
Cureton St SW1 115 D2 259 D3
Curie Gdns NW9 27 C1
Curie Ho 1 HA9 67 A5
Curlew Cl SE28 124 D6
Curlew Ct KT6 214 C5
Curlew Ho
Brockley SE4 141 A1
Enfield EN3 18 D6
7 Peckham SE15 139 D4
Curlew St SE1 117 D4 253 D2
Curlew Way UB4 84 D2
Curness St SE13 142 A1
Curnick's La SE27 183 A6
Curran Ave
Bexley DA15 167 D6
Hackbridge SM6 219 A5
Curran Ho SW3 257 A3
Currey Rd UB6 64 B2
Curricle St W3 111 C5
Currie Hill Cl SW19 179 B6
Currie Ho 13 SW12 159 D4
Curry Rise NW7 28 D4
Cursitor St EC4 94 C1 241 A2
Curtain Pl EC2 243 B6
Curtain Rd EC2 95 C3 243 B6
Curthwaite Gdns EN2 15 D6
Curtis Dr W3 89 B1
Curtis Field Rd SW16 182 C6
Curtis Ho
7 London N11 31 C5
Walworth SE17 262 C2
Curtis La HA0 66 A3
Curtis Rd
Twickenham TW4 151 B4
West Ewell KT19 215 A4
Curtis St SE1 117 D2 263 C4
Curtis Way
Bermondsey SE1 263 C4
7 Thamesmead SE28 124 B6
Curtlington Ho 3 HA8 27 A1
Curve Bldg The SE4 163 B6
Curve The Ealing W5 109 D4
Shepherd's Bush W12 112 A6
Curwen Ave E7 77 B4
Curwen & New Acad Gall★ W1 239 C3
Curwen Prim Sch E13 99 A5
Curwen Rd W12 112 A4
Curzon Ave
Enfield EN3 18 D6
Stanmore HA7 25 A2
Curzon Cl BR6 227 B4
Curzon Cres
Barking IG11 101 D4
Willesden NW10 67 C1
Curzon Ct SE9 167 A1
Curzon Gate W1 248 B3
Curzon Ho W5 87 B3
Curzon Pl HA5 40 C4
Curzon Rd Ealing W5 87 B3
Muswell Hill N10 31 B1
Thornton Heath CR7 204 C3
Curzon Sq W1 248 B3
Curzon St W1 115 B5 248 C4
Cusack Cl TW1 174 D6
Custance Ho N1 235 C3
Custance St N1 235 C2
CUSTOM HOUSE 121 C6
Custom House EC3 117 C6 253 A5
Custom House for ExCeL Sta E16 121 B6
Custom House Reach SE16 119 B3
Cutbush Ho N7 71 D3
Cutcombe Rd SE5 139 A3
Cuthberga Cl IG11 79 A1
Cuthbert Gdns SE25 205 C6
Cuthbert Harrowing Ho EC1 242 A5
Cuthbert Ho W2 236 C4
Cuthbert Rd
Croydon CR0 220 D6
8 Edmonton N18 34 A6
Walthamstow E17 54 A6
Cuthbert St W2 236 C5
Cuthill Wlk 3 SE5 139 B4
Cutlers Gdns EC2 243 B2
Cutlers Gdns Arc EC2 243 B2
Cutlers Sq E14 119 C2
Cutler St EC2 243 B2
Cut The SE1 116 C4 251 B2
Cutty Sark★ SE10 142 A6
Cutty Sark Ho 10 E14 119 D2
Cutty Sark Ret Development SE10 142 A6
Cutty Sark Sta SE10 142 A6
Cuxton BR5 211 A4
Cuxton Cl DA6 169 A6
Cuxton Ho SE17 263 B2
Cyclamen Cl 4 TW12 173 C4
Cyclamen Way KT19 215 A3
Cyclops Mews 12 E14 119 C2
Cygnet Ave TW14 150 D4
Cygnet Cl NW10 67 B3
Cygnet Ct EN3 7 A4
Cygnet Ho
Harrow HA7 24 D4
St John's Wood NW8 229 A6
Cygnet Hospl Harrow HA1 64 C6
Cygnet House N 18 E14 97 D1
Cygnet House S 19 E14 97 D1
Cygnet St E1 243 D6
Cygnets The TW13 173 A6
Cygnet Way UB4 84 D2
Cygnus Bsns Ctr NW10 67 D2
Cymbeline Ct 6 HA1 42 D3
Cyna Ct 5 E11 55 A3
Cynthia St N1 233 D3
Cyntra Pl 8 E8 74 B1
Cypress Ave
London N2 47 D6
Twickenham TW2 152 A4
Cypress Cl 9 E5 74 A6
Cypress Ct
Cheam SM1 217 C2
5 Leyton E11 76 B4
7 West Norwood SW16 182 C5
Cypress Gdns SE4 163 A6
Cypress Ho SE14 140 D4
Cypress Inf Sch SE25 183 C1
Cypress Jun Sch SE25 183 C1
Cypress Lo SE25 183 C1
Cypress Pl W1 239 B5
Cypress Rd
Harrow HA3 24 B1
South Norwood SE25 183 C1
Cypress Tree Cl DA15 167 D3
CYPRUS 122 C6
Cyprus Ave N3 29 A1
Cyprus Cl N4 50 C3
Cyprus Ct 9 N3 29 B1
Cyprus Gdns N3 29 A1
Cyprus Ho 10 N3 29 B1
Cyprus Pl
23 Bethnal Green E2 96 C5
Newham E6 122 C6
Cyprus Rd
Church End N3 29 B1
Edmonton N9 17 D2
Cyprus St E2 96 C5
Cyprus Sta E6 122 C6
Cyrena Rd SE22 161 D6
Cyril Jackson Prim Sch (North Bldg) 24 E14 119 B6
Cyril Jackson Prim Sch (South Bldg) 25 E14 119 B6
Cyril Lo 2 DA14 190 A6
Cyril Mans SW11 267 D1
Cyril Rd DA7 147 A3
Cyril Smith Ho N13 32 B5
Cyril Thatcher Ho SW6 265 B1
Cyrus Ho EC1 241 D6
Cyrus St EC1 94 D3 241 D6
Czar St SE8 141 C6

D

Daairy Mews N2 48 C5
Dabbs Hill La UB5 63 C3
Dabb's La EC1 241 B5
Dabin Cres SE10 142 A4
Dacca St SE8 141 B6
Dace Rd E3 97 C6
Dacre Cl UB6 85 D5
Dacre Gdns
Borehamwood WD6 11 B6
Lewisham SE13 142 C1
Dacre Ho SW3 266 D5
Dacre Pk SE13 142 C1
Dacre Pl SE13 142 C2
Dacre Rd
Leytonstone E11 54 D1
Newham E13 99 B6
Thornton Heath CR0 204 A2
Dacres Rd SE23 162 D1
Dacre St SW1 115 D3 259 C6
Dade Way UB2 107 B1
Daerwood Cl BR2 210 B1
Daffodil Cl CR0 206 D1
Daffodil Gdns IG1 78 D3
Daffodil Pl 7 TW12 173 C4
Daffodil St W12 111 D6
Dafforne Rd SW17 159 A1
DAGENHAM 81 D1
Dagenham Ave
Dagenham RM9 81 B1
Dagenham RM9 103 A6
Dagenham Dock Estate RM9 103 B3
Dagenham Dock Sta RM9 103 B5
Dagenham East Sta RM10 81 D3
Dagenham Heathway Sta RM9 81 B2
Dagenham Park Com Sch RM10 103 D6
Dagenham Rd
Dagenham RM10 81 D4
London E10 53 B1
Dagenham & Redbridge Football Grd RM10 81 D3
Dagenham Swimming Pool RM10 81 C6
Dagger La WD23 9 A6
Dagmar Ave HA9 66 B4
Dagmar Ct
Cubitt Town E14 120 A3
South Tottenham N15 51 B5
Dagmar Gdns NW10 90 D5
Dagmar Mews UB2 107 A3
Dagmar Pas N1 234 D6
Dagmar Rd
Camberwell SE5 139 C4
Finsbury Pk N4 50 C2
4 Kingston u T KT2 176 C3
Southall UB2 107 A3
South Norwood SE25 205 C4
West Green N15 51 B5
Wood Green N22 31 D2
Dagmar Terr N1 94 D6 234 D6
Dagnall Pk SE25 205 C4
Dagnall Rd SE25 205 C4
Dagnall St SW11 137 A4 268 A1
Dagnan Rd SW12 159 C4
Dagobert Ho 27 E1 96 C2
Dagonet Gdns BR1 165 A1
Dagonet Rd BR1 165 A1
Dahlia Gdns
Ilford IG1 78 D2
Mitcham CR4 203 D5
Dahlia Rd SE2 124 B2
Dahomey Rd SW16 181 C4
Daiglen Sch IG9 21 C2
Daimler Ho 8 E3 97 C3
Daimler Way SM6 220 A1
Daines Cl E12 78 B5
Dainford Cl BR1 186 B5
Dainton Cl 1 BR1 187 B2
Dainton Ho 22 W2 91 C2
Daintry Cl HA3 43 A5
Daintry Way E9 75 B2
Dairsie Ct 3 BR1 187 C1
Dairsie Rd SE9 144 C2
Dairy Cl Bromley BR1 187 B3
South Norwood CR7 183 A1
Willesden NW10 90 A6
Dairy La SE18 122 B2
Dairyman Cl NW2 69 A5
Dairy Meadow Prim Sch UB2 107 B3
Daisy Cl CR0 206 D1
Daisy Dormer Ct 11 SW9 138 B1
Daisy Ho IG3 58 A1
Daisy La SW6 135 C2
Daisy Rd Newham E16 98 C3
Woodford E18 37 B1
Dakin Pl 9 E1 97 A2
Dakota bldg 6 SE13 141 D4
Dakota Cl SM6 220 B1
Dakota Gdns UB5 85 A4
Dalberg Rd SW2 160 C6
Dalberg Way SE2 124 D3
Dalbury Ho 6 SW9 138 B1
Dalby Rd SW18 136 A1
Dalbys Cres N17 33 C4
Dalby St NW5 71 B2
Dalcross Rd TW4, TW5 129 A3
Dale Ave Edgware HA8 26 B1
Hounslow TW4 129 A2
Dalebury Rd SW17 158 D2
Dale Cl
Blackheath Pk SE3 143 A2
New Barnet EN5 13 D5
Pinner HA5 22 B2
Dale Croft N4 73 A5
Dale Ct
Cranley Gdns N8 49 C5
3 Kingston u T KT2 176 B3
Northolt UB5 63 B1
Wembley HA0 65 D4
Woodford E18 37 A1
Dale Dr UB4 83 D4
Dalefield IG9 21 D3
Dale Gdns IG8 37 B6
Dale Gr N12 30 A5
Dale Green Rd N11 15 B1
Dalehaed NW1 232 A3
Daleham Dr UB8 82 D1
Daleham Gdns NW3 70 B2
Daleham Mews NW3 70 B2
Dale Ho London SE4 141 A1
St John's Wood NW8 229 A6
Dale Lo N6 49 C3
Dalemain Ho 5 SW8 137 D3
Dalemain Mews 12 E16 121 A5
Dale Park Ave SM5 218 D6
Dale Park Rd SE19 183 B2
Dale Rd
Ashford TW16 171 D3
Camberwell SE17 138 D6
Cheam SM1 217 B4
Gospel Oak NW5 71 A3
Southall UB6 85 D2
Walton-on-T KT12 193 D2
Dale Row W11 91 A1
Daleside Rd
Streatham SW17 181 B5
West Ewell KT19 215 B2
Dales Path WD6 11 B6
Dales Rd WD6 11 B6
Dale St W4 111 C1
Dale The BR2 225 D4
Dale View Ave E4 20 A2
Dale View Cres E4 20 A1
Dale View Gdns E4 20 B1
Daleview Rd N15 51 C3
Dalewood Gdns KT4 216 B6
Dale Wood Rd BR6 211 C1

Daley Ho 6 W12 90 B1
Daley St E9 74 D2
Daley Thompson Way 7
SW8 137 B2
Dalgarno Gdns W10 90 C2
Dalgarno Way W10 90 C3
Daling Way E3 97 A5
Dali Universe★ SE1 250 C2
Dalkeith Ct SW1 259 D3
Dalkeith Gr HA7 26 A5
Dalkeith Ho 6 SW9 138 D4
Dalkeith Rd Ilford IG1 79 A5
West Norwood SE21 161 A4
Dallas Ct SM3 217 A2
Dallas Rd
Cheam SM3 217 A2
Ealing W5 88 B2
Forest Hill SE26 162 B1
Hendon NW4 46 A2
Dallas Terr UB3 105 D3
Dallega Cl UB3 105 B6
Dallinger Rd SE12 164 D5
Dalling Rd W6 112 B2
Dallington Sch
EC1 94 D3 241 D6
Dallington St
EC1 94 D3 241 D6
Dallin Rd Bexley DA6 146 D1
Woolwich SE18 144 D5
Dalmain Prim Sch
SE23 163 A3
Dalmain Rd SE23 162 D3
Dalmally Pas CR0 205 D2
Dalmally Passage
CR0 205 D3
Dalmally Rd CR0 206 A2
Dalmeny Ave
Thornton Heath
SW16 182 C1
Tufnell Pk N7 71 D4
Dalmeny Avenue Est 3
N7 71 D4
Dalmeny Cl HA0 65 C2
Dalmeny Cres TW3 130 B1
Dalmeny Ct 4 SW4 138 A3
Dalmeny Rd
Erith DA8 147 D4
New Barnet EN5 14 A5
North Cheam KT4 216 B5
Tufnell Pk N7 71 D4
Wallington SM5 219 A1
Dalmeyer Rd NW10 67 D2
Dalmore Ave KT10 212 D2
Dalmore Rd SE21 161 A2
Dalrymple Cl
Barnet N20 14 A4
London N14 15 D4
Dalrymple Rd SE4 141 A1
DALSTON 74 A2
Dalston Gdns HA7 26 A1
Dalston Jct E8 73 D2
Dalston Junction Sta
E8 73 C2
Dalston Kingsland Sta
E8 73 D3
Dalston La E8 74 A3
Dalton Ave CR4 180 C1
Dalton Cl Hayes UB4 83 B3
Orpington BR6 227 C5
Dalton Ho
7 Balham SW12 159 B4
10 Bow E3 97 A5
19 Deptford SE14 140 D6
Merton SW19 180 A2
Stanmore HA7 25 B5
Dalton St SE27 160 D1
Daltry Ho HA1 42 D5
Dalwood St SE5 139 C4
Daly Dr BR1 210 C6
Dalyell Rd SW9 138 B2
Damascene Wlk
SE21 161 A3
Damask Cres E16 98 C3
Damask Ct SM1 201 D1
Damer Ho 9 TW10 154 B5
Damer Terr SW10 266 B3
Dames Rd E7 77 A5
Dame St N1 95 A5 235 A4
Damien Ct 12 E1 96 B1
Damien St E1 96 B1
Damon Cl DA14 168 B1
Damon Ct DA14 168 B1
Damon Ho 2 N12 30 B5
Damory Ho 1 SE16 118 C2
Damson Dr UB3 106 A6
Damsonwood Rd
UB2 107 C3
Danbrook Rd SW16 182 A3
Dan Bryant Ho 5
SW12 159 C4
Danbury Cl RM6 58 D6
Danbury Mans 3
IG11 78 D1
Danbury Mews SM5,
SM6 219 B4
Danbury St
N1 94 D5 234 D4
Danbury Way IG8 37 C4
Danby Ct EN2 5 A2
Danby Ho
23 Hackney E9 74 C1
3 West Kilburn W10 91 B4
Danby St SE15 139 D2
Dancastle Ct 7 N3 29 C2
Dancer Rd
Fulham
SW6 135 B4 264 C1
Richmond TW9 132 C2
Dando Cres SE3 143 B2
Dandridge Cl SE10 120 D1
Dandridge Ho E1 243 C4
Danebury
New Addington CR0 223 D2
18 North Kensington
W10 90 C2
Danebury Ave SW15 155 D5
Daneby Rd SE6 164 A2
Dane Cl
Farnborough BR6 227 B3
Sidcup DA5 169 C4
Danecourt Gdns
CR0 221 D5
Danecroft Rd SE24 161 B6
Daneglen Ct 18 HA7 25 C5
Danegrove Prim Sch
(Ridgeway Ave)
EN4 14 D5
Danegrove Prim Sch
(Windsor Dr) EN4 14 C5
Danehill Wlk DA14 168 A1
Dane Ho
15 London SE5 139 A3
Upper Tooting SW17 180 A6
Danehurst TW8 131 C5
Danehurst Gdns IG4 56 B4
Danehurst St
SW6 135 A4 264 A2
Daneland EN4 14 D5
Danemead Gr UB5 63 D3
Danemere St SW15 134 C2
Dane Pl E3 97 B5
Dane Rd
Ashford TW15 171 B4
Ealing W13 109 C5
Ilford IG1 79 A3
Lower Edmonton N18 18 C1
Merton SW19 180 A2
Southall UB1 107 A6
Danesbury Rd TW13 150 B3
Danescombe SE12 165 A3
Danescourt Cres
SM1 218 A6
Danescroft
Hendon NW4 46 D4
3 North Finchley N12 30 A5
Danescroft Ave NW4 46 D4
Danescroft Gdns
NW4 46 D4
Danes Ct
Primrose Hill NW8 230 C5
Wembley HA9 66 D5
Danesdale Rd E9 75 A2
Danesfield SE5 139 C6
Danes Gate HA1 42 C6
Danes Ho 10 W10 90 C2
Dane St WC1 240 C3
Daneswood Ave SE6 164 A1
Danethorpe Rd HA0 65 D2
Danetree Cl KT19 215 A1
Danetree Rd KT19 215 A1
Danetree Sch KT19 215 A1
Danette Gdns RM8 81 B6
Daneville Rd SE5 139 B4
Danford Ho 9 N11 31 C5
Dangan Rd E11 55 A3
Daniel Almshouse
NW4 46 B5
Daniel Bolt Cl E14 97 D2
Daniel Cl London N18 34 C6
Daniel Cl *continued*
Twickenham TW4 151 B4
Upper Tooting SW17 180 C4
Daniel Ct Acton W3 111 C6
3 Beckenham BR3 185 C3
7 Edgware HA8 26 D5
10 Hendon NW9 27 C2
Daniel Gdns SE15 139 D5
Daniel Ho 1 HA5 22 C1
Daniell Ho N1 235 D4
Daniell Way CR0 204 B1
Daniel Pl NW4 46 B2
Daniel Rd W5 110 B6
Daniel's Rd SE15 140 C2
Dan Leno Wlk SW6 265 C3
Dansey Pl W1 249 C6
Dansington Rd
DA16 146 A1
Danson Cres DA16 146 B2
Danson House★
DA6 146 C1
Danson Intc DA5 168 C5
Danson La DA16 146 B1
Danson Mead DA16 146 C2
Danson Prim Sch
DA16 146 A1
Danson Rd DA5 168 D6
Danson Underpass
DA5 168 C5
Dante Pl SE11 261 D3
Dante Rd
SE11 116 D2 261 C4
Danube Ct 13 SE15 139 D5
Danube St
SW3 114 C1 257 B2
Danvers Ho 35 E1 96 A1
Danvers Rd N8 49 D5
Danvers St
SW3 136 B6 266 D5
Da Palma Ct SW6 265 A5
Daphne Ct Ealing W5 87 C1
Wembley HA0 65 D3
Worcester Pk KT4 215 C6
Daphne Gdns E4 20 A1
Daphne Ho N22 32 C2
Daphne St SW18 158 A5
Daplyn St 6 E1 96 A2
D'arblay St
W1 93 C1 239 B1
Darby Cres TW16 172 C1
Darby Gdns TW16 172 C1
Darcy Ave SM6 219 C4
Darcy Cl N20 14 B2
D'arcy Dr HA3 43 D5
D'arcy Gdns
Dagenham RM9 103 B6
Harrow HA3 44 A5
Darcy Ho E8 96 B6
D'arcy Pl BR2 209 A5
Darcy Rd
Isleworth TW7 131 A4
Thornton Heath
SW16 182 A1
D'arcy Rd SM3 216 D4
Dare Ct 2 E10 54 A2
Dare Gdns RM8 81 A5
Darell Prim Sch
TW9 132 C2
Darell Rd TW9 132 C2
Daren Ct N7 72 A4
Darent Ho
4 Catford BR1 186 B5
Lisson Gr NW8 236 D4
Darenth Rd
Stamford Hill N16 51 D1
Welling DA16 146 A4
Darfield NW1 232 A5
Darfield Rd SE4 163 B6
Darfield Way W10 90 D1
Darfur St 2 SW15 134 D2
Dargate Cl SE19 183 D3
Darien Ho
16 London SW11 136 B2
11 Stepney E1 96 D2
Darien Rd SW11 136 B2
Daring Ho 23 E3 97 A5
Darland Ho SE9 167 B5
Darlands Dr EN5 12 D6
Darlan Rd
SW6 135 B5 264 D3
Darlaston Rd SW19 179 A3
Darley Cl CR0 207 A3
Darley Dr KT3 177 B1
Darley Gdns SM4 201 D3
Darley Ho SE11 260 C1
Darley Rd
Clapham SW11 158 D5
Edmonton N9 17 D3
Darling Ho 12 TW1 153 D5
Darling Rd SE4 141 C2
Darling Row E1 96 B3
Darlington Ct 8
SE6 164 D3
Darlington Ho
South Lambeth SW8 269 D3
2 Surbiton KT6 197 D2
Darlington Rd SE27 182 D5
Darmaine Cl CR2 221 A1
Darnall Ho 4 SE10 142 A4
Darnay Ho 3 SE16 118 A3
Darndale Cl E17 35 B1
Darnell Ho 9 SE10 142 A5
Darnley Ho 7 E14 97 A1
Darnley Rd
Hackney E9 74 C2
Woodford IG8 37 B2
Darnley Terr 12
W11 112 D5
Darrell Ct BR2 208 C6
Darrell Rd SE22 162 A6
Darren Cl N4 50 B2
Darrick Wood Ho
BR6 227 A5
Darrick Wood Inf Sch
BR6 226 D5
Darrick Wood Jun Sch
BR6 226 D4
Darrick Wood Rd
BR6 227 B6
Darrick Wood Sch
BR6 226 D5
Darrick Wood Sports Ctr
BR6 227 A5
Darris Cl UB4 85 A3
Darsley Dr
SW8 138 A4 270 A2
Dartford Ave N9 18 D5
Dartford Gdns RM6 58 B4
Dartford Ho SE1 263 D4
Dartford St SE17 139 A6
Dartington NW1 232 B5
Dartington Ho
Bayswater W2 91 D2
7 London SW8 137 D3
Dartle Ct 29 SE16 118 A4
Dartmoor Wlk 18
E14 119 C2
Dartmouth Cl W11 91 C1
Dartmouth Ct SE10 142 A4
Dartmouth Gr SE10 142 A4
Dartmouth Hill SE10 142 A4
Dartmouth Ho
Dartmouth Pk N19 71 B6
11 Kingston u T KT2 176 A2
Lewisham SE10 142 A3
Thornton Heath CR0 204 D2
DARTMOUTH PARK 71 B5
Dartmouth Park Ave
NW5 71 B5
Dartmouth Park Hill
N19 71 B6
Dartmouth Park Rd
NW5 71 B5
Dartmouth Pl
Chiswick W4 133 C6
Forest Hill SE23 162 C2
Dartmouth Rd
Brondesbury NW2 68 D2
Forest Hill SE23,
SE26 162 C1
Hayes BR2 209 A2
Hendon NW4 46 A3
Ruislip HA4 62 A5
Dartmouth Row
SE10 142 A4
Dartmouth St
SW1 115 D4 249 D1
Dartmouth Terr
SE10 142 B4
Dartnell Rd CR0 205 D2
Darton Ct W3 111 A5
Dartrey Twr SW10 266 C4
Dartrey Wlk
SW10 136 A5 266 B4
Dart St W10 91 B4
Darul Uloom BR7 189 C4
Darville Rd N16 73 D5
Darwell Cl E6 100 C5
Darwen Pl E2 96 B6
Darwin Cl
Farnborough BR6 227 B3
Darwin Cl *continued*
New Southgate N11 15 B1
Darwin Ct
Eltham SE9 166 C5
Newham E13 99 B4
Primrose Hill NW1 231 B6
Darwin Ctr★ SW7 256 C5
Darwin Dr UB1 85 D1
Darwin Gdns WD19 22 C5
Darwin Ho
8 London SE13 142 A3
2 Wembley HA9 67 A5
Darwin Rd
Ealing W5 109 C2
Falconwood DA16 145 D2
Tottenham N22 32 D1
Darwin St
SE17 117 B2 262 D4
Daryngton Dr UB6 86 C5
Daryngton Ho SW8 270 A3
Dashwood Cl DA6 169 C6
Dashwood Ct TW3 130 A1
Dashwood Ho SE21 161 D1
Dashwood Rd N8 50 B3
Dassett Rd SE27 182 D5
Data Point Bsns Ctr
E16 98 B3
Datchelor Pl 14 SE5 139 B4
Datchet Ho NW1 231 D2
Datchet Rd SE6 163 B2
Datchett Ho 40 E2 95 D4
Datchwood Ct N4 73 A5
Datchworth Ct 7
EN1 17 C6
Datchworth Ho 8
N1 72 D1
Date St SE17 117 B1 262 C1
Daubeney Gdns N17 33 A3
Daubeney Pl TW12 173 D1
Daubeney Prim Sch
E5 75 A4
Daubeney Rd
Clapton Pk E5 75 A4
Tottenham N17 33 A3
Daubeney Twr 2
SE8 119 B1
Dault Rd SW18 158 A5
Dauney Ho SE1 251 C1
Dauphine Ct HA3 24 C1
Dave Adams Ho 8
E3 97 B5
Davenant Ho 20 E1 96 A2
Davenant Rd
Croydon CR0, CR9 220 D4
Upper Holloway N19 71 D6
Davenant St E1 96 A2
Davenport Cl TW11 175 A4
Davenport Ctr IG11 102 B5
Davenport Ho SE11 261 A5
Davenport Lo TW3 129 A5
Davenport Mews 6
W12 112 B5
Davenport Rd
London SE6 164 A5
Sidcup DA14 169 A2
Daventer Dr HA7 24 D3
Daventry Ave E17 53 C3
Daventry St
NW1 92 C2 237 A4
Dave Porter Hts
SW19 157 A4
Dave Ramsey Ho
SE18 123 B2
Daver Ct
Chelsea SW3 257 B1
Ealing W5 87 D3
Davern Cl SE10 120 D2
Davey Cl
Bowes Pk N13 32 B5
Islington N7 72 B2
Davey Ho HA9 67 A6
Davey Rd E9 75 C1
Davey's Ct WC2 250 A6
Davey St SE15 139 D6
David Ave UB6 86 C5
David Cl UB3 127 C5
David Coffer Ct
DA17 125 D2
David Ct N20 14 A1
David Devine Ho 7
E8 74 A3
David Game Coll
SW7 256 C3
Davidge Ho SE1 251 B1
Davidge St
SE1 116 D4 251 D1

David Henry Waring Ct TW14 149 A3
David Hewitt Ho 2 E3 97 D2
David Ho
8 Putney SW15 156 A6
South Lambeth SW8 270 A4
South Norwood SE25 206 A6
David Lee Point 4 E15 98 C6
David Livingstone Prim Sch CR7 183 A2
David Mews W1 237 D4
David Rd RM8 81 A6
Davidson Gdns SW8 138 A5 270 A4
Davidson Ho 7 N19 71 C4
Davidson Lo CR0 205 C2
Davidson Prim Sch CR0 205 D2
Davidson Rd CR0 205 D3
Davidson Terrs E7 77 B3
David's Rd SE23 162 C3
David St E15 76 B3
David Twigg Cl KT2 176 A2
Davies Cl CR0 206 A3
Davies La E11 76 D6
Davies Laing & Dick Coll W1 93 A1 238 B2
Davies Lane Prim Sch E11 76 D6
Davies Mews W1 248 C6
Davies St W1 115 B6 248 C6
Davies Walk TW7 130 B4
Davina Ho
Brondesbury NW2 69 B2
14 Hackney E5 74 B3
Da Vinci Ct 12 SE16 118 B1
Davington Ct 19 SM2 217 C1
Davington Gdns RM8 80 B3
Davington Rd RM8 80 B3
Davis Ct 1 N20 14 B2
Davis Ho 35 W12 112 B6
Davis Rd
Bedford Pk W3 111 D4
Chessington KT9 214 C4
Davis St E13 99 B5
Davisville Rd W12 112 A4
Davis Way DA14 191 A4
Davmor Ct TW8 109 C1
Dawes Ave TW7 131 A1
Dawe's Cl UB10 82 A5
Dawes Ho SE17 262 C3
Dawes Rd SW6 135 B5 264 C4
Dawe's Rd UB10 82 A5
Dawes St SE17 117 B1 262 D2
Dawley Ave UB8 83 A1
Dawley Par UB3 105 A6
Dawley Rd
Harlington UB3 105 C2
Hayes UB3 105 B6
Dawlish Ave
Bowes Pk N13 32 A5
Wandsworth SW18 157 D2
Wembley UB6 87 A5
Dawlish Dr Ilford IG3 79 D4
Pinner HA5 41 A3
Ruislip HA4 62 B6
Dawlish Prim Sch E10 54 A1
Dawlish Rd
Brondesbury NW2 68 D2
Leyton E10 76 A6
Tottenham Hale N17 52 A6
Dawnay Gdns SW18 158 B2
Dawnay Rd SW17, SW18 158 B2
Dawn Cl TW4 129 A2
Dawn Cres E15 98 B6
Dawn Wlk BR2 186 B1
Dawpool Rd NW2 67 D6
Daws La NW7 28 A5
Dawson Ave
Barking IG11 79 D1
St Paul's Cray BR5 190 B1
Dawson Cl Hayes UB3 83 B2
Woolwich SE18 123 A2
Dawson Gdns 10 IG11 79 D1
Dawson Ho
23 Bethnal Green E2 96 C4
5 Camberwell SE5 139 C4
Dawson Pl W2 113 C6 245 B6
Dawson Rd
Cricklewood NW2 68 C4
Kingston u T KT1 198 B6
Dawson St E2 95 D5
Dawson Terr N9 18 C4
Dax Ct TW16 194 C6
Daybrook Rd SW19 201 D6
Day Ho 2 SE5 139 A5
Daylesford Ave SW15 134 A1
Daymer Gdns HA5 40 C5
Daynor Ho 4 NW6 91 C6
Day's Armhouses HA8 26 B5
Daysbrook Rd SW2 160 B3
Days La DA15 167 C4
Days Lane Prim Sch DA15 167 D5
Daytone Ho SW20 178 D2
Dayton Gr SE15 140 C4
Deaconess Ct 5 N15 51 D5
Deacon Ho SE11 260 D3
Deacon Mews N1 73 B1
Deacon Rd
Kingston u T KT2 176 B2
Willesden NW2 68 A2
Deacons Cl HA5 22 B1
DEACONS HILL 10 C5
Deacon's Hill Rd WD6 10 C6
Deacons Hts WD6 10 C5
Deacons Leas BR6 227 B4
Deacons Rise N2 48 B4
Deacons Wlk TW12 173 C6
Deacon Way SE17 117 A2 262 B4
Deal Ct
13 Hendon NW9 27 D1
7 Southall UB1 86 A1
Deal Ho
Deptford SE15 140 D6
Walworth SE17 263 B2
Deal Porters Way SE16 118 D3
Deal Rd SW17 181 A4
Deal St E1 96 A2
Dealtry Rd SW15 134 C1
Deal Wlk 3 SW9 138 C5
Dean Bradley St SW1 260 A5
Dean Cl Hackney E9 74 C3
Hillingdon UB10 60 B1
Rotherhithe SE16 118 D5
Dean Coll of London 4 N7 72 B5
Deancross St E1 96 C1
Dean Ct Acton W3 89 B1
Ealing W13 109 B5
10 Kingston u T KT2 176 C3
South Lambeth SW8 270 A3
Wembley HA0 65 B5
Dean Dr HA7 26 A1
Deane Ave HA4 62 C3
Deane Croft Rd HA5 40 C3
Deanery Cl N2 48 C5
Deanery Mews W1 248 B4
Deanery Rd E15 76 C2
Deanery St W1 115 A5 248 B4
Deane Way HA4 40 B3
Dean Farrar St SW1 259 D6
Deanfield Gdns CR0 221 B4
Dean Gdns E17 54 B5
Deanhill Ct 2 SW14 132 D1
Deanhill Rd SW14 132 D1
Dean Ho London N4 51 A2
New Cross SE14 141 B5
Ruislip HA4 39 B1
Stamford Hill N16 51 D1
18 Stepney E1 96 C1
Dean Rd Croydon CR0 221 B4
Hampton TW12 173 C5
Hounslow TW3 151 D6
Thamesmead SE28 124 A6
Willesden NW2 68 C2
Dean Ryle St SW1 260 A4
Dean's Bldgs SE17 117 B2 262 D3
Deansbrook Cl HA8 27 A3
Deansbrook Jun & Inf Schs NW7 27 A4
Deansbrook Rd
Burnt Oak HA8 27 B4
Edgware HA8 26 D3
Deans Cl
Burnt Oak HA8 27 A4
Chiswick W4 132 D6
South Croydon CR0 221 D5
Deanscroft Ave NW9 45 A1
Deans Ct HA8 26 D4
Dean's Ct EC4 241 D1
Deans Dr N13 32 D4
Dean's Dr HA8 27 B5
Deansfield Prim Sch
Eltham SE9 144 C2
Ruislip HA4 62 D4
Deans Gate Cl SE23 162 D1
Dean's Gateway 9 SE10 141 C4
Deanshanger Ho 21 SE8 118 D2
Dean's La HA8 27 A4
Dean's Mews W1 238 D2
Deans Rd SM1 217 D5
Dean's Rd W7 108 D4
Dean St Forest Gate E7 77 A3
Soho W1 93 D1 239 C1
Dean Stanley St SW1 260 A5
Deansway
East Finchley N2 48 B5
Edmonton N9 17 C1
Deans Way HA8 27 A5
Deanswood N11 31 D4
Dean's Yd SW1 259 D6
Dean Trench St SW1 260 A5
Dean Way UB2 107 D4
Dean Wlk HA8 27 B3
Deanwood Ct N14 15 C3
Dearmer Ho 6 SW2 160 C4
Dearne Cl HA7 25 A5
De'arn Gdns CR4 202 C6
Dearsley Rd EN1 6 A2
Deason St E15 98 A6
Deauville Ct
14 London SW4 159 C5
4 Rotherhithe SE16 118 D4
Deauville Mans 13 SW4 159 C5
De Barowe Mews
4 Highbury N5 72 D4
1 London N5 72 D3
Debdale Ho 20 E2 96 A6
Debden N17 33 B1
Debden Cl
7 Edgware NW9 27 C2
Kingston u T KT2 175 D5
Woodford IG8 37 D3
De Beauvoir Cres N1 95 C6
De Beauvoir Ct N1 73 B1
De Beauvoir Pl 5 N1 73 C2
De Beauvoir Prim Sch 13 N1 73 C2
De Beauvoir Rd N1 73 C1
De Beauvoir Sq N1 73 C1
DE BEAUVOIR TOWN 73 C1
Debenham Ct
Barnet EN5 12 C6
Hackney E8 96 A6
Debham Ct NW2 68 C5
Debnams Rd SE16 118 C2
De Bohun Ave N14 15 B5
De Bohun Prim Sch N14 15 B6
Deborah Cl TW7 130 C4
Deborah Cres HA4 39 B2
Deborah Ct 7 E18 55 B6
Deborah Lo HA8 26 D2
De Broome Rd TW13 150 C3
De Burgh Ho 10 SW19 180 A3
Deburgh Rd SW19 180 A3
Debussy 9 NW9 27 D1
Decimal Ctr 1 UB2 107 C4
Decima St SE1 117 C3 263 A6
Decimus Cl 1 CR7 205 B5
Deck Cl SE16 118 D5
Decoy Ave NW11 47 A5
De Crespigny Pk SE5 139 B3
Dedham Ho 1 SE6 186 A6
Dee Ct W7 86 B1
Deeley Rd SW8 137 D4 269 C2
Deena Cl W3 88 B1
Deen City Farm★ SW19 180 A1
Deepdale Highbury N4 72 D5
Deepdale *continued*
Wimbledon SW19 178 D6
Deepdale Ave BR2 208 D5
Deepdale Cl N11 31 A4
Deepdene N12 30 C6
Deepdene Ave CR0 221 D5
Deepdene Cl E11 55 A5
Deepdene Ct
Beckenham BR2 208 C6
Southgate N21 16 D5
Deepdene Gdns SW2 160 B4
Deepdene Ho N16 51 B1
Deepdene Lo 5 SW2 160 B4
Deepdene Mans SW6 264 C2
Deepdene Point 9 SE26 162 D1
Deepdene Rd
London SE5, SE24 139 B1
Welling DA16 146 A2
Deepwell Cl TW7 131 A4
Deepwood La UB6 86 B4
Deerbrook Rd SE24, SW2 160 D3
Dee Rd TW9 132 B1
Deerdale Rd SE24 139 A1
Deerfield Cl NW9 45 D4
Deerhurst
7 Kingston u T KT2 176 D2
5 Streatham SW16 182 A5
Deerhurst Cl TW13 172 B6
Deerhurst Cres TW12 174 A5
Deerhurst Ct CR0 204 D1
Deerhurst Ho 6 SE15 140 A6
Deerhurst Rd
Brondesbury NW2 68 D2
Streatham SW16 182 B5
Deerings Ct 2 N20 14 B2
Deerings Dr HA5 40 A4
Deerleap Gr E4 19 D6
Deer Lo SW6 135 A2
Deer Park Cl KT2 176 D3
Deer Park Gdns CR4 202 B5
Deer Park Rd SW19 180 A1
Deer Park Way BR4 224 D6
Deesdale Ct CR2 221 B4
Deeside Rd SW17 158 B1
Dee St E14 98 A1
Defence Cl SE28 123 C5
Defiance Wlk SE18 122 B3
Defiant 18 NW9 27 D1
Defiant Way SM6 220 A1
Defoe Ave TW9 132 C5
Defoe Cl SW17 180 C4
Defoe Ho
Barbican EC2 242 A4
5 Stoke Newington N16 73 C5
Defoe Pl Barbican EC2 242 A4
Upper Tooting SW17 180 D6
Defoe Rd
Rotherhithe SE16 119 B4
Stoke Newington N16 73 C5
De Frene Rd SE26 163 A1
De Gama Pl 3 E14 119 C1
Degema Rd BR7 188 D5
Dehar Cres NW9 46 A2
De Haviland Dr 8 SE18 122 D1
Dehavilland Cl UB5 84 D4
De Havilland Rd
Edgware HA8 26 D1
Heston TW5 128 C5
De Havilland Sq IG1 57 B1
Dehavilland Studios E5 74 C6
De Havilland Way TW19 148 A5
Dekker Ho 19 SE5 139 B5
Dekker Rd SE21 161 C5
Delacourt Rd SE3 143 B5
Delafield Ho 28 E1 96 A1
Delafield Rd SE7 121 C1
Delaford Rd SE16 118 B1
Delaford St SW6 135 A6 264 B5
Delamare Cres CR0 206 C3
Delamere Gdns NW7 27 B4
Delamere Ho 4 N4 51 B2
Delamere Rd
Ealing W5 110 A4
Delamere Rd *continued*
Hayes UB4 106 D6
Wimbledon SW20 178 D2
Delamere St W2 236 A3
Delamere Terr W2 91 D2
Delancey Pas NW1 231 D5
Delancey St NW1 93 B6 231 D5
Delancey Studios NW1 231 D5
Delany Ho SE10 142 A6
Delarch Ho SE1 251 C1
De Laune St SE17 116 D1 261 C1
Delaware Rd W9 91 D3
Delawyk Cres SE24 161 B5
Delcombe Ave KT4 200 C1
Delft Ho 8 KT2 176 B3
Delft Way 2 SE22 161 C6
Delhi Rd EN1 17 D4
Delhi St N1 94 A6 233 B5
Delia St SW18 157 D4
Delisle Rd SE28 123 C5
Delius Cl WD6 9 C5
Delius Gr E15 98 A5
Dellafield N4 72 C6
Della Path E5 74 B5
Dellbow Rd TW14 150 B6
Dell Cl
Stratford Marsh E15 98 B6
Wallington SM6 219 D4
Woodford IG8 21 B1
Dellfield Cl BR3 186 A2
Dell La KT17 216 A3
Dellors Cl EN5 12 D6
Dellow Cl IG2 57 B2
Dellow Ho 6 E1 118 B6
Dellow St E1 118 B6
Dell Rd Enfield EN3 6 C5
Stoneleigh KT17 216 A2
West Drayton UB7 104 B3
Dells Cl Chingford E4 19 D4
Teddington TW11 174 D4
Dell's Mews SW1 259 B3
Dell The
Brentford TW8 131 C6
Feltham TW14 150 B4
Pinner HA5 22 D1
Plumstead Comm SE2 124 A1
South Norwood SE19 183 D2
Wembley HA0 65 B3
Woodford IG8 21 B1
Dell Way W13 87 C1
Dell Wlk KT3 177 C1
Dellwood Gdns IG5 56 C6
Delme Cres SE3 143 B3
Delmey Cl CR0 221 D5
Deloraine Ho SE8 141 C4
Deloraine St SE8 141 C4
Delorme St W6 134 D6
Delphian Ct 5 SW16 182 C6
Delroy Ct N20 14 A4
Delta Bldg 7 E14 98 A1
Delta Cl KT4 215 D5
Delta Ct NW2 68 A6
Delta Gr UB5 84 D4
Delta Ho N1 235 C2
Delta Pk SW18 135 D1
Delta Pk Ind Est EN3 7 B3
Delta Point 5 E2 96 A4
Delta Rd KT4 215 C5
Delta St 4 E2 96 A4
De Lucy Prim Sch SE2 124 B4
De Lucy St SE2 124 B2
Delvan Cl SE18 144 C5
Delverton Ho SE17 261 D2
Delverton Rd SE17 261 D1
Delvino Rd SW6 135 C4 265 B1
De Mandeville Gate EN1 6 B1
Demesne Rd SM6 219 D4
Demeta Cl HA9 67 A5
De Montfort Ct 1 SW16 160 A1
De Montfort Rd SW16 160 A2
De Morgan Rd SW6 135 D2
Dempster Cl KT6 197 C1
Dempster Rd SW18 158 A6
Denberry Dr DA14 168 B1

Denbigh Cl
Cheam SM1 .... 217 B3
Elmstead BR7 .... 188 B4
Notting Hill
W11 .... 113 B6 244 D6
Ruislip HA4 .... 61 D6
Southall UB1 .... 85 B1
Denbigh Ct
1 Ealing W7 .... 86 D2
Newham E6 .... 99 D4
Denbigh Dr UB3 .... 105 A4
Denbigh Gdns TW10 .... 154 B6
Denbigh Ho
Knightsbridge SW1 .... 257 D6
7 Notting Hill W11 .... 91 B1
Notting Hill W11 .... 244 D6
Denbigh Mews SW1 .... 259 A3
Denbigh Pl
SW1 .... 115 C1 259 A2
Denbigh Rd
Ealing W13 .... 87 B1
Hounslow TW3 .... 129 D3
Newham E6 .... 99 D4
Notting Hill
W11 .... 113 B6 244 D6
Southall UB1 .... 85 B1
Denbigh St
SW1 .... 115 C1 259 B2
Denbigh Terr
W11 .... 113 B6 244 D6
Denbridge Rd BR1,
BR7 .... 188 B1
Denbury Ho 48 E3 .... 97 D4
Denby Ct Barnet EN5 .... 1 D2
Lambeth SE11 .... 260 D4
Dence Ho 15 E2 .... 96 A4
Denchworth Ho 14
SW9 .... 138 C3
Den Cl BR2, BR3 .... 208 B6
Dencliffe 2 TW15 .... 170 C5
Dencora Centre The
EN3 .... 7 A2
Dendridge Cl EN1 .... 6 B6
Dene Ave
Blackfen DA15 .... 168 B4
Hounslow TW3 .... 129 B2
Dene Cl Brockley SE4 .... 141 A1
Hayes BR2 .... 208 D1
Leyton E10 .... 75 D6
Worcester Pk KT4 .... 215 D6
Denecroft Cres UB10 .... 82 D6
Dene Ct Ealing W5 .... 87 C2
Hanwell W7 .... 108 D4
Dene Gdns
Hinchley Wood KT7 .... 213 A6
Stanmore HA7 .... 25 C5
Dene Ho N14 .... 15 D4
Denehole Ho SE18 .... 124 A1
Denehurst Gdns
Acton W3 .... 110 D5
Hendon NW4 .... 46 C3
Richmond TW10 .... 132 C1
Twickenham TW2 .... 152 B4
Woodford IG8 .... 37 B6
Dene Mans 1 NW6 .... 69 C2
Dene Rd
Buckhurst Hill IG9 .... 21 D3
Friern Barnet N11 .... 14 D2
Denesmead SE24 .... 161 A6
Dene The Ealing W13 .... 87 B2
East Molesey KT12,
KT8 .... 195 B4
South Croydon CR0 .... 222 D4
Wembley HA9 .... 66 A4
Denewood EN5 .... 14 A6
Denewood Ho 6
SM1 .... 218 A4
Denewood Rd N6 .... 48 D2
Dengie Wlk N1 .... 235 A6
Denham Cl DA16 .... 146 C2
Denham Cres CR4 .... 202 D5
Denham Ct
Forest Hill SE26 .... 162 B1
Southall UB1 .... 108 A6
Denham Dr IG2 .... 57 A3
Denham Ho 32 W12 .... 112 B6
Denham Lo W5 .... 88 A1
Denham Rd
Feltham TW14 .... 150 C4
Friern Barnet N20 .... 14 D1
Denham St SE10 .... 121 A1
Denham Way IG11 .... 101 D6
Denholme Rd W9 .... 91 B4
Deniel Lo TW9 .... 153 C6
Denise Ct HA0 .... 65 C4
Denison Cl N2 .... 48 A6
Denison Rd Ealing W5 .... 87 C3
Feltham TW13 .... 171 D6
Mitcham SW19 .... 180 B4
Deniston Ave DA5 .... 169 A3
Denland Ho SW8 .... 270 D3
Denleigh Ct N14 .... 15 D4
Denleigh Gdns
Southgate N21 .... 16 C4
Thames Ditton KT7 .... 196 C3
Denman Dr
Ashford TW15 .... 170 D4
Claygate KT10 .... 213 A3
Hampstead Garden Suburb
NW11 .... 47 C4
Denman Dr N NW11 .... 47 C4
Denman Dr S NW11 .... 47 C4
Denman Ho 1 N16 .... 73 C6
Denman Rd SE15 .... 139 D3
Denman St W1 .... 249 C5
Denmark Ave SW19 .... 179 A3
Denmark Ct SM4 .... 201 C4
Denmark Gdns SM5 .... 218 D5
Denmark Gr N1 .... 234 A4
Denmark Hill SE5 .... 139 B3
Denmark Hill Dr NW9 .... 46 A6
Denmark Hill Sta
SE5 .... 139 B3
Denmark Ho 9 SE7 .... 122 A2
Denmark Mans 14
SE5 .... 139 A3
Denmark Pl
2 Bromley E3 .... 97 C4
Soho WC2 .... 239 D2
Denmark Rd
Bromley BR1 .... 187 B2
Camberwell SE5 .... 139 A3
Carshalton SM5 .... 218 D5
Croydon SE25 .... 206 B4
Ealing W13 .... 109 B6
Hornsey N8 .... 50 C5
Kilburn NW6 .... 91 B5
Kingston u T KT1 .... 198 A6
Twickenham TW2 .... 152 B1
Wimbledon SW19 .... 178 D4
Denmark St
8 Leyton E11 .... 76 C5
Newham E13 .... 99 B2
Soho WC2 .... 239 D2
Tottenham N17 .... 34 B3
Denmark Terr NW2 .... 48 D6
Denmead Ho SW15 .... 155 D5
Denmead Rd CR0 .... 204 D1
Denmead Sch TW12 .... 173 D3
Denmore Ct SM6 .... 219 B3
Dennan Rd KT6 .... 198 B1
Dennard Way BR6 .... 226 C4
Denner Rd E4 .... 19 C2
Denne Terr E8 .... 95 D6
Dennett Rd CR0 .... 204 C2
Dennett's Gr SE14 .... 140 D3
Dennett's Rd SE14 .... 140 C4
Denning Ave CR0 .... 220 C3
Denning Cl
Hampton TW12 .... 173 B5
St John's Wood
NW8 .... 92 A4 229 B1
Denning Mews
SW12 .... 159 A4
Denning Point E1 .... 243 D2
Denning Rd NW3 .... 70 B4
Dennington Cl 17 E5 .... 74 B6
**Dennington Park
Mansions** 12 NW6 .... 69 C3
Dennington Park Rd
NW6 .... 69 C2
Denningtons The
KT4 .... 215 C6
Dennis Ave HA9 .... 66 B3
Dennis Cl TW15 .... 171 B3
Dennis Ct
Chingford E17 .... 36 B1
Greenford UB6 .... 86 A1
Lewisham SE10 .... 142 A4
Dennis Gdns HA7 .... 25 C5
Dennis Ho 4 Bow E3 .... 97 B5
Sutton SM1 .... 217 C4
Dennis La HA7 .... 25 B6
Dennison Point E15 .... 76 A1
Dennis Par 1 N14 .... 15 D3
Dennis Park Cres
SW20 .... 179 A2
Dennis Rd KT8 .... 196 A5
Dennis Reeve Cl
CR4 .... 180 D2
Dennis Severs' House*
E1 .... 243 B4
Dennis Way SW4 .... 137 D2
Denny Cl 15 E6 .... 100 A2
Denny Cres SE11 .... 261 B2
Denny Gdns RM9 .... 80 B1
Denny Rd N9 .... 18 B3
Denny St
SE11 .... 116 C1 261 B2
Den Rd BR2 .... 208 B6
Densham Ho NW8 .... 229 D3
Densham Rd E15 .... 98 C6
Densole Cl BR3 .... 185 A2
Denstone Ho 5
SE15 .... 140 A6
Densworth Gr N9 .... 18 C2
Dent Ho SE17 .... 263 A3
Denton NW1 .... 71 A2
Denton Cl EN5 .... 12 C6
Denton Ct BR2 .... 210 C2
Denton Ho N1 .... 72 D1
Denton Rd
Bexley DA16 .... 146 C5
Edmonton N18 .... 33 C6
Hornsey N8 .... 50 B3
Twickenham TW1 .... 153 D5
Denton St SW18 .... 157 D5
Denton Way E5 .... 74 D5
Dents Rd SW11 .... 158 D5
Denvale Trade Pk
CR4 .... 202 B5
Denver Cl BR6 .... 211 C3
Denver Ct UB1 .... 107 B5
Denver Rd N16 .... 51 C2
Denwood SE23 .... 162 D1
Denyer Ho 1 NW5 .... 71 B4
Denyer St
SW3 .... 114 C2 257 B4
Denys Bldg EC1 .... 241 A4
Denziloe Ave UB10 .... 82 D4
Denzil Rd NW10 .... 67 D3
Deodar Rd SW15 .... 135 A1
Deodora Cl N20 .... 14 D1
Depot App NW2 .... 68 D4
Depot Rd
Isleworth TW3,
TW7 .... 130 B2
Shepherd's Bush W12 .... 112 C6
Depot St SE5 .... 139 B6
DEPTFORD 140 D6
Deptford Bridge
SE8 .... 141 C4
Deptford Bridge Sta
SE8 .... 141 C4
Deptford Broadway SE8,
SE14 .... 141 C4
Deptford Church St
SE8 .... 141 C5
Deptford Ferry Rd 24
E14 .... 119 C2
Deptford Gn SE8 .... 141 C6
Deptford Green Sch
SE14 .... 141 B5
Deptford Green Sch
(Annex) 12 SE14 .... 141 A5
Deptford High St
SE8 .... 141 C5
Deptford Park Prim Sch
2 SE8 .... 119 A1
Deptford Sta SE8 .... 141 C5
Deptford Trad Est
SE8 .... 141 A6
Deptford Wharf SE8 .... 119 B2
De Quincey Mews 3
E16 .... 121 A5
De Quincey Rd N17 .... 33 B2
Derby Ave
Harrow HA3 .... 24 B2
North Finchley N12 .... 30 A5
Romford RM7 .... 59 D3
Derby Ct
8 Clapton Pk E5 .... 74 D4
Woodford E18 .... 36 D2
Derby Gate SW1 .... 250 A2
Derby Hill SE23 .... 162 C2
Derby Hill Cres
SE23 .... 162 C2
Derby Ho
Hendon NW4 .... 46 C6
Lambeth SE11 .... 261 A4
Pinner HA5 .... 22 D1
4 Wallington SM6 .... 219 B3
Derby Lo N3 .... 29 B1
Derby Rd
Cheam SM1, SM2 .... 217 B2
Edmonton N18 .... 34 C5
Enfield EN3 .... 18 C6
Greenford UB6 .... 85 D6
Hounslow TW3 .... 129 D1
Merton SW19 .... 179 C3
Mortlake SW14 .... 132 D1
South Hackney E9 .... 96 D6
Surbiton KT5, KT6 .... 198 C1
Thornton Heath CR0 .... 204 D1
Upton E7 .... 77 D1
Woodford E18 .... 36 D2
Derby Rd Ind Est
TW3 .... 129 D1
Derbyshire St E2 .... 96 A4
Derby St W1 .... 248 B3
Dereham Ho 7 SE4 .... 140 D1
Dereham Pl EC2 .... 243 B6
Dereham Rd IG11 .... 79 D3
Derek Ave
Chessington KT19 .... 214 D3
Wallington SM6 .... 219 B4
Wembley HA9 .... 66 D1
Derek Cl KT19 .... 214 D3
Derek Walcott Cl
SE24 .... 160 D6
Dericote St E8 .... 96 B6
Deri Dene Cl 2
TW19 .... 148 A5
Derifall Cl E6 .... 100 B2
Dering Pl CR0 .... 221 A4
Dering Rd CR0 .... 221 A4
Dering St W1 .... 238 D1
Derinton Rd SW17 .... 181 A6
Derley Rd UB2 .... 106 D3
Dermody Gdns SE13 .... 164 B6
Dermody Rd SE13 .... 164 B6
Deronda Rd SE24,
SW2 .... 160 D3
Deroy Cl SM5 .... 218 D2
Derrick Gdns SE7 .... 121 C2
Derrick Ho 13 SW2 .... 160 C3
Derrick Rd BR3 .... 207 B5
Derrycombe Ho 18
W2 .... 91 C2
Derry Rd CR0, SM6 .... 220 A5
Derry St W8 .... 113 D4 245 C1
Dersingham Ave E12 .... 78 C4
Dersingham Inf Sch
E12 .... 78 C3
Dersingham Rd NW2 .... 69 A5
Derwent NW1 .... 232 A1
Derwent Ave
Barnet EN4 .... 14 D3
Burnt Oak NW7 .... 27 B4
Edmonton N18 .... 33 B5
Hyde The NW9 .... 45 C4
Kingston u T SW15 .... 177 C6
Pinner HA5 .... 23 A4
Uxbridge UB10 .... 60 C5
Derwent Cl
Claygate KT10 .... 212 D2
East Bedfont TW14 .... 149 D3
Derwent Cres
Bexleyheath DA7 .... 147 C3
Stanmore HA7 .... 25 C1
Whetstone N20 .... 14 A1
Derwent Ct
2 Hammersmith
W6 .... 112 A2
Hornsey N8 .... 50 A3
8 Rotherhithe SE16 .... 118 D4
Derwent Dr
Crofton BR5 .... 211 B2
Hayes UB4 .... 83 C2
Derwent Gdns
Redbridge IG4 .... 56 A5
Wembley HA9 .... 43 C2
Derwent Gr SE22 .... 139 D1
Derwent Ho
Penge SE20 .... 184 B1
South Kensington
SW7 .... 256 B4
Tower Hamlets E3 .... 97 B3
Derwent Lo
Hounslow TW7 .... 130 B3
North Cheam KT4 .... 216 B6
Derwent Rd
Ealing W5 .... 109 C3
Palmers Green N13 .... 16 B1
Penge SE20 .... 184 B1
Southall UB1 .... 85 B1
Twickenham TW2 .... 151 D5
West Barnes SM4 .... 200 D3
Derwent Rise NW9 .... 45 C3
Derwent St SE10 .... 120 C1
Derwentwater Mans 2
W3 .... 111 A5
Derwentwater Prim Sch
W3 .... 111 A5
Derwentwater Rd
W3 .... 111 A5
Derwent Wlk SM6 .... 219 B1
Derwent Yd W5 .... 109 C3
De Salis Rd UB10 .... 83 A3
Desborough Cl
Bayswater W2 .... 91 D2
Lower Halliford TW17 .... 192 C2
Desborough Ct SE25 .... 206 B5
Desborough Ho W14 .... 264 D6
Desenfans Rd SE21 .... 161 C5
Deseret Ho 6 CR4 .... 202 D6
Desford Rd E16 .... 98 C3
Desford Way TW15 .... 148 B2
Design Mus* SE1 .... 253 D2
Desmond Ho 4 EN4 .... 14 C5
Desmond St SE14 .... 141 A6
Desmond Tutu Dr
SE23 .... 163 A3
Despard Ho SW2 .... 160 C2
Despard Rd N19 .... 49 C1
Dessouter 19 NW9 .... 27 D1
Desvignes Dr SE13 .... 164 B5
Detherick Ct TW3 .... 130 A1
Dethick Ct E3 .... 97 A6
Detling Ho SE17 .... 263 A3
Detling Rd BR1 .... 187 A5
Detmold Rd E5 .... 74 C6
Devalls Cl E6 .... 122 C6
Devana End SM5 .... 218 D5
Devas Rd SW20 .... 178 C2
Devas St E3 .... 97 D3
Devema Cl BR7 .... 188 C2
Devenay Rd E15 .... 76 D1
Devenish Rd SE2 .... 124 A4
Deventer Cres 8
SE22 .... 161 C6
Deveraux Cl BR3 .... 208 A4
De Vere Cl SM6 .... 220 A1
De Vere Cotts W8 .... 256 A6
De Vere Ct 1 E5 .... 74 B5
De Vere Gdns
Kensington
W8 .... 114 A4 246 A1
Redbridge IG1 .... 56 B1
Deverell St
SE1 .... 117 B3 262 C5
De Vere Mews W8 .... 256 A6
Devereux Ct WC2 .... 241 A1
Devereux Ho 7
SW15 .... 156 A6
Devereux La SW13 .... 134 B5
Devereux Rd SW11 .... 158 D5
Deverill Ct SE20 .... 184 C2
Devey Cl KT2 .... 177 B5
Devitt Ho 5 E14 .... 119 D6
Devizes St N1 .... 235 D5
Devon Ave TW2 .... 152 A3
Devon Cl Chigwell IG9 .... 21 B2
Tottenham N17 .... 51 D6
Wembley UB6 .... 87 C6
Devoncroft Gdns
TW1 .... 153 A4
Devon Ct 3 Acton W3 .... 88 C1
2 Ealing W7 .... 86 D2
Hampton TW12 .... 173 C3
Devon Gdns N4 .... 50 D3
Devon Ho
9 Penge SE20 .... 184 B3
Walthamstow E17 .... 35 B1
6 Wanstead E11 .... 55 A4
Devonhurst Pl 4
W4 .... 111 B1
Devonia Gdns N18 .... 33 A4
Devonia Rd
N1 .... 94 D5 234 D4
Devon Mans SE1 .... 253 B2
Devon Par HA3 .... 43 C4
Devonport W2 .... 237 A2
Devonport Gdns IG1 .... 56 B3
Devonport Ho
Greenwich SE10 .... 142 A6
23 Paddington W2 .... 91 C2
Devonport Rd W12 .... 112 B4
Devonport St E1 .... 96 D1
Devon Rd IG11 .... 101 C6
Devon Rise N2 .... 48 B5
Devonshire Ave
SM2 .... 218 A1
Devonshire Cl
Edmonton N13 .... 32 C6

Devonshire Cl *continued*
Leyton E15 76 C4
Marylebone W1 238 C4
Devonshire Cres NW7 28 D3
Devonshire Ct
14 Balham SW12 159 B4
Croydon CR0 207 C1
Feltham TW13 150 B2
Pinner HA5 23 B2
6 Richmond TW9 132 B4
Tottenham N17 33 A4
Devonshire Dr
London SE10 141 D4
Long Ditton KT6 213 D6
Devonshire Gdns
Chiswick W4 133 A5
Edmonton N21 17 A4
Tottenham N17 33 A4
Devonshire Gr SE15 140 B6
Devonshire Hall 15 E9 74 C2
Devonshire Hill La N17 33 A4
Devonshire Hill Prim Sch N17 33 B4
Devonshire Ho
Brondesbury NW6 69 B2
Hounslow TW3 130 A2
Newington SE1 262 A6
Paddington W2 236 D4
2 Putney SW15 156 C4
10 Sutton SM2 218 A1
Westminster SW1 259 D2
Whetstone N12 14 A1
Devonshire House Prep Sch NW3 70 A3
Devonshire Mews 2 W4 111 C1
Devonshire Mews N W1 238 C4
Devonshire Mews S W1 238 C4
Devonshire Mews W W1 238 B4
Devonshire Pl
Child's Hill NW2 69 C5
Kensington W8 255 C5
Marylebone W1 93 A2 238 B4
Devonshire Place Mews W1 238 B4
Devonshire Prim Sch 18 SM2 218 A1
Devonshire Rd
Bexley DA6 147 A1
Chislehurst SE9 166 A2
Chiswick W4 111 C1
Ealing W5 109 C3
Eastcote HA5 40 C2
Edmonton N9 18 C3
Feltham TW13 173 A6
Forest Hill SE23 162 C4
Hackbridge SM5, SM6 219 A4
Harrow HA1 42 B3
Hatch End HA5 23 B2
Ilford IG2 57 C2
Mill Hill NW7 28 D3
Mitcham SW19 180 C3
Newham E16 99 B1
Palmers Green N13 32 C6
Southall UB1 85 C2
Sutton SM2 218 A1
Thornton Heath CR0 205 B2
Tottenham N17 33 A4
Walthamstow E17 53 C3
Devonshire Rd Nat Res* SE23 162 D4
Devonshire Row EC2 243 B3
Devonshire Row Mews W1 238 D5
Devonshire Sq
Bromley BR2 209 B5
Whitechapel EC2 95 C1 243 B2
Devonshire St
Chiswick W4 111 C1
Marylebone W1 93 B2 238 C4
Devonshire Terr W2 92 A1 236 B1
Devonshire Way
Croydon CR0, CR9 223 B6
Hayes UB4 84 B1
Devons Rd E3 97 D3
Devons Road Sta E3 97 D3
Devon St SE15 140 B6
Devon Way
Chessington KT9 213 C3
Ewell KT19 214 D3
Hillingdon UB10 82 B5
Devon Waye TW5 129 B5
De Walden Ho NW8 230 A4
De Walden St W1 238 B3
Dewar Ho 2 SW17 180 C5
Dewar St SE15 140 A2
Dewberry Gdns E6 100 A2
Dewberry St E14 98 A2
Dewey Rd
Dagenham RM10 81 D2
Islington N1 94 C5 234 A4
Dewey St SW17 180 D5
Dewhurst Rd W14 112 D3
Dewlands Ct 7 NW4 28 D1
Dewsbury Cl HA5 41 A3
Dewsbury Ct 5 W4 111 A2
Dewsbury Gdns KT4 216 A5
Dewsbury Rd NW10 68 A3
Dewsbury Terr NW1 231 D6
Dexter Ho 2 DA18 125 A3
Dexter Rd EN5 12 D5
Deyncourt Rd N17 33 A2
Deynecourt Gdns E11 55 C5
D'eynsford Rd SE5 139 B4
Dhonau Ho SE16 263 D4
Diadem Ct W1 239 C2
Dial Wlk The W8 113 D4 245 D2
Diameter Rd BR5 211 A3
Diamond Cl RM8 58 C1
Diamond Ct 8 W7 108 C5
Diamond Est SW17 158 C1
Diamond Ho 22 E3 97 A5
Diamond Rd HA4 63 A4
Diamond St
18 London NW10 67 B1
SE15 139 C5
Diamond Terr SE10 142 A4
Diana Cl
27 Deptford SE8 141 B6
Sidcup DA14 169 A2
Woodford E18 37 B2
Diana Ct SM5 219 A1
Diana Gdns KT6 214 B6
Diana Ho
Barnes SW13 133 D4
4 Brixton SW2 160 B6
Diana, Princess of Wales Mml Fountain* W2 114 C5 246 D2
Diana, Princess of Wales Mml Wlk W2 114 A5 246 A3
Diana Rd E17 53 B6
Dianne Ct SE12 165 A3
Dianne Way EN4 2 C1
Dianthus Cl SE2 124 B1
Dias Ho UB5 85 A6
Dibden Ho 8 SE5 139 C5
Dibden St N1 95 A6 235 A6
Dibdin Cl SM1 217 C5
Dibdin Ho W9 91 D5
Dibdin Rd SM1 217 C6
Dicey Ave NW2 68 C4
Dickens Ave
Finchley N3 30 A2
Hayes UB8 82 D1
Dickens Cl Erith DA8 147 D5
Hayes UB3 105 C2
Richmond TW10 154 A2
Dickens Ct
Clerkenwell EC1 241 C5
10 Wanstead E11 55 A5
Wembley HA0 65 C5
Dickens Dr BR7 189 A4
Dickens Ho
Bloomsbury WC1 240 A6
3 Erith DA17 125 B1
Hayes UB3 105 C2
Kennington SE17 261 D1
Kilburn NW6 91 C4
Paddington NW8 236 D6
Dickens La N18 33 C5
Dickenson Cl N9 18 A3
Dickenson Ho N8 50 B3
Dickenson Rd
Feltham TW13 172 D5
Hornsey N8 50 A2
Dickenson's La SE25 206 A3
Dickenson's Pl SE25 206 A3
Dickens Rd E6 99 D5
Dickens Sq SE1 117 A3 262 B6
Dickens St SW8 137 B3
Dickens Wood Cl SE19 182 D3
Dickerage Hill
Kingston u T KT3 177 A1
Kingston u T KT3 199 A6
Dickerage La KT3 199 A6
Dickerage Rd KT1, KT2, KT3 177 A1
Dickinson Ho 18 E2 96 A4
Dicksee Ho NW8 236 C5
Dick Shepherd Ct 17 SW2 160 C5
Dickson Fold HA5 40 D5
Dickson Ho
3 Charlton SE18 144 A4
4 Stepney E1 96 B1
Dickson Rd SE9 144 A2
Dick Turpin Way TW14 127 D1
Didbin Ho N7 72 B6
Didsbury Cl E6 100 B6
Digby Bsns Ctr E9 74 D2
Digby Cres N4 73 A6
Digby Gdns RM10 103 C6
Digby Mans W6 112 C1
Digby Pl CR0 221 D5
Digby Rd Barking IG11 79 D1
Homerton E9 74 D2
Digby St E2 96 C4
Diggon St E1 96 D2
Dighton Ct SE17 139 A6
Dighton Rd SW18 136 A1
Dignum St N1 234 A4
Digswell St N7 72 C2
Dilhorne Cl SE12 165 B1
Dilke St SW3 136 D6 267 D6
Dilloway Yd UB2 107 A4
Dillwyn Cl SE26 185 A6
Dilston Cl 1 UB5 84 C4
Dilston Gr SE16 118 C2
Dilton Gdns SW15 156 B3
Dilwyn Ct E17 35 A1
Dimes Pl 9 W6 112 B2
Dimmock Dr UB6 64 B3
Dimond Cl E7 77 A4
Dimsdale Dr
Enfield EN1 18 A5
Welsh Harp NW9 45 A1
Dimsdale Wlk 4 E13 99 A5
Dimson Cres E3 97 C4
Dinerman Ct NW8 229 B6
Dingle Cl EN5 11 D5
Dingle Ct 16 HA7 25 C5
Dingle Gdns E14 119 C6
Dingle Rd TW15 170 D5
Dingles Ct HA5 22 D1
Dingle The UB10 82 D4
Dingley La SW16 159 D2
Dingley Pl EC1 95 A4 235 B1
Dingley Rd EC1 95 A4 235 A1
Dingwall Ave CR0 221 A6
Dingwall Gdns NW11 47 C3
Dingwall Rd
South Croydon CR0 221 B6
Wandsworth SW18 158 A4
Dinmont Ho 27 E2 96 A5
Dinmont St 1 E2 96 B5
Dinmore Ho 6 E9 96 C6
Dinnington Ho 17 E1 96 B3
Dinorben SM6 219 C1
Dinsdale Ct EN5 13 D6
Dinsdale Gdns
New Barnet EN5 13 D6
South Norwood SE25 205 C4
Dinsdale Rd SE3 142 D6
Dinsmore Rd SW12 159 B4
Dinton Ho NW8 237 A6
Dinton Rd
Kingston u T KT2 176 B3
Mitcham SW19 180 B4
Dinwiddy Ho N1 233 C3
Dionis Ho SW6 135 C3
Diploma Ave N2 48 C5
Diploma Ct N2 48 C5
Diprose Lo SW17 180 B6
Dirleton Rd E15 98 D6
Disbrowe Rd W6 135 A6 264 B5
Discovery Bsns Pk 13 SE16 118 A3
Discovery Dock E E14 119 D4
Discovery Ho 1 E14 120 A6
Discovery Prim Sch SE28 123 C5
Dishforth La NW9 27 C2
Disley Ct 2 UB1 85 D1
Disney Pl SE1 252 B2
Disney St SE1 252 B2
Dison Cl EN3 6 D4
Disraeli Cl
1 Acton W4 111 B2
Thamesmead SE28 124 C5
Disraeli Gdns SW15 135 B1
Disraeli Rd
Acton NW10 89 B5
Ealing W5 109 D5
Putney SW15 135 A1
Upton E7 77 A2
Diss St E2 95 D4
Distaff La EC4 252 A6
Distillery La W6 112 C1
Distillery Rd W6 112 C1
Distillery Wlk 14 TW8 132 A6
Distin Ct 3 SM1 217 D3
Distin St SE11 116 C2 261 A3
District Rd HA0 65 B3
Ditchburn St E14 120 A6
Ditchfield Rd UB4 85 A3
Ditchley Ct W7 86 D2
Dittisham Rd SE9 188 A6
Ditton Cl KT7 197 A2
Dittoncroft Cl CR0 221 C4
Ditton Grange Cl KT6 197 D1
Ditton Grange Dr KT6 197 D1
Ditton Hill KT6 213 D6
Ditton Hill Rd KT6 197 C1
Ditton Ho 10 E5 74 B3
Ditton Lawn KT7 197 A1
Ditton Pl 6 SE20 184 B2
Ditton Rd Bexley DA6 169 A6
Southall UB2 107 B1
Surbiton KT6 198 B1
Ditton Reach KT7 197 B3
Divis Way SW15 156 B5
Dixon Cl 4 E6 100 B1
Dixon Clark Ct N1 72 D2
Dixon Ct N4 50 C3
Dixon Ho
20 North Kensington NW10 90 D1
West Heath SE2 124 C1
Dixon Pl BR4 207 D1
Dixon Rd
London SE14 141 A4
South Norwood SE25 205 D6
Dixon's Alley 10 SE16 118 B4
Dixon Way 9 NW10 67 C1
Dobbin Cl HA3 25 A1
Dobell Rd SE9 166 B6
Dobree Ave NW10 68 B1
Dobson Cl NW6 70 B1
Dobson Ho 18 SE14 140 D6
Doby Ct EC4 252 B6
Dockers Tanner Rd 26 E14 119 C2
Dockett Eddy La KT16, TW17 192 B1
Dockett Moorings KT16 192 B1
Dockhead SE1 117 D4 253 D1
Dockhead Wharf SE1 253 D2
Dock Hill Ave SE16 118 D4
Docklands Ct 20 E14 97 B1
Dockland St E16 122 C5
Docklands Visitor Ctr* E14 120 A4
Dockley Rd SE16 118 A3
Dockley Road Ind Est 11 SE16 118 A3
Dock Offices 12 SE16 118 C3
Dock Rd
Brentford TW8 131 D5
Canning Town E16 120 D6
Dockside Rd E16 121 D6
Dock St E1 118 A6
Dockwell Cl TW14 128 A1
Dockwell's Ind Est TW14 150 B6
Doctor Johnson Ho 2 SW16 181 D6
Doctors Cl SE26 184 C5
Doctor Spurstowe Almshouses 9 E8 74 B2
Docura Ho N7 72 B6
Docwras Bldgs N1 73 C2
Dodbrooke Rd SE27 160 D1
Dodd Ho 18 SE16 118 B2
Doddington Gr SE17 116 D1 261 D1
Doddington Pl 4 SE17 138 D6
Dodsley Pl N9 18 C1
Dodson St SE1 116 C4 251 B1
Dod St E14 97 C1
Doebury Wlk SE18 146 A6
Doel Cl SW19 180 A3
Dog & Duck Yd WC1 240 C4
Doggett Rd SE6 163 C4
Doggetts Ct EN4 14 C6
Doghurst Ave UB3 126 D5
Doghurst Dr UB7 126 D5
Dog Kennel Hill SE22 139 C2
Dog Kennel Hill Sch 23 SE22 139 C2
Dog La NW10 67 C4
Dogrose Ct 14 NW9 46 A5
Doherty Rd E13 99 A3
Dokal Ind Est UB2 107 A4
Doland Ct SW17 180 D4
Dolben Ct SW1 259 D3
Dolben St SE1 116 D5 251 D3
Dolby Rd SW6 135 B3
Doleman Ho 19 SE10 141 D4
Dolland Ho SE11 260 D1
Dolland St SE11 260 D1
Dollar Bay E14 120 A4
Dollary Ct KT3 198 D6
Dolliffe Cl CR4 180 D1
Dollis Ave N3 29 B2
Dollis Brook Wlk EN5 13 A5
Dollis Cres HA4 40 C1
Dolliscroft NW7 29 A3
Dollis Ct N3 29 B2
DOLLIS HILL 68 B5
Dollis Hill Ave NW2 68 B5
Dollis Hill Est NW2 68 A5
Dollis Hill La NW2 68 A5
Dollis Hill Sta NW2 68 A3
Dollis Hts NW2 68 B5
Dollis Jun & Inf Schs NW7 28 C3
Dollis Mews N3 29 C2
Dollis Pk N3 29 B2
Dollis Rd N3, NW7 29 B3
Dollis Valley Dr EN5 13 B6
Dollis Valley Way EN5 13 B5
Dolman Cl N3 30 A1
Dolman Rd W4 111 B2
Dolman St SW4 138 B1
Dolphin Cl
Kingston u T KT6 197 D4
2 Rotherhithe SE16 118 D4
Thamesmead SE28 102 D1
Dolphin Ct
London NW11 47 A3
Merton SW19 179 C3
Tufnell Pk N7 71 D4
2 Wallington SM6 219 B2
Dolphin Est The TW16 171 B2
Dolphin La E14 119 D6
Dolphin Rd
Charlton TW16 171 C2
Northolt UB5 85 B5
Dolphin Rd N TW16 171 C2
Dolphin Rd S TW16 171 C2
Dolphin Rd W TW16 171 C2
Dolphin Sch SW11 158 D6
Dolphin Sq SW1 115 C1 259 B1
Dolphin St KT2 176 A2
Dolphin Twr 21 SE8 141 B6
Dombey Ho
13 Bermondsey SE1 118 A4

Dombey Ho *continued*
[4] Shepherd's Bush W11 ... 112 D5
Dombey St WC1 ... 240 C4
Dome Hill Pk SE26 ... 183 D6
Domelton Ho SW18 ... 157 D5
Domett Cl SE5 ... 139 B1
Domfe Pl E5 ... 74 C4
Domingo St EC1 ... 242 A5
Dominica Cl [6] E6 ... 99 D5
Dominion Bsns Pk N9 ... 18 D2
Dominion Cl TW3 ... 130 B3
Dominion Ind Est UB2 ... 107 A4
Dominion Par HA1 ... 42 D4
Dominion Rd
Croydon CR0 ... 205 D2
Southall UB2 ... 107 A3
Dominion St EC2 ... 95 B2 242 D4
Dominion Wks RM8 ... 59 A1
Domonic Dr SE9 ... 166 D1
Domville Cl N20 ... 14 B2
Donaghue Cotts [11] E14 ... 97 A2
Donald Dr RM6 ... 58 C4
Donald Lynch Ho CR4 ... 180 D1
Donald Rd
Newham E13 ... 99 B6
Thornton Heath CR0 ... 204 B2
Donaldson Rd
Kilburn NW6 ... 91 B6
Shooters Hill SE18 ... 144 C4
Donald Woods Gdns KT5 ... 215 A6
Doncaster Dr UB5 ... 63 B3
Doncaster Gdns
London N4 ... 51 A3
Northolt UB5 ... 63 B3
Doncaster Gn WD19 ... 22 C5
Doncaster Rd N9 ... 18 B4
Doncel Ct E4 ... 20 B4
Donegal Ho [2] E1 ... 96 C3
Donegal St N1 94 B5 233 D3
Doneraile Ho SW1 ... 258 C1
Doneraile St SW6 ... 134 D4
Dongola Rd
Newham E13 ... 99 B4
Tottenham N17 ... 51 C6
Tower Hamlets E1 ... 97 A2
Dongola Rd W [5] E13 ... 99 B4
Don Gratton Ho [23] E1 ... 96 A2
Donhead Sch [19] SW19 ... 178 D3
Donington Ave IG6 ... 57 A4
Donkey Alley SE22 ... 162 A5
Donkey La EN1 ... 6 A3
Donkin Ho [15] SE16 ... 118 B2
Donne Ct SE24 ... 161 A5
Donnefield Ave HA8 ... 26 A3
Donne Ho
[18] Canonbury N16 ... 73 B4
[14] Deptford SE14 ... 140 D6
[11] Poplar E14 ... 97 C1
Donnelly Ct SW6 ... 264 B4
Donne Pl
Chelsea SW3 ... 114 C2 257 B4
Mitcham CR4 ... 203 B5
Donne Rd RM8 ... 80 C6
Donnington Ct
[11] Camden Town NW1 ... 71 B1
Willesden NW10 ... 68 B1
Donnington Ho [12] SW8 ... 137 D3
Donnington Prim Sch NW10 ... 90 B6
Donnington Rd
Harrow HA3 ... 43 D3
Willesden Green NW10 90 B6
Worcester Pk KT4 ... 216 A6
Donnybrook Rd SW16 ... 181 D3
Donoghue Bsns Pk NW2 ... 68 D5
Donovan Ave N10 ... 31 C1
Donovan Ct SW7 ... 256 C1
Donovan Ho [4] E1 ... 118 C6
Donovan Pl N21 ... 16 B6
Don Phelan Cl SE5 ... 139 B4
Doone Cl TW11 ... 175 A4
Doon St SE1 ... 116 C5 251 A4
Doradus Ct [20] SW19 156 D3
Dora Ho
[11] Shepherd's Bush W11 ... 112 D6
[1] Tower Hamlets E14 ... 97 B1
Doral Way SM5 ... 218 D3
Doran Ct E6 ... 100 B5
Dorando Cl W12 ... 112 B6
Doran Gr SE18 ... 145 C5
Doran Manor N2 ... 48 D4
Doran Wlk
Stratford E15 ... 76 A1
Stratford Marsh E15 ... 98 A6
Dora Rd SW19 ... 179 C6
Dora St E14 ... 97 B1
Dora Way SW9 ... 138 C3
Dorcas Ct [9] SW18 ... 136 B1
Dorchester Ave
Edmonton N13 ... 33 A6
Harrow HA2 ... 42 A3
Sidcup DA5 ... 168 D4
Dorchester Cl
Hinchley Wood KT10 ... 212 D6
Northolt UB5 ... 63 D3
St Paul's Cray BR5 ... 190 B3
Dorchester Ct
Cricklewood NW2 ... 68 D5
[1] De Beauvoir Town N1 ... 73 C1
East Barnet N14 ... 15 B4
Herne Hill SE24 ... 161 A6
Knightsbridge SW1 ... 257 D5
[1] Muswell Hill N10 ... 49 B6
[5] Streatham SW16 ... 160 A2
[2] Woodford E18 ... 36 D2
Dorchester Dr
Feltham TW14 ... 149 C5
Herne Hill SE24 ... 161 A6
Dorchester Gdns
Chingford E4 ... 35 C6
East Finchley NW11 ... 47 C5
Dorchester Gr W4 ... 111 D1
Dorchester Ho
Richmond TW9 ... 132 D5
Wallington SM5 ... 218 D3
Dorchester Mews
New Malden KT3 ... 199 B5
Twickenham TW1 ... 153 C5
Dorchester Prim Sch KT4 ... 200 C1
Dorchester Rd
Cheam SM4 ... 202 A2
North Cheam KT4 ... 200 C1
Northolt UB5 ... 63 D3
Dorchester Way HA3 ... 44 B3
Dorchester Waye
Hayes UB4 ... 84 B1
Hayes UB4 ... 84 C1
Dorcis Ave DA7 ... 147 A3
Dordrecht Rd W3 ... 111 C5
Dore Ave E12 ... 78 C3
Doreen Ave NW9 ... 45 B1
Doreen Capstan Ho [5] E11 ... 76 C5
Dore Gdns SM4 ... 201 D2
Dorell Cl UB1 ... 85 B2
Dorey Ho [7] TW8 ... 131 C5
Doria Rd SW6 ... 135 B3
Doric Ho [7] E2 ... 96 D5
Doric Way NW1 ... 93 D4 232 C2
Dorie Mews N12 ... 29 D6
Dorien Rd SW20 ... 178 D1
Doris Ashby Cl UB6 ... 87 A6
Doris Emmerton Ct SW18 ... 136 A1
Doris Rd
Ashford TW15 ... 171 B4
Upton E7 ... 77 A1
Dorking Cl
Deptford SE8 ... 141 B6
North Cheam KT4 ... 216 D6
Dorking Ct N17 ... 34 A2
Dorking Ho SE1 ... 262 D6
Dorland Ct SW15 ... 157 B5
Dorlcote Rd SW18 ... 158 C4
Dorleston Ct N1 ... 235 D6
Dorly Cl TW17 ... 193 C4
Dorman Pl [6] N9 ... 18 A2
Dorman Way NW8 ... 92 B6 229 C6
Dorman Wlk NW10 ... 67 B2
Dorma Trad Pk E10 ... 52 D1
Dormay St SW18 ... 157 D6
Dormer Cl Barnet EN5 ... 12 D6
Stratford E15 ... 76 D2
Dormer's Ave UB1 ... 85 C1
Dormers Lo EN4 ... 2 D3
Dormers Rise UB1 ... 85 D1
DORMER'S WELLS ... 107 C6
Dormer's Wells High Sch UB1 ... 85 C1
Dormers Wells Ho UB4 ... 84 C2
Dormer's Wells Inf Sch UB1 ... 107 D6
Dormer's Wells Jun Sch UB1 ... 107 D6
Dormer's Wells La UB1 ... 107 C5
Dormer's Wells L Ctr UB1 ... 107 D6
Dormer Wells L Ctr UB1 ... 85 D1
Dormstone Ho SE17 ... 263 A3
Dormywood HA4 ... 39 D4
Dornberg Cl SE3 ... 143 A5
Dornberg Rd SE3 ... 143 B5
Dorncliffe Rd SW6 ... 135 A3
Dorney NW3 ... 70 C1
Dorney Ct SW6 ... 135 A2
Dorney Rise BR5 ... 211 D5
Dorney Way TW4 ... 151 A6
Dornfell St NW6 ... 69 B3
Dornoch Ho [26] E3 ... 97 B5
Dornton Rd
South Croydon CR2 ... 221 C3
Upper Tooting SW12, SW17 ... 159 C2
Dorothy Ave HA0 ... 66 A1
Dorothy Barley Jun & Inf Schs RM8 ... 80 B3
Dorothy Charrington Ho [1] SE22 ... 162 A6
Dorothy Evans Cl DA7 ... 147 D1
Dorothy Gdns RM8 ... 80 B4
Dorothy Pettingel Ho [1] SM1 ... 217 D5
Dorothy Rd SW11 ... 136 D2
Dorothy Villas UB1 ... 107 C5
Dorrell Pl [18] SW9 ... 138 C2
Dorrien Wlk SW16 ... 159 D2
Dorrington Ct SE25 ... 183 C1
Dorrington Point [20] E3 ... 97 D4
Dorrington St EC1 ... 241 A4
Dorrington Way BR3 ... 208 A4
Dorrit Ho [2] W11 ... 112 D5
Dorrit Mews N18 ... 33 C5
Dorrit St SE1 ... 252 B2
Dorrit Way BR7 ... 189 A4
Dorryn Ct SE26 ... 184 D5
Dors Cl NW9 ... 45 B1
Dorset Ave
Falconwood DA16 ... 145 D1
Hayes UB4 ... 83 C4
Southall UB2 ... 107 C2
Dorset Bldgs EC4 ... 241 C1
Dorset Cl Hayes UB4 ... 83 C4
Marylebone NW1 ... 237 C4
Dorset Ct
[3] Ealing W7 ... 86 D2
[3] London N1 ... 73 C1
[4] Northolt UB5 ... 85 B4
Dorset Dr HA8 ... 26 B4
Dorset Gdns SW16 ... 204 B5
Dorset Hall SW19 ... 179 C2
Dorset Ho [1] SE20 ... 184 B2
Dorset Mans [2] W6 ... 134 D6
Dorset Mews
Belgravia SW1 ... 258 C6
Finchley N3 ... 29 C2
Dorset Pl E15 ... 76 B2
Dorset Rd
Ashford TW15 ... 148 A1
Chislehurst SE9 ... 166 A2
Ealing W5 ... 109 D3
Harrow HA1 ... 42 A3
Merton SW19 ... 179 C1
Mitcham CR4 ... 180 C1
Penge BR3 ... 206 D6
South Lambeth SW8 ... 138 B5 270 C4
Upton E7 ... 77 C1
West Green N15 ... 51 B5
Wood Green N22 ... 32 A2
Dorset Rise EC4 ... 94 D1 241 C1
Dorset Road Inf Sch [7] SE9 ... 166 A2
Dorset Sq NW1 ... 92 D3 237 C5
Dorset St W1 ... 92 D2 237 D3
Dorset Way
Hillingdon UB10 ... 82 B5
Twickenham TW2 ... 152 B3
Dorset Waye TW5 ... 129 B5
Dorton Cl [6] SE15 ... 139 C5
Dorton Villas UB7 ... 126 C4
Dorville Cres W6 ... 112 B3
Dorville Rd SE12 ... 165 A6
Dothill Rd SE18 ... 145 A5
Douai Gr TW12 ... 174 A2
Douay Martyrs RC Sch (Annexe) The UB10 ... 60 D3
Douay Martyrs RC Sch The UB10 ... 60 D4
Doughty Ct [11] E1 ... 118 B5
Doughty Mews WC1 ... 94 B3 240 C5
Doughty St WC1 ... 94 B3 240 C5
Douglas [20] NW9 ... 27 D1
Douglas Ave
Walthamstow E17 ... 35 C2
Wembley HA0 ... 66 A1
West Barnes KT3 ... 200 B5
Douglas Bader Ho N3 ... 29 D4
Douglas Bldgs SE1 ... 252 B2
Douglas Cl
Hadley Wood EN4 ... 2 B5
Stanmore HA7 ... 25 A5
Wallington SM6 ... 220 A2
Douglas Cres UB4 ... 84 D3
Douglas Ct London N3 ... 29 D1
[5] South Hampstead NW6 ... 69 C1
[1] Upper Tooting SW17 ... 180 C4
Douglas Dr CR0 ... 223 C5
Douglas Gracey Ho [1] SW18 ... 157 A4
Douglas Ho
Isleworth TW1 ... 153 B6
Putney SW15 ... 156 A5
Westminster SW1 ... 259 C3
Douglas Johnstone Ho SW6 ... 264 C5
Douglas Mews NW2 ... 69 A5
Douglas Path E14 ... 120 A1
Douglas Rd
Chingford E4 ... 20 C3
Hounslow TW3 ... 129 D2
Ilford IG3 ... 58 A3
Islington N1 ... 73 A1
Kilburn NW6 ... 91 B6
Kingston u T KT1 ... 176 D1
[5] Newham E16 ... 99 A2
Stanwell TW19 ... 148 A5
Surbiton KT6 ... 198 B1
Thames Ditton KT10 ... 212 A6
Welling DA16 ... 146 B4
Wood Green N22 ... 32 C2
Douglas Rd N N1 ... 73 A2
Douglas Rd S N1 ... 73 A2
Douglas Robinson Ct SW16 ... 182 A3
Douglas Sq SM4 ... 201 C3
Douglas St SW1 ... 115 D2 259 C3
Douglas Terr E17 ... 35 B2
Douglas Waite Ho NW6 ... 69 D1
Douglas Way SE8 ... 141 B5
Doulton Ho SE11 ... 260 D4
Doulton Mews [4] NW6 ... 69 D2
Dounesforth Gdns SW18 ... 157 D3
Douro Pl W8 ... 113 D3 255 D6
Douro St E3 ... 97 C5
Douthwaite Sq [11] E1 ... 118 A5
Dove App E6 ... 100 A2
Dove Cl Hendon NW7 ... 27 D3
Northolt UB5 ... 84 D3
Wallington SM6 ... 220 B1
Dovecot Cl HA5 ... 40 C4
Dovecote Gdns [8] SW14 ... 133 B2
Dove Ct
City of London EC2 ... 242 C1
Enfield EN3 ... 18 B6
Stanwell TW19 ... 148 A4
Dovedale Ave HA3 ... 43 C3
Dovedale Cl DA16 ... 146 A3
Dovedale Cotts [6] SW11 ... 136 D3
Dovedale Ho N16 ... 51 B2
Dovedale Rd SE22 ... 162 B5
Dovedale Rise CR4 ... 180 D3
Dovedon Cl N14 ... 16 A2
Dove House Gdns E4 ... 19 C2
Dovehouse Mead IG11 ... 101 B5
Dovehouse St SW3 ... 114 C1 257 A1
Dove Mews SW7 ... 114 A1 256 B2
Dove Pk HA5 ... 23 C3
Dover Cl NW2 ... 68 D6
Dovercourt Ave CR7 ... 204 C5
Dovercourt Gdns HA7 ... 26 A5
Dovercourt La SM1 ... 218 A5
Dovercourt Rd SE22 ... 161 D5
Dover Ct
Clerkenwell EC1 ... 241 C6
[17] Greenwich SE10 ... 141 D4
Sutton SM1 ... 218 B4
Dove Rd N1 ... 73 B2
Doverfield Rd SW2 ... 160 A4
Dover Flats SE1 ... 263 B3
Dover Gdns SM5 ... 218 D5
Dover Ho
[7] Beckenham BR3 ... 185 C3
Brixton SE5 ... 138 D4
[11] Deptford SE15 ... 140 C6
Edgware HA8 ... 26 B3
[14] Penge SE20 ... 184 B2
Dover House Rd SW15 ... 156 B6
Doveridge Gdns N13 ... 32 D6
Dover Mans [16] SW9 ... 138 C2
Dove Row E2 ... 96 A6
Dover Park Dr SW15 ... 156 B5
Dover Patrol SE3 ... 143 C3
Dover Rd
Dagenham RM6 ... 59 A3
Lower Edmonton N9 ... 18 C2
South Norwood SE19 ... 183 B4
Wanstead E12 ... 77 C6
Woolwich SE18 ... 145 A3
Dover St W1 ... 115 C5 249 A4
Dover Terr TW9 ... 132 C3
Dover Yd W1 ... 249 A4
Doves Cl BR2 ... 226 A6
Doves Yd N1 ... 94 C6 234 A5
Dovet Ct SW8 ... 270 C2
Doveton Ho [7] E1 ... 96 C3
Doveton Rd CR2 ... 221 B3
Doveton St [8] E1 ... 96 C3
Dove Wlk SW1 ... 258 A2
Dovey Lo [4] N1 ... 72 C1
Dowanhill Rd SE6 ... 164 B3
Dowd Cl N11 ... 15 A2
Dowdeny Cl [12] NW5 ... 71 C3
Dowdeswell Cl SW15 ... 133 C1
Dowding Ho N6 ... 49 A2
Dowding Pl HA7 ... 25 A4
Dowding Rd UB10 ... 60 B1
Dowe Ho SE3 ... 142 C2
Dowell Ho SE21 ... 161 D1
Dower Ho The DA14 ... 169 B1
Dowes Ho [18] SW16 ... 160 A1
Dowgate Hill EC4 ... 252 C6
Dowland Ho EN1 ... 5 D5
Dowland St W10 ... 91 A4
Dowlas St SE5 ... 139 C5
Dowlen Ct [14] E14 ... 119 C4
Dowler Ct [2] KT2 ... 176 B2
Dowler Ho [32] E1 ... 96 A1
Dowlerville Rd BR6 ... 227 D2
Dowling Ho DA17 ... 125 B3
Dowman Cl [2] SW19 ... 179 D3
Downage NW4 ... 46 C6
Downalong WD23 ... 8 B3
Down Barns Rd HA4 ... 62 D5
Downbarton Ho [11] SW9 ... 138 C4
Downbury Mews [13] SW18 ... 157 C6
Down Cl UB5 ... 84 B5

Downderry Prim Sch BR1 186 C6
Downderry Rd BR1 186 C6
Downe Cl DA16 146 C5
Downe Ho 9 SE7 143 C6
Downe Manor Prim Sch UB5 84 B4
Downend SE18 144 D5
Downend Ct 1 SE15 139 C6
Downe Rd CR4 180 D1
Downer's Cotts SW4 137 C1
Downes Cl TW1 153 B5
Downes Ct N21 16 C3
Downes Ho CR0 220 D4
Downey Ho 6 E1 96 D3
Downfield KT4 200 A1
Downfield Cl W9 91 D3
Downfield Ho KT3 199 B1
Down Hall Rd KT2 175 D2
DOWNHAM 186 C5
Downham Ct 1 N1 73 B1
Downham Ent Ctr SE6 164 D2
Downham La BR1 186 B5
Downham L Ctr BR1 187 A6
Downham Rd N1 73 B1
Downham Way BR1 186 C6
Downhills Ave N17 51 B6
Downhills Park Rd N17 51 A6
Downhills Prim Sch N15 51 B5
Downhills Way N17 33 A1
Downhurst Ave NW7 27 B5
Downhurst Ct NW4 46 C6
Downing Cl HA2 42 A6
Downing Ct N12 29 D5
Downing Dr UB6 86 C6
Downing Ho
9 Merton SW19 179 C3
2 North Kensington W10 90 D1
4 Putney SW15 156 A6
Downing Rd RM9 81 B1
Downings E6 100 C1
Downing St★ SW1 116 A4 250 A2
Downland Cl N20 14 A3
Downland Ct E11 76 C6
Downleys Cl SE9 166 B2
Downman Rd SE9 144 A2
Down Pl W6 112 B1
Down Rd TW11 175 B4
Down St Mews W1 248 C3
Downs Ave
Elmstead BR7 188 B5
Pinner HA5 41 B2
Downs Bridge Rd BR3 186 B2
Downs Ct
16 Hackney E8 74 B3
13 Wimbledon SW19 178 D3
Downsell Prim Sch E15 76 B4
Downsell Rd E15 76 B4
Downsfield Rd E17 53 A3
Downshall Ave IG3 57 C3
Downshall Ct IG3 57 C3
Downshall Prim Sch IG3 57 C2
Downs Hill BR2, BR3 186 B2
Downshire Hill NW3 70 B4
Downside
2 Putney SW15 157 A6
Sunbury TW16 172 A2
Twickenham TW1 152 D1
Downside Cl SW19 180 A4
Downside Cres
Ealing W13 87 A3
Maitland Pk NW3 70 C3
Downside Rd SM2 218 C2
Downside Wlk UB5 85 B4
Downs La 2 E5 74 B4
Downs Park Rd E5, E8 74 A3
Downs Rd
Beckenham BR3 185 D1
Enfield EN1 5 C1
Shacklewell E5, N16 74 A4
South Norwood CR7 183 A2
Down St
East Molesey KT8 195 C4
Mayfair W1 115 B5 248 C3
Downs The SW19, SW20 178 D3
Downs View TW7 131 A4
Downsview Gdns SE19 183 A3
Downs View Lo 9 KT6 198 A3
Downsview Prim Sch SE19 183 A3
Downsview Rd SE19 183 A3
Downsview Sch E5 74 B4
Downsway BR6 227 C3
Downton Ave SW2 160 B2
Downtown Rd SE16 119 A4
Downway N12 30 C3
Down Way UB5 84 B4
Dowrey St N1 234 A6
Dowsett Rd N17 34 A1
Dowson Cl SE5 139 B1
Dowson Ct SE13 142 B2
Dowson Ho 8 E1 96 D1
Doyce St SE1 252 A2
Doyle Gdns NW10 90 B6
Doyle Ho W3 110 D4
Doyle Rd SE25 206 A5
D'Oyley St SW1 258 A4
Doynton St N19 71 B6
Draco St SE17 139 A6
Dragon Ct WC2 240 B2
Dragonfly Cl E13 99 B4
Dragon Rd SE15 139 C6
Dragon Yd WC1 240 B2
Dragoon Rd SE8 119 B1
Dragor Rd NW10 89 A3
Drake Cl 30 SE16 118 D4
Drake Cres SE28 102 C1
Drake Croft N16 73 B6
Drake Ct
Dulwich SE19 183 D5
5 Hammersmith W12 112 B4
Kingston u T KT5 198 B5
Drakefell Rd SE4, SE14 140 D2
Drakefield Rd SW17 159 A1
Drake Hall 13 E16 121 B5
Drake Ho
2 Limehouse E14 119 A6
20 Stepney E1 96 C2
Drakeley Ct N5 72 D4
Drake Mews BR2 209 C5
Drake Rd
Brockley SE4 141 C2
Chessington KT9 214 C3
Harrow HA2 63 B6
Mitcham CR4 203 A3
Thornton Heath CR0 204 B2
Drakes Ct SE23 162 C3
Drakes Ctyd NW6 69 B1
Drake St Enfield EN2 5 B4
Holborn WC1 240 C3
Drakes Wlk E6 100 B6
Drakewood Rd SW16 181 D3
Drama Ctr London EC1 94 C3 241 B5
Draper Cl
Belvedere DA17 125 B2
Hounslow TW7 130 B3
Draper Ct BR1 210 A5
Draper Ho SE1 261 D4
Draper Pl N1 234 D6
Drapers Almhouses 5 E3 97 C4
Draper's Cottage Homes NW7 28 A6
Drapers Gdns EC2 242 D2
Drapers Rd Enfield EN2 4 D4
Leyton E15 76 B4
Tottenham N17 51 D6
Drappers Way 8 SE16 118 A2
Draven Cl BR2 208 D2
Drawell Cl SE18 123 C1
Drax Ave SW20 178 A3
Draxmont SW19 179 A4
Draycot Rd
Tolworth KT6 198 C1
Wanstead E11 55 B2
Draycott Ave
Chelsea SW3 114 C2 257 B3
Harrow HA3 43 C3
Draycott Cl
Camberwell SE5 139 B5
Cricklewood NW2 68 D5
Harrow HA3 43 B3
Draycott Ct SW11 267 A2
Draycott Ho SW3 257 C3
Draycott Pl SW3 114 D2 257 C3
Draycott Terr SW3 114 D2 257 D3
Drayford Cl W9 91 B3
Dray Gdns SW2 160 B6
Draymans Ct 4 SW9 138 B2
Draymans Mews SE15 139 D3
Draymans Way TW7 130 D2
Drayside Mews UB2 107 B4
Drayson Mews W8 113 C4 245 B1
Drayton Ave
Ealing W13 109 A6
Orpington BR6 210 D1
Drayton Bridge Rd
Ealing W7, W13 108 D6
Ealing W13 87 A1
Drayton Cl
Hounslow TW4 151 B6
Ilford IG1 57 B1
Drayton Ct
South Kensington SW10 256 B1
Tolworth KT5 214 D6
West Drayton UB7 104 B2
Drayton Gdns
Ealing W13 109 A6
Southgate N21 16 D4
South Kensington SW10 114 A1 256 B1
West Drayton UB7 104 A4
Drayton Gn W13 109 A6
Drayton Gr W13 109 A6
Drayton Green Prim Sch W13 109 A6
Drayton Green Rd W13 109 B6
Drayton Green Sta W7 86 D1
Drayton Ho
14 Camberwell SE5 139 B5
Leytonstone E11 54 B1
Drayton Lo E17 35 D1
Drayton Manor High Sch W7 86 D1
Drayton Park Mews 12 N5 72 C3
Drayton Park Prim Sch 13 N5 72 C3
Drayton Park Sta N5 72 C3
Drayton Pk N5, N7 72 C4
Drayton Rd
Croydon CR0 220 D6
Ealing W13 109 B6
Harlesden NW10 89 D6
Leytonstone E11 54 B1
Tottenham N17 33 C1
Drayton Waye HA3 43 B3
DRCA Business Pk SW11 137 A4 268 B1
Dreadnought Cl SW19 180 B1
Dreadnought St SE10 120 C3
Drenon Sq UB3 105 D6
Dresden Cl NW6 69 D2
Dresden Ho
5 Clapham SW11 137 A3
Lambeth SE11 260 D4
Dresden Rd N19 49 D1
Dressington Ave SE4 163 C5
Drew Ave NW7 29 A4
Drewery Ct SE3 142 C2
Drewett Ho 31 E1 96 A1
Drew Gdns UB6 64 D2
Drew Ho 12 SW16 160 A1
Drew Prim Sch E16 122 A5
Drew Rd E16 122 A5
Drewstead La SW16 159 D2
Drewstead Rd SW16 159 D2
Driberg Ct RM9 80 B2
Driffield Ct 4 NW9 27 C2
Driffield Rd E3 97 A5
Drift The BR2 225 D5
Driftway Ho 19 E3 97 B5
Driftway The CR4 181 A2
Drinkwater Ho 11 SE5 139 B5
Drinkwater Rd HA2 63 D6
Drive Ct HA8 26 C5
Drive Ho CR4 202 C5
Drive Mans 1 SW6 135 A3
Drive The Acton W3 89 A1
Ashford TW15 171 B3
Barking IG11 79 D1
Barking IG11 80 A2
Barnet EN5 1 A2
Beckenham BR3 185 C2
Bexley DA5 168 D4
Buckhurst Hill IG9 21 C4
Chingford E4 20 B4
Chislehurst BR7 189 D2
Edgware HA8 26 C5
Enfield EN2 5 B4
Erith DA8 147 D6
Feltham TW14 150 C4
Finchley N3 29 C3
Fortis Green N6 48 D4
Harlesden NW10 89 D6
Harrow HA2 41 C2
Hendon NW11 47 A2
Hounslow TW3, TW7 130 B3
Ickenham UB10 60 A5
Islington N7 72 B2
Kingston u T KT2 177 A3
Morden SM4 202 B4
New Barnet EN5 14 A5
Orpington BR6 227 D6
Redbridge IG1 56 B2
Sidcup DA14 190 B6
South Norwood CR7 205 B5
St Paul's Cray BR7 211 D6
Surbiton KT6 198 A2
Thames Ditton KT10 196 A1
Walthamstow E17 53 D6
Wanstead E18 55 A6
Wembley Pk HA9 67 A6
West Ewell KT19 215 D2
West Wickham BR4 208 B2
Wimbledon SW19, SW20 178 C3
Wood Green N11 31 D4
Dr Johnson Ave SW17 159 B1
Dr Johnson's House★ EC4 241 B1
Droitwich Cl SE26 162 A1
Dromey Gdns HA3 24 D3
Dromore Rd SW15 157 A5
Dronfield Gdns RM8 80 C3
Dron Ho E1 96 C2
Droop St W10 91 A3
Drovers Ct
3 Kingston u T KT1 176 A1
Lewisham SE13 142 A2
Drovers Pl SE15 140 B5
Drovers Rd CR2 221 B3
Drovers Way N7 72 A2
Dr Triplett's CE Jun & Inf Sch UB3 83 D1
Druce Rd SE21 161 C5
Druid St SE1 117 D4 253 C1
Druids Way BR2 208 B5
Drumaline Ridge KT4 215 C6
Drummer Lo N7 72 B5
Drummond Castle Ct E7 76 D4
Drummond Cres NW1 93 D4 232 C2
Drummond Ct
Finchley N12 30 C3
Harrow HA1 42 C2
Drummond Ctr CR0 221 A6
Drummond Dr HA7 24 D3
Drummond Gate SW1 259 D2
Drummond Ho
13 Bethnal Green E2 96 A5
Finchley N2 30 A1
Drummond Rd
Bermondsey SE16 118 B3
Croydon CR0 221 A6
Wanstead E11 55 C3
Drummonds Pl TW9 132 A1
Drummond St NW1 93 C3 239 A6
Drummonds The IG9 21 B2
Drum St E1 243 D2
Drury Cres CR0 220 C6
Drury Ho SW8 269 A2
Drury La WC2 94 A1 240 B1
Drury Rd HA1 42 A2
Drury Way NW10 67 B3
Drury Way Ind Est NW10 67 B3
Dryad St SW15 134 D2
Dryburgh Gdns NW9 44 C6
Dryburgh Ho SW1 258 D2
Dryburgh Mans SW15 134 C2
Dryburgh Rd SW15 134 C2
Dryden Ave W7 86 D1
Dryden Bldg 10 E1 96 A1
Dryden Cl SW4 159 D6
Dryden Ct
Lambeth SE11 261 B3
11 Richmond TW10 175 D6
Dryden Ho
Bromley Comm BR2 209 D4
6 Camberwell SE5 139 C4
16 Stoke Newington N16 73 C5
Dryden Rd
Bexley DA16 145 D4
Enfield EN1 17 D5
Harrow HA3 24 D2
Wimbledon SW19 180 A4
Dryden St WC2 240 B1
Dryer Ct 21 EN3 7 C6
Dryfield Cl NW10 67 A2
Dryfield Rd HA8 27 A4
Dryfield Wlk 1 SE8 141 C6
Dryhill Rd DA17 147 B6
Dryland Ave 5 BR6 227 D4
Drylands Rd N8 50 A3
Drysdale Ave E4 19 D5
Drysdale Flats 3 E8 73 D3
Drysdale Ho 19 E2 95 C4
Drysdale Pl N1 95 C4
Drysdale St N1 95 C4
Dublin Ave E8 96 A6
Du Burstow Terr W7 108 C4
Ducal St 25 E2 95 D4
Ducane Cl 6 W12 90 C1
Du Cane Ct SW12 159 A3
Du Cane Rd W12 90 A1
Ducavel Ho SW2 160 B3
Duchess Cl
London N11 31 B5
Sutton SM1 218 A4
Duchess Gr IG9 21 B2
Duchess Mews W1 238 D3
Duchess of Bedford Ho W8 245 A2
Duchess of Bedford's Wlk W8 113 C4 245 A1
Duchess St W1 93 B2 238 D3
Duchy Rd EN4 2 B5
Duchy St SE1 116 C5 251 B4
Ducie Ho
8 Charlton SE7 143 C6
2 Putney SW15 156 C6
Ducie St SW4 138 B1
Duckett Mews N4 50 D3
Duckett Rd N4 50 D3
Duckett St E1 97 A2
Duck La W1 239 C1
Duck Lees La EN3 7 A1
Ducks Hill Rd HA4, HA6 39 A5
DUCKS ISLAND 12 D5
Duck's Wlk TW1 153 C6
Du Cros Dr HA7 25 D4
Du Cros Rd W3 111 C5
DUDDEN HILL 68 A3
Dudden Hill La NW10 67 D3
Duddington Cl SE9 187 D6
Dudley Ave HA3 43 C6
Dudley Ct
Colney Hatch N12 30 C5
Marylebone W1 237 C1
St Giles WC2 240 A2
Temple Fortune NW11 47 B5
14 Wanstead E11 55 A4
Wembley HA0 65 D3
Dudley Dr Ruislip HA4 62 B3
West Barnes SM4 201 A2
Dudley Gdns
Ealing W13 109 B4
Harrow HA2 42 B1
Dudley Ho
13 Brixton SW9 138 C3
Edgware HA8 26 B3
Paddington W2 236 C3
Dudley Mews 14 SW2 160 C5

Dudley Pl UB3 ....105 B2
Dudley Rd
Ashford TW15 ....170 B6
East Bedfont TW14 ...149 B3
Finchley N3 ....29 D1
Harrow HA2............64 A6
Ilford IG1.............78 D4
Kilburn NW6 ....91 B5
Kingston u T KT1 .....198 B6
Richmond TW9........132 B3
Southall UB2 ....106 D3
Walthamstow E17 .....35 C1
Walton-on-T KT12....194 A2
Wimbledon SW19 .....179 C4
Dudley St W2.........236 C3
Dudlington Rd E5......74 C6
Dudmaston Mews
SW3 ....256 D2
Dudrich Cl N11, N12...30 D4
Dudsbury Rd DA14...190 B4
Dudset La TW5 ....128 A4
Duett Ct TW3 ....129 A5
Duffell Ho SE11 .....260 D1
Dufferin Ave EC1 .....242 C5
Dufferin Ct EC1......242 C5
Dufferin St
EC1.........95 A3 242 B5
Duffield Cl HA1.......42 D4
Duffield Dr N15.......51 D5
Duffield Ho N4 ....51 A2
Duff Miller Coll
SW7.......114 A3 246 B5
Duff St E14...........97 D1
Dufour's Pl W1 .....239 B1
Dugard Way
SE11.......116 D2 261 C3
Dugdale Ho 10 N7 ....71 D3
Duggan Dr BR7.....188 A4
Dugolly Ave HA9......66 D5
Duke Gdns IG6 ....57 B5
Duke Humphrey Rd
SE3...............142 C3
Duke Of Cambridge Cl
TW2...............152 B5
Duke Of Edinburgh Rd
SM1 ....218 B6
Duke Of Wellington Ave
SE18...............123 A3
Duke of Wellington Pl
SW1, W1........... 248 B2
Duke of York's Sq
SW3.......114 D2 257 D3
Duke of York St SW1 249 B4
Duke Rd Chiswick W4 .111 B1
Ilford IG6.............57 B5
Duke St Hill SE1 .... 252 D4
Duke St St James's
SW1.......115 C5 249 B4
Dukes Ave
Edgware HA8..........26 B5
Finchley N3 ....29 D2
Hornsey N10 ....49 C6
Hounslow TW4........ 129 A1
Kingston u T KT3 .... 199 D6
Northolt UB5 ....63 A1
Rayners La HA2, HA5 ...41 B3
Richmond KT2, TW10. 175 D6
Wealdstone HA1 ....42 C5
Duke's Ave W4 ....111 B1
Dukes Cl
Ashford TW15 .... 171 A6
Hampton TW12 ....173 B5
Dukes Ct Barking E6 ..100 C6
Beckenham BR3.......207 A6
Dulwich SE22........ 162 A3
Ealing W13............87 B2
East Dulwich SE22 ...162 B6
Lewisham SE13 ...... 142 A3
Mortlake SW14 ....133 B3
Dukes Gate 4 W4 ...111 A2
Dukes Green Ave
TW14 ....150 A6
Dukes Head Yd N6 .... 49 B1
Duke's Ho SW1 ..... 259 D4
Duke Shore Wharf
E14 ....119 B6
Dukes La W8 113 D4 245 C2
Dukes Mews N10 .....49 B6
Duke's Mews W1 ... 238 B2
Duke's Pl EC3..95 C1 243 B1
Dukes Point N6.......49 B1
Dukes Rd Acton W3....88 C3
Barking E6 .... 100 C6
Duke's Rd
WC1........93 D4 232 D1
Dukes Ride UB10 ......60 A4
Duke St
Marylebone
W1 ....93 A1 238 B1
Richmond TW10,
TW9 .... 153 D6
Sutton SM1 ....218 B4
Dukesthorpe Rd
SE26............. 184 D6
Duke Street Mans
W1 ....238 B1
Dukes Way
Coney Hall BR4 ..... 224 C5
Wembley HA9 ....66 A3
Duke's Yd W1....... 248 B6
Dulas St N4 ....50 B1
Dulford St
W11 ....113 A6 244 A6
Dulka Rd SW11 ..... 158 D6
Dulverton NW1 ......232 B5
Dulverton Ct 12 KT6..198 A4
Dulverton Mans
WC1............... 240 D5
Dulverton Prim Sch
SE9................167 B2
Dulverton Rd
New Eltham SE9......167 B2
Ruislip HA4 ....62 A6
DULWICH............161 C1
Dulwich Bsns Ctr
SE23.............. 162 D3
Dulwich Coll SE21 .. 161 C2
Dulwich Coll Prep Sch
SE21.............. 161 C1
Dulwich Com Hospl
SE22.............. 139 C1
Dulwich Comm
SE21...............161 C3
Dulwich Ct SE22 .....162 B3
Dulwich Hamlet Jun Sch
SE21...............161 B5
Dulwich Lawn Cl
SE22.............. 161 D6
Dulwich L Ctr SE22.. 140 A1
Dulwich Mead SE24..161 A5
Dulwich Mews
1 East Dulwich
SE22 .... 139 D1
East Dulwich SE22... 161 D6
Dulwich Oaks The
SE21.............. 161 D1
Dulwich Picture Gall★
SE21...............161 C4
Dulwich Rd SE24... 160 D5
DULWICH VILLAGE ..161 C4
Dulwich Village
SE21...............161 C5
Dulwich Village CE Inf
Sch SE21 .... 161 C5
Dulwich Wood Ave
SE19...............183 C5
Dulwich Wood Pk
SE19...............183 C6
Dumain Ct SE11 .... 261 C3
Du Maurier Ho 2
NW3...............70 D3
Dumbarton Ct 16
SW2...............160 A4
Dumbarton Rd SW2..160 A5
Dumbleton Cl KT2 .. 176 D2
Dumbreck Rd SE9 ...144 C2
Dumont Rd N16 ......73 C5
Dumphreys Ho 5
SW4 .... 159 D4
Dumpton Pl NW1.....71 A1
Dunally Pk TW17.....193 B2
Dunbar Ave
Beckenham BR3..... 207 A5
Dagenham RM10 ......81 C5
Thornton Heath
SW16 .... 182 C1
Dunbar Cl UB4........84 A2
Dunbar Ct
3 London N12 ....29 D6
Sutton SM1 ....218 B3
Walton-on-T KT12 ... 194 C1
Dunbar Gdns RM10 ...81 D3
Dunbar Rd
New Malden KT3 .... 199 A5
Tottenham N22 ....32 D2
Upton E7 ....77 A2
Dunbar St SE27 ......161 A1
Dunbar Wharf 20
E14...............119 B6
Dunblane Cl HA8 .....10 D2
Dunblane Rd SE9 ....144 A3
Dunboe Pl TW17 .....193 A2
Dunboyne Rd NW3....70 D3
Dunbridge Ho SW15 155 D5
Dunbridge St
Bethnal Green E2...........
Bethnal Green E2......96 B3
Duncan Cl EN5 ....2 A1
Duncan Ct
5 London N12 ....29 D5
3 Poplar E14 ....98 A2
Southgate N21.........16 D3
Duncan Gr W3........89 C1
Duncan Ho
Harrow HA2...........64 A5
3 Primrose Hill NW3 ..70 D1
Duncannon Ho SW1 259 D1
Duncannon St WC2 . 250 A5
Duncan Rd
Hackney E8 ....96 B6
Richmond TW9....... 132 A1
Duncan St N1 .94 D5 234 C4
Duncan Terr
N1.........94 D5 234 C4
Dunch St 33 E1 ....96 B1
Dunchurch Ho RM10..81 C1
Duncombe Hill SE23 .163 A4
Duncombe Ho 7
SW19 .... 156 D3
Duncombe Prim Sch
N19................50 A1
Duncombe Rd N19.....49 D1
Duncrievie Rd SE13..164 B5
Duncroft SE18.......145 C5
Dundalk Ho 2 E1.....96 C1
Dundalk Rd SE4 .....141 A2
Dundas Gdns KT8.... 195 D6
Dundas Ho 12 E2 .....96 C5
Dundas Mews 4 EN3 ..7 C6
Dundas Rd SE15 .....140 C3
Dundee Ct 36 E1......118 B5
Dundee Ho W9 ..... 229 A2
Dundee Rd
Croydon SE25........206 B4
Newham E13 ....99 B5
Dundee St E1........118 B5
Dundee Way EN3 ......7 A2
Dundee Wharf E14....119 B6
Dundela Gdns KT17,
KT4...............216 B4
Dundonald Cl 6 E6..100 A1
Dundonald Prim Sch
SW19..............179 B3
Dundonald Rd
Brondesbury Pk
NW10 ....90 D6
Merton SW19........179 B3
Dundonald Road Sta
SW19..............179 B3
Dundry Ho 8 SE26...162 A1
Duneaves HA1........64 C5
Dunedin Ho E16 .....122 B5
Dunedin Rd Ilford IG1 .57 A1
Leyton E10...........75 D5
Dunedin Way UB4 ....84 C3
Dunelm Gr SE27 .....161 A1
Dunelm St E1.........96 D1
Dunfield Gdns SE6.. 185 D5
Dunfield Rd SE6 .... 185 D5
Dunford Ct 9 HA5 ....23 B3
Dunford Rd N7 ....72 B4
Dungarvan Ave
SW15..............134 A1
Dungeness Ho
SW18..............136 A1
Dunheved Cl CR7.....204 C3
Dunheved Ct 2 CR7 .204 C3
Dunheved Rd N CR7. .204 C3
Dunheved Rd S CR7. .204 C3
Dunheved Rd W
CR7...............204 C3
Dunhill Point 12
SW15..............156 B3
Dunholme Gn N9 .....17 D1
Dunholme La N9......17 D1
Dunholme Rd N9 .....17 D1
Dunkeld Ho 15 E14.....98 B1
Dunkeld Rd
Dagenham RM8........80 C6
South Norwood SE25. .205 B5
Dunkery Rd SE9 .....166 A1
Dunkirk St 12 SE27....183 A6
Dunlace Rd E5.........74 D4
Dunleary Cl TW4.....151 B4
Dunley Dr CR0.......224 A2
Dunlin Ct 12 SE21.....161 B2
Dunlin Ho 18 SE16 ... 118 D2
Dunloe Ave N17 ......51 B6
Dunloe Ct 7 E2 ......95 D5
Dunloe St E2.........95 D5
Dunlop Pl
SE16...... 117 D3 263 D5
Dunmore Point 15 E2 .95 D4
Dunmore Rd
Kilburn NW6 ....91 A6
Wimbledon SW20 ... 178 D2
Dunmow Cl
Dagenham RM6.......58 C4
3 Feltham TW13......173 A6
Dunmow Ho
Dagenham RM9.......102 B6
Vauxhall SE11 ...... 260 D2
Dunmow Rd E15......76 B4
Dunmow Wlk N1 .... 235 A6
Dunnage Cres SE16 ..119 A2
Dunne Mews 11 NW5 .71 C3
Dunnet Ho 27 E3.......97 B5
Dunnico Ho SE17 ... 263 A2
Dunn Mead NW9......27 D3
Dunnock Cl N9 ....18 D3
Dunnock Ct 11 SE21..161 B2
Dunnock Rd E6.......100 A1
Dunn's Pas WC1 .... 240 B2
Dunn St E8...........73 D3
Dunollie Pl NW5......71 C3
Dunollie Rd NW5 .....71 C3
Dunoon Gdns SE23 . 162 D4
Dunoon Ho N1 ..... 233 C5
Dunoon Rd SE23.....162 C4
Dunraven Dr EN2 .....4 C3
Dunraven Ho 12
TW9 ....132 B4
Dunraven Rd W12.....112 A5
Dunraven Sch SW16 .160 B1
Dunraven St
W1....... 114 D6 247 D6
Dunrobin Ct NW3.....69 D3
Dunsany Rd W14.... 112 D3
Dunsfold Ct 14 SM2. 217 D1
Dunsfold Ho
10 Kingston u T
KT2............ 176 D4
4 Streatham SW2 ...160 B4
Dunsfold Way CR0 .. 223 D1
Dunsford Way SW15 .156 B5
Dunsmore Cl
Bushey WD23..........8 B5
Hayes UB4...........85 A3
Dunsmore Rd KT12 ..194 B3
Dunsmore Way WD23 .. 8 B5
Dunsmure Rd N16 ....51 C1
Dunstable Ct 8 SE3 .143 A5
Dunstable Mews W1 238 B4
Dunstable Rd
East Molesey KT8 ....195 B5
Richmond TW10,
TW9 .... 132 A1
Dunstall Ho 9 SE15..140 A4
Dunstall Rd SW19,
SW20 ....178 C4
Dunstall Way KT8.... 195 D6
Dunstall Welling Est
DA16..............146 B3
Dunstan Cl 2 N2.....48 A6
Dunstan Glade BR5 ..211 B3
Dunstan Ho SE4 .....141 B3
Dunstan Hos 5 E1.....96 C2
Dunstan Rd NW11.....47 C1
Dunstan's Gr SE22 ...162 B5
Dunstan's Rd SE22...162 A5
Dunster Ave SM4 ... 200 D1
Dunster Ct EC3 ..... 253 B6
Dunster Dr NW9 ......45 A1
Dunster Gdns NW6 ...69 B1
Dunster Ho SE6..... 163 D1
Dunsterville Way
SE1.............. 252 D1
Dunster Way
Carshalton CR4 ..... 203 A1
Harrow HA2...........63 A5
Dunston Rd
Clapham SW11 ..... 137 A3
Hackney E8 ....95 D6
Dunston St E8........95 D6
Dunton Cl KT6........198 A1
Dunton Ct 5 SE26 ...162 B2
Dunton Ho 14 SW16..160 A1
Dunton Rd
Bermondsey
SE1...... 117 D2 263 C3
Leyton E10...........53 D2
Duntshill Rd SW18.. 157 D3
Dunvegan Cl KT8.... 195 D5
Dunvegan Rd SE9....144 B1
Dunwich Ct 2 RM6 ...58 B4
Dunwich Rd DA7......147 B4
Dunworth Mews W11 . 91 B1
Duplex Ride SW1 ... 247 D1
Dupont Rd SW20.....178 D1
Duppas Ave CR0 .... 220 D4
Duppas Cl TW17 .....193 B4
Duppas Ct CR0 ..... 220 D5
Duppas Hill La CR0 .. 220 D4
Duppas Hill Rd CR0 . 220 D4
Duppas Hill Terr
CR0.............. 220 D5
Duppas Jun Sch
CR0...............220 D3
Duppas Rd CR0 ..... 220 D5
Dupree Rd SE7 ......121 B1
Dura Den Cl BR3.... 185 D3
Durand Cl SM5 ..... 202 D1
Durand Gdns
SW9.......138 B4 270 D1
Durand Prim Sch
SW9....... 138 B4 270 D2
Durand Way NW10....67 A1
Durants Lo EN3.........6 D2
Durants Park Ave EN3. .6 D1
Durants Rd EN3.........6 D1
Durants Sch EN3.........6 C4
Durant St E2 ....96 A4
Durban Ct E7..........77 D1
Durban Ho 28 W12 ...112 B6
Durban Rd
Beckenham BR3.......185 B1
Ilford IG2.............57 C1
Newham E15 ....98 C4
Tottenham N17 ....33 D4
Walthamstow E17 .....35 B2
West Norwood SE27 ..183 B6
Durbin Ho 18 N9.......18 A1
Durbin Rd KT9.......214 B4
Durdan Cotts UB5.....85 B1
Durdans Ho 3 NW1....71 C1
Durdans Park Prim Sch
UB1................85 B2
Durdans Rd UB1......85 B1
Durell Gdns RM9......80 D3
Durell Rd RM9 ....80 D3
Durfey Pl SE5.........139 B5
Durford Cres SW15 ..156 B3
Durham Ave
Beckenham BR2..... 208 D5
Hounslow TW5.......107 B1
Woodford IG8 ....37 D5
Durham Cl SW20......178 B1
Durham Ct
2 Barnet EN5...........1 B2
Brockley SE4 .... 141 C2
4 Kilburn NW6.........91 C5
Teddington TW11.... 174 C6
Durham Hill BR1.... 186 D6
Durham Ho
3 Barking IG11 ......80 A1
7 Dartmouth Pk NW5..71 C5
Edgware HA8..........26 B3
Lisson Gr NW8....... 230 B1
Durham House St
WC2...............250 B5
Durham Pl
Chelsea SW3 .... 257 C1
Ilford IG1.............79 A4
Durham Rd
Beckenham BR2..... 208 D6
Ealing W5.......... 109 D3
Edmonton N9 ....18 A2
Feltham TW14 ...... 150 C4
Harrow HA1...........41 D4
Lower Holloway N4, N7 72 B6
Manor Pk E12.........77 D4
Muswell Hill N2 ....48 D6
Newham E16 ....98 C3
Sidcup DA14..........190 B5
Wimbledon SW20 .....178 B2
Durham Rise SE18 ...123 B1
Durham Row E1 ......97 A2
Durham St
SE11.......138 B6 270 C6
Durham Terr W2......91 D1
Durham Wharf Dr
TW8...............131 C5
Durley Ave HA5.......41 A3
Durley Rd N16........51 C2
Durlock Ho 16 SW9 ..138 C4
Durlston Rd
Kingston u T KT2 .... 176 A4

Durlston Rd *continued*
Stoke Newington E5 74 A6
Durnford Ho SE6 163 D1
Durnford St
4 Greenwich SE10 142 A6
South Tottenham N15 51 C4
Durning Rd SE19 183 B5
Durnsford Ave SW18, SW19 157 C2
Durnsford Ct 5 EN3 7 A2
Durnsford Rd
London N11 31 D3
Wimbledon SW18, SW19 157 C1
Durnston Ct 2 SM1 217 D2
Durrant Ct HA3 24 C2
Durrant Way BR6 227 B3
Durrell Rd SW6 264 C1
Durrell Way TW17 193 B3
Durrels Ho W14 254 D4
Durrington Ave SW20 178 C3
Durrington Park Rd SW20 178 C2
Durrington Rd E5 75 A4
Durrington Twr 3 SW8 137 C3
Durrisdeer Ho NW2 69 B4
Dursley Cl SE3 143 C3
Dursley Gdns SE3 143 D4
Dursley Rd SE3 143 C3
Durston NW5 71 A3
Durston House Prep Sch W5 87 D1
Durston House Sch W5 87 D1
Durward St E1 96 B2
Durweston Mews W1 237 D4
Durweston St W1 237 D3
Dury Rd EN5 1 B3
Dutch Gdns KT2 176 D4
Dutch Yd SW18 157 C6
Dutton Ho SW2 160 D3
Dutton St SE10 142 A4
Duxberry Cl BR2 210 A4
Duxford 21 KT1 176 C1
Duxford Ho 10 SE2 124 D4
Dwight Ct 3 SW6 135 A3
Dycer Ho 19 E9 74 D2
Dye House La E3 97 C6
Dyer Ho
Hampton TW12 173 D2
New Cross SE4 141 A3
Dyer's Bldgs EC1 241 A3
Dyers Hall Rd
Leyton E11 76 B6
Leytonstone E11 54 C1
Dyer's La SW15 134 B1
Dykes Ct 11 SW2 160 B3
Dykes Way BR2 208 D6
Dylan Cl WD6 9 D4
Dylan Rd
Belvedere DA17 125 C3
2 Brixton SE24 138 D1
Dylways SE5 139 B1
Dymchurch Cl
Ilford IG5 56 C6
Orpington BR6 227 C4
Dymchurch Ho 12 E5 74 B3
Dymes Path SW19 156 D2
Dymock St SW6 135 D2
Dyneley Rd SE12 165 C1
Dyne Rd NW6 69 B1
Dynevor Rd
Richmond TW10 154 A6
Shacklewell N16 73 D5
Dynham Rd NW6 69 C1
Dyott St Soho WC1 239 D2
St Giles WC1, WC2 94 A1 240 A2
Dysart Ave KT2, TW10 175 C6
Dysart Sch KT6 198 B2
Dysart St EC2 95 C3 243 A5
Dyson Ct London NW2 46 C2
Wembley HA0 65 A4
Dyson Ho 3 SE10 120 D1
Dyson Rd
Leytonstone E11 54 C3
Stratford E15 76 D2
Dyson's Rd N18 34 B4

E

Eade Rd N4 51 A2
Eagans Cl N2 48 B6
Eagle Ave RM6 59 A3
Eagle Cl
Bermondsey SE16 118 C1
Enfield EN3 6 C1
Wallington SM6 220 A2
Eagle Ct
10 Dulwich SE21 161 B2
Edmonton N18 33 D4
Holborn EC1 241 C4
6 Wanstead E11 55 A5
Eagle Dr NW9 27 C1
Eagle Dwellings EC1 235 B2
Eagle Hill SE19 183 B4
Eagle Ho
22 Bethnal Green E1 96 B3
Finsbury Pk N7 72 B5
Eagle House Sch CR4 180 D1
Eagle Hts 10 SW11 136 C2
Eagle La E11 55 A5
Eagle Lo
Leytonstone E11 54 D5
London NW11 47 B2
Eagle Mans N16 73 D3
Eagle Mews N1 73 C2
Eagle Pl
South Kensington SW7 114 A1 256 B2
St James SW1 249 B5
Eagle Rd Hatton TW6 127 D2
Wembley HA0 65 D1
Eaglesfield Rd SE18 144 D4
Eagle St WC1 94 B2 240 C3
Eagle Star Ho SM1 217 D4
Eagle Terr IG8 37 B3
Eagle Trad Est CR4 202 D3
Eagle Wharf SE1 253 C3
Eagle Wharf Rd N1 95 A5 235 B4
Eagle Works E1 243 D5
Eagling Cl E3 97 C4
Ealcom Ct W5 110 B5
Ealdham Prim Sch SE9 143 C1
Ealdham Sq SE9 143 C1
EALING 109 D6
Ealing Broadway Ctr W5 109 D6
Ealing Broadway Sta W5 109 D6
Ealing Coll 1 W13 87 B1
Ealing Coll of Higher Ed W5 109 D5
Ealing Common W5 110 B6
Ealing Common Sta W5 110 B5
Ealing Court Man W5 109 D4
Ealing Gateway W5 109 C6
Ealing Gn W5 109 D5
Ealing, Hammersmith & West London Coll W14 113 A1 254 A2
Ealing Hospl UB1 108 B4
Ealing Ind Coll W5 109 C6
Ealing Park Gdns W5 109 C2
Ealing Park Lo UB6 87 A5
Ealing Park Mans W5 109 D3
Ealing Rd
Brentford TW8 109 D2
Northolt UB5 63 C1
Wembley HA0 66 A1
Ealing Road Trad Est TW8 109 D1
Ealing Studios* W5 109 D5
Ealing Village W5 88 A1
Ealing & West London Coll W5 109 D5
Eamann Casey Ho 34 SW9 138 C4
Eamont Cl HA4 38 D2
Eamont Ct NW8 230 B4
Eamont St NW8 92 C5 230 B4
Eardley Cres SW5 113 C1 255 B1
Eardley Point 9 SE18 122 D2
Eardley Rd
Belvedere DA17 125 C1
Streatham SW16 181 C4
Eardley Sch SW16 181 C4
Earl Cl N11 31 B5
Earldom Rd SW15 134 C1
Earle Gdns KT2 176 A3
Earle Ho SW1 259 D3
Earlham Gr
Forest Gate E7 77 A3
Wood Green N22 32 B3
Earlham Prim Sch
Stratford E7 76 D3
Wood Green N22 32 C3
Earlham St WC2 94 A1 240 A1
Earl Ho NW1 237 B5
Earlom Ho WC1 234 A1
Earl Rd SW14 133 A1
Earl Rise SE18 123 B2
EARL'S COURT 113 C1
Earl's Court Ex Ctr* SW5 113 C1 255 A1
Earl's Court Gdns SW5 113 D2 255 C3
Earl's Court Rd SW5, W8 113 C2 255 B4
Earl's Court Sq SW5 113 D1 255 C2
Earl's Court Sta SW5 113 C2 255 B3
Earls Cres HA1 42 C5
Earlsdown Ho 6 IG11 101 B5
Earlsferry Way N1 72 A1
EARLSFIELD 158 A3
Earlsfield Ho 16 KT2 175 D2
Earlsfield Prim Sch SW18 158 A2
Earlsfield Rd SW18 158 A4
Earlsfield Sta SW18 158 A3
Earlshall Rd SE9 144 C1
Earlsmead HA2 63 B4
Earlsmead Fst & Mid Sch HA2 63 B4
Earlsmead Prim Sch 3 N15 51 D5
Earlsmead Rd
Kensal Green NW10 90 C4
South Tottenham N15 51 D4
Earl St EC2 95 C2 243 A4
Earls Terr W8 254 D5
Earlsthorpe Mews 3 SW12 159 A5
Earlsthorpe Rd SE26 184 D6
Earlstoke St EC1 234 C2
Earlston Gr E9 96 B6
Earls Wlk
Dagenham RM8 80 B4
Kensington W8 113 C3 255 A5
Earlswood Ave CR7 204 C4
Earlswood Cl 10 SE10 120 C1
Earlswood Gdns IG5 56 C6
Earlswood Ho 2 SW2 160 B3
Earlswood St SE10 120 C1
Early Mews NW1 231 D6
Earnshaw Ho EC1 234 D1
Earnshaw St WC1, WC2 239 D2
Earsby St W14 254 B4
Earth Galleries* SW7 114 B3 256 D5
Easby Cres SM4 201 D3
Easebourne Rd RM8 80 C3
Easedale Ho TW7 152 D6
Eashing Point 5 SW15 156 B3
Easleys Mews W1 238 B2
East 10 Ent Pk E10 53 A1
EAST ACTON 111 C5
East Acton Arc W3 89 D1
East Acton Ct W3 111 C6
East Acton La W3 111 C6
East Acton Prim Sch W3 111 C6
East Acton Sta W12 89 D1
East Arbour St E1 96 D1
East Ave Croydon CR0 220 B3
East Finchley NW2 48 A6
Hayes UB3 106 A5
Plashet E12 78 A1
Southall UB1 107 B6
East Ave *continued*
Walthamstow E17 53 D5
East Bank N16 51 C2
Eastbank Cl 2 E17 53 D4
Eastbank Rd TW12 174 A5
EAST BARNET 14 D4
East Barnet Rd EN4 2 B1
East Barnet Sch
Barnet EN4 2 B2
East Barnet EN4 14 D5
East Beckton District Ctr E6 100 B2
EAST BEDFONT 149 C3
East Block 5 E1 118 D6
Eastbourne Ave W3 89 B1
Eastbourne Gdns SW14 133 A2
Eastbourne Mews W2 92 A1 236 B2
Eastbourne Rd
Brentford TW8 109 D1
Chiswick W4 133 A6
Feltham TW13 150 D2
South Tottenham N15 51 C3
Streatham SW17 181 A4
Wallend E6 100 C4
West Ham E15 98 C6
Eastbourne Terr W2 92 A1 236 B2
Eastbournia Ave N9 18 B1
Eastbrook Ave N9 18 C4
Eastbrook Rd SE3 143 B4
EASTBURY 22 A5
Eastbury Ave
Barking IG11 101 C6
Enfield EN1 5 D4
Mo Pk HA6 22 A5
Eastbury Comp Sch IG11 79 C2
Eastbury Ct
Barking IG11 101 C6
New Barnet EN5 14 A6
Eastbury Gr W4 111 C1
Eastbury Inf Sch IG11 79 D1
Eastbury Rd
Kingston u T KT2 176 A3
Newham E6 100 C3
Orpington BR5 211 B3
Eastbury Sq IG11 101 D6
Eastbury Terr E1 96 D3
Eastcastle St W1 93 C1 239 B2
Eastcheap EC3 117 C6 253 A6
East Churchfield Rd W3 111 B5
Eastchurch Rd TW6 127 C2
Eastchurch Road Rdbt TW6 127 C3
East Cl Cockfosters EN4 3 A1
Ealing W5 88 C3
Greenford UB6 86 A5
Eastcombe Ave SE7 143 B6
EASTCOTE 40 C3
Eastcote BR6 211 D1
Eastcote Ave
East Molesey KT8 195 C4
Harrow HA2 64 A6
Wembley UB6 65 A3
Eastcote Ind Est HA4 40 C2
Eastcote La
Harrow HA2 63 C5
Northolt UB5 63 B2
Eastcote La N UB5 63 C2
Eastcote Pl HA5 40 B3
Eastcote Prim Sch DA16 145 B2
Eastcote Rd
Bexley DA16 145 B3
Harrow HA2 64 A5
Pinner HA5 40 D4
Ruislip HA4 40 A3
Eastcote St SW9 138 B3
Eastcote Sta HA5 40 C2
Eastcote View HA5 40 C5
EASTCOTE VILLAGE 40 B4
Eastcott Cl KT2 177 A5
Eastcourt Ind Sch IG3 58 A1
East Cres Enfield EN1 17 D6
Friern Barnet N11 30 D6
Eastcroft Rd KT19 215 C1
East Cross Route
Bow E3 97 C6
Hackney Wick E9 75 B3
East Croydon Sta CR0 221 B6
East Ct
Sunbury TW16 172 C1
Wembley HA0 65 C6
Eastdown Ho E8 74 A4
Eastdown Pk SE13 142 B1
East Duck Lees La EN3 7 B1
EAST DULWICH 162 A6
East Dulwich Gr SE22 161 C6
East Dulwich Rd SE15, SE22 140 A1
East Dulwich Sta SE22 139 C1
East End Computing & Bsns Coll 37 E1 96 B1
East End Rd
East Finchley N2, N3 48 A6
Finchley N3 29 C1
East End Way HA5 41 A6
East Entrance RM10 103 D5
Eastern Ave
Gants Hill IG1, IG2, IG4 56 C3
Newbury Pk IG2 57 B3
Pinner HA5 40 D2
Wanstead E11 55 C3
Eastern Avenue W RM7 59 C5
Eastern Bsns Pk TW16 127 D3
Eastern Perimeter Rd TW14 127 D3
Eastern Quay 15 E16 121 B5
Eastern Rd
Brockley SE4 141 C1
Fortis Green N2 48 D5
Newham E13 99 B5
Walthamstow E17 54 A4
Wood Green N22 32 A2
Easternville Gdns IG2 57 A3
Eastern Way SE28 124 B4
East Ferry Rd E14 119 D2
Eastfield Gdns RM10 81 C4
Eastfield Prim Sch EN3 6 D5
Eastfield Rd
Dagenham RM9 81 B4
Dagenham RM10 81 C4
Enfield EN3 6 D5
Hornsey N8 50 A6
Walthamstow E17 53 C5
Eastfields HA5 40 C4
Eastfields Ave SW18 135 C1
Eastfields Rd
Acton W3 89 A2
Mitcham CR4 181 A1
Eastfield St E14 97 A2
EAST FINCHLEY 48 B5
East Finchley Sta N2 48 C5
Eastgate Bsns Pk E10 53 A1
Eastgate Cl SE28 102 D1
Eastgate Ct N3 29 C1
East Gdns SW17 180 C4
Eastglade HA5 41 B6
EAST HAM 100 A5
Eastham Cl EN5 13 B6
East Ham Ind Est E6 100 A2
East Ham L Ctr E6 100 B6
East Ham Manor Way E6 100 C1
East Ham Meml Hospl E7 77 D1
East Ham Sta E6 78 A1
East Harding St EC4 241 B2
East Heath Rd NW3 70 B5
East Hill
London SW18 158 A6
Wembley HA9 44 C1
Eastholm NW11 47 D5
Eastholme UB3 106 A5
East India Bldgs 9 E14 119 C6
East India Ct 7 SE16 118 C4
East India Dock Basin* E14 120 C6
East India Dock Rd E14 119 D6
East India Dock Road Tunnel 18 E14 98 B1

East India Sta E14 ... 120 B6
East India Way CR0 . 205 D1
East La
5 Bermondsey SE16 ... 118 A4
Bermondsey SE16 ... 118 A4
Kingston u T KT1 ... 197 D6
Wembley HA0, HA9 ... 65 D5
Eastlake Ho NW8 ... 236 D5
Eastlake Rd SE5 ... 139 A3
Eastland Ct 2 BR1 ... 187 C1
Eastlands Cres SE21 161 D5
East Lane Bsns Pk HA9 ... 65 D6
Eastlea Com Sch E16 . 98 C3
Eastlea Mews E16 ... 98 C3
Eastleigh Ave HA2 ... 63 D6
Eastleigh Cl
Belmont SM2 ... 217 D1
Neasden NW2 ... 67 C5
Eastleigh Rd E17 ... 35 B1
Eastleigh Way TW14 . 150 A3
Eastleigh Wlk 9 SW15 ... 156 A4
East London Coll 14 E11 ... 76 C6
Eastman Dental Hospl WC1 ... 94 B3 240 C6
Eastman Ho 7 SW4 .. 159 C5
Eastman Rd W3 ... 111 B4
East Mascalls 15 SE7 ... 143 C6
Eastmead IG3 ... 58 A2
East Mead HA4 ... 62 D5
Eastmead Ave UB6 ... 85 D4
Eastmead Cl BR1 ... 188 A1
Eastmearn Rd SE21, SE27 ... 161 A2
EAST MOLESEY ... 196 A4
Eastmont Rd KT10 .. 212 D6
Eastmoor Pl SE7 ... 121 D3
Eastmoor St SE7 ... 121 D3
East Mount St E1 ... 96 B2
Eastney Rd CR0 ... 204 D1
Eastney St SE10 ... 120 B1
Eastnor Rd SE9 ... 167 A3
Easton Ho 4 SE27 ... 160 D1
Easton St WC1 ... 241 A6
East Park Cl RM6 ... 59 A4
East Parkside SE10 . 120 D4
East Pas EC1 ... 242 A4
East Pl SE27 ... 183 A6
East Plaza E14 ... 119 D5
East Point 4 SE1 ... 118 A1
Eastpole Cotts N14 ... 3 D1
East Poultry Ave EC1 241 C3
East Putney Sta SW15 ... 157 A6
East Ramp TW6 ... 126 D4
East Rd Burnt Oak HA8 .. 27 A2
Chelsea SW1 115 A1 258 A1
Dagenham RM6 ... 59 A4
East Barnet EN4 ... 15 A3
East Bedfont TW14 ... 149 B4
Enfield EN3 ... 6 C5
Finchley N2 ... 30 C2
Kingston u T KT2 ... 176 A2
Newham E15 ... 99 A6
Shoreditch N1 . 95 B4 235 D2
Welling DA16 ... 146 B3
West Drayton UB7 ... 104 C2
Wimbledon SW19 ... 180 A4
East Rochester Way DA5, DA15, SE9 ... 168 C5
East Row
Kensal Town W10 ... 91 A3
Wanstead E11 ... 55 A3
Eastry Ave BR2 ... 208 D3
Eastry Ho SW8 ... 270 A3
Eastry Rd DA8 ... 147 C5
EAST SHEEN ... 133 B1
East Sheen Ave SW14 ... 133 B1
East Sheen Prim Sch SW14 ... 133 C1
Eastside Rd NW11 ... 47 B5
East Smithfield E1 ... 117 D6 253 D5
East St Barking IG11 ... 79 A1
Bexleyheath DA7 ... 147 C1
Brentford TW8 ... 131 C5
Bromley BR1 ... 187 A1
East St *continued*
Walworth SE17 ... 117 B1 262 C2
East Surrey Gr SE15 . 139 D5
East Tenter St E1 ... 95 D1 243 D1
East Terr DA15 ... 167 C3
East Thamesmead Bsns Pk DA18 ... 125 B4
East Towers HA5 ... 40 D3
Eastvale W3 ... 111 D5
East View Barnet EN5 ... 1 B2
Chingford E4 ... 36 A5
Hampstead NW3 ... 70 B6
Eastview Ave SE18 ... 145 C5
East View Ho 13 N2 ... 30 B1
Eastville Ave NW11 ... 47 B3
Eastway Hayes BR2 ... 209 A2
Merton SM4, SW20 .. 201 A5
South Hackney E3, E9 .. 97 A6
Wallington SM6 ... 219 C4
Wanstead E11 ... 55 B4
East Way
Croydon CR0 ... 223 A5
Hayes UB3 ... 106 A5
Ruislip HA4 ... 40 A1
Eastway Cres HA2 ... 63 D6
Eastwell Cl BR3 ... 185 A2
Eastwell Ho SE1 ... 262 D6
Eastwick Ct 2 SW19 ... 156 D3
EAST WICKHAM ... 146 A5
East Wickham Inf Sch DA16 ... 145 D4
East Wickham Jun Sch DA16 ... 146 A4
East Wlk
East Barnet EN4 ... 15 A3
Hayes UB3 ... 106 A5
Eastwood Cl
2 Islington N7 ... 72 C3
7 Tottenham N17 ... 34 B3
Woodford E18 ... 37 A1
Eastwood Rd
Ilford IG3 ... 58 A2
Muswell Hill N10 ... 31 A1
West Drayton UB7 ... 104 C4
Woodford E18 ... 37 A1
East Woodside DA5 .. 169 A3
Eastwood St SW16 .. 181 C4
Eatington Rd E10 ... 54 B4
Eaton Cl
Belgravia SW1 ... 258 A3
Stanmore HA7 ... 25 B6
Eaton Ct
Chislehurst BR7 ... 189 A4
Ealing W5 ... 87 D1
Edgware HA8 ... 26 C6
Southall UB1 ... 107 B6
Sutton SM2 ... 218 B2
6 Woodford E18 ... 37 A1
Eaton Dr
Brixton SW9 ... 138 D1
Kingston u T KT2 ... 176 C3
Eaton Gate SW1 ... 115 A2 258 A4
Eaton Gdns RM9 ... 81 A1
Eaton Ho
Battersea SW11 ... 266 D1
Ealing W5 ... 87 D1
23 Limehouse E14 ... 119 B6
Eaton House Sch SW1 ... 115 A2 258 A4
Eaton House The Manor Sch SW4 ... 137 B1
Eaton La SW1 ... 115 B3 258 D5
Eaton Lo SM2 ... 218 B2
Eaton Mans SW1 ... 258 A3
Eaton Mews N SW1 ... 115 A3 258 B5
Eaton Mews S SW1 ... 115 B3 258 C5
Eaton Mews W SW1 . 258 B4
Eaton Park Rd N13 ... 16 D2
Eaton Pl SW1 ... 115 A3 258 B5
Eaton Rd Enfield EN1 ... 5 C1
Hendon NW4 ... 46 C4
Isleworth TW3, TW7 .. 130 B1
Sidcup DA14 ... 168 D2
Sutton SM2 ... 218 B2
Eaton Rise Ealing W5 .. 87 D1
Wanstead E11 ... 55 C4
Eaton Row SW1 ... 115 B3 258 C5
Eatons Mead E4 ... 19 C2
Eaton Sq SW1 ... 115 A3 258 B5
Eaton Sq Pre-Prep Sch SW1 ... 115 B2 258 C4
Eaton Sq Prep Sch SW1 ... 115 C2 259 A4
Eaton Terr
Belgravia SW1 ... 115 A2 258 B4
Bow E3 ... 97 A4
Eaton Terr Mews SW1 ... 258 A4
Eatonville Rd SW17 . 158 D2
Eatonville Villas SW17 ... 158 D2
Ebb Ct E16 ... 123 A6
Ebbisham Dr SW8 ... 138 B6 270 C5
Ebbisham Rd KT4 ... 216 C6
Ebbsfleet Rd NW2 ... 69 A4
Ebdon Way SE3 ... 143 B2
Ebenezer Ho SE11 ... 261 C3
Ebenezer Mussel Ho 5 E2 ... 96 C5
Ebenezer St N1 ... 235 C2
Ebenezer Wlk CR4 ... 181 C2
Ebley Cl SE15 ... 139 D6
Ebner St SW18 ... 157 D6
Ebony Ct NW10 ... 67 D2
Ebony Ho
27 Bethnal Green E2 ... 96 A4
10 West Hampstead NW3 ... 69 D2
Ebor Cotts SW15 ... 155 C1
Ebor St E1, E2 ... 243 C6
Ebrington Rd HA3 ... 43 D3
Ebsworth St SE23 ... 162 D4
Eburne Rd N7 ... 72 A5
Ebury Bridge Rd SW1 ... 115 A1 258 B1
Ebury Cl BR2 ... 226 A5
Ebury Mews
Belgravia SW1 ... 115 B2 258 C4
West Norwood SE27 . 160 D1
Ebury Mews E SW1 . 258 C5
Ebury Sq SW1 ... 258 B3
Ebury St SW1 ... 115 B2 258 C4
Ecclesbourne Cl N13 .. 32 C5
Ecclesbourne Gdns N13 ... 32 C5
Ecclesbourne Inf Sch CR7 ... 205 A4
Ecclesbourne Jun Sch CR7 ... 205 A4
Ecclesbourne Rd
Islington N1 ... 73 A1
Thornton Heath CR7 . 205 A4
Eccles Ct SE11 ... 260 D1
Eccleshill 3 BR2 ... 208 D5
Eccles Rd SW11 ... 136 D1
Eccleston Cl
Cockfosters EN4 ... 2 D1
Crofton BR6 ... 211 B1
Eccleston Cres RM6 ... 58 B2
Ecclestone Ct HA9 ... 66 A3
Ecclestone Mews HA9 ... 66 A3
Ecclestone Pl HA9 ... 66 B3
Eccleston Ho 1 SW2 ... 160 C5
Eccleston Mews SW1 ... 115 A3 258 B5
Eccleston Pl SW1 ... 115 B2 258 C4
Eccleston Rd W13 ... 109 A5
Eccleston Sq SW1 ... 115 B2 258 D3
Eccleston Sq Mews SW1 ... 259 A3
Eccleston St SW1 ... 115 B2 258 C4
Echelforde Dr TW15 . 170 C6
Echelford Prim Sch The TW15 ... 170 D5
Echo Hts E4 ... 19 D3
Eckford St N1 ... 234 A4
Eckington Ho N15 ... 51 B3
Eckstein Rd SW11 ... 136 C1
Eclipse Rd E13 ... 99 B2
Ector Rd SE6 ... 164 C2
Edam Ct 11 DA14 ... 168 A1
Edans Ct W12 ... 111 D4
Edbrooke Rd W9 ... 91 C3
Eddinton Cl CR0 ... 224 A2
Eddisbury Ho 7 SE26 ... 162 A1
Eddiscombe Rd SW6 ... 135 B3
Eddison Ct N19 ... 72 A6
Eddy Cl RM7 ... 59 D3
Eddystone Rd SE4 ... 163 A6
Eddystone Twr SE8 ... 119 A1
Eddystone Wlk TW19 ... 148 A4
Ede Cl TW4 ... 129 B2
Edenbridge Cl 29 SE16 ... 118 B1
Edenbridge Rd
Enfield EN1 ... 17 C5
Hackney E9 ... 74 D1
Eden Cl
Child's Hill NW3 ... 69 C6
Enfield EN3 ... 7 C5
Kensington W8 ... 255 B6
Wembley HA0 ... 87 D6
Edencourt W5 ... 88 B1
Edencourt Rd SW16 .. 181 B4
Eden Ct 3 N3 ... 29 B1
Edendale W3 ... 110 D6
Edenfield Gdns KT4 . 215 D5
Eden Gr Islington N7 ... 72 B3
Walthamstow E17 ... 53 D4
Willesden NW10 ... 68 B2
Edenham High Sch CR0 ... 207 B2
Edenham Way W10 ... 91 B2
Eden High Sch 9 W6 ... 112 A1
Eden Ho
15 Battersea SW11 .. 136 C2
Lisson Gr NW8 ... 237 A5
Edenhurst Ave SW6 .. 135 B2
Eden Ind Sch UB5 ... 63 B2
Eden Lodge NW6 ... 68 D1
Eden Mews SW17 ... 158 A1
EDEN PARK ... 207 C5
Eden Park Ave BR3 .. 207 C4
Eden Park Sta BR3 .. 207 C4
Eden Rd Croydon CR0 . 221 B4
Penge BR3 ... 185 A2
Walthamstow E17 ... 53 D4
West Norwood SE27 . 182 D5
Edensmuir Ct SE3 ... 143 A5
Edensor Gdns W4 ... 133 C5
Edensor Rd W4 ... 133 C5
Eden St KT1, KT2 ... 176 A1
Edenvale Cl CR4 ... 181 A3
Edenvale Rd CR4 ... 181 A3
Edenvale St SW6 ... 136 A3
Eden Way
Beckenham BR3 ... 207 C3
Bow E3 ... 97 B6
Eden Wlk 5 KT1 ... 176 A1
Eden Wlk Sh Ctr KT2 ... 176 A1
Ederline Ave SW16 ... 182 C1
Edgar Ct KT3 ... 199 C6
Edgar Ho Homerton E9 . 75 A3
South Lambeth SW8 . 270 A4
Wanstead E11 ... 55 A2
Edgar Kail Way SE22 ... 139 C1
Edgarley Terr SW6 .. 264 A1
Edgar Rd Bromley E3 ... 97 D4
Dagenham RM6 ... 58 D2
Twickenham TW4 ... 151 B4
Yiewsley UB7 ... 104 A5
Edgar Wallace Cl 4 SE15 ... 139 C5
Edgbury Ct NW9 ... 45 A5
Edgcott Ho 2 W10 ... 90 C2
Edgeborough Way BR1 ... 187 D2
Edge Bsns Ctr NW2 ... 68 B6
Edgebury BR7, SE9 .. 188 D6
Edgebury Prim Sch BR7 ... 189 A6
Edgebury Wlk BR7 ... 167 A1
Edgecombe Cl KT2 ... 177 B3
Edgecombe Ho
4 London SE5 ... 139 C3
Putney SW19 ... 157 A4
Edgecoombe CR2 ... 222 C1
Edgecote Cl 7 W3 ... 111 A5
Edgecot Gr N15 ... 51 C4
Edgecumbe Ct 2 CR0 ... 206 A1
Edgefield Ave IG11 ... 79 D1
Edgefield Ct 3 IG11 .. 79 D1
Edge Hill
Shooters Hill SE18 ... 144 D6
Wimbledon SW19 ... 178 D3
Edge Hill Ave N3 ... 47 C5
Edgehill Ct KT12 ... 194 C1
Edge Hill Ct
Sidcup DA14 ... 189 D6
Wimbledon SW19 ... 178 D3
Edgehill Gdns RM10 ... 81 C4
Edgehill Ho 4 SW9 . 138 D3
Edgehill Rd
Ealing W13 ... 87 C2
Longlands BR7 ... 189 A6
Mitcham CR4 ... 181 B2
Edgeley La SW4 ... 137 D2
Edgeley Rd SW4 ... 137 D2
Edgel St SW18 ... 135 D1
Edge Point Cl SE27 ... 182 D5
Edge St W8 ... 113 C5 245 B4
Edgewood Dr BR6 .. 227 D3
Edgewood Gn CR0 .. 206 D1
Edgeworth Ave NW4 .. 46 A4
Edgeworth Cl NW4 ... 46 A4
Edgeworth Cres NW4 . 46 A4
Edgeworth Ct 10 EN4 .. 2 C1
Edgeworth Ho NW8 . 229 A6
Edgeworth Rd
Barnet EN4 ... 2 C1
Eltham SE9 ... 143 D1
Edgington Rd SW16 . 181 D4
Edgington Way DA14 ... 190 D3
Edgson Ho SW1 ... 258 C2
EDGWARE ... 26 C6
Edgware Acad WC2 . 240 B1
EDGWARE BURY ... 10 B3
Edgwarebury Ct HA8 .. 26 C5
Edgwarebury Gdns HA8 ... 26 C5
Edgwarebury La
Edgware Bury HA8 ... 10 C2
Edgware HA8 ... 26 C5
Edgware Community Hospl HA8 ... 26 D3
Edgware Ct HA8 ... 26 C4
Edgware Jewish Prim Sch HA8 ... 26 D5
Edgware Jun & Inf Schs HA8 ... 26 C4
Edgware Rd
Dollis Hill NW2 ... 68 C6
Paddington W1, W2, NW1, NW8 ... 92 C2 237 A3
Edgware Road Sta (Bakerloo) NW1 ... 92 C2 237 A3
Edgware Road Sta (Met, Distr, Circle) NW1 . 237 B3
Edgware Road The Hyde NW9 ... 45 C5
Edgware Road West Hendon Broadway NW9 ... 46 A2
Edgware Sta HA8 ... 26 D4
Edgware Way (Watford By-Pass) HA8 ... 27 A6
Edinburgh Cl
7 Bethnal Green E2 ... 96 C5
Pinner HA5 ... 41 A2
Uxbridge UB10 ... 60 D4
Edinburgh Ct
1 Catford SE6 ... 164 D3
2 Kingston u T KT1 .. 198 A6
Newham E13 ... 99 B5
10 Rotherhithe SE16 . 118 D5
West Barnes SM4 ... 200 D4
Edinburgh Dr UB10 ... 60 D4
Edinburgh Ho
3 Acton W3 ... 89 B1
Carshalton SM1 ... 218 B6
Hendon NW4 ... 46 C6
Maida Vale W9 ... 91 D4
Edinburgh Prim Sch E17 ... 53 B4
Edinburgh Rd
Carshalton SM1 ... 218 B6
Edmonton N18 ... 34 A5
Hanwell W7 ... 108 D4
Newham E13 ... 99 B5
Walthamstow E17 ... 53 C4
Edington 20 NW5 ... 71 A2
Edington Rd
Abbey Wood SE2 ... 124 B3
Enfield EN3 ... 6 C3
Edison Bldg 7 E14 .. 119 C4

Edison Cl
Walthamstow E17 ... 53 C4
West Drayton UB7 ... 104 B4
Edison Ct SE10 ... 120 D3
Edison Dr
Southall UB1 ... 85 D1
Wembley HA9 ... 66 A6
Edison Gr SE18 ... 145 D5
Edison Ho
Walworth SE1 ... 262 C4
7 Wembley HA9 ... 67 A5
Edison Rd
Bexley DA16 ... 145 D4
Brimsdown EN3 ... 7 B3
Bromley BR2 ... 187 A1
Crouch End N8 ... 49 D3
Edis St NW1 ... 93 A6 231 B6
Editha Mans SW10 ... 266 A5
Edith Cavell Cl 2 N19 ... 50 A2
Edith Cavell Way SE18 ... 144 A4
Edith Ct TW14 ... 149 B5
Edith Gdns KT5 ... 198 D2
Edith Gr SW10 ... 136 A5 266 B4
Edith Ho 6 W6 ... 112 C1
Edithna St SW9 ... 138 A2
Edith Nesbit Wlk SE9 ... 166 B6
Edith Neville Cotts NW1 ... 232 C2
Edith Neville Prim Sch NW1 ... 93 D5 232 C3
Edith Pond Ct SE9 ... 166 D2
Edith Ramsay Ho 2 E1 ... 97 A2
Edith Rd
Dagenham RM6 ... 58 D2
South Norwood SE25 ... 205 B4
Stratford New Town E15 ... 76 B3
Upton Pk E6 ... 77 D1
West Kensington W14 ... 113 A2 254 B3
Wimbledon SW19 ... 179 D4
Wood Green N11 ... 31 D3
Edith Row SW6 ... 265 D2
Edith St E2 ... 96 A5
Edith Summerskill Ho SW6 ... 264 C4
Edith Terr SW10 ... 136 A5 266 A4
Edith Villas W14 ... 113 B1 254 C2
Edith Yd SW10 ... 266 B4
Edmansons' Cl N17 ... 33 D2
Edmeston Cl E9 ... 75 A2
Edmond Ct SE14 ... 140 C4
Edmonscote W13 ... 87 A2
EDMONTON ... 33 D6
Edmonton Ct 5 SE16 ... 118 C3
Edmonton Cty Lower Sch N9 ... 17 C3
Edmonton Cty Upper Sch EN1 ... 17 D4
Edmonton Green Sh Ctr N9 ... 18 B2
Edmonton Green Sta N9 ... 18 A2
Edmonton Wharf N18 ... 34 D4
Edmund Gr TW13 ... 151 B2
Edmund Halley Way SE10 ... 120 C4
Edmund Ho
Kennington SE17 ... 261 D1
New Cross Gate SE14 ... 141 B4
Edmund Hurst Dr E6 ... 100 D2
Edmund Rd
Mitcham CR4 ... 202 C6
Welling DA16 ... 146 A2
Edmundsbury Ct Est 16 SW9 ... 138 B1
Edmunds Cl UB4 ... 84 C2
Edmund St SE5 ... 139 B5
Edmunds Wlk N2 ... 48 C5
Edmund Waller Prim Sch SE14 ... 140 D3
Ednam Ho SE15 ... 140 A6
Edna Rd SW20 ... 178 D1
Edna St SW11 ... 136 C4 267 A1
Edred Ho E9 ... 75 A4
Edrich Ho SW4 ... 270 A1
Edric Ho SW1 ... 259 D4
Edrick Rd HA8 ... 27 A4
Edrick Wlk HA8 ... 27 A4
Edric Rd SE14 ... 140 D5
Edridge Cl WD23 ... 8 A6
Edridge Ho 9 SE27 ... 160 D1
Edridge Rd CR0 ... 221 B5
Edward Alderton Theatre★ DA7 ... 146 D2
Edward Alleyn Ho SE21 ... 161 C4
Edward Ave
Chingford E4 ... 35 D4
Morden SM4 ... 202 B4
Edward Betham CE Prim Sch UB6 ... 86 A5
Edward Cl
Edmonton N9 ... 17 D4
Hampton TW12 ... 174 A5
Edward Ct
2 Ealing W5 ... 87 B3
Harrow HA1 ... 64 C6
2 Newham E16 ... 99 A2
Edward Dodd Ct N1 ... 235 D2
Edward Edward's Ho SE1 ... 251 C3
Edwardes Pl W8 ... 254 D5
Edwardes Sq W8 ... 113 B3 254 D5
Edward Friend Ho 6 N16 ... 73 C5
Edward Gr EN4 ... 14 B6
Edward Harvey Ct DA17 ... 125 B1
Edward Ho
Paddington W2 ... 236 C5
Vauxhall SE11 ... 260 D2
Edward Kennedy Ho 18 W10 ... 91 A3
Edward Mann Cl 13 E1 ... 96 D1
Edward Mans 8 IG11 ... 79 D1
Edward Mews NW1 ... 231 D3
Edward Pauling Ho TW14 ... 149 D4
Edward Pauling Prim Sch TW13 ... 149 C2
Edward Pinner Ct 5 KT6 ... 214 A6
Edward Pl SE8 ... 141 B6
Edward Rd
Bromley BR1 ... 187 C3
Chislehurst BR7 ... 188 D5
Croydon CR0 ... 205 C2
Dagenham RM6 ... 59 A3
Hampton TW12 ... 174 A5
Harrow HA2 ... 42 A6
Hatton TW14 ... 149 C6
New Barnet EN4 ... 14 B6
Northolt UB5 ... 84 C5
Penge SE20 ... 184 D4
Walthamstow E17 ... 52 D4
Edward Robinson Ho 3 SE14 ... 140 D5
Edward's Ave HA4 ... 62 C2
Edwards Cl 1 KT4 ... 216 D6
Edward's Cotts 11 N1 ... 72 D1
Edwards Dr N11 ... 31 D3
Edwards Ho 7 TW10 ... 153 C1
Edward's La N16 ... 73 C6
Edwards Language Sch 6 W5 ... 110 A6
Edwards Mews
Islington N1 ... 72 C1
Marylebone W1 ... 93 A1 238 A1
Edward Sq
Islington N1 ... 233 C5
1 Rotherhithe SE16 ... 119 A5
Edwards Rd DA17 ... 125 C2
Edward St
New Cross SE14 ... 141 B5
10 Newham E16 ... 99 A3
Edward Temme Ave E15 ... 76 D1
Edward Tyler Rd SE12 ... 165 C2
Edward VII Mans NW10 ... 90 D4
Edward Way TW15 ... 148 B2
Edward Wilson Prim Sch 2 W2 ... 91 D2
Edwina Ct SM1 ... 217 D4
Edwina Gdns IG4 ... 56 A4
Edwin Arnold Ct DA15 ... 189 D6
Edwin Ave E6 ... 100 C5
Edwin Cl DA7 ... 147 B6
Edwin Ho SE15 ... 140 A5
Edwin Pl 10 CR0 ... 205 B1
Edwin Rd
Burnt Oak HA8 ... 27 B4
Twickenham TW1, TW2 ... 152 C3
Edwin's Mead E9 ... 75 A4
Edwin St
Bethnal Green E1 ... 96 C3
Newham E16 ... 99 A2
Edwin Stray Ho TW13 ... 151 C1
Edwin Ware Ct 4 HA5 ... 22 C1
Edwy Ho E9 ... 75 B4
Edwyn Cl EN5 ... 12 D5
Edwyn Ho SW18 ... 157 D5
Eel Pie Island★ TW1 ... 153 A3
Effie Pl SW6 ... 265 B3
Effie Rd SW6 ... 135 C5 265 B3
Effingham Cl SM2 ... 217 D1
Effingham Ct SW19 ... 180 C3
Effingham Ho
37 Clapham SW8 ... 137 D3
9 Kingston u T KT2 ... 176 D4
Effingham Lo 1 KT6 ... 198 A4
Effingham Rd
Hornsey N8 ... 50 C5
Lewisham SE12 ... 164 D6
Thames Ditton KT6, KT7 ... 197 C2
Thornton Heath CR0 ... 204 B2
Effort St SW17 ... 180 C5
Effra Cl SW19 ... 179 D4
Effra Ct London SW2 ... 160 B6
South Norwood SE19 ... 183 C3
Effra Mans SW2 ... 160 C6
Effra Par SW2 ... 160 C6
Effra Rd London SW2 ... 160 C6
Wimbledon SW19 ... 179 D4
Effra Road Ret Pk SW2 ... 160 C6
EF International Language Sch SE1 ... 251 B3
Egan Way UB3 ... 105 C6
Egbert Ho E9 ... 75 A3
Egbert St NW1 ... 93 A6 231 A6
Egbury Ho SW15 ... 155 D5
Egerton Cl HA5 ... 40 A5
Egerton Cres SW3 ... 114 C2 257 B4
Egerton Ct
Leytonstone E11 ... 54 B2
5 Richmond TW10 ... 154 A6
Egerton Dr SE10 ... 141 D4
Egerton Gdns
Ealing W13 ... 87 B1
Hendon NW4 ... 46 B5
Ilford IG3 ... 79 D5
Knightsbridge SW3 ... 114 C3 257 A5
Willesden NW10 ... 90 C6
Egerton Gdns Mews SW3 ... 257 B5
Egerton Ho W4 ... 133 A6
Egerton Pl SW3 ... 257 B5
Egerton Rd
New Malden KT3 ... 199 D5
South Norwood SE25 ... 205 C6
Stamford Hill N16 ... 51 D2
Twickenham TW2 ... 152 C4
Wembley HA0 ... 66 B1
Egerton Terr SW3 ... 114 C3 257 B5
Egerton Way UB3 ... 126 D5
Eggardon Ct UB5 ... 64 A2
Egham Cl
Cheam SM3 ... 217 A6
Putney SW19 ... 157 A2
Egham Cres SM3 ... 217 A6
Egham Ct KT6 ... 197 D4
Egham Rd E13 ... 99 B2
Eglantine Rd SW18 ... 158 A6
Egleston Rd SM4 ... 201 D3
Eglington Ct SE17 ... 139 A6
Eglington Rd E4 ... 20 B4
Eglinton Hill SE18 ... 144 D5
Eglinton Prim Sch SE18 ... 144 C6
Eglinton Rd SE18 ... 144 D6
Egliston Mews SW15 ... 134 C2
Egliston Rd SW15 ... 134 C2
Egmont Ave KT6 ... 198 B1
Egmont Mews KT19 ... 215 B4
Egmont Rd
New Malden KT3 ... 199 D5
Sutton SM2 ... 218 A1
Tolworth KT6 ... 198 C1
Walton-on-T KT12 ... 194 B2
Egmont St SE14 ... 140 D5
Egremont Ho SE13 ... 141 D3
Egremont Rd SE27 ... 160 C1
Egret Ho 11 SE16 ... 118 D2
Egret Way UB4 ... 84 D2
Eider Cl Hayes UB4 ... 84 D2
Stratford E7 ... 76 D3
Eider Ct 38 SE8 ... 141 B6
Eighteenth Rd CR4 ... 204 A5
Eighth Ave
Hayes UB3 ... 106 A5
Ilford E12 ... 78 B4
Eileen Ct BR7 ... 188 C5
Eileen Rd SE25 ... 205 B4
Eindhoven Cl SM5 ... 203 A1
Einstein Ho HA9 ... 67 A5
Eisenhower Dr E6 ... 100 A2
Eisenhower Ho KT8 ... 175 C2
Elaine Ct 13 NW3 ... 70 D2
Elaine Gr NW5 ... 71 A3
Elaine Ho N4 ... 50 A1
Elam Cl SE5 ... 138 D3
Elam St SE5 ... 138 D3
Elan Ct E1 ... 96 B2
Eland Pl CR0 ... 220 D5
Eland Rd
Clapham SW11 ... 136 D2
Croydon CR0 ... 220 D5
Elba Pl SE17 ... 117 A2 262 B4
Elberon Ave CR0 ... 203 C3
Elbe St SW6 ... 136 A3
Elborough Rd SE25 ... 206 A4
Elborough St SW18 ... 157 C3
Elbourne Trad Est DA17 ... 125 D3
Elbury Dr E16 ... 99 A1
Elcho St SW11 ... 136 C5 267 B3
Elcot Ave SE15 ... 140 B5
Elder Ave N8 ... 50 A4
Elderberry Ct 2 EN2 ... 4 D3
Elderberry Gr 10 SE27 ... 183 A6
Elderberry Rd W5 ... 110 A4
Elder Cl Barnet N20 ... 13 D3
Sidcup DA15 ... 167 D3
Yiewsley UB7 ... 104 A6
Elder Ct WD23 ... 8 C2
Elderfield Ho 4 E14 ... 119 C6
Elderfield Pl SW17 ... 181 B6
Elderfield Rd E5 ... 74 C4
Elderfield Wlk E11 ... 55 B4
Elderflower Way E15 ... 76 C1
Elder Gdns 9 SE27 ... 183 A6
Elder Oak Cl SE20 ... 184 B2
Elder Rd SE27 ... 183 A5
Elderslie Cl BR3 ... 207 D3
Elderslie Rd SE9 ... 166 C6
Elder St E1 ... 95 D3 243 C5
Elderton Rd SE26 ... 185 A6
Eldertree Pl CR4 ... 181 C2
Eldertree Way CR4 ... 181 C2
Elder Wlk
Islington N1 ... 234 D6
2 Lewisham SE13 ... 142 A2
Elderwood Pl SE27 ... 183 A5
Eldon Ave
Croydon CR0 ... 222 C6
Heston TW5 ... 129 C5
Eldon Ct NW6 ... 91 C6
Eldon Gr NW3 ... 70 B3
Eldon Ho SW9 ... 138 D2
Eldon Jun & Inf Schs N9 ... 18 C3
Eldon Pk SE25 ... 206 B5
Eldon Rd Edmonton N9 ... 18 C3
Kensington W8 ... 113 D3 255 D5
Tottenham N22 ... 32 D2
Walthamstow E17 ... 53 B5
Eldon St EC2 ... 95 B2 242 D3
Eldonwall Est RM8 ... 59 B1
Eldon Way NW10 ... 88 D5
Eldred Rd IG11 ... 101 C6
Eldrick Ct TW14 ... 149 B3
Eldridge Cl TW14 ... 150 A3
Eldridge Ct
Bermondsey SE16 ... 118 A3
14 Dagenham RM10 ... 81 D2
Eleanor Cl
Rotherhithe SE16 ... 118 D4
South Tottenham N15 ... 51 D6
Eleanor Cres NW7 ... 28 D6
Eleanor Ct 13 E2 ... 96 A6
Eleanor Gdns
Barnet EN5 ... 12 D6
Dagenham RM8 ... 81 B6
Eleanor Gr
Mortlake SW13 ... 133 C2
Uxbridge UB10 ... 60 D5
Eleanor Ho
18 Hammersmith W6 ... 112 C1
1 Kentish Town NW5 ... 71 C3
6 Merton SW19 ... 179 D2
Eleanor Palmer Prim Sch 12 NW5 ... 71 C4
Eleanor Rathbone Ho 1 N6 ... 49 D2
Eleanor Rd
Bowes Pk N11 ... 32 A4
Hackney E8 ... 74 B1
Stratford E15 ... 76 D2
Eleanor Smith Sch 2 E13 ... 99 B5
Eleanor Smith Sch (West Beckton Site) E16 ... 99 C2
Eleanor St E3 ... 97 C4
Eleanor Wlk 24 SE18 ... 122 B2
Electra Ave TW6 ... 127 D2
Electra Ct 6 NW2 ... 68 C2
Electric Ave SW9 ... 138 C1
Electric Ho 13 Bow E3 ... 97 C4
Walthamstow E17 ... 53 C5
Electric La 2 SW9 ... 138 C1
Electric Mans 1 SW9 ... 138 C1
Electric Par Ilford IG3 ... 57 D1
Surbiton KT6 ... 197 D3
Woodford E18 ... 37 A1
Elenmore Ct BR1 ... 210 A5
Elephant & Castle
Newington SE1 ... 116 D3 261 D5
Newington SE1 ... 261 D4
Elephant & Castle Sh Ctr SE1 ... 117 A2 262 A4
Elephant & Castle Sta
Lambeth SE1 ... 116 D3 261 D5
Newington SE17 ... 117 A2 262 A4
Elephant La SE16 ... 118 C4
Elephant Rd SE17 ... 117 A2 262 A4
Elers Rd Ealing W13 ... 109 C4
Hayes UB3 ... 105 B2
Eley Rd N18 ... 34 D5
Eley's Est N18 ... 34 D6
Elfindale Rd SE24 ... 161 A6
Elfin Gr TW11 ... 174 D5
Elford Cl SE9 ... 143 C1
Elfort Rd N5 ... 72 C4
Elfrida Cres SE6 ... 185 C6
Elfrida Prim Sch SE6 ... 185 C6
Elf Row E1 ... 118 C6
Elfwine Rd W7 ... 86 C2
Elgal Cl BR6 ... 226 D3
Elgar N8 ... 50 A6
Elgar Ave Ealing W5 ... 110 A4
Thornton Heath SW16 ... 204 A6
Tolworth KT5, KT6 ... 198 D2
Willesden NW10 ... 67 B2
Elgar Cl
Buckhurst Hill IG9 ... 21 D2
Deptford SE8 ... 141 C5
Elstree WD6 ... 9 D4
Ickenham UB10 ... 60 C6
Newham E13 ... 99 C5
Elgar Ct W14 ... 254 A5
Elgar Ho Hayes UB4 ... 84 C2
Isleworth TW2 ... 152 B5

Elgar Ho *continued*
Pimlico SW1........ 258 D1
Southall UB1 ....85 C1
South Hampstead NW6 70 A1
Elgar St SE16........119 A3
Elgin Ave
Ashford TW15 ...... 171 A4
Hammersmith W12 ...112 B3
Harrow HA3..........25 B1
Westbourne Green W9 .91 D3
Elgin Cl W12.........112 B4
Elgin Cres
Hatton TW6 .... 127 C3
Notting Hill
W11 ......113 A6 244 B6
Elgin Ct
6 Croydon CR0..... 221 A4
Westbourne Green W9 .91 D3
Elgin Ho Northolt UB5 ..84 B5
8 Poplar E14 ....97 D1
Elgin Mans W9 ....91 D4
Elgin Mews W11.......91 A1
Elgin Mews N W9 ......91 D4
Elgin Mews S W9 ......91 D4
Elgin Rd
Croydon CR0 .... 221 D6
Ilford IG3............57 C2
Sutton SM1 .... 218 A5
Wallington SM6..... 219 C2
Wood Green N22......31 C1
Elgood Ave HA6 ......22 A3
Elgood Cl W11........ 244 A3
Elgood Ho NW8...... 229 D3
Elham Cl BR1....... 187 D3
Elham Ho 13 E5.......74 B3
Elia Mews N1. .94 D5 234 C3
Elias Pl SW8..........138 C6
Elia St N1 .....94 D5 234 C3
Elibank Rd SE9 ......144 C1
Elim Est SE1........ 263 A6
Elim St SE1......... 263 A6
Elim Way E13.........98 D4
Eliot Bank SE23,
SE26..............162 B2
Eliot Bank Prim Sch
SE26..............162 B2
Eliot Cotts SE3.......142 C3
Eliot Ct SW18.........157 D5
Eliot Dr HA2..........63 D6
Eliot Gdns SW15......134 A1
Eliot Hill SE13 ....142 A3
Eliot Ho 10 TW10......154 B5
Eliot Mews NW8..... 229 A3
Eliot Pk SE13 ....142 A3
Eliot Pl SE3..........142 C3
Eliot Rd RM9 ....80 D4
Eliot Vale SE3.........142 B3
Elis David Almshouses
CR0............... 220 D4
Elizabethan Ct N3 ....47 A6
Elizabeth Ave
Enfield EN2 ....4 D2
Ilford IG1............79 B6
Islington N1..........73 B1
Shoreditch N1 . 95 A6 235 B6
Elizabeth Barnes Ct 5
SW6............... 135 D3
Elizabeth Blackwell Ho
N22.................32 C2
Elizabeth Blount Ct 4
E14.................97 A1
Elizabeth Cl
Cheam SM1.........217 B4
Paddington W9 ..... 236 B5
12 Poplar E14 ....97 D1
Elizabeth Clyde Cl
N15.................51 C5
Elizabeth Cooper Lo
SW12..............159 A5
Elizabeth Cotts 5
TW9...............132 C4
Elizabeth Ct
Buckhurst Hill IG9 .....21 B3
Chelsea SW10....... 266 D5
East Dulwich SE22.... 140 A1
Kingston u T KT2 .... 176 A2
Marylebone NW8...... 237 B6
South Croydon CR0 .. 221 C5
Sunbury TW16 ...... 194 C6
3 Teddington TW11 .. 174 C5
Upper Tooting SW17 . 181 A5
West Barnes SM4 ... 201 A2
Westminster SW1 ... 259 D5
Elizabeth Ct *continued*
6 Woodford Green
E18 ....37 A2
2 Woodford Green
IG8 ....37 C3
10 Woolwich SE18.....122 B2
Elizabeth Finn Ho 1
W12 ....112 A3
Elizabeth Fry Ho
UB3............... 105 D2
Elizabeth Fry Pl
SE18...............144 A4
Elizabeth Garrett
Anderson Ho 9
DA17..............125 C3
Elizabeth Garrett
Anderson Hospl
NW1.........93 C3 239 B5
Elizabeth Garrett
Anderson Language
Coll N1 ......94 B5 233 D3
Elizabeth Gdns
East Acton W3 ...... 111 D5
Isleworth TW7....... 131 A1
Stanmore HA7........25 C5
Sunbury TW16 ...... 194 C6
Elizabeth Ho
Cheam SM3 .... 217 A2
Friern Barnet N20 ......14 D1
15 Hammersmith W6 112 C1
Lambeth SE11 ...... 261 B3
Stanmore HA7........26 A1
Wembley HA9 ....66 B3
Elizabeth Ind Est
SE14............... 140 D6
Elizabeth Kenny Ho
N1..................73 A2
Elizabeth Mews
28 Hackney E2........96 A5
Maitland Pk NW3......70 D2
Elizabeth Pl N15.......51 B5
Elizabeth Rd
Newham E6 ....99 D6
South Tottenham N15....51 C4
Elizabeth Ride N9 ....18 B4
Elizabeth Selby Inf Sch
31 E2................96 A4
Elizabeth Sq 13
SE16...............119 A6
Elizabeth St
SW1.......115 A2 258 B4
Elizabeth Terr SE9 ...166 B5
Elizabeth Way
Feltham TW13 ...... 172 C6
South Norwood SE19..183 B3
Elkanette Mews N20 ..14 A2
Elkington Point SE11 261 A3
Elkington Rd E13 .....99 B3
Elkstone Rd W10......91 B2
Ella Cl BR3 ....185 C1
Ellacombe Ho 1
SW2...............160 C4
Ellaline Rd W6....... 134 D6
Ella Mews NW3.......70 D4
Ellanby Cres N18 .....34 B5
Elland Cl EN5.........14 B6
Elland Ho 18 E14......97 B1
Elland Rd SE15 ....140 C1
Ella Rd N4, N8.........50 A2
Ellard Ct DA16 ....146 C2
Elle Ct N12 ....29 D5
Ellement Cl HA5 ......40 D4
Ellena Ct N14.........16 A1
Ellenborough Ct N22..32 D2
Ellenborough Ho 5
W12 ....112 B6
Ellenborough Pl
SW15...............134 A1
Ellenborough Rd
Sidcup DA14........ 191 A5
Tottenham N22 ....33 A2
Ellen Cl BR1......... 209 D6
Ellen Ct
4 Chingford E4.......20 A3
Lower Edmonton N9 ...18 C2
Ellen Miller Ho 2
E17.................54 A4
Ellen St E1 ....96 A1
Ellen Webb Dr HA3....42 C6
Ellen Wilkinson Ho
12 Dagenham RM10 ...81 C5
7 Globe Town E2 .....96 D4
West Brompton SW6. 264 D5
Ellen Wilkinson Prim Sch
E6................ 100 A2
Ellen Wilkinson Sch for
Girls W3.............88 B1
Elleray Rd TW11 .... 174 D4
Ellerby St SW6...... 134 D4
Ellerdale Cl 15 NW3...70 A4
Ellerdale Rd NW3.....70 A3
Ellerdale St SE13 ... 141 D2
Ellerdine Rd TW3 ....130 B1
Ellerker Gdns TW10 ..154 A5
Ellerman Ave TW2,
TW4 ....151 B3
Ellerslie Ct 6 SM6...219 B2
Ellerslie Gdns NW10 ..90 A6
Ellerslie Ind Est
SW2............... 160 A6
Ellerslie Rd W12 .....112 B5
Ellerton Ct W3....... 110 D4
Ellerton Gdns RM9....80 C1
Ellerton Lo N3.........29 C1
Ellerton Rd
Barnes SW13....... 134 A4
Dagenham RM9........80 C1
Surbiton KT6 ....198 B1
Wandsworth SW17,
SW18 ....158 B3
Wimbledon SW20 ... 178 A3
Ellery Cl 5 NW10.....89 D5
Ellery Ho SE17...... 262 D3
Ellery Rd SE19.......183 B3
Ellery St SE15........140 B3
Ellesborough Cl
WD19................22 C5
Ellesmere Ave
Beckenham BR3..... 185 D1
Edgware NW7 ....11 B1
Ellesmere Cl
Leytonstone E11 ......54 D4
Ruislip HA4 ....39 A2
Ellesmere Ct
Chiswick W4 ....133 B6
Lewisham SE12 ......165 A3
Penge SE20 ....184 B1
Ellesmere Gdns IG4...56 A3
Ellesmere Gr EN5......13 B6
Ellesmere Rd Bow E3..97 A5
Chiswick W4 ....133 B6
Greenford UB6........86 A3
Twickenham TW1.... 153 C5
Willesden NW10 ......68 A3
Ellesmere St E14 .....97 D1
Ellies Mews TW15.....148 A2
Ellingfort Rd E8 ......74 B1
Ellingham Prim Sch
KT9 .... 213 D1
Ellingham Rd
Chessington KT9.... 213 D2
Leyton E15............76 B4
Shepherd's Bush W12 112 A4
Ellington Ct N14.......15 D2
Ellington Ho SE1.... 262 B5
Ellington Rd
Cranley Gdns N10 .....49 B5
Feltham TW13 ...... 171 D6
Hounslow TW3....... 129 D3
Ellington St N7 ....72 C2
Elliot Cl Stratford E15 ..76 C1
Wembley HA9 ....66 C5
Woodford IG8 ....37 D4
Elliot Ct 6 N15 ....51 D5
Elliot Rd NW4 ....46 B3
Elliott Ave HA4 ....62 B6
Elliott Gdns TW17....192 C5
Elliott Ho 3 CR7.... 204 D5
Elliott Rd Acton W4 ...111 C2
Brixton SW9........ 138 D4
Bromley BR2 .... 209 D5
Camberwell SW9.... 138 D4
Stanmore HA7........25 A4
Thornton Heath CR7 . 204 D5
Elliott Sch SW15.... 156 C5
Elliott's Pl N1 ...... 234 D5
Elliott Sq NW3........70 C1
Elliott's Row
SE11...... 116 D2 261 D4
Ellis Cl Burnt Oak HA8 ..27 C4
New Eltham SE9..... 167 A2
Willesden NW10 ....68 C2
Elliscombe Mount 11
SE7................143 C6
Elliscombe Rd SE7....143 C6
Ellis Ct W7 ....86 D2
Ellisfield Dr SW15....156 A4
Ellis Franklin Ct
NW8............... 229 A4
Ellis Ho
Walthamstow E17 .....54 A4
Ellis Ho *continued*
Walworth SE17 ..... 262 C2
Ellison Gdns UB2 ....107 B2
Ellison Ho 1 SE13 ...142 A3
Ellison Rd
Barnes SW13....... 133 D3
New Eltham DA15 ....167 B3
Streatham SW16 .... 182 A3
Ellis Rd Mitcham CR4. 202 D3
Southall UB2 .... 108 A5
Ellis St SW1 ..115 A2 258 A4
Elliston Ho 8 SE18 ..122 C2
Ellora Rd SW16 ...... 181 D5
Ellswood Ct 18 KT6 . 197 D2
Ellsworth St E2.......96 B4
Ellwood Ct 1 W9......91 D3
Elmar Ct SW6.........135 A3
Elmar Rd N15.........51 B5
Elm Ave Ealing W5....110 B5
Ruislip HA4 ....40 B2
Elmbank N14.........16 A4
Elm Bank Dr BR1 ... 187 D1
Elm Bank Gdns
SW13..............133 C3
Elm Bank Mans
SW13..............133 C3
Elmbank Way W7 ......86 B2
Elmbourne Dr DA17. 125 D2
Elmbourne Rd SW17 159 B1
Elmbridge Ave KT5 ..199 A3
Elmbridge Cl HA4.....40 A3
Elmbridge Dr HA4 ....40 A3
Elmbridge Wlk E8 ....74 A1
Elmbridge Xcel Leisure
Complex KT12 ......194 B4
Elmbrook 3 E18......55 A6
Elmbrook Cl TW16 ...172 B2
Elmbrook Gdns SE9...144 A1
Elmbrook Rd SM1....217 B4
Elm Cl
Buckhurst Hill IG9 .....21 D2
Carshalton SM5..... 202 D1
Harrow HA2..........41 D3
Hayes UB3............84 A1
Hendon NW4 ....46 D4
South Croydon CR2 .. 221 C2
Tolworth KT5 .... 199 A2
Twickenham TW13,
TW2 .... 151 D2
Upper Holloway N19 ...71 C6
Wanstead E11 ....55 B3
West Barnes SW20 .. 200 C5
Elmcote HA5 ....22 D1
Elmcourt Rd SE21,
SE27............... 160 D2
Elm Court Sch SE27. 161 A2
Elm Cres Ealing W5 ...110 A4
Kingston u T KT2 .... 176 A2
Elmcroft Highgate N6 ..49 C2
Hornsey Vale N8 ....50 B4
Elmcroft Ave
Blackfen DA15...... 168 A5
Enfield N9 ....18 B5
Golders Green NW11...47 B2
Wanstead E11 ....55 B5
Elmcroft Cl
Chessington KT9.... 214 A5
Ealing W5............87 D1
Feltham TW14 ...... 149 D5
Wanstead E11 ....55 B5
Elmcroft Cres
Harrow HA2..........41 C6
Hendon NW11 ....47 A2
Elmcroft Dr
Ashford TW15 ...... 170 C5
Chessington KT9 .... 214 A5
Elmcroft Gdns NW9...44 C4
Elmcroft St E5........74 C4
Elmcroft Terr UB8.....82 C1
Elm Ct
5 Ashford TW16.... 171 D3
Brixton SW9........ 138 C4
Catford SE6 .... 163 D3
Chingford E4 ....36 A4
4 Finchley N3........29 C2
Lewisham SE13 ......142 B2
Mitcham CR4 .... 180 D1
42 Notting Hill W2.....91 C2
Strand EC4.......... 251 A6
Elm Ct Sch SE27 .....160 B4
Elmdale Rd N13 ....32 B5
Elmdene KT5.........199 A1
Elmdene Cl BR3 .....207 B4
Elmdene Rd SE18 ... 122 D1
Elmdon Rd
Hatton TW6 .... 127 D2
Elmdon Rd *continued*
Hounslow TW5....... 129 A3
Elm Dr Harrow HA2 ....41 D3
Sunbury TW16 ...... 172 C1
Elmer Cl EN2 ....4 B2
Elmer Ct HA1..........42 D3
Elmer Gdns
Edgware HA8..........26 D3
Isleworth TW7.......130 B2
Elmer Ho NW1...... 237 A4
Elmer Rd SE6.........164 A4
Elmer's Dr TW11 .....175 B4
ELMERS END 206 D6
Elmers End Rd BR3,
SE20...............206 C6
Elmers End Sta BR3. 206 D5
Elmerside Rd BR3 ...207 A5
Elmers Rd SE25......206 A2
Elmfield Ave
London N8 ....50 A4
1 Mitcham CR4 .... 181 A2
Teddington TW11.... 174 D5
Elmfield Cl HA1.......64 C6
Elmfield Ct DA16.....146 B4
Elmfield Ho
6 Canonbury N5......73 A3
22 London N2 ....30 B1
Paddington W9 ....91 C3
Elmfield Mans 5
SW17 ....159 A2
Elmfield Pk BR1 .....209 A6
Elmfield Rd
Bromley BR1 .... 209 A6
Chingford E4 ....20 B2
East Finchley N2 ......48 B6
Southall UB2 .... 107 A3
Upper Tooting SW17 ..159 B2
Walthamstow E17 .....52 D3
Elmfield Way
Paddington W9 ....91 C2
South Croydon CR2 .. 221 D1
Elm Friars Wlk NW1...71 D1
Elmgate Ave TW13 ...150 C1
Elmgate Ct HA8.......27 A5
Elmgate Gdns HA8....27 B6
Elm Gdns
Claygate KT10 ...... 212 D2
East Finchley N2 ......48 A6
Enfield EN2 ....5 B5
Mitcham CR4 .... 203 D5
Elm Gn W3 ....89 C1
Elm Gr
Cricklewood NW2 .....68 D4
Harrow HA2..........41 C2
Hornsey N8 ....50 A3
Kingston u T KT2 .... 176 A2
Orpington BR6....... 211 D1
Peckham SE15....... 140 A3
Sutton SM1 .... 217 D4
Wimbledon SW19 ... 179 A3
Woodford IG8 ....36 D5
Yiewsley UB7.........104 B6
Elmgreen Cl 8 E15 ...98 C6
Elmgreen Sch The
SE27...............160 B2
Elmgrove Cres HA1 ...43 A4
Elmgrove Fst & Mid Schs
HA3 ....43 A5
Elmgrove Gdns HA1...43 A4
Elm Grove Par SM6 ..219 A5
Elmgrove Rd
Croydon CR0 ....206 B2
Harrow HA1..........42 D4
Elm Grove Rd
Barnes SW13....... 134 A3
Ealing W5.......... 110 A4
Elm Hall Gdns E11 ....55 B3
Elm Hatch HA5 ....23 B3
Elm Ho
4 Cubitt Town E14 .. 120 A4
2 Kingston u T KT2...176 B3
Teddington TW11.... 175 C3
Elmhurst DA17 ......147 A6
Elmhurst Ave
London N2 ....48 B6
Mitcham CR4 ....181 B3
Elmhurst Cres N2.....48 B5
Elmhurst Ct
Carshalton SM5......218 B6
Croydon CR0 ....221 B3
Elmhurst Dr E18......37 A1
Elmhurst Lo 3 SM2..218 A1
Elmhurst Mans SW4 137 D2
Elmhurst Prim Sch
E7..................77 B1

Elmhurst Rd
Chislehurst SE9 ..... 166 A1
Enfield EN3 .... 6 C6
Tottenham N17 .... 33 D1
Upton E7 .... 77 B1
Elmhurst Sch for Boys
CR2 .... 221 B3
Elmhurst St SW4.... 137 D2
Elmhurst Villas
SE15 .... 140 C1
Elmington Cl DA5.. 169 D5
Elmington Rd SE5 ... 139 B5
Elmira St SE13...... 141 D2
Elm La SE6 .... 163 B2
Elm Lawn Cl UB8...... 60 A1
Elmlea Dr UB3........ 83 D2
Elm Lea Trad Est N17.. 34 B4
Elmlee Cl BR7 .... 188 B4
Elmley Cl 12 E6 .... 100 A2
Elmley St SE18....... 123 B2
Elm Lo SW6 .... 134 D4
Elmore Cl HA0........ 88 A5
Elmore Ho SW9..... 138 D3
Elmore Rd Enfield EN3 .. 6 D5
Leyton E11 .... 76 B5
Elmore St N1.......... 73 B1
Elm Park Ave N15..... 52 A3
Elm Park Ct HA5...... 40 C6
Elm Park Gdns
Chelsea
SW10 ..... 114 B1 256 C1
Hendon NW4 .... 46 D4
Elm Park Ho SW10.. 256 C1
Elm Park La
SW3 .... 114 B1 256 C1
Elm Park Mans
SW10 .... 266 B6
Elm Park Rd
Chelsea
SW3 ...... 136 B6 266 C6
Edmonton N21 .... 17 A4
Finchley N3 .... 29 B3
Pinner HA5 .... 40 D6
South Norwood SE25. 205 D6
Walthamstow E10 ..... 53 A1
Elm Pk Stanmore HA7 .. 25 C5
Streatham SW2 ...... 160 B4
Elm Pl Ashford TW15 .. 170 C5
SW7 .... 114 B1 256 C2
Elm Quay SW8 ...... 269 C5
Elm Rd Barnet EN5....... 1 B1
Beckenham BR3 ...... 185 B1
Chessington KT9 ..... 214 A4
Claygate KT10 ...... 212 D2
East Bedfont TW14 .. 149 B4
Hackbridge SM6 .... 203 A1
Kingston u T KT2 ..... 176 B2
Leyton E11 .... 76 B6
Mortlake SW14 ...... 133 A1
New Malden KT3 ..... 199 B6
Sidcup DA14 .... 190 A6
South Norwood CR7 .. 205 B5
Stoneleigh KT17 ..... 215 D2
Stratford E7 .... 76 D2
Tottenham N22 .... 32 D2
Walthamstow E17 ..... 54 A4
Wembley HA9 .... 66 A3
Elm Rd W SM4 .... 201 B2
Elm Row NW3 .... 70 A5
Elms Ave Hendon NW4 . 46 D4
Muswell Hill N10 ...... 49 B6
Elmscott Gdns N21 ... 17 A5
Elmscott Rd BR1 .... 186 D5
Elms Cotts 1 CR4 .. 180 D1
Elms Cres SW4 ...... 159 D5
Elms Ct
Merton SW19 .... 179 D3
Wembley HA0 .... 65 A4
Elmsdale Rd E17 ...... 53 B5
Elms Gdns
Dagenham RM9 .... 81 B4
Wembley HA0 .... 65 A4
Elmshaw Rd SW15 ... 156 A6
Elmside CR0 .... 223 D2
Elmside Rd HA9 ...... 66 C5
Elms La HA0 .... 65 A5
Elmsleigh Ave HA3 .... 43 C5
Elmsleigh Ct SM1 ... 217 D5
Elmsleigh Ho TW2 ... 152 B2
Elmsleigh Rd TW2 ... 152 B2
Elmslie Ct SE9 ...... 166 C5
Elmslie Point 2 E3 .... 97 B2
Elms Mews W2 ..... 246 C6
Elms Park Ave HA0 .... 65 A4
Elms Rd
Clapham Pk SW4 .... 159 C6
Elms Rd *continued*
Harrow HA3 .... 24 C3
Elm St WC1 .... 94 B3 240 D5
ELMSTEAD 188 A5
Elmstead Ave
Elmstead BR7 .... 188 B5
Wembley HA9 .... 66 B6
Elmstead Cl
Totteridge N20 .... 13 C2
West Ewell KT19 .... 215 C3
Elmstead Ct HA9 ...... 44 B1
Elmstead Gdns KT4 .. 216 A5
Elmstead Glade BR7 .. 188 B4
Elmstead La BR7 ..... 188 B5
Elmstead Rd IG3 .... 79 D6
Elmstead Woods Sta
BR7 .... 188 A4
Elmsted Cres DA16 .. 146 C6
Elms The
5 Ashford TW15 .... 170 C5
Barnes SW13 .... 133 D2
Claygate KT10 ...... 212 D1
Croydon CR0 .... 205 A1
3 Harlesden NW10 .... 89 C5
Kingsbury NW9 .... 45 A3
Plashet E12 .... 78 A2
Wallington SM6 ..... 219 C4
Elmstone Rd SW6 ... 265 A2
Elmsway TW15 ...... 170 C5
Elmsworth Ave TW3. 129 D3
Elm Terr
Child's Hill NW2 .... 69 C5
3 Eltham SE9 .... 166 C5
Harrow HA3 .... 24 B2
Elmton Ct NW8 ..... 236 C6
Elm Tree Ave KT10 .. 196 C2
Elm Tree Cl
Ashford TW15 ...... 170 D5
Northolt UB5 .... 85 B5
St John's Wood
NW8 .... 92 B4 229 C2
Elmtree Ct HA4 .... 40 A1
Elm Tree Ct
5 Camberwell SE5 .. 139 A4
18 Charlton SE7 ..... 143 C6
St John's Wood NW8 . 229 C2
Elmtree Rd TW11 .... 174 C5
Elm Tree Rd
NW8 .... 92 B4 229 C2
Elm View Ct UB2 ..... 107 C2
Elm Way London N11 ... 31 A4
North Cheam KT4 ... 216 C5
West Ewell KT19 .... 215 B3
Willesden NW10 ...... 67 C4
Elm Wlk
Child's Hill NW3 .... 69 C6
Orpington BR6 ...... 226 B5
West Barnes SW20 .. 200 D5
Elmwood Ave
Bowes Pk N13 .... 32 A5
Feltham TW13 .... 150 B1
Harrow HA3 .... 43 B3
Elmwood Cl
Hackbridge SM6 .... 219 B6
Stoneleigh KT17 ..... 216 A1
Elmwood Cres NW9 ... 45 A5
Elmwood Ct
Battersea SW11 .... 268 C2
Walthamstow E10 ..... 53 C1
Wembley HA0 .... 65 A5
Elmwood Dr
Sidcup DA5 .... 169 A4
Stoneleigh KT17 ..... 216 A1
Elmwood Gdns W7 .... 86 C1
Elmwood Ho
Enfield EN2 .... 4 D1
Feltham TW13 .... 150 B1
Elmwood Inf Sch
CR0 .... 204 D3
Elmwood Jun Sch
CR0 .... 204 D2
Elm Wood Prim Sch
SE27 .... 161 B1
Elmwood Rd
Chiswick W4 .... 133 A6
Herne Hill SE24 ..... 161 B6
Mitcham CR4 .... 202 D6
Thornton Heath CR0 . 204 D2
Elmworth Gr SE21 ... 161 B2
Elnathan Mews W9 ... 91 D3
Elphinstone Ct
SW16 .... 182 A4
Elphinstone Rd E17 ... 35 B1
Elphinstone St N5 .... 72 D4
Elrington Rd
Dalston E8 .... 74 A2
Elrington Rd *continued*
Woodford IG8 .... 37 A5
Elsa Ct BR3 .... 185 B2
Elsa Rd DA16 .... 146 C3
Elsa St E1 .... 97 A2
Elsdale Ho 14 E9 ...... 74 C2
Elsdale St E9 .... 74 C1
Elsden Mews E2 ...... 96 C5
Elsden Rd N17 .... 33 D2
Elsenham Rd E12 ..... 78 C3
Elsenham St SW18,
SW19 .... 157 B2
Elsfield NW5 .... 71 B3
Elsham Rd
Kensington
W14 ...... 113 A4 244 A1
Leyton E11 .... 76 C4
Elsham Terr W14 .... 244 A1
Elsiedene Rd N21 ..... 17 A4
Elsie Lane Ct W2 ...... 91 D2
Elsiemaud Rd SE4 ... 163 B6
Elsie Rd SE22 .... 139 D1
Elsinge Rd EN1 .... 6 B6
Elsinore Ave TW19 ... 148 A4
Elsinore Gdns NW2 ... 69 A5
Elsinore Ho
12 Camberwell SE5 .. 139 A3
Islington N1 .... 234 A5
7 Woolwich SE7 .... 122 A2
Elsinore Rd SE23 .... 163 A3
Elsinore Way TW9 ... 132 D2
Elsley Ct HA9 .... 66 D2
Elsley Prim Sch HA9 .. 66 B2
Elsley Rd SW11 ...... 137 A2
Elsley Sch 8 SW17 . 158 C2
Elspeth Rd
London SW11 .... 136 D1
Wembley HA0 .... 66 A3
Elsrick Ave SM4 ..... 201 C4
Elstan Way CR0 ...... 207 A2
Elstead Ct SM3 ...... 201 A1
Elstead Ho 9 SW2 ... 160 B4
Elsted St
SE17 .... 117 B2 262 D3
Elstow Cl Eltham SE9 .. 166 B6
Ruislip HA4 .... 40 D2
Elstow Gdns RM9 .... 103 A6
Elstow Grange NW6 ... 68 D1
Elstow Rd RM9 ...... 103 A6
ELSTREE 10 A5
Elstree Gdns
Abbey Wood DA17 ... 125 A2
Edmonton N9 .... 18 B3
Ilford IG1 .... 79 A3
Elstree Hill BR1 ..... 186 C3
Elstree Hill N WD6 ..... 9 D6
Elstree Hill S WD6 ..... 9 D4
Elstree Ho 3 HA7 ...... 25 C6
Elstree Pk WD6 .... 11 B5
Elstree Rd
Bushey WD23 .... 8 C4
Elstree WD6 .... 9 A5
Elswick Rd SE13 ..... 141 D3
Elswick St SW6 ...... 136 A3
Elsworth Cl TW14 ... 149 C3
Elsworthy KT7 .... 196 C3
Elsworthy Rd
NW3 .... 92 C6 230 A6
Elsworthy Rise NW3 ... 70 C1
Elsworthy Terr NW3 ... 70 C1
Elsynge Rd SW18 .... 158 B6
Elsynge Road Mans
SW18 .... 158 B6
ELTHAM 166 B6
Eltham CE Prim Sch
SE9 .... 166 B6
Eltham Coll SE9 .... 165 D2
Eltham Coll Jun Sch
SE9 .... 165 D3
Eltham Green Rd
SE9 .... 165 C6
Eltham Green Specialist
Sports Coll SE9 ... 165 D5
Eltham High St SE9 .. 166 B5
Eltham Hill SE9 ...... 166 A6
Eltham Hill Tech Coll
SE9 .... 166 A5
Eltham Pal★ SE9 ..... 166 A4
Eltham Palace Rd
SE9 .... 165 D5
Eltham Park Gdns
SE9 .... 144 C1
Eltham Rd SE9, SE12 .. 165 B6
Eltham Sta SE9 ...... 166 B6
Elthiron Rd
SW6 .... 135 C4 265 B1
Elthorne Ave W7 ..... 109 A4
Elthorne Ct
Feltham TW13 ...... 150 C3
Kingsbury NW9 .... 45 B3
Elthorne Park High Sch
W7 .... 108 D3
Elthorne Park Rd
W7 .... 109 A4
Elthorne Rd
London NW9 .... 45 B2
Upper Holloway N19 ... 71 D6
Elthorne Sp Ctr W7 . 108 D3
Elthorne Way NW9 ..... 45 B3
Elthruda Rd SE13 .... 164 B5
Eltisley Rd IG1 .... 78 D4
Elton Ave Barnet EN5 ... 13 B6
Wembley HA0 .... 65 B3
Wembley UB6 .... 64 D2
Elton Cl KT1 .... 175 C3
Elton Ho 3 E3 .... 97 B6
Elton Lo 4 W5 .... 110 A6
Elton Pl N16 .... 73 C3
Elton Rd KT2 .... 176 C2
Elton St 11 N16 .... 73 C3
Eltringham St SW18 .. 136 A1
Elvaston Ct EN5 .... 12 C6
Elvaston Mews SW7 256 B6
Elvaston Pl
SW7 .... 114 A3 256 B5
Elveden Ho 17 SW9 . 138 D1
Elveden Pl NW10 ...... 88 C5
Elveden Rd NW10 ..... 88 C5
Elvedon Rd TW13 ... 149 D1
Elvendon Rd N13 ...... 32 A4
Elver Gdns 10 E2 ...... 96 A4
Elverson Rd SE8 ..... 141 D3
Elverson Rd Sta SE8 141 D3
Elverton St
SW1 ...... 115 D2 259 C4
Elvin Ct NW9 .... 45 A2
Elvington Gn BR2 ... 208 D4
Elvington La NW9 ..... 27 C2
Elvin Ho 2 E9 .... 74 C2
Elvino Rd SE26 ...... 185 A5
Elvis Rd NW2 .... 68 C2
Elwill Way BR3 ...... 208 B5
Elwin St E2 .... 96 A4
Elwood Ho N5 .... 72 D5
Elwood St N4, N5 ...... 72 D5
Elworth Ho SW8 .... 270 D3
Elwyn Gdns SE12 .... 165 A4
Ely Cl SW20 .... 177 D1
Ely Cotts SW8 ...... 270 C3
Ely Court Flats SW6 . 264 A1
Ely Ct Holborn EC1 ... 241 B3
3 Maida Vale NW6 .... 91 C5
Ely Gdns
Borehamwood WD6 .... 11 B6
Redbridge IG1 .... 56 A2
Ely Ho Barnet EN4 .... 2 C1
Northolt UB5 .... 85 A6
22 Peckham SE15 ... 140 A5
Elyne Rd N4 .... 50 C3
Ely Pl EC1 ..... 94 C2 241 B3
Ely Rd Hatton TW6 ... 127 D3
Hounslow TW4 ...... 128 C2
Leyton E10 .... 54 A2
Thornton Heath CR0 . 205 B4
Elysan Pl CR2 .... 221 A1
Elysian Ave BR5 ..... 211 D3
Elysium Gate 7
SW6 .... 135 B3
Elysium Pl SW6 ...... 135 B3
Elysium St SW6 ...... 135 B3
Elystan Bsns Ctr
UB4 .... 106 C6
Elystan Ct SW15 ..... 156 B6
Elystan Pl
SW3 ...... 114 D1 257 C2
Elystan St
SW3 .... 114 C2 257 B3
Elystan Wlk N1 ..... 234 A5
Emanuel Ave W3 ...... 89 A1
Emanuel Ct Acton W3 .. 89 B1
10 Leyton E10 .... 53 D2
Emanuel Dr TW12 .... 173 B5
Emanuel Sch SW11 . 158 C6
Embankment SW15 . 134 D3
Embankment Gdns
SW3 ...... 136 D6 267 D6
Embankment Pier
WC2 .... 116 A5 250 B4
Embankment Pl
WC2 .... 250 B4
Embankment Sta
WC2 .... 116 A5 250 B4
Embankment The
TW1 .... 153 A3
Embassy Ct
Ealing W5 .... 110 B6
Kingston u T KT6 .... 197 D4
Sidcup DA14 .... 168 B1
St John's Wood NW8 . 229 D3
7 Wallington SM6 ... 219 B2
8 Wanstead E18 ...... 55 A6
Welling DA16 .... 146 B2
Wood Green N11 ...... 31 D4
Embassy Gdns BR3 .. 185 B2
Embassy Ho 2 NW6 .. 69 C1
Embassy Lo N3 .... 29 B1
Emba St SE16 .... 118 A4
Ember Cl BR5 .... 211 A2
Embercourt Rd KT10, KT7,
KT8 .... 196 C3
Ember Ct
2 Acton W12 ...... 111 C3
14 Hendon NW9 ...... 27 D1
Ember Farm Ave
KT8 .... 196 B3
Ember Farm Way
KT8 .... 196 B4
Ember Gdns KT10,
KT8 .... 196 C2
Ember Ho 8 BR1 .... 186 B5
Emberhurst Sch
KT10 .... 196 B2
Ember La KT10, KT8 .. 196 B2
Emberson Ho 7 E17 ... 54 A5
Emberton SE5 .... 139 C6
Emberton Ct EC1 .... 234 C1
Embleton Rd SE13 .. 141 D1
Embleton Wlk TW12 . 173 B5
Embry Cl HA7 .... 25 A6
Embry Dr HA7 .... 25 A4
Embry Way HA7 .... 25 A6
Emden Cl UB7 .... 104 C4
Emden St SW6 ...... 265 D2
Emerald Cl E16 ...... 100 A1
Emerald Ct N12 .... 30 A6
Emerald Gdns RM8 ... 59 C1
Emerald Rd NW10 ..... 89 B6
Emerald Sq UB2 .... 106 D3
Emerald St
WC1 .... 94 B2 240 C4
Emerson Apartments
N8 .... 50 B6
Emerson Ct 8
SW19 .... 179 A4
Emerson Gdns HA3 ... 44 B3
Emerson Ho N16 ...... 73 C3
Emerson Rd IG1 .... 56 C2
Emerson St
SE1 .... 117 A5 252 A4
Emerton Cl DA6 ..... 147 A1
Emery Hill St SW1 .. 259 B5
Emery St SE1 116 C3 261 B6
Emilia Cl EN3 .... 18 B6
Emily St 7 E16 .... 98 D1
Emirates Stad (Arsenal
FC) N7 .... 72 C4
Emlyn Gdns 3 W12 .. 111 C3
Emlyn Rd W12 ...... 111 D3
Emmanual Ho SE18 .. 123 B1
Emmanuel CE Prim Sch
NW6 .... 69 C3
Emmanuel Ct 3 EN4 .. 14 D3
Emmanuel Ho
Dulwich SE21 .... 161 B1
Lambeth SE11 ...... 261 A3
Emmanuel Rd
Northwood HA6 .... 22 A3
Streatham SW12 .... 159 D3
Emma Rd E13 .... 98 D5
Emma St E2 .... 96 B5
Emmeline Ct KT12 ... 194 C2
Emminster NW6 .... 91 D6
Emmott Ave IG6 .... 57 A4
Emmott Cl
London NW11 .... 48 A3
Mile End E1 .... 97 A3
Emperor's Gate
SW7 .... 114 A2 256 A4
Empingham Ho 20
SE8 .... 118 D2
Empire Ave N18 ...... 33 A4
Empire Ct HA9 .... 66 D5
Empire Ho
Brompton SW3 ..... 257 A5
Edmonton N18 .... 33 B4

Empire Par
Edmonton N18 33 B4
Wembley HA9 66 C5
Empire Rd UB6 65 C1
Empire Sq N19 72 A5
Empire Way HA9 66 C4
Empire Wharf E3 97 A6
Empire Wharf Rd E14 120 B2
Empress Ave
Chingford E4 35 D3
Ilford IG1 78 C6
Wanstead E12 77 D6
Woodford IG8 36 D3
Empress Dr BR7 188 D4
Empress Mews [36] SE5 139 A3
Empress Par E4 35 C3
Empress Pl SW5 113 C1 255 A1
Empress St SE17 139 A6
Empson St E3 97 D3
Emsworth Cl N9 18 C3
Emsworth St SW2 160 B2
Emu Rd SW8 137 B3
Ena Rd SW16 204 A6
Enard Ho [28] E3 97 B5
Enbrook St W10 91 A4
Enclave Ct EC1 241 D6
Endale Cl SM5 218 D6
Endeavour Way
Barking IG11 102 A5
Thornton Heath CR0 204 A2
Wimbledon SW19 179 D6
Endell St WC2 94 A1 240 A1
Enderby St SE10 120 C1
Enderfield Ct BR7 188 C2
Enderley Cl HA3 24 C2
Enderley Ho SE19 183 D2
Enderley Rd HA3 24 C2
Endersby Rd EN5 12 C6
Enders Cl EN2 4 C4
Endersleigh Gdns NW4 46 A5
Endlebury Ct E4 20 B2
Endlebury Rd E4 20 A2
Endlesham Ct [2] SW12 159 A4
Endlesham Rd SW12 159 A4
Endsleigh Gdns
Bloomsbury WC1 93 D3 239 C6
Ilford IG1 56 D1
Kingston u T KT6 197 C3
Endsleigh Ind Est UB2 107 B2
Endsleigh Mans [4] SW16 160 A1
Endsleigh Pl WC1 239 D6
Endsleigh Rd
Ealing W13 109 A6
Southall UB2 107 A2
Endsleigh St WC1 93 D3 239 D6
Endway KT5 198 D2
Endwell Rd SE4 141 A3
Endymion Rd
Harringay N4 50 D2
Tulse Hill SW2 160 B5
Energen Cl NW10 67 C2
ENFIELD 6 B2
Enfield Chase Sta EN2 5 A2
Enfield Cloisters [7] N1 95 C4
Enfield Coll EN3 6 C2
Enfield Cty Sch (Lower Sch) EN2 5 C5
Enfield Cty Sch (Upper Sch) EN2 5 B2
Enfield Gram Sch (Lower) EN1 5 B3
Enfield Gram Sch (Upper) EN2 5 B2
ENFIELD HIGHWAY 6 C3
Enfield Ho [24] SW9 138 A3
ENFIELD LOCK 7 B6
Enfield Lock Sta EN3 7 A6
Enfield Rd
Brentford TW8 109 D1
De Beauvoir Town E8, N1 73 C1
Enfield Rd *continued*
Enfield EN2 4 A2
Hatton TW6 127 C3
South Acton W3 110 D4
Enfield Ret Pk EN1 6 A2
Enfield Road Rdbt TW6 127 C3
ENFIELD TOWN 5 B1
Enfield Town Sta EN1 5 B2
ENFIELD WASH 6 D5
Enfield Wlk TW8 109 D1
Enford St W1 92 D2 237 C4
Engadine Cl CR0 221 D5
Engadine St SW18 157 C3
Engate St SE13 142 A1
Engel Pk NW7 28 C4
Engineer Cl SE18 144 C6
Engineers Way HA9 66 C4
England's La NW3 70 D2
England Way KT3 199 A5
Englefield
Bromley BR1 188 A1
Regent's Pk NW1 232 A1
Englefield Cl
Enfield EN2 4 C3
Orpington BR5 211 D5
Thornton Heath CR0 205 A3
Englefield Path BR5 211 D5
Englefield Rd N1 73 C1
Engleheart Dr TW14 149 D5
Engleheart Rd SE6 164 A4
Englewood Rd SW12 159 C5
English Gardening Sch The SW3 136 D6 267 C6
English Grounds SE1 253 A3
English Martyrs RC Prim Sch
Walworth SE17 117 B2 262 D3
Whitechapel E1 95 D1 243 D1
English St E3 97 B3
Enid St SE16 117 D3 263 D6
Enid Stacy Ho [11] N19 49 D2
Enmore Ave SE25 206 A4
Enmore Ct SW14 155 B6
Enmore Gdns SW14 155 B6
Enmore Rd
Croydon SE25 206 A4
Putney SW15 156 C6
Southall UB1 85 C3
Ennerdale Ave HA3, HA7 43 C6
Ennerdale Cl
Cheam SM1 217 B4
East Bedfont TW14 149 D3
Ennerdale Ct E11 55 A2
Ennerdale Dr NW9 45 C4
Ennerdale Gdns HA9 43 C1
Ennerdale Ho [3] N4 51 B2
Ennerdale Rd
Erith DA7 147 C4
Richmond TW9 132 B3
Ennersdale Rd SE13 164 B6
Ennis Ho [16] E14 97 D1
Ennismore Ave
Chiswick W4 111 D2
Greenford UB6 64 C3
Ennismore Gdns
Knightsbridge SW7 114 C3 257 A6
Thames Ditton KT7 196 C3
Ennismore Gdns Mews SW7 114 C3 257 A6
Ennismore Mews SW7 114 C3 257 A6
Ennismore St SW7 114 C3 257 A6
Ennis Rd London N4 50 C1
Shooters Hill SE18 145 A6
Ennor Ct KT4 216 C4
Ensbury Ho SW8 270 C4
Ensign Cl TW19 148 A3
Ensign Ct [12] E1 118 A6
Ensign Dr N13 17 A1
Ensign Ho [19] E14 119 C4
Ensign St E1 118 A6
Ensign Way
Stanwell TW19 148 A3
[2] Wallington SM6 220 A1
Enslin Rd SE9 166 C4
Ensor Mews SW7 256 C2
Enstone Rd Enfield EN3 7 A2
Enstone Rd *continued*
Ickenham UB10 60 B5
Enterprise Cl CR0 204 C1
Enterprise Ho IG11 101 D4
Enterprise Ho E4 20 A4
Enterprise Ho
[36] Hackney E9 74 C1
Walton-on-T KT12 194 B2
Enterprise Row N15 51 D4
Enterprise Way
College Pk NW10 90 A4
Teddington TW11 174 D4
Wandsworth SW18 135 C1
Enterprise Works EN3 7 B4
Enterprize Way SE8 119 B2
Enthoven Ho SE18 122 D2
Enton Pl TW3 129 D1
Enversham Ct SE23 163 A1
Envoy Ave TW6 127 D2
Epirus Mews SW6 265 A4
Epirus Rd SW6 135 B5 264 D4
Epping Cl
Millwall E14 119 C2
Romford RM7 59 D6
Epping Forest★ IG10 21 B6
Epping Glade E4 20 A5
Epping Ho [8] E5 74 A6
Epping New Rd IG9 21 B5
Epping Pl N1 72 C2
Epping Way E4 19 D5
Epple Rd SW6 135 B4 264 D2
Epsom Cl Erith DA7 147 D2
Northolt UB5 63 B3
Epsom & Ewell High Sch KT19 215 A3
Epsom Ho SM1 217 D4
Epsom Rd
Croydon CR0 220 C4
Ilford IG3 57 D3
Leyton E10 54 A3
Morden SM3, SM4 201 B2
Epsom Sq TW6 127 D3
Epstein Ct N1 234 D5
Epstein Rd SE28 124 B5
Epworth Rd TW7, TW8 131 B5
Epworth St EC2 95 B3 242 D5
Equity Sq [29] E2 95 D4
Erasmus St SW1 115 D2 259 D3
Erconwald St W12 89 D1
Erebus Dr SE28 123 B4
Eresby Dr BR3 207 C1
Eresby Ho SW7 247 B1
Eresby Pl NW6 69 C1
Erica Ct SW4 270 B1
Erica Gdns CR0 223 D5
Erica Ho London SE4 141 B2
[6] Wimbledon SW19 179 A3
Wood Green N22 32 C2
Erica St W12 112 A6
Eric Cl E7 77 A4
Eric Clarke La IG11 101 A4
Ericcson Cl SW18 157 C6
Eric Fletcher Ct [15] N1 73 A1
Eric Macdonald Ho SW6 265 B1
Eric Rd
Dagenham RM6 58 D2
Forest Gate E7 77 A4
Willesden NW10 67 D2
Eric Shipman Terr [2] E13 99 A3
Ericson Ho
London SE13 142 B1
Stamford Hill N16 51 D1
Eric St E3 97 B3
Eric Wilkins Ho [14] SE1 118 A1
Eridge Ho SE22 139 D2
Eridge House Sch [13] SW6 135 B3
Eridge Rd W4 111 B3
Erin Cl Bromley BR1 186 C3
Ilford IG3 58 A3
Erin Ct NW2 68 C2
Erindale SE18 145 B6
Erindale Ct [1] BR3 185 C2
Erindale Terr SE18 145 B6
ERITH 147 D6
Erith Rd
Belvedere DA17 125 D1
Erith Rd *continued*
Erith DA7 147 D2
Erlanger Rd SE14 140 D3
Erlesmere Gdns W13 109 A3
Ermine Cl TW4 128 C3
Ermine Ho [3] N17 33 D3
Ermine Rd
London SE13 141 D1
South Tottenham N15 51 D3
Ermine Side EN1 18 A6
Ermington Rd SE9 167 A2
Ernald Ave E6 100 A5
Erncroft Way TW1 152 D5
Ernest Ave SE27 182 D6
Ernest Bevin Coll SW17 158 C2
Ernest Cl BR3 207 C4
Ernest Cotts KT17 215 D1
Ernest Gdns W4 132 D6
Ernest Gr BR3 207 B4
Ernest Rd KT1 176 D1
Ernest Richards Twr E17 53 B3
Ernest Simmonds Ho SE14 140 C3
Ernest Sq KT1 176 D1
Ernest St E1 96 D3
Ernle Rd SW20 178 C3
Ernshaw Pl SW15 157 A6
Eros Ho SE6 163 D4
Eros (Shaftesbury Meml)★ W1 115 D6 249 C5
Erpingham Rd SW15 134 C2
Erridge Rd SW19 179 C1
Errington Manor [6] SM5 218 D5
Errington Rd W9 91 B3
Errol Gdns Hayes UB4 84 B3
West Barnes KT3 200 A5
Errol St EC1 95 A3 242 B5
Erskine Cl SM1 218 C5
Erskine Cres N17 52 B5
Erskine Hill NW11 47 C4
Erskine Ho
[7] Charlton SE7 143 C6
Pimlico SW1 259 A1
Erskine Rd
Carshalton SM1 218 B5
Primrose Hill NW3 70 D1
Walthamstow E17 53 B5
Erwood Rd SE7 122 A1
Esam Way SW16 182 C5
Escot Rd TW16 171 C3
Escott Gdns SE9 188 A6
Escot Way EN5 12 C6
Escreet Gr SE18 122 C2
Escuan Lo N5 73 A3
ESHER 212 A4
Esher Ave
Cheam SM3 216 D5
Walton-on-T KT12 194 A1
Esher CE Prim Sch KT10 212 A3
Esher Cl DA5 169 A3
Esher Coll KT7 196 C2
Esher Cres TW6 127 D3
Esher Gdns SW19 156 D2
Esher Ho [8] SW8 137 D3
Esher Mews [4] CR4 202 D6
Esher Park Ave KT10 212 A3
Esher Rd
East Molesey KT8 196 B4
Ilford IG3 79 C5
Esher Sta KT10 212 B6
Eskdale Enfield EN1 17 C6
Regent's Pk NW1 232 A3
Eskdale Ave UB5 85 B6
Eskdale Cl HA9 65 D6
Eskdale Rd DA7 147 C4
Esk Ho E3 97 B3
Eskmont Ridge SE19 183 C3
Esk Rd E13 99 B3
Esmar Cres NW9 46 A2
Esme Ho SW15 133 D1
Esmeralda Rd SE1 118 A2
Esmond Ct Barnet EN5 1 C1
Kensington W8 255 D6
Esmond Gdns W4 111 B2
Esmond Rd
Acton W4 111 B3
Kilburn NW6 91 B6
Esmond St SW15 135 A1
Esparto St SW18 157 D4
Espirit Ct E1 243 C3
Espirit Ho [6] SW15 157 A6
Essan Ho W13 87 B2
Essence Ct HA9 66 B6
Essenden Rd
Belvedere DA17 125 C1
South Croydon CR2 221 C1
Essendine Mans W9 91 C4
Essendine Prim Sch [11] W9 91 C4
Essendine Rd W9 91 C4
Essex Ave TW7 130 C2
Essex Cl Romford RM7 59 D5
Ruislip HA4 40 D1
Walthamstow E17 53 A5
West Barnes SM4 200 D2
Essex Ct
Barnes SW13 133 D3
Hammersmith W6 112 C3
Holborn EC4 241 A1
South Norwood SE19 183 B4
Essex Gdns N4 50 D3
Essex Gr SE19 183 B4
Essex Ho [4] Acton W3 88 C1
[2] Poplar E14 97 D1
Essex Lo [5] N10 31 B1
Essex Mans E11 54 B2
Essex Park Mews W3 111 C5
Essex Pk N3 29 D4
Essex Pl W4 111 A2
Essex Place Sq [5] W4 111 B2
Essex Prim Sch E12 78 A3
Essex Rd Acton W3 111 A6
Barking IG11 79 B1
Chingford E4 20 C3
Chiswick W4 111 B2
Enfield EN2 5 B1
Ilford RM6 58 C2
Islington N1 94 D6 234 D6
Leyton E10 54 A3
Plashet E12 78 A2
Romford RM7 59 D5
Walthamstow E17 53 A3
Willesden NW10 67 C1
Woodford E18 37 B1
Essex Rd S E11 54 B2
Essex Road Sta N1 73 A1
Essex St
Forest Gate E7 77 A3
Strand WC2 116 C6 251 A6
Essex Twr [4] SE20 184 B2
Essex Villas W8 113 C4 245 A1
Essian St E1 97 A2
Essington SW15 157 A5
Essoldo Way HA8 44 B6
Estate Way E10 53 B1
Estcourt Rd
Croydon SE25 206 B3
Fulham SW6 135 B5 264 C4
Estella Ave KT3 200 B5
Estella Ho [15] W11 112 D6
Estelle Rd NW3 70 D4
Esterbrooke St SW1 259 C3
Este Rd SW11 136 C2
Esther Cl N21 16 C4
Esther Doe Lo N21 16 C4
Esther Rd E11 54 C2
Estoria Cl [22] SW2 160 C4
Estreham Rd SW16 181 D4
Estridge Cl TW3 129 C1
Estuary Cl IG11 102 B4
Eswyn Rd SW17 180 D5
Etal Ho N1 72 D1
Etchingham Ct N12 30 A3
Etchingham Park Rd N3 29 D3
Etchingham Rd E15 76 A4
Eternit Wlk SW6 134 D4
Etfield Gr DA14 190 B5
Ethelbert Cl BR1 209 A6
Ethelbert Gdns IG2 56 C4
Ethelbert Ho E9 75 A4
Ethelbert Rd
Bromley BR1, BR2 209 A6
Wimbledon SW20 178 D2
Ethelbert St SW12 159 B3
Ethel Brooks Ho SE18 144 D6
Ethelburga St SW11 136 C4 267 B2

Ethelburga Twr SW11 . . . . 267 B2
Ethel Cotts RM6 . . . . 58 D6
Etheldene Ave N10 . . . . 49 C5
Ethelden Rd W12 . . . . 112 B5
Ethel Rankin Ct 8 SW6 . . . . 135 B3
Ethel Rd
Ashford TW15 . . . . 170 A5
Newham E16 . . . . 99 B1
Ethel St SE17 . . . . 262 B3
Ethelworth Ct 4 SW2 . . . . 160 C3
Etheridge Rd NW2 . . . . 46 C2
Etherley Rd N15 . . . . 51 A4
Etherow St SE22 . . . . 162 A4
Etherstone Gn SW16 . . . . 182 C6
Etherstone Rd SW16 . 182 C6
Ethnard Rd SE15 . . . . 140 B6
Ethronvi Rd DA7 . . . . 147 A2
Etienne Ho NW7 . . . . 28 C6
Etloe Ho E10 . . . . 53 C1
Etloe Rd E10 . . . . 75 C6
Eton Ave
East Barnet EN4 . . . . 14 C5
Finchley N12 . . . . 30 A3
Heston TW5 . . . . 129 C6
New Malden KT3 . . . . 199 B5
Primrose Hill NW3 . . . . 70 C1
Wembley HA0 . . . . 65 C4
Eton Cl SW18 . . . . 157 D4
Eton College Rd NW3 . 70 D2
Eton Ct
Hampstead NW3 . . . . 70 B1
Highgate N6 . . . . 49 B3
Wembley HA0 . . . . 65 C4
Eton Garages 11 NW3 . . . . 70 C2
Eton Gr
Lewisham SE13 . . . . 142 C2
Queensbury NW9 . . . . 44 C5
Eton Hall NW3 . . . . 70 D2
Eton Ho Hackney E9 . . . . 75 B2
Highbury N5 . . . . 72 D4
Eton Manor Ct E10 . . . . 75 C6
Eton Pl NW1 . . . . 71 A1
Eton Rd
Harlington UB3 . . . . 127 D5
Ilford IG1 . . . . 79 B4
Maitland Pk NW3 . . . . 70 D2
Eton Rise NW3 . . . . 70 D2
Eton St TW10 . . . . 154 A6
Eton Villas NW3 . . . . 70 D2
Etta St SE8 . . . . 141 A6
Ettrick Ho 8 E5 . . . . 74 B6
Ettrick St E14 . . . . 98 A1
Etwell Pl KT5 . . . . 198 B3
Euesden Cl N9 . . . . 18 B1
Eugene Cotter Ho SE17 . . . . 262 D3
Eugenia Rd SE16 . . . . 118 C2
Eugenie Mews BR7 . 188 D2
Eureka Rd 8 KT1 . . . . 176 C1
Euro Bsns Ctr 3 E15 . . 98 D6
Eurocentres SW1 . . . . 115 B2 258 D3
Euro Cl NW10 . . . . 68 A2
Eurolink Bsns Ctr SW2 . . . . 160 C6
Europa Pl EC1 . . . . 235 A1
European Coll 45 E1 . . 96 A1
Europe Rd SE18 . . . . 122 B3
Eustace Bldg SW8 . . 268 C5
Eustace Ho SE11 . . . . 260 C4
Eustace Pl SE18 . . . . 122 B2
Eustace Rd
Dagenham RM6 . . . . 58 D2
Newham E6 . . . . 100 A4
Walham Green SW6 . . . . 135 C5 265 A4
Euston Ct 5 HA0 . . . . 66 A2
Euston Rd
Fitzrovia NW1 . . . . 93 C3 239 B6
Thornton Heath CR0 . 204 C1
Euston Sq NW1 . . . . 232 C1
Euston Square Sta WC1 . . . . 93 C3 239 B6
Euston St NW1 . . . . 93 C4 232 B1
Euston Sta NW1 . . . . 93 D4 232 C1
Euston Underpass NW1 . . . . 239 A6
Evan Cook Cl SE15 . . . 140 C4
Evandale Rd SW9 . . . . 138 C3
Evangelist Rd NW5 . . . 71 B4
Evans Cl E8 . . . . 73 D2
Evans Gr TW13 . . . . 151 C2
Evans Ho
34 Shepherd's Bush W12 . . . . 112 B6
South Lambeth SW8 . 269 D3
Evans Rd SE6 . . . . 164 C2
Evanston Ave E4 . . . . 36 A3
Evanston Gdns IG4 . . . 56 A3
Eva Rd RM6 . . . . 58 D2
Eve Ct CR4 . . . . 181 A1
Evelina Mans 9 SE5 . . . . 139 B5
Evelina Rd
London SE15 . . . . 140 C3
Penge SE20 . . . . 184 D3
Eveline Ct N10 . . . . 49 B4
Eveline Lowe Prim Sch 23 SE1 . . . . 118 A1
Eveline Rd CR4 . . . . 180 D2
Evelyn Ave
London NW9 . . . . 45 B5
Ruislip HA4 . . . . 39 D2
Evelyn Cl TW2 . . . . 151 D4
Evelyn Cres TW16 . . . 171 D2
Evelyn Ct
Chislehurst SE9 . . . . 166 A2
Marylebone W1 . . . . 237 C1
Shacklewell E8 . . . . 74 A4
Shoreditch N1 . . . . 235 C3
Evelyn Denington Ct 2 N1 . . . . 72 D1
Evelyn Denington Rd E6 . . . . 100 A3
Evelyn Dr HA5 . . . . 22 D3
Evelyn Fox Ct W10 . . . . 90 C2
Evelyn Gdns
Richmond TW9 . . . . 132 A1
South Kensington SW7 . . . . 114 B1 256 C1
Evelyn Gr Ealing W5 . . . 110 B5
Southall UB1 . . . . 85 B1
Evelyn Grace Acad SW9 . . . . 138 C1
Evelyn Ho
Bedford Pk W12 . . . . 111 D4
3 Brixton SW2 . . . . 160 B6
Harrow HA1 . . . . 42 B4
18 Spitalfields E1 . . . . 96 A2
Evelyn Rd Acton W4 . . . 111 B3
Cockfosters EN4 . . . . 2 D1
Ham TW10 . . . . 153 C1
Newham E16 . . . . 121 B5
Richmond TW9 . . . . 132 A2
Walthamstow E17 . . . . 54 A5
Wimbledon SW19 . . . 179 D4
Evelyns Cl UB8 . . . . 82 C1
Evelyn St
Greenwich SE10 . . . . 142 A6
SE8 . . . . 119 A1
Evelyn Terr TW9 . . . . 132 A2
Evelyn Way
Sunbury TW16 . . . . 171 D2
Wallington SM6 . . . . 219 D4
Evelyn Wlk N1 95 B5 235 C3
Evelyn Yd W1 . . . . 239 C2
Evening Hill BR3 . . . . 186 A3
Evenlode Ho 5 SE2 . . 124 C4
Evenwood Cl SW15 . . 157 A6
Everard Ave BR2 . . . . 209 A1
Everard Ct N13 . . . . 16 B1
Everard Ho 33 E1 . . . . 96 A1
Everard Way HA9 . . . . 66 A5
Everatt Cl SW18 . . . . 157 B6
Eve Rd
Isleworth TW7 . . . . 131 A1
Leyton E11 . . . . 76 C4
Tottenham N17 . . . . 51 C6
West Ham E15 . . . . 98 C5
Everdale Ct N2 . . . . 48 C5
Everdon Rd SW13 . . . . 134 A6
Everest Ct
6 Chislehurst SE9 . . 166 A2
South Norwood SE19 . 183 C2
Everest Pl E14 . . . . 98 A2
Everest Rd
Eltham SE9 . . . . 166 B6
Stanwell TW19 . . . . 148 A4
Everett Cl Bushey WD23 . 8 C3
Pinner HA5 . . . . 39 D6
Everett Ho
Islington N7 . . . . 72 C4
Walworth SE17 . . . . 262 C2
Everett Wlk DA17 . . . . 125 B1
Everglade Ho E17 . . . . 35 B1
Everglades
Beckenham BR2 . . . . 208 C6
Hounslow TW3 . . . . 130 A2
Everglade Strand NW9 . . . . 27 D2
Evergreen Cl SE20 . . . 184 C3
Evergreen Ct 6 SM2 . . . . 218 A2
Evergreen Sq 3 E8 . . . 73 D1
Evergreen Way UB3 . 105 D6
Everilda St N1 . . . . 233 D5
Evering Rd E5, N16 . . . . 74 A5
Everington Rd N10 . . . . 30 D1
Everington St W6 . . . . 134 D6
Everitt Rd NW10 . . . . 89 B4
Everleigh St N4 . . . . 50 B1
Eversfield Ct SE12 . . . 165 B2
Eversfield Gdns HA8, NW7 . . . . 27 C3
Eversfield Rd TW9 . . . . 132 B3
Evershed Ho E1 . . . . 243 D2
Evershed Wlk W4 . . . . 111 B2
Eversholt Ct EN5 . . . . 14 A6
Eversholt St NW1 . . . . 93 D4 232 C2
Evershot Rd N4 . . . . 50 B1
Eversleigh Ct N3 . . . . 29 C3
Eversleigh Rd
Clapham SW11 . . . . 137 A3
Finchley N3 . . . . 29 B3
New Barnet EN5 . . . . 14 A6
Newham E6 . . . . 99 D6
Eversley Ave HA9 . . . . 66 C6
Eversley Cl N21 . . . . 16 B5
Eversley Cres
Hounslow TW7 . . . . 130 B4
Ruislip HA4 . . . . 61 D6
Southgate N21 . . . . 16 C5
Eversley Ho 12 E2 . . . . 96 A4
Eversley Mount N21 . . 16 B5
Eversley Park Rd N21 . 16 B5
Eversley Pk SW19 . . . . 178 B5
Eversley Prim Sch N21 . . . . 16 B5
Eversley Rd
Greenwich SE7 . . . . 143 B6
Kingston u T KT5 . . . . 198 B4
South Norwood SE19 . . 183 B3
Eversley Way CR0 . . . . 223 C5
Everthorpe Rd SE15 . 139 D2
Everton Bldgs NW1 . 232 A1
Everton Ct HA0 . . . . 65 D4
Everton Dr HA7 . . . . 44 A6
Everton Rd CR0 . . . . 206 A1
Evesham Ave E17 . . . . 35 C1
Evesham Cl
Belmont SM2 . . . . 217 C1
Greenford UB6 . . . . 85 D5
Evesham Ct
2 Ealing W13 . . . . 109 A5
2 Richmond TW10 . . . 154 B5
Evesham Gn SM4 . . . 201 D3
Evesham Ho
1 Bethnal Green E2 . . . 96 C5
Pimlico SW1 . . . . 258 D2
St John's Wood NW8 . 229 A5
Evesham Rd
London N11 . . . . 31 D5
Morden SM4 . . . . 201 D3
Stratford E15 . . . . 76 D1
Evesham St W11 . . . . 112 D6
Evesham Way
Clapham SW11 . . . . 137 A2
Ilford IG5 . . . . 56 C6
Evesham Wlk
Brixton SW9 . . . . 138 C3
Camberwell SE5 . . . . 139 B3
Evry Rd DA14 . . . . 190 C4
Ewald Rd SW6 . . . . 135 B3
Ewanrigg Terr IG8 . . . . 37 C5
Ewart Gr N22 . . . . 32 C2
Ewart Pl 13 E3 . . . . 97 B5
Ewart Rd SE23 . . . . 162 D4
Ewe Cl N7 . . . . 72 A2
EWELL 215 C1
Ewell By-Pass KT17 . . 216 A1
EWELL COURT 215 C2
Ewell Court Ave KT19 . . . . 215 C3
Ewell Park Gdns KT17 . . . . 216 A1
Ewell Park Way KT17 . . . . 216 A1
Ewell Rd
Cheam SM2, SM3 . . . . 216 D2
Ewell Rd *continued*
Surbiton KT6 . . . . 198 B2
Thames Ditton KT6, KT7 . . . . 197 B2
Tolworth KT6 . . . . 198 D1
Ewelme Rd SE23 . . . . 162 C3
Ewen Cres SW2 . . . . 160 C4
Ewen Henderson Ct 10 SE14 . . . . 141 A5
Ewen Ho N1 . . . . 233 C5
Ewer St SE1 . . . 117 A5 252 A3
Ewhurst 19 SW15 . . . 156 D5
Ewhurst Cl E1 . . . . 96 C2
Ewhurst Ct CR4 . . . . 202 B6
Ewhurst Rd SE4 . . . . 163 B5
Exbury Ho Hackney E9 . 74 C2
4 London SW9 . . . . 138 B1
Exbury Rd SE6 . . . . 163 C2
Excel Ct WC2 . . . . 249 D5
Excel Ex Ctr E16 . . . . 121 B6
Excelsior Cl KT1 . . . . 176 C1
Excelsior Coll N17 . . . . 33 C3
Excelsior Gdns SE13 . 142 A3
Excelsior Ind Est SE16 . . . . 140 C6
Exchange Apartments 4 BR2 . . . . 209 B5
Exchange Arc EC2 . . 243 B4
Exchange Cl N11 . . . . 15 A2
Exchange Ct WC2 . . . 250 B5
Exchange Mans 2 NW11 . . . . 47 B2
Exchange Pl EC2 . . . . 243 A4
Exchange The IG1 . . . . 78 D6
Exchange Wlk HA5 . . . . 41 A2
Exeforde Ave TW15 . . 170 C6
Exeter Cl E6 . . . . 100 B1
Exeter Ct Kilburn NW6 . . 91 C5
Kingston u T KT6 . . . . 198 A4
Mitcham SW19 . . . . 180 C3
Exeter Gdns IG1 . . . . 56 B1
Exeter Ho
7 Barking IG11 . . . . 80 A1
Feltham TW13 . . . . 151 C2
Paddington W2 . . . . 236 A2
11 Peckham SE15 . . . . 140 A6
Putney SW15 . . . . 156 C5
Exeter Mans NW2 . . . . 69 A2
Exeter Mews
Fulham SW6 . . . . 265 A4
12 Hampstead NW6 . . . 69 D2
Exeter Rd
Bexley DA16 . . . . 145 D3
Brondesbury NW2 . . . . 69 A2
Croydon CR0 . . . . 205 D2
Dagenham RM10 . . . . 81 D2
East Barnet N14 . . . . 15 B4
Enfield EN3 . . . . 6 D2
Harrow HA2 . . . . 63 A6
Hatton TW6 . . . . 127 C2
Lower Edmonton N9 . . . 18 C2
Newham E16 . . . . 99 A2
Twickenham TW13 . . . . 151 B1
Walthamstow E17 . . . . 53 C4
Exeter St WC2 . . . . 116 B6 250 C6
Exeter Way
Hatton TW6 . . . . 127 C3
2 New Cross SE14 . . . 141 B5
Exford Ct SW11 . . . . 266 D2
Exford Gdns SE12 . . . . 165 B3
Exford Rd SE12 . . . . 165 B3
Exhibition Cl W12 . . . . 112 C6
Exhibition Rd SW7 . . . . 114 B3 256 D6
Exit Rd N2 . . . . 30 B1
Exmoor Ho 25 E3 . . . . 97 A5
Exmoor St W10 . . . . 90 D2
Exmouth Ho
Clerkenwell EC1 . . . . 241 B6
6 Millwall E14 . . . . 119 D2
Exmouth Market EC1 . . . . 94 C3 241 B6
Exmouth Mews NW1 232 B1
Exmouth Pl E8 . . . . 74 B1
Exmouth Rd
Bexley DA16 . . . . 146 C5
Hayes UB4 . . . . 83 C4
Ruislip HA4 . . . . 62 C5
Walthamstow E17 . . . . 53 B4
Exmouth St E1 . . . . 96 C1
Exning Rd E16 . . . . 98 D3
Exonbury NW8 . . . . 91 D6
Exon St SE17 . 117 C2 263 A3
Explorer Ave TW19 . . . 148 A3
Explorers Ct 6 E14 . . 120 B6
Express Dr IG3 . . . . 58 B1
Express Wharf 10 E14 . . . . 119 C4
Exton Cres NW10 . . . . 67 A1
Exton Gdns RM8 . . . . 80 C3
Exton Rd NW10 . . . . 67 A1
Exton St SE1 . . 116 C5 251 A3
Eyebright Cl 3 CR0 . 206 D1
Eyhurst Cl NW2 . . . . 68 A6
Eylewood Rd SE27 . . . . 183 A5
Eynella Rd SE21 . . . . 161 D4
Eynham Rd W12 . . . . 90 C1
Eynsford Cl BR5 . . . . 211 A3
Eynsford Coll W1 . . . . 93 D1 239 C2
Eynsford Cres DA5 . . 168 D3
Eynsford Ho
Borough The SE1 . . . . 252 C2
12 Deptford SE15 . . . 140 C6
Walworth SE17 . . . . 263 A3
Eynsford Rd IG3 . . . . 79 C6
Eynsford Terr UB7 . . . . 82 B1
Eynsham Dr SE2 . . . . 124 B3
Eynswood Dr DA14 . . . 190 C5
Eyot Gdns W6 . . . . 111 D1
Eyot Gn W4 . . . . 111 D1
Eyre Ct NW8 . . . . 229 C4
Eyre St Hill EC1 . . . . 94 C3 241 A5
Eysham Ct 12 EN5 . . . . 13 D6
Eythorne Rd SW9 . . . . 138 C4
Ezra St E2 . . . . 95 D4

F

Faber Gdns NW4 . . . . 46 A4
Fabian Rd SW6 . . . . 135 B5 264 D4
Fabian St E6 . . . . 100 B3
Fabyc Ho TW9 . . . . 132 C5
Factory La
Croydon CR0 . . . . 220 D6
Tottenham N17 . . . . 33 D1
Factory Rd E16 . . . . 122 A5
Factory Yd W7 . . . . 108 C5
Fagg's Rd TW14 . . . . 150 A6
Fairacre
Hounslow TW7 . . . . 130 B4
Kingston u T KT3 . . . . 199 C6
Pinner HA5 . . . . 40 A5
Fairacres
Putney SW15 . . . . 134 A1
Ruislip HA4 . . . . 39 D2
Fair Acres BR2 . . . . 209 A4
Fairbairn Gn 1 SW9 . . . . 138 D4
Fairbairn Hall E13 . . . . 99 A3
Fairbank Ave BR6 . . . . 226 D6
Fairbanks Rd N17 . . . . 52 A6
Fairbourne Ho UB3 . . 105 A3
Fairbourne Rd N17 . . . 51 C6
Fairbriar Residence SW7 . . . . 256 B4
Fairbridge Rd N19 . . . . 71 D6
Fairbrook Cl N13 . . . . 32 C5
Fairbrook Rd N13 . . . . 32 C4
Fairburn Ct SW15 . . . . 157 A6
Fairburn Ho
9 Stamford Hill N16 . . . 51 C1
West Kensington SW5 254 D1
Fairby Ho SE1 . . . . 263 D4
Fairby Rd SE12 . . . . 165 B6
Faircharm Trad Est SE8 . . . . 141 D5
Fairchild Cl 6 SW11 . . . . 136 B3
Fairchild Ho
13 Hackney E9 . . . . 74 C1
Pimlico SW1 . . . . 259 B3
5 Shoreditch N1 . . . . 95 C4
Fairchild Pl EC2 . . . . 243 B5
Fairchild St EC2 . . . . 243 B5
Fairclough Cl UB5 . . . . 85 B3
Fairclough St E1 . . . . 96 A1
Faircourt 14 NW3 . . . . 70 D2
Faircroft
6 Forest Hill SE26 . . 184 C6
Stoke Newington N16 . . 51 B1
FAIR CROSS 79 D3
Fair Cross IG11 . . . . 79 C3
Faircross Ave IG11 . . . . 79 A2
Faircross Par IG11 . . . . 79 C3

Fairdale Gdns
Hayes UB3 106 A4
Putney SW15 134 B1
Fairdene Ct N7 72 A3
Fairey Ave UB3 105 D3
Fairfax Cl KT12 194 B1
Fairfax Gdns SE3 143 C4
Fairfax Ho
11 Brixton SW9 138 C3
5 Ealing W5 88 A4
6 Putney SW15 156 A6
Fairfax Mews
London N8 50 D5
Newham E16 121 B5
Putney SW15 134 C1
Fairfax Pl
Kensington W14 254 B5
South Hampstead NW6 70 A1
Fairfax Rd Acton W4 111 C3
Hornsey N8 50 C5
South Hampstead NW6 70 A1
Teddington TW11 175 B3
Fairfax Way N10 31 A3
Fairfield
Camden Town NW1 232 A5
Oakleigh Pk N20 14 B4
Pinner HA6 22 A1
4 Stepney E1 96 C2
Fairfield Ave
Edgware HA8 26 D3
Hendon NW4 46 B3
Ruislip HA4 39 A2
Twickenham TW2 151 D3
Fairfield Cl
Blackfen DA15 167 D5
Enfield EN3 7 A1
Mitcham SW19 180 C3
North Finchley N12 30 A6
West Ewell KT19 215 C3
Fairfield Cres HA8 26 D4
Fairfield Ct
Harlesden NW10 90 A6
1 London SW18 157 D6
Ruislip HA4 39 B1
8 Woodford IG8 37 A4
Fairfield Dr
Harrow HA2 42 A6
Wandsworth SW18 157 D6
Wembley UB6 87 C6
Fairfield E KT1 176 A1
Fairfield Gdns N8 50 A4
Fairfield Gr SE7 143 D6
Fairfield Ind Est KT1 198 B6
Fairfield N KT1, KT2 176 A1
Fairfield Path CR0 221 B5
Fairfield Pl KT1 198 A6
Fairfield Rd
Beckenham BR3 185 C1
Bexleyheath DA7 147 B3
Bow E3 97 C5
Edmonton N18 34 A6
Higham Hill E17 35 A1
Hornsey N8 50 A4
Ilford IG1 78 D2
Kingston u T KT1 176 A1
Petts Wood BR5 211 B3
Plaistow BR1 187 A3
Southall UB1 85 B1
South Croydon CR0 221 C5
Woodford IG8 37 A4
Yiewsley UB7 104 A6
Fairfields SE6 163 D4
Fairfield S KT1 176 B1
Fairfields Cl NW9 45 A4
Fairfields Cres NW9 45 A4
Fairfields Rd TW3 130 A2
Fairfield St SW18 157 D6
Fairfield W KT1 176 A1
Fairfield Way
Barnet EN5 13 C6
West Ewell KT19 215 C3
Fairfoot Rd E3 97 C3
Fairford SE6 163 C3
Fairford Ave CR0 206 D4
Fairford Cl CR0 207 A4
Fairford Ct SM2 217 D1
Fairford Gdns KT4 215 D5
Fairford Ho SE11 261 B3
Fairgreen EN4 2 D2
Fairgreen Ct EN4 2 D2
Fair Green Ct 1
CR4 202 D6
Fairgreen E EN4 2 D2
Fairgreen Rd CR7 204 D4
Fairhall Ct KT6 198 B2
Fairhaven Ave CR0 206 D3
Fairhaven Ct 7 CR2 221 A3
Fairhazel Gdns NW6 70 A1
Fairheathe SW15 156 D5
Fairholme TW14 149 C4
Fairholme Cl N3 47 A5
Fairholme Cres UB4 84 A3
Fairholme Gdns N3 47 A5
Fairholme Ho 4
KT3 199 C5
Fairholme Prim Sch
TW14 149 B3
Fairholme Rd
Ashford TW15 170 B5
Cheam SM1 217 B2
Harrow HA1 42 D4
Ilford IG1 56 C2
Thornton Heath CR0 204 C2
West Kensington
W14 113 A1 254 B1
Fairholt Cl N16 51 C1
Fairholt Rd N16 51 B1
Fairholt St SW7 257 B6
Fairhurst 4 NW6 70 A2
Fairland Ho BR2 209 B5
Fairland Rd E15 76 D1
Fairlands Ave
Sutton SM1 217 C6
Thornton Heath CR7 204 C4
Woodford IG9 21 A2
Fairlands Ct 6 SE9 166 C5
Fairlawn SE7 143 C6
Fairlawn Ave
Acton W4 111 A2
Bexley DA7 146 D3
East Finchley N2 48 C5
Fairlawn Cl
Claygate KT10 212 D2
Feltham TW13 173 B6
Kingston u T KT2 177 A4
Southgate N14 15 D5
Fairlawn Ct 3 W4 111 A2
Fairlawn Dr IG8 37 A3
Fairlawnes SM6 219 B3
Fairlawn Gdns UB1 107 B6
Fairlawn Gr W4 111 A2
Fairlawn Mans SE14 140 D4
Fairlawn Pk SE26 185 A5
Fairlawn Prim Sch
SE23 162 C4
Fairlawn Rd SW19 179 B3
Fairlawns
4 Bowes Pk N11 32 A4
10 Chingford E4 20 A2
Pinner HA5 22 D1
Putney SW15 156 D6
Sunbury TW16 194 A6
Twickenham TW1 153 C5
Fairlead Ho 6 E14 119 C3
Fairlea Pl W5 87 D3
Fair Lea Pl W5 87 C2
Fairleas 12 BR3 185 D1
Fairley Ct HA0 65 D3
Fairley House Sch
SW1 259 D2
Fairlie Ct
22 Bromley E3 97 D4
1 Tufnell Pk N7 71 D4
Fairlie Gdns SE23 162 C4
Fairlight TW12 173 D5
Fairlight Ave
Chingford E4 20 B2
Harlesden NW10 89 C5
Woodford IG8 37 A4
Fairlight Cl
Cheam KT4 216 C4
Chingford E4 20 B2
Fairlight Ct
Greenford UB6 86 B5
4 Harlesden NW10 89 C5
Fairlight Rd SW17 180 B6
Fairline Ct BR3 186 A1
Fairlop Ct E11 54 C1
Fairlop Pl NW8 229 D1
Fairlop Rd E11 54 B2
Fairmark Cl UB10 60 C2
Fairmead
Bromley BR1 210 B5
Tolworth KT5, KT6 198 D1
Fairmead Cl
Bromley BR1 210 B5
Heston TW5 128 D5
Kingston u T KT3 199 B6
Fairmead Cres HA8 11 A1
Fairmead Ct
3 Chingford E4 20 C4
Oakleigh Pk N20 14 A4
Fairmead Gdns IG4 56 A4
Fairmead Ho E9 75 A4
Fairmead Rd
Lower Holloway N7,
N19 72 A5
Thornton Heath CR0 204 C2
Fairmeadside IG10 21 C6
Fairmile Ave SW16 181 D5
Fairmile Ho
St Paul's Cray BR5 190 A1
Teddington TW11 175 A6
Fairmont Ave E14 120 B5
Fairmont Cl DA17 125 B1
Fairmont Ho 1 E3 97 C3
Fairmount Rd SW2 160 B5
Fairoak Cl BR5 210 D2
Fairoak Dr SE9 167 B6
Fairoaks Gr EN3 6 D6
Fairseat Cl WD23 8 C2
Fair St
Bermondsey
SE1 117 D4 253 C2
Hounslow TW3 130 A2
Fairstead Lo 4 IG8 37 A4
Fairstead Wlk N1 235 A6
Fairthorn Rd SE7,
SE10 121 A1
Fairview Ave HA0 65 D2
Fairview Cl SE26 185 A5
Fair View Cl E17 35 A2
Fairview Cres HA2 41 C1
Fairview Ct
Ashford TW15 170 C5
Hendon NW4 28 D1
Kingston u T KT2 176 D2
Fairview Dr
Littleton TW17 192 B4
Orpington BR6 227 B4
Fairview Gdns IG8 37 B2
Fairview Ho 14 SW2 160 B4
Fairview Pl SW2 160 B4
Fairview Rd
Carshalton SM1,
SM5 218 C3
Enfield EN2 4 C4
South Tottenham N15 51 D3
Thornton Heath
SW16 182 B2
Fairview Way HA8 26 C6
Fairwall Ho 9 SE5 139 C4
Fairwater Ave DA16 146 A1
Fairwater Ho TW11 175 A6
Fairway Bexley DA6 169 A6
Petts Wood BR5 211 B4
West Barnes SW20 200 C6
Woodford IG8 37 C5
Fairway Ave NW9 44 D6
Fairway Cl
Croydon CR0 207 A4
Heston TW4 150 C6
Hounslow TW4 150 D6
North End NW11 48 A2
West Ewell KT19 215 A4
Fairway Ct
Edgware NW7 11 B1
12 Eltham SE9 166 C5
New Barnet EN5 13 D5
13 Rotherhithe SE16 118 D4
Fairway Dr
Erith SE28 103 A1
Greenford UB6 63 D1
Fairway Est TW4 150 C6
Fairway Gdns
Ilford IG1 79 A3
West Wickham BR3 208 B3
Fairway Prim Sch
NW7 11 B2
Fairways
Ashford TW15 170 D4
10 Chingford E4 20 A3
4 Hounslow TW7 130 C4
Stanmore HA7 26 A1
Teddington TW11 175 D3
Walthamstow E17 54 A5
Fairways Bsns Pk
E10 75 A6
Fairway The Acton W3 89 C1
Bromley BR1, BR2 210 B4
East Molesey KT8 195 D6
Edgware NW7 11 B1
Edmonton N13 17 B1
Hillingdon UB10 82 B5
Kingston u T KT3 177 B2
Fairway The *continued*
New Barnet EN5 13 D5
Northolt UB5 64 A2
Ruislip HA4 62 D5
Southgate N14 15 C5
Wembley HA0 65 B6
Fairweather Cl N15 51 C5
Fairweather Ct N13 32 B6
Fairweather Ho N7 72 A4
Fairweather Rd N16 52 A3
Fairwood Ct E11 54 B2
Fairwyn Rd SE26 185 A6
Faith Ct NW2 68 B2
Faithfull Ho N5 73 A3
Fakenham Cl
Hendon NW7 28 A3
5 Northolt UB5 63 C2
Fakruddin St E1 96 A3
Falcon Ave BR1 210 A5
Falconberg Ct W1 239 D2
Falconberg Mews
W1 239 D2
Falconbrook Prim Sch 26
SW11 136 B2
Falcon Cl
Chiswick W4 133 A6
Lambeth SE1 251 D4
Falcon Cres EN3 18 D6
Falcon Ct
9 Dulwich SE21 161 B2
Holborn EC4 241 A1
Islington N1 234 D3
New Barnet EN5 2 A1
Ruislip HA4 61 C6
6 Wanstead E18 55 B6
Falcon Dr TW19 148 A5
Falconer Ct N17 33 A3
Falconer Wlk 12 N7 72 B6
Falcon Gr SW11 136 C2
Falcon Ho
11 London SE15 139 D4
9 Merton SW19 179 D2
Falconhurst 4 KT6 198 A4
Falcon La SW11 136 C2
Falcon Lo
11 Paddington W9 91 C2
West Hampstead NW3 69 D4
Falcon Pk Ind Est
NW10 67 C3
Falcon Point SE1 251 D5
Falcon Rd
Battersea SW11 136 C2
Enfield EN3 18 D6
Hampton TW12 173 B3
Falconry Ct KT1 198 A6
Falcon Sch for Girls The
W5 110 B5
Falcons Pre Prep Sch
The 1 W4 132 D6
Falcons Prep Sch for
Boys The TW9 132 A1
Falcons Sch for Girls The
W5 110 B5
Falcon St E13 99 A3
Falcon Terr SW11 136 C2
Falcon Way
Feltham TW14 150 B6
Harrow HA3 44 A3
Hendon NW9 27 C1
Millwall E14 119 D2
Sunbury TW16 171 C1
Wanstead E11 55 A5
FALCONWOOD 145 C1
Falconwood Ave
DA16 145 C3
Falconwood Ct SE3 142 D3
Falconwood Par
DA16 145 D1
Falconwood Rd CR0 223 C1
Falconwood Sta SE9 145 B1
Falcourt Cl SM1 217 D3
Falkener Ct SW11 268 B1
Falkirk Ct 11 SE16 118 D5
Falkirk Gdns WD19 22 D5
Falkirk Ho W9 91 D4
Falkirk St N1 95 C5
Falkland Ave
Finchley N3 29 C3
Friern Barnet N11 31 B6
Falkland Ho
Catford SE6 186 A6
Kensington W8 255 C5
West Kensington W14 254 C2
Falkland Park Ave
SE25 183 C1
Falkland Pl 2 NW5 71 C3
Falkland Rd Barnet EN5 1 A3
Hornsey N8 50 C5
Kentish Town NW5 71 C3
Falkner House Sch
SW7 256 B2
Fallaize Ave IG1 78 D4
Falling La UB7 104 A6
Falloden Ct NW11 47 C5
Falloden Way (Barnet By-
Pass) NW11 47 C5
Fallodon Ho
6 London SW8 137 D3
Paddington W11 91 B2
Fallow Court Ave
N12 30 A4
Fallow Ct 20 SE16 118 A1
Fallowfield
Lower Holloway N4 72 B6
Stanmore HA7 9 A1
Fallowfield Ct HA7 9 A1
Fallow Fields IG10 21 C4
Fallowfields Dr N12 30 C4
Fallows Cl N2 30 B1
Fallsbrook Rd SW16 181 C4
Falman Cl N9 18 A3
Falmer Rd Enfield EN1 5 C1
Walthamstow E17 53 D6
West Green N15 51 B4
Falmouth Ave E4 36 C5
Falmouth Cl
London SE12 164 D6
Wood Green N22 32 B3
Falmouth Gdns IG4 55 D5
Falmouth Ho
Bayswater W2 247 A6
Kennington SE11 261 B2
15 Kingston u T KT2 175 D2
6 Pinner HA5 23 B3
Falmouth Rd
SE1 117 A3 262 B5
Falmouth St E15 76 B3
Falmouth Way E17 53 B4
Falstaff Ct SE11 261 C3
Falstaff Ho 18 N1 95 C5
Falstaff Mews TW12 174 B5
Fambridge Cl SE26 185 B6
Fambridge Rd RM8 59 C1
Fane St W14 264 D6
Fan Mus The★ SE10 142 A5
Fann St EC1 95 A3 242 B5
Fanshawe Ave IG11 79 A2
Fanshawe Cres RM9 81 B3
Fanshawe Rd TW10 175 C6
Fanshaw Ho 6 E17 53 D6
Fanshaw St N1 95 C4
Fantail Cl SE28 102 C1
Fantail The BR6 226 B5
Fanthorpe St SW15 134 C2
Faraday Ave DA14 168 B2
Faraday Cl N7 72 B2
Faraday Ho
2 Balham SW12 159 B4
4 Belvedere DA17 125 C3
6 Gospel Oak NW5 71 B4
5 Hampton TW12 173 D4
Kensal Town W10 91 A2
6 Poplar E14 119 B6
Wembley HA9 67 A5
Faraday Lo SE10 120 D3
Faraday Pl KT8 195 C5
Faraday Rd
Acton W3 111 A6
East Molesey KT8 195 C5
Kensal Town W10 91 A2
Southall UB1 107 D6
Stratford E15 76 D2
Welling DA16 146 A2
Wimbledon SW19 179 D4
Faraday Way
Greenwich SE18 121 D3
Thornton Heath CR0 204 B1
Fareham Ho 13
SW15 156 A3
Fareham Rd TW14 150 C4
Fareham St W1 239 C2
Farendon Ho 15
SM2 218 A2
Farewell Pl CR4 180 C2
Faringdon Ave BR2 210 C3
Faringford Rd E15 76 C1
Farjeon Ho NW6 70 B1
Farjeon Rd SE3 143 D4
Farleigh Ave BR2 209 A2
Farleigh Ct CR2 221 A3
Farleigh Ho 7 KT2 176 D4
Farleigh Pl N16 73 D4

Farleigh Rd N16 . . . . . . 73 D4
Farleycroft 1 CR0 . . . 206 A1
Farley Croft BR2 . . . . . 186 C1
Farley Ct
Kensington W14 . . . . . 254 C6
Marylebone NW1 . . . . 238 A5
Farley Dr IG3 . . . . 57 C1
Farley Ho SE26 . . . . . . 162 B1
Farley Mews SE6 . . . . 164 A4
Farley Pl SE25 . . . . 206 A5
Farley Rd
Catford SE6 . . . . 164 A4
South Croydon CR2 . . . 222 B1
Farlington Pl SW15 . . 156 B4
Farlow Rd SW15 . . . . 134 D2
Farlton Rd SW18 . . . . . 157 D4
Farman Gr 2 UB5 . . . . 84 D4
Farman Terr HA3 . . . . . . 43 D5
Farm Ave
Child's Hill NW2 . . . . 69 B5
Harrow HA2, HA5 . . . . . 41 C3
Streatham SW16 . . . . . 182 A6
Wembley HA0 . . . . 65 C2
Farmborough Cl HA1 . 42 B2
Farm Cl Barnet EN5 . . . . 12 C6
Buckhurst Hill IG9 . . . . . 21 C1
Coney Hall BR4 . . . . . . 224 D5
Lower Halliford TW17 192 C2
Southall UB1 . . . . 107 D6
Sutton SM2 . . . . 218 B1
Uxbridge UB10 . . . . 60 D6
Walham Green SW6 . . 265 B4
Farmcote Rd SE12 . . . 165 A3
Farm Cotts E17 . . . . 53 A3
Farm Ct NW4 . . . . 46 A6
Farmdale Rd
Greenwich SE10 . . . . 121 A1
Sutton SM5 . . . . 218 C1
Farm Dr CR0 . . . . 223 B6
Farm End E4 . . . . 20 C6
Farmer Ho 4 SE16 . . . 118 B3
Farmer Rd E10 . . . . 53 D1
Farmers Mkt*
W8 . . . . 113 C5 245 B4
Farmers Rd SE5 . . . . 138 D5
Farmer St W8 . . . . . . 245 A4
Farmfield Rd BR1 . . . . 186 C5
Farm House Ct NW7 . . 28 A3
Farmhouse Rd
SW16 . . . . 181 C3
Farmilo Rd E17 . . . . 53 C2
Farmington Ave
SM1 . . . . 218 B5
Farm La Croydon CR0 . 223 B6
East Barnet N14 . . . . 15 B5
Walham Green
SW6 . . . . 135 C5 265 B4
Farmlands Enfield EN2 . . 4 C4
Pinner HA5 . . . . 40 A5
Farmlands The UB5 . . . 63 C2
Farmland Wlk BR7 . . 188 D5
Farm Lane Trad Ctr
SW6 . . . . 135 C6 265 B5
Farmleigh N14 . . . . 15 C4
Farmleigh Ho SW9 . . 160 D6
Farm Pl W8 . . . . 245 A4
Farm Rd Edgware HA8 . . 27 A5
Edmonton N21 . . . . 17 A3
Morden SM4 . . . . 201 D4
Stonebridge NW10 . . . . 89 B6
Sutton SM2 . . . . 218 B1
Thames Ditton KT10 . . 195 C1
Twickenham TW4 . . . . 151 A3
Farm St W1 . . . 115 B6 248 C5
Farmstead Ct 3
SM6 . . . . 219 B3
Farmstead Rd
Catford SE6 . . . . 185 D6
Harrow HA3 . . . . 24 B1
Farm Vale DA5 . . . . . . 169 D5
Farm View N3 . . . . 47 B6
Farmway RM8 . . . . 80 C5
Farm Way
Buckhurst Hill IG9 . . . . . 37 C6
North Cheam KT4 . . . . 216 C5
Farm Wlk NW11 . . . . . . 47 C4
Farnaby Ho 2 W10 . . . 91 B4
Farnaby Rd
Bromley BR1, BR2 . . . 186 C2
Kidbrooke SE9 . . . . . . 143 C1
Farnan Ave E17 . . . . 53 D6
Farnan Hall 6
SW16 . . . . 182 A5
Farnan Rd SW16 . . . . . 182 A5
FARNBOROUGH 227 B3
Farnborough Ave
South Croydon CR2 . . 223 A1
Walthamstow E17 . . . . . 53 A6
Farnborough Cl HA9 . . 66 D6
Farnborough Comm
Keston Mark BR2,
BR6 . . . . 226 B5
Orpington BR6 . . . . . . 226 C4
Farnborough Cres
3 Hayes BR2 . . . . . . 208 D1
South Croydon CR2 . . 223 A1
Farnborough Ct 2
BR6 . . . . 227 A3
Farnborough Hill
BR6 . . . . 227 C3
Farnborough Ho 1
SW15 . . . . 156 A3
Farnborough Prim Sch
BR6 . . . . 227 A3
Farnborough Way
BR6 . . . . 227 B3
Farncombe St SE16 . . 118 A4
Farndale Ave N13 . . . . . 17 A1
Farndale Cres UB6 . . . . 86 A4
Farndale Ho 3 NW6 . . 91 D6
Farnell Mews SW5 . . 255 C2
Farnell Pl W3 . . . . 110 D6
Farnell Rd TW7 . . . . . . 130 B2
Farnell's Almshouses
TW7 . . . . 130 D3
Farnfield Ho 12
SW2 . . . . 160 B6
Farnham Cl N20 . . . . . . 14 A4
Farnham Ct
2 Cheam SM3 . . . . . 217 A2
1 Southall UB1 . . . . 86 A1
2 Stamford Hill N16 . . . 51 C1
Farnham Gdns
SW20 . . . . 178 B1
Farnham Green Prim Sch
IG3 . . . . 58 A3
Farnham Ho
Borough The SE1 . . . . 252 A3
Marylebone NW1 . . . . 237 B5
Farnham Pl SE1 . . . . 251 D3
Farnham Rd
Bexley DA16 . . . . 146 C3
Ilford IG3 . . . . 57 D2
Farnham Royal
SE11 . . . . 116 B1 260 D1
Farnhurst Ho 7
SW11 . . . . 137 A3
Farningham Ct
SW16 . . . . 181 D3
Farningham Ho 9
N4 . . . . 51 B2
Farningham Rd N17 . . 34 A3
Farnley Ho 13 SW8 . . 137 D3
Farnley Rd
Chingford E4 . . . . 20 C4
South Norwood SE25 . . 205 B5
Farnsworth Ct SE10 . 120 D3
Farnsworth Ho 8
SW27 . . . . 182 D5
Farnworth Ho 5
E14 . . . . 120 B2
Faro Cl BR1 . . . . 188 C1
Faroe Rd W14 . . . . . . 112 D3
Farorna Wlk EN2 . . . . . . 4 C4
Farquhar Rd
Dulwich SE19 . . . . . . 183 D5
Wimbledon SW19 . . . 157 C1
Farquharson Rd
CR0 . . . . 205 A1
Farrance Rd RM6 . . . . . 59 A2
Farrance St E14 . . . . . . 97 C1
Farrans Ct HA3 . . . . 43 B2
Farrant Ave N22 . . . . . . 32 D1
Farrant Cl BR6 . . . . . . 227 D1
Farrant Ho 14 SW11 . . 136 B2
Farrants Ct BR1 . . . . . . 188 B1
Farr Ave IG11 . . . . 102 A5
Farrell Ho E1 . . . . 96 C1
Farren Rd SE23 . . . . . 163 A2
Farrer Ho SE8 . . . . . . 141 C5
Farrer Mews N8 . . . . . . 49 C5
Farrer Rd Harrow HA3 . . 44 A5
Hornsey N8 . . . . 49 D5
Farrer's Pl CR0 . . . . . 222 D4
Farrier Cl
Bromley BR1 . . . . 209 D6
Hillingdon UB8 . . . . 82 C1
Sunbury TW16 . . . . . . 194 A5
Farrier Pl SM1 . . . . . . 217 D6
Farrier Rd UB5 . . . . 85 C5
Farriers Ct
Belmont SM2 . . . . 217 A1
Wimbledon SW19 . . . 179 A3
Farriers Mews SE15 . . 140 C2
Farrier St NW1 . . . . 71 C1
Farriers Way WD6 . . . . 11 B6
Farrier Wlk
SW10 . . . . . . 136 A6 266 A6
Farringdon La
EC1 . . . . 94 C3 241 B5
Farringdon Rd
EC1 . . . . 94 C3 241 B5
Farringdon St
EC4 . . . . 94 D1 241 C2
Farringdon Sta
EC1 . . . . 94 D2 241 C4
Farrington Pl BR7 . . . 189 B3
Farringtons Sch
BR7 . . . . 189 B3
Farrins Rents SE16 . . . 119 A5
Farrow La SE14 . . . . . . 140 C5
Farrow Pl SE16 . . . . . . 119 A3
Farr Rd EN2 . . . . 5 B4
Farthingale Wlk E15 . . 76 B1
Farthing Alley 8
SE1 . . . . 118 A4
Farthing Ct 3 NW7 . . . 29 A3
Farthing Fields 8
E1 . . . . 118 B5
Farthings Cl
Chingford E4 . . . . 20 C1
Pinner HA5 . . . . 40 B3
Farthing St BR6 . . . . . . 226 B1
Farthings The 1
KT2 . . . . 176 C2
FARTHING STREET . . 226 B1
Farwell Rd DA14 . . . . . 190 C6
Farwig La BR1 . . . . 187 A2
Fashion Retail Acad The
W1 . . . . 239 C2
Fashion St E1 . 95 D2 243 D3
Fashion & Textile Mus*
SE1 . . . . 253 A2
Fashoda Rd BR2 . . . . . 209 D5
Fassett Rd Dalston E8 . . 74 A2
Kingston u T KT1 . . . . 198 A5
Fassett Sq E8 . . . . 74 A2
Fauconberg Ct W4 . . . 133 A6
Fauconberg Rd W4 . . . 133 A6
Faulkner Cl 6 RM8 . . . 58 D2
Faulkner Ho SW15 . . . 134 C3
Faulkner's Alley EC1 241 C4
Faulkner St SE14 . . . . 140 C4
Fauna Cl
Dagenham RM6 . . . . 58 C3
Stanmore HA7 . . . . 25 D6
Faunce Ho 1 SE17 . . 138 D6
Faunce St
SE17 . . . . 116 D1 261 C1
Favart Rd
SW6 . . . . 135 C4 265 B2
F Ave SE18 . . . . 122 D3
Faversham Ave
Chingford E4 . . . . 20 D3
Enfield EN1 . . . . 17 B5
Faversham Ct SE6 . . . 163 B3
Faversham Ho
Camden Town NW1 . . 232 B5
Walworth SE17 . . . . . 263 A1
Faversham Rd
Beckenham BR3 . . . . . 185 B1
Forest Hill SE6 . . . . . . 163 B3
Morden SM4 . . . . 201 D3
Fawcett Cl
London SW11 . . . . 136 B3
West Norwood SW16 182 C6
Fawcett Est E5 . . . . 52 A1
Fawcett Ho 25 SW9 . . 138 A3
Fawcett Rd
Croydon CR0 . . . . 221 A5
Willesden NW10 . . . . . . 67 D1
Fawcett St
SW10 . . . . . . 136 A6 266 A6
Fawcus Cl KT10 . . . . . 212 C2
Fawe Park Rd SW15 . . 135 B1
Fawe St E14 . . . . 97 D2
Fawkham Ho SE1 . . . 263 D3
Fawley Ct SE27 . . . . . 160 D2
Fawley Lo 2 E14 . . . . 120 B2
Fawley Rd NW6 . . . . . . 69 D3
Fawnbrake Ave
SE24 . . . . 161 A6
Fawn Rd E13 . . . . 99 C5
Fawns Manor Cl
TW14 . . . . 149 A3
Fawns Manor Rd
TW14 . . . . 149 B3
Fawood Ave NW10 . . . . 67 B1
Fayetville Ho 26 N19 . . 49 D2
Faygate Cres DA6 . . . . 169 C6
Faygate Ct CR2 . . . . . 220 D1
Faygate Rd SW2 . . . . . 160 B2
Fayland Ave SW16 . . . 181 C5
Fazal Laj IG1 . . . . 79 A6
Fazerley Ct 49 W2 . . . . 91 C2
Fearnley Cres TW12 . . 173 B4
Fearnley Ho SE5 . . . . . 139 C3
Fearon St SE10 . . . . . 121 A1
Featherbed La CR0 . . 223 B1
Feathers Pl SE10 . . . . . 142 B6
Featherstone Ave 4
SE23 . . . . 162 C2
Featherstone Ct NW7 28 A3
Featherstone High Sch
UB2 . . . . 107 A3
Featherstone Ho UB4 . 84 C2
Featherstone Ind Est
UB2 . . . . 107 A3
Featherstone Prim Sch
UB2 . . . . 106 C2
Featherstone Rd
Mill Hill NW7 . . . . 28 B4
Southall UB2 . . . . 107 A3
Featherstone St
EC1 . . . . 95 B3 242 C6
Featherstone Terr
UB2 . . . . 107 A3
Featley Rd SW9 . . . . . 138 D2
Federal Rd UB6 . . . . 87 C5
Federation Rd SE2 . . . 124 C2
Fee Farm Rd KT10 . . 212 D1
Felbridge Ave HA7 . . . . 25 B2
Felbridge Cl SW16 . . . 182 C6
Felbridge Ct
Croydon CR2 . . . . 221 A1
Feltham TW13 . . . . 150 B3
Harlington UB3 . . . . . . 127 B6
Felbridge Ho 21
SE22 . . . . 139 C2
Felbrigge Rd IG3 . . . . . 57 D1
Felday Rd SE13 . . . . . 163 D5
Felden Cl HA5 . . . . 23 A3
Felden St
SW6 . . . . 135 B4 264 C1
Feldman Cl N16 . . . . 52 A1
Feldspar Ct 6 EN3 . . . . . 7 A2
Felgate Mews 4
W6 . . . . 112 B2
Felhampton Rd SE9 . 166 D1
Felhurst Cres RM10 . . . 81 D4
Feline Ct 1 EN4 . . . . . . 14 C5
Felix Ave N8 . . . . 50 A3
Felix Ct E17 . . . . 53 D4
Felix La TW17 . . . . 193 D3
Felix Manor BR7 . . . . . 189 C4
Felix Neubergh Ct EN1 . 5 C1
Felix Rd Ealing W13 . . 109 A6
Walton-on-T KT12 . . . 194 A3
Felix St 19 E2 . . . . 96 B5
Felixstowe Ct E16 . . . 122 D5
Felixstowe Rd
Abbey Wood SE2 . . . . 124 B3
College Pk NW10 . . . . . 90 B4
Edmonton N9 . . . . 34 A6
Tottenham N17 . . . . 51 D6
Fellbrigg Rd SE22 . . . 161 D6
Fellbrigg St 21 E1 . . . . . 96 B3
Fellbrook TW10 . . . . . . 153 B1
Fell Ho 11 N19 . . . . 71 C5
Fellmongers Yd 1
CR0 . . . . 221 A5
Fellowes Cl UB4 . . . . . . 84 D3
Fellowes Ct UB3 . . . . . 127 B6
Fellowes Rd SM5 . . . . 218 C6
Fellows Ct E2 . . . . 95 D5
Fellows Rd NW3 . . . . . . 70 C1
Fell Rd CR0 . . . . 221 A5
Fells Haugh 6 W3 . . . . 89 A1
Felltram Way SE7 . . . . 121 A1
Fell Wlk HA8 . . . . 26 D2
Felmersham Cl 2
SW4 . . . . 137 D1
Felmingham Rd
SE20 . . . . 184 C1
Felnex Trad Est
SM6 . . . . 219 A6
Felpham Ct HA9 . . . . . . 65 D4
Felsberg Rd SW2 . . . . 160 A4
Fels Cl RM10 . . . . 81 D5
Felsham Ho 5
SW15 . . . . 134 D2
Felsham Mews 14
SW15 . . . . 134 D2
Felsham Rd SW15 . . . 134 D2
Felspar Cl SE18 . . . . . 123 D1
Felstead Cl N13 . . . . 32 C5
Felstead Rd E11 . . . . . . 55 A2
Felstead St E9 . . . . 75 B2
Felstead Wharf E14 . . 120 A1
Felsted Rd E16 . . . . 99 D1
FELTHAM 150 B2
Feltham Airparcs L Ctr
TW13 . . . . 150 D2
Feltham Arenas
TW14 . . . . 150 A4
Feltham Ave KT8 . . . . . 196 C5
Felthambrook Ind Est
TW13 . . . . 150 B1
Felthambrook Way
TW13 . . . . 172 B6
Feltham Bsns Complex
TW13 . . . . 150 B2
Feltham Com Sch
TW13 . . . . 150 C2
Feltham Corporate Ctr
TW13 . . . . 150 B1
FELTHAMHILL 171 D5
Feltham Hill Jun & Inf
Schs TW13 . . . . 149 D1
Feltham Hill Rd
Ashford TW15 . . . . . . 171 A4
Feltham TW13 . . . . . . 172 C5
Feltham Rd
Ashford TW15 . . . . . . 171 A6
Mitcham CR4 . . . . 181 A1
Feltham Sta TW13 . . . 150 B3
Felton Cl BR5 . . . . 210 D3
Felton Gdns IG11 . . . . 101 C5
Felton Ho
Kidbrooke SE9 . . . . . . 143 C1
Shoreditch N1 . . . . . . 235 D5
Felton Lea DA14 . . . . . 189 D5
Felton Rd
Barking IG11 . . . . 101 C5
Ealing W13 . . . . 109 C4
Felton St N1 . . . 95 B6 235 D5
Fenchurch Ave
EC3 . . . . 95 C1 243 A1
Fenchurch Bldgs
EC3 . . . . 243 B1
Fenchurch Pl EC3 . . . 253 B6
Fenchurch St
EC3 . . . . 117 C6 253 B6
Fenchurch Street Sta
EC3 . . . . 117 C6 253 B6
Fen Ct EC3 . . . . 253 A6
Fendall Rd KT19 . . . . . 215 A3
Fendall St
SE1 . . . . 117 C3 263 B5
Fender Ct 5 SW4 . . . . 138 A3
Fendt Cl 8 E16 . . . . 98 D1
Fendyke Rd SE2,
DA17 . . . . 124 D3
Fenelon Pl
W14 . . . . 113 B2 254 D3
Fen Gr DA15 . . . . 167 D5
Fenham Rd SE15 . . . . . 140 B5
Fenman Ct N17 . . . . 34 B2
Fenman Gdns IG3 . . . . 58 B1
Fenn Cl BR1 . . . . 187 A4
Fenn Ct HA1 . . . . 43 A4
Fennel Cl
Croydon CR0 . . . . 206 D1
Newham E16 . . . . 98 C3
Fennell St SE18 . . . . . 144 C6
Fenner Cl SE16 . . . . . . 118 B2
Fenner Ho 25 E1 . . . . . 118 B5
Fenner Sq 9 SW11 . . 136 B2
Fenn Ho TW7 . . . . 131 B4
Fenning Ct CR4 . . . . . 202 C5
Fenning St SE1 . . . . . 253 A2
Fenn St E9 . . . . 74 C3
Fen St E16 . . . . 120 D6
Fenstanton 3 N4 . . . . . 50 B1
Fenstanton Ave N12 . . 30 B5
Fenstanton Prim Sch 20
SW2 . . . . 160 C3
Fenswood Cl DA5 . . . . 169 C5
Fentiman Rd
SW8 . . . . 138 B5 270 C4
Fentiman Way HA2 . . . 63 D6
Fenton Cl
16 Dalston E8 . . . . 73 D2
Elmstead BR7 . . . . 188 B5

Fenton Cl *continued*
South Lambeth SW9 . . 138 B3
Fenton Ct TW3. . . . . . . 129 A5
Fenton Ho
Deptford SE14 . . . . . . 141 A5
Heston TW5. . . . . 129 C6
Fenton House* NW3 . 70 A5
Fenton Rd N17 . . . . 33 A3
Fentons SE3. . . . . 142 D5
Fenton's Ave E13 . . . . . 99 B5
Fenton St E1 . . . . 96 B1
Fenwick Cl 16 SE18 . . 144 C6
Fenwick Gr SE15. . . . . . 140 A2
Fenwick Pl
Croydon CR2 . . . . 220 D1
Stockwell SW9. . . . . . 138 A2
Fenwick Rd SE15 . . . . . 140 A2
Ferby Ct DA15 . . . . 189 D6
Ferdinand Ho 1
NW1. . . . . 71 B1
Ferdinand Pl NW1 . . . . 71 A1
Ferdinand St NW1 . . . . 71 A1
Ferguson Ave KT5 . . . 198 B4
Ferguson Cl BR2,
BR3. . . . . 208 B6
Ferguson Dr W3 . . . . . . 89 B1
Ferguson Ho SE10 . . . 142 A4
Ferguson's Cl E14 . . . 119 C2
Fergus Rd N5. . . . . 72 D3
Fermain Ct E N1 . . . . . . 95 C6
Fermain Ct N N1. . . . . . 95 C6
Fermain Ct W N1 . . . . . 95 C6
Ferme Park Rd N4,
N8. . . . . 50 B3
Fermor Rd SE23 . . . . . 163 A3
Fermoy Rd
Greenford UB6. . . . . . . 85 D3
West Kilburn W9 . . . . . . 91 B3
Fern Ave CR4 . . . . 203 D5
Fernbank IG9 . . . . 21 B3
Fernbank Ave
Walton-on-T KT12 . . . 195 A2
Wembley HA0 . . . . 64 D3
Fernbank Mews
SW12 . . . . 159 C5
Fernbrook Cres
SE13. . . . . 164 C5
Fernbrook Dr HA2 . . . . 41 D2
Fernbrook Rd SE13 . . 164 C5
Fern Cl 3 N1. . . . . 95 C5
Ferncliff Rd E8 . . . . 74 A3
Ferncroft Ave
London N12 . . . . 30 D4
Ruislip HA4 . . . . 62 C6
West Hampstead NW3 . 69 C4
Fern Ct
Bexleyheath DA7. . . . 147 C1
Chingford E4 . . . . 36 A4
New Cross Gate SE14 140 D3
Ferndale BR1. . . . . 187 C1
Ferndale Ave
Hounslow TW4. . . . . . . 129 A2
Walthamstow E17 . . . . . 54 B4
Ferndale Cl DA7 . . . . . 147 A4
Ferndale Com Sp Ctr
SW9. . . . . 138 B1
Ferndale Ct 3 SE3. . 142 D5
Ferndale Ho N16 . . . . . . 51 B1
Ferndale Rd
Ashford TW15 . . . . . . 170 A5
Brixton SW4, SW9 . . . . 138 B1
Croydon SE25. . . . . 206 B4
Enfield EN3 . . . . 7 A6
Leyton E11. . . . . 76 D6
South Tottenham N15. . . 51 D4
Upton E7 . . . . 77 B1
Ferndale St E6 . . . . . 100 D1
Ferndale Way BR6 . . . 227 B3
Ferndene NW9 . . . . 45 A4
Fern Dene W13 . . . . 87 B2
Ferndene Rd SE24 . . . 139 A1
Fernden Way RM7 . . . . 59 D3
Ferndown
5 Kingston u T
KT6. . . . . 198 A4
Pinner HA6. . . . . 22 A1
7 Wanstead E18. . . . . . . 55 A6
Ferndown Ave BR6. . . 211 B1
Ferndown Cl
Pinner HA5. . . . . 23 A3
Sutton SM2 . . . . 218 B2
Ferndown Ct 6 UB1 . . 86 A1
Ferndown Lo 17
E14. . . . . 120 A3
Ferndown Rd
Eltham SE9. . . . . 165 D4
South Oxhey WD19 . . . . . 22 C6
Ferney Meade Way
TW7 . . . . 131 A3
Ferney Rd EN4. . . . . 15 A3
Fern Gr TW14. . . . . 150 B4
Fernhall N12 . . . . 30 C5
Fernhall Dr IG4. . . . . . . 55 D4
Fernham Rd CR7. . . . . 205 A6
Fernhead 12 SM1 . . . . 218 A4
Fernhead Rd W9. . . . . . 91 B4
Fernhill Ct
Chingford E17 . . . . 36 B1
Kingston u T KT2 . . . . 175 D5
Fernhill Gdns KT2. . . . 176 A5
Fernhill Ho E5. . . . . 74 A6
Fern Hill Pl 3 BR6 . . . 227 A3
Fern Hill Prim Sch
KT2 . . . . 176 A4
Fernhill St E16. . . . . . . 122 B5
Fern Ho HA7. . . . . 24 D4
Fernholme Rd SE15 . 162 D6
Fernhurst Gdns HA8 . . 26 C4
Fernhurst Rd
Ashford TW15 . . . . . . 171 A6
Croydon CR0 . . . . 206 B1
Fulham SW6. . 135 A4 264 B2
Fernie Ho SE22 . . . . . 139 D2
Fern La TW5. . . . . 107 B1
Fernlea Ho NW10. . . . . . 88 B4
Fernlea Rd
Balham SW12 . . . . 159 B3
Mitcham CR4 . . . . 181 A2
Fernleigh Cl
Croydon CR0 . . . . 220 C4
West Kilburn W9 . . . . . . 91 B4
Fernleigh Ct
Harrow HA2. . . . . 23 D1
Wembley HA9 . . . . 44 A1
Fernleigh Rd N21 . . . . . 16 D2
Fern Lo 13 SW16. . . . . 182 C5
Fernly Cl HA5. . . . . 40 A5
Fernsbury St WC1. . . . 234 A1
Fernshaw Mans
SW10 . . . . 266 A5
Fernshaw Rd
SW10 . . . . . . 136 A6 266 A5
Fernside
Buckhurst Hill IG9 . . . . 21 B3
Golders Green NW11. . . 47 C1
Thames Ditton KT7. . . . 197 B1
Fernside Ave
Edgware NW7 . . . . 11 B1
Feltham TW13 . . . . 172 B6
Fernside Ct NW4. . . . . . 28 D1
Fernside Rd SW12 . . . 159 A4
Ferns Rd E15 . . . . 76 D2
Fern St E3. . . . . 97 C3
Fernthorpe Rd
SW16 . . . . 181 C4
Ferntower Rd N5 . . . . . 73 B3
Fernways IG1 . . . . 78 D4
Fern Wlk 18 SE16 . . . . 118 A1
Fernwood
Wandsworth SW19 . . . 157 B3
Wood Green N22 . . . . . . 32 A3
Fernwood Ave
Streatham SW16 . . . . . 181 D6
Wembley HA0 . . . . 65 C2
Fernwood Cl BR1. . . . . 187 C1
Fernwood Cres N20. . . . 14 D1
Fernwood Ct N14. . . . . . 15 D3
Ferny Hill EN4 . . . . 3 A5
Ferranti Cl SE18 . . . . . 121 D3
Ferraro Cl TW5 . . . . . . 129 C6
Ferrers Ave
Wallington SM6 . . . . . 219 D4
West Drayton UB7 . . . 104 A4
Ferrers Rd SW16. . . . . 181 D5
Ferrestone Rd N8. . . . . 50 B5
Ferrey Mews 19
SW9. . . . . 138 C3
Ferriby Cl N1 . . . . 72 C1
Ferrier Ind Est
SW18. . . . . 135 D1
Ferrier Point 6 E16 . . 99 A2
Ferrier St SW18. . . . . . 135 D1
Ferring Cl HA2. . . . . 42 A1
Ferrings SE21 . . . . 161 C1
Ferris Ave CR0. . . . . . . 223 B5
Ferris Rd SE22. . . . . . . 140 A1
Ferron Rd E5 . . . . 74 B5
Ferrour Ct N2 . . . . 48 B6
Ferrybridge Ho SE11 260 D5
Ferrydale Lo 4 NW4. . 46 C5
Ferry Ho E5 . . . . 52 B1
Ferry Island Ret Pk
N17 . . . . 52 A6
Ferry La
Barnes SW13. . . . . 133 D6
Brentford TW8. . . . . . 132 A6
Lower Halliford TW17 192 C1
Richmond TW9. . . . . . . 132 B6
Tottenham Hale N17 . . . 52 B5
Ferry Lane Ind Est
E17. . . . . 52 D5
Ferry Lane Prim Sch
N17 . . . . 52 B5
Ferrymead Ave UB6. . . 85 C5
Ferrymead Dr UB6. . . . 85 C5
Ferrymead Gdns UB6 . 86 A5
Ferrymoor TW10. . . . . 153 B1
Ferry Quays Ctyd 13
TW8 . . . . 131 D6
Ferry Rd
Barnes SW13. . . . . 134 A4
East Molesey KT8 . . . 195 C6
Richmond TW11. . . . . . 175 B5
Thames Ditton KT7. . . . 197 B3
Twickenham TW1. . . . . 153 B3
Ferry Sq
1 Brentford TW8 . . . . 132 A6
Lower Halliford TW17 192 D2
Ferry St E14 . . . . 120 A1
Ferry Wks TW17 . . . . 192 C1
Festing Rd SW15. . . . 134 D2
Festival Cl
Hillingdon UB10. . . . . . . 82 D6
Sidcup DA5. . . . . 168 D3
Festival Ct
Cheam SM1 . . . . 201 D1
5 Dalston E8 . . . . 73 D1
Festival Pier
SE1. . . . . 116 B5 250 C4
Festoon Way E16 . . . 121 D6
Fetherston Ct RM6. . . . 59 B3
Fetter La EC4 . . 94 C1 241 B2
Fettes Ho NW8 . . . . . 229 D3
Fews Lodge RM6 . . . . . 58 D5
Ffinch St SE8 . . . . 141 C5
Fidgeon Cl BR1 . . . . . 210 C6
Field Cl Bromley BR1. . . 187 C1
Buckhurst Hill IG9 . . . . 21 C1
Chessington KT9 . . . . 213 C3
Chingford E4 . . . . 35 D4
Cranford TW4 . . . . 128 B4
East Molesey KT8 . . . 195 D4
Harlington UB7 . . . . . . 127 A5
Ruislip HA4 . . . . 39 A1
Uxbridge UB10. . . . . 60 D6
Willesden NW2 . . . . 68 A6
Fieldcommon La
KT12. . . . . 195 B1
Field Ct
Hampstead NW3. . . . . . 70 A3
Holborn WC1 . . . . 240 D3
Lower Holloway N7 . . . . 72 A3
Wimbledon SW19 . . . 157 C1
Fieldend TW11. . . . . . . 174 D6
Field End HA4 . . . . 62 C2
Field End Jun & Inf Schs
HA4 . . . . 62 D6
Fieldend Rd SW16 . . . 181 C2
Field End Rd HA5,
HA4. . . . . 40 C1
Fielders Cl
2 Enfield EN1. . . . . 5 C1
Harrow HA2. . . . . 42 A1
Fieldfare Rd SE28. . . . 124 C6
Fieldgate Mans 25 E1 96 A2
Fieldgate St E1. . . . . . . 96 A2
Field Ho
4 Edmonton N9 . . . . . . 34 A6
Kensal Green NW10 . . . 90 D4
8 Richmond TW10 . . . 153 C1
Fieldhouse Cl E18 . . . . 37 B2
Fieldhouse Rd
SW12 . . . . 159 C3
Fielding Ave TW2 . . . . 152 A1
Fielding Ho
Chiswick W4 . . . . 133 C6
6 Kilburn NW6. . . . . . . 91 C4
St John's Wood NW8 . 229 A6
Fielding La BR2. . . . . . 209 C5
Fielding Mews
SW13 . . . . 134 B6
Fielding Prim Sch
W13. . . . . 109 B3
Fielding Rd
Acton W4 . . . . 111 C3
Hammersmith W14 . . . 112 D3
Fielding St SE17 . . . . . 139 A6
Fieldings The SE23. . . 162 C3
Fielding Terr W5. . . . . 110 B6
Field La
Brentford TW8. . . . . . . 131 C5
Teddington TW11. . . . . 175 A5
Field Lo NW10. . . . . 67 D2
Field Mead NW9,
NW7. . . . . 27 D3
Fieldpark Gdns CR0. . 207 A1
Field Pl KT3 . . . . 199 D3
Field Point E7 . . . . 77 A4
Field Rd
Feltham TW14 . . . . 150 B5
Forest Gate E7. . . . . 77 A4
Fulham W6. . 135 A6 264 A6
Tottenham N17 . . . . 51 C6
Fieldsend Rd SM3 . . . . 217 A3
Fields Est E8 . . . . 74 A1
Fieldside Cl BR6 . . . . . 227 A4
Fieldside Rd BR1 . . . . 186 B5
Fields Park Cres RM6 . 58 D4
Field St WC1. . . . . 233 C2
Fieldsway Ho N5 . . . . . 72 C3
Fieldview SW17,
SW18 . . . . 158 B3
Field View TW13 . . . . . 171 B6
Field View Cl RM7 . . . . . 59 C6
Fieldview Ct
2 Islington N5 . . . . 72 D3
London NW9 . . . . 44 C3
Fieldway
Dagenham RM8 . . . . 80 C4
Petts Wood BR5 . . . . . . 211 B3
Field Way
Greenford UB6. . . . . 85 D6
New Addington CR0 . . 223 D2
Ruislip HA4 . . . . 39 A1
Willesden NW10 . . . . . . 67 A1
Fieldway Cres N5, N7. . 72 C3
Fieldway Sta CR0. . . . 223 D1
Fieldwick Ho 14 E9 . . . 74 D2
Fiennes Cl RM8 . . . . 58 C1
Fife Ct 5 W3 . . . . 88 C1
Fifehead Cl TW15 . . . . 170 A4
Fife Rd
Kingston u T KT2 . . . . 176 A1
Mortlake SW14 . . . . . 155 A6
Newham E16 . . . . 99 A2
Tottenham N22 . . . . 32 D3
Fife Terr N1. . . . . 233 D4
Fifield Path SE23 . . . . 162 D1
Fifteenpenny Fields
SE9. . . . . 166 C6
Fifth Ave Hayes UB3 . 105 D5
Ilford E12. . . . . 78 B4
West Kilburn W10 . . . . . 91 A4
Fifth Cross Rd TW2. . . 152 B2
Fifth Way HA9 . . . . 66 D4
Figge's Rd CR4 . . . . . . 181 A3
Fig Tree Cl NW10. . . . . . 89 C6
Filanco Ct W7 . . . . 108 D5
Filby Rd KT9. . . . . 214 B2
Filey Ave N16. . . . . 52 A1
Filey Cl SM2. . . . . 218 A1
Filey Ho SW18 . . . . 136 A1
Filey Waye HA4 . . . . 62 B6
Filigree Ct SE16. . . . . . 119 B5
Fillebrook Ave EN1 . . . . 5 D3
Fillebrook Rd E11. . . . . 54 C1
Filmer Ho SW6 . . . . . . 264 B2
Filmer Mews SW6 . . . 264 B2
Filmer Rd
SW6 . . . . 135 B5 264 C3
Filston Rd DA8. . . . . . . 125 D1
Filton Cl NW9. . . . . 27 C1
Filton Ct 14 SE14. . . . . 140 C5
Finborough Rd
Upper Tooting
SW17 . . . . 180 D4
West Brompton
SW10 . . . . . . 135 D6 265 D6
Finchale Rd SE2 . . . . . 124 A3
Fincham Cl UB10 . . . . . 61 A5
Finch Ave SE27 . . . . . . 183 B6
Finch Cl Barnet EN5. . . . 13 C6
Willesden NW10 . . . . . . 67 B2
Finch Ct DA14 . . . . 168 B1
Finchdean Ho SW15 155 D4
Finch Dr TW14. . . . . . . 150 D4
Finch Gdns E4. . . . . 35 C5
Finch Ho 1 SE8 . . . . . 141 D5
Finchingfield Ave
IG8. . . . . 37 C3
Finch La EC2, EC3 . . . 242 D1
FINCHLEY 29 D3
Finchley Central Sta
N3 . . . . 29 C2
Finchley Ct N3. . . . . 29 D4
Finchley La NW4. . . . . . 46 D5
Finchley Lido L Ctr
N12 . . . . 30 B3
Finchley Lo N12 . . . . . . 29 D5
Finchley Meml Hospl
N12 . . . . 30 A3
Finchley Pk N12 . . . . . . 30 B6
Finchley Pl NW8 . . . . . 229 C4
Finchley RC High Sch
N12 . . . . 13 D1
Finchley Rd
Hampstead NW3 . . . . . . 70 A2
London NW11 . . . . 47 B3
St John's Wood NW8 . 229 C4
Finchley Road & Frognal
Sta NW3. . . . . 70 A3
Finchley Road Sta
NW3. . . . . 70 A2
Finchley Way N3. . . . . . 29 C3
Finch Lo 15 W9 . . . . 91 C2
Finch Mews 3
SE15. . . . . 139 D4
Finch's Ct 10 E14 . . . . 119 D6
Finden Rd E7. . . . . 77 C3
Findhorn Ave UB4 . . . . 84 B2
Findhorn St 8 E14. . . . . 98 A1
Findon Cl Harrow HA2 . 63 D5
Wandsworth SW18 . . . 157 C5
Findon Rd
Edmonton N9 . . . . 18 B3
Shepherd's Bush W12 112 A4
Fine Bush La HA4 . . . . . 38 D3
Fineran Ct 16 SW11 . . 136 B1
Fingal St SE10 . . . . . . 120 D1
Fingest Ho NW8 . . . . . 237 A6
Finians Cl UB10. . . . . . . 60 B1
Finland Rd SE4 . . . . . . 141 A2
Finland St SE16. . . . . . 119 A3
Finlays Cl KT9 . . . . . . 214 C3
Finlay St SW6. . . . . . . 134 D4
Finley Ct 21 SE5. . . . . 139 A5
Finmere Ho 1 N4 . . . . . 51 A2
Finnemore Ho N1. . . . 235 A6
Finney La TW7. . . . . . . 131 A4
Finn Ho N1 . . . . 235 D2
Finnis St E2 . . . . 96 B3
Finnymore Rd RM9 . . . 81 A1
FINSBURY 94 C4
Finsbury Ave EC2 . . . 242 D3
Finsbury Cir
EC2. . . . . 95 B2 242 D3
Finsbury Cotts N22 . . . 32 A3
Finsbury Ct EC2. . . . . 242 C4
Finsbury Ho N22. . . . . . 32 A2
Finsbury L Ctr
EC1. . . . . 95 A3 235 A1
Finsbury Market EC2 243 A4
Finsbury Mkt EC2. . . . 243 A5
FINSBURY PARK 72 C6
Finsbury Park Ave
N4. . . . . 51 A3
Finsbury Park Rd N4,
N5. . . . . 72 D6
Finsbury Park Sta N4 . 72 C6
Finsbury Pavement
EC2. . . . . 95 B2 242 D4
Finsbury Rd N22. . . . . . 32 B2
Finsbury Sq
EC2. . . . . 95 B2 242 D4
Finsbury St EC2. . . . . 242 C4
Finsbury Way DA5 . . . 169 B5
Finsen Rd SE5 . . . . . . 139 A2
Finstock Rd W10. . . . . . 90 D1
Finton House Sch
SW17. . . . . 158 D2
Finucane Ct TW9 . . . . 132 B2
Finucane Rise WD23 . . . 8 A2
Finwhale Ho E14. . . . . 119 D3
Fiona Ct Enfield EN2 . . . 4 D2
9 Kilburn NW6. . . . . . . 91 B5
Firbank Cl Enfield EN2 . . 5 A1
Newham E16 . . . . 99 D2
Firbank Rd SE15 . . . . . 140 B3
Fir Cl KT12 . . . . 194 A2
Fircroft N1 . . . . 94 D6 234 D6
Fircroft Gdns HA1. . . . . 64 C5
Fircroft Prim Sch
SW17. . . . . 158 D1

Fircroft Rd
Chessington KT9 214 B4
Upper Tooting SW17 158 D1
Firdene KT5 199 A1
Fir Dene BR6 226 C5
Fire Bell Alley KT6 198 A3
Firebell Mews KT6 198 A3
Fire Brigade Cotts HA5 41 C5
Fire Brigade Pier SE1 260 B4
Firecrest Dr NW3 69 D5
Firefly 7 NW9 27 D1
Firefly Gdns E6 100 A3
Firemans Cotts N10 49 A6
Fireman's Flats N22 32 A2
Firepower (The Royal Artillery Mus)★ SE18 122 D3
Fire Station Alley EN5 1 A3
Fire Station Flats TW7 130 C3
Fire Station Mews 4 BR3 185 D2
Firethorn Cl 4 HA8 27 A6
Fir Gr KT3 199 D3
Fir Grove Rd 25 SW9 138 C3
Firhill Rd SE6 163 C1
Fir Island NW7 28 C5
Firle Ho 7 W10 90 C2
Fir Lo SW15 134 B1
Firmans Ct E17 54 B5
Firmston Ho 9 SW14 133 B2
Fir Rd Cheam SM3 201 B1
Feltham TW13 172 D5
Firs Ave
Fortis Green N10 49 A5
Friern Barnet N11 31 A4
Mortlake SW14 133 A1
Firsby Ave CR0 207 A1
Firsby Rd N16 52 A1
Firs Cl Claygate KT10 212 C2
Forest Hill SE23 163 A4
Mitcham CR4 181 B2
Muswell Hill N10 49 A6
Firscroft N13 17 A1
Firs Dr TW5 128 B5
Firs Farm Prim Sch N13 17 B1
Firs Ho N22 32 C2
Firside Gr DA15 167 D3
Firs La N21, N13 17 A2
Firs Park Ave N21 17 B3
Firs Park Gdns N21 17 B3
First Ave Bexley DA7 146 C5
Chadwell Heath RM6 58 C4
Dagenham RM10 103 D5
East Acton W3 111 D5
East Molesey KT8 195 C5
Edmonton N18 34 C6
Enfield EN1 17 D6
Hayes UB3 105 D5
Hendon NW4 46 C5
Manor Pk E12 78 A3
Mortlake SW14 133 C2
Newham E13 99 A4
Walthamstow E17 53 D4
Walton-on-T KT12 194 B3
Wembley HA9 65 D6
West Kilburn W10 91 B3
First Cl KT8 196 A6
First Cross Rd TW2 152 C2
First Dr NW10 67 A1
Firs The
Belmont SM2 217 D1
Claygate KT10 212 C2
Ealing W5 87 D2
Forest Hill SE26 184 C5
Oakleigh Pk N20 14 B3
2 Penge SE26 184 B5
Sidcup DA15 167 D1
Upton Pk E6 78 A1
Wimbledon SW20 178 A3
Woodford IG8 37 C3
First St SW3 114 C2 257 B4
Firstway SW20 178 C1
First Way HA9 66 D4
Firs Wlk IG8 37 A5
Firswood Ave KT19 215 D3
Firth Gdns SW6 135 A4 264 A1
Firtree Ave CR4 181 A1
Fir Tree Ave UB7 104 C3
Fir Tree Cl Ealing W5 88 A1
Fir Tree Cl *continued*
Esher KT10 212 A3
5 Orpington BR6 227 D3
Streatham SW16 181 C5
Worcester Pk KT19 215 D4
Firtree Ct BR2 208 D6
Fir Tree Gdns CR0 223 C4
Fir Tree Gr SM5 218 D1
Firtree Ho SE13 164 B4
Fir Tree Ho 11 SE14 140 C5
Firtree Lodge N21 17 A2
Fir Tree Rd TW4 129 A1
Fir Trees Cl SE16 119 A5
Fir Tree Wlk EN1 5 B2
Fir Wlk KT17, SM3 216 D2
Fisher Cl
Croydon CR0 205 D1
Holdbrook EN3 7 C6
Southall UB6 85 C4
Fisherdene KT10 213 A1
Fisher Ho
Islington N1 234 A5
9 Shadwell E1 118 C6
2 Tufnell Pk N19 71 C5
Fisherman Cl TW10 175 C6
Fishermans Dr SE16 118 D4
Fishermans Wlk SE28 123 C4
Fisherman's Wlk E14 119 C5
Fisher Rd HA3 24 D1
Fishers Cl SW16 159 D1
Fishers Ct
London SE14 140 D4
6 Teddington TW11 174 D5
Fisher's La W4 111 B2
Fisher St
Holborn WC1 240 C3
Newham E16 99 A2
Fisherton St NW8 92 B3 236 D6
Fisherton Street Est NW8 92 B3 236 D5
Fishguard Way E16 122 D5
Fishlock Ct 6 SW4 138 A3
Fishponds Rd
Keston BR2 225 D3
Upper Tooting SW17 180 C6
Fish St Hill EC3 252 D5
Fisk Cl TW16 171 D4
Fiske Ct Barking IG11 101 B5
1 Merton SW19 180 A3
Sutton SM2 218 A1
Tottenham N17 34 A2
Fitch Ct London SW2 160 C6
8 Mitcham CR4 181 A1
Fitzalan Rd
Church End N3 47 B6
Claygate KT10 212 C1
Fitzalan St SE11 116 C2 261 A4
Fitzclarence Ho W11 244 A2
Fitzgeorge Ave KT2, KT3 177 B2
Fitz-George Ave W14 254 A3
Fitzgerald Ave SW14 133 C2
Fitzgerald Ct 1 E10 53 D1
Fitzgerald Ho
15 Brixton SW9 138 C3
Hayes UB3 106 B5
14 Poplar E14 97 D1
Fitzgerald Rd
Mortlake SW14 133 B2
Thames Ditton KT7 197 A3
Wanstead E11 55 A4
Fitzhardinge Ho
Beckenham BR3 185 D1
Marylebone W1 238 A2
Fitzhardinge St W1 238 A2
Fitzherbert Ho 11 TW10 154 B5
Fitzhugh Gr SW18 158 B5
Fitzjames Ave
Croydon CR0 222 A6
West Kensington W14 254 B3
Fitzjohn Ave EN5 1 B1
Fitzjohn's Ave NW3 70 B3
Fitzjohns Mans NW3 70 A2
Fitzjohns Prim Sch 4 NW3 70 B3
Fitzmaurice Ho 17 SE16 118 B2
Fitzmaurice Pl W1 248 D4
Fitzneal St W12 89 D1
FITZROVIA 93 C2
Fitzroy Cl N6 48 D1
Fitzroy Cres W4 133 B5
Fitzroy Ct London N6 49 C3
Marylebone W1 239 B5
Fitzroy Gdns SE19 183 C3
Fitzroy Ho
Bermondsey SE1 263 D2
12 Tower Hamlets E14 97 B1
Fitzroy Lo N21 16 D6
Fitzroy Mews W1 239 A5
Fitzroy Pk N6 48 D1
Fitzroy Rd NW1 93 A6 231 A6
Fitzroy Sq W1 239 A5
Fitzroy St W1 93 C3 239 A5
Fitzroy Yd NW1 231 A6
Fitzstephen Rd RM8 80 C3
Fitzwarren Gdns N19 49 C1
Fitzwilliam Ave TW9 132 B3
Fitzwilliam Cl 8 EN4 14 D3
Fitzwilliam Ho
4 Higham Hill E17 35 A1
Richmond TW9 131 D1
Fitzwilliam Hts 1 SE23 162 C2
Fitzwilliam Mews E16 121 A5
Fitzwilliam Rd SW4 137 C2
Fitzwygram Cl TW12 174 A5
Five Acre NW9 27 D1
Fiveacre Cl CR7 204 C3
Five Arch Bridge DA14 191 A6
Five Arches Bsns Pk DA14 190 D4
Five Elms Prim Sch RM8 81 B5
Five Elms Rd
Dagenham RM9 81 B5
Keston Mark BR2 225 C5
Five Oaks Mews BR1 165 A1
Fives Ct SE11 261 C5
Fiveways
Chislehurst SE9 166 D2
Croydon CR0 220 C4
Ruislip HA4 39 B1
Five Ways Bsns Ctr TW13 150 B1
Five Ways Cnr NW4 28 A2
Fiveways Rd SW9 138 C3
Flack Ct 15 E10 53 D2
Fladbury Rd N15 51 B3
Fladgate Rd E11 54 C3
Flag Cl CR0 206 D1
Flag Wlk HA5 40 A3
Flambard Rd HA1, HA3 43 A3
Flamborough Ho 12 SE15 140 A4
Flamborough Rd HA4 62 A5
Flamborough St E14 97 A1
Flamingo Ct 2 SE8 141 C5
Flamingo Gdns UB5 85 A4
Flamstead Gdns RM9 80 C1
Flamstead Rd RM9 80 C1
Flamsted Ave HA9 66 C2
Flamsteed Ct 15 SE13 141 D4
Flamsteed Ho★ SE10 142 B5
Flamsteed Rd SE7 122 A1
Flanchford Rd W12 111 D3
Flanders Cres SW17 180 D4
Flanders Ct E17 53 A3
Flanders Ho N16 73 C5
Flanders Mans 1 W4 111 D2
Flanders Rd
Acton W4 111 C2
Wallend E6 100 C5
Flanders Way E9 74 D2
Flandrian Cl EN3 7 D5
Flank St 9 E1 118 A6
Flansham Ho 2 E14 97 B1
Flash La EN2 5 A6
Flask Cotts 4 NW3 70 B4
Flask Wlk NW3 70 B4
Flatford Ho 2 SE6 186 A6
Flather Cl 12 SW16 181 C5
Flatiron Sq SE1 252 B3
Flatiron Yd SE1 252 B3
Flavell Mews SE10 120 C1
Flaxen Cl E4 19 D1
Flaxen Rd E4 19 D1
Flaxley Rd SM4 201 D2
Flaxman Ct
12 Belvedere DA17 125 C1
Soho W1 239 C1
Flaxman Ho
10 Chiswick W4 111 C1
Newington SE1 261 D6
Flaxman Rd SE5 138 D3
Flaxman Sp Ctr SE5 139 A3
Flaxman Terr WC1 93 D4 232 D1
Flaxman Villas N2 48 A6
Flaxmore Ct
Erith DA7 147 D2
South Norwood CR7 183 B1
Flaxton Rd SE18 145 C5
Flecker Cl HA7 24 D5
Flecker Ho 6 SE5 139 B5
Fleece Dr N9 34 A6
Fleecefield Prim Sch N18 34 A6
Fleece Rd KT6 197 C1
Fleece Wlk N7 72 A2
Fleeming Cl E17 35 B1
Fleeming Rd E17 35 B1
Fleet Cl
East Molesey KT8 195 B4
Ruislip HA4 39 A3
Fleet Ct 1 W12 111 C3
Fleetfield WC1 233 B2
Fleet Ho
6 Brixton SW2 160 C6
4 Limehouse E14 119 A6
Fleet Pl EC4 241 C2
Fleet Prim Sch 15 NW3 70 D3
Fleet Rd NW3 70 D3
Fleetside KT8 195 C4
Fleet Sq WC1 233 D1
Fleet St EC4 94 C1 241 B1
Fleet Street Hill 10 E1 96 A3
Fleet Terr SE6 164 A4
Fleetway WC1 233 B2
Fleetway West Bsns Pk UB6 87 B5
Fleet Wood 6 N16 73 D6
Fleetwood Cl
Chessington KT9 213 D1
Newham E16 99 D2
South Croydon CR0 221 D5
Fleetwood Ct
1 Newham E6 100 B2
Orpington BR6 226 C4
8 Stanwell TW19 148 A5
Fleetwood Rd
Kingston u T KT3 198 D6
Willesden NW10 68 A3
Fleetwood Sq KT3 198 D6
Fleetwood St N16 73 C6
Fleetwood Way WD19 22 C6
Fleming Cl 4 W9 91 C3
Fleming Ct
Croydon CR0 220 C3
Paddington W2 236 C4
Fleming Dr N21 16 B6
Fleming Ho
14 Bermondsey SE16 118 A4
Finsbury Pk N4 51 A1
5 Wembley HA9 67 A5
Fleming Mead CR4 180 D3
Fleming Rd
Camberwell SE17 138 D6
Southall UB1 86 A1
Fleming Way
Isleworth TW7 130 D1
Thamesmead SE28 124 D6
Fleming Wlk NW9 27 C1
Flemming Ave HA4 62 B6
Flempton Rd E10 53 A1
Fletcher Bldgs WC2 240 B1
Fletcher Cl E16 122 D6
Fletcher Ct 9 NW5 71 B4
Fletcher Ho 16 N16 73 C4
Fletcher La E10 54 A2
Fletcher Path 7 SE8 141 C5
Fletcher Rd W4 111 A3
Fletchers Cl BR2 209 B5
Fletcher St 16 E1 118 A6
Fletching Rd
Charlton SE7 143 D6
Lower Clapton E5 74 C5
Fletton Rd N11 32 A3
Fleur De Lis St E1 243 C5
Fleur Gates 7 SW19 156 D4
Flexmere Rd N17 33 C2
Flimwell Cl BR1 186 C5
Flinders Ho 28 E1 118 B5
Flint Cl
8 Green Street Green BR6 227 D2
1 Stratford E15 76 D1
Flint Ct CR0 204 B3
Flint Down Cl BR5 190 A2
Flintmill Cres SE3, SE9 144 A3
Flinton St SE17 117 C1 263 B2
Flint St SE17 117 B2 262 D3
Flitcroft St WC2 239 D1
Flitton Ho 7 N1 72 D1
Floathaven Cl SE28 124 A5
Flock Mill Pl SW18 157 D3
Flockton St
20 Bermondsey SE16 118 A4
3 Bermondsey SE16 118 A4
Flodden Rd SE5 139 A4
Flood La 5 TW1 153 A3
Flood St SW3 136 C6 267 B6
Flood Wlk SW3 136 C6 267 B6
Flora Cl Edgware HA7 10 A1
Poplar E14 97 D1
Flora Gardens Prim Sch 17 W6 112 B2
Flora Gdns
Dagenham RM6 58 C3
2 Hammersmith W6 112 B2
Floral St WC2 116 A6 250 A6
Flora St DA17 125 B1
Florence Ave
Enfield EN2 5 A2
Morden SM4 202 A4
Florence Cl KT12 194 B2
Florence Ct
18 New Barnet EN5 13 D6
St John's Wood W9 229 B1
Wanstead E11 55 C5
5 Wimbledon SW19 179 A4
Florence Dr EN2 5 A2
Florence Elson Cl E12 78 C4
Florence Gdns
Chiswick W4 133 A6
Ilford RM6 58 C2
Florence Ho
20 Bermondsey SE16 118 B1
2 Brixton SW2 160 B6
Kidbrooke SE18 144 B4
5 Kingston u T KT2 176 B3
10 Shepherd's Bush W11 112 D6
7 Wandsworth SW18 136 B1
Florence Mans
Fulham SW6 264 C2
4 Hendon NW4 46 B4
Florence Nightingale Ho 14 N1 73 A2
Florence Nightingale Mus★ SE1 250 D1
Florence Rd
Abbey Wood SE2 124 C2
Acton W4 111 B3
5 Beckenham BR3 185 A1
Bromley BR1 187 A2
Ealing W5 110 A6
Feltham TW13 150 B3
Finsbury Pk N4 50 C2
6 Kingston u T KT2 176 B3
New Cross Gate SE14 141 B4
Southall UB2 106 D3
7 Upton Pk E6 99 C6
Walton-on-T KT12 194 B2
West Ham E13 99 A5
Wimbledon SW19 179 D4
Florence Root Ho 3 IG4 56 B4
Florence St
Islington N1 72 D1
London NW4 46 C5

Florence St *continued*
Newham E16 . . . . 98 D3
Florence Terr
Kingston u T SW15 . . . 155 C1
New Cross Gate SE14 . 141 B4
Florence Way SW12. 158 D3
Florence White Ct N9 18 B1
Florentine Ho 3 IG1. . 78 D6
Flores Ho 13 E1. . . . . . 96 D2
Florey Sq N21 . . . . 16 B6
Florfield Rd E8 . . . . 74 B2
Florian SE5. . . . . 139 C4
Florian Ave SM1 . . . . . 218 B4
Florian Rd SW15. . . . . . 135 A1
Florida Cl WD23 . . . . 8 B2
Florida Ct BR2. . . . . . 208 D5
Florida Rd CR7 . . . . . . 182 D2
Florida St E2 . . . . 96 A4
Florida State Univ
WC1. . . . . 93 D2 239 D3
Florin Ct
Bermondsey SE1 . . . . . . 253 C1
Edmonton N18. . . . . 33 C6
8 St George in t East
SE1. . . . . 118 A6
Floris Pl 7 SW4 . . . . . 137 C2
Floriston Ave UB10. . . . 61 A1
Floriston Cl HA7 . . . . . . 25 B2
Floriston Ct UB5 . . . . . . 63 D3
Floriston Gdns HA7 . . . 25 B2
Florys Ct 7 SW19. . . . 157 A3
Floss St SW15 . . . . 134 C3
Flower & Dean Wlk
E1. . . . . 243 D3
Flower La NW7 . . . . 27 D4
Flower Mews NW11. . . . 47 A3
Flowerpot Cl N15 . . . . . 51 D3
Flower Pot Cl N15 . . . . 51 D3
Flowers Cl NW2 . . . . . . 68 A5
Flowersmead SW17. . 159 A2
Flowers Mews 1
N19. . . . . 71 C6
Flower Wlk The
SW7. . . . . . . 114 A4 246 B2
Floyd Rd SE7 . . . . 121 C1
Floyer Cl TW10. . . . . . . 154 B6
Fludyer St SE13. . . . . . 142 C1
Flynn Ct 19 E14 . . . . . 119 C6
Fogerty Cl EN3 . . . . 7 D6
Foley Cotts KT10. . . . . 212 D2
Foley Ct N12. . . . . 30 A5
Foley Ho 19 E1. . . . . 96 C1
Foley Mews KT10 . . . . 212 C2
Foley Rd KT10 . . . . 212 C1
Foley St W1 . . . . 93 C2 239 A3
Folgate St E1. . 95 D2 243 C4
Foliot Ho N1. . . . . 233 C4
Foliot St W12. . . . . 89 D1
Folkestone Ct UB5 . . . . 63 D3
Folkestone Rd
Edmonton N18. . . . . 34 A6
Wallend E6. . . . . 100 C4
Walthamstow E17 . . . . . 53 D5
Folkingham La 6
NW9. . . . . 27 C2
Folkington Cnr N12. . . 29 B5
Folland 6 NW9. . . . . 27 D1
Follett Ho SW10 . . . . 266 C4
Follett St E14. . . . . 98 A1
Folly La
Higham Hill E17 . . . . 35 A2
Walthamstow E4 . . . . . . 35 B3
Folly's End Christian Sch
CR2 . . . . 221 C4
Folly Wall E14 . . . . 120 A4
Fonda Ct 14 E14 . . . . . 119 C6
Fontaine Ct
3 Beckenham BR3 . . . 185 B2
Southgate N14. . . . . 15 D2
Fontaine Rd SW16 . . . 182 B3
Fontarabia Rd SW11 . 137 A1
Fontenelle SE5 . . . . . . 139 C4
Fontenoy Ho SE11 . . 261 C3
Fontenoy Rd SW12,
SW17 . . . . 159 C2
Fonteyne Gdns IG8 . . . 37 D1
Fonthill Cl SE20. . . . . . 184 A1
Fonthill Ct SE23 . . . . . 162 C4
Fonthill Ho
Kensington W14. . . . . 254 B6
Pimlico SW1. . . . . 258 D2
Fonthill Mews N4. . . . . . 72 B6
Fonthill Rd N4. . . . . 72 C6
Font Hills N2 . . . . 30 A1
Fontley Way SW15 . . . 156 A4
Fontmell Cl TW15 . . . . 170 C5
Fontmell Pk TW15 . . . 170 C5
Fontwell Cl
Harrow HA3. . . . . 24 C3
Northolt UB5 . . . . 63 C2
Fontwell Dr BR2 . . . . . 210 C4
Football La HA1 . . . . . . 42 C1
Footpath The SW15 . . 156 A6
FOOTS CRAY. 190 B4
Foots Cray High St
DA14. . . . . 190 D4
Foots Cray La DA14 . . 168 C3
Footscray Rd SE9 . . . 166 D3
Forber Ho 25 E2 . . . . . . 96 C4
Forbes Cl NW2 . . . . 68 A5
Forbes Ct SE19 . . . . . 183 C5
Forbes Ho 2 W4 . . . . 110 C1
Forbes St E1 . . . . 96 A1
Forbes Way HA4 . . . . . . 62 B6
Forburg Rd N16 . . . . . . 52 A1
Fordbridge Ct TW15. . 170 A4
Fordbridge Rd
Ashford TW15 . . . . 170 B5
Lower Halliford TW16,
TW17 . . . . 193 D3
Sunbury TW16 . . . . 194 A5
Fordbridge Rdbt
TW15 . . . . 170 A4
Ford Cl
Ashford TW15 . . . . 170 A4
12 Bow E3 . . . . 97 A5
Harrow HA1. . . . . 42 B2
Littleton TW17 . . . . 192 C4
Thornton Heath CR7 . 204 D4
Fordcombe 13 NW5. . . 71 A2
Forde Ave BR1. . . . . . . 209 C6
Fordel Rd SE6 . . . . 164 B3
Ford End IG8 . . . . 37 B4
Fordham 4 KT1 . . . . . . 176 C1
Fordham Cl
Cockfosters EN4 . . . . 2 C2
North Cheam KT4. . . . . 200 B1
Fordham Ho 11
SE14. . . . . 141 A5
Fordham Rd EN4. . . . . . . 2 C2
Fordham St 13 E1. . . . . 96 A1
Ford Ho
2 New Barnet EN5. . . . . 13 D6
2 Woolwich SE18. . . 122 D1
Fordhook Ave W5. . . . . 110 C6
Fordingley Rd W9. . . . . 91 B4
Fordington Ho 2
SE26 . . . . 162 B1
Fordington Rd N6 . . . . 48 D5
Fordmill Rd SE6 . . . . . 163 C2
Ford Rd
Ashford TW15 . . . . 170 B6
Bow E3. . . . . 97 B5
Dagenham RM10. . . . . . . 81 C1
Ford's Gr N21 . . . . 17 A3
Fords Park Rd E16 . . . . 99 A1
Ford Sq E1 . . . . 96 B2
Ford St Bow E3. . . . . 97 A5
Canning Town E16 . . . . . 98 D1
Fordwich Cl BR6. . . . . 211 D2
Fordwych Ct NW2. . . . . 69 A2
Fordwych Rd NW2. . . . 69 A3
Fordyce Ho 3
SW16 . . . . 181 C6
Fordyce Rd SE13. . . . . 164 A6
Fordyke Rd RM8 . . . . . . 81 B6
Forecastle Ct E14. . . . 119 C4
Foreign &
Commonwealth Office
SW1. . . . . 250 A2
Foreland Ct NW4 . . . . . 29 A2
Foreland Ho W11 . . . 244 A6
Foreland St SE18 . . . . 123 B2
Foreshore SE8. . . . . . . 119 B2
Fore St
Barbican EC2 . . 95 A2 242 B3
Edmonton N18. . . . . 34 A6
Pinner HA5. . . . . 40 A4
Forest App
Chingford E4 . . . . 20 C4
Woodford IG8 . . . . 37 A3
Forest Ave E4. . . . . 20 C4
Forest Bsns Pk E17 . . . 52 D2
Forest Cl
Brondesbury NW6. . . . . 69 A1
Chislehurst BR7. . . . . . 188 C2
Wanstead E11 . . . . 55 A4
Woodford IG8 . . . . 37 B6
Forest Ct Chingford E4. . 20 D3
Forest Ct *continued*
Leytonstone E11 . . . . . . 54 C5
14 Woodside Pk N12 . . . 29 D6
Forestdale N14 . . . . 31 D6
Forestdale Ctr The
CR0 . . . . 223 B1
Forestdale Prim Sch
CR0 . . . . 223 B1
Forest Dene Ct 2
SM2 . . . . 218 A2
Forest Dr
Ashford TW16 . . . . 171 D3
Chingford IG8 . . . . 36 C3
Keston Mark BR2. . . . . 226 A4
Wanstead E12 . . . . 77 D5
Forest Dr E E11. . . . . . . 54 B3
Forest Dr W E11 . . . . . . 54 B2
Forest Edge IG9 . . . . . . 21 D1
Forester Rd SE15 . . . . 140 B2
Foresters Cl SM6 . . . 219 D1
Foresters Cres DA7 . 147 D1
Foresters Dr
Wallington SM6 . . . . . 219 D1
Walthamstow E17 . . . . . 54 B5
Foresters Homes The
DA7. . . . . 147 D1
Foresters Prim Sch
SM6 . . . . 219 D1
FOREST GATE. 77 A3
Forest Gate NW9 . . . . . 45 C4
Forest Gate Com Sch
E7. . . . . 77 A3
Forest Gate Sta E7. . . . 77 A3
Forest Gdns N17. . . . . . 33 D1
Forest Glade
Chingford E4 . . . . 36 C5
Leytonstone E11 . . . . . . 54 C3
Forest Gr E8. . . . . 73 D2
FOREST HILL 163 A3
Forest Hill SE23. . . . . 162 C3
Forest Hill Bsns Ctr
SE23. . . . . 162 C2
Forest Hill Ct 6
SE26. . . . . 162 B1
Forest Hill Ind Est
SE23. . . . . 162 C2
Forest Hill Rd SE22. . . 162 B5
Forest Hill Sec Sch
SE23. . . . . 162 D1
Forest Hill Sta SE23. . 162 C2
Forest Ho 9 E4. . . . . . . 20 C4
Forestholme Cl
SE23. . . . . 162 C2
Forest Ho The SE23 . . 163 A3
Forest Hts IG9. . . . . 21 A2
Forest La E7, E15. . . . . 76 D3
Forest Lawns BR1. . . . 187 C2
Forest Lea 3 E11. . . . . 54 D2
Forest Lo 1 SE23. . . . 162 C1
Forest Mount Rd IG8. . 36 B3
Forest Point E7. . . . . . . 77 B3
Forest Rd Dalston E8. . . 73 D2
Edmonton N9 . . . . 18 B3
Feltham TW13 . . . . 150 C1
Forest Gate E7. . . . . 77 A4
Leytonstone E11 . . . . . . 54 B2
Morden SM3, SM4 . . . 201 C2
Richmond TW9. . . . . . . 132 C5
Romford RM7. . . . . 59 D6
Walthamstow E17 . . . . . 53 C6
Woodford IG8 . . . . 21 A1
Fore Street Ave EC2. . 242 C3
Forest Ridge
Beckenham BR3. . . . . . 207 C6
Bromley BR2 . . . . 226 B4
Forest Rise E17 . . . . . . 54 B5
Forest Sch E17 . . . . 54 C5
Forest Side
Buckhurst Hill IG9 . . . . 21 C3
Chingford E4 . . . . 20 D3
Forest Gate E7. . . . . 77 B4
New Malden KT4 . . . . . 199 D1
Forest St E7 . . . . 77 A3
Forest The E11. . . . . 54 C5
Forest Trad Est E17 . . . 52 D6
Forest View
Chingford E4 . . . . 20 B4
Leytonstone E11 . . . . . . 54 D2
Forest View Ave E10. . . 54 B4
Forest View Rd
Chingford E17 . . . . 36 A2
Manor Pk E12. . . . . 78 A4
Forest Way
Orpington BR5 . . . . . . 211 D4
Sidcup DA15. . . . . 167 B4
Forest Way *continued*
9 Upper Holloway
N19. . . . . 71 C6
Woodford IG8 . . . . 37 B6
Forest Wlk N10. . . . . . . 31 B2
Forfar Rd
London
SW11 . . . . . 137 A4 268 B2
Tottenham N22 . . . . 32 D2
Forge Cl
Harlington UB3 . . . . . . 127 B6
Hayes BR2. . . . . 209 A1
Forge Cotts W5. . . . . . 109 D5
Forge Dr KT10 . . . . 213 A1
Forge La
Belmont SM3. . . . . 217 A1
Feltham TW13 . . . . 173 A5
Richmond TW10. . . . . . 154 A3
Sunbury TW16 . . . . 194 A6
Forge Lane Prim Sch
TW13. . . . . 173 A5
Forge Lo 2 TW7. . . . . . 131 A2
Forge Mews
Addington CR0. . . . . . . 223 C3
Sunbury TW16 . . . . 194 A6
Forge Pl NW1. . . . . 71 A2
Forlong Path UB5. . . . . 63 A2
Forman Ct TW1 . . . . . 152 D3
Forman Ho SE4 . . . . . . 140 D1
Formby Ave HA3, HA7 . . 43 C6
Formby Ct 9 N7. . . . . . 72 C3
Formosa Ho 1 E1 . . . . 97 A3
Formosa St W9. . . . . 91 D3
Formunt Cl E16. . . . . . . 98 D2
Forres Gdns NW11. . . . 47 C3
Forrest Ct N7. . . . . 72 C2
Forrester Path SE26. . 184 C6
Forresters The HA5 . . . 40 B3
Forrest Gdns SW16 . . 204 B6
Forrest Ho SW15. . . . . 134 C3
Forris Ave UB3. . . . . . 105 D5
Forset Ct W1 . . . . 237 B2
Forset St W1 . . 92 C1 237 B2
Forstal Cl BR2 . . . . . . 209 A6
Forster Cl IG8 . . . . 36 B3
Forster Ho SE6 . . . . . . 164 B1
Forster Park Prim Sch
SE6. . . . . 164 C1
Forster Rd
Beckenham BR3. . . . . 207 A6
Streatham SW2 . . . . . . 160 A4
Thornton Heath CR0 . 205 A2
Tottenham N17 . . . . 51 D6
Walthamstow E17 . . . . . 53 A3
Forsters Cl RM6 . . . . . . 59 B3
Forsters Way UB4. . . . . 84 B1
Forston St N1 . . 95 A5 235 B4
Forsyte Cres SE19. . . 183 C2
Forsyte Ct KT2. . . . . . 176 D2
Forsyth Ct
13 Dagenham RM10 . . . 81 D2
Harrow HA1. . . . . 42 B3
Kingston u T KT3 . . . . 177 C1
Forsythe Shades
BR3. . . . . 186 A2
Forsyth Gdns SE17. . 138 D6
Forsyth Ho
14 Hackney E9. . . . . 74 C1
Pimlico SW1. . . . . 259 B3
Forsythia Cl IG1 . . . . . 78 D3
Forsythia Ho SE4 . . . 141 A2
Forsyth Pl EN1. . . . . 17 C6
Forterie Gdns IG3 . . . . 80 A4
Fortescue Ave
1 Hackney E8. . . . . 74 B1
Twickenham TW2. . . . 152 A1
Fortescue Rd
Burnt Oak HA8. . . . . 27 B3
Mitcham SW19 . . . . . . 180 B3
Fortess Gr NW5. . . . . . . 71 C3
Fortess Rd NW5 . . . . . . 71 C4
Fortess Wlk NW5 . . . . . 71 B3
Forthbridge Rd
SW11. . . . . 137 A1
Forth Ho 30 E3 . . . . 97 B5
Forties The 9 NW5 . . . 71 C3
Fortior Ct N6. . . . . 49 C2
Fortis Cl E16. . . . . 99 C1
Fortis Ct N10 . . . . 49 A6
Fortis Gn N2, N10 . . . . 48 D6
FORTIS GREEN. 48 D5
Fortis Green Ave N2 . . 48 D5
Fortis Green Cotts
N2. . . . . 48 D6
Fortismere Ave N10. . . 49 A6
Fortismere Sch N10 . . . 30 D1
Fortismere Sch (South
Wing) N10. . . . . 49 A6
Fortnam Rd N19. . . . . . 71 D6
Fortnums Acre HA7. . . 24 D4
Fort Rd
Bermondsey
SE1 . . . . . . 117 D2 263 D3
Northolt UB5 . . . . 63 C1
Fortrose Cl E14. . . . . . . 98 B1
Fortrose Gdns SW12,
SW2 . . . . 160 A3
Fort St Broadgate E1 . 243 B3
Newham E16 . . . . 121 B5
Fortuna Cl N7 . . . . 72 B2
Fortune Ave HA8. . . . . . 26 D2
Fortune Ct
Barking IG11 . . . . 102 B5
6 Dalston E8 . . . . 73 D1
Fortune Gate Rd
NW10. . . . . 89 C6
Fortune Green Rd
NW6. . . . . 69 C4
Fortune Ho
Lambeth SE11 . . . . . . 261 A3
St Luke's EC1 . . . . 242 B5
Fortune La WD6 . . . . 9 D5
Fortunes Mead UB5. . . 63 A2
Fortune St
EC1. . . . . 95 A3 242 B5
Fortune Way NW10 . . . 90 A4
Fortune Wlk 4
SE28. . . . . 123 B3
Forty Acre La E16. . . . . 99 A2
Forty Ave HA9 . . . . 66 B6
Forty Cl HA9. . . . . 66 B5
Forty Hall Mus & Gdns★
EN2 . . . . 5 D6
FORTY HILL. 5 D4
Forty Hill EN2 . . . . 5 D5
Forty Hill CE Prim Sch
EN2 . . . . 6 A6
Forty Hill Ho EN1 . . . . . . 5 D5
Forty La HA9 . . . . 66 D6
Forum Cl 7 E3. . . . . 97 C6
Forumside HA8. . . . . . . 26 C4
Forum The KT8 . . . . . . 195 D5
Forval Cl CR4. . . . . . . 202 D4
Forward Bsns Ctr The 3
E16. . . . . 98 B3
Forward Dr HA3 . . . . . . 42 D5
Fosbrooke Ho SW8 . . 270 A3
Fosbury Ho 7 SW9 . . 138 B1
Fosbury Mews W2. . . 245 D5
Foscote Mews W9 . . . . 91 C2
Foscote Rd NW4. . . . . . 46 B3
Foskett Ho 21 N2 . . . . . 30 B1
Foskett Rd SW6. . . . . . 135 B3
Foss Ave CR0, CR9 . . . 220 C3
Fossdene Prim Sch 4
SE7. . . . . 121 B1
Fossdene Rd SE7 . . . . 121 B1
Fossdyke Cl UB4. . . . . . 85 A2
Fosse Way W13. . . . . . . 87 A2
Fossil Rd SE13. . . . . . . 141 C2
Fossington Rd DA17 . 124 D2
Foss Rd SW17 . . . . 180 B6
Fossway RM8. . . . . 80 C6
Foster Ct
6 Camden Town
NW1 . . . . 71 C1
Canning Town E16 . . . 120 D6
Hendon NW4. . . . . 46 C5
Foster Ho SE14 . . . . . . 141 B4
Foster La EC2. . . 95 A1 242 A2
Foster Rd Acton W3. . . 111 C6
Chiswick W4 . . . . 111 B1
Newham E13 . . . . 99 A3
Fosters Cl
Elmstead BR7 . . . . 188 B5
Woodford E18 . . . . 37 B2
Fosters Old Sch
DA16. . . . . 146 B3
Foster's Prim Sch
DA16 . . . . 146 C2
Foster St NW4. . . . . 46 C5
Foster Wlk NW4 . . . . . . 46 C5
Fothergill Cl E13. . . . . . 99 A5
Fothergill Dr N21. . . . . 16 A6
Fotheringham Ct EN1 . . 5 D1
Fotheringham Rd EN1 . . 5 D1
Foubert's Pl W1 . . . . . 239 A1
Foulden Rd N16 . . . . . . 73 D4
Foulden Terr N16 . . . . . 73 D4
Foulis Terr
SW7 . . . . 114 B1 256 D2
Foulser Rd SW17 . . . . 159 A1

Foulsham Rd CR7 205 B6
Foundary Ho 6 E14 97 D2
Founder Cl 2 E6 100 D1
Founders Cl UB5 85 B4
Founders Ct EC2 242 C2
Founders Gdns SE19 183 A3
Founders Ho SW1 259 C2
Foundling Ct WC1 240 A6
Foundling Mus The★ WC1 94 A3 240 B6
Foundry Cl SE16 119 A5
Foundry Mews NW1 239 B6
Foundry Pl Stepney E1 96 C2
Wandsworth SW18 157 D4
Fountain Cl UB8 83 A2
Fountain Ct
Belgravia SW1 258 C3
Blackfen DA15 168 B5
New Malden KT3 199 A5
5 Penge SE26 184 C4
14 Shepherd's Bush W11 112 D4
Strand EC4 251 A6
Fountain Dr
Dulwich SE19 183 D6
Wallington SM5 218 D1
Fountain Green Sq 34 SE16 118 A4
Fountain Ho
33 Bermondsey SE16 118 A4
3 Brondesbury Pk NW6 69 A1
Mayfair W1 248 A4
5 Mitcham SW19 180 D1
Fountain Mews
1 Highbury N5 73 A4
Maitland Pk NW3 70 D2
Fountain Pl SW9 138 C4
Fountain Rd
South Norwood CR7 183 A1
Upper Tooting SW17 180 B6
Fountains Ave TW13 151 B1
Fountains Cl TW13 151 B1
Fountains Cres N14 16 A4
Fountains The
London N3 29 D3
Loughton IG10 21 D4
Fountayne Bsns Ctr N15 52 A5
Fountayne Rd
South Tottenham N15 52 A5
Stoke Newington N16 74 A6
Fount St SW8 137 D5 269 D3
Fouracres EN3 7 A4
Four Acres N12 29 D6
Fourland Wlk HA8 27 A4
Fournier St E1 95 D2 243 D4
Fourscore Mans E8 74 A1
Four Seasons Cl E3 97 C5
Four Seasons Cres SM3 217 B6
Four Square Ct TW4 151 C5
Fourth Ave
Hayes UB3 105 D5
Ilford E12 78 B4
West Kilburn W10 91 A4
Fourth Cross Rd TW2 152 B2
Fourth Way
Wembley HA9 66 D4
Wembley HA9 67 A4
Four Tubs The WD23 8 B4
Fourways 2 CR0 221 D6
Four Wents The E4 20 B2
Fovant Ct 5 SW8 137 C3
Fowey Ave IG4 55 D4
Fowey Cl E1 118 B5
Fowey Ho SE11 261 B2
Fowler Cl
London SW11 136 B2
Sidcup DA14 191 A5
Fowler Ho
5 Camberwell SE5 139 C3
Islington N1 94 D6 234 D6
South Lambeth SW8 269 D1
West Green N15 51 B4
Fowler Rd
Forest Gate E7 77 A4
Islington N1 94 D6 234 D6
Mitcham CR4 181 A1
Fowler's Wlk W5 87 D3
Fownes St SW11 136 C2
Fox and Knot St EC1 241 D4
Foxberry Ct SE4 141 B1
Foxberry Rd SE4 141 A2
Foxborough Gdns SE4 163 C6
Foxbourne Rd SW17 159 A2
Foxbury Ave BR7 189 B4
Foxbury Cl BR1 187 B4
Foxbury Rd BR1 187 B4
Fox Cl
Bethnal Green E1 96 C3
Elstree WD6 9 D5
Newham E16 99 A2
Foxcombe CR0 223 D2
Foxcombe Cl 1 E6 99 D5
Foxcombe Rd 6 SW15 156 A3
Foxcote SE5 263 B1
Foxcroft WC1 233 D3
Foxcroft Rd SE18 144 D4
Fox Ct EC1 241 A3
Foxdene Cl 12 E18 55 B6
Foxes Dale
Beckenham BR2 208 B6
Blackheath Pk SE3 143 A2
Foxfield NW1 231 D5
Foxfield Prim Sch SE18 123 A1
Foxfield Rd BR6 227 B6
Foxglove Cl
Bexley DA15 168 A5
Edmonton N9 18 C3
Southall UB1 107 A6
Foxglove Ct 11 HA0 88 A5
Foxglove Gdns E11 55 C5
Foxglove La KT9 214 C4
Foxglove Path SE28 123 C5
Foxglove St W12 111 D6
Foxglove Way SM6 203 B1
Fox Gr KT12 194 B2
Foxgrove N14 16 A1
Foxgrove Ave BR3 185 D3
Foxgrove Path WD19 22 D5
Foxgrove Rd BR3 186 A3
Foxham Rd N19 71 D5
Fox Hill Keston BR2 225 C3
Penge SE19 183 D3
Fox Hill Gdns SE19 183 D3
Fox Ho
2 London SW11 136 B1
Northolt UB5 85 A6
Foxhole Rd 2 SE9 166 A6
Fox Hollow Cl 1 SE18 123 C1
Fox Hollow Dr DA7 146 D2
Foxholt Gdns NW10 67 A1
Foxhome Cl BR7 188 C4
Fox House Rd DA17 125 D1
Fox La Ealing W5 88 A3
Keston BR2 225 C3
Palmers Green N13 16 B1
Foxlees HA0 65 A4
Foxley Cl E8 74 A3
Foxley Ct SM2 218 A1
Foxley Ho 4 E3 97 D4
Foxley Rd
Camberwell SW9 138 D5
Thornton Heath CR7 204 D5
Foxley Sq 3 SW9 138 D4
Foxmead Cl EN2 4 B2
Foxmore St SW11 267 C1
Fox Prim Sch W8 113 C5 245 A3
Fox Rd E16 98 D2
Foxs Path CR4 180 C1
Fox's Yd E2 243 D6
Foxtail Ho TW3 130 A4
Foxton KT1 198 C6
Foxton Gr CR4 180 B1
Foxton Ho E16 122 C4
Foxwarren KT10 212 D1
Foxwell Mews SE4 141 A2
Foxwell St SE4 141 A2
Foxwood Cl
Edgware NW7 27 C6
Feltham TW13 150 B1
Foxwood Green Cl EN1 17 C5
Foxwood Rd SE3 142 D1
Foyle Rd
Greenwich SE3 142 D6
Tottenham N17 34 A2
Fradel Lo N16 51 B1
Framfield Cl N12 13 C1
Framfield Ct EN1 17 C5
Framfield Rd
Ealing W7 86 D1
Islington N5 72 D3
Mitcham CR4 181 A3
Framlingham Cl 2 E5 74 C6
Framlingham Cres SE9 188 B6
Framlingham Ct 5 RM6 58 B4
Frampton NW1 71 D1
Frampton Cl SM2 217 C1
Frampton Ct 3 W3 111 A4
Frampton Ho NW8 236 D5
Frampton Park Rd E9 74 C1
Frampton Rd TW4 151 A6
Frampton St NW8 92 B3 236 D5
Francemary Rd SE4 163 C6
Frances Ct
South Norwood SE25 183 D1
Walthamstow E17 53 C3
Frances & Dick James Ct 2 NW7 29 A3
Frances Rd E4 35 C4
Frances St SE18 122 B2
Franche Court Rd SW17 158 A1
Francis Ave
Bexleyheath DA7 147 C3
Feltham TW13 150 A1
Ilford IG1 79 B6
Francis Barber Cl SW16 182 B6
Franciscan Prim Sch 3 SW17 181 A5
Franciscan Rd SW17 181 A6
Francis Chichester Way SW11 137 A4 268 B1
Francis Cl
6 Cubitt Town E14 120 B2
Littleton TW17 192 C5
West Ewell KT19 215 B4
Francis Ct
12 Deptford SE14 140 D6
Ealing W5 110 B6
Edgware NW7 27 D5
Kingston u T KT5 198 A5
Francis Gr SW19 179 B4
Francis Ho
Harlesden NW10 89 D6
11 Shoreditch N1 95 C6
Walham Green SW10 265 D4
Francis Holland Sch
Belgravia SW1 115 A2 258 B3
Marylebone NW1 92 D3 237 C6
Francis Rd
Fortis Green N2 48 D5
Harrow HA1 43 A4
Hounslow TW4 128 D3
Ilford IG1 79 B6
Leyton E10 76 A6
Pinner HA5 40 C4
Thornton Heath CR0 204 D2
Wallington SM6 219 C2
Wembley UB6 87 C6
Francis Snary Lo 11 SW18 157 C6
Francis St Ilford IG1 79 B6
Stratford E15 76 C3
Westminster SW1 115 C2 259 B4
Francis Terr N19 71 C5
Francis Terrace Mews 16 N19 71 C5
Francis Wlk N1 233 C6
Francklyn Gdns HA8 10 C1
Franconia Rd SW4 159 D6
Frank Bailey Wlk E12 78 C2
Frank Barnes Sch 13 NW3 70 B1
Frank Beswick Ho SW6 264 D5
Frank Burton Cl 5 SE7 121 B1
Frank Dixon Cl SE21 161 C3
Frank Dixon Way SE21 161 C3
Frankfurt Rd SE24 161 A6
Frank Godley Ct DA14 190 B5
Frankham Ho 8 SE8 141 C5
Frankham St SE8 141 C5
Frank Ho SW8 270 A4
Frankland Cl
Bermondsey SE16 118 B2
Woodford IG8 37 C5
Frankland Ho 4 SW12 159 B4
Frankland Rd
Brompton SW7 114 B3 256 C5
Chingford E4 35 C5
Franklin Bldg 5 E14 119 C4
Franklin Cl
Greenwich SE13 141 D4
Kingston u T KT1 198 C6
Oakleigh Pk N20 14 A4
West Norwood SE27 160 D1
Franklin Cres CR4 203 C5
Franklin Ho
Beckenham BR2 208 C6
New Cross SE4 141 A3
26 Wapping E1 118 B5
West Hendon NW9 45 D2
Franklin Ind Est SE20 184 C2
Franklin Pas SE9 144 A2
Franklin Pl SE13 141 D4
Franklin Rd
Bexleyheath DA7 147 A4
Penge SE20 184 C3
Walton-on-T KT12 194 A3
Franklins Mews HA2 64 A6
Franklin Sq SW5 254 D1
Franklin's Row SW3 114 D1 257 D2
Franklin St
43 Bromley E3 97 D4
South Tottenham N15 51 C3
Franklin Way CR0 204 A2
Franklyn Rd
Walton-on-T KT12 194 B3
Willesden NW10 67 D2
Franks Ave KT3 199 A5
Franks Ho TW7 131 B1
Frank Slater Ho 4 IG3 58 B1
Frank Soskice Ho SW6 264 D5
Frank St 5 E13 99 A3
Frankswood Ave
Hillingdon UB7 82 B1
Petts Wood BR2, BR5 211 A4
Frank Towell Ct TW14 150 A3
Frank Welch Ct HA5 40 C5
Frank Whymark Ho 4 SE16 118 C4
Franlaw Cres N13 33 A6
Frans Ct HA4 40 A1
Fransfield Gr SE26 162 B1
Frans Hals Ct E14 120 B3
Franshams WD23 8 C2
Frant Cl SE20 184 C3
Franthorne Way SE6 163 D1
Frant Rd CR7 204 D4
Fraserburgh Ho 29 E3 97 B5
Fraser Cl 3 E6 100 A1
Fraser Ct
Battersea SW11 267 A2
Heston TW3 129 A5
Fraser Ho
Brentford TW8 110 B1
40 Clapham SW8 137 D3
3 Woolwich SE18 122 C2
Fraser Rd
Edmonton N9 18 B1
Walthamstow E17 53 D3
Wembley UB6 87 C6
Fraser Regnart Ct 12 NW5 70 D3
Fraser St W4 111 C1
Frating Cres IG8 37 B4
Frazer Ave HA4 62 C3
Frazier St SE1 116 C4 251 A1
Freame Ho N21 17 B5
Frean St SE16 118 A3
Frearson Ho WC1 233 D2
Freda Corbett Cl 10 SE15 140 A5
Frederica Rd E4 20 B4
Frederica St 4 N7 72 B1
Frederick Blg N1 73 C2
Frederick Bremer Sec Sch E17 36 A1
Frederick Charrington Ho 4 E1 96 C3
Frederick Cl
Cheam SM1 217 B3
Marylebone W2 114 D6 247 C6
Frederick Cres
Camberwell SW9 138 D5
Enfield EN3 6 C3
Frederick Ct SW6 135 A2
Frederick Gdns
Cheam SM1 217 B3
Thornton Heath CR0 204 D3
Frederick Ho
Ashford TW15 170 A6
Southall UB1 107 B6
Woolwich SE7 122 A3
Frederick Pl SE18 122 D1
Frederick Rd SM1 217 B3
Frederick's Pl
City of London EC2 242 C1
North Finchley N12 30 A6
Frederick Sq 11 SE16 119 A6
Frederick's Row EC1 234 C2
Frederick St WC1 94 B4 233 C1
Frederick Terr E8 73 D1
Frederic Mews SW1 248 A1
Frederic St E17 53 A4
Fredora Ave UB4 83 D3
Fred Styles Ho SE7 143 C6
Fred Tibble Ct RM9 81 A4
Fred Wigg Twr E11 76 D6
Freedom Cl E17 53 A5
Freedom Rd N17 33 B1
Freedom St SW11 136 D3
Freegrove Rd N7 72 A3
Freehold Ind Ctr TW4 150 C6
Freeland Ct W5 110 B6
Freeland Pk N3 29 A1
Freeland Rd W5 110 B6
Freelands Ave CR2 222 D1
Freelands Gr BR1 187 B2
Freelands Rd BR1 187 B2
Freeling Ho NW8 229 C6
Freeling St 7 N1 72 B1
Freeman Cl
Northolt UB5 63 A1
Upper Halliford TW17 193 C5
Freeman Ct SW16 182 A1
Freeman Dr KT8 195 B5
Freeman Ho 13 SW2 160 A4
Freeman Rd SM4 202 B4
Freemans La UB3 105 C6
Freemantle Ave EN3 18 D6
Freemantle St SE17 117 C1 263 A2
Freemasons Pl 6 CR0 205 C1
Freemasons Rd E16 99 B1
Freemason's Rd CR0 205 C1
Freemens Hos 1 SW9 138 B1
Freesia Cl BR6 227 D3
Freethorpe Cl SE19 183 C2
Freezeland Way UB10 60 D2
Freke Rd SW11 137 A2
Fremantle Ho 14 E1 96 B3
Fremantle Rd
Belvedere DA17 125 C2
Ilford IG6 57 A6
Fremont St E9 96 C6
French Gdns KT12 195 B1
French Inst The SW7 114 B2 256 C4
French Pl E1 243 B6
French St TW16 172 C1
Frendsbury Rd SE4 141 A1
Frensham Cl UB1 85 B4
Frensham Ct
Canonbury N5 73 A3
6 London NW9 46 A5

Frensham Ct *continued*
Mitcham CR4 .... **202** B6
Frensham Dr
New Addington CR0 .. **224** A1
Roehampton SW15 .. **156** A2
Frensham Ho 7
KT6 .... **198** A4
Frensham Rd SE9 .... **167** B2
Frensham St SE15 ... **140** A6
Frere St 6 SW11 .. **136** C3
Fresham Ho BR2 .... **208** D6
Freshfield Ave E8 .... **73** D1
Freshfield Cl SE13 .. **142** B1
Freshfield Dr N14 ..... **15** B4
Freshfields CR0 ..... **207** B1
Freshford St SW17,
SW18 .... **158** A1
Freshwater Cl SW17 .**181** A4
Freshwater Ct UB1 .... **85** C4
Freshwater Rd
Dagenham RM8 .... **59** A1
Streatham SW17 .... **181** A4
Freshwell Ave RM6 .... **58** C5
Fresh Wharf Est
IG11 .... **100** D6
Fresh Wharf Rd
IG11 .... **100** D5
Freshwood Cl BR3 .. **185** D2
Freston Gdns EN4 ..... **15** A6
Freston Pk N3 .... **29** B1
Freston Rd W10,
W11 .... **112** D6
Freswick Ho 6 SE8 .. **119** A2
Freta Rd DA6 .... **169** B6
Freud Mus The★
NW3 .... **70** A2
Frewell Bldg EC1 ... **241** A4
Frewing Cl BR7 ..... **188** C5
Frewin Rd SW18 ..... **158** B3
Friar Mews SE27 .... **160** D1
Friar Rd UB4 .... **84** D3
Friars Ave London N20 .**30** C6
Putney SW15 .... **157** A6
Roehampton SW15 .. **155** D1
Friars Cl Chingford E4 .. **20** A1
Ilford IG1 .... **57** B1
Lambeth SE1 ...... **251** D3
16 Northolt UB5 ...... **84** D4
Friars Ct
5 Wallington SM6 ... **219** B4
Walthamstow E17 ..... **35** B2
Friars Gate Cl IG8 ..... **37** A6
Friars Gdns W3 .... **89** B1
Friars La TW9 .... **153** D6
Friars Mead E14 ..... **120** A3
Friars Mews SE9 ..... **166** C6
Friars Place La W3 ... **111** B6
Friars Prim Foundation
Sch SE1 ... **116** D4 **251** D1
Friar's Rd E6 .... **99** D6
Friars Stile Pl 9
TW10 .... **154** A5
Friars Stile Rd
TW10 .... **154** A5
Friar St EC4 .... **241** D1
Friars Way W3 .... **89** B1
Friars Wlk London N14 . **15** B4
West Heath SE2 ..... **124** D1
Friary Cl N12 .... **30** C5
Friary La IG8 .... **37** A6
Friary Park Ct 12 W3 .. **89** A1
Friary Rd Acton W3 .... **89** B1
London N12 .... **30** C6
Peckham SE15 ...... **140** A5
Friary Way N12 .... **30** C6
Friday Grove Mews 11
SW12 .... **159** C4
FRIDAY HILL **20** C1
Friday Hill E4 .... **20** C1
Friday Hill E E4 .... **20** C1
Friday Hill W E4 ...... **20** C2
Friday Rd CR4 ...... **180** D3
Friday St EC4 **117** A6 **252** A6
Frideswide Pl NW5 ... **71** C3
Friendly Pl 16 SE13 . **141** D4
Friendly St SE8 ...... **141** C4
Friendly Street Mews
SE8 .... **141** C3
Friendship Way E15 ... **98** A6
Friendship Wlk UB5 ... **84** D4
Friends' Rd CR0 ..... **221** B5
Friend St EC1 .. **94** D4 **234** C2
FRIERN BARNET **31** A6
Friern Barnet La N20 .. **30** C6
Friern Barnet Rd N11 .. **31** A5
Friern Barnet Sch
N11 .... **30** D5
Friern Bridge Ret Pk
N11 .... **31** B4
Friern Ct N20 .... **14** B1
Friern Mount Dr N20 .. **14** A4
Friern Pk N12 .... **30** B5
Friern Rd SE22 ...... **162** A5
Friern Watch Ave
N12 .... **30** B6
Frigate Ho 7 E14 .... **120** A2
Frigate Mews SE8 ... **141** C6
Frimley Ave SM6 ..... **220** B3
Frimley Cl
New Addington CR0 .. **224** A1
Putney SW19 .... **157** A2
Frimley Cres CR0 ... **224** A1
Frimley Ct DA14 ..... **190** C5
Frimley Gdns CR4 .... **202** C6
Frimley Ho CR4 ...... **202** C6
Frimley Rd
Chessington KT9 .... **214** A3
Ilford IG3 .... **79** C5
Frimley Way E1 .... **96** D3
Frinstead Ho 1
W10 .... **112** D6
Frinton Ct W13 .... **87** B2
Frinton Dr IG8 .... **36** B3
Frinton Mews IG2 ..... **56** C3
Frinton Rd
Newham E6 .... **99** D4
Sidcup DA14 .... **169** A2
South Tottenham N15 .. **51** C3
Streatham SW17 .... **181** A4
Friston St SW6 ..... **135** D3
Friswell Pl 1 DA6 ... **147** C1
Fritham Cl KT3 ...... **199** C3
Frith Ct NW7 .... **29** A3
Frith Ho
Bethnal Green E2 ...... **96** A4
Paddington NW8 .... **236** D5
Frith La NW7 .... **29** A4
Frith Manor Cotts
N12 .... **29** B5
Frith Manor Prim Sch
N12 .... **29** B5
Frith Rd Croydon CR0 . **221** A6
Leyton E11 .... **76** B4
Frith St W1 .... **93** D1 **239** C1
Frithville Ct 2 W12 .. **112** C5
Frithville Gdns W12 .. **112** C5
Frizlands La RM10 .... **81** D5
Frobisher Cl HA5 ...... **40** D2
Frobisher Cres
TW19 .... **148** A4
Frobisher Ct
Belmont SM2 .... **217** B1
6 Forest Hill SE23 ... **162** B2
1 Greenwich SE10 .. **142** B6
Hendon NW9 .... **27** C1
3 Shepherd's Bush
W12 .... **112** C4
Frobisher Gdns
TW19 .... **148** A4
Frobisher Ho
3 Ealing W5 .... **88** A4
27 Wapping E1 ...... **118** B5
Frobisher Mews EN2 ... **5** B1
Frobisher Pas E14 ... **119** C5
Frobisher Pl SE14 ... **140** C4
Frobisher Rd
London N8 .... **50** C5
Newham E6 .... **100** B1
Frobisher St SE10 ... **142** C6
Froghall Cotts EN5 .... **11** B5
Frogley Rd SE22 .... **139** D1
Frogmore SW18 ..... **157** C6
Frogmore Ave UB4 ..... **83** C3
Frogmore Cl SM3 .... **217** A5
Frogmore Ct UB2 .... **107** B2
Frogmore Est NW10 .. **89** A4
Frogmore Gdns
Cheam SM3 .... **217** A4
Hayes UB4 .... **83** C3
Frogmore Ind Est
Hayes UB3 .... **105** D4
Highbury N5 .... **73** A4
Frognal NW3 .... **70** A3
Frognal Ave
Harrow HA1 .... **42** D5
Sidcup DA14 .... **190** A4
Frognal Cl NW3 .... **70** A3
Frognal Cnr BR7 ..... **189** D4
Frognal Ct NW3 .... **70** A2
Frognal Gdns NW3 .... **70** A4
Frognal La NW3 .... **69** D3
Frognal Par NW3 ...... **70** A2
Frognal Pl DA14 ..... **190** A5
Frognal Rise NW3 ..... **70** A4
Frognal Way NW3 ..... **70** A4
Froissart Rd SE9 .... **166** A6
Frome Ho SE15 ...... **140** C1
Frome Rd N22 .... **50** D6
Frome St N1 ... **95** A5 **235** A4
Fromondes Rd SM3 .. **217** A3
Fromow's Cnr 14
W4 .... **111** A1
Frontenac NW10 ...... **68** B1
Frontier Works N17 ... **33** C4
Frosbery Ct 23 EN3 ..... **7** C6
Frostic Wlk E1 ...... **243** D3
Froude St SW8 ..... **137** B3
Fruen Rd TW14 ..... **149** D4
Fryatt Rd N17 .... **33** B3
Frye Ct 5 E3 .... **97** B4
Fryent Cl NW9 .... **44** C3
Fryent Cres NW9 ...... **45** C3
Fryent Ctry Park HA3, HA9,
NW9 .... **44** C2
Fryent Fields NW9 .... **45** C3
Fryent Gr NW9 .... **45** C3
Fryent Prim Sch NW9 **45** A2
Fryent Way HA9, NW9 .. **44** D2
Fry Ho E6 .... **77** C1
Frying Pan Alley E1 . **243** C3
Fry Rd
Harlesden NW10 ...... **89** D6
Upton Pk E6 .... **77** D1
Fryston Ave CR0 .... **222** A6
Fuchsia St SE2 ...... **124** B1
Fulbeck Dr NW9 .... **27** C2
Fulbeck Ho N7 .... **72** B2
Fulbeck Way HA2 ..... **24** A1
Fulbourn 9 KT1 ..... **176** C1
Fulbourne Rd E17 .... **36** A1
Fulbourne St E1 ...... **96** B2
Fulbrook Rd N19 ...... **71** C4
Fulcher Ct 40 SE8 ... **141** B6
Fulcher Ho
13 Deptford SE8 ..... **119** B1
10 Shoreditch N1 ...... **95** C6
Fulford Mans 3 N19 .. **72** A5
Fulford Rd KT19 .... **215** B1
Fulford St SE16 ..... **118** B4
FULHAM **134** D3
Fulham Broadway
SW6 .... **135** C5 **265** B3
Fulham Broadway Sh Ctr
SW6 .... **265** B3
Fulham Broadway Sta
SW6 .... **135** C5 **265** B4
Fulham Bsns Exchange
SW6 .... **266** B1
Fulham Cl UB10 .... **83** A3
Fulham Cross Girls Sec
Sch SW6 .. **135** A5 **264** A3
Fulham Ct
SW6 .... **135** C4 **265** A2
Fulham High St
SW6 .... **135** A3
Fulham Pal★ SW6 .. **135** A3
Fulham Palace Rd SW6,
W6 .... **134** D6
Fulham Park Gdns
SW6 .... **135** B3
Fulham Park Rd
SW6 .... **135** B3
Fulham Prep Sch
6 Fulham SW6 ..... **135** A3
Fulham W14 . **135** A6 **264** B6
Fulham Prim Sch
SW6 .... **135** C6 **265** A5
Fulham Rd
Chelsea
SW10 ..... **136** A6 **266** B6
Fulham SW6 . **135** B4 **264** D2
Fulke Ho E5 .... **74** B5
Fullbrooks Ave KT4 . **199** D1
Fuller Cl
4 Bethnal Green E2 ... **96** A3
Bushey WD23 .... **8** B4
Orpington BR6 ...... **227** D3
Fuller Rd RM8 .... **80** C4
Fullers Ave KT6 ..... **214** B6
Fuller's Ave IG8 ...... **36** D3
Fullers Ho 6 SW18 .. **157** C6
Fuller's Rd E18 .... **36** D3
Fuller St NW4 .... **46** C5
Fullers Way N KT6 ... **214** B5
Fullers Way S KT9 ... **214** A5
Fuller's Wood CR0 ... **223** C3
Fuller Terr IG1 .... **79** B3
Fullerton Ct TW11 ... **175** A4
Fullerton Rd
Croydon CR0 .... **205** D2
Wandsworth SW18 .. **158** A6
Fuller Way UB3 ..... **105** D1
Fullwood Prim Sch
IG6 .... **57** A5
Fullwood's Mews N1 **235** D2
Fulmar Ct
6 Dulwich SE21 ..... **161** B2
10 Ealing W13 .... **86** D3
Surbiton KT5 .... **198** B3
Fulmar Ho
12 Bermondsey
SE16 .... **118** D2
Marylebone NW8 ... **237** B5
Fulmead St SW6 .... **265** D1
Fulmer Cl TW12 ..... **173** A5
Fulmer Rd E16 .... **99** D2
Fulmer Way W13 .... **109** B3
Fulneck 1 E1 .... **96** C2
Fulready Rd E10 ...... **54** B4
Fulstone Cl TW4 .... **129** B1
Fulthorp Rd SE3 .... **143** A3
Fulton Ct EN3 .... **7** C5
Fulton Mews W2 .... **246** A6
Fulton Rd HA9 .... **66** C5
Fulwell Ct
Southall UB1 .... **108** A6
Teddington TW11 .... **174** C6
Fulwell Park Ave
TW2 .... **152** A2
Fulwell Rd TW11,
TW12 .... **174** B6
Fulwell Sta TW11 .... **174** B6
Fulwood Ave HA0 ..... **88** B5
Fulwood Cl UB3 ...... **83** D1
Fulwood Ct
Harrow HA3 .... **43** A3
Stanwell TW19 ...... **148** B5
Fulwood Gdns TW1 .. **153** A5
Fulwood Pl WC1 .... **240** D3
Fulwood Wlk SW19 .. **157** A3
Furber St W6 .... **112** B3
Furham Field HA5 .... **23** C3
Furley Ho 7 SE15 .... **140** A5
Furley Rd SE15 ..... **140** A5
Furlong Cl SM6 ..... **203** B1
Furlong Rd N7 .... **72** C2
Furmage St SW18 ... **157** D4
Furneaux Ave SE27 . **182** D5
Furness Ho SW1 .... **258** C2
Furness Lo 4 SW14 . **132** D1
Furness Prim Sch
NW10 .... **90** A5
Furness Rd
Harlesden NW10 ...... **90** A5
Harrow HA2 .... **41** D1
Morden SM4 .... **201** D3
Sands End SW6 .... **135** D3
Furnival St
EC4 .... **94** C1 **241** A2
Furrow La E9 .... **74** C3
Furrows The KT12 ... **194** C1
Fursby Ave N3 .... **29** C4
Fursecroft W1 ...... **237** C2
Further Acre NW9 .... **27** D1
Furtherfield Cl CR0 .. **204** C3
Further Green Rd
SE6 .... **164** C3
Furze Cl WD19 .... **22** C5
Furze Ct CR0 .... **222** A6
FURZEDOWN **181** B6
Furzedown Dr SW17 . **181** B5
Furzedown Prim Sch
SW17 .... **181** A4
Furzedown Rd
SW17 .... **181** B5
Furzefield Cl BR7 ... **188** D4
Furzefield Rd SE3 .... **143** B5
Furzeground Way
UB11 .... **105** A5
Furzeham Rd UB7 ... **104** A4
Furzehill Rd WD6 ..... **11** A6
Furze Inf Sch RM6 .... **59** A3
Furzeland Ho 2
KT3 .... **199** C2
Furze Rd CR7 .... **205** A6
Furze St E3 .... **97** C2
Furzewood TW16 .... **172** A2
Fuschia Ct IG8 .... **36** C4
Fuscia Ct TW13 ..... **149** D1
Fusion Ct SW15 ..... **155** C1
Futters Ct 1 NW10 ... **89** C5
Fyfe Way BR1 .... **187** A1
Fyfield N4 .... **72** C6
Fyfield Cl BR2, BR3 ... **208** B5
Fyfield Ct E7 .... **77** A2
Fyfield Ho RM9 .... **80** B1
Fyfield Rd
5 Brixton SW9 ...... **138** C2
Enfield EN1 .... **5** C2
Walthamstow E17 ..... **54** B6
Woodford IG8 .... **37** C3
Fynes St SW1 ...... **259** C4

G

Gable Cl HA5 .... **23** C3
Gable Ct SE26 ...... **184** B6
Gable Ho 12 W4 ..... **111** C2
Gable Lo
Hadley Wood EN4 .... **2** A5
5 North Finchley N12 .. **30** A5
West Wickham BR4 .. **208** A1
Gables Ave TW15 .... **170** B5
Gables Cl
Camberwell SE5 ..... **139** C4
Lewisham SE12 ..... **165** A3
Gables The
Barking IG11 .... **79** A2
Bromley BR1 .... **187** B3
3 Clapham SW4 ..... **137** C2
Ealing W13 .... **87** B1
Hampstead NW3 ...... **70** B6
Heston TW5 .... **129** C6
Mitcham CR4 .... **203** B6
Muswell Hill N10 ...... **49** A6
North Finchley N12 .... **29** D5
Wembley HA9 .... **66** B5
Gabriel Cl 1 TW13 .. **173** A6
Gabriel Ho SE11 .... **260** C4
Gabrielle Cl HA9 ...... **66** B5
Gabrielle Ct NW3 ..... **70** B2
Gabriel Mews NW2 ... **69** B6
Gabriel St SE23 ..... **163** A4
Gabriel's Wharf★
SE1 .... **251** A4
Gad Cl E13 .... **99** B4
Gaddesden Ave HA9 .. **66** B2
Gaddesden Ho EC1 . **235** D1
Gade Cl UB3 .... **106** B5
Gadesden Rd KT19 ... **215** A2
Gadsbury Cl NW9 ..... **45** D3
Gadsden Ho
6 Homerton E9 .... **74** D2
8 Kensal Town W10 ... **91** A3
Gadwall Cl E16 .... **99** B1
Gadwall Way SE28 ... **123** B4
Gagarin Ho SW11 .... **136** B2
Gage Rd E16 .... **98** C2
Gage St WC1 .... **240** B4
Gainford Ho 18 E2 .... **96** B4
Gainford St
N1 .... **94** C6 **234** A6
Gainsboro Gdns UB6 .. **64** C3
Gainsborough Ave
E12 .... **78** C3
Gainsborough Cl
Beckenham BR3 .... **185** C3
Thames Ditton KT10 .. **196** C1
Gainsborough Ct
11 Barnet EN5 .... **1** D1
6 Bermondsey SE16 . **118** B1
Bromley BR2 .... **209** C5
Dulwich SE21 ...... **161** C2
North Finchley N12 .... **29** D5
Shepherd's Bush W12 **112** C4
Gainsborough Gdns
Edgware HA8 .... **26** C1
Golders Green NW11 ... **47** B2
Hampstead NW3 ...... **70** B5
Isleworth TW7 ...... **152** B6
Gainsborough Ho
Dagenham RM8 .... **80** B4
Enfield EN1 .... **18** A6
Finsbury Pk N4 .... **50** B1
3 Hampstead NW3 ... **70** A4
5 Limehouse E14 ... **119** A6
Westminster SW1 ... **259** D3
Gainsborough Lodge
HA1 .... **42** C4
Gainsborough Mews 5
SE26 .... **162** B1
Gainsborough Prim Sch
Hackney Wick E9 ...... **75** C2
Newham E15 .... **98** C4
Gainsborough Rd
Bedford Pk W4 ...... **111** D2

Gainsborough Rd *continued*
Dagenham RM8 . . . . 80 B5
Hayes UB4 . . . . 83 B5
Leytonstone E11 . . . . . 54 C2
Newham E15 . . . . 98 C4
New Malden KT3 . . . . . 199 B2
North Finchley N12 . . . . 29 D5
Richmond TW9 . . . . 132 B2
Gainsborough Sq DA6 . . . . 146 D2
Gainsborough St 3 E9 . . . . 75 B2
Gainsborough Studios N1 . . . . 235 C5
Gainsborough Twr 7 UB5 . . . . 84 D5
Gainsfield Ct 3 E11 . . 76 C5
Gainsford Rd E17 . . . . . 53 B5
Gainsford St SE1 . . . . 117 D4 253 D2
Gairloch Ho 2 NW1 . . 71 D1
Gairloch Rd SE5 . . . . . 139 C3
Gaisford St NW5 . . . . . . 71 C2
Gaitskell Ct SW11 . . . . 136 C3
Gaitskell Ho
Camberwell SE17 . . . . . 139 B6
2 Newham E6 . . . . 99 D6
3 Walthamstow E17 . . . 53 D6
Gaitskell Rd SE9 . . . . . 167 A3
Gaitskell Way SE1 . . . 252 A2
Galahad Rd
Edmonton N9 . . . . 18 A1
Grove Pk BR1 . . . . 187 A6
Galata Rd SW13 . . . . . . 134 A5
Galatea Sq SE15 . . . . . 140 B2
Galaxy Bldg 6 E14 . . . 119 C2
Galaxy Ho EC2 . . . . . . 242 D6
Galba Ct 1 TW8 . . . . 131 D5
Galbraith St E14 . . . . . 120 A3
Galdana Ave EN5 . . . . . . 2 A2
Galeborough Ave IG8 36 B3
Gale Cl
Hampton TW12 . . . . . 173 A4
Mitcham CR4 . . . . 202 B6
Gale Ho
10 Brixton SW2 . . . . . . 160 B6
Carshalton SM5 . . . . . 218 C3
Galena Ho
5 Hammersmith W6 . . . . 112 B2
Plumstead Comm SE18 . . . . 123 D1
Galena Rd W6 . . . . 112 B2
Galen Pl WC1 . . . . 240 B3
Galesbury Rd SW18 . . 158 A5
Gales Gdns E2 . . . . 96 B4
Gale St
Dagenham RM9 . . . . 80 D1
Tower Hamlets E3 . . . . . 97 C2
Galgate Cl 4 SW19 . . 157 A3
Gallants Farm Rd EN4 . . . . 14 C3
Galleon Cl SE16 . . . . . 118 D4
Galleon Ho 8 E14 . . . 120 A2
Galleons Dr IG11 . . . . 102 A4
Galleries of Modern London★ EC1 . . . . . . 242 A3
Gallery Ct SW10 . . . . . 266 A5
Gallery Gdns UB5 . . . . . 84 D5
Gallery Rd SE21 . . . . . . 161 B3
Galleywall Rd SE16 . . . 118 B2
Galleywall Road Trad Est 12 SE16 . . . . 118 B2
Galleywood Ho 1 W10 . . . . 90 C2
Gallia Rd N5 . . . . 72 D3
Galliard Cl N9 . . . . 18 C5
Galliard Cres N9 . . . . . . 18 A4
Galliard Ct N9 . . . . 18 A5
Galliard Prim Sch N9 . 18 A4
Galliard Rd N9 . . . . 18 A5
Gallica Ct SM1 . . . . . . 201 D1
Gallions Cl IG11 . . . . . 102 A4
Gallions Mount Prim Sch SE18 . . . . 123 D1
Gallions Prim Sch E6 . . . . 100 D1
Gallions Rd E16 . . . . . 123 A6
Gallions Reach Shp Pk IG11 . . . . 101 A2
Gallions Reach Sta E16 . . . . 122 D6
Gallions View Rd SE28 . . . . 123 C4
Gallon Cl SE7 . . . . 121 C2
Gallop The
South Croydon CR2 . . . 222 B1
Sutton SM2 . . . . 218 A1
Gallosson Rd SE18 . . . 123 C2
Galloway Path CR0 . . . 221 B4
Galloway Rd W12 . . . . 112 A5
Gallus Cl N21 . . . . 16 B5
Gallus Sq SE3 . . . . 143 B2
Galpin's Rd CR4, CR7 . 204 B5
Galsworthy Ave
Ilford RM6 . . . . 58 B2
Tower Hamlets E14 . . . . 97 A2
Galsworthy Cl SE28 . . 124 B5
Galsworthy Cres SE3 . . . . 143 C4
Galsworthy Ct W3 . . 110 D3
Galsworthy Ho 4 W11 . . . . 91 A1
Galsworthy Rd
Cricklewood NW2 . . . . . 69 A4
Kingston u T KT2 . . . . 176 D2
Galton Ho SE18 . . . . . . 144 B4
Galton St W10 . . . . 91 A4
Galva Cl EN4 . . . . 3 A1
Galvani Way CR0 . . . . . 204 B1
Galveston Ho 2 E1 . . . 97 A3
Galveston Rd SW15 . . . 157 B6
Galway Cl 28 SE16 . . . 118 B1
Galway Ho
Finsbury EC1 . . . . 235 B1
7 Stepney E1 . . . . 96 D2
Galway St EC1 95 A4 235 B1
Galy 5 NW9 . . . . 27 D1
Gambetta St 3 SW8 . 137 B3
Gambia St SE1 . . . . 116 D5 251 D3
Gambler Ho EC1 . . . . 235 B1
Gambole Rd SW17 . . . 180 C6
Games Ho 6 SE7 . . . . 143 C6
Games Rd EN4 . . . . 2 D2
Gamlen Rd SW15 . . . . 134 D1
Gamma Ct 9 CR0 . . . 205 B1
Gamuel Cl E17 . . . . 53 C3
Gander Green Cres TW12 . . . . 173 C2
Gander Green La KT4, SM1, SM3 . . . . 217 B5
Gandhi Cl E17 . . . . 53 C3
Gandolfi St 5 SE15 . . 139 C6
Ganley Ct 18 SW11 . . 136 B2
Gannet Ct 5 SE21 . . . 161 B2
Gannet Ho SE15 . . . . 139 D4
Ganton St W1 . . . . . . 239 B1
Ganton Wlk WD19 . . . . . 22 D6
GANTS HILL 56 C3
Gants Hill IG2 . . . . 56 C3
Gantshill Cres IG2 . . . . 56 C4
Gants Hill Sta IG2 . . . . . 56 C3
Gap Rd SW19 . . . . 179 D5
Garage Rd W3 . . . . 88 C1
Garand Ct 2 N7 . . . . . . 72 B3
Garbett Ho 2 SE17 . . 138 D6
Garbutt Pl W1 . . . . . . 238 B3
Garden Ave
Bexleyheath DA7 . . . . 147 C2
Mitcham CR4 . . . . 181 B3
Garden City HA8 . . . . . . 26 C4
Garden Cl
Ashford TW15 . . . . . . 171 A4
Chingford E4 . . . . 35 C5
Grove Pk SE12 . . . . 165 B1
Hampton TW12 . . . . . . 173 B5
Northolt UB5 . . . . 85 A6
Roehampton SW15 . . . 156 B4
Ruislip HA4 . . . . 61 D6
Wallington SM6 . . . . . 220 A3
Garden Cotts BR5 . . . . 190 C1
Garden Ct
5 Belmont SM2 . . . . . 217 C1
10 Eltham SE9 . . . . . . 166 C5
Hampton TW12 . . . . . . 173 B5
North Finchley N12 . . . . 29 D5
4 Richmond TW9 . . . . . 132 B4
12 South Acton W4 . . 111 A3
South Croydon CR0 . . 221 D5
4 Stanmore HA7 . . . . . 25 C5
St John's Wood NW8 . 229 C2
Strand EC4 . . . . 251 A6
Wembley HA0 . . . . 65 C5
Wimbledon SW20 . . . . 178 D2
Gardeners Cl SE9 . . . . 166 A1
Gardeners Rd CR0 . . . 204 D1
Garden Flats SW16 . . 160 A1
Garden Ho
2 Finchley N2 . . . . 30 B1
Garden Ho *continued*
12 South Lambeth SW9 . . . . 138 A3
Garden Hospl The NW4 . . . . 46 C6
Garden House Sch SW3 . . . . . . 114 D1 257 D2
Gardenia Ct 1 BR3 . . 185 C3
Gardenia Rd
Bromley BR1 . . . . 210 C6
Enfield EN1 . . . . 17 C5
Gardenia Way IG8 . . . . 37 A5
Garden La
Bromley BR1 . . . . 187 B4
Streatham SW2 . . . . . . 160 B3
Garden Lodge Ct N2 . . 48 B6
Garden Mews W2 . . . . 245 B5
Garden Mus★ SE1 . . . 260 C5
Garden Pl 28 E2 . . . . . . 95 D6
Garden Prim Sch CR4 . . . . 203 D6
Garden Rd
Bromley BR1 . . . . 187 B4
Finchley N2 . . . . 30 B2
Penge SE20 . . . . 184 C2
Richmond TW9 . . . . . . 132 C2
St John's Wood NW8 . . . . 92 A4 229 B2
Walton-on-T KT12 . . . . 194 B2
Garden Row SE1 . . . . 116 D3 261 C6
Garden Royal 16 SW15 . . . . 156 D5
Garden St E1 . . . . 96 D2
Gardens The
Beckenham BR3 . . . . . 186 A2
East Bedfont TW14 . . . 149 B5
East Dulwich SE22 . . . . 140 A1
Harrow HA1, HA2 . . . . . 42 A3
Pinner HA5 . . . . 41 B3
Stamford Hill N16 . . . . . 51 D2
Garden Suburb Jun & Inf Schs NW11 . . . . 47 B4
Garden Terr
Knightsbridge SW7 . . 247 B1
Pimlico SW1 . . . . 259 C2
Garden Way NW10 . . . . 67 A2
Garden Wlk
Beckenham BR3 . . . . . . 185 B2
Shoreditch EC2 . . . . 95 C3 243 A6
Gardiner Ave NW2 . . . . 68 C3
Gardiner Cl
Chislehurst BR5 . . . . . 190 C1
Dagenham RM8 . . . . 80 D4
Enfield EN3 . . . . 18 D5
Gardiner Ct NW10 . . . . 89 B6
Gardiner Ho SW11 . . 267 A2
Gardner Cl E11 . . . . 55 B3
Gardner Ct
Highbury N5 . . . . 73 A4
Hounslow TW3 . . . . . . 129 C2
Tottenham N22 . . . . 32 D1
Gardner Ho
Feltham TW13 . . . . 151 B2
Southall UB1 . . . . 106 D6
Gardner Ind Est SE26 . . . . 185 B5
Gardner Pl TW14 . . . . . 150 B5
Gardner Rd E13 . . . . 99 B3
Gardners Cl N11 . . . . . . 15 A2
Gardners La EC4 . . . . 252 A6
Gardnor Mans 14 NW3 . . . . 70 A4
Gardnor Rd NW3 . . . . . . 70 B4
Gard St EC1 . . . . 234 D2
Garendon Gdns SM4 . . . . 201 D2
Garendon Rd SM4 . . 201 D2
Garenne Ct 8 E4 . . . . . 20 A3
Gareth Cl KT4 . . . . . . 216 D6
Gareth Ct SW16 . . . . . 159 D1
Gareth Gr BR1 . . . . 187 A6
Garfield Edmonton N9 . . 18 B3
Enfield EN2 . . . . 17 B6
Garfield Ho W2 . . . . . 237 C1
Garfield Mews 7 SW11 . . . . 137 A2
Garfield Prim Sch
London N11 . . . . 31 C5
Wimbledon SW19 . . . 180 A4
Garfield Rd
Chingford E4 . . . . 20 B3
Clapham SW11 . . . . . 137 A2
Enfield EN3 . . . . 6 C1
Newham E13 . . . . 98 D3
Garfield Rd *continued*
3 Twickenham TW1 . . 153 A3
Wimbledon SW19 . . . 180 A4
Garford St E14 . . . . 119 C6
Garganey Ct NW10 . . . . 67 B2
Garganey Wlk SE28 . . 124 C6
Garibaldi St SE18 . . . . 123 C2
Garland Ct 12 E14 . . . . 119 C6
Garland Dr TW3 . . . . . . 130 A3
Garland Ho
12 Kingston u T KT2 . . . . 176 A2
Stoke Newington N16 . . 73 B5
Garland Rd
Plumstead Comm SE18 . . . . 145 B5
Stanmore HA7 . . . . 26 A2
Garlands Ct CR0 . . . . . 221 B4
Garlands Ho NW8 . . . . . 91 D5
Garlands La HA1 . . . . . . 42 D1
Garlands The HA1 . . . . . 42 D2
Garlick Hill EC4 . . . . . . 117 A6 252 B6
Garlies Rd SE23 . . . . . 163 A1
Garlinge Ho 12 SW9 . . 138 C4
Garlinge Rd NW2 . . . . . 69 B2
Garman Cl N18 . . . . 33 B5
Garman Rd N17 . . . . 34 C3
Garnault Mews EC1 . . 234 B1
Garnault Pl EC1 . . . . . 234 B1
Garnault Rd EN1 . . . . 5 D5
Garner Cl RM8 . . . . 58 D1
Garner Rd E17 . . . . 36 A2
Garner St E2 . . . . 96 A5
Garnet Ct TW13 . . . . . . 149 C1
Garnet Ho KT4 . . . . 199 B1
Garnet Rd
South Norwood CR7 . . 205 B5
Willesden NW10 . . . . . . 67 C2
Garnet St E1 . . . . 118 C6
Garnett Cl SE9 . . . . 144 B2
Garnett Ho 5 NW3 . . . 70 D3
Garnett Rd NW3 . . . . . . 70 D3
Garnett Way 3 E17 . . . 35 A2
Garnet Wlk 8 E6 . . . . 100 A2
Garnham Cl 2 N16 . . . . 73 D6
Garnham St 1 N16 . . . 73 D6
Garnies Cl SE15 . . . . . 139 D5
Garrad's Rd SW16 . . 159 D1
Garrard Cl
Bexleyheath DA7 . . . . 147 C2
Chislehurst BR7 . . . . . 188 D5
Garrard Ho BR2 . . . . . . 209 C5
Garrard Wlk NW10 . . . . 67 C2
Garratt Cl CR0 . . . . 220 A4
Garratt Ho 8 N16 . . . . . 51 C1
Garratt La
Upper Tooting SW17, SW18 . . . . 180 C6
Wandsworth SW18 . . . 157 D3
Garratt Park Sec Specl Sch 6 SW18 . . . . . . 158 A2
Garratt Rd HA8 . . . . 26 C3
Garratts Rd WD23 . . . . . . 8 A4
Garratt Terr SW17 . . . . 180 C6
Garraway Ct SW13 . . . 134 C5
Garraway Ho SE21 . . 161 D1
Garrett Cl W3 . . . . 89 B2
Garrett Ho
8 Shepherd's Bush W12 . . . . 90 B1
Teddington TW11 . . . . . 175 B4
Garrett St EC1 . 95 A3 242 B6
Garrick Ave NW11 . . . . 47 A3
Garrick Cl Ealing W5 . . . 88 A3
1 Richmond TW9 . . . 153 D6
Wandsworth SW18 . . 136 A1
Garrick Cres CR0 . . . . 221 C6
Garrick Ct HA8 . . . . 26 B6
Garrick Dr
Hendon NW4 . . . . 28 C1
Plumstead SE18 . . . . . . 123 B3
Garrick Gdns KT8 . . . . 195 C6
Garrick Ho
Chiswick W4 . . . . 133 C6
2 Kingston u T KT1 . . 198 A5
Mayfair W1 . . . . 248 C3
7 Streatham SW16 . . 181 C5
Garrick Ind Ctr NW9 . . 45 D4
Garrick Pk NW4 . . . . . . 28 D1
Garrick Rd
Greenford UB6 . . . . 85 D3
Richmond TW9 . . . . . . 132 C3
West Hendon NW9 . . . . 45 D3
Garrick's Ait KT8 . . . . 174 A1
Garricks Ho KT1 . . . . 175 D1
Garrick St WC2 . . . . . . 116 A6 250 A6
Garrick's Villa TW12 . . 174 A1
Garrick Way NW4 . . . . . 46 D5
Garrick Yd WC2 . . . . . . 250 A6
Garrison Cl
Hounslow TW4 . . . . . . 151 B6
Shooters Hill SE18 . . . 144 C5
Garrison La KT9 . . . . . 214 A1
Garrowsfield EN5 . . . . . 13 B6
Garsdale Cl N11 . . . . . . 31 A4
Garsdale Terr SW5 . . 254 D2
Garside Cl
Hampton TW12 . . . . . 173 D4
Plumstead SE28 . . . . . . 123 B3
Garside Ct 5 N20 . . . . . 14 D2
Garsington Mews SE4 . . . . 141 B2
Garson Ho W2 . . . . . . 246 C6
Garston Ho 6 N1 . . . . . 72 D1
Garter Way SE16 . . . . 118 D4
Garth Cl
Kingston u T KT2 . . . . . 176 B5
Ruislip HA4 . . . . 40 D1
West Barnes SM4 . . . 200 D2
Garth Ct Chiswick W4 . 133 B6
11 Harrow HA1 . . . . 42 D3
Garth Dr N9 . . . . 18 A2
Garth Ho NW2 . . . . 69 B6
Garthland Dr EN5 . . . . . 12 C6
Garth Mews W5 . . . . . . 88 A3
Garthorne Rd SE23 . . 162 D4
Garth Rd
Child's Hill NW2 . . . . 69 B6
8 Chiswick W4 . . . . . . 111 B1
Kingston u T KT2 . . . . . 176 B5
West Barnes SM4 . . . 200 D2
Garth Road Ind Ctr The SM4 . . . . 200 D1
Garthside TW10 . . . . . . 176 A5
Garth The
Hampton TW12 . . . . . 173 D4
Harrow HA3 . . . . 44 B3
North Finchley N12 . . . . 29 D5
Garthway N12 . . . . 30 C4
Gartmoor Gdns SW19 . . . . 157 B3
Gartmore Rd IG3 . . . . . 79 D6
Garton Ho 6 N6 . . . . . . 49 D2
Garton Pl SW18 . . . . . . 158 A5
Gartons Cl EN3 . . . . 6 C1
Gartons Way SW11 . . . 136 A2
Garvary Rd E16 . . . . 99 B1
Garvens SE19 . . . . 183 C5
Garway Rd W2 . . . . 91 D1
Garwood Cl N17 . . . . . . 34 B2
Garwood Lo N22 . . . . . . 32 B3
Gascoigne Gdns IG8 . . 36 C3
Gascoigne Pl 17 E2 . . . 95 D4
Gascoigne Prim Sch IG11 . . . . 101 A6
Gascoigne Rd IG11 . . . 101 A5
Gascony Ave NW6 . . . . . 69 C1
Gascoyne Ho 2 E9 . . . 74 D1
Gascoyne Rd E9 . . . . . . 74 D1
Gaselee St E14 . . . . . . 120 A6
Gasholder Pl SE11 . . . . 116 B1 260 D1
Gaskarth Rd
Balham SW12 . . . . 159 B5
Burnt Oak HA8 . . . . 27 A1
Gaskell Rd N6 . . . . 48 D3
Gaskell St SW4 . . . . . . 138 A3
Gaskin Ho N16 . . . . 73 B5
Gaskin St N1 . . 94 D6 234 C6
Gaspar Cl SW7 . . . . . . 255 D4
Gaspar Mews SW5 . . 255 D4
Gassiot Rd SW17 . . . . 180 D6
Gassiot Way SM1 . . . . 218 B5
Gasson Ho 24 SE14 . . 140 D6
Gastein Rd W6 . . . . . . 134 D6
Gastigny Ho EC1 . . . . 235 B1
Gaston Bell Cl TW9 . . . 132 B2
Gaston Bridge Rd TW17 . . . . 193 B3
Gaston Gate SW8 . . . 270 C2
Gaston Rd CR4 . . . . . . 203 A6
Gaston Way TW17 . . . . 193 B4
Gataker Ho 5 SE16 . . . 118 B3
Gataker St 6 SE16 . . . 118 B3
Gatcliff Cl SW1 . . . . . 258 B1
Gatcombe Ct BR3 . . . . 185 C3

Gatcombe Ho 20 SE22 139 C2
Gatcombe Mews W5 110 B6
Gatcombe Rd
8 Newham E16 121 A5
Tufnell Pk N19 71 D5
Gatcombe Way EN4 2 D2
Gateacre Ct DA14 190 B6
Gate End HA6 22 A3
Gatefield Ct SE15 140 A2
Gateforth St NW8 237 A5
Gate Hill Ct W11 244 D4
Gatehill Rd HA6 22 A3
Gate Ho 4 KT6 198 A1
Gatehouse Cl KT2 177 A3
Gatehouse Sch 26 E2 96 D5
Gatehouse Sq SE1 252 B4
Gateley Ho 6 SE4 140 D1
Gateley Rd SW9 138 B2
Gate Mews SW7 114 C4 247 B1
Gater Dr EN2 5 B4
Gates 4 NW9 27 D1
Gatesborough St EC2 243 A6
Gates Ct SE17 262 A2
Gatesden WC1 233 B1
Gates Green Rd BR2, BR4 225 A4
Gateside Rd SW17 158 D1
Gate St WC2 94 B1 240 C2
Gatestone Ct 10 SE19 183 C4
Gatestone Rd SE19 183 C4
Gateway SE17 139 A6
Gateway Arc N1 234 C4
Gateway Bsns Ctr SE28 123 B3
Gateway Gdns E6 100 B4
Gateway Ho
Balham SW12 159 B5
3 Barking IG11 101 A6
3 Upper Tooting SW17 180 C4
Gateway Ind Est NW10 90 A3
Gateway Mews
Friern Barnet N11 31 C4
4 London E8 73 D3
Gateway Prim Sch NW8 92 B3 236 D6
Gateway Rd E15 75 D5
Gateway Ret Pk E6 100 D3
Gateways KT6 198 A4
Gateways Ct SM6 219 B3
Gateways The
Chelsea SW3 257 B3
Richmond TW9 131 D1
Gateway Trad Est NW10 89 D4
Gatfield Gr TW13 151 C2
Gatfield Ho TW13 151 C2
Gathorne Rd N22 32 C2
Gathorne St 19 E2 96 D5
Gatley Ave KT19 214 D3
Gatliff Rd SW1 115 B1 258 C1
Gatling Rd SE18, SE2 124 A1
Gatonby St SE15 139 D4
Gatting Cl HA8 27 A3
Gatting Way UB8 60 A2
Gatton Prim Sch SW17 180 C6
Gatton Rd SW17 180 C6
Gattons Way DA14 191 B6
Gatward Cl N21 16 D5
Gatward Gn N9 17 D2
Gatwick Ho 3 E14 97 B1
Gatwick Rd SW18 157 B4
Gauden Cl SW4 137 D2
Gauden Rd SW4 137 D2
Gaugin Ct 13 SE16 118 B1
Gauntlet 1 NW9 27 D1
Gauntlet Cl UB5 63 A1
Gauntlett Ct HA0 65 B3
Gauntlett Rd SM1 218 B3
Gaunt St SE1 262 A6
Gautrey Rd SE15 140 C3
Gautrey Sq 5 E6 100 B1
Gavel St SE17 262 D4
Gaven Ho N17 33 C1
Gaverick Mews 3 E14 119 C2
Gavestone Cres SE12 165 B4
Gavestone Rd SE12 165 B4
Gavestone Terr SE12 165 B4
Gaviller Pl 3 E5 74 B4
Gavina Cl SM4 202 C4
Gavin Ho 1 SE18 123 C2
Gawain Wlk N9 18 A1
Gawber St E2 96 C4
Gawsworth Cl E15 76 D3
Gawthorne Ct E3 97 C5
Gay Cl NW2 68 B3
Gaydon Ho W2 91 D2
Gaydon La NW9 27 C2
Gayfere Rd
Redbridge IG5 56 B6
Stoneleigh KT17 216 A3
Gayfere St SW1 116 A3 260 A5
Gayford Rd W12 111 D4
Gay Ho N16 73 C3
Gayhurst SE17 139 B6
Gayhurst Ct 9 UB5 84 C4
Gayhurst Ho NW8 237 B6
Gayhurst Prim Sch 5 E8 74 A1
Gayhurst Rd E8 74 A1
Gaylor Rd UB5 63 B3
Gaymead NW8 91 D6
Gaynesford Rd
Forest Hill SE23 162 D2
Wallington SM5 218 D1
Gay Rd E15 98 B5
Gaysham Ave IG2 56 D4
Gaysham Hall IG5 56 D6
Gaysley Ho SE11 261 A3
Gay St SW15 134 D2
Gayton Cres NW3 70 B4
Gayton Ct
3 Harrow HA1 42 D3
New Malden KT3 199 D4
Gayton Ho E3 97 C3
Gayton Rd
Abbey Wood SE2 124 C3
Hampstead NW3 70 B4
Harrow HA1 43 A3
Gayville Rd SW11 158 D5
Gaywood Cl SW2 160 C3
Gaywood Rd E17 53 C6
Gaywood St SE1 261 D5
Gaza St SE17 116 D1 261 C1
Gaze Ho 11 E14 98 B1
Gean Ct 3 E11 76 B4
Gearies Inf Sch IG2 56 D4
Gearies Jun Sch IG2 56 D4
Geariesville Gdns IG6 56 D5
Gearing Cl SW17 181 A6
Geary Ho N7 72 B3
Geary Rd NW10 68 A3
Geary St N7 72 B3
GEC Est HA9 65 D6
Geddes Pl 3 DA6 147 C1
Gedeney Rd N17 33 A2
Gedge Ct CR4 202 C5
Gedling Ho SE22 139 D2
Gedling Pl SE1 263 D6
Geere Rd E15 98 D6
Gees Ct W1 238 B1
Gee St EC1 95 A3 242 A6
Geffrey's Ct SE9 166 A1
Geffrye Ct N1 95 C5
Geffrye Mus★ E2 95 D5
Geffrye St E2 95 D5
Geldart Rd SE15 140 B5
Geldeston Rd E5 74 A6
Gellatly Rd SE14 140 D3
Gell Cl UB10 60 B5
Gemima Ct SM1 217 C3
Gemini Bsns Ctr E16 98 B3
Gemini Gr UB5 85 A4
Gemini Ho 11 E3 97 C6
Gemma Ct BR3 185 B1
Gems Hampshire Sch (Main Sch) SW7 257 A1
Gems Hampshire Sch (The Early Years) SW7 256 B3
General Gordon Pl SE18 122 D2
Generals Wlk The EN3 7 A6
General Wolfe Rd SE10 142 B4
Genesis Bsns Pk NW10 88 D5
Genesis Cl TW19 148 B3
Genesis Ho KT6 197 D1
Genesta Rd SE18 145 A6
Geneva Cl TW17 171 C1
Geneva Ct
Hendon NW9 45 D4
1 Putney SW15 156 D6
Stoke Newington N16 51 B1
Geneva Dr SW9 138 C1
Geneva Gdns RM6 59 A4
Geneva Rd
Kingston u T KT1 198 A5
Thornton Heath CR7 205 A4
Genever Cl E4 35 C5
Genista Rd N18 34 B5
Genoa Ave SW15 156 C6
Genoa Ho 19 E1 96 D3
Genoa Rd SE20 184 C2
Genotin Rd EN1 5 B2
Genotin Terr EN1 5 B2
Gentleman's Row EN2 5 A2
Gentry Gdns E13 99 A4
Geoffrey Cl SE5 139 A3
Geoffrey Ct SE4 141 B2
Geoffrey Gdns E6 100 A5
Geoffrey Ho SE1 262 D6
Geoffrey Jones Ct NW10 90 A6
Geoffrey Rd SE4 141 B2
George Akass Ho 5 SE18 123 A1
George Beard Rd 11 SE8 119 B2
George Beare Lo 9 SW4 159 C6
George Belt Ho 8 E2 96 D4
George Carver Ho E7 77 A3
George Comberton Wlk 4 E12 78 C3
George Cres N10 31 A3
George Ct
Buckhurst Hill IG9 21 D2
St James WC2 250 B5
George Davies Lodge IG6 57 A4
George Downing Est N16 73 D6
George Eliot Ho SW1 259 B3
George Eliot Jun & Inf Schs NW8 92 B6 229 C6
George Elliot Ho SE17 262 A2
George Elliston Ho 13 SE1 118 A1
George Eyre Ho NW8 229 D3
George Gange Way HA3 42 D6
George Green's Sch E14 120 A1
George Groves Rd SE20 184 A2
George Ho 8 SE26 184 B5
George Inn Yd SE1 252 C3
George La
Hayes BR2 209 B1
Lewisham SE13 164 A5
Wanstead E18 55 B6
Woodford E18 37 A1
George Lansbury Ho
7 Bow E3 97 B4
3 Willesden NW10 67 C1
Wood Green N22 32 C2
George Lashwood Ct 12 SW9 138 B1
George Leybourne Ho 15 E1 118 A6
George Lindgren Ho SW6 264 D4
George Loveless Ho 4 E2 95 D4
George Lovell Dr
Enfield EN3 7 A6
Holdbrook EN3 7 C6
George Mathers Rd SE11 261 C4
George Mews
27 Brixton SW9 138 C3
NW1 232 A1
George Mitchell Sch E10 53 D1
George Parr Ho N21 16 D4
George Peabody Ct NW1 237 A4
George Rd
Chingford E4 35 C4
Kingston u T KT2 177 A3
New Malden KT3 199 D4
George Row SE16 118 A4
Georges Mead WD6 10 A5
George Spicer Prim Sch EN1 5 D2
George Sq SW19 201 C6
George's Rd N7 72 B3
George's Sq SW6 264 D6
George St
Barking IG11 79 A1
6 Canning Town E16 98 D1
Ealing W7 108 C5
Hounslow TW3, TW5 129 B3
Marylebone W1 92 D1 237 D2
Richmond TW10 153 D6
Southall UB2 107 A2
South Croydon CR0 221 B6
George Street Sta CR0 221 A6
George Taylor CT N9 18 B1
George Tingle Ho SE1 263 D6
George Tomlinson Prim Sch E11 54 C1
Georgetown Cl 4 SE19 183 C5
Georgette Pl SE10 142 A5
George Vale Ho 35 E2 96 A5
George V Ave HA2, HA5 41 C6
Georgeville Gdns IG6 56 D5
George V Way UB6 87 B6
George Walter Ho 11 SE16 118 C2
George Wyver Cl SW18 157 A4
George Yd
City of London EC3 242 D1
Mayfair W1 115 A6 248 B6
Georgiana St NW1 93 C6 232 B6
Georgian Cl
Hayes BR2 209 B1
Ickenham UB10 60 A4
Stanmore HA7 25 A3
Georgian Ct
Croydon CR0 205 B1
12 Hackney E9 96 C6
3 Hendon NW4 46 B4
Wembley HA9 66 D2
Georgian Ho HA0 65 A5
Georgian Lo HA5 40 B4
Georgian Village The E17 54 A6
Georgian Way HA1 64 B6
Georgia Rd
New Malden KT3 199 A5
South Norwood CR7 182 D2
Georgina Ct 5 TW1 153 C5
Georgina Gdns 10 E2 95 D4
Geraint Rd BR1 187 A6
Geraldine Ct 6 NW9 46 A5
Geraldine Rd
Brentford W4 132 C6
Wandsworth SW18 158 A6
Geraldine St SE11 261 C5
Gerald Mews SW1 258 B4
Gerald Rd
Belgravia SW1 115 A2 258 B4
Dagenham RM8 59 B1
Newham E16 98 D3
Gerard Ave TW4 151 C4
Gerard Ct NW2 68 D3
Gerard Rd
Barnes SW13 133 D4
Harrow HA1 43 A3
Gerards Cl SE16 118 C1
Gerboa Ct 6 E4 36 B5
Gerda Rd SE9 167 A2
Germander Way E15 98 C4
German Sch The TW10 153 D3
Gernigan Ho SW18 158 B5
Gernon Rd E3 97 A5
Geron Way NW2 68 C6
Gerrard Gdns HA5 40 A4
Gerrard Ho 5 SE14 140 D5
Gerrard Pl W1 249 D6
Gerrard Rd N1 94 D5 234 D4
Gerrards Cl N14 15 C6
Gerrard's Ct W5 109 D3
Gerrard St W1 115 D6 249 D6
Gerridge Ct SE1 261 B6
Gerridge St SE1 116 C3 261 B6
Gerry Raffles Sq E15 76 B2
Gertrude Rd DA17 125 C2
Gertrude St SW10 136 A6 266 B5
Gervase Cl HA9 67 A5
Gervase Rd HA8 27 B2
Gervase St SE15 140 B5
Getters Talmud Torah 3 N16 51 B2
Ghent St SE6 163 C2
Ghent Way E8 73 D2
Giant Arches Rd SE24 161 A5
Giant Tree Hill WD23 8 B3
Gibbards Cott 1 IG11 79 D1
Gibbfield Cl RM6 59 A6
Gibbings Ho SE1 251 D1
Gibbins Rd E15 76 A1
Gibbon Ho NW8 236 D5
Gibbon Rd Acton W3 111 C6
Kingston u T KT2 176 A3
Nunhead SE15 140 C3
Gibbons Mews NW11 47 B4
Gibbons Rd NW10 67 C2
Gibbon's Rents SE1 253 A3
Gibbon Wlk SW15 134 A1
Gibbs Ave SE19 183 B5
Gibbs Cl SE19 183 B5
Gibbs Gn
Edgware HA8 27 A6
West Kensington W14 113 B1 254 D2
Gibbs Green Rd W14 113 B1 254 C2
Gibbs Green Specl Sch W14 113 B1 254 D2
Gibbs Ho
6 Balham SW12 159 B4
2 Bromley BR1 186 D2
Gibbs Rd N18 34 C6
Gibbs Sq SE19 183 B5
Gibraltar Ho NW10 89 C5
Gibraltar Wlk 28 E2 95 D4
Gibson Bsns Ctr 10 N17 33 D3
Gibson Cl
Bethnal Green E1 96 C3
Chessington KT9 213 C3
Isleworth TW7 130 B2
Southgate N21 16 C5
Gibson Ct
9 Friern Barnet N11 30 D5
Hinchley Wood KT10 212 D5
Gibson Gdns N16 73 D6
Gibson Ho
South Croydon CR2 221 A2
Sutton SM1 217 C4
Gibson Rd
Dagenham RM8 58 C1
Ickenham UB10 60 B4
Lambeth SE11 260 D3
Sutton SM1 217 D3
Gibson's Hill SW16 182 C3
Gibson Sq N1 94 C6 234 B6
Gibson St SE10 120 C1
Gideon Cl DA17 125 D2
Gideon Mews W5 109 D4
Gideon Rd SW11 137 A2
Giesbach Rd N19 71 D6
Giffard Rd N18 33 C4
Giffen Square Mkt★ SE8 141 C5
Giffin St SE8 141 C5
Gifford Gdns W7 86 C2
Gifford Ho
5 Clapham SW4 137 D1
Greenwich SE10 120 B1
Pimlico SW1 259 A1
Gifford Prim Sch UB5 85 B5
Gifford Rd NW10 67 C1
Gifford St N1 72 A1
Gift La E15 98 D6
Giggs Hill BR5 190 A2
Giggs Hill Gdns KT7 197 A1
Giggs Hill Rd KT7 197 A2

Gilbert Cl
Kidbrooke SE18 144 B4
1 Merton SW19 179 D2
Gilbert Ct W5 88 B1
Gilbert Gr HA8 27 B2
Gilbert Ho
Barbican EC2 242 B3
Deptford SE8 141 C6
5 Globe Town E2 96 D4
Pimlico SW1 258 D1
South Lambeth SW8 270 A4
5 Walthamstow E17 54 A6
Gilbert Pl
WC1 94 A2 240 A3
Gilbert Rd
Belvedere DA17 125 C3
Lambeth
SE11 116 C2 261 B4
Merton SW19 180 A3
Pinner HA5 40 D5
Plaistow BR1 187 A3
Gilbert Scott Prim Sch
CR2 223 A1
Gilbert Sheldon Ho
W2 236 D4
Gilbertson Ho 11
E14 119 C3
Gilbert St Enfield EN3 6 C6
Hounslow TW3 130 A2
Leyton E15 76 C4
Marylebone
W1 93 A1 238 B1
Gilbert White Cl UB6 87 A6
Gilbey Cl UB10 60 D4
Gilbey Rd SW17 180 C5
Gilbeys Yd NW1 71 A1
Gilbourne Rd SE18 145 D6
Gilby Ho 5 E9 74 D2
Gilda Ave EN3 19 A6
Gilda Cres N16 52 A1
Gilda Ct NW7 28 A2
Gildea Cl HA5 23 C3
Gildea St W1 238 D3
Gilden Cres NW5 71 A3
Gildersome St SE18 144 C6
Gilders Rd KT9 214 B2
Giles Coppice SE19 183 D6
Giles Ho
5 Bermondsey
SE16 118 A3
Notting Hill W11 91 C1
Gilesmead SE5 139 B4
Gilfrid Cl UB8 82 D1
Gilkes Cres SE21 161 C5
Gilkes Pl SE21 161 C5
Gillam Ho 9 SE16 118 C2
Gillan Ct SE12 165 B1
Gillan Gn WD23 8 A2
Gillards Mews 6 E17 53 C5
Gillards Way E17 53 C5
Gill Ave E16 99 A1
Gill Ct SE18 123 A2
Gillender St E3 98 A3
Gillespie Prim Sch
N5 72 D5
Gillespie Rd N4, N5 72 D5
Gillett Ave E6 100 A5
Gillette Cnr TW7 131 A5
Gillett Ho N8 50 A6
Gillett Pl 27 E8 73 C3
Gillett Rd CR7 205 B5
Gillett St E8, N16 73 C3
Gillfoot NW1 232 A3
Gillham Terr N17 34 A3
Gillian Ho HA3 24 C4
Gillian Park Rd SM3 201 B1
Gillian St SE13 163 D6
Gillies Ct
Sidcup DA14 189 C6
Southgate N21 16 B6
Gillies St NW5 71 A3
Gilling Ct 5 NW3 70 C2
Gillingham Ho SW1 259 A4
Gillingham Mews
SW1 259 A4
Gillingham Rd NW2 69 A5
Gillingham Row
SW1 259 A4
Gillingham St
SW1 115 C2 259 A4
Gillings Ct EN5 1 A1
Gillison Wlk 19 SE16 118 A3
Gillman Dr E15 98 D6
Gillman Ho 24 E2 96 A5
Gillray Ho
Chelsea SW10 266 C5
Gillray Ho *continued*
2 Sutton SM1 218 B3
Gills Ct 2 EN5 14 A6
Gill St E14 119 B6
Gillum Cl EN4 14 D3
Gilmore Cl UB10 60 C5
Gilmore Cres TW15 170 C4
Gilmore Ct N11 30 D5
Gilmore Ho SW4 136 D1
Gilmore Rd SE13 142 B1
Gilpin Ave SW14 133 B1
Gilpin Cl
Mitcham CR4 180 C1
Paddington W2 236 B4
Gilpin Cres
Edmonton N18 33 D5
Twickenham TW2 151 D4
Gilpin Ho
9 Edmonton N9 18 A1
New Malden KT3 199 C4
Gilpin Rd E5 75 A4
Gilpin Way UB3 127 B5
Gilray Ho W2 246 C6
Gilsland Rd CR7 205 B5
Gilson Pl N10 30 D3
Gilstead Ho IG11 102 B5
Gilstead Rd SW6 135 D3
Gilston Rd
SW10 114 A1 256 B1
Gilton Rd SE6 164 C1
Giltspur St
EC1 94 D1 241 D2
Gilwell Cl E4 7 D1
Gilwell Ct 7 E5 74 B4
Gippeswyck Cl HA5 22 D2
Gipsy Cnr W3 89 B2
Gipsy Hill SE19 183 C5
Gipsy Hill Sta SE19 183 C5
Gipsy La SW15 134 B2
Gipsy Rd
Bexley DA16 146 D3
West Norwood SE27 183 B6
Gipsy Road Gdns
SE27 183 A6
Giralda Cl E16 99 D2
Giraud St E14 97 D1
Girdlers Rd W14 112 D2
Girdlestone Wlk N19 71 C6
Girdwood Rd SW18,
SW19 157 A4
Girling Ho 9 N1 95 C6
Girling Way TW14 128 A2
Gironde Rd
SW6 135 B5 264 D3
Girtin Ho
6 Belmont SM2 217 D1
4 Northolt UB5 84 D5
Girton Ave NW9 44 C6
Girton Cl UB5 64 A2
Girton Gdns CR0 223 C5
Girton Ho SW15 156 D5
Girton Rd
Forest Hill SE26 184 D5
Northolt UB5 64 A2
Girton Villas 6 W10 90 D1
Gisbourne Cl SM6 219 D5
Gisburn Ho 23 SE15 140 A5
Gisburn Mans N8 50 B5
Gisburn Rd N8 50 B5
Gissing Wlk N1 72 C1
Gittens Cl BR1 186 D6
Given-Wilson Wlk
E13 98 D5
Glacier Way HA0 87 D5
Gladbeck Way EN2 4 D1
Gladding Rd E12 77 D4
Gladebury Ct 2
SW19 179 B4
Glade Cl KT6 213 D6
Glade Gdns CR0 207 A2
Glade La UB2 107 D4
Gladeside
Croydon CR0 206 D3
Southgate N21 16 B4
Gladeside Cl KT9 213 D1
Gladesmore Com Sch
N15 52 A4
Gladesmore Rd N15 51 D3
Glades Sh Ctr The
BR1 187 A1
Gladeswood Rd
DA17 125 D2
Glade The
Bromley BR1 187 D1
Charlton SE7 143 C5
Croydon CR0 206 D3
Glade The *continued*
Enfield EN2 4 C3
Hammersmith W12 112 B4
Southgate N21 16 B4
Stoneleigh KT17 216 A2
West Wickham BR4 223 D5
Woodford IG8 21 B1
Gladiator St SE23 163 A4
Glading Terr N16 73 D5
Gladioli Cl 6 TW12 173 C4
Gladsdale Dr HA5 40 B5
Gladsmuir Rd
Barnet EN5 1 A3
Upper Holloway N19 49 C1
Gladstone Ave
Feltham TW14 150 B5
Plashet E12 78 A1
Tottenham N22 32 D1
Twickenham TW2 152 B4
Gladstone Ct
12 Merton SW19 179 C3
Ruislip HA4 61 C6
Westminster SW1 259 D3
Willesden NW2 68 B3
Gladstone Gdns
TW3 130 A4
Gladstone Ho
6 Mitcham SW19 180 D1
16 Poplar E14 97 C1
Gladstone Mews
3 Penge SE20 184 C3
Wood Green N22 32 C1
Gladstone Par NW2 68 C5
Gladstone Park Gdns
NW2 68 B5
Gladstone Park Sch
NW10 68 B3
Gladstone Pl KT8 196 C4
Gladstone Rd
Acton W4 111 B3
Buckhurst Hill IG9 21 C3
Farnborough BR6 227 A3
Kingston u T KT1 198 C6
Merton SW19 179 C3
Southall UB2 107 A4
Surbiton KT6 214 A6
Thornton Heath CR0 205 B2
Gladstone St SE1 261 C6
Gladstone Terr SW8 268 D2
Gladstone Way HA3 42 C6
Gladwell Rd
London N8 50 B3
Plaistow BR1 187 A4
Gladwin Ho NW1 232 B3
Gladwyn Rd SW15 134 D2
Gladys Aylward Sch The
N18 33 B6
Gladys Dimson Ho
E7 76 D3
Gladys Rd NW6 69 C1
Glaisher St SE8 141 D6
Glamis Cres UB3 105 A3
Glamis Ct W3 110 D4
Glamis Est 3 E1 118 D6
Glamis Pl E1 118 C6
Glamis Rd E1 118 C6
Glamis Way UB5 64 A2
Glamorgan Cl CR4,
SW16 204 A6
Glamorgan Ct 4 W7 86 D2
Glamorgan Rd KT1 175 C3
Glandford Way RM6 58 B4
Glanfield Rd BR3 207 B5
Glanleam Rd HA7 25 D6
Glanville Ho 4
SW12 159 C4
Glanville Mews HA7 25 A5
Glanville Rd
Bromley BR2 209 B6
Clapham Pk SW2 160 A6
Glasbrook Ave TW2 151 B3
Glasbrook Rd SE9 165 D4
Glasbury Ho 5 SW9 138 B1
Glaserton Rd N16 51 C2
Glasford St SW17 180 D4
Glasfryn Ct HA2 64 B6
Glasgow Ho W9 91 D5
Glasgow Rd
Edmonton N18 34 B5
Newham E13 99 B5
Glasgow Terr
SW1 115 C1 259 A1
Glasier Ct 6 E15 76 C1
Glasse Cl W13 109 A6
Glasshill St
SE1 116 D4 251 D2
Glasshouse Cl UB8 82 D2
Glasshouse Fields
E1 118 D6
Glasshouse St
W1 115 C6 249 B5
Glasshouse The
SE13 142 A1
Glasshouse Wlk
SE11 116 B1 260 C2
Glasshouse Yd EC1 242 A5
Glasslyn Rd N8 49 D4
Glassmill La BR2 186 D1
Glass St 4 E2 96 B3
Glass Yd SE18 122 C3
Glastonbury Ave IG8 37 D4
Glastonbury Ct
12 Deptford SE14 140 C5
1 Ealing W13 109 A5
Glastonbury Ho
London SE12 164 D6
Pimlico SW1 258 C2
Glastonbury Pl 22 E1 96 C1
Glastonbury Rd
Edmonton N9 18 A3
Morden SM4 201 C2
Glastonbury St NW6 69 B3
Glaston Ct W5 109 D5
Glaucus St E3 97 D2
Glazbury Rd
W14 113 A1 254 B2
Glazebrook Cl SE21 161 B2
Glazebrook Rd
TW11 174 D3
Gleave Ct 7 N20 14 D2
Glebe Ave Enfield EN2 4 D2
Harrow HA3 44 A6
Mitcham CR4 180 C1
Ruislip HA4 62 B2
Uxbridge UB10 61 A4
Woodford IG8 37 A4
Glebe Cl
1 Chiswick W4 111 C1
Uxbridge UB10 61 A4
Glebe Cotts
Feltham TW13 151 C1
Sutton SM1 217 D4
Glebe Cres
Harrow HA3 44 A6
Hendon NW4 46 C5
Glebe Ct Ealing W5 109 D5
Hanwell W7 108 B6
Lewisham SE3 142 C2
Mitcham CR4 202 D6
Palmers Green N13 16 C1
Ruislip HA4 39 B2
Stanmore HA7 25 C5
Glebe Fst & Mid Sch
HA3 44 A5
Glebe Gdns KT3 199 C2
Glebe Ho
8 Bermondsey
SE16 118 B3
Feltham TW13 151 C1
7 Woolwich SE18 122 C2
Glebe House Dr BR2 209 B1
Glebehyrst SE19 183 C6
Glebe La Barnet EN5 12 A5
Harrow HA3 44 A5
Glebeland Gdns
TW17 193 A3
Glebelands
East Molesey KT8 195 D5
Leyton E10 75 D6
Mitcham CR4 202 C6
Glebelands Ave
Ilford IG2 57 B2
Woodford E18 37 A1
Glebelands Cl
Camberwell SE5 139 C2
Finchley N2 30 B2
Glebelands Rd
TW14 150 A4
Glebe Path CR4 202 D6
Glebe Pl
SW3 136 C6 267 A6
Glebe Prim Sch UB10 61 B4
Glebe Rd
Barnes SW13 134 A3
Belmont SM2 217 A1
Bromley BR1 187 A2
Dagenham RM10 81 D2
Dalston E8 73 D1
Finchley N3 30 A2
Hayes UB3 105 D5
Hornsey N8 50 B5
Stanmore HA7 25 C5
Glebe Rd *continued*
Wallington SM5 218 D2
Willesden NW10 68 A2
Glebe Sch BR4 224 B6
Glebe Side TW1 152 D5
Glebe Sq CR4 202 D6
Glebe St W4 111 C1
Glebe The
Chislehurst BR7 189 A2
Lewisham SE3 142 C2
New Malden KT4 199 D1
Streatham SW16 181 D6
West Drayton UB7 104 B2
Glebeway IG8 37 C5
Glebe Way
Feltham TW13 151 C1
West Wickham BR4 224 B6
Gledhow Gdns SW5 256 A3
Gledstanes Rd
W14 113 A1 254 B1
Gledwood Ave UB4 84 A2
Gledwood Cres UB4 83 D2
Gledwood Ct UB4 83 D2
Gledwood Dr UB4 83 D2
Gledwood Gdns UB4 84 A2
Gleed Ave WD23 8 B2
Gleeson Dr BR6 227 D4
Glegg Pl 3 SW15 134 D1
Glenaffric Ave E14 120 B2
Glen Albyn Rd
SW19 156 D2
Glenalla Rd HA4 39 D2
Glenalmond Ho
Ashford TW15 148 A1
2 Putney SW15 156 D5
Glenalmond Rd HA3 44 A5
Glenalvon Way 5
SE18 122 A2
Glena Mount SM1 218 A4
Glenarm Coll IG1 78 D6
Glenarm Rd E5 74 D4
Glen Ave TW15 170 C6
Glenavon Cl KT10 213 A1
Glenavon Ct KT4 216 B6
Glenavon Lo 5 E18 55 A6
Glenavon Rd E15 76 C1
Glenbarr Cl SE9 144 D2
Glenbow Rd BR1 186 C5
Glenbrook N EN2 4 B1
Glenbrook Prim Sch
SW4 159 D5
Glenbrook Rd NW6 69 C3
Glenbrook S EN2 4 B1
Glenbuck Ct 6 KT6 198 A3
Glenbuck Rd KT6 198 A3
Glenburnie Rd
SW17 158 D1
Glencairn Dr W5 87 C3
Glencairne Cl E16 99 D2
Glencairn Rd SW16 182 A3
Glen Cl TW17 192 C5
Glencoe Ave IG2 57 C2
Glencoe Dr RM10 81 C4
Glencoe Mans 6
SW9 138 C5
Glencoe Rd UB4 84 D3
Glencorse Gn WD19 22 D6
Glen Cres IG8 37 B4
Glencroft Ct SM1 217 C3
Glen Ct
6 Bromley BR1 186 D3
9 Penge SE20 184 B2
Sidcup DA14 190 A6
Glendale Ave
Edgware HA8 26 C6
Ilford RM6 58 C2
Wood Green N22 32 C3
Glendale Cl SE9 144 C2
Glendale Dr SW19 179 B5
Glendale Gdns HA9 44 A1
Glendale Mews BR3 185 D2
Glendale Way SE28 124 C6
Glendall St SW9 138 B1
Glendarvon St
SW15 134 D2
Glendevon Cl HA8 10 D1
Glendish Rd N17 34 B2
Glendor Gdns NW7 27 B6
Glendower Gdns 10
SW14 133 B2
Glendower Pl SW7 256 C4
Glendower Prep Sch
SW7 114 B2 256 C4

Glendower Rd
Chingford E4 .... 20 B3
Mortlake SW14 .... 133 B2
Glendown Ho 2 E8 ... 74 A3
Glendown Rd SE2 ..... 124 A1
Glendun Ct W3 .... 111 C6
Glendun Rd W3 .... 111 C6
Gleneagle Lo BR3 .... 185 C2
Gleneagle Mews
SW16 .... 181 D5
Gleneagle Rd SW16 . 181 D5
Gleneagles
Ealing W13 .... 87 B2
Stanmore HA7 .... 25 B4
Gleneagles Cl
21 Bermondsey
SE16 .... 118 B1
Crofton BR6 .... 211 B1
South Oxhey WD19 .... 22 D6
Gleneagles Ct 4
TW11 .... 175 A5
Gleneagles Gn 1
BR6 .... 211 B1
Gleneagles Twr 2
UB1 .... 86 A1
Gleneldon Mews
SW16 .... 182 A6
Gleneldon Rd SW16 . 182 A6
Glenelg Rd SW2 ...... 160 A6
Glenesk Rd SE9 ...... 144 D1
Glenfarg Rd SE6 ..... 164 B3
Glenfield Cres HA4 ... 39 B2
Glenfield Rd
Ashford TW15 .... 171 A4
Ealing W13 .... 109 B4
Streatham SW12 ..... 159 C3
Glenfield Terr W13 .. 109 B5
Glenfinlas Way SE5 . 138 D5
Glenforth St SE10 ... 120 D1
Glengall Ct SE23 ..... 163 A4
Glengall Gr E14 ...... 120 A3
Glengall Pass 2
NW6 .... 91 C6
Glengall Rd
Bexley DA7 .... 147 A2
Camberwell SE15 .... 139 D6
Edgware HA8 .... 10 D1
Kilburn NW6 .... 91 B6
Woodford IG8 .... 37 B4
Glengall Terr SE15 .. 139 D6
Glengarnock Ave
E14 .... 120 A2
Glengarry Rd SE22 .. 161 D6
Glen Gdns CR0 .... 220 C4
Glenham Dr IG2 .... 56 D4
Glenhead Cl SE9 .... 144 D2
Glenhill Cl N3 .... 29 C1
Glen Ho
6 Newham E16 ...... 122 C5
Wallington SM6 ..... 219 C4
Glenhouse Rd SE9 .. 166 C6
Glenhurst 4 BR3 .... 186 A2
Glenhurst Ave
Gospel Oak NW5 ...... 71 A4
Ruislip HA4 .... 39 A1
Sidcup DA5 .... 169 B3
Glenhurst Ct 1
SE19 .... 183 D5
Glenhurst Rd
Brentford TW8 ...... 109 C1
North Finchley N12 .... 30 B5
Glenhurst Rise SE19 183 A3
Glenilla Rd NW3 .... 70 C2
Glenister Ho UB3 .... 106 B5
Glenister Park Rd
SW16 .... 181 D3
Glenister Rd SE10 ... 120 D1
Glenister St E16 ..... 122 C5
Glenkerry Ho 1 E14 ... 98 A1
Glenlea Rd SE9 ...... 166 C6
Glenloch Ct 2 NW3 ... 70 C2
Glenloch Rd
Enfield EN3 .... 6 C3
Maitland Pk NW3 ...... 70 C3
Glenluce Rd SE3 ..... 143 A6
Glenlyon Rd SE9 ..... 166 C6
Glenmead IG9 .... 21 C3
Glenmere Ave NW7 ... 28 A4
Glenmere Row
Lee SE12 .... 165 A5
Lewisham SE12 ..... 164 D5
Glen Mews E17 .... 53 B4
Glenmill TW12 .... 173 B5
Glenmore SW15 .... 156 D5
Glenmore Ho 6
TW10 .... 154 A5
Glenmore Lawns
W13 .... 87 A1
Glenmore Rd
Bexley DA16 .... 145 D4
Maitland Pk NW3 ...... 70 C2
Glenmore Way IG11 . 102 A5
Glenmount Path 1
SE18 .... 123 A1
Glennie Ct SE21 ..... 162 A3
Glennie Ho SE10 ..... 142 A4
Glennie Rd SE27,
SW16 .... 160 C1
Glenny Rd IG11 .... 79 A2
Glenorchy Cl UB4 ..... 85 A2
Glenpark Ct W13 .... 109 A6
Glenparke Rd E7 ...... 77 B2
Glen Rd
Chessington KT9 .... 214 A5
Newham E13 .... 99 C3
Walthamstow E17 ..... 53 B4
Glenridding NW1 ... 232 B3
Glen Rise IG8 .... 37 B4
Glenrosa St SW6 .... 136 A3
Glenrose Ct DA14 ... 190 B5
Glenrose Ho 9 SM1 . 218 A4
Glenroy St W12 .... 90 C1
Glensdale Rd SE4 ... 141 B2
Glenshaw Mans 7
SW9 .... 138 C5
Glenshiel Rd SE9 .... 166 C6
Glentanner Way
SW17 .... 158 B1
Glentham Gdns
SW13 .... 134 B6
Glentham Rd SW13 .. 134 B6
Glen The
Beckenham BR2 ..... 186 C1
Eastcote Village HA5 ... 40 B4
Enfield EN2 .... 4 D1
Locksbottom BR6 .... 226 C5
Rayners La HA5 .... 41 A2
Southall UB2 .... 107 B1
South Croydon CR0 .. 222 D5
Wembley HA9 .... 65 D4
Glenthorne Ave CR0 . 206 C1
Glenthorne Cl SM3 .. 201 C1
Glenthorne Gdns
Cheam SM3 .... 201 C1
Ilford IG6 .... 56 D5
Glenthorne High
Specialist Arts Coll
SM3 .... 201 C1
Glenthorne Mews
W6 .... 112 B2
Glenthorne Rd
Friern Barnet N11 ..... 31 A5
Hammersmith W6 .... 112 B2
Kingston u T KT1 .... 198 B5
Walthamstow E17 ..... 53 A4
Glenthorpe SW15 .... 134 A1
Glenthorpe Rd SM4 . 200 D4
Glenton Rd SE13 ..... 142 C1
Glentrammon Ave
BR6 .... 227 D2
Glentrammon Cl
BR6 .... 227 D3
Glentrammon Gdns
BR6 .... 227 D2
Glentrammon Rd
BR6 .... 227 D2
Glentworth Ct HA8 .... 26 B5
Glentworth St
NW1 .... 92 D3 237 D5
Glenure Rd SE9 ...... 166 C6
Glenview SE2 .... 146 D6
Glen View Rd BR1 ... 187 D1
Glenville Ave EN2 .... 5 A5
Glenville Gr SE8 ..... 141 B5
Glenville Mews
SW18 .... 157 C4
Glenville Rd KT2 ..... 176 C2
Glen Wlk TW7 .... 152 B6
Glenwood Ave NW9 ... 45 C1
Glenwood Cl HA1 ..... 42 D4
Glenwood Ct
7 Sidcup DA14 ..... 190 A6
6 Wanstead E18 ...... 55 A6
Glenwood Gdns IG2 .. 56 C4
Glenwood Gr NW9 .... 45 A1
Glenwood Ho 3 EN5 .. 13 D6
Glenwood Rd
Edgware NW7 .... 11 C1
Forest Hill SE6 ...... 163 C3
Glenwood Rd *continued*
Harringay N15 .... 50 D4
Hounslow TW3 .... 130 B2
Stoneleigh KT17 .... 216 A2
Glenwood Way CR0 . 206 D3
Glenworth Ave E14 .. 120 B2
Gliddon Rd
W14 .... 113 A1 254 A2
Glimpsing Gn DA18 .. 125 A3
Glisson Rd UB10 ...... 82 C5
Globe Acad The
SE1 .... 117 B3 262 C5
Globe Ct SE18 .... 145 A6
Globe Pond Rd
SE16 .... 119 A5
Globe Prim Sch 37
E2 .... 96 C4
Globe Rd
Bethnal Green E1, E2 ... 96 C3
Stratford E15 .... 76 D3
Woodford IG8 .... 37 C4
Globe St SE1 . 117 B4 252 C1
Globe Terr 9 E2 .... 96 C4
Globe Theatre The★
SE1 .... 117 A5 252 A5
GLOBE TOWN 96 D4
Globe View EC4 ..... 252 A6
Globe Yd W1 .... 238 C1
Glossop Ho TW7 .... 131 A1
Gloster Rd KT3 ...... 199 C5
Gloucester W14 .... 254 D3
Gloucester Ave
Camden Town
NW1 .... 93 A6 231 B6
Falconwood DA16 ... 145 D1
Sidcup DA15 .... 167 C2
Gloucester Cir SE10 . 142 A5
Gloucester Cl
Thames Ditton KT7 ... 197 A1
Willesden NW10 .... 67 B1
Gloucester Cres
Camden Town
NW1 .... 93 B6 231 C6
Staines TW18 .... 170 A4
Gloucester Ct
6 Acton W3 .... 88 C1
10 Belmont SM2 .... 217 C1
Borough The SE1 .... 262 B6
City of London EC3 ... 253 B5
Dulwich SE22 .... 162 A3
5 Ealing W7 .... 86 D2
Golders Green NW11 ... 47 B2
Harrow HA1 .... 42 C6
Redbridge IG1 .... 56 B2
Richmond TW9 ...... 132 C5
8 Surbiton KT6 ..... 197 D2
Gloucester Dr
Finsbury Pk N4 .... 72 D6
London NW11 .... 47 C5
Gloucester Gate
NW1 .... 231 C4
Gloucester Gate Mews
NW1 .... 231 C4
Gloucester Gdns
Cockfosters EN4 ...... 15 A6
Golders Green NW11 ... 47 B2
Paddington W2 ..... 236 A2
Redbridge IG1 .... 56 A2
Sutton SM1 .... 217 D6
Gloucester Gr HA8 .... 27 B2
Gloucester Ho
Kilburn NW6 .... 91 C5
Richmond TW10 ..... 154 C6
Gloucester Lo 9
CR0 .... 221 D6
Gloucester Mews
Paddington W2 ..... 236 B1
Walthamstow E17 ..... 53 C2
Gloucester Mews W
W2 .... 236 B1
Gloucester Par
Bexley DA15 .... 168 A6
Hayes UB3 .... 105 A3
Gloucester Pk SW7 . 256 A4
Gloucester Pl
W1 .... 92 D2 237 D4
Gloucester Pl Mews
W1 .... 92 D2 237 D3
Gloucester Prim Sch
SE15 .... 139 C5
Gloucester Rd
Acton W3 .... 111 A4
Croydon CR0 .... 205 C2
Ealing W5 .... 109 C4
Edmonton N18 .... 33 D5
Enfield EN2 .... 5 A5
Gloucester Rd *continued*
Erith DA17 .... 125 B1
Feltham TW13 .... 150 C3
Hampton TW12 ...... 173 D3
Harrow HA1 .... 41 D4
Higham Hill E17 .... 34 D1
Hounslow TW4 .... 129 A1
Ilford E12 .... 78 B4
Kingston u T KT1, KT2 . 176 D1
Leyton E10 .... 53 C2
New Barnet EN5 ...... 14 A6
Richmond TW9 ...... 132 C5
South Kensington
SW7 .... 114 A2 256 A4
Teddington TW11 .... 174 C5
Tottenham N17 .... 51 B6
Twickenham TW2 .... 152 A3
Wanstead E11 .... 55 C4
Gloucester Road Sta
SW7 .... 114 A2 256 A4
Gloucester Sq
6 Hackney E2 .... 96 A6
Paddington
W2 .... 92 C1 237 A1
Gloucester St
SW1 .... 115 C1 259 A2
Gloucester Terr
W2 .... 92 A1 236 B1
Gloucester Way EC1 234 B1
Gloucester Wlk
W8 .... 113 C4 245 B2
Glover Cl SE2 .... 124 C2
Glover Dr N18 .... 34 C4
Glover Ho
London SE15 .... 140 B1
2 South Hampstead
NW6 .... 70 A1
Glover Rd HA5 .... 40 D3
Glovers Gr HA4 .... 38 D2
Glovers Lo 24 TW10 . 153 D6
Glowhill Ct N12 .... 30 A3
Gloxinia Wlk TW12 ... 173 C4
Glycena Rd SW11 ... 136 D2
Glyn Ave EN4 .... 2 B1
Glyn Cl SE25 .... 183 C2
Glyn Ct Stanmore HA7 .. 25 B4
West Norwood SE27 . 160 C1
Glyndale Grange
SM2 .... 217 D2
Glyndebourne Ct 5
UB5 .... 84 C4
Glyndebourne Pk
BR6 .... 226 D6
Glynde Mews SW3 .. 257 B5
Glynde Rd DA7 .... 147 A2
Glynde Reach WC1 .. 233 B1
Glynde St SE4 .... 163 B5
Glyndon Rd SE18 .... 123 B2
Glyn Dr DA14 .... 190 B6
Glynfield Rd NW10 .... 67 C1
Glyn Mans W14 ..... 254 B4
Glynne Rd N22 .... 32 C1
Glyn Rd Clapton Pk E5 .. 74 D4
Enfield EN3 .... 6 C1
North Cheam KT4,
SM3 .... 216 D6
Glyn St SE11 .... 260 C1
Glynwood Ct 7
SE23 .... 162 C2
Goater's Alley SW6 . 264 D3
Goat La EN1 .... 5 D5
Goat Rd CR4 .... 202 D2
Goat Wharf TW8 .... 132 A6
Godalming Ave SM6 . 220 B3
Godalming Rd E14 .... 97 D2
Godbold Rd E15 .... 98 C4
Goddard Cl TW17 ... 192 B6
Goddard Ct HA3 .... 25 A1
Goddard Ho SW19 .. 156 D2
Goddard Pl N19 .... 71 C5
Goddard Rd BR3 .... 207 A5
Goddards Way IG1 .... 57 B1
Goddarts Ho E17 ...... 53 C6
Godfrey Ave
Northolt UB5 .... 85 A6
Twickenham TW2 .... 152 B4
Godfrey Hill SE18 ... 122 A2
Godfrey Ho EC1 ..... 235 C1
Godfrey Rd SE18 .... 122 B2
Godfrey St
Chelsea
SW3 .... 114 C1 257 B2
Mill Meads E15 .... 98 A5
Godfrey Way TW4 ... 151 B4
Goding St
SE11 .... 116 A1 260 B1
Godley Rd SW18 ..... 158 B3
Godliman St EC4 .... 252 A6
Godman Rd SE15 .... 140 B3
Godolphin Cl N13 ..... 32 D4
Godolphin Ho
Primrose Hill NW3 ..... 70 C1
7 Streatham SW2 .. 160 C3
Godolphin & Latymer
Sch 16 W6 .... 112 B2
Godolphin Pl W3 .... 111 B6
Godolphin Rd W12 .. 112 B4
Godson Rd CR0 ..... 220 C5
Godson St N1 .... 234 A4
Godstone Ct 1 N16 ... 51 C1
Godstone Ho
Borough The SE1 .... 262 D6
1 Kingston u T KT2 .. 176 D4
Godstone Rd
Sutton SM1 .... 218 A4
Twickenham TW1 .... 153 B5
Godstow Rd SE2 ..... 124 C4
Godwin Cl
Shoreditch N1 ...... 235 B4
West Ewell KT19 .... 215 A2
Godwin Ct NW1 ..... 232 B4
Godwin Ho
2 Haggerston E2 ...... 95 D5
Kidbrooke SE18 ..... 144 B4
Kilburn NW6 .... 91 D5
Godwin Jun Sch E7 ... 77 B4
Godwin Prim Sch
RM9 .... 81 A1
Godwin Rd
Bromley BR1, BR2 ... 209 C6
Forest Gate E7 .... 77 B4
Godwyn Ho 13 KT6 .. 198 A3
Goffers Ho SE3 ...... 142 C3
Goffers Rd SE3, SE13 . 142 C3
Goffs Rd TW15 ...... 171 B4
Goffton Ho 14 SW9 ... 138 B3
Goidel Cl SM6 .... 219 D4
Golborne Gdns
5 Kensal Town W10 ... 91 A3
West Kilburn W10 ..... 91 B3
Golborne Mews 9
W10 .... 91 A2
Golborne Rd W10 ..... 91 A2
Golda Cl EN5 .... 12 D5
Golda Ct N3 .... 29 B1
Goldbeaters Gr HA8 .. 27 C3
Goldbeaters Prim Sch
HA8 .... 27 B2
Goldcliff Cl SM4 .... 201 C2
Goldcrest Cl
Newham E16 .... 99 D2
Woolwich SE28 ..... 124 C6
Goldcrest Mews W5 .. 87 D2
Goldcrest Way
Bushey WD23 .... 8 A3
New Addington CR0 ... 224 B1
Golden Cres UB3 .... 105 D5
Golden Cross Mews 2
W11 .... 91 B1
Golden Ct
4 Barnet EN4 .... 2 C1
Ealing W7 .... 108 C6
Hounslow TW3 ...... 130 B3
10 Richmond TW9 ... 153 D6
Golden Hinde The★
SE1 .... 252 C4
Golden Hind Pl 5
SE8 .... 119 B2
Golden La EC1 95 A3 242 B5
Golden Lane Campus
EC1 .... 95 A3 242 B5
Golden Lane L Ctr
EC1 .... 95 A3 242 A5
Golden Manor W7 ... 108 C6
Golden Mews SE20 .. 184 C2
Golden Par 2 E17 ..... 54 A6
Golden Plover Cl E16 . 99 A1
Golden Sq
W1 .... 115 C6 249 B6
Golders Cl HA8 .... 26 D5
Golders Ct NW11 ..... 47 B2
Golders Gdns NW11 ... 47 B2
GOLDERS GREEN 47 B2
Golders Green Coll
NW11 .... 47 C1
Golders Green Cres
NW11 .... 47 C2
Golders Green Rd
NW11 .... 47 A2
Golders Green Sta
NW11 .... 47 C1

Golders Hill Sch NW11 47 C2
Golderslea NW11 47 C1
Golders Manor Dr NW11 47 A3
Golders Park Cl NW11 47 C1
Golders Rise NW4 46 D4
Golders Way NW11 47 B2
Golderton 2 NW4 46 C5
Goldfinch Rd SE28 123 B3
Goldhawk Ind Est W6 112 B3
Goldhawk Mews 2 W12 112 B4
Goldhawk Rd W12 112 A3
Goldhawk Road Sta W12 112 C4
Goldhaze Cl IG8 37 D3
Gold Hill HA8 27 B4
Goldhurst Terr NW6 70 A1
Goldie Ho N19 49 D2
Goldie Leigh Hospl SE2 146 C6
Golding Cl KT9 213 C2
Golding Ct 7 IG1 78 C5
Golding St E1 96 A1
Goldington Cres NW1 232 C4
Goldington Ct NW1 232 C5
Goldington St NW1 93 D5 232 C4
Gold La HA8 27 B4
Goldman Cl E2 96 A3
Goldmark Ho SE3 143 B2
Goldney Rd W9 91 C3
Goldrill Dr N11 15 A2
Goldsboro Rd SW8 137 D5 269 D3
Goldsborough Cres E4 20 A2
Goldsborough Ho SW8 269 D1
Goldsdown Cl EN3 7 A3
Goldsdown Rd EN3 7 A3
Goldsmid St 2 SE18 123 C1
Goldsmith Ave
Acton W3 111 B6
Dagenham RM7 59 C2
Hyde The NW9 45 C3
Plashet E12 78 A2
Goldsmith Cl HA2 41 D1
Goldsmith Ct
Edgware HA8 26 B6
St Giles WC1 240 B2
Goldsmith Ho W3 111 B6
Goldsmith La NW9 45 A5
Goldsmith Rd
Acton W3 111 B5
Friern Barnet N11 30 D5
Higham Hill E17 34 D1
Leyton E10 53 D1
Peckham SE15 140 A4
Goldsmiths Bldgs W3 111 B5
Goldsmiths Cl W3 111 B5
Goldsmiths Coll, Univ of London SE14 141 A4
Goldsmith's Ct N6 49 B3
Goldsmith's Pl 6 NW6 91 D6
Goldsmith's Row E2 96 A5
Goldsmith's Sq 17 E2 96 A5
Goldsmith St EC2 242 B2
Goldthorpe NW1 232 A5
Goldwell Ho SE22 139 C1
Goldwell Rd CR7 204 B5
Goldwin Cl SE14 140 C4
Goldwing Cl E16 99 A1
Golf Cl
South Norwood SW16 182 C2
Stanmore HA7 25 C3
Golf Club Dr KT2 177 B3
Golfe Ho IG1 79 B5
Golfe Rd IG1 79 B5
Golfers View N12 30 B6
Golf Rd Bromley BR1 210 C6
Ealing W5 88 B1
Golf Side TW2 152 B1
Golfside Cl N20 14 C1
Golf Side Cl KT3 177 C1
Gollogly Terr 9 SE7 121 C1
Gomer Gdns TW11 175 A4
Gomer Pl TW11 175 A4
Gomm Rd SE16 118 C3
Gomshall Ave SM6 220 A3
Gondar Gdns NW6 69 B3
Gondar Mans NW6 69 B3
Gonson St SE8 141 D6
Gonston Cl SW19 157 A2
Gonville Cres UB5 63 D2
Gonville Ct 6 EN4 14 D3
Gonville Ho 6 SW15 156 D5
Gonville Prim Sch CR7 204 B4
Gonville Rd CR7 204 B4
Gonville St SW6 135 A2
Gooch Ho
Holborn EC1 241 A4
Lower Clapton E5 74 B5
Goodall Ho 10 SE4 140 D1
Goodall Rd E11 76 A5
Goodbehere Ho 7 SE27 183 A6
Gooden Ct HA1 64 C5
Goodenough Coll WC1 94 B3 240 C6
Goodenough Rd SW19 179 B3
Goodey Rd IG11 79 D1
Goodfaith Ho 18 E14 119 D6
Goodge Pl W1 239 B3
Goodge St W1 93 C2 239 B3
Goodge Street Sta W1 93 D2 239 C4
Goodhall Cl HA7 25 B4
Goodhall St NW10 89 D4
Good Hart Pl E14 119 A6
Goodhart Way BR4 208 C3
Goodhew Rd CR0 206 A3
Goodhope Ho 17 E14 119 D6
Gooding Cl KT3 199 A4
Goodinge Cl N7 72 A2
Goodinge Rd N7 72 A2
Gooding Ho 4 SE7 121 C1
Goodison Cl WD23 8 A6
Goodland Ho 1 KT3 199 C2
Goodman Cres
Streatham SW2 159 D2
Thornton Heath CR0 205 A3
Goodman Rd E10 54 A2
Goodmans Ct HA0 65 D4
Goodman's Stile 17 E1 96 A1
Goodman's Yd E1, EC3 117 D6 253 C6
GOODMAYES 58 B1
Goodmayes Ave IG3 58 A1
Goodmayes Hospl IG3 58 A4
Goodmayes La IG3 80 A5
Goodmayes Lodge RM8 80 A4
Goodmayes Prim Sch IG3 58 B1
Goodmayes Rd IG3 58 A1
Goodmayes Ret Pk RM6 58 B2
Goodmayes Sta IG3 58 A1
Goodrich Com Prim Sch SE22 162 A5
Goodrich Ct 9 W10 90 D1
Goodrich Ho
20 Bethnal Green E2 96 C5
Stamford Hill N16 51 C2
Goodrich Rd SE22 162 A5
Goodridge Ho E17 36 A3
Good Shepherd RC Prim Sch
Catford BR1 186 D6
New Addington CR0 223 D1
Good Shepherd RC Prim Sch The W12 111 D4
Goodson Ho SM4 202 A2
Goodson Rd NW10 67 C1
Goodspeed Ho 20 E14 119 D6
Goodsway NW1 94 A5 233 A4
Goodway Gdns E14 98 B1
Goodwill Ho 22 E14 119 D6
Goodwin Cl
Bermondsey SE16 117 D3 263 D5
Mitcham CR4 202 B6
Goodwin Ct
East Barnet EN4 14 C5
Hornsey N8 50 A6
2 Mitcham SW19 180 C3
Goodwin Dr DA14 168 D2
Goodwin Gdns CR0, CR2 220 D2
Goodwin Ho
Edmonton N9 18 C3
2 Peckham SE15 140 B2
Goodwin Rd
Croydon CR0 220 D3
Edmonton N9 18 D3
Shepherd's Bush W12 112 A4
Goodwins Ct WC2 250 A6
Goodwin St N4 72 C6
Goodwood Ave EN3 6 C6
Goodwood Cl
Morden SM4 201 C5
11 Stanmore HA7 25 C5
Goodwood Ct W1 238 D4
Goodwood Dr UB5 63 C2
Goodwood Ho
3 Acton Green W4 111 A1
Penge SE26 184 B4
Goodwood Lo 1 SM6 219 D5
Goodwood Mans 3 SW9 138 C2
Goodwood Par BR3 207 A5
Goodwood Rd SE14 141 A5
Goodwyn Ave NW7 27 C5
Goodwyn Sch NW7 28 A5
Goodwyn's Vale N10 31 B2
Goodyear Ho 8 N2 30 B1
Goodyers Gdns NW4 46 D4
Goosander Ct 34 NW9 27 D1
Goosander Way SE18, SE28 123 B3
Gooseacre La HA3 43 D4
Goose Green Cl BR5 190 A1
Goose Green Prim Sch SE22 139 D1
Goose Green Trad Est SE22 140 A1
Gooseley La E6 100 C4
Goose Sq 8 E6 100 B1
Goossens Cl 1 SM1 218 A3
Gophir La EC4 252 C6
Gopsall St N1 95 B6 235 D5
Gordon Ave
Chingford E4 36 C4
Isleworth TW1 153 B6
Mortlake SW14 133 C1
Stanmore HA7 25 A4
Gordonbrock Prim Sch SE4 163 C6
Gordonbrock Rd SE4 163 C6
Gordon Cl E17 53 C3
Gordon Cres
Croydon CR0 205 D1
Hayes UB3 106 A2
Gordon Ct
Edgware HA8 26 B5
Hampton TW12 174 A5
5 Shepherd's Bush W12 90 C1
18 Wimbledon SW20 178 D3
Gordondale Rd SW18, SW19 157 C2
Gordon Dr TW17 193 B2
Gordon Gdns HA8 26 D1
Gordon Gr SE5 138 D3
Gordon Hill EN2 5 A4
Gordon Hill Sta EN2 4 D4
Gordon Ho
2 Ealing W5 88 A4
Lee SE12 165 A4
17 Shadwell E1 118 C6
Gordon Hospl SW1 115 D2 259 C3
Gordon House Rd NW5 71 A4
Gordon Inf Sch IG1 79 B5
Gordon Lo N16 51 B1
Gordon Mans
3 Barnet EN5 1 B1
Marylebone WC1 239 C5
Gordon Pl W8 113 C4 245 B2
Gordon Prim Sch SE9 144 B1
Gordon Rd
Ashford TW15 148 A1
Gordon Rd *continued*
Avery Hill DA15 167 C6
Barking IG11 101 C6
Beckenham BR3 207 B6
Chingford E4 20 C4
Chiswick W4 132 D6
Claygate KT10 212 C1
Dagenham RM6 59 B3
Ealing W13 109 C6
Edmonton N9 18 B2
Enfield EN2 5 B3
Finchley N3 29 B3
Harrow HA3 42 C6
Ilford IG1 79 B5
Isleworth TW3 130 A1
Kingston u T KT2 176 B2
Leyton E15 76 A4
Peckham SE15 140 B3
Richmond TW9 132 B3
Shepperton TW17 193 B3
Southall UB2 107 A2
Surbiton KT5 198 B2
Wallington SM5 218 D2
Wanstead E11 55 A3
Woodford E18 37 B2
Wood Green N11 31 D3
Yiewsley UB7 104 A6
Gordon Sq WC1 93 D3 239 D6
Gordon St
Bloomsbury WC1 93 D3 239 C6
Newham E13 99 A4
Gordon Way
Barnet EN5 1 B1
Bromley BR1 187 A2
Gore Ct NW9 44 C4
Gorefield Ho NW6 91 C5
Gorefield Pl NW6 91 C5
Gore Rd Hackney E9 96 C6
Merton SW20 178 C1
Goresbrook L Ctr RM9 102 D6
Goresbrook Rd RM9 102 D6
Gore St SW7 114 A3 256 B6
Gorham Ho 12 SW4 159 C5
Gorham Pl W11 244 A5
Goring Gdns RM8 80 C4
Goring Rd N11 32 A4
Goring St EC3 243 B2
Goring Way UB6 86 A5
Gorleston Rd N15 51 B4
Gorleston St W14 113 A2 254 B4
Gorman Rd SE18 122 B2
Gorringe Park Ave CR4 181 A3
Gorringe Park Prim Sch CR4 181 A2
Gorse Cl E16 99 A1
Gorsefield Ho 6 E14 119 C6
Gorse Rd CR0 223 C5
Gorse Rise SW17 181 A5
Gorse Wlk UB7 82 A1
Gorst Rd
London SW11 158 D5
North Acton NW10 89 B3
Gorsuch Pl 1 E2 95 D4
Gorsuch St E2 95 D4
Gosberton Rd SW12 159 A3
Gosbury Hill KT9 214 A4
Gosfield Rd RM8 59 C1
Gosfield St W1 93 C2 239 A3
Gosford Gdns IG4 56 B4
Gosford Ho 25 E3 97 B5
Goshawk Gdns UB4 83 C5
Goslett Yd WC2 239 D2
Gosling Cl UB6 85 C4
Gosling Ho 2 E1 118 C6
Gosling Way SW9 138 C4
Gosmore Ct N9 18 B2
Gospatric Home Ho SW14 133 C2
Gospatrick Rd N17 33 A2
GOSPEL OAK 71 A4
Gospel Oak Prim Sch NW5 71 A4
Gospel Oak Sta NW5 71 A4
Gosport Ho 9 SW15 156 A3
Gosport Rd E17 53 B4
Gosport Wlk N17 52 B5
Gossage Rd
Hillingdon UB10 60 B1
Gossage Rd *continued*
Plumstead SE18 123 B1
Gosset St E2 96 A4
Gosshill Rd BR7 188 C1
Gossington Cl BR7 188 D6
Gosterwood St SE8 141 A6
Gostling Rd TW2 151 C3
Goston Gdns CR7 204 C6
Goswell Pl EC1 234 D1
Goswell Rd EC1 94 D4 234 D2
Gothic Ct
17 Camberwell SE5 139 A5
Harlington UB3 127 B6
Gothic Rd TW2 152 B2
Gottfried Mews NW5 71 C4
Goudhurst Ho 7 SE20 184 C3
Goudhurst Rd BR1 186 D5
Gough Ho
Islington N1 234 D6
4 Kingston u T KT1 176 A1
Gough Rd Enfield EN1 6 B3
Stratford E15 76 D4
Gough Sq EC4 94 C1 241 B2
Gough St WC1 94 B3 240 D5
Gough Wlk 14 E14 97 C1
Gould Ct SE19 183 C5
Goulden Ho SW11 136 C3
Goulding Gdns CR7 183 A1
Gouldman Ho 33 E1 96 C3
Gould Rd
East Bedfont TW14 149 C4
Twickenham TW2 152 C3
Gould's Gn UB8 104 D6
Gould Terr 26 E8 74 B3
Goulston St E1 95 D1 243 C2
Goulton Rd E5 74 B4
Gourley Pl N15 51 C4
Gourley St N15 51 C4
Gourock Rd SE9 166 C6
Govan St E2 96 A6
Gover Ct 8 SW4 138 A3
Government Row EN3 7 C6
Govett Ave TW17 193 A4
Govier Cl E15 76 C1
Gowan Ave SW6 135 A4 264 A2
Gowan Ho 22 E2 95 D4
Gowan Lea 4 E18 55 A5
Gowan Rd NW10 68 B2
Gower Cl SW4 159 C5
Gower Ct WC1 239 C6
Gower Ho
2 Barking IG11 79 A1
Hayes UB3 105 C6
Upper Tooting SW17 180 B4
12 Walthamstow E17 53 D6
Walworth SE17 262 B2
Gower House Sch NW9 67 A6
Gower Mews WC1 239 D4
Gower Pl NW1, WC1 93 D3 239 C6
Gower Rd
Hounslow TW7 130 D6
Upton E7 77 A2
Gower Sch The 4 N7 72 A2
Gower St WC1 93 D3 239 C5
Gower's Wlk E1 96 A1
Gowland Pl BR3 185 B1
Gowlett Rd SE15 140 A2
Gowlland Cl CR0 206 A2
Gowrie Rd SW11 137 A2
Graburn Way KT8 196 B6
Grace Ave DA7 147 B3
Grace Bsns Ctr CR4 202 D3
Gracechurch St EC2, EC4 252 D6
Grace Cl
Burnt Oak HA8 27 A3
Mottingham SE9 165 D1
Grace Ct
5 Croydon CR0 220 D5
Twickenham TW2 152 C2
Gracedale Rd SW16 181 B5
Gracedyer Ho N22 32 A3
Gracefield Gdns SW16 160 A1
Gracehill 2 E1 96 C2

Grace Ho
Kennington SE11 270 D6
Penge SE26 184 B5
Grace Jones Cl E8 74 A2
Grace Path 2 SE26 184 C6
Grace Pl E3 97 D4
Grace Rd CR0 205 A3
Graces Alley 14 SE1 118 A6
Graces Mews NW8 229 B3
Grace's Mews SE5 139 C3
Grace's Rd SE5 139 C3
Grace St E3 97 D4
Gradient The SE26 184 A6
Graeme Ct UB6 85 D4
Graeme Rd EN1 5 C3
Graemesdyke Ave SW14 132 D1
Grafton Cl Ealing W13 87 A1
Twickenham TW4 151 B3
Worcester Pk KT4 215 C5
Grafton Cres NW1 71 B2
Grafton Ct
10 Dalston E8 74 A3
East Bedfont TW14 149 B3
Grafton Gdns
Dagenham RM8 81 A6
Harringay N4 51 A3
Grafton Ho 16 Bow E3 97 C4
12 Deptford SE8 119 B1
Grafton Jun & Inf Schs RM8 81 B6
Grafton Mans SW4 137 C1
Grafton Mews W1 239 A5
Grafton Park Rd KT4 215 C6
Grafton Pl NW1 93 D4 232 D1
Grafton Prim Sch 5 N7 72 A5
Grafton Rd Acton W3 111 A6
Dagenham RM8 81 A6
Enfield EN2 4 B2
Gospel Oak NW5 71 A3
Harrow HA1 42 A4
Kingston u T KT3 199 C6
Thornton Heath CR0 204 C1
Worcester Pk KT4 215 C5
Grafton Sq SW4 137 C2
Grafton St W1 115 B6 248 D5
Grafton Terr NW5 71 A3
Grafton Way
East Molesey KT8 195 B5
Marylebone W1 239 B5
Grafton Yd NW5 71 B2
Graham Ave
Ealing W13 109 B4
Mitcham CR4 181 A2
Graham Cl CR0 223 C6
Graham Ct
Bromley BR1 187 B3
5 Deptford SE14 140 D6
Northolt UB5 63 B3
GRAHAME PARK 27 C2
Grahame Park Way NW7, NW9 27 D2
Grahame White Ho HA3 43 D6
Graham Gdns KT6 198 A1
Graham Ho
5 Balham SW12 159 B4
6 Barnet EN5 1 D1
Edmonton N9 18 C3
6 Tufnell Pk N19 71 D4
Woolwich SE18 144 D5
Graham Lo
Edgware HA8 26 B4
Hendon NW4 46 B3
Graham Mans
11 Barking IG11 80 A1
2 Hackney E8 74 B2
Graham Rd
Acton W4 111 B3
Bexleyheath DA6 147 C1
Dalston E8 74 A2
Hampton TW12 173 C6
Harringay N15 50 D6
Harrow HA3 42 C6
Hendon NW4 46 B3
Merton SW19 179 B3
Mitcham CR4 181 A2
Newham E13 99 A3
Graham St N1 94 D5 234 D3
Graham Terr SW1 115 A2 258 B3
Graham Twr W3 110 D3
Grainger Cl UB5 64 A3
Grainger Ct 22 SE5 139 A5
Grainger Rd
Isleworth TW7 130 D3
Tottenham N22 33 A2
Gramer Cl E11 76 B6
Grampian Cl
Harlington UB3 127 B5
Orpington BR6 211 D3
15 Sutton SM2 218 A1
Grampian Gdns NW2 47 A1
Grampians The 10 W14 112 D4
Gramsci Way SE6 163 D1
Granada St SW17 180 D5
Granard Ave SW15 156 B6
Granard Bsns Ctr NW7 27 C4
Granard Ho 20 E9 74 D2
Granard Prim Sch SW15 156 B5
Granard Rd SW11, SW12 158 D4
Granary Cl N9 18 C4
Granary Ct 3 RM6 58 D2
Granary Mans SE28 123 A4
Granary Rd E1 96 B3
Granary Sq N1 72 C2
Granary St NW1 93 D6 232 C5
Granary The SE8 141 C5
Granby Ho 13 SE18 122 B2
Granby Pl SE1 251 A1
Granby Rd
Eltham SE9 144 B2
Woolwich SE18 122 D3
Granby St
Bethnal Green E2 96 A3
Shoreditch E2 243 D6
Granby Terr NW1 93 C5 232 A3
Grand Arc N12 30 A5
Grand Ave
Clerkenwell EC1 241 D4
Fortis Green N10 49 A5
Tolworth KT5 198 D3
Wembley HA9 66 C3
Grand Ave E HA9 66 D3
Grand Avenue Prim Sch KT5 199 A3
Grand Ct RM8 81 A5
Grand Depot Rd SE18 122 C1
Grand Dr
Southall UB2 108 A4
West Barnes SM4, SW20 200 C5
Granden Rd SW16 182 A1
Grandfield Ct W4 133 B6
Grandison Rd
London SW11 158 D6
North Cheam KT4 216 C5
Grand Junction Wharf N1 235 A3
Grand Par London N4 50 D3
Mortlake SW14 133 A1
Tolworth KT6 198 C1
Wembley HA9 66 C6
Grand Union Cl W9 91 B2
Grand Union Cres E8 96 A6
Grand Union Ind Est NW10 88 D5
Grand Union Way UB2 107 C4
Grand Vitesse Ind Est SE1 251 D3
Granfield St SW11 266 D1
Grange Ave
East Barnet EN4 14 D3
North Finchley N12 30 A5
South Norwood SE25 183 C1
Stanmore HA7 25 C1
Totteridge N20 13 A4
Twickenham TW2 152 C2
Woodford IG8 37 A3
Grange Cl
East Molesey KT8 195 D5
Edgware HA8 27 A5
Hayes UB3 83 C2
Heston TW5 129 B6
Sidcup DA15 168 A1
Woodford IG8 37 A3
Grangecliffe Gdns SE25 183 C1
Grangecourt Rd N16 51 C1
Grange Cres SE28 102 C1
Grange Ct
Belmont SM2 217 D1
4 Finchley N12 30 A4
Hackbridge SM6 219 B5
Harrow HA1 64 D5
Ilford IG6 57 A6
Littleton TW17 192 C5
Loughton IG10 21 D6
Northolt UB5 84 C5
Peckham SE15 139 D3
Pinner HA5 41 A6
Strand WC2 240 D1
Wembley HA0 65 C3
1 Willesden NW10 67 C4
Grange Dr BR7 188 B4
Grange Farm Cl HA2 64 A6
Grange Farm Est TW17 193 C6
Grangefield NW1 72 A1
Grange Fst & Mid Schs HA2 41 D1
Grange Gdns
London N14 15 D3
Pinner HA5 41 A5
South Norwood SE25 183 C1
West Hampstead NW3 69 D5
Grange Gr N1 73 A2
Grange Hill
Edgware HA8 27 A5
South Norwood SE25 183 C1
Grangehill Pl SE9 144 B2
Grangehill Rd SE9 144 B1
Grange Ho
6 Barking IG11 101 B6
Bermondsey SE1 263 C5
Willesden NW10 68 B1
Grange La SE21 161 D2
Grange Lo SW19 178 D4
Grange Mans KT17 215 D1
Grangemill 11 NW5 71 B4
Grangemill Rd SE6 163 C2
GRANGE MILLS 113 C3
Grange Mills SW12 159 C3
Grangemill Way SE6 163 C2
GRANGE PARK 16 C6
Grange Park Ave N21 17 A5
Grange Park Jun & Inf Schs UB4 83 D3
Grange Park Pl SW20 178 B3
Grange Park Prep Sch N21 16 D5
Grange Park Prim Sch N21 4 C1
Grange Park Rd
Leyton E10 53 D1
South Norwood CR7 205 B6
Grange Park Sta N21 16 D5
Grange Pk W5 110 A5
Grange Pl NW6 69 C1
Grange Prim Sch
Bermondsey SE1 117 C3 263 A5
Ealing W5 109 D4
Newham E13 98 D4
Grange Rd
Barnes SW13 134 A4
Belmont SM2 217 C1
Bermondsey SE1 117 D3 263 C5
Borehamwood WD6 10 B6
Burnt Oak HA8 27 B4
Chessington KT9 214 A4
Ealing W5 110 A5
East Molesey KT8 195 D5
Greenhill HA1 43 A4
Gunnersbury W4 110 D1
Hayes UB3 83 C1
Highgate N6 49 A3
Ilford IG1 79 A4
Kingston u T KT1 198 A6
Leyton E10 53 C1
Newham E13 98 D4
Orpington BR6 227 A6
Roxeth HA2 64 B6
Southall UB1 107 A4
South Norwood SE19, SE25 183 B1
Tottenham N17 34 A4
Walthamstow E17 53 A4
Willesden NW10 68 B2
Grange St N1 235 D5
Grange The
Bermondsey SE1 117 D3 263 C5
Cockfosters EN4 2 D2
Croydon CR0 223 B6
Ealing W13 87 C2
7 Gunnersbury W4 110 D1
Hammersmith W12 112 B3
19 Maitland Pk NW3 70 D2
South Acton W3 110 D4
3 Walthamstow E17 53 A4
4 Wanstead E18 55 A6
Wembley HA0 66 C1
West Barnes KT3 200 A4
West Ewell KT19 215 B4
West Kensington W14 113 B2 254 C3
Wimbledon SW19 178 D4
Grange Vale SM2 217 D1
Grange View Rd N20 14 A3
Grangeway
London N12 29 D6
South Hampstead NW6 69 C1
Woodford IG8 37 C6
Grangeway Gdns IG4 56 A4
Grangeway The N21 16 D5
Grange Wlk SE1 117 D3 263 C5
Grangewood DA5 169 B3
Grangewood Cl HA5 40 A4
Grangewood Ind Sch E7 77 D1
Grangewood La BR3 185 B4
Grangewood Sch HA5 39 D4
Grangewood St E6 99 D6
Grange Yd SE1 117 D3 263 C5
Granham Gdns N9 17 D2
Granite Apts E15 76 B2
Granite St SE18 123 D1
Granleigh Rd E11 76 C6
Grannary The 10 SE16 118 C4
Gransden Ave E8 74 B1
Gransden Ho 1 SE8 119 B1
Gransden Rd W12 111 D4
Grantbridge St N1 94 D5 234 D4
Grantchester 12 KT1 176 C1
Grantchester Cl HA1 64 D5
Grant Cl London N14 15 C4
Shepperton TW17 192 D3
Tottenham N17 33 C1
Grant Ct
2 Chingford E4 20 A3
11 Hendon NW9 27 D1
Grantham Cl HA8 10 A1
Grantham Ct
Dagenham RM6 59 B2
Kingston u T KT2 175 D5
9 Rotherhithe SE16 118 D4
Grantham Gdns RM6 59 B2
Grantham Gn WD6 11 A6
Grantham Ho
Ashford TW16 171 C3
12 Peckham SE15 140 A6
Grantham Pl W1 248 C3
Grantham Rd
Chiswick W4 133 C5
Little Ilford E12 78 C4
South Lambeth SW9 138 A3
Grant Ho
38 Clapham SW8 137 D3
Clerkenwell EC1 241 D4
Grantley Ho
2 Deptford SE14 140 D6
5 Putney SW19 156 D3
Grantley Pl KT10 212 A3
Grantley Rd TW4, TW5 128 C3
Grantley St E1 96 D3
Grant Mus of Zoology★ WC1 93 D3 239 C5
Grantock Rd E17 36 B2
Granton Prim Sch SW16 181 C3
Granton Rd Ilford IG3 58 A1
Sidcup DA14 190 C4
Streatham SW16 181 C2
Grant Pl 2 CR0 205 D1
Grant Rd
Battersea SW11 136 C2
Croydon CR0 205 D1
Grant Rd *continued*
Harrow HA3 42 D6
Grants Cl NW7 28 D3
Grants Cotts KT10 212 B6
Grant St Islington N1 234 A4
Newham E13 99 A4
Grantully Rd W9 91 D4
Grant Way TW7 131 A6
Granville Ave
Feltham TW13 150 A2
Hounslow TW3, TW4 151 C6
Lower Edmonton N9 18 C1
Granville Cl CR0 221 C6
Granville Ct
8 Deptford SE14 141 A5
Hornsey N4 50 B3
Shoreditch N1 235 D6
Granville Gdns
Ealing W5 110 B5
South Norwood SW16 182 B3
Granville Gr SE13 142 A2
Granville Ho 18 E14 97 C1
Granville Ind Est NW2 69 B6
Granville Mans 8 W12 112 C4
Granville Mews DA14 190 A6
Granville Pk SE13 142 B2
Granville Pl
London N12 30 A3
Marylebone W1 93 A1 238 A1
Pinner HA5 40 D6
Walham Green SW6 265 C3
Granville Point NW2 69 B6
Granville Rd
Bexley DA16 146 C2
Bowes Pk N13 32 B4
Child's Hill NW2 69 B6
Finchley N12 30 A3
Hayes UB3 105 D2
Hillingdon UB10 60 D2
Hornsey N4, N8 50 B3
Ilford IG1 78 D6
Kilburn NW6 91 C5
Merton SW19 179 C3
Sidcup DA14 190 B6
Tottenham N22 32 D2
Walthamstow E17 53 D3
Wandsworth SW18 157 B4
Woodford E18 37 B1
Granville Sq
3 Camberwell SE15 139 C5
Finsbury WC1 94 B4 233 D1
Granville St WC1 233 D1
Granwood Ct 5 TW7 130 C4
Grape St WC2 240 A2
Grapsome Cl KT9 213 C1
Grasdene Rd SE18 146 A5
Grasgarth Cl W3 111 A6
Grasmere NW1 231 D1
Grasmere Ave
Acton W3 111 B6
Kingston u T SW15 177 C6
Locksbottom BR6 226 D5
Merton SW19 201 C6
Ruislip HA4 39 A2
Twickenham TW3 151 D5
Wembley HA9 43 D1
Grasmere Cl TW14 149 D3
Grasmere Ct
Barnes SW13 134 A6
Bowes Pk N22 32 B4
Forest Hill SE26 184 A5
7 Sutton SM2 218 A2
Grasmere Gdns
Harrow HA3 25 A1
Locksbottom BR6 226 D5
Redbridge IG4 56 B4
Grasmere Ho 20 N16 73 B4
Grasmere Point 2 SE15 140 C5
Grasmere Prim Sch N16 73 B4
Grasmere Rd
Bromley BR1 186 D3
Croydon SE25 206 B4
Locksbottom BR6 226 D5
Muswell Hill N10 31 B2
3 Newham E13 99 A5
Streatham SW16 182 B5
Tottenham N17 34 A4

Green La *continued*
New Malden KT3 199 A4
New Malden KT4 200 A1
Penge SE20 184 D3
Shepperton TW17 193 A4
South Norwood CR7, SW16 182 C2
Stanmore HA7 25 B5
Greenland Cres UB2 106 D3
Greenland Ho
Bermondsey SE8 118 D1
4 Mile End E1 97 A3
Greenland Mews SE8 118 D1
Greenland Pl NW1 231 D6
Greenland Quay SE16 118 D2
Greenland Rd
Barnet EN5 12 C5
Camden Town NW1 93 C6 232 A6
Greenlands
Borehamwood WD6 11 B5
Chessington KT19 214 D3
Greenland St NW1 231 D6
Greenland Way CR0 203 D2
Green Lane Bsns Pk SE9 166 C2
Green Lane Cotts HA7 25 B6
Green Lane Gdns CR7 183 A1
Green Lane Mews SM4 201 D3
Green Lane Prim Sch KT4 200 B2
Green Lanes
London N4, N8, N15 50 D2
Palmers Green N13 16 C1
West Ewell KT19 215 C1
Greenlaw Ct W5 87 D1
Greenlaw Gdns KT3 199 D2
Greenlawn La TW8 109 D2
Greenlawns N12 29 D4
Green Lawns
Ruislip HA4 40 C1
8 Woolwich SE18 122 D2
Greenlaw St SE18 122 C3
Green Leaf Ave SM6 219 D4
Greenleaf Cl 8 SW2 160 C4
Greenleaf Ct N20 14 B3
Greenleafe Dr IG6 56 D6
Greenleaf Prim Sch E17 53 B6
Greenleaf Rd
5 Newham E6 99 C6
Walthamstow E17 53 B6
Greenleaf Way HA3 42 D6
Greenlea Pk SW19 180 C2
Green Leas
Ashford TW16 171 D4
Kingston u T KT1 198 A6
Green Leas Cl TW16 171 D4
Greenleaves Ct TW15 170 D4
Green Link Wlk TW9 132 D4
Green Man Gdns W13 109 A6
Green Man Intc E11 54 D2
Green Man La
Ealing W13 109 A5
Hatton TW14 128 A1
Greenman St N1 95 A6 235 A6
Greenmead Cl SE25 206 A4
Greenmead Prim Sch SW15 156 B6
Green Moor Link N21 16 D4
Greenmoor Rd EN3 6 C3
Greenoak Pl EN4 2 D3
Green Oaks UB2 106 D2
Greenoak Way SW19 178 D6
Greenock Rd
Mitcham SW16 181 D2
11 South Acton W3 111 A3
Greeno Cres TW17 192 C4
Green Park★ SW1, W1 115 B4 248 D2
Greenpark Ct HA0 65 C1
Green Park Sta W1 115 C5 249 A4
Green Park Way UB6 86 C6
Green Pond Cl E17 53 B6
Green Pond Rd E17 53 A6
Green Pt E15 76 C2
Green Rd
East Barnet N14 15 B5
Whetstone N20 14 A1
Green Ride IG10, E4 21 A6
Greenroof Way SE10 120 D3
Green Sch (Girls) The TW7 131 A4
Greens Ct Soho W1 249 C6
Wembley HA9 65 D5
Green's Ct W11 244 C3
Greens End SE18 122 D2
Greenshank Cl E17 35 A3
Greenshaw High Sch SM1 218 A6
Greenshields Ind Est E16 121 B5
Greenside
Dagenham RM8 58 C1
Sidcup DA5 169 A3
Greenside Cl
Catford SE6 164 B2
Whetstone N20 14 B2
Greenside Prim Sch W12 112 A4
Greenside Rd
Shepherd's Bush W12 112 A4
Thornton Heath CR0 204 C2
Greenslade Prim Sch SE18 145 B6
Greenslade Rd IG11 79 B1
Greensleeves Ho UB2 107 D2
Greensleeves Manor SM2 217 D2
Green St Enfield EN3 6 D3
Mayfair W1 115 A6 248 A6
Newham E13 99 C6
Sunbury TW16 172 A1
Upton E7 77 C1
Greenstead Ave IG8 37 C4
Greenstead Cl IG8 37 C4
Greenstead Gdns
Putney SW15 156 B6
Woodford IG8 37 C4
Greenstone Mews E11 55 A3
GREEN STREET GREEN 227 C2
Green Street Green Prim Sch BR6 227 D2
Greenstreet Hill SE4 140 D2
Greensward Ho SW6 136 A3
Green Terr EC1 234 B1
Green The Acton W3 89 C1
Buckhurst Hill IG9 21 B3
Chingford E4 20 B3
Claygate KT10 212 D2
Ealing W5 109 D6
Edmonton N9 18 A2
Erith DA7 147 C4
Falconwood DA16 145 C1
Feltham TW13 150 B2
Grove Pk BR1 165 A1
Hackbridge SM6 219 A6
Hayes BR2 209 A2
Heston TW5 129 C6
Kingston u T KT3 177 A1
Merton SM4 201 A5
Palmers Green N14 15 D1
Richmond TW9 131 D1
7 Richmond TW9 153 D6
Sidcup DA14 190 A5
Southall UB2 107 B4
Southgate N21 16 C4
St Paul's Cray BR5 190 B3
Stratford E15 76 D2
Sutton SM1 217 D5
Tottenham N17 33 A4
Twickenham TW2 152 C2
Upper Halliford TW17 193 C5
Uxbridge UB10 61 A6
Wallington SM5 219 A4
Wanstead E11 55 B3
Wembley HA0 65 A6
Wimbledon SW19 178 D5
Woodford IG8 37 A5
Green Vale
Bexley DA6 168 D6
Ealing W5 88 B1
Greenvale Rd SE9 144 C1
Greenvale Sch SE23 164 C1
Green Verges HA7 25 D3
Green View KT9 214 B1
Greenview Ave CR0 207 A3
Greenview Cl W3 111 C5
Greenview Ct
Ashford TW15 170 B6
East Dulwich SE22 140 A1
Oakleigh Pk N20 14 A4
Wandsworth SW18 158 C4
Greenway
Chislehurst BR7 188 D5
Dagenham RM8 58 C1
Harrow HA3 44 A4
Hayes UB4 84 B3
Palmers Green N14 16 A2
Pinner HA5 22 B1
Totteridge N20 13 C2
Wallington SM6 219 C4
West Barnes SW20 200 C5
Woodford IG8 37 C5
Green Way
Bromley Comm BR2 210 A3
Eltham SE9 165 D6
Sunbury TW16 194 A5
Greenway Ave E17 54 B5
Greenway Cl
Finsbury Pk N4 73 A6
Friern Barnet N11 31 A4
Hendon NW9 27 B1
2 South Tottenham N15 51 D5
Totteridge N20 13 C2
Greenway Ct
Hayes UB4 84 B3
Ilford IG1 56 D1
2 Newham E15 98 C5
Greenway Gdns
Croydon CR0 223 B5
Greenford UB6 85 D4
Hendon NW9 27 B1
Green Way Gdns HA3 24 C1
Greenways
Beckenham BR3 185 C1
5 Forest Hill SE26 184 C6
Hinchley Wood KT10 212 C4
Greenways The 1 TW1 153 A5
Greenway The
Harrow HA3 24 C2
Hendon NW9 27 B1
Hounslow TW4 129 B1
Pinner HA5 41 B3
Uxbridge UB8 82 A5
West Ruislip UB10 61 A6
Greenwell St W1 238 D5
GREENWICH 142 C6
Greenwich Acad SE10 141 D4
Greenwich Borough Mus★ SE18 123 D1
Greenwich Bsns Ctr SE10 141 D5
Greenwich Bsns Pk SE10 141 D5
Greenwich Church St SE10 142 A6
Greenwich Coll 17 SE10 142 A5
Greenwich Com Coll Plumstead Ctr SE18 123 A2
Greenwich Cres E6 100 A2
Greenwich Ct 11 E1 96 B1
Greenwich Heritage Ctr★ SE18 122 D3
Greenwich High Rd SE10 141 D5
Greenwich Ho SE13 164 B5
Greenwich Hts SE18 144 A5
Greenwich Ind Est SE10 141 D5
Greenwich London Coll 15 SE18 122 C2
Greenwich Mkt 2 SE10 142 A6
Greenwich Mkt★ SE10 142 A6
Greenwich Park★ SE10 142 C5
Greenwich Park St SE10 142 B6
Greenwich Quay SE8 141 D6
Greenwich Sh Pk SE7 121 B2
Greenwich South St SE10 142 A4
Greenwich Sta SE10 141 D5
Greenwich View Pl E14 119 D3
Green Wlk
Bermondsey SE1 263 A5
Hampton TW12 173 B4
Hendon NW4 46 D4
Ruislip HA4 39 D1
Southall UB2 107 C1
Green Wlk The E4 20 B3
Greenwood
8 Putney SW19 156 D4
3 Woodford IG8 37 A3
Green Wood NW5 71 C3
Greenwood Ave
Dagenham RM10 81 D4
Enfield EN3 7 A4
Greenwood Cl
Bushey WD23 8 C3
Merton SM4 201 A5
Orpington BR5 211 C3
Sidcup DA15 168 A2
Thames Ditton KT7 197 A1
Greenwood Dr E4 36 B5
Greenwood Gdns N13 16 D1
Greenwood Ho
Finsbury WC1 234 A1
8 Nunhead SE4 140 D1
Wood Green N22 32 C2
Greenwood La TW12 173 D5
Greenwood Mans 9 IG11 80 A1
Greenwood Pk KT2 177 C3
Greenwood Pl NW5 71 B3
Greenwood Prim Sch UB5 64 A3
Greenwood Rd
Dalston E8 74 A2
Hinchley Wood KT7 213 A6
Isleworth TW7 130 D2
Mitcham CR4 203 D6
Thornton Heath CR0 205 A2
West Ham E13 98 D5
Greenwoods The HA2 64 A5
Greenwood Terr NW10 89 B5
Green Wrythe Cres SM5 202 C1
Green Wrythe La SM5 202 C2
Green Wrythe Prim Sch SM5 202 B3
Green Yd WC1 240 D6
Greer Rd HA3 24 A2
Greet Ho SE1 251 B1
Greet St SE1 116 C5 251 B3
Greg Cl E10 54 A3
Gregor Mews SE3 143 A5
Gregory Cres SE9 165 D4
Gregory Ho SE3 143 B3
Gregory Pl W8 245 C2
Gregory Rd
Dagenham RM6 58 D5
Southall UB2 107 C3
Greig City Acad 6 N8 50 A5
Greig Cl N8 50 A4
Greig Ho 9 TW10 153 C1
Greig Terr SE17 138 D6
Grenaby Ave CR0 205 B2
Grenaby Rd CR0 205 B2
Grenada Ho 18 E14 119 B6
Grenada Rd SE7 143 C5
Grenade St E14 119 B6
Grenadier St E16 122 C5
Grena Gdns TW9 132 B1
Grena Rd TW10, TW9 132 B1
Grenard Cl SE15 140 A5
Grendon Gdns HA9 66 C6
Grendon Ho
29 Hackney E9 74 C1
Pentonville N1 233 C3
Grendon St NW8 92 C3 237 A6
Grenfell Ct NW7 28 B4
Grenfell Gdns
Harrow HA3 44 A2
Grenfell Gdns *continued*
Ilford IG2 57 D4
Grenfell Ho SE5 139 A5
Grenfell Rd
Mitcham CR4, SW17 180 D4
Shepherd's Bush W11 112 D6
Grenfell Twr 5 W11 112 D6
Grenfell Wlk 4 W11 112 D6
Grengate Lodge 2 E13 99 B4
Grenier Apartments 11 SE15 140 B5
Grennell Cl SM1 218 B6
Grennell Rd SM1 218 A6
Grenoble Gdns N13 32 C4
Grenville Cl
Church End N3 29 B2
Tolworth KT5 199 A1
Grenville Ct
3 Dulwich SE19 183 D5
Ealing W13 87 B2
Edgware HA8 26 D6
Grenville Gdns IG8 37 C3
Grenville Ho
26 Bow E3 97 A5
4 Deptford SE8 141 C6
Grenville Lo N6 49 C2
Grenville Mans WC1 240 A6
Grenville Mews
Hampton TW12 173 D5
South Kensington SW7 256 A3
Grenville Pl
Burnt Oak NW7 27 B5
South Kensington SW7 114 A2 256 A4
Grenville Rd N19 50 A1
Grenville St WC1 240 B5
Gresham Almshouses 3 SW9 138 B1
Gresham Ave N20 30 D6
Gresham Cl Enfield EN2 5 A2
Sidcup DA5 169 B5
Gresham Coll EC1 94 C2 241 B3
Gresham Ct TW3 130 A4
Gresham Dr RM6 58 B3
Gresham Gdns NW11 47 A1
Gresham Ho
4 Teddington TW11 174 D5
3 Thames Ditton KT7 197 A2
West Barnes KT3 200 B5
Gresham Lo E17 53 D4
Gresham Pl 2 N19 71 D6
Gresham Rd
Beckenham BR3 185 A1
Brixton SW9 138 C2
Canning Town E16 99 B1
Croydon SE25 206 A5
East Ham E6 100 B5
Edgware HA8 26 B4
Hampton TW12 173 C4
Hillingdon UB10 82 C5
Hounslow TW3, TW5 130 A4
Willesden NW10 67 B3
Gresham St EC2 95 A1 242 B2
Gresham Way SW19 157 C1
Gresham Way Est SW19 157 D1
Gresley Cl London N15 51 B5
Walthamstow E17 53 A3
Gresley Ho SW8 269 D2
Gresley Rd N19 49 C2
Gressenhall Rd SW18 157 B4
Gressenham Ct 7 HA7 25 C6
Gresse St W1 93 D1 239 C2
Gresswell Cl DA14 168 A1
Greswell St SW6 134 D4
Greta Ho SE3 142 D6
Gretton Ho 2 E2 96 C4
Gretton Rd N17 33 D3
Greville Cl TW1 153 B4
Greville Ct
Harrow HA1 64 C4
3 Lower Clapton E5 74 B5
Greville Hall NW6 91 D5

Greville Ho
Harrow HA2 . . . 42 B1
Knightsbridge SW1 . . 258 A6
Putney SW15 . . . 134 D2
Greville Lo
5 Bayswater W2 . . . 91 D1
16 London N12 . . . 29 D6
Greville Mews 5
NW6 . . . 91 D6
Greville Pl W9 . . . 91 D5
Greville Rd
Kilburn NW6 . . . 91 D5
Richmond TW10 . . . 154 B5
Walthamstow E17 . . . 54 A5
Greville St
EC1 . . . 94 C2 241 B4
Grey Cl NW11 . . . 48 A3
Grey Coat Hospital The
SW1 . . . 115 D2 259 C3
SW1 . . . 115 D3 259 C5
Greycoat Pl
SW1 . . . 115 D3 259 C5
Greycoat St
SW1 . . . 115 D3 259 C5
Greycot Rd BR3 . . . 185 C5
Grey Court Sch
TW10 . . . 153 C1
Grey Eagle St
E1 . . . 95 D3 243 D5
Greyfell Cl HA7 . . . 25 B5
Greyfriars 16 SE26 . . . 162 A1
Greyfriars Ho SE3 . . . 142 D6
Grey Ho 27 W12 . . . 112 B6
Greyhound Ct WC2 . . . 251 A6
Greyhound Hill NW4 . . 46 B6
Greyhound La SW16 181 D4
Greyhound Rd
College Pk NW10 . . . 90 B4
Fulham W6 . . 135 A6 264 A6
Sutton SM1 . . . 218 A3
Tottenham N17 . . . 51 C6
Greyhound Terr
SW16 . . . 181 C2
Greyladies Gdns
SE10 . . . 142 A3
Greys Park Cl BR2 . . . 225 D3
Greystead Rd SE23 . . . 162 C4
Greystoke Ave HA5 . . . 41 C6
Greystoke Ct W5 . . . 88 B3
Greystoke Dr HA4 . . . 38 D3
Greystoke Gdns
Ealing W5 . . . 88 B3
Enfield EN2 . . . 3 D1
Greystoke Ho
Ealing W5 . . . 88 A3
Peckham SE15 . . . 140 A6
Greystoke Lo W5 . . . 88 B3
Greystoke Park Terr
W5 . . . 88 A4
Greystoke Pl EC4 . . . 241 B2
Greystone Gdns HA3 . . 43 C3
Greystones TW2 . . . 152 A2
Greyswood St SW16 . . 181 B4
Greytiles TW11 . . . 174 D4
Grey Turner Ho W12 . . . 90 A1
Grice Ct N1 . . . 73 A2
Grierson Ho SW16 . . . 181 C6
Grierson Rd
Forest Hill SE23 . . . 162 D4
Forest Hill SE23 . . . 163 A5
Griffin Cl NW10 . . . 68 B3
Griffin Ct
8 Brentford TW8 . . . 132 A6
Chiswick W4 . . . 111 D1
Shepherd's Bush W12 . 112 B5
Griffin Ctr TW14 . . . 150 B5
Griffin Ctr The KT1 . . 175 D1
Griffin Gate 1
SW15 . . . 134 D2
Griffin Lo N12 . . . 30 A6
Griffin Manor Way
SE28 . . . 123 B3
Griffin Park (Brentford
FC) TW8 . . . 131 D6
Griffin Rd
Plumstead SE18 . . . 123 B1
Tottenham N17 . . . 33 C1
Griffins Cl N21 . . . 17 B4
Griffin Way
Sunbury TW16 . . . 172 A1
Woolwich SE28 . . . 123 C3
Griffith Cl RM8 . . . 58 C1
Griffiths Cl KT4 . . . 216 B6
Griffiths Ho 2 SE18 . . 144 D6
Griffiths Rd SW19 . . . 179 D3
Griffon Ho 3 SW11 . . 136 C2
Griggs App IG1 . . . 79 A6
Griggs Cl IG1 . . . 79 C4
Grigg's Pl SE1 . . . 263 B5
Griggs Rd E10 . . . 54 A3
Grilse Cl N9 . . . 34 B6
Grimaldi Ho N1 . . . 233 C4
Grimsby Gr E16 . . . 122 D5
Grimsby St
8 Bethnal Green E2 . . . 96 A3
Shoreditch E2 . . . 243 D6
Grimsdell Mill Hill Pre
Prep Sch NW7 . . . 28 B5
Grimsdyke Fst & Mid Sch
HA5 . . . 23 B4
Grimsdyke Rd HA5 . . . 23 A3
Grimsel Path SE5 . . . 138 D5
Grimshaw Cl N6 . . . 49 A2
Grimston Rd SW6 . . . 135 B3
Grimthorpe Ho EC1 . 241 C6
Grimwade Ave CR0 . . 222 A5
Grimwade Cl SE15 . . . 140 C2
Grimwood Rd TW1 . . 152 D4
Grindall Cl CR0 . . . 220 D4
Grindall Ho 26 E1 . . . 96 B3
Grindal St SE1 . . . 251 A1
Grindleford Ave N11 . . 15 A2
Grindley Gdns CR0 . . 205 D3
Grindley Ho 3 E3 . . . 97 B2
Grinling Gibbons Prim
Sch 42 SE8 . . . 141 B6
Grinling Ho 6 SE18 . . 122 C2
Grinling Pl SE8 . . . 141 C6
Grinstead Rd SE8 . . . 119 A1
Grisedale NW1 . . . 232 A2
Grittleton Ave HA9 . . . 66 D2
Grittleton Rd W9 . . . 91 C3
Grizedale Terr 8
SE23 . . . 162 B2
Grogan Cl TW12 . . . 173 B4
Groombridge Cl
DA16 . . . 168 A6
Groombridge Ho 1
SE20 . . . 184 D3
Groombridge Rd E9 . . 74 D1
Groom Cl BR2 . . . 209 B5
Groom Cres SW18 . . . 158 B4
Groome Ho SE11 . . . 260 D3
Groomfield Cl SW17 . 181 A6
Groom Pl
SW1 . . . 115 A3 258 B6
Grooms Dr HA5 . . . 40 A4
Grosmont Rd SE18 . . 123 D1
Grosse Way SW15 . . . 156 B5
Grosslea SM4 . . . 202 B4
Grosvenor Ave
Canonbury N5 . . . 73 A3
Harrow HA2 . . . 41 D3
Hayes UB4 . . . 83 D5
Mortlake SW14 . . . 133 C2
Richmond TW10 . . . 154 A6
Wallington SM5, SM6 . 219 A2
Grosvenor Bridge
SW1 . . . 137 B6 268 D6
Grosvenor Cotts
SW1 . . . 258 A4
Grosvenor Court Mans
W2 . . . 237 C1
Grosvenor Cres
Hillingdon UB10 . . . 82 D6
Queensbury NW9 . . . 44 C5
Westminster
SW1 . . . 115 A4 248 B1
Grosvenor Cres Mews
SW1 . . . 248 A1
Grosvenor Ct
4 Acton W3 . . . 110 C5
Brondesbury Pk NW6 . . 90 D6
3 Ealing W5 . . . 110 A6
3 Edgware NW7 . . . 27 B5
Gunnersbury W4 . . . 110 D1
Leyton E10 . . . 53 D1
Morden SM4 . . . 201 C5
Oakwood N14 . . . 15 C4
Penge SE19 . . . 183 D4
22 Poplar E14 . . . 97 B1
Putney SW15 . . . 157 A6
1 Sutton SM2 . . . 218 A2
Teddington TW11 . . . 175 A4
3 Wanstead E11 . . . 55 B4
2 Wimbledon SW19 . 179 A4
Grosvenor Gdns
Cricklewood NW2 . . . 68 C3
Hornsey N10 . . . 49 C6
Kingston u T KT2 . . . 175 D4
Mortlake SW14 . . . 133 C2
Newham E6 . . . 99 D4
Grosvenor Gdns *continued*
Southgate N14 . . . 15 D6
Temple Fortune NW11 . . 47 B4
Wallington SM6 . . . 219 C1
Westminster
SW1 . . . 115 B3 258 D5
Woodford IG8 . . . 37 B4
Grosvenor Gdns Mews E
SW1 . . . 258 D6
Grosvenor Gdns Mews N
SW1 . . . 258 C5
Grosvenor Gdns Mews S
SW1 . . . 258 D5
Grosvenor Hill
Mayfair W1 . . 115 B6 248 C6
Wimbledon SW19 . . . 179 A4
Grosvenor Hill Ct
W1 . . . 248 C6
Grosvenor Ho
5 Sutton SM1 . . . 217 D3
Upper Clapton E5 . . . 52 A1
Grosvenor Hts E4 . . . 20 C4
Grosvenor Lo
London N20 . . . 14 A1
4 Woodford E18 . . . 36 D1
Grosvenor Par 1
W5 . . . 110 C5
Grosvenor Park SE5 . . 139 A5
Grosvenor Park Rd
E17 . . . 53 D4
Grosvenor Pier SW1 269 C6
Grosvenor Pk SE5 . . . 139 A6
Grosvenor Pl
SW1 . . . 115 B4 248 C1
Grosvenor Rd
Acton Green W4 . . . 111 A1
Bexley DA6 . . . 169 A6
Brentford TW8 . . . 131 D6
Croydon SE25 . . . 206 A5
Dagenham RM8 . . . 59 B1
Ealing W7 . . . 109 A5
Edmonton N9 . . . 18 B3
Erith DA17 . . . 147 C6
Finchley N3 . . . 29 C3
Hounslow TW3, TW4 . . 129 B2
Ilford IG1 . . . 79 A5
Leyton E10 . . . 54 A1
Muswell Hill N10 . . . 31 B2
Newham E6 . . . 99 D6
Orpington BR6 . . . 211 C3
Pimlico SW1 . . 137 C6 269 B6
Richmond TW10 . . . 154 A6
Southall UB2 . . . 107 B3
Twickenham TW1 . . . 153 A3
Upton E7 . . . 77 B2
Wallington SM6 . . . 219 B3
Wanstead E11 . . . 55 B4
West Wickham BR4 . . 223 D6
Grosvenor Residences 1
W14 . . . 112 D3
Grosvenor Rise E E17 . 53 D4
Grosvenor Sq
W1 . . . 115 A6 248 B6
Grosvenor St
W1 . . . 115 B6 248 C6
Grosvenor Terr SE5 . . 139 A6
Grosvenor The NW11 . . 47 D2
Grosvenor Vale HA4 . . . 61 D6
Grosvenor Way E5 . . . 74 C6
Grosvenor Wharf Rd
E14 . . . 120 B2
Grote's Bldgs SE3 . . . 142 C3
Grote's Pl SE3 . . . 142 C3
Groton Rd SW18 . . . 157 D2
Grotto Ct SE1 . . . 252 A2
Grotto Pas W1 . . . 238 A4
Grotto Rd TW1 . . . 152 D2
Grove Ave
Cheam SM1 . . . 217 C2
Ealing W7 . . . 86 C1
Finchley N3 . . . 29 C3
Pinner HA5 . . . 41 A5
Twickenham TW1 . . . 152 D3
Wood Green N10 . . . 31 C1
Grovebury Ct
Bexley DA6 . . . 169 D6
Southgate N14 . . . 15 D4
Grovebury Rd SE2 . . . 124 B4
Grove Cl
Forest Hill SE23 . . . 163 A3
Hayes BR2 . . . 225 A6
Ickenham UB10 . . . 60 C3
Kingston u T KT1 . . . 198 B5
Grove Cres
Feltham TW13 . . . 173 A6
Kingsbury NW9 . . . 45 B5
Grove Cres *continued*
Kingston u T KT1 . . . 198 A6
Walton-on-T KT12 . . . 194 B2
Woodford E18 . . . 36 D1
Grove Crescent Rd
E15 . . . 76 B2
Grove Ct Barnet EN5 . . . 1 B2
Camberwell SE5 . . . 139 C3
Clapham SW4 . . . 137 C2
Ealing W5 . . . 110 A5
East Molesey KT8 . . . 196 B4
3 Forest Hill SE26 . . 185 A6
Hounslow TW3 . . . 129 C1
8 Kingston u T KT1 . . 198 A6
New Malden KT3 . . . 199 C6
Penge SE20 . . . 184 B3
Seething Wells KT6 . . 197 D4
South Kensington
SW10 . . . 256 B1
St John's Wood NW8 . 229 C2
Grovedale Rd N19 . . . 71 D6
Grove Dwellings E1 . . . 96 C2
Grove End
Gospel Oak NW5 . . . 71 B4
Woodford E18 . . . 36 D1
Grove End Gdns
NW8 . . . 229 B3
Grove End Ho NW8 . . 229 C1
Grove End La KT10 . . 196 B1
Grove End Rd
NW8 . . . 92 B4 229 C1
Grove Farm Ct CR4 . . 202 D4
Grovefield 1 N11 . . . 31 B6
Grove Footpath KT5 . . 198 A5
Grove Gdns Enfield EN3 . 6 D5
Hendon NW4 . . . 46 A5
Lisson Gr NW8 92 C4 230 B1
Teddington TW11 . . . 175 A6
Grove Glade Shop Hall
W13 . . . 109 A5
Grove Green Rd E11 . . . 76 B6
Grove Hall Ct Bow E3 . . 97 C5
St John's Wood
NW8 . . . 92 A4 229 B2
Grove Hill Harrow HA1 . 42 C2
Woodford E18 . . . 36 D1
Grovehill Ct BR1 . . . 186 D4
Grove Hill Rd
Camberwell SE5 . . . 139 C2
Harrow HA1 . . . 42 D2
Grove Ho
Blackheath SE3 . . . 142 D3
Chelsea SW3 . . . 267 B6
Hendon N3 . . . 46 D6
Grove House Rd N8 . . . 50 A5
Grove La
Camberwell SE5 . . . 139 C2
Hillingdon UB8 . . . 82 B3
Kingston u T KT1 . . . 198 A5
Groveland Ave
SW16 . . . 182 B3
Groveland Ct EC4 . . . 242 B1
Groveland Rd BR3 . . . 207 B6
Grovelands
East Molesey KT8 . . . 195 C5
Kingston u T KT1 . . . 197 D5
Grovelands Cl
Camberwell SE5 . . . 139 C3
Harrow HA2 . . . 63 D5
Grovelands Ct N14 . . . 15 D4
Grovelands Rd
Palmers Green N13 . . . 16 B1
South Tottenham N15 . . . 52 A3
St Paul's Cray BR5 . . . 190 A3
Grovelands Sch
KT12 . . . 194 B3
Groveland Way KT3 . . 199 B4
Grove Lane Terr
SE5 . . . 139 B3
Groveley Ho 7 N4 . . . 51 A2
Groveley Rd TW13,
TW16 . . . 171 D5
Grove Lo
Clapham SW4 . . . 137 C1
Cranley Gdns N10 . . . 49 C5
Grove Mans
London SW4 . . . 136 D1
2 Shepherd's Bush
W6 . . . 112 C4
3 Stamford Hill N16 . . . 52 A1
Grove Market Pl
SE9 . . . 166 B5
Grove Mews W6 . . . 112 C3
Grove Mill CR4 . . . 202 C4
Grove Mill Pl SM5 . . . 219 A5
GROVE PARK SE9 . . . 165 B1
GROVE PARK *continued*
W4 . . . 133 A4
Grove Park Ave E4 . . . 35 D3
Grove Park Bridge
W4 . . . 133 A5
Grove Park Gdns
W4 . . . 133 A5
Grove Park Mews
W4 . . . 133 A5
Grove Park Prim Sch
W4 . . . 133 A6
Grove Park Rd
Chiswick W4 . . . 132 D5
Mottingham SE9,
SE12 . . . 165 D2
South Tottenham N15 . . . 51 C5
Grove Park Sch NW9 . . 45 A5
Grove Park Sta SE12 . 165 B1
Grove Park Terr W4 . 132 D6
Grove Pk
Camberwell SE5 . . . 139 C3
Kingsbury NW9 . . . 45 B5
Wanstead E11 . . . 55 B4
Grove Pl Acton W3 . . . 111 A5
Balham SW12 . . . 159 B5
Hampstead NW3 . . . 70 B5
Grove Prim Sch RM6 . . 58 C4
Grover Ct SE13 . . . 141 D3
Grove Rd Acton W3 . . . 111 A5
Barnes SW13 . . . 133 D3
Belmont SM2 . . . 217 C2
Bow E3 . . . 97 A5
Brentford TW8 . . . 109 C1
Chingford E4 . . . 20 A1
Cockfosters EN4 . . . 2 C2
Dagenham RM6 . . . 58 C3
Ealing W5 . . . 109 D6
East Molesey KT8 . . . 196 B5
Edgware HA8 . . . 26 C4
8 Erith DA17 . . . 147 B6
Friern Barnet N11 . . . 31 B5
Hounslow TW3 . . . 129 C1
Kingston u T KT6 . . . 197 D4
Leytonstone E11 . . . 54 D2
Merton SW19 . . . 180 A3
Mitcham CR4 . . . 181 B1
North Finchley N12 . . . 30 B5
Pinner HA5 . . . 41 B4
Richmond TW10 . . . 154 B5
Shepperton TW17 . . . 193 A3
South Tottenham N15 . . . 51 C4
Spring Gr TW7 . . . 130 C4
Thornton Heath CR7 . . 204 C5
Twickenham TW2 . . . 152 B1
Uxbridge UB8 . . . 60 A1
Walthamstow E17 . . . 53 D4
Willesden NW2 . . . 68 C2
Woodford E18 . . . 36 D1
Grove Rd Prim Sch
TW3 . . . 129 C1
Grove Rd W EN3 . . . 6 C6
Grover Ho
4 London SW4 . . . 159 C6
Vauxhall SE11 . . . 260 D1
Groves Ho UB4 . . . 84 B4
Groveside Cl
Acton W3 . . . 88 C1
Carshalton SM5 . . . 218 C6
Groveside Ct SW11 . . . 136 B3
Groveside Rd E4 . . . 20 C1
Grove St
Deptford SE8 . . . 119 B1
Edmonton N18 . . . 33 D4
Grovestile Waye
TW14 . . . 149 B4
Grove Terr
Gospel Oak NW5 . . . 71 B4
Southall UB1 . . . 107 C6
Teddington TW11 . . . 175 A6
Grove Terrace Mews
NW5 . . . 71 B5
Grove The
Bexley DA6 . . . 146 D1
Dulwich SE21 . . . 162 A3
Ealing W5 . . . 110 A5
Edgware HA8 . . . 26 D6
Edmonton N13 . . . 32 C6
Enfield EN2 . . . 4 C3
Finchley N3 . . . 29 C3
Hendon NW11 . . . 47 A2
Highgate N6 . . . 49 A1
Hornsey N8 . . . 49 D4
Hounslow TW7 . . . 130 C4

Grove The *continued*
Ickenham UB10 . . . . **60** C3
Kingsbury NW9 . . . . **45** B4
Sidcup DA14 . . . . **191** A6
Southall UB6 . . . . **86** A1
Stratford E15 . . . . **76** C2
Stroud Green N4 . . . . . . **50** B2
Teddington TW11 . . . . **175** A6
1 Twickenham TW1 . . . **153** B5
Walton-on-T KT12 . . . . **194** B2
West Wickham BR4 . . **224** A6
Grove Vale
Chislehurst West
BR7 . . . . **188** C4
East Dulwich SE22 . . . **139** D1
Groveway
Dagenham RM8 . . . . **80** D4
South Lambeth
SW9 . . . . **138** B4 **270** D1
Grove Way
Thames Ditton KT10 . . **196** A1
Wembley HA9 . . . . **67** A3
Grovewood 9 TW9 . . **132** C4
Grove Wood Cl BR1 . . **210** C6
Grovewood Ct 6
TW7 . . . . **130** C4
Grovewood Ho NW2 . . **69** B6
Grummant Rd SE15 . **139** D4
Grundy St E14 . . . . **97** D1
Gruneisen Rd N3 . . . . . **29** D3
Guardian Angels RC Prim Sch 9 E3 . . . . **97** A4
Guardian Ct SE12 . . . . **164** C6
Guards Mus The★
SW1 . . . . **115** C4 **249** B1
Gubyon Ave SE24 . . . **160** D6
Gudden Dr E5 . . . . **74** B4
Guerin Sq E3 . . . . **97** B4
Guernsey Cl TW5 . . . . **129** C5
Guernsey Gr SE24 . . . . **161** A4
Guernsey Ho
10 Canonbury N1 . . . . . . **73** A2
Enfield EN3 . . . . **6** D5
Guernsey Rd
11 Canonbury N1 . . . . . . **73** A2
Leytonstone E11 . . . . . . **54** B1
Guibal Rd SE12 . . . . . . **165** B3
Guildersfield Rd
SW16 . . . . **182** A3
Guildford Ave TW13 . . **150** A2
Guildford Gr SE10 . . . **141** D4
Guildford Ho 23 SE5 . . **139** A3
Guildford Rd
Chingford E17 . . . . **36** A2
Ilford IG3 . . . . **79** C6
Newham E6 . . . . **100** B1
South Lambeth
SW8 . . . . . **138** A4 **270** B2
Thornton Heath CR0 . . . **205** B3
Guildford Way SM6 . . **220** A3
Guildhall Art Gall★
EC2 . . . . **95** A1 **242** B2
Guildhall Ho EC2 . . . . . **242** C2
Guildhall Sch Music & Drama EC2 . . **95** A2 **242** B4
Guildhall Yd EC2 . . . . . **242** B2
Guild Ho SW19 . . . . . . **179** B4
Guildhouse St
SW1 . . . . **115** C2 **259** A3
Guildown Ave N12 . . . . **29** D6
Guild Rd SE7 . . . . **143** D6
Guildsway E17 . . . . **35** B2
Guilford Ave KT5 . . . . . **198** B4
Guilford Pl WC1 . . . . . **240** C5
Guilford St
WC1 . . . . **94** A3 **240** B5
Guilfoyle 2 NW9 . . . . . **27** D1
Guillemot Ct 28 SE8 . . **141** B6
Guinness Cl
Hayes UB3 . . . . **105** B3
Homerton E9 . . . . **75** A1
Guinness Ct
Chelsea SW3 . . . . **257** C3
6 Croydon CR0 . . . . **221** D6
Finsbury EC1 . . . . **235** B1
Primrose Hill NW8 . . . **230** B5
Whitechapel E1 . . . . . **243** D1
Guinness Sq SE1 . . . . . **263** A4
Guinness Trust Bldgs
Bermondsey SE1 . . . . **253** A2
7 Bethnal Green E2 . . . **96** A5
Chelsea SW3 . . . . **257** C3
Hammersmith W6 . . . **112** C1
Guinness Trust Bldgs *continued*
Kennington SE11 . . . . **261** C2
Guion Rd SW6 . . . . **135** B3
Gujarat Ho 1 N16 . . . . **73** C5
Gulland Cl WD23 . . . . **8** A6
Gulland Wlk 21 N1 . . . . . **73** A2
Gullane Ho 24 E3 . . . . . **97** B5
Gull Cl SM6 . . . . **220** A1
Gulliver Cl UB5 . . . . **85** B6
Gulliver Ct CR2 . . . . . **220** D1
Gulliver Rd DA15 . . . . **167** C2
Gulliver St SE16 . . . . . **119** B3
Gulston Wlk SW3 . . . . **257** D3
Gumleigh Rd W5 . . . . . **109** C2
Gumley Gdns TW7 . . . . **131** A2
Gumley House Convent Sch (Girls) TW7 . . . **131** A2
Gumping Rd BR5 . . . . **227** A6
Gundulph Rd BR2 . . . . **209** C6
Gunmakers La E3 . . . . . **97** A6
Gunnel Cl SE20 . . . . . . **184** A6
Gunnell Cl SE25 . . . . . . **206** A3
Gunnell Ct 3 CR4 . . . . **180** C2
Gunnels Ct & Hastingwood Ct 6
IG9 . . . . **21** C2
Gunner Dr 9 EN3 . . . . . . **7** C6
Gunner La SE18 . . . . . . **122** C1
GUNNERSBURY **110** D2
Gunnersbury Avenue (North Circular Rd)
W3 . . . . **110** C3
Gunnersbury Cl 8
W4 . . . . **110** D1
Gunnersbury Cres
W3 . . . . **110** C4
Gunnersbury Ct 8
W3 . . . . **110** D4
Gunnersbury Dr W5 . . **110** B4
Gunnersbury Gdns
W3 . . . . **110** C4
Gunnersbury La W3 . . **110** C4
Gunnersbury Manor
W5 . . . . **110** B5
Gunnersbury Mews 6
W4 . . . . **110** D1
Gunnersbury Park
W3 . . . . **110** C3
Gunnersbury Park Mus★
W3 . . . . **110** C3
Gunnersbury RC Sch
TW8 . . . . **109** C1
Gunnersbury Sta
W4 . . . . **110** D1
Gunnersbury Triangle Nat Res★ W12 . . . . . **111** A2
Gunners Gr E4 . . . . **20** A1
Gunners Rd SW18 . . . . **158** B2
Gunnery Terr SE18 . . . **123** A3
Gunning St SE18 . . . . . **123** C2
Gunpowder Sq EC4 . . . **241** B2
Gun St E1 . . . . **243** C3
Gunstor Rd N16 . . . . **73** C4
Gunter Gr
Chelsea
SW6 . . . . . **136** A5 **266** A4
Hendon HA8 . . . . **27** B2
Gunterstone Rd
W14 . . . . **113** A1 **254** B2
Gunthorpe St
E1 . . . . **95** D1 **243** D2
Gunton Rd
Streatham SW17 . . . . **181** A4
Upper Clapton E5 . . . . . . **74** B6
Gunwhale Cl SE16 . . . **118** D5
Gun Wharf
Old Ford E3 . . . . **97** A6
Wapping E1 . . . . **118** C5
Gurdon Ho 7 E14 . . . . . **97** C1
Gurdon Rd SE7 . . . . . . **121** A1
Gurnell Gr W13 . . . . **86** D3
Gurnell L Ctr W13 . . . . . **86** D4
Gurney Cl
Barking IG11 . . . . **78** D2
Higham Hill E17 . . . . **34** D2
Stratford E15 . . . . **76** C3
Gurney Cres CR0 . . . . . **204** B1
Gurney Dr N2 . . . . **48** A5
Gurney Ho
3 Bayswater W2 . . . . . . **91** D1
14 Bethnal Green E2 . . . **96** A5
Hayes UB3 . . . . **105** C2
Gurney Rd
London SW6 . . . . **136** A2
Northolt UB5 . . . . **84** C4
Gurney Rd *continued*
Stratford E15 . . . . **76** C3
Wallington SM5 . . . . . **219** A4
Guru Nanak Sikh Prim & Sec Schs UB4 . . . . . **106** C5
Guthrie Ct SE1 . . . . . . **251** B1
Guthrie St SW3 . . . . . . **257** A2
Gutter La EC2 . . **95** A1 **242** A2
Guyatt Gdns CR4 . . . . . **181** A1
Guy Barnett Gr SE3 . . **143** A2
Guy Rd SM6 . . . . **219** D5
Guyscliff Rd SE13 . . . . **164** A6
Guy's Hospl
SE1 . . . . **117** B4 **252** D2
Guy's Retreat IG9 . . . . . **21** C4
Guy St SE1 . . . **117** B4 **252** D2
Gwalior Ho N14 . . . . **15** C5
Gwalior Rd SW15 . . . . **134** D2
Gwendolen Ave
SW15 . . . . **156** D6
Gwendolen Cl SW15 **156** D6
Gwendolen Ho
TW19 . . . . **148** A3
Gwendoline Ave E13 . . **99** B6
Gwendoline Ct
TW15 . . . . **170** A6
Gwendwr Rd
W14 . . . . **113** A1 **254** B2
Gwent Ct 13 SE16 . . . . **118** D5
Gwillim Cl DA15 . . . . . **168** A6
Gwilym Maries Ho 11
E2 . . . . **96** B4
Gwydor Rd BR3 . . . . . . **206** D6
Gwydyr Rd BR2 . . . . . . **208** D6
Gwyn Cl SW6 . **136** A5 **266** A3
Gwyn Jones Prim Sch
E11 . . . . **54** B2
Gwynne Ave CR0 . . . . . **206** D2
Gwynne Cl W4 . . . . **133** D6
Gwynne Ho
Finsbury WC1 . . . . **234** A1
6 Streatham SW2 . . . . **160** B3
3 Wanstead E11 . . . . **55** A4
Whitechapel E1 . . . . **96** B2
Gwynne Pl WC1 . . . . . . **233** D1
Gwynne Rd SW11 . . . . **136** B3
Gye Ho 2 SW4 . . . . . . **138** A1
Gylcote Cl SE5 . . . . **139** B1
Gyles Pk HA7 . . . . **25** C2
Gyllyngdune Gdns
IG3 . . . . **79** D5

H

Haarlem Rd 12 W14 . . **112** D3
Haberdasher Pl 4
N1 . . . . **95** C4
Haberdashers' Aske's Hatcham Coll SE4 . **141** A3
Haberdashers' Aske's Knights Acad BR1 . **187** A6
Haberdasher St
N1 . . . . **95** B4 **235** D2
Haccombe Rd SW19 . **180** A4
HACKBRIDGE **219** B6
Hackbridge Park Gdns
SM5 . . . . **218** D6
Hackbridge Prim Sch
SM5 . . . . **203** A1
Hackbridge Rd SM5,
SM6 . . . . **219** A6
Hackbridge Sta SM6 . **219** B6
Hackford Rd
SW9 . . . . **138** B4 **270** D2
Hackford Wlk SW9 . . . **138** C4
Hackforth Cl EN5 . . . . . **12** B6
Hackington Cres
BR3 . . . . **185** C4
HACKNEY **74** B2
Hackney Central Sta
E8 . . . . **74** B2
Hackney Cl WD6 . . . . . . **11** B6
Hackney Com Coll 33
N1 . . . . **95** C4
Hackney Downs Sta
E8 . . . . **74** B3
Hackney Empire E8 . . . **74** B2
Hackney Free & Parochial CE Sec Sch
18 E9 . . . . **74** C2
Hackney Gr E8 . . . . **74** B2
Hackney Rd E2 . . . . **96** A5
HACKNEY WICK **75** C2
Hackney Wick E9 . . . . . **75** B2
Hackney Wick Sta E9 . **75** C2
Hackworth Point 24
E3 . . . . **97** D4
Hacon Sq 12 E8 . . . . **74** B1
Hadar Cl N20 . . . . **13** D3
Haddenham Ct
SW17 . . . . **180** B6
Hadden Rd SE28 . . . . . **123** C3
Hadden Way UB6 . . . . . . **64** B2
Haddington Rd BR1 . . **186** B6
Haddo Ho
Gospel Oak NW5 . . . . . . **71** B4
Greenwich SE10 . . . . . **141** D6
Haddon Cl Enfield EN1 . **18** A5
New Malden KT3 . . . . **199** D4
Haddon Ct
East Acton W3 . . . . . . **111** D6
Hendon NW4 . . . . **46** C6
Haddon Gr DA15 . . . . . **168** A4
Haddon Rd SM1 . . . . . **217** D4
Haddo St SE10 . . . . . . **142** A6
Haden Ct N4 . . . . **72** C6
Hadfield Cl UB1 . . . . **85** B4
Hadfield Ho
Edgware NW7 . . . . **28** C6
37 Whitechapel E1 . . . . . **96** A1
Hadleigh Cl
17 Bethnal Green E1 . . . **96** C3
Merton SW20 . . . . **179** B1
Hadleigh Ct 8 E4 . . . . . **20** C4
Hadleigh Ho 16 E1 . . . . **96** C3
Hadleigh Lo 5 IG8 . . . . **37** A4
Hadleigh Rd N9 . . . . **18** B4
Hadleigh St E2 . . . . **96** C4
Hadleigh Wlk 1 E6 . . . **100** A1
HADLEY **1** B2
Hadley Cl
Borehamwood WD6 . . . . **10** B5
Southgate N21 . . . . **16** C5
Hadley Ct
1 London N3 . . . . **29** D3
Stamford Hill N16 . . . . . **52** A1
Hadley Gdns
Chiswick W4 . . . . **111** B1
Southall UB2 . . . . **107** B1
Hadley Gn W EN5 . . . . . . **1** B3
Hadley Gr EN5 . . . . **1** A3
Hadley Green Rd EN5 . . . **1** B3
Hadley Hall N21 . . . . **16** C3
Hadley Highstone EN5 . . **1** B4
Hadley Ho BR5 . . . . . . **189** D1
Hadley Hts EN5 . . . . **1** D3
Hadley Rd Barnet EN5 . . . **1** D2
Belvedere DA17 . . . . . . **125** B2
Enfield EN2 . . . . **4** A5
Mitcham CR4 . . . . **203** D5
Hadley Ridge EN5 . . . . . . **1** B2
Hadley St NW1 . . . . **71** B2
Hadleyvale Ct EN5 . . . . . **1** D2
Hadley View 9 EN5 . . . . . **1** D1
Hadley Way N21 . . . . **16** C5
HADLEY WOOD **2** B5
Hadley Wood Prim Sch
EN4 . . . . **2** A5
Hadley Wood Rd
Barnet EN4 . . . . **2** A3
Barnet EN5 . . . . **1** C3
Hadley Wood Sta EN4 . . **2** A5
Hadlow Coll (Mottingham Ctr)
SE12 . . . . **165** C3
Hadlow Ho SE17 . . . . . **263** B2
Hadlow Pl SE19 . . . . . . **184** A3
Hadlow Rd
Bexley DA16 . . . . **146** C5
Sidcup DA14 . . . . **190** A6
Hadrian Cl
5 Old Ford E3 . . . . **97** C6
Stanwell TW19 . . . . **148** A4
Hadrian Ct Barnet EN5 . . **1** D1
11 Belmont SM2 . . . . . **217** D1
Brockley SE4 . . . . **141** C2
Hadrian Est 33 E2 . . . . . **96** A5
Hadrian's Ride EN1 . . . **17** D6
Hadrian St SE10 . . . . . . **120** C1
Hadrian Way TW19 . . . **148** A4
Hadstock Ho NW1 . . . **232** D2
Hadyn Park Ct 13
W12 . . . . **112** A4
Hadyn Park Rd W12 . . **112** A4
Hafer Rd SW11 . . . . . . **136** D1
Hafton Rd SE6 . . . . **164** C2
Haggard Rd TW1 . . . . . **153** B4
Hagger Ct E17 . . . . **54** B6
HAGGERSTON **95** D5
Haggerston Rd E8 . . . . . **95** D6
Haggerston Sch 15
E2 . . . . **95** D5
Haggerston Sta E2 . . . . **95** D6
Haggerston Studios 30
E8 . . . . **95** D6
Hague Prim Sch 21
E2 . . . . **96** B3
Hague St 30 E2 . . . . **96** A4
Ha-Ha Rd SE7, SE18 . . **144** B6
Haig Ct BR7 . . . . **188** D5
Haig Ho 4 E2 . . . . **96** A5
Haig Pl SM4 . . . . **201** C3
Haig Rd Hillingdon UB8 . **83** A2
Stanmore HA7 . . . . **25** C5
Haig Rd E E13 . . . . **99** C5
Haig Rd W E13 . . . . **99** C4
Haigville Gdns IG6 . . . . **56** D5
Hailes Cl SW19 . . . . . . **180** A4
Haileybury Ave EN1 . . . **17** D5
Hailey Rd DA18 . . . . . . **125** C4
Hailey Rd Bsns Pk
DA18 . . . . **125** C4
Hailing Mews BR2 . . . . **209** B6
Hailsham Ave SW2 . . . **160** B2
Hailsham Cl KT6 . . . . . **197** D2
Hailsham Dr HA1 . . . . . . **42** B6
Hailsham Rd SW17 . . . **181** A4
Hailsham Terr N18 . . . . . **33** B5
Haimo Prim Sch
SE9 . . . . **165** D6
Haimo Rd SE9 . . . . **165** D6
Hainault Bldgs E10 . . . . **54** A1
Hainault Bridge Par 5
IG1 . . . . **78** D6
Hainault Ct E17 . . . . **54** B5
Hainault Gore RM6 . . . . **59** A4
Hainault Rd
Dagenham RM6 . . . . **59** B3
Ilford RM6 . . . . **58** B6
Leytonstone E11 . . . . **54** B2
Hainault St Ilford IG1 . . **78** D6
New Eltham SE9 . . . . . . **166** D3
Haines Wlk SM4 . . . . . . **201** D2
Hainford Cl SE4 . . . . . . **140** D1
Haining Cl 3 W4 . . . . . **110** C1
Hainthorpe Rd SE27 . **182** D6
Hainton Cl E1 . . . . **96** B1
Halberd Mews E5 . . . . . . **74** B6
Halbutt Gdns RM9 . . . . **81** B5
Halbutt St RM9 . . . . **81** B4
Halcomb St N1 . . . . **95** C6
Halcot Ave DA6 . . . . . . **169** D6
Halcroft Ct SM1 . . . . . . **218** B4
Halcrow St E1 . . . . **96** B2
Halcyon Ho 8 EN1 . . . . **17** C6
Haldane Cl
Holdbrook EN3 . . . . **7** D5
Muswell Hill N10 . . . . **31** B3
Haldane Pl SW18 . . . . . **157** D3
Haldane Rd
Fulham
SW6 . . . . . **135** B6 **264** D5
Newham E6 . . . . **100** A4
Southall UB1 . . . . **86** A1
Thamesmead SE28 . . . . **124** D6
Haldan Rd E4 . . . . **36** A4
Haldon Rd SW18 . . . . . . **157** B5
Hale Cl Chingford E4 . . . **20** A1
Edgware HA8 . . . . **27** A5
Orpington BR6 . . . . **227** A4
Hale Ct HA8 . . . . **27** A5
Hale Dr NW7 . . . . **27** B4
HALE END **36** C4
Hale End Cl HA4 . . . . **40** A3
Hale End Rd E17 . . . . **36** B2
Halefield Rd N17 . . . . . . **34** B2
Hale Gdns Acton W3 . . **110** C5
Tottenham Hale N17 . . . **52** A6
Hale Grove Gdns
NW7 . . . . **27** C5
Hale Ho Enfield EN3 . . . . . **6** D6
Westminster SW1 . . . . **259** D2
Hale La NW7, HA8 . . . . . **27** B5
Hale Lo HA1 . . . . **42** C2
Hale Rd Newham E6 . . . **100** A3
Tottenham Hale N17 . . . **52** A6
Hales Ct 6 TW11 . . . . . **175** A5
Hales Ho 3 SW12 . . . . . **159** B4
Halesowen Rd SM4 . . . **201** D2
Hales Prior N1 . . . . **233** C3
Hales St SE8 . . . . **141** C5
Hale St E14 . . . . **119** D6
Halesworth Cl 3 E5 . . . **74** C6
Halesworth Rd SE13 . **141** D2
Hale The Chingford E4 . . **36** B3
Tottenham Hale N17 . . . **52** A6

Hale Wlk W7 . . . . 86 C2
Haley Rd NW4 . . . . 46 C3
Halfacre 14 HA3 . . . . 25 C5
Half Acre
Brentford TW8 . . . . . 131 D6
2 Wanstead E18 . . . . . 55 A6
Half Acre Mews
TW8 . . . . 131 D6
Half Acre Rd W7 . . . . . . 108 C5
Half Moon Cres N1 . . . . 233 D4
Half Moon Ct EC1 . . . . . 242 A3
Half Moon La SE24 . . . 161 A5
Halfmoon Pas E1 . . . . . 243 D1
Half Moon St
W1 . . . . . . 115 B5 248 D3
Halford Cl HA8 . . . . 26 D1
Halford Ct KT9 . . . . 214 A1
Halford Ho 9 SW15 . 156 D6
Halford Rd
Ickenham UB10 . . . . . . 60 C3
Leyton E10 . . . . 54 B4
Richmond TW10 . . . . 154 A6
West Brompton
SW6 . . . . . . 135 C6 265 A5
Halfway St DA15 . . . . . . 167 C3
Haliburton Rd TW1,
TW7 . . . . 131 A1
Haliday Ho N1 . . . . 73 B2
Haliday Wlk 4 N1 . . . . . 73 B2
Halidon Cl E9 . . . . 74 C3
Halifax 8 NW9 . . . . 27 D1
Halifax Cl TW11 . . . . . . 174 C4
Halifax Rd Enfield EN2 . . 5 B3
Greenford UB6 . . . . . . 85 D6
Halifax St SE26 . . . . . . 162 B1
Halkett Dr DA17 . . . . . 125 A3
Haling Gr CR2 . . . . 220 D1
Haling Manor High Sch
CR2 . . . . 220 D1
Haling Park Gdns
CR2 . . . . 220 D2
Haling Park Rd
Croydon CR2 . . . . . . 220 D3
South Croydon CR2 . . 221 A2
Haling Rd CR2 . . . . 221 B2
Haliwell Ho 10 NW6 . . . 91 D6
Halkett Ho 1 E2 . . . . 96 C6
Halkin Arc
SW1 . . . . . . 114 D3 257 D6
Halkin Mews SW1 . . . . 258 A6
Halkin Pl SW1 . . . . 258 A6
Halkin St
SW1 . . . . . . 114 A3 248 B1
Hallam Cl BR7 . . . . 188 B5
Hallam Ct W1 . . . . 238 D4
Hallam Gdns HA5 . . . . . 23 A3
Hallam Ho
6 London SW9 . . . . 138 C4
Pimlico SW1 . . . . 259 B1
Hallam Mews W1 . . . . . 238 D4
Hallam Rd
Barnes SW13 . . . . . . 134 B2
Harringay N15 . . . . . . 50 D5
Hallam St W1 . . 93 B2 238 D4
Hallane Ho SE27 . . . . . 183 A5
Hall Cl W5 . . . . 88 A2
Hall Ct TW11 . . . . 174 D5
Hall Dr Ealing W7 . . . . . 86 C1
Forest Hill SE26 . . . . 184 C5
Halley Gdns SE13 . . . . 142 B1
Halley Ho
8 Bethnal Green E2 . . 96 A5
8 Cubitt Town SE10 . . 120 D1
Halley Prim Sch E14 . . 97 A2
Halley Rd E7,E12 . . . . . 77 D2
Halley St E14 . . . . 97 A2
Hall Farm Cl HA7 . . . . . 25 B6
Hall Farm Dr TW2 . . . . 152 B4
Hallfield Jun & Inf Schs
2 W2 . . . . 91 D1
Hallgate SE3 . . . . 143 A2
Hall Gate NW8 . . 92 A4 229 B2
Hall Gdns E4 . . . . 35 B6
Halliards The KT12 . . . . 194 A3
Halliday Ho 10 E1 . . . . . 96 A6
Halliday Sq UB2 . . . . . 108 B5
Halliford Cl TW17 . . . . 193 C6
Halliford Rd
Sunbury TW16 . . . . . 194 A5
Upper Halliford TW16,
TW17 . . . . 193 D5
Halliford Sch TW17 . . 193 A2
Halliford St N1 . . . . 73 B1
Hallingbury Ct 1
E17 . . . . 53 D6
Halling Ho SE1 . . . . . . 252 D1

Hallings Wharf Studios
2 E15 . . . . 98 B6
Halliwell Ct 4 SE22 . . 162 A6
Halliwell Rd SW2 . . . . 160 B5
Halliwick Court Par 2
N12 . . . . 30 D5
Halliwick Ct 1 N12 . . . 30 D5
Halliwick Ho N21 . . . . . 17 B5
Halliwick Rd N10 . . . . . 31 A2
Hall La
Chingford Hatch E4 . . 35 B5
Harlington UB3 . . . . . 127 B5
Hendon NW4 . . . . 28 A1
Hall Lane E4 . . . . 35 A5
Hallmark Trad Ctr
HA9 . . . . 47 C2
Hallmead Rd SM1 . . . 217 D5
Hall Oak Wlk NW6 . . . . 69 C2
Hallowell Ave CR0 . . . . 220 A4
Hallowell Cl CR4 . . . . . 203 A6
Hallowfield Way
CR4 . . . . 202 C6
Hallows Gr TW16 . . . . . 171 D5
Hall Pl W2 . . . . 92 B3 236 C5
Hall Rd
Dagenham RM6 . . . . . 58 D3
Isleworth TW7 . . . . . 152 B6
Leyton E15 . . . . 76 B4
Newham E6 . . . . 100 B6
St John's Wood
NW8 . . . . . . 92 A4 229 B3
Halls Bsns Ctr UB3 . . 106 A3
Hall Sch SW20 . . . . . . 178 D2
Hall Sch The NW3 . . . . . 70 B2
Hall Sch Wimbledon
SW15 . . . . 156 A1
Hallside Rd EN1 . . . . 5 D5
Hall St
Finsbury EC1 . . 94 D4 234 D2
North Finchley N12 . . . 30 A5
Halls Terr UB10 . . . . . . 82 D3
Hallsville Prim Sch
E16 . . . . 99 A1
Hallsville Rd E16 . . . . . 98 D1
Hallswelle Par 1
NW11 . . . . 47 B4
Hallswelle Rd NW11 . . 47 B4
Hall The SE3 . . . . 143 A2
Hall Twr W2 . . . . 236 D4
Hall View SE9 . . . . 165 D3
Hallywell Cres E6 . . . . 100 B2
Halons Rd SE9 . . . . . . 166 C4
Halpin Pl
SE17 . . . . . . 117 B2 262 D3
Halsbrook Rd SE3 . . . 143 D2
Halsbury Cl HA7 . . . . . . 25 B6
Halsbury Ct HA7 . . . . . . 25 B6
Halsbury Ho N7 . . . . . . 72 B4
Halsbury Rd W12 . . . . 112 B5
Halsbury Rd E UB5 . . . 64 A4
Halsbury Rd W UB5 . . . 63 D3
Halsend UB3 . . . . 106 B5
Halsey St
SW3 . . . . . . 114 D2 257 C4
Halsham Cres IG11 . . . 79 D3
Halsmere Rd SE5 . . . . 138 D4
Halstead Ct 2 CR0 . . . 221 A5
Halstead Ct
Shoreditch N1 . . . . . 235 D3
Walthamstow E17 . . . 53 B2
Halstead Gdns N21 . . . 17 B3
Halstead Rd
Edmonton N13 . . . . . . 17 B3
Enfield EN1 . . . . 5 C1
Wanstead E11 . . . . . . 55 B4
Halston Cl SW11 . . . . 158 D5
Halstow Prim Sch 5
SE10 . . . . 121 A1
Halstow Rd
Greenwich SE3,
SE10 . . . . 121 A1
Kensal Green NW10 . . 90 D4
Halsway UB3 . . . . 106 A5
Halter Cl WD6 . . . . 11 B6
Halton Cl N11 . . . . 30 D4
Halton Cross St
N1 . . . . 94 D6 234 D6
Haltone Ho 1 SW4 . . . 137 D3
Halton Ho 22 N1 . . . . . 72 D1
Halton Mans N1 . . . . . . 72 D1
Halton Pl N1 . . . . 235 A6
Halton Rd N1 . . 94 D6 234 D6
Halton Rd N5 . . . . 72 D4
Halt Robin La DA17 . . 125 D2
Halt Robin Rd DA17 . . 125 D2
Halyard Ho E14 . . . . . 120 A3

HAM 153 C1
Hamara Ghar E13 . . . . . 99 C5
Hambalt Rd SW4 . . . . 159 C6
Hamble Cl HA4 . . . . 61 C6
Hamble Ct KT1 . . . . . . 175 D3
Hambledon SE17 . . . . 139 B6
Hambledon Chase
N4 . . . . 50 A2
Hambledon Cl UB8 . . . . 82 D3
Hambledon Ct
5 Ealing W5 . . . . . . 110 A6
9 Wallington SM6 . . 219 B2
Hambledon Gdns
SE25 . . . . 205 D6
Hambledon Ho
2 Kingston u T
KT2 . . . . 176 D4
Lower Clapton E5 . . . . 74 B4
Hambledon Pl SE21 . . 161 D3
Hambledon Rd
SW18 . . . . 157 B4
Hambledown Rd
DA15 . . . . 167 C4
Hamble St SW6 . . . . . 135 D2
Hambleton Cl KT4 . . . . 216 C6
Hamble Wlk UB5 . . . . . 85 C5
Hambley Ho 5 SE16 . . 118 B2
Hamblin Rd UB1 . . . . . 107 A6
Hambly Mans SW16 . . 182 A4
Hamblyn Cts N16 . . . . . 51 D2
Hambridge Way
SW2 . . . . 160 C4
Hambro Ave BR2 . . . . 209 A1
Hambrook Ct 12 NW5 . 71 B4
Hambrook Rd SE25 . . 206 B6
Hambro Rd SW16 . . . . 181 D5
Hambrough Ho UB4 . . . 84 C2
Hambrough Prim Sch
UB1 . . . . 107 B5
Hambrough Rd UB1 . . 107 A5
Ham Comm TW10 . . . 153 D1
Ham Croft Cl TW13 . . 150 A1
Ham Ct 12 NW9 . . . . . . 27 D1
Hamden Cres RM10 . . . 81 D5
Hamel Cl HA3 . . . . 45 A5
Hamers Ho 9 SW2 . . . 160 C4
Hameway E6 . . . . 100 C3
Ham Farm Rd KT2,
TW10 . . . . 176 A6
Hamfrith Rd E15 . . . . . . 76 D2
Ham Gate Ave TW10 . 176 A6
Ham Ho★ TW10 . . . . 153 C2
Hamilton Ave
Cheam SM3 . . . . 217 A6
Edmonton N9 . . . . . . 18 A4
Ilford IG6 . . . . 57 A4
Tolworth KT6, SM3 . . 214 C6
Hamilton Cl
Ashford TW15 . . . . . 171 D5
Cockfosters EN4 . . . . . 2 D1
Rotherhithe SE16 . . . 119 B3
St John's Wood
NW8 . . . . . . 92 A4 229 C1
Croydon CR0 . . . . . . 206 A1
Ealing W5 . . . . 110 B6
St John's Wood W9 . . 229 A2
Hamilton Gdns
NW8 . . . . . . 92 A4 229 A2
Hamilton Ho
20 Bow E3 . . . . 97 B4
Chiswick W4 . . . . . . 133 C6
Kensington W8 . . . . 245 C2
Oakleigh Pk N20 . . . . 14 A4
1 Poplar E14 . . . . . 119 B6
Putney SW15 . . . . . 156 A6
10 Richmond TW9 . . 132 C4
St John's Wood NW8 . 229 C2
Hamilton La N5 . . . . . . 72 D4
Hamilton Lo 37 E1 . . . . 96 C3
Hamilton Mews W1 . . 248 C2
Hamilton Pk N5 . . . . . . 72 D4
Hamilton Pk W N5 . . . . 72 D4
Hamilton Pl
Mayfair W1 . . 115 A5 248 B3

Hamilton Pl continued
Sunbury TW16 . . . . . 172 B3
Tottenham N17 . . . . . 33 D1
Hamilton Rd
Acton W4 . . . . 111 C4
Barnet EN4 . . . . 2 C1
Bexleyheath DA7 . . . 147 A3
Brentford TW8 . . . . 131 D6
Ealing W5 . . . . 110 A6
East Finchley N2 . . . . 48 A6
Edmonton N9 . . . . . . 18 A4
Feltham TW13 . . . . . 171 D6
Harrow HA1 . . . . 42 C4
Hayes UB3 . . . . 106 B6
Hendon NW11 . . . . . 47 A2
Higham Hill E17 . . . . 35 A1
Ilford IG1 . . . . 78 D4
Merton SW19 . . . . . 179 D3
Newham E15 . . . . 98 C4
Sidcup DA15 . . . . . . 190 A6
Southall UB1 . . . . . . 107 B5
South Norwood CR7 . 205 B6
Stamford Hill N2 . . . 152 C3
Twickenham TW2 . . . 152 C3
West Norwood SE27 . 183 B6
Willesden NW10 . . . . 68 A3
Hamilton Road Ind Est
SE27 . . . . 183 B6
Hamilton Road Mews 1
SW19 . . . . 179 D3
Hamilton Sq
Bermondsey SE1 . . . 252 D2
Finchley N12 . . . . . . 30 A4
Hamilton St SE8 . . . . . 141 C6
Hamilton Terr
NW8 . . . . . . 92 A4 229 B2
Hamilton Way
Edmonton N13 . . . . . 32 D6
Finchley N3 . . . . 29 C4
Hamlea Cl SE12 . . . . . 165 A6
Hamlet Cl SE13 . . . . . 142 C1
Hamlet Ct
14 Enfield EN1 . . . . . 17 C6
1 Hammersmith W6 . 112 A2
Kensington SE11 . . . 261 C2
Hamlet Gdns W6 . . . . 112 A2
Hamlet Ho SE9 . . . . . 166 C6
Hamleton Terr RM9 . . . 80 C1
Hamlet Rd SE19 . . . . . 184 A3
Hamlet Sq NW2 . . . . . . 69 A5
Hamlets Way E3 . . . . . 97 B3
Hamlet The SE5 . . . . . 139 B2
Hamlet Way SE1 . . . . 252 D2
Hamlin Cres HA5 . . . . . 40 C4
Hamlyn Cl HA8 . . . . . . 10 A1
Hamlyn Gdns SE19 . . 183 C3
Hamlyn Ho 3 TW13 . . 150 B3
Hammelton Ct 2
BR1 . . . . 186 D2
Hammelton Gn 2
SW9 . . . . 138 D4
Hammelton Rd BR1 . . 187 A2
Hammers La NW7 . . . . 28 A6
Hammersley Ho 8
SE14 . . . . 140 C5
HAMMERSMITH 112 C2
Hammersmith Bridge Rd
W6,SW13 . . . . 112 C1
Hammersmith
Broadway
Hammersmith W6 . . 112 C1
3 Hammersmith W6 112 C2
Hammersmith Flyover
W6 . . . . 112 C1
Hammersmith Gr
W6 . . . . 112 C3
Hammersmith Hospl
W12 . . . . 90 B1
Hammersmith Rd
Hammersmith W6 . . 112 C2
Kensington W14 . . . 254 B4
Hammersmith Sta
W6 . . . . 112 C2
Hammersmith Terr 6
W6 . . . . 112 A1
Hammet Cl UB4 . . . . . . 84 D2
Hammett St EC3 . . . . 253 C6
Hammond Ave CR4 . . 181 B1
Hammond Cl
Barnet EN5 . . . . 13 B6
Greenford UB6 . . . . . 64 B3
Hampton TW12 . . . . 173 C2
Hammond Ct
1 Leyton E10 . . . . . . 75 D6
1 Walthamstow E17 . . 53 A4

Hal–Ham 355

Hammond Ho
10 Deptford SE14 . . . 140 C5
Millwall E14 . . . . . . 119 D3
9 Wembley HA9 . . . 91 C2
Hammond Rd
Enfield EN1 . . . . 6 B3
Southall UB2 . . . . . . 107 A3
Hammonds Cl RM8 . . . 80 C5
Hammonds Ho
TW19 . . . . 148 B3
Hammond St NW5 . . . . 71 C2
Hammond Way
SE28 . . . . 124 B6
Hamonde Cl HA8 . . . . . 10 D2
Hamond Sq N1 . . . . . . 95 C5
Ham Park Rd E15 . . . . . 76 D1
Hampden Ave BR3 . . . 185 A1
Hampden Cl NW1 . . . . 232 D4
Hampden Ct
Harrow HA1 . . . . 42 A5
10 Muswell Hill N10 . 31 A3
Hampden Gurney CE
Prim Sch W1 92 C1 237 B2
Hampden Gurney St
W1 . . . . 237 C1
Hampden Ho SW9 1 147 A2
Hampden Rd
Beckenham BR3 . . . . 185 A1
Harrow HA3 . . . . 24 A1
Hornsey N8 . . . . 50 C5
Kingston u T KT1 . . . 198 C6
Muswell Hill N10 . . . . 31 A3
Tottenham N17 . . . . . 34 A1
Upper Holloway N19 . 71 D6
Hampden Sq N14 . . . . 15 B3
Hampden Way N14 . . . 15 B2
Hampshire Cl N18 . . . . 34 B5
Hampshire Ct
6 Barnes SW13 . . . . 133 D3
Hendon NW4 . . . . . . 46 C4
Hampshire Ho HA8 . . . 26 B3
Hampshire Hog La
3 Hammersmith
W6 . . . . 112 B1
11 Hammersmith W6 . 112 B1
Hampshire Rd N22 . . . 32 B3
Hampshire Sch The
SW7 . . . . 256 B4
Hampson Way
SW8 . . . . . . 138 B4 270 C2
HAMPSTEAD 70 B3
Hampstead Cl SE28 . 124 B5
Hampstead Coll of Fine
Arts & Humanities 2
NW3 . . . . 70 C2
Hampstead Com Mkt★
NW3 . . . . 70 B4
HAMPSTEAD GARDEN
SUBURB. 47 C4
Hampstead Gate
NW3 . . . . 70 A3
Hampstead Gdns
NW11 . . . . 47 C3
Hampstead Grn NW3 . 70 C3
Hampstead Gr NW3 . . 70 A5
Hampstead Heath★
NW3 . . . . 70 B6
Hampstead Heath Pre
Prep Sch NW3 . . . . . 70 C3
Hampstead Heath Sta
NW3 . . . . 70 A4
Hampstead High Sch 3
NW3 . . . . 70 B4
Hampstead High St
NW3 . . . . 70 B4
Hampstead Hill Gdns
NW3 . . . . 70 C4
Hampstead Hts N2 . . . 48 A6
Hampstead La N6 . . . . 48 C2
Hampstead Parochial CE
Sch NW3 . . . . 70 B4
Hampstead Rd
NW1 . . . . . . 93 C4 232 A2
Hampstead Sch NW2 69 A4
Hampstead Sq 1
NW3 . . . . 70 B5
Hampstead Sta NW3 . 70 A4
Hampstead West 4
NW6 . . . . 69 C2

Hampstead Wlk 1 E3 97 B6
HAMPTON 173 C1
Hampton Cl
Borehamwood WD6 11 A6
Friern Barnet N11 31 B5
Kilburn NW6 91 C4
Wimbledon SW20 178 C3
Hampton Com Coll TW12 173 C5
Hampton Court Ave KT8 196 C3
Hampton Court Cres KT8 196 B6
Hampton Court Landing Stage KT8 196 C6
Hampton Court Pal★ KT8 196 D6
Hampton Court Par KT8 196 C5
Hampton Court Rd KT1, KT8 197 B6
Hampton Court Sta KT8 196 C5
Hampton Court Way KT10, KT7, KT8 196 C3
Hampton Ct
Hampton KT8 196 C6
1 Islington N1 72 D2
19 Rotherhithe SE16 118 D5
Wood Green N22 31 C2
Hampton Ct House Sch KT8 174 C1
Hampton Farm Ind Est TW13 151 A1
HAMPTON HILL 174 A5
Hampton Hill Bsns Pk TW12 174 A5
Hampton Hill Jun Sch TW12 174 A5
Hampton Ho DA7 147 D3
Hampton Inf Sch TW12 173 C3
Hampton Jun Sch TW12 173 C2
Hampton La TW13 173 A6
Hampton Pool (Open Air) TW12 174 A3
Hampton Rd
Chingford Hatch E4 35 B5
Forest Gate E7 77 C3
Ilford IG1 79 A4
Leytonstone E11 54 B1
North Cheam KT4 216 B6
Teddington TW11, TW12 174 C5
Thornton Heath CR0 205 A3
Twickenham TW2 152 B1
Hampton Rd E TW13 151 B1
Hampton Rd W TW13 151 A1
Hampton Rise HA3 44 A3
Hampton Road Ind Pk CR0 205 A3
Hampton Sch TW12 173 C5
Hampton St SE1 116 D2 261 D3
Hampton Sta TW12 173 C2
HAMPTON WICK 175 D3
Hampton Wick Inf Sch TW11 175 D3
Hampton Wick Sta KT1 175 C2
Ham Ridings TW10 176 B5
Ham Shades Cl 1 DA15 168 A1
Hamson Ct HA2 64 B6
Ham St TW10 153 C1
Hamstead Gates 11 NW5 71 B2
Ham The TW8 131 C5
Ham View CR0 207 A3
Ham Yd W1 249 C6
Hanameel St E16 121 B5
Hana Mews E5 74 B4
Hanbury Cl NW4 46 C6
Hanbury Ct HA1 42 D3
Hanbury Dr
2 Leyton E11 54 D2
Southgate N21 16 B6
Hanbury Ho
8 Bethnal Green E1 96 A2
South Lambeth SW8 270 B5
Hanbury Mews N1 235 B5
Hanbury Rd
South Acton W3 110 D4
Tottenham N17 34 B1
Hanbury St E1 95 D2 243 D4
Hancocke Ho 4 E17 53 D6
Hancock Nunn Ho 1 NW3 70 D1
Hancock Rd
Bromley E3 98 A4
South Norwood SE19 183 B4
Handa Wlk 3 N1 73 A2
Handcroft Rd CR0 204 D1
Hand Ct WC1 240 D3
Handel Cl HA8 26 B4
Handel Ho TW2 152 B5
Handel House Museum★ W1 115 B6 248 D6
Handel Mans
Barnes SW13 134 C5
Bloomsbury WC1 240 B6
Handel Par HA8 26 C3
Handel Pl NW10 67 B2
Handel St WC1 94 A3 240 B6
Handel Way HA8 26 C3
Handen Rd SE12 164 D6
Handforth Rd
Brixton SW9 138 C5
6 Ilford IG1 78 D5
Handley Gr NW2 68 D5
Handley Page Rd SM6 220 B1
Handley Rd E9 96 C6
Handowe Cl NW4 46 A5
Handside Cl KT4 200 D1
Hands Wlk E16 99 A1
Handsworth Ave E4 36 B4
Handsworth Prim Sch E4 36 B4
Handsworth Rd N17 51 B6
Handtrough Way IG11 100 D5
Hanford Cl SW18 157 C3
Hanford Row SW19 178 C4
Hanger Ct W5 88 C3
Hanger Gn W5 88 C3
Hanger Lane Sta W5 88 A4
Hanger La (North Circular Rd) W5 88 B2
Hanger Vale La W5 88 B1
Hanger View Way W3 88 C2
Hangmans Cnr BR7 188 D2
Hankey Pl SE1 117 B4 252 D1
Hankins La NW7 11 C1
Hanley Ct N4 50 B1
Hanley Gdns N4 50 B1
Hanley Pl BR3 185 C3
Hanley Rd N4, N19 50 A1
Hanmer Wlk N7 72 B6
Hannah Cl
Beckenham BR3 208 A6
Wembley NW10 67 A4
Hannah Ct
Palmers Green N13 16 B2
5 Sutton SM1 217 D2
Wimbledon SW19 178 D3
Hannah Mary Way 17 SE1 118 A2
Hannah Mews SM6 219 C1
Hannay La N8 49 D2
Hannay Wlk SW16 159 D2
Hannell Rd SW6 135 A5 264 B4
Hannen Ho SE5 139 B2
Hannen Rd SE27 160 D1
Hannibal Rd
Stanwell TW19 148 A4
Stepney E1 96 C2
Hannibal Way CR0 220 B2
Hanning Lo TW3 130 A1
Hannington Rd SW4 137 B2
Hanno Cl SM6 219 D1
Hanover Ave
Feltham TW13 150 A2
Newham E16 121 A5
Hanover Circ UB3 83 B1
Hanover Cl
Cheam SM3 217 B4
Richmond TW9 132 C5
Hanover Ct
Colindale NW9 45 C6
Harrow HA1 42 B2
1 Penge SE19 184 A3
Hanover Ct *continued*
11 Pinner HA5 23 B3
Shepherd's Bush W12 112 A5
Stamford Hill N16 51 D2
Hanover Dr BR7 189 A6
Hanover Gate Mans NW1 237 B6
Hanover Gdns SE11 138 C6
Hanover Ho
1 New Barnet EN5 2 A1
St John's Wood NW8 230 A3
Tolworth KT6 198 C1
Hanover Lo N21 16 D6
Hanover Mans 5 SW2 160 C6
Hanover Mead NW11 47 A3
Hanover Pk SE15 140 A4
Hanover Pl 16 Bow E3 97 B4
St Giles WC2 240 B1
Hanover Prim Sch N1 95 A5 235 A4
Hanover Rd
Merton SW19 180 A3
South Tottenham N15 51 D5
Willesden NW10 90 C6
Hanover Sq W1 93 B1 238 D1
Hanover St
Croydon CR0 220 D5
Marylebone W1 93 B1 238 D1
Hanover Stps W2 237 B1
Hanover Terr
Isleworth TW7 131 A4
Lisson Gr NW1 92 D4 230 C1
Hanover Terrace Mews NW1 92 C4 230 B1
Hanover Way DA6 146 D2
Hanover West Ind Est NW10 89 B4
Hanover Yd N1 235 A4
Hansard Mews W14 112 D4
Hansart Way EN2 4 C4
Hanscomb Mews SW4 137 C1
Hans Cres SW1 114 D3 257 C6
Hanselin Cl HA7 24 D5
Hansen Dr N21 16 B6
Hanshaw Dr HA8 27 B2
Hansler Ct 14 SW19 157 A3
Hansler Gr KT8 196 B5
Hansler Rd SE22 161 D6
Hansol Rd DA6 169 A6
Hanson Cl
Balham SW12 159 B4
Beckenham BR3 185 D4
Mortlake SW14 133 A2
West Drayton UB7 104 B3
Hanson Ct E17 53 D3
Hanson Gdns UB1 107 A4
Hanson Ho 2 E1 118 A6
Hanson St W1 93 C2 239 A4
Hans Pl SW1 114 D3 257 C6
Hans Rd SW3 114 D3 257 C6
Hans St SW1 114 D3 257 D5
Hanway Ho 25 SW9 138 C4
Hanway Pl W1 239 C2
Hanway Rd W7 86 C1
Hanway St W1 239 C2
HANWELL 108 D5
Hanwell Sta W7 108 C6
HANWORTH 172 D6
Hanworth Ho SE5 138 D5
Hanworth Rd
Ashford TW16 172 A3
Feltham TW13 150 B3
Hampton TW12 173 C5
Hounslow TW3, TW4 129 D1
Twickenham TW4 151 B4
Hanworth Terr TW3 129 D1
Hanworth Trad Est TW13 151 A1
Hapgood Cl UB6 64 B3
Harben Rd NW6 70 A1
Harberson Rd
Balham SW12 159 B3
West Ham E15 98 D6
Harberton Rd N19 49 C1
Harbet Rd
Highams Pk N18 35 A4
Paddington W2 92 B2 236 D3
Harbex Cl DA5 169 D4
Harbinger Prim Sch 11 E14 119 D2
Harbinger Rd E14 119 D2
Harbin Ho 5 SW2 160 C3
Harbledown Ho SE1 252 C1
Harbledown Rd SW6 265 A2
Harbord Cl
Camberwell SE15 139 C5
London SE5 139 B3
Harbord Ho 5 SE16 118 D2
Harbord St SW6 134 D4
Harborne Cl WD19 22 C5
Harborough Ave DA15 167 D4
Harborough Rd SW16 182 B6
Harbour Ave SW10 136 A4 266 B1
Harbour Cl 2 CR4 181 A2
Harbour Exchange Sq E14 119 D4
Harbour Rd SE5 139 A2
Harbridge Ave SW15 156 A4
Harbury Rd SM5 218 C1
Harbut Rd SW11 136 B1
Harcombe Rd N16 73 C5
Harcourt Ave
Edgware HA8 11 A1
Little Ilford E12 78 B3
Sidcup DA15 168 C4
Wallington SM6 219 B4
Harcourt Cl TW7 131 A2
Harcourt Field SM6 219 B4
Harcourt Ho
5 Chingford E4 36 B5
27 Clapham SW8 137 D3
Marylebone W1 238 C2
4 Willesden NW10 68 C2
Harcourt Lo 2 SM6 219 B4
Harcourt Rd
Bexley DA6 147 A1
Brockley SE4 141 B2
Bushey WD23 8 A6
Merton SW19 179 C3
Thornton Heath CR7 204 C3
Wallington SM6 219 B4
West Ham E15 98 D5
Wood Green N22 31 D2
Harcourt St W1 92 C2 237 B3
Harcourt Terr SW10 113 D1 255 D1
Hardcastle Cl SE25 206 A3
Hardcastle Ho
3 New Cross Gate SE14 141 A4
8 Peckham SE15 140 A4
Hardcourts Cl BR4 223 D5
Hard Ct IG8 37 C4
Hardel Rise SW2 160 D3
Hardel Wlk SE24, SW2 160 C4
Harden Ct 1 SE7 122 A2
Harden Ho SE5 139 C3
Harders Rd SE15 140 B3
Hardess St SE24 139 A2
Hardham Ho 5 SW2 160 C5
Hardie Cl NW10 67 B3
Harding Cl
Camberwell SE17 139 A6
South Croydon CR0 221 D5
Harding Ct SE25 183 D1
Hardinge Cl UB8 82 D1
Hardinge Cres SE18 123 A3
Hardinge Rd
Edmonton N18 33 C4
Willesden NW10 90 C6
Hardinge St
Stepney E1 96 C1
Woolwich SE18 122 D3
Harding Ho
Barnes SW13 134 B6
Hayes UB3 84 B1
14 Woolwich SE18 122 B2
Harding Pl SE23 163 A4
Harding Rd DA7 147 B3
Hardings Cl KT2 176 B2
Hardings La SE20 184 D4
Hardington 2 NW1 71 A1
Hardman Rd
Greenwich SE7 121 B1
Kingston u T KT2 176 A1
Hardwick Cl 7 HA7 25 C5
Hardwick Ct 8 E11 55 A3
Hardwicke Ave TW5 129 C4
Hardwicke Ho 14 E3 97 D4
Hardwicke Mews WC1 233 D1
Hardwicke Rd
Acton W4 111 B2
Bowes Pk N13 32 A4
Richmond TW10 175 C6
Hardwicke St IG11 101 A6
Hardwick Gn W13 87 B2
Hardwick Ho
14 London SW8 137 D3
Marylebone NW8 237 B6
Hardwick St EC1 94 C4 234 B1
Hardwick's Way SW18 157 C6
Hardwidge St SE1 253 A2
Hardy Ave
4 Newham E16 121 A5
Ruislip HA4 62 B3
Hardy Cl Barnet EN5 13 A6
Pinner HA5 40 D2
Rotherhithe SE16 118 D4
Hardy Cotts 2 SE10 142 B6
Hardy Ct
Greenwich SE3 142 D6
9 Wanstead E11 55 A5
Hardyng Ho 4 E17 53 A5
Hardy Pas N22 32 C1
Hardy Rd
Greenwich SE3 142 D6
Merton SW19 179 D3
Walthamstow E4 35 B4
Hardys Mews KT8 196 C5
Hardy Way EN2 4 C4
Hare and Billet Rd SE3 142 B3
Harebell Dr E6 100 C2
Harecastle Cl UB4 85 A3
Harecourt Rd N1 73 A2
Hare Ct EC4 241 A1
Haredale Ho 24 SE16 118 A4
Haredale Rd SE24 139 A1
Haredon Cl SE23 162 D4
Harefield KT10 212 C5
Harefield Cl EN2 4 C4
Harefield Ct 4 SW19 179 C3
Harefield Mews SE4 141 B2
Harefield Rd
Brockley SE4 141 B2
Hornsey N8 49 D4
Sidcup DA14 168 D1
South Norwood SW16 182 B3
Uxbridge UB8 60 A3
Hare La KT10 212 C2
Hare Marsh E2 96 A3
Harenc Sch DA14 190 C5
Harepit Cl CR2 220 D1
Hare Pl EC4 241 B1
Hare Row E2 96 B5
Haresfield Rd RM10 81 C2
Hare St SE18 122 C3
Harestone Ct CR2 221 C2
Hare Wlk N1 95 C5
Harewood Ave
Lisson Gr NW1 92 C3 237 B5
Northolt UB5 63 B1
Harewood Cl UB5 63 B1
Harewood Ct HA3 24 C2
Harewood Pl W1 238 D1
Harewood Rd
Hounslow TW7 130 D4
Mitcham SW19 180 C4
South Croydon CR2 221 C2
Harewood Row NW1 237 B4
Harewood Terr UB2 107 B2
Harfield Gdns 1 SE5 139 C2
Harfield Rd TW16 172 D1
Harfleur Ct SE11 261 C3
Harford Cl E4 19 D4
Harford Ho
Camberwell SE5 139 A6
Notting Hill W11 91 B2
Harford Mews 6 N19 71 D5
Harford Rd E4 19 D4
Harford St E1 97 A3
Harford Wlk N2 48 B5
Hargood Cl HA3 44 A3
Hargood Rd SE3 143 C4

Hargrave Mans 3
N19 ....71 D6
Hargrave Park Prim Sch
14 N19 ....71 C6
Hargrave Pk N19 ....71 C6
Hargrave Pl N7 .....71 D3
Hargrave Rd N19 ....71 C6
Hargraves Ho 14
W12 ....112 B6
Hargwyne St SW9 ..138 B2
Haringey Pk N8 ......50 A3
Haringey Rd N8 ......50 A5
Haringey Sixth Form Ctr
N17 ....33 D4
Harington Terr N18 ..17 B1
Harkett Cl HA3 ......24 D1
Harkett Ct HA3 ......24 D1
Harkness Ct SM1 ...201 D1
Harkness Ho 30 E1 ...96 A1
Harland Ave
Sidcup DA15 ....167 C2
South Croydon CR0 .222 A5
Harland Cl SW19 ....201 D6
Harland Rd SE12 ....165 A3
Harlands Gr BR6 ....226 D4
Harlech Cl 1 SE23 ..162 C3
Harlech Gdns TW5 ..128 C5
Harlech Rd N14 ......16 A1
Harlech Twr 5 W3 ...111 A4
Harlequin Ave TW8 .131 A6
Harlequin Cl
Hayes UB4 ....84 D2
Isleworth TW7 ......152 C6
Harlequin Ct
Croydon CR2 ....221 A1
Ealing W5 ....109 C6
Willesden NW10 .....67 B2
Harlequin Ho 1
DA18 ....125 A3
Harlequin Rd TW11 .175 B3
Harlescott Rd SE15 .140 D1
HARLESDEN 89 D6
Harlesden Gdns
NW10 ....89 C6
Harlesden Plaza 2
NW10 ....89 C6
Harlesden Prim Sch
NW10 ....89 C5
Harlesden Rd NW10 ..90 A6
Harlesden StanW10 ..89 C5
Harleston Cl 4 E5 ....74 C6
Harley BR7 ....189 B2
Harley Cl HA0 ....65 D2
Harley Cres HA1 .....42 B5
Harley Ct Harrow HA1 .42 B5
Wanstead E11 ....55 A2
Whetstone N20 ......14 A1
Harleyford BR1 .....187 C2
Harleyford Ct
Kennington SW8 ....270 C6
Wembley HA0 ....65 A4
Harleyford Manor 8
W3 ....111 A5
Harleyford Rd
SE11 ....138 B6 270 C6
Harleyford St SE11 .138 C6
Harley Gdns
Orpington BR6 .....227 C4
South Kensington
SW10 ....114 A1 256 B1
Harley Gr E3 ....97 B4
Harley Ho
Leytonstone E11 .....54 B2
Marylebone NW1 ...238 B5
Harley Pl W1 ...93 B2 238 C3
Harley Rd
Hampstead NW3 .....70 B1
Harlesden NW10 .....89 C5
Harrow HA1 ....42 B5
Harley St W1 ...93 B2 238 C2
Harley Villas NW10 ..89 C5
Harling Ct 3 SW11 .136 D3
Harlinger St SE18 ...122 A3
HARLINGTON 127 A6
Harlington Cl UB7 ...127 A5
Harlington Cl 3 UB7 .127 B4
Harlington Com Sch
UB3 ....105 B2
Harlington Rd
Bexley DA7 ....147 A2
Hillingdon UB8 ......82 C3
Harlington Rd E TW13
TW14 ....150 C3
Harlington Rd W
TW14 ....150 B5
Harlow Ho 13 E8 ....95 D6

Harlow Mans 2 IG11 .78 D1
Harlow Rd N13 ......17 A1
Harlyn Dr HA5 ......40 B6
Harlyn Prim SchHA5 ..40 B6
Harlynwood 10 SE5 .139 A5
Harman Ave IG8 .....36 D4
Harman Dr
10 Bermondsey
SE1 ....118 A1
Chingford E4 ....36 B6
Cricklewood NW2 ....69 A5
Harman Dr
Blackfen DA15 .....167 D5
Cricklewood NW2 ....69 A4
Harman Rd EN1 ......17 D6
HARMONDSWORTH
...........126 A6
Harmondsworth La
UB7 ....126 A6
Harmondsworth Rd
UB7 ....104 A2
Harmon Ho 7 SE8 .119 B2
Harmony Terr HA4 ...47 A4
Harmony Way
Bromley BR1 ....187 A1
Hendon NW4 ....46 C5
Harmood Gr NW1 ....71 B1
Harmood Ho 2 NW1 .71 B1
Harmood St NW1 ....71 B1
Harmsworth St
SE17 ....116 D1 261 C1
Harmsworth Way
N20 ....10 D3
Harnage Ho TW8 ...110 A1
Harney Ct SE14 ....141 A4
Harold Ave
Erith DA17 ....125 B1
Hayes UB3 ....105 D3
Harold Ct
14 Rotherhithe
SE16 ....118 D4
6 Teddington TW11 .174 C5
Harold Est SE1 .....263 B5
Harold Gibbons Ct 3
SE7 ....143 C6
Harold Ho 10 E2 ....96 D5
Harold Laski Ho EC1 .234 D1
Harold Maddison Ho
SE17 ....261 D2
Harold Rd
Chingford E4 ....20 A1
Hornsey N8 ....50 B5
Leytonstone E11 .....54 C1
Newham E13 ....99 B6
North Acton NW10 ...89 B4
South Norwood SE19 .183 B3
South Tottenham N15 ..51 D4
Sutton SM1 ....218 A4
Woodford IG8 ....37 A2
Haroldstone Rd E17 ..53 A4
Harold Wilson Ho
SW6 ....264 D5
Haronton Ct E10 ....76 A6
Harp Alley EC4 .....241 C2
Harp Bsns Ctr The
NW2 ....68 A6
Harpenden Rd
Wanstead E12 ......77 C6
West Norwood SE27,
SW16 ....160 D2
Harpenmead Point
NW2 ....69 B6
Harper Cl N14 ......15 C6
Harper Ho 3 SW9 ..138 D2
Harper Mews SW17 .158 A1
Harper Rd
Bermondsey
SE1 ....117 A3 262 B6
Newham E6 ....100 B1
Harper's Yd N17 .....33 D2
Harp Island Cl NW11 ..67 B6
Harp La EC3 ....253 A5
Harpley Sq E1 ....96 D3
Harpour Rd IG11 ....79 A2
Harp Rd W7 ....86 D3
Harpsden St SW11 ..268 A1
Harpur Mews WC1 ..240 C4
Harpur St
WC1 ....94 B2 240 C4
Harraden Rd SE3 ...143 C4
Harrier Ave E11 .....55 B3
Harrier CtTW4 .....129 A3
Harrier Ho 3 SW11 .136 C2
Harrier Mews SE28 .123 B4
Harrier Rd NW9 .....27 C1
Harriers Cl W5 .....110 A6

Harrier Way E6 ......100 B2
Harries Rd UB4 .....84 C3
Harriet Cl E8 ....96 A6
Harriet Gdns CR0 ...222 A6
Harriet Ho
Walham Green SW6 .265 D3
1 Walthamstow E17 ..53 D6
Harriet Mews DA16 .146 B3
Harriet St
SW1 ....114 D4 247 D1
Harriet Tubman Cl 3
SW2 ....160 C4
Harriet Way WD23 ....8 B4
Harriet Wlk
SW1 ....114 D4 247 D1
HARRINGAY 50 D4
Harringay Gdns N8 ...50 D5
Harringay Green Lanes
StaN4 ....50 D3
Harringay Rd N15 ....50 D3
Harringay StaN4 ....50 D3
Harrington Cl
6 South Croydon
CR0 ....221 B6
South Kensington
SW7 ....256 C4
2 West Kilburn W9 ...91 A4
Harrington Gdns
SW7 ....114 A2 256 A3
Harrington Hill E5 ...52 B1
Harrington Hill Prim Sch
E5 ....52 B1
Harrington Ho
2 Bromley BR1 .....187 A2
Regent's Pk NW1 ...232 A2
Upper Clapton E5 ....52 C1
Westminster SW1 ...259 D2
Harrington Rd
Croydon SE25 ......206 B5
Leytonstone E11 .....54 C1
South Kensington
SW7 ....114 B2 256 C4
Harrington Road Sta
SE25 ....206 C6
Harrington Sq
NW1 ....93 C5 232 A3
Harrington St
NW1 ....93 C4 232 A2
Harrington Way
SE18 ....121 D3
Harriott Cl SE10 ....120 D2
Harriott Ho 11 E1 ....96 C1
Harris Acad at Peckham
SE15 ....139 D4
Harris Acad Bermondsey
SE1 ....117 D2 263 D4
Harris Acad Falconwood
DA16 ....145 C1
Harris Acad Merton Sch
CR4 ....203 B6
Harris Acad South
Norwood SE25 ......205 D6
Harris City Acad Crystal
PalaceSE19 ....183 D2
Harris Cl Enfield EN2 ...4 A4
Heston TW5 ....129 C4
Harris Cotts 1 E15 ...98 D6
Harris CtHA9 ....66 B5
Harris Girl's Acad
SE15 ....139 A5
Harris Ho 1 Bow E3 ..97 C4
7 Brixton SW9 .....138 C2
Lo SE6 ....164 A3
Harrison Cl N20 ....14 C3
Harrison Dr BR1 ....210 D5
Harrison Ho SE17 ...262 A2
Harrison Rd
Dagenham RM10 .....81 D2
Stonebridge NW10 ...89 B6
Harrisons Ct 1
SE14 ....140 D6
Harrison's Rise CR0 .220 D5
Harrison St
WC1 ....94 A4 233 B1
Harrison Way E17 .192 D4
Harris Rd
Dagenham RM9 .....81 B3
Erith DA7 ....147 B4
Harris St
Camberwell SE5 ....139 B5
Walthamstow E17 ....53 B2
Harriet Way TW16 ..171 C2

Harrodian Sch The
SW13 ....133 D5
Harrods Gn HA8 .....26 C5
Harrogate Ct
2 Forest Hill SE26 ...162 A1
9 New Southgate N11 ..31 A4
Harrold Ho 1 NW3 ...70 A1
Harrovian Bsns Village
1 HA1 ....42 C2
HARROW 42 B3
Harrow Arts Ctr*
HA5 ....23 C3
Harrow Ave EN1 ....17 D5
Harroway Rd SW11 .136 B3
Harrowby St
W1 ....92 C1 237 B2
Harrow Cl KT9 .....213 D1
Harrow Coll HA1, ...42 C2
Harrow Coll (Harrow
Weald Campus)
HA3 ....24 C4
Harrowdene Cl HA0 ..65 D4
Harrowdene Ct
SW19 ....179 A5
Harrowdene Gdns
TW11 ....175 A5
Harrowdene Rd HA0 .65 D4
Harrow Dr N9 ....17 D7
Harrowes Meade
...........16 C1
Harrow Fields Gdns
HA1 ....64 C5
Harrowgate Rd 22 E9 .74 D2
Harrowgate Rd E9 ...75 A1
Harrow Gn E11 .....76 C5
Harrow High Sch
HA1 ....43 A3
Harrow La E14 .....120 A6
Harrow Lo SM2 ....218 B2
Harrow Manor Way
SE2 ....124 C3
Harrow Mus & Her Ctr*
HA2 ....42 A6
HARROW ON THE
HILL 42 C1
Harrow-on-the-Hill Sta
HA1 ....42 C1
Harrow Pk HA1 .....64 C6
Harrow Pl E1 ...95 C1 243 B2
Harrow Rd
Ashford TW15 .....148 C2
Barking IG11 ....101 C6
Carshalton SM5 ....218 C2
Ilford IG1 ....79 A4
Leyton E11 ....76 D5
Little Venice
...........92 A2 236 B3
2 Newham E6 ......100 A6
Sudbury HA0 ....66 C2
Wembley HA0 ....65 D3
Westbourne Green W2,
W9 ....91 C3
Harrow SchHA1 ....42 C1
Harrow St NW1 ....237 A4
Harrow View
Harrow HA1, HA2 ...42 B5
Hayes UB3 ....84 A1
Hillingdon UB10 .....83 A4
Harrow View Rd W5 .87 B3
Harrow Way
Charlton NW7 ......171 A1
South Oxhey WD19 ...23 A6
HARROW WEALD 24 B2
Harrow Weald Pk
HA3 ....24 B4
Harrow & Wealdstone
StaHA1, ...42 C5
Harry Cl CR7, ...205 A3
Harry Ct 8 NW9 .....45 A5
Harry Gosling Prim Sch
1 E1 ....96 A1
Harry Hinkins Ho
SE17 ....262 B1
Harry Lambourn Ho 10
SE15 ....140 B5
Harston 13 KT1 .....176 C1
Harston Dr EN3 ......7 C5
Hart Cl E12 ....78 C1
Harte Rd TW3, ...129 B3
Hartfield Ave
Borehamwood WD6, ..10 C6
Northolt UB5 ....84 B5
Hartfield Cl WD6, ...10 C6

Hartfield Cres
Coney Hall BR4 .....225 A5
Merton SW19, ...179 B3
Hartfield Ct CR2 ....220 D1
Hartfield Gr SE20 ...184 C2
Hartfield Ho UB5 ....84 B5
Hartfield Rd
Chessington KT9 ....213 D3
Hayes BR4 ....225 A4
Merton SW19, ...179 C3
Hartfield Terr E3 ....97 C5
Hartford Ave HA3 ...43 B6
Hartford Rd
Old Bexley DA5 .....169 C5
West Ewell KT19 ...214 D2
Hart Gr Ealing W5, ..110 C5
Southall UB1 ....85 C2
Hartgrove Ct NW9 ...45 A5
Hart Grove Ct 3
W5 ....110 C5
Hartham Cl
Isleworth TW7 .....131 A4
Lower Holloway N7 ...72 A3
Hartham Rd
Isleworth TW7 .....131 A4
Lower Holloway N7 ...72 A3
...N7 ....33 D1
Hart Ho Hayes UB4 ...83 B2
Streatham SW2 ....160 C3
Harting Rd SE9 .....166 A1
Hartington Cl
Farnborough BR6, ..227 A3
Harrow HA1, ...64 C4
Hartington Ct
Chiswick W4 ....132 D5
South Lambeth SW8 .270 A2
Hartington Rd
Chiswick W4 ....133 A4
Ealing W13, ...109 B6
Newham E16 ....99 B1
Southall UB1 ....102 A3
South Lambeth
SW8 ....138 A3 270 A2
Twickenham TW1, ...153 B5
Walthamstow E17 ....53 A3
Hartismere Rd
SW6 ....135 B5 264 D4
Hartlake Rd E9 ......75 A2
Hartland NW1 ......232 B5
Hartland Cl
Edgware HA8 ....10 C2
Enfield N21 ....17 A5
Hartland Cl 5 N11, ...30 D5
Hartland Dr
Edgware HA8 ....10 C2
Ruislip HA4 ....62 B4
Hartland Rd
Camden Town NW1 ..71 B1
Cheam SM4 ....201 D2
Friern Barnet N11 ....30 D5
Hampton TW12 .....173 D6
Isleworth TW7 ......131 A2
Kilburn NW6 ....91 B6
Stratford E15, ...76 D1
Hartlands Ct DA5 ...169 B5
HartlandsThe TW5 ..128 C6
Hartland Way
Croydon CR0 ....223 A6
Morden SM4 ....201 B2
Hartlepool Ct E16, ..122 D5
Hartley Ave
Edgware NW7 ....27 C5
Newham E6 ....100 A6
Hartley Cl
Bickley BR1 ....188 B1
Edgware NW7 ....27 D5
Hartley Ct Ealing W5, .110 C5
5 Mitcham CR4 ....180 C2
Hartley Ho
Bermondsey SE1 ...263 D4
Finchley N3 ....29 D4
Putney SW15 ......156 A6
Hartley Prim Sch 7
E6 ....100 A6
Hartley Rd
Bexley DA16, ...146 C5
Leytonstone E11 .....54 D1
Thornton Heath CR0 .205 A2
Hart Lo SE1 ....1 A2
Hartmann Rd E16, ..122 A5
Hartmoor Mews EN3, ...7 C3
Hartnoll Ho 4 N7, ...72 C3

Hartnoll St N7 . . . . 72 B3
Harton Cl BR1 . . . . . . 187 D2
Harton Lodge 2
SE8 . . . . 141 C4
Harton Rd N9 . . . . 18 B2
Harton St SE8 . . . . 141 C4
Hartopp Ct 20 N16 . . . . 73 C5
Hartopp Point SW6 . 264 B4
Hartsbourne Ave
WD23 . . . . 8 B2
Hartsbourne Cl WD23 . . 8 B2
Hartsbourne Ct 5
UB1 . . . . 86 A1
Hartsbourne Pk WD23 . . 8 C2
Hartsbourne Prim Sch
WD23 . . . . 8 B2
Hartsbourne Rd WD23 . 8 B2
Harts Gr IG8 . . . . 37 A5
Hartshill Cl UB10 . . . . . 60 D2
Hartshorn Alley EC3 243 B1
Hartshorn Gdns E6 . . 100 C3
Harts La IG11 . . . . 78 D2
Hart's La SE14 . . . . . . 141 A4
Hartslock Dr SE2 . . . 124 D4
Hartsmead Rd SE9 . . . 166 B2
Hart Sq SM4 . . . . 201 C3
Hart St EC3 . . . . 253 B6
Hartsway EN3 . . . . 6 C1
Hartswood Gn WD23 . . . 8 B2
Hartswood Ho 10
SW2 . . . . 160 A3
Hartswood Rd W12 . 111 D3
Hartsworth Cl E13 . . . . 98 D5
Hartville Rd SE18 . . . . 123 C2
Hartwell Cl 12 SW2 . . . 160 B3
Hartwell Ct SE22 . . . . 140 A1
Hartwell Dr E4 . . . . 36 A4
Hartwell Ho 2 SE7 . . . 121 B1
Hartwell St E8 . . . . 73 D2
Harvard Ct
9 Eltham SE9 . . . . . . 166 C5
West Hampstead NW6 . 69 D3
Harvard Hill W4 . . . . 132 D6
Harvard Ho
3 Camberwell
SE17 . . . . 138 D6
Putney SW15 . . . . 156 D5
Harvard Mans 18
SW11 . . . . 136 B1
Harvard Rd
11 Acton Green W4 . . 111 A1
Gunnersbury W4 . . . . . 110 D1
Hounslow TW7 . . . . . 130 C4
Lewisham SE13 . . . . . 164 A6
Harvel Cres SE2 . . . . 124 D1
Harvel Ct SE2 . . . . 125 A1
Harvest Bank Rd
BR4 . . . . 225 A5
Harvest Ct
Beckenham BR3 . . . . . 185 C3
Littleton TW17 . . . . . . 192 C5
Harvesters Cl TW7 . . . 152 B6
Harvest La
Loughton IG10 . . . . 21 D4
Thames Ditton KT7 . . . 197 A3
Harvest Rd TW13 . . . . 150 A1
Harvey Ct
Battersea SW11 . . . . . 267 B2
Walthamstow E17 . . . . . 53 C4
Harvey Dr TW12 . . . . . 173 C2
Harvey Gdns
Greenwich SE7 . . . . . 121 C1
Leytonstone E11 . . . . . . 54 D1
Harvey Ho
1 Barking IG11 . . . . . . 79 A1
10 Bethnal Green E1 . . . 96 B3
Brentford TW8 . . . . . . 110 A1
Dagenham RM6 . . . . 58 D5
Hornsey N8 . . . . 50 A6
Pimlico SW1 . . . . 259 D1
Shoreditch N1 . . . . 235 D5
Wembley Pk HA9 . . . . . . 66 D6
Harvey Lo 8 W9 . . . . . . 91 C2
Harvey Mews N8 . . . . . . 50 B4
Harvey Point 7 E16 . . . . 99 A2
Harvey Rd
15 Camberwell SE5 . . . 139 B4
Hillingdon UB10 . . . . . . 82 C5
Hornsey Vale N8 . . . . . . 50 B4
Ilford IG1 . . . . 78 D3
Leytonstone E11 . . . . . . 54 D1
Ruislip UB5 . . . . 62 C1
Twickenham TW4 . . . . . 151 B4
Harvey Rd *continued*
Walton-on-T KT12 . . . 194 A2
Harvey St N1 . . . . 235 D5
Harvill Rd
Newyears Green UB9 . . 38 A2
Sidcup DA14 . . . . 191 A5
Harvil Rd UB9, UB10 . . . 38 A2
Harvington Sch W5 . . . 87 D1
Harvington Wlk E8 . . . . 74 A1
Harvist Rd NW6 . . . . 91 A5
Harwell Cl HA4 . . . . 39 B1
Harwood Ave
Bromley BR1 . . . . 187 B1
Mitcham CR4 . . . . 202 C6
Harwood Cl
London N12 . . . . 30 C4
Wembley HA0 . . . . 65 D4
Harwood Ct
Putney SW15 . . . . 134 C1
Shoreditch N1 . . . . 235 D5
Harwood Dr UB10 . . . . . 82 B6
Harwood Point SE16 119 B4
Harwood Rd
SW6 . . . . . . 135 D5 265 C3
Harwoods Yd N21 . . . . . 16 C4
Harwood Terr
SW6 . . . . . . 135 D4 265 C2
Hascombe Ho 11
SW15 . . . . 156 B3
Hascombe Terr 2
SE5 . . . . 139 B3
Haselbury Rd N9 . . . . . 17 C1
Haseley End SE23 . . . 162 C4
Haselrigge Rd SW4 . 137 D1
Haseltine Prim Sch
SE26 . . . . 185 B6
Haseltine Rd SE26 . . . 185 B6
Haselwood Dr EN2 . . . . . 4 D1
Haskard Rd RM9 . . . . . . 80 D4
Hasker St
SW3 . . . . . . 114 C2 257 B4
Haslam Ave SM3 . . . . . 201 A1
Haslam Cl Islington N1 72 C1
Uxbridge UB10 . . . . 61 A6
Haslam Ct N11 . . . . 31 B6
Haslam Ho 12 N1 . . . . . 73 A1
Haslam St SE15 . . . . . 139 D4
Haslemere Ave
Barnet EN4 . . . . 14 D3
Cranford TW5 . . . . 128 C3
Ealing W13 . . . . 109 A3
Hendon NW4 . . . . 46 D3
Mitcham CR4, SW19 . . 180 B1
Wandsworth SW18 . . . 157 D2
Haslemere Bsns Ctr
EN1 . . . . 18 B6
Haslemere Cl
Hampton TW12 . . . . . . 173 B5
Wallington SM6 . . . . . 220 A3
Haslemere Ct 5 N16 . . . 51 C1
Haslemere Gdns N3 . . . 47 B5
Haslemere & Heathrow
Est The TW4 . . . . 128 B3
Haslemere Ind Est
Feltham TW14 . . . . . . 150 A6
Wandsworth SW18 . . . 157 D2
Haslemere Prim Sch
CR4 . . . . 180 B1
Haslemere Rd
Bexleyheath DA7 . . . . 147 C3
Hornsey N8 . . . . 50 A2
Ilford IG3 . . . . 79 D6
Southgate N21 . . . . 16 D3
Thornton Heath CR7 . 204 D4
Hasler Cl SE28 . . . . . . 124 C6
Hasler Ct E12 . . . . 78 A4
Haslett Rd TW17 . . . . 171 C1
Hasluck Gdns EN5 . . . . 14 A5
Hasmonean High Sch
(Boys) NW4 . . . . 28 D1
Hasmonean High Sch
(Girls) NW7 . . . . 28 A2
Hasmonean Prim Sch 1
NW4 . . . . 46 D4
Hassard St E2 . . . . 95 D5
Hassendean Rd SE3 . . 143 B5
Hassett Rd E9 . . . . 75 A2
Hassocks Cl SE23,
SE26 . . . . 162 B1
Hassocks Rd SW16 . . 181 D2
Hassock Wood BR2 . 225 D4
Hassop Rd NW2 . . . . . . 68 D4
Hassop Wlk SE9 . . . . . 188 A6
Hasted Rd SE7 . . . . . . 121 D1
Hasting Ct TW11 . . . . 174 B5
Hastings Ave IG6 . . . . . 57 A5
Hastings Cl
New Barnet EN5 . . . . 2 A1
17 Peckham SE15 . . . . 140 A5
Wembley HA0 . . . . 65 C4
Hastings Dr KT6 . . . . . 197 C3
Hastings Ho
Ealing W13 . . . . 109 B6
Enfield EN3 . . . . 6 C3
18 Shepherd's Bush
W12 . . . . 112 B6
Tottenham N17 . . . . 34 A2
6 Woolwich SE18 . . . . 122 B2
Hastings Hos WC1 . . 233 A1
Hastings Pl 1 CR0 . . 205 D1
Hastings Rd
Croydon CR0 . . . . 205 D1
Ealing W13 . . . . 109 B6
Keston Mark BR2 . . . . 226 A6
Tottenham N17 . . . . 51 B6
Wood Green N11 . . . . . . 31 D5
Hastings St
St Pancras
WC1 . . . . 94 A4 233 A1
Woolwich SE18 . . . . . 123 A3
Hastingwood Ct
1 Newham E6 . . . . . . 100 B5
Walthamstow E17 . . . . . 53 D4
Hastingwood Trad Est
N18 . . . . 35 A4
Hastoe Cl UB4 . . . . 85 A3
Hasty Cl CR4 . . . . 181 A2
Hatcham Mews Bsns Ctr
SE14 . . . . 140 D4
Hatcham Park Mews
SE14 . . . . 140 D4
Hatcham Park Rd
SE14 . . . . 140 D4
Hatcham Rd SE15 . . . . 140 C6
Hatchard Rd N19 . . . . . 72 A6
Hatchcroft NW4 . . . . . . 46 B6
HATCH END 23 A3
Hatch End High Sch
HA3 . . . . 23 D2
Hatch End Sta HA5 . . . . 23 C3
Hatchers Mews SE1 . 253 B1
Hatchett Rd TW14 . . . . 149 A3
Hatchfield Ho 8 N15 . . 51 C3
Hatch Gr RM6 . . . . 59 A5
Hatch Ho
9 Muswell Hill N10 . . . 31 A3
14 Richmond TW10 . . 153 C1
Hatch La E4 . . . . 20 C1
Hatch Pl KT2 . . . . 176 B5
Hatch Rd SW16 . . . . . . 182 A1
Hatch The EN3 . . . . 6 D4
Hatchwoods IG8 . . . . . . 36 D6
Hatcliffe Almshouses 8
SE10 . . . . 120 C1
Hatcliffe Cl SE3 . . . . . 142 D2
Hatcliffe St SE10 . . . . 120 D1
Hatfield Cl
Deptford SE14 . . . . . . 140 D5
Ilford IG6 . . . . 56 D6
Mitcham CR4 . . . . 202 B5
Hatfield Ct
Greenwich SE3 . . . . . . 143 A5
8 Northolt UB5 . . . . 84 C4
Hatfield Ho
16 Kingston u T
KT6 . . . . 198 A4
Leytonstone E11 . . . . . . 54 D2
St Luke's EC1 . . . . 242 A5
Hatfield Mead SM4 . . 201 C4
Hatfield Mews RM9 . . . 81 A1
Hatfield Prim Sch
SM4 . . . . 201 A3
Hatfield Rd
Acton W4 . . . . 111 B4
Dagenham RM9 . . . . 81 A1
10 Ealing W13, W7 . . . 109 A5
Stratford E15 . . . . 76 C3
Hatfields SE1 116 C5 251 B4
Hathaway Cl
Bromley BR2 . . . . 210 B1
Ruislip HA4 . . . . 61 D4
Stanmore HA7 . . . . 25 A5
Hathaway Cres E12 . . . 78 C2
Hathaway Gdns
Ealing W13 . . . . 87 A2
Ilford RM6 . . . . 58 D4
Hathaway Ho 3 N1 . . . . 95 C4
Hathaway Prim Sch
W13 . . . . 86 D2
Hathaway Rd CR0 . . . 204 D2
Hatherleigh Cl
Barnet EN4 . . . . 1 D4
Hatherleigh Cl *continued*
Chessington KT9 . . . . 213 D3
Edgware NW7 . . . . 28 D3
Morden SM4 . . . . 201 C5
Hatherleigh Ho SM4 . 201 C5
Hatherleigh Rd HA4 . . . 62 A6
Hatherley Cres
DA14 . . . . 168 A2
Hatherley Ct 6 W2 . . . . 91 D1
Hatherley Gdns
London N8 . . . . 50 A3
Newham E6 . . . . 99 D4
Hatherley Gr W2 . . . . . . 91 D1
Hatherley Ho 2 E17 . . . 53 C5
Hatherley Mews E17 . . 53 C5
Hatherley Rd
Richmond TW9 . . . . . . 132 B4
Sidcup DA14 . . . . 168 A1
Walthamstow E17 . . . . . 53 C5
Hatherley St SW1 . . . . 259 B3
Hathern Gdns SE9 . . . 188 C6
Hatherop Rd TW12 . . . 173 B3
Hathersage Ct N1 . . . . . 73 B3
Hathersley Ho 3
SW2 . . . . 160 C4
Hathorne Cl 3 SE15 . 140 B3
Hathway Ho 3 SE15 . 140 C3
Hathway St 4 SE15 . . 140 C3
Hatley Ave IG6 . . . . 57 A5
Hatley Cl N11 . . . . 30 D5
Hatley Rd N4, N7 . . . . . 72 B6
Hat & Mitre Ct EC1 . . 241 D5
Hatstone Ct 2 NW3 . . . 70 A3
Hatteraick St 6
SE16 . . . . 118 C4
Hattersfield Cl DA17 . 125 B2
HATTON 127 D1
Hatton Cl SE18 . . . . . . 145 B5
Hatton Cross Rdbt
TW6 . . . . 127 D2
Hatton Cross Sta
TW6 . . . . 127 D1
Hatton Ct BR7 . . . . 188 B3
Hatton Gdn
EC1 . . . . 94 C2 241 B4
Hatton Gdns CR4 . . . 202 D4
Hatton Gn TW14 . . . . 128 A1
Hatton Ho 17 E1 . . . . . 118 A6
Hatton Pl EC1 . . . . 241 B4
Hatton Rd
Hatton TW14, TW6 . . . 149 C6
Thornton Heath CR0 . 204 C1
Hatton Row NW8 . . . . 236 D5
Hatton Sch IG8 . . . . 55 D6
Hatton St NW8 . . . . . . 236 D5
Hatton Wall
EC1 . . . . 94 C2 241 B4
Haughmond 4 N12 . . . . 29 D6
Haunch of Venison Yd
W1 . . . . 238 C1
Hauteville Court Gdns 2
W6 . . . . 111 D3
Havana Rd SW18,
SW19 . . . . 157 C2
Havannah St E14 . . . . 119 C4
Havant Rd E17 . . . . 54 A6
Havelock Cl 13 W12 . . 112 B6
Havelock Ct
8 Peckham SE15 . . . . 140 B5
Southall UB2 . . . . 107 B3
Havelock Hall 8
CR0 . . . . 205 D1
Havelock Ho
4 Croydon CR0 . . . . . . 205 D1
Forest Hill SE23 . . . . . 162 C3
Havelock Pl HA1 . . . . . . 42 C3
Havelock Prim Sch
UB2 . . . . 107 B3
Havelock Rd
Belvedere DA17 . . . . . 125 B2
Bromley BR2 . . . . 209 C5
Croydon CR0 . . . . 221 D6
Harrow HA3 . . . . 42 C6
Southall UB2 . . . . 107 C3
Tottenham N17 . . . . 34 A1
Wimbledon SW19 . . . . 180 A5
Havelock St Ilford IG1 . 78 D6
Islington N1 . . . 94 A6 233 B6
Havelock Terr
SW8 . . . . . . 137 B5 268 D3
Havelock Wlk SE23 . . 162 C2
Haven Cl
Chislehurst SE9 . . . . . . 166 B1
Hayes UB4 . . . . 83 C3
Hinchley Wood KT10 . 212 C6
Sidcup DA14 . . . . 190 C4
Haven Cl *continued*
Wimbledon SW19 . . . 156 D1
Haven Ct
Beckenham BR3 . . . . . 186 A1
Hinchley Wood KT10 . 212 C6
Thornton Heath CR7 . 204 C6
Haven Gn W5 . . . . 87 D1
Haven Green Ct W5 . . . 87 D1
Havenhurst Rise EN2 . . . 4 C3
Haven La W5 . . . . 88 A1
Haven Lo
15 Enfield EN1 . . . . 17 C6
Temple Fortune NW11 . . 47 B4
7 Woolwich SE18 . . . . 122 D2
Haven Pl Ealing W5 . . . 109 D6
Hinchley Wood KT10 . 212 C6
Havenpool NW8 . . . . . . 91 D6
Haven Rd TW15 . . . . . 148 D1
Haven St 18 NW1 . . . . . 71 B1
Havenswood Ct 14
KT2 . . . . 176 D4
Haven The
Ashford TW16 . . . . . . 172 A3
East Barnet N14 . . . . 15 B5
Richmond TW9 . . . . . . 132 C2
Havenwood HA9 . . . . . . 66 D5
Havercourt 3 NW3 . . . . 70 C2
Haverfield Gdns
TW9 . . . . 132 C5
Haverfield Rd E3 . . . . . 97 A4
Haverford Way HA8 . . . 26 B2
Havergal Villas N15 . . . 50 D6
Haverhill Rd
Chingford E4 . . . . 20 A3
Streatham SW12 . . . . 159 C3
Havering 8 NW1 . . . . . . 71 B1
Havering Gdns RM6 . . . 58 D4
Havering Ho N4 . . . . . . 51 A2
Havering St E1 . . . . 96 D1
Havering Way IG11 . . 102 B4
Haverley 15 SW20 . . . 178 D3
Haversham Cl TW1 . . 153 D5
Haversham Ct UB6 . . . . 64 D2
Haversham Lo NW2 . . . 68 D3
Haversham Pl N6 . . . . . 70 D6
Haverstock Ct 2
BR5 . . . . 190 B1
Haverstock Hill NW3 . . 70 D2
Haverstock Rd NW5 . . . 71 A3
Haverstock Sch 22
NW1 . . . . 71 A2
Haverstock St
N1 . . . . 94 D5 234 D3
Haverthwaite Rd
BR6 . . . . 227 B5
Havilland Ct HA8 . . . . . 26 B6
Havil St SE5 . . . . 139 C4
Havisham Ho 25
SE16 . . . . 118 A4
Havisham Pl SW16 . . 182 D3
Hawarden Gr SE24 . . . 161 A4
Hawarden Hill NW2 . . . 68 A5
Hawarden Rd E17 . . . . . 52 D5
Hawberry Lo N7 . . . . . . 72 A2
Hawbridge Rd E11 . . . . 54 B1
Hawes Down Inf Sch
BR4 . . . . 208 B1
Hawes Down Jun Sch
BR4 . . . . 208 B1
Hawes La BR4 . . . . 224 C6
Hawes Rd
Bromley BR1 . . . . 187 B2
Edmonton N18 . . . . 34 B4
Hawes St N1 . . . . 72 D1
Haweswater Ho
TW1 . . . . 152 D6
Hawfinch 29 NW9 . . . . . 27 D2
Hawgood St E3 . . . . 97 C2
Hawkdene E4 . . . . 20 A5
Hawke Ct UB4 . . . . 84 C3
Hawkedale Inf Sch
TW16 . . . . 193 D6
Hawke Ho 20 E1 . . . . . . 96 D3
Hawke Park Rd N22 . . . 50 D6
Hawke Pl 29 SE16 . . . 118 D4
Hawker 28 NW9 . . . . 27 D2
Hawker Ct 14 KT2 . . . . 176 C3
Hawker Ctr The KT2 . 175 D5
Hawke Rd SE19 . . . . . . 183 C4
Hawker Pl E4 . . . . 36 A1
Hawker Rd CR0 . . . . . 220 C2
Hawkesbury Rd
SW15 . . . . 156 B6
Hawkesdown House Sch
W2 . . . . 113 C5 245 B3

Hawkesfield Rd SE23 163 B2
Hawkesley Cl TW1 175 A6
Hawkes Rd
Feltham TW14 150 A4
Mitcham CR4 180 D2
Hawkesworth Ho 5 SW4 159 C5
Hawke Twr 4 SE14 141 A6
Hawkewood Rd TW16 194 A6
Hawkfield Ct TW7 130 C3
Hawk Ho 7 SW11 136 C2
Hawkhurst Gdns KT9 214 A4
Hawkhurst Rd SW16 181 D2
Hawkhurst Way
New Malden KT3 199 B4
West Wickham BR4 223 D6
Hawkinge N17 33 B1
Hawkins Cl
Burnt Oak NW7 27 B5
Harrow HA1 42 B2
Hawkins Ho
3 Deptford SE8 141 C6
10 Richmond TW10 153 C1
Hawkins Rd
Teddington TW11 175 B4
Willesden NW10 67 C1
Hawkins Way SE6 185 C5
Hawkley Gdns SE27 160 D2
Hawkridge 19 NW5 71 A2
Hawkridge Cl RM6 58 C3
Hawksbrook La BR3 208 A3
Hawkshaw Cl 28 SW2 160 A4
Hawkshead NW1 232 A2
Hawkshead Cl BR1 186 C3
Hawkshead Rd
Acton W4 111 C4
Willesden NW10 67 D1
Hawkslade Rd SE15 162 D6
Hawksley Rd N16 73 C5
Hawks Mews 10 SE10 142 A5
Hawksmoor Cl
2 Newham E6 100 A1
Plumstead Comm SE18 123 C1
Hawksmoor Mews E1 118 B6
Hawksmoor Pl 2 E2 96 A3
Hawksmoor Prim Sch SE28 124 B6
Hawksmoor St 5 W6 134 D6
Hawksmouth E4 20 A4
Hawks Rd KT1 176 B1
Hawkstone Rd SE16 118 C2
Hawkwell Ct E4 20 A1
Hawkwell Ho RM8 81 C6
Hawkwell Wlk N1 235 B6
Hawkwood Cres E4 19 D5
Hawkwood La BR7 189 A2
Hawkwood Mount 1 E5 52 B1
Hawlands Dr HA5 41 A2
Hawley Cl TW12 173 B4
Hawley Cres NW1 71 B1
Hawley Inf Sch 23 NW1 71 B1
Hawley Mews 4 NW1 71 B1
Hawley Rd
3 Camden Town NW1 71 B1
London N18 34 D5
Hawley St NW1 71 B1
Hawley Way TW15 170 D5
Haworth Ho 7 SW2 160 C5
Hawstead Rd SE6 163 D5
Hawsted IG9 21 B4
Hawthorn Ave
Bowes Pk N13 32 A5
South Norwood CR7 182 D2
Hawthorn Cl
Cranford TW5 128 B5
Hampton TW12 173 C5
Petts Wood BR5 211 B3
Hawthorn Cres SW17 181 A5
Hawthorn Ct
Littleton TW15 171 A3
2 Pinner HA5 22 C1
Putney SW15 134 B2
Redbridge IG5 56 B6
Hawthorn Ct *continued*
Richmond TW9 132 D4
Sutton SM1 217 C4
8 West Norwood SW16 182 C5
Hawthorn Ctr HA1 43 A4
Hawthornden Cl N12 30 C4
Hawthorndene Cl BR2 225 A6
Hawthorndene Rd BR2 225 A6
Hawthorn Dr
Coney Hall BR4 224 C4
Harrow HA2 41 C3
Hawthorne Ave
Harrow HA3 43 A3
Mitcham CR4 180 B1
Old Ford E3 97 B6
Ruislip HA4 40 B2
Wallington SM5 219 A1
Hawthorne Cl
Bickley BR1 210 B6
Kingsland N1 73 C2
Sutton SM1 218 A6
Hawthorne Cres UB7 104 B4
Hawthorne Ct
Chingford E4 35 D4
Ealing W5 110 A5
Pinner HA6 22 A1
Hawthorne Gr NW9 45 A2
Hawthorne Ho SW1 259 B1
Hawthorne Mews UB6 86 A1
Hawthorne Rd
Bickley BR1 210 B6
Edmonton N18 33 D5
Walthamstow E17 53 C6
Hawthorne Way N9 17 D2
Hawthorn Farm Ave UB5 85 A6
Hawthorn Gdns W5 109 D3
Hawthorn Gr
Edgware EN5 11 D5
Enfield EN2 5 B5
Penge SE20 184 B2
Hawthorn Hatch TW8 131 B5
Hawthorn Ho SE14 141 B4
Hawthorn Mews NW7 29 A2
Hawthorn Pl UB3 105 D6
Hawthorn Rd
Bexleyheath DA6 147 B1
Brentford TW8 131 B5
Carshalton SM1 218 C2
Feltham TW14 150 A3
Hornsey N8 50 A6
Wallington SM5, SM6 219 B1
Willesden NW10 68 A1
Woodford IG9 37 D6
Hawthorns IG8 21 A1
Hawthorns The
2 Cheam SM2 217 C2
Edgware NW7 27 B4
Stoneleigh KT17 216 A1
Hawthorn Terr DA15 167 D6
Hawthorn Way TW17 193 B5
Hawthorn Wlk W10 91 A3
Hawtrey Ave UB5 84 D5
Hawtrey Dr HA4 40 A2
Hawtrey Rd NW3 70 C1
Haxted Rd BR1 187 B2
Haybridge Ho 1 E5 74 C6
Hay Cl E15 76 D1
Haycroft Gdns NW10 90 B6
Haycroft Mans NW10 90 A6
Haycroft Rd
London SW2 160 A6
Surbiton KT6 214 A6
Hay Currie St E14 97 D1
Hayday Rd E16 99 A2
Hayden Piper Ho SW3 267 C6
Hayden's Pl W11 91 B1
Haydock Ave UB5 63 C2
Haydock Gn UB5 63 C2
Haydock Green Flats 2 UB5 63 C2
Haydock Lo 2 SM6 219 D5
Haydon Cl Enfield EN1 17 C6
Kingsbury NW9 45 A5
Haydon Ct NW9 45 A5
Haydon Dr HA5 40 A5
Haydon Ho W7 108 D5
Haydon Park Rd SW19 179 D5
Haydon Rd RM8 80 C6
Haydon Sch HA5 39 D6
Haydon's Rd SW19 180 A4
Haydons Road Sta SW19 180 A5
Haydon St E1, EC3 117 D6 253 C6
Haydon Way SW11 136 B1
Haydon Wlk E1 243 D1
HAYES BR2 209 A2
UB3 83 C1
Hayes Bridge Ret Pk UB4 106 D6
Hayes Chase BR4 208 C3
Hayes Cl BR2 225 A6
Hayes Cres
Cheam SM3 216 D4
Temple Fortune NW11 47 B4
Hayes Ct
23 Camberwell SE5 139 A5
Streatham SW12 160 A3
Wimbledon SW19 179 A4
HAYES END 83 B3
Hayes End Cl UB4 83 B2
Hayes End Dr UB4 83 B3
Hayesend Ho SW17 180 A6
Hayes End Rd UB4 83 B3
Hayesford Park Dr BR2 208 D4
Hayes Gdn BR2 209 A1
Hayes Gr SE15, SE22 139 D1
Hayes & Harlington Sta UB3 105 D3
Hayes Hill BR2 208 C1
Hayes Hill Rd BR2 208 D1
Hayes La
Beckenham BR2, BR3 208 B5
Hayes BR2 209 A4
Hayes Mead Rd BR2 208 C1
Hayes Park Sch UB4 83 D3
Hayes Pl NW1 237 B5
Hayes Prim Sch BR2 209 B1
Hayes Rd
Bromley BR2 209 A5
Southall UB2 106 B2
Hayes Sch BR2 225 B6
Hayes St BR2 209 B1
Hayes Sta BR2 208 D1
Hayes Stadium Sp Ctr UB3 83 B1
HAYES TOWN 106 B5
Hayes Way BR3 208 B5
Hayes Wood Ave BR2 209 B1
Hayfield Pas E1 96 C3
Hayfield Yd 43 E1 96 C3
Hayford Ct NW2 68 D5
Haygarth Pl 2 SW19 178 D5
Haygreen Cl KT2 176 D4
Hay Hill W1 115 B6 248 D5
Hayhurst N1 234 D6
Hay La NW9 45 B5
Hayland Cl NW9 45 B5
Hay Lane Sch NW9 45 A5
Hayles Bldgs SE11 261 D4
Hayles St SE11 116 D2 261 C4
Haylett Gdns KT1 197 D5
Hayley Ho DA17 147 C6
Hayling Ave TW13 150 A1
Hayling Cl 20 N16 73 C3
Hayling Ct SM3 216 C4
Haymaker Cl UB10 60 B1
Hayman Cres UB4 83 B5
Haymans Point SE11 260 C2
Haymarket SW1 115 D6 249 C5
Haymeads Dr KT10 212 A2
Haymer Gdns KT4 216 A5
Haymerle Ho 6 SE15 140 A5
Haymerle Rd SE15 140 A6
Haymerle Sch 15 SE15 140 A6
Haymill Cl UB6 86 D4
Haymills Ct W5 88 B3
Hayne Ho W11 244 A4
Hayne Rd BR3 185 B2
Haynes Cl
Friern Barnet N11 15 A1
Lewisham SE3 142 C2
Tottenham N17 34 B3
Haynes Dr N9 18 B1
Haynes Ho 3 E9 74 D2
Haynes La SE19 183 C4
Haynes Rd HA0 66 A1
Hayne St EC1 94 D2 241 D4
Haynt Wlk SW20 201 A6
Hay's Galleria★ SE1 253 A4
Hay's La SE1 253 A4
Haysleigh Gdns SE20 184 A1
Haysleigh Ho SE20 184 B1
Hay's Mews W1 115 B5 248 C4
Hay St E2 96 A6
Haystall Cl UB4 83 C5
Hayter Ct E11 77 B6
Hayter Ho W12 112 A6
Hayter Rd SW2 160 B6
Haythorn Ho SW11 136 B4 266 D1
Hayton Cl 11 E8 73 D2
Hayward Cl SW19 179 D2
Hayward Ct
14 London SW4 138 A3
Mitcham CR4 180 B1
Hayward Gallery★ SE1 116 B5 250 D4
Hayward Gdns SW15 156 C5
Hayward Ho
Islington N1 234 A4
Lower Clapton E5 74 B5
Hayward Rd
London N20 14 A2
Thames Ditton KT7 196 D1
Haywards Cl RM6 58 C4
Haywards Pl EC1 241 C6
Hayward's Pl EC1 241 C6
Haywood Cl HA5 22 D1
Haywood Ct N11 31 D4
Haywood Lo 23 N7 71 D3
Haywood Rd BR2 209 D5
Haywood Rise BR6 227 C3
Hazel Ave UB7 104 C3
Hazelbank KT5 199 A1
Hazel Bank SE25 183 C1
Hazelbank Rd SE6 164 C2
Hazelbourne Rd SW12 159 B5
Hazelbury Cl SW19 179 C1
Hazelbury Gn N9 17 C1
Hazelbury Inf Sch N9 17 C1
Hazelbury Jun Sch N9 17 C1
Hazelbury La N9 17 C1
Hazel Cl
Brentford TW8 131 B5
Croydon CR0 206 D1
Edmonton N13 17 B1
Hendon NW9 27 D1
Mitcham CR4 203 D5
Peckham SE15 140 A3
Twickenham TW2 152 A4
Upper Holloway N19 71 C6
Hazelcroft HA5 23 D4
Hazelcroft Cl UB10 60 B1
Hazel Ct Ealing W5 110 A6
8 Rotherhithe SE16 119 A5
9 West Norwood SW16 182 C5
Hazeldean Rd NW10 67 B1
Hazeldene Dr HA5 40 C6
Hazeldene Gdns UB10 83 A6
Hazeldene Rd
Bexley DA16 146 C3
Ilford IG3 80 B6
Hazeldon Rd SE4 163 A6
Hazel Gdns HA8 26 D6
Hazel Gr
Dagenham RM6 59 A6
Enfield EN1 18 A5
Feltham TW14 150 A3
Forest Hill SE26 184 D6
Orpington BR6 226 D6
Wembley HA0 88 A6
Hazelgreen Cl N21 16 D3
Hazel Ho London SE4 141 B2
12 Maitland Pk NW3 70 D2
Hazelhurst BR3 186 B2
Hazelhurst Ct SE6 186 A5
Hazelhurst Rd SW17 180 B6
Hazellville Rd N19 49 D1
Hazel Mead EN5 12 B6
Hazelmere Cl
Feltham TW14 149 C5
Hazelmere Cl *continued*
Northolt UB5 85 B5
Hazelmere Ct 10 SW2 160 B3
Hazelmere Dr UB5 85 B5
Hazelmere Rd
Kilburn NW6 91 B6
Northolt UB5 85 B5
Petts Wood BR5 211 B5
Hazelmere Way BR2 209 A3
Hazelmere Wlk UB5 85 B5
Hazel Rd
Kensal Green NW10 90 C4
Stratford E15 76 C3
Hazeltree La UB5 85 A4
Hazel Way
Bermondsey SE1 263 C4
Walthamstow E4 35 B4
Hazel Wlk BR2 210 C3
Hazelwood IG10 21 D6
Hazelwood Ave SM4 201 D5
Hazelwood Cl
Clapton Pk E5 75 A5
Ealing W5 110 A4
Harrow HA2 41 D5
Hazelwood Cres N13 32 C6
Hazelwood Ct
1 Edmonton N13 32 C6
Surbiton KT6 198 A3
1 Willesden NW10 67 C5
Hazelwood Dr HA5 22 B1
Hazelwood Ho
Beckenham BR2 208 C6
Chingford E4 20 B4
11 Deptford SE8 119 A2
Edmonton N13 32 D6
2 Sutton SM1 218 A4
Hazelwood Jun & Inf Schs N13 32 C6
Hazelwood La N13 32 C6
Hazelwood Lo BR4 208 A2
Hazelwood Mans SW6 264 C2
Hazelwood Rd
Enfield EN1 17 D5
Walthamstow E17 53 A4
Hazlebury Rd SW6 135 D3
Hazledean Rd CR0 221 B6
Hazledene Rd W4 133 A6
Hazlemere 3 DA14 190 A6
Hazlemere Gdns KT4 200 A1
Hazlewell Rd SW15 156 C6
Hazlewood Cres W10 91 A3
Hazlewood Twr W10 91 B3
Hazlitt Cl TW13 173 A6
Hazlitt Ct 4 SE28 124 C5
Hazlitt Mews W14 254 A5
Hazlitt Rd W14 113 A3 254 A5
Heacham Ave UB10 61 A5
Headbourne Ho SE1 262 D6
Headcorn 10 NW5 71 A2
Headcorn Pl CR7 204 B5
Headcorn Rd
Plaistow BR1 187 A5
Thornton Heath CR7 204 B5
Tottenham N17 33 D3
Headfort Pl SW1 115 A4 248 B1
Headingley Dr BR3 185 C4
Headington Rd SW18 158 A2
Headlam Rd SW4 159 D4
Headlam St E1 96 B3
Headley App IG2 56 D4
Headley Ave CR0, SM6 220 B3
Headley Cl KT19 214 C2
Headley Ct SE26 184 C5
Headley Dr Ilford IG2 56 D3
New Addington CR0 224 A1
Headley Ho 5 BR5 190 B1
Heads Mews W11 91 C1
Head St E1 96 D1
Headstart Montessori Sch SW17 180 A6
HEADSTONE 41 D5
Headstone Dr HA1, HA3 42 C6
Headstone Gdns HA2 42 A5
Headstone La
Harrow HA2, HA3 23 D2

Headstone La *continued*
Headstone HA2 41 D5
Headstone Lane Sta
HA3 23 D2
Headstone Manor★
HA2 42 A6
Headstone Rd HA1 42 C3
Headway Cl TW10 175 C6
Heald St SE8, SE14 141 C4
Healey Ho RM6 59 A5
Healey St NW1 71 B2
Healy Ct EN5 12 D5
Healy Dr 1 BR6 227 D4
Healy Ho
12 Kennington SW9 138 C5
2 Tower Hamlets E3 97 C3
Heanor Ct 4 E5 74 D4
Hearne Rd W4 132 C6
Hearn Rise UB5 84 D6
Hearn's Bldgs SE17 262 D3
Hearnshaw St 1 E14 97 A1
Hearn St EC2 95 C3 243 B5
Hearnville Rd SW12 159 A3
Heart Hospl The
W1 93 A2 238 B3
Heart Raido W11 112 D6
Heart The KT12 193 D1
Heatham Pk TW2 152 D4
Heath Ave DA7 146 D6
Heathbourne Rd WD23 8 D3
Heathbrook Prim Sch 11
SW4 137 C3
Heath Brow NW3 70 A5
Heath Bsns Ctr The
TW3 130 A1
Heath Cl
Croydon CR2 220 D2
Ealing W5 88 B3
Golders Green NW11 47 D2
Harlington UB3 127 B5
Heathcote Gr E4 20 A2
Heathcote Point 25
E9 74 D2
Heathcote Rd TW1 153 B6
Heathcote Sch E4 20 C2
Heathcote St
WC1 94 B4 233 C1
Heathcroft Ealing W5 88 B3
Golders Green NW11 47 D1
Heathcroft Ave
TW16 171 D3
Heathcroft Gdns E4 36 B2
Heath Ct
Carshalton SM5 218 B6
Eltham SE9 167 A3
2 Hampstead NW3 70 A2
Leytonstone E11 54 D3
Stoke Newington N16 51 B1
Uxbridge UB8 60 A1
Heathdale Ave TW4 129 A2
Heathdene N14 15 C4
Heathdene Dr DA17 125 D2
Heathdene Rd
South Norwood
SW16 182 B3
Wallington SM5, SM6 219 B1
Heath Dr
West Barnes SW20 200 C5
West Hampstead NW3 69 D4
Heathedge SE23,
SE26 162 B2
Heath End Ct WD23 8 C2
Heatherbank
Chislehurst BR7 188 C1
Eltham SE9 144 B3
Heather Cl
Clapham SW8 137 B2
Hampton TW12 173 B2
Hillingdon UB8 82 B2
Hither Green SE13 164 B4
Isleworth TW7 152 B6
Newham E6 100 C1
Heather Ct
South Lambeth SW4 270 B1
6 West Norwood
SW16 182 C6
Heatherdale Cl KT2 176 D3
Heatherdene Cl
London N12 30 A2
Mitcham CR4 202 C5
Heatherdene Ct CR4 202 B5
Heatherdene Mans 2
TW1 153 D5
Heather Dr EN2 4 D3
Heatherfold Way HA5,
HA6 39 D6
Heather Gdns
Belmont SM2 217 C2
Hendon NW11 47 A3
Heather Ho 11 E14 98 A1
Heather La UB7 82 A1
Heatherlands TW16 172 A4
Heatherlea Gr KT4 200 B1
Heatherley Ct N16 74 A5
Heatherley Dr IG5 56 B6
Heatherley Sch of Fine
Art SW10 266 B3
Heather Lo N16 51 C1
Heather Park Dr HA0 66 C1
Heather Park Par
HA0 66 B1
Heather Rd
Dollis Hill NW2 67 D6
Lewisham SE12 165 A3
Walthamstow E4 35 B4
Heatherset Cl KT10 212 A3
Heatherset Gdns
SW16 182 B3
Heatherside Rd
Sidcup DA14 168 C1
West Ewell KT19 215 B1
Heathers The TW19 148 B4
Heather Way HA7 24 D4
Heather Wlk
Edgware HA8 26 D5
Twickenham TW4 151 C4
West Kilburn W10 91 A3
Heatherwood Cl E12 77 C6
Heatherwood Dr UB4 83 B5
Heathfield
Chingford E4 20 A1
Chislehurst BR7 189 A4
Heathfield Ave
SW18 158 B4
Heathfield Cl
Keston BR2 225 C3
Newham E16 99 D2
Heathfield Ct
Ashford TW15 148 A1
3 Bow E3 97 C5
5 Chiswick W4 111 B1
Penge SE20 184 C3
Sidcup DA14 190 B5
8 Sutton SM2 218 A2
Wandsworth SW18 158 B4
Heathfield Dr CR4 180 C2
Heathfielde N2 48 A4
Heathfield Gdns
Acton Green W4 111 A1
Blackheath SE3 142 C3
Croydon CR0 221 B4
Hendon NW11 46 D3
Wandsworth SW18 158 B5
Heathfield Ho SE3 142 C3
Heathfield House Sch 15
W4 111 A1
Heathfield Inf Sch
TW2 151 C3
Heathfield Jun Sch
TW2 151 C3
Heathfield La BR7 189 A4
Heathfield N TW1,
TW2 152 D4
Heathfield Park Dr
RM6 58 B4
Heathfield Pk NW2 68 C2
Heathfield Rd
Bexleyheath DA6 147 B1
Bromley BR1 186 D3
Croydon CR0 221 B4
Keston BR2 225 D3
South Acton W3 110 D4
Wandsworth SW18 158 B5
Heathfield Rise HA4 39 A2
Heathfield S TW1,
TW2 152 D4
Heathfield Sch HA5 40 D2
Heathfield Sq SW18 158 B4
Heathfield Terr
Chiswick W4 111 B1
Plumstead Comm
SE18 145 D6
Heathfield Vale CR2 223 A1
Heathgate NW11 47 D3
Heathgate Pl NW3 70 D4
Heath Gdns TW1 152 D2
Heath Gr
Ashford TW16 171 D3
Penge SE20 184 C3
Heath Ho
Thornton Heath
CR7 204 C4
Uxbridge UB10 60 D4
Heath House Prep Sch
1 SE8 142 D3
Heath Hurst Rd NW3 70 C4
Heath La SE3 142 B3
Heathland Rd N16 51 C1
Heathland Sch The
TW4 151 B5
Heathlands Cl
Sunbury TW16 172 A1
Twickenham TW1 152 D3
Heathlands Ct
Hounslow TW4 151 A6
Mitcham CR4 203 A6
Heathlands Way
TW4 151 A6
Heathlee Rd SE3 142 D1
Heathley End BR7 189 A4
Heath Lo WD23 8 B3
Heath Mans
5 Hampstead NW3 70 A4
Putney SW15 156 D5
Heathman's Rd
SW6 135 B4 264 D1
Heath Mead SW19 156 D1
Heathmere Prim Sch
SW15 156 A3
Heath Park Dr BR1 210 A6
Heath Park Gdns
NW3 69 D5
Heath Park Ind Est
RM8 59 A1
Heathpool Ct 8 E1 96 B3
Heath Rd
Clapham SW8 137 B3
Dagenham RM6 59 A2
Harrow HA1 42 A2
Hillingdon UB10 83 A3
Isleworth TW3, TW7 130 A1
South Norwood CR7 205 A6
Twickenham TW1 152 D3
Heath Rise
Hayes BR2 209 A3
Putney SW15 156 D5
Heathrow Airport
London TW6 126 D3
Heathrow Bvd UB7 126 B5
Heathrow Causeway Est
TW4 128 B2
Heathrow International
Trad Est TW4 128 B2
Heathrow Prim Sch
UB7 126 B6
Heathrow Terminal 4 Sta
TW6 149 A5
Heathrow Terminals 1, 2,
3 Sta TW6 126 D2
Heath Royal SW15 156 D5
Heath's Cl EN1 5 C3
Heathshott 8 TW10 154 A5
Heathside
Hampstead NW3 70 B4
Hinchley Wood KT10 212 C5
Twickenham TW4 151 B4
Heath Side BR5 211 A2
Heathside Ave DA7 147 A3
Heathside Cl
Hinchley Wood
KT10 212 C5
Ilford IG2 57 B4
Heathside Prep Sch 32
NW3 70 A4
Heath St NW3 70 A5
Heathstan Rd W12 90 A1
Heath Terr RM6 58 D2
Heath The W7 108 C5
Heath View
Gospel Oak NW5 71 A4
London N2 48 A5
Heath View Cl N2 48 A5
Heathview Ct SW19 156 D2
Heath View Dr SE2 146 D6
Heathview Gdns
SW15 156 C4
Heathview Rd CR7 204 C5
Heath Villas
Hampstead NW3 70 B5
Plumstead Comm
SE18 123 D1
Heathville Rd N4, N19 50 A2
Heathwall St SW11 136 D2
Heathway
Croydon CR0 223 B5
Heathway *continued*
Dagenham RM10 81 C2
Dagenham RM10 103 C6
Greenwich SE3 143 A5
Woodford IG8 37 C5
Heathway Ct NW3 69 C6
Heathway Ind Est
RM10 81 D4
Heathwood Ct
1 Hounslow TW3 129 D1
Streatham SW12 159 C3
Heathwood Gdns
SE7 122 A1
Heathwood Point 7
SE26 162 D1
Heaton Cl E4 20 A1
Heaton Ct 3 N20 14 D2
Heaton Ho
Chelsea SW10 266 B6
6 Peckham SE15 140 B3
Heaton Rd
London SE15 140 B3
Mitcham CR4 181 A3
Heaven Tree Cl N1 73 A3
Heaver Rd 23 SW11 136 B2
Heavers Farm Prim Sch
SE25 205 D4
Heavitree Cl SE18 123 B1
Heavitree Ct E17 35 D2
Heavitree Rd 2
SE18 123 B1
Hebble Ho UB5 85 A6
Hebden Ct 24 E2 95 D6
Hebden Terr N17 33 C4
Hebdon Rd SW17 158 C1
Hebe Ct SM1 218 A4
Heber Prim Sch
SE22 161 D5
Heber Rd
Cricklewood NW2 68 D4
East Dulwich SE22 161 D5
Hebron Rd W6 112 B3
Hecham Cl E17 35 A2
Heckfield Pl
SW6 135 C5 265 A3
Heckford Ho E14 97 D1
Heckford St E1 118 D6
Hector 31 NW9 27 D2
Hector Cl 8 N9 18 A2
Hector Ct
1 London SW9 138 C4
Putney SW15 156 D6
Hector Ho 14 E2 96 B5
Hector St SE18 123 C2
Heddington Gr N7 72 B3
Heddon Cl TW7 131 A1
Heddon Court Ave
EN4 14 D6
Heddon Court Par
EN4 15 A6
Heddon Ct EN4 15 A6
Heddon Rd EN4 14 D6
Heddon St W1 249 A6
Hedge Hill EN2 4 D4
Hedge La N13 17 A1
Hedgeley IG4 56 B5
Hedgemans Rd RM9 81 A1
Hedgemans Way
RM9 81 A2
Hedgemoor Ct 1 E4 36 B5
Hedgerley Gdns UB6 86 A5
Hedgerow La EN5 12 B6
Hedger's Gr E9 75 A2
Hedger St SE11 261 C4
Hedge Wlk SE6 185 D6
Hedgewood Gdns
IG5 56 C4
Hedgewood Sch UB4 83 C4
Hedgley Mews SE12 164 D6
Hedgley St SE12 164 D6
Hedingham Cl 6 N1 73 A1
Hedingham Ho 7
KT2 176 A2
Hedingham Rd RM8 80 B3
Hedley Ct SW15 156 D5
Hedley Ho E14 120 A3
Hedley Rd TW4 151 C4
Hedley Row N5, N16 73 B3
Hedsor Ho E2 243 C6
Heenan Cl IG11 79 A2
Heene Rd EN2 5 B4
Heidegger Cres
SW13 134 B5
Heigham Rd E6 78 A1
Heighton Gdns CR0 220 D3
Heights Cl SW20 178 B3
Heights The
Beckenham BR3 186 A3
Greenwich SE7 121 C1
Hampstead NW3 70 A4
Northolt UB5 63 C3
Stroud Green N4 50 C3
Heiron St SE17 138 D6
Helby Rd SW4 159 D5
Heldar Ct SE1 252 D1
Helder Gr SE12 164 D4
Helder St CR2 221 B2
Heldmann Cl TW7 130 B1
Helegan Cl BR6 227 D4
Helena Cl EN4 2 B5
Helena Ct W5 87 D2
Helena Pl 3 E9 96 C6
Helena Rd Ealing W5 87 D2
Newham E13 99 A5
Walthamstow E17 53 C4
Willesden NW10 68 B3
Helena Sq 12 SE16 119 A6
Helen Ave TW14 150 B4
Helen Cl
East Finchley N2 48 A6
East Molesey KT8 195 D5
Helen Clare Ct EN2 4 D2
Helen Ct N3 47 A6
Helen Gladstone Ho
SE1 251 C2
Helen Ho 9 E2 96 B5
Helen Mackay Ho 10
E14 98 B1
Helen Peele Cotts 10
SE16 118 C3
Helenslea Ave NW11 47 C1
Helen's Pl E2 96 C4
Helen St SE18 122 D2
Helen Taylor Ho 5
SE16 118 A2
Helen Way WD19 22 D6
Helford Cl HA4 61 C6
Helgiford Gdns
TW16 171 C3
Helios Rd CR4 203 A1
Heliport Ind Est
SW11 136 B3
Helix Ct 17 W11 112 D5
Helix Gdns SW2 160 B5
Helix Ho TW7 131 B3
Helix Rd SW2 160 B5
Helix The SW19 156 D2
Hellings St E1 118 A5
Helme Cl SW19 179 B5
Helmet Row EC1 242 B6
Helmore Rd IG11 79 D1
Helmsdale Cl UB4 85 A3
Helmsdale Ho NW6 91 D5
Helmsdale Rd SW16 181 D2
Helmsley 11 E18 55 A6
Helmsley Pl E8 74 B1
Helmsley St 7 E8 74 B1
Helperby Rd NW10 67 C1
Helsby Ct NW8 236 C6
Helsinki Sq SE16 119 A3
Helston NW1 232 B4
Helston Cl HA5 23 B3
Helston Ct N15 51 C4
Helston Ho SE11 261 B2
Helvetia St SE6 163 B2
Helwys Ct E4 36 A4
Hemans Est
SW8 137 D5 269 D3
Hemans St
SW8 137 D5 269 D3
Hemberton Rd SW9 138 A2
Hemery Rd UB6 64 B3
Hemingford Cl N12 30 B5
Hemingford Rd
Cheam SM3 216 C4
Islington N1 94 B6 233 D6
Heming Rd HA8 26 D3
Hemington Ave N11 30 D5
Hemlock Cl SW16 181 D1
Hemlock Rd W12 111 D6
Hemmen La UB3 83 D1
Hemming Cl 6
TW12 173 C2
Hemmings Cl DA14 168 B2
Hemmings Ct HA8 27 A3
Hemmings Mead
KT19 215 A2
Hemming St E1 96 A3
Hemmingway Cl NW5 71 A4
Hempstead Cl IG9 21 A2
Hempstead Rd E17 36 B1
Hemp Wlk SE17 262 D4

Hemsby Rd KT9 ... 214 B2
Hemstal Rd NW6 ... 69 C1
Hemswell Dr NW9 ... 27 C2
Hemsworth Ct N1 ... 95 C5
Hemsworth St N1 ... 95 C5
Hemus Pl SW3 ... 257 B1
Henchman St W12 ... 89 D1
Hendale Ave NW4 ... 46 B6
Hendale Ho 13 E5 ... 74 B6
Henderson Cl NW10 .. 67 A2
Henderson Ct
8 Deptford SE14 ... 140 D6
Hampstead NW3 ... 70 B3
Wandsworth SW18 .. 158 C4
Woodside Pk N12 ... 29 D6
Henderson Dr
NW8 ... 92 B3 236 C6
Henderson Ho 7
RM10 ... 81 C5
Henderson Rd
Edmonton N9 ... 18 B3
Forest Gate E7 ... 77 C2
Hayes UB4 ... 84 A4
Thornton Heath CR0 . 205 B3
Wandsworth SW18 .. 158 C4
Hendfield Ct 5 SM6 . 219 B2
Hendham Rd SW17 .. 158 D2
HENDON ... 46 C3
Hendon Ave N3 ... 29 A2
Hendon Central NW4 . 46 B4
Hendon Central Sta
NW4 ... 46 B4
Hendon Hall Ct NW4 .. 46 D6
Hendon Ho NW4 ... 46 D4
Hendon La N3 ... 29 B1
Hendon L Ctr NW2 ... 46 D2
Hendon Lo NW4 ... 46 B6
Hendon Park Mans
NW4 ... 46 C4
Hendon Park Row
NW11 ... 47 B3
Hendon Pk Cotts
NW7 ... 11 D2
Hendon Prep Sch
NW4 ... 46 D6
Hendon Rd N9 ... 18 A2
Hendon Sch NW4 ... 46 D4
Hendon Sta NW4 ... 46 A3
Hendon Terr TW15 ... 171 B4
Hendon Way NW2,
NW4 ... 46 C3
Hendon Wood La
NW7 ... 12 A3
Hendre Ho SE1 ... 263 B3
Hendren Cl UB6 ... 64 B3
Hendre Rd
SE1 ... 117 C2 263 B3
Hendrick Ave SW12 . 158 D4
Heneage La EC3 ... 243 B1
Heneage Pl EC3 ... 243 B1
Heneage St
E1 ... 95 D2 243 D4
Henfield Cl
London N19 ... 49 C1
Old Bexley DA5 ... 169 C5
Henfield Rd SW19 ... 179 B2
Hengelo Gdns CR4 ... 202 B5
Hengist Rd
Eltham SE12 ... 165 B4
Erith DA8 ... 147 D5
Hengist Way
Beckenham BR2,
BR3 ... 208 C5
Wallington SM6 ... 219 D1
Hengrave Rd SE23 .. 162 D4
Hengrove Ct DA5 ... 169 A3
Henley Ave SM3 ... 217 A5
Henley Cl
Greenford UB6 ... 86 A5
Hounslow TW7 ... 130 D4
Rotherhithe SE16 ... 118 C4
Henley Ct
Brondesbury NW2 ... 68 D2
Hendon NW4 ... 46 A6
Ilford IG1 ... 78 D4
Mitcham CR4 ... 203 A6
Oakwood N14 ... 15 C4
Peckham SE15 ... 140 A2
Sidcup DA5 ... 169 B4
Henley Dr
Bermondsey
SE1 ... 117 D2 263 D4
Kingston u T KT2 ... 177 D3
Henley Gdns
Dagenham RM6 ... 59 A4
Pinner HA5 ... 40 B6

Henley Ho London N12 . 30 B5
Shoreditch E2 ... 243 D6
Henley Lo
South Norwood
SE25 ... 205 D5
Walthamstow E17 ... 53 B4
Henley Prior N1 ... 233 C3
Henley Rd
Edmonton N18 ... 33 C6
Ilford IG1 ... 79 B4
Newham E16 ... 122 B4
Willesden NW10 ... 90 C6
Henleys Cnr NW11 ... 47 B5
Henleys Rdbt TW5 ... 128 C3
Henley St SW11 ... 137 A3
Henley Way TW13 ... 172 D5
Henlow Pl TW10 ... 153 D2
Hennel Cl SE23 ... 162 C1
Hennessy Rd N9 ... 18 C2
Henniker Gdns E6 .. 100 A4
Henniker Mews SW3 266 C6
Henniker Point E15 ... 76 C3
Henniker Rd E15 ... 76 B3
Henningham Rd N17 .. 33 B2
Henning St
SW11 ... 136 C4 267 A1
Henrietta Barnett Sch
NW11 ... 47 D3
Henrietta Cl SE8 ... 141 C6
Henrietta Ho
11 Hammersmith
W6 ... 112 C1
3 New Barnet EN5 ... 2 A1
3 South Tottenham
N15 ... 51 C3
Henrietta Mews
WC1 ... 240 B6
Henrietta Pl
W1 ... 93 B1 238 C2
Henrietta St
Strand
WC2 ... 116 A6 250 B6
Stratford New Town
E15 ... 76 A3
Henriques St E1 ... 96 A1
Henry Addlington Cl
E6 ... 100 D2
Henry Cavendish Prim
Sch 2 SW12 ... 159 C3
Henry Cl EN2 ... 5 C5
Henry Compton Sch
SW6 ... 135 A4 264 A2
Henry Cooper Way
SE12 ... 187 D6
Henry Darlot Dr NW7 . 29 A5
Henry Dent Cl SE5 ... 139 B2
Henry Dickens Ct
W11 ... 244 A4
Henry Doulton Dr
SW17 ... 181 B6
Henry Fawcett Prim Sch
15 SE11 ... 138 C6
Henry Green Prim Sch
RM8 ... 80 D6
Henry Hatch Ct SM2 . 218 A1
Henry Ho
Lambeth SE1 ... 251 B3
South Lambeth SW8 . 270 A4
St John's Wood NW8 . 230 A4
Henry Jackson Ho 4
SW15 ... 134 D2
Henry Jackson Rd
SW15 ... 134 D2
Henry Macaulay Ave 13
KT2 ... 175 D2
Henry Maynard Inf Sch
E17 ... 54 A4
Henry Maynard Jun Sch
E17 ... 54 A4
Henry Peters Dr
TW11 ... 174 C5
Henry Rd London N4 ... 51 A1
New Barnet EN4 ... 14 B6
Newham E6 ... 100 A5
Henry's Ave IG8 ... 36 D5
Henryson Rd SE4 ... 163 C6
Henry St BR1 ... 187 B2
Henry Tate Mews
SW16 ... 182 C5
Henry Wise Ho SW1 . 259 B3
Henshall Point 19 E3 .. 97 D4
Henshall St N1 ... 73 B2
Henshawe Rd RM8 ... 80 D5
Henshaw St
SE17 ... 117 B2 262 C4
Hensley Point 28 E9 ... 74 D2

Henslowe Rd SE22 ... 162 A6
Henslow Ho 12 SE15 . 140 A5
Henson Ave NW2 ... 68 C3
Henson Cl BR6 ... 226 D6
Henson Ct 3 N5 ... 73 A4
Henson Path HA3 ... 43 D6
Henson Pl UB5 ... 84 C6
Henstridge Pl NW8 . 230 A5
Henty Cl
SW11 ... 136 C4 267 B2
Henty Wlk SW15 ... 156 B6
Henville Rd BR1 ... 187 B2
Henwick Prim Sch
SE9 ... 144 A2
Henwick Rd SE9 ... 144 A2
Hepburn Gdns BR2 . 208 D1
Hepburn Mews
SW11 ... 158 D6
Hepple Cl TW7 ... 131 B3
Hepplestone Cl
SW15 ... 156 B5
Hepscott Rd E9 ... 75 C1
Hepworth Ct
Barking IG11 ... 80 A3
Cheam SM3 ... 201 C1
Chelsea SW1 ... 258 C1
Islington N1 ... 234 C6
Hepworth Gdns IG11 .. 80 A3
Hepworth Ho IG8 ... 21 A1
Hepworth Rd SW16 .. 182 A3
Hepworth Way KT12 193 D1
Heracles 30 NW9 ... 27 D2
Heracles Cl SM6 ... 220 A1
Hera Ct 15 E14 ... 119 C2
Herald Gdns SM6 ... 219 B5
Heralds Pl SE11 ... 261 C4
Herald St 5 E2 ... 96 B3
Herbal Hill EC1 ... 241 B5
Herbert Chapman Ct
N5 ... 72 D4
Herbert Cres SW1 .. 257 D6
Herbert Ct 4 KT5 ... 198 B3
Herbert Gdns
Chiswick W4 ... 132 D6
Dagenham RM6 ... 58 D2
Willesden Green NW10 90 B5
Herbert Ho E1 ... 243 C2
Herbert Mews 15
SW2 ... 160 C5
Herbert Morrison Ho
SW6 ... 264 C5
Herbert Morrison Prim
Sch SW8 ... 138 A5 270 A3
Herbert Pl
Hounslow TW3 ... 130 B3
Shooters Hill SE18 ... 144 D6
Herbert Rd
Bexleyheath DA7 ... 147 A3
Bromley BR2 ... 210 A4
Hendon NW9 ... 46 A3
Ilford IG3 ... 79 C6
Kingston u T KT1 ... 198 B6
Manor Pk E12 ... 78 A4
Merton SW19 ... 179 B3
Shooters Hill SE18 ... 144 D6
Southall UB1 ... 107 B5
South Tottenham N15 ... 51 D4
Walthamstow E17 ... 53 B2
Wood Green N11 ... 32 A3
Herbert St
Camden Town NW5 ... 71 A2
Newham E13 ... 99 A5
Herbrand Est
WC1 ... 94 A3 240 A6
Herbrand St
WC1 ... 94 A3 240 A6
Hercies Rd UB10 ... 60 C2
Hercules Ct 7 SE14 . 141 A6
Hercules Pl N7 ... 72 A5
Hercules Rd
SE1 ... 116 B3 260 D5
Hercules St N7 ... 72 A5
Hereford Ave EN4 ... 14 D3
Hereford Bldgs SW3 266 D6
Hereford Ct
20 Belmont SM2 ... 217 C1
6 Croydon CR0 ... 205 D1
6 Ealing W7 ... 86 D2
Harrow HA1 ... 42 C6
Hereford Gdns
London SE13 ... 164 C6
Pinner HA5 ... 41 A4
Redbridge IG1 ... 56 A2
Twickenham TW2 ... 152 A3
Hereford Ho
7 Acton W3 ... 88 C1

Hereford Ho *continued*
5 Brixton SW2 ... 138 C1
25 Camberwell SE5 .. 139 A3
Edgware HA8 ... 26 B3
Knightsbridge SW3 .. 257 B6
Walham Green SW10 . 265 D4
Hereford Mans 10
W2 ... 91 C1
Hereford Mews 11
W2 ... 91 C1
Hereford Pl SE14 ... 141 B5
Hereford Rd
Acton W3 ... 111 A6
Bayswater
W2 ... 113 C6 245 B6
Ealing W5 ... 109 C3
Feltham TW13 ... 150 C3
Wanstead E11 ... 55 B4
Hereford Retreat 5
SE15 ... 140 A5
Hereford Sq
SW7 ... 114 A2 256 B3
Hereford St E2 ... 96 A3
Hereford Way KT9 .. 213 D3
Herent Dr IG5 ... 56 B6
Hereward Gdns N13 .. 32 C5
Hereward House Sch
NW3 ... 70 B2
Hereward Rd SW17 . 180 D6
Herga Ct HA1 ... 64 C6
Herga Rd HA3 ... 42 D5
Heriot Ave E4 ... 19 C2
Heriot Rd NW4 ... 46 C4
Heriots Cl HA7 ... 25 A6
Heritage Ave NW9 ... 27 D1
Heritage Cl
London SW9 ... 138 D2
Sunbury TW16 ... 172 A2
Heritage Ct SE8 ... 118 D1
Heritage Hill BR2 ... 225 C3
Heritage Ho
22 Putney SW19 ... 156 D3
3 Twickenham TW1 . 153 A4
Heritage View HA1 ... 64 D5
Herlwyn Ave HA4 ... 61 C5
Herlwyn Gdns SW17 180 D6
Herm Cl TW7 ... 130 A5
Hermes Cl 5 W9 ... 91 C3
Hermes Ct 4 SW9 ... 138 C4
Hermes Ho BR3 ... 185 A2
Hermes St N1 ... 234 A3
Hermes Wlk UB5 ... 85 C5
Herm Ho EN3 ... 6 D5
Hermiston Ave N8 ... 50 A4
Hermiston Ct
3 Hornsey N8 ... 50 A4
7 North Finchley N12 .. 30 B5
Hermitage Cl
1 Abbey Wood
SE2 ... 124 C3
Claygate KT10 ... 213 A2
Enfield EN2 ... 4 D3
Littleton TW17 ... 192 C5
Snaresbrook E18 ... 54 D5
Hermitage Ct
2 Child's Hill NW2 ... 69 C5
Colney Hatch N11 ... 30 D4
3 Wanstead E18 ... 55 A5
13 Wapping E1 ... 118 A5
Hermitage Gdns
Child's Hill NW2 ... 69 C5
South Norwood SE19 . 183 A3
Hermitage La
Child's Hill NW2 ... 69 C5
Croydon CR0 ... 206 A3
South Norwood SW16 182 B3
Hermitage Prim Sch 19
E1 ... 118 A5
Hermitage Rd
London N4, N15 ... 51 A3
South Norwood SE19 .. 183 B4
Hermitage Row 9
E8 ... 74 A3
Hermitage St W2 ... 236 C3
Hermitage The
Barnes SW13 ... 133 D4
Feltham TW13 ... 149 D1
Forest Hill SE23 ... 162 C3
Kingston u T KT1 ... 197 D5
Richmond TW10 ... 154 A6
Uxbridge UB8 ... 60 A2
Hermitage Villas
SW6 ... 265 A6
Hermitage Wall E1 .. 118 A5
Hermitage Way HA7 .. 25 A2
Hermitage Wlk E18 ... 54 D5

Hermit Pl NW6 ... 91 D6
Hermit Rd E16 ... 98 D3
Hermit St EC1 ... 234 C2
Hermon Gr UB3 ... 106 A5
Hermon Hill E11 ... 55 A5
Herndon Rd SW18 ... 158 A6
Herne Cl Hayes UB3 ... 83 D1
Willesden NW10 ... 67 B3
Herne Ct WD23 ... 8 A4
HERNE HILL ... 161 A6
Herne Hill SE24 ... 139 A1
Herne Hill Ho SE24 .. 160 D5
Herne Hill Mans
SE24 ... 161 A5
Herne Hill Rd SE24 ... 139 A1
Herne Hill Sch SE24 . 161 A6
Herne Hill Sta SE24 . 160 D5
Herne Hill Velodrome
SE24 ... 161 B5
Herne Mews N18 ... 34 A6
Herne Pl SE24 ... 160 D6
Herne Rd KT6 ... 214 A6
Heron Cl
Buckhurst Hill IG9 ... 21 A3
Cheam SM1 ... 217 B3
Walthamstow E17 ... 35 B1
Willesden NW10 ... 67 C2
Heron Cres DA14 ... 189 C6
Heron Ct
Bromley BR2 ... 209 C5
16 Cubitt Town E14 .. 120 A3
7 Dulwich SE21 ... 161 B2
9 Forest Hill SE23 ... 162 C3
Ilford IG1 ... 78 D6
5 Kingston u T KT1 ... 198 A6
Merton SW20 ... 178 C1
Mitcham CR4 ... 180 C2
Ruislip HA4 ... 61 B6
Stanwell TW19 ... 148 A3
Herondale Ave
SW18 ... 158 C3
Heron Dr N4 ... 73 A6
Herongate N1 ... 235 B6
Herongate Rd E12 ... 77 C6
Heron Hill DA17 ... 125 B2
Heron Ho
Battersea SW11 ... 267 B2
Ealing W13 ... 87 A3
Peckham SE15 ... 139 D4
Sidcup DA14 ... 168 B1
St John's Wood NW8 . 230 A3
Teddington KT1 ... 175 C2
Heron Mead EN3 ... 7 C5
Heron Mews IG1 ... 78 D6
Heron Pl
Marylebone W1 ... 238 B2
Rotherhithe SE16 ... 119 A5
Heron Quays E14 ... 119 C5
Heron Quays Sta
E14 ... 119 C5
Heron Rd
Croydon CR0 ... 221 C6
Herne Hill SE24 ... 139 A1
Isleworth TW1 ... 131 B1
Heronsforde W13 ... 87 C1
Heronsgate HA8 ... 26 C5
Heronsgate Prim Sch
SE28 ... 123 B3
Heron's Lea N6 ... 48 D3
Heronslea Dr HA7 ... 26 A5
Herons Pl TW7 ... 131 B2
Heron Sq 27 TW10 .. 153 D6
Herons Rise EN4 ... 2 C1
Herons The E11 ... 54 D3
Heron Trad Est W3 ... 88 D2
Heronway IG8 ... 37 C6
Heron Way
Hatton TW14 ... 128 A1
Wallington SM6 ... 219 D1
Herrick Ct 4 TW10 .. 175 D6
Herrick Ho
18 Camberwell SE5 ... 139 B5
17 Canonbury N16 ... 73 B4
Herrick Rd N5 ... 73 A5
Herrick St
SW1 ... 115 D2 259 D3
Herries St W10 ... 91 A5
Herringham Rd SE7 .. 121 C3
Herrongate Cl EN1 ... 5 D3
Hersant Cl NW10 ... 90 A6
Herschell Rd SE23 ... 163 A4
Herschell's Mews
SE5 ... 139 A2

Hersham Cl SW15 ... 156 A4
Hersham Rd KT12 ... 194 A1
Hershell Ct 1 SW14 132 D1
Hertford Ave SW14 ... 133 C1
Hertford Cl EN4 ... 2 B2
Hertford Ct
16 London SW11 ... 136 C2
Newham E6 ... 100 B4
Palmers Green N13 ... 16 C1
Hertford Ho 5 UB5 ... 85 B3
Hertford Lo 10
SW19 ... 157 A3
Hertford Pl W1 ... 239 B5
Hertford Rd
Barking IG11 ... 78 D1
Barnet EN4 ... 2 A2
East Finchley N2 ... 48 C6
Edmonton N9 ... 18 B3
Enfield EN3 ... 6 C5
Ilford IG2 ... 57 C3
Shoreditch N1 ... 95 C6
Hertford Rd High St
EN3 ... 18 C6
Hertford St
W1 ... 115 B5 248 C3
Hertford Way CR4 ... 204 A5
Hertford Wlk 13
DA17 ... 125 C1
Hertmitage The 5
SE13 ... 142 A3
Hertslet Rd N7 ... 72 B5
Hertsmere Rd E14 ... 119 C6
Hertswood Ct 1 EN5 ... 1 A1
Hervey Cl N3 ... 29 C2
Hervey Park Rd E17 ... 53 A5
Hervey Rd SE3 ... 143 B4
Hesa Rd UB3 ... 106 A6
Hesewall Cl SW4 ... 137 C3
Hesketh Pl W11 ... 244 A5
Hesketh Rd E7 ... 77 A5
Heslop Ct 1 SW12 ... 159 A3
Heslop Rd SW12 ... 158 D3
Hesper Mews
SW5 ... 113 D2 255 C3
Hesperus Cres E14 ... 119 D2
Hessel Rd W13 ... 109 B4
Hessel St E1 ... 96 B1
Hestercombe Ave
SW6 ... 135 A4 264 B1
Hester Ct SW16 ... 181 C5
Hesterman Way CR0 ... 204 B1
Hester Rd
Battersea
SW11 ... 136 C5 267 A3
Edmonton N18 ... 34 A5
Hester Terr TW9 ... 132 C2
Hestia Ho SE1 ... 253 A1
HESTON ... 129 B5
Heston Ave TW5 ... 129 A5
Heston Com Sch
TW5 ... 129 C5
Heston Ctr The TW5 ... 106 C1
Heston Grange TW5 ... 129 B6
Heston Grange La
TW5 ... 129 B6
Heston Ho
Gunnersbury W4 ... 110 D1
5 St Johns SE8 ... 141 C4
Heston Ind Mall
TW5 ... 129 B5
Heston Inf Sch TW5 ... 129 C5
Heston Jun Sch
TW5 ... 129 C5
Heston Phoenix
Distribution Pk
TW5 ... 128 C6
Heston Pool TW5 ... 129 B6
Heston Rd TW5 ... 129 C5
Heston St SE14 ... 141 C4
Hetherington Rd
Charlton TW17 ... 171 A1
Stockwell SW2, SW4 ... 138 A1
Hetherington Way
UB10 ... 60 A4
Hethpool Ho W2 ... 236 C5
Hetley Gdns 1
SE19 ... 183 D3
Hetley Rd W12 ... 112 B4
Heton Gdns NW4 ... 46 A5
Hetty Rees Ct 6 N19 ... 50 A2
Hevelius Cl SE10 ... 120 D1
Hever Croft SE9 ... 188 C6
Heverfield Ct CR4 ... 180 D3
Hever Gdns BR1 ... 188 C1
Heverham Rd SE18 ... 123 C2
Hever Ho SE15 ... 140 D6
Heversham Ho SE15 ... 140 C6
Heversham Rd DA7 ... 147 C4
Hevingham Dr RM6 ... 58 C4
Heward Ct SE13 ... 142 A3
Hewens Rd UB4 ... 83 A3
Hewer Ho 6 SW4 ... 159 C6
Hewer St W10 ... 90 D2
Hewes Ho E17 ... 52 D5
Hewett Cl HA7 ... 25 B6
Hewett Ho
Putney SW15 ... 134 C3
7 Woolwich SE18 ... 122 D1
Hewett Rd RM8 ... 80 D4
Hewetts Quay 6
IG11 ... 101 A6
Hewett St EC2 ... 95 C3 243 B5
Hewish Rd N18 ... 33 C6
Hewison St E3 ... 97 B5
Hewitt Ave N22 ... 32 D1
Hewitt Cl CR0 ... 223 C5
Hewitt Ho 2 E4 ... 36 B5
Hewitt Rd N8 ... 50 D4
Hewlett Rd E3 ... 97 A5
Hewling Ho 1 N16 ... 73 C3
Hexagon Bsns Ctr
UB4 ... 106 C6
Hexagon The N6 ... 48 D1
Hexal Rd SE6 ... 164 C1
Hexham Gdns TW7 ... 131 A5
Hexham Rd Barnet EN5 ... 1 D1
Cheam SM4 ... 201 D1
West Norwood SE27 ... 161 A2
Hexton Ct N4 ... 73 A6
Heybourne Rd N17 ... 34 B3
Heybridge 9 NW1 ... 71 B2
Heybridge Ave
SW16 ... 182 B4
Heybridge Dr IG6 ... 57 B6
Heybridge Way E10 ... 53 B1
Heydon Ct BR4 ... 224 C6
Heydon Ho 3 SE14 ... 140 C4
Heyford Ave
Merton SW20 ... 201 B6
South Lambeth
SW8 ... 138 A5 270 B4
Heyford Rd CR4 ... 180 C1
Heyford Terr SW8 ... 270 B4
Heygate St
SE17 ... 117 A2 262 B4
Heylyn Sq E3 ... 97 B4
Heynes Rd RM8 ... 80 C4
Heysham Dr WD19 ... 22 D5
Heysham La NW3 ... 69 D5
Heysham Rd N15 ... 51 B3
Heythorp St SW18 ... 157 B2
Heythrop Coll
W8 ... 113 D3 255 C6
Heythrop Dr UB10 ... 60 B4
Heyward Ct SM2 ... 217 C2
Heywood Ave NW9 ... 27 C2
Heywood Ct 2 HA7 ... 25 C5
Heywood Ho
11 Deptford SE14 ... 140 D6
6 Tulse Hill SW2 ... 160 C5
Heyworth Rd
Lower Clapton E5 ... 74 B4
Stratford E15 ... 76 D4
Hibbert Ho 13 E14 ... 119 C3
Hibbert Rd
Harrow HA3 ... 24 D1
Walthamstow E17 ... 53 B2
Hibbert St SW11 ... 136 B2
Hibernia Gdns TW3 ... 151 C6
Hibernia Point 9
SE2 ... 124 D4
Hibernia Rd TW3 ... 129 C1
Hibiscus Cl 6 HA8 ... 27 A6
Hibiscus Lo 5 E15 ... 76 C1
Hichisson Rd SE15 ... 162 C6
Hicken Rd SW2 ... 160 B6
Hickes Ho 6 NW6 ... 70 B1
Hickey's Almshouses 7
TW9 ... 132 B1
Hickin Cl SE7 ... 121 D2
Hickin St 2 E14 ... 120 A3
Hickleton NW1 ... 232 B5
Hickling Ho 10 SE16 ... 118 B3
Hickling Rd IG1 ... 78 D3
Hickman Ave E4 ... 36 A4
Hickman Cl E16 ... 99 D2
Hickman Rd RM6 ... 58 C2
Hickmore Wlk SW4 ... 137 C2
Hickory Cl N9 ... 18 A4
Hicks Ave UB6 ... 86 C4
Hicks Cl SW11 ... 136 C2
Hicks Ct RM10 ... 81 D5
Hicks St SE8 ... 119 A1
Hidaburn Ct 7
SW16 ... 181 C6
Hidcote Gdns SW20 ... 200 B6
Hidcote Ho 11 SM2 ... 218 A1
Hide E6 ... 100 C1
Hide Pl SW1 ... 115 D2 259 C3
Hider Ct SE3 ... 143 C5
Hide Rd HA1 ... 42 B5
Hide Twr SW1 ... 259 C3
Hieover SE21 ... 161 A2
Higgins Ho 7 N1 ... 95 C6
Higginson Ho 2
NW3 ... 70 D1
Higgins Wlk TW12 ... 173 A4
Higgs Ind Est 9
SE24 ... 138 D2
High Acre EN2 ... 4 D2
Higham Ct 9 IG8 ... 37 A4
HIGHAM HILL ... 35 A2
Higham Hill Ho E17 ... 34 D2
Higham Hill Rd E17 ... 35 A1
Higham Ho E4 ... 35 C4
Higham Mews UB5 ... 85 B3
Higham Pl E17 ... 53 A6
Higham Rd
Tottenham N17 ... 51 B6
Woodford IG8 ... 37 A4
Highams Lodge Bsns Ctr
E17 ... 52 D6
HIGHAMS PARK ... 36 A3
Highams Park Sch E4 ... 36 B4
Highams Park Sta E4 ... 36 B4
Higham St E17 ... 53 A6
Higham Station Ave
E4 ... 35 D4
Highams The E17 ... 36 A2
High Ashton 11 KT2 ... 176 D3
Highbanks Cl DA16 ... 146 B5
Highbanks Rd HA5 ... 23 D4
Highbank Way N8 ... 50 C3
HIGH BARNET ... 1 B2
High Barnet Sta EN5 ... 1 C1
Highbarrow Rd CR0 ... 206 A1
High Beech
South Croydon CR2 ... 221 C1
Southgate N21 ... 16 B5
High Beeches DA14 ... 191 A5
High Birch Ct 7 EN4 ... 2 C1
Highbridge Ct 13
SE14 ... 140 C5
Highbridge Rd IG11 ... 100 D6
High Bridge Wharf
SE10 ... 120 B1
Highbrook Rd SE3 ... 143 D2
High Broom Cres
BR4 ... 207 D2
Highburty Mans 24
N1 ... 72 D1
HIGHBURY ... 72 D4
Highbury Ave CR7 ... 182 D1
Highbury Cl
New Malden KT3 ... 199 A4
West Wickham BR4 ... 223 D6
Highbury Cnr N5 ... 72 D2
Highbury Corner N5 ... 72 D2
Highbury Cres N5 ... 72 C3
Highbury Fields Sch 4
N5 ... 72 D3
Highbury Gdns IG3 ... 79 C6
Highbury Gr N5 ... 72 D3
Highbury Grange N5 ... 73 A4
Highbury Grove Ct
N5 ... 72 D2
Highbury Grove Sch 7
N5 ... 73 A3
Highbury Hill N5 ... 72 D4
Highbury & Islington Sta
N1 ... 72 D2
Highbury New Pk N5 ... 73 A4
Highbury Pk N5 ... 72 D4
Highbury Pl N5 ... 72 D3
Highbury Pool N5 ... 72 D2
Highbury Quadrant
N5 ... 73 A5
Highbury Quadrant Prim
Sch N5 ... 73 A4
Highbury Rd SW19 ... 179 A5
Highbury Sq N14 ... 15 C3
Highbury Station Rd
N1 ... 72 C2
Highbury Terr N5 ... 72 D3
Highbury Terrace Mews
N5 ... 72 D3
High Cedar Dr SW20 ... 178 B3
Highclears 6 IG9 ... 21 B2
Highclere Rd KT3 ... 199 B6
Highclere St SE26 ... 185 A6
Highcliffe
Beckenham BR3 ... 185 D2
Ealing W13 ... 87 B2
Highcliffe Dr SW15 ... 155 D5
Highcliffe Gdns IG4 ... 56 A4
Highcombe SE7 ... 143 B6
Highcombe Cl SE9 ... 166 A3
High Coombe Pl
KT2 ... 177 B3
Highcroft Highgate N6 ... 49 A3
Hyde The NW9 ... 45 C4
2 Kingston u T KT5 ... 198 B4
Highcroft Ave HA0 ... 88 C6
Highcroft Gdns NW11 ... 47 B3
Highcroft Point E17 ... 35 D2
Highcroft Rd N19 ... 50 A2
High Cross Ctr The
N15 ... 52 A5
High Cross Rd N17 ... 52 A6
Highcross Way 4
SW15 ... 156 A3
Highdaun Dr SW16 ... 204 B5
High Dene EN2 ... 4 D2
Highdown KT4 ... 215 D6
Highdown Rd SW15 ... 156 B5
High Dr KT2, KT3 ... 177 A1
High Elms IG8 ... 37 A5
High Elms Ctry Pk*
BR6 ... 227 A1
High Elms Rd BR6 ... 227 A1
Highfield WD23 ... 8 C2
Highfield Ave
Erith DA8 ... 147 D6
Greenford UB6 ... 64 D3
Hendon NW11 ... 47 A2
Kingsbury NW9 ... 45 A4
Orpington BR6 ... 227 D3
Pinner HA5 ... 41 B4
Wembley HA9 ... 66 B5
Highfield Cl
Hither Green SE13 ... 164 B5
Kingsbury NW9 ... 45 A4
Long Ditton KT6 ... 197 C1
Wood Green N22 ... 32 C2
Highfield Ct
7 Barnet EN5 ... 1 D1
Hendon NW11 ... 47 A3
Mitcham CR4 ... 202 C5
Southgate N14 ... 15 C5
Wanstead E12 ... 77 C6
Highfield Dr
Beckenham BR2 ... 208 D5
Ickenham UB10 ... 60 A5
West Ewell KT19 ... 215 D2
West Wickham BR4 ... 224 A5
Highfield Gdns NW11 ... 47 A3
Highfield Hill SE19 ... 183 C3
Highfield Ho N21 ... 16 D3
Highfield Inf Sch
BR2 ... 208 C5
Highfield Jun Sch
BR2 ... 208 C5
Highfield Mews NW6 ... 69 D1
Highfield Prim Sch
Edmonton N21 ... 17 A3
Hillingdon UB10 ... 82 D4
Highfield Rd
Acton W3 ... 89 A2
Bexley DA6 ... 169 B6
Bromley BR1 ... 210 B5
Carshalton SM1 ... 218 C3
Edmonton N21 ... 16 D2
Feltham TW13 ... 150 A2
4 Feltham TW13 ... 150 B3
Hendon NW11 ... 47 A3
Hounslow TW7 ... 130 D4
Orpington BR5, BR7 ... 211 D6
St Paul's Cray BR5,
BR7 ... 211 D6
Tolworth KT5 ... 199 A2
Upper Halliford TW16 ... 193 D4
Walton-on-T KT12 ... 194 A1
Highfields SM1 ... 217 C6
Highfields Gr N6 ... 48 D1
High Foleys KT10 ... 213 B1
High Gables
Beckenham BR2 ... 186 C1
Loughton IG10 ... 21 D6
High Garth KT10 ... 212 A2
HIGHGATE ... 49 A2
Highgate Archway
N6 ... 49 C1
Highgate Ave N6 ... 49 B2
Highgate Cemetery*
N19 ... 71 B6
Highgate Cl N6 ... 49 A2
High Gate Edge N2 ... 48 C4
Highgate High St N6 ... 49 B1
Highgate Hill N19 ... 49 C1
Highgate Ho 11
SE26 ... 162 A1
Highgate Hts N6 ... 49 C3
Highgate Pre-Prep &
Jun Sch N6 ... 48 D2
Highgate Prim Sch
N6 ... 48 D3
Highgate (Private) Hospl
N6 ... 48 D3
Highgate Rd NW5 ... 71 B4
Highgate Sch N6 ... 49 A2
Highgate Spinney N8 ... 49 D3
Highgate Sta N6 ... 49 B3
Highgate West Hill
Highgate N6 ... 49 A1
London N6 ... 71 A6
Highgate Wlk SE23 ... 162 C2
Highgate Wood Sch
N8 ... 49 C4
High Gr Bromley BR1 ... 187 D2
Woolwich SE18 ... 145 B4
Highgrove Cl
London N11 ... 31 A5
Widmore BR7 ... 188 A2
Highgrove Ct BR3 ... 185 C3
Highgrove Ho HA4 ... 40 A3
Highgrove Mews
SM5 ... 218 D5
Highgrove Point 2
NW3 ... 70 A4
Highgrove Rd RM8 ... 80 C4
Highgrove Way HA4 ... 40 A2
High Hill Ferry 3 E5 ... 52 B1
High Holborn
WC1 ... 94 B2 240 C3
High Holborn Ho
WC1 ... 240 D3
High La W7 ... 86 B1
Highland Ave W7 ... 86 C1
Highland Cotts SM6 ... 219 C4
Highland Croft BR3 ... 185 D4
Highland Ct E18 ... 37 B2
Highland Dr WD23 ... 8 A4
Highland Lo 3
SE19 ... 183 D3
Highland Pk TW13 ... 171 D6
Highland Rd
Bexley DA6 ... 147 C1
Bromley BR1 ... 186 D2
Pinner HA6 ... 22 A1
West Norwood SE19 ... 183 C4
Highlands N20 ... 14 B2
Highlands Ave
Acton W3 ... 111 A6
Southgate N21 ... 16 B6
Highlands Cl
Hornsey N4 ... 50 A2
Hounslow TW3 ... 129 D4
Highlands Ct SE19 ... 183 C4
Highlands Gdns IG1 ... 56 B1
Highlands Heath
SW15 ... 156 C4
Highlands Prim Sch
IG1 ... 56 B1
Highlands Rd EN5 ... 13 C6
Highlands Sch N21 ... 4 C1
Highlands The
Barnet EN5 ... 1 D1
Edgware HA8 ... 26 D1
Highlawn Hall HA1 ... 64 C5
Highlea Cl NW9 ... 27 C2
High Level Dr SE26 ... 184 A6
Highlever Rd W10 ... 90 C2
High Limes 2 SE19 ... 183 C4
High London 5 N6 ... 49 D2
Highmead
9 Edmonton N18 ... 34 A5
Plumstead Comm
SE18 ... 145 D5
High Mead
Harrow HA1 ... 42 D4
West Wickham BR4 ... 224 C6
Highmead Cres HA0 ... 66 B1
High Meadow Cl HA5 ... 40 C5
High Meadow Cres
NW9 ... 45 B4
High Meads Rd E16 ... 99 D1

Highmore Rd SE3 142 C5
High Mount
Hendon NW4 46 A3
11 Hornsey N4 50 A2
High Oaks EN2 4 B5
High Oaks Lo 9 E18 37 A1
High Park Ave TW9 132 C4
High Park Rd TW9 132 C4
High Par The SW16 160 A1
High Path SW19 180 A2
Highpoint EN5 14 A6
High Point
Chislehurst SE9 166 D1
Highgate N6 49 A2
High Range SW20 178 C3
High Rd
Buckhurst Hill IG9, IG10 21 C5
Bushey WD23 8 B3
Chadwell Heath RM6 58 C2
East Finchley N2 48 C6
Finchley N2, N12 30 A3
Friern Barnet N11 31 B5
Harrow HA3 24 C3
Ilford IG1 78 D6
Leyton E10 53 D3
Oakleigh Pk N20 14 A4
Seven Kings IG1, IG3 79 C6
South Tottenham N15, N17 51 D5
Tottenham N17 33 D2
Wembley HA0, HA9 66 A3
Willesden NW10 68 A2
Woodford E18 37 A2
Wood Green N22 32 B3
High Ridge N10 31 B2
Highridge Pl EN2 4 B5
High Road Buckhurst Hill 5 IG9 21 B2
High Road Eastcote HA5 40 B4
High Road, Ickenham UB10 61 A6
High Road Leyton E10 75 D6
High Road Leytonstone E11 76 C6
High Road Woodford Gn IG8 37 A6
High St Mews SW19 179 A5
High St N
Newham E6 100 A6
Plashet E12 78 A2
High St S E6 100 B4
High Sheldon N6 48 D3
Highshore Rd SE15 139 D3
Highshore Sch 16 SE15 139 D4
High Silver IG10 21 D6
High St Acton W3 110 D5
Barnet EN5 1 B1
Beckenham BR3 185 C1
Brentford TW8 132 A6
Bromley BR1 187 A1
Cheam SM1, KT17 217 A2
Claygate KT10 212 D2
Cranford TW5 128 B5
Croydon CR0 221 A5
Ealing W5 109 D6
East Molesey KT8 195 C5
Edgware HA8 26 C4
Elstree WD6 9 D5
Farnborough BR6 227 A3
Feltham TW13 150 A2
Green Street Green BR6 227 D2
Hampton TW12 174 A4
Harlington UB3 127 B6
Harrow on t H HA1 42 C1
Hornsey N8 50 B5
Hounslow TW3 129 D2
Ilford IG6 57 A6
Kingston u T KT1 175 D2
Kingston u T KT1 197 D6
Mill Hill NW7 28 B5
Newham E13 99 A5
New Malden KT3 199 C5
Palmers Green N14 15 D2
Penge SE20 184 D3
Pinner HA5 41 A6
Ruislip HA4 39 C1
Shepperton TW17 193 A3
Sidcup DA14 190 A6
Southall UB1 107 B5
South Norwood CR7 205 B5
South Norwood SE25 206 A5
High St *continued*
Stratford Marsh E15 98 A6
Sutton SM1 217 D4
Sutton SM1, SM2 217 D3
Teddington TW11 175 A5
Thames Ditton KT7 197 A3
Twickenham TW2 152 A4
Wallington SM5 219 A4
Walthamstow E17 53 B5
Walton-on-T KT12 194 A1
Wanstead E11 55 A4
Wealdstone HA3 24 C1
Wealdstone HA3 42 C6
Wembley HA9 66 B4
West Wickham BR4 207 D1
Wimbledon SW19 178 D5
Yiewsley UB7 104 A6
Highstone Ave E11 55 A3
Highstone Ct E11 54 D3
High Street Collier's Wood SW17, SW19 180 B4
High Street Harlesden NW10 89 D5
High Street Harlington TW6 127 B5
High Street Kensington Sta W8 113 D4 245 C1
High The SW16 160 A1
High Timber St EC4 252 A6
High Tor Cl BR1 187 B3
High Tor View SE28 123 C5
High Trees
Cheam SM3 201 B2
Croydon CR0 207 A1
East Barnet EN4 14 C6
Streatham SW2 160 C3
Uxbridge UB10 61 A6
Whetstone N20 14 A1
Hightrees Ct W7 108 C6
Hightrees Ho SW12 159 A5
Highview
Crouch End N6 49 C3
Hornsey N8 50 A2
Northolt UB5 85 A4
Woolwich SE18 144 D5
High View
6 Penge SE19 183 D3
Pinner HA5 40 C6
Highview Ave HA8 27 A6
High View Ave CR0, SM6 220 B3
High View Cl
Loughton IG10 21 C6
South Norwood SE19 183 D1
Highview Ct 2 SW19 157 A3
High View Ct HA3 24 C3
Highview Gdns
Edgware HA8 27 A6
Hendon N3 47 A6
New Southgate N11 31 C5
Highview Ho
1 Buckhurst Hill IG9 21 D1
2 Buckhurst Hill IG9 21 D1
High View Ho RM6 59 A5
High View Par 1 IG4 56 B4
High View Prim Sch
1 London SW11 136 B1
Wallington SM6 220 A3
Highview Rd
Ealing W13 87 A1
Sidcup DA14 190 B6
High View Rd
London N10 30 D2
Snaresbrook E18 54 D6
South Norwood SE19 183 B4
Highway Bsns Pk The 7 E1 118 D6
Highway The
Shadwell E1 118 C6
Stanmore HA7 25 A3
Highway Trad Ctr The 6 E1 118 D6
High Wigsell TW11 175 A5
Highwood IG8 36 D6
Highwood Ave N12 30 A6
Highwood Cl
Dulwich SE22 162 A3
Orpington BR6 227 A6
Highwood Ct
Barnet EN5 13 C6
Whetstone N12 14 A1
Highwood Dr BR6 227 A6
Highwood Gdns IG5 56 B5
Highwood Gr NW7 27 B5
Highwood Hill NW7 11 D2
Highwood Rd N19 72 A5
High Worple HA2 41 B1
Highworth Rd N11 31 D5
Highworth St NW1 237 B4
Hilary Ave CR4 203 A6
Hilary Cl Bexley DA8 147 D4
Walham Green SW6 265 C4
Hilary Ct N9 18 D3
Hilary Rd W12 111 D6
Hilbert Rd SM3 216 D5
Hilborough Cl SW19 180 A3
Hilborough Ct 1 E8 95 D6
Hilborough Rd 1 E8 73 D1
Hilborough Way BR6 227 B3
Hilda Rd Newham E16 98 C3
Upton Pk E6 77 D1
Hilda Terr 2 SW9 138 C3
Hilda Vale Cl BR6 226 D4
Hilda Vale Rd BR6 226 D4
Hildenborough Gdns BR1 186 D4
Hildenbrough Ho BR3 185 B3
Hildenlea Pl BR2 186 C1
Hilditch Ho 7 TW10 154 B5
Hildred Ho SW1 258 C4
Hildreth St 6 SW12 159 B3
Hildreth Street Mews 2 SW12 159 B3
Hildyard Rd SW6 265 B6
Hiley Rd NW10 90 C4
Hilfield La WD23 8 C6
Hilgrove Rd NW6 70 A1
Hiliary Gdns HA7 25 C1
Hillary Cres KT12 194 C1
Hillary Ct
3 Chislehurst SE9 166 A2
13 Shepherd's Bush W12 112 C4
Stanwell TW19 148 A3
Hillary Dr TW7 152 D6
Hillary Rd UB2 107 C3
Hillary Rise EN5 1 C1
Hillbeck Cl
Deptford SE15 140 C5
Deptford SE15 140 C6
Hillbeck Way UB6 86 B6
Hillborne Cl UB3 106 A1
Hillboro Ct
Leytonstone E11 54 B2
1 Woodford E18 36 D2
Hillborough Ct HA1 42 C2
Hillbrook Prim Sch SW17 181 A6
Hillbrook Rd SW17 181 A6
Hillbrow
Kingston u T KT3 199 D6
7 Richmond TW10 154 A5
Hill Brow BR1 187 D2
Hillbrow Ct KT10 212 A4
Hillbrow Rd
Catford BR1 186 C4
Esher KT10 212 A4
Hill Bunker's DA17 125 C2
Hillbury Ave HA3 43 B4
Hillbury Rd SW17 159 B1
Hill Cl Barnet EN5 12 C6
Chislehurst BR7 188 D5
Dollis Hill NW2 68 B5
Hampstead Garden Suburb NW11 47 C3
Harrow HA1 64 C5
Stanmore HA7 25 B6
Hillcote Ave SW16 182 C3
Hillcourt N6 49 C3
Hillcourt Ave N12 29 D4
Hillcourt Rd SE22 162 B5
Hill Cres Harrow HA1 43 A4
Kingston u T KT5 198 B4
North Cheam KT4 216 C6
Totteridge N20 13 D2
Hillcrest
Camberwell SE24 139 B1
Highgate N6 49 A2
Notting Hill W11 244 C5
Southgate N21 16 C4
Hill Crest DA15 168 B4
Hillcrest Ave
Edgware HA8 26 D6
Pinner HA5 40 D5
Temple Fortune NW11 47 B4
Hillcrest Cl
Beckenham BR3 207 B3
Forest Hill SE26 184 A6
Hillcrest Ct
Brondesbury NW2 69 A3
8 Edgware HA8 26 D5
Lewisham SE6 164 B4
Sutton SM2 218 B2
Hillcrest Gdns
Dollis Hill NW2 68 A5
Hendon N3 47 A5
Hinchley Wood KT10 212 D5
Hillcrest Hts W5 88 A3
Hillcrest Rd
Acton W3 110 D5
Chingford E17 36 B1
Ealing W5 88 A2
Grove Pk BR1 187 A6
Loughton IG10 21 D5
Woodford E18 37 A1
Hillcrest View BR3 207 B3
Hillcroft Ave HA5 41 B3
Hillcroft Coll KT6 198 A3
Hillcroft Cres
Ealing W5 87 D1
Ruislip HA4 62 D5
Wembley HA9 66 B4
Hillcroft Rd E6 100 D2
Hillcroome Rd SM2 218 B2
Hillcross Ave SM4 201 A4
Hillcross Prim Sch SM4 201 B5
Hill Ct Barnet EN4 2 C1
Ealing W5 88 B3
Hampstead NW3 70 C4
8 Norbiton KT2 176 D3
Northolt UB5 63 C3
Putney SW15 156 D6
14 Surbiton KT6 198 A4
Wembley HA0 65 A4
9 Wimbledon SW19 179 A4
Hilldale Rd SM1 217 B4
Hilldown Ct SW16 182 A3
Hilldown Rd
Hayes BR2 208 D1
South Norwood SW16 182 B3
Hill Dr London NW9 45 A1
Thornton Heath SW16 204 B6
Hilldrop Cres N7 71 D3
Hilldrop La N7 71 D3
Hilldrop Rd
Bromley BR1 187 B4
Kentish Town N7 71 D3
Hill End
Orpington BR6 227 D6
Shooters Hill SE18 144 C4
Hillersdon Ave
Barnes SW13 134 A3
Edgware HA8 26 B5
Hillersdon Ho SW1 258 C2
Hillery Cl SE17 262 D3
Hill Farm Rd W10 90 D2
Hillfield Ave
Colindale NW9 45 C5
Hornsey N8 50 A5
Mitcham SM4 202 C4
Wembley HA0 66 B1
Hillfield Cl HA2 42 A5
Hillfield Ct NW3 70 C3
Hillfield Ho N5 73 A3
Hillfield La S WD23 8 D5
Hillfield Lo SW17 180 D5
Hillfield Mans NW3 70 C3
Hillfield Par SM4 202 B3
Hillfield Park Mews N10 49 B5
Hillfield Pk
London N10 49 B5
Southgate N21 16 C2
Hillfield Rd
Hampton TW12 173 B2
West Hampstead NW6 69 C3
Hillgate Pl
Balham SW12 159 B4
Kensington W8 113 C5 245 A4
Hillgate St W8 245 A4
Hill Gate Wlk N6 49 C3
Hill Gr TW13 151 B2
Hill Ho Southall UB1 85 C1
Stanmore HA7 9 A1
Upper Clapton E5 52 B1
Woolwich SE28 123 C5
Hill House Ave HA7 24 D3
Hill House Cl N21 16 C4
Hill House Dr TW12 173 C2
Hill House International Jun Sch SW1 114 D3 257 D5
Hill House Rd SW16 182 B5
Hilliard Ct SM6 219 D2
Hilliard Ho 15 E1 118 B5
Hilliard's Ct E1 118 C5
Hillier Cl EN5 13 D5
Hillier Gdns CR0 220 C3
Hillier Ho 1 NW1 71 D1
Hillier Lo TW12 174 B5
Hillier Pl KT9 213 D2
Hillier Rd SW11 158 D5
Hilliers Ave UB8 82 C4
Hillier's La CR0, SM6 220 A5
HILLINGDON 82 D5
Hillingdon Ave TW19 148 A3
Hillingdon Circus UB10 60 D2
HILLINGDON HEATH 82 D2
Hillingdon Hill UB10 82 B4
Hillingdon Hospl UB8 82 B2
Hillingdon Manor Sch UB8 82 D2
Hillingdon Manor Upper Sch UB3 83 D1
Hillingdon Par 6 UB10 82 D3
Hillingdon Prim Sch UB10 82 D4
Hillingdon Rd UB10 82 A5
Hillingdon St SE17 138 D6
Hillingdon Sta UB10 60 D3
Hillington Gdns IG8 37 D1
Hill La HA4 39 A1
Hill Lo SW11 136 B1
Hillman Cl UB8 60 A3
Hillman Dr 12 NW10 90 C3
Hillman St E8 74 B2
Hillmarton Rd N7 72 A3
Hillmead Dr SW9 138 D1
Hill Mead Prim Sch 23 SW9 138 D1
Hillmont Rd KT10 212 C5
Hillmore Ct SE13 142 B2
Hillmore Gr SE26 185 A5
Hill Rd
Carshalton SM5 218 C2
Finchley N10 30 D2
Harrow HA1 43 A4
Mitcham CR4 181 B3
Pinner HA5 41 A3
St John's Wood NW8 92 A5 229 B3
Sutton SM1 217 D3
Wembley HA0 65 B5
Hillreach SE7, SE18 122 B1
Hillrise KT12 193 D2
Hill Rise
East Finchley NW11 47 D5
Enfield N9 18 B5
Forest Hill SE23 162 B3
Greenford UB6 86 A6
Hinchley Wood KT10 213 B6
Richmond TW10 153 D6
Ruislip HA4 39 B1
Hillrise Mans N19 50 A2
Hillrise Rd N19 50 A2
Hillsboro Rd SE22 161 C6
Hillsborough Ct 13 NW6 91 D6
Hillsde 6 SM1 218 B3
Hillsgrove Cl DA16 146 C5
Hillsgrove Prim Sch DA16 146 C5
Hillside Barnet EN5 14 A6
Crouch End N8 49 D3
Greenwich SE10 142 B5
Kingsbury NW9 45 B5
Stonebridge NW10 89 B6
Wimbledon SW19 178 D4
Hill Side EN5 14 A6
Hillside Ave
London N11 30 D4
Wembley HA9 66 B4
Woodford IG8 37 C5
Hillside Cl
Merton SM4 201 A5
St John's Wood NW8 91 D5
Woodford IG8 37 C5
Hillside Cres
Enfield EN2 5 B5

Hillside Cres *continued*
Harrow HA2 . . . 42 A1
Northwood HA6 . . . 22 A2
Hillside Ct
Hampstead NW3 . . . 69 D3
7 Kingston u T KT2 . . 176 D3
Hillside Dr HA8 . . . 26 C5
Hillside Gdns
Chipping Barnet EN5 . . . 1 A1
Edgware HA8 . . . 26 B6
Friern Barnet N11 . . . 31 C4
Harrow HA3 . . . 44 A2
Highgate N6 . . . 49 B3
Northwood HA6 . . . 22 B2
Streatham SW2 . . . 160 C2
Wallington SM6 . . . 219 C1
Walthamstow E17 . . . 54 B6
Hillside Glen CR0 . . . 220 D4
Hillside Gr
Hendon NW7 . . . 28 A3
Southgate N14 . . . 15 D4
Hillside Ho CR0 . . . 220 D4
Hillside Jun & Inf Schs
HA6 . . . 22 A3
Hillside La BR2 . . . 224 D6
Hillside Mans EN5 . . . 1 B1
Hillside Rd
Beckenham BR2 . . . 208 D6
Belmont SM2 . . . 217 B1
Croydon CR0 . . . 220 D4
Ealing W5 . . . 88 A2
Northwood HA6, HA5 . . . 22 B3
Southall UB1 . . . 85 C3
South Tottenham N15 . . . 51 C3
Streatham SW2 . . . 160 C2
Surbiton KT5 . . . 198 C4
Hillside Rise HA6 . . . 22 A3
Hillsleigh Rd
W14 . . . 113 B5 244 D4
Hillsley DA14 . . . 190 A6
Hills Mews 2 W5 . . . 110 A6
Hills Pl W1 . . . 239 A1
Hill's Rd IG9 . . . 21 B3
Hill St
Mayfair W1 . . 115 B5 248 C4
Richmond TW10 . . . 153 D6
Hillstone Ct 5 E3 . . . 97 D3
Hillstowe St E5 . . . 74 C5
Hilltop 7 E17 . . . 53 D6
Hill Top Cheam SM3 . . . 201 B2
East Finchley NW11 . . . 47 D5
Hilltop Ave NW10 . . . 67 A1
Hilltop Ct
12 London SW18 . . . 136 B1
South Hampstead NW8 70 A1
South Norwood SE19 . . 183 B2
Hilltop Gdns
Hendon NW4 . . . 28 B1
Orpington BR6 . . . 227 C6
Hilltop Ho 7 N6 . . . 49 D2
Hilltop Rd NW6 . . . 69 C1
Hilltop Way HA7 . . . 9 A1
Hillview SW20 . . . 178 B3
Hill View
Mitcham CR4 . . . 204 A5
Primrose Hill NW1 . . . 230 D6
Hillview Ave HA3 . . . 44 A4
Hillview Cl Pinner HA5 . 23 B4
Wembley HA9 . . . 66 B6
Hillview Cres
Orpington BR6 . . . 211 D1
Redbridge IG1 . . . 56 B3
Hillview Ct SE19 . . . 183 C6
Hill View Dr
Bexley DA16 . . . 145 C3
Woolwich SE28 . . . 123 C5
Hillview Gdns
Harrow HA2 . . . 41 C5
Hendon NW4 . . . 46 D5
Hill View Gdns NW9 . . . 45 B4
Hillview Rd
Carshalton SM1 . . . 218 B5
Chislehurst BR7 . . . 188 D6
Mill Hill NW7 . . . 28 D6
Pinner HA5 . . . 23 B4
Hill View Rd
Claygate KT10 . . . 213 A1
Orpington BR6 . . . 227 D6
Twickenham TW1 . . . 153 A5
Hillway Highgate N6 . . . 71 A6
London NW9 . . . 45 C1
Hill Wood Ho NW1 . . 232 C3
Hillworth 7 BR3 . . . 185 D1
Hillworth Rd SW2 . . . 160 C4
Hillyard Rd W7 . . . 86 C2
Hillyard St SW9 . . . 138 C4
Hillyfield E17 . . . 35 A1
Hillyfield Cl E9 . . . 75 A3
Hillyfield Prim Sch
E17 . . . 53 A6
Hilly Fields Cres
SE4 . . . 141 C2
Hilly Mead SW19 . . . 179 A3
Hilsea Point 7
SW15 . . . 156 B3
Hilsea St E5 . . . 74 C4
Hilton Ave N12 . . . 30 B5
Hilton Ho
4 Ealing W13 . . . 87 C1
12 Finchley N2 . . . 30 B1
Lower Holloway N7 . . . 72 A4
9 Nunhead SE4 . . . 140 D1
Hilversum Cres 10
SE22 . . . 161 C6
Himley Rd SW17 . . . 180 D4
Hinchley Manor
KT10 . . . 212 D5
Hinchley Cl KT10 . . . 212 D5
Hinchley Dr KT10 . . . 212 D5
Hinchley Way KT10 . . . 213 A5
HINCHLEY WOOD . . 212 D6
Hinchley Wood Prim Sch
KT10 . . . 213 A6
Hinchley Wood Sch
KT10 . . . 213 A6
Hinchley Wood Sta
KT10 . . . 212 D5
Hinckley Rd SE15 . . . 140 A1
Hind Ct EC4 . . . 241 B1
Hinde Mews W1 . . . 238 B2
Hindes Rd HA1 . . . 42 C4
Hinde St W1 . . . 93 A1 238 B2
Hind Gr E14 . . . 97 C1
Hindhead Cl UB8 . . . 82 D2
Hindhead Gdns UB5 . . 85 A6
Hindhead Gn WD19 . . . 22 C5
Hindhead Point 6
SW15 . . . 156 B3
Hindhead Way SM6 . . 220 A3
Hind Ho
13 Deptford SE14 . . . 140 D6
Islington N7 . . . 72 C4
Hindhurst Ct NW9 . . . 45 A5
Hindle Ho E8 . . . 73 D3
Hindley Ho N7 . . . 72 B5
Hindlip Ho SW8 . . . 269 C1
Hindmans Rd SE22 . . . 162 A6
Hindmans Way RM9 . . 103 B3
Hindmarsh Cl E1 . . . 118 A6
Hindrey Rd E5 . . . 74 B3
Hindsley's Pl SE23 . . . 162 C2
Hines Ct HA1 . . . 43 A4
Hinkler Rd HA3 . . . 43 D6
Hinksey Path SE2 . . . 124 D3
Hinstock NW6 . . . 91 D6
Hinstock Rd SE18 . . . 145 A5
Hinton Ave TW4 . . . 128 D1
Hinton Cl SE9 . . . 166 A3
Hinton Ct 3 E10 . . . 75 D6
Hinton Rd
Brixton SE24 . . . 138 D2
Edmonton N18 . . . 33 C6
Wallington SM6 . . . 219 C2
Hippisley Ct TW7 . . . 130 D2
Hippodrome Mews
W11 . . . 244 A5
Hippodrome Pl W11 . 244 B5
Hirst Cres HA9 . . . 66 A5
Hirst Ct SW1 . . . 258 C1
Hispano Mews 17 EN3 . . 7 C6
Hitcham Rd E17 . . . 53 B2
Hitchcock Cl TW17 . . . 192 B6
Hitchin Sq E3 . . . 97 A5
Hithe Gr 15 SE16 . . . 118 C3
Hitherbroom Rd
UB3 . . . 106 A6
Hither Farm Rd SE3 . . 143 C2
Hitherfield Prim Sch
SW16 . . . 160 C2
Hitherfield Rd
Dagenham RM8 . . . 81 A6
Streatham SW16,
SW27 . . . 160 C1
HITHER GREEN . . . 164 C5
Hither Green La
SE13 . . . 164 B5
Hither Green Prim Sch
SE13 . . . 164 B5
Hither Green Sta
SE13 . . . 164 C5
Hitherlands SW12 . . . 159 B2
Hitherwell Dr HA3 . . . 24 B2
Hitherwood Ct SE21 . 183 D6
Hitherwood Dr SE19 183 D6
Hive Cl WD23 . . . 8 B2
Hive Rd WD23 . . . 8 C2
Hive Wood Ho E7 . . . 77 A2
HM Prison Wormwood
Scrubs W12 . . . 90 A1
HMS Belfast★ SE1 . . 253 B4
Hoadly Rd SW16 . . . 159 D2
Hobart Cl
East Barnet N20 . . . 14 C2
Hayes UB4 . . . 84 D3
Hobart Ct Harrow HA1 . 42 C2
Woodford IG8 . . . 36 D6
Hobart Dr UB4 . . . 84 D3
Hobart Gdns CR7 . . . 205 B6
Hobart Ho 24 KT6 . . . 198 A4
Hobart La UB4 . . . 84 D3
Hobart Pl
Richmond TW10 . . . 154 B4
Westminster
SW1 . . . 115 B3 258 C6
Hobart Rd
Dagenham RM9 . . . 80 D4
Hayes UB4 . . . 84 D3
North Cheam KT4 . . . 216 B5
Hobbayne Prim Sch
W7 . . . 86 D1
Hobbayne Rd W7 . . . 86 B1
Hobbes Wlk SW15 . . . 156 B6
Hobb's Ct SE1 . . . 253 D2
Hobbs Gn N2 . . . 48 A6
Hobbs Mews IG3 . . . 79 D6
Hobbs' Pl N1 . . . 95 C6
Hobbs Rd 5 SE27 . . . 183 A6
Hobby St EN3 . . . 18 D6
Hobday St E14 . . . 97 D1
Hobhouse Ct SW1 . . 249 D5
Hobill Wlk KT5 . . . 198 B3
Hoblands End BR7 . . . 189 C4
Hobsons Pl 7 E1 . . . 96 A2
Hobury St
SW10 . . . 136 B6 266 C5
Hockenden La BR5,
BR8 . . . 191 D1
Hocker St 41 E2 . . . 95 D4
Hockett Cl SE8 . . . 119 B2
Hockington Ct 7
EN5 . . . 13 D6
Hockley Ave E6 . . . 100 A5
Hockley Ct 2 E18 . . . 37 A2
Hockley Ho 4 E9 . . . 74 C2
Hockley Mews IG11 . . 101 C5
Hockliffe Ho 5 W10 . . 90 C2
Hockney Ct 1 SE16 . . 118 B1
Hockworth Ho 7
N16 . . . 51 C1
Hocroft Ave NW2 . . . 69 B5
Hocroft Ct NW2 . . . 69 B5
Hocroft Rd NW2 . . . 69 B5
Hocroft Wlk NW2 . . . 69 B5
Hodder Dr UB6 . . . 86 D5
Hoddesdon Rd DA17 . 125 C1
Hodford Lo NW11 . . . 69 C6
Hodford Rd NW11 . . . 47 B1
Hodgkins Cl SE28 . . . 124 D6
Hodgkins Mews HA7 . . 25 B5
Hodister Cl 28 SE5 . . . 139 A5
Hodnet Gr SE16 . . . 118 C2
Hodson Cl HA2 . . . 63 B5
Hodson Pl EN3 . . . 7 C5
Hoecroft Ct EN3 . . . 6 C5
Hoe La EN1 . . . 6 B5
Hoe St E17 . . . 53 C4
Hoffman Gdns CR2 . . 222 B1
Hoffman Sq N1 . . . 235 D2
Hofland Rd
W14 . . . 113 A3 254 A6
Hogan Mews W2 . . . 236 C4
Hogan Way E5 . . . 74 A6
Hogarth Ave TW15 . . . 171 A4
Hogarth Bsns Pk
W4 . . . 133 C6
Hogarth Cl Ealing W5 . . 88 A2
Newham E16 . . . 99 D2
Hogarth Cres
Mitcham SW19 . . . 180 B2
Thornton Heath CR0 . . 205 A2
Hogarth Ct
8 Camden Town
NW1 . . . 71 C1
City of London EC3 . . . 253 B6
Hogarth Ct *continued*
Dulwich SE19 . . . 183 D6
Heston TW5 . . . 129 A5
24 Whitechapel E1 . . . 96 A1
Hogarth Gdns TW5 . . 129 C5
Hogarth Hill NW11 . . . 47 B5
Hogarth Ho
Enfield EN1 . . . 18 A6
12 Northolt UB5 . . . 84 D5
1 Sutton SM1 . . . 218 B3
Westminster SW1 . . . 259 D3
6 West Norwood
SE27 . . . 183 A6
Hogarth Ind Est
NW10 . . . 90 A3
Hogarth La W4 . . . 133 C6
Hogarth Pl SW5 . . . 255 C3
Hogarth Rd
Barking RM8 . . . 80 B3
Earl's Ct
SW5 . . . 113 D2 255 C3
Edgware HA8 . . . 26 C1
Hogarth Roundabout
W4 . . . 133 C6
Hogarth's House★
W4 . . . 133 C6
Hogarth Way TW12 . . 174 A2
Hogsmill Way KT19 . . 215 A4
Holbeach Cl 8 NW9 . . 27 C2
Holbeach Gdns
DA15 . . . 167 D5
Holbeach Mews 1
SW12 . . . 159 B3
Holbeach Prim Sch
SE6 . . . 163 C4
Holbeach Rd SE6 . . . 163 D4
Holbeck Row SE15 . . . 140 A5
Holbein Ho
Chelsea SW1 . . . 258 A2
10 Stanmore HA7 . . . 25 C5
Holbein Mews
SW1 . . . 115 A1 258 A2
Holbein Pl
SW1 . . . 115 A2 258 A3
Holberry Ho 5
SE21 . . . 183 C6
Holberton Gdns
NW10 . . . 90 B4
HOLBORN . . . 94 C2
Holborn EC1 . . . 94 C2 241 B3
Holborn Cir
EC1 . . . 94 C2 241 B3
Holborn Coll SE18 . . 121 D2
Holborn Ho 1 W12 . . . 90 B1
Holborn Pl WC1 . . . 240 C3
Holborn Rd E13 . . . 99 B3
Holborn Sta
WC1 . . . 94 B2 240 C3
Holborn Viaduct
EC1 . . . 94 D2 241 C3
Holborn Way CR4 . . . 180 D1
Holbrook Cl Enfield EN1 . 6 A5
Highgate N19 . . . 49 B1
Holbrook Ct W7 . . . 108 C6
Holbrooke Ct N7 . . . 72 A4
Holbrooke Pl 25
TW10 . . . 153 D6
Holbrook Ho
Acton W3 . . . 89 B2
Chislehurst BR7 . . . 189 B2
5 Streatham SW2 . . . 160 B3
Holbrook La BR7 . . . 189 B3
Holbrook Rd E15 . . . 98 D5
Holbrook Way BR2 . . . 210 B4
Holburne Cl SE3 . . . 143 C4
Holburne Gdns SE3 . 143 D4
Holburne Rd SE3 . . . 143 D4
Holcombe Hill NW7 . . . 12 A1
Holcombe Ho SW9 . . . 138 A2
Holcombe Pl SE4 . . . 141 A2
Holcombe Rd
Ilford IG1 . . . 56 C2
Tottenham Hale N17 . . . 52 A6
1 Tottenham N17 . . . 51 D6
Holcombe St W6 . . . 112 B2
Holcote Cl DA17 . . . 125 A3
Holcroft Ct W1 . . . 239 A4
Holcroft Ho
Battersea SW11 . . . 136 B2
Lewisham SE10 . . . 142 A4
Holcroft Rd E9 . . . 74 C1
Holden Ave
North Finchley N12 . . . 29 D5
Welsh Harp NW9 . . . 45 A1
Holdenby Rd SE4 . . . 163 A6
Holden Cl RM8 . . . 80 B5
Holden Ho
12 Deptford SE8 . . . 141 C5
Islington N1 . . . 235 A5
Holden Hts N12 . . . 13 D1
Holdenhurst Ave N12 . 30 A3
Holden Lo N11 . . . 31 C5
Holden Point E15 . . . 76 B2
Holden Rd
East Barnet N11 . . . 15 B1
London N12 . . . 29 D6
Holden St SW11 . . . 137 A3
Holdernesse Rd
Isleworth TW7 . . . 131 A4
6 Upper Tooting
SW17 . . . 159 A2
Holderness Ho SE5 . . 139 C2
Holderness Way
SE27 . . . 182 D5
Holders Hill Ave NW4 . 46 D6
Holders Hill Cres
NW4 . . . 28 D1
Holders Hill Dr NW4 . . 28 D1
Holders Hill Gdns
NW4 . . . 29 A1
Holders Hill Par NW7 . 29 A2
Holders Hill Rd
Church End NW4,
NW7 . . . 29 A2
Hendon NW4 . . . 28 D1
Holdsworth Ho 5
SW2 . . . 160 C4
Holford Ho
6 Bermondsey
SE16 . . . 118 B2
Finsbury WC1 . . . 233 D2
Holford Pl WC1 . . . 233 D2
Holford Rd NW3 . . . 70 A5
Holford St WC1 . . . 234 A2
Holford Yd WC1 . . . 234 A3
Holgate Ave SW11 . . . 136 B2
Holgate Ct HA8 . . . 26 B6
Holgate Gdns RM10 . . . 81 C2
Holgate Rd RM10 . . . 81 C3
Holgate St SE7 . . . 121 D3
Holkham Ho 6 EN5 . . . 1 A2
Hollam Ho N8 . . . 50 B5
Holland Ave
Belmont SM2 . . . 217 C1
Wimbledon SW20 . . . 177 D2
Holland Cl
Coney Hall BR2 . . . 224 D6
New Barnet EN5 . . . 14 B4
Stanmore HA7 . . . 25 B5
Holland Ct
Ashford TW15 . . . 170 B4
Hendon NW7 . . . 28 A4
6 Walthamstow E17 . . . 54 A5
Holland Dr SE23 . . . 163 A1
Holland Gdns
Brentford TW8 . . . 132 A6
Kensington W14 . . . 254 B6
Holland Gr SW9 . . . 138 C5
Holland Ho E4 . . . 36 A6
Holland House Sch
HA8 . . . 26 D6
Holland Park
W11 . . . 113 B5 244 C3
Holland Park Ave
Ilford IG3 . . . 57 D4
Notting Hill
W11 . . . 113 A5 244 B3
Holland Park Ct W14 244 B2
Holland Park Gdns
W14 . . . 113 A4 244 A2
Holland Park Mews
W11 . . . 113 B5 244 C3
Holland Park Pre Prep
Sch W14 . . . 113 B3 254 C5
Holland Park Rd
W14 . . . 113 B3 254 D5
Holland Park Rdbt
W12 . . . 112 D4
Holland Park Sch
W8 . . . 113 B4 244 D2
Holland Park Sta
W11 . . . 113 B5 244 C3
Holland Pas N1 . . . 235 A6
Holland Pl W8 . . . 245 C2
Holland Rd
Croydon SE25 . . . 206 A4
Newham E15 . . . 98 C4
Wallend E6 . . . 78 C1
Wembley HA0 . . . 65 D2
West Kensington
W14 . . . 113 A3 254 B6
Willesden Green NW10 90 B5

Holland Rise Ho SW9 270 D3
Holland St
Kensington W8 113 C4 245 B2
Lambeth SE1 116 D5 251 D4
Hollands The
Feltham TW13 172 D6
New Malden KT4 199 D1
Holland Villas Rd W14 113 A4 244 A1
Holland Way BR2 224 D6
Holland Wlk
Kensington W14 113 B4 244 D1
Stanmore HA7 25 A5
Upper Holloway N19 49 D1
Hollar Rd N16 73 D5
Hollen St W1 239 C2
Holles Cl TW12 173 C5
Holles Ho 8 SW9 138 C3
Holles St W1 93 B1 238 D2
Holley Rd W3 111 C4
Hollickwood Ave N12 30 D4
Hollickwood JMI Sch N10 31 B3
Holliday Sq 6 SW11 136 B2
Hollidge Way RM10 81 D1
Hollies Ave DA15 167 D3
Hollies Cl
South Norwood SW16 182 C4
Twickenham TW1 152 D2
Hollies End NW7 28 B5
Hollies Rd W5 109 C2
Hollies The
Harrow HA3 43 A5
Oakleigh Pk N20 14 B3
Upper Tooting SW12 159 C2
9 Wanstead E11 55 A4
Wood Green N11 31 D4
Hollies Way 1 SW12 159 A4
Holligrave Rd BR1 187 A2
Hollingbourne Ave DA7 147 B4
Hollingbourne Gdns W13 87 B2
Hollingbourne Rd SE24 161 A6
Hollingsworth Ct 7 KT6 197 D2
Hollingsworth Rd CR0 222 B2
Hollington Cres KT3 199 D3
Hollington Ct BR7 188 D4
Hollington Rd
Newham E6 100 B4
Tottenham N17 34 A1
Hollingworth Cl KT8 195 B5
Hollingworth Rd BR2, BR5 210 D2
Hollins Ho N7 72 A4
Hollisfield WC1 233 B1
Hollman Gdns SW16 182 D4
Holloway Cl UB7 104 A1
Holloway La UB7 104 B1
Holloway Rd
Leyton E11 76 B5
Lower Holloway N7 72 B4
Newham E6 100 B4
Upper Holloway N19 71 D6
Holloway Road Sta N7 72 B3
Holloway Sch N7 71 D3
Holloway St TW3 129 D2
Hollow Combe SE20 184 B6
Hollowfield Wlk UB5 63 A2
Hollow The IG8 36 D6
Holly Ave London N2 47 D6
Stanmore HA7 26 A1
Walton-on-T KT12 194 D1
Hollybank Cl TW12 173 C5
Holly Berry La 8 NW3 70 A4
Hollybrake Cl BR7 189 B3
Hollybush Cl
Harrow HA3 24 C2
Wanstead E11 55 A4
Hollybush Gdns E2 96 B4
Hollybush Hill E11 54 D3
Holly Bush Hill 4 NW3 70 A4
Hollybush Ho 23 E2 96 B4
Holly Bush La TW12 173 C3
Hollybush Pl E2 96 B4
Hollybush Rd KT2 176 A4
Hollybush St E13 99 B4
Holly Bush Steps 6 NW3 70 A4
Holly Bush Vale 10 NW3 70 A4
Holly Cl
Beckenham BR3 208 A5
Buckhurst Hill IG9 21 D1
Feltham TW13 173 A5
Wallington SM6 219 B1
Willesden NW10 67 C1
Holly Cottage Mews UB8 82 C2
Holly Cotts KT7 197 A1
Holly Cres
Beckenham BR3 207 B4
Chingford IG8 36 B3
Hollycroft Ave
Child's Hill NW3 69 C5
Wembley HA9 66 B5
Hollycroft Cl
Harmondsworth UB7 126 C6
South Croydon CR2 221 C3
Hollycroft Gdns UB7 126 C6
Holly Ct
16 Belmont SM2 217 C1
Catford SE6 164 A1
4 Sidcup DA14 190 B6
South Tottenham N15 51 C5
Hollydale Cl UB5 63 D4
Hollydale Dr BR2 226 B5
Hollydale Prim Sch 7 SE15 140 C3
Hollydale Rd SE15 140 C3
Hollydene
Bromley BR1 186 D2
Hither Green SE13 164 B5
5 Peckham SE15 140 B4
Hollydown Way E11 76 B5
Holly Dr E4 19 D4
Holly Farm Rd UB2 107 A1
Hollyfield Ave N11 30 D5
Hollyfield Rd KT5 198 B2
Hollyfield Sch & Sixth Form Ctr The KT6 198 A4
Holly Gdns UB7 104 B4
Holly Gr
Kingsbury NW9 45 A2
Peckham SE15 140 A3
Pinner HA5 23 A2
Hollygrove WD23 8 B4
Hollygrove Cl TW3 129 B1
Hollyhedge Ho SE3 142 B3
Holly Hedge Terr SE13 164 B6
Holly Hill
Hampstead NW3 70 A4
Southgate N21 16 B5
Holly Hill Rd DA8, DA17 125 D1
Holly Ho
Brentford TW8 131 C6
Ilford IG3 58 A1
Holly House (Private) Hospl IG9 21 B2
Holly Lo
Cottenham Pk SW20 178 B1
Harrow HA1 42 B4
Kensington W8 245 A2
Southgate N21 16 C3
4 Wimbledon SW19 179 A4
Holly Lodge
Lewisham SE13 142 B1
Southall UB2 107 B2
Holly Lodge Gdns N6 49 A1
Holly Lodge Mans N6 71 A6
Hollymead SM5 218 D5
Holly Mews SW10 256 B1
Holly Mount NW3 70 A4
Hollymount Cl 9 SE10 142 A4
Hollymount Sch SW20 178 C2
Holly Park Est N4 50 B2
Holly Park Gdns N3 47 C6
Holly Park JMI Sch N11 31 A5
Holly Park Rd
Ealing W7 108 D5
Friern Barnet N11 31 A5
Holly Pk
East Finchley N3 47 C6
Hornsey N4 50 B2
Holly Pl NW3 70 A4
Holly Rd
6 Chiswick W4 111 B2
Hampton TW12 174 A4
Hounslow TW3 129 D1
Leytonstone E11 54 D2
Twickenham TW1 153 A3
Holly St E8 73 D1
Holly Terr N6 49 A1
Hollytree Cl SW19 156 D3
Holly Tree Ho SE4 141 B2
Holly Tree Lo EN2 4 D3
Hollyview Cl NW4 46 A3
Holly Village N6 71 B6
Holly Way CR4 203 D6
Holly Wlk Enfield EN2 5 B2
Hampstead NW3 70 A4
Hollywood Ct W5 110 B6
Hollywood Gdns UB4 84 B1
Hollywood Lofts E1 243 C5
Hollywood Mews SW10 266 A6
Hollywood Rd
Chelsea SW10 136 A6 266 A6
Highams Pk E4 35 A5
Hollywood Way IG8 36 B4
Holman Ho 2 E2 96 D4
Holman Hunt Ho W14 254 A1
Holman Rd
London SW11 136 B3
West Ewell KT19 215 A3
Holmbank Dr TW17 193 C5
Holmbridge Gdns EN3 6 D1
Holmbrook NW1 232 B3
Holmbrook Dr NW4 46 D4
Holmbury Cl WD23 8 C2
Holmbury Ct
Mitcham SW19 180 C3
Upper Tooting SW17 158 D1
Holmbury Gdns UB3 105 D5
Holmbury Gr CR0 223 B1
Holmbury Ho SW9 160 D6
Holmbury Manor 9 DA14 190 A6
Holmbury Pk BR7 188 A3
Holmbury View 2 E5 52 B1
Holmbush Ct NW4 46 D4
Holmbush Rd SW15 157 A5
Holmcote Gdns N5 73 A3
Holmcroft Ho 10 E17 53 D5
Holmcroft Way BR2 210 B4
Holm Ct SE12 165 B1
Holmdale Gdns NW4 46 D4
Holmdale Rd
Chislehurst BR7 189 A5
South Hampstead NW6 69 C3
Holmdale Terr N15 51 C3
Holmdene N12 29 D5
Holmdene Ave
Harrow HA2 41 D6
Hendon NW7 28 A4
Herne Hill SE24 161 A6
Holmdene Cl BR3 186 A1
Holmdene Ct BR1 210 A6
Holmead Rd SW6 135 D5 265 D3
Holme Ct 12 TW7 131 A2
Holmefield Ct 4 NW3 70 C2
Holmefield Ho W10 91 A3
Holme Lacey Rd SE12 164 D5
Holmeleigh Ct EN3 6 C1
Holme Rd E6 100 A6
Holmes Ave
Mill Hill NW7 29 A5
Walthamstow E17 53 B6
Holmes Cl SE22 140 A1
Holmes Ct
Chingford E4 20 B2
18 South Acton W4 111 A3
18 South Lambeth SW4 138 A3
Holmesdale Ave SW14 132 D1
Holmesdale Cl SE25 205 D6
Holmesdale Ho 12 NW6 91 C6
Holmesdale Rd
Bexley DA7 146 D3
Highgate N6 49 B2
Richmond TW9 132 B4
South Norwood SE25 205 C5
Teddington TW11 175 C4
Holmesdale Rd *continued*
Thornton Heath CR0 205 B4
Holmesley Rd SE23 163 A5
Holmes Pl SW10 266 B6
Holmes Rd
Kentish Town NW5 71 B3
Merton SW19 180 A3
Twickenham TW1 152 D2
Holmes Terr SE1 251 A2
Holmeswood 1 SM2 217 D1
Holmeswood Ct 3 N22 32 C1
Holme Way HA7 24 D4
Holmewood Gdns SW2 160 B4
Holmewood Rd
South Norwood SE25 205 C6
Streatham SW2 160 B4
Holmfield Ave NW4 46 D4
Holmfield Ho E17 54 B5
Holm Gr UB10 60 C1
Holmhurst
London SE13 164 B5
Wimbledon SW19 178 C3
Holmhurst Rd DA17 125 D1
Holmlea Ct CR0 221 B4
Holmleigh Prim Sch N16 51 C1
Holmleigh Rd N16 51 C1
Holm Oak Cl SW15 157 B5
Holmoaks Ho BR3 186 A1
Holmsbury Ho 6 N7 71 D3
Holmsdale Ho
6 London N11 31 B6
24 Poplar E14 119 D6
Holmshaw Cl SE26 185 A6
Holmside Ct SW12 159 A5
Holmside Rd SW12 159 A5
Holmsley Cl KT3 199 D2
Holmsley Ho SW15 155 D4
Holmstall Ave HA8 27 A1
Holmstall Par HA8 27 A1
Holm Wlk SE3 143 A3
Holmwood 2 KT5 198 B3
Holmwood Cl
Cheam SM2 216 D1
Harrow HA2 42 A6
Northolt UB5 63 D2
Holmwood Ct
Kingston u T KT3 199 B6
Sidcup DA14 189 D5
3 Stamford Hill N16 51 D2
Holmwood Gdns
London N3 29 C1
Wallington SM6 219 B2
Holmwood Gr NW7 27 B5
Holmwood Mans W3 110 C5
Holmwood Rd
Chessington KT9 214 A3
Ilford IG3 79 C6
Holne Chase
London N2 48 A3
Morden SM4 201 C3
Holne Lo N6 49 C3
Holness Rd E15 76 D2
Holocaust Meml Gdn* W2 114 D4 247 D2
Holroyd Rd SW15 156 C6
Holsgrove Ct W3 111 C5
Holstein Way 6 DA18 125 A3
Holst Mans SW13 134 C5
Holstock Rd IG1 79 A6
Holsworth Cl HA2 42 A4
Holsworthy Ho 49 E3 97 D4
Holsworthy Sq WC1 240 D5
Holsworthy Way KT9 213 C3
Holt Cl London N10 49 A5
Sidcup DA14 191 A6
Woolwich SE28 124 C6
Holt Ct SE10 142 A6
Holt Ho SW2 160 C5
Holtoake Ct 1 W5 87 C3
Holtoake Ho 3 W5 87 C3
Holton St E1 96 D3
Holt Rd Newham E16 122 A5
Wembley HA0 65 C5
Holt The
Morden SM4 201 C5
Wallington SM6 219 C4
Holtwhite Ave EN2 5 A3
Holtwhite's Hill EN2 4 D4
Holwell Pl HA5 41 A5
Holwood Park Ave BR2, BR6 226 B4
Holwood Pl 7 SW4 137 D1
Holybourne Ave SW15 156 A4
Holy Cross Prep Sch KT2 177 A3
Holy Cross Prim Sch SW6 135 C4 265 A2
Holy Cross RC Prim Sch SE6 164 A3
Holy Cross Sch The 4 KT3 199 C4
Holy Family RC Prim Sch
Kidbrooke SE9 143 C1
23 Poplar E14 119 C6
Holy Family Tech Coll E17 54 A5
Holy Ghost RC Prim Sch 4 SW12 159 A4
Holyhead Cl Bow E3 97 C4
3 Newham E6 100 B2
Holyhead Ct KT1 197 D5
Holy Innocents RC Prim Sch BR6 227 D5
Holyoake Ct SE16 119 B4
Holyoake Wlk
Ealing W5 87 C3
East Finchley N2 48 A6
Holyoak Rd SE11 116 D2 261 D3
Holyport Rd SW6 134 D5
Holyrood Ave HA2 63 B4
Holyrood Gdns HA8 26 D1
Holyrood Ho N4 51 A1
Holyrood Mews
6 Greenwich SE7 121 A1
10 Newham E16 121 A5
Holyrood Rd EN5 14 B5
Holyrood St SE1 117 C5 253 A3
Holy Trinity CE Jun Sch 1 SM6 219 C4
Holy Trinity CE Prim Sch
Belgravia SW1 115 A2 258 A4
Dalston E8 73 D2
East Finchley N2 48 B6
10 Forest Hill SE26 162 C2
10 Hampstead NW3 70 A2
Richmond TW10 132 C1
Streatham SW2 160 B4
Wimbledon SW19 179 D4
Holy Trinity Coll Prep Sch BR1 187 C2
Holy Trinity Lamorbey CE Prim Sch DA15 168 A3
Holy Trinity & Saint Silas CE Prim Sch 22 NW1 71 B1
Holywell Cl
35 Bermondsey SE16 118 B1
2 Greenwich SE3 143 A6
Stanwell TW19 148 A3
Holywell La EC2 243 B6
Holywell Lo EN2 4 B5
Holywell Row EC2 95 C3 243 A5
Holywell Way TW19 148 A3
Homan Ct N12 30 A6
Homan Ho 6 SW4 159 D4
Homebush Ho E4 19 D4
Homecedars Ho WD23 8 B3
Homecherry Ho 3 IG10 21 D6
Home Cl
Carshalton SM5 218 D6
Northolt UB5 85 B4
Homecoppice Ho 1 BR1 186 D3
Homecroft Rd
Forest Hill SE26 184 C5
Tottenham N22 33 A2
Homecross Ho 7 W4 111 B2
Home Ct KT6 197 D4
Homedale Ho SM1 217 D4

Home Farm Cl
Thames Ditton KT7... 196 D2
Upper Halliford TW17 193 C5
Home Farm Cotts
BR5... 190 D2
Homefarm Rd W7... 86 D1
Homefield SM4... 201 C5
Home Field EN5... 13 B6
Homefield Ave IG2... 57 C4
Homefield Cl
Hayes UB4... 84 D3
Willesden NW10... 67 A2
Homefield Ct NW4... 46 C5
Homefield Gdns
London N2... 48 B6
Mitcham CR4, SW19.. 180 B1
Homefield Ho SE23.. 162 D1
Homefield Pk SM1, SM2... 217 D2
Homefield Pl 4 SW19... 178 D5
Homefield Prep Sch SM1... 217 C3
Homefield Rd
Bromley BR1... 187 C2
Burnt Oak HA8... 27 B4
Chiswick W4... 111 D1
Walton-on-T KT12... 195 A2
Wembley HA0... 65 B4
Wimbledon SW19... 179 A4
Homefield St 14 N1... 95 C5
Homefirs Ho HA9... 66 B5
Homeheather Ho 5 IG4... 56 B4
Homelands Dr SE19.. 183 C3
Home Lea BR6... 227 D3
Homeleigh Ct 8 SW16... 160 A1
Homeleigh Rd SE15.. 162 D6
Homemead SW12... 159 B2
Home Mead HA7... 25 C2
Homemead Rd
Bromley BR2... 210 B4
Wallington CR0... 203 C3
Home Office SW1... 259 D5
Home Park Rd SW19... 157 B1
Home Park Terr KT1... 175 D1
Home Park Wlk KT1. 197 D5
Home Rd SW11... 136 C3
Homer Dr E14... 119 C2
Homer Rd
Croydon CR0... 206 D3
Homerton E9... 75 A2
Homer Row W1... 237 B3
Homersham Rd KT1. 176 D1
Homer St W1... 92 C2 237 B3
HOMERTON... 74 D1
Homerton Ct 2 EN4.. 14 D3
Homerton Gr E9... 74 D3
Homerton High St E9. 74 D3
Homerton Rd E9... 75 B3
Homerton Row E9... 74 C3
Homerton Sta E9... 74 D2
Homerton Terr E9... 74 C2
Homerton University Hospl E9... 74 D3
Homesdale Cl E11... 55 A4
Homesdale Rd
Bromley BR1, BR2... 209 C6
Orpington BR5... 211 C2
Homesfield NW11... 47 C4
Homes Of Rest (CE Temperance Society) IG1... 79 B5
Homestall Rd SE22... 162 C6
Homestead Ct EN5... 13 C6
Homestead Gdns KT10... 212 C3
Homestead Paddock N14... 15 B6
Homestead Pk NW2... 67 D5
Homestead Rd
Dagenham RM8... 81 B6
Fulham SW6. 135 B5 264 D3
Homesteads The BR3... 185 D4
Homestead The N11.. 31 B6
Homewalk Ho 1 SE26... 184 C6
Homewaters Ave TW16... 171 D2
Homewillow Cl N21... 16 D5
Homewood Cl TW12. 173 B4
Homewood Cres BR7... 189 C4
Homewood Gdns SE25... 205 C4
Homewoods 2 SW12... 159 C4
Homildon Ho 10 SE26... 162 A1
Homington Ct KT2... 176 A3
Honduras St EC1... 242 A6
Honeybourne Rd NW6... 69 D3
Honeybourne Way BR5... 211 B1
Honeybrook Rd SW12, SW4... 159 C4
Honey Cl RM10... 81 D2
Honeycroft Hill UB10.. 60 A1
Honeyden Rd DA14... 191 A4
Honeyfield N4... 72 C6
Honey Hill UB10... 60 B1
Honey La EC2... 242 B1
Honey Lane Ho SW10... 265 D6
Honeyman Cl NW6... 68 D1
Honeypot Bsns Ctr HA7... 26 A2
Honeypot Cl NW9... 44 B5
Honeypot La
Stanmore HA3, HA7, NW9... 44 B6
Stanmore HA7... 25 D3
Honeysett Rd 3 N17.. 33 D1
Honeysuckle Cl UB1. 107 A6
Honeysuckle Ct
Ilford IG1... 78 D2
2 Lee SE12... 165 A4
6 Sutton SM2... 217 D2
Honeysuckle Gdns CR0... 206 D1
Honeywell Jun & Inf Schs 3 SW11... 158 D5
Honeywell Rd SW11. 158 D5
Honeywood Ho 5 SE15... 140 A4
Honeywood Mus★ SM5... 218 D4
Honeywood Rd
Harlesden NW10... 89 D5
Isleworth TW7... 131 A1
Honeywood Wlk SM5... 218 D4
Honister Cl HA7... 25 B2
Honister Gdns HA7... 25 B2
Honister Pl HA7... 25 B2
Honiton Gdns
Edgware NW7... 28 D3
1 Nunhead SE15... 140 C3
Honiton Ho 29 SE5... 139 A3
Honiton Rd
Bexley DA16... 145 D3
Kilburn NW6... 91 B5
Honley Rd SE6... 163 D4
Honnor Gdns TW7... 130 B3
HONOR OAK... 162 C6
Honor Oak Park Sta SE23... 162 D5
Honor Oak Pk SE23.. 162 D5
Honor Oak Rd SE23.. 162 C4
Honor Oak Rise SE23... 162 C5
Honwell Ho 24 W2... 91 C2
Hood Ave
East Barnet N14... 15 B5
Mortlake SW14... 155 A6
Hood Cl CR0... 204 D1
Hoodcote Gdns N21.. 16 D4
Hood Ct N7... 72 B5
Hood Ho 17 SE5... 139 B5
Hood Lo E11... 77 B6
Hood Rd SW20... 177 D3
HOOK... 214 A4
Hook KT6... 214 A5
Hooke Ct SE10... 142 A4
Hooke Ho 32 E3... 97 A5
Hooker's Rd E17... 52 D6
Hook Farm Rd BR2.. 209 D4
Hookham Ct SW8... 269 C2
Hook Ho 9 SW27... 182 D5
Hooking Gn HA2... 41 D4
Hook La DA16... 146 A1
Hook Lane Prim Sch DA16... 146 A2
Hook Rd KT19, KT17.. 215 A1
Hook Rise N
Surbiton KT6... 214 A5
Tolworth KT6... 214 D6
Hook Rise S KT6, KT9... 214 D6
Hook Rise S Ind Est KT6... 214 C5
Hook Rise South KT6... 214 A5
Hook Rise South Ind Pk KT6... 214 C5
Hooks Cl SE15... 140 B4
Hookstone Way IG8... 37 D3
Hook The EN5... 14 B5
Hook Underpass KT6... 214 A5
Hook Wlk HA8... 27 A4
Hooper Dr UB8... 82 D2
Hooper Ho 9 SW18.. 157 B6
Hooper Rd E16... 99 A1
Hooper's Ct SW1... 247 C1
Hooper's Mews 4 W3... 111 A5
Hooper St E1... 96 A1
Hoop La NW11... 47 C2
Hoover Ho 5 SE6... 186 A6
Hope Cl
2 Brentford TW8... 110 A1
Canonbury N1... 73 A2
Dagenham RM6... 58 D5
Grove Pk SE12... 165 B1
Sutton SM1... 218 A3
1 Woodford IG8... 37 C4
Hope Ct 1 SE1... 118 A1
Hopedale Rd SE7... 143 B6
Hopefield 3 W7... 108 D5
Hopefield Ave NW6... 91 A5
Hope Gdns 10 W3... 110 D4
Hope Pk BR1... 186 D3
Hopes Cl TW5... 129 C6
Hope St SW11... 136 B2
Hopetown St E1... 243 D3
Hopewell Sch IG11... 79 B2
Hopewell St SE5... 139 B5
Hop Gdns WC2... 250 A5
Hopgood St 5 W12.. 112 C5
Hopkins Cl N10... 31 A3
Hopkins Ho 17 E14... 97 C1
Hopkins Mews E15... 98 D6
Hopkinson Ho 1 SW11... 137 A3
Hopkinson's Pl NW1 231 A6
Hopkins Rd E10... 53 D2
Hopkins St W1... 93 D1 239 C1
Hopley Ho W13... 109 B6
Hoppers Rd N21... 16 C2
Hoppett Rd E4... 20 C2
Hopping La N1... 72 D2
Hoppingwood Ave KT3... 199 C6
Hoppner Rd UB4... 83 B5
Hop St SE10... 120 D2
Hopton Ct BR2... 209 A1
Hopton Gdns KT3... 200 A3
Hopton Ho 5 SW9... 138 D3
Hopton Par 2 SW16... 182 A5
Hopton Rd
Streatham SW16... 182 A5
Woolwich SE18... 122 D3
Hopton's Gdns SE1.. 251 D4
Hopton St SE1... 116 D5 251 D4
Hoptree Cl N12... 29 D6
Hopwood Cl SW17... 158 A1
Hopwood Rd SE17... 139 B6
Hopwood Wlk E8... 74 A1
Horace Rd
Forest Gate E7... 77 B4
Ilford IG6... 57 A6
Kingston u T KT1... 198 B6
Horatio Ho
13 Haggerston E2... 95 D5
4 Merton SW19... 179 D3
Horatio Pl
9 Canary Wharf E14... 120 A5
Merton SW19... 179 C2
Horatio St 11 E2... 95 D5
Horatius Way CR0... 220 B2
Horbury Cres W11... 113 C6 245 A5
Horbury Lo TW12... 173 C3
Horbury Mews W11... 113 B6 244 D5
Horder Rd SW6... 135 A4 264 B1
Hordle Prom E 15 SE15... 139 D5
Hordle Prom N 4 SE15... 139 D5
Hordle Prom S 7 SE15... 139 D5
Horizon Bldg 22 E14. 119 C6
Horizon Ind Est SE15... 140 A5
Horizon Sch N16... 73 C4
Horle Wlk SE5... 138 D3
Horley Cl DA6... 169 C6
Horley Rd SE9... 188 A6
Hormead Rd W9... 91 B3
Hornbeam Cl
Barking IG11... 102 B3
Buckhurst Hill IG9... 21 D1
Edgware NW7... 11 D1
Ilford IG1... 79 B3
Lambeth SE11... 261 A4
Northolt UB5... 63 B3
Hornbeam Cres TW8... 131 B5
Hornbeam Gdns KT3... 200 A3
Hornbeam Gr E4... 20 D1
Hornbeam Ho
1 Buckhurst Hill IG9... 21 D1
2 Maitland Pk NW3... 70 D2
6 Penge SE20... 184 D3
6 Sidcup DA15... 168 A1
Hornbeam La E4... 20 C6
Hornbeam Rd
Buckhurst Hill IG9... 21 D1
Hayes UB4... 84 C2
Hornbeam Sq 8 E3... 97 B6
Hornbeams Rise N11. 31 A4
Hornbeam Terr SM5. 202 C1
Hornbeam Way BR2. 210 C3
Hornblower Cl 2 SE16... 119 A2
Hornbuckle Cl HA2... 64 B6
Hornby Cl NW3... 70 B1
Hornby Ho
6 Kennington SE11... 138 C6
13 Richmond TW10... 153 C1
Horncastle Cl SE12.. 165 A4
Horncastle Rd SE12. 165 A4
Hornchurch N17... 33 B1
Hornchurch Cl KT2. 175 D6
Horndean Cl 3 SW15... 156 A3
Horne Ho 4 SE18... 144 A4
Horner Ct E11... 76 B5
Horne Rd TW17... 192 C5
Horner Hos 18 N1... 95 C6
Horner La 3 CR4... 180 B1
Horne Way SW15... 134 C3
Hornfair Rd SE7... 143 D5
Horniman Dr SE23... 162 C4
Horniman Grange 7 SE23... 162 C3
Horniman Mus & Gdns★ SE23... 162 B3
Horniman Prim Sch SE23... 162 B3
Horning Cl SE9... 188 A6
Horn La Acton W3... 89 A1
Greenwich SE10... 121 A2
Woodford IG8... 37 A3
Horn Link Way SE10. 121 A2
Horn Park Cl SE12... 165 B6
Horn Park La SE12... 165 B5
Horn Park Prim Sch SE12... 165 B4
Hornsby House Sch 7 SW12... 159 A3
Horns Croft IG11... 79 C1
Hornscroft Cl IG11... 79 C1
Horns End Pl HA5... 40 C4
HORNSEY... 50 A5
Hornsey La N6... 49 C2
Hornsey Lane Gdns N6... 49 C2
Hornsey Park Rd N8.. 50 B6
Hornsey Rd N7, N19... 72 B6
Hornsey Rise Gdns N19... 50 A2
Hornsey Sch for Girls N8... 50 B4
Hornsey St N7... 72 B3
Hornsey Sta N8... 50 B5
HORNSEY VALE... 50 B4
Hornshay St SE15... 140 C6
Horns Rd IG2, IG6... 57 A4
Hornton Ct W8... 245 B1
Hornton Pl W8... 245 B1
Hornton St W8... 113 C4 245 B2
Horrocks Ho SW15... 156 B6
Horsa Rd
Eltham SE12... 165 C4
Erith DA8... 147 D5
Horsebridge Cl RM9. 103 A6
Horsecroft Rd HA8... 27 B3
Horse & Dolphin Yd W1... 249 D6
Horse Fair KT1... 175 D1
Horseferry Pl SE10... 142 A6
Horseferry Rd
Limehouse E14... 119 A6
Westminster SW1... 115 D2 259 D4
Horseferry Rd Est SW1... 259 C5
Horse Guards Ave SW1... 116 A5 250 A3
Horse Guards Par★ SW1... 115 D5 249 D3
Horse Guards Rd SW1... 115 D4 249 D2
Horse Leaze E6... 100 C1
Horsell Rd
Islington N5... 72 C3
St Paul's Cray BR5... 190 B2
Horselydown La SE1... 117 D5 253 C3
Horselydown Mans SE1... 253 C2
Horsemongers Mews SE1... 252 B1
Horsenden Ave UB6... 64 D3
Horsenden Cres UB6.. 64 D3
Horsenden La N UB6.. 64 D1
Horsenden La S UB6.. 87 A6
Horsenden Prim Sch UB6... 64 C2
Horsendon Ho 11 N7.. 71 D3
Horseshoe Cl
Cubitt Town E14... 120 A1
Dollis Hill NW2... 68 B6
Horse Shoe Cres UB5. 85 C5
Horseshoe Dr UB8... 82 C1
Horse Shoe Gn SM1. 217 D6
Horseshoe La
Barnet N20... 12 D3
Enfield EN2... 5 A2
Horse Yd N1... 234 D6
Horsfeld Gdns 1 SE9... 166 A6
Horsfeld Rd SE9... 165 D6
Horsfield Ho 13 N1... 73 A1
Horsford Rd SW2... 160 B6
Horsham Ave N12... 30 C5
Horsham Ct N17... 34 A2
Horsham Rd
Bexley DA6... 169 C6
East Bedfont TW14... 149 A5
Horsley Ct SW1... 259 D3
Horsley Dr
Kingston u T KT2... 175 D5
New Addington CR0.. 224 A1
Horsley Ho 11 SE4... 140 D1
Horsley Rd
Bromley BR1... 187 B2
Chingford E4... 20 A2
Horsley St 3 SE17... 139 B6
Horsman Ho SE5... 139 A6
Horsman St SE5... 139 A6
Horsmonden Cl BR6 211 D2
Horsmonden Rd SE4... 163 B5
Horston Ho N4... 51 A2
Hortensia Ho SW10.. 266 A4
Hortensia Rd SW10... 136 A5 266 A4
Horticultural Pl 6 W4... 111 B1
Horton Ave NW2... 69 A4
Horton Bridge Rd UB7... 104 B5
Horton Cl UB7... 104 B5
Horton Ctry Pk KT19 214 C1
Horton Ho
13 Deptford SE15... 140 C6
South Lambeth SW8... 270 C4
West Kensington W14 254 A1
Horton Ind Pk UB7... 104 B5

Horton La KT19 215 A1
Horton Par UB7 104 A5
Horton Rd Hackney E8 74 B2
Yiewsley UB7 104 B5
Horton Road Ind Est UB7 104 B5
Horton St SE13 141 D2
Horton Way CR0 206 D4
Hortus Rd
Chingford E4 20 A2
Southall UB2 107 B4
Horwood Ho
24 Bethnal Green E2 96 B4
Marylebone NW8 237 B6
Hosack Rd SW12, SW17 159 A2
Hoser Ave SE12 165 A2
Hosier La EC1 94 D2 241 D3
Hoskins Cl UB3 105 D1
Hoskin's Cl E16 99 C1
Hoskins St SE10 120 B1
Hospital Bridge Rd TW2 151 D3
Hospital Bridge Rdbt TW2 151 D2
Hospital of the Holy Trinity (Almshouses) 5 CR0 221 A6
Hospital Rd
Hounslow TW3 129 C2
Leytonstone E10, E11 54 B4
Hospital Way SE13 164 B4
Hospl for Tropical Diseases NW1 93 C3 239 B5
Hospl of St John & St Elizabeth NW8 92 B5 229 C3
Hotham Cl KT8 195 C6
Hotham Prim Sch SW15 134 D1
Hotham Rd
Merton SW19 180 A3
Putney SW15 134 C2
Hotham Road Mews 12 SW19 180 A3
Hotham St E15 98 C6
Hothfield Pl SE16 118 C3
Hotspur Ind Est N17 34 B4
Hotspur Rd UB5 85 C5
Hotspur St SE11 116 C1 261 A2
Houblon Rd TW10 154 A6
Houghton Cl
10 Dalston E8 73 D2
Hampton TW12 173 A4
Houghton Rd N15 51 D5
Houghton Sq SW9 138 A2
Houghton St WC2 240 D1
Houlder Cres CR0 220 D2
Houndsden Rd N21 16 C5
Houndsditch EC3 95 C1 243 B2
Houndsfield Prim Sch N9 18 B4
Houndsfield Rd N9 18 B4
HOUNSLOW 129 C3
Hounslow Ave TW3 151 D6
Hounslow Bsns Pk TW3 129 D1
Hounslow Central Sta TW3 129 D2
Hounslow Ctr The TW3 129 D2
Hounslow East Sta TW3 130 A3
Hounslow Gdns TW3 151 D6
Hounslow Heath Jun & Inf Schs TW4 129 A2
Hounslow Heath Nature Reserve TW4 151 A5
Hounslow Manor Sch TW3 130 A2
Hounslow Rd
Feltham TW14 150 B4
Hanworth TW13 151 A2
Twickenham TW2, TW3 152 A5
Hounslow Sta TW3 151 D6
Hounslow Town Prim Sch TW3 130 B2
Hounslow Urban Farm* TN14 150 A6
HOUNSLOW WEST 128 D2
Hounslow West Sta TW3 129 A3
Household Cavalry Mus* SW1 250 A3
Houseman Way 20 SE5 139 B5
House Mill The* E3 98 A4
Houses of Parliament* SW1 116 A3 260 B6
Houston Ct 3 CR0 205 C1
Houston Pl KT10 196 C1
Houston Rd
Forest Hill SE23 163 A1
Thames Ditton KT6 197 B3
Houstoun Ct TW5 129 B5
Hove Ave E17 53 B4
Hoveden Rd NW2 69 A3
Hove Gdns SM1 201 D1
Hovenden Ho 6 SE21 183 C6
Hoveton Rd SE28 102 C1
Howard Ave DA5 168 C4
Howard Bldg SW8 268 C5
Howard Cl Acton W3 88 D1
Ashford TW16 171 D4
Brunswick Pk N11 15 A2
Bushey WD23 8 C4
Cricklewood NW2 69 A4
Hampton TW12 174 A4
Howard Ct
12 Barking IG11 101 B6
Beckenham BR3 186 A1
Lewisham SE10 142 A4
Peckham SE15 140 A2
Howard Ho
6 Brixton SW9 138 C2
14 Deptford SE8 141 B6
Fitzrovia W1 238 D5
Penge SE20 184 C2
6 Upper Clapton E5 74 C6
Howard Mans E17 53 D6
Howard Mews N5 72 D4
Howard Prim Sch CR0 221 A4
Howard Rd
Barking IG11 101 B6
Canonbury N16 73 B4
Cricklewood NW2 68 D4
Croydon SE25 206 A3
Ilford IG1 78 D4
Isleworth TW7 130 D2
Leyton E11 76 C5
Newham E6 100 B5
New Malden KT3 199 D5
Penge SE20 184 C2
Plaistow BR1 187 A3
Southall UB1 85 D1
South Tottenham N15 51 C3
Surbiton KT5 198 B3
Walthamstow E17 53 D6
Howards Cl HA5 22 B1
Howards Crest Cl BR3 186 A1
Howard's La SW15 134 C1
Howard's Rd E13 99 A4
Howard St KT7 197 B3
Howard Way EN5 12 D6
Howard Wlk N2 48 B5
Howarth Rd SE2 124 A2
Howberry Cl HA8 25 D4
Howberry Rd
South Norwood CR7 183 B1
Stanmore HA7, H8 25 D4
Howbury Rd SE15 140 C2
Howcroft Cres N3 29 C3
Howcroft Ho 3 E3 97 B4
Howcroft La UB6 86 B4
Howden Cl SE28 124 D6
Howden Ct SE25 183 D1
Howden Rd SE25 183 D1
Howden St SE15 140 A2
Howell Cl RM6 58 D4
Howell Ct 2 E10 53 D2
Howell Ho 5 N7 71 D3
Howell Wlk SE1 261 D3
Howe Lo TW1 153 A4
Howerd Way SE18 144 A4
Howes Cl N3 47 C6
Howeth Ct 7 N11 31 A4
Howfield Pl N17 51 D6
Howgate Rd SW14 133 B2
Howick Mans SE18 122 A3
Howick Pl SW1 115 C3 259 B5
Howie St SW11 136 C5 267 A3
Howitt Cl
6 Maitland Pk NW3 70 C2
Stoke Newington N16 73 C4
Howitt Rd NW3 70 C2
Howland Ho 9 SW16 160 A1
Howland Mews E W1 239 B4
Howland St W1 93 C2 239 B4
Howland Way SE16 119 A4
Howletts La HA4 39 A3
Howletts Rd SE24 161 A5
Howley Pl W2 92 A2 236 B4
Howley Rd CR0 221 A5
Howmic Ct 1 TW1 153 C5
Howsman Rd SW13 134 A6
Howson Rd SE4 141 A1
Howson Terr TW10 154 A5
How's St E2 95 D5
Howton Pl WD23 8 B3
HOXTON 95 C5
Hoxton Mkt 10 N1 95 C4
Hoxton Point EC1 95 C4
Hoxton Sq N1 95 C4
Hoxton St N1 95 C5
Hoxton Sta E2 95 D5
Hoylake Cres UB10 60 D6
Hoylake Gdns
Mitcham CR4 203 C6
Ruislip HA4 40 B1
South Oxhey WD19 22 D6
Hoylake Rd W3 89 C1
Hoyland Cl 4 SE15 140 B5
Hoyle Rd SW17 180 C5
Hoy St E16 98 D1
Hubbard Dr KT9 213 D2
Hubbard Rd SE27 183 A6
Hubbards Cl UB8 82 D1
Hubbard St E15 98 C6
Hub Buildings The 4 SW12 159 B3
Hub E15 E15 97 D5
Huberd Ho SE1 262 D6
Hubert Gr SW9 138 A2
Hubert Ho NW8 237 A5
Hubert Rd E6 99 D4
Hucknall Ct NW8 236 C6
Huddart St 6 E3 97 B2
Huddleston Cl E2 96 C5
Huddlestone Rd
Forest Gate E7 76 D4
Willesden NW2 68 B2
Huddleston Rd N7 71 C4
Hudson 27 NW9 27 D2
Hudson Cl
Newham E15 99 A6
15 Shepherd's Bush W12 112 B6
Hudson Ct
Croydon SE25 206 A5
1 Isle Of Dogs E14 119 C1
4 Merton SW19 179 D2
Hudson Ho
Chelsea SW10 266 A4
5 Notting Hill W11 91 A1
Hudson Pl SE18 123 A1
Hudson Rd Erith DA7 147 B4
Harlington UB7 127 B6
Hudsons Ho N1 235 D1
Hudson's Pl SW1 115 C2 259 A4
Hudson Way N9 18 C2
Huggin Ct EC4 252 B6
Huggin Hill EC4 252 B6
Huggins Ho 3 E3 97 C4
Huggins Pl SW2 160 B3
Hughan Rd E15 76 B3
Hugh Astor Ct SE1 261 D6
Hugh Clark Ho 13 W13 109 A5
Hugh Dalton Ave SW6 264 C5
Hughenden Ave HA3 43 B4
Hughenden Gdns UB5 84 C4
Hughenden Ho NW8 237 A6
Hughenden Rd KT4 200 A2
Hughendon EN5 1 D1
Hughendon Terr E15 76 A4
Hughes Cl N12 30 A5
Hughes Ho
26 Bethnal Green E2 96 C4
Camberwell SE5 139 A4
15 Deptford SE8 141 C6
Newington SE17 261 D3
Hughes Mans E1 96 A3
Hughes Rd
Ashford TW15 171 A4
Hayes UB3 106 B6
Hughes Terr 6 E16 98 D2
Hughes Wlk CR0 205 A2
Hugh Gaitskell Cl SW6 264 C5
Hugh Gaitskell Ho
Stoke Newington N16 73 D6
Willesden NW10 67 D1
Hugh Herland KT1 198 A6
Hugh Mews SW1 258 D3
Hugh Morgan Ho 5 SW4 137 D2
Hugh Myddelton Prim Sch EC1 94 C4 234 B1
Hugh Platt Ho 29 E2 96 B5
Hugh St SW1 115 B2 258 D3
Hugo Ho SW1 257 D6
Hugon Rd SW6 135 D2
Hugo Rd N19 71 C4
Huguenot Ct 9 E1 96 A2
Huguenot Pl
London SW18 158 A6
Spitalfields E1 243 D4
Huguenot Sq SE15 140 B2
Hullbridge Mews N1 235 C6
Hull Cl SE16 118 D5
Hull Ct SE5 139 B3
Hull Pl E16 123 A5
Hull St EC1 235 A1
Hulme Pl SE1 252 B1
Hulse Ave IG11 79 C2
Humber Ct W7 86 B1
Humber Dr W10 90 D3
Humber Rd
Dollis Hill NW2 68 B6
Greenwich SE3 142 D6
Humberstone Rd E13 99 C4
Humberton Cl E9 75 A3
Humber Trad Est NW2 68 B6
Humbolt Rd W6 135 A6 264 A5
Hume Ct N1 72 D1
Hume Ho 14 W11 112 D5
Humes Ave W7 108 D4
Hume Terr E16 99 B1
Hume Way HA4 40 A3
Humphrey Ct SW11 266 D1
Humphrey St SE1 117 D1 263 C2
Humphries Cl RM9 81 B4
Humphry Ho 10 SW15 156 D6
Hundred Acre NW9 27 D1
Hungerdown E4 20 A3
Hungerford Bridge WC2 250 C4
Hungerford Ho SW1 269 B6
Hungerford La WC2 250 B4
Hungerford Prim Sch 19 N7 71 D2
Hungerford Rd
12 Camden Town N7 71 D2
Lower Holloway N7 72 A3
Hungerford St 21 E1 96 B1
Hunsdon Cl RM9 81 A2
Hunsdon Ho E5 74 B5
Hunsdon Rd SE14 140 D5
Hunslett St 26 E2 96 C5
Hunstanton Ho NW1 237 B4
Hunston Rd SM4 201 D1
Hunt Cl W11 112 D5
Hunt Ct London N14 15 B4
10 Northolt UB5 84 D5
Hunter Cl
Borehamwood WD6 11 A6
Borough The SE1 262 D5
Upper Tooting SW12 159 A3
3 Wallington SM6 220 A1
Huntercombe-Roehampton Hospl The SW15 156 A4
Huntercrombe Gdns WD19 22 C5
Hunter Ct
8 London SE5 139 B1
27 Streatham SW2 160 C4
11 Wanstead E11 55 A4
Hunter Ho
Bloomsbury WC1 240 B6
Feltham TW14 150 A3
Lambeth SE1 251 D1
South Lambeth SW8 269 D3
Hunter Ho *continued*
1 Tufnell Pk N19 71 C5
West Brompton SW5 255 B1
Hunterian Mus* WC2 94 B1 240 D2
Hunter Lo 9 W9 91 C2
Hunter Rd
South Norwood CR7 205 B6
Wimbledon SW20 178 C2
Hunters Ct 5 TW9 153 D6
Hunters Gr
Harrow HA3 43 C5
Hayes UB3 106 A4
Hunter's Gr BR6 227 A4
Hunters Hall Prim Sch RM10 81 D3
Hunters Hall Rd RM10 81 C3
Hunters Hill HA4 62 D5
Hunters Lo
9 Edgware HA8 26 D5
10 Sidcup DA15 168 A1
Hunters Mdw SE19 183 C6
Hunters Rd
Chessington KT9 214 A4
Ilford IG1 78 D3
Hunters Sq RM10 81 C4
Hunter St WC1 94 A3 240 B6
Hunters The 2 BR3 186 A2
Hunters Way
Enfield EN2 4 C4
South Croydon CR0 221 C4
Hunter Wlk
Borehamwood WD6 11 B6
Newham E13 99 A5
Huntingdon Cl
Mitcham CR4, SW16 204 A5
Northolt UB5 63 C2
Huntingdon Ct
3 Barnet EN5 1 B2
Mortlake SW14 133 A2
Huntingdon Gdns
Chiswick W4 133 A5
North Cheam KT4 216 C5
Huntingdon Ho SW5 255 B4
Huntingdon Rd
East Finchley N2 48 C6
Edmonton N9 18 C3
Huntingdon St
Canning Town E16 98 D1
Islington N1 72 B1
Huntingfield CR0 223 B1
Huntingfield Rd SW15 156 A6
Huntingford Ho SW15 134 C3
Hunting Gate Cl EN2 4 C2
Hunting Gate Dr KT9 214 A1
Hunting Gate Mews
Sutton SM1 217 D5
Twickenham TW2 152 C3
Huntings Farm IG1 79 C6
Huntings Rd RM10 81 C2
Huntington Ho NW2 68 C2
Huntley Cl TW19 148 A4
Huntley Ho 7 SE21 183 C6
Huntley St WC1 93 D3 239 C5
Huntley Way SW20 178 A1
Huntly Dr N3 29 C4
Huntly Rd SE25 205 C5
Hunton St E1 96 A2
Hunt Rd UB2 107 C3
Hunts Cl SE3 143 A3
Hunt's Ct WC2 249 D5
Huntshaw Ho 37 E3 97 D4
Hunt's La E15 98 A5
Huntsmans Cl TW13 172 B6
Huntsman St SE17 263 A3
Hunts Mead EN3 6 D2
Hunts Medde Cl BR7 188 B3
Huntsmoor Rd KT19 215 B3
Huntspill St SW17 158 A1
Hunts Slip Rd SE21 161 C2
Huntsworth Ct SE6 163 C3
Huntsworth Mews NW1 92 D3 237 C5
Huon Ct N20 14 C2
Hurdwick Ho NW1 232 A4

- Hurdwick Pl NW1 232 A4
- Hurleston Ho 11 SE8 119 B1
- Hurley Cres SE16 118 D4
- Hurley Ct 1 W5 87 C1
- Hurley Ho
  - Lambeth SE11 261 B3
  - 34 Shoreditch E2 95 D4
- Hurley Lo SE22 162 C5
- Hurley Rd UB6 85 D2
- Hurlingham Bsns Pk SW6 135 C2
- Hurlingham & Chelsea Sec Sch SW6 135 C2
- Hurlingham Court Mans SW6 135 C3
- Hurlingham Ct SW6 135 B2
- Hurlingham Gdns SW6 135 B2
- Hurlingham Rd
  - Erith DA7 147 B5
  - Fulham SW6 135 B3
- Hurlingham Sch SW15 135 B1
- Hurlingham Sq SW6 135 D2
- Hurlock Ho 1 N5 72 D5
- Hurlock St N5 72 D5
- Hurlstone Rd SE25 205 C4
- Hurn Court Rd TW5 128 D3
- Hurn Ct TW5 128 D3
- Huron Cl 5 BR6 227 D2
- Huron Rd SW17 159 A1
- Huron Univ WC1 94 A2 240 A4
- Hurren Cl SE3 142 C2
- Hurricane Rd SM6 220 B1
- Hurricane Trad Ctr NW9 28 A2
- Hurry Cl E15 76 C1
- Hursley Ct 11 KT6 197 D2
- Hurst Ave
  - Chingford E4 19 C1
  - Highgate N6 49 C3
- Hurstbourne KT10 212 D2
- Hurstbourne Cotts DA5 169 D4
- Hurstbourne Gdns IG11 79 C2
- Hurstbourne Ho SW15 155 D5
- Hurstbourne Priors CR2 221 C2
- Hurstbourne Rd SE23 163 A3
- Hurst Cl
  - Chessington KT9 214 C3
  - Chingford E4 19 C1
  - Hampstead Garden Suburb NW11 47 D3
  - Hayes BR2 208 D1
  - Northolt UB5 63 B3
- Hurstcombe IG9 21 A2
- Hurstcourt Rd SM1 217 D6
- Hurst Ct
  - Beckenham BR3 185 C3
  - Newham E6 99 D2
  - South Norwood SE25 205 D5
  - Woodford IG8 37 B4
- Hurstdene Ave BR2 208 D1
- Hurstdene Gdns N15 51 C2
- Hurstfield BR2 209 A4
- Hurstfield Cres UB4 83 C2
- Hurstfield Rd KT8 195 C6
- Hurst Gr KT12 193 D1
- Hurst Ho
  - 7 Penge SE26 184 B5
  - Pentonville WC1 233 D3
  - West Heath SE2 124 D1
- Hurst La
  - East Molesey KT8 196 A6
  - West Heath SE2 124 D1
- Hurst Lo London N8 49 D3
  - Wembley HA0 66 B1
- Hurstmead Ct HA8 26 D6
- Hurstmere Foundation Sch DA15 168 C3
- HURST PARK 174 A1
- Hurst Park Prim Sch KT8 195 C6
- Hurst Pl Erith SE2 146 D6
  - Woolwich SE2 124 C1
- Hurst Pool The KT8 195 D6
- Hurst Prim Sch DA5 168 D3
- Hurst Rd
  - Buckhurst Hill IG9 21 D3
  - Croydon CR0 221 B3
  - East Molesey KT8, KT12 195 C6
  - Sidcup DA5, DA15 168 C3
  - Southgate N21 16 C3
  - Walthamstow E17 53 D6
  - Walton-on-T KT8&KT12 194 D5
- Hurst Rise EN5 1 C2
- Hurst Springs DA5 169 A3
- Hurst St SE24 160 D5
- Hurst View Grange CR2 220 D1
- Hurst View Rd CR2 221 C1
- Hurst Way CR2 221 C2
- Hurstway Wlk 2 W11 112 D6
- Hurstwood Ave
  - Sidcup DA5 169 A3
  - Wanstead E18 55 B5
- Hurstwood Ct
  - Colney Hatch N12 30 C4
  - Temple Fortune NW11 47 B5
- Hurstwood Dr BR1 210 B6
- Hurstwood Rd NW11 47 B5
- Hurtwood Rd KT12 195 B2
- Husbourne Ho 8 SE8 119 A2
- Huson Cl NW3 70 C1
- Hussain Cl HA1 64 D4
- Hussars Cl TW4 129 A2
- Husseywell Cres BR2 209 A1
- Hutching's St E14 119 C4
- Hutching's Wharf 11 E14 119 C4
- Hutchings Wlk NW11 47 D5
- Hutchins Cl E15 76 A1
- Hutchins Ho 8 SW4 159 D4
- Hutchinson Ct RM6 58 D5
- Hutchinson Ho 9 SE14 140 C5
- Hutchinson Terr HA9 65 D5
- Hutchins Rd SE28 124 A5
- Hutton Cl
  - Greenford UB6 64 B3
  - Woodford IG8 37 B4
- Hutton Ct
  - 1 Ealing W5 87 C2
  - Edmonton N9 18 C4
  - 4 Finsbury Pk N4 50 B1
- Hutton Gdns HA3 24 A3
- Hutton Gr N12 29 D5
- Hutton Ho 19 E2 96 A4
- Hutton La HA3 24 A3
- Hutton Row 4 HA8 27 A3
- Hutton St EC4 241 B1
- Hutton Wlk HA3 24 A3
- Huxbear St SE4 163 B6
- Huxley Cl UB5 85 A6
- Huxley Dr RM6 58 B2
- Huxley Gdns NW10 88 B5
- Huxley Ho
  - 4 London SW9 138 B3
  - Paddington NW8 236 D5
  - West Heath SE2 124 D1
- Huxley Par N18 33 B5
- Huxley Pl N13 16 D1
- Huxley Rd
  - Edmonton N18 33 C6
  - Falconwood DA16 145 D2
  - Leyton E10 76 A6
- Huxley Sayze N18 33 B5
- Huxley South N18 33 B5
- Huxley St W10 91 A4
- Hyacinth Cl
  - 3 Hampton TW12 173 C4
  - Ilford IG1 78 D2
- Hyacinth Ct 2 HA5 40 C6
- Hyacinth Dr UB10 60 A1
- Hyacinth Rd SW15 156 A3
- Hyde Cl
  - Ashford TW16 171 C4
  - Barnet EN5 1 B2
  - Newham E13 99 A5
- Hyde Cres NW9 45 C4
- Hyde Ct
  - Forest Hill SE23 163 A2
  - Hounslow TW4 151 B6
  - Kingsbury NW9 45 B2
  - Whetstone N20 14 B1
- Hyde Estate Rd NW9 45 D4
- Hyde Farm Mews SW12 159 D3
- Hydefield Cl N21 17 B3
- Hydefield Ct N9 17 C2
- Hyde Ho
  - 12 Ealing W13 109 A5
  - Hounslow TW3 130 A2
- Hyde Ind Est The NW9 45 D4
- Hyde La SW11 136 C4 267 A2
- Hyde Park★ W2 114 D5 247 C3
- Hyde Park Ave N21 17 B3
- Hyde Park Cnr SW1 248 B2
- Hyde Park Corner Sta SW1 115 A4 248 B2
- Hyde Park Cres W2 92 C1 237 A1
- Hyde Park Gate Mews SW7 246 B1
- Hyde Park Gdns
  - Bayswater W2 114 B6 246 D6
  - Edmonton N21 17 A3
- Hyde Park Gdns Mews W2 114 C6 247 A6
- Hyde Park Mans NW1 237 A3
- Hyde Park Pl W2 247 B6
- Hyde Park Sq W2 92 C1 237 A1
- Hyde Park Square Mews W2 237 A1
- Hyde Park St W2 92 C1 237 A1
- Hyde Park Twrs W2 246 A5
- Hyderabad Way E15 76 C1
- Hyde Rd
  - Bexleyheath DA7 147 B3
  - Richmond TW10 154 B6
  - Shoreditch N1 95 C6
- Hyde Sch The NW9 45 D4
- Hydeside Gdns N9 17 D2
- Hyde's Pl 12 N1 72 D1
- Hyde St SE8 141 C6
- Hyde Terr TW15, TW16 171 C4
- HYDE THE 45 D4
- Hydethorpe Ave N9 17 D2
- Hydethorpe Rd SW12 159 C3
- Hyde Vale SE10 142 A5
- Hyde Way
  - Edmonton N9 17 D2
  - Hayes UB3 105 D2
- Hyde Wlk SM4 201 C2
- Hydon Ct N11 30 D5
- Hyh Ho E17 35 D2
- Hyland House Sch E17 36 B1
- Hylands Rd E17 36 B1
- Hylda Ct NW5 71 A5
- Hylton St SE18 123 D2
- Hyndewood 14 SE23 162 D1
- Hyndman Ho
  - 5 Dagenham RM10 81 C5
  - 4 Tufnell Pk N19 71 D4
- Hyndman St SE15 140 B6
- Hynton Rd RM8 80 C6
- Hyperion Ho
  - 27 Bow E3 97 A5
  - Streatham SW2 160 B4
- Hyrstdene CR0 220 D4
- Hyrst The CR0 207 A1
- Hyson Rd SE16 118 B1
- Hythe Ave DA7 147 B5
- Hythe Cl N18 34 A6
- Hythe Ho 14 SE16 118 C4
- Hythe Rd
  - College Pk NW10 90 A3
  - South Norwood CR7 183 B1
- Hythe Road Ind Est NW10 90 A3
- Hyver Hill NW7 11 B4

I

- Ian Ct SE23 162 C2
- Ian Hamilton Ho NW1 232 C2
- Ian Mikardo Sch 52 E3 97 D4
- Ian Sq EN3 6 D4
- Ibberton Ho
  - Kensington W14 254 B5
  - South Lambeth SW8 270 C4
- Ibbotson Ave E16 98 D1
- Ibbott St 22 E1 96 C3
- Iberia Ho 17 N19 49 D2
- Iberian Ave CR0, SM6 220 A4
- Ibex Ho E15 76 C3
- Ibis Ct 16 SE8 141 B6
- Ibis Ho E12 78 B4
- Ibis La W4 133 A4
- Ibis Way UB4 84 D1
- Ibrox Ct 3 IG9 21 C2
- Ibsley Gdns SW15 156 A3
- Ibsley Way EN4 2 C1
- Ibstock Place Sch SW15 155 C5
- Icarus Ho 21 E3 97 B4
- Iceland Rd E3 97 C6
- Iceland Wharf SE16 119 A2
- Iceni Ct 23 Bow E3 97 B6
  - Buckhurst Hill IG9 21 B3
- Ice Wharf NW1 233 B4
- Ickburgh Est E5 74 B6
- Ickburgh Rd E5 74 B5
- Ickburgh Sch E5 74 B5
- ICKENHAM 60 C4
- Ickenham Cl HA4 61 B6
- Ickenham Rd HA4 39 B1
- Ickenham Sta UB10 61 A4
- Ickleton Rd SE9 188 A6
- Icknield Dr IG2 56 D4
- Ickworth Park Rd E17 53 A5
- Icough Ct SE3 143 B5
- Idaho Bldg 7 SE13 141 D4
- Ida Rd N15 51 B5
- Ida St E14 98 A1
- Iden Cl BR2 208 C6
- Identity & Passport Office SW1 115 B2 258 D4
- Idlecombe Rd SW17 181 A4
- Idmiston Rd
  - New Malden KT4 199 D2
  - Stratford E15 76 D3
  - West Norwood SE21, SE27 161 A2
- Idmiston Sq KT4 199 D2
- Idol La EC3 117 C6 253 A5
- Idonia St SE8 141 C5
- Iffley Ho 47 E2 95 D4
- Iffley Rd W6 112 B3
- Ifield Ho SE17 263 B2
- Ifield Rd SW10 135 D6 265 D6
- Ifor Evans Pl E1 96 D3
- Ightham Ho
  - Beckenham BR3 185 B3
  - Walworth SE17 263 A3
- Ightham Rd DA8 147 C5
- Ikon Ho 21 E1 118 C6
- Ilbert St W10 91 A4
- Ilchester Gdns W2 245 C6
- Ilchester Mans W8 255 A6
- Ilchester Pl W14 113 B3 254 D6
- Ilchester Rd RM8 80 C3
- Ildersly Gr SE21 161 B2
- Ilderton Prim Sch 16 SE16 118 C1
- Ilderton Rd SE15, SE16 140 C6
- Ilex Cl TW16 172 C1
- Ilex Rd NW10 67 D2
- Ilex Way SW16 182 C5
- ILFORD 78 D6
- Ilford Chambers 10 IG1 78 D5
- Ilford Hill IG1 78 C5
- Ilford Ho 14 N1 73 B2
- Ilford Interchange IG1 78 C5
- Ilford Jewish Prim Sch IG6 57 B6
- Ilford La IG1 78 D4
- Ilford Mus★ IG1 78 D5
- Ilford Prep Sch IG3 58 A1
- Ilford Ret Pk IG1 79 A6
- Ilford Sta IG1 78 D6
- Ilford Ursuline High Sch IG1 78 D6
- Ilford Ursuline Prep Sch 7 IG1 78 D6
- Ilfracombe Flats SE1 252 B2
- Ilfracombe Gdns RM6 58 B2
- Ilfracombe Rd BR1 164 D1
- Iliffe St SE17 116 D1 261 D2
- Iliffe Yd SE17 116 D1 261 D2
- Ilkeston Ct 7 E5 74 D4
- Ilkley Cl SE19 183 B4
- Ilkley Ct N11 31 A4
- Ilkley Rd Newham E16 99 C2
  - South Oxhey WD19 22 D5
- Illingworth Cl CR4 202 B6
- Illingworth Way EN1 17 C6
- Ilmington Rd HA3 43 D3
- Ilminster Gdns SW11 136 C1
- Ilsley Ct 8 SW8 137 C3
- Iman Zakaria Acad 2 E7 77 C3
- Imber Cl London N14 15 C4
  - Thames Ditton KT7 196 B1
- Imber Court Trad Est KT8 196 B3
- Imber Cross KT7 196 D3
- Imber Ct 4 SE9 166 C5
- Imber Gr KT10 196 B2
- Imber Park Rd KT10 196 B1
- Imber St N1 235 C5
- Immanuel CE Prim Sch SW16 182 A4
- Immanuel Coll WD23 8 C4
- Impact Ct SE20 184 B1
- Imperial Ave 5 N16 73 C4
- Imperial Cl
  - Harrow HA2 41 C3
  - Willesden NW2 68 B3
- Imperial College London (Charing Cross) W6 112 D1
- Imperial College London (Chelsea & Westminster) SW10 136 A6 266 B5
- Imperial College London (Hammersmith) W12 90 B1
- Imperial College London (Northwick Park) HA1 43 A1
- Imperial College London (Royal Brompton) SW3 114 C1 257 A2
- Imperial College London (South Kensington) SW7 114 B3 256 C6
- Imperial College London (St Mary's) W2 92 B1 236 D2
- Imperial College Rd SW7 114 B3 256 C6
- Imperial Cres SW6 136 A3
- Imperial Ct
  - Chislehurst BR7 188 D4
  - Harrow HA2 41 C2
  - St John's Wood NW8 230 B4
  - Wembley HA9 66 C5
  - Whetstone N20 14 A1
- Imperial Dr HA2 41 C3
- Imperial Gdns CR4 203 B6
- Imperial Ho
  - 1 Bow E3 97 A4
  - 2 Poplar E14 119 B6
  - Strand WC2 240 C1
- Imperial Mews 5 E6 99 D5
- Imperial Pl BR7 188 C2
- Imperial Rd
  - East Bedfont TW14 149 C4
  - Walham Green SW6 265 D1
  - Wood Green N22 32 A2
- Imperial Sq SW6 265 D2
- Imperial St E3 98 A4
- Imperial Twrs 3 NW3 70 A2
- Imperial War Mus★ SE1, SE11 116 C3 261 B5
- Imperial Way
  - Croydon CR0, CR9 220 C2
  - Harrow HA3 44 A3
  - Longlands BR7 167 A1
- Imperial Wharf Sta SW10 136 A4 266 B1
- Impington 19 KT1 176 C1
- Imre Cl W12 112 B5
- Inca Dr SE9 166 D4
- Ince Terr 3 N15 50 D6
- Inchbald Sch of Design (Garden Design) SW1 115 B2 258 D3

Inchbald Sch of Design (Interior Design) SW1 115 A2 258 A4
Inchmery Rd SE6 164 A3
Inchwood BR4, CR0 223 D4
Independant Jewish Day Sch 2 NW4 46 D4
Independence Ho 4 SW19 180 B2
Independent Ind Est UB7 104 C5
Independent Pl E8 73 D3
Independents Rd SE3 142 D2
Inderwick Rd N8 50 B4
Indescon Ct E14 119 D4
Indiana Bldg 7 SE8 141 C4
India St EC3 243 C1
India Way W12 112 B6
Indigo Ct TW13 149 D1
Indigo Mews N16 73 B5
Indoor Go Karting Arena (The Raceway) SE7 121 C3
Indoor Sports Arena E14 120 A5
Indus Ct 16 SE15 139 D5
Indus Rd SE7 143 C5
Ingal Rd E13 99 A3
Ingate Pl SW8 137 B4 268 D1
Ingatestone Rd
Croydon SE25 206 B5
Wanstead E12 55 C1
Woodford IG8 37 B3
Ingelow Ho W8 245 C2
Ingelow Rd SW8 137 B3
Ingersoll Rd
Enfield EN3 6 C5
Shepherd's Bush W12 112 B5
Ingestre Pl W1 239 B1
Ingestre Rd
Forest Gate E7 77 A4
Gospel Oak NW5 71 B4
Ingham Rd NW6 69 C4
Inglebert St EC1 94 C4 234 A2
Ingleborough EN2 4 C3
Ingleborough St SW9 138 C3
Ingleby Ct N21 16 D3
Ingleby Dr HA1 64 B5
Ingleby Rd
Dagenham RM10 81 D2
Ilford IG1 56 D1
Lower Holloway N7 72 A5
Ingleby Way
Chislehurst West BR7 188 C5
Wallington SM6 219 D1
Ingle Cl HA5 41 B6
Ingledew Rd SE18 123 B1
Inglefield Sq 12 E1 118 B5
Ingle Ho 3 SW12 159 D3
Inglehurst Gdns IG4 56 B4
Inglemere Ct CR4, SW17 180 D3
Inglemere Rd
Forest Hill SE23 162 D1
Mitcham CR4, SW17 180 D3
Inglesham Wlk E9 75 B2
Ingleside Cl BR3 185 C3
Ingleside Gr SE3 142 D6
Inglethorpe Ho 6 E5 74 A6
Inglethorpe St SW6 134 D4
Ingleton Ave DA16 168 A6
Ingleton Rd N18 34 A4
Ingleton St SW9 138 C3
Ingleway N12 30 C4
Inglewood BR7 189 B4
Inglewood Cl E14 119 C2
Inglewood Copse BR1 188 B1
Inglewood Ct 4 BR1 186 D3
Inglewood Mans 11 NW6 69 C3
Inglewood Mews KT6 198 C1
Inglewood Rd NW6 69 C3
Inglis Ct W5 110 B6
Inglis Ho 1 SW15 156 C6
Inglis Rd
Croydon CR0 205 D1
Ealing W5 110 B6
Inglis St SE5 138 D4
Ingram Ave NW11 48 A2
Ingram Cl
Lambeth SE11 260 D4
Stanmore HA7 25 C5
Ingram Ct EN1 17 D5
Ingram Ho
7 Harrow HA1 42 D4
Old Ford E3 97 A6
Teddington KT8 175 C2
Ingram Lo 8 SW4 159 D5
Ingram Rd London N2 48 C5
South Norwood CR7 183 A2
Ingram Way UB6 86 B6
Ingrave Ho RM9 102 B6
Ingrave St SW11 136 C2
Ingrebourne Ct E4 19 D2
Ingrebourne Ho
2 Catford BR1 186 B5
Lisson Gr NW8 236 D4
Ingress St 4 W4 111 C1
Inigo Jones Rd SE7 144 A5
Inigo Pl WC2 250 A6
Inkerman Rd NW5 71 B2
Inkerman Terr W8 255 B5
Inks Gn E4 36 A5
Inkster Ho 8 SW11 136 C2
Inkwell Cl N12 14 A1
Inman Rd
Harlesden NW10 89 C6
Wandsworth SW18 158 A4
Inmans Row IG8 37 A6
Innellan House Sch HA5 41 A6
Inner Circ NW1 93 A4 231 A2
Inner Park Rd SW19 156 D2
Inner Ring E TW6 126 D2
Inner Ring W TW6 126 C2
Inner Temple★ EC4 251 A6
Inner Temple La EC4 241 A1
Innes Cl SW20 179 A1
Innes Gdns SW15 156 B5
Innes Lo SE23 162 D1
Innes Yd CR0 221 A5
Innisfree Ho NW2 68 D2
Innis Ho SE17 263 A2
Inniskilling Rd E13 99 C5
Innova Bsns Pk EN3 7 B3
Innovation Cl HA0 88 A6
Inskip Cl E10 75 D6
Inskip Rd RM8 58 D1
Insley Ho 13 E3 97 D4
Institute of Cancer Research The SW7 114 A1 256 B2
Institute Pl 31 E8 74 B3
Institute The N2 48 C5
Inst of Child Health WC1 94 B3 240 C5
Inst of Neurology
Bloomsbury WC1 94 A2 240 B4
St Pancras WC1 94 A3 240 B5
Int Coll of Accountancy The SW17 158 D1
Integer Gdns E11 54 B2
Interchange The
Kentish Town NW5 71 B3
Thornton Heath CR0 204 D2
International Ave TW5 106 C1
International Com Sch W1 93 A3 238 B5
International House Language Sch WC2 94 A1 240 B2
International Sch of Bsns Studies HA2 41 C2
International Sch of London W3 110 C2
International Trad Est UB2 106 B3
International Univ of America (London Campus) 15 SE18 122 D2
International Way TW16 171 C2
Inverary Pl SE18 145 B6
Inver Cl E5 74 C6
Inverclyde Gdns RM6 58 D5
Inver Ct
11 Bayswater W2 91 D1
4 Hammersmith W6 112 A3
Inveresk Gdns KT4 216 A5
Inverey Ho 2 N12 29 D5
Inverforth Cl NW3 70 A6
Inverforth Ho NW3 70 A6
Inverforth Rd N11 31 B5
Invergarry Ct 11 EN5 13 D6
Invergarry Ho NW6 91 D5
Inverine Rd SE7 121 B1
Invermead Cl W6 112 A2
Invermore Pl SE18 123 A2
Inverness Ave EN1 5 C4
Inverness Ct
8 Acton W3 88 C1
10 Catford SE6 164 D3
Inverness Gdns W8 245 C3
Inverness Mews
Bayswater W2 245 D6
Newham E16 122 D5
North Woolwich E16 123 A5
Inverness Pl W2 245 D6
Inverness Rd
Edmonton N18 34 B5
Hounslow TW3 129 C1
North Cheam KT4 200 D1
Southall UB2 107 A2
Inverness St NW1 231 D6
Inverness Terr W2 113 D6 245 D6
Inverton Rd SE15 140 D1
Invicta Cl
Chislehurst West BR7 188 C5
East Bedfont TW14 149 D3
21 Tower Hamlets E3 97 C2
Invicta Ct KT9 214 B3
Invicta Ctr The IG11 102 A6
Invicta Gr UB5 85 B4
Invicta Plaza SE1 251 C4
Invicta Prim Sch SE3 143 A5
Invicta Rd SE3, SE7 143 A6
Inville Rd SE17 117 B1 262 D1
Inwen Ct SE8 119 A1
Inwood Ave TW3 130 A2
Inwood Bsns Pk TW3 129 D1
Inwood Cl CR0 223 A6
Inwood Ct 12 NW1 71 C1
Inwood Ho 19 SE22 139 C2
Inwood Rd TW3 130 A1
Inworth St SW11 136 C3
Inworth Wlk N1 235 A6
Io Ctr Barking IG11 101 D3
Woolwich SE18 123 A3
Iona Cl Catford SE6 163 C4
Morden SM4 201 D2
Ion Ct 8 E2 96 A5
Ionian Bldg 19 E14 119 A6
Ionian Ho 22 E1 96 D3
Ipsden Bldgs SE1 251 B2
Ipswich Ho SE4 162 D6
Ipswich Rd SW17 181 A4
Iqra Ind Sch SW9 138 C2
Irby Ho SW2 160 C5
Ireland Cl E6 100 B2
Ireland Pl N22 32 A3
Ireland Yd EC4 241 D1
Irene Rd
Broom Hill BR6 211 D2
Parsons Green SW6 135 C4 265 B1
Ireton Cl N10 31 A3
Ireton Ho 22 SW9 138 C3
Ireton St 12 E3 97 C3
Iris Ave DA5 169 A5
Iris Cl Croydon CR0 206 D1
Newham E6 100 A3
Surbiton KT6 198 B2
Iris Cres DA7 147 B6
Iris Ct Dagenham IG11 80 B1
8 Peckham SE15 140 B3
4 Pinner HA5 40 C6
Iris Rd KT19 214 D3
Iris Way E4 35 B4
Iris Wlk 1 HA8 27 A6
Irkdale Ave EN1 5 D4
Iroko Ho 7 NW3 69 D2
Iron Bridge Cl
Southall UB2 108 A5
Willesden NW10 67 C3
Iron Bridge Ho NW3 70 D1
Iron Bridge Rd N UB11 104 C5
Iron Bridge Rd S UB7 104 C4
Irongate Ho EC3 243 B2
Iron Mill Pl SW18 157 D5
Iron Mill Rd SW18 157 D5
Ironmonger La EC2 95 B1 242 C1
Ironmonger Pas EC1 235 B1
Ironmonger Row EC1 95 A4 235 B1
Ironmonger Row Baths EC1 235 B1
Ironmongers Pl E14 119 C2
Ironmonger's Pl 22 E14 119 C2
Ironside Cl SE16 118 D4
Ironside Ho E9 75 A4
Ironworks 1 E3 97 C6
Irvine Ave HA3 43 B6
Irvine Cl N20 14 C2
Irvine Ct
Marylebone W1 239 B5
Thornton Heath CR7 204 C3
Irvine Ho N7 72 B2
Irvine Way BR6 211 D2
Irving Ave UB5 84 D6
Irving Ct N22 32 D2
Irving Gr SW9 138 B3
Irving Ho SE17 261 C1
Irving Mews N1 73 A2
Irving Rd W14 112 D3
Irving St WC2 249 D5
Irwell Ct W7 86 B1
Irwell Est 31 SE16 118 C4
Irwin Ave SE18 145 C5
Irwin Cl UB10 60 C5
Irwin Gdns NW10 90 B6
Isabel Hill Cl TW12 173 C2
Isabella Cl N14 15 C4
Isabella Ct 8 TW10 154 B5
Isabella Dr BR6 227 A4
Isabella Ho
19 Hammersmith W6 112 C1
Kennington SE11 261 C2
Isabella Mews 11 E8 73 C2
Isabella Pl KT2 176 B5
Isabella Rd E9 74 C3
Isabel St SW9 270 D2
Isambard Mews E14 120 A3
Isambard Pl SE16 118 C5
Iseldon Ct N7 72 A4
Isel Way 4 SE22 161 C6
Isham Rd SW16 182 A1
Isis Cl Putney SW15 134 C1
Ruislip HA4 39 A3
Isis Ct W4 132 D5
Isis Ho
2 Edmonton N18 33 D4
Paddington NW8 236 D5
Isis St SW18 158 A2
Islamia Girls' High Sch NW6 91 A6
Islamia Prim Sch NW6 91 A6
Islamic Coll for Advanced Studies 2 NW10 68 B2
Islamic Shaksiyah Foundation Sch N15 51 B4
Island Centre Way 16 EN3 7 C6
Island Farm Ave KT8 195 B4
Island Farm Rd KT8 195 C4
Island Gardens Sta E14 120 A1
Island Ho Bromley E14 98 A4
Morden SW19 202 A5
Island Rd
Deptford SE16 118 D2
Mitcham CR4 180 D3
Island Row E14 97 B1
Isla Rd SE18 145 A6
Islay Gdns TW4 150 D6
Islay Wlk 17 N1 73 A2
Isleden Ho N1 235 A6
Isledon Rd N4, N7 72 C5
Islehurst Cl BR7 188 C2
ISLE OF DOGS 120 A2
ISLEWORTH 131 B2
Isleworth Bsns Complex TW7 130 D3
Isleworth Sta TW7 130 D3
Isleworth & Syon Sch for Boys TW7 130 C5
Isleworth Town Prim Sch TW7 131 A3
ISLINGTON 72 D2
Islington Arts & Media Sch 6 N4 50 B1
Islington Bsns Ctr N1 235 B6
Islington Est N1 95 A6 235 A6
Islington Gn N1 94 D6 234 C5
Islington High St N1 94 D5 234 C4
Islington Mus★ WC1 94 D4 234 C1
Islington Park Mews 1 N1 72 D1
Islington Park St N1 72 D1
Islington Tennis Ctr N7 72 A2
Islip Gdns
Burnt Oak HA8 27 B3
Northolt UB5 63 A1
Islip Manor Rd UB5 63 A1
Islip St NW5 71 C3
Ismailia Rd E7 77 B1
Isobel Ho
10 Ashford TW16 171 D3
Harrow HA1 42 D4
Isokon Flats 3 NW3 70 D3
Isom Cl E13 99 B4
Issac Way SE1 252 B2
Issa Rd TW3 129 B1
Italia Conti Acad of Theatre Arts EC1 242 A5
Ithell Ct HA0 65 D3
Ivanhoe Dr HA3 25 B1
Ivanhoe Ho
11 Balham SW12 159 B4
34 Bow E3 97 A5
Ivanhoe Rd
Hounslow TW4 128 D2
Peckham SE5 139 D2
Ivatt Pl W14 113 B1 254 D1
Ivatt Way N17 50 D6
Ivax Quays E16 123 A6
Iveagh Ave NW10 88 C5
Iveagh Cl Ealing NW10 88 C5
South Hackney E9 96 D6
Iveagh Ct
4 Beckenham BR3 207 D6
Whitechapel EC3 243 C1
Iveagh Ho
2 Brixton SW9 138 D3
Chelsea SW10 266 B4
Ivebury Ct 9 W10 90 C1
Ivedon Rd DA16 146 C3
Ive Farm Cl E10 75 C6
Ive Farm La E10 75 C6
Iveley Rd SW4 137 C3
Iver Ct N1 73 A2
Ivere Dr EN5 13 D5
Iverhurst Cl DA6 168 D6
Iverna Ct W8 255 B6
Iverna Gdns
Hatton TW14 149 B6
Kensington W8 113 C3 255 B6
Iverson Rd NW6 69 C2
Ivers Way CR0 223 D1
Ives Rd E16 98 C2
Ives St SW3 114 C2 257 B4
Ivestor Terr SE23 162 C4
Ivimey St E2 96 A4
Ivinghoe Cl EN1 5 C4
Ivinghoe Ho 14 N7 71 D3
Ivinghoe Rd
Barking RM8 80 B3
Bushey WD23 8 B4
Ivor Ct Hendon N3 47 A6
Hornsey N8 50 A3
Lisson Gr NW1 237 C6
Ivor Gr SE9 166 D3
Ivor Ho DA14 190 C5
Ivories The N1 73 A1
Ivor Mayor Lo SW12 159 A5
Ivor Pl NW1 92 D3 237 C5
Ivor St NW1 71 C1
Ivory Ct TW13 150 A3
Ivorydown BR1 187 A6
Ivory Ho
9 London SW11 136 A2
St George in t East E1 253 D4
Ivory Sq 15 SW18 136 A2

Ivybridge Cl
2 Twickenham TW1 ... 153 A4
Uxbridge UB8 ... 82 A4
Ivybridge Ct 1 BR7 ... 188 C2
Ivybridge Ho 18 SE22 ... 139 C2
Ivybridge La WC2 ... 250 B5
Ivybridge Prim Sch TW1 ... 152 D5
Ivybridge Ret Pk TW7 ... 152 D6
Ivychurch Cl SE20 ... 184 C3
Ivy Church La SE1, SE17 ... 263 C2
Ivy Cl Harrow HA2 ... 63 B4
Pinner HA5 ... 40 C2
Sunbury TW16 ... 172 C1
Ivy Cotts UB10 ... 82 C4
Ivy Cres W4 ... 111 A2
Ivy Ct
19 Bermondsey SE16 ... 118 A1
Lewisham SE3 ... 142 D1
Ivydale Prim Sch SE15 ... 140 D1
Ivydale Rd
Carshalton SM5 ... 218 D6
Nunhead SE15 ... 140 D1
Ivyday Gr SW16 ... 160 B1
Ivydene KT12, KT8 ... 195 B4
Ivydene Cl SM1 ... 218 A4
Ivy Gdns London N8 ... 50 A3
Mitcham CR4 ... 203 D6
Ivy Ho Croydon CR0 ... 206 D1
6 Upper Clapton E5 ... 52 B1
Ivyhouse Rd RM9 ... 81 A2
Ivy House Rd UB10 ... 60 D5
Ivy La TW4 ... 129 B1
Ivy Lo W8 ... 245 A4
Ivymount Rd SE27 ... 160 C1
Ivy Rd Brockley SE4 ... 141 C1
Cricklewood NW2 ... 68 C4
Hounslow TW3 ... 129 D1
Newham E16 ... 99 A1
Southgate N14 ... 15 D4
Tolworth KT6 ... 198 C1
Upper Tooting SW17 ... 180 C5
Walthamstow E17 ... 53 C3
Ivy St N1 ... 95 C5
Ivy Terr 2 IG2 ... 57 A3
Ivy Wlk RM9 ... 81 A2
Ixworth Pl SW3 ... 114 C2 257 A3
Izane Rd DA6 ... 147 B1

J

Jacaranda Cl KT3 ... 199 C6
Jacaranda Gr E8 ... 73 D1
Jack Ashley Ct 5 NW9 ... 27 C2
Jackass La BR2 ... 225 C2
Jack Barnett Way N22 ... 32 B1
Jack Clow Rd E15 ... 98 C5
Jack Cook Ho 9 IG11 ... 78 D1
Jack Cornwell St E12 ... 78 C4
Jack Dash Gdns E6 ... 100 A3
Jack Goodchild Way KT3 ... 198 D6
Jack & Jill Sch Hampton TW12 ... 173 C4
1 Twickenham TW2 ... 152 C2
Jack Jones Way RM9 ... 103 B5
Jacklin Gn IG8 ... 37 A6
Jackman Ho 24 E1 ... 118 B5
Jackman Mews NW2 ... 67 C5
Jackman St E8 ... 96 B6
Jackson Cl
Hackney E9 ... 74 D1
Uxbridge UB10 ... 60 A1
Jackson Ct
Forest Gate E7 ... 77 B2
Wanstead E11 ... 55 B1
Jackson Ho
15 London SW11 ... 136 B2
13 New Southgate N11 ... 31 C5
Jackson Rd
Barking IG11 ... 101 B6
Jackson Rd *continued*
Bromley BR2 ... 226 B6
East Barnet EN4 ... 14 C5
Lower Holloway N7 ... 72 B4
Uxbridge UB10 ... 60 A1
Jackson's La N6 ... 49 B2
Jackson's Pl CR0 ... 205 C1
Jackson St SE18 ... 144 C6
Jackson's Way CR0 ... 223 C5
Jackson Way UB2 ... 107 D4
Jack Taylor Sch NW8 ... 92 A6 229 A6
Jack Tizard Sch W12 ... 112 B5
Jack Walker Ct N5 ... 72 D4
Jacob Ct 24 EN3 ... 7 C6
Jacob Ho 14 DA18 ... 124 D4
Jacobin Lo N7 ... 72 A3
Jacob Mans 15 E1 ... 96 B1
Jacobs Cl RM10 ... 81 D4
Jacobs Ho E13 ... 99 C4
Jacobson Ct SW11 ... 267 B1
Jacobson Ho E1 ... 243 C2
Jacob St SE1 ... 118 A4
Jacob's Well Mews W1 ... 238 B2
Jacotts Ho W10 ... 90 C3
Jacqueline Cl UB5 ... 85 A6
Jacqueline Ho 8 E1 ... 96 D2
Jacques Prevert Sch 3 W6 ... 112 D2
Jade Cl
Dagenham RM8 ... 58 C1
Hendon NW2 ... 46 D2
Newham E16 ... 99 D1
Jaffe Rd IG1 ... 57 B1
Jaffray Rd BR2 ... 209 D5
Jaggard Way SW12 ... 158 D4
Jagger Ho SW11 ... 267 C2
Jago Cl SE18 ... 145 A6
Jago Wlk SE5 ... 139 B5
Jamahirya Sch SW3 ... 136 C6 267 A6
Jamaica Rd
Bermondsey SE1 ... 253 D1
Bermondsey SE16 ... 118 B3
Thornton Heath CR7 ... 204 D3
Jamaica St E1 ... 96 C2
James Allen's Girls' Sch 12 SE22 ... 161 C6
James Allen's Pre-Prep Sch SE21 ... 161 B5
James Allen's Prep Sch 13 SE22 ... 161 C6
James Anderson Ct 29 E2 ... 95 C5
James Ave
Cricklewood NW2 ... 68 C3
Dagenham RM8 ... 59 B1
James Bedford Cl HA5 ... 22 C1
James Boswell Cl 1 SW16 ... 182 C6
James Brine Ho 6 E2 ... 95 D4
James Campbell Ho 2 E2 ... 96 C5
James Cl
London NW11 ... 47 A3
8 Newham E13 ... 99 A5
James Collins Cl W9 ... 91 B3
James Ct Chingford E4 ... 20 B2
Finchley N12 ... 30 C3
Hendon NW9 ... 27 C1
Northolt UB5 ... 85 A5
3 Woodford E18 ... 37 B1
James Dixon Prim Sch SE20 ... 184 A2
James Docherty Ho 4 E2 ... 96 C5
James Dudson Ct NW10 ... 67 A1
James Est CR4 ... 180 D1
James Gdns N22 ... 32 D3
James Hammett Ho 9 E2 ... 95 D5
James Ho Mile End E1 ... 97 A3
33 Rotherhithe SE16 ... 118 D4
James Joyce Wlk 7 SE24 ... 138 D1
James La E10, E11 ... 54 B3
James Lee Sq EN3 ... 7 C5
James Leicester Hall of Residence N7 ... 72 A2
James Lind Ho 6 SE8 ... 119 B2
James Middleton Ho 20 E2 ... 96 B4
James Newman Ct SE9 ... 166 C1
Jameson Ct 6 E2 ... 96 C5
Jameson Ho SE11 ... 260 C2
Jameson Lo N6 ... 49 C3
Jameson Pl 11 W3 ... 111 A4
Jameson St W8 ... 245 B4
James Pl N17 ... 33 D2
James's Cotts TW9 ... 132 C5
James St Barking IG11 ... 79 A1
Enfield EN1 ... 17 D6
Hounslow TW3 ... 130 B2
Marylebone W1 ... 93 A1 238 B1
Strand WC2 ... 116 A6 250 B6
James Stewart Ho NW6 ... 69 B1
James Stroud Ho SE17 ... 262 B1
Jamestown Rd NW1 ... 93 B6 231 C6
Jamestown Way E14 ... 120 B6
James Voller Way 30 E1 ... 96 C1
James Way WD19 ... 22 D6
James Wolfe Prim Sch 16 SE10 ... 142 A5
Jamiatul Ummah Sch 40 E1 ... 96 B1
Jamieson Ho TW4 ... 151 B5
Jamuna Cl E14 ... 97 A2
Jane Austen Hall 14 E16 ... 121 B5
Jane St E1 ... 96 B1
Janet Ct
4 Bexleyheath DA7 ... 147 C1
Wood Green N22 ... 32 B2
Janet St E14 ... 119 C3
Janeway Pl 2 SE16 ... 118 B4
Janeway St SE16 ... 118 A4
Janice Mews 3 IG1 ... 78 D5
Jansen Ho 5 SW15 ... 156 A6
Jansen Wlk SW11 ... 136 B1
Janson Cl
Stratford E15 ... 76 C3
Willesden NW10 ... 67 C5
Janson Rd E15 ... 76 C3
Jansons Rd N15 ... 51 C6
Japan Cres N4 ... 50 B1
Japanese Sch The W3 ... 110 C6
Japan Rd RM6 ... 58 D3
Jaquets Ct DA5 ... 169 C2
Jardine Ho HA1 ... 42 C2
Jardine Rd E1 ... 118 D6
Jarman Ho
Bermondsey SE16 ... 118 D2
16 Stepney E1 ... 96 C2
Jarrett Cl SW2 ... 160 D3
Jarrow Cl SM4 ... 201 D4
Jarrow Rd
Bermondsey SE16 ... 118 C1
Dagenham RM6 ... 58 C3
Tottenham Hale N17 ... 52 B5
Jarrow Way E9 ... 75 A4
Jarvis Cl
1 Barking IG11 ... 101 B6
Barnet EN5 ... 12 D6
Jarvis Ho 3 SE15 ... 140 A4
Jarvis Rd
London SE22 ... 139 C1
South Croydon CR2 ... 221 B2
Jasmin SE1 ... 253 D3
Jasmine Cl Ilford IG1 ... 78 D3
Orpington BR6 ... 226 D6
Southall UB1 ... 107 A6
Jasmine Ct Lee SE12 ... 165 A5
11 Wallington SM6 ... 219 B2
Wimbledon SW19 ... 179 C5
Jasmine Gdns
Harrow HA2 ... 63 C6
West Wickham CR0 ... 223 D5
Jasmine Gr SE20 ... 184 B2
Jasmine Sq 15 E3 ... 97 B6
Jasmine Terr UB7 ... 104 C4
Jasmine Way KT7 ... 196 C5
Jasmin Ho SE4 ... 141 B2
Jasmin Lo 17 SE16 ... 118 B1
Jasmin Rd KT19 ... 214 D3
Jason Ct
2 London SW9 ... 138 C4
Marylebone W1 ... 238 B2
Jason Ho UB5 ... 84 B4
Jason Wlk SE9 ... 188 C6
Jasper Cl EN3 ... 6 C5
Jasper Ho KT4 ... 199 B1
Jasper Rd
Newham E16 ... 99 D1
Penge SE19 ... 183 D4
Jasper Wlk N1 ... 235 C2
Java Wharf SE1 ... 253 D2
Javelin Ct HA7 ... 25 B5
Javelin Way UB5 ... 84 D4
Jawahar Bagh SW16 ... 182 D4
Jaycroft EN2 ... 4 C4
Jay Gdns BR7 ... 188 B6
Jay Ho SW15 ... 134 C3
Jay Mews SW7 ... 114 A4 246 B1
Jayson Ct 7 CR0 ... 206 A1
Jazzfern Terr HA0 ... 65 A3
Jean Batten Cl SM6 ... 220 B1
Jean Darling Ho SW10 ... 266 C5
Jean Ho 3 SW17 ... 180 C5
Jean Humbert Ho 2 SE27 ... 183 B6
Jean Pardies Ho 23 E1 ... 96 C2
Jebb Ave SW2 ... 160 A5
Jebb St E3 ... 97 C5
Jedburgh Rd E13 ... 99 C4
Jedburgh St SW11 ... 137 A1
Jeddo Mews W12 ... 111 D4
Jeddo Rd W12 ... 111 D4
Jefferies Ho 13 NW10 ... 67 B1
Jefferson Bldg 3 E14 ... 119 C4
Jefferson Cl
Ealing W13 ... 109 B3
Ilford IG2 ... 56 D4
Jefferson Wlk 13 SE18 ... 144 C6
Jeffrey Row SE12 ... 165 B6
Jeffrey's Ct 2 SW4 ... 138 A3
Jeffrey's Pl NW1 ... 71 C1
Jeffreys Rd EN3 ... 7 B1
Jeffrey's Rd SW4 ... 138 A3
Jeffrey's St NW1 ... 71 C1
Jeffs Cl TW12 ... 173 D4
Jeffs Rd SM1 ... 217 B4
Jeff Wooller Coll WC1 ... 94 A2 240 B4
Jefton Ct SM6 ... 219 C3
Jeger Ave E2 ... 95 D6
Jeken Rd SE9 ... 143 C1
Jelf Rd SW2 ... 160 C6
Jellicoe Ct E4 ... 36 B4
Jellicoe Gdns HA7 ... 25 A4
Jellicoe Ho
5 Bethnal Green E2 ... 96 A5
Fitzrovia NW1 ... 238 D5
11 Putney SW15 ... 156 D6
Jellicoe Rd
4 Newham E13 ... 99 A3
Tottenham N17 ... 33 B3
Jemmett Cl KT2 ... 176 D2
Jemotts Ct 9 SE14 ... 140 D6
Jem Paterson Ct HA1 ... 64 C4
Jengar Cl SM1 ... 217 D4
Jenkins Ho SW8 ... 269 C2
Jenkins La IG11 ... 101 A4
Jenkinson Ho 12 E2 ... 96 D4
Jenkins Rd E13 ... 99 B3
Jenner Ave W3 ... 89 B2
Jenner Cl DA14 ... 190 A6
Jenner Ct N21 ... 16 A6
Jenner Ho
5 Belvedere DA17 ... 125 C3
Greenwich SE3 ... 142 C6
Jenner Pl SW13 ... 134 B6
Jenner Rd N16 ... 73 D5
Jennett Rd CR0 ... 220 C5
Jennifer Ho SE11 ... 261 B3
Jennifer Rd BR1 ... 164 D1
Jennings Cl KT6 ... 197 C2
Jennings Ho SE10 ... 120 B1
Jennings Rd SE22 ... 161 D5
Jenny Hammond Cl E11 ... 76 D5
Jenny Hammond Prim Sch E11 ... 76 C4
Jensen Ho 10 E3 ... 97 C3
Jenson Way SE19 ... 183 D3
Jenton Ave DA7 ... 147 A3
Jephson Ct 17 SW4 ... 138 A3
Jephson Ho 6 SE17 ... 138 D6
Jephson Rd E7 ... 77 C1
Jephson St SE5 ... 139 B4
Jephtha Rd SW18 ... 157 C5
Jeppo's La CR4 ... 202 D5
Jerdan Pl SW6 ... 265 A4
Jeremiah St 11 E14 ... 97 D1
Jeremy Bentham Ho 24 E2 ... 96 A4
Jeremy's Gn N18 ... 34 C6
Jermyn St SW1 ... 115 C5 249 B4
Jerningham Ct SE14 ... 141 A4
Jerningham Rd SE14 ... 141 A4
Jerome Cres NW8 ... 92 C3 237 A6
Jerome Ct 2 N11 ... 31 C5
Jerome Ho
Kingston u T KT1 ... 175 D1
Lisson Gr NW1 ... 237 B4
Jerome Pl KT1 ... 175 D1
Jerome St E1 ... 95 D3 243 C5
Jerome Twr 5 W3 ... 110 D4
Jerrard St SE13 ... 141 D2
Jerrold Lo SW15 ... 134 C2
Jerrold St 24 N1 ... 95 C5
Jersey Ave HA7 ... 25 C1
Jersey Ct UB2 ... 107 B3
Jersey Dr BR5 ... 211 B3
Jersey Ho
15 Canonbury N1 ... 73 A2
Enfield EN3 ... 6 D5
Jersey Rd
Canonbury N1 ... 73 A2
Ealing W7 ... 109 A4
Hounslow TW5, TW7 ... 130 B5
Ilford IG1 ... 78 D4
Leytonstone E11 ... 54 B1
Mitcham SW17 ... 181 B4
Newham E16 ... 99 C1
Jersey St E2 ... 96 B4
Jerusalem Pas EC1 ... 241 C5
Jervis Bay Ho 9 E14 ... 98 B1
Jervis Ct
9 Dagenham RM10 ... 81 D2
2 Greenwich SE10 ... 142 A4
Marylebone W1 ... 238 D1
Jerviston Gdns SW16 ... 182 C4
Jesmond Ave HA9 ... 66 B2
Jesmond Cl CR4 ... 203 B6
Jesmond Ct HA9 ... 66 C2
Jesmond Rd CR0 ... 205 D2
Jesmond Way HA7 ... 26 A5
Jessam Ave E5 ... 52 B1
Jessamine Rd W7 ... 108 D5
Jessel Ho
St Pancras WC1 ... 233 A1
Westminster SW1 ... 259 D4
Jesse Rd E10 ... 54 A1
Jessica Rd SW18 ... 158 A6
Jessie Blythe La 4 N19 ... 50 A2
Jessie Duffett Ho 11 SE5 ... 139 A5
Jessie's Cotts E17 ... 53 A3
Jessiman Terr TW17 ... 192 C4
Jesson Ho SE17 ... 262 C3
Jessop Ave UB2 ... 107 B2
Jessop Ct N1 ... 234 D3
Jessop Ho 9 W4 ... 111 B2
Jessop Pl CR4 ... 202 C5
Jessop Sq E14 ... 119 C5
Jessops Way CR0 ... 203 C3
Jessops Wharf 4 TW8 ... 131 C5
Jessup Cl SE18 ... 123 A2
Jeston Ho 10 SE27 ... 160 D1
Jethou Ho 16 N1 ... 73 A2
Jetstar Way UB5 ... 85 A4
Jevington Way SE12 ... 165 B3
Jevons Ho 9 NW8 ... 70 B1
Jewell Ho 3 SW12 ... 159 C4
Jewel Rd E17 ... 53 C6
Jewish Free Sch HA3 ... 44 C3
Jewish Mus The★ NW1 ... 93 B6 231 D5
Jewry St EC3 ... 95 D1 243 C1
Jews Row SW18 ... 136 A1
Jews Wlk SE26 ... 184 B6
Jeymer Ave NW2 ... 68 C3
Jeymer Dr UB6 ... 86 A6
Jeypore Rd SW18 ... 158 A5
Jillian Cl TW12 ... 173 C3

Jim Bradley Cl 10 SE18 122 C2
Jim Griffiths Ho SW6 264 D5
Jimis Coll HA9 65 C5
Jim Veal Dr 3 N17 72 A2
Joan Cres SE9 165 D4
Joan Gdns RM8 81 A6
Joanna Ho 7 W6 112 C1
Joanne Ct EN1 17 C5
Joan Player Ho EN3 6 D6
Joan Rd RM8 81 A6
Joan St SE1 116 D5 251 C3
Joan Villas IG2 57 A2
Jocelin Ho N1 233 D5
Jocelyn Rd TW9 132 A2
Jocelyn St SE15 140 A4
Jockey's Fields WC1 94 B2 240 D4
Jodane Rd SE8 119 B2
Jodrell Cl TW7 131 A4
Jodrell Rd E3 75 B1
Joe Hunte Ct 2 SW27 182 D5
Joel St HA5, HA6 40 A5
Johanna Prim Sch SE1 116 C4 251 A1
Johanna St SE1 251 A1
John Adam St WC2 116 A6 250 B5
John Aird Ct W2 92 A2 236 B4
John Aldis Ho N22 32 B1
John Archer Way SW18 158 B5
John Ashby Cl SW2 160 A5
John Austin Cl KT2 176 B2
John Baird Ct SE26 184 D6
John Baird Ho 11 SE20 184 C3
John Ball Prim Sch SE3 142 C3
John Barker Ct NW6 69 A1
John Barker Ho IG1 79 B6
John Barnes Wlk E15 76 D2
John Barter Ho TW3 129 B3
John Betts' Ho W12 112 A3
John Betts Prim Sch W6 112 B3
John Bond Ho 2 E3 97 B5
John Bradshaw Rd N14 15 D3
John Brent Ho 8 SE8 118 D2
John Buck Ho NW10 89 D6
John Burns Dr IG11 79 C1
John Burns Prim Sch 17 SW11 137 A3
Johnby Cl EN3 7 A6
John Campbell Rd 26 N16 73 C3
John Carpenter St EC4 251 C6
John Cartwright Ho 7 E2 96 B4
John Chilton Sch UB5 63 A1
John Clifford Ho N8 50 A3
John Clynes Ct SW15 134 B1
John Conwey Ho 23 SW2 160 C5
John Cornwell VC Ho 6 E12 78 C4
John Day Ho TW7 131 B2
John Dee Ho 3 SW14 133 B2
John Donne Prim Sch 13 SE15 140 B4
John Drinkwater Cl E11 54 D2
John Dwight Ho SW6 135 D2
John Fearon Wlk 5 W10 91 A4
John Felton Rd 19 SE16 118 A4
John Fielden Ho 10 E2 96 B4
John Fisher St E1 118 A6
John F Kennedy Specl Sch 6 E15 98 B6
John Gooch Dr EN2 4 D4
John Harris Ho SE15 140 A2
John Harrison Way SE10 120 D3
John Hunt Ct 5 SE9 166 A2
John Islip St SW1 116 A2 260 A3
John Kaye Ct TW17 192 C4
John Keall Ho 3 SW15 134 D2
John Keats Ho N22 32 B2
John Keats Lo EN2 5 B4
John Keble CE Prim Sch NW10 89 D6
John Kelly Tech Colls NW2 67 D5
John Kennedy Ct 1 N1 73 B2
John Kennedy Ho 1 SE16 118 D2
John Kennedy Lo 2 N1 73 B2
John King Ct 5 N19 71 D6
John Kirk Ho
21 Battersea SW11 136 B2
Beckenham BR3 207 A5
5 Streatham SW16 160 A1
John Knight Lo SW6 265 B4
John Lamb Ct HA3 24 C2
John Loughborough Sch 9 N17 33 D1
John Lyon Sch The HA2 42 B1
John McDonald Ho 3 E14 120 A3
John McKenna Wlk 17 SE16 118 A3
John Masefield Ho N15 51 B3
John Maurice Cl SE17 117 B2 262 C4
John Nettleford Ho 14 E2 96 B4
John Newton Ct DA16 146 B2
John Orwell Sports Ctr E1 118 B5
John Parker Cl RM10 81 D1
John Parker Sq 7 SW11 136 B2
John Parry Ct 28 N1 95 C5
John Paul II Sch 9 SW19 156 D4
John Penn Ho SE8 141 B5
John Penn St SE13 141 D4
John Perrin Pl HA3 44 A2
John Perryn Prim Sch W3 89 C1
John Prince's St W1 238 D2
John Pritchard Ho 16 E1 96 A3
John Ratcliffe Ho 8 NW6 91 C4
John Rennie Wlk 1 E1 118 C5
John Roan Sch SE3 142 C5
John Roll Way SE16 118 A3
John Ruskin Coll CR2 223 A1
John Ruskin Prim Sch SE5 139 A6
John Ruskin St SE5 139 A6
John's Ave NW4 46 C5
Johns Cl TW15 171 A6
John Scurr Ho 18 E14 97 A1
John Scurr Prim Sch 46 E1 96 C3
John Silkin La SE8 118 D1
Johns La SM4 202 A4
John's Mews WC1 94 B3 240 D5
John Smith Ave SW6 135 B5 264 C4
John Smith Mews E14 120 B6
Johnson Cl E8 96 A6
Johnson Ct
Hendon NW4 46 A6
10 Wandsworth SW18 136 B1
Johnson Ho
Belgravia SW1 258 B3
23 Bethnal Green E2 96 A4
Somers Town NW1 232 B3
South Lambeth SW8 269 D3
Johnson Lo 12 W9 91 C2
Johnson Rd
Bromley Comm BR2 209 D4
Heston TW5 128 C5
Stonebridge NW10 89 B6
Thornton Heath CR0 205 B2
Johnson's Cl SM5 218 D5
Johnsons Ct EC4 241 B1
Johnsons Dr TW12 174 A2
Johnson's Ind Est UB3 106 A3
Johnson's Pl SW1 115 C1 259 A1
Johnson St
Southall UB2 106 D3
Stepney E1 96 C1
Johnsons Way NW10 88 D3
John Spencer Sq N1 72 D2
John's Pl E1 96 B1
John St
Croydon SE25 206 A5
Enfield EN1 17 D6
Finsbury WC1 94 B3 240 D5
Hounslow TW3, TW5 129 A3
West Ham E15 98 D6
John Stainer Prim Sch SE4 141 A2
John's Terr CR0 205 C1
Johnston Cl SW9 270 D1
Johnstone Ho SE13 142 B2
Johnstone Rd E6 100 B4
Johnston Rd IG8 37 A5
John Strachey Ho SW6 264 D5
John Strype Ct E10 53 D1
John Trundle Ct EC4 242 A4
John Tucker Ho 3 E14 119 C3
John Walsh Twr E11 76 D6
John Wesley Cl 4 E6 100 B4
John Wesley Ct 6 TW1 153 A3
John Wesley's House & Mus of Methodism★ EC1 242 D6
John Wheatley Ho
14 London N19 49 D2
West Brompton SW6 264 D5
John William Cl 12 KT2 175 D2
John Williams Cl SE14 140 D6
John Wilson St SE18 122 C2
John Wooley Cl SE13 142 C1
Joiners Arms Yd 1 SE5 139 B4
Joiners Ct 5 N20 14 D1
Joiner St SE1 252 D3
Joiners Yd N1 233 B3
Joint Rd N10 30 C2
Jolles Ho 9 E3 97 D4
Jollys La Harrow HA2 42 B1
Hayes UB4 84 D2
Jonathan Ct 9 W4 111 C2
Jonathan St SE11 116 B1 260 C2
Jones Ho
4 South Bromley E14 98 B1
Stamford Hill N16 51 C1
Jones Rd E13 99 B3
Jones St W1 248 C5
Jones Wlk 6 TW10 154 B5
Jonquil Gdns 5 TW12 173 C4
Jonson Cl Hayes UB4 84 A2
Mitcham CR4 203 B6
Jonson Ho
Borough The SE1 262 D5
16 Canonbury N16 73 B4
Jordan Cl HA2 63 B5
Jordan Ct SW15 134 D1
Jordan Hill N10 30 C2
Jordan Ho
12 London SE4 140 D1
Shoreditch N1 235 D5
Jordan Lo SW17 180 C5
Jordan Rd UB6 87 C6
Jordans Cl
Dagenham RM10 81 D4
Hounslow TW7 130 C4
Jordans Ho NW8 237 A5
Jordans Mews TW11 152 C2
Jo Richardson Com Sch RM9 102 D6
Joscoyne Ho 5 E1 96 B1
Josef Perrin Ho 1 SE27 183 B6
Joseph Ave W3 89 B1
Joseph Clarke Specl Sch E4 36 B4
Joseph Conrad Ho SW1 259 B3
Joseph Ct N16 51 C2
Joseph Hardcastle Cl SE14 140 D5
Joseph Hood Prim Sch SW20 201 A6
Josephine Ave SW2 160 B6
Joseph Irwin Ho 11 E14 119 B6
Joseph Lister Ct E7 77 A1
Joseph Lister Lo E11 55 B1
Joseph Powell Cl 1 SW12 159 C5
Joseph Priestley Ho 12 E2 96 B4
Joseph Ray Rd E11 76 C6
Joseph St E3 97 B3
Joseph Trotter Cl EC1 234 B1
Joshua Cl
Croydon CR2 220 D1
Muswell Hill N10 31 B3
Joshua St E14 98 A1
Joslings Cl W12 112 A6
Joslyn Cl EN3 7 C5
Josseline Ct 9 E3 97 A5
Joubert Mans SW3 257 B2
Joubert St SW11 136 D3
Jowett Ho 27 SW9 138 A3
Jowett St SE15 139 D5
Joyce Ave N18 33 D5
Joyce Butler Ho N22 32 B2
Joyce Dawson Way SE28 124 A6
Joyce Lattimore Ct N9 18 B1
Joyce Page Cl SE7 143 D6
Joy Ct NW2 68 D5
Joydon Dr RM6 58 B3
Joyner Ct UB1 107 B6
Joyners Cl RM9 81 B4
Joystone Ct 8 EN4 2 C1
Jubb Powell Ho N15 51 C3
Jubet Ho 9 N16 73 B4
Jubilee Ave
Chingford E4 36 A4
Romford RM7 59 D4
Twickenham TW2 152 A3
Jubilee Bldgs NW8 229 C4
Jubilee Cl
4 Harlesden NW10 89 D5
Kingsbury NW9 45 B3
Pinner HA5 22 C1
Romford RM7 59 D4
Teddington KT1 175 C2
Jubilee Cres
Cubitt Town E14 120 A3
Edmonton N9 18 A3
Jubilee Ct
Harrow HA3 44 A2
Hounslow TW3 129 D2
Islington N1 233 B6
Muswell Hill N10 49 A6
12 Sutton SM2 218 A2
Thornton Heath CR7 204 C5
Jubilee Dr HA4 63 A4
Jubilee Gdns UB1 85 C1
Jubilee Hall Mkt★ WC2 250 B6
Jubilee Ho
3 Hampton TW12 173 C2
Lambeth SE11 261 B3
Jubilee Hts NW2 69 B2
Jubilee JMI Sch N16 52 A1
Jubilee Lo HA7 25 A5
Jubilee Mans 10 E1 96 C1
Jubilee Par IG8 37 C4
Jubilee Park Ctry Pk BR2 210 C4
Jubilee Pl SW3 114 C1 257 B2
Jubilee Prim Sch
London SW2 160 C5
Woolwich SE28 124 C6
Jubilee Rd
Cheam SM3 216 D1
Wembley UB6 87 B6
Jubilee St E1 96 C2
Jubilee The 2 SE10 141 D5
Jubilee Villas KT10 196 C1
Jubilee Way
East Bedfont TW14 150 A3
Merton SW19 179 D2
Sidcup DA14 168 A2
Tolworth KT4, KT9 214 D5
Jubilee Wks SW19 180 A1
Jubilee Wlk WD19 22 B6
Jubilee Yd SE1 253 C2
Judd St WC1 94 A4 233 A1
Jude St E16 98 D1
Judge Heath La UB3 83 B1
Judges' Wlk NW3 70 A5
Judge Wlk KT10 212 C2
Juer St SW11 136 C5 267 B3
Jules Thorn Ave EN1 6 A1
Julia Ct E17 53 D4
Julia Garfield Mews 4 E16 121 B5
Julia Gdns IG11 102 D5
Juliana Cl N2 48 A6
Julian Ave W3 110 D6
Julian Cl EN5 1 D2
Julian Ct SW13 133 D4
Julian Hill HA1 64 C6
Julian Ho SE21 183 C6
Julian Pl E14 119 D1
Julian's Prim Sch SW16 182 C6
Julian Taylor Path 7 SE23 162 B2
Julia St NW5 71 A3
Julien Rd W5 109 C3
Juliet Ho 11 N1 95 C5
Juliette Rd E13 99 A5
Julius Caesar Way HA7 9 D1
Julius Ct TW8 132 A5
Julius Ho 8 E14 98 B1
Julius Nyerere Cl N1 233 C5
Junction App
Battersea SW11 136 C2
Lewisham SE13 142 A2
Junction Mews W2 237 A2
Junction Pl W2 236 D2
Junction Rd
Ashford TW15 171 B5
Brentford TW8 109 D2
Croydon CR2 221 B3
Dartmouth Pk N19 71 C5
Edmonton N9 18 A3
Harrow HA1 42 C3
Newham E13 99 B5
Tottenham Hale N17 52 A6
Junction Rd E RM6 59 A2
Junction Rd W RM6 59 A2
Junction Wembley Ret Pk The HA9 66 D4
Juniper Cl Barnet EN5 12 D6
Chessington KT9 214 B3
Wembley HA9 66 C3
Juniper Cres NW1 71 A1
Juniper Ct
Dagenham RM6 58 C3
Harrow HA3 24 D2
Hounslow TW3 129 D1
Stoke Newington N16 73 B6
Thornton Heath CR0 204 C3
Juniper Dr SW18 136 A1
Juniper Gdns
Ashford TW16 171 D4
Streatham CR4 181 C2
Juniper Ho
12 Ealing W5 87 C2
6 Peckham SE14, SE15 140 C5
9 Richmond TW9 132 D4
Juniper La E6 100 A2
Juniper Rd IG1 78 D4
Juniper St 16 E1 118 C6
Juniper Way UB3 105 C6
Juno Ct 11 SW9 138 C5
Juno Ho 2 E3 97 C6
Juno Way SE14 140 D6
Juno Way Ind Est SE14 140 D6
Jupiter Ct
10 Brixton SW9 138 C5
8 Northolt UB5 84 D4
Jupiter Hts UB10 82 B6
Jupiter Way N7 72 B2

Jupp Rd E15 ... 76 B1
Jupp Rd W E15 ... 98 B6
Jura Ho SE16 ... 119 A2
Jurston Ct SE1 ... 251 B1
Justice Wlk SW3 ... 267 A5
Justin Cl TW8 ... 131 D5
Justin Ct [3] CR7 ... 204 C4
Justines Pl E2 ... 96 D4
Justin Plaza CR4 ... 202 C5
Justin Rd E4 ... 35 B4
Jute La EN3 ... 7 A2
Jutland Cl N19 ... 50 A1
Jutland Ho
[4] London SE5 ... 139 A3
[10] Woolwich SE7 ... 122 A2
Jutland Rd
Catford SE6 ... 164 A4
Newham E13 ... 99 A3
Jutsums Ave RM7 ... 59 D3
Jutsums Ct RM7 ... 59 D3
Jutsums La RM7 ... 59 D2
Juxon Cl HA3 ... 23 D2
Juxon St
SE11 ... 116 B2 260 D4
JVC Bsns Pk NW2 ... 46 A1

K

Kaduna Cl HA5 ... 40 B4
Kaine Pl CR0 ... 207 A2
Kaizen Prim Sch E13 ... 99 B3
Kale Rd DA18 ... 125 A4
Kambala Rd SW11 ... 136 B2
Kangley Bridge Ctr
SE26 ... 185 B5
Kangley Bridge Rd
SE26 ... 185 B5
Kaplan Dr N21 ... 16 B6
Karachi Ho E15 ... 76 C2
Kara Way NW2 ... 68 D4
Karen Ct
Bromley BR1 ... 186 D2
[2] Camberwell SE5 ... 139 C2
Forest Hill SE23 ... 163 A5
Karen Ho [7] N16 ... 73 B4
Karens Ct EN3 ... 6 D6
Karen Terr Ilford IG2 ... 57 B4
Leyton E11 ... 76 D6
Karenza Ct HA9 ... 43 C2
Kariba Cl N9 ... 18 C1
Karman Ct HA3 ... 42 C6
Karma Way HA2 ... 41 C1
Karoline Gdns UB6 ... 86 B5
Karyatis Ct EN1 ... 17 D6
Kashgar Rd SE18 ... 123 D2
Kashmir Rd SE7 ... 143 D5
Kasmin Ct NW10 ... 68 A1
Kassala Rd
SW11 ... 136 D4 267 D1
Katella Trad Est
IG11 ... 101 C4
Kates Cl EN5 ... 12 A6
Katharine Rd [1]
TW1 ... 153 A3
Katharine St CR0 ... 221 A5
Katherine Cl [3]
SE16 ... 118 D5
Katherine Ct
[10] Forest Hill SE23 ... 162 C3
Penge SE20 ... 184 C2
Katherine Gdns SE9 ... 143 D1
Katherine Ho
[15] Kensal Town W10 ... 91 A3
[6] South Croydon
CR0 ... 221 A5
South Norwood SE19 ... 183 C4
Katherine Rd E6, E7 ... 77 C1
Katherine Sq W11 ... 244 A4
Kathleen Ave
Acton W3 ... 89 A2
Wembley HA0 ... 66 A1
Kathleen Ferrier Ct [4]
N17 ... 33 D3
Kathleen Godfree Ct
SW19 ... 179 C5
Kathleen Moore Ct
BR4 ... 224 A6
Kathleen Rd SW11 ... 136 D2
Katrine Ct NW2 ... 68 C5
Kayemoor Rd SM2 ... 218 C2
Kay Rd SW9 ... 138 B3
Kays Ct EN3 ... 6 D1
Kay St E2 ... 96 A5
Keadby Ho [2] UB5 ... 85 B4
Kean Ho [5] SE17 ... 138 D6
Kean St WC2 ... 94 B1 240 C1
Keates Est N16 ... 73 D6
Keatley Gn E4 ... 35 B4
Keats Ave E16 ... 121 B5
Keats Cl
Bermondsey SE1 ... 263 C3
Enfield EN3 ... 18 D6
Hampstead NW3 ... 70 C4
Hayes UB4 ... 84 A2
Mitcham SW19 ... 180 B4
Wanstead E11 ... 55 B4
Keats Ct HA0 ... 65 C5
Keats Gr NW3 ... 70 C4
Keats Ho
[7] Beckenham BR3 ... 185 D4
[22] Bethnal Green E2 ... 96 C4
[30] Camberwell SE5 ... 139 A5
Chelsea SW1 ... 269 B6
Harrow HA2 ... 64 C6
Keats House Mus★
NW3 ... 70 C4
Keats Par [3] N9 ... 18 A2
Keats Pl EC2 ... 242 C3
Keats Rd DA16 ... 145 D4
Keats Way
Croydon CR0 ... 206 C3
Southall UB6 ... 85 D2
West Drayton UB7 ... 104 B2
Kebbell Terr E7 ... 77 B3
Keble Cl
New Malden KT4 ... 199 D1
Northolt UB5 ... 64 A3
Keble Ct SW19 ... 179 C4
Keble Ho [4] SW15 ... 156 D5
Keble Pl SW13 ... 134 B6
Keble Prep Sch N21 ... 16 C4
Keble St SW17 ... 180 A6
Kechill Gdns BR2 ... 209 A2
Kedelston Ct E5 ... 75 A4
Kedeston Ct SM1 ... 201 D1
Kedge Ho [16] E14 ... 119 C3
Kedleston Dr BR5 ... 211 D4
Kedleston Wlk [21] E2 ... 96 B4
Kedyngton Ho [5]
HA8 ... 27 A1
Keeble Cl SE18 ... 144 D6
Keedonwood Rd
BR1 ... 186 D5
Keel Cl Barking IG11 ... 102 C5
Rotherhithe SE16 ... 118 D5
Keel Ct [8] E14 ... 120 B6
Keeley Rd CR0 ... 221 A6
Keeley St WC2 ... 94 B1 240 C1
Keeling [2] TW11 ... 174 C5
Keeling Ct CR0 ... 220 D4
Keeling Ho [4] E2 ... 96 B5
Keeling Rd SE9 ... 165 D6
Keelson Ho [9] E14 ... 119 C3
Keely Cl EN4 ... 14 C6
Keemor Cl SE18 ... 144 C5
Keens Cl SW16 ... 181 D5
Keen's Rd CR0 ... 221 A4
Keen's Yd N1 ... 72 D2
Keepers Ct [4] CR2 ... 221 A3
Keepers Mews
TW11 ... 175 C4
Keeper Wharf E1 ... 118 D6
Keepier Wharf [15]
E1 ... 118 D6
Keep The
Forest Hill SE6 ... 163 C3
Kidbrooke SE3 ... 143 A3
Kingston u T KT2 ... 176 B3
Keeton's Rd SE16 ... 118 B3
Keevil Dr SW19 ... 157 A4
Keighley Cl N7 ... 72 A4
Keightley Dr SE9 ... 167 A3
Keilder Cl UB10 ... 82 C5
Keildon Rd SW11 ... 136 D1
Keir Hardie Est E5 ... 52 B1
Keir Hardie Ho
[6] Belvedere DA17 ... 125 C3
Fulham W6 ... 134 D6
[15] Upper Holloway
N19 ... 49 D2
Willesden NW10 ... 67 D1
Keir Hardie Way
Barking IG11 ... 80 A1
Hayes UB4 ... 84 A4
Keir Hardy Prim Sch [13]
E16 ... 99 A2
Keir The SW19 ... 178 C5
Keith Connor Cl [5]
SW8 ... 137 B2
Keith Gr W12 ... 112 A5
Keith Ho NW6 ... 91 D5
Keith Park Rd UB10 ... 60 B1
Keith Rd
Barking IG11 ... 101 B5
Hayes UB3 ... 105 C3
Walthamstow E17 ... 35 B2
Keith Sutton Ho [3]
SE9 ... 167 A2
Kelbrook Rd SE3 ... 144 A2
Kelby Ho N7 ... 72 B2
Kelceda Cl NW2 ... 68 A6
Kelf Gr UB3 ... 83 D1
Kelfield Ct [1] W10 ... 90 D1
Kelfield Gdns W10 ... 90 D1
Kelfield Mews W10 ... 90 D1
Kelham Ho [10] SE18 ... 144 D6
Kelland Cl [1] N8 ... 49 D4
Kelland Rd E13 ... 99 A3
Kellaway Rd SE3 ... 143 D3
Keller Cres E12 ... 77 D4
Kellerton Rd SE13 ... 164 C6
Kellett Ho N1 ... 235 D5
Kellett Rd SW2 ... 138 C1
Kelling Gdns CR0 ... 204 D2
Kellino St SW17 ... 180 D6
Kellner Rd SE28 ... 123 D3
Kellow Ho SE1 ... 252 C2
Kell St SE1 ... 116 D3 261 D6
Kelly Ave SE15 ... 139 D4
Kelly Cl
Upper Halliford
TW17 ... 171 C1
Willesden NW10 ... 67 B5
Kelly Ct [18] E14 ... 119 C6
Kelly Mews [4] W9 ... 91 B3
Kelly Rd NW7 ... 29 A4
Kelly St NW1 ... 71 B2
Kelly Way RM6 ... 59 A3
Kelman Cl SW4 ... 137 D3
Kelmore Gr SE22 ... 140 A1
Kelmscott [5] SE23 ... 162 D1
Kelmscott Cl E17 ... 35 B2
Kelmscott Ct [2] HA7 ... 25 C6
Kelmscott Gdns
W12 ... 112 A3
Kelmscott House★
W6 ... 112 B2
Kelmscott L Ctr E17 ... 53 B3
Kelmscott Rd SW11 ... 158 D6
Kelmscott Sch E17 ... 53 B3
Kelross Rd N5 ... 73 A4
Kelsall Cl SE3 ... 143 B3
Kelsall Mews TW9 ... 132 D4
Kelsey Gate [8] BR3 ... 185 D1
Kelsey La BR3 ... 207 C6
Kelsey Park Ave
BR3 ... 185 D1
Kelsey Park Man
BR3 ... 207 D6
Kelsey Park Rd BR3 ... 185 C1
Kelsey Park Sp Coll
BR3 ... 207 C6
Kelsey Rd BR5 ... 190 B1
Kelsey Sq BR3 ... 185 C1
Kelsey St E2 ... 96 A3
Kelsey Way BR3 ... 207 C6
Kelshall Ct N4 ... 73 A6
Kelso Ct SE20 ... 184 B3
Kelso Lo E18 ... 37 B1
Kelson Ho E14 ... 120 A3
Kelso Pl W8 ... 113 D3 255 D6
Kelso Rd SM5 ... 202 A2
Kelvedon Cl KT2 ... 176 C4
Kelvedon Ct HA4 ... 62 C4
Kelvedon Ho SW8 ... 270 B2
Kelvedon Rd
SW6 ... 135 B5 264 D3
Kelvin Ave N13 ... 32 B4
Kelvinbrook KT8 ... 195 D6
Kelvin Cl KT19 ... 214 C2
Kelvin Cres HA3 ... 24 C3
Kelvin Ct
Chiswick W4 ... 133 A5
Harrow HA2 ... 42 A1
Isleworth TW7 ... 130 C3
Notting Hill W11 ... 245 A5
[7] Penge SE20 ... 184 B2
[8] Twickenham TW1 ... 153 B5
Kelvin Dr TW1 ... 153 B5
Kelvin Gdns
Southall UB1 ... 85 C1
Thornton Heath CR0 ... 204 A2
Kelvin Gr
Forest Hill SE26 ... 162 B1
Surbiton KT6 ... 214 A5
Kelvin Grove Prim Sch [7]
SE26 ... 162 B1
Kelvington Cl CR0 ... 207 A2
Kelvington Rd SE15 ... 162 D6
Kelvin Ho [3] DA17 ... 125 C3
Kelvin Ind Est UB6 ... 85 D6
Kelvin Par BR6 ... 211 C1
Kelvin Rd Highbury N5 ... 73 A4
Welling DA16 ... 146 A2
Kelyway Ho [20] SW2 ... 160 C4
Kember St N1 ... 72 B1
Kemble Dr BR2 ... 226 A5
Kemble Ho
London SW9 ... 138 D2
Stanmore HA7 ... 24 D5
Kemble Rd
Croydon CR0 ... 220 D5
Forest Hill SE23 ... 162 D3
Tottenham N17 ... 34 A2
Kemble St
WC2 ... 94 B1 240 C1
Kemerton Rd
Beckenham BR3 ... 185 D1
Camberwell SE5 ... 139 A2
Croydon CR0 ... 205 D2
Kemey's St E9 ... 75 A3
Kemnal Rd BR7 ... 189 B5
Longlands BR7, SE9 ... 167 B1
Kemnal Tech Coll
DA14 ... 190 B3
Kemnal Warren BR7 ... 189 B4
Kemp [24] NW9 ... 27 D2
Kemp Ct SW8 ... 270 A3
Kempe Ho SE1 ... 262 D5
Kempe Rd NW6 ... 90 D5
Kemp Gdns CR0 ... 205 A3
Kemp Ho
Finsbury EC1 ... 235 C1
[1] Globe Town E2 ... 96 D5
Wallend E6 ... 78 C2
Kempis Way [5]
SE22 ... 161 C6
Kemplay Rd NW3 ... 70 B4
Kemp Rd RM8 ... 58 D1
Kemps Ct NW2 ... 68 D5
Kemp's Ct W1 ... 239 C1
Kemps Dr E14 ... 119 C6
Kempsford Gdns
SW5 ... 113 C1 255 B1
Kempsford Rd
Lambeth SE11 ... 261 B3
Newington SE11 ... 261 C3
Kemps Gdns SE13 ... 164 A6
Kempshott Rd SW16 ... 182 A3
Kempson Rd
SW6 ... 135 C5 265 B3
Kempthorne Rd SE8 ... 119 B2
Kempton Ave
Northolt UB5 ... 63 C3
Sunbury TW16 ... 172 B2
Kempton Cl UB10 ... 61 A4
Kempton Ct
Stepney E1 ... 96 B2
Sunbury TW16 ... 172 B2
Kempton Ho [13] N1 ... 95 C6
Kempton Lo [3] SM6 ... 219 D5
Kempton Park Race
Course TW16 ... 172 C3
Kempton Park Sta
TW16 ... 172 B3
Kempton Rd E6 ... 100 B6
Kempton Wlk CR0 ... 207 A3
Kempt St SE18 ... 144 C6
Kemsing Cl
Coney Hall BR2 ... 224 D6
Sidcup DA5 ... 169 A4
South Norwood CR7 ... 205 A5
Kemsing Ho SE1 ... 252 D1
Kemsing Rd SE10 ... 121 A1
Kemsley SE13 ... 163 D6
Kemsley Ct
Ealing W13 ... 109 C5
St Paul's Cray BR5 ... 190 B2
Kenbrook Ho
Kensington W14 ... 254 D5
[5] Kentish Town NW5 ... 71 C3
Kenbury Cl UB10 ... 60 C5
Kenbury Gdns [10]
SE5 ... 139 A3
Kenbury Mans [18]
SE5 ... 139 A3
Kenbury St SE5 ... 139 A3
Kenchester Cl
SW8 ... 138 A5 270 B3
Kencot Cl DA18 ... 125 B4
Kencot Way DA18 ... 125 B4
Kendal NW1 ... 231 D2
Kendal Ave Acton W3 ... 88 D2
Barking IG11 ... 101 C6
Edmonton N18 ... 33 B6
Kendal Cl
Camberwell SE5 ... 138 D5
East Barnet N20 ... 14 C2
East Bedfont TW14 ... 149 D3
Hayes UB4 ... 83 C5
Woodford IG8 ... 20 D2
Kendal Ct Acton W3 ... 88 C2
Brondesbury NW2 ... 69 A3
[9] Chingford E4 ... 20 A3
Kendale Rd BR1 ... 186 C5
Kendal Gdns
Edmonton N18 ... 33 B6
Sutton SM1 ... 218 A6
Kendal Ho
Edgware HA8 ... 27 A6
Forest Hill SE23 ... 163 B3
[32] Hackney E9 ... 74 C1
Islington N1 ... 233 D4
Penge SE20 ... 184 B1
Kendall Ave BR3 ... 185 A1
Kendall Ct
[3] London SE22 ... 162 A6
Mitcham SW19 ... 180 B4
[5] Penge SE19 ... 183 D3
Sidcup DA15 ... 168 A1
Kendall Ho SE12 ... 164 D4
Kendall Lo [5] BR1 ... 187 B2
Kendall Pl W1 ... 238 A3
Kendall Rd
Beckenham BR3 ... 185 A1
Isleworth TW7 ... 131 A3
Kidbrooke SE18 ... 144 A4
Kendalmere Cl N10 ... 31 B2
Kendal Par N18 ... 33 B6
Kendal Pl SW15 ... 157 B6
Kendal Rd NW10 ... 68 A4
Kendal St W2 ... 92 C1 237 B1
Kendal Stps W2 ... 237 B1
Kender Prim Sch
SE14 ... 140 C4
Kender St SE14 ... 140 C4
Kendoa Rd [1] SW4 ... 137 D1
Kendon Cl E11 ... 55 B4
Kendon Ho E15 ... 76 B1
Kendra Ct CR2 ... 220 D1
Kendra Hall Rd CR2 ... 220 D1
Kendrey Gdns TW2 ... 152 C4
Kendrick Ct [12] SE15 ... 140 B4
Kendrick Mews SW7 ... 256 C3
Kendrick Pl SW7 ... 256 C3
Kenelm Cl HA1 ... 65 A5
Kenerne Dr EN5 ... 13 A6
Kenilford Rd SW12 ... 159 B4
Kenilworth Ave
Harrow HA2 ... 63 B4
Walthamstow E17 ... 53 C6
Wimbledon SW19 ... 179 C6
Kenilworth Cres EN1 ... 5 C4
Kenilworth Ct
[7] Chingford E4 ... 20 A2
Fulham SW6 ... 135 A2
Twickenham TW2 ... 152 C2
Kenilworth Gdns
Hayes UB4 ... 83 D2
Ilford IG3 ... 79 D6
Southall UB1 ... 85 B4
South Oxhey WD19 ... 22 C5
Woolwich SE18 ... 144 D3
Kenilworth Ho HA7 ... 25 B3
Kenilworth Rd
Ashford TW15,
TW19 ... 148 A1
Bow E3 ... 97 A5
Ealing W5 ... 110 A5
Edgware HA8 ... 11 A1
Kilburn NW6 ... 91 B6
Orpington BR5 ... 211 A3
Penge SE20 ... 184 D2
Stoneleigh KT17 ... 216 A3
Kenilworth Terr [3]
SM2 ... 217 C1
Kenley N17 ... 33 B1
Kenley Ave NW9 ... 27 C2
Kenley Cl Barnet EN4 ... 2 C1
Sidcup DA5 ... 169 C4
St Paul's Cray BR7 ... 211 C6
Kenley Gdns CR7 ... 204 D5

Kenley Ho
5 Croydon CR0 206 A1
6 St Paul's Cray BR5 190 B1
Kenley Rd
Kingston u T KT1, KT3 176 D1
Merton SW19 201 C6
Twickenham TW1 153 B5
Kenley Wlk
Cheam SM3 216 D4
Notting Hill W11 244 A5
Kenlor Ct 6 HA8 26 D5
Kenlor Rd SW17 180 B5
Kenmare Ct 5 HA7 25 C6
Kenmare Dr
Mitcham CR4 180 D3
1 Tottenham N17 33 D1
Kenmare Gdns N13 33 A6
Kenmare Rd CR7 204 C3
Kenmere Gdns HA0 88 C6
Kenmere Rd DA16 146 C3
Kenmont Gdns NW10 90 B4
Kenmont Prim Sch NW10 90 B4
Kenmore Ave HA3 43 A6
Kenmore Cl TW9 132 C5
Kenmore Cres UB4 83 D4
Kenmore Ct NW6 69 C1
Kenmore Gdns HA8 26 D1
Kenmore Park Fst & Mid Schs HA3 44 A6
Kenmore Rd HA3 43 D5
Kenmure Mans W5 87 C3
Kenmure Rd E8 74 B3
Kenmure Yd E8 74 B3
Kennacraig Cl 6 E16 121 A5
Kennard Ho 12 SW11 137 A3
Kennard Mans 6 N11 30 D5
Kennard Rd
London N11 30 D5
Stratford E15 76 B1
Kennard St
9 London SW11 137 A3
Newham E16 122 B5
Kennedy Ave EN3 18 C5
Kennedy Cl
Crofton BR5 211 B1
1 Mitcham CR4 181 A1
Newham E13 99 A5
Pinner HA5 23 B4
Kennedy Cox Ho 9 E16 98 D2
Kennedy Ct
Ashford TW15 171 A5
Bushey WD23 8 B2
Kennedy Ho SE11 260 C2
Kennedy Path W7 86 D3
Kennedy Rd
Barking IG11 101 C6
Ealing W7 86 C2
Kennedy Wlk SE17 262 D3
Kennet Cl SW11 136 B1
Kennet Ct 47 W2 91 C2
Kennet Dr UB4 85 A2
Kenneth Ave IG1 78 D4
Kenneth Campbell Ho NW8 236 D6
Kenneth Cres NW2 68 B3
Kenneth Ct SE11 261 B4
Kenneth Gdns HA7 25 A4
Kenneth More Rd 4 IG1 78 D5
Kennet Ho NW8 236 D5
Kenneth Rd RM6 59 A2
Kenneth Robbins Ho 1 N17 34 B3
Kenneth Younger Ho SW6 264 D5
Kennet Rd
Isleworth TW7 130 D2
West Kilburn W9 91 B3
Kennet Sq CR4 180 C2
Kennet St E1 118 A5
Kennett Ho HA1 64 D6
Kennett Wharf La EC4 252 B6
Kenninghall N18 34 C5
Kenninghall Rd
London N18 34 C5
Lower Clapton E5 74 B5
Kenning Ho 6 N1 95 C6
Kenning St 18 SE16 118 C4
Kennings Way SE11 116 C1 261 B2
KENNINGTON 116 C1
Kennington Ent Ctr SE17 261 C1
Kennington La SE11 116 B1 260 D1
Kennington Oval SE11 138 B6 270 D5
Kennington Palace Ct SE11 261 A2
Kennington Park Gdns SE17 138 D6
Kennington Park Ho SE11 261 B1
Kennington Park Pl SE11 138 D6
Kennington Park Rd SE11 116 D1 261 C2
Kennington Rd SE11 116 C2 261 A3
Kennington Sta SE17 116 D1 261 C2
Kennoldes SE21 161 B2
Kennyland Ct NW4 46 B3
Kenrick Pl W1 238 A3
KENSAL GREEN 90 C4
Kensal Green Cemy (All Souls)* NW10 90 C4
Kensal Green Sta NW10 90 C4
Kensal Ho W10 90 D3
Kensal Rd W10 91 A3
KENSAL RISE 90 D5
Kensal Rise Prim Sch NW6 90 D5
Kensal Rise Sta NW10 90 D5
KENSAL TOWN 91 A3
KENSINGTON 113 C4
Kensington Acad SW6 256 C3
Kensington Ave
Plashet E12 78 B2
South Norwood CR7 182 C2
Kensington Avenue Prim Sch CR7 182 C2
Kensington & Chelsea Coll
Chelsea SW10 136 A5 266 A4
14 Kensal Town W10 91 A2
Kensington Church Ct W8 245 C1
Kensington Church St W8 113 C5 245 B3
Kensington Church Wlk W8 245 C1
Kensington Cl N11 31 A4
Kensington Court Mans W8 245 D1
Kensington Court Mews W8 255 D6
Kensington Court Pl W8 113 D3 255 D6
Kensington Ct
2 Burnt Oak NW7 27 B5
Enfield EN2 5 C5
Hendon NW4 28 C1
Kensington W8 113 D4 245 D1
Kensington Ct Gdns W8 255 D6
Kensington Dr IG8 37 D1
Kensington Gardens* W2 114 A5 246 B3
Kensington Gate W8 114 A3 256 A6
Kensington Gdns
Kingston u T KT1 197 D6
Redbridge IG1 56 B1
Kensington Gdns Sq W2 91 D1
Kensington Gore SW7 114 B4 246 C1
Kensington Hall Gdns W14 254 C2
Kensington High St W8 113 C3 255 B6
Kensington Ho 3 NW5 71 C3
Kensington Hts
Harrow HA1 42 D3
Kensington W8 245 A3
Kensington L Ctr W11 113 A6 244 A6
Kensington Lodge UB5 85 C5
Kensington Mall W8 245 B4
Kensington Mans SW5 255 B2
Kensington Olympia Sta W14 113 A3 254 A6
Kensington Pal* W8 113 D5 245 D3
Kensington Palace Gdns W8 113 D5 245 C4
Kensington Park Gdns W11 113 B6 244 D5
Kensington Park Mews W11 91 B1
Kensington Park Rd W11 113 B6 244 D6
Kensington Pl W8 113 C5 245 A4
Kensington Prep Sch SW6 135 B4 264 D2
Kensington Prim Sch E12 78 B2
Kensington Rd
Kensington SW7 114 A4 246 B1
Northolt UB5 85 C5
Kensington Sq W8 113 D4 245 C1
Kensington Terr CR2 221 B1
Kensington Village W14 113 B2 254 D3
Kensington W W14 254 A4
Kensit Meml Coll N3 29 A1
Kensworth Ho EC1 235 D1
Kent Ave
Bexley DA16 167 D6
Dagenham RM9 103 C3
Ealing W13 87 B2
Kent Cl
Mitcham CR4, SW16 204 A5
Orpington BR6 227 C2
Kent Ct Acton W3 88 B1
3 Haggerston E2 95 D5
Hendon NW9 27 C1
Kent Dr
Cockfosters EN4 15 A6
Teddington TW11 174 C5
Kentford Way UB5 85 A6
Kent Gate Way CR0 223 D3
Kent Gdns Ealing W13 87 B2
Ruislip HA4 40 B3
Kent Ho
Camberwell SE1 263 D1
13 Chiswick W4 111 C1
Edgware HA8 26 B3
Marylebone W1 239 A2
Pimlico SW1 259 C1
Richmond TW10 154 C6
Kent House La BR3 185 A5
Kent House Rd BR3 185 A4
Kent House Sta BR3 185 A2
Kent House Station App BR3 184 D2
Kentish Bldgs SE1 252 C3
Kentish Rd DA17 125 C2
KENTISH TOWN 71 C3
Kentish Town CE Prim Sch 13 NW5 71 C3
Kentish Town City Farm* NW5 71 A3
Kentish Town Rd NW1 71 B2
Kentish Town Sta NW5 71 C3
Kentish Town West Sta NW5 71 B2
Kentish Way BR1, BR2 209 B6
Kentlea Rd SE28 123 C4
Kent Lo 9 SW19 156 D3
Kentmere Ho SE15 140 C6
Kentmere Rd SE18 123 C2
KENTON 43 C3
Kenton Ave
Harrow HA1 42 D2
Southall UB1 107 C6
Sunbury TW16 173 A1
Kenton Ct
2 Forest Hill SE26 185 A6
Harrow HA3 43 B3
3 Richmond TW10 153 D5
Kenton Ct *continued*
West Kensington W14 254 C5
Kenton Gdns HA3 43 C4
Kenton Grove Ho HA3 44 B4
Kenton Ho
20 Globe Town E1 96 C3
Highbury N5 72 C5
Kenton La
Harrow HA3 24 D3
Kenton HA3 43 C6
Kenton Park Ave HA3 43 D5
Kenton Park Cl HA3 43 C4
Kenton Park Cres HA3 43 D5
Kenton Park Mans HA3 43 C4
Kenton Park Par HA3 43 D4
Kenton Park Rd HA3 43 C5
Kenton Rd
Harrow HA3 43 C4
Homerton E9 74 D2
Kenton St WC1 240 A6
Kenton Sta HA3 43 B3
Kenton Way UB4 83 C4
Kent Pas NW1 237 C6
Kent Pk Ind Est SE15 140 B6
Kent Rd
Dagenham RM10 81 D3
East Molesey KT8 196 A5
Kingston u T KT1 197 D6
Richmond TW9 132 C5
South Acton W4 111 A3
Southgate N21 17 B4
West Wickham BR4 207 D1
Kent St Haggerston E2 95 D5
Newham E13 99 B4
Kent Terr NW1 92 C4 230 B1
Kent Twr SE20 184 B3
Kent View Gdns IG3 79 C6
Kent Way KT6 214 B6
Kentwell Cl SE4 141 A1
Kentwins N14 15 B6
Kentwode Gn SW13 134 A5
Kent Yard SW7 247 B1
Kenver Ave N12 30 B4
Kenward Rd SE9 165 D6
Ken Way HA9 67 A5
Kenway Rd SW5 113 D2 255 C3
Ken Wilson Ho 19 E2 96 A5
Kenwood Ave N14 15 D6
Kenwood Cl
North End NW3 48 B1
Sipson UB7 126 C6
Kenwood Ct NW9 45 A5
Kenwood Dr BR3 208 A6
Kenwood Gdns
Ilford IG2 56 C4
2 Wanstead E18 55 B6
Kenwood Ho
15 Brixton SW9 138 D1
Enfield EN1 17 C5
Kenwood Ho* NW3 48 C1
Kenwood Rd
Edmonton N9 18 A3
Highgate N6 48 D3
Kenworthy Rd E9 75 A2
Kenwrick Ho N1 233 D5
Kenwyn Dr NW2 67 D5
Kenwyn Rd
Clapham SW4 137 D1
Wimbledon SW20 178 C2
Kenya Rd SE7 143 D5
Kenyngton Dr TW16 172 A5
Kenyngton Manor Prim Sch TW16 172 A4
Kenyngton Pl HA3 43 C4
Kenyon Ho 31 SE5 139 A5
Kenyon St SW6 134 D4
Keogh Rd E15 76 D2
Kepler Ho 9 SE10 120 D1
Kepler Rd SW2, SW4 138 A1
Keppel Ho
Brompton SW3 257 A3
5 Deptford SE8 119 B1
Keppel Rd
Dagenham RM9 81 A4
Newham E6 100 B6
Keppel Row SE1 252 A3
Keppel St WC1 239 D4
Kerala Ct N17 33 D2
Kerbela St 8 E2 96 A3
Kerbey St E14 97 D1
Kerem Sch N2 48 B4
Kerfield Cres SE5 139 B4
Kerfield Pl SE5 139 B4
Kerridge Ct 10 N1 73 C2
Kerrier Ho SW10 266 B3
Kerrington Ct 7 W12 112 C4
Kerrison Pl W5 109 D5
Kerrison Rd
Battersea SW11 136 C2
Ealing W5 109 D5
Mill Meads E15 98 B6
Kerrison Villas W5 109 D5
Kerry N7 72 A2
Kerry Ave HA7 25 D6
Kerry Cl Newham E16 99 B1
Palmers Green N13 16 B2
Kerry Ct HA7 25 D6
Kerry Ho 5 E1 96 C1
Kerry Path SE8 141 B6
Kerry Rd SE8 141 B6
Kerscott Ho 30 E3 97 D4
Kersey Gdns SE9 188 A6
Kersfield Ho SW15 156 D5
Kersfield Rd SW15 156 D5
Kershaw Cl SW18 158 B5
Kershaw Ho 7 SE27 160 D1
Kershaw Rd RM10 81 C5
Kersley Mews SW11 267 C1
Kersley Rd N16 73 C5
Kersley St SW11 136 D3
Kerstin Cl UB3 105 D6
Kerswell Cl N15 51 C4
Kerwick Cl 1 N7 72 B1
Keslake Mans NW10 90 D5
Keslake Rd NW6 90 D5
Kessock Cl N17 52 B4
Kestlake Rd DA5 168 C5
KESTON 225 D4
Keston Ave BR2 225 C3
Keston CE Prim Sch BR2 225 D3
Keston Cl
Bexley DA16 146 C5
Edmonton N18 17 B1
Keston Ct DA5 169 B4
Keston Gdns BR2 225 C4
Keston Ho SE17 263 B2
KESTON MARK 225 D6
Keston Mark BR2 226 A5
Keston Park Cl BR2 226 B5
Keston Rd
East Dulwich SE15 140 A2
Thornton Heath CR7 204 C3
West Green N17 51 B5
Kestrel Ave
East Ham E6 100 A2
Herne Hill SE24 161 A6
Kestrel Cl
Grahame Pk NW9 27 C1
Kingston u T KT2 175 D6
Neasden NW10 67 B3
Kestrel Ct
Higham Hill E17 34 D1
Ruislip HA4 61 B6
South Croydon CR2 221 A2
Wallington SM6 219 C3
Kestrel Ho
4 Battersea SW11 136 C2
Enfield EN3 19 A6
Finsbury EC1 235 A2
Kestrel Pl SE14 141 A6
Kestrel Way UB3 105 B4
Keswick Apartments 4 N17 51 D6
Keswick Ave
Kingston u T KT2, SW15 177 C5
Merton SW19 179 C1
Upper Halliford TW17 193 C6
Keswick Broadway 1 SW15 157 B6
Keswick Cl SM1 218 A4
Keswick Ct
18 Catford SE6 164 D3
2 East Dulwich SE22 162 A6
Keswick Dr EN3 6 C6
Keswick Gdns
Redbridge IG4 56 A5
Ruislip HA4 39 B3
Wembley HA9 66 A4
Keswick Ho 8 SE5 139 A4

Keswick Hts 9 SW15 157 A6
Keswick Lo E8 73 D2
Keswick Mews W5 110 A5
Keswick Rd
Bexleyheath DA7 147 C4
Broom Hill BR6 211 D1
Putney SW15 157 A6
Twickenham TW2 152 A5
West Wickham BR4 224 C6
Kettering Ct CR7 205 A5
Kettering Rd EN3 6 D6
Kettering St SW16 181 C4
Kett Gdns SW2 160 B6
Kettlebaston Rd E10 53 B1
Kettleby Ho SW9 138 D2
Kettlewell Cl N11 31 A4
Ketton Ho 11 W10 90 C3
Kevan Ct 6 E17 53 D5
Kevan Ho SE5 139 A5
Kevelioc Rd N17 33 A2
Kevin Cl TW4 128 D3
Kevington Cl BR5 211 D5
Kevington Dr BR5, BR7 211 D5
KEW 132 C6
Kew Bridge TW8 110 B1
Kew Bridge Ct W4 110 C1
Kew Bridge Distribution Ctr TW8 110 B1
Kew Bridge Rd TW8 110 B1
Kew Bridge Sta TW8 110 B1
Kew Bridge Steam Mus* TW8 110 B1
Kew Coll TW9 132 C5
Kew Cres SM3 217 B5
Kew Ct KT2 176 A2
Kew Foot Rd TW9 132 A2
Kew Gardens Rd TW9 132 C4
Kew Gardens (Royal Botanic)* TW9 132 A4
Kew Gardens Sta TW9 132 C4
Kew Gn TW9 132 B6
Kew Green TW9 132 C6
Kew Green Prep Sch TW9 132 B6
Kew Lo 11 TW9 132 B4
Kew Obsy* TW9 131 C2
Kew Pal* TW9 132 A5
Kew Pier TW9 132 C6
Kew Rd Finchley N2 30 C2
Richmond TW9, W4 132 B4
Kew Ret Pk TW9 132 D4
Kew Riverside Prim Sch TW9 132 D3
Key Cl E1 96 B3
Keyes Ct SE22 162 A6
Keyes Rd NW2 68 D3
Keyham Ho 31 W2 91 C2
Key Ho 9 SE11 138 C6
Keymer Rd SW2 160 B2
Keynes Cl N2 48 D6
Keynes Ct 9 SE28 124 B6
Keynsham Ave IG8 36 C6
Keynsham Gdns SE9 166 A6
Keynsham Ho 2 N4 51 A2
Keynsham Rd
Cheam SM4 201 D1
Eltham SE9 166 A6
Keynsham Wlk SM4 201 D1
Keysham Ave TW5 128 A4
Keysham Ct HA9 66 A6
Keystone Cres N1 233 B3
Keywood Dr TW16 172 A4
Keyworth Cl E5 75 A4
Keyworth Pl SE1 261 D6
Keyworth Prim Sch SE17 116 D1 261 C2
Keyworth St SE1 116 D3 261 D6
Kezia St SE8 119 A1
Khalsa Coll London HA1 42 B3
Khalsa Ct N22 32 D2
Khama Rd SW17 180 C6
Khartoum Rd
Ilford IG1 78 D3
Newham E13 99 B4
Upper Tooting SW17 180 B6
Khyber Rd SW11 136 C3
Kibworth St SW8 138 B5 270 C3
KIDBROOKE 143 C3
Kidbrooke Gdns SE3 143 A4
Kidbrooke Gr SE3 143 B4
Kidbrooke Interchange SE3 143 C2
Kidbrooke La SE9 144 A1
Kidbrooke Park Cl SE3 143 B4
Kidbrooke Park Prim Sch SE3 143 C4
Kidbrooke Park Rd SE12, SE3 143 B2
Kidbrooke Sch SE3 143 D3
Kidbrooke Sta SE3 143 B2
Kidbrooke Way SE3 143 B3
Kiddens BR8 191 D1
Kidderminster Pl CR0 204 D1
Kidderminster Rd CR0 205 A2
Kidderpore Ave NW3 69 C4
Kidderpore Gdns NW3 69 C4
Kidd Ho RM9 81 B4
Kidd Pl SE7 122 A1
Kidlington Way NW9 27 C2
Kidspace Indoor Adventure Pk* CR0 220 C2
Kierbeck Bsns Complex E16 121 B4
Kiffen St EC2 242 D6
Kilberry Cl TW7 130 B4
Kilbrennan Ho 9 E14 98 A1
KILBURN 91 C6
Kilburn Bridge 14 NW6 91 C6
Kilburn Gate NW6 91 D5
Kilburn High Rd NW6 91 C6
Kilburn High Road Sta NW6 91 D6
Kilburn Ho 11 W9 91 B4
Kilburn La W10 91 A5
Kilburn Park Rd NW6 91 C4
Kilburn Park Sch 10 NW6 91 B5
Kilburn Park Sta NW6 91 C5
Kilburn Pl NW6 91 C6
Kilburn Priory NW6 91 D6
Kilburn Sq NW6 91 C6
Kilburn Sta NW2 69 B2
Kilburn Vale NW6 91 D6
Kilburn Vale Est 13 NW6 91 C6
Kilby Ct SE10 120 D3
Kildare Cl HA4 40 C1
Kildare Ct W2 91 C1
Kildare Gdns W2 91 C1
Kildare Rd E16 99 A2
Kildare Terr W2 91 C1
Kildare Wlk E14 97 C1
Kildoran Rd SW2 160 A6
Kildowan Rd IG3 58 A1
Kilgour Rd SE23 163 A5
Kilkie St SW6 136 A3
Killarney Rd SW18 158 A5
Killburns Mill Cl SM6 219 B6
Killearn Rd SE6 164 B3
Killester Gdns KT17, KT4 216 B4
Killick Ho SM1 217 D4
Killick Mews 6 SM3 217 A2
Killick St N1 94 B5 233 C3
Killieser Ave SW2 160 A2
Killigrew Ho TW16 171 C3
Killip Cl E16 98 D1
Killoran Ho 9 E14 120 A3
Killowen Ave UB5 64 A3
Killowen Rd E9 74 D2
Killyon Rd SW8 137 C3
Kilmaine Rd SW6 135 A5 264 B3
Kilmarnock Gdns RM8 80 C5
Kilmarnock Rd WD19 22 D6
Kilmarsh Rd W6 112 C2
Kilmartin Ave SW16 204 C6
Kilmartin Rd IG3 80 A6
Kilmington Rd SW13 134 A6
Kilmiston Ave TW17 193 A3
Kilmiston Ho TW17 193 A3
Kilmore Ho 17 E14 97 D1
Kilmorey Gdns TW1 131 B1
Kilmorey Rd TW1 131 B1
Kilmorie Prim Sch SE23 163 A2
Kilmorie Rd SE23 163 A2
Kilmuir Ho SW1 258 B3
Kiln Cl UB3 127 B6
Kiln Ct E14 119 B6
Kilner Ho 3 SE11 138 C6
Kilner St E14 97 C2
Kiln Mews SW17 180 B5
Kiln Pl NW5 71 A3
Kilnsey Ct 8 N11 31 A4
Kilnside KT10 213 A1
Kiloh Ct 1 SW11 136 C2
Kilpatrick Ct N16 51 D1
Kilpatrick Way UB4 85 A2
Kilpeck Ho 3 N4 51 A2
Kilravock Ho SE25 205 C6
Kilravock St W10 91 A4
Kilronan 5 W3 89 B1
Kilross Rd TW14 149 C3
Kilsby Wlk RM9 80 B2
Kilsha Rd KT12 194 C3
Kilvinton Dr EN2 5 B5
Kimbell Gdns SW6 135 A4 264 A1
Kimbell Pl SE9 143 C1
Kimber Ctr The SW18 157 C4
Kimber Ho 11 SE18 144 D6
Kimberley Ave
Ilford IG2 57 C2
Newham E6 100 A5
Nunhead SE15 140 C2
Kimberley Ct
Belvedere DA17 125 B2
Kilburn NW6 91 A6
Kimberley Dr DA14 168 D2
Kimberley Gate 3 BR1 186 D3
Kimberley Gdns
Enfield EN1 5 D2
Harringay N4 50 D4
Kimberley Ho 7 E14 120 A3
Kimberley Ind Est E17 35 B2
Kimberley Rd
Chingford E4 20 C3
Edmonton N18 34 B4
Kilburn NW6 91 A6
Leyton E11 76 B6
Newham E16 98 D3
Penge BR3 184 D1
Stockwell SW9 138 A2
Thornton Heath CR0 204 D3
Tottenham N17 34 A1
Walthamstow E17 35 B2
Kimberley Way E4 20 C3
Kimberley Wlk KT12 194 B2
Kimber Pl TW4 151 C4
Kimber Rd SW18 157 D4
Kimble Cres WD23 8 A4
Kimble Ho
Lisson Gr NW8 237 B6
1 Lower Holloway N7 72 A3
Kimble Rd SW17 180 B4
Kimbolton Cl SE12 164 D5
Kimbolton Row SW3 257 A3
Kimmeridge Gdns 3 SE9 188 A6
Kimmeridge Rd SE9 188 A6
Kimm Ho 18 E17 53 D6
Kimpton Ct 12 SE5 139 B4
Kimpton Ho SW15 156 A4
Kimpton Link Bsns Ctr SM3 217 B6
Kimpton Park Way SM3 217 B6
Kimpton Rd
Camberwell SE5 139 B4
Cheam SM3 217 B6
Kimpton Trade & Bsns Ctr SM3 217 B6
Kinburn St SE16 118 D4
Kincaid Rd SE15 140 B5
Kincardine Gdns W9 91 C3
Kinch Gr HA3, HA9 44 B2
Kincraig BR7 188 C2
Kindell Ho 4 SW14 133 B2
Kinder Cl SE28 124 D6
Kinder Ho N1 235 D4
Kindersley Ho 38 E1 96 A1
Kinder St 19 E1 96 B1
Kinderton Cl N14 15 C3
Kinefold Ho N7 72 A2
Kinfauns Rd Ilford IG3 58 B1
Streatham SW2 160 C2
King Alfred Ave
Catford SE6 163 C1
Catford SE6 185 C6
King Alfred Sch NW11 47 D1
King Arthur Cl SE15 140 C5
King Athelstan Prim Sch KT1 198 B6
King Charles Cres KT5 198 B2
King Charles Ct 16 SE17 138 D6
King Charles Ho SW6 265 D4
King Charles' Rd KT5, KT6 198 B3
King Charles St SW1 116 A4 250 A2
King Charles Terr 11 E1 118 B6
King Charles Wlk 6 SW19 157 A3
King Ct 16 E10 53 D2
Kingcup Cl CR0 206 D1
King David La E1 118 C6
Kingdom St W2 92 A2 236 A3
Kingdon Ho 8 E14 120 A3
Kingdon Rd NW6 69 C2
Kingdown Cl W10 90 D1
King Edward Dr KT6 214 A5
King Edward Mans 12 E8 96 B6
King Edward Mews SW13 134 A4
King Edward Rd
Barnet EN5 1 D1
Leytonstone E10 54 A1
Walthamstow E17 53 A6
King Edward's Gdns W3 110 C5
King Edward's Gr TW11 175 C4
King Edwards Mans SW6 265 A3
King Edwards Pl 5 W3 110 C5
King Edwards Rd HA4 39 B1
King Edward's Rd
Barking IG11 101 B5
Edmonton N9 18 B4
Enfield EN3 6 D1
South Hackney E9 96 C6
King Edward St EC1 242 A2
King Edward The Third Mews 11 SE16 118 B4
King Edward VII Hospl for Officers W1 93 A2 238 B4
King Edward Wlk SE1 116 C3 261 B6
King Fahad Acad The W5 109 C2
King Fahed Acad W3 111 D6
Kingfield Rd W5 87 D3
Kingfield St E14 120 A2
Kingfisher Ave E11 55 B3
Kingfisher Cl
Harrow HA3 24 D3
Woolwich SE28 124 C6
Kingfisher Ct
11 Battersea SW11 136 C2
Cheam SM1 217 B3
17 Cubitt Town E14 120 A4
East Molesey KT8 196 C5
Enfield EN2 4 B5
Hounslow TW3 151 D6
Merton SW19 179 B3
Putney SW19 157 A2
Spring Gr TW3 130 B3
Kingfisher Dr TW10 175 B6
Kingfisher Ho
16 Battersea SW18 136 A2
Peckham SE15 139 D4
West Kensington W14 254 C6
Kingfisher L Ctr KT1 176 A1
Kingfisher Lo TW11 175 A6
Kingfisher Mews SE13 163 D6
Kingfisher Sq 19 SE8 141 B6
Kingfisher St E6 100 A2
Kingfisher Way
Croydon CR0 206 D4
Neasden NW10 67 B3
Kingfisher Wlk NW9 27 C1
King Frederick IX Twr SE16 119 B3
King Garth Mews SE23 162 C2
King Gdns CR0 220 D3
King George Ave
Ilford IG2 57 B3
Newham E16 99 D1
Walton-on-T KT12 194 D1
King George Cl TW16 171 C5
King George Hospl IG3 58 A4
King George Sq TW10 154 B5
King George St SE10 142 A5
King George's Trad Est KT9 214 C4
King George VI Ave CR4 202 D5
King George V Sta E16 122 C5
Kingham Cl
3 Shepherd's Bush W11 112 D4
Wandsworth SW18 158 A4
Kingham Ind Est NW10 89 B4
King Harolds Way DA7 147 A5
King Henry Mews
Harrow HA2 42 C1
7 Orpington BR6 227 D3
King Henry's Mews EN3 7 C6
King Henry's Rd
Kingston u T KT1, KT3 198 D6
Primrose Hill NW3 70 C1
King Henry's Reach W6 134 C6
King Henry St N16 73 C3
King Henry's Wlk N1 73 C2
King Henry's Yd 5 N16 73 C3
King Henry Terr 10 E1 118 B6
King Ho 5 W12 90 B1
Kinghorn St EC1 242 A3
King James Ct SE1 251 D1
King James St SE1 116 D4 251 D1
King John Ct EC2 243 B6
King John St E1 96 D2
King John's Wlk SE9 166 A5
Kinglake St SE17 117 C1 263 B2
Kinglet Cl E7 77 A2
Kingly Ct W1 249 B6
Kingly St W1 115 C6 249 A6
King & Queen Cl 4 SE9 188 A6
King & Queen St SE17 117 A1 262 B2
Kingsand Rd SE12 165 A2
Kings Arbour UB2 107 A1
King's Arms Ct E1 96 A2
King's Arms Yd EC2 242 C2
Kingsash Dr UB4 85 A3
Kings Ave
Bromley BR1 186 D4
Clapham Pk SW4 160 A5
Dagenham RM6 59 B3
Ealing W5 87 D1
Muswell Hill N10 49 A6
New Malden KT3 199 D5
Wallington SM5 218 D1
King's Ave
Ashford TW16 171 D4
Buckhurst Hill IG9 21 D2
Hounslow TW3, TW5 129 D4
Southall UB1 85 D1
Southgate N21 16 D3
Woodford IG8 37 C5

Kings Avenue Sch
SW4 . . . . 160 A6
King's Bench St
SE1 . . . . . 116 D4 251 D2
King's Bench Wlk
EC4 . . . . 241 B1
Kingsbridge N16 . . . . . 51 B1
Kingsbridge Ave W3 . 110 B4
Kingsbridge Cres
UB1 . . . . 85 B2
Kingsbridge Ct
Edmonton N21 . . . . 16 D2
Millwall E14 . . . . 119 C2
Kingsbridge Dr NW7 . . 28 D3
Kingsbridge Ho 10
SE20 . . . . 184 B2
Kingsbridge Ind Est
IG11 . . . . 101 C4
Kingsbridge Rd
Barking IG11 . . . . 101 B5
North Kensington W10 . . 90 C1
Southall UB2 . . . . 107 B2
Walton-on-T KT12 . . . . 194 B2
West Barnes SM4 . . . 200 D2
Kingsbridge Way
UB4 . . . . 83 C4
KINGSBURY 45 B3
Kingsbury Green Prim
Sch NW9 . . . . 44 D4
Kingsbury High Sch
(Lower Sch) NW9 . . . 45 A5
Kingsbury High Sch
(Upper Sch) NW9 . . . 44 D5
Kingsbury Rd
Kingsbury NW9 . . . . 44 D4
Kingsland N1 . . . . 73 C2
Kingsbury Sta NW9 . . . 44 C4
Kingsbury Terr N1 . . . . 73 C2
Kingsbury Trad Est
NW9 . . . . 45 B3
Kings Chase KT8 . . . . . 196 A6
Kings Chase View EN2 . . 4 C3
Kings Cl Hendon NW4 . . 46 D5
Walthamstow E10 . . . . . 53 D2
Walton-on-T KT12 . . . . 194 B1
King's Cl KT7 . . . . 197 A2
Kingsclere Cl SW15 . . 156 A4
Kingsclere Ct
Colney Hatch N12 . . . . . 30 C5
New Barnet EN5 . . . . . . 14 A6
Kingsclere Pl EN2 . . . . . 5 A3
Kingscliffe Gdns
SW19 . . . . 157 B3
King's Coll SE24 . . . . . 161 B5
Kings College Ct
NW3 . . . . 70 C1
King's College Hospl
SE5 . . . . 139 B3
Kings College Rd
Primrose Hill NW3 . . . . . 70 B1
Ruislip HA4 . . . . 39 D3
King's Coll Jun Sch
SW19 . . . . 178 D4
King's Coll London
(Denmark Hill Campus)
SE5 . . . . 139 A2
King's Coll London
School of Medicine
SE1 . . . . . . 117 B5 252 D3
King's Coll London
(Strand Campus)
WC2 . . . . . . 116 B6 250 D6
King's Coll London (St
Thomas' Campus)
SE1 . . . . 116 B3 260 C5
King's Coll London
(Waterloo Campus)
SE1 . . . . . . 116 C5 251 A3
King's Coll Sch
SW19 . . . . 178 D4
Kingscote NW11 . . . . . . 47 B1
Kingscote Rd
Bedford Pk W4 . . . . . . 111 B3
Croydon CR0 . . . . 206 B2
Kingston u T KT3 . . . . 199 B6
Kingscote St EC4 . . . . 251 C6
Kings Court Mews
KT8 . . . . 196 B4
King's Court N SW3 . 257 A1
Kingscourt Rd SW16 . 160 A1
King's Court S SW3 . 257 A1
King's Cres N4, N5 . . . . 73 A5
Kingscroft SW4 . . . . . . 160 A5
Kingscroft Rd NW2 . . . 69 B2
KING'S CROSS 94 A5
King's Cross
WC1 . . . . 94 A4 233 B2
King's Cross Bridge
WC1 . . . . 233 B2
King's Cross Rd
WC1 . . . . 94 B4 233 D1
King's Cross, St Pancras
N1 . . . . 94 A4 233 A2
King's Cross Sta
N1 . . . . 94 A5 233 B3
Kings Ct
6 Barnsbury N7 . . . . . . 72 B1
2 Buckhurst Hill IG9 . . 21 D2
Chiswick W6 . . . . 112 A2
East Dulwich SE22 . . . . 140 A1
16 Kingston u T KT2 . . 176 C3
Newham E13 . . . . 99 B6
Primrose Hill NW8 . . . 230 C5
10 Putney SW15 . . . . 156 A4
3 Wallington SM6 . . . . 219 B2
Wembley Pk HA9 . . . . . . 66 D6
King's Ct
Beckenham BR3 . . . . . 207 D6
9 Ealing W5 . . . . 87 C2
Wimbledon SW19 . . . 179 C4
Kingsdale Ct EN4 . . . . . . 2 D3
Kingsdale Gdns
W11 . . . . 112 D5
Kingsdale Rd
Penge SE20 . . . . 184 D3
Plumstead Comm
SE18 . . . . 145 D6
Kingsdale Sch SE21 . 161 C1
Kingsdown SW19 . . . . 178 D3
Kingsdown Ave
East Acton W3 . . . . . . 111 C6
West Ealing W13 . . . . . 109 B4
Kingsdown Cl
26 Deptford SE16 . . . . 118 B1
8 Notting Hill W11 . . . . 91 A1
Kingsdown Ct SW11 . 158 C5
Kingsdowne Rd KT6 . 198 B2
Kingsdown Ho 1 E8 . . 74 A3
Kingsdown Rd
Cheam SM3 . . . . 217 A3
Leyton E11 . . . . 76 C5
4 Upper Holloway
N19 . . . . 72 A6
Kingsdown Way
BR2 . . . . 209 A3
Kings Dr Edgware HA8 . 26 B6
Surbiton KT5 . . . . 198 C3
Wembley Pk HA9 . . . . . . 66 D6
King's Dr KT7 . . . . 197 B2
Kingsend HA4 . . . . 39 C1
Kingsend Ct HA4 . . . . . 39 C1
Kings Farm E17 . . . . . . 35 D2
Kings Farm Ave
TW10 . . . . 132 C1
Kingsfield Ave HA1,
HA2 . . . . 42 A4
Kingsfield Ct HA1 . . . . 42 B2
Kingsfield Ho
Mottingham SE9 . . . . 165 D1
7 Muswell Hill N10 . . . . 31 A3
18 Stoke Newington
N16 . . . . 73 C5
Kingsfield Rd HA1 . . . . 42 B2
Kingsford Com Sch
E6 . . . . 100 B1
Kingsford St NW5 . . . . . 70 D3
Kingsford Way E6 . . . . 100 B2
Kingsgate HA9 . . . . 67 A5
Kingsgate Ave N3 . . . . . 47 C6
Kingsgate Bsns Ctr
KT2 . . . . 176 A2
Kingsgate Cl
Erith DA7 . . . . 147 A4
Sidcup BR5 . . . . 190 C1
Kingsgate Est N1 . . . . . 73 C2
Kingsgate Ho 29
SW9 . . . . 138 C4
Kingsgate Par SW1 . 259 B5
Kingsgate Pl NW6 . . . . 69 C1
Kingsgate Prim Sch
NW6 . . . . 69 C1
Kingsgate Rd
Hampstead NW6 . . . . . . 69 C1
Kingston u T KT2 . . . . 176 A2
Kings Gdns IG1 . . . . 57 B1
King's Gdns 6 NW6 . . . 69 C1
King's Gr
Peckham SE15 . . . . 140 B4
Peckham SE15 . . . . 140 B5
Kings Grange HA4 . . . . 39 D1
Kingsground SE9 . . . . 166 A5
Kingshall Mews
SE13 . . . . 142 A2
Kings Hall Rd BR3 . . . . 185 A2
Kings Head Hill E4 . . . . 19 D4
King's Head Yd SE1 . 252 C3
King's Highway
SE18 . . . . 145 D6
Kingshill SE17 . . . . . . 262 B4
Kingshill Ave
Harrow HA3 . . . . 43 B5
Hayes UB4 . . . . 83 D4
New Malden KT4 . . . . . 200 B2
Northolt UB5 . . . . 84 B4
Kingshill Cl UB4, UB5 . . 84 A4
Kingshill Ct 8 EN5 . . . . . 1 A1
Kingshill Dr HA3 . . . . . . 43 B6
Kings Ho
19 Limehouse E14 . . . . 119 B6
South Lambeth SW8 . 270 B4
Kingshold Rd E9 . . . . . . 74 C1
Kingsholm Gdns
SE9 . . . . 144 A1
King's House Sch
TW10 . . . . 154 B6
King's House Sch (Jun)
TW10 . . . . 154 B6
Kingshurst Rd SE12 . 165 A4
Kings Keep KT6 . . . . . 198 A5
King's Keep 6
SW15 . . . . 156 D6
King's La SM1 . . . . . . 218 B3
KINGSLAND 73 C2
Kingsland
NW8 . . . . 92 C6 230 B5
Kingsland Gn 1 E8,
N1 . . . . 73 C2
Kingsland High St E8 . 73 D3
Kingsland Pas 2 E8 . . 73 C2
Kingsland Rd
Hoxton E2 . . . . 95 C5
Newham E13 . . . . 99 C4
Kingsland Sh Ctr 12
E8 . . . . 73 D2
Kingslawn Cl SW15 . . 156 B6
Kingslee Ct 4 SM2 . . 217 D1
Kingsleigh Cl TW8 . . 131 D6
Kingsleigh Pl CR4 . . 202 D6
Kingsleigh Wlk BR2 . 208 D5
Kingsley Ave
Ealing W13 . . . . 87 A1
Hounslow TW3 . . . . . 130 A3
Southall UB1 . . . . 107 C6
Sutton SM1 . . . . 218 B4
Kingsley Cl
Dagenham RM10 . . . . . . 81 D4
East Finchley N2 . . . . . . 48 A4
Kingsley Ct
Bexley DA6 . . . . 147 C1
Edgware HA8 . . . . 10 D2
Snaresbrook E11 . . . . . . 54 D3
1 Thamesmead
SE28 . . . . 124 C5
Willesden NW2 . . . . 68 B2
Wood Green N22 . . . . . . 32 B3
Worcester Pk KT4 . . . 215 D6
Kingsley Dr KT4 . . . . 215 D6
Kingsley Flats SE1 . . 263 B3
Kingsley Gdns E4 . . . . . 35 C5
Kingsley Grange 1
E11 . . . . 55 A4
Kingsley High Sch
HA3 . . . . 24 A3
Kingsley Ho
Chelsea SW3 . . . . 266 D5
3 Clapham SW4 . . . . . 137 D3
East Finchley NW11 . . . . 48 A3
8 Kingston u T KT6 . . 198 A4
Kingsley Mews
Chislehurst West
BR7 . . . . 188 D4
Dagenham RM9 . . . . 80 D4
4 Ilford IG1 . . . . 78 D6
Kensington W8 . . . . . 255 D5
15 St George in t East
E1 . . . . 118 B6
Kingsley Pl N6 . . . . 49 A2
Kingsley Prim Sch
CR9 . . . . 204 C1
Kingsley Rd
Chingford E17 . . . . 36 A1
Edmonton N13 . . . . 32 D6
Harrow HA2 . . . . 64 A5
Hounslow TW3 . . . . . . 130 A3
Kilburn NW6 . . . . 91 B6
Orpington BR6 . . . . . . 227 D1
Pinner HA5 . . . . 41 B5
Kingsley Rd *continued*
Thornton Heath CR0 . 204 C1
Upton E7 . . . . 77 A1
Wimbledon SW19 . . . 179 D5
Kingsley St SW11 . . . 136 D2
Kingsley Way N2 . . . . . 48 A4
Kingsley Wood Dr
SE9 . . . . 166 B1
Kings Lo HA4 . . . . 39 C1
Kingslyn Cres SE19 . . 183 C2
Kings Mall Sh Ctr
W6 . . . . 112 C2
Kingsman Par SE18 . . 122 B3
King's Mans SW3 . . . 267 A5
Kingsman St SE18 . . . 122 B2
Kingsmead Barnet EN5 . . 1 C1
Richmond TW10 . . . . . 154 B5
Kingsmead Ave
Edmonton N9 . . . . 18 B3
Kingsbury NW9 . . . . 45 B2
Mitcham CR4 . . . . 203 C6
North Cheam KT4 . . . . 216 B5
Sunbury TW16 . . . . . . 172 C1
Tolworth KT6 . . . . 214 C6
Kingsmead Cl
Sidcup DA15 . . . . 168 A2
Teddington TW11 . . . . 175 B4
West Ewell KT19 . . . . 215 B1
Kingsmead Cotts
BR2 . . . . 210 A1
Kingsmead Ct
Bromley BR1 . . . . 186 D3
Crouch End N6 . . . . 49 D2
Kingsmead Dr UB5 . . . . 63 B1
Kingsmead Ho E9 . . . . 75 A4
Kingsmead Lo
9 Chingford E4 . . . . . . 20 A2
Sutton SM2 . . . . 218 B2
Kings Mead Pk
KT10 . . . . 212 C1
Kingsmead Prim Sch
E9 . . . . 75 A4
Kingsmead Rd SW2 . . 160 C2
Kingsmead Sch EN1 . . . 6 A2
King's Mead Way E5,
E9 . . . . 75 A4
Kingsmere
Catford SE6 . . . . 163 D3
Widmore BR7 . . . . 188 A2
Kingsmere Cl 13
SW15 . . . . 134 D2
Kingsmere Ct NW9 . . . 44 D1
Kingsmere Pk NW9 . . . 45 A1
Kingsmere Pl N16 . . . . 51 B1
Kingsmere Rd SW19 156 D2
King's Mews
1 Clapham Pk
SW4 . . . . 160 A6
Gray's Inn
WC1 . . . . 94 B3 240 D5
Kingsmill
NW8 . . . . 92 B5 229 D4
Kingsmill Bsns Pk
KT1 . . . . 198 B6
Kingsmill Gdns RM9 . . 81 B3
Kingsmill Rd RM9 . . . . 81 B3
Kingsmill Terr
NW8 . . . . 92 B5 229 D4
Kingsmount Ct SM1 . 217 D4
Kingsnorth Ho 12
W10 . . . . 90 D1
Kingsnympton Pk
KT2 . . . . 176 D4
Kings Oak RM7 . . . . . . 59 C6
Kings Oak Hospl
(Private) The EN2 . . . . 4 C5
King Solomon Acad
NW1 . . . . 92 C2 237 A4
King's Orch SE9 . . . . 166 A5
King's Paddock
TW12 . . . . 174 A2
King's Par
3 Hammersmith
W12 . . . . 112 A3
Willesden NW10 . . . . . . 90 C6
Kingspark Bsns Ctr
KT3 . . . . 199 A6
Kingspark Ct E18 . . . . 55 A6
King's Penny Ho 4
KT2 . . . . 176 A3
Kings Pl
Acton Green W4 . . . . . 111 A2
Buckhurst Hill IG9 . . . . 21 D2
Kings Pl★ N1 . . 94 A5 233 B4
Kings Pl IG10 . . . . 21 D4
King's Pl SE1 . . . . . . 252 A1
King Sq EC1 . . . 95 A4 235 A1
King's Quay SW10 . . 266 B2
Kings Rd Ealing W5 . . . . 87 D2
Feltham TW13 . . . . . . 150 C3
Harrow HA2 . . . . 63 B6
Mitcham CR4 . . . . 203 A6
Orpington BR6 . . . . . . 227 D4
Richmond TW10, TW9 . 154 B6
Walton-on-T KT12 . . . 194 B1
West Drayton UB7 . . . 104 B4
Willesden NW10 . . . . . . 68 B1
Wood Green N22 . . . . . . 32 B2
King's Rd Barking IG11 79 A1
Chelsea SW3 . . . . 257 B1
Chelsea
SW10 . . . . . . 136 B6 266 C5
Chingford E4 . . . . 20 B3
Edmonton N18 . . . . 34 A6
Kingston u T KT2 . . . . 176 B3
Leytonstone E11 . . . . . . 54 C2
Long Ditton KT6 . . . . . 197 C1
Mortlake SW14 . . . . . . 133 B2
Newham E6 . . . . 99 C6
South Norwood SE25 . 206 A6
Teddington TW11,
TW12 . . . . 174 B5
Tottenham N17 . . . . 33 D2
Twickenham TW1 . . . . 153 B5
Wimbledon SW19 . . . 179 C4
Kings Ride Gate
TW10 . . . . 132 C1
Kingsridge SW19 . . . . 157 A2
Kings Road Bglws
HA2 . . . . 63 B5
King's Scholars' Pas
SW1 . . . . 259 A4
King St Acton W3 . . . . 111 A5
East Finchley N2 . . . . . . 48 B6
Hammersmith W6 . . . . 112 A2
Newham E13 . . . . 98 D3
Newham E13 . . . . 99 A3
Richmond TW9 . . . . . . 153 D6
Southall UB2 . . . . 107 A3
St James
SW1 . . . . . . 115 C5 249 B4
Strand WC2 . . . . 250 A6
Tottenham N17 . . . . 33 D2
Twickenham TW1 . . . . 153 A3
Whitechapel
EC2 . . . . 95 A1 242 B1
King Stairs Cl SE16 . . . 118 B4
King's Terr
Camden Town
NW1 . . . . 93 C6 232 A5
10 Isleworth TW7 . . . . 131 A2
Kingsthorpe Rd
SE26 . . . . 184 D6
Kingston Ave
Cheam SM3 . . . . 217 A5
Feltham TW14 . . . . . . 149 D5
Yiewsley UB7 . . . . 104 B6
Kingston Bsns Ctr
KT9 . . . . 214 B5
Kingston By-Pass KT6, KT7,
KT9 . . . . 213 C5
Kingston Cl
Dagenham RM6 . . . . 59 A6
Northolt UB5 . . . . 85 B6
Teddington TW11 . . . . 175 B4
Kingston Coll
Kingston u T KT1 . . . . 197 D6
Kingston u T KT2 . . . . 176 A2
Kingston Cres BR3 . . . 185 B2
Kingston Ct HA3 . . . . . . 44 B4
Kingston Gdns CR0 . . 220 A5
Kingston Gram Sch
KT2 . . . . 176 B1
Kingston Hall Rd
KT1 . . . . 197 D6
Kingston Hill KT2 . . . . 177 A5
Kingston Hill Ave
RM6 . . . . 59 A6
Kingston Hill Pl KT2,
TW10 . . . . 177 A6
Kingston Ho 4 NW6 . . 69 A1
Kingston Ho E SW7 . 247 A1
Kingston Ho N SW7 . 247 A1
Kingston Ho S SW7 . 247 A1
Kingston Hospl KT2 . 176 D2
Kingston House Est
KT6 . . . . 197 B3
Kingston La
Teddington TW11 . . . . 175 B4

Kingston La continued
Uxbridge UB8 82 A4
West Drayton UB7 104 B4
Kingston Lo 2 KT3 199 C5
Kingston Mus★ KT1 176 A1
Kingston Pl HA3 24 D3
Kingston Rd
Ashford TW15 170 A4
Ashford TW15 170 B4
Edmonton N9 18 A2
Ewell KT17 215 D1
Ilford IG1 79 A4
Kingston u T KT1, KT3 199 A5
Merton SW19, SW20 179 B1
New Barnet EN4 14 B6
Roehampton SW15, SW19 156 B3
Southall UB2 107 B4
Teddington TW11 175 B4
Kingston Sq SE19 183 B5
Kingston Sta KT2 176 A2
Kingston Univ (Kingston Hill) KT2 177 B5
Kingston Univ (Knights Park) KT1 198 A6
Kingston Univ (Penrhyn Road) KT1 198 A6
Kingston Univ (Roehampton Vale) SW15 155 D1
KINGSTON UPON THAMES 197 C6
KINGSTON VALE 177 B6
Kingston Vale SW15 155 C1
Kingstown St NW1 93 A6 231 A6
King Street Cloisters 8 W6 112 B2
King Street Coll 10 W12 112 C2
King Street Par 7 TW1 153 A3
Kings View Ct 1 SW20 178 D3
Kingswater Pl SW11 267 A3
Kingsway
Coney Hall BR4 224 D5
Enfield EN3 18 B6
Hayes UB3 83 A2
Mortlake SW14, TW9 132 D2
North Finchley N12 30 A4
Petts Wood BR5 211 B4
Stanwell TW19 148 A3
St Giles WC2 94 B1 240 C2
Wembley HA9 66 A4
West Barnes KT3 200 C4
Woodford IG8 37 C5
Kings Way
Croydon CR0 220 B3
Harrow HA1 42 C5
Kingsway Bsns Pk TW12 173 B2
Kingsway Coll 12 NW5 71 B2
Kingsway Cres HA2 42 A5
Kingsway Est N18 34 D4
Kingsway Mans WC1 240 C4
Kingsway Pl EC1 241 C6
Kingsway Rd SM3 217 A1
Kingswear Ho 5 SE23 162 C2
Kingswear Rd
Dartmouth Pk NW5 71 B5
Ruislip HA4 62 A6
Kings Well 25 NW3 70 A4
Kings Wlk Sh Mall SW3 114 D1 257 C2
Kingswood 31 E2 96 C5
Kingswood Ave
Beckenham BR2, BR3 208 C5
Belvedere DA17 125 B2
Hampton TW12 173 D4
Hounslow TW3, TW5 129 B3
Kensal Rise NW6 91 A5
Thornton Heath CR7 204 C4
Kingswood Cl
Ashford TW15 171 B5
Crofton BR6 211 B2
East Barnet N20 14 A4
Enfield EN1 17 D6
New Malden KT3 199 D3
South Lambeth SW8 270 B3
Kingswood Cl continued
Surbiton KT6 198 A2
Kingswood Ct
Chingford E4 35 C5
Hither Green SE13 164 B5
7 Richmond TW10 154 B6
Kings Wood Ct 4 NW6 69 C1
Kingswood Dr
Carshalton SM5 202 D1
Dulwich SE19, SE21 183 D6
Kingswood Ho 3 KT2 176 D4
Kingswood Mans 14 SM2 217 C1
Kingswood Pk N3 29 B1
Kingswood Pl SE13 142 C1
Kingswood Prim Sch SE27 183 B5
Kingswood Rd
Beckenham BR2 208 C6
Ilford IG3 58 A2
Leytonstone E11 54 C2
Merton SW19 179 B2
Penge SE20 184 C4
South Acton W4 111 A3
Streatham SW2 160 A4
Wembley HA9 66 C5
Kingswood Terr W4 111 A3
Kingswood Way SM6 220 A3
Kingsworth Cl BR3 207 A4
Kingsworthy Cl KT1 198 B6
Kings Yd E15 75 C2
Kingthorpe Rd NW10 67 B1
Kingthorpe Terr 2 NW10 67 B1
Kington Ho 18 NW6 91 D6
Kingward Ho E1 96 A2
Kingwell Rd EN4 2 B5
Kingweston Cl NW2 69 A5
King William IV Gdns SE20 184 C4
King William La 3 SE10 120 C1
King William St EC4 117 B6 252 D6
King William Wlk SE10 142 A6
Kingwood Rd SW6 135 A5 264 A3
Kinlet Rd SE18 145 A4
Kinloch Dr NW9 45 C2
Kinloch St N7 72 B5
Kinloss Ct NW3 47 B5
Kinloss Gdns NW3 47 B5
Kinloss Rd SM5 202 A2
Kinnaird Ave
Bromley BR1 186 D4
Chiswick W4 133 A5
Kinnaird Cl BR1 186 D4
Kinnear Ct 2 SW20 178 D2
Kinnear Rd W12 111 D4
Kinnerton Pl N SW1 247 D1
Kinnerton Pl S SW1 247 D1
Kinnerton St SW1 115 A4 248 A1
Kinnerton Yd SW1 248 A1
Kinnoull Mans 10 E5 74 B4
Kinnoul Rd W6 135 A6 264 A6
Kinross Ave KT4 216 A6
Kinross Cl
Ashford TW16 171 D5
Edgware HA8 10 D2
Harrow HA3 44 B4
Kinross Ct 1 SE6 164 D2
Kinross Dr TW16 171 D5
Kinross Ho N1 233 C6
Kinross Terr E17 35 B1
Kinsale Grange 10 SM2 218 A2
Kinsale Rd SE15 140 A2
Kinsella Gdns SW19 178 B5
Kinsey Ho SE21 183 C6
Kinsham Ho 5 E2 96 A3
Kintore Way SE1 263 C4
Kintyre Cl SW16 204 B6
Kintyre Ct 17 SW2 160 A4
Kintyre Ho 6 E14 120 A5
Kinveachy Gdns SE7 122 A1
Kinver Ho N4 51 B2
Kinver Rd SE26 184 C6
Kipling Ct W7 108 D6
Kipling Dr SW17 180 B4
Kipling Ho 29 SE5 139 A5
Kipling Pl HA7 24 D4
Kipling Rd DA7 147 A4
Kipling St SE1 117 B4 252 D2
Kipling Terr N9 17 B2
Kipling Twr 3 W3 111 A3
Kippington Dr SE9 165 D3
Kirby Cl KT19 215 D3
Kirby Est SE16 118 B3
Kirby Gr SE1 117 C4 253 A2
Kirby St EC1 94 C2 241 B4
Kirby Way
Hillingdon UB8 82 B3
Walton-on-T KT12 194 C3
Kirchen Rd W13 109 B6
Kirkby Cl N11 31 A4
Kirkdale SE26 162 B1
Kirkdale Rd E11 54 C2
Kirkeby Bldg EC1 241 A4
Kirkfield Cl W13 109 B5
Kirkham Rd E6 100 A1
Kirkham St SE18 145 C6
Kirk Ho HA9 66 A5
Kirk La SE18 145 A6
Kirkland Cl DA15 167 C5
Kirkland Dr EN2 5 A4
Kirkland Terr BR3 185 C4
Kirkland Wlk 4 E8 73 D2
Kirkleas Rd KT6 198 A1
Kirklees Rd
Dagenham RM8 80 C3
Thornton Heath CR7 204 C4
Kirkley Ho N16 51 C1
Kirkley Rd SW19 179 C2
Kirkman Ho W1 239 C3
Kirkman Pl W1 239 C3
Kirkmichael Rd E14 98 A1
Kirk Rd E17 53 B3
Kirk Rise SM1 217 D5
Kirkside Rd SE3 143 A6
Kirk St WC1 240 D5
Kirkstall Ave N17 51 B5
Kirkstall Gdns SW2 160 A3
Kirkstall Ho SW1 258 C2
Kirkstall Rd SW2 160 A3
Kirkstead Ct E5 75 A4
Kirksted Rd SM4 201 D1
Kirkstone NW1 232 A2
Kirkstone Way BR1 186 C3
Kirkton Rd N15 51 C5
Kirkwall Pl E2 96 C4
Kirkwood Rd SE15 140 B3
Kirn Rd W13 109 B6
Kirrane Cl KT3 199 D4
Kirtley Ho SW8 269 B2
Kirtley Rd SE26 185 A6
Kirtling St SW8 137 C5 269 A4
Kirton Cl W4 111 B2
Kirton Gdns 23 E2 95 D4
Kirton Rd E13 99 C5
Kirton Wlk HA8 27 A3
Kirwin Way SE5 138 D5
Kisharon Sch NW11 47 B3
Kismul Sch KT6 213 C6
Kitcat Terr E3 97 C4
Kitchener Rd
Dagenham RM10 81 D2
East Finchley N2 48 C6
South Norwood CR7 205 B6
Tottenham N17 51 C6
Upton E7 77 B2
Walthamstow E17 35 D2
Kite Ho 5 SW11 136 C2
Kite Pl 9 E2 96 A4
Kitley Gdns SE19 183 D2
Kitson Rd
Barnes SW13 134 A4
Camberwell SE5 139 A5
Kittiwake Ct 26 SE8 141 B6
Kittiwake Pl SM1 217 B3
Kittiwake Rd UB5 84 D4
Kittiwake Way UB4 84 D2
Kitto Rd SE14 140 D3
KITTS END 1 A5
Kitt's End Rd EN5 1 A6
Kiver Rd N19 72 A6
Klea Ave SW4 159 C5
Kleffens Ct 2 SE3 142 D5
Kleine Wharf 30 N1 95 C6
Knaggs Ho 1 TW11 174 C5
Knapdale Cl SE23 162 B2
Knapmill Rd SE6 163 D2
Knapmill Way SE6 163 D2
Knapp Cl NW10 67 C2
Knapp Rd
Ashford TW15 170 B6
Bow E3 97 C3
Knapton Mews SW17 181 A4
Knaresborough Dr SW18 157 D3
Knaresborough Ho 4 N4 51 A2
Knaresborough Pl SW5 113 D2 255 C4
Knatchbull Rd
Brixton SE5 138 D4
Stonebridge NW10 89 B6
Knebworth Ave E17 35 C2
Knebworth Cl EN5 1 D1
Knebworth Ho
South Lambeth SW8 269 D1
2 Stoke Newington N16 73 C4
Walthamstow E17 35 C2
Knebworth Rd 3 N16 73 C4
Knee Hill SE2 124 C1
Knee Hill Cres SE2 124 C2
Kneller Gdns TW7 152 B5
Kneller Ho 9 SW8 137 D3
Kneller Rd
Brockley SE4 141 A1
Isleworth TW2 152 B5
New Malden KT3 199 C2
Knevett Terr TW3 129 C1
Knight Cl RM8 80 C6
Knight Ct N15 51 C4
Knighten St E1 118 B5
Knighthead Point 26 E14 119 C4
Knight Ho
Walworth SE17 263 A3
Worcester Pk KT4 216 A6
Knightland Ho E5 74 B6
Knightland Rd E5 74 B6
Knightleas Ct NW2 68 C2
Knightleys Ct E10 53 A1
Knighton Cl
Croydon CR2 220 D1
Woodford IG8 37 B6
Knighton Dr IG8 37 B6
Knighton Gn IG9 21 B2
Knighton La IG9 21 B2
Knighton Park Rd SE26 184 D5
Knighton Rd E7 77 A4
Knightrider Ct EC4 252 A6
Knightrider St EC4 251 D6
Knights Arc SW1 247 C1
Knight's Ave W5 110 A4
KNIGHTSBRIDGE 114 C4
Knightsbridge SW1, SW7 114 D4 247 C1
Knightsbridge Ct SW1 247 D1
Knightsbridge Gn SW1 247 C1
Knightsbridge Mews BR7 188 B3
Knightsbridge Sch SW11 114 D3 257 C5
Knightsbridge Sta SW1 114 D4 247 C1
Knightsbridge Under Sch SW7 256 B3
Knights Cl
East Molesey KT8 195 B4
Lower Clapton E9 74 C3
Knights Ct
Bushey WD23 8 B3
11 Friern Barnet N11 30 D5
Kingston u T KT1 198 A6
Penge BR3 185 A2
Knight's Ct BR1 164 D1
Knightshayes Ho 8 NW4 28 D1
Knight's Hill SE19, SE27 182 D6
Knight's Hill Sq SE27 182 D6
Knights Ho
Bermondsey SE1 253 C2
South Lambeth SW8 270 B3
West Kensington SW5 254 C2
Knight's Ho SW10 266 A4
Knight's Pk KT1 198 A6
Knight's Pl TW2 152 C3
Knights Rd
Newham E16 121 A4
Knights Rd continued
Stanmore HA7 25 C6
Knight's Wlk SE11 261 C3
Knightswood Cl HA8 11 A2
Knightswood Ct N6 49 D2
Knightswood Ho N12 30 A4
Knightwood Cres KT3 199 C3
Knivet Rd SW6 135 C6 265 A5
Knockholt Rd SE9 165 D6
Knole Cl CR0 206 C3
Knole Ct UB5 84 C4
Knole Gate DA15 167 C1
Knole The SE9 188 C6
Knoll Ct
Dulwich SE19 183 D5
Orpington BR6 227 D6
Knoll Dr N14 15 A4
Knoll Ho NW8 229 A4
Knoll Lo EN5 14 A6
Knollmead KT4, KT5 199 A1
Knollmead Prim Sch KT5 215 A6
Knoll Rd Bexley DA5 169 C5
Sidcup DA14 190 B6
Wandsworth SW18 158 A6
Knoll Rise BR6 211 D1
Knolls Cl KT4 216 B5
Knoll The
Beckenham BR3 185 D2
Ealing W13 87 C2
Hayes BR2 209 A1
Knolly's Cl SE27, SW16 160 C1
Knolly's Rd SE27, SW16 160 C1
Knot Ho SE1 253 C3
Knottisford St E2 96 C4
Knotts Green Mews E10 54 A3
Knotts Green Rd E10 54 A3
Knowlden Ho 5 E1 118 C6
Knowle Ave DA7 147 B5
Knowle Cl SW9 138 C2
Knowledge Point Sch 6 N7 72 B2
Knowle Lo BR7 188 B4
Knowle Rd
Bromley BR2 226 A6
Twickenham TW2 152 C3
Knowles Cl UB7 104 A5
Knowles Ct 7 HA1 42 D3
Knowles Hill Cres SE13 164 B6
Knowles Ho
Wandsworth SW18 157 D5
Willesden Green NW10 90 A6
Knowles Wlk SW4 137 C2
Knowl Pk WD6 10 A6
Knowlton Gn 1 BR2 208 D4
Knowlton Ho 32 SW9 138 C4
Knowl Way WD6 10 B6
Knowsley Ave UB1 107 D5
Knowsley Rd SW11 136 D3
Knox Ct 16 SW4 138 A3
Knox Ho SW15 134 C3
Knox Rd E7 77 A2
Knox St W1 92 D2 237 C4
Knoyle Ho W14 254 B6
Knoyle St SE14 141 A6
Kobi Nazrul Prim Sch 43 E1 96 A1
Koblenz Ho N8 50 A6
Kohat Rd SW19 179 D5
Korda Cl TW17 192 B6
Kossuth St SE10 120 C1
Kotree Way 16 SE1 118 A2
Kramer Mews SW5 255 C1
Kreedman Wlk 8 E8 74 A3
Kreisel Wlk TW9 132 B6
Krishna Avanti Prim Sch HA8 26 C2
Kristina Ct 5 SM2 217 C2
Kuala Gdns SW16 182 B2
Kubrick Bsns Est E7 77 B4
Kuhn Way E7 77 A3
Kwesi Johnson Ct 4 N22 32 C1
Kydbrook Cl BR5 211 A2
Kyle Ho TW12 174 A2
Kylemore Cl 3 E6 99 D5
Kylemore Ct 4 W12 112 A4
Kylemore Rd NW6 69 C1

Kylestrome Ho SW1. 258 B3
Kymberley Rd HA1 42 C3
Kynance Gdns HA7 25 C2
Kynance Mews SW7 113 D3 255 D5
Kynance Pl SW7 256 A5
Kynaston Ave CR7 205 A4
Kynaston Cl HA3 24 B3
Kynaston Cres CR7 205 A4
Kynaston Ho 7 SW2 160 B3
Kynaston Rd
Enfield EN2 5 B4
Plaistow BR1 187 A5
Stoke Newington N16 73 C5
Thornton Heath CR7 205 A4
Kynaston Wood HA3 24 B3
Kynersley Cl 1 SM5 218 D5
Kynoch Rd N18 34 D6
Kyrle Rd SW11 159 A5
Kyverdale Rd N16 51 D1

L

Laburnam Ct 12 SW16 182 C5
Laburnham Ct
Child's Hill NW2 69 B6
Sutton SM1 217 C3
Laburnham Pl SE9 166 C6
Laburnum Ave
Carshalton SM1 218 C5
Edmonton N9 17 D2
Tottenham N17 33 B3
Yiewsley UB7 104 B6
Laburnum Cl
Friern Barnet N11 31 A4
5 Nunhead SE15 140 C5
Walthamstow E4 35 B4
Wembley HA0 88 C6
Laburnum Cres TW16 172 B2
Laburnum Ct
26 Haggerston E2 95 D6
Harrow HA1 41 D3
5 Mitcham CR4 181 A1
Stanmore HA7 25 C6
Laburnum Gdns
Croydon CR0 206 D1
Edmonton N21 17 A2
Laburnum Gr
Edmonton N21 17 A2
Hounslow TW3 129 B1
Kingsbury NW9 45 A2
Kingston u T KT3 177 B1
Ruislip HA4 39 B3
Southall UB1 85 B3
Laburnum Ho
Dagenham RM10 81 C6
New Cross SE4 141 B3
6 Stoke Newington N16 73 B6
Laburnum Lo 2 N3 29 B1
Laburnum Rd
Hayes UB3 105 D2
Merton SW19 180 A3
Mitcham CR4 181 A1
Laburnum St E2 95 D6
Laburnums The E6 100 A3
Laburnum Way
Southborough BR2 210 D2
Stanwell TW19 148 B3
Lacebark Cl DA15 167 D4
Lacewing Cl E13 99 A4
Lacey Cl N9 18 A2
Lacey Dr
Dagenham RM8 80 C5
Edgware HA8 26 B6
Hampton TW12 173 B2
Lacey Ho 7 SE13 142 A3
Lacey Mews 9 E3 97 C5
Lacine Ct 12 SE16 118 D4
Lackington St EC2 242 D4
Lackland Ho SE1 263 D2
Lacland Ho SW10 266 C4
Lacock Cl SW19 180 A4
Lacock Ct 3 W13 109 A5
Lacon Rd SE22 140 A1
Lacrosse Way SW16 181 D2
Lacy Rd SW15 134 D1
Ladas Rd SE27 183 A5
Ladbroke Cres W11 91 A1
Ladbroke Gdns W11 113 B6 244 C6
Ladbroke Gr
Kensal Town W10 91 A2
Notting Hill W11 113 B6 244 C6
Ladbroke Grove Ho W11 244 C6
Ladbroke Grove Sta W10 91 A1
Ladbroke Ho E1 243 D3
Ladbroke Mews W11 244 B3
Ladbroke Rd
Enfield EN1 17 D5
Notting Hill W11 113 B5 244 C4
Ladbroke Sq W11 113 B6 244 D5
Ladbroke Terr W11 113 B5 244 D4
Ladbroke Wlk W11 113 B5 244 D4
Ladbrook Cl HA5 41 B4
Ladbrooke Cres DA14 168 D1
Ladbrook Rd SE25 205 B5
Ladderstile Ride KT2, TW10 176 D5
Ladderswood Way N11 31 C5
Ladlands SE22 162 A4
Lady Alesford Ave HA7 25 B5
Lady Bankes Jun & Inf Schs HA4 62 A6
Lady Booth Rd 7 KT1 176 A1
Ladybower Ct 6 E5 74 D4
Ladycroft Gdns 6 BR6 227 A3
Ladycroft Rd SE13 141 D2
Ladycroft Way BR6 227 A3
Ladycroft Wlk HA7 25 D1
Lady Eleanor Holles Sch (Jun Girls) The TW12 173 D5
Lady Eleanor Holles Sch (Senior Girls) The TW12 173 D5
Lady Elizabeth Ho SW14 133 A2
Ladyfern Ho 19 E3 97 C2
Lady Florence Ctyd 15 SE8 141 C5
Ladygate La HA4 39 A3
Lady Hay KT4 215 D6
Lady Helen Seymour Ho 14 E13 99 A5
Lady Margaret Prim Sch UB1 85 B2
Lady Margaret Rd
Kentish Town NW5 71 C3
Southall UB1 85 B2
Lady Margaret Sch SW6 135 C4 265 A1
Lady Shaw Ct N13 16 B1
Ladysmith Ave
Ilford IG2 57 C2
Newham E6 100 A5
Ladysmith Cl NW7 28 A3
Ladysmith Rd
Edmonton N18 34 B5
Eltham SE9 166 C5
Enfield EN1 5 D3
Harrow HA3 24 C1
Newham E16 98 D4
Tottenham N17 34 A1
Lady Somerset Rd NW5 71 B4
LADYWELL 163 C6
Ladywell Arena SE13 163 D5
Ladywell Cl SE4 141 C1
Ladywell Ho 7 BR5 190 B1
Ladywell Hts SE4 163 B5
Ladywell Rd SE13 163 D6
Ladywell St 4 E15 98 D6
Ladywell Sta SE13 163 D6
Ladywell Water Twr SE4 163 C6
Ladywood Ave BR5 211 C4
Ladywood Rd KT6 214 C6
Lafitte Ho 22 N19 49 D2
Lafone Ave TW13 150 C2
Lafone Ho 11 SW2 160 A4
Lafone St SE1 117 D4 253 C2
Lagado Mews SE16 118 D5
Lagonda Ho 11 E3 97 C3
Lagonier Ho EC1 235 B1
Laidlaw Dr N21 16 B6
Laindon Ho 6 N16 51 D1
Laing Dean UB5 84 C6
Laing Ho SE5 139 A5
Laings Ave CR4 180 D1
Laings Cnr CR4 180 D2
Lainlock Pl TW3 129 D4
Lainson St SW18 157 C4
Lairdale Cl SE21 161 A4
Laird Ho SE5 139 A5
Lairs Cl N7 72 A2
Lait Ho 3 BR3 185 D2
Laitwood Rd SW12 159 B3
Lakanal 14 SE5 139 C4
Lake Ave BR1 187 A4
Lake Bsns Ctr N17 34 A3
Lake Cl
Dagenham RM8 80 D5
6 Wimbledon SW19 179 B5
Lakedale Ct IG11 102 A3
Lakedale Rd SE18 123 C1
Lake Dr WD23 8 B2
Lake Farm Ctry Pk UB3 105 C5
Lakefield Cl SE20 184 B3
Lakefield Rd N22 32 D1
Lake Gdns
Dagenham RM10 81 C3
Hackbridge SM6 219 B5
Richmond TW10 153 B2
Lakehall Gdns CR7 204 D4
Lakehall Rd CR7 204 D4
Lake Ho
Borough The SE1 252 A1
4 West Norwood SW27 182 D5
Lake House Rd E11 77 A6
Lakehurst Rd KT19 215 C3
Lakeland Cl HA3 24 B4
Lakeman Ct CR7 183 A1
Lakenheath N14 15 D6
Laker Ct SW4 138 A3
Lake Rd Croydon CR0 223 B6
Dagenham RM6 58 D5
Wimbledon SW19 179 B5
Laker Pl SW15 157 A5
Lakeside
Beckenham BR3 207 D6
Deacons Hill WD6 10 C6
Ealing W13 87 C1
Enfield EN2 3 D1
Finchley N3 29 D1
10 Kingston u T KT2 176 D3
Wallington SM6 219 B4
West Ewell KT19 215 C2
Lakeside Ave
Redbridge IG4 55 D5
Thamesmead SE28 124 A5
Lakeside Cl
Ruislip HA4 39 B5
Sidcup DA15 168 C6
South Norwood SE25 184 A1
Lakeside Complex The SE2 124 D5
Lakeside Cres EN4 14 D6
Lakeside Ct N4 51 A1
Lakeside Dr
Acton NW10 88 B4
Esher KT10 212 A2
Keston Mark BR2 226 A5
Lakeside Lo NW4 47 A5
Lakeside Rd
Brook Green W14 112 D3
Palmers Green N13 16 B1
Lakeside Way HA9 66 C4
Lakes Rd BR2 225 C3
Lakeswood Rd BR5 211 A3
Lake The WD23 8 B3
Lakeview 23 E3 96 D5
Lake View HA8 26 B5
Lakeview Ct E4 36 B4
Lake View Ct SW1 258 D6
Lakeview Rd
Bexley DA16 146 B1
West Norwood SE27 182 D5
Lake View Terr N18 33 D6
Lakis Cl NW3 70 A4
Laleham Ave NW7 11 B1
Laleham Ho E2 243 C6
Laleham Rd
Catford SE6 164 A4
Littleton TW17 192 C4
Lalor St SW6 135 A3
Lambarde Ave SE9 188 C6
Lambard Ho 4 SE10 142 A5
Lamb Cl UB5 85 A4
Lamb Ct 16 E14 119 A6
Lamberhurst Ho 14 SE15 140 C6
Lamberhurst Rd
Dagenham RM8 59 B1
West Norwood SE27 182 C5
Lambert Ave TW9 132 D2
Lambert Ho
16 Brixton SW9 138 C3
19 Crouch End N19 49 D2
Lambert Lo TW8 109 D1
Lambert Rd
Clapham Pk SW2 160 B6
Newham E16 99 B1
North Finchley N12 30 B5
Lambert's Pl CR0 205 B1
Lambert's Rd KT6 198 B4
Lambert St N1 72 C1
Lambert Way N12 30 A5
Lambert Wlk HA9 65 D5
LAMBETH 116 B4
Lambeth Acad SW4 159 C6
Lambeth Coll SW16 160 A1
Lambeth Coll (Brixton Ctr) SW2 160 B6
Lambeth Coll (Clapham Ctr) SW4 159 C6
Lambeth Coll (Vauxhall Ctr) SW8 137 D4 269 C2
Lambeth Ct 8 SW18 157 C6
Lambeth High St SE1 116 B2 260 C4
Lambeth Hill EC4 252 A6
Lambeth Hospl SW9 138 B2
Lambeth North Sta SE1 116 C3 261 A6
Lambeth Pal* SE1 116 B3 260 C5
Lambeth Palace Rd SE1 116 B3 260 C6
Lambeth Pier SE1 260 B5
Lambeth Prospect SE19 183 B4
Lambeth Rd
Lambeth SE1 116 C3 261 B5
Thornton Heath CR0 204 D1
Lambeth Twrs SE11 261 A5
Lambeth Wlk SE11 116 B2 260 D4
Lambfold Ho N7 72 A2
Lamb Ho
28 Camberwell SE5 139 A5
11 Camberwell SE5 139 B4
Greenwich SE10 142 A6
Lamb La E8 74 B1
Lamble St NW5 71 A4
Lambley Rd RM9 80 B2
Lamb Office Ct WC1 240 C4
Lambolle Pl NW3 70 C2
Lambolle Rd NW3 70 C2
Lambourn Cl
Hanwell W7 108 D4
9 Kentish Town NW5 71 C4
Lambourne Ave SW19 179 B6
Lambourne Ct 5 IG8 37 C3
Lambourne Gdns
5 Barking IG11 79 D1
Chingford E4 19 C2
Enfield EN1 5 D3
Lambourne Gr
Deptford SE16 118 D1
Kingston u T KT1 176 D1
Lambourne Ho NW8 236 D4
Lambourne Pl SE3 143 B4
Lambourne Rd
Barking IG11 79 D1
Ilford IG3 79 C6
Leytonstone E11 54 A2
Lambourn Ho BR1 188 A3
Lambourn Rd SW4 137 B2
Lambrook Ho 13 SE15 140 A4
Lambrook Terr SW6 135 A4 264 A2
Lamb's Bldgs EC1 242 C5
Lamb's Cl N9 18 A2
Lamb's Conduit Pas WC1 240 C4
Lamb's Conduit St WC1 94 B3 240 C5
Lambscroft Ave SE9, SE12 165 D1
Lambs Mdw IG8 37 D1
Lamb's Mews N1 234 C5
Lamb's Pas EC1 95 B3 242 C5
Lamb St E1 95 D2 243 C4
Lamb's Terr N9 17 B2
Lambs Wlk EN2 5 A3
Lambton Ct 2 N19 50 A1
Lambton Mews 4 N19 50 A1
Lambton Pl W11 244 D6
Lambton Rd
Finsbury Pk N19 50 A1
Wimbledon SW20 178 C2
Lamb Wlk SE1 253 A1
Lamerock Rd BR1 186 D6
Lamerton Lo 10 TW9 132 B4
Lamerton St 8 SE8 141 C6
Lamford Cl N17 33 B3
Lamington St 3 W6 112 B2
Lamlash St SE11 261 C4
Lamley Ho SE10 141 D5
Lammas Ave CR4 181 A1
Lammas Gn SE26 162 B1
Lammas Park Gdns W5 109 C5
Lammas Park Rd W5 109 D4
Lammas Rd
Homerton E9 74 D1
Richmond TW10 175 C6
Walthamstow E10 53 A1
Lammas Sch E10 53 B1
Lammermoor Rd SW12 159 B4
Lamont Rd SW10 136 B6 266 C5
Lamont Rd Pas SW10 266 C5
Lamorbey Cl DA15 167 D2
Lamorna Cl E17 36 A2
Lamorna Gr HA7 25 D1
Lampard Gr N16 51 D1
Lampern Sq 8 E2 96 A4
Lampeter Cl NW9 45 C3
Lampeter Sq W6 264 A5
Lamplighter Cl 34 E1 96 C3
Lampmead Rd SE12 142 D1
Lamport Cl SE18 122 B2
Lampson Ho 6 N19 71 C4
LAMPTON 129 D4
Lampton Ave TW5 129 D4
Lampton Ct TW5 129 D4
Lampton House Cl SW19 178 D6
Lampton Park Rd TW3 129 D3
Lampton Rd TW3, TW5 129 D3
Lampton Sch TW5 129 C4
Lampton Sp Ctr TW5 129 C4
Lanacre Ave NW9 27 C2
Lanadron Cl 5 TW7 130 D3
Lanain Ct SE12 164 D4
Lanark Cl W5 87 C2
Lanark Ct UB5 63 C3
Lanark Ho 12 SE1 118 A1
Lanark Mans
Paddington W9 236 B6
15 Shepherd's Bush W12 112 C4
Lanark Mews NW8 229 B1
Lanark Pl W9 92 A3 236 B6
Lanark Rd W9 92 A4 229 A1
Lanark Sq E14 119 D3
Lanata Wlk UB4 84 D3
Lanbury Rd SE15 140 D1
Lancashire Ct W1 248 D6
Lancaster Ave
Barking IG11 101 C6
Croydon CR4 204 A5
Hadley Wood EN4 2 B5
Wanstead E18 55 B5
West Norwood SE21, SE27 161 A2
Wimbledon SW19 178 D5
Lancaster Cl
Ashford TW15 170 A6
Beckenham BR2 208 D5

Lancaster Cl continued
　10 De Beauvoir Town
　N1 . . . . .73 C1
Grahame Pk NW9 . . . . . .27 D3
Kensington W2 . . . . . . .245 C5
Kingston u T KT2 . . . . . .175 D5
New Malden KT4 . . . . . .200 B2
Stanwell TW19 . . . . . . .148 A5
Tottenham N17 . . . . . . .34 A3
Lancaster Cotts 1
　TW10 . . . . .154 A5
Lancaster Ct
Bayswater W2 . . . . .246 B6
　1 Belmont SM2 . . . . .217 C1
Parsons Green SW6 . . . .264 D3
Stanwell TW19 . . . . . . .148 A3
Walton-on-T KT12 . . . . .194 B2
West Norwood SE27 . . .160 D2
Lancaster Dr
Canary Wharf E14 . . . . .120 A5
Maitland Pk NW3 . . . . . .70 C2
Lancaster Gate
W2 . . . . .114 B6 246 C6
Lancaster Gate Sta
W2 . . . . .114 B6 246 C6
Lancaster Gdns
Bromley BR1 . . . . .210 A4
Kingston u T KT2 . . . . .175 D5
West Ealing W13 . . . . . .109 B4
Wimbledon SW19 . . . . .179 A6
Lancaster Gr NW3 . . . .70 C2
Lancaster Hall 14
E16 . . . . .121 A5
Lancaster Ho
Enfield EN3 . . . . .5 B4
Putney SW15 . . . . .134 C3
Stanmore HA7 . . . . .9 A1
Lancaster Ho SW1 . . .249 A2
Lancaster Ho NW8 . .157 D4
Lancasterian Prim Sch
N17 . . . . .33 D2
Lancaster Lo 2 W11 . .91 A1
Lancaster Mews
Bayswater
　W2 . . . . .114 A6 246 B6
　3 Richmond TW10 . .154 A3
　3 Wandsworth
　SW18 . . . . .157 C5
Lancaster Pl
Hounslow TW5 . . . . . . .128 D3
Ilford IG1 . . . . .79 A4
Strand WC2 . . . . . . .116 B6 262 C6
Twickenham TW1 . . . . .153 A4
　1 Wimbledon SW19 . .178 D5
Lancaster Rd
Bowes Pk N11 . . . . .31 D4
Dudden Hill NW10 . . . . . .68 A3
Edmonton N18 . . . . .33 D5
Enfield EN2 . . . . .5 B4
Finsbury Pk N4 . . . . .50 C2
Harrow HA2 . . . . .42 A1
Higham Hill E17 . . . . . . .34 D1
Leytonstone E11 . . . . . . .76 C6
New Barnet EN4 . . . . . . .14 B6
Northolt UB5 . . . . .64 A2
Notting Hill W11 . . . . . . .31 A3
Southall UB1 . . . . .107 A6
South Norwood SE25 . . .206 A6
Upton E7 . . . . .77 A1
Wimbledon SW19 . . . . .178 D5
Lancaster Road Ind Est
　2 EN4 . . . . .14 B6
Lancaster St
SE1 . . . . .116 D4 251 D1
Lancaster Stables 3
NW3 . . . . .70 C2
Lancaster Terr
W2 . . . . .114 B6 246 C6
Lancaster Wlk
Hayes UB3
　Knightsbridge 83 A1
　W2 . . . . .114 A5 246 B6
Lancastrian Rd SM6 . .220 B1
Lancefield Ho SE15 . .140 B2
Lancefield St W10 . . . .91 B4
Lancell St N16 . . . . .73 C6
Lancelot Ave HA0 . . . . .65 D4
Lancelot Cres HA0 . . . .65 D4
Lancelot Gdns EN4 . . .15 A4
Lancelot Ho SM5 . . . . .202 C1

Lancelot Pl
SW7 . . . . .114 D4 247 C1
Lancelot Rd
Welling DA16 . . . . .146 A2
Wembley HA0 . . . . .65 D3
Lance Rd HA1 . . . . .42 A2
Lancer Sq W8 . . . . . . .245 C2
Lancey Cl SE7 . . . . . . .122 A2
Lanchester Ct W2 . . . .237 C1
Lanchester Rd N6 . . . . .48 D4
Lanchester Way
SE14 . . . . .140 D4
Lancing Gdns N9 . . . . .17 D3
Lancing Rd
Ealing W13 . . . . .109 B6
Feltham TW13 . . . . .149 D2
Ilford IG2 . . . . .57 B2
Thornton Heath CR0 . . .204 B2
Lancing St NW1 . . . . . .232 C1
Lancresse Ct N1 . . . . . .95 C6
Landale Ct SE10 . . . . .142 A4
Landale Ho 13 SE16 . .118 C3
Landau Ct 13 CR2 . . . .221 C1
Landcroft Rd SE22 . . .161 D5
Landells Rd SE22 . . . .162 A5
Lander Ct EN5 . . . . .14 A6
Landford Rd SW15 . . .134 C2
Landgrove Rd SW19 . .179 C5
Landin Ho 1 E14 . . . . . .97 C1
Landleys Field 2 N7 . . .71 D3
Landmann Ho 6
SE16 . . . . .118 B2
Landmann Way
SE14 . . . . .118 D1
Landmark Commercial
　Ctr N18 . . . . .33 C4
Landmark Hts E5 . . . . .75 A4
Landon Pl SW1 . . . . . .247 C6
Landons Cl E14 . . . . . .120 A5
Landon Way 5 TW10 . .154 A4
Landor Ct N16 . . . . .73 C3
Landor Ho 4 SE5 . . . . .139 B5
Landor Rd SW9 . . . . . .138 A2
Landor Wlk 1 W12 . . . .112 A4
Landra Gdns N21 . . . . .16 D5
Landrake NW1 . . . . . . .232 B5
Landridge Dr EN1 . . . . . .6 B5
Landridge Rd SW6 . . .135 B3
Landrock Rd N8 . . . . . . .50 B3
Landscape Rd IG8 . . . . .37 B3
Landsdown Cl 8 EN5 . . .2 A1
Landseer Ave E12 . . . . .78 C3
Landseer Cl
Edgware HA8 . . . . .26 C1
Mitcham SW19 . . . . . . .180 B2
Landseer Ct
Hayes UB4 . . . . .83 B5
　10 Upper Holloway
　N19 . . . . .72 A6
Landseer Ho
Battersea SW11 . . . . . .268 B1
　10 Northolt UB5 . . . . .64 B3
Paddington NW8 . . . . . .236 D6
Westminster SW1 . . . . .259 D3
Landseer Rd
Cheam SM1 . . . . .217 C2
Enfield EN1 . . . . .18 A6
New Malden KT3 . . . . . .199 B2
Upper Holloway N19 . . . .72 A6
Lands' End W10 . . . . . . .91 C3
Landstead Rd SE18 . . .145 B5
Landulph Ho SE11 . . . .261 B2
Landward Ct W1 . . . . . .237 B2
Lane Cl NW2 . . . . .68 B4
Lane Ct SW11 . . . . .158 C4
Lane End DA7 . . . . .147 D2
Lane Gdns
Bushey Heath WD23 . . . .8 C4
Claygate KT10 . . . . .212 D1
Lane Mews E12 . . . . . . .78 B5
Lanercost Cl SW2 . . . .160 C2
Lanercost Gdns N14 . . .16 A4
Lanercost Rd SW2 . . . .160 C2
Laneside
Chislehurst BR7 . . . . . .189 A5
Edgware HA8 . . . . .27 A5
Laneside Ave RM8 . . . . .59 B2
Lane The
Blackheath Pk SE3 . . . .143 A2
St John's Wood
　NW8 . . . . .92 A5 229 A4
Laneway SW15 . . . . . .156 B6
Laney Bldg EC1 . . . . . .241 A4
Lanfranc Ct HA1 . . . . . .64 D5
Lanfranc Rd E3 . . . . .97 A5

Lanfrey Pl W14 . . . . . .254 C1
Langbourn Ct E17 . . . . .53 A3
Langbourne Ave N6 . . . .71 A6
Langbourne Ho 7
　SW2 . . . . .160 C6
Langbourne Mans N6 . .71 A6
Langbourne Pl E14 . . . .119 C1
Langbourne Prim Sch
SE21 . . . . .161 C1
Langbourne Way
KT10 . . . . .213 A2
Langbrook Rd SE3 . . . .143 D3
Langcroft Cl SM5 . . . . .218 D5
Langdale NW1 . . . . . . .232 A2
Langdale Ave CR4 . . . .202 D6
Langdale Cl
Camberwell SE17 . . . . .139 A6
Dagenham RM8 . . . . . . .58 C1
Locksbottom BR6 . . . . .226 D5
Mortlake SW14 . . . . . . .132 C1
Langdale Cres DA7 . . .147 C4
Langdale Ct
　8 Ealing W5 . . . . . . .87 C2
　9 Ilford IG1 . . . . .78 D5
Ruislip HA4 . . . . .62 B3
Langdale Dr UB4 . . . . . .83 C5
Langdale Gdns UB6 . . . .87 B4
Langdale Ho SW1 . . . . .259 A1
Langdale Par 8
　CR4 . . . . .202 D6
Langdale Rd
Greenwich SE10 . . . . . .142 A5
Thornton Heath CR7 . . .204 C5
Langdale St 12 E1 . . . . .96 B1
Langdon Cres E6 . . . . .100 C5
Langdon Ct
Finsbury EC1 . . . . .234 D3
Harlesden NW10 . . . . . . .89 C6
Langdon Ho **3** NW9 . . . .45 A1
Langdon Ho 3 E14 . . . . .98 A1
Langdon Park Sch
E14 . . . . .98 A1
Langdon Park Sta
E14 . . . . .97 D1
Langdon Pk TW11 . . . .175 C3
Langdon Pk L Ctr
E14 . . . . .98 A1
Langdon Pl SW14 . . . . .133 A2
Langdon Rd
Barking E6 . . . . .100 C6
Bromley BR2 . . . . .209 B6
Morden SM4 . . . . .202 A4
Langdon Sch E6 . . . . . .100 C6
Langdon Way 22
SE1 . . . . .118 A2
Langdon Wlk SM4 . . . .202 A4
Langford Cl
Shacklewell E8 . . . . .74 A3
　7 South Tottenham
　N15 . . . . .51 C3
St John's Wood NW8 . . .229 B4
Langford Cres EN4 . . . . . .2 D1
Langford Ct NW8 . . . . .229 B3
Langford Gn SE5 . . . . .139 C2
Langford Ho 5 SE8 . . . .141 C6
Langford Pl
Sidcup DA14 . . . . .168 A1
St John's Wood
　NW8 . . . . .92 A5 229 B4
Langford Prim Sch
SW6 . . . . .135 D3
Langford Rd
Cockfosters EN4 . . . . .2 D1
　4 Sands End SW6 . .135 D3
Woodford IG8 . . . . .37 C4
Langfords IG9 . . . . .21 D2
Langham Cl 1 N15 . . . . .50 D6
Langham Ct
Hendon NW4 . . . . .46 D4
Merton SW20 . . . . .178 C1
　4 Putney SW15 . . . .156 D6
Ruislip HA4 . . . . .62 B3
　12 Twickenham TW1 .153 C5
Langham Dr RM6 . . . . . .58 B3
Langham Gdns
Burnt Oak HA8 . . . . .27 A3
Ealing W13 . . . . .109 B6
Richmond TW10 . . . . . .175 C6
Southgate N21 . . . . .16 D6
Wembley HA0 . . . . .65 C2

Langham Ho
Clapham Pk SW4 . . . . .159 C6
　3 Wanstead E11 . . . .55 B5
Langham House Cl
　TW10 . . . . .175 C3
Langham Mans SW5 . .255 C1
Langham Park Pl
　BR2 . . . . .208 D5
Langham Pl
Chiswick W4 . . . . .133 C6
Fitzrovia W1 . . . .93 B2 238 D3
Noel Pk N15 . . . . .50 D6
Langham Rd
Burnt Oak HA8 . . . . .27 A4
Teddington TW11 . . . . .175 B4
West Green N15 . . . . . . .51 A6
Wimbledon SW20 . . . . .178 C2
Langham St
W1 . . . . .93 B2 238 C3
Langhedge Cl N18 . . . . .33 D4
Langhedge La N18 . . . . .33 D4
Langhedge Lane Ind Est
N18 . . . . .33 D4
Lang Ho
South Lambeth SW8 . . .270 A3
Stanwell TW19 . . . . . . .148 A3
　3 Tufnell Pk N19 . . . .71 C5
Langholm Cl SW12 . . .159 D4
Langholme WD23 . . . . . .8 A3
Langhorn Dr TW2 . . . . .152 C4
Langhorne Ct 10
NW8 . . . . .70 B1
Langhorne Ho 5
SE7 . . . . .143 C6
Langhorne Rd RM10 . . .81 C1
Langhurst Ho 10
SW11 . . . . .137 A3
Langland Cres HA7 . . . .25 D1
Langland Dr HA5 . . . . . .23 A3
Langland Gdns
Croydon CR0 . . . . .223 B6
West Hampstead NW3 . . .69 B3
Langland Ho 10 SE5 . .139 B5
Langland Mans NW3 . . .69 B3
Langler Rd NW10 . . . . . .90 C5
Langley Ave
North Cheam KT4,
　SM3 . . . . .216 D6
Ruislip HA4 . . . . .62 B6
Surbiton KT6 . . . . .198 A1
Langley Cres
Dagenham RM9 . . . . . . .80 D1
Edgware HA8 . . . . .11 A1
Harlington UB3 . . . . . . .127 D5
Wanstead E11 . . . . .55 C2
Langley Ct
South Croydon CR2 . . . .221 B1
Strand WC2 . . . . .250 A3
　18 Sutton SM2 . . . . .218 A2
Langley Dr
South Acton W3 . . . . . .110 C4
Wanstead E11 . . . . .55 B2
Langley Gdns
Bromley BR2 . . . . .209 C5
Dagenham RM9 . . . . . . .80 D1
Southborough BR5 . . . .210 D3
Langley Gr KT3 . . . . . .177 C1
Langley Ho
　1 Lower Clapton E5 . .74 B3
　36 Paddington W2 . . .91 C2
Langley La
SW8 . . . . .138 A6 270 B6
Langley Lawns SM2 . .218 B1
Langley Manor BR3 . . .208 A4
Langley Mans SW8 . . .270 B6
Langley Park Rd SM1,
　SM2 . . . . .218 A1
Langley Park Sch for
　Boys BR3 . . . . .207 D3
Langley Park Sch for
　Girls BR3 . . . . .208 A3
Langley Pk NW7 . . . . . .27 C4
Langley Pl 4 KT4 . . . . .216 D6
Langley Rd
Beckenham BR3 . . . . . .207 A5
Isleworth TW7 . . . . .130 C3
Merton SW19 . . . . .179 C2
Surbiton KT6 . . . . .198 A2
West Heath DA16 . . . . .146 C6
Langley Row EN5 . . . . . .1 B4
Langley St
WC2 . . . . .94 A1 240 A1
Langley Way BR4 . . . . .208 C2
Langmead Dr WD23 . . . . .8 B3
Langmead Ho 34 E3 . . . .97 D4

Langmead St SE27 . . .183 A6
Langmore Ct DA6 . . . . .146 D2
Langmore Ho 16 E1 . . . .96 A1
Langport Ct KT12 . . . . .194 C1
Langport Ho 1
SW9 . . . . .138 D3
Langridge 16 NW5 . . . . .71 A2
Langridge Mews
TW12 . . . . .173 B4
Langroyd Rd SW17 . . .158 D2
Langside Ave SW15 . . .134 A1
Langside Cres N14 . . . .15 D3
Lang St E1 . . . . .96 C3
Langstone Way NW7 . . .28 D3
Langston Hughes Cl 5
SE24 . . . . .138 D1
Langthorn Ct EC2 . . . . .242 D2
Langthorne Ct 3
SE6 . . . . .186 A6
Langthorne Ho UB3 . . .105 C2
Langthorne Lo 30
SW2 . . . . .160 C4
Langthorne Rd E11 . . . .76 B5
Langthorne St SW6 . . .134 D5
Langton Ave
Oakleigh Pk N20 . . . . . .14 B4
Wallend E6 . . . . .100 C4
Langton Cl
WC1 . . . . .94 B3 240 D6
Langton Ct SW15 . . . . .157 B5
Langton Ho
Harrow HA2 . . . . .64 C6
Lambeth SE11 . . . . .260 D4
　5 Streatham SW16 . .181 C6
Langton Pl SW18 . . . . .157 C3
Langton Rd
Camberwell SW9 . . . . . .138 D5
Cricklewood NW2 . . . . . .68 C5
West Barnsey KT8 . . . . .196 A5
Harrow Weald HA3 . . . . .24 A3
Langton Rise SE22,
SE23 . . . . .162 B4
Langton St
SW10 . . . . . . .136 A6 266 B5
Langton Way
Greenwich SE3 . . . . . . .143 A5
South Croydon CR0 . . . .221 C4
Langtry Ho BR1 . . . . . .187 B3
Langtry Pl SW6 . . . . . .265 B6
Langtry Rd
Northolt UB5 . . . . .84 D5
Paddington NW8 . . . . . . .91 D6
Langtry Wlk
NW8 . . . . .92 A6 229 A6
Langwood Chase
TW11 . . . . .175 C4
Langworth Dr UB4 . . . . .84 B1
Langworthy HA5 . . . . . .23 C4
Lanherne Ho 7
SW19 . . . . .178 D3
Lanhill Rd W9 . . . . .91 C3
Lanier Rd SE13 . . . . . .164 B5
Lanigan Dr TW3 . . . . . .151 D6
Lankaster Gdns N2 . . . .30 B2
Lankers Dr HA2 . . . . . . .41 B3
Lankton Cl BR3 . . . . . .186 A2
Lanner Ho 8 SW11 . . . .136 C2
Lannock Cl 2 SW17 . . .180 C4
Lannock Rd UB3 . . . . . .105 D5
Lannoy Point SW6 . . . .264 A4
Lannoy Rd SE9 . . . . . . .167 A3
Lanrick Rd E14 . . . . .98 C1
Lanridge Rd SE2 . . . . . .124 D3
Lansan Ct EL1 . . . . .76 C6
Lansbury Ave
Barking IG11 . . . . .80 A1
Dagenham RM6 . . . . . . .59 A4
Edmonton N18 . . . . .33 C5
Feltham TW14 . . . . . . .150 B5
Lansbury Cl NW10 . . . . .67 A3
Lansbury Dr UB4 . . . . . .84 B3
Lansbury Est 8
E14 . . . . .98 B1
Lansbury Gdns 1
E14 . . . . .98 B1
Lansbury Ho 5
DA17 . . . . .125 B1
Lansbury Lawrence
　Prim Sch 3 E14 . . . . .98 B1
Lansbury Rd EN3 . . . . . . .6 D4
Lansbury Way N18 . . . .33 C5
Lanscombe Wlk SW8 . .270 C5
Lansdell Ho 9 SW2 . . .160 C5
Lansdell Rd CR4 . . . . . .181 A1
Lansdown Cl KT12 . . . .194 C1
Lansdowne Ave
Orpington BR6 . . . . .210 D1

Lansdowne Ave *continued*
West Heath DA7 .... 146 D5
Lansdowne Cl
Tolworth KT5 .... 214 D6
Twickenham TW1 ...... 152 D3
Wimbledon SW20 .... 178 D3
Lansdowne Coll W2. 245 C5
Lansdowne Copse 1
KT4 .... 216 A6
Lansdowne Cres
W11 .... 113 A6 244 B5
Lansdowne Ct
Redbridge IG5 .... 56 A6
2 Worcester Pk KT4. 216 A6
Lansdowne Dr E8 ...... 74 A1
Lansdowne Gdns
SW8 .... 138 A4 270 A2
Lansdowne Gr NW10 .. 67 C4
Lansdowne Hill
SE27 .... 160 D1
Lansdowne Ho
19 Belmont SM2 .... 217 D1
Enfield EN2 .... 4 C3
Notting Hill W11 ..... 244 C4
Lansdowne La SE7 .. 121 D1
Lansdowne Mews
Greenwich SE7 ..... 121 D1
Notting Hill W11 ..... 244 C4
Lansdowne Pl
Borough The SE1 .... 262 D6
Penge SE19 .... 183 D3
Lansdowne Rd
Chingford E4 .... 19 C2
Croydon CR0 .... 205 B1
Finchley N3 .... 29 C3
Harrow HA1 .... 42 C2
Hayes UB8 .... 83 A1
Hounslow TW3 ...... 129 D2
Ilford IG3 .... 57 D2
Leytonstone E11 ...... 76 D6
Muswell Hill N10 ...... 31 C1
Notting Hill
W11 .... 113 A6 244 B5
Stanmore HA7 .... 25 C4
Sundridge BR1 .... 187 B3
Tottenham N17 .... 34 A2
Walthamstow E17 ..... 53 C3
Wanstead E18 .... 55 A6
West Ewell KT19 ..... 215 B1
Wimbledon SW19,
SW20 .... 178 C3
Lansdowne Rise
W11 .... 113 A6 244 B5
Lansdowne Row W1 248 D4
Lansdowne Sch 5
SW9 .... 138 B2
Lansdowne Terr
WC1 .... 240 B5
Lansdowne Way SW4,
SW8 .... 138 A4 270 B1
Lansdowne Wlk
W11 .... 113 B5 244 C4
Lansdowne Wood Cl 11
SE27 .... 160 D1
Lansdowne Workshops
SE7 .... 121 D1
Lansdown Ho 28
SE5 .... 139 A3
Lansdown Rd
Sidcup DA14 .... 168 B1
Upton E7 .... 77 C1
Lansfield Ave N18 ..... 34 A6
Lanson Ho HA8 .... 26 C4
Lantern Cl
Orpington BR6 ...... 226 D4
Putney SW15 .... 134 A1
Wembley HA0 .... 65 D3
Lantern Ct
Southgate N14 .... 15 D3
4 Wimbledon SW20. 178 D2
Lantern Ho
Millwall E14 .... 119 C4
Woolwich SE18 ..... 122 C1
Lantern of Knowledge
Boys Sec Sch 1
E10 .... 76 A6
Lanterns Ct E14 ...... 119 C3
Lanterns The N12 ..... 29 D4
Lantern Way UB7 .... 104 B4
Lant Ho SE1 .... 252 A1
Lantry Ct 1 W3 ..... 110 D5
Lant St SE1 ..... 117 A4 252 B1
Lanvanor Rd SE15 .... 140 C3
Lanyard Ho 4 SE8 ... 119 B2
Lapford Cl W9 .... 91 B3
Lapponum Wlk UB4 ... 84 D2
Lapsang SE1 .... 253 D3
Lapse Wood Wlk
SE22 .... 162 B3
Lapstone Gdns HA3 ... 43 C3
Lapwing Ct
Grahame Pk NW9 ..... 27 C1
Tolworth KT6 .... 214 C5
Lapwing Terr E7 .... 77 D3
Lapwing Twr 31 SE8 .. 141 B6
Lapwing Way UB4 .... 84 D1
Lapworth 2 N11 ...... 31 B6
Lapworth Ct W2 .... 91 D2
Lara Cl
Chessington KT9 .... 214 A1
Lewisham SE13 ..... 164 A5
Lara Lo SM1 .... 217 C3
Larbert Rd SW16 ..... 181 C3
Larch Ave W3 .... 111 C5
Larch Cl
Balham SW12 .... 159 B2
Colney Hatch N11 ..... 31 A3
15 Deptford SE8 ..... 141 B6
Newham E13 .... 99 C3
10 Upper Holloway
N19 .... 71 C6
Larch Cres Hayes UB4 .. 84 D2
West Ewell KT19 .... 214 D2
Larch Ct 41 W2 .... 91 C2
Larch Dene BR6 ..... 226 C6
Larches Ave SW14 ... 133 B1
Larches The
Edmonton N13 .... 17 A1
Hillingdon UB10 ...... 82 D5
Larchfield Ho 2 N5 ... 73 A3
Larch Gn NW9 .... 27 C2
Larch Gr DA15 ...... 167 D3
Larch Ho Hayes UB4 ... 84 C2
23 Rotherhithe SE16 . 118 C4
Larchmont HA4 .... 39 B2
Larchmore Ct N19 .... 72 A6
Larch Rd
Criclewood NW2 ...... 68 C4
Leyton E10 .... 75 C6
Larch Tree Way CR0 .. 223 C5
Larchvale Ct 20
SM2 .... 217 D1
Larch Way BR2 ...... 210 C2
Larchwood Rd SE9 .. 166 D2
Larcombe Cl CR0 ... 221 D4
Larcom St
SE17 .... 117 A2 262 B3
Larden Rd W3 .... 111 C4
La Retraite RC Girls Sch
SW12 .... 159 C4
Largewood Ave KT6 .. 214 C6
Larissa St SE17 ..... 262 D3
Larix Ct NW10 .... 90 A6
Larkbere Rd SE26 ... 185 A6
Larken Cl WD23 .... 8 A3
Larken Dr WD23 .... 8 A3
Larkfield Ave HA3 ..... 43 B6
Larkfield Cl BR2 ..... 225 A6
Larkfield Rd
Longlands DA14 ..... 167 D1
Richmond TW9 ...... 132 A1
Larkhall La
SW4 .... 138 A4 270 A1
Lark Hall Prim Sch
SW4 .... 137 D3
Larkhall Rise SW4 .. 137 D3
Larkham Cl TW13 .... 149 C1
Lark Row E2 .... 96 C6
Larksfield Gr EN1 ...... 6 B4
Larks Gr IG11 .... 79 C1
Larkshall Bsns Ctr E4 . 20 B2
Larkshall Cres E4 ..... 36 A6
Larkshall Ct E4 .... 36 A5
Larkshall Rd E4 ...... 36 B6
Larkspur Cl
Kingsbury NW9 .... 44 D4
4 Newham E6 ...... 100 A2
Ruislip HA4 .... 39 A2
Tottenham N17 .... 33 B3
Larkspur Ct SM6 ..... 219 B1
Larkspur Gr HA8 ...... 27 A6
Larkspur Way KT19 .. 215 A3
Larkswood Ct E4 ..... 36 B5
Larkswood L Ctr E4 .. 36 A6
Larkswood Prim Sch
E4 .... 35 D6
Larkswood Rd E4 ..... 35 D6
Larkswood Rise HA5 .. 40 C5
Lark Way SM5 ...... 202 C2
Larkway Cl NW9 ...... 45 B5
Larmenier & Sacred
Heart RC Prim Sch 4
W6 .... 112 D2
Larnaca Ho SE1 ..... 263 C6
Larnach Rd W6 ..... 134 D6
Larne Rd HA4 .... 39 D2
Larpent Ave SW15 ... 156 C6
Larwood Cl UB6 .... 64 B3
La Saint Union RC Sec
Sch NW5 .... 71 A5
Lascelles Ave HA1 .... 42 B2
Lascelles Cl E11 ...... 76 B6
Lascelles Ho NW1 ... 237 B5
Lascott's Rd N22 ..... 32 B4
Laseron Ho 1 N15 .... 51 D5
Lashford Ho HA8 ..... 27 A4
Lassa Rd SE9 .... 166 B6
Lassell St SE10 ..... 120 B1
Lasseter Pl SE3 ..... 142 D6
Latchett Rd E18 ...... 37 B2
Latchingdon Ct E17 ... 52 D5
Latchmere Cl KT2,
TW10 .... 176 A5
Latchmere La KT2,
TW10 .... 176 B5
Latchmere L Ctr
SW11 .... 136 D3
Latchmere Prim Sch
KT2 .... 176 B4
Latchmere Rd
Battersea SW11 .... 136 D3
Kingston u T KT2 ... 176 B4
Latchmere St 5
SW11 .... 136 D3
Lateward Rd TW8 ... 131 D6
Latham Cl
Newham E6 .... 100 A1
6 Twickenham TW1 . 153 A4
Latham Ct
3 Bowes Pk N11 ...... 32 A4
7 Northolt UB5 .... 84 D4
Latham Ho Stepney E1 . 96 D1
18 Walthamstow E17 ... 53 D6
Latham Rd
Bexleyheath DA6 .... 169 C6
Twickenham TW1 .... 152 D4
Latham's Way CR0 ... 220 B6
Lathkill Cl EN1 .... 18 A4
Lathkill Ct BR3 ...... 185 B2
Lathom Jun Sch E6 ... 78 A1
Lathom Rd E6 .... 78 B1
Lathwood Ho 6
SE26 .... 184 B5
Latimer SE17 .... 263 A1
Latimer Ave E6 ..... 100 B6
Latimer Cl
North Cheam KT4 .... 216 B4
Pinner Green HA5 ..... 22 C2
Latimer Gdns HA5 .... 22 C2
Latimer Ho
11 Homerton E9 ...... 74 D2
Notting Hill W11 ..... 244 D5
Latimer Ind Est 1
NW10 .... 90 C1
Latimer Pl W10 .... 90 C1
Latimer Rd Barnet EN5 .. 1 D2
1 Croydon CR0 ..... 220 D5
Forest Gate E7 .... 77 B4
North Kensington W10 . 90 C1
South Tottenham N15 .. 51 C3
Teddington TW11 .... 174 D5
Wimbledon SW19 .... 179 D4
Latimer Road Sta
W10 .... 112 D6
Latitude Ct E16 ..... 123 A6
Latitude Ho NW1 ... 231 C5
Latona Rd SE15 ..... 140 A6
La Tourne Gdns
BR6 .... 227 A5
Lattimer Pl W4 ...... 133 C6
Latton Cl KT12 ...... 195 A2
Latvia Ct SE17 ..... 262 B1
Latymer All Saints CE
Prim Sch N9 .... 17 D2
Latymer Ct W6 ...... 112 D2
Latymer Rd N9 .... 17 D3
Latymer Sch The N9 .. 17 C2
Latymer Upper Sch 14
W6 .... 112 A2
Latymer Way N9 ...... 17 C2
Laubin Cl TW1 ...... 131 B1
Lauder Cl UB5 .... 84 D5
Lauder Ct N14 .... 16 A4
Lauderdale Dr
TW10 .... 153 D1
Lauderdale Mans W9 . 91 D4
Lauderdale Rd W9 .... 91 D4
Lauderdale Twr EC2 . 242 A4
Laud St Croydon CR0 .. 221 A5
Vauxhall
SE11 .... 116 B1 260 C2
Laughton Ho 11
SW2 .... 160 C5
Laughton Rd UB5 ..... 84 D6
Launcelot Prim Sch
BR1 .... 187 A6
Launcelot Rd BR1,
SE12 .... 187 A6
Launcelot St SE1 .... 251 A1
Launceston Ct CR7 .. 204 C3
Launceston Gdns
UB6 .... 65 C1
Launceston Pl
W8 .... 114 A3 256 A5
Launceston Rd UB6 ... 87 C6
Launch St E14 ...... 120 A3
Laundress La N16 .... 74 A5
Laundry La 7 N1 ..... 73 A1
Laundry Mews SE23 . 162 D4
Laundry Rd
W6 .... 135 A6 264 A5
Launton Dr DA6 .... 146 D1
Laura Cl Enfield EN1 ... 17 C6
Wanstead E11 .... 55 C4
Laura Ct HA2 .... 24 A1
Lauradale Rd N2 ...... 48 D5
Laura Pl E5 .... 74 C4
Laurel Ave TW1 ..... 152 D3
Laurel Bank Gdns 3
SW6 .... 135 B3
Laurel Bank Rd EN2 .... 5 B4
Laurel Cl
Sidcup DA14 .... 168 A1
8 Upper Holloway
N19 .... 71 C6
Upper Tooting SW17 . 180 C5
Laurel Cres CR0 ..... 223 C5
Laurel Ct Dalston E8 ... 73 D1
2 Putney SW15 ..... 156 D6
9 Rotherhithe SE16 . 119 A5
South Norwood SE25 . 205 C4
8 Wembley HA0 ...... 88 A5
Laurel Dr N21 .... 16 C4
Laurel Gdns
Bromley BR1 .... 210 A5
Chingford E4 .... 19 D4
Ealing W7 .... 108 C5
Edgware NW7 .... 11 B1
Hounslow TW4 ...... 129 A1
Laurel Gr
Forest Hill SE26 ..... 185 A6
Penge SE20 .... 184 C3
Laurel Ho
Brentford W5 .... 109 C2
9 Deptford SE8 ..... 141 B6
5 Hamstead NW3 ..... 69 D2
Morden SM4 .... 201 D4
Laurel La UB7 ...... 104 A2
Laurel Manor SM2 ... 218 A1
Laurel Mead Ct 8
E18 .... 37 A2
Laurel Pk HA3 .... 24 D3
Laurel Rd
Barnes SW13 .... 134 A3
Teddington TW12 .... 174 B5
Wimbledon SW20 .... 178 B2
Laurel St E8 .... 73 D2
Laurels The
8 Belvedere DA17 .. 125 C1
2 Buckhurst Hill IG9 .. 21 C3
Bushey WD23 .... 8 C2
Finchley N3 .... 29 D4
Shortlands BR2 ..... 209 A5
9 Sundridge BR1 .... 187 B2
Laurel View N12 ...... 13 D1
Laurel Way
Snaresbrook E18 ...... 54 D5
Woodside Pk N20 ...... 13 C1
Laurence Ct E10 ...... 53 D2
Laurence Mews 12
W12 .... 112 A4
Laurence Pountney Hill
EC4 .... 252 C6
Laurence Pountney La
EC4 .... 252 D6
Laurie Gr SE14 ...... 141 A4
Laurie Ho
Newington SE1 ..... 261 D5
Notting Hill
W8 ...... 113 C5 245 A3
Laurie Rd W7 .... 86 C2
Laurier Rd
Croydon CR0 .... 205 D2
Dartmouth Pk NW5 .... 71 B5
Laurimel Cl HA7 ...... 25 B4
Laurino Pl WD23 .... 8 A2
Lauriston Apartments 6
N17 .... 51 D6
Lauriston Ho 6 E9 .... 74 D1
Lauriston Lo NW6 ..... 69 B2
Lauriston Prim Sch 6
E9 .... 96 D6
Lauriston Rd
Homerton E9 .... 74 D1
Wimbledon SW19 .... 178 D4
Lausanne Rd
Hornsey N8 .... 50 C5
St Johns SE15 ...... 140 C4
Lavehham Ho E17 .... 35 D2
Lavell St N16 .... 73 B4
Lavender Ave
Mitcham CR4 .... 180 D2
North Cheam KT4,
SM3 .... 216 C5
Welsh Harp NW9 ...... 45 A1
Lavender Cl
Bromley Comm BR2 .. 210 A3
Chingford E4 .... 35 C6
South Kensington
SW3 .... 266 D5
Wallington SM5 ...... 219 B4
Lavender Ct
Colney Hatch N12 ..... 30 C4
East Molesey KT8 ... 195 D6
Edgware HA8 .... 27 A5
Feltham TW14 .... 150 B5
South Lambeth SW4 . 270 B1
Sutton SM2 .... 218 A1
Lavender Gdns
Clapham SW11 ..... 136 D1
Enfield EN2 .... 4 D4
Stanmore HA3 .... 24 C4
Lavender Gr
Dalston E8 .... 74 A1
Mitcham CR4 .... 180 C2
Lavender Hill
Clapham SW11 ..... 137 A2
Enfield EN2 .... 4 D4
Lavender Ho
8 Richmond TW9 ... 132 D4
14 Rotherhithe SE16 . 118 D5
Lavender Pl IG1 ...... 78 D3
Lavender Prim Sch
EN2 .... 5 C5
Lavender Rd
Battersea SW11 ..... 136 B2
Enfield EN2 .... 5 B4
Hillingdon UB8 .... 82 B2
Rotherhithe SE16 .... 119 A5
Sutton SM1 .... 218 B4
Thornton Heath CR0 .. 204 B3
Wallington SM5 ..... 219 A4
West Ewell KT19 ..... 214 D2
Lavender Rise UB7 ... 104 C4
Lavender St E15 ...... 76 C2
Lavender Sweep
SW11 .... 136 D1
Lavender Terr 12
SW11 .... 136 C2
Lavender Vale SM6 .. 219 D2
Lavender Way CR0 .. 206 D3
Lavender Wlk SW11 . 136 D1
Lavendon Ho NW8 .. 237 B6
Lavengro Rd SE27 ... 161 A2
Lavenham Rd SW18 .. 157 C3
Lavernock Rd DA7 ... 147 C3
Lavers Rd N16 .... 73 C5
Laverstoke Gdns
SW15 .... 156 A4
Laverton Mews SW5 255 D3
Laverton Pl SW5 .... 255 D3
Lavidge Rd SE9 ..... 166 B2
Lavina Gr N1 .... 233 C4
Lavington Cl E9 ...... 75 B2
Lavington Rd
Ealing W13 .... 109 B5
Wallington CR0 ..... 220 B4
Lavington St
SE1 .... 116 D5 251 D3
Lavinia Ct BR1 ...... 186 C3
Lavisham Ho BR1 .... 187 B5
Lawdale Jun Sch 32
E2 .... 96 A4
Lawdon Gdns CR0 .. 220 D4

Lawford Rd
Chiswick W4 133 A5
De Beauvoir Town N1 73 C1
Kentish Town NW5 71 C2
Lawfords Wharf 18
NW1 71 C1
Law Ho IG11 102 A5
Lawless Ho 5 E14 120 A6
Lawless St 12 E14 119 D6
Lawley Ho 11 TW1 153 D5
Lawley Rd N14 15 B4
Lawley St E5 74 C4
Lawman Ct 2 TW9 132 B4
Lawn Cl Edmonton N9 17 D4
Kingston u T KT3 177 C1
Ruislip HA4 61 D5
Sundridge BR1 187 B3
Lawn Cres TW9 132 C3
Lawn Farm Gr RM6 59 A5
Lawnfield Ct NW6 68 D1
Lawn Gdns W7 108 C5
Lawn House Cl E14 120 A4
Lawn La SW8 138 B6 270 C6
Lawn Mans EN5 1 B1
Lawn Rd
Beckenham BR3 185 B3
Maitland Pk NW3 70 D3
Lawns Ct HA9 66 C6
Lawnside SE3 142 D1
Lawns The
Belmont SM2 217 A1
Blackheath SE3 142 D2
Chingford E4 35 C5
Harrow HA5 23 D3
Sidcup DA14 190 B6
South Norwood SE19 183 B2
Stoke Newington N16 73 C3
1 Wimbledon SW19 179 B5
Lawn Terr SE3 142 C2
Lawn The UB2 107 C1
Lawn Vale HA5 23 A1
Lawrence Ave
Edmonton N13 32 D6
Higham Hill E17 34 D2
Little Ilford E12 78 C4
Mill Hill NW7 27 D6
New Malden KT3 199 C2
Stonebridge NW10 89 B6
Lawrence Bldgs 1
N16 73 D5
Lawrence Camp Cl
N20 14 B1
Lawrence Cl Bow E3 97 C5
6 Shepherd's Bush
W12 112 B6
West Green N15 51 C5
Lawrence Cres
Dagenham RM10 81 D5
Edgware HA8 26 C1
Lawrence Ct
Hornsey N10 49 C6
Mill Hill NW7 27 C5
4 South Acton W3 111 A3
Stoke Newington N16 73 D5
5 Woodford IG8 37 C4
Lawrence Dr UB10 61 A4
Lawrence Est TW4 128 C1
Lawrence Gdns NW7 11 D1
Lawrence Hall E13 99 B3
Lawrence Hill E4 19 C2
Lawrence Ho
Bowes Pk N22 32 B4
20 Camden Town NW1 71 B1
Westminster SW1 259 D3
Lawrence La EC2 242 B2
Lawrence Mans SW3 267 A5
Lawrence Pl N1 233 B6
Lawrence Rd
Coney Hall BR4 225 A4
Ealing W5 109 D2
Edmonton N18 34 B6
Erith DA8 147 D5
Hampton TW12 173 B3
Hillingdon UB4 83 A5
Hounslow TW4 128 C1
Pinner HA5 40 D4
Richmond TW10 175 C6
South Norwood SE25 205 D5
Tottenham N15 51 C5
Upton Pk E6 100 A6
West Ham E13 99 B6
Lawrence St
Canning Town E16 98 D2

Lawrence St *continued*
Chelsea SW3 136 C6 267 A5
Mill Hill NW7 27 D6
Lawrence Trad Est
SE10 120 C2
Lawrence Univ SW7 256 B3
Lawrence Way NW10 67 B5
Lawrence Weaver Cl
SM4 201 C3
Lawrence Yd N15 51 C5
Lawrie Ct HA3 24 D3
Lawrie Park Ave
SE26 184 B5
Lawrie Park Cres
SE26 184 B5
Lawrie Park Gdns
SE26 184 B5
Lawrie Park Rd
SE26 184 C5
Laws Cl SE25 205 B5
Lawson Cl Ilford IG1 79 B3
Newham E16 99 C2
Wimbledon SW19 156 D1
Lawson Ct
1 Finsbury Pk N4 50 B1
13 Surbiton KT6 197 D2
Lawson Gdns HA5 40 B6
Lawson Ho
17 Shepherd's Bush
W12 112 B6
1 Woolwich SE18 144 C6
Lawson Rd Enfield EN3 6 C4
Southall UB1 85 C3
Law St SE1 117 B3 262 D6
Lawton Rd Barnet EN4 2 B2
Bow E3 97 A4
Leytonstone E10 54 A1
Laxcon Cl NW10 67 B3
Laxey Rd BR6 227 D2
Laxfield Ct E8 96 A6
Laxley Cl SE5 138 D5
Laxmi Ct N3 29 B2
Laxton Ct CR7 205 A5
Laxton Path 1 SE4 140 D1
Laxton Pl NW1 238 D6
Layard Rd Enfield EN1 5 D4
Rotherhithe SE16 118 B2
South Norwood CR7 183 B1
Layard Sq SE16 118 B2
Laybourne Ho 18
E14 119 C4
Laycock Prim Sch 5
N1 72 D2
Laycock St N1 72 C2
Layer Gdns W3 110 C6
Layfield Cl NW4 46 B2
Layfield Cres NW4 46 B2
Layfield Ho 1 SE10 121 A1
Layfield Rd NW4 46 B2
Laymarsh Cl DA17 125 B3
Laymead Cl UB5 63 A2
Laystall Ct EC1 241 A5
Laystall St EC1 241 A5
Layton Cres CR0 220 D3
Layton Ct TW8 109 D1
Layton Pl TW9 132 C4
Layton Rd
Brentford TW8 109 D1
Hounslow TW3 129 D1
Layton's La TW16 171 D1
Layzell Wlk SE9 165 D3
Lazar Wlk 2 N7 72 B6
Leabank Cl HA1 64 C5
Leabank Sq E9 75 C2
Leabank View N15 52 A3
Leabourne Rd N16 52 A2
LEA BRIDGE 74 D5
Lea Bridge Rd E10 53 C2
Lea Cl TW2 151 B4
Lea Cotts 10 CR4 181 A1
Lea Cres HA4 61 D4
Leacroft Ave SW12 158 D4
Leacroft Cl
Southgate N21 16 D2
3 Yiewsley UB7 104 A6
Lea Ct
3 Bedford Pk W12 111 C4
1 Chingford E4 20 A2
3 Hillingdon UB10 82 D3
2 Newham E13 99 A4
Leadale Ave E4 19 C2
Leadale Rd N16 52 A3
Leadbeaters Cl 8
N11 30 D5
Leadbetter Ct 12
NW10 67 B1

Leadenhall Mkt★
EC3 243 A1
Leadenhall Pl EC3 243 A1
Leadenhall St
EC3 95 C1 243 A1
Leadenham Ct 15 E3 97 C3
Leader Ave E12 78 C3
Leadings The HA9 67 A5
Leaf Cl KT7, KT8 196 C4
Leaf Gr SE27 182 C5
Leaf Ho Barnet EN5 1 D1
9 Harrow HA1 42 D4
Leafield Cl SW16 182 D4
Leafield La DA14 169 B1
Leafield Rd
Merton SW19,
SW20 201 B6
Sutton SM1 217 C6
Leafy Gr BR2 225 C3
Leafy Oak Rd SE12 165 C1
Leafy Way CR0 221 D6
Lea Gdns HA9 66 B4
Leagrave St E5 74 C5
Lea Hall Gdns E10 53 C1
Lea Hall Rd E10 53 C1
Lea Ho
2 Edmonton N9 18 A1
Lisson Gr NW8 237 A5
Upper Clapton E5 52 C1
Leaholme Waye HA4 39 A3
Leahurst Rd SE13 164 B6
Lea Int E9 75 C3
Leake St Lambeth SE1 251 A1
South Bank
SE1 116 B4 250 D2
Lealand Rd N15 51 D3
Leamington Ave
Bromley BR1 187 C5
Farnborough BR6 227 C4
Merton SM4 201 B5
Walthamstow E17 53 C4
Leamington Cl
Bromley BR1 187 C5
Hounslow TW3 152 A6
Plashet E12 78 A3
Leamington Cres HA2 63 B5
Leamington Ct
4 Forest Hill SE26 162 A1
North Acton W3 89 B2
Leamington Gdns
IG3 79 D6
Leamington Ho
Edgware HA8 26 B5
4 Kensal Town W11 91 B2
Leamington Pk W3 89 B2
Leamington Pl UB4 83 D3
Leamington Rd UB2 106 D2
Leamington Rd Villas
W11 91 B2
Leamington Villas
SE13 164 C6
Leamore St W6 112 C2
Leamouth Rd
Newham E6 100 A2
South Bromley E14 98 B1
Leander Ct
11 Edgware NW9 27 C2
27 Hackney E9 74 C1
St Johns SE8 141 C4
5 Surbiton KT6 197 D2
Leander Rd
Northolt UB5 85 C5
Thornton Heath CR7 204 B5
Tulse Hill SW2 160 C5
Lea Park Trad Est
E10 53 B1
Lea Rd
2 Beckenham BR3 185 C1
Enfield EN2 5 B4
Southall UB2 107 A2
Learner Dr HA2 63 C6
Learoyd Gdns E6 122 C6
Leary Ho SE11 260 D1
Leas Cl KT9 214 B1
Leas Dale SE9 166 C1
Leas Gn BR7 189 D4
Leaside Ave N10 49 A5
Leaside Bsns Ctr EN3 7 B3
Leaside Ct UB10 82 D4
Leaside Ho 4 E5 52 B1
Leaside Mans N10 49 A6
Leaside Rd E5 52 C1
Leasowes Rd E10 53 C1
Lea Sq 22 E3 97 B6
Leas The SE18 144 D4

Leatherbottle Gn
DA18 125 B3
Leather Cl CR4 181 A1
Leatherdale St
32 Bethnal Green E1 96 C3
19 Globe Town E1 96 D4
Leather Gdns E15 98 C6
Leatherhead Cl N16 51 D1
Leatherhead Rd
KT9 213 D1
Leather La
EC1 94 C2 241 B4
Leather La Mkt★
EC1 94 C2 241 B4
Leathermarket Ct
SE1 253 A1
Leathermarket St
SE1 117 C4 253 A1
Leather Rd SE16 118 D2
Leathersellers Cl 5
EN5 1 A2
Leathsale Rd HA2 63 D5
Leathwaite Rd
SW11 158 D6
Leathwell Rd SE8 141 D3
Lea Valley Athletics Stad
N9 18 D3
Lea Valley Prim Sch
N17 34 A3
Lea Valley Rd EN3 19 B5
Lea Valley Technopark
N17 52 A6
Lea Valley Trad Est
N18 34 D5
Leaveland Cl BR3 207 C5
Leaver Gdns UB6 86 C5
Leavesden Rd HA7 25 A4
Lea View Ho E5 52 B1
Lebanon Ave TW13 172 D5
Lebanon Ct 10 TW1 153 B4
Lebanon Gdns
SW18 157 C5
Lebanon Park Mans
TW1 153 B4
Lebanon Pk TW1 153 B4
Lebanon Rd
Croydon CR0 205 C1
Wandsworth SW18 157 C6
Lebanon Road Sta
CR0 221 C6
Lebrun Sq SE3 143 B2
Lebus Ho NW8 230 A3
Le Chateau CR0 221 B5
Lechmere App IG8 37 D1
Lechmere Ave IG8 37 D1
Lechmere Rd NW2 68 B2
Leckford Rd SW18 158 A3
Leckhampton Pl 23
SW2 160 C4
Leckwith Ave DA7 147 A6
Lecky Ho NW2 68 B4
Lecky St
SW7 114 B1 256 C2
Leclair Ho SE3 143 B2
L'Ecole des Petits Sch
SW6 135 D3
Leconfield Ave SW13,
SW15 133 D2
Leconfield Ho SE5 139 C2
Leconfield Rd N5 73 B4
Lector Ct EC1 241 B5
Leda Ave EN3 6 D5
Leda Ct 9 SW9 138 C5
Ledalle Ho NW2 68 B5
Ledam Bldg EC1 241 A4
Leda Rd SE18 122 B3
Ledbury Ho 12 SE22 139 C2
Ledbury Mews N
W11 91 C1
Ledbury Mews W
W11 245 A6
Ledbury Pl 10 CR0 221 A4
Ledbury Rd
Croydon CR0 221 B4
Kensington W11 91 C1
Ledbury St SE15 140 A5
Ledo Ho 1 N16 73 B4
Ledrington Rd SE19 184 A4
Ledway Dr HA9 44 B2
LEE 164 D5
Lee Ave RM6 59 A3
Leechcroft Ave
DA15 167 D6
Leechcroft Rd SM6 219 A5
Lee Church St SE13 142 C1
Lee Cl Higham Hill E17 34 D2

Lee Cl *continued*
New Barnet EN5 2 A1
Lee Conservancy Rd
E9 75 B3
Leecroft Rd EN5 1 A1
Lee Ct SE13 142 B1
Leeds Ct
7 Carshalton SM5 218 D5
Catford SE6 163 D1
Clerkenwell EC1 241 C6
Leeds Rd IG1 57 B1
Leeds St N18 34 A5
Leegate SE12 164 D6
Leegate Sh Ctr SE12 164 D6
Lee Green SE12 142 D1
Lee High Rd SE12,
SE13 142 C1
Lee Ho
3 Kentish Town N19 71 D3
Wimbledon SW19 179 D4
Leeke St WC1 94 B4 233 C2
Leeland Mans 15
W13 109 A5
Leeland Rd W13 109 A5
Leeland Terr W13 109 A5
Leeland Way NW10 67 D4
Lee Manor Prim Sch
SE13 164 C5
Lee Mews BR3 207 A6
Lee Park Way N9, N18 19 A1
Lee Pk SE3 142 D2
Lee Rd Enfield EN1 18 A5
Lewisham SE3 142 D1
Merton SW19 179 D2
Mill Hill NW7 28 D3
Wembley UB6 87 C6
Leerdam Dr E14 120 A3
Lees Ct W1 248 A6
Lees Ho SE17 262 D1
Leeside EN5 13 A5
Leeside Cres NW11 47 C3
Leeside Ind Est N17 34 B3
Leeside Rd N17 34 B4
Leeside Trad Est N17 34 C3
Leeside Works N17 34 C3
Leeson Ho 7 TW1 153 B4
Leeson Rd 12 SE24 138 C1
Leesons Hill BR5,
BR7 211 D6
Leesons Way BR5 189 D1
Lees Par UB10 82 D3
Lees Pl W1 115 A6 248 A6
Lees Rd UB8 82 D3
Lee St E8 95 D6
Lee Sta SE12 165 A5
Lees The CR0 223 B6
Leet Ct N16 73 B4
Lee Terr SE3 142 C2
Lee Valley Athletics Ctr
N9 18 D3
Lee Valley Country Pk
EN3 7 C4
Lee Valley Ice Ctr
E10 74 D6
Lee Valley Leisure
Complex N9 19 A3
Lee Valley Riding Ctr
E10 52 D1
Leeve Ho 7 W9 91 B4
Lee View EN2 4 D4
Leeview Ct 5 E4 20 A3
Leeward Ct 3 E1 118 A5
Leeward Gdns SW19 179 B5
Leeway SE8 119 B1
Leeway Cl HA5 23 B3
Leewood Cl SE12 165 A5
Lefevre Wlk E3 97 C6
Leffern Rd W12 112 A4
Leff Ho 9 NW6 69 A1
Lefroy Ho SE1 252 A1
Lefroy Rd W12 111 D4
Legard Rd N5 72 D5
Legat Ct N4 51 A4
Legatt Rd SE9 165 D6
Leggatt Rd E15 98 A5
Legge St SE13 164 A6
Leghorn Rd
Plumstead SE18 123 B1
Willesden Green NW10 90 A5
Legion Cl N1 72 C1
Legion Ct SM4 201 C3
Legion Rd UB6 86 A5
Legion Terr E3 97 C6
Legion Way N12 30 C3
Legrace Ave TW4,
TW5 128 D3

Leicester Ave CR4 204 A5
Leicester Cl KT4 216 C4
Leicester Ct
[46] Paddington W2 91 C2
St James WC2 249 D6
[5] Twickenham TW1 153 D5
Leicester Gdns IG3 57 C2
Leicester Ho
[4] Brixton SW9 138 D2
Carshalton SM5 218 C5
[5] Putney SW15 156 C4
[2] Thames Ditton KT7 197 A2
Leicester Mews N2 48 C6
Leicester Pl WC2 249 D6
Leicester Rd
Barnet EN5 1 D1
Croydon CR0 205 C2
East Finchley N2 48 C6
Stonebridge NW10 67 B1
Wanstead E11 55 B4
Leicester Sq★ WC2 115 D6 249 D5
Leicester Square Sta WC2 115 D6 249 D6
Leicester St WC2 249 D6
Leigham Ave SW16 160 A1
Leigham Cl
[5] Streatham SW16 160 B1
Streatham SW16 182 B6
[9] Wallington SM6 219 C2
Leigham Court Rd SW16 182 C6
Leigham Dr TW7 130 C5
Leigham Hall [3] SW16 160 A1
Leigham Hall Par [2] SW16 160 A1
Leigham Vale SE27, SW16, SW2 160 C2
Leigh Ave IG4 55 D5
Leigh Cl KT3 199 B5
Leigh Cl Ind Est KT3 199 B5
Leigh Close Ind Est KT3 199 B5
Leigh Cres CR0 223 D1
Leigh Ct Harrow HA2 42 C1
[22] Tulse Hill SW2 160 C5
[3] Woodford E18 37 A1
Leighfield Ho [5] N4 51 A2
Leigh Gdns NW10 90 C5
Leigh Ho
[4] Kingston u T KT2 176 D4
[9] Putney SW15 156 A6
Leigh Hunt Dr N14 15 D3
Leigh Orchard Cl SW16 160 B1
Leigh Pl
Feltham TW13 150 C3
Holborn EC1 241 A4
Welling DA16 146 A3
Leigh Rd Highbury N5 72 D4
Isleworth TW3 130 B1
Leytonstone E10 54 A2
Wallend E6 78 C2
Leigh St WC1 94 A4 233 A1
Leigh The KT2 177 C3
Leighton Ave
Little Ilford E12 78 C3
Pinner HA5 41 A6
Leighton Cl HA8 26 C1
Leighton Cres NW5 71 C3
Leighton Ct NW7 28 D3
Leighton Gdns
Thornton Heath CR0 204 D1
Willesden Green NW10 90 C5
Leighton Gr NW5 71 C3
Leighton Ho [7] KT6 198 A3
Leighton House (Art Gall & Mus)★ W14 254 D6
Leighton Pl NW5 71 C3
Leighton Rd
Ealing W13 109 A4
Enfield EN1 18 A6
Harrow HA3 24 B1
Kentish Town NW5 71 C3
Leighton St CR0 204 D1
Leila Parnell Pl [14] SE7 143 C6
Leinster Ave SW14 133 A1
Leinster Gdns W2 114 A6 246 A6
Leinster Mews
[7] Barnet EN5 1 A2
Bayswater W2 246 A6
Leinster Pl W2 236 A1
Leinster Rd N10 49 B5
Leinster Sq W2 91 D1
Leinster Terr W2 246 A6
Leisure Way N12 30 B3
Leitch Ho [8] NW8 70 B1
Leith Cl NW9 45 B1
Leithcote Gdns SW16 182 B6
Leithcote Path SW16 160 B1
Leith Hill BR5 190 A2
Leith Hill Gn BR5 190 A2
Leith Ho
[7] Kentish Town N7 71 D3
[13] Streatham SW2 160 B4
Leith Mans W9 91 D4
Leith Rd N22 32 D2
Leith Towers [7] SM2 217 D1
Leith Yd [3] NW6 91 C6
Lela Ave TW4, TW5 128 C3
Lelitia Cl E8 96 A6
Lely Ho [3] UB5 84 D5
Leman St E1 96 A1
Lemark Cl HA7 25 C4
Le May Ave SE12 165 B1
Lemmon Rd SE10 142 C6
Lemna Ct E11 54 C2
Lemna Rd E11 54 C2
Le Moal Ho [28] E1 96 C2
Lemon Gr TW14 150 A3
Lemonwell Ct SE9 167 A6
Lemonwell Dr SE9 167 A6
Lemsford Cl N15 52 A4
Lemsford Ct N4 73 A6
Lena Cres N9 18 C2
Lena Gardens Prim Sch W6 112 C3
Lena Gdns W6 112 C3
Lena Kennedy Cl E4 36 A4
Lenan Ct W13 109 C5
Len Clifton Ho [12] SE18 122 B2
Lendal Terr [7] SW4 137 D2
Lenelby Rd KT6 198 C1
Len Freeman Pl SW6 264 C5
Lenham [11] NW5 71 A2
Lenham Ho SE1 252 D1
Lenham Rd Erith DA7 147 B6
Lewisham SE12 142 D1
South Norwood CR7 183 B1
Sutton SM1 218 A3
Lennard Ave BR4 224 C6
Lennard Cl BR4 224 C6
Lennard Rd
Bromley BR2 210 B1
Croydon CR0 205 A1
Penge BR3 185 A4
Lennon Rd NW2 68 C2
Lennox Gdns
Croydon CR0 220 D4
Knightsbridge SW1 114 D3 257 C5
Redbridge IG1 56 B1
Willesden NW10 67 D4
Lennox Gdns Mews SW1 257 C4
Lennox Ho
[7] Belvedere DA17 125 C3
[10] Hackney E9 74 C2
[4] Twickenham TW1 153 D5
Lennox Rd
Finsbury Pk N4, N7 72 C6
Walthamstow E17 53 C3
Lenor Cl DA6 147 A1
Lensbury Way SE2 124 D3
Lens Rd E7 77 C1
Lenthall Ho SW1 259 B1
Lenthall Rd E8 74 A1
Lenthorp Rd SE10 120 D2
Lentmead Rd BR1 164 D1
Lenton Rise TW9 132 A2
Lenton St SE18 123 B2
Len Williams Ct NW6 91 C5
Leo Ct [4] TW8 131 D5
Leof Cres SE6 185 D5
Leominster Rd SM4 202 A3
Leominster Wlk SM4 202 A3
Leonard Ave SM4 202 A4
Leonard Ct
Bloomsbury WC1 240 A6
Leonard Ct *continued*
Harrow HA3 24 C3
Kensington W8 255 A6
Leonard Day Ho [3] NW5 71 B2
Leonard Ho [10] E17 54 A5
Leonard Pl [6] N16 73 C4
Leonard Rd
Chingford E4 35 C4
Edmonton N9 18 A1
Forest Gate E7 77 A4
Mitcham CR4, SW16 181 C2
Southall UB2 106 D2
Leonard Robbins Path [3] SE28 124 B6
Leonard St
Broadgate EC2 95 B3 242 D6
Newham E16 122 A5
Leonora Ho W9 236 A6
Leontine Cl SE15 140 A5
Leopards Ct EC1 241 A4
Leopold Ave SW19 179 B5
Leopold Bldgs [14] E2 95 D4
Leopold Ct [12] SW19 179 B5
Leopold Mews E9 96 C6
Leopold Prim Sch NW10 67 D1
Leopold Rd
Ealing W5 110 B5
East Finchley N2 48 B6
Edmonton N18 34 B5
Walthamstow E17 53 C4
Willesden NW10 67 C1
Wimbledon SW19 179 B5
Leopold St E3 97 B2
Leopold Terr SW19 179 C5
Leopold Wlk SE11 260 C1
Leo St SE15 140 B5
Leo Yd EC1 241 D5
Leppoc Rd SW4 159 D6
Leroy St SE1 117 C2 263 A4
Lerry Cl W14 264 D6
Lerwick Ct [4] EN1 17 C6
Lerwick Ho SW18 136 A1
Lescombe Cl SE23 163 A1
Lescombe Rd SE23, SE6 163 A1
Lesley Cl DA5 169 D4
Lesley Ct
[8] Wallington SM6 219 B4
Westminster SW1 259 C5
Leslie Gdns SM2 217 C1
Leslie Gr CR0 205 C1
Leslie Grove Pl CR0 205 C1
Leslie Park Rd CR0 205 C1
Leslie Prince Ct [8] SE5 139 B5
Leslie Rd
East Finchley N2 48 B6
Leyton E11 76 B4
Newham E16 99 B1
Leslie Smith Sq [7] SE18 144 C6
Lessar Ave SW4 159 C5
Lessar Ct SW4 159 C5
Lessingham Ave
Ilford IG5 56 C6
Upper Tooting SW17 181 A6
Lessing St SE23 163 A4
Lessness Ave DA7 146 D5
LESSNESS HEATH 125 D1
Lessness Heath Prim Sch DA17 125 C1
Lessness Pk DA17 125 C1
Lessness Rd
Belvedere DA17 125 C1
Morden SM4 202 A4
Lester Ave E16 98 C3
Lester Ct [42] E3 97 D4
Lester Ho IG8 36 B3
Lestock Cl [2] SE25 206 A6
Lestock Ho SE3 143 D4
Lestor Ct TW7 130 D2
Leswin Pl N16 73 D5
Leswin Rd N16 73 D5
Letchford Gdns NW10 90 A4
Letchford Mews NW10 90 A4
Letchmore Ho [7] W10 90 C3
Letchworth Ave TW14 149 D4
Letchworth Cl
Bromley BR2 209 A4
Letchworth Cl *continued*
South Oxhey WD19 22 D5
Letchworth Dr BR2 209 A4
Letchworth St SW17 180 D6
Lethaby Ho [15] SW4 138 B1
Lethbridge Cl SE13 142 A3
Letterstone Rd SW6 264 C3
Lettice St SW6 135 B4 264 D1
Lett Rd E15 76 B1
Lettsom St SE5 139 C3
Lettsom Wlk [1] E13 99 A5
Leucha Rd E17 53 A4
Levana Cl SW19 157 A3
Levant Ho [17] E1 96 D3
Levehurst Ho SE27 183 A5
Levehurst Way SW4, SW9 138 A3
Leven Cl WD19 22 D5
Levendale Rd SE23 163 B2
Leven Rd E14 98 B1
Leven Way UB3 83 C1
Lever Ct [15] E9 74 D2
Leverett St SW3 257 B4
Leverholme Gdns SE9 188 C6
Leverington Pl N1 235 D1
Leverson St SW16 181 C4
Lever St EC1 95 A4 235 A1
Leverstock Ho SW3 257 B2
Leverton Pl NW5 71 C3
Leverton St NW5 71 C3
Levett Gdns IG3 80 A5
Levett Ho [8] SW16 181 C5
Levett Rd IG11 79 C2
Levine Gdns IG11 102 D5
Levison Way [2] N19 49 D1
Levita Ho NW1 232 D2
Levyne Ct EC1 241 A6
Lewes Cl UB5 63 C2
Lewes Ct [3] CR4 202 D6
Lewesdon Cl [13] SW19 156 D3
Lewes Ho
Bermondsey SE1 253 B2
Peckham SE15 140 A6
Lewes Rd
Bromley BR1 187 D1
Colney Hatch N12 30 C5
Leweston Pl N16 51 D2
Lewey Ho E3 97 B3
Lewgars Ave NW9 45 A3
Lewin Ct
[4] Plumstead SE18 123 C2
Streatham SW16 182 A4
Lewing Cl BR6 211 C1
Lewington Ct EN3 6 D6
Lewin Rd Bexley DA6 147 A1
Mortlake SW14 133 B2
Streatham SW16 181 D4
Lewin Terr TW14 149 B4
Lewis Ave E17 35 C2
Lewis Cl N14 15 C4
Lewis Cres NW10 67 B3
Lewis Ct [5] SE16 118 B1
Lewis Gdns London N2 30 B1
South Tottenham N15, N16 51 D3
Lewis Gr SE13 142 A2
LEWISHAM 142 A1
Lewisham Bridge Prim Sch [3] SE13 141 D2
Lewisham Bsns Ctr SE14 140 D6
Lewisham Coll (Deptford Campus) [12] SE8 141 C4
Lewisham Coll (Lewisham Way Campus) SE4 141 C3
Lewisham Ct EN3 7 C5
Lewisham Ctr SE13 142 A2
Lewisham High St SE13 163 D6
Lewisham Hill SE13 142 A3
Lewisham Hospl SE13 163 D6
Lewisham Pk SE13 164 A5
Lewisham Rd SE13 142 A3
Lewisham St SW1 249 D1
Lewisham Sta SE13 142 A2
Lewisham Way SE4, SE14 141 B4
Lewis Ho [2] E4 35 C5
Lewis King Ho BR1 187 B3
Lewis Pl E8 74 A3
Lewis Rd
Bexley DA16 146 C2
Mitcham CR4 180 C1
[19] Richmond TW10 153 D6
Sidcup DA14 168 C1
Southall UB1 107 A4
Sutton SM1 217 D4
Lewis Silkin Ho [9] SE15 140 C6
Lewis Sports & L Ctr SE19 183 D2
Lewis St NW1 71 B2
Lewiston Cl KT4 200 B2
Lewis Way RM10 81 D2
Lexden Dr RM6 58 B3
Lexden Rd Acton W3 110 D5
Mitcham CR4 203 D5
Lexdon Ct RM6 58 B3
Lexfield Ho N5 73 A4
Lexham Ct UB6 86 B6
Lexham Gardens Mews W8 255 D5
Lexham Gdns W8 113 D2 255 C4
Lexham Ho [9] IG11 101 B6
Lexham Mews W8 113 C2 255 B4
Lexham Wlk W8 255 D5
Lexington Pl KT1 175 D2
Lexington St W1 115 C6 249 B6
Lexton Gdns SW12 159 D3
Leyborne Ave W13 109 C4
Leyborne Pk TW9 132 C4
Leybourne Cl BR2 209 A3
Leybourne Ct [1] SE25 206 A6
Leybourne Ho [20] SE15 140 C6
Leybourne Rd
[17] Camden Town NW1 71 B1
Hillingdon UB10 83 A6
Leytonstone E11 54 D1
Queensbury NW9 44 C4
Leybourne St [5] NW1 71 B1
Leybridge Ct SE12 165 A6
Leyburn Cl E17 53 D5
Leyburn Gdns CR0 221 C6
Leyburn Gr N18 34 A4
Leyburn Rd N18 34 B4
Leyden Mans [7] N19 50 A2
Leyden St E1 95 D2 243 C3
Leydon Cl
Rotherhithe SE16 118 D5
SE16 118 D5
Leyes Rd E16 99 D1
Leyfield KT4 199 D1
Ley Ho SE1 252 A1
Leyland Ave EN3 7 A3
Leyland Ct [8] N11 31 B6
Leyland Gdns IG8 37 C5
Leyland Ho
[6] Canary Wharf E14 119 D6
[12] Richmond TW10 153 C1
Leyland Rd SE12 165 A6
Leylands SW18 157 B5
Leylang Rd SE14 140 D5
Leys Cl Finchley N12 30 C3
Harrow HA1 42 B4
Leys Ct [9] SW9 138 C3
Leysdown [9] NW5 71 A2
Leysdown Ho SE17 263 B2
Leysdown Rd SE9 166 B2
Leysfield Rd W12 112 A4
Leys Gdns EN4 15 A6
Leyspring Rd E11 54 D1
Leys Rd E EN3 7 A4
Leys Rd W EN3 7 A4
Ley St Ilford IG1 78 D6
Newbury Pk IG1, IG2 57 B1
Leys The
East Finchley N2 48 A5
Harrow HA3 44 B3
Leyswood Dr IG2 57 C4
Leythe Rd W3 111 A4
LEYTON 76 B5
Leyton Bsns Ctr E10 75 C6
Leyton Ct SE23 162 C3
Leyton Grange E10 53 C1
Leyton Green Rd E10 54 A3

Leyton Green Twrs E10 54 A3
Leyton Ind Village E10 52 D2
Leyton Leisure Lagoon E10 54 A2
Leyton Link Est E10 53 A2
Leyton Midland Road Sta E10 54 A1
Leyton Mill Ret Pk E10 76 A4
Leyton Mills E10 76 A4
Leyton Park Rd E10 76 A5
Leyton Rd
 Merton SW19 180 A3
 Stratford E15 76 B2
Leyton Sixth Form Coll E10 54 B3
Leyton Sta E11 76 A5
LEYTONSTONE 54 D1
Leytonstone High Road Sta E11 76 C6
Leytonstone Rd E15 76 C3
Leytonstone Sch E11 54 C3
Leytonstone Sta E11 54 C1
Leyton Town Ctr E10 76 A5
Leywick St E15 98 C5
Lezayre Rd BR6 227 D2
Liardet St SE14 141 A6
Liberia Rd N5 72 D2
Libert Cl N18 33 D6
Liberty Ave SW19 180 B2
Liberty Cl KT4 200 C1
Liberty Ct IG11 102 C5
Liberty Ctr HA0 88 B6
Liberty Ho 11 E1 118 A6
Liberty Mews
 Balham SW12 159 B5
 Orpington BR6 227 D6
 Wood Green N22 32 D2
Liberty Sch CR4 180 C1
Liberty St SW9 138 B4 270 D2
Libra Rd 7 Bow E3 97 B5
 Newham E13 99 A5
Library Ct N17 51 D6
Library Mans 4 W12 112 C4
Library Par NW10 89 C6
Library Pl E1 118 B6
Library St SE1 116 D4 251 D1
Library Way 1 TW2 152 A4
Libro Ct E4 35 C6
Lichen Ct IG6 56 D6
Lichfield Cl EN4 2 D2
Lichfield Ct
 Kingston u T KT6 198 A4
 Richmond TW9 132 A1
Lichfield Gdns TW10, TW9 154 A6
Lichfield Gr N3 29 C1
Lichfield Ho 27 SE5 139 A3
Lichfield Rd
 Dagenham RM8 80 C5
 Edmonton N9 18 A2
 Hounslow TW4 128 C2
 Mile End E3 97 A4
 Newham E6 99 D4
 Northwood HA6 40 A6
 Richmond TW9 132 B4
 West Hampstead NW2 69 A4
 Woodford IG8 36 C6
Lichfield Terr 1 TW9 154 A6
Lichlade Cl 7 BR6 227 D4
Lickey Ho W14 264 D6
Lidbury Rd NW7 29 A4
Lidcote Gdns 22 SW9 138 B3
Liddall Way UB7 104 B5
Liddell Cl HA3 43 D6
Liddell Gdns NW10 90 C5
Liddell Rd NW6 69 C2
Lidding Rd HA3 43 D4
Liddington Rd E15 98 D6
Liddlesdale Ho E 6 KT2 176 D2
Liddlesdale Ho W 5 KT2 176 D2
Liddon Rd
 Bromley BR1 209 D6
 Newham E13 99 B4
Liden Cl E10, E17 53 B1
Lidfield Rd N16 73 B4
Lidgate Rd 22 SE15 139 D5
Lidiard Rd SW18 158 A2
Lidlington Pl NW1 232 B3
Lido Sq N17 33 B1
Lido The★ W2 114 A4 247 A3
Lidyard Rd N19 49 C1
Liffey Ct Edmonton N9 18 C1
 Willesden NW10 68 A1
Liffler Rd SE18 123 C1
Liffords Pl SW13 133 D3
Lifford St SW15 134 D1
Lightcliffe Rd N13 16 C1
Lighted Lady★ IG11 78 D1
Lighter Cl 16 SE16 119 A2
Lighterman Mews 15 E1 96 D1
Lighterman's Rd E14 119 D4
Lighterman's Wlk SW18 135 C1
Lightfoot Rd N8 50 A4
Light Horse Ct SW1 258 A1
Lightley Cl
 Wembley HA0 66 B1
 Wembley HA0 88 B6
Ligonier St E2 243 C6
Lilac Cl E4 35 B4
Lilac Ct
 Colney Hatch N12 30 C4
 3 Newham E13 99 C6
 Teddington TW11 174 D6
Lilac Gdns
 Croydon CR0 223 C5
 Ealing W5 109 D3
 Hayes UB3 83 C1
Lilac Ho SE4 141 B2
Lilac Pl
 Vauxhall SE11 116 B2 260 C3
 Yiewsley UB7 104 B6
Lilac St W12 112 A6
Lilah Mews BR2 186 D1
Lilburne Gdns SE9 166 A6
Lilburne Rd SE9 166 A6
Lilburne Wlk NW10 67 A2
Lile Cres W7 86 C2
Lilestone Est NW8 236 D5
Lilestone Ho NW8 236 D6
Lilestone St NW8 92 C3 237 A6
Lilford Ho 21 SE5 139 A3
Lilford Rd SE5 138 D3
Lilian Barker Cl SE12 165 A6
Lilian Baylis Ho N1 73 A2
Lilian Baylis Tech Sch SE11 116 B1 260 D1
Lilian Board Way UB6 64 B3
Lilian Gdns IG8 37 B2
Lilian Rd SW16 181 C2
Lilian Rolfe Ho 5 SE27 183 B6
Lillechurch Rd RM8 80 C2
Lilleshall Rd SM4 202 B3
Lilley Cl E1 118 A5
Lillian Ave W3 110 C4
Lillian Cl 14 N16 73 C5
Lillian Rd SW13 134 B6
Lillie Ho N5 72 C3
Lillie Rd SW6 135 B6 264 C5
Lillie Road Mans SW6 264 B5
Lillieshall Rd SW4 137 C2
Lillie Yd SW6 135 C6 265 A6
Lillingston Ho N7 72 C4
Lilliput Ave UB5 85 B6
Lillywhite 21 NW9 27 D2
Lily Albon Ct RM9 81 B4
Lily Cl W14 112 D2
Lily Gdns HA0 87 C5
Lily Ho 7 HA9 66 A3
Lily Pl EC1 241 B4
Lily Rd E17 53 C3
Lilyville Rd SW6 135 B4 264 C2
Limavady Ho 12 SE18 122 C2
Limborough Ho 5 E14 97 C2
Limbourne Ave RM8 59 B2
Limburg Rd SW11 136 C1
Lime Ave UB7 104 B6
Limeburner La EC4 94 D1 241 C2
Lime Cl Bromley BR1 210 A5
 Buckhurst Hill IG9 21 D2
 Carshalton SM5 218 D6
 Harrow HA3 25 A1
 Pinner HA5 39 D6
 Wapping E1 118 A5
Lime Cres TW16 172 C1
Limecroft Cl KT19 215 B1
Lime Ct
 9 Harrow HA1 42 D3
 Hendon NW4 28 C1
 Kingston u T KT3 198 D6
 9 Leyton E11 76 C6
 Mitcham CR4 180 B1
 Putney SW15 134 B2
Limedene Cl HA5 22 D2
Lime Gr Barnet N20 13 B3
 Blackfen DA15 167 D5
 Hayes UB3 105 B6
 Kingston u T KT3 199 C6
 Orpington BR6 226 D6
 Ruislip HA4 40 B2
 Shepherd's Bush W12 112 C4
 Twickenham TW1 153 A5
 Walthamstow E4 35 B4
Limeharbour E14 119 D4
Lime Ho 7 TW9 132 D4
LIMEHOUSE 119 A6
Limehouse Cswy E14 119 B6
Limehouse Ct 5 E14 97 C1
Lime House Ct 23 E14 97 B1
Limehouse Cut 4 E14 97 D2
Limehouse Fields Est 14 E14 97 A2
Limehouse Link (Tunnel) E14 119 B6
Limehouse Sta E14 97 A1
Lime Kiln Dr SE7 143 B6
Limekiln Pl SE19 183 D3
Limekiln Wharf 21 E14 119 B6
Limeleaf Ct HA8 27 A6
Lime Lo 3 TW16 171 D3
Limerick Cl SW12 159 C4
Limerick Ct 1 SW12 159 C4
Lime Row DA18 125 B3
Limerston St SW10 136 A6 266 B5
Lime St Pas EC3 253 A6
Limes Ave
 Barnes SW13 133 D3
 Carshalton SM5 202 D1
 Croydon CR0 220 C5
 Edgware NW7 27 C4
 Golders Green NW11 47 A2
 North Finchley N12 30 A6
 Penge SE20 184 B3
 Wanstead E11 55 B5
Limes Ave The N11 31 C5
Limes Cl
 Ashford TW15 170 C5
 3 Friern Barnet N11 31 C5
Limes Ct
 Beckenham BR3 185 D1
 Willesden NW6 68 D1
Limesdale Gdns HA8 27 A1
Limes Field Rd SW14 133 C2
Limesford Rd SE15 140 D1
Limes Gdns SW18 157 C5
Limes Gr SE13 142 A1
Limes Rd
 Beckenham BR3 185 D1
 Thornton Heath CR0 205 B2
Limes Row BR6 226 D3
Lime St
 Walthamstow E17 53 A5
 Whitechapel EC3 95 C1 243 A1
Limes The
 Camberwell SE5 139 C2
 3 Cheam SM2 217 C2
 East Molesey KT8 195 D5
 Kensington W2 245 B5
 Keston Mark BR2 226 A6
 Stanmore HA7 9 B2
Limestone Wlk 12 DA18 124 D4
Limes Wlk Ealing W5 109 D4
 Nunhead SE15 140 C1
Lime Terr W7 108 C6
Lime Tree Ave KT10, KT7 196 C1
Limetree Cl SW2 160 B3
Lime Tree Cl E11 55 C5
Limetree Ct HA5 23 C3
Lime Tree Ct
 East Barnet EN4 14 C6
 East Finchley N2 47 D6
 14 Poplar E3 97 C2
 South Croydon CR2 221 A2
Lime Tree Gr CR0 223 B5
Limetree Pl CR4 181 B2
Lime Tree Rd TW5 129 D4
Limetree Wlk 2 SW17 181 A5
Lime Tree Wlk
 Bushey WD23 8 C2
 Coney Hall BR4 224 D4
 Enfield EN2 5 A5
Lime Wlk 11 E15 98 C6
Limewood Cl
 Beckenham BR3 208 A4
 Ealing W13 87 B1
 Walthamstow E17 53 B5
Limewood Ct IG4 56 B4
Limpsfield Ave
 Putney SW19 156 D2
 Thornton Heath CR7 204 B4
Limscott Ho 35 E3 97 D4
Linacre Cl SE15 140 B2
Linacre Ct W6 112 D1
Linacre Rd NW2 68 B2
Linale Ho N1 235 C3
Linberry Wlk 3 SE8 119 B2
Linchmere Rd SE12 164 D4
Lincoln Ave
 Osidge N14 15 C2
 Twickenham TW2 152 A2
 Wimbledon SW19 156 D1
Lincoln Cl
 Croydon SE25 206 B3
 Greenford UB6 86 A6
 Harrow HA2 41 B4
Lincoln Cres EN1 17 D6
Lincoln Ct
 Borehamwood WD6 11 B6
 Enfield EN2 5 B1
 Grove Pk SE12 165 C1
 Hampton TW12 173 B5
 Hendon NW4 46 B5
 Mitcham CR4 204 A4
 Redbridge IG1 56 B2
 5 South Croydon CR2 221 A3
 Stoke Newington N16 51 B2
Lincoln Gdns IG1 56 A2
Lincoln Green Rd BR5 211 D4
Lincoln Ho
 Bloomsbury WC1 240 D3
 9 Dartmouth Pk NW5 71 C5
 2 Islington N1 73 A1
 Knightsbridge SW1 247 C1
Lincoln Lo 10 BR3 185 D1
Lincoln Mews NW6 91 B6
Lincoln Rd
 Croydon SE25 206 B6
 East Finchley N2 48 C6
 Enfield EN1, EN3 17 D6
 Harrow HA2, HA5 41 B4
 Kingston u T KT3 199 A6
 Mitcham CR4 204 A4
 Newham E13 99 B3
 North Cheam KT4 200 B1
 Northwood HA6 39 D6
 Plashet E7 77 D2
 Sidcup DA14 190 B5
 Twickenham TW13 151 B1
 Wembley HA0 65 D2
 Woodford E18 37 A2
Lincoln's Inn★ WC2 94 B1 240 D2
Lincoln's Inn Fields WC2 94 B1 240 D2
Lincoln St
 Chelsea SW3 257 C3
 Leyton E11 76 C6
Lincolns The NW7 11 D1
Lincoln Terr 4 SM2 217 C1
Lincoln Way
 Charlton TW16 171 C2
 Enfield EN1 18 B6
Lincombe Rd BR1 164 D1
Linda Ct KT9 213 D4
Lindal Cres EN2 4 B1
Lindal Ct 1 E18 37 A2
Lindale SW19 157 A2
Lindales The N17 33 D4
Lindal Rd SE4 163 B6
Lindbergh Rd SM6 220 A1
Linden Ave Enfield EN1 6 A4
 Hounslow TW3 151 D6
 Kensal Rise NW10 90 D5
 Ruislip HA4 40 A1
 Thornton Heath CR7 204 D5
 Wembley HA9 66 B3
Linden Bridge Sch KT4 215 C5
Linden Cl Ruislip HA4 40 A1
 Southgate N14 15 C5
 Stanmore HA7 25 B5
 Thames Ditton KT7 197 A2
Linden Cotts 6 SW19 179 A4
Linden Cres
 Kingston u T KT1 176 B1
 Wembley UB6 64 D2
 Woodford IG8 37 B4
Linden Ct
 8 Battersea SW18 136 B1
 1 Beckenham BR3 207 D6
 2 Bromley BR1 186 D3
 Edgware NW7 27 B5
 Penge SE20 184 B3
 1 Shepherd's Bush W12 112 C5
 Sidcup DA14 189 C6
 11 Sutton SM2 218 A2
Lindenfield BR7 188 D1
Linden Gate SW20 200 C6
Linden Gdns
 Chiswick W4 111 B1
 Enfield EN1 6 A4
 Notting Hill W2 113 C6 245 B5
Linden Gr
 Kingston u T KT3 199 C6
 Nunhead SE15 140 C2
 Penge SE20 184 C4
 Teddington TW11 174 D5
Linden Ho
 Bromley BR1 187 B3
 10 Deptford SE8 141 B6
 Hampton TW12 173 D4
 Walthamstow E17 35 B1
Linden Lawns HA9 66 B4
Linden Lea N2 48 A4
Lindenlea Ct E17 53 B5
Linden Leas BR4 224 B6
Linden Lo N21 16 B4
Linden Lodge Sch SW19 157 A3
Linden Mans N6 49 B1
Linden Mews
 Kensington W2 245 B5
 Stoke Newington N1 73 B3
Linden Pl CR4 202 C5
Linden Rd
 Brunswick Pk N11 15 A2
 Cranley Gdns N10 49 B5
 Hampton TW12 173 C2
 Tottenham N15 51 A5
Lindens The
 Chiswick W4 133 A4
 New Addington CR0 224 A2
 North Finchley N12 30 B5
 5 Walthamstow E17 53 D5
Linden Way
 Shepperton TW17 193 A4
 Southgate N14 15 C5
Lindeth Cl HA7 25 B4
Lindfield Gdns NW3 70 A3
Lindfield Hts NW3 70 A3
Lindfield Rd
 Croydon CR0 205 D3
 Ealing W5 87 C3
Lindfield St E14 97 C1
Lindhill Cl EN3 6 D3
Lindholme Ct 3 NW9 27 C2
Lindisfarne Rd
 Dagenham RM8 80 C5
 Wimbledon SW20 178 A3
Lindisfarne Way E9 75 A4
Lindley Ct KT1 175 C2
Lindley Ho
 13 Peckham SE15 140 A5
 9 Stepney E1 96 C2
Lindley Pl TW9 132 C4
Lindley Rd E10 76 A6
Lindley St E1 96 C2

Lindon Bennett Sch The TW13 172 D5
Lindop Ho 8 E1 97 A3
Lindore Rd SW11 136 D1
Lindores Rd SM5 202 A1
Lindo St SE15 140 C3
Lind Rd SM1 218 A3
Lindrop St SW6 136 A3
Lindsay Cl KT9 214 A1
Lindsay Ct
Battersea SW11 266 D1
Sutton SM1 217 C3
Lindsay Dr
Harrow HA3 44 B4
Shepperton TW17 193 B3
Lindsay Ho 2 SE18 122 C2
Lindsay Rd
Hampton TW12 173 D6
North Cheam KT4 216 B6
Lindsay Sq
SW1 115 D1 259 D2
Lindsell St 6 SE10 142 A4
Lindsey Cl
Bickley BR1 210 A6
Mitcham CR4, SW16 204 A5
Lindsey Ct N13 16 C1
Lindsey Gdns TW14 149 B4
Lindsey Ho W5 109 D2
Lindsey Ho* SW10 266 D4
Lindsey Mews 18 N1 73 A1
Lindsey Rd RM8 80 C5
Lindsey St
EC1 94 D2 241 D4
Lind St SE8 141 D3
Lindum Rd TW11 175 C3
Lindums The BR3 185 B4
Lindway SE27 182 D5
Lindwood Cl 8 E6 100 B2
Linear View HA9 66 D6
Linfield WC1 233 C1
Linfield Cl NW4 46 C5
Linford Christie Stadium The W12 90 B2
Linford Ct 1 CR4 180 C2
Linford Ho 17 E2 96 A6
Linford Rd E17 54 A6
Linford St
SW8 137 C4 269 A1
Linford Street Bsns Est
SW8 269 A2
Lingard Ho 11 E14 120 A3
Lingards Rd SE13 142 A1
Lingey Cl DA15 167 D2
Lingfield Ave KT1, KT5 198 A5
Lingfield Cl EN1 17 C5
Lingfield Cres SE9 145 B1
Lingfield Ct
Northolt UB5 85 C5
Wimbledon SW19 178 D4
Lingfield Gdns N9 18 B4
Lingfield Ho
5 Acton Green W4 111 A1
Lambeth SE1 251 D1
Penge SE26 184 B4
Lingfield Rd
North Cheam KT4 216 C5
Wimbledon SW19 178 D4
Lingham St SW9 138 B3
Lingholm Way EN5 12 D6
Ling Rd E16 99 A2
Lingrove Gdns IG9 21 B2
Ling's Coppice SE21 161 B2
Lingwell Rd SW17 158 C1
Lingwood DA7 147 D3
Lingwood Gdns TW7 130 C5
Lingwood Rd E5 52 A2
Linhope St
NW1 92 D3 237 C5
Link Day Prim Sch The CR0 220 A4
Linkenholt Mans 3 W6 111 D2
Linkfield KT8 195 D6
Link Field BR2 209 A3
Linkfield Rd TW7 130 D3
Link La SM6 220 A2
Linklea Cl NW9 27 C3
Link Rd
Dagenham RM9 103 D5
East Bedfont TW14 149 D4
Friern Barnet N11 31 A6
Hackbridge SM6 203 A1
Links Ave SM4 201 C5
Linkscroft Ave TW15 170 D4
Links Ct N20 14 B1
Links Dr N20 13 D3
Link Sec Sch The CR0 220 B4
Links Gdns SW16 182 C3
Linkside Finchley N12 29 C4
Kingston u T KT3 177 C1
Linkside Cl EN2 4 C2
Linkside Gdns EN2 4 B2
Links Ind Est TW13 151 A1
Links Prim Sch SW17 181 A4
Links Rd Acton W3 88 C1
Ashford TW15 170 A5
Mitcham SW16, SW17 181 A4
West Wickham BR4 208 A1
Willesden NW2 67 D6
Woodford IG8 37 A5
Links Side EN2 4 C2
Link St E9 74 C3
Links The E17 53 A5
Linksview N2 48 D4
Links View Finchley N3 29 B3
Shooters Hill SE18 144 D4
Links View Cl HA7 25 A4
Links View Rd
Croydon CR0 223 C5
Hampton TW12 174 A6
Linksway NW4 28 D1
Links Way
Beckenham BR3 207 C3
Streatham SW17 181 A4
Links Yd
10 Spitalfields E1 96 A2
Spitalfields E1 243 D4
Link The Acton W3 88 D1
Chislehurst SE9 166 C1
Enfield EN3 7 A4
Hendon NW2 46 A1
Northolt UB5 63 B3
Pinner HA5 40 C2
Teddington TW11 174 D4
Wembley HA0 43 C1
Linkway
Dagenham RM8 80 C4
Pinner HA5 22 D2
Stoke Newington N4 51 A2
West Barnes SW20 200 B5
Link Way
Bromley BR2 210 A2
Richmond TW10 153 B2
Linkway The EN5 13 D5
Linkwood Wlk NW1 71 D1
Linley Cres RM7 59 D6
Linley Ct
1 Dulwich SE21 183 C6
Sutton SM1 218 A4
Linley House Sch KT5 198 B3
Linley Rd N17 33 C1
Linnell Cl NW11 47 D3
Linnell Dr NW11 47 D3
Linnell Ho
Spitalfields E1 243 C4
St John's Wood NW8 229 A6
Linnell Rd
Camberwell SE5 139 C3
Edmonton N18 34 A5
Linnet Cl Bushey WD23 8 A3
Lower Edmonton N9 18 D3
Woolwich SE28 124 C6
Linnet Ct CR4 180 C2
Linnet Mews SW12 159 A4
Linnett Cl E4 36 A6
Linom Rd SW4 138 A1
Linscott Rd E5 74 C4
Linsdell Rd IG11 101 A6
Linsey St
Bermondsey SE16 118 A2
Bermondsey SE16 118 A3
Linslade Cl
Hounslow TW4 151 A6
Pinner HA5 40 B6
Linslade Ho
10 Hackney E2 96 A6
Marylebone NW8 237 B6
Linstead St 1 NW6 69 C1
Linstead Way SW18, SW19 157 A4
Linsted Ct SE9 167 C5
Linster Gr WD6 11 A6
Lintaine Cl W6 264 B5
Linthorpe Ave HA0 65 C2
Linthorpe Rd
Cockfosters EN4 2 C2
Stamford Hill N16 51 C2
Linton Cl
Carshalton CR4 202 D2
2 Greenwich SE7 121 C1
Welling DA16 146 B4
Linton Gdns E6 100 A1
Linton Gr SE27 183 A5
Linton Ho
Lower Holloway N7 72 B4
2 Tower Hamlets E3 97 C2
Linton Mead Prim Sch SE28 124 B6
Linton Rd IG11 79 A1
Linton St N1 95 A6 235 B5
Lintons The
Barking IG11 79 A1
Finchley N3 29 B2
Linver Rd SW6 135 C3
Linwood Cl SE5 139 D3
Linwood Cres EN1 6 A4
Linzee Rd N8 50 A5
Lion Ave TW1 152 D3
Lion Cl Ladywell SE4 163 C5
Littleton TW17 192 A6
Lion Ct 12 NW9 46 A5
Lion Ctr The TW13 151 A1
Lionel Gdns SE9 165 D6
Lionel Ho
Bowes Pk N22 32 B4
5 Kensal Town W10 91 A2
Lionel Mans 14 W14 112 D3
Lionel Mews 13 W10 91 A2
Lionel Rd SE9 165 D6
Lionel Road N TW8 110 A2
Lionel Road Prim Sch TW8 110 A2
Lionel Road S TW8 110 B1
Lion Gate Gdns TW9 132 B2
Lion Gate Mews SW18 157 C4
Lion House Sch SW15 134 D1
Lion Mills 36 E2 96 A5
Lion Park Ave KT9 214 C4
Lion Rd
Bexleyheath DA6 147 B1
Edmonton N9 18 A2
Newham E6 100 B2
Thornton Heath CR0 205 A4
Twickenham TW1, TW2 152 D3
Lions Cl SE12 165 D1
Lion Way TW8 131 D5
Lion Wharf Rd TW7 131 B2
Lion Yd SW4 137 D1
Liphook Cres SE23 162 C4
Liphook Rd WD19 22 D6
Lipton Cl SE28 124 C6
Lipton Ct N14 15 C4
Lipton Rd 9 E1 96 D1
Lisa Lo 5 EN5 13 D6
Lisbon Ave TW2 152 A2
Lisbon Cl E17 35 B1
Lisburne Rd NW3 70 D4
Lisford St SE15 139 D4
Lisgar Terr W14 113 B2 254 C4
Liskeard Cl BR7 189 A4
Liskeard Gdns SE3 143 A4
Liskeard Ho SE11 261 B2
Lisle Cl SW17 181 B6
Lisle Ct NW2 69 A5
Lisle St WC2 115 D6 249 D6
Lismirrane Ind Pk WD6 9 B5
Lismore 9 SW19 179 B5
Lismore Cir NW5 71 A3
Lismore Cl TW7 131 A3
Lismore Rd
South Croydon CR2 221 C2
Tottenham N17 51 B6
Lismore Wlk 4 N1 73 A2
Lissant Cl KT6 197 D2
Lisselton Ho 3 NW4 46 D5
Lissenden Gdns NW5 71 A4
Lissenden Mans NW5 71 A4
Lisson Cotts NW1 237 B4
Lisson Gr NW1, NW8 92 C3 237 A6
LISSON GROVE 92 B3
Lisson Ho NW1 237 A4
Lisson St NW1 92 C2 237 A4
Lister Cl
Dagenham W3 89 B2
Lister Cl *continued*
Mitcham SW19 180 C2
Lister Com Sch 1 E13 99 B5
Lister Cotts WD6 9 A6
Lister Ct Hendon NW9 27 C1
Stoke Newington N16 73 C6
Lister Gdns N18 33 A5
Lister Ho
Greenwich SE3 142 C6
Hayes UB3 105 C2
Marylebone W1 238 C2
Spitalfields E1 96 A2
6 Wembley HA9 67 A5
West Heath SE2 124 D1
Lister Hospl SW1 115 B1 258 C1
Lister Mews N7 72 B4
Lister Rd E11 54 D1
Lister Wlk SE28 124 D6
Liston Ho N21 16 B6
Liston Rd
Clapham SW4 137 C2
Tottenham N17 34 A2
Liston Way 1 IG8 37 C3
Listowel Cl 2 SW9 138 C5
Listowel Rd RM10 81 C5
Listria Lo N16 73 D6
Listria Pk N16 73 D6
Litcham Ho 23 E1 96 D4
Litchfield Ave
Morden SM4 201 B2
Stratford E15 76 C2
Litchfield Ct E17 53 C3
Litchfield Gdns NW10 68 A2
Litchfield Rd SM1 218 A4
Litchfield St WC2 249 D6
Litchfield Way NW11 48 A4
Lithgow's Rd TW14, TW6 127 D1
Lithos Rd NW3 70 A2
Little Acre BR3 207 C6
Little Albany St NW1 238 D6
Little Argyll St W1 239 A1
Littleberry Ct NW7 28 C6
Little Birches DA15 167 C2
Little Boltons The SW10 255 D1
Little Bornes SE21 183 C6
Littlebourne 2 SE13 164 C4
Little Britain EC1 242 A3
Littlebrook Cl CR0 206 D3
Little Brownings SE23 162 B2
Littlebury Rd SW4 137 D2
Little Bury St N9 17 C4
Little Bushey La WD23 8 B5
Little Cedars N12 30 A6
Little Chelsea Ho SW10 266 B5
Little Chester St SW1 258 C6
Little Cloisters SW1 260 A6
Little College St SW1 260 A6
Littlecombe SE7 143 B6
Little Combe Cl 13 SW15 156 D5
Little Common HA7 9 A1
Littlecote Cl SW19 157 A4
Littlecote Pl HA5 23 B2
Little Cottage Pl SE10 141 D5
Littlecroft SE9 144 C2
Little Ct Harrow HA1 42 C2
West Wickham BR4 224 C6
Littledale SE2 146 A6
Little David's Sch CR0 223 D2
Little Deans Yd SW1 260 A6
Little Dell Lo 8 N3 29 B1
Little Dimocks SW12 159 B2
Little Dorrit Ct SE1 252 B2
Little Ealing La W5 109 C2
Little Ealing Prim Sch 2 W5 109 C3
Little Edward St NW1 231 D2
Little Elms UB3 127 B5
Little Essex St WC2 251 A6
Little Ferry Rd TW1 153 B3
Littlefield Cl
9 Kingston u T KT1 176 A1
Littlefield Cl *continued*
Tufnell Pk N19 71 C4
Littlefield Ct UB7 126 A5
Littlefield Ho KT1 176 A1
Littlefield Rd HA8 27 A3
Little Friday Rd E4 20 C2
Little Gearies IG6 56 D5
Little George St SW1 250 A1
Little Gn TW9 131 D1
Little Grange UB6 87 A4
Little Green St NW5 71 B4
Littlegrove EN4 14 C5
Littlegrove Ct 3 EN4 14 C5
Little Halliards KT12 194 A3
LITTLE HEATH 58 B5
Little Heath
Ilford RM6 58 B5
Woolwich SE7 122 A1
Littleheath Rd CR2 222 B1
Little Heath Rd DA7 147 B5
Little Heath Sch RM6 58 B5
Little Holt 10 E11 55 A4
LITTLE ILFORD 78 C3
Little Ilford La E12 78 B4
Little Ilford Sch E12 78 B3
Littlejohn Rd W7 86 D1
Little Larkins EN5 13 A5
Little London Cl UB8 82 D2
Little Marlborough St W1 239 A1
Littlemead KT10 212 B4
Littlemede SE9 166 B1
Littlemoor Rd IG1 79 B5
Littlemore Rd SE2 124 A4
Little Moss La HA5 23 A1
Little Newport St WC2 249 D6
Little New St EC4 241 B2
Little Oak Cl TW17 192 B5
Little Orchard Cl
Esher KT10 212 A5
Pnr HA5 23 A1
Little Oxhey La WD19 23 A6
Little Park Dr TW13 151 A2
Little Park Gdns EN2 5 B2
Little Pluckett's Way IG9 21 D3
Little Portland St W1 239 A2
Little Potters WD23 8 C4
Little Queens Rd TW11 174 D4
Little Rd UB3 105 D4
Little Redlands BR1 188 A1
Littlers Cl SW19 180 B2
Little Russell St WC1 240 A3
Little St James's St SW1 249 A3
Little St Leonards SW14 133 A2
Little Sanctuary SW1 250 A1
Little Smith St SW1 259 D6
Little Somerset St E1 243 C1
LITTLE STANMORE 26 B2
Little Stanmore Fst & Mid Sch HA8 26 B2
Littlestone Cl BR3 185 C4
Little Strand NW9 27 D1
Little Thrift BR5 211 A5
Little Titchfield St W1 239 A3
LITTLETON 192 C6
Littleton Ave E4 20 D3
Littleton CE Inf Sch TW17 192 C6
LITTLETON COMMON 171 B3
Littleton Cres HA1 64 D6
Littleton Ho TW15 171 A3
Littleton La TW17, TW18 192 A4
Littleton Rd
Harrow HA1 64 D6
Littleton TW15, TW17 171 A3
Littleton St SW18 158 A2
Little Trinity La EC4 252 B6
Little Turnstile WC1 240 C3
LITTLE VENICE 92 A2
Little Venice* W9 92 A2 236 A4
Littlewood SE13 164 A5
Littlewood Cl W13 109 B3

Little Wood Cl BR5...190 A2
Littleworth Ave
KT10..............212 B3
Littleworth Common Rd
KT10..............212 B5
Littleworth La KT10..212 B4
Littleworth Pl KT10..212 B4
Littleworth Rd KT10..212 C5
Livermere Ct [3] E8....95 D6
Livermere Rd E8......95 D6
Liverpool Gr
SE17.......117 B1 262 C1
Liverpool Ho N7......72 C2
Liverpool Rd
Ealing W5..........109 D4
Islington N1.........234 B5
Islington N1, N7.......72 C1
Kingston u T KT2 ....176 C3
Leytonstone E10 ......54 A3
Newham E16 ....98 C2
South Norwood CR7..205 A6
Liverpool St
EC2.........95 C2 243 A3
Liverpool Street Sta
EC2 ....95 C2 243 A3
Livesey Cl
Kingston u T KT1 .....198 B6
Woolwich SE28 ......123 A3
Livesey Pl SE15......140 A6
Livingstone Ct
Barnet EN5 ....1 A3
Leytonstone E10 ......54 A3
Stanwell TW19.......148 A3
Livingstone Ho [16]
SE5...............139 A5
Livingstone Lo
[13] Paddington W9.....91 C2
Walthamstow E17 .....35 C1
Livingstone Pl E14...120 A1
Livingstone Prim Sch
EN4..................2 B2
Livingstone Rd
[13] Battersea SW11...136 B2
Bowes Pk N13 ....32 A5
Isleworth TW3.......130 A1
Mill Meads E15 ....98 A6
Southall UB1 ....106 D6
South Norwood CR7...183 B1
Walthamstow E17 .....53 D3
Livity Sch The SW2..160 A6
Livonia St W1.......239 B1
Lizard St EC1..95 A4 235 B1
Lizban St SE3........143 B5
Llandovery Ho [1]
E14................120 A4
Llanelly Rd NW2......69 B6
Llanover Rd
Shooters Hill SE18...144 C5
Wembley HA9 ....65 D4
Llanthony Rd SM4...202 B4
Llanvanor Rd NW2.....69 B6
Llewellyn Ct SE20....184 C2
Llewellyn Ho [10] N19...71 C5
Llewellyn St SE16....118 A4
L'lle aux Enfants NW5 71 A3
Lloyd Ave SW16......182 A2
Lloyd Baker St
WC1........94 C4 234 A1
Lloyd Ct
Ladywell SE13 ......163 D6
Pinner HA5...........40 D4
[6] West Norwood
SE27 ....160 D1
Lloyd Ho
[3] Beckenham BR3...185 D4
Bromley BR1 ....187 B5
Stoke Newington N16..73 B5
Lloyd Mews EN3........7 C5
Lloyd Park Ave CR0 .221 D4
Lloyd Park Ho E17 ....53 C6
Lloyd Park Sta CR0..221 D4
Lloyd Rd
Dagenham RM9........81 B1
Newham E6 ....100 B6
North Cheam KT4,
SM3...............216 D5
Walthamstow E17 .....52 D5
Lloyd's Ave EC3......243 B1
Lloyd's Bldg★
EC3 ....95 C1 243 A1
Lloyd's Pl SE3 ....142 C3
Lloyd Sq WC1..94 C4 234 A2
Lloyd's Row
EC1...........94 D4 234 C1
Lloyd St WC1..94 C4 234 A2
Lloyds Way BR3......207 B4
Lloyd Villas SE4......141 C3
Lloyd Williamson Sch [17]
W10...............91 A2
Loampit Hill SE13...141 D3
Loampit Vale SE13 ...142 A2
Loanda Cl [17] E8 ......95 D6
Loats Rd SW2........160 A5
Lobelia Cl [5] E6 .....100 A2
Locarno Cl [15] SW16..181 C5
Locarno Rd
[6] Acton W3 ....111 A5
Greenford UB6........86 B3
Lochaber Rd SE13 ...142 C1
Lochaline St W6......134 C6
Lochan Cl UB4........85 A3
Lochbie [9] N4 ....50 A2
Lochinvar St SW12....159 B4
Lochleven Ho [9] N2...30 B1
Lochmere Cl DA8...147 D6
Lochmore Ho SW1...258 B3
Lochnagar St E14.....98 A2
Lockbridge Ct [3] W9...91 C2
Lock Chase SE3......142 C2
Lock Cl UB2 ....108 A4
Locke Ho
Nine Elms SW8 .....269 A2
Stamford Hill N16 .....51 D1
Lockesfield Pl E14..119 D1
Lockesley Dr BR5...211 D3
Lockesley Sq KT6...197 D3
Locket Rd HA3.........24 D1
Locket Rd Ms HA3 ....42 C6
Lockfield Ave EN3 .....7 B4
Lockgate Cl E9 ....75 B3
Lockhart Cl
Barnsbury N7.........72 B2
Enfield EN3 ....18 B6
Lockhart Lo [4] E4 .....20 C4
Lockhart St E3.........97 B3
Lockhurst St E5 ......74 D4
Lockier Wlk HA9......65 D5
Lockington Rd
SW8........137 B4 268 D2
Lockmead Rd
Lewisham SE13.....142 A2
South Tottenham N15...52 A3
Lock Mews [9] NW1 ....71 D2
Lock Rd TW10 ....175 C6
LOCKSBOTTOM......226 D5
Lockside [17] E14 .....119 A6
Lock's La CR4 ....181 A1
Locksley St E14.......97 B2
Locksmeade Rd
TW10..............175 C6
Lock View Ct [9] E14..119 A6
Lockwell Rd RM10 ....81 C5
Lockwood Cl
Barnet EN4 ....2 D1
Forest Hill SE26.....184 D6
Lockwood Ct KT3....199 A5
Lockwood Ho [10]
SE11..............138 C6
Lockwood Ind Pk
N17 ....52 B6
Lockwood Pl E4 ......35 C4
Lockwood Sq SE16...118 B3
Lockwood Way
Chessington KT9 ....214 C3
Higham Hill E17 ....34 D1
Lockyer Cl EN3 ....7 D5
Lockyer Est SE1 ....252 D1
Lockyer Ho
[7] Greenwich SE10..120 D1
[10] Putney SW15 ....134 D2
South Lambeth SW8 .270 A4
Lockyer St SE1 .....252 D1
Locomotive Dr
TW14..............150 A3
Locton Gn [4] E3 ......97 B6
Lodden Lo [13] SM2 ...218 A1
Loddiges Ho [5] E9....74 C1
Loddiges Rd E9.......74 C1
Loddon Ho NW8 ....236 D5
Loder St SE15........140 C5
Lodge Ave
Borehamwood WD6....10 B6
Croydon CR0 ....220 C5
Dagenham RM8, RM9,
IG11 ....80 B3
Harrow HA3...........44 A5
Mortlake SW14 .....133 C2
Lodge Cl Edgware HA8 .26 C4
Lodge Cl *continued*
Edmonton N18........33 A5
Hackbridge SM6 ....203 A1
Isleworth TW7.......131 B4
Lodge Ct [3] HA0 ......66 A3
Lodge Dr N13..........32 C6
Lodge Gdns BR3.....207 B4
Lodge Hill
East Wickham DA16...146 B5
Redbridge IG4.........56 A5
Lodgehill Park Cl
HA2................63 D6
Lodge La Bexley DA5. 168 D5
New Addington CR0..223 D1
North Finchley N12 ....30 A5
Lodge Mead Ct [5]
N3..................29 D3
Lodge Pl SM1.......217 D3
Lodge Rd
Bromley BR1 ....187 C3
Hendon NW4 ....46 C5
Lisson Gr NW8 92 C4 230 A1
Sutton SM1 ....217 D3
Thornton Heath CR0 .204 D2
Wallington SM6......219 B3
Lodge The
[9] Chiswick W4.....111 C3
[1] Sutton SM1......218 A4
Lodge Villas IG8 ......36 D4
Lodge Way
Charlton TW17.......171 A1
Stanwell TW15.......148 A2
Lodore Gdns NW9 ....45 C4
Lodore Gn UB10 ......60 A5
Lodore St E14.........98 A1
Lodsworth Ho SW11 268 A1
Lofthouse Pl KT9 ....213 C2
Loftie St SE16........118 A4
Lofting Ho [8] N1.......72 C1
Lofting Rd N1 ....72 C1
Lofts on the Park [24]
E9..................74 D2
Loftus Rd
Barking IG11.........79 A2
Shepherd's Bush W12 .112 B5
Loftus Rd (Queens Park
Rangers FC) W12...112 B5
Logan Cl Enfield EN3 ...6 D4
Hounslow TW4.......129 B2
Logan Mews W8.....255 A4
Logan Pl W8..113 C2 255 A4
Logan Rd
Edmonton N9.........18 B2
Wembley HA9 ....66 A6
Loggetts SE21 ....161 C2
Logs Hill BR1, BR7...188 A2
Logs Hill Cl BR7......188 A2
Lohmann Ho [5]
SE11...............138 C6
Lois Dr TW17 ....192 D4
Lolesworth Cl E1 ...243 D3
Lolland Ho [8] SE7 ...122 A2
Lollard St
SE11......116 C2 261 A3
Lollards Twr SE1 ....260 C5
Loman St
SE1.......116 D4 251 D2
Lomas Cl CR0.......224 A1
Lomas Dr [10] E8.......73 D1
Lomas St E1..........96 A2
Lombard Ave
Enfield EN3 ....6 C4
Ilford IG3............57 C1
Lombard Bsns Pk
Merton SW19........179 D1
Thornton Heath CR0 ..204 B2
Lombard Ct
[14] Acton W3 ....110 D5
City of London EC3...252 D6
Lombard La EC4 ....241 B1
Lombard Rd
Battersea SW11 .....136 B3
Friern Barnet N11 .....31 B5
Merton SW19........179 D1
Lombard Rdbt CR0...204 B2
Lombard St
EC3.........95 B1 242 D1
Lombard Trad Est
SE7...............121 B2
Lombard Wall SE7 ..121 B2
Lombardy Pl W2.....245 D5
Lombardy Ret Pk
UB3 ....106 B6
Lomley Ho [10] SW2...160 C5
Lomond Cl
Tottenham N15 ....51 C4
Lomond Cl *continued*
Wembley HA0 ....66 B1
Lomond Ct HA3.......42 D6
Lomond Gdns CR2...223 A1
Lomond Gr SE5......139 B5
Lomond Ho [10] SE5...139 B4
Loncroft Rd SE5 .....139 C6
Londesborough Ho [1]
N16.................73 C4
Londesborough Rd
N16.................73 C4
London Acadamy
HA8 ....26 B6
London Acad for Higher
Education The E15 ..98 B6
London Acad of
Computing &
Electronics SW17 . 158 D1
London Bridge EC4,
SE1........117 B6 252 D5
London Bridge City Pier
SE1........117 C5 253 A4
London Bridge
Experience The
SE1...............252 D4
London Bridge Hospl
SE1........117 B5 252 D4
London Bridge St
SE1........117 B5 252 D3
London Bridge Sta
SE1........117 B5 252 D3
London Bridge Wlk
SE1...............252 D4
London Britannia Coll
N1..........95 B4 235 C2
London Business Sch
NW1........92 D3 237 C6
London Canal Mus★
N1..........94 A5 233 B4
London Central
Mosque★
NW8........92 C4 230 B1
London Chest Hospl
E2..................96 C5
London Christian Sch
SE16.............118 C3
London City Airport
E16...............122 B5
London City Airport Sta
E16...............122 A5
London City Sh Ctr
EC1 ....242 B5
London Clinic (Hospl)
NW1........93 A3 238 B5
London Coll of Advanced
Studies SE1.......252 C3
London Coll of Beauty
Therapy W1..93 C1 239 B1
London Coll of Bsns &
Computer Studies [12]
SW4..............137 D1
London Coll of
Communication (Sch of
Printing & Publishing)
SE11.......116 D3 261 D5
London Coll of
Economics & Science
NW10..............89 A3
London Coll of Fashion
(Curtain Rd)
EC2 ....95 C3 243 B6
London Coll of Fashion
(Davies St) W1....238 C1
London Coll of Fashion
(Golden La)
EC1 ....95 A3 242 A5
London Coll of Fashion
(John Prince's St)
W1...............238 D2
London Coll of Fashion
(Lime Grove) [18]
W6...............112 C4
London Coll of Fashion
(Mare St) E8........74 C1
London Coll of
International Business
Studies WC1 ....240 B3
London Coll of Tech
IG2.................56 C3
London Ct [3] SW18 ..157 C6
London Dungeon The★
SE1........117 B5 252 D4
London Electronics Coll
SW5.......113 D1 255 C2
London Eye (Millennium
Wheel)★
SE1........116 B4 250 C2
London Fields East Side
E8..................74 B1
London Fields Prim Sch
[15] E8...............96 B6
London Fields Sta E8 .74 B1
London Fields West Side
E8..................74 A1
London Fire Brigade
Mus★ SE1 ....252 A2
London Glassblowing
Workshop SE1....253 A1
London Group Bsns Pk
NW2................46 A1
London Ho
Edgware HA8.........26 A6
[13] Hammersmith W6 112 A2
London Ho TW9.......132 B2
London Ho NW8 ....230 B4
London Hospital Dental
Inst [5] E1...........96 B2
London Independent
Hospl The E1........96 D2
London Inst The
SW17..............181 B5
London International
Film Sch
WC2.........94 A1 240 A1
London Irish Rifles
Mus★ SW9 ....139 A4
London Jewish Girls
High Sch NW4 ......46 C4
London La
Bromley BR1 ....186 D3
Hackney E8 ....74 B1
London Meridian Coll [2]
N7..................72 B5
London Metrocity Coll [21]
E3..................97 E3
London Metropolitan
Univ
Islington N7..........72 C3
Whitechapel
E1.........95 D1 243 C1
Whitechapel
E1.........95 D1 243 C2
London Metropolitan
Univ (Central Ho) [44]
E1..................96 A1
London Metropolitan
Univ (Commercial Rd)
[42] E1...............96 A1
London Metropolitan
Univ (Ladbrook Ho) [5]
N5..................72 D3
London Metropolitan
Univ (Moorgate)
EC2 ....95 B2 242 D3
London Metropolitan
Univ (Tower Hill)
EC3 ....253 C6
London Metropolitan
Univ (Spring Ho) [1]
N7..................72 C2
London Mews W2....236 D2
London Motorcycle
Mus★ UB6...........86 A4
London Nautical Sch
SE1........116 C5 251 B4
London Oratory Sch The
SW6........135 C5 265 B4
London Oratory The★
SW7........114 C3 257 A5
London Rd
Ashford TW15, TW18,
TW19, TW14.......148 B2
Brentford TW7, TW8 ..131 B4
Bromley BR1 ....186 D3
Carshalton CR4 .....203 A2
Enfield EN2 ....5 B1
Forest Hill SE22,
SE23 ....162 C3
Hackbridge SM6, CR4 .219 B6
Harrow HA1...........64 C6
Hounslow TW3, TW7, TW1,
TW8 ....130 B3
Kingston u T KT1, KT2..176 B1
Lambeth SE1 116 D3 261 D6
Mitcham CR4 ....180 D2
Morden SM4 ....201 C5
Newham E13 ....99 A5
Romford RM7, RM8....59 C5
Stanmore HA7........25 D6

London Rd *continued*
Stoneleigh KT17, KT4, SM3 216 B3
Thornton Heath CR0, CR7, SW16 204 C3
Twickenham TW1 153 A4
Wembley HA9 66 A2
London Road Rdbt TW1 153 A5
London Sch of Economics & Political Science WC2 94 B1 240 D1
London Sch of Jewish Studies 5 NW4 46 D5
London South Bank Univ SE1 116 D3 261 D6
London St
City of London EC3 253 B6
Paddington W2 92 B1 236 C1
London Stile 5 W4 110 C1
London Stock Exchange★ EC2 242 A2
London Stone Bsns Est 15 SW11 137 A3
London Terr 1 E2 96 A5
London Tottenham Coll 12 N17 33 D3
London Transport Mus★ WC2 250 B6
London Trocadero★ W1 249 C5
London Wall EC2 95 B2 242 D3
London Wall Bldgs EC2 242 D3
London Wetland Ctr★ SW13 134 B5
London Wetland Visitor Ctr★ SW13 134 B4
London Wharf 4 E2 96 B6
London Zoo★ NW1 93 A5 231 A4
Lonesome Prim Sch CR4 181 B1
Lonesome Way CR4 181 C2
Long Acre WC2 94 A1 240 B1
Long Acre Ct W13 87 A2
Longacre Pl SM5 219 A2
Longacre Rd E17 36 B2
Longbeach Rd SW11 136 D2
Longberrys NW2 69 B5
Longboat Row UB1 85 B1
Longbridge Ho RM8 80 B4
Longbridge Rd
Barking IG11 79 C3
Dagenham RM8 80 B4
Longbridge Way SE13 164 A6
Longbury Dr BR5 190 B1
Longchamp Ct 13 HA7 25 C5
Longcliffe Ho SW18 157 D6
Longcroft SE9 166 C1
Longcrofte Rd HA8 25 D3
Long Deacon Rd E4 20 C3
LONG DITTON 197 C1
Long Ditton City Inf Sch KT6 197 C1
Longdon Wood BR2 226 A4
Longdown Rd SE6 185 C6
Long Dr Dagenham W3 89 C1
Greenford UB6 85 D6
Ruislip HA4 62 D4
Long Elmes HA3 24 A2
Longfellow Rd
North Cheam KT4 200 B1
Walthamstow E17 53 B3
Longfellow Way SE1 263 D3
Longfield
3 Bromley BR1 186 D2
Loughton IG10 21 C6
Long Field NW9 27 D3
Longfield Ave
Ealing W5 109 C6
Enfield EN3 6 C5
Hackbridge SM6 203 A1
Hendon NW7 28 A3
Walthamstow E17 53 A5
Wembley HA9 44 A1
Longfield Cres SE23, SE26 162 C1
Longfield Ct 4 N2 48 A6
Longfield Dr
Mitcham SW19 180 C2
Mortlake SW14 154 D6
Longfield Est SE1 263 D3
Longfield Fst & Mid Schs HA2 41 C3
Longfield Ho
Ealing W5 109 C6
Walthamstow E17 53 B4
Longfield Rd W5 87 C1
Longfield St SW18 157 C4
Longford Ave
Feltham TW14 149 D5
Southall UB1 107 D6
Stanwell TW19 148 A3
Longford Cl
Feltham TW13 151 A1
Hampton TW12 173 C6
Hayes UB4 106 D6
Longford Com Sch TW14 149 D4
Longford Ct
1 Bedford Pk W12 111 C4
2 Clapton Pk E5 74 D4
Hampton TW12 173 D4
9 Hendon NW4 46 C5
Southall UB1 107 C5
West Ewell KT19 215 A4
Longford Gdns
Hayes UB4 106 D6
Sutton SM1 218 A6
Longford Ho
1 Catford BR1 186 B5
Hampton TW12 173 C6
7 Stepney E1 96 C1
Longford Ind Est TW12 173 D4
Longford Rd TW2 151 D3
Longford St NW1 93 B3 238 D6
Longford Way TW19 148 A3
Longford Wlk 9 SW2 160 C4
Longhayes Ave RM6 58 D5
Longhayes Ct RM6 58 D5
Longheath Gdns CR0 206 C4
Longhedge Ho SE26 184 A6
Longhedge St SW11 137 A3
Longhill Rd SE6 164 B1
Long Ho SM5 218 C6
Longhook Gdns UB5 84 B4
Longhope Cl SE15 139 D6
Longhurst Ho 8 W9 91 B4
Longhurst Rd
Croydon CR0 206 B3
Lewisham SE13 164 C6
Long La
Bermondsey SE1 117 B4 252 D1
Croydon CR0 206 C3
East Finchley N2 48 B6
Erith DA7 147 B4
Finchley N3 29 D2
Hillingdon UB10 82 D6
Holborn EC1 94 D2 241 D4
Stanwell TW15, TW19 148 B3
Longland Ct
Bermondsey SE1 118 A1
Hackney E9 75 A3
Longland Dr N20 13 D2
LONGLANDS 167 B1
Longlands Ct
Higham Hill E17 35 A2
Mitcham CR4 181 A2
Notting Hill W11 244 D6
Sidcup DA15 167 D1
Longlands Park Cres DA15 167 C2
Longlands Prim Sch DA15 167 C1
Longlands Rd DA15 167 D1
Longleat Ct 3 DA6 147 A1
Longleat Ho SW1 259 C2
Longleat Rd EN1 17 C6
Longleat Way TW14 149 B4
Longleigh Ho 8 SE5 139 C4
Longleigh La SE2, DA7 146 C6
Longlents Ho 3 NW10 89 B6
Longley Ave HA0 88 B6
Longley Ho 5 N19 71 C4
Longley Rd
Harrow HA1 42 B5
Longley Rd *continued*
Thornton Heath CR0 204 D2
Upper Tooting SW17 180 D4
Long Leys E4 36 A4
Longley St SE1 118 A2
Longley Way NW2 68 C5
Longman Ho
9 Globe Town E2 96 D5
10 Shoreditch E8 95 D6
Long Mark Rd 5 E16 99 D2
Longmarsh La SE28 123 C5
Longmead BR7 188 C1
Long Mead NW9 27 D2
Longmead Dr DA14 168 D2
Longmead Ho SE27 183 A5
Long Meadow 20 N7 71 D3
Long Meadow Cl BR3, BR4 208 A2
Longmeadow Rd DA15 167 C3
Longmead Prim Sch UB7 104 A2
Longmead Rd
Hayes UB3 105 D6
Thames Ditton KT7 196 D2
Upper Tooting SW17 180 D5
Longmoor Point 14 SW15 156 B3
Longmore Ave EN4, EN5 14 B5
Longmore St SW1 115 C2 259 A3
Longnor Rd E1 96 D4
Long Pond Rd SE3 142 C4
Long Rd SW4 137 C1
Longreach Ct IG11 101 B5
Long Reach Rd IG11 101 D3
Longridge Ho SE1 262 B5
Longridge La UB1 85 D1
Longridge Rd SW5 113 C2 255 B3
Long Ridges N2 49 A6
Longs Ct 2 TW9 132 B1
Long's Ct W1 249 D5
Longshaw Prim Sch E4 20 B1
Longshaw Rd E4 20 B1
Longshore SE8 119 B2
Long St E2 95 D4
Longstaff Cres SW18 157 C4
Longstaff Rd SW18 157 C5
Longstone Ave NW10 89 D6
Longstone Rd SW17 181 B5
Longthorne Ho 18 E3 97 B4
Longthornton Rd SW16 181 D1
Longthorpe Ct 9 W6 112 A2
Longton Ave SE26 184 A6
Longton Gr SE26 184 B6
Longville Rd SE11 261 D4
Longwalk Rd UB11 104 D5
Long Wlk
Bermondsey SE1 263 B6
Kingston u T KT3 199 A6
Shooters Hill SE18 144 D6
Longwood Bsns Pk TW16 193 D4
Longwood Dr SW15 156 A5
Longwood Gdns IG2, IG6, IG5 56 C6
Longwood Par IG6 56 D6
Longworth Cl SE28 102 D1
Long Yd WC1 94 B3 240 C5
Loning The Enfield EN3 6 C5
Hyde The NW9 45 D5
Lonsdale Ave
Newham E6 100 A3
Wembley HA9 66 A3
Lonsdale Cl
Edgware HA8 26 B5
Hillingdon UB8 83 A2
Mottingham SE12 165 D1
Newham E6 100 A3
Pinner HA5 23 A2
Lonsdale Cres IG2 56 D3
Lonsdale Dr EN2 16 A6
Lonsdale Dr N EN2 4 A1
Lonsdale Gdns CR7, SW16 204 B5
Lonsdale Ho
Fulham SW6 135 C2
6 Stoke Newington N4 51 A2
Lonsdale Mews
Notting Hill W11 91 B1
4 Richmond TW9 132 C4
Lonsdale Pl N1 72 C1
Lonsdale Rd
Barnes SW13 133 D5
Bexley DA7 147 B3
Chiswick W4 111 D2
Croydon SE25 206 B5
Kilburn NW6 91 B6
Leytonstone E11 54 D2
Notting Hill W11 91 B1
Southall UB2 106 D3
Lonsdale Sq
Islington N1 72 C1
Islington N1 234 B6
Loobert Rd N15 51 C6
Looe Gdns IG6 56 D6
Loop Rd BR7 189 A4
Lopen Rd N18 33 C6
Lopen Works N18 33 C6
Lopez Ho 4 SW9 138 A2
Lorac Ct 13 SM2 217 C1
Loraine Cl EN3 18 C6
Loraine Ct BR7 188 D5
Loraine Ho 1 SM5 219 B4
Loraine Rd
Chiswick W4 132 D6
Islington N7 72 B4
Lord Ave IG5 56 B6
Lord Chancellor Wlk KT2 177 A2
Lord David Pitt Ho 8 SE24 138 C1
Lordell Pl SW19 178 C4
Lorden Wlk 13 E2 96 A4
Lord Gdns IG5 56 B5
Lord Hills Rd W2 91 D2
Lord Holland La 5 SW9 138 C3
Lord Knyvetts Ct 3 TW19 148 A5
Lord Napier Pl W6 112 A1
Lord North St SW1 260 A5
Lord Roberts Mews SW6 265 C3
Lord Roberts Terr SE18 122 C1
Lords Cl
Feltham TW13 151 A2
West Norwood SE21 161 A2
Lord's Cricket Mus★ NW8 92 B4 229 D1
Lords Ct 3 HA8 27 A3
Lordship Gr N16 73 B6
Lordship Ho 3 N16 73 B6
Lordship La
Dulwich Village SE22 161 D5
Tottenham N22 33 B2
Lordship Lane Prim Sch 1 N22 33 A2
Lordship Park Mews N16 73 A6
Lordship Pk N16 73 B6
Lordship Pl SW3 267 A5
Lordship Rd
Northolt UB5 63 A1
Stoke Newington N16 73 B6
Lordship Terr N16 73 B6
Lord's Indoor Cricket Sch NW8 230 A2
Lord's (MCC & Middlesex Cty Cricket Ground)★ NW8 92 B4 229 D2
Lordsmead Rd N17 33 C1
Lord St E16 122 A5
Lord's View NW8 229 D1
Lord Warwick St SE18 122 B3
Loreburn Ho 2 N7 72 B4
Lorenzo St N1, WC1 233 C2
Loretto Gdns HA3 44 A5
Lorian Cl N12 29 D6
Loring Rd
East Barnet N20 14 C2
Isleworth TW7 130 D3
Loris Rd W6 112 C3
Lorn Ct SW9 138 C3
Lorne Ave CR0 206 D2
Lorne Cl NW8 92 C4 230 B1
Lorne Ct Harrow HA1 42 C2
Putney SW15 156 D5
Lorne Gdns
Croydon CR0 206 D2
Lorne Gdns *continued*
5 Hammersmith W11 112 D4
Wanstead E11 55 C5
Lorne Ho
Friern Barnet N11 31 B5
Hornsey N4 50 B2
7 Tower Hamlets E1 97 A2
Lorne Rd
Finsbury Pk N4 50 B1
Forest Gate E7 77 C4
Harrow HA3 24 D1
3 Richmond TW10 154 B6
Walthamstow E17 53 C4
Lorn Rd SW9 138 C3
Lorraine Ct
Beckenham BR3 186 A2
9 Belmont SM2 217 C1
10 Camden Town NW1 71 B1
Lorraine Pk HA3 24 C3
Lorrimore Rd SE17 138 D6
Lorrimore Sq SE17 138 D6
Lorton Ho 9 NW6 91 C6
Loseberry Rd KT10 212 B3
Lostock Ho 10 SW8 137 D3
Lothair Rd W5 109 D4
Lothair Rd N N4 50 D3
Lothair Rd S N4 50 D2
Lothbury EC2 95 B1 242 C2
Lothian Ave UB4 84 B2
Lothian Cl HA0 65 A5
Lothian Rd SW9 138 D4
Lothrop St W10 91 A4
Lots Rd SW10 136 A5 266 B3
Loubet St SW17 180 D4
Loudoun Ave IG6 56 D4
Loudoun Rd NW8 92 A6 229 B5
Loudwater Cl TW16 194 A5
Loudwater Rd TW16 194 A5
Loughborough Ct 7 SW9 138 D2
Loughborough Junction Sta SW9 138 D2
Loughborough Pk SW9 138 D1
Loughborough Prim Sch SW9 138 D3
Loughborough Rd SE5, SW9 138 D3
Loughborough St SE11 116 B1 260 D1
Lough Rd N7 72 B2
LOUGHTON 21 D5
Loughton Way IG9 21 D3
Louie Black Ho 4 SW19 179 A3
Louisa Cl E9 96 D6
Louisa Ct
Twickenham TW2 152 C2
Wood Green N11 31 D3
Louisa Gdns E1 96 D3
Louisa Ho SW15 133 D1
Louisa St E1 96 D3
Louis Ct 3 RM10 81 D2
Louise Bennett Cl 9 SE24 138 D1
Louise Ct
7 Bexley DA6 147 A1
4 Wanstead E11 55 B4
Wood Green N22 32 C2
Louise De Marillac Ho 26 E1 96 C2
Louise Graham Ho 5 IG11 101 B6
Louise Rd E15 76 C2
Louise White Ho 1 N19 49 D1
Louis Gdns BR7 188 B6
Louis Mews N10 31 B2
Louisville Rd SW17 159 A1
Lousada Lo N14 15 C5
Louvaine Rd SW11 136 B1
Lovage App E6 100 A2
Lovat Cl NW2 67 D5
Lovat La EC3 253 A5
Lovatt Cl HA8 26 D4
Lovatt Ct SW12 159 B3
Lovatt Dr HA4 39 D4
Lovat Wlk TW5 129 A5
Loveday Ho 2 SW2 160 C3
Loveday Rd W13 109 B5

Lovegrove St SE1 . . . . 140 A6
Lovegrove Wlk E14 . . 120 A5
Lovekyn Cl KT2 . . . . . . 176 B1
Love La Cheam SM3 . . . 217 A2
City of London EC2 . . . . . . 95 A1 242 B2
Croydon SE25 . . . . 206 B6
Long Ditton KT6 . . . . . . 213 D6
Mitcham CR4 . . . . 202 C6
Morden SM4 . . . . 201 D2
Old Bexley DA5 . . . . . 169 C5
Pinner HA5 . . . . 41 A6
Tottenham N17 . . . . 33 D3
Woolwich SE18 . . . . . 122 D2
Lovelace Ave BR2 . . . . 210 C3
Lovelace Gdns
Barking IG11 . . . . 80 A4
Surbiton KT6 . . . . 197 D2
Lovelace Gn SE9 . . . . . . 144 B2
Lovelace Ho 12 E8 . . . . 95 D6
Lovelace Prim Sch KT9 . . . . 213 C3
Lovelace Rd
East Barnet EN4 . . . . 14 C4
Surbiton KT6 . . . . 197 D2
West Norwood SE21 . 161 A3
Loveland Mans 7 IG11 . . . . 79 D1
Lovel Ave DA16 . . . . . . 146 A3
Lovelinch Cl SE15 . . . . 140 C6
Lovell Ho Hackney E8 . . 96 A6
4 Merton SW19 . . . . 180 A2
Lovell Pl SE16 . . . . 119 A3
Lovell Rd
Richmond TW10 . . . . . 153 C1
Southall UB1 . . . . 85 D1
Loveridge Mews NW6 69 B2
Loveridge Rd NW6 . . . . 69 B2
Lover's Wlk W1 . . . . 115 A5 248 A3
Lovett Dr SM5 . . . . 202 B2
Lovette Ho 4 E3 . . . . . . 97 C4
Lovetts Pl SW18 . . . . 135 D1
Lovett Way NW10 . . . . . 67 A3
Love Wlk SE5 . . . . 139 B3
Lovibonds Ave
Hillingdon UB7 . . . . 82 B1
Locksbottom BR6 . . . . 226 D5
Lowbrook Rd IG1 . . . . . . 78 D4
Low Cross Wood La SE21 . . . . 161 D1
Lowdell Cl UB7 . . . . 82 A1
Lowden Rd
Edmonton N9 . . . . 18 B3
Herne Hill SE24 . . . . . . 139 A1
Southall UB1 . . . . 107 A6
Lowder Ho 6 E1 . . . . . 118 B5
Lowe Ave E16 . . . . 99 A2
Lowell Ho 10 SE5 . . . . 139 A5
Lowell St E14 . . . . 97 A1
Lower Addiscombe Rd CR0 . . . . 205 C1
Lower Addison Gdns W14 . . . . 113 A4 244 A1
Lower Belgrave St SW1 . . . . 115 B3 258 C5
Lower Boston Rd W7 . . . . 108 C4
Lower Broad St RM10 . . . . 103 C6
Lower Camden BR7 . . 188 B2
Lower Church St CR0 . . . . 220 D6
LOWER CLAPTON 74 C4
Lower Clapton Rd E5 . 74 C4
Lower Clarendon Wlk 9 W11 . . . . 91 A1
Lower Comm S SW15 . . . . 134 B2
Lower Coombe St CR0 . . . . 221 A4
Lower Downs Rd SW20 . . . . 178 D2
LOWER EDMONTON . . 18 B1
LOWER FELTHAM . . 149 D1
Lower Fosters NW4 . . . 46 C4
Lower George St 13 TW10 . . . . 153 D6
Lower Gn W CR4 . . . . . . 202 C6
Lower Gravel Rd BR2 . . . . 210 B1
LOWER GREEN 195 C1
Lower Green Gdns KT4 . . . . 200 A1
Lower Green Rd KT10 . . . . 212 A6
Lower Grosvenor Pl SW1 . . . . 115 B3 258 D6
Lower Grove Rd TW10 . . . . 154 B6
LOWER HALLIFORD 193 C3
Lower Hall La E4 . . . . . . 35 A6
Lower Hampton Rd TW12, TW16 . . . . 172 D1
Lower Ham Rd KT2 . 175 D4
LOWER HOLLOWAY . . 72 A3
Lower James St W1 . . 249 B6
Lower John St W1 . . 249 B6
Lower Kenwood Ave EN2 . . . . 16 A6
Lower Kings Rd KT2 . . 176 A3
Lower Lea Crossing E14, E16 . . . . 120 C6
Lower Maidstone Rd N11 . . . . 31 C4
Lower Mall W6 . . . . . . 112 B1
Lower Marsh SE1 . . . . 116 C4 251 A1
Lower Marsh La KT1, KT5 . . . . 198 C5
Lower Merton Rise NW3 . . . . 70 C1
LOWER MORDEN . . . 201 A2
Lower Morden La SM4 . . . . 201 A3
Lower Mortlake Rd TW9 . . . . 132 B2
Lower Park Rd
Belvedere DA17 . . . . . 125 C2
Friern Barnet N11 . . . . . 31 C5
2 Loughton IG10 . . . . . 21 D6
Lower Pk Acton W3 . . . . 89 A3
5 Putney SW15 . . . . 156 D6
LOWER PLACE 89 A5
Lower Place Bsns Ctr NW10 . . . . 89 A5
Lower Queen's Rd IG9 . . . . 21 D2
Lower Rd
Belvedere DA17 . . . . . 125 D3
Finchley N2 . . . . 30 B2
Harrow HA2 . . . . 42 B1
Rotherhithe SE16 . . . . 118 C4
Sutton SM1 . . . . 218 A4
Lower Richmond Rd
Mortlake SW14, TW9 . . . . 132 D2
Putney SW15 . . . . 134 C2
Lower Robert St WC2 . . . . 250 B5
Lower Sand Hills KT6 . . . . 197 C2
Lower Sloane St SW1 . . . . 115 A1 258 A2
Lower Sq TW7 . . . . 131 B2
Lower Strand NW9 . . . . 27 D1
Lower Sunbury Rd TW12 . . . . 173 C1
LOWER SYDENHAM 185 A6
Lower Sydenham Sta SE26 . . . . 185 B5
Lower Teddington Rd KT1 . . . . 175 D2
Lower Terr NW3 . . . . . . 70 A5
Lower Thames St EC3 . . . . 117 C6 253 A5
Lower Tub WD23 . . . . 8 B4
Lowerwood Ct W11 . . . 91 A1
Lower Wood Rd KT10 . . . . 213 B2
Lowestoft Cl 5 E5 . . . . 74 C6
Lowestoft Mews E16 . . . . 122 D4
Loweswater Cl HA9 . . . 65 D6
Loweswater Ho E3 . . . . 97 B3
Lowfield Rd
Dagenham W3 . . . . 89 A1
Hampstead NW6 . . . . 69 C1
Low Hall Cl E4 . . . . 19 D4
Low Hall La E17 . . . . 53 A3
Lowick Rd HA1 . . . . 42 C4
Lowland Gdns RM7 . . . . 59 D3
Lowlands NW3 . . . . 70 C2
Lowlands Ct NW7 . . . . . . 27 D5
Lowlands Rd
Harrow HA1 . . . . 42 C2
Pinner HA5 . . . . 40 C3
Lowman Rd N7 . . . . 72 B4
Lowndes Cl SW1 . . . . 258 B5
Lowndes Ct
Knightsbridge SW1 . . 257 D6
Marylebone W1 . . . . . 239 A1
Lowndes Lo Barnet EN5 1 D2
SW1 . . . . 257 D6
Lowndes Pl SW1 . . . . 115 A3 258 A5
Lowndes Sq SW1 . . . . 114 D4 247 D1
Lowndes St SW1 . . . . 115 A3 258 A6
Lownds Ct BR1 . . . . . . 187 A1
Lowood Ct SE19 . . . . . 183 D5
Lowood Ho 12 E1 . . . . 118 C6
Lowood St E1 . . . . 118 B6
Lowry Cres CR4 . . . . . . 180 C1
Lowry Ct 3 SE16 . . . . 118 B1
Lowry Ho N17 . . . . 33 D2
Lowry Lo 1 HA0 . . . . . . 65 D3
Lowry Rd RM8 . . . . 80 B3
Lowther Cl WD6 . . . . . . 10 B6
Lowther Dr EN2 . . . . 4 A1
Lowther Hill SE23 . . . . 163 A4
Lowther Ho
Pimlico SW1 . . . . 259 B1
11 Shoreditch E8 . . . . . . 95 D6
Lowther Prim Sch SW13 . . . . 134 A6
Lowther Rd
Barnes SW13 . . . . 133 D4
Higham Hill E17 . . . . 35 A1
Islington N7 . . . . 72 C3
Kingston u T KT2 . . . . . 176 B2
Stanmore HA7 . . . . 44 B6
Lowth Rd SE5 . . . . 139 A3
Lowton Lo E17 . . . . 53 A6
LOXFORD 79 A3
Loxford Ave E6 . . . . 99 D5
Loxford Ho SW1 . . . . 258 B3
Loxford La IG1 . . . . 79 B3
Loxford Rd IG11 . . . . 78 D2
Loxford Sch of Science & Tech IG1 . . . . 79 B3
Loxham Rd E4 . . . . 35 D3
Loxham St WC1 . . . . . 233 B1
Loxley Cl SE26 . . . . 184 D5
Loxley Hall E11 . . . . 54 C2
Loxley Ho HA9 . . . . 66 A5
Loxley Rd
Feltham TW12 . . . . 173 B6
Wandsworth SW18 . . . 158 B3
Loxton Rd SE23 . . . . . . 163 A3
Loxwood Cl TW14 . . . . 149 B3
Loxwood Rd N17 . . . . . . 51 C6
Loyola Prep Sch IG9 . . 21 C3
LTC Coll London W1 239 A2
Lubavitch Boys Prim Sch 6 E5 . . . . 51 D2
Lubavitch Girls Prim Sch 8 N16 . . . . 51 D2
Lubavitch House Sch (Jun Boys) 9 E5 . . . . . 51 D2
Lubbock Ct BR7 . . . . . 188 B3
Lubbock Ho
21 Canary Wharf E14 . . . . 119 D6
Orpington BR6 . . . . . . 227 C6
Lubbock Rd BR7 . . . . . 188 B3
Lubbock St SE14 . . . . . 140 C5
Lucan Ho N1 . . . . 235 D5
Lucan Pl SW3 . . . . 114 C2 257 B3
Lucan Rd EN5 . . . . 1 A2
Lucas Ave Harrow HA2 . 63 C6
Newham E13 . . . . 99 B6
Lucas Ct
Battersea SW11 . . . . 268 B1
Forest Hill SE26 . . . . . 185 A5
Lucas Gdns N2 . . . . 30 A1
Lucas Ho
2 Clapham SW8 . . . . . 137 C3
Walham Green SW10 . 265 D4
Lucas Rd SE20 . . . . 184 C4
Lucas Sq NW11 . . . . 47 C3
Lucas St SE4, SE8 . . . . 141 C4
Lucas Vale Prim Sch 10 SE8 . . . . 141 C4
Lucerne Cl N14 . . . . 16 A1
Lucerne Ct
5 Abbey Wood DA18 . . . . 125 A3
8 Beckenham BR3 . . . 185 C3
Lucerne Gr E17 . . . . 54 B5
Lucerne Mews W8 . . . 245 B4
Lucerne Rd
Highbury N5 . . . . 72 D4
Orpington BR6 . . . . . . 211 D1
South Norwood CR7 . . 205 A5
Lucey Rd SE16 . . . . 118 A3
Lucey Way SE16 . . . . . 118 A2
Lucie Ave TW15 . . . . . . 170 D4
Lucien Rd
Upper Tooting SW17 . . . . 181 A6
Wandsworth SW18 . . 157 D2
Lucille Ho SE26 . . . . . . 184 B4
Lucknow St SE18 . . . . 145 C5
Lucorn Cl SE12 . . . . . 164 D5
Lucraft Ho 12 SW2 . . . . 160 A4
Luctons Ave IG9 . . . . . . 21 C3
Lucy Ashe Ho SE17 . . 261 D3
Lucy Brown Ho SE1 . . 252 B3
Lucy Cres W3 . . . . 89 A3
Lucy Gdns RM8 . . . . 81 A5
Luddesdon Rd DA8 . . 147 C5
Ludford Cl
Croydon CR0 . . . . 220 D4
Edgware NW9 . . . . 27 C1
Ludgate Broadway EC4 . . . . 241 D1
Ludgate Cir EC4 . . . . 94 D1 241 C1
Ludgate Hill EC4 . . . . 94 D1 241 D1
Ludgate Ho EC4 . . . . 241 C1
Ludgate Sq EC4 . . . . . 241 D1
Ludgrove Ct EN4 . . . . 2 C1
Ludgrove Hall EN4 . . . . . 2 C2
Ludham NW5 . . . . 70 D3
Ludham Cl SE28 . . . . . . 102 C1
Lud Lo TW15 . . . . 148 A2
Ludlow Cl
Bromley BR2 . . . . 209 A6
Harrow HA2 . . . . 63 B4
Ludlow Ct Acton W3 . . 111 A4
East Barnet EN4 . . . . 14 C6
Ludlow Rd Ealing W5 . . 87 C3
Feltham TW13 . . . . 172 A6
Ludlow St EC1 . . . . . . 242 A6
Ludlow Way N2 . . . . 48 A5
Ludovick Wlk SW15 . . 133 C1
Ludwell Ho W14 . . . . . 254 B6
Ludwick Mews SE14 . 141 A5
Luffield Rd SE2 . . . . . . 124 B3
Luffman Rd SE12 . . . . 165 B1
Lugard Ho 2 W12 . . . 112 B5
Lugard Rd SE15 . . . . . . 140 B4
Lugg App E12 . . . . 78 C5
Luke Ho 32 E1 . . . . 96 B1
Lukes Ct N3 . . . . 47 C6
Luke St EC2 . . . . 95 C3 243 A6
Lukin Cres E4 . . . . 20 B1
Lukin St E1 . . . . 96 C1
Lullingstone Cl BR5 . . 190 B3
Lullingstone Cres BR5 . . . . 190 B3
Lullingstone Ho 21 SE15 . . . . 140 C6
Lullingstone La SE13 . . . . 164 B5
Lullingstone Rd 3 DA17 . . . . 147 B6
Lullington Garth
Borehamwood WD6 . . . . 10 D6
Bromley BR1 . . . . 186 C3
Finchley N12 . . . . 29 B5
Lullington Rd
Dagenham RM9 . . . . 81 A1
Penge SE20 . . . . 184 A3
Lulot Gdns N19 . . . . 71 B6
Lulworth
Camden Town NW1 . . . . 71 D1
Walworth SE17 . . . . . 262 C2
Lulworth Ave
Hounslow TW5, TW7 . . . . 130 A5
Wembley HA9 . . . . 43 C2
Lulworth Cl HA2 . . . . . . 63 B5
Lulworth Cres CR4 . . . 180 C1
Lulworth Ct N14 . . . . . . 16 A1
Lulworth Dr HA5 . . . . . . 41 A2
Lulworth Gdns HA2 . . . 63 B6
Lulworth Ho SW8 . . . . 270 C3
Lulworth Rd
Bexley DA16 . . . . 145 D3
Chislehurst SE9 . . . . . 166 A2
Peckham SE15 . . . . 140 B3
Lulworth Waye UB4 . . . 84 B1
Lumen Rd HA9 . . . . 65 D6
Lumiere Bldg The E7 . . 77 D3
Lumiere Ct 7 SW17 . . 159 A2
Lumina Bldg 1 E14 . . 120 A5
Lumley Cl DA17 . . . . . . 125 C1
Lumley Ct WC2 . . . . . . 250 B5
Lumley Flats SW1 . . . 258 A2
Lumley Gdns SM3 . . . . 217 A3
Lumley Ho KT3 . . . . 199 B1
Lumley Rd SM1, SM3 . . 217 A3
Lumley St W1 . . . . 238 B1
Lumsdon NW8 . . . . 91 D6
Luna Ho 6 SE16 . . . . . 118 A4
Lunan Ho 14 E3 . . . . 97 B5
Luna Rd CR7 . . . . 205 A6
Lundin Wlk WD19 . . . . . 22 D6
Lund Point E15 . . . . 98 A6
Lundy Dr UB3 . . . . 105 C2
Lunham Rd SE19 . . . . . 183 C4
Luntley Pl E1 . . . . 96 A2
Lupin Cl Croydon CR0 206 D1
Streatham SW2 . . . . . 160 D2
Lupin Cres IG11 . . . . . . 78 D2
Lupino Ct SE11 . . . . . 260 D4
Lupin Point SE1 . . . . 253 D1
Lupton Cl SE12 . . . . . . 187 B6
Lupton St NW5 . . . . 71 C4
Lupus Ct SE19 . . . . 183 B2
Lupus St SW1 . . . . 115 C1 259 B1
Luralda Gdns E14 . . . 120 B1
Lurgan Ave W6 . . . . . 134 D6
Lurline Gdns SW11 . . . . . . 137 A4 268 B2
Luscombe Ct BR2 . . . . 186 C1
Luscombe Ho SW18 . . 157 B6
Luscombe Way SW8 . . . . 138 A5 270 A4
Lusher Ho SW15 . . . . 156 D5
Lushington Ho KT12 . 194 C3
Lushington Rd
Catford SE6 . . . . 185 D5
Willesden Green NW10 90 B5
Lushington Terr 11 E8 . . . . 74 A3
Lutea Ho SM2 . . . . 218 A1
Luther Cl HA8 . . . . 11 A2
Luther King Cl E17 . . . . 53 A3
Luther Mews 2 TW11 . . . . 174 D5
Luther Rd TW11 . . . . . 174 D5
Luton Pl SE10 . . . . 142 A5
Luton Rd Newham E13 . 99 A3
Sidcup DA14 . . . . 168 C1
Walthamstow E17 . . . . . 53 B6
Luton St NW8 . . . 92 B3 236 D5
Luttrell Ave SW15 . . . . 156 B6
Lutwyche Rd SE6 . . . . 163 B2
Lutyens Ho SW1 . . . . 259 A1
Luxborough Ho W1 . 238 A4
Luxborough St W1 . . . . 93 A2 238 A4
Luxborough Twr W1 . 238 A4
Luxembourg Mews 2 E15 . . . . 76 C3
Luxemburg Gdns W6 . . . . 112 D2
Luxfield Rd SE9 . . . . . . 166 A3
Luxford St SE16 . . . . . 118 D2
Luxmore St SE4 . . . . . 141 B4
Luxor St SE5 . . . . 139 A2
Lyall Ave SE21 . . . . . . 183 D6
Lyall Mews SW1 . . . . 115 A3 258 A5
Lyall Mews W SW1 . . 258 A5
Lyall St SW1 . . 115 A3 258 A5
Lyal Rd E3 . . . . 97 A5
Lycett Ho 10 SW2 . . . . 160 A4
Lycett Pl 3 W12 . . . . . 112 A4
Lychgate Ct 4 N12 . . . . 30 B5
Lychgate Manor HA1 . . 42 C2
Lych Gate Wlk UB3 . . 105 D6
Lyconby Gdns CR0 . . . 207 A2
Lycott Gr SE22 . . . . . . 161 D6
Lydd Cl DA14 . . . . 167 C1
Lydden Ct SE9 . . . . 167 C5
Lydden Gr SW18 . . . . . 157 D4
Lydden Rd SW18 . . . . 157 D4
Lydd Rd DA7 . . . . 147 B5
Lydeard Rd E6 . . . . 78 B1
Lydford NW1 . . . . 232 B5
Lydford Cl 22 N16 . . . . . 73 C3
Lydford Rd
Brondesbury NW2 . . . . . 68 D2
Paddington W9 . . . . 91 B3
Tottenham N15 . . . . 51 B4
Lydgate Ho 8 N16 . . . . 73 C3
Lydhurst Ave SW2 . . . 160 B2

Lydia Ct 2 N12 . . . . .30 A4
Lydia Lodge HA1. . . . . .64 C4
Lydney Cl
Camberwell SE15. . . . 139 C5
Putney SW19. . . . . . . 157 A2
Lydon Rd SW4. . . . . . .137 C2
Lydstep Rd BR7. . . . . .188 C6
Lydwell Ho 29 SW8. . 137 D3
Lyford Rd SW18. . . . . .158 C3
Lyford St SE18. . . . . . .122 A2
Lygoe Ho 18 N6. . . . . . .49 D2
Lygoe Rd N2. . . . . .30 B2
Lygon Ho 2 E2. . . . . . .96 A4
Lygon Pl SW1. . . . . . . 258 C5
Lyham Cl SW2 . . . . . .160 A5
Lyham Rd SW2 . . . . . .160 A5
Lyle Cl CR4. . . . . .203 A2
Lyle Ct SM4. . . . . .202 B3
Lyle Pk SW15. . . . . . . 156 D5
Lyly Ho SE1. . . . . 262 D5
Lyme Farm Rd SE12. .143 B1
Lyme Gr E9. . . . . .74 C1
Lyme Grove Ho 2 E9 .74 C1
Lymer Ave SE19. . . . . 183 D5
Lyme Rd DA16 . . . . . . .146 B4
Lymescote Gdns
SM1 . . . . .217 C6
Lyme St NW1. . 93 C6 232 A6
Lyminge Cl DA14. . . . 189 D6
Lyminge Gdns SW17,
SW18. . . . . .158 C3
Lymington Ave N22. . .32 D1
Lymington Cl
Mitcham SW16 . . . . . 181 D1
2 Newham E6 . . . . . .100 B2
Lymington Ct SM1 . . .218 A5
Lymington Dr HA4. . . .61 B6
Lymington Gdns
KT19. . . . . 215 D3
Lymington Mans
NW6. . . . . .69 D2
Lymington Rd
Dagenham RM8. . . . . . .58 D1
Hampstead NW6. . . . . .69 D2
Lyminster Cl UB4 . . . . .85 A2
Lympne N17. . . . . .33 B1
Lympstone Gdns
SE15. . . . . .140 A5
Lynbridge Gdns N13 . .32 D6
Lynbrook Gr SE15. . . .139 C5
Lynchen Cl TW5 . . . . .128 B4
Lynch Wlk 2 SE8. . . . .141 B6
Lyncott Cres SW4. . . . .137 B1
Lyncourt SE3. . . . . . . .142 B3
Lyncroft Ave HA5 . . . . .41 A4
Lyncroft Gdns
Ealing W13. . . . . 109 C5
Hampstead NW6. . . . . .69 C3
Hounslow TW3. . . . . . . 152 A6
Lyncroft Mans 4
NW6. . . . . .69 C3
Lyndale NW2. . . . . .69 B5
Lyndale Ave NW2. . . . . .69 B5
Lyndale Cl SE3. . . . . . . 142 D6
Lyndean Ind Est SE2 124 C3
Lynde Ho
2 Clapham SW4. . . . 137 D2
Walton-on-T KT12 . . . 194 C3
Lynden Gate SW15. . .156 B4
Lyndenhurst SE3 . . . . 142 D2
Lynden Hyrst CR0. . . . 221 D6
Lyndhurst BR7. . . . . . 188 D4
Lyndhurst Ave
Colney Hatch N12 . . . . .30 D4
Edgware NW7 . . . . .27 C4
Mitcham SW16 . . . . . 181 D1
Pinner HA5. . . . . .22 B2
Southall UB1 . . . . 107 D5
Sunbury TW16 . . . . . . 194 A6
Tolworth KT5 . . . . 198 D1
Twickenham TW2,
TW4 . . . . 151 C3
Lyndhurst Cl
Bexleyheath DA7 . . . . 147 D2
Neasden NW10 . . . . . . .67 B5
Orpington BR6. . . . . . . 226 D4
South Croydon CR0 . . 221 D5
Lyndhurst Ct
8 Belmont SM2 . . . . 217 C1
11 Woodford E18. . . . . .37 A2
Lyndhurst Dr
Leytonstone E10 . . . . . .54 A2
New Malden KT3 . . . . 199 D2
Lyndhurst Gdns
Barking IG11 . . . . .79 C2
Enfield EN1 . . . . .5 C1
Lyndhurst Gdns *continued*
Hampstead NW3 . . . . . .70 B3
Hendon N3. . . . . .29 A2
Ilford IG2. . . . . .57 B3
Pinner HA5. . . . . .22 B2
Lyndhurst Gr SE5,
SE15. . . . . 139 D3
Lyndhurst Ho 2
SW15 . . . . .156 A4
Lyndhurst House Prep
Sch NW3 . . . . .70 B3
Lyndhurst Lo 3 E14 .120 B2
Lyndhurst Rd
Bexleyheath DA7 . . . . 147 D2
Chingford E4 . . . . .36 A3
Edmonton N18. . . . . . . .34 A6
Greenford UB6. . . . . . . .85 D3
Hampstead NW3 . . . . . .70 B3
Thornton Heath CR7 . 204 C5
Tottenham N22 . . . . . . .32 C4
Lyndhurst Sch SE5. . .139 B3
Lyndhurst Sq SE15. . 139 D4
Lyndhurst Terr NW3. . .70 B3
Lyndhurst Way
Belmont SM2. . . . . . . 217 C1
Camberwell SE15. . . . 139 D3
Lyndon Ave
Bexley DA15. . . . . 167 D6
Hackbridge SM6 . . . . 219 A5
Pinner HA5. . . . . .23 A4
Lyndon Rd DA17 . . . . .125 C2
Lyndon Yd SW17 . . . . 179 D6
Lyndum Ct N22 . . . . . . .32 C2
Lyne Cres E17 . . . . .35 B2
Lyne Ct NW9. . . . . .45 B2
Lynegrove Ave
TW15 . . . . .171 A5
Lyneham Wlk
Hackney E5 . . . . .75 A3
Pinner HA5. . . . . .39 D6
Lynette Ave SW4. . . . .159 C5
Lynfield Ct SE23 . . . . 162 D4
Lynford Cl
Barnet Gate EN5 . . . . . .11 D6
Burnt Oak HA8. . . . . . . .27 A2
Lynford French Ho
SE17. . . . . 262 A2
Lynford Gdns
Edgware HA8. . . . . .10 D1
Ilford IG3. . . . . .79 D6
Lynford Terr N9. . . . . . .17 D3
Lyngham Ct 10 N4 . . . .50 A2
Lynhurst Cres UB10. . .61 B1
Lynhurst Ct NW8. . . . 229 C5
Lynhurst Rd UB10. . . . .61 A1
Lynmere Rd DA16. . . .146 B3
Lyn Mews 12 E3 . . . . . .97 B4
Lynmouth Ave
Enfield EN1 . . . . .17 D5
West Barnes SM4 . . . 200 D2
Lynmouth Dr HA4. . . . .62 B5
Lynmouth Gdns
Heston TW5. . . . . 128 D4
Wembley UB6 . . . . .65 B1
Lynmouth Rd
Fortis Green N2. . . . . . .48 D5
Stamford Hill N16 . . . . .51 D1
Walthamstow E17 . . . . .53 A4
Wembley UB6 . . . . .87 B6
Lynn Cl
Ashford TW15 . . . . . . .171 B5
Harrow HA3. . . . . .24 B1
Lynn Ct SW16. . . . . . . 181 D5
Lynne Cl 7 BR6 . . . . . 227 D2
Lynne Ct
Forest Hill SE23 . . . . . .163 B4
Hampstead NW6. . . . . .69 D1
South Croydon CR2 . . 221 C4
Wimbledon SW20 . . . . .178 B2
Lynnett Ct E9. . . . . .75 A2
Lynnett Rd RM8. . . . . . .58 D1
Lynne Way UB5 . . . . . . .84 D5
Lynne Wlk KT10. . . . . .212 A3
Lynn Ho SE15. . . . . . . .140 A6
Lynn Mews E11. . . . . . . .76 C6
Lynn Rd
Balham SW12 . . . . . . .159 B4
Ilford IG2. . . . . .57 B2
Leyton E11. . . . . .76 C5
Lynn St EN2 . . . . .5 B4
Lynsted Cl
Bexley DA6. . . . . 169 D6
Bromley BR1 . . . . 187 C1
Lynsted Ct 4 BR3. . . .185 A1
Lynsted Gdns SE9. . . 143 D2
Lynton KT7. . . . . .197 A2
Lynton Ave
Ealing W13. . . . . .87 A1
Hyde The NW9 . . . . . . .45 D5
North Finchley N12 . . . .30 B6
Lynton Cl
Chessington KT9 . . . . 214 A4
Isleworth TW7. . . . . . . 130 D1
Willesden NW10 . . . . . .67 D3
Lynton Cres IG2 . . . . . .56 D3
Lynton Ct
Bowes Pk N13 . . . . .32 A5
9 Dagenham W3 . . . . .89 A1
Penge SE20 . . . . .184 B2
Sutton SM2 . . . . .218 A2
Lynton Est SE1. . . . . . .118 A2
Lynton Gdns
Enfield EN1 . . . . .17 C4
Friern Barnet N11 . . . . .31 D4
Lynton Grange N2 . . . .48 D6
Lynton Ho 16 W2. . . . . .91 D1
Lynton Lo N5. . . . . .72 D3
Lynton Mans SE1 . . . . 261 A6
Lynton Mead N20. . . . .13 D2
Lynton Rd Acton W3 . 110 D6
Bermondsey SE1 . . . . . 117 D2
Chingford E4 . . . . .35 D5
Harrow HA2. . . . . .63 A6
Hornsey N8 . . . . .50 A4
New Malden KT3 . . . . .199 B4
Paddington NW6 . . . . . .91 B5
Thornton Heath CR0 . 204 C3
Lynton Terr 4 W3. . . . .89 A1
Lynton Wlk UB4 . . . . . .83 C4
Lynwood Cl
Harrow HA2. . . . . .63 A5
Woodford E18 . . . . .37 C2
Lynwood Ct TW15. . . . .170 B5
Lynwood Dr KT4 . . . . .216 A6
Lynwood Gdns
Southall UB1 . . . . .85 B1
Wallington CR0 . . . . . .220 B4
Lynwood Gr
Orpington BR6. . . . . . . 211 C1
Southgate N21. . . . . . . .16 C3
Lynwood Rd
Ealing W5. . . . . .88 A3
Thames Ditton KT7. . . . 196 D1
Upper Tooting SW17 . 180 D6
Lynx Terr SW19 . . . . . .157 C1
Lynx Way E16. . . . . . . 121 D6
Lyon Bsns Pk IG11. . 101 C5
Lyon Ct HA4 . . . . .39 D1
Lyon Ho NW8. . . . . . . 237 A5
Lyon Meade HA7. . . . . .25 C2
Lyon Park Ave HA0. . . .66 B2
Lyon Park Jun & Inf Schs
HA0 . . . . .66 B1
Lyon Rd Harrow HA1. . .42 D3
Merton SW19. . . . . 180 A2
Lyonsdown Ave EN5 . .14 A5
Lyonsdown Ct EN5. . . .14 A6
Lyonsdown Rd EN5 . . .14 A6
Lyonsdown Sch EN5 . .14 A6
Lyons Pl NW8. . 92 B3 236 C5
Lyon St N1 . . . . .72 B1
Lyons Wlk W14 . . . . . 254 A4
Lyon Way UB6 . . . . .86 C6
Lyoth Rd BR5 . . . . . . .227 A6
Lyric Dr UB6. . . . . .85 D3
Lyric Mews SE26. . . . .184 C6
Lyric Rd SW13 . . . . . . 133 D4
Lysander 20 NW9 . . . . .27 D2
Lysander Ct 8 EN5 . . . .13 D6
Lysander Gdns KT5 . .198 B3
Lysander Gr N19. . . . . .49 D1
Lysander Ho 10 E2. . . . .96 B5
Lysander Mews N19 . . .49 C1
Lysander Rd
Ruislip HA4 . . . . .61 B6
Wallington CR0 . . . . . .220 B2
Lysander Way BR6 . . .227 A5
Lysia Ct SW6 . . . . 134 D5
Lysias Rd SW12. . . . . .159 B5
Lysia St SW6. . . . . 134 D5
Lysons Wlk SW15 . . . .156 A6
Lytchet Rd BR1 . . . . . .187 B3
Lytchet Way EN3. . . . . . .6 C4
Lytchgate Cl CR2 . . . .221 C1
Lytcott Dr KT8 . . . . . . .195 B6
Lytham Ave WD19. . . . .22 D5
Lytham Cl SE28 . . . . . .103 A1
Lytham Ct 5 UB1. . . . . .85 D1
Lytham Gr W5 . . . . .88 B4
Lytham St
SE17. . . . . . . 117 B1 262 C1
Lyttelton Cl NW3. . . . . .70 C1
Lyttelton Ct N2 . . . . . . .48 A4
Lyttelton Rd
Hampstead Garden Suburb
N2. . . . . .48 A4
Leyton E10. . . . . .76 A5
Lytten Ct 6 W12. . . . . .112 A4
Lyttleton Ct UB4 . . . . . .84 C3
Lyttleton Ho 10 E9 . . . .74 C1
Lyttleton Rd N8. . . . . . .50 C6
Lytton Ave Enfield EN3 . . 7 A5
Southgate N13. . . . . . . .16 C2
Lytton Cl
Hampstead Garden Suburb
N2. . . . . .48 B4
Northolt UB5 . . . . .63 B1
Lytton Ct WC1 . . . . 240 B3
Lytton Gdns SM6. . . . 219 D4
Lytton Gr SW15 . . . . . .157 A5
Lytton Ho 3 TW12 . . 173 D4
Lytton Rd
Leytonstone E11 . . . . . .54 C2
New Barnet EN5 . . . . . . .2 A1
Pinner HA5. . . . . .23 A3
Lytton Strachey Path 8
SE28. . . . . .124 B6
Lyveden Rd
Greenwich SE3 . . . . . .143 B5
Mitcham SW17,
SW19 . . . . 180 D4

M

Mabbett Ho 2 SE18. .144 C6
Mabel Crout Ct SE9 . . .145 B1
Mabel Evetts Ct UB3 . .106 B6
Mabel Thornton Ho 12
N16. . . . . .73 B4
Maberley Cres SE19. . .184 A3
Maberley Ct SE19. . . .184 A3
Maberley Rd SE19 . . .182 C2
Mabledon Pl NW1,
WC1 . . . . 232 D1
Mablethorpe Rd
SW6. . . . . 264 A3
Mabley St E9. . . . . .75 A3
Mablin Lo 3 IG9 . . . . . .21 C3
Mcadam Dr EN2 . . . . . . .4 D3
Macallister Ho 8
SE18. . . . . 144 D6
Macaret Cl N20. . . . . . .14 A4
Macarthur Cl
London E7 . . . . .77 A2
Wembley HA9 . . . . .66 D2
MacArthur Ho 4
SW2. . . . . .160 A4
Macartney Ho SE10 . . .142 B5
Macaulay Ave KT10 . . .212 C6
Macaulay CE Prim Sch
SW4. . . . . .137 B1
Macaulay Ct SW4 . . . .137 B2
Macaulay Ho
2 Kensal Town W10 . . .91 A2
10 Stoke Newington
N16. . . . . .73 C5
Macaulay Rd
Clapham SW4 . . . . . . .137 B2
Newham E6 . . . . .99 D5
Macaulay Sq SW4. . . . 137 B1
Macaulay Way 2
SE28. . . . . .124 B5
McAuley Cl
Eltham SE9. . . . . 166 C6
Lambeth SE1 116 C3 261 A6
Macauley Mews
SE13. . . . . .142 A3
McAusland Ho 5 E3. . .97 B5
Macbean St SE18 . . . 122 D3
Macbeth Ho 4 N1. . . . .95 C5
Macbeth St W6. . . . . . .112 B1
McBride Ho 6 E3 . . . . .97 B5
McCall Cl SW4. . . . . . .138 A3
McCall Cres SE7 . . . . .122 A1
McCall Ho N7 . . . . .72 A4
Mccarthy Ct SW11 . . 267 B1
McCarthy Rd TW13. . . 172 D5
Macclesfield Rd
Croydon SE25. . . . . . . 206 C4
Shoreditch
EC1 . . . . 95 A4 235 A2
Macclesfield St W1. . 249 D6
McClintock Pl EN3. . . . . .7 D6
McCoid Way SE1. . . . 252 A1
Mcconnell Ho SW8 . . 269 C1
McCormick Ho 9
SW2. . . . . .160 C3
McCrone Mews 3
NW3. . . . . .70 B2
McCullum Rd E3. . . . . .97 B6
McDermott Cl SW11 .136 C2
McDermott Rd SE15 .140 A2
Macdonald Ave RM10 .81 D5
Macdonald Ct TW3. . .130 A1
McDonald Ho 1
KT2. . . . . .176 B3
Macdonald Ho 2
SW11 . . . . .137 A3
Macdonald Rd
Chingford E17 . . . . .36 A1
Dartmouth Pk N19. . . . .71 C6
Forest Gate E7. . . . . . . .77 A4
Friern Barnet N11 . . . . .30 D5
McDonough Cl KT9 . .214 A4
McDougall Ct TW9. . .132 C3
Mcdougall Ho E2 . . . . .96 A4
McDowall Cl E16 . . . . .98 D2
McDowall Rd SE5. . . .139 A4
Macduff Rd
SW11 . . . . . . 137 A4 268 B2
Mace Cl E1. . . . . 118 B5
Mace Ho 2 E17 . . . . . .53 D6
McEntee Ave E17 . . . . .35 A2
Mace St E2. . . . . .96 D5
McEwan Way E15. . . . .98 B6
Macey Ho
Battersea SW11 . . . . 267 A1
10 Greenwich SE10. . 142 A6
Macfarlane La TW7 . . .131 A6
Macfarlane Rd W12. . .112 C5
Macfarren Ho 7
W10 . . . . .91 A4
MacFarren Pl NW1. . 238 B5
McGlashon Ho 15 E1. . 96 A3
McGrath Rd E15 . . . . . .76 D2
McGregor Ct 8 N1 . . . .95 C4
MacGregor Ho 2
SW12 . . . . 159 D3
McGregor Rd W11 . . . .91 B2
Macgregor Rd E16. . . .99 C2
Mcguffie Ct E17 . . . . . .53 B6
Machell Rd SE15. . . . .140 C2
McIndoe Ct N1 . . . . . . 235 C6
McIntosh Cl SM6. . . . .220 A1
McIntosh Ho 14
SE16. . . . . .118 C2
McIntyre Ct 19 SW4. . .138 A3
Mackay Ho 33 W12. . .112 B6
McKay Rd SW20 . . . . .178 C4
Mackay Rd SW4 . . . . .137 B2
McKellar Cl WD23. . . . . .8 A2
McKenna Ho 3 E3. . . . .97 B5
Mackennal St
NW8. . . . . 92 C5 230 B4
Mackenzie Cl 7
W12 . . . . .112 B6
Mackenzie Ho
5 Dollis Hill NW2. . . . .68 A5
1 Hornsey N8. . . . . . . .50 A5
Mackenzie Rd
Barnsbury N7. . . . . .72 B2
Penge BR3 . . . . 184 D1
Mackenzie Wlk E14. .119 C5
McKerrell Rd SE15. . . .140 A4
Mackeson Rd NW3. . . . .70 D4
Mackie Ho 18 SW2. . . .160 C4
Mackie Rd SW2. . . . . .160 C4
McKiernan Ct 2
SW11 . . . . .136 C3
Mc Killop Way DA14. .190 C3
McKinlay Ct
Beckenham BR3. . . . . .185 B1
Bexley DA16. . . . . 146 C2
McKinnon Wood Ho 16
E2. . . . . .96 A4
Mackintosh La E9. . . . .74 D3
Macklin Ho SE23. . . . .162 B2
Macklin St
WC2 . . . . 94 A1 240 B2
Mackonochie Ho
EC1. . . . . 241 A4
Mackrow Wlk 11
E14. . . . . .120 A6
Macks Rd SE16 . . . . . .118 A2
Mackworth Ho NW1 . 232 A2
Mackworth St NW1 . 232 A2
Mac Laren Mews
SW15 . . . . .134 C1
Maclean Rd SE23 . . . .163 A5
Mcleod Ct SE21. . . . . .162 A3

McLeod Ho 3 SE23 162 C2
McLeod Rd SE2 124 B2
Macleod Rd N21 16 A6
McLeod's Mews SW7 113 D2 255 D4
Macleod St SE17 117 A1 262 B1
Maclise Rd W14 113 A3 254 A5
McManus Ho 2 SW11 136 B2
McMillan Ct 2 SE6 164 D3
Macmillan Ct HA2 41 C1
Mcmillan Ho SE4 141 A2
Macmillan Ho
- Cricklewood NW4 68 B4
- Lisson Gr NW8 230 B1
McMillan St SE8 141 C6
Macmillan Way SW17 181 B6
Mcmorran Ho 4 N7 72 A4
McNair Rd UB2 107 D3
Macnamara Ho SW10 266 C4
Mcneil Rd SE5 139 C3
McNicol Dr NW10 89 A5
Macoma Rd SE18 145 B6
Macoma Terr SE18 145 B6
Maconochies Rd 9 E14 119 D1
Macquarie Way E14 119 D2
McRae La CR4 202 D2
Macready Ho W1 237 B3
Macready Pl 2 N7 72 A4
Macroom Ho W9 91 B4
Macroom Rd W9 91 B4
Mac's Pl EC4 241 B2
Madame Tussaud's* NW1 93 A3 238 A5
Madani Girls Sch 36 E1 96 B1
Mada Rd BR6 226 D5
Maddams St E3 97 D3
Madderfields Ct N11 31 D2
Maddison Cl
- Finchley N2 30 A1
- Teddington TW11 174 D4
Maddison Ct NW4 28 C1
Maddocks Cl DA14 191 A5
Maddocks Ho 3 E1 118 B6
Maddock Way SE17 138 D6
Maddox Ct 1 E4 20 B3
Maddox St W1 248 D6
Madeira Ave BR1 186 C3
Madeira Gr IG8 37 C4
Madeira Rd
- Edmonton N13 16 D1
- Leytonstone E11 54 C1
- Mitcham CR4 202 D5
- Streatham SW16 182 A5
Madeleine Cl RM6 58 C3
Madeleine Ct RM6 58 C3
Madeley Ct W5 88 A1
Madeley Rd W5 88 A1
Madeline Gr IG1 79 B3
Madeline Rd SE20 184 A3
Madge Gill Way 4 E6 100 A6
Madge Hill W7 108 C6
Madinah Rd
- 7 Dalston E8 74 A2
- London E8 74 A3
Madingley 11 KT1 176 C1
Madingley Ct TW1 153 C6
Madison Apartments N11 31 D3
Madison Cl SM2 218 B1
Madison Cres DA7 146 C5
Madison Ct 15 RM10 81 D2
Madison Gdns
- Beckenham BR2 208 D6
- Bexley DA7 146 C5
Madison Ho E3 98 A4
Madras Ho IG1 78 D4
Madras Pl N7 72 C2
Madras Rd IG1 78 D4
Madrid Rd SW13 134 A5
Madron St SE17 117 C1 263 B2
Mafeking Ave
- Brentford TW8 132 A6
- Ilford IG2 57 B2
- Newham E6 100 A5
Mafeking Rd
- Enfield EN1 5 D2
- Newham E16 98 D3
- Tottenham N17 34 A1
Magdala Ave N19 71 C6
Magdala Rd
- Isleworth TW7 131 A2
- South Croydon CR2 221 B1
Magdalen Ct SE25 206 A4
Magdalene Cl 7 SE15 140 B3
Magdalene Gdns
- 7 East Barnet N11 14 D3
- Newham E6 100 C3
Magdalene Ho 7 SW15 156 D5
Magdalene Rd TW17 192 B6
Magdalen Pas E1 253 D6
Magdalen Rd SW18 158 B3
Magdalen St SE1 253 A3
Magee St SE11 138 C6
Magellan Bvd E16 123 A6
Magellan Ct 11 NW10 67 B1
Magellan Ho 16 E1 96 D3
Magellan Pl 25 E14 119 C2
Magna Ct UB6 86 B4
Magnaville Rd WD23 8 D4
Magnetic Cres EN3 7 B6
Magnet Rd HA9 65 D6
Magnin Cl 5 E8 96 A6
Magnolia Cl
- Kingston u T KT2 176 D4
- Leyton E10 75 C6
Magnolia Ct
- 13 Belmont SM2 217 D1
- Feltham TW14 150 A3
- 2 Finchley N12 29 D6
- Forest Hill SE26 184 C5
- Harrow HA3 44 B2
- Hillingdon UB10 60 D2
- Northolt UB5 85 A3
- Richmond TW9 132 D4
- Wallington SM6 219 B3
- Wandsworth SW11 158 D5
Magnolia Gdns HA8 27 A6
Magnolia Ho 18 SE8 141 B6
Magnolia Lo E4 19 D1
Magnolia Pl
- Clapham Pk SW4 160 A6
- Ealing W5 87 D2
Magnolia Rd W4 132 D6
Magnolia Way KT19 215 A3
Magnolia Wharf W4 132 D6
Magpie Cl
- Edgware NW9 27 C1
- Enfield EN1 6 A4
- Forest Gate E7 76 D3
Magpie Hall Cl BR2 210 A3
Magpie Hall La BR2 210 B3
Magpie Hall Rd WD23 8 C2
Magpie Ho 7 E3 97 B6
Magpie Pl SE14 141 A6
Magri Wlk 22 E1 96 C2
Maguire Dr TW10 175 C6
Maguire St SE1 117 D4 253 D2
Mahatma Gandhi Ind Est 1 SE24 138 D1
Mahlon Ave HA4 62 B2
Mahogany Cl SE16 119 A5
Mahon Cl EN1 5 D4
Mahoney Ho SE14 141 B4
Maida Ave
- Chingford E4 19 D4
- Little Venice W2 92 A3 236 B5
Maida Rd DA17 125 C3
MAIDA VALE 91 D4
Maida Vale W9 92 A4 229 A1
Maida Vale Sta W9 91 D4
Maida Way E4 19 D4
Maiden Erlegh Ave DA5 169 A3
Maiden La
- Borough The SE1 117 A5 252 B4
- Camden Town NW1 71 D1
- Strand WC2 116 A6 250 B6
Maiden Rd E15 76 C1
Maidenstone Hill SE10 142 A4
Maids of Honour Row 4 TW9 153 D6
Maidstone Bldgs SE1 252 C3
Maidstone Ct N11 31 D4
Maidstone Ho 4 E14 97 D1
Maidstone Rd
- Friern Barnet N11 31 D4
- Ruxley DA14 191 C3
Mail Coach Yd 23 E2 95 C4
Main Ave EN1 17 D6
Main Dr HA9 65 D5
Main Rd
- Chislehurst BR5 190 C1
- Sidcup DA14 167 C1
Mainridge Rd BR7, SE9 188 C6
Main St TW13 172 D5
Mainwaring Ct 3 CR4 181 A1
Main Yd E9 75 C2
Mais Ho SE26 162 B2
Maismore St SE15 140 A6
Maison Alfort HA3 24 C2
Maisonettes The SM1 217 B3
Maitland Cl
- 3 Greenwich SE10 141 D5
- Hounslow TW4 129 B2
Maitland Ct W2 246 C6
Maitland Ho
- Chelsea SW1 269 A6
- 16 South Hackney E2 96 C5
MAITLAND PARK 70 D2
Maitland Park Rd NW3 70 D2
Maitland Park Villas NW3 70 D2
Maitland Pl E5 74 C4
Maitland Rd
- Penge SE26 184 D4
- Stratford E15 76 D2
Majendie Rd SE18 123 B1
Majestic Ct N4 50 D1
Majestic Way CR4 180 D1
Major Cl SW9 138 D2
Majorie Mews 6 E1 96 D1
Major Rd
- 22 Bermondsey SE16 118 A3
- Stratford New Town E15 76 B3
Makepeace Ave N6 71 A6
Makepeace Mans N6 71 A6
Makepeace Rd
- Northolt UB5 85 A6
- Wanstead E11 55 A5
Makinen Ho 5 IG9 21 C3
Makins St SW3 257 B3
Malabar Ct 20 W12 112 B6
Malabar St E14 119 C4
Malam Ct SE11 261 A3
Malam Gdns 3 E14 119 D6
Malatia CR2 221 A2
Malay Ho 2 E1 118 C5
Malborough Ho 3 N20 14 D1
Malbrook Rd SW15 134 B1
Malbury Ct N22 32 A3
Malcolm Cl SE20 184 C3
Malcolm Cres NW4 46 A3
Malcolm Ct Ealing W5 88 B3
- Hendon NW4 46 A3
- Stanmore HA7 25 C5
- Stratford E7 76 D2
Malcolm Dr KT6 198 A1
Malcolm Ho 13 N1 95 C5
Malcolm Pl E2 96 C3
Malcolm Prim Sch SE20 184 C3
Malcolm Rd
- Bethnal Green E1 96 C3
- Croydon SE25 206 A3
- Ickenham UB10 60 B4
- Penge SE20 184 C3
- Wimbledon SW19 179 A4
Malcolmson Ho SW1 259 D1
Malcolms Way N14 15 C6
Malcolm Way E11 55 A5
Malden Ave
- Croydon SE25 206 B6
- Northolt UB6 64 C2
Malden Cres NW1 71 A2
Malden Ct
- Stoke Newington N4 51 A3
- West Barnes KT3 200 B6
Malden Ctr The KT3 199 D5
Malden Green Ave KT4 200 A1
Malden Hill KT3 199 D6
Malden Hill Gdns KT3 199 D6
Malden Junc KT3 199 D4
Malden Manor Prim Sch KT3 199 C2
Malden Manor Sta KT3 199 C2
Malden Parochial Prim Sch KT4 199 C1
Malden Pk KT3 199 D3
Malden Pl NW5 71 A3
Malden Rd
- Camden Town NW5 71 A2
- Cheam KT4, SM3 216 D4
- New Malden KT3, KT4 199 D2
Malden Way KT3 200 A5
Malden Way (Kingston By-Pass) KT3, KT5 199 C4
Maldon Cl
- Camberwell SE5 139 C2
- Shoreditch N1 235 B6
- Stratford New Town E15 76 B3
Maldon Ct
- Barking E6 100 C6
- Wallington SM6 219 C3
Maldon Rd Acton W3 111 A6
- Edmonton N9 17 D1
- Wallington SM6 219 B3
Maldon Wlk IG8 37 C4
Malet Pl WC1 239 C5
Malet St WC1 93 D2 239 D4
Maley Ave SE27 160 D2
Malford Ct E18 37 A1
Malford Gr E18 54 D6
Malfort Rd SE5 139 C2
Malham Cl N11 31 A4
Malham Rd SE23 162 D3
Malham Road Ind Est SE23 162 D3
Malindi Ct N8 49 D4
Malins Cl EN5 12 C6
Malins Ct SW12 159 A5
Mallaig Ct HA8 10 D2
Mallams Mews 1 SW9 138 D2
Mallard Cl
- 1 Hackney E9 75 B2
- Hanwell W7 108 C4
- Kilburn NW6 91 C6
- New Barnet EN5 14 B5
- Twickenham TW4 151 C4
Mallard Ct
- Chingford E4 20 B4
- Ilford IG1 79 A6
- Kingsbury NW9 45 A2
- Little Ilford E12 78 B3
- 16 Richmond TW10 153 D5
- Walthamstow E17 54 B6
Mallard Ho
- 8 Camberwell SE15 139 D4
- St John's Wood NW8 230 A3
Mallard Path 3 SE28 123 B3
Mallard Pl TW1 153 A1
Mallard Point 6 E3 97 C4
Mallards E11 55 A2
Mallards Rd
- Barking IG11 102 A3
- Woodford IG8 37 B3
Mallard Way NW9 45 A2
Mallard Wlk
- Beckenham BR3 206 D4
- Sidcup DA14 190 C4
Mall Ct W5 110 A6
Mallet Dr UB5 63 B3
Mallet Ho 11 SW15 156 A6
Mallet Rd SE13 164 B5
Mall Galleries* SW1 249 D4
Malling SE13 163 D6
Malling Cl CR0 206 C3
Malling Gdns SM4 202 A3
Malling Ho 9 BR3 185 C3
Malling Way BR2 208 D2
Mallinson Ct 2 E11 76 C6
Mallinson Rd
- Wallington SM6 219 D5
- Wandsworth SW11 158 D6
Mallinson Sp Ctr N6 48 D2
Mallon Gdns E1 243 D3
Mallord St SW3 136 B6 266 D6
Mallory Bldgs EC1 241 C5
Mallory Cl
- London SE4 141 A1
- South Bromley E14 98 C3
Mallory Gdns EN4 15 A4
Mallory St NW8 92 C3 237 B6
Mallow Cl CR0 206 D1
Mallow Ct
- Colney Hatch N12 30 C4
- Lewisham SE13 142 A3
Mallow Mead NW7 29 A3
Mallow St EC1 242 C6
Mallows The UB10 60 D5
Mall Rd W6 112 B1
Mall Sh Ctr The RM10 81 C2
Mall Studios 9 NW3 70 D3
Mall The
- 6 Bexley DA6 147 C1
- Brentford TW8 131 D6
- 4 Bromley BR1 209 A6
- Ealing W5 110 A6
- Harrow HA3 44 B3
- Kingston u T KT6 197 D4
- Mortlake SW14 155 A6
- Palmers Green N14 16 A1
- St James SW1 115 D5 249 C3
Mall The N22 32 C1
Mall The (Sch) TW2 152 B1
Malmains Cl BR3 208 B5
Malmains Way BR3 208 B5
Malmesbury 30 E2 96 C5
Malmesbury Cl HA5 40 A5
Malmesbury Prim Sch
- Morden SM4 202 A3
- 25 Tower Hamlets E3 97 B4
Malmesbury Rd
- Bow E3 97 B5
- Morden SM4 202 A3
- Newham E16 98 C2
- Woodford E18 36 D2
Malmesbury Terr E16 98 D2
Malmsey Ho SE11 260 D2
Malmsmead Ho E9 75 A3
Malorees Jun & Inf Schs NW6 68 D1
Malory Cl BR3 185 A1
Malpas Dr HA5 40 D4
Malpas Rd
- Dagenham RM9 80 D2
- Hackney E8 74 B2
- New Cross SE4 141 B3
Malta Rd E10 53 C2
Malta St EC1 241 D6
Maltby Dr EN1 6 B5
Maltby Rd KT9 214 C2
Maltby St SE1 117 D3 263 C6
Maltham Terr N18 34 B4
Malthouse Dr
- Chiswick W4 133 D6
- Feltham TW13 172 D5
Malthouse Pas SW13 133 C3
Malthus Path 7 SE28 124 C5
Malting Ho E14 119 B6
Maltings W4 110 C1
Maltings Cl
- Barnes SW13 133 C3
- South Bromley E3 98 C3
Maltings Lo W4 133 C5
Maltings Pl
- Bermondsey SE1 253 B2
- Parsons Green SW6 265 D1
Maltings The BR6 211 D1
Malting Way TW7 130 D2
Malt Mill SE1 253 C3
Malton Ho SE25 205 C5
Malton Mews
- 1 Notting Hill W10 91 A1
- Plumstead Comm SE18 145 C6
Malton Rd W10 91 A1
Malton St SE18 145 C6
Maltravers St WC2 251 A6
Malt St SE1 140 A6
Malva Cl SW18 157 D6
Malvern Ave
- Chingford E4 36 B3
- Erith DA7 147 A5
- Harrow HA2 63 B5

Malvern Cl
Bushey WD23 8 A5
Ickenham UB10 60 C6
Mitcham CR4 203 C6
Notting Hill W10 91 B2
Penge SE20 184 A1
Surbiton KT6 198 A1
Malvern Ct
Belmont SM2 217 C1
5 East Barnet N20 14 C2
15 Shepherd's Bush W12 112 A4
South Kensington SW7 256 D4
3 Surbiton KT6 198 A1
Malvern Dr
Feltham TW13 172 D5
Ilford IG3 79 D4
Woodford IG8 37 C6
Malvern Gdns
Cricklewood NW2 69 A6
Harrow HA3 44 A5
Malvern Ho
London N16 51 D1
SE17 262 B1
Malvern Lo N12 30 B6
Malvern Mews NW6 91 C4
Malvern Pl NW6 91 B4
Malvern Rd
Dalston E8 74 A1
Enfield EN3 7 A6
Hampton TW12 173 C3
Harlington UB3 127 C5
Hornsey N8 50 C6
Leytonstone E11 76 D6
Maida Vale NW6 91 C4
Newham E6 100 A6
Surbiton KT6 198 A1
Thornton Heath CR7 204 C5
Tottenham Hale N17 52 A6
Upper Holloway N19 49 D1
Malvern Terr
Edmonton N9 17 D3
Islington N1 234 A6
Malvern Way W13 87 B2
Malwood Rd SW12 159 B5
Malyons Rd SE13 163 D6
Malyons Terr SE13 163 D6
Malyons The TW17 193 B3
Managers St 8 E14 120 A5
Manatee Pl SM6 219 D5
Manaton Cl SE15 140 B2
Manaton Cres UB1 85 C1
Manbey Gr E15 76 C2
Manbey Park Rd E15 76 C2
Manbey Rd E15 76 C2
Manbey St E15 76 C2
Manbre Rd W6 134 C6
Manbrough Ave E6 100 C4
Manchester Ct E16 99 B1
Manchester Dr W10 91 A3
Manchester Gr E14 120 A1
Manchester Ho SE17 262 B2
Manchester Mans N19 49 D2
Manchester Mews W1 238 A3
Manchester Rd
Cubitt Town E14 120 A3
South Norwood CR7 205 A6
Tottenham N15 51 B3
Manchester Sq W1 93 A1 238 B2
Manchester St W1 93 A2 238 A3
Manchester Way RM10 81 D4
Manchuria Rd SW11 159 A5
Manciple St SE1 117 B3 262 D6
Mandalay Ho 6 N16 73 B4
Mandalay Rd SW4 159 C6
Mandarin Ct
6 Deptford SE8 141 C6
Willesden NW10 67 B2
Mandarin Way UB4 84 D1
Mandela Cl
36 Shepherd's Bush W12 112 B6
Stonebridge NW10 67 A1
Mandela Ho
Plumstead Comm SE18 145 B6
18 Spitalfields E2 95 D4
Mandela Rd E16 99 A1
Mandela St
Camden Town NW1 93 C6 232 B6
Kennington SW9 138 C5
Mandela Way SE1 117 C2 263 B4
Manderville Ho SE1 263 D2
Mandeville Cl
5 Greenwich SE3 142 D5
Merton SW19 179 A2
Mandeville Ct
Hampstead NW3 69 D3
Highams Pk E4 35 A6
Mandeville Ctyd SW11 268 A1
Mandeville Dr KT6 197 D1
Mandeville Ho 8 SW4 159 C6
Mandeville Pl W1 238 B2
Mandeville Prim Sch E5 74 D5
Mandeville Rd
Enfield EN3 7 A6
Isleworth TW7 131 A3
Littleton TW17 192 C4
Northolt UB5 63 C1
Osidge N14 15 C2
Mandeville Sch UB5 63 B2
Mandeville St E5 75 A5
Mandrake Rd SW17 158 D1
Mandrake Way 3 E15 76 C1
Mandrell Rd SW2 160 A6
Manesty Ct N14 15 D4
Manette St W1 239 D1
Manfred Ct 7 SW15 157 B6
Manfred Rd SW15 157 B6
Manger Rd N7 72 A2
Mangold Way 4 DA18 125 A3
Manilla Ct RM6 58 B3
Manilla St E14 119 C4
Manister Rd SE2 124 A3
Manitoba Ct 29 SE16 118 C4
Manitoba Gdns 6 BR6 227 D2
Manley Ct N16 73 D5
Manley Ho SE11 261 A2
Manley St NW1 231 A6
Manly Dixon Dr EN3 7 A6
Mann Cl 3 CR0 221 A5
Manneby Prior N1 233 D3
Mannering Ho 16 SW2 160 B6
Manning Ct 3 SE28 124 B5
Manningford Cl EC1 234 C2
Manning Gdns
Croydon CR0 206 B2
Harrow HA3 43 D2
Manning Ho
3 Notting Hill W11 91 A1
6 Walthamstow E17 54 A6
Manning Pl TW10 154 B5
Manning Rd
Dagenham RM10 81 C1
Walthamstow E17 53 A4
Manningtree Cl SW19 157 A3
Manningtree Rd HA4 62 B4
Manningtree St 2 E1 96 A1
Mannin Rd RM6 58 B2
Mannock Cl NW9 45 B6
Mannock Mews IG8 37 B2
Mannock Rd N22 50 D6
Mann's Cl TW7 152 D6
Manns Rd HA8 26 C4
Manny Shinwell Ho SW6 264 D5
Manoel Rd TW2 152 A2
Manor Ave
Hounslow TW4 128 D3
New Cross SE4 141 B3
Northolt UB5 63 B1
Manorbrook SE12, SE3 143 A1
Manor Circus TW9 132 C2
Manor Cl Barnet EN5 1 A1
Edgware NW7 27 B5
Higham Hill E17 35 A1
Kingsbury NW9 44 D4
New Malden KT4 199 C1
Ruislip HA4 39 D1
Thamesmead SE28 102 C1
Manor Cottages App N2 30 A1
Manor Cotts N2 30 A1
Manor Court Lo 12 E18 37 A2
Manor Court Rd W7 108 C6
Manor Cres KT5 198 C3
Manor Croft HA8 26 C4
Manor Ct
4 Barking IG11 79 D1
7 Brixton SW2 160 B6
Camberwell SE15 139 D4
Chingford E4 20 C3
Fortis Green N2 48 D4
Friern Barnet N20 14 D1
Gunnersbury W3 110 C2
5 Hackbridge SM6 219 A5
Harrow HA1 42 D3
Kingston u T KT2 176 C2
Osidge N14 15 D2
Parsons Green SW6 265 D1
Streatham SW16 160 A1
Surbiton KT5 198 C3
8 Sutton SM1 218 A4
Twickenham TW2 152 A2
Walthamstow E10 53 D1
5 Wembley HA9 66 A3
Manordene Cl KT7 197 A1
Manordene Rd SE28 102 D1
Manor Dr
East Barnet N14 15 B3
Edgware NW7 27 B5
Feltham TW13 172 D5
Friern Barnet N20 14 D1
Hinchley Wood KT10 213 A5
Sunbury TW16 172 A1
Surbiton KT5 198 C3
Wembley HA9 66 B4
West Ewell KT19 215 C2
Manor Dr N KT3, KT4 199 B2
Manor Dr The KT4 199 D1
Manor Farm Ave TW17 192 D3
Manor Farm Cl KT4 199 C1
Manor Farm Ct E6 100 B4
Manor Farm Dr E4 20 C1
Manor Farm Rd
Thornton Heath CR7, SW16 182 C1
Wembley HA0 87 D5
Manorfield Cl 3 N19 71 C4
Manorfield Prim Sch 8 E14 97 D2
Manorfields Cl BR7 211 D6
Manor Gate UB5 63 A1
Manorgate Rd KT2 176 C2
Manor Gdns
8 Chiswick W4 111 C1
Clapham SW4 137 C3
Gunnersbury W3 110 C2
Hampton TW12 174 A3
Merton SW20 179 B1
Richmond TW10, TW9 132 B1
Ruislip HA4 62 C3
South Croydon CR2 221 D2
Sunbury TW16 172 A1
Upper Holloway N7 72 A5
Manor Gr
Beckenham BR3 185 D1
Deptford SE15 140 C6
Richmond TW9 132 C2
Manor Gt SW15 157 A6
Manor Hall Ave NW4 28 D1
Manor Hall Dr NW4 28 D1
Manor Hall Gdns E10 53 C1
Manor Ho
Brentford TW8 109 C1
Manor Pk E12 77 D4
Osidge N14 15 D3
Paddington NW1 237 B4
Twickenham TW2 152 C2
Wallington SM6 219 B3
Manor Ho The
Bexley DA5 169 D3
Chislehurst SE9 188 A5
Manor House Ct
Lower Halliford TW17 192 D2
Paddington W9 236 A5
Manor House Dr NW6 68 D1
Manor House Est HA7 25 B5
Manor House Gdns E11 55 B3
Manor House Sta N4 50 D1
Manor House Way TW7 131 B2
Manor Jun & Inf Schs IG11 79 D2
Manor La
Feltham TW13 150 A2
Harlington UB3 127 B6
Hither Green SE12 164 C5
Sunbury TW16 172 B1
Sutton SM1 218 A3
Manor Lane Terr SE13 164 C6
Manor Lo NW2 68 D2
Manor Mans
7 Hampstead NW3 70 C2
Tufnell Pk N7 72 A5
Manor Mead Sch TW17 192 D4
Manor Mews
New Cross SE4 141 B3
Paddington NW6 91 C5
Manor Mount SE23 162 C3
Manor Oak Mans SE22 162 B5
Manor Par
Harrow HA1 42 D3
Stoke Newington N16 73 D6
MANOR PARK 78 A4
Manor Park Cl BR4 207 D1
Manor Park Cres HA8 26 C4
Manor Park Dr HA2 41 D6
Manor Park Gdns HA8 26 C4
Manor Park Par SE13 142 B1
Manor Park Prim Sch 8 SM1 218 A3
Manor Park Rd
Chislehurst BR7 189 B2
Dagenham NW10 89 D6
East Finchley N2 48 B6
Manor Pk E12 77 D4
Sutton SM1 218 A3
West Wickham BR4 207 D1
Manor Park Sta E12 77 D4
Manor Pk
Chislehurst BR7 189 B2
Lewisham SE13 164 C6
Richmond TW9 132 B1
Manor Pl
Chislehurst BR7 189 B1
East Bedfont TW14 150 A3
Mitcham CR4 203 C6
Newington SE17 117 A1 262 A2
Sutton SM1 217 D4
Walton-on-T KT12 194 A2
Manor Prim Sch E15 98 C5
Manor Rd
Ashford TW15 170 C5
Barking IG11 79 D2
Barnet EN5 1 A1
Beckenham BR3 185 D1
Belmont SM2 217 B1
Bowes Pk N22 32 A4
Dagenham RM6 58 D3
Ealing W13 109 A6
East Molesey KT8 196 B5
Enfield EN2 5 B3
Harrow HA1 43 A3
Hayes UB3 84 A1
Higham Hill E17 35 A1
Loughton IG10 21 B5
Merton SW20 179 B1
Mitcham CR4 203 C6
Newham E15, E16 98 C4
Old Bexley DA5 169 D3
Richmond TW10, TW9 132 B1
Ruislip HA4 39 B1
Sidcup DA15 168 A1
South Norwood SE25 206 A6
Stamford Hill N16 51 C1
Teddington TW11 175 B5
Tottenham N17 34 B2
Twickenham TW2 152 B2
Wallington SM5, SM6 219 B3
Walthamstow E10 53 C2
Walton-on-T KT12 193 D2
West Wickham BR4 223 D6
Manor Rd N
Hinchley Wood KT7 213 A6
Wallington SM5, SM6 219 B4
Manor Rd S KT10 212 C4
Manor Road Ho HA1 43 A3
Manorside EN5 1 A1
Manorside Cl SE2 124 D2
Manorside Prim Sch N3 30 A2
Manor Specl Sch NW10 90 C6
Manor Sq RM8 80 C6
Manor Street Est SW3 267 B6
Manor The
Dulwich SE23 162 C4
Mayfair W1 248 C5
Manor Vale TW8 109 C1
Manor View N3 29 D1
Manorway Enfield EN1 17 C4
Woodford IG8 37 C5
Manor Way
Beckenham BR3 207 C6
Bromley BR2 210 A3
Chingford E4 36 B6
Colindale NW9 45 C5
Greenwich SE3 143 A1
Gunnersbury W3 110 C2
Harrow HA2 41 D5
Mitcham CR4 203 C6
New Malden KT4 199 D1
Orpington BR5 211 A5
Ruislip HA4 39 D1
Sidcup DA5 169 C3
Southall UB2 106 D2
South Croydon CR2 221 D2
Manor Waye UB8 82 A6
Manor Way The SM6 219 B4
Manpreet Ct E12 78 B3
Manray Ct 2 N8 50 A4
Manresa Rd SW3 114 C1 257 A1
Mansard Beeches SW17 181 A5
Mansard Cl HA5 40 D6
Mansard Manor 4 SM2 218 A1
Manse Cl UB3 127 B6
Manse Ct DA14 190 C5
Mansel Ct SW11 267 B1
Mansel Gr E17 35 C2
Mansell Ho SW8 269 B2
Mansell Rd
Acton W3 111 B4
Southall UB6 85 D2
Mansell St E1 95 D1 243 D1
Mansel Rd SW19 179 B4
Manse Rd N16 73 D5
Mansergh Cl SE18 144 A5
Mansfield Ave
East Barnet EN4 15 A5
Ruislip HA4 40 B1
Tottenham N15 51 B5
Mansfield Cl N9 18 A5
Mansfield Ct 27 E2 95 D6
Mansfield Dr UB4 83 C3
Mansfield Hill E4 19 D3
Mansfield Ho SW15 156 D5
Mansfield Hts N2 48 D4
Mansfield Mews W1 238 C3
Mansfield Pl 28 NW3 70 A4
Mansfield Rd
Acton W3 88 D3
Chessington KT9 213 D3
Ilford IG1 78 C6
Maitland Pk NW3 70 D4
South Croydon CR2 221 B2
Walthamstow E17 53 B5
Wanstead E11 55 B3
Mansfield St W1 93 B2 238 C3
Mansford St E2 96 A5
Manship Rd CR4 181 A2
Mansion Cl SW9 138 C4
Mansion Gdns NW3 69 D5
Mansion Ho* EC4 242 C1
Mansion House Pl EC3, EC4 242 C1
Mansion House St EC2 242 C1
Mansion House Sta EC4 117 A6 252 B6
Mansions The NW6 69 B3
Manson Mews SW7 114 B2 256 C3
Manson Pl SW7 114 B2 256 C3
Manstead Gdns RM6 58 C2

Manston
Camden Town NW1 71 C1
Tottenham N17 33 B1
Manston Ave UB2 107 C2
Manston Cl SE20 184 C2
Manstone Rd NW2 69 A3
Manston Gr KT2 175 D5
Manston Ho W14 254 B5
Mantell Ho SW4 159 C6
Manthorpe Rd SE18 123 A1
Mantilla Rd SW17 181 A6
Mantle Rd SE4 141 A2
Mantlet Cl SW16 181 C3
Mantle Way E15 76 C1
Manton Ave W7 109 A4
Manton Cl UB3 105 C6
Manton Ho N16 73 B5
Manton Rd
Holdbrook EN3 7 C5
Plumstead SE2 124 A2
Mantua St 22 SW11 136 B2
Mantus Cl
Bethnal Green E1 96 C3
19 Stepney E1 96 C3
Mantus Rd E1 96 C3
Manus Way N20 14 A3
Manville Gdns SW17 159 B1
Manville Rd SW17 159 B1
Manwood Rd SE4 163 B5
Manwood St E16 122 B5
Manygate La TW17 193 A3
Many Gates SW12 159 B2
Mapesbury Ct NW2 69 A3
Mapesbury Mews 1 NW9 46 A3
Mapesbury Rd NW2 69 A2
Mapeshill Pl NW2 68 C2
Mapes Ho 7 NW6 69 A1
Mape St E2 96 B3
Maple Ave
East Acton W3 111 C5
Harrow HA2 63 D6
Walthamstow E4 35 B4
Yiewsley UB7 104 B6
Maple Cl
Buckhurst Hill IG9 21 D1
Clapham Pk SW4 159 D5
Finchley N3 29 C4
Hampton TW12 173 B4
Hayes UB4 84 D4
Mitcham CR4 181 B2
Petts Wood BR5 211 B4
Ruislip HA4 40 B3
South Tottenham N16 52 A3
Maple Cres DA15 168 A5
Maplecroft Cl E6 100 A1
Maple Ct
Ashford TW15 171 B3
Catford SE6 163 D3
2 Croydon CR0 221 A4
7 Dagenham RM8 58 D2
Kingston u T KT3 199 B6
Newham E6 100 C2
6 Pinner HA5 22 C1
Sidcup DA14 190 B5
11 West Norwood SW16 182 C5
3 Willesden NW2 68 D4
Mapledale Ave CR0 222 A5
Mapledene BR7 189 A5
Mapledene Est E8 74 A1
Mapledene Rd E8 74 A1
Mapledown Sch NW2 46 C2
Mapledurham Ct 3 N13 32 C6
Maple Gdns
Grahame Pk HA8 27 C3
Stanwell TW19 148 A2
Maple Gr
Brentford TW8 131 B5
Ealing W5 109 D3
Kingsbury NW9 45 A2
Southall UB1 85 B2
Maple Gr Bsns Ctr TW4 128 C1
Maple Ho
2 Kingston u T KT6 198 A4
11 Maitland Pk NW3 70 D2
5 New Cross SE8 141 B5
4 Richmond TW9 132 D4
Teddington KT1 175 C3
13 Walthamstow E17 53 D6
Maple House Ind Montessori Sch 3 CR7 205 A6
Maplehurst 2 BR2 186 C1
Maplehurst Cl KT1 198 A5
Maple Ind Est TW13 150 A1
Maple Inf Sch KT6 197 D4
Maple Leaf Dr DA15 167 D3
Mapleleafe Gdns IG6 56 D6
Maple Leaf Sq 27 SE16 118 D4
Maple Lo
Buckhurst Hill IG9 21 D3
Putney SW15 157 A5
Welsh Harp NW9 67 B6
Maple Mews
Paddington NW6 91 D5
Streatham SW16 182 B5
Maple Pl
Marylebone W1 239 B5
3 Tottenham N17 34 A3
Yiewsley UB7 104 B6
Maple Rd Hayes UB4 84 D4
Kingston u T KT6 197 D4
Leytonstone E11 54 C3
Penge SE20 184 C2
Maples Pl E1 96 B2
Maple St
5 Bethnal Green E2 96 B5
Fitzrovia W1 93 C3 239 B5
Maplestead Rd
Dagenham RM9 102 B6
Streatham SW2 160 B4
Maples The 4 KT1 175 C3
Maplethorpe Rd CR7 204 D5
Mapleton Cl BR2 209 A3
Mapleton Cres
Enfield EN3 6 C5
Wandsworth SW18 157 D5
Mapleton Rd
Chingford E4 20 A1
Enfield EN1 6 B3
Wandsworth SW18 157 D5
Maple Tree Pl 7 SE3 144 A4
Maple Way TW13 150 B1
Maple Wlk W10 90 D3
Maplin Cl N21 16 B5
Maplin Ho 7 SE2 124 D4
Maplin Rd E16 99 B1
Maplin St E3 97 B4
Mapperley Cl 3 E11 55 A3
Mapperley Dr IG8 36 C3
Marabou Cl E12 78 A3
Marada Ho NW6 69 A1
Marais W4 133 A5
Maran Way DA18 124 D3
Marathon Way SE28 123 D4
Marban Rd W9 91 B4
Marble Arch★ W1 114 D6 247 D6
Marble Arch Sta W1 92 D1 237 D1
Marble Cl W3 110 D5
Marble Dr NW2 46 D2
Marbleford Ct 4 N6 49 D2
Marble Hill Cl TW1 153 B4
Marble Hill Gdns TW1 153 B4
Marble Hill House★ TW1 153 C4
Marble Ho
Paddington W9 91 B3
Plumstead Comm SE18 123 D1
Marble Quay SE1 118 A5
Marbrook Ct SE12 165 C1
Marcella Rd SW9 138 C3
Marcellina Way BR6 227 D5
March 23 NW9 27 D2
Marchant Cl NW7 27 C3
Marchant Ho 13 SW2 160 B6
Marchant Rd E11 76 B6
Marchant St SE14 141 A6
Marchbank Rd W14 135 B6 264 D6
March Ct SW15 134 B1
Marchmont Ho 10 SW16 181 C5
Marchmont Rd
Richmond TW10 154 B6
Wallington SM6 219 C1
Marchmont St WC1 94 A3 240 A6
March Rd 7 TW1 153 A4
Marchside Cl TW5 128 D4
Marchwood Cl 9 SE5 139 C5
Marchwood Cres W5 87 D1
Marcia Rd SE1 117 C2 263 B3
Marcilly Rd SW18 158 B6
Marcol Ho W1 238 D2
Marcon Ct 29 E8 74 B3
Marconi Pl N11 31 B6
Marconi Rd E10 53 C1
Marconi Way UB1 85 D1
Marcon Pl E8 74 B3
Marco Rd W6 112 C3
Marcourt Lawns W5 88 A3
Marcus Ct
Brentford TW8 132 A5
Newham E15 98 C6
Marcus Garvey Mews SE22 162 B6
Marcus Garvey Way 9 SE24 138 C1
Marcus Ho 14 SE15 139 D4
Marcus St
Wandsworth SW18 157 D5
West Ham E15 98 D6
Marcus Terr SW18 157 D5
Mardale Ct NW7 28 A3
Mardale Dr NW9 45 B4
Mardell Rd CR0 206 D4
Marden Ave BR2 209 A3
Marden Cres CR0 204 B3
Marden Ho 6 E8 74 B3
Marden Rd
Thornton Heath CR0 204 B3
Tottenham N17 33 C1
Marden Sq SE16 118 B3
Marder Rd W13 109 A4
Mardon HA5 23 B3
Mardyke Ho SE17 262 D4
Marechal Niel Ave DA15 167 B1
Marechal Niel Par DA15 167 B1
Maresby Ho E4 19 D2
Maresfield CR0 221 C5
Maresfield Gdns NW3 70 A2
Mare St E8 74 B1
Marey Ct 10 CR2 221 A3
Marfleet Cl SM5 218 C6
Margaret Ave E4 19 D5
Margaret Bondfield Ave IG11 80 A1
Margaret Bondfield Ho
5 Bow E3 97 A5
22 Kentish Town N7 71 D3
Margaret Ct Barnet EN4 2 B1
Marylebone W1 239 A2
Margaret Gardner Dr SE9 166 B2
Margaret Herbison Ho SW6 264 D5
Margaret Hill Ho 1 N8 50 A4
Margaret Ho
16 Hammersmith W6 112 C1
2 Sutton SM1 217 D5
Margaret Ingram Cl SW6 264 C5
Margaret Lockwood Cl KT5 198 B5
Margaret Mcmillan Ho 10 N19 49 D2
Margaret Rd
Barnet EN4 2 B1
Bexley DA5 168 D5
Stamford Hill N16 51 D1
Margaret Rutherford Pl 3 SW12 159 C3
Margarets Ct HA8 26 D5
Margaret's Ct E11 54 B2
Margaret St W1 93 C1 239 A2
Margaretta Terr SW3 136 C6 267 B6
Margaretting Rd E12 55 C1
Margaret Way IG4 56 A3
Margaret White Ho NW1 232 C2
Margate Rd SW2 160 A6
Margery Fry Ct N7 72 A5
Margery Park Rd E7 77 A2
Margery Rd RM8 80 D5
Margery St WC1 94 C4 234 A1
Margin Dr SW19 178 D6
Margravine Gdns
Hammersmith W6 112 D1
West Kensington W14 254 A2
Margravine Rd W6 135 A6 264 A6
Marham Dr 17 NW9 27 C2
Marham Gdns
Morden SM4 202 A3
Wandsworth SW17, SW18 158 C3
Mar Ho 4 SE7 143 C6
Maria Cl 18 SE1 118 A2
Maria Fidelis Convent Sch (Lower) NW1 93 C4 232 B1
Maria Fidelis Convent Sch (Upper) NW1 93 D4 232 C2
Marian Cl UB4 84 D3
Marian Ct Hackney E9 74 C3
1 Sutton SM1 217 D3
Marian Lo 5 SW20 178 D3
Marian Pl E2 96 B5
Marian Rd SW16 181 C2
Marian Sq E2 96 B5
Marian St 2 E2 96 B5
Marian Vian Prim Sch BR3 207 A4
Marian Way NW10 67 D1
Maria Terr E1 96 D3
Maria Theresa Cl KT3 199 B4
Maribor 13 SE10 142 A5
Maricas Ave HA3 24 B2
Marie Curie SE5 139 C4
Marie Lloyd Ct 13 SW9 138 B1
Marie Lloyd Gdns 1 N19 50 A2
Marie Lloyd Ho N1 235 C3
Marien Ct E4 36 B5
Marie Stopes Ct 3 N19 50 A2
Marigold Cl UB1 107 A6
Marigold Rd N17 34 C3
Marigold St SE16 118 B4
Marigold Way CR0 206 D1
Marilea Ct W5 109 D4
Marillic Ho NW7 28 C6
Marina App UB4 85 A2
Marina Ave KT3 200 B4
Marina Cl 1 BR2 209 A6
Marina Ct 12 Bow E3 97 C4
Greenford UB6 85 D5
Marina Dr DA16 145 C3
Marina Gdns RM7 59 D4
Marina Pl KT1 175 D2
Marina Point 4 E14 119 D3
Marina Way TW11 175 D3
Marine Dr
Barking IG11 102 B4
5 Woolwich SE18 122 B2
Marinefield Rd SW6 135 D3
Marinel Ho 25 SE5 139 A5
Mariner Gdns TW10 153 C1
Mariner Rd E12 78 C4
Mariners Mews E14 120 B2
Marine St SE16 118 A3
Marine Twr 29 SE8 141 B6
Marion Ave TW17 192 D4
Marion Ct 4 SW17 180 C5
Marion Gr IG8 36 C6
Marion Rd
Mill Hill NW7 28 A5
Thornton Heath CR0 205 B4
Marion Richardson Prim Sch 17 E1 96 D1
Marischal Rd SE13 142 B2
Maritime Greenwich Coll 18 SE8 141 C5
Maritime Ho
5 Clapham SW4 137 C2
14 Woolwich SE18 122 D2
Maritime Ind Est SE7 121 B2
Maritime Quay 5 E14 119 C1
Maritime St E3 97 B3
Marius Mans 3 SW17 159 A2
Marius Rd SW17 159 A2
Marjorie Gr SW11 136 D1
Marjorie McClure Sch BR7 189 A2
Marjory Kinnon Sch TW14 149 C6
Markab Rd HA6 22 A5
Mark Ave E4 19 D5
Mark Cl
Bexleyheath DA7 147 A4
Keston Mark BR2 226 A4
Southall UB1 107 D5
Markeston Gn WD19 22 D6
Market Ct W1 239 A2
Market Ctr The UB2 106 B2
Market La
Burnt Oak HA8 27 A2
Shepherd's Bush W12 112 C4
Market Mews W1 115 B5 248 C3
Market Par
Croydon SE25 206 A5
1 Edmonton N9 18 A2
Feltham TW13 151 A2
Leyton E10 53 D3
Walthamstow E17 53 B6
Market Pavilion E10 75 C5
Market Pl
3 Acton W3 111 A5
1 Bermondsey SE16 118 B2
2 Bexleyheath DA6 147 C1
Brentford TW8 131 C5
East Finchley N2 48 C6
Enfield EN2 5 B2
Kingston u T KT1 175 D1
Marylebone W1 239 A2
Market Pl The NW11 47 D5
Market Rd
Barnsbury N7 72 A2
Richmond TW9 132 C2
Market Sq
Bromley BR1 187 A1
Poplar E14 97 D1
Market Sq The N9 18 B2
Market St
Spitalfields E1 243 C4
Wallend E6 100 C5
Woolwich SE18 122 C2
Market Studios 14 W12 112 C4
Market The SM1, SM5 202 A1
Market Way
Poplar E14 97 D1
2 Wembley HA0 66 A3
Market Yd Mews SE1 263 A6
Markfield Beam Engine & Mus★ N15 52 A4
Markfield Gdns E4 19 D4
Markfield Ho N15 52 A4
Markfield Rd N15 52 A4
Markham Ct NW4 46 C6
Markham Ho
1 Dagenham RM10 81 C5
9 Dulwich SE21 183 C6
Markham Pl SW3 257 C2
Markham Sq SW3 114 D1 257 C2
Markham St SW3 114 C1 257 B2
Mark Ho 3 E2 96 D5
Markhole Cl TW12 173 B3
Markhouse Ave E17 53 A3
Markhouse Pas E17 53 B3
Markhouse Rd E17 53 B3
Mark La EC3 117 C6 253 B6
Markland Ho W10 112 D6
Mark Lo 9 EN4 2 C1
Markmanor Ave E17 53 B2
Mark Mans W12 112 A4
Mark Rd N22 32 D1
Marksbury Ave TW9 132 C2
Marks Gate Jun & Inf Schs RM6 59 A6
Mark Sq EC2 243 A6
Mark St
Broadgate EC2 243 A6
Stratford E15 76 C1
Markstone Ho SE1 251 C1
Mark Wade Cl E12 55 D1
Markway The TW16 172 C1
Markwell Cl SE26 184 B6
Markyate Ho 6 W10 90 C3
Markyate Rd RM8 80 B3
Marland Ho SW1 257 D6
Marlands Rd IG5 56 B6
Marlang Ct BR3 186 B2

Marlborough
11 Putney SW19 . . . . 156 D3
St John's Wood W9 . . 229 A2
Marlborough Ave
Edgware HA8. . . . . 10 D1
3 Hackney E8. . . . . 96 A6
New Southgate N14. . . . 15 C1
Ruislip HA4 . . . . 39 B3
Marlborough Cl
Broom Hill BR6. . . . . . 211 D3
Friern Barnet N20 . . . . . 14 D1
Mitcham SW19 . . . . . 180 C4
Newington SE17 . . . . . 261 D3
Marlborough Cres
Bedford Pk W4. . . . . . 111 C3
Harlington UB3 . . . . . . 127 B5
Marlborough Ct
6 Beckenham BR3 . . . 185 C2
7 Bromley BR1. . . . . . 186 D3
7 Buckhurst Hill IG9 . . 21 C2
Harrow HA1. . . . . 42 B5
Kensington W8. . . . . . 255 A4
Marylebone W1 . . . . . 239 A1
Wallington SM6 . . . . . 219 C1
Marlborough Dr IG5 . . 56 A6
Marlborough Flats
SW3 . . . . 257 B4
Marlborough Fst & Mid Sch HA1 . . . . 42 C5
Marlborough Gdns
Friern Barnet N20 . . . . . 14 D1
Surbiton KT6 . . . . 197 D2
Marlborough Gr
SE1. . . . . 118 A1
Marlborough Hill
Harrow HA1. . . . . 42 C5
St John's Wood
NW8 . . . . 92 A6 229 B5
Marlborough Ho
Marylebone NW1. . . . 238 D6
Richmond TW10. . . . . . 154 C6
Stoke Newington N4 . . . 51 A1
Marlborough Ho
SW1. . . . . 249 B3
Marlborough Ho
SW19. . . . . 156 D1
Marlborough La
SE7. . . . . 143 C5
Marlborough Lo
36 Stepney E1 . . . . 96 C3
St John's Wood NW8 . 229 A3
Marlborough Mans 5
NW6. . . . . 69 C3
Marlborough Mews 18
SW2. . . . . 138 B1
Marlborough Par 1
UB10. . . . . 82 D3
Marlborough Park Ave
DA15. . . . . 168 A3
Marlborough Pl
NW8. . . . . 92 A5 229 B4
Marlborough Prim Sch
Chelsea
SW3 . . . . . . 114 C2 257 B3
Isleworth TW7. . . . . 131 A4
Marlborough Rd
Acton Green W4. . . . . 111 A1
Ashford TW15 . . . . . . 170 A5
Bexley DA7. . . . . 146 D2
Bowes Pk N22 . . . . 32 B4
Brentford TW7. . . . . . . 131 B5
Bromley BR2 . . . . 209 C5
Chingford E4 . . . . 35 D4
Dagenham RM8. . . . . . . 80 C4
Ealing W5. . . . . 109 D4
Edmonton N9. . . . . 18 A3
Feltham TW13 . . . . . . 150 D2
Hampton TW12 . . . . . 173 C4
Hillingdon UB10. . . . . . . 82 D4
Leyton E15. . . . . 76 C4
Mitcham SW19 . . . . . 180 C4
Richmond TW10. . . . . . 154 B5
Romford RM7. . . . . 59 D5
Southall UB2 . . . . 106 C3
South Croydon CR2 . . 221 A1
St James
SW1 . . . . . . 115 C5 249 B3
Sutton SM1 . . . . 217 C6
Upper Holloway N19 . . . 72 A6
Upton E7 . . . . 77 C1
Wanstead E18 . . . . 55 A6
Woolwich SE18 . . . . . . 123 A3
Marlborough Sch
DA15 . . . . 168 A4
Marlborough St
SW3. . . . . . . 114 C2 257 B3
Marlborough Trad Est
TW9. . . . . 132 D4
Marlborough Yd N19. . 71 D6
Marlbury NW8. . . . . . . 91 D6
Marler Rd SE23 . . . . . . 163 B3
Marlesford Ct SM6 . . . 219 C4
Marlex Lo N3. . . . . 29 D2
Marley Ave DA7. . . . . 146 D6
Marley Cl
Harringay N15. . . . . 50 D5
Southall UB6 . . . . 85 C4
Marley Ho 14 W11 . . 112 D6
Marley Wlk NW2. . . . . . . 68 C3
Marlfield Cl KT4 . . . . . 200 A1
Marlfield Ct KT3 . . . . . 199 D2
Marlin Cl TW16 . . . . . 171 C4
Marlin Ct 5 DA14. . . . 190 A6
Marling Ct TW12. . . . . 173 B4
Marlingdene Cl
TW12 . . . . 173 C4
Marlings Cl BR7 . . . . . 211 C5
Marlings Park Ave
BR7. . . . . 211 C6
Marlin Ho SW15 . . . . . 157 A6
Marlins Cl 3 SM1. . . . 218 A3
Marloes Cl HA0 . . . . 65 D4
Marloes Rd
W8 . . . . 113 D3 255 C5
Marlow Cl SE20. . . . . . 206 B6
Marlow Cres TW1. . . . 152 D5
Marlow Ct
Colindale NW9. . . . . 45 D6
1 Ealing W7 . . . . 108 C5
6 Finchley N3. . . . . 29 C2
Harrow HA1. . . . . 42 A3
Osidge N14 . . . . 15 C4
Willesden NW6 . . . . 68 D1
Marlow Dr SM3. . . . . 216 D5
Marlowe Bsns Ctr 2
SE14. . . . . 141 A5
Marlowe Cl BR7 . . . . . 189 B4
Marlowe Ct
Chelsea SW3. . . . . . . 257 B3
2 Dulwich SE19 . . . . 183 D5
6 Kingston u T KT2. . 175 D6
Marlowe Gdns SE9. . . 166 C5
Marlowe Ho
Kingston u T KT1 . . . . 197 D5
15 Stoke Newington
N16. . . . . 73 C4
Marlowe Lo CR0 . . . . . 223 A6
Marlowe Rd E17 . . . . . . 54 A5
Marlowe Sq CR4 . . . . . 203 C5
Marlowes The
NW8. . . . . 92 B6 229 C6
Marlowe Way CR0 . . . 220 A6
Marlow Gdns UB3. . . . 105 B3
Marlow Ho
Bermondsey SE1 . . . . 263 C6
15 Kensington W2. . . . . 91 D1
44 Spitalfields E2. . . . . . 95 D4
Teddington TW11. . . . . 175 A6
Wallington CR0 . . . . . 220 A5
Marlow Rd
Newham E6 . . . . 100 B4
Penge SE20 . . . . 184 B1
Southall UB2 . . . . 107 B3
Marlow Studio Workshops 43 E2. . . 95 D4
Marlow Way SE16. . . . 118 D4
Marl Rd SW18 . . . . . . 136 A1
Marlston NW1. . . . . . 231 D1
Marlton St SE10 . . . . 120 D1
Marlwood Cl DA15 . . . 167 C2
Marmadon Rd SE18,
SE2. . . . . 123 D2
Marmara Apts 4
E16. . . . . 121 A6
Marmion App E4 . . . . . . 35 C6
Marmion Ave E4. . . . . . 35 B6
Marmion Cl E4 . . . . 35 B6
Marmion Ho 13
SW12 . . . . 159 B4
Marmion Mews 4
SW11 . . . . 137 A2
Marmion Rd SW11 . . . 137 A1
Marmont Rd SE15. . . . 140 A5
Marmora Ho E1 . . . . . . 97 A2
Marmora Rd SE22. . . . 162 C5
Marmot Rd TW4 . . . . . 128 D2
Marncrest Ct KT5 . . . . 198 B4
Marne Ave
Friern Barnet N11 . . . . . 31 B6
Welling DA16. . . . . 146 A2
Marnell Way TW4 . . . . 128 D2
Marner Prim Sch 6
E3. . . . . 97 D3
Marne St W10 . . . . 91 A4
Marney Rd SW11. . . . . 137 A1
Marnfield Cres SW2. . 160 B3
Marnham Ave NW2 . . . . 69 A4
Marnham Cres UB6 . . . . 85 D5
Marnham Ct HA0 . . . . . . 65 C3
Marnie Ct 11 E11 . . . . . 76 C6
Marnock Ho SE17. . . . 262 C2
Marnock Rd SE4. . . . . 163 B6
Maroon St E14. . . . . 97 A2
Maroons Way SE6. . . . 185 C5
Marqueen Twrs 1
SW16 . . . . 182 B3
Marquess Rd N1. . . . . . 73 B2
Marquis Cl HA0 . . . . 66 B1
Marquis Ct
Barking IG11. . . . . 79 C3
Finsbury Pk N4. . . . . 50 B1
1 Kingston u T KT1 . . 198 A5
Stanwell TW19. . . . . . 148 A3
Marquis Rd
Bowes Pk N22 . . . . 32 B4
Finsbury Pk N4. . . . . 50 C1
Kentish Town NW1. . . . . 71 D2
Marrabon Cl DA15 . . . 168 A3
Marrick Cl SW15. . . . . 134 A1
Marrick Ho 19 NW6 . . . . 91 D6
Marrilyne Ave EN3 . . . . . 7 B5
Marriner Ct UB3 . . . . . 105 C6
Marriott Cl TW14. . . . . 149 B5
Marriott Ho 8 SE6. . . 186 A6
Marriott Rd
Finsbury Pk N4. . . . . 50 B1
Muswell Hill N10 . . . . . . 30 D2
Newham E15 . . . . 98 C6
Marriotts Cl NW9 . . . . . 45 D3
Marryat Cl TW3 . . . . . . 129 B1
Marryat Ct 12 W6 . . . . 112 B2
Marryat Ho SW1 . . . . 259 A1
Marryat Pl SW19 . . . . 179 A6
Marryat Rd SW19 . . . . 179 A6
Marryat Sq SW6 . . . . 264 A2
Marryatt Ct W5 . . . . 88 B1
Marryfields Way
SE6. . . . . 163 D4
Marsala Rd SE13. . . . . 141 D1
Marsalis Ho 3 E3 . . . . 97 C4
Marsden Rd
Camberwell SE15. . . . . 139 D2
Edmonton N9. . . . . 18 B2
Marsden St NW5. . . . . . 71 A2
Marsden Way 2
BR6. . . . . 227 D4
Marshall Cl
Brunswick Pk N11 . . . . . 15 B1
Harrow HA1. . . . . 42 B2
Hounslow TW4. . . . . . . 151 B6
Wandsworth SW18 . . 158 A5
Marshall Ct SW4. . . . . 270 B1
Marshall Dr UB4 . . . . . . 83 D2
Marshall Ho
5 New Malden
KT3 . . . . 199 C5
Paddington NW6 . . . . . . 91 B5
Shoreditch N1 . . . . . . 235 D4
Walworth SE17 . . . . . . 262 C2
Marshall Path 10
SE28. . . . . 124 B6
Marshall Rd
Leyton E10. . . . . 75 D4
Tottenham N17 . . . . 33 B2
Marshall St L Ctr
W1. . . . . 93 C1 239 B1
Marshalls Gr SE18 . . . 122 A2
Marshall's Pl SE16 . . 263 D5
Marshall's Rd SM1. . . 217 D4
Marshall St
W1. . . . . 93 C1 239 B1
Marshalsea Rd
SE1. . . . . 117 A4 252 B2
Marsham Cl BR7. . . . . 188 D5
Marsham Ct
19 Putney SW19 . . . . 156 D3
Westminster SW1 . . . 259 D4
Marsham St
SW1 . . . . . . 115 D2 259 D4
Marsh Ave CR4 . . . . . . 181 A1
Marshbrook Cl SE3 . . 143 D2
Marsh Cl NW7 . . . . 11 D1
Marsh Ct Dalston E8 . . . 74 A2
3 Merton SW19. . . . . 180 A2
Marsh Dr NW9. . . . . 45 D3
Marsh Farm Rd
TW2. . . . . 152 D3
Marshfield St E14. . . . 120 A3
Marsh Gate Bsns Ctr
E15. . . . . 98 A5
Marshgate Sch
TW10. . . . . 154 B6
Marsh Green Prim Sch
RM10. . . . . 103 C5
Marsh Green Rd
RM10 . . . . 103 C6
Marsh Hall HA9. . . . . . . 66 B5
Marsh Hill E9. . . . . 75 A3
Marsh Ho
Nine Elms SW8 . . . . . 269 B2
Pimlico SW1. . . . . 259 D1
Marsh La
Edgware NW7 . . . . 11 C1
Leyton E10. . . . . 75 C6
Stanmore HA7 . . . . 25 C4
Tottenham N17 . . . . 34 B2
Marsh Point HA5 . . . . . 41 B5
Marsh Rd Pinner HA5 . . 41 A5
Wembley HA0 . . . . 87 D5
Marshside Cl N9. . . . . . 18 C3
Marsh St E14 . . . . 119 D2
Marsh Wall E14. . . . . . 119 D4
Marshwood Ho 10
NW6. . . . . 91 C6
Marsland Cl SE17 . . . 261 D1
Marsom Ho N1 . . . . . . 235 C3
Marston SE17 . . . . . . 262 B4
Marston Ave
Chessington KT9 . . . . 214 A2
Dagenham RM10. . . . . . 81 C5
Marston Cl
Dagenham RM10. . . . . . 81 C5
South Hampstead NW6 70 A1
Marston Ct
Barnet EN5 . . . . 13 C6
Sidcup DA14. . . . . 189 D6
Walton-on-T KT12 . . . . 194 C1
Marston Ho 23 SW9. . 138 C3
Marston Rd TW11. . . . 175 B5
Marston Way SE19. . . . 183 A3
Marsworth Ave HA5. . . . 22 D2
Marsworth Cl UB4 . . . . . 85 A2
Marsworth Ho 8 E2 . . . 96 A6
Martaban Rd N16. . . . . . 73 D6
Martello St E8. . . . . 74 B1
Martello Terr E8 . . . . . . 74 B1
Martell Rd SE21. . . . . . 161 B1
Martel Pl E8. . . . . 73 D2
Marten Rd E17. . . . . 35 C1
Martens Ave DA7 . . . . 147 D1
Martham Cl SE28 . . . . 124 D6
Martha Rd E15. . . . . 76 C2
Martha's Bldgs EC1. . 242 C6
Martha St E1 . . . . 96 C1
Marthorne Cres HA3 . . 24 B1
Martin Bowes Rd
SE9. . . . . 144 B2
Martinbridge Trad Est
EN1 . . . . 18 A6
Martin Cl
Lower Edmonton N9 . . . 18 D3
Uxbridge UB10. . . . . 82 A5
Martin Cres CR0 . . . . . 204 C1
Martin Ct
15 Cubitt Town E14 . . 120 A4
Lewisham SE12 . . . . . 164 D4
Merton SW19. . . . . 179 C3
Southall UB2 . . . . 107 B4
Martindale SW14 . . . . 155 A6
Martindale Ave 2
E16. . . . . 121 A6
Martindale Ho 23
E14. . . . . 119 D6
Martindale Rd
Balham SW12 . . . . 159 B4
Hounslow TW4. . . . . . . 129 A2
Martin Dene DA6 . . . . 169 B6
Martin Dr UB5 . . . . 63 B3
Martineau Cl KT10 . . . 212 B4
Martineau Dr TW1 . . . 131 B1
Martineau Ho SW1. . . 259 A1
Martineau Mews N5 . . . 72 D4
Martineau Rd N5 . . . . . 72 D4
Martingale Cl TW16 . . 194 A5
Martingales Cl
TW10 . . . . 153 D1
Martin Gdns RM8 . . . . . 80 D4
Martin Gr SM4. . . . . . . 201 C6
Martin Ho
Newington SE1 . . . . . 262 B5
7 New Malden KT3 . 199 C5
South Lambeth SW8 . 270 A4
Martini Dr EN3 . . . . 7 C6
Martin La EC4 . . . . 252 D6
Martin Prim Sch N2. . . 30 C1
Martin Rd RM8 . . . . 80 D4
Martin Rise DA6 . . . . . 169 B6
Martins Cl BR4 . . . . . . 224 B6
Martins Mount EN5 . . . . . 1 D1
Martins Pl SE28. . . . . . 123 C5
Martin's Rd BR2 . . . . 186 D1
Martin St SE28. . . . . . . 123 C5
Martins The
Penge SE26 . . . . 184 B5
Wembley HA9 . . . . 66 B5
Martins Wlk
Muswell Hill N10 . . . . . . 31 A2
Woolwich SE28 . . . . . 123 C5
Martin Way SW20,
SM4 . . . . 201 B6
Martlesham N17. . . . . . . 33 C1
Martlesham Wlk
NW9. . . . . 27 C2
Martlet Gr 5 UB5. . . . . 84 D4
Martlett Ct WC2 . . . . 240 B1
Martlett Lo NW3. . . . . . 69 D4
Martley Dr IG2 . . . . 56 D4
Martley Ho SW8 . . . . 269 B2
Martock Cl HA3. . . . . . . 43 A5
Martock Ct 10 SE15 . . 140 B4
Martock Gdns N11. . . . . 31 A5
Marton Cl SE6 . . . . . . 163 C1
Marton Rd 2 N16. . . . . 73 C5
Martyn Ct HA8. . . . . 26 B6
Martyn Ho SE2. . . . . . 146 D6
Martynside 22 NW9 . . . 27 D2
Marvel Ho 5 SE5 . . . . 139 B5
Marvell Ave UB4 . . . . . . 84 A2
Marvels Cl SE12 . . . . . 165 B2
Marvels La SE12. . . . . 165 C1
Marvels Lane Prim Sch
SE12. . . . . 187 C6
Marville Rd
SW6 . . . . 135 B5 264 C3
Marvin Ho 9 SE18 . . . 144 D6
Marvin St 3 E8. . . . . . . 74 B2
Marwell Cl BR4 . . . . . 224 D6
Marwell Ct SE3 . . . . . . 142 B3
Marwick Rd UB7 . . . . . 104 B4
Marwood Cl DA16. . . . . 146 B2
Marwood Ct N3. . . . . 29 D3
Marwood Dr NW7. . . . . . 28 D3
Mary Adelaide Cl
Kingston u T SW15. . . 155 C1
Kingston u T SW15. . . 177 C6
Mary Adelaide Ho
W2 . . . . 236 D4
Mary Ann Bldgs SE8 . 141 C6
Maryatt Ave HA2. . . . . . 63 D6
Marybank SE18. . . . . . 122 B2
Mary Cl HA7 . . . . 44 B5
Mary Datchelor Cl
SE5. . . . . 139 B4
Mary Dine Ct SW8 . . 270 D3
Mary Gn NW8. . . . . 91 D6
Marygold Ho TW3. . . . 130 A4
Mary Ho
8 Hammersmith
W6 . . . . 112 C1
6 Stockwell SW9 . . . . 138 B3
Mary James Ho 32
E2. . . . . 96 A5
Mary Jones Ho 20
E14. . . . . 119 C6
Maryland Ct KT1. . . . 176 D1
Maryland Pk E15 . . . . . 76 C3
Maryland Point E15. . . 76 C2
Maryland Prim Sch
E15. . . . . 76 C3
Maryland Rd
Paddington W9 . . . . 91 C3
South Norwood CR7. . 182 D2
Stratford New Town
E15 . . . . 76 B3
Tottenham N22 . . . . 32 C4
Marylands Ind Est
E15. . . . . 76 C3
Maryland Sq E15 . . . . . 76 C3
Marylands Rd W9. . . . . 91 D3
Maryland St E15. . . . . . 76 C3
Maryland Sta E15. . . . . 76 C2
Maryland Way TW16 . 172 A1
Maryland Wlk N1 . . . 235 A6
Mary Lawrenson Pl 1
SE3 . . . . 143 A5
MARYLEBONE 93 B1

Marylebone Ct 3 HA0 ... 66 A2
Marylebone Flyover NW1 ... 92 C2 237 A3
Marylebone High St W1 ... 93 A2 238 B4
Marylebone La W1 ... 93 A1 238 B2
Marylebone Mews W1 ... 238 C3
Marylebone Pas W1 239 B2
Marylebone Rd NW1 ... 92 D2 237 D4
Marylebone St W1 ... 93 A2 238 B3
Marylebone Sta NW1 ... 92 D3 237 C5
Marylee Way SE11 ... 116 B2 260 D3
Mary McArthur Ho 12 N19 ... 49 D2
Mary Macarthur Ho
 8 Belvedere DA17 ... 125 C3
 11 Dagenham RM10 ... 81 C5
 15 Globe Town E2 ... 96 D4
 W14 ... 264 A6
Marymount International Sch KT2 ... 177 A3
Maryon Gr SE7 ... 122 A2
Maryon Mews NW3 ... 70 C4
Maryon Rd SE7 ... 122 A2
Mary Peters Dr UB6 ... 64 B3
Mary Pl W11 .. 113 A6 244 A5
Mary Rose Cl TW12 ... 173 C2
Mary Rose Mall E6 ... 100 B2
Maryrose Way N20 ... 14 B3
Mary's Ct NW8 ... 237 B6
Mary Seacole Villas 19 NW10 ... 67 B1
Mary Secole Cl 21 E8 .. 95 D6
Mary Smith Ct SW5 . 255 B3
Mary St
 5 Canning Town E16 ... 98 D2
 Shoreditch N1 . 95 A6 235 B5
Mary's Terr TW1 ... 153 A4
Mary Tates Cotts CR4 ... 202 D5
Mary Terr NW1 ... 232 A5
Maryville DA16 ... 145 D3
Mary Way WD19 ... 22 C6
Mary Wharrie Ho 4 NW3 ... 70 D1
Marzena Ct TW2 ... 152 A6
Masbro' Rd W14 ... 112 D3
Mascalls Ct 13 SE7 ... 143 C6
Mascalls Rd SE7 ... 143 C6
Mascotte Rd 2 SW15 ... 134 D1
Mascotts Cl NW2 ... 68 B5
Masefield Ave
 Borehamwood WD6 ... 10 D6
 Southall UB1 ... 107 C6
 Stanmore HA7 ... 24 D5
Masefield Cres N14 ... 15 C5
Masefield Ct
 New Barnet EN5 ... 2 A1
 Stoke Newington N5 ... 73 B3
 19 Surbiton KT6 ... 197 D2
Masefield Gdns E6 ... 100 C3
Masefield Ho 4 NW6 . 91 C4
Masefield La UB4 ... 84 C3
Masefield Rd TW13 ... 173 B6
Masefield View BR6 .. 227 A5
Masefield Way TW19 ... 148 B3
Masham Ho 13 DA18 ... 124 D4
Mashie Rd W3 ... 89 C1
Maskall Cl SW2 ... 160 C3
Maskani Wlk SW16 ... 181 C3
Maskell Rd SW17 ... 158 A1
Maskelyne Cl SW11 ... 136 C4 267 B2
Mason Cl
 Bermondsey SE16 ... 118 A1
 Bexleyheath DA7 ... 147 D2
 Hampton TW12 ... 173 B2
 Newham E16 ... 121 A6
 Wimbledon SW20 ... 178 D2
Mason Ct
 4 Penge SE19 ... 183 D3
 Wembley HA9 ... 66 C6
Mason Ho
 15 Bermondsey SE1 ... 118 A2
 8 Friern Barnet N11 ... 31 C5
 16 Hackney E9 ... 74 C1
Mason Rd
 Sutton SM1 ... 217 D3
 Woodford IG8 ... 36 C6
Mason's Arms Mews W1 ... 248 D6
Masons Ave HA3 ... 42 D5
Mason's Ave
 City of London EC2 ... 242 C2
 Croydon CR0 ... 221 A5
Masons Hill
 Bromley BR2 ... 209 B5
 13 Woolwich SE18 ... 122 D2
Masons Ho NW9 ... 44 D4
Mason's Pl
 Finsbury EC1 ... 235 A2
 Mitcham CR4 ... 180 D2
Mason St SE17 ... 117 B2 262 D4
Mason's Yd
 Finsbury EC1 ... 234 D2
 St James SW1 ... 249 B4
 Wimbledon SW19 ... 178 D5
Massey Cl N11 ... 31 B5
Massey Ct 6 E6 ... 99 C6
Massie Rd E8 ... 74 A2
Massingberd Way SW17 ... 181 B6
Massinger St SE1, SE17 ... 263 A3
Massingham St E1 ... 96 D3
Masson Ave HA4 ... 62 C2
Mast Ct 17 SE16 ... 119 A2
Master Gunner's Pl 1 SE18 ... 144 A4
Masterman Ho 1 SE5 ... 139 B5
Masterman Rd E6 ... 100 A4
Masters Cl SW16 ... 181 C4
Masters Ct HA4 ... 61 C6
Masters Dr SE16 ... 118 B1
Masters Lo 24 E1 ... 96 C1
Master's St 16 E1 ... 96 D2
Mast House Terr E14 ... 119 C2
Mastin Ho SW18 ... 157 C3
Mastmaker Rd E14 ... 119 C4
Maswell Park Cres TW3 ... 152 A6
Maswell Park Rd TW3 ... 130 A1
Matara Mews SE17 .. 262 A1
Matcham Rd E11 ... 76 D5
Matching Ct 14 E3 ... 97 C4
Matchless Dr SE18 ... 144 C5
Matchroom Stadium (Brisbane Rd) (Leyton Orient FC) E10 ... 75 D5
Matfield Cl BR2 ... 209 A4
Matfield Rd DA17 ... 147 C6
Matham Gr SE22 ... 139 D1
Matham Rd KT8 ... 196 B4
Mathart Ct E4 ... 36 B4
Matheson Lang Ho SE1 ... 251 A1
Matheson Rd W14 ... 113 B2 254 C3
Mathews Ave E6 ... 100 C5
Mathews Park Ave E15 ... 76 D2
Mathews Yd WC2 ... 240 A1
Mathieson Ct SE1 ... 251 D1
Mathieson Ho 10 E4 .. 20 C4
Mathilda Marks-Kennedy Jewish Prim Sch 5 NW7 ... 27 B5
Mathison Ho SW10 .. 266 A4
Matilda Cl SE19 ... 183 B3
Matilda Gdns 10 E3 ... 97 C5
Matilda Ho E1 ... 118 A5
Matilda St N1 .. 94 B6 233 D6
Matlock Cl Barnet EN5 . 12 D6
 Herne Hill SE24 ... 139 A1
Matlock Cres SM3 ... 217 A4
Matlock Ct
 7 Herne Hill SE5 ... 139 B1
 St John's Wood NW8 . 229 A4
 Woodford IG8 ... 36 D2
Matlock Gdns SM1, SM3 ... 217 A4
Matlock Pl SM1, SM3 . 217 A4
Matlock Rd E10 ... 54 A3
Matlock St E14 ... 97 A1
Matlock Way KT3 ... 177 B2
Maton Ho SW6 ... 264 C4
Matson Ct IG8 ... 36 C3
Matson Ho
 9 Bermondsey SE16 ... 118 B3
 16 Homerton E9 ... 74 D2
Matthew Cl W10 ... 90 D3
Matthew Ct
 Mitcham CR4 ... 203 D4
 4 Walthamstow E17 ... 54 A6
Matthew Parker St SW1 ... 249 D1
Matthews Ct N5 ... 73 A4
Matthews Ho 8 E14 ... 97 C2
Matthews Rd UB6 ... 64 B3
Matthews St SW11 . 136 D3
Matthias Ct 12 TW10 ... 154 A5
Matthias Ho 2 N16 ... 73 C3
Matthias Rd N16 ... 73 C3
Mattingly Way 8 SE15 ... 139 D5
Mattison Rd N4 ... 50 D3
Mattock La W5, W13 .. 109 C5
Maud Cashmore Way SE18 ... 122 B3
Maude Ho 8 E2 ... 96 A5
Maude Rd
 Camberwell SE5 ... 139 C4
 Walthamstow E17 ... 53 A4
Maudesville Cotts W7 ... 108 C5
Maude Terr E17 ... 53 A5
Maud Gdns
 Barking IG11 ... 101 D5
 Newham E13 ... 98 D5
Maudlins Gn E1 ... 118 A5
Maud Rd Leyton E10 ... 76 A5
 Newham E13 ... 98 D5
Maudslay Rd SE9 ... 144 B2
Maudsley Ho TW8 ... 110 A1
Maudsley Hospl SE5 . 139 B3
Maud St E16 ... 98 D2
Maud Wilkes Cl 10 NW5 ... 71 C3
Maugham Ct 5 W3 .. 111 A3
Mauleverer Rd SW2 .. 160 A6
Maultway Ct KT19 ... 215 B3
Maundeby Wlk NW10 . 67 C2
Maunder Rd 4 W7 . 108 D5
Maunsel St SW1 ... 115 D2 259 C4
Maureen Campbell Ct TW17 ... 192 D4
Maurer Ct 2 SE10 .. 120 D3
Mauretania Bldg 11 E1 ... 118 D6
Maurice Ave N22 ... 32 D1
Maurice Browne Cl NW7 ... 28 D4
Maurice Ct
 3 Brentford TW8 ... 131 D5
 4 Mile End E1 ... 97 A4
 Wood Green N22 ... 32 C2
Maurice Ho
 Hither Green SE12 ... 164 D5
 1 Stockwell SW9 ... 138 B3
Maurice St W12 ... 90 B1
Maurice Wlk NW11 ... 48 A5
Maurier Cl UB5 ... 84 C6
Mauritius Rd SE10 ... 120 C2
Maury Rd N16 ... 74 A5
Mausoleum Rd N2 ... 30 C2
Mauveine Gdns TW3 ... 129 C1
Mavelstone Cl BR1 .. 188 A2
Mavelstone Rd BR1 .. 188 A2
Maverton Rd E3 ... 97 C6
Mavery Ct 5 BR1 ... 186 D3
Mavis Ave KT19 ... 215 C3
Mavis Cl KT19 ... 215 C3
Mavis Ct 33 NW9 ... 27 D1
Mavis Wlk 9 E6 ... 100 A2
Mavor Ho N1 ... 233 D5
Mawbey Ho SE1 ... 263 D1
Mawbey Pl SE1 ... 117 D1 263 D1
Mawbey Rd SE1 ... 263 D1
Mawbey St SW8 ... 270 A3
Mawdley Ho SE1 ... 251 B1
Mawney Cl RM7 ... 59 D6
Mawney Rd RM7 ... 59 D6
Mawson Cl SW20 ... 179 A1
Mawson Ct N1 ... 235 D5
Mawson Ho EC1 ... 241 A4
Mawson La W4 ... 133 D6
Maxden Ct SE15 ... 140 A2
Maxey Gdns RM9 ... 81 A4
Maxey Rd
 Dagenham RM9 ... 81 A4
 Plumstead SE18 ... 123 A2
Maxfield Cl N20 ... 14 A4
Maxim Apartments 3 BR2 ... 209 B5
Maxim Rd N21 ... 16 C5
Maxted Pk HA1 ... 42 C2
Maxted Rd SE15 ... 139 D2
Maxwell Cl
 Croydon CR0 ... 204 A1
 Hayes UB3 ... 106 A6
Maxwell Ct SE21 ... 162 A3
Maxwell Gdns BR6 .. 227 D5
Maxwell Ho
 Bowes Pk N22 ... 32 B4
 Chislehurst BR7 ... 188 D3
 12 Shooters Hill SE18 144 D6
Maxwell Rd
 Ashford TW15 ... 171 A4
 Fulham SW6 . 135 D5 265 D3
 Welling DA16 ... 146 A2
 West Drayton UB7 ... 104 B2
Maxwelton Ave NW7 ... 27 B5
Maxwelton Cl NW7 ... 27 B5
Maya Angelou Ct E4 .. 36 A6
Maya Cl SE15 ... 140 B3
Mayall Cl EN3 ... 7 C5
Mayall Rd SE24 ... 160 D6
Maya Pl N11 ... 31 D3
Maya Rd N2 ... 48 A5
Maybank Ave
 Wembley HA0 ... 65 A3
 Woodford E18 ... 37 B1
Maybank Gdns HA5 ... 40 A4
Maybank Rd E18 ... 37 C2
May Bate Ave KT2 ... 175 D2
Maybells Commercial Est IG11 ... 102 D5
Mayberry Pl KT5 ... 198 B2
Maybourne Cl SE26 .. 184 B5
Maybourne Grange CR0 ... 221 C6
Maybrook Ct E11 ... 77 B6
Maybury Cl Enfield EN1 .. 6 B5
 Petts Wood BR5 ... 210 D4
Maybury Ct
 Beckenham BR3 ... 185 B3
 Croydon CR2 ... 220 D3
 Harrow HA1 ... 42 B3
 Marylebone W1 ... 238 B3
Maybury Gdns NW10 .. 68 B2
Maybury Mews N6 ... 49 C2
Maybury Rd
 Barking IG11 ... 102 A5
 Newham E13 ... 99 C3
Maybury St SW17 ... 180 C5
Maychurch Cl HA7 ... 25 D3
May Cl KT9 ... 214 B2
Maycroft
 2 Hayes BR2 ... 208 D1
 Pinner HA5 ... 22 B1
Maycross Ave SM4 ... 201 C5
May Ct 2 SW19 ... 180 A2
Mayday Gdns SE3 ... 144 A3
Mayday Rd CR0, CR7 . 204 D3
Mayday University Hospl CR7 ... 204 D3
Maydeb Ct RM6 ... 59 B3
Maydew Ho SE16 ... 118 C2
Maydwell Ho 6 E14 .. 97 C2
Mayerne Rd SE9 ... 165 D6
Mayesbrook Rd
 Barking IG11 ... 101 D6
 Dagenham RM8, IG3 ... 80 B5
Mayesford Rd RM6 ... 58 C2
Mayespark Prim Sch IG3 ... 80 A5
Mayes Rd N22 ... 32 B1
Mayeswood Rd SE12 ... 187 C6
MAYFAIR ... 115 B6
Mayfair Ave
 Bexley DA7 ... 146 D4
 Dagenham RM6 ... 58 D3
 Ilford IG1 ... 56 C1
 New Malden KT4 ... 200 A1
 Twickenham TW2 ... 152 A4
Mayfair Cl
 Beckenham BR3 ... 185 D2
 Surbiton KT6 ... 198 A1
Mayfair Ct
 2 Beckenham BR3 .. 185 D2
 7 Croydon CR0 ... 221 D6
 Edgware HA8 ... 26 B5
 13 Wimbledon SW19 . 179 A3
Mayfair Gdns
 Tottenham N17 ... 33 B4
 Woodford IG8 ... 37 A3
Mayfair Ho 11 SE1 ... 118 A2
Mayfair Pl W1 ... 248 D4
Mayfair Terr N14 ... 15 D4
Mayfield DA7 ... 147 B2
Mayfield Ave
 Broom Hill BR6 ... 211 D2
 Chiswick W4 ... 111 C2
 Harrow HA3 ... 43 B4
 North Finchley N12 ... 30 B6
 Osidge N14 ... 15 D2
 West Ealing W13 ... 109 B4
 Woodford IG8 ... 37 A4
Mayfield Cl
 Ashford TW15 ... 170 D4
 Clapham Pk SW4 ... 159 D6
 Dalston E8 ... 73 D2
 Hillingdon UB10 ... 82 D4
 Long Ditton KT7 ... 197 B1
 Penge SE20 ... 184 B2
Mayfield Cres
 Enfield N9 ... 18 B5
 Thornton Heath CR7 .. 204 B4
Mayfield Ct SM2 ... 218 A1
Mayfield Dr HA5 ... 41 B5
Mayfield Gdns
 Ealing W7 ... 86 C2
 Hendon NW4 ... 46 D3
Mayfield Ho
 31 Bethnal Green E2 ... 96 B5
 Stamford Hill N16 ... 51 C2
Mayfield Mans SW15 ... 157 B6
Mayfield Prim Sch W7 ... 86 B1
Mayfield Rd
 Acton W3 ... 110 D6
 Bedford Pk W12 ... 111 C4
 Bromley BR1 ... 210 A4
 Chingford E4 ... 20 B2
 Dagenham RM8 ... 58 C1
 Dalston E8 ... 73 D1
 Enfield EN3 ... 6 D3
 Higham Hill E17 ... 35 A1
 Hornsey Vale N8 ... 50 B3
 Merton SW19 ... 179 B2
 Newham E13 ... 98 D3
 South Croydon CR2 ... 221 B1
 Sutton SM2 ... 218 B2
 Thornton Heath CR7 .. 204 B4
Mayfields HA9 ... 66 C6
Mayfield Sch & Coll RM8 ... 58 C1
Mayfields Cl HA9 ... 66 C6
Mayfield Villas DA14 ... 190 C4
Mayflower Cl
 Bermondsey SE16 ... 118 D2
 Ruislip HA4 ... 39 A3
Mayflower Ho 2 IG11 ... 101 B6
Mayflower Lo
 Hendon N3 ... 47 B6
 Muswell Hill N10 ... 31 A2
Mayflower Prim Sch 22 E14 ... 97 D1
Mayflower Rd SW9 ... 138 A2
Mayflower St 1 SE16 ... 118 C4
Mayfly Cl HA5 ... 40 C2
Mayfly Gdns 12 UB5 ... 84 D4
Mayford NW1 ... 232 B4
Mayford Cl
 Balham SW12 ... 158 D4
 Penge BR3 ... 206 D6
Mayford Rd SW12 ... 159 A4
May Gdns Elstree WD6 .. 9 D5
 Wembley HA0 ... 87 C4
Maygood Ho N1 ... 234 A4
Maygood St N1 ... 94 C5 234 A4
Maygrove Rd NW6 ... 69 B2
Mayhew Cl E4 ... 19 C1
Mayhew Ct 2 SE5 ... 139 B1
Mayhill Rd Barnet EN5 . 13 A5
 Greenwich SE7 ... 143 B6
Mayland Mans 4 IG11 ... 78 D1
Maylands Dr DA14 .. 168 D1

Maylands Ho SW3 .. 257 B3
Maylands Rd WD19 ... 22 C6
Maylie Ho 4 SE16 ... 118 B4
Maynard Cl
Fulham
SW6 ..... 135 D5 265 D3
Tottenham N15 .... 51 C4
Maynard Ct EN3 .... 7 C5
Maynard Ho
Mile End E1 .... 97 A4
2 Plumstead SE18 .. 123 A2
Maynard Rd E17 ...... 54 A4
Maynards Quay E1... 118 C6
Mayne Ct E8.......... 74 A4
Maynooth Gdns CR4 202 D2
Mayo Ct W13 .... 109 B3
Mayo Ho 10 E1 .... 96 C2
Mayola Rd E5......... 74 C4
Mayo Rd
Thornton Heath CR0 .. 205 B4
Walton-on-T KT12 .... 194 A2
Willesden NW10 ...... 67 C2
Mayow Rd SE23,
SE26 .... 184 D6
Mayplace Cl DA7 ... 147 D2
Mayplace La SE18... 144 D6
Mayplace Rd W DA7 . 147 C1
Maypole Ct UB2 ..... 107 B4
May Rd Chingford E4 ... 35 C4
Newham E13 .... 99 A5
Twickenham TW2.... 152 C3
Mayroyd Ave KT6 .... 214 C6
May's Buildings Mews
SE10............... 142 B5
Mays Ct WC2 .... 250 A5
May's Ct SE10 .... 142 B5
May's Hill Rd BR2.... 208 C6
May's La EN5.......... 12 C5
Maysoule Rd SW11 .. 136 B1
Mays Rd TW11, TW12.. 174 B5
May St W14.......... 254 D1
Maystocks E18 .... 55 C6
Mayston Mews 3
SE10............... 121 A1
May Terr IG1 .... 78 D4
Maythorne Cotts
SE13............... 164 B5
Mayton St N7......... 72 B5
Maytree Cl HA8....... 11 A1
Maytree Ct
Mitcham CR4 .... 203 A6
Northolt UB5 .... 85 A4
May Tree Ho SE4..... 141 B2
Maytree La HA7...... 24 D3
Maytree Wlk SW2.... 160 C2
Mayville Prim Sch
E11................. 76 C6
Mayville Rd Ilford IG1 . 78 D3
Leyton E11 .... 76 C6
Mayward Ho 7 SE5.. 139 C4
May Wlk E13 .... 99 B5
Maywood Cl BR3.... 185 D3
May Wynne Ho E16 ... 99 B1
Maze Hill SE10, SE3.. 142 C6
Maze Hill Lodge 7
SE10............... 142 B6
Maze Hill Sta SE10.. 142 C6
Mazenod Ave NW6.... 69 C1
Maze Rd TW9......... 132 C5
Mead Cl
3 Camden Town
NW1 .... 71 A1
Harrow HA3.......... 24 B2
Mead Cres
Carshalton SM1..... 218 C4
Chingford E4 .... 36 A6
Meadcroft Ho 4
KT3................ 199 C2
Meadcroft Rd SE17 . 138 D6
Mead Ct NW9.......... 45 B4
Meade Cl W4 .... 132 C6
Meader Ct SE14..... 140 D5
Meadfield HA8 .... 10 D2
Mead Field HA2 ...... 63 B5
Meadfield Gn HA8 .... 10 D2
Meadfoot Rd SW16 .. 181 C2
Mead Gr RM6......... 58 D6
Mead Ho W11 .... 244 C4
Mead House La UB4... 83 B3
Meadhurst Club
TW16.............. 171 D5
Meadhurst Pk TW16.. 171 C4
Mead Inf Sch The
KT19 .... 215 D4
Meadlands Dr TW10. 153 D2
Meadlands Prim Sch
TW10.............. 175 C6
Mead Lo W4......... 111 B4
Meadow Ave CR0 ... 206 D3
Meadowbank
Lewisham SE3 ...... 142 D2
Primrose Hill NW3..... 70 D1
Southgate N21........ 16 B5
Surbiton KT5 .... 198 B3
Meadow Bank 8
SW15 .... 157 B6
Meadowbank Cl
SW6 .... 134 C5
Meadowbank Gdns
TW5 .... 128 B4
Meadowbank Rd
NW9................ 45 B2
Meadowbanks EN5 ... 12 A6
Meadowbrook Ct
TW7 .... 130 D2
Meadow Cl
Barking IG11 .... 80 A1
Barnet EN5 .... 13 B5
Bexley DA6........... 169 B6
Catford SE6 .... 185 C5
Chingford E4 .... 19 D3
Chislehurst BR7..... 188 D5
Enfield EN3 .... 7 A5
Hackney E9 .... 75 B3
Hinchley Wood KT10 . 212 D5
Hounslow TW4....... 151 C5
Northolt UB5 .... 85 C5
Richmond TW10..... 154 A3
Ruislip HA4 .... 39 D3
Sutton SM1 .... 218 A6
West Barnes SW20 .. 200 C5
Meadowcourt Rd
SE3................ 142 D1
Meadowcroft 8 W4 . 110 C1
Meadow Croft BR1.... 210 B6
Meadowcroft Rd N13 . 16 C2
Meadow Dr
Hendon NW4 .... 28 C1
Muswell Hill N10 ...... 49 B6
Meadowford Cl
SE28 .... 124 A6
Meadow Garth NW10 . 67 B2
Meadow Gate HA2 ... 63 D5
Meadowgate Cl NW7.. 27 D5
Meadowgate Sch
SE4................ 141 A2
Meadow Gdns HA8.... 27 A4
Meadow High Sch
UB8 .... 82 A2
Meadow Hill KT3 .... 199 C3
Meadow La SE12..... 165 B1
Meadow Mews SW8 270 C5
Meadow Pl
Chiswick W4 .... 133 C5
South Lambeth
SW8 ...... 138 A5 270 B4
Meadow Rd
Ashford TW15 .... 171 B5
Barking IG11.......... 80 A1
Beckenham BR2..... 186 C1
Carshalton SM1..... 218 C3
Claygate KT10 ...... 212 C2
Dagenham RM9........ 81 B2
Feltham TW13 ...... 151 A2
Merton SW19......... 180 A3
Pinner HA5............ 41 A5
Southall UB1 .... 107 B6
South Lambeth
SW8 ...... 138 B5 270 C4
Meadow Row SE1... 262 A5
Meadows Cl E10....... 75 C6
Meadows Ct DA14 ... 190 B4
Meadows End TW16.. 172 A2
Meadowside
Eltham SE9.......... 143 C1
Twickenham TW1.... 153 D4
Meadow Stile CR0 ... 221 A5
Meadowsweet Cl
3 Newham E16 ...... 99 D2
West Barnes KT3.... 200 C5
Meadow The BR7 ... 189 A4
Meadowview TW17 .. 193 A2
Meadow View
Blackfen DA15....... 168 B4
Harrow HA1.......... 42 C1
Meadowview Rd
Catford SE6 .... 185 C5
Sidcup DA5.......... 169 B5
West Ewell KT19 .... 215 C1
Meadow View Rd
Hayes UB4........... 83 B3
Meadow View Rd
continued
Thornton Heath CR7 . 204 D4
Meadow Way
Kingsbury NW9 .... 45 B4
Locksbottom BR6..... 226 C5
Ruislip HA4 .... 40 B3
Wembley HA9 .... 65 D4
Meadow Waye TW5 .. 129 A5
Meadow Way The
HA3................. 24 C2
Meadow Wlk
Dagenham RM9....... 81 B2
Hackbridge SM6 .... 219 B5
Wanstead E18 .... 55 A5
West Ewell KT17,
KT19 .... 215 D1
Meadow Wood Sch
WD23................ 8 A6
Mead Pl Croydon CR0 . 205 A1
Hackney E9 .... 74 C2
Mead Plat NW10...... 67 A2
Mead Rd
Chislehurst BR7..... 189 A4
Edgware HA8......... 26 C4
Richmond TW10..... 153 C1
Mead Road Inf Sch
BR7 .... 189 A4
Mead Row
SE1....... 116 C3 261 A6
Meads Ct E15......... 76 D2
Meadside Cl BR3 .... 185 A2
Meads La IG3......... 57 D2
Meads Rd Enfield EN3 ... 7 A4
Tottenham N22 .... 32 D1
Meads The
Cheam SM3......... 217 A5
Edgware HA8......... 27 B4
Hillingdon UB8........ 82 A3
Mead The
Beckenham BR3..... 186 A2
Ealing W13........... 87 B2
Finchley N2 .... 30 A1
Ickenham UB10........ 60 C6
Wallington SM6..... 219 D2
West Wickham BR4 ... 208 B1
Meadvale Rd
Croydon CR0 .... 206 A3
Ealing W5............ 87 C3
Meadway
Ashford TW15 ...... 170 C6
Barnet EN5 .... 1 C1
Beckenham BR3..... 186 A2
Enfield EN3 .... 6 D6
Esher KT10 .... 212 A1
Hampstead Garden Suburb
NW11 .... 47 D3
Ilford IG3............ 79 C4
Palmers Green N14.... 16 A2
Tolworth KT5 .... 199 A1
Twickenham TW2..... 152 B3
West Barnes SW20 .. 200 C5
Woodford IG8 .... 37 C5
Mead Way
Croydon CR0 .... 223 A6
Hayes BR2.......... 209 A3
Ruislip HA4 .... 39 B3
Meadway Cl
Barnet EN5 .... 1 C1
Hampstead Garden Suburb
NW11 .... 47 D3
Pinner HA5............ 23 D4
Meadway Ct
Dagenham RM8....... 81 B6
Ealing W5............ 88 B2
Hampstead Garden Suburb
NW11 .... 47 D3
Meadway Gate NW11 . 47 C3
Meadway Gdns HA4... 39 B3
Meadway The
Buckhurst Hill IG9 ..... 21 D3
Lewisham SE3 ...... 142 B3
Meaford Way SE20... 184 B3
Meakin Est SE1..... 263 A6
Meakin Ho N7......... 72 B3
Meanley Rd E12 ...... 78 A3
Meard St W1 .... 239 C1
Meath Cres E1, E2..... 96 D4
Meath Ho SE24 ..... 160 D5
Meath Rd Ilford IG1 ... 79 A5
Newham E15 .... 98 D5
Meath St
SW11 ..... 137 B4 268 C2
Mecklenburgh Pl
WC1............. 240 C6
Mecklenburgh Sq
WC1........ 94 B3 240 C6
Mecklenburgh St
WC1............. 240 C6
Medburn St NW1 ... 232 C4
Medcalf Rd EN3 .... 7 B6
Medcroft Gdns
SW14.............. 133 A1
Medebourne Cl SE3.. 143 A2
Mede Ho BR1........ 187 B5
Medesenge Way N13. 32 D4
Medfield St SW15.... 156 B4
Medhurst Cl 19 E3 .... 97 A5
Medhurst Dr BR1 .... 186 C5
Median Rd E5 .... 74 C3
Medici Cl IG3.......... 58 A3
Medina Ave KT10 ... 212 C5
Medina Ct N7......... 72 C5
Medina Gr N7 .... 72 C5
Medina Ho SE15 ..... 140 C1
Medina Rd N7 .... 72 C5
Medlar Cl 1 UB5 ...... 84 D5
Medlar Ho 3 DA15 ... 168 A1
Medlar St SE5 .... 139 A4
Medley Rd NW6....... 69 C2
Medora Rd SW2 ..... 160 B4
Medresco Ho NW3.... 70 B3
Medusa Rd SE6,
SE13............... 163 D5
Medway Bldgs E3..... 97 A5
Medway Cl
Croydon CR0 .... 206 C3
Ilford IG1............ 79 A3
Medway Ct
South Norwood
SE25 .... 205 C4
St Pancras WC1..... 233 A1
Medway Dr UB6 ...... 86 D5
Medway Gdns HA0.... 65 A4
Medway Ho
Bermondsey SE1 .... 252 D1
6 Kingston u T KT2.. 175 D2
Paddington NW8 .... 237 A4
Stoke Newington N16 .. 73 B4
Medway Mews 35 E3.. 97 A5
Medway Par 1 UB6... 86 D5
Medway Rd E3 .... 97 A5
Medway St
SW1 ...... 115 D3 259 D5
Medwin St SW4...... 138 B1
Meecham Ct 1
SW11 .... 136 C3
Meerbrook Rd SE3... 143 C2
Meers Ct SW20 ...... 178 C2
Meeson Rd E15....... 76 D1
Meeson St E5 .... 75 A4
Meeting House Alley 7
E1.................. 118 B5
Meeting House La
SE15............... 140 B5
Mehetabel Rd E9 ..... 74 C3
Meister Cl IG1......... 57 B1
Melanda Cl BR7 ..... 188 B5
Melanie Cl DA7 ..... 147 A4
Melba Way SE13 ..... 141 D4
Melbourne Ave
Bowes Pk N13 .... 32 B4
Ealing W13......... 109 A5
Pinner HA2, HA5 ...... 41 D6
Melbourne Cl
Broom Hill BR6...... 211 C2
Ickenham UB10....... 60 C4
Wallington SM6..... 219 C3
Melbourne Ct
Hackney E5 .... 75 A4
Muswell Hill N10 ...... 31 B3
Paddington W9 ..... 236 B6
Penge SE20 .... 184 A3
Twickenham TW2..... 152 B3
Melbourne Gdns RM6 59 A4
Melbourne Gr SE22 . 139 D1
Melbourne Ho
Hayes UB4........... 84 C3
Kensington W8...... 245 A3
South Norwood SE25. 205 D5
Melbourne Mews
Brixton SW9......... 138 C4
Catford SE6 .... 164 A4
Melbourne Pl WC2.. 240 D1
Melbourne Rd
Ilford IG1............ 56 D1
Leyton E10........... 53 D2
Merton SW19........ 179 C2
Newham E6 .... 100 B5
Teddington TW11.... 175 C4
Wallington SM6..... 219 C3
Melbourne Rd *continued*
Walthamstow E17 ...... 53 A5
Melbourne Sq 21
SW9............... 138 C4
Melbourne Way EN1 .. 17 D5
Melbray Mews 11
SW6 .... 135 B3
Melbreak Ho 11
SE22 .... 139 C2
Melbury Ave UB2 ... 107 D3
Melbury Cl
Claygate KT10 ...... 213 B2
Elmstead BR7 ...... 188 B4
Melbury Ct
W8 .... 113 B3 254 D6
Melbury Dr SE5...... 139 C5
Melbury Gdns SW20 . 178 B2
Melbury Grange
BR1................ 188 A2
Melbury Ho
South Lambeth SW8 . 270 C4
Twickenham TW2..... 152 B2
Melbury Rd
Harrow HA3.......... 44 B4
Kensington
W14 ...... 113 B3 254 D6
Melchester 5 W11 .... 91 B1
Melchester Ho 1
N19................. 71 D5
Melcombe Ct NW1.. 237 C4
Melcombe Gdns HA3.. 44 B3
Melcombe Ho SW8 . 270 C3
Melcombe Pl NW1... 237 C4
Melcombe Prim Sch 6
W6................. 134 D6
Melcombe St
NW1....... 92 D3 237 D5
Meldex Cl NW7 .... 28 C4
Meldon Cl SW6 ..... 265 D2
Meldone KT3 .... 199 B1
Meldone Cl KT5..... 198 D3
Meldrum Rd IG3....... 80 A6
Melfield Gdns SE6 .. 186 A5
Melford Ave IG11 ..... 79 D2
Melford Cl KT9 ...... 214 B3
Melford Ct
Bermondsey SE1 .... 263 B6
Dulwich SE22....... 162 A4
Hackney E5 .... 74 B5
2 Sutton SM2....... 218 A1
Melford Rd
Dulwich SE21, SE22.. 162 A3
Ilford IG1............ 79 B6
Leyton E11 .... 76 C6
Newham E6 .... 100 B4
Walthamstow E17 ..... 53 B5
Melfort Ave CR7 .... 204 D6
Melfort Rd CR7 ..... 204 D6
Melgund Rd N5....... 72 C3
Melina Cl UB3 .... 83 B2
Melina Ct
Putney SW15....... 134 A2
St John's Wood NW8 . 229 C1
Melina Pl
NW8....... 92 B4 229 C1
Melina Rd W12 ...... 112 B4
Melior Ct N6 .... 49 C3
Melior Pl SE1....... 253 A2
Melior St
SE1....... 117 C4 253 A2
Meliot Rd SE6 .... 164 B2
Melisa Ct N6 .... 49 D2
Meller Cl SM6 .... 220 A5
Mellifont Cl SM5..... 202 B2
Melling Dr EN1 .... 6 A4
Melling St SE18...... 145 C6
Mellington Ct 2 N16 . 74 A5
Mellis Ave TW9 ..... 132 D4
Mellish Cl IG11 ..... 101 D6
Mellish Ct KT6...... 198 A3
Mellish Flats E10 ..... 53 C2
Mellish Gdns IG8 ..... 37 A5
Mellish Ho 2 E1...... 96 B1
Mellish Ind Est SE18 121 D3
Mellish St E14 ...... 119 C3
Mellison Rd SW17 ... 180 C5
Mellitus St W12....... 89 D1
Mellor Cl KT12....... 195 B2
Mellor Ct 2 SW19 ... 180 A3
Mellor Ho 2 SE21 ... 183 C6
Mellow La E UB4...... 83 A3
Mellow Lane Sch
UB4 .... 83 A3

Mellow La W UB10 83 A4
Mellows Rd
Redbridge IG5 56 B6
Wallington SM6 219 D3
Mells Cres SE9 188 B6
Mell St 6 SE10 120 C1
Melody La N5 73 A3
Melody Rd SW18 158 A6
Melon Pl W8 245 B2
Melon Rd Leyton E11 76 C5
Peckham SE15 140 A4
Melrose Ave
Borehamwood WD6 10 D6
Cricklewood NW2 68 C3
Greenford UB6 85 D5
Mitcham CR4 181 B3
Thornton Heath SW16 204 C6
Tottenham N22 32 D2
Twickenham TW2 151 D4
Wimbledon SW19 157 C1
Melrose Cl
Greenford UB6 85 D5
Grove Pk SE12 165 B3
Hayes UB4 84 A2
Melrose Cres BR6 227 B3
Melrose Ct
5 Ealing W13 109 A5
Wandsworth SW18 157 B5
Melrose Dr UB1 107 C5
Melrose Gdns
Edgware HA8 26 D1
Hammersmith W6 112 C3
Kingston u T KT3 199 B6
Melrose Ho
Maida Vale NW6 91 C4
Pimlico SW1 258 D2
Melrose Rd
1 Barnes SW13 133 D3
Merton SW19 179 C2
Pinner HA5 41 B5
Wandsworth SW18 157 B5
Melrose Specl Sch 2 CR4 202 C6
Melrose Terr W6 112 C3
Melrose Tudor SM6 220 A3
Melsa Rd SM4 202 A3
Melthorne Dr HA4 62 C5
Melthorpe Gdns SE3 144 A4
Melton Cl HA4 40 C1
Melton Ct
11 Croydon CR0 221 D6
South Kensington SW7 256 D3
Sutton SM2 218 A1
1 Twickenham TW1 153 B4
Melton Ho E5 74 A6
Melton St NW1 93 D4 232 C1
Melville Ave
Greenford UB6 64 D3
South Croydon CR2 221 D3
Wimbledon SW20 178 A3
Melville Cl UB10 61 B5
Melville Court Flats 8 W12 112 B4
Melville Ct
4 Brentford W4 110 C1
Rotherhithe SE8 119 A2
Melville Gdns N13 32 D5
Melville Ho
Lewisham SE10 142 A4
New Barnet EN5 14 B5
Melville Pl 4 N1 73 A1
Melville Rd
Barnes SW13 134 A4
Sidcup DA14 168 C2
Stonebridge NW10 67 B1
Walthamstow E17 53 B6
Melville Villas Rd W3 111 B5
Melvin Ct 11 TW9 132 C4
Melvin Rd SE20 184 C2
Melwood Ho 23 E1 96 B1
Melyn Cl N7 71 C4
Memel Ct EC1 242 A5
Memel St EC1 242 A5
Memess Path 4 SE18 144 C6
Memorial Ave E15 98 C4
Memorial Cl TW5 129 B6
Memorial Hospl SE18 144 C3
Memorial Hts IG2 57 B3
Menai Pl 2 E3 97 C5
Menard Ct EC1 235 B1
Mendham Ho SE1 263 A6
Mendip Cl
Forest Hill SE26 184 C6
Harlington UB3 127 B5
North Cheam KT4 216 C6
Mendip Ct
12 Battersea SW11 136 A2
Deptford SE14 140 C6
1 East Barnet N20 14 C2
Mendip Dr NW2, NW11 69 A6
Mendip Ho
Harrow HA3 43 A3
2 Stoke Newington N4 51 B2
Mendip Hos 12 E2 96 C4
Mendip Rd
Battersea SW11 136 A2
Bushey WD23 8 A5
Ilford IG2 57 C4
Mendora Rd SW6 135 B5 264 C4
Menelik Rd NW2 69 B4
Menin Wks CR4 180 D1
Menlo Gdns SE19 183 B3
Mennie Ho SE18 144 B4
Mennis Ho SM5 218 C6
Menon Dr N9 18 B1
Menorah Foundation Sch 8 HA8 27 A3
Menorah Gram Sch HA8 27 A3
Menorah High Sch for Girls NW2 68 A5
Menorah Prim Sch NW11 47 A2
Menotti St 6 E2 96 A3
Menteath Ho 9 E14 97 C1
Mentmore Cl HA3 43 C3
Mentmore Terr E8 74 B1
Mentone Ct SW8 270 B2
Meon Ct TW7 130 C3
Meon Rd W3 111 A4
Meopham Rd CR4, SW16 181 C2
Mepham Cres HA3 24 A3
Mepham Gdns HA3 24 A3
Mepham St SE1 116 C5 251 A3
Mera Dr DA7 147 D1
Merantun Way SW19 180 A2
Merbury Cl
Lewisham SE13 164 B6
Woolwich SE28 123 B5
Merbury Rd SE28 123 C4
Mercator Pl 4 E14 119 C1
Mercator Rd SE13 142 B1
Mercer Cl KT7 196 D2
Merceron Ho 3 E2 96 C4
Merceron St E1 96 B3
Mercer Pl HA5 22 C1
Mercers Cl SE10 120 D2
Mercer's Cotts 8 E3 97 A1
Mercers Mews N7 71 D4
Mercers Pl W6 112 D2
Mercers Rd N19 71 D5
Mercer St WC2 94 A1 240 A1
Merchant Ct E1 118 C5
Merchants Cl SE25 206 A5
Merchants Ho SE10 120 B1
Merchants Lo 5 E17 53 C5
Merchant Sq W2 236 C3
Merchant St E3 97 B4
Merchant Taylors' Almshouses SE13 142 C1
Merchant Taylors Hall★ EC3 242 D1
Merchiston Rd SE6 164 B2
Merchland Rd SE9 167 A3
Merchon Ho N7 71 C4
Mercia Gr SE13 142 A1
Mercia Ho
9 Camberwell SE5 139 A3
Charlton TW15 171 A2
Mercie Ct SE22 162 A3
Mercier Rd SW15 157 A6
Mercury 25 NW9 27 D2
Mercury Ct
8 Brixton SW9 138 C4
Mercury Ct *continued*
10 Millwall E14 119 C2
Mercury Ctr TW14 150 A6
Mercury Ho
Brentford TW8 109 D1
6 Old Ford E3 97 C6
Mercury Rd 2 TW8 109 C1
Mercury Way SE14 140 D6
Mercy Terr SE13 163 D6
Merebank La CR0, SM6 220 B3
Mere Cl
Orpington BR6 226 D6
Putney SW15, SW19 156 D4
Meredith Ave NW2 68 C3
Meredith Cl HA5 22 D3
Meredith Ho 17 N16 73 C3
Meredith Mews SE4 141 B1
Meredith St
Finsbury EC1 234 C1
Newham E13 99 A4
Meredith Twr W3 110 D3
Meredyth Rd SW13 134 A3
Mere End CR0 206 D2
Mere Rd TW17 192 D3
Mereside BR6 226 C6
Mereside Pk TW15 171 A6
Meretone Cl SE4 141 A1
Mereton Mans 6 SE8 141 C4
Meretune Ct SM4 201 B6
Merevale Cres SM4 202 A3
Mereway Industry TW2 152 C4
Mereway Rd TW2 152 C3
Merewood Cl BR1 188 C1
Merewood Gdns CR0 206 D2
Mereworth Cl BR2 208 D4
Mereworth Dr SE18 145 A5
Mereworth Ho 3 SE15 140 C6
Merganser Ct 17 SE8 141 B6
Merganser Gdns SE28 123 B3
Meridan Ct SE13 142 B1
Meriden Cl BR1 187 D3
Meriden Ct SW3 257 A1
Meriden Ho
4 Barnet EN5 1 A1
25 Hoxton N1 95 C6
Meridian Building★ SE10 142 B5
Meridian Cl NW7 27 B6
Meridian Ct
4 Bermondsey SE16 118 A4
4 Catford SE6 164 D3
Croydon CR0 220 C4
Meridian Ho SE10 120 C2
Meridian Pl E14 120 A4
Meridian Prim Sch 9 SE10 142 B6
Meridian Rd SE7 143 D5
Meridian Sq E15 76 B1
Meridian Trad Est SE7 121 B2
Meridian Way
Enfield EN3 19 A5
Lower Edmonton N9, N18 18 D1
Meridian Wlk N17 33 C4
Merifield Rd SE9 143 C1
Merino Cl E11 55 C5
Merino Pl DA15 168 A6
Merioneth Ct 7 W7 86 D2
Merivale Rd
Harrow HA1 42 A2
Putney SW15 135 A1
Merlewood Dr BR7 188 B2
Merley Ct NW9 45 A1
Merlin 26 NW9 27 D2
Merlin Cl
Mitcham CR4 202 C6
4 Northolt UB5 84 C4
South Croydon CR0 221 C4
Wallington SM6 220 B2
Merlin Cres HA8 26 B2
Merlin Ct
Beckenham BR2 208 D5
6 Ealing W7 86 D3
Mitcham CR4 180 C2
Ruislip HA4 61 B6
Stanmore HA7 25 B5
Wood Green N22 32 C2
Merling Cl KT9 213 D3
Merlin Gdns BR1 165 A1
Merlin Gr BR3 207 C4
Merlin Ho
7 Chiswick W4 111 B1
Enfield EN3 18 D6
West Hampstead NW3 69 D4
Merlin Prim Sch BR1 165 A1
Merlin Rd
Bexley DA16 146 A1
Wanstead E12 77 D6
Merlin Rd N DA16 146 A1
Merlins Ave HA2 63 B5
Merlin Sch The 11 SW15 157 A6
Merlins Ct WC1 234 A1
Merlin St EC1 94 C4 234 A1
Mermaid Ct
Bermondsey SE1 117 B4 252 C2
Rotherhithe SE16 119 B5
Stroud Green N4 50 C3
Mermaid Ho 8 E14 120 A6
Mermaid Twr 22 SE8 141 B6
Meroe Ct N16 73 C6
Merredene St SW2 160 B5
Merriam Ave 2 E9 75 B2
Merriam Cl E4 36 A5
Merrick Rd UB2 107 B3
Merricks Ct 5 SW14 132 D1
Merrick Sq SE1 117 B3 262 C6
Merridale SE12 164 D6
Merridene N21 16 D5
Merrielands Cres RM9 103 B5
Merrielands Ret Pk RM9 103 B5
Merrilands Rd KT4 200 C1
Merrilees Rd DA15 167 C4
Merrilyn Cl KT10 213 A2
Merriman Rd SE3 143 C4
Merrington Rd SW6 265 B6
Merrion Ave HA7 25 D5
Merritt Gdns KT9 213 C2
Merritt Rd SE4 163 B6
Merrivale
Camden Town NW1 232 B5
Southgate N14 15 D6
Merrivale Ave IG4 55 D5
Merrow Ct CR4 180 B1
Merrow St SE17 117 B1 262 C1
Merrow Way CR0 224 A2
Merrow Wlk SE17 262 D2
Merrydown Way BR7 188 B2
Merry Fiddlers RM8 81 B6
Merryfield SE3 142 D3
Merryfield Gdns HA7 25 C5
Merryfield Ho SE12 165 C1
Merryhill Cl E4 19 D4
Merry Hill Rd WD23 8 A3
Merryhills Ct N14 15 C6
Merryhills Dr EN2 4 A1
Merryhills Prim Sch EN2 4 B1
Merryweather Ct
13 Dartmouth Pk N19 71 C5
1 New Malden KT3 199 C4
Mersea Ho IG11 78 D2
Mersey Ct 10 KT2 175 D2
Mersey Ho 10 N7 72 C3
Mersey Rd E17 53 B6
Mersey Wlk UB5 85 C5
Mersham Dr NW9 44 D4
Mersham Pl
Penge SE20 184 B2
South Norwood CR7 183 B1
Mersham Rd CR7 183 B1
Merstone Ho SW18 157 D5
Merten Rd RM6 59 A2
Merthyr Terr SW13 134 B6
MERTON 179 C2
Merton Abbey Mills Mkt★ SW19 180 A2
Merton Abbey Prim Sch SW19 179 D2
Merton Ave
Chiswick W4 111 D2
Hillingdon UB10 60 D1
Northolt UB5 64 A3
Merton Coll SM4 201 B4
Merton Court Prep Sch DA14 190 C6
Merton Ct Barnet EN5 1 D1
Welling DA16 146 B3
Merton Gdns BR5 210 D4
Merton Hall Gdns SW20 179 A2
Merton Hall Rd SW19 179 A2
Merton High St SW19 180 A3
Merton Ho SW18 157 C3
Merton Ind Pk SW19 180 A2
Merton La N6 70 D6
Merton Lo
New Barnet EN5 14 A6
3 Streatham SW16 182 A5
Merton Mans SW20 178 D1
MERTON PARK 179 C1
Merton Park Par SW19 179 B2
Merton Park Prim Sch SW19 179 C1
Merton Park Sta SW19 179 C2
Merton Pl 9 SW19 180 A3
Merton Rd
Barking IG11 79 D1
Croydon CR0 205 D3
Croydon SE25 206 A4
Enfield EN2 5 B5
Harrow HA2 42 A1
Ilford IG3 57 D2
Leytonstone E17 54 A3
Merton SW19 179 D3
Wandsworth SW18 157 C4
Merton Rise NW3 70 C1
Merton Road Ind Est SW18 157 C4
Merton Way
East Molesey KT8 196 A6
Hillingdon UB10 60 D1
Merttins Rd SE15 162 D6
Meru Cl NW5 71 A3
Mervan Rd SW2 138 C1
Mervyn Ave SE9 167 A2
Mervyn Ct SE18 145 C6
Mervyn Rd
Brentford W13 109 A3
Shepperton TW17 193 A2
Mervyn Stockwood Ho 1 SE9 167 A2
Messaline Ave W3 89 A1
Messent Rd SE9 165 D6
Messer Ct CR0 220 D4
Messeter Pl SE9 166 C5
Messina Ave NW6 69 C1
Messiter Ho N1 233 D5
Met Appts The SE12 164 D6
Metcalfe Ho 28 SW8 137 D3
Metcalfe Wlk 2 TW13 173 A6
Metcalf Rd TW15 170 D5
Meteor St SW11 137 A1
Meteor Way SM6 220 A1
Metford Cres EN3 7 C5
Metherell Ho N21 17 B5
Metheringham Way NW9 27 C2
Methley Ho 8 N7 72 B6
Methley St SE11 116 C1 261 B1
Methodist Central Hall★ SW1 115 D4 249 D1
Methuen Cl HA8 26 C3
Methuen Pk N10 49 B6
Methuen Rd
Belvedere DA17 125 D2
Bexleyheath DA6 147 B1
Edgware HA8 26 C3
Methwold Rd W10 90 D2
Metro Bsns Ctr The SE26 185 B5
Metro Ctr UB4 106 C6
Metro Ho E7 77 B2
Metro Ind Ctr TW7 130 C3
Metropolis Apartments 5 SW12 159 B3
Metropolitan Benefit Societies Almshouses 3 N1 73 C2
Metropolitan Bsns Ctr 9 N1 73 C1

Metropolitan Cl [23] E14 97 C2
Metropolitan Ctr The UB6 85 D6
Metro Trad Ctr HA9 66 D4
Meudon Ct KT6 197 D4
Mews Pl IG8 37 A6
Mews St E1 118 A5
Mews The
Beckenham BR3 185 C2
Hampton TW12 174 A4
Hornsey N8 50 C5
Redbridge IG4 55 D4
Shoreditch N1 235 B6
Thornton Heath SW16 182 B2
Tottenham N15 51 C5
[5] Upper Holloway N19 50 A1
Woolwich SE18 122 D1
Mexborough NW1 232 A5
Mexfield Rd SW15 157 B6
Meyer Gn EN1 6 A5
Meyer Ho [1] SW12 159 B4
Meymott St SE1 116 D5 251 C3
Meynell Cres E9 74 D1
Meynell Gdns E9 74 D1
Meynell Rd E9 74 D1
Meyrick Ct CR7 204 C3
Meyrick Ho [8] E14 97 C2
Meyrick Rd
Battersea SW11 136 C2
Willesden NW10 68 A2
Miah Terr [9] E1 118 A5
Miall Wlk SE26 185 A6
Micawber Ave UB8 82 C3
Micawber Ct N1 235 B2
Micawber Ho [27] SE16 118 A4
Micawber St N1 95 A4 235 B2
Michael Cliffe Ho EC1 234 B1
Michael Faraday Ho SE17 262 D1
Michael Faraday Prim Sch SE17 117 B1 262 D1
Michael Gaynor Cl W7 108 D5
Michael Manley Ind Est [12] SW8 137 C3
Michael Marshall Ho [2] SE9 167 A2
Michaelmas Cl SW20 200 C6
Michael Rd
Leytonstone E11 54 D1
Parsons Green SW6 135 D4 265 D2
South Norwood SE25 205 C6
Michaels Cl SE13 142 C1
Michael Sobell Sinai Sch HA3 44 C3
Michaelson Ho [4] SE21 183 C6
Michael Tippett Sch The SE24 139 A1
Michelangelo Ct [14] SE16 118 B1
Micheldever Rd SE12 164 D5
Michelham Gdns TW1 152 D1
Michelle Ct
Acton W3 111 B6
North Finchley N12 30 A5
Michell Ho TW1 152 D3
Michels Almshouses [11] TW10 154 A6
Michelsdale Dr [3] TW9 132 A1
Michelson Ho SE11 260 D3
Michel's Row [2] TW9 132 A1
Michel Wlk SE18 122 D1
Michigan Ave E12 78 B4
Michigan Ho E14 119 C3
Michleham Down N12 29 B6
Mickledore NW1 232 B3
Micklefield Ct CR0 204 D3
Mickleham Cl BR5 190 A1
Mickleham Gdns SM3 217 A2
Mickleham Rd BR5 190 A1
Mickleham Way CR0 224 B1
Micklethwaite Rd SW6 135 C6 265 B5
Mickleton Ho [30] W2 91 C2
Midas Bsns Ctr RM10 81 D4
Midas Metro Ctr SM4 200 D2
Midcroft HA4 39 C1
Middle Dene NW7 11 B1
Middlefield NW8 92 B6 229 C6
Middlefielde W13 87 B2
Middlefield Gdns IG2 56 D3
Middle Green Cl [3] KT5 198 B3
Middleham Gdns N18 34 A4
Middleham Rd N18 34 A4
Middle La Hornsey N8 50 A4
Teddington TW11 174 D4
Middle Lane Mews N8 50 A4
Middle Mill KT5 198 B6
Middle Park Ave SE9 165 D4
Middle Park Prim Sch SE9 165 D4
Middle Rd
East Barnet EN4 14 C5
Finchley N10 30 C2
Harrow HA2 42 B1
Mitcham SW16 181 D1
[12] Newham E13 99 A5
Middle Row W10 91 A3
Middle Row Prim Sch [21] W10 91 A3
Middlesborough Rd N18 34 A4
Middlesex Bsns Ctr UB2 107 B4
Middlesex Cl UB6 85 D3
Middlesex Ct
[5] Chiswick W4 111 D2
[6] Harrow HA1 42 D4
Middlesex Cty Cricket Sch N3 29 D1
Middlesex Ho
Marylebone W1 239 B4
[4] Penge SE20 184 C3
Wembley HA0 87 D6
Middlesex Pas EC1 241 D3
Middlesex Pl [13] E9 74 C2
Middlesex Rd CR4 204 A4
Middlesex Sch of Complementary Medicine HA7 26 A1
Middlesex St E1 95 D1 243 C2
Middlesex Univ (Archway Campus) [15] N19 71 C6
Middlesex Univ (Cat Hill) EN4 15 A6
Middlesex Univ (Chase Farm Hospl) EN2 4 C5
Middlesex Univ (Hendon Campus) NW4 46 B5
Middlesex Univ (Trent Park) EN4 3 C3
Middle St
Croydon CR0 221 A5
Holborn EC1 242 A4
Middle Temple* EC4 251 A6
Middle Temple La EC4 116 C6 251 A6
Middleton Ave
Chingford Green E4 19 B1
Greenford UB5 86 B5
Sidcup DA14 190 C5
Middleton Cl E4 19 B1
Middleton Ct
Bromley BR1 187 B3
New Barnet EN5 2 A1
Middleton Dr
Bermondsey SE16 118 D4
Pinner HA5 40 A6
Middleton Gdns IG2 56 D3
Middleton Gr N7 72 A3
Middleton Ho
Dalston E8 73 D1
Newington SE1 262 C5
Middleton Mews N7 72 A3
Middleton Pl W1 239 A3
Middleton Rd
Carshalton CR4, SM5 202 B2
Dalston E8 73 D1
Middleton Rd *continued*
Golders Green NW11 47 C2
Hayes UB3 83 B2
Middleton St E2 96 B4
Middleton Way SE13 142 B1
Middleway NW11 47 D4
Middle Way
Hayes UB4 84 C3
Mitcham SW16 181 D1
Middle Way The HA3 24 D1
Middlewich Ho [7] UB5 85 B3
Middle Yd SE1 253 A4
Midfield Prim Sch BR5 190 A3
Midfield Way BR5 190 B2
Midford Ho [1] NW4 46 D5
Midford Pl W1 239 B5
Midholm
East Finchley NW11 47 D5
Wembley HA9 44 C1
Midholm Cl NW11 47 D5
Midholm Rd CR0 223 A6
Midhope Ho WC1 233 B1
Midhope St WC1 233 B1
Midhurst [1] SE26 184 C4
Midhurst Ave
Muswell Hill N10 49 A6
Thornton Heath CR0 204 C2
Midhurst Ct N8 50 A2
Midhurst Gdns UB10 61 A1
Midhurst Hill DA6 169 C6
Midhurst Ho [6] E14 97 B1
Midhurst Par N10 49 A6
Midhurst Rd W13 109 A3
Midhurst Way E5 74 A4
Midland Pl E14 120 A1
Midland Rd
Leytonstone E10 54 A2
St Pancras NW1 94 A4 233 A2
Midland Terr NW10 89 C3
Midlea Ho EN3 6 C4
Midleton Rd KT3 177 A1
Midlothian Ho NW2 68 B4
Midlothian Rd E3 97 B3
Midmoor Rd
Merton SW19 179 A2
Streatham SW12 159 C3
Midship Cl SE16 118 D5
Midship Point E14 119 C4
Midstrath Rd NW10 67 C4
Midsummer Apartments [7] SM2 217 C1
Midsummer Ave TW4 129 B1
Midsummer Ct
Blackheath Pk SE12 143 A1
Edgware HA8 10 D1
Harrow HA1 42 B4
Midway SM3 201 B2
Midway Ho EC1 234 D2
Midwinter Cl [3] DA16 146 A2
Midwood Cl NW2 68 B5
Mighell Ave IG4 55 D4
Milan Ct N11 31 D2
Milan Rd UB1 107 B4
Milborne Gr SW10 256 B1
Milborne Ho [11] E9 74 C2
Milborne St E9 74 C2
Milborough Cres SE12 164 C5
Milbourne La KT10 212 A3
Milbourne Lodge Jun Sch KT10 212 A2
Milbourne Lodge Sch KT10 212 B2
Milbrook KT10 212 A2
Milbrook Ct NW3 48 A1
Milburn Dr [1] UB7 104 A6
Milburn Ho SW20 178 B1
Milcote St SE1 251 D1
Mildenhall Rd E5 74 C5
Mildmay Ave N1 73 B2
Mildmay Ct N1 73 B3
Mildmay Gr N N1 73 B3
Mildmay Gr S N1 73 B3
Mildmay Ho [6] SW15 156 C6
Mildmay Mission Hospl E2 95 D4
Mildmay Pk N1 73 B3
Mildmay Rd Ilford IG1 78 D5
Stoke Newington N1 73 C3
Mildmay St N1 73 B2
Mildon Ho EN3 6 C3
Mildred Ave
Hayes UB3 105 B3
Northolt UB5 63 D3
Mildura Ct N8 50 B5
MILE END 97 A3
Mile End Hospl E2 96 D4
Mile End Park L Ctr & Stad E3 97 B2
Mile End Pl E1 96 D3
Mile End Rd E1, E3 96 D3
Mile End Sta E3 97 B4
Mile End The E17 34 D2
Mile Rd
Hackbridge SM6 203 A1
Wallington CR0, CR4, CR9 203 D1
Miles Bldgs NW1 237 A4
Miles Cl SE28 123 B5
Miles Coverdale Prim Sch [16] W12 112 C4
Miles Ct Croydon CR0 220 D6
Stepney E1 96 B1
Miles Dr SE28 123 C5
Miles Ho [5] SE10 120 C1
Miles Lo Harrow HA1 42 B4
Stratford New Town E15 76 B3
Milespit Hill NW7 28 C5
Miles Pl NW8 236 D4
Miles Rd Hornsey N8 50 A6
Mitcham CR4 202 C6
Miles St SW8 138 A6 270 B5
Milestone Cl
Edmonton N9 18 A2
Sutton SM2 218 B1
Milestone Ct TW7 131 A4
Milestone Green SW14 133 B1
Milestone Ho KT1 197 D5
Milestone Rd SE19 183 D4
Miles Way N20 14 C2
Milfoil St W12 112 A6
Milford Cl SE2 147 A6
Milford Ct
Southall UB1 107 C5
[3] Stamford Hill N16 51 C1
Milford Gdns
Croydon CR0 206 D4
Edgware HA8 26 C3
Wembley HA0 65 D3
Milford Gr SM1 218 A4
Milford La WC2 116 C6 251 A6
Milford Mews SW16 160 B1
Milford Rd
Ealing W13 109 B5
Southall UB1 107 C6
Milk St Bromley BR1 187 B4
City of London EC2 95 A1 242 B2
Newham E16 122 D5
Milkwell Gdns IG8 37 B3
Milkwell Yd [7] SE5 139 A4
Milkwood Rd SE24 138 D1
Milk Yd E1 118 C6
Millais Ave E12 78 C3
Millais Cres KT19 215 C3
Millais Ct [9] UB5 84 D5
Millais Gdns HA8 26 C1
Millais Rd Enfield EN1 17 D6
Leyton E11 76 B4
New Malden KT3 199 C2
Millais Way KT19 215 A4
Milland Ho [11] SW15 156 A3
Millard Cl [21] N16 73 C3
Millard Rd SE8 119 B1
Millard Terr RM10 81 C2
Millars Meadow Cl SE12 165 A6
Millbank
Wallington SM6 219 D3
Westminster SW1 116 A2 260 A3
Millbank Ho KT6 198 B2
Millbank Prim Sch SW1 115 D2 259 D3
Millbank Way SE12 165 A6
Millbourne Rd TW13 173 A6
Mill Bridge EN5 13 B5
Millbrook [1] E18 55 A6
Millbrook Ave DA16 145 B1
Millbrooke Ct [7] SW15 157 A6
Millbrook Gdns RM6 59 A3
Millbrook Ho [4] SE15 140 A6
Millbrook Pl NW1 232 A4
Millbrook Rd
Brixton SW9 138 D2
Edmonton N9 18 B3
Mill Cl SM5 219 A6
Mill Cnr EN5 1 B4
Millcroft Ho SE6 185 D6
Mill Ct Hendon NW7 29 A2
Leyton E10 76 A5
[14] Thamesmead SE28 124 B6
Millender Wlk SE16 118 C2
Millennium Bridge* SE1, EC4 252 A5
Millennium Bsns Ctr NW2 68 B6
Millennium City Acad W1 238 D3
Millennium Cl E16 99 B1
Millennium Dr E14 120 B2
Millennium Harbour E14 119 C4
Millennium Ho E17 52 D4
Millennium Pl [27] E2 96 B5
Millennium Prim Sch The SE10 120 D3
Millennium Sq SE1 253 D2
Millennium Way SE10 120 C3
Miller Ave EN3 7 C5
Miller Cl
Bromley BR1 187 B5
Carshalton CR4 202 D2
Pinner HA5 22 C1
Miller Ct
Bexleyheath DA7 147 D2
[8] Hendon NW9 46 A5
Miller Ho
Harringay N15 50 D5
[9] Streatham SW2 160 A4
Miller Rd
Mitcham SW19 180 B4
Thornton Heath CR0 204 C1
Miller's Ave E8, N16 73 D3
Millers Cl NW7 28 A6
Millers Ct [3] HA0 88 A5
Miller's Ct [1] W4 111 D1
Millers Green Cl EN2 4 D2
Millers Mead Ct SW19 180 B3
Miller St NW1 232 A4
Miller's Terr [1] E8 73 D3
Miller's Way W6 112 C4
Millers Wharf Ho E1 118 A5
Millers Yd N3 29 D3
Miller Wlk SE1 251 B3
Millet Rd UB6 85 D5
Mill Farm Ave TW16 171 C3
Millfarm Bsns Pk TW4 151 A4
Mill Farm Cl HA5 22 C1
Mill Farm Cres TW4 151 A3
Millfield
Charlton TW16 171 B2
Finsbury Pk N4 72 C6
Kingston u T KT1 198 B6
Millfield Ave E17 35 B2
Millfield La N6 70 D6
Millfield Pl N6 71 A6
Millfield Rd
Hendon HA8 27 A1
Twickenham TW4 151 B3
Millfields Com Sch E5 74 C4
Millfields Rd E5 74 C5
Mill Gdns SE26 162 B1
Mill Gn CR4 203 A2
Mill Green Bsns Pk CR4 203 A2
Mill Green Rd CR4 203 A2
Millgrove St [6] SW11 137 A3
Millharbour E14 119 D4
Millhaven Cl RM6 58 B3
MILL HILL 28 B5
Mill Hill SW13 134 A2
Mill Hill Broadway Sta NW7 27 C4
Mill Hill Circus NW7 27 D5

Mill Hill Cty High Sch NW7 . . . 11 C2
Mill Hill East Sta NW7 . . . 29 A3
Mill Hill Gr 11 W3 . . . 110 D5
Mill Hill Ind Est NW7 . . 27 D4
Mill Hill Rd
Barnes SW13 . . . 134 A3
South Acton W3 . . . 110 D4
Mill Hill Sch NW7 . . . 28 B6
Mill Hill Terr 9 W3 . . 110 D5
Mill Ho
4 Lewisham SE13 . . 142 A2
Morden SM4 . . . 202 A5
Woodford IG8 . . . 36 D5
Millhouse Pl SE27 . . 182 D6
Millicent Fawcett Ct N17 . . . 33 D2
Millicent Gr N13 . . . 32 D5
Millicent Preston Ho 4 IG11 . . . 101 B6
Millicent Rd E10 . . . 53 B1
Milligan Ho SE23 . . . 163 B3
Milligan St E14 . . . 119 B6
Milliners Ho SW18 . . 135 C1
Milling Rd HA8 . . . 27 B3
Millington Ho N16 . . . 73 B5
Millington Rd UB3 . . . 105 C3
Mill La
Brondesbury NW6 . . . 69 B3
Carshalton SM5 . . . 219 A5
Croydon CR0 . . . 220 C5
Dagenham RM6 . . . 59 A3
Sewardstone E4 . . . 7 D2
Woodford IG8 . . . 36 D5
Woolwich SE18 . . . 122 C1
Mill Lane Trad Est CR0 . . . 220 B5
Millman Ct
Bloomsbury WC1 . . . 240 C5
Greenwich SE3 . . . 143 B5
Millman Mews WC1 . 240 C5
Millman Pl WC1 . . . 240 D5
Millman St WC1 . . . 94 B3 240 C5
Millmark Gr SE14 . . . 141 A3
Millmarsh La EN3 . . . 7 B3
Millmead Bsns Ctr N17 . . . 52 B6
Millmead Ind Ctr N17 . 52 B6
Mill Mead Rd N17 . . . 52 B6
MILL MEADS . . . 98 B5
Millner Ct SE4 . . . 141 B3
Mill Pl
Chislehurst BR7 . . . 188 D2
Kingston u T KT1 . . . 198 B6
Limehouse E14 . . . 97 A1
Mill Plat TW7 . . . 131 A3
Mill Plat Ave TW7 . . . 131 A3
Mill Pond Cl SW8 . . . 137 D5 269 D3
Millpond Est SE16 . . . 118 B4
Millpond Pl 2 SM6 . . 219 A5
Mill Rd Ilford IG1 . . . 78 C5
Merton SW19 . . . 180 A3
Newham E16 . . . 121 B5
Twickenham TW2 . . . 152 A2
Mill Ridge HA8 . . . 26 C5
Mill River Trad Est EN3 . . . 7 A1
Mill Row N1 . . . 95 C6
Mills Cl UB10 . . . 82 C5
Mills Ct 9 Leyton E11 . . 76 C5
Shoreditch EC2 . . . 95 C4
Mills Gr Hendon NW4 . . 46 D6
1 South Bromley E14 . . 98 A2
Mills Ho
Nine Elms SW8 . . . 269 B2
Walthamstow E17 . . . 54 B6
Millshott Cl SW6 . . . 134 C4
Millside SM5 . . . 218 D6
Millside Pl TW7 . . . 131 B3
Millson Cl N20 . . . 14 B2
Mills Row W4 . . . 111 B2
Mill St
Bermondsey SE1 . . . 117 D4 253 D2
Kingston u T KT1 . . . 198 A6
Mayfair W1 . . . 249 A6
Millstone Cl E15 . . . 76 B2
Millstream Cl N13 . . . 32 C5
Millstream Ho 14 SE16 . . . 118 B4
Millstream Rd SE1 . . . 117 D4 253 C1
Mill Trad Est The NW10 . . . 89 A4
Mill Vale BR2 . . . 186 D1
Mill View Cl KT17 . . . 215 D1
Mill View Gdns CR0 . . 222 D5
MILLWALL . . . 119 C3
Millwall Dock Rd E14 . . . 119 C3
Mill Way
Edgware NW7 . . . 27 C5
Feltham TW14 . . . 150 B6
Millway Gdns UB5 . . . 63 B2
Millwood Rd TW3, TW7 . . . 152 A6
Millwood St 10 W10 . . . 91 A2
Mill Yd E1 . . . 118 A6
Milman Cl HA5 . . . 40 D6
Milman Rd NW6 . . . 91 A5
Milman's Ho SW10 . . 266 C5
Milman's St SW10 . . . 136 B6 266 C5
Milne Ct Enfield EN2 . . . 4 C3
4 Woodford E18 . . . 37 A2
Milne Field HA5 . . . 23 C3
Milne Gdns SE9 . . . 166 A6
Milne Ho 18 SE18 . . . 122 B2
Milner Bldg N16 . . . 73 B5
Milner Dr TW2 . . . 152 B4
Milner Ho
1 Battersea SW11 . . . 136 B2
Hayes UB4 . . . 84 B4
Milner Pl N1 . . . 94 C6 234 B6
Milner Rd
Dagenham RM8 . . . 80 C6
Kingston u T KT1 . . . 197 D6
Merton SW19 . . . 179 D2
Morden SM4 . . . 202 B4
Newham E15 . . . 98 C4
South Norwood CR7 . . . 205 B6
Milner Sq N1 . . . 72 D1
Milner St SW3 . . . 114 D2 257 C4
Milner Wlk SE9 . . . 167 B3
Milnthorpe Rd W4 . . . 133 B6
Milo Rd SE22 . . . 161 D5
Milrood Ho 5 E1 . . . 96 D2
Milroy Wlk SE1 . . . 251 C4
Milson Rd W14 . . . 113 A3 254 A6
Milsted Ho 23 E5 . . . 74 B3
Milton Ave Barnet EN5 . 13 B6
Becontree NW10 . . . 89 B6
Carshalton SM1 . . . 218 C4
Crouch End N6 . . . 49 C2
Kingsbury NW9 . . . 45 A6
Plashet E6 . . . 78 A1
Stonebridge NW10 . . . 89 A6
Thornton Heath CR0 . . 205 B2
Milton Cl
Bermondsey SE1 . . . 117 D2 263 C3
Carshalton SM1 . . . 218 B5
Hampstead Garden Suburb N2 . . . 48 A3
Hayes UB4 . . . 84 A1
Milton Court Rd SE14 . . . 141 A6
Milton Cres IG2 . . . 57 A3
Milton Ct
Fulham SW6 . . . 135 A2
Ilford RM6 . . . 58 C2
Kingston u T KT2 . . . 176 A6
St Luke's EC2 . . . 242 C4
Twickenham TW2 . . . 152 C1
Uxbridge UB10 . . . 60 D5
9 Wandsworth SW18 . . . 157 C6
Milton Dr
Borehamwood WD6 . . . 10 D6
Littleton TW17 . . . 192 A5
Milton Gdns TW19 . . . 148 B3
Milton Gr
Friern Barnet N11 . . . 31 D5
Stoke Newington N16 . . 73 C4
Milton Ho
12 Beckenham BR3 . . 185 C3
19 Bethnal Green E2 . . . 96 C4
2 Camberwell SE5 . . . 139 B5
5 Kingston u T KT2 . . . 176 D4
Sutton SM1 . . . 217 C5
Milton House Mans E8 . . . 73 D4
Milton Lo
4 Sidcup DA14 . . . 190 A6
Milton Lo *continued*
Southgate N21 . . . 16 D3
Twickenham TW1 . . . 152 D4
Milton Pk N6 . . . 49 C2
Milton Pl 3 N7 . . . 72 C3
Milton Rd Acton W3 . . . 111 B5
Belvedere DA17 . . . 125 C2
Bexley DA16 . . . 145 D4
Crouch End N6 . . . 49 C2
Ealing W7 . . . 108 D6
Hampton TW12 . . . 173 C3
Harrow HA1 . . . 42 C5
1 Hendon NW9 . . . 46 A2
Mill Hill NW7 . . . 28 A5
Mitcham CR4 . . . 181 A3
Mortlake SW14 . . . 133 B2
Sutton SM1 . . . 217 C4
Thornton Heath CR0 . . 205 B2
Tottenham N15 . . . 50 D6
Tulse Hill SE24 . . . 160 D6
Uxbridge UB10 . . . 60 D4
Wallington SM6 . . . 219 D2
Walthamstow E17 . . . 53 C5
Wimbledon SW19 . . . 180 A4
Milton St EC1, EC2 . . . 95 B2 242 C4
Milton Way UB7 . . . 104 B2
Milverton NW5 . . . 71 A3
Milverton Dr UB10 . . . 61 A4
Milverton Gdns IG3 . . . 79 D6
Milverton Ho SE23 . . . 163 A1
Milverton Rd NW6 . . . 68 C1
Milverton St SE11 . . . 116 C1 261 B1
Milverton Way SE9 . . . 188 C6
Milward St E1 . . . 96 B2
Milward Wlk 14 SE18 . . . 144 C6
Mimosa N15 . . . 51 B4
Mimosa Ct
Colney Hatch N12 . . . 30 C4
South Lambeth SW4 . . 270 B1
Mimosa Ho UB4 . . . 84 C2
Mimosa Rd UB4 . . . 84 C2
Mimosa St SW6 . . . 135 B4 264 D1
Mina Rd
Merton SW19 . . . 179 C2
Walworth SE17 . . . 117 C1 263 B2
Minard Rd SE6 . . . 164 C3
Minchenden Cres N14 . . . 15 D1
Minchenden Ct N14 . . . 15 D2
Minchin Ho 10 E14 . . . 97 C1
Mincing La EC3 . . . 117 C6 253 A6
Minden Rd
Cheam SM3 . . . 217 B6
Penge SE20 . . . 184 B2
Minehead Ct HA2 . . . 63 C6
Minehead Rd
Harrow HA2 . . . 63 C5
Streatham SW16 . . . 182 B5
Mineral Cl EN5 . . . 12 C6
Mineral St SE18 . . . 123 C2
Minera Mews SW1 . . 258 B4
Minerva Cl
Kennington SW9 . . . 138 C5
Sidcup DA14 . . . 189 C6
Minerva Rd
Becontree NW10 . . . 89 B4
Chingford E4 . . . 35 D3
Kingston u T KT1 . . . 176 B1
Minerva St E2 . . . 96 B5
Minerva Wlk EC1 . . . 241 D2
Minet Ave NW10 . . . 89 C5
Minet Ctry Pk UB2, UB3, UB4 . . . 106 C5
Minet Dr UB3 . . . 106 A5
Minet Gdns
Dagenham NW10 . . . 89 C5
Hayes UB3 . . . 106 B5
Minet Ho 20 E1 . . . 96 A1
Minet Jun & Inf Schs UB3 . . . 106 B5
Minet Rd SE5, SW9 . . 138 D3
Minetta Ct 19 EN5 . . . 13 D6
Minford Gdns W14 . . . 112 D4
Mingard Wlk N7 . . . 72 B5
Ming St E14 . . . 119 C6
Minimax Cl TW14 . . . 150 A5
Ministry Way SE9 . . . 166 B2
Mink Ct TW4 . . . 128 C3
Minnie Bennett Ho SE3 . . . 143 C5
Minniedale KT5 . . . 198 B4
Minnow Wlk SE17 . . . 263 B3
Minories EC3 117 D6 253 C6
Minshaw Ct DA14 . . . 189 D6
Minshull Pl 23 BR3 . . . 185 C3
Minshull St SW8 . . . 269 C1
Minson Rd E9 . . . 96 D6
Minstead Gdns SW15 . . . 155 D4
Minstead Way KT3 . . . 199 C3
Minster Ave SM1 . . . 217 C6
Minster Ct EC3 . . . 253 B6
Minster Dr CR0 . . . 221 C4
Minster Gdns KT8 . . . 195 B5
Minsterley Ave TW16, TW17 . . . 193 C5
Minster Rd
Bromley BR1 . . . 187 B3
Brondesbury NW2 . . . 69 A3
Minster Wlk N8 . . . 50 A5
Minstrel Ct HA3 . . . 24 C1
Minstrel Gdns KT5 . . . 198 B5
Mint Bsns Pk 12 E16 . . . 99 A2
Mint Cl UB10 . . . 82 D4
Mintern Cl N13 . . . 16 D1
Minterne Ave UB2 . . . 107 C2
Minterne Rd HA3 . . . 44 B4
Minterne Waye UB4 . . . 84 C1
Mintern St N1 . 95 B5 235 D4
Minton Ho SE11 . . . 261 A4
Minton Mews 3 NW6 . . . 69 D2
Mint Rd SM5, SM6 . . . 219 B4
Mint St SE1 . . . 252 B2
Mint Wlk CR0 . . . 221 A5
Mirabel Rd SW6 . . . 135 B5 264 D4
Mirage Ctr The HA9 . . . 66 D4
Miranda Cl 10 E1 . . . 96 C2
Miranda Ct W3 . . . 88 B1
Miranda Ho
6 Belvedere DA17 . . . 125 C1
17 Hoxton N1 . . . 95 C5
Miranda Rd N19 . . . 49 C1
Mirfield Ct SE20 . . . 184 A1
Mirfield St SE7 . . . 121 D3
Miriam Ct DA14 . . . 190 B6
Miriam Rd SE18 . . . 123 C1
Mirravale Ct 11 IG9 . . . 21 C2
Mirravale Trad Est RM8 . . . 59 A2
Mirren Cl HA2 . . . 63 B5
Mirror Path SE12 . . . 165 C1
Misbourne Rd UB10 . . . 82 C6
Missenden SE17 . . . 262 D1
Missenden Cl TW14 . . 149 D3
Missenden Gdns SM4 . . . 202 A3
Missenden Ho NW8 . 237 A6
Mission Gr E17 . . . 53 A4
Mission Grove Prim Sch E17 . . . 53 B5
Mission Pl SE15 . . . 140 A4
Mission Sq 13 TW8 . . . 132 A6
Mission The
13 Bermondsey SE16 . . . 118 B4
14 Poplar E14 . . . 97 B1
Missouri Ct HA5 . . . 40 C3
Misterton Ct SW11 . . . 266 D2
Mistletoe Cl CR0 . . . 206 D1
Mistley Thorn IG1 . . . 56 C2
Mistral SE5 . . . 139 C4
Mistral Ct E4 . . . 19 D1
Mistys Field KT12 . . . 194 C1
Mitali Pas 21 E1 . . . 96 A1
MITCHAM . . . 202 D5
Mitcham Eastfields Sta CR4 . . . 181 A1
Mitcham Garden Village CR4 . . . 203 A4
Mitcham Ho 9 SE5 . . . 139 A4
Mitcham Ind Est CR4 . . . 181 A2
Mitcham Junction Sta CR4 . . . 203 A4
Mitcham La SW16 . . . 181 C5
Mitcham Pk CR4 . . . 202 C5
Mitcham Rd
Ilford IG3 . . . 57 D2
Newham E6 . . . 100 A4
Upper Tooting SW17 . . 180 D5
Mitcham Sta CR4 . . . 202 C5
Mitchell 19 NW9 . . . 27 D2
Mitchell Brook Prim Sch NW10 . . . 67 C2
Mitchellbrook Way NW10 . . . 67 B2
Mitchell Cl
Abbey Wood SE2 . . . 124 C2
Belvedere DA17 . . . 125 D3
Mitchell Ct SW14 . . . 133 C1
Mitchell Ho
Gunnersbury W4 . . . 110 D1
6 Islington N1 . . . 72 C1
31 Shepherd's Bush W12 . . . 112 B6
Mitchell Rd
Edmonton N13 . . . 33 A5
Orpington BR6 . . . 227 D4
Mitchell's Pl SE21 . . . 161 C4
Mitchell St EC1 . . . 95 A3 242 B6
Mitchell Way
1 Bromley BR1 . . . 187 A2
Tokyngton NW10 . . . 67 A2
Mitchell Wlk E6 . . . 100 B2
Mitchison Rd N1 . . . 73 B2
Mitchley Rd N17 . . . 52 A6
Mitford Cl KT9 . . . 213 C2
Mitford Rd N19 . . . 72 A6
Mitre Bridge Ind Pk W10 . . . 90 B3
Mitre Cl
Shepperton TW17 . . . 193 B3
Sutton SM2 . . . 218 B1
Mitre Ct
Belvedere DA17 . . . 125 C1
1 Ilford RM6 . . . 58 B2
9 Woodford E18 . . . 37 A2
Mitre Ho RM7 . . . 59 D5
Mitre Rd
Lambeth SE1 . . . 116 C4 251 B2
Newham E15 . . . 98 C5
Mitre Sq EC3 . . . 243 B1
Mitre St EC3 . . . 95 C1 243 B1
Mitre The 9 E14 . . . 119 B6
Mitre Way W10 . . . 90 B2
Mizzen Ct E14 . . . 119 C4
Moatbridge Sch SE9 . . . 165 D5
Moat Cl BR6 . . . 227 D2
Moat Cres N3 . . . 47 D6
Moat Croft DA16 . . . 146 C2
Moat Ct Eltham SE9 . . . 166 B5
Sidcup DA15 . . . 167 D1
Moat Dr Harrow HA1 . . . 42 B5
5 Newham E13 . . . 99 C5
Ruislip HA4 . . . 39 C2
Moat Farm Rd UB5 . . . 63 B1
Moatfield NW6 . . . 69 A1
Moat Lodge The HA1 . . 64 C6
Moat Pl Acton W3 . . . 88 D1
Stockwell SW9 . . . 138 B2
Moat Sch The 7 SW6 . . . 135 A3
Moat Side Enfield EN3 . . . 6 D1
Feltham TW13 . . . 172 C6
Moat The KT3 . . . 177 C2
Moberly Rd SW4 . . . 159 D4
Mobey Ct SW4 . . . 270 A1
Moby Dick RM6 . . . 59 B5
Mocatta Ho 9 E1 . . . 96 B3
Modbury Gdns NW5 . . 71 A2
Modder Pl SW15 . . . 134 D1
Model Cotts SW14 . . . 133 A2
Model Farm Cl SE9 . . 166 A1
Modling Ho 8 E2 . . . 96 D5
Modoc Ho EN3 . . . 18 D6
Moelwyn Hughes Ct N7 . . . 71 D3
Moelyn Mews HA1 . . . 43 A4
Moffat Ct
Upper Tooting SW17 . . . 180 C6
Wimbledon SW19 . . . 179 C5
Moffat Ho 24 SE5 . . . 139 A5
Moffat Rd
Bowes Pk N13 . . . 32 A4
South Norwood CR7 . . . 183 B1
Upper Tooting SW17 . . 180 D6
Mogden La TW7 . . . 152 D6
Mohammedi Pk Complex UB5 . . . 85 C6
Mohawk Ho 33 E3 . . . 97 A5
Mohmmad Khan Rd E11 . . . 54 D1
Mohr Ct N22 . . . 32 B3
Moidart Ct HA8 . . . 10 D2
Moineau 18 NW9 . . . 27 D2
Moira Cl N17 . . . 33 C1

Moira Ct SW17 . . . . 159 A2
Moira Ho 13 SW9 . . . . 138 C4
Moira Rd SE9 . . . . 144 B1
Molasses Ho 1 SW11 . . . . 136 A2
Molasses Row 2 SW11 . . . . 136 A2
Mole Abbey Gdns KT8 . . . . 195 D6
Mole Ct
2 Bedford Pk W12 . 111 C4
West Ewell KT19 . . . . 215 A4
Mole Ho NW8 . . . . 236 D5
Molember Ct KT7 . . . . 196 C5
Molember Rd KT8 . . . 196 C4
Molescroft SE9 . . . . . . 167 A1
Molesey Ave KT12, KT8 . . . . 195 B4
Molesey Bsns Ctr KT8 . . . . 195 B4
Molesey Dr SM3 . . . . . 217 A5
Molesey Ho E2 . . . . . 243 C6
Molesey Hospl KT8 . 195 C4
Molesey Park Ave KT8 . . . . 195 D4
Molesey Park Cl KT8 . . . . 196 A4
Molesey Park Rd KT8 . . . . 196 A4
Molesey Rd KT12 . . 195 A2
Molesford Rd SW6 . . 265 A1
Molesham Cl KT8 . . . 195 D6
Molesham Way KT8 195 D6
Molesworth Ho 9 SE17 . . . . 138 D6
Molesworth St SE13 . 142 A2
Moliner Ct 4 BR3 . . . 185 C3
Mollie Davis Ct SE19 . . . . 183 D4
Mollison Ave EN3 . . . . . . 7 B5
Mollison Dr SM6 . . . . . 220 A1
Mollison Sq SM6 . . . . . 219 D1
Mollison Way HA8 . . . . 26 C1
Molly Huggins Cl SW12 . . . . 159 C4
Molton Ho N1 . . . . . . 233 D5
Molvic Ct BR3 . . . . . . 185 B1
Molyneux Dr SW17 . . . 181 B6
Molyneux Ho W1 . . . . 237 B2
Molyneux St W1 . . . . . 92 C2 237 B3
Monarch Cl
Coney Hall BR4 . . . . . 224 D4
East Bedfont TW14 . . 149 C4
Monarch Ct Ealing W5 . 87 C2
Hampstead Garden Suburb N2 . . . . 48 A4
Monarch Dr E16 . . . . . . 99 D2
Monarch Mews
Walthamstow E17 . . . . . 53 D3
West Norwood SW16 182 C5
Monarch Par CR4 . . . 180 D1
Monarch Pl
Buckhurst Hill IG9 . . . . . 21 C2
Sutton SM1 . . . . 218 B3
Monarch Rd DA17 . . . . 125 C3
Monarchs Ct
1 Edgware NW7 . . . . . 27 B5
Harrow HA2 . . . . 41 C2
Monarchs Way HA4 . . . 39 C1
Monarch Way IG2 . . . . 57 B3
Mona Rd SE15 . . . . 140 C3
Mona St E16 . . . . 98 D2
Monastery Gdns EN2 . . . 5 B3
Monaveen Gdns KT8 . . . . 195 D6
Monck's Row SW18 . . 157 B5
Monck St SW1 . . . . 115 D3 259 D5
Monckton Ct W14 . . . 254 C6
Monclar Rd SE5 . . . . . 139 B1
Moncorvo Cl SW7 . . . . 114 C4 247 A1
Moncrieff Cl 4 E6 . . . 100 A1
Moncrieff St SE15 . . . 140 A3
Mondial Way UB7 . . . . 127 A5
Mondragon Ho SW8 . 270 B2
Monega Prim Sch E12 . . . . 77 D2
Monega Rd E7, E12 . . . . 77 D2
Monet Ct 15 SE16 . . . . 118 B1
Moneyer Ho N1 . . . . . 235 C2
Monica Ct SW16 . . . . 181 D4
Monica James Ho 12 DA14 . . . . 168 A1
Monica Shaw Ct NW1 . . . . 232 D3
Monier Rd E3 . . . . 75 C1
Monivea Rd BR3 . . . . . 185 B3
Monkbretton Ho E2 . . . 96 A4
Monk Ct W12 . . . . 112 A5
Monk Dr E16 . . . . 121 A6
MONKEN HADLEY 1 A3
Monken Hadley CE Prim Sch EN4 . . . . 1 C4
Monkfrith Ave N14 . . . . 15 B5
Monkfrith Cl N14 . . . . . 15 B4
Monkfrith Prim Sch N14 . . . . 15 A4
Monkfrith Way N14 . . . 15 B4
Monkham's Ave IG8 . . . 37 B5
Monkham's Dr IG8 . . . . 37 B5
Monkham's La IG8 . . . . 37 B6
Monkleigh Rd SM4, SW20 . . . . 201 A5
Monkridge 3 N8 . . . . . 49 D2
Monks Ave
East Molesey KT8 . . . . 195 B4
New Barnet EN5 . . . . . . 14 A5
Monks Cl
Abbey Wood SE2 . . . . 124 D2
Enfield EN2 . . . . 5 A3
Harrow HA2 . . . . 63 D6
Ruislip HA4 . . . . 62 D4
Monks Cres KT12 . . . . 194 B1
Monksdene Gdns SM1 . . . . 217 D5
Monks Dr W3 . . . . 88 C1
Monksfield N4 . . . . 72 C6
Monks Hill Sp Ctr CR2 . . . . 222 D1
MONKS ORCHARD . . 207 A3
Monks Orchard Rd BR3, CR0 . . . . 207 C2
Monks Orchard Sch CR0 . . . . 206 D4
Monks Park Gdns HA9 . . . . 66 D1
Monks Pk HA9 . . . . 67 A2
Monks Rd EN2 . . . . 5 A3
Monk St SE18 . . . . 122 C2
Monks Way
Beckenham BR3 . . . . . 207 C3
Crofton BR5 . . . . 211 B1
Harmondsworth UB7 . 126 A6
Temple Fortune NW11 . . 47 B5
Monkswell Ct N10 . . . . 31 A2
Monkswell Ho E2 . . . . . 96 A4
Monkswood Gdns
Borehamwood WD6 . . . . 11 B6
Ilford IG5 . . . . 56 C6
Monk Terr SE23 . . . . . . 163 B2
Monkton Ho
32 Bermondsey SE16 . . . . 118 D4
22 Hackney E5 . . . . 74 B3
Monkton Rd DA16 . . . 145 D3
Monkton St SE11 . . . . . . 116 C2 261 B4
Monkville Ave NW11 . . . 47 B5
Monkville Par 1 NW11 . . . . 47 B5
Monkwell Sq EC2 . . . . 242 B3
Monmouth Ave
Teddington KT1 . . . . . 175 C3
Wanstead E18 . . . . 55 B6
Monmouth Cl
Bedford Pk W4 . . . . . . 111 B3
Bexley DA16 . . . . 146 A1
Mitcham CR4, SW16 . 204 A5
Monmouth Ct 9 W7 . . . 86 D2
Monmouth Gr TW8 . . . 110 A2
Monmouth Ho
5 Camden Town NW5 . . . . 71 B2
Wandsworth SW18 . . 157 C5
Monmouth Pl W2 . . . . . 91 D1
Monmouth Rd
Dagenham RM9 . . . . 81 B3
Hayes UB3 . . . . 105 D2
Lower Edmonton N9 . . . 18 C2
Newham E6 . . . . 100 B4
Notting Hill W2 . . . . 91 C1
Monmouth St WC2 . . . . 94 A1 240 A1
Monnery Rd N19 . . . . . . 71 C5
Monnow Rd SE1 . . . . . 118 A2
Mono La TW13 . . . . . . 150 B2
Monoux Almshouses E17 . . . . 53 D5
Monoux Gr E17 . . . . 35 C2
Monroe Cres EN1 . . . . . . 6 B4
Monroe Dr SW14 . . . 154 D6
Monroe Ho
16 Crouch End N19 . . . . 49 D2
Lisson Gr NW8 . . . . . . 230 B1
Monro Gdns HA3 . . . . . 24 C3
Monro Ho
16 Hampstead NW3 . . . 70 A4
Putney SW15 . . . . 156 B6
Monro Way E5 . . . . 74 A4
Monsal Ct E5 . . . . 75 A4
Monsell Ct 4 N4 . . . . . 72 D5
Monsell Rd N4, N5 . . . . 72 D5
Monson Rd
Deptford SE14 . . . . . . 140 D5
Willesden Green NW10 90 B5
Mons Way BR2 . . . . . . 210 A3
Montacute Rd
Bushey WD23 . . . . 8 C4
Carshalton SM4 . . . . . . 202 B3
Forest Hill SE6 . . . . 163 B4
Montagu Cres N18 . . . . 34 B6
Montagu Ct W1 . . . . . 237 D3
Montague Ave
Brockley SE4 . . . . 141 C1
Ealing W7 . . . . 108 D5
Montague Cl
4 Barnet EN5 . . . . 1 B1
Borough The SE1 . . . . 252 C4
Walton-on-T KT12 . . . . 194 A2
Montague Fell HA0 . . . 64 D4
Montague Gdns W3 . . 110 C6
Montague Pl WC1 . . . . 93 D2 239 D4
Montague Rd
Ealing W13 . . . . 87 B1
Hanwell W7 . . . . 108 D4
Hornsey Vale N8 . . . . . . 50 B4
Hounslow TW3 . . . . . . 129 D2
Leytonstone E11 . . . . . . 76 D6
Merton SW19 . . . . 179 D3
Richmond TW10 . . . . . 154 A5
Shacklewell E8 . . . . 74 A3
Southall UB2 . . . . 107 A2
Thornton Heath CR0 . 204 D1
Tottenham Hale N15 . . . 52 A5
Uxbridge UB8 . . . . 60 A1
Montague Sq SE15 . . . 140 C5
Montague St
Bloomsbury WC1 . . . . 94 A2 240 A4
City of London EC1 . . . 242 A3
Montague Terr 1 BR2 . . . . 209 A5
Montague Waye UB2 . . . . 107 A3
Montague Works HA0 . . . . 88 B5
Montagu Gdns
Edmonton N18 . . . . 34 B6
Wallington SM6 . . . . . 219 C4
Montagu Ind Est N18 . . 34 C6
Montagu Mans W1 . . . . 92 D2 237 D3
Montagu Mews N W1 . . . . 237 D3
Montagu Mews S W1 . . . . 237 D2
Montagu Mews W W1 . . . . 237 D2
Montagu Pl W1 . . . . 92 D2 237 D3
Montagu Rd
Hendon NW4 . . . . 46 A3
Lower Edmonton N9, N18 . . . . 18 C1
Montagu Row W1 . . . 237 D3
Montagu Sq W1 . . . . 92 D1 237 D2
Montagu St W1 . . . . 92 D1 237 D2
Montaigne Cl SW1 . . . 259 D3
Montalt Ho IG8 . . . . 36 D6
Montalt Rd IG8 . . . . 36 D5
Montana Bldg 4 SE13 . . . . 141 D4
Montana Gdns
Penge SE26 . . . . 185 B5
5 Sutton SM1 . . . . . . 218 A3
Montana Rd
Upper Tooting SW17 . . . . 159 A1
Wimbledon SW20 . . . 178 C2
Montbelle Prim Sch SE9 . . . . 188 C6
Montbelle Rd SE9 . . . 166 D1
Montcalm Cl
Hayes BR2 . . . . 209 A3
Yeading UB4 . . . . 84 B4
Montcalm Ho E14 . . . . 119 C3
Montcalm Rd SE7 . . . 143 D5
Montclair Ct 21 N12 . . . 29 D6
Montclare St E2 . . . . 95 D3 243 C6
Monteagle Ave IG11 . . 79 A2
Monteagle Ct
Barking IG11 . . . . 79 A1
27 Hoxton N1 . . . . 95 C5
Monteagle Prim Sch RM9 . . . . 102 B6
Monteagle Way
Nunhead SE15 . . . . 140 B2
Shacklewell E5 . . . . 74 A5
Montefiore Ct 2 N16 . 51 D1
Montefiore St 2 SW8 . . . . 137 B3
Montego Cl 10 SW2 . . 138 C1
Montem Prim Sch 5 N7 . . . . 72 B5
Montem Rd
Forest Hill SE23 . . . . . 163 B4
New Malden KT3 . . . . 199 C5
Montem St N4 . . . . 50 B1
Montenotte Rd N8 . . . . 49 C4
Monteray Studios W10 . . . . 91 A5
Monterey Cl NW7 . . . . . 27 C5
Montesole Ct 7 HA5 . . 22 C1
Montesquieu Terr 3 E16 . . . . 98 D1
Montford Pl
Kennington SE11 . . . . 138 C6
Kennington SE11 . . . . 261 A1
Montford Rd TW16 . . 194 A5
Montfort Ho
4 Bethnal Green E2 . . . 96 C4
Cubitt Town E14 . . . . . 120 A3
Montfort Pl SW19 . . . 156 D3
Montgolfier Wlk UB5 . 85 A4
Montgomerie Ct 2 BR3 . . . . 185 C2
Montgomery Ave KT10 . . . . 212 C6
Montgomery Cl
Blackfen DA15 . . . . . . 167 D5
Mitcham CR4 . . . . 204 A5
Montgomery Ct W4 . 133 A6
Montgomery Gdns SM2 . . . . 218 B1
Montgomery Ho 5 SW14 . . . . 133 B2
Montgomery Lo 38 E1 . . . . 96 C3
Montgomery Rd
Acton W4 . . . . 111 A2
Edgware HA8 . . . . 26 B4
Montgomery St E14 . 119 D5
Montholme Rd SW11 . . . . 158 D5
Monthope Rd 17 E1 . . . 96 A2
Montolieu Gdns SW15 . . . . 156 B6
Montpelier Ave
Ealing W5 . . . . 87 C2
Sidcup DA5 . . . . 168 D4
Montpelier Cl UB10 . . . 82 C6
Montpelier Ct
5 Beckenham BR2 . . 208 D5
Ealing W5 . . . . 87 D2
Montpelier Gdns
Ilford RM6 . . . . 58 C2
Newham E6 . . . . 99 D4
Montpelier Gr NW5 . . . 71 C3
Montpelier Mews SW7 . . . . 257 B6
Montpelier Pl
Knightsbridge SW7 . . 257 B6
21 Stepney E1 . . . . 96 C1
Montpelier Prim Sch W5 . . . . 87 D2
Montpelier Rd
Ealing W5 . . . . 87 D2
Finchley N3 . . . . 30 A2
Peckham SE15 . . . . . . 140 B4
Sutton SM1 . . . . 218 A4
Montpelier Rise
Golders Green NW11 . . . 47 A2
Wembley HA9 . . . . 43 D1
Montpelier Row
Blackheath Vale SE3 . . . . 142 D3
Twickenham TW1 . . . . 153 C4
Montpelier Sq SW7 . . . . 114 C4 247 B1
Montpelier St SW7 . . . . 114 C3 257 B6
Montpelier Terr SW7 . . . . 247 B1
Montpelier Vale SE3 . . . . 142 D3
Montpelier Way NW11 . . . . 47 A2
Montpelier Wlk SW7 . . . . 114 C3 257 B6
Montpellier Ct KT12 . . 194 B3
Montrave Rd SE20 . . . 184 C3
Montreal Ho
Catford SE6 . . . . 163 D3
Hayes UB4 . . . . 84 B4
Montreal Pl WC2 . . . . 250 C6
Montreal Rd IG1 . . . . . . 57 A2
Montrell Rd SW2 . . . . 160 A3
Montrose Ave
Falconwood DA16 . . . . 145 C2
Hendon HA8 . . . . 27 B2
Kensal Rise NW6 . . . . . . 91 A5
Sidcup DA15 . . . . 168 A4
Twickenham TW2 . . . . 151 D4
Montrose Cl
Ashford TW15 . . . . 171 A5
Falconwood DA16 . . . . 145 D2
Woodford IG8 . . . . 37 A6
Montrose Cres
Finchley N12 . . . . 30 A4
1 Wembley HA0 . . . . . . 66 A2
Montrose Ct
2 Catford SE6 . . . . . . 164 D2
Hendon NW9 . . . . 27 A1
Knightsbridge SW7 . . . . . 114 B4 246 D1
Temple Fortune NW11 . . 47 B5
Montrose Gdns
Mitcham CR4 . . . . 180 D1
Sutton SM1 . . . . 217 D6
Montrose Ho
Belgravia SW1 . . . . . . 248 B1
Millwall E14 . . . . 119 C3
Twickenham TW2 . . . . 151 D4
Montrose Pl SW1 . . . . . . 115 A4 248 B1
Montrose Rd
East Bedfont TW14 . . . 149 B5
Harrow HA3 . . . . 24 D1
Montrose Villas 5 W6 . . . . 112 A1
Montrose Way SE23 . 162 D3
Montserrat Ave IG8 . . . 36 B3
Montserrat Cl SE19 . . 183 B5
Montserrat Rd SW15 . . . . 135 A1
Montway Hts SW19 . 179 D3
Monument* EC3 . . . 252 D6
Monument Gdns SE13 . . . . 164 A6
Monument St EC3 . . . . 117 B6 252 D6
Monument Sta EC3 . . . . 117 B6 252 D6
Monument Way N17 . . 51 D6
Monza Bldg The E1 . . 118 C6
Monza St E1 . . . . 118 C6
Moodkee St SE16 . . . . 118 C3
Moody Rd SE15 . . . . . . 139 D4
Moody St E1 . . . . 96 D4
Moolintock Pl EN3 . . . . . 7 D6
Moon Ct SE12 . . . . 143 A1
Moon Ho HA1 . . . . 42 D5
Moon La EN5 . . . . 1 B2
Moon St N1 . . . 94 D6 234 C6
Moorcroft HA8 . . . . 26 D2
Moorcroft Ct 4 N3 . . . . 29 B1
Moorcroft Gdns BR1 . . . . 210 A4
Moorcroft La UB8 . . . . . 82 C2
Moorcroft Rd SW16 . . 160 A1
Moorcroft Sch UB8 . . . 82 B1
Moorcroft Way HA5 . . . 41 A4
Moordown SE18 . . . . . 144 D4
Moore Cl
Mitcham CR4 . . . . 181 B1
Mortlake SW14 . . . . . . 133 A2
Wallington SM6 . . . . . 220 A1
Moore Cres RM9 . . . . . 102 B6
Moore Ct N1 . . . . 234 C5
Moorefield Rd N17 . . . 33 D1

Moorehead Way
SE3 . . . . .143 B2
Moore Ho
1 Bethnal Green E2 . . . .96 C4
7 Greenwich SE10 . . . 120 D1
Hornsey N8 . . . . .50 A5
2 Shadwell E1 . . . . . . 118 C6
1 West Norwood
SE27 . . . . 183 A6
Mooreland Rd BR1 . . 187 A2
Moore Park E2 . . . . . .265 D4
Moore Park Rd
SW6 . . . . .135 D5 265 C3
Moore St SE19 . . . . . .183 A4
Moore St
SW3 . . . . .114 D2 257 C4
Moorey Cl **2** E15 . . . . .98 D6
Moorfield Ave W5 . . . .87 D3
Moorfield Rd
Chessington KT9 . . . . 214 A3
Enfield EN3 . . . . .6 D4
Moorfields
EC2 . . . . .95 B2 242 C3
Moorfields Ct **6**
SW16 . . . . 181 C6
Moorfields Eye Hospl
EC1 . . . . .95 B4 235 C1
Moorfields Highwalk
EC2 . . . . .242 C3
Moorgate EC2 . 95 B2 242 C3
Moorgate Pl EC2 . . . .242 C2
Moorgate Sta
EC2 . . . . .95 B2 242 C3
Moorgreen Ho EC1 . .234 C2
Moorhouse
NW9 . . . . .27 D2
Moorhouse Rd
Harrow HA3 . . . . .43 D6
Notting Hill W2 . . . . . . .91 C1
Moorings Ho **3**
TW8 . . . . .131 C5
Moorings The **5** E16 . .99 C2
Moor La
Broadgate
EC2 . . . . .95 B2 242 C3
Chessington KT9 . . . . 214 A3
Moorland Cl TW4 . . . .151 C4
Moorland Ct N21 . . . . .16 B5
Moorland Rd SW9 . . .138 C5
Moorlands
Chislehurst BR7 . . . . . 188 D3
Northolt UB5 . . . . .85 A6
3 Wallington SM6 . . . 219 B2
Moorlands Ave NW7 . .28 D4
Moormead Dr KT19 . .215 C3
Moor Mead Rd TW1 . .153 A5
Moor Park Gdns
KT2 . . . . .177 C3
Moor Pl EC2 . . . . . . .242 C3
Moorside Ct W13 . . . .109 A5
Moorside Rd BR1 . . . .186 D6
Moor St W1 . . . . .239 D1
Moortown Rd WD19 . . .22 D1
Moot Ct NW9 . . . . .44 C4
Morant Ho SW9 . . . . .138 B3
Morant Pl N22 . . . . . . .32 B2
Morant St E14 . . . . . . .99 C6
Mora Prim Sch NW2 . .68 C4
Mora Rd NW2 . . . . . . .68 C4
Mora St EC1 . . .95 A4 235 B1
Morat St
SW9 . . . . .138 B4 270 D2
Moravian Cl SW3 . . . .266 D5
Moravian Pl
SW10 . . . . .136 B6 266 D5
Moravian Tower **12** E2 . .96 D4
Moray Ave UB3 . . . . . .105 D5
Moray Cl HA8 . . . . .10 D2
Moray Ho
1 Kingston u T
KT6 . . . . .198 A4
3 Mile End E1 . . . . . . .97 A3
Moray Mews N4, N7 . . .72 B6
Moray Rd N4, N7 . . . . .72 B6
Mordaunt Ho
5 Becontree NW10 . .89 B6
3‑4 Clapham SW8 . . . 137 D3
Mordaunt Rd NW10 . . .89 B6

Mordaunt St SW9 . . . .138 B2
MORDEN 201 D3
Morden Court Par
SM4 . . . . .201 D5
Morden Ct SM4 . . . . . .201 D5
Morden Gdns
Greenford UB6 . . . . . . .64 D3
Mitcham CR4 . . . . . . .202 B5
Morden Hall SW19 . . .201 D6
Morden Hall Rd
SM4 . . . . .202 A5
Morden Hill SE13 . . . .142 A3
Morden Ho
Morden SM4 . . . . .201 C5
1 Tulse Hill SW2 . . . . 160 C5
Morden La SE13 . . . . .142 A4
Morden Lo BR2 . . . . . .186 B1
Morden Mount Prim Sch
1 SE13 . . . . .141 D3
MORDEN PARK 201 A3
Morden Park Pools
SM4 . . . . .201 B4
Morden Prim Sch
SM4 . . . . .201 C4
Morden Rd
Dagenham RM6 . . . . . .59 A2
Kidbrooke SE3 . . . . . . 143 A3
Merton SW19 . . . . . . .179 D1
Mitcham CR4, SM4 . . .202 B5
Morden Road Mews
SE3 . . . . .143 A3
Morden Road Sta
SW19 . . . . .179 D1
Morden South Sta
SM4 . . . . .201 C4
Morden St SE13 . . . . .141 D4
Morden Sta SW19 . . . .201 D6
Morden Way SM3 . . . .201 C2
Morden Wharf Rd
SE10 . . . . .120 C3
Mordern Ho **1** NW1 . .237 B5
Mordon Rd IG3 . . . . . . .57 D2
Mordred Rd SE6 . . . . .164 C2
Morecambe Cl **8** E1 . .96 D2
Morecambe Gdns
HA7 . . . . .25 D6
Morecambe St
SE17 . . . . .117 A1 262 B2
Morecambe Terr N18 . .33 B6
More Cl
Canning Town E16 . . . .98 D1
West Kensington
W14 . . . . .113 A2 254 A3
Morecoombe Cl
KT2 . . . . .176 D3
Morecroft TW2 . . . . . .152 A2
Moredown Ho **3** E8 . .74 A3
More Way N18 . . . . . . .34 A6
More House Sch
SW1 . . . . .114 D3 257 D5
Moreland Ct **1** NW2 . .69 C5
Moreland Prim Sch
EC1 . . . . .94 D4 234 D1
Moreland St
EC1 . . . . .94 D4 234 D2
Moreland Way **4** E4 . .20 A1
Morella Rd SW11,
SW12 . . . . .158 D4
Morell Ho **5** SW9 . . . .138 B3
Morello Ave UB8 . . . . . .82 D2
Moredown Ho **3** E8 . .74 A3
More London Pl SE1 . .253 A3
Moremead Rd SE6 . . .185 C6
Morena St SE6 . . . . . .164 D4
Moresby Ave KT5 . . . .198 D2
Moresby Rd E5 . . . . . . .52 B1
Moresby Wlk **2**
SW8 . . . . .137 B3
More's Gdn SW3 . . . .266 D5
Moreton Ave TW7 . . . .130 C4
Moreton Cl
Mill Hill NW7 . . . . .28 C4
Tottenham N15 . . . . . . .51 B3
Upper Clapton E5 . . . . .52 C1
Moreton Ho
Bermondsey SE16 . . . .118 B3
Upper Tooting SW17 . .180 B6
Moreton Pl
SW1 . . . . .115 C1 259 B2
Moreton Rd
Croydon CR2 . . . . .221 B3
North Cheam KT4 . . . .216 B6
Tottenham N15 . . . . . . .51 B3
Moreton St
SW1 . . . . 115 D1 259 C2

Moreton Terr
SW1 . . . . .115 C1 259 B2
Moreton Terr Mews N
SW1 . . . . .259 B2
Moreton Terr Mews S
SW1 . . . . .259 B2
Moreton Twr **3** W3 . .110 D5
Morford Cl HA4 . . . . . . .40 B2
Morford Way HA4 . . . . .40 B2
Morgan Ave E17 . . . . . .54 B5
Morgan Ct RM10 . . . . . .81 C1
Morgan Ct
Ashford TW15 . . . . 170 D5
5 Battersea SW11 . . .136 B3
Carshalton SM5 . . . . . 218 D4
Morgan Ho
Nine Elms SW8 . . . . . .269 B2
Pimlico SW1 . . . . .259 B3
Morgan Rd
Islington N7 . . . . .72 C3
Notting Hill W10 . . . . . .91 B2
Plaistow BR1 . . . . .187 A3
Morgans La SE1 . . . . . .253 A3
Morgan's La UB3 . . . . . .83 B2
Morgan St
Canning Town E16 . . . .98 D2
Globe Town E3 . . . . . . .96 D4
Morgan's Wlk SW11 . .267 A3
Morgan Terr RM6 . . . . .58 C4
Moriah Jewish Day Sch
HA5 . . . . .41 A1
Moriarty Cl BR1 . . . . . .210 D5
Moriatry Cl N7 . . . . .72 A4
Morie St SW18 . . . . . .157 D6
Morieux Rd E10 . . . . . . .53 B1
Moring Rd SW17 . . . . .181 A6
Morkyns Wlk SE21 . . .161 C1
Morland Ave CR0 . . . .205 C1
Morland Ct
Golders Green NW11 . .47 D1
Hampton TW12 . . . . . . 173 B5
Mitcham CR4 . . . . . . .202 C6
Morland Ct **2** W12 . . .112 B4
Morland Est E8 . . . . . . .74 A1
Morland Gdns
Southall UB1 . . . . .107 D5
Stonebridge NW10 . . . .67 B1
Morland Ho
Kilburn NW6 . . . . .91 C6
Notting Hill W11 . . . . . .91 A1
Somers Town NW1 . . .232 B3
Westminster SW1 . . . .260 A4
Morland Mews N1 . . . .72 C1
Morland Rd
Croydon CR0 . . . . .205 D2
Dagenham RM10 . . . . . .81 C1
Harrow HA3 . . . . .44 A5
Ilford IG1 . . . . .78 B5
Penge SE20 . . . . .184 D4
Sutton SM1 . . . . .218 A3
Walthamstow E17 . . . . .52 D4
Morley Ave
Chingford E4 . . . . .36 B3
Edmonton N18 . . . . . . .34 A4
Wood Green N22 . . . . . .32 D1
Morley Cl BR6 . . . . . . .226 D6
Morley Coll
SE1 . . . . .116 C3 261 B6
Morley Cres
Edgware HA8 . . . . .11 A2
Ruislip HA4 . . . . .62 C6
Morley Cres E HA7 . . . .43 D6
Morley Cres W HA7 . . .43 C6
Morley Ct
Bromley BR3 . . . . .186 B2
Chingford Hatch E4 . . . .35 B5
Lewisham SE13 . . . . . .142 A1
Shortlands BR2 . . . . . .208 D5
Morley Hill EN2 . . . . . . .5 B5
Morley Ho
Stoke Newington N16 . .74 A6
Streatham SW2 . . . . . .160 A4
Morley Rd
Barking IG11 . . . . .101 B6
Cheam SM3 . . . . .201 B1
Chislehurst BR7 . . . . . 189 A2
Dagenham RM6 . . . . . .59 A4
Lewisham SE13 . . . . . .142 A1
Leytonstone E10 . . . . . .54 A1
Newham E15 . . . . .98 D5
Twickenham TW1 . . . . .153 B5
Morley St
SE1 . . . . .116 C4 251 B1
Morna Rd SE5 . . . . . . .139 A3
Morning La E9 . . . . .74 C2

Morningside Prim Sch **17**
E9 . . . . .74 C2
Morningside Rd KT4 . .216 C6
Mornington Ave
Bromley BR1 . . . . .209 D6
Ilford IG1 . . . . .56 C2
West Kensington
W14 . . . . .113 B2 254 D3
Mornington Avenue
Mans W14 . . . . .254 C3
Mornington Cl IG8 . . . .37 A6
Mornington Cres
Camden Town
NW1 . . . . .93 C5 232 A4
Cranford TW5 . . . . 128 B7
NW1 . . . . .232 A4
Mornington Crescent Sta
NW1 . . . . .93 C5 232 A4
Mornington Ct NW1 . .232 A4
Mornington Gr E3 . . . . .97 C4
Mornington Lo EN1 . . . .17 C6
Mornington Mews **2**
SE5 . . . . .139 A4
Mornington Pl
1 New Cross SE8 . . .141 B5
Regent's Pk NW1 . . . . .232 A4
Mornington Rd
Ashford TW15 . . . . 171 A5
Chingford E4 . . . . .20 B6
Greenford UB6 . . . . . . .85 D3
Leytonstone E11 . . . . . .54 D1
New Cross SE14, SE8 . .141 B5
Woodford IG8 . . . . .36 D5
Mornington St
NW1 . . . . .93 B5 231 D4
Mornington Terr
NW1 . . . . .93 B5 231 D4
Mornington Wlk
TW10 . . . . .175 C6
Morocco St
SE1 . . . . .117 C4 253 A1
Morpeth Gr E9 . . . . . . .96 D5
Morpeth Rd E9 . . . . . . .96 C6
Morpeth Sch **2** E2 . . .96 C4
Morpeth St E2 . . . . . . .96 D4
Morpeth Terr
SW1 . . . . .115 C2 259 A4
Morpeth Wlk N17 . . . . .34 B3
Morphou Rd NW7 . . . . .29 A5
Morrab Gdns IG3 . . . . .79 D5
Morrel Cl EN5 . . . . .2 D2
Morrel Cl **2** E12 . . . . . .96 A5
Morris Ave E12 . . . . . . .78 B3
Morris Blitz Ct **1**
N16 . . . . .73 D4
Morris Cl
Croydon CR0 . . . . .207 A4
Orpington BR6 . . . . . . .227 C5
Morris Ct CR0 Chingford E4 . . .19 D1
Croydon CR0 . . . . .220 D4
3 Herne Hill SE5 . . . .139 B1
Morris Gdns SW18 . . .157 C5
Morris Ho
17 Bethnal Green E2 . .96 C4
Lisson Gr NW8 . . . . . . .230 D1
3 Stockwell SW4 . . . .138 A1
10 Tufnell Pk N19 . . . .71 C4
Morrish Rd SW2 . . . . .160 A4
Morrison Ave
Chingford E4 . . . . .35 C4
Tottenham N17 . . . . . . .51 C6
Morrison Bldgs **3** E1 . .96 A1
Morrison Ct
7 Barnet EN5 . . . . . .1 A1
Finchley N12 . . . . .30 D5
Morrison Ho SW2 . . . .160 C3
Morrison Rd
Barking IG11 . . . . .103 A5
5 Brixton SW9 . . . . .138 C3
Hayes UB4 . . . . .84 B4
Morrison St SW11 . . . .137 A2
Morrison Yd N17 . . . . . .33 D1
Morris Pl N4 . . . . .72 C6
Morris Rd
Bow Common E14 . . . . .97 D2
Dagenham RM8 . . . . . . .81 B6
Isleworth TW7 . . . . . . .130 D2
Leyton E15 . . . . .76 C4
Morriss Ho
9 Bermondsey
SE16 . . . . .118 B4
5 Upper Clapton E5 . .74 B6
Morris St E1 . . . . .96 B1
Morris Stephany Ho **8**
SE27 . . . . .182 D6
Morriston Cl WD19 . . . .22 C5

Morritt Ho **2** HA0 . . . . .65 D3
Morse Cl E13 . . . . .99 A4
Morshead Mans W9 . . .91 C4
Morshead Rd W9 . . . . .91 C4
Morson Rd EN3 . . . . . . .19 A5
Morston Gdns SE9 . . .188 B6
Mortain Ho **9** SE16 . .118 B2
Morten Cl SW4 . . . . . .159 D5
Morteyne Rd N17 . . . . .33 B2
Mortgramit Sq SE18 .122 C3
Mortham St E15 . . . . . .98 C6
Mortimer Cl
1 Child's Hill NW2 . . .69 B5
Streatham SW16 . . . . .159 D2
Mortimer Cres
Paddington NW6 . . . . . .91 D6
Worcester Pk KT4 . . . .215 B5
Mortimer Ct
St John's Wood
NW8 . . . . .229 B3
4 Whetstone N20 . . .14 A2
Mortimer Dr EN1 . . . . .17 C6
Mortimer Est NW6 . . . .91 D6
Mortimer Ho
5 Shepherd's Bush
W11 . . . . .112 D5
West Kensington W14 .254 B3
Mortimer Lo **11**
SW19 . . . . .157 A3
Mortimer Market
WC1 . . . . .239 B5
Mortimer Pl NW6 . . . . .91 D6
Mortimer Rd
De Beauvoir Town N1 . .73 C1
Ealing W13 . . . . .87 C1
Kensal Green NW10 . . .90 C4
Mitcham CR4 . . . . .180 D2
Newham E6 . . . . .100 B4
Mortimer Sq W11 . . . .112 D6
Mortimer St
W1 . . . . .93 C2 239 B3
Mortimer Terr NW5 . . .71 B4
MORTLAKE 133 A2
Mortlake Cl CR0 . . . . .220 A5
Mortlake Dr CR4 . . . . .180 C2
Mortlake High St
SW14 . . . . .133 B2
Mortlake Ho **7** W4 . . .111 A2
Mortlake Rd
Ilford IG1 . . . . .79 B4
Newham E16 . . . . .99 B1
Richmond SW14,
TW9 . . . . .132 C4
Mortlake Sta SW14 . . .133 A2
Mortlake Terr TW9 . . .132 C5
Mortlock Cl SE15 . . . .140 B4
Mortlock Ct E12 . . . . . . .77 D4
Morton Cl
Hillingdon UB8 . . . . . . .82 B3
20 Stepney E1 . . . . . .96 C1
Wallington SM6 . . . . . .220 B1
Morton Cres N14 . . . . .31 C6
Morton Ct UB5 . . . . .64 A3
Morton Gdns SM6 . . . .219 C3
Morton Ho
Kennington SE17 . . . . .138 D6
West Norwood SE27 . .183 B5
Morton Mews SW5 . . .255 C3
Morton Pl SE1 . . . . . . .261 A5
Morton Rd
Islington N1 . . . . .73 A1
Morden SM4 . . . . .202 B4
Stratford E15 . . . . .76 D1
Morton Way N14 . . . . . .31 C6
Morvale Cl DA17 . . . . .125 B2
Morval Rd SW2 . . . . . .160 C6
Morven Rd SW17 . . . .158 D1
Morville Ho SW18 . . . .158 B5
Morville St E3 . . . . .97 C5
Morwell St WC1 . . . . . .239 D3
Moscow Pl W2 . . . . . . .245 C6
Moscow Rd
W2 . . . . .113 D6 245 C6
Mosedale NW1 . . . . . .231 D1
Moseley Row SE10 . . .120 D2
Moselle Ave N22 . . . . . .32 C1
Moselle Cl N8 . . . . .50 B6
Moselle Ct **9** N19 . . . . .18 C1
Moselle Ho **2** N17 . . . .33 D3
Moselle Pl N17 . . . . . . .33 D3
Moselle Sch (Upper)
N17 . . . . .51 A6
Moselle Specl Sch
N17 . . . . .33 C1
Moselle St N17 . . . . . . .33 D3

Mosque Tower 26 E1 . . 96 A2
Mosquito Cl 5 SM6 . . 220 A1
Mossborough Cl N12 . . 29 D4
Mossbourne Com Acad E8 . . 74 A3
Mossbury Rd SW11 . . 136 C2
Moss Cl Pinner HA5 . . 23 A1
Spitalfields E1 . . 96 A2
Mossdown Cl DA17 . . 125 C2
Mossford Ct IG6 . . 56 D6
Mossford Gn IG6 . . 57 A6
Mossford St E3 . . 97 B3
Moss Gdns
Feltham TW13 . . 150 A2
South Croydon CR2 . . 222 D1
Moss Hall Cres N12 . . 30 A4
Moss Hall Ct N12 . . 29 D4
Moss Hall Gr N12 . . 29 D4
Moss Hall Inf Sch 1 N12 . . 29 D4
Moss Hall Jun Sch N3 . . 29 D4
Mossington Gdns SE16 . . 118 C2
Moss La HA5 . . 23 A1
Mosslea Rd
Bromley Comm BR2 . . 209 D4
Orpington BR6 . . 227 A5
Penge SE20 . . 184 C4
Mossop St SW3 . . 114 C2 257 B4
Moss Rd RM10 . . 81 C1
Mossville Gdns SM4 . . 201 B5
Mosswell Ho 4 N10 . . 31 A3
Moston Cl UB3 . . 105 D1
Mostyn Ave HA9 . . 66 B3
Mostyn Gdns NW10 . . 90 D5
Mostyn Gr E3 . . 97 C5
Mostyn Lo N5 . . 73 A4
Mostyn Rd
Brixton SW9 . . 138 C4
Bushey WD23 . . 8 A6
Grahame Pk HA8 . . 27 C3
Merton SW19 . . 179 B1
Mosul Way BR2 . . 210 A3
Motcomb St SW1 . . 115 A3 258 A6
Moth Cl SM6 . . 220 A1
Mothers Sq The 13 E5 . . 74 B4
Motley Ave EC2 . . 243 A6
Motley St SW8 . . 137 C3
MOTSPUR PARK . . 200 A3
Motspur Park Sta KT3 . . 200 B4
Motspur Pk KT3 . . 200 A3
MOTTINGHAM . . 165 D2
Mottingham Ct SE9 . . 166 B3
Mottingham Gdns SE9 . . 165 D3
Mottingham La SE9 . . 165 C3
Mottingham Nature Reserve* SE12 . . 165 C3
Mottingham Prim Sch SE9 . . 166 B1
Mottingham Rd
Chislehurst SE9 . . 166 B1
Ponders End N9 . . 18 D4
Mottingham Sta SE9 . . 166 B3
Mottisfont Rd SE2 . . 124 B2
Moules Ct SE5 . . 139 A5
Moulins Rd E9 . . 74 C1
Moulsford Ho
5 Lower Holloway N7 . . 72 A3
32 Paddington W2 . . 91 C2
Moulton Ave TW3, TW5 . . 129 B3
Moundfield Rd N16 . . 52 A3
Mound The SE9 . . 166 C1
Mounsey Ho 18 W10 . . 91 A4
Mountacre Cl SE26 . . 183 D6
Mount Adon Pk SE21, SE22 . . 162 A4
Mountague Pl 2 E14 . . 120 A6
Mountain Ho SE11 . . 260 C2
Mountaire Ct NW9 . . 45 B4
Mount Angelus Rd SW15 . . 155 D4
Mount Ararat Rd TW10 . . 154 A6
Mount Arlington 3 BR2 . . 186 C1
Mount Ash Rd SE26 . . 162 B1
Mount Ave
Chingford E4 . . 19 D1
Ealing W5 . . 87 D2
Southall UB1 . . 85 C1
Mountbatten Cl
Plumstead Comm SE18 . . 145 C6
6 West Norwood SE19 . . 183 C5
Mountbatten Ct 8 IG9 . . 21 D2
Mountbatten Gdns BR3 . . 207 A5
Mountbatten Ho N6 . . 49 A2
Mountbatten Mews SW18 . . 158 A3
Mountbel Rd HA7 . . 25 A1
Mount Carmel 3 N7 . . 72 B3
Mount Carmel RC Tech Coll for Girls 6 N19 . . 49 D1
Mount Cl
Bromley BR1 . . 188 A2
Cockfosters EN4 . . 3 A1
Ealing W5 . . 87 C2
Mountcombe Cl KT6 . . 198 A2
Mountcombe Ho SW17 . . 180 B5
Mount Ct
6 Kingston u T KT2 . . 176 D3
West Wickham BR4 . . 224 C6
Mount Culver Ave DA14 . . 190 D4
Mount Dr Bexley DA6 . . 169 A6
Harrow HA2, HA5 . . 41 B4
Welsh Harp HA9 . . 67 A6
Mountearl Gdns SW16, SW2 . . 160 B1
Mount Eaton Ct W5 . . 87 C2
Mount Echo Ave E4 . . 19 D3
Mount Echo Dr E4 . . 19 D3
Mount Ephraim La SW16 . . 159 D1
Mount Ephraim Rd SW16 . . 159 D1
Mount Felix KT12 . . 193 D1
Mountfield NW2 . . 69 B6
Mountfield Cl SE6 . . 164 B4
Mountfield Ct SE13 . . 164 B5
Mountfield Rd
Ealing W5 . . 88 A1
East Finchley N3 . . 47 C6
Wallend E6 . . 100 C4
Mountford Ho EN2 . . 4 D1
Mount Ford St E1 . . 96 A1
Mountfort Cres N1 . . 72 C1
Mountfort Terr 1 N1 . . 72 C1
Mount Gdns SE26 . . 162 B1
Mount Gr HA8 . . 27 B6
Mountgrove Rd N5 . . 73 A5
Mount Holme KT7 . . 197 B2
Mounthurst Rd BR2 . . 208 D2
Mountier Ct 12 E11 . . 55 A4
Mountington Park Cl HA3 . . 43 D3
Mountjoy Cl SE2 . . 124 B4
Mountjoy Ho EC2 . . 242 A3
Mount Lo N6 . . 49 C3
Mount Lodge SW4 . . 137 D1
Mount Mews TW12 . . 173 D2
Mount Mills EC1 . . 234 D1
Mount Nod Rd SW16, SW2 . . 160 B1
Mount Olive Ct W7 . . 108 C4
Mount Par EN4 . . 2 C1
Mount Park Ave HA1 . . 64 C6
Mount Park Cres W5 . . 87 D1
Mount Park Rd
Ealing W5 . . 87 D1
Harrow HA1 . . 64 B5
Pinner HA5 . . 40 A4
Mount Pk SM5 . . 219 A1
Mount Pl 7 W3 . . 110 D5
Mount Pleasant
Cockfosters EN4 . . 2 D1
Finsbury WC1 . . 94 C3 241 A5
Ilford IG1 . . 79 A3
Ruislip HA4 . . 62 D6
Wembley HA0 . . 88 B6
West Norwood SE27 . . 183 A6
Mount Pleasant Cotts
Osidge N14 . . 15 D4
Southall UB1 . . 85 C1
Mount Pleasant Cres N4 . . 50 B2
Mount Pleasant Hill E5 . . 74 C6
Mount Pleasant La E5 . . 52 B1
Mount Pleasant Pl SE18 . . 123 B2
Mount Pleasant Rd
Ealing W5 . . 87 C3
Higham Hill E17 . . 35 A1
Kingston u T KT3 . . 199 A6
Lewisham SE13 . . 164 A5
Tottenham N17 . . 33 C1
Willesden NW10 . . 90 C6
Mount Pleasant Villas N4 . . 50 B2
Mount Prim Sch The KT3 . . 199 A6
Mount Rd
Bexley DA6 . . 169 A6
Chessington KT9 . . 214 B3
Dagenham RM8 . . 59 B1
Dollis Hill NW2 . . 68 C5
East Barnet EN4 . . 14 C6
Feltham TW13 . . 151 A1
Hayes UB3 . . 106 A4
Hendon NW4 . . 46 A3
Kingston u T KT3 . . 199 B6
Mitcham CR4 . . 180 C1
South Norwood SE19 . . 183 B4
Wimbledon SW18, SW19 . . 157 D2
Mount Row W1 . . 115 B6 248 C5
Mount Sch The NW7 . . 28 C5
Mountside HA7 . . 25 A2
Mounts Pond Rd SE3, SE13 . . 142 B3
Mount Sq The 3 NW3 . . 70 A5
Mount St W1 . . 115 A6 248 B5
Mount Stewart Ave HA3 . . 43 D2
Mount Stewart Jun & Inf Schs HA3 . . 43 D2
Mount Terr E1 . . 96 B2
Mount The
Bexley DA6 . . 169 D6
Cheam SM1 . . 217 C2
Chislehurst BR7 . . 188 C2
Finchley N2 . . 30 C1
Hampstead NW3 . . 70 A5
Harrow HA1 . . 64 C6
Kensington W8 . . 245 A3
Kingston u T KT3 . . 199 D6
North Cheam KT4 . . 216 B4
Northolt UB5 . . 63 D3
6 South Croydon CR2 . . 221 A3
Upper Clapton E5 . . 74 B6
Welsh Harp HA9 . . 67 A6
Whetstone N20 . . 14 A2
Mount Tyndal NW3 . . 48 B1
Mount Vernon NW3 . . 70 A4
Mountview
Edgware NW7 . . 11 B1
Northwood HA6 . . 22 A4
5 Streatham SW16 . . 160 B1
Mount View
Ealing W5 . . 87 D3
Enfield EN2 . . 4 B5
Southall UB2 . . 106 D2
Mountview Cl NW11 . . 48 A1
Mountview Cotts EN5 . . 11 D5
Mountview Ct
Harringay N8 . . 50 D5
3 Whetstone N20 . . 14 A2
Mount View Rd
Chingford E4 . . 20 B4
Claygate KT10 . . 213 B1
Hornsey Vale N4 . . 50 B3
Kingsbury NW9 . . 45 B4
Mount Villas SE27 . . 160 D1
Mountwood KT8 . . 195 D6
Mountwood Ho W5 . . 87 D3
Mourne Ho NW3 . . 70 A2
Movers La IG11 . . 101 C6
Movers Lane (Flyover) IG11 . . 101 C5
Movieum The* SE1 . . 250 C2
Mowat Ct KT4 . . 215 D6
Mowatt Cl N19 . . 49 D1
Mowbray Ct
South Norwood SE19 . . 183 D2
Wood Green N22 . . 32 C2
Mowbray Gdns UB5 . . 85 C6
Mowbray Ho 5 N2 . . 30 B1
Mowbray Rd
Brondesbury NW6 . . 69 A1
Edgware HA8 . . 26 C6
New Barnet EN5 . . 14 A6
Richmond TW10 . . 153 C1
South Norwood SE19 . . 183 D2
Mowlem Prim Sch 36 E2 . . 96 C5
Mowlem St E2 . . 96 B5
Mowlem Trad Est N17 . . 34 C3
Mowll St SW9 . . 138 C5
Moxon Cl E13 . . 98 D5
Moxon St Barnet EN5 . . 1 B2
Marylebone W1 . . 93 A2 238 A3
Moye Cl 10 E2 . . 96 A5
Moyers Rd E10 . . 54 A2
Moylan Rd W6 . . 135 A6 264 B5
Moyle Ho SW1 . . 269 B6
Moyne Ho 16 SW9 . . 138 D1
Moyne Pl NW10 . . 88 C5
Moynihan Dr N21 . . 16 A6
Moys Cl CR0 . . 204 A3
Moyser Rd SW16 . . 181 B5
Mozart St W10 . . 91 B4
Mt Carmel RC Prim Sch 1 W5 . . 109 C3
Muchelney Rd SM4 . . 202 A3
Mudchute Pk & Farm* E14 . . 120 A2
Mudchute Sta E14 . . 119 D2
Mudie Ho 8 SW2 . . 160 A4
Mudlarks Blvd 3 SE10 . . 120 D3
Muggeridge Cl CR2 . . 221 B3
Muggeridge Rd RM10 . . 81 D4
Muirdown Ave SW14 . . 133 B1
Muir Dr SW18 . . 158 C5
Muirfield W3 . . 89 C1
Muirfield Cl
23 Bermondsey SE16 . . 118 B1
South Oxhey WD19 . . 22 C6
Muirfield Cres E14 . . 119 D3
Muirfield Gn WD19 . . 22 C6
Muirfield Rd WD19 . . 22 C6
Muirhead Quay IG11 . . 101 A5
Muirkirk Rd SE6 . . 164 A3
Muir Rd E5 . . 74 A5
Muir St E16 . . 122 A5
Mulbarton Ct BR7 . . 189 B4
Mulberry Ave TW19 . . 148 A3
Mulberry Bsns Ctr SE16 . . 118 D4
Mulberry Cl Barnet EN4 . . 2 B1
Charlton SE7 . . 143 D6
Chelsea SW3 . . 266 D5
Chingford E4 . . 19 C2
East Dulwich SE22 . . 162 A5
Hampstead NW3 . . 70 B4
Hendon NW4 . . 46 C6
Hornsey N8 . . 50 A4
Northolt UB5 . . 85 A5
Streatham SW16 . . 181 C6
Mulberry Cres
Brentford TW8 . . 131 C5
West Drayton UB7 . . 104 C4
Mulberry Ct
Barking IG11 . . 79 D1
Bexley DA16 . . 145 D3
Finchley N2 . . 48 C6
Finsbury EC1 . . 234 D1
Islington N5 . . 72 D3
1 Leyton E11 . . 76 B4
10 Paddington W9 . . 91 B4
4 Surbiton KT6 . . 197 D2
Twickenham TW1 . . 152 D1
Willesden NW10 . . 67 B2
Mulberry Ho
1 Bethnal Green E2 . . 96 C4
8 Deptford SE8 . . 141 B6
Mulberry House Sch NW2 . . 69 A3
Mulberry La CR0 . . 205 D1
Mulberry Mews
New Cross SE14 . . 141 B4
2 Wallington SM6 . . 219 C2
Mulberry Par UB7 . . 104 C4
Mulberry Pl
Chiswick W6 . . 112 A1
Greenwich SE9 . . 143 D1
Mulberry Prim Sch N17 . . 34 A1
Mulberry Rd E8 . . 73 D1
Mulberry Sch for Girls
39 Stepney E1 . . 96 B1
16 St George in t East E1 . . 118 B6
Mulberry St 7 E1 . . 96 A1
Mulberry Trees TW17 . . 193 B2
Mulberry Way
Ilford IG6 . . 57 A5
Woodford E18 . . 37 B1
Mulberry Wlk SW3 . . 136 B6 266 D6
Mulgrave Chambers SM2 . . 217 D2
Mulgrave Hall SM2 . . 217 D2
Mulgrave Ho 19 SE18 . . 122 B2
Mulgrave Manor SM2 . . 217 D2
Mulgrave Prim Sch SE18 . . 122 C2
Mulgrave Rd
Belmont SM2 . . 217 C2
Ealing W5 . . 87 D3
Harrow HA1 . . 65 A6
South Croydon CR0 . . 221 B5
West Kensington W14 . . 264 C6
Willesden NW10 . . 67 D4
Woolwich SE18 . . 122 C2
Mulholland Cl CR4 . . 181 B1
Mulkern Rd N19 . . 49 D1
Mullard Ho WC1 . . 239 C4
Mullards Cl CR4 . . 202 D1
Mullens Ho 7 SW15 . . 156 C6
Mullen Twr EC1 . . 241 A5
Muller Ho SE18 . . 122 C1
Muller Rd SW4 . . 159 D5
Mullet Gdns 7 E2 . . 96 A4
Mulletsfield WC1 . . 233 B1
Mull Ho 17 E3 . . 97 B5
Mullins Path SW14 . . 133 B2
Mullion Cl HA3 . . 23 D2
Mullion Wlk WD19 . . 22 D6
Mulready St NW8 . . 237 A5
Multi Way W3 . . 111 C4
Multon Ho E9 . . 74 C1
Multon Rd SW18 . . 158 B4
Mulvaney Way SE1 . . 252 D1
Mumford Rd SE24 . . 160 D6
Muncaster Cl TW15 . . 170 C6
Muncaster Rd
Ashford TW15 . . 170 D5
Balham SW11 . . 159 A6
Muncies Mews SE6 . . 164 A2
Mundania Ct SE22 . . 162 B5
Mundania Rd SE22 . . 162 C5
Munday Ho SE1 . . 262 C5
Munday Rd E16 . . 121 A6
Munden Ho 5 E3 . . 97 D4
Munden St W14 . . 113 A2 254 A4
Mundford Rd E5 . . 74 C6
Mundon Gdns IG1 . . 57 B1
Mundsley Cl WD19 . . 22 C6
Mund St W14 . . 113 B1 254 D1
Mundy Ho 6 W10 . . 91 A4
Mundy St N1 . . 95 C4
Mungo-Park Cl WD23 . . 8 A2
Munnery Way BR6 . . 226 D6
Munning Ho 12 E16 . . 121 B5
Munnings Gdns TW7 . . 152 B6
Munro Dr N11 . . 31 C4
Munro Ho
Bermondsey SE1 . . 252 D1
Lambeth SE1 . . 251 A1
Munro Mews W10 . . 91 A2
Munro Rd WD23 . . 8 A6
Munslow Gdns SM1 . . 218 B4
Munstead Ct 12 SM2 . . 218 A1
Munster Ave TW4 . . 151 A6
Munster Ct
Fulham SW6 . . 135 B3
Teddington TW11 . . 175 C4
Munster Gdns N13 . . 33 A6
Munster Ho N17 . . 33 D2

Munster Rd
Fulham
SW6 135 A5 264 B4
Teddington TW11 175 C4
Munster Residences
SW6 264 B2
Munster Sq
NW1 93 B3 238 D6
Munton Rd SE1,
SE17 117 A2 262 B4
Murchison Ave DA5 169 A3
Murchison Ho 1
W10 91 A2
Murchison Rd E10 76 A6
Murdoch Ho 4
SE16 118 C3
Murdock Cl E16 98 D1
Murdock St SE15 140 B6
Murfett Cl SW19 157 A2
Muriel Ct 18 E10 53 D2
Muriel St N1 94 B6 233 D6
Murillo Rd SE13 142 C1
Murley Ct N21 17 A4
Murphy Ho SE1 261 D6
Murphy St
SE1 116 C4 251 A1
Murray Ave
Bromley BR1 187 B1
Hounslow TW3 151 D6
Murray Cl SE28 123 C5
Murray Cres HA5 22 D2
Murray Ct
5 Harrow HA1 42 D3
Southall TW7 108 C3
Twickenham TW2 152 A2
Murray Gr N1 95 B5 235 C3
Murray Grey Ho UB4 83 B2
Murray Ho
1 North Finchley
N12 30 B5
20 Woolwich SE18 122 B2
Murray Mews NW1 71 D1
Murray Rd
Brentford W5 109 C2
Richmond TW10 153 C2
Wimbledon SW19 178 D4
Murray Sq E16 121 B6
Murray St NW1 71 D1
Murray Terr NW3 70 B4
Musard Rd
W6 135 A6 264 B6
Musbury St E1 96 C1
Muscal W6 264 A6
Muscatel Pl SE5 139 C4
Muschamp Prim Sch
SM5 218 C6
Muschamp Rd
Camberwell SE15 139 D2
Carshalton SM5 218 C6
Muscott Ho 15 E2 96 A6
Muscovy Ho DA18 125 A4
Muscovy St EC3 253 B6
Museum & Galleries of Modern London★
EC2 242 A2
Museum Ho 7 E2 96 C4
Museum La SW7 256 C5
Museum Mans WC1 240 A3
Museum of Brands, Packaging & Advertising★ W11 91 B1
Museum of Childhood (V&A)★ E2 96 C4
Museum of Culinary History & Alimentation★
NW1 93 C5 232 B4
Museum of Domestic Design & Architecture (MoDA)★ EN4 15 A6
Museum of Instruments★
SW7 256 C6
Museum of London★
EC2 95 A2 242 A3
Museum of London Docklands★ E14 119 C6
Museum of Richmond★
TW10 153 D6
Museum of the Great Eastern Rly★ E16 122 C4
Museum of the Order of St John★
EC1 94 D3 241 C5
Museum St
WC1 94 A1 240 A2
Museum Way W3 110 C4
Musgrave Cl EN4 2 A4
Musgrave Cres
SW6 135 C4 265 B2
Musgrave Ct SW11 267 A2
Musgrave Rd TW7 130 D4
Musgrove Ho 1 E9 74 D2
Musgrove Rd SE14 141 A4
Musical Mus The★
TW8 132 B6
Musjid Rd 7 SW11 136 B3
Muslim Coll The
W5 110 C6
Mus of the Royal Pharmaceutical Society★ SE1 260 C4
Musquash Way TW4 128 C3
Muston Rd E5 74 B6
Mustow Pl 2 SW6 135 B3
Muswell Ave N10 31 B1
MUSWELL HILL 49 A6
Muswell Hill N10 49 C6
Muswell Hill Broadway
N10 49 B6
Muswell Hill Pl N10 49 B5
Muswell Hill Prim Sch
N10 49 B6
Muswell Hill Rd N10 49 A4
Muswell Mews N10 49 B6
Muswell Rd N10 31 B1
Mutrix Rd NW6 91 C6
Mutton Pl NW1 71 A2
Muybridge Rd KT3 177 A1
Myatt Garden Prim Sch
SE4 141 B3
Myatt Ho SE5 138 D3
Myatt Rd SW9 138 D4
Myatts Field Ct SE5 139 A4
Mycenae Rd SE3 143 A6
Mychell Ho 8 SW19 180 A3
Myddelton Ave EN1 5 C5
Myddelton Cl EN1 5 D4
Myddelton Gdns N21 17 A4
Myddelton Ho N8 50 A6
Myddelton Pas
EC1 94 C4 234 B2
Myddelton Pk N20 14 B2
Myddelton Rd N8 50 A5
Myddelton Sq
EC1 94 C4 234 B2
Myddelton St
EC1 94 C4 234 B1
Myddleton Ave N4 73 A6
Myddleton Cl HA7 9 A2
Myddleton Ho 14 N2 30 B1
Myddleton Mews
N22 32 A3
Myddleton Rd N22 32 B3
Myers Ho 5 SE5 139 A5
Myers La SE14 140 D6
Myherin Ct SE23 163 B2
Mylis Cl SE26 184 B6
Mylius Cl SE14 140 C4
Mylne Cl W6 112 A1
Mylne Ho N21 17 B5
Mylne St EC1 234 A3
Mynterne Ct 16
SW19 156 D3
Myra St SE2 124 A2
Myrdle Ct 14 E1 96 A1
Myrdle St E1 96 A1
Myrna Cl SW19 180 C3
Myron Pl SE13 142 A2
Myrtle Alley SE18 122 C3
Myrtle Ave
Hatton TW14 149 C6
Ruislip HA4 40 B2
Myrtle Cl Barnet EN4 14 D3
Hillingdon UB8 82 B2
West Drayton UB7 104 B3
Myrtledene Rd SE2 124 A1
Myrtle Gdns W7 108 C5
Myrtle Gr Enfield EN2 5 B5
Kingston u T KT3 177 A1
Myrtle Ho SE14 140 D4
Myrtle Rd Acton W3 111 A5
Croydon CR0 223 C5
Edmonton N13 17 B1
Hampton TW12 174 A4
Hounslow TW3 130 A3
Ilford IG1 78 D6
Myrtle Rd *continued*
Newham E6 100 A6
Sutton SM1 218 A3
Walthamstow E17 53 A3
Myrtle Wlk 20 N1 95 C5
Mysore Rd SW11 136 D1
Myton Rd SE21 161 B1
Mytton Ho SW8 270 C3

N

N1 Shopping Ctr
N1 94 C5 234 B4
Nacton Ct 2 RM6 58 C4
Nadine St SE7 121 C1
Nadir Ct E11 55 A2
Naffenton Rise IG10 21 D6
Nagle Cl E17 36 B1
Nags Head N7 72 B4
Nags Head Ct EC1 242 B5
Nag's Head La DA16 146 B2
Nags Head Rd EN3 6 D1
Nags Head Sh Ctr The
N7 72 B4
Naima Jewish Prep Sch
4 NW6 91 D5
Nainby Ho SE11 261 A3
Nairn Ct
3 Wallington SM6 219 C2
Wimbledon SW19 179 D4
Nairne Gr SE5, SE24 139 B1
Nairn Rd HA4 62 C2
Nairn St E14 98 A2
Naish Ho SW19 201 D6
Naldera Gdns SE3 143 A6
Nallhead Rd TW13 172 C5
Nalton Ho 4 NW6 70 A1
Namba Roy Cl SW16 182 B6
Namco Sta★ SE1 250 C2
Namton Dr CR7,
SW16 204 B5
Nan Clark's La NW7 11 D2
Nancy Reuben Prim Sch
8 NW4 46 D5
Nankin St E14 97 C1
Nansen Ct 1 E11 76 C6
Nansen Ho 8 NW10 67 B1
Nansen Rd SW11 137 A2
Nansen Village 5
N12 29 D6
Nant Ct NW2 69 B6
Nantes Cl SW18 136 A1
Nant Rd NW2 69 B6
Nant St E2 96 B4
Naomi Watts Ho 11
SW19 179 A3
Naoroji St WC1 234 A1
Napier 15 NW9 27 D2
Napier Ave
Deptford E14 119 C1
Fulham SW6 135 B2
Napier Cl
New Cross SE14,
SE8 141 B5
West Drayton UB7 104 B3
West Kensington W14 254 C6
Napier Ct
13 Croydon CR0 221 D6
Fulham SW6 135 B2
Grove Pk SE12 165 B1
Hayes UB4 84 C3
Shoreditch N1 235 C4
1 Surbiton KT6 197 D2
12 Wallington SM6 219 B2
Wembley HA0 65 D2
Napier Gr N1 95 A5 235 B4
Napier Ho
Eltham SE12 165 B1
Kennington SE17 138 D6
Napier Lo TW15 171 B4
Napier Pl
W14 113 B3 254 C5
Napier Rd
Ashford TW15 171 B3
Belvedere DA17 125 B2
Bromley BR2 209 B5
College Pk NW10 90 B4
Croydon SE25 206 B5
Enfield EN3 18 D6
Isleworth TW7 131 A1
Kensington
W14 113 B3 254 C5
Leyton E11 76 C5
Newham E15 98 C5
South Croydon CR2 221 B1
Napier Rd *continued*
Tottenham N17 51 C6
Wallend E6 100 C5
Wembley HA0 65 D2
Napier Terr N1 72 D1
Napier Wlk TW15 171 B3
Napoleon Rd
Hackney E5 74 B5
Twickenham TW1 153 B4
Napton Cl UB4 85 A3
Narbonne Ave SW4 159 C6
Narborough Cl UB10 61 A6
Narborough St SW6 135 D3
Narcissus Rd NW6 69 C3
Nardini 12 NW9 27 D2
Naresby Fold HA7 25 C4
Narford Rd E5 74 A6
Narrow Boat Cl
SE28 123 B4
Narrow St
6 Acton W3 110 D5
Limehouse E14 119 A6
Narrow Way BR2 210 A3
Nascot St W12 90 C1
Naseby Cl
Hounslow TW7 130 C4
South Hampstead NW6 70 A1
Naseby Ct DA14 189 D6
Naseby Rd
Dagenham RM10 81 C5
South Norwood SE19 183 B4
NASH 225 A2
Nash Cl SM1 218 B5
Nash Coll of FE BR4 224 D4
Nash Ct HA3 43 B3
Nashe Ho SE1 262 C5
Nash Gn BR1 187 A4
Nash Ho
5 Millwall E14 119 C3
Pimlico SW1 258 D1
1 Walthamstow E17 53 D5
Nash La BR2 225 A2
Nash Rd
Brockley SE4 163 A6
Dagenham RM6 58 D5
Lower Edmonton N9 18 C2
Nash St NW1 231 D2
Nash Way HA3 43 B3
Nasmyth St W6 112 B3
Nassau Path 6
SE28 124 C5
Nassau Rd SW13 133 D4
Nassau St W1 239 A3
Nassington Rd NW3 70 D4
Natalie Cl TW14 149 B4
Natalie Mews TW2 152 B1
Natal Rd
Bowes Pk N11 32 A4
Ilford IG1 78 D4
South Norwood CR7 205 B6
Streatham SW16 181 D4
Nathan Ct N9 18 C4
Nathan Ho SE11 261 B3
Nathaniel Cl E1 243 D3
Nathaniel Ct E17 53 A3
Nathans Rd HA0 65 C6
Nathan Way SE28,
SE18 123 D3
National Archives The
TW9 132 D5
National Army Mus★
SW3 136 D6 267 D6
National Construction Coll & National Skills Acad E16 123 A5
National Gallery★
W1 115 D6 249 D5
National Hospl for Neurology & Neurosurgery
WC1 94 A3 240 B5
National Maritime Mus★
SE10 142 B6
National Physical Laboratory TW11 174 C4
National Portrait Gallery★ W1 249 D5
National Portrait Gallery (Annexe)★ SW1 249 D4
National Theatre★
SE1 116 B5 250 D4
National Wks TW4 129 B2
Nation Way E4 20 A3
Natural History Mus★
SW7 114 B3 256 C5
Nautilus Bldg The
EC1 234 B2
Naval Row E14 120 A6
Navarino Gr E8 74 A2
Navarino Mans E8 74 A2
Navarino Rd E8 74 A2
Navarre Rd E6 100 A5
Navarre St E2 243 C6
Navenby Wlk 13 E3 97 C3
Navestock Cl E4 20 A1
Navestock Cres IG8 37 C3
Navestock Ho IG11 102 B5
Navigation Ct E16 123 A6
Navigator Dr UB2 108 A4
Navy St SW4 137 D2
Naxos Bldg 9 E14 119 C4
Nayland Ho SE6 186 A6
Naylor Bldg W 4 E1 96 A1
Naylor Gr EN3 18 D6
Naylor Ho
33 Clapham SW8 137 D3
Walworth SE17 262 D2
5 West Kilburn W10 91 B4
Naylor Rd
Peckham SE15 140 B5
Whetstone N20 14 A2
Nayor Bldg E 6 E1 96 A1
Nazareth Cl SE15 140 B3
Nazrul St E2 95 D4
Neal Ave UB1 85 B3
Neal Cl HA6 22 A2
Nealden St SW9 138 B2
Neale Cl N2 48 A6
Neale Ct
Dagenham RM9 80 B2
Muswell Hill N10 31 B3
Neal St WC2 94 A1 240 A1
Neal's Yd WC2 240 A1
Near Acre NW9 27 D2
NEASDEN 67 B4
Neasden Cl NW10 67 C3
Neasden Junc NW10 67 C4
Neasden La
Church End NW10 67 C3
Neasden NW10 67 B5
Neasden La N NW10 67 C5
Neasden Sta NW10 67 C3
Neasham Rd RM8 80 B3
Neath Gdns SM4 202 A3
Neathouse Pl SW1 259 A4
Neats Acre HA4 39 B2
Neatscourt Rd E16 99 D2
Nebraska Bldg 11
SE13 141 D4
Nebraska St
SE1 117 B4 252 C1
Neckinger
SE16 117 D3 263 D6
Neckinger Est SE16 263 D6
Neckinger St SE1 263 D6
Nectarine Way SE13 141 D3
Nedahall Ct 4 NW11 47 B2
Needham Ct 20 EN3 7 C6
Needham Ho SE11 261 A3
Needham Rd W11 91 C1
Needham Terr NW2 68 D5
Needleman St SE16 118 D4
Needwood Ho N4 51 A1
Neela Cl UB10 60 D4
Neeld Cres
Hendon NW4 46 B4
Wembley HA9 66 C3
Neeld Ct HA9 66 C3
Neeld Par HA9 66 B3
Neil Cl TW15 171 A5
Neilson-Terry Ct 9
SW9 138 B1
Neil Wates Cres 17
SW2 160 C3
Nelgarde Rd SE6 163 C4
Nella Rd W6 134 D6
Nelldale Rd SE16 118 C2
Nellgrove Rd UB10 82 D3
Nell Gwynn Ave
TW17 193 B3
Nell Gwynn Ho SW3 257 B3
Nello James Gdns
SE27 183 B6
Nelson Cl
East Bedfont TW14 149 D3
Hillingdon UB10 82 D4
2 Paddington NW6 91 C4
Thornton Heath CR0 204 D1
Walton-on-T KT12 194 B1
Nelson Ct
5 Carshalton SM5 218 D5

Nelson Ct *continued*
Rotherhithe SE16. . . . .119 B5
Nelson Docks SE16 . .119 B5
Nelson Gdns
Bethnal Green E2. . . . . .96 A4
Twickenham TW3, TW4 . . . . 151 C5
Nelson Grove Rd
SW19. . . . . .180 A2
Nelson Ho 1 W5 . . . . . .88 A4
Nelson Hospl SW20. .179 B1
Nelson La UB10. . . . . . .82 D4
Nelson Mandela Cl
N10. . . . . .31 A1
Nelson Mandela Rd
SE3. . . . . .143 C2
Nelson Pas EC1. . . . . 235 B2
Nelson Pl N1 . . . . 234 D3
Nelson Prim Sch
Twickenham TW2. . . . 151 D5
Wallend E6. . . . . 100 C5
Nelson Rd
Ashford TW15 . . . . . . 170 A5
Bromley BR2 . . . . 209 C5
Chingford E4 . . . . .35 D4
Edmonton N9. . . . . .18 B2
Enfield EN3 . . . . .18 D5
Erith DA17 . . . . .125 B1
Greenwich SE10 . . . . . 142 A6
Harmondsworth TW6 .126 B4
Harrow HA1. . . . . .42 C1
Hillingdon UB10. . . . . . .82 D4
Hornsey Vale N8 . . . . . .50 B3
Merton SW19. . . . . . . 180 A3
New Malden KT3 . . . . .199 B4
Sidcup DA14. . . . . 190 A6
Stanmore HA7 . . . . .25 C4
Tottenham N15 . . . . . . .51 C5
Twickenham TW2, TW4 . . . . 151 C5
Wanstead E11 . . . . .55 B5
Nelson's Monument★
WC2. . . . . . . .116 A5 250 A4
Nelson Sq
SE1. . . . . . . 116 D4 251 C2
Nelsons Row SW4 . . . 137 D1
Nelson St Barking E6. .100 C6
Canning Town E16 . . . 120 D6
Newham E6 . . . . .100 B5
Stepney E1. . . . . .96 B1
Nelsons Yd NW1 . . . 232 A4
Nelson Terr N1 . . . . . 234 D3
Nelson Trad Est
SW19. . . . . 179 D2
Nemoure Rd W3. . . . .111 A6
Nene Gdns TW13. . . . .151 B2
Nene Rd TW6, UB7 . . . 126 D4
Nene Road Rdbt
TW6 . . . . 126 D4
Nepaul Rd 17 SW11 . .136 C2
Nepean St SW15. . . . .156 A4
Neptune Ct
Dagenham IG11. . . . . .102 B4
13 Millwall E14 . . . . . 119 C2
Neptune Ho
2 Rotherhithe SE16 . . . . 118 C3
14 Stoke Newington N16. . . . . .73 C3
Neptune Rd
Harlington TW6 . . . . . 127 A4
Harrow HA1. . . . . .42 B3
Neptune St SE16. . . . .118 C3
Nero Ct 6 TW8 . . . . . 131 D5
Nesbit Cl SE3. . . . . . . .142 C2
Nesbit Rd SE9 . . . . . . 143 D1
Nesbitt Ho DA6 . . . . . 169 D6
Nesbitt Sq SE19. . . . . .183 C3
Nesham Ho 14 N1. . . . .95 C6
Nesham St E1 . . . . . . .118 A5
Ness St 9 SE16. . . . . . .118 A3
Nesta Rd IG8 . . . . .36 D4
Nestle's Ave UB3. . . . 105 D3
Nestor Ave N21 . . . . . . .16 D5
Nestor Ho 18 E2 . . . . . .96 B5
Netheravon Rd
Chiswick W4 . . . . 111 D1
Ealing W7. . . . . 108 D5
Netheravon Rd S
W4 . . . . 111 D1
Netherbury Rd W5. . 109 D3
Netherby Gdns EN2 . . . .4 A1
Netherby Ho 23
SW8 . . . . 137 D3
Netherby Rd SE23. . . .162 C4
Nether Cl N3 . . . . .29 C3
Nethercombe Ho 1
SE3. . . . . .143 A6
Nethercott Ho 27 E3 . .97 D4
Nethercourt Ave N3. . .29 C4
Netherfield Gdns
IG11. . . . . .79 B1
Netherfield Rd
Finchley N12 . . . . .29 D5
Upper Tooting SW17 . 159 A1
Netherford Rd SW4 . .137 C3
Netherhall Gdns NW3 70 A3
Netherhall Int Coll
NW3. . . . . .70 A2
Netherhall Way NW3. .70 A3
Netherlands Rd EN5 . .14 B5
Netherleigh Cl N6 . . . .49 B1
Nether St Finchley N3 . .29 D4
North Finchley N12 . . . .30 A5
Netherton Gr
SW10 . . . . . .136 A6 266 B5
Netherton Ho 1 UB5 . .85 B4
Netherton Rd
Isleworth TW1. . . . . . .153 B6
Tottenham N15 . . . . . . .51 B3
Netherwood 24 N2. . . .30 B1
Netherwood Rd
W14 . . . . 112 D4
Netherwood St NW6 . .69 C2
Nethewode Ct DA17. 125 D3
Netley 13 SE5. . . . . . . .139 C4
Netley Cl Cheam SM3 216 D3
New Addington CR0. . 224 A1
Netley Ct IG2. . . . . .57 B4
Netley Dr KT12. . . . . . .195 B2
Netley Gdns SM4 . . . .202 A2
Netley Prim Sch
NW1. . . . . .93 C4 232 A1
Netley Rd
Brentford TW8. . . . . . 132 A6
Cheam SM4 . . . . 202 A2
Ilford IG2. . . . . .57 B4
Walthamstow E17 . . . . . .53 B4
Netley St NW1 93 C4 232 A1
Nettlecombe NW1 . . . .71 D1
Nettleden Ave HA9. . . .66 C2
Nettleden Ho SW3 . . 257 B3
Nettlefold Pl SE27 . . 160 D1
Nettlestead Cl 16
BR3. . . . . .185 C3
Nettleton Rd
Harlington TW6 . . . . . 126 D4
Ickenham UB10. . . . . . .60 B4
New Cross Gate SE14 140 D4
Nettlewood Rd
SW16 . . . . 181 D3
Neuchatel Rd SE6. . . .163 B2
Nevada Cl KT3. . . . . . .199 A5
Nevada St SE10. . . . . .142 A6
Nevena Ct 3 SW2 . . .160 C6
Nevern Mans SW5 . . 255 A2
Nevern Pl
SW5 . . . . . . .113 C2 255 B3
Nevern Rd SW5. . . . . 255 A3
Nevern Sq
SW5 . . . . . . .113 C2 255 B3
Nevil Ho 7 SW9. . . . . 138 D3
Nevill Ct SW10. . . . . . 266 A4
Neville Ave KT3. . . . . .177 B2
Neville Cl Acton W3. . .111 A4
Hounslow TW3. . . . . . 129 D3
Leyton E11. . . . . .76 D5
Paddington NW6 . . . . . .91 B5
Peckham SE15. . . . . . 140 A4
Sidcup DA15. . . . . 189 D6
Somers Town NW1. . . 232 D3
Neville Ct 10 SW12. . .159 C4
Neville Dr N2. . . . . .48 A3
Neville Gdns RM8. . . . .80 D5
Neville Gill Cl SW18. 157 D5
Neville Ho
Friern Barnet N11 . . . . .31 A6
5 Twickenham TW1 . 153 A4
Neville Pl N22 . . . . .32 B2
Neville Rd
Dagenham RM8. . . . . . .80 D5
Ealing W5. . . . . .87 D3
Forest Gate E7. . . . . . . .77 B1
Kingston u T KT1 . . . . 176 C1
Paddington NW6 . . . . . .91 B5
Richmond TW10. . . . . 153 C2
Thornton Heath CR0 . .205 B2
Neville's Ct NW2. . . . . .68 A5
Neville St
SW7 . . . . . . .114 B1 256 C2
Neville Terr SW7 . . . . 256 C2
Neville Wlk SM5 . . . . .202 C2
Nevill Rd N16. . . . . .73 C5
Nevin Dr E4 . . . . .19 D3
Nevin Ho UB3. . . . . . . .105 A3
Nevinson Cl SW18 . . .158 B5
Nevis Rd SW17. . . . . . .159 A2
Nevitt Ho N1 . . . . 235 D3
New Acres Rd SE28 . .123 C5
NEW ADDINGTON. . . .224 B1
Newall Ho SE1. . . . . . 262 B6
Newall Rd TW6 . . . . . .127 A4
Newark Cres NW10 . . .89 B4
Newark Ct KT12. . . . . .194 C1
Newark Ho 3 SW9 . 138 D3
Newark Knok E6. . . . . .100 C2
Newark Rd CR2. . . . . .221 B2
Newark St E1. . . . . .96 B2
Newark Way NW4. . . . .46 A6
New Ash Cl N2. . . . . . . .48 B6
New Atlas Wharf
E14 . . . . .119 C3
New Barn Cl SM6 . . . .220 B2
NEW BARNET. 14 A6
New Barnet Sta EN5 . .14 B6
New Barns Ave CR4 . 203 D5
New Barn St E13. . . . . .99 B3
NEW BECKENHAM . .185 A4
New Beckenham Sta
BR3 . . . . .185 B3
New Belmont Ho 4
SE23. . . . . .162 C3
New Bentham Ct 10
N1. . . . . .73 A1
Newbery Ho N1. . . . . . .73 A1
Newbiggin Path
WD19. . . . . .22 C6
Newbold Cotts 4 E1. .96 C1
Newbolt Ave SM3 . . . 216 D3
Newbolt Ho SE17 . . . 262 C2
Newbolt Rd HA7 . . . . . .24 D5
New Bond St
W1 . . . . .115 B6 248 D6
Newborough Gn
KT3. . . . . .199 B5
Newborough Ho
SW19 . . . . .180 B3
New Brent St NW4 . . . .46 C4
Newbridge Ct SW17. .180 A6
Newbridge Point 3
SE23. . . . . 162 D1
Newbridge Sch RM6 . .58 B4
New Bridge St
EC4. . . . . . . .94 D1 241 C1
New Broad St
EC2. . . . . . . .95 C2 243 A3
New Broadway
Ealing W5. . . . . 109 D6
7 Hillingdon UB10 . . . .82 D3
Teddington TW12. . . . .174 B5
New Bsns Ctr The
NW10. . . . . .89 D4
Newburgh Rd W3. . . .111 A5
Newburgh St W1 . . . 239 B1
New Burlington Mews
W1 . . . . 249 A6
New Burlington Pl
W1 . . . . 249 A6
New Burlington St
W1 . . . . 249 A6
Newburn Ct N12. . . . . . .30 A3
Newburn Ho SE11 . . 260 D2
Newburn St
SE11. . . . . . .116 B1 260 D2
Newbury Ave EN3. . . . . .7 B6
Newbury Cl UB5 . . . . . .63 B2
Newbury Cotts 3
IG2 . . . . .57 A3
Newbury Ct
Hackney E5 . . . . .75 A3
Sidcup DA14. . . . . 189 D6
7 Wanstead E11. . . . . .55 A5
Newbury Gdns KT19 215 D4
Newbury Ho
Barnet EN4 . . . . .2 B1
Brixton SW9. . . . . 138 D3
13 Kensington W2 . . . . .91 D1
Wood Green N22. . . . . .32 A2
Newbury Mews NW5. .71 A2
NEWBURY PARK 57 B3
Newbury Park Prim Sch
IG2. . . . . .57 B3
Newbury Park Sta
IG2. . . . . .57 B3
Newbury Rd
Bromley BR2 . . . . 209 A6
Chingford E4 . . . . .36 A4
Harmondsworth TW6 .126 B4
Newbury Rd *continued*
Ilford IG2. . . . . .57 C3
Newbury St EC1 . . . . 242 A4
Newbury Way UB5 . . . .63 B2
New Butt La SE8 . . . . .141 C5
Newby NW1 . . . . 232 A2
Newby Cl EN1 . . . . .5 C3
Newby Pl E14. . . . . . . .120 A6
Newby St SW8. . . . . . .137 B2
New Caledonian Mkt★
SE1. . . . . .117 C3 263 B6
New Caledonian Wharf
SE16. . . . . .119 B3
New Campden Ct 9
NW3 . . . . .70 A4
Newcastle Cl EC4. . . . 241 C2
Newcastle Ct EC4. . . 252 B6
Newcastle Ho W1. . . 238 A4
Newcastle Pl
W2 . . . . .92 B2 236 D4
Newcastle Row EC1. 241 B5
New Cavendish St
W1 . . . . .93 B2 238 C3
New Change
EC4. . . . . . . .95 A1 242 A1
New Chapel Sq
TW13 . . . . .150 B3
New Charles St EC1. 234 D2
NEW CHARLTON 121 C2
New Church Ct 3
SE19. . . . . .184 A3
New Church Rd
32 Camberwell SE5. . 139 A5
Camberwell SE5. . . . . .139 B6
New City Prim Sch
E13. . . . . .99 C4
New City Rd E13 . . . . . .99 C4
New Cl
Feltham TW13 . . . . . . 173 A5
Morden SW19 . . . . . . 202 A6
New Colebrooke Ct
SM5 . . . . .219 A1
New College Ct 6
NW3. . . . . .70 A2
New College Mews 7
N1. . . . . .72 C1
New College Par 1
NW3. . . . . .70 B1
Newcombe Gdns
TW3 . . . . .129 B1
Newcombe Ho N5 . . . .73 A3
Newcombe Pk
Edgware NW7 . . . . .27 C5
Wembley HA0 . . . . .88 B6
Newcombe Rise UB7. .82 A1
Newcombe St W8. . . 245 B4
Newcome Gdns
SW16 . . . . .182 A6
Newcome Ho E5. . . . . .74 B5
Newcomen Ho 5
NW5. . . . . .71 B4
Newcomen Rd
Battersea SW11 . . . . .136 B2
Leyton E11. . . . . .76 D5
Newcomen St
SE1. . . . . . . .117 B4 252 C2
New Compton St
WC2 . . . . .94 A1 240 A1
New Concordia Wharf
SE1. . . . . 253 D2
Newcourt Ho 26 E2 . . . .96 B4
Newcourt St
NW8 . . . . .92 C5 230 A3
New Covent Garden Flower Market★
SW8. . . . . . . .138 A6 270 A5
New Covent Garden Fruit & Vegetable Mkt★
SW8. . . . . . . 137 D5 269 C3
New Crane Pl E1. . . . . .118 C5
New Crescent Yd 1
NW10 . . . . .89 D5
Newcroft Cl UB8. . . . . .82 B2
Newcroft Ho 10
NW10 . . . . .67 B1
NEW CROSS 141 B4
New Cross SE14 . . . . .141 B5
NEW CROSS GATE . 140 D4
New Cross Gate
SE14 . . . . 140 D4
New Cross Gate Sta
SE14. . . . . 141 A5
New Cross Rd SE14 . .141 A4
New Cross Sta SE14. .141 B5
New Ct
City of London EC4. . . 241 A1
New Ct *continued*
26 Hampstead NW3 . . .70 A4
Northolt UB5 . . . . .63 D3
Stoke Newington N16 . . .51 B1
Newdales Cl N9 . . . . . .18 A2
Newdene Ave UB5 . . . .84 D5
New Den (Millwall FC)
The SE16 . . . . 118 C1
Newdigate Ho
6 Kingston u T KT2 . . . . 176 D4
5 Poplar E14 . . . . .97 B1
Newell St E14 . . . . .97 B1
NEW ELTHAM. 167 A2
New Eltham Sta
SE9. . . . . 166 D3
New End NW3 . . . . .70 A5
New End Prim Sch 33
NW3. . . . . .70 A4
New End Sq NW3 . . . . .70 B4
New England Est
IG11. . . . . 101 A5
Newent Cl
Camberwell SE15. . . . 139 C5
Carshalton SM5 . . . . . 202 D1
New Farm Ave BR2. . .209 A5
New Ferry App SE18 .122 C3
New Fetter La
EC4. . . . . . . .94 C1 241 B2
Newfield Cl TW12. . . .173 C2
Newfield Prim Sch
NW10. . . . . .67 D1
Newfield Rise NW2 . . .68 B5
Newgale Gdns HA8 . . .26 B2
New Garden Dr UB7. .104 A4
Newgate CR0. . . . . . . .205 A1
Newgate Cl TW13 . . . .151 A1
Newgate St
Chingford E4 . . . . .20 C1
Holborn EC1. . .94 D1 241 D2
New Globe Wlk SE1. . 252 A4
New Goulston St E1. 243 C2
New Green Pl SE19. . .183 C4
NEWHAM. 98 D4
Newham Acad of Music
8 E6. . . . . 100 A6
Newham City Farm★
E6. . . . . .99 D1
Newham Coll of FE 3
E6. . . . . .100 B5
Newham Coll of FE (Stratford Campus)
E15. . . . . .76 C1
Newham Ctr for Mental Health E13. . . . . .99 D3
Newham Gn N22. . . . . .32 C2
Newham L Ctr E13 . . . .99 C2
Newham Sixth Form Coll
E13. . . . . .99 B3
Newham Sixth Form Coll (Stratford Ctr) 7
E15. . . . . .76 B1
Newham's Row SE1. 253 B1
Newham Training & Ed Ctr E15 . . . . .76 C2
Newham University Hospl E13. . . . . .99 C3
Newham Way
Beckton E6. . . . . .100 B3
Canning Town E13 . . . . .99 B2
Newhaven Cl UB3. . . . 105 D2
Newhaven Cres
TW15 . . . . .171 B5
Newhaven Gdns
SE9. . . . . 143 D1
Newhaven La 3 E16 . . .99 A2
Newhaven Rd SE25 . .205 B4
New Heston Rd TW5 .129 B5
New Hope Christian Sch
1 SE22. . . . . 139 D1
New Horizons Ct
TW8 . . . . .131 A6
Newhouse 5 KT3. . . . .199 C2
Newhouse Ave RM6. . .58 D6
Newhouse Cl KT3. . . .199 C2
Newhouse Wlk SM4. .202 A2
Newick Cl DA5. . . . . . 169 D5
Newick Rd E5 . . . . .74 C5
Newing Gn BR1. . . . . . 187 D3
NEWINGTON. 116 D2
Newington Barrow Way
N7. . . . . .72 B5

Newington Butts SE1, SE11 116 D2 261 D3
Newington Cswy SE1 117 A3 262 A6
Newington Gn N16 73 B3
Newington Green Mans N16 73 B3
Newington Green Prim Sch 1 N16 73 B3
Newington Green Rd N1 73 B3
Newington Ind Est SE17 262 A3
New Inn Broadway EC2 243 B6
New Inn Ct The KT8 196 B4
New Inn Sq EC2 243 B6
New Inn St EC2 243 B6
New Inn Yd EC2 95 C3 243 B6
New James Ct SE15 140 B2
New Jubilee Ct 1 IG8 37 A3
New Kelvin Ave TW11 174 C4
New Kent Rd SE1 117 A2 262 B4
New King's Prim Sch 12 SW6 135 B3
New King's Rd SW6 135 C4 265 B1
New King St SE8 141 C6
Newland Cl HA5 23 B4
Newland Ct
St Luke's EC1 242 C6
Wembley HA9 66 C6
Newland Dr EN1 6 B4
Newland Gdns W13 109 A4
Newland Ho
17 Deptford SE14 140 D6
Hornsey N8 50 A6
Newland House Sch TW1 174 D6
Newland Rd N8 50 A6
Newlands NW1 232 A2
Newlands Ave KT7 196 C1
Newlands Cl
Edgware HA8 10 A1
Southall UB2 107 A1
Wembley HA0 65 C2
Newlands Croft SE20 184 D4
Newlands Ct
8 Eltham SE9 166 C5
6 Penge SE26 184 C4
Streatham SW16 182 A5
Newlands Pk SE26 184 D5
Newlands Pl EN5 12 D6
Newlands Quay E1 118 C6
Newlands Rd
Thornton Heath SW16 182 A1
Woodford IG8 20 D2
Newland St E16 122 B5
Newlands The
Thames Ditton KT7 196 C1
Wallington SM6 219 D1
Newlands Way KT9 213 C3
New Life Christian Sch CR0 220 D6
Newling Cl E6 100 B1
New London St EC3 253 B6
New Lydenburg Commercial Est SE7 121 C3
New Lydenburg St SE7 121 C3
Newlyn NW1 232 B5
Newlyn Cl
Hillingdon UB8 82 C2
Orpington BR6 227 D4
Newlyn Gdns HA2 41 B2
Newlyn Ho
7 Pinner HA5 23 B3
7 Sutton SM1 218 A4
Newlyn Rd Barnet EN5 1 B1
Bexley DA16 145 D3
Tottenham N17 33 D2
NEW MALDEN 199 D5
New Malden Sta KT3 199 C6
Newman Ct
3 Bromley BR1 187 A2
Newman Ct *continued*
8 Finchley N3 29 C2
Newman Ho 11 TW10 153 C1
Newman Pas W1 239 B3
Newman Rd
Bromley BR1 187 A2
Harmondsworth UB7 126 C4
Hayes UB3 106 B6
Newham E13 99 B4
Thornton Heath CR0 204 B1
Walthamstow E17 52 D4
Newman's Ct EC3 242 D1
Newmans La 15 KT6 198 A3
Newman's Row WC2 240 D3
Newman St W1 93 C2 239 B3
Newman's Way EN4 2 A4
Newman Terr 9 CR4 202 D6
Newmarket Ave UB5 63 D3
Newmarket Gn SE9 165 D4
Newmarsh Rd SE28 123 D5
Newmill Ho E3 98 A3
New Mill Rd BR5 190 C2
Newminster Rd SM4 202 A3
Newmount NW3 70 B3
New Mount St E15 76 B1
Newnes Path SW15 134 B1
Newnham Ave HA4 40 C1
Newnham Cl
Loughton IG10 21 D5
Northolt UB5 64 A2
South Norwood CR7 183 A1
Newnham Gdns UB5 64 A2
Newnham Ho
Catford SE6 164 A1
Loughton IG10 21 D5
9 Putney SW15 156 D5
Newnham Jun & Inf Schs HA4 40 C1
Newnham Lo 10 DA17 125 C1
Newnham Mews N22 32 C2
Newnham Rd N22 32 C2
Newnhams Cl BR1 210 B6
Newnham Terr SE1 261 A6
Newnham Way HA3 44 A4
New North Com Sch N1 95 A6 235 A6
New North Pl EC2 243 A6
New North Rd N1 95 B6 235 C5
New North Road Bridge N1 235 C5
New North St WC1 94 B2 240 C4
Newnton Cl N4 51 B2
New Oak Rd N2 30 A1
New Oxford St WC1 94 A1 240 A2
New Palace Yd SW1 116 A4 250 A1
New Par
Ashford TW15 170 B6
Yiewsley UB7 104 A5
New Park Ave N13 17 B1
New Park Cl UB5 63 A2
New Park Ct 26 SW2 160 A4
New Park Ho N13 32 B6
New Park Par 14 SW2 160 A4
New Park Rd
Ashford TW15 171 A5
Streatham SW2 160 A4
New Pl CR0 223 C2
New Place Sq SE16 118 B3
New Plaistow Rd E15 98 C6
New Pond Par HA4 62 A5
Newport Ave
Blackwall E14 120 B6
Newham E13 99 B3
Newport Cl EN3 7 A6
Newport Ct WC2 249 D6
Newport Ho 2 E3 97 A4
Newport Lo 2 EN1 17 C6
Newport Mead WD19 22 D6
Newport Pl WC2 249 D6
Newport Rd
Barnes SW13 134 A4
Harmondsworth TW6 126 C4
Hayes UB4 83 B2
Leyton E10 76 B6
Walthamstow E17 53 A5
Newport Sch E10, E11 76 A6
Newport St SE11 116 B2 260 D4
New Priory Ct 9 NW6 69 C1
New Providence Wharf E14 120 B5
Newquay Cres HA2 63 A6
Newquay Ho SE11 261 A2
Newquay Rd SE6 164 A2
New Quebec St W1 237 D1
New Rd
Brentford TW8 109 D1
Carshalton CR4 203 A1
Chingford E4 36 A6
Dagenham RM10 103 D5
East Bedfont TW14 149 B5
East Molesey KT8 195 C6
Edmonton N9 18 B2
Elstree WD6 9 D5
Esher KT10 212 A4
feltham TW14 150 B3
Finchley N10 30 C2
Hanworth TW13 173 A5
Harlington TW6, UB7 127 A5
Harrow HA1 64 D4
Hendon NW7 29 A3
Hillingdon UB8 83 A2
Hornsey N8 50 A4
Hounslow TW3 129 D1
Ilford IG3 79 C6
Kingston u T KT2 176 C3
Littleton TW17 192 D6
Richmond TW10 175 C6
Stepney E1 96 B2
Tottenham N22 33 A2
Welling DA16 146 B3
West Heath SE2 124 D1
New River Ave N8 50 B6
New River Cres N13 32 D6
New River Ct N5 73 B4
New River Stad N22 32 D3
New River Way N4 51 B2
New Row WC2 116 A6 250 A6
New Rush Hall Sch IG1 79 A6
Newry Rd TW1 153 A6
New St Sq EC4 94 C1 241 B2
Newsam Ave N15 51 B4
New Scotland Yard★ SW1 115 D3 259 C6
New Shepherd's Bush Mkt★ 6 W12 112 C4
Newsholme Dr N21 16 B6
NEW SOUTHGATE 31 C6
New Southgate Ind Est 10 N11 31 C5
New Southgate Sta N11 31 B5
New Spitalfields Mkt E10 75 C5
New Spring Gdns Wlk SE11 260 B1
New Sq
East Bedfont TW14 149 A3
St Giles WC2 94 B1 240 D2
New Square Pas WC2 241 A2
New St EC2 95 C2 243 B3
Newstead Ave BR6 227 C6
Newstead Cl N12 30 C4
Newstead Ct UB5 85 A4
Newstead Ho
Edmonton N9 17 D1
Islington N1 234 B4
Newstead Rd SE12 164 D4
Newstead Way SW19 178 D6
Newstead Wlk SM5 202 A2
Newstead Wood Sch for Girls BR6 227 B5
New Street Hill BR1 187 C5
Newton Ave
Acton W3 111 A4
Muswell Hill N10 31 B2
Newton Cl
Harrow HA2 63 C6
Walthamstow E17 53 A3
Newton Farm Ecology Pk HA2 63 C6
Newton Farm Fst & Mid Sch HA2 63 B6
Newton Gr W4 111 C2
Newton Ho
22 Clapham SW8 137 D3
Paddington NW8 91 D6
Newton Ho *continued*
1 Stepney E1 118 B6
10 Walthamstow E17 54 A6
Newton Ind Est RM6 58 D5
Newton Pl E14 119 C2
Newton Point 1 E16 98 D1
Newton Prep Sch SW8 137 B4 268 D2
Newton Rd
Acton W3 111 A4
Cricklewood NW2 68 C5
Harmondsworth UB7 126 B4
Harrow HA3 24 C1
Isleworth TW7 130 D3
Kensington W2 91 D1
South Tottenham N15 52 A4
Stratford New Town E15 76 B3
Welling DA16 146 A2
Wembley HA0 66 B1
Wimbledon SW19 179 A3
Newton St WC2 94 A1 240 B2
Newton's Yd 14 SW18 157 C6
Newton Terr BR2 209 D3
Newton Way N18 33 A5
Newton Wlk HA8 26 D2
New Tower Bldgs 21 E1 118 B5
Newtown Ct
Battersea SW11 268 C1
Clapham SW4 159 B6
New Trinity Rd 1 N2 30 B1
New Union Cl E14 120 A3
New Union St EC2 242 C3
New Victoria Hospl KT3 177 C2
New Wanstead E11 55 A3
New Way Rd NW9 45 C5
New Wharf Rd N1 94 A5 233 B4
New Woodlands Sch BR1 186 C6
NEWYEARS GREEN 38 B3
Newyears Green La UB9 38 B3
New Zealand Ave KT12 193 D1
Nexus Ct E11 54 C2
Niagara Ave W5 109 C2
Niagara Cl N1 235 B4
Niagara Ct 6 SE16 118 C3
Niagara Ho W5 109 C2
Nibthwaite Rd HA1 42 C4
Nicholas Cl UB6 85 D5
Nicholas Ct
Chiswick W4 133 C5
Golders Green NW11 47 C2
Lewisham SE12 165 A3
Newham E13 99 B4
Nicholas Gdns W5 109 D4
Nicholas Ho
Ealing W13 87 C1
Penge SE26 184 B4
2 Putney SW15 156 A6
Nicholas La EC2, EC4 252 D6
Nicholas Pas EC3 252 D6
Nicholas Rd
Bethnal Green E1 96 C3
Borehamwood WD6 10 B6
Dagenham RM8 81 B5
20 Shepherd's Bush W11 112 D6
Wallington CR0 220 A4
Nicholas Stacey Ho 3 SE7 121 B1
Nicholay Rd N19 49 D1
Nichol Cl N14 15 D3
Nicholes Rd TW3 129 C1
Nichol La BR1 187 A3
Nicholl Ho N4 51 A1
Nicholls Almshouses NW7 28 B5
Nicholls Ave UB8 82 C3
Nicholls Point 4 E15 99 A6
Nicholl St E2 96 A6
Nichols Cl
Chessington KT9 213 C2
Finsbury Pk N4 50 C1
Nichols Ct E2 95 D5
Nichols Gn W5 88 A2
Nicholson Ct 9 N17 51 D6
Nicholson Ho SE17 262 C2
Nicholson Mews KT1 198 A5
Nicholson Rd CR0 205 D1
Nicholson St SE1 251 C3
Nickelby Cl SE28 102 C1
Nickleby Cl UB8 82 D1
Nickleby Ho
18 Bermondsey SE1 118 A4
7 Shepherd's Bush W11 112 D5
Nickols Wlk SW18 135 D1
Nicola Cl Harrow HA3 24 B1
South Croydon CR2 221 A2
Nicola Terr DA7 147 A4
Nicol Cl 6 TW1 153 B5
Nicole Ho SE25 206 A6
Nicoll Ct
Dagenham NW10 89 C6
Muswell Hill N10 31 B3
Nicoll Pl NW4 46 B2
Nicoll Rd NW10 89 C6
Nicoll Way WD6 11 B6
Nicolson 14 NW9 27 D2
Nicolson Dr WD23 8 A2
Nicosia Rd SW18 158 C4
Niederwald Rd SE26 185 A6
Nield Rd UB3 105 D4
Nigel Bldg EC1 241 A4
Nigel Cl UB5 85 A6
Nigel Ct N3 29 D3
Nigel Fisher Way KT9 213 D1
Nigel Mews IG1 78 D4
Nigel Playfair Ave W6 112 B1
Nigel Rd
Forest Gate E7 77 C3
Peckham SE15 140 A2
Nigeria Rd SE7 143 D5
Nighthawk 16 NW9 27 D2
Nightingale Ave
Chingford E4 36 C5
Harrow HA1 43 B1
Nightingale Cl
Carshalton SM5 219 A6
Chingford E4 36 C6
Chiswick W4 133 A6
Pinner HA5 40 C4
Nightingale Ct
14 Cubitt Town E14 120 A3
Finsbury Pk N4 72 B6
1 Harrow HA1 42 D3
Penge SE19 183 D4
Sutton SM1 218 A3
1 Wanstead E11 55 B4
Nightingale Dr KT19 214 D2
Nightingale Gr SE13 164 B6
Nightingale Ho
Hayes UB3 105 D2
21 Hoxton E1 95 C6
4 North Kensington W12 90 C1
7 St George in t East E1 118 A5
Woolwich SE18 122 C1
Nightingale La
Balham SW11, SW12 159 A5
Bromley BR1 187 D1
Hornsey N8 50 A6
Richmond TW10 154 A4
Wanstead E11 55 B4
Nightingale Lo
Edgware HA8 27 A4
5 Paddington W9 91 C2
Nightingale Mans 4 SW12 159 A5
Nightingale Mews
1 Bow E3 97 A5
Newington SE11 261 C4
8 Wanstead E11 55 B4
Nightingale Pl
Shooters Hill SE18 144 D6
West Brompton SW10 136 A6 266 B6
Nightingale Prim Sch
Shacklewell E5 74 A4
Wanstead E18 55 C5
Wood Green N22 32 B2
Woolwich SE18 122 D1
Nightingale Rd
22 Canonbury N1 73 A2
Carshalton SM5 219 A6
Dagenham NW10 89 D5
Ealing W7 108 D5
East Molesey KT8 195 D4
Hackney E5 74 B5

Nightingale Rd continued
Hampton TW12 ..... 173 C4
Orpington BR5 ...... 211 A3
Ponders End N9 ...... 18 C4
Walton-on-T KT12 .... 194 B2
Wood Green N22 ...... 32 B3
Nightingale Sch SW17 ...... 158 C2
Nightingale Sq SW12 ...... 159 A4
Nightingales The TW19 ...... 148 B3
Nightingale Vale SE18 ...... 144 C6
Nightingale Way E6 .. 100 A2
Nightingale Wlk SW18, SW4 ...... 159 B5
Nile Cl N16 ...... 73 D5
Nile Ct N12 ...... 30 C4
Nile Dr N9 ...... 18 C2
Nile Ho N1 ...... 235 C2
Nile Path 6 SE18 .... 144 C6
Nile Rd E13 ...... 99 C5
Nile St N1 ..... 95 B4 235 C2
Nile Terr SE1, SE15 ...... 117 D1 263 D1
Nimegen Way 9 SE22 ...... 161 C6
Nimmo Dr WD23 ...... 8 B4
Nimrod 12 NW9 ...... 27 C2
Nimrod Cl UB5 ...... 84 D4
Nimrod Pas 4 N1 .... 73 C2
Nimrod Rd SW16 .... 181 B5
Nina Mackay Cl 10 E15 ...... 98 C6
Nine Acres Cl
Hayes UB3 ...... 105 A3
London E12 ...... 78 A3
NINE ELMS 137 C5
Nine Elms Cl TW14 .. 149 D3
Nine Elms La SW8 ...... 137 D6 269 C5
Nineteenth Rd CR4 .. 204 A5
Ninhams Wood BR6 .. 226 C4
Ninth Ave UB3 ...... 106 A6
Nisbet 13 NW9 ...... 27 C2
Nisbet Ho E9 ...... 74 D3
Nisbett Wlk DA14 .... 190 A6
Nita Ct SE12 ...... 165 A3
Nithdale Rd SE18 .... 145 A5
Nithsdale Gr UB10 .... 61 A5
Niton Cl EN5 ...... 12 D5
Niton Rd TW9 ...... 132 C2
Niton St SW6 ...... 134 D5
No 1 St SE18 ...... 122 D3
No 2 Willow Rd★ NW3 ...... 70 C4
Noam Prim Sch HA9 .. 66 B5
Nobel Dr TW6 ...... 127 C5
Nobel Ho 8 SE5 ...... 139 A3
Nobel Rd N18 ...... 34 C6
Noble Cnr TW5 ...... 129 C4
Noble Ct
Mitcham CR4 ...... 180 B1
Stepney E1 ...... 118 B6
Noblefield Hts N2 ..... 48 D4
Noble Ho 18 E1 ...... 118 A6
Noble St EC2 .. 95 A1 242 A2
Noel 13 NW9 ...... 27 D2
Noel Baker Ct 5 E11 .. 76 C6
Noel Coward Ho SW1 ...... 259 B3
Noel Ct TW4 ...... 129 B2
Noel Dene W5 ...... 109 C1
Noel Ho 3 NW3 ...... 70 B1
NOEL PARK 32 D1
Noel Park Prim Sch N22 ...... 32 C1
Noel Park Rd N22 ..... 32 C1
Noel Rd Acton W3 ..... 88 D1
Islington N1 .. 94 D5 234 D4
Newham E6 ...... 100 A3
Noel Sq RM8 ...... 80 C4
Noel St W1 .... 93 C1 239 B1
Noel Terr
Forest Hill SE23 ..... 162 C2
Sidcup DA14 ...... 190 B6
Noko NW10 ...... 90 D4
Nolan Way E5 ...... 74 A4
Noll Ho N7 ...... 72 B6
Nolton Pl HA8 ...... 26 B2
Nonsuch Ct SM3 ...... 217 A2
Nonsuch High Sch for Girls SM3 ...... 216 D1
Nonsuch Ho 5 SW19 ...... 180 B2
Nonsuch Prim Sch KT17 ...... 216 B3
Nook The SW19 ...... 180 A1
Noor Ul Islam Prim Sch E10 ...... 76 A6
Nora Gdns NW4 ...... 46 D5
NORBITON 176 C1
Norbiton Ave KT1, KT2 ...... 176 C1
Norbiton Common Rd KT1, KT3 ...... 198 D6
Norbiton Hall KT2 ... 176 B1
Norbiton Rd E14 ...... 97 B1
Norbiton Sta KT1 .... 176 C2
Norbreck Gdns NW10 .. 88 B4
Norbreck Par NW10 .. 88 B4
Norbroke St W12 ... 111 D6
Norburn St W10 ...... 91 A2
NORBURY 182 C2
Norbury Ave
Isleworth TW3 ...... 130 B1
Thornton Heath CR7, SW16 ...... 182 C1
Norbury Cl SW16 ... 182 D2
Norbury Court Rd SW16 ...... 182 A1
Norbury Cres SW16 .. 182 C1
Norbury Cross SW16 ...... 204 A6
Norbury Ct N12 ...... 30 A6
Norbury Fst & Mid Sch HA1 ...... 42 C4
Norbury Gdns RM6 .... 58 D4
Norbury Gr NW7 ...... 11 C1
Norbury Hill SW16 .. 182 D3
Norbury Manor Bsns & Enterprise Coll For Girls CR7 ...... 182 C2
Norbury Manor Prim Sch SW16 ...... 182 A2
Norbury Rd
Chingford E4 ...... 35 C5
Feltham TW13 ...... 149 D1
South Norwood CR7 .. 205 A6
Norbury Rise SW16 .. 204 A6
Norbury Sta SW16 ... 182 B2
Norbury Trad Est SW16 ...... 182 B1
Norcombe Gdns HA3 .. 43 C4
Norcombe Ho 2 N19 .. 71 D5
Norcott Cl UB4 ...... 84 C3
Norcott Rd N16 ...... 74 A5
Norcroft Gdns SE22 .. 162 A4
Norcutt Rd TW2 ...... 152 C3
Norden Ho 25 E2 ...... 96 B4
Norden Point NW2 ..... 46 C1
Nore Ct NW10 ...... 68 A1
Norfolk Ave
Edmonton N13 ...... 32 D4
South Tottenham N15 ... 51 D3
Norfolk Cl
Cockfosters EN4 ...... 3 A1
East Finchley N2 ...... 48 C6
Edmonton N13 ...... 32 D4
5 Twickenham TW1 .. 153 B5
Norfolk Cres
Paddington W2 ...... 92 C1 237 B2
Sidcup DA15 ...... 167 C4
Norfolk Ct
5 Barnet EN5 ...... 1 A1
4 Ilford RM6 ...... 58 B4
Surbiton KT5 ...... 198 B3
Wembley HA0 ...... 65 C2
Norfolk Gdns DA7 .... 147 B4
Norfolk Ho
13 Acton W3 ...... 88 C1
Beckenham BR2 ...... 208 D5
City of London EC4 ... 252 A6
Edgware HA8 ...... 26 B3
Greenwich SE3 ...... 142 C6
11 Merton SW19 ...... 180 A3
Penge SE20 ...... 184 C2
4 Putney SW15 ...... 156 C4
Richmond TW10 ...... 154 C6
Shacklewell E8 ...... 73 D4
2 South Croydon CR0 ...... 221 B6
3 Stanmore HA7 ...... 25 C5
St Johns SE8 ...... 141 C4
Westminster SW1 ... 259 D4
Norfolk House Rd SW16 ...... 160 A1
Norfolk House Sch N10 ...... 31 B1
Norfolk Mans
Battersea SW11 .... 267 D1
10 Wandsworth SW18 ...... 157 C6
Norfolk Mews 12 W10 ...... 91 A2
Norfolk Pl
Paddington W2 ...... 92 B1 236 D2
Welling DA16 ...... 146 A3
Norfolk Rd
Barking IG11 ...... 79 C1
Barnet EN5 ...... 1 C2
Claygate KT10 ...... 212 C3
Dagenham RM10 ...... 81 D3
Enfield EN3 ...... 18 B6
Feltham TW13 ...... 150 C3
Harrow HA1 ...... 41 D4
Higham Hill E17 ...... 34 D1
Ilford IG3 ...... 57 C2
Mitcham SW19 ...... 180 C4
Newham E6 ...... 100 B6
South Norwood CR7 .. 205 A6
St John's Wood NW8 ...... 92 B6 229 D5
Willesden NW10 ...... 67 C1
Norfolk Row SE1, SE11 ...... 116 B2 260 C4
Norfolk Sq W2 ...... 92 B1 236 D2
Norfolk Sq Mews W2 ...... 236 D1
Norfolk St E7 ...... 77 A3
Norgrove St SW12 ... 159 A4
Norhyrst Ave SE25 .. 205 D6
Norland Ho 13 W11 .. 112 D5
Norland Pl W11 ...... 113 A5 244 B3
Norland Place Sch W11 ...... 113 A5 244 A3
Norland Rd 16 W11 .. 112 D5
Norlands Cres BR7 .. 188 D2
Norland Sq W11 ...... 113 A5 244 B3
Norley Vale SW15 .... 156 A3
Norlington Rd E10, E11 ...... 54 B1
Norlington Sch E10 ... 54 B1
Norman Ave
Feltham TW13 ...... 151 B2
Southall UB1 ...... 107 A6
Tottenham N22 ...... 33 A2
Twickenham TW1 ...... 153 C4
Norman Butler Ho 10 W10 ...... 91 A3
Normanby Cl SW15 .. 157 B6
Normanby Rd NW10 .. 67 D4
Norman Cl
Orpington BR6 ...... 227 A5
Tottenham N22 ...... 33 A2
Norman Cres
Heston TW5 ...... 128 D5
Pinner HA5 ...... 22 C2
Norman Ct
Dulwich SE22 ...... 162 A4
5 Finchley N3 ...... 29 C2
Finsbury Pk N4 ...... 50 C2
8 Hampton TW12 ... 173 C2
Ilford IG2 ...... 57 B2
West Norwood SW16 182 C5
Willesden NW10 ...... 68 A1
Woodford IG8 ...... 37 B5
Normand Croft Com Sch W14 ...... 135 B6 264 D6
Normand Mews W14 264 B6
Normand Rd W14 ...... 135 B6 264 C6
Normandy Ave EN5 .... 1 B1
Normandy Cl SE26 ... 163 A1
Normandy Dr UB3 .... 83 A1
Normandy Ho
8 Cubitt Town E14 .. 120 A4
4 Hendon NW4 ...... 28 D1
Normandy Rd SW9 ... 138 C4
Normandy Terr E16 .... 99 B1
Norman Gr E3 ...... 97 A5
Norman Hay Trad Est UB7 ...... 126 B4
Norman Ho
1 Cheam SM1 ...... 217 C2
Feltham TW13 ...... 151 B2
7 Leyton E11 ...... 76 C6
Lower Halliford TW17 192 C2
South Lambeth SW8 .. 270 A4
Normanhurst TW15 .. 170 C5
Normanhurst Ave DA7 ...... 146 D4
Normanhurst Dr TW1 ...... 153 B6
Normanhurst Rd
St Paul's Cray BR5 .... 190 B1
Streatham SW2 ...... 160 B2
Walton-on-T KT12 ... 194 D1
Normanhurst Sch E4 .. 20 B4
Norman Par DA14 ... 168 D2
Norman Rd
Ashford TW15 ...... 171 B4
Belvedere DA17 ...... 125 D3
Greenwich SE10 .... 141 D5
Ilford IG1 ...... 78 D3
Leyton E11 ...... 76 C6
Merton SW19 ...... 180 A3
Newham E6 ...... 100 B3
South Tottenham N15 ... 51 D4
Sutton SM1 ...... 217 C3
Thornton Heath CR7 .. 204 D4
Normans Cl
Hillingdon UB8 ...... 82 A2
Willesden NW10 ...... 67 B2
Normansfield Ave KT1, KT8 ...... 175 C3
Normanshire Dr E4 .... 35 D6
Normans Mead NW10 67 B2
Norman St EC1 ...... 95 A4 235 B1
Normanton Ave SW18, SW19 ...... 157 C2
Normanton Ct CR2 ... 221 C3
Normanton Ho 6 SW4 ...... 159 C5
Normanton Pk E4 ...... 20 C2
Normanton Rd CR2 .. 221 C2
Normanton St SE23 .. 162 D2
Norman Way
Acton W3 ...... 88 D1
Palmers Green N14 .... 16 A2
Normington Cl SW16 ...... 182 C5
Norrice Lea N2 ...... 48 B4
Norris 11 NW9 ...... 27 D2
Norris Ho
12 Hoxton N1 ...... 95 C6
15 South Hackney E9 .. 96 C6
Norris St SW1 ...... 249 C5
Norroy Rd SW15 .... 134 D1
Norrys Cl EN4 ...... 2 D1
Norrys Rd EN4 ...... 2 D1
Norse Ho 13 SE5 ...... 139 A3
Norseman Cl 3 IG3 ... 58 B1
Norseman Way UB6 ... 85 D6
Norstead Pl SW15 .... 156 A2
North Access Rd E17 .. 52 D3
North Acre NW9 ...... 27 C2
NORTH ACTON 89 B4
North Acton Rd NW10 ...... 89 B4
North Acton Sta W3 ... 89 B2
Northala Fields UB5 .. 85 B6
Northampton Gr N1 .. 73 B3
Northampton Pk N1 .. 73 B2
Northampton Rd
Croydon CR0 ...... 222 A6
Enfield EN3 ...... 7 A1
Finsbury EC1 .. 94 C3 241 B6
Northampton Sq EC1 ...... 94 D4 234 C1
Northampton St N1 ... 73 A1
Northanger Rd SW16 ...... 182 A4
North Audley St W1 ...... 115 A6 248 A6
North Ave Ealing W13 .. 87 B2
Edmonton N18 ...... 34 A6
Harrow HA2 ...... 41 D3
Hayes UB3 ...... 106 A6
8 Richmond TW9 ... 132 C4
Southall UB1 ...... 107 B6
Wallington SM5 ...... 219 A1
Northaw Ho 4 W10 ... 90 C3
North Bank NW8 ...... 92 C4 230 A1
Northbank Rd E17 ..... 36 A1
North Beckton Prim Sch E6 ...... 100 B2
North Birkbeck Rd E11 ...... 76 B5
North Block 19 E1 ... 118 C6
Northborough Rd SW16 ...... 182 A1
Northbourne BR2 .... 209 A2
Northbourne Ho
21 Hackney E5 ...... 74 B3
Osidge N14 ...... 15 D4
Northbourne Rd SW4 ...... 159 D6
North Bridge House Sch 13 NW3 ...... 70 A2
North Bridge House Senior Sch NW1 ...... 93 B6 231 C5
Northbrook CE Sch SE12 ...... 164 B6
Northbrook Rd
Barnet EN5 ...... 13 A5
Ilford IG1 ...... 78 C6
Lewisham SE13 ...... 164 C6
Thornton Heath CR0 .. 205 B4
Wood Green N22 ...... 32 A3
Northburgh St EC1 ...... 94 D3 241 D6
Northbury Inf & Jun Schs IG11 ...... 79 A2
North Carriage Dr W2 ...... 114 C6 247 B6
NORTH CHEAM 216 C6
Northchurch SE17 .. 262 D2
Northchurch Ho 19 E2 ...... 96 A6
Northchurch Rd
De Beauvoir Town N1 ... 73 B1
Wembley HA9 ...... 66 C2
Northchurch Terr N1 .. 73 C1
North Circular Rd
Edmonton N13 ...... 32 C5
Finchley N2 ...... 30 B2
Highams Pk E17 ...... 35 D2
Ilford IG1, E12 ...... 78 C4
Neasden NW2, NW10 .. 67 C3
Temple Fortune N3, NW2, NW4 ...... 47 A4
Woodford E18 ...... 37 C1
North Cl Barnet EN5 ... 12 C6
Bexley DA6 ...... 146 D1
Dagenham RM10 .... 103 C6
East Bedfont TW14 .... 149 B5
Merton SM4 ...... 201 A5
Northcliffe Cl KT4 ... 215 C5
Northcliffe Dr N20 .... 13 B3
North Colonnade The E14 ...... 119 D5
North Common Rd
Ealing W5 ...... 110 A6
Uxbridge UB8 ...... 60 A3
Northcote 3 HA5 ...... 22 C1
Northcote Ave
Ealing W5 ...... 110 A6
Isleworth TW7 ...... 153 A6
Southall UB1 ...... 107 A6
Tolworth KT5 ...... 198 D2
Northcote Ho UB4 .... 84 D2
Northcote Lodge Sch SW11 ...... 158 D5
Northcote Rd
Isleworth TW7 ...... 153 A6
Kingston u T KT3 ...... 199 B6
Sidcup DA14 ...... 189 C6
Thornton Heath CR0 .. 205 B3
Walthamstow E17 ...... 53 A5
Wandsworth SW11 .. 158 D6
Willesden NW10 ...... 67 C1
Northcott Ave N22 .... 32 A2
North Countess Rd E17 ...... 35 B2
Northcourt W1 ...... 239 B4
NORTH CRAY 169 B1
North Cray Rd DA14 . 191 A5
North Cres
Finchley N3 ...... 29 B1
Marylebone WC1 .... 239 C4
Newham E16 ...... 98 B3
Northcroft Ct 3 W12 ...... 112 A4
Northcroft Rd
Brentford W13 ...... 109 B3
West Ewell KT19 .... 215 C1
North Crofts SE21 ... 162 B3
North Cross Rd
East Dulwich SE22 ... 162 A6
Ilford IG6 ...... 57 A5
North Ct SW1 ...... 260 A5
North Dene
Edgware NW7 ...... 11 B1
Hounslow TW5 ...... 129 D4

Northdene Gdns N15 .. 51 D3
Northdown Cl HA4 .... 61 D5
Northdown Gdns IG2 . 57 C4
Northdown Rd DA16 . 146 C3
Northdown St
N1 .... 94 B5 233 C3
North Dr
Beckenham BR3 ..... 207 D5
Hounslow TW3, TW7 . 130 A3
Orpington BR6 ...... 227 C4
Ruislip HA4 .... 39 C2
Streatham SW16 .... 181 C6
North Dulwich Sta
SE21 .... 161 B6
North Ealing Prim Sch
W5 .... 87 B3
North Ealing Sta W3 .. 88 B1
NORTH END 70 A6
North End
Buckhurst Hill IG9 ..... 21 C4
Croydon CR0 .... 221 A6
North End NW3 .... 70 A6
North End Ave NW3 ... 70 A6
North End Cres
W14 .... 113 B2 254 C3
North End Ho
W14 .... 113 A2 254 B3
North End La BR6 ... 226 D1
Northend Lodge 2
HA5 .... 40 D6
North End Par W14 . 254 B3
North End Rd
Golders Green NW11 .. 47 D1
Wembley HA9 .... 66 D5
West Kensington
W14 ..... 113 B1 254 D1
North End Way NW3 .. 70 A6
Northern Ave N9 ...... 17 D2
Northernhay Wlk
SM4 .... 201 A5
Northern Hts N8 ...... 49 D2
Northern Perimeter Rd
TW6 .... 127 C4
Northern Perimeter Rd
(W) TW6 .... 126 B4
Northern Rd E13 ...... 99 B5
Northern Relief Rd
IG11 .... 79 A2
Northern Star Ho
N11 .... 31 B5
Northesk Ho 6 E1 .... 96 B3
North Eyot Gdns 5
W6 .... 111 D1
Northey St E14 ..... 119 A6
NORTH FELTHAM ... 150 B6
North Feltham Trad Est
TW14 .... 128 B1
Northfield IG10 .... 21 D6
Northfield Ave
Pinner HA5 .... 40 D5
West Ealing W13, W5 . 109 B4
Northfield Cl
Bromley BR1 .... 188 A2
Hayes UB3 .... 105 D3
Northfield Cres SM3 . 217 A4
Northfield Gdns RM9 .. 81 B4
Northfield Hall N6 .... 49 A2
Northfield Ho
2 Newham E13 ...... 99 C5
3 Peckham SE15 ... 140 A6
Northfield Ind Est
HA0 .... 88 C6
Northfield Par UB3 . 105 D3
Northfield Path RM9 .. 81 B4
Northfield Pk UB3 .. 105 D3
Northfield Rd
Cockfosters EN4 .... 2 C2
Dagenham RM9 .... 81 B4
Enfield EN3 .... 18 B6
Heston TW5 .... 128 D5
Plashet E6 .... 78 B1
Stamford Hill N16 ..... 51 C2
West Ealing W13 .... 109 B4
Northfields SW18 ... 135 C1
Northfields Prospect
SW18 .... 135 C1
Northfields Rd W3 .... 89 A2
Northfields Sta W5 . 109 C3
NORTH FINCHLEY ... 30 A6
Northfleet Ho SE1 .. 252 C2
North Flower Wlk
W2 .... 114 B6 246 C5
North Gate
NW8 .... 92 C5 230 A3
Northgate Bsns Ctr
EN1 .... 6 B1
Northgate Ct 14
SW9 .... 138 C2
Northgate Dr NW9 .... 45 C3
North Gates N12 ...... 30 A2
North Gdns SW19 ... 180 B3
North Glade The
DA5 .... 169 B3
North Gn NW9 .... 27 C3
North Gower St
NW1 .... 93 C4 232 B1
North Gr Highgate N6 .. 49 A2
Tottenham N15 .... 51 B4
North Greenwich Sta
SE10 .... 120 C4
North Harringay Prim
Sch N8 .... 50 C5
NORTH HARROW 41 D2
North Harrow Sta
HA2 .... 41 D4
North Hill N6 .... 49 A3
North Hill Ave N6 ..... 48 D3
North Hill Ct N6 ...... 49 A2
NORTH HILLINGDON . 61 A2
North Ho 3 SE8 ..... 119 B1
NORTH HYDE 107 A1
North Hyde Gdns UB2,
UB3 .... 106 A3
North Hyde La UB2 .. 107 A1
North Hyde Rd UB3 . 105 D3
Northiam Finchley N12 . 29 C6
St Pancras WC1 ..... 233 B1
Northiam St E9 .... 96 B6
Northington St
WC1 .... 94 B3 240 D5
NORTH
KENSINGTON 90 D2
North Kingston Ctr
KT2 .... 176 A4
North La TW11 ...... 174 D4
Northlands 4 BR1 ... 187 C1
Northlands Ave BR6 .. 227 C4
Northlands St SE5 ... 139 A3
Northleigh Ho 36 E3 .. 97 D4
North Lo
Clapham SW4 .... 137 B1
Muswell Hill N22 ...... 31 D1
New Barnet EN5 ...... 14 A6
North Lodge Cl
SW15 .... 156 D6
North London Bsns Pk
N11 .... 15 A1
North London Coll 13
N17 .... 51 D6
North London Collegiate
Sch HA7, HA8 .... 26 A5
North London Int Sch (IB
Diploma Ctre) 15
N11 .... 30 D5
North London Int Sch
(Lower Sch)
5 North Finchley
N12 .... 14 A1
24 North Finchley N12 .. 29 D6
North London Int Sch
(Lower School) 24
N12 .... 29 D6
North London Int Sch
(Upper Sch) 14 N11 . 30 D5
North London Rudolf
Steiner Sch 7 N8 ... 50 A5
North London Science
Ctr 12 N1 .... 72 C1
North Mall The N9 .... 18 B2
North Mews
WC1 .... 94 B3 240 D5
North Middlesex
University Hospl
N18 .... 33 C5
Northmoor 4 SE23 . 162 D1
North Mount N20 ..... 14 A2
Northolm HA8 .... 27 B6
Northolme Gdns HA8 . 26 C2
Northolme Rd N5 ..... 73 A4
Northolme Rise BR6 . 227 C6
NORTHOLT 63 C1
Northolt N17 .... 33 C1
Northolt Aerodrome
HA4 .... 61 D3
Northolt Ave HA4 ..... 62 B3
Northolt Gdns UB6 .... 64 D3
Northolt High Sch
UB5 .... 63 B2
Northolt Park Sta
HA2 .... 63 D4
Northolt Rd HA2 ...... 64 A5
Northolt Sta UB5 ..... 63 C2
Northolt Trad Est
UB5 .... 63 D1
Northover BR1 ..... 164 D1
North Par
Chessington KT9 .... 214 B3
Edgware HA8 .... 26 C1
Southall UB1 .... 85 C1
North Pas SW18 .... 157 C6
North Pk SE9 .... 166 C5
North Pl
Mitcham SW19 ...... 180 D3
Teddington TW11 ... 174 D4
Northpoint BR1 ..... 187 A2
North Point UB7 .... 104 A5
Northpoint Cl SM1 .. 218 A5
Northpoint Sq 8
NW1 .... 71 D2
North Pole La BR2 .. 225 A2
North Pole Rd W10 ... 90 C2
Northport St N1 .... 235 D5
North Prim Sch UB1 . 107 B6
North Rd
Barnsbury N7 .... 72 A2
Brentford TW8 ..... 132 A6
Bromley BR1 .... 187 B2
Dagenham RM6 ...... 59 A4
Ealing W5 .... 109 D3
East Bedfont TW14 .. 149 B5
Edgware HA8 .... 26 D2
Edmonton N9 .... 18 B3
Erith DA17 .... 125 D4
Finchley N2 .... 30 C2
Hayes UB3 .... 83 B2
Highgate N6 .... 49 A2
Ilford IG3 .... 79 C6
Plumstead SE18 .... 123 C2
Richmond TW9 ..... 132 C3
Southall UB1 .... 107 C6
Surbiton KT6 .... 197 D3
West Drayton UB7 .. 104 B3
1 West Wickham
BR4 .... 207 D1
Wimbledon SW19 ... 180 A4
North Residence IG3 . 58 B4
North Ride
W2 .... 114 C6 247 A5
North Rise W2 ...... 237 B1
Northrop Rd TW6 ... 127 C4
North Row
W1 .... 115 A6 248 A6
NORTH SHEEN 132 C3
North Sheen Sta
TW10 .... 132 C1
Northside Prim Sch
N12 .... 30 A5
Northside Rd BR1 ... 187 A2
North Side Wandsworth
Comm SW18 ...... 158 B6
Northspur Rd SM1 .. 217 C5
North Sq Edmonton N9 . 18 B2
Hampstead Garden Suburb
NW11 .... 47 C4
North St Barking IG11 .. 79 A1
Bexleyheath DA7 .... 147 C1
Bromley BR1 .... 187 A2
Carshalton SM5 .... 218 D4
Clapham SW4 ...... 137 C2
Hendon NW4 .... 46 C4
Isleworth TW7 ..... 131 A2
Newham E13 .... 99 B5
Northstead Rd SW2 . 160 C2
North Tenter St E1 .. 243 D1
North Terr SW3 .... 257 A5
Northumberland Alley
EC3 .... 243 B1
Northumberland Ave
Enfield EN1 .... 6 B4
Falconwood DA16 ... 145 C2
Hounslow TW7 ..... 130 D4
Wanstead E12 .... 55 C1
Westminster
WC2 ...... 116 A5 250 A4
Northumberland Cl
TW19 .... 148 A5
Northumberland Cres
TW14 .... 149 C5
Northumberland Ct
3 Hounslow TW3 ... 129 D1
South Croydon CR2 .. 221 C3
Northumberland Gdns
Brentford TW7 ..... 131 A5
Bromley BR1 .... 210 C5
Edmonton N9 .... 17 D1
Mitcham CR4 .... 203 D4
Northumberland Gr
N17 .... 34 B3
Northumberland Heath
Prim Sch DA8 ..... 147 D5
Northumberland Ho
Finchley N12 .... 29 D4
Kentish Town NW5 .... 71 C2
Northumberland Mans
E5 .... 74 C4
Northumberland Park
Com Sch 2 N17 ..... 34 A3
Northumberland Park
Ind Est N17 .... 34 B3
Northumberland Park
Resource Ctr N17 ... 34 A3
Northumberland Park
Sta N17 .... 34 B3
Northumberland Pk
Erith DA8 .... 147 D5
Tottenham N17 .... 34 A3
Northumberland Pl
Notting Hill W2 ...... 91 C1
26 Richmond TW10 .. 153 D6
Northumberland Rd
Harrow HA2 .... 41 C4
New Barnet EN5 ...... 14 A4
Newham E6 .... 100 A1
Walthamstow E17 ..... 53 C2
Northumberland St
WC2 .... 250 A4
Northumbria Ct 10
TW9 .... 132 A1
Northumbria St E14 .. 97 C1
North Verbena Gdns 2
W6 .... 112 A1
Northview 1 N7 ...... 72 A5
North View Ealing W5 .. 87 C3
Pinner HA5 .... 40 C2
Wimbledon SW19 ... 178 C5
Northview Cres
NW10 .... 67 D4
Northview Dr IG8 ..... 37 D1
Northview Prim Sch
NW10 .... 67 D4
North View Rd N8 .... 49 D6
North Villas NW1 ..... 71 D2
Northway
Hampstead Garden Suburb
NW11 .... 47 D4
Merton SM4 .... 201 A5
Wallington SM6 .... 219 C4
North Way
Friern Barnet N11 ..... 31 C4
Lower Edmonton N9 ... 18 D2
Pinner HA5 .... 40 D5
Queensbury NW9 ..... 44 D6
Uxbridge UB10 .... 60 A1
Northway Cir NW7 .... 27 B6
Northway Cres NW7 .. 27 C6
Northway Ct NW7 ..... 27 B6
Northway Rd
Camberwell SE5 .... 139 A2
Croydon CR0 ...... 205 D2
Northway Sch NW7 ... 11 B1
Northways Par 2
NW3 .... 70 B1
North Weald La KT2 . 175 D5
NORTH WEMBLEY ... 65 C6
North Wembley Sta HA0,
HA9 .... 65 D5
North Western Ave
(Tylers Way) WD23 ... 8 C6
North Western Ave
(Watford By-Pass)
WD6 .... 9 B4
North West London
Jewish Day Sch
NW6 .... 69 A1
Northwest Pl N1 .... 234 B4
North Wharf Rd
W2 .... 92 B2 236 C3
Northwick Ave HA3 ... 43 B3
Northwick Circ HA3 ... 43 C3
Northwick Cl
Harrow HA1 .... 43 B1
Lisson Gr NW8 92 B3 236 C6
Northwick Ho NW8 . 236 B6
Northwick Park Hospl
HA1 .... 43 A2
Northwick Park Rd
HA1 .... 42 D3
Northwick Park Sta
HA3 .... 43 B2
Northwick Rd
South Oxhey WD19 .... 22 C6
Wembley HA0 .... 87 D6
Northwick Terr
NW8 .... 92 B3 236 C6
North Wlk
Bayswater
W2 ...... 114 A6 246 A5
New Addington CR0 .. 224 A3
Northwold Dr HA5 .... 40 C6
Northwold Prim Sch
E5 .... 74 A6
Northwold Rd E5, N16 . 74 A6
NORTHWOOD 22 A3
Northwood Gdns
Greenford UB6 .... 64 D3
Ilford IG5 .... 56 C5
North Finchley N12 .... 30 B5
NORTHWOOD HILLS . 22 A1
Northwood Hills Cir
HA6 .... 22 A2
Northwood Hills Sta
HA6 .... 22 A1
North Wood Lo NW3 .. 69 D4
Northwood Pl DA18 .. 125 B3
Northwood Prim Sch
DA18 .... 125 B3
Northwood Rd
Forest Hill SE23 .... 163 B3
Highgate N6 .... 49 B2
South Norwood CR7 .. 183 A1
Wallington SM5 .... 219 A2
Northwood Sch HA6 .. 22 A2
Northwood Twr 1
E17 .... 54 A5
Northwood Way
Northwood HA6 .... 22 A3
1 West Norwood
SE19 .... 183 C4
NORTH
WOOLWICH 122 D4
North Woolwich Rd
E16 .... 121 B5
North Woolwich Rdbt
E16 .... 121 D5
North Worple Way
SW14 .... 133 B2
Norton Ave KT5 .... 198 D2
Norton Cl Chingford E4 35 C5
Enfield EN1 .... 6 B3
Norton Ct
Beckenham BR3 .... 185 B2
Ilford IG2 .... 57 B3
Norton Folgate E1 .. 243 B4
Norton Gdns SW16 .. 182 A1
Norton Ho
14 Globe Town E2 ..... 96 D5
6 New Malden KT3 . 199 C5
30 Stepney E1 .... 96 B1
16 Stockwell SW9 ... 138 B3
Norton Rd
Walthamstow E10 ..... 53 B1
Wembley HA0 .... 65 D2
Norval Gn 1 SW9 ... 138 C3
Norval Rd HA0 .... 43 B1
Norvic Ho 5 SE5 ... 139 A3
Norway Gate SE16 .. 119 A3
Norway Pl E14 .... 97 B1
Norway St SE10 .... 141 D6
Norwegian Sch The 6
SW20 .... 178 C3
Norwich Cres RM6 .... 58 B4
Norwich Ho 6 E14 .... 97 D1
Norwich Mews IG3 ... 58 A1
Norwich Rd
Forest Gate E7 .... 77 A3
Greenford UB6 .... 85 D6
Northwood HA6 .... 39 D6
South Norwood CR7 .. 205 A6
Norwich St
EC4 .... 94 C1 241 A2
Norwich Wlk HA8 ..... 27 A3
Norwood Ave HA0 .... 88 B5
Norwood Cl
Cricklewood NW2 ..... 69 A5
Southall UB2 .... 107 C2
Twickenham TW2 ... 152 B2
Norwood Dr HA2 ..... 41 C3
Norwood Gdns
Hayes UB4 .... 84 C3
Southall UB2 .... 107 B2
NORWOOD GREEN . 107 C2
Norwood Green Inf Sch
UB2 .... 107 B1

Norwood Green Jun Sch UB2 107 A1
Norwood Green Rd UB2 107 C2
Norwood Heights Sh Ctr 13 SE19 183 C4
Norwood High St SE27 183 A6
Norwood Ho 25 E14 119 D6
Norwood Junction Sta SE25 206 A5
NORWOOD NEW TOWN 183 A4
Norwood Park Rd SE27 183 A5
Norwood Rd
  Southall UB2 107 C2
  West Norwood SE24, SE27 160 D3
Norwood Sch SE19 183 A5
Norwood Terr UB2 107 D2
Notley St SE5 139 B5
Notre Dame RC Girls Sch SE1 116 D3 261 D5
Notre Dame RC Prim Sch SE18 144 D6
Notson Rd SE25 206 B5
Notting Barn Rd W10 90 D3
Nottingdale Sq W11 244 A4
Nottingham Ave E16 99 C1
Nottingham Ct WC2 240 A1
Nottingham Ho
  33 Camberwell SE5 139 A3
  Stoke Newington N4 51 A1
Nottingham Pl W1 93 A2 238 A4
Nottingham Rd
  Croydon CR2 221 A3
  Isleworth TW7 130 D3
  Leytonstone E10 54 A3
  Upper Tooting SW17 158 D3
Nottingham St W1 238 A4
Nottingham Terr NW1 238 A5
NOTTING HILL 113 B6
Notting Hill & Ealing High Sch W13 87 B2
Notting Hill Gate W11 113 C5 245 A4
Notting Hill Gate Sta W11 113 C5 245 A4
Notting Hill Prep Sch 17 W11 91 A1
Nottingwood Ho W11 244 A6
Nova Bldg 1 E14 119 C2
Nova Ct E 3 E14 120 A5
Nova Ct W 2 E14 120 A5
Nova Mews SM4 201 A2
Novar Cl BR6 211 D2
Nova Rd CR0 205 A2
Novar Rd SE9 167 A3
Novello St SW6 135 C4 265 A2
Nowell Rd SW13 134 A6
Nower Ct HA5 41 B5
NOWER HILL 41 B6
Nower Hill HA5 41 B5
Nower Hill High Sch HA5 41 C5
Noyna Rd SW17 158 D1
Nubia Way SE6 164 C1
Nucleus NW10 89 A4
Nuding Cl SE13 141 C2
Nuffield Ct TW5 129 B5
Nuffield Lo 14 W9 91 C2
Nugent Ct
  Streatham SW16 181 C6
  3 Upper Holloway N19 50 A1
Nugent Rd
  Finsbury Pk N19 50 A1
  South Norwood SE25 205 D6
Nugents Ct HA5 23 A2
Nugent's Pk HA5 23 B2
Nugent Terr NW8 92 A5 229 B3
Numa Ct TW8 131 D5
Nun Ct EC2 242 C2
Nuneaton Rd RM9 81 A1
Nuneham SW16 181 D6
NUNHEAD 140 C1
Nunhead Cres SE15 140 B2
Nunhead Gn SE15 140 B2
Nunhead Gr SE15 140 C2
Nunhead La SE15 140 B2
Nunhead Sta SE15 140 C3
Nunnington Cl SE9 166 A1
Nunn's Rd EN2 5 A3
Nupton Dr EN5 12 C5
Nurse Cl HA8 27 A2
Nursery Ave
  Bexleyheath DA7 147 B2
  Croydon CR0 222 D6
  Finchley N3 30 A1
Nursery Cl
  Broom Hill BR6 211 D2
  Croydon CR0 222 D6
  Dagenham RM6 58 D3
  Enfield EN3 6 D4
  Feltham TW14 150 B4
  New Cross SE4 141 B3
  Putney SW15 134 D1
  Woodford IG8 37 B5
Nursery Ct Ealing W13 87 A2
  8 Tottenham N17 33 D3
Nursery Gdns
  Chislehurst BR7 188 D4
  Enfield EN3 6 D4
  Hampton TW13 173 B6
  Hounslow TW4 151 B6
  Sunbury TW16 171 D1
Nursery La
  Forest Gate E7 77 A2
  North Kensington W10 90 C2
  Shoreditch E2 95 D6
Nurserymans Rd N11 15 A2
Nursery Rd
  Finchley N2 30 B2
  Hackney E9 74 C2
  Loughton IG10 21 C6
  Merton SW19 179 D1
  Mitcham CR4 202 C6
  Osidge N14 15 C4
  Pinner HA5 40 C6
  South Norwood CR7 205 B5
  Stockwell SW9 138 B1
  Sunbury TW16 171 D1
  Sutton SM1 218 A4
  Wimbledon SW19 179 A3
Nursery Row SE17 262 C3
Nursery St N17 33 D3
Nursery Walk Ct NW4 46 B6
Nursery Wlk NW4 46 C6
Nurstead Rd DA8 147 C5
Nutborn Ho SW19 178 D4
Nutbourne St W10 91 A4
Nutbrook St SE15 140 A2
Nutbrowne Rd RM9 103 B6
Nutchford EN1 17 C5
Nutcroft Rd SE15 140 B5
Nutfield Cl
  Carshalton SM5 218 C5
  Edmonton N18 34 A4
Nutfield Gdns
  Ilford IG3 80 A6
  Northolt UB5 84 C5
Nutfield Pl 1 CR7 204 D5
Nutfield Rd
  Dollis Hill NW2 68 A5
  East Dulwich SE22 139 D1
  Leyton E15 76 A4
  Thornton Heath CR7 204 D5
Nutfield Way BR6 226 D6
Nutford Pl W1 92 D1 237 C2
Nuthatch Cl TW19 148 B3
Nuthatch Gdns SE28 123 B4
Nuthurst Ave SW2 160 B2
Nutkin Wlk UB8 60 A1
Nutley Terr NW3 70 B2
Nutmeg Cl E16 98 C3
Nutmeg La E14 98 B1
Nuttall St N1 95 C5
Nutter La E11 55 C4
Nutt Gr HA8 9 D2
Nutt St SE15 139 D5
Nutty La TW17 193 A6
Nutwell St SW17 180 C5
Nuxley Rd DA17 125 C1
Nyanza St SE18 145 B6
Nye Bevan Est E5 74 D5
Nye Bevan Ho SW6 264 C4
Nye's Wharf SE1, SE15 140 A6
Nylands Ave TW9 132 C3
Nymans Gdns SW20 200 B6
Nynehead St SE14 141 A5
Nyon Gr SE6 163 B2
Nyton Cl N19 50 A1

O

O2 Ctr NW6 70 A2
O2 Millennium Dome The★ SE10 120 C5
Oak Apple Ct SE12 165 A3
Oak Ave Croydon CR0 223 D6
  Enfield EN2 4 B5
  Hampton TW12, TW13 173 A4
  Heston TW5 129 A5
  Hornsey N8 50 A5
  Muswell Hill N10 31 B3
  Tottenham N17 33 C3
  Uxbridge UB10 60 D6
  West Drayton UB7 104 C3
Oak Bank CR0 224 A2
Oakbank Ave KT12 195 B2
Oakbank Gr SE24 139 A1
Oakbark Ho 10 TW8 131 C5
Oakbrook 3 BR3 185 D1
Oakbrook Cl BR1 187 B6
Oakbury Rd SW6 135 D3
Oak Cl East Barnet N14 15 B4
  Sutton SM1 218 A6
Oakcombe Cl KT3 177 C2
Oak Cottage Cl 11 SE6 164 D3
Oak Cotts W7 108 C4
Oakcourt 17 SE15 139 D5
Oak Cres E16 98 C2
Oakcroft SE12 165 B1
Oakcroft Bsns Ctr KT9 214 B4
Oakcroft Cl HA5 22 B1
Oakcroft Ct SE3 143 A4
Oakcroft Ho 3 KT3 199 C2
Oakcroft Rd
  Chessington KT9 214 B4
  Lewisham SE13 142 B3
Oakcroft Villas KT9 214 B4
Oak Ct Bickley BR1 188 B1
  Chingford E4 35 D4
Oakdale
  Beckenham BR3 186 A1
  East Barnet N14 15 B3
Oakdale Ave
  Harrow HA3 44 A4
  Pinner HA6 22 A1
Oakdale Cl WD19 22 C6
Oakdale Ct
  Chingford E4 36 A5
  Upper Holloway N19 72 A6
Oakdale Gdns E4 36 A5
Oakdale Inf Sch E18 37 B1
Oakdale Jun Sch E18 37 B1
Oakdale Lo NW4 29 A2
Oakdale Rd
  Leyton E11 76 B6
  Nunhead SE15 140 C2
  South Oxhey WD19 22 C6
  Streatham SW16 182 A5
  Tottenham N4 51 B3
  Upton E7 77 B1
  Woodford E18 37 B1
Oakdale Way CR4 203 A2
Oakdene Ealing W13 87 B2
  3 Peckham SE15 140 B4
  1 West Norwood SE19 183 C5
Oakdene Ave
  Chislehurst West BR7 188 C5
  Thames Ditton KT7 197 A1
Oakdene Cl HA5 23 B3
Oakdene Ct
  Feltham TW12 173 B6
  1 Streatham SW16 182 A5
Oakdene Dr KT5 199 A1
Oakdene Ho
  Enfield EN2 4 D2
  11 Stamford Hill N16 51 C1
Oakdene Lo 3 SE20 184 B3
Oakdene Mews SM3 201 B1
Oakdene Pk N3 29 B3
Oakdene Rd
  Hillingdon UB10 82 D5
  Orpington BR5 211 D4
Oakden St SE11 116 C2 261 B4
Oakeford Ho W14 254 B5
Oakend Ho 10 N4 51 B2
Oaken Dr KT10 212 D2
Oakenholt Ho 1 SE2 124 D4
Oaken La KT10 212 C3
Oakenshaw Cl KT6 198 A2
Oakes Cl E6 100 B1
Oakeshott Ave N6 71 A6
Oakey La SE1 261 A6
Oak Farm WD6 11 A6
Oak Farm Jun & Inf Schs UB10 82 D6
Oakfield E4 35 D5
Oakfield Ave HA3 43 B6
Oakfield Cl
  New Malden KT3 199 D4
  Ruislip HA4 39 D3
Oakfield Ct
  Clapham Pk SW4 160 A5
  2 Ealing W5 110 C5
  Finchley N3 29 D2
  Finsbury Pk N8 50 A2
  Hendon NW2 46 D2
  South Croydon CR2 221 A2
Oakfield Gdns
  Beckenham BR3 207 C4
  Carshalton SM5 202 D1
  Edmonton N18 33 C6
  Greenford UB6 86 B4
  3 West Norwood SE19 183 C5
Oakfield Ho 2 IG1 78 D5
Oakfield La BR2 225 C4
Oakfield Lo 8 IG1 78 D5
Oakfield Prep Sch SE21 161 B3
Oakfield Rd
  Ashford TW15 170 D5
  Croydon CR0 205 A1
  Finchley N3 29 D2
  Finsbury Pk N4 50 C2
  Higham Hill E17 35 A1
  Ilford IG1 78 D5
  Newham E6 100 A6
  Palmers Green N14 16 A2
  Penge SE20 184 B3
  Wimbledon SW19 156 D1
Oakfield Road Ind Est 11 SE20 184 B3
Oakfields KT12 194 A1
Oakfields Rd NW11 47 A3
Oakfield St SW10 136 A6 266 A6
Oakford Rd NW5 71 C4
Oak Gdns
  Croydon CR0 223 C6
  Hendon HA8 27 A1
Oak Gr Ruislip HA4 40 B1
  Sunbury TW16 172 B3
  West Hampstead NW2 69 A4
  West Wickham BR4 208 A1
Oak Grove Rd SE20 184 C1
Oakhall Ct
  Ashford TW16 171 D5
  Wanstead E11 55 B3
Oakhall Dr TW16 171 D5
Oak Hall Rd E11 55 B3
Oakham Cl
  Cockfosters EN4 2 D2
  Forest Hill SE6 163 B2
Oakham Dr BR2 208 D5
Oakham Ho 5 W10 90 C3
Oakhampton Rd NW7 28 D3
Oakhill KT10 213 A2
Oak Hill Chingford IG8 36 C3
  Surbiton KT6 198 A2
Oakhill Ave
  Pinner HA5 23 A1
  West Hampstead NW3 69 D4
Oak Hill Cl IG8 36 B3
Oak Hill Cres
  Chingford IG8 36 C3
  Surbiton KT6 198 A2
Oakhill Ct
  Honor Oak SE23 162 C5
  Putney SW15 157 B6
  8 Surbiton KT6 198 A3
  Wimbledon SW19 178 D3
Oak Hill Ct IG8 36 C3
Oak Hill Gdns E4 36 C2
Oak Hill Gr KT6 198 A3
Oakhill Ho BR5 190 A2
Oak Hill Lo NW3 69 D4
Oakhill Mans EN4 14 C5
Oak Hill Park Mews NW3 70 A4
Oak Hill Pk NW3 69 D4
Oakhill Pl SW15 157 C6
Oakhill Prim Sch IG8 36 C4
Oakhill Rd
  Beckenham BR3 186 A1
  Orpington BR6 227 D6
  Putney SW15 157 B6
  Sutton SM1 218 A5
  Thornton Heath SW16 182 B2
Oak Hill Rd KT6 198 A3
Oak Hill Theological Coll N14 15 A5
Oak Hill Way NW3 70 A4
Oak Ho
  13 Cubitt Town E14 120 A4
  11 Finchley N2 30 B1
  8 Maitland Pk NW3 70 D2
  Penge SE20 184 B1
  2 Richmond TW9 132 D4
  13 Sidcup DA15 168 A1
  9 Stoke Newington N16 73 B6
  Teddington TW11 175 C4
  Wood Green N22 32 A3
Oakhouse Rd DA6 169 C6
Oak Hts Ind Sch 1 TW3 129 D2
Oakhurst Ave
  East Barnet EN4 14 C4
  Erith DA7 147 A5
Oakhurst Cl
  Chislehurst BR7 188 B2
  Snaresbrook E17 54 C5
  4 Teddington TW11 174 C5
Oakhurst Ct E17 54 C5
Oakhurst Gdns
  Chingford E4 20 D3
  Erith DA7 147 A5
  Snaresbrook E11, E17 54 C5
Oakhurst Gr SE22 140 A1
Oakhurst Rd KT19 215 B2
Oakington 14 KT1 176 C1
Oakington Ave
  Harrow HA2 41 C2
  Hayes UB3 105 B2
  Wembley HA9 66 B5
Oakington Cl TW16 172 C1
Oakington Ct 1 EN2 4 D3
Oakington Dr TW16 172 C1
Oakington Manor Dr HA9 66 C3
Oakington Manor Sch HA9 66 D3
Oakington Rd W9 91 C3
Oakington Way N8 50 A2
Oak La Finchley N2 30 B1
  Friern Barnet N11 31 D4
  Isleworth TW7 130 C1
  Limehouse E14 119 B6
  Twickenham TW1 153 A4
  Woodford IG8 36 D6
Oakland Pl IG9 21 A2
Oakland Rd E15 76 C4
Oaklands
  Chislehurst BR7 189 B4
  Croydon CR0 220 D3
  Ealing W13 87 A2
  Southgate N21 16 B2
  Twickenham TW2 152 A4
Oaklands Ave
  Enfield N9 18 B5
  Hounslow TW7 130 D6
  Sidcup DA15 167 D4
  Thames Ditton KT10 196 B1
  Thornton Heath CR7 204 C5
  West Wickham BR4 223 D5
Oaklands Cl
  Bexley DA6 169 B6
  Chessington KT9 213 C4
  Orpington BR5 211 C3
Oaklands Ct
  Beckenham BR3 186 A1
  Dagenham NW10 89 C6
  Orpington BR6 227 A6
  5 Shepherd's Bush W12 112 B5
  Wembley HA0 65 D3
Oaklands Dr TW2 152 A4
Oaklands Gr W12 112 A5
Oaklands Ho SE4 141 B2
Oaklands Mews 1 NW2 68 D4
Oaklands Park Ave IG1 79 A6
Oaklands Pas NW2 68 D4

Oaklands Pl 8 SW4. 137 D1
Oaklands Prim Sch
W7 108 D4
Oaklands Rd
Barnet N20 13 B4
Bexley DA6 169 B6
Bromley BR1 186 C3
Cricklewood NW2 68 D4
Ealing W7 108 D4
Mortlake SW14 133 B2
West Ealing W7, W13. 109 A4
Oaklands Sch
Hounslow TW3 130 B2
Loughton IG10 21 D6
Oaklands Sec Sch 31
E2 96 B4
Oaklands Way SM6 219 D1
Oakland Way KT19 215 C2
Oaklawn Ct HA7 25 B4
Oakleafe Gdns IG6 56 D6
Oaklea Pas KT1 197 D6
Oakleigh Ave
East Barnet N20 14 C3
Edgware HA8 26 D2
Tolworth KT6 214 D6
Oakleigh Cl N20 14 D1
Oakleigh Cres N20 14 C1
Oakleigh Ct
East Barnet EN4 14 C5
Hendon HA8 27 A1
7 Penge SE20 184 B3
Southall UB1 107 B5
Surbiton KT6 214 B6
Oakleigh Gdns
Edgware HA8 26 B5
Oakleigh Pk N20 14 B3
Orpington BR6 227 C4
Oakleigh Lodge IG3 80 A5
Oakleigh Mews 2
N20 14 A2
OAKLEIGH PARK 14 B3
Oakleigh Park Ave
BR7 188 C2
Oakleigh Park Sta
EN4 14 C4
Oakleigh Pk N N20 14 B3
Oakleigh Pk S N20 14 C3
Oakleigh Rd
Hillingdon UB10 61 A1
Pinner HA5 23 B4
Oakleigh Rd N N20 14 C2
Oakleigh Rd S N11 31 A6
Oakleigh Sch N20 14 D1
Oakleigh Way
Mitcham CR4 181 B2
1 Tolworth KT6 198 D1
Oakley Ave
Barking IG11 79 D1
Ealing W5 110 C6
Wallington CR0 220 A4
Oakley Cl Chingford E4 20 A1
Ealing W7 108 C6
Hounslow TW7 130 B4
7 Newham E6 100 A1
Oakley Cres EC1 234 D3
Oakley Ct
Carshalton CR4 203 A2
Harlington UB7 127 A5
Wembley HA0 65 A4
Oakley Dr
Keston Mark BR2 226 A5
Lewisham SE13 164 B5
New Eltham SE9 167 B3
Oakley Gdns
Chelsea
SW3 136 C6 267 B6
Hornsey Vale N8 50 B4
Oakley Ho
Chelsea SW1 257 D4
Ealing W5 110 C6
Oakley Pk DA5 168 C4
Oakley Pl
SE1 117 D1 263 C1
Oakley Rd
Croydon SE25 206 B4
De Beauvoir Town N1 73 B1
Harrow HA1 42 C3
Keston Mark BR2 226 A6
Oakley Sq
NW1 93 C5 232 B4
Oakley St
SW3 136 C6 267 A6
Oakley Wlk W6 134 D6
Oak Lo
4 Ashford TW16 171 D3
Southgate N21 16 B5
10 Sutton SM1 218 A4
Wanstead E11 55 A2
6 Wembley HA0 65 D3
Oak Lodge 14 SE21 161 B2
Oak Lodge Cl HA7 25 C5
Oak Lodge Dr BR4 207 D2
Oak Lodge Prim Sch
BR4 207 D2
Oak Lodge Sch
Balham SW12 159 A4
East Finchley N2 48 A5
Oaklodge Way NW7 27 D4
Oakman Ho 29
SW19 156 D3
Oakmead HA1 64 B5
Oakmead Ave BR2 209 A3
Oakmead Ct HA7 25 C6
Oakmeade HA5 23 C4
Oakmead Gdns HA8 27 B6
Oakmead Pl CR4 180 C2
Oakmead Rd
Balham SW12 159 B3
Wallington CR0 203 D3
Oakmere Rd SE2 146 A6
Oakmont Pl 6 BR6 211 B1
Oak Park Gdns
SW19 156 D3
Oak Park Mews N16 73 D5
Oak Rd Ealing W5 109 D6
Kingston u T KT3 177 B1
Oakridge Dr N2 48 B6
Oakridge La BR1 186 B5
Oakridge Rd BR1 186 C6
Oak Rise IG9 21 D1
Oak Row CR4 181 C1
Oaks Ave
Feltham TW13 151 A2
North Cheam KT4 216 B4
West Norwood SE19 183 C5
Oaksford Ave SE26 162 B1
Oaks Gr E4 20 C2
Oakshade Rd BR1 186 B6
Oakshaw Rd SW18 157 D4
Oakshott Ct NW1 232 C3
Oaks La Ilford IG2 57 C5
South Croydon CR0 222 C5
Oaks Park High Sch
IG2 57 C4
Oaks Rd CR0 222 C4
Oaks Sh Ctr The W3 111 A5
Oaks The
Brondesbury Pk NW6 68 D1
Chingford IG8 36 C3
Enfield EN2 4 D2
Finchley N12 29 D6
Hayes UB4 83 A5
Long Ditton KT6 213 C5
Ruislip HA4 39 C2
Southborough BR2 210 C3
Wallington SM6 219 C4
Willesden NW10 68 B1
Wimbledon SW19 179 A4
Woolwich SE18 123 A1
Oaks Way
Surbiton KT6 197 D1
Wallington SM5 218 D1
Oakthorpe Ct N13 33 A5
Oakthorpe Prim Sch
N13 33 A5
Oakthorpe Rd N13 32 C5
Oaktree Ave N13 16 D1
Oak Tree Ave N2 47 D6
Oak Tree Cl Ealing W5 87 C1
Stanmore HA7 25 C3
Oak Tree Ct
Acton W3 110 D6
8 Clapham Pk SW4 160 A6
Elstree WD6 9 D5
Oak Tree Dell NW9 45 B4
Oak Tree Dr N20 13 D3
Oak Tree Gdns BR1 187 B5
Oaktree Gr IG1 79 B3
Oak Tree Ho W9 91 D3
Oak Tree Rd
NW8 92 C4 230 A1
Oaktree Sch EN4 15 A5
Oaktrees Hostel HA8 11 A2
Oakview Gdns N2 48 B5
Oakview Gr CR0 207 A1
Oakview Lo NW11 47 B2
Oakview Rd SE6 185 D5
Oak Village NW5 71 A4
Oakway
Beckenham BR2 186 B1
West Barnes SW20 200 C5
Oak Way
Croydon CR0 206 D3
East Acton W3 111 C5
East Barnet N14 15 B4
East Bedfont TW14 149 C3
Oakway Cl DA5 169 A5
Oakways SE9 166 D5
Oakwell Ho 24 SW8 137 D3
Oak Wlk CR4 203 A1
OAKWOOD 15 D6
Oakwood Ave
Beckenham BR2,
BR3 186 A1
Bromley BR2 209 B6
Chessington KT9 214 B1
Mitcham CR4 180 B1
Osidge N14 15 D4
Southall UB1 107 C6
Oakwood Cl
Chislehurst West
BR7 188 C4
Lewisham SE13 164 B5
Southgate N14 15 C5
Oakwood Cres
Southgate N21 16 B5
Wembley UB6 65 B2
Oakwood Ct
Beckenham BR3 186 A1
6 Chingford E4 20 C4
Kensington
W14 113 B3 254 C6
1 Newham E6 100 A6
17 Sutton SM1 218 A4
Oakwood Dr
Burnt Oak HA8 27 A4
West Norwood SE19 183 C4
Oakwood Gdns
Ilford IG3 79 D6
Orpington BR6 227 A6
Sutton SM1 217 C6
Oakwood La
W14 113 B3 254 C6
Oakwood Park Rd
N14 16 A5
Oakwood Pl CR0 204 C3
Oakwood Rd
Hampstead Garden Suburb
NW11 47 D4
Orpington BR6 227 A6
Pinner HA5 22 B1
Thornton Heath CR0 204 C3
Wimbledon SW20 178 A2
Oakwood Sta N14 15 C6
Oakwood View N14 15 D4
Oakworth Rd W10 90 D2
Oarsman Pl KT8 196 C5
Oasis The 6 BR1 187 C1
Oast Ct 8 E14 119 B6
Oast Lo W4 133 C5
Oates Cl BR2 208 B6
Oatfield Ho 1 N15 51 C3
Oatfield Rd BR6 211 D1
Oat La EC2 95 A1 242 B2
Oatland Rise E17 35 A1
Oatlands Ct 3
SW19 156 D3
Oatlands Dr KT13 193 C1
Oatlands Rd EN3 6 C4
Oatwell Ho SW3 257 B3
Oban Cl E13 99 C3
Oban Ct HA8 10 D2
Oban Ho
5 Barking IG11 101 B5
South Bromley E14 98 B1
Oban Rd Newham E13 99 C4
South Norwood SE25 205 B5
Oban St E14 98 B1
Oberon Ho 5 N1 95 C5
Oberon Way TW17 192 A6
Oberstein Rd 15
SW11 136 B1
Oborne Cl SE24 160 D6
O'Brian Ho 10 E1 96 D4
Observatory Gdns
W8 245 B2
Observatory Mews
E14 120 B2
Observatory Rd
Kensington SW7 256 C5
Mortlake SW14 133 A1
Occupation La
Brentford W5 109 D2
Shooters Hill SE18 144 D4
Occupation Rd
Newington
SE17 117 A1 262 A2
West Ealing W13 109 B4
Ocean St E1 96 D2
Ocean Wharf E14 119 C4
Ochre Ct TW13 149 D1
Ockbrook 3 E1 96 C2
Ockendon Rd N1 73 B2
Ockham Dr BR5 190 A3
Greenford UB6 64 B1
Ockley Ct
Sidcup DA14 167 C1
Sutton SM1 218 A4
Ockley Ho 8 KT2 176 D4
Ockley Rd
Streatham SW16 160 A1
Thornton Heath CR0 204 B2
Octagon Arc EC2 243 A3
Octagon The NW3 69 C4
Octavia Cl CR4 202 C4
Octavia Ho
Catford SE6 163 D4
Kensal Town W10 91 A3
Octavia Mews 1 W9 91 B3
Octavia Rd TW7 130 D2
Octavia St
SW11 136 C4 267 B1
Octavia Way 12
SE28 124 B6
Octavius St SE8 141 C5
October Ct BR2 208 D6
October Pl NW4 46 D6
Odard Rd KT8 195 C5
Odell Cl IG11 79 D1
Odell Wlk SE13 142 A2
Odeon Ct
Dagenham NW10 89 C6
1 Newham E16 99 A2
Odeon Par
Eltham SE9 144 A1
Wembley UB6 65 B2
Odeon The IG11 79 B1
Odessa Inf Sch E7 77 A3
Odessa Rd Leyton E7 76 D4
Willesden Green NW10 90 A5
Odessa St SE16 119 B3
Odette Ct N20 14 A1
Odette Duval Ho 29
E1 96 C2
Odette Ho 6 SE27 183 B6
Odger St SW11 136 D3
Odhams Wlk WC2 240 B1
Odin Ho 6 SE5 139 A3
O'Donnell Ct WC1 240 B6
O'Driscoll Ho 4 W12 90 B1
Odyssey Bsns Pk HA4 62 B3
Offa's Mead E9 75 A4
Offenbach Ho 12 E2 96 D5
Offenham Rd BR7,
SE9 188 B6
Offers Ct KT1 198 B6
Offerton Rd SW4 137 C2
Offham Ho SE17 263 A3
Offham Slope N12 29 B5
Offley Ho 10 E9 74 D2
Offley Pl TW7 130 B3
Offley Rd SW9 138 C5
Offord Cl N17 34 A4
Offord Rd N1 72 B1
Offord St N1 72 B1
Ogden Ho TW13 173 A6
Ogilby St SE18 122 B2
Ogilvie Ho 12 E1 96 D1
Oglander Rd SE15 139 D2
Ogle St W1 93 C2 239 A4
Oglethorpe Rd RM10 81 C5
O'Gorman Ho SW10 266 B4
O'Grady Ct 17 W13 109 A5
O'Grady Ho 17 E17 53 D6
Ohio Bldg 13 SE13 141 D4
Ohio Rd E13 98 D3
Oil Mill La W6 112 A1
Okeburn Rd SW17 181 A5
Okehampton Cl N12 30 B5
Okehampton Cres
DA16 146 C4
Okehampton Rd
NW10 90 D6
Okeover Manor
SW4 137 B1
Olaf Palme Ho
TW13 150 B1
Olaf St W11 112 D6
Old Bailey
EC4 94 D1 241 D1
Old Bailey (Central
Criminal Court)★
EC4 94 D1 241 D2
Old Barn Cl SM2 217 A1
Old Barrack Yd SW1 248 A1
Old Barrowfield 7
E15 98 C6
Old Bellgate Wharf
E14 119 C3
Oldberry Rd HA8 27 B4
Old Bethnal Green Rd
E2 96 B4
OLD BEXLEY 169 D4
Old Bexley Bsns Pk
DA5 169 D4
Old Bexley CE Prim Sch
DA5 169 B3
Old Billingsgate Wlk
EC3 253 A5
Old Bldgs WC2 241 A2
Old Bond St
W1 115 C6 249 A5
Oldborough Rd HA0 65 C5
Old Brewery Mews
NW3 70 B4
Old Bridge Cl UB5 85 C5
Old Bridge St KT1 175 D1
Old Broad St
EC2 95 B1 242 D2
Old Bromley Rd BR1 186 B5
Old Brompton Rd SW5,
SW7 114 A2 256 B3
Old Burlington St
W1 115 C6 249 A5
Oldbury Ct E9 75 A3
Oldbury Pl W1 93 A2 238 B4
Oldbury Rd EN1 6 A3
Old Castle St
E1 95 D1 243 D2
Old Cavendish St
W1 238 C1
Old Change Ct EC4 242 A1
Old Chapel Pl 2 N10 49 B6
Old Charlton Rd
TW17 193 A4
Old Chiswick Yd W4 133 C6
Old Church Ct N11 31 B5
Old Church La
Ealing UB6 87 A4
Stanmore HA7 25 C4
Welsh Harp NW9 67 B6
Old Church Path
KT10 212 A4
Old Church Rd
Chingford E4 19 C1
Stepney E1 96 D1
Old Church St SW3 256 D1
Old Claygate La
KT10 213 A3
Old Clem Sq 12
SE18 144 C6
Old College Ct DA17 125 D1
Old Compton St
W1 93 D1 239 C1
Old Cople La SE26 184 A5
Old Cote Dr TW5 129 C6
Old Court Ho W8 245 C1
Old Court (Mus & Liby)★
HA0 65 C3
Old Court Pl
W8 113 D4 245 C1
Old Covent Gdn★
WC2 116 A6 250 B6
Old Ctyd The BR1 187 B2
Old Cty H★ SE1 250 C2
Old Dairy Mews
5 Balham SW12 159 A3
4 Camden Town NW5 71 B2
Old Dairy Sq The N21 16 C4
Old Deer Park Gdns
TW9 132 A2
Old Devonshire Rd
SW12 159 B4
Old Dock Cl TW9 132 C6
Old Dover Rd SE3 143 B5
Oldegate Ho 1 E6 99 D6
Old Farm Ave
Osidge N14 15 C4
Sidcup DA15 167 C2
Old Farm Cl TW4 129 B1
Old Farm Ct UB2 107 D2
Old Farm Rd
Hampton TW12 173 C4
London N2 30 B2
Old Farm Rd E DA15 168 A2

Old Farm Rd W DA15. . . . . 167 D2
Oldfield Cl
Bromley BR1 . . . . 210 B5
Greenford UB6. . . . 64 C2
Stanmore HA7 . . . . 25 A5
Oldfield Farm Gdns UB6. . . . 86 B6
Oldfield Gr SE16 . . . . 118 D2
Oldfield Ho
14 Chiswick W4. . . . 111 C1
Streatham SW16 . . . . 181 B6
Oldfield House Specl Sch TW12. . . . 173 B2
Oldfield La N UB6 . . . . 64 B1
Oldfield La S UB6 . . . . 86 A4
Oldfield Mews N6. . . . 49 C2
Oldfield Prim Sch UB6 . . . . 86 B5
Oldfield Rd
Bedford Pk W3, W12 . . . . 111 D4
Bexleyheath DA7 . . . . 147 A3
Bromley BR1 . . . . 210 B5
Hampton TW12 . . . . 173 B2
Stoke Newington N16 . . 73 C5
Willesden NW10 . . . . 67 D1
Wimbledon SW19 . . . 179 A4
Oldfields Cir UB5 . . . . 64 A2
Oldfields Rd SM1, SM3 . . . . 217 C6
Oldfields Trad Est SM1. . . . 217 C5
Old Fire Station The SE18. . . . 144 D5
Old Fish St Hill EC4 . 252 A6
Old Fleet La EC4 . . 241 C2
Old Fold Cl EN5. . . . 1 B4
Old Fold La EN5. . . . 1 B4
OLD FORD 97 B6
Old Ford Ho CR0. . . . 220 A5
Old Ford Prim Sch 38 E3. . . . 97 B5
Old Ford Rd E2, E3 . . . . 96 D5
Old Ford Trad Est E3 . . 97 C6
Old Forge Cl HA7 . . . . 25 A6
Old Forge Cres TW17 . . . . 192 D3
Old Forge Mews W12 . . . . 112 B4
Old Forge Rd
Enfield EN1 . . . . 5 D5
Upper Holloway N19 . . . 71 D6
Old Forge Way DA14. . . . 190 B6
Old Gloucester St WC1. . . . 94 A2 240 B4
Old Hall Cl HA5 . . . . 23 A2
Old Hall Dr HA5. . . . 23 A2
Oldham Ho 10 SE21 . . 183 C6
Oldham Terr W3 . . . . 111 A5
Old Hatch Manor HA4. . . . 40 A2
Old Hill
Chislehurst BR7. . . . 188 C2
Orpington BR6. . . . 227 C2
Oldhill St N16 . . . . 52 A1
Old Homesdale Rd BR2. . . . 209 C5
Old Hospital Cl SW12, SW17 . . . . 158 D3
Old Ho The BR7 . . . . 189 B2
Old House Cl SW19 . . 179 A5
Old House Gdns 9 TW1 . . . . 153 C5
Old Howlett's La HA4 . 39 B3
Olding Ho 6 SW12. . . 159 C4
Old Jamaica Bsns Est 23 SE16. . . . 118 A3
Old Jamaica Rd SE16. . . . 118 A3
Old James St SE15 . . . 140 B2
Old Jewry EC2 95 B1 242 C1
Old Kenton La NW9 . . . 44 D4
Old Kent Rd
Deptford SE1, SE15 . . . 140 B6
Walworth SE1 . . . . 117 C1 263 B2
Old Kingston Rd KT4. . . . 215 A5
Old Laundry The 14 SW18. . . . 136 B1
Old Lodge Pl 7 TW1 . . . . 153 B5
Old Lodge Way HA7 . . . 25 A5
Old London Rd KT2 . . 176 A1
Old Maidstone Rd BR8, DA14. . . . 191 B3
OLD MALDEN 199 C1
Old Malden La KT4. . 215 C6
Oldman Ct SE12 . . . . 165 B2
Old Manor Ct NW8. . . 229 B4
Old Manor Dr TW7 . . . 152 A5
Old Manor House Mews TW17 . . . . 192 C6
Old Manor Rd UB2 . . 106 D2
Old Manor Way BR7, SE9. . . . 188 B5
Old Manor Yd SW5. . 255 C3
Old Market Ct SM1. . . 217 D4
Old Market Sq 11 E2 . . 95 D4
Old Marylebone Rd NW1. . . . 92 C2 237 B3
Oldmead Ho 8 RM10 . 81 D2
Old Mill Ct E18. . . . 55 C6
Old Mill Rd SE18 . . . . 145 B6
Old Mitre Ct EC4 . . . . 241 B1
Old Montague St E1 . . 96 A2
Old Nichol St E2. . . . 95 D3 243 C6
Old North St WC1 . . . 240 C4
Old Nursery Pl TW15 . . . . 170 D5
OLD OAK COMMON . . 89 D3
Old Oak Common La NW10. . . . 89 C3
Old Oak La NW10 . . . . 89 D4
Old Oak Prim Sch W12. . . . 89 D1
Old Oak Rd W3 . . . . 111 D6
Old Orch TW16. . . . 172 C1
Old Orchard Cl
Hadley Wood EN4. . . . 2 B5
Hillingdon UB8. . . . 82 C1
Old Orch The NW3 . . . 70 D4
Old Palace La TW9 . . . 153 C6
Old Palace of John Whitgift Sch (Juniors) CR2 . . . . 221 D3
Old Palace of John Whitgift Sch (Seniors) 11 CR9. . . . 220 D5
Old Palace Prim Sch 51 E3. . . . 97 D4
Old Palace Rd CR0 . . 221 A5
Old Palace Terr 8 TW9 . . . . 153 D6
Old Palace Yd 2 TW9 . . . . 153 D6
Old Paradise St SE11. . . . 116 B2 260 C4
Old Park Ave
Balham SW12 . . . . 159 A5
Enfield EN2 . . . . 5 A1
Old Park Gr EN2. . . . 5 A1
Old Park Ho N13. . . . 32 B6
Old Park La W1. . . . 115 B5 248 C3
Old Park Mews TW5. . 129 B5
Old Park Rd
Enfield EN2 . . . . 4 D2
Palmers Green N13 . . . . 32 B6
Plumstead Comm SE2 124 A1
Old Park Rd S EN2 . . . . 4 D1
Old Park Ridings N21 . 17 A6
Old Park View EN2 . . . . 4 D2
Old Pearson St SE10. . . . 141 D5
Old Perry St BR7 . . . . 189 C3
Old Post Office La SE3. . . . 143 B2
Old Pound Cl TW7 . . . 131 A4
Old Priory UB9 . . . . 38 D2
Old Pye St SW1 . . . . 259 C6
Old Pye Street Est SW1. . . . 259 C5
Old Quebec St W1 . . 237 D1
Old Queen St SW1. . . . 115 D4 249 D1
Old Rd Enfield EN3 . . . . 6 C4
Lewisham SE13 . . . . 142 C1
Old Rectory Gdns HA8. . . . 26 C4
Old Redding HA3 . . . . 24 A6
Oldridge Rd SW12 . . . 159 B4
Old Royal Free Pl N1 234 B5
Old Royal Free Sq N1. . . . 94 C6 234 B5
Old Ruislip Rd UB5. . . . 84 C5
Old St Andrews Mans NW9. . . . 67 B6
Old School Cl
3 Beckenham BR3 . . 185 A1
Merton SW19. . . . 179 C1
Old School Cres E7 . . . 77 A2
Old School Ct 8 N17. . 51 D6
Old School Ho CR4. . 202 C6
Old School Ho The EN2. . . . 4 D2
Old School Pl CR0 . . . 220 C4
Old School Rd UB8. . . . 82 B3
Old School Sq
12 Poplar E14 . . . . 97 C1
Thames Ditton KT7. . . 196 D3
Old School The
Bloomsbury WC1. . . . 240 D4
Merton SW19. . . . 179 C1
Old Seacoal La EC4 . . 241 C1
Old South Cl HA5 . . . . 22 D2
Old South Lambeth Rd SW8 . . . . 138 A5 270 B4
Old Spitalfields Mkt★ E1. . . . 95 D2 243 D4
Old Sq WC2. . . . 241 A2
Old St
Broadgate EC1 . . . . 95 B3 242 D6
Newham E13 . . . . 99 B5
Old Stable Mews N5 . . 73 A5
Old Station Rd UB3 . 105 D3
Old Station Yard The 11 E17. . . . 54 A5
Oldstead Rd BR1. . . . 186 B6
Old Street Sta EC1 . . . . 95 B3 242 D6
Old Studio Cl CR0. . . . 205 B2
Old Sun Wharf E14. . . 119 A6
Old Swan Wharf SW11 . . . . 266 D2
Old Swan Yd SM5 . . . 218 D4
Old Theatre Ct SE1. . 252 B4
Old Town
Clapham SW4 . . . . 137 C2
Croydon CR0 . . . . 220 D5
Old Tramyard SE18. . . 123 C2
Old Twelve Cl W7 . . . . 86 C3
Old Vicarage Sch 13 TW10. . . . 154 A5
Old Vicarage The CR4. . . . 202 C6
Old Woolwich Rd SE10. . . . 120 B1
Old York Rd SW18. . . 157 D6
Oleander Cl BR6. . . . 227 B3
O'Leary Sq E1 . . . . 96 C2
Oleastor Ct IG5. . . . 56 A6
Olga Prim Sch 37 E3. . 97 A5
Olga St 20 E3. . . . 97 A5
Olinda Rd N16. . . . 51 D3
Oliphant St W10 . . . . 91 A4
Olive Blythe Ho 14 W10 . . . . 91 A3
Oliver Ave SE25. . . . 205 D6
Oliver Bsns Pk NW10. . 89 A5
Oliver Cl W4. . . . 132 D6
Oliver Ct
Isleworth TW7. . . . 130 D2
2 Penge SE26 . . . . 184 C4
Plumstead SE18. . . . 123 A2
Olive Rd
Cricklewood NW2 . . . . 68 C4
Ealing W5. . . . 109 D3
3 Merton SW19. . . . 180 A3
Newham E13 . . . . 99 C4
Oliver Gdns E6 . . . . 100 A2
Oliver Goldsmith Prim Sch
18 Camberwell SE5. . 139 D4
Kingsbury NW9 . . . . 45 B4
Oliver Gr SE25 . . . . 205 D5
Oliver Ho
22 Bermondsey SE16 . . . . 118 A4
Notting Hill W11. . . . 244 A5
South Lambeth SW8 . . 270 A4
Oliver House Prep Sch 1 SW4 . . . . 159 B5
Oliver Mews SE15. . . . 140 A3
Oliver Rd
Kingston u T KT3 . . . . 177 A1
Leyton E10. . . . 75 D5
Sutton SM1 . . . . 218 B4
Walthamstow E17 . . . . 54 A4
Oliver's Yd EC1 . . . . 242 D6
Olive Tree Ho
7 Deptford SE15 . . . 140 C6
Olive Tree Ho *continued*
Stroud Green N4 . . . . 50 C3
Olive Tree Sch The SE13. . . . 163 D5
Olivette St 1 SW15 . 134 D1
Olive Waite Ho NW6 . . 69 D1
Olivia Ct 1 EN5. . . . 1 B1
Ollard's Gr IG10 . . . . 21 D6
Ollerton Gn E3 . . . . 97 B6
Ollerton Rd N11 . . . . 31 D5
Olley Cl SM6. . . . 220 A2
Ollgar Cl W12. . . . 111 D5
Olliffe St E14 . . . . 120 A3
Olmar St SE1 . . . . 140 A6
Olney Ho NW8. . . . 237 B6
Olney Rd SE17 . . . . 139 A6
Olron Cres DA6 . . . . 169 A6
Olven Rd SE18 . . . . 145 A6
Olveston Wlk SM5 . . . 202 B3
Olwen Mews HA5 . . . . 22 D1
Olyffe Ave DA16. . . . 146 A3
Olyffe Dr BR3. . . . 186 A2
Olympia Ex Ctr★ W14. . . . 113 A3 254 B5
Olympia Ind Est N22 . . 50 B6
Olympian Ct 8 E14 . . 119 C2
Olympia Way W14. . . . 113 A3 254 B5
Olympia Yd W2. . . . 245 D5
Olympic Ho 10 W10 . . . 90 C1
Olympic Ret Pk HA9 . . 66 D4
Olympic Way
Greenford UB6. . . . 85 D6
Wembley HA9 . . . . 66 C4
Olympus Gr N22 . . . . 32 C2
Olympus Sq E5 . . . . 74 A5
Oman Ave NW2. . . . 68 C4
Oman Ct NW4 . . . . 68 B4
Ombersley Ho N4. . . . 51 A2
Omeara St SE1 . . . . 252 B3
Omega Cl E14 . . . . 119 D3
Omega Ho SW10. . . . 266 B4
Omega Pl N1. . . . 233 B3
Omega St SE14 . . . . 141 C4
Omega Works E3. . . . 75 C1
Ommaney Rd SE14. . . 141 A4
Omnibus Bsns Ctr N7 . 72 A3
Omnibus Way E17 . . . . 35 C1
Ondine Rd SE15. . . . 139 D1
Onedin Point 10 E1 . . 118 A6
Onega Gate SE16 . . . 119 A3
O'Neill Ho NW8. . . . 229 D3
O'Neill Path 11 SE18 . 144 C6
One Tree Cl SE23. . . . 162 C5
Ongar Cl RM6. . . . 58 C4
Ongar Ho 15 N1. . . . 73 B2
Ongar Rd SW6 . . . . 135 C6 265 B6
Onra Rd E17. . . . 53 C2
Onslow Ave TW10. . . . 154 A6
Onslow Avenue Mans 10 TW10 . . . . 154 A6
Onslow Cl
Chingford E4 . . . . 20 B2
Notting Hill W9. . . . 91 B4
Thames Ditton KT7. . . 196 C1
Onslow Cres BR7 . . . 188 D2
Onslow Ct SW10. . . . 256 B1
Onslow Dr DA14 . . . . 168 D2
Onslow Gdns
Chelsea SW7 . . . . 114 B1 256 C2
Cranley Gdns N10 . . . . 49 B4
Southgate N21. . . . 16 C6
Thames Ditton KT7. . . 196 C1
Wallington SM6 . . . . 219 C1
Wanstead E18. . . . 55 C6
Onslow Ho 1 KT2 . . . 176 B2
Onslow Lo 28 SW2 . . . 160 C4
Onslow Mews E SW7 256 C3
Onslow Mews W SW7 . . . . 256 C3
Onslow Par N14 . . . . 15 B3
Onslow Rd
Richmond TW10. . . . 154 A5
Thornton Heath CR0 . . 204 C1
West Barnes KT3. . . . 200 A5
Onslow Sq SW7 . . . . 114 B2 256 D3
Onslow St EC1. . . . 241 B5
Onslow Way KT7. . . . 196 C1
Ontario St SE1. . . . 116 D3 261 D6
Ontario Way E14. . . . 119 C6
Onyx Ct N11. . . . 31 D3
Onyx Ho KT4. . . . 199 B1
Onyx Mews 4 E15 . . . . 76 D2
Opal Cl E16. . . . 99 D1
Opal Ct N11 . . . . 31 D3
Opal Ho KT4 . . . . 199 B1
Opal Mews 2 IG1 . . . . 78 D6
Opal St SE11. 116 D1 261 C2
Open Air Theatre, Regent's Pk★ NW1 231 A1
Openshaw Rd SE2 . . . 124 B2
Openview SW17, SW18 . . . . 158 B2
Opera Ct 7 N19 . . . . 71 D5
Operating Theatre Mus & Herb Garret The★ SE1. . . . 117 B5 252 D3
Ophelia Gdns NW2. . . . 69 A5
Ophir Terr SE15 . . . . 140 A4
Opie Ho NW8 . . . . 230 B4
Opossum Way TW4 . . 128 C2
Oppenheim Rd SE13 . 142 A3
Oppidan Apartments NW6. . . . 69 C2
Oppidans Rd NW3 . . . . 70 D1
Opus Studios E13. . . . 99 A5
Orange Gr E11. . . . 76 C5
Orange Hill Rd HA8 . . . 27 A3
Orange Pl SE16 . . . . 118 C3
Orangery Gallery The★ W8. . . . 113 B4 244 C1
Orangery La SE9. . . . 166 B6
Orangery The TW10 . . 153 C2
Orange St WC2. . . . 115 D6 249 D5
Orange Yd WC2. . . . 239 D1
Oransay Rd 25 N1. . . . 73 A2
Oratory La SW3. . . . 256 D2
Oratory RC Prim Sch SW3. . . . 114 C1 257 A2
Orbain Rd SW6 . . . . 135 A5 264 B3
Orbel St SW11 . . . . 136 C4 267 A1
Orb St SE17. . . . 117 B2 262 C3
Orchard Ave
Ashford TW15 . . . . 171 A4
Carshalton CR4 . . . . 203 A1
Croydon CR0 . . . . 207 A1
East Finchley N3 . . . . 47 C6
Erith DA17 . . . . 147 B6
Hatton TW14 . . . . 149 B6
Heston TW5. . . . 129 A5
Hinchley Wood KT7 . . 213 A6
Kingston u T KT3 . . . . 199 C6
Osidge N14 . . . . 15 C4
Southall UB1 . . . . 107 B5
Whetstone N20 . . . . 14 B2
Orchard Bsns Ctr SE26. . . . 185 B5
Orchard Cl
Ashford TW15 . . . . 171 A4
Bexleyheath DA7 . . . . 147 A4
Bushey WD23. . . . 8 B3
Chingford E4 . . . . 35 C6
Dollis Hill NW2. . . . 68 A5
Edgware HA8. . . . 26 A4
Honor Oak SE23. . . . 162 C5
21 Islington N1 . . . . 73 A1
Kensal Town W10. . . . 91 A2
Northolt UB5 . . . . 64 A2
Ruislip HA4 . . . . 39 A2
Thames Ditton KT7. . . 197 B2
Walton-on-T KT12 . . . 194 B2
Wanstead E11 . . . . 55 B5
Wembley HA0 . . . . 88 A6
West Barnes SW20 . . 200 C5
West Ewell KT19 . . . . 214 D2
Orchard Cotts
Chislehurst BR7. . . . 189 C4
Hayes UB3. . . . 105 C4
Orchard Cres
Edgware HA8. . . . 27 A5
Enfield EN1 . . . . 5 D4
Orchard Ct
Barnes SW13. . . . 133 D2
Barnet EN5 . . . . 1 D2
Croydon BR3 . . . . 207 C1
Edgware HA8. . . . 26 B5
Hounslow TW7. . . . 130 B5
Marylebone W1 . . . . 238 A2
New Malden KT4 . . . . 200 A1
Penge SE26 . . . . 184 D5
Southgate N14. . . . 15 C5
Wallington SM6 . . . . 219 B3

Orchard Ct *continued*
Walthamstow E10 . . . . . 53 D1
1 Walton-on-T KT12. 193 D1
Wood Green N22 . . . . . . 32 A3
Orchard Dr
Blackheath Vale
SE3 . . . . 142 C3
Edgware HA8. . . . . 26 B5
Upper Halliford TW17 193 C6
Orchard Gate
Colindale NW9. . . . . 45 C5
Thames Ditton KT10. . . 196 B1
Wembley UB6 . . . . 65 B2
Orchard Gdns
Chessington KT9 . . . . 214 A4
Sutton SM1 . . . . 217 C3
Orchard Gn
Bromley BR1 . . . . 187 C2
Orpington BR6. . . . . . 227 C6
Orchard Gr BR6. . . . . 227 D6
Croydon CR0 . . . . 207 A2
Edgware HA8. . . . . 26 D2
Harrow HA3. . . . . 44 B4
Orpington BR6 . . . . . . 211 D1
Penge SE20 . . . . 184 A3
Orchard Hill SE13. . . 141 D4
Orchard Hill Coll 18
SM6. . . . . 219 B2
Orchard Ho
Camberwell SE5. . . . . 139 A4
11 Rotherhithe SE16. 118 C3
Shepherd's Bush W12 112 A5
Orchard House Sch 15
W4. . . . . 111 C2
Orchard La
Thames Ditton KT8. . . . 196 B3
Wimbledon SW20 . . . 178 B2
Woodford IG8 . . . . 37 C6
Orchardleigh Ave EN3. . 6 C3
Orchard Lo N12. . . . . . . 14 A1
Orchard Mead Ho
NW11. . . . . 69 C6
Orchardmede N21. . . . . 17 B5
Orchard Mews N1 . . . . 73 B1
Orchard Pl
Canning Town E14 . . . 120 C6
Tottenham N17 . . . . 33 D3
Orchard Prim Sch
DA14 . . . . 190 B5
41 London E9. . . . . 74 C1
Orchard Prim Sch The
TW3. . . . . 151 C6
Orchard Rd Barnet EN5 . 1 B1
Belvedere DA17. . . . . . 125 C2
Brentford TW8. . . . . . . 131 C6
Bromley BR1 . . . . 187 C2
Carshalton CR4 . . . . . 203 A1
Chessington KT9 . . . . 214 A4
Dagenham RM10. . . . . 103 C6
Enfield EN3 . . . . 18 C6
Farnborough BR6. . . . 226 D3
Feltham TW14 . . . . . . 150 A3
Hampton TW12 . . . . . . 173 B3
Hayes UB3. . . . . 106 A6
Highgate N6. . . . . 49 B2
Hounslow TW4. . . . . . . 151 C6
Isleworth TW1. . . . . . . 153 B6
Kingston u T KT1 . . . . 176 A1
Richmond TW9. . . . . . . 132 C2
Sidcup DA14. . . . . 189 C6
Sunbury TW16 . . . . . . 172 B3
Sutton SM1 . . . . 217 C4
Welling DA16. . . . . 146 B2
Orchard Rise
Croydon CR0 . . . . 207 B1
Kingston u T KT2 . . . . 177 A2
Mortlake TW10 . . . . . 132 D1
Pinner HA5. . . . . 39 D6
Orchard Rise E
DA15. . . . . 167 D6
Orchard Rise W
DA15. . . . . 167 C6
Orchard Sch HA3 . . . . . 44 B4
Orchard Sch The
KT8 . . . . 196 B5
Orchardson Ho NW8 236 D5
Orchardson St
NW8. . . . . 92 B3 236 D5
Orchard Sq W14 . . . . 254 C1
Orchard St
Marylebone W1 . . . . . 238 B2
Walthamstow E17 . . . . . 53 A5
Orchard Terr EN1 . . . . . 18 A5
Orchard The
Acton Green W4. . . . . . 111 B2
Ealing W5. . . . . 87 D2
East Barnet N14. . . . . . . 15 B6
Edgware HA8. . . . . 26 C5
Enfield N21 . . . . 17 B5
Ewell KT17. . . . . 215 D1
Hampstead Garden Suburb
NW11 . . . . 47 C4
Hounslow TW3. . . . . . 130 A3
Lewisham SE3 . . . . . . 142 B3
Totteridge N20. . . . . 13 D3
Orchard Villas BR7 . . . 189 C4
Orchard Way
Ashford TW15 . . . . 148 B2
Croydon BR3, CR0 . . . 207 A3
Enfield EN1 . . . . 5 C2
Esher KT10 . . . . 212 A2
Sutton SM1 . . . . 218 B4
Orchard Way Prim Sch
CR0 . . . . 207 A2
Orchestra Ct HA8 . . . . . 26 D3
Orchid Cl
Chessington KT9 . . . . 213 C1
Lewisham SE13 . . . . . 164 B6
1 Newham E6 . . . . . 100 A2
Southall UB1 . . . . 85 A1
Orchid Ct
Catford BR1. . . . . 164 B1
Harrow HA3. . . . . 24 C2
Wembley HA9 . . . . 66 A6
Orchid Gdns TW3 . . . . 129 B1
Orchid Grange N14 . . . . 15 C4
Orchid Lo N14 . . . . 15 C4
Orchid Rd N14. . . . . 15 C4
Orchid St W12. . . . . . . 112 A6
Orch Sch The 15
SW2. . . . . 160 B3
Orde 6 NW9 . . . . 27 D2
Orde Hall St
WC1 . . . . 94 B2 240 C4
Orde Ho 10 N16. . . . . . . 73 B4
Ordell Ct 36 E3 . . . . 97 B5
Ordell Rd E3. . . . . 97 B5
Ordnance Cl TW13 . . . 150 A2
Ordnance Cres SE10 . 120 C4
Ordnance Hill
NW8. . . . . 92 B6 229 D5
Ordnance Mews
NW8. . . . . 229 D4
Ordnance Rd
Canning Town E16 . . . . . 98 D2
Enfield EN3 . . . . 7 B6
Shooters Hill SE18. . . . 144 C6
Oregano Cl UB7 . . . . . 104 B6
Oregano Dr E14 . . . . 98 B1
Oregon Ave E12 . . . . 78 B4
Oregon Bldg 5
SE13. . . . . 141 D4
Oregon Cl KT3. . . . . . . 199 A5
Oregon Sq BR6 . . . . . . 211 B1
Orestes Ct 9 E18. . . . . . 55 A6
Orestes Mews 1
NW6. . . . . 69 C3
Orford Ct
Stanmore HA7. . . . . 25 C4
Wallington SM6. . . . . . 219 C3
West Norwood SE27 . 160 D2
Orford Gdns TW1 . . . 152 D2
Orford Rd
Catford SE6 . . . . 163 D1
Walthamstow E17 . . . . . 53 D4
Wanstead E18 . . . . 55 B6
Organ Crossroads
KT17. . . . . 216 A1
Oriana Ct CR0 . . . . 221 B1
Oriana Ho 3 E14 . . . . 119 B6
Oriel Cl CR4 . . . . 203 D6
Oriel Ct
6 Croydon CR0. . . . . . 205 B1
Hampstead NW3 . . . . 70 A4
Oriel Dr SW13 . . . . 134 C6
Oriel Gdns IG5 . . . . 56 B6
Oriel Prim Sch
TW13. . . . . 151 A1
Oriel Rd Hackney E9 . . . 75 A2
Homerton E9 . . . . 74 D2
Oriel Way UB5 . . . . 63 D1
Oriental Rd E16. . . . . . 121 D5
Orient Ind Pk E10. . . . . . 75 C6
Orient St
SE11. . . . . . . 116 D2 261 C4
Orient Way
Lea Bridge E5. . . . . 74 D5
Leyton E10. . . . . 75 B6
Oriole Way SE28 . . . . . 124 B6
Orion Bsns Ctr SE14. 118 D1
Orion Ct 10 HA8. . . . . . . 26 D5
Orion Ctr The CR0. . . . 220 A6
Orion Ho 20 E1 . . . . 96 B3
Orion Mews SM4 . . . . 201 C5
Orion Point 5 E14. . . . 119 C2
Orion Prim Sch The
NW9. . . . . 27 D2
Orion Rd N11. . . . . 31 A4
Orion Way HA6 . . . . 22 A6
Orissa Rd SE18 . . . . . . 123 C1
Orkney Ho N1 . . . . . . 233 C6
Orkney St SW11 . . . . . 137 A3
Orlando Rd SW4 . . . . . 137 C2
Orleans Cl KT10. . . . . . 212 B6
Orleans Ct 9 TW1 . . . . 153 B4
Orleans House Gallery*
TW1. . . . . 153 B3
Orleans Inf Sch TW1 . . 153 B4
Orleans Park Sch
TW1. . . . . 153 B4
Orleans Rd
South Norwood
SE19 . . . . 183 B4
Twickenham TW1. . . . 153 C4
Orleston Mews N7. . . . 72 C2
Orleston Rd N7. . . . . . . 72 C2
Orley Farm Rd HA1. . . . 64 C5
Orley Farm Sch HA1 . . 64 B5
Orlop St SE10. . . . . 120 C1
Ormanton Rd SE26. . . . 184 A6
Orme Ct W2 . 113 D6 245 C5
Orme Ct Mews W2. . . 245 D5
Orme Ho 8 E8 . . . . 95 D6
Orme La W2 . 113 D6 245 C5
Ormeley Rd SW12. . . . 159 B3
Orme Rd
Kingston u T KT1,
KT3. . . . . 176 D1
Sutton SM1 . . . . 217 D2
Ormerod Gdns CR4 . . 181 A2
Ormerod Ho 3
SW9. . . . . 138 A2
Ormesby Cl SE28. . . . . 124 D6
Ormesby Way HA3 . . . . 44 B4
Orme Sq W2. . . . . 245 C5
Ormiston Gr W12 . . . . 112 B5
Ormiston Rd SE10 . . . . 121 A1
Ormond Ave
Hampton TW12 . . . . . . 173 D2
23 Richmond TW10. . 153 D6
Ormond Cl WC1. . . . . . 240 B4
Ormond Cres TW12 . . 173 D2
Ormond Dr TW12 . . . . 173 D3
Ormonde Ave BR6 . . . 227 A6
Ormonde Ct
Hendon NW4 . . . . 46 D6
Putney SW15. . . . . 134 C1
Ormonde Gate
SW3 . . . . . . 114 D1 257 D1
Ormonde Mans WC1 240 B4
Ormonde Pl SW1 . . . . 258 B3
Ormonde Rd SW14. . . 133 A2
Ormonde Rise IG9 . . . . 21 C3
Ormonde Terr
NW8. . . . . 92 D6 230 C5
Ormond Ho 7 N16. . . . . 73 B6
Ormond Mans WC1 . 240 C5
Ormond Mews WC1. 240 B5
Ormond Rd
Finsbury Pk N4, N19. . . . 50 A1
Richmond TW10. . . . . . 153 D6
Ormond Yd SW1 . . . . . 249 B4
Ormrod Ct W11 . . . . 91 B1
Ormsby SM2. . . . . 217 D1
Ormsby Gdns UB6 . . . . 86 A5
Ormsby Lo 7 W4 . . . . 111 C3
Ormsby Pl N16 . . . . 73 D5
Ormsby Point 6
SE18. . . . . 122 D2
Ormsby St E2. . . . . 95 D5
Ormside St SE15. . . . . 140 C6
Ormskirk Rd WD19. . . . . 22 D5
Ornan Rd NW3. . . . . 70 C3
Orpen Ho SW5. . . . . . . 255 B3
Orpen Wlk N16 . . . . 73 C5
Orpheus Ho 25 N19 . . . 49 D2
Orpheus St SE5. . . . . . 139 B4
ORPINGTON 227 D6
Orpington Gdns N18 . . 17 C1
Orpington Hospl
BR6 . . . . 227 D4
Orpington Mans N21. . 16 C3
Orpington Rd
Southgate N21. . . . . 16 D3
St Paul's Cray BR7 . . . 211 C6
Orpington Sta BR6. . 227 C6
Orpwood Cl TW12. . . . 173 B4
Orsett Mews
W2 . . . . 92 A1 236 A2
Orsett St
SE11. . . . . . . 116 B1 260 D2
Orsett Terr
Bayswater
W2 . . . . 92 A1 236 A2
Woodford IG8 . . . . 37 C3
Orsman Rd N1. . . . . 95 C6
Orton Gr EN1 . . . . 6 A4
Orton St E1. . . . . 118 A5
Orville Rd SW11 . . . . . 136 B3
Orwell Cl UB3 . . . . 105 C6
Orwell Ct Hackney E8 . . 96 A6
Highbury N5. . . . . 73 A4
Northolt UB5 . . . . 85 A6
Orwell Ho W12 . . . . . . 112 A6
Orwell Lo 2 E18. . . . . . . 55 A5
Orwell Rd E13 . . . . 99 C6
Osbaldeston Rd N16 . . 52 A1
Osberton Rd SE12. . . . 165 A6
Osbert St SW1 . . . . . . 259 C3
Osborn Cl E8 . . . . 96 A6
Osborne Ave TW19. . . 148 B3
Osborne Cl
Beckenham BR3. . . . . . 207 A5
Cockfosters EN4 . . . . 2 D2
Feltham TW13 . . . . . . 172 D5
Osborne Ct Ealing W5. . 88 A2
10 Surbiton KT6. . . . . 198 A3
17 Walthamstow E10. . . 53 D2
Osborne Gdns CR7. . . 183 A1
Osborne Gr E17. . . . . . . 53 B5
Osborne Mews E17 . . . 53 B5
Osborne Pl SM1 . . . . . 218 B3
Osborne Rd
Buckhurst Hill IG9. . . . . 21 B3
Dagenham RM9. . . . . . . 81 B3
Enfield EN3 . . . . 7 A3
Erith DA17 . . . . 147 B6
Finsbury Pk N4. . . . . 50 C1
Forest Gate E7. . . . . 77 B3
Hackney E9 . . . . 75 B2
Hounslow TW3, TW4 . . 129 B2
Kingston u T KT2 . . . . 176 A3
Leyton E10. . . . . 75 D6
Palmers Green N13. . . . 16 C1
South Acton W3 . . . . . 110 D4
Southall UB1 . . . . 86 A1
South Norwood CR7. . 183 A1
Walton-on-T KT12 . . . 194 A1
Willesden NW2 . . . . 68 B2
Osborne Sq RM9. . . . . . 81 B4
Osborne Terr 1
SW17. . . . . 181 A5
Osborne Way KT9. . . . 214 B3
Osborn Gdns NW7 . . . . 28 D3
Osborn La SE23. . . . . . 163 A4
Osborn St E1 . . 95 D2 243 D4
Osborn Terr SE3 . . . . . 142 D1
Osbourne Ct HA2 . . . . . 41 D5
Osbourne Ho
Richmond TW10. . . . . 154 C6
Twickenham TW2. . . . . 152 A2
Oscar Faber Pl 8 N1. . 73 C1
Oscar St SE8. . . . . 141 C3
Oseney Cres NW5. . . . . 71 D2
Osgood Ave BR6 . . . . 227 D3
Osgood Gdns 1
BR6. . . . . 227 D3
OSIDGE 15 B2
Osidge Ct N14 . . . . 15 B3
Osidge La N14 . . . . 15 B3
Osidge Prim Sch N14 . 15 C3
Osier Cres N10 . . . . 30 D2
Osier Ct E1. . . . . 96 D3
Osier La SE10. . . . . . . 120 D3
Osier Mews W4. . . . . . 133 D6
Osiers Ct 3 KT1. . . . . 175 D2
Osiers Rd SW18. . . . . . 135 C1
Osier St E1. . . . . 96 C3
Osier Way Leyton E10 . . 75 D5
Mitcham CR4 . . . . 202 D4
Oslac Rd SE6 . . . . 185 D5
Oslo Ct
Mitcham SW19 . . . . . . 180 B3
St John's Wood NW8. . 230 A3
Oslo Ho 2 SE5 . . . . . . 139 A3
Oslo Sq SE16 . . . . 119 A3
Oslow Cl W10. . . . . 91 B4
Osman Cl N15 . . . . 51 B3
Osmani Prim Sch E1. . 96 A2
Osman Rd
Edmonton N9. . . . . 18 A1
Osman Rd *continued*
Hammersmith W6 . . . . 112 C3
Osmington Ho SW8. . 270 D3
Osmond Cl HA2. . . . . . . 64 A6
Osmond Gdns SM6. . . 219 C3
Osmund St W12 . . . . . . 89 D2
Osnaburgh St
NW1. . . . . 93 B3 238 D6
Osnaburgh Terr
NW1. . . . . 238 D6
Osney Ho 4 SE2. . . . . 124 D4
Osney Wlk SM5. . . . . . 202 B3
Osprey 7 NW9 . . . . 27 D2
Osprey Cl
Cheam SM1. . . . . 217 B3
Higham Hill E17 . . . . 35 A3
Keston Mark BR2. . . . . 210 A1
Newham E6 . . . . 100 A2
Wanstead E11 . . . . 55 A5
West Drayton UB7. . . 104 A4
Osprey Ct
7 Ealing W7 . . . . 86 D3
Hampstead NW3 . . . . . . 69 D3
Thornton Heath
SW16 . . . . 182 B1
Osprey Ho
Camberwell SE15. . . . 139 D4
Isleworth TW7. . . . . . . 131 B2
3 Limehouse E14. . . 119 A6
Walthamstow E4 . . . . . . 35 B4
Osprey Mews EN3. . . . . 18 B6
Ospringe Cl 6 SE20. . 184 C3
Ospringe Ct SE9 . . . . . 167 B5
Ospringe Ho SE1. . . . . 251 B3
Ospringe Rd NW5. . . . . 71 C4
Osram Ct W6 . . . . 112 C3
Osram Rd HA9 . . . . 65 D5
Osric Path 8 N1. . . . . . 95 C5
Ossian Mews N4. . . . . . 50 B2
Ossian Rd N4. . . . . 50 B2
Ossie Garvin Rdbt
UB4. . . . . 106 C6
Ossington Bldgs W1 238 A3
Ossington Cl W2. . . . . 245 B5
Ossington St
W2 . . . . 113 D6 245 C5
Ossory Rd SE1 . . . . . . 140 A6
Ossulston St
NW1. . . . . 93 D5 232 D4
Ossultan Pl N2 . . . . 48 A6
Ossulton Way N2 . . . . . 48 A5
Ostade Rd SW2 . . . . . . 160 B4
Ostell Cres EN3 . . . . 7 C5
Osten Mews
SW7 . . . . . . 113 D3 255 D5
OSTERLEY. 130 B5
Osterley Ave TW7 . . . . 130 B5
Osterley Cl BR5 . . . . . 190 A2
Osterley Cres TW7 . . 130 D4
Osterley Ct
Hounslow TW7. . . . . . . 130 B4
7 Northolt UB5. . . . . . . 84 C4
Osterley Gdns
Southall UB2 . . . . 108 A4
South Norwood CR7. . 183 A1
Osterley Ho 5 E14. . . . 97 D1
Osterley La
Isleworth TW7. . . . . . . 108 C1
Southall UB2, TW7 . . . 107 D1
Osterley Lo 1 TW7. . . 130 C4
Osterley Park* TW7 . 108 B1
Osterley Park Rd
UB2. . . . . 107 B3
Osterley Park View Rd
W7 . . . . 108 C4
Osterley Rd
Hounslow TW7. . . . . . 130 C4
Stoke Newington N16 . . 73 C4
Osterley Sta TW7 . . . . 130 B5
Osterley Views UB2 . . 108 B4
Osterly Lodge UB2. . . 107 B3
Oster Terr E17 . . . . 52 D4
Ostlers Dr TW15 . . . . . 171 A5
Ostliffe Rd N13 . . . . 33 A5
Oswald Bldg SW8. . . . 268 C5
Oswald Rd UB1 . . . . . . 107 A5
Oswald's Mead E9. . . . 75 A4
Oswald St E5 . . . . 74 D5
Oswald Terr NW2 . . . . . 68 C5
Osward Pl N9. . . . . 18 B2
Osward Rd SW12,
SW17. . . . . 158 D2
Oswell Ho 9 E1 . . . . . 118 B5
Oswin St
SE11. . . . . . . 116 D2 261 D4
Oswyth Rd SE5 . . . . . . 139 C3

Otford Cl Bexley DA5 169 D5
Bromley BR1 210 C6
Penge SE20 184 C2
Otford Cres SE4 163 B5
Otford Ho
Bermondsey SE1 252 D1
6 Deptford SE15 140 C6
Otha Ho 13 SW9 138 A3
Othello Cl SE11 261 C2
Otho Ct 5 TW8 131 D5
Otis St E3 98 A4
Otley App IG2 56 D3
Otley Ct N11 31 A4
Otley Dr IG2 56 D3
Otley Ho N5 72 D5
Otley Rd E16 99 C1
Otley Terr E5 74 D5
Ottawa Ho 4 HA4 40 C1
Ottaway Ct E5 74 A5
Ottaway St E5 74 A5
Otterbourne Rd
Chingford E4 20 B1
1 Croydon CR0 221 A6
Otterburn Gdns
TW7 131 A5
Otterburn Ho 12
SE5 139 A5
Otterburn St SW17 180 D4
Otter Cl E15 98 A6
Otterden Cl BR6 227 C4
Otterden St SE6 185 C6
Otterfield Rd UB7 104 A6
Otter Rd UB6 86 A3
Ottershaw Ho BR5 190 B2
Otto Cl SE26 162 B1
Ottoman Ct W5 109 D2
Otto St SE17 138 D6
Otway Ct N4 50 B3
Otway Gdns WD23 8 C4
Oulton Cl Erith SE28 102 C1
Upper Clapton E5 74 C6
Oulton Cres IG11 79 D3
Oulton Rd N15 51 B4
Oulton Way WD19 23 B6
Oundle Ave WD23 8 A5
Our Lady Immaculate RC
Prim Sch KT6 198 D1
Our Lady of Dolours RC
Prim Sch 1 W2 91 D2
Our Lady of Grace RC Inf
Sch NW2 68 C6
Our Lady of Grace RC
Jun Sch NW2 68 B5
Our Lady of Grace RC
Prim Sch 4 SE7 143 B6
Our Lady of Lourdes RC
Prim Sch
1 Finchley N12 30 A2
Friern Barnet N11 31 C5
1 Lewisham SE13 142 B2
London NW10 89 A6
Our Lady of Lourds RC
Prim Sch E11 55 A3
Our Lady of Muswell
Prim Sch N10 49 A6
Our Lady of Muswell RC
Prim Sch N10 31 A1
Our Lady of the Rosary
RC Prim Sch DA15 167 C5
Our Lady of the
Visitation RC Combined
Prim Sch UB6 86 A3
Our Lady of Victories
RC Prim Sch
7 Putney SW15 134 D1
South Kensington
SW7 114 A2 256 B3
Our Lady Queen of
Heaven RC Prim Sch 10
SW19 156 D4
Our Lady RC Prim Sch
Camden Town
NW1 93 C6 232 B6
28 Poplar E14 97 B1
Our Lady & St John's RC
Jun & Inf Sch 4
TW8 109 C1
Our Lady & St Joseph RC
Prim Sch 14 N1 73 C2
Our Lady & St Philip Neri
RC Infants Sch 16
SE23 162 D1
Our Lady & St Philip Neri
RC Prim Sch 6
SE26 185 A6
Our Lady's Convent RC
High Sch 3 N15 51 C2
Ouseley Rd SW12 158 D3
Outer Circ
NW8 92 D5 230 D3
Outgate Rd NW10 67 D1
Outram Pl N1 94 A6 233 B6
Outram Rd
Croydon CR0 221 D6
Muswell Hill N22 31 D2
Newham E6 100 A6
Outwich St EC3 243 B2
Outwood Ct CR2 221 A1
Outwood Ho 3
SW2 160 B4
Oval Ct Burnt Oak HA8 27 A3
8 Teddington TW11 174 D5
Oval Mans SE11 270 D6
Oval Pl SW8 138 B5 270 D4
Oval Prim Sch CR0 205 C1
Oval Rd
Camden Town
NW1 93 B6 231 C6
Croydon CR0 205 C1
Oval Rd N RM10 103 D6
Oval Rd S RM10 103 D5
Oval Sta SE11 138 C6
Oval The Hackney E2 96 B5
Sidcup DA15 168 A4
Oval Way
SE11 116 B1 260 D1
Overbrae BR3 185 C5
Overbrook Wlk HA8 26 C3
Overbury 1 BR3 208 A6
Overbury Ave BR3 208 A6
Overbury Ho 3 E5 74 D4
Overbury Rd N4, N15 51 B3
Overbury St E5 74 D4
Overcliff Rd SE13 141 C2
Overcourt Cl DA15 168 B5
Overdale Ave KT3 177 B1
Overdale Rd W5 109 C3
Overdown Rd SE6 185 D6
Overhill Rd SE21,
SE22 162 A4
Overhill Way BR3 208 B4
Overlea Rd E5 52 A2
Overmead DA15 167 B4
Oversley Ho 17 W2 91 C2
Overstand Cl BR3 207 C4
Overstone Gdns CR0 207 B2
Overstone Ho 19 E14 97 C1
Overstone Rd W6 112 C2
Overstrand Mans
SW11 268 A1
Overton Cl
1 Hounslow TW7 130 D4
Tokyngton NW10 67 A2
Overton Ct E11 55 A2
Overton Dr Ilford RM6 58 C2
Wanstead E11 55 B2
Overton Grange Sch
SM2 217 D1
Overton Ho SW15 155 D4
Overton Rd
Abbey Wood SE2 124 D3
Belmont SM2 217 C1
Brixton SW9 138 C3
Southgate N14 16 A6
Walthamstow E10 53 A1
Overton's Yd CR0 221 A5
Overy Ho SE1 251 C1
Ovesdon Ave HA2 41 B1
Ovett Cl SE19 183 C4
Ovex Cl E14 120 A4
Ovington Ct SW3 257 B5
Ovington Gdns SW3 257 B5
Ovington Mews SW3 257 B5
Ovington Sq
SW3 114 C3 257 B5
Ovington St
SW3 114 C2 257 B4
Owen Cl Hayes UB4 84 B4
Northolt UB5 63 A2
Thamesmead SE28 124 C5
Thornton Heath CR0 205 B3
Owen Ct UB4 84 B4
Owen Ho
Feltham TW14 150 A4
11 Tufnell Pk N19 71 C4
5 Twickenham TW1 153 B4
Owenite St SE2 124 B2
Owen Rd
Edmonton N13 33 A5
Hayes UB4 84 B4
Owen's Ct EC1 234 C2
Owens Mews 10 E11 76 C6
Owen's Row EC1 234 C2
Owen St EC1 234 C3
Owens Way SE23 163 A4
Owen Way NW10 67 A3
Owen Wlk 7 SE20 184 A3
Owgan Cl SE5 139 B5
Oxberry Ave SW6 135 A3
Oxbridge Ct 4 W4 110 D1
Oxendon St SW1,
W1 115 D6 249 C5
Oxenford St SE15 139 D2
Oxenham Ho 13 SE8 141 C6
Oxenholme NW1 232 B3
Oxenpark Ave HA9 44 A2
Oxestalls Rd SE8 119 A1
Oxford Ave
Harlington TW6 127 D5
Hounslow TW5 107 C1
Merton SW20 179 A1
Southgate N14 15 C3
Oxford & Cambridge
Mans NW1 237 B3
Oxford Cir W1 93 C1 239 A1
Oxford Circus Ave
W1 239 A1
Oxford Circus Sta
W1 93 C1 239 A1
Oxford Cl
Edmonton N9 18 B2
Littleton TW15, TW17 171 A3
Mitcham CR4 203 C6
Oxford Cres KT3 199 B3
Oxford Ct
16 Acton W3 88 C1
City of London EC4 252 C6
8 Ealing W7 86 D2
Gunnersbury W4 110 D1
17 Kingston u T KT6 198 A4
48 Paddington W2 91 C2
Sidcup DA14 189 D6
Oxford Dr
Bermondsey SE1 253 A3
Ruislip HA4 62 C6
Oxford Gardens Prim
Sch 21 W10 90 D1
Oxford Gate W6 112 D2
Oxford Gdns
Brentford W4 132 C6
Edmonton N21 17 A4
North Kensington W10 90 D1
Oakleigh Pk N20 14 B3
Oxford Ho N4 50 C1
Oxford Mews DA5 169 C4
Oxford Rd
Carshalton SM5 218 C3
Ealing W5 109 D6
Edmonton N9 18 B2
Enfield EN3 18 B6
Finsbury Pk N4 50 C1
Harrow HA1 42 A3
Ilford IG1 79 A3
Paddington NW6 91 C5
Putney SW15 135 A1
Sidcup DA14 190 B5
South Norwood SE19 183 B4
Stratford E15 76 B2
Teddington TW11,
TW12 174 B5
Wallington SM6 219 C3
Wealdstone HA3 42 D6
Woodford IG8 37 D5
Oxford Rd N W4 110 D1
Oxford Rd S W4 110 D1
Oxford Sq W2 92 C1 237 B1
Oxford St W1 93 B1 238 D1
Oxford Way TW13 172 D6
Oxford Wlk UB1 107 B5
Oxgate Ct NW2 68 A6
Oxgate Ct Par NW2 68 A6
Oxgate Ctr NW2 68 B6
Oxgate Gdns NW2 68 B6
Oxgate La NW2 68 B6
Oxhawth Cres BR2 210 D3
Oxhey Dr WD19 22 B6
Oxhey Dr S HA6 22 B5
Oxhey La HA5 23 C5
Oxhey Ridge Cl HA6 22 B5
Oxhey Wood Prim Sch
WD19 22 C6
Oxleas E6 100 D1
Oxleas Cl DA16 145 B3
Oxleay Rd HA2 41 C1
Oxleigh Cl KT3 199 C4
Oxley Cl SE1 118 A1
Oxleys Rd NW2 68 B5
Oxlip Cl 2 CR0 206 D1
Oxlow La RM10 81 C4
Oxonian St SE22 139 D1
Oxo Tower Wharf
SE1 251 B5
Oxo Twr★ SE1 251 B5
Oxted Cl CR4 202 B6
Oxted Ct N16 51 C1
Oxtoby Way SW16 181 D2
Oyster Catchers Cl
E16 99 B1
Oyster Catcher Terr
IG5 56 C6
Oyster Row E1 96 C1
Ozolins Way E16 99 A1

P

Pablo Neruda Cl 4
SE24 138 D1
Pace Pl E1 96 B1
Pacific Cl TW14 149 D3
Pacific Ho 15 E1 96 D3
Pacific Hts BR3 185 C3
Pacific Rd E16 99 A1
Pacific Wharf IG11 78 D1
Pacific Wharf SE16 118 D5
Packenham Ho
24 Crouch End N19 49 D2
21 Spitalfields E2 95 D4
Packham Ct KT4 216 C5
Packington Sq
N1 95 A6 235 A6
Packington St
N1 94 D6 234 D5
Packmores Rd SE9 167 B6
Padbury SE17 263 B1
Padbury Cl TW14 149 B3
Padbury Ct E2 95 D4
Padbury Ho NW8 237 B6
Padden Ct NW7 28 D3
Paddenswick Ct 2
W6 112 B3
Paddenswick Rd
W6 112 A3
PADDINGTON 92 A2
Paddington Acad 7
W9 91 C3
Paddington Cl UB4 84 D3
Paddington Ct
10 Ealing W7 86 D2
7 Wembley HA0 66 A2
Paddington Gn
W2 92 B2 236 C4
Paddington Green Prim
Sch NW8 92 B3 236 C5
Paddington St W1 238 A4
Paddington Sta
W2 92 B1 236 C2
Paddock Cl
Forest Hill SE26 184 D6
Kidbrooke SE3 143 A3
New Malden KT4 199 C1
Northolt UB5 85 C5
Orpington BR6 226 D4
Paddock Ct SW20 200 C5
Paddock Gdns SE19 183 C4
Paddock Lo 13 EN1 17 C6
Paddock Prim Sch
SW11 137 A1
Paddock Rd
Bexley DA6 147 A1
Dollis Hill NW2 68 A6
Ruislip HA4 62 D5
Paddock Sch SW15 133 D1
Paddocks Cl HA2 63 D4
Paddocks Gn NW9 44 D1
Paddocks The
Addington CR0 223 C2
Cockfosters EN4 2 D2
Preston HA9 66 D6
Paddock The
Muswell Hill N10 49 B6
Uxbridge UB10 60 D4
Paddock Way
Chislehurst BR7 189 B3
11 Putney SW15 156 C4
Padelford La HA7 9 A2
Padfield Ct HA9 66 B5
Padfield Rd SE5 139 A2
Padley Cl KT9 214 B3
Padnall Ct RM6 58 D6
Padnall Rd RM6 58 D5
Padstone Ho 50 E3 97 D4
Padstow Cl BR6 227 D4
Padstow Ho 12 E14 119 B6
Padstow Rd EN2 4 D4
Padstow Wlk TW14 149 D3
Padua Rd SE20 184 C2
Pagden St SW8 268 D2
Pageant Ave NW9 27 C2
Pageant Cres SE16 119 B5
Pageantmaster Ct
EC4 241 C1
Pageant Wlk CR0 221 C5
Page Cl
Dagenham RM9 81 A3
Hampton TW12 173 A4
Harrow HA3 44 B3
Page Cres CR0 220 D3
Page Ct NW7 28 A3
Page Green Rd N15 52 A4
Page Green Terr N15 51 D4
Page Heath La BR1 209 D6
Page Heath Villas
BR1 209 D6
Page High N22 50 C6
Page Ho SE10 142 A6
Pagehurst Rd CR0 206 B2
Page Mdw NW7 28 A3
Page Rd TW14 149 B5
Page's Ct N10 31 A1
Page's Hill N10 31 A1
Page's La N10 31 A1
Page St Hendon NW7 28 A3
Westminster
SW1 115 D2 259 D4
Page's Wlk
SE1 117 C3 263 B5
Page's Yd W4 133 C6
Paget Ave SM1 218 B5
Paget Cl TW12 174 B6
Paget Ct UB7 104 A4
Paget Gdns BR7 188 D2
Paget Ho 15 E2 96 C5
Paget La TW7 130 C2
Paget Pl
Kingston u T KT2 177 A4
Thames Ditton KT7 196 D1
Paget Rd
Hillingdon UB10 83 A3
Ilford IG1 78 D4
Stoke Newington N16 51 B1
Paget Rise SE18 144 C5
Paget St EC1 234 C2
Paget Terr SE18 144 D6
Pagham Ho 8 W10 90 C3
Pagin Ho N15 51 C4
Pagitts Gr EN4 1 D4
Pagnell St SE14 141 B5
Pagoda Ave TW9 132 B2
Pagoda Gdns SE3 142 B3
Pagoda Gr SE27 161 A2
Paignton Rd
Ruislip HA4 62 A5
Tottenham N15 51 C3
Paine Ct SE3 142 D6
Paines Cl HA5 41 A6
Paine's La HA5 23 A1
Pain's Cl CR4 181 B1
Painsthorpe Rd 3
N16 73 C5
Painswick Ct 1
SE15 139 D5
Painters Mews SE16 118 A2
Painters Rd IG2, RM6 58 A6
Paisley Rd
Carshalton SM5 202 B1
Tottenham N22 32 D2
Paisley Terr SM5 202 B2
Pakeman Ho SE1 251 D2
Pakeman Prim Sch 1
N7 72 B5
Pakeman St N7 72 B5
Pakenham Cl SW12 159 A3
Pakenham St
WC1 94 B3 240 D6
Pakington Ho 22
SW9 138 A3
Palace Ave
W8 113 D4 245 D2
Palace Cl 4 E9 75 B2
Palace Court Gdns
N10 49 C6

Palace Ct
Bromley BR1 . . . . **187** B2
Eltham SE9 . . . . **166** B3
Hampstead NW3 . . . . **69** D3
Harrow HA3 . . . . **44** D3
Kensington
W2 . . . . **113** D6 **245** C5
2 South Norwood
CR7 . . . . **205** B5
Streatham SW2 . . . . **160** C3
Palace Exchange EN2 . **5** B1
Palace Garden Mews
W8 . . . . **245** B4
Palace Gate
Hampton KT8 . . . . . . **196** C6
Knightsbridge
W8 . . . . **114** A4 **246** A1
Palace Gate Mews 4
N8 . . . . **50** A5
Palace Gates Rd N11 . **31** C5
Palace Gdns EN2 . . . . **21** D3
Palace Gdns Mews
W8 . . . . **113** D5 **245** D5
Palace Gdns Sh Ctr
EN2 . . . . **5** B1
Palace Gn
Kensington
W8 . . . . **113** D5 **245** D5
New Addington CR0 . . **223** B1
Palace Gr
Bromley BR1 . . . . **187** B2
Penge SE19 . . . . **183** D3
Palace Mans 4 . . . **254** B4
Palace Mews
Belgravia SW1 . . . . . **258** B3
Fulham SW6 . . . . **264** D4
1 Walthamstow E17 . . **53** C5
Palace Par E17 . . . . . **53** C5
Palace Pl SW1 . . . . . **259** A6
Palace Rd
Bromley BR1 . . . . **187** B2
East Molesey KT8 . . . **196** B6
Hornsey N8 . . . . **49** D4
Kingston u T KT1 . . . . **197** D5
Penge SE19 . . . . **183** D3
Ruislip HA4 . . . . **63** A4
Streatham SE27, SW16,
SW2 . . . . **160** C2
Wood Green N11 . . . . **32** A3
Palace Sq SE19 . . . . **183** D3
Palace St
SW1 . . . . **115** C3 **259** A6
Palace View
Bromley BR1 . . . . **209** B6
Croydon CR0 . . . . **223** B4
Grove Pk SE12 . . . . . **165** A2
Palace View Rd E4 . . . **37** C4
Palamos Rd E10 . . . . **53** C1
Palatine Ave N1 . . . . **73** C4
Palatine Rd N16 . . . . **73** C4
Palazzo Apartments 11
N1 . . . . **235** A5
Palemead Cl SW6 . . . **134** D4
Palermo Rd NW10 . . . **21** C3
Palestine Gr SW19 . . **180** B2
Palewell Cl BR5 . . . . **190** B1
Palewell Common Dr
SW14 . . . . **155** B6
Palewell Pk SW14 . . **133** B1
Palfrey Pl
SW8 . . . . **138** B5 **270** D4
Palgrave Gdns
NW1 . . . . **92** C3 **237** B6
Palgrave Ho
7 Camberwell SE5 . . **139** A5
4 Maitland Pk NW3 . . **70** D3
Twickenham TW2 . . . **152** A4
Palgrave Rd W12 . . . **111** D3
Palissy St 55 E2 . . . . **95** D4
Palladino Ho 6
SW17 . . . . **180** C5
Pallant Ho SE1 . . . . . **262** D5
Pallant Way BR6 . . . . **226** C5
Pallester Ct NW11 . . . **47** A1
Pallet Way SE18 . . . . **144** A4
Palliser Ct W14 . . . . **254** A2
Palliser Ho
3 Greenwich SE10 . . **142** B6
1 Stepney E1 . . . . . . **96** D3
Palliser Rd
W14 . . . . **113** A1 **254** A1
Pallister Terr SW15 . . **155** D5
Pall Mall
SW1 . . . . **115** D5 **249** C3
Pall Mall E
SW1 . . . . **115** D5 **249** D4
Pall Mall Pl SW1 . . . **249** B3
Palmar Cres DA7 . . . **147** C3
Palmar Rd DA7 . . . . **147** C3
Palm Ave DA14 . . . . **190** D4
Palm Cl E10 . . . . **75** D5
Palm Ct
Beckenham BR3 . . . . **207** B6
11 Camberwell SE15 . **139** D5
Stoke Newington N16 . **73** B6
Wood Green N22 . . . . **32** B3
Palmeira Rd DA7 . . . **146** D2
Palmer Ave KT4,
SM3 . . . . **216** C4
Palmer Cl
Heston TW5 . . . . **129** C4
Northolt UB5 . . . . **63** A2
West Wickham BR4 . . **224** B6
Palmer Cres KT1 . . . **198** A6
Palmer Gdns EN5 . . . **12** C6
Palmer Ho
6 Deptford SE14 . . . . **141** A5
8 Kentish Town NW5 . **71** C4
5 Tufnell Pk N7 . . . . . **71** C5
Palmer Pl N7 . . . . **72** C3
Palmer Rd
Dagenham RM8 . . . . . **58** D1
Newham E13 . . . . **99** B3
Palmer's Ct 11 N11 . . **31** C5
Palmers Gr KT8 . . . . **195** C5
PALMERS GREEN . . **16** A1
Palmers Green High Sch
N21 . . . . **16** C2
Palmers Green Sta
N13 . . . . **32** B6
Palmers La EN3 . . . . . **6** C4
Palmers Rd
Globe Town E2 . . . . . . **96** D5
Mortlake SW14 . . . . . **133** A2
Thornton Heath
SW16 . . . . **182** B1
Palmer St N11 . . . . . . **31** C5
Palmer St SW1 . . . . **259** C6
Palmerston Cres
Bowes Pk N13 . . . . . . **32** B5
Woolwich SE18 . . . . **145** A6
Palmerston Ho
2 Buckhurst Hill IG9 . **21** C2
22 Globe Town E13 . . . **96** D5
7 Surbiton KT6 . . . . **197** D2
9 Sutton SM1 . . . . . . **218** A3
Walthamstow E17 . . . **53** B5
Palmerston Ctr HA3 . **42** D6
Palmerston Gr 11
SW19 . . . . **179** C3
Palmerston Rd
Battersea SW11 . . . . **268** B1
Kensington W8 . . . . **245** A3
Palmerston Rd
Acton Green W3 . . . . **111** A3
Bowes Pk N22 . . . . . . **32** B4
Brondesbury NW6 . . . **69** B1
Buckhurst Hill IG9 . . . **21** C3
Farnborough BR6 . . . **227** A3
Hampstead NW6 . . . . **69** C1
Harrow HA1 . . . . **42** D6
Hounslow TW3 . . . . . **130** A4
Merton SW19 . . . . . . **179** C3
Mortlake SW14 . . . . . **133** A1
Sutton SM1 . . . . **218** C3
Thornton Heath CR0 . **205** B4
Twickenham TW2 . . . **152** C5
Upton E7 . . . . **77** B2
Wallington SM5 . . . . **219** A4
Walthamstow E17 . . . **53** B5
Palmerston Way
SW8 . . . . **268** D3
Palm Gr W5 . . . . **110** A3
Palm Tree Cl 5 N17 . . **33** D1
Palm Tree Ho 2
SE14 . . . . **140** D5
Pamela Ct
Finchley N12 . . . . **29** D4
Willesden NW10 . . . . **20** A4
Pamela Gdns HA5 . . . **40** B2
Pamela Ho 11 E8 . . . . **95** D6
Pamir Ct 10 SM2 . . . **217** D2
Pamlion Ct N4 . . . . . . **50** A2
Pams Way KT19 . . . . **215** B3
Panama Ho 8 E1 . . . . **96** D2
Panbro Ho SE18 . . . . **144** B4
Pancras La EC2 . . . . **242** C1
Pancras Rd
NW1 . . . . **93** D5 **232** D4
Pancras Way Bow E3 . **98** C5
Old Ford E3 . . . . **97** C5
Pandian Way 4 NW5 . **71** D2
Pandora Ct 4 KT6 . . . **198** A3
Pandora Rd NW6 . . . . **69** C2
Panfield Mews IG2 . . . **56** C3
Panfield Rd SE2 . . . . **124** A3
Pangbourne NW1 . . . **232** A1
Pangbourne Ave
W10 . . . . **90** C2
Pangbourne Ct
Oakleigh Pk N20 . . . . **14** A4
Upper Tooting SW17 . **180** A6
Pangbourne Dr HA7 . **26** A5
Pangbourne Ho 7
N7 . . . . **72** A3
Panhard Pl 11 UB1 . . **107** D6
Pank Ave EN5 . . . . . . **14** A6
Pankhurst Ave 8
E16 . . . . **121** B5
Pankhurst Cl
7 Deptford SE14 . . . **140** D5
Isleworth TW7 . . . . . **130** D2
Pankhurst Ho
2 Kensington NW10 . **90** C1
Streatham SW16 . . . **181** D5
Pankhurst Rd KT12 . . **194** C2
Panmuir Rd SW20 . . . **178** B2
Panmure Cl N5 . . . . . . **72** D2
Panmure Ct 11 UB1 . . **86** A1
Panmure Rd SE26 . . **162** B1
Panorama Ct N6 . . . . **49** C3
Pan Peninsula Sq
E14 . . . . **119** D4
Pansy Gdns W12 . . . **112** A6
Panther Dr NW10 . . . . **67** B3
Pantiles Cl N13 . . . . . **32** D5
Pantiles The
Bickley BR1 . . . . **210** A6
Bushey WD23 . . . . **8** B3
Erith DA7 . . . . **147** B5
Temple Fortune NW11 . **47** B4
Panton Cl CR0 . . . . . **242** A6
Panton St SW1 . . . . **249** C5
Panyer Alley EC2 . . . **242** A2
Papermill Cl SM5 . . . **219** A4
Paper Mill Wharf
E14 . . . . **119** A6
Papillons Wlk SE3 . . **143** A2
Papworth Gdns N7 . . **72** B3
Papworth Way SW2 . **160** C4
Parade Mans
10 Camberwell SE5 . . **139** A3
2 Hendon NW4 . . . . . **46** B4
Parade Mews SE27,
SW2 . . . . **160** D2
Parade The
Ashford TW16 . . . . . **171** D3
Battersea
SW11 . . . . . . **136** D5 **267** C4
Claygate KT10 . . . . . **212** C2
Ilford IG2 . . . . **57** B3
Thornton Heath CR0 . **204** A3
Thornton Heath CR7 . **204** C6
Waddon CR0 . . . . . . **220** B3
Wembley UB6 . . . . . . **65** B3
Paradise Pas 6 N7 . . **72** C3
Paradise Pl 18 SE17 . **261** A2
Paradise Rd
Richmond TW10 . . . . **154** A6
South Lambeth SW4 . **138** A3
Paradise Row E2 . . . . **96** B4
Paradise St SE16 . . . **118** B4
Paradise Wlk
SW3 . . . . **136** D6 **267** D6
Paragon N8 . . . . **50** C5
Paragon Christian Acad
E5 . . . . **74** D4
Paragon Cl E16 . . . . . **99** A1
Paragon Ct NW4 . . . . **29** A2
Paragon Gr KT5 . . . . **198** B3
Paragon Ho SE3 . . . . **142** D3
Paragon Mews SE1 . **262** D4
Paragon Pl
Blackheath Vale
SE3 . . . . **142** D3
Surbiton KT5 . . . . . . **198** B3
Paragon Rd E9 . . . . . . **74** C2
Paragon The
Kidbrooke SE3 . . . . . **143** A3
Walworth SE17 . . . . **261** C4
Paramount Bldg EC1 . **241** C6
Paramount Ct WC1 . . **239** B5
Paramount Ho 10
E11 . . . . **76** C5
Parbury Rd SE23 . . . **163** A5
Parbury Rise KT9 . . . **214** A2
Parchmore Rd CR7 . . **205** A6
Parchmore Way
CR7 . . . . **182** D1
Pardes House Gram Sch
11 N3 . . . . **29** B1
Pardes House Prim Sch
11 N3 . . . . **29** B1
Pardoner St
SE1 . . . . **117** B3 **262** D6
Pardon St EC1 . . . . . **241** D6
Parfett St E1 . . . . **96** A1
Parfew Ct 2 SE22 . . **162** B2
Parfitt Cl NW11 . . . . . **48** A1
Parfrey St W6 . . . . . **134** C6
Pargraves Ct HA9 . . . **66** C6
Parham Dr IG2 . . . . . . **56** D4
Paris Gdn
SE1 . . . . **116** D5 **251** C4
Parish CE Prim Sch
E11 . . . . **187** B3
Parish Church CE Inf Sch
11 CR0 . . . . **220** D5
Parish Church CE Jun
Sch 9 CR0 . . . . **220** D5
Parish Ct KT6 . . . . . . **198** A3
Parish Gate Dr
DA15 . . . . **167** C5
Parish La SE20 . . . . . **184** D3
Paris Ho 2 E2 . . . . **96** B5
Parish Wharf 1
SE7 . . . . **122** A2
Park App SE16 . . . . . **146** B1
Park Ave Barking IG11 . **79** A2
Bromley BR6 . . . . . . **226** C6
Edmonton N18 . . . . . . **34** A6
Enfield EN1 . . . . **17** C5
Finchley N3 . . . . **29** D2
Golders Green NW11 . . **47** D1
Ilford IG1 . . . . **56** C1
Mitcham CR4 . . . . . . **181** B3
Mortlake SW14 . . . . . **133** B1
Palmers Green N13 . . **16** C1
Plaistow BR1 . . . . . . **187** A4
Ruislip HA4 . . . . **39** C3
Southall UB1 . . . . . . **107** C5
Stratford E15 . . . . **76** C2
Twickenham TW3 . . . **151** B5
Upper Halliford TW17 . **193** C6
Wallend E6 . . . . **100** C5
Wallington SM5 . . . . **219** A2
West Barnes SM4 . . . **177** A5
Willesden NW2 . . . . . . **68** C2
Woodford IG8 . . . . **37** B5
Wood Green N22 . . . . **32** B2
Park Ave E KT17 . . . **216** A2
Park Ave N
Dudden Hill NW10 . . . **68** B3
Hornsey N8 . . . . **49** D5
Park Avenue Mews 7
CR4 . . . . **181** B3
Park Avenue Rd N17 . **34** B3
Park Ave S N8 . . . . . . **49** D5
Park Ave W KT17 . . . **216** A2
Park Chase HA9 . . . . . **66** B4
Park Cl Dollis Hill NW2 . **68** B4
Ealing NW10 . . . . **88** B4
Hampton TW12 . . . . . **174** A2
Harrow HA3 . . . . **24** C2
Isleworth TW3, TW7 . **152** A6
Kensington
W14 . . . . **113** B3 **256** D6
Kingston u T KT2 . . . **176** C2
Knightsbridge SW1 . . **247** D4
North Finchley N12 . . . **30** B6
13 South Hackney E9 . . **96** C6
Wallington SM5 . . . . **218** D2
Park Cotts 2 NW1 . . **231** C6
Park Cres Enfield EN2 . **5** B3
Finchley N3 . . . . **30** A3
Harrow HA3 . . . . **24** C2
Regent's Pk
W1 . . . . **93** B3 **238** C5
Twickenham TW2 . . . **152** B3
Park Crescent Mews E
W1 . . . . **238** C5
Park Crescent Mews W
W1 . . . . **238** C5
Park Croft HA8 . . . . . . **27** A2
Parkcroft Rd SE12 . . **164** B4
Park Ct
Battersea SW11 . . . . **268** C2
2 Beckenham BR3 . . **207** D6

Park Ct continued
2 Chingford E4 . . . . . . **20** A2
Clapham Pk SW4 . . . **159** D6
Dulwich SE21 . . . . . . **161** B1
12 Hammersmith W6 **112** A2
New Barnet EN5 . . . . . **14** B4
New Malden KT3 . . . . **199** B5
North Finchley N12 . . . **30** B5
Teddington KT1 . . . . . **175** C2
Twickenham TW4 . . . **151** D6
Upper Tooting SW12 . **159** A3
Wallington SM6 . . . . **220** A3
Walthamstow E17 . . . . **53** D4
Wembley HA9 . . . . **66** A3
Wood Green N11 . . . . . **31** D3
Parkdale N11 . . . . **31** D4
Parkdale Cres KT4 . . **215** B5
Parkdale Rd SE18 . . **123** C1
Park Dr Acton W3 . . . **110** C3
Enfield N21 . . . . **17** A5
Golders Green NW11 . . **47** D1
Harrow HA2 . . . . **41** C2
Mortlake SW14 . . . . . **133** B1
Stanmore HA3 . . . . . . **24** C4
Woolwich SE7 . . . . . **144** A6
Park Dwellings 7
NW3 . . . . **70** D3
Park End
Bromley BR1 . . . . **186** D2
Hampstead NW3 . . . . . **70** C4
Parker Cl
Newham E16 . . . . **122** A5
Wallington SM5 . . . . **218** D2
Parker Ct
Shoreditch N1 . . . . . . **235** B6
South Lambeth SW8 . **270** A1
Wimbledon SW19 . . . **179** A3
Parke Rd
Barnes SW13 . . . . . . **134** A4
Sunbury TW16 . . . . . **194** A5
Parker Ho 4 SE18 . . . **122** D1
Parker Mews WC2 . . **240** B2
Parker Rd CR0 . . . . . **221** A4
Parkers Rd N10 . . . . . **30** C2
Parkers Row 15
SE16 . . . . **118** A4
Parker's Row SE1 . . **253** D1
Parker St
Newham E16 . . . . **122** A5
St Giles WC2 . . **94** A1 **240** B2
Park Farm Cl
East Finchley N2 . . . . . **48** A6
Pinner HA5 . . . . **40** B4
Park Farm Ct UB3 . . **105** C6
Park Farm Rd
Bromley BR1 . . . . **187** D2
Kingston u T KT2 . . . **176** C4
Parkfield 3 TW7 . . . . **130** C4
Parkfield Ave
Feltham TW13 . . . . . **150** A1
Harrow HA2 . . . . **24** A1
Hillingdon UB10 . . . . . **82** D4
Mortlake SW14 . . . . . **133** C1
Northolt UB5 . . . . **84** D5
Parkfield Cl
Edgware HA8 . . . . **26** D4
Northolt UB5 . . . . **85** A5
Parkfield Cres
Feltham TW13 . . . . . **150** A1
Harrow HA2 . . . . **24** A1
Ruislip HA4 . . . . **63** A5
Parkfield Ct SE14 . . . **141** B4
Parkfield Dr UB5 . . . . **84** D5
Parkfield Gdns HA2 . . **41** D6
Parkfield Ho 2
N8 . . . . **23** D2
Parkfield Ind Est
SW11 . . . . **137** A3
Parkfield Par TW13 . . **150** A1
Parkfield Prim Sch
NW4 . . . . **46** B2
Parkfield Rd
Feltham TW13 . . . . . **150** A1
Harrow HA2 . . . . **64** A5
New Cross SE14 . . . . **141** B4
Northolt UB5 . . . . **85** A5
Uxbridge UB10 . . . . . . **60** D6
Willesden NW10 . . . . . **68** B1
Parkfields
Croydon CR0 . . . . . . **207** B3
Putney SW15 . . . . . . **134** C1
Parkfields Ave
Welsh Harp NW9 . . . . **45** B1
Wimbledon SW20 . . . **178** B1
Parkfields Cl SM5 . . . **219** A4
Parkfields Rd KT2 . . . **176** B5

Parkfield St
N1 ... 94 C5 234 B4
Parkfield Way BR2 ... 210 B4
Park Flats N6 ... 48 C2
Parkgate SE3 ... 142 D2
Park Gate Ealing W5 ... 87 D2
East Finchley N2 ... 48 B6
Southgate N21 ... 16 B4
Parkgate Ave EN4 ... 2 A4
Parkgate Cl KT2 ... 176 D4
Parkgate Cres EN4 ... 2 A4
Park Gate Ct TW12 ... 174 A5
Parkgate Gdns
SW14 ... 155 B6
Parkgate House Sch
SW11 ... 137 A1
Parkgate Mews N6 ... 49 C2
Parkgate Rd
Battersea
SW11 ... 136 C5 267 B3
Wallington SM5, SM6 ... 219 B3
Park Gates HA2 ... 63 C4
Park Gdns
Kingston u T KT2 ... 176 B5
Queensbury NW9 ... 44 D6
Park Gr Bromley BR1 ... 187 B2
Edgware HA8 ... 26 B5
Newham E15 ... 99 A6
Wood Green N11 ... 31 D3
Park Grove Rd E11 ... 76 C6
Park Hall SE10 ... 142 B5
Park Hall Rd
Dulwich SE21 ... 161 B1
East Finchley N2 ... 48 C5
Park Hall Road Trad Est
SE21 ... 161 B1
Parkham Ct BR2 ... 186 C1
Parkham St
SW11 ... 136 C4 267 A1
Parkham Way N10 ... 31 C1
Park Heights Ct 21
E14 ... 97 B1
Park High Sch HA7 ... 25 D1
Park Hill
Bromley BR1 ... 210 B5
Clapham Pk SW4 ... 159 D6
Ealing W5 ... 87 D2
Forest Hill SE23 ... 162 C3
Loughton IG10 ... 21 D6
Richmond TW10 ... 154 B5
Wallington SM5 ... 218 D2
Park Hill Cl SM5 ... 218 C3
Park Hill Ct
Croydon CR0 ... 221 C6
Ealing W5 ... 87 D2
Upper Tooting SW17 ... 158 D1
Parkhill Ho 1 SW16 ... 182 C5
Parkhill Inf Sch IG5 ... 56 C6
Park Hill Inf Sch
CR0 ... 221 C5
Parkhill Jun Sch IG5 ... 56 C6
Park Hill Jun Sch
CR0 ... 221 C5
Parkhill Rd
Chingford E4 ... 20 A4
Maitland Pk NW3 ... 70 D3
Old Bexley DA5 ... 169 B4
Sidcup DA15 ... 167 C1
Park Hill Rd
Beckenham BR2 ... 186 C1
South Croydon CR0 ... 221 C5
Wallington SM6 ... 219 B1
Park Hill Rise CR0 ... 221 D5
Park Hill Sch 17
KT2 ... 176 C3
Park Hill Wlk 10 NW3 ... 70 D3
Park Ho
8 Camberwell SE5 ... 139 B4
Finsbury Pk N4 ... 72 D6
Forest Hill SE26 ... 184 A5
35 Hackney E9 ... 74 C1
Richmond TW10 ... 154 A5
Sidcup DA14 ... 190 A5
Southgate N21 ... 16 B4
Parkholme Rd E8 ... 74 A2
Park House Gdns
TW1 ... 153 C6
Parkhouse St SE5 ... 139 B5
Park Hts NW4 ... 46 B6
Parkhurst Ct N7 ... 72 A4
Parkhurst Gdns 2
DA5 ... 169 C4
Parkhurst Rd
Bowes Pk N22 ... 32 B4
Friern Barnet N11 ... 31 A5
Little Ilford E12 ... 78 C4
Parkhurst Rd *continued*
Lower Holloway N7 ... 72 A4
Sidcup DA5 ... 169 C4
Sutton SM1 ... 218 B4
Tottenham N17 ... 34 A1
Walthamstow E17 ... 53 A5
Parkin Ho SE20 ... 184 D3
Parkinson Ct
Finsbury N1 ... 235 C1
Shoreditch EC1 ... 235 D2
Parkinson Ho 6 E9 ... 74 C1
Park La Cheam SM3 ... 217 A2
Cranford TW5 ... 128 A5
Dagenham RM6 ... 58 D3
Edmonton N9 ... 17 D1
Harrow HA2 ... 63 D5
Hayes UB4 ... 83 C3
Mayfair W1 ... 115 A6 248 A5
Mill Meads E15 ... 98 B6
Richmond TW9 ... 131 D1
South Croydon CR0 ... 221 B5
Stanmore HA7 ... 9 A1
Teddington TW11 ... 174 D4
Tottenham N17 ... 34 A3
Wallington SM5, SM6 ... 219 A3
Wembley HA9 ... 66 A4
Parkland Ct
Kensington W14 ... 244 A2
Stratford E15 ... 76 C3
Parkland Gdns 12
SW19 ... 156 D3
Parkland Gr
Ashford TW15 ... 170 C6
Hounslow TW7 ... 130 D4
Parkland Mead BR1 ... 210 D6
Parkland Rd
Ashford TW15 ... 170 C6
Woodford IG8 ... 37 B3
Wood Green N22 ... 32 B1
Parklands
Bushey WD23 ... 8 A5
East Dulwich SE22 ... 162 B6
Highgate N6 ... 49 B2
Kingston u T KT5 ... 198 B4
5 Whetstone N20 ... 14 A2
Parklands Cl
Hadley Wood EN4 ... 2 B5
Ilford IG2 ... 57 A2
Mortlake SW14 ... 155 A6
Parklands Ct TW5 ... 128 D3
Parklands Dr N3 ... 47 A6
Parklands Par TW5 ... 128 D3
Parklands Pl HA8 ... 26 B6
Parklands Rd SW16 ... 181 B5
Parklands Way KT4 ... 215 C6
Park Lane Cl N17 ... 34 A3
Park Lane Mans
CR0 ... 221 B5
Park Lane Prim Sch
HA9 ... 66 A4
PARK LANGLEY ... 208 B4
Park Lawn CR7 ... 183 A1
Parklea Cl NW9 ... 27 C2
Park Lea Ct N16 ... 51 C2
Parkleigh Ct SW19 ... 179 D1
Parkleigh Rd SW19 ... 179 D1
Parkleys KT2, TW10 ... 175 D6
Parklife Oxford St
W1 ... 238 A1
Park Lo 3 Ealing W5 ... 87 B3
North Finchley N12 ... 30 A5
11 South Hampstead
NW8 ... 70 B1
10 Wapping E1 ... 118 B5
Willesden NW2 ... 68 C4
Park Lodge Ave UB7 ... 104 B4
Park Lofts 9 SW4 ... 160 A6
Park Lorne NW8 ... 230 B1
Park Mans
Battersea SW11 ... 267 C1
Bedford Pk W6 ... 111 D3
Forest Hill SE26 ... 162 C1
Fulham SW6 ... 264 B1
5 Hendon NW4 ... 46 B4
Knightsbridge SW1 ... 247 C1
St John's Wood NW8 ... 230 A3
Vauxhall SW8 ... 270 B6
Parkmead SW15 ... 156 B5
Park Mead
Blackfen DA15 ... 168 B5
Harrow HA2 ... 63 D5
Parkmead Gdns NW7 ... 27 D4
Park Mews
Chislehurst BR7 ... 188 D4
Greenwich SE10 ... 120 D1
Hornsey N8 ... 50 A3
Park Mews *continued*
Kensal Rise W10 ... 91 A5
Stanwell TW19 ... 148 B4
Parkmore BR7 ... 188 D3
Parkmore Cl IG8 ... 37 A6
Park Nook Gdns EN2 ... 5 B6
Park Par Acton W3 ... 110 C3
Dagenham NW10 ... 89 D5
Hayes UB3 ... 83 C1
Kingsbury NW9 ... 45 B6
Park Piazza 3 SE13 ... 164 B5
Park Pl
Canary Wharf E14 ... 119 C5
Ealing W5 ... 109 D5
Gunnersbury W3 ... 110 C2
Hampton TW12 ... 174 A4
Shoreditch N1 ... 235 D6
St James
SW1 ... 115 C5 249 A4
Wembley HA9 ... 66 B4
Park Place Dr W3 ... 110 C3
Park Place Ho 8
SE10 ... 142 B6
Park Place Villas W2 ... 236 B4
Park Prim Sch E15 ... 76 D1
Park Rd
Ashford TW15 ... 170 D5
Beckenham BR3 ... 185 C3
Bromley BR1 ... 187 B2
Cheam SM3 ... 217 A2
Chipping Barnet EN5 ... 1 B1
Chislehurst BR7 ... 188 D4
Chiswick W4 ... 133 B6
Cockfosters EN4 ... 2 C1
Dagenham NW10 ... 89 C6
Ealing W7 ... 108 D6
East Finchley N2 ... 48 B6
East Molesey KT8 ... 196 A5
Edmonton N18 ... 34 A6
Feltham TW13 ... 172 D6
Hackbridge SM6 ... 219 B6
Hampton TW12 ... 174 A5
Hampton Wick KT1 ... 175 C2
Harringay N8, N15 ... 50 D5
Hayes UB4 ... 83 C2
Hendon NW4 ... 46 B3
Hornsey N8 ... 49 D4
Hounslow TW3, TW7 ... 152 A6
Ilford IG1 ... 79 B5
Isleworth TW7 ... 131 B3
Kingsbury NW9 ... 45 B2
Kingston u T KT2,
TW10 ... 176 C3
Leyton E10 ... 53 C1
Lisson Gr NW1,
NW8 ... 92 C3 237 B6
Lower Halliford TW17 ... 192 C1
Mitcham SW19 ... 180 C4
Newham E15 ... 99 A6
New Malden KT3 ... 199 B5
Osidge N14 ... 15 D4
Richmond TW10 ... 154 B5
South Norwood SE25 ... 205 C5
Sunbury TW16 ... 172 B3
Teddington TW11 ... 174 D4
Twickenham TW1 ... 153 C5
Upton Pk E6 ... 99 C6
Uxbridge UB8 ... 60 A2
Wallington SM6 ... 219 B3
Walthamstow E17 ... 53 B4
Wanstead E12 ... 77 B6
Wembley HA0 ... 66 A2
Wood Green N11 ... 31 D3
Park Rd E Acton W3 ... 111 A4
Uxbridge UB10 ... 82 A5
Park Rd N
Chiswick W4 ... 111 B1
South Acton W3 ... 110 D4
Park Ridings N8 ... 50 C6
Park Rise
Forest Hill SE23 ... 163 A3
Harrow HA3 ... 24 C2
Park Rise Rd SE23 ... 163 A3
Park Road E 11 W3 ... 110 D4
Park Road Ho 3
KT2 ... 176 C3
Park Row SE10 ... 142 B6
PARK ROYAL ... 88 D4
Park Royal NW10 ... 88 D6
Park Royal Bsns Ctr
NW10 ... 89 A3
Park Royal Metro Ctr
NW10 ... 88 D3
Park Royal Rd NW10,
W3 ... 89 A3
Park Royal Sta W5 ... 88 C3
Park S SW11 ... 268 A1
Park St James NW8 ... 230 C5
Park Sch for Girls
IG1 ... 56 D1
Park Sheen 3
SW14 ... 132 D1
Parkshot TW9 ... 132 A1
Parkside
1 Beckenham BR3 ... 185 D1
Cheam SM3 ... 217 A2
Ealing W5 ... 110 A6
East Acton W3 ... 111 C5
Finchley N3 ... 29 D3
Greenwich SE3 ... 142 D5
Hampton TW12 ... 174 A5
Hayes UB3 ... 105 C6
Hendon NW7 ... 28 A4
Sidcup DA14 ... 168 B2
Wimbledon SW19 ... 178 D6
Park Side Chigwell IG9 ... 21 B2
Dollis Hill NW2 ... 68 B4
Parkside Ave
Bromley BR1 ... 210 A5
Wimbledon SW19 ... 178 D5
Parkside Bsns Est
SE8 ... 141 A6
Parkside Cl SE20 ... 184 C3
Parkside Cres
Highbury N7 ... 72 C5
Tolworth KT5 ... 199 A3
Parkside Ct
Bowes Pk N22 ... 32 B4
2 Wanstead E11 ... 55 A3
Parkside Dr HA8 ... 10 C1
Parkside Est E9 ... 96 D6
Parkside Gdns
East Barnet EN4 ... 15 A4
Wimbledon SW19 ... 178 D6
Parkside Lo DA17 ... 125 D1
Parkside Prep Sch 2
N17 ... 33 C2
Parkside (Private) Hospl
SW19 ... 156 D1
Parkside Rd
Belvedere DA17 ... 125 D2
Hounslow TW3 ... 151 D6
Parkside St SW11 ... 268 A1
Parkside Terr N18 ... 33 B6
Parkside Way HA2 ... 42 A5
Park Sq E
NW1 ... 93 B3 238 D6
Park Square Mews
NW1 ... 238 C5
Park Sq W
NW1 ... 93 B3 238 C5
Park St
Borough The
SE1 ... 117 A5 252 B4
Croydon CR0 ... 221 A6
Mayfair W1 ... 115 A6 248 A5
Teddington TW11 ... 174 C4
Parkstead Rd SW15 ... 156 B6
Parkstone Ave N18 ... 33 D5
Parkstone Rd
5 Peckham SE15 ... 140 A3
Walthamstow E17 ... 54 A6
Park Stps W2 ... 247 B6
Park Terr
Carshalton SM5 ... 218 C5
Enfield EN3 ... 7 A5
New Malden KT4 ... 200 A1
Park The Ealing W5 ... 109 D5
Forest Hill SE23 ... 162 C3
Golders Green NW11 ... 47 D1
Highgate N6 ... 49 A3
Sidcup DA14 ... 190 A5
Wallington SM5 ... 218 D3
Parkthorne Cl HA2 ... 41 D3
Parkthorne Dr HA2 ... 41 D3
Parkthorne Rd
SW12 ... 159 D4
Park Twrs W1 ... 248 C3
Parkview UB6 ... 87 A4
Park View
Dagenham W3 ... 89 A2
Highbury N5 ... 73 A4
Kingston u T KT3 ... 199 D6
Morden SM4 ... 202 B4
Pinner HA5 ... 23 B2
Southgate N21 ... 16 B4
Wembley HA9 ... 66 D3
Willesden NW2 ... 68 C4
Yiewsley UB7 ... 104 A6
Park View Acad N15 ... 51 A5
Park View Cl SM5 ... 219 A1
Parkview Cres KT4 ... 200 C1
Park View Cres N11 ... 31 B6
Parkview Ct
Fulham SW6 ... 135 A3
Harrow HA3 ... 24 C3
Ilford IG2 ... 57 C3
Penge SE20 ... 184 B2
Twickenham TW1 ... 153 C4
Park View Ct
Colney Hatch N12 ... 30 C6
Kingsbury NW9 ... 45 A5
Wandsworth SW18 ... 157 C5
Park View Dr CR4 ... 180 B1
Park View Gdns
Hendon NW4 ... 46 D4
Redbridge IG4 ... 56 B5
Wood Green N22 ... 32 C2
Park View Ho
Chingford E4 ... 35 C5
Hampton TW12 ... 174 A5
Streatham SE24 ... 160 D5
Parkview Lo BR3 ... 207 D6
Park View Mans N4 ... 50 D2
Park View Mews 24
SW9 ... 138 B3
Parkview Rd
Chislehurst SE9 ... 166 D2
Croydon CR0 ... 206 A1
Park View Rd
Bexley DA16 ... 146 C2
Ealing W5 ... 88 A2
Finchley N3 ... 29 D2
Hillingdon UB8 ... 82 C1
Pinner HA5 ... 22 B3
Southall UB1 ... 107 C5
Tottenham N17 ... 34 A1
Tottenham N17 ... 34 B2
Willesden NW10 ... 67 D4
Park Village E
NW1 ... 93 B5 231 D3
Park Village W
NW1 ... 93 B5 231 C4
Park Villas RM6 ... 58 D3
Parkville Rd
SW6 ... 135 B5 264 C3
Park Vista SE10 ... 142 B6
Park Vista Apartments
E13 ... 98 D4
Park Walk Prim Sch
SW10 ... 136 B6 266 C5
Parkwat Cres E15 ... 76 A3
Parkway
Abbey Wood DA18 ... 125 A3
Camden Town
NW1 ... 93 B6 231 C5
Hillingdon UB10 ... 60 D1
Ilford IG3 ... 79 D5
Palmers Green N14 ... 16 A2
West Barnes SW20 ... 200 D5
Woodford IG8 ... 37 C5
Park Way
East Molesey KT8 ... 195 D6
Edgware HA8 ... 26 D2
Enfield EN2 ... 4 C3
Feltham TW14 ... 150 B4
Friern Barnet N20 ... 30 D6
Gunnersbury W3 ... 110 C2
Ruislip HA4 ... 40 A1
Temple Fortune NW11 ... 47 A4
Park Way Ct HA4 ... 39 D1
Parkway Ho SW14 ... 133 B1
Parkway Prim Sch
DA18 ... 125 A3
Parkway The
Cranford TW5 ... 128 B5
Hayes UB2, UB3, UB4,
TW5 ... 106 B3
Yeading UB4 ... 84 D2
Parkway Trad Est
TW5 ... 128 C6
Park West W2 ... 92 C1 237 B1
Park West Pl W1,
W2 ... 92 C1 237 B2
Park Wlk
Chelsea
SW10 ... 136 B6 266 C6
Highgate N6 ... 49 A2
Parkwood
Beckenham BR3 ... 185 C3
Primrose Hill NW8 ... 230 C5
Parkwood Ave KT10 ... 196 A1
Parkwood Gr TW16 ... 194 A6
Parkwood Mews N6 ... 49 B3

Parkwood Prim Sch 1 N4 ... 72 D6
Parkwood Rd
Hounslow TW7 ... 130 D4
Old Bexley DA5 ... 169 B4
Wimbledon SW19 ... 179 B5
Parliament Ct NW3 ... 70 C4
Parliament Hill NW3 .. 70 C4
Parliament Hill Mans NW5 ... 71 A4
Parliament Hill Sch NW5 ... 71 A4
Parliament Mews SW14 ... 133 A3
Parliament Sq* SW1 ... 116 A4 250 A1
Parliament St SW1 ... 116 A4 250 A2
Parliament View Apartments SE11 . 260 C4
Parma Cres SW11 .. 136 D1
Parminter Ind Est 24 E2 ... 96 B5
Parmiter St E2 ... 96 B5
Parmoor Ct EC1 ... 242 A6
Parnall Ho 11 SE19 ... 183 C6
Parnell Cl
Edgware HA8 ... 27 A6
Hammersmith W12 ... 112 B3
Parnell Ho WC1 ... 239 D2
Parnell Rd E3 ... 97 B6
Parnham Cl BR1 ... 210 D6
Parnham St E14 ... 97 A1
Parolles Rd N19 ... 49 C1
Paroma Rd DA17 ... 125 C3
Parr Cl N9 ... 34 B6
Parr Ct
Feltham TW13 ... 172 C6
Shoreditch N1 ... 235 C4
Parrington Ho 1 SW4 ... 159 D5
Parr Pl W4 ... 111 D2
Parr Rd Newham E6 ... 99 D6
Stanmore HA7 ... 26 A2
Parr's Pl TW12 ... 173 C3
Parr St N1 ... 95 B5 235 C4
Parry Ave E6 ... 100 B1
Parry Cl KT17 ... 216 A1
Parry Ho 32 E1 ... 118 B5
Parry Pl SE18 ... 122 D2
Parry Rd
South Norwood SE25 ... 205 C6
West Kilburn W10 ... 91 A4
Parry St SW8 . 138 A6 270 B6
Parsifal Coll 1 NW3 .. 69 C4
Parsifal Ho NW3 ... 69 C4
Parsifal Rd NW6 ... 69 C3
Parsley Gdns CR0 ... 206 D1
Parsloes Ave RM9 ... 81 A3
Parsloes Prim Sch RM9 ... 81 B2
Parsonage Cl UB3 ... 83 D1
Parsonage Ct WD6 ... 11 A6
Parsonage Gdns EN2 ... 5 A3
Parsonage La
Enfield EN2 ... 5 B3
Sidcup DA14 ... 191 B6
Parsonage Manorway DA17 ... 147 C6
Parsonage St E14 ... 120 A2
Parsons Cl SM1 ... 217 D5
Parsons Cres HA8 ... 10 C1
Parsons Gn SW6 ... 135 C4 265 A1
PARSONS GREEN ... 135 C4
Parsons Green La SW6 ... 135 C4 265 A2
Parsons Green Sta SW6 ... 135 C4 265 A1
Parsons Hill SE18 ... 122 C3
Parsons Ho
Paddington W2 ... 236 C5
21 Streatham SW12 . 160 A4
Parsons Lo NW6 ... 69 D1
Parsons Mead KT8 ... 196 A6
Parson's Mead CR0 . 204 D1
Parsons Rd
Edgware HA8 ... 10 C1
Newham E13 ... 99 C5
Parson St NW4 ... 46 C6
Parthenia Rd SW6 ... 135 C4 265 B1
Partingdale La NW7 .. 28 D5
Partington Cl N19 ... 49 D1
Parton Lo 14 E8 ... 73 D2
Partridge Cl
Barnet EN5 ... 12 C5
Bushey WD23 ... 8 A3
1 Newham E16 ... 99 D2
Stanmore HA7 ... 26 A6
Partridge Ct EC1 ... 241 C6
Partridge Dr BR6 ... 227 A5
Partridge Gn SE9 ... 166 C1
Partridge Ho 22 E3 ... 97 B5
Partridge Rd
8 Hampton TW12 ... 173 C4
Sidcup DA14 ... 189 C6
Partridge Sq 3 E6 ... 100 A2
Partridge Way N22 ... 32 A2
Pasadena Cl UB3 ... 106 B4
Pascall Ho SE17 ... 139 A6
Pascals Coll BR3 ... 185 C1
Pascal St SW8 ... 137 D5 269 D4
Pascoe Rd SE13 ... 164 B6
Pasley Cl SE17 ... 262 A1
Pasquier Rd E17 ... 53 A6
Passey Pl SE9 ... 166 B5
Passfield Dr E14 ... 97 D2
Passfield Ho SE18 ... 123 B2
Passfield Path 13 SE28 ... 124 B6
Passfields
Catford SE6 ... 164 A1
West Kensington W14 254 C1
Passing Alley EC1 ... 241 D5
Passingham Ho TW5 ... 129 C6
Passmore Edwards Ho N11 ... 31 D3
Passmore Gdns N11 ... 31 D4
Passmore Ho 12 N9 ... 18 A1
Passmore St SW1 ... 115 A1 258 A2
Pasters Ct EN1 ... 17 D5
Pasteur Cl NW9 ... 27 C1
Pasteur Gdns N18 ... 33 A5
Paston Cl SM6 ... 219 C5
Paston Cres SE12 ... 165 B4
Pastor Ct N6 ... 49 C3
Pastor St SE1, SE11 ... 116 D2 261 D4
Pasture Cl
Bushey WD23 ... 8 A4
Wembley HA0 ... 65 B5
Pasture Rd
Catford SE6 ... 164 D3
Dagenham RM9 ... 81 B3
Wembley HA0 ... 65 B5
Pastures Mead UB10 ... 60 C2
Pastures Path E11 ... 54 C1
Pastures The N20 ... 13 B3
Patcham Terr SW8 .. 268 D2
Patch Cl UB10 ... 82 B6
Patching Way UB4 ... 85 A2
Pat Drew Ho BR1 ... 187 C2
Patent Ho E14 ... 97 D2
Paternoster La EC4 ... 94 D1 241 D2
Paternoster Sq EC4 ... 94 D1 241 D2
Pater St W8 .. 113 C3 255 A5
Pates Manor Dr TW14 ... 149 B4
Pathfield Rd SW16 ... 181 D4
Path The SW19 ... 179 D2
Pathway Ho SW17 ... 180 D4
Pathway Lo CR4 ... 180 D2
Patience Rd SW11 ... 136 C3
Patience Villas SE13 .. 142 B2
Patio Cl SW4 ... 159 D5
Patmore Ho 9 N16 ... 73 C3
Patmore St SW8 ... 137 C4 269 B2
Patmos Rd SW9 ... 138 D4
Paton Cl E3 ... 97 C4
Paton Ho 3 SW9 ... 138 B3
Paton St EC1 ... 235 A1
Patricia Ct
Chislehurst BR7 ... 189 B2
Woolwich DA16 ... 146 B5
Patrick Coman Ho EC1 ... 234 C1
Patrick Connolly Gdns 41 E3 ... 97 D4
Patrick Rd E13 ... 99 C4
Patriot Sq E2 ... 96 B5
Patrol Pl SE6 ... 163 D5
Pat Shaw Ho 2 E1 ... 96 D3
Patshull Pl NW5 ... 71 C2
Patshull Rd NW5 ... 71 C2
Patson Cl E5 ... 74 D5
Pattenden Rd SE6 ... 163 B3
Patten Ho N4 ... 51 A1
Patten Rd SW18 ... 158 C4
Patterdale NW1 ... 231 D1
Patterdale Cl BR1 ... 186 C4
Patterdale Rd SE15 .. 140 C5
Patterson Ct SE19 ... 183 D4
Patterson Rd SE19 ... 183 D4
Pattina Wlk SE16 ... 119 A5
Pattinson Point 10 E16 ... 99 A2
Pattison Ho
Borough The SE1 ... 252 B2
1 Stepney E1 ... 96 D1
Pattison Rd NW2 ... 69 C5
Pattison Wlk SE18 ... 123 A1
Pat Williams Ho SE27 ... 161 A1
Paul Byrne Ho 3 N2 .. 48 A6
Paul Cl E15 ... 76 C1
Paul Ct
7 Edmonton N18 ... 34 A6
Hendon N3 ... 29 A1
Paul Daisley Ct 2 NW6 ... 69 A1
Paulet Rd SE5 ... 138 D4
Paul Gdns CR0 ... 221 D6
Paulhan Rd HA3 ... 43 D5
Paul Ho 13 W10 ... 91 A3
Paulin Dr N21 ... 16 C4
Pauline Cres TW2 ... 152 A3
Pauline Ho 21 E1 ... 96 A2
Paulinus Cl BR5 ... 190 C1
Paul Julius Cl E14 ... 120 B6
Paul Robeson Cl E6 .. 100 C4
Paulson Ho 7 IG11 ... 78 D1
Paul St
Broadgate EC2 ... 95 C3 243 A6
Newham E15 ... 98 C6
Paultons Ho SW3 ... 266 D6
Paultons Sq SW3 ... 136 B6 266 D6
Paultons St SW3 ... 136 B6 266 D5
Pauntley Ho 6 N19 ... 49 C1
Pauntley St 4 N19 ... 49 C1
Pavan Ct 29 E2 ... 96 C4
Paved Ct 9 TW9 ... 153 D6
Paveley Ct NW7 ... 28 D3
Paveley Dr SW11 ... 136 C5 267 A3
Paveley Ho N1 ... 233 C3
Paveley St NW8 ... 92 C3 237 B6
Pavement Mews 1 RM6 ... 58 D2
Pavement Sq CR0 ... 206 A1
Pavement The
Brentford W5 ... 110 A3
Clapham SW4 ... 137 C1
Leytonstone E11 ... 54 A1
11 West Norwood SE27 ... 183 A6
Pavet Cl RM10 ... 81 D2
Pavilion Ct
Dagenham RM9 ... 103 A6
7 Hampstead NW3 ... 70 A4
Hampstead NW3 ... 70 B3
3 Paddington NW6 ... 91 C4
5 South Norwood SW16 ... 182 B3
3 Wimbledon SW19 . 179 A3
Pavilion L Ctr The BR1 ... 187 A1
Pavilion Lo HA2 ... 42 B1
Pavilion Mans 10 SW9 ... 138 B1
Pavilion Mews N3 ... 29 C1
Pavilion Rd
Knightsbridge SW1 ... 114 D3 257 D5
Redbridge IG1 ... 56 B2
Pavilion Sq SW17 ... 158 D1
Pavilion St SW1 ... 257 D5
Pavilions The BR3 ... 185 C4
Pavilion Terr
Ilford IG2 ... 57 C4
8 North Kensington W12 ... 90 C1
Pavilion Way
Burnt Oak HA8 ... 27 A3
Pavilion Way *continued*
Ruislip HA4 ... 62 C6
Pavillion Ct SW1 ... 268 C6
Pavitt Ct NW10 ... 68 A1
Pawleyne Cl SE20 ... 184 C3
Pawsey Cl E13 ... 99 A6
Pawson's Rd CR0 ... 205 A4
Paxford Rd HA0 ... 65 B6
Paxton Cl
Richmond TW9 ... 132 B3
Walton-on-T KT12 ... 194 C2
Paxton Ct
1 Forest Hill SE26 .. 185 A6
Grove Pk SE9 ... 165 C1
Mitcham CR4 ... 180 D1
Paxton Ho SE17 ... 262 B2
Paxton Pl SE27 ... 183 C6
Paxton Prim Sch 14 SE19 ... 183 C4
Paxton Rd
Chiswick W4 ... 133 C6
Forest Hill SE23 ... 163 A1
Plaistow BR1 ... 187 A3
Tottenham N17 ... 34 A3
Paxton Terr SW1 ... 268 D6
Paymal Ho 33 E1 ... 96 C2
Payne Cl IG11 ... 79 D1
Payne Ho N1 ... 233 D5
Paynell Ct SE3 ... 142 C2
Payne Rd E3 ... 97 D5
Paynesfield Ave SW14 ... 133 B2
Paynesfield Rd WD23 .. 8 D4
Payne St SE8 ... 141 B6
Paynes Wlk W6 ... 135 A6 264 A5
Payzes Gdns IG8 ... 36 D5
Peabody Ave SW1 ... 115 B1 258 D1
Peabody Bldgs
6 Camberwell SE5 ... 139 B4
Walworth SE17 ... 262 C3
Peabody Cl
Croydon CR0 ... 206 C1
SW1 ... 268 D6
Peabody Cotts N17 ... 33 C2
Peabody Ct
9 Camberwell SE5 ... 139 B4
25 Enfield EN3 ... 7 C6
St Luke's EC1 ... 242 B5
Peabody Est
18 Bethnal Green E2 ... 96 B5
Borough The SE1 ... 252 A3
Fulham SW6 . 135 B6 264 D6
17 Hammersmith W6 112 C1
Holborn EC1 ... 241 B5
Lambeth SE1 ... 251 B3
North Kensington W10 . 90 C2
4 Ratcliff E1 ... 118 D6
7 St George in t East E1 ... 118 A6
St Luke's EC1 ... 242 B5
Strand WC2 ... 240 C1
Streatham SE24 ... 161 A4
Westminster SW1 ... 259 B4
Peabody Hill SE21 ... 161 A3
Peabody Sq SE1 ... 251 C1
Peabody Twr EC1 ... 242 B5
Peabody Yd N1 ... 235 A6
Peace Cl
East Barnet N14 ... 15 B6
Greenford UB6 ... 86 B6
South Norwood SE25 . 205 C5
Peace Ct 10 NW9 ... 46 A5
Peace Gr HA9 ... 66 D5
Peacehaven Ct 8 N10 ... 31 A3
Peace Pagoda* SW3 ... 267 D4
Peace St SE18 ... 144 C6
Peach Ct E4 ... 35 C6
Peaches Cl SM2 ... 217 A1
Peaches Ct SM2 ... 217 A1
Peach Gr E11 ... 76 B5
Peach Rd
Feltham TW14 ... 150 A3
London W10 ... 91 A4
Peach Tree Ave UB7 ... 82 B1
Peachum Rd SE3 ... 142 D6
Peach Walk Mews 24 E3 ... 96 D5
Peacock Ave TW14 ... 149 B3
Peacock Cl
Dagenham RM8 ... 80 C6
Finchley NW7 ... 29 A5
Walthamstow E4 ... 35 B3
Peacock Ct EN1 ... 17 C5
Peacock Ind Est N17 ... 33 D3
Peacock St SE17 ... 116 D2 261 D3
Peacock Wlk E16 ... 99 B1
Peacock Yd SE17 ... 261 D3
Peaketon Ave IG4 ... 55 D4
Peak Hill SE26 ... 184 C6
Peak Hill Ave SE26 ... 184 C6
Peak Hill Gdns SE26 ... 184 C6
Peak Ho N4 ... 51 A1
Peak The SE26 ... 162 C1
Peal Gdns W13 ... 87 A3
Peall Rd CR0 ... 204 B3
Peall Rd Ind Est CR0 . 204 B3
Pearce Cl 2 CR4 ... 181 A1
Pearcefield Ave 5 SE23 ... 162 C3
Pearce Ho
Camden Town N19 ... 71 C5
7 Streatham SW2 ... 160 A4
Westminster SW1 ... 259 D3
Pear Cl Kingsbury NW9 . 45 B5
New Cross Gate SE14 141 A5
Pearcroft Rd E11 ... 76 B6
Pear Ct 21 SE15 ... 139 D5
Peardon St SW8 ... 137 B3
Peareswood Gdns HA7 ... 25 D2
Pearfield Ho 1 N5 ... 73 A3
Pearfield Rd SE23 ... 163 A1
Pearing Cl 2 KT4 ... 216 D6
Pearl Cl Hendon NW2 .. 46 D2
Newham E6 ... 100 C1
Pearl Ct 18 NW9 ... 46 A5
Pearl Rd E17 ... 53 C6
Pearl St E1 ... 118 B5
Pearlstones Ct RM10 ... 103 C6
Pearmain Cl TW17 .. 192 D4
Pearmain Ho 9 SE13 ... 142 A3
Pearman St SE1 ... 116 C4 251 B1
Pear Pl SE1 ... 251 A2
Pear Rd E11 ... 76 C5
Pears Ave TW17 ... 193 C6
Pearscroft Ct SW6 ... 135 D4 265 D1
Pearscroft Rd SW6 ... 135 D4 265 D1
Pearse St 3 SE15 ... 139 C6
Pearson Cl Barnet EN5 . 1 D2
4 Camberwell SE5 .. 139 A4
Pearson Ct SM4 ... 201 D4
Pearson Ho SW15 ... 134 C3
Pearson's Ave SE8, SE14 ... 141 C4
Pearson St E2 ... 95 D5
Pearson Way CR4 ... 181 A2
Pears Rd TW3 ... 130 A2
Peartree Ave SW17 ... 158 A1
Pear Tree Ave UB7 ... 82 B1
Peartree Cl BR2 ... 209 D4
Pear Tree Cl
Chessington KT9 ... 214 C3
Mitcham CR4 ... 180 C1
23 Shoreditch E2 ... 95 D6
Pear Tree Ct
Holborn EC1 ... 241 B5
Putney SW15 ... 134 B1
Woodford IG8 ... 37 B2
Peartree Gdns RM8 ... 80 B4
Pear Tree Ho
Brockley SE4 ... 141 B1
Hayes UB8 ... 83 A1
Peartree La E1 ... 118 C6
Peartree Rd EN1 ... 5 C2
Pear Tree Rd TW15 ... 171 A5
Peartree St EC1 ... 95 A3 242 A6
Peartree Way SE10 ... 121 A2
Peary Ho 4 NW10 ... 67 B1
Peary Pl E2 ... 96 C4
Peaslake Ct SM2 ... 218 A1
Peas Mead Terr E4 ... 36 A6
Peatfield Cl DA15 ... 167 C1
Pebworth Lo
2 Belmont SM2 ... 217 D1
South Norwood SE25 . 205 D5
Pebworth Rd HA1 ... 65 A6
Peckarmans Wood SE21, SE26 ... 162 A1
Peckett Sq 3 N5 ... 72 D4
Peckford Pl SW9 ... 138 C3
PECKHAM ... 140 A4

Peckham Gr SE15...139 C5
Peckham High St
SE15...140 A4
Peckham Hill St
SE15...140 A5
Peckham Park Prim Sch
25 SE15...140 A5
Peckham Park Rd
SE15...140 A5
Peckham Rd SE5...139 C4
Peckham Rye
East Dulwich SE22...140 A1
Peckham SE15, SE22...140 B1
Peckham Rye Sta
SE15...140 A3
Peckwater Ho 2
NW5...71 D2
Peckwater St NW5...71 C3
Pedlars Wlk N7...72 A3
Pedley Rd RM8...58 C1
Pedley St E1...95 D3 243 D5
Pedro St E5...74 D4
Pedworth Gdns 4
SE16...118 C2
Peebles Ct UB1...86 A1
Peek Cres SW19...178 D5
Peel Centre
(Metropolitan Police
Training
Establishment)
NW9...45 D6
Peel Cl Chingford E4...19 D2
Edmonton N9...18 A1
Peel Ct UB6...86 A4
Peel Dr Colindale NW9...45 D6
Redbridge IG5...56 A6
Peel Gr E2...96 C5
Peel Pass W8...245 A3
Peel Pl IG5...37 D1
Peel Prec NW6...91 C5
Peel Rd
Farnborough BR6...227 A3
Harrow HA3...42 D6
Wembley HA0, HA9...65 D5
Woodford E18...36 D2
Peel St W8...113 C5 245 A3
Peel Way UB8...82 A2
Peel Yates Ho 13
SE7...122 A2
Peerglow Est EN3...18 C6
Peerless St
EC1...95 B4 235 C1
Pegamoid Rd N18...18 C1
Pegasus Cl N16...73 B4
Pegasus Ct
11 Acton W3...89 A1
Brentford TW8...110 B1
6 Buckhurst Hill IG9...21 D2
College Pk NW10...90 B4
Edmonton N21...17 A4
Harrow HA3...43 D4
Kingston u T KT1...197 D6
Sutton SM1...217 D6
Pegasus Ho 9 E1...96 D3
Pegasus Lo N21...17 A4
Pegasus Pl 2 SE11...138 C6
Pegasus Rd CR0,
CR9...220 C2
Pegasus Way N11...31 B4
Peggotty Way UB8...82 D1
Pegg Rd TW5...128 D5
Peggy Quirke Ct 2
HA0...66 A2
Pegley Gdns SE12...165 A2
Pegwell Ho 19 E5...74 B3
Pegwell St SE18...145 C5
Pekin St E14...97 C1
Pekoe SE1...253 D3
Peldon Ct TW10...154 B6
Pele Ct N17...33 B3
Pelham Ave IG11...101 D6
Pelham Cl SE5...139 C2
Pelham Cotts DA5...169 D3
Pelham Cres SW7...257 A3
Pelham Ct SW3...257 A3
Pelham Ho W14...254 C3
Pelham Pl
Chelsea SW7...257 A3
8 Ealing W7...86 D3
Pelham Prim Sch
Bexleyheath DA7...147 C2
15 Merton SW19...179 C3
Pelham Rd
Bexleyheath DA7...147 C2
Ilford IG1...79 B6
Merton SW19...179 C3
Pelham Rd *continued*
Penge BR3, SE20...184 C1
Tottenham N15...51 D5
Wanstead E18...55 B6
Wood Green N22...32 C1
Pelham St
SW7...114 B2 256 D4
Pelican Ho 8 SE8...119 B2
Pelican Pas 3 E1...96 C3
Pelier St SE17...139 A6
Pelinore Rd SE6...164 C2
Pella Ho SE11...260 D2
Pellant Rd
SW6...135 A5 264 B4
Pellatt Gr N22...32 C2
Pellatt Rd
East Dulwich SE22...161 D6
Wembley HA9...66 A6
Pellerin Rd N16...73 C3
Pellew Ho 15 E1...96 B3
Pellings Cl BR2...208 C6
Pelling St E14...97 C1
Pellipar Cl N13...16 C1
Pellipar Gdns SE18...122 B1
Pellipar Rd SE18...122 B1
Pellow Cl EN5...13 B5
Pelly Ct 4 E17...54 A5
Pelly Rd E13...99 A5
Pelter St E2...95 D4
Pelton Ct CR2...221 A2
Pelton Rd SE10...120 C1
Pembar Ave E17...53 A6
Pemberley Chase
KT19...214 D3
Pemberley Cl KT19...214 D3
Pemberley Ho KT19...214 D3
Pember Rd NW10...90 D4
Pemberton Cl TW19...148 A3
Pemberton Ct 18 E1...96 D4
Pemberton Gdns
Camden Town N19...71 C5
Dagenham RM6...59 A4
Pemberton Ho SE26...184 A6
Pemberton Pl
Esher KT10...212 A5
2 Hackney E8...74 B1
Pemberton Rd
East Molesey KT8...196 A5
Harringay N4...50 D4
Pemberton Row EC4...241 B2
Pemberton Terr N19...71 C5
Pembridge Ave TW4...151 B3
Pembridge Cres
W11...113 C6 245 A6
Pembridge Gdns
W2...113 C6 245 A5
Pembridge Hall Prep Sch
for Girls
W2...113 C6 245 B5
Pembridge Mews
W11...113 C6 245 A6
Pembridge Pl
Notting Hill
W2...113 C6 245 B6
1 Wandsworth
SW15...157 C6
Pembridge Rd
W11...113 C6 245 A5
Pembridge Sq
W2...113 C6 245 B5
Pembridge Villas
W11...113 C6 245 A6
Pembroke W14...254 D3
Pembroke Ave
Enfield EN1...6 B4
Harrow HA3...43 B6
Islington N1...94 A6 233 B6
Surbiton KT5...198 D4
Pembroke Bldgs
NW10...90 A4
Pembroke Cl SW1...248 B1
Pembroke Ct 11 W7...86 D2
Pembroke Gdns
Dagenham RM10...81 D5
West Kensington
W8...113 B2 254 D4
Pembroke Gdns Cl
W8...255 A5
Pembroke Hall NW4...46 C6
Pembroke Ho
Acton W3...111 A4
Chelsea SW1...258 A5
5 Clapham Pk SW2...160 A6
17 Kensington W2...91 D1
Putney SW15...156 A6
Upper Tooting SW17...180 B5
Pembroke Lo 2
SW16...160 B1
Pembroke Mews
8 Bow E3...97 A4
Kensington W8...255 A5
Muswell Hill N10...31 A2
Pembroke Pl
Edgware HA8...26 C3
Isleworth TW7...130 C3
Kensington W8...255 A5
Pembroke Rd
Bromley BR1...187 D1
Edmonton N13...17 A1
Greenford UB6...85 D3
Hornsey N8...50 A5
Ilford IG3...57 D2
Kensington
W8...113 C2 255 A4
Mitcham CR4...181 A1
Muswell Hill N10...31 A3
Newham E6...100 B2
Ruislip HA4...39 D1
South Norwood SE25...205 C5
South Tottenham N15...51 D4
Walthamstow E17...53 D4
Wembley HA9...65 D5
Pembroke Sq
W8...113 C3 255 A5
Pembroke St
N1...94 A6 233 B6
Pembroke Studios
W8...254 D5
Pembroke Terr NW8...229 C5
Pembroke Villas
Kensington W8...255 A4
Richmond TW9...131 D1
Pembroke Way UB3...105 A3
Pembroke Wlk W8...255 A4
Pembry Cl SW9...138 C4
Pembury Ave KT4...200 A2
Pembury Cl
Hackney E5...74 B3
Hayes BR2...208 D2
Pembury Cres DA14...169 A2
Pembury Ct UB3...127 B6
Pembury Ho
Camberwell SE5...139 C3
Keston Mark BR2...210 A1
Pembury Pl 15 E5, E8...74 B3
Pembury Rd
Croydon SE25...206 A5
Erith DA7...147 A6
Hackney E5...74 B3
Tottenham N17...33 D1
Pemdevon Rd CR0...204 C2
Pemell Cl 30 E1...96 C3
Pemell Ho 31 E1...96 C3
Pemerich Cl UB3...105 D1
Pempath Pl HA9...65 D6
Penair Lodge HA1...64 C5
Penally Pl N1...235 D6
Penang St E1...118 B5
Penard Rd UB2...107 D3
Penarth Ct SM2...218 A1
Penarth Ctr The
SE15...140 C6
Penarth St SE15...140 C6
Penates KT10...212 B4
Penberth Rd SE6...164 A3
Penbury Rd UB2...107 B1
Penceat Ct SE20...184 C1
Pencombe Mews
W11...244 D6
Pencraig Way SE15...140 B6
Pendall Cl EN4...2 C1
Penda Rd DA8...147 D5
Pendarves Rd SW20...178 C2
Penda's Mead E9...75 A4
Pendell Ave UB3...127 D5
Pendennis Ho 15
SE8...119 A2
Pendennis Rd
Streatham SW16...182 A6
Tottenham N17...51 B6
Penderel Rd TW3...151 C6
Penderry Rise SE6...164 B2
Penderyn Way N7...71 D4
Pendlebury Ho 5
SE18...144 A4
Pendle Ho 13 SE26...162 A1
Pendle Rd SW16...181 B5
Pendlestone Rd E17...53 D4
Pendlewood Cl 13
W5...87 C2
Pendley Ho 18 E2...96 A6
Pendolino Way NW10...66 D1
Pendragon Rd BR1...165 A1
Pendragon Sch BR1...165 A1
Pendragon Wlk NW9...45 C3
Pendrell Ho WC2...239 D1
Pendrell Rd SE4...141 A3
Pendrell St SE18...145 B6
Pendula Dr UB4...84 D3
Penelope Ho 20
SW9...138 C4
Penerley Rd SE6...163 D3
Penfield Lo 7 W9...91 C2
Penfields Ho N7...72 A2
Penfold Cl CR0...220 C5
Penfold Ct 7 CR4...181 A1
Penfold Ho 14 SE18...144 D6
Penfold La DA5...168 D3
Penfold Pl
NW1...92 C2 237 A4
Penfold Rd N9...18 D3
Penfold St
NW8...92 B3 236 D5
Penford Gdns SE9...143 D2
Penford St SE5...138 D3
Pengarth Rd DA5...168 D5
PENGE...184 D4
Penge East Sta
SE20...184 C4
Penge La SE20...184 D3
Penge Rd
Newham E13...99 C6
South Norwood SE25...206 A6
Penge West Sta
SE20...184 B4
Penhall Rd SE7...121 D2
Penhill Rd DA5...168 C4
Penhurst Mans SW6...264 C2
Penifather La UB6...86 B4
Peninsula Ct E14...119 D3
Peninsular Cl TW14...149 C5
Peninsular Park Rd
SE7...121 A2
Penistone Rd SW16...182 A3
Penketh Dr HA1...64 B5
Penmayne Ho SE11...261 B2
Penmon Rd SE2...124 A3
Pennack Rd SE15...139 D6
Penn Almshouses 1
SE10...142 A4
Pennant Mews
W8...113 D2 255 C4
Pennant Terr E17...35 B1
Pennard Mans 5
W12...112 C4
Pennard Rd W12...112 C4
Pennards The TW16...194 C6
Penn Cl
Greenford UB6...85 D5
Harrow HA3...43 C5
Penn Ct NW9...45 B6
Pennefather Ho N1...73 B2
Pennells Ct TW5...129 C6
Penner Cl SW19...157 A2
Penners Gdns KT6...198 A2
Pennethorne Cl E9...96 C6
Pennethorne Ho
SW11...136 B2
Pennethorne Rd
SE15...140 B5
Penn Gdns BR7...188 D1
Penn Ho
7 Edmonton N9...18 A1
Lisson Gr NW8...237 A5
Pennine Dr NW2...68 D6
Pennine La NW2...69 A6
Pennine Mans NW2...69 A6
Pennine Par NW2...69 A6
Pennine Way UB7...127 B5
Pennington Cl 10
SE27...183 B6
Pennington Ct
4 Rotherhithe
SE16...119 A5
23 St George in t East
E1...118 A6
Pennington Dr N21...16 A6
Pennington Lo 18
KT5...198 A4
Pennington St E1...118 B6
Pennington Way
SE12...165 B2
Penniston Cl N17...33 A1
Penniwell Cl HA8...26 B6
Penn La Bexley DA5...168 D5
Sidcup DA5...169 A5
Penn Rd N7...72 A4
Penn St N1...95 B6 235 D5
Penny Ct SW10...266 B6
Pennyfields E14...119 C6
Pennyford Ct NW8...236 C6
Penny La TW17...193 C2
Penny Mews SW12...159 B4
Pennymore Wlk W9...91 B3
Penny Rd NW10...88 D4
Penny Royal SM6...219 D2
Pennyroyal Ave E6...100 C1
Penpoll Rd E8...74 B2
Penpool La DA16...146 B2
Penray EN5...1 A2
Penrhyn Ave E17...35 C2
Penrhyn Cres
Mortlake SW14...133 A1
Walthamstow E17...35 C2
Penrhyn Gdns KT1...197 D5
Penrhyn Gr E17...35 C2
Penrhyn Rd KT1...198 A6
Penrith Cl
Beckenham BR3...185 D2
Putney SW15...157 A6
Penrith Pl SE27...160 D2
Penrith Rd
New Malden KT3...199 B5
South Norwood CR7...183 A1
Tottenham N15...51 B4
Penrith St SW16...181 C4
Penrose Gr
SE17...117 A1 262 A1
Penrose Ho
Camberwell SE17...262 A1
Southgate N21...16 B6
Penrose St
SE17...117 A1 262 A1
Penryn Ho SE11...261 C2
Penryn St
NW1...93 D5 232 C4
Penry St SE1...263 B3
Pensbury Pl SW8...137 C3
Pensbury St SW8...137 C3
Pensford Ave TW9...132 C3
Penshurst 2 NW5...71 A2
Penshurst Ave DA15...168 A5
Penshurst Ct
Croydon CR2...220 D1
1 Edgware HA8...26 D5
Penshurst Gdns HA8...26 D5
Penshurst Gn BR2...208 D4
Penshurst Ho 1
SE15...140 C6
Penshurst Rd
Erith DA7...147 B4
Homerton E9...74 D1
Thornton Heath CR7...204 D4
Tottenham N17...33 D3
Penshurst Way SM2...217 C1
Penshurst Wlk 4
BR2...208 D4
Pensilver Cl EN4...2 C1
Penstemon Cl N3...29 C4
Pentavia Retail Pk
NW7...27 D3
Pentelow Gdns
TW14...150 A5
Pentire Rd E17...36 B2
Pentland Ave
Edgware HA8...10 D2
Littleton TW17...192 C4
Pentland Cl
Cricklewood NW11...69 A6
Lower Edmonton N9...18 C2
Pentland Gdns
SW18...158 A5
Pentland Ho
17 Camden Town
NW5...71 A2
7 Stamford Hill N16...51 D1
Pentland Pl UB5...85 A6
Pentland Rd
Bushey WD23...8 A5
1 Maida Vale NW6...91 C4
Pentlands BR3...186 A2
Pentlands Cl CR4...203 B6
Pentland St SW18...158 A5
Pentland Way UB10...61 A5
Pentlow St SW15...134 C2
Pentney Rd
5 Chingford E4...20 B3
Merton SW19, SW20...179 A2
Streatham SW12...159 C3
Penton Gr N1...234 A3

Penton Ho
3 Abbey Wood SE2 124 D4
Islington N1 234 A3
Sutton SM2 218 A1
Penton Pl SE17 116 D1 261 D2
Penton Rise WC1 94 B4 233 D2
Penton St N1 94 C5 234 A3
PENTONVILLE 94 B5
Pentonville Rd WC1 94 B5 233 C3
Pentrich Ave EN1 6 A5
Pentridge St SE15 139 D5
Pentyre Ave N18 33 B5
Penwerris Ave TW5, TW7 130 A5
Penwerris Ct TW7 130 A5
Penwith Rd SW18 157 D2
Penwood Ct HA5 41 B5
Penwood Ho SW15 155 D5
Penwortham Ct 1 N22 32 C1
Penwortham Prim Sch SW17 181 B4
Penwortham Rd SW16 181 C4
Penylan Pl HA8 26 C3
Penywern Rd SW5 113 C1 255 B2
Penzance Ho SE11 261 B2
Penzance Pl W11 113 A5 244 B4
Penzance St W11 113 A5 244 A4
Peony Ct IG8 36 C3
Peony Gdns W12 112 A6
Peperfield WC1 233 C1
Pepler Ho 17 W10 91 A3
Pepler Mews SE1 263 C1
Peploe Rd NW6 90 D5
Pepper Cl E6 100 B2
Peppercorn Cl CR7 183 B1
Peppermead Sq SE13 163 C6
Peppermint Cl CR0 204 A2
Peppermint Pl 7 E11 76 C5
Pepper St
Borough The SE1 252 A2
Millwall E14 119 D3
Peppie Cl N16 73 C6
Pepys Cl UB10 60 D4
Pepys Cres
Barnet EN5 12 C6
2 Newham E16 121 A5
Pepys Ct SW20 178 C1
Pepys Ent Ctr 13 SE8 119 B2
Pepys Ho
14 Bethnal Green E2 96 C4
Clapham Pk SW4 159 D6
Pepys Rd
New Cross Gate SE14 140 D3
Wimbledon SW20 178 C2
Pepys Rise BR6 211 D1
Pepys St EC3 117 C6 253 B6
Perak Ct KT5 199 A2
Peralte Terr CR4 204 A5
Perceval Ave NW3 70 C3
Perceval Ct UB5 63 C3
Percheron Cl TW7 130 D2
Percheron Ct 3 SW9 138 B2
Percheron Rd WD6 11 B5
Perch St E8 73 D4
Percival Ct N17 33 D3
Percival Gdns RM6 58 C3
Percival Ho 3 IG8 37 A6
Percival Rd Enfield EN1 5 D1
Feltham TW13 149 D2
Mortlake SW14 133 A1
Orpington BR6 226 D6
Percival St EC1 94 D4 234 D1
Percival Way KT19 215 B4
Percy Ave TW15 170 C5
Percy Bilton Ct TW5 129 D4
Percy Bryant Rd TW16 171 C3
Percy Bush Rd UB7 104 B3
Percy Cir WC1 94 B4 233 D2
Percy Ct 1 KT5 198 B3
Percy Gdns
Enfield EN3 18 D6
Hayes UB4 83 C4
5 Isleworth TW7 131 A2
New Malden KT4 199 C1
Percy Ho 4 SW16 181 C6
Percy Laurie Ho 6 SW15 134 D1
Percy Mews W1 239 C3
Percy Pas W1 239 C3
Percy Rd
Bexleyheath DA7 147 A3
Carshalton CR4 203 A2
Croydon SE25 206 A4
Edmonton N21 17 A4
Hampton TW12 173 C3
Ilford IG3 58 A2
Isleworth TW7 131 A1
Leytonstone E11 54 C2
Newham E16 98 C2
North Finchley N12 30 A5
Penge SE20 184 D2
Romford RM7 59 D6
Shepherd's Bush W12 112 A4
Twickenham TW2 152 A3
Percy St W1 93 D2 239 C3
Percy Terr BR1 210 D6
Percy Way TW2 152 A3
Peregrine Cl NW10 67 B3
Peregrine Ct
Bexley DA16 145 D4
Streatham SW16 182 B6
Peregrine Gdns CR0 223 A6
Peregrine Ho
6 Battersea SW11 136 C2
Finsbury EC1 234 D2
Peregrine Rd
Sunbury TW16 171 D1
Tottenham N17 33 B3
Peregrine Way SW19, SW20 178 C3
Perham Rd W14 113 A1 254 B1
Peridot St E6 100 A2
Perifield SE21 161 A3
Perimeade Rd UB6 87 C5
Period Wks E10 53 A1
Periton Rd SE9 143 D1
PERIVALE 87 B5
Perivale UB6 86 D5
Perivale Gdns W13 87 B3
Perivale Grange UB6 87 A4
Perivale Ind Pk UB6 87 B5
Perivale La UB6 87 A4
Perivale Lo UB6 87 A4
Perivale New Bsns Ctr UB6 87 C5
Perivale Pk Athletics Tk UB6 86 C4
Perivale Prim Sch UB6 87 C5
Perivale Sta UB6 87 A5
Periwood Cres UB6 87 A6
Perkin Cl
Hounslow TW3 129 D1
Wembley HA0 65 B3
Perkins Ct TW15 170 B5
Perkins Ho 15 E14 97 B2
Perkins Rd IG2 57 B4
Perkins Rents SW1 259 C5
Perkins Sq SE1 252 B4
Perks Cl SE3 142 C2
Perley Ho 9 E3 97 B2
Perotti Ho SW6 135 D2
Perpins Rd SE9 167 C5
Perran Rd SE24, SW2 160 D2
Perren St NW5 71 B2
Perrers Rd W6 112 B2
Perrin Cl TW15 170 B5
Perrin Ct TW15 170 C6
Perring Est E3 97 C2
Perrin Grange HA9 66 B6
Perrin Rd HA0 65 B4
Perrins Ct HA3 44 B2
Perrin's Ct 20 NW3 70 A4
Perrin's La NW3 70 A4
Perrin's Wlk NW3 70 A4
Perronet Ho SE1 261 D5
Perry Ave W3 89 B1
Perry Cl UB8 82 D1
Perry Ct
6 Isle of Dogs E14 119 C1
2 Kingston u T KT2 176 A1
Perry Ct *continued*
Sutton SM1 217 C3
2 Tottenham N15 51 C3
Perryfield Way
Richmond TW10 153 B2
West Hendon NW9 45 D3
Perry Garth UB5 84 C6
Perry Gdns N9 17 C1
Perry Hall Prim Sch BR6 211 D3
Perry Hill SE6 163 B1
Perry Ho 24 SW2 160 A4
Perry How KT4 199 D1
Perryman Ho
Barking IG11 101 A6
Tottenham N17 34 B3
Perrymans Farm Rd IG2 57 B4
Perry Mead
Bushey WD23 8 A5
Enfield EN2 4 D3
Perrymead St SW6 135 D4 265 C1
Perrymount Prim Sch 5 SE23 162 D2
Perryn Ct 1 TW1 153 A4
Perryn Ho W3 111 C6
Perryn Rd Acton W3 111 B6
1 Bermondsey SE16 118 B3
Perry Rd RM9 103 B2
Perry Rise SE23 163 A1
Perry's Pl W1 239 C2
Perry St BR7 189 C4
Perry Street Gdns BR7 189 C4
Perry Vale SE23 162 D2
Perrywood Ho 17 E5 74 B3
Persant Rd SE6 164 C2
Perseverance Pl SW9 138 C5
Perseverance Works 17 E2 95 C4
Pershore Cl IG2 56 D4
Pershore Gr SM5 202 B3
Pershore Ho 11 W13 109 A5
Pert Cl N10 31 B4
Perth Ave Hayes UB4 84 C3
Kingsbury NW9 45 B2
Perth Cl Northolt UB5 63 C3
Wimbledon SW20 178 A1
Perth Ct 5 SE5 139 B1
Perth Ho 12 Acton W3 88 C1
Barnsbury N1 72 B1
Perth Rd
Barking IG11 101 B6
Beckenham BR3 186 A1
Finsbury Pk N4 50 C1
Ilford IG2 56 D3
Newham E13 99 B5
Tottenham N22 32 D2
Walthamstow E10 53 B1
Perth Terr IG2 57 A2
Perwell Ave HA2 41 B1
Perystreete SE23 162 C2
Petavel Rd TW11 174 C4
Petchey Acad The E8 73 D3
Peter Ave NW10 68 B1
Peter Best Ho 1 E1 96 B1
Peterboat Cl SE10 120 C2
Peterborough Ct EC4 241 B1
Peterborough Gdns IG1 56 A2
Peterborough Mews SW6 135 C3
Peterborough Rd
Carshalton SM5 202 C3
Fulham SW6 135 C2
Harrow HA1 42 D2
Leytonstone E10 54 B3
Peterborough & St Margarets High Sch HA7 8 C1
Peterborough Villas SW6 265 C2
Peter Bradley Ct RM9 81 B1
Peter Butler Ho 9 SE1 118 A4
Peterchurch Ho SE15 140 B6
Peter Fagan Ho UB3 105 C3
Petergate SW11 136 A1
Peterhead Ct 12 UB1 86 A1
Peter Heathfield Ho 4 E15 98 B6
Peter Hills Ho 6 SE16 118 A2
Peter Hills Sch 29 SE16 118 D5
Peter Ho SW8 270 A4
Peter James Bsns Ctr UB3 106 A4
Peter James Ent Ctr NW10 89 A4
Peter Kennedy Ct CR0 207 B3
Peterley Bsns Ctr 21 E2 96 B5
Peter Lyell Ct HA4 62 B6
Peters Cl
Bexley DA16 145 C3
Dagenham RM8 58 D1
Stanmore HA7 25 D4
Peters Ct 9 W2 91 D1
Peter's Ct SW4 160 A5
Petersfield Cl N18 33 A5
Petersfield Rd W3 111 A4
Petersfield Rise SW15 156 B3
PETERSHAM 154 A3
Petersham Cl
Richmond TW10 153 D2
Sutton SM1 217 C3
Petersham Dr BR5 190 A1
Petersham Gdns BR5 189 D1
Petersham Ho SW7 256 C4
Petersham La SW7 256 A6
Petersham Mews SW7 114 A3 256 B5
Petersham Pl SW7 114 A3 256 B6
Petersham Rd TW10 154 A3
Petersham Terr CR0 220 A5
Peter's La EC1 241 D4
Peter's Lo HA8 26 B4
Peter's Path SE26 184 B6
Peter St W1 115 D6 249 C6
Peterstone Rd SE2 124 B4
Peterstow Cl SW19 157 A2
Peterwood Pk CR9 220 B6
Peterwood Way CR0 220 B6
Petherton Ct
Brondesbury Pk NW10 90 D6
10 Harrow HA1 42 D3
Petherton Ho N4 51 A1
Petherton Rd N5 73 A3
Petiver Cl 26 E9 74 C1
Petley Rd W6 134 D5
Peto Pl NW1 238 D6
Peto St N E16 98 D1
Petrel Ct 8 SE21 161 B2
Petrie Cl NW2 69 A2
Petrie Ho 3 SE18 144 C6
Petrie Mus of Egyptian Archaeology★ WC1 93 D3 239 C5
Petros Gdns 1 NW3 70 A2
Pettacre Cl SE28 123 A3
Petticoat Lane Mkt★ EC2 95 D2 243 C3
Petticoat Sq E1 243 C2
Petticoat Twr E1 243 C2
Pettit's Pl RM10 81 C3
Pettit's Rd RM10 81 C3
Pettiward Cl SW15 134 C1
Pettman Cres SE18, SE28 123 B3
Pettsgrove Ave HA0 65 C3
Pett's Hill UB5 63 D3
Petts Hill Prim Sch UB5 63 D3
Petts La TW17 192 C5
Pett St SE18 122 A2
PETTS WOOD 211 B5
Petts Wood Rd BR5 211 B4
Petts Wood Sta BR5 211 A4
Petty France SW1 115 D3 259 C6
Petty Wales EC3 253 B5
Petworth Cl UB5 63 B1
Petworth Gdns
Hillingdon UB10 83 A6
West Barnes SW20 200 B6
Petworth Ho 16 SE22 139 C2
Petworth Rd
Bexley DA6 169 C6
Colney Hatch N12 30 C5
Petworth St SW11 136 C4 267 B2
Petyt Pl SW3 136 C6 267 A5
Petyward SW3 114 C2 257 B3
Pevensey Ave
Enfield EN1 5 C3
Friern Barnet N11 31 D5
Pevensey Cl TW7 130 A5
Pevensey Ct
4 South Acton W3 110 D4
West Norwood SW16 160 C1
10 Woodford E18 37 A2
Pevensey Ho 5 E1 97 A2
Pevensey Rd
Feltham TW13 151 A3
Forest Gate E7 77 A4
Upper Tooting SW17 180 B6
Peverel E6 100 C1
Peverel Ho RM10 81 C6
Peverett Cl N11 31 B5
Peveril Dr TW11 174 B5
Peveril Ho SE1 262 D5
Pewsey Cl E4 35 C5
Pewsham Ho N4 51 A1
Pewterers Ct N3 29 B2
Peyton Ho N11 31 A6
Peyton Pl SE10 142 A5
Pharamond NW2 68 D2
Pharaoh Cl CR4 202 D2
Pheasant Cl E16 99 B1
Phelps Ho 11 SW15 134 D2
Phelp St SE17 139 B6
Phelps Way UB3 105 D2
Phene St SW3 136 C6 267 B6
Philadelphia Ct SW10 266 B3
Philbeach Gdns SW5 113 C1 255 A2
Phil Brown Pl 3 SW8 137 B2
Philchurch Pl 36 E1 96 A1
Philia Ho 4 NW1 71 C1
Philimore Cl SE18 123 C1
Philip Blairman Ho E1 243 C5
Philip Ct Enfield EN2 5 B4
Paddington W2 236 C4
Philip Gdns CR0 223 B6
Philip Ho
East Barnet N20 14 D2
12 Paddington NW6 91 D6
Philip La N15 51 C6
Philipot Almshouse SE9 166 B5
Philipot Path SE9 166 B5
Philippa Gdns SE9 165 D6
Philips Cl CR4 203 A1
Philip St E13 99 A3
Philip Turner Est 28 E9 74 C1
Philip Wlk SE15 140 A2
Phillimore Ct W8 245 B1
Phillimore Gardens Cl W8 113 C3 255 A6
Phillimore Gdns
Kensington W8 113 C4 245 A1
Willesden NW10 90 C6
Phillimore Pl W8 113 C4 245 A1
Phillimore Terr W8 255 B6
Phillimore Wlk W8 113 C3 255 B6
Phillip Ho E1 243 D3
Phillipp St N1 95 C6
Phillips Ct
Edgware HA8 26 C4
Hayes UB4 84 B4
Phillipson Ho 6 N12 29 D5
Philpot La EC3 253 A6
Philpot Sq SW6 135 D2
Philpot St E1 96 B1
Philson Mans 13 E1 96 B1
Phineas Pett Rd SE9 144 A2
Phipp's Bridge Rd CR4, SW19 202 B6
Phipps Bridge Sta CR4 202 B6
Phipps Hatch La EN2 5 A5
Phipps Ho
1 Greenwich SE7 121 B1

Phipps Ho *continued*
16 Shepherd's Bush W12 .... 112 B6
Phipp St EC2 .. 95 C3 243 A6
Phoebeth Rd SE4 .... 163 C6
Phoenix Acad 2 N9 .. 18 B3
Phoenix Bsns Ctr 22 E3 .... 97 C2
Phoenix Cl
18 Shoreditch E8 ...... 95 D6
Walthamstow E17 ..... 35 B1
West Wickham BR4 .. 224 C6
Phoenix Ct
4 Brentford TW8 ... 110 A1
Chingford E4 .... 19 D1
Croydon SE25 .... 206 A4
2 Deptford SE14 ... 141 A6
Enfield EN3 .... 6 C5
Feltham TW13 ...... 171 C6
Millwall E14 .... 119 C2
8 New Barnet EN5 ...... 2 A1
Phoenix Ctr The 1 SM6 .... 220 A1
Phoenix Dr BR2 ..... 225 D5
Phoenix High Sch W12 .... 112 A6
Phoenix Ho
Chelsea SW1 .... 258 A4
Kingston u T KT3 .... 199 D6
Phoenix Ind Est HA1 .. 42 D5
Phoenix Lodge Mans 1 W6 .... 112 C2
Phoenix Pk NW2 ...... 68 A6
Phoenix Pl WC1 .... 94 B3 240 D6
Phoenix Rd
Penge SE20 .... 184 C4
Somers Town NW1 ...... 93 D4 232 C2
Phoenix Sch The 12 NW3 .... 70 A2
Phoenix Sec & Prim Sch 26 E3 .... 97 B4
Phoenix St WC2 ..... 239 D1
Phoenix Trad Est UB6 .... 87 D6
Phoenix Trad Pk TW8 .... 109 D1
Phoenix Way TW5 .... 128 D6
Phoenix Wharf Rd SE1 .... 253 D1
Phyllis Ave KT3 ...... 200 B4
Phyllis Ho CR0 ...... 220 D4
Phyllis Hodges Ho NW1 .... 93 D5 232 C3
Physic Pl SW3 ...... 136 D6 267 C6
Picador Ho 1 RM10 .. 81 D2
Picardy Manorway DA17 .... 125 D4
Picardy Rd DA17 ..... 125 C2
Picardy St DA17 ..... 125 C3
Piccadilly W1 .... 115 C5 249 A4
Piccadilly Arc SW1 .. 249 A4
Piccadilly Cir★ W1 ...... 115 D6 249 C5
Piccadilly Circus Sta SW1 ...... 115 D6 249 C5
Piccadilly Ct 5 N7 .... 72 B2
Piccadilly Pl W1 .... 249 B5
Pickard Cl N14 .... 15 D3
Pickard St EC1 ...... 234 D2
Pickering Ave E6 .... 100 C4
Pickering Cl E9 .... 74 D1
Pickering Ct N22 ..... 32 D2
Pickering Gdns
Croydon SE25 ...... 205 D3
Friern Barnet N11 ..... 31 A4
Pickering Ho
Brentford W5 .... 109 C2
18 Kensington W2 .... 91 D1
Stoke Newington N4 ... 51 B2
4 Woolwich SE18 ... 122 C2
Pickering Mews 9 W2 .... 91 D1
Pickering Pl SW1 .... 249 B3
Pickering St N1 ..... 234 D6
Pickets Cl WD23 .... 8 C3
Pickets St SW12 ..... 159 B4
Pickett Croft HA7 ..... 25 D2
Pickett's Lock La N9 .. 18 D2
Pickford Cl DA7 ...... 147 A3
Pickford La DA7 ..... 147 A3
Pickford Rd DA7 ..... 147 A2
Pickfords Wharf N1 . 235 A3
Pickhurst Gn BR2 ... 208 D2
Pickhurst Inf Sch BR2 .... 208 D3
Pickhurst Jun Sch BR2 .... 208 D3
Pickhurst La BR2, BR3, BR4 .... 208 C2
Pickhurst Mead BR2 .... 208 D2
Pickhurst Pk BR2 ... 208 D4
Pickhurst Rise BR4 .. 208 B1
Pickwick Cl TW4 ..... 151 A6
Pickwick Ct SE9 ..... 166 B3
Pickwick Ho
21 Bermondsey SE16 .... 118 A4
3 Shepherd's Bush W11 .... 112 D5
Pickwick Mews N18 .. 33 C5
Pickwick Pl HA1 ...... 42 C2
Pickwick Rd SE21 .... 161 C4
Pickwick St SE1 ..... 252 A1
Pickwick Way BR7 ... 189 A4
Pickworth Cl SW8 .. 270 B3
Picton Ho 1 SW4 .... 160 A4
Picton Pl
Marylebone W1 ..... 238 B1
Tolworth KT6 .... 198 C1
Picton St SE5 .... 139 B5
Picture Ho 6 SW16 .. 160 A2
Pied Bull Ct WC1 .... 240 B3
Pied Bull Yd WC1 .... 240 B3
Piedmont Rd SE18 ... 123 B1
Pield Heath Ave UB8 .. 82 C3
Pield Heath Rd UB8 ... 82 B3
Pield Heath Sch UB8 .. 82 A3
Pier Head E1 .... 118 B5
Pierhead Wharf 37 E1 .... 118 B5
Pier Ho SW3 .... 267 B5
Piermont Pl BR1 ..... 188 A1
Piermont Rd SE22 ... 162 B6
Pier Par 3 E16 ...... 122 C5
Pierpoint Bldg 4 E14 .... 119 C4
Pier Rd
Feltham TW14 .... 150 B6
Newham E16 .... 122 C4
Pierrepoint SE25 .... 205 C6
Pierrepoint Rd W3 .. 110 D6
Pierrepoint Row N1 . 234 C4
Pierson Ho 12 SE19 .. 183 C6
Pier St E14 .... 120 A2
Pier Terr SW18 ...... 136 A1
Pier Way SE18 ...... 123 B3
Pigeon Ct E4 .... 36 A4
Pigeon La TW12 ..... 173 C6
Piggott Ho 2 E2 ...... 96 D5
Pigott St E14 .... 97 C1
Pike Cl Bromley BR1 .. 187 B5
Hillingdon UB10 ...... 82 B6
Pike Rd NW7 .... 27 B6
Pike's End HA5 ...... 40 B5
Pikestone Cl UB4 ..... 85 A3
Pikethorne 1 SE23 . 162 D2
Pilgrimage St SE1 ...... 117 B4 252 C1
Pilgrim Cl SM4 ..... 201 D2
Pilgrim Hill SE27 .... 183 A6
Pilgrim Ho SE1 ..... 262 D5
Pilgrims Cl
Northolt UB5 .... 64 A3
Palmers Green N13 .... 32 B6
Pilgrims Cloisters 10 SE5 .... 139 C5
Pilgrims Ct Enfield EN1 .. 5 B3
Greenwich SE3 ..... 143 A4
Pilgrim's La NW3 ..... 70 B4
Pilgrims Mews 12 E14 .... 120 B6
Pilgrim's Pl 6 NW3 ... 70 B4
Pilgrim's Rise EN4 .... 14 C6
Pilgrim St EC4 ...... 241 C1
Pilgrims Way
5 Newham E6 ..... 100 A6
Upper Holloway N19 ... 49 D1
Wembley HA9 .... 44 D1
Pilgrim's Way CR2 .. 221 D3
Pilgrims Way Prim Sch 22 SE15 .... 140 C6
Pilkington Ct 1 NW9 . 46 A5
Pilkington Rd
Orpington BR6 ...... 227 A6
4 Peckham SE15 .... 140 B3
Pillions La UB4 .... 83 B3
Pilot Ind Ctr NW10 .... 89 C3
Pilsden Cl SW19 .... 156 D3
Piltdown Rd WD19 .... 22 D6
Pilton Est The CR0 .. 220 D6
Pilton Pl SE17 ...... 262 B2
Pimento Ct W5 ..... 109 D3
Pimilico Sta SW1 .... 115 D1 259 C2
PIMLICO 115 C1
Pimlico Acad SW1 .... 115 C1 259 B1
Pimlico Rd SW1 .... 115 A1 258 B2
Pimlico Wlk 1 N1 .... 95 C4
Pinchbeck Rd BR6 .. 227 D2
Pinchin St E1 .... 118 A6
Pincombe Ho SE17 .. 262 C2
Pincott Pl SE4 ...... 140 D2
Pincott Rd
7 Bexley DA6 ...... 147 C1
Merton SW19 .... 180 A2
Pindar St EC2 .. 95 C2 243 A4
Pindock Mews W9 .... 91 D3
Pine Apple Ct SW1 .. 259 A6
Pine Ave
Stratford New Town E15 .... 76 B3
West Wickham BR4 .. 207 D1
Pine Cl
11 Dartmouth Pk N19 .... 71 C6
London E10 .... 75 D6
Osidge N14 .... 15 C4
3 Penge SE20 ..... 184 C2
Stanmore HA7 .... 25 B6
Pine Coombe CR0 .. 222 D4
Pinecrest Gdns BR6 . 226 D4
Pinecroft
East Wickham DA16 .. 146 A5
Harrow HA3 .... 44 B4
Pinecroft Cres EN5 .... 1 A1
Pine Ct UB5 .... 85 A4
Pinedene 2 SE15 .... 140 B4
Pinefield Cl E14 ..... 119 C6
Pine Gdns Ruislip HA4 .. 62 B6
Surbiton KT5 .... 198 C3
Pine Glade BR6 ..... 226 B4
Pine Gr
Finsbury Pk N4, N19 .... 72 B6
Totteridge N20 .... 13 C3
Wimbledon SW19 ..... 179 B5
Pine Ho Bow E3 .... 97 A6
21 Rotherhithe SE16 . 118 C4
Pinehurst
Chislehurst BR7 ..... 188 D4
Stanmore HA7 .... 25 A5
Pinehurst Ct 6 W11 .. 91 B1
Pinehurst Wlk 4 BR6 .... 211 B1
Pinelands Cl 7 SE3 . 142 D5
Pine Lo SW15 .... 157 A5
Pinemartin Cl NW2 ... 68 C5
Pine Pl UB4 .... 83 D3
Pine Rd
Brunswick Pk N11 ..... 15 A2
Cricklewood NW2 ..... 68 D4
Pine Ridge SM5 ..... 219 A1
Pines Ct 14 SW19 ... 156 D3
Pines Rd BR1 .... 188 A1
Pine St EC1 .... 94 C3 241 A6
Pines The
Southgate N14 .... 15 C6
South Norwood SE19 . 182 D4
Sunbury TW16 ...... 194 A6
Surbiton KT6 .... 214 A5
Woodford IG8 .... 21 A1
Pine Tree Cl TW5 .... 128 B4
Pine Tree Ho SE14 .. 140 D5
Pine Tree Lo BR2 ... 208 D5
Pine Trees Dr UB10 .... 60 A4
Pine Tree Way 1 SE13 .... 141 D2
Pineview Ct 3 E4 .... 20 A3
Pine Wlk KT5 .... 198 C3
Pinewood BR7 ...... 188 C4
Pine Wood TW16 .... 172 A2
Pinewood Ave
Hillingdon UB8 .... 82 B1
Pinner HA5 .... 23 D4
Sidcup DA15 .... 167 C3
Pinewood Cl
Crofton BR6 .... 211 B1
Croydon CR0 .... 223 A5
Pinner HA5 .... 23 D4
South Oxhey HA6 ..... 22 B5
Pinewood Ct
Clapham Pk SW4 .... 159 D5
Pinewood Ct *continued*
Enfield EN2 .... 4 D2
Merton SW19 .... 179 D3
Pinewood Dr BR6 ... 227 C3
Pinewood Gr W5 ..... 87 C1
Pinewood Lo WD23 .... 8 B3
Pinewood Pl KT19 ... 215 B4
Pinewood Rd
Bromley BR2 .... 209 A5
Feltham TW13 ...... 150 B1
West Heath SE2 ..... 146 D6
Pinfold Rd SW16 .... 182 A6
Pinglestone Cl UB7 .. 126 A5
Pinkcoat Cl TW13 .... 150 B1
Pinkerton Ct KT2 ... 176 D1
Pinkerton Pl SW16 .. 181 D6
Pinkham Mans W4 ... 110 C1
Pinkham Way (North Circular Rd) N12 ...... 31 A4
Pinkwell Ave UB3 .... 105 B2
Pinkwell La UB3 ..... 105 B2
Pinkwell Prim Sch UB3 .... 105 A2
Pinley Gdns RM9 .... 102 B6
Pinnace Ho E14 ..... 120 A3
Pinnacle Hill DA7 ... 147 D1
Pinnacle Hill N DA7 . 147 D1
Pinnacle Ho EC3 .... 253 A5
Pinnacle The
Dagenham RM6 ...... 59 A3
7 Kingsland N1 ...... 73 B2
Pinnata Cl EN2 .... 5 A4
Pinnell Rd SE9 ..... 143 D1
PINNER 41 A6
Pinner Ct NW8 ...... 236 C6
Pinner Gn HA5 .... 22 C1
Pinner Gr HA5 .... 41 A4
PINNER GREEN 22 C1
Pinner Hill HA5 .... 22 B3
Pinner Hill Rd HA5 .... 22 C1
Pinner Ho
30 Camberwell SE5 .. 139 A3
Pinner HA5 .... 41 A6
Pinner Park Ave HA2 .. 24 A1
Pinner Park Fst & Mid Schs HA5 .... 41 D6
Pinner Park Gdns HA2 .... 24 A1
Pinner Rd
Harrow HA1, HA2 ..... 42 A3
Northwood HA6 .... 22 A1
Pinner HA2, HA5 ..... 41 C5
Pinner Sta HA5 .... 41 A5
Pinner View HA1, HA2 . 42 A4
PINNERWOOD PARK . 22 C3
Pinner Wood Sch HA5 .... 22 C2
Pinn Way HA4 .... 39 C2
Pintail Cl E6 .... 100 A2
Pintail Ct 39 SE8 .... 141 B6
Pintail Rd IG8 .... 37 B3
Pintail Way UB4 ...... 84 D2
Pinter Ho 30 SW9 ... 138 A3
Pinto Cl WD6 .... 11 B5
Pinto Way SE3 ...... 143 B1
Pioneer Cl
10 Bow Comm E14 ..... 97 D2
London W12 .... 90 B1
Pioneers Ind Pk CR0 .... 204 A1
Pioneer St SE15 ..... 140 A4
Pioneer Way W12 ..... 90 C1
Piper Cl N7 .... 72 B3
Piper Rd KT1 .... 198 C6
Pipers Gdns CR0 .... 207 A2
Pipers Gn NW9 .... 45 A4
Pipers Green La HA8 .. 10 A1
Pipers Ho SE10 ...... 120 B1
Piper Way IG1 .... 57 B1
Pipewell Rd SM5 .... 202 C3
Pippenhall SE9 ..... 166 D5
Pippin Cl
Croydon CR0 .... 207 B1
Dollis Hill NW2 .... 68 B5
Pippin Ct 5 EN4 .... 2 C1
Pippin Ho 17 W10 ... 112 D6
Pippins Ct TW15 .... 170 D4
Piquet Rd SE20 ..... 184 C1
Pirate Castle The★ NW1 .... 71 A1
Pirbright Cres CR0 .. 224 A2
Pirbright Ho 11 KT2 . 176 D4
Pirbright Rd SW18 .. 157 C3
Pirie St 6 E16 ...... 121 B5
Pitcairn Cl RM7 .... 59 C5
Pitcairn Ct CR4 ..... 180 D3
Pitcairne Ct N21 ...... 16 B6
Pitcairn Ho 1 E9 ..... 74 C1
Pitcairn Rd CR4 ..... 180 D3
Pitchford St E15 ...... 76 C1
Pitfield Cres SE28 ... 124 A5
Pitfield Ho N5 .... 73 A3
Pitfield St N1 .... 95 C5
Pitfield Way
Enfield EN3 .... 6 C4
Tokyngton NW10 ...... 67 A2
Pitfold Cl SE12 ...... 165 B5
Pitfold Rd SE12 ..... 165 A4
Pit Ho NW10 .... 67 B5
Pitlake CR0 .... 220 D6
Pitman Ho
Southgate N21 .... 16 B6
4 St Johns SE8 ..... 141 C4
Pitman St SE5 ...... 139 A5
Pitmaston Ho 2 SE13 .... 142 A3
Pitsea Pl E1 .... 96 D1
Pitsea St E1 .... 96 D1
Pitshanger Ct 2 W5 .. 87 C3
Pitshanger La W5 ..... 87 C3
Pitt Cres SW19 ..... 179 D6
Pitt Ho 4 SW11 ..... 136 B1
Pittman Gdns IG1 ..... 79 A3
Pitt Rd Harrow HA2 .... 64 A6
Orpington BR6 ...... 227 A4
Thornton Heath CR0, CR7 .... 205 A4
Pitt's Head Mews W1 .... 248 B3
Pittsmead Ave BR2 .. 209 A2
Pitt St W8 .... 113 C4 245 B2
Pittville Gdns SE25 .. 206 A6
Pitzhanger Manor House & Gallery★ W5 .... 109 D5
Pixfield Ct BR2 ..... 186 D1
Pixham Ct 5 SW19 .. 179 B5
Pixley St E14 .... 97 B1
Pixton 14 NW9 .... 27 C2
Pixton Way CR2 ..... 223 B1
Place Farm Ave BR5, BR6 .... 211 B1
Plains The 7 E4 ...... 20 C4
PLAISTOW BR1 ..... 187 A4
E13 .... 99 B4
Plaistow Gr
Bromley BR1 .... 187 B3
West Ham E15 .... 98 D6
Plaistow La BR1 .... 187 C2
Plaistow Park Rd E13 . 99 B5
Plaistow Prim Sch E13 .... 99 B5
Plaistow Rd E13, E15 .. 98 D5
Plaistow Sta E13 ..... 98 D5
Plane St SE26 ...... 162 B1
Plane Tree Cres TW13 .... 150 B1
Planetree Ct W6 .... 112 D2
Plane Tree Ho
Deptford SE8 .... 141 A6
Greenwich SE7 ..... 121 D1
Plane Tree Wlk 4 SE19 .... 183 C4
Plantagenet Cl KT19 . 215 B4
Plantagenet Gdns RM6 .... 58 D2
Plantagenet Ho SE18 .... 122 B3
Plantagenet Pl RM6 ... 58 D2
Plantagenet Rd EN5 .... 2 A1
Plantain Gdns E11 .... 76 B5
Plantain Pl SE1 ..... 252 C2
Plantation La EC3 ... 253 A6
Plantation The SE3 .. 143 A3
Plasel Ct E13 .... 99 B6
PLASHET 78 A2
Plashet Gr E6 .... 77 D1
Plashet Rd E13 .... 77 B1
Plashet Sch E6 .... 78 A1
Plassy Rd SE6 ...... 163 D4
Platehouse The 3 E14 .... 119 D1
Platina St EC2 ...... 242 D6
Platinum Ct RM7 ...... 59 D6
Plato Pl 1 SW6 ..... 135 B3
Plato Rd SW2 .... 138 A1
Platt Halls (a) 35 NW9 .... 27 D1
Platt Halls (b) 37 NW9 .... 27 D1

Platt Halls (c) 38 NW9 . . . 27 D1
Platt's Eyot TW12 . . . 173 C1
Platt's La NW3 . . . 69 C5
Platts Rd EN3 . . . 6 C4
Platt St NW1 . . . 232 C4
Plaxdale Ho SE17 . . . 263 A3
Plaxtol Cl BR1 . . . 187 C2
Plaxtol Rd DA8 . . . 147 C5
Plaxton Ct E11 . . . 76 D5
Playfair St W6 . . . 112 C1
Playfield Cres SE22 . 161 D6
Playfield Rd HA8 . . . 27 A1
Playford Rd
Finsbury Pk N4 . . . 72 B6
Finsbury Pk N4 . . . 72 C6
Playgreen Way SE6 . 185 C6
Playground Cl BR3 . 184 D1
Playhouse Yd EC4 . . . 241 C1
Plaza Bsns Ctr EN3 . . . 7 B3
Plaza Hts E10 . . . 76 A5
Plaza Sh Ctr W1 . . . 93 C1 239 B2
Plaza Wlk NW9 . . . 45 A6
Pleasance Rd
Putney SW15 . . . 156 B6
St Paul's Cray BR5 . . . 190 B1
Pleasance The SW15 . . . 134 B1
Pleasant Gr CR0 . . . 223 B5
Pleasant Pl N1 . . . 72 D1
Pleasant Row NW1 . 231 D5
Pleasant View BR6 . . . 227 A3
Pleasant View Pl BR6 . . . 227 A3
Pleasant Way HA0 . . . 87 C5
Pleasaunce Ct SE9 . . . 144 B1
Plender Ct NW1 . . . 232 B5
Plender St NW1 . . . 93 C6 232 B5
Pleshey Rd N7 . . . 71 D4
Plevna Cres N15 . . . 51 C3
Plevna Ho 1 N9 . . . 18 A1
Plevna Rd
Edmonton N9 . . . 18 B1
Hampton TW12 . . . 173 D2
Plevna St E14 . . . 120 A3
Pleydell Ave
Chiswick W6 . . . 111 D2
Penge SE19 . . . 183 D3
Pleydell Ct EC4 . . . 241 B1
Pleydell Gdns SE19 . 183 D4
Pleydell St EC4 . . . 241 B1
Plimsoll Cl E14 . . . 97 D1
Plimsoll Rd N4 . . . 72 D5
Plough Ct EC3 . . . 252 D6
Plough Farm Cl HA4 . . 39 B3
Plough La
Dulwich Village SE22 . . . 161 D5
7 Teddington TW11 . 175 A5
Wallington CR0, SM6 . 220 A3
Wimbledon SW17, SW19 . . . 180 A6
Plough Lane Cl CR0, SM6 . . . 220 A3
Ploughmans Cl NW1 232 C6
Ploughmans End TW7 . . . 152 B6
Plough Mews 19 SW11 . . . 136 B1
Plough Pl EC4 . . . 241 B2
Plough Rd
Battersea SW11 . . . 136 B1
West Ewell KT19 . . . 215 B1
Plough St 16 E1 . . . 96 A1
Plough Terr SW11 . . . 136 B1
Plough Way SE16 . . . 119 A2
Plough Yd EC2 . . . 243 B5
Plover Ho 4 SW9 . . . 138 C5
Plover Way
Hayes UB4 . . . 84 D2
Rotherhithe SE16 . . . 119 A3
Plowman Cl N18 . . . 33 B5
Plowman Ho SW19 . . 156 D2
Plowman Way RM8 . . . 58 C1
Plumbers Row E1 . . . 96 A1
Plumbridge St 7 SE10 . . . 142 A4
Plum Cl TW14 . . . 150 A3
Plumcroft Prim Sch SE18 . . . 145 A6
Plume Ho SE10 . . . 141 D6
Plum Garth TW8 . . . 109 D2
Plum La SE18 . . . 145 A5
Plummer Ct SE13 . . . 163 D5
Plummer La CR4 . . . 180 D1
Plummer Rd SW4 . . . 159 D4
Plumpton Cl UB5 . . . 63 C2
Plumpton Ct SE23 . . . 163 A4
Plumpton Lo E5 . . . 74 D5
Plumpton Way SM5 . . 218 C5
PLUMSTEAD . . . 123 C2
PLUMSTEAD COMMON . . . 145 D6
Plumstead Common Rd SE18 . . . 145 A6
Plumstead High St SE18, SE2 . . . 123 C2
Plumstead Manor Sch SE18 . . . 145 B6
Plumstead Rd SE18, SE28 . . . 123 A2
Plumstead Road Covered Mkt* SE18 . . . 122 D2
Plumstead Sta SE18 . 123 B2
Plumtree Cl
Dagenham RM10 . . . 81 D2
Wallington SM6 . . . 219 D1
Plumtree Ct EC4 . . . 241 C2
Plymen Ho KT8 . . . 195 C4
Plymouth Ho
10 Barking IG11 . . . 80 A1
20 Lewisham SE10 . . 141 D4
Plymouth Rd
Bromley BR1 . . . 187 B2
Newham E16 . . . 99 A2
Plymouth Wharf E14 . . . 120 B2
Plympton Ave NW6 . . . 69 B1
Plympton Cl 8 DA17 . . . 125 A3
Plympton Pl NW1 . . . 237 A5
Plympton Rd NW6 . . . 69 B1
Plympton St NW8 . . . 237 A5
Plymstock Rd DA16 . . 146 C5
Pocklington Cl NW9 . . 27 C1
Pocklington Ct SW15 . . . 156 A3
Pocklington Lo 6 W12 . . . 112 A3
Pocock Ave UB7 . . . 104 B3
Pocock St SE1 . . . 116 D4 251 D2
Podmore Rd SW18 . . . 136 A1
Poets Cnr* SW1 . . . 260 A6
Poets Mews 3 SE24 . . . 160 D6
Poet's Rd N5 . . . 73 B3
Poets Way HA1 . . . 42 C5
Pointalls Cl N3 . . . 30 A1
Point Cl SE10 . . . 142 A4
Pointer Cl SE28 . . . 102 D1
Pointer Sch The SE3 . . . 143 A5
Pointers Cl E14 . . . 119 D1
Point Hill SE10 . . . 142 A4
Point Ho SE10 . . . 142 A4
Point Pl HA9 . . . 66 D1
Point Pleasant SW18 . . . 135 C1
Point Terr E7 . . . 77 B3
Point The HA4 . . . 62 A4
Point Wharf La TW8 . . 132 A5
Poland Ho 3 E15 . . . 98 B6
Poland St W1 . . 93 C1 239 B1
Polaris Ct EN4 . . . 14 B6
Polebrook Rd SE3 . . . 143 C2
Polecroft La SE6 . . . 163 B2
Polehamptons The TW12 . . . 174 A2
Pole Hill Rd
Chingford E4 . . . 20 A4
Hillingdon UB4 . . . 83 A4
Polesden Gdns SW20 . . . 178 B1
Polesworth Ho 16 W2 . . . 91 C2
Polesworth Rd RM9 . . . 80 D1
Polish Inst & Sikorski Mus* SW7 . . . 246 D1
Polish Univ Abroad 16 W6 . . . 112 A2
Polish War Meml HA4 . . . 62 C2
Pollard Cl Islington N7 . 72 B4
Newham E16 . . . 121 A6
Pollard Ct SM4 . . . 202 C4
Pollard Ho
Cheam KT4 . . . 216 C4
Islington N1 . . . 233 C3
Pollard Rd
East Barnet N20 . . . 14 C2
Morden SM4 . . . 202 B4
Pollard Row E2 . . . 96 A4
Pollards Cl IG10 . . . 21 C6
Pollards Cres SW16 . . 204 A6
Pollards Hill E SW16 . 204 B6
Pollards Hill N SW16 . . . 204 B6
Pollards Hill S SW16 . 204 B6
Pollards Hill W SW16 . . . 204 B6
Pollard St E2 . . . 96 A4
Pollards Wood Rd SW16 . . . 204 A6
Pollard Wlk DA14 . . . 190 C4
Pollen St W1 . . . 238 D1
Pollitt Dr NW8 92 B3 236 D6
Pollock Ho W10 . . . 91 A3
Pollock's Toy Mus* W1 . . . 239 B4
Polperro Cl BR6 . . . 211 D3
Polperro Mans 3 NW6 . . . 69 C3
Polperro Mews SE11 261 C4
Polsted Rd SE6 . . . 163 B4
Polsten Mews 2 EN3 . . 7 C6
Polthorne Gr SE18 . . . 123 B2
Polworth Rd SW16 . . . 182 A5
Polygon Rd NW1 . . . 93 D5 232 C3
Polygon The
1 Clapham SW4 . . . 137 C1
St John's Wood NW8 . 229 D6
Polytechnic St SE18 . . 122 C2
Pomell Way E1 . . . 243 D2
Pomeroy Cl TW1 . . . 131 B1
Pomeroy Ct W11 . . . 91 A1
Pomeroy Ho 5 E2 . . . 96 D5
Pomeroy St SE14 . . . 140 C4
Pomfret Rd SE5 . . . 138 D2
Pomoja La N19 . . . 72 A6
Pomona Ho 10 SE8 . . . 119 A2
Pond Cl
Colney Hatch N12 . . . 30 C4
Kidbrooke SE3 . . . 143 A3
Pond Cottage La BR3, BR4 . . . 207 C1
Pond Cotts SE21 . . . 161 C3
PONDERS END . . . 18 D6
Ponders End Ind Est EN3 . . . 19 A6
Ponders End Sta EN3 . 19 A6
Ponder St 5 N7 . . . 72 B1
Pond Farm Est E5 . . . 74 C5
Pondfield End IG10 . . . 21 C4
Pondfield Ho
4 Islington N5 . . . 73 A3
West Norwood SE27 . 183 A5
Pondfield Rd
Dagenham RM10 . . . 81 D3
Locksbottom BR6 . . . 226 D5
West Wickham BR2 . . 208 C1
Pond Gn HA4 . . . 61 C6
Pond Hill Gdns SM3 . . 217 A2
Pond Ho Chelsea SW3 257 A3
Stanmore HA7 . . . 25 B4
Pond Mead SE21 . . . 161 B5
Pond Path BR7 . . . 188 D4
Pond Pl SW3 . 114 C2 257 A3
Pond Rd
Blackheath Vale SE3 . . . 142 D3
Newham E15 . . . 98 C5
Pondside Ave KT4 . . . 200 C1
Pondside Cl UB3 . . . 127 B6
Pond Sq N6 . . . 49 A1
Pond St NW3 . . . 70 C3
Pond Way TW11 . . . 175 C4
Pondwood Rise BR6 . 211 C2
Ponler St E1 . . . 96 B1
Ponsard Rd NW10 . . . 90 B4
Ponsford St E9 . . . 74 C2
Ponsonby Ho 13 E2 . . . 96 C5
Ponsonby Pl SW1 . . . 115 D1 259 D2
Ponsonby Rd SW15 . . 156 B4
Ponsonby Terr SW1 . 259 D2
Pontefract Ct UB5 . . . 63 D3
Pontefract Rd BR1 . . 186 D5
Ponton Ho SW2 . . . 160 C3
Ponton Rd SW8 . . . 137 D6 269 D5
Pontoon Dock Sta E16 . . . 121 C5
Pont St Mews SW1 . . 257 C5
Pont St SW1 . 114 D3 257 D5
Pontypool Pl SE1 . . . 251 C2
Pool Cl
Beckenham BR3 . . . 185 C5
East Molesey KT8 . . . 195 B4
Pool Ct SE6 . . . 163 C2
Poole Cl HA4 . . . 61 C6
Poole Court Rd TW5 . . . 129 A3
Poole Ct
De Beauvoir Town N1 . . 73 C1
Hounslow TW5 . . . 129 A3
Poole Ho SE11 . . . 260 D5
Pool End Cl TW17 . . . 192 C4
Poole Rd Homerton E9 . 74 D2
West Ewell KT19 . . . 215 B2
Pooles Bldgs EC1 . . . 241 A5
Pooles Ct IG3 . . . 80 A5
Pooles La SW10 . . . 266 A3
Pooles Park Prim Sch 16 N4 . . . 72 B6
Pooles Pk N4 . . . 72 C6
Poole St N1 . . . 95 B6 235 C5
Poole Way UB4 . . . 83 C4
Pooley Ho E1 . . . 96 D4
Pool Ho NW8 . . . 236 D4
Poolmans St SE16 . . 118 D4
Pool Rd
East Molesey KT12, KT8 . . . 195 B4
Harrow HA1 . . . 42 B2
Poolsford Rd NW9 . . . 45 C5
Poonah St E1 . . . 96 C1
Pope Cl
East Bedfont TW14 . . 149 D3
Mitcham SW17, SW19 . . . 180 B4
Pope Ct 10 KT2 . . . 175 D6
Pope Ho
7 Bermondsey SE16 . . . 118 B2
3 Camberwell SE5 . . . 139 B5
Pope John Prim Sch W12 . . . 112 B6
Pope Rd BR2 . . . 209 D4
Pope's Ave TW2 . . . 152 C2
Popes Ct TW2 . . . 152 C2
Popes Dr N3 . . . 29 C2
Popes Gr CR0 . . . 223 B5
Pope's Gr TW1, TW2 . 152 D2
Pope's Head Alley EC3 . . . 242 D1
Pope's La W5 . . . 110 A3
Pope's Rd SW9 . . . 138 C2
Pope St SE1 . . . 253 B1
Pope Street Ct SE9 . . . 166 B3
Popham Cl TW13 . . . 151 B1
Popham Ct N16 . . . 73 C5
Popham Gdns TW9 . . 132 D2
Popham Rd N1 . . . 95 A6 235 A6
Popham St
Islington N1 . . . 234 D6
Shoreditch N1 . 95 A6 235 A6
Pop In Bsns Ctr HA9 . . 66 D3
POPLAR . . . 97 C1
Poplar Ave
Mitcham CR4 . . . 180 D2
Orpington BR6 . . . 226 D6
Southall UB2 . . . 107 D3
Yiewsley UB7 . . . 104 B6
Poplar Bath St 11 E14 . . . 119 D6
Poplar Bsns Pk E14 . 120 A6
Poplar Cl Hackney E9 . . 75 B3
Pinner HA5 . . . 22 D2
Poplar Cres KT19 . . . 215 A2
Poplar Ct Chingford E4 . 35 D4
Northolt UB5 . . . 84 C5
4 Streatham SW16 . . 160 B1
13 Twickenham TW1 . 153 C5
Wimbledon SW19 . . . 179 C5
Poplar Farm Cl KT19 . . . 215 A2
Poplar Gdns KT3 . . . 177 B1
Poplar Gr
Friern Barnet N11 . . . 31 A4
Hammersmith W6 . . . 112 C4
Kingston u T KT3 . . . 199 B6
Wembley HA9 . . . 67 A5
Poplar High St E14 . . 119 D6
Poplar Ho
Brockley SE4 . . . 141 B1
Poplar Ho *continued*
19 Rotherhithe SE16 . 118 D4
Poplar La BR3 . . . 207 D4
Poplar Mews 4 W12 . . . 112 C5
Poplar Mount DA17 . 125 D2
Poplar Pl Hayes UB3 . . 106 A6
Kensington W2 . . . 113 D6 245 D6
Woolwich SE28 . . . 124 C6
Poplar Prim Sch SW19 . . . 201 C6
Poplar Rd
Ashford TW15 . . . 171 A5
Cheam SM3 . . . 201 B1
Herne Hill SE24 . . . 139 A1
Merton SW19 . . . 179 C1
Poplar Rd S SW19 . . . 201 C6
Poplars Cl HA4 . . . 39 C1
Poplars Ho 14 E17 . . . 53 D6
Poplars Rd E17 . . . 53 D3
Poplar Sta E14 . . . 119 D6
Poplars The
East Barnet N14 . . . 15 B6
Kentish Town NW5 . . . 71 C3
Poplar View HA9 . . . 65 D6
Poplar Way
Feltham TW13 . . . 150 B1
Ilford IG6 . . . 57 A5
Poplar Wlk
Croydon CR0 . . . 205 A1
Herne Hill SE24 . . . 139 A1
Poppins Ct EC4 . . . 241 C1
Poppleton Rd E11 . . . 54 C3
Poppy Cl
Belvedere DA17 . . . 125 D4
Hackbridge SM6 . . . 203 A1
Northolt UB5 . . . 63 B2
Poppy Ct HA3 . . . 42 C6
Poppy La CR0 . . . 206 C1
Porchester Ct W2 . . . 91 D1
Porchester Gate W2 246 A5
Porchester Gdn Mews W2 . . . 91 D1
Porchester Gdns W2 . . . 113 D6 245 D6
Porchester Ho 8 E1 . . 96 B1
Porchester Mead BR3 . . . 185 D4
Porchester Mews W2 . . . 91 D1
Porchester Pl W2 . . . 237 B1
Porchester Rd
Kensington W2 . . . 91 D1
Kingston u T KT1 . . . 176 D1
Porchester Sq W2 . . . 91 D1
Porchester Terr W2 . . . 114 A6 246 A6
Porchester Terr N W2 . . . 91 D1
Porch Way N20 . . . 14 D1
Porcupine Cl SE9 . . . 166 A2
Porden Rd SW2 . . . 138 B1
Porland Ct SE1 . . . 262 C6
Porlock Ave HA1, HA2 . 42 A1
Porlock Ho 5 SE26 . . 162 A1
Porlock Rd EN1 . . . 17 D4
Porlock St SE1 . . . 117 B4 252 D2
Porrington Cl BR7 . . 188 C2
Porson Ct SE13 . . . 141 D2
Portal Cl
Hillingdon UB10 . . . 60 B1
Ruislip HA4 . . . 62 B4
West Norwood SE27 . 160 C1
Portal Way W3 . . . 89 B2
Portbury Cl 17 SE15 . . 140 A4
Portchester Cl SE24 . . 139 B1
Port Cres E13 . . . 99 B3
Portcullis Lodge Rd EN1 . . . 5 B2
Porte 10 NW9 . . . 27 D2
Portelet Ct 1 N1 . . . 95 C6
Portelet Rd E1 . . . 96 D4
Porten Hos W14 . . . 254 A5
Porten Rd W14 . . . 254 A5
Porter Rd E6 . . . 100 B1
Porters Ave RM8, RM9 . 80 C3
Porter Sq N19 . . . 50 A1
Porter St
Borough The SE1 . . . 117 A5 252 B4
Marylebone W1 . . . 237 D4
Porters & Walters Almshouses N22 . . . 32 B3
Porters Way UB7 . . . 104 B4

Porteus Rd W2 236 B4
Portfleet Pl 34 N1 95 C6
Portgate Cl W9 91 B3
Porthallow Cl BR6 227 D4
Porthcawe Rd SE26 185 B6
Porthkerry Ave DA16 146 A1
Port Ho 6 SW11 136 A2
Port House The 6 E14 119 D1
Portia Ct 12 IG11 80 A1
Portia Way E3 97 B3
Porticos The SW3 266 C5
Portinscale Rd SW15 157 B6
Portishead Ho 29 W2 91 C2
Portland Ave
Blackfen DA15 168 A5
New Malden KT3 199 D2
Stamford Hill N16 51 D2
Portland Cl
Dagenham RM6 59 A4
New Malden KT4 200 B2
Portland Commercial Est IG11 102 C5
Portland Cotts
Feltham TW13 173 A5
Wallington CR0 203 D2
Portland Cres
1 Chislehurst SE9 166 A2
Feltham TW13 171 B6
Southall UB6 86 A2
Stanmore HA7 25 D1
Portland Cres W HA7 43 D6
Portland Ct
7 De Beauvoir Town N1 73 C1
1 Deptford SE14 141 A6
1 Sutton SM2 217 D2
Portland Dr EN2 5 C5
Portland Gdns
Harringay N4 50 D3
Ilford RM6 58 D4
Portland Gr SW8 138 B4 270 C2
Portland Ho 19 SW2 160 C3
Portland Hospl for Women & Children The W1 238 D5
Portland Mans SE25 206 B4
Portland Mews W1 239 B1
Portland Pl
Croydon SE25 206 A5
Marylebone W1 93 B2 238 D3
Portland Place Sch W1 93 B2 238 D4
Portland Rd
Ashford TW15 148 A1
Bromley BR1 187 C5
Chislehurst SE9 166 A2
Croydon SE25 206 B4
Hayes UB4 83 C4
Kingston u T KT1 198 B5
Kingston u T KT1 198 B6
Mitcham CR4 180 C1
Notting Hill W11 113 A5 244 B4
Notting Hill W11 113 A6 244 A5
Southall UB2 107 B3
Tottenham N15 51 D5
Portland Rise N4 51 A1
Portland Sq 4 E1 118 B5
Portland St SE17 117 B1 262 C1
Portland Terr
Edgware HA8 26 C3
Richmond TW9 131 D1
Portland Village W6 112 C3
Portman Ave SW14 133 B2
Portman Cl
Bexley DA7 147 A2
Marylebone W1 93 A1 238 A2
Portman Dr IG8 37 D1
Portman Gate NW1 237 B5
Portman Gdns
Hendon NW9 27 B1
Hillingdon UB10 60 C1
Portman Hall HA3 24 B5
Portman Hts 1 NW3 69 C5
Portman Lo N21 16 D6
Portman Mews S W1 238 A1
Portman Pl E2 96 C4
Portman Rd KT1 176 B1
Portman Sq W1 93 A1 238 A2
Portman St W1 93 A1 238 A1
Portman The NW11 47 C2
Portman Twrs W1 237 D2
Portmeadow Wlk SE2 124 D4
Portmeers Cl E17 53 C3
Portnall Rd W9 91 B4
Portobello Ct Est W11 91 B1
Portobello Ho 6 SW27 182 D5
Portobello Mews W11 245 A5
Portobello Rd W11 113 B6 244 D6
Portobello Road Mkt* W10 91 A2
Porton Ct KT6 197 C3
Portpool La EC1 94 C2 241 A4
Portree Cl N22 32 B3
Portree St E14 98 B1
Port Royal Pl 3 N16 73 C3
Portrush Ct 9 UB1 86 A1
Portsdown HA8 26 C5
Portsdown Ave NW11 47 B3
Portsdown Mews NW11 47 B3
Portsea Hall W2 237 B1
Portsea Ho 3 SW15 156 B3
Portsea Mews W2 237 B1
Portsea Pl W2 237 B1
Portslade Rd SW8 137 C3
Portsmouth Ave KT7 197 A2
Portsmouth Mews 16 E16 121 B5
Portsmouth Rd
Esher KT10 212 A5
Putney SW15 156 C4
Thames Ditton KT6, KT7 197 C3
Portsmouth St WC2 240 D1
Portsoken St E1, EC3 253 C6
Portswood Pl SW15 155 D5
Portugal Gdns TW2 152 A2
Portugal St WC2 94 B1 240 D1
Portway E15 98 D6
Portway Gdns SE18 143 D5
Portway Prim Sch 7 E13 99 A6
Poseidon Ct
Dagenham IG11 102 B4
9 Millwall E14 119 C2
Postern Gn EN2 4 C2
Postern The EC2 242 B3
Post La TW2 152 B3
Postmasters Lodge HA5 41 A2
Postmill Cl CR0 222 D5
Post Office App E7 77 B3
Post Office Way SW8 137 D5 269 C4
Post Rd UB2 107 D3
Postway Mews 1 IG1 78 D5
Potier St SE1 262 D5
Potter Cl CR4 181 B1
Potteries The EN5 13 C6
Potterill Ct TW11 175 B3
Potterne Cl 5 SW19 156 D4
Potters Cl
5 Camberwell SE15 139 C5
Croydon CR0 207 A1
Pottersfield EN1 5 C1
Potters Fields SE1 117 C5 253 B3
Potters Gr KT3 199 A5
Potters Heights Cl HA5 22 B3
Potter's La Barnet EN5 1 C1
Streatham SW16 181 D4
Potters Lo E14 120 A1
Potters Mews WD6 9 D5
Potters Rd SW6 136 A3
Potter's Rd EN5 1 D1
Potter St HA5 22 B2
Potter Street Hill HA5 22 B3
Pottery La W11 113 A5 244 B4
Pottery Rd TW8 132 A6
Pottery St SE16 118 B4
Pott St E2 96 B4
Poulett Gdns TW1 153 A3
Poulett Rd E6 100 B5
Poullett Ho SW2 160 D3
Poulters Wood BR2 225 D3
Poulton Ave SM1 218 B5
Poulton Cl E8 74 B2
Poultry EC2 95 B1 242 C1
Pound Cl
Long Ditton KT6 197 C1
Orpington BR6 227 B6
Pound Court Dr BR6 227 B6
Pound Farm Cl KT10 196 B1
Pound Green Ct 4 DA5 169 C4
Pound La NW10 68 A2
Pound Park Rd SE7 121 D2
Pound Pl SE9 166 C5
Pound St SM5 218 D3
Pountney Rd SW11 137 A2
Poverest Rd BR5 211 D4
Povey Ho
Tulse Hill SW2 160 C5
Walworth SE17 263 A3
Powder Mill La TW2, TW4 151 C3
Powell Cl
Chessington KT9 213 D3
Edgware HA8 26 B4
Wallington SM6 220 A1
Powell Ct
Croydon CR2 221 A4
19 Walthamstow E17 53 D6
Powell Gdns RM10 81 C4
Powell Ho 10 SW19 179 A4
Powell Rd
Buckhurst Hill IG9 21 C4
Hackney E5 74 B5
Powell's Wlk W4 133 D6
Powell Terr CR4 204 A5
Powergate Bsns Pk NW10 89 B4
Power Ho 13 TW9 132 C4
Power Ho The W4 111 D2
Power Rd W4 110 C2
Powerscroft Rd
Lower Clapton E5 74 C4
Sidcup DA14 190 C4
Powers Ct TW1 153 D4
Powis Ct Bushey WD23 8 B3
Edgware HA8 26 B6
Powis Gdns
Golders Green NW11 47 B2
Notting Hill W11 91 B1
Powis Ho WC2 240 B2
Powis Mews W11 91 B1
Powis Pl WC1 94 A3 240 B5
Powis Rd E3 97 D4
Powis Sq W11 91 B1
Powis St SE18 122 D2
Powis Terr W11 91 B1
Powlesland Ct 21 E14 97 A1
Powle Terr IG1 79 B3
Powlett Ho NW1 71 B2
Powlett Pl NW1 71 B1
Pownall Gdns TW3 129 D1
Pownall Rd
Hackney E8 96 A6
Hounslow TW3 129 D1
Pownsett Terr IG1 79 A3
Powrie Ho 4 SW11 136 B3
Powster Rd BR1 187 B5
Powys Cl DA7 146 D6
Powys Ct N11 32 A5
Powys La
Bowes Pk N13 32 A5
Palmers Green N14 32 A6
Poynder Ct 3 N7 72 A3
Poynder Lo TW7 131 A4
Poynders Ct 9 SW4 159 C5
Poynders Gdns SW12 159 C4
Poynders Rd SW12, SW4 159 D4
Poynings Rd N19 71 C5
Poynings Way N12 29 C5
Poyntell Cres BR7 189 B2
Poynter Ct 11 UB5 84 D5
Poynter Ho
Paddington NW8 236 C6
10 Shepherd's Bush W11 112 D5
Poynter Rd EN1 18 A6
Poynton Rd N17 34 A1
Poyntz Rd SW11 136 D3
Poyser St E2 96 B5
Praed Mews W2 236 D2
Praed St W2 92 B1 236 D2
Pragel St E13 99 C5
Pragnell Rd SE12 165 B2
Prague Pl SW2 160 A6
Prah Rd N4 72 C6
Prairie St SW8 137 B3
Pratt Mews NW1 232 A5
Pratt St NW1 93 C6 232 A6
Pratt Wlk SE1, SE11 116 B2 260 D4
Prayle Gr NW2 46 D1
Preachers Ct EC1 241 D5
Prebend Gdns W4, W6 111 D2
Prebend Mans 4 W4 111 D2
Prebend St N1 95 A6 235 A6
Precinct Rd UB3 106 A6
Precincts The SM4 201 C3
Precinct The
Islington N1 235 A5
Islington N5 72 D3
Premier Corner NW6 91 B5
Premier Ct EN3 6 D5
Premier Ho 25 N1 72 D1
Premier Lo N3 29 C2
Premier Park Rd NW10 88 D5
Premier Pk NW10 88 D5
Premier Pl 17 E14 119 C6
Prendergast Ho 7 SW4 159 D4
Prendergast Ladywell Fields Coll SE4 163 C5
Prendergast Rd SE3 142 C2
Prendergast Sch SE4 141 C1
Prentice Ct 2 SW19 179 B5
Prentis Rd SW16 181 D6
Prentiss Ct SE7 121 D2
Presburg Rd KT3 199 C4
Prescelly Pl HA8 26 B2
Prescot St E1 117 D6 253 D6
Prescott Ave BR5 210 D3
Prescott Ho
Croydon CR0 220 C5
13 Kennington SE17 138 D6
Prescott Pl SW4 137 D1
Presentation Mews SW2 160 B3
Preshaw Cres CR4 202 C6
President Dr E1 118 B5
President Ho EC1 234 D1
President St EC1 235 A2
Prespa Cl N9 18 C2
Press Ho NW10 67 B5
Press Rd NW10 67 B5
Prestage Way 13 E14 120 A6
Prestbury Rd E7 77 C1
Prestbury Sq SE9 188 B6
Prested Rd SW11 136 C1
PRESTON 44 A1
Preston Ave E4 36 B4
Preston Cl
Twickenham TW2 152 C1
Walworth SE1 263 A4
Preston Ct
5 New Barnet EN5 2 A1
Northwood Hills HA6 22 A1
Sidcup DA14 189 D6
Walton-on-T KT12 194 C1
Preston Dr
Bexley DA7 146 D4
Wanstead E11 55 C4
West Ewell KT19 215 D2
Preston Gdns
Enfield EN3 7 A6
Redbridge IG1 56 A3
Willesden NW10 67 C2
Preston Hill HA3 44 B3
Preston Ho
Bermondsey SE1 263 C6
3 Dagenham RM10 81 C5
Walworth SE1 263 A4
1 Woolwich SE18 122 C2
Preston Manor High Sch HA9 66 B6
Preston Park Prim Sch HA9 43 D1
Preston Pl
Richmond TW10 154 A6
Willesden NW2 68 A2
Preston Rd
Leytonstone E11 54 C3
Littleton TW17 192 C4
South Norwood SE19 182 D4
Wembley HA3, HA9 66 A6
Wimbledon SW20 177 D3
Preston Road Sta HA3 44 A1
Prestons Rd BR2 225 A6
Preston's Rd E14 120 A5
Preston Waye HA3 44 A1
Prestwich Terr SW4 159 D6
Prestwick Cl UB2 107 A1
Prestwick Ct
Southall UB1 108 A6
Tottenham N17 34 A3
Prestwick Rd WD19 22 D6
Prestwood Ave HA3 43 B5
Prestwood Cl
East Wickham SE18 146 A6
Harrow HA3 43 B5
Prestwood Gdns CR0 205 A2
Prestwood Ho 3 SE16 118 B3
Prestwood St N1 235 B3
Pretoria Ave E17 53 A5
Pretoria Cres E4 20 A3
Pretoria Ho 3 HA4 40 C1
Pretoria Rd
Chingford E4 20 B3
Ilford IG1 78 D3
Leytonstone E11 54 B1
Newham E16 98 D3
Streatham SW16 181 C5
Tottenham N17 33 D4
Pretoria Rd N N18 33 D4
Pretty Cnr HA6 22 A5
Prevost Rd N11 15 A2
Priam Ho 17 E2 96 B5
Price Cl Finchley NW7 29 A4
Upper Tooting SW17 158 D1
Price Ct HA1 43 A4
Price Ho N1 235 A5
Price Rd CR0 220 D3
Prices Ct SW11 136 B2
Price's St SE1 251 D4
Price's Yd N1 233 D5
Price Way TW12 173 A4
Prichard Ct
Battersea SW11 266 D1
Islington N7 72 B3
Pricklers Hill EN5 13 D5
Prickley Wood BR2 208 D1
Priddy's Yd 4 CR0 221 A6
Prideaux Ho WC1 233 D2
Prideaux Pl
Acton W3 111 B6
St Pancras WC1 94 B4 233 D2
Prideaux Rd SW9 138 A2
Pride Ct N1 234 B4
Pridham Rd CR7 205 B5
Priestfield Rd SE23 163 A1
Priestlands Park Rd DA15 167 D1
Priestley Cl N16 51 D2
Priestley Gdns RM6 58 B3
Priestley Ho
2 Camden Town NW5 71 B2
St Luke's EC1 242 B6
3 Wembley HA9 67 A5
Priestley Rd CR4 181 A1
Priestley Way
Hendon NW2 46 A1
Walthamstow E17 52 D6
Priestman Point 25 E3 97 D4
Priestmead Fst & Mid Schs HA3 43 B6
Priest Park Ave HA2 63 C6
Priests Bridge SW14 133 C2
Priest's Ct EC2 242 A2
Prima Rd SW9 138 C5
Primrose Ave
Enfield EN2 5 C4
Ilford RM6 58 B2

Primrose Cl
6 Bow E3 97 C5
Catford SE6 186 A5
Finchley N3 29 D1
Hackbridge SM6 203 B1
Harrow HA2 63 B5
Primrose Ct
2 Child's Hill NW2 69 B5
New Malden KT4 200 A2
Primrose Hill NW8 230 C5
11 Streatham SW12 159 D4
Primrose Gdns
Hampstead NW3 70 C2
Ruislip HA4 62 C3
PRIMROSE HILL 70 D1
Primrose Hill EC4 241 B1
Primrose Hill Ct NW3 70 D1
Primrose Hill Rd
Primrose Hill NW1, NW3 70 D1
Primrose Hill NW1, NW3 230 C6
Primrose Hill Sch
NW1 93 A6 231 B6
Primrose Hill Studios
NW1 231 A6
Primrose Ho
7 Peckham SE15 140 A4
1 Richmond TW9 132 B4
Primrose La CR0 206 D1
Primrose Mans
SW11 268 A2
Primrose Mews 9
NW1 70 D1
Primrose Pl 4 TW7 130 D3
Primrose Rd
Walthamstow E10 53 D1
Woodford E18 37 B1
Primrose Sq E9 96 C6
Primrose St
EC2 95 C2 243 B4
Primrose Way HA0 87 D5
Primrose Wlk
Ewell KT17 215 D1
6 New Cross Gate SE14 141 A5
Primula St W12 90 A1
Prince Albert Ct
Primrose Hill NW8 230 C5
Sunbury TW16 171 C3
Prince Albert Rd
NW8 92 D6 230 C5
Prince Arthur Ct 18
NW3 70 A4
Prince Arthur Mews 17
NW3 70 A4
Prince Arthur Rd
NW3 70 A3
Prince Charles Dr
NW2 46 C2
Prince Charles Rd
SE3 142 D4
Prince Charles Way
SM6 219 B5
Prince Consort Dr
BR7 189 B2
Prince Consort Ho
SE1 260 B2
Prince Consort Rd
SW7 114 B3 256 C6
Princedale Rd
W11 113 A5 244 B4
Prince Edward Mans
W2 245 B6
Prince Edward Rd E9 75 B2
Prince George Ave
N14 15 D6
Prince George Rd
N16 73 C4
Prince George's Ave
SW20 178 C1
Prince Georges Rd
SW19 180 B2
Prince Henry Rd
SE7 143 D5
Prince Imperial Rd
Chislehurst BR7 188 D3
Kidbrooke SE18 144 B4
Prince John Rd SE9 166 A6
Princelet St
E1 95 D2 243 D4
Prince of Orange La 3
SE10 142 A5
Prince Of Wales Cl
NW4 46 B5
Prince of Wales Dr
SW11 137 A4 268 A2
Prince of Wales Mans
Battersea SW11 268 B2
Clapham SW4 159 B6
Prince of Wales Pas
NW1 232 A1
Prince of Wales Prim Sch EN3 7 B6
Prince of Wales Rd
Blackheath Vale SE3 142 D4
Camden Town NW5 71 A2
Newham E16 99 C1
Prince Of Wales' Rd
SM1 218 B6
Prince Of Wales Terr
Chiswick W4 111 C1
Kensington W8 245 D1
Prince Rd SE25 205 C4
Prince Regent E16 99 C2
Prince Regent Ct 2
SE16 119 A5
Prince Regent La E13 99 C3
Prince Regent Mews
NW1 232 A1
Prince Regent Rd
TW3 130 A2
Prince Regent Sta
E16 121 C6
Prince Rupert Rd
SE9 144 B1
Princes Arc SW1 249 B4
Princes Ave
Acton W3 110 C3
Edmonton N13 32 C5
Finchley N3 29 D2
Muswell Hill N10 49 B6
Orpington BR5 211 C4
Queensbury NW9 44 D5
Tolworth KT6 214 C6
Wallington SM5 218 D1
Woodford IG8 37 C6
Wood Green N22 31 D2
Prince's Ave UB1 85 D1
Princes Cir
WC2 94 A1 240 A2
Princes Cl
Edgware HA8 26 C5
Finsbury Pk N4 50 D1
Queensbury NW9 44 C5
Sidcup DA14 168 D1
Prince's Cl TW11, TW12 174 B6
Princes Coll WC1 240 A2
Princes Court Bsns Ctr
14 E1 118 B6
Princes Ct
Brondesbury NW2 69 A3
Hampstead NW3 70 B4
Kingston u T KT3 199 D6
Stepney E1 118 B6
Wembley HA9 66 A3
Prince's Ct SE16 119 B3
Princes Dr HA1 42 C6
Princes Gate
SW7 114 B4 246 D1
Prince's Gate
SW7 114 C4 247 A1
Princes Gate Ct SW7 246 D1
Princes Gate Mews
SW7 114 B3 256 D6
Princes Gdns
Acton W3 88 C2
Brompton SW7 114 B3 256 D6
Ealing W5 87 C3
Princes Ho W11 245 A5
Princes La N10 49 B6
Princes Mews TW3 129 C1
Prince's Mews
1 Hammersmith W6 112 B1
Kensington W2 113 D6 245 C6
Princes Par NW11 47 A3
Princes Park Ave
Hayes UB3 105 B6
Temple Fortune NW11 47 A4
Princes Park Circ
UB3 105 B6
Princes Park Cl UB3 105 B6
Princes Park La UB3 105 B6
Princes Park Par
UB3 105 B6
Princes Pl
Notting Hill W11 113 A5 244 A4
St James SW1 249 B4
Prince's Plain BR2 210 A1
Princes Plain Prim Sch
BR2 210 A2
Princes Rd
Ashford TW15 170 B5
Buckhurst Hill IG9 21 C2
Ealing W13 109 B5
Edmonton N18 34 C6
Feltham TW13 149 D1
Ilford IG6 57 B5
Kew TW9 132 B4
Kingston u T KT2 176 C3
Penge SE20 184 D4
Richmond TW10 154 B6
Prince's Rd
Mortlake SW14 133 B2
Teddington TW11, TW12 174 B6
Wimbledon SW19 179 C4
Princes Rise SE13 142 A3
Princes Riverside Rd 7
SE16 118 D5
Princessa Ct EN2 17 B6
Princess Alexandra School of Nursing The
6 E1 96 B2
Princess Alice Ho 1
W10 90 C3
Princess Alice Way
SE28 123 B4
Princess Ave HA9 66 A6
Princess Beatrice Ho
SW10 255 C1
Princess Cl SE28 102 D1
Princess Cres N4 72 D6
Princess Ct
Catford BR1 186 C4
3 Croydon CR0 221 D6
Hampstead NW6 69 D1
Hounslow TW4 128 C2
Kensington W2 245 D6
Marylebone W1 237 C3
11 Wimbledon SW19 178 D3
Princess Frederica CE Jun & Inf Sch NW10 90 C5
Princess Grace Hospl The W1 93 A3 238 A5
Princess La HA4 39 C1
Princess Louise Cl
W2 236 D4
Princess Mary Ho
SW1 259 D3
Princess May Prim Sch
6 N16 73 D4
Princess May Rd N16 73 C4
Princess Mews
Hampstead NW3 70 B2
Kingston u T KT1 198 B6
Princess Par
Dagenham RM10 103 C5
Locksbottom BR6 226 C5
Princess Park Manor
N11 31 A5
Prince's Sq
W2 113 D6 245 C6
Princess Rd
Camden Town NW1 93 A6 231 B6
Paddington NW6 91 C5
Thornton Heath CR0 205 A3
Princess Royal University Hospl BR6 226 C5
Princess St
Bexley DA7 147 B2
Newington SE1 261 D5
Princes St
Bexleyheath DA7 147 B1
Marylebone W1 238 D1
Sutton SM1 218 B4
Tottenham N17 33 C4
Prince's St
City of London EC2 95 B1 242 C1
Richmond TW10, TW9 154 A6
Prince St SE8 141 B6
Prince's Terr E13 99 B6
Princes Way
Acton W3 110 C3
Buckhurst Hill IG9 21 C2
Princes Way *continued*
Coney Hall BR4 224 D5
Croydon CR0 220 B3
Putney SW15, SW19 157 A3
Ruislip HA4 63 A4
Princes Yd W11 244 B3
Princethorpe Ho W2 91 D2
Princethorpe Rd
SE26 184 D6
Princeton Ct 12
SW15 134 D2
Princeton Mans WC1 240 C3
Princeton Mews 3
KT2 176 C2
Princeton St
WC1 94 B2 240 C4
Prince William Ct
TW15 170 B5
Principal Cl N14 15 C3
Principal Sq E9 74 D3
Pringle Gdns SW16 181 C6
Pringle Ho N21 16 B6
Printers Mews E3 97 A6
Printer St EC4 241 B2
Printinghouse La
UB3 105 C4
Printing House Yd 16
E2 95 C4
Printon Ho 16 E3 97 B2
Print Village Ind Est
SE15 139 D3
Priolo Rd SE7 121 C1
Prior Ave SM2, SM5 218 C1
Prior Bolton St N1 72 D2
Prioress Ho 2 E3 97 D4
Prioress Rd SE27 160 D1
Prioress St SE1 262 D5
Prior Rd IG1 78 C5
Priors Croft E17 35 B1
Priors Field UB5 63 A2
Priors Gdns HA4 62 C3
Priors Lo 4 TW10 154 A5
Priors Mead EN1 5 C4
Prior St SE10 142 A5
Priors Wood KT10 212 D6
Prior Weston Prim Sch
EC1 95 B3 242 C6
Priory Ave
Bedford Pk W4 111 C3
Cheam SM3 216 D4
Chingford E4 19 C1
Hornsey N8 49 D5
Petts Wood BR5 211 B3
Walthamstow E17 53 C4
Wembley HA0 64 D4
Priory CE Prim Sch
SW19 179 D5
Priory Cl
Ashford TW16 172 A3
Barnet N20 13 B4
Beckenham BR3 207 A6
Chingford Green E4 19 B1
Chislehurst BR7 188 B2
East Barnet N14 15 B6
Finchley N3 29 B2
Hampton TW12 173 B2
Hayes UB3 106 B6
3 Merton SW19 179 D2
Ruislip HA4 39 D1
Stanmore HA7 8 D1
Wembley HA0 64 D4
Woodford E18 37 A2
Priory Cres
Cheam SM3 216 D4
South Norwood SE19 183 A3
Wembley HA0 65 A5
Priory Ct Bushey WD23 8 A3
Cheam SM3 217 A4
City of London EC4 241 D1
Hampton TW12 173 C3
Highgate N6 49 B3
Homerton E9 74 D3
Hounslow TW3 129 D2
Ilford RM6 58 B3
Newham E6 99 D6
Nunhead SE15 140 C1
Roehampton SW15 133 D1
South Lambeth SW8 137 D4 269 D2
Walthamstow E17 35 B1
4 Wembley HA0 88 A5
Priory Dr Stanmore HA7 8 D1
West Heath SE2 124 D1
Priory Field Dr HA8 26 D6
Priory Gdns
Ashford TW15 171 B5
Priory Gdns *continued*
Barnes SW13 133 D2
6 Chiswick W4 111 C2
Ealing W5 88 A4
Hampton TW12 173 B2
Highgate N6 49 B3
South Norwood SE25 205 D5
Wembley HA0 65 A4
Priory Gn N1 233 C4
Priory Gr Barnet EN5 13 C6
South Lambeth SW8 138 A4 270 A1
Priory Grange N2 48 D6
Priory Hill HA0 65 A4
Priory Ho
3 Charlton SE7 143 C6
Clerkenwell EC1 241 C6
Pimlico SW1 259 C2
Spitalfields E1 243 C4
Priory Hospl Grange Roehampton
SW15 133 D1
Priory Hospl Hayes Grove The BR2 225 A6
Priory Hospl North London The (Grovelands) N14 16 A3
Priory House Ct SE6 163 D3
Priory Hts N1 233 D4
Priory La
East Molesey KT8 195 D5
Roehampton SW15 155 D6
Priory Leas SE9 166 A3
Priory Lo
7 Brentford W4 110 C1
Coney Hall BR4 224 C5
Ealing W5 87 C1
Priory Mans
17 Maitland Pk NW3 70 D2
South Kensington SW10 256 B1
Priory Park Rd
Kilburn NW6 91 B6
Wembley HA0 65 A4
Priory Pk SE3 142 D2
Priory Rd Barking IG11 79 B1
Bedford Pk W4 111 B3
Cheam SM3 216 D4
Chessington KT9 214 A5
Hampstead NW6 69 D1
Hampton TW12 173 C3
Hornsey N8 49 D5
Hounslow TW3 152 A6
Mitcham SW19 180 B3
Newham E6 99 D5
Richmond TW9 132 C5
Thornton Heath CR0 204 C2
Priory Ret Pk SW19 180 B3
Priory Specl Sch
SE25 205 D5
Priory St 16 E3 97 D4
Priory Terr NW6 91 D6
Priory The
Croydon CR0 220 C5
Hornsey N8 49 D5
21 Kingston u T KT6 198 A4
Lambeth SE1 251 C1
Lewisham SE3 142 D1
Priory View WD23 8 C4
Priory Villas N11 30 D5
Priory Way
Harmondsworth UB7 126 A6
Harrow HA2 41 D5
Southall UB2 106 D3
Priory Wlk
South Kensington SW10 114 A1 256 B1
Sunbury TW16 172 A3
Priscilla Cl N15 51 A4
Priscilla Ho 8
TW16 171 D3
Pritchard Ho 38 E2 96 A5
Pritchard's Rd E2 96 A5
Pritchett Cl 13 EN3 7 C6
Priter Rd SE16 118 A3
Priter Road Hostel 14
SE16 118 A3
Private Rd EN1 17 C6
Probert Rd SW2 160 C6
Probyn Ho SW1 259 D4
Probyn Rd SW2 160 D2
Procter Ho 12 SE5 139 B5
Procter St
WC1 94 B2 240 C3

Proctor Cl CR4 181 A2
Proctor Ho 5 SE1 118 A1
Proctors Cl TW14 150 A3
Prodger 8 NW9 27 D2
Progress Bsns Pk CR9 220 B6
Progress Way
Croydon CR0 220 B6
Enfield EN1 18 A6
Wood Green N22 32 C2
Prologis Pk
Hounslow TW4 128 C1
Wallington CR0 203 D2
Prome Ho 3 N16 73 B4
Promenade Approach Rd W4 133 C5
Promenade Mans HA8 26 C5
Promenade The W4 133 C4
Pronto Trad Est UB4 83 C2
Prospect Cl
Belvedere DA17 125 C2
Bushey WD23 8 B4
Forest Hill SE26 184 B6
Hounslow TW5 129 B4
Ruislip HA4 40 D2
Prospect Cotts SW18 135 C1
Prospect Cres TW2 152 A5
Prospect Hill E17 53 D5
Prospect Ho
1 Dalston E8 73 D2
Islington N1 234 A3
3 Mitcham SW19 180 B2
Newington SE1 261 D5
14 North Kensington W10 90 D1
9 Walthamstow E17 54 A6
Prospect House Sch 11 SW15 156 D4
Prospect Pl
Bromley BR2 209 B6
5 Child's Hill NW2 69 B5
2 Chiswick W4 111 B1
6 Deptford SE8 141 B6
East Finchley N2 48 B5
12 Hampstead NW3 70 A4
7 Lower Holloway N7 72 A4
Tottenham N17 33 C3
Wapping E1 118 C5
Wimbledon SW20 178 B3
Prospect Quay SW18 135 C1
Prospect Rd
Barnet EN5 1 D1
Child's Hill NW2 69 C5
Kingston u T KT6 197 C3
Woodford IG8 37 C5
Prospect Ring N2 48 B6
Prospect St SE16 118 B4
Prospect Vale SE18 122 A2
Prospect Wharf E1 118 C6
Prospero Ho 7 DA17 125 C1
Prospero Rd N19 49 D1
Protea Cl E16 98 D3
Protheroe Ho 11 N17 51 D6
Prothero Gdns NW4 46 B4
Prothero Ho 15 NW10 67 B1
Prothero Rd SW6 135 B5 264 C4
Proud Ho 16 E1 96 B1
Prout Gr NW10 67 D4
Prout Rd E5 74 B5
Provence St N1 235 A4
Providence 1 SE16 118 A4
Providence Ave HA2 41 C1
Providence Cl E9 96 D6
Providence Ct
Harlington UB3 127 B5
Islington N1 234 C5
Mayfair W1 248 B6
Providence La UB3 127 B5
Providence Pl N1 234 C5
Providence Rd UB7 104 B5
Providence Row N1 233 C3
Providence Row Cl 30 E1 96 B4
Providence Sq 36 SE1 118 A4
Providence Yd 1 E2 96 A4
Provident Ind Est UB3 106 A4
Provincial Terr 2 SE20 184 D3
Provost Ct NW3 70 D2
Provost Rd NW3 70 D1
Provost St N1 95 B4 235 C2
Prowse Ave WD23 8 A2
Prowse Pl NW1 71 C1
Prudence La BR6 226 C4
Pruden Cl N14 15 C2
Prudent Pas EC2 242 B1
Prusom's Island 8 E1 118 C5
Prusom St E1 118 B5
Pryors The NW3 70 B5
Puccinia Ct TW19 148 A3
Pudding La EC3 252 D6
Pudding Mill La E15 97 D6
Pudding Mill Lane Sta E15 97 D6
Puddle Dock EC4 116 D6 251 D6
Puffin Cl
Barking IG11 102 B4
Beckenham BR3 206 D4
Puffin Ct 9 W13 86 D3
Puffin Terr IG5 56 C6
Puget Ct N12 30 A5
Pugin Ct N1 72 C1
Pulborough Rd SW18 157 B4
Pulborough Way TW4 128 C1
Pulford Rd N15 51 B3
Pulham Ave N2 48 B5
Pulham Ho SW8 270 C3
Puller Rd EN5 1 A3
Pulleyns Ave E6 100 A4
Pullman Ct SW2 160 B3
Pullman Gdns SW15 156 C5
Pullman Mews SE12 165 B1
Pullman Pl SE9 166 A6
Pulross Rd SW9 138 B2
Pulteney Cl
3 Isleworth TW7 131 A2
20 Old Ford E3 97 B6
Pulteney Gdns 9 E18 55 B6
Pulteney Rd E18 55 B6
Pulteney Terr N1 94 B6 233 D6
Pulton Ho SE4 141 A1
Pulton Pl SW6 135 C5 265 A3
Puma Ct E1 243 C4
Puma Trade Pk CR4 202 B5
Pump Alley 8 TW8 131 D5
Pump Cl UB5 85 C5
Pump Ct EC4 241 A1
Pump House Cl
Bromley BR2 186 D1
Rotherhithe SE16 118 C4
Pumphouse Educational Mus The★ SE16 119 A5
Pump House Gall★ SW11 137 A5 268 A3
Pumping Ho 8 E14 120 B6
Pumping Station Rd W4 133 C6
Pump La
Deptford SE14 140 C5
Hayes UB3 106 A4
Pump Pail N CR0 221 A5
Pump Pail S CR0 221 A5
Punchard Cres EN3 7 D5
Punderson's Gdns E2 96 B4
Puran Ho E13 99 C5
Purbeck Ave KT3 199 D3
Purbeck Ct 2 N20 14 C2
Purbeck Dr NW2 68 D6
Purbeck Ho SW8 270 C3
Purbrook Est SE1 253 B1
Purbrook Ho 2 SW15 156 B3
Purbrook St SE1 263 B6
Purcell Cres SW6 135 A5 264 A4
Purcell Ho
Chelsea SW10 266 C5
Isleworth TW2 152 B5
Southall UB1 85 C1
Purcell Mews 2 NW10 67 C1
Purcell Rd UB6 85 D2
Purcells Ave HA8 26 C5
Purcell St N1 95 C5
Purchese St NW1 93 D5 232 D3
Purday Ho 4 W10 91 B4
Purdey Ct 3 KT4 200 A1
Purdon Ho 11 SE15 140 A4
Purdy St E3 97 D3
Purkis Cl UB3 105 A6
Purland Cl RM8 59 B1
Purland Rd SE28, SE18 123 D4
Purley Ave NW2 69 A6
Purley Oaks Prim Sch CR2 221 B1
Purley Pl N1 72 D1
Purley Rd
Edmonton N9 17 C1
South Croydon CR2 221 B1
Purley View Terr CR2 221 B1
Purley Way
Croydon CR0, CR9 220 C3
Thornton Heath CR0 204 B1
Purley Way Cres CR0 204 B2
Purneys Rd SE9 143 D1
Purrett Rd SE18 123 D1
Purser Ho 3 SW2 160 C5
Pursers Cross Rd SW6 135 B4 264 D2
Pursewardens Cl W13 109 C5
Pursley Rd NW7 28 B3
Purves Rd NW10 90 C5
Purvis Ho CR0 205 B2
Pusey Ho 20 E14 97 C1
Puteaux Ho 6 E2 96 D5
PUTNEY 156 C6
Putney Bridge App SW6 135 A2
Putney Bridge Rd SW15 135 B1
Putney Bridge Sta SW6 135 B2
Putney Comm SW15 134 C2
Putney Exchange Shopping Ctr SW15 134 D1
Putney Gdns RM6 58 B4
PUTNEY HEATH 156 C4
Putney Heath SW15 156 C5
Putney Heath La SW15 156 D5
Putney High Sch SW15 156 D6
Putney High St SW15 135 A1
Putney Hill
12 Putney SW15 156 C4
Putney SW15 156 D6
Putney L Ctr SW15 134 C1
Putney Park Ave SW15 134 A1
Putney Park La SW15 156 B6
Putney Park Sch SW15 134 B1
Putney Pier SW15 135 A2
Putney School of Art & Design SW15 135 A1
Putney Sta SW15 135 A1
PUTNEY VALE 156 A1
Putney Wharf Twr SW15 135 A2
Pycombe Cnr N12 29 B6
Pycroft Way N9 34 A6
Pykewell Lo 13 E8 74 A3
Pylbrook Rd SM1 217 D5
Pylon Trad Est E16 98 B2
Pylon Way CR0 204 A1
Pym Cl EN4 14 B6
Pymers Mead SE21 161 A3
Pymmes Brook Dr EN4 2 C1
Pymmes Brook Ho 3 N10 31 A3
Pymmes Cl
Bowes Pk N13 32 B5
Tottenham N17 34 B2
Pymmes Gdns N N9 17 D1
Pymmes Gdns S N9 17 D1
Pymmes Green Rd N11 15 C1
Pymmes Mews N13 32 A5
Pymmes Rd N13 32 A5
Pynchester Cl UB10 60 C6
Pyne Rd KT6 198 C1
Pynfolds SE16 118 B4
Pynham Cl SE2 124 B3
Pynnacles Cl HA7 25 B5
Pynnersmead SE24 161 A6
Pyramid Ho N12 30 A6
Pyrford Ho 12 SW9 138 D1
Pyrland Rd
Richmond TW10 154 B5
Stoke Newington N5 73 B3
Pyrmont Gr SE27 160 D1
Pyrmont Rd W4 132 C6
Pytchley Cres SE19 183 A4
Pytchley Rd SE22 139 C2

Q

Quadrangle Cl SE1 263 A4
Quadrangle Ho The E15 76 C2
Quadrangle Lo SW19 179 C4
Quadrangle The
Chelsea SW10 266 B2
Fulham SW6 264 A3
Herne Hill SE24 161 A6
3 North Kensington W12 90 C1
Paddington W2 237 A2
Stanmore HA7 25 C3
Walthamstow E17 35 B1
Quadrant Arc W1 249 B5
Quadrant Bsns Ctr NW6 91 A6
Quadrant Cl NW4 46 B4
Quadrant Gr NW5 70 D3
Quadrant Ho E15 98 C4
Quadrant Rd
Finchley N2 30 C2
Richmond TW9 131 D1
Thornton Heath CR7 204 D5
Quadrant The
4 Kensal Green W10 90 D4
Richmond TW9 132 A1
Sutton SM2 218 A2
West Heath DA7 146 D5
Wimbledon SW20 179 A2
Quad Rd HA9 65 D5
Quaggy Wlk SE3 143 A1
Quainton Hall Sch HA1 42 C4
Quainton St NW10 67 B5
Quaker Ct EC1 242 B6
Quaker La UB2 107 C3
Quakers Course NW9 27 D2
Quakers La TW7 131 A4
Quaker's Pl E7 77 D3
Quaker St E1 95 D3 243 C5
Quakers Wlk N21 17 B5
Quality Ct WC2 241 A2
Quantock Cl UB3 127 B5
Quantock Ct
4 East Barnet N20 14 C2
Greenford UB6 64 C3
Quantock Dr KT4 216 C6
Quantock Gdns NW2 68 D6
Quantock Ho N16 51 D1
Quantock Mews 3 SE15 140 A3
Quarles Park Rd RM6 58 C3
Quarrendon St SW6 135 C3
Quarr Rd SM5 202 C3
Quarry Park Rd SM1 217 B2
Quarry Rd SW18 158 A5
Quarry Rise SM1 217 B2
Quarterdeck The E14 119 C4
Quartermain Ho SM4 202 A4
Quartermile La E10 75 D4
Quayside Ct 6 SE16 118 D5
Quay West Ct TW11 175 B5
Quebec & Crown Wharves E14 97 B1
Quebec Ind Est SE16 119 A3
Quebec Mews W1 237 D1
Quebec Rd Hayes UB4 84 C1
Ilford IG1 57 A2
Quebec Way SE16 119 A4
Quebec Wharf 32 E8 95 C6
Quedgeley Ct 3 SE15 139 D6
Queen Adelaide Ct SE20 184 C4
Queen Adelaide Rd SE20 184 C3
Queen Alexandra Mans WC1 233 A1
Queen Alexandra's Ct SW19 179 B5
Queen Anne Ave BR2 208 D6
Queen Anne Dr KT10 212 C1
Queen Anne Gate DA7 146 D2
Queen Anne Mews W1 238 D3
Queen Anne Rd E9 74 D2
Queen Annes Cl TW2 152 B1
Queen Anne's Gate SW1 115 D4 249 C1
Queen Anne's Gdns
Bedford Pk W4 111 C3
Ealing W5 110 A4
Enfield EN1 17 C5
Mitcham CR4 202 D6
Queen Anne's Gr
Bedford Pk W4 111 C3
Ealing W5 110 A4
Enfield EN1 17 C5
Queen Anne's Pl EN1 17 C5
Queen Anne St W1 93 B2 238 C3
Queen Anne Terr 9 E1 118 B6
Queenborough Gdns
Chislehurst BR7 189 B4
Ilford IG2 56 C5
Queen Caroline St W6 112 C1
Queen Charlotte's & Chelsea Hospl W12 90 A1
Queen Ct WC1 240 B5
Queen Elizabeth Ct
Barnet EN5 1 B1
5 Kingsland N1 73 B2
Queen Elizabeth Gdns SM4 201 C5
Queen Elizabeth Hall & Purcell Room★ SE1 250 D4
Queen Elizabeth Ho SW12 159 A4
Queen Elizabeth Hospl SE18 144 A5
Queen Elizabeth II Con Ctr SW1 249 D1
Queen Elizabeth II Jubilee Sch 5 W9 91 B3
Queen Elizabeth II Pier SE10 120 D5
Queen Elizabeth Rd
Kingston u T KT2 176 B1
Walthamstow E17 53 A6
Queen Elizabeth's Cl N16 73 B6
Queen Elizabeth's Coll 15 SE10 142 A5
Queen Elizabeth's Dr N14 16 A3
Queen Elizabeth's Girls Sch EN5 1 B1
Queen Elizabeth's Hunting Lodge Mus★ E4 20 D4
Queen Elizabeth St SE1 117 D4 253 C2
Queen Elizabeth's Wlk
Stoke Newington N16 73 B6
Wallington SM6 219 D4
Queen Elizabeth Wlk SW13 134 B4
Queenhithe EC4 252 B6
Queen Margaret Flats 22 E2 96 B4
Queen Margarets Ct N1 73 C3
Queen Margaret's Gr N1 73 C3
Queen Mary Ave SM4 200 D4
Queen Mary Cl KT9 214 C5
Queen Mary Ct TW19 148 A3
Queen Mary Rd
Charlton TW17 171 A1
South Norwood SE19 182 D4
Queen Mary's Ave SM5 218 D1
Queen Mary's Gdns★ NW1 231 A1

Queen Mary's Hospl
DA14 . . . . 190 A4
Queen Mary's Univ Hospl
SW15 . . . . 156 A5
Queen Mary, Univ of
London E1 . . . . 97 A3
Queen Mother Sp Ctr
SW1 . . . . 259 A4
Queen of Denmark Ct
SE16 . . . . 119 B3
Queens Acre SM3 . . . 217 A1
Queen St Pl EC4 . . . . 252 B6
Queens Ave
Feltham TW13 . . . . . . 172 C6
Muswell Hill N10 . . . . . . 49 B6
Stanmore HA7 . . . . 25 C1
Whetstone N20 . . . . 14 B2
Queen's Ave
Finchley N3 . . . . 30 A2
Southall UB1 . . . . 86 A1
Southgate N21 . . . . 16 D3
Woodford IG8 . . . . 37 B5
Queensberry Ho 6
TW9 . . . . 153 D6
Queensberry Mews W
SW7 . . . . 256 C4
Queensberry Pl
Chelsea
SW7 . . . . . . 114 B2 256 C4
Plashet E12 . . . . 78 A3
Queensberry Way
SW7 . . . . 256 C4
Queensborough Ct
N3 . . . . 47 B5
Queensborough Mews
W2 . . . . 246 A6
Queensborough Pas
W2 . . . . 246 A6
Queensborough Terr
W2 . . . . 113 D6 245 D6
Queensbridge Ct 1
E2 . . . . 95 D5
Queensbridge Inf Sch 11
E8 . . . . 73 D1
Queensbridge Pk
TW7 . . . . 152 C6
Queensbridge Rd
Dalston E8 . . . . 73 D1
Shoreditch E2, E8 . . . . . 95 D6
QUEENSBURY 44 B6
Queensbury IG9 . . . . . . 21 B3
Queensbury Circ Par
HA3 . . . . 44 A6
Queensbury Ct CR7 . . 183 A1
Queensbury Rd
Kingsbury NW9 . . . . 45 B2
Wembley HA0 . . . . 88 B5
Queensbury St 22 N1 . 73 A1
Queensbury Sta HA7,
HA8 . . . . 44 B6
Queensbury Station Par
HA8 . . . . 44 B6
Queen's CE Prim Sch The
TW9 . . . . 132 C5
Queen's Cir
SW11 . . . . . . 137 B5 268 C3
Queen's Cl
Edgware HA8 . . . . 26 C5
Wallington SM6 . . . . . . 219 B3
Queen's Club Gdns
W14 . . . . 135 A6 264 B6
Queen's Club The
W14 . . . . 113 A1 254 B1
Queen's Coll
W1 . . . . 93 B2 238 C3
Queen's Coll Prep Sch
W1 . . . . 238 C4
Queenscourt HA9 . . . . . 66 A4
Queens Cres TW10 . . . 154 B6
Queen's Cres NW5 . . . . 71 A2
Queenscroft Rd SE9 . 165 D5
Queens Ct
Battersea SW11 . . . . 268 C2
Beckenham BR3 . . . . . 185 D3
Camberwell SE5 . . . . . 139 C3
Leyton E10 . . . . 53 C2
4 Limehouse E14 . . . . 119 B6
Sidcup DA14 . . . . 190 A6
Stanmore HA7 . . . . 25 B1
8 Temple Fortune
NW11 . . . . 47 B4
Walthamstow E17 . . . . . 53 C4
Queen's Ct
Barnes SW13 . . . . 134 A2
Beckenham BR3 . . . . . 185 C2
Croydon CR2 . . . . 221 A3
8 Ealing W5 . . . . 87 C2
Hampstead Garden Suburb
NW11 . . . . 47 C4
Kensington W2 . . . . . . 245 D5
1 Kingston u T KT2 . . 176 C3
Leytonstone E11 . . . . . . 54 C2
3 Richmond TW10 . . . 154 B5
St John's Wood NW8 . 229 C4
Thornton Heath CR7 . . 204 C4
Queensdale W11 . . . . 112 D5
Queensdale Cres
W11 . . . . 112 D5
Queensdale Pl W11 . 244 A3
Queensdale Rd
Notting Hill W11 . . . . . 112 D5
Notting Hill
W11 . . . . 113 A5 244 A3
Queensdale Wlk
W11 . . . . 244 A3
Queensdown Rd E5 . . . 74 B4
Queens Dr
Surbiton KT5 . . . . 198 C3
Walthamstow E10 . . . . . 53 C2
Queen's Dr Acton W3 . . 88 C1
Finsbury Pk N4 . . . . 72 D6
Thames Ditton KT7 . . . 197 A3
Queen's Elm Par
SW3 . . . . 256 D2
Queen's Elm Sq SW3 256 D1
Queensferry Wlk N17 . 52 B5
Queensfield Ct SM3 . . 216 C4
Queen's Gallery*
SW1 . . . . 115 B4 248 D1
Queens Gate IG4 . . . . . 56 B5
Queen's Gate
SW7 . . . . 114 A3 256 B5
Queensgate Ct N12 . . . 29 D5
Queensgate Gdns
SW15 . . . . 134 B1
Queens Gate Gdns
BR7 . . . . 189 B2
Queen's Gate Gdns
SW7 . . . . 114 A3 256 B5
Queensgate Ho 34 E3 . 97 B5
Queen's Gate Jun Sch
SW7 . . . . 256 C4
Queen's Gate Mews
SW7 . . . . 114 A3 256 B6
Queensgate Pl 10
NW6 . . . . 69 C1
Queen's Gate Pl
SW7 . . . . 114 A3 256 B5
Queen's Gate Pl Mews
SW7 . . . . 114 A3 256 B5
Queen's Gate Terr
SW7 . . . . 114 A3 256 B6
Queens Gate Villas
E9 . . . . 75 A1
Queens Gdns NW4 . . . 46 C4
Queen's Gdns
Bayswater
W2 . . . . 114 A6 246 A6
Ealing W5 . . . . 87 C3
Heston TW5 . . . . 129 A4
Queen's Gr
NW8 . . . . 92 B6 229 D5
Queen's Grove Rd E4 . 20 B3
Queen's Head Pas
EC2 . . . . 242 A2
Queen's Head St
N1 . . . . 94 D6 234 D5
Queen's Head Yd
SE1 . . . . 252 C3
Queens Ho 1 SE17 . . 139 B6
Queen's Ho TW11 . . . 174 D4
Queen's House The*
SE10 . . . . 142 B6
Queens Keep 10
TW1 . . . . 153 C5
Queens La
2 Ashford TW15 . . . . . 170 B6
Muswell Hill N10 . . . . . . 49 B6
Queensland Ave
Edmonton N18 . . . . 33 A4
Merton SW19 . . . . 179 D2
Queensland Cl E17 . . . . 35 B1
Queensland Ct N10 . . . . 31 B3
Queensland Ho 2
E16 . . . . 122 C5
Queensland Rd N7 . . . . 72 C4
Queens Lo HA7 . . . . 25 A5
Queens Manor Sch
SW6 . . . . 134 D5
Queens Mans
Hampstead NW6 . . . . . . 69 D3
Hendon NW4 . . . . 46 B4
Queen's Mans
Brook Green W6 . . . . 112 D2
Muswell Hill N10 . . . . . . 49 A6
Queensmead
Ashford TW15 . . . . . . 170 B5
St John's Wood
NW8 . . . . 92 B6 229 D6
Queens Mead HA8 . . . . 26 B4
Queen's Mead Rd
BR2 . . . . 186 D1
Queensmead Sch
HA4 . . . . 62 D4
Queensmead Sp Ctr
HA4 . . . . 62 D3
Queensmere 4
SM1 . . . . 217 D3
Queensmere Cl
SW19 . . . . 156 D2
Queensmere Ct
SW13 . . . . 134 A6
Queensmere Rd
SW19 . . . . 156 D2
Queens Mews 5 IG9 . 21 C2
Queen's Mews
W2 . . . . 113 D6 245 C6
Queensmill Rd SW6 . 134 D5
Queensmill Sch
SW6 . . . . 135 C3
Queen's Mkt* E13 . . . . 99 C6
Queens Par Ealing W5 . 88 B1
7 Hendon NW4 . . . . . . 46 B4
3 Willesden NW2 . . . . . 68 C2
Queen's Par
3 Friern Barnet N11 . . 30 D5
Wood Green N11 . . . . . . 32 A3
Queens Parade Cl
N11 . . . . 30 D5
Queens Park Com Sch
NW6 . . . . 90 D6
Queens Park Ct 5
W10 . . . . 90 D4
Queens Park Gdns
TW13 . . . . 149 D1
Queen's Park Prim Sch
20 W10 . . . . 91 A3
Queen's Park Sta
NW6 . . . . 91 B5
Queen's Pas BR7 . . . 188 D4
Queen's Pl SM4 . . . . . 201 C5
Queen Sq
WC1 . . . . 94 A2 240 B4
Queen's Quay EC4 . . 252 B6
Queens Rd Hayes UB3 . 83 C1
Morden SM4 . . . . 201 C5
Twickenham TW1 . . . . 153 A3
West Drayton UB7 . . . 104 B4
Queen's Rd
Barking IG11 . . . . 79 A2
Beckenham BR3 . . . . . 185 A1
Bowes Pk N11 . . . . 32 A4
Bromley BR1 . . . . 187 A1
Buckhurst Hill IG9 . . . . 21 C2
Chislehurst BR7 . . . . . 188 D4
Ealing W5 . . . . 88 A1
Edmonton N9 . . . . 18 B2
Enfield EN1 . . . . 5 C1
Feltham TW13 . . . . . . 150 B3
Finchley N3 . . . . 30 A2
Hampton TW12 . . . . . 173 D6
Hendon NW4 . . . . 46 C4
Hounslow TW3 . . . . . . 129 D2
Kingston u T KT2 . . . . 176 C3
Leytonstone E11 . . . . . . 54 C2
Mitcham CR4 . . . . 202 B6
Mortlake SW14 . . . . . . 133 B2
New Cross Gate SE14,
SE15 . . . . 140 C4
Newham E13 . . . . 99 C6
New Malden KT3 . . . . 199 D4
Richmond KT2, TW10 . 176 C5
Richmond TW10 . . . . . 154 B5
Southall UB2 . . . . 107 A4
Teddington TW11 . . . . 174 D4
Thames Ditton KT7 . . . 196 D4
Thornton Heath CR0 . . 205 A3
Wallington SM6 . . . . . . 219 B3
Walthamstow E17 . . . . . 53 C3
Welling DA16 . . . . 146 B3
Wimbledon SW19 . . . . 179 C4
Queen's Rd W E13 . . . . 99 B5
Queens Reach KT8 . . 196 C5
Queen's Ride SW13 . . 134 B2
Queen's Rise TW10 . . 154 B5
Queen's Road Sta
SE15 . . . . 140 C4
Queen's Row SE17 . . . 139 B6
Queen St
Bexleyheath DA7 . . . . 147 B2
City of London
EC4 . . . . 117 A6 252 B6
Croydon CR0 . . . . 221 A4
Mayfair W1 . . 115 B5 248 C4
Tottenham N17 . . . . 33 C4
Queens Terr
Harrow HA3 . . . . 24 C1
Newham E13 . . . . 99 B6
St John's Wood
NW8 . . . . 92 B5 229 C4
Queen's Terr TW7 . . . 131 A1
Queens Terr Cotts
W7 . . . . 108 C4
Queensthorpe Rd
SE26 . . . . 184 D6
Queenstown Mews
SW8 . . . . 268 C1
Queenstown Rd
SW8 . . . . 137 B5 268 C4
Queenstown Road
(Battersea) Sta
SW8 . . . . 137 B4 268 D2
Queensville Rd SW12,
SW4 . . . . 159 D4
Queens Walk Ho W5 . . 87 C2
Queensway
Coney Hall BR4 . . . . . 224 D4
Croydon CR0 . . . . 220 B3
Enfield EN3 . . . . 6 C1
Kensington
W2 . . . . 113 D6 245 D6
Orpington BR5 . . . . . . 211 A3
Sunbury TW16 . . . . . . 172 B1
Queens Way
Feltham TW13 . . . . . . 172 C6
Hendon NW4 . . . . 46 C4
Queensway Bsns Ctr
EN3 . . . . 6 C1
Queensway Sta
W2 . . . . 113 D6 245 D5
Queens Well Ave N20 . 30 C6
Queenswell Jun & Inf
Schs N20 . . . . 14 B2
Queens Wlk
Ashford TW15 . . . . . . 170 A6
Chingford E4 . . . . 20 B3
Harrow HA1 . . . . 42 C5
Ruislip HA4 . . . . 62 C5
Welsh Harp NW9 . . . . . 67 A6
Queen's Wlk
Ealing W5 . . . . 87 C2
St James
SW1 . . . . 115 C5 249 A3
Queenswood Ave
Chingford E17 . . . . 36 A2
Hampton TW12 . . . . . 173 D4
Hounslow TW3, TW5 . . 129 B3
Thornton Heath CR7 . 204 C4
Wallington CR0, SM6 . 219 D4
Queenswood Ct
7 Clapham Pk
SW4 . . . . 160 A6
11 West Norwood
SE27 . . . . 183 B6
Queenswood Gdns
E11 . . . . 55 B1
Queenswood Pk N3 . . . 29 A2
Queenswood Rd
Blackfen DA15 . . . . . . 167 D5
Forest Hill SE23 . . . . . 163 A1
Queen's Wood Rd N6 . 49 B3
Queens Yd E9 . . . . 75 C2
Queen's Yd W1 . . . . . 239 B5
Queen Victoria Ave
HA0 . . . . 65 D1
Queen Victoria Meml*
SW1 . . . . 249 A2
Queen Victoria St
EC4 . . . . 117 A6 252 A6
Queen Victoria Terr 12
E1 . . . . 118 B6
Quelch Ho 2 N19 . . . . 71 D3
Quemerford Rd N7 . . . 72 B3
Quendon Ho 9 W10 . . 90 C3
Quenington Ct 5
SE15 . . . . 139 D6
Quenington Mans
SW6 . . . . 264 C2
Quennel Ho 7
SW12 . . . . 159 C4
Quentin Pl SE13 . . . . 142 C2
Quentin Rd SE13 . . . . 142 C2
Quernmore Cl BR1 . . . 187 A4
Quernmore Rd
Plaistow BR1 . . . . 187 A4
Stroud Green N4 . . . . . . 50 C3
Querrin St SW6 . . . . . 136 A3
Quested Ct 27 E8 . . . . . 74 B3
Quex Mews NW6 . . . . . 91 C6
Quex Rd NW6 . . . . 91 C6
Quick Rd W4 . . . . 111 C1
Quicks Rd SW19 . . . . 179 D3
Quick St N1 . . . 94 D5 234 D3
Quick Street Mews
N1 . . . . 234 C3
Quickswood NW3 . . . . . 70 C1
Quiet Nook BR2 . . . . . 225 D5
Quill La SW15 . . . . 134 D1
Quill St Ealing W5 . . . . . 88 A5
Highbury N4 . . . . 72 C5
Quilp St SE1 . . . . 252 A2
Quilters Pl SE9 . . . . . . 167 A3
Quilter St
Bethnal Green E2 . . . . . . 96 A4
Plumstead Comm
SE18 . . . . 123 D1
Quilting Ct 23 SE16 . . 118 D4
Quince Ho TW13 . . . . 150 A3
Quince Rd SE13 . . . . . 141 D3
Quinnel Cl SE18 . . . . . 123 D1
Quinta Dr EN5 . . . . 12 C6
Quintin Ave SW20 . . . 179 B2
Quintin Cl HA5 . . . . 40 B4
Quintin Ct W4 . . . . . . 133 A5
Quintin Kynaston Sch
NW8 . . . . 92 B6 229 C5
Quintock Ho 2
TW9 . . . . 132 C4
Quinton Cl
Beckenham BR3 . . . . . 208 A6
Cranford TW5 . . . . 128 B5
Wallington SM6 . . . . . . 219 B4
Quinton Ho SW8 . . . . 270 A4
Quinton Rd KT7 . . . . . 197 A1
Quinton St SW18 . . . . 158 A2
Quixley St 1 E14 . . . . 120 B6
Quorn Rd SE22 . . . . . . 139 C2
Quwwatul Islam Girls
Sch E7 . . . . 77 B2

R

Rabbit Row W8 . . . . . 245 B4
Rabbits Rd E12 . . . . 78 A4
Rabbs Farm Prim Sch
UB7 . . . . 104 A6
Rabinal Ho EN3 . . . . 18 D6
Rabournmead Dr
UB5 . . . . 63 A3
Raby Rd KT3 . . . . 199 B5
Raby St E14 . . . . 97 A1
Raccoon Way TW4 . . . 128 C3
Rachel Cl IG6 . . . . 57 B6
Rachel Ct SM2 . . . . . . 218 B1
Racine 15 SE5 . . . . . . 139 C4
Rackham Cl DA16 . . . . 146 B3
Rackham Mews
SW16 . . . . 181 C4
Racs Flats 9 SE1 . . . . 118 A2
Racton Rd
SW6 . . . . 135 C6 265 A5
Radbourne Ave W5 . . 109 C2
Radbourne Cl E5 . . . . . 74 D4
Radbourne Cres E17 . . 36 B1
Radbourne Ct HA3 . . . . 43 B3
Radbourne Rd
SW12 . . . . 159 D3
Radcliff Bldg EC1 . . . 241 A4
Radcliffe Ave
Enfield EN2 . . . . 5 A4
Willesden Green NW10 90 A5
Radcliffe Coll
Marylebone
W1 . . . . 93 C1 239 A1
Soho W1 . . . . . 93 D1 239 C2
Radcliffe Gdns SM5 . . 218 C1
Radcliffe Ho 10
SE16 . . . . 118 B2
Radcliffe Path 5
SW8 . . . . 137 B3
Radcliffe Rd
Bermondsey SE1 . . . . 263 B6
Harrow HA3 . . . . 25 A1

Radcliffe Rd *continued*
South Croydon CR0 221 D5
Southgate N21 16 D3
Radcliffe Sq SW15 156 D5
Radcliffe Way UB5 84 D4
Radcliff Mews TW12 174 A5
Radcot Point 2 SE23 162 D1
Radcot St SE11 261 B1
Raddington Rd W10 91 A2
Radfield Way DA15 167 B4
Radford Ho
7 Bow Comm E14 97 D2
Islington N7 72 B3
Radford Rd SE13 164 A5
Radford Way IG11 101 D4
Radipole Rd SW6 135 B4 264 C2
Radius Pk TW6 127 D1
Radland Rd E16 99 A1
Radlet Ave SE23 162 B2
Radlett Cl E7 76 D2
Radlett Pl NW8 92 C6 230 A6
Radley Ave IG3 80 A4
Radley Cl TW14 149 D3
Radley Ct
4 Catford BR1 186 A6
25 Rotherhithe SE16 118 D4
Radley Gdns HA3 44 A5
Radley Ho
11 Abbey Wood SE2 124 D4
Marylebone NW1 237 C6
Radley Lo 30 SW19 156 D3
Radley Mews W8 255 B5
Radley Rd N17 33 C1
Radley's La E18 37 A1
Radleys Mead RM10 81 D2
Radley Sq E5 74 C6
Radley Terr 1 E16 98 D2
Radlix Rd E10 53 C1
Radnor Ave
Bexley DA16 168 B6
Harrow HA1 42 C4
Radnor Cl
Chislehurst BR7 189 C4
Mitcham CR4 204 A5
Radnor Cres
Redbridge IG4 56 B4
Woolwich SE18 146 A5
Radnor Ct Ealing W7 86 D1
6 Forest Hill SE23 162 D1
Harrow HA3 24 D2
Radnor Gdns
Enfield EN1 5 C4
Twickenham TW1 152 D2
Radnor Gr UB10 82 C5
Radnor Ho
East Molesey KT8 196 B5
Thornton Heath SW16 182 B1
Radnor Lo W2 236 D1
Radnor Mews W2 92 B1 236 D1
Radnor Pl W2 92 C1 237 A1
Radnor Rd
Harrow HA1 42 C4
Kensal Rise NW6 91 A6
Peckham SE15 140 A5
Twickenham TW1 152 D2
Radnor St EC1 95 A4 235 B1
Radnor Terr W14 113 B2 254 C4
Radnor Way NW10 88 D3
Radnor Wlk
Chelsea SW3 114 D1 257 C1
Croydon CR0 207 A3
21 Millwall E14 119 C2
Radstock Ave HA3 43 B6
Radstock Cl N11 31 A4
Radstock St SW11 267 A3
Radway Ho 38 W2 91 C2
Radwell Ho SW2 160 C6
Raebarn Ct 6 SW16 160 A1
Raebarn Gdns EN5 12 B6
Raeburn Ave KT5 198 D3
Raeburn Cl
Hampstead Garden Suburb NW11 48 A3
Teddington KT1 175 D3
Raeburn Ho
5 Belmont SM2 217 D1
6 Northolt UB5 84 D5
Raeburn Rd
Edgware HA8 26 C2
Hayes UB4 83 B5
Sidcup DA15 167 C5
Raeburn St SW2 138 A1
Raffles Ct HA8 26 B6
Raffles Ho NW4 46 B5
Rafford Way BR1 209 B6
RAF Mus★ NW9 28 A1
Ragged School Mus★ E3 97 A2
Raggleswood BR7 188 C2
Raglan Cl TW4 151 B6
Raglan Ct
Brixton SW9 138 C2
Croydon CR0, CR2 220 D3
Lee SE12 165 A6
Wembley HA9 66 C5
Raglan Jun & Inf Schs EN1 17 C4
Raglan Prim Sch BR2 209 D5
Raglan Rd
Belvedere DA17 125 B2
Bromley BR2 209 C5
Enfield EN1 17 D4
Walthamstow E17 54 B4
Woolwich SE18 123 A1
Raglan St NW5 71 B2
Raglan Terr HA2 63 D4
Raglan Way UB5 64 A2
Ragley Cl W3 111 A4
Ragwort Ct 1 SE26 184 B5
Rahere Ho EC1 235 A2
Railey Mews NW5 71 C3
Railshead Rd TW1, TW7 131 B1
Railton Rd SE24 160 D6
Railway App
Bermondsey SE1 252 D4
Harrow HA1, HA3 42 D5
Stroud Green N4 50 C3
11 Twickenham TW1 153 A4
Wallington SM6 219 B3
Railway Ave SE16 118 C4
Railway Cotts
Hammersmith W6 112 C4
Ilford IG6 57 B6
Railway Gr SE14 141 B5
Railway Pl DA17 125 C3
Railway Rd TW11 174 D6
Railway Rise SE22 139 C1
Railway Side SW13 133 C2
Railway St Ilford RM6 58 C2
King's Cross N1 233 B3
Railway Terr
Chingford E17 36 A2
Feltham TW13, TW14 150 A3
Ladywell SE13 163 D6
Rainborough Cl NW10 67 A2
Rainbow Ave E14 119 D1
Rainbow Ct 3 SE14 141 A6
Rainbow Ind Est SW20 178 B1
Rainbow Montessori Sch NW6 69 D1
Rainbow Quay SE16 119 A3
Rainbow Sch 5 SW17 158 A2
Rainbow St SE5 139 C5
Rainbow Works N15 52 A4
Raine Gdns 4 IG8 37 A6
Raines Ct N16 73 D6
Raine's Foundation Lower Sch 32 E2 96 B4
Raine's Foundation Sch 34 E2 96 C5
Raine St E1 118 B5
Rainford Ho 9 N7 72 B6
Rainham Cl
Sidcup SE9 167 C5
Wandsworth SW11 158 C5
Rainham Ho NW1 232 B5
Rainham Rd NW10 90 C4
Rainham Rd N RM10 81 D6
Rainham Rd S RM10 81 D4
Rainhill Way E3 97 C4
Rainsborough Ave SE8 119 A2
Rainsford Cl HA7 25 C5
Rainsford Ct NW10 88 D5
Rainsford Ho 14 SW2 160 B6
Rainsford Rd NW10 88 D5
Rainsford St W2 237 A2
Rainstar Est N18 34 C6
Rainton Rd SE7 121 A1
Rainville Rd W6 134 C6
Raisins Hill HA5 40 C6
Raith Ave N14 15 D1
Raleigh Ave
Hayes UB4 84 B2
Wallington SM6 219 D4
Raleigh Cl
Hendon NW4 46 C4
Pinner HA5 40 D2
Ruislip HA4 61 D6
Raleigh Ct
Beckenham BR3 185 D2
4 Dulwich SE19 183 D5
Ealing W13 87 B2
7 Hammersmith W12 112 B4
2 Rotherhithe SE16 118 D5
Wallington SM6 219 B2
Raleigh Dr
East Barnet N20 14 C1
Esher KT10 212 B3
Tolworth KT5 199 A1
Raleigh Gdns
Mitcham CR4 202 D6
Tulse Hill SW2 160 B5
Raleigh Ho
30 Clapham SW8 137 D3
Isle of Dogs E14 119 D4
1 Thames Ditton KT7 197 A2
Raleigh Mews
Islington N1 234 D5
6 Orpington BR6 227 D3
Raleigh Rd Enfield EN2 5 B1
Feltham TW13 149 D2
Finchley N10 30 C2
Hornsey N8 50 C5
Penge SE20 184 D3
Richmond TW9 132 B2
Southall UB2 107 A1
Raleigh St N1 94 D6 234 D5
Raleigh Way
Feltham TW13 172 C5
Southgate N14 16 A3
Ralph Ct 8 W2 91 D1
Ralph Perring Ct BR3 207 C5
Ralston St SW3 257 C1
Ramac Ind Est SE7 121 B1
Rama Cl SW16 182 A3
Rama Ct HA1 64 C6
Ramac Way SE7 121 B1
Rama La SE19 183 D3
Ramar Ho 12 E1 96 A2
Rambler Cl SW16 181 C6
Rambler Ct 11 NW9 46 A5
Rame Cl SW17 181 A5
Ramilles Cl SW2 160 A5
Ramillies Ho W1 239 B1
Ramillies Pl W1 93 C1 239 A1
Ramillies Rd
Bedford Pk W4 111 B3
Blackfen DA15 168 B5
Edgware NW7 11 C2
Ramillies St W1 239 A1
Ramney Dr EN3 7 A6
Rampart St E1 96 B1
Ram Pas KT1 175 D1
Rampayne St SW1 259 C2
Rampton Cl E4 19 C1
Ramsay Ho NW8 230 A4
Ramsay Rd
Acton W3 111 A4
Leyton E7 76 D4
Ramscroft Cl N9 17 C4
Ramsdale Rd SW17 181 A5
Ramsdean Ho 1 SW15 156 B3
Ramsden Rd
Balham SW12 159 A4
Friern Barnet N11 30 D5
Ramsey Cl
Greenford UB6 64 B3
West Hendon NW9 45 D3
Ramsey Ct
Croydon CR0 220 D6
Hornsey N8 49 D4
Putney SW15 156 C5
6 Upper Holloway N19 71 D6
Ramsey Ho
5 Battersea SW11 136 B1
14 Kennington SW9 138 C5
Ramsey Ho *continued*
7 Merton SW19 179 D2
Ramsey Rd CR7 204 B3
Ramsey St E2 96 A3
Ramsey Way N14 15 C4
Ramsey Wlk N1 73 B2
Ramsfort Ho 4 SE16 118 B2
Ramsgate Cl 10 E16 121 B5
Ramsgate St E8 73 D2
Ramsgill App IG2 57 D5
Ramsgill Dr IG2 57 D5
Rams Gr RM6 59 A5
Ram St SW18 157 D6
Ramulis Dr UB4 84 D3
Ramus Wood Ave BR6 227 C3
Rance Ho 12 SE7 122 A2
Rancliffe Gdns SE9 144 A1
Rancliffe Rd E6 100 A5
Randal Cremer JMI Sch 16 E2 95 D5
Randall 9 NW9 27 D2
Randall Ave NW2 67 D5
Randall Cl SW11 136 C4 267 A2
Randall Ct NW7 28 A3
Randall Pl SE10 142 A5
Randall Rd SE11 116 B2 260 C3
Randall Row SE11 260 C3
Randell's Rd N1 94 A6 233 B6
Randisbourne Gdns SE6 163 D1
Randle Rd TW10 175 C6
Randlesdown Rd SE6 163 D1
Randmore Ct 6 BR3 185 C3
Randolf Ct
Paddington NW6 91 D5
St John's Wood NW8 229 A5
Randolf Rd BR2 210 B1
Randolph App E16 99 C1
Randolph Ave W9 92 A4 229 A1
Randolph Cl KT2 177 A5
Randolph Cres W9 92 A3 236 A6
Randolph Ct HA5 23 C3
Randolph Gdns NW6 91 D5
Randolph Gr RM6 58 C4
Randolph Mews W9 92 A3 236 B5
Randolph Rd
Paddington W9 92 A3 236 B5
Southall UB1 107 B4
Walthamstow E17 53 D4
Randolph St NW1 71 C1
Randon Cl HA2 23 D1
Ranelagh Ave
Barnes SW13 134 A3
Fulham SW6 135 B2
Ranelagh Cl HA8 26 C6
Ranelagh Ct HA8 26 C6
Ranelagh Dr
Edgware HA8 26 C6
Twickenham TW1 153 C6
Ranelagh Gardens Mans SW6 135 A2
Ranelagh Gardens (site of Chelsea Flower Show)★ SW1 115 A1 258 B1
Ranelagh Gdns
3 Bedford Pk W6 111 D3
Chiswick W4 133 A5
Fulham SW6 135 B2
Ilford IG1 56 C1
Wanstead E11 55 C4
Ranelagh Gr SW1 115 A1 258 B2
Ranelagh Ho SW3 257 C2
Ranelagh Mans 4 SW6 135 B3
Ranelagh Pl KT3 199 C4
Ranelagh Prim Sch E15 98 C5
Ranelagh Rd
Dagenham NW10 89 D5
Ealing W5 109 D4
Leyton E11 76 C4
Newham E15 98 C5
Pimlico SW1 115 C1 259 B1
Ranelagh Rd *continued*
Southall UB1 106 D5
Tottenham N17 51 C6
Wallend E6 100 C5
Wembley HA0 65 D2
Wood Green N22 32 B2
Ranfurly Rd SM1 217 C6
Rangdon St EC3 243 C1
Rangefield Prim Sch BR1 186 C5
Rangefield Rd BR1 186 D5
Rangemoor Rd N15 51 D4
Ranger's House (The Wernher Collection)★ SE10 142 B4
Ranger's Rd
Buckhurst Hill IG9, IG10 21 A4
Chingford E4 20 D4
Rangers Sq SE10 142 B4
Range Villas TW17 192 A2
Range Way TW17 192 C2
Rangeworth Pl DA15 167 D1
Rangoon Ho 5 N16 73 B4
Rankin Cl NW9 45 C6
Rankine Ho SE1 262 A5
Ranleigh Gdns DA7 147 B5
Ranmere St SW12 159 B3
Ranmoor Cl HA1 42 B5
Ranmoor Gdns HA1 42 C5
Ranmore Ave CR0 221 D5
Ranmore Ct
Kingston u T KT6 197 D4
3 Wimbledon SW20 178 D2
Rann Ho 1 SW14 133 B2
Rannoch Cl HA8 10 D2
Rannoch Ct 9 KT6 198 A4
Rannoch Rd W6 134 D6
Rannock Ave NW9 45 C2
Ransford Ho 16 SE21 183 C6
Ransomes Dock Bsns Ctr SW11 267 B3
Ransomes Mews SW11 267 B4
Ransom Rd 1 SE7 121 C1
Ranston St NW1 237 A4
Ranulf Rd NW2 69 B4
Ranwell Cl 18 E3 97 B6
Ranwell Ho 17 E3 97 B6
Ranworth Rd N9 18 C2
Ranyard Cl KT9 214 B5
Raphael Ct 9 SE16 118 B1
Raphael Dr KT7 196 D2
Raphael St SW7 247 C1
Rapide 15 NW9 27 C2
Rapley Ho 14 E2 96 A4
Rashleigh Ct 8 SW8 137 B2
Rashleigh Ho WC1 233 A1
Rasper Rd N20 14 A2
Rastell Ave SW12 159 D3
RATCLIFF 118 D6
Ratcliffe Cl SE12 165 A4
Ratcliffe Cross St E1 96 D1
Ratcliffe Ho 10 E14 97 A1
Ratcliffe La 16 E14 97 A1
Ratcliffe Orch 9 E1 118 D6
Ratcliff Rd E7 77 C3
Rathbone Ho
5 Canning Town E16 98 D1
Kilburn NW6 91 C6
10 Wimbledon SW19 178 D3
Rathbone Mkt★ 3 E16 98 D2
Rathbone Pl W1 93 D1 239 C2
Rathbone St
Canning Town E16 98 D1
Fitzrovia W1 93 C2 239 B3
Rathcoole Ave N8 50 B4
Rathcoole Gdns N8 50 B4
Rathfern Prim Sch SE6 163 B3
Rathfern Rd SE6 163 B3
Rathgar Ave W13 109 C5
Rathgar Cl N3 29 B1
Rathgar Rd SW9 138 D2
Rathmell Dr SW4 159 D5
Rathmore Rd SE7 121 B1
Ratier 16 NW9 27 C2

Rattray Ct **3** SE6 . . . . . . **164** D2
Rattray Rd SW2 . . . . **160** C6
Raul Rd SE15 . . . . **140** A4
Raveley St NW5 . . . . **71** C4
Raven CI NW9 . . . . **27** C1
Ravendale Rd TW16 . **171** C1
Ravenet Ct
 Battersea SW11 . . . . . **268** C1
 Clapham SW4 . . . . . . **159** B6
Ravenet St
 SW11 . . . . . **137** B4 **268** C1
Ravenfield Rd SW17 **158** D1
Ravenhill Rd E13 . . . . . **99** C5
Raven Ho **10** SE16 . . . **118** D2
Ravenings Pge IG3 . . . **58** A1
Ravenna Rd SW15 . . **156** D6
Ravenor Ct UB6 . . . . . . **85** D3
Ravenor Park Rd UB6 **84** A4
Ravenor Prim Sch
 UB6 . . . . **85** C4
Raven Row E1 . . . . **96** B2
Ravensbourne Ho
 Bromley BR2, BR3 . . . **186** C5
 Catford BR1 . . . . **186** B3
 Stanwell TW19 . . . . . **148** A3
Ravensbourne Bsns Ctr
 BR3 . . . . **225** D4
Ravensbourne Coll of
 Design &
 Communication
 BR7 . . . . **188** B5
Ravensbourne Ct
 SE6 . . . . **163** C4
Ravensbourne Gdns
 W13 . . . . **87** B2
Ravensbourne Ho
 10 Catford BR1 . . . . **186** B5
 Paddington NW8 . . . **237** A4
 1 Twickenham TW1 . **153** C5
Ravensbourne Mans **9**
 SE8 . . . . **141** C6
Ravensbourne Park Cres
 SE6 . . . . **163** B4
Ravensbourne Pk
 SE6 . . . . **163** B4
Ravensbourne Pl
 SE13 . . . . **141** D3
Ravensbourne Rd
 Bromley BR1, BR2 . . **209** A6
 Forest Hill SE23 . . . . **163** A3
 Twickenham TW1 . . . **153** C5
Ravensbourne Sch The
 BR2 . . . . **209** B6
Ravensbourne Sta
 BR3 . . . . **186** B3
Ravensbury Ave
 SM4 . . . . **202** A4
Ravensbury Ct CR4 . . **202** B5
Ravensbury Gr CR4 . . **202** B5
Ravensbury La CR4 . . **202** B5
Ravensbury Rd
 Orpington BR5 . . . . . **211** D5
 Wandsworth SW18 . . **157** D2
Ravensbury Terr
 SW18 . . . . **157** D2
Ravenscar NW1 . . . . . . **82** A3
Ravenscar Lo **14**
 SW19 . . . . **178** D3
Ravenscar Rd
 Catford BR1 . . . . **186** C6
 Surbiton KT6 . . . . . . **214** B6
Ravens CI
 Bromley BR2 . . . . . . **186** D1
 Enfield EN1 . . . . **5** C3
 Kingston u T KT1 . . . **197** D5
 Kingston u T KT6 . . . **197** D3
Ravenscourt
 1 Shacklewell N16 . . **74** A3
 Sunbury TW16 . . . . . **171** D2
Ravenscourt Ave
 W6 . . . . **112** A3
Ravenscourt CI HA4 . . **39** A2
Ravenscourt Gdns
 W6 . . . . **112** A3
Ravenscourt Ho **13**
 W6 . . . . **112** B2
Ravenscourt Park Mans
 7 W6 . . . . **112** A3
Ravenscourt Park Prep
 Sch W6 . . . . **112** A2
Ravenscourt Park Sta
 W6 . . . . **112** B2

Ravenscourt Pk W6 . . **112** A4
Ravenscourt Pl W6 . . **112** B2
Ravenscourt Rd
 Hammersmith W6 . . . **112** B2
 St Paul's Cray BR5 . . **190** B1
Ravenscourt Sq W6 . . **112** A3
Ravenscourt Theatre Sch
 10 W6 . . . . **112** B2
Ravenscraig Rd N11 . **31** C6
Ravenscroft Ave
 Golders Green NW11 . **47** B2
 Wembley HA9 . . . . . . **44** B2
Ravenscroft CI **4**
 E16 . . . . **99** A2
Ravenscroft Cres
 SE9 . . . . **166** B1
Ravenscroft Ct NW11 . **47** B2
Ravenscroft Pk EN5 . . **1** A1
Ravenscroft Point **20**
 E9 . . . . **74** D2
Ravenscroft Prim Sch **21**
 E16 . . . . **99** A3
Ravenscroft Rd
 Acton W4 . . . . **111** A2
 Newham E16 . . . . **99** A2
 Penge BR3 . . . . **184** D1
Ravenscroft Sch N20 . **13** B4
Ravenscroft St E2 . . **99** C4
Ravensdale Ave N12 . **30** A6
Ravensdale Commercial
 Est N16 . . . . **52** A3
Ravensdale Gdns
 Hounslow TW4 . . . . . **129** A2
 South Norwood SE19 . **183** B3
Ravensdale Mans N8 . **50** A3
Ravensdale Rd
 Hounslow TW4 . . . . . **129** A2
 South Tottenham N16 . **51** D3
Ravensdon St
 SE11 . . . . . **116** C1 **261** B1
Ravensfield CI RM9 . . **80** D4
Ravensfield Gdns
 KT19 . . . . **215** C4
Ravenshaw St NW6 . . **69** B3
Ravenshill BR7 . . . . . . **188** D2
Ravens Ho KT1 . . . . . . **175** D1
Ravenshurst Ave
 NW4 . . . . **46** C5
Ravenside CI N18 . . . . **34** D5
Ravenside Ret Pk
 N18 . . . . **34** D5
Ravenslea Rd SW11,
 SW12 . . . . **158** D4
Ravensleigh Gdns
 BR1 . . . . **187** B5
Ravensmead Rd
 BR2 . . . . **186** B3
Ravensmede Way
 W4 . . . . **111** D2
Ravensroost SE19 . . . **183** B2
Ravenstone
 SE17 . . . . . **117** C1 **263** B1
Ravenstone Prim Sch
 SW12 . . . . **159** A2
Ravenstone Rd
 Hornsey N8 . . . . **50** C6
 West Hendon NW9 . . . **45** D3
Ravenstone St
 SW12 . . . . **159** A3
Ravensview CI KT6 . . **197** D4
Ravens Way SE3,
 SE12 . . . . **165** A6
Ravenswood
 Bowes Pk N22 . . . . . **32** B4
 Sidcup DA5 . . . . **169** A3
Ravenswood Ave
 Tolworth KT6 . . . . . . **214** C6
 West Wickham BR4 . . **208** A1
Ravenswood Ct
 Harrow HA2 . . . . **63** B6
 West Wickham BR4 . . **208** A1
Ravenswood Gdns
 TW7 . . . . **130** C4
Ravenswood Ind Est **9**
 E17 . . . . **54** A5
Ravenswood Pk HA6 . **26** A2
Ravenswood Rd
 Balham SW12 . . . . . . **159** B4
 Croydon CR0 . . . . . . **220** D5
 Walthamstow E17 . . . **54** A5
Ravens Wood Sch
 BR2 . . . . **225** D5
Ravensworth Ct SW6 **265** A3
Ravensworth Rd
 Chislehurst SE9 . . . . **188** B6

Ravensworth Rd continued
 College Pk NW10 . . . . **90** B4
Raven Wharf SE1 . . **253** C2
Ravey St EC2 . . **95** C3 **243** A6
Ravine Gr SE18 . . . . . **145** C6
Raw Pinter CI N16 . . **51** C2
Rawlings CI
 Beckenham BR3 . . . . **208** A4
 3 Orpington BR6 . . . **227** D3
Rawlings Cres HA9 . . **66** D5
Rawlings St
 SW3 . . . . . . **114** D2 **257** C4
Rawlins CI Hendon N3 . **47** A6
 South Croydon CR2 . . **221** A2
Rawlinson Ct NW2 . . **46** C2
Rawlinson Ho SE13 . . **142** B1
Rawlinson Point **8**
 E16 . . . . **98** D2
Rawnsley Ave CR4 . . **202** C4
Rawreth Wlk N1 . . . **235** B6
Rawson Ct SW11 . . . **268** B1
Rawson St
 SW11 . . . . . **137** B4 **268** B1
Rawsthorne CI E16 . . **122** B5
Rawstone Wlk **5** E13 . **99** A5
Rawstorne Pl EC1 . . **234** C2
Rawstorne St
 EC1 . . . . **94** D4 **234** C2
Raybell Ct **7** TW7 . . **130** D3
Rayburne Ct
 1 Buckhurst Hill IG9 . **21** C3
 West Kensington W14 **254** A6
Ray CI KT9 . . . . **213** C2
Ray Ct Ealing W13 . . **109** B5
 Stanmore HA7 . . . . . . **25** B5
 Woodford IG8 . . . . . . **37** D4
Raydean Rd EN5 . . . . **13** D6
Raydons Pk RM9 . . . . **81** A3
Raydons Rd RM9 . . . . **81** A3
Raydon St N19 . . . . . . **71** B1
Rayfield CI BR2 . . . . . **210** A3
Rayford Ave SE12 . . . **164** D4
Ray Gdns
 Barking IG11 . . . . . . **102** A5
 Stanmore HA7 . . . . . . **25** B5
Ray Ho
 7 North Kensington
 W10 . . . . **90** D1
 Shoreditch N1 . . . . . **235** D5
Rayleas CI SE18 . . . . **144** D4
Rayleigh Ave TW11 . . **174** C4
Rayleigh CI N13 . . . . . **17** B1
Rayleigh Ct
 2 Kingston u T KT1 . **176** B1
 Tottenham N22 . . . . . **33** A2
Rayleigh Rd
 Edmonton N13 . . . . . . **17** B1
 Merton SW19 . . . . . . **179** B2
 5 Newham E16 . . . . **121** B5
 Woodford IG8 . . . . . . **37** C3
Rayleigh Rise CR2 . . **221** C2
Ray Lodge Prim Sch
 IG8 . . . . **37** D4
Ray Lodge Rd IG8 . . . **37** D4
Ray Massey Way **3**
 E6 . . . . **100** A4
Raymead Ave CR4 . . **204** C4
Raymede Twr **2**
 W10 . . . . **90** D2
Raymere Gdns SE18 . **145** C5
Raymond Ave
 Brentford W13 . . . . . **109** A3
 Woodford E18 . . . . . . **36** D1
Raymond Bldgs WC1 **240** D4
Raymond CI SE26 . . **184** C5
Raymond Ct N10 . . . . **31** A3
Raymond Postgate Ct **5**
 SE28 . . . . **124** B6
Raymond Rd
 Beckenham BR3 . . . . **207** A5
 Ilford IG2 . . . . **57** B2
 Newham E13 . . . . **99** C6
 Wimbledon SW19 . . . **179** A4
Raymond Way KT10 . **213** A2
Raymouth Rd SE16 . . **118** B2
Raynald Ho **15**
 SW16 . . . . **160** A1
Rayne Ct
 Bermondsey SE1 . . **253** C2
 Snaresbrook E18 . . . . **54** D5
Rayne Ho
 1 Balham SW12 . . . **159** A5
 Paddington W9 . . . . . **91** D3
Rayner Ct **6** W12 . . . **112** C4
Rayners CI HA0 . . . . . **65** D3
Rayners Cres UB5 . . . **84** B4

Rayners Gdns UB5 . . **84** B4
Rayners La
 Harrow HA2 . . . . **63** D6
 Pinner HA5 . . . . **41** B3
RAYNERS LANE **41** B1
Rayners Lane Sta
 HA5 . . . . **41** B2
Rayner's Rd SW15 . . **157** A6
Rayner Twrs E10 . . . . **53** C2
Raynes Ave E11 . . . . . **55** C2
Raynes CI NW2 . . . . . **69** A4
Raynesfield SW20 . . **200** C6
RAYNES PARK **200** C6
Raynes Park High Sch
 SW20 . . . . **200** B6
Raynes Park Sta
 SW20 . . . . **178** C1
Raynham **2** **237** A2
Raynham Ave N18 . . . **34** A5
Raynham Ho **1** E1 . . **96** D3
Raynham Prim Sch
 N18 . . . . **34** A5
Raynham Rd
 Edmonton N18 . . . . . **34** A5
 Hammersmith W6 . . . **112** B2
Raynham Terr N18 . . . **34** A5
Raynor CI UB1 . . . . . **107** B5
Raynor Pl
 20 Canonbury N1 . . **73** A1
 N1 . . . . **235** B6
Raynton CI
 Harrow HA2 . . . . **41** A2
 Hayes UB4 . . . . **83** D3
Raynton Dr
 Hayes UB4 . . . . **83** C5
 Hayes UB4 . . . . **83** D3
Raynton Rd EN3 . . . . . **6** D6
Ray Rd KT8 . . . . **195** D4
Rays Ave N18 . . . . **34** C6
Rays Rd Edmonton N18 **34** C6
 West Wickham BR4 . . **208** A2
Ray St EC1 . . . . **95** C1
Ray Wlk N7 . . . . **72** B6
Raywood **17** GM7 . . **127** A5
Reachview CI **17**
 NW1 . . . . **71** C1
Read CI KT7 . . . . **197** A1
Read Ct E17 . . . . **53** D3
Reade Ct **9** W3 . . . . **111** A3
Reade Wlk **5** NW10 . **67** C1
Read Ho
 Friern Barnet N11 . . . **30** D6
 4 Kennington SE11 . **138** C6
Reading Ho
 Paddington W2 . . . **236** A1
 Peckham SE15 . . . . . **140** A6
Reading La E8 . . . . **74** B2
Reading Rd
 Northolt UB5 . . . . **64** A3
 Sutton SM1 . . . . **218** A3
Reading Way NW7 . . . **29** A5
Readman Ct **8** SE20 **184** B2
Reads CI IG1 . . . . **78** D5
Reapers CI NW1 . . . **232** C6
Reapers Way TW7 . . **152** B6
Reardon Ho **6** E1 . . **118** B5
Reardon Path **31** E1 . **118** B5
Reardon St E1 . . . . . **118** B5
Reaston St SE14 . . . **140** C5
Reay Prim Sch
 SW9 . . . . . . **138** B5 **270** D3

Rebecca Ct
 3 Beckenham BR3 . **185** C2
 Sidcup DA14 . . . . . . **190** B6
Rebecca Ho **8** N12 . . **29** C6
Reckitt Rd W4 . . . . . . **111** C1
Record St SE16 . . . . . **140** C6
Recovery St SW17 . . **180** C5
Recreation Rd
 Bromley BR2 . . . . . . **186** D1
 Forest Hill SE26 . . . . **184** D6
 Southall UB2 . . . . . . **107** A2
Recreation Way CR4,
 SW16 . . . . **202** B6
Rector St N1 . . **95** A6 **235** A5
Rectory Bsns Ctr **5**
 DA14 . . . . **190** B6
Rectory CI
 Chingford E4 . . . . **19** C1
 Finchley N3 . . . . **29** B2
 Littleton TW17 . . . . . **192** C6
 Long Ditton KT6 . . . . **197** C1
 Sidcup DA14 . . . . . . **190** B6
 Stanmore HA7 . . . . . . **25** B5
 West Barnes SW20 . . **200** C5
Rectory Cres E11 . . . . **55** C3

Rectory Ct
 Cranford TW5 . . . . . **128** C3
 Feltham TW13 . . . . . **172** C6
 Leyton E11 . . . . **76** D5
 Wallington SM6 . . . . **219** C4
 West Drayton UB7 . . **104** A4
 Woodford E18 . . . . . . **36** D2
Rectory Field Cres
 SE7 . . . . **143** C5
Rectory Gdns
 Beckenham BR3 . . . . **185** C2
 6 Clapham SW4 . . **137** C2
 Hornsey N8 . . . . **50** A5
 Northolt UB5 . . . . **85** B6
Rectory Gn BR3 . . . . **185** B2
Rectory Gr
 Clapham SW4 . . . . . **137** C2
 Croydon CR0 . . . . . . **220** D6
 Hampton TW12,
 TW13 . . . . **173** B6
Rectory La
 Edgware HA8 . . . . **26** C4
 Long Ditton KT6 . . . . **197** C1
 Sidcup DA14 . . . . . . **190** C6
 Stanmore HA7 . . . . . . **25** B5
 Upper Tooting SW17 . **181** A5
 Wallington SM6 . . . . **219** C4
Rectory Orch SW19 . **179** A6
Rectory Park Ave
 UB5 . . . . **85** B4
Rectory Pl SE18 . . . . **122** C2
Rectory Rd
 Barnes SW13 . . . . . . **134** A3
 Beckenham BR3 . . . . **185** C2
 Cranford TW5 . . . . . **128** C3
 Dagenham RM10 . . . . **81** D1
 Hayes UB3 . . . . **84** A1
 Keston BR2 . . . . **225** D1
 Little Ilford E12 . . . . . **78** B3
 1 London W3 . . . . . **111** A5
 Shacklewell N16 . . . . **73** D5
 Southall UB2 . . . . . . **107** B3
 Sutton SM1 . . . . **217** D5
 Walthamstow E17 . . . **53** D5
Rectory Road Sta
 N16 . . . . **73** D5
Rectory Sq E1 . . . . . . **96** D2
Rectory Way UB10 . . **60** D5
Reculver Ho **2**
 SE15 . . . . **140** C6
Reculver Mews N18 . . **34** A6
Reculver Rd SE16 . . . **118** D1
Red Anchor CI SW3 . **267** A5
Redan Pl W2 . . . . **91** D1
Redan St W14 . . . . . . **112** D3
Redan Terr SE5 . . . . . **138** C2
Red Barracks Rd **4**
 SE18 . . . . **122** C2
Redberry Gr SE23,
 SE26 . . . . **162** C1
Redbourne Ave N3 . . **29** C2
Redbourne Dr SE28 . **102** D1
Redbourne Ho
 Finchley N3 . . . . **29** C2
 2 Poplar E14 . . . . . . **97** B1
Redbourn Ho **10** W10 . **90** C3
REDBRIDGE **55** C3
Redbridge CoII RM6 . . **58** B4
Redbridge Ct IG1 . . . . **55** D3
Redbridge Ent Ctr
 IG1 . . . . **79** A6
Redbridge Foyer IG1 . **79** A6
Redbridge Gdns
 SE5 . . . . **139** C5
Redbridge La E IG4 . . **56** A4
Redbridge La W E11 . . **55** C3
Redbridge Prim Sch
 IG4 . . . . **56** A4
Redbridge Rdbt IG1 . . **55** D3
Redbridge Sta IG4 . . . **55** D3
Redburn St
 SW3 . . . . . . **136** D6 **267** C6
Redburn Trad Est
 EN3 . . . . **18** D5
Redcar CI UB5 . . . . . . **63** D2
Redcar Ho SE26 . . . . **184** B4
Redcar St SE5 . . . . . **139** A5
Redcastle CI E1 . . . . **118** C6
Red Cedars Rd BR6 . **211** C2
Redchurch St
 E2 . . . . **95** D3 **243** C6
Redcliffe CI SW5 . . **255** C1
Redcliffe Ct **2** E5 . . **74** B5
Redcliffe Gdns
 Chiswick W4 . . . . . . **132** D5

Redcliffe Gdns continued
Fulham
SW10 .... 135 D6 265 D6
Ilford IG1 ... 56 C1
Redcliffe Mews
SW10 ... 255 D1
Redcliffe Pl SW10 ... 266 A5
Redcliffe Rd
SW10 ... 136 A6 266 B6
Redcliffe Sch
SW10 ... 136 A6 266 A6
Redcliffe Sq
SW10 ... 113 D1 255 D1
Redcliffe St SW10 ... 265 D6
Redclose Ave SM4 ... 201 C4
Redclyffe Rd E6 ... 99 C6
Redclyffe Terr 2
SM2 ... 217 C1
Redclyf Ho 13 E1 ... 96 C3
Redcroft 5 NW6 ... 69 C2
Redcroft Rd UB1 ... 86 A1
Red Cross Cotts SE1 252 B2
Redcross Way
SE1 ... 117 A5 252 B3
Reddiford Sch HA5 ... 41 A5
Redding Ho SE18 ... 122 A3
Reddings Ave WD23 ... 8 A6
Reddings Cl NW7 ... 27 D6
Reddings The NW7 ... 11 D1
Reddins Rd SE15 ... 140 A6
Reddons Rd BR3 ... 185 A3
Rede Pl W2 ... 113 C6 245 B6
Redesdale Gdns
TW7 ... 131 A5
Redesdale St SW3 ... 267 C6
Redfern Ave TW2,
TW4 ... 151 C4
Redfern Ho 6 E13 ... 98 D6
Redfern Rd
Catford SE6 ... 164 A4
Willesden NW10 ... 67 C1
Redfield La
SW5 ... 113 D2 255 C4
Redfield Mews SW5. 255 B4
Redfiff Est SE16 ... 119 B3
Redford Ave
Thornton Heath CR7 .. 204 B5
Wallington SM6 ... 220 A2
Redford Cl TW13 ... 149 D2
Redford Wlk N1 ... 235 A6
Redgate Dr BR2 ... 225 B6
Red Gates Sch CR9 .. 220 C3
Redgate Terr SW15 .. 156 D5
Redgrave Cl SE25 .. 205 D3
Redgrave Rd SW15 .. 134 D2
Red Hill BR7 ... 188 D5
Redhill Ct SW2 ... 160 C2
Redhill Dr HA8 ... 27 A1
Red Hill Prim Sch
BR7 ... 188 D5
Redhill St
NW1 ... 93 B4 231 D2
Red House★ DA6 ... 147 A1
Red House La DA6 ... 147 A1
Red House Rd CR0 ... 203 D3
Red House Sq 20 N1 ... 73 A1
Redif Ho RM10 ... 81 D4
Redington Gdns NW3 .69 D4
Redington Ho N1 ... 233 D4
Redington Rd NW3 ... 69 D4
Redknap Ho TW10 ... 153 C1
Red La KT10 ... 213 A2
Redland Gdns KT8 ... 195 B5
Redlands
Teddington TW11 ... 175 A4
Tottenham N15 ... 51 B5
Redlands Ct BR1 ... 186 D3
Redlands Prim Sch 35
E1 ... 96 C2
Redlands Rd EN3 ... 7 A4
Redlands The 5
BR3 ... 185 D1
Redlands Way SW2 .. 160 B4
Redleaf Cl DA17 ... 147 C6
Redleaves Ave
TW15 ... 170 D4
Redlees Cl TW7 ... 131 A1
Red Leys UB8 ... 60 A1
Red Lion Bsns Ctr
KT6 ... 214 B5
Red Lion Cl 9 SE17 ... 139 B6
Red Lion Ct
Holborn EC4 ... 241 B1
Hounslow TW3 ... 129 D2
Red Lion Hill N2 ... 30 B1
Red Lion La SE18 ... 144 C4
Red Lion Pl SE18 ... 144 C4
Red Lion Rd KT6 ... 214 C6
Red Lion Row SE17 .. 139 A6
Red Lion Sq
WC1 ... 94 B2 240 C3
Red Lion St
Gray's Inn
WC1 ... 94 B2 240 C3
Richmond TW10 ... 153 D6
Red Lion Yd W1 ... 248 B4
Red Lo Ealing W5 ... 88 A2
West Wickham BR4 .. 208 A2
Red Lodge Rd BR3,
BR4 ... 208 B2
Redlynch Ct
W14 ... 113 A4 244 B1
Redlynch Ho 27
SW9 ... 138 C4
Redman Bldg EC1 ... 241 A4
Redman Cl UB5 ... 84 C5
Redman Ho SE1 ... 252 B1
Redman's Rd E1 ... 96 C2
Redmayne Ho 15
SW9 ... 138 B3
Redmead La E1 ... 118 A5
Redmead Rd UB3 ... 105 C2
Redmill Ho 24 E1 ... 96 B3
Redmond Ho N1 ... 233 D5
Redmore Rd W6 ... 112 B2
Red Oak Cl BR6 ... 226 D6
Redo Ho 3 E12 ... 78 C3
Red Pl W1 ... 248 A6
Redpoll Way DA18 .. 124 D3
Red Post Hill SE21,
SE24 ... 161 B6
Red Post Ho E6 ... 77 D1
Redriffe Rd E13 ... 98 D6
Redriff Prim Sch
SE16 ... 119 A4
Redriff Rd SE16 ... 119 A3
Redroofs Cl BR3 ... 185 D2
Redrose Trad Ctr 1
EN4 ... 14 B6
Red Rover SW13 ... 134 A2
Redrup Ho 21 SE14 .. 140 D6
Redruth Cl N22 ... 32 B3
Redruth Gdns KT10 . 212 D1
Redruth Ho SM2 ... 217 D1
Redruth Rd E9 ... 96 C6
Red Sq The N16 ... 73 B5
Redstart Cl
New Cross Gate
SE14 ... 141 A5
Newham E6 ... 100 A2
Redston Rd N8 ... 49 D5
Redvers Rd N22 ... 32 C1
Redvers St E2 ... 95 C4
Redwald Rd E5 ... 74 D4
Redway Dr TW2 ... 152 A4
Redwing Path SE28 .. 123 B4
Redwing Rd SM6 ... 220 B1
Redwood Cl
4 Bow E3 ... 97 C5
Chigwell IG9 ... 21 B2
Hillingdon UB10 ... 82 D5
Osidge N14 ... 15 D4
Rotherhithe SE16 ... 119 A5
Sidcup DA15 ... 168 A3
South Oxhey WD19 ... 22 D6
Redwood Ct
Brondesbury NW6 ... 69 A1
Crouch End N19 ... 49 D2
Northolt UB5 ... 85 A4
10 Surbiton KT6 ... 197 D2
Redwood Est TW5 ... 128 B6
Redwood Gdns E4 ... 19 D5
Redwood Gr W5 ... 109 B2
Redwood Mews
Ashford TW15 ... 171 B3
2 Clapham SW4 ... 137 B2
Redwoods SW15 ... 156 A3
Redwood Way EN5 ... 12 D6
Redwood Wlk KT6 .. 197 D1
Reece Mews SW7 ... 256 C4
Reed Ave BR6 ... 227 C5
Reed Cl Lee SE12 ... 165 A6
Newham E16 ... 99 A2
Reede Gdns RM10 ... 81 D3
Reede Rd RM10 ... 81 D2
Reede Way RM10 ... 81 D2
Reedham Cl N17 ... 52 B5
Reedham St SE15 ... 140 A2
Reed Ho SW15 ... 156 A5
Reedholm Villas N16 .. 73 B4
Reed Mans 6 E11 ... 55 A3
Reed Pl
Battersea SW11 ... 136 C1
Clapham SW4 ... 137 D1
Lower Halliford TW17 .192 B1
Reed Rd N17 ... 33 D1
Reedsfield Cl TW15 . 148 D1
Reedsfield Rd TW15. 170 D6
Reed's Pl NW1 ... 71 C1
Reedworth St
SE11 ... 116 C2 261 B3
Reef Ho E14 ... 120 A3
Reenglass Rd HA7 ... 25 D6
Rees Dr HA7 ... 26 A6
Rees Gdns CR0 ... 205 D3
Rees Ho 6 N17 ... 33 D3
Reesland Cl E12 ... 78 C2
Rees St N1 ... 95 A6 235 B5
Reets Farm Cl NW9 ... 45 C3
Reeves Ave NW9 ... 45 B2
Reeves Cnr CR0 ... 220 D6
Reeves Cnr Sta CR0. 220 D6
Reeves Ho
Lambeth SE1 ... 251 A1
Mayfair W1 ... 248 A5
Reeves Mews
W1 ... 115 A6 248 B5
Reeves Rd Bromley E3. 97 D3
Shooters Hill SE18 ... 144 D6
Reflection Ho 9 E2 ... 96 A3
Reflection The E16 .. 122 D4
Reflex Apartments 1
BR2 ... 209 B5
Reform Row N17 ... 33 D1
Reform St SW11 ... 136 D3
Regal Cl Ealing W5 ... 87 D2
Spitalfields E1 ... 96 A2
Regal Cres SM6 ... 219 B5
Regal Ct
Edmonton N18 ... 33 D5
2 Mitcham CR4 ... 202 D6
Wembley HA0 ... 65 D4
Regal Dr N11 ... 31 B5
Regal Ho IG2 ... 57 B3
Regal Int Coll HA9 ... 66 A3
Regal La NW1 ... 231 B5
Regal Pl
8 Tower Hamlets E3 .. 97 B4
Walham Green SW6 .. 265 D3
Regal Way HA3 ... 44 A3
Regan Ho 1 N18 ... 33 D4
Regan Way N1 ... 95 C5
Regatta Ho TW11 ... 175 A6
Regatta Point TW8 ... 132 B6
Regel Ct NW7 ... 29 A2
Regency Cl Ealing W5 .. 88 A1
Hampton TW12 ... 173 B5
Regency Cres 3
NW4 ... 28 D1
Regency Ct 9 Bow E3 . 97 B5
Enfield EN1 ... 17 B6
4 Kingston u T KT5 ... 198 B4
4 Penge SE19 ... 184 A3
14 South Hackney E9 ... 96 C6
Sutton SM1 ... 217 D5
Wimbledon SW19 ... 179 B3
7 Woodford E18 ... 37 A1
Regency Dr HA4 ... 39 C1
Regency Gdns KT12 .. 194 C1
Regency Ho
Finchley N3 ... 29 B1
Marylebone NW1 ... 238 D6
Regency Lo
1 Buckhurst Hill
IG9 ... 21 D2
Harrow HA3 ... 42 C6
South Hampstead NW3 70 B1
Regency Mews
Beckenham BR3 ... 186 A2
Camberwell SW9 ... 138 D5
Isleworth TW7 ... 152 C6
1 Willesden NW10 ... 68 A2
Regency Pl SW1 ... 259 D4
Regency St
SW1 ... 115 D2 259 D3
Regency Terr SW7 .. 256 C2
Regency Way DA6 ... 147 A2
Regency Wlk
Croydon CR0 ... 207 B3
8 Richmond TW10 .. 154 A6
Regeneration Rd
SE16 ... 118 D1
Regent Ave UB10 ... 60 D1
Regent Bsns Ctr
UB3 ... 106 A4
Regent Cl
Cranford TW4 ... 128 B4
Regent Cl continued
Harrow HA3 ... 44 A3
North Finchley N12 ... 30 A5
Regent Ct
4 Finchley N3 ... 29 D3
Lisson Gr NW8 ... 230 A1
South Norwood SE19. 182 D4
1 Stamford Hill N16 ... 51 D2
Regent Gdns IG3 ... 58 A2
Regent Ho W14 ... 254 A4
Regent Pl
Croydon CR0 ... 205 D1
St James W1 ... 249 B6
Wimbledon SW19 ... 180 A5
Regent Rd
Surbiton KT5 ... 198 C4
Tulse Hill SE24 ... 160 D6
Regents Ave N13 ... 32 C5
Regents Bridge Gdns
SW8 ... 270 B4
Regents Canal Ho 19
E14 ... 97 A1
Regents Cl Hayes UB4 . 83 C2
South Croydon CR2 .. 221 C2
Regent's Coll
NW1 ... 93 A3 238 A6
Regents Ct
22 Beckenham BR3 .. 185 C3
Bromley BR1 ... 186 D3
Edgware HA8 ... 26 A6
Hackney E8 ... 96 A6
1 Kingston u T KT2 .. 176 A2
Regent's Ct HA5 ... 22 D1
Regents Dr BR2 ... 225 D3
Regents Gate Ho 20
E14 ... 119 A6
Regents Lo 9 SW2 .. 160 B3
Regents Mews
NW8 ... 92 A5 229 B4
REGENT'S PARK ... 93 B4
Regent's Park★
NW1 ... 93 A5 231 A3
Regent's Park Barracks
NW1 ... 231 D3
Regent's Park Rd
Camden Town
NW1 ... 93 A6 231 A6
Hendon N3 ... 47 B6
Primrose Hill NW3 ... 71 A1
Regent's Park Sta
NW1 ... 93 B3 238 C5
Regent's Park Terr
NW1 ... 231 C6
Regents Pl IG10 ... 21 D4
Regent's Pl SE3 ... 143 A3
Regents Plaza 2
NW6 ... 91 D5
Regent Sq
Belvedere DA17 ... 125 D2
23 Bromley E3 ... 97 D4
St Pancras
WC1 ... 94 A4 233 B1
Regent's Row E8 ... 96 A6
Regent St
Brentford W4 ... 110 C1
7 Kensal Green
NW10 ... 90 D4
Mayfair W1 . 115 C6 249 A6
Regents Wharf
3 Hackney E2 ... 96 B6
Islington N1 ... 233 C4
Regina Coeli RC Prim
Sch CR2 ... 220 D1
Regina Ct TW11 ... 174 C5
Reginald Ct BR3 ... 186 A2
Reginald Pl 6 SE8 ... 141 C5
Reginald Rd
Deptford SE8 ... 141 C5
Forest Gate E7 ... 77 A2
Reginald Sorenson Ho
E11 ... 54 B2
Reginald Sq SE8 ... 141 C5
Regina Point SE16 ... 118 C3
Regina Rd
Ealing W13 ... 109 A5.
Finsbury Pk N4 ... 50 B1
Southall UB2 ... 107 A2
South Norwood SE25. 206 A6
Regina Terr W13 ... 109 B5
Regis Ct
East Bedfont TW14 ... 149 B5
Hornsey N8 ... 50 B5
Marylebone NW1 ... 237 C4
Mitcham SW19 ... 180 C2
Regis Pl 17 SW2 ... 138 B1
Regis Rd NW5 ... 71 B3
Regnart Bldgs NW1. 232 B1
Regnolruf Ct KT12 ... 194 A2
Reid Cl Hayes UB3 ... 83 C1
Pinner HA5 ... 40 A5
Reid Ct SW14 ... 133 A3
Reidhaven Rd SE18 ... 123 C2
Reigate Ave SM1 ... 201 D1
Reigate Rd
Catford BR1 ... 164 D1
Grove Pk BR1, SE12 .. 165 A2
Ilford IG3 ... 79 D6
Reigate Way SM6 ... 220 A3
Reighton Rd E5 ... 74 A6
Reinckendorf Ave
SE9 ... 167 A5
Reindeer Cl 5 E13 ... 99 A6
Reizel Cl N16 ... 51 D1
Relay Rd W12 ... 112 C5
Relf Rd SE15 ... 140 A2
Reliance Sq E2 ... 243 B6
Relko Gdns SM1 ... 218 B3
Relton Ct W3 ... 110 C4
Relton Mews SW7 ... 257 B6
Rembrandt Cl E14 ... 120 B3
Rembrandt Ct
10 Bermondsey
SE16 ... 118 B1
Harrow HA3 ... 43 A3
West Ewell KT19 ... 215 D2
Rembrandt Rd
Edgware HA8 ... 26 C1
Lewisham SE13 ... 142 C1
Rembrant Cl SW1 ... 258 A3
Remembrance Ave
N2 ... 47 D6
Remington Rd
Newham E6 ... 100 A1
Tottenham N15 ... 51 B3
Remington St
N1 ... 94 D5 234 D3
Remnant St WC2 ... 240 C2
Remsted Ho 7 NW6 ... 91 D6
Remus Rd E3 ... 75 C1
Renaissance Ct SM1 .202 A1
Renaissance Wlk 4
SE10 ... 120 D3
Renbold Ho 5 SE10 .. 142 A4
Rendlebury Ho 17
SE18 ... 122 B2
Rendle Cl CR0 ... 206 A4
Rendlesham Ho 3 E5,
N16 ... 74 A5
Rendlesham Rd
Enfield EN2 ... 4 D4
Shacklewell E5 ... 74 A5
Renforth St SE16 ... 118 C4
Renfree Way TW17 ... 192 C2
Renfrew Cl E6 ... 122 C6
Renfrew Ct TW5 ... 129 A3
Renfrew Ho
Paddington NW6 ... 91 D5
Walthamstow E17 ... 35 B1
Renfrew Rd
Hounslow TW5 ... 129 A3
Kingston u T KT2 ... 177 A3
Newington
SE11 ... 116 D2 261 C3
Renmuir St SW17 ... 180 D4
Rennell Ho 18 E9 ... 74 D2
Rennell St SE13 ... 142 A2
Renness Rd E17 ... 53 A6
Rennets Cl SE9 ... 167 C6
Rennets Wood Ho
SE9 ... 167 B6
Rennets Wood Rd
SE9 ... 167 B6
Rennie Cotts 29 E1 ... 96 C3
Rennie Ct
Holdbrook EN3 ... 7 C5
Lambeth SE1 ... 251 C4
Rennie Ho SE1 ... 262 A5
Rennie St
SE1 ... 116 D5 251 C4
Renoir Ct 7 SE16 ... 118 B1
Renovation The E16. 122 D4
Renown Cl CR0 ... 204 D1
Rensburg Rd E17 ... 52 D3
Rensburg Villas E17 ... 52 D4
Renshaw Cl 7 DA17 ... 147 B6
Renshaw Cnr CR4 ... 181 A2
Renshaw Ct SW19 ... 179 A6
Renshaw Ho 11
SW27 ... 182 D5

Renters Ave NW4 .... 46 C3
Renton Cl SW2 .... 160 B5
Renwick Rd IG11 .... 102 B4
Repens Way UB4 .... 84 D3
Rephidim St SE1 .... 263 A5
Replingham Rd
  SW18 .... 157 C3
Reporton Rd
  SW6 .... 135 A5 264 B3
Repository Rd SE7,
  SE18 .... 122 B1
Repton Ave
  Hayes UB3 .... 105 B2
  Wembley HA0 .... 65 C4
Repton Cl SM5 .... 218 C3
Repton Ct
  Beckenham BR3 .... 185 D2
  Southgate N21 .... 16 C3
Repton Ho N21 .... 259 B3
Repton Rd
  Harrow HA3 .... 44 B5
  Orpington BR6 .... 227 D5
Repton St E14 .... 97 A1
Reserve Rd N2 .... 30 C2
Reservoir Cl 3 CR7 .205 B5
Reservoir Rd
  New Cross Gate
    SE4 .... 141 A3
  Ruislip HA4 .... 39 B5
  Southgate N14 .... 15 C6
Reservoir Studios 14
  E1 .... 96 D1
Resham Cl SE2 .... 106 C3
Resolution Way 14
  SE8 .... 141 C5
Resolution Wlk
  SE18 .... 122 B3
Restell Cl SE3 .... 142 C6
Restmor Way SM5,
  SM6 .... 219 A6
Reston Pl SW7 .... 246 A1
Restons Cres DA15,
  SE9 .... 167 C5
Restoration Sq
  SW11 .... 266 D1
Restormel Cl TW3 .. 151 C6
Retcar Pl N19 .... 71 B6
Retford St E2 .... 95 C5
Retingham Way E4 .. 19 D2
Retlas Ct HA1 .... 42 B2
Retreat Cl HA3 .... 43 C4
Retreat Cvn Site The
  IG9 .... 21 A3
Retreat Ho 1 E9 .... 74 C2
Retreat Pl E9 .... 74 C2
Retreat Rd TW9 .. 153 D6
Retreat The
  Harrow HA2 .... 41 C2
  Kingsbury NW9 .... 45 B4
  Mortlake SW14 .... 133 C2
  North Cheam KT4 . 216 B6
  South Norwood CR7 205 B5
  Surbiton KT5 .... 198 B3
Reunion Row E1 .. 118 B6
Reveley Sq SE16 . 119 A4
Revell Rd
  Cheam SM1 .... 217 B2
  Kingston u T KT1 .. 176 D2
Revell Rise SE18 .. 123 D1
Revelon Rd SE4 .. 141 A2
Revelstoke Rd SW18,
  SW19 .... 157 C2
Reventlow Rd SE9 .167 A3
Reverdy Rd SE1 .. 118 A2
Reverend Cl HA2 .... 63 D5
Revesby Rd SM5 .. 202 C3
Review Lo RM10 .. 103 D5
Review Rd
  Dagenham RM10 .. 103 D6
  Willesden NW2 .... 67 D6
Rewell St
  SW6 .... 136 A5 266 A4
Rewley Rd SM4 .. 202 B3
Rew Lo 25 N2 .... 30 B1
Rex Ave TW15 .... 170 C5
Rex Ho TW13 .... 151 A1
Rex Par 2 IG8 .... 37 C4
Rex Pl W1 ... 115 A5 248 B5
Reydon Ave E11 .... 55 C3
Reygate Ct N4 .... 51 A3
Reynard Cl
  Brockley SE4 .... 141 A2
  Bromley BR1 .... 210 C6

Reynard Dr SE19 .... 183 D3
Reynard Mills Trad Est
  TW8 .... 109 C1
Reynard Pl 1 SE14 .. 141 A6
Reynardson Rd N17 .. 33 A3
Reynardson's Ct 10
  N17 .... 51 D6
Reynola Gdns SE7 .. 121 B1
Reynolds Ave
  Chessington KT9 .. 214 A1
  Ilford RM6 .... 58 C2
  Little Ilford E12 .... 78 C3
Reynolds Cl
  Carshalton SM5 .... 202 D1
  Golders Green NW11 .. 47 D2
  Mitcham SW19 .... 180 B2
Reynolds Ct
  Ilford RM6 .... 58 D6
  Leyton E11 .... 76 D5
Reynolds Dr HA8 .... 44 B6
Reynolds Ho
  Enfield EN1 .... 18 A6
  Finsbury Pk N4 .... 50 A1
  19 South Hackney E2 .. 96 C5
  St John's Wood NW8 229 D3
  Westminster SW1 .. 259 D3
Reynolds Pl
  Greenwich SE3 .... 143 B5
  12 Richmond TW10 .. 154 B5
Reynolds Rd
  Acton Green W4 .... 111 A3
  Hayes UB4 .... 84 C3
  New Malden KT3 .. 199 B2
  Nunhead SE15 .... 140 C1
  Reynolds Sp Ctr W3 .110 C4
  Rffra Rd Ret Pk
    SW2 .... 160 C6
Rheidol Mews N1 .. 235 A4
Rheidol Terr
  N1 .... 95 A6 235 A5
Rhein Ho N8 .... 50 A6
Rheola Cl N17 .... 33 D2
Rhizotron & Xstrata
  Treetop Walkway★
    TW9 .... 132 A4
Rhoda St E2 ... 95 D3 243 D6
Rhodes Ave N22 .... 31 C2
Rhodes Avenue Prim Sch
  N22 .... 31 C2
Rhodes Ho
  Shepherd's Bush
    W12 .... 112 B5
  Shoreditch N1 .... 235 C2
Rhodesia Rd
  Leyton E11 .... 76 B6
  Stockwell SW9 .. 138 A3
Rhodes-Moorhouse Ct
  SW4 .... 201 C3
Rhodes St N7 .... 72 B3
Rhodeswell Rd E14 .. 97 B1
Rhodrons Ave KT9 .. 214 A3
Rhondda Gr E3 .... 97 B4
Rhyl Prim Sch 21
  NW5 .... 71 A2
Rhyl Rd UB6 .... 86 D5
Rhyl St NW5 .... 71 A2
Rhys Ave N11 .... 31 D3
Rialto Rd CR4 .... 181 A1
Ribble Cl IG8 .... 37 C4
Ribblesdale Ave
  Friern Barnet N11 .. 31 A4
  Northolt UB5 .... 63 D2
Ribblesdale Ho 11
  NW6 .... 91 C6
Ribblesdale Rd
  Hornsey N8 .... 50 C5
  Streatham SW16 .. 181 B5
Ribbon Dance Mews
  SE5 .... 139 B4
Ribchester Ave UB6 .. 86 D4
Ribston Cl BR2 .... 210 C1
Ribstone Ho 12 E9 .. 74 D2
Ricardo Path 5
  SE28 .... 124 C5
Ricardo St E14 .... 97 D1
Ricards Lodge High Sch
  SW19 .... 179 B5
Ricards Rd SW19 .. 179 B5
Riccall Ct 2 NW9 .... 27 C2
Riceyman Ho C1 .. 234 A1
Richard Alibon Prim Sch
  RM10 .... 81 C3
Richard Anderson Ct 4
  SE14 .... 140 D5

Richard Atkins Prim Sch
  20 SW2 .... 160 A4
Richard Burbidge Mans
  SW13 .... 134 C6
Richard Burton Ct 4
  IG9 .... 21 C2
Richard Challoner Sch
  KT3 .... 199 B2
Richard Cl SE18 .. 122 A2
Richard Cloudesley Sch
  (Prim Dept)
    EC1 ... 95 A3 242 B5
Richard Cloudesley Sch
  (Secondary Dept)
    EC1 ... 95 A3 242 A5
Richard Cobden Prim
  Sch NW1 .93 C6 232 B5
Richard Fell Ho 3
  E12 .... 78 C4
Richard Fox Ho N4 .. 73 A5
Richard Ho 10 SE16 .. 118 C2
Richard House Dr
  E16 .... 100 A1
Richard Knight Ho
  SW6 .... 265 B2
Richard Neale Ho 2
  E1 .... 118 B6
Richard Neve Ho 2
  SE18 .... 123 C2
Richards Cl
  Bushey WD23 .... 8 B4
  Harlington UB3 .... 127 B6
  Harrow HA1 .... 43 A4
  Uxbridge UB10 .... 82 C6
Richards Ct BR3 .. 184 D2
Richard Sharples Ct 3
  SM2 .... 218 A1
Richardson Cl 10 E8 .. 95 D6
Richardson Ct 20
  SW4 .... 138 A3
Richardson Gdns 12
  RM10 .... 81 D2
Richardson Ho
  Isleworth TW7 .. 130 D2
  10 Poplar E14 .... 97 C2
Richardson Rd E15 .. 98 C5
Richardson's Mews
  W1 .... 239 A5
Richards Pl SW3 .. 257 C6
Richard's Pl SW3 .. 257 B4
Richard St 20 E1 .... 96 B1
Richbell WC1 .... 240 B4
Richbell Pl WC1 .. 240 C4
Richborne Terr
  SW8 .... 138 B5 270 C4
Richborough Ho
  10 Deptford SE15 .. 140 C6
  14 Hackney E5 .... 74 C4
Richborough Rd NW2 .69 A4
Richbourne Ct W1 .. 237 B2
Richens Cl TW3 .. 130 B3
Riches Rd IG1 .... 79 A6
Richfield Ct
  18 Beckenham BR3 .185 B2
  Wembley HA0 .... 66 A2
Richfield Rd WD23 .. 8 A4
Richford Gate W6 .. 112 C5
Richford Rd E15 .... 98 D6
Richford Street W6 .112 C3
Richill Lodge TW2 .. 181 C5
Rich Ind Est SE15 .. 140 B6
Richings Ho BR5 .. 190 A2
Rich La SW5 .... 255 C2
Richland Ho 4
  SE15 .... 140 A4
Richlands Ave KT17 216 A4
Richman Ho 10 SE8 .118 B1
RICHMOND 131 C1
Richmond Adult Com
  Coll TW9 .... 131 C1
Richmond American Int
  Univ in London
    TW10 .... 154 A4
Richmond Ave
  Chingford E4 .... 36 B5
  Feltham TW14 .... 149 C5
  Hillingdon UB10 .. 60 D2
  Islington N1 .. 94 B6 233 D6
  Willesden NW10 .. 68 C2
  Wimbledon SW20 . 179 A2
Richmond Bdgs W1 239 C1
Richmond Bridge
  TW1 .... 153 D5

Richmond Bridge Mans
  1 TW1 .... 153 D5
Richmond Circus
  TW9 .... 132 A1
Richmond Cl
  Borehamwood WD6 ... 11 B6
  Walthamstow E17 .. 53 B3
Richmond Coll
  W8 .... 113 D3 255 D6
Richmond Cres
  Chingford E4 .... 36 B5
  Edmonton N9 .... 18 A3
  Islington N1 .. 94 C6 233 A6
Richmond Ct
  Bromley BR1 .... 187 B3
  12 Knightsbr u T KT2 . 176 C3
  Knightsbridge SW1 . 247 D1
  Mitcham CR4 .... 202 B6
  6 New Southgate N11 31 A4
  Wembley HA9 .... 66 B6
  Wimbledon SW20 . 178 B2
Richmond Dr TW17 .193 B3
Richmond Gate
  TW10 .... 154 B4
Richmond Gdns
  Harrow HA3 .... 23 D2
  Hendon NW4 .... 46 A4
Richmond Gn CR0 .. 220 A5
Richmond Gr
  Islington N1 .... 72 D1
  Surbiton KT5 .... 198 B3
Richmond Healthcare
  Hamlet Hospl TW9 132 A2
RICHMOND HILL .. 154 A5
Richmond Hill TW10 .154 A5
Richmond Hill Ct 5
  TW10 .... 154 A5
Richmond Ho
  15 Forest Hill SE26 .. 162 A1
  Regent's Pk NW1 . 231 D3
  Walworth SE17 .. 262 C2
Richmond Ho (Hampton
  Com Coll) TW12 ...173 B5
Richmond International
  Bsns Ctr 9 TW9 .. 132 B1
Richmond Mans
  Earl's Ct SW5 .... 255 C2
  Putney SW15 .... 135 A2
  13 Twickenham TW1 . 153 D5
Richmond Mews V1 239 C1
Richmond Park ★
  TW10 .... 155 A3
Richmond Park Rd
  Kingston u T KT2 .. 176 A3
  Mortlake SW14 .... 133 B1
Richmond Pk IG10 .. 21 C4
Richmond Pl SE18 .. 123 A2
Richmond Rd
  Bowes Pk N11 .... 32 A4
  Chingford E4 .... 20 A6
  Dalston E8 .... 74 A1
  Ealing W5 .... 110 A4
  Finchley N2 .... 30 A1
  Forest Gate E7 .... 77 B3
  Ilford IG1 .... 79 A5
  Isleworth TW7 .. 131 A2
  Kingston u T KT2 .. 176 A4
  Leyton E11 .... 76 B6
  New Barnet EN5 .. 14 A6
  Thornton Heath CR7 . 204 D5
  Tottenham N15 .. 51 C3
  Twickenham TW1 . 153 C4
  Wallington CR0 .. 220 A5
Richmond St E13 .. 99 A5
Richmond Sta TW9 . 132 A1
Richmond Terr
  SW1 .... 116 A4 250 A2
Richmond upon Thames
  Coll TW2 .... 152 C4
Richmond Way
  Hammersmith W12,
    W14 .... 112 D4
  Wanstead E11 .... 55 A3
Richmount Gdns
  SE3 .... 143 A2
Rich St E14 .... 119 B6
Rickard Cl
  Hendon NW4 .... 46 A5
  Streatham SW2 .. 160 C3
Rickards Cl KT6 .... 214 A6
Rickett St SW6 .... 265 B6
Rickman Ho 20 E2 .. 96 C3
Rickman St 2 E1 .... 96 C3

Rickmansworth Rd
  HA5 .... 22 C1
Rick Roberts Way
  E15 .... 98 B5
Rickthorne Rd 7
  N19 .... 72 A6
Rickyard Path SE9 .. 144 A1
Riddell Ct SE1 .... 263 C2
Riddell Lo EN2 .... 4 D3
Ridding La UB6 .... 64 D3
Riddons Rd SE12 .. 187 C6
Rideout St SE18 .. 122 B2
Rider Cl DA15 .... 167 C5
RideThe
  Brentford TW8 .. 109 C1
  Enfield EN3 .... 6 D2
Ridgdale St E3 .... 97 D5
Ridge Ave N21 .... 17 B4
Ridgebrook Rd SE3,
  SE9 .... 143 D2
Ridge Cl Hendon NW4 .28 D1
  Kingsbury NW9 .. 45 B5
  Plumstead SE28 .. 123 B4
Ridge Crest EN2 .... 4 B4
Ridge Hill NW11 .... 47 A1
Ridge Ho 2 KT2 .... 176 D3
Ridgeleigh Ct 3 EN5 .. 1 A2
Ridgemead Cl N13,
  N14 .... 16 A2
Ridgemont Gdns HA8 .27 A6
Ridgemount Ave
  CR0 .... 206 D1
  13 Islington N7 .... 72 B4
Ridgemount Cl 4
  SE20 .... 184 B3
Ridgemount Gdns EN2 .4 B3
Ridgeon Ct N22 .... 32 B4
Ridge Rd Cheam SM3 .201 B1
  Child's Hill NW2 .... 69 B5
  Edmonton N21 .... 17 B3
  Hornsey Vale N8 .. 50 B3
  Mitcham CR4 .... 181 B3
RidgesThe E4 .... 35 C6
Ridge's Yd 8 CR0 .. 220 D5
RidgeTerr N21 .... 17 A4
RidgeThe Barnet EN5 . 13 B6
  Old Bexley DA5 .. 169 B4
  Orpington BR6 .. 227 B6
  Surbiton KT5 .... 198 C4
  Twickenham TW2 . 152 B4
Ridgeview Cl EN5 .. 12 D5
Ridgeview Ct EN4 .. 14 C6
Ridgeview Rd N20 .. 14 A1
Ridgeway Hayes BR2 .225 A6
  8 Richmond TW10 . 154 A5
  Walton-on-T KT12 . 193 D1
  Woodford IG8 .... 37 C6
Ridge Way
  Feltham TW13 .... 151 A1
  7 West Norwood
    SE19 .... 183 C4
Ridgeway Ave EN4 .. 14 D5
Ridgeway Cres BR6 . 227 C5
Ridgeway Crescent Gdns
  BR6 .... 227 C5
RidgewayThe
  Acton W3 .... 110 C3
  Grove Pk BR1 .... 187 A6
  1 Chingford E4 .... 20 A3
  Enfield EN2 .... 4 B5
  Finchley N3 .... 29 D3
  Friern Barnet N11 .. 30 D6
  Golders Green NW11. . 47 B1
  Kenton HA3 .... 43 C3
  Kingsbury NW9 .. 45 B5
  Mill Hill NW7 .... 28 B6
  North Harrow HA2 . 41 D3
  Palmers Green N14 . 16 A2
  Pinner HA2 .... 41 B4
  Ruislip HA4 .... 40 A2
  Stanmore HA7 .... 25 C4
  Wallington CR0 .. 220 B5
Ridgeway W DA15 .. 167 D6
Ridgeway Wlk UB5 .. 63 A2
RidgewellCl
  Dagenham RM10 .. 103 D6
  Forest Hill SE26 .. 185 B6
  Shoreditch N1 .... 235 B6

Ridgmount Gdns WC1 93 D2 239 C4
Ridgmount Pl WC1 239 C4
Ridgmount Rd SW18 157 D6
Ridgmount St WC1 93 D2 239 C4
Ridgway SW19, SW20 178 D4
Ridgway Ct SW19 178 D4
Ridgway Gdns SW19 178 D3
Ridgway Pl SW19 179 A4
Ridgway Rd SW9 138 D2
Ridgway The SM2 218 B1
Ridgwell Rd E16 99 C2
Riding House St W1 93 C2 239 A3
Ridings Ave N21 17 A6
Ridings Cl N6 49 C2
Ridings The Ealing W5 88 B3
Oakleigh Pk EN4 14 B4
Sunbury TW16 172 A2
Surbiton KT5 198 C4
Riding The NW11 47 B2
Ridler Rd EN1 5 C5
Ridley Ave W13 109 B3
Ridley Cl IG11 79 D1
Ridley Ct
Orpington BR6 227 A4
Streatham SW16 182 A4
Ridley Ho 14 SW11 136 C2
Ridley Rd
Beckenham BR2 208 D6
Dalston E8 73 D3
Forest Gate E7 77 C4
Merton SW19 179 D3
Welling DA16 146 B4
Willesden Green NW10 90 A5
Ridley Road Mkt* E8 73 D3
Ridsdale Rd SE20 184 B2
Riefield Rd SE9 167 A6
Riesco Dr CR0 222 C2
Riffel Rd NW2 68 C3
Rifle Ct SE11 138 C6
Rifle Pl W11 112 D5
Rifle St E14 97 D2
Riga Ho 12 E1 96 D2
Rigault Rd SW6 135 A3
Rigby Cl CR0 220 C5
Rigby Ho 2 N17 51 D6
Rigby La UB3 105 A4
Rigby Mews IG1 78 C6
Rigby Pl 8 EN3 7 C6
Rigden St E14 97 D1
Rigeley Rd NW10 90 A4
Rigg App E10 53 A1
Rigge Pl SW4 137 D1
Rigg Ho 2 SW4 160 A4
Riggindale Rd SW16 181 D6
Rignold Ho 6 SE5 139 C3
Riley Ho 9 Bow E3 97 C3
Chelsea SW10 266 C5
1 Streatham SW4 159 D4
Riley Rd
Bermondsey SE1 117 D3 263 C6
Enfield EN3 6 C5
Riley St SW10 136 B5 266 C4
Rill Ho 16 SE5 139 C5
Rimini Ct SW12 158 D3
Rinaldo Rd SW12 159 B4
Ring Cl BR1 187 B3
Ringcroft St N7 72 C3
Ringer's Rd BR1 209 A6
Ringford Ho SW18 157 B6
Ringford Rd SW18 157 C5
Ring Ho 15 E1 118 C6
Ringlet Cl E16 99 B2
Ringlewell Cl EN1 6 B3
Ringmer Ave SW6 135 A4 264 B1
Ringmer Gdns 3 N19 72 A6
Ringmer Ho 15 SE22 139 C2
Ringmer Pl N21 17 B6
Ringmer Way BR1 210 B4
Ringmore Rise SE23 162 B4
Ring Rd W12 112 C5
Ringsfield Ho SE17 262 B1
Ringslade Rd N22 32 B1
Ringstead Bldgs SE6 163 D4
Ringstead Ct SM1 218 B3
Ringstead Rd
Catford SE6 163 D4
Sutton SM1 218 B3
Ringway UB2 107 A1
Ring Way N11 31 C4
Ringwold Cl BR3 185 A3
Ringwood Ave
Muswell Hill N2 48 D6
Thornton Heath CR0 204 A2
Ringwood Cl HA5 40 C6
Ringwood Gdns
17 Millwall E14 119 C2
Roehampton SW15 156 A3
Ringwood Rd E17 53 B3
Ringwood Way
Hampton TW12 173 C6
Southgate N21 16 D4
Ripley Cl
Bromley BR1 210 B4
New Addington CR0 224 A2
Ripley Ct 1 CR4 180 B1
Ripley Gdns
Mortlake SW14 133 B2
Sutton SM1 218 A4
Ripley Ho
13 Kingston u T KT2 176 D4
Mortlake SW14 133 C2
Nine Elms SW1 269 A6
5 Penge SE26 184 B5
Ripley Mews E11 54 C3
Ripley Rd
Belvedere DA17 125 C2
Enfield EN2 5 A4
Hampton TW12 173 C3
Ilford IG3 79 D6
Newham E16 99 C1
Ripley's Believe It or Not!* SW1 249 C5
Riplington Ct SW15 156 B4
Ripon Cl UB5 63 C2
Ripon Ct 10 N11 31 A4
Ripon Gdns
Chessington KT9 213 D3
Redbridge IG1 56 A2
Ripon Rd Edmonton N9 18 B4
Shooters Hill SE18 144 D6
Tottenham N17 51 B6
Ripon Way WD6 11 B6
Rippersley Rd DA16 146 A4
Ripple Ct 10 IG11 101 B6
Ripple Jun & Inf Schs IG11 79 C1
Ripple Rd
Barking IG11 79 A1
Barking IG11 101 C6
Castle Green RM9 102 A6
Rippleside Commercial Est IG11 102 C5
Ripplevale Gr N1 72 B1
Rippolson Rd SE18 123 D1
Ripston Rd TW15 171 B5
Risborough SE17 262 A4
Risborough Cl 4 N10 49 B6
Risborough Ct 5 N10 49 B6
Risborough Dr KT4 200 A2
Risborough Ho NW8 237 B6
Risborough St SE1 251 D2
Risdon Ho 26 SE16 118 C4
Risdon St 27 SE16 118 C4
Risedale Rd DA7 147 D2
Riseholme Ct E9 75 B2
Riseholme Ho 14 SE22 139 C2
Riseldine Rd SE23 163 A5
Rise The
Borehamwood WD6 10 B6
Buckhurst Hill IG9 21 D4
Chingford E4 20 C3
Edgware HA8 26 D5
Edmonton N13 32 C6
Harrow HA2 24 A1
Hendon NW7 27 D4
Hillingdon UB10 82 B5
Neasden NW10 67 B5
Sidcup DA5 168 C4
Wanstead E11 55 A4
Wembley HA0, UB6 65 A3
Risinghill St N1 234 A4
Risingholme Cl HA3 24 C2
Risingholme Rd HA3 24 C1
Risings The E17 54 B5
Rising Sun Ct EC1 241 D3
Risley Ave N17 33 B2
Risley Avenue Prim Sch 1 N17 33 C2
Risley Ho 7 E9 74 D2
Rita Rd SW8 138 B5 270 C4
Ritches Rd N15 51 A4
Ritchie Ho
Crouch End N19 49 D2
8 Rotherhithe SE16 118 C3
12 South Bromley E14 98 B1
Ritchie Rd CR0 206 B3
Ritchie St N1 94 C5 234 B4
Ritchings Ave E17 53 A5
Ritherdon Rd SW17 159 B2
Ritson Ho N1 233 C5
Ritson Rd E8 74 A2
Ritter St SE18 144 C6
Ritz Par W5 88 B3
Rivaz Pl E9 74 C2
Riven Ct 10 W2 91 D1
Rivenhall Gdns E11, E18 54 D5
Riverains The SW11 266 C1
River Ave
Southgate N13 16 D1
Thames Ditton KT7 197 A2
Riverbank KT8 196 C5
River Bank
Edmonton N21 17 A4
Thames Ditton KT7 196 D4
Riverbank Rd BR1 165 A1
Riverbank Way TW8 131 C6
River Barge Cl E14 120 A4
River Brent Bsns Pk W7 108 C3
River Cl Ruislip HA4 39 D3
Southall UB2 108 A4
Wanstead E11 55 C3
River Cotts BR5 190 C1
Rivercourt Rd W6 112 B1
River Crane Way TW13 151 B2
River Ct
Kingston u T KT6 197 D4
Lambeth SE1 251 C5
Shepperton TW17 193 A2
Wanstead E11 55 C3
Riverdale Cl IG11 102 B3
Riverdale Ct N21 17 B6
Riverdale Dr SW18 157 D3
Riverdale Gdns TW1 153 C6
Riverdale Rd
Erith DA8 125 D1
Feltham TW13 173 B6
Plumstead Comm SE18 123 D1
Sidcup DA5 169 B5
Twickenham TW1 153 C5
Riverdene HA8 11 A1
Riverdene Rd IG1 78 D5
Riverfleet WC1 233 B2
Riverford Ho 28 W2 91 C2
River Front EN1 5 C2
River Gdns
Carshalton SM5 219 A5
Feltham TW14 150 B6
River Gdns Bsns Ctr TW14 128 B1
River Grove Pk BR3 185 B2
Riverhead Cl E17 34 D1
Riverhill Mews KT4 215 B5
River Ho
Barnes SW13 133 C3
1 Forest Hill SE26 162 B1
Riverholme KT8 196 C6
Riverhope Mans SE18 122 A3
River House Montessori Sch E14 119 D4
Riverine Lo HA7 25 A5
River La TW10 153 D3
Riverleigh Ct E4 35 A5
Riverly Prim Sch E10 53 C1
Rivermead
East Molesey KT8 196 A6
Kingston u T KT6 197 D4
Rivermead Cl TW11 175 B5
Rivermead Ct
Ealing UB6 87 A4
Fulham SW6 135 B2
Rivermead Ho
Hackney E9 75 A3
Sunbury TW16 194 C6
River Meads Ave TW13, TW2 151 D1
River Mole Bsns Pk KT10 195 C1
River Mount KT12 193 D2
Rivernook Cl KT12 194 C4
River Park Gdns BR2 186 B3
River Park Rd N22 32 B1
River Pl N1 73 A1
River Plate Ho EC2 242 D3
River Rd
Barking IG11 101 D3
Buckhurst Hill IG9 21 D3
River Reach TW11 175 C5
River Road Bsns Pk IG11 101 D4
Riversdale Gdns N22 32 C2
Riversdale Prim Sch SW18 157 C3
Riversdale Rd
Highbury N5 73 A5
Thames Ditton KT7 197 A3
Riversdene N5 73 A5
Riversfield Rd EN1 5 C2
Rivers Ho 10 TW8 110 C1
Riverside
Battersea SW11 267 B4
Forest Hill SE6 185 B6
Greenwich SE7 121 B3
Hendon NW4 46 B2
Oatlands Pk TW17 193 C2
Richmond TW9 153 D6
11 Rotherhithe SE16 118 C4
St Pancras WC1 233 B2
Sunbury TW16 172 D1
Twickenham TW1 153 B3
Riverside Apartments N13 32 B5
Riverside Ave KT8 196 B4
Riverside Bsns Ctr SW18 157 D3
Riverside Bsns Pk SW19 180 A2
Riverside Cl
Chislehurst BR5 190 C1
Ealing W7 86 C3
Hackbridge SM6 219 B5
Kingston u T KT1 197 D5
Upper Clapton E5 74 C6
Riverside Ct
Chingford E4 19 D5
Lewisham SE12 142 D1
Nine Elms SW8 269 D6
Richmond TW11 175 C5
Riverside Dr
Chiswick W4 133 C4
Mitcham CR4 202 C4
Richmond TW10 153 B1
Temple Fortune NW11 47 A3
Riverside Est EN3 19 A5
Riverside Gdns
Enfield EN2 5 A3
Hammersmith W6 112 B1
Hendon N3 47 A6
Wembley HA0 88 A5
Riverside Health & Racquets Club Chiswick The W4 133 C4
Riverside Ho
Finchley N12 29 D6
14 Islington N1 73 A1
Morden SW19 202 A5
30 Richmond TW10 153 D6
Riverside Ind Est IG11 102 A4
Riverside Mans 4 E1 118 C5
Riverside Pl
New Southgate N11 15 C1
Stanwell TW19 148 A5
Riverside Prim Sch 37 SE16 118 A4
Riverside Rd
Mill Meads E15 98 A5
Sidcup DA14 169 A2
South Tottenham N15 52 A3
Stanwell TW19 148 A5
Wandsworth SW17, SW19 158 A1
Riverside Sch BR5 190 C1
Riverside The KT8 196 B6
Riverside Wlk
Isleworth TW7 130 C2
3 West Wickham BR4 207 D1
Riverside Wlk Mkt* WC2 116 B5 250 D4
Riverside Works IG11 78 D1
Riverside Workshops SE1 252 B4
River St EC1 94 C4 234 A2
Riverstone Cl HA2 64 B6
Riverstone Ct KT2 176 B2
Riverston Sch SE12 165 A6
River Terr
London W6 112 C1
St James SW1 250 C5
Riverton Cl W9 91 B4
Riverview TW17 193 B2
River View EN2 5 A2
Riverview CE Prim Sch KT19 215 B4
Riverview Ct 14 DA17 125 C1
Riverview Gdns SW13 134 B6
River View Gdns TW1 152 D2
Riverview Gr W4 132 D6
Riverview Hts SE18 144 D5
Riverview Lo NW9 67 B6
Riverview Pk SE6 163 C2
Riverview Rd
Chiswick W4 132 D6
West Ewell KT19 215 B4
Riverway N13 32 C6
River Way
Canning Town SE10 120 D3
Twickenham TW13, TW2 151 D2
West Ewell KT19 215 C3
River Wlk KT12 194 A3
Riverwood La BR7 189 B2
Rivet Ho SE1 263 D2
Rivington Ave IG8 37 D1
Rivington Cres NW7 27 D3
Rivington Ct
17 Dagenham RM10 81 D2
Willesden Green NW10 90 A6
Rivington Pl EC2 95 C4
Rivington St EC2 95 C4
Rivington Wlk 4 E8 96 A6
Rivulet Rd N17 33 A3
Rixon Ho SE18 144 D6
Rixon St N7 72 C5
Rixsen Rd E12 78 A3
Roach Rd E3 75 C1
Roads Pl N19 72 A6
Roan Ind Est CR4 180 D2
Roan St SE10 142 A6
Robart Ho 2 N12 30 A5
Robarts Cl HA5 40 B4
Robbins Hall EN3 18 D5
Robb Rd HA7 25 A4
Robert Adam St W1 238 A2
Roberta St E2 96 A4
Robert Bell Ho 2 SE16 118 A2
Robert Blair Prim Sch N7 72 A2
Robert Browning Prim Sch SE17 117 B1 262 C2
Robert Burns Ho N17 34 B3
Robert Cl
Barking IG11 79 A2
Paddington W9 236 B5
Robert Clack Sch
Dagenham RM8 59 C1
Dagenham RM8 81 B6
Robert Dashwood Way SE17 262 A3
Robert Gentry Ho W14 254 B1
Robert Gerard Ho 7 SE27 183 B6
Robert Ho 12 HA1 42 D4
Robert Jones Ho 3 SE16 118 A2
Robert Keen Cl 18 SE15 140 A4
Robert Lowe Cl SE14 140 D5
Roberton Dr BR1 187 C2
Robert Owen Ho
Fulham SW6 134 D4
8 Spitalfields E2 95 D4
Robert Owen Lo 4 E5 74 B4
Robertsbridge Rd SM5 202 B2

Roman Sq SE28 124 A5
Roman Way
Barnsbury N7 72 B2
Croydon CR0 220 D6
4 Deptford SE15 140 C5
Enfield EN1 17 D6
Romany Gdns
Cheam SM3 201 C2
1 Higham Hill E17 35 A2
Romany Ho 8 N9 18 A1
Romany Prospect
SE19 183 B4
Romany Rise BR5 211 A1
Roma Rd E17 53 A6
Roma Read Cl SW15 156 B4
Romayne Ho SW4 137 D2
Romberg Rd SW17 159 A1
Romborough Gdns
SE13 164 A6
Romborough Way
SE13 164 A6
Romeland WD6 9 D5
Romeland Ct WD6 9 D5
Romer Ho 9 SW2 160 B6
Romero Cl SW9 138 B2
Romero Sq SE9 143 C1
Romeyn Rd SW16 160 B1
ROMFORD 59 D4
Romford Ho 17 N1 73 B2
Romford Rd
Forest Gate E7, E12 77 C3
Stratford E15 76 D2
Romford St E1 96 B2
Romilly Dr WD19 23 A6
Romilly Rd N4 72 D6
Romilly St W1 249 D6
Romily Ct 2 SW6 135 A3
Rommany Ct SE27 183 B6
Rommany Rd SE27 183 B6
Romney Cl
Ashford TW15 171 A5
Chessington KT9 214 A4
7 Deptford SE14 140 C5
Harrow HA2 41 C2
North End NW11 48 A1
Tottenham N17 34 B2
Romney Ct
9 Hammersmith W12 112 C4
9 Hampstead NW3 70 C2
15 Northolt UB5 84 D5
Romney Dr
Bromley BR1 187 D3
Harrow HA2 41 C2
Romney Gdns DA7 147 B4
Romney Ho
2 Blackwall E14 120 B6
Enfield EN1 18 A6
Sutton SM2 217 D2
Romney Mews W1 238 A4
Romney Par UB4 83 B5
Romney Rd
Greenwich SE10 142 B6
Hayes UB4 83 B5
New Malden KT3 199 B3
10 Woolwich SE18 123 A3
Romney Row NW2 68 D6
Romney St
SW1 116 A3 260 A5
Romola Rd SE24, SW2 160 D3
Romsey Cl BR6 226 D4
Romsey Gdns RM9 102 D6
Romsey Rd
Dagenham RM9 102 D6
Ealing W13 109 A6
Romulus Ct 7 TW8 131 D5
Ronald Ave E15 98 C4
Ronald Cl BR3 207 B4
Ronald Ct EN5 1 D2
Ronald Ho
Eltham SE9 143 C1
4 Sutton SM1 218 B3
Ronald Ross Prim Sch 6 SW19 157 A4
Ronaldshay N4 50 C1
Ronalds Rd
Bromley BR1 187 A2
Islington N5 72 C3
Ronald St E1 96 C1
Ronaldstone Rd
DA15 167 C5
Rona Rd NW3 71 A4
Ronart St HA3 42 D6
Rona Wlk 20 N1 73 B2
Rondu Rd NW2 69 A3
Ronelean Rd KT6 214 B5
Ron Leighton Way
E6 100 A6
Ronnie La E12 78 C4
Ron Todd Cl RM10 103 C6
Ronver Lo E4 20 C1
Ronver Rd SE12 164 D3
Rood La EC3 117 C6 253 A6
Rookby Ct N21 16 D2
Rook Cl HA9 66 D5
Rookeries Cl TW13 150 C1
Rookery Cl NW9 45 D4
Rookery Cotts EN4 3 B2
Rookery Cres RM10 81 D1
Rookery Dr BR7 188 C2
Rookery La BR2 209 D3
Rookery Rd SW4 137 C1
Rookery Way NW9 45 D4
Rooke Way SE10 120 D1
Rookfield Ave N10 49 C5
Rookfield Cl N10 49 C5
Rook Lo IG1 55 D3
Rooks Heath Coll Bsns & Enterprise HA2 63 C5
Rooksmead Rd
TW16 172 A1
Rooks Terr UB7 104 A4
Rookstone Rd SW17 180 D5
Rook Wlk E6 100 A1
Rookwood Ave
Wallington SM6 219 D4
West Barnes KT3 200 A5
Rookwood Gdns E4 20 D2
Rookwood Ho 2
IG11 101 B5
Rookwood Rd N16 52 A2
Roosevelt Ct 15
SW19 157 A3
Rootes Dr W10 90 D2
Ropemaker Rd SE16 119 A3
Ropemaker's Fields 7
E14 119 B6
Ropemaker St
EC2 95 B2 242 C4
Roper Ho 13 SE21 183 C6
Roper La SE1 117 C4 253 B1
Ropers Ave E4 36 A5
Roper's Orch SW3 267 A5
Roper St 1 SE9 166 C5
Ropers Wlk 13 SE24 160 C4
Roper Way CR4 181 A1
Ropery Bsns Pk SE7 121 C2
Ropery St E3 97 B3
Rope St SE16 119 A3
Ropewalk Gdns 18
E1 96 A1
Rope Yard Rails
SE18 122 D3
Ropley St 6 E2 96 A5
Rosa Alba Mews N5 73 A4
Rosa Ave TW15 170 C6
Rosa Freedman Ctr
NW2 46 C1
Rosalind Ct 6 IG11 80 A1
Rosalind Ho 25 N1 95 C5
Rosaline Rd
SW6 135 A5 264 B3
Rosaline Terr SW6 264 B3
Rosamond St SE26 162 B1
Rosamund Cl CR2 221 B4
Rosamun St UB2 107 A2
Rosa Parks Ho 8
SW9 138 B3
Rosary Cl TW3, TW5 129 A3
Rosary Ct 17 E1 96 D2
Rosary Gdns
Ashford TW15 170 D6
Bushey WD23 8 C4
South Kensington
SW7 114 A2 256 B3
Rosary RC Inf Sch
TW5 129 C6
Rosary RC Jun Sch
TW5 129 C6
Rosary RC Prim Sch
NW3 70 C3
Rosaville Rd
SW6 135 B5 264 C3
Rosbury SW15 157 A5
Roscastle Rd SE4 163 A6
Roscoe St EC1 95 A3 242 B5
Roscoff Cl HA8 27 A2
Roscommon Ho 2
NW3 70 B3
Roseacre Cl
Ealing W13 87 B2
Roseacre Cl *continued*
Littleton TW17 192 C4
Roseacre Lo EN3 6 C1
Roseacre Rd DA16 146 B2
Rose Alley
Borough The SE1 252 B4
Broadgate EC2 243 B3
Rose Ave
Mitcham CR4 180 D2
Morden SM4 202 A4
Woodford E18 37 B1
Rosebank
2 Dagenham W3 89 B1
Fulham SW6 134 C5
Penge SE20 184 B3
Rosebank Ave HA0 64 D4
Rosebank Cl
Colney Hatch N12 30 C5
Teddington TW11 175 A4
Rosebank Gdns
Bow E3 97 B5
1 Dagenham W3 89 B1
Rosebank Gr E17 53 B6
Rosebank Rd
Hanwell W7 108 C4
Walthamstow E17 53 D3
Rosebank Villas E17 53 C5
Rosebank Way W3 89 B1
Rosebank Wlk
Camden Town NW1 71 D1
14 Woolwich SE7 122 A2
Rose Bates Dr NW9 44 C5
Rosebay Ho 20 E3 97 C2
Roseberry Gdns
Harringay N4 50 D3
Orpington BR6 227 C5
Roseberry Pl E8 73 D2
Roseberry St SE16 118 B2
Rosebery Ave
Finsbury EC1 94 C4 234 B1
Harrow HA2 63 B4
Kingston u T KT3 199 D6
Plashet E12 78 B2
Sidcup DA15 167 C4
South Norwood CR7 183 A1
Tottenham N17 34 A1
Rosebery Cl SM4 200 D3
Rosebery Ct
Chessington KT9 214 B3
Holborn EC1 241 A6
Mayfair W1 248 C4
Rosebery Gdns
Ealing W13 87 A1
Hornsey N8 50 A4
Sutton SM1 217 D4
Rosebery Ho 21 E2 96 C5
Rosebery Ind Pk N17 34 B1
Rosebery Mews N10 31 C1
Rosebery Rd
Cheam SM1, SM2 217 B2
Clapham Pk SW2 160 A5
Isleworth TW3, TW7 152 A6
Kingston u T KT1 176 D1
Muswell Hill N10 31 C1
Rosebery Sq
Holborn EC1 241 A5
Kingston u T KT1 176 D1
Rosebine Ave TW2 152 B4
Rosebriars KT10 212 A3
Rose Bruford Coll
DA15 168 B3
Rosebury Ct SW16 182 B2
Rosebury Rd SW6 135 D3
Rosebury Vale HA4 62 A6
Rose Bush Ct NW3 70 D3
Rose Cotts KT10 212 B3
Rosecourt Rd CR0 204 B3
Rosecroft N22 32 B2
Rosecroft Ave NW3 69 C5
Rosecroft Gdns
Dollis Hill NW2 68 A5
Twickenham TW2 152 B3
Rosecroft Rd UB1 85 C3
Rosecroft Wlk
Pinner HA5 40 D4
Wembley HA0 65 D3
Rose & Crown Ct
EC2 242 A2
Rose & Crown Yd
SW1 249 B3
Rose Ct 7 Dalston E8 73 D1
Harrow HA2 64 A6
Ilford IG1 78 D2
Islington N1 234 C5
Muswell Hill N10 31 B3
3 Pinner HA5 40 C6
Rose Ct *continued*
Spitalfields E1 243 D3
7 Wembley HA0 88 A5
10 Wimbledon SW19 179 B5
Rose Dale BR6 226 D6
Rosedale Ave UB3 83 B2
Rosedale Cl
Abbey Wood SE2 124 B3
Hanwell W7 108 D4
Stanmore HA7 25 B4
Rosedale Cnr BR7 188 B2
Rosedale Coll UB3 83 C1
Rosedale Ct N5 72 D4
Rosedale Dr RM9 80 B1
Rosedale Gdns RM9 80 B1
Rosedale Ho N16 51 B1
Rosedale Lo N14 15 B4
Rosedale Pl CR0 206 D2
Rosedale Rd
Dagenham RM9 80 B1
Forest Gate E7 77 C3
Richmond TW9 132 A1
Stoneleigh KT17 216 A3
Rosedale Terr W6 112 B3
Rosedene NW6 90 D6
Rosedene Ave
Morden SM4 201 C4
Southall UB6 85 C4
Streatham SW16 160 B1
Thornton Heath CR0 204 A2
Rosedene Ct HA4 39 C1
Rosedene Gdns IG2 56 C5
Rosedene Terr E10 75 D6
Rosedew Rd W6 134 D6
Rose End KT4 200 D1
Rosefield Cl SM5 218 C3
Rosefield Ct EN4 2 D1
Rosefield Gdns E14 119 C6
Roseford Ct 16 W12 112 D4
Rose Garden Cl HA8 26 A4
Rosegate Ho 32 E3 97 B5
Rose Gdns
Ealing W5 109 D3
Feltham TW13 150 A2
Southall UB1 85 C3
Rose Glen NW9 45 B5
Rosehart Mews 8
W11 91 C1
Rosehatch Ave RM6 58 D6
Roseheath Rd TW4 151 B6
ROSEHILL 202 A1
Rosehill
Claygate KT10 213 A2
Hampton TW12 173 C2
Rose Hill
Carshalton SM4, SM5 202 A2
Cheam SM1 201 D1
Rosehill Ave SM1, SM5 202 A1
Rosehill Ct SM4 202 A2
Rosehill Gdns
Greenford UB6 64 D3
Sutton SM1 218 A6
Rose Hill Park W
SM1 218 A6
Rosehill Rd SW18 158 A6
Rose Joan Mews
NW6 69 C4
Rose La RM6 59 A5
Roseland Cl N17 33 B3
Roseland Ho SW6 135 A2
Rose Lawn WD23 8 A3
Roseleigh Ave N5 72 D4
Roseleigh Cl 15
TW1 153 D5
Roselle Ct W5 88 A1
Rosemary Ave
East Finchley NW2 47 D5
East Molesey KT8 195 C5
Edmonton N9 18 B3
Enfield EN2 5 C4
Finchley N3 29 D1
Hounslow TW4 128 D3
Rosemary Branch Bridge
N1 235 D6
Rosemary Cl
Hillingdon UB8 82 C2
Thornton Heath CR0 204 A3
Rosemary Cotts 4
SW19 178 C3
Rosemary Ct 35 SE8 141 B6
Rosemary Dr
Redbridge IG4 55 D4
16 South Bromley E14 98 B1
Rosemary Gdns
Chessington KT9 214 A4
Dagenham RM8 59 B1
Mortlake SW14 133 A2
Rosemary Ho
Shoreditch N1 235 D5
Willesden NW10 90 B6
Rosemary La SW14 133 A2
Rosemary Rd
Bexley DA16 145 D4
Camberwell SE15 139 D5
Wandsworth SW17 158 A1
Rosemary St N1 235 D6
Rosemary Works Sch
N1 95 B6 235 D5
Rosemead NW9 46 A2
Rosemead Ave
Feltham TW13 149 D2
Mitcham CR4 181 C1
Wembley HA9 66 A3
Rosemead Prep Sch
SE27 161 A2
Rose Mews N18 34 B6
Rosemont Ave N12 30 A4
Rosemont Mans 11
NW3 69 D2
Rosemont Rd
Acton W3 110 D6
Kingston u T KT3 199 A6
Richmond TW10 154 A5
South Hampstead NW3 70 A2
Wembley HA0 88 A6
Rosemoor Ho 14
W13 109 A5
Rosemoor St
SW3 114 D2 257 C3
Rosemount Ct
2 Acton W3 110 D5
South Norwood SE25 205 C6
Rosemount Dr BR1 210 B5
Rosemount Lo W3 110 D6
Rosemount Point 10
SE23 162 D1
Rosemount Rd W13 87 A1
Rosemount Twrs 5
SM6 219 C2
Rosenau Cres SW11 267 C1
Rosenau Rd
SW11 136 D4 267 C2
Rosendale Prim Sch
SE21 161 A4
Rosendale Rd SE21, SE24 161 A3
Roseneath Ave N21 16 D3
Roseneath Pl 2
SW16 182 B6
Roseneath Rd SW11 159 A5
Roseneath Wlk EN1 5 C1
Rosens Wlk HA8 10 D1
Rosenthal Ho SE6 163 D5
Rosenthal Rd SE6 164 A5
Rosenthorpe Rd
SE15 162 D6
Roserton St E14 120 A4
Rosery The CR0 206 D3
Rose Sq SW7 256 D2
Rose St Holborn EC4 241 D2
Strand WC2 116 A6 250 A6
Roses The IG8 36 D3
Rose Theatre SE1 252 A4
Rosethorn Cl SW12 159 D4
Rosetree Pl TW12 173 C4
Rosetta Cl SW8 270 B3
Rosetta Ct SE19 183 C3
Rosetta Prim Sch E16 99 B2
Rosetti Terr RM8 80 B4
Roseveare Rd SE12 187 C6
Roseville N21 16 C3
Roseville Ave TW3, TW4 151 C6
Roseville Rd UB3 106 A2
Rosevine Rd SW20 178 C2
Rosewall Ct SW19 179 D5
Roseway
7 Edgware HA8 27 A6
London SE21 161 B5
Rose Way
Edgware HA8 27 A6
Lee SE12 165 A6
Rosewell Cl SE20 184 B3
Rose Wlk
Surbiton KT5 198 D4
West Wickham BR4 224 B6

Rosewood Ave UB6 65 A2
Rosewood Cl DA14 168 C1
Rosewood Ct
Bromley BR1 187 D2
Dagenham RM6 58 C4
Kingston u T KT2 176 C3
2 Leyton E11 76 B4
Rosewood Dr TW17 192 B4
Rosewood Gdns
SE13 142 A3
Rosewood Gr SM1 218 A6
Rosewood Ho 9
NW3 69 D2
Rosewood Sq W12 90 A1
Rosher Cl E15 76 B1
Roshni Ho SW17 180 C4
Rosh Pinah Prim Sch
HA8 10 D1
Rosina Ct SW17 180 C5
Rosina St E9 74 D2
Roskeen Ct 1
SW19 178 C3
Roskell Rd SW15 134 D2
Roskild Ct HA9 66 B4
Roslin Ho 2 E1 118 D6
Roslin Rd W3 110 D3
Roslin Way BR1 187 A5
Roslyn Cl CR4 180 B1
Roslyn Rd N15 51 C4
Rosmead Rd
W11 113 A6 244 B6
Rosoman Pl EC1 241 B6
Rosoman St EC1 234 B1
Rossal Ct 2 SE20 184 B3
Rossall Cres NW10 88 B4
Rossanne Ho N3 29 D3
Ross Ave RM8 59 B1
Ross Cl Harrow HA3 24 A3
Hayes UB3 105 B2
Northolt UB5 64 B4
Ross Ct
Chislehurst BR7 188 B3
Colindale NW9 45 C6
Ealing W13 87 B2
Edgware HA8 10 D2
1 Hackney E5 74 B4
4 Putney SW15 156 D4
South Croydon CR2 221 A2
Rossdale SM1 218 C3
Rossdale Dr
Ponders End N9 18 C5
Welsh Harp NW9 45 A1
Rossdale Rd SW15 134 C1
Rosse Gdns SE13 164 B5
Rosse Mews SE3 143 B4
Rossendale Cl EN2 4 D6
Rossendale Ho 7 E5 74 B6
Rossendale St E5 74 B6
Rossendale Way
NW1 93 C6 232 B6
Rossendon Ct 1
SM6 219 C2
Rossetti Ct WC1 239 C4
Rossetti Gdns Mans
SW3 267 C6
Rossetti Ho SW1 259 D3
Rossetti Mews NW8 229 D5
Rossetti Rd SE16 118 B1
Rossetti Studios
SW3 267 B6
Ross Ho
2 Kidbrooke SE18 144 A4
Twickenham TW2 151 D2
18 Wapping E1 118 B5
Rossignol Gdns SM5 219 A6
Rossindel Rd TW3 151 C6
Rossington Cl EN1 6 B5
Rossington St E5 74 A6
Rossiter Cl SE19 183 A3
Rossiter Fields EN5 13 B5
Rossiter Rd SW12 159 B3
Rossland Cl DA6 169 D6
Rosslyn Ave
Barnes SW13 133 D2
Chingford E4 20 D2
Dagenham RM8 59 C2
East Barnet EN4 14 C5
Feltham TW14 150 A5
Rosslyn Cl
Ashford TW16 171 C4
Coney Hall BR4 224 D5
Hayes UB3 83 B2
Rosslyn Cres
Harrow HA1 42 D5
Wembley HA9 66 A4
Rosslyn Ct NW3 70 C3
Rosslyn Hill NW3 70 B3
Rosslyn Ho 8 TW9 132 B4
Rosslyn Mans
8 Hampstead NW3 70 A2
South Hampstead NW6 70 A2
Rosslyn Mews 7
NW3 70 B4
Rosslyn Park Mews
NW3 70 B3
Rosslyn Rd
Barking IG11 79 B1
Twickenham TW1 153 C5
Walthamstow E17 54 A5
Rossmore Cl EN3 6 D1
Rossmore Ct NW1 237 C6
Rossmore Rd
NW1 92 C3 237 B6
Ross Par SM6 219 B2
Ross Rd
South Norwood
SE25 205 C6
Twickenham TW2 152 A3
Wallington SM6 219 C3
Ross Way SE9 144 A2
Rossway Dr WD23 8 B6
Rosswood Gdns
SM6 219 C2
Rosswood Ho 13
SM6 219 B2
Rosswood Lo CR0 222 D6
Rostella Rd SW17 180 B6
Rostrever Gdns UB3 105 C5
Rostrevor Ave N15 51 D3
Rostrevor Gdns UB2 107 A1
Rostrevor Mans SW6 264 C2
Rostrevor Mews
SW6 264 C1
Rostrevor Rd
Fulham
SW6 135 B4 264 C2
Wimbledon SW19 179 C5
Rotary Ct KT8 196 C6
Rotary Lo 12 SE27 160 D1
Rotary St SE1 261 D6
Rothay NW1 231 D2
Rothbury Gdns TW7 131 A5
Rothbury Rd E9 75 C1
Rothbury Wlk N17 34 A3
Rotheley Ho 39 E9 74 C1
Rotherfield Ct
De Beauvoir Town N1 73 B1
Shoreditch N1 95 B6 235 C6
Rotherfield Prim Sch
N1 95 A6 235 B6
Rotherfield Rd
Enfield EN3 6 D6
Wallington SM5 219 A3
Rotherfield St
Islington N1 73 A1
Shoreditch N1 95 A6 235 B6
Rotherham Wlk SE1 251 C3
Rotherhill Ave
SW16 181 D4
ROTHERHITHE 118 D3
Rotherhithe Bsns Est 6
SE16 118 C2
Rotherhithe New Rd
SE16 118 B1
Rotherhithe Old Rd
SE16 118 D2
Rotherhithe Prim Sch 24
SE16 118 D2
Rotherhithe St SE16 118 C4
Rotherhithe Sta
SE16 118 C4
Rotherhithe Tunnel
SE16 118 D5
Rother Ho SE15 140 B1
Rotherwick Hill W5 88 B3
Rotherwick Rd NW11 47 C2
Rotherwood Cl
SW20 179 A2
Rotherwood Rd
SW15 134 D2
Rothery St N1 234 D6
Rothesay Ave
Merton SW20 179 A1
Mortlake SW14,
TW10 132 D1
Northolt UB6 64 B2
Rothesay Ct
4 Catford SE6 164 D2
Rothesay Ct *continued*
Grove Pk SE12 165 B1
13 Kennington SE11 138 C6
Rothesay Rd SE25 205 C5
Rothley Ct NW8 236 C6
Rothsay Rd E7 77 C2
Rothsay St
SE1 117 C3 263 A5
Rothsay Wlk 19 E14 119 C2
Rothschild Rd W4 111 A3
Rothschild St SE27 182 D6
Rothwell Ct
2 Bromley BR1 187 B2
4 Harrow HA1 42 D4
Rothwell Gdns RM9 102 C6
Rothwell Ho TW5 129 C6
Rothwell Rd RM9 102 C6
Rothwell St
10 Hampstead NW1 70 D1
Primrose Hill NW1 230 D6
Roth Wlk N7 72 B6
Rotten Row
SW1 114 D4 247 C2
Rotterdam Dr E14 120 A3
Rouel Rd
Bermondsey SE16 118 A2
Bermondsey SE16 118 A3
Rougemont Ave
SM4 201 C3
Roundabout Ho HA6 22 A2
Roundacre SW19 156 D2
Roundel Cl SE4 141 B1
Roundell Ho 14
SE21 183 C6
Rounders Ct 7 RM10 81 D2
Round Gr CR0 206 D2
Roundhay Cl SE23 162 D2
Roundhedge Way EN2 4 B5
Round Hill SE23 162 C1
Roundhill Dr EN2 4 B1
ROUNDSHAW 220 B1
Roundshaw Ctr SM6 220 A1
Roundtable Rd BR1 164 D1
Roundtree Rd HA0 65 B3
Roundways HA4 61 D5
Roundway The
Claygate KT10 212 D2
Tottenham N17 33 B2
Roundwood BR7 188 D1
Roundwood Ave
UB11 105 A5
Roundwood Cl HA4 39 B2
Roundwood Rd
NW10 67 D1
Rounton Rd E3 97 C3
Rountree Ct 9 UB1 85 D1
Roupell Ho 9 KT2 176 B3
Roupell Rd SW2 160 B3
Roupell St
SE1 116 C5 251 B3
Rousden St NW1 71 C1
Rouse Gdns SE21 183 C6
Routemaster Cl E13 99 B4
Routh Ct TW14 149 B3
Routh Rd SW18 158 C4
Routh St E6 100 B2
Rover Ho 26 N1 95 C6
Rowallan Ct 3 SE6 164 D3
Rowallan Rd
SW6 135 A5 264 A3
Rowallen Par RM8 58 C1
Rowan N10 31 B1
Rowan Ave E4 35 B4
Rowan Cl Ealing W5 110 A4
Harrow HA7 24 D4
Ilford IG1 79 B3
Kingston u T KT3 177 C1
Streatham SW16 181 C2
Wembley HA0 65 A5
Rowan Cres SW16 181 C2
Rowan Ct
19 Camberwell
SE15 139 D5
Forest Hill SE26 184 C6
11 Kingston u T KT2 176 C3
Newham E13 99 B5
Twickenham TW4 151 D6
Wandsworth SW11 158 D5
Wimbledon SW20 178 B1
Rowan Dr NW9 46 A6
Rowan Gdns CR0 221 D5
Rowan Ho 9 Bow E3 97 B6
Dagenham NW10 89 C3
East Bedfont TW14 149 B5
Ilford IG1 79 B3
5 Maitland Pk NW3 70 D2
Rowan Ho *continued*
Sidcup DA14 167 D1
Rowan Pl UB3 105 D6
Rowan Pre Prep Sch
KT10 212 C1
Rowan Prep Sch
KT10 212 D1
Rowan Rd
Brentford TW8 131 B5
Brook Green W6 112 D2
DA7 147 A2
Mitcham SW16 181 C1
West Drayton UB7 104 A2
Rowans Sch The
SW20 178 A3
Rowans The
Ashford TW16 171 D5
Edmonton N13 17 A1
7 Sutton SM2 217 D2
Rowan Terr W6 112 D2
Rowantree Cl N21 17 B3
Rowantree Rd
Edmonton N21 17 B3
Enfield EN2 4 D3
Rowan Way RM6 58 C6
Rowan Wlk BR2 226 B5
7 Dartmouth Pk N19 71 C6
Hampstead Garden Suburb
N2 48 A4
Kensal Town W10 91 A3
1 New Barnet EN5 13 D6
Rowanwood Ave
DA15 168 A3
Rowanwood Mews
EN2 4 D3
Rowben Cl N20 13 D3
Rowberry Cl SW6 134 C5
Rowcross St
SE1 117 D1 263 D2
Rowdell Rd UB5 85 C6
Rowden Par E4 35 C4
Rowden Park Gdns
E4 35 C4
Rowden Rd
Beckenham BR3 185 B2
Chingford E4 35 D4
West Ewell KT19 215 A4
Rowditch La SW11 137 A3
Rowdon Ave NW10 68 B1
Rowdowns Rd RM9 81 B1
Rowe Gdns IG11 102 A5
Rowe Ho E9 74 C2
Rowe La E9 74 C3
Rowena Cres SW11 136 C3
Rowe Wlk HA2 63 C5
Rowfant Rd SW12,
SW17 159 A2
Rowhill Mans 11 E5 74 B4
Rowhill Rd E5 74 B4
Rowington Cl W2 91 D2
Rowland Ave HA3 43 C6
Rowland Ct E16 98 D3
South Croydon CR0 221 C6
Rowland Gr SE26 162 B1
Rowland Hill Almshouses
7 TW15 170 C5
Rowland Hill Ave N17 33 B4
Rowland Hill Ho SE1 251 C2
Rowland Hill St NW3 70 C3
Rowlands Ave HA5 23 D4
Rowlands Cl
Hendon NW7 28 A3
Highgate N6 49 A3
Rowlands Rd RM8 81 B6
Rowland Way
Ashford TW15 171 B3
Merton SW19 179 D2
Rowley Ave DA15 168 B4
Rowley Cl HA0 66 B1
Rowley Ct EN1 17 C6
Rowley Gdns N4 51 A2
Rowley Green Rd
EN5 12 A6
Rowley Ho SE8 141 C6
Rowley Ind Pk W3 110 D3
Rowley La EN5 11 D6
Rowley Rd N15 51 A4
Rowley Way NW8 229 A6
Rowlheys Pl UB7 104 A3
Rowlls Rd KT1 198 B6
Rowney Gdns RM9 80 C2
Rowney Rd RM9 80 B2
Rowntree Cl NW6 69 C2
Rowntree Clifford Cl 7
E13 99 B4
Rowntree Path 1
SE28 124 B5
Rowntree Rd TW2 152 C3
Rowse Cl E15 98 A6
Rowsham Ct HA1 64 C5
Rowsley Ave NW4 46 C6
Rowstock 1 NW5 71 D2
Rowstock Gdns N7 71 D3
Rowton Rd SE18 145 A5
Roxborough Ave
Harrow HA1 42 C2
Hounslow TW7 130 D5
Roxborough Pk HA1 42 C2
Roxborough Rd HA1 42 B3
Roxbourne Cl UB5 62 D2
Roxbourne Fst & Mid
Schs HA2 63 A6
Roxburgh Rd SE27 182 D5
Roxburn Way HA4 61 D5
Roxby Pl
SW6 135 C6 265 B6
ROXETH 64 A6
Roxeth Ct 6 TW15 170 C5
Roxeth Fst & Mid Sch
HA2 64 B6
Roxeth Gr HA2 63 D4
Roxeth Green Ave
HA2 63 D6
Roxeth Hill HA2 64 C6
Roxeth Manor Fst & Mid
Schs HA2 63 C5
Roxeth Mead Sch
HA2 64 B6
Roxford Cl TW17 193 C4
Roxford Ho 2 E3 97 D3
Roxley Rd SE13 163 D5
Roxton Gdns CR0 223 C3
Roxwell 10 NW1 71 B2
Roxwell Rd
Barking IG11 102 A5
Shepherd's Bush W12 112 A4
Roxwell Trad Pk E10 53 A2
Roxwell Way IG8 37 C3
Roxy Ave RM6 58 C2
Royal Academy of
Dramatic Art★
WC1 93 D2 239 C4
Royal Acad of Arts★
W1 115 C6 249 A5
Royal Acad of Dance
SW11 266 D1
Royal Acad of Music
NW1 238 B5
Royal Albert Hall★
SW7 114 B4 246 C1
Royal Albert Sta
E16 122 A6
Royal Albert Way
E6 122 B6
Royal Arc W1 249 A5
Royal Armouries The★
E1 253 C5
Royal Ave
SW3 114 D1 257 C2
Worcester Pk KT4 215 C6
Royal Avenue Ho
SW3 257 C2
Royal Ballet Sch (White
Lodge) The TW10 155 B3
Royal Ballet Upper Sch
The WC2 94 A1 240 B1
Royal Brompton Hospl
Chelsea
SW3 114 B1 256 C2
Chelsea SW3 114 C1 257 A2
Royal Cir SE27 160 D1
Royal Cl Deptford SE8 141 B6
Hillingdon UB7 82 B1
Ilford IG3 58 A2
Locksbottom BR6 226 D4
Putney SW19 156 D2
Stamford Hill N16 51 C1
Worcester Pk KT4 215 C6
Royal College of
Physicians Liby
NW1 93 B3 238 D6
Royal College St
NW1 93 C6 232 B6
Royal Coll of
Anaesthetists WC1 240 C3
Royal Coll of Art
SW7 114 B4 246 C1
Royal Coll of Art
Sculpture Sch
SW11 136 C5 267 A3

Royal Coll of Midwives W1 93 B2 238 C3
Royal Coll of Music SW7 114 B3 256 C6
Royal Coll of Obstetricians & Gynaecologists NW1 92 D3 230 C1
Royal Coll of Ophthalmologists NW1 238 A5
Royal Coll of Paediatrics & Child Health W1 240 D4
Royal Coll of Pathologists SW1 115 D5 249 C3
Royal Coll of Physicians NW1 93 B3 238 D6
Royal Coll of Radiologists W1 238 D4
Royal Coll of Science SW7 114 B3 256 C6
Royal Coll of Speech Language Therapists SE1 252 C3
Royal Coll of Surgeons WC2 94 B1 240 D2
Royal Coll of Veterinary Surgeons SW1 116 A3 260 A5
Royal Connaught Apts E16 121 D5
Royal Courts of Justice WC2 94 C1 241 A1
Royal Cres Ilford IG2 57 B3
Ruislip HA4 63 A5
W11 113 A5 244 A3
Royal Crescent Mews W11 112 D5
Royal Crest Ho SM2 217 A1
Royal Ct
City of London EC3 242 D1
Enfield EN1 17 C5
9 Kingston u T KT2 176 D3
Mottingham SE9 166 B3
Rotherhithe SE16 119 B3
Ruislip HA4 40 A2
Royal Dock Com Sch The E16 99 C1
Royal Docks Rd E6 100 D2
Royal Dr N11 31 A5
Royal Duchess Mews 16 SW12 159 B4
Royal Exchange★ EC3 242 D1
Royal Exchange Bldgs EC3 242 D1
Royal Festival Hall★ SE1 116 B5 250 D3
Royal Free Hospl NW3 70 C3
Royal Fusiliers Mus★ E1 253 C5
Royal Gdns W7 109 A3
Royal Geographical Society SW7 246 D1
Royal Hill SE10 142 A5
Royal Hill Ct 2 SE10 142 A5
Royal Horticultural Society (Lawrence Hall & Conf Ctr) SW1 259 C5
Royal Horticultural Society (Lindley Hall) SW1 259 C4
Royal Hospital Chelsea The★ SW1 115 A1 258 A1
Royal Hospital Rd SW3 114 D1 257 D1
Royal Hospl for Neuro-Disability The SW15 157 A5
Royal Hospl Mus★ SW3 257 D1
Royal Institute of British Architects W1 93 B2 238 D4
Royal Institution Mus The★ SW1 249 A5
Royal La
Hillingdon UB7 82 B1
Hillingdon UB8 82 B3
Royal Langford Apartments 3 NW6 91 D5
Royal London Est N17 34 B4
Royal London Est The NW10 89 B5
Royal London Homeopathic Hospl WC1 94 A2 240 B4
Royal London Hospl Mus★ E1 96 B2
Royal London Hospl (Whitechapel) The E1 96 B2
Royal Marsden Hospl SW3 114 B1 256 D2
Royal Mews KT8 196 C6
Royal Mews The★ SW1 115 B3 258 D6
Royal Military Sch of Music (Kneller Hall) TW2 152 B5
Royal Mint Pl 6 E1 118 A6
Royal Mint St E1 117 D6 253 D6
Royal National Orthopaedic Hospl
Regent's Pk W1 93 B3 238 D5
Stanmore HA7 9 C2
Royal National TNE Hospl The WC1 94 B4 233 C2
Royal Naval Pl SE14 141 B5
Royal Oak Ct
Dagenham RM8 80 C6
9 Shoreditch N1 95 C4
Royal Oak Mews 9 TW11 175 A5
Royal Oak Pl SE22 162 B5
Royal Oak Rd
Bexley DA6 147 C1
DA6 169 B6
5 Hackney E8 74 B2
Royal Oak Sta W2 91 D2
Royal Oak Yd SE1 253 A1
Royal Observatory The★ SE10 142 B5
Royal Opera Arc SW1 249 C4
Royal Orchard Cl SW18 157 A4
Royal Par
Blackheath Vale SE3 142 D3
Chislehurst BR7 189 A3
11 Dagenham RM10 81 D2
Ealing W5 88 A4
Fulham SW6 264 A4
12 Richmond TW9 132 C4
Royal Park Prim Sch DA14 169 A1
Royal Pl 11 SE10 142 A5
Royal Rd
Kennington SE17 138 D6
Newham E16 99 D1
Sidcup DA14 168 D1
Teddington TW11 174 B5
Royal Route HA9 66 B4
Royal Russell Sch CR0 222 B3
Royal Sch Hampstead The 8 NW3 70 B4
Royal St SE1 116 B3 260 D6
Royal Tower Lo 3 SE1 118 A6
Royalty Ho W1 239 C1
Royalty Mews W1 239 C1
Royalty Studios W11 91 A1
Royal United Services Mus★ SW1 250 A3
Royal Veterinary Coll NW1 93 D6 232 C5
Royal Victoria Pl 7 E16 121 B5
Royal Victoria Sq E16 121 B6
Royal Victoria Sta E16 121 A6
Royal Victor Pl E3 96 D5
Royal Wlk SM6 219 B5
Roycraft Ave IG11 101 D5
Roycroft Cl
Streatham SW2 160 C3
Woodford E18 37 B2
Roydene Rd SE18 123 C1
Roydon Cl 7 SW11 136 D3
Roy Gdns IG2 57 D4
Roy Gr TW12 173 D4
Royle Cres W13 87 A3
Roymount Ct TW2 152 C1
Roy Ridley Ho 6 SW4 137 D2
Roy Sq E14 119 A6
Royston Ave
Carshalton SM1 218 B5
Chingford E4 35 D5
Wallington SM6 219 D4
Royston Cl
Cranford TW5 128 B4
Walton-on-T KT12 194 A1
Royston Ct
Hinchley Wood KT10 212 D6
New Cross SE4 141 B3
1 Newham E13 99 A6
Redbridge IG1 55 D3
3 Richmond TW9 132 B4
Ruislip HA5 40 C2
Tolworth KT6 214 C6
Royston Gdns IG1 55 D3
Royston Gr HA5 23 C4
Royston Ho
Friern Barnet N11 31 A6
14 SE15 140 A6
Royston Lo SW19 180 A4
Royston Par IG1 55 D3
Royston Park Rd HA5 23 C5
Royston Prim Sch SE20 184 D2
Royston Rd
Penge SE20 184 D2
Richmond TW10 154 A6
Royston St 24 E2 96 C5
Roystons The KT5 198 D4
Rozel Ct 3 N1 95 C6
Rozelle Ct 1 CR7 204 C3
Rozel Rd SW4 137 C2
Rubastic Rd UB2 106 C3
Rubens Rd UB5 84 D5
Rubens St SE6 163 B2
Rubin Pl 14 EN3 7 C6
Ruby Ct TW13 149 D1
Ruby Rd E17 53 C6
Ruby St SE15 140 B6
Stonebridge NW10 67 A1
Ruby Triangle SE15 140 B6
Ruckholt Cl E10 75 D5
Ruckholt Rd
London E10 75 D5
Temple Mills E9, E10 75 C4
Rucklidge Ave NW10 90 A5
Rudall Cres NW3 70 B4
Rudbeck Ho 11 SE15 140 A5
Ruddington Cl E5 75 A4
Ruddock Cl HA8 27 A3
Ruddstreet Cl SE18 123 A2
Rudge Ho 1 SE16 118 A3
Rudgwick Terr NW8 92 C6 230 B5
Rudhall Ho 4 SW2 160 C5
Rudland Rd DA7 147 D2
Rudloe Rd SW12 159 C4
Rudolf Pl SW8 270 B5
Rudolph Ct SE22 162 B4
Rudolph Rd E13 98 D5
Paddington NW6 91 C5
Rudstone Ho 10 E3 97 D4
Rudyard Ct SE1 252 D1
Rudyard Gr NW7 27 A4
Ruegg Ho 5 SE18 144 C6
Ruffetts Cl CR2 222 B1
Ruffetts The CR2 222 B1
Ruffle Cl UB7 104 B4
Rufford Cl HA3 43 A3
Rufford St N1 94 A6 233 B6
Rufford Street Mews N1 72 A1
Rufford Twr 5 W3 110 D5
Rufforth Ct 1 NW9 27 C2
Rufus Bsns Ctr SW18 157 D2
Rufus Cl HA4 63 A5
Rufus Ho SE1 263 D6
Rufus St N1 95 C4
Rugby Ave
Edmonton N9 17 D3
Northolt UB6 64 B2
Wembley HA0 65 C4
Rugby Cl HA1 42 C5
Rugby Gdns RM9 80 C2
Rugby Mans W14 254 B4
Rugby Rd
Bedford Pk W4 111 C4
Dagenham RM9 80 C2
Queensbury NW9 44 D5
Twickenham TW1, TW2, TW7 152 C5
Rugby St WC1 94 B3 240 C5
Rugg St E14 119 C6
Rugless Ho 2 E14 120 A4
Rugmere 4 NW1 71 A1
RUISLIP 39 B2
Ruislip Cl UB6 85 D3
RUISLIP COMMON 39 B4
Ruislip Ct HA4 61 D6
RUISLIP GARDENS 61 D5
Ruislip Gardens Prim Sch HA4 61 D4
Ruislip Gardens Sta HA4 62 A4
Ruislip High Sch HA4 62 A5
Ruislip Lido★ HA4, HA5 39 B5
Ruislip Lido Rly★ HA4 39 B5
RUISLIP MANOR 40 A1
Ruislip Manor Sta HA4 40 A1
Ruislip Rd UB6, UB5 85 C4
Ruislip Rd E
Ealing UB6, W7 86 D3
Greenford UB6 86 B3
Ruislip St SW17 180 D6
Ruislip Sta HA4 39 D1
Rumball Ho 14 SE5 139 C5
Rumbold Rd SW6 135 D5 265 D3
Rum Cl E1 118 C6
Rumford Ho SE1 262 A5
Rumsey Cl TW12 173 B4
Rumsey Rd SW9 138 B2
Runacres Ct SE17 262 A1
Runbury Circ NW9 67 B6
Runcorn Cl N17 52 B5
Runcorn Pl W11 244 A6
Rundell Cres NW4 46 B4
Rundell Twr SW8 270 C2
Runes Cl CR4 202 C5
Runnelfield HA1 64 C5
Running Horse Yd 12 TW8 132 A6
Runnymede SW19 180 B2
Runnymede Cl TW2 151 D4
Runnymede Cres SW16 182 A2
Runnymede Ct
Roehampton SW15 156 A3
1 Wallington SM6 219 B2
Runnymede Gdns
Greenford UB6 86 C5
Twickenham TW2 151 D4
Runnymede Ho
Hackney E9 75 A4
Richmond TW10 154 C6
Runnymede Rd TW2 151 D5
Runway The HA4 62 C3
Rupack St 3 SE16 118 C4
Rupert Ave 6 HA9 66 A3
Rupert Ct W1 249 C6
Rupert Gdns SW9 138 D3
Rupert Ho SE11 261 B3
8 Upper Holloway N19 71 D5
Rupert Rd
Bedford Pk W4 111 C3
Paddington NW6 91 B5
Upper Holloway N19 71 D6
Rupert St W1 115 D6 249 C6
Rural Way SW16 181 B3
Rusbridge Cl E8 74 A3
Ruscoe Ho 12 SW27 182 D5
Ruscoe Rd E16 98 D1
Ruscombe Way TW14 149 D4
Rusham Rd SW12 158 D4
Rushbridge Cl CR0 205 A3
Rushbrook Cres E17 35 B2
Rushbrook Ho 20 SW8 137 D3
Rushbrook Rd SE9 167 A2
Rushbury Ct 4 TW12 173 C2
Rushby Ct SW4 270 A1
Rush Common Mews 18 SW2 160 B4
Rushcroft Rd
Brixton SW2, SW9 138 C1
Chingford E4 35 D3
Rush Croft Sch E4 35 D3
Rushcutters Ct 18 SE16 119 A2
Rushden Cl SE19 183 B3
Rushdene SE2 124 D3
Rushdene Ave EN4 14 C4
Rushdene Cl UB5 84 C5
Rushdene Cres UB5 84 C4
Rushdene Rd HA5 40 D3
Rushden Gdns
Ilford IG5 56 C6
Mill Hill NW7 28 C4
Rushen Wlk SM5 202 B1
Rushet Rd BR5 190 A1
Rushett Cl KT7 197 B1
Rushett Rd KT7 197 B2
Rushey Cl KT3 199 B5
Rushey Gn SE6 163 D4
Rushey Green Prim Sch SE6 163 D3
Rushey Hill EN2 4 B1
Rushey Mead SE4 163 C6
Rushford Rd SE4 163 B5
Rush Green Rd RM7, RM8, RM10 59 D1
Rushgrove Ave NW9 45 D5
Rushgrove Ct NW9 45 C4
Rushgrove St SE18 122 B2
Rush Hill Mews 3 SW11 137 A2
Rush Hill Rd SW11 137 A2
Rushlake Ho 3 SW11 137 A3
Rushley Cl BR2 226 A4
Rushman Villas KT3 199 D5
Rushmead
5 Bethnal Green E2 96 B4
Richmond TW10 153 B1
Rushmead Cl CR0 221 D4
Rushmere Ct KT4 216 A6
Rushmere Ho 2 SW15 156 A3
Rushmere Pl SW19 178 D5
Rushmon Pl SM3 217 A2
Rushmoor Cl HA5 40 B5
Rushmore Cl BR1 210 A6
Rushmore Cres 9 E5 74 D4
Rushmore Ho
9 Kentish Town N7 71 D3
W14 254 B5
Rushmore Prim Sch 12 E5 74 D4
Rushmore Rd
Clapton Pk E5 74 D4
Hackney E5 75 A4
Rusholme Ave RM10 81 C5
Rusholme Gr SE19 183 C5
Rusholme Rd SW15 157 A5
Rushout Ave HA3 43 B3
Rush The SW20 179 B2
Rushton Ho 26 SW8 137 D3
Rushton St N1 95 B5 235 D4
Rushworth St SE1 116 D4 251 D1
Rushy Meadow La SM5 218 C5
Rushy Meadow Prim Sch SM5 218 C5
Ruskin Ave DA16 146 A3
Feltham TW14 149 D5
Plashet E12 78 A2
Richmond TW9 132 C5
Ruskin Cl NW11 47 D3
Ruskin Ct
Herne Hill SE5 139 B2
SE9 166 B5
Southgate N21 16 B4
Ruskin Dr
North Cheam KT4 216 C6
Orpington BR6 227 C5
Welling DA16 146 A2
Ruskin Gdns
Ealing W5 87 D3
Harrow HA3 44 B5
Ruskin Gr DA16 146 A3
Ruskin Ho SW1 259 D3
Ruskin Par CR0 221 B3
Ruskin Park Ho SE5 139 B2

Ruskin Rd
Belvedere DA17 125 C2
Croydon CR0 220 D6
Isleworth TW7 130 D2
Southall UB1 107 A6
Tottenham N17 33 D2
Wallington SM5 219 A3
Ruskin Way SW19 180 B2
Ruskin Wlk BR2 210 B3
Edmonton N9 18 A2
Herne Hill SE24 161 A6
Rusland Ave BR6 227 B5
Rusland Hts HA1 42 C5
Rusland Park Rd HA1 42 C5
Rusper Cl
Cricklewood NW2 68 C5
Stanmore HA7 25 C6
Rusper Ct SW9 138 A3
Rusper Rd
Dagenham RM9 80 C2
Tottenham N17, N22 51 A6
Russel Cl BR3 208 A6
Russel Ct N14 15 D6
Russell Ave N22 32 D1
Russell Cl
Bexleyheath DA7 147 C1
Chiswick W4 133 D6
Greenwich SE7 143 C5
Ruislip HA4 62 C6
Stonebridge NW10 67 A1
Russell Ct
Battersea SW11 268 B1
Bloomsbury WC1 240 A5
Bromley BR1 186 D3
12 New Barnet EN5 2 A1
5 Peckham SE15 140 B3
St James SW1 249 B3
Streatham SW16 182 B5
Surbiton KT6 198 A2
Wallington SM6 219 C3
4 Walthamstow E10 53 D2
Wembley HA0 66 A1
Russell Gdns
East Barnet N20 14 C2
Ilford IG2 57 B2
Richmond TW10 153 C2
Temple Fortune NW11 47 A3
W14 113 A3 254 A6
West Drayton UB7 104 C1
Russell Gdns Mews
W14 113 A3 254 A6
Russell Gr
33 Brixton SW9 138 C4
Edgware NW7 27 C6
Russell Ho
21 Poplar E14 97 C1
SW1 259 A2
Russell Kerr Cl W4 133 A5
Russell La N20 14 D2
Russell Lo
5 Chingford E4 20 A2
SE1 262 C6
Russell Mans WC1 240 B4
Russell Mead HA3 24 D2
Russell Par NW11 47 A3
Russell Pickering Ho 2
SW4 138 A2
Russell Pl
Hampstead NW3 70 C3
Rotherhithe SE16 119 A3
Russell Prim Sch The
TW10 153 D3
Russell Rd
Bowes Pk N13 32 B4
Buckhurst Hill IG9 21 C3
Chingford Hatch E4 35 B6
Crouch End N8 49 D3
East Barnet N20 14 C2
Enfield EN1 5 D5
Leyton E10 53 D3
Merton SW19 179 C3
Mitcham CR4 202 C6
Newham E16 99 B1
Northolt UB5 64 A3
Shepperton TW17 193 A2
Tottenham N15 51 C4
Twickenham TW1,
TW2 152 D5
W14 113 A3 254 B5
Walthamstow E17 53 B6
Walton-on-T KT12 194 A3
West Hendon NW9 45 D3
Russell Sq
WC1 94 A3 240 A5
Russell Square Ho
WC1 240 A5
Russell Square Mans
WC1 240 B4
Russell Square Sta
WC1 94 A3 240 A5
Russell St
WC2 116 A6 250 B6
Russell's Wharf 2
W9 91 B3
Russell Way SM1 217 D3
Russell Wlk 4
TW10 154 B5
Russell Yd SW15 135 A1
Russet Ave TW16,
TW17 193 C6
Russet Cl UB10 83 A3
Russet Cres N7 72 B3
Russet Ct
6 Barnet EN4 2 C1
Dollis Hill NW2 68 B5
Feltham TW13 149 C1
Russet Dr CR0 207 A1
Russet Ho TW3 129 B1
Russet House Sch EN1 6 B4
Russets Cl E4 36 B6
Russettings 1 HA5 23 B3
Russett Way SE13 141 D3
Russia Dock Rd
SE16 119 A5
Russia La E2 96 C5
Russia Row EC2 242 B1
Russington Rd
TW17 193 B3
Rusthall Ave W4 111 B3
Rusthall Cl CR0 206 C3
Rusthall Mans 3
W4 111 B2
Rustic Ave SW16 181 B3
Rustic Pl HA0 65 D4
Rustic Wlk E16 99 B1
Rustington Wlk SM4 201 B2
Ruston Ave KT5 198 D2
Ruston Gdns N14 15 A5
Ruston Mews W11 91 A1
Ruston Rd SE18 122 A3
Ruston St E3 97 B6
Rust Sq SE5 139 B5
Rutford Rd SW16 182 A5
Ruth Cl HA7 44 B5
Ruth Ct 16 E3 97 A5
Rutherford Cl
Hillingdon UB8 82 B3
Sutton SM2 218 B2
Rutherford Ct
Mitcham SW19 180 B3
Southgate N21 16 B6
Rutherford Ho
12 Bethnal Green E1 96 B3
Teddington TW11 174 D5
4 Wembley HA9 67 A5
Rutherford Sch CR2 221 D3
Rutherford St
SW1 115 D2 259 C4
Rutherford Twr 8
UB1 85 D1
Rutherford Way
Bushey WD23 8 C3
Wembley HA9 66 C4
Rutherglen Rd SE2 146 A6
Rutherwyke Cl KT17 216 A2
Ruth Ho W10 91 A3
Ruthin Cl NW9 45 C3
Ruthin Rd SE3 143 A6
Ruthven St E9 96 D6
Rutland Ave DA15 168 A4
Rutland Cl
Chessington KT9 214 B2
DA5 168 D3
Mitcham SW19 180 C3
Mortlake SW14 133 A2
Rutland Ct
15 Acton W3 88 C1
Chislehurst BR7 188 C2
Enfield EN3 18 B6
Herne Hill SE5 139 B1
Sidcup SE9 167 A2
SW7 247 B1
Twickenham TW2 152 C1
Rutland Dr
Morden SM4 201 C2
Richmond TW10 154 A3
Rutland Gate
Beckenham BR2 208 D5
Rutland Gate *continued*
Belvedere DA17 125 D1
SW7 114 C4 247 B1
Rutland Gate Mews
SW7 247 A1
Rutland Gdns
Dagenham RM8 80 C3
Ealing W13 87 A2
South Croydon CR0 221 C4
Stoke Newington N4 51 A3
SW7 114 C4 247 B1
Rutland Gdns Mews
SW7 247 B1
Rutland Gr W6 112 B1
Rutland Ho
Edgware HA8 26 B4
6 Northolt UB5 63 C2
2 Penge SE20 184 C2
10 Putney SW15 156 C4
Tolworth KT6 198 C1
W8 255 C5
15 Woolwich SE18 122 B2
Rutland Lo
Forest Hill SE6 163 B2
Teddington TW11 174 C5
Rutland Mews 21
NW8 91 D6
Rutland Mews E
SW7 257 B6
Rutland Mews S
SW7 257 A6
Rutland Mews W
SW7 257 A6
Rutland Park Gdns 1
NW2 68 C2
Rutland Park Mans 2
NW2 68 C2
Rutland Pk
Forest Hill SE6 163 B2
Willesden NW2 68 C2
Rutland Pl
Bushey WD23 8 B3
EC1 241 D4
Rutland Rd
Forest Gate E7 77 D1
Harrow HA1 42 A3
Hayes UB3 105 B2
Ilford IG1 78 D5
Mitcham SW19 180 C3
Southall UB1 85 C2
South Hackney E9 96 D6
Twickenham TW2 152 B2
Walthamstow E17 53 C3
Wanstead E11 55 B4
Rutland St SW7 257 B6
Rutland Studios
NW10 90 A4
Rutland Wlk SE6 163 B2
Rutley Cl SE11 138 D6
Rutlish Rd SW19 179 C2
Rutlish Sch SW20 179 B1
Rutter Gdns CR4 202 B5
Rutters Cl UB7 104 C4
Rutt's Terr SE14 140 D4
Rutts The WD23 8 B3
Ruvigny Gdns SW15 134 D2
Ruvigny Mans 7
SW15 134 D2
Ruxbury Ct TW15 148 A1
RUXLEY 191 A3
Ruxley Cl
Chessington KT19 214 D3
Sidcup DA14 191 A4
Ruxley Cnr DA14 191 A4
Ruxley Corner Ind Est
DA14 190 D4
Ruxley Cres KT10 213 B1
Ruxley Ct KT19 215 A3
Ruxley Gdns TW17 193 A4
Ruxley La KT19 215 B3
Ruxley Mews KT19 214 D3
Ruxley Ridge KT10 213 A1
Ryall's Ct N20 14 D1
Ryan Cl Ruislip HA4 40 B1
SE9 143 C1
Ryan Ct SW16 182 A3
Ryan Dr TW8 131 A6
Ryan Ho 3 HA1 42 D4
Ryarsh Cres BR6 227 C4
Rycott Path SE22 162 A4
Rycroft Way N17 51 D6
Ryculff Sq SE3 142 D3
Rydal Cl NW4 29 A2
Rydal Cres UB6 87 C5
Rydal Ct Edgware HA8 26 B5
Wembley HA9 44 A2
Rydal Dr DA7 147 C4
West Wickham BR4 224 C6
Rydal Gdns
Kingsbury NW9 45 C4
Kingston u T SW15 177 C5
Twickenham TW2,
TW3 151 D5
Wembley HA9 43 C1
Rydal Ho 25 SW8 137 D3
Rydal Lo N17 34 A3
Rydal Rd SW16 181 D6
Rydal Water NW1 232 A1
Rydal Way Enfield EN3 18 C5
Ruislip HA4 62 C4
Ryde Ho 1 NW6 91 C6
Rydens Ho SE9 165 C1
Rydens Rd KT12 194 D1
Ryde Pl TW1 153 D5
Ryder Cl BR1 187 B5
Ryder Ct Leyton E10 75 D6
SW1 249 B4
Ryder Dr SE16 118 B1
Ryder Ho
18 Bethnal Green E1 96 C3
5 Merton SW19 179 D2
Ryder St SW1 249 B4
Ryder's Terr
NW8 92 A5 229 A4
Ryder Yd SW1 249 B4
Ryde Vale Rd SW12 159 C2
Rydon Mews SW19 178 C3
Rydons Cl SE9 144 A2
Rydon St N1 235 B6
Rydston Cl 2 N7 72 B1
Rye Cl DA5 169 D5
Ryecotes Mead
SE21 161 C3
Ryecroft Ave TW2 151 D3
Ryecroft Cres EN5 12 B6
Ryecroft Rd BR5 211 B3
Lewisham SE13 164 A6
South Norwood SW16 182 C4
Ryecroft St
SW6 135 D4 265 C1
Rye Ct BR3 185 B2
Ryedale SE22 162 B5
Ryedale Ct 7 TW12 173 C2
Ryefield Ave UB10 60 D1
Ryefield Cres HA5,
HA6 22 A1
Ryefield Ct HA6 22 A1
Ryefield Jun & Inf Sch
UB10 83 B6
Ryefield Path 7
SW15 156 A3
Ryefield Rd SE19 183 A4
Ryegates 2 SE15 140 B3
Ryehill Ct KT3 199 D2
Rye Hill Pk SE15 140 C1
Rye Ho 17 SE16 118 C4
Rye La SE15 140 A3
Ryeland Cl UB7 82 A1
Ryelands Cres SE12 165 C5
Ryelands Prim Sch
SE25 206 B4
Rye Lane Mkt★
SE15 140 A3
Rye Oak Sch 7
SE15 140 B2
Rye Rd SE15 140 D1
Rye The N14 15 C4
Rye Way HA8 26 B4
Rye Wlk SW15 156 D6
Ryfold Rd SW19 157 C1
Ryhope Rd N11 31 B6
Ryland Cl TW13 171 D6
Rylandes Rd NW2 68 A5
Ryland Ho 11 SW16 181 C5
Ryland Rd NW5 71 B2
Rylett Cres W12 111 D3
Rylett Rd W12 111 D3
Rylston Rd
Edmonton N13 17 B1
SW6 135 B6 264 C5
Rylton Ho KT12 194 A1
Rymer Rd CR0 205 C2
Rymer St SE24 160 D5
Rymill St E16 122 C5
Rysbrack St SW1 257 C6
Rythe Cl
Chessington KT9 213 C1
Claygate KT10 212 C3
Rythe Ct KT7 197 A2
Rythe Ho 7 BR1 186 B5
Rythe Rd KT10 212 C3

S

Saatchi Gallery Duke of York's HQ★
SW3 114 D1 257 D2
Sabah Ct TW15 170 C6
Sabbarton St 9 E16 98 D1
Sabella Ct E3 97 B5
Sabine Rd SW11 137 A2
Sable Cl TW4 128 C2
Sable Ct 3 KT3 199 C4
Sable St N1 72 D1
Sach Rd E5 74 B6
Sacketts Ho 24 SW9 138 C4
Sackville Ave BR2 209 A1
Sackville Cl HA2 64 B5
Sackville Gdns IG1 56 B1
Sackville Ho
Hornsey N8 50 A5
16 Streatham SW16 160 A1
Sackville Rd SM2 217 C1
Sackville St
W1 115 C6 249 B5
Sacred Heart High Sch
9 W6 112 C2
Sacred Heart Language
Coll HA3 24 C1
Sacred Heart Prim Sch,
Battersea SW11 136 C3
Sacred Heart RC Prim
Sch
East Barnet N20 14 C2
Putney SW15 156 A6
Ruislip HA4 61 C6
Teddington TW11 175 B3
West Barnes KT3 200 A5
Sacred Heart RC Sec Sch
10 SE5 139 A4
Sacred Heart Sch N7 72 B3
Saddlebrook Pk
TW16 171 C3
Saddlers Cl
Barnet EN5 12 B6
Borehamwood WD6 11 B5
Pinner HA5 23 C5
Saddlers Mews SW8 270 B2
Teddington KT1 175 C2
Wembley HA0 64 D4
Saddlers Path WD6 11 B6
Saddlescombe Way
N12 29 C5
Sadler Cl CR4 180 D1
Sadler Ho
17 Bromley E3 97 D4
EC1 234 C2
Sadlers Ho EN1 17 C6
Sadlers Ride KT8 174 A1
Saffron Ave E14 120 B6
Saffron Cl
Temple Fortune
NW11 47 B3
Thornton Heath CR0 204 A3
Saffron Ct
East Bedfont TW14 149 A4
10 Kingsland N1 73 B2
Stratford E15 76 C3
Saffron Hill
EC1 94 C2 241 B4
Saffron Ho 6 TW9 132 D4
Saffron St EC1 241 B4
Saffron Way KT6 197 D1
Saffron Wharf SE1 253 D2
Sage Cl 7 E6 100 B2
Sage Mews SE22 161 D6
Sage St E1 118 C6
Sage Way WC1 233 C1
Sage Yd KT6 198 B1
Sahara Ct UB1 107 A6
Saigasso Cl E16 99 D1
Sailacre Ho 10 SE10 120 D1
Sail Ct 10 E14 120 B6
Sailmakers Ct SW6 136 A2
Sail St SE11 116 B2 260 D4
Saimet 3 NW9 27 D2
Sainfoin Rd SW17 159 A2
Sainsbury Rd SE19 183 C5
St Agatha's Dr KT2 176 B4
St Agatha's Gr SM5 202 D1
St Agatha's RC Prim Sch
KT2 176 B4
St Agnes Cl E9 96 C6
St Agnes Pl SE11 138 D6
St Agnes RC Prim Sch
15 E3 97 D4
London NW2 69 A5

St Aidans Ct IG11 ....102 B5
St Aidan's Prim Sch N4 ....50 C2
St Aidan's RC Prim Sch IG1 ....57 B1
St Aidan's Rd
East Dulwich SE22 ....162 B6
West Ealing W13 ....109 B4
St Aiden's Ct W13 ....109 C4
St Albans Ave
Bedford Pk W4 ....111 B3
Feltham TW13 ....172 D5
St Alban's Ave E6 ....100 C4
St Alban's CE Prim Sch EC1 ....94 C2 241 A4
St Alban's Cl NW11 ...47 C1
St Albans Cres N22 ...32 C2
St Alban's Cres IG8 ...37 A2
St Alban's Gdns TW11 ....175 A5
St Alban's Gr
Carshalton SM5 ....202 C2
W8 ....113 D3 255 D6
St Albans Ho 2 SW16 ....182 C6
St Albans La NW11 ....47 C1
St Albans Mans W8 . 255 D6
St Alban's Pl N1 ....94 D6 234 C5
St Alban's RC Aided Prim Sch KT8 ....196 A4
St Albans Rd
Barnet EN5 ....1 A3
Cheam SM1 ....217 B4
Ilford IG3 ....57 D2
Kingston u T KT2 ....176 A4
St Alban's Rd
Dagenham NW10 ....89 C6
Dartmouth Pk NW5 ....71 B5
Woodford IG8 ....37 A3
St Alban's St SW1 ....249 C5
St Albans Studios W8 ....255 D6
St Albans Terr W6 ....264 A6
St Alban's Villas NW5 .71 A5
St Alfege Pas SE10 ...142 A6
St Alfege Rd SE7 ....143 D6
St Alfege with St Peter's CE Prim Sch SE10 . 142 A6
St Aloysius Convent NW1 ....93 D4 232 C2
St Aloysius RC Coll 9 N19 ....49 C1
St Aloysius RC Inf Sch NW1 ....93 D4 232 C2
St Aloysius RC Jun Sch NW1 ....93 D5 232 C3
St Alphage Ct NW9 ....45 B6
St Alphage Gdn EC2 . 242 B3
St Alphage Highwalk EC2 ....242 B3
St Alphage Wlk HA8 ...27 A1
St Alphege Rd N9 ....18 C4
St Alphonsus Rd SW4 ....137 D1
St Amunds Cl SE6 ....185 C6
St Andrew & St Francis CE Prim Sch 6 NW2 ....68 A2
St Andrews Ave HA0 ..65 A4
St Andrew's (Barnsbury) Prim Sch N1 94 B6 233 D6
St Andrew's CE Prim Sch
Enfield EN1 ....5 C3
Osidge N14 ....15 D3
St Andrew's CE VA Prim Sch N20 ....13 B2
St Andrews Chambers W1 ....239 B2
St Andrews Cl
25 Bermondsey SE16 ....118 B1
Erith SE28 ....102 D1
Long Ditton KT7 ....197 B1
Ruislip HA4 ....62 D6
Stanmore HA7 ....25 C1
Wimbledon SW19 ....179 D4
St Andrew's Cl
Dollis Hill NW2 ....68 B5
2 Hounslow TW7 ....130 C4
North Finchley N12 ....30 A6
Upper Halliford TW17 .193 B5
St Andrews Ct W4 ....133 A4
St Andrew's Ct
Carshalton SM5 ....218 C5
St Andrew's Ct *continued*
2 Higham Hill E17 ....35 A1
Kingston u T KT3 ....199 D6
2 Wandsworth SW18 ....158 A2
St Andrews Dr HA7 ...25 C2
St Andrew's Gr N16 ...51 B1
St Andrew's Greek Sch NW1 ....71 C2
St Andrew's High Sch CR0 ....220 D4
St Andrew's Hill EC4 ....94 D1 241 D1
St Andrews Ho
11 Bermondsey SE16 ....118 B3
Bromley BR1 ....187 B4
St Andrews Mans 9 E5 ....74 B4
St Andrew's Mans W1 ....238 A3
St Andrews Mews
Greenwich SE3 ....143 A5
4 Streatham SW12 . 159 D3
St Andrew's Mews N16 ....51 C1
St Andrew's Pl NW1 . 238 D6
St Andrew's Prim Sch 33 SW9 ....138 A3
St Andrews RC Prim Sch SW16 ....182 A5
St Andrews Rd
Carshalton SM5 ....218 C5
DA14 ....168 D1
Dagenham W3 ....89 C1
Higham Hill E17 ....35 A1
Ponders End N9 ....18 C4
Uxbridge UB10 ....60 B1
Welsh Harp NW9 ....45 B1
St Andrew's Rd
3 Croydon CR0 ....221 A4
Enfield EN1 ....5 B2
Hanwell W7 ....108 C4
Hillingdon UB10 ....82 B6
Leytonstone E11 ....54 C3
Newham E13 ....99 B4
Redbridge IG1 ....56 B2
Surbiton KT6 ....197 D3
Temple Fortune NW11 ..47 B3
W14 ....264 B6
Willesden NW2 ....68 B2
St Andrew's & St Mark's CE Jun Sch KT6 ....197 D4
St Andrew's Sq
Notting Hill W11 ....91 A1
Surbiton KT6 ....197 D3
St Andrew St EC4 ....241 B3
St Andrews Terr WD19 ....22 C5
St Andrew's Twr UB1 ....108 A6
St Andrews Way E3 ...97 D3
St Andrew's Wharf SE1 ....253 D2
St Angela's & St Bonaventure's Sixth Form Ctr E7 ....77 B2
St Angela's Ursuline Sch E7 ....77 B2
St Anna Rd EN5 ....12 D6
St Anne RC Prim Sch 18 E1 ....96 A3
St Annes Catholic High Sch N13 ....32 C6
St Anne's CE Prim Sch 6 SW18 ....157 D6
St Annes Cl WD19 ....22 C6
St Anne's Cl N6 ....71 A5
St Annes Ct 8 SM2 . 217 D2
St Anne's Ct
Kensal Rise NW6 ....91 A6
W1 ....239 C1
St Anne's Flats NW1 232 C2
St Annes Gdns NW10 ..88 B4
St Anne's Independent PRU CR0 ....205 B3
St Anne's Pas E14 ....97 B1
St Anne's RC High Sch for Girls EN2 ....5 B1
St Anne's RC Prim Sch SE11 ....138 B6 270 C6
St Anne's Rd
Leyton E11 ....76 B6
Wembley HA0 ....65 D3
St Anne's Row E14 ....97 B1
St Anne St E14 ....97 B1
St Anne's Trad Est 25 E14 ....97 B1
St Ann's IG11 ....101 A6
St Ann's CE Prim Sch N15 ....51 B4
St Ann's Cres SW18 ..158 A5
St Ann's Ct NW4 ....46 B6
St Ann's Ctr HA1 ....42 C3
St Ann's Gdns NW5 ...71 A2
St Ann's Hill SW18 ...158 A5
St Ann's Ho WC1 ....234 A1
St Ann's Hospl N4, N15 ....51 A4
St Ann's La SW1 ....259 D5
St Ann's Park Rd SW18 ....158 A5
St Anns Rd
Barnes SW13 ....133 D4
Shepherd's Bush W11 ....112 D6
St Ann's Rd
1 Barking IG11 ....101 A6
Edmonton N9 ....17 D3
Harrow HA1 ....42 C3
Tottenham N15 ....51 B4
St Ann's Sch 9 W7 . 108 C5
St Ann's Specl Sch SM4 ....201 D4
St Ann's St SW1 ....115 D3 259 D6
St Ann's Terr NW8 ....92 B5 229 D4
St Ann's Villas W11 ....113 A5 244 A3
St Ann's Way CR2 ....220 D2
St Anselm RC Prim Sch UB2 ....107 B3
St Anselm's Ct SW16 ....182 A5
St Anselm's Pl W1 ..248 C6
St Anselm's RC Prim Sch
Harrow HA1 ....42 C2
Upper Tooting SW17 . 159 A1
St Anselms Rd UB3 . 105 D4
St Anthony's Ave IG8. .37 C3
St Anthonys Cl 5 SW17 ....158 C2
St Anthony's Cl
8 E1 ....118 A5
5 Hackney Wick E9 ....75 B2
St Anthony's Ct
2 Balham SW12 ....159 A5
Orpington BR6 ....226 D6
Upper Tooting SW17 . 159 A2
St Anthony's Flats NW1 ....232 C3
St Anthony's Hospl SM3 ....200 D1
St Anthony's RC Prim Sch
East Dulwich SE22 ... 162 A5
4 Penge SE20 ....184 C2
Upton E7 ....77 B1
St Anthony's Sch 8 NW3 ....70 B3
St Anthony's Way TW14 ....127 D1
St Antony's RC Prim Sch IG8 ....37 A6
St Antony's Rd E7 ....77 B1
St Arvans Cl CR0 ....221 C5
St Asaph Ct SE4 ....140 D2
St Asaph Rd SE4 ....140 D2
St Aubins Ct N1 ....235 D6
St Aubyns E18 ....54 D5
St Aubyn's Ave
Hounslow TW3, TW4 ....151 C6
Wimbledon SW19 ....179 B5
St Aubyns Cl BR6 ....227 D5
St Aubyn's Ct SW19 ..179 A4
St Aubyns Gdns BR6 227 D6
St Aubyn's Rd SE19 . 183 D4
St Aubyn's Sch IG8 ...36 D3
St Audrey Ave DA7 ...147 C3
St Augustine's Ave
BR1, BR2 ....210 A4
Ealing W5 ....88 A4
South Croydon CR2 .. 221 A1
Wembley HA9 ....66 A5
St Augustine's CE High Sch 5 NW6 ....91 C5
St Augustine's CE Prim Sch DA17 ....125 B2
St Augustines Ct
Beckenham BR3 ....185 A1
4 New Barnet EN5 ....14 A6
St Augustine's Ct E11 .54 D1
St Augustine's Ho NW1 ....232 C2
Upper Tooting SW17 . 180 D6
St Augustine's Prim Sch 5 NW6 ....91 D5
St Augustines Priory Sch W5 ....88 B2
St Augustine's RC Prim Sch
Catford SE6 ....186 A5
1 Ilford IG2 ....56 D4
W6 ....135 A6 264 B5
St Augustine's Rd
Camden Town NW1 ....71 D1
DA17 ....125 B2
St Austell Cl HA8 ....26 B1
St Austell Rd SE13 ...142 B3
St Awdry's Rd IG11 ...79 B1
St Barnabas CE Prim Sch SW1 ....115 A1 258 B2
St Barnabas Cl
Beckenham BR3 ....186 A1
11 Dulwich Village SE22 ....161 C6
St Barnabas Ct HA3 ...24 A2
St Barnabas' Gdns KT8 ....195 C4
St Barnabas Ho CR4 ..181 A3
St Barnabas Rd
Mitcham CR4 ....181 A3
Sutton SM1 ....218 B3
Walthamstow E17 ....53 C3
Woodford IG8 ....37 C3
St Barnabas & St Philip CE Prim Sch W8 ....113 C3 255 A5
St Barnabas St SW1 . 258 B2
St Barnabas Terr E9 ...74 D3
St Barnabas Villas SW8 ....138 A4 270 B2
St Bartholomew's CE Prim Sch SE26 ....184 C6
St Bartholomew's Cl SE26 ....184 C6
St Bartholomews Ct 6 E6 ....100 A6
St Bartholomew's Hospl EC1 ....94 D2 241 D3
St Bartholomew's Mus* EC1 ....241 D3
St Bartholomew's Rd E6 ....100 B5
St Bede's RC Inf Sch SW12 ....159 D3
St Bede's RC Prim Sch RM6 ....58 C4
St Benedict's Cl SW17 ....181 A5
St Benedict's Jun Sch 15 W5 ....87 C2
St Benedict's Sch W5 87 D2
St Benets Cl 6 SW17 ....158 C2
St Benet's Gr SM5 ...202 A2
St Benet's Pl EC3 ....252 D6
St Bernadette RC Jun Sch 12 SW12 ....159 C4
St Bernadette's Fst & Mid Sch HA3 ....44 B5
St Bernadette's RC Prim Sch UB10 ....82 D6
St Bernard Ho 6 E14 ....120 A3
St Bernards CR0 ....221 C5
St Bernards Cl 8 SE27 ....183 B6
St Bernards Ho 1 KT6 ....214 A6
St Bernard's Rd E6 ....99 D6
St Blaise Ave BR1 ....187 B1
St Bonaventure's Sch E7 ....77 A1
St Boniface RC Prim Sch 1 SW17 ....180 D5
St Botolph St E1, EC3 ....95 D1 243 C2
St Brelades Ct N1 ....235 D6
St Bride's EC4 ....241 C1
St Bride's Ave EC4 ....241 C1
Edgware HA8 ....26 B2
St Brides Cl DA18 ....124 D4
St Bride's Pas EC4 ....241 C1
St Bride St EC4 ....94 D1 241 C2
St Catherines Cl
Chessington KT9 ....213 D2
7 Upper Tooting SW17 ....158 C2
St Catherines Ct TW13 ....150 A3
St Catherine's Ct 8 W4 ....111 C3
St Catherine's Dr SE14 ....140 D3
St Catherines Farm Ct HA4 ....39 A3
St Catherines Mews SW3 ....257 C4
St Catherine's RC Sch EN5 ....1 C1
St Catherine's RC Sch for Girls DA6 ....169 D6
St Catherines Rd
Chingford E4 ....19 C2
Ruislip HA4 ....39 B3
St Catherine's Sch TW1 ....153 A2
St Catherines Twr 5 E10 ....53 D2
St Cecilia's CE Sch SW18 ....157 B3
St Cecilia's Cl SM3 ..201 A1
St Cecilia's RC Prim Sch SM3 ....216 D6
St Chads Cl KT6 ....197 C2
St Chad's Gdns RM6 ..59 A2
St Chad's Pl WC1 ....233 C2
St Chad's RC Prim Sch SE25 ....205 C4
St Chad's Rd RM6 ....59 A2
St Chad's St WC1 ....233 B2
St Charles' Hospl W10 ....90 D2
St Charles Pl W10 ....91 A2
St Charles RC Prim Sch 7 W10 ....90 D2
St Charles RC Sixth Form Coll 8 W10 ....90 D2
St Charles Sq W10 ....90 D2
St Christina's RC Prep Sch NW8 ....92 C5 230 B4
St Christopher's Cl TW7 ....130 C4
St Christophers Ct 15 N19 ....71 C5
St Christophers Dr UB3 ....106 B6
St Christophers Gdns CR7 ....204 C6
St Christopher's Ho NW1 ....232 C3
St Christopher's Mews SM6 ....219 C3
St Christopher's Pl W1 ....238 B2
St Christopher's Sch
Beckenham BR3 ....186 A1
5 Hampstead NW3 ....70 B3
Wembley HA9 ....66 B5
St Clair Dr KT4 ....216 B4
St Clair Ho 17 E3 ....97 B4
St Clair Rd E13 ....99 B5
St Clair's Rd CR0 ....221 C6
St Clare Bsns Pk TW12 ....174 A4
St Clare St EC3 ....243 C1
St Clement Danes CE Prim Sch WC2 ....94 B1 240 C1
St Clement & St James CE Prim Sch W11 ....113 A5 244 A4
St Clements Ct
Barnsbury N7 ....72 B2
7 SE14 ....140 D6
8 Shepherd's Bush W11 ....112 D6
St Clement's Ct EC3 . 252 D6
St Clements Ho E1 ..243 C3
Walton-on-T KT12 ....194 A2
St Clement's Hts SE26 ....184 A6
St Clement's La WC2 240 D1
St Clements Mans 3 SW6 ....134 D6

St Clements St N7 ... 72 C1
St Cloud Rd SE27 ... 183 B6
St Columba's Ct E15 ... 76 C4
St Columbas Ho 2
E17 ... 53 D5
St Columba's RC Boys Sch DA6 ... 169 D6
St Columb's Ho 11
W10 ... 91 A2
St Crispins Cl NW3 ... 70 C4
St Crispin's Cl UB1 ... 85 B1
St Crispins Ct 1 UB1 ... 85 B1
St Cross St
EC1 ... 94 C2 241 B4
St Cuthberts Gdns 2
HA5 ... 23 B3
St Cuthberts Rd N13 ... 32 C4
St Cuthbert's Rd NW2 69 B2
St Cuthbert with St Matthias CE Prim Sch
SW5 ... 113 D1 255 C2
St Cyprian's Greek Orthodox Prim Sch
CR7 ... 183 A2
St Cyprian's St
SW17 ... 180 D6
St Davids Cl
27 Bermondsey SE16 ... 118 B1
Wembley HA9 ... 67 A5
St David's Cl BR4 ... 207 D2
St David's Coll BR4 . 207 D2
St Davids Ct 5 E11 ... 55 B4
St David's Ct
Bromley BR1 ... 210 D6
8 Southall UB1 ... 86 A1
1 Walthamstow E17 ... 54 A6
St David's Dr HA8 ... 26 B2
St David's Pl NW4 ... 46 B2
St David's Sch TW15 . 148 B1
St David's Sq E14 ... 119 D1
St Denis Rd SE27 ... 183 B6
St Dionis Rd
Fulham SW6 ... 135 B3
Wanstead E12 ... 78 A5
St Domingo Ho
SE18 ... 122 B3
St Dominic RC Prim Sch
14 NW5 ... 70 D3
St Dominics RC Prim Sch
6 E9 ... 75 A2
St Dominic's Sixth Form Coll HA1 ... 64 C6
St Donatt's Rd
London SE14 ... 141 B4
New Cross Gate SE4 ... 141 B3
St Dunstan Ave W3 ... 111 B6
St Dunstan Gdns
W3 ... 111 B6
St Dunstans SM1 ... 217 B2
St Dunstan's Alley
EC3 ... 253 A5
St Dunstan's CE Prim Sch
2 SM3 ... 217 A1
St Dunstans Cl UB3 . 105 D2
St Dunstan's Coll
SE6 ... 163 C3
St Dunstan's Ct EC4. 241 B1
St Dunstan's Hill
Cheam SM1, SM3 ... 217 A3
EC3 ... 253 A5
St Dunstan's La
Beckenham BR3 ... 208 A4
EC3 ... 253 A5
St Dunstans Rd E7 ... 77 C2
St Dunstan's Rd
Cranford TW5 ... 128 B3
Feltham TW13 ... 149 D1
Hammersmith W6 ... 112 D1
Hanwell W7 ... 108 C4
South Norwood SE25. 205 D5
St Edmunds Ave HA4 ... 39 B3
St Edmunds Cl
DA18 ... 124 D4
3 Upper Tooting SW17 ... 158 C2
St Edmund's Cl NW8 230 C5
St Edmund's Ct NW8 230 C5
St Edmunds Dr HA7 ... 25 A2
St Edmund's La
TW2 ... 151 D4
St Edmunds RC Prim Sch
E14 ... 119 C2
St Edmund's RC Prim Sch
1 Edmonton N9 ... 18 B3
Twickenham TW2 ... 151 D4
St Edmunds Rd N9 ... 18 A4
St Edmund's Rd IG1 ... 56 B3
St Edmund's Sq
SW13 ... 134 C6
St Edmund's Terr
NW8 ... 92 D6 230 C5
St Edward's CE Comp Sch RM7 ... 59 C3
St Edward's Cl NW11 ... 47 C3
St Edwards Ct 3 E10 ... 54 A2
St Edward's Ct NW11 ... 47 C3
St Edwards RC Prim Sch
10 E6 ... 99 C6
St Edward's RC Prim Sch
NW1 ... 92 C3 237 B5
St Egberts Way E4 ... 20 A3
St Elizabeth Ct
North Finchley N12 ... 30 A6
9 Walthamstow E10 ... 53 D2
St Elizabeth RC Prim Sch
33 E2 ... 96 C5
St Elizabeth's RC Prim Sch TW10 ... 154 B5
St Elmo Rd W12 ... 111 D4
St Elmos Rd SE16 ... 119 A4
St Elphege's RC Sch
SM6 ... 220 A2
SS Peter & Paul's Prim Sch CR4 ... 202 D5
SS Peter & Paul's RC Prim Sch IG1 ... 79 B5
St Erkenwald Mews
IG11 ... 101 B6
St Erkenwald Rd
IG11 ... 101 B6
St Ermin's Hill SW1 . 259 C6
St Ervan's Rd W10 ... 91 B2
St Eugene de Mazenod RC Prim Sch 12
NW6 ... 69 C1
St Faith's CE Prim Sch 1
SW18 ... 158 A6
St Faith's Cl EN2 ... 5 A4
St Faith's Rd SE24 ... 160 D3
St Fillans Rd SE6 ... 164 A4
St Francesca Cabrini RC Prim Sch SE23 ... 162 C5
St Francis Cl BR5 ... 211 C3
St Francis de Sales RC Jun & Inf Sch 12
N17 ... 33 D3
St Francis' Ho NW1 . 232 C3
St Francis Lodge
HA0 ... 64 D5
St Francis of Assisi Prim Sch 19 W11 ... 112 D6
St Francis Pl SW12 ... 159 B5
St Francis RC Prim Sch
28 SE15 ... 140 A5
Stratford E15 ... 76 C3
St Francis Rd SE22 ... 139 C1
St Francis Way IG1 ... 79 B4
St Francis Xavier Coll
SW12 ... 159 B5
St Frideswides Mews 5
E14 ... 98 A1
St Gabriel's CE Prim Sch
SW1 ... 115 C1 259 A1
St Gabriels Cl 3 E14 ... 97 D2
St Gabriel's Cl E11 ... 55 B1
St Gabriels Ct N11 ... 31 D3
St Gabriel's Rd NW2 ... 68 D3
St George Ho SW11 . 268 B1
ST GEORGE IN THE EAST ... 118 A6
St George's Ave
Ealing W5 ... 109 D4
Kingsbury NW9 ... 45 B5
Southall UB1 ... 107 B6
Tufnell Pk N7 ... 71 D4
Upton E7 ... 77 B1
St George's Bldgs
SE11 ... 261 D5
St George's Cath
NW1 ... 231 D2
St George's Cath RC Prim Sch
SE1 ... 116 D3 261 C6
St George's CE Prim Sch
BR1 ... 187 D1
18 SE5 ... 139 C5
St George's CE Prim Sch *continued*
SW8 ... 137 C5 269 B3
St George's Circ
SE1 ... 116 D3 261 C6
St Georges Cl
Erith SE28 ... 102 D1
Nine Elms SW8 ... 269 B2
Wembley HA0 ... 65 A5
St George's Cl NW11 ... 47 B3
St Georges Coll N7 ... 72 C5
St Georges Ct
Harrow HA3 ... 43 A3
Newham E6 ... 100 B3
Penge SE20 ... 184 B2
Putney SW15 ... 135 B1
Walthamstow E17 ... 54 B4
St George's Ct
Brompton SW3 ... 257 A4
Kensington SW7 ... 256 A5
Newington SE1 ... 261 C5
St George's Dr
Ickenham UB10 ... 60 B6
South Oxhey WD19 ... 23 A6
SW1 ... 115 C1 259 A2
St George's Field
W2 ... 92 C1 237 B1
St George's Gdns
KT6 ... 214 D6
St George's Gr
SW17 ... 158 B1
St Georges Hanover Sq Sch W1 ... 115 A6 248 B5
St George's Ho NW1 232 B3
St George's Hospl
SW17 ... 180 B5
St Georges Ind Est
N22 ... 32 D3
St George's Ind Est
KT2 ... 175 D5
St George's La EC3 ... 253 A6
St Georges Lo N10 ... 49 C5
St Georges Mews 11
NW1 ... 70 D1
St George's Mews
2 Rotherhithe SE8 ... 119 B2
SE1 ... 261 B6
St Georges Pl N7 ... 71 D4
St George's Pools
E1 ... 118 B6
St George's RC Cath
SE1 ... 116 C3 261 B6
St George's RC Prim Sch
Enfield EN2 ... 5 B3
Harrow HA1 ... 64 D5
St George's RC Sec Sch
W9 ... 91 D5
St Georges Rd
Acton W4 ... 111 B4
Bickley BR1 ... 210 B6
Dagenham RM9 ... 81 A4
Petts Wood BR5 ... 211 B3
St George's Rd
Beckenham BR3 ... 185 D2
Ealing W7 ... 108 D5
Enfield EN1 ... 5 D5
Feltham TW13 ... 172 D6
Isleworth TW1 ... 153 B6
2 Kingston u T KT2 ... 176 C3
Leyton E10 ... 76 A5
Mitcham CR4 ... 203 B6
Newington
SE1 ... 116 D3 261 C5
Palmers Green N13 ... 16 B2
Redbridge IG1 ... 56 B2
Richmond TW9 ... 132 B2
Sidcup DA14 ... 190 D4
Temple Fortune NW11 ... 47 B3
Upton E7 ... 77 B2
Wallington SM6 ... 219 B3
Wimbledon SW19 ... 179 B4
St Georges Rd Ctr
RM9 ... 81 B4
St Georges Rd W
BR1 ... 188 A1
St George's Residences
4 SW2 ... 160 C6
St Georges's Ct EC4. 241 C2
St George's Sh Ctr
HA1 ... 42 C3
St Georges Sq 1
E14 ... 119 A6
St George's Sq
Kingston u T KT3 ... 199 C6
Rotherhithe SE8 ... 119 B2
St George's Sq *continued*
SW1 ... 115 D1 259 C1
Upton E7 ... 77 B1
St George's Square Mews SW1 ... 259 C1
St George St
W1 ... 115 B6 248 D6
St Georges Terr
Hampstead NW1 ... 70 D1
NW1 ... 230 D6
St Georges Univ of London SW17 ... 180 B5
St George's Way
SE15 ... 139 C6
St George's Wlk
CR0 ... 221 A5
St George the Martyr CE Prim Sch
WC1 ... 94 B3 240 D5
St George Wharf
SW8 ... 270 A6
St Gerards Cl SW4 ... 159 C6
St German's Pl SE3 ... 143 A4
St German's Rd
SE23 ... 163 A3
St Gildas' RC Jun Sch 13
N8 ... 50 A2
ST GILES ... 94 A1
St Giles Ave
Dagenham RM10 ... 81 D1
Uxbridge UB10 ... 61 A4
St Giles Cir
WC1 ... 93 D1 239 D2
St Giles Cl BR6 ... 227 B3
Dagenham RM10 ... 81 D1
Heston TW3 ... 129 A5
St Giles Coll
Highgate N6 ... 49 C3
WC1 ... 94 A2 240 B4
St Giles Ct
Ealing W13 ... 109 C5
WC2 ... 240 A2
St Giles High St
WC2 ... 93 D1 239 D2
St Giles Ho
2 New Barnet EN5 ... 2 A1
Streatham SW16 ... 160 A1
St Giles Pas WC2 ... 239 D1
St Giles Rd SE5 ... 139 C4
St Giles' Specl Sch
CR2 ... 220 D2
St Giles Terr EC1 ... 242 B3
St Giles Twr 3 SE5 ... 139 C4
St Gilles Ho 15 E2 ... 96 D5
St Gothard Rd SE21,
SE27 ... 183 B6
St Gregor High Sch
HA3 ... 43 D4
St Gregory Cl HA4 ... 62 C4
St Gregory's RC Prim Sch
14 W5 ... 87 D2
St Helena Ho WC1 ... 234 A1
St Helena Pier TW9 . 153 D6
St Helena Rd SE16 ... 118 D2
St Helena St WC1 ... 234 A1
St Helena Terr 31
TW9 ... 153 D6
St Helens KT7 ... 196 D2
St Helens Coll UB10 ... 60 C1
St Helen's Cres
SW16 ... 182 B2
St Helens Gdns W10 ... 90 D1
St Helens Pl E10 ... 53 A2
St Helen's Pl EC3 ... 243 A2
St Helen's RC Inf Sch
E17 ... 54 A4
St Helen's RC Prim Sch
E13 ... 99 A3
St Helen's RC Sch 17
SW9 ... 138 C2
St Helens Rd 5
DA18 ... 124 D4
St Helen's Rd
Ealing W13 ... 109 C5
Redbridge IG1 ... 56 B3
Thornton Heath
SW16 ... 182 B2
ST HELIER ... 202 B2
St Helier Ave SM4 ... 202 A3
St Helier Ct 4 N1 ... 95 C6
St Helier Hospl SM5 202 A1
St Heliers Ave TW3,
TW4 ... 151 C6
St Helier's Rd E10 ... 54 A3
St Helier Sta SM4 ... 201 C3
St Hilary's Ct BR1 ... 210 D6
St Hilda's Ave TW15 ... 170 A5
St Hildas Cl 2
SW17 ... 158 C2
St Hilda's Cl NW6 ... 68 D1
St Hilda's Rd SW13 ... 134 B6
St Hildas Wharf E1 ... 118 C5
St Hubert's Ho 2
E14 ... 119 C3
St Hughes Cl 4
SW17 ... 158 C2
St Hugh's Rd SE20 ... 184 B3
St Ignatius Coll EN1 ... 6 B6
St Ignatius RC Prim Sch
TW16 ... 172 A2
St Ignatius' RC Prim Sch
N15 ... 51 D3
St Ives Ct NW2 ... 69 A2
St Ivian Ct 3 N10 ... 31 B1
ST JAMES ... 115 C5
St James Apartments 2
E17 ... 53 A4
St James Ave
East Barnet N20 ... 14 C1
Sutton SM1 ... 217 C3
St James' Ave W13 ... 109 A5
St James' CE Jun & Inf Sch 24 SE16 ... 118 A3
St James CE Jun Sch
E7 ... 77 A3
St James CE Prim Sch
EN3 ... 6 C3
St James Cl Barnet EN4 . 2 B1
East Barnet N20 ... 14 C1
St James' Cl
New Malden KT3 ... 199 D4
Ruislip HA4 ... 62 C6
St James Ct
26 Bethnal Green E2 ... 96 A4
9 Brentford W4 ... 110 C1
1 Bromley BR2 ... 187 A1
Forest Hill SE23 ... 163 A3
SE3 ... 143 B4
Thornton Heath CR0 . 204 D2
Wanstead E12 ... 77 C6
St James' Ct
Bedford Pk W4 ... 111 B3
7 Kingston u T KT1 ... 198 A6
SW1 ... 259 B6
St James Gate IG9 ... 21 B3
St James Gdns IG6 ... 58 B5
St James' Gdns HA0 ... 66 A1
St James Ho N5 ... 72 C3
St James Hts 3
SE18 ... 123 A1
St James Independent Schs W14 ... 113 A2 254 B4
St James Ind Mews 16
SE1 ... 118 A1
St James Ind Sch for Boys TW1 ... 153 A2
St James' Mans NW6 ... 69 C1
St James Mews E14 ... 120 A3
St James' RC High Sch
NW9 ... 27 D2
St James RC Prim Sch
BR5 ... 210 D4
St James Rd
Carshalton SM5 ... 218 C5
Kingston u T KT1 ... 175 D1
Sutton SM1, SM2 ... 217 C3
St James' Rd
Edmonton N9 ... 18 B2
Forest Gate E15 ... 76 D3
Mitcham CR4 ... 181 A3
Surbiton KT6 ... 197 D3
Sutton SM1 ... 217 C2
St James's SE14 ... 141 A4
St James & St Michael's CE Prim Sch
W2 ... 114 A6 246 B6
St James's App EC2. 243 A5
St James's Ave
Beckenham BR3 ... 207 A6
Hampton TW12 ... 174 A5
South Hackney E2 ... 96 C5
St James's CE Prim Sch
Cranley Gdns N10 ... 49 A5
London SE14 ... 141 A4
St James School Flats 5
N7 ... 72 C3
St James's Cl NW8 ... 230 C5
Upper Tooting SW17 . 158 D2
Woolwich SE18 ... 123 A1
St James's Cloisters 2
SE22 ... 139 D1

St James's Cotts 14
TW10 153 D6
St James's Cres
SW9 138 C2
St James's Ct
8 Edmonton N18 34 A5
Harrow HA1 43 A3
St James's Dr
Balham SW12,
SW17 158 D4
Upper Tooting SW17 158 D3
St James's Gdns
W11 113 A5 244 A4
St James's Gr SW11 136 D3
St James's La N10 49 B5
St James's Market
SW1 249 C5
St James's Mews E17 53 A4
St James's Pal★
SW1 115 C5 249 B3
St James's Park Sta
SW1 115 D3 259 C6
St James's Pas EC3 243 B1
St James's Pk★ SW1 249 C2
St James's Pk CR0 205 A2
St James's Pl
SW1 115 C5 249 A3
St James's RC Prim Sch
TW2 152 C1
St James's Rd
Bermondsey SE1,
SE16 118 A2
Hampton TW12 173 D5
Peckham SE1 140 A6
Thornton Heath CR0 205 B2
St James's Sq
SW1 115 C5 249 B4
St James's St
SW1 115 C5 249 A4
Walthamstow E17 53 A4
St James St W6 112 C1
St James's Terr NW8 230 C6
2 Upper Tooting
SW12 159 A3
St James's Terrace Mews
NW8 230 C5
St James Street Sta
E17 53 A4
St James The Great RC
Prim Sch
17 Camberwell
SE15 139 D4
South Norwood CR7 182 D1
St James Way DA14 191 A5
St James Wlk EC1 241 C6
St Jerome's Gr UB3 83 A1
St Joachim's RC Prim
Sch 1 E16 99 C1
St Joan of Arc RC Prim
Sch N5 73 A4
St Joan's Rd N9 17 D2
St John Baptist CE Prim
Sch BR1 186 A6
St John Fisher RC Fst &
Mid Sch HA5 41 C5
St John Fisher RC Prim
Sch
DA18 125 A3
Wembley UB6 87 C5
West Barnes SW20 200 D4
St John of Jerusalem CE
Prim Sch 42 E9 74 C1
ST JOHN'S 141 C3
St John & St James CE
Prim Sch
Edmonton N18 33 D5
1 Hackney E9 74 C3
St John's Angell Town
CE Prim Sch 28
SW9 138 C3
St John's Ave
Dagenham NW10 89 D6
Friern Barnet N11 30 D5
Putney SW15 156 D6
St John's CE First Sch
HA7 25 A6
St John's CE Prim Sch
Buckhurst Hill IG9 21 B3
Croydon CR0 222 D5
Enfield EN2 4 D6
Kingston u T KT1 198 A6
London N11 30 D6
12 Penge SE20 184 C3
35 South Hackney E2 96 C5
St John's CE Prim Sch
continued
Whetstone N20 14 A2
St John's CE Sch HA7 25 A6
St John's CE Walham
Green Prim Sch
SW6 135 A4 264 B2
St John's Church Rd
E9 74 C3
St Johns Cl N14 15 C5
St John's Cl SW6 265 A4
Wembley HA9 66 A3
St John's Concert Hall★
SW1 260 A5
St John's Cotts 2
SE20 184 C3
St John's Cres SW9 138 C2
St Johns Ct 39 E1 118 B5
St John's Ct
Buckhurst Hill IG9 21 B3
Finsbury Pk N4 72 D6
Hammersmith W6 112 B2
2 Harrow HA1 42 D3
Isleworth TW7 130 D3
Kingston u T KT1 198 A5
Lewisham SE13 142 A3
Leytonstone E11 54 D1
5 South Hampstead
NW3 70 A2
Saint John's Ct N5 72 D4
St Johns Dr KT12 194 C1
St John's Dr SW18 157 D3
St John's Est SE1 253 C1
St John's Gdns
W11 113 B6 244 C5
St John's Gr
3 Barnes SW13 133 D3
1 Richmond TW9 132 A1
Upper Holloway N19 71 C6
St John's Highbury Vale
CE Prim Sch N5 72 D5
St John's Hill SW11 136 B1
St John's Hill Gr
SW11 136 B1
St Johns Ho 5 SE17 139 B6
Streatham SW16 182 A4
St John's Ho 1 E14 120 A2
St John's La
EC1 94 D2 241 D4
St John's Lodge 8
SE8 141 C4
St John's Mans E5 74 C3
St John's Par
Ealing W13 109 B5
3 Sidcup DA14 190 B6
St John's Park Mans
N19 71 C5
St John's Path EC1 241 C5
St John's Pk SE3 143 A5
St John's Pl EC1 241 C5
St John's Prim Sch
W13 109 A6
St John's RC Prim Sch
SE16 119 A4
St Johns Rd Ilford IG2 57 C2
Kingston u T KT3 199 A6
St John's Rd
Barking IG11 101 C6
Battersea SW11 136 C1
Canning Town E16 99 A1
Carshalton SM5 218 C5
Chingford E4 35 D6
Croydon CR0 220 D5
DA16 146 B2
East Ham E6 100 A6
East Molesey KT8 196 B5
Feltham TW13 173 B6
Harrow HA1 42 D3
Isleworth TW7 130 D3
Orpington BR5 211 C3
Penge SE20 184 C4
Richmond TW9 132 A1
Sidcup DA14 190 B6
Southall UB2 107 A3
Sutton SM1 217 D6
Teddington KT1 175 C1
Temple Fortune NW11 47 B3
Tottenham N15 51 C3
Walthamstow E17 36 A1
Wembley HA9 66 A3
Wimbledon SW19 179 A4
St John's & St Clements
CE Jun & Inf Sch 4
SE15 140 A2
St John's Sch HA6 22 B4
St John's Sq
EC1 94 D3 241 C5
St Johns Sta SE8 141 C3
St John St
EC1 94 D3 241 C6
St John's Terr
Enfield EN2 5 B6
North Kensington W10 90 D3
SE18 145 B6
Upton E7 77 B2
St John's Therapy Ctr
SW11 136 B1
St Johnstone Ho 17
N12 29 D6
St John's Upper
Holloway CE Prim Sch
7 N19 71 D6
St John's Vale SE8 141 C3
St John's Villas
4 Friern Barnet N11 30 D5
Upper Holloway N19 71 D6
W8 255 D5
St John's Walworth CE
Prim Sch
SE17 117 A2 262 B3
St John's Way N19 49 D1
ST JOHN'S WOOD 92 B5
St John's Wood Ct
NW8 229 D1
St John's Wood High St
NW8 92 C5 230 A3
St John's Wood Park
NW8 92 B6 229 C6
St John's Wood Pre-
Prep Sch
NW8 92 C4 230 A2
St John's Wood Rd
NW8 92 B4 229 D1
St John's Wood Sta
NW8 92 B5 229 C4
St John's Wood Terr
NW8 92 C5 230 A4
St John the Baptist CE
Jun Sch KT1 175 D3
St John the Baptist VA
CE Prim Sch
N1 95 B5 235 D3
St John the Divine CE
Jun & Inf Sch SE5 138 D5
St John the Evangelist
RC Prim Sch
N1 94 D5 234 C4
St John Vianney RC Prim
Sch 4 N8 50 D5
St Josephs Cl BR6 227 D4
St Joseph's Cl W10 91 A2
St Joseph's Convent Sch
9 E11 55 A3
St Josephs Ct
3 Dagenham NW10 89 D5
20 Walthamstow E10 53 D2
St Joseph's Ct E4 20 B4
St Joseph's Dr UB1 107 B5
St Joseph's Flats
NW1 232 C2
St Josephs Gr NW4 46 B5
St Joseph's Ho W6 112 D2
St Joseph's Hospice E9,
E8 96 B6
St Joseph's RC Coll
SW16 182 D4
St Joseph's RC Fst & Mid
Sch HA3 25 A1
St Joseph's RC Inf &
Jun Schs
Hendon NW4 46 B5
36 SE5 139 A5
St Joseph's RC Inf Sch
Leyton E10 75 C6
South Norwood SE19 183 A4
St Joseph's RC Jun & Inf
Schs HA9 66 B3
St Joseph's RC Jun Sch
South Norwood
SE19 183 A4
Walthamstow E10 53 D1
St Josephs RC Prim Sch
10 W7 108 C5
St Joseph's RC Prim
Sch
Barking IG11 101 A6
39 Bermondsey SE16 118 A4
Bromley BR1 187 B3
Chelsea SW3 114 D2 257 C3
Dagenham RM9 81 B4
19 Deptford SE8 141 C5
St Joseph's RC Prim Sch
continued
11 Greenwich SE10 120 C1
Kingston u T KT1 176 B1
Paddington
W9 92 A4 229 A1
Rotherhithe SE16 118 C3
St Giles WC2 94 A1 240 B2
Upper Holloway N19 49 B1
16 Wandsworth
SW18 157 C6
8 Willesden NW10 67 C1
St Joseph's Rd N9 18 C3
St Joseph's St SW8 268 D2
St Joseph's Vale
SE3 142 B2
St Jude & St Paul's CE
Prim Sch 12 N1 73 C2
St Jude's CE Prim Sch
4 London SE24 160 D6
SE1 116 D3 261 C5
St Judes Ho 6 W10 91 B4
St Jude's Rd E2 96 B5
St Jude St N16 73 C3
St Julian's Cl SW16 182 C6
St Julian's Farm Rd SE27,
SW16 182 D6
St Julian's Rd NW6 91 C6
St Katharine's Ho N1 234 A4
St Katharine's Prec
NW1 231 C4
St Katharine's Way
E1 117 D5 253 D4
St Katherines Rd
DA18 124 D4
St Katherine's Row
EC3 243 B1
St Katherine's Wlk 1
W11 112 D5
St Keverne Rd SE9 188 A6
St Kilda Rd BR6 211 D1
Ealing W13 109 A4
St Kilda's Rd
Harrow HA1 42 C3
Stamford Hill N16 51 C1
St Kitts Terr SE19 183 C5
St Laurence's Cl NW6 90 D6
St Lawrence Bsns Ctr
TW13 150 B2
St Lawrence Cl HA8 26 B3
St Lawrence Ct N1 235 D6
St Lawrence Dr HA5 40 B4
St Lawrence Ho SE1 263 B6
St Lawrence Jun Sch
KT8 196 B5
St Lawrence RC Prim
Sch TW13 150 B2
St Lawrence St E14 120 A5
St Lawrence Terr
W10 91 A2
St Lawrence Way
SW9 138 C3
St Leonards Ave HA3 43 C4
St Leonard's Ave E4 36 B4
St Leonard's CE Prim Sch
SW16 181 D5
St Leonards Cl 4
DA16 146 A2
St Leonards Ct
SW14 133 A2
St Leonard's Ct N1 235 D2
St Leonards Gdns
IG1 79 A3
St Leonard's Gdns
TW5 129 A4
St Leonard's Hospl
N1 95 C5
St Leonards Rd
SW14 133 A2
St Leonard's Rd
Becontree NW10 89 B3
Claygate KT10 212 D2
Croydon CR0 220 D5
Ealing W13 109 C6
Kingston u T KT6 197 D4
South Bromley E14 98 A2
Thames Ditton KT7 197 A2
St Leonards Rise
BR6 227 C4
St Leonard's Sq
Camden Town NW5 71 A2
Kingston u T KT6 197 D4
St Leonard's St E3 97 D4
St Leonard's Terr
SW3 114 D1 257 D1
St Leonard's Wlk
SW16 182 B3
St Loo Ave
SW3 136 C6 267 B6
St Loo Ct SW3 267 C6
St Louis Rd SE27 183 B6
St Loy's Rd N17 51 D6
St Lucia Dr E15 98 D6
St Luke Prim CE Sch 9
E16 98 D1
ST LUKE'S 95 A3
St Luke's Ave
Clapham SW4 137 D1
Enfield EN2 5 B5
Ilford IG1 78 D3
St Luke's CE Prim Sch
7 Cubitt Town E14 120 B2
Kingston u T KT2 176 B2
Paddington W9 91 B4
Shoreditch EC1 95 A4 235 B1
West Norwood SE27 183 A5
St Luke's Cl
Croydon SE25 206 B3
St Luke's EC1 95 A3 242 B6
St Lukes Ct 6 E10 53 D2
St Luke's Ct W11 91 B1
St Luke's Mews W11 91 B1
St Luke's Path 1 IG1 78 D3
St Luke's RC Sixth Form
Coll DA14 189 D5
St Luke's Rd
Notting Hill W11 91 B2
Uxbridge UB10 60 A1
St Luke's Sq E16 98 D1
St Luke's St SW3 257 B2
St Luke's Woodside
Hospl N10 49 A5
St Malo Ave N9 18 C1
St Margaret Clitherow
RC Prim Sch
Neasden NW10 67 B4
Woolwich SE28 124 B5
St Margaret Lee CE Prim
Sch SE13 142 C1
ST MARGARETS 153 A5
St Margarets IG11 101 B6
St Margarets Ave
Ashford TW15 170 D5
DA15 167 B1
Hillingdon UB8 82 C3
Whetstone N20 14 A3
St Margaret's Ave
Cheam SM3 217 A5
Harringay N8, N15 50 D5
Harrow HA2 64 A5
St Margarets Bsns Ctr 11
TW1 153 B5
St Margaret's CE Prim
Sch
Barking IG11 79 A1
Woolwich SE18 123 A1
St Margaret's Cres
SW15 156 B6
St Margaret's Ct
Leyton E15 76 C4
Putney SW15 134 B1
SE1 252 C3
9 Twickenham TW1 153 B5
St Margaret's Dr
TW1 153 B6
St Margaret's Gr
Leyton E11 76 D5
SE18 145 A6
Twickenham TW1 153 A5
St Margaret's La
W8 113 D3 255 C5
St Margarets Lo W3 110 D4
St Margaret's Pass
SE13 142 C2
St Margaret's Path 4
SE18 123 A1
St Margarets Rd
Edgware HA8 26 D5
Ruislip HA4 39 B3
St Margaret's Rd
Brockley SE4 141 B1
Hanwell W7 108 C4
Isleworth TW1 153 B6
Kensal Green NW10 90 C4
Tottenham N17 51 C6
Wanstead E12 77 C6

St Margarets Rdbt
TW1 . . . . 153 B6
St Margaret's Sch
NW3 . . . . 69 D4
St Margaret's Sch
TW1 . . . . 153 B5
St Margaret St SW1 . 250 A1
St Margaret's Terr
SE18 . . . . 123 A1
St Margret's Ct N11 . . . 31 A6
St Mark's CE Acad
CR4 . . . . 181 B1
St Mark's CE Prim Sch
Bromley BR2 . . . . 209 B6
3 Croydon SE25 . . . . . 206 A5
Kennington
SE11 . . . . 138 B6 270 C6
St Marks Cl 5 SE10 . 142 A3
St Mark's Cres
NW1 . . . . 93 A6 231 B6
St Mark's Ct
Hanwell W7 . . . . 108 C4
6 Walthamstow E10 . . 53 D2
St Marks Gate E9 . . . . 75 B1
St Mark's Gr
SW10 . . . . 135 D5 266 D4
St Marks Hill KT6 . . . 198 A3
St Marks Ho 6
SE17 . . . . 139 B6
St Mark's Ho 8 E17 . . . 54 A5
St Mark's Hospl HA1 . . 43 B2
St Mark's Hts 2
KT6 . . . . 198 A4
St Marks Ind Est
E16 . . . . 121 D5
St Mark's Mans 14 N4 . 72 B6
St Marks Pl RM10 . . . . 81 D2
St Mark's Pl
Notting Hill W11 . . . . . . .91 A1
Wimbledon SW19 . . . . . 179 B4
St Mark's Prim Sch
Hanwell W7 . . . . 108 C4
8 Mitcham CR4 . . . . . . 180 D1
11 Upper Holloway
N19 . . . . 72 A6
St Mark's Rise
TW3 . . . . 129 C2
St Marks Rd
15 North Kensington
NW10 . . . . 90 D1
North Kensington W10 . 90 D2
St Mark's Rd
Bromley BR2 . . . . 209 B6
Croydon SE25 . . . . 206 A5
Ealing W5 . . . . 110 A5
Enfield EN1 . . . . 17 D6
Hanwell W7 . . . . 108 C4
Mitcham CR4 . . . . 181 A1
Notting Hill W11 . . . . . . .91 A1
Teddington TW11 . . . . . 175 B3
St Mark's Rise E8 . . . . . . 73 D3
St Marks Sq NW1 . . . 231 A5
St Mark St E1 . . 95 D1 243 D1
St Martha's Convent Jun
Sch **11** EN5 . . . . 1 A1
St Martha's Senior Sch
EN4 . . . . 1 A1
St Martin-in-the-Fields
High Sch **1** SW2 . . . 160 C3
St Martin of Porres Prim
Sch N11 . . . . 31 C4
St Martin's Almshouses
NW1 . . . . 232 A6
St Martins App HA4 . . 39 C2
St Martin's Ave E6 . . . 99 D5
St Martins Cl D18 . . . 124 D4
South Oxhey WD19 . . . . 22 C6
St Martin's Cl
Enfield EN1 . . . . 18 D2
NW1 . . . . 232 A6
St Martins Cl N1 . . . . 95 C6
St Martin's Ct WC2 . . 250 A5
West Norwood SE27 . . 160 D2
St Martins La BR3 . . . 207 D4
St Martin's La
WC2 . . . . 6 A6 250 A5
St Martin's Le Grand
EC1 . . . . 242 A2
St Martin's Pl WC2 . . 250 A5
St Martin's Sch
Edmonton N9 . . . . .18 B2

St Martin's Rd continued
Finchley N2 . . . . 30 B2
Stockwell SW9 . . . . . . 138 B3
St Martin's Sch NW7 . . 27 B5
St Martin's St WC2 . 249 D5
St Martin's Way
SW17 . . . . 158 A1
St Mary Abbots CE Prim
Sch W8 . . . 113 D4 245 C1
St Mary Abbot's Ct
W14 . . . . 254 C5
St Mary Abbot's Pl
W8 . . . . 254 D5
St Mary Abbots Terr
W14 . . . . 254 D5
St Mary at Hill
EC3 . . . . 117 C6 253 A5
St Mary Ave SM6 . . . 219 B5
St Mary Axe
EC3 . . . . 95 C1 243 B2
St Marychurch St
SE16 . . . . 118 C4
St Mary Graces Ct
E1 . . . . 253 D5
St Marylebone CE Sch
The W1 . . . . 93 A2 238 B4
St Mary le Bone Church*
EC2 . . . . 242 B1
St Mary - le-Park Ct
SW11 . . . . 267 B3
St Mary Magdalene Acad
N7 . . . . 72 C2
St Mary Magdalene
Prim Sch
3 Paddington W2 . . . . 91 D2
10 Peckham SE15 . . . . 140 B3
18 Woolwich SE18 . . . . 122 C2
St Mary Magdalen's CE
Prim Sch
Brockley SE4 . . . . 141 A1
14 Mortlake SW14 . . . . 133 B2
St Mary Magdelen's RC
Jun Sch **3** NW2 . . . . . 68 B2
St Mary Newington CE
Prim Sch
SE17 . . . . 263 B2
St Mary RC Prim Sch **2**
W10 . . . . .91 A4
St Mary Rd E17 . . . . . 53 D5
St Marys Rd E11 . . . 101 B6
St Mary & St Michael
Prim Sch **11** E1 . . . . 96 C1
St Mary & St Pancras CE
Prim Sch
NW1 . . . . . . 83 D5 232 C3
St Marys App E12 . . . . 61 A1
St Marys Ave UB2 . . 107 D2
St Marys Ave
Beckenham BR2 . . . . . 208 C6
Finchley N3 . . . . 29 B1
Teddington TW11 . . . . . 174 D4
Wanstead E11 . . . . 55 B2
St Mary's CE Inf Sch **3**
N8 . . . . 46 C6
St Mary's CE Jun Sch **5**
N8 . . . . 50 A5
St Mary's CE Prim Sch
Chessington KT9 . . . . . 214 B2
East Barnet EN4 . . . . . 14 C5
Finchley N3 . . . . 29 B1
Islington N1 . . 94 D6 234 D6
London SE13 . . . . 163 D6
Long Ditton KT7 . . . . . 197 B1
18 Putney SW15 . . . . 134 D2
Walthamstow E17 . . . . . 53 D5
Willesden NW10 . . . . . 67 C2
St Mary's CE Prim Sch
(Inf) **12** TW1 . . . . 153 A4
St Mary's Ch Sch BR5 . 190 B1
Chessington KT9 . . . . . 214 B1
Ewell KT17 . . . . 215 D1
Sunbury TW16 . . . . . . 194 A5
Tottenham N17 . . . . 34 A2
St Mary's ColTW1 . . . 152 D1

St Mary's Cres
Hayes UB3 . . . . 105 A6
Hendon NW4 . . . . 46 B6
Hounslow TW7 . . . . . . 130 C5
St Marys Ct
Abbey Wood SE2 . . . . 124 D2
Newham E6 . . . . 100 B3
SE7 . . . . 143 D5
St Mary's Ct
Bedford Pk W6 . . . . . . 111 D3
Ealing W5 . . . . 109 D4
Finchley N12 . . . . .30 A3
Kingston u T KT3 . . . . 199 C6
Leytonstone E11 . . . . . . 54 D1
Wallington SM6 . . . . . . 219 C4
St Mary's Dr TW14 . . . 149 A4
St Mary's Est 2
SE16 . . . . 118 C4
St Mary's Flats NW1 . 232 C2
St Mary's Gate W8 . . 255 C5
St Mary's Gdns SE11 . 261 B4
St Mary's Gn 1 N2 . . . 48 A6
St Mary's Ho
Ealing W5 . . . . 109 D3
N1 . . . . 234 D6
St Mary's Hospl
W2 . . . . 92 B1 236 D2
St Mary's Hospl Medical
Sch W2 . . . . . 92 B1 236 D2
St Mary's Kilburn CE
Prim Sch **10** NW6 . . . . 91 C6
St Mary's Lo E11 . . . . . 55 B3
St Mary's Mans
Dagenham RM10 . . . . . 89 C6
Paddington
W2 . . . . 92 B2 236 C4
St Mary's Mews NW6 .69 D1
St Mary's Path 1 . . . 234 D6
St Mary's Pl
Ealing W5 . . . . 109 D4
Eltham SE9 . . . . 166 C5
Kensington
W8 . . . . 113 D3 255 C5
St Mary's RC High Sch
CR0 . . . . 205 A1
St Mary's RC Inf Sch
SM5 . . . . 218 D4
St Mary's RC Jun & Inf
Sch
Croydon CR0 . . . . 205 B1
London N15 . . . . 51 B4
St Mary's RC Jun Sch
Wallington SM5 . . . . . 218 D3
Walthamstow E17 . . . . . 54 A6
St Michael & All Angels
CE Acad **15** SE5 . . . 139 A5
St Michael-at-Bowes CE
Jun Sch N13 . . . . 32 C4
St Michael & St Martin
RC Prim Sch **1**
TW4 . . . . 129 B2
St Michael's Alley
EC3 . . . . 253 C2
St Michaels Ave N9 . . 18 C4
St Michael's Ave HA9 . 66 C2
St Michael's CE Prim
Sch
Camden Town
NW1 . . . . . . 93 C6 232 A6
DA16 . . . . 146 C4
Enfield EN2 . . . . 5 A4
5 Forest Hill SE26 . . 185 A6
Highgate N6 . . . . 49 A2
Wandsworth SW18 . . . 157 B4
Wood Green N22 . . . . . 32 B2
St Michaels BR1 . . . . . 210 A6
4 Newham E16 . . . . . 99 C2
Worcester Pk KT4 . . . 215 D6
St Michael's Cl
Colney Hatch N12 . . . . 30 C5
DA18 . . . . 124 D4
Finchley N3 . . . . 29 B1
St Michael's Cres
HA5 . . . . 41 A3
St Michaels Ct 2
E14 . . . . 98 A2
St Michael's Flats
NW1 . . . . 232 C3
St Michael's Gdns
W10 . . . . .91 A2

St Mary's Sch Hampstead
NW3 . . . . 70 B3
St Mary's Sq
Ealing W5 . . . . 109 D4
W2 . . . . 236 C3
St Mary's Stoke
Newington CE Prim Sch
2 N16 . . . . 73 C6
St Mary St SE18 . . . . 122 C2
St Mary's Terr W2 . . 236 C4
St Marys Twr EC1 . . 242 B5
St Marys View HA3 . . 43 C4
St Mary's Wlk
Hayes UB3 . . . . 105 A6
SE11 . . . . 261 B4
St Matthew Acad
SE3 . . . . 142 C2
St Matthew's Ave
KT6 . . . . 198 B1
St Matthew's CE Prim
Sch
Enfield EN3 . . . . 18 C6
Surbiton KT6 . . . . 198 A2
Wimbledon SW20 . . . . 178 A2
Yiewsley UB7 . . . . 104 A5
St Matthews CE Sch
SW1 . . . . 115 D3 259 D6
St Matthews Ct
Muswell Hill N10 . . . . . . 31 A1
SE1 . . . . 262 A5
2 Stratford E15 . . . . . 76 C1
7 Walthamstow E10 . . 53 D1
St Matthew's Ct 1
TW15 . . . . 170 C2
St Matthews Dr BR1 . 210 B6
St Matthew's Ho 8
SE17 . . . . 139 B6
St Matthew's Lo
NW1 . . . . 232 B4
St Matthew's Rd
Clapham Pk SW2 . . . . 160 B6
Ealing W5 . . . . 110 A5
St Matthew's Row 2 E2 . 96 A3
St Matthew St SW1 . 259 C5
St Matthias CE Prim Sch
E2 . . . . 95 D3 243 D6
St Matthias Cl NW9 . . 45 D4
St Matthias CE Prim
Sch **11** N16 . . . . 73 C4
St Mauritius Ho
SE13 . . . . 164 A6
St Maur Rd
SW6 . . . . 135 B4 264 D1
St Mellion Cl SE28 . . 102 D1
St Merryn Cl SE18 . . 145 B5
St Merryn St BR3 . . . 185 C3
St Michael & All Angels
CE Acad **15** SE5 . . . 139 A5
St Michael-at-Bowes CE
Jun Sch N13 . . . . 32 C4

St Michaels Ho SE26 . 185 B6
St Michael's Hospl EN2 5 B4
St Michael's RC Gram
Sch **13** N12 . . . . .30 A5
St Michael's RC Prim Sch
SE6 . . . . 100 D5
St Michael's RC Sec Sch
NW15 . . . . 170 C5
St Michaels Rd
Cricklewood NW2 . . . . . 68 C4
Croydon CR0 . . . . 205 A3
DA16 . . . . 146 B2
Stockwell SW9 . . . . . . 138 B3
Wallington SM6 . . . . . . 219 C2
St Michael's Rise
DA16 . . . . 146 B4
St Michael's St
W2 . . . . 92 C1 237 A2
St Michael Steiner Sch
The **18** SW18 . . . . . . 157 C6
St Michael's Terr N22 .32 A2
St Mildred's Ct EC2 . 242 C1
St Mildreds Rd SE12,
SE6 . . . . 164 D4
St Mirren Cl 8 EN5 . . 14 A6
St Monica's RC Prim
Sch
Palmers Green N14 . . . .16 A1
21 Shoreditch N1 . . . . 95 C4
St Nicholas CE Prim Sch
TW17 . . . . 192 D3
St Nicholas Cl WD6 . . . 9 D5
St Nicholas Ct E4 . . . .36 A4
St Nicholas Ctr **7**
SM1 . . . . 217 D3
St Nicholas Dr
TW17 . . . . 192 C2
St Nicholas Flats
NW1 . . . . 232 C3
St Nicholas Glebe
SW17 . . . . 181 A4
St Nicholas Ho SE8 . 141 C6
St Nicholas Mans
SW17 . . . . 158 D2
St Nicholas Rd
Elst WD6 . . . . 9 D5
London NW9 . . . . 67 A6
St Nicholas St SE8 . . 141 C4
St Nicholas Way
SM1 . . . . 217 D3
St Nicolas La BR7 . . 188 A2
St Ninian's Ct N20 . . 14 D1
St Norbert Gn SE4 . . 141 A1
St Norbert Rd SE4 . . 141 A1
St Olaf's Rd
SW6 . . . . 135 A4 264 B3
St Olaves Ct W2 . . . 245 C5
St Olave's Ct EC2 . . 242 C1
St Olave's Est SE1 . . 253 B2
St Olave's Gdns SE11 261 A4
St Olave's Mans
SE11 . . . . 261 A4
St Olaves Prep Sch
SE9 . . . . 166 D2
St Olave's Rd E6 . . . 100 C6
St Olave's Wlk SW16 181 D1
St Olav's Sq 12 SE16 . 118 C4
St Osmund's RC Prim
Sch SW13 . . . . 133 D4
St Oswald's Pl
SE11 . . . . 116 B1 260 C1
St Oswald's Rd
SW16 . . . . 182 D2
St Oswulf St SW1 . . 259 D3
St Owen Ho SE1 . . . 263 B6
ST PANCRAS 94 A4
St Pancras Almshouses
13 NW5 . . . . 70 D3
St Pancras Commercial
Ctr NW1 . . . . 232 B6
St Pancras Ct
Finchley N2 . . . . 30 B1
8 Wembley HA0 . . . . . 66 A2
St Pancras Hospl
NW1 . . . . 93 D6 232 C5
St Pancras International
Sta WC1 . . . . 94 A4 233 A2

St Pancras Way NW1 .... 93 D6 232 C6
St Patrick's Coll W1 .... 93 D1 239 C2
St Patricks Ct IG8 ..... 36 C3
St Patrick's RC Prim Sch
Camden Town NW5 .... 71 B3
Plumstead SE18 ...... 123 B2
6 Walthamstow E17 ... 53 A5
St Paul's Acad SE2 .. 146 A6
St Paul's & All Hallows CE Jun & Inf Schs 1 N17 .... 34 A3
St Paul's Ave
Harrow HA3 .... 44 B5
Rotherhithe SE16 .... 118 D5
Willesden NW2 .... 68 C2
St Paul's Cath★ EC4 .... 95 A1 242 A1
St Paul's Cath Sch EC4 .... 95 A1 242 A1
St Paul's CE Jun Sch 18 KT2 .... 176 C3
St Pauls CE Prim Sch
14 Brentford TW8 ... 131 D6
1 Friern Barnet N11 ... 31 B5
St Paul's CE Prim Sch
Chessington KT9 .... 214 A4
24 E1 .... 118 A6
1 Friern Barnet N11 ... 31 B5
23 Hammersmith W6 112 C1
Hampstead NW3 ...... 70 D1
Mill Hill NW7 .... 28 B6
SE17 .... 117 A1 262 A2
Southgate N21 .... 16 D4
St Paul's Church Yd EC4 .... 95 A1 242 A1
St Pauls Cl
Ealing W5 .... 110 B4
Hayes UB3 .... 105 B1
St Paul's Cl
Ashford TW15 ...... 171 A5
Borehamwood WD6 .... 11 A6
Carshalton SM5 ..... 202 C1
Chessington KT9 .... 213 D4
Greenwich SE7 ...... 121 D1
Hounslow TW3, TW4 . 129 A3
ST PAUL'S CRAY 190 A1
St Paul's Cray Rd BR7 .... 189 B2
St Pauls Cres NW1 ..... 71 D1
St Paul's Ct
Clapham SW4 ...... 137 D1
Hounslow TW4 ...... 129 A2
6 Upper Holloway N19 .... 72 A6
St Paul's Dr E15 ...... 76 B3
St Paul's Girls' Sch 1 W6 .... 112 D2
St Pauls Ho N17 ...... 34 A3
St Pauls Mews NW1 ... 71 D1
St Paul's Pl N1 .... 73 B2
St Paul's RC Coll TW16 .... 172 A2
St Paul's RC Prim Sch
Thames Ditton KT7 ... 196 C2
2 Wood Green N22 ... 32 B1
St Pauls Rd
Barking IG11 .... 101 A6
Richmond TW9 ...... 132 B2
St Paul's Rd
Brentford TW8 ...... 131 D6
Canonbury N1 .... 73 A2
South Norwood CR7 .. 205 A6
Tottenham N17 .... 34 A2
St Pauls Rise N13 ..... 32 D4
St Paul's Sch SW13 . 112 A1
St Paul's Sq BR2 ..... 187 A1
St Paul's Sta EC2 .... 95 A1 242 A2
St Pauls Steiner Sch 22 N1 .... 73 B2
St Paul St N1 .... 235 B5
St Paul's Terr SE17 ... 138 D6
St Paul's Twr 14 E10 ... 53 D2
St Pauls View WC1 .. 234 A1
St Paul's Way
Finchley N3 .... 29 D3
Tower Hamlets E3 ..... 97 C2
St Paul's Way Com Sch 25 E3 .... 97 C2
St Paul's with St Michael's Prim Sch 24 E8 .... 96 A6
St Paul's Wood Hill BR5 .... 189 D1
St Paul with St Luke CE Prim Sch 18 E3 ...... 97 B2
St Peter Chanel RC Prim Sch DA14 .... 190 C5
St Peter in Chains RC Inf Sch N8 .... 50 A3
St Peter & Paul RC Prim Sch BR5 .... 189 C1
St Peter & St Paul RC Prim Sch EC1 .... 94 D3 241 D6
St Peter & St Paul RC Sch CR4 .... 202 D5
St Peter's Alley EC3 . 242 D1
St Peters Ave N12 ..... 30 C3
St Peter's Ave
Edmonton N18 .... 34 A6
37 Hackney E2 .... 96 A5
Walthamstow E17 ..... 54 C5
St Petersburgh Mews W2 .... 245 C6
St Petersburgh Pl W2 .... 113 D6 245 C5
St Peter's CE Prim Sch
15 Chiswick W6 ..... 112 A2
9 E1 .... 118 C5
6 Paddington W9 ...... 91 C3
SE17 .... 117 B1 262 C1
SW1 .... 115 B3 258 D5
St Peter's Church Ct N1 .... 234 D5
St Peters Cl BR7 ..... 189 B3
Ilford IG2 .... 57 D5
1 Upper Tooting SW17 .... 158 C2
St Peter's Cl
Barnet EN5 .... 12 B6
Bushey WD23 .... 8 B3
Hackney E2 .... 96 A5
Ruislip HA4 .... 62 D6
St Peters Ct
East Molesey KT8 ... 195 C5
New Cross SE4 ...... 141 B3
28 Stepney E1 .... 96 C3
St Peter's Ct
Hendon NW4 .... 46 C4
Lewisham SE12 ..... 164 D6
St Peter's Gdns SE27 .... 160 C1
St Peter's Gr W6 ..... 112 A2
St Peters Ho
Tottenham Hale N15 ... 52 A5
WC1 .... 233 B1
St Peter's Ho
4 SE17 .... 139 B6
Stamford Hill N16 ..... 51 C2
St Peters La BR5 ..... 190 A1
St Peters Mews N4 .... 50 D4
St Peter's Pl W9 ...... 91 D3
St Peter's Prim Sch CR2 .... 221 C2
St Peter's RC Prim Sch
Dagenham RM9 ...... 103 B6
Woolwich SE18 ..... 122 D2
St Peters Rd KT1 ..... 176 C1
St Peter's Rd
Chiswick W6 .... 112 A1
Croydon CR0 .... 221 B4
East Molesey KT8 ... 195 C5
Edmonton N9 .... 18 B3
Isleworth TW1 ...... 153 B6
Southall UB1 .... 85 C2
St Peter's Sq
Chiswick W6 .... 111 D1
Hackney E2 .... 96 A5
St Peter's St
Croydon CR2 .... 221 B3
Islington N1 ... 94 D6 234 D5
St Peter's Street Mews N1 .... 234 D4
St Peter's Terr SW6 . 264 B3
St Peter's Villas 5 W6 .... 112 A2
St Peters Way UB3 ... 105 B1
St Peter's Way
De Beauvoir Town N1 ... 73 C1
Ealing W5 .... 87 D2
St Peter's Wharf 8 W6 .... 112 A1
St Philip Ho WC1 .... 234 A1
St Philip's Ave KT4 ... 216 B6
St Philips Gate KT4 .. 216 B6
St Philip Sq 1 SW8 .. 137 B3
St Philip's Rd
Dalston E8 .... 74 A2
Surbiton KT6 .... 197 D3
St Philip's Sch
Chessington KT9 .... 213 D2
SW7 .... 114 A2 256 B3
St Philip St SW8 ..... 137 B3
St Philip's Way N1 .. 235 B5
St Philomena's RC High Sch SM5 .... 218 C3
St Quentin Ho SW18 . 158 B5
St Quentin Rd DA16 . 145 D2
St Quintin Ave W10 ... 90 D2
St Quintin Gdns 21 W10 .... 90 C2
St Quintin Rd E13 ..... 99 B5
St Raphaels Ho W13 . 109 C5
St Raphael's RC Prim Sch UB5 .... 84 B5
St Raphael's Way NW10 .... 67 A3
St Regis Cl N10 .... 31 B1
St Regis Hts NW3 ..... 69 D5
St Richards Ct TW10 . 153 B1
St Richard's Ho NW1 232 C2
St Richard's with St Andrew's CE Prim Sch TW10 .... 153 B1
St Robert Southwell RC Prim Sch NW9 ...... 45 A3
St Ronan's 2 N3 ..... 29 C2
St Ronans Cl EN4 ...... 2 B5
St Ronans Cres IG8 ... 37 A3
St Rule St SW8 .... 137 C3
St Savior's CE Inf Sch 3 W5 .... 109 D6
St Saviours SW4 ..... 137 B1
St Saviour & St Olaves CE Sch SE1 117 B3 262 D5
St Saviour's CE Prim Sch
9 Bow Comm E14 ..... 97 D2
Camberwell SE24 .... 139 A2
26 Paddington W9 ..... 91 D3
Walthamstow E17 ..... 53 B2
St Saviour's Coll SE27 .... 183 B6
St Saviours Ct
Harrow HA1 .... 42 C4
Muswell Hill N22 ...... 31 D1
St Saviours Ho 35 SE1 .... 118 A4
St Saviour's RC Prim Sch SE13 .... 142 A1
St Saviour's Rd
Clapham Pk SW2 ..... 160 B6
Thornton Heath CR0 . 205 A3
St Saviour's Wharf SE1 .... 253 D2
St Scholastica's RC Prim Sch 6 E5 .... 74 A5
Saints Cl SE27 ...... 182 D6
Saints Dr E7 .... 77 D3
St Silas Pl NW5 .... 71 A2
St Simon's Ave SW15 .... 156 C6
St Stephens Ave E17 .. 54 A4
St Stephen's Ave
Ealing W13 .... 87 B1
Shepherd's Bush W12 . 112 B4
St Stephen's CE Jun Sch TW1 .... 153 B5
St Stephen's CE Prim Sch
Paddington W2 .... 91 C2
17 Shepherd's Bush W12 .... 112 C4
2 St Johns SE8 ..... 141 C3
SW8 .... 138 B5 270 C4
St Stephens Cl E17 ... 53 D4
St Stephen's Cl
Maitland Pk NW5 ..... 70 D3
NW8 .... 230 B5
Southall UB1 .... 85 C2
St Stephen's Cres
Notting Hill W2 .... 91 C1
Thornton Heath CR7 . 204 C6
St Stephens Ct
Ealing W13 .... 87 B1
Enfield EN1 .... 17 C5
Hornsey Vale N8 ...... 50 B3
St Stephen's Gdns
Notting Hill W2 .... 91 C1
4 Putney SW15 ..... 157 B6
Twickenham TW1 .... 153 C5
St Stephen's Gr SE13 .... 142 A2
St Stephens Ho 7 SE17 .... 139 B6
St Stephen's Mews 34 W2 .... 91 C2
St Stephens Par E6 ... 77 C1
St Stephens Prim Sch E6 .... 77 C1
St Stephen's RC Prim Sch DA16 .... 146 A3
St Stephens Rd
Barnet EN5 .... 12 D6
Upton E6 .... 77 C1
Walthamstow E17 ..... 53 D4
St Stephen's Rd
Bow E3 .... 97 B5
Ealing W13 .... 87 C1
Enfield EN3 .... 6 D6
Hounslow TW3, TW4 . 151 C6
Yiewsley UB7 .... 104 A5
St Stephen's Row EC4 .... 242 C1
St Stephen's Terr SW8 .... 270 C3
St Stephen's Wlk SW7 .... 256 A4
St Swithin's La EC4 .... 117 B6 252 C6
St Swithun's Rd SE13 .... 164 B6
St Swithun Wells RC Prim Sch HA4 .... 62 D5
St Teresa's RC Fst & Mid Sch HA3 .... 24 A2
St Teresa's RC Prim Sch SM4 .... 202 B3
St Teresa's RC Prim Sch The RM8 .... 80 C4
St Theresa Ct E4 ..... 20 B4
St Theresas Cl E9 ..... 75 C4
St Theresa's RC Prim Sch N3 .... 47 D6
St Theresa's Rd TW14 .... 127 D1
St Thomas a Beckett RC Prim Sch SE2 ...... 124 A3
St Thomas Becket RC Prim Sch 4 SE25 . 206 A3
St Thomas' CE Prim Sch 23 W10 .... 91 A3
St Thomas' Cl KT6 .... 198 B1
St Thomas Ct
14 Camden Town NW1 .... 71 C1
Sidcup DA5 .... 169 C4
11 Walthamstow E10 ... 53 D2
St Thomas' Ct HA5 ..... 23 A2
St Thomas' Dr BR5 ... 211 A1
Pinner HA5 .... 23 A2
St Thomas Gdns IG1 .. 79 A2
St Thomas Ho 2 E1 .... 96 D1
St Thomas More Language Coll SW3 .... 114 D2 257 C3
St Thomas More RC Prim Sch
Bexley DA7 .... 147 B3
SE9 .... 144 A2
St Thomas More RC Sch
SE9 .... 166 C5
Wood Green N22 ...... 32 C3
St Thomas of Canterbury RC Prim Sch
Mitcham CR4 .... 203 A6
SW6 .... 135 B5 264 C4
St Thomas Rd
Newham E16 .... 99 A1
Osidge N14 .... 15 D4
St Thomas' Rd W4 ... 133 A6
St Thomas's Gdns NW5 .... 71 A2
St Thomas's Hospl SE1 .... 116 B3 260 C6
St Thomas's Pl 20 E9 .. 74 C1
St Thomas's Rd
Dagenham NW10 ...... 89 C6
Highbury N4, N5 ...... 72 C5
St Thomas's Sq E9 .... 74 C1
St Thomas St SE1 .... 117 B5 252 D3
St Thomas's Way SW6 .... 135 B5 264 D4
St Thomas the Apostle Coll SE15 .... 140 C4
St Timothy's Mews 3 BR1 .... 187 B2
St Ursula Gr HA5 ...... 41 A4
St Ursula Rd UB1 ..... 85 C1
St Ursula's Convent Sch SE10 .... 142 B5
St Vincent Cl SE27 ... 182 D5
St Vincent De Paul Ho 24 E1 .... 96 C2
St Vincent De Paul RC Prim Sch SW1 .... 115 C3 259 B6
St Vincent Ho SE1 ... 263 C6
St Vincent Rd TW2 ... 152 A5
St Vincents La NW7 ... 28 C6
St Vincent's Nursing Home HA5 .... 39 D6
St Vincents RC Prim Sch SE9 .... 188 A6
St Vincent's RC Prim Sch
Acton W3 .... 110 D6
Dagenham RM8 .... 80 C6
London NW7 .... 28 C5
Marylebone W1 .... 93 A2 238 B3
St Vincent St W1 .... 238 B3
St Wilfrid's Cl EN4 .... 14 C6
St Wilfrid's Rd EN4 .... 14 C6
St William of York Prim Sch SE23 .... 163 A3
St Winefride's Ave E12 .... 78 B3
St Winefride's RC Prim Sch E12 .... 78 B3
St Winifred's RC Inf Sch SE12 .... 164 C6
St Winifred's RC Jun Sch SE12 .... 164 D4
St Winifred's Rd TW11 .... 175 B4
Sakura Dr N22 .... 31 D2
Sala Ho SE3 .... 143 B1
Salamanca Pl SE1 .. 260 C3
Salamanca St SE1, SE11 .... 116 B2 260 C3
Salamander Cl KT2 .. 175 C5
Salamander Quay KT1 .... 175 D2
Salcombe Dr
Dagenham RM6 .... 59 B3
North Cheam SM4 ... 200 D1
Salcombe Gdns
Clapham SW4 ...... 137 B1
Mill Hill NW7 .... 28 C4
Salcombe Ho 6 SE23 .... 162 C2
Salcombe Lo NW5 .... 71 A4
Salcombe Pk IG10 .... 21 D6
Salcombe Prep Sch (Infant Dept) N14 ... 15 B6
Salcombe Prep Sch (Junior Dept) 1 N14 .... 15 B4
Salcombe Rd
Ashford TW15 ...... 148 A1
23 Stoke Newington N16 .... 73 C3
Walthamstow E17 ..... 53 B2
Salcombe Villas 13 TW10 .... 154 A6
Salcombe Way
Hayes UB4 .... 83 C4
Ruislip HA4 .... 62 A6
Salcot N4 .... 72 B6
Salcott Rd
Wallington CR0 ..... 220 B4
Wandsworth SW11 .. 158 D6
Salehurst Cl HA3 ..... 44 A4
Salehurst Rd SE4 .... 163 B5
Salem Ho 13 E9 .... 74 D2
Salem Pl CR0 .... 221 A5
Salem Rd W2 .... 113 D6 245 D6
Sale Pl W2 ..... 92 C1 237 A2
Salesian Coll SW11 .... 136 C4 267 A1
Sale St E2 .... 96 A3
Salford Ho 5 E14 .... 120 A2
Salford Rd SW12, SW2 .... 159 D3

Salhouse Cl SE28 .... 102 C1
Salisbury Ave
Barking IG11 .... 79 C1
Cheam SM1, SM2 .... 217 B2
Hendon N3 .... 47 B6
Salisbury Cl SE17 .... 262 C4
Worcester Pk KT4 ... 215 D5
Salisbury Ct
15 Bermondsey
SE16 .... 118 A3
Chiswick W4 .... 111 C2
EC4 .... 241 C1
Edgware HA8 .... 26 B6
Enfield EN2 .... 5 B1
Finchley N3 .... 29 B1
Hackney E9 .... 75 A3
Northolt UB5 .... 63 D3
Salisbury Gdns
5 Buckhurst Hill
IG9 .... 21 D2
Wimbledon SW19 ... 179 A3
Salisbury Hall Gdns
E4 .... 35 C4
Salisbury Ho
2 Islington N1 .... 72 D2
Islington N1 .... 234 C6
3 Poplar E14 .... 97 D1
1 Ruislip HA4 .... 40 C1
Stanmore HA7 .... 25 A4
5 Wallington SM6 ... 219 B3
Westminster SW1 ... 259 D2
Wimbledon SW19 ... 156 D1
Salisbury Lower Sch
N9 .... 18 C4
Salisbury Mans
Edmonton N9 .... 18 A1
Harringay N4, N15 ..... 50 D4
Salisbury Mews
Bromley Comm BR2 .. 210 A4
Fulham SW6 .... 264 C3
Salisbury Pl
Camberwell SW9 ..... 138 D5
Marylebone W1 ..... 237 C4
Salisbury Prim Sch 1
E12 .... 78 A3
Salisbury Rd
Barnet EN5 .... 1 A2
Bromley Comm BR2 .. 210 A4
Chingford E4 .... 19 C1
Croydon SE25 .... 206 A3
Dagenham RM10 ...... 81 D2
East Bedfont TW6 ... 149 A5
Enfield EN3 .... 7 B6
Feltham TW13 ...... 150 C3
Forest Gate E7 .... 77 A2
Harringay N4 .... 50 D4
Harrow HA1 .... 42 B4
Hounslow TW4 ...... 128 C2
Ilford IG3 .... 79 C6
Kingston u T KT3 ..... 199 B6
Leyton E10 .... 76 A6
Old Bexley DA5 ..... 169 C3
Pinner HA5 .... 40 A5
Plashet E12 .... 77 D3
Richmond TW9 ...... 132 A1
Southall UB2 .... 107 A2
Tottenham N22 .... 32 D1
Wallington SM5 ..... 218 D2
Walthamstow E17 ..... 54 A4
West Ealing W13 ..... 109 B4
Wimbledon SW19 ... 179 A3
Worcester Pk KT4 ... 215 C5
Salisbury Sq EC4 .... 241 B1
Salisbury St
10 Acton W3 .... 111 A4
NW8 .... 237 A5
Salisbury Terr SE15 . 140 C2
Salisbury Upper Sch
N9 .... 18 C4
Salisbury Wlk N19 .... 71 C6
Salix Cl TW16 .... 172 B3
Salix Ct N3 .... 29 C4
Salliesfield TW2 ..... 152 B5
Sally Murray Cl E12 .. 78 C4
Salmen Rd E13 .... 98 D5
Salmond Cl HA7 ...... 25 A4
Salmon La E14 .... 97 A1
Salmon Rd DA17 ..... 125 C1
Salmons Brook Ho
EN2 .... 4 D2
Salmons Rd
Chessington KT9 .... 214 A2
Edmonton N9 .... 18 A3
Salmon St
Kingsbury NW9 .... 45 A2
13 Poplar E14 .... 97 B1
Salomons Rd 2 E13 .... 99 C2
Salop Rd E17 .... 52 D3
Saltash Cl SM1 ...... 217 B4
Saltash Rd DA16 .... 146 C4
Saltcoats Rd W4 ..... 111 C4
Saltcroft Cl HA9 ...... 44 D1
Saltdene N4 .... 50 B1
Salter Cl HA2 .... 63 B4
Salterford Rd SW17 . 181 A4
Salter Ho 8 SW16 .... 181 C6
Saltern Ct IG11 ...... 102 B4
Salter Rd
Rotherhithe SE16 .... 118 D5
SE16 .... 119 A5
Salters' Hall Ct EC4 . 252 C6
Salter's Hill SE19 .... 183 B5
Salters Rd
North Kensington
W10 .... 90 D3
Walthamstow E17 ..... 54 B5
Salter St
College Pk NW10 ...... 90 A4
11 Poplar E14 .... 119 C6
Salterton Rd N7 ...... 72 B5
Salt Hill Cl UB8 .... 60 A3
Saltley Cl E6 .... 100 A1
Saltoun Rd SW2,
SW9 .... 138 C1
Saltram Cl N15 .... 51 D5
Saltram Cres W9 ...... 91 C4
Saltwell St E14 ...... 119 C6
Saltwood Gr SE17 ... 262 C1
Saltwood Ho 19
SE15 .... 140 C6
Salusbury Prim Sch
NW6 .... 91 B6
Salusbury Rd NW6 ... 91 A6
Salutation Rd SE10 .. 120 C2
Salvador SW17 ..... 180 D5
Salvatorian Coll HA3 . 24 C1
Salvia Gdns UB6 ...... 87 A5
Salvin Rd SW15 ..... 134 D2
Salway Cl IG8 .... 37 A3
Salway Ho E10 .... 75 D6
Salway Pl E15 .... 76 C2
Salway Rd E15 .... 76 B2
Salween Ho 2 N16 .... 73 B4
Samantha Cl E17 ..... 53 B2
Samantha Ct E11 ..... 54 C2
Sam Bartram Cl SE7 . 121 C1
Sambrooke Ct EN1 .... 17 D6
Sambrook Ho 25 E1 .... 96 C2
Sambruck Mews
SE6 .... 163 D3
Samels Ct W6 .... 112 A1
Samford Ho N1 ...... 234 A5
Samford St NW8 ..... 237 A5
Samira Cl 1 E17 ...... 53 C3
Sam Manners Ho 7
SE10 .... 120 C1
Sam March Ho 5
E14 .... 98 B1
Samos Rd SE20 ...... 184 B1
Sampson Ave EN5 .... 12 D6
Sampson Cl DA17 .... 125 A3
Sampson Ct TW17 .... 193 A4
Sampson St E1 ...... 118 A5
Samson Ct 5 DA17 .... 125 C2
Samson Ho SE18 ..... 123 A2
Samson St E13 .... 99 C5
Samuel Cl Bushey HA7 ... 9 A2
SE14 .... 140 D6
Shoreditch E8 .... 95 D6
Woolwich SE18 ...... 122 A2
Samuel Ct
Beckenham BR3 ..... 207 D6
Shoreditch N1 .... 95 C4
Samuel Gray Gdns
KT2 .... 175 D2
Samuel Ho
15 Shoreditch E8 ...... 95 D6
3 West Norwood
SE27 .... 182 D6
Samuel Johnson Cl
SW16 .... 182 B6
Samuel Jones Ind Est 7
SE15 .... 139 C5
Samuel Lewis Bldgs
N1 .... 72 C2
Samuel Lewis Trust Dwellings
6 Camberwell SE5 .. 139 A4
Samuel Lewis Trust Dwellings *continued*
Chelsea SW3 .... 257 A3
Walham Green
SW6 ..... 135 C5 265 B4
West Kensington W14 254 B4
Samuel Lewis Trust Est
N15 .... 51 C3
Samuel Lo N3 .... 29 B1
Samuel Rhodes Sch
N1 .... 94 C6 234 A6
Samuel Richardson Ho
W14 .... 254 C3
Samuel's Cl 2 W6 .... 112 C2
Samuel St SE15 ..... 139 D5
Woolwich SE18 ...... 122 B2
Sancroft Cl NW2 ...... 68 B5
Sancroft Ct SW11 ... 267 B2
Sancroft Ho SE11 ... 260 D2
Sancroft Rd HA3 ...... 25 A1
Sancroft St
SE11 ...... 116 B1 260 D2
Sanctuary Mews 15
E8 .... 73 D2
Sanctuary Rd TW19,
TW6 .... 148 C5
Sanctuary St SE1 ... 252 B2
Sanctuary The
Morden SM4 .... 201 C3
Sidcup DA5 .... 168 D5
35 Wapping E1 ...... 118 B5
Westminster
SW1 .... 115 D3 259 D6
Sandale Cl N16 .... 73 B5
Sandall Cl W5 .... 88 A3
Sandall Ho 7 E3 ...... 97 A5
Sandall Rd Ealing W5 .. 88 A3
Kentish Town NW5 ..... 71 C2
Sandal Rd
Edmonton N18 .... 34 A5
New Malden KT3 .... 199 C5
Sandal St E15 .... 98 C6
Sandalwood Cl
Borehamwood EN5 .... 11 D6
11 E1 .... 97 A3
Sandalwood Dr HA4 .. 39 A2
Sandalwood Ho
DA15 .... 167 D1
6 Hampstead NW3 ... 69 D2
Sandalwood Rd
TW13 .... 150 B1
Sandbach Pl SE18 ... 123 A1
Sandbourne
4 Kensington W11 .... 91 C1
14 Paddington NW8 ... 91 D6
Sandbourne Ave
SW19 .... 179 D1
Sandbourne Rd SE4 . 141 A3
Sandbrook Cl NW7 .... 27 B4
Sandbrook Rd N16 .... 73 C5
Sandby Ct BR3 ...... 185 B2
Sandby Gn SE9 ..... 144 A2
Sandby Ho
11 Camberwell SE5 .. 139 C4
6 Kilburn NW6 .... 91 C6
Sandcroft Cl N13 ..... 32 D4
Sandells Ave
Ashford TW15 ...... 171 A6
Ashford TW15 ...... 171 A6
Sandell St SE1 ...... 251 A2
Sanderling Ct
20 SE8 .... 141 B6
Woolwich SE28 ..... 124 C6
Sanders Cl TW12 ..... 174 A5
Sanders Ho
Streatham SW16 .... 182 A4
WC1 .... 234 A2
Sanders La NW7 ...... 28 C3
Sanderson Cl NW5 .... 71 B4
Sanderson Ho 7
SE8 .... 119 B1
Sanderson Sq BR1 ... 210 C6
Sanderstead Ave
NW2 .... 69 A6
Sanderstead Cl
SW12 .... 159 C4
Sanderstead Rd
South Croydon CR2 ... 221 B1
Walthamstow E10 ..... 53 A1
Sanders Way 3 N19 ... 49 D1
Sandfield WC1 ...... 233 B1
Sandfield Gdns CR7 . 204 D6
Sandfield Pl CR7 ..... 205 A6
Sandfield Rd CR7 .... 204 D6
Sandford Ave N22 .... 33 A2
Sandford Cl E6 ...... 100 B3
Sandford Ct Barnet EN5 1 D2
Stamford Hill N16 ..... 51 C1
Sandford Rd
Bexley DA7 .... 147 A2
BR2 .... 209 A5
Newham E6 .... 100 B4
Sandford Row SE17 . 262 D2
Sandford St SW6 ... 265 D3
Sandgate Ho
14 Beckenham BR3 .. 185 C3
Ealing W5 .... 87 C2
15 Hackney E5 .... 74 B4
Sandgate La SW17,
SW18 .... 158 C3
Sandgate Rd DA16 ... 146 C5
Sandgate St SE15 ... 140 B6
Sandgate Trad Est
SE15 .... 140 B6
Sandham Ct SW4 ... 270 B1
Sandham Point 10
SE18 .... 122 D2
Sandhills CR0, SM6 .. 219 D4
Sandhills Mdw
TW17 .... 193 A2
Sandhills The SW10 . 266 B6
Sandhurst Ave
Harrow HA2 .... 41 D3
Tolworth KT5 .... 198 D2
Sandhurst Cl
Queensbury NW9 ..... 44 C6
South Croydon CR2 ... 221 C1
Sandhurst Ct SW2 ... 138 A1
Sandhurst Dr IG3 ..... 79 D4
Sandhurst Ho 12 E1 .... 96 C2
Sandhurst Jun & Inf Schs
SE6 .... 164 C3
Sandhurst Mkt SE6 .. 164 A3
Sandhurst Rd
Bexley DA5 .... 168 D6
Catford SE6 .... 164 B3
DA15 .... 168 A1
Ponders End N9 ...... 18 D5
Queensbury HA8, NW9 . 44 C6
Sandhurst Way CR2 .. 221 C1
Sandifer Dr NW2 ...... 68 D5
Sandiford Rd SM3 ... 217 B6
Sandiland Cres BR2 . 224 D6
Sandilands CR0 ..... 222 A5
Sandilands Rd
SW6 ..... 135 D4 265 C1
Sandilands Sta CR0 . 221 D6
Sandison St SE15 .... 140 A2
Sandland St WC1 ... 240 D3
Sandling Rise SE9 ... 166 C1
Sandlings Cl SE15 ... 140 B3
Sandlings The
Tottenham N22 .... 50 D6
5 Wood Green N22 ... 32 C1
Sandmartin Way
CR4 .... 203 A1
Sandmere Rd SW4 ... 138 A1
Sandon Cl KT10 ...... 196 B1
Sandon Ct IG3 .... 80 A5
Sandon Ho 5 SW2 ... 160 A4
Sandow Commercial Est
UB3 .... 105 D3
Sandow Cres UB3 ... 105 D3
Sandown Ave KT10 .. 212 A3
Sandown Cl TW5 .... 128 A4
Sandown Ct 12 SM2 . 217 D1
Sandown Gate KT10 . 212 B5
Sandown Ho
2 Acton Green W4 ... 111 A1
Esher KT10 .... 212 A4
Penge SE26 .... 184 B4
Sandown Park KT10 212 A6
Sandown Rd
Croydon SE25 ...... 206 B4
Esher KT10 .... 212 A4
Sandown Way UB5 .... 63 B3
Sandpiper Cl
Higham Hill E17 .... 34 D3
Rotherhithe SE16 .... 119 B4
Sandpiper Ct
13 Cubitt Town E14 .. 120 A3
1 SE8 .... 141 C5
Sandpiper Rd SM1 ... 217 B3
Sandpiper Terr IG5 ... 56 D6
Sandpit Pl SE7 ...... 122 A1
Sandpit Rd BR1 ..... 186 C5
Sandpits Rd
Richmond TW10 .... 153 D2
South Croydon CR0 .. 222 D4
Sandra Cl
Hounslow TW3 ...... 151 D6
Tottenham N17 .... 33 A2
Sandra Ho KT8 ...... 196 B4
Sandridge Cl
Hadley Wood EN4 ...... 2 C6
Harrow HA1 .... 42 C5
Sandridge St 3 N19 .. 71 C6
Sandringham Ave
SW20 .... 179 A1
Sandringham Cl
Enfield EN1 .... 5 C3
Ilford IG6 .... 57 A6
1 Putney SW19 ... 156 D3
Sandringham Cres
HA2 .... 63 D6
Sandringham Ct
3 Beckenham BR3 .. 186 A2
Edgware HA8 .... 26 D6
Hillingdon UB10 ...... 83 A3
Kingston u T KT2 .... 176 A2
Marylebone W1 ..... 239 B1
Putney SW15 .... 156 D5
18 Rotherhithe SE16 . 118 D5
St John's Wood W9 .. 229 B1
2 Twickenham TW1 . 153 A3
Sandringham Dr
Ashford TW15 ...... 170 A6
DA16 .... 145 C3
Sandringham Flats
WC2 .... 249 D6
Sandringham Gdns
Cranford TW5 ...... 128 A4
East Molesey KT8 ... 195 C5
Finchley N12 .... 30 B4
Hornsey Vale N8 ...... 50 A3
Ilford IG6 .... 57 A6
Sandringham Ho
Richmond TW10 ..... 154 C6
W14 .... 254 A4
Sandringham Lo
BR6 .... 226 C4
Sandringham Mews
1 Ealing W5 .... 109 D6
Hampton TW12 ..... 173 B2
Sandringham Prim Sch
1 E7 .... 77 C3
Sandringham Rd
Barking IG11 .... 79 D2
BR1 .... 187 A5
Dalston E8 .... 73 D3
Forest Gate E7 .... 77 C3
Golders Green NW11 .. 47 A2
Leytonstone E10 ...... 54 B3
Northolt UB5 .... 63 C1
Stanwell TW19, TW6 . 148 A6
Thornton Heath CR0 . 205 A4
Tottenham N22 .... 33 A1
Willesden NW2 .... 68 B2
Worcester Pk KT4 ... 216 A5
Sandrock Pl CR0 .... 222 D4
Sandrock Rd SE13 ... 141 C2
SANDS END 136 A2
Sands End La
SW6 ..... 135 D4 265 D2
Sandstone TW9 ...... 132 C5
Sandstone La E16 .... 121 B6
Sandstone Pl N19 ..... 71 B6
Sandstone Rd SE12 .. 165 B2
Sandtoft Rd SE7 ..... 143 B6
Sandways 6 TW9 ..... 132 C4
Sandwell Cres 2
NW6 .... 69 C2
Sandwell Mans 3
NW6 .... 69 C2
Sandwich Ho
15 Rotherhithe
SE16 .... 118 C4
WC1 .... 233 A1
Sandwich St
WC1 .... 94 A4 233 A1
Sandwick Cl NW7 ..... 28 A3
Sandy Bury BR6 ..... 227 B5
Sandycombe Ctr
TW9 .... 132 C2
Sandycombe Rd
East Bedfont TW14 .. 150 A3
Richmond TW9 ...... 132 C3
Sandycoombe Rd
TW1 .... 153 C5
Sandycroft SE2 ...... 146 A6
Sandy Dr TW14 ...... 149 C3
Sandy Hill Ave SE18 . 122 D1
Sandy Hill La SE18 .. 122 D2
Sandyhill Rd IG1 ...... 78 D4
Sandy Hill Rd SE18 .. 122 D1
Sandy La
Belmont SM2 .... 217 A1
BR5 .... 190 D2

Sandy La *continued*
Eastbury HA6 .... 22 A6
Harrow HA3 .... 44 C3
Mitcham CR4 .... 181 A2
Richmond TW10 ..... 153 D2
Teddington KT8, TW11 .... 175 B3
Walton-on-T KT12 .... 194 C3
Sandy Lane N SM6 .. 219 D3
Sandy Lane S SM6 .. 219 C1
Sandy Lo N6 .... 49 C2
Sandymount Ave HA7 25 D5
Sandy Rd NW3 .... 69 D6
Sandy Ridge BR7 .... 188 C4
Sandy's Row E1 .... 243 B3
Sandy Way
Croydon CR0 .... 223 B5
Walton-on-T KT12 .... 193 D1
Sanford La 3 N16 .... 73 D6
Sanford St SE14, SE8 . 141 A6
Sanford Terr N16 .... 73 D5
Sanford Wlk SE14 .... 141 A6
4 Stoke Newington N16 .... 73 D6
Sangam Cl UB2 .... 107 A3
Sanger Ave KT9 .... 214 B4
Sangley Rd
Catford SE6 .... 164 A3
South Norwood SE25 . 205 C5
Sangora Rd 17 SW11 .... 136 B1
San Ho 29 E9 .... 74 D2
Sankey Ho 22 E2 .... 96 C5
Sansom Rd E11 .... 76 D6
Sansom St
Camberwell SE5 .... 139 B4
SE5 .... 139 B5
Sans Wlk EC1 .. 94 D3 241 C6
Santana SE18 .... 144 D5
Santley Ho SE1 .... 251 B1
Santley St SW4 .... 138 B1
Santos Rd SW18 .... 157 C6
Sapcote Trad Ctr NW10 .... 67 D2
Saperton Wlk SE11 . 260 D4
Saphora Cl BR6 .... 227 B3
Sapperton Ct EC1 ... 242 A6
Sapphire Cl
Dagenham RM8 .... 58 C1
Newham E6 .... 100 C1
Sapphire Ct 13 E1 .... 118 A6
Sapphire Rd
Rotherhithe SE8 .... 119 A2
Willesden NW10 .... 67 A1
Saracen Cl CR0 .... 205 B3
Saracen's Head Yd EC2 .... 243 B1
Saracen St E14 .... 97 C1
Sarah Bonnell Sch E15 .... 76 C2
Sarah Ct UB5 .... 85 B6
Sarah Ho
Roehampton SW15 .. 133 D1
8 Stepney E1 .... 96 B1
Sarah Swift Ho SE1 . 252 D2
Sarah Turnbull Ho 2 SE18 .... 122 B2
Sara Lane Ct 31 N1 .... 95 C5
Saratoga Rd E5 .... 74 C4
Sardeson Ho 13 SW27 .... 182 D5
Sardinia Ho WC2 .... 240 C1
Sardinia St WC2 .... 240 C2
Sargents Hill N2 .... 30 C2
Sarita Cl HA3 .... 24 B1
Sarjant Path SW19 .. 156 D2
Sark Cl TW5 .... 129 C5
Sark Ho
9 Canonbury N1 .... 73 A2
Enfield EN3 .... 6 D5
Sark Twr SE28 .... 123 A4
Sark Wlk E16 .... 99 B1
Sarnersfield Ho SE15 .... 140 B6
Sarnes Ct 4 N11 .... 31 B6
Sarnesfield Rd EN2 .... 5 B2
Sarratt Ho 6 W10 .... 90 C2
Sarre Rd NW2 .... 69 B3
Sarsden Bldgs W1 .. 238 B1
Sarsen Ave TW3 .... 129 C3
Sarsfeld Rd SW12, SW17 .... 158 D3
Sarsfield Rd UB6 .... 87 C5
Sartor Rd SE15 .... 140 D1
Sarum Hall Sch NW3 .. 70 C1
Sarum Ho W11 .... 244 D5
Sarwan Ho 1 E7 .... 77 C1
Sassoon 4 NW9 .... 27 D2
Sassoon Ho SE15 .... 140 C3
Satanita Cl E16 .... 99 D1
Satchell Mead NW9 .... 27 D2
Satchwell Rd 17 E2 .... 96 A4
Satin Ct NW9 .... 45 D5
Saturn Ho 4 E3 .... 97 C6
Saul Ct 4 SE15 .... 139 D6
Sauls Gn E11 .... 76 C5
Saunders Cl Ilford IG1 57 B1
14 Limehouse E14 .... 119 B6
Saunders Ho 11 SW2 .... 160 C3
Saunders Ness Rd E14 .... 120 B2
Saunders Rd
Hillingdon UB10 .... 82 B6
Plumstead Comm SE18 .... 123 D1
Saunders St SE11 .... 261 A4
Saunders Way SE28 .. 124 B6
Saunderton Rd HA0 .... 65 B3
Saunton Ave UB3 .... 127 D5
Saunton Ct UB1 .... 108 A6
Savage Gdns EC3 .... 253 B6
Newham E6 .... 100 B1
Savana N16 .... 73 C6
Savannah Cl 9 SE15 .... 139 D5
Savera Cl UB2 .... 106 C3
Savernake Ct HA7 .... 25 B4
Savernake Ho N4 .... 51 B2
Savernake Rd
Enfield N9 .... 18 A5
Maitland Pk NW3 .... 70 D4
Savery Dr KT6 .... 197 C2
Savile Cl
New Malden KT3 .... 199 C4
Thames Ditton KT7 .... 197 A1
Savile Gdns CR0 .... 221 D6
Savill Ct IG8 .... 36 D4
Saville Cres TW15 .... 171 B4
Saville Ho E16 .... 122 D5
Saville Rd
Bedford Pk W4 .... 111 B3
Dagenham RM6 .... 59 B2
Newham E16 .... 122 A5
Twickenham TW1 .... 152 D3
Saville Row Enfield EN3 . 6 D3
Hayes BR2 .... 208 D1
W1 .... 115 C6 249 A6
Savill Gdns SW20 .... 200 A6
Savill Ho 2 SW4 .... 159 D5
Savill Row IG8 .... 36 D4
Savin Lo 7 SM2 .... 218 A1
Savona Cl 16 SW19 .. 178 D3
Savona Ct SW20 .... 178 D2
Savona St SW8 .... 137 C5 269 A3
Savoy Ave UB3 .... 105 C1
Savoy Circus W3 .... 111 D6
Savoy Cl Edgware HA8 .. 26 C5
Newham E15 .... 98 C6
Savoy Ct
Earl's Ct SW5 .... 255 B4
Strand WC2 .... 250 B5
Savoy Hill WC2 .... 250 C5
Savoy Mews SW9 .... 138 A2
Savoy Par EN1 .... 5 C2
Savoy Pier WC2 .... 250 C5
Savoy Pl WC2 .... 116 B6 250 C5
Savoy Row WC2 .... 250 C6
Savoy St WC2 .... 116 B6 250 C5
Savoy Stps WC2 .... 250 C5
Savoy Way WC2 .... 250 C5
Sawbill Cl UB4 .... 84 D2
Sawkins Cl SW19 .... 157 A2
Sawley Rd W12 .... 112 A5
Sawmill Yd E3 .... 97 A6
Sawtry Cl SM5 .... 202 C2
Sawyer Cl N9 .... 18 A2
Sawyer Ho 15 SE21 .. 183 C6
Sawyer's Hill TW10 .. 154 B4
Sawyers Lawn W13 .... 87 A1
Sawyer St SE1 .... 117 A4 252 A2
Saxby Rd SW2 .... 160 A4
Saxham Rd IG11 .... 101 D5
Saxlingham Rd E4 .... 20 B1
Saxon Ave TW13 .... 151 B2
Saxon Bsns Ctr SW19 .... 180 A2
Saxonbury Ave TW16 .... 172 B1
Saxonbury Cl CR4 .... 202 B6
Saxonbury Ct
16 Kentish Town N7 .... 71 D3
2 Lower Holloway N7 .. 72 A3
Saxonbury Gdns KT6 .... 197 C1
Saxon Cl
Hillingdon UB8 .... 82 A2
Surbiton KT6 .... 197 D3
Walthamstow E17 .... 53 C2
Saxoncroft Ho SW16 .... 159 D1
Saxon Ct
Colney Hatch N12 .... 30 C5
4 Edgware HA8 .... 26 D5
Saxon Dr W3 .... 88 D2
Saxonfield Cl SW2 .... 160 B4
Saxon Gdns UB1 .... 107 A6
Saxon Hall W2 .... 245 C5
Saxon Ho
4 Clapham SW4 .... 137 D1
Feltham TW13 .... 151 B2
Saxon Prim Sch TW17 .... 192 C4
Saxon Rd
Ashford TW15 .... 171 B4
Bow E3 .... 97 B5
Bromley BR1 .... 186 D3
Ilford IG1 .... 78 D3
Kingston u T KT2 .... 176 A2
Newham E6 .... 100 B3
Southall UB1 .... 107 A6
South Norwood SE25 .. 205 B4
Tottenham N22 .... 32 D2
Wembley HA9 .... 67 A5
Saxon Terr SE6 .... 163 B2
Saxon Way N14 .... 15 D5
Saxon Wlk DA14 .... 190 C4
Saxony Par UB3 .... 83 A2
Saxton Cl SE13 .... 142 B2
Saxville Rd BR5 .... 190 B1
Sayer Ho SE4 .... 141 A1
Sayers Ho 4 N2 .... 30 B1
Sayer's Wlk TW10 .... 154 B4
Sayesbury La N18 .... 34 A5
Sayes Court St SE8 .. 141 B6
Sayes Ct SE8 .... 141 B6
Sayline Ct CR0 .... 221 B5
Scadbury Gdns BR5 .. 190 A1
Scadbury Park★ BR7 .... 189 D4
Scads Hill Cl BR6 .... 211 D3
Scafell NW1 .... 232 A2
Scala St W1 .... 239 B4
Scales Rd N17 .... 52 A6
Scampston Mews 5 W10 .... 90 D1
Scandrett St 38 E1 .... 118 B5
Scarba Wlk N1 .... 73 B2
Scarborough Rd
East Bedfont TW6 .... 149 A5
Finsbury Pk N4 .... 50 C1
Leytonstone E11 .... 54 B1
Ponders End N9 .... 18 C4
Scarborough St E1 .. 243 D1
Scarbrook Rd CR0 .... 221 A5
Scardale Ho 12 E5 .... 74 B6
Scarle Rd HA0 .... 65 D2
Scarlet Rd SE6 .... 164 C1
Scarlette Manor Wlk 10 SE24 .... 160 C4
Scarsbrook Ho 2 SW2 .... 160 C5
Scarsbrook Rd SE3 .. 143 D2
Scarsdale Pl W8 .... 255 C6
Scarsdale Rd HA2 .... 64 A5
Scarsdale Villas W8 .... 113 C3 255 B5
Scarth Rd SW13 .... 133 D2
Scawen Cl SM5 .... 219 A4
Scawen Rd SE8 .... 119 A1
Scawfell St E2 .... 95 D5
Scaynes Link N12 .... 29 C6
Sceptre Ho 10 E1 .... 96 C3
Sceptre Rd E2 .... 96 C4
Schiller International Univ SE1 ... 116 C5 251 A3
Schofield Wlk SE3 .... 143 A5
Sch of Pharmacy WC1 .... 94 A3 240 B6
Sch of the Islamic Republic of Iran The 6 NW6 .... 91 C5
Scholars Cl EN5 .... 1 A1
Scholars Ct 5 N19 .... 49 D1
Scholars Ho 6 E4 .... 20 B3
Scholars Rd
Chingford E4 .... 20 B3
Streatham SW12 .... 159 C3
Scholefield Rd N19 .... 71 D6
Scholey Ho SW11 .... 136 C2
Schomberg Ho SW1 259 D4
Schonfeld Sq N16 .... 51 B1
School App 21 E2 .... 95 C4
Schoolbank Rd SE10 .... 120 D2
School Bell Cloisters 17 E3 .... 97 A5
Schoolbell Mews 18 E3 .... 97 A5
School Cotts
Bromley BR1 .... 187 A3
Sidcup DA14 .... 190 C5
School Flats SW8 .... 270 A1
School Ho SE1 .... 263 A4
Schoolhouse La E1 . 118 D6
School House La TW11 .... 175 C3
Schoolhouse Yd 9 SE18 .... 122 D1
School La
Lower Halliford TW17 .... 192 D2
Pinner HA5 .... 41 A5
Surbiton KT6 .... 198 B1
Teddington KT1 .... 175 C2
School Pas
3 Kingston u T KT1 .. 176 B1
Southall UB1 .... 107 B6
School Rd
Ashford TW15 .... 170 D4
Becontree NW10 .... 89 B3
BR7 .... 189 A3
Dagenham RM10 .... 103 D6
East Molesey KT8 .... 196 B5
Hampton TW12 .... 174 A4
Hounslow TW3 .... 130 A2
Ilford E12 .... 78 B4
Littleton TW15 .... 170 D3
Teddington KT1 .... 175 C2
School Road Ave TW12 .... 174 A4
School Sq SE10 .... 120 D3
Schoolway N12 .... 30 B4
School Way RM8 .... 80 C5
School Wlk TW16 .... 193 D6
Schooner Cl
Barking IG11 .... 102 B4
Cubitt Town E14 .... 120 B3
1 Rotherhithe SE16 . 118 D4
Schubert Rd
Elstree WD6 .... 9 D5
Putney SW15 .... 157 B6
Science Mus★ SW7 .... 114 B3 256 C5
Scilly Isles KT10 .... 212 C6
Sclater St E1 .... 243 D6
Scoles Cres SW2 .... 160 C3
Scope Way KT1 .... 198 A5
Scoresby St SE1 .... 251 C3
Scoresdale SE19 .... 183 C2
Scorton Ave UB6 .... 87 A5
Scorton Ho 2 N1 .... 95 C5
Scotch Comm W13 .... 87 B2
Scotch Ho SW1 .... 114 D4 247 C1
Scoter Cl IG8 .... 37 B3
Scoter Ct 23 SE8 .... 141 B6
Scot Gr HA5 .... 22 D3
Scotia Bldg 10 E1 .... 118 D6
Scotia Ct 3 SE16 .... 118 C3
Scotia Rd 24 SW2 .... 160 C4
Scotland Gn N17 .... 33 D1
Scotland Green Rd EN3 .... 18 D6
Scotland Green Rd N EN3 .... 7 A1
Scotland Pl SW1 .... 250 A3
Scotland Rd IG9 .... 21 C3
Scotney Cl BR6 .... 226 C4
Scotney Ho E9 .... 74 C2
Scots Cl TW19 .... 148 A3
Scotsdale Cl
Belmont SM3 .... 217 A1
BR5 .... 211 C5
Scotsdale Rd SE12 .... 165 B6
Scotson Ho SE11 .... 261 A3
Scotswood St EC1 .... 94 C3 241 B6
Scotswood Wlk N17 .. 34 A3
Scott Ave SW15, SW18 .... 157 A5
Scott Cl
Thornton Heath SW16 .... 182 B2
West Drayton UB7 .... 104 B2
West Ewell KT19 .... 215 A3
Scott Ct Acton W4 .... 111 B4
4 Clapham SW11 .... 137 B3
17 Stoke Newington N16 .... 73 C5
Scott Ellis Gdns NW8 .... 92 B4 229 C1
Scottes La RM8 .... 58 D1
Scott Farm Cl KT7 .... 197 B1
Scott Gdns TW5 .... 128 D5
Scott Ho
2 Barnsbury N7 .... 72 B2
3 Edmonton N18 .... 34 A5
4 Erith DA17 .... 125 B1
Islington N1 .... 235 C6
Lisson Gr NW8 .... 237 A5
17 Millwall E14 .... 119 C4
6 Newham E13 .... 99 A5
Richmond TW10 .... 153 C2
3 Stonebridge NW10 .. 67 B1
Scott Lidgett Cres SE16 .... 118 A4
Scott Rd HA8 .... 26 D1
Scott's Ave
Ashford TW16 .... 171 C3
Beckenham BR2 .... 186 B1
Scotts Ct 6 W12 .... 112 B4
Scotts Dr TW12 .... 173 D3
Scotts Farm Rd KT19 .... 215 A2
Scotts Ho DA16 .... 146 C4
Scott's La BR2, BR3 ... 186 B1
Scotts Park Prim Sch BR1 .... 187 C2
Scotts Rd BR1 .... 187 A3
Southall UB2 .... 106 D3
Scott's Rd
Leytonstone E10 .... 54 A1
Shepherd's Bush W12 . 112 B4
Scott's Sufferance Wharf SE1 .... 253 D1
Scott St E1 .... 96 B3
Scott's Way TW16 .... 171 C3
Scott's Yd EC4 .... 252 C6
Scott Trimmer Way TW3 .... 129 A3
Scottwell Dr NW9 .... 45 D4
Scott Wilkie Prim Sch E16 .... 99 C1
Scoulding Ho 12 E14 .... 119 C3
Scoulding Rd E16 .... 99 A1
Scouler St E14 .... 120 B6
Scout App NW10 .... 67 C4
Scout La SW4 .... 137 C2
Scout Way NW7 .... 27 B6
Scovell Cres SE1 .... 252 A1
Scovell Rd SE1 .... 252 A1
Scratchwood Nature Trail★ NW7 .... 11 B4
Scrattons Terr IG11 ... 103 A5
Scriven Ct 2 E8 .... 95 D6
Scriven St E8 .... 95 D6
Scrooby St SE6 .... 163 D5
Scrope Bldg EC1 .... 241 A4
Scrubs La NW10, W10, W12 .... 90 B3
Scrutton Cl SW12 ... 159 D4
Scrutton St EC2 .... 95 C3 243 A5
Scudamore La NW9 ... 45 A5
Scutari Rd SE22 .... 162 C6
Scylla Cres TW6&TW14 .... 148 D4
Scylla Rd
East Bedfont TW14, TW6 .... 148 D5
Nunhead SE15 .... 140 B2
Seabright St 27 E2 .... 96 B4
Seabrook Dr BR4 .... 224 C6
Seabrook Gdns RM7 .. 59 C2
Seabrook Rd RM8 .... 80 D5
Seacole Cl W3 .... 89 B2
Seacole Ct N15 .... 51 D4
Seacole Lo N21 .... 16 B6
Seacon Twr 8 E14 ... 119 C4
Seacourt Rd SE2 .... 124 D4

Seacroft Gdns WD19 . . 22 D6
Seafield Rd N11 . . . . . . 31 D6
Seaford Cl HA4 . . . . 61 B6
Seaford Ho 13 SE16 . . 118 C4
Seaford Rd
Ealing W13 . . . . 109 B5
Enfield EN1 . . . . 5 C1
Tottenham N15 . . . . 51 C4
Walthamstow E17 . . . . . 53 D6
Seaford St WC1 . . . . . . 233 B1
Seaforth Ave KT3 . . . . 200 B5
Seaforth Cres N5 . . . . . 73 A3
Seaforth Gdns
Southgate N21 . . . . 16 C3
Woodford IG8 . . . . 37 C5
Worcester Pk KT19 . . 215 D3
Seaforth Lo 2
SW13 . . . . 133 D3
Seaforth Pl SW1 . . . . 259 B6
Seagrave Lo SW6 . . . 265 B6
Seagrave Rd
SW6 . . . . . 135 C6 265 B6
Seagrove Cl E1 . . . . 96 D2
Seagry Rd E11 . . . . 55 B2
Seagull Cl IG11 . . . . . . 102 A4
Seagull La E16 . . . . 121 A6
Sealand Rd TW6 . . . . . 148 C5
Sealand Wlk UB5 . . . . . 85 A4
Seal Ho SE1 . . . . 262 D6
Sea Life London Aquarium★ SE1 . . . 250 C1
Seal St E8 . . . . 73 D4
Searle Ct 2 CR4 . . . . . 180 C2
Searle Pl N4 . . . . 50 B1
Searles Cl
SW11 . . . . . 136 C5 267 B3
Searles Dr E6 . . . . 100 D2
Searles Rd SE1 . . . . . 262 D4
Searson Ho SE17 . . . 261 D3
Sears Ret Pk UB6 . . . . . 86 C6
Sears St SE5 . . . . 139 B5
Seasalter Ho 10
SW9 . . . . 138 C4
Seasprite Cl 10 UB5 . . . 84 D4
Seath Ho 4 SE26 . . . . 184 B5
Seaton Ave IG3 . . . . 79 D3
Seaton Cl
Isleworth TW2 . . . . 152 B5
6 Newham E13 . . . . . . 99 A3
Roehampton SW15 . . . . 156 B4
Seaton Dr TW15 . . . . . 148 A2
Seaton Gdns HA4 . . . . . 62 A6
Seaton Point E5 . . . . 74 A4
Seaton Rd
Bexley DA16 . . . . 146 C5
Hayes UB3 . . . . 105 B3
Mitcham CR4 . . . . 180 C1
Twickenham TW2 . . . . 152 A5
Wembley HA0 . . . . 88 A5
Seaton Sq NW7 . . . . 28 D3
Seaton St N18 . . . . 34 A5
Seavington Ho 3
SE5 . . . . 139 C2
Sebastian Ct 11 IG11 . . 79 D1
Sebastian Ho 22 N1 . . . . 95 C5
Sebastian St
EC1 . . . . 94 D4 234 D1
Sebastopol Rd N9 . . . . 34 A6
Sebbon St N1 . . . . 72 D1
Sebergham Gr NW7 . . . 28 A3
Sebert Rd E7 . . . . 77 B4
Sebright Ho 22 E2 . . . . 96 A5
Sebright Pas 29 E2 . . . . 96 A5
Sebright Rd EN5 . . . . 1 A2
Sebright Sch 39 E2 . . . 96 A5
Secker Cres HA3 . . . . . . 24 A2
Secker Ho SW9 . . . . . . 138 D3
Secker St SE1 . . . . . . 251 A3
Second Ave
Chadwell Heath RM6 . . . 58 C4
Dagenham RM10 . . . . 103 D5
East Acton W3 . . . . . . 111 D5
Edmonton N18 . . . . 34 C6
Enfield EN1 . . . . 17 D6
Hayes UB3 . . . . 105 D5
Hendon NW4 . . . . 46 D5
Kensal Town W10 . . . . . 91 A3
Manor Pk E12 . . . . 78 A3
Mortlake SW14 . . . . . 133 C2
Newham E13 . . . . 99 A4
Walthamstow E17 . . . . . 53 C4
Walton-on-T KT12 . . . . 194 B3
Wembley HA9 . . . . 65 D6
Second Cl KT8 . . . . 196 A5
Second Cross Rd
TW2 . . . . 152 C2
Second Way HA9 . . . . . 66 D4
Secrett Ho 6 TW10 . . 153 C1
Sedan Way
SE17 . . . . 117 C1 263 A2
Sedcombe Cl DA14 . . 190 C6
Sedcote Rd EN3 . . . . . . 18 D6
Sedding St SW1 . . . . 258 A4
Seddon Ho EC2 . . . . . 242 A4
Seddon Rd SM4 . . . . . . 202 B4
Seddon St
WC1 . . . . 94 B4 233 D1
Sedgebrook Rd SE3 . 143 D2
Sedgecombe Ave
HA3 . . . . 43 C4
Sedgefield Ct UB5 . . . . 63 D3
Sedgeford Rd W12 . . 111 D5
Sedgehill Rd SE6 . . . 185 D5
Sedgehill Sch SE6 . . . 185 D5
Sedgemere Ave N2 . . . 48 A6
Sedgemere Rd SE2 . . . 124 C3
Sedgemoor Dr RM10 . . 81 C4
Sedge Rd N17 . . . . 34 C3
Sedgeway SE6 . . . . . . 164 D3
Sedgewick Ho
SW19 . . . . 156 D2
Sedgewood Cl BR2 . . 208 D2
Sedgley Ho N4 . . . . 72 B6
Sedgmoor Pl SE5 . . . . 139 C5
Sedgwick Ave UB10 . . . 60 D1
Sedgwick Rd E10 . . . . . 76 A6
Sedgwick St E9 . . . . 74 D3
Sedleigh Rd SW18 . . . 157 B5
Sedlescombe Rd
SW6 . . . . . 135 C6 265 A6
Sedley Cl EN1 . . . . 6 B5
Sedley Ct SE26 . . . . . . 162 B2
Sedley Ho SE11 . . . . . 260 D2
Sedley Pl W1 . . . . 238 C1
Sedum Cl NW9 . . . . 44 D4
Seeley Dr SE21 . . . . . . 183 C6
Seelig Ave NW9 . . . . 46 A2
Seely Rd SW17 . . . . . . 181 A4
Seething La
EC3 . . . . 117 C6 253 B6
SEETHING WELLS . . 197 D3
Seething Wells Halls of Residence KT6 . . . . 197 C3
Seething Wells La
KT6 . . . . 197 C3
Sefton Ave
Edgware NW7 . . . . 27 B5
Harrow HA3 . . . . 24 B2
Sefton Cl BR5 . . . . 211 D5
Sefton Ct TW5 . . . . . . 129 D4
Sefton Lo 2 TW1 . . . . 153 C5
Sefton Rd
Croydon CR0 . . . . 206 A1
Orpington BR5 . . . . . . 211 D5
Sefton St SW15 . . . . . . 134 C2
Segal Cl SE23 . . . . 163 A4
Sekforde St
EC1 . . . . 94 D3 241 C6
Sekhon Terr TW13 . . . . 151 C1
Selan Gdns UB4 . . . . . . 84 B2
Selbie Ave NW10 . . . . . . 67 D3
Selborne 2 SW11 . . . . 137 A2
Selborne Ave DA5 . . . 169 A3
Little Ilford E12 . . . . . . 78 C4
Walthamstow E17 . . . . . 53 B5
Selborne Gdns
Hendon NW4 . . . . 46 A5
Wembley UB6 . . . . 87 A5
Selborne Ho SE1 . . . . 252 C1
Selborne Prim Sch
UB6 . . . . 86 D5
Selborne Rd
1 Camberwell SE5 . . . 139 B3
Ilford IG1 . . . . 78 C6
Kingston u T KT3 . . . . 177 C1
Palmers Green N14 . . . . 16 A1
Sidcup DA14 . . . . 190 B6
South Croydon CR0 . . . 221 D5
Walthamstow E17 . . . . . 53 C4
Wood Green N22 . . . . . . 32 B2
Selborne Wlk E17 . . . . . 53 B5
Selborne Wlk Sh Ctr
E17 . . . . 53 B5
Selbourne Ave KT6 . . 214 C5
Selbridge Ct SW19 . . . 179 C4
Selby Chase HA4 . . . . . 62 B6
Selby Cl BR7 . . . . 188 C4
Chessington KT9 . . . . 214 A1
14 Newham E6 . . . . . 100 A2
Selby Ct TW2 . . . . 152 B2
Selby Gdns UB1 . . . . . . 85 C3
Selby Gn SM5 . . . . 202 C2
Selby Ho 10 SW4 . . . . 159 C5
Selby Rd
Ashford TW15 . . . . . . 171 A4
Carshalton SM5 . . . . . 202 C2
Ealing W5 . . . . 87 C3
Leyton E11 . . . . 76 C5
Newham E13 . . . . 99 B2
Penge SE20 . . . . 184 A1
Tottenham N17 . . . . 33 C4
Selby Sq 1 W10 . . . . . . 91 A4
Selby St E1 . . . . 96 A3
Selden Ho 2 SE15 . . . 140 C3
Selden Rd SE15 . . . . . 140 C3
Selden Wlk N7 . . . . 72 B6
Seldon Ho
Nine Elms SW8 . . . . . 269 A3
Pimlico SW1 . . . . 259 A1
Selena Ct N20 . . . . 14 D1
SELHURST 205 B4
Selhurst Cl SW19 . . . 156 D3
Selhurst New Ct
SE25 . . . . 205 C3
Selhurst New Rd
SE25 . . . . 205 C3
Selhurst Park (Crystal Palace FC) SE25 . . . 205 C5
Selhurst Pl SE25 . . . . 205 C3
Selhurst Rd
Edmonton N9 . . . . 17 C1
South Norwood SE25 . 205 C5
Selhurst Sta SE25 . . . 205 C4
Selina Ho NW8 . . . . . 236 D6
Selinas La RM8 . . . . 59 B2
Selkirk Ct N17 . . . . 33 C1
Selkirk Ho N1 . . . . . . 233 C6
4 Stoke Newington
N16 . . . . 73 C5
Selkirk Rd
Twickenham TW2 . . . . 152 A3
Upper Tooting SW17 . 180 C6
Sellers Hall Cl N3 . . . . . 29 C3
Sellincourt Prim Sch
SW17 . . . . 180 C4
Sellincourt Rd
SW17 . . . . 180 C4
Sellindge Cl BR3 . . . . 185 B3
Sellons Ave NW10 . . . . . 89 D6
Sellsby Ct N11 . . . . 31 B5
Sellwood Dr EN5 . . . . . . 12 D6
Selma Ho 7 W12 . . . . . 90 B1
Selman Ho 3 E9 . . . . . 75 A2
SELSDON 223 A1
Selsdon Ave CR2 . . . . 221 B2
Selsdon Cl KT6 . . . . . 198 A4
Selsdon High Sch
CR2 . . . . 222 D1
Selsdon Park Rd CR0, CR2 . . . . 223 B1
Selsdon Rd
Newham E13 . . . . 99 C5
South Croydon CR2 . . . 221 B2
Wanstead E11 . . . . 55 A2
West Norwood SE27 . 182 D6
Willesden NW2 . . . . 67 D6
Selsdon Road Ind Est
CR2 . . . . 221 B2
Selsdon Way E14 . . . 119 D3
Selsea Pl N16 . . . . 73 C3
Selsey Cres DA16 . . . 146 D4
Selsey St E14 . . . . 97 C2
Selvage La NW7 . . . . . . 27 B6
Selway Cl HA5 . . . . 40 B6
Selway Ho SW8 . . . . . 270 B2
Selwood Ho
Chislehurst BR7 . . . . 189 A4
1 Stoke Newington
N4 . . . . 51 B2
Selwood Pl
SW7 . . . . 114 B1 256 C2
Selwood Rd
Cheam SM3 . . . . 201 B1
Chessington KT9 . . . . 213 D4
Croydon CR0 . . . . 206 B1
Selwood Terr SW7 . . 256 C2
Selworthy Cl E11 . . . . . 55 A4
Selworthy Ho SW11 . 266 D2
Selworthy Rd SE6 . . . . 163 B1
Selwyn Ave
Chingford E4 . . . . 36 A4
Ilford IG3 . . . . 57 D3
Richmond TW9 . . . . . . 132 B2
Selwyn Cl TW4 . . . . . . 129 A1
Selwyn Cres DA16 . . . 146 B1
Selwyn Ct
Edgware HA8 . . . . 26 D3
Lewisham SE3 . . . . . . 142 D2
8 Richmond TW10 . . . 154 B6
Walthamstow E17 . . . . . 53 C4
Wembley HA9 . . . . 67 A5
Selwyn Ho 3 SW15 . 156 D5
Selwyn Prim Sch
Chingford E4 . . . . 36 A4
6 Newham E13 . . . . . . 99 A6
Selwyn Rd Bow E3 . . . . 97 B5
Newham E13 . . . . 99 B6
New Malden KT3 . . . . 199 B4
Willesden NW10 . . . . . . 67 C1
Semley Gate E9 . . . . . . 75 B2
Semley Ho SW1 . . . . . 258 C3
Semley Pl
SW1 . . . . 115 B2 258 C3
Thornton Heath
SW16 . . . . 182 B1
Semley Rd SW16 . . . . 182 A1
Senate St SE15 . . . . . 140 C3
Senators Lo 31 E3 . . . . 97 A5
Senator Wlk 2
SE28 . . . . 123 B3
Sencler Ho SE2 . . . . . 146 D6
Sendall Ct 12 SW11 . . 136 B2
Seneca Rd CR7 . . . . . . 205 A5
Senga Rd SM6 . . . . . . 203 A1
Senhouse Rd SM3 . . . 216 D5
Senior St W2 . . . . 91 D2
Senlac Rd SE12 . . . . . 165 B3
Sennen Rd EN1 . . . . 17 D4
Sennen Wlk SE9 . . . . . 166 A1
Senrab St E1 . . . . 96 D1
Sentinel Cl UB5 . . . . . . 85 A3
Sentinel Ho NW4 . . . . . 46 C5
Sentinel Sq NW4 . . . . . 46 C5
September Ct UB1 . . 107 D5
September Way HA7 . . 25 B4
Sequoia Cl WD23 . . . . . . 8 B3
Sequoia Gdns BR6 . . 211 D2
Sequoia Pk HA5 . . . . . . 23 D4
Seraph Ct EC1 95 A4 235 A2
Serbin Cl E10 . . . . 54 A2
Serenaders Rd 20
SW9 . . . . 138 C3
Sergeant Ind Est The
SW18 . . . . 157 D5
Serica Ct 14 SE10 . . . 142 A5
Serjeants' Inn EC4 . . 241 B1
Serlby Ct W14 . . . . . . 254 C6
Serle St WC2 . . 94 B1 240 D2
Sermon La EC4 . . . . 242 A1
Serpentine Ct 10
SE16 . . . . 118 D4
Serpentine Gallery★
W2 . . . . 114 B4 246 D2
Serpentine Rd
W2 . . . . 114 D5 247 C3
Serpentine The★
W2 . . . . 114 C5 247 B3
Service Route No 1
E15 . . . . 76 B1
Service Route No 2 1
E15 . . . . 76 B1
Service Route No 3 2
E15 . . . . 76 B1
Serviden Dr BR1 . . . . 187 D2
Servite Ho
Beckenham BR3 . . . . . 185 B2
Bromley BR1 . . . . 188 B1
East Barnet N14 . . . . . . 15 B6
Lewisham SE13 . . . . . 141 D4
Penge SE26 . . . . 184 C4
Worcester Pk KT4 . . . 215 D6
Servite RC Prim Sch
SW10 . . . . . 136 A6 266 A6
Servius Ct 2 TW8 . . . 131 D5
Sessions Terr CR4 . . . 180 D2
Setchell Rd
SE1 . . . . 117 D2 263 C4
Setchell Way SE1 . . . 263 C4
Seth St 25 SE16 . . . . . 118 C4
Seton Ct 3 NW9 . . . . . . 46 A5
Seton Gdns RM9 . . . . . . 80 C1
Settle Point 11 E13 . . . 99 A5
Settlers Ct 11 E14 . . . 120 B6
Settles St E1 . . . . 96 A1
Settrington Rd SW6 . 135 D3
Seven Acres
Carshalton SM5 . . . . . 218 C6
Northwood HA6 . . . . 22 A4
Seven Dials
WC2 . . . . 94 A1 240 A1
Seven Islands L Ctr
SE16 . . . . 118 C3
SEVEN KINGS 57 D2
Seven Kings High Sch
IG2 . . . . 57 B2
Seven Kings Rd IG3 . . . 79 D6
Seven Kings Sta IG3 . . 57 C1
Seven Kings Way
KT2 . . . . 176 A2
Seven Mills Prim Sch 27
E14 . . . . 119 C4
Sevenoaks Cl DA7 . . 147 D1
Sevenoaks Rd BR6 . . 227 D4
Catford SE4 . . . . 163 B5
Sevenoaks Way BR5 . 190 C1
Seven Seas Rd TW6 . . 149 A5
Seven Sisters N15 . . . . 51 D4
Seven Sisters Prim Sch
N15 . . . . 51 B4
Seven Sisters Rd
Finsbury Pk N4 . . . . 72 D6
Stoke Newington N4, N7, N15 . . . . 51 A2
Seven Sisters Sta
N15 . . . . 51 C4
Seven Stars Cnr
W12 . . . . 112 A3
Seven Stars Yd E1 . . 243 D4
Seventh Ave
Hayes UB3 . . . . 106 A5
Ilford E12 . . . . 78 B4
Seven Ways Par IG2 . . 56 C4
Severnake Cl E14 . . . . 119 C2
Severn Ave 2 W10 . . . . 91 A4
Severn Ct 11 KT2 . . . 175 D2
Severn Dr Enfield EN1 . . . 6 A5
Hinchley Wood KT10 . 213 A6
Severn Way NW10 . . . . 67 D3
Severus Rd SW11 . . . . 136 C1
Seville Ho 10 E1 . . . . . 118 A5
Seville Mews N1 . . . . . 73 C1
Seville St SW1 . . . . . . 247 D1
Sevington Rd NW4 . . . . 46 B3
Sevington St W9 . . . . . . 91 D3
Seward Rd
Penge BR3 . . . . 184 D1
West Ealing W7 . . . . . 109 A4
Seward St EC1 95 A4 235 A1
SEWARDSTONEBURY
. . . . 20 C6
Sewardstone Gdns
E4 . . . . 19 D6
Sewardstone Rd
Chingford E4 . . . . 19 D6
South Hackney E2 . . . . . 96 C5
Sewdley St E5 . . . . 74 D5
Sewell Ho 7 N16 . . . . . 73 C3
Sewell Rd SE2 . . . . . . 124 B4
Sewell St E13 . . . . 99 A4
Sextant Ave E14 . . . . . 120 B2
Sexton Ct 7 E14 . . . . . 120 B6
Sexton's Ho 5 SE13 . 142 A6
Seychelle Ct BR3 . . . 185 D3
Seymour Ave
Tottenham N17 . . . . 34 A1
West Barnes SM4 . . . 200 D2
Seymour Cl
East Molesey KT8 . . . 196 A4
Pinner HA5 . . . . 23 B2
Seymour Ct
Chingford E4 . . . . 20 D2
Dollis Hill NW2 . . . . 68 B6
Muswell Hill N10 . . . . . . 31 A1
Putney SW15 . . . . 134 B1
Southgate N21 . . . . 16 B5
Upper Clapton N16 . . . . 52 A1
Seymour Dr BR2 . . . . . 210 B1
Seymour Gdns
Brockley SE4 . . . . 141 A2
Feltham TW13 . . . . . . 172 C6
Kingston u T KT5 . . . . 198 B4
Redbridge IG1 . . . . 56 B1
Ruislip HA4 . . . . 40 D1
Twickenham TW1 . . . . 153 B4
Seymour Ho
Bloomsbury WC1 . . . . 240 A6
1 Clapham SW8 . . . . 137 C3
Ruislip HA4 . . . . 40 A5
Somers Town NW1 . . . 232 D1
Seymour Lo 14 KT1 . 175 D2
Seymour Mews W1 . . 238 A2
Seymour Pl
Croydon SE25 . . . . . . 206 B5
Paddington
W1 . . . . 92 D1 237 C2

Seymour Rd
Acton W4 . . . . 111 A2
Carshalton CR4 . . . . . 203 A2
Chingford E4 . . . . 19 D3
East Molesey KT8 . . . 196 A4
Edmonton N9 . . . . 18 B2
Finchley N3 . . . . 29 D3
Hampton TW12 . . . . . 174 A5
Harringay N8 . . . . 50 D4
Newham E6 . . . . 99 D6
Teddington KT1 . . . . . 175 D2
Wallington SM5 . . . . . 219 A3
Walthamstow E10 . . . . . 53 B1
Wandsworth SW18 . . . 157 B5
Wimbledon SW19 . . . 156 D1
Seymour St
Paddington
W1 . . . . 92 D1 237 D1
Woolwich SE18 . . . . . . 123 A3
Seymour Terr SE20 . . 184 B2
Seymour Villas SE20 . 184 A2
Seymour Way TW16 . . 171 C3
Seymour Wlk
SW10 . . . . . . 136 A6 266 A6
Seyssel St E14 . . . . . . 120 A2
Shaa Rd W3 . . . . 111 B6
Shabana Ct 3 W12 . . 112 B5
Shacklegate La
TW11 . . . . 174 C6
Shackleton Cl SE23 . . 162 B2
Shackleton Ct
3 Dulwich SE21 . . . . . 161 B2
2 Isle of Dogs E14 . . 119 C1
4 Shepherd's Bush
W12 . . . . 112 B4
7 Stanwell TW19 . . . . 148 A5
Shackleton Ho
5 Stonebridge
NW10 . . . . 67 B1
5 Wapping E1 . . . . . . 118 C5
Shackleton Lo
SW16 . . . . 181 D5
Shackleton Rd UB1 . . 107 B6
SHACKLEWELL 73 D4
Shacklewell Ho 3
E8 . . . . 73 D4
Shacklewell La E8 . . . . 73 D3
Shacklewell Prim Sch 5
E8 . . . . 73 D4
Shacklewell Rd N16 . . 73 D4
Shacklewell Row E8 . . 73 D4
Shacklewell St 30 E2 . . 95 D4
Shadbolt Ave E4 . . . . . . 35 A5
Shadbolt Cl KT4 . . . . 215 D6
Shad Thames
SE1 . . . . 117 D4 253 D2
SHADWELL 118 C6
Shadwell Ct UB5 . . . . . . 85 B5
Shadwell Dr UB5 . . . . . 85 B4
Shadwell Gdns E1 . . . 118 C6
Shadwell Pierhead
E1 . . . . 118 C6
Shadwell Pl 1 E1 . . . 118 C6
Shadwell Sta E1 . . . . . 118 B6
Shady Bush Cl WD23 . . . 8 A4
Shaef Way TW11 . . . . . 175 A3
Shaftesbury Ave
Enfield EN3 . . . . 6 D3
Feltham TW14 . . . . . . 150 A5
Kenton HA3 . . . . 44 A3
New Barnet EN5 . . . . 2 A1
Southall UB2 . . . . 107 C3
W1 . . . . 115 D6 249 D6
West Harrow HA1,
HA2 . . . . 42 A1
Shaftesbury Circ HA2 . 42 A1
Shaftesbury Ct
Borough The SE1 . . . . 262 C6
1 Herne Hill SE5 . . . . . 139 B1
Ilford RM6 . . . . 58 C2
Newham E6 . . . . 100 C1
Shoreditch N1 . . . . 235 C3
Streatham SW16 . . . . 159 D1
3 Thamesmead
SE28 . . . . 124 C5
Shaftesbury Ctr
NW10 . . . . 90 D3
Shaftesbury Gdns
NW10 . . . . 89 C3
Shaftesbury High Sch
HA3 . . . . 23 D2
Shaftesbury Ho
11 Canning Town
E16 . . . . 98 D1
Croydon SE25 . . . . 206 A3
Shaftesbury Ho *continued*
13 Stoke Newington
N16 . . . . 73 C5
Upper Tooting SW17 . . 180 B6
W2 . . . . 245 D6
Shaftesbury Lo 9
E14 . . . . 97 D1
Shaftesbury Mews
2 Clapham Pk
SW4 . . . . 159 C6
W8 . . . . 255 B5
Shaftesbury Park Chambers 1
SW11 . . . . 137 A2
Shaftesbury Point
E13 . . . . 99 B5
Shaftesbury Prim Sch
E7 . . . . 77 C1
Shaftesbury Rd
Beckenham BR3 . . . . . 185 B1
Carshalton SM5 . . . . . 202 C2
Chingford E4 . . . . 20 B3
Edmonton N18 . . . . 33 D4
Finsbury Pk N4, N19 . . . . 50 A1
Leyton E10 . . . . 53 C1
Richmond TW9 . . . . . . 132 A2
Upton E7 . . . . 77 C1
Walthamstow E17 . . . . . 53 D3
Shaftesbury St N1 . . 235 C3
Shaftesburys The
IG11 . . . . 101 A5
Shaftesbury Way
TW2 . . . . 152 B1
Shaftesbury Waye
UB4 . . . . 84 C1
Shafteswood Ct
SW17 . . . . 158 D1
Shafto Mews SW1 . . 257 D5
Shafton Rd E9 . . . . 96 D6
Shaftsbury Park Prim
Sch 16 SW11 . . . . . . 137 A3
Shafts Ct EC3 . . . . 243 A1
Shahjalal Ho 18 E2 . . . . 96 A5
Shakespeare Ave
7 Becontree NW10 . . . 89 B6
Feltham TW14 . . . . 150 A5
Friern Barnet N11 . . . . . 31 C5
Hayes UB4 . . . . 84 B2
Shakespeare Cl HA3 . . 44 C2
Shakespeare Cres
E12 . . . . 78 B2
Shakespeare Ct EN5 . . . 1 D2
Shakespeare Dr HA3 . . 44 B3
Shakespeare Gdns
N2 . . . . 48 D5
Shakespeare Ho
1 Erith DA17 . . . . 125 B1
3 Hackney E9 . . . . 74 C1
Osidge N14 . . . . 15 D2
Shakespeare Rd
Acton W3 . . . . 111 A5
Brixton SE24 . . . . 138 D1
DA7 . . . . 147 A4
Ealing W7 . . . . 108 D6
Finchley N3 . . . . 29 C2
Higham Hill E17 . . . . 34 D1
Mill Hill NW7 . . . . 28 A6
Stonebridge NW10 . . . . 89 B6
Shakespeare's Globe
Theatre (site of)★
SE1 . . . . 252 B4
Shakespeare Twr
EC2 . . . . 242 B4
Shakespeare Way
TW13 . . . . 172 C6
Shakspeare Mews 7
N16 . . . . 73 C4
Shakspeare Wlk N16 . . 73 C4
Shalbourne Sq E9 . . . . 75 B2
Shalcomb St
SW10 . . . . . . 136 A6 266 B5
Shalden Ho SW15 . . . 155 D5
Shaldon Dr
Ruislip HA4 . . . . 62 C5
West Barnes SM4 . . . . 201 A4
Shaldon Rd HA8 . . . . . . 26 B1
Shalfleet Dr W10 . . . 112 D6
Shalford
Willesden Green
NW10 . . . . 90 A6
3 Woodford IG8 . . . . . . 37 C4
Shalford Cl BR6 . . . . . 227 A4
Shalford Ct N1 . . . . . . 234 C4
Shalford Ho SE1 . . . . 262 D6
Shalimar Gdns W3 . . . 111 A6
Shalimar Lo W3 . . . . . 111 A6
Shalimar Rd W3 . . . . . 111 A6
Shallons Rd SE9 . . . . 188 D6
Shalstone Rd SW14,
TW9 . . . . 132 D2
Shalston Villas KT5,
KT6 . . . . 198 B3
Shamrock Ct E7 . . . . . . 77 D3
Shamrock Ho
East Barnet N14 . . . . . . 15 B4
Forest Hill SE26 . . . . . 184 A6
Shamrock Rd CR0 . . . 204 B3
Shamrock St SW4 . . . 137 D2
Shamrock Way N14 . . . 15 B3
Shandon Ct SE4 . . . . . 141 A3
Shandon Rd SW4 . . . . 159 C5
Shand St SE1 117 C4 253 B2
Shandy St E1 . . . . 96 D3
Shane Ct EN2 . . . . 5 A3
Shan Ho WC1 . . . . 240 C5
Shanklin Gdns WD19 . . 22 C6
Shanklin Ho E17 . . . . . . 35 B1
Shanklin Rd
Hornsey N8 . . . . 49 D4
Tottenham Hale N15 . . . 52 A5
Shannon Cl UB2 . . . . . 106 D1
Shannon Cnr KT3 . . . . 200 A5
Shannon Cnr Ret Pk
KT3 . . . . 200 A5
Shannon Commercial Ctr
KT3 . . . . 200 A5
Shannon Ct
Croydon CR0 . . . . 205 A1
11 Peckham SE15 . . . . 139 D5
Stoke Newington N16 . . 73 C5
Willesden NW10 . . . . . . 68 A2
Shannon Gr SW9 . . . . 138 B1
Shannon Pl
NW8 . . . . 92 C5 230 B4
Shannon Way BR3 . . . 185 D4
Shanti Ct SW18 . . . . . 157 C3
Shap Cres SM5 . . . . . . 202 D1
Shapland Way N13 . . . . 32 B5
Shapla Prim Sch 25
E1 . . . . 118 A6
Shapwick Cl N11 . . . . . 30 D5
Shardcroft Ave
SE24 . . . . 160 D6
Shardeloes Rd SE14 . . 141 B3
Shard's Sq SE15 . . . . . 140 A6
Sharebourne Ho
SW2 . . . . 160 C6
Sharland Cl CR7 . . . . . 204 C3
Sharman Ct DA14 . . . . 190 A6
Sharman Ho 13 E14 . . . 98 A1
Sharnbrooke Cl
DA16 . . . . 146 C2
Sharnbrook Ho W6 . . 265 A6
Sharon Cl KT6 . . . . 197 C1
Sharon Ct 1 N12 . . . . . . 30 A4
Sharon Gdns E9 . . . . . . 96 C6
Sharon Rd
Chiswick W4 . . . . 111 B1
Enfield EN3 . . . . 7 A3
Sharpe Cl W7 . . . . 86 D2
Sharp Ho SW8 . . . . . . 137 B2
Sharples Hall St 8
NW1 . . . . 70 D1
Sharpness Cl UB4 . . . . . 85 A2
Sharpness Ct 2
SE15 . . . . 139 D5
Sharps La HA4 . . . . 39 B2
Sharratt St SE15 . . . . . 140 C6
Sharsted St
SE17 . . . . . . 116 D1 261 C1
Sharvel La UB5 . . . . . . 84 B6
Sharwood WC1 . . . . . . 233 D3
Shaver's Pl SW1 . . . . 249 C5
Shaw Ave IG11 . . . . . . 103 A5
Shawbrooke Rd SE9 . 143 D1
Shawbury Cl 9 NW9 . . 27 C2
Shawbury Ct SE22 . . . 161 D6
Shawbury Rd SE22 . . . 161 D6
Shaw Cl Bushey WD23 . . . 8 C2
Woolwich SE28 . . . . . . 124 B5
Shaw Cotts SE23 . . . . 163 A1
Shaw Cres 6 E14 . . . . . 97 A1
Shaw Ct
8 Acton Green W3 . . 111 A3
11 Battersea SW11 . . . 136 B2
Cheam SM4 . . . . 202 A2
Upper Holloway N19 . . . 72 A6
Shaw Dr KT12 . . . . 194 C2
Shawfield Ct UB7 . . . . 104 A3
Shawfield Pk BR1 . . . 187 D1
Shawfield St
SW3 . . . . 114 C1 257 B1
Shawford Ct 8
SW15 . . . . 156 A4
Shawford Rd KT19 . . . 215 B2
Shaw Gdns IG11 . . . . . 103 A5
Shaw Ho
6 Erith DA17 . . . . 125 B1
5 Newham E16 . . . . . 122 C5
Shaw Path BR1 . . . . . 164 D1
Shaw Rd
Camberwell SE22 . . . . 139 C1
Catford BR1 . . . . 164 D1
Enfield EN3 . . . . 6 D4
Shaw Sq E17 . . . . 35 A2
Shaws Wood Cotts
EN4 . . . . 3 C3
Shaw Way SM6 . . . . . . 220 A1
Shearing Dr SM4 . . . . 202 A2
Shearling Way N7 . . . . . 72 A2
Shearman Rd SE3 . . . 142 D2
Shears Ct TW16 . . . . . 171 C3
Shearsmith Ho 19
E1 . . . . 118 A6
Shears The TW16 . . . . 171 C3
Shears Way TW16 . . . . 171 C2
Shearwater Cl IG11 . . 102 A4
Shearwater Ct 24
SE8 . . . . 141 B6
Shearwater Rd SM1 . . 217 B3
Shearwater Way UB4 . 84 D1
Sheaveshill Ave NW9 . . 45 C5
Sheaveshill Ct NW9 . . . 45 C5
Sheaveshill Par NW9 . . 45 C5
Sheba Ct N17 . . . . 34 A4
Sheba Pl E1 . . . . 243 D5
Sheen Common Dr SW14,
TW10 . . . . 154 C6
Sheen Court Rd
TW10 . . . . 132 C1
Sheen Ct TW10 . . . . . . 132 C1
Sheendale Rd TW9 . . . 132 B1
Sheenewood SE26 . . . 184 B6
Sheen Gate Gdns
SW14 . . . . 133 A1
Sheengate Mans
SW14 . . . . 133 B1
Sheen Gr N1 . . 94 C6 234 A6
Sheen La SW14 . . . . . . 133 A1
Sheen Mount Prim Sch
SW14 . . . . 154 D6
Sheen Pk TW10,
TW9 . . . . 132 A1
Sheen Rd
Orpington BR5 . . . . . . 211 D5
Richmond TW10, TW9 . 132 B1
Sheen Way SM6 . . . . . 220 B3
Sheen Wood SW14 . . . 155 A6
Sheepcote Cl TW5 . . . 128 A5
Sheepcote La SW11 . 136 D3
Sheepcote Rd HA1 . . . . 42 D3
Sheepcotes Rd RM6 . . 59 A5
Sheephouse Way
KT3 . . . . 199 C2
Sheep La E8 . . . . 96 B6
Sheepwalk TW17 . . . . 192 B3
Sheep Walk Mews 7
SW19 . . . . 179 A4
Sheerness Mews
E16 . . . . 122 D4
Sheerwater Rd E16 . . . 99 D2
Sheffield Ho 15
SE15 . . . . 139 D4
Sheffield Rd TW14,
TW6 . . . . 149 A6
Sheffield Sq 2 E3 . . . . 97 B4
Sheffield St WC2 . . . . 240 C1
Sheffield Terr
W8 . . . . 113 C5 245 B3
Sheffield Way TW14,
TW6 . . . . 149 B6
Shefton Rise HA6 . . . . . 22 A3
Shelbey Ct BR1 . . . . . . 186 D2
Shelbourne Cl HA5 . . . 41 B6
Shelbourne Ho 20
N19 . . . . 49 D2
Shelbourne Rd N17 . . . 34 B2
Shelburne Ct SW15 . . 156 D6
Shelburne Dr TW4 . . . 151 C5
Shelburne Ho 9
SW16 . . . . 181 C5
Shelburne Rd N7 . . . . . 72 B4
Shelbury Cl DA14 . . . . 168 A1
Shelbury Rd SE22 . . . 162 B6
Sheldon Ave N6 . . . . . . 48 D3
Sheldon Cl
Penge SE20 . . . . 184 B2
SE12 . . . . 165 B6
Sheldon Ct Barnet EN5 . . 1 D1
SW8 . . . . 270 A3
Sheldon Ho
Chingford E4 . . . . 36 C4
9 Homerton E9 . . . . . . 74 D2
Teddington TW11 . . . . 175 A4
Sheldon Pl E2 . . . . 96 B5
Sheldon Rd
Cricklewood NW2 . . . . . 68 D4
DA7 . . . . 147 B4
Dagenham RM9 . . . . 81 A1
Edmonton N18 . . . . 33 C6
Sheldon Sq W2 . . . . . 236 B3
Sheldon St CR0 . . . . . 221 A5
Sheldrake Cl E16 . . . . 122 B5
Sheldrake Ho 15
SE16 . . . . 118 D2
Sheldrake Pl
W8 . . . . 113 C4 245 A2
Sheldrick Cl CR4 . . . . 180 B1
Shelduck Cl E15 . . . . . . 76 D3
Shelduck Ct 37 SE8 . . 141 B6
Sheldwich Terr BR2 . . 210 A3
Shelford 20 KT1 . . . . . 176 C1
Shelford Ct 7 E5 . . . . . 52 B1
Shelford Pl N16 . . . . . . 73 B5
Shelford Rd EN5 . . . . . . 12 C5
Shelford Rise SE19 . . 183 D3
Shelgate Rd SW11 . . . 158 D6
Shell Cl BR2 . . . . 210 A3
Shell Ctr SE1 . . . . 250 D3
Shellduck Cl NW9 . . . . . 27 C1
Shelley N8 . . . . 50 A6
Shelley Ave
Greenford UB6 . . . . 86 B4
Plashet E12 . . . . 78 A2
Shelley Cl BR6 . . . . . . 227 C5
Edgware HA8 . . . . 26 C6
Greenford UB6 . . . . 86 B4
Hayes UB4 . . . . 84 A2
Peckham SE15 . . . . . . 140 B3
Shelley Cres
Heston TW5 . . . . 128 D4
Southall UB1 . . . . 85 B1
Shelley Ct
Finsbury Pk N4 . . . . 50 B1
9 Kingston u T KT2 . . 175 D6
SW3 . . . . 267 D6
13 Walthamstow E10 . . 53 D2
8 Wanstead E11 . . . . . . 55 A5
Wembley HA0 . . . . 65 C4
West Barnes KT3 . . . . 200 A4
Shelley Dr DA16 . . . . . 145 C4
Shelley Gdns HA0 . . . . . 65 C6
Shelley Ho
21 Bethnal Green E2 . . . 96 C4
Chelsea SW1 . . . . 269 A6
9 Stoke Newington
N16 . . . . 73 C4
Walworth SE17 . . . . . 262 B2
Shelley Rd NW10 . . . . . 89 B6
Shelley Way SW17 . . . 180 B4
Shellgrove Rd 31 N16 . 73 C3
Shellness Rd E5 . . . . . . 74 B3
Shell Rd SE13 . . . . . . 141 D2
Shellwood Rd SW11 . 136 D3
Shelly Lo EN2 . . . . 5 B4
Shelmerdine Cl E3 . . . . 97 C2
Shelson Ave TW13 . . . 171 D6
Shelton Ct N21 . . . . 16 C4
Shelton Rd SW19 . . . . 179 C2
Shelton St
WC2 . . . . 94 A1 240 A1
Shene Bldg EC1 . . . . 241 A4
Shene Sch SW14 . . . . 133 C1
Shenfield Ho 3
SE18 . . . . 143 D5
Shenfield Rd IG8 . . . . . 37 B3
Shenfield St N1 . . . . . . 95 C5
Shenley Ave HA4 . . . . . 39 D1
Shenley Ho 3 SW16 . 182 B6
Shenley Rd
Camberwell SE5 . . . . . 139 C4
Heston TW5 . . . . 129 A4
Shenstone W13 . . . . . . 109 C5
Shenstone Gdns IG2 . . 57 D4
Shenstone Ho SW16 . 181 C5
Shepard Ho 17
SW11 . . . . 136 B2
Sheperdess Pl N1 . . . 235 B2
Shepherd Cl
Feltham TW13 . . . . . . 173 A6
W1 . . . . 248 A6

Shepherdess Wlk
N1 95 A5 235 B3
Shepherd Ho
Barnsbury N7 72 A2
10 Poplar E14 97 D1
Shepherd Mkt W1 248 C3
SHEPHERD'S BUSH 112 B5
Shepherd's Bush Gn
W12 112 C4
Shepherd's Bush Market
W12 112 C4
Shepherd's Bush Mkt Sta
W12 112 C5
Shepherd's Bush Overground Sta
W12 112 D4
Shepherd's Bush Pl
W12 112 D4
Shepherd's Bush Rd
W6 112 C3
Shepherd's Bush Sta
W12 112 D4
Shepherds Cl
Dagenham RM6 58 D5
Orpington BR6 227 D5
Shepperton TW17 192 D3
Stanmore HA7 25 A5
Shepherd's Cl N6 49 B3
Shepherds Ct
8 Hammersmith W12 112 D4
13 Harrow HA1 42 D3
Shepherds Gn BR7 189 B3
Shepherd's Hill N6 49 C3
Shepherds La SE28 123 C5
Shepherd's La E9 74 D2
Shepherds Leas SE9 145 B1
Shepherds Path UB5 63 A2
Shepherds Pl W1 248 A6
Shepherd St
W1 115 B5 248 C3
Shepherds Way CR2 222 D1
Shepherds Wlk
Bushey WD23 8 B2
Dollis Hill NW2 68 A6
Shepherd's Wlk NW3 70 B4
Shepiston La UB3 105 A1
Shepley Cl SM5 219 A5
Shepley Ct SW16 181 C6
Shepley Mews EN3 7 C6
Sheppard Cl
Enfield EN1 6 B5
Kingston u T KT6 198 A5
Sheppard Dr SE16 118 B1
Sheppard Ho
31 Hackney E2 96 A5
8 Streatham SW2 160 C3
Sheppard's Ct
Harrow HA1 42 C2
Wembley UB6 64 D2
Sheppard St E16 98 D3
SHEPPERTON 193 A3
Shepperton Bsns Park
TW17 193 A4
Shepperton Court Dr
TW17 192 D4
Shepperton Ct
TW17 192 D3
SHEPPERTON GREEN 192 D5
Shepperton Rd
Littleton TW17, TW18 192 A5
Orpington BR5 211 A3
Shoreditch N1 95 B6 235 C6
Shepperton Sta
TW17 193 A4
Shepperton Studios
TW17 192 B6
Sheppey Gdns RM9 80 C1
Sheppey Ho 16 E5 74 B4
Sheppey Rd RM9 80 C1
Shepton Ct SW11 266 D2
Shepton Hos 11 E2 96 C4
Sherard Ct N19 72 A5
Sherard Ho 24 E9 74 C1
Sherard Rd SE9 166 A6
Sheraton Bsns Ctr
UB6 87 C5
Sheraton Cl WD6 10 B6
Sheraton Ho SW1 268 D6
Sheraton Lo HA3 42 C6
Sheraton St W1 239 C1
Sheraton The 22
KT6 198 A4
Sherborne Ave
Enfield EN3 6 C3
Southall UB2 107 C2
Sherborne Cl UB4 84 C1
Sherborne Cres
SM5 202 C2
Sherborne Ct SE20 184 C1
Sherborne Gdns
Ealing W13 87 B2
Queensbury NW9 44 C6
Sherborne Ho
Pimlico SW1 258 D2
South Lambeth SW8 270 C3
Sherborne La EC4 252 D6
Sherborne Rd BR5 211 D4
Cheam SM3 201 C1
Chessington KT9 214 A3
East Bedfont TW14 149 B3
Sherborne St
N1 95 B6 235 C6
Sherboro Rd 1 N15 51 D3
Sherbourne Ct
1 Hampton TW12 173 C2
9 Sutton SM2 218 A2
SW5 255 C4
Sherbourne Gdns
TW17 193 C2
Sherbourne Pl HA7 25 A4
Sherbrooke Cl DA7 147 C1
Sherbrooke Ho 9 E2 96 C5
Sherbrooke Rd
SW6 135 A5 264 B3
Sherbrooke Terr
SW6 264 B3
Sherbrooke Way
KT4 200 B2
Sherbrook Gdns N21 16 D4
Sherbrook Ho 2 N3 29 D3
Shere Cl KT9 213 D3
Sheredan Rd E4 36 C5
Shere Ho SE1 262 C6
Shere Lo 1 SW19 180 C3
Shere Rd IG2 56 C4
Sherfield Cl KT3 198 D5
Sherfield Gdns
SW15 155 D5
Sheridan N8 50 C5
Sheridan Bldgs WC2 240 B1
Sheridan Cl UB10 83 A3
Sheridan Cres BR7 188 D1
Sheridan Ct
Ealing W7 108 D6
Earl's Ct SW5 255 C3
Harrow HA1 42 B3
Hounslow TW4 151 A6
South Hampstead NW6 70 A1
South Lambeth SW9 270 D1
Sheridan Gdns HA3 43 D3
Sheridan Ho SE11 261 B3
7 Stoke Newington N16 73 C5
Sheridan Lo
Barnet EN5 1 D1
Bromley BR2 209 C5
East Barnet N14 15 B4
Sheridan Mews E11 55 B3
Sheridan Pl
Barnes SW13 133 D2
Bromley BR1 187 D1
Hampton TW12 174 A2
Harrow HA1 42 C2
Sheridan Rd
Belvedere DA17 125 C2
DA7 147 A2
Leyton E7 76 D5
Little Ilford E12 78 B3
Merton SW19 179 B2
Richmond TW10 153 C1
Sheridan St 34 E1 96 B1
Sheridan Terr UB5 63 D3
Sheridan Way 5
BR3 185 B2
Sheridan Wlk
Golders Green NW11 47 C3
Wallington SM5 218 D3
Sheringdale Prim Sch
SW18 157 B3
Sheringham NW8 229 D6
Sheringham Ave
Feltham TW13 150 A1
Little Ilford E12 78 B3
Southgate N14 15 D5
Twickenham TW2 151 C3
Sheringham Ct 1 N3 29 C2
Sheringham Dr IG11 80 A3
Sheringham Ho NW1 237 B4
Sheringham Jun Sch
E12 78 B4
Sheringham Mews 4
SW18 158 A2
Sheringham Rd
Islington N7 72 C2
Penge SE20 206 C6
Sheringham Twr
UB1 107 D6
Sherington Ave HA5 23 C3
Sherington Prim Sch 3
SE7 143 B6
Sherington Rd SE7 143 B6
Sheriton Ct SM1 217 C5
Sherland Rd TW1 152 D3
Sherleys Ct HA4 61 C6
Sherlies Ave BR6 227 C6
Sherlock Ct NW8 229 C6
Sherlock Holmes Mus*
NW1 92 D3 237 D5
Sherlock Mews W1 238 A4
Sherman Gdns RM6 58 C3
Sherman Rd BR1 187 A2
Shernhall St E17 54 A5
Shernwood Ho 1
E18 55 A5
Sherrard Rd E7, E12 77 D2
Sherrards Way EN5 13 D5
Sherren Ho 35 E1 96 C3
Sherrick Green Rd
NW10 68 B3
Sherriff Ct NW6 69 C2
Sherriff Rd NW6 69 C2
Sherringham Ave
N17 34 A1
Sherrin Rd E10 75 D4
Sherrock Gdns NW4 46 A5
Sherry Mews IG11 79 B1
Sherston Ct
Finsbury WC1 234 A1
Newington SE1 261 D4
Sherwin Ho 1 SE11 138 C6
Sherwin Rd SE14 140 D4
Sherwood
3 Barnet EN5 1 D1
Brondesbury NW6 69 A1
Long Ditton KT6 213 D6
Sherwood Ave
Greenford UB6 64 C3
Hayes UB4 84 B3
Mitcham SW16 181 D2
Ruislip HA4 39 C3
Wanstead E18 55 B6
Sherwood Cl
Barnes SW13 134 B2
DA5 168 C5
Ealing W13 109 B5
Walthamstow E17 35 B1
Sherwood Ct
11 Battersea SW11 136 A2
Colney Hatch N12 30 C5
2 South Croydon CR2 221 A3
St Johns SE13 141 D3
Sutton SM1 217 C3
W1 237 C3
6 West Wickham BR4 207 D1
Sherwood Gdns
Barking IG11 79 B1
Bermondsey SE16 118 B1
Millwall E14 119 C2
Sherwood Hall 7 N2 48 A6
Sherwood Ho N4 51 A2
Sherwood Park Ave
DA15 168 B5
Sherwood Park Prim Sch
DA15 168 B5
Sherwood Park Rd
Mitcham CR4 203 D5
Sutton SM1 217 C3
Sherwood Park Sch
SM6 219 D5
Sherwood Rd
Croydon CR0 206 B1
DA16 145 C2
Hampton TW12 174 A5
Harrow HA2 64 A6
Hendon NW4 46 C6
Ilford IG6 57 B5
Merton SW19 179 B3
Sherwood Sch CR4 203 C5
Sherwood St W1 249 B6
Whetstone N20 14 B1
Sherwood Terr N20 14 B1
Sherwood Way BR4 224 A6
Shetland Cl WD6 11 B5
Shetland Rd Bow E3 97 B5
East Bedfont TW6 149 A5
Shield Dr TW8 131 A6
Shieldhall St SE2 124 C2
Shield Rd TW15 171 B6
Shifford Path SE23 162 D1
Shillaker Ct W3 111 D5
Shillibeer Ct N18 34 B5
Shillibeer Pl W1 237 B3
Shillingford Cl NW7 28 D3
Shillingford Ho 40 E3 97 D4
Shillingford St 23 N1 72 D1
Shilling Pl TW8 109 A5
Shillingstone Ho
W14 254 B5
Shine Ho 3 N3 29 D3
Shinfield St W12 90 C1
Shinglewell Rd DA8 147 C5
Shinners Cl SE25 206 A4
Shipka Rd SW12 159 B3
Ship La SW14 133 A3
Shiplake Ct SW17 180 B6
Shiplake Ho 45 E2 95 D4
Shipley Ct SE20 184 A1
Shipley Ho 32 SW8 137 D3
Shipman Rd
Forest Hill SE23 162 D2
Newham E16 99 C1
Ship & Mermaid Row
SE1 253 A2
Ship St SE8 141 C4
Ship Tavern Pas EC3 253 A6
Shipton Cl RM8 80 D5
Shipton Ho
7 Camden Town NW5 71 A2
14 Haggerston E2 95 D5
Shipton Rd UB8 60 B4
Shipton St E2 95 D4
Shipwright Rd SE16 119 A4
Shipwright Yd SE1 253 A3
Shirburn Cl SE23 162 C4
Shirbutt St E14 119 D6
Shirebrook Rd SE3 143 D2
Shire Ct DA18 124 D3
Ewell KT17 215 D1
Shirehall Cl NW4 46 D3
Shirehall Gdns NW4 46 D3
Shirehall La NW4 46 D3
Shirehall Pk NW4 46 D3
Shire Ho E11 76 D5
Shire Horse Way
TW7 130 D2
Shire La BR6 227 B2
Shiremeade WD6 10 B6
Shire Mews TW2 152 A5
Shire Pl
12 Brentford TW8 131 C5
Wandsworth SW18 158 A4
Shires The TW10 176 A6
Shirland Mews W9 91 B4
Shirland Rd W9 91 C3
SHIRLEY 206 C1
Shirley Ave
Carshalton SM1 218 C4
Croydon CR0 206 D1
DA5 168 D3
Shirley Church Rd
CR0 223 A5
Shirley Cl
Hounslow TW3 152 A6
Walthamstow E17 53 D4
Shirley Cres BR3 207 A5
Shirley Ct
8 Ealing W13 109 A5
Ilford IG2 57 B4
Kingsbury NW9 45 B4
2 South Norwood SW16 182 B3
Thornton Heath SW16 204 B6
Shirley Dr TW3 152 A6
Shirley Gdns
Barking IG11 79 C2
Ealing W7 108 D5
Shirley Gr
Clapham SW11 137 A2
Ponders End N9 18 D4
Shirley High Sch
CR0 222 D5
Shirley Hills Rd CR0 222 D3
Shirley Ho 13 SE5 139 B5
Shirley House Dr
SE7 143 C5
Shirley Hts 6 DA6 147 A1
Shirley Lo 4 SE26 185 A6
SHIRLEY OAKS 207 A1
Shirley Oaks Hospl
CR0 206 C2
Shirley Oaks Rd
CR0 222 D6
Shirley Park Rd CR0 206 C1
Shirley Rd Acton W4 111 B4
Croydon CR0 206 B1
Enfield EN2 5 A2
Sidcup DA15 167 C1
Stratford E15 76 C1
Shirley St E16 98 D1
Shirley Way CR0 223 B5
Shirlock Rd NW3 70 D4
Shirwell Cl NW7 28 D3
Shobden Rd N17 33 B2
Shobroke Cl NW2 68 C5
Shoebury Rd E6 78 B1
Shoe La EC4 94 C1 241 B2
Shoelands Ct NW9 45 B6
Shona Ho E16 99 C2
Shooters Ave HA3 43 C5
SHOOTERS HILL 145 A4
Shooters Hill SE18 144 B4
Shooters Hill Post 16 Campus SE18 144 C4
Shooters Hill Rd
Blackheath Vale SE3, SE10 142 C4
SE18, SE3, SE7 143 D5
Shooters Rd EN2 4 D4
Shoot-Up Hill NW2 69 A2
Shopstop SW11 136 C1
Shore Bsns Ctr 31 E9 74 C1
Shore Cl
Feltham TW14 150 A4
Hampton TW12 173 A5
Shorediche Cl UB10 60 B5
SHOREDITCH 95 B5
Shoreditch Ct 2 E8 73 D1
Shoreditch High St Sta
E2 95 D3 243 C5
Shoreditch High St
E2 95 C3 243 B6
Shoreditch Ho N1 235 D1
Shore Gr TW13 151 C2
Shoreham Cl
Croydon CR0 206 C3
DA5 168 D3
Wandsworth SW18 157 D6
Shoreham Rd BR5 190 B1
Shoreham Rd (E)
TW6 148 A6
Shoreham Rd (W)
TW6 148 A6
Shoreham Way BR2 209 A3
Shore Ho SW8 137 B2
Shore Mews 30 E9 74 C1
Shore Pl E9 74 C1
Shore Point 2 IG9 21 B2
Shore Rd E9 74 C1
Shore Way 26 SW9 138 C3
Shorncliffe Rd
SE1 117 D1 263 C2
Shorndean St SE6 164 A3
Shorne Cl 3 DA15 168 B5
Shornefield Cl BR1 210 C6
Shornells Way SE2 124 C1
Shorrolds Rd
SW6 135 B5 264 D4
Shortcroft Mead Ct
NW10 68 A3
Shortcroft Rd KT17 215 D1
Shortcrofts Rd RM9 81 B2
Shorter St
EC3 117 D6 253 D6
Shortgate N12 29 B6
Short La TW15, TW19 148 B3
SHORTLANDS 208 C6
Shortlands
Brook Green W6 112 D2
Harlington UB3 127 B6
Shortlands Cl DA17 125 B3
Edmonton N18 17 B1
Shortlands Gdns
BR2 186 C1
Shortlands Gr BR2 208 B6
Shortlands Rd
Beckenham BR2, BR3 208 C6
Kingston u T KT2 176 B3

Shortlands Rd *continued*
Walthamstow E10 .....53 D2
Shortlands Sta BR2. 186 C1
Short Path SE18 .... 144 D6
Short Rd
Chiswick W4 .... 133 C6
Leyton E11 ....76 C6
Stanwell TW19 ...... 148 A5
Shorts Croft NW9 .....44 D5
Shorts Gdns
WC2 ....94 A1 240 A1
Shorts Rd SM5 ....218 C3
Short St
7 Hendon NW4 ......46 C5
SE1 .... 251 B2
Shortway SE9 ....144 A2
Short Way
Colney Hatch N12 .....30 C4
Twickenham TW2 ..... 152 A4
Shotfield SM6 ....219 B2
Shott Cl SM1 ....218 A3
Shottendane Rd
SW6 ....135 C4 265 A2
Shottery Cl SE9 ......166 A1
Shottfield Ave SW14 .133 C1
Shottsford 1 W11 ....91 C1
Shoulder of Mutton Alley
10 E14 ....119 A6
Shouldham St
W1 ....92 C2 237 B3
Showers Way UB3 ....106 A5
Shrapnel Cl SE18 .....144 A5
Shrapnel Rd SE9 ......144 B2
Shreveport Ho 23
N19 ....49 D2
Shrewsbury Ave
Harrow HA3 ....44 A5
Mortlake SW14 ......133 B1
Shrewsbury Cl KT6 ..214 A6
Shrewsbury Cres
NW10 ....89 B6
Shrewsbury Ho
Chelsea SW3 .... 267 A5
Kennington SE11 .... 270 D5
Shrewsbury House Sch
KT6 .... 214 A6
Shrewsbury La SE18 144 D4
Shrewsbury Mews 33
W2 ....91 C2
Shrewsbury Rd
Beckenham BR3 ..... 207 A6
Carshalton SM5 ..... 202 C2
Friern Barnet N11 .....31 D4
Harlington TW14,
TW6 ....149 B5
Notting Hill W2 ....91 C1
Plashet E7 ....77 D2
Shrewsbury St W10 ...90 C3
Shrewsbury Wlk 9
TW7 ....131 A2
Shrewton Rd SW17 . 180 D3
Shri Swaminarayan
Mandir★ NW10 .....67 B2
Shroffold Rd BR1 .... 164 D1
Shropshire Cl CR4 ...204 A5
Shropshire Ct W7 .....86 D1
Shropshire Ho WC1 . 239 B5
Shropshire Rd N22 ....32 B3
Shroton St
NW1 ....92 C2 237 B4
Shrubberies The
Ilford IG2 ....57 D4
Woodford E18 ....37 A1
Shrubbery Cl N1 .... 235 B5
Shrubbery Gdns N21 ..16 D4
Shrubbery Rd
Edmonton N9 ....18 A1
Southall UB1 .... 107 C5
Streatham SW16 .... 182 A6
Shrubbery The
2 Surbiton KT6 ..... 198 A1
7 Wanstead E11 ......55 B4
Shrub Ct 5 SM2 .....218 A2
Shrubland Gr KT4 ....216 C5
Shrubland Rd
Hackney E8 ....96 A6
Leyton E10 ....53 C2
Walthamstow E17 .....53 C4
Shrublands Ave CR0 .223 C4
Shrublands Cl
Forest Hill SE26 ..... 162 C1
Whetstone N20 ....14 B2
Shrubsall Cl SE9 .....166 A3
Shrubs Ho SW1 ..... 259 D3
Shurland Ave EN4 .....14 B5
Shurland Gdns SE15 139 D5
Shurlock Dr BR6 .....227 A4
Shuters Sq W14 .... 254 C1
Shuttle Cl DA15 ......167 D4
Shuttlemead DA5 ....169 B4
Shuttle St E1 ....96 A3
Shuttleworth Rd
SW11 ....136 C3
Siamese Mews 11 N3 .29 C2
Sibella Rd SW4 ...... 137 D3
Sibford Ct 5 CR4 ... 202 D6
Sibley Cl Bexley DA6 ..169 A6
Bromley BR1 .... 210 A4
Sibley Ct
Beckenham BR3 ..... 186 C1
Hillingdon UB8 ....83 A2
Sibley Gr E12 ....78 A1
Sibthorpe Rd SE12 ...165 C4
Sibthorp Rd 2 CR4 . 180 D1
Sibton Rd SM5 ....202 C2
Sicilian Ave WC1 .... 240 B3
Sidbury St
SW6 ....135 A4 264 A2
SIDCUP 190 A5
Sidcup By-Pass Rd
Sidcup DA14 .... 189 C6
St Paul's Cray BR5, BR7,
DA14 ....190 B3
Sidcup Hill DA14 .....190 B5
Sidcup Hill Gdns
DA14 ....190 C5
Sidcup Pl DA14 ......190 A5
Sidcup Rd SE9 ....166 A3
Sidcup Sta DA15 ..... 168 A2
Sidcup Tech Ctr
DA14 .... 190 D4
Siddeley Dr TW4 .....129 A3
Siddons Ct WC2 ..... 240 C1
Siddons Ho 8 NW3 ...70 D3
Siddons La
NW1 ....92 D3 237 D5
Siddons Rd
Croydon CR0 .... 220 D5
Forest Hill SE23 ..... 163 A2
Tottenham N17 ....34 A2
Side Rd E17 ....53 B4
Sidewood Rd SE9 ....167 B3
Sidford Ho SE1 ..... 260 D5
Sidford Pl
SE1 ....116 B3 260 D5
Sidgwick Ho 26
SW9 ....138 A3
Sidi Ct 2 N15 ....50 D6
Sidings Mews N7 .....72 C4
Sidings The E11 ....54 A1
Sidlaw Ho N16 ....51 D1
Sidmouth Ave TW7 ...130 C3
Sidmouth Dr HA4 .....62 A5
Sidmouth Ho
18 Camberwell
SE15 .... 140 A5
Marylebone W1 ..... 237 B2
26 Streatham SW2 .. 160 C4
Sidmouth Mews
WC1 .... 233 C1
Sidmouth Par NW2 ...68 C1
Sidmouth Rd
Bexley DA16 .... 146 C5
Leyton E10 ....76 A5
Willesden NW2 ....68 C1
Sidmouth St
WC1 ....94 B4 233 C1
Sidney Ave N13 ....32 B5
Sidney Boyd Ct NW6 ..69 C1
Sidney Elson Way
E6 ....100 C5
Sidney Gdns TW8 ... 131 D6
Sidney Godley (VC) Ho
31 E2 ....96 C4
Sidney Gr EC1 ...... 234 C3
Sidney Ho
4 Globe Town E2 .....96 D5
SE18 ....144 B4
Sidney Miller Ct 8
W3 .... 110 D5
Sidney Rd
Beckenham BR3 ..... 185 A1
Croydon SE25 .... 206 A4
Harrow HA2 ....42 A6
Stockwell SW9 ....138 B3
Twickenham TW1 .....153 B5
Walton-on-T KT12 ....194 B1
Wanstead E7 ....77 A5
Wood Green N22 ......32 B3
Sidney Sq E1 ....96 C2
Sidney St E1 ....96 C2
Sidworth St 6 E8 .....74 B1
Siebert Rd SE3 ......143 A6
Siedle Ho 9 SE18 ....144 C6
Siege Ho 14 E1 ....96 B1
Siemens Rd SE18 ....121 D3
Sienna SE28 .... 123 D3
Sienna Cl KT9 ...... 213 D2
Sienna Ct TW13 ..... 149 D1
Sierra Dr RM9, RM10 . 103 D5
Sigdon Rd E8 ....74 A3
Sigers The HA5 .... 40 B3
Signal Ho
9 London E8 ....74 B1
SE1 .... 252 A1
Signmakers Yd NW1 231 D5
Sigrist Sq 4 KT2 .....176 A2
Silbury Ave CR4 .....180 C2
Silbury Ho 9 SE26 ...162 A1
Silbury St N1 .... 235 C2
Silchester Ct
Stanwell TW15 ...... 148 A2
Thornton Heath CR7 . 204 C5
Silchester Rd W10 ....90 D1
Silecroft Rd DA7 .....147 C4
Silesia Bldgs E8 ......74 B1
Silex St SE1 . 116 D4 251 D1
Silicone Bsns Ctr
UB6 ....87 C5
Silk Cl SE12 ....165 A5
Silkfield Rd NW9 ......45 C4
Silk Ho NW9 ....45 B6
Silkin Mews 24
SE15 .... 140 A5
Silk Mews SE11 ..... 261 B1
Silk Mills Path SE13 .142 A2
Silk Mills Sq E9 ....75 B2
Silks Ct E11 ....54 C1
Silk St EC2 .....95 A2 242 B4
Silkstream Par HA8 ...27 A2
Silkstream Rd HA8 ....27 A2
Sillitoe Ho N1 ...... 235 D5
Silsoe Ho NW1 ..... 231 D3
Silsoe Rd N22 ....50 B6
Silverbell Ct 1 N12 ...29 D5
Silver Birch Ave E4 ...35 B4
Silver Birch Cl
Forest Hill SE6 ....163 B1
Friern Barnet N11 .....31 A4
Ickenham UB10 ....60 A4
SE28 ....124 A5
Silver Birch Ct EN3 ....18 D6
Silver Birch Gdns
E6 ....100 B3
Silverbirch Wlk 1
NW3 ....71 A2
Silverburn Ho 4
SW9 .... 138 D4
Silver Cl Harrow HA3 ...24 B3
SE14 .... 141 A5
Silvercliffe Gdns EN4 ..2 C1
Silver Cres W4 ...... 110 D2
Silver Ct N19 ....71 C5
Silverdale Enfield EN2 ...4 A1
Forest Hill SE26 ..... 184 C6
NW1 .... 232 A2
Silverdale Ave IG3 ....57 D4
Silverdale Cl
Cheam SM1 ....217 B4
1 Ealing W7 .... 108 D5
Northolt UB5 ....63 B3
Silverdale Ct EC1 ... 241 D6
Silverdale Dr
Chislehurst SE9 ..... 166 A2
Sunbury TW16 ....172 B1
Silverdale Factory Ctr
UB3 .... 106 A3
Silverdale Gdns UB3 .106 A4
Silverdale Ind Est
UB3 .... 106 A4
Silverdale Par IG3 ....57 D4
Silverdale Rd
Bexleyheath DA7 .... 147 D3
Chingford E4 ....36 B4
Hayes UB3 .... 106 A4
Petts Wood BR5 ..... 211 A5
Silverhall St TW7 ....131 A2
Silverholme Cl HA3 ...44 A2
Silver Ind Est N17 .....33 D1
Silver Jubilee Way
TW4 ....128 B3
Silver La BR4 ....224 B6
Silverland St E16 ....122 B5
Silverleigh Rd CR7 ...204 B4
Silvermead 7 E18 .....37 A2
Silvermere Rd SE6 .. 163 D5
Silver Pl W1 .... 249 B6
Silver Rd
Shepherd's Bush
W12 .... 112 D6
St Johns SE13 ...... 141 D2
Silvers 4 IG9 ....21 C3
Silver Spring Cl
DA8 .... 147 D6
Silver St
Edmonton N18 ....33 C6
Enfield EN1 ....5 B2
Silverstone Ct 8
BR1 ....187 C1
Silverston Way HA7 ...25 C4
Silver Street Sta N18 ..33 D5
Silverthorn 17 NW6 ...91 D6
Silverthorne Lo EN1 ..17 C6
Silverthorne Rd
SW8 ....137 B3
Silverthorn Gdns E4 ..19 C2
Silverton Lo SE19 ....183 C3
Silverton Rd W6 .... 134 D6
SILVERTOWN 121 B4
Silvertown Way E16 . 121 A5
Silvertree La UB6 .....86 B4
Silver Way
Hillingdon UB10 ....82 D5
Romford RM7 ....59 D6
Silver Wing Ind Est
CR0 ....220 B2
Silver Wlk SE16 ......119 B5
Silverwood Cl BR3 ...185 C3
Silvester Ho
27 Bethnal Green E2 ...96 C4
1 Notting Hill W11 .....91 B1
Pinner HA5 ....40 A5
6 Stepney E1 ....96 B1
Silvester Rd SE22 ... 161 D6
Silvester St SE1 .... 252 C1
Silwex Ho E1 .... 243 C5
Silwood St SE16 .....118 C1
Simba Ct TW1 ...... 152 D3
Simla Ho SE1 ...... 252 D1
Simmil Rd KT10 ......212 C3
Simmonds Ct SW5 .. 255 C3
Simmons Cl
Chessington KT9 .... 213 C2
East Barnet N20 ....14 C3
Simmons Dr RM8 ......81 A5
Simmons Gate KT10 .212 A3
Simmons Ho
20 Bethnal Green E2 ...96 A4
Finsbury Pk N7 ....72 B6
Simmons La E4 ....20 B2
Simmons Rd SE18 .. 122 D1
Simmons' Way N20 ...14 C2
Simms Cl SM5 ....218 C6
Simms Ct SW6 ....135 A2
Simms Gdns N2 ......30 A1
Simms Rd SE1 ....118 A2
Simnel Rd SE12 ......165 B4
Simon Cl
W11 ....113 B6 244 D6
Simon Ct
Paddington W9 ....91 C4
5 Woolwich SE28 .....124 B5
Simonds Rd E10 ......75 C6
Simone Cl BR1 ...... 187 D2
Simon Lo 31 SW19 .. 156 D3
Simon Marks Jewish
Prim Sch 8 N16 ....73 D6
Simons Wlk E15 ......76 B3
Simpson Cl
Southgate N21 ....16 B6
Thornton Heath CR0 . 205 A3
Simpson Dr W3 ....89 B1
Simpson Ho
Lisson Gr NW8 ...... 230 A1
Vauxhall SE11 ...... 260 C1
Wembley HA9 ....65 D6
Simpson Rd
Hounslow TW4 ....151 B5
Richmond TW10 ..... 175 C6
Simpson's Rd BR2 ...209 A6
Poplar E14 .... 119 D6
Simpson St SW11 ....136 C3
Simpson Way KT6 ...197 C3
Sim's Cotts KT10 .... 212 D2
Sims Wlk SE3 ...... 142 D1
Sinclair Ct
21 Beckenham BR3 .. 185 C3
Canonbury N5 ....73 A2
5 Croydon CR0 ..... 221 D6
Sinclair Gdns W14 .. 112 D4
Sinclair Gr NW11 .....46 D3
Sinclair Ho
Harrow HA7 ....24 D4
Sinclair Ho *continued*
3 South Norwood
SW16 ....182 B3
1 Streatham SW12 . 159 D3
Sinclair Mans 13
W12 .... 112 D4
Sinclair Pl SE4 ....163 C5
Sinclair Rd
Chingford Hatch E4 ....35 B5
W14 ....113 A3 254 A6
Sinclairs Ho 18 E3 ....97 B5
Sinclare Cl EN1 ....5 D4
Singapore Rd W13 ...109 A5
Singer St EC2 .... 235 D1
Singlegate Prim Sch
SW19 ....180 B3
Singleton Cl
Mitcham SW17 ..... 180 D3
Thornton Heath CR0 . 205 A2
Singleton Rd RM9 ....81 B3
Singleton Scarp N12 ..29 C5
Sinnott Rd E17 ....34 D2
Sion Ct TW1 ....153 B3
Sion Ho SE13 ....142 A1
Sion-Manning RC Sch
for Girls
16 Kensal Town W10 ...91 A2
6 North Kensington
W10 ....90 D2
Sion Rd TW1 ....153 B3
Sippetts Ct IG1 ....57 B1
SIPSON 126 C6
Sipson Cl UB7 ....126 C6
Sipson La UB3, UB7 .. 126 D6
Sipson Rd
Harmondsworth
UB7 .... 126 C6
West Drayton UB7 ....104 B2
West Drayton UB7 ... 104 C1
Sipson Way UB7 .....126 C5
Sir Abraham Dawes
Cotts SW15 ....135 A1
Sir Alexander Cl
W3 .... 111 D5
Sir Alexander Rd
W3 .... 111 D5
Sir Arthur Bliss Ct 4
SW19 .... 180 D1
Sir Cyril Black Way 2
SW19 ....179 C3
Sirdar Rd
Mitcham CR4 .... 181 A4
Tottenham N22 ....33 A1
W11 ....113 A6 244 A5
Sir Francis Drake Prim
Sch 1 SE8 .... 119 A1
Sir George Monoux Coll
E17 ....35 D1
Sir Henry Floyd Ct HA7 . 9 B2
Sirinham Point SW8 270 D5
Sirius Bldg 13 E1 .... 118 D6
Sir James Barrie Prim
Sch SW8 ....137 C4 269 B1
Sir John Cass
Foundation & Redcoat
CE Sec Sch 19 E1 ....96 D2
Sir John Cass's
Foundation Prim Sch
EC3 ....95 C1 243 B1
Sir John Heron Prim Sch
E12 ....78 B4
Sir John Kirk Cl 33
SE5 ....139 A5
Sir John Lillie Prim Sch
SW6 ....135 A6 264 B5
Sir John Soane's Mus★
WC2 ....94 B1 240 C2
Sir Martin Bowes Ho 9
SE18 ....122 C2
Sir Oswald Stoll
Foundation The
SW6 .... 265 C4
Sir Thomas Abney Prim
Sch N16 ....51 B1
Sir Thomas More Est
SW3 ....136 B6 266 D5
Sirus Rd HA6 ....22 A5
Sir William Burrough
Prim Sch 27 E14 .....97 B1
Sir William Powell's
Almshos SW6 .....135 A2
Sise La EC4 .... 242 C1

Siskin Ho
Edmonton N9 18 D3
14 Rotherhithe SE16 118 D2
Sisley Rd IG11 101 D6
Sispara Gdns SW18 157 B5
Sissinghurst Cl BR1 186 C5
Sissinghurst Ho 17
SE15 140 C6
Sissinghurst Rd CR0 206 A2
Sissulu Ct 8 E6 99 C6
Sister Mabel's Way 15
SE15 140 A5
Sisters Ave SW11 136 D1
Sisters of St Marcellina Sch 34 NW3 70 A4
Sistova Rd SW12 159 B3
Sisulu Pl SW9 138 C2
Sitarey Ct 4 W12 112 B5
Site of Changing of the Guard★ SW1 249 A1
Sittingbourne Ave
EN1 17 B5
Sitwell Gr HA7 24 D5
Siverst Cl UB5 63 D2
Sivill Ho 9 E2 95 D4
Siviter Way RM10 81 D1
Siward Rd
Bromley BR2 209 C6
Tottenham N17 33 B2
Wandsworth SW17 158 A1
Six Bridges Ind Est 15
SE1 118 A1
Sixpenny Ct IG11 79 A2
Sixth Ave Hayes UB3 105 D5
Ilford E12 78 B4
West Kilburn W10 91 A4
Sixth Cross Rd TW2 152 A1
Skardu Rd NW2 69 A3
Skeena Hill SW18,
SW19 157 A4
Skeffington Rd E6 100 B6
Skeffington St SE18 123 A3
Skeggs Ho 5 E14 120 A3
Skegness Ho 3 N7 72 B1
Skelbrook St SW18 158 A2
Skelgill Rd SW15 135 B1
Skelley Rd E15 76 D1
Skelton Cl 7 E8 73 D2
Skelton Ho N16 73 C3
Skelton Rd E7 77 A2
Skeltons La E10 53 D2
Skelwith Rd W6 134 C6
Skenfrith Ho SE15 140 B6
Skerne Rd KT2 175 D2
Skerne Wlk KT2 175 D2
Sketchley Gdns
SE16 118 D1
Sketty Rd EN1 5 D2
Skiers St E15 98 C6
Skiffington Cl SW2 160 C3
Skillen Lodge HA5 22 D2
Skinner Ct E17 53 C4
Skinner Pl SW1 258 A3
Skinners Almshouses
N13 16 C1
Skinners Company Sch (Upper) 10 N16 51 D2
Skinner's Company's Lower Sch 8 E5 52 B1
Skinners La EC4 252 B6
Hounslow TW5 129 D4
Skinner St
EC1 94 C3 241 B6
Skip La UB9 38 A1
Skipper Ct 5 IG11 101 A6
Skipsea Ho SW18 158 B5
Skipsey Ave E6 100 B4
Skipton Cl N11 31 A4
Skipton Dr UB3 105 A3
Skipton Ho SE4 141 A1
Skipwith Bldg EC1 241 A4
Skipworth Rd E9 96 C6
Skua Ct 33 SE8 141 B6
Skyline Ct SE1 263 C5
Skyline Plaza Bldg 19
E1 96 A1
Skylines E14 120 A4
Sky Peals Rd IG8 36 B3
Sky Studios E16 122 C4
Sladebrook Rd SE3 143 D2
Slade Ct Barnet EN5 1 D2
Brondesbury NW2 69 A3
Muswell Hill N10 31 B3
Sladedale Rd SE18 123 C1
Slade Ho TW4 151 B5
Sladen Pl 12 E5 74 B4
Slades Cl EN2 4 C2
Slades Dr BR7 189 A6
Slades Gdns EN2 4 C2
Slades Hill EN2 4 C2
Slades Rise EN2 4 C2
Slade The SE18 145 C6
Slade Twr E10 75 C6
Slade Way CR4 181 A2
Slagrove Pl SE13 163 D6
Slaidburn St
SW10 136 A6 266 B5
Slaithwaite Rd SE13 142 A1
Slaney Ct NW10 68 C1
Slaney Pl 1 N7 72 C3
Slater Cl 13 SE18 122 C2
Slatter 1 NW9 27 D2
Slattery Rd TW13 150 C3
Sleaford Ho 16 E3 97 C3
Sleaford Ind Est
SW8 137 C5 269 B3
Sleaford St
SW8 137 C5 269 B3
Sleat Ho 11 E3 97 B5
Sledmere Ct TW14 149 C3
Slievemore Cl 8
SW4 137 D2
Sligo Ho 8 E1 96 D3
Slingsby Pl WC2 250 A6
Slippers Pl SE16 118 B3
Slipway Ho 1 E14 119 D1
Sloane Ave
SW3 114 C2 257 B3
Sloane Avenue Mans
SW3 257 C3
Sloane Ct E SW3 258 A2
Sloane Ct W SW3 258 A2
Sloane Gate Mans
SW1 258 A4
Sloane Gdns
Belgravia
SW1 115 A2 258 A3
Orpington BR6 227 A5
Sloane Ho 7 E9 74 C1
Sloane Hospl BR3 186 B2
Sloane Sq SW1 257 D3
Sloane Square Sta
SW1 115 A2 258 A3
Sloane St
SW1 114 D3 257 D5
Sloane Terr SW1 258 A4
Sloane Terr Mans
SW1 258 A4
Sloane Wlk CR0 207 B3
Sloan Ho RM10 81 D1
Slocum Cl SE28 124 C6
Slough La NW9 45 A3
Sly St 17 E1 96 B1
Smaldon Cl UB7 104 C3
Smallberry Ave
TW7 130 D3
Smallberry Green Prim Sch TW7 131 A3
Smallbrook Mews
W2 236 C1
Smallbugh Mans HA0 65 B4
Smalley Cl N16 73 D5
Smallwood Prim Sch
SW17 180 B6
Smallwood Rd
SW17 180 B6
Smarden Cl DA17 125 C1
Smarden Gr SE9 188 B6
Smart's Pl
Edmonton N18 34 A5
WC1, WC2 240 B2
Smart St E2 96 D4
Smeaton Cl KT9 213 D2
Smeaton Ct SE1 262 A5
Smeaton Rd
Holdbrook EN3 7 C6
Wandsworth SW18 157 C4
Smeaton St E1 118 B5
Smedley St SW4 137 D3
Smeed Rd E3 75 C1
Smiles Pl SE13 142 A3
Smith Cl SE16 118 D5
Smithers Ho 3
SE20 184 D3
Smithfield Mkt★
EC1 94 D2 241 D3
Smithfield St
EC1 94 D2 241 C3
Smithies Rd SE2 124 B2
Smith's Ct W1 249 C6
Smithson Rd N17 33 B2
Smiths Point E13 99 A6
Smith Sq
SW1 116 A3 260 A5
Smith St
Surbiton KT5 198 B3
SW3 114 D1 257 C1
Smith's Yd
7 Croydon CR0 221 A5
Wandsworth SW18 158 A2
Smith Terr
SW3 114 D1 257 C1
Smithwood Cl SW19 157 A2
Smithy St E1 96 C2
Smithy Street Sch 34
E1 96 C2
Smock Wlk CR0 205 A3
Smoothfield TW3 129 C1
Smtyhe Cl N9 18 A2
Smugglers Way
SW18 135 D1
Smyrk's Rd
SE17 117 C1 263 B1
Smyrna Mans 8
NW6 69 C1
Smyrna Rd NW6 69 C1
Smythe St E14 119 D6
Snakes La EN4, N14 3 C1
Snakes La E IG8 37 C4
Snakes La W IG8 37 B4
Snakey La TW13 172 B6
SNARESBROOK 54 D6
Snaresbrook Coll Prep Sch 10 E18 37 A1
Snaresbrook Dr HA7 26 A6
Snaresbrook Hall 12
E18 55 A6
Snaresbrook Ho E18 54 D5
Snaresbrook Prim Sch
E18 55 A5
Snaresbrook Rd E11 54 D5
Snaresbrook Sta E11 55 A4
Snarsgate St W10 90 C2
Sneath Ave NW11 47 B2
Snell's Pk N18 33 D4
Sneyd Rd NW2 68 C4
Snowberry Cl E11 76 B4
Snowbury Rd 6
SW6 135 D3
Snow Ct 4 HA0 65 D3
Snowden Ave UB10 82 D5
Snowden St
EC2 95 C3 243 A5
Snowdon Cres UB3 105 A3
Snowdon Dr NW9 45 C3
Snowdon Rd TW6 149 A5
Snowdown Cl SE20 184 D2
Snowdrop Cl 2
TW12 173 C4
Snowe Ho SE27 160 D1
Snow Hill EC1 94 D2 241 C3
Snowman Ho NW6 91 D6
Snowsfields
SE1 117 B4 252 D2
Snowsfields Prim Sch
SE1 117 C4 253 A2
Snowshill Rd E12 78 A3
Snowy Fielder Waye
TW7 131 B3
Soames St SE15 139 D2
Soames Wlk KT3 177 C2
Soane Cl W5 109 D4
Soane Ct 10 NW1 71 C1
Soane Ho SE17 262 D1
Soaphouse La TW8 132 A5
Sobell L Ctr N7 72 B5
Soham Rd EN3 7 B6
SOHO 93 D1
Soho★ W1 93 D1 239 C2
Soho Mills SM6 203 B1
Soho Parish CE Prim Sch
W1 115 D6 249 C6
Soho Sq W1 93 D1 239 C2
Soho St W1 239 C2
Sojourner-Truth Cl 11
E8 74 B2
Sola Ct 8 CR0 205 B1
Solander Gdns
13 Shadwell E1 118 C6
Stepney E1 118 B6
Solar Ct N3 29 D3
Soldene Ct N7 72 B2
Solebay St E1 97 A3
Solent Ct SW16 182 B1
Solent Ho 6 E1 97 A2
Solent Rd NW6 69 C3
Solent Rise E13 99 A4
Soley Mews WC1 234 A2
Solidarity Ho 5
NW10 68 C2
Solna Ave SW15 156 C6
Solna Rd N21 17 B4
Solomon Ave N9 34 A6
Solomons Ct N12 30 A3
Solomon's Pas SE15 140 B1
Solon New Rd SW4 138 A1
Solon Rd SW2 138 A1
Solway Cl TW4 129 A2
Solway Ho 12 E1 96 D3
Solway Rd
East Dulwich SE22 140 A1
Tottenham N22 32 D2
Somaford Gr EN4 14 B5
Somali Rd NW2 69 B3
Somborne Ho 11
SW15 156 A4
Sombrook Ho SE11 261 A3
Somerby Rd IG11 79 B1
Somercoates Cl EN4 2 C2
Somer Ct SW6 265 A5
Somerfield Rd N4 72 D6
Somerfield St SE16 118 D1
Somerford Cl HA5 40 A5
Somerford Gr
Shacklewell N16 73 D4
Tottenham N17 34 A3
Somerford Grove Est
N16 73 D4
Somerford St E1 96 B3
Somerford Way
SE16 119 A4
Somerhill Ave DA15 168 B4
Somerhill Rd DA16 146 B3
Somerleyton Rd
SW9 138 C1
Somersby Est SE20 184 C3
Somersby Gdns IG4 56 B4
Somers Cl NW1 232 C4
Somers Cres W2 237 A1
Somerset Ave
Chessington KT9 213 D4
DA16 145 D1
Wimbledon SW20 178 B1
Somerset Cl
New Malden KT3 199 C3
North Cheam KT4 216 C5
Tottenham N17 33 B1
Woodford IG8 37 A2
Somerset Ct
10 Buckhurst Hill IG9 21 C2
Ealing W7 86 D1
2 Hampton TW12 173 C2
Somerset Gdns
Highgate N6 49 A2
St Johns SE13 141 D3
Teddington TW11 174 C5
Thornton Heath
SW16 204 B6
Tottenham N17 33 C3
Somerset Hall N17 33 C3
Somerset Ho
WC2 116 B6 250 D6
Somerset Ho SW19 157 A1
Somerset Lo
9 Brentford TW8 131 D6
5 New Barnet EN5 14 A6
Putney SW15 134 B1
Somerset Rd
Bedford Pk W4 111 B3
Brentford TW8 131 C6
Ealing W13 109 C5
Edmonton N18 33 D5
Harrow HA1 42 A4
Hendon NW4 46 C5
Holdbrook EN3 7 C5
Kingston u T KT1 176 B1
New Barnet EN5 14 A6
Southall UB1 85 C2
Teddington TW11 174 C5
Tottenham N17 51 D6
Walthamstow E17 53 C3
Wimbledon SW19 157 A1
Somerset Sq
W14 113 B4 244 C1
Somerset Waye
TW5 129 A5
Somersham Rd DA7 147 A3
Somers Pl SW2 160 B4
Somers Rd
Tulse Hill SW2 160 B5
Walthamstow E17 53 B5
SOMERSTOWN 93 D4
Somers Town Est
NW1 93 C5 232 B3
Somers Way WD23 8 A4
Somerton Ave TW9 132 D2
Somerton Rd
Cricklewood NW2 69 A5
Nunhead SE15 140 B1
Somertrees Ave
SE12 165 B2
Somervell Rd HA2 63 C3
Somerville Ave
SW13 134 C6
Somerville Cl SW9 138 B3
Somerville Ct SW16 181 D4
Somerville Ho 10
SW15 156 D5
Somerville Point
SE16 119 B4
Somerville Rd
Dagenham RM6 58 C4
Penge SE20 184 D3
Sonderburg Rd 13 N7 72 B6
Sondes St SE17 139 B6
Songhurst Cl CR0 204 B3
Sonia Ct Edgware HA8 26 B3
North Finchley N12 30 A6
Sonia Gdns
Heston TW5 129 C5
North Finchley N12 30 A6
Willesden NW10 67 D4
Sonning Ct CR0 222 A6
Sonning Gdns TW12 173 A4
Sonning Ho 32 E2 95 D4
Sonning Rd CR0 206 A3
Soper Cl
Chingford Hatch E4 35 B5
4 Forest Hill SE23 162 D2
Soper Mews EN3 7 C5
Sophia Cl N7 72 B2
Sophia Ho
10 Hammersmith
W6 112 C1
Tottenham N15 51 D5
Sophia Rd
Newham E13 99 B2
Walthamstow E10 53 D1
Sophia Sq 14 SE16 119 A6
Sopwith 2 NW9 27 D2
Sopwith Ave KT9 214 A3
Sopwith Cl KT2 176 B5
Sopwith Rd TW5 128 C5
Sopwith Way
Battersea
SW8 137 B5 268 C4
Kingston u T KT2 176 A2
Sorbus Ct EN2 4 D3
Sorensen Ct 2 E10 75 D6
Sorrel Cl SE28 124 A5
Sorrel Gdns E6 100 A2
Sorrel Ho TW3 130 A4
Sorrel La 17 E14 98 B1
Sorrell Cl
6 Brixton SW9 138 C3
SE14 141 A5
Sorrento Rd SM1 217 D5
Soseki Mus★ SW4 137 B2
Sotheby Rd N5 73 A4
Sotheran Cl E8 96 A6
Sotheron Pl SW6 265 D3
Soudan Rd
SW11 136 D4 267 C1
Souldern Rd 10
W14 112 D3
South Access Rd E17 53 A3
South Acre NW9 27 D1
Southacre Way HA5 22 C2
SOUTH ACTON 110 D3
South Acton Sta W3,
W4 111 A3
South Africa Rd
W12 112 B6
SOUTHALL 107 A5
Southall Ct UB1 107 B6
Southall Ent Ctr
UB2 107 C4
Southall La TW5 106 B1
Southall Norwood Hospl
UB2 107 B3
Southall Pl SE1 252 C1
Southall Sp Ctr UB1 107 B5
Southall Sta UB1 107 B4
Southall & West London Coll UB1 107 A5
Southam Ho 9 W10 91 A3

- **Southampton Bldgs** WC2 241 A3
- **Southampton Gdns** CR4 204 A4
- **Southampton Mews** E16 121 B5
- **Southampton Pl** WC1 240 B3
- **Southampton Rd**
  - Maitland Pk NW5 70 D3
  - Stanwell TW19, TW6 148 A5
- **Southampton Rd E** TW6 148 B5
- **Southampton Rd W** TW6 148 B5
- **Southampton Row** WC1 94 A2 240 B4
- **Southampton St** WC2 250 B6
- **Southampton Way** SE5 139 C5
- **Southam St** W10 91 A3
- **South Audley St** W1 115 A5 248 B4
- **South Ave**
  - Chingford E4 20 A4
  - East Finchley NW11 47 D5
  - Richmond TW9 132 C3
  - Southall UB1 107 B6
  - Wallington SM5 219 A1
- **South Avenue Gdns** UB1 107 B6
- **Southbank** KT7 197 B2
- **SOUTH BANK** 116 B4
- **South Bank** KT6 198 A3
- South Bank Bsns Ctr SW8 137 D6 269 D5
- Southbank International Sch 14 NW3 70 A2
- Southbank International Sch (Westminster Campus) W1 93 B2 238 C4
- Southbank Int Sch W11 113 C6 245 A5
- **South Bank Lo** 2 KT6 198 A3
- **South Bank Terr** KT6 198 A3
- South Bank Univ SW8 137 D4 269 D2
- South Bank University (Erlang House) SE1 116 D4 251 C1
- **SOUTH BEDDINGTON** 219 C2
- South Bermondsey Sta SE16 118 C1
- **South Birkbeck Rd** E11 76 B5
- **South Black Lion La** 7 W6 112 A1
- **South Bldg** SW1 259 B6
- **South Block** 20 E1 118 C6
- **South Bolton Gdns** SW10 255 D2
- **SOUTHBOROUGH**
  - BR2 210 B3
  - KT6 197 D1
- **Southborough Cl** KT6 197 D1
- **Southborough Ho** SE17 263 B2
- **Southborough La** BR1, BR2 210 B4
- Southborough Prim Sch BR2 210 C4
- **Southborough Rd**
  - Bromley BR1, BR2 210 A5
  - South Hackney E9 96 D6
  - Surbiton KT6 198 A1
- **Southborough Rd (The Lane)** KT6 198 A1
- Southborough Sch KT6 214 A5
- **Southbourne** BR2 209 A2
- **Southbourne Ave** NW9 27 B1
- **Southbourne Cl** HA5 41 A2
- **Southbourne Cres** NW4 47 A5
- **Southbourne Ct** NW9 27 A1
- **Southbourne Gdns**
  - Ilford IG1 79 A3
  - Ruislip HA4 40 B1
  - SE12 165 B6
- **Southbridge Pl** CR0 221 A4
- **Southbridge Rd** CR0 221 A4
- **Southbridge Way** UB2 107 A4
- **SOUTH BROMLEY** 98 B2
- **Southbrook Mews** SE12 164 D5
- **Southbrook Rd**
  - Hither Green SE12 164 D5
  - Thornton Heath SW16 182 A2
- South Building★ SE10 142 B5
- **Southbury** NW8 229 B6
- **Southbury Ave** EN1 6 A1
- Southbury Prim Sch EN3 6 C1
- **Southbury Rd**
  - Enfield EN1 5 D2
  - Enfield EN1, EN3 6 B1
- Southbury Sta EN3 6 B1
- South Camden Com Sch NW1 93 D5 232 C4
- **South Carriage Dr** SW1, SW7 114 D4 247 C2
- South Chelsea Coll 22 SW9 138 B1
- **Southchurch Ct**
  - Bowes Pk N13 32 B5
  - Newham E6 100 B5
- **Southchurch Rd** E6 100 B5
- **South Cl** Barnet EN5 1 B2
  - DA6 146 D1
  - Dagenham RM10 103 C6
  - Highgate N6 49 B3
  - Morden SM4 201 C3
  - Pinner HA5 41 B2
  - Twickenham TW2 151 C1
  - West Drayton UB7 104 C3
- **South Colonnade The** E14 119 D5
- **Southcombe St** W14 254 A4
- **South Common Rd** UB8 60 A2
- **Southcote Ave**
  - Feltham TW13 150 A2
  - Tolworth KT5 198 D2
- **Southcote Rd**
  - Croydon SE25 206 B3
  - Tufnell Pk N19 71 C4
  - Walthamstow E17 53 A4
- **Southcote Rise** HA4 39 B2
- **Southcott Ho**
  - 31 Bromley E3 97 D4
  - W9 236 B5
- **South Countess Rd** E17 53 B6
- **South Cres**
  - Newham E16 98 B3
  - WC1 239 C3
- **Southcroft**
  - Carshalton SM1 218 C3
  - 8 Stonebridge NW10 89 B6
- **Southcroft Ave**
  - DA16 145 C2
  - West Wickham BR4 224 A6
- **Southcroft Rd** BR6 227 C5
  - Streatham SW17 181 A4
- **South Cross Rd** IG6 57 A4
- **South Croxted Rd** SE21 183 B6
- **SOUTH CROYDON** 221 B1
- South Croydon Sta CR2 221 B3
- **South Ct** 17 SW15 156 D5
- **Southdean Gdns** SW19 157 B2
- **South Dene** NW7 11 B1
- **Southdene Ct** N11 15 C1
- **Southdown** N7 72 A2
- **Southdown Ave** W7 109 A3
- **Southdown Cres**
  - Harrow HA2 42 A1
  - Ilford IG2 57 C4
- **Southdown Dr** SW20 178 D3
- **Southdown Rd** SW20 178 D2
- **South Dr**
  - Orpington BR6 227 C3
  - Ruislip HA4 39 C1
- **South Ealing Cemy** W5 109 D2
- **South Ealing Rd** W5 109 D3
- South Ealing Sta W5 109 D3
- **South Eastern Ave** N9 17 D1
- South Eastern Univ 3 N7 72 B5
- **South Eaton Pl** SW1 115 A2 258 B4
- **South Eden Park Rd** BR3 207 D4
- **South Edwardes Sq** W8 255 A5
- **SOUTHEND** 186 B6
- **South End**
  - Croydon CR0 221 A4
  - W8 113 D3 255 D6
- **Southend Cl** SE9 166 D5
- **South End Cl** NW3 70 C4
- **Southend Cres** SE9 166 D5
- **South End Gn** NW3 70 C4
- **Southend Ho** SE9 166 C4
- **Southend La** SE6 185 C6
- **Southend Rd**
  - Beckenham BR3 185 C2
  - Plashet E6 78 B1
  - Woodford IG8 37 D1
- **South End Rd** NW3 70 C4
- **Southend Road (North Circular Rd)** E17, E18 36 B2
- **South End Row** W8 113 D3 255 D6
- **Southern Ave**
  - East Bedfont TW14 150 A3
  - South Norwood SE25 205 D6
- **Southerngate Way** SE14 141 A5
- **Southern Gr** E3 97 B3
- **Southernhay** IG10 21 D6
- **Southern Perimeter Rd**
  - Hatton TW14, TW6 149 B6
  - West Bedfont TW19, TW6 148 C5
- **Southern Rd**
  - Fortis Green N2 48 D5
  - Newham E13 99 B5
- Southern Road Prim Sch E13 99 B5
- **Southern Row** W10 91 A3
- **Southern St** N1 233 C4
- **Southern Way**
  - Greenwich SE10 120 D3
  - Romford RM7 59 C3
- **Southerton Rd** W6 112 C2
- **South Esk Rd** E7 77 C2
- **Southey Ho** SE17 262 B2
- **Southey Mews** E16 121 A5
- **Southey Rd**
  - Brixton SW9 138 C4
  - Merton SW19 179 C3
  - Tottenham N15 51 C4
- **Southey St** SE20 184 D3
- **Southfield** EN5 12 D5
- **Southfield Cl** UB8 82 C4
- **Southfield Cotts** W7 108 D4
- **Southfield Ct** E11 76 D5
- **Southfield Gdns** TW1, TW2 174 D6
- **Southfield Lo** W4 111 B4
- **Southfield Pk** HA2 41 D5
- Southfield Prim Sch W4 111 C4
- **Southfield Rd**
  - Acton W4 111 B4
  - Enfield EN3 18 C5
  - St Paul's Cray BR7 211 D6
- **SOUTHFIELDS** 157 D3
- **Southfields**
  - Hendon NW4 46 B6
  - Thames Ditton KT8 196 C3
- **Southfields Ave** TW15 170 D4
- Southfields Com Coll SW18 157 C3
- **Southfields Ct** SM3 217 C6
- **Southfields Rd** SW18 157 C5
- Southfields Sta SW18 157 B3
- **Southfleet Rd** BR6 227 C4
- **SOUTHGATE** 16 B4
- **South Gate Ave** TW13 171 B6
- **Southgate Cir** 3 N14 15 D3
- Southgate Coll N14 15 D2
- **Southgate Ct** N1 73 B1
- **Southgate Gr** N1 73 B1
- **Southgate Ho** 7 E17 54 A6
- **Southgate Rd** N1 95 B6 235 D6
- **South Gate Rd** E12 77 D5
- Southgate Sch EN4 15 B6
- Southgate Sta N14 15 D3
- **Southgate Way** N2 30 C2
- **South Gdns**
  - Mitcham SW19 180 B3
  - Wembley HA9 66 C6
- **South Gipsy Rd** DA16 146 D2
- **South Glade The** DA5 169 B3
- **South Gn** NW9 27 C2
- **South Gr** Highgate N6 49 A1
  - Tottenham N15 51 B4
  - Walthamstow E17 53 B4
- South Greenford Sta UB6 86 C4
- **South Grove Ho** N6 49 A1
- South Grove Prim Sch E17 53 B3
- **SOUTH HACKNEY** 96 C6
- **SOUTH HAMPSTEAD** 70 A1
- South Hampstead High Sch 11 NW3 70 B2
- South Hampstead Sta NW8 70 A1
- South Harringay Jun & Inf Schs 1 N4 50 D4
- **SOUTH HARROW** 63 D5
- South Harrow Sta HA2 64 A5
- **South Hill** BR7 188 B4
- **South Hill Ave** HA1, HA2 64 B5
- **South Hill Gr** HA1 64 C4
- **South Hill Pk** NW3 70 C4
- **South Hill Pk Gdns** NW3 70 C4
- **South Hill Rd**
  - Beckenham BR2 208 C5
  - 6 Beckenham BR2 208 D5
- **Southholme Cl** SE19 183 C2
- **Southill La** HA5 40 B5
- **Southill Rd** BR7 188 B3
- **Southill St** E14 97 D1
- **South Island Pl** SW9 138 C5
- **SOUTH KENSINGTON** 114 A1
- South Kensington Sta SW7 114 B2 256 D4
- **South Kensington Station Arc** SW7 256 D4
- South Kenton Sta HA9 43 C1
- **South La**
  - Kingston u T KT1 197 D6
  - New Malden KT3 199 B3
- **SOUTH LAMBETH** 138 A4
- **South Lambeth Pl** SW8 270 B6
- **South Lambeth Rd** SW8 138 A5 270 B4
- **Southland Rd** SE18 145 D5
- **Southlands Ave** BR6 227 C3
- **Southlands Ct** BR2 209 D5
- **Southlands Dr** SW19 156 D2
- **Southlands Gr** BR1 210 A6
- **Southlands Rd** BR1, BR2 209 D5
- **Southland Way** TW7 152 B6
- **South La W** KT3 199 B5
- **South Lo**
  - 6 New Barnet EN5 13 D6
  - NW8 229 C2
  - Twickenham TW2 152 A5
- **South Lodge Ave** CR4, CR7, SW16 204 A5
- **South Lodge Cres** EN2 3 D1
- **South Lodge Dr** N14 15 D6
- South London Gall★ SE5 139 C4
- South London Montessori Sch SW11 267 A1
- **South Mall The** N9 18 A1
- **South Mead**
  - Grahame Pk NW9 27 D2
  - West Ewell KT19 215 D1
- Southmead Prim Sch 16 SW19 157 A3
- **Southmead Rd** SW19 157 A3
- South Merton Sta SW20 201 B6
- **South Molton La** W1 93 B1 238 C1
- **South Molton Rd** E16 99 A1
- **South Molton St** W1 93 B1 238 C1
- **Southmont Rd** KT10 212 C5
- **Southmoor Way** E9 75 B3
- **South Mount** N20 14 A2
- **SOUTH NORWOOD** 205 C6
- South Norwood Ctry Pk★ SE25 206 C5
- **South Norwood Hill** SE19, SE25 183 D1
- South Norwood Pools & L Ctr SE25 206 B4
- South Norwood Prim Sch SE25 206 A5
- **South Oak Rd** SW16 182 B6
- **Southold Rise** SE9 166 B1
- **Southolm St** SW11 137 B4 268 D1
- **South Ordnance Rd** EN3 7 C5
- **Southover** BR1 187 A5
  - Finchley N12 29 C6
- **SOUTH OXHEY** 22 B6
- **South Par**
  - Acton Green W4 111 B2
  - Edgware HA8 26 C1
  - Wallington SM6 219 C2
- **South Parade** SW3 114 B1 256 D2
- South Park Bsns Ctr IG3 79 C6
- **South Park Cres**
  - Catford SE6 164 D3
  - Ilford IG1 79 C5
- **Southpark Ct** SW19 179 C4
- **South Park Ct** 24 BR3 185 C3
- **South Park Dr** IG3 79 C4
- **South Park Gr** KT3 199 A5
- **South Park Hill Rd** CR2 221 B4
- **South Park Mews** SW6 135 D2
- South Park Prim Sch IG3 79 C5
- **South Park Rd**
  - Ilford IG1 79 B5
  - Wimbledon SW19 179 D4
- **South Park Terr** IG1 79 C5
- **South Park Villas** IG3 79 C4
- **South Park Way** HA4 62 C3
- **South Pl**
  - Broadgate EC2 95 B2 242 D3
  - Enfield EN3 18 C6
  - Surbiton KT5 198 B2
- **South Pl Mews** EC2 242 D3
- **Southport Rd** SE18 123 B2
- **South Quay Plaza** E14 119 D4
- South Quay Sta E14 119 D4
- **South Rd**
  - Brentford W5 109 D2
  - Edgware HA8 26 D2
  - Edmonton N9 18 A3
  - Feltham TW13 172 D5
  - Forest Hill SE23 162 D2
  - Hampton TW12 173 B4
  - Heston TW5 128 D6
  - Mitcham SW19 180 B4
  - Southall UB1 107 B5
  - Twickenham TW2 152 B1
  - West Drayton UB7 104 C3
- **South Residence** IG3 58 B4
- **South Ridge** BR2 209 C5
- **Southridge Pl** SW20 178 D3
- **South Rise** W2 247 B6
- South Rise Prim Sch 3 SE18 123 B1
- **South Rise Way** SE18 123 B2
- **South Row** SE3 142 D3
- **SOUTH RUISLIP** 62 D4
- South Ruislip Sta HA4 62 C3
- **Southsea Rd** KT1 198 A5
- **South Sea St** SE16 119 B3
- **Southside** N7 71 D4

South Side W6 ... 111 D3
Southside Comm SW19 ... 178 D4
Southside Ind Est SW8 ... 269 A2
Southside Quarter 4 SW11 ... 136 D3
Southside Sh Ctr SW18 ... 157 D5
Southspring DA15 ... 167 B4
South Sq
Hampstead Garden Suburb NW11 ... 47 D3
WC1 ... 241 A3
South St
Bromley BR1 ... 187 A1
Enfield EN3 ... 18 D6
Isleworth TW7 ... 131 A2
Mayfair W1 ... 115 A5 248 B4
South Tenter St E1 ... 95 D1 243 D1
South Terr
Muswell Hill N22 ... 31 D1
Surbiton KT6 ... 198 A3
SW7 ... 114 C2 257 A4
South Thames Coll (Putney Ctr) 12 SW15 ... 156 D6
South Thames Coll (Roehampton Ctr) SW15 ... 156 A5
South Thames Coll (Tooting Ctr) 7 SW17 ... 180 C5
South Thames Coll (Wandsworth Ctr) 7 SW18 ... 157 D6
SOUTH TOTTENHAM ... 51 D3
South Tottenham Sta N15 ... 51 D4
South Vale
Harrow HA1 ... 64 C4
West Norwood SE19 ... 183 C4
Southvale Rd SE3 ... 142 C3
South View BR1 ... 187 C1
Wimbledon SW19 ... 178 D4
Southview Ave NW10 ... 67 D3
Southview Cl SW17 ... 181 A5
South View Cl DA5 ... 169 B5
South View Cres IG2 ... 56 D3
South View Ct
8 Forest Hill SE23 ... 162 C3
South Norwood SE19 ... 183 A3
Southview Dr E18 ... 55 B6
Southview Gdns SM6 ... 219 C1
Southview Rd BR1 ... 186 B6
South View Rd
Hornsey N8 ... 50 A6
Pinner HA5 ... 22 B4
South Villas NW1 ... 71 D2
Southville
London SW8 ... 137 D4 269 D1
South Lambeth SW8 ... 137 A4
Southville Cl
East Bedfont TW14 ... 149 C3
West Ewell KT19 ... 215 B1
Southville Cres TW14 ... 149 C3
Southville Jun & Inf Schs TW14 ... 149 D3
Southville Rd
East Bedfont TW14 ... 149 C4
Thames Ditton KT7 ... 197 B2
SOUTHWARK ... 117 B5
Southwark Bridge SE1, EC4 ... 117 A6 252 B5
Southwark Bridge Rd SE1 ... 117 A5 252 B3
Southwark Cath* SE1 ... 117 B5 252 C4
Southwark Coll SE1 ... 116 D4 251 C2
Southwark Coll (Blackfriars Ctr) SE1 ... 251 C3
Southwark Coll (Camberwell Ctr) 17 SE5 ... 139 C5
Southwark Coll (Grange Ctr) SE1 ... 263 B5
Southwark Coll (Surrey Docks Ctr) 12 SE16 ... 118 B3
Southwark Park Est 11 SE16 ... 118 B2
Southwark Park Prim Sch 19 SE16 ... 118 B2
Southwark Park Rd SE16 ... 118 A2
Southwark Pk Sports Complex SE16 ... 118 C2
Southwark Pl BR1 ... 210 B6
Southwark St SE1 ... 117 A5 252 A3
Southwark Sta SE1 ... 116 D5 251 C3
Southwater Cl
Beckenham BR3 ... 185 D3
8 Poplar E14 ... 97 B1
Southway
Hampstead Garden Suburb NW11 ... 47 D4
Hayes BR2 ... 209 A2
Totteridge N20 ... 13 C2
Wallington SM6 ... 219 C4
West Barnes SW20 ... 200 D5
South Way
Croydon CR0 ... 223 A5
Friern Barnet N11 ... 31 C4
Harrow HA2 ... 41 C5
Lower Edmonton N9 ... 18 C2
Wembley HA9 ... 66 C3
Southway Cl 9 W12 ... 112 B4
Southwell Ave UB5 ... 63 C2
Southwell Gdns SW7 ... 256 A3
Southwell Grove Rd E11 ... 76 C6
Southwell Ho
8 Bermondsey SE16 ... 118 B2
13 Stoke Newington N16 ... 73 C3
Southwell Rd
Camberwell SE5 ... 139 A2
Harrow HA3 ... 43 D3
Thornton Heath CR0 ... 204 C3
South Western Rd TW1 ... 153 B5
Southwest Rd E11 ... 54 B1
South Wharf Rd W2 ... 92 B1 236 D2
Southwick Mews W2 ... 236 D2
Southwick Pl W2 ... 237 A1
Southwick St W2 ... 92 C1 237 A2
Southwick Yd W2 ... 237 A1
SOUTH WIMBLEDON ... 179 D4
South Wimbledon Sta SW19 ... 179 D3
South Wlk
Coney Hall BR4 ... 224 C5
Hayes UB3 ... 83 B2
Southwold Dr IG11 ... 80 A3
Southwold Mans W9 ... 91 C4
Southwold Prim Sch E5 ... 74 B6
Southwold Rd DA5 ... 169 D5
Upper Clapton E5 ... 74 C6
Southwood Ave
Highgate N6 ... 49 B2
Kingston u T KT2, KT3 ... 177 A2
Southwood Cl BR1 ... 210 B5
North Cheam KT4 ... 200 D1
Southwood Ct EC1 ... 234 C1
Hampstead Garden Suburb NW11 ... 47 D4
Southwood Dr KT5 ... 199 A1
South Woodford 10 E18 ... 37 A1
South Woodford Sta E18 ... 37 B1
Southwood Gdns
Hinchley Wood KT10 ... 213 A5
Ilford IG2 ... 56 D5
Southwood Hall N6 ... 49 B3
Southwood Ho
New Eltham SE9 ... 166 D2
Notting Hill W11 ... 244 A6
Southwood Hts N6 ... 49 B2
Southwood La N6 ... 49 A2
Southwood Lawn Rd N6 ... 49 B2
Southwood Mans N6 ... 49 B3
Southwood Park N6 ... 49 A2
Southwood Prim Sch RM9 ... 81 A4
Southwood Rd SE9 ... 166 D2
Woolwich SE28 ... 124 B5
Southwood Smith Ho 4 E2 ... 96 B4
Southwood Smith St N1 ... 234 C5
South Worple Ave SW14 ... 133 C2
Southwyck Ho SW9 ... 138 C1
South Yd EC1 ... 242 C4
Sovereign Bsns Ctr EN3 ... 7 B2
Sovereign Cl
Ealing W5 ... 87 C2
Ruislip HA4 ... 39 C1
Stepney E1 ... 118 B6
Sovereign Cres SE16 ... 119 A6
Sovereign Ct BR2 ... 210 B3
East Molesey KT8 ... 195 B5
Harlington UB7 ... 126 D5
3 Richmond TW9 ... 132 B1
13 Stepney E1 ... 118 B6
Sovereign Gr HA0 ... 65 D5
Sovereign Ho
Ashford TW15 ... 170 A6
23 Bethnal Green E1 ... 96 B3
Chislehurst BR7 ... 189 B3
Edgware NW7 ... 27 B6
3 Wimbledon SW19 ... 179 A4
Woolwich SE18 ... 122 B3
Sovereign Mews
Barnet EN4 ... 2 D2
6 Haggerston E2 ... 95 D5
Sovereign Pk NW10 ... 88 D3
Sovereign Pl HA1 ... 42 D4
Sovereign Rd IG11 ... 102 C4
Sovreign Ct HA6 ... 22 A2
Sowerby Cl SE9 ... 166 B6
Spa at Beckenham The BR3 ... 185 A2
Space Apartments N22 ... 32 B3
Space Bsns Pk NW10 ... 88 D4
Spa Central 1 SW16 ... 182 A3
Space Waye TW14 ... 150 B6
Spa Cl SE19 ... 183 C2
Spa Ct
12 Bermondsey SE16 ... 118 A3
Streatham SW16 ... 182 B6
Spafield St EC1 ... 241 A6
Spa Hill CR7, SE19 ... 183 B2
Spalding Cl HA8 ... 27 C3
Spalding Ct HA8 ... 26 B6
Spalding Ho SE4 ... 163 A6
Spalding Rd
Hendon NW4 ... 46 C3
Streatham SW17 ... 181 B5
Spanby Rd E3 ... 97 C3
Spangate SE3 ... 142 D2
Spaniards Cl NW11 ... 48 B1
Spaniards End NW3 ... 48 B1
Spaniards Rd NW3 ... 70 A6
Spanish Billingual Sch W10 ... 91 A2
Spanish Pl W1 ... 238 B2
Spanish Rd SW18 ... 158 A6
Spanswick Lo 2 N15 ... 50 D5
Spa Rd SE16 ... 117 D3 263 D5
Sparkbridge Rd HA1 ... 42 C5
Sparkes Cl BR2 ... 209 B5
Sparke Terr 2 E16 ... 98 D1
Sparkford Gdns N11 ... 31 A5
Sparkford Ho SW11 ... 266 D2
Sparks Cl Acton W3 ... 89 B1
Dagenham RM8 ... 80 D6
Hampton TW12 ... 173 A4
Sparrow Cl TW12 ... 173 A4
Sparrow Ct E4 ... 36 A4
Sparrow Dr BR5 ... 211 B1
Sparrow Farm Com Jun Sch KT17 ... 216 B4
Sparrow Farm Dr TW14 ... 150 D4
Sparrow Farm Inf Sch TW14 ... 150 C4
Sparrow Farm Jun Sch TW14 ... 150 C4
Sparrow Farm Rd KT17, KT4 ... 216 B4
Sparrow Gn RM10 ... 81 D5
Sparrows Herne WD23 ... 8 A4
Sparrows La SE9 ... 167 A3
Sparrows Way WD23 ... 8 A4
Sparsholt Rd
Barking IG11 ... 101 C6
Finsbury Pk N19 ... 50 B1
Sparta St SE10 ... 142 A4
Spa Sch SE1 ... 118 A2
Spa View 6 SW16 ... 160 B1
Speakers' Corner* W1 ... 114 D6 247 D6
Speaker's Ct 3 CR0 ... 205 B1
Speakman Ho SE4 ... 141 A2
Spearman St 8 SE18 ... 144 C6
Spear Mews SW5 ... 113 C2 255 B3
Spearpoint Gdns IG2 ... 57 D5
Spears Rd N19 ... 50 A1
Speart La TW5 ... 129 A5
Spectacle Works E13 ... 99 C4
Spectrum Ho NW5 ... 71 A4
Spectrum Twr 1 IG1 ... 79 A6
Spedan Cl NW3 ... 70 A5
Speechly Mews E8 ... 73 D3
Speed Ho EC2 ... 242 C4
Speedwell Ct 9 N12 ... 29 D6
Speedwell Ho 11 N12 ... 29 D6
Speedwell St 5 SE8 ... 141 C5
Speedy Pl WC1 ... 233 A1
Speer Rd KT7 ... 196 D3
Speirs Cl KT3 ... 199 D3
Spekehill SE9 ... 166 B1
Speke Rd CR7 ... 183 B1
Speldhurst Cl 2 BR2 ... 208 D4
Speldhurst Rd
Bedford Pk W4 ... 111 B3
Homerton E9 ... 74 D1
Spellbrook Wlk N1 ... 235 B6
Spelman Ho 15 E1 ... 96 A2
Spelman St E1 ... 96 A2
Spelthorne Gr TW16 ... 171 D3
Spelthorne Inf Sch TW15 ... 171 B4
Spelthorne Jun Sch TW15 ... 171 B4
Spelthorne La TW15, TW17 ... 171 A2
Spelthorne Sports Club TW16 ... 171 B3
Spence Cl SE16 ... 119 B4
Spencer Ave
Bowes Pk N13 ... 32 B4
Hayes UB4 ... 84 A2
Spencer Cl BR6 ... 227 D6
Church End N3 ... 29 C1
Ealing NW10 ... 88 B4
Woodford IG8 ... 37 C5
Spencer Ct 5 BR6 ... 227 A3
6 Finchley N3 ... 29 D3
Wimbledon SW20 ... 178 B2
Spencer Dr N2 ... 48 A3
Spencer Gdns SW14 ... 155 A6
Spencer Hill SW19 ... 179 A3
Spencer Hill Rd SW19 ... 179 A3
Spencer Ho
31 Clapham SW8 ... 137 D3
Hendon NW4 ... 46 B4
24 Putney SW19 ... 156 D3
Vale of Health NW3 ... 70 B5
Wimbledon SW19 ... 156 D1
Spencer House Mus* SW1 ... 115 C5 249 A3
Spencer Mews
Fulham W6 ... 264 A6
South Lambeth SW9 ... 270 C1
Spencer Park Ct SW18 ... 158 B6
Spencer Pk
East Molesey KT8 ... 196 A4
Wandsworth SW18 ... 158 B6
Spencer Pl
16 Islington N1 ... 72 D1
SW1 ... 259 B5
Thornton Heath CR0 ... 205 B2
Spencer Rd
Acton W3 ... 111 A5
Bromley BR1 ... 186 D3
Carshalton CR4 ... 203 A2
Chingford E17 ... 36 A1
Chiswick W4 ... 133 A5
East Molesey KT8 ... 196 A4
Friern Barnet N11 ... 31 B6
Harrow HA3 ... 24 C1
Spencer Rd *continued*
Hornsey Vale N8 ... 50 B4
Hounslow TW3, TW5, TW7 ... 130 A4
Ilford IG3 ... 57 D1
Mitcham CR4 ... 203 A6
Newham E6 ... 99 D6
South Croydon CR2 ... 221 C3
Tottenham N17 ... 34 A2
Twickenham TW2 ... 152 C2
Wandsworth SW18 ... 158 B6
Wembley HA0 ... 65 C6
Wimbledon SW20 ... 178 B2
Spencer Rise NW5 ... 71 B5
Spencer St
Finsbury EC1 ... 94 D4 234 C1
Southall UB2 ... 106 D4
Spencer Way 35 E1 ... 96 B1
Spencer Wlk
23 Hampstead NW3 ... 70 A4
Putney SW15 ... 134 D1
Spencer Yd SE3 ... 142 D3
Spenlow Ho 2 SE16 ... 118 A3
Spenser Ct 5 TW10 ... 175 D6
Spenser Gr N16 ... 73 C4
Spenser Mews SE21 ... 161 B3
Spenser Rd SE24 ... 160 D6
Spenser St SW1 ... 259 B6
Spens Ho WC1 ... 240 C5
Spensley Wlk N16 ... 73 B5
Speranza St SE18 ... 123 D1
Sperling Rd N17 ... 33 C1
Spert St E14 ... 119 A6
Speyside N14 ... 15 C5
Spey St E14 ... 98 A2
Spezia Rd NW10 ... 90 A5
Spice Ct
10 Battersea SW11 ... 136 A2
2 St George in t East E1 ... 118 A5
Spice Quay Htss SE1 ... 253 D3
Spicer Cl
Brixton SE5, SW9 ... 138 D3
Walton-on-T KT12 ... 194 C3
Spicer Ct EN1 ... 5 C2
Spicer Ho E2 ... 96 A4
Spices Yd CR0 ... 221 A4
Spigurnell Rd N17 ... 33 B2
Spikes Bridge Rd UB1 ... 107 A6
Spilsby Cl NW9 ... 27 C1
Spindle Cl SE18 ... 122 A3
Spindle Ho 8 DA15 ... 168 A1
Spindlewood Gdns CR0 ... 221 C4
Spindrift Ave E14 ... 119 D2
Spinel Cl SE18 ... 123 D1
Spinnaker Cl IG11 ... 102 B4
Spinnaker Ct 2 KT1 ... 175 D2
Spinnaker Ho 21 E14 ... 119 C4
Spinnells Rd HA2 ... 41 B1
Spinney Cl
Beckenham BR3 ... 207 D5
New Malden KT3 ... 199 C4
Worcester Pk KT4 ... 215 D6
Yiewsley UB7 ... 104 A6
Spinney Dr TW14 ... 149 A4
Spinney Gdns
Dagenham RM9 ... 81 A3
Dulwich SE19 ... 183 D5
Spinney Oak BR1 ... 188 A1
Spinneys The BR1 ... 188 B1
Spinney The
Barnes SW13 ... 134 B6
Barnet EN5 ... 1 D3
Cheam SM3 ... 216 C4
DA14 ... 191 A5
Edgware HA7 ... 26 A6
Southgate N21 ... 16 C4
Streatham SW16 ... 159 D1
Sunbury TW16 ... 172 A2
Wembley HA0 ... 65 A5
Spire Bushey Hospl WD23 ... 8 D3
Spire Ct 10 TW10 ... 154 A5
Spire Ho W2 ... 246 B6
Spire Roding Hospl IG4 ... 55 D6
Spires The EN5 ... 1 A2
Spirit Quay E1 ... 118 B5
SPITALFIELDS ... 95 D2
Spital Sq E1 ... 95 C2 243 B4
Spital St E1 ... 96 A2
Spital Yd E1 ... 243 B4

Spitfire Bsns Pk
  CRO 220 C2
Spitfire EstThe
  TW5.....................106 C1
Spitfire Rd SM6.........220 A1
Spitfire Way TW5.......106 C1
Splendour Ho SE16 ...118 C1
Spode Ho SE11..........261 A5
Spode Wlk NW3 ....69 D3
Spondon Rd N15.........52 A5
Spoonbill Way UB4 ....84 D2
Spooner 8 NW9...........27 D3
Spooner Ho TW5.........129 C6
Spooner Wlk SM6......219 D3
Sporle Ct 5 SW11.....136 B2
Sportsbank St SE6.....164 A4
Spottons Gr N17..........33 A2
Spout Hill CRO............223 C3
Spratt Hall Rd E11......55 A3
Spray St SE18..............122 C2
Spreighton Rd E8..195 D5
Sprewell SW15..........157 A5
Spriggs Ho 14 N1......72 C1
Sprimont Pl
  SW3.........114 D1 257 C2
Springall St 9 SE15..140 B5
Springalls Wharf 2
  SE16.......................118 A4
Springbank N21...........16 B5
Springbank Rd SE13..164 C5
Springbank Wlk NW1 .71 D1
Springbourne Ct
  BR3.........................186 A2
Spring Bridge Rd
  W5..........................109 D6
Spring Cl Barnet EN5...12 C6
  Dagenham RM8........60 C4
Springclose La SM3..217 A2
Spring Cott TW13.....149 D1
Spring Cott 10 W12 ..112 A4
Spring Cotts KT6 ......197 D4
Spring Court Rd EN2....4 C5
Springcroft Ave N2....48 D5
Spring Ct
  Brondesbury NW2.....69 B2
  Ealing W7................108 B6
  10 Wanstead E18......55 B6
Spring Ct Rd EN2 ....4 B5
Springdale Rd N16.....73 B4
Spring Dr HA5..........40 A3
Springett Ho 15
  SW2.......................160 B6
Springfield
  Bushey WD23.............8 B3
  South Norwood SE25..206 A6
  Upper Clapton E5.......52 B1
Springfield Ave
  Hampton TW12.......173 D4
  Hornsey N10...........49 C6
  Merton SW20..........201 B6
Springfield Christian Sch
  SE6...........................163 B1
Springfield Cl
  Finchley N12.............29 D5
  Stanmore HA7............9 A1
Springfield Com Prim
  Sch N16 ....52 A3
Springfield Ct
  7 Dagenham W3 ......39 A1
  1 Friern Barnet N20..14 D1
  Hampstead NW3.......70 C1
  2 Ilford IG1..............71 A2
  2 Kingston u KT1 198 A6
  Upper Clapton E5......52 B1
  Wallington SM6.......219 B3
Springfield Dr IG2.....57 A3
Springfield Gdns
  BR1..........................210 B5
  Kingsbury NW9.........45 B4
  Ruislip HA4...............40 C6
  Upper Clapton E5......52 B1
  West Wickham BR4 ..223 D6
  Woodford IG8 ....37 C3
Springfield Gr SE7..143 C6
  Sunbury TW16.........172 A2
Springfield Ho
  Acton W3...................111 A5
  1 Camberwell SE5...139 C3
  13 Dalston E8 ....73 D2
Springfield La NW6...91 D6
Springfield Mount
  NW9..........................45 B4
Springfield Par Mews
  N13............................32 C6
Springfield Pl KT3 ..199 A5

Springfield Prim Sch
  TW16......................171 D1
Springfield Rd
  Ashford TW15..........170 B5
  Bexleyheath DA7 ....147 D1
  Bromley BR1...........210 B5
  Chingford E4 ....20 C4
  Ealing W7...............108 C5
  Friern Barnet N11 ....31 C5
  Harrow HA1.............118 A6
  Kingston u KT1........198 A6
  Newham E6.............98 C4
  Penge SE20..........184 B5
  Plashet E6................78 B1
  South Norwood CR7...183 A2
  St John's Wood
    NW8 ......92 A6 229 B5
  8 Teddington TW1..152 C3
  Tottenham Hale N15 ..52 A5
  Twickenham TW2....151 C3
  Wallington SM6.......219 B3
  Walthamstow E17 ....53 B3
  Welling DA16..........146 B2
Springfield Rise
  SE26........................162 B1
Springfields 10 EN5...13 D6
Springfield University
  Hosp SW17 ....158 C1
Springfield Wlk
  3 NW6.....................211 B1
  Paddington NW6.......91 D6
Spring Gdns
  East Molesey KT8 ...196 A4
  Islington N5..............73 A3
  SW1..........116 A5 250 A4
  Wallington SM6.......219 C3
  Woodford IG8 ....37 C3
Spring Gr
  Brentford W4..........132 C6
  Hampton TW12......173 D2
  Loughton IG10..........21 D5
  Mitcham CR4...........181 A2
Spring Grove Cres
  TW3.........................130 C3
Spring Grove Prim Sch
  TW7.........................130 B3
Spring Grove Rd
  Hounslow TW3, TW5,
  TW7 ....130 C3
  Richmond TW10.......154 B6
Springhallow Sch
  W13............................87 A1
Spring Hill
  Forest Hill SE26......184 C6
  Upper Clapton E5.....52 B2
Springhill Ct 5 E5...139 B2
Spring Ho
  Merton SW19..........179 B2
  WC1..........................234 A1
Springhurst Cl CR0 ..223 B4
Spring La
  Croydon SE25..........206 B3
  Muswell Hill N10 .....49 A6
  Upper Clapton E5......52 B2
Spring Lake HA7......9 A1
Spring Mews W1 .....237 D4
Spring Park Ave
  CR0.........................222 D6
Springpark Dr
  Beckenham BR3.......208 A6
  Stoke Newington N4...51 A1
Spring Park Prim Sch
  CR0..........................223 C5
Spring Park Rd CR0..222 D6
Spring Path NW3......70 B2
Springpond Rd RM9..81 B2
Spring Rd TW13......149 B2
Springrice Rd SE13..164 B5
Spring Shaw Rd
  BR5...........................190 A2
Spring St W2...92 B1 236 C1
Spring Terr TW9......154 A6
Springtide Cl 10
  SE15.........................140 B5
Spring Vale DA7 ......147 D1
Springvale Ave TW8..136 A4
Springvale Ct SE12...143 A1
Springvale Terr 5
  W14..........................112 D1

Spring Villa Rd HA8 ...26 C3
Springwater WC1......240 C4
Springwater
  SE18.......................144 C4
Springway HA1........147 A2
Springwell Ave NW10..89 D6
Springwell Cl SW16..182 B6
Springwell CtTW5...128 B3
Springwell Jun & Inf
  Schs TW5................129 A5
Springwell Rd
  Heston TW5..............129 D6
  West Norwood SW16 182 C5
Spring Wlk E1............96 A2
Springwood Cl 8 E3...97 C5
Springwood Cres
  HA8..........................11 A2
Springwood CtCr2...221 C4
Sproggit Ind Est
  TW19.....................148 B5
Sprowston Mews E7..77 A3
Sprowston Rd E7.......77 A3
Spruce Ct W5...........110 A3
Sprucedale Gdns
  CR0.........................222 D4
Spruce Hills Rd E17...36 A1
Spruce Ho
  2 Brentford TW8 .....131 C5
  15 Rotherhithe SE16..118 D4
Spruce Pk BR2..........208 D5
Sprules Rd SE4.........141 A3
Spurfield E15............195 D6
Spurgeon Ave SE19..183 B3
Spurgeon Rd SE19....183 B3
Spurgeon's Coll
  SE25........................183 C1
Spurgeon St
  SE1...........117 B3 262 C6
Spur Ho 10 SW19 ....179 D2
Spurling Rd
  Dagenham RM9........81 B2
  East Dulwich SE22...139 D4
Spur Rd
  Brentford TW7.........131 B5
  Edgware HA8.............26 A6
  Feltham TW14 ....128 D1
  SE1............116 C4 251 A2
  Tottenham N15.........51 B5
Spurstowe Rd E8.......74 B2
Spurstowe Terr E8.....74 B3
Spurway Pr 22 SE2...162 B4
Square Rigger Row 7
  SW11......................136 A2
Square,The
  Hammersmith W6 ...112 C1
  Hayes UB11............105 B5
  Ilford IG1...................56 C2
  Leyton E10.................76 A5
  8 Richmond TW10...153 D6
  SW6.........................265 A1
  Wallington SM5.......219 A3
  Woodford IG8 ....37 A5
Squarey St SW17 .....158 A1
Squire Ct 2 CR0.......205 C1
Squire Gdns NW8.....229 C1
Squire's Almshouses 7
  E17............................53 D5
Squires Bridge Rd
  KT17........................192 B5
Squires Ct Finchley N3 .30 A2
  Wimbledon SW19 ....179 C6
Squires Ho 5 SE18 ..144 D6
Squires La N3............30 A2
Squire's Mount NW3...70 B5
Squire's RdTW17 ....192 C5
Squires Way RM7 ....59 D3
Squires WkTW15 ....171 B3
Squires Wood Dr
  BR7..........................188 B3
Squirrel CtW4...........128 C2
Squirrel Mews W13 ..109 A6
Squirrels Cl
  Hillingdon UB10.......60 C1
  North Finchley N12 ...30 A6
  Orpington BR6..........211 C1
Squirrels Ct14 ....215 D6
Squirrels Gn KT4.......216 A6
Squirrel's La IG9.......21 D1
Squirrels,The
  Bushey WD23..............8 B5
  Lewisham SE13 ......142 B2
  Pinner HA5................41 B6
Squirrels Trad Est
  UB3.........................105 D3

Squirries St E2...........96 A4
Stable Cl
  Kingston u KT2.......176 B4
  Northolt UB5.............85 C5
Stable Ct SM6...........219 A5
Stable Ho 9 SE16.....118 C4
Stable La DA5 ....169 D2
Stable Mews
  Twickenham TW1....152 D3
  West Norwood SE27 .183 A5
Stables End BR6.......227 A5
StablesThe IG9..........21 C4
Stables Way
  SE11..........116 C1 261 A2
Stable WayW10..........90 C1
Stable Wlk N2.............30 B2
Stable Yd Rd
  SW1...........115 C4 249 B2
Staburn Ct HA8..........27 A1
Stacey Ave N18..........34 C6
Stacey Cl E10.............54 B4
Stacey St Highbury N7...72 C5
  Soho WC2 ....93 D1 239 D1
Stack Ho SW1...........258 B3
Stackhouse St SW1 ..257 C6
Stacy Path 12 SE5....139 C5
Staddon Ct BR3.........207 A5
Stadium Bsns Ctr
  HA9............................66 D5
Stadium Rd
  Hendon NW2............46 C2
  SE7, SE18...............144 B6
Stadium Rd E NW2...46 C2
Stadium Ret Pk HA9 ..66 C5
Stadium St
  SW10 ....136 A5 266 B3
Stadium Way HA9......66 C4
Staffa Rd E10............53 A3
Stafford Cripps Ho
  2 Bethnal Green E2 ..96 C4
  SW6.........................264 D5
Stafford Cross CR0...220 B3
Stafford Cross Bsns Pk
  CR0..........................220 B3
Stafford Ct
  Croydon CR0 ....220 C4
  Ealing W7...................86 D1
  Kensington W8..........255 B6
  South Lambeth SW8 .270 A2
Stafford Gdns CR0....220 B3
Stafford Ho SE1 ....263 D2
Stafford Mans
  1 Hammersmith
    W14 ....112 D3
  10 Stockwell SW4 ...138 A1
  SW1.........................267 C3
Stafford Morris Ho
  E15.............................98 C5
Stafford Pl
  Richmond TW10......154 B4
  SW1...........115 C3 258 A6
Stafford Rd Bow E3...97 B5
  Harrow HA3...............24 A3
  Kingston u KT3 ....199 A6
  Maida Vale NW6 ....91 C4
  Plashet E7...................78 B1
  Ruislip HA4.................61 D4
  Sidcup DA14............189 C4
  Wallington CR0, SM6..220 A3
Staffordshire Ho N3...47 A6
Staffordshire St
  Peckham SE15.........140 A4
  Peckham SE15.........140 B4
Stafford St
  W8.............113 C3 255 A6
Stag Cl HA8.................27 A1
Stag Ct 18 SM6 ....219 B2
Stag Hill EN4..............2 C6
Stag Hts E11 ....21 B2
Stag La Chigwell IG9...21 B2
  Edgware HA8, NW9.....45 B4
  Roehampton SW15 ...155 D2
Stag Lane Fst & Mid
  Schs HA8....................26 C1
Stags Ct KT7...........197 A2
Stagshaw Ho 17
  SE22........................139 C2
Stags WayTW7 ....130 D6
Stainbank Rd CR4....203 B6
Stainby Cl UB7.........104 A3

Stainby Rd N15..........51 D5
Staincliffe Ho 5
  SM1.........................218 A4
Stainer Ho SE9 ....143 C1
Stainer St SE1..........252 C1
Staines Ave SM3......216 D6
Staines By-Pass
  TW15......................170 A4

Staines Rd E TW12,
  TW16......................172 C2
Staines Rd W TW15 ..171 B3
Staines Wlk DA14....190 C4
Stainford Cl TW15....171 B3
Stainforth Rd
  Ilford IG2....................57 B2
  Walthamstow E17 ....53 C5
Staining La EC2........242 B2
Stainmore Cl BR7 ....207 C3
Stainsbury St 22 E2...96 C5
Stainsby Rd E14.........97 C1
Stainton Rd Enfield EN3 .6 B1
  Lewisham SE13 ......164 B4
Stalbridge Flats W1...238 B1
Stalbridge Ho NW1 ..232 A3
Stalbridge St NW1....237 B4
Stalham St SE16 ....118 B3
Stambourne Ho SW8 270 B2
Stambourne Way
  Penge SE19.............183 D3
  West Wickham BR4 ..224 B5
Stambourne Woodland
  Wlk 8 SE19 ....183 D3
Stamford Bridge
  Stadium (Chelsea FC)
  SW6...........135 D3 265 C4
Stamford Brook Ave
  W6..........................111 C3
Stamford Brook Gdns
  4 W6........................111 C3
Stamford Brook Mans 2
  W6..........................111 C2
Stamford Brook Rd
  W6..........................111 C3
Stamford Brook Sta
  W6..........................111 C3
Stamford Cl
  Harrow HA3................24 C3
  2 London NW3.........70 A5
  Southall UB1 ....107 C6
  Tottenham Hale N15 ..52 A5
Stamford Cotts
  SW10 ....265 D4
Stamford Ct
  Chiswick W6 ....112 A2
  Edgware HA8.............26 B6
Stamford Dr BR2.......208 D3
Stamford Gdns RM9...80 C1
Stamford Gr E 1
  N16............................52 A1
Stamford Gr W 4
  N16............................52 A1
STAMFORD HILL 51 D1
Stamford Hill N16......51 D1
Stamford Hill Mans 1
  N16............................51 D1
Stamford Hill Prim Sch
  N16............................51 B3
Stamford Hill Sta
  N16............................51 C2
Stamford Lo 2 N16....51 D2
Stamford Mans 2
  N16............................52 A1
Stamford Rd
  Dagenham RM9........80 C1
  Kingsland N1............73 C2
  Newham E6 ....100 A6
  South Tottenham N15..51 C3
Stamford St
  SE1 ....116 C5 251 B4
Stamp Pl E2................95 D4
Stanard Cl N16...........51 C2
Stanborough Cl
  TW12......................173 B2

Stanborough Ho 4
E3 . . . . .97 D3
Stanborough Pas E8 . . .73 D2
Stanborough Rd TW3,
TW7 . . . . .130 B2
Stanbridge Mans
SW15 . . . . .134 C2
Stanbridge Pl N21 . . . .16 D2
Stanbridge Rd
SW15 . . . . .134 C2
Stanbrook Ct W1 . . . . 249 A4
Stanbrook Rd SE2 . . . 124 B4
Stanbury Ct E NW3 . . .70 D2
Stanbury Rd
Nunhead SE15 . . . . . . 140 C3
Peckham SE15 . . . . 140 B3
Stancroft NW9 . . . . 45 C4
Standale Gr HA4 . . . . . .39 A4
Standard Ind Est
E16 . . . . 122 B4
Standard Pl 13 EC2 . . .95 E4
Standard Rd
Becontree NW10 . . . . . .89 B3
Belvedere DA17 . . . . . 125 C1
DA6 . . . . 147 A1
Enfield EN3 . . . . .7 A6
Hounslow TW4 . . . . . . 129 A2
Standen Rd SW18 . . . 157 C4
Standfield Gdns
RM10 . . . . .81 C2
Standfield Rd RM10 . . .81 C3
Standish Ho
6 Chiswick W6 . . . . . . 112 A2
SE9 . . . . 143 B1
Standish Rd W6 . . . . . 112 A2
Standlake Point 1
SE23 . . . . 162 D1
Standon Ho 7 CR4 . . 202 D6
Stane Cl SW19 . . . . . . 179 D3
Stanedge Ct SW16 . . 182 A5
Stane Gr SW4 . . . . 138 A3
Stanesgate Ho 20
SE15 . . . . .140 A5
Stanetta Ct 3 RM6 . . .58 B3
Stane Way SE18 . . . . 144 A5
Stanfield Ho
8 Northolt UB5 . . . . . . 84 D5
NW8 . . . . 236 B4
Stanfield Rd 14 E3 . . .97 A5
Stanford Cl
Hampton TW12 . . . . . . 173 B4
Romford RM7 . . . . .59 D3
Ruislip HA4 . . . . .39 A3
Stanford Ct
Friern Barnet N11 . . . . .31 A5
Kensington W8 . . . . . . 255 D5
Walham Green SW6 . . 265 D1
Stanford Ho IG11 . . . 102 B5
Stanford Pl
SE1 . . . . 117 C2 263 A3
Stanford Prim Sch
SW16 . . . . 181 D2
Stanford Rd
Friern Barnet N11 . . . . .30 D1
Thornton Heath
SW16 . . . . .182 A1
W8 . . . . 113 D3 255 D5
Stanford St SW1 . . . . 259 C3
Stanford Way SW16 . 181 D1
Stangate SE1 . . . . 261 C5
Stangate Cres WD6 . . .11 C6
Stangate Gdns HA7 . .25 B6
Stangate Lo N21 . . . . . .16 B4
Stangate Mansi
TW1 . . . . 152 D1
Stanger Rd SE25 . . . . 206 A5
Stanhope Ave
Harrow HA3 . . . . .24 B2
Hayes BR2 . . . . 209 A1
Hendon N3 . . . . .47 B6
Stanhope Cl 28
SE16 . . . . .118 D4
Stanhope Ct N3 . . . . . . 29 B1
Stanhope Gate W1 . . 248 B4
Stanhope Gdns
Crouch End N6 . . . . .49 C3
Dagenham RM8 . . . . . . .81 B5
Edgware NW7 . . . . .27 D5
Ilford IG1 . . . . .56 B4
Stoke Newington N4 . . .51 A3
SW7 . . . . .114 A2 256 B4

Stanhope Gr BR3 . . . . 207 B5
Stanhope Ho
Crouch End N6 . . . . .49 C3
6 Friern Barnet N11 . . .31 B6
8 Putney SW15 . . . . . 156 C6
SE8 . . . . 141 B5
Stanhope Mews E
SW7 . . . . .114 A2 256 B4
Stanhope Mews S
SW7 . . . . 256 B3
Stanhope Mews W
SW7 . . . . .114 A2 256 B4
Stanhope Par NW1 . . 232 A2
Stanhope Pl W2 . . . . . 237 C1
Stanhope Park Rd
UB6 . . . . .86 A3
Stanhope Pl W2 . . . . . 237 C1
Stanhope Prim Sch
UB6 . . . . .86 A3
Stanhope Rd
Barnet EN5 . . . . .12 D5
Crouch End N6 . . . . .49 C2
DA7 . . . . 147 A3
Dagenham RM8 . . . . . . .81 B5
North Finchley N12 . . . .30 A5
Sidcup DA15 . . . . 190 A6
Southall UB6 . . . . .86 A2
South Croydon CR0 . . 221 C5
Wallington SM5 . . . . . . 219 A1
Walthamstow E17 . . . . .53 D4
Stanhope Row W1 . . 248 C3
Stanhope St
NW1 . . . . .93 C4 232 A1
Stanhope Terr
W2 . . . . .114 B6 246 D6
Stanier Cl SW5 . . . . . 254 D1
Stanlake Mews 7
W12 . . . . 112 C5
Stanlake Rd W12 . . . . 112 C5
Stanlake Villas 7
W12 . . . . 112 C5
Stanley Ave
Barking IG11 . . . . 101 D5
Beckenham BR2, BR3 . 208 A6
Dagenham RM8 . . . . . . .59 B2
Greenford UB6 . . . . .86 A4
Wembley HA0 . . . . .66 A1
West Barnes KT3 . . . . 200 A4
Stanley Cl
Eltham SE9 . . . . 167 A3
SW8 . . . . 270 C5
Wembley HA0 . . . . .66 A1
Stanley Cohen Ho
EC1 . . . . 242 A5
Stanley Cres
W11 . . . . .113 B6 244 C6
Stanleycroft Cl TW7 . 130 C4
Stanley Ct
Belmont SM2 . . . . 217 D1
11 Ealing W5 . . . . .87 C2
Wallington SM5 . . . . . . 219 A1
Wimbledon SW19 . . . . 179 C4
Stanley Gardens Rd
TW11 . . . . 174 C5
Stanley Gdns
Bedford Pk W3 . . . . . . 111 C4
Cricklewood NW2 . . . . .68 C3
Mitcham CR4 . . . . 181 A4
W11 . . . . 244 C6
Wallington SM6 . . . . . . 219 C2
Stanley Glynn Ct
BR7 . . . . 188 C5
Stanley Gr
Clapham SW11 . . . . . . 137 A3
Thornton Heath CR0 . . 204 C3
Stanley Ho
5 Clapham SW8 . . . . . 137 D3
Leytonstone E11 . . . . . .54 C3
22 Poplar E14 . . . . . . .97 C1
Wembley HA0 . . . . .66 A1
Stanley Holloway Ct
E16 . . . . .99 A1
Stanley Inf Sch
KT11 . . . . 174 C6
Stanley Jun Sch
KT11 . . . . 174 C6
Stanley Mans SW10 . 266 B6
Upper Tooting SW17 . . 158 D2
Stanley Park Dr HA0 . .66 B1
Stanley Park High Sch
SM5 . . . . 219 A2
Stanley Park Inf Sch
SM5 . . . . 218 D1
Stanley Park Jun Sch
SM5 . . . . 218 D1
Stanley Park Rd SM5,
SM6 . . . . 219 A1

Stanley Rd
Acton Green W3 . . . . . 111 A3
Ashford TW15 . . . . 170 A5
Belmont SM2 . . . . 217 D1
BR6 . . . . 211 D1
Bromley BR2 . . . . 209 C5
Chingford E4 . . . . .20 B3
East Finchley N2 . . . . . .48 B6
Edmonton N9 . . . . .17 D2
Enfield EN1 . . . . .5 C2
Friern Barnet N11 . . . . .31 D5
Harringay N15 . . . . .50 D5
Harrow HA2 . . . . .64 A6
2 Hendon NW9 . . . . . . .46 A2
Ilford IG1 . . . . .79 B6
Isleworth TW3 . . . . 130 A1
Mill Meads E15 . . . . . . .98 B6
Mitcham CR4 . . . . 181 A3
Morden SM4 . . . . 201 C5
Mortlake SW14 . . . . . . 132 D1
Muswell Hill N10 . . . . . .31 B3
Northwood HA6 . . . . . . .22 A2
Plashet E12 . . . . 78 A3
Sidcup DA14 . . . . 168 A1
Southall UB1 . . . . 107 A6
Teddington TW11,
TW2 . . . . 174 C5
Thornton Heath CR0 . . 204 C3
Twickenham TW2 . . . . 152 B1
Wallington SM5 . . . . . . 219 A1
Walthamstow E10 . . . . .53 B5
Wembley HA0 . . . . .66 B2
Wimbledon SW19 . . . . 179 C4
Woodford E18 . . . . .36 D2
Stanley Sq SE14, SE8 . 141 B5
Stanley Studios
SW10 . . . . 266 B6
Stanley Terr 13 N19 . .72 A6
Stanliff Ho 8 E14 . . . . 119 C3
Stanmer St SW11 . . . 136 C3
STANMORE 25 A5
Stanmore Coll HA7 . . .25 C4
Stanmore Gdns
Richmond TW9 . . . . . . 132 B2
Sutton SM1 . . . . 218 A5
Stanmore Hill HA7 . . . .24 A6
Stanmore Ho 21
SW8 . . . . 137 D3
Stanmore Lo HA7 . . . . .25 B6
Stanmore Pl NW1 . . . 231 D6
Stanmore Rd
Harringay N15 . . . . .50 D5
Leytonstone E11 . . . . . .54 D1
Richmond TW9 . . . . . . 132 B2
Stanmore St
N1 . . . . .94 B4 233 C6
Stanmore Sta HA7 . . . .25 C6
Stanmore Terr 3
BR3 . . . . 185 C1
Stannard Cl E10 . . . . . .35 A4
Stannard Cotts 27 E1 . .96 C3
Stannard Ct SE6 . . . . . 163 D3
Stannard Mews E8 . . . .74 A2
Stannard Rd E8 . . . . . . .74 A2
Stannary Pl SE11 . . . . 261 B1
Stannary St
SE11 . . . . .116 C1 261 B1
Stannet Way SM6 . . . 219 C4
Stansbury Sq 3 W10 . .91 A4
Stansfeld Rd E6 . . . . . 100 A1
Stansfeld Rd E6 . . . . . 263 D3
Stansfield Rd
Cranford TW4, TW5 . . 128 B3
Stockwell SW9 . . . . . . 138 B2
Stansgate Rd RM10 . . .81 C5
Stanstead Cl BR2 . . . . 208 D3
Stanstead Gr SE23 . . . 163 B3
Stanstead Ho E3 . . . . . .98 A3
Stanstead Manor
SM1 . . . . 217 C2
Stanstead Rd
Forest Hill SE23,
SE6 . . . . 163 A3
Wanstead E11 . . . . .55 B4
Stansted Cres DA5 . . . 168 D3
**Stansted Express
Terminal E2** 243 A4
Stansted Rd TW6 . . . . 148 B5
Stanswood Gdns
SE5 . . . . 139 C5
Stanthorpe Cl SW16 . 182 A5
Stanthorpe Rd
SW16 . . . . 182 A5
Stanton Ave TW11 . . . 174 C4
Stanton Cl
Chessington KT19 . . . . 214 D3

Stanton Cl continued
North Cheam KT4 . . . . 200 D1
Stanton Ct 5 DA15 . . . 168 A1
Finchley N3 . . . . .29 C2
6 Stoke Newington N16 . 51 B2
Stanton Ho 9 SE10 . . 142 A6
Stanton Rd
Barnes SW13 . . . . 133 D3
Thornton Heath CR0 . . 205 A2
Wimbledon SW20 . . . . 178 D2
Sutton Sq SE26 . . . . . . 185 B6
Stanton Way SE26 . . . 185 B6
Stanway Ct 22 N1 . . . .95 D5
Stanway Gdns
Acton W3 . . . . 110 C5
Edgware HA8 . . . . .27 A5
Stanway St N1 . . . . .95 C5
STANWELL 148 A3
**Stanwell Fields CE Prim
Sch** TW15 . . . . 148 A4
Stanwell Rd
Ashford TW15 . . . . 170 A6
East Bedfont TW14, TW19,
TW6 . . . . 148 D4
Stanwell TW15 . . . . . . 148 A1
Stanwick Rd
W14 . . . . .113 B2 254 C3
Stanworth Ct TW5 . . . 129 C5
Stanworth St SE1 . . . . 253 D1
Stanyhurst SE23 . . . . . 163 A3
Stapenhill Rd HA0 . . . .65 B5
Staplefield Cl
Pinner HA5 . . . . .23 A3
3 Streatham SW2 . . . . 160 A3
Stapleford N17 . . . . . . .33 C1
Stapleford Ave IG2 . . . .57 C4
Stapleford Cl
Chingford E4 . . . . .20 A1
Kingston u T KT1 . . . . . 198 C6
Putney SW19 . . . . 157 A4
Stapleford Rd HA0 . . . .65 D1
Stapleford Way
IG11 . . . . 102 B4
Staplehurst Ct 1
SW11 . . . . 158 D5
Staplehurst Ho 18 E5 . .74 B3
Staplehurst Rd
Lewisham SE13 . . . . . . 164 C6
Sutton SM5 . . . . 218 C1
Staple Inn WC2 . . . . . . 241 A3
Staple Inn Bldgs
WC2 . . . . 241 A3
Staples Cl SE16 . . . . . . 119 A5
Staples Corner Bsns Pk
NW2 . . . . .46 B1
Staples Corner (East)
NW2 . . . . .46 B1
Staples Corner Ret Pk
NW2 . . . . .46 B1
Staples Corner (West)
NW2 . . . . .46 B1
Staple St SE1 . . 117 B4 252 D1
Stapleton Gdns CR0 . . 220 C3
Stapleton Hall N4 . . . . .50 B2
Stapleton Hall Rd N4 . .50 B2
Stapleton Ho 10 E2 . . . .96 B4
Stapleton Rd
Orpington BR6 . . . . 227 D5
Upper Tooting SW17 . . 159 A1
Stapley Rd DA17 . . . . . 125 C1
Stapylton Rd EN5 . . . . . .1 A2
Star Alley EC3 . . . . 253 B6
Star and Garter Hill
TW10 . . . . 154 A4
Starboard Way E14 . . . 119 C3
Starbuck Cl SE9 . . . . . . 166 C4
Star Cl EN3 . . . . 18 C5
Starcross St
NW1 . . . . .93 C4 232 B2
Stardome * NW1 . . . . . 230 A5
Starfield Rd W12 . . . . . 112 A4
Star & Garter Mans 6
SW15 . . . . 134 D2
Starks Field Prim Sch
N9 . . . . .17 C2
Star La E16 . . . . .98 C3
Starliner Ct N7 . . . . .72 C2
Starling Cl
Beckenham BR3 . . . . . 207 B3
Buckhurst Hill IG9 . . . . .21 A3
Pinner HA5 . . . . .40 C6
Starling Ct E13 . . . . 99 B6
Starling Ho NW8 . . . . . 230 A4
Starling Wlk TW12 . . . 173 A5
Starmans Cl RM9 . . . . 103 A6

Star Path UB5 . . . . .85 C5
Star Pl E1 . . . . 118 A6
Star Prim Sch E16 . . . . .98 C3
Star Rd
Hillingdon UB10 . . . . . . .83 A3
Hounslow TW7 . . . . . . 130 B3
W14 . . . . 113 B1 254 C1
Star St W2 . . . . .92 C1 237 A2
Starts Cl BR6 . . . . 226 C5
Starts Hill Ave BR6 . . . 226 D4
Starts Hill Rd BR6 . . . . 226 D4
Starveall Cl UB7 . . . . . . 104 B3
Star Works NW10 . . . . . .90 A4
Star Yd WC2 . . . . 94 C1 241 A2
State Farm Ave BR6 . . 227 A4
Stateland Ct 10 N11 . . .31 B6
Staten Gdns TW1 . . . . 152 D3
Statham Ct N7 . . . . .72 A5
Statham Gr
Edmonton N18 . . . . .33 C5
Stoke Newington N16 . .73 B5
Statham Ho SW8 . . . . . 269 A2
Station App
Ashford TW15 . . . . 170 B6
Belmont SM2 . . . . 217 A1
Bexleyheath DA7 . . . . . 147 A4
Chislehurst BR7 . . . . . 188 C1
Dagenham RM10 . . . . . .89 A4
Elmstead BR7 . . . . 188 A4
20 Finchley N12 . . . . . .29 D6
Forest Gate E7 . . . . 77 B4
Friern Barnet N11 . . . . .31 B5
Fulham SW6 . . . . 135 A2
Greenford UB6 . . . . .64 B1
Hampton TW12 . . . . . . 173 C2
Harrow HA1 . . . . .42 C2
Hayes BR2 . . . . 209 A1
Hayes Town UB3 . . . . . 105 D3
Hinchley Wood KT10 . . 212 D5
4 Kingston u T KT1,
KT2 . . . . 176 C2
Lewisham SE3 . . . . 143 B2
Mottingham SE9 . . . . . 166 B3
New Barnet EN5 . . . . 2 A1
6 New Malden KT4 . . . 200 A1
Orpington BR6 . . . . 227 D6
Penge SE26 . . . . 185 B5
Pinner HA5 . . . . .41 A6
Richmond TW9 . . . . . . 132 C4
Ruislip HA4 . . . . .39 D1
Shepperton TW17 . . . . 193 A4
3 South Croydon
CR0 . . . . 221 B6
South Ruislip HA4 . . . . .62 B3
Streatham SW16 . . . . . 181 D5
Sunbury TW16 . . . . 172 A2
1 Surbiton KT6 . . . . . . 198 A3
Walthamstow E17 . . . . .53 C4
Wanstead E11 . . . . .55 A4
Welling DA16 . . . . 146 A3
Wembley HA0 . . . . .65 B2
22 Woodford E18 . . . . .37 B1
Woodford IG8 . . . . .37 B4
Woodford IG9 . . . . .37 D5
Worcester Pk KT19 . . . 216 A3
Yiewsley UB7 . . . . 104 A5
Station Approach Rd
W4 . . . . 133 A5
Station Ave
5 Brixton SW9 . . . . . . 138 D2
Kingston u T KT3 . . . . . 199 C6
14 Richmond TW9 . . . 132 C4
West Ewell KT19 . . . . . 215 D1
Station Bldgs
Catford SE6 . . . . 163 D6
Merton SW20 . . . . 178 C1
Station Blgs W5 . . . . . 110 B5
Station Cl Finchley N3 . .29 C2
Hampton TW12 . . . . . . 173 C2
Station Cres
Ashford TW15 . . . . 170 A6
Greenwich SE3 . . . . . . 121 A1
Tottenham N15 . . . . . . .51 B5
Wembley HA0 . . . . .65 B2
Station Ct
Mitcham CR4 . . . . 202 C5
5 Nunhead SE15 . . . . . 140 C3
South Tottenham N15 . .51 D4
Wembley Park HA9 . . . .43 C1
Stationers Hall Ct
EC4 . . . . 241 D1
Station Est BR3 . . . . . . 206 D5
Station Est 1 E18 . . . . . .37 B1
Station Estate Rd
TW14 . . . . 150 B3
Station Gdns W4 . . . . . 133 A5

Station Gr HA0 66 A2
Station Hill BR2 225 A6
Station House Mews N9 34 A6
Station Mans 9 N3 29 C2
Station Mews Terr 4 SE3 121 A1
Station Par Acton W3 88 C1
1 Ashford TW15 170 B6
Barking IG11 79 A1
Belmont HA3 25 A1
Cockfosters EN4 3 A1
Cricklewood NW2 68 C2
Dagenham RM10 81 C2
Ealing W5 110 B5
Edgware HA8 26 A3
Feltham TW14 150 B4
Northolt UB5 63 D4
4 Osidge N14 15 D3
Richmond TW9 132 C4
Ruislip HA4 61 B6
South Harrow HA2 63 D4
4 Upper Tooting SW12 159 A3
2 Wanstead E11 55 A4
Woodford IG9 37 D6
Station Pas
New Cross Gate SE15 140 C4
Woodford E18 37 B1
Station Pl N4 72 C6
Station Rd
Ashford TW15 170 B6
Barkingside IG6 57 B6
Barnes SW13 133 D3
Beckenham BR2 186 C1
Belvedere DA17 125 C3
Bexleyheath DA7 147 A2
Bromley BR1 187 A2
Camden Town N19 71 C5
Carshalton SM5 218 D4
Chadwell Heath RM6 58 D2
Chessington KT9 214 A3
Chingford E4 20 B3
Church End N3 29 C1
Claygate KT10 212 C3
Croydon CR0 205 A1
Edgware HA8 26 C4
Edgware NW7 27 C4
Esher KT10 212 B6
Forest Gate E7 77 A4
Friern Barnet N11 31 B5
Greenhill HA1 42 D4
Hampton TW12 173 D2
Hampton Wick KT1 175 D2
Hanwell W7 108 C5
Harlesden NW10 89 D5
Hayes UB3 105 C2
Hendon NW4 46 A4
Hounslow TW3 129 D1
Ilford IG1 78 D5
Kingston u T KT2 176 C2
Lewisham SE13 142 A2
Leyton E10 76 A5
Manor Pk E12 78 A4
Merton SW19 180 A2
New Barnet EN5 13 D6
North Harrow HA1, HA2 41 D4
Orpington BR6 227 D6
Penge SE20 184 C4
Shepperton TW17 193 A4
Sidcup DA14, DA15 168 A1
Southgate N21 16 D3
South Norwood SE25 205 D5
Sunbury TW16 172 A3
Teddington TW11 175 A4
Thames Ditton KT7 196 D2
Tottenham Hale N17 52 A6
Twickenham TW1 152 D4
Walthamstow E17 53 A4
West Acton W5 88 B1
West Barnes KT3 200 B4
West Drayton UB7 104 A4
West Wickham BR4 208 A1
Wood Green N22 32 B1
Station Rd N DA17 125 D3
Station Rise SE27 160 D2
Station Sq BR5 211 A4
Station St
Newham E16 122 D5
Stratford E15 76 B1
Station Terr
Camberwell SE5 139 A4
Kensal Rise NW10 90 D5
Station View UB6 86 B6
Station Way
Cheam SM2, SM3 217 A1
Claygate KT10 212 C2
Woodford IG9 37 D6
Station Yd TW1 153 A4
Staton Ct 1 E10 53 D2
Staunton Ho SE17 263 A3
Staunton Rd KT2 176 B3
Staunton St SE8 141 B6
Staveley NW1 232 A2
Staveley Cl
Hackney E9 74 C3
Lower Holloway N7 72 A4
New Cross Gate SE15 140 C4
8 Peckham SE15 140 B4
Staveley Ct 4 E11 55 A4
Staveley Gdns W4 133 B4
Staveley Ho SE4 163 A6
Staveley Rd
Ashford TW15 171 B4
Chiswick W4 133 B5
Stavers Ho 31 E3 97 B5
Staverton Rd NW2 68 C1
Stave Yard Rd SE16 119 A5
Stavordale Lo W14 254 D6
Stavordale Rd
Carshalton SM5 202 A2
Highbury N5 72 D4
Stayner's Rd E1 96 D3
Stayton Rd SM1 217 C5
Steadfast Rd KT1 175 D2
Steadman Ct EC1 242 B6
Steadman Ho 4 RM10 81 C5
Stead St SE17 117 B2 262 C3
Steam Farm La TW14 127 D1
Stean St E8 95 D6
Stebbing Ho 8 W11 112 D5
Stebbing Way IG11 102 A5
Stebondale St E14 120 A2
Stebon Prim Sch 26 E14 97 C2
Stedham Pl WC1 240 A2
Stedman Cl UB10 60 C5
Steedman St SE17 117 A2 262 A3
Steeds Rd N10 30 D2
Steel App IG11 102 B5
Steele Rd
Acton Green W4 111 A3
Becontree NW10 89 A5
Isleworth TW7 131 A1
Leyton E11 76 C4
Tottenham N17 51 C6
Steele's Mews N NW3 70 D2
Steele's Mews S NW3 70 D2
Steele's Rd NW3 70 D2
Steele Wlk DA8 147 D5
Steel's La 23 E1 96 C1
Steen Way 7 SE22 161 C6
Steep Cl BR6 227 D2
Steep Hill
South Croydon CR0 221 C4
Streatham SW16 159 D1
Steeple Cl
Fulham SW6 135 A3
Wimbledon SW19 179 A5
Steeple Ct
19 Bethnal Green E1 96 B3
Wimbledon SW19 179 A5
Steeplestone Cl N18 33 A5
Steepleton Ct E11 54 A1
Steeple Wlk N1 235 B6
Steerforth St SW18 158 A2
Steering Cl N9 18 C3
Steers Mead CR4 180 D2
Steers Way SE16 119 A4
Steetley Ct 14 SM2 218 A1
Steinman Ct TW7 130 D2
Stelfax Ho WC1 233 D2
Stella Cl UB8 82 D2
Stella Rd SW17 180 D4
Stellar Ho 4 N17 33 D4
Stellman Cl E5 74 A5
Stembridge Rd SE20 184 B1
Sten Cl 12 EN3 7 C6
Stephan Cl E8 96 A6
Stephen Cl BR6 227 D5
Stephen Ct 18 SW19 156 D3
Stephendale Rd SW6 136 A3
Stephen Fox Ho 7 W4 111 C1
Stephen Hawking Sch 23 E14 97 A1
Stephen Mews W1 239 C3
Stephen Pl SW4 137 C2
Stephen Saunders Ct SW11 158 C6
Stephens Collection The★ N3 29 C1
Stephens Ct
Brockley SE4 141 A2
E16 98 D3
Stephens Lo N12 14 A1
Stephenson Ct SM2 217 B1
Stephenson Ho
2 Gospel Oak NW5 71 B4
6 Maitland Pk NW3 70 D3
Newington SE1 262 A6
West Heath SE2 124 D1
Stephenson Rd
Ealing W7 86 D1
Twickenham TW4 151 C4
Walthamstow E17 53 A4
Stephenson St
Dagenham NW10 89 D4
Newham E16 98 C2
Stephenson Way NW1 93 C3 239 B6
Stephen's Rd E15 98 C6
Stephen St W1 239 C3
STEPNEY 96 D2
Stepney City E1 96 C2
Stepney Cswy E1 96 D1
Stepney Gn E1 96 D2
Stepney Greencoat CE Prim Sch The 26 E14 97 B1
Stepney Green Ct 4 E1 96 D2
Stepney Green Maths & Computing Coll 18 E1 96 D2
Stepney Green Sta E1 96 D3
Stepney High St E1 96 D2
Stepney Way
Mitcham CR4 181 A2
Stepney E1 96 C2
Stepping Stones Farm★ E1 96 D2
Sterling Ave HA8 26 B6
Sterling Cl NW10 68 A1
Sterling Gdns SE14 141 A6
Sterling Ho SE9 143 B1
Sterling Ind Est RM10 81 D4
Sterling Pl W5 110 A2
Sterling Rd EN2 5 B5
Sterling St SW7 257 B6
Sterling Way (North Circular Rd) N18 33 C5
Stern Cl IG11 102 C5
Sterndale Rd W14 112 D3
Sterne St W12 112 D4
Sternhall La SE15 140 A2
Sternhold Ave SW12, SW2 159 D2
Sterry Cres RM10 81 C3
Sterry Dr
Thames Ditton KT7 196 C3
Worcester Pk KT19 215 C4
Sterry Gdns RM10 81 C2
Sterry Rd
Barking IG11 101 D6
Dagenham RM10 81 C3
Sterry St SE1 252 C1
Steucers La SE23 163 A3
Stevanne Ct 1 DA17 125 C1
Steve Biko Ct W10 90 D3
Steve Biko La SE6 185 C6
Steve Biko Lodge 13 E13 99 A5
Steve Biko Rd N7 72 C5
Steve Biko Way TW3 129 C2
Stevedale Rd DA16 146 C3
Stevedore St 3 E1 118 B5
Stevenage Rd
Fulham SW6 134 D4
Wallend E6 78 C2
Stevens Ave E9 74 C2
Stevens Cl
Beckenham BR3 185 C4
Hampton TW12 173 B4
Pinner HA5 40 C4
Stevens Ct BR3 185 C4
Stevens Gn WD23 8 A3
Stevens Ho KT1 175 D1
Stevens' La KT10 213 A2
Stevenson Cl EN5 14 B4
Stevenson Cres SE16 118 B1
Stevenson Ho
1 Battersea SW11 136 D3
6 Clapham Pk SW2 160 A6
NW8 229 A6
Wembley HA9 65 D6
Stevens Rd RM8 80 C5
Stevens St SE1 263 B6
Steventon Rd W12 111 D6
Stewards Holte Wlk 3 N11 31 B6
Stewart Ave TW17 192 C5
Stewart Cl BR7 188 D6
Hampton TW12 173 A4
Kingsbury NW9 45 A3
Stewart Fleming Prim Sch SE20 206 C6
Stewart Headlam Prim Sch 28 E1 96 B3
Stewart Ho SE1 263 A5
Stanmore HA7 25 B5
Stewart Quay UB3 105 C4
Stewart Rainbird Ho 1 E12 78 C3
Stewart Rd E15 76 B4
Stewartsby Cl N18 33 A5
Stewart's Gr SW3 114 C1 257 A2
Stewart's Rd SW8 137 C4 269 A2
Stewart St E14 120 A4
Stew La EC4 252 A6
Steyne Ho
15 Acton W3 110 D5
11 Acton W3 111 A5
Steyne Rd W3 110 D5
Steyning Gr SE9 188 B6
Steynings Way N12 29 C5
Steyning Way TW4 128 C1
Steynton Ave DA5 168 D2
Stickland Rd DA17 125 C2
Stickleton Cl UB6 85 D4
Stifford Ho E1 96 C2
Stilecroft Gdns HA0 65 B5
Stile Hall Gdns W4 110 C1
Stile Hall Par 6 W4 110 C1
Stileman Ho 4 E3 97 B2
Stile Path TW16 194 A5
Stiles Cl BR2 210 B3
Erith DA8 125 D1
Stillingfleet Rd SW13 134 A6
Stillington St SW1 115 C2 259 B4
Stillness Jun & Inf Schs SE23 163 A5
Stillness Rd SE23 163 B5
Stilwell Dr UB8 82 B3
Stilwell Rdbt UB8 104 D6
Stipularis Dr UB4 84 D3
Stirling Ave
Pinner HA5 41 A2
Upper Halliford TW17 193 C6
Wallington SM6 220 A1
Stirling Cl
Sidcup DA14 189 D6
Streatham SW16 181 C2
Stirling Cnr EN5, WD6 11 B5
Stirling Ct
Clerkenwell EC1 241 C6
Ealing W13 109 B6
Strand WC2 240 C1
Stirling Gr TW3 130 A3
Stirling Ho 5 SE18 122 D1
Stirling Ind Ctr WD6 11 B6
Stirling Lo 7 EN5 14 A6
Stirling Mans NW6 70 A2
Stirling Rd
Harrow HA3 42 D6
Hayes UB3 106 B6
Newham E13 99 B5
South Acton W3 110 D3
Stanwell TW19, TW6 148 B5
Stockwell SW9 138 A3
Tottenham N17 34 A2
Twickenham TW2 151 D4
Walthamstow E17 53 A6
Wood Green N22 32 D2
Stirling Ret Pk WD6 11 B5
Stirling Way
Borehamwood WD6 11 B6
Thornton Heath CR0 204 A2
Stiven Cres HA2 63 B5
Stoatley Ho 10 SW15 156 A3
Stockbeck NW1 232 B3
Stockbridge Ho EN2 4 D3
Stockbury Rd CR0 206 C3
Stockdale Rd RM8 81 B6
Stockdove Way UB6 86 D4
Stocker Gdns RM9 80 C1
Stockfield Rd
Claygate KT10 212 C3
Streatham SW16 160 B1
Stockford Ave NW7 28 D3
Stockholm Ho E1 118 A6
Stockholm Rd SE16 118 C1
Stockholm Way E1 118 A5
Stockhurst Cl SW15 134 D3
Stockingswater La EN3 7 B2
Stockleigh Hall NW8 230 B4
Stockley Acad UB8 82 B1
Stockley Cl UB7 104 D4
Stockley Ctry Pk UB7 104 C6
Stockley Farm Rd UB7 104 D3
Stockley Park Bsns Pk UB11 105 A5
Stockley Rd UB7, UB8, UB11 104 D4
Stock Orchard Cres N7 72 B3
Stock Orchard St N7 72 B3
Stockport Rd SW16 181 D2
Stocks Ct 5 E1 96 D3
Stocksfield Rd E17 54 A6
Stocks Pl
Hillingdon UB10 82 C6
16 Limehouse E14 119 B6
Stock St E13 99 A5
Stockton Cl EN5 2 A1
Stockton Gdns
Edgware NW7 11 C1
Tottenham N17 33 A3
Stockton Ho 16 E2 96 B4
Harrow HA2 41 C1
Stockton Rd
Edmonton N18 34 B4
Tottenham N17 33 A3
STOCKWELL 138 A2
Stockwell Ave SW9 138 B2
Stockwell Cl BR1 187 B1
Stockwell Gdns SW9 138 B4 270 C1
Stockwell Gn SW9 138 B3
Stockwell La SW9 138 B3
Stockwell Park Cres SW9 138 B3
Stockwell Park Rd SW9 138 B4 270 D1
Stockwell Park Sch SW9 138 B4 270 C1
Stockwell Park Wlk SW9 138 C2
Stockwell Prim Sch 6 SW9 138 B2
Stockwell Rd SW9 138 B3
Stockwell St SE10 142 A6
Stockwell Sta SW4 138 A3
Stockwell Terr SW9 270 C1
Stodart Rd SE20 184 C2
Stoddart Ho SW8 270 D5
Stodmarsh Ho 28 SW9 138 C4
Stofield Gdns SE9 165 D1
Stoford Cl 4 SW19 157 A4
Stokenchurch St SW6 135 D4 265 C1
STOKE NEWINGTON 73 C6
Stoke Newington Church St N16 73 C6
Stoke Newington Comm N16 73 D6
Stoke Newington High St N16 73 D5
Stoke Newington Rd N16 73 D4
Stoke Newington Sch N16 73 B5

Stoke Newington Sta N16 73 D6
Stoke Pl NW10 89 D4
Stoke Rd KT2 177 A3
Stokesby Rd KT9 214 B2
Stokes Ct N2 48 C5
Stokesley St W12 89 D1
Stokes Rd
Croydon CR0 206 D3
Newham E6 100 A3
Stokley Ct N8 50 A5
Stoll Cl NW2 68 C5
Stoms Path SE6 185 C5
Stonard Rd
Dagenham RM8 80 B4
Palmers Green N13 16 C1
Stondon Pk SE23 163 A5
Stondon Wlk [4] E6 99 D5
Stonebanks KT12 194 A2
Stone Bldgs WC2 94 B2 240 D3
STONEBRIDGE 89 A6
Stonebridge Ct [9] NW10 67 B1
Stonebridge Ctr [6] NW10 89 B6
Stonebridge Ctr The N15 52 A4
Stonebridge Park HA9 66 D1
Stonebridge Park Sta NW10 66 D1
Stonebridge Pk NW10 67 B1
Stonebridge Prim Sch NW10 89 B6
Stonebridge Rd N15 51 D4
Stonebridge Way HA9 66 D2
Stonechat Sq [6] E6 100 A2
Stone Cl
Clapham SW4 137 C3
Dagenham RM8 81 B6
Yiewsley UB7 104 B5
Stonecot Cl SM3 201 A1
Stonecot Hill SM3 201 A1
Stone Cres TW14 149 D4
Stonecroft Way CR0 204 A2
Stonecrop Cl NW9 45 B6
Stone Ct
Southgate N21 16 B6
[4] Stratford E15 76 D1
Stonecutter St EC4 241 C2
Stonefield N4 72 B6
Stonefield Cl DA7 147 C2
Ruislip HA4 63 A3
Stonefield Mans N1 234 A5
Stonefield St N1 94 C6 234 B6
Stonefield Way
Ruislip HA4 63 A3
SE7 143 D5
Stonegate [8] NW5 71 A2
Stone Gr HA8 26 B5
Stone Grove Ct HA8 26 B5
Stonegrove Gdns HA8 26 A5
Stonegrove Ho HA8 26 B5
Stonehall Ave IG1 56 A3
Stone Hall Rd N21 16 C4
Stoneham Rd N11 31 C5
Stonehaven BR3 185 D1
Stonehill Bsns Pk N18 34 D5
Stonehill Cl SW14 155 B6
Stonehill Ct E4 19 D4
Stonehill Rd
Brentford W4 110 C1
Mortlake SW14 155 B6
Stonehills Ct SE21 161 C1
Stonehill's Mans [3] SW16 160 A2
Stonehill Woods Pk DA14 191 D4
Stonehorse Rd EN3 18 C6
Stonehouse NW1 232 B5
Stonehouse Ct EC2 243 B2
Stonehouse Ho [27] W2 91 C2
Stone Lake Ind Pk SE7 121 C2
Stone Lake Ret Pk SE7 121 C2
STONELEIGH 216 A3
Stoneleigh Ave
Enfield EN1 6 B4
North Cheam KT17, KT4 216 A5
Stoneleigh Broadway KT17 216 A3
Stoneleigh Cres KT19 215 D3
Stoneleigh Ct
Redbridge IG5 56 A6
[6] Tottenham N17 33 D1
Stoneleigh Fst Sch KT17 216 B4
Stoneleigh Lo [13] TW9 132 B4
Stoneleigh Mews [15] E3 97 A5
Stoneleigh Park Ave CR0 206 D3
Stoneleigh Park Rd KT19, KT4 216 A3
Stoneleigh Pl W11 112 D6
Stoneleigh Rd
Bromley BR1 210 D6
Carshalton SM5 202 C2
Redbridge IG5 56 B6
Tottenham N17 33 D1
Stoneleigh St W11 112 D6
Stoneleigh Sta KT19 216 A3
Stoneleigh Terr N19 71 B6
Stonell's Rd SW11 158 D6
Stonemasons Cl N15 51 B5
Stonenest St N4 50 B1
Stone Park Ave BR3 207 D5
Stone Pl KT4 216 A6
Stone Rd BR2 208 D4
Stones End St SE1 252 A1
Stonewall E6 100 C2
Stoneworth Ct SE25 206 A3
Stoneyard La E14 119 D6
Stoneycroft Cl SE12 164 D4
Stoney Deep TW11 175 A6
Stoneydown E17 53 A5
Stoneydown Ave E17 53 A5
Stoneydown Ho [2] E17 53 A5
Stoneydown Park Sch [5] E17 53 A5
Stoneyfields Gdns HA8 27 A6
Stoneyfields La HA8 27 A6
Stoney La EC3 243 B2
Penge SE19 183 D4
Stoney St SE1 117 B5 252 C4
Stonhouse St SW4 137 D1
Stonor Rd W14 113 B2 254 C3
Stonycroft Cl EN3 7 A3
Stopes St SE15 139 D5
Stopford Rd
Newham E13 99 A6
SE17 261 D1
Stopher Ho SE1 251 D1
Storace Ho [6] SW4 138 A1
Store Rd E16 122 C4
Storers Quay E14 120 B2
Store St
Bloomsbury WC1 93 D2 239 C4
Stratford New Town E15 76 B3
Storey Ct NW8 229 C1
Storey Ctr The E16 122 C5
Storey Ho [13] E14 119 D6
Storey Rd Highgate N6 48 D3
Walthamstow E17 53 B5
Storey's Gate SW1 115 D4 249 D1
Storey St E16 122 C4
Stories Rd SE5 139 C2
Stork Rd E7 77 A2
Storksmead Rd HA8 27 C3
Storks Rd SE16 118 A3
Stormont House Sch E5 74 B4
Stormont Rd
Clapham SW11 137 A1
Highgate N6 48 D2
Stormont Way KT9 213 C3
Stormount Dr UB3 105 A4
Storrington WC1 233 B1
Storrington Rd CR0 205 D1
Story St N1 72 B1
Stotfold BR1 188 A2
Stothard Ho [25] E1 96 C3
Stothard Pl E2 243 B4
Stothard St [12] E1 96 C3
Stott Cl SW18 158 B5
Stoughton Ave SM3 217 A3
Stoughton Cl
Roehampton SW15 156 A3
SE11 260 D3
Stour Ave UB2 107 C3
Stourbridge Ho [8] UB5 85 B3
Stour Cl BR2 225 C4
Stourcliffe Cl W1 237 C2
Stourcliffe St W1 237 C1
Stour Ct UB1 86 B1
Stourhead Cl [6] SW19 156 D4
Stourhead Gdns SW20 200 A6
Stour Rd
Dagenham RM10 81 C6
Hackney Wick E3 75 C1
Stourton Ave TW13 173 B6
Stowage SE8 141 D6
Stow Cres E17 35 A3
Stowe Cres HA4 39 A3
Stowe Gdns N9 17 D3
Stowe Ho
Hampstead Garden Suburb NW11 48 A3
[11] Stoke Newington N16 73 C5
Stowell Ho [2] N8 50 A5
Stowe Rd W12 112 B4
Stowford Coll SM2 218 A1
Stowting Rd BR6 227 C4
Stox Mead HA3 24 B2
Stracey Rd
Becontree NW10 89 B6
Forest Gate E7 77 A4
Strachan Pl SW19, SW20 178 C4
Stradbroke Gr
Buckhurst Hill IG9 21 D3
Redbridge IG5 56 C6
Stradbroke Rd N5 73 A4
Stradbrook Cl HA2 63 B5
Stradella Rd SE24 161 A5
Straffan Lo [8] NW3 70 C2
Strafford Ho [9] SE8 119 B1
Strafford Rd
Acton W3 111 A4
Barnet EN5 1 A2
Hounslow TW3 129 B2
Twickenham TW1 153 A4
Strafford St E14 119 C4
Strahan Rd E3 97 A4
Straightsmouth SE10 142 A5
Straight The UB2 107 A4
Strait Rd E6 122 B6
Straker's Rd SE15 140 B1
Strale Ho [17] N1 95 C6
STRAND 116 B6
Strand
Strand WC2 116 B6 250 C6
Strand WC2 240 D1
Strand Ct SE18 123 D1
Strand Dr TW9 132 D5
Strandfield Cl SE18 123 C1
Strand Ho SE28 123 B5
Strand La WC2 250 D6
STRAND ON THE GREEN 132 C6
Strand-on-the-Green W4 132 C6
Strand-on-the-Green Schs [5] W4 132 C6
Strand Pl N18 33 C6
Strang Ho N1 235 A5
Strangways Terr W14 254 C5
Stranraer Way
Barnsbury N1 72 A1
[1] Stanwell TW6 148 A5
Strasburg Rd SW11 137 B4 268 C1
Stratfield Ho SE12 165 A2
Stratfield Park Cl N21 16 D4
STRATFORD 76 A2
Stratford Ave UB10 82 B5
Stratford Bus Sta E15 76 B1
Stratford Cl IG11 80 A1
Stratford Coll (Newham 6th Form Coll) E15 76 B2
Stratford Ct KT3 199 B5
Stratford Gr SW15 134 D1
Stratford House Ave BR1 210 A6
Stratford International Sta E15 76 A2
STRATFORD MARSH 97 D6
STRATFORD NEW TOWN 76 A3
Stratford Office Village The [1] E15 76 C1
Stratford Pl W1 238 C1
Stratford Rd
Harlington TW6 149 A6
Hayes UB4 84 B3
Hendon NW4 46 D5
Newham E13 99 A6
Southall UB2 107 A2
Thornton Heath CR7 204 D6
W8 113 C3 255 B5
Stratford Sch E7 77 A1
Stratford Sh Ctr E15 76 B1
Stratford Sta E15 76 B1
Stratford Studios W8 255 C5
Stratford Villas NW1 71 D1
Stratford Workshops E15 98 B6
Strathan Cl SW18 157 A5
Strathaven Rd SE12 165 B5
Strathblaine Rd SW11 136 B1
Strathbrook Rd SW16 182 B3
Strathcona Rd HA9 65 D6
Strathdale SW16 182 B5
Strathdon Dr SW17 158 B1
Strathearn Ave
Harlington UB3 127 D5
Twickenham TW2 152 A3
Strathearn Ho W2 247 A6
Strathearn Pl W2 114 C6 247 A6
Strathearn Rd
Sutton SM1 217 C3
Wimbledon SW19 179 C6
Stratheden Par SE3 143 A5
Stratheden Rd SE3 143 A5
Strathfield Gdns IG11 79 B2
Strathleven Rd SW2 160 A6
Strathmore Ct NW8 230 A2
Strathmore Gdns
Edgware HA8 26 D1
Finchley N3 29 D2
W8 245 B4
Strathmore Rd
Teddington TW11, TW2 174 C6
Thornton Heath CR0 205 B2
Wimbledon SW19 157 C1
Strathmore Sch TW10 153 D2
Strathnairn St SE1 118 A2
Strathray Gdns NW3 70 C2
Strath Terr SW11 136 C1
Strathville Rd SW18 157 D2
Strathyre Ave SW16 204 C6
Stratton Ave EN2 5 B6
Stratton Cl DA7 147 A2
Edgware HA8 26 B4
Heston TW5 129 C4
Merton SW19 179 C1
Walton-on-T KT12 194 C1
Stratton Ct
[4] De Beauvoir Town N1 73 C1
[10] Kingston u T KT6 198 A4
[10] Pinner HA5 23 B3
Strattondale St E14 120 A3
Stratton Dr IG11 79 D2
Stratton Gdns UB1 85 C1
Stratton Ho HA8 26 B6
Stratton Lo [10] EN5 1 D1
Stratton Rd DA7 147 A2
Merton SW19 179 C1
Sunbury TW16 171 D1
Stratton St W1 115 B5 248 D4
Strauss Rd W4 111 B4
Strawberry Fields BR6 226 D3
STRAWBERRY HILL 152 D1
Strawberry Hill Cl TW1 152 D1
Strawberry Hill Rd TW1 152 D1
Strawberry Hill Sta TW2 152 D1
Strawberry La SM5 219 A5
Strawberry Terr N10 30 D2
Strawberry Vale
Finchley N2 30 B2
Twickenham TW1 153 A1
Strayfield Rd EN2 4 D6
Streakes Field Rd NW2 68 A6
Streamdale SE2 146 B6
Stream La HA8 26 D5
Streamline Mews SE22 162 A3
Streamside Cl BR2 209 A5
Edmonton N9 17 D3
Stream Way DA17 147 C6
Streatfeild Ave E6 100 B6
Streatfield Rd HA3, HA7 43 D6
STREATHAM 182 A4
Streatham Cl SW16 160 A2
Streatham & Clapham High Sch SW16 159 D1
Streatham Common N SW16 182 B5
Streatham Common S SW16 182 B4
Streatham Common Sta SW16 181 D3
Streatham Ct SW16 160 A1
Streatham High Rd SW16, SW2 182 A5
STREATHAM HILL 160 A3
Streatham Hill SW2 160 A3
Streatham Hill & Clapham High Sch [14] SW2 160 B3
Streatham Hill Sta SW2 160 A2
Streatham L Ctr & Ice Arena SW16 181 D5
STREATHAM PARK 181 C6
Streatham Pl SW2 160 A4
Streatham Rd CR4 181 A2
Streatham St WC1 240 A2
Streatham Sta SW16 181 D5
STREATHAM VALE 181 D3
Streatham Vale SW16 181 D3
Streathbourne Rd SW17 159 A1
Streathem Wells Prim Sch SW2 160 C2
Streatleigh Par [4] SW16 160 A2
Streatley Pl
[27] Hampstead NW3 70 A4
Hampstead NW3 70 B4
Streatley Rd NW6 69 B1
Streeters La SM6 219 D5
Streetfield Mews SE3 143 A2
Streimer Rd E15 98 A5
Strelley Way W3 111 C6
Stretford Ct [1] SW19 179 A3
Stretton Lo W13 109 B6
Stretton Mans [16] SE8 141 C6
Stretton Rd
Croydon CR0 205 C2
Richmond TW10 153 C2
Strickland Ct SE15 140 A2
Strickland Ho [26] E2 95 D4
Strickland Row SW18 158 B4
Strickland St SE8 141 C4
Strickland Way [4] BR6 227 D4
Stride Rd E13 98 D5
Strimon Cl N9 18 C2
Stringer Hos [19] N1 95 C6
Strode Cl N10 31 A3
Strode Ho [3] SW2 160 C3
Strode Rd
Forest Gate E7 77 A4
SW6 135 A5 264 A4
Tottenham N17 33 C1
Willesden NW10 68 A2
Strome Ho NW6 91 D5
Strone Rd E7, E12 77 D2
Strone Way UB4 85 A3

Strongbow Cres SE9 . . 166 B6
Strongbow Rd SE9 . . 166 B6
Strongbridge Cl HA2 . . 41 C1
Stronsa Rd W12 . . 111 D4
Strood Ho
9 Penge SE20 . . 184 C3
SE1 . . 252 D1
Stroud Cres SW15 . . 156 A1
Stroudes Cl KT4 . . 199 D2
Stroud Field UB5 . . 63 A2
Stroud Gate HA2 . . 63 D4
STROUD GREEN . . 50 C3
Stroud Green Gdns
CR0 . . 206 C2
Stroud Green Prim Sch
N4 . . 50 C1
Stroud Green Rd N4 . . 50 C1
Stroud Green Way
CR0 . . 206 C3
Stroudley Ho SW8 . . 269 B2
Stroudley Wlk E3 . . 97 D4
Stroud Rd
Croydon SE25 . . 206 A3
Wimbledon SW19 . . 157 C1
Strouds Cl RM6 . . 58 B4
Stroud Way TW15 . . 171 A4
Strout's Pl 2 E2 . . 95 D4
Struan Ho 15 E11 . . 55 A4
Strudwick Ct SW4 . . 270 B1
Strutton Ground
SW1 . . 115 D3 259 C5
Strype St E1 . . 243 C3
Stuart Ave Ealing W5 . . 110 B4
Harrow HA2 . . 63 B5
Hayes BR2 . . 209 A1
Hendon NW9 . . 46 A2
Walton-on-T KT12 . . 194 B1
Stuart Cl UB10 . . 60 C2
Stuart Cres
Croydon CR0 . . 223 B5
Hayes UB3 . . 83 A1
Wood Green N22 . . 32 B2
Stuart Ct Chingford E4 . . 20 D2
6 Croydon CR0 . . 220 D5
2 Elstree WD6 . . 9 D5
Stuart Evans Cl
DA16 . . 146 C2
Stuart Gr TW11 . . 174 C5
Stuart Ho
Hammersmith W6 . . 112 C3
1 Homerton E9 . . 74 D1
Queensbury NW9 . . 44 C5
5 Stockwell SW4 . . 138 A1
W14 . . 254 A4
Stuart Lo SE25 . . 183 C1
Stuart Mill Ho N1 . . 233 C3
Stuart Pl CR4 . . 180 D2
Stuart Rd Acton W3 . . 111 A5
Barking IG11 . . 79 D1
DA16 . . 146 B4
East Barnet EN4 . . 14 D4
Harrow HA3 . . 42 D6
Maida Vale NW6 . . 91 C4
Nunhead SE15 . . 140 C1
Richmond TW10 . . 153 B1
South Norwood CR7 . . 205 A5
Wimbledon SW19 . . 157 C1
Stubbs Cl NW9 . . 45 A4
Stubbs Dr SE16 . . 118 B1
Stubbs Ho
Finsbury Pk N4 . . 50 B1
1 Globe Town E2 . . 96 D4
Stubbs Mews RM8 . . 80 B4
Stubbs Point E13 . . 99 B3
Stubbs Way SW19 . . 180 B2
Stucley Pl 19 NW1 . . 71 B1
Stucley Rd TW5,
TW7 . . 130 A5
Studdridge St SW6 . . 135 C3
Studd St N1 . . 94 D6 234 C6
Studholme Ct NW3 . . 69 C4
Studholme St SE15 . . 140 B5
Studio Mews 5 NW4 . . 46 C5
Studio Pl SW1 . . 247 D1
Studios NW8 . . 229 A4
Studios Rd TW17 . . 192 B6
Studios The
4 Clapham SW4 . . 137 C1
SW8 . . 269 D1
Studland SE17 . . 262 C2
Studland Cl DA15 . . 167 D1
Studland Ho E14 . . 97 A1
Studland Rd
Ealing W7 . . 86 C1
Forest Hill SE26 . . 184 D5
Kingston u T KT2 . . 176 A4
Studland St W6 . . 112 B2
Studley Ave E4 . . 36 B3
Studley Cl E5 . . 75 A3
Studley Ct
13 Blackwall E14 . . 120 B6
DA14 . . 190 B5
Redbridge IG4 . . 55 D3
Studley Dr IG4 . . 55 D3
Studley Grange Rd
W7 . . 108 D4
Studley Rd
Dagenham RM9 . . 80 D1
South Lambeth SW4 . . 138 A3
Upton E7 . . 77 B2
Study Prep Sch The
(Spencer House)
SW19 . . 178 D5
Study Prep Sch The
(Wilberforce House)
SW19 . . 178 C5
Study Sch The KT3 . . 199 C4
Stukeley Rd E7 . . 77 B1
Stukeley St
WC2 . . 94 A1 240 B2
Stumps Hill La BR3 . . 185 C4
Stunell Ho 23 SE14 . . 140 D6
Sturdee Ho 2 E2 . . 96 A5
Sturdy Ho 28 E3 . . 97 A5
Sturdy Rd SE15 . . 140 B3
Sturge Ave E17 . . 35 D1
Sturgeon Rd
SE17 . . 117 A1 262 A1
Sturges Field BR7 . . 189 B4
Sturgess Ave NW4 . . 46 B2
Sturge St
SE1 . . 117 A4 252 A2
Sturmer Way N7 . . 72 B3
Sturminster Cl UB4 . . 84 C1
Sturminster Ho SW8 . . 270 D3
Sturrock Cl N15 . . 51 B5
Sturry St E14 . . 97 D1
Sturt St N1 . . 235 B3
Stutfield St E1 . . 96 A1
Stuttle Ho 14 E1 . . 96 A3
Styles Gdns SW9 . . 138 D2
Styles Ho SE1 . . 251 C3
Styles Way BR3 . . 208 A5
Stylus Apartments 25
E1 . . 96 C1
Sudbourne Prim Sch 18
SW2 . . 160 B6
Sudbourne Rd SW2 . . 160 B6
Sudbrooke Rd SW12 . . 159 A5
Sudbrook Gdns
TW10 . . 154 A1
Sudbrook La TW10 . . 154 A2
SUDBURY . . 65 A4
Sudbury E6 . . 100 C1
Sudbury Ave HA0 . . 65 D4
Sudbury Court Dr
HA1 . . 65 A5
Sudbury Court Rd
HA1 . . 65 A5
Sudbury Cres BR1 . . 187 A5
Wembley HA0 . . 65 B3
Sudbury Croft HA0 . . 64 D4
Sudbury Ct
1 Ilford RM6 . . 58 B4
SW8 . . 269 D2
Sudbury Gdns CR0 . . 221 C4
Sudbury & Harrow Road
Sta HA0 . . 65 B3
Sudbury Heights Ave
UB6 . . 65 A3
Sudbury Hill HA1 . . 64 C5
Sudbury Hill Cl HA0 . . 64 D5
Sudbury Hill Harrow Sta
HA1 . . 64 C4
Sudbury Hill Sta HA1 . . 64 C4
Sudbury Ho SW18 . . 157 D6
Sudbury Prim Sch
HA0 . . 65 B4
Sudbury Rd IG11 . . 79 D3
Sudbury Town Sta
UB6 . . 65 B2
Sudeley St N1 . . 94 D5 234 D3
Sudlow Rd SW18 . . 157 C6
Sudrey St SE1 . . 252 A1
Suez Ave UB6 . . 86 D5
Suez Rd EN3 . . 7 A2
Suffah Prim Sch
TW3 . . 129 B1
Suffield Ho SE17 . . 261 D2
Suffield Rd
Chingford E4 . . 35 D6
Penge SE20 . . 184 C1
Suffield Rd *continued*
2 South Tottenham
N15 . . 51 D4
Suffolk Cl WD6 . . 11 B6
Suffolk Ct
3 Dagenham RM6 . . 58 C4
Ilford IG3 . . 57 C3
Walthamstow E17 . . 53 C2
3 West Norwood
SW16 . . 182 C6
Suffolk Ho
11 Acton W3 . . 88 C1
Beckenham BR2 . . 208 D5
8 Dartmouth Pk NW5 . . 71 C5
Edgware HA8 . . 26 B4
Penge SE20 . . 184 C2
4 South Croydon
CR0 . . 221 B6
Suffolk La EC4 . . 252 C6
Suffolk Park Rd E17 . . 53 A5
Suffolk Pl SW1 . . 249 D4
Suffolk Rd
Barking IG11 . . 79 B1
Barnes SW13 . . 134 A5
Dagenham RM10 . . 81 D3
Enfield EN3 . . 18 B6
Harrow HA2 . . 41 C4
Ilford IG3 . . 57 C3
4 Newham E13 . . 99 A4
Sidcup DA14 . . 190 C4
South Norwood SE25 . . 205 D5
Tottenham N15 . . 51 B3
Willesden NW10 . . 67 C1
Worcester Pk KT4 . . 215 D6
Suffolks Prim Sch EN1 . . 6 B3
Suffolk St
Forest Gate E7 . . 77 A4
SW1 . . 115 D5 249 D4
Sugar House La E15 . . 98 A5
Sugar Loaf Wlk 6 E2 . . 96 C4
Sugden Rd
Clapham SW11 . . 137 A1
Long Ditton KT7 . . 197 B1
Sugden Way IG11 . . 101 D5
Sulby Ho SE4 . . 141 A1
Sulgrave Gdns 11
W6 . . 112 C4
Sulgrave Rd W6 . . 112 C3
Sulina Rd SW2 . . 160 A4
Sulivan Ct SW6 . . 135 C3
Sulivan Ent Ctr SW6 . . 135 C2
Sulivan Prim Sch
SW6 . . 135 C3
Sulivan Rd SW6 . . 135 C2
Sulkin Ho 11 E2 . . 96 D4
Sullivan Ave E16 . . 99 D2
Sullivan Cl
Battersea SW11 . . 136 C2
Hayes UB4 . . 84 C2
Sullivan Ct
4 Croydon CR0 . . 206 A1
Stamford Hill N16 . . 51 D1
SW5 . . 255 B4
Sullivan Ho
Chelsea SW1 . . 268 D6
Isleworth TW2 . . 152 B5
Vauxhall SE11 . . 260 D3
Sullivan Rd
SE11 . . 116 C2 261 B4
Sullivans Reach
KT12 . . 193 D2
Sullivan Way WD6 . . 9 C5
Sultan Ho SE1 . . 118 A1
Sultan Rd E11 . . 55 B5
Sultan St Penge BR3 . . 184 D1
SE5 . . 139 A5
Sumal Ct E9 . . 76 B6
Sumatra Rd NW6 . . 69 C2
Sumburgh Rd SW12 . . 159 A5
Summer Ave KT8 . . 196 C4
Summercourt Rd E1 . . 96 C1
Summer Crossing
KT7 . . 196 C4
Summerene Cl
SW16 . . 181 C3
Summerfield 6 BR1 . . 187 B2
Summerfield Ave
Colney Hatch N12 . . 30 C4
Kensal Rise NW6 . . 91 A5
Summerfield Ho RM9 . . 80 D4
Summerfield La
KT6 . . 213 D6
Summerfield Rd
Ealing W5 . . 87 B3
Loughton IG10 . . 21 D5
Summerfield St
SE12 . . 164 D4
Summer Gdns KT8 . . 196 C4
Summer Gr WD6 . . 9 D5
Summer Hill
Borehamwood WD6 . . 10 C6
BR7 . . 188 C1
Summerhill Cl BR6 . . 227 C5
Summerhill Gr EN1 . . 17 C5
Summerhill Rd N15 . . 51 B5
Summerhill Villas
BR7 . . 188 D2
Summerhill Way
CR4 . . 181 A2
Summer Ho SE13 . . 142 B1
Summerhouse Ave
TW5 . . 129 A4
Summerhouse Rd
N16 . . 73 C6
Summerland Gdns
N10 . . 49 B6
Summerland Grange
N10 . . 49 B6
Summerlands Ave
W3 . . 111 A6
Summerlands Lo
BR6 . . 226 C4
Summerlee Ave N2 . . 48 D5
Summerlee Gdns N2 . . 48 D5
Summerley St SW18 . . 157 D2
Summer Rd
East Molesey KT8 . . 196 B4
Thames Ditton KT7,
KT8 . . 196 D4
Summersby Rd N6 . . 49 B3
Summers Cl
Belmont SM2 . . 217 C1
Wembley HA9 . . 44 D1
Summersell Ho
SE27 . . 183 B5
Summerside Prim Sch
N12 . . 30 B4
Summerskille Cl N9 . . 18 B2
Summers La N12 . . 30 B3
Summers Row N12 . . 30 C4
Summers St EC1 . . 241 A5
SUMMERSTOWN . . 158 A1
Summerstown
SW17 . . 180 A6
Summerswood Prim Sch
WD6 . . 10 D6
Summerton Way
SE28 . . 102 D1
Summer Trees
TW16 . . 172 B2
Summerville Gdns
SM1 . . 217 B2
Summerwood Rd TW1,
TW7 . . 152 D5
Summit Ave NW9 . . 45 B4
Summit Bsns Pk
TW16 . . 172 A3
Summit Cl
Edgware HA8 . . 26 C3
Kingsbury NW9 . . 45 B5
Osidge N14 . . 15 C2
Summit Ct
5 Barnet EN5 . . 1 B2
Brondesbury NW2 . . 69 A3
Summit Dr IG8 . . 37 D1
Summit Est N16 . . 52 A2
Summit Rd
Northolt UB5 . . 63 C1
Walthamstow E17 . . 53 D5
Summit Way
Brunswick Pk N14 . . 15 B2
South Norwood SE19 . . 183 C3
Sumner Ave SE15 . . 139 D4
Sumner Bldgs SE1 . . 252 A4
Sumner Cl BR6 . . 227 A4
Sumner Ct SW8 . . 270 A2
Sumner Gdns CR0 . . 204 C1
Sumner Ho 1 E3 . . 97 D2
Sumner Pl
SW7 . . 114 B2 256 D3
Sumner Place Mews
SW7 . . 256 D3
Sumner Rd
Harrow HA1 . . 42 A2
SE15 . . 139 D5
Thornton Heath CR0 . . 204 D1
Sumner Rd S CR0 . . 204 C1
Sumner St
SE1 . . 117 A5 252 A4
Sumpter Cl NW3 . . 70 A2
Sun Alley 6 TW9 . . 132 A1
Sun Alliance Ho
WC2 . . 241 A2
Sunbeam Cres W10 . . 90 C3
Sunbeam Rd NW10 . . 89 B3
SUNBURY . . 194 B6
Sunbury Ave
Edgware NW7 . . 27 B6
Mortlake SW14 . . 133 B1
Sunbury Cl KT12 . . 194 A3
SUNBURY
COMMON . . 171 D3
Sunbury Court Island
TW16 . . 194 D6
Sunbury Court Mews
TW16 . . 172 D1
Sunbury Court Rd
TW16 . . 172 C1
Sunbury Cres TW13 . . 171 D6
Sunbury Cross
TW16 . . 172 A3
Sunbury Cross Ctr 9
TW16 . . 171 D3
Sunbury Ct
3 Barnet EN5 . . 1 A1
3 SE14 . . 140 D6
Sunbury TW16 . . 172 D1
Sunbury Ct (Con Ctr)
TW16 . . 172 D1
Sunbury Gdns NW7 . . 27 B5
Sunbury Ho 38 E2 . . 95 D4
Sunbury Int Bsns Ctr
TW16 . . 171 C2
Sunbury La
Battersea
SW11 . . 136 B4 266 D2
Walton-on-T KT12 . . 194 A3
Sunbury L Ctr TW16 . . 171 D2
Sunbury Manor Sch
TW16 . . 171 D2
Sunbury Rd
Cheam SM3 . . 217 A5
Feltham TW13 . . 171 D6
Sunbury St SE18 . . 122 B3
Sunbury Sta TW16 . . 172 A2
Sunbury Walled Gdn★
TW16 . . 194 B6
Sunbury Way TW13 . . 172 C5
Sunbury Workshops 39
E2 . . 95 D4
Suncroft Pl SE26 . . 162 C1
Sun Ct EC3 . . 242 D1
Sundeala Cl TW16 . . 172 A3
Sunderland Ct
Dulwich SE22 . . 162 A4
12 Stanwell TW19 . . 148 A5
Sunderland Ho 26
W2 . . 91 C2
Sunderland Mount
SE23 . . 162 D2
Sunderland Point
E16 . . 123 A5
Sunderland Rd
Ealing W5 . . 109 D3
Forest Hill SE23 . . 162 D2
Sunderland Terr W2 . . 91 D1
Sunderland Way E12 . . 77 D6
Sundew Ave W12 . . 112 A6
Sundew Ct 9 HA0 . . 88 A5
Sundial Ave SE25 . . 205 D6
Sundial Ct KT5 . . 214 D6
Sundorne Rd SE7 . . 121 C1
Sundown Rd TW15 . . 171 A5
Sundra Wlk 26 E1 . . 96 D3
SUNDRIDGE . . 187 C4
Sundridge Ave
Bromley BR1, BR7 . . 188 A3
DA16 . . 145 B2
Sundridge Ho
Bromley BR1 . . 187 B5
4 Homerton E9 . . 74 D1
Sundridge Par BR1 . . 187 B3
Sundridge Park Sta
BR1 . . 187 B3
Sundridge Pl 8
CR0 . . 206 A1
Sundridge Rd CR0 . . 206 A1
Sunfields Pl SE3 . . 143 B5
Sun in the Sands
SE3 . . 143 B5
Sunken Rd CR0 . . 222 C3
Sun La SE3 . . 143 B5
Sunland Ave DA6 . . 147 A1
Sunleigh Ct HA0 . . 88 A6

Sunleigh Rd HA0......88 A6
Sunley Gdns UB6......87 A6
Sunley Ho UB1 .... 243 D3
Sun Life Trad Est
TW14....................1 B3
Sunlight Cl SW19 ...180 A4
Sunlight Sq ⓔ E2.....67 A6
Sunmead Rd TW16..194 A6
Sunna Gdns TW16...172 B1
Sunna Lo TW16 .....171 D3
Sunniholme Ct CR2 ..221 A3

Sunningdale
W13........................87 B2
Friern Barnet N14...31 D5
Sunningdale Ave
Barking IG11 ....79 B1
East Acton W3 ......111 C6
Feltham TW13 ....151 A2
Ruislip HA4 ....40 C1

Sunningdale Cl
㉖ Bermondsey
SE16 ....118 B1
Erith DA8 ....103 A1
❶ Newham E6 ......100 B4
Stanmore HA7 ....25 A3
⑧ Surbiton KT6 .....214 A6

Sunningdale Ct
⑬ Kingston u T
KT2 ....176 C3
⑮ Southall UB1......86 A1

Sunningdale Gdns
Kingsbury NW9 ......45 A4
W8........................255 B5
Sunningdale Lo HA8..26 B5

Sunningdale Rd
BR1, BR2 ....210 A4
Cheam SM1 ....217 B4

Sunningfields Cres
NW4 ....46 B6

Sunningfields Rd
NW4 ....46 B6

Sunninghill Ct ⑨
W3........................111 A4

Sunninghill Gdns IG2 57 B4
Sunninghill Rd SE13 141 D3
Sunny Bank SE25 ...206 A6
Sunny Cres NW10....67 A1

Sunnycroft Rd
Hounslow TW3 ......129 D3
Southall UB1...........85 C2
South Norwood SE25.206 A5
Sunnydale BR6 .....226 C6
Sunnydale Gdns NW7 27 C4
Sunnydale Rd SE12 .165 B6

Sunnydene
Chingford E4 ....36 B5
Ruislip HA4 ....62 A6
Sunnydene Gdns HA0 65 C2
Sunnydene St SE26..185 A6
Sunnyfield NW7 .....27 C6

Sunnyfields Prim Sch
NW4 ....46 B6

Sunny Gardens Par
NW4 ....28 B1

Sunny Gardens Rd
NW4 ....46 C6
Sunny Hill NW4 ......46 B6
Sunnyhill Cl E5 ....75 A4
Sunnyhill Ct N3 ......11 D1

Sunnyhill Prim Sch
SW16....................182 B6
Sunnyhill Rd SW16..182 A6
Sunnyhurst Cl SM1..217 C5

Sunnymead Ave
CR4 ....203 D6
Sunnymead Ct W5...109 D2

Sunnymead Rd
Kingsbury NW9 ......45 B2
Putney SW15 ....156 B6

Sunnymede Ave
KT19 ....215 C1
Sunnymede Dr IG6 ..56 D5

Sunny Nook Gdns
CR2 ....221 B2
Sunny Pl NW4 ....46 C5
Sunny Rd The EN3 ....6 D4

Sunnyside
❹ Child's Hill NW2 ....9 B3
Walton-on-T KT12 ..194 C4
Wimbledon SW19 ...179 A4
Sunnyside Dr E4 ......20 A4
Sunnyside Ho ⑥
NW2 ....69 B5

Sunnyside Pl SW19 .179 A4

Sunnyside Rd
Crouch End N19 ......49 D2
Ealing W5 ....109 D5
Ilford IG1...............79 B5
Teddington TW11 ...174 B6
Walthamstow E10 ...53 C1
Sunnyside Rd E N18..18 A1
Sunnyside Rd N N9 ..18 A1
Sunnyside Rd S N9 ..18 A1
Sunny View NW9 ....45 B4
Sunny Way N12 ......30 C3
Sun Pas ⑧ SE18 ....118 A3
Sunray Ave BR2 .....210 B3
Herne Hill SE5, SE24 .139 B1
Tolworth KT5 ....214 D6
Sun Rd W14 ....113 B1
Sunrise CI TW13 ....151 B1
Sunrise Sch N7 ....34 A4
Sunrise View NW7 ...27 D4

Sun St Pas
EC2 ....95 C2 243 A3
Sunset Ave
Chingford E4 ....19 D3
Woodford IG8 ....36 D6
Sunset Ct ⓔ IG8......37 C3
Sunset Gdns SE25...183 D1
Sunset Ho HA3 ....42 C6

Sunset Rd
Herne Hill SE5 ......139 B1
SE28.....................124 A5
Wimbledon SW19 ...178 B5
Sunset View NN5 .....1 A3
Sunshine CW4 ....180 D1
Sun St EC2 ....95 B2 242 D4
Sunwell Cl SE15 ....140 B4
Superior Dr ⓐ BR6 .227 D2
Suraj Ho ⓐ N22 .....32 C1
SURBITON........198 A2
Surbiton Boys Prep Sch
KT6 ....198 A4
Surbiton Cres KT1,
KT6 ....198 A5
Surbiton Ct KT6 .....197 D3
Surbiton Ct Mews
KT6 ....197 D3
Surbiton Hall Cl KT1 198 A5
Surbiton Hgh Sch Jun
Girls Sch ❸ KT1...198 A5
Surbiton High Senior
Sch ❸ KT1,.........198 A5
Surbiton Hill Pk KT5 198 C4
Surbiton Hill Rd
KT6 ....198 A6
Surbiton Hospl KT6 .198 A4
Surbiton Par ❶ KT6 .198 A4
Surbiton Rd KT1 ....198 A5
Surbiton Sta KT6 ...198 A3
Surcot Ho ⓔ SW4...137 D3
Surlingham Cl SE28 124 D6
Surma Cl E1 ....96 A3
Surmans Rd RM9 ...102 C6
Surrendale Pl W9 ....91 C3
Surrey Canal Rd
SE8........................140 C6
Surrey Cl N3 ....47 A6
Surrey Cres ❶ W4 .110 C1
Surrey Ct SE16★ ...219 B2
Surrey Docks Farm★
SE16.....................119 B4
Surrey Docks
Watersports Ctr
SE8........................119 B2
Surrey Gdns N4 ....51 A3
Surrey Gr
Carshalton SM1......218 B5
SE17.....................263 A1
Surrey Ho
Edgware HA8 ....26 B4
❸ Rotherhithe SE16 118 D5
Surrey La
SW11 ....136 C4 267 B1
Surrey Lo SW20 .....178 C1
Surrey Mews SE27..183 C6
Surrey Mount SE23 162 B3
Surrey Quays Ctr
SE16.....................118 D4
Surrey Quays Sh Ctr
SE16.....................118 D3
Surrey Quays Sta
SE16.....................118 D2
Surrey Rd
Barking IG11 ....79 C1
Dagenham RM10 ....81 D3
Harrow HA1............42 A4
Honor Oak SE15 ....162 D6

Surrey Rd continued
West Wickham BR4 . 207 D1
Surrey Row
SE1.............116 C4 251 D2
Surrey Sq
SE17............117 C1 263 B2
Surrey Square Inf Sch
SE17............117 C1 263 A2
Surrey Square Jun Sch
SE17............117 C1 263 A2
Surrey St
Croydon CR0 ....221 A5
❶ Newham E13......99 B4
WC2 ....116 B6 250 D6
Surrey Terr SE17 ...263 B2
Surrey Water Rd
SE16.....................118 D5
Surrey Wharf SE1, SE40 A6
Surridge Ct ⑮ SW9 .138 A3
Surridge Gdns SE19 183 B4
Surr St N7................72 A3
Sury Basin KT2 ......176 A2
Susan Constant Ct ⑱
E14.......................120 B6
Susan Lawrence Ho ❹
E12 ....78 C3
Susannah St E14......98 A1
Susan Rd SE3.........143 B3
Susan Wood BR7 ...188 C2
Sussex Ave KT3 .....199 C5
Sussex Cl
New Malden KT3 ...199 C5
Redbridge IG4 ....56 B4
❶ Twickenham TW1 153 B5
Upper Holloway N19 ..72 A6
Sussex Cres UB5.....63 C2
Sussex Ct
❹ Barnes SW13 ....133 D3
Greenwich SE10 ....142 A6
Mitcham CR4 ....204 A4
Paddington W2 .....236 C1
Sussex Gdns
Chessington KT9 ...213 D2
Fortis Green N6 ......48 D4
Harringay N4 ....51 A4
Paddington
W2 ....92 B3 236 D1
Sussex Ho
Edgware HA8 ....26 B4
Hampstead NW3 .....70 C2
Richmond TW9 ......132 B3
Sussex House Sch
SW3 ....114 D2 257 C4
Sussex Mans
South Kensington
SW7 ....256 C3
Strand WC2 ....250 B6
Sussex Mews SE6...163 C3
Sussex Mews E W2 .236 D1
Sussex Mews W W2. 246 D6
Sussex Pl
❷ Hammersmith
W6 ....106 C1
Lisson Gr NW1 92 D3 237 C6
New Malden KT3 ...199 C5
Paddington
W2 ....92 B3 236 D1
Sussex Rd
Barking IG11 ....100 C6
Erith DA8 ....147 D5
Harrow HA1............42 A4
Mitcham CR4 ....204 A4
New Malden KT3 ...199 C5
Sidcup DA14 ....190 B5
Southall UB2 ....106 D3
South Croydon CR2 221 B2
Uxbridge UB10.......61 A3
Wallington SM5 .....218 D2
West Wickham
BR4 ....207 D1
Sussex Ring N12.....29 C5
Sussex Sq
W2 ....114 B6 246 D6
Sussex St Newham E13 99 B2
SW1 ....258 D2 C2
Sussex Way
Cockfosters EN4 ....15 B6
Upper Holloway N7 .72 B5
Upper Holloway N7,
N19.......................72 A6
Sutcliffe Cl NW11....47 D4
Sutcliffe Ho UB3 ....84 A1

Sutcliffe Rd
Bexley DA16..........146 C3
SE18.....................145 C6
Sutherland Ave
Ealing W13 ....87 B1
Falconwood DA16 ..145 C1
Hayes UB3 ....106 A2
Orpington BR5 ......211 D4
Paddington
W9 ....92 A3 236 A6
Sunbury TW16 ......171 D1
Sutherland Ct EN5 ....1 A1
Sutherland Ct
Kingsbury NW9 ......44 D1
❸ Paddington W9 ...91 C3
Stoke Newington N16 ..73 B4
Sutherland Dr SW19 180 B2
Sutherland Gdns
Mortlake SW14 .....133 C2
North Cheam KT4...200 B1
Sunbury TW16 ......171 D1
Sutherland Gr
Putney SW18,
SW19 ....157 B4
Teddington TW11....174 C5
Sutherland Ho
❹ South Hampstead
NW6 ....69 A2
❸ South Kensington
W8........................255 C5
Kidbrooke SE18 ....144 B4
❼ Putney SW15 ....156 C4
Richmond TW10 ....153 C2
Sutherland Pl W2 ....91 C1
Sutherland Point ❸
E5 ....74 B4
Sutherland Rd
Belvedere DA17 ....125 C3
Chiswick W4 ....133 C6
Ealing W13 ....87 A1
Edmonton N9 ....18 B3
Enfield EN3 ....18 C6
Southall UB1...........85 B1
Thornton Heath CR0 204 C2
Tottenham N17 ....34 A2
Walthamstow E17 ...53 A6
Sutherland Row
SW1 ....258 D2
Sutherland Sq
SE17............117 A1 262 A1
Sutherland St
SW1 ....115 B1 258 D2
Sutherland Wlk SE17 262 B1
Sutterton St N7 ....72 B2
SUTTON 218 A2
Sutton Arena L Ctr
SM5 ....202 B2
Sutton Cl
Beckenham BR3....185 D2
Pinner HA5 ....40 A4
Sutton Coll of Learning
for Adults ❿ SM1 . 217 D3
Sutton Common Rd
Cheam SM1 ....201 C1
Sutton SM1, SM3 ...217 D6
Sutton Common Sta
SM1 ....217 D6
Sutton Courtenay Ho
SW17.....................180 B6
Sutton Court Mans
W4........................133 A4
Sutton Court Rd
Chiswick W4 ....133 A6
Hillingdon UB10.....62 A4
Sutton E13 ....99 C4
Sutton SM1 ....218 A2
Sutton Cres EN5 ....12 C4
Sutton Ct
Chiswick W4 ....133 A4
Ealing W5..............110 A5
East Molesey KT8 ..195 B4
Sutton E5................74 B4
Penge SE19 ....183 D3
Sutton SM2 ....218 A2
Sutton Dene TW3 ...129 D4
Sutton Est The ⑧
W10 ....90 C2
Sutton Gdns
Barking IG11 ....101 C6
Croydon CR0 ....205 D4
Sutton Gn IG11 .....101 C6
Sutton Gr SM1 ......218 B4
Sutton Gram Sch For
Boys ❸ SM1 ....218 A3
Sutton Hall Rd TW5 129 C5

Sutton High Sch
SM1 ....217 D2
Sutton Ho N21........16 B6
Sutton House★ E9...74 C3
Sutton Hts SM2......218 B1
Sutton La EC1 ....241 D5
Hounslow TW3, TW4,
TW5 ....129 B3
Sutton La N W4 .....111 A1
Sutton La S W4 .....133 A6
Sutton Par NW4 .....46 C5
Sutton Park Rd SM1,
SM2 ....217 D2
Sutton Pl E9............74 C3
Sutton Rd
Barking IG11 ....101 C6
E13.........................98 D3
Heston TW5..........129 C4
Higham Hill E17 .....32 C4
Muswell Hill N10 ...31 A2
Sutton Row W1 .....239 D2
Sutton Sq Hackney E9 74 C3
Hounslow TW5 .....129 B4
Sutton St E1 ....96 C1
Sutton Sta SM2 .....218 A2
Suttons Way EC1 ...242 B5
Sutton Way
Hounslow TW5......129 B4
North Kensington W10..90 C2
Sutton Wlk
SE1.............116 B5 250 D3
Swaby Rd SW17,
SW18 ....158 A4
Swaffham Ct ❶ RM6..58 C4
Swaffield Prim Sch
SW18.....................158 A4
Swaffield Rd SW18..158 A4
Swain Cl SW16.......181 B4
Swain Ho NW6 ......71 C6
Swain Rd CR7 ....205 A4
Swains Cl UB7 ....104 A4
Swain's La N6 ....71 B6
Swainson Rd N7 .....72 C4
Swainson Rd W3.....111 D4
Swains Rd CR4,
SW17.....................180 D3
Swain St NW8 .92 C3 237 A6
Swakeleys Dr UB10 ..60 C3
Swakeleys Rd UB10 ..60 C5
Swakeleys Rdbt UB8,
UB10......................60 A4
Swakeleys Sch UB10..82 D5
Swaledale Cl N11 ...31 A1
Swallands Rd SE6 ..163 C1
Swallowbrook Bsns Ctr
UB4 ....106 D5
Swallow Cl
Bushey WD23..........8 A3
New Cross Gate SE14 140 D4
Swallow Ct
Chingford IG8 ....36 B3
Ilford IG2.................56 D4
❹ Paddington W9 ...91 C2
❺ Ruislip HA4 ....40 C1
❶ SE12 ....165 A4
Swallow Dr
Northolt UB5 ....85 C5
Willesden NW10 .....67 B2
Swallowfield NW1...232 D1
Swallowfield Rd
SE7.......................121 B1
Swallowfield Way
UB3.......................105 B4
Swallow Gdns SW16 181 D5
Swallow Ho
Hornsey N8 ....50 B6
NW8.....................230 A4
Swallow Pk KT6 .....214 B5
Swallow Pl
❷❹ Poplar E14 ....97 B1
W1......................238 D1
Swallows Ct ❸
SE20......................184 D3
Swallow St
Newham E6 ....100 A4
W1.............116 C6 249 B5
Swaminarayan Sch The
NW10.....................67 B2
Swanage Cl ❶ N11 ..73 C1
Swanage Ho SW8 ..270 C3
Swanage Rd
Chingford E4 ....36 A3
Wandsworth SW18 .158 A5
Swanage Waye UB4..84 C1
Swan and Pike Rd
EN3 ....7 C5

Swan App E6 . . . . 100 A2
Swanbourne SE17 . . 262 A3
Swanbourne Ho
NW8 . . . . 237 A6
Swanbridge Rd DA7 . 147 C4
Swan Bsns Ctr 8
W4 . . . . 111 B2
Swan Cl Croydon CR0 . . 205 C2
Feltham TW13 . . . . . 173 A6
Higham Hill E17 . . . . . . 35 A3
Swan Ct Chelsea SW3 257 B1
Parsons Green SW6 . 265 A3
Poplar E14 . . . . 97 B1
Whetstone N20 . . . . 14 A2
Swan Ctr SW17 . . . . . . 158 A1
Swandon Way SW18 135 D1
Swan Dr NW9 . . . . 27 C1
Swanfield St E2 . . . . . . 95 D4
Swan Ho
De Beauvoir Town N1 . . . 73 B1
Enfield EN3 . . . . 18 C6
Swan La EC4 . 117 B6 252 D5
Loughton IG10 . . . . 21 C4
Whetstone N20 . . . . 14 A1
Swan Lane Pier
EC4 . . . . 117 B6 252 C5
Swanlea Sch E1 . . . . 96 B3
Swanley Ho SE17 . . . 263 B2
Swanley Rd DA16 . . . . 146 C4
Swan Mead
SE1 . . . . 117 C3 263 A5
Swan Mews
Stockwell SW9 . . . . . . 138 B3
SW6 . . . . 265 A2
Swanmore Ct SE18 . . 158 A5
Swann Ct 8 TW7 . . . . 131 A2
Swanne Ho 12 SE10 . . 142 A5
Swan Pas 5 E1 . . . . . . 118 A6
Swan Pl SW13 . . . . . . 133 D3
Swan Rd
Feltham TW13 . . . . . . 173 A6
Greenwich SE18 . . . . 121 D3
Rotherhithe SE16 . . . . 118 C4
Southall UB1 . . . . 85 D1
West Drayton UB7 . . . 104 A4
Swanscombe Ho
1 BR5 . . . . 190 B1
11 Shepherd's Bush
W11 . . . . 112 D5
Swanscombe Point 7
E16 . . . . 98 D2
Swanscombe Rd
5 Chiswick W4 . . . . . 111 C1
Shepherd's Bush
W11 . . . . 112 D5
Swansea Ct E16 . . . . 122 D5
Swansea Rd
Enfield EN3 . . . . 6 C1
Harlington TW14,
TW6 . . . . 149 B5
Swansland Gdns 2
E17 . . . . 35 A2
Swan St
Isleworth TW7 . . . . 131 B2
SE1 . . . . 117 A4 252 B1
Swanston Ct TW1 . . . 152 D4
Swan The BR4 . . . . . . 224 A6
Swanton Gdns
SW19 . . . . 156 D3
Swanton Rd DA8 . . . . 147 D5
Swan Way EN3 . . . . 6 D3
Swanwick Cl SW15 . . 155 D4
Swan Wlk
Oatlands Pk TW17 . . . 193 C2
SW3 . . . . 136 D6 267 C6
Swan Yd N1 . . . . 72 D2
Swaton Rd E3 . . . . 97 C3
Swaylands Rd DA17 . . 147 C6
Swaythling Cl N18 . . . . 34 B6
Swaythling Ho
SW15 . . . . 155 D5
Swedenborg Gdns
E1 . . . . 118 B6
Sweden Gate SE16 . . . 119 A2
Swedish Quays
SE16 . . . . 119 A3
Swedish Sch The
SW13 . . . . 134 A6
Sweeney Cres SE1 . . 253 D1
Sweet Briar Gn N9 . . . . 17 D1
Sweet Briar Gr N9 . . . . 17 D1
Sweet Briar Wlk N18 . . 33 D6
Sweetcroft La UB10 . . . 60 C1
Sweetmans Ave HA5 . . 40 D6
Sweets Way N20 . . . . . . 14 B2
Swell Ct E17 . . . . 53 D3
Swetenham Wlk
SE18 . . . . 123 A1
Swete St E13 . . . . 99 A5
Sweyn Pl SE3 . . . . 143 A3
Swift Cl Harrow HA2 . . . 63 D6
Hayes UB3 . . . . 83 D1
Higham Hill E17 . . . . . . 35 A3
Thamesmead SE28 . . . 124 B6
Swift Ct SM2 . . . . 217 D1
Swift Ctr CR0 . . . . 220 B1
Swift Ho
16 Stepney E1 . . . . 96 C1
15 Stoke Newington
N16 . . . . 73 C5
1 SW9 . . . . 138 C5
8 Wanstead E18 . . . . . . 55 B6
Swift Rd
Feltham TW13 . . . . 173 A6
Southall UB2 . . . . 107 B3
Swiftsden Way BR1 . . 186 C4
Swift St SW6 . 135 B4 264 C2
Swinbrook Rd W10 . . . 91 A2
Swinburne Cres
CR0 . . . . 206 C3
Swinburne Ct 4
SE5 . . . . 139 B1
Swinburne Ho 15 E2 . . 96 C4
Swinburne Rd SW15 . 134 A1
Swinderby Rd HA0 . . . . 66 A2
Swindon Cl IG3 . . . . 57 C1
Swindon Rd TW6 . . . . 149 A6
Swindon St W12 . . . . . 112 C5
Swinfield Cl TW13 . . . 173 A6
Swinford Gdns SW9 . 138 D2
Swingate La SE18 . . . 145 C5
Swingfield Ct BR2 . . . 209 D4
Swingfield Ho 4 E9 . . 96 C6
Swinley Ho NW1 . . . . 231 D2
Swinnerton St E9 . . . . . 75 A3
Swinson Ho 12 N11 . . . 31 C5
Swinton Cl HA9 . . . . . . 44 D1
Swinton Ho 21 E2 . . . . . 96 A4
Swinton Pl WC1 . . . . . 233 C2
Swinton St
WC1 . . . . 94 B4 233 C2
Swires Shaw BR2 . . . . 225 D4
Swiss Cottage NW3 . . . 70 B1
Swiss Cottage L Ctr
NW3 . . . . 70 B1
Swiss Cottage Sch
14 South Hampstead
NW3 . . . . 70 B1
St John's Wood
NW8 . . . . 92 B6 229 D6
Swiss Cottage Sta
NW3 . . . . 70 B1
Swiss Ct SW1 . . . . 249 D5
Swiss Re Building★
EC2 . . . . 95 C1 243 B2
Swiss Terr 7 NW3 . . . . 70 B1
Switch Ho 4 E14 . . . . 120 B6
Swithland Gdns SE9 . 188 C6
Swyncombe Ave W5 . 109 B2
Swynford Gdns 7
NW4 . . . . 46 A5
Sybil Elgar Sch UB2 . . 107 B3
Sybil Mews N4 . . . . 50 D3
Sybil Phoenix Cl
SE8 . . . . 118 D1
Sybil Thorndike Casson
Ho SW5 . . . . 255 B1
Sybil Thorndike Ho 12
N1 . . . . 73 A2
Sybourn Inf Sch E17 . . 53 B2
Sybourn Inf Sch
(Annexe) E10 . . . . 53 A1
Sybourn St E17 . . . . 53 B2
Sycamore Ave DA15 . 167 D5
Ealing W5 . . . . 109 D3
East Finchley N3 . . . . . . 47 D6
Hayes UB3 . . . . 105 C6
Old Ford E3 . . . . 97 B6
Sycamore Cl
Carshalton SM5 . . . . . 218 D4
Chislehurst SE9 . . . . . 166 A2
East Acton W3 . . . . 111 C5
2 Edgware HA8 . . . . . . 27 A6
Edmonton N9 . . . . 34 A6
Feltham TW13 . . . . 150 A1
New Barnet EN4 . . . . . . 14 B5
Newham E16 . . . . 98 C3
Northolt UB5 . . . . 85 A6
South Croydon CR2 . . 221 C3
Yiewsley UB7 . . . . 104 B6
Sycamore Ct
4 Beckenham BR3 . . 185 C2
Sycamore Ct *continued*
Forest Gate E7 . . . . 77 A2
3 Forest Hill SE26 . . 184 C6
Golders Green NW11 . . 47 A3
Hendon NW4 . . . . 28 C1
Hillingdon UB8 . . . . 82 C3
Hounslow TW4 . . . . . . 129 A1
Kilburn NW6 . . . . 91 C6
Surbiton KT6 . . . . 198 A2
Tufnell Pk N19 . . . . 71 D5
10 West Norwood
SW16 . . . . 182 C5
Sycamore Gdns
Hammersmith W6,
W12 . . . . 112 B3
Mitcham CR4 . . . . 180 B1
Tottenham N15 . . . . 51 D5
Sycamore Gr
Kingsbury NW9 . . . . 45 A2
Kingston u T KT3 . . . . 199 C6
Lewisham SE6 . . . . . . 164 A5
Penge SE20 . . . . 184 A2
Sycamore Hill N11 . . . . 31 A4
Sycamore Ho
4 Buckhurst Hill
IG9 . . . . 21 D2
23 Finchley N2 . . . . 30 B1
10 Maitland Pk NW3 . . . 70 D2
Penge SE20 . . . . 184 D4
17 Rotherhithe SE16 . 118 D4
3 Shepherd's Bush
W6 . . . . 112 B4
2 Stoke Newington
N16 . . . . 73 B6
Teddington TW11 . . . . 175 C3
Twickenham TW1 . . . . 152 D2
Sycamore Lo
7 Ashford TW16 . . . . 171 D3
Putney SW15 . . . . 134 B2
Sycamore Lodge HA2 . 64 B6
Sycamore Mews 4
SW4 . . . . 137 C2
Sycamore Rd SW19,
SW20 . . . . 178 C4
Sycamore St EC1 . . . 242 A5
Sycamore Way
TW11 . . . . 175 C4
Sycamore Wlk
Ilford IG6 . . . . 57 A5
1 Kensal Town W10 . . . 91 A3
Sydcote SE21 . . . . 161 A3
Sydenham Ave
Penge SE26 . . . . 184 B5
Southgate N21 . . . . 16 B6
Sydenham Girls Sch
SE26 . . . . 162 B1
Sydenham High Sch Jun
Dept SE26 . . . . 184 B6
Sydenham High Sch
(Sec) 13 SE26 . . . . . . 184 B5
Sydenham Hill SE21, SE22,
SE23, SE26, SE19 . . . 162 A1
Sydenham Hill Sta
SE21 . . . . 161 D1
Sydenham Hill Wood
Nature Reserve
SE26 . . . . 162 A1
Sydenham Ho 16
KT6 . . . . 197 D2
Sydenham Ind Est
SE26 . . . . 185 B5
Sydenham Park Mans 2
SE26 . . . . 162 C1
Sydenham Park Rd SE23,
SE26 . . . . 162 C1
Sydenham Pk SE26 . . 162 C1
Sydenham Rd
Forest Hill SE26 . . . . . 185 A6
Thornton Heath CR0 . . 205 B2
Sydenham Rise
SE23 . . . . 162 B2
Sydenham Sta SE26 . 184 C6
Sydenham Station App
4 SE26 . . . . 184 C6
Sydmons Ct SE23 . . . 162 C4
Sydner Mews N16 . . . . 73 D4
Sydner Rd N16 . . . . 73 D4
Sydney Chapman Way
EN5 . . . . 1 B3
Sydney Cl SW3 . . . . . 256 D3
Sydney Cotts KT10 . . 212 D2
Sydney Cres TW15 . . 170 D4
Sydney Ct Hayes UB4 . . 84 C3
Surbiton KT6 . . . . 214 A6
Sydney Gr NW4 . . . . 46 C4
Sydney Ho
4 Chiswick W4 . . . . . 111 C2
Muswell Hill N10 . . . . . . 31 B3
Sydney Mews SW3 . . 256 D3
Sydney Pl SW7 . . . . . 257 A3
Sydney Rd
Abbey Wood SE2 . . . . 124 D3
Bexley DA6 . . . . 146 D1
Ealing W13 . . . . 109 A4
East Bedfont TW14 . . . 150 A3
Hornsey N8 . . . . 50 C5
Muswell Hill N10 . . . . . . 31 B3
Richmond TW10,
TW9 . . . . 132 A1
Sidcup DA14 . . . . 189 C6
Sutton SM1 . . . . 217 C4
Teddington TW11 . . . . 174 D5
Wanstead E11 . . . . 55 B3
West Barnes SW20 . . 178 D1
Woodford IG8 . . . . 37 A6
Sydney Russell Sch The
RM9 . . . . 80 D3
Sydney St
SW3 . . . . 114 C1 257 A2
Sydney Terr KT10 . . . 212 D2
Sylva Cotts 3 SE8 . . . 141 C4
Sylva Ct 3 SW15 . . . . 156 D4
Sylvana Cl UB10 . . . . . . 82 B6
Sylvan Ave
Church End N3 . . . . 29 C1
Dagenham RM6 . . . . . . 59 B3
Edgware NW7 . . . . 27 D4
Wood Green N22 . . . . . . 32 C3
Sylvan Ct Finchley N12 . 29 D6
1 Kilburn NW6 . . . . 91 D6
South Croydon CR2 . . 221 A2
Sylvan Gdns KT6 . . . . 197 D2
Sylvan Gr
Hampstead NW2 . . . . . . 68 D4
SE15 . . . . 140 B6
Sylvan Hill SE19 . . . . 183 C2
Sylvan Ho N21 . . . . 16 B6
Sylvan Rd Ilford IG1 . . . 79 A6
South Norwood SE19 . 183 D2
Upton E7 . . . . 77 B2
Walthamstow E17 . . . . . 53 C4
Wanstead E11 . . . . 55 A4
Sylvan Way
Coney Hall BR4 . . . . . 224 C4
Dagenham RM8 . . . . . . 80 B5
Sylvan Wlk BR1 . . . . . 210 B6
Sylverdale Rd CR0 . . 220 D5
Sylvester Ave BR7 . . . 188 B4
Sylvester Ct HA0 . . . . . 65 D3
Sylvester Ho 7 E8 . . . . 74 B2
Sylvester Path 8 E8 . . 74 B2
Sylvester Rd
Finchley N2 . . . . 30 B1
Hackney E8 . . . . 74 B2
Walthamstow E17 . . . . . 53 B2
Wembley HA0 . . . . 65 C3
Sylvestrus Cl KT1 . . . . 176 C1
Sylvia Ave HA5 . . . . 23 B4
Sylvia Ct N1 . . . . 235 C3
Wembley HA9 . . . . 66 D1
Sylvia Gdns HA9 . . . . . 66 D1
Sylvia Lawla Ct N22 . . . 32 B1
Sylvia Pankhurst Ho
10 Dagenham RM10 . . . 81 C5
14 Globe Town E2 . . . . 96 D4
Sylvia Young Theatre
Sch NW1 . . . . 92 C3 237 B5
Symes Mews NW1 . . . 232 A4
Symington Ho SE1 . . . 262 C5
Symington Mews E9 . . 74 D3
Symister Mews N1 . . . . 95 C4
25 Shoreditch N1 . . . . . 95 C4
Symons Cl 6 SE15 . . . 140 C3
Symons St
SW3 . . . . 114 D2 257 D3
Symphony Cl HA8 . . . . 26 D3
Symphony Mews 15
W10 . . . . 91 A4
Syon Gate Way TW7,
TW8 . . . . 131 B5
Syon Ho & Pk★
TW8 . . . . 131 C4
Syon La
Brentford TW7,
TW8 . . . . 131 B5
Hounslow TW7 . . . . . . 130 D6
Syon Lane Sta TW7 . . 131 A5
Syon Lo 6 SE12 . . . . . 165 A4
Syon Park Cotts
TW8 . . . . 131 C4
Syon Park Gdns
TW7 . . . . 130 D5
Syracuse Univ
W11 . . . . 113 B6 244 C5
Syringa Ho SE4 . . . . . . 141 B2

T

Tabard Ct 6 E14 . . . . . 98 A1
Tabard Ho SE1 . . . . . . 262 D6
Teddington KT1 . . . . . 175 C2
Tabard St
SE1 . . . . 117 B3 262 C6
Tabernacle Ave 7
E13 . . . . 99 A3
Tabernacle St
EC2 . . . . 95 B3 242 D6
Tableer Ave SW4 . . . . 159 D6
Tabley Rd N7 . . . . 72 A4
Tabor Ct 3 SM3 . . . . . 217 A2
Tabor Gdns SM2,
SM3 . . . . 217 B1
Tabor Gr SW19 . . . . . . 179 B3
Tabor Rd W6 . . . . 112 B3
Tachbrook Est
SW1 . . . . 115 D1 259 D1
Tachbrook Mews
SW1 . . . . 259 A4
Tachbrook Rd
East Bedfont TW14 . . 149 D4
Southall UB2 . . . . 106 D2
Tachbrook St
SW1 . . . . 115 C2 259 B3
Tack Mews SE4 . . . . . 141 C2
Tadbourne Ct 1 HA8 . . 27 A3
Tadema Ho NW8 . . . . 236 D5
Tadema Rd
SW10 . . . . 136 A5 266 B3
Tadlow KT1 . . . . 198 C6
Tadmor Cl TW16 . . . . 193 D5
Tadmor St W12 . . . . . 112 D5
Tadworth Ave KT3 . . . 199 D4
Tadworth Ct 5 N11 . . . 31 A4
Tadworth Ho SE1 . . . . 251 C1
Tadworth Rd NW2 . . . . 68 A6
Taeping St E14 . . . . . 119 D2
Taffrail Ho 2 E14 . . . . 119 D1
Taffy's How CR4 . . . . 202 C6
Taft Way 44 E3 . . . . 97 D4
Taggs Ho KT1 . . . . 175 D1
Tailors Ct 9 SW16 . . . 181 C6
Tailworth St 16 E1 . . . . 96 A2
Tait 7 NW9 . . . . 27 D3
Tait Ct 16 Old Ford E3 . . . 97 B6
SW8 . . . . 269 D2
Tait Ho SE1 . . . . 251 B3
2 Tufnell Pk N19 . . . . . 71 C4
Tait Rd CR0 . . . . 205 C2
Tait Rd Ind Est CR0 . . 205 C2
Takhar Mews SW11 . . 136 C3
Talacre Com Sp Ctr
NW5 . . . . 71 B2
Talacre Rd NW5 . . . . . . 71 A2
Talbot Ave N2 . . . . 48 B6
Talbot Cl N15 . . . . 51 D5
Talbot Cres NW4 . . . . . 46 A4
Talbot Ct EC3 . . . . 252 D6
Neasden NW9 . . . . 67 B5
Talbot Gdns IG3 . . . . . . 80 A6
Talbot Grove Ho 10
W11 . . . . 91 A1
Talbot Ho Highbury N7 . 72 C5
Poplar E14 . . . . 97 D1
Talbot Pl SE3 . . . . 142 C3
Talbot Rd
Ashford TW15 . . . . . . 170 A5
Camberwell SE22 . . . . 139 C1
Dagenham RM9 . . . . . . 81 B1
Ealing W13 . . . . 109 A5
Forest Gate E7 . . . . 77 A4
Harrow HA3 . . . . 24 D1
Highgate N6 . . . . 49 A3
Isleworth TW1, TW7 . 131 A1
Notting Hill W2 . . . . 91 C1
Notting Hill W11 . . . . . . 91 B1
Southall UB2 . . . . 107 A2
South Norwood CR7 . . 205 B5
Tottenham N15 . . . . 51 D5
Twickenham TW2 . . . . 152 D3
Wallend E6 . . . . 100 C5
Wallington SM5 . . . . . 219 A3
Wembley HA0 . . . . 65 D2

Talbot Rd *continued*
Wood Green N22 31 C2
Talbot Sq W2 92 B1 236 C1
Talbot Wlk
Notting Hill W11 91 A1
Willesden NW10 67 C2
Talbot Yd SE1 252 C3
Talcott Path 12 SW2 160 C3
Talehangers Cl DA6 146 D1
Talfourd Pl SE15 139 D4
Talfourd Rd SE15 139 D4
Talgarth Rd
Hammersmith W6 112 C1
W14 113 A1 254 B2
Talgarth Wlk NW9 45 C4
Talia Ho E14 120 A3
Talisman Cl 2 IG3 58 B1
Talisman Sq SE26 184 A6
Talisman Way HA9 66 B5
Tallack Cl HA3 24 C3
Tallack Rd E10 53 B1
Tall Elms Cl BR2 208 D4
Talleyrand Ho SE5 139 A3
Tallis Cl E16 99 B1
Tallis Gr SE7 143 B6
Tallis St EC4 251 B6
Tallis View NW10 67 B2
Tallow Cl RM9 81 A2
Tallow Rd TW8 131 C5
Tall Trees SW16 204 B6
Talma Gdns TW2 152 C4
Talmage Cl SE23 162 C4
Talman Gr HA7 25 D4
Talma Rd SW2 138 C1
Talmud Torah Machzikei Hadass Sch E5 52 A2
Talmud Torah Tiferes Shlomo 1 NW11 47 A2
Talmud-Torah Yetev-Lev 6 N16 52 A1
Talwin St E3 97 D4
Tamar Cl 24 E3 97 B6
Tamar Ho
10 Cubitt Town E14 120 A4
SE11 261 B2
Tamarind Ct 8 W3 89 A1
Tamarind Ho 4
SE15 140 A5
Tamarind Yd 5 E1 118 A5
Tamarisk Sq W12 111 D6
Tamar Sq IG8 37 B4
Tamar St SE7 122 A2
Tamar Way N17 52 A6
Tame Ho 3 UB5 85 B4
Tamesa Ho TW17 192 C2
Tamesis Gdns KT4 215 C6
Tamian Ind Est TW4 128 C1
Tamian Way TW4 128 C1
Tamil Ho SE6 163 C2
Tamworth N7 72 A2
Tamworth Ave IG8 36 C4
Tamworth La CR4 203 B6
Tamworth Pk CR4 203 B6
Tamworth Pl 3 CR0 221 A6
Tamworth Rd CR0 221 A6
Tamworth St
SW6 135 C6 265 A5
Tancred Rd N4 50 D3
Tandem Ctr SW19 180 B2
Tandridge Ct SM2 217 D2
Tandridge Dr BR6 211 B1
Tandridge Pl 2 BR6 211 B1
Tanfield Ave NW2 67 D5
Tanfield Rd CR0 221 A4
Tangier Rd TW10 132 D2
Tangleberry Cl BR1 210 B5
Tangle Tree Cl N3 29 D1
Tanglewood Cl
Hillingdon UB10 82 C3
South Croydon CR0 222 C5
Stanmore HA7 8 C2
Tanglewood Lo HA8 27 A4
Tanglewood Way
TW13 150 B1
Tangley Gr SW15 155 D4
Tangley Park Rd
TW12 173 B4
Tanglyn Ave TW17 192 D4
Tangmere
Tottenham N17 33 B1
WC1 233 C1
Tangmere Gdns UB5 84 C5
Tangmere Gr KT2 175 D5
Tangmere Way NW9 27 C1
Tanhurst Ho 27
SW2 160 A4
Tanhurst Wlk SE2 124 D3
Tankerton Rd KT6 214 B6
Tankerton St WC1 233 B1
Tankerton Terr CR0 204 B3
Tankerville Rd
SW16 182 A3
Tankridge Rd NW2 68 B6
Tanner Ho
1 Merton SW19 180 A2
SE1 253 B1
Tanner Point 8 E13 99 A6
Tanners Cl KT12 194 B3
Tanners End La N18 33 C5
Tanner's Hill SE8 141 C4
Tanners La IG6 57 A6
Tanners Mews SE8 141 B4
Tanner St
Barking IG11 79 A2
SE1 117 C4 253 B1
Tanners Yd 33 E2 96 B5
Tannery Cl
Beckenham BR3,
CR0 206 D4
Dagenham RM10 81 D5
Tannery Ho 22 E1 96 A2
Tannington Terr N5 72 C5
Tannsfeld Rd SE26 184 D5
Tansley Cl N7 71 D3
Tanswell St SE1 251 A1
Tansy Cl E6 100 C1
Tantallon Rd SW12 159 A3
Tant Ave E16 98 D1
Tantony Gr RM6 58 D6
Tanworth Gdns HA5 22 C1
Tanyard Ho 8 TW8 131 C5
Tan Yard La DA5 169 C4
Tanza Rd NW3 70 D4
Tapestry Cl SM2 217 D1
Tapley Ho 11 SE1 118 A4
Taplow NW3 70 B1
Taplow Ct CR4 202 C5
Taplow Ho 36 E2 95 D4
Taplow Rd N13 33 A6
Taplow St N1 95 A5 235 B3
Tappesfield Rd
SE15 140 C2
Tapping Cl 5 KT2 176 C3
Tapp St E1 96 B3
Tapster St EN5 1 B2
Tara Ct 4 BR3 185 D1
Tara Mews N8 50 A3
Taranto Ho 14 E1 96 D2
Tarati Ct HA0 65 D1
Tarbert Rd SE22 161 C6
Tarbert Wlk E1 118 C6
Target Cl TW14 149 C5
Target Ho W13 109 B5
Target Rdbt UB5 85 B6
Tariff Rd N17 34 A4
Tarleton Ct 2 N22 32 C1
Tarleton Gdns SE23 162 B3
Tarling Cl DA14 168 B1
Tarling Rd
Canning Town E16 98 D1
Finchley N2 30 A1
Tarling St E1 96 C1
Tarnbank EN2 16 A6
Tarnbrook Ct SW1 258 A3
Tarn St SE1 117 A3 262 A5
Tarns The NW1 232 A2
Tarnwood Pk SE9 166 B3
Tarplett Ho 22 SE14 140 D6
Tarquin Ho SE26 184 A6
Tarragon Cl SE14 141 A5
Tarragon Gr SE26 184 D4
Tarranbrae NW6 69 A1
Tarrant Ho E2 96 C4
Tarrant Pl W1 237 C3
Tarrantt Ho W14 254 A6
Tarriff Cres SE8 119 B2
Tarrington Cl SW16 159 D1
Tartan Ho 12 E14 98 A1
Tarver Rd
SE17 116 D1 261 D2
Tarves Way SE10 141 D5
Tashbar of Edgware Prim Sch HA8 26 C6
Tash Pl N11 31 B5
Tasker Cl UB7 127 A5
Tasker Ho
3 Barking IG11 101 B5
17 Poplar E14 97 B2
Tasker Lo W8 245 A2
Tasker Rd NW3 70 D3
Tasman Ct
Ashford TW16 171 C3
9 Cubitt Town E14 119 D2
Tasman Ho 17 E1 118 B5
Tasmania Terr N18 33 A4
Tasman Rd SW9 138 A2
Tasman Wlk E16 99 D1
Tasso Rd W6 135 A6 264 A6
Tasso Yd W6 264 A5
Tatam Rd NW10 67 B1
Tatchbury Ho SW15 155 D5
Tate Britain★
SW1 116 A2 260 A3
Tate Gdns WD23 8 C4
Tate Ho 13 E2 96 D5
Tate Modern★
EC4 116 D5 251 D4
Tate Rd Newham E16 122 B5
Sutton SM1 217 C3
Tatham Pl
NW8 92 B5 229 D4
Tatnell Rd SE23 163 A5
Tattersall Cl SE9 166 A6
Tatton Cres E5, N16 51 D2
Tatum St
SE17 117 B2 262 D3
Tauheed Cl N4 73 A6
Taunton Ave
Hounslow TW3 130 A3
Wimbledon SW20 178 B1
Taunton Cl SM3 201 C1
Taunton Dr Enfield EN2 4 C2
Finchley N2 30 A1
Taunton Ho W2 236 A1
Taunton Mews NW1 237 C5
Taunton Pl
NW1 92 D3 237 C6
Taunton Rd
Greenford UB6 85 D6
Lewisham SE12 164 D6
Taunton Way HA7 26 A1
Tavern Cl SM5 202 C2
Tavern Ct SE1 262 B5
Taverner Ho N16 73 B5
Taverners Cl W11 244 A3
Taverners Ct HA9 66 B6
Taverners Lo EN4 15 A6
Taverner Sq 4 N5 73 A4
Taverners Way E4 20 C3
Tavern La SW9 138 C3
Tavistock Ave
Mill Hill NW7 28 D3
Walthamstow E17 53 A6
Wembley UB6 87 A5
Tavistock Cl N16 73 C3
Tavistock Cres
Mitcham CR4 204 A5
Notting Hill W11 91 B2
Tavistock Ct
1 Croydon CR0 205 B1
WC1 239 D6
Tavistock Gdns IG3 79 C4
Tavistock Gr CR0 205 B2
Tavistock Ho 3 W11 91 B2
Tavistock Mews 3
W11 91 B1
Tavistock Pl
Bloomsbury
WC1 94 A3 240 A6
East Barnet N14 15 B5
Tavistock Rd
4 Beckenham BR2 208 D5
Carshalton SM5 202 B1
Croydon CR0 205 B1
DA16 146 C4
Dagenham NW10 89 D5
Edgware HA8 26 C2
Leyton E7 76 D4
Notting Hill W11 91 B2
Stratford E15 76 D2
Tottenham N4, N15 51 B3
Uxbridge UB10 61 A3
Wanstead E18 55 A6
Tavistock Sq
WC1 93 D3 239 D6
Tavistock St
WC2 116 A6 250 B6
Tavistock Terr N19 71 D5
Tavistock Twr SE16 119 A3
Tavistock Wlk SM5 202 B1
Taviton St
WC1 93 D3 239 C6
Tavy Bridge SE2 124 C4
Tavy Cl SE11 261 B2
Tawhid Boys Sch
N16 73 D6
Tawney Rd SE28 124 B6
Tawny Cl Ealing W13 109 B5
Feltham TW13 150 A1
Tawny Way SE16 118 D2
Tayben Ave TW2 152 C5
Taybridge Rd SW11 137 A1
Tayburn Cl E14 98 A1
Tayfield Cl UB10 61 A5
Tay Ho 10 E3 97 B5
Tayler Ct NW8 229 C6
Taylor Ave TW9 132 D3
Taylor Cl
Deptford SE8 141 B6
Hampton TW12 174 A5
Hounslow TW3 130 A4
3 Orpington BR6 227 D4
Tottenham N17 34 A3
Taylor Ct Ealing W13 109 C5
Penge SE20 184 C1
Taylor Ho
Carshalton SM5 218 C6
10 Streatham SW2 160 C3
Taylor Rd
Mitcham CR4 180 C3
Wallington SM6 219 B3
Taylor's Bldgs SE18 122 D2
Taylors Cl DA14 167 D1
Taylors Ct TW13 150 A2
Taylor's Gn W3 89 C1
Taylor's La Barnet EN5 1 B4
Forest Hill SE26 184 B6
Willesden NW10 67 C1
Taylorsmead NW7 28 A5
Taymount Grange 2
SE23 162 C2
Taymount Ri SE23 162 B2
Taymount Rise SE23 162 C2
Tayport Cl N1 72 A1
Tayside Ct 6 SE5 139 B1
Tayside Dr HA8 10 D2
Taywood Rd UB5 85 B3
Tayyibah Girls Sch 5
E5 52 B1
Teak Cl SE16 119 A5
Tealby Ct N7 72 B2
Teal Cl Enfield EN3 6 C6
Newham E16 99 D2
Teal Ct 30 SE8 141 B6
Wallington SM6 219 C3
Willesden NW10 67 B2
Teale St E2 96 A5
Tealing Dr KT19 215 B4
Teal Pl SM1 217 B3
Teal St 1 SE10 120 D3
Teasel Cl CR0 206 D1
Teasel Cres SE28 123 C5
Teasel Way E15 98 C4
Teather St 12 SE5 139 C5
Tebbs Ho 14 SW2 160 C4
Tebworth Rd N17 33 D3
Technology Pk NW9 45 C6
Teck Cl TW7 131 A3
Tedder 5 NW9 27 D3
Tedder Cl
Chessington KT9 213 C3
Hillingdon UB10 60 B1
Ruislip HA4 62 B3
Tedder Rd CR2 222 D1
TEDDINGTON 175 C5
Teddington Bsns Pk
TW11 174 D4
Teddington Meml Hospl
TW11 174 C4
Teddington Park Rd
TW11 174 D6
Teddington Pk
TW11 174 D5
Teddington Sch
TW11 175 C4
Teddington Sta
TW11 175 A4
Ted Hennem Ho
RM10 81 D5
Tedman Ct SE13 142 A1
Ted Roberts Ho 25
E2 96 B5
Tedworth Gdns SW3 257 C1
Tedworth Sq
SW3 114 D1 257 C1
Tees Ave UB6 86 D5
Tees Ct W7 86 B1
Teesdale Ave TW7 131 A4
Teesdale Cl E2 96 B5
Teesdale Gdns
Isleworth TW7 131 A4
South Norwood SE25 183 C1
Teesdale Rd E11 54 D2
Teesdale St E2 96 B5
Teesdale Yd 34 E2 96 B5
Teeswater Ct DA18 124 D3
Tee The W3 89 C1
Teevan Cl CR0 206 A2
Teevan Rd CR0 206 A2
Tegan Cl SM2 217 C1
Teign Mews SE9 166 A2
Teignmouth Cl
6 Clapham SW4 137 D1
Edgware HA8 26 B1
Teignmouth Gdns
UB6 87 A4
Teignmouth Par UB6 87 B5
Teignmouth Rd
Bexley DA16 146 C3
Brondesbury NW2 68 D2
Tejas Ct N3 47 A5
Tej Ct E7 77 D3
Telcote Way HA4 40 C2
Telegraph Hill NW3 69 D5
Telegraph La KT10 212 D3
Telegraph Mews IG3 58 A1
Telegraph Pl E14 119 D2
Telegraph Rd SW15 156 C4
Telegraph St EC2 242 C2
Telemann Sq SE3 143 B2
Telephone Pl SW6 264 D6
Telfer Cl 4 W3 111 A4
Telfer Ho
8 Dulwich SE21 183 C6
EC1 234 D1
Telferscot Prim Sch 5
SW12 159 D3
Telferscot Rd SW12 159 D3
Telford Ave SW12,
SW2 160 A3
Telford Avenue Mans 7
SW2 160 A3
Telford Cl
Penge SE19 183 D4
Walthamstow E17 53 A2
Telford Ct EN5 13 C6
Telford Dr KT12 194 C2
Telford Ho
2 Belvedere DA17 125 C3
8 Kensal Town W10 91 A2
SE1 262 A6
Telford Parade Mans 8
SW2 160 A3
Telford Rd
3 Hendon NW9 46 A3
Kensal Town W10 91 A2
Sidcup SE9 167 B2
Southall UB1 85 D1
Twickenham TW4 151 C4
Telford Rd (North Circular Rd) N11 31 C5
Telford's Yd 21 SE1 118 A6
Telford Terr SW1 269 A6
Telford Way
Dagenham W3 89 C2
Hayes UB4 85 A2
Telham Rd E6 100 C5
Tell Gr SE22 139 D1
Tellson Ave SE18 144 A4
Telscombe Cl BR6 227 C6
Telscombe Ho SW11 268 A1
Temair Ho 1 SE10 142 A5
Temeraire Pl TW8 110 B1
Temeraire St SE16 118 C4
Tempelhof Ave NW2 46 C2
Temperley Rd SW12 159 A4
Templar Ct RM7 59 D5
Templar Dr SE28 102 D1
Templar Ho
Hampstead NW2 69 B2
7 Upper Clapton E5 74 C6
Templar Pl TW12 173 C3
Templars Ave NW11 47 B3
Templars Cres N3 29 C1
Templars Dr HA3 24 B4
Templar St SE5 138 D3
Temple Ave
Croydon CR0 223 B5
Dagenham RM8 59 C1
EC4 116 C6 251 B6
Oakleigh Pk N20 14 B4
Temple Bar★ EC4 241 D1
Temple Cl Finchley N3 29 B1
Leytonstone E11 54 C2
Woolwich SE18 123 A3

Templecombe Rd E9 .. 96 C6
Templecombe Way SM4 ... 201 A4
Templecroft TW15 ... 171 B4
Temple Ct Stepney E1 .. 96 D2
SW8 ... 270 A3
Templedene BR2 ... 186 B1
Temple Dwellings 7 E2 ... 96 B5
TEMPLE FORTUNE ... 47 A4
Temple Fortune Ct 9 NW11 ... 47 B4
Temple Fortune Hill NW11 ... 47 C4
Temple Fortune Ho 3 NW11 ... 47 B4
Temple Fortune La NW11 ... 47 C3
Temple Fortune Par 5 NW11 ... 47 B4
Temple Gdns
Dagenham RM8 ... 80 D5
Edmonton N21 ... 16 D2
Temple Fortune NW11 .. 47 B3
Temple Gr Enfield EN2 .. 4 D2
Golders Green NW11 .. 47 C3
Temple Gr Hatcham Sch SE14 ... 141 A3
Temple Hall Ct E4 ... 20 B2
Temple Ho
13 Battersea SW11 .. 136 C2
4 Tufnell Pk N7 ... 71 C5
11 Walthamstow E17 ... 53 D6
Temple La EC4 ... 94 C1 241 B1
Temple Lo EN5 ... 14 B4
Templeman Rd W7 ... 86 D2
Templemead Cl W3 ... 89 C1
Temple Mead Cl HA7 .. 25 B4
Templemead Ho E9 ... 75 A4
TEMPLE MILLS ... 75 D3
Temple Mills La
London E10, E15 ... 76 A4
Stratford E15 ... 75 D4
Temple Mills Rd E9 ... 75 C4
Templemore DA14 ... 190 B5
Temple Par EN5 ... 14 B4
Temple Pk UB8 ... 82 C4
Temple Pl WC2 ... 116 B6 250 D6
Temple Rd
Acton Green W4 ... 111 A3
Cricklewood NW2 ... 68 C5
Croydon CR0 ... 221 B4
Ealing W5 ... 109 D3
Hornsey N8 ... 50 B5
Isleworth TW3 ... 130 A1
Newham E6 ... 100 A6
Richmond TW9 ... 132 B2
Temple Sheen SW14 ... 155 A6
Temple Sheen Rd SW14 ... 133 A1
Temple St E2 ... 96 B5
Temple Sta WC2 ... 116 C6 251 A6
Temple Terr N22 ... 32 C1
Templeton Ave E4 ... 35 D6
Templeton Cl
South Norwood SE19 ... 183 B2
25 Stoke Newington N16 ... 73 C3
Templeton Ct
Enfield EN3 ... 6 C5
Walthamstow E10 ... 53 D1
Templeton Pl SW5 ... 113 C2 255 B3
Templeton Rd N4, N15 ... 51 B3
Temple Way SM1 ... 218 B5
Temple West Mews SE11 ... 261 C5
Templewood W13 ... 87 B2
Templewood Ave NW3 ... 69 D5
Templewood Gdns NW3 ... 69 D5
Templewood Point NW2 ... 69 B6
Tempsford Cl EN2 ... 5 A2
Tempsford Ct HA1 ... 42 D3
Temsford Cl HA2 ... 24 A1
Ten Acre Wood Nature Reserve UB4 ... 83 D6
Tenbury Cl E7 ... 77 D3
Tenbury Ct SW12 ... 159 D3
Tenby Ave HA3 ... 25 B1
Tenby Cl
Dagenham RM6 ... 59 A3
Tottenham N15 ... 51 D5
Tenby Ct E17 ... 53 A4
Tenby Gdns UB5 ... 63 C2
Tenby Ho Hayes UB3 .. 105 A3
Islington N7 ... 72 C4
W2 ... 236 A1
Tenby Rd DA16 ... 146 D4
Dagenham RM6 ... 59 A3
Edgware HA8 ... 26 B1
Enfield EN3 ... 6 C1
Walthamstow E17 ... 53 A4
Tench St E1 ... 118 B5
Tenda Rd SE16 ... 118 B2
Tendring Ho SW2 ... 160 C5
Tendring Way RM6 ... 58 C4
Tenham Ave SW2 ... 159 D2
Tenison Ct W1 ... 249 A6
Tenison Way SE1 ... 251 A3
Tenniel Cl W2 ... 245 D6
Tennison Ave WD6 ... 10 D6
Tennison Rd SE25 ... 205 D4
Tennis St SE1 ... 117 B4 252 C2
Tenniswood Rd EN1 ... 5 C4
Tennyson Ave
Kingsbury NW9 ... 45 A6
Plashet E12 ... 78 A1
Twickenham TW1 ... 152 D3
Wanstead E11 ... 55 A2
West Barnes KT3 ... 200 B4
Tennyson Cl DA16 ... 145 D4
Enfield EN3 ... 18 D6
Feltham TW14 ... 150 A5
Tennyson Ct 3 TW10 ... 175 D6
Tennyson Ho
2 Erith DA17 ... 125 B1
SE17 ... 262 B2
Southall UB1 ... 85 C1
Tennyson Rd
Ashford TW15 ... 170 A5
Ealing W7 ... 108 D6
Hounslow TW3 ... 130 A3
Kilburn NW6 ... 91 B6
Leyton E10 ... 75 D6
Mill Hill NW7 ... 28 A5
Penge SE20 ... 184 D3
Stratford E15 ... 76 C1
Walthamstow E17 ... 53 B3
Wimbledon SW19 ... 180 A4
Tennyson St SW8 ... 137 B3
Tensing Ct TW19 ... 148 A3
Tensing Ho N1 ... 72 D2
Tensing Rd UB2 ... 107 C3
Tentelow La UB2 ... 107 D3
Tenterden Cl
Hendon NW4 ... 46 D6
SE9 ... 188 B6
Tenterden Dr NW4 ... 46 D6
Tenterden Gdns
Croydon CR0 ... 206 A2
Hendon NW4 ... 46 D6
Tenterden Gr NW4 ... 46 D6
Tenterden Ho SE17 . 263 B2
Tenterden Rd
Croydon CR0 ... 206 A2
Dagenham RM8 ... 81 B6
Tottenham N17 ... 33 D3
Tenterden St W1 ... 238 D1
Tenter Ground E1 ... 243 C3
Tent Peg La BR5 ... 211 A4
Tent St E1 ... 96 B3
Tenzing Ct 4 SE9 ... 166 A2
Tequila Wharf E14 ... 97 A1
Terborch Way 6 SE22 ... 161 C6
Tercelet Terr NW3 ... 70 A4
Teredo St SE16 ... 118 D3
Terence Ct 6 DA17 .. 147 B6
Teresa Mews E17 ... 53 C5
Teresa Wlk N10 ... 49 B4
Terling Cl E11 ... 76 D5
Terling Ho 9 W10 ... 90 C2
Terling Rd RM8 ... 81 C6
Terling Wlk N1 ... 235 A6
Terminal Four Rdbt TW6 ... 149 A5
Terminus Pl SW1 ... 258 D5
Tern Ho 9 SE15 ... 139 D4
Terrace Gdns SW13 . 133 D3
Terrace Ho 2 N20 ... 14 A1
Terrace La TW10 ... 154 A5
Terrace Rd
Hackney E9 ... 74 C1
Newham E13 ... 99 B6
Walton-on-T KT12 ... 194 B3
Terraces The 6 SW20 ... 178 D3
Terrace The
Barnes SW13, SW14 ... 133 C3
Chingford E4 ... 20 C1
Cranley Gdns N2 ... 49 A5
EC4 ... 241 B1
Kilburn NW6 ... 91 C6
10 Rotherhithe SE8 ... 119 B2
1 Woodford IG8 ... 37 A4
Terrace Wlk RM9 ... 81 A3
Terrall Apartments 7 N17 ... 51 D6
Terrano Ho 1 TW9 ... 132 D4
Terrapin Ct SW17 ... 159 B1
Terrapin Rd SW17 ... 159 B1
Terrapins KT6 ... 197 D2
Terrence McMillan Stad E13 ... 99 C3
Terrick Rd N22 ... 32 A2
Terrick St W12 ... 90 B1
Terrilands HA5 ... 41 B6
Territorial Ho SE11 .. 261 B3
Terront Rd N15 ... 51 A5
Terry Ct 8 SM6 ... 219 C2
Terry Ho SW2 ... 160 C3
Terry Lodge 2 CR7 ... 204 C4
Tersha St TW9 ... 132 B1
Tessa Sanderson Pl 6 SW8 ... 137 B2
Tessa Sanderson Way UB6 ... 64 B3
Testerton Wlk 3 W11 ... 112 D6
Testwood Ct W7 ... 108 C6
Tetcott Rd SW10 ... 136 A5 266 A3
Tetherdown N10 ... 49 A6
Tetherdown Prim Sch N10 ... 49 A5
Tetty Way BR1, BR2 ... 187 A1
Teversham La SW8 ... 138 A4 270 B2
Teviot Cl DA16 ... 146 B4
Teviot St E14 ... 98 A2
Tewkesbury Ave
Forest Hill SE23 ... 162 B4
Pinner HA5 ... 41 A4
Tewkesbury Cl
Barnet EN4 ... 2 B1
Tottenham N15 ... 51 B3
Tewkesbury Ct N11 ... 31 D4
Tewkesbury Gdns NW9 ... 44 D6
Tewkesbury Rd
Carshalton SM5 ... 202 B1
Ealing W13 ... 109 A6
Tottenham N15 ... 51 B3
Tewkesbury Terr N11 .. 31 D4
Tewson Rd SE18 ... 123 C1
Teyham Ct 2 SW11 .. 158 D5
Teynham Ave EN1 ... 17 B5
Teynham Ct N12 ... 30 A6
Teynham Gn BR2 ... 209 A4
Teynham Ho SE9 ... 167 B5
Teynton Terr N17 ... 33 A2
Thackeray Ave N17 ... 34 A1
Thackeray Cl
Hayes UB8 ... 82 D1
Isleworth TW7 ... 131 A3
Wimbledon SW19 ... 178 D3
Thackeray Ct
Chelsea SW3 ... 257 C2
Ealing W5 ... 88 B1
West Kensington W14 254 A5
Thackeray Dr RM6 ... 58 B2
Thackeray Ho
College Pk NW10 ... 90 A4
WC1 ... 240 A6
Thackeray Manor SM1 ... 218 A3
Thackeray Mews 6 E8 ... 74 A2
Thackeray Rd
Clapham SW8 ... 137 B3
Newham E6 ... 99 D5
Thackeray's Almshouses SE6 ... 163 D5
Thackeray St W8 ... 255 D6
Thackery Lo TW14 ... 149 B5
Thackrah Cl N2 ... 30 A1
Thakeham Cl SE26 ... 184 B5
Thalia Cl SE10 ... 142 B6
Tham Cl 10 SE24 ... 138 D2
Thame Rd SE16 ... 118 D4
Thames Ave
Dagenham RM9 ... 103 D3
North Cheam KT4 ... 200 C1
Sands End SW10 ... 136 A4 266 B2
Wembley UB6 ... 86 D5
Thames Bank SW14 .. 133 A3
Thamesbank Pl SE28 ... 102 C1
Thames Barrier Visitor Ctr★ SE18 ... 121 D3
Thames Christian Coll 25 SW11 ... 136 B2
Thames Circ E14 ... 119 C2
Thames Cl TW12 ... 173 D1
Thames Cnr TW16 ... 194 C6
Thames Cres W4 ... 133 C5
Thames Ct Ealing W7 .. 86 C1
Edmonton N9 ... 18 C1
10 SE15 ... 139 D5
West Molesey KT8 ... 173 D1
THAMES DITTON ... 197 B2
Thames Ditton Inf Sch KT7 ... 196 D3
Thames Ditton Island KT7 ... 197 A3
Thames Ditton Jun Sch KT7 ... 196 D2
Thames Ditton Sta KT7 ... 196 D2
Thames Dr HA4 ... 39 A3
Thames Eyot 8 TW1 ... 153 A3
Thamesfield Ct TW17 ... 193 A2
Thamesfield Ho TW17 ... 193 A2
Thamesfield Mews TW17 ... 193 A2
Thamesgate Cl TW10 ... 175 B6
Thames Gateway Pk RM9 ... 103 B4
Thames Haven KT6 . 197 D4
Thames Hts SE1 ... 253 C2
Thameside TW11 ... 175 D3
Thameside Ctr TW8 .. 132 B6
Thameside Ind Est E16 ... 121 D4
Thameside Pl KT1 .. 175 D2
Thames Link Ho 7 TW9 ... 132 A1
Thames Mdw KT12, TW17 ... 193 C1
THAMESMEAD ... 124 A5
Thames Mead KT12 .. 194 A3
Thames Meadow KT8 ... 195 C6
Thamesmead Sch TW17 ... 193 B3
Thamesmead Sh Ctr SE28 ... 124 A6
Thamesmere Dr SE28 ... 124 A6
Thames Pl SW15 ... 134 D2
Thamespoint TW11 . 175 D3
Thames Quay
Millwall E14 ... 119 D4
SW10 ... 266 B1
Thames Rd
Barking IG11 ... 102 A4
Chiswick W4 ... 132 D6
Newham E16 ... 121 D5
Thames Reach
Fulham W6 ... 134 C6
Woolwich SE28 ... 123 C4
Thames Road Ind Est E16 ... 121 D4
Thames Row TW9 ... 132 B6
Thames Side
Teddington KT1 ... 175 D2
Thames Ditton KT7 ... 197 B3
Thames St
Hampton TW12 ... 173 D1
Kingston u T KT1, KT2. 175 D1
SE10 ... 141 D6
Sunbury TW16 ... 194 B6
Walton-on-T KT12 ... 193 D2
Thamesvale Cl TW3 .. 129 C3
Thames Valley Univ W5 ... 109 D5
Thames Valley Univ (Ealing Campus) W5 ... 109 D5
Thames Valley Univ (Walpole House) W5 ... 109 C6
Thames View 2 IG1 .. 79 A6
Thames View Ho TW12 ... 194 A3
Thames View Inf Sch IG11 ... 102 A5
Thames View Jun Sch IG11 ... 101 D5
Thames View Lo IG11 ... 101 C4
Thames Village W4 .. 133 A4
Thames Wlk SW11 ... 136 C5 267 A4
Thane Mans N7 ... 72 B5
Thanescroft Gdns CR0 ... 221 C5
Thanet Ct 14 W3 ... 88 C1
Thanet Dr BR2 ... 225 D5
Thanet Ho WC1 ... 233 A1
1 West Norwood SE27 ... 160 D1
Thanet Lo NW2 ... 69 A2
Thanet Pl CR0 ... 221 A4
Thanet Rd DA5 ... 169 C4
Thanet St WC1 ... 94 A4 233 A1
Thane Villas N7 ... 72 B5
Thane Works N7 ... 72 B5
Thanington Ct DA15 . 167 C5
Thant Cl E10 ... 75 D5
Tharp Rd SM6 ... 219 D3
Thatcham Ct N20 ... 14 A4
Thatcham Gdns N20 .. 14 A4
Thatcher Cl UB7 ... 104 A4
Thatchers Way TW7 .. 152 B6
Thatches Gr RM6 ... 59 A5
Thavies Inn EC4 ... 241 B2
Thaxted Ct N1 ... 235 D3
Thaxted Ho
Bermondsey SE16 ... 118 C2
Dagenham RM10 ... 81 D1
Thaxted Lo 8 E18 ... 55 B6
Thaxted Pl 9 SW20 . 178 D3
Thaxted Rd
Buckhurst Hill IG9 ... 21 D4
SE9 ... 167 A2
Thaxton Rd W14 ... 135 B6 264 D6
Thayers Farm Rd BR3 ... 185 A2
Thayer St W1 .. 93 A1 238 B2
Theatre Royal★ E10 .. 76 B2
Theatre Sq E15 ... 76 B2
Theatre St SW11 ... 136 D2
Theberton St N1 ... 94 D6 234 C6
Theed St SE1 . 116 C5 251 B3
Thelbridge Ho 28 E3 .. 97 D4
Thelma Gdns SE3 ... 144 A4
Thelma Gr TW11 ... 175 A4
Theobald Cres HA3 ... 24 A2
Theobald Rd
Croydon CR0 ... 220 D6
Walthamstow E17 ... 53 C2
Theobalds Ave N12 ... 30 A6
Theobalds Ct N4 ... 73 A6
Theobalds Park Rd EN2 ... 4 D6
Theobald's Rd WC1 ... 94 B2 240 C4
Theobald St SE1 ... 262 C5
Theodora Way HA5 ... 39 D6
Theodore Ct SE13 ... 164 B5
Theodore Ho 1 SW15 ... 156 A6
Theodore Rd SE13 ... 164 B5
Therapia La
Thornton Heath CR0 ... 204 A2
Thornton Heath CR0 . 204 A3
Wallington CR0 ... 203 D2
Therapia Lane Sta CR0 ... 204 A2
Therapia Rd SE22 ... 162 C5
Theresa Rd W6 ... 112 A2
Therfield Ct N4 ... 73 A6
Thermopylae Gate E14 ... 119 D2

Theseus Ho
2 South Bromley
E14 98 B1
2 E14 98 B1
Theseus Wlk N1 234 D3
Thesiger Rd SE20 184 D3
Thessaly Ho SW8 269 A3
Thessaly Rd
SW8 137 C4 269 B2
Thetford Cl N13 32 D4
Thetford Ct
3 Dulwich SE21 162 B2
New Malden KT3 199 C4
Thetford Gdns RM9 103 A6
Thetford Ho SE1 263 C6
Thetford Rd
Ashford TW15 148 A1
Dagenham RM9 80 D1
New Malden KT3 199 C4
Thetis Terr TW9 132 C6
Theydon Gr IG8 37 C4
Theydon Rd E5 74 C6
Theydon St E17 53 B2
Thicket Cres SM1 218 A4
Thicket Ct 14 SM1 218 A4
Thicket Gr
Dagenham RM9 80 C2
Penge SE20 184 A3
Thicket Rd
Penge SE20 184 B3
Sutton SM1 218 A4
Thicket The UB7 82 A1
Third Ave
Chadwell Heath RM6 58 C3
Dagenham RM10 103 D5
East Acton W3 111 D5
Enfield EN1 17 D6
Hayes UB3 105 D5
Little Ilford E12 78 B3
3 Newham E13 99 A4
Walthamstow E17 53 C4
Wembley HA9 65 D6
West Kilburn W10 91 A4
Third Cl KT8 196 A5
Third Cross Rd TW2 152 B2
Thirleby Rd
Hendon HA8 27 B2
SW1 115 C3 259 B5
Thirlestane Ct N10 31 A1
Thirlestane Ho
TW12 173 D6
Thirlmere NW1 231 D2
Thirlmere Ave UB6 87 C4
Thirlmere Gdns HA9 43 D1
Thirlmere Ho
Isleworth TW1 152 D6
19 Stoke Newington
N16 73 B4
Thirlmere Rd
Muswell Hill N10 31 B2
Streatham SW16 181 D6
Thirlmere Rise BR1 186 D4
Thirsk Cl UB5 63 C2
Thirsk Rd
Clapham SW11 137 A1
Mitcham CR4 181 A3
South Norwood SE25 205 B5
Thistlebrook SE2 124 C3
Thistlebrook Ind Est
SE2 124 C4
Thistlecroft Gdns
HA7 25 D1
Thistle Ct N17 52 B5
Thistledene KT7 196 C3
Thistledene Ave HA2 63 A5
Thistledown Ct
SE25 205 C6
Thistlefield Cl DA5 168 D3
Thistle Gr SW7 256 B1
Thistle Ho 10 E14 98 A1
Thistlemead BR7 188 D1
Thistlewaite Rd E5 74 B5
Thistlewood Cl 3 N7 72 B6
Thistleworth Cl TW7 130 B5
Thistley Cl N12 30 C4
Thistly Ct SE8 141 D6
Thomas a' Beckett Cl
HA0 64 D4
Thomas Arnold Prim Sch
RM9 81 B1
Thomas Baines Rd
SW11 136 B2
Thomas Burt Ho 9
E2 96 B4
Thomas Buxton Jun & Inf
Sch 17 E1 96 A3
Thomas Cribb Mews
E6 100 B1
Thomas Crowell Ct 29
N1 73 C3
Thomas Ct RM8 80 C6
Thomas Dean Rd
SE26 185 B6
Thomas Dinwiddy Rd
SE12 165 B2
Thomas Doyle St
SE1 261 D6
Thomas Fairchild Com
Sch N1 95 A5 235 B4
Thomas Gamuel Prim
Sch E17 53 C3
Thomas Hardy Ho
N22 32 B2
Thomas Hewlett Ho
HA1 64 C4
Thomas Ho
9 Belmont SM2 217 D1
3 Hackney E9 74 C2
4 Stockwell SW4 138 A1
Thomas Hollywood Ho 3
E2 96 C5
Thomas Jacomb Pl 2
E17 53 B5
Thomas Jones Prim Sch
16 W11 91 A1
Thomas Knyvett Coll
TW15 148 A1
Thomas' La SE6 163 C4
Thomas Lo E17 53 D4
Thomas London Ind Day
Sch W8 113 D3 255 D6
Thomas Milner Ho 8
SE15 140 A5
Thomas More Bldg The
HA4 39 C1
Thomas More Ho
EC2 242 A3
Thomas More Sq E1 118 A6
Thomas More St E1 118 A5
Thomas More Way
N2 48 A6
Thomas Neal's Ctr
WC1 94 A1 240 A1
Thomas North Terr 4
E16 98 D2
Thomas Pl W8 255 C5
Thomas Pooley Ct
KT6 198 A2
Thomas Rd E14 97 C2
Thomas Road Ind Est 2
E14 97 C1
Thomas Shearley Ct
DA5 169 D4
Thomas's Prep Sch
Clapham SW11 158 D6
Thomas's Prep Schs
SW11 136 B4 266 D1
Thomas St SE18 122 D2
Thomas Tallis Sch
SE3 143 B2
Thomas Wall Cl
SM1 217 D3
Thomas Watson Cottage
Homes The EN5 13 A6
Thompson Ave
Richmond TW9 132 C2
6 SE5 139 A5
Thompson Cl
Ilford IG1 79 A6
Morden SM3 201 C1
Thompson Ho
11 Kensal Town W10 91 A3
SE14 140 D6
Southall UB1 107 A6
Thompson Rd
Dagenham RM9 81 B5
Dulwich Village SE22 161 D5
Hounslow TW3 129 D1
Uxbridge UB10 60 A1
Thomson Cres CR0 204 C1
Thomson Ct 4 E8 74 A2
Thomson Ho
Pimlico SW1 259 D1
Walworth SE17 263 A3
Thomson Rd HA3 42 C6
Thorburn Ho SW1 248 A1
Thorburn Sq SE1 118 A2
Thorburn Way SW19 180 B2
Thoresby Ho N16 73 B5
Thoresby St
N1 95 A4 235 B2
Thorkhill Gdns KT7 197 B1
Thorkhill Rd KT7 197 B2
Thornaby Gdns N18 34 B5
Thornaby Ho 15 E2 96 B4
Thorn Ave WD23 8 A3
Thornbill Ho 1
SE15 140 A5
Thornbridge Ct 10
EN5 13 D6
Thornbury 3 NW4 46 C5
Thornbury Ave TW7 130 B5
Thornbury Cl
Edgware NW7 28 D3
Stoke Newington N16 73 C3
Thornbury Ct
Croydon CR2 221 B3
Hounslow TW7 130 C5
W11 245 A6
Thornbury Ho N6 49 C1
Thornbury Lo EN2 4 D2
Thornbury Rd
Clapham Pk SW2 160 A5
Hounslow TW7 130 B4
Thornbury Sq N6 49 C1
Thornby Rd E5 74 C5
Thorn Cl BR2 210 C3
Northolt UB5 85 B4
Thorncliffe Ct SW2 160 A5
Thorncliffe Rd
Clapham Pk SW2 160 A5
Southall UB2 107 B1
Thorncombe Rd
SE22 161 C6
Thorncroft HA2 64 A5
Thorncroft Rd SM1 217 D4
Thorncroft St
SW8 138 A5 270 A3
Thorndale BR7 188 B3
Thorndale Ho 10 N16 51 C1
Thorndean St SW18 158 A2
Thorndene Ave N11 15 A3
Thorndike Ave UB5 84 D6
Thorndike Cl
SW10 136 A5 266 A4
Thorndike Ho SW1 259 C2
Thorndike Rd 21 N1 73 B2
Thorndike St
SW1 115 D2 259 C3
Thorndon Cl BR5 189 D1
Thorndon Gdns
KT19 215 C4
Thorndon Rd BR5 189 D1
Thorndyke Ct HA5 23 B3
Thorne Cl
Claygate KT10 213 A1
DA8 147 D6
Leyton E11 76 C4
Littleton TW15 171 A3
Newham E16 99 A1
Thorne Ho
34 Bethnal Green E2 96 C4
4 Cubitt Town E14 120 A3
Thorneloe Gdns CR0,
CR9 220 D3
Thorne Pas 7
SW13 133 D3
Thorne Rd
SW8 138 A5 270 B3
Thorne's Cl BR3 208 A6
Thorness Ct SW18 158 A5
Thorne St SW13,
SW14 133 C2
Thornet Wood Rd
BR1 210 C6
Thornewill Ho 8
E1 118 C6
Thorney Cres
SW11 136 B5 266 D3
Thorneycroft Cl
KT12 194 C3
Thorneycroft Dr EN3 7 C6
Thorneycroft Ho 11
W4 111 C1
Thorney Ct W8 246 A1
Thorney Hedge Rd
W4 110 D2
Thorney St
SW1 116 A2 260 A4
Thornfield Ave NW7 29 A2
Thornfield Ct NW7 29 A2
Thornfield Ho 5
E14 119 C6
Thornfield Par NW7 29 A3
Thornfield Rd W12 112 B4
Thornford Rd SE13 164 A6
Thorngate Rd W9 91 C3
Thorngrove Rd E13 99 B6
Thornham Gr E15 76 B3
Thorn Ham Ho SE1 262 D6
Thornham St SE10 141 D6
Thornhaugh St WC1 239 D5
Thornhill Ave SE18 145 C5
Surbiton KT6 214 A6
Thornhill Bridge Wharf
N1 233 C5
Thornhill Cres N1 72 B1
Thornhill Ct N8 49 D3
Thornhill Gdns
Barking IG11 79 C1
Leyton E10 75 D6
Thornhill Gr N1 72 C1
Thornhill Ho
12 Chiswick W4 111 C1
Islington N1 72 C1
Thornhill Mews
SW15 135 B1
Thornhill Prim Sch 11
N1 72 C1
Thornhill Rd
Ickenham UB10 60 C4
Islington N1 94 C6 234 A6
Leyton E10 75 D6
Surbiton KT6 214 B6
Thornton Heath CR0 205 A2
Thornhill Sq N1 72 B1
Thornhill Way TW17 192 C4
Thornicroft Ho 12
SW9 138 B3
Thornlaw Rd SE27 182 D6
Thornley Cl N17 34 A3
Thornley Dr HA2 63 D6
Thornley Pl 2 SE10 120 C1
Thornsbeach Rd
SE6 164 A2
Thornsett Pl SE20 184 B1
Thornsett Rd
Penge SE20 184 B1
Wandsworth SW18 157 D3
Thornsett Terr SE20 184 B1
Thornton Ave
Chiswick W4 111 C2
Streatham SW2 159 D3
Thornton Heath CR0 204 B3
West Drayton UB7 104 B3
Thornton Cl UB7 104 B3
Thornton Ct
Lower Holloway N7 72 A3
West Barnes SW20 200 D4
Thornton Dene BR3 185 C1
Thornton Gdns
SW12 159 D3
Thornton Gr HA5 23 C4
THORNTON HEATH 204 D3
Thornton Heath L Ctr
CR7 205 A5
Thornton Heath Pond
CR7 204 C4
Thornton Heath Sta
CR7 205 A5
Thornton Hill SW19 179 A3
Thornton Ho SE17 263 A3
7 Wanstead E11 55 A3
Thornton Lo
South Norwood CR7 205 A6
8 Wimbledon SW19 179 A3
Thornton Pl W1 237 D4
Thornton Rd
Barnet EN5 1 A2
Belvedere DA17 125 D2
BR1 187 A5
Carshalton SM5 202 B1
Ilford IG1 78 D4
Leyton E11 76 B6
Lower Edmonton N18 18 C1
Mortlake SW14 133 B2
Streatham SW12,
SW2 159 D3
Thornton Heath CR0,
CR7 204 B3
Wimbledon SW19 178 D3
Thornton Rd E
SW19 178 D4
Thornton Rd Ind Est
CR0 204 B3
Thornton Row CR7 204 C4
Thornton St SW9 138 C3
Thornton Way NW11 47 D4
Thorntree Ct W5 88 A2
Thorntree Prim Sch
SE7 121 D1
Thorntree Rd SE7 121 D1
Thornville Gr CR4 180 B1
Thornville St SE8 141 C4
Thornwell Ct W7 108 C4
Thornwood Cl E18 37 B1
Thornwood Gdns
W8 245 A2
Thornwood Lo W8 245 A2
Thornwood Rd SE13 164 C6
Thornycroft Ct TW9 132 B3
Thorogood Gdns E15 76 C3
Thorold Ho SE1 252 A2
6 Streatham SW2 160 A4
Thorold Rd Ilford IG1 57 A1
Wood Green N22 32 A3
Thorparch Rd
SW8 137 D5 269 D3
Thorpebank Rd
W12 112 A5
Thorpe Cl BR6 227 C6
Forest Hill SE26 184 D6
Notting Hill W10 91 A1
Thorpe Coombe Hospl
E17 54 A6
Thorpe Cres E17 35 B1
Thorpe Ct Enfield EN2 4 D2
Upper Tooting SW17 180 C6
Thorpedale Gdns IG6 56 D5
Thorpedale Rd N4 50 B1
Thorpe Hall W5 87 D2
Thorpe Hall Prim Sch
E17 36 B2
Thorpe Hall Rd E17 36 A2
Thorpe Ho N1 233 D5
Thorpe Rd
Barking IG11 79 B1
Chingford E17 36 A1
Kingston u T KT2 176 A3
Leyton E7 76 D4
Newham E6 100 B6
Tottenham N15 51 C3
Thorpewood Ave SE23,
SE26 162 B2
Thorpland Ave UB10 61 A5
Thorsden Way 2
SE19 183 C5
Thorverton Rd NW2 69 A5
Thoydon Rd E3 97 A5
Thrale Almshouses
SW16 182 A5
Thrale Rd SW16 181 C5
Thrale St SE1 252 B3
Thrasher Cl 20 E8 95 D6
Thrawl St E1 95 D2 243 D3
Thrayle Ho 2 SW9 138 B2
Threadgold Ho 8 N1 73 B2
Threadneedle St EC2,
EC3 95 B1 242 D1
Three Bridges Bsns Ctr
UB2 108 A4
Three Bridges Prim Sch
UB2 107 D3
Three Colts La E2 96 B3
Three Colt St E14 119 B6
Three Corners DA7 147 D3
Three Cups Yd WC1 240 D3
Three Kings Yd W1 248 C6
Three Meadows Mews
HA7 24 D2
Three Mill La E3 98 A4
Three Mills Studios*
E14 98 A4
Three Nun Ct EC2 242 B2
Three Oak La SE1 253 C2
Three Oaks Cl UB10 60 B5
Threshers Pl W11 244 A6
Thriffwood SE23,
SE26 162 D1
Thrigby Rd KT9 214 B2
Thring Ho 2 SW9 138 B3
Throckmorten Rd
E16 99 B1
Throgmorton Ave
EC2 95 B1 242 D2
Throgmorton St
EC2 95 B1 242 D2
Throwley Cl SE2 124 C3
Throwley Rd SM1 217 D3
Throwley Way SM1 217 D3
Thrupp Cl CR4 181 B1
Thrush Gn HA2 41 C5
Thrush St SE17 262 A2
Thunderer Rd RM9 103 B3
Thurbarn Rd SE6 185 D5

Thurbin Ho UB4 83 B2
Thurland Ho 3
SE16 118 B2
Thurland Rd SE16 118 A3
Thurlby Cl HA1 43 A3
Thurlby Croft NW4 46 C6
Thurlby Rd
Wembley HA0 65 D2
West Norwood SE27 182 C6
Thurleigh Ave SW12 159 A5
Thurleigh Ct SW12 159 A5
Thurleigh Rd SW12 159 A5
Thurleston Ave SM4 201 A4
Thurlestone Ave
Colney Hatch N12 30 D4
Ilford IG3 79 D4
Thurlestone Cl
TW17 193 A3
Thurlestone Ct 1
UB1 85 D1
Thurlestone Par
TW17 193 A3
Thurlestone Rd
SE27 182 C6
Thurloe Cl SW7 257 A4
Thurloe Ct SW3 257 A3
Thurloe Pl
SW7 114 B2 256 D4
Thurloe Place Mews
SW7 256 D4
Thurloe Sq
SW7 114 C2 257 A4
Thurloe St
SW7 114 B2 256 D4
Thurlow Cl E4 35 D4
Thurlow Ct 5 E11 55 A4
Thurlow Gdns HA0 65 D3
Thurlow Hill SE21 161 A2
Thurlow Ho 17
SW16 160 A1
Thurlow Park Rd SE21,
SE24 161 A2
Thurlow Rd
Hampstead NW3 70 B3
West Ealing W7 109 A4
Thurlow St
SE17 117 C1 263 A1
Thurlow Terr NW5 71 A3
Thurlow Twrs SE27 160 C1
Thurlow Wlk SE17 263 A1
Thurlston Rd HA4 62 A5
Thurnby Ct TW2 152 C1
Thurnscoe NW1 232 A5
Thursland Rd DA14 191 A5
Thursley Cres CR0 224 B1
Thursley Gdns
SW19 156 D2
Thursley Ho
3 Kingston u T
KT2 176 D3
10 Streatham SW2 160 B4
Thursley Rd SE9 166 B1
Thurso Ho NW6 91 D5
Thurso St SW17 180 B6
Thurstan Rd SW20 178 B3
Thurston Ho 4 BR3 185 D4
Thurston Ind Est
SE13 141 D2
Thurston Rd
Southall UB1 85 B1
St Johns SE8, SE13 141 D3
Thurtle Rd E2 95 D5
Thurza Ct 3 TW7 130 D3
Thyer Cl BR6 227 A4
Thyme Cl SE3 143 C2
Thyme Ct NW7 29 A3
Thyra Gr N12 29 D4
Tibbatt's Rd E3 97 D3
Tibbenham Pl SE6 163 C2
Tibbenham Wlk E13 98 D5
Tibberton Sq N1 235 A6
Tibbets Cl SW19 156 D3
Tibbet's Corner
SW19 156 D4
Tibbet's Ride SW19 156 D4
Tiber Cl 10 E3 97 C6
Tiber Gdns N1 233 B5
Ticehurst Cl BR5 190 A3
Ticehurst Rd SE23 163 A2
Tickford Cl SE2 124 C4
Tickford Ho NW8 230 A1
Tidal Basin Rd E16 120 D6
Tidbury Ct SW8 269 A3
Tide Cl 3 CR4 181 A2
Tideham Ho SE28 123 B5
Tidelock Ho SE28 123 B4
Tidemill Prim Sch 20
SE8 141 C5
Tidenham Gdns CR0 221 C5
Tideside Ct SE18 122 A3
Tideslea Path SE28 123 B5
Tideslea Twr SE28 123 A4
Tideswell 10 NW5 71 B4
Tideswell Rd
Croydon CR0 223 C5
Putney SW15 134 C1
Tideway Cl TW10 175 C6
Tideway Ct 9 SE16 118 D5
Tideway Ho E14 119 C4
Tideway Ind Est
SW8 137 C6 269 B5
Tideway Wharf
SW13 133 C3
Tideway Yd SW13 133 C3
Tidey St E3 97 C2
Tidford Rd DA16 145 D3
Tidworth Ho 13
SE22 139 C2
Tidworth Rd E3 97 C3
Tiepigs La BR2, BR4 208 D1
Tierney Ct 4 CR0 221 D6
Tierney Rd SW2 160 A3
Tierney Terr SW2 160 A3
Tiffin Girls' Sch KT2 176 A4
Tiffin Sch KT2 176 B1
Tiger Ho WC1 232 D1
Tiger La BR2 209 B5
Tiger Way E5 74 B4
Tignel Ct W3 110 C4
Tigris Cl N9 18 C2
Tilbrook Rd SE3 143 C2
Tilbury Cl
14 Camberwell
SE15 139 D5
12 Pinner HA5 23 B3
St Paul's Cray BR5 190 B1
Tilbury Ho 4 SE14 140 D6
Tilbury Rd
Leytonstone E10 54 A2
Newham E6 100 B5
Tildesley Rd SW15 156 C5
Tile Farm Rd BR6 227 B5
Tilehurst NW1 231 D1
Tilehurst Point 2
SE2 124 C4
Tilehurst Rd
Cheam SM3 217 A3
Wandsworth SW17,
SW18 158 B3
Tile Kiln La
Edmonton N13 33 A5
Harefield UB9 38 D2
Upper Holloway N6 49 C1
Tileyard Rd N7 72 A1
Tilford Ave CR0 224 A1
Tilford Gdns SW19 156 D3
Tilford Ho 8 SW2 160 B4
Tilia Cl SM1 217 B3
Tilia Rd E5 74 B4
Tilia Wlk 21 SW9 138 D1
Tiller Ho 28 N1 95 C6
Tiller L Ctr E14 119 C3
Tiller Rd E14 119 C3
Tillet Sq SE16 119 A4
Tillett Cl NW10 67 A2
Tillet Way 6 E2 96 A4
Tilley Rd TW14 150 A3
Tillingbourne Gdns
N3 47 B6
Tillingbourne Way
N3 47 B5
Tillingham Way N12 29 D6
Tilling Ho 1 SE15 140 B2
Tilling Rd NW2 46 C2
Tilling Way HA9 65 D6
Tillman Ho 8 SW2 160 B3
Tillman St E1 96 B1
Tilloch St 9 N1 72 B1
Tillotson Ct SW8 269 D3
Tillotson Rd
Edmonton N9 17 D2
Harrow HA3 23 D3
Ilford IG1 56 C2
Tilney Ct EC1 242 B6
Kingston u T KT6 197 D4
Woodford IG9 21 A2
Tilney Dr IG9 21 A2
Tilney Gdns 12 N1 73 B2
Tilney Rd
Dagenham RM9 81 B2
Southall UB2 106 C2
Woodford IG9 21 A2
Tilney St W1 248 B4
Tilson Cl 2 SE15 139 C5
Tilson Gdns SW2,
SW4 160 A4
Tilson Ho SW2 160 A4
Tilson Rd N17 34 A2
Tilston Cl E11 76 D5
Tilton St SW6 264 B5
Tiltwood The W3 111 A6
Tilt Yard App SE9 166 B5
Timber Cl BR7 188 C1
Timbercroft KT19 215 C4
Timbercroft La SE18 145 C5
Timbercroft Prim Sch
SE18 145 C5
Timberdene NW4 28 D1
Timberland Cl 16
SE15 140 A5
Timberland Rd E1 96 B1
Timber Mill Way
SW4 137 D2
Timber Pond Rd
SE16 118 D4
Timber St EC1 242 A6
Timberwharf Rd N16 52 A3
Time Sq E8 73 D3
Times Sq SM1 217 D3
Times Sq Sh Ctr
SM1 217 D3
Timms Cl BR1 210 B5
Timor Ct UB1 107 D5
Timothy Cl
Bexley DA6 169 A6
1 Clapham Pk SW4 159 C6
Timothy Ho DA18 125 A4
Timsbury Wlk 5
SW15 156 A3
Tina Ct
Forest Hill SE6 163 B4
West Norwood SW16 160 C1
Tindal St SW9 138 D4
Tinniswood Cl N5 72 C3
Tinsley Cl SE25 206 B6
Tinsley Rd E1 96 C2
Tintagel Cres SE22 139 D1
Tintagel Ct EC1 241 C6
Tintagel Dr HA7 25 D6
Tintagel Ho SE20 184 A3
Tintern Ave NW9 44 D6
Tintern Cl
Putney SW15 157 A6
Wimbledon SW19 180 A4
Tintern Ct W13 109 A6
Tintern Gdns N14 16 A4
Tintern Ho
Belgravia SW1 258 C3
Regent's Pk NW1 231 D3
Tintern Path NW9 45 C3
Tintern Rd
Carshalton SM5 202 B1
Tottenham N22 33 A2
Tintern St SW4 138 A1
Tintern Way HA2 41 D1
Tinto Rd E16 99 A3
Tinwell Mews WD6 11 B6
Tinworth St
SE11 116 A1 260 B2
Tippett Ct 2 E6 100 B5
Tippetts Cl EN2 5 A4
Tipthorpe Rd SW11 137 A2
Tipton Dr CR0 221 C4
Tiptree 7 NW1 71 B1
Tiptree Cl E4 20 A1
Tiptree Cres IG5 56 C6
Tiptree Ct EN2 5 B1
Tiptree Dr EN2 5 B1
Tiptree Rd HA4 62 B4
Tirlemont Rd CR2 221 A1
Tirrell Rd CR0 205 A3
Tisbury Ct W1 249 C6
Tisbury Rd SW16 182 A1
Tisdall Pl
SE17 117 B2 262 D3
Tissington Ct 4
SE16 118 D2
Titan Bsns Est 3
SE8 141 C5
Titan Ct TW8 110 B1
Titchborne Row W2 237 B1
Titchfield Rd
Carshalton SM5 202 B1
Enfield EN3 7 A6
Paddington
NW8 92 D6 230 C6
Titchfield Wlk SM5 202 B2
Titchwell Rd SW18 158 B3
Tite St SW3 136 D6 267 C6
Tithe Barn Cl KT2 176 B2
Tithe Barn Way UB5 84 B5
Tithe Cl Hayes UB4 83 D2
Hendon NW7 28 A2
Walton-on-T KT12 194 B3
Tithe Ct NW4 28 A2
Tithe Farm Ave HA2 63 C5
Tithe Farm Cl HA2 63 C5
Tithe Wlk NW7 28 A2
Titian Ave WD23 8 C4
Titley Cl E4 35 C5
Titmus Cl UB8 83 A1
Titmuss Ave SE28 124 B6
Titmuss St W12 112 C4
Tivendale N8 50 A6
Tiverton Ave IG5 56 C6
Tiverton Cl CR0 205 D2
Tiverton Dr SE9 167 A3
Tiverton Prim Sch
N15 51 B3
Tiverton Rd
Brondesbury Pk NW6,
NW10 90 D6
Edgware HA8 26 B1
Edmonton N18 33 C5
Hounslow TW3 130 A3
Ruislip HA4 62 A5
Tottenham N4, N15 51 B3
Wembley HA0 88 A5
Tiverton St
SE1 117 A3 262 A6
Tiverton Way
Chessington KT9 213 D3
Edgware NW7 28 D3
Tivoli Ct SE16 119 B5
Tivoli Gdns 11 SE18 122 A2
Tivoli Rd Hornsey N8 49 D4
Hounslow TW4 129 A1
West Norwood SE27 183 A5
Toad La TW4 129 B1
Tobago St 12 E14 119 C4
Tobin Cl NW3 70 C1
Toby Ct N9 18 C4
Toby La E1 97 A3
Toby Way KT5, KT6 214 D6
Todber Ho W14 254 A6
Todd Ho 3 N2 30 B1
Todds Wlk N7 72 B6
Tokenhouse Yd EC2 242 C2
Token Yd SW15 135 A1
TOKYNGTON 66 D2
Tokyngton Ave HA9 66 C2
Toland Sq SW15 156 A6
Tolcairn Ct 2 DA17 125 C1
Tolcarne Dr HA5 40 B6
Tolchurch 2 W11 91 C1
Toldos Sch N16 51 C1
Toley Ave HA3, HA9 44 A2
Tolhurst Dr 4 W10 91 A4
Tollbridge Cl W10 91 A3
Tollesbury Gdns IG6 57 B6
Tollet St E1 96 D3
Tollgate Dr
Dulwich SE21 161 C2
Hayes UB4 106 D6
Tollgate Ho 1 NW6 91 D5
Tollgate Prim Sch
E13 99 C3
Tollgate Rd E6 100 A2
Tollhouse Way N19 71 C6
Tollington Ct N4 72 B6
Tollington Ho 4 N19 72 A5
Tollington Pk N4 72 B6
Tollington Pl N4 72 B6
Tollington Rd N7 72 B4
Tollington Way N7 72 A5
Tolmers Sq
NW1 93 C3 239 B6
Tolpaide Ho SE11 261 A3
Tolpuddle Ave 1 E13 99 C6
Tolpuddle St
N1 94 C5 234 A4
Tolsford Rd E5 74 B3
Tolson Ho 4 TW7 131 A2
Tolson Rd TW7 131 A2
Tolverne Rd SW20 178 C2
TOLWORTH 214 C6
Tolworth Cl KT6 198 D1
Tolworth Gdns RM6 58 D4
Tolworth Girls' Sch
KT6 214 B5
Tolworth Hospl KT6 214 C6
Tolworth Inf Sch
KT6 198 B1
Tolworth Junc KT6 214 D6
Tolworth Jun Sch
KT6 198 B1
Tolworth Par RM6 59 A4
Tolworth Park Rd
KT6 214 B6
Tolworth Rd KT6 214 A6
Tolworth Recn Ctr
KT6 214 B5
Tolworth Rise N
KT5 198 D1
Tolworth Rise S
KT5 198 D1
Tolworth Sta KT5 214 D6
Tolworth Underpass KT5,
KT6 214 D6
Tomahawk Gdns 4
UB5 84 D4
Tom Blau Gallery*
SE1 250 C2
Tom Coombs Cl SE9 144 A1
Tom Cribb Rd SE18,
SE28 123 B3
Tom Groves Cl E15 76 B3
Tom Hood Cl E15 76 B3
Tom Hood Sch E11 76 D5
Tom Jenkinson Rd 5
E16 121 A5
Tomkyns Ho SE11 261 A3
Tomline Ho SE1 252 A3
Tomlin's Gr E3 97 C4
Tomlinson Cl
5 Gunnersbury
W4 110 D1
Spitalfields E2 95 D4
Tomlins Orch IG11 101 A6
Tomlin's Terr E14 97 A1
Tomlins Wlk 4 N7 72 B6
Tom Mann Cl IG11 101 C6
Tom Nolan Cl E15 98 C5
Tompion Ho EC1 241 D6
Tompion St EC1 234 D1
Tom Smith Cl SE10 142 C6
Tom Smith Ho 3 E17 54 A4
Tomson Ho SE1 263 C6
Tom Williams Ho
SW6 264 C5
Tonbridge Cres HA3 44 A5
Tonbridge Hos WC1 233 A1
Tonbridge Rd KT12,
KT8 195 B5
Tonbridge St
WC1 94 A4 233 A1
Toneborough 16
NW8 91 D6
Tonfield Rd SM3 201 B1
Tonge Cl BR3 207 C4
Tonsley Hill SW18 157 D6
Tonsley Pl SW18 157 D6
Tonsley Rd SW18 157 D6
Tonsley St SW18 157 D6
Tonstall Rd CR4 181 A1
Tony Law Ho SE12 165 A6
Tooke Cl HA5 23 A2
Tookey Cl HA3 44 B2
Took's Ct EC4 241 A2
Tooley St
SE1 117 C5 253 A3
Toorack Rd HA3 24 B1
Tooting Bec Gdns
SW16 181 D6
Tooting Bec Lido
SW16 181 C6
Tooting Bec Rd
Furzedown SW17 181 B6
Streatham SW16 181 C5
Tooting Bec Sta
SW17 159 A1
Tooting Broadway
SW17 180 D5
Tooting Broadway Sta
SW17 180 C5
Tooting Gr SW17 180 C5
TOOTING
GRAVENEY 180 B5
Tooting High St SW17,
SW19 180 C5
Tooting L Ctr SW17 180 B6
Tooting Mkts*
SW17 180 D6
Tooting Sta SW17 180 D4
Tootswood Rd BR2,
BR3 208 C5
Topaz Ct TW13 149 D1

Topaz Ho KT4 199 B1
Topaz Wlk NW2 46 D2
Topcliffe Dr BR6 227 B4
Topham Ho 8 SE10 142 A5
Topham Sq N17 33 A2
Topham St EC1 241 A6
Top House Rise E4 20 A4
Topiary Sq TW9 132 B2
Topley St SE9 143 D1
Topmast Point 23 E14 119 C4
Top Pk BR3 208 C4
Topsfield Cl N8 49 D4
Topsfield Par N8 50 A3
Topsfield Rd N8 50 A4
Topsham Rd SW17 181 A6
Tora Ct 9 IG9 21 C2
Torah Vodaas NW11 47 B1
Tora Temimah Prim Sch NW2 68 B4
Torbay Ct 13 NW1 71 B1
Torbay Mans NW6 91 B6
Torbay Rd
Brondesbury NW6 69 B1
Harrow HA2 63 A6
Torbay St 15 NW1 71 B1
Torbitt Way IG2 57 D4
Torbridge Cl HA8 26 A3
Torbrook Cl DA5 169 A5
Torcross Dr SE23 162 C2
Torcross Rd HA4 62 C5
Tor Ct W8 245 B2
Torfell 5 E18 36 D1
Tor Gdns W8 113 C4 245 A2
Tor Gr SE28 123 C5
Tor Ho N6 49 B3
Tormead Cl SM1 217 C2
Tormount Rd SE18 145 C6
Tornay Ho Hackney E9 74 C1
N1 233 C4
Toronto Ave E12 78 B4
Toronto Rd IG1 57 A1
Torquay Gdns IG4 55 D5
Torquay Ho 1 SM6 219 D3
Torquay St W2 91 D2
Tor Rd DA16 146 C4
Torrence Ho 6 N19 71 C6
Torrens Ct SE5 139 B2
Torrens Rd
Clapham Pk SW2 160 B6
Stratford E15 76 D2
Torrens Sq E15 76 D2
Torrens St EC1 94 D5 234 C3
Torres Sq E14 119 C1
Torre Wlk SM5 202 C1
Torrey Dr SW9 138 C3
Torriano Ave NW5 71 D3
Torriano Cotts NW5 71 C3
Torriano Jun & Inf Schs 24 NW5 71 D3
Torriano Mews NW5 71 C3
Torridge Gdns SE15 140 C1
Torridge Rd CR7 204 D4
Torridon Ct HA8 10 D2
Torridon Ho NW6 91 D5
Torridon Jun & Inf Schs SE6 164 B2
Torridon Rd SE13, SE6 164 B3
Torrington Ave N12 30 B5
Torrington Cl
Claygate KT10 212 C2
North Finchley N12 30 B6
Torrington Ct
Forest Hill SE26 184 A5
Harrow HA2 63 D5
North Finchley N12 30 B6
Torrington Dr HA2 63 D5
Torrington Gdns
Friern Barnet N11 31 C4
Wembley UB6 65 C1
Torrington Gr N12 30 C5
Torrington Pk N12 30 B6
Torrington Pl
Bloomsbury WC1 93 D2 239 C4
St George in t East E1 118 A5
Torrington Rd
Claygate KT10 212 C2
Dagenham RM8 59 B1
Ruislip HA4 62 A5
Wanstead E18 55 A6
Torrington Rd *continued*
Wembley UB6 87 C6
Torrington Sq
Bloomsbury WC1 93 D3 239 D5
Thornton Heath CR0 205 B2
Torrington Way SM4 201 C3
Torr Rd SE20 184 D3
Tortington Ho 1 SE15 140 B5
Torver Rd HA1 42 C5
Torver Way BR6 227 B5
Torwood Rd SW15 156 A6
Totham Lo SW20 178 B2
Tothill Ho SW1 259 D4
Tothill St SW1 115 D4 249 D1
Totland Ho SW18 157 D5
Totnes Rd DA16 146 C5
Totnes Villas N11 31 C5
Totnes Wlk N2 48 B5
Tottan Terr E1 96 D1
Tottenhall 5 NW1 71 A1
Tottenhall Inf Sch N13 32 C4
Tottenhall Rd N13 32 D4
TOTTENHAM 33 D1
Tottenham Court Rd W1 93 C2 239 B4
Tottenham Court Road Sta W1 93 D1 239 D2
Tottenham Gn E 3 N15 51 D5
Tottenham Gn E South Side 4 N15 51 D5
Tottenham Gn L Ctr N17 51 B5
TOTTENHAM HALE 52 A6
Tottenham Hale N15 52 A5
Tottenham Hale Ret Pk N15 52 A5
Tottenham Hale Sta N17 52 B6
Tottenham La N8 50 B4
Tottenham Mews W1 239 B4
Tottenham Rd N1 73 C2
Tottenham St W1 93 C2 239 B4
Totterdown St SW17 180 D5
TOTTERIDGE 13 C3
Totteridge Comm N20 12 C3
Totteridge Gn N20 13 C2
Totteridge Ho
Barnet N20 13 B3
Battersea SW11 136 B3
Totteridge La N20 13 D3
Totteridge Pk N20 12 D3
Totteridge Rd EN3 6 D6
Totteridge Village N20 13 B3
Totteridge & Whetstone Sta N20 14 A2
Totternhoe Cl HA3 43 C4
Totton Rd CR7 204 C6
Toucan Cl NW10 88 C4
Touchard Ho N1 235 D1
Toulmin St SE1 117 A4 252 A1
Toulon St SE5 139 A5
Toulouse Ct 2 SE16 118 B1
Tounson Ct SW1 259 D3
Tournay Rd SW6 135 B5 264 D4
Toussaint Wlk 18 SE16 118 A3
Tovil Cl SE20 184 B1
Tovy Ho 6 SE1 118 A1
Towcester Rd E3 98 A3
Tower 42★ EC2 95 C1 243 A2
Tower Bldgs 22 E1 118 B5
Tower Br App E1, EC3 253 C5
Tower Bridge★ E1, EC3, SE1 117 D5 253 C4
Tower Bridge Bsns Complex SE16 118 B3
Tower Bridge Bsns Sq SE16 118 B2
Tower Bridge Ex★ E1 253 C4
Tower Bridge Mews HA0 64 D4
Tower Bridge Piazza SE1 253 C3
Tower Bridge Prim Sch SE1 117 D4 253 C2
Tower Bridge Rd SE1 117 C4 253 A1
Tower Bridge Sq SE1 253 C2
Tower Bridge Wharf SE1 118 A5
Tower Cl
Hampstead NW3 70 B3
Orpington BR6 227 D5
Penge SE20 184 B3
Tower Ct
Brockley SE4 141 A1
Stamford Hill E5 51 D2
St Giles WC2 240 A1
St John's Wood NW8 230 B4
Tower Gardens Rd N17 33 B2
Towergate SE1 263 A4
Towergate Cl UB8 60 A3
Towergate Ho 35 E3 97 B5
Tower Gateway Sta EC3 117 D6 253 C6
Tower Gdns KT10 213 A1
Tower Gr KT13 193 C1
TOWER HAMLETS 97 B2
Tower Hamlets Coll
25 Poplar E14 97 D1
27 Poplar E14 119 D6
16 Stepney E1 96 D1
Tower Hamlets Rd
Forest Gate E7 76 D3
Walthamstow E17 53 C6
Tower Hill EC3 117 D6 253 D5
Tower Hill Sta EC3 117 D6 253 C6
Tower House Sch SW14 133 A1
Tower La HA9 65 D5
Tower Mans SE1 263 C5
Tower Mews
Hackney E5 75 A3
Walthamstow E17 53 C5
Tower Millennium Pier EC3 117 C5 253 B4
Tower Mill Rd
7 Camberwell SE15 139 C6
1 SE15 139 C5
Tower Pl E EC3 253 B5
Tower Pl W EC3 253 B5
Tower Rd DA7 147 D1
Orpington BR6 227 D5
Twickenham TW1, TW2 152 D1
Willesden NW10 68 A1
Tower Rise TW9 132 A2
Tower Royal EC4 252 C6
Towers Ave UB10 83 A4
Towers Bsns Pk HA9 66 D4
Towers Ct UB10 83 A4
Towers Pl TW10 154 A6
Towers Rd Pinner HA5 23 A2
Southall UB1 85 C3
Tower St WC2 240 A1
Towers The
Dartmouth Pk NW5 71 B5
1 Richmond TW9 132 B1
Tower Terr
Brockley SE4 141 A1
Wood Green N22 32 B1
Tower The★ EC3 117 D6 253 C5
Towerview SE13 163 C6
Tower View
Bushey WD23 8 C4
Croydon CR0 207 A2
Tower Wharf SE1 253 C2
Tower Wlk SE1 263 A4
Towfield Ct TW13 151 B2
Towfield Rd TW13 151 B2
Towncourt Cres BR5 211 B5
Towncourt La BR5 211 B2
Towncourt Path N4 51 A1
Townend Ct 6 BR1 186 D2
Towney Mead UB5 85 B5
Towney Mead Ct UB5 85 B5
Townfield Rd UB3 105 D5
Townfield Sq UB3 105 D6
Town Field Way TW7 131 A3
Town Hall Approach Rd N15 51 D5
Townhall Ave 3 W4 111 B1
Town Hall Rd SW11 136 D2
Townholm Cres W7 108 D3
Town Hos EC1 241 D5
Town La TW19 148 A2
Townley Ct E15 76 D2
Townley Gram Sch for Girls DA6 169 B6
Townley Rd DA6 169 B6
Dulwich Village SE22 161 C6
Townley St SE17 117 B1 262 C2
Townmead Bsns Ctr SW6 136 A2
Town Meadow TW8 131 D5
Townmead Rd
Richmond TW9 132 D3
Sands End SW6 136 A3
Town Quay IG11 100 D6
Town Quay Wharf IG11 100 D6
Town Rd N9 18 B2
Townsend Ave N14 31 D6
Townsend Ct NW9 45 B2
Townsend Ho 14 SE1 118 A2
Townsend Ind Est NW10 89 A5
Townsend La NW9 45 B3
Townsend Mews 3 SW18 158 A2
Townsend Prim Sch SE17 117 C2 263 A4
Townsend Rd
Ashford TW15 170 A5
Regents Park NW8 92 C5 230 B4
Southall UB1 107 A5
South Tottenham N15 51 D4
Townsend St SE1, SE17 117 C2 263 A4
Townsend Way HA6 22 A3
Townsend Yd N6 49 B1
Townshend Cl DA14 190 C4
Townshend Ct NW8 230 B4
Townshend Est NW8 92 C5 230 A4
Townshend Ho 16 SE18 122 B2
Townshend Rd
Chislehurst BR7 188 D5
Primrose Hill NW8 92 C6 230 A5
Richmond TW9 132 B1
Townshend Terr TW9 132 B1
Towns Ho 4 SW4 137 D2
Townson Ave UB5 84 B5
Townson Way UB5 84 A5
Town The EN2 5 B2
Town Tree Rd TW15 170 C5
Towpath TW17 192 B1
Towpath Way CR0 205 D4
Towpath Wlk E9 75 B3
Towton Rd SE27 161 A2
Toxteth Ho N4 51 A2
Toynbec Cl BR7 188 D6
Toynbee Rd SW19, SW20 179 A2
Toynbee St E1 95 D2 243 C3
Toynbee Studios★ E1 243 D3
Toyne Way N6 48 D3
Tracey Ave NW2 68 C3
Tracy Ct HA7 25 C3
Tracy Ho 15 E3 97 B4
Trade Cl N13 32 C6
Trader Rd E6 100 D1
Tradescant Ho 15 E9 74 C1
Tradescant Rd SW8 138 A5 270 B3
Trade Twr 8 SW11 136 A2
Trade Winds Ct 1 E1 118 A5
Trading Estate Rd NW10 89 A3
Traemore Ct SW16 160 C1
Trafalgar Ave
North Cheam KT4, SM3, SM4 200 D1
SE15 139 D6
Tottenham N17 33 C4
Trafalgar Bsns Ctr IG11 101 D3
Trafalgar Cl 1 SE16 119 A2
Trafalgar Ct
Barking E6 100 C6
Hounslow TW3 129 B2
West Barnes KT3 200 B6
Trafalgar Gdns
Stepney E1 96 D2
W8 255 D6
Trafalgar Gr SE10 142 B6
Trafalgar Ho
Barking IG11 102 B4
SE17 262 B2
Trafalgar Inf Sch TW2 152 B2
Trafalgar Jun Sch TW2 152 B2
Trafalgar Mews E9 75 B2
Trafalgar Pl
Edmonton N18 34 A5
Wanstead E11 55 A5
Trafalgar Point 2 N1 73 B1
Trafalgar Rd
Greenwich SE10 120 C1
Merton SW19 180 A3
Twickenham TW2 152 B2
Trafalgar Sq★ SW1 115 D5 249 D4
Trafalgar St SE17 117 B1 262 D2
Trafalgar Terr HA1 42 C1
Trafalgar Trad Est EN3 7 A1
Trafalgar Way
Canary Wharf E14 120 A5
Croydon CR0 220 C6
Trafford Ho N1 235 D4
Trafford Rd CR7 204 B4
Trafford Villas CR0 204 B4
Tragail SW15 157 A6
Traherne Lo 5 TW11 174 D5
Trahorn Cl E1 96 B3
Traitors Gate★ EC3 117 D5 253 C4
Tralee Ct 31 SE16 118 B1
Tramsheds Ind Est The CR0, CR4 203 D2
Tramway Ave
Ponders End N9 18 C4
Stratford E15 76 B1
Tramway Cl SE20 184 C2
Tramway Path CR4 202 C5
Trance Way W3 110 C3
Tranmere Ct 5 SM2 218 A1
Tranmere Ho 7 N7 72 C3
Tranmere Rd
Edmonton N9 17 D4
Twickenham TW2 151 D4
Wandsworth SW17, SW18 158 A2
Tranquil Pas SE3 142 D3
Tranquil Vale SE3 142 C3
Transept St NW1 237 B3
Transmere Cl BR5 211 A3
Transmere Rd BR5 211 A3
Transom Cl SE16 119 A2
Transom Sq E14 119 D1
Transport Ave TW8 131 B6
Tranton Rd SE16 118 B3
Trappes Ho 2 SE16 118 B2
Traps La KT2, KT3 177 C2
Travellers Way TW5 128 C3
Travers Cl E17 34 D2
Travers Ho 6 SE10 142 B6
Travers Rd N7 72 C5
Travis Ho SE10 142 A4
Treacy Cl WD23 8 A2
Treadgold Ho 7 W11 112 D6
Treadgold St W11 112 D6
Treadway St E2 96 B5
Treasury Bldgs SW1 250 A2
Treasury Cl SM6 219 D3
Treaty Ctr TW3 129 D2
Treaty St N1 94 B6 233 C5
Trebeck St W1 248 C3
Treborough Ho W1 238 A4
Trebovir Rd SW5 113 C2 255 B3
Treby St E3 97 B3
Trecastle Way 2 N7 71 D4
Tredegar Mews 10 E3 97 B4
Tredegar Rd Bow E3 97 B5

Tredegar Rd *continued*
Wood Green N11 .... 31 D3
Tredegar Sq E3 .... 97 B4
Tredegar Terr E3 .... 97 B4
Trederwen Rd E8 .... 96 A6
Tredown Rd SE26 .... 184 C5
Tredwell Cl BR2 .... 210 A5
Tredwell Rd SE27 .... 182 D6
Tree Cl TW10 .... 153 D3
Treehouse Sch N10 .... 49 A5
Treen Ave SW13 .... 133 D2
Tree Rd E16 .... 99 C1
Trees The N16 .... 51 B2
Tree Tops 1 IG8 .... 37 A6
Treetops Cl SE2 .... 125 A1
Treetops Ct CR7 .... 205 A4
Treetops View IG10 .... 21 D4
Treeview Cl SE19 .... 183 C2
Treewall Gdns BR1 .... 187 B6
Trefgarne Rd RM10 .... 81 C6
Trefil Wlk N7 .... 72 A4
Trefoil Ho DA18 .... 125 A4
Trefoil Rd SW18 .... 158 A6
Trefusis Ct TW5 .... 128 B4
Tregaron Ave N8 .... 50 A3
Tregaron Gdns KT3 .... 199 C5
Tregarvon Rd SW11 .... 137 A1
Tregenna Ave HA2 .... 63 C4
Tregenna Cl 1 N14 .... 15 C6
Tregenna Ct HA2 .... 63 C4
Trego Rd E9 .... 75 C1
Tregothnan Rd SW9 .... 138 A2
Tregunter Rd
SW10 .... 114 A1 256 A1
Treherne Ct
Brixton SW9 .... 138 D4
Upper Tooting SW17 .... 181 A6
Trehern Rd 12 SW14 .... 133 B2
Trehurst St E5 .... 75 A3
Trelawney Cl E17 .... 53 D5
Trelawney Est E9 .... 74 C2
Trelawney Ho SE1 .... 252 A2
Trelawn Rd
Leyton E10 .... 76 A5
Tulse Hill SW2 .... 160 C6
Trellis Ho SW19 .... 180 A3
Trellis Sq 1 E3 .... 97 B4
Treloar Gdns SE19 .... 183 B4
Tremadoc Rd SW4 .... 137 D1
Tremaine Cl SE4 .... 141 C3
Tremaine Rd SE20 .... 184 B1
Trematon Ho SE11 .... 261 B2
Trematon Pl TW11 .... 175 C3
Tremlett Gr N19 .... 71 C5
Tremlett Mews 17
N19 .... 71 C5
Trenance Gdns IG3 .... 80 A5
Trenchard Ave HA4 .... 62 B4
Trenchard Cl
Grahame Pk NW9 .... 27 C2
Stanmore HA7 .... 25 B4
Trenchard Ct SM4 .... 201 C3
Trenchard St SE10 .... 120 B1
Trenchold St
SW8 .... 138 A6 270 A5
Trend Ct W13 .... 109 B5
Trendell Ho 8 E14 .... 97 C1
Trenholme Cl 6
SE20 .... 184 B3
Trenholme Rd SE20 .... 184 B3
Trenholme Terr
SE20 .... 184 B3
Trenmar Gdns NW10 .... 90 B4
Trent Ave W5 .... 109 C3
Trent CE Prim Sch
EN4 .... 2 D1
Trent Ct
1 South Croydon
CR2 .... 221 A3
Wanstead E11 .... 55 A4
Trent Ctry Pk* EN4 .... 3 A3
Trent Gdns N14 .... 15 B5
Trentham Ct W3 .... 89 B2
Trentham Lo 8 EN1 .... 17 C6
Trentham St SW18 .... 157 C3
Trent Ho
4 Kingston u T
KT2 .... 175 D2
Nunhead SE15 .... 140 C1
Trent Rd
Buckhurst Hill IG9 .... 21 B3
Clapham Pk SW2 .... 160 B6
Trent Way Hayes UB4 .... 83 C4
North Cheam KT4 .... 216 C5
Trentwood Side EN2 .... 4 B2
Treport St SW18 .... 157 D4
Tresco Cl BR1 .... 186 C4
Trescoe Gdns HA2 .... 41 A2
Tresco Gdns IG3 .... 80 A6
Tresco Ho SE11 .... 261 A2
Tresco Rd SE15 .... 140 B1
Tresham Cres
NW8 .... 92 C3 237 A6
Tresham Rd IG11 .... 79 D1
Tresham Wlk E9 .... 74 C3
Tresidder Ho 10
SW4 .... 159 D4
Tresilian Ave N21 .... 16 B6
Tressel Cl 20 N1 .... 72 D1
Tressillian Cres SE4 .... 141 C2
Tressillian Rd SE4 .... 141 C2
Trestis Cl UB4 .... 84 D2
Treswell Rd RM9 .... 103 A6
Tretawn Gdns NW7 .... 11 C1
Tretawn Pk NW7 .... 27 C6
Trevallyn Lo 1 KT2 .... 176 D2
Trevanion Rd W14 .... 254 B2
Treve Ave HA1 .... 42 B2
Trevelyan Ave E12 .... 78 B4
Trevelyan Cres HA3 .... 43 D2
Trevelyan Ct KT3 .... 199 D2
Trevelyan Gdns
NW10 .... 90 C6
Trevelyan Ho
16 Globe Town E2 .... 96 D4
SE5 .... 138 D5
6 Twickenham TW1 .... 153 C5
Trevelyan Rd
Leyton E15 .... 76 D4
Upper Tooting SW17 .... 180 D4
Trevenna Ho 13
SE23 .... 162 D1
Trevera Ct EN3 .... 19 A6
Treveris St SE1 .... 251 D3
Treversh Ct 7 BR1 .... 186 D2
Treverton St W10 .... 90 D3
Treverton Twr 1
W10 .... 90 D2
Treves Cl N21 .... 16 B6
Treves Ho E1 .... 96 A3
Treville St SW15 .... 156 B4
Treviso Rd SE23 .... 163 A2
Trevithick Cl TW14 .... 149 D3
Trevithick Ho
13 Bermondsey
SE16 .... 118 B2
3 Gospel Oak NW5 .... 71 B4
SW8 .... 269 C2
Trevithick St SE8 .... 141 C6
Trevone Gdns HA5 .... 41 A3
Trevor Cl Harrow HA3 .... 24 D3
Hayes BR2 .... 209 A2
Isleworth TW7 .... 152 D6
New Barnet EN4 .... 14 B5
Northolt UB5 .... 84 C5
Trevor Cres HA4 .... 61 D4
Trevor Gdns
Hendon HA8 .... 27 B2
Northolt UB5 .... 84 C5
Ruislip HA4 .... 62 A4
Trevor Pl
SW7 .... 114 C4 247 B1
Trevor Rd Hayes UB3 .... 105 C4
Hendon HA8 .... 27 B2
Wimbledon SW19 .... 179 A3
Woodford IG8 .... 37 A3
Trevor Roberts Sch
NW8 .... 70 B1
Trevor Sq
SW7 .... 114 C4 247 B1
Trevor St
SW7 .... 114 C4 247 B1
Trevose Ho SE11 .... 260 D2
Trevose Rd E17 .... 36 B2
Trewenna Dr KT9 .... 213 D3
Trewince Rd SW20 .... 178 C2
Trewint St SW18 .... 158 A2
Trewsbury Ho 2
SE2 .... 124 D4
Trewsbury Rd SE26 .... 184 D5
Triandra Way UB4 .... 84 D2
Triangle Ct
4 Newham E16 .... 99 C2
SE1 .... 252 B3
Triangle Ctr UB1 .... 108 B5
Triangle Est The
SE11 .... 261 A1
Triangle Ho SE1 .... 253 C2
Triangle Pl SW4 .... 137 D1
Triangle Rd 7 E8 .... 96 B6
Triangle The
Barking IG11 .... 79 A2
Triangle The *continued*
Crouch End N19 .... 49 D2
EC1 .... 241 D6
16 Hackney E8 .... 96 B6
Kingston u T KT3 .... 177 A1
Tribune Ct 16 NW9 .... 46 A5
Tricorn Ho SE28 .... 123 B5
Trident Bsns Ctr
SW17 .... 180 D5
Trident Gdns 6 UB5 .... 84 D4
Trident Ho
14 South Bromley
E14 .... 98 A1
Woolwich SE28 .... 123 B5
Trident St SE16 .... 118 D2
Trident Way UB2 .... 106 B3
Trieste Ct SW12 .... 158 D3
Trig La EC4 .... 252 A6
Trigon Rd
SW8 .... 138 B5 270 D4
Trilby Rd SE23 .... 162 D2
Trillington Ho W12 .... 112 A5
Trillo Ct IG1 .... 57 C2
Trimdon NW1 .... 232 B5
Trimmer Ct TW7 .... 130 D2
Trimmer Wlk 11
TW8 .... 132 A6
Trim St SE8 .... 141 B6
Trinder Gdns N19 .... 50 A1
Trinder Mews 10
TW11 .... 175 A5
Trinder Rd Barnet EN5 .... 12 C6
Finsbury Pk N4, N19 .... 50 A1
Tring Ave Ealing W5 .... 110 B5
Southall UB1 .... 85 B1
Wembley HA9 .... 66 C2
Tring Cl IG2 .... 57 B4
Tring Ct TW1 .... 175 A6
Trinidad Ho 17 E14 .... 119 B6
Trinidad St E14 .... 119 B6
Trinity Ave
East Finchley N2 .... 48 B6
Enfield EN1 .... 17 D5
Trinity Church Rd
SW13 .... 134 B6
Trinity Church Sq
SE1 .... 117 A3 262 B6
Trinity Cl
3 Clapham SW4 .... 137 C1
Hounslow TW4 .... 129 A1
Keston Mark BR2 .... 210 A1
Lewisham SE13 .... 142 B1
Leyton E11 .... 76 C6
Trinity Coll London
SE1 .... 116 A1 260 B1
Trinity Coll of Music
SE10 .... 142 B6
Trinity Cotts TW9 .... 132 B2
Trinity Cres SW17 .... 159 A2
Trinity Ct
8 Chingford E4 .... 20 A2
Edmonton N18 .... 33 D4
Eltham SE9 .... 166 D5
Finsbury WC1 .... 240 C6
Forest Hill SE23 .... 162 C1
Greenwich SE7 .... 121 D2
2 Hoxton N1 .... 95 C6
Rotherhithe SE16 .... 119 A4
Southgate N21 .... 16 D3
Thornton Heath SE25 .... 205 C3
Twickenham TW2 .... 152 C2
Wallington SM6 .... 219 C1
Willesden NW2 .... 68 C3
Wimbledon SW19 .... 179 C4
Trinity Dr UB8 .... 83 A1
Trinity Gdns E16 .... 98 D2
Stockwell SW2, SW9 .... 138 B1
11 Wanstead E18 .... 55 B6
Trinity Gn E1 .... 96 C2
Trinity Gr 8 SE10 .... 142 A4
Trinity Ho SE1 .... 262 B6
5 Walthamstow E17 .... 53 D6
Trinity Homes 14
SW2 .... 138 B1
Trinity Mews
Penge SE20 .... 184 B2
SE9 .... 167 B5
Wandsworth SW18 .... 157 C3
Trinity Par TW3 .... 129 D2
Trinity Pl
Bexleyheath DA6 .... 147 B1
City of London EC3 .... 253 C5
Trinity RC High Sch
(Lower) IG8 .... 37 A6
Trinity RC High Sch
(Upper) IG8 .... 37 A6
Trinity RC High Sch
(Upper Sch) IG8 .... 36 D6
Trinity Rd
East Finchley N2 .... 48 B6
Ilford IG6 .... 57 A6
Richmond TW9 .... 132 B2
Southall UB1 .... 107 A5
Wandsworth SW17,
SW18 .... 158 C4
Wimbledon SW19 .... 179 C4
Wood Green N22 .... 32 A3
Wood Green N22 .... 32 B2
Trinity Rise SE24,
SW2 .... 160 D4
Trinity St Mary's Prim
Sch 8 SW12 .... 159 A3
Trinity Sch
Croydon CR0 .... 222 C6
Dagenham RM10 .... 81 C4
Trinity Sq
EC3 .... 117 C6 253 B6
Trinity St Enfield EN2 .... 5 A3
9 Newham E16 .... 99 A2
SE1 .... 117 B3 262 C6
Trinity Terr IG9 .... 21 B4
Trinity Way
East Acton W3 .... 111 D6
Walthamstow E4 .... 35 B4
Trio Pl SE1 .... 117 A4 252 B1
Triscott Ho UB3 .... 106 A5
Tristan Ct 34 SE8 .... 141 B6
Tristan Sq SE3 .... 142 C2
Tristram Cl E17 .... 54 B6
Tristram Dr N9 .... 18 A1
Tristram Rd BR1 .... 186 D6
Triton Ct EC2 .... 242 D5
Woodford IG9 .... 21 A2
Triton Ho 2 E14 .... 119 D2
Tritton Ave CR0 .... 220 A4
Tritton Ho N21 .... 17 B5
Tritton Rd SE21,
SE27 .... 161 B1
Triumph Cl UB7 .... 127 A4
Triumph Ho IG11 .... 102 A4
Triumph Rd E6 .... 100 B1
Triumph Trad Est
N17 .... 34 A4
Trocette Mans SE1 .... 263 B6
Trojan Ct
Brondesbury NW6 .... 69 A1
9 Ealing W7 .... 109 A5
Trojan Ind Est NW10 .... 67 D2
Trojan Way CR0 .... 220 B5
Troon Cl
34 Bermondsey
SE16 .... 118 B1
Erith SE28 .... 102 D1
Troon Ct UB1 .... 108 A6
Troon Ho 9 E14 .... 97 A1
Troon St E1 .... 97 A1
Tropical Ct 2 W10 .... 90 D4
Trosley Rd DA17 .... 147 C6
Trossachs Rd SE22 .... 161 C6
Trothy Rd SE1 .... 118 A2
Trotman Ho 1 SE14 .... 140 C4
Trott Rd N10 .... 31 A3
Trott St
SW11 .... 136 C4 267 A1
Trotwood Ho 3
SE16 .... 118 B4
Troubridge Ct 12
W4 .... 111 A1
Troughton Rd SE7 .... 121 B1
Troutbeck NW1 .... 231 D1
Troutbeck Rd SE14 .... 141 A4
Trouville Rd SW4 .... 159 C5
Trowbridge Est 6
E15 .... 75 B2
Trowbridge Rd E9 .... 75 B2
Trower Ho 5 E9 .... 75 A2
Trowlock Ave TW11 .... 175 C4
Trowlock Island
TW11 .... 175 D4
Trowlock Way
TW11 .... 175 D4
Troy Ct W8 .... 255 A6
5 Woolwich SE18 .... 122 D2
Troyes Ho NW3 .... 70 D3
Troy Rd SE19 .... 183 B4
Troy Town SE15 .... 140 A2
Troy Town Flats
SE15 .... 140 A2
Trubshaw Rd UB2 .... 107 D3
Trulock Ct N17 .... 34 A3
Trulock Rd N17 .... 34 A3
Truman Cl 2 HA8 .... 27 A3
Truman's Rd 24 N16 .... 73 C3
Trumpers Way W7 .... 108 D3
Trumpeters Inn
TW9 .... 153 C6
Trumpington Rd E7 .... 76 D4
Trump St EC2 .... 242 B1
Trundlers Way WD23 .... 8 C3
Trundle St SE1 .... 252 A2
Trundleys Rd SE8 .... 141 A6
Trundley's Rd SE8 .... 118 D1
Trundley's Terr SE8 .... 118 D2
Truro Ct 2 N8 .... 49 D4
Truro Gdns IG1 .... 56 A2
Truro Ho
25 Paddington W2 .... 91 C2
Pinner HA5 .... 23 B2
Truro Rd
Walthamstow E17 .... 53 B5
Wood Green N22 .... 32 B3
Truro St NW5 .... 71 A2
Truro Way UB4 .... 83 C4
Truscott Ho 3 CR7 .... 204 C3
Trusedale Rd E6 .... 100 B1
Truslove Rd SE27 .... 182 D5
Trussley Rd W6 .... 112 C3
Trust Wlk SE21 .... 160 D3
Tryfan Cl IG4 .... 55 D4
Tryon Cres E9 .... 96 C6
Tryon St
SW3 .... 114 D1 257 C2
Trystings Cl KT10 .... 213 A2
Tuam Rd SE18 .... 145 B6
Tubbenden Cl BR6 .... 227 C5
Tubbenden Dr BR6 .... 227 B4
Tubbenden Jun & Inf
Schs BR6 .... 227 B4
Tubbenden La BR6 .... 227 C5
Tubbenden La S
BR6 .... 227 B3
Tubbs Rd NW10 .... 89 D5
Tudor Ave
Hampton TW12 .... 173 C3
North Cheam KT4 .... 216 B4
Tudor Cl
Ashford TW15 .... 170 A6
BR7 .... 188 B2
Cheam SM3 .... 217 A2
Chessington KT9 .... 214 A3
Crouch End N6 .... 49 C2
Hampstead NW3 .... 70 C2
Hampton TW12 .... 174 A5
Hendon NW7 .... 28 A4
Pinner HA5 .... 40 A4
Tulse Hill SW2 .... 160 B5
Wallington SM6 .... 219 C1
Welsh Harp NW9 .... 67 A6
Woodford IG8 .... 37 B5
Tudor Coll WC1 .... 233 A1
Tudor Court N HA9 .... 66 C3
Tudor Court S HA9 .... 66 C3
Tudor Cres EN2 .... 5 A4
Tudor Ct 2 Barnet EN5 .... 1 B1
3 Ealing W13 .... 87 C1
Feltham TW13 .... 172 C6
Kingsland N1 .... 73 C2
5 Rotherhithe SE16 .... 118 D5
Sidcup DA14 .... 168 A1
South Acton W5 .... 110 C4
4 Stanwell TW19 .... 148 A5
Teddington TW11 .... 174 D4
Walthamstow E17 .... 53 B2
Tudor Dr
Kingston u T KT2 .... 176 A5
Walton-on-T KT12 .... 194 D1
West Barnes SM4 .... 201 A3
Tudor Ent Pk HA3 .... 42 B6
Tudor Est NW10 .... 88 D5
Tudor Gables NW7 .... 27 D6
Tudor Gdns Acton W3 .... 88 C1
Harrow HA3 .... 24 B1
Mortlake SW14 .... 133 C2
Twickenham TW1 .... 152 D3
Welsh Harp NW9 .... 67 A6
West Wickham BR4 .... 224 A5
Tudor Gr E9 .... 74 C1
Tudor Ho
Brook Green W14 .... 112 D2
Feltham TW13 .... 172 C6
34 Hackney E9 .... 74 C1
Mitcham CR4 .... 181 A2
6 Muswell Hill N10 .... 31 A3
Queensbury NW9 .... 44 C5
Tolworth KT6 .... 198 C1

Tudor Lo 4 N12 29 D5
Tudor Mews
Walthamstow E17 53 B5
2 Willesden NW10 68 A2
Tudor Par
Dagenham RM6 58 D2
SE9 144 A1
Tudor Pl SW19 180 C3
Tudor Prim Sch
Finchley N3 30 A2
Southall UB1 107 A6
Tudor Rd
Ashford TW15 171 B4
Barking IG11 101 D6
Barnet EN5 1 D2
Beckenham BR3 208 A6
Chingford E4 35 D4
Croydon SE25 206 B4
Hackney E9 96 B6
Hampton TW12 173 C3
Harrow HA3 24 B1
Hayes UB3 83 B1
Isleworth TW3 130 B1
Kingston u T KT2 176 C3
Newham E6 99 C6
Penge SE19 183 D3
Pinner HA5 22 C1
Ponders End N9 18 C4
Southall UB1 107 A6
Tudor Sq UB3 83 B2
Tudor St EC4 116 C6 251 B6
Tudors The 2 BR3 185 D1
Tudor Way BR5 211 B3
Hillingdon UB10 60 C2
Osidge N14 15 D3
South Acton W3 110 C4
Tudor Well Cl HA7 25 B5
Tudor Wlk DA5 169 A5
Tudway Rd SE3, SE9 143 C1
Tufnell Ct 19 E3 97 B6
Tufnell Mans 7 N7 71 D4
TUFNELL PARK 71 D4
Tufnell Park Mans 2 N7 72 A5
Tufnell Park Prim Sch N7 71 D4
Tufnell Park Rd N19, N7 71 D4
Tufnell Park Sta N19 71 C4
Tufton Ct SW1 260 A5
Tufton Gdns KT8 173 D1
Tufton Rd E4 35 C6
Tufton St SW1 116 A3 260 A5
Tugboat St SE28 123 C4
Tugela Rd CR0 205 B3
Tugela St SE6 163 B2
Tugmutton Cl BR6 226 D4
Tuke Sch SE15 140 B4
Tulip Cl Croydon CR0 206 D1
Hampton TW12 173 B4
5 Newham E6 100 B2
Southall UB2 108 A4
Tulip Ct 1 HA5 40 C6
Tulip Gdns
Chingford E4 20 B1
Ilford IG1 78 D2
Tullis Ho 12 E9 74 C1
Tull St CR4 202 D2
Tulse Cl BR3 208 A6
TULSE HILL 160 D4
Tulse Hill
Tulse Hill SW2 160 C4
Tulse Hill SW27 160 D2
Tulse Hill Sta SE27 160 D2
Tulse Ho SW2 160 C5
Tulsemere Rd SE21, SE27 161 A2
Tumbling Bay KT12 194 A3
Tummons Gdns SE25 183 C1
Tump Ho SE28 123 C5
Tunbridge Ct 1 SE26 162 A1
Tunbridge Ho EC1 234 C2
Tuncombe Rd N18 33 C6
Tunis Rd W12 112 B5
Tunley Gn 12 E14 97 B2
Tunley Rd
Dagenham NW10 89 C6
Upper Tooting SW12, SW17 159 A2
Tunmarsh La E13 99 C4
Tunnan Leys E6 100 C1
Tunnel Avenue Trad Est SE10 120 B4
Tunnel Gdns N11 31 C3
Tunnel Link Rd TW6 148 C5
Tunnel Rd SE16 118 C4
Tunnel Rd E TW6 126 D3
Tunnel Rd W TW6 126 D4
Tunstall Cl BR6 227 C4
Tunstall Ct 14 TW9 132 B4
Tunstall Rd
Croydon CR0 205 C1
Stockwell SW9 138 B1
Tunstall Wlk 10 TW8 132 A6
Tunstock Way DA17 125 A3
Tunworth Cl NW9 45 A3
Tunworth Cres SW15 155 D5
Tun Yd SW8 137 B2
Tupelo Rd E10 75 D6
Tupman Ho 26 SE16 118 A4
Tuppy St SE28 123 A3
Turberville Ho 1 SW9 138 B2
Turenne Cl SW18 136 A1
Turin Gr Sch N9 18 C4
Turin Rd N9 18 C4
Turin St E2 96 A4
Turkey Oak Cl SE19 183 C2
Turkey St EN1, EN3 6 C6
Turkey Street Sta EN3 6 C6
Turks Cl UB8 82 C4
Turk's Head Yd EC1 241 C4
Turks Row SW3 114 D1 257 D2
Turle Rd
Finsbury Pk N4 72 B6
Thornton Heath SW16 182 A1
Turlewray Cl N4 50 B1
Turley Cl E15 98 C6
Turnagain La EC4 241 C2
Turnage Rd RM8 59 A1
Turnant Rd N17 33 A2
Turnberry Cl
24 Bermondsey SE16 118 B1
Hendon NW4 28 D1
Turnberry Quay 1 E14 119 D3
Turnberry Way BR6 211 B1
Turnbull Ho N1 234 D6
Turnbury Cl SE28 102 D1
Turnchapel Mews 1 SW4 137 B2
Turner Ave
Mitcham CR4 180 D2
Tottenham N15 51 C5
Twickenham TW2 152 A1
Turner Cl
7 Brixton SW9 138 D4
Hampstead Garden Suburb NW11 47 D3
Hillingdon UB4 83 A4
Wembley HA0 65 D2
Turner Cres CR7 205 A3
Turner Ct
9 Herne Hill SE5 139 B1
24 Rotherhithe SE16 118 C4
Turner Dr NW11 47 D3
Turner Ho
Finsbury Pk N4 50 B1
24 Millwall E14 119 C4
St John's Wood NW8 230 A4
Strand WC2 250 B5
6 Twickenham TW1 153 D5
Westminster SW1 259 D3
Turner Lo 10 SW19 156 D3
Turner Mews SM2 217 D1
Turner Pl SW11 158 C6
Turner Rd
Edgware HA8 26 B1
New Malden KT3 199 B2
Walthamstow E17 54 A6
Turners Cl N20 14 D1
Turners Ct Leyton E15 76 A4
New Barnet EN5 13 D5
Tottenham N15 51 B4
Turners Meadow Way BR3 185 B2
Turner's Rd E3 97 B2
Turner St
Canning Town E16 98 D1
Stepney E1 96 B2
Turners Way CR0 220 C6
Turneville Rd W14 135 B6 264 C6
Turney Rd SE21 161 B4
Turney Sch SE21 161 A4
Turnham Green Sta W4 111 C2
Turnham Green Terr W4 111 C2
Turnham Ho SE4 141 A1
Turnham Prim Sch 1 SE4 141 A1
Turnham Rd SE4 141 A1
Turnmill Ho 8 SW2 160 C6
Turnmill St EC1 94 D2 241 C4
Turnour Ho 31 E1 96 B1
Turnpike Cl SE8 141 B5
Turnpike Ct DA6 146 D1
Turnpike Ho EC1 234 D1
Turnpike La
Hornsey N8 50 C6
Sutton SM1 218 A3
Uxbridge UB10 82 A5
Turnpike Lane Sta N15 50 D6
Turnpike Link CR0 221 C6
Turnpike Mews N8 50 C6
Turnpike Way TW7 131 A4
Turnpin La 3 SE10 142 A6
Turnstone Cl
Edgware NW9 27 C1
Newham E13 99 A4
Uxbridge UB10 60 D3
Turnstone Terr 11 W13 86 D3
Turpentine La SW1 115 B1 258 D1
Turpin Cl 15 EN3 7 C6
Turpington Cl BR2 210 A2
Turpington La BR2 210 A3
Turpin Ho SW11 268 C2
Turpin Rd TW14 149 D5
Turpin Way
Upper Holloway N19 49 D1
Wallington SM6 219 B1
Turquand St SE17 262 B3
Turret Gr SW4 137 C2
Turret Ho KT2 176 A4
Turton Ho 5 SE18 144 D6
Turton Rd HA0 66 A3
Turville Ho NW8 237 A6
Turville St E2 243 C6
Tuscan Ho 36 E2 96 C4
Tuscan Rd SE18 123 B1
Tuscany Ho E17 35 B1
Tuskar St SE10 120 C1
Tuttlebee La IG9 21 A2
Tuttle Ho SW1 259 D1
Tweed Ct W7 86 C1
Tweeddale Gr UB10 61 A5
Tweeddale Prim Sch SM5 202 B2
Tweeddale Rd SM5 202 B1
Tweed Ho E14 98 A3
Tweedmouth Rd E13 99 B5
Tweedy Cl EN1 17 D6
Tweedy Rd BR1 187 A2
Tweezer's Alley WC2 251 A6
Twelve Acre Ho 5 E12 78 C5
Twelvetrees Bsns Pk E16 98 B3
Twelvetrees Cres E3 98 A3
Twentyman Cl IG8 37 A5
TWICKENHAM 152 D4
Twickenham Bridge TW9 153 C6
Twickenham Cl CR0 220 B5
Twickenham Gdns
Harrow HA3 24 C3
Wembley UB6 65 A3
Twickenham Mus The★ TW1 153 A3
Twickenham Pl KT7 212 D6
Twickenham Prep Sch TW12 174 A2
Twickenham Rd
Isleworth TW1, TW7 131 A2
Leyton E11 76 B6
Richmond TW1, TW9 131 C1
Teddington TW11 175 A6
Twickenham TW13 151 B1
Twickenham Sta TW1 153 A4
Twickenham Stad (Rugby Football Union) TW2 152 C5
Twickenham Stoop Stadium TW2 152 D4
Twickenham Trad Ctr TW1 152 D5
Twickenham Trad Est TW1 152 D5
Twig Folly Cl 21 E2 96 D5
Twilley St SW18 157 D4
Twine Cl IG11 102 B4
Twine Ct E1 118 C6
Twineham Gn N12 29 C6
Twining Ave TW2 152 B1
Twinings Mus★ WC2 241 A1
Twinn Rd NW7 29 A4
Twin Tumps Way SE28 124 A6
Twisden Rd NW5 71 B4
Twiss Ho 6 SE18 122 D1
Twist Ho E10 75 D6
Two Bridges Ind Est CR0 221 B2
Twybridge Way NW10 67 A1
Twycross Mews SE10 120 C2
Twyford Abbey Rd NW10 88 B4
Twyford Ave
Acton W3 110 C6
Muswell Hill N2 48 D6
Twyford CE High Sch W3 110 D5
Twyford Cres W3 110 C5
Twyford Ct
Acton W3 110 C6
Muswell Hill N10 49 A6
6 Wembley HA0 88 A5
Twyford Ho
Highbury N5 72 D5
6 Tottenham N15 51 C3
Twyford Par KT6 198 C1
Twyford Rd
Carshalton SM5 202 B1
Harrow HA2 41 D2
Ilford IG1 79 A3
Twyford Sp Ctr W3 110 D5
Twyford St N1 94 B6 233 C6
Twynholm Mans SW6 264 A4
Tyas Rd E16 98 D3
Tybenham Rd SW19 201 C6
Tyberry Rd EN3 6 C2
Tyburn La HA1 42 D2
Tyburn Tree (site of)★ W2 247 C6
Tyburn Way W1 247 D6
Tye La BR6 227 A3
Tyer's Est SE1 253 A2
Tyers Gate SE1 117 C4 253 A1
Tyers Ho 1 SW16 181 C5
Tyers St SE11 116 B1 260 C2
Tyers Terr SE11 116 B1 260 D1
Tyeshurst Cl SE2 125 A1
Tylecroft Rd SW16 182 A1
Tylehurst Gdns IG1 79 A3
Tyler Cl Erith DA8 147 D5
Haggerston E2 95 D5
Tyler Ho SE3 142 B3
Tyler Rd UB2 107 D3
Tylers Ct
4 Walthamstow E17 53 C5
5 Wembley HA0 88 A5
Tylers Gate HA3 44 A3
Tylers Path SM5 218 D4
Tyler St
Greenwich SE10 120 C1
SE10 142 C6
Tylney Ave SE19 183 D5
Tylney Ho 10 E1 96 B1
Tylney Rd BR1 187 D1
Forest Gate E7 77 C4
Tymperley Ct SW19 157 A3
Tynamara KT1 197 D5
Tynan Cl TW14 150 A3
Tyndale La N1 72 D1
Tyndale Mans N1 72 D1
Tyndale Terr 13 N1 72 D1
Tyndall Gdns E10 76 A6
Tyndall Rd DA16 145 D2
Leyton E10 76 A6
Tyne Ct W7 86 C1
Tyneham Cl 10 SW11 137 A2
Tyneham Rd SW11 137 A2
Tyne Ho 8 KT2 175 D2
Tynemouth Cl E6 100 D1
Tynemouth Dr EN1 6 A5
Tynemouth Rd
Mitcham CR4 181 A3
Plumstead Comm SE18 123 C1
Tottenham N15 51 D5
Tynemouth St SW6 136 A3
Tynemouth Terr 9 N15 51 D5
Tyne St E1 243 D2
Tynsdale Rd NW10 67 C2
Tynte Ct E9 75 A3
Tynwald Ho 14 SE26 162 A1
Type St E2 96 D5
Tyrawley Rd SW6 265 C2
Tyrell Cl HA1 64 C4
Tyrell Ct SM5 218 D4
Tyrells Ct 3 SE15 140 B2
Tyrols Rd SE23 162 D3
Tyrone Ct SW16 181 D5
Tyrone Rd E6 100 B4
Tyron Way DA14 189 D5
Tyrrell Ave DA16 168 B6
Tyrrell Ho
Catford BR3 185 D5
SW1 269 B6
Tyrrell Rd SE22 140 A1
Tyrrell Sq CR4 180 C2
Tyrrel Way NW9 46 A2
Tyrwhitt Rd SE4 141 C2
Tysoe Ave EN3 7 B6
Tysoe St EC1 234 B1
Tyson Rd SE23 162 C4
Tyssen Com Prim Sch N16 52 A1
Tyssen Rd N16 73 D5
Tyssen St Dalston E8 73 D2
Hoxton N1 95 C5
Tysson Ho E9 75 A1
Tytherton 29 E2 96 C5
Tytherton Rd N19 71 D5

U

Uamvar St E14 97 D2
Uckfield Gr CR4 181 A2
Uckfield Rd EN3 6 D6
Udall St SW1 259 B3
Udimore Ho 11 W10 90 C2
Udney Park Rd TW11 175 A4
Uffington Rd
West Norwood SE27 182 C6
Willesden Green NW10 90 B6
Ufford Cl HA3 23 D3
Ufford Rd HA3 23 D3
Ufford St SE1 116 C4 251 B2
Ufton Ct UB5 84 D4
Ufton Gr N1 73 B1
Ufton Rd N1 73 C1
Uhura Sq 19 N16 73 C5
Ujima Ct
Finsbury Pk N19 50 A1
Streatham SW16 182 A6
Ujima Ho SW16 182 A6
UK Coll of Bsns & Computing IG2 56 C3
Uk Cotts UB3 105 B4
Ullathorne Rd SW16 181 C6
Ulleswater Rd N14 16 B1
Ullin St E14 98 A2
Ullswater SW15 156 D5
Ullswater Cl
Bromley BR1 186 C3
Hayes UB4 83 C5
Kingston u T KT2, SW15 177 B6
Ullswater Cres SW15 177 B6
Ullswater Ct
Harrow HA2 41 C2
2 Woodford E18 37 A1
Ullswater Ho SE15 140 C6
Ullswater Rd
Barnes SW13 134 A5
West Norwood SE27, SW16 160 D2
Ulster Ct KT2 175 D4
Ulster Gdns N13 33 A6

Ulster Pl NW1 ...... 238 C5
Ulster Terr NW1 ..... 238 C6
Ulundi Rd SE3 .... 142 C6
Ulva Rd SW15 .... 134 D1
Ulverscroft Rd SE22 .. 162 A6
Ulverstone Rd SE27 . 160 D2
Ulverston Rd E17 ..... 36 B1
Ulysses Rd NW6 ...... 69 B3
Umberston St E1 ...... 96 B1
Umbria St SW15 ..... 156 A5
Umfreville Rd N4 ..... 50 D3
Umoja Ho N22 .... 32 B1
Una Ho 7 NW5 .... 71 B2
Undercliff SE10 ...... 142 A4
Undercliff Rd SE13 .. 141 D2
UNDERHILL 13 C6
Underhill EN5 .... 13 C6
Underhill Ct EN5 ...... 13 C6
Underhill Ho 7 E14 .. 97 C2
Underhill Jun & Inf Schs
EN5 .... 13 A6
Underhill Pas NW1 .. 231 D6
Underhill Rd SE21,
SE22 .... 162 B4
Underhill St NW1 .... 231 D5
Underne Ave N14 ..... 15 B2
Undershaft
EC3 .... 95 C1 243 A1
Undershaw Rd BR1 . 164 D1
Underwood CR0 ..... 224 A3
Underwood Ct 3
E10 .... 53 D1
Underwood Ho
East Molesey KT8 ... 195 C4
Hammersmith W6 .... 112 B3
Underwood Rd
Bethnal Green E1 ...... 96 A3
Chingford E4 .... 35 D5
Woodford IG8 .... 37 D3
Underwood Row N1 235 B2
Underwood St
N1 .... 95 A4 235 B2
Underwood The SE9 . 166 B2
Undine Rd E14 ...... 119 D2
Undine St SW17 ..... 180 D5
Uneeda Dr UB6 .... 86 B6
Unicorn Bldg 14 E1 . 118 D6
Unicorn Prim Sch
BR3 .... 207 D4
Unicorn Sch TW9 .... 132 B4
Unicorn Works N17 ... 34 C3
Union Cl E11 .... 76 B4
Union Ct
45 Paddington W2 ..... 91 C2
2 Richmond TW10 .. 154 A6
South Lambeth SW4 . 138 A3
Whitechapel EC2 .... 243 A2
Union Dr E1 .... 97 A3
Union Gr SW8 ...... 137 D3
Union Mews 32
SW9 .... 138 A3
Union Pk 11 SE10 ... 120 D1
Union Rd BR2 .... 209 D4
Clapham SW8 .... 137 D3
Friern Barnet N11 ..... 31 D4
Northolt UB5 .... 85 C5
Thornton Heath CR0 . 205 A2
Wembley HA0 .... 66 A2
Union Sq N1 ... 95 A6 235 B5
Union St Barnet EN5 .... 1 A2
Kingston u T KT1 .... 175 D1
Mill Meads E15 .... 98 B6
SE1 .... 117 A5 252 A3
Union Terr HA2 .... 41 C1
Union Wharf N1 .... 235 B4
Union Wlk E2 .... 95 C4
Union Yd W1 .... 238 D1
United International Coll
W1 .... 238 D3
Unity Cl
West Norwood
SE19 .... 183 A5
Willesden NW10 ...... 68 A2
Unity Mews NW1 ... 232 C4
Unity Rd EN3 .... 6 C6
Unity Terr HA2 .... 63 D6
Unity Way SE18 ..... 121 D3
Univ Coll Jun Sch 31
NW3 .... 70 A4
Univ Coll London
Bloomsbury
WC1 .... 93 D3 239 C6
Bloomsbury
WC1 .... 94 A3 240 B6
Univ Coll London
(Windeyer Inst)
W1 .... 93 C2 239 B4
Univ Coll London
(Wolfson Ho)
NW1 .... 93 C4 232 B1
University Cl NW7 ... 27 D3
University Coll Hospl
WC1 .... 93 C3 239 B6
University Coll Sch
NW3 .... 70 A3
University Gdns DA5 . 169 B4
University Mans 9
SW15 .... 134 D2
University Pl DA8 ... 147 D5
University Rd SW19 .. 180 B4
University St
WC1 .... 93 C3 239 B5
University Way E16 . 122 D6
Univ of California
WC1 .... 93 D2 239 D3
Univ of East London
Barking RM8 .... 80 A4
Newham E16 .... 122 C6
Stratford E15 .... 76 C2
Univ of East London
(Duncan Ho) 7 E15 98 B6
Univ of East London
(Holbrook Ctr) E15 .. 98 D5
Univ of Greenwich
SE10 .... 142 B6
Univ of Greenwich Avery
Hill Campus Mansion
Site SE9 .... 167 A5
Univ of Greenwich Avery
Hill Campus
Southwood Site
SE9 .... 167 B4
Univ of London
WC1 .... 93 D3 239 D5
Univ of London (King's
Coll Hall) SE5 ...... 139 B2
Univ of London Obsy
NW7 .... 27 D4
Univ of London (Queen
Mary & Westfield Coll)
E1 .... 97 A3
Univ of Notre Dame
SW1 .... 115 D6 249 D5
Univ of Notre Dame
SW1 .... 249 D4
Univ of Westminster
(Cavendish Campus)
W1 .... 93 C2 239 A4
Univ of Westminster
(Harrow Campus)
HA1 .... 43 A2
Univ of Westminster
(Marylebone Campus)
W1 .... 93 A2 238 A4
Univ of Westminster
(Regent Campus)
W1 .... 93 C2 239 A3
Univ of Westminster
(Regent Campus, Univ
HQ) W1 ...... 93 B1 238 D2
Univ of Westminster
(Wigram House Halls of
Residence)
SW1 .... 115 C3 259 B5
Uno Apartments 4
BR1 .... 187 A2
Unwin Ave TW14 ..... 149 B6
Unwin Cl SE15 ...... 140 A6
Unwin Rd
Isleworth TW7 ...... 130 C2
SW7 .... 114 B3 256 D6
Upbrook Mews
W2 .... 92 A1 236 B1
Upcerne Rd
SW10 ...... 136 A5 266 B3
Upchurch Cl 8
SE20 .... 184 B3
Upcott Ho
33 Bromley E3 .... 97 D4
4 Hackney E9 .... 74 C1
Upcroft Ave HA8 ...... 27 A6
Updale Rd DA14 .... 189 D6
Upfield CR0 .... 222 B5
Upfield Rd W7 .... 86 D2
Upgrove Manor Way 12
SE24 .... 160 C4
Uphall Prim Sch IG1 .. 78 D3
Uphall Rd IG1 .... 78 D3
Upham Park Rd W4 .. 111 C2
Uphill Dr
Edgware NW7 .... 27 C5
Kingsbury NW9 .... 45 A4
Uphill Gr NW7 .... 27 C6
Uphill Rd NW7 .... 27 C6
Upland Ct SE23 ..... 162 C2
Upland Prim Sch
DA7 .... 147 B2
Upland Rd
Croydon CR2 .... 221 B3
DA7 .... 147 B2
East Dulwich SE22 ... 162 A5
8 Newham E13 ...... 99 A3
Sutton SM2 .... 218 B1
Uplands
Beckenham BR3 ..... 185 C1
Woolwich SE18 ...... 122 D1
Uplands Ave E17 ...... 34 D1
Uplands Bsns Pk E17 . 52 D6
Uplands Cl SW14 ... 154 D6
Uplands Ct N21 .... 16 C4
Uplands Park Rd EN2 .. 4 C3
Uplands Rd
East Barnet EN4 ...... 15 A3
Hornsey Vale N8 ...... 50 B4
Ilford RM6 .... 58 D6
Woodford IG8 .... 37 D3
Uplands The HA4 ..... 40 A1
Uplands Way N21 ..... 16 C6
Upnall Ho 16 SE15 ... 140 C6
Upney Ct 2 IG11 ..... 79 D1
Upney La IG11 .... 79 D1
Upney Sta IG11 .... 79 D1
Upnor Way SE17 .... 263 B2
Uppark Dr IG2 .... 57 A3
Upper Abbey Rd
DA17 .... 125 C2
Upper Addison Gdns
W14 .... 113 A4 244 A2
Upper Bank St E14 .. 119 D5
Upper Bardsey Wlk 7
N1 .... 73 A2
Upper Belgrave St
SW1 .... 115 A3 258 B6
Upper Berkeley St
W1 .... 92 D1 237 D1
Upper Beulah Hill
SE19 .... 183 C2
Upper Brighton Rd
KT6 .... 198 A2
Upper Brockley Rd
SE4 .... 141 B3
Upper Brook St
W1 .... 115 A6 248 A6
Upper Butts TW8 .... 131 C6
Upper Caldy Wlk 18
N1 .... 73 A2
Upper Camelford Wlk 14
W10 .... 91 A1
Upper Cavendish Ave
N3 .... 47 C6
Upper Cheyne Row
SW3 .... 136 C6 267 A6
UPPER CLAPTON 52 B1
Upper Clapton Rd E5 . 74 B6
Upper Clarendon Wlk 12
W11 .... 91 A1
Upper Dengie Wlk
N1 .... 235 A6
UPPER EDMONTON .. 34 B5
UPPER ELMERS
END 207 B3
Upper Elmers End Rd
BR3 .... 207 A4
Upper Farm Rd KT8 .. 195 B5
Upper Fosters NW4 ... 46 C5
Upper Gn W CR4 .... 180 D1
Upper Gr SE25 ...... 205 D5
Upper Grosvenor St
W1 .... 115 A6 248 A5
Upper Grotto Rd
TW1 .... 152 D2
Upper Ground
SE1 .... 116 C5 251 A4
Upper Grove Rd
DA17 .... 147 B6
Upper Gulland Wlk 23
N1 .... 73 A2
UPPER HALLIFORD . 193 B5
Upper Halliford Rd
TW17 .... 193 C6
Upper Halliford Sta
TW16 .... 171 C1
Upper Hampstead Wlk 29
NW3 .... 70 A4
Upper Ham Rd KT2,
TW10 .... 175 D6
Upper Handa Wlk 2
N1 .... 73 A2
Upper Harley St
NW1 .... 238 B5
Upper Hawkwell Wlk
N1 .... 235 B6
UPPER HOLLOWAY ... 71 D6
Upper Holloway Sta
N19 .... 71 D6
Upper Holly Hill Rd
DA17 .... 125 D1
Upper James St W1 . 249 B6
Upper John St W1 .. 249 B6
Upper Lismore Wlk 8
N1 .... 73 A2
Upper Lodge Mews
TW12 .... 174 A4
Upper Mall W6 ...... 112 B1
Upper Marsh
SE1 .... 116 B3 260 D6
Upper Montague St
W1 .... 92 D2 237 C3
Upper Mulgrave Rd
SM2 .... 217 A1
Upper North St E3,
E14 .... 97 C2
UPPER NORWOOD .. 183 C3
Upper Park Rd
Belvedere DA17 ..... 125 D2
BR1 .... 187 C2
Friern Barnet N11 ..... 31 C5
Kingston u T KT2 .... 176 C4
Maitland Pk NW3 ..... 70 D3
Upper Phillimore Gdns
W8 .... 113 C4 245 A1
Upper Pk IG10 .... 21 D6
Upper Ramsey Wlk 19
N1 .... 73 B2
Upper Rawreth Wlk
N1 .... 235 B6
Upper Rd Finchley N2 .. 30 C2
Newham E13 .... 99 A4
Wallington SM6 ..... 219 D3
Upper Richmond Rd
SW15 .... 134 C1
Upper Richmond Rd W
TW10, SW14, SW15 . 133 A1
UPPER RUXLEY 191 C3
Upper St Martin's La
WC2 .... 250 A6
Upper Selsdon Rd
CR2 .... 221 D1
Upper Sheridan Rd 3
DA17 .... 125 C2
UPPER SHIRLEY ... 222 D4
Upper Shirley Rd
CR0 .... 222 D5
Upper Sq TW7 .... 131 A2
Upper St N1 ... 94 D6 234 C5
Upper Sunbury Rd
TW12 .... 173 C2
Upper Sutton La
TW5 .... 129 C4
UPPER SYDENHAM . 184 A6
Upper Tachbrook St
SW1 .... 259 B4
Upper Talbot Wlk 7
W10 .... 91 A1
Upper Teddington Rd KT1,
KT8 .... 175 C2
Upper Terr NW3 ...... 70 A5
Upper Thames St
EC4 .... 117 A6 252 B6
Upper Tollington Pk
N4 .... 50 C1
Upperton Rd DA14 .. 189 D5
Upperton Rd E E13 ... 99 C4
Upperton Rd W E13 ... 99 C4
UPPER TOOTING ... 158 D1
Upper Tooting Park
Mans 1 SW17 ...... 159 A2
Upper Tooting Pk
SW17 .... 158 D2
Upper Tooting Rd
SW17 .... 158 D1
Upper Town Rd UB6 ... 85 D3
Upper Tulse Hill
SW2 .... 160 B3
Upper Vernon Rd
SM1 .... 218 B3
UPPER
WALTHAMSTOW ... 54 C6
Upper Walthamstow Rd
E17 .... 54 B6
Upper Wickham La
DA16 .... 146 B4
Upper Wimpole St
W1 .... 93 A2 238 B4
Upper Woburn Pl NW1,
WC1 .... 93 D4 232 D1
Uppingham Ave HA7 .. 25 C1
Upsdell Ave N13 ...... 32 C4
Upshire Ho E17 .... 35 B1
Upstall St SE5 ...... 138 D4
UPTON 77 B1
Upton Ave E7 .... 77 A1
Upton Cl
Cricklewood NW2 ..... 69 A5
Sidcup DA5 .... 169 B5
Upton Cross E13 ...... 99 A6
Upton Cross Prim Sch
E13 .... 99 B6
Upton Ct Penge SE20 . 184 C3
Southall UB1 .... 107 D5
4 Wimbledon SW19 . 178 D3
Upton Day Hospl
DA6 .... 147 A1
Upton Dene SM2 .... 217 D1
Upton Gdns HA3 ...... 43 C3
Upton Hts E7 .... 77 A1
Upton La E7 .... 77 A1
Upton Lo E7 .... 77 A2
Upton Lodge Cl WD23 .. 8 A4
UPTON PARK 99 D6
Upton Park Rd E7 ..... 77 B1
Upton Park Sta E13 ... 99 C6
Upton Prim Sch
DA5 .... 169 B6
Upton Rd Bexley DA6 . 169 A6
Edmonton N18 .... 34 A5
Hounslow TW3 ...... 129 C2
SE18 .... 145 A6
South Norwood CR7 .. 183 B1
Upton Rd S DA5 ..... 169 B5
Upton Villas 4 DA6 . 147 A1
Upway N12 .... 30 C4
Upwood Rd SE12 .... 165 A5
Thornton Heath
SW16 .... 182 A2
Urban Mews N4 ...... 50 D2
Urlwin St SE5 .... 139 A6
Urlwin Wlk SW9 .... 138 D4
Urmston Dr SW19 ... 157 A3
Urmston Ho 4 E14 .. 120 A2
Urquhart Ct BR3 .... 185 B3
Ursula Lo DA14 ..... 190 B5
Ursula Mews N4 ...... 51 A1
Ursula St
SW11 ...... 136 C4 267 A1
Ursuline High Sch
SW20 .... 178 D2
Ursuline Prep Sch 20
SW19 .... 178 D3
Urswick Gdns RM9 .... 81 A1
Urswick Rd
Dagenham RM9 .... 81 A1
Hackney E5, E9 .... 74 C3
Usborne Mews SW8 270 D4
Usher Hall NW4 ...... 46 B5
Usher Rd E3 .... 97 B5
Usk Rd SW11 .... 136 A1
Usk St E2 .... 96 D4
Utah Bldg 3 SE13 .. 141 D4
Utopia Ho 3 NW2 .... 68 A2
Utopia Village
NW1 .... 93 A6 231 A6
Uvedale Rd
Dagenham RM10 ...... 81 C5
Enfield EN2 .... 17 B6
Uverdale Rd
SW10 ...... 136 A5 266 B3
UXBRIDGE 82 A6
Uxbridge Coll
Hayes UB3 .... 106 A6
Uxbridge UB8 .... 60 A2
Uxbridge High Sch
UB8 .... 82 A5
Uxbridge Rd
Acton W3, W5 ...... 110 C5
Ealing W13 .... 109 C6
Feltham TW13 ...... 150 D2
Hampton TW12,
TW13 .... 173 D5
Hayes UB4 .... 106 C6
Hillingdon UB10, UB4 .. 83 C2
Kingston u T KT1, KT6 . 197 D4
Shepherd's Bush W12 . 112 B5

Uxbridge Rd *continued*
Southall UB1, UB2, W5, W7 ... 108 B5
Stanmore HA7 ... 25 A5
Uxbridge Road (Harrow Weald) HA3 ... 24 B3
Uxbridge Road (Hatch End) HA5 ... 23 B3
Uxbridge Road (Pinner) HA5 ... 22 D1
Uxbridge St W8 ... 113 C5 245 A4
Uxendon Cres HA3, HA9 ... 44 A1
Uxendon Hill HA9 ... 44 B2
Uxendon Manor JMI Sch HA3 ... 44 A4

V

Vadnie Bish Ho NW5 ... 71 C2
Vaine Ho [4] E9 ... 75 A2
Valance Ave E4 ... 20 D3
Valan Leas BR2 ... 208 C6
Vale Ave WD6 ... 10 D6
Vale Cl Muswell Hill N2 ... 48 D6
Orpington BR6 ... 226 C4
St John's Wood W9 ... 92 A4 229 A1
Twickenham TW1 ... 153 A1
Vale Cres SW15 ... 177 C6
Vale Croft
Claygate KT10 ... 212 D1
Pinner HA5 ... 41 A4
Vale Ct Barnet EN5 ... 1 D1
East Acton W3 ... 111 D5
St John's Wood W9 ... 92 A4 229 A1
Wembley HA0 ... 65 C5
Vale Dr EN5 ... 13 C6
Vale End SE22 ... 139 D1
Vale Est The W3 ... 111 C5
Vale Farm Sports Ctr HA0 ... 65 B4
Vale Gr Acton W3 ... 111 B5
Stoke Newington N4 ... 51 A2
Vale La W3 ... 88 C2
Vale Lo SE23 ... 162 C2
Valence Ave RM8 ... 80 D6
Valence Cir RM8 ... 81 A5
Valence House Mus★ RM8 ... 81 A6
Valence Prim Sch RM8 ... 80 D6
Valence Wood Rd RM8 ... 81 A5
Valencia Rd HA7 ... 25 C6
Valens Ho [1] SW2 ... 160 C3
Valentia Pl SW9 ... 138 C1
Valentine Ave DA5 ... 169 A3
Valentine Ct
Elstree WD6 ... 9 D5
[3] Forest Hill SE23 ... 162 D2
Valentine Ho
[11] Clapham Pk SW4 ... 159 C5
[26] Old Ford E3 ... 97 B6
Valentine Pl SE1 ... 116 D4 251 C2
Valentine Rd
Harrow HA2 ... 64 A5
Homerton E9 ... 74 D2
Valentine Row SE1 ... 251 C1
Valentines High Sch IG2 ... 56 C3
Valentines Rd IG1 ... 56 D1
VALE OF HEALTH ... 70 B5
Vale of Health NW3 ... 70 B5
Vale Rd BR1 ... 188 C1
Claygate KT10 ... 212 D1
Mitcham CR4 ... 203 D5
Stoke Newington N4 ... 51 A2
Sutton SM1 ... 217 D4
Upton E7 ... 77 B2
Worcester Pk KT19, KT4 ... 215 D5
Vale Rd N KT6 ... 214 A6
Vale Rd S KT6 ... 214 A6
Valerian Way E15 ... 98 C4
Valerian Wlk N11 ... 15 A2
Valerie Ct
Belmont SM2 ... 217 D1
Valerie Ct *continued*
Bushey WD23 ... 8 A4
Vale Rise NW11 ... 47 B1
Vale Row N5 ... 72 D5
Vale Royal N7 ... 72 A1
Valery Pl TW12 ... 173 C3
Vale Sch The SW7 ... 256 A5
Valeside Ct [2] EN5 ... 1 D1
Valeswood Rd BR1 ... 186 D5
Vale Terr N4 ... 51 A3
Vale The
Ashford TW16 ... 172 A4
Cricklewood NW11 ... 69 A6
Croydon CR0 ... 222 D6
East Acton W3 ... 111 C5
Feltham TW14 ... 150 B5
Heston TW5 ... 129 A6
Muswell Hill N10 ... 31 A2
Ruislip HA4 ... 62 C4
Southgate N14 ... 16 A4
SW3 ... 136 B6 266 D6
Woodford IG8 ... 37 A3
Valetta Gr E13 ... 99 A5
Valetta Rd W3 ... 111 D4
Valette Ct N10 ... 49 B5
Valette Ho E9 ... 74 C2
Valette St E8 ... 74 B2
Valiant Cl [13] UB5 ... 84 D4
Valiant Ho
[9] Cubitt Town E14 ... 120 A4
[5] Greenwich SE7 ... 121 C1
SW11 ... 266 D1
Valiant Way E6 ... 100 B2
Vallance Rd
Bethnal Green E1 ... 96 A3
Muswell Hill N22 ... 31 C1
Vallentin Rd E17 ... 54 A5
Valley Ave N12 ... 30 B6
Valley (Charlton Athletic FC) The SE7 ... 121 C1
Valley Cl HA5 ... 22 B1
Valley Ct IG8 ... 37 B3
Valley Dr NW9 ... 44 D3
Valleyfield Rd SW16 ... 182 B5
Valley Fields Cres EN2 ... 4 C3
Valley Gdns
Mitcham SW19 ... 180 B3
Wembley HA0 ... 66 B1
Valley Gr SE7 ... 121 C1
Valley Ho
[4] Edmonton N9 ... 18 A1
Upper Clapton E5 ... 52 C1
Valleylink Est EN3 ... 19 A5
Valley Mews TW1 ... 153 A2
Valley Pl KT6 ... 198 A3
Valley Point Ind Est CR0 ... 204 A2
Valley Prim Sch BR2 ... 186 D1
Valley Prospect [3] SE19 ... 183 C4
Valley Rd
Beckenham BR2 ... 186 C1
BR5 ... 190 B2
Streatham SW16 ... 182 B6
Uxbridge UB10 ... 82 A5
Valleyside SE7 ... 121 D1
Valley Side E4 ... 19 C3
Valley Side Par E4 ... 19 C2
Valley View EN5 ... 13 A5
Valley Wlk CR0 ... 222 C6
Valliere Rd NW10 ... 90 A4
Valliers Wood Rd DA15 ... 167 C3
Vallis Way
Chessington KT9 ... 213 D4
Ealing W13 ... 87 A2
Val McKenzie Ave N7 ... 72 C5
Valmar Rd SE5 ... 139 A4
Valmar Trad Est SE5 ... 139 A4
Valnay St SW17 ... 180 D5
Valognes Ave E17 ... 35 A2
Valois Ho SE1 ... 263 C6
Valonia Gdns SW18 ... 157 B5
Vambery Rd SE18 ... 145 A6
Vanbern Ho NW5 ... 71 A2
Vanborough Ct [4] SM2 ... 218 A2
Vanbrough Cres UB5 ... 84 C6
Vanbrugh Ct SE11 ... 261 B3
Vanbrugh Dr KT12 ... 194 C3
Vanbrugh Fields SE3 ... 142 D5
Vanbrugh Hill SE10, SE3 ... 142 D6
Vanbrugh Ho [8] E9 ... 74 C1
Vanbrugh Mews KT12 ... 194 C2
Vanbrugh Park Rd SE3 ... 142 D5
Vanbrugh Park Rd W SE3 ... 142 D5
Vanbrugh Pk SE3 ... 142 D5
Vanbrugh Rd W4 ... 111 B3
Vanbrugh Terr SE3 ... 142 D4
Vanburgh Cl
[2] Newham E16 ... 99 D2
Orpington BR6 ... 211 C1
Vanburgh Ct [6] EN5 ... 1 A1
Vanburgh Ho E1 ... 243 C4
Vancouver Rd
Edgware HA8 ... 26 D2
Forest Hill SE23 ... 163 B2
Hayes UB4 ... 84 B3
Richmond TW10 ... 175 C6
Vancover Ho [33] E1 ... 118 B5
Vanderbilt Rd SW18 ... 158 A3
Vanderbilt Villas [1] W12 ... 112 D4
Vanderville Gdns N2 ... 30 B1
Vandome Cl E16 ... 99 B1
Vandon Ct SW1 ... 259 B6
Vandon Pas SW1 ... 259 B6
Vandon St SW1 ... 259 B6
Van Dyck Ave KT3 ... 199 B2
Vandyke Cl SW15 ... 156 D5
Vandyke Cross SE9 ... 166 A6
Vandy St EC2 ... 243 A5
Vane Cl
Hampstead NW3 ... 70 B4
Harrow HA3 ... 44 B3
Vane Ho [18] N2 ... 30 B1
Vanessa Cl DA17 ... 125 C1
Vane St SW1 ... 259 B4
Vanfame Ct KT3 ... 199 D6
Vange Ho [12] W10 ... 90 C2
Van Gogh Cl [11] TW7 ... 131 A2
Van Gogh Ct E14 ... 120 B3
Vanguard Bldg [6] E14 ... 119 C4
Vanguard Cl
Newham E16 ... 99 B2
Thornton Heath CR0 ... 204 D1
Vanguard Ho
[11] Hackney E8 ... 74 B1
[7] Merton SW19 ... 180 A3
[6] Stanwell TW19 ... 148 A5
Vanguard St SE8 ... 141 C4
Vanguard Way
Hatton TW6 ... 127 C3
Wallington SM6 ... 220 A1
Van Lang Ho EN3 ... 18 D6
Vanneck Sq SW15 ... 156 A6
Vanner Point [27] E9 ... 74 D2
Vanoc Gdns BR1 ... 187 A6
Vanquish Cl TW2 ... 151 C4
Vansittart Rd E7 ... 77 A4
Vansittart St [7] SE14 ... 141 A5
Vanston Pl SW6 ... 135 C5 265 B4
Vantage Ct
Harlington UB3 ... 127 C5
[4] South Norwood SW16 ... 182 B3
Vantage Mews [7] E14 ... 120 A5
Vantage Pl W8 ... 255 B5
Vant Rd SW17 ... 180 D5
Vantrey Ho SE11 ... 261 A3
Varcoe Rd SE16 ... 118 C1
Vardens Rd SW11 ... 136 B1
Varden St E1 ... 96 B1
Vardon Cl W3 ... 89 B1
Vardon Ho SE10 ... 142 A4
Vardy Ho HA7 ... 25 B5
Varey Ho E1 ... 97 A4
Varley Ho [5] NW6 ... 91 C6
Varley Par NW9 ... 45 C5
Varley Rd E16 ... 99 B1
Varley Way CR4 ... 180 B1
Varma Ct SE3 ... 143 A4
Varna Rd
Hampton TW12 ... 173 D2
SW6 ... 135 B5 264 C3
Varndell St NW1 ... 93 C4 232 A2
Varnishers Yard N1 ... 233 B3
Varsity Dr TW1, TW7 ... 152 D5
Varsity Row SW14 ... 133 A3
Vartry Rd N15 ... 51 C3
Vascroft Est NW10 ... 88 D3
Vassall Ho [3] E3 ... 97 A4
Vassall Rd SW9 ... 138 C5
Vat Ho SW8 ... 270 B4
Vauban Est SE16 ... 263 D5
Vauban St SE16 ... 117 D3 263 D5
Vaudeville Ct N4 ... 72 C6
Vaughan Almshouses TW15 ... 170 D5
Vaughan Ave
Chiswick W6 ... 111 D2
Hendon NW4 ... 46 A4
Vaughan Cl TW12 ... 173 A4
Vaughan Est [3] E2 ... 95 D4
Vaughan Fst & Mid Sch HA1 ... 42 A3
Vaughan Gdns IG1 ... 56 B2
Vaughan Ho SE1 ... 251 C2
Vaughan Rd
Camberwell SE5 ... 139 A2
DA16 ... 145 D3
Harrow HA1 ... 42 B3
Stratford E15 ... 76 D2
Thames Ditton KT7 ... 197 B2
Vaughan St SE16 ... 119 B4
Vaughan Way E1 ... 118 A5
Vaughan Williams Cl SE8 ... 141 C5
VAUXHALL ... 116 A1
Vauxhall Bridge Rd SW1 ... 115 C2 259 B3
Vauxhall City Farm★ SE1 ... 260 C1
Vauxhall Cross SE1, SW8 ... 116 A1 260 B1
Vauxhall Gdns CR2 ... 221 A2
Vauxhall Gr SW8 ... 138 B6 270 C6
Vauxhall Prim Sch SE11 ... 116 B1 260 D2
Vauxhall St SE11 ... 116 B1 260 D2
Vauxhall Sta SE11 ... 116 A1 260 B1
Vauxhall Wlk SE11 ... 260 C2
Vawdrey Cl E1 ... 96 C3
Vaynor Ho N7 ... 72 A4
Veals Mead CR4 ... 180 C2
Vectis Ct SW18 ... 157 D5
Vectis Gdns SW17 ... 181 B4
Vectis Rd SW17 ... 181 B4
Veda Rd SE13 ... 141 C1
Vega Cres HA6 ... 22 A5
Vega Rd WD23 ... 8 A4
Veitch Cl TW14 ... 149 D4
Veldene Way HA2 ... 63 B5
Velde Way [1] SE22 ... 161 C6
Vellacott Ho [3] W12 ... 90 B1
Velletri Ho [17] E2 ... 96 D5
Vellum Dr SM5 ... 219 A5
Velocity Way EN3 ... 7 B6
Venables Cl RM10 ... 81 D4
Venables St NW8 ... 92 B2 236 D4
Vencourt Pl W6 ... 112 A2
Venetian Rd SE5 ... 139 A3
Venetia Rd
Ealing W5 ... 109 D4
Harringay N4 ... 50 D3
Venice Ct [14] SE5 ... 139 A5
Venita Manor SE27 ... 182 C5
Venmead Ct [7] DA17 ... 125 C2
Venner Rd SE26 ... 184 C5
Venn Ho N1 ... 233 D5
Venn St SW4 ... 137 C1
Ventnor Ave HA7 ... 25 B1
Ventnor Dr N20 ... 13 D2
Ventnor Gdns IG11 ... 79 C2
Ventnor Mans IG11 ... 79 C2
Ventnor Rd
Belmont SM2 ... 217 D1
SE14 ... 140 D5
Ventnor Terr N15 ... 52 A5
Ventura Ho [12] SW2 ... 138 A1
Venture Cl DA5 ... 169 A4
Venture Ct [3] SE12 ... 165 A4
Venue St E14 ... 98 A2
Venus Ho
[7] Millwall E14 ... 119 C2
[8] Old Ford E3 ... 97 C6
Venus Mews CR4 ... 202 C6
Venus Rd SE18 ... 122 B3
Vera Ave N21 ... 16 C6
Vera Ct
[1] Kensington W2 ... 91 D1
Tottenham N22 ... 32 D2
Vera Lynn Cl [5] E7 ... 77 A4
Vera Rd SW6 ... 135 A4 264 B2
Verbena Cl E16 ... 98 D3
Verbena Gdns [4] W6 ... 112 A1
Verdant Ct [3] SE6 ... 164 C4
Verdant La SE6 ... 164 C3
Verdayne Ave CR0 ... 222 D6
Verdun Rd
Barnes SW13 ... 134 A5
SE18 ... 146 A6
Vere Bank SW19 ... 157 B3
Vereker Dr TW16 ... 194 A6
Vereker Rd W14 ... 254 B1
Vere St W1 ... 93 B1 238 C1
Verity Cl W11 ... 91 A1
Verity Ct N9 ... 18 D3
Verity Ho [20] E3 ... 97 B4
Vermeer Ct E14 ... 120 B3
Vermillion Ct TW13 ... 149 D1
Vermont Cl EN2 ... 4 D1
Vermont Ho E17 ... 35 B1
Vermont Rd
Sutton SM1 ... 217 D5
Wandsworth SW18 ... 157 D5
West Norwood SE19 ... 183 C4
Verne Ct [9] W3 ... 111 A3
Verneer Gdns SE15 ... 140 C1
Verney Gdns RM9 ... 81 A4
Verney Ho
Isleworth TW3 ... 130 A1
Lisson Gr NW8 ... 237 A6
South Kensington SW10 ... 266 A6
Verney Rd
Bermondsey SE16 ... 118 B1
Dagenham RM9 ... 81 A4
Verney St NW10 ... 67 B5
Verney Way SE16 ... 118 B1
Vernham Rd SE18 ... 145 A6
Vernon Ave Ilford E12 ... 78 B4
West Barnes SW20 ... 178 D1
Woodford IG8 ... 37 B3
Vernon Cl
Stanwell TW19 ... 148 A3
West Ewell KT19 ... 215 A2
Vernon Cres EN4 ... 15 A5
Vernon Ct
Child's Hill NW2 ... 69 B5
Ealing W5 ... 109 C6
Stanmore HA7 ... 25 B2
Vernon Dr HA7 ... 25 A2
Vernon Ho
Hyde The NW9 ... 45 D4
SE11 ... 260 D1
Vernon House Specl Sch NW10 ... 67 B3
Vernon Mews W14 ... 254 B3
Vernon Pl WC1 ... 240 B3
Vernon Rd Bow E3 ... 97 B5
Feltham TW13 ... 149 D2
Hornsey N8 ... 50 C6
Ilford IG3 ... 57 D1
Leytonstone E11 ... 54 C1
Mortlake SW14 ... 133 B2
Stratford E15 ... 76 C1
Sutton SM1 ... 218 B3
Walthamstow E17 ... 53 B4
Vernon Rise
Greenford UB6 ... 64 B3
WC1 ... 233 D2
Vernon Sq WC1 ... 233 D2
Vernon St W14 ... 113 A2 254 B3
Vernon Yd W11 ... 113 B6 244 C6
Veroan Rd DA7 ... 147 A3
Verona Ct
Chiswick W4 ... 111 C1
[10] SE14 ... 140 D6
Verona Dr KT6 ... 214 A6
Verona Rd E7 ... 77 A1
Veronica Gdns CR4, SW16 ... 181 C2
Veronica Ho
Brockley SE4 ... 141 B2
[46] Bromley E3 ... 97 D4
Veronica Rd SW17 ... 159 B2
Veronique Gdns IG6 ... 57 A4
Verran Rd SW12 ... 159 B4
Versailles Rd SE20 ... 184 A3
Verulam Ave E17 ... 53 B2
Verulam Bldgs WC1 ... 240 D4

Verulam Ct
Hendon NW9 . . . . 46 A2
4 Southall UB1 . . . . 86 A1
Verulam Ho 1 W6 . . . 112 C4
Verulam Rd UB6 . . . . . . 85 C3
Verulam St
EC1 . . . . . . 94 C2 241 A4
Vervain Ho 2 SE15 . . 140 A5
Verwood Dr EN4 . . . . 2 D2
Verwood Ho SW8 . . . . 270 D3
Verwood Lo 1 E14 . . . 120 B2
Verwood Rd HA2 . . . . . 24 A1
Veryan Ct 3 N8 . . . . . . 49 D4
Vesage Ct EC1 . . . . . . 241 B3
Vesey Path 15 E14 . . . . 97 D1
Vespan Rd W12 . . . . . . 112 A4
Vesta Ct SE1 . . . . 253 A1
Vesta Ho 9 E3 . . . . 97 C6
Vesta Rd SE4, SE14 . . . 141 A3
Vestris Rd SE23 . . . . . 162 D2
Vestry House (Mus)★
E17 . . . . 53 D5
Vestry Mews 12 SE5 . . 139 C4
Vestry Rd
Camberwell SE5 . . . . . 139 C4
Walthamstow E17 . . . . . 53 D5
Vestry St N1 . . . 95 B4 235 C2
Vevey St SE23, SE6 . . . . 163 B2
Veysey Gdns RM10 . . . . 81 C5
Viaduct Pl 28 E2 . . . . . . 96 B4
Viaduct Rd N2 . . . . 30 C1
Viaduct St E2 . . . . 96 B4
Viaduct The
Harrow HA2 . . . . 64 A5
Woodford E18 . . . . 37 B1
Vian St SE13 . . . . 141 D2
Vibart Gdns SW2 . . . . . 160 B4
Vibart Wlk N1 . . . . 233 B6
Vicarage Ave SE3 . . . . 143 A5
Vicarage Cl
New Malden KT4 . . . . 199 C1
Northolt UB5 . . . . 63 B1
Ruislip HA4 . . . . 39 B2
Vicarage Cres
SW11 . . . . . 136 B4 266 C1
Vicarage Ct
Beckenham BR3 . . . . . 207 A6
East Bedfont TW14 . . 149 A4
Finchley N12 . . . . 29 D5
7 Putney SW15 . . . . . 156 A4
W8 . . . . 245 C2
Vicarage Dr
Barking IG11 . . . . 79 A1
Beckenham BR3 . . . . . . 185 C2
Mortlake SW14 . . . . . . 155 B6
Vicarage Farm Ct
TW5 . . . . 129 B5
Vicarage Farm Rd TW3,
TW4, TW5 . . . . 129 A4
Vicarage Fields
KT12 . . . . 194 C3
Vicarage Field Sh Ctr
The IG11 . . . . 79 A1
Vicarage Gate
W8 . . . . . . 113 D5 245 C3
Vicarage Gdns
Mitcham CR4 . . . . 202 C6
Mortlake SW14 . . . . . . 155 B6
W8 . . . . 245 B3
Vicarage Gr SE5 . . . . . 139 B4
Vicarage Ho 1 KT1 . . 176 B1
Vicarage La Ilford IG1 . 57 B1
Stratford E15 . . . . 76 D1
Wallend E6 . . . . 100 C4
Vicarage Mans N15 . . . 51 A5
Vicarage Pk SE18 . . . . 123 A1
Vicarage Prim Sch 5
E6 . . . . 100 B4
Vicarage Rd
Ashford TW16 . . . . . . 171 D4
Croydon CR0 . . . . 220 C5
DA5 . . . . 169 D3
Dagenham RM10 . . . . . . 81 D1
Hampton Wick KT1 . . . 175 C2
Hendon NW4 . . . . 46 A3
Kingston u T KT1 . . . . 175 D1
Mortlake SW14 . . . . . . 155 B6
Old Bexley DA5 . . . . . 169 D2
Stratford E15 . . . . 76 D1
Sutton SM1 . . . . 217 D5
Teddington TW11 . . . . 175 A5
Tottenham N17 . . . . 34 A2
Walthamstow E10 . . . . . 53 D1
Woolwich SE18 . . . . . 123 A1
Vicarage The N8 . . . . . . 50 B3
Vicarage Way
Harrow HA2 . . . . 41 C2
Neasden NW10 . . . . 67 B5
Vicarage Wlk
SW11 . . . . . . 136 B4 266 D2
Vicars Bridge Cl HA0 . . 88 A5
Vicar's Cl Enfield EN1 . . . 5 C3
Newham E15 . . . . 99 A6
South Hackney E9 . . . . . 96 C6
Vicar's Green Prim Sch
HA0 . . . . 87 C5
Vicars Hill SE13 . . . . . 141 D1
Vicar's Moor La N21 . . 16 D4
Vicars Oak Rd SE19 . . 183 C4
Vicar's Rd NW5 . . . . 71 A3
Vicar's Wlk RM8 . . . . . . 80 B5
Viceroy Cl N2 . . . . 48 C6
Viceroy Ct
5 Croydon CR0 . . . . . 205 B1
NW8 . . . . 230 B4
Viceroy Lo 6 KT6 . . . . 198 A4
Viceroy Par N2 . . . . 48 C6
Viceroy Rd
SW8 . . . . . . 138 A4 270 A2
Vic Johnson Ho 21
E3 . . . . 97 B6
Vickers Cl SM6 . . . . . . 220 B1
Vickers Ct 10 TW19 . . 148 A5
Vickery Ct EC1 . . . . . . 242 B6
Vickery Ho 13 SW4 . . . 138 A1
Vickery's Wharf 3
E14 . . . . 97 C1
Victor Cazalet Ho N1 234 C6
Victor Gr HA0 . . . . 66 A1
Victor Ho 2 N20 . . . . . . 14 D1
Victoria & Albert Mus★
SW7 . . . . 114 B3 256 D5
Victoria Arc SW1 . . . . 258 D5
Victoria Ave Barnet EN4 . 2 B1
East Molesey KT8 . . . 195 D6
EC2 . . . . 243 B3
Finchley N3 . . . . 29 B2
Hackbridge SM5, SM6 219 A5
Hillingdon UB10 . . . . . . 60 D1
Hounslow TW3, TW4 . 151 C6
Newham E6 . . . . 99 D6
Surbiton KT6 . . . . 197 D3
Wembley HA9 . . . . 66 D2
Victoria Bglws DA14 . 191 B3
Victoria Bldgs 13 E8 . . 96 B6
Victoria Bsns Ctr
DA16 . . . . 146 B3
Victoria Chambers
EC2 . . . . 243 A6
Victoria Cl Barnet EN4 . . 2 B1
East Molesey KT8 . . . 195 C6
Harrow HA1 . . . . 42 D3
Hayes UB3 . . . . 83 B1
Victoria Coach Sta
SW1 . . . . 115 B2 258 C3
Victoria Coll WC2 . . . 241 A2
Victoria Cotts
Ilford IG6 . . . . 57 A4
Muswell Hill N10 . . . . . . 31 A1
7 Richmond TW9 . . . . 132 C4
3 Spitalfields E1 . . . . . . 96 A2
Victoria Cres
Tottenham N15 . . . . 51 C4
West Norwood SE19 . 183 C4
Victoria Ct
5 Clapham Pk
SW4 . . . . 159 D5
3 Penge SE26 . . . . . . 184 C4
South Acton W3 . . . . . 110 C4
4 St George in t East
E1 . . . . 118 A6
1 Wanstead E18 . . . . . . 55 B6
Wembley HA9 . . . . 66 C2
Victoria Dock Rd
E16 . . . . 121 B6
Victoria Dr SW19 . . . . 156 D3
Victoria Emb
WC2 . . . . 116 C6 251 A5
Victoria Gdns
Heston TW5 . . . . 129 A4
W11 . . . . 113 C5 245 A4
Victoria Gr
North Finchley N12 . . . . 30 B5
W8 . . . . 114 A3 256 A6
Victoria Gr Mews
W2 . . . . 245 C5
Victoria Hall 15 E16 . . 121 A5
Victoria Ho
6 Clapham Pk
SW4 . . . . 159 D5
Edgware HA8 . . . . 26 D4
Victoria Ho continued
2 Shepherd's Bush
W12 . . . . 112 A4
SW1 . . . . 258 C2
Victoria Ind Est W3 . . . 89 C2
Victoria Jun Sch
TW13 . . . . 150 B3
Victoria La Barnet EN5 . . 1 B1
Hayes UB3 . . . . 105 B1
Victoria Lo 5 SW19 . . 178 C3
Victoria Mans
8 Islington N7 . . . . 72 C3
Willesden NW10 . . . . . . 68 B1
Victoria Mews
Kilburn NW6 . . . . 91 C6
Wandsworth SW18 . . 158 A3
Victoria Mills 1 E15 . . 98 B6
Victorian Gr N16 . . . . . . 73 C5
Victorian Hts 7
SW8 . . . . 137 B3
Victorian Rd N16 . . . . . . 73 D5
Victoria Park Ct 11
E9 . . . . 74 C1
Victoria Park Ind Ctr
E9 . . . . 75 B1
Victoria Park Lofts
E9 . . . . 96 D6
Victoria Park Rd E9 . . . 74 D1
Victoria Park Sq E2 . . . 96 C4
Victoria Pas NW8 . . . 236 C6
Victoria Pl 17 TW10 . 153 D6
Victoria Place Sh Ctr
SW1 . . . . 115 B2 258 D4
Victoria Point 10 E13 . . 99 A5
Victoria Rd
Barking IG11 . . . . 78 D2
Barnet EN4 . . . . 2 B1
Bexley DA6 . . . . 147 C1
Bromley Comm BR2 . . 209 D4
Buckhurst Hill IG9 . . . . 21 D2
Chingford E4 . . . . 20 C3
Chislehurst West BR7 188 C5
Dagenham RM10 . . . . . . 81 D3
Ealing W5 . . . . 87 B2
Edgware NW7 . . . . 27 D5
Edmonton N9 . . . . 17 D1
Feltham TW13 . . . . 150 B3
Finsbury Pk N4 . . . . 50 B1
Hendon NW4 . . . . 46 D5
Kensington
W8 . . . . 114 A3 256 A6
Kilburn NW6 . . . . 91 B6
Kingston u T KT1 . . . . 176 B1
Leyton E11 . . . . 76 C4
Mitcham CR4 . . . . 180 D3
Mortlake SW14 . . . . . . 133 B2
Muswell Hill N22 . . . . . . 31 D2
Newham E13 . . . . 99 A5
North Acton NW10 . . . . 89 C3
Ruislip HA4 . . . . 62 B4
Sidcup DA15 . . . . 168 A1
Southall UB2 . . . . 107 B3
Surbiton KT6 . . . . 197 D3
Sutton SM1 . . . . 218 B3
Teddington TW11 . . . . 175 A4
Tottenham Hale N15 . . . 52 A5
Twickenham TW1 . . . . 153 B4
Walthamstow E17 . . . . . 36 A1
Wanstead E18 . . . . 55 B6
Victoria Ret Pk HA4 . . . 62 D3
Victoria Rise SW4 . . . . 137 B2
Victoria Sq SW1 . . . . . 258 D6
Victoria St
Erith DA17 . . . . 125 B1
Stratford E15 . . . . 76 C1
SW1 . . . . 115 C3 259 B5
Victoria Sta
SW1 . . . . 115 B2 258 D4
Victoria Terr
Dagenham NW10 . . . . . . 89 C3
Finsbury Pk N4 . . . . 50 C1
Harrow HA1 . . . . 42 C1
Victoria (Underground)
SW1 . . . . 115 B3 258 D5
Victoria Villas TW9 . . . 132 B1
Victoria Way SE7 . . . . 143 C6
Victoria Wharf E14 . . . 119 A6
Victoria Yd 28 E1 . . . . . 96 A1
Victor Mills Cotts
BR8 . . . . 191 C3
Victor Rd
College Pk NW10 . . . . . 90 B4
Harrow HA2 . . . . 42 A6
Penge SE20 . . . . 184 D3
Teddington TW11 . . . . 174 C6
Victors Dr TW12 . . . . . 173 A4
Victor Seymour Inf Sch
6 SM5 . . . . 219 A5
Victors Way EN5 . . . . 1 B2
Victor Villas N9 . . . . 17 B1
Victory Ave SM4 . . . . . 202 A4
Victory Bsns Ctr
TW7 . . . . 130 D1
Victory Cl TW19 . . . . . 148 A3
Victory Ct IG11 . . . . . . 102 B4
Victory Pl
6 Limehouse E14 . . . . 119 A6
SE17 . . . . 117 B2 262 C4
West Norwood SE19 . 183 C4
Victory Prim Sch
SE17 . . . . 117 A2 262 B4
Victory Rd
Merton SW19 . . . . 180 A3
Wanstead E11 . . . . 55 B5
Victory Road Mews 5
SW19 . . . . 180 A3
Victory Way
Hounslow TW5 . . . . . . 106 C1
Rotherhithe SE16 . . . . 119 A4
Victory Wlk SE8 . . . . . 141 C4
Video Ct N4 . . . . 50 A2
Vidler Cl KT9 . . . . 213 C2
Vienna Cl IG5 . . . . 37 D1
Vietory Day Sch 3
CR7 . . . . 205 A6
View Cl Harrow HA1 . . . . 42 B5
Highgate N6 . . . . 48 D2
View Cres N8 . . . . 49 D4
Viewfield Cl HA3 . . . . . . 44 A2
Viewfield Rd DA5 . . . . 168 C3
Wandsworth SW18 . . . 157 B5
Viewland Rd SE18 . . . 123 D1
Viewpoint Ealing W5 . . 110 B6
3 Islington N5 . . . . 72 D3
View Point N20 . . . . 14 A4
Viewpoint Ct 8 HA5 . . 22 C1
View Rd N6 . . . . 48 D3
Viewside Lo N6 . . . . 49 C3
View The SE2 . . . . 125 A1
Viga Rd N21 . . . . 16 C5
Vigilant Cl SE26 . . . . . 184 A6
Vignoles Rd RM7 . . . . . 59 C2
Vigo St W1 . . . 115 C6 249 A5
Vi & John Rubens Ho
IG2 . . . . 56 C3
Viking Cl 13 E3 . . . . 97 A5
Viking Ct
Hampton TW12 . . . . . 173 D2
New Barnet EN4 . . . . . . 14 B6
Viking Gdns E6 . . . . . . 100 A3
Viking Ho
3 Camberwell SE5 . . . 139 A3
3 Woolwich SE18 . . . 122 A2
Viking Pl E10 . . . . 53 B1
Viking Prim Sch UB5 . . 84 D4
Viking Rd UB1 . . . . 107 A6
Villacourt Rd SE18 . . . 146 A6
Village Arc The 2 E4 . . . 20 B3
Village Cl Chingford E4 . 36 A5
Hampstead NW3 . . . . . . 70 B3
Village Ct
Blackheath SE3 . . . . . 142 C2
Walthamstow E17 . . . . . 53 D4
Village Gate TW17 . . 192 D4
Village Home The
IG6 . . . . 57 A6
Village Hts IG8 . . . . 36 D5
Village Inf Sch RM10 . . 81 C1
Village Mount 19
NW3 . . . . 70 A4
Village Park Cl EN1 . . . 17 C5
Village Rd Enfield EN1 . . 17 C6
Hendon N3 . . . . 29 A1
Village Row SM2 . . . . . 217 C1
Village Sch The NW3 . . 70 D2
Village The
Battersea SW11 . . . . . 136 D2
SE7 . . . . 143 D6
Village Way
Ashford TW15 . . . . . . 170 C6
Beckenham BR3 . . . . . 207 C6
Dulwich Village SE21 . 161 B5
Ilford IG6 . . . . 57 A6
Pinner HA5 . . . . 41 B2
Willesden NW10 . . . . . . 67 B4
Village Way E HA2 . . . . 41 C2
Villa Rd SW9 . . . . 138 C2
Villas On The Heath
NW3 . . . . 70 A5
Villas Rd SE18 . . . . . . 123 A2
Villa St SE17 . . 117 B1 262 D1
Villiers Ave
Kingston u T KT5 . . . . 198 B5
Twickenham TW2 . . . . 151 B3
Villiers Cl
Kingston u T KT5 . . . . 198 B5
Leyton E10 . . . . 75 C6
Villiers Ct
Oakleigh Pk N20 . . . . . . 14 A4
SW11 . . . . 267 B2
Villiers High Sch
UB1 . . . . 107 B5
Villiers Ho W5 . . . . 109 D6
Villiers Rd
Isleworth TW7 . . . . . . 130 C3
Kingston u T KT1 . . . . 198 B6
Penge BR3 . . . . 184 D1
Southall UB1 . . . . 107 B5
Willesden NW2 . . . . 68 A2
Villiers St WC2 . . . . . . 250 B4
Vimy Cl TW4 . . . . 151 B6
Vincam Cl TW2 . . . . . . 151 C4
Vince Ct N1 . . . . 235 D1
Vincent Ave KT5 . . . . . 215 A6
Vincent Cl
Avery Hill DA15 . . . . . 167 C3
Barnet EN5 . . . . 1 D2
Bromley BR2 . . . . 209 B5
Harmondsworth UB7 . 126 C6
Vincent Ct
Finsbury Pk N4 . . . . 50 A1
Hendon NW4 . . . . 46 D5
Marylebone W1 . . . . . 237 C2
Ruislip HA4 . . . . 62 B3
South Lambeth SW9 . 270 D1
Vincent Dr
Hillingdon UB10 . . . . . . 82 B6
Upper Halliford TW17 193 C6
Vincent Gdns NW2 . . . . 67 D5
Vincent Ho KT3 . . . . . . 199 D5
Vincent Mews 1 E3 . . . 97 C5
Vincent Rd
Acton Green W3 . . . . . 111 A3
Chingford E4 . . . . 36 B4
Croydon CR0 . . . . 205 C2
Dagenham RM9 . . . . 81 A1
Hounslow West TW4 . 128 D2
Kingston u T KT1 . . . . 198 C6
Osterley TW7 . . . . 130 B4
Tottenham N15 . . . . 51 A5
Wembley HA0 . . . . 66 B1
Wood Green N22 . . . . . . 32 C1
Woolwich SE18 . . . . . . 122 D2
Vincent Row TW12 . . . 174 A5
Vincents Cl SE16 . . . . . 119 A4
Vincents Path UB5 . . . . 63 A2
Vincent Sq
SW1 . . . . 115 D2 259 C4
Wood Green N22 . . . . . . 32 C1
Vincent St
Canning Town E16 . . . . 98 D2
Westminster
SW1 . . . . 115 D2 259 D4
Vincent Terr
N1 . . . . 94 D5 234 D4
Vince St EC1 . . . 95 B4 235 D1
Vine Cl Shacklewell E5 . . 74 A4
Surbiton KT5 . . . . 198 B3
Sutton SM1 . . . . 218 A5
West Drayton UB7 . . . 104 C2
Vine Cotts
3 Ealing W7 . . . . 108 C5
Southall UB2 . . . . 107 D2
Vine Ct Harrow HA3 . . . . 44 A3
Spitalfields E1 . . . . 96 A2
Vinegar St E1 . . . . 118 B5
Vinegar Yd SE1 . . . . . . 253 A2
Vine Gdns IG1 . . . . 79 A3
Vine Gr UB10 . . . . 60 C1
Vine Hill EC1 . . . . 241 A5
Vine La
Hillingdon UB10 . . . . . . 82 B6
SE1 . . . . 117 C5 253 B3
Uxbridge UB10 . . . . 60 B1
Vine Lo N12 . . . . 30 A4
Vine Pl Ealing W5 . . . . . 110 A5
Hounslow TW3 . . . . . . 129 D1
Vine Rd
Barnes SW13 . . . . 133 D2
BR6 . . . . 227 D2
East Molesey KT8 . . . 196 A5
Stratford E15 . . . . 76 D1
Vineries Bank NW7 . . . 28 B5

Vineries Cl
Dagenham RM9 .... 81 B2
Harmondsworth UB7. 126 C6
Vineries The
Enfield EN1 .... 5 C2
Southgate N14 .... 15 C5
Viners Cl KT12 .... 194 C3
Vine St Bridge EC1 .. 241 B5
Vines Ave N3 .... 29 D2
Vine Sq W14 .... 254 D1
Vine St W1 .... 249 B5
Whitechapel
EC3 .... 95 D1 243 C1
Vinewood Ct E17 ...... 54 B4
Vineyard Ave NW7 .... 29 A3
Vineyard Cl
Forest Hill SE6 ...... 163 C3
Kingston u T KT1 ..... 198 B6
Vineyard Gr N3 .... 29 D2
Vineyard Hill Rd
SW19 .... 179 C6
Vineyard Path SW14 . 133 B2
Vineyard Prim Sch The
TW10 .... 154 A5
Vineyard Rd TW13 .... 150 A1
Vineyard Row KT1,
KT8 .... 175 C2
Vineyards The TW13 . 150 A1
Vineyard Studios [3]
E7 .... 77 C1
Vineyard The TW10 .. 154 A6
Vineyard Wlk EC1 ... 241 A6
Viney Ct [9] SW4 ..... 159 D5
Vine Yd SE1 .... 252 B2
Viney Rd SE13 .... 141 D2
Vining St SW2, SW9 .. 138 C1
Vinlake Ave UB10 ...... 60 C5
Vinson Ho N1 .... 235 D3
Vinter Ct TW17 .... 192 C4
Vintners Ct EC4 ..... 252 B6
Vintry Mews [3] E17 ... 53 C5
Viola Ave
Feltham TW14 ...... 150 C5
SE2 .... 124 B1
Stanwell TW19 ...... 148 A3
Viola Ct HA8 .... 26 D3
Viola Sq W12 .... 111 D6
Violet Ave Enfield EN2 ... 5 B5
Hillingdon UB8 .... 82 B2
Violet Cl Cheam SM3 . 201 A1
Hackbridge SM6 .... 203 A1
Newham E16 .... 98 C3
[32] SE8 .... 141 B6
Violet Ct [2] E15 .... 76 C1
Violet Gdns CR0 .... 220 D3
Violet Hill
NW8 .... 92 A5 229 A3
Violet Hill Ho NW8 .. 229 A3
Violet La CR0 .... 220 D3
Violet Rd Bromley E3 ... 97 D3
Walthamstow E17 ...... 53 C3
Woodford E18 .... 37 B1
Violet St E2 .... 96 B3
Violet Terr UB8 .... 82 C2
Violette Szabo Ho [4]
SE27 .... 183 B6
VIP Trad Est SE7 .... 121 C2
Virgil Pl W1 .... 237 C3
Virgil St SE1 .. 116 B3 260 D6
Virginia Cl
Beckenham BR2 ..... 208 C6
New Malden KT3 .... 199 A5
Virginia Ct
Ashford TW15 ...... 170 A6
[7] Rotherhithe SE16 . 118 D4
Virginia Ho
[3] Blackwall E14 .... 120 A6
Teddington TW11 .... 175 A5
Virginia Prim Sch [48]
E2 .... 95 D4
Virginia Rd
South Norwood CR7 .. 182 D2
[19] Spitalfields E2 ...... 95 D4
Virginia St E1 .... 118 A6
Virginia Wlk SW2 .... 160 B5
Virgo Fidelis Convent
Senior Sch SE19 ... 183 B4
Virgo Fidelis Prep Sch
SE19 .... 183 B4
Viridian Ct TW13 .... 149 D1
Viscount Cl N11 .... 31 B5
Viscount Ct
[9] Kensington W11 .... 91 C1
Viscount Ct *continued*
[1] Littleton TW15 ... 171 A3
Viscount Dr E6 .... 100 B2
Viscount Gr [3] UB5 ... 84 D4
Viscount Point [6]
SW19 .... 179 C3
Viscount Rd TW19 .... 148 A3
Viscount St EC1 ..... 242 A4
Viscount Way TW6 ... 127 C1
Vision Coll of Theology
E9 .... 75 C2
Vista Ave EN3 .... 6 D3
Vista Bldgs [10] E3 ..... 97 B4
Vista Bldg The [14]
SE18 .... 122 C2
Vista Dr IG4 .... 55 D4
Vista Ho [2] SW19 ..... 180 B2
Vista Hts SE23 .... 163 A4
Vista The Chingford E4 .. 20 B4
SE9 .... 165 D4
Sidcup DA14 .... 189 D5
Vista Way HA3 .... 44 A3
Vitae Apartments [7]
W6 .... 112 A3
Vita Et Pax Sch N14 ... 15 B6
Vittoria Ho N1 ...... 233 D5
Vittoria Prim Sch
N1 .... 94 C5 234 A4
Viveash Cl UB3 ..... 105 D3
Vivian Ave
Hendon NW4 .... 46 B4
Wembley HA9 .... 66 C2
Vivian Comma Cl [3]
N4 .... 72 D5
Vivian Ct Finchley N12 .. 29 D5
Paddington NW6 ...... 91 D5
Vivian Gdns HA9 ...... 66 C3
Vivian Ho N4 .... 51 B2
Vivian Mans [1] NW4 .. 46 B4
Vivian Rd E3 .... 97 A5
Vivian Sq SE15 ...... 140 B2
Vivian Way N2 .... 48 B4
Vivien Cl KT9 .... 214 A1
Vivienne Cl TW1 .... 153 D5
Voce Rd SE18 .... 145 B5
Voewood Cl KT3 .... 199 D3
Vogans Mill SE1 .... 253 D2
Vogler Ho [3] E1 ..... 118 C6
Vogue Ct [8] BR1 ..... 187 B2
Vollasky Ho [5] E1 ..... 96 A2
Volta Cl N9 .... 18 C1
Voltaire
[2] Camberwell SE5 .. 139 D4
[15] Richmond TW9 .... 132 B4
Voltaire Ct [13] SW11 .. 137 A3
Voltaire Rd SW4 .... 137 D2
Voltaire Way UB3 .... 105 C6
Volt Ave NW10 .... 89 C4
Volta Way CR0 .... 204 B1
Voluntary Pl E11 ...... 55 A3
Vora Ho HA0 .... 65 D2
Vorley Rd N19 .... 71 C6
Voss Ct SW16 .... 182 A4
Voss St E2 .... 96 A4
Voyager Bsns Est [10]
SE16 .... 118 A3
Voyagers Cl IG11 ..... 102 C1
Voysey Cl N3 .... 47 A6
Vulcan Cl E6 .... 100 C1
Vulcan Gate EN2 .... 4 C3
Vulcan Rd SE4 .... 141 B3
Vulcan Sq E14 .... 119 C2
Vulcan Terr SE4 ...... 141 B3
Vulcan Way N7 .... 72 B2
Vyne Ho SM5 .... 218 D2
Vyner Ct E5 .... 74 A6
Vyner Rd W3 .... 111 B6
Vyners Sch UB10 .... 60 B4
Vyner St E2 .... 96 B6
Vyners Way UB10 ..... 60 C3
Vyne The DA7 .... 147 D2
Vyvyan Ho SE18 ..... 144 C4

W

Wadbrook St KT1 ... 175 D1
Wadcroft Ct SE4 ..... 141 B2
Waddesdon Lo HA3 ... 43 A3
Wadding St
SE17 .... 117 B2 262 C3
Waddington Cl EN1 ...... 5 C1
Waddington Rd E15 ... 76 B2
Waddington St E15 ... 76 B2
Waddington Way
SE19 .... 183 B2
WADDON 220 C4
Waddon Cl CR0 ...... 220 C5
Waddon Court Rd
CR0 .... 220 C5
Waddon Inf Sch
CR9 .... 220 C3
Waddon Marsh Sta
CR0 .... 220 C6
Waddon Marsh Way
CR0 .... 204 B1
Waddon New Rd
CR0 .... 220 D6
Waddon Park Ave
CR0 .... 220 C5
Waddon Rd CR0 .... 220 D5
Waddon Sta CR0 .... 220 C4
Waddon Way CR0, CR2,
CR9 .... 220 D2
Wade Ct
Muswell Hill N10 ...... 31 B3
Wembley HA0 .... 65 D5
Wade Ho
[16] Bermondsey
SE1 .... 118 A4
[1] Enfield EN1 .... 17 C6
Wade's Gr N21 .... 16 C4
Wade's Hill N21 .... 16 C4
Wade's La TW11 ...... 175 A5
Wadeson St E2 .... 96 B5
Wade's Pl E14 .... 119 D6
Wadeville Ave RM6 .... 59 B2
Wadeville Cl DA17 ... 125 C1
Wadham Ave E17 ...... 35 D3
Wadham Cl TW17 .... 193 A2
Wadham Gdns
Greenford UB6 .... 64 B2
Primrose Hill
NW3 .... 92 C6 230 A6
Wadham Ho N18 .... 33 D5
Wadham Rd
Chingford E4 .... 36 A2
Highams Pk E17 .... 35 D2
Putney SW15 .... 135 A1
Wadhurst Cl SE20 .... 184 B1
Wadhurst Ct E6 ...... 100 C5
Wadhurst Rd W4 ..... 111 B3
Wadley Rd E11 .... 54 C2
Wadsworth Bsns Ctr
UB6 .... 87 C5
Wadsworth Cl
Enfield EN3 .... 18 D6
Wembley UB6 .... 87 C5
Wadsworth Ct E10 .... 54 A3
Wadsworth Rd UB6 ... 87 C5
Wager St E3 .... 97 B3
Waggoners Rdbt
TW5 .... 128 B4
Waggon Mews N14 ... 15 C3
Waggon Rd EN4 .... 2 B6
Waghorn Rd
Harrow HA3 .... 43 D6
Newham E13 .... 99 C6
Waghorn St SE15 .... 140 A2
Wagner St SE15 ...... 140 C5
Wagon Rd EN4, EN5 ..... 1 D6
Wagstaff Gdns RM9 ... 80 C1
Wagtail Cl Enfield EN1 ... 6 B4
NW9 .... 27 C1
Wagtail Wlk BR3 ..... 208 A4
Waights Ct KT2 .... 176 A2
Waikato Lo IG9 .... 21 C3
Wainford Cl SW19 .. 156 D3
Wainwright Gr TW7 .. 130 B1
Wainwright Ho [3]
E1 .... 118 C5
Waite Davies Rd
SE12 .... 164 D4
Waitelands Ho KT3 .. 199 B5
Waite St SE15 .... 139 D6
Waithman St EC4 ... 241 C1
Wakefield Ct [4]
SE26 .... 184 C4
Wakefield Gdns
Redbridge IG1 .... 56 A3
South Norwood SE19 . 183 C3
Wakefield Ho
Dulwich SE22 .... 162 B3
[6] Peckham SE15 ... 140 A4
Wakefield Mews
WC1 .... 233 B1
Wakefield Rd
Friern Barnet N11 ..... 31 D5
[20] Richmond TW10 .. 153 D6
South Tottenham N15 .. 51 D4
Wakefield St
Edmonton N18 .... 34 A5
Wakefield St *continued*
Newham E6 .... 100 A6
St Pancras
WC1 .... 94 A4 233 B1
Wakeford Cl
London SW4 .... 159 C6
Sidcup OP5 .... 168 D3
Wakehams Hill HA5 ... 41 B6
Wakeham St [9] N1 .... 73 B2
Wakehurst Rd SW11 158 D6
Wakeling Ct E7 .... 77 C2
Wakeling Ho [8]
SE27 .... 160 D1
Wakeling La HA0 ...... 65 B5
Wakeling Rd W7 .... 86 D2
Wakeling St [11] E14 ... 97 A1
Wakelin Ho
Forest Hill SE23 ..... 163 A4
[10] Islington N1 .... 72 D1
Wakelin Rd E15 .... 98 C5
Wakeman Ho HA8 ..... 26 A6
Wakeman Rd NW10 ... 90 D4
Wakemans Hill Ave
NW9 .... 45 B4
Wakering Rd IG11 .... 79 A1
Wakerley Cl [6] E6 .... 100 B1
Wakley St EC1 . 94 D4 234 C2
Walberswick St SW8 270 B3
Walbrook EC4 .... 252 C6
[10] Wanstead E18 ...... 55 A6
Walbrook Ct [32] N1 .... 95 C5
Walbrook Ho N9 .... 18 C2
Walbrook Wharf EC4 252 C6
Walburgh St E1 .... 96 B1
Walcorde Ave SE17 . 262 B3
Walcot Ct CR0 .... 222 A6
Walcot Gdns SE11 .. 261 A4
Walcot Ho [9] SE22 ... 139 C2
Walcot Rd EN3 .... 7 B3
Walcot Sq
SE11 .... 116 C2 261 B4
Walcott St SW1 ..... 259 B4
Waldair Ct E16 ...... 122 D4
Waldeck Gr SE27 ... 160 D1
Waldeck Rd
Brentford W4 .... 132 C6
Ealing W13 .... 87 B1
Mortlake SW14 ..... 133 A2
Tottenham N15 .... 50 D6
Waldeck Terr SW14 . 133 A2
Waldegrave Ct
[11] Barking IG11 ..... 101 B6
[1] Teddington TW11 . 174 D5
Waldegrave Gdns
TW1 .... 152 D1
Waldegrave Girls Sch
TW2 .... 152 B1
Waldegrave Ho [5]
SW15 .... 156 C6
Waldegrave Pk TW1 . 174 D6
Waldegrave Rd BR1 . 210 B5
Dagenham RM8 .... 80 C6
Ealing W5 .... 110 B6
Hornsey N8 .... 50 C6
Penge SE19 .... 183 D3
Teddington TW11 .... 174 D6
Waldegrove CR0 .... 221 D5
Waldemar Ave
Ealing W13 .... 109 C5
Fulham SW6 .... 135 A3
Waldemar Avenue Mans
SW6 .... 264 A1
Waldemar Rd SW19 .. 179 C5
Walden Ave BR7 ..... 188 B6
Edmonton N13 .... 33 A6
Walden Cl DA17 ..... 125 B1
Walden Ct SW8 ...... 269 D2
Walden Gdns CR7,
SW16 .... 204 B5
Walden Ho Barnet EN4 .. 2 C1
[8] Clapham SW11 ... 137 A3
SW1 .... 258 B3
Walden Rd BR7 ...... 188 B4
Tottenham N17 .... 33 B2
Waldenshaw Rd
SE23 .... 162 C3
Walden St E1 .... 96 B1
Walden Way NW7 ..... 28 D4
Waldo Cl SW4 .... 159 C6
Waldo Ind Est BR1 ... 209 D6
Waldo Pl SW19 ...... 180 C3
Waldo Rd BR1 .... 209 D6
College Pk NW10 ...... 90 B4
Waldorf Cl CR2 ...... 220 D1
Waldorf Sch of S W
London SW16 ..... 159 D2
Waldram Cres SE23 .. 162 C3
Waldram Park Rd
SE23 .... 162 D3
Waldram Pl [6] SE23 .. 162 C3
Waldrist Way DA18 ... 125 B4
Waldron Gdns BR2 .. 208 B6
Waldron Ho [17] SW2 .. 160 B6
Waldronhyrst CR0,
CR2 .... 220 D4
Waldron Mews SW3 266 D6
Waldron Rd
Harrow HA1, HA2 ..... 42 C1
Wandsworth SW18 ... 158 A1
Waldrons The CR0 .. 221 A4
Waldron's Yd HA2 ..... 64 B6
Waldstock Rd SE28 .. 124 A6
Waleran Cl HA7 .... 24 D4
Walerand Rd SE13 ... 142 A3
Waleran Flats SE1 .. 263 A4
Wales Ave SM5 ...... 218 C3
Wales Cl SE15 .... 140 B6
Wales Farm Rd W3 .... 89 B2
Waleton Acres SM6 . 219 C2
Waley St [1] E1 .... 97 A2
Walfield Ave N20 ...... 13 D4
Walfield Ho N20 .... 14 A4
Walford Ho [28] E1 ...... 96 B1
Walford Rd N16 .... 73 C4
Walfrey Gdns RM9 ..... 81 A1
Walham Ct [15] NW3 ... 70 D2
Walham Gr
SW6 .... 135 C5 265 A4
WALHAM GREEN ... 135 D5
Walham Green Arc
SW6 .... 265 B4
Walham Rise [1]
SW19 .... 179 A4
Walham Yd SW6 .... 265 A4
Walkden Rd BR7 .... 188 C5
Walker Cl Ealing W7 .. 108 C5
East Bedfont TW14 .. 149 D4
Friern Barnet N11 ..... 31 C6
Hampton TW12 ...... 173 B4
Plumstead SE18 ..... 123 A2
Walker Ho NW1 ..... 232 C3
Walker Mews [9]
SW2 .... 160 C6
Walker Prim Sch N14 . 15 D2
Walkerscroft Mead
SE21 .... 161 A3
Walker's Ct W1 ...... 249 C6
Walkers Lo [18] E14 ... 120 A4
Walker's Pl SW15 .... 135 A1
Walkinshaw Ct [9] N1 . 73 A1
Walks The N2 .... 48 B6
Walk The
Ashford TW16 ...... 171 D3
Palmers Green N13 .... 16 C1
Walkynscroft [1]
SE15 .... 140 B3
Wallace Cl SE28 ..... 124 D6
Upper Halliford TW17 . 193 B5
Uxbridge UB10 .... 82 A5
Wallace Collection*
W1 .... 238 A2
Wallace Cres SM5 ... 218 D3
Wallace Ct
[19] Enfield EN3 .... 7 C6
NW1 .... 237 B3
Wallace Ho N7 .... 72 B2
Wallace Lo N4 .... 50 C1
Wallace Rd N1, N5 .... 73 A2
Wallasey Cres UB10 ... 60 C5
Wallbrook Bsns Ctr
TW4 .... 128 B2
Wallbutton Rd SE4 ... 141 A3
Wallcote Ave NW2 ..... 46 D1
Wall Ct N4 .... 50 B1
Walled Garden Cl
BR3 .... 207 D5
WALLEND 100 C6
Wall End Ct E6 .... 100 C6
Wall End Rd E6 .... 78 C1
Waller Dr HA6 .... 22 A2
Waller Rd SE14 ...... 140 D3
Wallers Cl RM9 ...... 103 B6
Wallett Ct [11] NW1 .... 71 C1
Wallflower St W12 .. 111 D6
Wallgrave Rd SW5 .. 255 C3
Wallingford Ave W10 . 90 D1
WALLINGTON 219 A2
Wallington Cl HA4 .... 39 A3
Wallington Ct [10]
SM6 .... 219 B2
Wallington Cty Gram Sch
SM6 .... 219 B5

Wallington Green SM6 219 B4
Wallington Rd IG3 57 D2
Wallington Sq 4 SM6 219 C2
Wallington Sta SM6 219 B2
Wallis Alley SE1 252 B2
Wallis Cl SW11 136 B2
Wallis Ho
5 New Cross Gate SE14 141 A4
Ruislip HA4 39 A1
Ruislip HA4 39 B1
Wallis Rd
Hackney Wick E9 75 C2
Southall UB1 85 D1
Wallman Pl N22 32 B2
Wallorton Gdns SW14 133 B1
Wallside EC2 242 B3
Wall St N1 73 B2
Wallwood Rd E11 54 B2
Wallwood St E14 97 B2
Walmar Cl EN4 2 B4
Walmer Cl BR6 227 B4
Chingford E4 19 D2
Walmer Gdns W13 109 A4
Walmer Ho
8 North Kensington W10 90 D1
8 Penge SE20 184 C3
Walmer Pl W1 237 C4
Walmer Rd
North Kensington W10 90 C1
W11 113 A6 244 A5
Walmer Terr SE18 123 B2
Walmgate Rd UB6 87 B6
Walmington Fold N12 29 C4
Walm La NW2 68 C2
Walmsley Ho 1 SW16 181 C6
Walney Wlk 6 N1 73 A2
Walnut Ave UB7 104 C3
Walnut Cl Hayes UB3 105 C6
Ilford IG6 57 A5
SE8 141 B6
Wallington SM5 218 D3
Walnut Ct 2 E17 54 A5
Walnut Gdns E15 76 C3
Walnut Gr EN1 17 B6
Walnut Ho 11 E3 97 B6
Walnut Mews SM2 218 A1
Walnut Rd E10 75 D6
Walnut Tree Ave CR4 202 C6
Walnut Tree Cl
Barnes SW13 133 D4
Chislehurst BR7 189 A2
Walnut Tree Cotts SW19 179 A5
Walnut Tree Ho SW10 265 D6
Walnut Tree Rd
Brentford TW8 132 A6
Charlton TW17 171 A1
Dagenham RM8 81 A6
Greenwich SE10 120 C1
Heston TW5 129 B6
Walnut Tree Walk Prim Sch SE11 116 C2 261 A4
Walnut Tree Wlk SE11 116 C2 261 A4
Walnut Way
Buckhurst Hill IG9 21 D1
Ruislip HA4 62 C2
Walpole Ave TW9 132 B3
Walpole Cl Pinner HA5 23 C4
West Ealing W13 109 C4
Walpole Cres 10 TW11 174 D5
Walpole Ct
Ealing W5 109 D5
7 Hammersmith W14 112 D3
South Hampstead NW6 70 A1
Twickenham TW2 152 C2
2 Wallington SM6 219 B3
Walpole Gdns
Acton Green W4 111 A1
Twickenham TW2 152 C1
Walpole Ho
Chislehurst BR7 189 B2
East Molesey KT8 195 C4
Walpole Lo W13 109 C5
Walpole Mews NW8 229 C5
Walpole Pl
9 Teddington TW11 174 D5
3 Woolwich SE18 122 D2
Walpole Rd BR2 209 D4
Mitcham SW19 180 B4
South Croydon CR0 221 B6
Surbiton KT6 198 A3
Teddington TW11 174 D5
Tottenham N17 33 A1
Tottenham N17 51 A6
Twickenham TW2 152 C2
Upton E6 77 C1
Walthamstow E17 53 A5
Woodford E18 36 D2
Walpole St SW3 114 D1 257 D2
Walrond Ave HA9 66 A3
Walsham Cl SE28 124 D6
Upper Clapton N16 52 A1
Walsham Ho
New Cross Gate SE14 140 D3
SE17 262 C2
Walsham Rd
Feltham TW14 150 B4
New Cross Gate SE14 140 D3
Walsh Lodge HA4 40 B3
Walsingham NW8 229 D6
Walsingham Gdns KT19 215 D3
Walsingham Ho
Chingford E4 20 B4
Twickenham TW2 152 B2
Walsingham Lo SW13 134 A4
Walsingham Mans SW6 265 D4
Walsingham Pk BR7 189 B1
Walsingham Pl SW4, SW11 159 A5
Walsingham Rd BR5 190 B2
Ealing W13 109 A5
Enfield EN2 17 B6
Mitcham CR4 202 D4
Shacklewell E5 74 A5
Walsingham Wlk DA17 147 C6
Walter Besant Ho 20 E1 96 D4
Walter Ct 3 W3 89 A1
Walter Green Ho SE15 140 C4
Walter Ho SW10 266 C4
Walter Hurford Par 5 E12 78 C4
Walter Northcott Ho 2 NW6 69 C3
Walter Rodney Cl E12 78 B2
Walter Savill Twr 2 E17 53 C3
Walters Cl
Hayes UB3 105 D4
SE17 262 B3
Walters Ho
3 Camberwell SE5 139 C3
Islington N1 234 D6
10 Kennington SE17 138 D6
Walter Sickert Hall N1 235 A3
Walters Rd EN3 6 C1
Walter's Rd SE25 205 C5
Walter St
Globe Town E2 96 D4
2 Kingston u T KT2 176 A2
Walters Way SE23 162 D5
Walters Yd BR1 187 A1
Walter Taylor Ct SE4 141 B1
Walter Terr E1 96 D1
Walterton Rd W9 91 C3
Walter Wlk HA8 27 A4
Waltham Ave
Hayes UB3 105 B3
Preston NW9 44 C3
Waltham Ct
Chingford E17 36 A2
Whetstone N20 14 B1
Waltham Dr HA8 44 C6
Waltham Forest Coll E17 35 D1
Waltham Forest Pool & Tk E17 35 D1
Waltham Gdns EN3 6 C6
Waltham Green Ct SW6 265 C3
Waltham Ho NW8 229 A6
10 Stockwell SW9 138 B3
Waltham Park Way E17 35 C3
Waltham Pk E17 35 C2
Waltham Rd
Carshalton SM5 202 C1
Southall UB2 107 A3
WALTHAMSTOW 53 D6
Walthamstow Acad E17 35 B2
Walthamstow Ave E4 35 C3
Walthamstow Ave (North Circular Rd) E4 35 B4
Walthamstow Bsns Ctr E17 36 A1
Walthamstow Central Sta E17 53 C4
Walthamstow Marshes Country Pk E10 52 C1
Walthamstow Mkt* E17 53 C5
Walthamstow Queens Road Sta E17 53 C4
Walthamstow Sch for Girls E17 53 D5
Waltham Way E4 19 C2
Waltheof Ave N17 33 B2
Waltheof Gdns N17 33 B2
Walton Ave
Cheam SM3 217 B5
Harrow HA2 63 B4
New Malden KT3 199 D5
Wembley HA9 66 D5
Walton Bridge Rd KT12, TW17 193 C2
Walton Cl
Dollis Hill NW2 68 B6
Harrow HA1 42 B5
Lea Bridge E5 74 D5
SW8 138 A5 270 B4
Walton Croft HA1 64 C4
Walton Ct EN5 14 A6
Walton Dr
Harrow HA1 42 B5
Willesden NW10 67 B2
Walton Gdns
Acton W3 88 D2
Feltham TW13 171 D6
Wembley HA9 66 A6
Walton Gn CR0 224 A1
Walton Ho E2 243 D6
Ealing W5 109 D2
1 Edmonton N9 34 A6
1 Kingston u T KT2 176 A3
Upper Holloway N7 72 B5
10 Walthamstow E17 53 D6
Wandsworth SW18 157 C5
Walton La
Oatlands Pk KT13, TW17 193 B1
Shepperton TW17 193 B2
Walton Oak Sch KT12 194 C1
WALTON-ON-THAMES 194 C2
Walton Pl SW3 257 C6
Walton Rd
East Molesey KT8, KT12 195 C5
Harrow HA1 42 B5
Little Ilford E12 78 C4
Newham E13 99 C5
Sidcup DA14 168 C1
Tottenham N15 51 D5
Walton-on-T KT12&KT8 194 D4
Walton St Enfield EN2 5 B4
SW3 114 C3 257 B5
Walton Way Acton W3 88 D2
Mitcham CR4 203 C5
Walt Whitman Cl 6 SE24 138 D1
WALWORTH 117 B1
Walworth Acad (Lower School) SE17 117 B1 262 D2
Walworth Acad (Upper School) SE17 117 C1 263 B1
Walworth Pl SE17 117 A1 262 B1
Walworth Rd SE17 117 A1 262 B2
Walwyn Ave BR1 209 D6
Wanborough Dr SW15 156 B3
Wanderer Dr IG11 102 C4
Wandle Bank
Mitcham SW19 180 B3
Wallington CR0 220 A5
Wandle Court Gdns CR0 220 A5
Wandle Ct
4 Bedford Pk W12 111 C4
Wallington CR0 220 A5
West Ewell KT19 215 A4
Wandle Ho
6 Catford BR1 186 B5
NW8 237 A4
Wandsworth SW18 157 D4
Wandle Ind Mus* CR4 202 D6
Wandle Lo CR0 220 A5
Wandle Lodge SM6 219 B6
Wandle Pk Sta CR0 220 C6
Wandle Rd
Croydon CR0 221 A5
Hackbridge SM6 219 B6
Morden SM4 202 B4
Upper Tooting SW17 158 C2
Wallington CR0 220 A5
Wandle Side
Hackbridge SM6 219 B5
Wallington CR0 220 B5
Wandle Tech Pk CR4 202 D2
Wandle Trad Est CR4 202 D2
Wandle Valley Sch SM5 202 C2
Wandle Way
Mitcham CR4 202 D4
Wandsworth SW18 157 D3
Wandon Rd SW6 135 D5 265 D3
WANDSWORTH 157 C5
Wandsworth Bridge Rd SW6 135 D4 265 C1
Wandsworth Common Sta SW12 158 D4
Wandsworth Common West Side SW18 158 A6
Wandsworth Gyratory SW18 157 D6
Wandsworth High St SW18 157 D6
Wandsworth Plain SW18 157 D6
Wandsworth Rd SW8 138 A5 270 A3
Wandsworth Road Sta SW4 137 C3
Wandsworth Town Sta SW18 135 D1
Wangey Rd RM6 58 D2
Wangford Ho 13 SW9 138 D1
Wanless Rd SE24 139 A2
Wanley Rd SE5 139 B1
Wanlip Rd E13 99 B3
Wansbeck Ct EN2 4 D2
Wansbeck Rd E3, E9 75 B1
Wansdown Pl SW6 135 D5 265 C4
Wansdworth Riverside Quarter Pier SW6 135 C2
Wansey St SE17 117 A2 262 B3
Wansford Rd IG8 37 C2
WANSTEAD 55 C3
Wanstead CE Prim Sch E11 55 A4
Wanstead Cl BR1 187 C1
Wanstead High Sch E11 55 C3
Wanstead Hts 8 E11 55 A4
Wanstead La IG1 56 A3
Wanstead L Ctr E11 55 C3
Wanstead Park Ave E12 77 D6
Wanstead Park Rd IG1 56 A1
Wanstead Park Sta E7 77 B4
Wanstead Pl E11 55 A4
Wanstead Rd BR1 187 C1
Wanstead Sta E11 55 B3
Wantage Rd SE12 164 D6
Wantz Rd RM10 81 D3
WAPPING 118 B5
Wapping Dock St 19 E1 118 B5
Wapping High St E1 118 B5
Wapping La E1 118 B5
Wapping Sta E1 118 C5
Wapping Wall E1 118 C5
Warbank La KT2 177 D3
Warbeck Rd W12 112 B4
Warberry Rd N22 32 B1
Warboys App KT2 176 D4
Warboys Cres E4 36 A5
Warboys Rd KT2 176 D4
Warburg Ho E2 96 A4
Warburton Cl
6 Kingsland N1 73 C2
Stanmore HA3 24 B4
Warburton Ct
Peckham SE15 140 A2
Ruislip HA4 62 A6
Warburton Ho 5 E8 96 B6
Warburton Rd
8 Hackney E8 96 B6
Twickenham TW2 151 D3
Warburton St 6 E8 96 B6
Warburton Terr E17 35 D1
Wardalls Ho 12 SE8 141 B6
Ward Cl CR2 221 C3
Wardell Cl NW7 27 C3
Wardell Ct N2 48 B6
Wardell Field 18 NW9 27 C2
Wardell Ho 7 SE10 142 A6
Warden Ave HA2 41 B1
Warden Rd NW5 71 A2
Wardens Field Cl 2 BR6 227 D2
Wardens Gr SE1 252 A3
Wardle St E9 74 D3
Wardley Lo E11 54 D3
Wardley St SW18 157 D4
Wardlow 8 NW5 71 B4
Wardo Ave SW6 135 A4 264 A2
Wardour Mews W1 239 B1
Wardour St W1 93 D1 239 C1
Ward Point SE11 261 A3
Ward Rd
Camden Town N19 71 C5
Mill Meads E15 98 B6
Wardrew Ct 9 EN5 14 A6
Wardrobe Pl EC4 241 D1
Wardrobe Terr EC4 251 D6
Wardrobe The 3 TW9 153 D6
Wards Cotts TW19 148 B4
Wards Rd IG2 57 B2
Wards Wharf App E16 121 D4
Ware Ct Cheam SM1 217 B4
Edgware HA8 26 A6
Wareham Cl TW3 129 D1
Wareham Ct 2 N1 73 C1
Wareham Ho SW8 270 C4
Warehouse W E16 121 B6
Waremead Rd IG2 56 D4
Ware Point Dr SE28 123 B4
Warfield Rd
East Bedfont TW14 149 C4
Hampton TW12 173 D2
Kensal Green NW10 90 D4
Warfield Yd 6 NW10 90 D4
Wargrave Ave N15 51 D3
Wargrave Ho 46 E2 95 D4
Wargrave Rd HA2 64 A5
Warham Rd
Croydon CR2 221 A3
Harringay N4 50 D4
Harrow HA3 24 D1
Warham St SE5 138 D5
Waring Cl BR6 227 D2
Waring Dr BR6 227 D2
Waring Ho 25 E2 96 A4
Waring Rd DA14 190 C4
Waring St SE27 183 A6
Warkworth Gdns TW7 131 A5
Warkworth Rd N17 33 B3
Warland Rd SE18 145 C5
Warley Ave
Dagenham RM8 59 B2
Hayes UB4 84 A1

Warley Cl E10 .... 53 B1
Warley Ho N1 .... 73 B2
Warley Rd Hayes UB4 .. 84 A2
Lower Edmonton N9 ... 18 C2
Woodford IG8 .... 37 B3
Warley St E2 .... 96 D4
Warlingham Rd CR7 204 D5
Warlock Rd W9 .... 91 C3
Warlow Cl 6 EN3 ...... 7 C6
Warlters Cl N7 .... 72 A4
Warlters Rd N7 .... 72 A4
Warltersville Mans
N19 .... 50 A2
Warltersville Rd N4, N8,
N19 .... 50 A2
War Meml Homes
W4 .... 133 B5
Warming Cl E5 .... 74 D5
Warmington Rd
SE24 .... 161 A5
Warmington St 3
E13 .... 99 A3
Warminster Gdns
SE25 .... 184 A1
Warminster Rd
SE25 .... 184 A1
Warminster Sq SE25 . 184 A1
Warminster Way
CR4 .... 181 B1
Warmsworth NW1 .. 232 A6
Warmwell Ave NW9 ... 27 C2
Warndon St SE16 .... 118 C2
Warneford Rd HA3 .... 44 A6
Warneford St E9 ..... 96 B6
Warne Pl 4 DA15 .... 168 B5
Warner Ave SM3 ..... 217 A6
Warner Cl
Hadley Wood EN4 ...... 2 C6
Hampton TW12 ...... 173 B5
Harlington UB3 ..... 127 B5
Hendon NW9 .... 46 A2
Stratford E15 .... 76 C3
Warner Ct SM3 ...... 217 A6
Warner Ho
1 Beckenham BR3 .. 185 D4
Harrow HA1 .... 42 B2
4 Homerton E9 ...... 74 D2
Lewisham SE13 ..... 141 D3
NW8 .... 229 A2
Warner Pl E2 .... 96 A4
Warner Rd
Bromley BR1 .... 186 D3
Camberwell SE5 ..... 139 A4
Hornsey N8 .... 49 D5
Walthamstow E17 .... 53 A5
Warners Cl IG8 ...... 37 A5
Warner St EC1 94 C3 241 A5
Warner Yd EC1 ...... 241 A5
Warnford Ho SW15 .. 155 C5
Warnford Ind Est
UB3 .... 105 C4
Warnford Rd BR6 ... 227 D3
Warnham WC1 ...... 233 C1
Warnham Court Rd
SM5 .... 218 D1
Warnham Ho 6
SW2 .... 160 B4
Warnham Rd N12 ..... 30 C5
Warple Mews W3 .... 111 C4
Warple Way W3,
W12 .... 111 C4
Warren Ave
Bromley BR1 .... 186 C3
Leyton E11 .... 76 B5
Mortlake SW14,
TW10 .... 132 D1
Orpington BR6 ...... 227 D3
South Croydon CR2 .. 222 D1
Warren Cl DA6 ...... 169 C6
Esher KT10 .... 212 A4
Hayes UB4 .... 84 C2
Ponders End N9 ...... 18 D4
Wembley HA9 .... 65 D6
West Norwood SE21 . 161 A4
Warren Comp Sch
RM6 .... 59 B4
Warren Cres N9 ...... 17 D4
Warren Ct
17 Beckenham BR3 .. 185 C3
5 Croydon CR0 ..... 205 C1
6 Ealing W5 .... 87 C2
Greenwich SE7 ..... 143 C6
N1 .... 234 A4
Warren Ct *continued*
Tottenham Hale N17 ... 52 A6
Warren Cutting KT2 .. 177 B3
Warrender Prim Sch
HA4 .... 39 D2
Warrender Rd N19 .... 71 C4
Warrender Way HA4 .. 40 A2
Warren Dr
Greenford UB6 .... 86 A3
Ruislip HA4 .... 40 D2
Warren Dr N KT5,
KT6 .... 198 D1
Warren Dr S KT5 .... 199 A1
Warren Dr The E11 .... 55 C2
Warren Farm Cotts
RM6 .... 59 B5
Warren Fields HA7 .... 25 C6
Warren Gdns E15 ..... 76 B3
Warren Hill IG10 ..... 21 C6
Warren Ho 21 E3 ...... 97 D4
Warren Jun Sch RM6 .. 59 B4
Warren La
Stanmore HA7 .... 9 A2
Woolwich SE18 ..... 122 D3
Warren La Gate
SE18 .... 122 D3
Warren Mews W1 ... 239 A5
Warren Park Rd
SM1 .... 218 C2
Warren Pk KT2 ...... 177 A4
Warren Pond Rd E4 ... 20 D4
Warren Rd
Ashford TW15 ...... 171 C3
Bexleyheath DA6 .... 169 C6
Bushey WD23 .... 8 B3
Chingford E4 .... 20 A2
Croydon CR0 .... 205 D1
Hayes BR2 .... 225 A6
Ickenham UB10 ...... 60 B4
Ilford IG6 .... 57 B4
Isleworth TW2 ...... 152 B5
Kingston u T KT2 .... 177 A4
Leyton E10 .... 76 A5
Mitcham SW19 ..... 180 C4
Sidcup DA14 .... 168 C1
Wanstead E11 .... 55 C2
Willesden NW2 .... 67 D6
Warren Rise KT3 .... 177 B2
Warren Road Prim Sch
BR6 .... 227 D4
Warrens Shawe La
HA8 .... 10 D2
Warren St W1 . 93 C3 239 A5
Warren Street Sta
NW1 .... 93 C3 239 B6
Warren Terr RM6 ..... 58 D5
Warren The
Hayes UB4 .... 84 A1
Heston TW5 .... 129 B5
Manor Pk E12 .... 78 A4
Worcester Pk KT19 .. 215 B5
Warren Way HA8 ..... 26 D1
Warren Wlk 1 SE7 ... 143 C6
Warren Wood Cl
BR2 .... 225 A6
Warriner Dr N9 .... 18 A1
Warriner Gdns
SW11 ...... 137 A4 268 A1
Warrington Cres
W9 .... 92 A3 236 A6
Warrington Ct
4 Croydon CR0 ..... 220 D5
13 Merton SW19 .... 179 C3
Warrington Gdns
W9 .... 236 A5
Warrington Rd
Croydon CR0 .... 220 D5
Dagenham RM8 ...... 81 A6
Harrow HA1 .... 42 C4
22 Richmond TW10 .. 153 D6
Warrington Sq RM8 ... 80 D6
Warrior Cl SE28 ..... 123 C5
Warrior Sq E12 .... 78 C4
Warsaw Cl HA4 .... 62 B2
Warspite Ho 3 E14 . 119 D2
Warspite Rd SE18 ... 122 A3
Warton Rd E15 .... 98 A6
Warwall E6 .... 100 D1
Warwick
W14 .... 113 B2 254 D3
Warwick Ave
Edgware HA8 .... 11 A1
Harrow HA2 .... 63 B4
Paddington
W9 .... 92 A3 236 A5
Warwick Avenue Sta
W9 .... 92 A3 236 A5
Warwick Bldg SW8 .. 268 C5
Warwick Chambers
W8 .... 255 A6
Warwick Cl
Bushey WD23 .... 8 C4
DA5 .... 169 B4
Hampton TW12 ...... 174 A3
New Barnet EN4 ...... 14 B6
Warwick Cres
Hayes UB4 .... 83 D3
Little Venice
W2 .... 92 A2 236 A4
Warwick Ct
1 Beckenham BR2 .. 186 C1
Ealing W7 .... 86 D1
5 East Finchley N2 ... 48 A6
Friern Barnet N11 .... 31 D4
Harrow HA1 .... 42 C6
Merton SW19 .... 179 B2
13 New Barnet EN5 .... 13 D6
Northolt UB5 .... 63 C3
Surbiton KT6 .... 214 A6
3 Upper Clapton E5 ... 74 B6
WC1 .... 240 D3
Warwick Dene W5 ... 110 A5
Warwick Dr SW15 .... 134 B2
Warwick Gdns
Harringay N4 .... 51 A4
Ilford IG1 .... 56 D1
Thames Ditton KT7 ... 196 D4
Thornton Heath CR7 . 204 C5
W14 .... 113 B2 254 D4
Warwick Gr
Surbiton KT5 .... 198 B2
Upper Clapton E5 ..... 52 B1
Warwick Ho
9 Acton W3 .... 88 C1
10 Brixton SW9 ..... 138 C3
6 Kingston u T KT2 .. 176 A2
6 Putney SW15 ..... 156 C4
Stoke Newington N4 ... 51 A1
5 Wimbledon SW19 . 179 A3
Warwick House St
SW1 .... 249 D4
Warwick La
EC4 .... 94 D1 241 D1
Warwick Lo
Brondesbury NW2 ..... 69 A3
Cheam SM1 .... 217 B4
Twickenham TW2 .... 151 D1
Warwick Mans SW5 . 255 A4
Warwick Par HA7 ..... 25 B1
Warwick Pas EC4 ... 241 D2
Warwick Pl
Ealing W5 .... 109 D4
Little Venice
W9 .... 92 A2 236 A4
Warwick Pl N SW1 .. 259 A3
Warwick Rd
Ashford TW15 ...... 170 A5
Barnet EN5 .... 1 D1
Bexley DA16 .... 146 C2
Chingford E4 .... 35 C5
Ealing W5 .... 110 A5
Edmonton N18 .... 33 D6
Enfield EN3 .... 7 B6
Friern Barnet N11 .... 31 D4
Hounslow TW4 ...... 128 B2
Kingston u T KT3 .... 199 A6
Penge SE20 .... 206 B6
Plashet E12 .... 78 A3
Sidcup DA14 .... 190 B5
Southall UB2 .... 107 B3
Stratford E15 .... 76 D2
Sutton SM1 .... 218 A3
Teddington KT1 ..... 175 C2
Thames Ditton KT7 ... 196 D4
Thornton Heath CR7 . 204 C6
Twickenham TW2 .... 152 C3
Walthamstow E17 .... 35 B1
Wanstead E11 .... 55 B4
West Kensington W14,
SW5 ...... 113 B2 254 D4
Yiewsley UB7 .... 104 A5
Warwick Row
SW1 ...... 115 B3 258 D6
Warwick Sch for Boys
E17 .... 54 A5
Warwickshire Path
SE8 .... 141 B5
Warwick Sq
Holborn EC4 .... 241 D2
Pimlico SW1 . 115 C1 259 A2
Warwick Sq Mews
SW1 .... 259 A3
Warwick St
W1 .... 115 C6 249 B6
Warwick Terr
Leytonstone E17 ...... 54 B4
SE18 .... 145 B6
Warwick Way
SW1 ...... 115 B2 258 D4
Warwick Yd EC1 .... 242 B5
Wasdale NW1 ...... 231 D1
Washbourne Ct N9 ... 18 A2
Washbrook Ho SW2 . 160 C5
Washington Ave E12 .. 78 B4
Washington Bldg 1
SE13 .... 141 D4
Washington Cl 45 E3 .. 97 D4
Washington Ct
SW17 .... 180 D4
Washington Ho SW1 247 C1
Walthamstow E17 .... 35 B1
Washington Rd
Barnes SW13 .... 134 A5
Kingston u T KT1 .... 176 C1
North Cheam KT4 ... 200 B1
Upton E6 .... 77 C1
2 Woodford E18 ...... 36 D1
Wastdale Rd SE23 ... 162 D3
Watchfield Ct 7
W4 .... 111 A1
Watcombe Cotts
TW9 .... 132 C6
Watcombe Rd SE25 . 206 B4
Waterbank Rd SE6 .. 186 A6
Waterbeach Rd RM9 .. 80 C2
Water Brook La NW4 .. 46 C4
Watercress Pl 12 N1 .. 73 C1
Waterdale Rd SE2 ... 146 A6
Waterden Rd E15 ..... 75 C2
Waterer Ho 7 SE6 ... 186 A6
Waterer Rise SM6 ... 219 D2
Waterfall Cl N14 ..... 15 C1
Waterfall Cotts
SW19 .... 180 B4
Waterfall Rd
Mitcham SW19 ..... 180 B4
New Southgate N11,
N14 .... 15 C1
Waterfall Terr SW17 . 180 C4
Waterfield Cl
Belvedere DA17 .... 125 C3
Woolwich SE28 ..... 124 B5
Waterfield Gdns
SE25 .... 205 C4
Waterford Ct 16
W13 .... 109 A5
Waterford Rd
SW6 ...... 135 D5 265 C3
Waterford Way NW10 . 68 A3
Watergardens The
Kingston u T KT2 .... 177 A4
Woodford IG8 .... 37 A5
Water Gardens The
W2 .... 92 C1 237 B2
Watergate EC4 ..... 251 C6
Watergate Ho 5
SE18 .... 122 C2
Watergate Sch SE6 . 185 D5
Watergate St SE8 ... 141 C6
Watergate Wlk WC2 . 250 B4
Water Gdns HA7 ..... 25 B4
Waterglade Ctr The
W5 .... 109 D6
Waterhall Ave E4 .... 36 C6
Waterhall Cl E17 ..... 34 D2
Waterhead NW1 .... 232 A2
Waterhedge Mews
EN1 .... 17 D6
Waterhouse Cl
Hammersmith W6 ... 112 D1
Hampstead NW3 ...... 70 B3
Newham E16 .... 99 D2
Waterhouse Ct 7
TW11 .... 174 D5
Waterhouse Sq EC1 . 241 A3
Wateridge Cl E14 ... 119 C3
Wateringbury Cl
BR5 .... 190 B1
Water La
16 Camden Town
NW1 .... 71 B1
Edmonton N9 .... 18 B4
Ilford IG3 .... 79 D5
Richmond TW10,
TW9 .... 153 D6
SE14 .... 140 C5
Water La *continued*
Sidcup DA14 .... 169 B2
Stratford E15 .... 76 C2
Teddington KT1 ..... 175 D2
Twickenham TW1 .... 153 A3
Water Lane Ho 29
TW10 .... 153 D6
Water Lily Cl UB2 ... 108 A4
Waterloo Bridge SE1,
WC2 ...... 116 B6 250 D5
Waterloo Cl
East Bedfont TW14 .. 149 D3
Hackney E9 .... 74 C3
Waterloo Ct 4 HA0 ... 66 A2
Waterloo East Sta
SE1 ...... 116 C5 251 B3
Waterloo Gdns
26 Islington N1 .... 72 D1
South Hackney E2 ..... 96 C5
Waterloo Millennium
Pier SE1 .... 250 C2
Waterloo Pl
Kew TW9 .... 132 C6
9 Richmond TW9 ... 132 A1
SW1 ...... 115 D5 249 C4
Waterloo Rd
Dollis Hill NW2 ...... 68 A6
Forest Gate E7 .... 76 D3
SE1 .... 116 C4 251 B2
Sutton SM1 .... 218 B3
Upton E6 .... 77 C1
Walthamstow E10 .... 53 C2
Waterloo Sta
SE1 .... 116 C4 251 A2
Waterloo Terr N1 ..... 72 D1
Waterlow Ct NW11 .... 47 D2
Waterlow Rd N19 ..... 49 C1
Waterman Bldg 2
E14 .... 119 C4
Watermans Arts Ctr*
TW8 .... 132 A6
Watermans Ct
12 Brentford TW8 ... 131 D6
2 Brentford TW8 ... 132 A6
Watermans Mews 1
W5 .... 110 A6
Waterman St SW15 . 134 D2
Waterman Way E1 ... 118 B5
Watermark Ct RM6 ... 58 B3
Watermead TW14 ... 149 C3
Watermead Ho E9 .... 75 B3
Watermead La CR4 . 202 D2
Watermeadow La
SW6 .... 136 A3
Watermead Rd SE6 . 186 A6
Watermead Way N17 .. 34 B1
Watermen's Sq 1
SE20 .... 184 C3
Water Mews SE15 ... 140 C1
Watermill Bsns Ctr
EN3 .... 7 B3
Watermill Cl TW10 .. 153 C1
Watermill Ct SE13 .. 141 D2
Watermill La N18 ..... 33 C5
Watermill Way
SW19 .... 180 A2
Water Mill Way
TW13 .... 151 C2
Watermint Quay N16 .. 52 A2
Water Rd HA0 .... 88 B6
Watersedge KT19 ... 215 A4
Water's Edge SW6 .. 134 C4
Watersfield Way HA8 . 26 A3
Waters Gdns RM10 ... 81 C3
Watershipdown Ho 4
E11 .... 54 D2
Waterside
11 Beckenham BR3 .. 185 C2
N1 .... 235 A3
Walthamstow E17 .... 52 C3
Waterside Ave BR3 . 207 D4
Waterside Bsns Ctr
TW7 .... 131 B1
Waterside Cl
Barking IG11 .... 80 A4
30 Bermondsey SE16 118 A4
Northolt UB5 .... 85 B4
Old Ford E3 .... 97 B6
Surbiton KT6 .... 214 A6
Woolwich SE28 ..... 123 D5
Waterside Ct
3 Hackbridge SM6 .. 219 A5
Lewisham SE13 ..... 142 B1
Waterside Dr KT12 . 194 B4
Waterside Pl NW1 .. 231 B6

Waterside Point SW11 267 B4
Waterside Prim Sch SE18 123 B1
Waterside Rd UB2 107 C3
Waterside Trad Ctr W7 108 C3
Waterside Way SW17 180 A5
Watersmeet Way SE28 102 D1
Waterson St E2 95 D4
Waters Pl SW15 134 C3
Watersplash Cl KT1 198 A6
Watersplash La
Hayes UB3 106 A2
Southall TW5 106 B1
Watersplash Rd
Littleton TW17 192 C5
Littleton TW17 192 C6
Waters Rd
Catford SE6 164 C1
Kingston u T KT1 176 D1
Waters Sq KT1 198 D6
Water St WC2 251 A6
Water Tower Cl UB8 60 A3
Water Tower Hill CR0 221 B4
Water Tower Pl N1 234 C5
Water View Cl DA6 168 D6
Waterview Ho 13 E14 97 A2
Waterville Lo 6 N12 30 A5
Waterway Ave 2 SE13 141 D2
Waterways Bsns Ctr EN3 7 C5
Waterworks Cnr E17 36 C1
Waterworks Ctr* E10 75 A6
Waterworks La E5 74 D6
Waterworks Nature Reserve E10 75 A6
Waterworks Rd SW2 160 B5
Waterworks Yd 4 CR0 221 A5
Watery La DA14 190 B4
Hayes UB3 105 B1
Merton SW19, SW20 179 B1
Northolt UB5 84 C5
Wates Way CR4 202 D3
Wateville Rd N17 33 A2
Watford Cl SW11 267 B2
Watford Rd
Elstree WD6 9 C5
Harrow HA1 43 A1
Newham E16 99 A2
Northwood HA6 22 A4
Sudbury HA0, HA1 65 B4
Watford Way NW4 46 A5
Watford Way (Barnet By-Pass) NW9 27 D3
Watkin Mews 18 EN3 7 C6
Watkin Rd HA9 66 D5
Watkins Ho
11 Cubitt Town E14 120 A4
Harrow HA1 42 D4
Watkinson Rd N7 72 B2
Watling Ave HA8 27 B2
Watling Ct EC4 242 B1
1 Elstree WD6 9 D5
Watling Farm Cl HA7, WD6 9 C3
Watling Gate NW9 45 C5
Watling Gdns NW2 69 A2
Watling Ho 10 SE18 144 C6
Watlings Cl CR0 207 A3
Watling St
Bexleyheath DA7 147 D1
4 Camberwell SE15 139 C6
City of London EC4 95 A1 242 B1
Elstree WD6 9 D6
Watlington Gr SE26 185 A5
Watney Cotts SW14 133 A2
Watney Mkt* E1 96 B1
Watney Rd SW14 133 A2
Watneys Rd CR4 203 D4
Watney St E1 96 B1
Watson Ave
Cheam SM3 217 A6
Wallend E6 78 C1
Watson Cl
Mitcham SW19 180 C3
Stoke Newington N16 73 B3
Watson Ho 3 SW2 160 A4
Watsons Lo 4 RM10 81 D2
Watsons Mews W1 237 B3
Watsons Rd N22 32 B2
Watson's St SE8 141 C5
Watson St E13 99 B5
Wattisfield Rd E5 74 C5
Watts Cl N15 51 C4
Wattsdown Cl E13 99 A6
Watts Gr E3 97 D2
Watts Ho 6 W10 91 A2
Watt's La
Chislehurst BR7 189 A2
Teddington TW11 175 A5
Watts Rd KT7 197 A2
Watts St SE15 139 D4
Wapping E1 118 B5
Wat Tyler Ho N8 50 A6
Wat Tyler Rd SE10 142 B4
Wauthier Cl N13 32 D5
Wavel Ct
7 Streatham SW16 160 A1
7 Wapping E1 118 C5
Wavell Dr DA15 167 C5
Wavell Ho N6 49 A3
Wavel Mews
Hampstead NW6 69 D1
Hornsey N8 49 D5
Wavel Pl SE26 183 D6
Wavendon Ave W4 111 B1
Waveney Ave SE15 140 B1
Waveney Cl 20 E1 118 A5
Waveney Ho SE15 140 B1
Waverley Ave
Chingford Hatch E4 35 B6
Sutton SM1 217 D6
Tolworth KT5 199 A3
Twickenham TW2, TW4 151 C3
Walthamstow E17 54 B6
Wembley HA9 66 B3
Waverley Cl BR2 209 D4
East Molesey KT8 195 C4
Hayes UB3 105 B2
Woodford E18 37 C1
Waverley Cres SE18 123 B1
Waverley Ct
5 Brondesbury NW6 69 A1
Enfield EN2 5 A2
North Finchley N12 30 B6
W1 238 B4
Waverley Gdns
Barking IG11 101 C5
Ealing NW10 88 B5
Ilford IG6 57 B6
Newham E6 100 A2
Northwood HA6 22 A2
Waverley Gr N3 47 A6
Waverley Ind Pk HA1 42 B6
Waverley Pl
Finsbury Pk N4 50 D1
St John's Wood NW8 92 B5 229 C4
Waverley Rd
Croydon SE25 206 B6
Enfield EN2 4 D2
Finsbury Pk N8 50 A2
Harrow HA2 41 A1
Plumstead SE18 123 B1
Southall UB1 107 C6
Stoneleigh KT17, KT4 216 B3
Tottenham N17 34 B3
Walthamstow E17 54 A6
Woodford E18 37 C2
Waverley Sch EN3 6 C1
Waverley Way SM5 218 C2
Waverly Ct NW3 70 D2
Waverton Ho 2 E3 97 B6
Waverton Rd SW18 158 A4
Waverton St W1 115 B5 248 C4
Wavertree Ct 9 SW2 160 A3
Wavertree Rd
Streatham SW2 160 B3
Woodford E18 37 A1
Waxham NW5 70 D3
Waxlow Cres UB1 85 C1
Waxlow Ho UB4 84 C2
Waxlow Rd NW10 89 B5
Waxlow Way UB5 85 B3
Waxwell Cl HA5 22 D1
Waxwell La HA5 22 D1
Wayatt Point 1 SE28 123 A3
Wayborne Gr HA4 39 A3
Waye Ave TW5 128 A4
Wayfarer Rd UB5 85 A4
Wayfield Link SE9 167 B5
Wayford St SW11 136 C3
Wayland Ave E8 74 A3
Wayland Ho 12 SW9 138 C3
Waylands UB3 83 B2
Waylands Ct IG1 79 B4
Waylands Mead BR3 185 D2
Waylett Ho SE11 261 A1
Waylett Pl
Wembley HA0 65 D4
West Norwood SE27 160 D1
Wayman Ct E8 74 B2
Wayne Cl BR6 227 D5
Waynflete Ave CR0 220 D5
Waynflete Sq
18 North Kensington W10 90 D1
16 Shepherd's Bush W10 112 D6
Waynflete St SW18 158 A2
Wayside
Chislehurst BR7 189 B2
Golders Green NW11 47 A1
Mortlake SW14 155 A6
New Addington CR0 223 D2
Wayside Ave WD23 8 B5
Wayside Cl N14 15 C5
Wayside Commercial Est IG11 102 A5
Wayside Ct
Isleworth TW7 130 C3
Twickenham TW1 153 C5
Wembley HA9 66 C5
Wayside Gdns RM10 81 C3
Wayside Gr BR7, SE9 188 B6
Wayside Mews IG2 56 C4
Weald Cl
16 Bermondsey SE16 118 B1
BR2 226 A6
Weald Fst & Mid Schs HA3 24 D3
Weald La HA3 24 B2
Weald Rd UB10 82 C5
Weald Rise HA3 24 D2
Weald Sq E5 74 B6
WEALDSTONE 42 D6
Wealdstone Rd SM3 217 B6
Weald The BR7 188 B4
Weald Way Hayes UB4 83 C4
Romford RM7 59 D3
Wealdwood Gdns HA5 23 D4
Weale Rd E4 20 B1
Weall Ct HA5 41 A5
Weardale Ct EN5 12 C6
Weardale Gdns EN2 5 B4
Weardale Ho N4 51 A2
Weardale Rd SE13 142 B1
Wearmouth Ho 1 E3 97 B2
Wear Pl 13 E2 96 B4
Wearside Rd SE13 141 D1
Weatherbury 6 W2 91 C1
Weatherbury Ho 3 N19 71 D5
Weatherill Ct SE25 206 B3
Weatherley Cl E3 97 B2
Weathersfield Ct SE9 166 B5
Weaver Cl
Newham E16 122 D6
South Croydon CR0 221 D4
Weaver Ct 2 E2 96 B3
Weaver Ho
12 Bethnal Green E1 96 A3
1 Northolt UB5 85 B3
Weavers Cl TW7 130 C1
Weavers Ho 4 E11 55 A3
Weaver's La SE1 117 C5 253 B3
Weaver St E1 96 A3
Weavers Way
6 Camden Town NW1 71 D1
NW1 232 C6
Weaver Wlk SE27 182 D6
Webb Cl NW10 90 C3
Webb Ct 6 SE28 124 B6
South Acton W3 110 D4
Webber Cl WD6 9 D5
Webber Ho 6 IG11 78 D1
Webber Row SE1 116 D4 251 C1
Webber St SE1 116 D4 251 C1
Webb Est E5 52 A2
Webb Gdns 1 E13 99 A3
Webb Ho
2 Dagenham RM10 81 C5
Feltham TW13 151 A1
SW8 269 D3
Webb Pl NW10 89 D4
Webb Rd SE3 142 D6
Webbscroft Rd RM10 81 D4
Webbs Rd UB4 84 B4
Webb's Rd SW11 158 D6
Webb St SE1 117 C3 263 A5
Webheath 6 NW6 69 B1
Webley Ct 22 EN3 7 C6
Webster Gdns W5 109 D5
Webster Ho 16 N16 73 C3
Webster Rd
Bermondsey SE16 118 A3
Leyton E11 76 A5
Weddell Ho 23 E1 96 D3
Wedderburn Rd
Barking IG11 101 C6
Hampstead NW3 70 B3
Wedgewood Ct
1 Beckenham BR2 208 D5
DA5 169 B4
Wedgewood Ho
SW1 259 A1
Thames Ditton KT7 196 D1
Wedgewood Mews W1 239 D1
Wedgewood Wlk NW3 69 D3
Wedgwood Ho
17 Globe Town E2 96 D4
SE11 261 A5
Wedgwood Way SE19 183 A3
Wedlake St W10 91 A3
Wedmore Gdns N19 71 D6
Wedmore Mews N19 71 D5
Wedmore Rd UB6 86 B4
Wedmore St N19 71 D5
Weech Rd NW6 69 C4
Weedington Rd NW5 71 A3
Weedon Ho W12 90 A1
Weekley Sq SW11 136 B2
Weeks Ho TW10 175 C6
Weigall Rd SE12, SE3 143 A1
Weighhouse St W1 238 B1
Weighton Rd
Harrow HA3 24 B2
Penge SE20 184 B1
Weihurst Ct SM1 218 C3
Weihurst Gdns SM1 218 B3
Weimar St SW15 135 A2
Weirdale Ave N20 14 D2
Weir Hall Ave N18 33 B4
Weir Hall Gdns N18 33 B5
Weir Hall Rd N18 33 B4
Weir Ho 8 SW12 159 C4
Weir Rd Sidcup DA5 169 D4
Streatham SW12 159 C4
Walton-on-T KT12 194 A3
Wimbledon SW18, SW19 157 D1
Weiss Rd SW15 134 D2
Welbeck Ave
Grove Pk BR1 187 B6
Hayes UB4 84 B3
Sidcup DA15 168 A3
Welbeck Cl
New Malden KT3 199 D4
North Finchley N12 30 B5
Stoneleigh KT17 216 A1
Welbeck Ct
Hayes UB4 84 B3
W14 254 C4
Welbeck Mans 10 NW6 69 C3
Welbeck Rd
Carshalton SM1 218 B6
Carshalton SM5 202 C1
East Barnet EN4 14 C5
Harrow HA2 41 D1
Newham E6 99 D4
Welbeck St W1 93 B1 238 C2
Welbeck Villas N21 17 A3
Welbeck Way W1 238 C2
Welbeck Wlk SM5 202 B1
Welbourne Prim Sch 2 N17 52 A6
Welbury Ct E8 73 C1
Welby Ho N19 49 D2
Welby St SE5 138 D4
Welch Pl HA5 22 C2
Welcome Ct E17 53 C2
Weldon Cl HA4 62 B2
Weldon Ct
Southgate N21 16 B6
St Johns SE8 141 C3
7 Sutton SM1 218 B3
Thornton Heath CR7 204 D4
Weldon Dr KT8 195 B5
Weld Pl N11 31 B5
Welfare Rd E15 76 C1
Welford Cl E5 74 D5
Welford Ct
12 Camden Town NW1 71 B1
7 Clapham SW8 137 C3
Welford Ho 4 UB5 85 B3
Welford Pl SW19 179 A6
Welham Rd SW16, SW17 181 B4
Welhouse Rd SM5 202 C1
Wellacre Rd HA3 43 B3
Wellan Cl DA15, DA16 168 B6
Welland Ct SE6 163 B2
Welland Gdns UB6 86 D5
Welland Ho SE15 140 C1
Welland Mews 21 E1 118 A5
Wellands Cl BR1 188 B1
Welland St SE10 142 A6
Well App EN5 12 C6
Wellbrook Rd BR6 226 C4
Wellby Cl N9 18 A3
Wellby Ct 1 E13 99 C5
Well Cl Ruislip HA4 63 A5
Streatham SW16 182 B6
Wellclose Sq E1 118 A6
Wellclose St 20 E1 118 A6
Well Cottage Cl E11 55 C2
Well Ct EC4 242 B1
Wellday Ho 2 E9 75 A2
Welldon Cres HA1 42 C3
Welldon Ct
Harrow HA1 42 C4
1 West Dulwich SE21 161 B2
Welldon Park Fst Sch HA2 64 A4
Welldon Park Mid Sch HA2 64 A4
Weller Ho 23 SE16 118 A4
Weller Mews 6 BR2 209 B5
Weller St SE1 252 A2
Welles Ct 15 E14 119 C6
Wellesley Ave W6 112 B3
Wellesley Cl 8 SE7 121 C1
Wellesley Court Rd 1 CR0 221 B6
Wellesley Cres TW2 152 C1
Wellesley Ct
Cheam SM3 201 A1
St John's Wood W9 92 A4 229 A2
Twickenham TW2 152 C1
Wellesley Gr CR0 221 B6
Wellesley Ho NW1 232 C1
12 Wimbledon SW19 179 A3
Wellesley Park Mews EN2 4 D3
Wellesley Pl
Camden Town NW5 71 A3
NW1 232 C1
Wellesley Rd
Croydon CR0 205 A1
Gospel Oak NW5 71 A3
Gunnersbury W4 110 D1
Harrow HA1 42 C4
Ilford IG1 57 A1
Sutton SM2 218 A2
Twickenham TW2 152 C1
Walthamstow E17 53 C3
Wanstead E11 55 A4
Wood Green N22 32 C1
Wellesley Road Sta CR0 221 B6
Wellesley St E1 96 D2

Wellesley Terr N1 95 A4 235 B2
Wellfield Ave N10 49 B6
Wellfield Rd SW16 182 B6
Wellfit St 6 SE24 138 D2
Wellgarth UB6 65 B2
Wellgarth Rd NW11 47 D1
Well Gr N20 14 B3
Wellgrove Sch N20 14 B3
Well Hall Par SE9 144 B1
Well Hall Pleasaunce* SE9 144 A1
Well Hall Rd SE9 144 B1
Well Ho 11 N9 18 A1
Wellhouse Rd BR3 207 C5
Wellhurst Cl BR6 227 D1
WELLING 146 B2
Wellingfield Ct 1 DA16 146 A2
Welling High St DA16 146 B2
Welling Sch DA16 146 B4
Wellings Ho UB3 106 B5
Welling Sta DA16 146 A3
Wellington
1 Grahame Pk NW9 27 D3
Hornsey N8 50 A5
Wellington Arch* SW1 248 B2
Wellington Ave
Chingford E4 19 D2
DA15 168 A5
Edmonton N9 18 B1
Hounslow TW3, TW4 151 C6
North Cheam KT4 216 C5
Pinner HA5 23 B2
South Tottenham N15 52 A3
Wellington Bldgs
15 Bow E3 97 C4
SW1 258 B1
Wellington Cl
Kensington W11 91 C1
New Cross Gate SE14 140 D4
Walton-on-T KT12 193 D1
Wellington Cres KT3 199 A6
Wellington Ct
Ashford TW15 170 A6
Knightsbridge SW1 247 C1
Stanwell TW19 148 A4
St John's Wood NW8 229 D3
Strand WC2 250 A6
5 Surbiton KT6 198 A3
Teddington TW12 174 B5
4 Upper Tooting SW17 180 C4
Wandsworth SW18 158 C6
Wellington Gdns
Greenwich SE7 121 C1
Teddington TW12, TW2 174 B6
Wellington Gr SE10 142 B5
Wellington Ho
4 Ealing W5 88 A4
18 Maitland Pk NW3 70 D2
Northolt UB5 63 C1
6 Ruislip HA4 40 C1
Stanmore HA7 9 A1
Wellington Hospl The NW8 92 B5 229 D3
Wellington Mans
Shacklewell N16 73 D4
1 Walthamstow E10 53 C1
Wellington Mews
East Dulwich SE22 140 A1
3 Islington N7 72 B2
SE7 143 C6
Streatham SW16 159 D1
Wellington Par DA15 168 A6
Wellington Park Est NW2 68 A6
Wellington Pas 7 E11 55 A4
Wellington Pl
East Finchley N2 48 C4
St John's Wood NW8 92 B4 229 D2
Wellington Prim Sch
20 Bow E3 97 C4
Chingford E4 19 D2
Hounslow TW3 129 B3
Wellington Rd
Ashford TW15 170 A5
Bexley DA5 168 D6
Brentford W5 109 C3
Bromley BR2 209 C5
Enfield EN1 17 C6
Erith DA17 125 B1
Harrow HA3 42 C6
Hatton TW14 149 C6
Kensal Green NW10 90 D4
Leyton E7 76 D4
Newham E6 100 B5
Pinner HA5 23 B2
St John's Wood NW8 92 B5 229 D3
Teddington TW12, TW2 174 B6
Thornton Heath CR0 204 D2
Walthamstow E10 53 A1
Walthamstow E17 53 A5
Wanstead E11 55 A4
Wimbledon SW19 157 C2
Wellington Rd N TW4 129 B2
Wellington Rd S TW4 151 B6
Wellington Row E2 96 A4
Wellington Sq
Islington N1 233 B6
SW3 114 D1 257 C2
Wellington St
WC2 116 B6 250 C6
Woolwich SE18 122 C2
Wellington Terr
Harrow HA1 42 B1
2 Wapping E1 118 B5
Wellington Way E3 97 C4
Welling Way DA16 145 B2
Well La SW14 155 A6
Wellmead IG3 58 A2
Wellmeadow Rd
Brentford W7 109 A2
Catford SE13, SE6 164 C3
Wellow Wlk SM5 202 B1
Well Rd Barnet EN5 12 C6
Vale of Health NW3 70 B5
Wells Cl
2 Northolt UB5 84 C4
South Croydon CR2 221 C3
Wells Ct
21 Hampstead NW3 70 A4
4 Mitcham CR4 180 C2
1 Paddington NW6 91 C5
Stoke Newington N1 73 C3
Wells Dr NW9 45 B1
Wells Gdns
Dagenham RM10 81 D3
Redbridge IG1 56 A2
Wells Ho
4 Barking IG11 80 A1
Ealing W5 109 D6
Finsbury EC1 234 C2
12 Kensal Town W10 91 A3
New Cross Gate SE4 141 A3
Plaistow BR1 187 B5
9 Rotherhithe SE16 118 C3
Wells Ho The 2 NW3 70 B4
Wells House Rd NW10 89 C2
Wellside Gdns SW14 155 A6
Wells Mews W1 239 B2
Wellsmoor Gdns BR1 210 C6
Wells Park Ct SE26 184 B6
Wells Park Rd SE26 184 B6
Wells Pl SW18 158 A4
Wells Prim Sch IG8 37 A6
Wellspring Cres HA9 66 D5
Wells Rd BR1 188 B1
Hammersmith W12 112 C4
Wells Rise NW8 92 D6 230 C5
Wells Sq WC1 233 D1
Wells St W1 93 C1 239 B2
Well St Hackney E9 74 C1
Stratford E15 76 C2
Wellstead Ave N9 18 D4
Wellstead Rd E6 100 C5
Wells Terr N4 72 C6
Wells The N14 15 D4
Wells Way
Brompton SW7 114 B3 256 C6
Camberwell SE5 139 C6
Well Wlk NW3 70 B5
Wellwood Ct SW15 134 C1
Wellwood Rd IG3 58 A2
Welmar Works SW4 137 D1
Welsby Ct W5 87 C2
Welsford St SE1 118 A2
Welsh Cl E13 99 A4
Welsh Harp Field Centre NW9 45 B1
Welsh Ho 14 E1 118 B5
Welshpool Ho 22 E8 96 A6
Welshpool St 1 E8 96 B6
Welshside NW9 45 C3
Welshside Wlk NW9 45 C3
Welstead Ho 20 E1 96 B1
Welstead Way W4 111 D2
Weltje Rd W6 112 A1
Welton Ct SE5 139 C4
Welton Ho E1 96 D2
Welton Rd SE18 145 C5
Welwyn Ave TW14 149 D5
Welwyn St E2 96 C4
Welwyn Way UB4 83 C3
WEMBLEY 65 D2
Wembley HA0 65 D2
Wembley Arena HA9 66 C4
Wembley Central Sta HA9 66 A3
Wembley Commercial Ctr HA9 65 D6
Wembley Conference Ctr HA9 66 C4
Wembley Exhibition Halls HA9 66 C4
Wembley High Tech Coll HA0 65 C5
Wembley Hill Rd HA9 66 B4
Wembley Mkt
1 Wembley HA0 66 A3
1 Wembley Pk HA9 66 C4
WEMBLEY PARK 66 C5
Wembley Park Bsns Ctr
Wembley HA9 66 C5
Wembley HA9 66 D5
Wembley Park Dr HA9 66 B5
Wembley Park Sta HA9 66 C5
Wembley Prim Sch HA9 66 A5
Wembley Rd TW12 173 C2
Wembley Stadium HA9 66 C3
Wembley Stadium Ind Est HA9 66 D4
Wembley Stadium Sta HA9 66 B3
Wembley Way HA9 66 D2
Wemborough Rd HA7 25 C3
Wembury Mews N6 49 C2
Wembury Rd N6 49 B2
Wemyss Rd SE3 142 D3
Wendela Ct HA1 64 C6
Wendell Park Prim Sch W12 111 D4
Wendell Rd W12 111 D4
Wenderholme CR2 221 B3
Wendle Ct SW8 270 A5
Wendling NW5 70 D3
Wendling Rd SM1 218 B6
Wendon Ct 13 SM6 219 C2
Wendon St E3 97 B6
Wendover SE17 117 C1 263 A1
Wendover Cl UB4 85 A3
Wendover Ct
Acton W3 88 D3
Becontree W3 89 A3
Bromley BR2 209 B6
4 Child's Hill NW2 69 C5
W1 238 A3
Wendover Dr KT3 199 D3
Wendover Ho
Bowes Pk N22 32 B5
W1 238 A3
Wendover Lo NW9 45 D3
Wendover Rd
Blackheath SE9 143 D2
Bromley BR1, BR2 209 B6
Dagenham NW10 89 D5
Wendover Way
Bexley DA16 146 A1
Bushey WD23 8 A5
Wendy Cl EN1 17 D5
Wendy Ho 3 N12 30 B5
Wendy Way HA0 88 A6
Wengham Ho W12 112 A6
Wenham Ho SW8 269 A3
Wenlake Ho EC1 242 A6
Wenlock Ct N1 235 D3
Wenlock Gdns 13 NW4 46 A5
Wenlock Rd
Burnt Oak HA8 27 A4
Shoreditch N1 95 A5 235 B3
Wenlock St N1 95 B5 235 C3
Wennington Rd E3 96 D5
Wensdale Ho E5 74 A6
Wensley Ave IG8 37 A3
Wensley Cl
6 Barnet N11 31 A4
SE9 166 B5
Wensleydale Gdns TW12 173 D3
Wensleydale Ho 8 N4 51 A2
Wensleydale Rd TW12 173 D3
Wensley Rd N18 34 B4
Wentland Cl SE6 164 B2
Wentland Rd SE6 164 B2
Wentway Ct W13 87 A3
Wentwood Ho 1 E5 74 B6
Wentworth Ave
Borehamwood WD6 10 B6
Finchley N3 29 C3
Wentworth Cl
Ashford TW15 170 D6
Finchley N3 29 D3
Hayes BR2 225 A6
Long Ditton KT6 213 D6
Morden SM4 201 C2
Orpington BR6 227 C3
Thamesmead SE28 102 D1
Wentworth Cres
Hayes UB3 105 B3
SE15 140 A5
Wentworth Ct
Barnet EN5 1 A2
7 Chingford E4 36 B5
20 Kingston u T KT6 198 A4
Southall UB2 106 C2
2 Surbiton KT6 214 A6
Twickenham TW2 152 C1
W6 264 A5
Wandsworth SW18 157 D5
Wentworth Dr
Pinner HA5 40 A4
South Oxhey WD19 22 D5
Wentworth Dwellings E1 243 C2
Wentworth Gdns N13 16 D1
Wentworth Hall NW7 28 C5
Wentworth Hill HA9 44 B1
Wentworth Ho
Enfield EN1 17 C5
4 Greenwich SE3 143 A5
Wentworth Lo N3 29 D3
Wentworth Mews E3 97 B4
Wentworth Pk N3 29 D3
Wentworth Pl HA7 25 B4
Wentworth Rd
Manor Pk E12 77 D4
Southall UB2 106 D2
Temple Fortune NW11 47 B3
Thornton Heath CR0 204 C2
Wentworth St E1 95 D2 243 D3
Wentworth Tutorial Coll NW11 46 D3
Wentworth Way HA5 41 A5
Wenvoe Ave DA7 147 D3
Wepham Cl UB4 84 D2
Wernbrook St SE18 145 A6
Werndee Rd SE25 206 A5
Werneth Hall Rd IG5 56 C6
Werrington St NW1 93 C5 232 B3
Werter Rd SW15 135 A1
Wesleyan Pl NW5 71 B4
Wesley Ave
Becontree NW10 89 B4
Hounslow TW3 129 B3
Newham E16 121 B5
Wesley Cl
Finsbury Pk N7 72 B6
Harrow HA2 64 A6
SE17 261 D3
Wesley Ct W1 238 B3
Wesley Ho SE24 161 B5
Wesley Rd
Becontree NW10 89 A6
Finchley N10 30 C2
Hayes UB3 84 A1
Leytonstone E10 54 A2
Wesley Sq W11 91 A1
Wesley St W1 238 B3
Wessex Ave SW19 201 C6
Wessex Cl
Hinchley Wood KT10, KT7 212 D6
Ilford IG3 57 C3
Kingston u T KT1, KT2 176 D2
Wessex Ct
Putney SW15 156 D6
5 Stanwell TW19 148 A5
Wembley HA9 66 B6
Wessex Dr HA5 23 A3
Wessex Gardens Prim Sch NW11 47 A1
Wessex Gdns NW11 47 A1
Wessex Ho SE1 263 D1
4 Tufnell Pk N19 71 D5
Wessex La UB6 86 B5
Wessex St E2 96 C4
Wessex Way NW11 47 A1
Wesson Ho 3 CR0 206 A1
West 12 Sh Ctr W12 112 D4
Westacott UB4 83 C2
Westacott Cl N19 49 D1
WEST ACTON 88 C1
West Acton Prim Sch W3 88 D1
West Acton Sta W3 88 C1
West App BR5 211 A4
West Arbour St E1 96 D1
West Ave
East Finchley N2 47 D6
Finchley N3 29 C4
Hayes UB3 105 D6
Hendon NW4 46 D4
Pinner HA5 41 B2
Southall UB1 107 B6
Wallington SM6 220 A3
Walthamstow E17 53 D4
West Avenue Rd E17 53 D5
West Bank
Barking IG11 100 D6
Enfield EN2 5 A3
Stamford Hill N16 51 C2
Westbank Rd TW12 174 A4
WEST BARNES 200 C4
West Barnes La KT3, SW20 200 B5
WEST BEDFONT 148 B4
Westbeech Rd N22 50 C6
Westbere Ct HA7 25 D5
Westbere Dr HA7 25 D5
Westbere Rd NW2 69 A3
West Block 18 E1 118 C6
Westbourne Ave
Cheam SM3 217 A6
Dagenham W3 89 B1
Westbourne Cl UB4 84 C3
Westbourne Cres W2 246 C6
Westbourne Ct
Cheam SM3 217 A6
W2 236 A2
Westbourne Dr SE23 162 D2
Westbourne Gdns W2 91 D1
Westbourne Gr
Notting Hill W2, W11 91 C1
W11 113 B6 244 D6
WESTBOURNE GREEN 91 D3
Westbourne Gr Mews 7 W11 91 C1
Westbourne Gr Terr W2 91 D1
Westbourne Ho
Heston TW5 129 C6
SW1 258 C2
8 Twickenham TW1 153 B4
Westbourne Par 4 UB10 82 D3
Westbourne Park Rd
Notting Hill W2 91 C1
Notting Hill W11 91 B1
Westbourne Park Sta W11 91 B2
Westbourne Park Villas W2 91 D2
Westbourne Pl N9 18 B1

Westbourne Prim Sch SM1 217 C5
Westbourne Rd
Barnsbury N7 72 B2
Croydon CR0 205 D3
DA7 147 A5
Feltham TW13 149 D1
Hillingdon UB8 82 D3
Penge SE26 184 D4
Westbourne St W2 114 B6 246 C6
Westbourne Terr W2 92 A1 236 B2
Westbourne Terrace Mews W2 236 A2
Westbourne Terrace Rd W2 92 A2 236 A3
Westbridge Cl W12 112 A5
Westbridge Prim Sch SW11 267 A2
Westbridge Rd SW11 136 C4 267 A2
WEST BROMPTON 135 D6
West Brompton Sta SW5 113 C1 255 B1
Westbrook Ave TW12 173 B3
Westbrook Cl EN4 2 B2
Westbrook Cres EN4 2 B2
Westbrook Ct SE3 143 B4
Westbrooke Cres DA16 146 C2
Westbrooke Rd
Bexley DA16 146 C2
DA15 167 B2
Westbrooke Sch DA16 146 D2
Westbrook Ho
[5] Bethnal Green E2 96 C4
[5] Clapham Pk SW4 159 C6
Westbrook Rd
Heston TW5 129 B5
SE3 143 B4
South Norwood CR7 183 B1
Westbrook Sq EN4 2 B2
West Brow BR7 188 D5
Westbury Ave
Claygate KT10 212 D2
Southall UB1 85 C3
Tottenham N22 32 D1
Wembley HA0 66 A1
Westbury Cl
Ruislip HA4 40 A2
Shepperton TW17 192 D3
Westbury Ct
[3] Barking IG11 101 B6
Beckenham BR3 185 D2
[1] Buckhurst Hill IG9 21 C2
Clapham SW4 159 B5
[11] New Barnet EN5 14 A6
Tottenham N22 33 A1
Westbury Gr N12 29 C4
Westbury Ho
[1] Walthamstow E17 53 C5
[6] Willesden NW10 67 C1
Westbury House Sch KT3 199 B4
Westbury La IG9 21 C2
Westbury Lodge Cl HA5 40 D6
Westbury Pl [2] TW8 131 D6
Westbury Rd
Barking IG11 101 B6
Beckenham BR3 207 A6
Bowes Pk N11 32 A4
Bromley BR1 187 D2
Buckhurst Hill IG9 21 C3
Ealing W5 88 A1
Feltham TW13 150 D3
Finchley N12 29 D5
Ilford IG1 78 C6
New Malden KT3 199 B4
Penge SE20 184 D2
Thornton Heath CR0 205 B3
Upton E7 77 B2
Walthamstow E17 53 C5
Wembley HA0 66 A1
Westbury Terr E7 77 B2
Westbush Ct [1] W12 112 B4
West Carriage Dr W2 114 C5 247 A4
West Central St WC1 240 A2
West Chantry HA3 23 D2
Westchester Ct NW4 46 D6
Westchester Dr NW4 46 D6
Westchester Ho W2 237 C1
West Cl
Ashford TW15 170 A6
Barnet EN5 12 B6
Cockfosters EN4 3 A1
Edmonton N9 17 D1
Greenford UB6 86 A5
Hampton TW12 173 A4
Wembley HA9 44 B1
Westcliff Ho [13] N1 73 B2
Westcombe Ave CR0 204 B2
Westcombe Ct [1] SE3 142 D5
Westcombe Dr EN5 13 C6
Westcombe Hill SE3, SE10 143 A6
Westcombe Lodge Dr UB4 83 B2
Westcombe Park Rd SE3 142 D5
Westcombe Park Sta SE3 121 A1
West Common Rd BR2 225 B5
Westcoombe Ave SW20 177 D2
Westcote Rd SW16 181 C5
Westcote Rise HA4 39 A2
Westcott Cl BR1 210 A4
[2] South Tottenham N15 51 D3
Westcott Cres W7 86 C2
Westcott Ho [1] E14 119 D6
Westcott Rd SE17 138 D6
West Cotts NW6 69 C3
Westcroft [1] SM5 219 A4
Westcroft Cl
Enfield EN3 6 C5
West Hampstead NW2 69 A4
Westcroft Ct
[3] Chiswick W6 112 A2
Kingsbury NW9 44 D4
Westcroft Gdns SM4 201 B5
Westcroft Ho [2] SM5 219 A4
Westcroft L Ctr SM5 219 A4
Westcroft Rd SM5, SM6 219 A4
Westcroft Sq W6 112 A2
Westcroft Way NW2 69 A4
West Cromwell Rd W14 113 B1 254 D2
West Cross Ctr TW8 131 B6
West Cross Route W10, W11 112 D6
West Cross Way TW8 131 B6
West Croydon Sta CR9 205 A1
West Ct
Hounslow TW7 130 A5
Sunbury TW16 172 B1
Walthamstow E17 53 D5
Wembley HA0 65 C6
Westdale Rd SE18 144 D6
Westdean Ave SE12 165 C3
Westdean Cl SW18 157 D5
Westdown Rd
Catford SE6 163 C4
Leyton E15 76 A4
West Dr Stanmore HA3 24 B4
Streatham SW16 181 C6
WEST DRAYTON 104 B4
West Drayton Park Ave UB7 104 A3
West Drayton Prim Sch UB7 104 A4
West Drayton Rd UB8 82 D1
West Drayton Sta UB7 104 A5
West Drive Gdns HA3 24 B4
WEST DULWICH 161 A2
West Dulwich Sta SE21 161 B3
WEST EALING 109 B5
West Ealing Bsns Ctr W13 109 A6
West Ealing Sta W13 109 B6
West Eaton Pl SW1 258 A4
West Eaton Pl Mews SW1 258 A4
West Ella Rd NW10 67 C1
West End Ave
Leytonstone E10 54 B4
Pinner HA5 40 D5
West End Cl
Stonebridge NW10 67 A1
Willesden NW10 67 A1
West End Ct
Hampstead NW6 69 D1
Pinner HA5 40 D5
West End Gdns UB5 84 C5
West End La
Hampstead NW6 69 D2
Harlington UB7 127 A5
Pinner HA5 40 D5
West End Rd
Ruislip HA4, UB5 62 A4
Ruislip UB5 62 C1
Southall UB1 107 A5
Westerdale Ct N5 72 D4
Westerdale Rd [2] SE10 121 A1
Westerfield Rd [1] N15 51 D4
Westergate W5 88 A2
Westergate Rd SE2 147 A6
Westerham
[13] Kingston u T KT6 198 A4
NW1 232 A5
Westerham Ave N9 17 C1
Westerham Dr DA15 168 C5
Westerham Ho SE1 262 D6
Westerham Lo [10] BR3 185 C3
Westerham Rd
Keston BR2 225 D2
Walthamstow E10 53 D2
Westerley Cres SE26 185 B5
Westerley Ct HA4 62 B3
Western Ave
Dagenham W3 89 B1
Hendon NW11 46 D3
Hillingdon HA4, UB4, UB5, UB10 61 C1
Northolt UB5, UB6 85 B6
Ruislip UB8, UB9, UB10 60 B3
Wembley UB6 87 C4
Western Avenue Bsns Pk W3 88 D3
Western Beach Apts E16 121 A5
Western Ct
[4] Dagenham W3 89 B1
Finchley N3 29 C4
[3] Kilburn W9 91 B5
Southall UB2 107 A3
Western Dr TW17 193 B3
Western Eye Hospl The NW1 92 D2 237 C4
Western Gateway E16 121 A6
Western Gdns W5 110 C6
Western Ho [3] W9 91 B3
Western Hts SM1 217 C3
Western International Market UB2 106 B2
Western La SW12 159 A4
Western Mews W9 91 B3
Western Par EN5 13 D6
Western Pl [19] SE16 118 C4
Western Rd
Becontree NW10 89 A3
Brixton SW9 138 C2
Ealing W5 109 D6
Fortis Green N2 48 D5
Mitcham CR4, SW19 180 C1
Newham E13 99 C5
Southall UB2 106 D2
Sutton SM1 217 C3
Walthamstow E17 54 A4
Wood Green N22 32 B1
Western Terr [3] W6 112 A1
Western View UB3 105 D4
Westernville Gdns IG2 57 A2
Western Way
New Barnet EN5 13 D5
Plumstead SE28 123 C4
Western Wharf [2] SE15 140 A6
WEST EWELL 215 C1
West Ewell Inf Sch KT19 215 B3
West Farm Ct EN4 2 D2
Westferry Cir E14 119 C5
Westferry Rd E14 119 C3
Westferry Sta E14 119 C6
Westfield [1] BR6 227 A3
Loughton IG10 21 C6
West Hampstead NW3 69 C4
Westfield Cl
Cheam SM1 217 B4
Enfield EN3 7 A2
Kingsbury NW9 45 A6
SW10 266 A3
Westfield Ct
[1] Kensal Green W10 90 D4
Kingston u T KT6 197 D4
Westfield Dr HA3 43 D5
Westfield Gdns
Harrow HA3 43 D5
Ilford RM6 58 C3
Westfield Ho [6] SE16 118 D2
Westfield La HA3 43 D5
Westfield London Sh Ctr W12 112 D5
Westfield Pk HA5 23 B3
Westfield Rd
Beckenham BR3 185 B1
Cheam SM1 217 B4
Croydon CR0 220 D6
Dagenham RM9 81 B4
Ealing W13 109 A5
Edgware NW7 11 C1
Kingston u T KT6 197 D4
Mitcham CR4 180 D1
Walton-on-T KT12 195 A2
Westfields SW13 133 D2
Westfields Ave SW13 133 C2
Westfields Rd W3 88 D2
Westfield St SE18 121 D3
Westfield Way
Mile End E1 97 A3
Ruislip HA4 61 D5
West Finchley Sta N3 29 D4
West Garden Pl W2 237 B1
West Gate W5 88 A4
Westgate Bsns Ctr
[2] Kensal Town W10 91 A3
North Kensington W10 90 D3
Westgate Ct
[6] Beckenham BR3 186 A2
[15] Brixton SW9 138 C2
Lewisham SE12 165 A3
Westgate Est TW14 148 D3
Westgate Rd
Beckenham BR3 186 A2
Croydon SE25 206 B5
Westgate St E8 96 B6
Westgate Terr SW10 135 D6 265 D6
West Gdns
Mitcham SW19 180 C4
Stepney E1 118 B6
Westglade Ct HA3 43 D4
West Gr
Lewisham SE10 142 B4
Woodford IG8 37 C5
WEST GREEN 51 A5
West Green Pl UB6 86 B6
West Green Prim Sch N15 51 A5
West Green Rd N15 51 B5
Westgrove La SE10 142 A4
West Grove Prim Sch N14 15 D4
West Halkin St SW1 115 A3 258 A6
West Hallowes SE9 166 A3
West Hall Rd TW9 132 D4
WEST HAM 99 B6
West Ham Church Prim Sch [7] E15 98 D6
West Ham La E15 76 C1
WEST HAMPSTEAD 69 C4
West Hampstead Mews NW6 69 D2
West Hampstead Sta NW6 69 C2
West Hampstead Thameslink Sta NW6 69 C2
West Ham Sta E15 98 C4
West Harding St EC4 241 B2
WEST HARROW 42 A2
West Harrow Sta HA1 42 A3
West Hatch Manor HA4 39 D2
Westhaven SM1 217 C3
Westhay Gdns SW14 154 D6
WEST HEATH 146 D6
West Heath Ave NW11 47 C1
West Heath Cl NW3 69 C5
West Heath Ct NW11 47 C1
West Heath Dr NW11 47 C1
West Heath Gdns NW3 69 C5
West Heath Rd
SE2, DA7 146 D6
West Hampstead NW3 69 D5
WEST HENDON 45 D3
WEST HILL 157 B5
West Hill Harrow HA2 64 C6
Putney SW15 157 A5
South Croydon CR2 221 C1
Wembley HA9 44 B1
Westhill Ct W11 244 D6
West Hill Ct N6 71 A5
West Hill Hall HA2 64 C6
Westhill Pk
Dartmouth Pk N6 71 A6
Highgate N6 70 D6
West Hill Prim Sch [17] SW18 157 C6
West Hill Rd SW18 157 B5
West Hill Way N20 13 D3
West Ho Barking IG11 78 D2
[4] Penge SE20 184 D3
[9] Streatham SW12 159 C4
Westholm NW11 47 D5
Westholme BR6 211 D2
Westholme Gdns HA4 40 A1
Westhope Ho [28] E2 96 A4
Westhorne Ave SE9, SE12 165 C5
Westhorpe Gdns NW4 46 C6
Westhorpe Rd SW15 134 C2
West House Cl SW19 157 A3
Westhurst Dr BR7 188 D5
West India Ave E14 119 C5
West India Dock Rd E14 119 C6
West India Ho [1] E14 119 C6
West India Quay Sta E14 119 C6
WEST KENSINGTON 113 A2
West Kensington Ct W14 254 C2
West Kensington Mans W14 254 C1
West Kensington Sta W14 113 B1 254 C2
WEST KILBURN 91 A4
West La SE16 118 B4
Westlake [12] SE16 118 C2
Westlake Cl
Hayes UB4 85 A3
Palmers Green N13 16 C1
Westlake Rd HA9 65 D6
Westland Cl TW19 148 A5
Westland Ct [5] UB5 84 D4
Westland Dr BR2, BR4 224 D6
Westland Ho [1] E16 122 C5
Westland Lo [1] BR1 187 C1
Westland Pl N1 235 C2
Westlands Cl UB3 106 A2
Westlands Ct KT8 196 C5
Westlands Terr [3] SW12 159 C5
Westlea Rd W7 109 A3
West Lea Sch N9 17 C1
Westleigh Ave SW15 156 C6
Westleigh Ct
Finchley N12 29 D4
[16] Wanstead E11 55 A4
Westleigh Dr BR1 188 A2
Westleigh Gdns HA8 26 C1
West Links HA0 87 D4
Westlinton Cl NW7 29 A4
West Lodge Ave W3 110 C5

West Lodge Ct W3 ... 110 C5
West Lodge Fst & Mid Schs HA5 ... 40 D5
West Lodge Sch DA15 ... 168 A1
West London Acad
Northolt UB5 ... 63 A1
Northolt UB5 ... 85 A6
West London Shooting Sch UB5 ... 84 B6
Westly Ct NW2 ... 68 D2
Westly Ho N9 ... 18 B3
Westmacott Dr TW14 ... 149 D3
Westmacott Ho NW8 236 D5
West Mall W11 ... 245 B4
Westmark Point 13 SW15 ... 156 B3
Westmead SW15 ... 156 B5
West Mead
Ruislip HA4 ... 62 C4
West Ewell KT19 ... 215 C2
Westmead Cnr SM5 ... 218 C4
Westmead Rd SM1 ... 218 B4
Westmeath Ho NW2 ... 68 A5
Westmere Dr NW7 ... 11 B1
West Mersea Cl 9 E16 ... 121 B5
West Mews SW1 ... 259 A3
West Middlesex Univ Hosp TW7 ... 131 A3
Westmill Ct N4 ... 73 A6
WESTMINSTER ... 115 C4
Westminster Abbey* SW1 ... 116 A3 260 A6
Westminster Abbey Choir Sch SW1 ... 115 D3 259 D6
Westminster Acad W2 ... 91 C2
Westminster Acad (Sch of English) W1 ... 93 C1 239 B2
Westminster Ave CR7 ... 182 D1
Westminster Boating Base SW1 ... 269 C6
Westminster Bridge SE1, SW1 ... 116 A4 250 B1
Westminster Bridge Rd SE1 ... 116 B4 250 C1
Westminster Cath* SW1 ... 115 C3 259 A5
Westminster Cath Choir Sch SW1 ... 115 C2 259 B4
Westminster Cath RC Prim Sch SW1 ... 115 D1 259 D2
Westminster City Hall SW1 ... 259 B6
Westminster City Sch SW1 ... 259 B6
Westminster Cl
East Bedfont TW14 ... 150 A3
Teddington TW11 ... 175 A5
Westminster Coll W1 ... 115 D6 249 C6
Westminster Ct
22 Rotherhithe SE16 ... 118 D5
South Norwood CR7 ... 183 A1
5 Wandsworth SW18 ... 157 C6
Wanstead E11 ... 55 B3
Westminster Dr N13 ... 32 A5
Westminster Dragoons Mus* SW6 ... 135 A2
Westminster Gdns
Barking IG11 ... 101 C5
Chingford E4 ... 20 C3
SW1 ... 260 A4
Westminster Ind Est SE18 ... 121 D3
Westminster Kingsway Coll (King's Cross Centre) WC1 94 B4 233 C1
Westminster Kingsway Coll (Regent's Park Ctr) NW1 ... 93 C3 239 A6
Westminster Kingsway Coll (Victoria Centre) SW1 ... 115 D2 259 C4
Westminster Pier SW1 ... 250 B1
Westminster Rd
Carshalton SM1 ... 218 B6
Ealing W7 ... 108 C5
Edmonton N9 ... 18 B3
Westminster Sch SW1 ... 116 A3 260 A6
Westminster Sta SW1 ... 116 A4 250 B1
Westminster Under Sch SW1 ... 115 D2 259 C3
Westmoat Cl BR3 ... 186 A3
WEST MOLESEY ... 195 C5
Westmont Rd KT10 ... 212 C6
Westmoor Gdns EN3 ... 6 D3
Westmoor Rd EN3 ... 6 D3
Westmoor St SE7 ... 121 D3
Westmore Ct SW15 ... 157 A6
Westmoreland Ave DA16 ... 145 C1
Westmoreland Dr SM2 ... 217 D1
Westmoreland Ho NW10 ... 90 A4
Westmoreland Pl
5 Bromley BR1 ... 209 A6
Ealing W5 ... 87 D2
Pimlico SW1 ... 258 D1
Westmoreland Rd
Barnes SW13 ... 134 A4
Beckenham BR2, BR3 208 D5
Bromley BR2 ... 209 A5
Camberwell SE17 ... 139 B6
Queensbury NW9 ... 44 B5
Westmoreland St W1 ... 238 B3
Westmoreland Terr
10 Penge SE20 ... 184 B3
SW1 ... 115 B1 258 D1
Westmorland Cl
3 Twickenham TW1 ... 153 B5
Wanstead E12 ... 77 D6
Westmorland Ct
12 Surbiton KT6 ... 197 D2
Sutton SM1 ... 218 A5
Westmorland Rd
BR2 ... 209 A5
Harrow HA1 ... 41 D4
Walthamstow E17 ... 53 C3
Westmorland Way CR4 ... 203 D4
Westmount Ct W5 ... 88 B2
Westmount Rd SE9 ... 144 C1
WEST NORWOOD ... 161 A1
West Norwood Sta SE27 ... 160 D1
West Oak BR3 ... 186 B2
Westoe Rd N9 ... 18 B2
Weston A?e
East Molesey KT8 ... 195 B5
Thames Ditton KT10, KT7 ... 196 C2
Westonbirt Ct 6 SE15 ... 139 D6
Weston Ct
Highbury N4 ... 73 A5
3 Kingston u T KT1 ... 198 A6
Oakleigh Pk N20 ... 14 A4
Weston Dr HA7 ... 25 B2
West One Ho W1 ... 239 A3
Westone Mans 6 IG11 ... 79 D1
West One Sh Ctr W1 ... 93 B1 238 C1
Weston Gdns TW7 ... 130 C4
Weston Gn
Dagenham RM9 ... 81 B4
Thames Ditton KT7 ... 196 C1
Weston Gr 1 BR1 ... 186 D2
WESTON GREEN ... 196 D1
Weston Green Rd KT7 ... 196 C2
Weston Green Sch KT7 ... 196 C1
Weston Ho
6 Brondesbury NW6 ... 69 A1
8 South Hackney E9 ... 96 C6
Weston Lo KT7 ... 196 D1
Weston Park Cl KT7 ... 196 C1
Weston Park Prim Sch N8 ... 50 B4
Weston Pk
Hornsey Vale N8 ... 50 B3
Weston Pk *continued*
Kingston u T KT1 ... 176 A1
Thames Ditton KT10, KT7 ... 196 C1
Weston Rd
Acton Green W4 ... 111 A3
Bromley BR1 ... 186 D3
Dagenham RM9 ... 81 A4
Enfield EN2 ... 5 B3
Thames Ditton KT7 ... 196 C1
Weston Rise N1, WC1 ... 94 B4 233 D2
Weston St SE1 ... 117 B4 252 D2
Weston Wlk 3 E8, E9 ... 74 B1
Westover Hill NW3 ... 69 C6
Westover Rd SW18 ... 158 A5
Westow Hill SE19 ... 183 D4
Westow St SE19 ... 183 C4
Westpark W5 ... 87 D1
West Park Ave TW9 ... 132 D4
West Park Cl
Heston TW5 ... 129 B6
Ilford RM6 ... 58 D4
West Park Rd
Richmond TW9 ... 132 C4
Southall UB2 ... 108 B5
West Parkside
Greenwich SE10 ... 120 D3
Greenwich SE10 ... 121 A2
West Pk SE9 ... 166 A3
West Pl SW19 ... 178 C5
West Plaza E14 ... 119 D5
Westpoint
Beckenham BR2 ... 208 B6
Putney SW15 ... 156 D5
West Point 2 SE1 ... 118 A1
Westpoint Apartments N8 ... 50 B5
Westpoint Trad Est W3 ... 88 D2
Westpole Ave EN4 ... 3 B1
Westport Ct UB4 ... 84 C3
Westport Rd E13 ... 99 B3
Westport St E1 ... 96 D1
West Poultry Ave EC1 ... 241 C3
West Quarters W12 ... 90 A1
West Quay Dr UB4 ... 85 A2
West Ramp TW6 ... 126 C4
West Rd
Chelsea SW3 ... 136 D6 267 D6
Clapham Pk SW4 ... 159 D6
Dagenham RM6 ... 59 A3
Ealing W5 ... 88 A2
East Barnet EN4 ... 15 A3
East Bedfont TW14 ... 149 B4
Finchley N2 ... 30 B2
Kingston u T KT2, KT3 ... 177 A2
Tottenham N17 ... 34 B4
West Drayton UB7 ... 104 B3
West Ham E15 ... 98 D6
West Ridge Gdns UB6 ... 86 A5
Westrow SW15 ... 156 C5
West Row W10 ... 91 A3
Westrow Dr IG11 ... 80 A2
Westrow Gdns IG3 ... 79 D5
WEST RUISLIP ... 61 B6
West Ruislip Ct HA4 ... 61 B6
West Ruislip Elementary Sch UB10 ... 61 A5
West Ruislip Sta HA4 ... 61 A6
West Sheen Vale TW9 ... 132 B1
Westside
11 Hammersmith W6 ... 112 A2
Hendon NW4 ... 28 B1
Muswell Hill N2 ... 48 D6
West Side Comm SW19 ... 178 C5
Westside Ct 1 W9 ... 91 C3
West Silvertown Sta E16 ... 121 A5
West Smithfield EC1 ... 94 D2 241 D3
West Sq SE11 ... 116 D3 261 C5
West St
30 Bethnal Green E2 ... 96 B5
Bexleyheath DA7 ... 147 B2
Bromley BR1 ... 187 A1
Carshalton SM5 ... 218 D4
Croydon CR0 ... 221 A4
West St *continued*
Harrow HA1 ... 42 C1
Leyton E11 ... 76 C5
Soho WC2 ... 93 D1 239 D1
Sutton SM1 ... 217 D3
Walthamstow E17 ... 53 D4
West Street La SM5 ... 218 D4
West Street Pl 1 CR0 ... 221 A4
West Surrey Est TW15 ... 171 A2
West Sutton Sta SM1 ... 217 C4
West Temple Sheen SW14 ... 154 D6
West Tenter St E1 ... 95 D1 243 D1
West Terr DA15 ... 167 C3
West Thames Coll TW7 ... 130 C4
West Thamesmead Bsns Pk SE28 ... 123 D3
West Thornton Prim Sch CR0 ... 204 B3
West Towers HA5 ... 40 D3
West Twyford Prim Sch NW10 ... 88 C5
Westvale Mews W3 ... 111 C4
Westview W7 ... 86 C1
West View
Dagenham RM6 ... 58 C4
East Bedfont TW14 ... 149 A4
Westview Cl
North Kensington W10 ... 90 C1
Willesden NW10 ... 67 D3
Westview Cres N9 ... 17 C4
Westview Ct
3 Elstree WD6 ... 9 D5
1 Whetstone N20 ... 14 A2
Westview Dr IG8 ... 37 D1
West View Gdns WD6 ... 9 D5
Westville Rd
Shepherd's Bush W12 ... 112 A4
Thames Ditton KT7 ... 197 A2
Westward Rd E4 ... 35 B5
Westward Way HA3 ... 44 A3
West Warwick Pl SW1 ... 259 A3
Westway
Shepherd's Bush W10, W12 ... 112 A6
West Barnes SW20 ... 200 C5
West Way BR5 ... 211 B4
Burnt Oak HA8 ... 27 A4
Croydon CR0 ... 223 A5
Edmonton N18 ... 33 B6
Hounslow TW5 ... 129 B4
Neasden NW10 ... 67 B5
Pinner HA5 ... 40 D5
Ruislip HA4 ... 39 D1
Shepperton TW17 ... 193 B3
West Wickham BR4 ... 208 C3
Westway Cl SW20 ... 200 B6
Westway Ct UB5 ... 85 C6
Westway (Elevated Rd) W10 ... 91 B2
West Way Gdns CR0 ... 222 D6
Westway Lo 35 W2 ... 91 C2
Westways KT19 ... 215 D4
West Ways HA6 ... 22 A1
Westwell 4 NW5 ... 71 A2
Westwell Rd SW16 ... 182 A4
Westwell Road App SW16 ... 182 A4
Westwick 7 KT1 ... 176 C1
Westwick Gdns
Cranford TW4, TW5 ... 128 B3
Hammersmith W14 ... 112 D4
WEST WICKHAM ... 224 C6
West Wickham Sta BR3 ... 208 A2
West Wimbledon Prim Sch SW20 ... 200 B6
West Wlk
East Barnet EN4 ... 15 A3
Hayes UB3 ... 106 A5
Westwood Ave
Harrow HA2 ... 63 D4
South Norwood SE19 ... 183 A2
Westwood Bsns Ctr NW10 ... 89 C3
Westwood Cl BR1 ... 209 D6
Esher KT10 ... 212 A5
Ruislip HA4 ... 38 D3
Westwood Ct
Enfield EN1 ... 17 C5
3 Forest Hill SE23 ... 162 C3
7 Wimbledon SW19 ... 179 B5
Westwood Gdns SW13 ... 133 D2
Westwood Hill SE26 ... 184 B6
Westwood Ho
6 Shepherd's Bush W12 ... 112 C5
5 Stoke Newington N4 ... 51 B2
Westwood La DA16 ... 145 D1
Westwood Language College for Girls SE19 ... 183 B3
Westwood Lo N12 ... 30 C5
Westwood Park Trad Est W3 ... 88 D3
Westwood Pk SE23 ... 162 B4
Westwood Pl SE26 ... 184 A6
Westwood Rd
Barnes SW13 ... 133 D2
Ilford IG3 ... 58 A2
Westwood Sch WD23 ... 8 B2
West Woodside DA5 ... 169 A3
Wetheral Ct SW17 ... 180 B6
Wetheral Dr HA7 ... 25 C1
Wetherby Cl UB5 ... 63 D2
Wetherby Ct SE25 ... 183 C1
Wetherby Gdns SW5 ... 114 A2 256 A3
Wetherby Mans SW5 255 C2
Wetherby Mews SW5 ... 255 D2
Wetherby Pl SW7 ... 114 A2 256 B3
Wetherby Prep Sch W11 ... 113 C6 245 A6
Wetherby Rd EN2 ... 5 A4
Wetherby Way KT9 ... 214 A1
Wetherden St E17 ... 53 B2
Wetherell Rd E9 ... 96 D6
Wetherill Rd N10 ... 31 A2
Wevco Wharf SE15 ... 140 B6
Wexford Ho 11 E1 ... 96 C2
Wexford Rd SW12 ... 158 D4
Weybourne St SW18 ... 158 A2
Weybridge Ct 19 SE16 ... 118 B1
Weybridge Ho N4 ... 51 A2
Weybridge Point 11 SW11 ... 136 D3
Weybridge Rd CR7 ... 204 C5
Wey Ct KT19 ... 215 A4
Weydown Cl SW19 ... 157 A3
Weyhill Ho 28 SE5 ... 139 A3
Weyhill Rd 11 E1 ... 96 A1
Wey Ho
6 Northolt UB5 ... 85 B3
NW8 ... 236 D5
Weylands Cl KT12 ... 195 B1
Weylond Rd RM8 ... 81 B5
Weyman Rd SE3 ... 143 C4
Weymarks The N17 ... 33 B4
Weymouth Ave
Brentford W5 ... 109 C3
Edgware NW7 ... 27 C5
Weymouth Cl 1 E6 ... 100 D1
Weymouth Ct
Belmont SM2 ... 217 C1
5 Haggerston E2 ... 95 D5
15 Streatham SW2 ... 160 B4
Weymouth Ho
Bromley BR2 ... 186 D1
Edgware HA8 ... 26 B4
Fitzrovia W1 ... 238 D4
South Lambeth SW8 ... 270 C3
Weymouth Mews W1 ... 93 B2 238 C4
Weymouth Rd UB4 ... 83 C4
Weymouth St W1 ... 93 B2 238 C4
Weymouth Terr E2 ... 95 D5
Weymouth Wlk HA7 ... 25 A4
Whadcoat St N4 ... 72 C6
Whaddon Ho
10 Camberwell SE5 ... 139 C2
SW1 ... 247 D1
Whalebone Ave RM6 ... 59 B3
Whalebone Gr RM6 ... 59 B3
Whalebone La E15 ... 76 C1
Whalebone Lane N RM6 ... 59 A6
Whalebone Lane S RM6, RM8 ... 59 B2

Whales Yd E15 ... 76 C1
Wharfdale Cl N11 ... 31 A4
Wharfdale Rd
N1 ... 94 A5 233 B4
Wharfedale Ct 5 E5 ... 74 D4
Wharfedale Gdns CR7,
SW16 ... 204 B6
Wharfedale St SW10 255 C1
Wharf La
19 Poplar E14 ... 97 B1
Twickenham TW1 ... 153 A3
Wharf Pl E2 ... 96 B6
Wharf Rd Enfield EN3 ... 19 A5
King's Cross
NW1 ... 93 D6 232 D5
Shoreditch N1 . 95 A5 235 A3
Wharf Road
NW1 ... 94 A5 233 A4
Wharfside HA0 ... 88 A6
Wharfside Rd E16 ... 98 C2
Wharf St E16 ... 98 C2
Wharf View Ct 15
E14 ... 98 A1
Wharncliffe Dr UB1 ... 108 B5
Wharncliffe Gdns
SE25 ... 183 C1
Wharncliffe Ho 3
SW15 ... 156 C6
Wharncliffe Rd
SE25 ... 183 C1
Wharton Cl NW10 ... 67 C2
Wharton Ho SE1 ... 263 C6
Wharton Rd BR1 ... 187 B2
Wharton St
WC1 ... 94 B4 233 D1
Whateley Rd
East Dulwich SE22 ... 161 D6
Penge SE20 ... 184 D3
Whatley Ave SW20 ... 201 A6
Whatman Ho 10 E14 ... 97 B1
Whatman Rd SE23 ... 162 D4
Wheatcroft Ct SM1 ... 201 D1
Wheatfields Enfield EN3 . 7 A3
Newham E6 ... 100 D1
Wheatfield Way KT1 . 176 A1
Wheathill Ho SE20 ... 184 B1
Wheathill Rd SE20 ... 206 B6
Wheat Ho TW19 ... 148 A3
Wheatland Ho 7
SE22 ... 139 C2
Wheatlands TW5 ... 129 C6
Wheatlands Rd
SW17 ... 159 A1
Wheatley Cl NW4 ... 28 A1
Wheatley Cres UB3 ... 106 A6
Wheatley Gdns N9 ... 17 C2
Wheatley Ho
Gospel Oak NW5 ... 71 B4
3 Putney SW15 ... 156 A4
Wheatley Mans 8
IG11 ... 80 A1
Wheatley Rd TW7 ... 130 D2
Wheatley St W1 ... 238 B3
Wheatsheaf Cl UB5 ... 63 A3
Wheat Sheaf Cl E14 . 119 D2
Wheatsheaf La
Fulham SW6 ... 134 C5
SW8 ... 270 B4
Wheatsheaf Par 7
BR4 ... 207 D1
Wheatsheaf Terr
SW6 ... 264 D3
Wheatstone Cl
SW19 ... 180 C2
Wheatstone Ho 7
W10 ... 91 A2
Wheatstone Rd W10 ... 91 A2
Wheeler 2 NW9 ... 27 D3
Wheeler Ct 4 SW11 . 136 B2
Wheeler Gdns N1 ... 233 B6
Wheeler La E1 ... 243 C4
Wheeler Pl 2 BR2 ... 209 B5
Wheelers Cross
IG11 ... 101 B5
Wheelers Dr HA4 ... 39 A3
Wheeler's St SM1 ... 217 C5
Wheelhouse The 4
E14 ... 119 D1
Wheelock Cl DA8 ... 147 D5
Wheelwright St N7 ... 72 B1
Whelan Way SM6 ... 219 D5
Wheldon Ct SE1 ... 253 C2
Wheler Ho E1 ... 243 C5
Wheler St E1 . 95 D3 243 C5
Whellock Rd W4 ... 111 C3
Whernside Cl SE28 ... 124 C6
WHETSTONE ... 14 A2
Whetstone Cl N20 ... 14 B2
Whetstone Park
WC2 ... 94 B1 240 C2
Whetstone Rd SE3 ... 143 D4
Whewell Rd N19 ... 72 A6
Whichcote St SE1 ... 251 A3
Whidborne Bldgs
WC1 ... 233 A1
Whidborne Cl SE8 ... 141 C3
Whidborne St WC1 ... 233 B1
Whimbrel Cl SE28 ... 124 C6
Whimbrel Way UB4 ... 84 D2
Whinchat Rd SE18,
SE28 ... 123 B3
Whinfell Cl SW16 ... 181 D5
Whinyates Rd SE9 ... 144 A2
Whippendell Cl BR5 . 190 B2
Whippendell Way
BR5 ... 190 B1
Whippingham Ho 22
E3 ... 97 B4
Whipps Cross E17 ... 54 B4
Whipps Cross Ho E17 . 54 B4
Whipps Cross Hospl E10,
E11 ... 54 B3
Whipps Cross Rd E11 . 54 C3
Whiskin St
EC1 ... 94 D4 234 C1
Whisperwood Cl HA3 . 24 C3
Whistler Gdns HA8 ... 26 B1
Whistler Mews
Dagenham RM8 ... 80 B3
23 SE15 ... 139 D5
Whistlers Ave
SW11 ... 136 B5 266 D3
Whistler St N5 ... 72 D3
Whistler Twr SW10 ... 266 A3
Whistler Wlk SW10 ... 266 B4
Whiston Ho 18 N1 ... 72 D1
Whiston Rd E2 ... 96 A6
Whitakers Lo EN2 ... 5 B4
Whitbread Cl N17 ... 34 A2
Whitbread Ctr EC1 ... 242 C5
Whitbread Rd SE4 ... 141 B1
Whitburn Rd SE13 ... 142 A1
Whitby Ave NW10 ... 88 D4
Whitby Ct
6 Lower Holloway
N7 ... 72 A4
3 New Southgate N11 31 A4
Whitby Gdns
Carshalton SM1 ... 218 B6
Queensbury NW9 ... 44 C6
Whitby Ho NW8 ... 229 A5
Whitby Par HA4 ... 62 C6
Whitby Rd
Carshalton SM1 ... 218 B6
Harrow HA2 ... 64 A5
Ruislip HA4 ... 62 C6
Woolwich SE18 ... 122 B2
Whitby St E1 ... 243 C6
Whitcher Cl SE14 ... 141 A6
Whitcher Pl NW1 ... 71 C2
Whitchurch Ave HA8 ... 26 B3
Whitchurch Cl HA8 ... 26 B4
Whitchurch Ct
SW17 ... 180 B6
Whitchurch Fst Sch
HA7 ... 25 D3
Whitchurch Gdns
HA8 ... 26 B4
Whitchurch Ho
Catford SE6 ... 164 A1
16 North Kensington
W10 ... 90 D1
Whitchurch La HA8 ... 26 B3
Whitchurch Par HA8 ... 26 C3
Whitchurch Rd W11 . 112 D6
Whitcomb Ct W1 ... 249 D5
Whitcomb St
WC2 ... 115 D6 249 D5
Whitcome Mews
TW9 ... 132 D4
Whiteacre Mews
SE11 ... 261 B1
Whiteadder Way
E14 ... 119 D2
Whitear Wlk E15 ... 76 B2
Whitebarn La RM10 ... 103 C6
Whitebeam Ave BR2 . 210 C3
Whitebeam Cl SW9 ... 270 D3
Whitebeam Ho 3
NW3 ... 70 D2
White Bear Pl 1
NW3 ... 70 B4
White Bear Yd EC1 ... 241 A5
White Bridge Ave
CR4 ... 202 B6
White Bridge Cl
TW14 ... 149 D5
White Butts Rd HA4 ... 62 D5
WHITECHAPEL ... 95 D1
Whitechapel Bell
Foundry★ E1 ... 96 A2
Whitechapel Gall★
E1 ... 243 D2
Whitechapel High St
E1 ... 95 D1 243 D2
Whitechapel Mkt★
E1 ... 96 A2
Whitechapel Rd E1 ... 96 B2
Whitechapel Sta E1 ... 96 B2
Whitechurch La 3
E1 ... 96 A1
Whitechurch Pas 1
E1 ... 96 A1
White City W10 ... 90 C1
White City Cl W12 ... 112 C6
White City Est W12 ... 112 B6
White City Rd W12 ... 112 C6
White City Sta W12 . 112 C6
Whitecliff Ho SW18 . 157 D5
White Conduit St N1 234 B4
Whitecote Rd UB1 ... 86 A1
White Craig Cl HA5 ... 23 C5
Whitecroft Cl BR3 ... 208 B5
Whitecroft Way BR3 . 208 B5
Whitecross Pl EC2 ... 242 D4
Whitecross St
EC1 ... 95 A3 242 B5
White Cube The, Art
Gallery★ N1 ... 95 C4
Whitefield Ave NW2 ... 46 C1
Whitefield Cl SW15 ... 157 A5
Whitefield Sch NW2 ... 46 D2
Whitefield Sch & Ctr
E17 ... 36 A1
Whitefoot La BR1 ... 164 B1
Whitefoot Terr BR1 ... 164 D1
Whitefriars Ave HA3 ... 24 C1
Whitefriars Ct 9 N12 . 30 B5
Whitefriars Dr HA3 ... 24 C1
Whitefriars Fst & Mid
Sch HA3 ... 24 C1
Whitefriars St
EC4 ... 94 C1 241 B1
Whitefriars Trad Est
HA3 ... 24 B1
White Gate Gdns
HA3 ... 24 D3
Whitegates 4 EN5 ... 13 D6
White Gates 5 KT7 ... 197 A2
White Gdns RM10 ... 81 C2
Whitehall SW1 ... 250 A2
Whitehall Cres KT9 ... 213 D3
Whitehall Ct
SW1 ... 116 A5 250 B3
Whitehall Gdns
Acton W3 ... 110 C5
Chingford E4 ... 20 C3
Chiswick W4 ... 132 D6
SW1 ... 250 A3
Whitehall La IG9 ... 21 A2
Whitehall Lo
Muswell Hill N10 ... 49 A6
Woodford IG8 ... 21 A1
Whitehall Mans 3
N19 ... 49 C1
Whitehall Park Rd
W4 ... 132 D6
Whitehall Pk N19 ... 49 C1
Whitehall Pl
Wallington SM5 ... 219 B4
WC2, SW1 ... 116 A5 250 A3
Whitehall Prim Sch
E4 ... 20 C2
Whitehall Rd
Bromley BR2 ... 209 D5
Chingford E4 ... 20 C2
Harrow HA1 ... 42 C2
Thornton Heath CR7 . 204 C4
West Ealing W7 ... 109 A4
Woodford IG8 ... 21 A1
Whitehall St N17 ... 33 D3
White Hart Ave SE28,
SE18 ... 123 D3
White Hart Ct EC2 ... 243 A3
White Hart La
Mortlake SW13 ... 133 C2
Willesden NW10 ... 67 D2
White Hart Lane Sta
N17 ... 33 D3
White Hart Lane
(Tottenham Hotspur
FC) N17 ... 34 A3
Whitehart Lo SW19 ... 180 A4
White Hart Rd SE18 ... 123 C2
White Hart Rdbt UB5 ... 84 D5
White Hart St
Holborn EC4 ... 241 D2
Kennington
SE11 ... 116 C1 261 B2
White Hart Terr N17 ... 33 D3
White Hart Yd SE1 ... 252 C3
Whitehaven Cl BR2 ... 209 A5
Whitehaven Ct 5
DA6 ... 147 A1
Whitehaven St NW8 . 237 A5
Whitehead Cl
Edmonton N18 ... 33 B5
Wandsworth SW18 ... 158 A4
Whitehead Ct
Muswell Hill N10 ... 31 A2
Twickenham TW1 ... 152 D4
Whitehead Ho 8
SW15 ... 156 D6
Whitehead's Gr
SW3 ... 114 C2 257 B3
White Heart Ave UB8 ... 83 A2
Whiteheath Ave HA4 ... 39 A2
Whiteheath Inf Sch
HA4 ... 39 A3
Whiteheath Jun Sch
HA4 ... 39 A2
White Heron Mews
TW11 ... 174 D4
White Ho
2 Battersea SW11 ... 136 B3
Lower Edmonton N9 ... 18 C2
3 Streatham SW4 ... 159 D4
Whitehorn Ho 6 E1 ... 118 C5
White Horse Hill BR7,
SE9 ... 188 C6
Whitehorse La SE25 ... 205 C5
White Horse La E1 ... 96 D2
Whitehorse Manor Inf
Sch 6 CR7 ... 205 B5
Whitehorse Manor Jun
Sch 5 CR7 ... 205 B5
Whitehorse Mews
SE1 ... 261 C6
Whitehorse Rd
South Norwood CR0,
CR7 ... 205 B3
Tower Hamlets E1 ... 97 A2
White Horse Rd
Limehouse E1 ... 97 A1
Newham E6 ... 100 B4
White Horse St
W1 ... 115 B5 248 D3
White Horse Yd EC2 . 242 C2
White Ho The NW1 ... 238 D6
Tottenham N17 ... 51 C6
Upper Tooting SW17 . 180 D5
White House Ct
1 Beckenham BR3 ... 186 A2
Osidge N14 ... 15 D2
White House Dr HA7 ... 25 C6
Whitehouse Est E10 ... 54 A3
White House La EN2 ... 5 A4
White House Prep Sch
SW12 ... 159 D3
Whitehouse Way N14 . 15 B1
White Kennett St E1 243 B2
Whitelands Cres
SW18 ... 157 A4
Whitelands Ho SW3 . 257 D2
Whiteledges W13 ... 87 C1
Whitelegg Rd E13 ... 98 D5
Whiteley Ho 9 SW4 159 D4
Whiteley Rd SE19 ... 183 B5
Whiteleys Ctr 19 W2 ... 91 D1
Whiteleys Ho TW13 ... 151 C1
Whiteleys Par 5
UB10 ... 82 D3
Whiteleys Way
TW13 ... 151 C1
White Lion Ct EC3 ... 243 A1
White Lion Hill
EC4 ... 116 D6 251 D6
White Lion St
N1 ... 94 C5 234 B3
White Lo 7 Ealing W5 . 87 C2
Golders Green NW11 ... 47 B1
South Norwood SE19 . 182 D3
Whitelock Ho 21 E9 ... 74 D2
White Lodge Cl
Hampstead Garden Suburb
N2 ... 48 B3
Isleworth TW7 ... 131 A3
Sutton SM2 ... 218 A1
White Lodge Ct
TW16 ... 172 C2
Whitely Ct TW13 ... 151 B1
White Lyon Ct EC2 ... 242 A4
Whiteness Ho 18
SW9 ... 138 C4
White Oak Dr BR3 ... 186 A1
White Oak Gdns
DA15 ... 167 D4
Whiteoak Ho SE19 ... 183 A3
Whiteoaks La UB6 ... 86 B5
White Orchards
Barnet N20 ... 13 B3
Stanmore HA7 ... 25 A5
White Post La E9 ... 75 C2
White Post St SE14,
SE15 ... 140 C5
White Rd
Broadgate EC2 ... 243 A3
London E15 ... 76 C1
Whites Ave IG2 ... 57 C3
Whites Dr BR2 ... 208 D2
White's Grounds
SE1 ... 117 C4 253 B2
White's Grounds Est
SE1 ... 253 B2
White's Mdw BR1 ... 210 C5
Whitespar DA14 ... 189 D6
White's Row
E1 ... 95 D2 243 C3
White's Sq SW4 ... 137 D1
White St UB1 ... 106 D4
Whitestile Rd TW8 ... 109 D1
Whitestone La NW3 ... 70 A5
Whitestone Wlk NW3 . 70 A5
Whitethorn Ave UB7 . 104 B6
Whitethorn Gdns
Croydon CR0 ... 222 B6
Enfield EN2 ... 17 B6
Whitethorn Pl UB7 ... 104 B5
Whitethorn St E3 ... 97 C2
White Twr Way E1 ... 97 A2
Whiteways NW4 ... 46 D5
Whitewebbs Way
BR5 ... 189 D2
Whitfield Ct
3 Dulwich SE21 ... 183 C6
Redbridge IG1 ... 56 B2
SW4 ... 270 A1
West Barnes SW20 ... 178 D1
Whitfield Gdns W1 ... 239 B4
Whitfield Ho NW8 ... 237 A5
Whitfield Pl W1 ... 239 B5
Whitfield Rd DA7 ... 147 B5
Upton E6 ... 77 C1
Whitfield St
W1 ... 93 C2 239 B4
Whitford Gdns CR4 . 202 D6
Whitgift Ave CR2 ... 221 A3
Whitgift Ct CR2 ... 221 A3
Whitgift Ctr CR0 ... 221 A6
Whitgift Ho
Battersea SW11 ... 267 A2
Croydon CR2 ... 221 A3
Lambeth SE11 ... 260 C4
Whitgift Sch CR2 ... 221 A3
Whitgift St
Croydon CR0 ... 221 A5
SE11 ... 116 B2 260 C4
Whiting Ave IG11 ... 78 D1
Whitings Hill Prim Sch
EN5 ... 12 C6
Whitings Rd EN5 ... 12 C6
Whitings The IG2 ... 57 C4
Whitings Way E6 ... 100 C2
Whitington Ave EC3 . 243 A1
Whitland Rd SM5 ... 202 B1
Whitley Cl TW19 ... 148 A5
Whitley Ho SW1 ... 269 B6
Whitley Rd N17 ... 33 C1
Whitlock Dr SW19 ... 157 A3
Whitman Ho 20 E2 ... 96 C4
Whitman Rd E3 ... 97 A3
Whitmead Cl CR2 ... 221 C2
Whitmore Cl N11 ... 31 B5
Whitmore Gdns
NW10 ... 90 C5

Whitmore High Sch HA1, HA2 42 A1
Whitmore Ho
Friern Barnet N11 30 D6
20 Hoxton E1 95 C6
Whitmore Prim Sch N1 95 B6 235 D5
Whitmore Rd
Beckenham BR3 207 B6
Harrow HA1 42 A2
Hoxton N1 95 C6
Whitnell Ct 7 SW15 156 D6
Whitnell Way SW15 156 D6
Whitney Ave IG4 55 D5
Whitney Ho 6 SE22 139 C2
Whitney Rd E10 53 D2
Whitney Wlk DA14 191 A4
Whitstable Cl
Beckenham BR3 185 B2
Ruislip HA4 61 C6
Whitstable Ho 11 W10 90 D1
Whitstable Pl 9 CR0 221 A4
Whitsters Ho SE1 253 C2
Whitstone La BR3 207 D4
Whittaker 3 NW9 27 D3
Whittaker Ave TW10, TW9 153 D6
Whittaker Ct SW4 270 B1
Whittaker Pl 28 TW10 153 D6
Whittaker Rd
Cheam SM3 217 B5
Forest Gate E6 77 D1
Whittaker St SW1 258 A3
Whittaker Way 19 SE1 118 A2
Whittam Ho SE27 183 A5
Whitta Rd E12 77 D4
Whittell Gdns SE26 162 C1
Whitten Lo N12 30 C6
Whittingham 6 N17 34 B3
Whittingham Com Prim Sch E17 35 A2
Whittingham Ct W4 133 C5
Whittingstall Mans SW6 264 D1
Whittingstall Rd SW6 135 B4 264 D1
Whittington Ave UB4 83 D2
Whittington Ct
Fortis Green N2 48 D4
Penge SE20 184 B1
Whittington Hospl The N19 71 C6
Whittington Mews N12 30 A6
Whittington Rd N22 32 A3
Whittington Way HA5 41 A4
Whittle 4 NW9 27 D3
Whittlebury Cl SM5 218 D1
Whittlebury Ho N4 51 A2
Whittle Cl
Southall UB1 85 D1
Walthamstow E17 53 A2
Whittle Rd
Heston TW5 128 C5
Southall UB2 107 D4
Whittlesea Cl HA3 24 A3
Whittlesea Path HA3 24 A2
Whittlesea Rd HA3 24 A2
Whittlesey St SE1 116 C5 251 B3
WHITTON 152 A4
Whitton NW3 70 D1
Whitton Ave W UB5, UB6 64 B3
Whitton Cl UB6 65 B2
Whitton Dene TW3, TW7 152 B6
Whitton Dr UB6 65 A2
Whitton Manor Rd TW7 152 A5
Whitton Rd
Hounslow TW3 151 D6
Twickenham TW1 153 A4
Whitton Road Rdbt TW1 152 D5
Whitton Sch TW2 151 D2
Whitton Sta TW2 152 A4
Whitton Waye TW2, TW3 151 C5
Whitton Wlk E3 97 C4
Whitwell Ho 11 E5 74 B6
Whitwell Rd E13 99 A4
Whitworth Cres 1 EN3 7 C6
Whitworth Ho SE1 262 B5
Whitworth Rd SE18 144 C5
South Norwood SE25 205 D5
Whitworth St SE10 120 C1
Whorlton Rd SE15 140 B2
Whychcote Point NW2 46 C2
Whymark Ave N22 50 D6
Whytecroft TW5 128 D5
Whyte Mews 5 SM3 217 A2
Whyteville Ho E7 77 B2
Whyteville Rd E7 77 B2
Whytlaw Ho 10 E3 97 B2
Wickersley Rd SW11 137 A3
Wickers Oake SE19 183 D6
Wicker St 24 E1 96 B1
Wicket Rd UB6 87 A4
Wickets The TW15 170 A6
Wicket The CR0 223 C3
Wickfield Ho 32 SE16 118 A4
Wickford Ho 5 E1 96 C3
Wickford St E1 96 C3
Wickford Way E17 52 D5
Wickham Ave
Cheam KT4, SM3 216 C3
Croydon CR0 207 A1
Wickham Chase BR4 208 C2
Wickham Cl Enfield EN3 6 C2
New Malden KT3 199 D4
Stepney E1 96 C2
Wickham Common Prim Sch BR4 225 A4
Wickham Court Rd BR4 224 A6
Wickham Court Sch BR4 224 B4
Wickham Cres BR4 224 A6
Wickham Ct DA16 145 C3
Wickham Gdns SE4 141 B2
Wickham Ho SW15 156 D5
Wickham La SE2 146 A6
Wickham Mews SE4 141 B3
Wickham Rd
Beckenham BR3 207 D6
Brockley SE4 141 B2
Chingford E4 36 A3
Croydon CR0 207 B1
Harrow HA3 24 B1
Wickham St
Bexley DA16 145 C3
Vauxhall SE11 116 B1 260 C2
Welling DA16 146 A4
Wickham Way BR3 208 A4
Wick Ho 1 KT1 175 D2
Wick La Hackney E3 75 B1
Stratford Marsh E3 97 C6
Wickliffe Ave N3 29 A1
Wickliffe Gdns HA9 66 D6
Wicklow Ct SE26 184 C5
Wicklow Ho N16 51 D1
Wicklow St WC1 94 B4 233 C2
Wick Rd Hackney E9 74 D2
Hackney E9 75 A2
Teddington TW11 175 C3
Wicks Cl SE12 187 D6
Wickstead Ho TW8 110 B1
Wicksteed Ho SE1 262 B5
Wick Village 7 E15 75 B2
Wickway Ct 7 SE15 139 D6
Wickwood St SE5 138 D3
Widdenham Rd N7 72 B4
Widdicombe Ave HA2 63 A6
Widdin St E15 76 C1
Widecombe Ct N2 48 B4
Widecombe Gdns IG4 56 A5
Widecombe Ho 32 SE5 139 A3
Widecombe Rd SE9 166 A1
Widecombe Way N2 48 B5
Widegate St E1 243 B3
Widenham Cl HA5 40 C4
Wide Way CR4 203 D6
Widewing Cl TW11 175 B3
Widford 8 NW1 71 B2
Widford Ho N1 234 C3
Widgeon Cl E16 99 B1
Widgeon Path SE28 123 B3
Widley Rd W9 91 C3
Widmer Ct TW5 129 A3
WIDMORE 188 A1
Widmore Lodge Rd BR1 187 D1
Widmore Rd BR1 187 C1
Hillingdon UB8 82 D3
Widnes Ho 6 N7 72 C3
Wieland Rd HA6 22 A3
Wigeon Way UB4 84 D1
Wiggins La TW10 153 C2
Wiggins Mead NW9 27 D3
Wigginton Ave HA9 66 D2
Wigham Ho IG11 79 A1
Wightman Rd N4, N8 50 C4
Wighton Mews TW7 130 C3
Wigley Rd TW13 150 D3
Wigmore Ct 4 W13 109 A5
Wigmore Hall* W1 238 C2
Wigmore Pl W1 93 B1 238 C2
Wigmore Rd SM5 202 C1
Wigmore St W1 93 A1 238 B2
Wigmore Wlk SM5 218 B6
Wigram Ct SW11 267 A2
Wigram Ho 7 E14 119 D6
Wigram Rd E11 55 C3
Wigram Sq E17 54 A6
Wigston Cl N18 33 C5
Wigston Rd E13 99 B3
Wigton Gdns HA7 26 A2
Wigton Pl SE11 261 B1
Wigton Rd E17 35 B2
Wilberforce Ct
Edgware HA8 26 B6
2 SE28 124 C5
Wilberforce Ho 3 SW11 136 B2
Wilberforce Mews 9 SW4 137 D1
Wilberforce Prim Sch W10 91 A4
Wilberforce Rd
Finsbury Pk N4 72 D6
Hendon NW9 46 A3
Highbury N4, N5 73 A5
Wilberforce Way SW19 178 D4
Wilbraham Ho SW8 270 A3
Wilbraham Pl SW1 258 A4
Wilbury Prim Sch N18 33 B5
Wilbury Way N18 33 B5
Wilby Mews W11 113 B5 244 D4
Wilcox Cl SW8 270 B4
Wilcox Gdns TW17 192 B6
Wilcox Ho 5 E3 97 B2
Wilcox Pl SW1 259 B5
Wilcox Rd
Sutton SM1 217 D4
SW8 138 A5 270 A4
Teddington TW11 174 B6
Wildcroft Gdns HA8 25 D4
Wildcroft Manor SW15 156 C4
Wildcroft Rd SW15 156 C4
Wild Ct WC2 94 B1 240 C2
Wilde Cl E8 96 A6
Wilde Pl
Edmonton N13 32 D4
Wandsworth SW18 158 B4
Wilder Cl HA4 40 B1
Wilde Rd DA8 147 D5
Wilderness Mews SW4 137 B1
Wilderness Rd BR7 188 D3
Wilderness The
East Molesey KT8 196 A4
Hampton TW12 173 D6
Wilderton Rd N16 51 C2
Wildes Cotts SM3 217 A2
Wildfell Rd SE6 163 D4
Wild Goose Dr SE14 140 C4
Wild Hatch NW11 47 C3
Wilding Ho 17 E9 74 D2
Wild Marsh Ct EN3 7 A6
Wild's Rents SE1 117 C3 263 A6
Wild St WC2 94 B1 240 C1
Wildwood Cl SE12 164 D4
Wildwood Gr NW3 48 A1
Wildwood Rd NW11 48 A2
Wildwood Rise NW11 48 A1
Wildwood Terr NW3, NW11 48 A1
Wilford Cl EN2 5 B2
Wilford Ho 3 SE18 122 D1
Wilford Rd CR0 205 A2
Wilfred Fienburgh Ho N7 71 D4
Wilfred Owen Cl SW19 180 A4
Wilfred St SW1 115 C3 259 A6
Wilfrid Gdns W3 89 A2
Wilkes Rd 3 TW8 132 A6
Wilkes St E1 95 D2 243 D4
Wilkie Ho SW1 259 D2
Wilkin St Mews NW1 71 B2
Wilkins Cl
Hayes UB3 105 D1
Mitcham CR4 180 C2
Wilkins Ho SW1 269 A6
Wilkinson Cl UB10 83 A6
Wilkinson Ct SW17 180 B6
Wilkinson Gdns CR7 183 C2
Wilkinson Ho
Isleworth TW7 130 D2
N1 235 D3
Twickenham TW2 152 B2
Wilkinson Rd E16 99 C1
Wilkinson St SW8 138 B5 270 C3
Wilkinson Way W4 111 B4
Wilkin St NW5 71 B2
Wilks Gdns CR0 207 A1
Wilks Pl N1 95 C5
Willan Rd N17 33 C1
Willan Wall E16 120 D6
Willard St SW8 137 B2
Willbury Ho 4 N7 71 D3
Willcocks Cl KT9 214 A5
Willcott Rd W3 110 D5
Will Crooks Gdns SE9 143 D1
Willenfield Rd NW10 89 A5
Willenhall Ave EN5 14 A5
Willenhall Ct EN5 14 A5
Willenhall Dr UB3 105 C6
Willenhall Rd SE18 122 D1
Willersley Ave
Blackfen DA15 167 D4
Orpington BR6 227 B5
Willersley Cl DA15 167 D3
WILLESDEN 67 D1
Willesden Community Hospl The NW10 68 A1
WILLESDEN GREEN 90 B6
Willesden Green Sta NW2 68 C2
Willesden Junction Sta NW10 89 D4
Willesden La NW2, NW6 68 D2
Willesden Sports Ctr NW10 90 B6
Willes Rd NW5 71 B2
Willett Cl BR5 211 C3
3 Northolt UB5 84 C4
Willett Ho
7 Newham E13 99 A5
Stockwell SW9 138 A2
Willett Pl CR7 204 C4
Willett Rd CR7 204 C4
Willett Way BR5 211 C3
William Allen Ho HA8 26 B3
William Ash Cl RM9 80 B2
William Atkinson Ho N17 33 C3
William Banfield Ho 10 SW6 135 B3
William Barefoot Dr SE9 166 C1
William Bellamy Jun & Inf Schs RM10 81 C6
William Blake Ho 2 SE15 140 A3
William Bonney Est 10 SW4 137 D1
William Booth Meml Training Coll SE5 139 B3
William Booth Rd SE20 184 A2
William Brown Ct SE27 160 D2
William Byrd Sch UB3 127 A6
William Carey Way HA1 42 C3
William Caslon Ho 28 E2 96 B5
William Channing Ho 6 E2 96 B4
William C Harvey Specl Sch N17 33 B1
William Cl
26 Finchley N2 30 B1
Lewisham SE13 142 A2
Southall UB2 108 A4
William Covell Cl EN2 4 B5
William Ct
4 Belvedere DA17 125 C2
4 Ealing W5 87 C2
Ilford IG6 57 B5
William Davies Prim Sch E7 77 D2
William Davis Prim Sch 19 E2 96 A3
William Dr HA7 25 B5
William Dromey Ct NW6 69 B1
William Dunbar Ho NW6 91 B5
William Dyce Mews 1 SW16 181 D6
William Ellis Sch NW5 71 A5
William Ellis Way 16 SE16 118 A3
William Evans Ho 9 SE8 118 D2
William Ford CE Jun Sch RM10 81 C1
William Foster La DA16 146 A3
William Gdns SW15 156 B6
William Guy Gdns 47 E3 97 D4
William Harvey Ho 1 SW19 157 A3
William Ho N13 32 D4
William Hogarth Sch The 15 W4 111 C1
William Hunt Mans SW13 134 C6
William IV St WC2 116 A6 250 A5
William Margrie Cl 1 SE15 140 A3
William Marsden Ho 2 SE27 182 D6
William Mews SW1 114 D4 247 D1
William Morley Cl E6 99 D6
William Morris Acad W6 112 D1
William Morris Cl E17 53 B6
William Morris Gallery* E17 53 C6
William Morris Ho W6 134 D6
William Morris Prim Sch CR4 203 D6
William Morris Sch E17 35 A2
William Morris Way SW6 136 A3
William Patten Prim Sch 9 N16 73 D6
William Perkin Ct UB6 64 C2
William Pl 37 E3 97 B5
William Rainbird Ho 9 N17 33 D3
William Rathbone Ho 3 E2 96 B4
William Rd
Regent's Pk NW1 93 C4 232 A1
Sutton SM1 218 A3
Wimbledon SW19 179 A3
William Rushbrooke Ho 4 SE16 118 A2
Williams Ave E17 35 B2
William Saville Ho 2 NW6 91 B5
William's Bldgs 1 E2 96 C3
Williams Cl SW6 135 A5 264 B4
Williams Coll EC1 241 B3

Williams Dr TW3 129 C1
Williams Gr
Kingston u T KT6 197 C3
Wood Green N22 32 C2
Williams Ho
10 Bow E3 97 C4
9 Hackney E9 96 B6
14 Streatham SW2 160 C3
7 Tottenham N17 33 D3
Willesden NW2 68 C5
Williams La
Morden SM4 202 A4
Mortlake SW14 133 A3
William Smith Ho 10
DA17 125 C3
Williamson Cl SE10 120 D1
Williamson Ct SE17 262 A1
Williamson Rd N4 50 D3
Williamson St N7 72 A4
William Sq 15 SE16 119 A6
Williams Rd UB2 107 A2
William's Rd W13 109 A5
William St
Barking IG11 79 A1
Carshalton SM5 218 D5
SW1 114 D4 247 D1
Tottenham N17 33 D3
Walthamstow E10 53 D3
Williams Terr CR0 220 C2
William Torbitt Prim Sch
IG2 57 D4
William Tyndale Prim
Sch 27 N1 72 D1
William Wilberforce Ho
1 SE27 182 D6
William Winter Ct 29
SW2 160 C4
William Wood Ho 3
SE26 162 C1
Willifield Way NW11 47 C4
Willingale Cl IG8 37 C4
Willingdon Rd N22 32 D1
Willingham Cl 4
NW5 71 C3
Willingham Terr
NW5 71 C3
Willingham Way
KT1 176 C1
Willington Ct E5 75 A5
Willington Rd SW9 138 A2
Willington Sch 13
SW19 179 B5
Willis Ave SM2, SM5 218 C2
Willis Ct CR7 204 C3
Willis Ho 2 Ilford E12 78 C5
8 Poplar E14 119 D6
Willis Rd E15 98 D5
Thornton Heath CR0 205 A2
Willis St E14 97 D1
Willis Yd N14 15 D4
Willlows The CR0 223 A6
Will Miles Ct 6
SW19 180 A3
Willmore End SW19 179 D1
Willoughby Ave CR0 220 B4
Willoughby Gr N17 34 B3
Willoughby Ho EC2 242 C3
34 Wapping E1 118 B5
Willoughby La N17 34 B3
Willoughby Mews
N17 34 B3
Willoughby Park Rd
N17 34 B3
Willoughby Rd
Hampstead NW3 70 B4
Hornsey N8 50 C5
Kingston u T KT2 176 B2
Twickenham TW1 153 D6
Willoughby St WC1 240 A3
Willoughbys The
SW14 133 C1
Willoughby Way
SE7 121 B2
Willow Ave
Barnes SW13 133 D3
DA15 168 A5
Yiewsley UB7 104 B6
Willowbank SW6 135 A2
Willow Bank TW10 153 B1
Willowbank Rd
SE15 139 D6
Willowbay Cl EN5 12 D5
Willow Bridge Rd N1 73 A2
Willow Brook Prim Sch
E10 53 C1
Willowbrook Rd
Southall UB2 107 C3
Stanwell TW19 148 A2
Willow Bsns Ctr
CR4 202 D3
Willow Bsns Pk
SE26 162 C1
Willow Cl BR2 210 B4
Brentford TW8 131 C6
Buckhurst Hill IG9 21 D1
12 Catford SE6 164 D3
Sidcup DA5 169 B5
Willow Cotts
Carshalton CR4 202 D2
Feltham TW13 151 A1
Richmond TW9 132 C6
Willowcourt Ave HA3 43 B4
Willowcroft SE3 142 D1
Willow Ct
Ashford TW16 171 C3
5 Beckenham BR3 185 C2
Brixton SW9 138 C4
Chiswick W4 133 C5
8 Dagenham RM8 58 D2
EC2 243 A6
Edgware HA8 26 A6
6 Finchley N12 29 D6
Harrow HA3 24 D2
Headstone HA2 24 A1
Ilford IG1 79 A3
Islington N7 72 B3
Kingston u T KT3 198 D6
8 London E11 76 C6
Mitcham CR4 202 C5
40 Paddington W2 91 C2
3 Streatham SW16 160 B1
Thornton Heath CR7 205 B4
Willow Ctr The CR4 202 D3
Willow Dean HA5 22 D1
Willowdene
Highgate N6 48 D2
1 Peckham SE15 140 B4
5 SE15 140 B5
Willow Dene WD23 8 C4
Willowdene Cl TW2 152 A4
Willowdene Ct N20 14 A4
Willow Dene Sch
SE18 145 C4
Willow Dr EN5 1 A1
Willow End
Northwood HA6 22 A4
Surbiton KT6 198 A1
Totteridge N20 13 C2
Willow Farm La
SW15 134 B2
Willowfield Sch E17 52 D6
Willowfields Cl
SE18 123 C1
Willow Gdns
Heston TW5 129 C4
Ruislip HA4 61 D6
Willow Gn
Borehamwood WD6 11 B6
Grahame Pk NW9 27 C2
Willow Gr BR7 188 D4
Newham E13 99 A5
Ruislip HA4 39 D1
Willow Hall NW3 70 B4
Willowhayne Dr
KT12 194 B2
Willowhayne Gdns
KT4 216 C4
Willow Ho TW14 150 B6
Willow Ho
17 Finchley N2 30 B1
9 Maitland Pk NW3 70 D2
North Kensington W10 90 D3
Teddington TW11 175 C3
Willow La
Mitcham CR4 202 D3
Woolwich SE18 122 C2
Willow Lo
6 Ashford TW16 171 D3
Fulham SW6 134 D4
New Barnet EN5 14 A6
Putney SW15 134 B2
Willow Lodge 10
SW8 137 B2
Willow Manor SM1 217 B4
Willowmead Cl W5 87 D2
Willowmere
Esher KT10 212 A4
Ladywell SE13 163 D6
Willow Mount CR0 221 C5
Willow Pl
SW1 115 C2 259 B4
Willow Rd
Dagenham RM6 59 A3
Ealing W5 110 A4
Enfield EN1 5 C3
Hampstead NW3 70 B4
New Malden KT3 199 A5
Wallington SM6 219 B1
Willows Ave SM4 201 D4
Willows Cl HA5 22 C1
Willows Ct 3 SW19 179 C3
Willows Sch The UB4 84 D3
Willow St
Broadgate
EC2 95 C3 243 A6
Chingford E4 20 B4
Willows Terr NW10 89 D5
Willows The
Beckenham BR3 185 C2
Claygate KT10 212 C2
Loughton IG10 21 D6
Wallend E12 78 C1
Whetstone N20 14 A1
Willowtree Cl UB10 61 A5
Willow Tree Cl
Hayes UB4 84 C3
Northolt UB5 63 A2
14 Old Ford E3 97 B6
Wandsworth SW18 157 D3
Willow Tree Ct
DA14 189 D5
5 Wembley HA0 65 D3
Willow Tree La UB4 84 C3
Willow Tree Prim Sch
UB5 63 A2
Willow Tree Rd UB4 84 D2
Willowtree Way
SW16 182 C2
Willow Tree Wlk
BR1 187 B2
Willow Vale BR7 188 D4
Shepherd's Bush W12 112 A5
Willow View SW19 180 B2
Willow Way
Finchley N3 29 D3
Forest Hill SE26 162 C1
9 Shepherd's Bush
W11 112 D6
Sunbury TW16 194 A5
Twickenham TW2 151 D2
Wembley HA0 65 A5
West Ewell KT19 215 B2
Willow Wlk
Bermondsey
SE1 117 D2 263 C4
Cheam SM1, SM3 217 B5
15 Finchley N2 30 B1
Harringay N15 50 D5
Locksbottom BR6 226 D5
Southgate N21 16 B5
Walthamstow E17 53 B4
Willow Wood Cres
SE25 205 C3
Willridge Ct E11 54 B2
Willrose Cres SE2 124 B1
Willsbridge Ct 1
SE15 139 D6
Wills Cres TW3 151 D5
Wills Gr NW7 28 B5
Will Thorne Pav The
E16 100 A1
Wilman Gr E8 74 A1
Wilmar Cl UB4 83 B3
Wilmar Gdns BR4 207 D1
Wilmcote Ho W2 91 D2
Wilment Ct NW2 68 C5
Wilmer Cl KT2 176 B5
Wilmer Cres KT2 176 B5
Wilmer Gdns 22 N1 95 C6
Wilmer Ho 6 E3 97 A5
Wilmer Lea Cl E15 76 B1
Wilmer Pl N16 73 D6
Wilmers Ct 5 NW10 89 B6
Wilmer Way N14 31 D5
Wilmington Ave W4 133 B5
Wilmington Ct
SW16 182 A3
Wilmington Gdns
IG11 79 C1
Wilmington Sq
WC1 94 C4 234 A1
Wilmington St WC1 234 A1
Wilmot Cl Finchley N2 30 A1
SE15 140 A5
Wilmot Ho 14 SM2 218 A2
Wilmot Pl
Camden Town NW1 71 C1
Wilmot Pl *continued*
Ealing W7 108 C5
Wilmot Rd Leyton E10 75 D6
Tottenham N17 51 B6
Wallington SM5 218 D3
Wilmot St E2 96 B3
Wilmount St SE18 122 D2
Wilna Rd SW18 158 A4
Wilnett Ct 4 RM6 58 B2
Wilnett Villas 5 RM6 58 B2
Wilsham St
W11 113 A5 244 A4
Wilshaw Cl NW4 46 A6
Wilshaw Ho 10 SE8 141 C5
Wilshaw St SE14 141 C4
Wilsmere Dr
Harrow HA3 24 C3
Northolt UB5 63 A3
Wilson Ave CR4 180 C2
Wilson Cl
Croydon CR2 221 B3
Wembley HA9 44 B2
Wilson Ct 9 SE28 123 A3
Wilson Dr HA9 44 B2
Wilson Gdns HA1 42 A2
Wilson Gr SE16 118 B4
Wilson Ho
30 Clapham SW8 137 D3
2 SE7 143 C6
South Hampstead NW6 70 A1
Wilson Rd
Camberwell SE5 139 C4
Chessington KT9 214 B2
Newham E6 99 D4
Redbridge IG1 56 B2
Wilson's Ave 4 N17 33 D1
Wilson's Pl E14 97 B1
Wilson's Rd W6 112 D1
Wilson's Sch SM6 220 A2
Wilson St
Broadgate
EC2 95 B2 242 D4
Southgate N21 16 C4
Walthamstow E17 54 A4
Wilstone Cl UB4 85 A3
Wiltern Ct NW2 69 A2
Wilthorne Gdns
RM10 81 D1
Wilton Ave W4 111 C1
Wilton Cres
Merton SW19 179 B2
SW1 115 A4 248 A1
Wilton Ct
3 Edgware HA8 26 D5
Muswell Hill N10 31 A1
4 Richmond TW10 154 A6
7 Stepney E1 96 B1
7 Woodford IG8 37 A4
Wilton Est E8 74 A2
Wilton Gdns
East Molesey KT8 195 C6
Walton-on-T KT12 194 D1
Wilton Gr
Merton SW19 179 B2
New Malden KT3 199 D3
Wilton Ho
8 Camberwell
SE22 139 C2
Chislehurst BR7 189 B2
Ealing W13 109 B6
Wilton Mews
SW1 115 A3 258 B6
Wilton Par TW13 150 B2
Wilton Pl
2 Beckenham BR3 208 A6
4 Harrow HA1 42 D3
SW1 115 A4 248 A1
Wilton Rd
Abbey Wood SE2 124 C2
Cockfosters EN4 2 D1
Hounslow TW4 128 D2
Mitcham SW19 180 C3
Muswell Hill N10 31 A1
Westminster
SW1 115 C2 259 A4
Wilton Row SW1 248 A1
Wilton Sq N1 95 B6 235 C6
Wilton St
SW1 115 B3 258 C6
Wilton Terr SW1 258 A6
Wilton Villas N1 235 C5
Wilton Way E8 74 A2
Wiltshire Cl
Edgware NW7 27 D5
SW3 257 C3
Wiltshire Ct
Barking IG11 79 A2
2 Finsbury Pk N4 50 B1
Wiltshire Gdns
Stoke Newington N4 51 A3
Twickenham TW2 152 A3
Wiltshire La
Pinner HA5 40 A5
Ruislip HA4 39 D6
Wiltshire Rd
Brixton SW9 138 C2
Thornton Heath CR7 204 C6
Wiltshire Row
N1 95 B6 235 D5
Wilverley Cres KT3 199 C3
Wimbart Rd SW2 160 B4
WIMBLEDON 179 B4
Wimbledon Bridge
SW19 179 B4
Wimbledon Central
SW19 179 B4
Wimbledon Chase Prim
Sch 2 SW20 179 A2
Wimbledon Chase Sta
SW20 179 A1
Wimbledon Cl 2
SW20 178 D3
Wimbledon Coll
SW19 178 D3
Wimbledon Common★
SW19 178 B6
Wimbledon Common
Prep Sch SW19 178 D3
Wimbledon High Sch
SW19 179 A4
Wimbledon Hill Rd
SW19 179 B4
Wimbledon Lawn Tennis
Mus★ SW19 157 A1
Wimbledon L Ctr
SW19 179 D4
Wimbledon Mus★
SW19 179 A4
Wimbledon Park Ct
SW19 157 B3
Wimbledon Park
Montessori Sch
SW18 157 C2
Wimbledon Park Prim
Sch SW19 157 D2
Wimbledon Park Rd SW18,
SW19 157 B3
Wimbledon Park Side
SW19 156 D3
Wimbledon Park Sta
SW19 157 C1
Wimbledon Rd
SW17 180 A6
Wimbledon Sch of Art 1
SW19 179 A2
Wimbledon Sch of Art
Annexe 14 SW19 179 C3
Wimbledon Sta
SW19 179 B4
Wimbledon Stad
SW17 180 A6
Wimbledon Stadium
Bsns Ctr SW17 157 D1
Wimbledon Windmill
Mus★ SW19 156 C1
Wimbolt St E2 96 A4
Wimborne 2 DA14 190 B6
Wimborne Ave
Hayes UB4 84 B1
Southall UB2 107 C2
St Paul's Cray BR5,
BR7 211 D5
Wimborne Cl
Buckhurst Hill IG9 21 C2
Lewisham SE12 164 D6
North Cheam KT4 200 C1
Wimborne Ct 1 UB5 63 C2
Wimborne Dr
Pinner HA5 41 A2
Queensbury NW9 44 C6
Wimborne Gdns W13 87 B2
Wimborne Ho
Canning Town E16 120 D6
Croydon CR0 206 C4
Marylebone NW1 237 B5
South Lambeth SW8 270 D3
Upper Tooting SW12 159 C1

Wimborne Rd
Edmonton N9 . . . . 18 A2
Tottenham N17 . . . . 33 C1
Wimborne Way BR3 . . 207 A5
Wimbourne Ct
Mitcham SW19 . . . . . . 180 B3
N1 . . . . 235 C4
South Croydon CR2 . . 221 C2
Wimbourne St
N1 . . . . 95 B5 235 C4
Wimbush Ho 3 N12 . . 29 D5
Wimpole Cl
Bromley BR2 . . . . 209 C5
1 Kingston u T KT1 . . 176 C1
Wimpole Mews
W1 . . . . 93 B2 238 C3
Wimpole St
W1 . . . . 93 B1 238 C2
Wimshurst Cl CR0 . . . 204 A1
Winans Wlk SW9 . . . . 138 C3
Winant Ho 19 E14 . . . 119 D6
Wincanton Cres UB5 . . 63 C3
Wincanton Ct 2 N11 . . 31 A4
Wincanton Gdns IG6 . . 56 D6
Wincanton Rd SW18 . 157 B4
Winchcombe Rd
SM5 . . . . 202 C1
Winchcomb Gdns
SE9 . . . . 143 D2
Winchelsea Ave
DA7 . . . . 147 B5
Winchelsea Cl
SW15 . . . . 156 D6
Winchelsea Ho 16
SE16 . . . . 118 C4
Winchelsea Rd
Becontree NW10 . . . . . . 89 B6
Forest Gate E7 . . . . 77 A4
Tottenham N17 . . . . 51 C6
Winchelsey Rise
CR2 . . . . 221 D2
Winchendon Rd
Fulham
SW6 . . . . . 135 B4 264 D2
Teddington TW11,
TW12 . . . . 174 B6
Winchester Ave
Brondesbury NW6 . . . . . 69 A1
Heston TW5 . . . . 129 B6
Queensbury NW9 . . . . . 44 C6
Winchester Cl
Beckenham BR2 . . . . . 208 D6
Enfield EN1 . . . . 17 C6
Kingston u T KT2 . . . . 176 D3
11 Newham E6 . . . . . . 100 B1
SE17 . . . . 261 D3
Winchester Ct
15 Belvedere DA17 . . 125 C1
5 Higham Hill E17 . . . . 35 A2
Richmond TW9 . . . . 132 B2
W8 . . . . 245 C2
Winchester Dr HA5 . . . 40 D4
Winchester Ho
5 Barking IG11 . . . . . . 80 A1
Bayswater W2 . . . . . . 236 A1
Chelsea SW3 . . . . 266 D5
1 Greenwich SE18 . . 143 D5
24 Tower Hamlets E3 . . . 97 B4
Twickenham TW1 . . . . 153 C4
Winchester Mews
KT4 . . . . 216 D6
Winchester Pal★
SE1 . . . . 252 C4
Winchester Pk BR2 . 208 D6
Winchester Pl
6 Dalston E8 . . . . 73 D3
Highgate N6 . . . . 49 B1
Winchester Rd
Beckenham BR2 . . . . . 208 D6
Bexley DA7 . . . . 146 D3
Chingford E4 . . . . 36 A3
Edmonton N9 . . . . 18 A3
Harlington UB3 . . . . . 127 C5
Harrow HA3 . . . . 44 A5
Highgate N6 . . . . 49 B1
Ilford IG1 . . . . 79 B5
Northwood HA6 . . . . . . 40 A6
South Hampstead NW3 70 B1
St Margarets TW1 . . . . 153 B5
Twickenham TW13 . . . . 151 B1
Walton-on-T KT12 . . . 194 A1
Winchester Sq SE1 . 252 C4
Winchester St
Acton W3 . . . . 111 A4
SW1 . . . . 115 B1 258 D2
Winchester Wlk SE1 252 C4
Winchet Wlk CR0 . . . 206 C3
Winchfield Cl HA3 . . . 43 C3
Winchfield Ho
SW15 . . . . 155 D5
Winchfield Rd SE26 . . 185 A5
Winch Ho
Isle of Dogs E14 . . . . . 119 D3
SW10 . . . . 266 B4
Winchilsea Cres
KT8 . . . . 174 A1
Winchilsea Ho NW8 . 229 D1
WINCHMORE HILL . . . 16 D4
Winchmore Hill Rd N14,
N21 . . . . 16 A4
Winchmore Hill Sta
N21 . . . . 16 D4
Winchmore Sch N21 . . 17 A2
Winchmore Villas
N21 . . . . 16 B4
Winchstone Cl
TW17 . . . . 192 B5
Winckley Cl HA3 . . . . . 44 B4
Wincott St
SE11 . . . . 116 C2 261 B3
Wincrofts Dr SE9 . . . 145 B1
Windall Cl SE20 . . . . . 184 A2
Windborough Rd
SM5 . . . . 219 A1
Windcott Ct HA3 . . . . . 43 C2
Windermere NW1 . . 231 D2
12 Putney SW15 . . . . 156 D5
Windermere Ave
Golders Green N3 . . . . . 47 C6
Kensal Rise NW6 . . . . . 91 A6
Merton SW19 . . . . 201 D6
Ruislip HA4 . . . . 40 D2
Wembley HA9 . . . . 43 C1
Windermere Cl BR6 . 226 D5
East Bedfont TW14 . . 149 D3
Stanwell TW19 . . . . . . 148 A2
Windermere Ct
Barnes SW13 . . . . 133 D6
Barnet EN5 . . . . 1 D1
Carshalton SM5 . . . . . 219 A5
Wembley HA9 . . . . 43 C2
Windermere Gdns
IG4 . . . . 56 A4
Windermere Gr HA9 . . 43 C1
Windermere Hall
HA8 . . . . 26 B5
Windermere Ho
Isleworth TW1 . . . . . . 152 D6
Tower Hamlets E3 . . . . 97 B3
Windermere Point 3
SE15 . . . . 140 C5
Windermere Rd
Brentford W5 . . . . 109 C3
Croydon CR0 . . . . 205 D1
Kingston u T SW15 . . . 177 C5
Mitcham SW16 . . . . . 181 D1
Muswell Hill N10 . . . . . 31 B2
Southall UB1 . . . . 85 B2
Upper Holloway N19 . . . 71 C6
West Wickham BR4 . . 224 C6
Windermere Way
UB7 . . . . 104 B5
Winders Rd SW11 . . . 136 C3
Windfield Cl SE26 . . . 184 D6
Windham Rd TW9 . . . 132 B2
Winding Way RM8 . . . 80 C5
Windlass Pl SE8 . . . . 119 A2
Windlesham Gr
SW19 . . . . 156 D3
Windley Cl SE23 . . . . 162 C2
Windmill WC1 . . . . . . 240 C4
Windmill Alley 7
W4 . . . . 111 C2
Windmill Ave UB2 . . . 108 A4
Windmill Bridge Ho 1
CR0 . . . . 205 C1
Windmill Bsns Ctr
UB2 . . . . 108 A5
Windmill Bsns Village
TW16 . . . . 171 C2
Windmill Cl
Ashford TW16 . . . . . . 171 C3
12 Bermondsey SE1 . 118 A2
Kingston u T KT6 . . . . 197 C2
4 Lewisham SE13 . . 142 A3
Windmill Ct
Brentford W5 . . . . 109 C2
Brondesbury NW2 . . . . . 69 A2
Windmill Ct *continued*
Bushey WD23 . . . . 8 B3
Windmill Dr
Clapham SW4 . . . . 159 B6
Cricklewood NW2 . . . . . 69 A5
Windmill Gdns
Brixton SW2 . . . . 160 B5
Enfield EN2 . . . . 4 C2
Windmill Gr CR0 . . . . 205 A3
Windmill Hill
Enfield EN2 . . . . 5 A2
1 Hampstead NW3 . . . 70 A4
Hampstead NW3 . . . . . . 70 A5
Ruislip HA4 . . . . 39 D1
Windmill Ho
4 Millwall E14 . . . . . 119 C2
SE1 . . . . 251 B3
Windmill La
Barnet Gate EN5 . . . . . 11 D5
BR2 . . . . 225 C4
Bushey WD23 . . . . 8 C3
Greenford UB6 . . . . 86 A2
Isleworth TW7, UB2,
W7 . . . . 108 C2
Southall UB2 . . . . 108 A4
Stratford E15 . . . . 76 B2
Thames Ditton KT7 . . . 197 B2
Windmill Lo TW16 . . . 171 C2
Windmill Pas 10 W4 . . 111 C2
Windmill Pl UB1 . . . . . 108 A5
Windmill Rd
Brentford TW8, W5 . . 109 C1
Charlton TW16 . . . . . . 171 C2
Chiswick W4 . . . . 111 C2
Edmonton N18 . . . . 33 B6
Hampton TW12 . . . . . . 174 A5
Mitcham CR4 . . . . 203 C5
Roehampton SW19 . . . 156 B1
Thornton Heath CR0 . 205 A2
Wandsworth SW18 . . . 158 B5
Windmill Rd W
TW16 . . . . 171 C1
Windmill Rise KT2 . . 176 D3
Windmill Row SE11 . 261 A1
Windmill St
Bloomsbury
W1 . . . . 93 D2 239 C3
Bushey WD23 . . . . 8 C3
Windmill Terr TW17 . . 193 C2
Windmill Trad Est
CR4 . . . . 203 C5
Windmill Way HA4 . . . 39 D1
Windmill Wlk SE1 . . . 251 B2
Windmore Cl HA0 . . . . 65 A3
Windover Ave NW9 . . . 45 B5
Windrose Cl SE16 . . . 118 D4
Windrush KT3 . . . . . . 199 A5
Windrush Cl
Battersea SW11 . . . . . 136 B1
Chiswick W4 . . . . 133 A5
4 Hackney E8 . . . . 74 A1
Ickenham UB10 . . . . . . 60 B4
Tottenham N17 . . . . 33 C2
Windrush Ho NW8 . . 236 D4
Windrush La SE23 . . 162 D1
Windrush Prim Sch
SE28 . . . . 124 B5
Windrush Rd NW10 . . . 89 B6
Windrush Sq SW9 . . . 138 C1
Windsock Cl 1
SE16 . . . . 119 B2
Windsor Ave
Cheam SM3 . . . . 217 A5
East Molesey KT8 . . . 195 C6
Edgware HA8 . . . . 10 D1
Higham Hill E17 . . . . . . 35 A1
Hillingdon UB10 . . . . . . 60 D1
Merton SW19 . . . . 180 A2
New Malden KT3 . . . . 199 A4
Windsor Cl
Brentford TW8 . . . . . . 131 B6
Chislehurst BR7 . . . . . 188 D5
Harrow HA2 . . . . 63 C5
Hendon N3 . . . . 29 A1
Pinner HA6 . . . . 22 A1
West Norwood SE27 . 183 A6
Windsor Cres
Harrow HA2 . . . . 63 C5
Wembley HA9 . . . . 66 D5
Windsor Ct
Battersea SW11 . . . . . 136 B3
Bayswater W2 . . . . 245 C6
Bickley BR1 . . . . 210 A6
Bushey WD23 . . . . 8 A4
Chelsea SW3 . . . . 257 B2
2 Clapham SW4 . . . . 137 C1
Windsor Ct *continued*
Edgware HA8 . . . . 26 B3
Friern Barnet N11 . . . . . 30 D5
Fulham SW6 . . . . 135 A2
Northolt UB5 . . . . 63 B3
Osidge N14 . . . . 15 C4
20 Rotherhithe SE16 . 118 D5
South Norwood SE19 . 183 C2
Sunbury TW16 . . . . . . 172 A3
Temple Fortune NW11 . . 47 A3
Walthamstow E17 . . . . . 53 B6
4 Wandsworth
SW18 . . . . 157 C6
West Hampstead NW3 . 69 C4
5 West Wickham
BR4 . . . . 207 D1
Windsor Ctr The
SE27 . . . . 183 A6
Windsor Dr EN4 . . . . . 14 D5
Windsor Gdns
Hayes UB3 . . . . 105 B3
Paddington W9 . . . . 91 C3
Wallington CR0 . . . . . 220 A5
Windsor Gr SE27 . . . . 183 A6
Windsor Hall 11 E16 . 121 B5
Windsor Ho
4 Acton Green W4 . . 111 A1
Brondesbury NW2 . . . . 69 A2
4 Globe Town E2 . . . . 96 D4
2 Hendon NW4 . . . . . . 28 D1
7 Northolt UB5 . . . . . . 63 C2
Queensbury NW9 . . . . . 44 C5
Regent's Pk NW1 . . . . 231 D2
Shoreditch N1 . . . . . . 235 B4
Stanmore HA7 . . . . 25 B5
Stoke Newington N4 . . . 51 A1
Windsor Lo KT3 . . . . . 199 A4
Windsor Mews
Catford SE6 . . . . 164 A3
Forest Hill SE23 . . . . . 163 A3
Windsor Park Rd
UB3 . . . . 127 D5
Windsor Pk SW19 . . . 180 A2
Windsor Pl SW1 . . . . 259 B4
Windsor Rd
Ashford TW16 . . . . . . 172 A4
Barnet EN5 . . . . 12 D5
Chingford E4 . . . . 35 D6
Cranford TW4, TW5 . . 128 C3
DA6 . . . . 147 A1
Dagenham RM8 . . . . . . 81 A5
Ealing W5 . . . . 110 A6
Forest Gate E7 . . . . 77 C3
Harrow HA3 . . . . 24 B2
Hendon N3 . . . . 29 A1
Ilford IG1 . . . . 79 A4
Kingston u T KT2 . . . . 176 A3
Leyton E10 . . . . 75 D6
Palmers Green N13 . . . . 16 C1
Richmond TW9 . . . . . . 132 B3
Southall UB2 . . . . 107 B3
South Norwood CR7 . . 182 D1
Teddington TW11 . . . . 174 B5
Tottenham N17 . . . . 34 A1
Upper Holloway N7 . . . . 72 A5
Wanstead E11 . . . . 77 A6
Willesden NW2 . . . . 68 B2
Worcester Pk KT4 . . . 216 A6
Windsor St
N1 . . . . 94 D6 234 D6
Windsor Terr
N1 . . . . 95 A4 235 B2
Windsor Way
W14 . . . . . . 113 A2 254 A4
Windsor Wharf E9 . . . . 75 B3
Windsor Wlk
Camberwell SE5 . . . . . 139 B3
Walton-on-T KT12 . . . 194 D1
Windspoint Dr SE15 . . 140 B6
Windus Rd N16 . . . . . . 51 D1
Windus Wlk N16 . . . . . 51 D1
Windy Ridge BR1 . . . 188 A2
Windy Ridge Cl
SW19 . . . . 178 D5
Wine Cl E1 . . . . 118 C6
Wine Office Ct EC4 . . 241 B2
Winery La KT1 . . . . . . 198 B6
Winey Cl KT9 . . . . 213 C1
Winfield Ho 3
SW11 . . . . 136 B3
Winford Ct 16 SE15 . . 140 A4
Winford Ho E3 . . . . 75 B1
Winford Par 6 UB1 . . . 85 D1
Winforton St SE10 . . . 142 A4
Winfrith Rd SW18 . . . 158 A3
Wingate Cres CR0 . . . 204 A3
Wingate Ho
26 Bromley E3 . . . . 97 D4
8 Stoke Newington
N16 . . . . 73 B4
Wingate Rd
Hammersmith W6 . . . . 112 B3
Ilford IG1 . . . . 78 D3
Sidcup DA14 . . . . 190 C4
Wingate Trad Est 11
N17 . . . . 33 D3
Wingfield Ct
5 Blackwall E14 . . . . 120 B6
Sidcup DA15 . . . . 167 D3
Wingfield Ho
Paddington NW6 . . . . . 91 D5
16 Spitalfields E2 . . . . 95 D4
Wingfield Mews
SE15 . . . . 140 A2
Wingfield Prim Sch
SE3 . . . . 143 B2
Wingfield Rd
Kingston u T KT2 . . . . 176 C4
Leyton E15 . . . . 76 C4
Walthamstow E17 . . . . . 53 D4
Wingfield St SE15 . . . 140 A2
Wingfield Way HA4 . . . 62 B2
Wingford Rd SW2 . . . . 160 A5
Wingham 3 NW5 . . . . . 71 A2
Wingham Ho 3
SE26 . . . . 184 B5
Wingmore Rd SE24 . . 139 A2
Wingrad Ho 18 E1 . . . . 96 C2
Wingrave SE17 . . . . . 262 C3
Wingrave Rd W6 . . . . 134 C6
Wingreen 15 NW8 . . . . 91 D6
Wingrove Ho E4 . . . . . 19 D4
Wingrove Rd SE6 . . . . 164 C2
Wings Cl SM1 . . . . 217 C4
Winicotte Ho W2 . . . 236 D4
Winifred Cl EN5 . . . . . . 11 D5
Winifrede Paul Ho 7
NW5 . . . . 71 B4
Winifred Pl N12 . . . . . . 30 A5
Winifred Rd
Dagenham RM8 . . . . . . 59 A1
Hampton TW12 . . . . . . 173 C6
Merton SW19 . . . . 179 C2
Winifred St E16 . . . . . 122 B5
Winifred Terr
Enfield EN1 . . . . 17 D4
15 Newham E13 . . . . . . 99 A5
Winkfield Rd
Newham E13 . . . . 99 B5
Wood Green N22 . . . . . 32 C2
Winkley Ct
Cranley Gdns N10 . . . . . 49 B5
Harrow HA2 . . . . 63 C5
Winkley St 6 E2 . . . . . 96 B5
Winkworth Cotts 14
E1 . . . . 96 C3
Winlaton Rd BR1 . . . . 186 B6
Winmill Rd RM8 . . . . . 81 B5
Winn Bridge Cl IG8 . . . 37 D2
Winn Common Rd
SE18 . . . . 145 C6
Winnett St W1 . . . . . . 249 C6
Winningales Ct IG5 . . . 56 A6
Winnings Wlk UB5 . . . . 63 A2
Winnington Cl N2 . . . . 48 B3
Winnington Ho
19 Kensal Town W10 . . . 91 A3
8 SE5 . . . . 139 A5
Winnington Rd
Enfield EN3 . . . . 6 C6
Hampstead Garden Suburb
N2 . . . . 48 B3
Winnipeg Dr 3 BR6 . 227 D2
Winnipeg Ho UB4 . . . . 84 B3
Winn Rd SE12 . . . . 165 B3
Winns Ave E17 . . . . 53 B6
Winns Mews N15 . . . . . 51 C5
Winns Prim Sch E17 . . . 35 B1
Winns Terr E17 . . . . . . 53 C6
Winsbeach E17 . . . . . . 36 B1
Winscombe Cres W5 . . 87 D3
Winscombe Ct W5 . . . . 87 D3
Winscombe St N19 . . . 71 B6
Winscombe Way HA7 . 25 A5
Winsford Rd SE6 . . . . 163 B1
Winsford Terr N18 . . . . 33 B5
Winsham Gr SW11 . . . 159 A6
Winsham Ho NW1 . . . 232 D2
Winslade Ho 4 E5 . . . . 74 B6
Winslade Rd SW2 . . . 160 A6
Winslade Way SE6 . . 163 D4
Winsland Mews W2 . . 236 C2

Winsland St
W2 92 B1 236 C2
Winsley St W1 239 B2
Winslow SE17 263 A1
Winslow Cl
2 Neasden NW10 67 C5
Pinner HA5 40 B3
Winslow Gr E4 20 C2
Winslow Rd W6 134 C6
Winslow Way TW13 151 A1
Winsmoor Ct EN2 4 D2
Winsor Prim Sch E6 100 C1
Winsor Terr E6 100 C2
Winstanley Rd SW11 136 B2
Winston Ave NW9 45 C2
Winston Churchill Britain at War Experience★
SE1 253 A3
Winston Cl
Harrow HA3 24 D4
Romford RM7 59 D5
Winston Ct 7 BR1 187 B2
Harrow HA3 23 D3
Winston Ho WC1 239 D6
Winston House Prep Sch
E18 37 A1
Winston Rd N16 73 B4
Winston Way IG1 79 A5
Winston Way Prim Sch
IG1 78 D5
Winston Wlk 2 W4 111 B2
Winter Ave E6 100 A6
Winterberry Ct 22
N12 29 D6
Winterborne Ave
BR6 227 B5
Winterbourne Ho
W11 244 A5
Winterbourne Inf Sch
CR7 204 C5
Winterbourne Jun Boys' Sch CR7 204 C5
Winterbourne Jun Girls' Sch CR7 204 C5
Winterbourne Rd
Dagenham RM8 80 C6
Forest Hill SE6 163 B3
Thornton Heath CR7 204 C5
Winter Box Wlk
TW10 154 B6
Winterbrook Rd
SE24 161 A5
Winterburn Cl N11 31 A4
Winterfold Cl SW19 157 A2
Wintergreen Cl 7
E6 100 A2
Winterleys 7 NW6 91 B5
Winter Lo 17 SE16 118 A1
Winter's Ct E4 19 D1
Winterslow Ho 20
SE5 139 A3
Winters Rd KT7 197 B2
Winterstoke Gdns
NW7 28 A5
Winterstoke Rd SE6 163 B3
Winterton Ct KT1 175 D2
Winterton Ho 15 E1 96 C1
Winterton Pl SW10 266 B6
Winterwell Rd SW2 160 A6
Winthorpe Rd SW15 135 A1
Winthrop Ho 10
W12 112 B6
Winthrop St E1 96 B2
Winthrop Wlk HA9 66 A5
Winton Ave N11 31 C3
Winton Cl N9 18 D4
Winton Ct 15 KT6 197 D2
Winton Gdns HA8 26 B3
Winton Prim Sch
N1 94 B5 233 C3
Winton Rd BR6 226 D4
Winton Way SW16 182 C5
Wintour Ho HA9 65 D6
Wirrall Ho 15 SE26 162 A1
Wirral Wood Cl BR7 188 C4
Wisbeach Rd CR0 205 B4
Wisbech 5 N4 50 B1
Wisden Ho SW8 270 D5
Wisdom Ct 7 TW7 131 A2
Wisdom Sch 1 N15 51 B5
Wisdons Cl RM7, RM9 59 D1
Wise La NW7 28 A4
Wiseman Ct 12 SE19 183 C5
Wiseman Rd E10 75 C6
Wise Rd E15 98 B6
Wiseton Rd SW17 158 D3
Wishart Rd SE3 143 D3
Wishaw Wlk N13 32 A4
Wisley Ho SW1 259 C2
Wisley Rd
Balham SW11 159 A6
St Paul's Cray BR5 190 B3
Wistaria Cl BR6 226 D6
Wisteria Cl
Edgware NW7 27 D4
Ilford IG1 78 D3
Wisteria Ho SE4 141 A2
Wisteria Rd SE13 142 B1
Wistow Ho 14 E2 96 A6
Witanhurst La N6 49 A1
Witan St E2 96 B4
Witchwood Ho 10
SW9 138 C2
Witcombe Point 14
SE15 140 A4
Witechapel Sp Ctr E1 96 C2
Witham Ct Leyton E10 75 D5
Upper Tooting SW17 158 D1
Witham Ho 34 SE5 139 A3
Witham Rd
Dagenham RM10 81 C3
Ealing W13 109 B5
Hounslow TW7 130 B4
Penge SE20 206 C6
Witherby Cl CR0 221 C4
Witherington Rd N5 72 C3
Withers Cl KT9 213 C2
Withers Mead NW9 27 D2
Withers Pl EC1 242 B6
Witherston Way SE9 166 C1
Withington Rd N2 30 C2
Withycombe Rd
SW19 156 D4
Withy Ho 4 E1 96 D3
Withy La HA4 39 A4
Withy Mead E4 20 B1
Witley Cres CR0 224 A2
Witley Ct
Southall UB2 107 B2
WC1 240 A5
Witley Gdns UB2 107 B2
Witley Ho 2 SW2 160 B4
Witley Ind Est UB2 107 B2
Witley Point 8
SW15 156 B3
Witley Rd N19 71 C6
Witney Cl
Ickenham UB10 60 B4
Pinner HA5 23 B4
Witney Path SE23 162 D1
Wittenham Way E4 20 B1
Witten Ho KT3 199 B1
Wittering Cl KT2 175 D5
Wittering Ho 9
SW11 136 D3
Wittersham Rd BR1 186 D5
Witts Ho KT2 198 B6
Wivenhoe Cl SE15 140 B2
Wivenhoe Ct TW4 129 B1
Wivenhoe Rd IG11 102 B5
Wiverton Rd SE26 184 C5
Wixom Ho SE9 143 C1
Wix Prim Sch SW4 137 B1
Wix Rd RM9 102 D6
Wix's La SW4 137 B1
Woburn W13 87 B2
Woburn Cl
Bushey WD23 8 A5
SE28 102 D1
Wimbledon SW19 180 A4
Woburn Ct
32 Bermondsey
SE16 118 B1
Croydon CR0 205 A1
1 DA6 147 A1
Richmond TW9 132 B2
4 Woodford E18 37 A1
Woburn Pl
WC1 94 A3 240 A5
Woburn Rd
Carshalton SM5 202 C1
Croydon CR0 205 A1
Woburn Sq
WC1 93 D3 239 D5
Woburn Twr 14 UB5 84 D4
Woburn Wlk WC1 232 D1
Wodeham Gdns 1
E1 96 B2
Wodehouse Ave
SE15 139 D4
Wodehouse Ct 10
W3 111 A3
Woffington Cl KT1,
KT8 175 C2
Woking Cl SW15 133 D1
Wolcot Ho NW1 232 B3
Woldham Pl BR2 209 C5
Woldham Rd BR2 209 C5
Wolds Dr BR6 226 C4
Wolfe Cl Hayes BR2 209 A3
Yeading UB4 84 B4
Wolfe Cres
Greenwich SE7 121 D1
34 Rotherhithe SE16 118 D4
Wolfe Ho 19 W12 112 B6
Wolferton Rd E12 78 B4
Wolffe Gdns 2 E15 76 D2
Wolf Fields Prim Sch
UB2 107 B2
Wolfington Rd SE27 182 D6
Wolfram Cl SE13 164 C6
Wolfson Ct
4 Barnet EN4 14 D3
Golders Green NW11 47 A2
SE1 253 D2
Wolfson Hillel Prim Sch
N14 15 D5
Wolftencroft Cl
SW11 136 B2
Wollaston Cl SE1 262 A4
Wollotan Ho N1 234 B4
Wolmer Cl HA8 26 D6
Wolmer Gdns HA8 10 C1
Wolmer Rd HA8 26 D6
Wolseley Ave SW18,
SW19 157 C2
Wolseley Gdns W4 132 D6
Wolseley Rd
Acton W4 111 A2
Carshalton CR4 203 A2
Harrow HA3 42 C6
Hornsey N8 49 D4
Upton E7 77 B1
Wood Green N22 32 B2
Wolseley St
SE1 117 D4 253 D1
Wolsey Ave
Thames Ditton KT7 196 D4
Wallend E6 100 C4
Walthamstow E17 53 B6
Wolsey Cl
Isleworth TW3 130 A1
Kingston u T KT2 176 D2
Southall UB2 108 A3
Wimbledon SW20 178 B3
Worcester Pk KT19,
KT4 216 A4
Wolsey Cres SM4 201 B2
Wolsey Ct
Bromley BR1 186 D3
SE9 166 B5
South Hampstead NW6 70 A1
Wolsey Dr
Kingston u T KT2 176 A4
Walton-on-T KT12 194 D1
Wolsey Gr HA8 27 B3
Wolsey Ho
2 Hampton TW12 173 D4
3 Kentish Town NW5 71 D2
Wolsey Inf Sch CR0 224 A1
Wolsey Jun Sch
CR0 224 A1
Wolsey Mews
Kentish Town NW5 71 C2
Orpington BR6 227 D3
Wolsey Rd
Ashford TW15 170 B6
East Molesey KT8 196 B5
Enfield EN1 6 B3
Hampton TW12 174 A4
Stoke Newington N1 73 B3
Sunbury Comm TW16 171 D4
Wolsey St E1 96 C2
Wolsey Way KT9 214 C3
Wolstenholme HA7 25 B5
Wolstonbury N12 29 C5
Wolvercote Rd SE2 124 D4
Wolverley St E2 96 B4
Wolverton SE17 263 A2
Wolverton Ave KT2 176 C2
Wolverton Gdns
Brook Green W6 112 D2
Ealing W5 110 B6
Wolverton Mans W5 110 B5
Wolverton Rd HA7 25 B3
Wolverton Way N14 15 C6
Wolves La N22 32 C4
Woman's Liby The★
EC2 243 C2
Womersley Rd N4, N8 50 B3
Wonford Cl KT2, KT3 177 C2
Wontner Cl 5 N1 73 A1
Wontner Rd SW12,
SW17 158 D2
Wooburn Cl UB8 82 D3
Wooburn Ct N14 15 D3
Woodall Cl
Chessington KT9 213 D2
15 Poplar E14 119 D6
Woodall Ho TW7 130 D2
Woodall Rd EN3 18 D5
Woodbank Rd BR1 164 D1
Woodbastwick Rd
SE26 185 A5
Woodberry Ave
Edmonton N21 16 D2
Harrow HA2 42 A5
Woodberry Cl
Ashford TW16 172 A4
Mill Hill NW7 28 D3
Woodberry Cres N10 49 B6
Woodberry Down N4 51 A2
Woodberry Down Com
Prim Sch N4 51 A2
Woodberry Gdns N12 30 A4
Woodberry Gr
Finchley N12 30 A4
Stoke Newington N4 51 A2
Woodberry View N6 49 A3
Woodberry Way
Chingford E4 20 A4
Finchley N12 30 A4
Woodbine Cl TW2 152 B2
Woodbine Gr
Enfield EN2 5 B5
Penge SE20 184 B3
Woodbine La KT4 216 C5
Woodbine Pl E11 55 A3
Woodbine Rd DA15 167 C3
Woodbines Ave KT1 197 D6
Woodbine Terr E9 74 C2
Woodborough Rd
SW15 134 B1
Woodbourne Ave
SW16 159 D1
Woodbourne Cl
SW16 160 A1
Woodbourne Dr
KT10 212 D2
Woodbourne Gdns
SM6 219 B1
Woodbridge Cl
4 Dollis Hill NW2 68 A5
10 Finsbury Pk N7 72 B6
Woodbridge Ct
Forest Gate E7 77 D3
Stoke Newington N16 73 B5
Woodbridge High Sch
IG8 37 B3
Woodbridge Ho E11 54 D1
Woodbridge Rd IG11 79 D3
Woodbridge St
EC1 94 D3 241 C6
Woodbrook Rd SE2 146 B6
Woodburn Cl NW4 46 D4
Woodbury Cl
Croydon CR0 221 D6
Wanstead E11 55 B5
Woodbury Ct 1 W13 87 B3
Woodbury Gdns
Bromley SE12 187 B6
Eltham SE12 165 B1
Woodbury Ho 4
SE26 162 B1
Woodbury Park Rd
W13 87 B3
Woodbury Rd E17 53 D5
Woodbury St SW17 180 C5
Woodchester Sq W2 91 D2
Woodchurch Cl
DA14 167 B1
Woodchurch Dr
BR1 187 D3
Woodchurch Ho 15
SW9 138 C4
Woodchurch Rd NW6 69 D1
Wood Cl
Bethnal Green E2 96 A3
Harrow HA1 42 B2
Kingsbury NW9 45 B2
Woodclyffe Dr BR7 188 C1
Woodcock Ct HA3 44 A2
Woodcock Dell Ave
HA3 43 D2
Woodcock Hill HA3 43 C3
Woodcock Ho 4 E14 97 C2
Woodcocks E16 99 D2
Woodcombe Cres
SE23 162 C3
Woodcote Ave
Mill Hill NW7 28 C4
Thornton Heath CR7 204 D5
Wallington SM6 219 B1
Woodcote Cl
Enfield N9 18 C5
Kingston u T KT2 176 B5
Woodcote Ct 14
SM6 219 B2
Woodcote Dr BR6 211 B2
Woodcote Ho 4
SE8 141 B6
Woodcote Mews
Loughton IG10 21 D4
Wallington SM6 219 B2
Woodcote Pl 1
SE27 182 D5
Woodcote Rd
Wallington SM6 219 C1
Wanstead E11 55 A2
Woodcott Ho 1
SW15 156 A4
Woodcroft SE9 166 B1
South Croydon CR0 221 C5
Southgate N21 16 C3
17 Stanmore HA7 25 C5
Wembley UB6 65 A2
Woodcroft Ave
Edgware NW7 27 C4
Stanmore HA7 25 A2
Woodcroft Cres UB10 82 D6
Woodcroft Mews
SE8 119 A2
Woodcroft Prim Sch
HA8 27 C3
Woodcroft Rd CR7 204 D3
Wood Dene 6 SE15 140 B4
Wood Dr BR7 188 A4
Woodedge Cl E4 20 D3
Woodend
South Norwood
SE19 183 A4
Sutton SM1 218 A6
Thames Ditton KT10 212 A6
WOOD END 83 D1
Wood End UB3 83 C1
Wood End Ave HA2 64 A4
Wood End Cl UB5 64 B3
Woodend Gdns EN2 4 A1
Wood End Gdns UB5 64 A3
WOOD END GREEN 83 C2
Wood End Green Rd
UB3 83 C1
Wood End Inf Sch
UB5 64 B3
Wood End Jun Sch
UB6 64 B3
Wood End La UB5 63 D3
Wood End Park Com Sch
UB3 105 A6
Woodend Rd E17 36 A1
Wood End Rd HA1,
UB5 64 B4
Wood End Way UB5 64 A3
Wooder Gdns E7 77 A4
Wooderson Cl SE25 205 C5
Wooderson Ct 9
BR3 185 C2
Woodfall Ave EN5 13 B6
Woodfall Rd N4 72 C6
Woodfall St SW3 257 C1
Woodfarrs SE5 139 B1
Woodfield SW16 182 B2
Wood Field NW3 70 D3
Woodfield Ave
Colindale NW9 45 C5
Ealing W5 87 C3
Streatham SW16 159 D1
Wallington SM5 219 A1
Wembley HA0 65 C5
Woodfield Cl
1 Enfield EN1 5 C1
South Norwood SE19 183 A3
Woodfield Cres W5 87 D3
Woodfield Ct SW16 159 D1
Woodfield Dr EN4 15 A3

Woodfield Gdns KT3 199 D4
Woodfield Gr SW16 159 D1
Woodfield Ho
11 Forest Hill SE23 162 D1
Hinchley Wood KT7 212 D6
New Malden KT3 199 D4
6 Upper Clapton E5 74 B6
Wood Green N11 31 D4
Woodfield La SW16 159 D1
Woodfield Pl W9 91 B3
Woodfield Rd
Cranford TW4, TW5 128 B3
Ealing W5 87 C3
Hinchley Wood KT10, KT7 212 D6
Kensal Town W9 91 B2
Woodfield Rise WD23 8 B4
Woodfield Sch NW9 45 C1
Woodfields Ct SM1 218 A5
Woodfield Way N11 31 D3
WOODFORD 37 D5
Woodford Ave IG2, IG4, IG5, IG8 56 B5
Woodford Bridge Rd IG4 56 A5
Woodford Cres HA5 22 B1
Woodford Ct 15 W12 112 D4
Woodford Cty High Sch for Girls IG8 36 D4
Woodforde Ct UB3 105 B1
WOODFORD GREEN 37 B3
Woodford Green Prep Sch IG8 37 A4
Woodford Green Sch IG8 36 D5
Woodford Ho
13 SE18 144 D6
5 Wanstead E18 55 A5
Woodford New Rd
Upper Walthamstow E17 54 C6
Woodford E18 36 D3
Woodford Pl HA9 44 A1
Woodford Rd
Forest Gate E7 77 B4
Wanstead E18 55 A6
Woodford Sta IG8 37 B4
Woodford Trad Est IG8 37 D1
WOODFORD WELLS 21 B1
Woodgate Ave KT9 213 D3
Woodgate Cres HA6 22 A4
Woodgate Dr SW16 181 D3
Woodgate Ho 12 KT6 198 A3
Woodger Rd W12 112 C4
Woodget Cl E6 100 A1
Woodglen SM4 202 C4
Woodgrange Ave
Ealing W5 110 C5
Enfield EN1 18 A5
Finchley N12 30 B4
Harrow HA3 43 D4
Woodgrange Cl HA3 43 D4
Woodgrange Ct 1 BR2 208 D1
Woodgrange Gdns EN1 18 A5
Woodgrange Ho W5 110 B5
Woodgrange Inf Sch E7 77 B4
Woodgrange Mans HA3 43 C4
Woodgrange Park Sta E12 77 D3
Woodgrange Rd E7 77 A3
Woodgrange Terr EN1 18 A5
WOOD GREEN 32 B2
Wood Green Sh City N22 32 C1
Wood Green Sta N22 32 C1
Woodhall NW1 232 A1
Woodhall Ave
Dulwich SE21 161 D1
Pinner HA5 23 A2
Woodhall Dr
Dulwich SE21 161 D1
Pinner HA5 23 A2
Woodhall Gate HA5 22 D3
Woodhall Ho SW18 158 B5
Woodhall La WD19 23 A6
Woodhall Rd HA5 22 D4
Woodhall Sch WD19 23 A6
Woodham Ct E11 54 D5
Woodham Rd SE6 164 A1
Woodhatch Cl 16 E6 100 A2
Woodhaven Gdns IG6 57 A5
Woodhayes BR7 188 D4
Woodhayes Rd SW19, SW20 178 C4
Woodhead Dr BR6 227 C6
Woodheyes Rd NW10 67 C3
Woodhill SE7, SE18 122 A2
Woodhill Cres HA3 43 D3
Woodhill Prim Sch SE18 122 A2
Wood Ho
4 Clapham SW4 137 D3
6 Paddington NW6 91 B5
Woodhouse Ave UB6 86 D5
Woodhouse Cl
Hayes UB3 105 C3
Wembley UB6 86 D5
Woodhouse Coll N12 30 B4
Woodhouse Eaves HA6 22 A5
Woodhouse Gr E12 78 A2
Woodhouse Rd
Colney Hatch N12 30 C4
Leyton E11 76 D5
Woodhurst Ave BR5 211 A3
Woodhurst Rd
Acton W3 111 A6
SE2 124 A2
Woodington Cl SE9 166 C5
Woodison St E3 97 A3
Woodknoll Dr BR7 188 B2
Wood La
Dagenham RM10 81 A5
Highgate N6 49 B3
Hounslow TW7 130 D5
Kingsbury NW9 45 B2
Ruislip HA4 61 C6
Shepherd's Bush W12 112 C6
Stanmore HA7 9 B2
Woodford IG8 36 D5
Woodland App UB6 65 A2
Woodland Cl
Kingsbury NW9 45 A3
Uxbridge UB10 60 D6
West Ewell KT19 215 C2
West Norwood SE19 183 C4
Woodford IG8 21 B1
Woodland Cres
18 Rotherhithe SE16 118 D4
SE10 142 C6
Woodland Ct
Cheam SM1 217 C2
Temple Fortune NW4 47 A4
13 Wanstead E11 55 A4
Woodland Gdns
Cranley Gdns N10 49 B4
Isleworth TW7 130 C2
Woodland Gr SE10 120 C1
Woodland Hill SE19 183 C4
Woodland Hts SE3 142 C6
Woodland Mews SW16 160 A1
Woodland Rd
Chingford E4 20 A3
Friern Barnet N11 31 B5
Penge SE19 183 D4
Thornton Heath CR7 204 C5
Woodland Rise
Cranley Gdns N10 49 B5
Wembley UB6 65 A2
WOODLANDS 130 C2
Woodlands
Beckenham BR3 185 D3
Bexley DA6 169 D6
Clapham SW4 137 B1
Finchley N12 30 A4
Harrow HA2 41 C5
Temple Fortune NW11 47 A4
Walthamstow E11 54 B2
West Barnes SW20 200 D5
Woodlands Ave
Acton W3 110 D5
DA15 167 C3
Dagenham RM6 59 A2
Finchley N3 30 A2
Kingston u T KT3 177 B2
Ruislip HA4 40 D2
Wanstead E11 55 B1
Woodlands Ave *continued*
Worcester Pk KT4 216 A6
Woodlands Cl BR1 188 B1
Claygate KT10 212 D1
Temple Fortune NW11 47 A4
Woodlands Ct
9 Bromley BR1 186 D2
Brondesbury Pk NW10 90 D6
Dulwich SE22 162 B4
Southall UB1 107 C6
Woodlands Dr
Harrow HA7 24 D4
Sunbury TW16 172 C1
Woodlands Fst & Mid Sch HA8 26 B2
Woodlands Gdns E17 54 C5
Woodlands Gr TW7 130 C3
Woodlands Gt SW15 157 B6
Woodlands Jun & Inf Schs IG1 79 B3
Woodlands Par TW15 171 A4
Woodlands Park Rd
SE10 142 C6
Tottenham N15 51 A4
Woodlands Rd
Barnes SW13 133 D2
Bexleyheath DA7 147 A2
Bickley BR1 188 B1
Enfield EN2 5 B4
Harrow HA1 42 D4
Ilford IG1 79 A5
Isleworth TW7 130 C3
Lower Edmonton N9 18 C3
Southall UB1 106 D5
Surbiton KT6 197 D2
Walthamstow E17 54 A6
Woodlands St SE13 164 B4
Woodland St 2 E8 73 D2
Woodlands The
East Barnet N14 15 B3
Harrow HA1 64 C6
Highbury N5 73 A4
12 Hornsey N8 50 A2
Isleworth TW7 130 D3
Lewisham SE13 164 B4
Mitcham CR4 203 A6
South Norwood SE19 183 A3
Stanmore HA7 25 B5
Thames Ditton KT10 212 A6
Woodlands Way SW15 157 B6
Woodland Terr SE7 122 A2
Woodland Way
Abbey Wood SE2 124 D2
Croydon CR0 207 A1
Edgware NW7 27 D4
Merton SM4 201 B5
Mitcham CR4 181 A3
Petts Wood BR5 211 A4
Southgate N21 16 C2
Tolworth KT5 214 D6
West Wickham BR4 224 A5
Woodford IG8 21 B1
Woodland Wlk
Chessington KT19 214 C2
9 Greenwich SE10 120 C1
Hampstead NW3 70 C3
Wood Lane High Sch W12 90 B1
Wood Lane Sta W12 112 C6
Wood La Sp Ctr RM8 59 D1
Wood La Sta W12 112 C6
Woodlawn Cl SW15 157 B6
Woodlawn Cres TW2 151 D2
Woodlawn Dr TW13 150 D2
Woodlawn Rd SW6 134 D4
Woodlea Dr BR2 208 C4
Woodlea Lo EN1 17 C5
Woodlea Rd N16 73 C5
Woodleigh
1 Kingston u T KT5 198 B4
3 Woodford E18 37 A2
Woodleigh Ave N12 30 C4
Woodleigh Ct N22 32 B2
Woodleigh Gdns SW16 160 A1
Woodley Cl SW17 180 D3
Woodley La SM1, SM5 218 C5
Woodlodge 4 SW19 179 B5
Wood Lodge Gdns BR1 188 A3
Wood Lodge La BR4 224 A5
Woodman La E4 20 C6
Woodman Mews TW9 132 D4
Woodman Par 4 E16 122 C5
Woodmans Ct HA7 44 A6
Woodmans Gr NW10 67 D3
Woodmans Mews W12 90 B2
Woodman St E16 122 C5
Woodmansterne Prim Sch SW16 181 D2
Woodmansterne Rd
Mitcham SW16 181 D2
Sutton SM5 218 C1
Wood Mead N17 34 A4
Woodmere SE9 166 B3
Woodmere Ave CR0 206 D2
Woodmere Cl
11 Clapham SW11 137 A2
Croydon CR0 206 D2
Woodmere Ct N14 15 B4
Woodmere Gdns CR0 206 D2
Woodmere Way BR3 208 B4
Woodmill Rd E5 74 C6
Woodnook Rd SW16 181 B5
Woodpecker Cl
Bushey WD23 8 A3
Enfield N9 18 B5
Harrow HA3 24 D2
Woodpecker Ct TW2 151 D4
Woodpecker Ho E17 53 C6
Woodpecker Mews SE13 142 B1
Woodpecker Rd
6 SE14 141 A6
Woolwich SE28 124 C6
Wood Point 8 E16 99 A2
Woodquest Ave SE24 161 A6
Wood Rd
Littleton TW17 192 C5
Willesden NW10 67 A1
Wood Retreat SE18 145 B5
Wood Ride Barnet EN4 2 B4
Orpington BR5 211 C5
Woodridge Cl EN2 4 C4
Woodridge Prim Sch N12 13 C1
Woodridings Ave HA5 23 B2
Woodridings Cl HA5 23 B3
Woodridings Ct N22 31 D2
Woodriffe Rd E11 54 B2
Wood Rise HA5 40 A4
Woodrow SE18 122 B2
Woodrow Ave UB4 83 D3
Woodrow Cl UB6 65 B1
Woodrow Ct 3 N17 34 B3
Woodruff Ho 12 SW2 160 C5
Woodrush Cl 4 SE14 141 A5
Woodrush Way RM6 58 D5
Woodseer St E1 96 A2
Woodsford SE17 262 C1
Woodsford Sq W14 113 A4 244 B2
Woodshire Rd RM10 81 D5
Woods Ho SW8 269 A2
WOODSIDE 206 A4
Woodside
Buckhurst Hill IG9 21 C2
Hampstead Garden Suburb NW11 47 C4
Muswell Hill N10 49 A6
Walton-on-T KT12 194 A1
Wimbledon SW19 179 B5
Woodside Ave
Chislehurst BR7 189 A5
Croydon SE25 206 B4
Fortis Green N6 48 D5
North Finchley N12 30 A6
Thames Ditton KT10 196 C2
Wembley HA0 88 A6
Woodside Cl
Ruislip HA4 39 B3
Stanmore HA7 25 B5
Tolworth KT5 199 A2
Wembley HA0 88 A6
Woodside Court Rd CR0 206 A2
Woodside Cres DA15 167 C1
Woodside Ct
Ealing W5 110 A5
Enfield EN2 4 D4
10 Finchley N12 29 D6
Palmers Green N13 16 C1
Wanstead E12 55 C1
Woodside End HA0 88 A6
Woodside Gdns
Chingford E4 35 D4
Tottenham N17 33 D1
Woodside Gn SE25 206 A3
Woodside Gr N12 14 A1
Woodside Grange Rd N12 29 D6
Woodside High Sch N22 32 D3
Woodside Ho SW19 179 B4
Woodside Jun & Inf Sch CR0 206 A2
Woodside La DA5 168 D5
Whetstone N12 14 A1
WOODSIDE PARK 29 C6
Woodside Park Ave E17 54 B5
Woodside Park Rd N12 30 A6
Woodside Pk SE25 206 B3
Woodside Pk Sta N12 29 D6
Woodside Pl HA0 88 A6
Woodside Prim Sch E17 54 A6
Woodside Rd BR1 210 A4
Coombe KT3 177 C1
Croydon SE25 206 B3
Kingston u T KT2 176 A3
Newham E13 99 C3
Northwood HA6 22 A3
Sidcup DA15 167 C1
Sutton SM1 218 A5
Woodford IG8 37 A6
Wood Green N22 32 C3
Woodside Sch DA17 125 D2
Woodside Sta SE25 206 B3
Woodside Way
Croydon CR0 206 C3
Streatham CR4 181 C2
Wood's Mews W1 115 A6 248 A6
Woodsome Rd NW5 71 B5
Wood's Pl SE1 263 B5
Woodspring Rd SW19 157 A2
Wood's Rd SE15 140 B4
Wood St Barnet EN5 1 A1
Carshalton CR4 203 A2
Chiswick W4 111 C1
City of London EC2 95 A1 242 B2
Custom Ho E16 121 B6
Kingston u T KT1 175 D1
Kingston u T KT2 176 A2
Walthamstow E17 54 B5
Woodstar Ho 3 SE15 140 A5
Woodstead Gr HA8 26 A4
Woods The
Eastbury HA6 22 A5
Uxbridge UB10 60 D4
Woodstock Ave
Brentford W13 109 A3
Cheam SM3 201 B2
Golders Green NW11 47 A2
Isleworth TW7 153 A6
Southall UB1 85 B4
Woodstock Cl DA5 169 B3
Stanmore HA7 26 A1
Woodstock Cres N9 18 B5
Woodstock Ct
Kingston u T KT2 176 D1
Lee SE12 165 A5
Vauxhall SE11 260 D2
Woodstock Dr UB10 60 B4
Woodstock Gdns
Beckenham BR3 185 D3
Hayes UB4 83 D2
Ilford IG3 80 A6
Woodstock Gr W12 112 D4
Woodstock Grange W5 110 A5
Woodstock Ho
Hayes UB3 83 B2
2 Highbury N5 73 A4

Woodstock Lane N
KT6 . . . 213 C6
Woodstock Lane S KT6,
KT9, KT10 . . . 213 C4
Woodstock Mews
W1 . . . 238 B3
Woodstock Rd
Bedford Pk W4 . . . 111 C3
Bushey WD23 . . . 8 D4
Chingford E17 . . . 36 B1
Finsbury Pk N4 . . . 50 C1
Golders Green NW11 . . . 47 B1
South Croydon CR0 . . . 221 B5
Upton E7 . . . 77 C1
Wallington SM5, SM6. 219 A3
Wembley HA0 . . . 66 B1
Woodstock Rise
SM3 . . . 201 B2
Woodstock St W1 . . . 238 C1
Woodstock Studios [17]
W12 . . . 112 D4
Woodstock Terr
E14 . . . 119 D6
Woodstock The SM3 . 201 B2
Woodstock Way
CR4 . . . 181 C1
Woodstone Ave KT17,
KT4 . . . 216 A3
Wood Street Sta E17 . . 54 B5
Woodsyre SE26 . . . 183 D6
Woodthorpe Rd
Ashford TW15 . . . 170 A6
Putney SW15 . . . 134 B1
Woodtree Cl NW4 . . . 28 C1
Wood Vale
Cranley Gdns N10 . . . 49 C4
Dulwich SE22 . . . 162 B4
Woodvale Ave SE25. 183 D1
Woodvale Ct BR1 . . . 187 B1
South Norwood SE25. 205 D6
Woodvale Way NW11 . 68 D5
Woodvale Wlk SE27 . . 183 A5
Woodview Ave E4 . . . 36 A6
Woodview Cl
Finsbury Pk N4 . . . 50 D2
Kingston u T SW15 . . . 177 B6
Orpington BR6 . . . 227 A6
Woodville SE3 . . . 143 B4
Woodville Cl SE12 . . . 165 A6
Teddington TW11 . . . 175 A6
Woodville Ct
[3] Lewisham SE10 . . 142 A4
Southgate N14 . . . 15 C6
Woodville Gdns
Ealing W5 . . . 88 A1
Hendon NW11 . . . 46 D2
Ilford IG6 . . . 56 D5
Ruislip HA4 . . . 39 A2
Surbiton KT6 . . . 197 D2
Woodville Gr [2]
DA16 . . . 146 A2
Woodville Ho SE1 . . . 263 C6
Sutton SM1 . . . 217 D4
Woodville Rd
Barnet EN5 . . . 1 D2
Ealing W5 . . . 87 D1
Golders Green NW11 . . . 47 A2
Leytonstone E11 . . . 54 D1
Morden SM4 . . . 201 C5
Paddington NW6 . . . 91 B5
Richmond TW10 . . . 153 C1
South Norwood CR7 . . . 205 B6
Stoke Newington N16 . . 73 C3
Walthamstow E17 . . . 53 B5
Woodford E18 . . . 37 B1
Woodville St [16]
SE18 . . . 122 A2
Woodville The W5 . . . 87 D1
Woodward Ave NW4 . . 46 A4
Woodward Cl KT10 . . 212 D2
Woodwarde Rd
SE22 . . . 161 C5
Woodward Gdns
Dagenham RM9 . . . 80 C1
Harrow HA7 . . . 24 D3
Woodward Rd RM9 . . . 80 C1
Wood Way BR6 . . . 226 C6
Woodway Cres HA1 . . . 43 A3
Woodwell St SW18 . . . 158 A6
Wood Wharf SE10 . . . 142 A6
Woodyard Cl NW5 . . . 71 A3
Woodyard La SE21 . . . 161 C4
Woodyates Rd SE12 . . 165 B4
Woolacombe Rd
SE3 . . . 143 C3
Woolacombe Way
UB3 . . . 105 C2
Woolands Rd E11 . . . 76 C6
Woolcombes Ct [4]
SE16 . . . 118 D5
Woolden Ho [2] E4 . . . 20 C4
Wooler St
SE17 . . . 117 B1 262 D2
Woolf Cl SE28 . . . 124 B5
Woolf Ct [7] W3 . . . 111 A3
Woolf Mews WC1 . . . 240 A6
Woollaston Rd N4 . . . 50 D3
Woolley Ho SW9 . . . 138 D2
Woollon Ho [1] E1 . . . 96 C1
Woolmead Ave NW9 . . 46 A2
Woolmer Gdns N18 . . . 34 A5
Woolmer Ho [2] E5 . . . 74 B6
Woolmer Rd N18 . . . 34 A5
Woolmore Prim Sch [14]
E14 . . . 120 A6
Woolmore St E14 . . . 120 A6
Woolneigh St SW6 . . 135 D3
Woolpack Ho [1] E9 . . . 74 C2
Wool Rd SW20 . . . 178 B4
Woolridge Cl TW14 . . . 149 A3
Woolridge Way E9 . . . 74 C1
Woolstaplers Way
SE16 . . . 118 A2
Woolston Cl E17 . . . 34 D1
Woolstone Ho [7] E2 . . . 96 A6
Woolstone Rd SE23 . . 163 A2
Woolven Ho SE3 . . . 142 D6
WOOLWICH . . . 122 D3
Woolwich Arsenal Sta
SE18 . . . 122 D2
Woolwich Church St SE7,
SE18 . . . 122 A3
Woolwich Comm
SE18 . . . 144 C6
Woolwich Ct EN3 . . . 7 C5
Woolwich Dockyard Ind
Est SE18 . . . 122 A3
Woolwich Dockyard Sta
SE18 . . . 122 B2
Woolwich High St
SE18 . . . 122 C3
Woolwich Manorway
E16 . . . 122 D4
Woolwich Manor Way
Beckton E6 . . . 100 C1
North Woolwich E16 . 122 D5
Woolwich New Rd
SE18 . . . 122 D2
Woolwich Poly Sch
SE28 . . . 124 A5
Woolwich Rd
Belvedere DA17 . . . 125 C1
DA7 . . . 147 C2
Erith SE2 . . . 125 B1
Greenwich SE7, SE10. 121 C2
Woolwich Tramshed
The★ [16] SE18 . . . 122 D2
Wooster Gdns E14 . . . 98 B1
Wooster Mews HA2 . . . 42 A6
Wooster Pl SE1 . . . 262 D4
Wootton KT10 . . . 212 A4
Wootton Gr N3 . . . 29 C2
Wootton Ho SE9 . . . 167 B5
Wootton St
SE1 . . . 116 C5 251 B3
Worbeck Rd SE20 . . . 184 C1
Worcester Ave N17 . . . 34 A3
Worcester Cl
Croydon CR0 . . . 223 C6
Dollis Hill NW2 . . . 68 B5
Mitcham CR4 . . . 181 A1
Worcester Cres
Edgware NW7 . . . 11 C1
Woodford IG8 . . . 37 C6
Worcester Ct
Ashford TW15 . . . 170 D5
Ealing W7 . . . 86 D1
Finchley N12 . . . 29 D5
Harrow HA1 . . . 42 C6
[44] Paddington W2 . . . 91 C2
[12] Sutton SM2 . . . 217 D2
Walton-on-T KT12 . . . 194 C1
Worcester Pk KT4 . . . 215 C5
Worcester Dr
Ashford TW15 . . . 170 D5
Bedford Pk W4 . . . 111 C4
Worcester Gdns
Northolt UB6 . . . 64 B2
Redbridge IG1 . . . 56 A2
Wandsworth SW11 . . 158 D6
Worcester Pk KT4 . . . 215 C5
Worcester Ho
Bayswater W2 . . . 236 A1
[3] Islington N1 . . . 73 A1
Lambeth SE11 . . . 261 A5
[9] Putney SW15 . . . 156 C4
Worcester Mews [2]
NW6 . . . 69 D2
WORCESTER PARK . 215 C4
Worcester Park Rd
KT4 . . . 215 B5
Worcester Park Sta
KT4 . . . 200 A1
Worcester Rd
Belmont SM2 . . . 217 D1
Higham Hill E17 . . . 34 D1
Ilford E12 . . . 78 B4
[11] Wimbledon SW19 . . 179 B5
Worcesters Ave EN1 . . . 6 A5
Worcesters Prim Sch
EN1 . . . 5 D5
Wordsworth N8 . . . 50 C5
Wordsworth Ave
Greenford UB6 . . . 86 B5
Plashet E12 . . . 78 A1
Snaresbrook E18 . . . 54 D6
Wordsworth Ct
Harrow HA1 . . . 42 B2
New Barnet EN5 . . . 14 A6
Wordsworth Dr KT4,
SM3 . . . 216 C4
Wordsworth Gdns
WD6 . . . 10 C6
Wordsworth Ho
Maida Vale NW6 . . . 91 C4
[15] SE18 . . . 144 C6
Wordsworth Par [1]
N15 . . . 50 D5
Wordsworth Pl [11]
NW5 . . . 70 D3
Wordsworth Rd
Bermondsey SE1 . . . 263 D3
Bexley DA16 . . . 145 C4
Hampton TW12,
TW13 . . . 173 B6
Penge SE20 . . . 184 D3
Stoke Newington N16 . . 73 C4
Wallington SM6 . . . 219 D2
Wordsworth Way
UB7 . . . 104 B2
Wordsworth Wlk
NW11 . . . 47 C5
Worfield St
SW11 . . . 136 C5 267 B3
Worgan St
Rotherhithe SE16 . . . 118 D2
SE11 . . . 116 B1 260 C2
Working Men's Coll The
NW1 . . . 93 C5 232 B4
Worland Rd E15 . . . 76 C1
World Bsns Ctr TW6. 127 A4
World Rugby Mus★
TW1 . . . 152 C5
WORLD'S END . . . 4 C1
Worlds End La BR6 . . 227 D1
World's End La EN2 . . . 4 B1
World's End Pas
SW10 . . . 266 C4
World's End Pl SW10 266 B4
World Trade Ctr London
E14 . . . 119 D4
Worley Ct NW2 . . . 68 D5
Worleys Dr BR6 . . . 227 B4
Worlidge St W6 . . . 112 C1
Worlingham Rd
SE22 . . . 139 D1
Wormholt Park Prim Sch
W12 . . . 112 A6
Wormholt Rd W12 . . . 112 A5
Wormwood St EC2 . . 243 A2
Wornington Rd W10 . . 91 A2
Woronzow Rd
NW8 . . . 92 C6 230 A5
Worple Ave
Isleworth TW7 . . . 153 A6
Wimbledon SW19 . . . 178 D3
Worple Cl HA2 . . . 41 B1
Worple Ct SW19 . . . 179 A4
Worple Prim Sch
TW7 . . . 131 A1
Worple Rd
Isleworth TW7 . . . 131 A1
Wimbledon SW19,
SW20 . . . 178 D2
Worple Road Mews
SW19 . . . 179 B4
Worple St SW14 . . . 133 B2
Worple Way
Harrow HA2 . . . 41 B1
Richmond TW10 . . . 132 A1
Worship St
EC2 . . . 95 C3 243 A5
Worslade Rd SW17 . . . 180 B6
Worsley Bridge Jun Sch
[25] BR3 . . . 185 C3
Worsley Bridge Rd BR3,
SE6 . . . 185 C5
Worsley Ct N3 . . . 29 D4
Worsley Gr E5 . . . 74 A4
Worsley Grange
BR7 . . . 189 A4
Worsley Ho [9] SE23 . . 162 B2
Worsley Rd E11 . . . 76 C4
Worsopp Dr SW4 . . . 159 C6
Worth Cl BR6 . . . 227 C4
Worthfield Cl KT19 . . . 215 B1
Worth Gr SE17 . . . 262 C1
Worthing Cl [5] E15 . . . 98 C6
Worthing Rd TW5 . . . 129 B6
Worthington Cl CR4 . . 203 B6
Worthington Ho EC1 234 B2
[16] Streatham SW2 . . 160 C4
Worthington Rd KT6 . 198 B1
Wortley Rd
Forest Gate E6 . . . 77 D1
Thornton Heath CR0 . 204 C2
Worton Ct TW7 . . . 130 C1
Worton Gdns TW7 . . . 130 B3
Worton Hall Ind Est
TW7 . . . 130 C1
Worton Rd TW7 . . . 130 C2
Worton Way TW3,
TW7 . . . 130 B3
Wotton Ct [14] E14 . . . 120 B6
Wotton Rd
Cricklewood NW2 . . . 68 C5
[18] SE8 . . . 141 B6
Wouldham Rd E16 . . . 98 D1
Wragby Rd E11 . . . 76 C5
Wrampling Pl N9 . . . 18 A3
Wrangthorne Wlk
CR0 . . . 220 C4
Wray Ave IG5 . . . 56 C6
Wrayburn Ho [28]
SE16 . . . 118 A4
Wray Cres N4 . . . 72 B6
Wray Ct N4 . . . 72 B6
Wrayfield Rd SM3 . . . 216 D5
Wray Ho [11] SW2 . . . 160 A3
Wraysbury Cl TW4 . . . 151 A6
Wrays Way UB4 . . . 83 C3
Wrekin Rd SE18 . . . 145 A5
Wren Acad N12 . . . 30 B5
Wren Ave
Cricklewood NW2 . . . 68 C4
Southall UB2 . . . 107 B2
Wren Cl E16 . . . 98 D1
Lower Edmonton N9 . . . 18 D3
Wren Cres WD23 . . . 8 A3
Wren Ct
[1] Barnet EN4 . . . 14 D3
Croydon CR0 . . . 221 B4
Wren Gdns RM9 . . . 80 D3
Wren Ho [29] Bow E3 . . . 97 A5
[4] Hampton TW12 . . . 173 D4
SW1 . . . 259 C1
Wren Landing E14 . . . 119 C5
Wrenn Ho SW13 . . . 134 C6
Wren Path SE28 . . . 123 B4
Wren Rd
Camberwell SE5 . . . 139 B4
Dagenham RM9 . . . 80 D3
Sidcup DA14 . . . 168 C1
Wrens Ave TW15 . . . 171 A6
Wren's Park Ho E5 . . . 74 B6
Wren St WC1 . . 94 B3 240 D6
Wrentham Ave NW10 . 90 D5
Wrenthorpe Rd BR1 . 186 C6
Wren View N6 . . . 49 C1
Wrenwood Way HA5 . . 40 B5
Wrestlers Ct EC3 . . . 243 A2
Wrexham Rd E3 . . . 97 C5
Wricklemarsh Rd
SE3 . . . 143 D4
Wrigglesworth St
SE14 . . . 140 D5
Wright Cl SE13 . . . 142 B1
Wright Gdns TW17 . . . 192 C4
Wright Ho SW15 . . . 156 B6
Wrighton Ct SM1 . . . 217 B2
Wright Rd TW5 . . . 128 C5
Wrights Cl RM10 . . . 81 D4
Wright's Gn SW4 . . . 137 D1
Wright's La
W8 . . . 113 D3 255 C6
Wrights Pl NW10 . . . 67 A2
Wrights Rd SE25 . . . 205 C6
Wright's Rd E3 . . . 97 B5
Wright's Row SM5 . . . 219 B4
Wrights Wlk SW14 . . . 133 B2
Writtle Ho [36] NW9 . . . 27 D1
Wrotham Ho
Beckenham BR3 . . . 185 B3
SE1 . . . 262 D6
Wrotham Rd
Barnet EN5 . . . 1 A3
[13] Camden Town NW1 . . 71 C1
DA16 . . . 146 C4
Ealing W13 . . . 109 C5
Wrottesley Rd SE18 . . 145 A6
Willesden Green NW10 90 A5
Wroughton Rd
SW11 . . . 158 D5
Wroughton Terr NW4 . 46 B5
Wroxall Rd RM9 . . . 80 C2
Wroxham Gdns N11 . . . 31 D3
Wroxham Rd SE28 . . 124 D6
Wroxton Rd SE15 . . . 140 C3
Wrythe Gn [2] SM5 . . 218 D5
Wrythe Green Rd
SM5 . . . 218 D5
Wrythe La SM1, SM5,
SM4 . . . 218 C5
WRYTHE THE . . . 218 D6
Wulfstan St W12 . . . 89 D1
Wyatt Cl Bushey WD23 . . 8 C4
Feltham TW13 . . . 150 D3
Hayes UB4 . . . 84 A2
Rotherhithe SE16 . . . 119 B4
Wyatt Ct HA0 . . . 66 A1
Wyatt Dr SW13 . . . 134 B5
Wyatt Ho
Blackheath Vale
SE3 . . . 142 D3
NW8 . . . 236 D5
Wyatt Park Mans [1]
SW2 . . . 160 A2
Wyatt Park Rd SW2 . . 160 B2
Wyatt Rd
Forest Gate E7 . . . 77 A2
Highbury N5 . . . 73 A5
Wyatt's La E17 . . . 54 A6
Wybert St NW1 . . . 239 A6
Wyborne Ho NW10 . . . 67 A1
Wyborne Prim Sch
SE9 . . . 166 D3
Wyborne Way NW10 . . 67 A1
Wyburn Ave EN5 . . . 1 B2
Wyche Gr CR2 . . . 221 A1
Wycherley Cl SE3 . . . 142 D5
Wycherley Cres EN5 . . 13 D5
Wychwood Ave
Edgware HA8 . . . 25 D4
South Norwood CR7 . . 205 A6
Wychwood Cl
Ashford TW16 . . . 172 A4
Edgware HA8 . . . 25 D4
Wychwood End N6 . . . 49 C2
Wychwood Gdns IG5 . . 56 C5
Wychwood Ho N4 . . . 51 A2
Wychwood Way
SE19 . . . 183 B4
Wyclif Ct EC1 . . . 234 C1
Wycliffe Cl DA16 . . . 145 D4
Wycliffe Ho [13] N16 . . . 73 C4
Wycliffe Rd
Battersea SW11 . . . 137 A3
Wimbledon SW19 . . . 179 D4
Wyclif St EC1 . . . 234 C1
Wycombe Ct SE3 . . . 143 A5
Wycombe Gdns
NW11 . . . 69 C6
Wycombe Ho NW8 . . 237 A6
Wycombe Pl SW18 . . . 158 A5
Wycombe Rd
Redbridge IG2 . . . 56 B4
Tottenham N17 . . . 34 A2
Wembley HA0 . . . 88 C6
Wycombe Sq W8 . . . 245 A3
Wydehurst Rd CR0 . . . 206 B2
Wydell Cl SM4 . . . 200 D3
Wydeville Manor Rd
SE12 . . . 187 B6
Wye Cl Ashford TW15. 170 D6
BR6 . . . 211 D2
Ruislip HA4 . . . 39 A3

Wye Ct W13 87 B2
Wyemead Cres E4 20 C2
Wyersdale Ho N4 51 A2
Wye St SW11 136 B3
Wyevale Cl HA5 40 A6
Wyfold Ho 8 SE2 124 D4
Wyfold Rd
SW6 135 A5 264 A3
Wyke Cl TW7 130 D6
Wyke Gdns W7 109 A3
Wykeham Ave RM9 80 C2
Wykeham Cl UB7 126 C6
Wykeham Ct
Chislehurst BR7 189 C4
Hendon NW4 46 C4
Wykeham Gn RM9 80 C2
Wykeham Hill HA9 44 B1
Wykeham Ho SW19 179 C2
Wykeham Prim Sch
NW10 67 C5
Wykeham Rd
Harrow HA3 43 B5
Hendon NW4 46 C4
Wykeham Rise N20 13 A3
Wykehurst Ho SW17 180 B5
Wyke Rd
Hackney Wick E3 75 C1
Merton SW20 178 C1
Wylchin Cl HA5 39 D6
Wyldes Cl NW11 48 A1
Wyldfield Gdns N9 17 D2
Wyld Way HA9 66 D2
Wyleu St SE23 163 A4
Wylie Rd UB2 107 C3
Wyllen Cl E1 96 C3
Wylo Dr EN5 12 A5
Wymering Mans 9
W9 91 C4
Wymering Rd W9 91 C4
Wymondham Ct
NW8 229 D6
Wymond St SW15 134 C2
Wynan Rd E14 119 D1
Wynash Gdns SM5 218 C3
Wynaud Ct N22 32 B4
Wynbourne Ct SE20 184 B1
Wyncham Ave DA15 167 C3
Wynchgate
Harrow HA3 24 C3
Southgate N14 16 A4
Wyncroft Cl BR1 210 B6
Wyndale Ave NW9 44 C3
Wyndcliff Rd SE7 143 B6
Wyndcroft Cl EN2 4 D2
Wyndham Cl
Belmont SM2 217 C1
Orpington BR6 211 A1
Wyndham Cres
Camden Town N19 71 C5
Hounslow TW4 151 C5
Wyndham Ct
Brentford W7 109 A2
1 Thornton Heath
CR0 204 D3
Wyndham Deedes Ho 30
E2 96 A5
Wyndham Ho SW1 258 A3
Wyndham Lo TW7 130 C4
Wyndham Mews W1 237 C3
Wyndham Pl W1 237 C3
Wyndham Rd
Barnet EN4 14 D3
Brentford W13 109 B3
Forest Gate E6 77 D1
Kingston u T KT2 176 B3
SE5 139 A5
Wyndhams Ct 4 E8 73 D1
Wyndham St
W1 92 D2 237 C4
Wyndham Yd W1 237 C3
Wyndhurst Cl CR2 220 D1
Wyneham Rd SE24 161 B6
Wynell Rd SE23 162 D1
Wynford Pl DA17 147 C6
Wynford Rd
N1 94 B5 233 D4
Wynford Way SE9 166 B1
Wynlie Gdns HA5 22 B1
Wynndale Rd E18 37 B2
Wynne Ct 6 TW7 131 A2
Wynne Ho SE14 140 D4
Wynne Rd SW9 138 C3
Wynn's Ave DA15 168 A6
Wynnstay Gdns
W8 113 C3 255 B6
Wynter Ho 20 SW9 138 B3
Wynter St SW11 136 A1
Wynton Gdns SE25 205 D4
Wynton Pl W3 88 D1
Wynyard Ho SE11 260 D2
Wynyard Terr SE11 260 D2
Wynyatt Ho EC1 234 C2
Wynyatt St
EC1 94 D4 234 C2
Wyre Gr Edgware HA8 10 D1
Hayes UB3 106 A2
Wyresdale Cres UB6 86 D4
Wyteleaf Cl HA4 39 A3
Wytham Ho NW8 236 D5
Wythburn Ct W1 237 C2
Wythburn Pl W1 237 C2
Wythenshawe Rd
RM10 81 C5
Wythens Wlk SE9 166 D5
Wythes Cl BR1 188 B1
Wythes Rd E16 122 A5
Wythfield Rd SE9 166 B5
Wyvenhoe Rd HA2 64 A5
Wyvern Est The KT3 200 A5
Wyvil Prim Sch
SW8 138 A5 270 B4
Wyvil Rd
SW8 138 A5 270 A4
Wyvis St E14 97 D2

X

Xavier Ho E17 35 B1

Y

Yabsley St E14 120 A5
Yaldam Ho SE1 263 A3
Yalding Ho 20 E5 74 B3
Yalding Rd SE16 118 A2
Yale Cl TW4 151 B6
Yale Ct NW6 69 D3
Yarborough Rd 1
SW19 180 B2
Yardley Cl E4 19 D6
Yardley Ct SM3 216 D4
Yardley La E4 19 D6
Yardley Prim Sch E4 20 A5
Yardley St WC1 234 A1
Yard The N1 233 B3
Yarlington Ct N11 31 A5
Yarmouth Cres N17 52 B4
Yarmouth Pl W1 248 C3
Yarnfield Sq 15
SE15 140 A4
Yarnton Way DA17,
DA18 125 B3
Yarrow Cres E6 100 A2
Yarrow Ho
12 Cubitt Town E14 120 A3
16 North Kensington
W10 90 C2
Yateley St SE18 121 D3
Yatesbury Ct E5 75 A3
Yates Ct NW2 68 D2
Yates Ho 22 E2 96 A4
Yatton Ho 15 W10 90 C2
YEADING 84 D3
Yeading Ave HA2 41 A1
Yeading Ct UB4 84 C3
Yeading Fork UB4 84 C3
Yeading Gdns UB4 84 B2
Yeading Ho UB4 84 D2
Yeading Jun & Inf Schs
UB4 84 C2
Yeading La Hayes UB4 84 B2
Northolt UB4, UB5 84 C4
Yeadon Ho 14 W10 90 C2
Yeames Cl W13 87 A1
Yearby Ho W10 90 C3
Yeate St N1 73 B1
Yeatman Rd N6 48 D3
Yeats Cl Ealing W7 108 D6
London NW10 67 C2
Yeend Cl KT8 195 C5
Yeldham Ho W6 112 D1
Yeldham Rd W6 112 D1
Yellowhammer Ct
NW9 27 C1
Yelverton Lo TW1 153 C4
Yelverton Rd SW11 136 B3
Ye Market CR0 221 B3
Yenston Cl SM4 201 C3
Yeoman Cl
Newham E16 122 D6
West Norwood SE27 160 D1
Yeoman Ct
Heston TW5 129 B5
8 Sutton SM1 218 B3
Yeoman Dr TW19 148 A3
Yeoman Rd UB5 63 A1
Yeomans Acre HA4 40 A3
Yeomans Mews
TW7 152 B6
Yeoman's Row
SW3 114 C3 257 B5
Yeoman St SE8 119 A2
Yeomans Way EN3 6 C3
Yeoman's Yd E1 253 D6
Yeo St E3 97 D2
Yeovil Cl BR6 227 C6
Yeovil Ho
Finsbury Pk N7 72 B6
North Kensington W10 90 C3
Yeovilton Pl KT2 175 C5
Yerbury Prim Sch
N19 71 D5
Yerbury Rd N19 71 D5
Yeshivo Horomo
Talmudical Coll N16 51 B1
Yesodey Hatorah Jun
Sch for Girls 7 N16 51 D2
Yesodey Hatorah Sec
Sch for Girls 5 N16 51 D2
Yester Dr BR7 188 A3
Yester Pk BR7 188 B4
Yester Rd BR7 188 B3
Yet Lev Ct E5 52 A1
Yew Ave UB7 104 A6
Yew Cl IG9 21 D2
Yewdale Cl BR1 186 C4
Yewfield Rd NW10 67 D2
Yew Gr NW2 68 D4
Yew Ho SE14 141 B3
Yews The TW15 170 D6
Yew Tree Ave N2 47 D6
Yewtree Cl
Harrow HA2 41 D5
Wood Green N22 31 C2
Yew Tree Cl DA16 146 A4
3 Lewisham SE13 142 A2
New Malden KT4 199 C1
Southgate N21 16 C4
Yew Tree Cotts
KT10 212 B6
Yew Tree Ct
Elstree WD6 9 D5
8 Stoke Newington
N16 73 B6
8 Sutton SM2 218 A1
4 Temple Fortune
NW11 47 B4
Yew Tree Gdns RM6 59 A4
Yew Tree Grange 2
W5 109 C6
Yew Tree Ho
New Malden KT4 199 C1
5 Surbiton KT6 198 A1
Yew Tree Lo 10
SW16 181 C6
Yewtree Rd BR3 207 B6
Yew Tree Rd
East Acton W12 111 D6
Hillingdon UB10 82 B6
Yew Trees TW17 192 B5
Yew Tree Wlk TW4 151 B6
Yew Wlk HA1 42 C1
YIEWSLEY 104 A6
Yiewsley Ct UB7 104 A5
Yoakley Rd N16 73 C6
Yoke Cl N7 72 A2
Yolande Gdns SE9 166 A6
Yonge Pk N4, N7 72 C5
York Ave Ealing W7 108 C5
Hayes UB3 83 A1
Mortlake SW14 155 A6
Sidcup DA15 167 D2
Stanmore HA7 25 B1
Walworth SE17 262 B2
York Bldgs
WC2 116 A6 250 B5
York Bridge
NW1 93 A3 238 A6
York Cl
17 Camberwell SE5 139 A3
Ealing W7 108 C5
Morden SM4 201 D5
Newham E6 100 B1
York Ct
Beckenham BR3 186 B2
Kingston u T KT2 175 D4
Palmers Green N13 16 A1
Wallington SM6 219 C3
York Gate NW1 238 B5
Southgate N14 16 A4
York Gr SE15 140 C4
York Hall L Ctr E2 96 C5
York Hill SE27, SW16 160 D1
York Ho Acton W3 111 A6
Chelsea SW3 257 D2
Chingford E4 35 C6
Edgware HA8 26 B4
Enfield EN2 5 B4
Forest Hill SE26 184 C5
1 Hendon NW4 28 D1
1 Ilford IG1 78 D6
Islington N5 72 C3
Kensington W8 245 C2
11 Kentish Town N7 71 D2
Kew TW9 132 C4
4 Kingston u T KT2 176 B3
Lambeth SE1 116 B3 260 D5
Marylebone W1 237 C4
Pentonville N1 233 C3
Richmond TW10 154 C6
South Norwood SE25 205 C5
10 West Acton W3 88 C1
York House Pl
W8 113 D4 245 C2
Yorkland Ave DA16 145 D1
Yorkley Ho 3 W10 90 C3
York Mans
Battersea SW11 268 B2
2 Hendon NW9 46 A3
Marylebone W1 238 A4
Walworth SE17 262 B2
York Mews
Camden Town NW5 71 B3
Ilford IG1 78 C5
York Par
Brentford TW8 109 D1
Hendon NW9 46 A3
York Pl
Battersea SW11 136 B2
Ilford IG1 78 C6
WC2 250 B5
York Place Mans
NW1 237 D4
York Rd
Battersea SW11,
SW18 136 B2
Belmont SM1, SM2 217 C1
Brentford TW8 109 D1
Chingford E4 35 C5
Dagenham W3 89 B1
Ealing W5 109 C3
Edmonton N18 34 B5
Forest Gate E7 77 A2
Friern Barnet N11 31 D4
Hounslow TW3 129 D2
Ilford IG1 78 C6
Kingston u T KT2 176 B3
Leyton E10 76 A5
New Barnet EN5 14 B6
Pinner HA6 22 A1
4 Richmond TW10 154 B6
SE1 116 B4 250 D2
Southgate N21 17 B4
Teddington TW11 174 C6
Thornton Heath CR0 204 C2
York Rd *continued*
Walthamstow E17 52 D4
Wimbledon SW19 180 A4
York Rise BR6 227 C6
Dartmouth Pk NW5 71 B5
York Road Bsns Ctr
SW11 136 B3
York St Chambers
W1 237 C4
Yorkshire Cl N16 73 C5
Yorkshire Gdns N18 34 B5
Yorkshire Grey SE9 165 D6
Yorkshire Grey Pl 13
NW3 70 A4
Yorkshire Grey Yd
WC1 240 C3
Yorkshire Rd
Limehouse E14 97 A1
Mitcham CR4 204 A5
York Sq 12 E14 97 A1
York St
Carshalton CR4 203 A2
Paddington
W1 92 D2 237 D4
Twickenham TW1 153 A3
York Terr EN2 5 A5
York Terr E
NW1 93 A3 238 B5
York Terr W
NW1 93 A3 238 A5
Yorkton St E2 96 A5
York Way
Barnsbury N1, N7,
NW1 72 A1
Chessington KT9 214 A1
Friern Barnet N20 14 D1
N1 233 B5
Twickenham TW13 151 B1
York Way Ct
Islington N1 233 C5
Islington N1 233 B5
York Wr Gate★ SW1 250 B4
Youngmans Cl EN2 5 A4
Young Rd E16 99 C1
Young's Bldgs EC1 242 B6
Youngs Brewery Visitor
Ctr★ SW18 157 D6
Youngs Ct SW11 268 B1
Youngs Rd IG2 57 B4
Young St W8 113 D4 245 C1
Yoxall Ho 2 W10 90 C3
Yoxford Ct 6 RM6 58 B4
Yoxley App IG2 57 A3
Yoxley Dr IG2 57 A3
Yukon Rd SW12 159 B4
Yunus Khan Cl E17 53 C4

Z

Zambezie Dr N9 18 C1
Zampa Rd SE16 118 C1
Zander Ct E2 96 A4
Zangwill Ho NW6 91 B5
Zangwill Rd SE18,
SE3 143 D4
Zaskin Coll 13 HA1 42 D3
Zealand Ave UB7 126 A5
Zealand Ho
11 Camberwell SE5 139 A3
4 Woolwich SE18 122 A2
Zealand Rd E3 97 A5
Zenith Lo 7 N3 29 D3
Zennor Rd SW12 159 C3
Zenoria St SE22 139 D1
Zermatt Rd CR7 205 A5
Zetland Ho W8 255 C6
Zetland St E14 98 A2
Zeus Ho N1 235 C1
Zion Ho 6 E1 96 C1
Zion Pl CR7 205 B5
Zion Rd CR7 205 B5
Zircon Ct N11 31 D3
ZK Pk CR0 220 B5
Zoar St SE1 117 A5 252 A4
Zodiac Ct CR0 204 D1
Zodiac Ho 3 E3 97 C3
Zoffany St N19 71 D6

List of numbered locations

In some busy areas of the maps it is not always possible to show the name of every place.

Where not all names will fit, some smaller places are shown by a number. If you wish to find out the name associated with a number, use this listing.

The places in this list are also listed conventionally in the Index.

Page number	→	10
Grid square	→	C1 2 Sunset Square
Location number	→	
Place name	→	

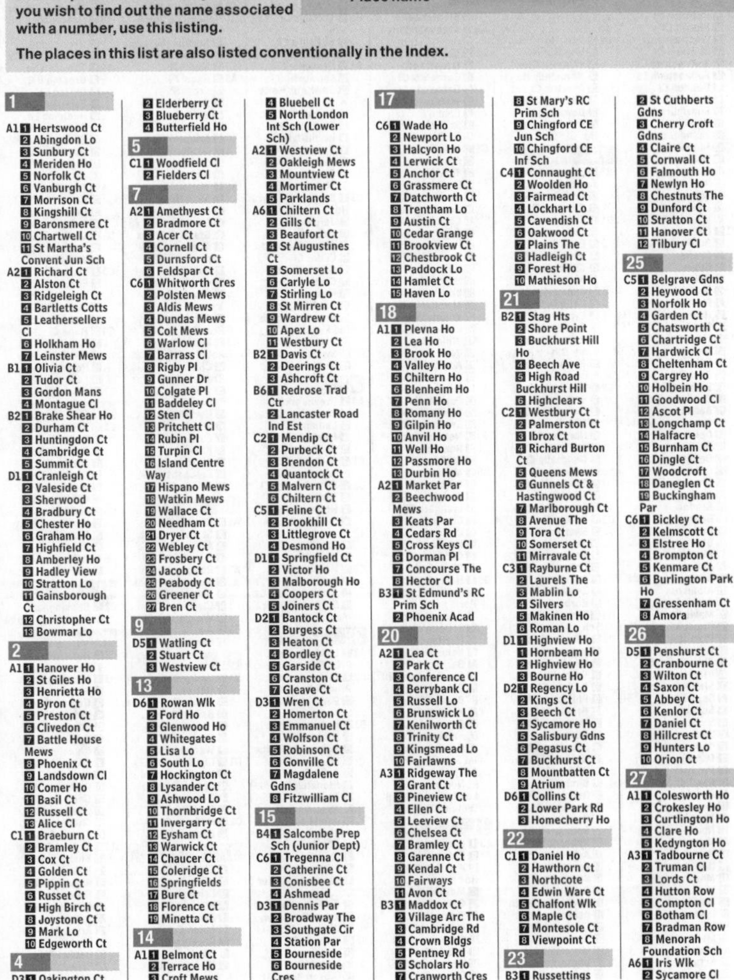

1

A1 1 Hertswood Ct
2 Abingdon Lo
3 Sunbury Ct
4 Meriden Ho
5 Norfolk Ct
6 Vanburgh Ct
7 Morrison Ct
8 Kingshill Ct
9 Baronsmere Ct
10 Chartwell Ct
11 St Martha's Convent Jun Sch
A2 1 Richard Ct
2 Alston Ct
3 Ridgeleigh Ct
4 Bartletts Cotts Cl
5 Leathersellers Cl
6 Holkham Ho
7 Leinster Mews
B1 1 Olivia Ct
2 Tudor Ct
3 Gordon Mans
4 Montague Cl
B2 1 Brake Shear Ho
2 Durham Ct
3 Huntingdon Ct
4 Cambridge Ct
5 Summit Ct
D1 1 Cranleigh Ct
2 Valeside Ct
3 Sherwood
4 Bradbury Ct
5 Chester Ho
6 Graham Ho
7 Highfield Ct
8 Amberley Ho
9 Hadley View
10 Stratton Lo
11 Gainsborough Ct
12 Christopher Ct
13 Bowmar Lo

2

A1 1 Hanover Ho
2 St Giles Ho
3 Henrietta Ho
4 Byron Ct
5 Preston Ct
6 Clivedon Ct
7 Battle House Mews
8 Phoenix Ct
9 Landsdown Ct
10 Comer Ho
11 Basil Ct
12 Russell Ct
13 Alice Cl
C1 1 Braeburn Ct
2 Bramley Ct
3 Cox Ct
4 Golden Ct
5 Pippin Ct
6 Russet Ct
7 High Birch Ct
8 Joystone Ct
9 Mark Lo
10 Edgeworth Ct

4

D3 1 Oakington Ct
2 Elderberry Ct
3 Blueberry Ct
4 Butterfield Ho

5

C1 1 Woodfield Cl
2 Fielders Cl

7

A2 1 Amethyest Ct
2 Bradmore Ct
3 Acer Ct
4 Cornell Ct
5 Durnsford Ct
6 Feldspar Ct
C6 1 Whitworth Cres
2 Polsten Mews
3 Aldis Mews
4 Dundas Mews
5 Colt Mews
6 Warlow Ct
7 Barrass Ct
8 Rigby Pl
9 Gunner Dr
10 Colgate Pl
11 Baddeley Cl
12 Sten Cl
13 Pritchett Cl
14 Rubin Pl
15 Turpin Ct
16 Island Centre Way
17 Hispano Mews
18 Watkin Mews
19 Wallace Ct
20 Needham Ct
21 Dryer Ct
22 Webley Ct
23 Frosbery Ct
24 Jacob Ct
25 Peabody Ct
26 Greener Ct
27 Bren Ct

9

D5 1 Watling Ct
2 Stuart Ct
3 Westview Ct

13

D6 1 Rowan Wlk
2 Ford Ho
3 Glenwood Ho
4 Whitegates
5 Lisa Lo
6 South Lo
7 Hockington Ct
8 Lysander Ct
9 Ashwood Lo
10 Thornbridge Ct
11 Invergarry Ct
12 Eysham Ct
13 Warwick Ct
14 Chaucer Ct
15 Coleridge Ct
16 Springfields
17 Bure Ct
18 Florence Ct
19 Minetta Ct

14

A1 1 Belmont Ct
2 Terrace Ho
3 Croft Mews
4 Bluebell Ct
5 North London Int Sch (Lower Sch)
A2 1 Westview Ct
2 Oakleigh Mews
3 Mountview Ct
4 Mortimer Ct
5 Parklands
A6 1 Chiltern Ct
2 Gills Ct
3 Beaufort Ct
4 St Augustines Ct
5 Somerset Lo
6 Carlyle Lo
7 Stirling Lo
8 St Mirren Ct
9 Wardrew Ct
10 Apex Lo
11 Westbury Ct
B2 1 Davis Ct
2 Deerings Ct
3 Ashcroft Ct
B6 1 Redrose Trad Ctr
2 Lancaster Road Ind Est
C2 1 Mendip Ct
2 Purbeck Ct
3 Brendon Ct
4 Quantock Ct
5 Malvern Ct
6 Chiltern Ct
C5 1 Feline Ct
2 Brookhill Ct
3 Littlegrove Ct
4 Desmond Ho
D1 1 Springfield Ct
2 Victor Ho
3 Malborough Ho
4 Coopers Ct
5 Joiners Ct
D2 1 Bantock Ct
2 Burgess Ct
3 Heaton Ct
4 Bordley Ct
5 Garside Ct
6 Cranston Ct
7 Gleave Ct
D3 1 Wren Ct
2 Homerton Ct
3 Emmanuel Ct
4 Wolfson Ct
5 Robinson Ct
6 Gonville Ct
7 Magdalene Gdns
8 Fitzwilliam Ct

15

B4 1 Salcombe Prep Sch (Junior Dept)
C6 1 Tregenna Ct
2 Catherine Ct
3 Conisbee Ct
4 Ashmead
D3 1 Dennis Par
2 Broadway The
3 Southgate Cir
4 Station Par
5 Bourneside
6 Bourneside Cres

17

C6 1 Wade Ho
2 Newport Lo
3 Halcyon Ho
4 Lerwick Ct
5 Anchor Ct
6 Grassmere Ct
7 Trentham Ct
8 Datchworth Ct
9 Austin Ct
10 Cedar Grange
11 Brookview Ct
12 Chestbrook Ct
13 Paddock Lo
14 Hamlet Ct
15 Haven Lo

18

A1 1 Plevna Ho
2 Lea Ho
3 Brook Ho
4 Valley Ho
5 Chiltern Ho
6 Blenheim Ho
7 Penn Ho
8 Romany Ho
9 Gilpin Ho
10 Anvil Ho
11 Well Ho
12 Passmore Ho
13 Durbin Ho
A2 1 Market Par
2 Beechwood Mews
3 Keats Par
4 Cedars Rd
5 Cross Keys Cl
6 Dorman Pl
7 Concourse The
8 Hector Ct
B3 1 St Edmund's RC Prim Sch
2 Phoenix Acad

20

A2 1 Lea Ct
2 Park Ct
3 Conference Cl
4 Berrybank Ct
5 Russell Lo
6 Brunswick Lo
7 Kenilworth Ct
8 Trinity Ct
9 Kingsmead Lo
10 Fairlawns
A3 1 Ridgeway The
2 Grant Ct
3 Pineview Ct
4 Ellen Ct
5 Leeview Ct
6 Chelsea Ct
7 Bramley Ct
8 Garenne Ct
9 Kendal Ct
10 Fairways
11 Avon Ct
B3 1 Maddox Ct
2 Village Arc The
3 Cambridge Rd
4 Crown Bldgs
5 Pentney Rd
6 Scholars Ho
7 Cranworth Cres

21

C1 1 Daniel Ho
2 Hawthorn Ho
3 Northcote
4 Edwin Ware Ct
5 Chalfont Wlk
6 Maple Ct
7 Montesole Ct
8 Viewpoint Ct

23

B3 1 Russettings

24

B2 1 St Mary's RC Prim Sch
9 Chingford CE Jun Sch
10 Chingford CE Inf Sch
C4 1 Connaught Ct
2 Woolden Ho
3 Fairmead Ct
4 Lockhart Lo
5 Cavendish Ct
6 Oakwood Ct
7 Plains The
8 Hadleigh Ct
9 Forest Ho
10 Mathieson Ho

18

B2 1 Stag Hts
2 Shore Point
3 Buckhurst Hill Ho
4 Beech Ave
5 High Road Buckhurst Hill
6 Highclears
C2 1 Westbury Ct
2 Palmerston Ct
3 Ibrox Ct
4 Richard Burton Ct
5 Queens Mews
6 Gunnels Ct & Hastingwood Ct
7 Marlborough Ct
8 Avenue The
9 Tora Ct
10 Somerset Ct
11 Mirravale Ct
C3 1 Rayburne Ct
2 Laurels The
3 Mablin Lo
4 Silvers
5 Makinen Ho
6 Roman Lo
D1 1 Highview Ho
2 Hornbeam Ho
3 Highview Ho
4 Bourne Ho
D2 1 Regency Lo
2 Kings Ct
3 Beech Ct
4 Sycamore Ho
5 Salisbury Gdns
6 Pegasus Ct
7 Buckhurst Ct
8 Mountbatten Ct
9 Atrium
D6 1 Collins Ct
2 Lower Park Rd
3 Homecherry Ho

25

C5 1 Belgrave Gdns
2 Heywood Ct
3 Norfolk Ho
4 Garden Ct
5 Chatsworth Ct
6 Chartridge Ct
7 Hardwick Ct
8 Cheltenham Ct
9 Cargrey Ho
10 Holbein Ho
11 Goodwood Ct
12 Ascot Pl
13 Longchamp Ct
14 Hallace
15 Burnham Ct
16 Dingle Ct
17 Woodcroft
18 Daneglen Ct
19 Buckingham Par
C6 1 Bickley Ct
2 Kelmscott Ct
3 Elstree Ho
4 Brompton Ct
5 Kenmare Ct
6 Burlington Park Ho
7 Gressenham Ct
8 Amora

26

D5 1 Penshurst Ct
2 Cranbourne Ct
3 Wilton Ct
4 Saxon Ct
5 Abbey Ct
6 Kenlor Ct
7 Daniel Ct
8 Hillcrest Ct
9 Hunters Lo
10 Orion Ct

27

A1 1 Colesworth Ho
2 Crokesley Ho
3 Curtlington Ho
4 Clare Ho
5 Kedyngton Ho
A3 1 Tadbourne Ct
2 Truman Ct
3 Lords Ct
4 Hutton Row
5 Compton Ct
6 Botham Ct
7 Bradman Row
8 Menorah Foundation Sch
A6 1 Iris Wlk
2 Sycamore Cl

A6
- 3 Aster Ct
- 4 Firethorn Cl
- 5 Berberry Cl
- 6 Hibiscus Cl
- 7 Roseway

B5
- 1 Monarchs Ct
- 2 Kensington Ct
- 3 Grosvenor Ct
- 4 Chasewood Ct
- 5 Mathilda Marks-Kennedy Jewish Prim Sch

C2
- 1 Rufforth Ct
- 2 Riccall Ct
- 3 Lindholme Ct
- 4 Driffield Ct
- 5 Jack Ashley Ct
- 6 Folkingham La
- 7 Debden Ct
- 8 Holbeach Cl
- 9 Shawbury Ct
- 10 Daniel Ct
- 11 Leander Ct
- 12 Nimrod
- 13 Nisbet
- 14 Pixton
- 15 Rapide
- 16 Ratier
- 17 Marham Dr
- 18 Wardell Field

D1
- 1 Gauntlet
- 2 Guilfoyle
- 3 Grebe
- 4 Gates
- 5 Galy
- 6 Folland
- 7 Firefly
- 8 Halifax
- 9 Debussy
- 10 Crosbie
- 11 Grant Ct
- 12 Ham Ct
- 13 Deal Ct
- 14 Ember Ct
- 15 Canterbury Ct
- 16 Beaumont Ct
- 17 Cirrus
- 18 Defiant
- 19 Dessouter
- 20 Douglas
- 21 Cobham
- 22 Camm
- 23 Bradon
- 24 Boarhound
- 25 Bodmin
- 26 Bleriot
- 27 Blackburn
- 28 Audax
- 29 Anson
- 30 Albatross
- 31 Arran Ct
- 32 Mavis Ct
- 33 Goosander Ct
- 34 Platt Halls (a)
- 35 Writtle Ho
- 36 Platt Halls (b)
- 37 Platt Halls (c)

D2
- 1 Slatter
- 2 Sopwith
- 3 Saimet
- 4 Sassoon
- 5 Roe
- 6 Orde
- 7 Osprey
- 8 Prodger
- 9 Randall
- 10 Porte
- 11 Norris
- 12 Nardini
- 13 Noel
- 14 Nicolson
- 15 Napier
- 16 Nighthawk
- 17 Moorhouse
- 18 Moineau
- 19 Mitchell
- 20 Lysander
- 21 Lillywhite
- 22 Martynside
- 23 March
- 24 Kemp
- 25 Mercury
- 26 Merlin
- 27 Hudson
- 28 Hawker
- 29 Hawfinch
- 30 Heracles
- 31 Hector
- 32 Concourse The

D3
- 1 Wellington
- 2 Wheeler
- 3 Whittaker
- 4 Whittle
- 5 Tedder
- 6 Cranwell Ct
- 7 Tait
- 8 Spooner

28

D1
- 1 York Ho
- 2 Windsor Ho
- 3 Regency Cres
- 4 Normandy Ho
- 5 Allerton Ct
- 6 Beaulieu Ho
- 7 Dewlands Ct
- 8 Knightshayes Ho

29

A3
- 2 Frances & Dick James Ct
- 3 Farthing Ct
- 4 Coniston Ct

B1
- 1 Carlisle Ho
- 2 Laburnum Lo
- 3 Eden Ct
- 4 Moorcroft Ct
- 5 Clifford Lo
- 6 Acacia Lo
- 7 Cumberland Ct
- 8 Little Dell Lo
- 9 Cyprus Ct
- 10 Cyprus Ho
- 11 Pardes House Gram Sch
- 12 Pardes House Prim Sch

C2
- 1 Sheringham Ct
- 2 St Ronan's
- 3 Crescent Rise
- 4 Elm Ct
- 5 Norman Ct
- 6 Marlow Ct
- 7 Dancastle Ct
- 8 Newman Ct
- 9 Station Mans
- 10 Alice Ct
- 11 Siamese Mews

D3
- 1 Hadley Ct
- 2 Sherbrook Ho
- 3 Shine Ho
- 4 Regent Ct
- 5 Lodge Mead Ct
- 6 Spencer Ct
- 7 Zenith Lo

D4
- 1 Moss Hall Inf Sch

D5
- 1 Silverbell Ct
- 2 Inverey Ho
- 3 Wimbush Ho
- 4 Tudor Lo
- 5 Duncan Ct
- 6 Philipson Ho

D6
- 1 Brookfield Ct
- 2 Magnolia Ct
- 3 Dunbar Ct
- 4 Haughmond
- 5 Nansen Village
- 6 Willow Ct
- 7 Birch Ct
- 8 Beechcroft Ct
- 9 Speedwell Ct
- 10 Woodside Ct
- 11 Speedwell Ho
- 12 Rebecca Ho
- 13 Ashbourne Ct
- 14 Forest Ct
- 15 Beecholme
- 16 Greville Lo
- 17 St Johnstone Ho
- 18 Ashbourne Cl
- 19 Clements Ct
- 20 Station App
- 21 Montclair Ct
- 22 Winterberry Ct
- 23 Caroline Ct

30

A2
- 1 Our Lady of Lourdes RC Prim Sch

A4
- 1 Sharon Ct
- 2 Lydia Ct
- 3 Beatrice Lo
- 4 Grange Ct
- 5 Blissland Ct

A5
- 1 Archgate Bsns Ctr
- 2 Robart Ho
- 3 Danescroft
- 4 Cornelius Ct
- 5 Gable Lo
- 6 Waterville Lo
- 7 Sarnes Ct
- 8 St Michael's RC Gram Sch

B1
- 1 New Trinity Rd
- 2 Garden Ho
- 3 Todd Ho
- 4 Sayers Ho
- 5 Mowbray Ho
- 6 Bouchier Ho
- 7 Goodyear Ho
- 8 Lochleven Ho
- 9 Berwick Ho
- 10 Oak Ho
- 11 Hilton Ho
- 12 East View Ho
- 13 Myddleton Ho
- 14 Willow Wlk
- 15 Craven Ho
- 16 Willow Ho
- 17 Vane Ho
- 18 Adelphi Ct
- 19 Annette White Lo
- 20 Foskett Ho
- 21 Elmfield Ho
- 22 Sycamore Ho
- 23 Netherwood
- 24 Rew Lo
- 25 William Ct

B5
- 1 Murray Ho
- 2 Damon Ho
- 3 Wendy Ho
- 4 Lychgate Ct
- 5 Clarence Ct
- 6 Carley Ct
- 7 Herniston Ct
- 8 Cardrew Ct
- 9 Whitefriars Ct

D5
- 1 Halliwick Ct
- 2 Halliwick Court Par
- 3 Queen's Par
- 4 St John's Villas
- 5 Hartland Ct
- 6 Kennard Mans
- 7 Bensley Cl
- 8 Leadbeaters Cl
- 9 Gibson Ct
- 10 Burton Ct
- 11 Knights Ct
- 12 Constable Cl
- 13 Alderman Ct
- 14 North London Int Sch (Upper Sch)
- 15 North London Int Sch (IB Diploma Ctre)

31

A3
- 1 Campe Ho
- 2 Betsylne Ho
- 3 Pymmes Brook Ho
- 4 Mosswell Ho
- 5 Cavendish Ho
- 6 Tudor Ho
- 7 Kingsfield Ho
- 8 Hatch Ho
- 9 Hampden Ct

24 North London Int Sch (Lower Sch)

25 North London Int Sch (Lower School)

D31
- 1 Carlisle Lo *(see note)*

B6
- 1 Grovefield
- 2 Lapworth
- 3 Stewards Holte Wlk
- 4 Stanhope Ho
- 5 Holmsdale Ho
- 6 Crosby Ct
- 7 Leyland Ct
- 8 Boundary Ct
- 9 Stateland Ct

C5
- 1 Barbara Martin Ho
- 2 Jerome Ct
- 3 Limes Cl
- 4 Arnos Grove Ct
- 5 Cedar Ct
- 6 Betspath Ho
- 7 Curtis Ho
- 8 Mason Ho
- 9 Danford Ho
- 10 New Southgate Ind Est
- 11 Palmer's Ct
- 12 Swinson Ho
- 13 Jackson Ho

32

A4
- 1 Brownlow Ct
- 2 Brownlow Ct
- 3 Latham Ct
- 4 Fairlawns
- 5 Beaumaris

B1
- 1 St Paul's RC Prim Sch

C1
- 1 Penwortham Ct
- 2 Tarleton Ct
- 3 Holmeswood Ct
- 4 Kwesi Johnson Ct
- 5 Sandlings The
- 6 Suraj Ho

C6
- 1 Hazelwood Ct
- 2 Ashbourne Ct
- 3 Mapledurham Lo
- 4 Springfield Par Mews

33

A2
- 1 Lordship Lane Prim Sch

C2
- 1 Risley Avenue Prim Sch
- 2 Parkside Prep Sch

D1
- 1 Kenmare Dr
- 2 Ashling Ho
- 3 Honeysett Ho
- 4 Wilson's Ave
- 5 Palm Tree Ct
- 6 Stoneleigh Ct
- 7 Brook St
- 8 Assunah Sch
- 9 John Loughborough Sch

D3
- 1 Charles Ho
- 2 Moselle Ho
- 3 Ermine Ho
- 4 Kathleen Ferrier Ct
- 5 Concord Ho
- 6 Rees Ho
- 7 Williams Ho
- 8 Nursery Ct
- 9 William Rainbird Ho
- 10 Gibson Bsns Ctr

A4
- 1 Cheddar Cl
- 2 Wincanton Ct
- 3 Whitby Ct
- 4 Richmond Ct
- 5 Tadworth Ct
- 6 Wensley Cl
- 7 Howeth Ct
- 8 Kilnsey Ct
- 9 Harrogate Ct
- 10 Ripon Ct

B1
- 1 Cedar Ct
- 2 Carisbrook
- 3 St Ivian Ct
- 4 Barrington Ct
- 5 Essex Lo

B5
- 1 St Pauls CE Prim Sch
- 2 St Paul's CE Prim Sch

11 Wingate Trad Est

2 London Tottenham Coll

3 St Francis de Sales RC Jun & Inf Sch

D4
- 1 Regan Ho
- 2 Isis Ho
- 3 Boundary Ct
- 4 Stellar Ho
- 5 Cooperage Cl

34

A3
- 1 St Paul's & All Hallows CE Jun & Inf Schs
- 2 Northumberland Park Com Sch
- 3 Maple Pl

A5
- 1 Angel Pl
- 2 Cross St
- 3 Scott Ho
- 4 Beck Ho
- 5 Booker Rd
- 6 Bridport Ho
- 7 Cordwain Ho
- 8 St James's Ct
- 9 Highmead

A6
- 1 Walton Ho
- 2 Alma Ho
- 3 Brompton Ho
- 4 Field Ho
- 5 Bradwell Mews
- 6 Angel Corner Par
- 7 Paul Ct
- 8 Cuthbert Rd
- 9 Brockenhurst Mews
- 10 Brettenham Prim Sch

B3
- 1 Kenneth Robbins Ho
- 2 Charles Bradlaugh Ho
- 3 Woodrow Ct
- 4 Cheviot
- 5 Corbridge
- 6 Whittingham
- 7 Eastwood Cl
- 8 Alnwick
- 9 Bamburgh
- 10 Bellingham
- 11 Briaris Cl

35

A1
- 1 Clayton Ct
- 2 St Andrew's Ct
- 3 Aranya Ct
- 4 Fitzwilliam Ho

A2
- 1 Romany Gdns
- 2 Swansland Gdns
- 3 Garnett Way
- 4 Claymore Ct
- 5 Winchester Ct

C5
- 1 Ainslie Ho
- 2 Lewis Ho

36

B5
- 1 Hedgemoor Ct
- 2 Hewitt Ho
- 3 Castle Ho
- 4 Bailey Ct
- 5 Harcourt Ho
- 6 Gerboa Ct
- 7 Wentworth Ct

D1
- 1 Chatham Rd
- 2 Washington Ho
- 3 Cherry Tree Ct
- 4 Grosvenor Lo
- 5 Torfell

D2
- 1 Hillboro Ct
- 2 Dorchester Ct

37

A1
- 1 Chiltons The
- 2 Ullswater Ct
- 3 Leigh Ct
- 4 Woburn Ct
- 5 Alveston Sq
- 6 Eaton Ct
- 7 Regency Ct
- 8 Cowley Ct
- 9 High Oaks Lo

10 Snaresbrook Coll Prep Sch

10 South Woodford

A2
- 1 Lindal Ct
- 2 Hockley Ct
- 3 Woodleigh
- 4 Milne Ct
- 5 Cedar Ct
- 6 Elizabeth Ct
- 7 Silvermead
- 8 Laurel Mead Ct
- 9 Mitre Ct
- 10 Pevensey Ct
- 11 Lyndhurst Ct
- 12 Manor Court Lo

A3
- 1 New Jubilee Ct
- 2 Chartwell Ct
- 3 Greenwood
- 4 Clementine Wlk

A4
- 1 Terrace The
- 2 Broomhill Ct
- 3 Clifton Ct
- 4 Fairstead Lo
- 5 Hadleigh Ct
- 6 Broadmead Ct
- 7 Wilton Ct
- 8 Fairfield Ct
- 9 Higham Ct
- 10 Aston Ct

A6
- 1 Tree Tops
- 2 Cranfield Ct
- 3 Percival Ho
- 4 Raine Gdns

B1
- 1 Station Est
- 2 Station App
- 3 James Ct

C3
- 1 Liston Way
- 2 Elizabeth Ct
- 3 Coopersale Cl
- 4 Sunset Ct
- 5 Lambourne Ct

C4
- 1 Hope Ct
- 2 Rex Par
- 3 Shalford
- 4 Rodings The
- 5 Lawrence Ct
- 6 Cowan Lo

40

C1
- 1 Salisbury Ho
- 2 Rodwell Cl
- 3 Pretoria Ho
- 4 Ottawa Ho
- 5 Swallow Ct
- 6 Wellington Ho
- 7 Canberra Ho

C6
- 1 Tulip Ct
- 2 Hyacinth Ct
- 3 Rose Ct
- 4 Iris Ct

D6
- 1 Ashburton Ct
- 2 Northend Lodge

41

C2
- 1 Buckingham College Prep Sch

42

C2
- 6 Harrovian Bsns Village

D3
- 1 Nightingale Ct
- 2 St John's Ct
- 3 Gayton Ct
- 4 Wilton Pl
- 5 Murray Ct
- 6 Cymbeline Ct
- 7 Knowles Ct
- 8 Charville Ct
- 9 Lime Ct
- 10 Petherton Ct
- 11 Garth Ct
- 12 Chalfont Ct
- 13 Shepherds Ct
- 14 Zaskin Coll

D4
- 1 Crystal Cctr The
- 2 Blue Point Ct
- 3 Ryan Ho
- 4 Rothwell Ct
- 5 Bruce Ho
- 6 Middlesex Ct
- 7 Ingram Ho
- 8 Arless Ho
- 9 Leaf Ho
- 10 Becket Fold
- 11 Brandan Ho
- 12 Robert Ho

46
A2 1 Milton Rd
2 Stanley Rd
A3 1 Mapesbury Mews
2 York Mans
3 Telford Rd
4 Beis Soroh Schneirer (Sch)
A5 1 Pilkington Ct
2 Cousins Ct
3 Seton Ct
4 Frensham Ct
5 Chatton Ct
6 Geraldine Ct
7 Swynford Gdns
8 Miller Ct
9 Roffey Ct
10 Peace Ct
11 Rambler Ct
12 Lion Ct
13 Wenlock Gdns
14 Dogrose Ct
15 Harry Ct
16 Tribune Ct
17 Bonville Gdns
18 Pearl Ct
B4 1 Vivian Mans
2 Parade Mans
3 Georgian Ct
4 Florence Mans
5 Park Mans
6 Cheyne Cl
7 Queens Par
8 Central Mans
C5 1 Courtney Ho
2 Golderton
3 Thornbury
4 Ferrydale Lo
5 Studio Mews
6 Brampton La
7 Short St
8 Belle Vue Rd
9 Longford Ct
10 Ashwood Ho
D4 1 Hasmonean Prim Sch
2 Independant Jewish Day Sch
D5 1 Midford Ho
2 Rockfield Ho
3 Lisselton Ho
4 Acrefield Ho
5 London Sch of Jewish Studies
6 Beth Jacob Gram Sch
7 Bell Lane Prim Sch
8 Nancy Reuben Prim Sch

47
A2 1 Talmud Torah Tiferes Shlomo
B2 1 Berkeley Ct
2 Exchange Mans
3 Beechcroft Ct
4 Nedahall Ct
B3 1 Charlton Lo
2 Clifton Gdns
B4 1 Hallswelle Par
2 Belmont Par
3 Temple Fortune Ho
4 Yew Tree Ct
5 Temple Fortune Par
6 Courtleigh
7 Arcade Ho
8 Queens Ct
9 Temple Fortune Ct
10 Crispin Mews
B5 1 Monkville Par
2 Ashbourne Par

48
A6 1 St Mary's Gn
2 Dunstan Cl
3 Paul Byrne Ho
4 Longfield Ct
5 Warwick Ct
6 Branksome Ct
7 Sherwood Hall

49
B6 1 Dorchester Ct
2 Old Chapel Pl
3 Athenaeum Pl
4 Risborough Cl
5 Risborough Ct
C1 1 Calvert Ct
2 Academy The
3 Whitehall Mans
4 Pauntley St
5 Archway Hts
6 Pauntley Ho
7 St Aloysius RC Coll
D1 1 Louise White Ho
2 Levison Way
3 Sanders Way
4 Birbeck Ho
5 Scholars Ct
6 Mount Carmel RC Tech Coll for Girls
D2 1 Eleanor Rathbone Ho
2 Christopher Lo
3 Monkridge
4 Marbleford Ct
5 High London
6 Garton Ho
7 Hilltop Ho
8 Caroline Martyn Ho
9 Arthur Henderson Ho
10 Margaret Mcmillan Ho
11 Enid Stacy Ho
12 Mary McArthur Ho
13 Bruce Glasier Ho
14 John Wheatley Ho
15 Keir Hardie Ho
16 Monroe Ho
17 Iberia Ho
18 Lygoe Ho
19 Lambert Ho
20 Shelbourne Ho
21 Arkansas Ho
22 Lafitte Ho
23 Shreveport Ho
24 Packenham Ho
25 Orpheus Ho
26 Fayetville Ho
27 Bayon Ho
D4 1 Kelland Cl
2 Truro Ct
3 Veryan Ct
4 Coulsdon Ct

50
A1 1 Beeches The
2 Lambton Ct
3 Nugent Ct
4 Lambton Mews
5 Mews The
A2 1 Marie Lloyd Gdns
2 Edith Cavell Cl
3 Marie Stopes Ct
4 Jessie Blythe La
5 Barbara Rudolph Ct
6 Hetty Rees Ct
7 Leyden Mans
8 Brambledown
9 Lochbie
10 Lyngham Ct
11 High Mount
12 Woodlands The
13 St Gildas' RC Jun Sch
A4 1 Margaret Hill Ho
2 Manray Ct
3 Hermiston Ct
4 Carleton Ho
5 Rokesly Jun & Inf Schs
A5 1 Mackenzie Ho
2 Stowell Ho
3 Campsbourne Ho
4 Palace Gate Mews
5 St Mary's CE Jun Sch
6 Greig City Acad
7 North London Rudolf Steiner Sch
B1 1 Lawson Ct
2 Wiltshire Ct
3 Fenstanton
4 Hutton Ct
5 Wisbech
6 Islington Arts & Media Sch
B5 3 St Mary's CE Inf Sch
D4 1 South Harringay Jun & Inf Schs
D5 1 Wordsworth Par
2 Spanswick Lo
3 Barker Ho
4 St John Vianney RC Prim Sch
D6 1 Langham Cl
2 Sidi Ct
3 Ince Terr

51
A2 1 Finmere Ho
2 Keynsham Ho
3 Kilpeck Ho
4 Knaresborough Ho
5 Leighfield Ho
6 Lonsdale Ho
7 Groveley Ho
8 Wensleydale Ho
9 Badminton Ct
B2 1 Selwood Ho
2 Bnois Jerusalem Girls Sch
3 Mendip Ho
3 Ennerdale Ho
3 Getters Talmud Torah
4 Delamere Ho
5 Westwood Ho
6 Bernwood Ho
7 Allerdale Ho
8 Chattenden Ho
9 Farningham Ho
10 Oakend Ho
B5 1 Wisdom Sch
C1 1 Godstone Ct
2 Farnham Ct
3 Milford Ct
4 Cranleigh Ct
5 Haslemere Ct
6 Belmont Ct
7 Hockworth Ho
8 Garratt Ho
9 Fairburn Ho
10 Thorndale Ho
11 Oakdene Ho
12 Briardale Ho
C2 1 Beis Rochel d'Satmar Girls Sch
3 Our Lady's Convent RC High Sch
C3 1 Oatfield Ho
2 Perry Ct
3 Henrietta Ho
4 Bournes Ho
5 Chisley Rd
6 Twyford Ho
7 Langford Cl
8 Hatchfield Ho
D1 1 Stamford Hill Mans
2 Montefiore Ct
3 Berwyn Ho
4 Clent Ho
5 Chiltern Ho
6 Laindon Ho
7 Pentland Ho
D2 1 Regent Ct
2 Stamford Lo
3 Holmwood Ct
4 Bobov Foundation Sch
5 Yesodey Hatorah Sec Sch for Girls
6 Lubavitch Boys Prim Sch
7 Yesodey Hatorah Jun Sch for Girls
8 Lubavitch Girls Prim Sch
9 Lubavitch House Sch (Jun Boys)
10 Skinners Company Sch (Upper)
D3 1 Sherboro Rd
2 Westcott Cl
3 Cadoxton Ave
D4 1 Westerfield Rd
2 Suffield Rd
D5 1 Laseron Ho
2 Greenway Cl
3 Earlsmead Prim Sch
3 Tottenham Gn E
4 Tottenham Gn E South Side
5 Deaconess Ct
6 Elliot Ct
7 Bushmead Cl
8 Beaufort Ho
9 Tynemouth Terr
10 Green CE Sch Holy Trinity (Inf Annexe) The
D6 1 Holcombe Rd
2 Rigby Ho
3 Chaplin Rd
4 Keswick Apartments
5 Ambleside Cl
6 Lauriston Apartments
7 Terrall Apartments
8 Old School Ct
9 Nicholson Ct
10 Reynardson's Ct
11 Protheroe Ho
13 North London Coll
14 Green CE Prim Sch The

52
A1 1 Stamford Gr E
2 Stamford Mans
3 Grove Mans
4 Stamford Gr W
6 Talmud-Torah Yetev-Lev
A6 2 Welbourne Prim Sch
B1 1 Hawkwood Mount
2 Holmbury View
3 High Hill Ferry
4 Leaside Ho
5 Courtlands
6 Tayyibah Girls Sch
6 Ivy Ho
7 Shelford Ct
8 Skinner's Company's Lower Sch

53
A4 1 Hammond Ct
2 St James Apartments
3 Grange The
A5 1 Bristol Park Rd
2 Stoneydown Ho
3 Callonfield
4 Hardyng Ho
5 Stoneydown Park Sch
6 St Patrick's RC Prim Sch
B5 1 Palace Mews
2 Thomas Jacomb Pl
C1 1 Wellington Mans
2 Clewer Ct
3 Cochrane Ct
C3 1 Samira Cl
2 Walter Savill Twr
3 Boston Rd
C5 1 Westbury Ho
2 Hatherley Ho
3 Vintry Mews
4 Tylers Ct
5 Merchants Lo
6 Gillards Mews
7 Blacksmiths Ho
8 Central Par
D1 1 Fitzgerald Ct
2 Bechervaise Ct
3 Underwood Ct
D2 1 Staton Ct
2 Howell Ct
3 Atkinson Ct
4 Russell Ct
5 St Catherines Twr
6 St Lukes Ct
7 St Matthews Ct
8 St Mark's Ct
9 St Elizabeth Ct
10 Emanuel Ct
11 St Thomas Ct
12 Beaumont Ho
13 Shelley Ct
14 St Paul's Twr
15 Flack Ct
16 King Ct
17 Osborne Ct
18 Muriel Ct
19 All Saints Twr
20 St Josephs Ct
D4 1 Harriet Ho
2 Eastbank Cl
D5 1 Nash Ho
2 St Columbas Ho
3 Attlee Terr
4 Astins Ho
5 Lindens The
6 Kevan Ct
7 Squire's Almshouses
8 Berry Field Cl
9 Connaught Ct
10 Holmcroft Ho
11 St Mary's Church Ho
D6 1 Hallingbury Ct
2 Mace Ho
3 Gaitskell Ho
4 Hancocke Ho
5 Trinity Ho
6 Fanshaw Ho
7 Hilltop
8 Batten Ho
9 Bradwell Ho
10 Walton Ho
11 Temple Ho
12 Gower Ho
13 Maple Ho
14 Poplars Ho
15 Cedars Ho
16 Kimm Ho
17 O'Grady Ho
18 Latham Ho
19 Powell Ct
20 Crosbie Ho

54
A2 1 Ayerst Ct
2 Dare Ct
3 St Edwards Ct
A4 1 Collard's Almshouses
2 Ellen Miller Ho
3 Tom Smith Ho
A5 1 Northwood Twr
2 Walnut Ct
3 Albert Whicher Ho
4 Pelly Ct
5 Ravenswood Ind Est
6 Holland Ct
7 Emberson Ho
8 St Mark's Ho
9 Alfred Villas
10 Leonard Ho
11 Old Station Yard The
A6 1 St David's Ct
2 Golden Par
3 Chestnuts Ct
4 Matthew Ct
5 Gilbert Ho
6 Manning Ho
7 Southgate Ho
8 Boyden Ho
9 Prospect Ho
10 Newton Ho
C1 2 Connaught Sch for Girls
D2 1 Buxton Ct
2 Hanbury Dr
3 Forest Lea
4 Watershipdown Ho

55
A3 1 Aldham Hall
2 Parkside Ct
3 Mapperley Cl
4 Weavers Ho
5 Cyna Ct
6 Reed Mans
7 Thornton Ho
8 Hardwick Ct
9 St Joseph's Convent Sch
A4 1 Kingsley Grange
2 Station Par
3 Gwynne Ho
4 Staveley Ct
5 Thurlow Ct
6 Devon Ho
7 Wellington Pas
8 Wanstead Hts
9 Hollies The
10 Little Holt
11 Hunter Ct
12 Mountier Ct
13 Woodland Ct
14 Dudley Ct
15 Struan Ho
16 Westleigh Ct
A5 1 Shernwood Ho
2 Orwell Lo
3 Hermitage Ct
4 Gowan Lea
5 Woodford Ho
6 Eagle Ct
7 Newbury Ct
8 Shelley Ct
9 Hardy Ct
10 Dickens Ct
11 Byron Ct
A6 1 Millbrook
2 Half Acre
3 Elmbrook
4 Grange The
5 Glenavon Lo
6 Glenwood Ct
7 Ferndown
8 Embassy Ct
9 Orestes Ct
10 Walbrook
11 Helmsley
12 Snaresbrook Hall
B4 1 Nightingale Ct
2 Chelston Ct
3 Grosvenor Ct
4 Louise Ct
5 St Davids Ct
6 Cedar Ct
7 Shrubbery The
8 Nightingale Mews
B5 1 Great Hall The
2 Clock Ct
3 Langham Ho
B6 1 Victoria Ct
2 Kenwood Gdns
3 Thaxted Lo
4 Albert Rd
5 Albert Ho
6 Falcon Ct
7 Deborah Ct
8 Swift Ho
9 Pulteney Gdns
10 Spring Ct
11 Trinity Gdns
12 Foxdene Cl

56
B4 1 High View Par
2 Spurway Par
3 Florence Root Ho
4 Rohan Pl
5 Homeheather Ho
D4 1 St Augustine's RC Prim Sch

57
A3 1 Catherine Ct
2 Ivy Terr
3 Newbury Cotts

58

B1
1 Caledonian Cl
2 Talisman Cl
3 Norseman Cl
4 Frank Slater Ho
5 Brook's Mans
6 Brook's Par

B2
1 Mitre Ct
2 Coppins The
3 Stanetta Ct
4 Wilnett Ct
5 Wilnett Villas

B4
1 Sudbury Ct
2 Dunwich Ct
3 Cromer Terr
4 Norfolk Ct
5 Framlingham Ct
6 Yoxford Ct

C4
1 Swaffham Ct
2 Nacton Ct
3 Suffolk Ct

D2
1 Pavement Mews
2 Chadview Ct
3 Granary Ct
4 Bedwell Ct
5 Chapel La
6 Faulkner Ct
7 Maple Ct
8 Willow Ct
9 Cedar Terr

63

C2
1 Wimborne Ct
2 Haydock Green Flats
3 Brighton Dr
4 Blaydon Ct
5 Fakenham Ct
6 Rutland Ho
7 Windsor Ho

65

D3
1 Lowry Lo
2 Morritt Ho
3 Charles Goddard Ho
4 Snow Ct
5 Willow Tree Ct
6 Oak Lo

66

A2
1 Montrose Cres
2 Peggy Quirke Ct
3 Marylebone Ct
4 Waterloo Ct
5 Euston Ct
6 St Pancras Ct
7 Paddington Ct
8 Copland Mews
9 Coronet Par
10 Aylestone Ct
11 Charlotte Ct

A3
1 Wembley Mkt
2 Market Way
3 Lodge Ct
4 Central Sq
5 Manor Ct
6 Rupert Ave
7 Lily Ho

C4
1 Wembley Mkt

67

A5
1 Curie Ho
2 Darwin Ho
3 Priestley Ho
4 Rutherford Ho
5 Fleming Ho
6 Lister Ho
7 Edison Ho

B1
1 Biko Ho
2 Kingthorpe Terr
3 Scott Ho
4 Peary Ho
5 Shackleton Ho
6 Amundsen Ho
7 Brentfield Ho
8 Nansen Ho
9 Stonebridge Ct
10 Newcroft Ho
11 Magellan Ho
12 Leadbetter Ct
13 Jefferies Ho
14 Cowan Ct
15 Prothero Ho
16 Crawford St
17 Clark Ct
18 Diamond St
19 Mary Seacole Villas

C1
1 Beveridge Rd
2 Purcell Mews
3 George Lansbury Ho
4 Charles Hobson Ho
5 Reade Wlk
6 Westbury Ho
7 Bridge Ct
8 St Joseph's RC Prim Sch
9 Dixon Way
10 Armstrong Rd
11 Brittage Rd

C4
1 Grange Ct
2 Green Ct

C5
1 Hazelwood Ct
2 Winslow Cl

68

A2
1 Regency Mews
2 Tudor Mews
3 Utopia Ho
4 Bell Flats
5 Angel Ct
6 St Andrew & St Francis CE Prim Sch

A5
1 Bourne Ho
2 Carton Ho
3 Bidwell Ho
4 Woodbridge Cl
5 Mackenzie Ho
6 Banting Ho

B2
1 St Mary Magdalen's RC Jun Sch
2 Islamic Coll for Advanced Studies

C2
1 Rutland Park Gdns
2 Rutland Park Mans
3 Queens Par
4 Harcourt Ho
5 Solidarity Ho
6 Electra Ct
7 Cassandra Ct
8 Carlton Ct
9 Convent of Jesus & Mary RC Inf Sch

D4
1 Oaklands Mews
2 Acer Ct
3 Maple Ct
4 Argyle Mans

69

A1
1 Christ Church Ct
2 Paul Daisley Ct
3 Fountain Ho
4 Kingston Ho
5 Waverley Ct
6 Weston Ho
7 Mapes Ho
8 Athelstan Gdns
9 Leff Ho
10 Brondesbury Coll for Boys

B1
1 Alma Birk Ho
2 Brooklands Ct
3 Brooklands Court Apartments
4 Cleveland Mans
5 Buckley Ct
6 Webheath

B5
1 Mortimer Cl
2 Primrose Ct
3 Sunnyside Ho
4 Sunnyside
5 Prospect Pl

C1
1 Linstead St
2 Embassy Ho
3 Acol Ct
4 Kings Wood Ct
5 Douglas Ct
6 King's Gdns
7 Carlton Mans
8 Smyrna Mans
9 New Priory Ct
10 Queensgate Pl
11 Brondesbury Mews
12 St Eugene de Mazenod RC Prim Sch

C2
1 Dene Mans
2 Sandwell Ct
3 Sandwell Mans
4 Hampstead Mans
5 Redcroft

C3
1 Orestes Mews
2 Walter Northcott Ho
3 Polperro Mans
4 Lyncroft Mans
5 Marlborough Mans
6 Alexandra Mans
7 Cumberland Mans
8 Cavendish Mans
9 Ambassador Ct
10 Welbeck Mans
11 Inglewood Mans
12 Dennington Park Mansions

C4
1 Parsifal Coll

C5
1 Portman Hts
2 Hermitage Ct
3 Moreland Ct
4 Wendower Ct

D2
1 Beswick Mews
2 Worcester Mews
3 Minton Mews
4 Doulton Mews
5 Laurel Ho
6 Sandalwood Ho
7 Iroko Ho
8 Banyan Ho
9 Rosewood Ho
10 Ebony Ho
11 Rosemont Mans
12 Exeter Mews

70

A1
1 Harrold Ho
2 Glover Ho
3 Byron Ct
4 Nalton Ho

A2
1 Petros Gdns
2 Heath Ct
3 Imperial Twrs
4 Fairhurst
5 St John's Ct
6 New College Ct
7 Chalford
8 Rosslyn Mans
9 Sutherland Ho
10 Holy Trinity CE Prim Sch
11 Phoenix Sch
12 North Bridge House Sch
13 Southbank International Sch

A3
1 Arkwright Mans
2 Hatstone Ct
3 Hampstead High Sch

A4
1 Windmill Hill
2 Highgrove Point
3 Gainsborough Ho
4 Holly Bush Hill
5 Heath Mans
6 Holly Bush Steps
7 Pavilion Ct
8 Holly Berry La
9 New Campden Ct
10 Holly Bush Vale
11 Benham's Pl
12 Prospect Pl
13 Yorkshire Grey Pl
14 Gardnor Mans
15 Ellerdale Cl
16 Monro Ho
17 Prince Arthur Mews
18 Prince Arthur Ct
19 Village Mount
20 Perrin's Ct
21 Wells Ct
22 Bakers Pas
23 Spencer Wlk
24 Bird In Hand Yd
25 Kings Well
26 New Ct
27 Streatley Pl
28 Mansfield Pl
31 Upper Hampstead Wlk
50 Hampstead Parochial CE Prim Sch

C2
1 New End Prim Sch
30 Univ Coll Jun Sch
32 Heathside Prep Sch
33 New End Prim Sch
34 Sisters of St Marcellina Sch

A5
1 Hampstead Sq
2 Stamford Cl
3 Mount Sq The

B1
1 New College Par
2 Northways Par
3 Noel Ho
4 Campden Ho
5 Centre Hts
6 Hickes Ho
7 Swiss Terr
8 Leitch Ho
9 Jevons Ho
10 Langhorne Ct
11 Park Lo
12 Avenue Lo
13 Frank Barnes Sch
14 Swiss Cottage Sch

B2
1 Belsize Park Mews
2 Baynes Mews
3 McCrone Mews
4 South Hampstead High Sch

B3
1 Belsize Court Garages
2 Roscommon Ho
3 Akenside Ct
4 Fitzjohns Prim Sch
5 St Christopher's Sch
6 St Anthony's Sch

B4
1 White Bear Pl
2 Wells Ho The
3 Boades Mews
4 Flask Cotts
5 Coach House Yd
6 Pilgrim's Pl
7 Rosslyn Mews
8 Royal Sch Hampstead The
9 Academy Sch The

C2
1 Banff Ho
2 Glenloch Ct
3 Havercourt
4 Holmefield Ct
5 Gilling Ct
6 Howitt Cl
7 Manor Mans
8 Straffan Lo
9 Romney Ct
10 Lancaster Stables
11 Eton Garages
12 Hampstead Coll of Fine Arts & Humanities

C3
1 Hampstead High Sch

D1
1 Hancock Nunn Ho
2 Higginson Ho
3 Duncan Ho
4 Mary Wharrie Ho
5 Rockstraw Ho
6 Cleaver Ho
7 Chamberlain St
8 Sharples Hall St
9 Primrose Mews
10 Rothwell St
11 St Georges Mews

D2
1 Alder Ho
2 Hornbeam Ho
3 Whitebeam Ho
4 Aspen Ho
5 Rowan Ho
6 Beech Ho
7 Chestnut Ho
8 Oak Ho
9 Willow Ho
10 Sycamore Ho
11 Maple Ho
12 Hazel Ho
13 Elaine Ct
14 Faircourt
15 Walham Ct
16 Stanbury Ct
17 Priory Mans
18 Wellington Ho
19 Grange The

D3
1 Cayford Ho
2 Du Maurier Ho
3 Isokon Flats
4 Palgrave Ho
5 Garnett Ho
6 Stephenson Ho
7 Park Dwellings
8 Siddons Ho
9 Mall Studios
10 Park Hill Wlk
11 Wordsworth Pl
12 Fraser Regnart Ct
13 St Pancras Almshouses
14 St Dominic RC Prim Sch
15 Fleet Prim Sch

71

A1
1 Bridge Ho
2 Hardington
3 Mead Cl
4 Rugmere
5 Tottenhall
6 Beauvale
7 Broomfield
8 Camden Coll of English

A2
1 Silverbirch Wlk
2 Penshurst
3 Wingham
4 Westwell
5 Chislet
6 Burmarsh
7 Shipton Ho
8 Stonegate
9 Leysdown
10 Headcorn
11 Lenham
12 Halstow
13 Fordcombe
14 Cannington
15 Langridge
16 Athlone Ho
17 Pentland Ho
18 Beckington
19 Hawkridge
20 Edington
21 Rhyl Prim Sch
22 Haverstock Sch

B1
1 Ferdinand St
2 Harmood Ho
3 Hawley Rd
4 Hawley Mews
5 Leybourne St
6 Barling
7 Tiptree
8 Havering
9 Candida Ct
10 Lorraine Ct
11 Donnington Ct
12 Welford Ct
13 Torbay Ct
14 Bradfield Ct
15 Torbay St
16 Water La
17 Leybourne Rd
18 Haven St
19 Stucley Ho
20 Lawrence Ho
21 Chalcot Sch
22 Holy Trinity & Saint Silas CE Prim Sch
23 Hawley Inf Sch

B2
1 Ashington
2 Priestley Ho
3 Leonard Day Ho
4 Old Dairy Mews
5 Monmouth Ho
6 Alpha Ct
7 Una Ho
8 Widford
9 Heybridge
10 Roxwell
11 Hampstead Gates
12 Kingsway Coll

B4
1 Denyer Ho
2 Stephenson Ho
3 Trevithick Ho
4 Brunel Ho
5 Newcomen Ho
6 Faraday Ho
7 Winifrede Paul Ho
8 Wardlow
9 Fletcher Ct
10 Tideswell
11 Grangehill
12 Hambrook Ct
13 Calver

C1
1 Cherry Tree Ct
2 Chichester Ct
3 Durdans Ho
4 Philia Ho
5 Bernard Shaw Ct
6 Foster Ct
7 Bessemer Ct
8 Hogarth Ct
9 Rochester Ct
10 Soane Ct
11 Wallett Ct
12 Inwood Ct
13 Wrotham Rd
14 St Thomas Ct
15 Caulfield Ct
16 Bruges Pl
17 Reachview Ct
18 Lawfords Wharf

C3
1 Eleanor Ho
2 Falkland Ho
3 Kensington Ho
4 Willingham Cl
5 Kenbrook Ho
6 Aborfield
7 Great Field
8 Appleford
9 Forties The
10 Maud Wilkes Cl
11 Dunne Mews
12 Dowdeny Cl
13 Kentish Town CE Prim Sch

C4
1 Benson Ct
2 Tait Ho
3 Manorfield Cl
4 Greatfield Cl
5 Longley Ho
6 Lampson Ho
7 Davidson Ho
8 Palmer Ho
9 Lambourn Cl
10 Morris Ho
11 Owen Ho
12 Eleanor Palmer Prim Sch

C5
1 Hunter Ho
2 Fisher Ho
3 Lang Ho
4 Temple Ho
5 Palmer Ho
6 Carlisle Ho
7 Durham Ho
8 Suffolk Ho
9 Lincoln Ho
10 Llewellyn Ho
11 Fell Ho
12 Aveling Ho
13 Merryweather Ct
14 Brennands Ct
15 St Christophers Ct
16 Francis Terrace Mews
17 Tremlett Mews

C6
1 Flowers Mews
2 Archway Cl
3 Sandridge St
4 Bovingdon Ct
5 Cavell Ct
6 Torrence Ho
7 Rowan Wlk
8 Laurel Ct
9 Forest Way
10 Larch Ct
11 Pine Ct
12 Alder Mews
13 Aspen Cl
14 Hargrave Park Prim Sch
15 Middlesex Univ (Archway Campus)

D1
1 Hillier Ho
2 Gairloch Ho

3 Cobham Mews
4 Bergholt Mews
5 Blakeney Cl
5 Weavers Way
6 Allensbury Pl
D2 1 Rowstock
2 Peckwater Ho
3 Wolsey Ho
4 Pandian Way
5 Busby Mews
6 Caledonia Sq
7 Canal Bvd
8 Northpoint Sq
9 Lock Mews
10 Carters Cl
11 York Ho
12 Hungerford Rd
13 Cliff Road Studios
14 Cliff Ct
15 Camelot Ho
16 Church Studios
17 Camden Terr
18 Brecknock Prim Sch
19 Hungerford Prim Sch
D3 1 Blake Ho
2 Quelch Ho
3 Lee Ho
4 Willbury Ho
5 Howell Ho
6 Holmsbury Ho
7 Leith Ho
8 Betchworth Ho
9 Rushmore Ho
10 Dugdale Ho
11 Horsendon Ho
12 Colley Ho
13 Coombe Ho
14 Ivinghoe Ho
15 Buckhurst Ho
16 Saxonbury Ct
17 Charlton Ct
18 Apollo Studios
19 Barn Cl
20 Long Meadow
21 Landleys Field
22 Margaret Bondfield Ho
23 Haywood Lo
24 Torriano Jun & Inf Schs
D4 1 Fairlie Ct
2 Trecastle Way
3 Dalmeny Avenue Est
4 Hyndman Ho
5 Carpenter Ho
6 Graham Ho
7 Tufnell Mans
D5 1 Melchester Ho
2 Norcombe Ho
3 Weatherbury Ho
4 Wessex Ho
5 Archway Bsns Ctr
6 Harford Mews
7 Opera Ct
8 Rupert Ho
9 All Saints Church
D6 1 Bowerman Ct
2 Gresham Pl
3 Hargrave Mans
4 Church Garth
5 John King Ct
6 Ramsey Ct
7 St John's Upper Holloway CE Prim Sch
8 Byam Shaw Sch of Art

72
A2 1 Clock Tower Pl
2 Clock View Cres
3 Jim Veal Dr
4 Gower Sch The
A3 1 Kimble Ho
2 Saxonbury Ct
3 Poynder Ct
4 Pangbourne Ho
5 Moulsford Ho
A4 1 Arcade The
2 Macready Pl
3 Cardwell Rd
4 Mcmorran Ho

5 Crayford Ho
6 Whitby Ct
7 Prospect Pl
8 City & Islington Coll (Ctr for Bsns, Arts & Technology)
A5 1 Northview
2 Tufnell Park Mans
3 Fulford Mans
4 Tollington Ho
5 Grafton Prim Sch
A6 1 Bracey Mews
2 Christie Ct
3 Ringmer Gdns
4 Kingsdown Rd
5 Cottenham Ho
6 St Paul's Ct
7 Rickthorne Rd
8 Stanley Terr
9 Arundel Lo
10 Landseer Ct
11 St Mark's Prim Sch
B1 1 Kerwick Cl
2 Rydston Cl
3 Skegness Ho
4 Frederica St
5 Ponder St
6 Kings Ct
7 Freeling St
8 Coatbridge Ho
9 Tilloch St
B2 1 Burns Ho
2 Scott Ho
3 Wellington Mews
4 Roman Ct
5 Piccadilly Ct
6 Knowledge Point Sch
B3 1 Culverin Ct
2 Garand Ct
3 Mount Carmel
B4 1 Buckmaster Ho
2 Loreburn Ho
3 Cairns Ho
4 Halsbury Ho
5 Chelmsford Ho
6 Cranworth Ho
7 City & Islington Coll (Ctr for Health, Social & Child Care)
B5 1 Pakeman Prim Sch
2 London Meridian Coll
3 American Univ in London The
4 South Eastern Univ
5 Dean Coll of London
6 Montem Prim Sch
B6 1 Berkeley Wlk
2 Lazar Wlk
3 Thistlewood Cl
4 Tomlins Wlk
5 Andover Ho
6 Barmouth Ho
7 Christ the King RC Prim Sch
8 Methley Ho
9 Rainford Ho
10 Woodbridge Cl
11 Allerton Wlk
12 Falconer Wlk
13 Bardolph Rd
14 St Mark's Mans
15 Athol Ct
16 Pooles Park Prim Sch
C1 1 Mountfort Terr
2 Avon Ho
3 Buckland Ho
4 Dovey Lo
5 Carfree Cl
6 Mitchell Ho
7 New College Mews
8 Lofting Ho
9 Brooksby Ho
10 Cara Ho
11 Thornhill Prim Sch

12 North London Science Ctr
C2 1 London Metropolitan Univ (Spring Ho)
C3 1 Slaney Rd
2 Eastwood Cl
3 Milton Pl
4 Hartnoll Ho
5 St James School Flats
6 Widnes Ho
7 Tranmere Ho
8 Victoria Mans
9 Formby Ct
10 Mersey Ho
11 Birkenhead Ho
12 Drayton Park Mews
13 Drayton Park Prim Sch
C6 1 Brookfield
2 Churchfield
3 Cornwallis Sq
D1 1 Islington Park Mews
2 Evelyn Denington Ct
3 Bassingbourn Ho
4 Cadmore Ho
5 Adstock Ho
6 Garston Ho
7 Flitton Ho
8 Datchworth Ho
9 Battishill St
10 Almeida St
11 Edward's Cotts
12 Hyde's Pl
13 Tyndale Terr
14 Spriggs Ho
15 Barratt Ho
16 Spencer Pl
17 Chadston Ho
18 Whiston Ho
19 Wakelin Ho
20 Tressel Cl
21 Canonbury St
22 Halton Ho
23 Shillingford St
24 Highbury Mans
25 Premier Ho
26 Waterloo Gdns
27 William Tyndale Prim Sch
D2 1 Hampton Ct
2 Salisbury Ho
3 Canonbury Prim Sch
4 Laycock Prim Sch
D3 1 De Barowe Mews
2 Fieldview Ct
3 Viewpoint
4 Ashurst Lo
5 Highbury Fields Sch
6 London Metropolitan Univ (Ladbroke Ho)
7 Robinswood Mews
D4 1 Chestnuts The
2 Bowen Ct
3 Peckett Sq
4 De Barowe Mews
D5 1 Hurlock Ho
2 Blackstock Ho
3 Vivian Comma Cl
4 Monsell Ct
D6 1 Parkwood Prim Sch
2 Ambler Prim Sch
3 City & Islington Coll (Ctr for Lifelong Learning)

73
A1 1 Astey's Row
2 Lincoln Ho
3 Worcester Ho
4 Melville Pl
5 Wontner Cl
6 Hedingham Cl
7 Laundry La
8 Base Apartments
9 Walkinshaw Ct
10 New Bentham Ct

11 Bentham Ct
12 Haslam Ho
13 Horsfield Ho
14 Riverside Ho
15 Eric Fletcher Ct
16 Annette Cres
17 Ashby Ho
18 Lindsey Mews
19 Cardigan Wlk
20 Red House Sq
21 Orchard Ct
22 Queensbury St
23 Raynor Pl
A2 1 Crowline Wlk
2 Upper Handa Wlk
3 Handa Wlk
4 Lismore Wlk
5 Bardsey Wlk
6 Walney Wlk
7 Upper Bardsey Wlk
8 Upper Lismore Wlk
9 Sark Ho
10 Guernsey Ho
11 Guernsey Ho
12 Sybil Thorndike Ho
13 Clephane Rd
14 Florence Nightingale Ho
15 Jersey Ho
16 Jethou Ho
17 Islay Wlk
18 Upper Caldy Wlk
19 Caldy Wlk
20 Alderney Ho
21 Gulland Wlk
22 Nightingale Rd
23 Upper Gulland Wlk
24 Church Rd
25 Oransay Rd
26 Canonbury Yd E
A3 1 Pearfield Ho
2 Larchfield Ho
3 Beresford Terr
4 Pondfield Ho
5 Ashfield Ho
6 Elmfield Ho
7 Highbury Grove Sch
A4 1 Fountain Mews
2 Woodstock Ho
3 Henson Ct
4 Taverner Sq
B1 1 Trafalgar Point
2 John Kennedy Ct
2 John Kennedy Lo
3 Ball's Pond Pl
4 Haliday Wlk
5 Queen Elizabeth Ct
6 Canonbury Hts
7 Pinnacle The
8 Threadgold Ho
9 Wakeham St
10 Saffron Ct
11 Callaby Terr
12 Tilney Gdns
13 Westcliff Ho
14 Ilford Ho
15 Greenhills Terr
16 Romford Ho
17 Bute Wlk
18 Upper Ramsey Wlk
19 Rona Wlk
20 Thorndike Rd
21 St Pauls Steiner Sch
B3 1 Newington Green Prim Sch
B4 1 Ledo Ho
2 Salween Ho
3 Prome Ho
4 Arakan Ho
5 Rangoon Ho
6 Mandalay Ho
7 Karen Ho
8 Wingate Ho
9 Jubet Ho
10 Orde Ho
11 Chindit Ho

12 Mabel Thornton Ho
13 Crawshay Ho
14 Avon Ho
15 Connaught Mans
16 Jonson Ho
17 Herrick Ho
18 Donne Ho
19 Thirlmere Ho
20 Grasmere Ho
B5 1 Betty Layward Prim Sch
B6 1 Chestnut Cl
2 Sycamore Ho
3 Lordship Ho
4 Clissold Ho
5 Beech Ho
6 Laburnum Ho
7 Ormond Ho
8 Yew Tree Ct
9 Oak Ho
C1 1 Dorchester Ct
2 Wareham Ho
3 Dorset Ct
4 Stratton Ct
5 Swanage Ct
6 Blandford Ct
7 Portland Ct
8 Oscar Faber Pl
9 Metropolitan Bsns Ctr
10 Lancaster Cl
11 Palazzo Apartments
12 Watercress Pl
C2 1 Kingsland Pas
2 Kingsland Pas
3 Metropolitan Benefit Societies Almshouses
4 Nimrod Pas
5 De Beauvoir Pl
6 Warburton Ct
7 Buckingham Mews
8 Aztec Ct
9 Kerridge Ct
10 Isabella Mews
11 St Jude & St Paul's CE Prim Sch
12 De Beauvoir Prim Sch
13 Our Lady & St Joseph RC Prim Sch
14 Childrens House Upper Sch
C3 1 Hewling Ho
2 Matthias Ho
3 Port Royal Pl
4 Cressington Ct
5 King Henry's Yd
6 Bronte Ho
7 Sewell Ho
8 Lydgate Ho
9 Patmore Ho
10 Congreve Ho
11 Elton St
12 Conrad Ho
13 Southwell Ho
14 Neptune Ho
15 Campion Ho
16 Webster Ho
17 Meredith Ho
18 Beckford Ho
19 Ashley Ct
20 Hayling Ct
21 Millard Ct
22 Lydford Ct
23 Salcombe Rd
24 Truman's Ho
25 Templeton Cl
26 John Campbell Rd
27 Gillett Pl
28 Bradbury St
29 Thomas Crowell Ct
30 Shellgrove Rd
C4 1 Londesborough Ho
2 Knebworth Ho
3 Knebworth Rd
4 Bransby Ct
5 Imperial Ave
6 Leonard Pl

7 Shakspeare Mews
8 Binyon Ho
9 Shelley Ho
10 Browning Ho
11 Burns Ho
12 Andrew Marvell Ho
13 Wycliffe Ho
14 Blake Ho
15 Marlowe Ho
16 Fletcher Ho
17 Chaucer Ct
18 St Matthias's CE Prim Sch
C5 1 Gujarat Ho
2 Marton Rd
3 Painsthorpe Rd
4 Selkirk Ho
5 Defoe Ho
6 Edward Friend Ho
7 Sheridan Ho
8 Barrie Ho
9 Arnold Ho
10 Macaulay Ho
11 Stowe Ho
12 Carlyle Ho
13 Shaftesbury Ho
14 Lillian Cl
15 Swift Ho
16 Dryden Ho
17 Scott Ct
18 Kingsfield Ho
19 Uhura Sq
20 Hartopp Ct
C6 1 Denman Ho
2 St Mary's Stoke Newington CE Prim Sch
D1 1 Hilborough Rd
2 Shoreditch Ct
3 Evergreen Sq
4 Wyndhams Ct
5 Festival Ct
6 Fortune Ct
7 Rose Ct
8 Ability Plaza
9 Briar Ct
10 Lomas Dr
11 Queensbridge Inf Sch
D2 1 Prospect Ho
2 Woodland St
3 Crosby Wlk
4 Kirkland Wlk
5 Bowness Cl
6 Carlisle Wlk
7 Skelton Cl
8 Cameron Cl
9 Buttermere Wlk
10 Houghton Cl
11 Hayton Cl
12 Kingsland Sh Ctr
13 Springfield Ho
14 Parton Lo
15 Sanctuary Mews
16 Fenton Cl
D3 1 Miller's Terr
2 Chow Sq
3 Drysdale Flats
4 Gateway Mews
5 Birkbeck Mews
6 Winchester Pl
D4 1 Coronation Ave
2 Morris Blitz Ct
3 Shacklewell Ho
4 Alexandra St
5 Shacklewell Prim Sch
6 Princess May Prim Sch
D5 1 Lawrence Bldgs
2 Cottage Wlk
3 Batley Pl
D6 1 Garnham St
2 Garnham Cl
3 Sanford La
4 Sanford Wlk
5 Abney Gdns
6 Fleet Wood
7 Simon Marks Jewish Prim Sch

8 Rutherford Twr
9 Rountree Ct

86

A1 1 Farnham Ct
2 Gleneagles Twr
3 Birkdale Ct
4 Verulam Ct
5 Hartsbourne Ct
6 Ferndown Ct
7 Deal Ct
8 St David's Ct
9 Portrush Ct
10 Alnmouth Ct
11 Panmure Ct
12 Peterhead Ct
13 Sunningdale Ct
D2 1 Denbigh Ct
2 Devon Ct
3 Dorset Ct
4 Glamorgan Ct
5 Gloucester Ct
6 Hereford Ct
7 Merioneth Ct
8 Oxford Ct
9 Monmouth Ct
10 Paddington Ct
11 Pembroke Ct
12 Chadwick Cl
13 Cotts Cl
D3 1 Berkshire Ct
2 Buckingham Ct
3 Cardigan Ct
4 Carmarthen Ct
5 Cornwall Ct
6 Merlin Ct
7 Osprey Ct
8 Pelham Pl
9 Puffin Ct
10 Fulmar Ct
11 Turnstone Terr
D5 1 Medway Par
2 Brabstone Ho
3 Cotswold Ct

87

B1 1 Ealing Coll
2 Avenue House Sch
B3 1 Woodbury Ct
2 Edward Ct
3 Park Lo
C1 1 Hurley Ct
2 Amherst Gdns
3 Tudor Ct
4 Hilton Ho
C2 1 Hutton Ct
2 Cain Ct
3 Langdale Ct
4 William Ct
5 Castlebar Ct
6 Warren Ct
7 White Lo
8 Queen's Ct
9 King's Ct
10 Cheriton Cl
11 Stanley Ct
12 Juniper Ho
13 Pendlewood Cl
15 St Benedict's Jun Sch
C3 1 Holtoake Ct
2 Pitshanger Ct
3 Holtoake Ho
D2 14 St Gregory's RC Prim Sch

88

A4 1 Nelson Ho
2 Gordon Ho
3 Frobisher Ho
4 Wellington Ho
5 Fairfax Ho
A5 1 Carlyon Mans
2 Ainslie Ct
3 Millers Ct
4 Priory Ct
5 Tylers Ct
6 Twyford Ct
7 Rose Ct
8 Laurel Ct
9 Sundew Ct
10 Campion Ct
11 Foxglove Ct
C1 1 Buckingham Ho
2 Chester Ct
3 Devon Ct
4 Essex Ho
5 Fife Ct
6 Gloucester Ct
7 Hereford Ho
8 Inverness Ct
9 Warwick Ho
10 York Ho
11 Suffolk Ho
12 Perth Ho
13 Norfolk Ho
14 Thanet Ct
15 Rutland Ct
16 Oxford Ct

89

A1 1 Avon Ct
2 Bromley Lo
3 Walter Ct
4 Lynton Terr
5 Acton Ho
6 Fells Haugh
7 Springfield Ct
8 Tamarind Ct
9 Lynton Ct
10 Aspen Ct
11 Pegasus Ct
12 Friary Park Ct
B1 1 Rosebank Gdns
2 Rosebank
3 Edinburgh Ho
4 Western Ct
5 Kilronan
B6 1 Carlyle Rd
2 Bernard Shaw Ho
3 Longlents Ho
4 Mordaunt Ho
5 Wilmers Ct
6 Stonebridge Ctr
7 Shakespeare Ave
8 Southcroft
9 Brent Adult Comm Education Service Coll
C5 1 Futters Ct
2 Barrett Ct
3 Elms The
4 Fairlight Ct
D5 1 New Crescent Yd
2 Harlesden Plaza
3 St Josephs Ct
4 Jubilee Cl
5 Ellery Cl

90

B1 1 Holborn Ho
2 Clement Danes Ho
3 Vellacott Ho
4 O'Driscoll Ho
5 King Ho
6 Daley Ho
7 Selma Ho
8 Garrett Ho
C1 1 Latimer Ind Est
2 Pankhurst Ho
3 Quadrangle The
4 Nightingale Ho
5 Gordon Ct
6 Ducane Cl
7 Browning Ho
8 Pavilion Terr
9 Ivebury Ct
10 Olympic Ho
C2 1 Galleywood Ho
2 Edgcott Ho
3 Cuffley Ho
4 Addlestone Ho
5 Hockliffe Ho
6 Sarratt Ho
7 Firle Ho
8 Sutton Est The
9 Terling Ho
10 Danes Ho
11 Udimore Ho
12 Vange Ho
13 Binbrook Ho
14 Yeadon Ho
15 Yatton Ho
16 Yarrow Ho
17 Clement Ho
18 Danebury
19 Coronation Ct
20 Calderon Pl
21 St Quintin Gdns
C3 1 Princess Alice Ho
2 Yoxall Ho
3 Yorkley Ho
4 Northaw Ho
5 Oakham Ho
6 Markyate Ho
7 Letchmore Ho
8 Pagham Ho
9 Quendon Ho
10 Redbourn Ho
11 Ketton Ho
12 Hillman Dr
D1 1 Kelfield Ct
2 Downing Ho
3 Crosfield Ct
4 Robinson Ho
5 Scampston Mews
6 Girton Villas
7 Ray Ho
8 Walmer Ho
9 Goodrich Ct
10 Arthur Ct
11 Whitstable Ho
12 Kingsnorth Ho
13 Bridge Cl
14 Prospect Ho
15 St Marks Rd
16 Whitchurch Ho
17 Blechynden Ho
18 Waynflete Sq
19 Bramley Ho
20 Dixon Ho
21 Oxford Gardens Prim Sch
22 Bassett House Sch
D2 1 Treverton Twr
2 Raymede Twr
3 Bruce Ho
4 Balfour Ho
5 Burleigh Ho
6 Sion-Manning RC Sch for Girls
7 St Charles RC Prim Sch
8 St Charles RC Sixth Form Coll
D4 1 Westfield Ct
2 Tropical Ct
3 Chamberlayne Mans
4 Quadrant The
5 Queens Park Ct
6 Warfield Yd
7 Regent St
8 Cherrytree Ho
9 Artisan Mews
10 Artisan Quarter

91

A1 1 Malton Mews
2 Lancaster Lo
3 Manning Ho
4 Galsworthy Ho
5 Hudson Ho
6 Cambourne Mews
7 Upper Talbot Wlk
8 Kingsdown Cl
9 Lower Clarendon Wlk
10 Talbot Grove Ho
11 Clarendon Wlk
12 Upper Clarendon Wlk
13 Camelford Wlk
14 Upper Camelford Wlk
15 Camelford Ct
16 Thomas Jones Prim Sch
17 Notting Hill Prep Sch
A2 1 Murchison Ho
2 Macaulay Ho
3 Chesterton Ho
4 Chiltern Ho
5 Lionel Ho
6 Watts Ho
7 Wheatstone Ho
8 Telford Ho
9 Golborne Mews
10 Millwood St
11 St Columb's Ho
12 Norfolk Mews
13 Lionel Mews
14 Kensington & Chelsea Coll
15 Bevington Prim Sch
16 Sion-Manning RC Sch for Girls
17 Lloyd Williamson Sch
A3 1 Sycamore Wlk
2 Westgate Bsns Ctr
3 Buspace Studios
4 Bosworth Ho
5 Golborne Gdns
6 Appleford Ho
7 Adair Twr
8 Gadsden Ho
9 Southam Ho
10 Norman Butler Ho
11 Thompson Ho
12 Wells Ho
13 Paul Ho
14 Olive Blythe Ho
15 Katherine Ho
16 Breakwell Ct
17 Pepler Ho
18 Edward Kennedy Ho
19 Winnington Ho
20 Queen's Park Prim Sch
21 Middle Row Prim Sch
22 St Mary RC Prim Sch
23 St Thomas' CE Prim Sch
A4 1 Selby Sq
2 Severn Ave
3 Stansbury Sq
4 Tolhurst Dr
5 John Fearon Wlk
6 Mundy Ho
7 Macfarren Ho
8 Bantock Ho
9 Banister Ho
10 Batten Ho
11 Croft Ho
12 Courtville Ho
13 Mounsey Ho
14 Bliss Mews
15 Symphony Mews
B1 1 Silvester Ho
2 Golden Cross Mews
3 Tavistock Mews
4 Clydesdale Ho
5 Colville Prim Sch
5 Melchester
6 Pinehurst Ct
7 Denbigh Ho
B2 1 Blagrove Rd
2 All Saints Ho
3 Tavistock Ho
4 Leamington Ho
B3 1 Octavia Mews
2 Russell's Wharf
3 Western Ho
4 Kelly Mews
5 Queen Elizabeth II Jubilee Sch
B4 1 Boyce Ho
2 Farnaby Ho
3 Danby Ho
4 Purday Ho
5 Naylor Ho
6 St Judes Ho
7 Leeve Ho
8 Longhurst Ho
9 Harrington Ct
10 Mulberry Ct
11 Kilburn Ho
12 Carlton Vale Inf Sch
B5 1 Claremont Ct
2 William Saville Ho
3 Western Ct
4 Bond Ho
5 Crone Ct
6 Wood Ho
7 Winterleys
8 Carlton Ho
9 Fiona Ct
10 Kilburn Park Sch
C1 1 Shottsford
2 Tolchurch
3 Casterbridge
4 Sandbourne
5 Anglebury
6 Weatherbury
7 Westbourne Gr Mews
8 Rosehart Mews
9 Viscount Ct
10 Hereford Mans
11 Hereford Mews
12 St Mary of the Angels RC Prim Sch
C2 1 Ascot Ho
2 Ashgrove Ct
3 Lockbridge Ct
4 Swallow Ct
5 Nightingale Lo
6 Hammond Lo
7 Penfield Lo
8 Harvey Lo
9 Hunter Lo
10 Barnard Lo
11 Falcon Lo
12 Johnson Lo
13 Livingstone Lo
14 Nuffield Lo
15 Finch Lo
16 Polesworth Ho
17 Oversley Ho
18 Derrycombe Ho
19 Buckshead Ho
20 Combe Ho
21 Culham Ho
22 Dainton Ho
23 Devonport Ho
24 Honwell Ho
25 Truro Ho
26 Sunderland Ho
27 Stonehouse Ho
28 Riverford Ho
29 Portishead Ho
30 Mickleton Ho
31 Keyham Ho
32 Moulsford Ho
33 Shrewsbury Mews
34 St Stephen's Mews
35 Westway Lo
36 Langley Ho
37 Brindley Ho
38 Radway Ho
39 Astley Ho
40 Willow Ct
41 Larch Ct
42 Elm Ct
43 Beech Ct
44 Worcester Ct
45 Union Ct
46 Leicester Ct
47 Kennet Ct
48 Oxford Ct
49 Fazerley Ct
C3 1 Westside Ct
2 Byron Mews
3 Sutherland Ct
4 Fleming Cl
5 Hermes Cl
6 St Peter's CE Prim Sch
7 Paddington Acad
C4 1 Pentland Rd
2 Nelson Cl
3 Pavilion Ct
4 Masefield Ho
5 Austen Ho
6 Fielding Ho
7 Argo Bsns Ctr
8 John Ratcliffe Ho
9 Wymering Mans
10 City of Westminster Coll, Queens Park Ctr
11 Essendine Prim Sch
C5 1 Wells Ct
2 Cambridge Ct
3 Ely Ct
4 Durham Ct
5 St Augustine's CE High Sch
6 Sch of the Islamic Republic of Iran The
C6 1 Ryde Ho
2 Glengall Pass
3 Leith Yd
4 Daynor Ho
5 Varley Ho
6 Sandby Ho
7 Colas Mews
8 Bishopsdale Ho
9 Lorton Ho
10 Marshwood Ho
11 Ribblesdale Ho
12 Holmesdale Ho
13 Kilburn Vale Est
14 Kilburn Bridge
15 Coll of NW London
16 St Mary's Kilburn CE Prim Sch
D1 1 Vera Ct
2 Alexander Mews
3 Gurney Ho
4 Burdett Mews
5 Greville Lo
6 Hatherley Ct
7 Bridge Field Ho
8 Ralph Ct
9 Peters Ct
9 Pickering Mews
10 Riven Ct
11 Inver Ct
12 Cervantes Ct
13 Bishops Ct
14 Newbury Ho
15 Marlow Ho
16 Lynton Ho
17 Pembroke Ho
18 Pickering Ho
19 Whiteleys Ctr
20 College Park Sch
21 Hallfield Jun & Inf Schs
D2 1 Our Lady of Dolours RC Prim Sch
2 Edward Wilson Prim Sch
3 St Mary Magdalene CE Prim Sch
D3 1 Ellwood Ct
26 St Saviour's CE Prim Sch
D4 1 City of Westminster Coll, Maida Vale Ctr
D5 1 Tollgate Ho
2 Regents Plaza
3 Royal Langford Apartments
4 Naima Jewish Prep Sch
5 St Augustine's Prim Sch
D6 1 Sylvan Ct
2 Birchington Ct
3 Farndale Ho
5 Greville Mews
6 Goldsmith's Pl
7 Remsted Ho
8 Bradwell Ho
9 Cheshunt Ho
10 Haliwell Ho
11 Broadoak Ho
12 Philip Ho
13 Hillsborough Ct
14 Sandbourne
15 Wingreen
16 Toneborough
17 Silverthorn
18 Kington Ho
19 Marrick Ho
21 Rutland Mews

95

C4 1 Pimlico Wlk
2 Aske Ho
3 Hathaway Ho
4 Haberdasher Pl
5 Fairchild Ho
6 Burtt Ho
7 Enfield Cloisters
8 McGregor Ct
9 Royal Oak Ct
10 Hoxton Mkt

4 Millicent Preston Ho
5 Louise Graham Ho
6 Grange Ho
7 Basing Ho
8 Barnes Ho
9 Lexham Ho
10 Ripple Ct
11 Waldegrave Ho
12 Howard Ct

104
A6 1 Milburn Dr
2 Cousins Ct
3 Leacroft Cl

107
C4 1 Decimal Ctr
2 Bridge Bsns Ctr The

108
C5 1 Marlow Ct
2 Andrewes Ct
3 Vine Cotts
4 Benjamin Ct
5 Broadway Bldgs
6 Clocktower Mews
7 Amberley Ho
8 Diamond Ct
9 St Ann's Sch
10 St Josephs RC Prim Sch
D5 1 Silverdale Ct
2 Burdett Cl
3 Hopefield
4 Maunder Rd
5 Clare Ho

109
A5 1 Glastonbury Ct
2 Evesham Ct
3 Lacock Ct
4 Wigmore Ct
5 Melrose Ct
6 Brownlow Rd
7 Chignell Pl
8 Shirley Ct
9 Trojan Ct
10 Hatfield Rd
11 Pershore Ho
12 Hyde Ho
13 Hugh Clark Ho
14 Rosemoor Ho
15 Leeland Mans
16 Waterford Ct
17 O'Grady Ct
C1 1 Barrow Wlk
2 Mercury Rd
3 Our Lady & St John's RC Jun & Inf Sch
C3 1 Mt Carmel RC Prim Sch
2 Little Ealing Prim Sch
C6 1 Abbey Lo
2 Yew Tree Grange
3 Abinger Ct
D6 1 Sandringham Mews
2 St Savior's CE Inf Sch

110
A1 1 Burford Ho
2 Hope Cl
3 Centaur Ct
4 Phoenix Ct
A6 1 Watermans Mews
2 Hills Mews
3 Grosvenor Ct
4 Elton Lo
5 Hambledon Ct
6 Edwards Language Sch
C1 1 Surrey Cres
2 Forbes Ho
3 Haining Cl
4 Melville Ct
5 London Stile
6 Stile Hall Par
7 Priory Lo
8 Meadowcroft
9 St James Ct

10 Rivers Ho
C5 1 Grosvenor Par
2 Oakfield Ct
3 Hart Grove Ct
4 Grosvenor Ct
5 King Edwards Pl
D1 1 Churchdale Ct
2 Cromwell Ct
3 Cambridge Rd S
4 Oxbridge Ct
5 Tomlinson Cl
6 Gunnersbury Mews
7 Grange The
8 Gunnersbury Cl
9 Bellgrave Ct
D4 1 Cheltenham Pl
2 Beaumaris Twr
3 Arundel Ho
4 Pevensey Ct
5 Jerome Twr
6 Anstey Ct
7 Bennett Ct
8 Gunnersbury Ct
9 Barrington Ct
10 Hope Gdns
11 Park Road E
D5 1 Lantry Ct
2 Rosemount Ct
3 Disraeli Ct
4 Acton Central Ind Est
5 Rufford Twr
6 Narrow St
7 Mount Pl
8 Sidney Miller Ct
9 Mill Hill Terr
10 Cheltenham Pl
11 Mill Hill Gr
12 Benjamin Ho
13 Arlington Ct
14 Lombard Ct
15 Steyne Ho
16 Acton & West London Coll

111
A1 1 Arlington Park Mans
2 Sandown Ho
3 Goodwood Ho
4 Windsor Ho
5 Lingfield Ho
6 Ascot Ho
7 Watchfield Ct
8 Belgrave Ct
9 Beverley Ct
10 Beaumont Ct
11 Harvard Rd
12 Troubridge Ct
13 Branden Lo
14 Fromow's Cnr
15 Heathfield Ho Sch
A2 1 Chiswick Green Studios
2 Bell Ind Est
3 Fairlawn Ct
4 Dukes Gate
5 Dewsbury Ct
6 Chiswick Terr
7 Mortlake Ho
A3 1 Blackmore Twr
2 Bollo Ct
3 Kipling Twr
4 Lawrence Ct
5 Maugham Ct
6 Reade Ct
7 Woolf Ct
8 Shaw Ct
9 Verne Ct
10 Wodehouse St
11 Greenock Rd
12 Garden Ct
13 Barons Gate
14 Cleveland Rd
15 Carver Cl
16 Chapter Cl
17 Beauchamp Cl
18 Holmes Ct
19 Copper Mews
A4 1 Belgrave Ct
2 Buckland Wlk
3 Frampton Ct
4 Telfer Cl
5 Harlech Twr

6 Corfe Twr
7 Barwick Ho
8 Charles Hocking Ho
9 Sunninghill Ct
10 Salisbury St
11 Jameson Pl
12 Castle Cl
A5 1 Rectory Rd
2 Derwentwater Mans
3 Market Pl
4 Hooper's Mews
5 Cromwell Pl
6 Locarno Rd
7 Edgecote Cl
8 Harleyford Manor
9 Coopers Ct
10 Avingdor Ct
11 Steyne Ho
B1 1 Chatsworth Lo
2 Prospect Pl
3 Townhall Ave
4 Devonhurst Pl
5 Heathfield Ct
6 Horticultural Pl
7 Merlin Ho
8 Garth Rd
9 Autumn Rise
B2 1 Winston Wlk
2 Rusthall Mans
3 Bedford Park Mans
4 Essex Place Sq
5 Holly Rd
6 Homecross Ho
7 Swan Bsns Ctr
8 Jessop Ho
9 Belmont Prim Sch
C1 1 Glebe Ct
2 Devonshire Mews
3 Binns Terr
4 Ingress St
5 Swanscombe Rd
6 Brackley Terr
7 Stephen Fox Ho
8 Manor Gdns
9 Coram Ho
10 Flaxman Ho
11 Thorneycroft Ho
12 Thornhill Ho
13 Kent Ho
14 Oldfield Ho
15 William Hogarth Sch The
C2 1 Chestnut Ho
2 Bedford Ho
3 Sydney Ho
4 Bedford Cnr
5 Bedford Park Cnr
6 Priory Gdns
7 Windmill Alley
8 Castle Pl
9 Jonathan Ct
10 Windmill Pas
11 Chardin Rd
12 Gable Ho
13 Chiswick & Bedford Park Prep Sch
14 Arts Educational Sch The
15 Orchard House Sch
C3 1 Fleet Ct
2 Ember Ct
3 Emlyn Gdns
4 Clone Ct
5 Brent Ct
6 Abbey Ct
7 Ormsby Lo
8 St Catherine's Ct
9 Lodge The
C4 1 Longford Ct
2 Mole Ct
3 Lea Ct
4 Wandle Ct
5 Beverley Ct
6 Roding Ct
7 Crane Ct
D1 1 Miller's Ct
2 British Grove Pas
3 British Grove S
4 Berested Rd

5 North Eyot Gdns
D2 1 Flanders Mans
2 Stamford Brook Ho
3 Linkenholt Mans
4 Prebend Mans
5 Middlesex Ct
D3 1 Stamford Brook Gdns
2 Hauteville Court Gdns
3 Ranelagh Gdns

112
A1 1 Chisholm Ct
2 North Verbena Gdns
3 Western Terr
4 Verbena Gdns
5 Montrose Villas
6 Hammersmith Terr
7 South Black Lion La
8 St Peter's Wharf
9 Eden High Sch
A2 1 Hamlet Ct
2 Derwent Ct
3 Westcroft Ct
4 Black Lion Mews
5 St Peter's Villas
6 Standish Ho
7 Chambon Pl
8 Court Mans
9 Longthorpe Ct
10 Charlotte Ct
11 Westside
12 Park Ct
13 London Ho
14 Latymer Upper Sch
A3 1 St Peter's CE Prim Sch
2 Polish Univ Abroad
A3 1 Elizabeth Finn Ho
2 Aschurch Ct
3 King's Par
4 Inver Ct
5 Ariel Ct
6 Pocklington Lo
7 Vitae Apartments
A4 1 Becklow Gdns
2 Victoria Ho
3 Lycett Pl
4 Kylemore Ct
5 Alexandra Ct
6 Lytten Ct
7 Becklow Mews
8 Northcroft Ct
9 Bailey Ct
10 Spring Cott
11 Landor Wlk
12 Laurence Mews
13 Hadyn Park Ct
14 Askew Mans
15 Malvern Ct
B1 1 Prince's Mews
2 Aspen Gdns
3 Hampshire Hog La
4 Blades Ct
B2 1 Albion Gdns
2 Flora Gdns
3 Lamington St
4 Felgate Mews
5 Galena Ho
6 Albion Mews
7 Albion Ct
8 King Street Cloisters
9 Dimes Pl
10 Clarence Ct
11 Hampshire Hog La
12 Marryat Ct
13 Ravenscourt Ho
14 Ravenscourt Theatre Sch
15 Cambridge Sch
16 Godolphin & Latymer Sch
17 Flora Gardens Prim Sch
B3 1 Ravenscourt Park Mans

2 Paddenswick Ct
3 Ashbridge Ct
4 Brackenbury Prim Sch
B4 1 Westbush Ct
2 Goldhawk Mews
3 Sycamore Ho
4 Shackleton Ct
5 Drake Ct
6 Scotts Ct
7 Raleigh Ct
8 Melville Court Flats
9 Southway Cl
B5 1 Arlington Ho
2 Lurgard Ho
3 Shabana Ct
4 Sitarey Ct
5 Oaklands Ct
6 Davenport Mews
B6 1 Abercrombie Ho
2 Bathurst Ho
3 Brisbane Ho
4 Bentinck Ho
5 Ellenborough Ho
6 Lawrence Cl
7 Mackenzie Cl
8 Carteret Ho
9 Calvert Ho
10 Winthrop Ho
11 Auckland Ho
12 Blaxland Ho
13 Havelock Cl
14 Hargraves Ho
15 Hudson Cl
16 Phipps Ho
17 Lawson Ho
18 Hastings Ho
19 Wolfe Ho
20 Malabar Ct
21 Commonwealth Ave
22 Charnock Ho
23 Canning Ho
24 Cornwallis Ho
25 Commonwealth Ave
26 Champlain Ho
27 Grey Ho
28 Durban Ho
29 Baird Ho
30 Campbell Ho
31 Mitchell Ho
32 Denham Ho
33 Mackay Ho
34 Evans Ho
35 Davis Ho
36 Mandela Cl
C1 1 Bridge Avenue Mans
2 Bridgeview
3 College Ct
4 Beatrice Ho
5 Amelia Ho
6 Edith Ho
7 Joanna Ho
8 Mary Ho
9 Adela Ho
10 Sophia Ho
11 Henrietta Ho
12 Charlotte Ho
13 Alexandra Ho
14 Bath Pl
15 Elizabeth Ho
16 Margaret Ho
17 Peabody Est
18 Eleanor Ho
19 Isabella Ho
20 Caroline Ho
21 Chancellors Wharf
22 Sussex Pl
23 St Paul's CE Prim Sch
C2 1 Phoenix Lodge Mans
2 Samuel's Cl
3 Broadway Arc
4 Brook Ho
5 Hammersmith Broadway
6 Broadway Ctr The
7 Cambridge Ct
8 Ashcroft Sq
9 Sacred Heart High Sch

C4 1 Verulam Ho
2 Grove Mans
3 Frobisher Ct
4 Library Mans
5 Pennard Mans
6 New Shepherd's Bush Mkt
7 Kerrington Ct
8 Granville Mans
9 Romney Ct
10 Rayner Ct
11 Sulgrave Gdns
12 Bamborough Gdns
13 Hillary Ct
14 Market Studios
15 Lanark Mans
16 Miles Coverdale Prim Sch
17 St Stephen's CE Prim Sch
18 London Coll of Fashion (Lime Grove)
C5 1 Linden Ct
2 Frithville Ct
3 Blomfield Mans
4 Poplar Mews
5 Hopgood St
6 Westwood Ho
7 Stanlake Mews
8 Stanlake Villas
9 Alexandra Mans
D2 1 St Paul's Girls' Sch
2 Bute House Prep Sch
3 Jacques Prevert Sch
4 Larmenier & Sacred Heart RC Prim Sch
D3 1 Grosvenor Residences
2 Blythe Mews
3 Burnand Ho
4 Bradford Ho
5 Springvale Terr
6 Ceylon Rd
7 Walpole Ct
8 Bronte Ct
9 Boswell Ct
10 Souldern Rd
11 Brook Green Flats
12 Haarlem Rd
13 Stafford Mans
14 Lionel Mans
15 Barradell Ho
D4 1 Vanderbilt Villas
2 Bodington Ct
3 Kingham Cl
4 Clearwater Terr
5 Lorne Gdns
6 Cameret Ct
7 Bush Ct
8 Shepherds Ct
9 Rockley Ct
10 Grampians The
11 Charcroft Ct
12 Addison Park Mans
13 Sinclair Mans
14 Fountain Ct
15 Woodford Ct
16 Roseford Ct
17 Woodstock Studios
D5 1 St Katherine's Wlk
2 Dorrit Ho
3 Pickwick Ho
4 Dombey Ho
5 Caranday Villas
6 Mortimer Ho
7 Nickleby Ho
8 Stebbing Ho
9 Boxmoor Ho
10 Poynter Ho
11 Swanscombe Ho
12 Darnley Terr
13 Norland Ho

11 Hazelwood Ho
12 Cannon Wharf Bsns Ctr
13 Bence Ho
14 Clement Ho
15 Pendennis Ho
16 Lighter Cl
17 Mast Ct
18 Rushcutters Ct
19 Boat Lifter Way
A5 1 Edward Sq
2 Prince Regent Ct
3 Codrington Ct
4 Pennington Ct
5 Cherry Ct
6 Ash Ct
7 Beech Ct
8 Hazel Ct
9 Laurel Ct
A6 1 St Georges Sq
2 Drake Ho
3 Osprey Ho
4 Fleet Ho
5 Gainsborough Ho
6 Victory Pl
7 Challenger Ho
8 Conrad Ho
9 Lock View Ct
10 Shoulder of Mutton Alley
11 Frederick Sq
12 Helena Sq
13 Elizabeth Sq
14 Sophia Sq
15 William Sq
16 Lamb Ct
17 Lockside
18 Adriatic Bldg
19 Ionian Bldg
20 Regents Gate Ho
B1 1 Gransden Ho
2 Daubeney Twr
3 North Ho
4 Rochfort Ho
5 Keppel Ho
6 Camden Ho
7 Sanderson Ho
8 Berkeley Ho
9 Strafford Ho
10 Richman Ho
11 Hurleston Ho
12 Grafton Ho
13 Fulcher Ho
14 Citrus Ho
B2 1 Windsock Cl
2 St George's Mews
3 Linberry Wlk
4 Lanyard Ho
5 Golden Hind Pl
6 James Lind Ho
7 Harmon Ho
8 Pelican Ho
9 Bembridge Ho
10 Terrace The
11 George Beard Rd
12 Colonnade The
13 Pepys Ent Ctr
B6 1 Hamilton Ho
2 Imperial Ho
3 Oriana Ho
4 Queens Ct
5 Brightlingsea Pl
6 Faraday Ho
7 Ropemaker's Fields
8 Oast Ct
9 Mitre The
10 Bate St
11 Joseph Irwin Ho
12 Padstow Ho
13 Bethlehem Ho
14 Saunders Cl
15 Roche Ho
16 Stocks Pl
17 Trinidad Ho
18 Grenada Ho
19 Kings Ho
20 Dunbar Wharf
21 Limekiln Wharf
22 Belgrave Ct
23 Eaton Ho
24 Cyril Jackson Prim Sch (North Bldg)

25 Cyril Jackson Prim Sch (South Bldg)
C1 1 Hudson Ct
2 Shackleton Ct
3 De Gama Pl
4 Mercator Pl
5 Maritime Quay
6 Perry Ct
7 Amundsen Ct
C2 1 Nova Bldg
2 Apollo Bldg
3 Gaverick Mews
4 Windmill Ho
5 Orion Point
6 Galaxy Bldg
7 Venus Ho
8 Olympian Ct
9 Poseidon Ct
10 Mercury Ct
11 Aphrodite Ct
12 Cyclops Mews
13 Neptune Ct
14 Artemis Ct
15 Hera Ct
16 Ares Ct
17 Ringwood Gdns
18 Dartmoor Wlk
19 Rothsay Wlk
20 Ashdown Wlk
21 Radnor Wlk
22 Ironmonger's Pl
23 Britannia Rd
24 Deptford Ferry Rd
25 Magellan Pl
26 Dockers Tanner Rd
C3 1 Bowsprit Point
2 St Hubert's Ho
3 John Tucker Ho
4 Broadway Wlk
5 Nash Ho
6 Fairlead Ho
7 Crosstrees Ho
8 Stanliff Ho
9 Keelson Ho
10 Clara Grant Ho
11 Gilbertson Ho
12 Scoulding Ho
13 Hibbert Ho
14 Cressall Ho
15 Alexander Ho
16 Kedge Ho
C4 1 Anchorage Point
2 Waterman Bldg
3 Jefferson Bldg
4 Pierpoint Bldg
5 Franklin Bldg
6 Vanguard Bldg
7 Edison Bldg
8 Seacon Twr
9 Naxos Bldg
10 Express Wharf
11 Hutching's Wharf
12 Tobago St
13 Bellamy Ct
14 Dowlen Ct
15 Cochrane Ho
16 Beatty Ho
17 Scott Ho
18 Laybourne Ho
19 Ensign Ho
20 Beaufort Ho
21 Spinnaker Ho
22 Bosun Cl
23 Topmast Point
24 Turner Ho
25 Constable Ho
26 Knighthead Point
27 Seven Mills Prim Sch
C6 1 West India Ho
2 Berber Pl
3 Birchfield Ho
4 Elderfield Ho
5 Thornfield Ho
6 Gorsefield Ho
7 Arborfield Ho
8 Colborne Ho
9 East India Bldgs
10 Compass Point
11 Salter St
12 Garland Ct
13 Bogart Ct
14 Fonda Ct

3 Welles Ct
4 Rogers Ct
5 Premier Pl
6 Kelly Ct
7 Flynn Ct
20 Mary Jones Ho
21 Cannon Dr
22 Horizon Bldg
23 Holy Family RC Prim Sch
D1 1 Slipway Ho
2 Taffrail Ho
3 Platehouse The
4 Wheelhouse The
5 Chart House The
6 Port House The
7 Beacon Ho
8 Blasker Wlk
9 Maconochies Rd
D2 1 Brassey Ho
2 Triton Ho
3 Warspite Ho
4 Rodney Ho
5 Conway Ho
6 Exmouth Ho
7 Akbar Ho
8 Arethusa Ho
9 Tasman Ct
10 Cutty Sark Ho
11 Harbinger Prim Sch
D3 1 Turnberry Quay
2 Balmoral Ho
3 Aegon Ho
4 Marina Point
D6 1 Westcott Ho
2 Corry Ho
3 Malam Gdns
4 Blomfield Ho
5 Devitt Ho
6 Leyland Ho
7 Wigram Ho
8 Willis Ho
9 Balsam Ho
10 Finch's Ct
11 Poplar Bath St
12 Lawless St
13 Storey Ho
14 Abbot Ho
15 Woodall Cl
16 Landon Wlk
17 Goodhope Ho
18 Goodfaith Ho
19 Winant Ho
20 Goodspeed Ho
21 Lubbock Ho
22 Goodwill Ho
23 Martindale Ho
24 Holmsdale Ho
25 Norwood Ho
26 Constant Ho
27 Tower Hamlets Coll

120
A2 1 St John's Ho
2 Betty May Gray Ho
3 Castleton Ho
4 Urmston Ho
5 Salford Ho
6 Capstan Ho
7 Frigate Ho
8 Galleon Ho
9 Barons Lo
A3 1 Cardale St
2 Hickin St
3 John McDonald Ho
4 Thorne Ho
5 Skeggs Ho
6 St Bernard Ho
7 Kimberley Ho
8 Kingdon Ho
9 Killoran Ho
10 Alastor Ho
11 Lingard Ho
12 Yarrow Ho
13 Sandpiper Ct
14 Nightingale Ct
15 Robin Ct
16 Heron Ct
17 Ferndown Lo
18 Crosby Ho
A4 1 Llandovery Ho
2 Rugless Ho

3 Ash Ho
4 Elm Ho
5 Cedar Ho
6 Castalia Sq
7 Aspect Ho
8 Normandy Ho
9 Valiant Ho
10 Tamar Ho
11 Watkins Ho
12 Alice Shepherd Ho
13 Oak Ho
14 Ballin Ct
15 Martin Ct
16 Grebe Ct
17 Kingfisher Ct
18 Walkers Lo
19 Antilles Bay
A5 1 Lumina Bldg
2 Nova Ct W
3 Nova Ct E
4 Aurora Bldg
5 Arran Ho
6 Kintyre Ho
7 Vantage Mews
8 Managers St
9 Horatio Pl
10 Concordia Wharf
A6 1 Discovery Ho
2 Mountague Pl
3 Virginia Ho
4 Collins Ho
5 Lawless Ho
6 Carmichael Ho
7 Commodore Ho
8 Mermaid Ho
9 Bullivant St
10 Anderson Ho
11 Mackrow Wlk
12 Robin Hood Gdns
13 Prestage Way
14 Woolmore Prim Sch
B2 1 Verwood Lo
2 Fawley Lo
3 Lyndhurst Lo
4 Blyth Cl
5 Farnworth Ho
6 Francis Cl
7 St Luke's CE Prim Sch
B6 1 Quixley St
2 Romney Ho
3 Pumping Ho
4 Switch Ho
5 Wingfield Ct
6 Explorers Ct
7 Sexton Ct
8 Keel Ct
9 Bridge Ct
10 Sail Ct
11 Settlers Ct
12 Pilgrims Mews
13 Studley Ct
14 Wotton Ct
15 Cape Henry Ct
16 Bartholomew Ct
17 Adventurers Ct
18 Susan Constant Ct
C1 1 Bellot Gdns
2 Thornley Pl
3 King William La
4 Bolton Ho
5 Miles Ho
6 Mell St
7 Sam Manners Ho
8 Hatcliffe Almshouses
9 Woodland Wlk
10 Earlswood Ct
11 St Joseph's RC Prim Sch
D1 1 Baldrey Ho
2 Christie Ho
3 Dyson Ho
4 Cliffe Ho
5 Moore Ho
6 Collins Ho
7 Lockyer Ho
8 Halley Ho
9 Kepler Ho
10 Sailacre Ho
11 Union Pk
D3 1 Teal St

2 Maurer Ct
3 Mudlarks Blvd
4 Renaissance Wlk
5 Alamaro Lo

121
A1 1 Layfield Ho
2 Westerdale Rd
3 Mayston Mews
4 Station Mews Terr
5 Halstow Prim Sch
6 Holyrood Mews
A5 1 Capulet Mews
2 Pepys Cres
3 De Quincey Mews
4 Hardy Ave
5 Tom Jenkinson Rd
6 Kennacraig Cl
7 Charles Flemwell Mews
8 Gatcombe Rd
9 Badminton Mews
10 Holyrood Mews
11 Britannia Gate
12 Dalemain Mews
13 Bowes-Lyon Hall
14 Lancaster Hall
15 Victoria Hall
A6 1 Clements Ave
2 Martindale Ave
3 Balearic Apts
4 Marmara Apts
5 Baltic Apts
6 Coral Apts
7 Aegean Apts
8 Capital East Apts
B1 1 Phipps Ho
2 Hartwell Ho
3 Nicholas Stacey Ho
4 Fossdene Prim Sch
5 Frank Burton Ct
B5 1 Beaulieu Ave
2 Charles Whincup Rd
3 Audley Dr
4 Julia Garfield Mews
5 Rayleigh Rd
6 Pirie St
7 Royal Victoria Pl
8 Pankhurst Ave
9 West Mersea Cl
10 Ramsgate Cl
11 Windsor Hall
12 Munning Ho
13 Drake Hall
14 Jane Austen Hall
15 Eastern Quay
16 Portsmouth Mews
17 Britannia Village Prim Sch
C1 1 Ransom Rd
2 Linton Ct
3 Cedar Pl
4 Gooding Ho
5 Valiant Ho
6 Chaffey Ho
7 Benn Ho
8 Wellesley Ho
9 Gollogly Terr

122
A2 1 Harden Ct
2 Albion Ct
3 Viking Ho
4 Zealand Ho
5 Glenalvon Way
6 Parish Wharf
7 Elsinore Ho
8 Lolland Ho
9 Denmark Ho
10 Jutland Ho
11 Tivoli Gdns
12 Rance Ho
13 Peel Yates Ho
14 Rosebank Wlk
15 Paradise Pl
16 Woodville St
B2 1 Bowling Green Row

123 A2 489

2 Sarah Turnbull Ho
3 Brewhouse Rd
4 Red Barracks Rd
5 Marine Dr
6 Hastings Ho
7 Centurion Ct
8 Cambridge Ho
9 Churchill Ct
10 Elizabeth Ct
11 Cambridge Barracks Rd
12 Len Clifton Ho
13 Granby Ho
14 Harding Ho
15 Rutland Ho
16 Townshend Ho
17 Rendlebury Ho
18 Milne Ho
19 Mulgrave Ho
20 Murray Ho
21 Chatham Ho
22 Biddulph Ho
23 Carew Ho
24 Eleanor Wlk
25 Cardwell Prim Sch
C2 1 Preston Ho
2 Lindsay Ho
3 Fraser Ho
4 Pickering Ho
5 Watergate Ho
6 Grinling Ho
7 Glebe Ho
8 Elliston Ho
9 Sir Martin Bowes Ho
10 Jim Bradley Cl
11 Bathway
12 Limavady Ho
13 Slater Cl
14 Vista Bldg The
15 Greenwich London Coll
16 St Mary Magdalene CE Prim Sch
C5 1 Westland Ho
2 Queensland Ho
3 Pier Par
4 Woodman Par
5 Shaw Ho
6 Glen Ho
7 Brocklebank Ho
D1 1 Branham Ho
2 Ford Ho
3 Wilford Ho
4 Parker Ho
5 Stirling Ho
6 Twiss Ho
7 Hewett Ho
8 De Haviland Dr
9 Schoolhouse Yd
D2 1 Beresford Ho
2 Central Ct
3 Walpole Pl
4 Anglesea Ave
5 Troy Ct
6 Ormsby Point
7 Haven Lo
8 Green Lawns
9 Eardley Point
10 Sandham Point
11 Bingham Point
12 Anglesea Mews
13 Masons Hill
14 Maritime Ho
15 Univ of America (London Campus)
16 Woolwich Tramshed The

123
A1 1 Glenmount Path
2 Claymill Ho
3 St James Hts
4 St Margaret's Path
5 George Akass Ho
A2 1 Abel Ho
2 Maynard Ho
3 Crown Ho

A3
1 Wayatt Point
2 Albert Ho
3 Building 50
4 Building 49
5 Building 48
6 Building 47
7 Building 36
8 Blenheim Ho
9 Wilson Ct
10 Romney Rd
B1
1 Bert Reilly Ho
2 Heavitree Rd
3 South Rise Prim Sch
B3
1 Apollo Way
2 Senator Wlk
3 Mallard Path
4 Fortune Wlk
C1
1 Fox Hollow Cl
2 Goldsmid St
C2
1 Gavin Ho
2 Richard Neve Ho
3 Bateson St
4 Lewin Ct
5 Conway Prim Sch

124

B5
1 Rowntree Path
2 Macaulay Way
3 Manning Ct
4 Chadwick Ct
5 Simon Ct
B6
1 Beveridge Ct
2 Hammond Way
3 Leonard Robbins Path
4 Lansbury Ct
5 Raymond Postgate Ct
6 Webb Ct
7 Curtis Way
8 Lytton Strachey Path
9 Keynes Ct
10 Marshall Path
11 Cross Ct
12 Octavia Way
13 Passfield Path
14 Mill Ct
15 Besant Ct
C3
1 Hermitage Ct
2 Chantry Cl
C4
1 Binsey Wlk
2 Tilehurst Point
3 Blewbury Ho
4 Coralline Wlk
5 Evenlode Ho
C5
1 Kingsley Cl
2 Wilberforce Ct
3 Shaftesbury Ct
4 Hazlitt Cl
5 Ricardo Path
6 Nassau Path
7 Malthus Path
8 Bright Ct
9 Cobden Ct
D4
1 Oakenholt Ho
2 Trewsbury Ho
3 Penton Ho
4 Osney Ho
5 St Helens Rd
6 Clewer Ho
7 Maplin Ho
8 Wyfold Ho
9 Hibernia Point
10 Duxford Ho
11 Radley Ho
12 Limestone Wlk
13 Masham Ho
14 Jacob Ho

125

A3
1 Harlequin Ho
2 Dexter Ho
3 Argali Ho
4 Mangold Way
5 Lucerne Ct
6 Holstein Way
7 Abbotswood Cl
8 Plympton Cl
9 Benedict Cl
B1
1 Shakespeare Ho
2 Tennyson Ho

3 Dickens Ho
4 Scott Ho
5 Lansbury Ho
6 Shaw Ho
7 Chestnuts The
C1
1 Stevanne Ct
2 Tolcairn Ct
3 Chalfont Ct
4 Alonso Ho
5 Ariel Ct
6 Miranda Ho
7 Prospero Ho
8 Laurels The
9 Camden Ct
10 Newnham Lo
11 Court Lo
12 Flaxman Ct
13 Hertford Wlk
14 Riverview Ct
15 Winchester Ct
C2
1 Brushwood Ct
2 Bletchington Ct
3 Upper Sheridan Rd
4 William Ct
5 Samson Ct
6 Cowper Rd
7 Venmead Ct
C3
1 Cressingham Ct
2 Telford Ho
3 Kelvin Ho
4 Faraday Ho
5 Jenner Ho
6 Keir Hardie Ho
7 Lennox Ho
8 Mary Macarthur Ho
9 Elizabeth Garrett Anderson Ho
10 William Smith Ho
11 Baden Powell Ho
12 Baird Ho
13 Boyle Ho

129

B2
1 St Michael & St Martin RC Prim Sch
2 Bellview Ct
3 Heathwood Ct
4 Aldermead
5 Northumberland Ct
D2
1 Oak Hts Ind Sch

130

C4
1 Osterley Lo
2 St Andrew's Cl
3 Parkfield
4 Fairways
5 Granwood Ct
6 Grovewood Ct
D3
2 Beechen Cliff Way
4 Thurza Ct
5 Primrose Pl
6 Lanadron Cl
D4
1 Overton Cl

131

A2
1 Brewery Mews Bsns Ctr
2 Forge Lo
3 Pulteney Ct
4 Tolson Ho
5 Percy Gdns
6 Wynne Ct
7 Wisdom Ct
8 Swann Ct
9 Shrewsbury Wlk
10 King's Terr
11 Van Gogh Ct
12 Holme Ct
13 St Mary's RC Prim Sch
C5
1 Canute Ho
2 Spruce Ho
3 Moorings Ho
4 Jessops Wharf
5 Corsell Ho
6 Barnes Qtr
7 Dorey Ho
8 Tanyard Ho
9 Booth Ho
10 Oakbark Ho
11 Bordeston Ct
12 Shire Pl

D5
1 Galba Ct
2 Servius Ct
3 Maurice Ct
4 Leo Ct
5 Otho Ct
6 Nero Ct
7 Romulus Ct
8 Caxton Mews
D6
1 Brockshot Cl
2 Westbury Pl
3 Brook La N
4 Braemar Ct
5 Brook Cs
6 Clifden Ho
7 Cedar Ct
8 Cranbrook Ct
9 Somerset Lo
10 Alexandra Rd
11 Berkeley Ho
12 Watermans Ct
13 Ferry Quays Ctyd
14 St Pauls CE Prim Sch

132

A1
1 St John's Gr
2 Michel's Row
3 Michelsdale Dr
4 Blue Anchor Alley
5 Clarence St
6 Sun Alley
7 Thames Link Ho
8 Benns Wlk
9 Waterloo Pl
10 Northumbria Ct
A6
1 Ferry Sq
2 Watermans Ct
3 Wilkes Rd
4 Albany Par
5 Charlton Ho
6 Albany Ho
7 Alma Ho
8 Griffin Ct
9 Cressage Ho
10 Tunstall Wlk
11 Trimmer Wlk
12 Running Horse Yd
13 Distillery Wlk
B1
1 Towers The
2 Longs Ct
3 Sovereign Ct
4 Calvert Ct
5 Bedford Ct
6 Hickey's Almshouses
7 Church Estate Almshouses
8 Richmond International Bsns Ctr
9 Abercorn Mews
B4
1 Primrose Ho
2 Lawman Ct
3 Royston Ct
4 Garden Ct
5 Capel Lo
6 Devonshire Ct
7 Celia Ct
8 Rosslyn Ho
9 Branstone Ct
10 Lamerton Lo
11 Kew Lo
12 Dunraven Ct
13 Stoneleigh Lo
14 Tunstall Ct
15 Voltaire
C4
1 Clarendon Ct
2 Quintock Ho
3 Broome Ct
4 Lonsdale Mews
5 Elizabeth Cotts
6 Sandways
7 Victoria Cotts
8 North Ave
9 Grovewood
10 Hamilton Ho
11 Melvin Ct
12 Royal Par
13 Power Ho
14 Station Ave
15 Blake Mews
C6
5 Strand-on-the-Green Schs

D1
1 Hershell Ct
2 Deanhill Ct
3 Park Sheen
4 Furness Lo
5 Merricks Ct
D4
1 Terrano Ho
2 Oak Ho
3 Aura Ho
4 Maple Ho
5 Cedar Ho
6 Saffron Ho
7 Lime Ho
8 Lavender Ho
9 Juniper Ho
D6
1 Falcons Pre Prep school The

133

B2
1 Rann Ho
2 Craven Ho
3 John Dee Ho
4 Kindell Ho
5 Montgomery Ho
6 Avondale Ho
7 Addington Ct
8 Dovecote Gdns
9 Firmston Ho
10 Glendower Gdns
11 Trehern Ave
12 Rock Ave
13 St Mary Magdalen's RC Prim Sch
D3
1 Melrose Rd
2 Seaforth Lo
3 St John's Gr
4 Sussex Ct
5 Carmichael Ct
6 Hampshire Ct
7 Thorne Pas
8 Brunel Ct
9 Beverley Path

134

D1
1 Olivette St
2 Mascotte Rd
3 Glegg Pl
4 Crown Ct
5 Charlwood Terr
6 Percy Laurie Ho
7 Our Lady of Victories RC Prim Sch
D2
1 Griffin Gate
2 Darfur St
3 John Keall Ho
4 Henry Jackson Ho
5 Felsham Ho
6 Ardshiel Cl
7 Ruvigny Mans
8 Star & Garter Mans
9 University Mans
10 Lockyer Ho
11 Phelps Ho
12 Princeton Ct
13 Kingsmere Cl
14 Felsham Mews
15 St Mary's CE Prim Sch
D6
1 Cobb's Hall
2 Dorset Mans
3 St Clements Mans
4 Bothwell St
5 Hawksmoor St
6 Melcombe Prim Sch

135

A3
1 Drive Mans
2 Romily Ct
3 Dwight Ct
4 Burlington Gdns
5 Fulham Prep Sch
6 Moat Sch The
7 All Saints CE Prim Sch
B3
1 Plato Pl
2 Mustow Pl
3 Laurel Bank Gdns
4 Ranelagh Mans
5 Churchfield Mans
6 Bear Croft Ho

7 Elysium Gate
8 Ethel Rankin Ct
9 Arthur Henderson Ho
10 William Banfield Ho
11 Melbray Mews
12 New King's Prim Sch
Be Eridge House Sch
D3
1 Brightwells
2 Broughton Road App
3 Bulow Ct
4 Langford Rd
5 Elizabeth Barnes Ct
6 Snowbury Rd

136

A2
1 Molasses Ho
2 Molasses Row
3 Cinnamon Row
4 Calico Ho
5 Calico Row
6 Port Ho
7 Square Rigger Row
8 Trade Twr
9 Ivory Ho
10 Spice Ct
11 Sherwood Ct
12 Mendip Ct
13 Chalmers Ho
14 Coral Row
15 Ivory Sq
16 Kingfisher Ho
B1
1 High View Prim Sch
2 Centre Acad
3 Fox Ho
4 Buxton Ho
5 Pitt Ho
6 Ramsey Ho
7 Beverley Cl
8 Florence Ho
9 Linden Ct
10 Dorcas Ct
11 Johnson Ct
12 Agnes Ct
13 Hilltop Ct
14 Courtyard The
15 Old Laundry The
16 Oberstein Rd
17 Fineran Ct
18 Sangora Rd
19 Harvard Mans
20 Plough Mews
B2
1 Milner Ho
2 McManus Ho
3 Wilberforce Ho
4 Wheeler Ct
5 Sporle Ct
6 Holliday Sq
7 John Parker Sq
8 Carmichael Ct
9 Fenner Sq
10 Clark Lawrence Ct
11 Shaw Ct
12 Sendall Ct
13 Livingstone St
14 Farrant Ho
15 Jackson Ho
16 Darien Ho
17 Shepard Ho
18 Ganley Ct
19 Arthur Newton Ho
20 Chesterton Ho
21 John Kirk Ho
22 Mantua St
23 Heaver Rd
24 Candlemakers
25 Thames Christian Coll
26 Falconbrook Prim Sch
B1
1 Archer Ho
2 White Ho
3 Winfield Ho
4 Powrie Ho
5 Morgan Ct
6 Fairchild Cl
7 Musjid Rd

C2
1 Kiloh Ct
2 Lanner Ho
3 Griffon Ho
4 Kestrel Ho
5 Kite Ho
6 Peregrine Ho
7 Hawk Ho
8 Inkster Ho
9 Harrier Ho
10 Eagle Hts
11 Kingfisher Ct
12 Lavender Terr
13 Temple Ho
14 Ridley Ho
15 Eden Ho
16 Hertford Ct
17 Nepaul Rd
C3
1 Meecham Ct
2 McKiernan Ct
3 Colestown St
4 Crombie Mews
5 Frere St
D3
1 Stevenson Ho
2 Ambrose Mews
3 Harling Ct
4 Southside Quarter
5 Latchmere St
6 Dovedale Cotts
7 Royden Cl
8 Castlemaine
9 Wittering Ho
10 Berry Ho
11 Weybridge Point

137

A2
1 Shaftesbury Park Chambers
2 Selborne
3 Rush Hill Mews
4 Marmion Mews
5 Crosland Pl
6 Craven Mews
7 Garfield Mews
8 Audley Cl
9 Basnett Rd
10 Tyneham Cl
11 Woodmere Cl
A3
1 Hopkinson Ho
2 Macdonald Ho
3 Rushlake Ho
4 Bishopstone Ho
5 Dresden Ho
6 Millgrove St
7 Farnhurst Ho
8 Walden Ho
9 Kennard St
10 Langhurst Ho
11 Atkinson Ho
12 Kennard Ho
13 Voltaire Ct
14 Barloch Ho
15 London Stone Bsns Est
16 Shaftsbury Park Prim Sch
17 John Burns Prim Sch
B2
1 Turnchapel Mews
2 Redwood Mews
3 Phil Brown Pl
4 Bev Callender Cl
5 Keith Connor Cl
6 Tessa Sanderson Pl
7 Daley Thompson Way
8 Rashleigh Ct
9 Abberley Mews
10 Willow Lodge
11 Beaufoy Rd
B3
1 St Philip Sq
2 Montefiore St
3 Gambetta St
4 Scott Ct
5 Radcliffe Path
6 Moresby Wlk
7 Victorian Hts
C1
1 Polygon The
2 Windsor Ct
3 Trinity Cl
4 Studios The
5 Bourne Ho
C2
1 Clapham Manor Ct

2 Clarke Ho
3 Gables The
4 Sycamore Mews
5 Maritime Ho
6 Rectory Gdns
7 Floris Pl
8 Clapham Manor Prim Sch
C3 1 Seymour Ho
2 Lucas Ho
3 Durrington Twr
4 Amesbury Twr
5 Fovant Ct
6 Allington Ct
7 Welford Ct
8 Ilsley Ct
9 Blake Ct
10 Brooklands Ct
11 Heathbrook Prim Sch
12 Michael Manley Ind Est
D1 1 Kendoa Rd
2 Felmersham Cl
3 Abbeville Mews
4 Saxon Ho
5 Gifford Ho
6 Teignmouth Cl
7 Holwood Pl
8 Oaklands Pl
9 Wilberforce Mews
10 William Bonney Est
11 London Coll of Bsns & Computer Studies
D2 1 Chelsham Ho
2 Lynde Ho
3 Greener Ho
4 Towns Ho
5 Hugh Morgan Ho
6 Roy Ridley Ho
7 Lendal Terr
8 Slievemore Cl
9 Cadmus Cl
10 Clapham North Bsns Ctr
D3 1 Haltone Ho
2 Surcot Ho
3 Kingsley Ho
4 Wood Ho
5 Dalemain Ho
6 Fallodon Ho
7 Dartington Ho
8 Esher Ho
9 Kneller Ho
10 Lostock Ho
11 Croxteth Ho
12 Donnington Ho
13 Farnley Ho
14 Hardwick Ho
15 Bradfield Ho
16 Brocket Ho
17 Colchester Ho
18 Clive Ho
19 Chessington Ho
20 Rushbrook Ho
21 Stanmore Ho
22 Newton Ho
23 Netherby Ho
24 Oakwell Ho
25 Rydal Ho
26 Rushton Ho
27 Harcourt Ho
28 Metcalfe Ho
29 Lydwell Ho
30 Raleigh Ho
31 Spencer Ho
32 Shipley Ho
33 Naylor Ho
34 Mordaunt Ho
35 Stanley Ho
36 Alderley Ho
37 Effingham Ho
38 Grant Ho
39 Wilson Ho
40 Fraser Ho

138

A1 1 Morris Ho
2 Gye Ho
3 Clowes Ho
4 Thomas Ho
5 Stuart Ho
6 Storace Ho
7 Bedford Ho
8 Ascot Ct
9 Ascot Par
10 Ashmere Ho
11 Ashmere Gr
12 Ventura Ho
13 Vickery Ho
14 Stafford Mans
15 Beresford Ho
A2 1 Callingham Ho
2 Russell Pickering Ho
3 Ormerod Ho
4 Lopez Ho
5 Coachmaker Mews
6 Brixton Day Coll
A3 1 Barling Ct
2 Jeffrey's Ct
3 Brooks Ct
4 Dalmeny Ct
5 Fender Ct
6 Fishlock Ct
7 Bedser Ct
8 Gover Ct
9 Clarence Wlk
10 Barton Ct
11 Allom Ct
12 Garden Ho
13 Otha Ho
14 Hayward Ct
15 Surridge Ct
16 Knox Ct
17 Jephson Ct
18 Holmes Ct
19 McIntyre Ct
20 Richardson Ct
21 Cassell Ho
22 Pakington Ho
23 Bain Ho
24 Enfield Ho
25 Fawcett Ho
26 Sidgwick Ho
27 Jowett Ho
28 Beckett Ho
29 Arden Ho
30 Pinter Ho
31 Barrington Ct
32 Union Mews
33 St Andrew's Prim Sch
B1 1 Freemens Hos
2 Roger's Almshouses
3 Gresham Almshouses
4 Exbury Ho
5 Glasbury Ho
6 Dalbury Ho
7 Fosbury Ho
8 Chalbury Ho
9 Neilson-Terry Ct
10 Pavilion Mans
11 Daisy Dormer Ct
12 George Lashwood Ct
13 Marie Lloyd Ct
14 Trinity Homes
15 Lethaby Ho
16 Edmundsbury Ct Est
17 Regis Pl
18 Marlborough Mews
19 Alpha Ho
20 Beta Pl
21 Cedars Ho
22 South Chelsea Coll
B2 1 Turberville Ho
2 Thrayle Ho
3 Percheron Ct
4 Draymans Ct
5 Lansdowne Sch
6 Stockwell Prim Sch
B3 1 Maurice Ho
2 Thring Ho
3 Paton Ho
4 Huxley Ho
5 Morell Ho
6 Mary Ho
7 Beale Ho
8 Rosa Parks Ho
9 Birrell Ho
10 Waltham Ho
11 Burford Ho
12 Thornicroft Ho
13 Addington Ho
14 Goffton Ho
15 Redmayne Ho
16 Norton Ho
17 Aytoun Ct
18 Colwall Ho
19 Burrow Ho
20 Wynter Ho
21 Crowhurst Ho
22 Lidcote Gdns
23 Cumnor Cl
24 Park View Mews
C1 1 Electric Mans
2 Electric La
3 Connaught Mans
4 Clifton Mans
5 Hereford Ho
6 Chaplin Ho
7 Brixton Oval
8 Lord David Pitt Ho
9 Marcus Garvey Way
10 Montego Cl
11 Bob Marley Way
12 Leeson Rd
C2 1 Buckmaster Cl
2 Albemarle Ho
3 Goodwood Mans
4 Angell Park Gdns
5 Fyfield Rd
6 Howard Ho
7 Harris Ho
8 Broadoak Ct
9 Burgate Ct
10 Witchwood Ho
11 Blacktree Mews
12 Chartham Ct
13 Chilham Ct
14 Northgate Ct
15 Westgate Ct
16 Dover Mans
17 St Helen's RC Sch
18 Dorrell Pl
C3 1 Norval Gn
2 Hilda Terr
3 Burton La
4 Church Gn
5 Lord Holland La
6 Sorrell Cl
7 Burton Rd
8 Holles Ho
9 Leys Ct
10 Warwick Ho
11 Fairfax Ho
12 Wayland Ho
13 Dudley Ho
14 Denchworth Ho
15 Fitzgerald Ho
16 Lambert Ho
17 Chute Ho
18 Bedwell Ho
19 Ferrey Mews
20 Serenaders Rd
21 Boatemah Wlk
22 Ireton Ho
23 Marston Ho
24 Morrison Rd
25 Fir Grove Rd
26 Shore Way
27 George Mews
28 St John's Angell Town CE Prim Sch
C4 1 Hector Ct
2 Jason Ct
3 Creon Ct
4 Hermes Ct
5 Argos Ct
6 Cadmus Ct
7 Appollo Ct
8 Mercury Ct
9 County Ho
10 Seasalter Ho
11 Downbarton Ho
12 Garlinge Ho
13 Moira Ho
14 Alvanley Ho
15 Woodchurch Ho
16 Durlock Ho
17 Hallam Ho
18 Whiteness Ho
19 Bromstone Ho
20 Penelope Ho
21 Melbourne Sq
22 Cloisters The
23 Cliffsend Ho
24 Sacketts Ho
25 Hanway Ho
26 Brickworth Ho
27 Redlynch Ho
28 Stodmarsh Ho
29 Kingsgate Ho
30 Chardin Ho
31 Annesley Ho
32 Knowlton Ho
33 Russell Gr
34 Eamann Casey Ho
35 Christ Church CE Prim Sch
C5 1 Swift Ho
2 Listowel Cl
3 Deal Wlk
4 Plover Ho
5 Aigburth Mans
6 Glencoe Mans
7 Glenshaw Mans
8 Cleveland Mans
9 Leda Ct
10 Jupiter Ct
11 Juno Ct
12 Healy Ho
13 Ashton Ho
14 Ramsey Ho
15 Annesley Ho
16 Cowley Rd
C6 1 Sherwin Ho
2 Pegasus Pl
3 Kilner Ho
4 Read Ho
5 Lohmann Ho
6 Hornby Ho
7 Abel Ho
8 Blythe Ho
9 Key Ho
10 Lockwood Ho
11 Alverstone Ho
12 Blades Ho
13 Rothesay Ct
14 Henry Fawcett Prim Sch
D1 1 Mahatma Gandhi Ind Est
2 Dylan Rd
3 Bessemer Park Ind Est
4 Pablo Neruda Cl
5 Langston Hughes Cl
6 Walt Whitman Cl
7 James Joyce Wlk
8 Alice Walker Cl
9 Louise Bennett Cl
10 Chadacre Ho
11 Burwood Ho
12 Pyrford Ho
13 Wangford Ho
14 Ashford Ho
15 Kenwood Ho
16 Moyne Ho
17 Elveden Ho
18 Carrara Cl
19 Broughton Dr
20 Angela Davis Ind Est
21 Tilia Wlk
22 County Ho
23 Hill Mead Prim Sch
D2 1 Mallams Mews
2 Amberley Ct
3 Harper Ho
4 Leicester Ho
5 Station Ave
6 Wellfit St
7 Loughborough Ct
8 Belinda Rd
9 Higgs Ind Est
10 Tham Cl
D3 1 Langport Ho
2 Iveagh Ho
3 Newark Ho
4 Edgehill Ho
5 Hopton Ho
6 Ashby Ho
7 Nevil Ho
D4 1 Fairbairn Gn
2 Hammelton Gn
3 Foxley Sq
4 Silverburn Ho
5 Butler Ho
6 Dalkeith Ho
7 Turner Cl
8 Bathgate Ho
9 Black Roof Ho
10 Charles Edward Brooke Sch (Dennen Site)
11 Charles Edward Brooke Sch
D6 1 Faunce Ho
2 Garbett Ho
3 Harvard Ho
4 Doddington Pl
5 Kean Ho
6 Jephson Ho
7 Cornish Ho
8 Bateman Ho
9 Molesworth Ho
10 Walters Ho
11 Cruden Ho
12 Brawne Ho
13 Prescott Ho
14 Chalmer's Wlk
15 Copley Cl
16 King Charles Ct

139

A3 1 Bergen Ho
2 Oslo Ho
3 Viking Ho
4 Jutland Ho
5 Norvic Ho
6 Odin Ho
7 Baltic Ho
8 Nobel Ho
9 Mercia Ho
10 Kenbury Gdns
11 Zealand Ho
12 Elsinore Ho
13 Norse Ho
14 Denmark Mans
15 Dane Ho
16 Canterbury Cl
17 York Cl
18 Kenbury Mans
19 Parade Mans
20 Winterslow Ho
21 Lilford Ho
22 Bartholomew Ho
23 Guildford Ho
24 Boston Ho
25 Hereford Ho
26 Weyhill Ho
27 Lichfield Ho
28 Lansdown Ho
29 Honiton Ho
30 Pinner Ho
31 Baldock Ho
32 Widecombe Ho
33 Nottingham Ho
34 Witham Ho
35 Barnet Ho
36 Empress Mews
A4 1 Bertha Neubergh Ho
2 Mornington Mews
3 Badsworth Rd
4 Pearson Cl
5 Elm Tree Ct
6 Samuel Lewis Trust Dwellings
7 Milkwell Yd
8 Keswick Ho
9 Mitcham Ho
10 Sacred Heart RC Sec Sch
A5 1 Boundary Ho
2 Day Ho
3 Burgess Ho
4 Carlyle Ho
5 Myers Ho
6 Thompson Ave
7 Palgrave Ho
8 Winnington Ho
9 Brantwood Ho
10 Lowell Ho
11 Jessie Duffett Ho
12 Otterburn Ho
13 Crossmount Ho
14 Venice Ct
15 Bowyer St
16 Livingstone Ho
17 Gothic Ct
18 Coniston Ho
19 Harlynwood
20 Carey Ct
21 Finley Ct
22 Grainger Ct
23 Hayes Ct
24 Moffat Ho
25 Marinel Ho
26 Hodister Cl
27 Arnot Ho
28 Lamb Ho
29 Kipling Ho
30 Keats Ho
31 Kenyon Ho
32 New Church Rd
33 Sir John Kirk Cl
34 Comber Grove Prim Sch
35 St Michael & All Angels CE Acad
36 St Joseph's RC Inf & Jun Schs
B1 1 Shaftesbury Ct
2 Mayhew Ct
3 Morris Ct
4 Swinburne Ct
5 Perth Ct
6 Tayside Ct
7 Matlock Ct
8 Hunter Ct
9 Turner Ct
B3 1 Selborne Rd
2 Hascombe Terr
B4 1 Joiners Arms Yd
2 Butterfly Wlk
3 Cuthill Wlk
4 Colonades The
5 Artichoke Mews
6 Peabody Bldgs
7 Brighton Ho
8 Park Ho
9 Peabody Ct
10 Lomond Ho
11 Lamb Ho
12 Kimpton Ct
13 Belham Wlk
14 Datchelor Pl
15 Harvey Rd
B5 1 Masterman Ho
2 Milton Ho
3 Pope Ho
4 Chester Ct
5 Marvel Ho
6 Flecker Ho
7 Landor Ho
8 Leslie Prince Ct
9 Evelina Mans
10 Langland Ho
11 Drinkwater Ho
12 Procter Ho
13 Shirley Ho
14 Drayton Ho
15 Bridges Ho
16 Cunningham Ho
17 Hood Ho
18 Herrick Ho
19 Dekker Ho
20 Houseman Way
21 Coleby Path
22 Brunswick Park Prim Sch
B6 1 Queens Ho
2 Arnside Ho
3 Horsley St
4 St Peter's Ho
5 St Johns Ho
6 St Marks Ho
7 St Stephens Ho
8 St Matthew's Ho
9 Red Lion Cl
10 Boyson Rd
11 Bradenham
C2 1 Harfield Gdns
2 Karen Ct
3 Seavington Ho
4 Appleshaw Ho
5 Birdsall Ho
6 Whitney Ho
7 Wheatland Ho
8 Wilton Ho
9 Walcot Ho
10 Whaddon Ho
11 Melbreak Ho
12 Ledbury Ho
13 Tidworth Ho

12 Clipper Appts
B2 1 Our Lady of Lourdes RC Prim Sch
B6 1 Frobisher Ct
2 Hardy Cotts
3 Palliser Ho
4 Bernard Angell Ho
5 Corvette Sq
6 Travers Ho
7 Maze Hill Lodge
8 Park Place Ho
9 Meridian Prim Sch
D3 1 Heath House Prep Sch
D5 1 Westcombe Ct
2 Kleffens Ct
3 Ferndale Ct
4 Combe Mews
5 Mandeville Cl
7 Pinelands Cl

143

A5 1 Mary Lawrenson Pl
2 Bradbury Ct
3 Dunstable Ct
4 Wentworth Ho
A6 1 Nethercombe Ho
2 Holywell Cl
B6 1 Capella Ho
2 Collington Ho
3 Sherington Prim Sch
4 Our Lady of Grace RC Prim Sch
C6 1 Warren Wlk
2 Wilson Ho
3 Priory Ho
4 Mar Ho
5 Langhorne Ho
6 Games Ho
7 Erskine Ho
8 Ducie Ho
9 Downe Ho
10 Bayeux Ho
11 Elliscombe Mount
12 Harold Gibbons Ct
13 Mascalls Ct
14 Leila Parnell Pl
15 East Mascalls
16 Birch Tree Ho
17 Cherry Tree Ct
18 Elm Tree Ct
19 Cedar Ct
D5 1 Winchester Ho
2 Brentwood Ho
3 Shenfield Ho
4 Chesterford Ho

144

A4 1 Master Gunner's Pl
2 Ross Ho
3 Dickson Ho
4 Horne Ho
5 Pendlebury Ho
6 Roberts Ho
7 Maple Tree Pl
8 Berber Par
9 Centurian Sq
C6 1 Lawson Ho
2 Mabbett Ho
3 Petrie Ho
4 Memess Path
5 Ruegg Ho
6 Nile Path
7 Leslie Smith Sq
8 Spearman St
9 Siedle Ho
10 Watling Ho
11 O'Neill Path
12 Old Clem Sq
13 Jefferson Wlk
14 Milward Wlk
15 Wordsworth Ho
16 Fenwick Cl
D6 1 Acworth Ho
2 Griffiths Ho
3 Squires Ho
4 Cowen Ho
5 Turton Ho
6 Alford Ho
7 Boxshall Ho
8 Macallister Ho
9 Marvin Ho
10 Kelham Ho
11 Kimber Ho
12 Maxwell Ho
13 Woodford Ho
14 Penfold Ho
15 Butterfield Mews

146

A2 1 Wellingfield Ct
2 Woodville Gr
3 Midwinter Cl
4 St Leonards Cl

147

A1 1 Woburn Ct
2 Arundel Ct
3 Longleat Ct
4 Upton Villas
5 Whitehaven Ct
6 Shirley Hts
7 Louise Ct
8 Bethany Ct
B6 1 Bevercote Wlk
3 Lullingstone Rd
4 Benjamin Ct
5 Charton Cl
6 Terence Ct
7 Renshaw Cl
8 Grove Rd
C1 1 Friswell Pl
2 Market Pl
3 Geddes Pl
4 Janet Ct
5 Broadway Sh Ctr
6 Mall The
7 Pincott Rd

148

A5 1 Stranraer Way
2 Deri Dene Cl
3 Lord Knyvetts Ct
4 Tudor Ct
5 Wessex Ct
6 Vanguard Ho
7 Shackleton Ct
8 Fleetwood Ct
9 Clifton Ct
10 Vickers Ct
11 Bristol Ct
12 Sunderland Ct

150

B3 1 Bergenia Ho
2 Azalea Ho
3 Hamlyn Ho
4 Highfield Rd
5 Cardinal Road Inf Sch

152

A4 1 Library Way
C2 1 Jack & Jill Sch
2 Archdeacon Cambridge's CE Prim Sch

153

A3 1 Katharine Rd
2 Sandringham Ct
3 Garfield Rd
4 Arragon Rd
5 Flood La
6 John Wesley Ct
7 King Street Par
8 Thames Eyot
A4 1 Perryn Ct
2 Ivybridge Cl
3 Heritage Ho
4 Brook Ho
5 Neville Ho
6 Latham Cl
7 March Rd
8 Berkley Ct
9 Cole Court Lo
10 Cheltenham Ave
11 Railway App
12 St Mary's CE Prim Sch (Inf)
A5 1 Greenways The
2 Cole Park View
B4 1 Melton Ct
2 Amyand Park Gdns
3 Crown Ct
4 Burrell Ho
5 Owen Ho
6 Brentford Ho
7 Leeson Ho
8 Westbourne Ho
9 Orleans Ct
10 Lebanon Ct
B5 1 Grove The
2 Cumberland Cl
3 Westmorland Cl
4 Sussex Cl
5 Norfolk Cl
6 Nicol Cl
7 Old Lodge Pl
8 Kelvin Ct
9 St Margaret's Ct
10 Park Cotts
11 St Margarets Bsns Ctr
12 Amyand Cotts
C1 1 Benson Ho
2 Bowes Lyon Ho
3 Cavendish Ho
4 Bentinck Ho
5 Clarke Ho
6 Secrett Ho
7 Edwards Ho
8 Field Ho
9 Greig Ho
10 Hawkins Ho
11 Newman Ho
12 Leyland Ho
13 Hornby Ho
14 Hatch Ho
C5 1 Howmic Ct
2 Sefton Lo
3 Ravensbourne Ho
4 Arlington Ct
5 Georgina Ct
6 Trevelyan Ho
7 Caradon Ct
8 Green Hedges
9 Old House Gdns
10 Queens Keep
11 Beresford Ct
12 Langham Ct
13 Poplar Ct
D5 1 Richmond Bridge Mans
2 Heatherdene Mans
3 Kenton Ct
4 Lennox Ho
5 Leicester Ct
6 Turner Ho
7 Blanchard Ho
8 Arosa Rd
9 Ashe Ho
10 Bevan Ct
11 Lawley Ho
12 Darling Ho
13 Richmond Mans
14 Beaulieu Cl
15 Roseleigh Cl
16 Mallard Ct
D6 1 Garrick Cl
2 Old Palace Yd
3 Wardrobe The
4 Maids of Honour Row
5 Hunters Ct
6 Queensberry Ho
7 Green The
8 Old Palace Terr
9 Paved Ct
10 Golden Ct
11 Brewers La
12 Square The
13 Lower George St
14 St James's Cotts
15 Church Wlk
16 Church Ct
17 Victoria Pl
18 Castle Yd
19 Lewis Rd
20 Wakefield Rd
21 Church Terr
22 Warrington Rd
23 Ormond Ave
24 Glovers Lo
25 Holbrooke Pl
26 Northumberland Pl
27 Heron Sq
28 Whittaker Pl
29 Water Lane Ho
30 Riverside Ho
31 St Helena Terr

154

A5 1 Lancaster Cotts
2 Lancaster Mews
3 Bromwich Ho
4 Priors Lo
5 Richmond Hill Ct
6 Glenmore Ho
7 Hillbrow
8 Heathshott
9 Friars Stile Pl
10 Spire Ct
11 Ridgeway
12 Matthias Ct
13 Old Vicarage Sch
A6 1 Lichfield Terr
2 Union Ct
3 Carrington Lo
4 Wilton Ct
5 Egerton Ct
6 Beverley Lo
7 Bishop Duppa's Almshouses
8 Regency Wlk
9 Clear Water Ho
10 Onslow Avenue Mans
11 Michels Almshouses
12 Albany Pas
13 Salcombe Villas
B5 1 Chester Cl
2 Evesham Ct
3 Queen's Ct
4 Russell Wlk
5 Charlotte Sq
6 Jones Wlk
7 Hilditch Ho
8 Isabella Ct
9 Damer Ho
10 Eliot Ho
11 Fitzherbert Ho
12 Reynolds Pl
13 Chisholm Rd
B6 1 Alberta Ct
2 Beatrice Rd
3 Lorne Rd
4 York Rd
5 Connaught Rd
6 Albany Terr
7 Kingswood Ct
8 Selwyn Ct
9 Broadhurst Cl

156

A3 1 Farnborough Ho
2 Rushmere Ho
3 Horndean Cl
4 Highcross Way
5 Timsbury Wlk
6 Foxcombe Rd
7 Ryefield Path
8 Greatham Wlk
9 Gosport Ho
10 Stoatley Ho
11 Milland Ho
12 Clanfield Ho
13 Fareham Ho
14 Grayswood Point
A4 1 Woodcott Ho
2 Lyndhurst Ho
3 Wheatley Ho
4 Allbrook Ho
5 Bordon Wlk
6 Chilcombe Ho
7 Vicarage Ct
8 Shawford Ct
9 Eastleigh Wlk
10 Kings Ct
11 Somborne Ho
A6 1 Theodore Ho
2 Nicholas Ho
3 Bonner Ho
4 Downing Ho
5 Jansen Ho
6 Fairfax Ho
7 Devereux Ho
8 David Ho
9 Leigh Ho
10 Clipstone Ho
11 Mallet Ho
12 Arton Wilson Ho
B3 1 Ramsdean Ho
2 Purbrook Ho
3 Portsea Ho
4 Blendworth Point
5 Eashing Point
6 Hindhead Point
7 Hilsea Point
8 Witley Point
9 Buriton Ho
10 Grateley Ho
11 Hascombe Ho
12 Dunhill Point
13 Westmark Point
14 Longmoor Point
15 Cadnam Point
C4 1 Cumberland Ho
2 Devonshire Ho
3 Cornwall Ho
4 Norfolk Ho
5 Leicester Ho
6 Warwick Ho
7 Sutherland Ho
8 Carmarthen Ho
9 Worcester Ho
10 Rutland Ho
11 Paddock Way
12 Putney Hill
C6 1 Inglis Ho
2 Ducie Ho
3 Wharncliffe Ho
4 Stanhope Ho
5 Waldegrave Ho
6 Mildmay Ho
7 Mullens Ho
D3 1 Sandringham Cl
2 Eastwick Ct
3 Oatlands Ct
4 Banning Ho
5 Grantley Ho
6 Caryl Ho
7 Duncombe Ho
8 Chilworth Ct
9 Kent Lo
10 Turner Lo
11 Marlborough
12 Parkland Gdns
13 Lewesdon Cl
14 Pines Ct
15 Ashtead Ct
16 Mynterne Ct
17 Arden
18 Stephen Ct
19 Marsham Ct
20 Doradus Ct
21 Acorns The
22 Heritage Ho
23 Conifer Ct
24 Spencer Ho
25 Chartwell
26 Blenheim
27 Chivelston
28 Greenfield Ho
29 Oakman Ho
30 Radley Lo
31 Simon Lo
32 Admirals Ct
33 Augustus Rd
D4 1 Brett Ho
2 Brett House Cl
3 Sylva Ct
4 Ross Ct
5 Potterne Cl
6 Stourhead Cl
7 Fleur Gates
8 Greenwood
9 John Paul II Sch
10 Our Lady Queen of Heaven RC Prim Sch
11 Prospect House Sch
D5 1 Balmoral Cl
2 Glenalmond Ho
3 Selwyn Ho
4 Keble Ho
5 Bede Ho
6 Gonville Ho
7 Magdalene Ho
8 Armstrong Ho
9 Newnham Ho
10 Somerville Ho
11 Balliol Ho
12 Windermere
13 Little Combe Cl
14 Classinghall Ho
15 Chalford Ct
16 Garden Royal
17 South Ct
18 Anne Kerr Ct
19 Ewhurst
D6 1 Geneva Ct
2 Laurel Ct
3 Cambalt Ho
4 Langham Ct
5 Lower Pk
6 King's Keep
7 Whitnell Ct
8 Whitehead Ho
9 Halford Ho
10 Humphry Ho
11 Jellicoe Ho
12 South Thames Coll (Putney Ctr)

157

A3 1 William Harvey Ho
2 Highview Ct
3 Cameron Ct
4 Galgate Cl
5 Green Ho The
6 King Charles Wlk
7 Florys Ct
8 Augustus Ct
9 Albert Ct
10 Hertford Lo
11 Mortimer Lo
12 Allenswood
13 Ambleside
14 Hansler Ct
15 Roosevelt Ct
16 Southmead Prim Sch
A4 1 Douglas Gracey Ho
2 Aman Dalvi Ho
3 Andrew Reed Ho
4 Stoford Cl
6 Ronald Ross Prim Sch
A6 1 Claremont
2 Downside
3 Cavendish Cl
4 Ashcombe Ct
5 Carltons The
6 Espirit Ho
7 Millbrooke Ct
8 Coysh Ct
9 Keswick Hts
10 Avon Ct
11 Merlin Sch The
B6 1 Keswick Broadway
2 Burlington Mews
3 Cambria Lo
4 St Stephen's Gdns
5 Atlantic Ho
6 Burton Lo
7 Manfred Ct
8 Meadow Bank
9 Hooper Ho
10 Aspire Bld
C6 1 Pembridge Pl
2 Adelaide Rd
3 London Ct
4 Windsor Ct
5 Westminster Ct
6 Fullers Ho
7 Bridge Pk
8 Lambeth Ct
9 Milton Ct
10 Norfolk Mans
11 Francis Snary Lo
12 Bush Cotts
13 Downbury Mews
14 Newton's Yd
15 Roche Sch The
16 St Joseph's RC Prim Sch
17 West Hill Prim Sch
18 St Michael Steiner Sch The
D6 1 Fairfield Ct
2 Blackmore Ho
3 Lancaster Mews
4 Cricketers Mews

494 157 D6

5 College Mews
6 Arndale Wlk
8 St Anne's CE
Prim Sch
7 South Thames
Coll (Wandsworth
Ctr)

158

A2 1 Bremans Row
2 St Andrew's Ct
3 Townsend Mews
4 Sheringham
Mews
5 Rainbow Sch
6 Garratt Park Sec
Specl Sch
A6 1 St Faith's CE Prim
Sch
C2 2 St Peters Cl
3 St Hildas Cl
4 St Edmunds Cl
5 St Hughes Cl
6 St Anthonys Cl
8 St Benets Cl
9 St Catherines Cl
7 Elsley Sch
D5 1 Staplehurst Ct
2 Teyham Ct
3 Honeywell Jun &
Inf Schs
D6 1 Clapham Computer & Secretarial
Coll

159

A2 1 Upper Tooting
Park Mans
2 Cecil Mans
3 Marius Mans
4 Boulevard The
5 Elmfield Mans
6 Holdernesse Rd
7 Lumiere Ct
A3 1 Heslop Ct
2 St James's Terr
3 Boundaries Mans
4 Station Par
5 Old Dairy Mews
6 Chestnut Grove
Sch
7 Hornsby House
Sch
8 Trinity St Mary's
Prim Sch
A4 1 Hollies Way
2 Endlesham Ct
3 Broomwood Hall
Sch (Upper Sch)
4 Holy Ghost RC
Prim Sch
A5 1 Rayne Ho
2 St Anthony's Ct
3 Earlsthorpe
Mews
4 Nightingale Mans
5 Broomwood Hall
(Lower Sch)
B3 1 Holbeach Mews
2 Hildreth Street
Mews
3 Coalbrook Mans
4 Hub Buildings
The
5 Metropolis
Apartments
6 Hildreth St
B4 1 Meyer Ho
2 Faraday Ho
3 Hales Ho
4 Frankland Ho
5 Graham Ho
6 Gibbs Ho
7 Dalton Ho
8 Ainslie Wlk
9 Rokeby Ho
10 Caistor Ho
11 Ivanhoe Ho
12 Catherine Baird
Ct
13 Marmion Ho
14 Devonshire Ct

15 Blueprint
Apartments
16 Royal Duchess
Mews
17 Alderbrook Prim
Sch
B5 1 Oliver House
Prep Sch
C3 2 Henry Cavendish
Prim Sch
3 Margaret
Rutherford Pl
C4 1 Limerick Ct
2 Homewoods
3 Jewell Ho
4 Glanville Ho
5 Dan Bryant Ho
6 Olding Ho
7 Quennel Ho
8 Weir Ho
9 West Ho
10 Neville Ct
11 Friday Grove
Mews
12 St Bernadette RC
Jun Sch
C5 1 Joseph Powell Cl
2 Cavendish Mans
3 Westlands Terr
4 Cubitt Ho
5 Hawkesworth Ho
6 Normanton Ho
7 Eastman Ho
8 Couchman Ho
9 Poynders Ct
10 Selby Ho
11 Valentine Ho
12 Gorham Ho
13 Deauville Mans
14 Deauville Ct
C6 1 Timothy Cl
2 Shaftesbury
Mews
3 Brook Ho
4 Grover Ho
5 Westbrook Ho
6 Hewer Ho
7 Batten Ho
8 Mandeville Ho
9 George Beare Lo
D3 1 Sinclair Ho
2 MacGregor Ho
3 Ingle Ho
4 St Andrews Mews
5 Telferscot Prim
Sch
D4 1 Riley Ho
2 Bennett Ho
3 White Ho
4 Rodgers Ho
5 Dumphreys Ho
6 Homan Ho
7 Prendergast Ho
8 Hutchins Ho
9 Whiteley Ho
10 Tresidder Ho
11 Primrose Ct
12 Angus Ho
13 Currie Ho
D5 1 Farrington Ct
2 Savill Ho
3 Blackwell Ho
4 Bruce Ho
5 Victoria Ct
6 Victoria Ho
7 Belvedere Ct
8 Ingram Lo
9 Viney Ct
10 Bloomsbury Ho
11 Belgravia Ho
12 Barnsbury Ho

160

A1 1 De Montfort Ct
2 Leigham Hall Par
3 Leigham Hall
4 Endsleigh Mans
5 John Kirk Ho
6 Raeburn Ct
7 Wavel Ct
8 Homeleigh Ct
9 Howland Ho
10 Beauclerk Ho
11 Bertrand Ho

12 Drew Ho
13 Dowes Ho
14 Dunton Ho
15 Raynald Ho
16 Sackville Ho
17 Thurlow Ho
18 Astoria Mans
A2 1 Wyatt Park Mans
2 Broadlands Mans
3 Stonehill's Mans
4 Streatleigh Par
5 Dorchester Ct
6 Picture Ho
A3 1 Beaumont Ho
2 Christchurch Ho
3 Staplefield Cl
4 Chipstead Ho
5 Coulsdon Ho
6 Conway Ho
7 Telford Avenue
Mans
8 Telford Parade
Mans
9 Wavertree Ct
10 Hartswood Ho
11 Wray Ho
A4 1 Picton Ho
2 Rigg Ho
3 Watson Ho
4 MacArthur Ho
5 Sandon Ho
6 Thorold Ho
7 Pearce Ho
8 Mudie Ho
9 Miller Ho
10 Lycett Ho
11 Lafone Ho
12 Lucraft Ho
13 Freeman Ho
14 New Park Par
15 Argyll Ho
16 Dumbarton Ct
17 Kintyre Ct
18 Cotton Ho
19 Crossman Hos
20 Camford Ct
21 Parsons Ho
22 Brindley Ho
23 Arkwright Ho
24 Perry Ho
25 Brunel Ho
26 New Park Ct
27 Tanhurst Ho
28 Hawkshaw Cl
29 Richard Atkins
Prim Sch
A6 1 King's Mews
2 Clapham Court
Terr
3 Clapham Cl
4 Clapham Park
Terr
5 Pembroke Ho
6 Stevenson Ho
7 Queenswood Ct
8 Oak Tree Ct
9 Park Lofts
10 Ashby Mews
B1 1 Carisbrooke Ct
2 Pembroke Lo
3 Willow Ct
4 Poplar Ct
5 Leigham Cl
6 Mountview
7 Spa View
B3 1 Charlwood Ho
2 Earlswood Ho
3 Balcombe Ho
4 Claremont Cl
5 Holbrook Ho
6 Gwynne Ho
7 Kynaston Ho
8 Tillman Ho
9 Regents Lo
10 Hazelmere Ct
11 Dykes Ct
12 Hartwell Ct
13 Christ Church
Streatham CE Prim
Sch
14 Streatham Hill &
Clapham High Sch
15 Orch Sch The
B4 1 Archbishop's Pl
2 Witley Ho
3 Outwood Ho

4 Dunsfold Ho
5 Deepdene Lo
6 Warnham Ho
7 Albury Lo
8 Tilford Ho
9 Elstead Ho
10 Thursley Ho
11 Brockham Ho
12 Capel Lo
13 Leith Ho
14 Fairview Ho
15 Weymouth Ct
16 Ascalon Ct
17 China Mews
18 Rush Common
Mews
B6 1 Beatrice Ho
2 Florence Ho
3 Evelyn Ho
4 Diana Ho
5 Brixton Hill Ct
6 Austin Ho
7 Manor Ct
8 Camsey Ho
9 Romer Ho
10 Gale Ho
11 Byrne Ho
12 Farnfield Ho
13 Marchant Ho
14 Rainsford Ho
15 Springett Ho
16 Mannering Ho
17 Waldron Ho
18 Sudbourne Prim
Sch
19 Corpus Christi RC
Prim Sch
C3 1 Valens Ho
2 Loveday Ho
3 Strode Ho
4 Ethelworth Ct
5 Harbin Ho
6 Brooks Ho
7 Godolphin Ho
8 Sheppard Ho
9 McCormick Ho
10 Taylor Ho
11 Saunders Ho
12 Talcott Path
13 Derrick Ho
14 Williams Ho
15 Baldwin Ho
16 Churston Ct
17 Neil Wates Cres
18 Burnell Ho
19 Portland Ho
20 Fenstanton Prim
Sch
21 St Martin-in-the-
Fields High Sch
C4 8 Ellacombe Ho
2 Booth Ho
3 Hathersley Ho
4 Brereton Ho
5 Holdsworth Ho
6 Dearmer Ho
7 Cherry Cl
8 Greenleaf Cl
9 Longford Wlk
10 Scarlette Manor
Wlk
11 Chandlers Way
12 Upgrove Manor
Way
13 Ropers Wlk
14 Tebbs Ho
15 Bell Ho
16 Worthington Ho
17 Courier Ho
18 Mackie Ho
19 Hamers Ho
20 Kelyway Ho
21 Harriet Tubman
Cl
22 Estoria Cl
23 Leckhampton Pl
24 Scotia Rd
25 Charles Haller St
26 Sidmouth Ho
27 Hunter Ct
28 Onslow Lo
29 William Winter Ct
30 Langthorne Lo
C5 1 Eccleston Ho
2 Scarsbrook Ho
3 Purser Ho

4 Rudhall Ho
5 Hardham Ho
6 Heywood Ho
7 Haworth Ho
8 Birch Ho
9 Lansdell Ho
10 Lomley Ho
11 Laughton Ho
12 Woodruff Ho
13 Bascome St
14 Dudley Mews
15 Herbert Mews
16 Blades Lo
17 Dick Shepherd Ct
18 Charman Ho
19 Morden Ho
20 Bishop Ct
21 Blackburn Ct
22 Leigh Ct
23 John Conwey Ho
24 Bristowe Ct
C6 1 Crownstone Ct
2 Brockwell Ct
3 Nevena Ct
4 St George's
Residences
5 Hanover Mans
6 Fleet Ho
7 Langbourne Ho
8 Turnmill Ho
9 Walker Mews
10 Cossar Mews
11 Carter Ho
12 Arengo Mews
D1 1 Thanet Ho
2 Chapman Ho
3 Beaufoy Ho
4 Easton Ho
5 Roberts Ho
6 Lloyd Ct
7 Kershaw Ho
8 Wakeling Ho
9 Edridge Ho
10 Jeston Ho
11 Lansdowne Wood
Cl
2 Rotary Lo
D6 3 Poets Mews
4 St Jude's CE Prim
Sch

161

A1 1 Welldon Ct
2 Coppedhall
3 Shackleton Ct
4 Bullfinch Ct
5 Gannet Ct
6 Fulmar Ct
7 Heron Ct
8 Petrel Ct
9 Falcon Ct
10 Eagle Ct
11 Dunnock Ct
12 Dunlin Ct
13 Cormorant Ct
14 Oak Lodge
15 Corfe Lodge
C6 1 Velde Way
2 Delft Way
3 Arnhem Way
4 Isel Way
5 Kempis Way
6 Terborch Way
7 Steen Way
8 Deventer Cres
9 Nimegen Way
10 Hilversum Cres
11 St Barnabas St
12 James Allen's
Girls' Sch
13 James Allen's
Prep Sch

162

A1 1 Tunbridge Ct
2 Harrogate Ct
3 Bath Ct
4 Leamington Ct
5 Porlock Ho
6 Cissbury Ho
7 Eddisbury Ho
8 Dundry Ho
9 Silbury Ho
10 Homildon Ho
11 Highgate Ho
12 Richmond Ho

18 Pendle Ho
14 Tynwald Ho
15 Wirrall Ho
19 Greyfriars
A6 1 Dorothy Charrington Ho
2 Keswick Ct
3 Kendall Ct
4 Halliwell Ct
B1 1 River Ho
2 Fordington Ho
3 Arbury Terr
4 Woodbury Ho
5 Gainsborough
Mews
6 Forest Hill Ct
7 Kelvin Grove
Prim Sch
B2 1 Bromleigh Ct
2 Parfew Ct
3 Thetford Ct
4 Attleborough Ct
5 Dunton Ct
6 Frobisher Ct
7 Julian Taylor
Path
8 Grizedale Terr
9 Worsley Ho
C1 1 Forest Lo
2 Sydenham Park
Mans
3 William Wood Ho
C2 1 Fitzwilliam Hts
2 Taymount Grange
3 McLeod Ho
4 Featherstone Ave
5 Kingswear Ho
6 Salcombe Ho
7 Glynwood Ct
8 Holy Trinity CE
Prim Sch
C3 1 Harlech Ct
2 Angela Ct
3 Westwood Ct
4 New Belmont Ho
5 Pearcefield Ave
6 Waldram Pl
7 Horniman Grange
8 South View Ct
9 Heron Ct
10 Katherine Ct
D1 1 Standlake Point
2 Radcot Point
3 Newbridge Point
4 Northmoor
5 Kelmscott
6 Radnor Ct
7 Heathwood Point
8 Ashleigh Point
9 Deepdene Point
10 Rosemount Point
11 Woodfield Ho
12 Clairville Point
13 Trevenna Ho
14 Hyndewood
15 Brent Knoll Sch
16 Our Lady & St
Philip Neri RC
Infants Sch
D2 1 Pikethorne
2 Andrew Ct
3 Valentine Ct
4 Soper Cl
5 Perrymount Prim
Sch
6 Christ Church CE
Prim Sch

164

B5 1 Park Piazza
2 Birdwood Ave
C4 1 Beaumont Terr
2 Littlebourne
3 Verdant Ct
D2 1 Kinross Ct
2 Montrose Ct
3 Rattray Ct
4 Rothesay Ct
D3 1 Edinburgh Ct
2 McMillan Ct
3 Rowallan Ct
4 Meridian Ct
5 Braemar Ct
6 Barrow Ct
7 Blair Ct
8 Darlington Ct

496 182 B6

4 Blytheswood Pl
C5
1 Parkhill Ho
2 Ash Ct
3 Alder Ct
4 Beech Ct
5 Acacia Ct
6 Blackthorn Ct
7 Cypress Ct
8 Hawthorn Ct
9 Hazel Ct
10 Sycamore Ct
11 Maple Ct
12 Laburnam Ct
13 Fern Lo
14 Colyton La
C6
1 James Boswell Cl
2 St Albans Ct
3 Suffolk Ct
4 Rockhampton Cl
5 Delphian Ct
6 Heather Ct
D5
1 Woodcote Pl
2 Joe Hunte Ct
3 Cork Tree Ho
4 Lake Ho
5 Cedars Ho
6 Portobello Ho
7 Cooper Ho
8 Farnsworth Ho
9 Hook Ho
10 Crest The
11 Renshaw Ho
12 Ruscoe Ho
13 Sardeson Ho
D6
1 William Wilberforce Ho
2 William Marsden Ho
3 Samuel Ho
4 Morris Stephany Ho
5 Church Ct

183
A6
1 Moore Ho
2 Chaucer Ho
3 Bushell Ho
4 Bligh Ho
5 Hobbs Rd
6 Hogarth Ho
7 Goodbehere Ho
8 Astley Ho
9 Elder Gdns
10 Elderberry Ct
11 Pavement The
12 Dunkirk St
B6
1 Josef Perrin Ho
2 Jean Humbert Ho
3 Charles Staunton Ho
4 Violette Szabo Ho
5 Lilian Rolfe Ho
6 Odette Ho
7 Robert Gerard Ho
8 St Bernards Cl
9 Champness Cl
10 Pennington Ct
C4
1 Queenswood Ct
2 Northwood Rd
3 High Limes
4 Valley Prospect
5 Plane Tree Wlk
6 City Prospect
7 Bankside Way
8 Ridge Way
9 Rochdale
10 Barrington Wlk
11 Gatestone Ct
12 Childs La
13 Carberry Rd
14 Norwood Heights Sh Ctr
15 Paxton Prim Sch
C5
1 Oakdene
2 Thorsden Way
3 Oakfield Gdns
4 Georgetown Cl
5 Bridgetown Cl
6 Mountbatten Cl
7 Brabourne Cl
8 Alexandra Wlk
9 Compton Ct
10 Battenburg Wlk
11 Burma Terr
12 Wiseman Ct
C6
1 Linley Ct
2 Mellor Ho
3 Whitfield Ct
4 Michaelson Ho
5 Holberry Ho
6 Hovenden Ho
7 Huntley Ho
8 Telfer Ho
9 Markham Ho
10 Oldham Ho
11 Parnall Ho
12 Pierson Ho
13 Roper Ho
14 Roundell Ho
15 Sawyer Ho
16 Ransford Ho
17 Carmichael Ho
18 Bonne Marche Terr Mews
D3
1 Hetley Gdns
2 Claybourne Mews
3 Highland Lo
4 Mason Ct
5 Kendall Ct
6 High View
7 Stambourne Woodland Wlk
D5
1 Glenhurst Ct
2 Marlowe Ct
3 Grenville Ct
4 Raleigh Ct
5 Beechwoods Ct
6 Burntwood View

184
A3
1 Hanover Ct
2 Brunswick Ct
3 New Church Ct
4 Regency Ct
5 Owen Wlk
6 Bargrove Ct
7 Beaver Ct
B2
1 Dorset Ho
2 Collingwood Ct
3 Chartwell Way
4 Essex Twr
5 Appletree Ct
6 Ditton Pl
7 Kelvin Ct
8 Readman Ct
9 Glen Ct
10 Kingsbridge Ho
11 Carlton Ct
12 Benhurst Ct
13 Carole Ho
14 Dover Ho
15 Bettswood Ct
B3
1 Avery Ct
2 Rossal Ct
3 Oakdene Lo
4 Ridgemount Cl
5 Blakewood Ct
6 Trenholme Ct
7 Upchurch Ct
8 Devon Ho
9 Westmoreland Terr
10 Oakfield Road Ind Est
B5
1 Ragwort Ct
2 Firs The
3 Wingham Ho
4 Seath Ho
5 Ripley Ho
6 Lathwood Ho
7 Hurst Ho
8 George Ho
9 Browne Ho
10 Beacon Ho
11 Bailey Ho
12 Agate Ho
13 Sydenham High Sch (Sec)
C2
1 Challin St
2 Rutland Ho
3 Pine Cl
4 St Anthony's RC Prim Sch
C3
1 Watermen's Sq
2 St John's Cotts
3 Gladstone Mews
4 Middlesex Ho
5 Bethesda Ct
6 Ospringe Cl
7 Goudhurst Ho
8 Walmer Ho
9 Strood Ho
10 Greatstone Ho
11 John Baird Ho
12 St John's CE Prim Sch
C4
1 Midhurst
2 Oliver Ct
3 Victoria Ct
4 Wakefield Ct
5 Fountain Ct
6 Newlands Ct
D3
1 Homewalk Ho
2 Grace Path
3 Sycamore Ct
4 Sydenham Station App
5 Greenways
6 Faircroft
D3
1 Groombridge Ho
2 Provincial Terr
3 Smithers Ho
4 West Ho
5 Swallows Ct
6 Hornbeam Ho
7 Blenheim Centre

185
A1
1 Clock House Ct
2 Blandford Ave
3 Old School Ct
4 Lynsted Ct
5 Florence Rd
A6
1 Paxton Ct
2 Kenton Ct
3 Grove Ct
4 Shirley Lo
5 St Michael's CE Prim Sch
6 Our Lady & St Philip Neri RC Prim Sch
B2
1 Ashton Ct
2 Coombe Ct
3 Fontaine Ct
4 Richfield Ct
5 Sheridan Way
C1
1 Christ Church Ct
2 Lea Rd
3 Stanmore Terr
C2
1 Erindale Ct
2 Montgomerie Ct
3 Rebecca Ct
4 Sycamore Ct
5 Willow Ct
6 Marlborough Ct
7 Bearsted Terr
8 Berwick Ct
9 Wooderson Ct
10 Beck River Pk
11 Waterside
C3
1 Gardenia Ct
2 Brackendale Ct
3 Daniel Ct
4 Moliner Ct
5 Chartwell Lo
6 Randmore Ct
7 Dover Ho
8 Lucerne Ct
9 Malling Ho
10 Westerham Lo
11 Brasted Lo
12 Milton Ho
13 Bradsole Ho
14 Sandgate Ho
15 Adelaide Ct
16 Nettlestead Ct
17 Warren Ct
18 Alton Ct
19 Rockingham Ct
20 Camellia Ct
21 Sinclair Ct
22 Regents Ct
23 Minshull Pl
24 South Park Ct
25 Worsley Bridge Jun Sch
D1
1 Parkside
2 Tudors The
3 Oakbrook
4 Tara Ct
5 Redlands The
6 Cambria
7 Hillworth
8 Kelsey Gate
9 Burrells
10 Lincoln Lo
11 Courtlands
12 Fairleas
13 Ashdown Ct
14 Barons
D2
1 Clifton Ct
2 Mayfair Ct
3 Lait Ho
4 Fire Station Mews
5 Bromley Road Inf Sch
D4
1 Warner Ho
2 Clifford Ho
3 Lloyd Ho
4 Thurston Ho
5 Byron Ho
6 Blake Ho
7 Keats Ho

186
A2
1 White House Ct
2 Hunters The
3 Sandringham Ct
4 Glenhurst
5 Copperfields
6 Westgate Ct
A6
1 Dedham Ho
2 Flatford Ho
3 Langthorne Ct
4 Radley Ct
5 Hoover Ho
6 Brunner Ho
7 Waterer Ho
8 Marriott Ho
9 Bourbon Ho
B5
1 Longford Ho
2 Ingrebourne Ho
3 Brent Ho
4 Darent Ho
5 Beverley Ho
6 Wandle Ho
7 Rythe Ho
8 Ember Ho
9 Crane Ho
10 Ravensbourne Ho
C1
1 Warwick Ct
2 Maplehurst
3 Mount Arlington
4 Arundel Ct
D2
1 Weston Gr
2 Gibbs Ho
3 Longfield
4 Hammelton Ct
5 Bracken Hill Ct
6 Townend Ct
7 Treversh Ct
8 Cameron Ho
9 Woodlands Ct
10 Blythwood Pk
11 Bromley Pk
D3
1 Homecoppice Ho
2 Linden Ct
3 Kimberley Gate
4 Inglewood Ct
5 Mavery Ct
6 Glen Ct
7 Marlborough Ct
8 Cawston Ct
9 Blendon Path

187
A1
1 St James Ct
2 Court St
A2
1 Mitchell Way
2 Harrington Ho
3 Newman Ct
4 Uno Apartments
5 Bromley Ho
B2
1 Dainton Cl
2 Rothwell Ct
3 St Timothy's Mews
4 Andringham Lo
5 Kendall Lo
6 Summerfield
7 Winston Ct
8 Vogue Ct
9 Laurels The
10 Westland Ct
11 Eastland Ct
12 Dairsie Ct
13 Northlands
5 Beechfield Cotts
6 Oasis The
7 Cromarty Ct
8 Silverstone Ct

188
A6
1 Beaconsfield Par
2 Cranley Par
3 Kimmeridge Gdns
4 King & Queen Cl
5 Ballantyne Ct
C2
1 Ivybridge Ct
2 Greenbank Lo

190
A6
1 Cyril Lo
2 Hazlemere
3 Milton Lo
4 Marlin Ct
5 Conroy Ct
6 Glenwood Ct
7 Culverton Ct
8 Holmbury Manor
B1
1 Swanscombe Ho
2 Haverstock Ct
3 Arrandene Ho
4 Broomfield Ho
5 Headley Ho
6 Kenley Ho
7 Ladywell Ho
B6
1 Chudleigh
2 St John's Par
3 Holly Ct
4 Rectory Bsns Ctr

193
D1
1 Orchard Ct
2 Bridge Ct

197
A2
1 Raleigh Ho
2 Leicester Ho
3 Gresham Ho
4 White Gates
D2
1 Napier Ct
2 Darlington Ho
3 Charminster Ct
4 Mulberry Ct
5 Leander Ct
6 Clinton Ho
7 Hollingsworth Ct
8 Gloucester Ct
9 Palmerston Ct
10 Redwood Ct
11 Hursley Ct
12 Westmorland Ct
13 Lawson Ct
14 Alexander Ct
15 Winton Ct
16 Sydenham Ho
17 Caroline Ct
18 Ellswood Ct
19 Masefield Ct

198
A1
1 Ash Tree Cl
2 Shrubbery The
3 Malvern Ct
4 Gate Ho
5 Yew Tree Ho
A3
1 Station App
2 South Bank Lo
3 Bramshot Ct
4 Pandora Ct
5 Wellington Ct
6 Glenbuck Ct
7 Leighton Ho
8 Oakhill Ct
9 Downs View Lo
10 Osborne Ct
11 Surbiton Par
12 Woodgate Ho
13 Godwyn Ho
14 Ashby Ho
15 Newmans La
A4
1 Effingham Ho
2 Maple Ho
3 Channon Ct
4 Falconhurst
5 Ferndown
6 Viceroy Lo
7 Frensham Ho
8 Kingsley Ho
9 Rannoch Ct
10 Stratton Ct
11 Moray Ho
12 Dulverton Ct
13 Westerham
14 Hill Ct
15 Assheton-Bennett Ho
16 Hatfield Ho
17 Oxford Ct
18 Pennington Lo
19 Austin Ho
20 Wentworth Ct
21 Priory The
22 Sheraton The
23 Christopher Ct
24 Hobart Ho
25 St Mark's Hts
26 Surbiton Boys Prep Sch
A5
1 Marquis Ct
2 Garrick Ho
3 Surbiton High Sch Jun Girls Sch
4 Surbiton High Senior Sch
A6
1 College Rdbt
2 Edinburgh Ct
3 Weston Ct
4 Grebe Terr
5 Heron Ct
6 Agar Ho
7 St James' Ct
8 Grove Ct
9 Springfield Ct
10 College Wlk
B3
1 Percy Ct
2 Holmwood
3 Middle Green Cl
4 Herbert Ct
5 Alfriston Ct
B4
1 Woodleigh
2 Highcroft
3 Caernarvon Ct
4 Regency Ct
D1
1 Oakleigh Way
2 Chandler Ct

199
C2
1 Goodland Ho
2 Furzeland Ho
3 Oakcroft Ho
4 Meadcroft Ho
5 Newhouse
C4
1 Merryweather Ct
2 Roebuck Ct
3 Sable Ct
4 Holy Cross Sch The
C5
1 Acacia Ho
2 Kingston Lo
3 Carrington Ct
4 Fairholme Ho
5 Marshall Ho
6 Norton Ho
7 Martin Ho

200
A1
1 Brookside Cres
2 Beverley Gdns
3 Purdey Ct
4 Avenue The
5 Briarwood Ct
6 Station App

202
C6
1 Cricket Green Specl Sch
2 Melrose Specl Sch
D6
1 Fair Green Ct
2 Regal Ct
3 Lewes Ct
4 Esher Mews
5 Sibford Ct
6 Deseret Ho
7 Standor Ho
8 Langdale Par
9 Newman Terr

204
A2
1 Barcom Trad Est
2 Croydon Valley Trade Pk
C3
1 Rozelle Ct
2 Dunheved Ct
3 Truscott Ho
C4
1 Brigstock Par

2 Terry Lodge
3 Justin Ct
D3 1 Wyndham Ct
2 Byrne Cl
D5 1 Nutfield Pl
2 Braidwood Ho
3 Elliott Ho

205

A6 1 Beulah Jun Sch
2 Beulah Inf Sch
3 Maple House Ind Montessori Sch
4 Victory Day Sch
B1 1 Tavistock Ct
2 Chartwell Ct
3 Speaker's Ct
4 Cumberland Ct
5 Viceroy Ct
6 Oriel Ct
7 Cherry Orchard Gdns
8 Sola Ct
9 Gamma Ct
10 Croydon Coll Annexe
11 Edwin Pl
B5 1 Decimus Cl
2 Palace Ct
3 Reservoir Cl
4 Broxholme Cl
5 Whitehorse Manor Jun Sch
6 Whitehorse Manor Inf Sch
C1 1 Windmill Bridge Ho
2 Squire Ct
3 Houston Ct
4 Warren Ct
5 Freemasons Pl
6 Al Khair Prim & Sec Sch
7 Croydon Prim Independant Sch
D1 1 Hastings Pl
2 Grant Pl
3 Clive Ho
4 Havelock Ho
5 Bellmore Ct
6 Hereford Ct
7 Chequers Ct
8 Havelock Hall

206

A1 1 Farleycroft
2 Edgecumbe Ct
3 Wesson Ho
4 Sullivan Ct
5 Kenley Ho
6 Christopher Ct
7 Jayson Ct
8 Sundridge Ct
A3 4 St Thomas Becket RC Prim Sch
A5 3 St Mark's CE Prim Sch
A6 1 Leybourne Ct
2 Lestock Cl
3 Croftside The
D1 1 Cottongrass Cl
2 Oxlip Cl
3 Eyebright Cl

207

D1 1 North Rd
2 Sussex Rd
3 Riverside Wlk
4 Christie Ho
5 Windsor Ct
6 Sherwood Ct
7 Wheatsheaf Par
D6 1 Linden Ct
2 Park Ct

3 Chilchester Ct
4 Iveagh Ct

208

A6 1 Overbury
2 Wilton Pl
D1 1 Woodgrange Ct
2 Maycroft
3 Farnborough Cres
D4 1 Knowlton Gn
2 Speldhurst Cl
3 Bidborough Cl
4 Penshurst Wlk
D5 1 Wedgewood Ct
2 Birches The
3 Eccleshill
4 Tavistock Rd
5 Montpelier Ct
6 South Hill Rd

209

A5 1 Montague Terr
2 Chatsworth Ho
A6 1 Marina Ct
2 Cheveney Wlk
3 Bromley Manor Mans
4 Mall The
5 Westmoreland Ct
B5 1 Reflex Apartments
2 Wheeler Pl
3 Maxim Apartments
4 Exchange Apartments
5 Axiom Apartments
6 Weller Mews

211

B1 1 Gleneagles Gn
2 Tandridge Pl
3 Springfield Wlk
4 Pinehurst Wlk
5 Cromer Pl
6 Oakmont Pl

214

A6 1 St Bernards Ho
2 Wentworth Ho
3 Sunningdale Cl
4 Arklow Mews
5 Edward Pinner Ct

216

A6 1 Lansdowne Copse
2 Lansdowne Ct
D6 1 Edwards Cl
2 Pearing Cl
3 Churchlands Way
4 Langley Pl

217

A1 2 St Dunstan's CE Prim Sch
C1 1 Cheam Court Flats
2 Farnham Ct
3 Tabor Ct
4 Whyte Mews
5 Killick Mews
C1 1 Lancaster Ct
2 Redclyffe Terr
3 Kenilworth Terr
4 Lincoln Terr
5 Garden Ct
6 Ashwood Pk
7 Midsummer Apartments
8 Lyndhurst Ct
9 Lorraine Ct

10 Gloucester Ct
11 Banbury Ct
12 Camilla Ct
13 Lorac Ct
14 Kingswood Mans
15 Claremont Ho
16 Holly Ct
17 Castle Ho
18 Balmoral Ct
19 Davington Ct
20 Hereford Ct
C2 1 Norman Ho
2 Hawthorns The
3 Limes The
4 Alexa Ct
5 Kristina Ct
6 Beverley Ct
7 Chestnut Ct
D1 1 Holmeswood
2 Pebworth Lo
3 Addison Ct
4 Kingslee Ct
5 Raeburn Ho
6 Girtin Ho
7 Leith Towers
8 Courtlands
9 Thomas Ho
10 Grayshott Ct
11 Hadrian Ct
12 Sandown Ct
13 Magnolia Ct
14 Dunsfold Ct
15 Camberley Ct
16 Berrylands Ct
17 Brockham Ct
18 Alford Ct
19 Lansdowne Ho
20 Larchvale Ct
D2 1 Portland Ct
2 Durnston Ct
3 Barton Ct
4 Aplin Ct
5 Hannah Ct
6 Honeysuckle Ct
7 Rowans The
8 St Annes Ct
9 Bonnington Ho
10 Pamir Ct
11 Bradbourne Ct
12 Worcester Ct
D3 1 Marian Ct
2 Robin Hood Ct
3 Distin Ct
4 Queensmere
5 Grosvenor Ho
6 Cromer Mans
7 St Nicholas Ctr
8 Robin Hood Jun Sch
9 Sutton Coll of Learning for Adults
D5 1 Dorothy Pettingel Ho
2 Margaret Ho
3 All Saints' Benhilton CE Prim Sch

218

A1 1 Beauclere Ho
2 Melford Ct
3 Elmhurst Lo
4 Mansard Manor
5 Tranmere Ct
6 Beechcroft Lo
7 Savin Lo
8 Yew Tree Ct
9 Avondale Ct
10 Devonshire Ho
11 Hidcote Ho
12 Munstead Ct
13 Lodden Lo
14 Steetley Ct
15 Grampian Cl

16 Richard Sharples Ct
17 Devonshire Prim Sch
A2 1 Grosvenor Ct
2 Forest Dene Ct
3 Cedar Ct
4 Vanborough Ct
5 Shrub Ct
6 Evergreen Ct
7 Grasmere Ct
8 Heathfield Ct
9 Sherbourne Ct
10 Kinsale Grange
11 Linden Ct
12 Jubilee Ct
13 Langley Ct
14 Wilmot Ho
15 Farendon Ho
16 Alexander Ho
A3 1 Goossens Cl
2 Cliffe Wlk
3 Marlins Ct
4 Clowser Ct
5 Montana Gdns
6 Bournemouth Ct
7 Palmerston Ct
8 Manor Park Prim Sch
9 Sutton Gram Sch For Boys
A4 8 Lodge The
2 Hazelwood Ho
3 Chesterton Ho
4 Clevedon Ho
5 Staincliffe Ho
6 Denewood Ho
7 Newlyn Ho
8 Manor Ct
9 Glenrose Ho
10 Oak Lo
11 Briar The
12 Fernhead
13 Branch Ho
14 Thicket Ct
15 Adam Ct
16 Arndell Ho
17 Oakwood Ct
B3 1 Hogarth Ho
2 Gillray Ho
3 Cramhurst Ho
4 Ronald Ho
5 Blythewood
6 Hillside
7 Weldon Ct
8 Yeoman Ct
D5 1 Kynersley Cl
2 Wrythe Gn
3 Bedford Villas
4 Chateau The
5 Nelson Ct
6 Errington Manor
7 Leeds Ct
8 Blair Ct

219

A4 1 Westcroft
2 Westcroft Ho
A5 1 Burnside Ct
2 Millpond Ct
3 Waterside Ct
4 Stable Ct
5 Manor Ct
6 Victor Seymour Inf Sch
B2 1 Runnymede Ct
2 Dolphin Ct
3 Kings Ct
4 Cheyne Ct
5 Henfield Ct
6 Ellersile Ct
7 Embassy Ct
8 Chandler Ct
9 Hambledon Ct

10 Wallington Ct
11 Jasmine Ct
12 Napier Ct
13 Rosswood Ho
14 Woodcote Ct
15 Surrey Ct
16 Stag Ct
17 Moorlands
18 Orchard Hill Coll
B3 1 Cornelion Cotts
2 Walpole Ct
3 Farmstead Ct
4 Derby Ho
5 Salisbury Ho
6 Chatham Ho
7 Collingwood Sch
B4 1 Loraine Ho
2 Harcourt Ct
3 Coniston Ct
4 Alcester Ct
5 Friars Ct
6 Campbell Ho
7 Brodie Ho
8 Lesley Ct
9 Birch Ct
10 Airborne Ho
C2 1 Rossendon Ct
2 Mulberry Mews
3 Nairn Ct
4 Wallington Sq
5 Rosemount Twrs
6 Connell Ho
7 Ashby Grange
8 Terry Ct
9 Leigham Cl
10 Clyde Works
11 Chandos Bsns Ctr
12 Beech Ho
13 Wendon Ct
C4 1 Holy Trinity CE Jun Sch
D3 1 Torquay Ho
2 Ashburton Ho
D5 1 Goodwood Lo
2 Haydock Lo
3 Kempton Lo

220

A1 1 Phoenix Ctr The
2 Ensign Way
3 Hunter Ct
4 Cirrus Cl
5 Mosquito Cl
D5 1 Latimer Rd
2 Cromwell Ct
3 Arundel Ct
4 Warrington Ct
5 Grace Ct
6 Stuart Ct
7 Bridge Par
8 Ridge's Yd
9 Parish Church CE Jun Sch
10 Parish Church CE Inf Sch
11 Old Palace of John Whitgift Sch (Seniors)

221

A3 1 Trent Ct
2 Sherwood Ct
3 Archers Ct
4 Keepers Ct
5 Lincoln Ct
6 Mount The
7 Fairhaven Ct
8 Brockham Ct
9 Chelwood Ct
10 Marey Ct
11 Landau Ct
A4 1 West Street Pl
2 Maple Ct
3 St Andrew's Rd

227 D4 **497**

4 Albury Ct
5 Chestnut Ct
6 Elgin Ct
7 Beechfield Ct
8 Barham Ct
9 Whitstable Pl
10 Ledbury Pl
A5 1 Fellmongers Yd
2 Halstead Ct
3 Mann Cl
4 Waterworks Yd
5 Chanderia Ct
6 Katherine Ho
7 Smith's Yd
A6 1 Otterbourne Rd
2 Charrington Rd
3 Tamworth Pl
4 Priddy's Yd
5 Hospital of the Holy Trinity (Almshouses)
B1 1 Wellesley Court Rd
2 Norfolk Ho
3 Station App
4 Suffolk Ho
5 Cherry Orchard Gdns
6 Harrington Ct
D6 1 Cheyne Ct
2 Fourways
3 Princess Ct
4 Tierney Ct
5 Sinclair Ct
6 Guinness Ct
7 Mayfair Ct
8 Bishopscourt
9 Gloucester Lo
10 Beverley Hyrst
11 Melton Ct
12 Cecil Ct
13 Napier Ct

227

A3 1 Westfield
2 Farnborough Ct
3 Fern Hill Pl
4 Churchill Ct
5 Spencer Ct
6 Ladycroft Gdns
7 Crabbs Croft Cl
8 Clifton Cl
D2 1 Brittenden Cl
2 Wardens Field Cl
3 Winnipeg Dr
4 Superior Dr
5 Huron Ct
6 Manitoba Gdns
7 Lynne Ct
8 Flint Cl
9 Bakers Mews
D3 1 Osgood Gdns
2 Amberley Cl
3 Rawlings Cl
4 Beblets Cl
5 Fir Tree Cl
6 Raleigh Mews
7 King Henry Mews
D4 1 Healy Dr
2 Marsden Way
3 Taylor Cl
4 Strickland Way
5 Dryland Ave
6 Adcot Wlk
7 Lichlade Cl

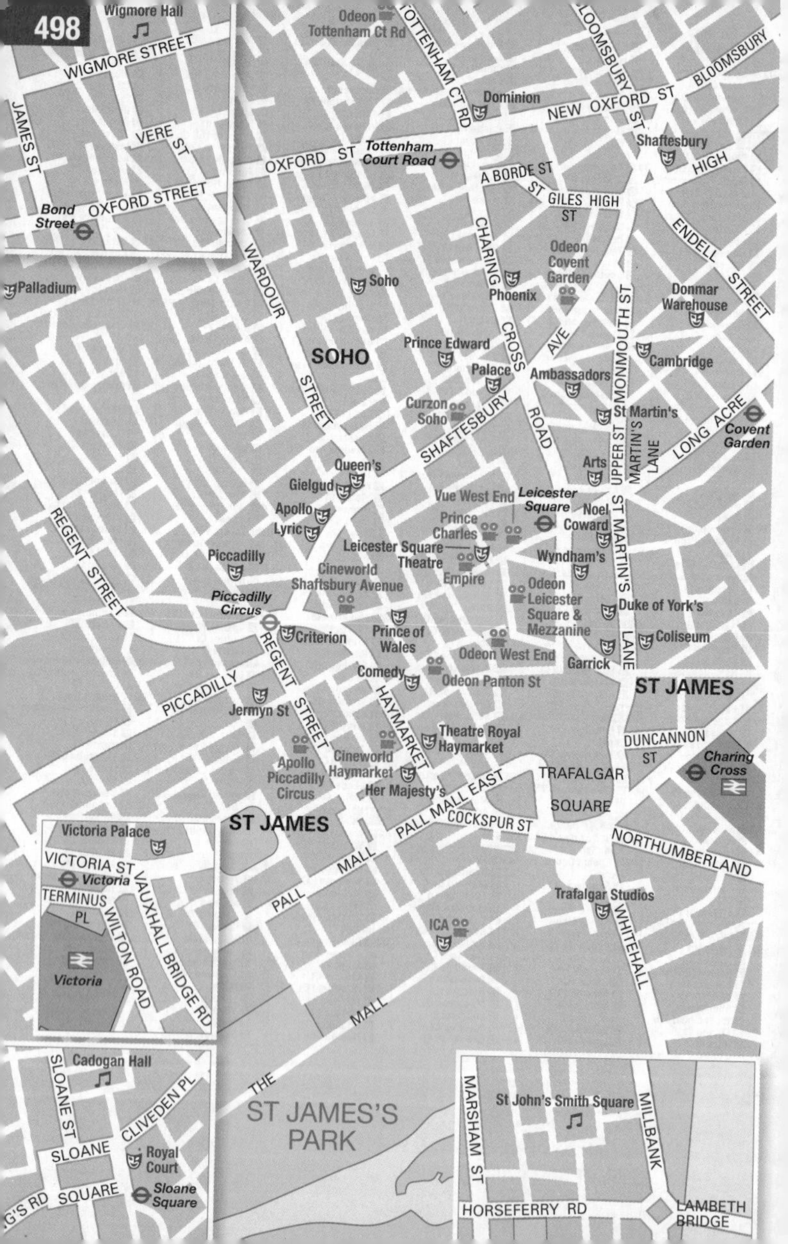
Wigmore Hall
WIGMORE STREET
JAMES ST
VERE ST
OXFORD STREET
Bond Street
Odeon Tottenham Ct Rd
TOTTENHAM CT RD
BLOOMSBURY ST
BLOOMSBURY
Dominion
NEW OXFORD ST
OXFORD ST
Tottenham Court Road
A BORDE ST
ST GILES HIGH ST
Shaftesbury
HIGH
ENDELL STREET
WARDOUR STREET
CHARING CROSS ROAD
Palladium
Soho
Phoenix
Odeon Covent Garden
Donmar Warehouse
MONMOUTH ST
SOHO
Prince Edward
Palace
AVE
Ambassadors
Cambridge
Curzon Soho
SHAFTESBURY
St Martin's
LONG ACRE
Covent Garden
UPPER ST MARTIN'S LANE
Arts
Queen's
Gielgud
Apollo
Lyric
Vue West End
Leicester Square
Noel Coward
Prince Charles
Leicester Square Theatre
Empire
REGENT STREET
Piccadilly
Cineworld Shaftsbury Avenue
Wyndham's
Odeon Leicester Square & Mezzanine
ST MARTIN'S LANE
Piccadilly Circus
Duke of York's
Criterion
Prince of Wales
Coliseum
Odeon West End
Garrick
Comedy
Odeon Panton St
ST JAMES
PICCADILLY
Jermyn St
HAYMARKET
Theatre Royal Haymarket
DUNCANNON ST
Apollo Piccadilly Circus
Cineworld Haymarket
Her Majesty's
TRAFALGAR SQUARE
Charing Cross
PALL MALL EAST
COCKSPUR ST
ST JAMES
NORTHUMBERLAND
Victoria Palace
VICTORIA ST
Victoria
TERMINUS PL
WILTON ROAD
VAUXHALL BRIDGE RD
PALL MALL
Trafalgar Studios
ICA
WHITEHALL
THE MALL
Cadogan Hall
SLOANE ST
CLIVEDEN PL
SLOANE SQUARE
Royal Court
Sloane Square
G'S RD
ST JAMES'S PARK
MARSHAM ST
St John's Smith Square
MILLBANK
HORSEFERRY RD
LAMBETH BRIDGE

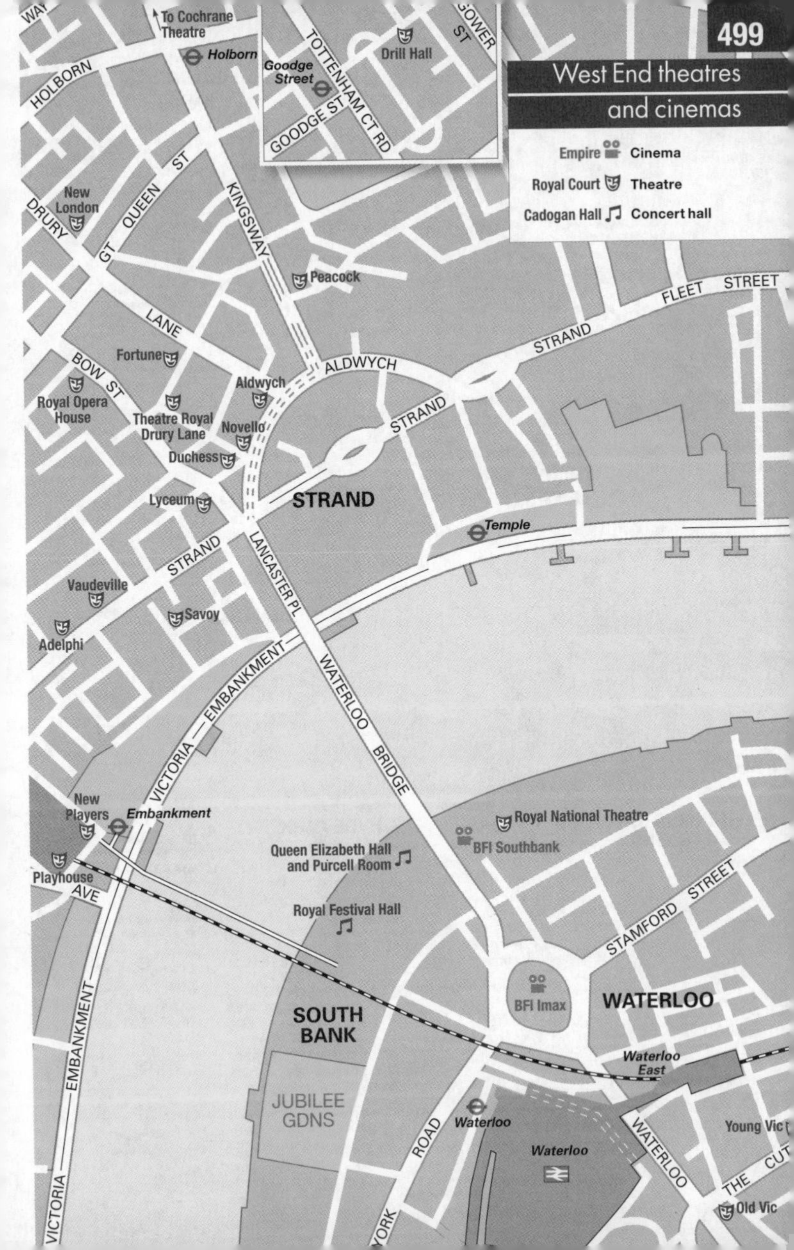

West End theatres and cinemas

Empire ▦	**Cinema**
Royal Court ☺	**Theatre**
Cadogan Hall ♫	**Concert hall**

To Cochrane Theatre

WAY

HOLBORN

⊖ Holborn

Drill Hall

GOWER ST

TOTTENHAM CT RD

Goodge Street

GOODGE ST

⊖ Goodge Street

New London ☺

DRURY

GT QUEEN ST

QUEEN ST

KINGSWAY

LANE

⊖ Peacock

FLEET STREET

Fortune ☺

BOW ST

Aldwych ☺

STRAND

STRAND

Royal Opera House

Theatre Royal Drury Lane

Novello ☺

STRAND

Duchess ☺

Lyceum ☺

STRAND

⊖ Temple

Vaudeville ☺

STRAND

Savoy ☺

Adelphi ☺

LANCASTER PL

WATERLOO BRIDGE

VICTORIA EMBANKMENT

New Players ☺

⊖ Embankment

Royal National Theatre ☺

Queen Elizabeth Hall and Purcell Room ♫

▦ BFI Southbank

Playhouse ☺

AVE

Royal Festival Hall ♫

STAMFORD STREET

EMBANKMENT

SOUTH BANK

▦ BFI Imax

WATERLOO

JUBILEE GDNS

YORK ROAD

⊖ Waterloo

Waterloo East

Young Vic

Waterloo ⇆

WATERLOO

VICTORIA

THE CUT

Old Vic ☺

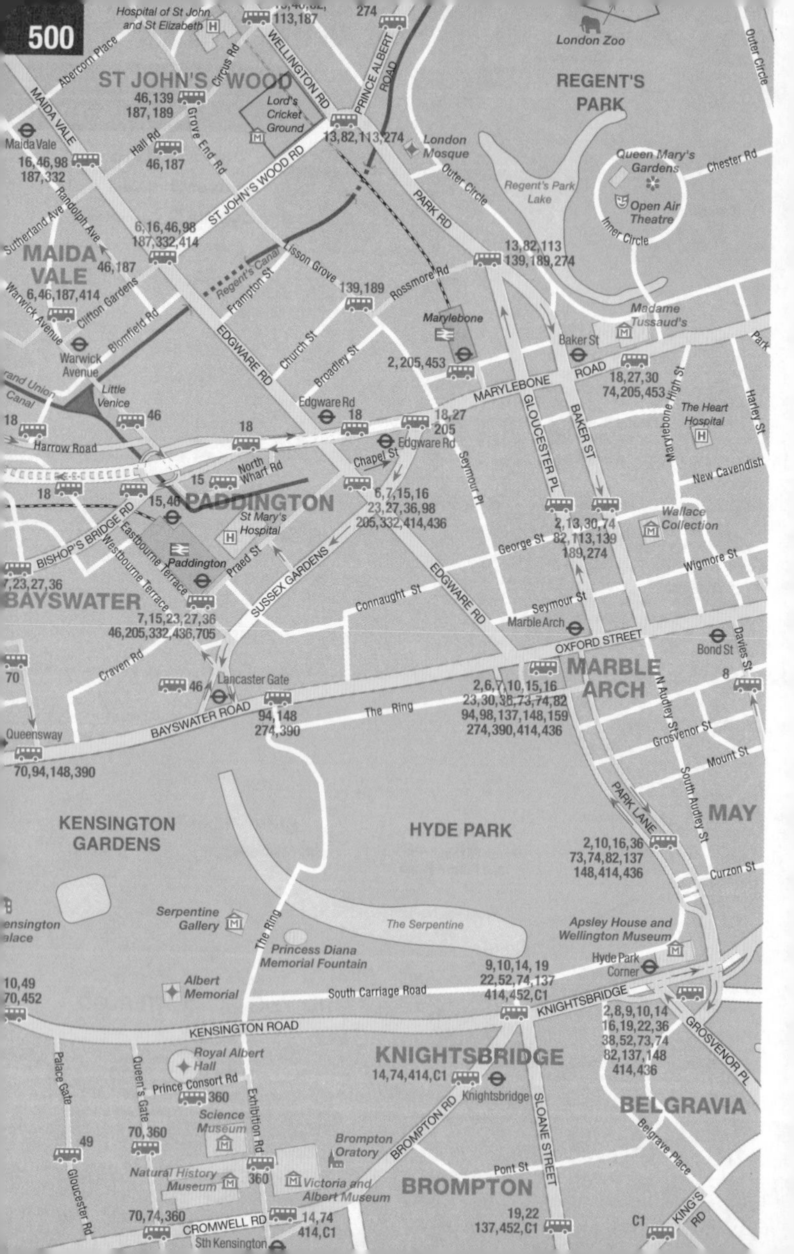

Hospital of St John and St Elizabeth
113,187
274
London Zoo
Outer Circle
Abercorn Place
ST JOHN'S WOOD
Circus Rd
WELLINGTON RD
PRINCE ALBERT ROAD
REGENT'S PARK
Lord's Cricket Ground
46,139
187,189
MAIDA VALE
Grove End Rd
Maida Vale
Hall Rd
13,82,113,274
London Mosque
Queen Mary's Gardens
Chester Rd
16,46,98
187,332
46,187
ST JOHN'S WOOD RD
Outer Circle
Regent's Park Lake
Open Air Theatre
Randolph Ave
PARK RD
Inner Circle
Sutherland Ave
6,16,46,98
187,332,414
13,82,113
139,189,274
MAIDA VALE
46,187
Regent's Canal
Lisson Grove
Frampton St
Rossmore Rd
Warwick Avenue
6,46,187,414
Clifton Gardens
139,189
Madame Tussaud's
Blomfield Rd
Marylebone
Baker St
Park
Warwick Avenue
EDGWARE RD
Church St
Broadley St
2,205,453
ROAD
18,27,30
74,205,453
Grand Union Canal
Little Venice
Marylebone High St
MARYLEBONE
Harley St
Edgware Rd
18
18,27
205
GLOUCESTER PL
BAKER ST
The Heart Hospital
18
46
18
Harrow Road
Edgware Rd
Chapel St
Seymour Pl
North Wharf Rd
15
New Cavendish
18
6,7,15,16
23,27,36,98
205,332,414,436
PADDINGTON
15,46
St Mary's Hospital
2,13,30,74
82,113,139
189,274
Wallace Collection
BISHOP'S BRIDGE RD
Eastbourne Terrace
Westbourne Terrace
Paddington
Praed St
SUSSEX GARDENS
George St
Wigmore St
7,23,27,36
BAYSWATER
EDGWARE RD
Connaught St
Seymour St
7,15,23,27,36
46,205,332,436,705
Marble Arch
OXFORD STREET
Bond St
Davies St
Craven Rd
MARBLE ARCH
70
46
Lancaster Gate
2,6,7,10,15,16
23,30,36,73,74,82
94,98,137,148,159
274,390,414,436
8
BAYSWATER ROAD
94,148
274,390
The Ring
N Audley St
Grosvenor St
Queensway
Mount St
70,94,148,390
PARK LANE
South Audley St
MAY
KENSINGTON GARDENS
HYDE PARK
2,10,16,36
73,74,82,137
148,414,436
Curzon St
Serpentine Gallery
Kensington Palace
The Serpentine
The Ring
Apsley House and Wellington Museum
Princess Diana Memorial Fountain
Hyde Park Corner
10,49
70,452
Albert Memorial
9,10,14,19
22,52,74,137
414,452,C1
South Carriage Road
KNIGHTSBRIDGE
2,8,9,10,14
16,19,22,36
38,52,73,74
82,137,148
414,436
GROSVENOR PL
KENSINGTON ROAD
Royal Albert Hall
KNIGHTSBRIDGE
14,74,414,C1
Palace Gate
Queen's Gate
Prince Consort Rd
360
Exhibition Rd
Knightsbridge
SLOANE STREET
BELGRAVIA
Science Museum
BROMPTON RD
70,360
49
Brompton Oratory
Belgrave Place
Natural History Museum
360
Victoria and Albert Museum
Pont St
BROMPTON
Gloucester Rd
70,74,360
CROMWELL RD
14,74
414,C1
19,22
137,452,C1
C1
KING'S RD
Sth Kensington

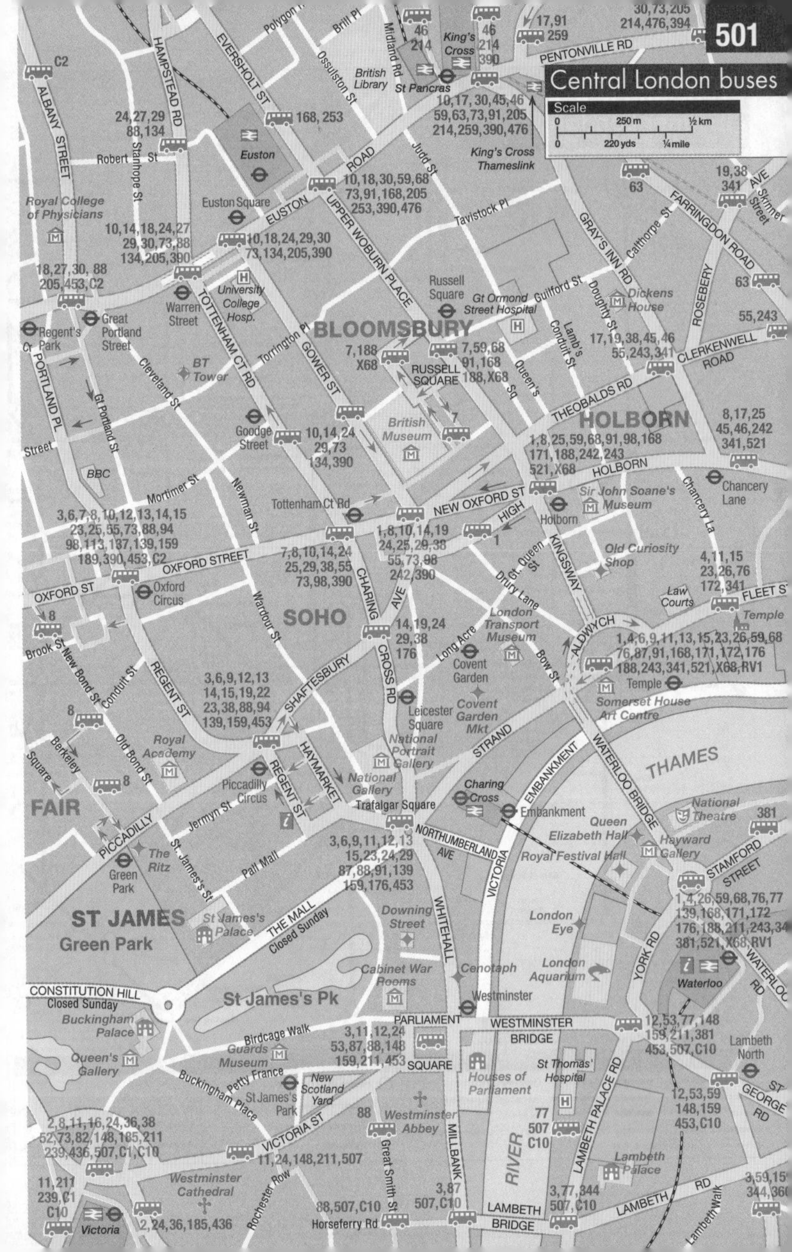
Central London buses
Scale
0
250 m
½ km
220 yds
¼ mile
King's Cross
St Pancras
King's Cross Thameslink
British Library
PENTONVILLE RD
Euston
Euston Square
EUSTON ROAD
HAMPSTEAD RD
EVERSHOLT ST
ALBANY STREET
Robert St
Stanhope St
Royal College of Physicians
Warren Street
Great Portland Street
Regent's Park
University College Hosp.
TOTTENHAM CT RD
UPPER WOBURN PLACE
GOWER ST
Torrington Pl
Tavistock Pl
BLOOMSBURY
Russell Square
RUSSELL SQUARE
Gt Ormond Street Hospital
Guilford St
GRAY'S INN RD
FARRINGDON ROAD
ROSEBERY AVE
Dickens House
CLERKENWELL ROAD
THEOBALDS RD
HOLBORN
Chancery Lane
Sir John Soane's Museum
BT Tower
Cleveland St
PORTLAND PL
Gt Portland St
Goodge Street
British Museum
BBC
Mortimer St
Newman St
Tottenham Ct Rd
NEW OXFORD ST
HIGH
Holborn
KINGSWAY
Old Curiosity Shop
Law Courts
FLEET ST
Temple
OXFORD STREET
Oxford Circus
Wardour St
SOHO
CHARING CROSS RD
SHAFTESBURY AVE
Long Acre
Covent Garden
London Transport Museum
Drury Lane
Bow St
ALDWYCH
Somerset House Art Centre
Brook St
New Bond St
Conduit St
REGENT ST
Leicester Square
Covent Garden Mkt
Royal Academy
National Portrait Gallery
STRAND
Berkeley Square
Old Bond St
Piccadilly Circus
HAYMARKET
National Gallery
Trafalgar Square
Charing Cross
Embankment
EMBANKMENT
WATERLOO BRIDGE
THAMES
National Theatre
FAIR
PICCADILLY
Jermyn St
The Ritz
Green Park
St James's St
Pall Mall
NORTHUMBERLAND AVE
VICTORIA
Queen Elizabeth Hall
Hayward Gallery
Royal Festival Hall
STAMFORD STREET
ST JAMES
Green Park
St James's Palace
THE MALL Closed Sunday
Downing Street
WHITEHALL
London Eye
YORK RD
Cabinet War Rooms
Cenotaph
London Aquarium
Waterloo
WATERLOO RD
CONSTITUTION HILL Closed Sunday
St James's Pk
Westminster
Buckingham Palace
Birdcage Walk
PARLIAMENT SQUARE
WESTMINSTER BRIDGE
Lambeth North
Queen's Gallery
Guards Museum
Houses of Parliament
St Thomas' Hospital
LAMBETH PALACE RD
ST GEORGE RD
Buckingham Place
Petty France
New Scotland Yard
St James's Park
Westminster Abbey
MILLBANK
RIVER
VICTORIA ST
Great Smith St
Lambeth Palace
Westminster Cathedral
Rochester Row
Horseferry Rd
LAMBETH BRIDGE
LAMBETH RD
Lambeth Walk
Victoria

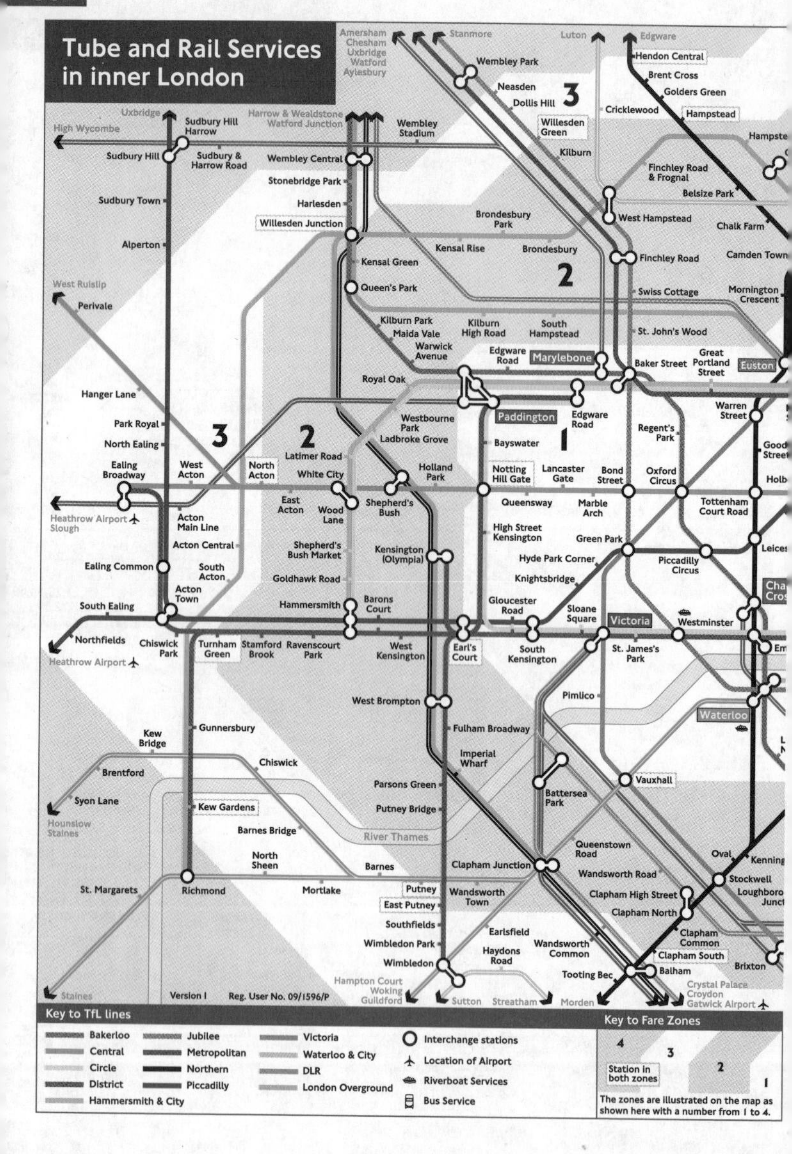
Tube and Rail Services in inner London
Amersham
Chesham
Uxbridge
Watford
Aylesbury
Stanmore
Luton
Edgware
Wembley Park
Hendon Central
Brent Cross
Golders Green
Hampstead
Neasden
Dolls Hill
3
Cricklewood
Willesden Green
Kilburn
Uxbridge
High Wycombe
Harrow & Wealdstone
Watford Junction
Sudbury Hill Harrow
Wembley Stadium
Sudbury Hill
Sudbury & Harrow Road
Wembley Central
Finchley Road & Frognal
Belsize Park
Stonebridge Park
Sudbury Town
Harlesden
West Hampstead
Chalk Farm
Willesden Junction
Brondesbury Park
Alperton
Kensal Rise
Brondesbury
Finchley Road
Camden Town
Kensal Green
2
West Ruislip
Queen's Park
Swiss Cottage
Mornington Crescent
Perivale
Kilburn Park
Kilburn High Road
South Hampstead
St. John's Wood
Maida Vale
Warwick Avenue
Edgware Road
Marylebone
Great Portland Street
Baker Street
Euston
Royal Oak
Hanger Lane
Warren Street
Westbourne Park
Paddington
Edgware Road
Park Royal
3
2
Ladbroke Grove
Bayswater
1
Regent's Park
North Ealing
Latimer Road
Ealing Broadway
West Acton
North Acton
White City
Holland Park
Notting Hill Gate
Lancaster Gate
Bond Street
Oxford Circus
East Acton
Wood Lane
Shepherd's Bush
Queensway
Marble Arch
Tottenham Court Road
Heathrow Airport
Slough
Acton Main Line
High Street Kensington
Green Park
Acton Central
Shepherd's Bush Market
Kensington (Olympia)
Hyde Park Corner
Piccadilly Circus
Ealing Common
South Acton
Knightsbridge
Goldhawk Road
Acton Town
Gloucester Road
Sloane Square
Barons Court
South Ealing
Hammersmith
Victoria
Westminster
Northfields
Chiswick Park
Turnham Green
Stamford Brook
Ravenscourt Park
West Kensington
Earl's Court
South Kensington
St. James's Park
Heathrow Airport
Pimlico
West Brompton
Waterloo
Gunnersbury
Fulham Broadway
Kew Bridge
Imperial Wharf
Chiswick
Brentford
Parsons Green
Battersea Park
Vauxhall
Syon Lane
Kew Gardens
Putney Bridge
Hounslow
Staines
Barnes Bridge
River Thames
Queenstown Road
North Sheen
Oval
Barnes
Clapham Junction
Wandsworth Road
Stockwell
St. Margarets
Richmond
Mortlake
Putney
Wandsworth Town
Clapham High Street
East Putney
Clapham North
Southfields
Earlsfield
Clapham Common
Wimbledon Park
Wandsworth Common
Haydons Road
Clapham South
Wimbledon
Brixton
Tooting Bec
Balham
Hampton Court
Woking
Guildford
Crystal Palace
Croydon
Gatwick Airport
Staines
Version 1
Reg. User No. 09/1596/P
Sutton
Streatham
Morden
Key to TfL lines
Bakerloo
Central
Circle
District
Hammersmith & City
Jubilee
Metropolitan
Northern
Piccadilly
Victoria
Waterloo & City
DLR
London Overground
Interchange stations
Location of Airport
Riverboat Services
Bus Service
Key to Fare Zones
4
3
2
1
Station in both zones
The zones are illustrated on the map as shown here with a number from 1 to 4.

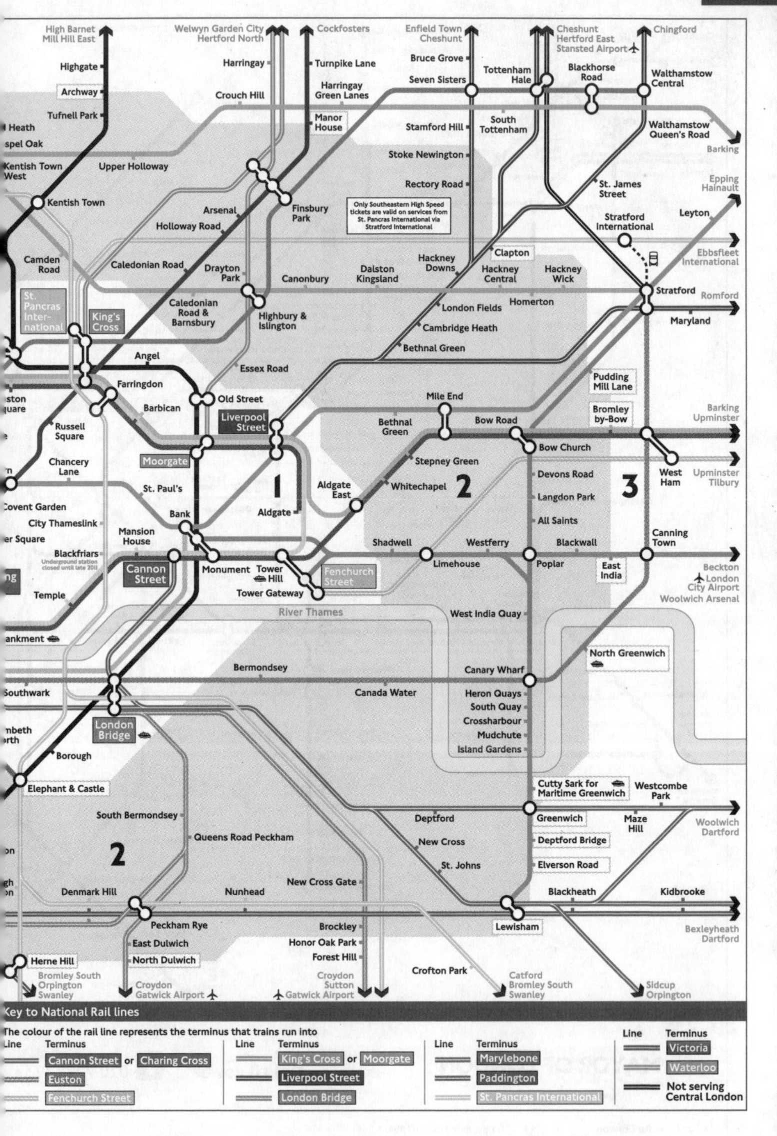

Key to National Rail lines

The colour of the rail line represents the terminus that trains run into

Line	Terminus	Line	Terminus	Line	Terminus	Line	Terminus
	Cannon Street or Charing Cross		King's Cross or Moorgate		Marylebone		Victoria
	Euston		Liverpool Street		Paddington		Waterloo
	Fenchurch Street		London Bridge		St. Pancras International		Not serving Central London

Only Southeastern High Speed tickets are valid on services from St. Pancras International via Stratford International

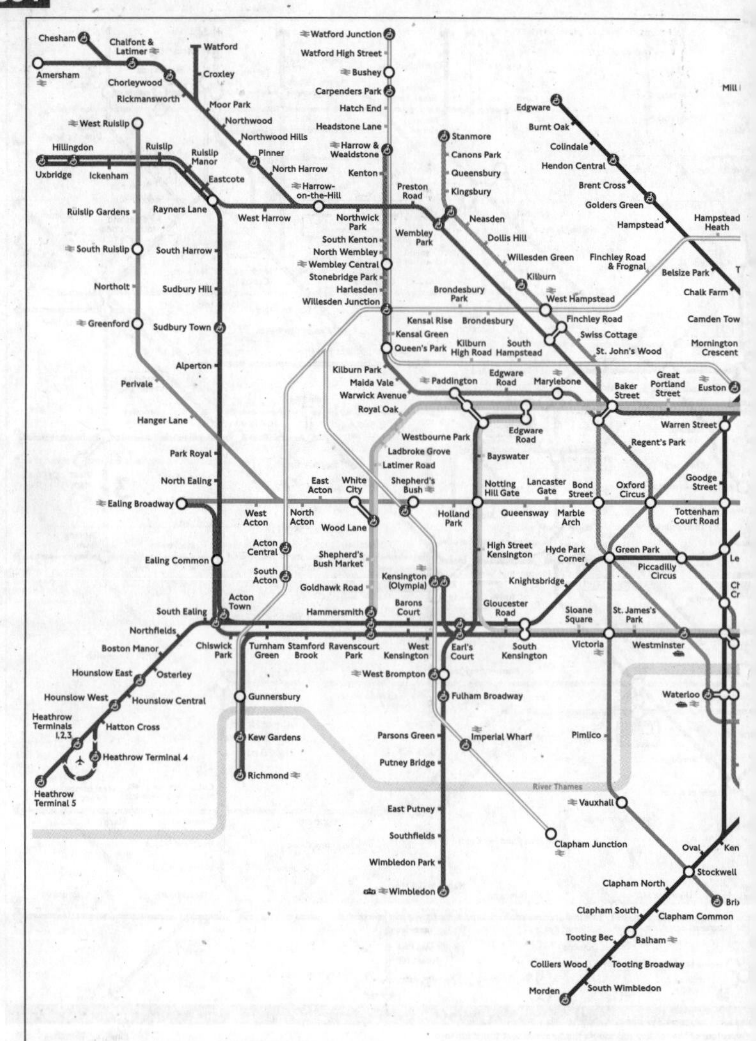

Chesham
Chalfont & Latimer
Watford
Amersham
Croxley
Chorleywood
Rickmansworth
Moor Park
Northwood
Northwood Hills
West Ruislip
Hillingdon
Ruislip
Ruislip Manor
Pinner
North Harrow
Uxbridge
Ickenham
Eastcote
Harrow-on-the-Hill
Ruislip Gardens
Rayners Lane
West Harrow
South Ruislip
South Harrow
Northolt
Sudbury Hill
Greenford
Sudbury Town
Alperton
Perivale
Hanger Lane
Park Royal
North Ealing
Ealing Broadway
West Acton
North Acton
East Acton
White City
Wood Lane
Ealing Common
Acton Central
South Acton
Acton Town
South Ealing
Northfields
Boston Manor
Chiswick Park
Turnham Green
Stamford Brook
Ravenscourt Park
Hounslow East
Osterley
Hounslow West
Hounslow Central
Heathrow Terminals 1,2,3
Hatton Cross
Heathrow Terminal 4
Heathrow Terminal 5
Gunnersbury
Kew Gardens
Richmond
Watford Junction
Watford High Street
Bushey
Carpenders Park
Hatch End
Headstone Lane
Harrow & Wealdstone
Kenton
Preston Road
Northwick Park
South Kenton
North Wembley
Wembley Park
Wembley Central
Stonebridge Park
Harlesden
Willesden Junction
Stanmore
Canons Park
Queensbury
Kingsbury
Neasden
Dollis Hill
Willesden Green
Kilburn
Brondesbury Park
Kensal Rise
Brondesbury
Kensal Green
Queen's Park
Kilburn High Road
South Hampstead
Kilburn Park
Maida Vale
Warwick Avenue
Paddington
Royal Oak
Westbourne Park
Ladbroke Grove
Latimer Road
Shepherd's Bush
Shepherd's Bush Market
Goldhawk Road
Hammersmith
Kensington (Olympia)
Barons Court
West Kensington
Earl's Court
West Brompton
Fulham Broadway
Parsons Green
Putney Bridge
East Putney
Southfields
Wimbledon Park
Wimbledon
Imperial Wharf
Clapham Junction
Edgware
Burnt Oak
Colindale
Hendon Central
Brent Cross
Golders Green
Hampstead
Hampstead Heath
Finchley Road & Frognal
Belsize Park
Chalk Farm
West Hampstead
Finchley Road
Swiss Cottage
St. John's Wood
Mornington Crescent
Edgware Road
Marylebone
Baker Street
Great Portland Street
Euston
Warren Street
Regent's Park
Goodge Street
Bayswater
Notting Hill Gate
Lancaster Gate
Bond Street
Oxford Circus
Tottenham Court Road
Holland Park
Queensway
Marble Arch
High Street Kensington
Hyde Park Corner
Green Park
Piccadilly Circus
Knightsbridge
Gloucester Road
South Kensington
Sloane Square
St. James's Park
Victoria
Westminster
Waterloo
Pimlico
River Thames
Vauxhall
Oval
Stockwell
Clapham North
Clapham South
Clapham Common
Tooting Bec
Balham
Colliers Wood
Tooting Broadway
Morden
South Wimbledon

MAYOR OF LONDON

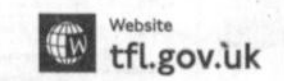

Website
tfl.gov.uk

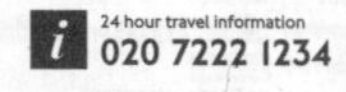

24 hour travel information
020 7222 1234